KEY FIGURES IN MEDIEVAL EUROPE

AN ENCYCLOPEDIA

KEY FIGURES IN MEDIEVAL EUROPE

AN ENCYCLOPEDIA

Richard K. Emmerson

Editor

Sandra Clayton-Emmerson

Associate Editor

Routledge
Taylor & Francis Group
New York   London

Published in 2006 by
Routledge
Taylor & Francis Group
270 Madison Avenue
New York, NY 10016

Published in Great Britain by
Routledge
Taylor & Francis Group
2 Park Square
Milton Park, Abingdon
Oxon OX14 4RN

© 2006 by Taylor & Francis Group, LLC
Routledge is an imprint of Taylor & Francis Group

Printed in the United States of America on acid-free paper
10 9 8 7 6 5 4 3 2 1

International Standard Book Number-10: 0-415-97385-6 (Hardcover)
International Standard Book Number-13: 978-0-415-97385-4 (Hardcover)

Library of Congress Cataloging-in-Publication Data

Catalog record is available from the Library of Congress

Taylor & Francis Group is the Academic Division of Informa plc.

Visit the Taylor & Francis Web site at
http://www.taylorandfrancis.com

and the Routledge Web site at
http://www.routledge-ny.com

CONTENTS

INTRODUCTION

Key Figures in Medieval Europe: An Encyclopedia provides a broad introduction to the biographical knowledge collected and investigated by modern scholarship over the past several decades regarding the persons whose actions, beliefs, creations, and writings shaped the Middle Ages, roughly that period in European history stretching from about 500 to 1500.

The geographic and chronological range of this volume is therefore extensive and impressive, as are the lives and accomplishments of the 587 figures it discusses. Although the historical record tends to favor persons born into or achieving the higher estates of the Middle Ages, such as the princes of church and state, these entries include a wide range of individuals, from emperors and queens to businessmen and traveling performers, from popes and university scholars to visionary women and heretics, from one of the greatest poets of all times, Dante, who during the later Middle Ages was known internationally, to Caedmon, a little known oral poet living on the edge of civilized Europe during the early Middle Ages. These are the people who influenced, motivated, and were shaped by the artistic, economic, intellectual, literary, political, religious, and social history of one of the most fascinating periods of world history, the Middle Ages. It is worth noting that the Islamic world receives attention in *Key Figures in Medieval Europe,* most of all because of its important place in medieval Iberia.

The 587 entries included in *Key Figures in Medieval Europe* are drawn from the following eight previously published volumes in the *Routledge Encyclopedias of the Middle Ages* series, initiated by Garland.

- *Medieval Scandinavia: An Encyclopedia,* edited by Phillip Pulsiano and Kirsten Wolf (Garland, 1993)
- *Medieval France: An Encyclopedia,* edited by William W. Kibler, Grover A. Zinn, John Bell Henneman, Jr., and Lawrence Earp (Garland, 1995)
- *Medieval England: An Encyclopedia,* edited by Paul E. Szarmach, M. Teresa Tavormina, and Joel T. Rosenthal (Garland, 1998)
- *Trade, Travel, and Exploration in the Middle Ages: An Encyclopedia,* edited by John Block Friedman and Kristen Mossler Figg (Garland, 2000)
- *Medieval Germany: An Encyclopedia,* edited by John M. Jeep (Garland, 2001)
- *Medieval Jewish Civilization: An Encyclopedia,* edited by Norman Roth (Routledge, 2002)
- *Medieval Iberia: An Encyclopedia,* edited by E. Michael Gerli (Routledge, 2003)
- *Medieval Italy: An Encyclopedia*, edited by Christopher Kleinhenz (Routledge, 2003).

The entries comprising *Key Figures in Medieval Europe* were carefully selected amongst the biographical entries found in the above volumes to provide a source for quick and ready information. The present volume is intended not only for students, librarians, teachers, and the general public, who may be interested in the Middle Ages but do not wish to purchase or sift through numerous individual encyclopedias, but also for medievalists and other scholars who want to have a reliable reference work easily at hand. By drawing on previously published entries, the volume gathers the best of scholarship scattered over eight volumes into one easy to use biographical resource. To preserve the integrity of the scholarship, the entries are published as they originally appeared.

The strength of the entries is evident in the quality of the scholarship that informed the original volumes and that drew on the wide knowledge of hundreds of scholars selected by the editors of the volumes for their expertise in the areas of medieval studies assigned to them. The entries, therefore, are reliable accounts of the medieval figures discussed and can be used with confidence by all readers.

INTRODUCTION

A compilation that seeks to combine entries from several geographically-based volumes into a single Europe-wide volume is bound to have slight inconsistencies. The entries are arranged alphabetically according to the spelling of the name in the source volume, but entries drawn from other volumes may refer to these individuals by somewhat different names or spellings. There is also some variation in length. Readers should not assume that the length of an entry represents the importance of a subject, because the source volumes vary in the size of their entries.

Given the thousands of individuals included in the eight encyclopedias, it was necessary to establish some reasonably consistent criteria for selecting the entries included in *Key Figures in Medieval Europe*. Obviously, word length could not be the primary criterion. However, within individual encyclopedias length could be used as a rough gauge of importance, especially within certain categories, such as political figures. But such distinctions in length within a single volume could not be used as an absolute, because of the nature of historical knowledge and available evidence. We simply know much more about political figures (particularly members of the nobility) than we know about commoners, which means that entries on emperors, kings, and caliphs, for example, will, with a very few exceptions (e.g., Dante), be longer than entries on musicians, painters, and poets. Similarly, because of the international nature of the Christian church and its omnipresence, we often know much more about religious figures than secular ones, even when they were attached to courts and cathedrals. As in the modern world, gender structures also affected the status of men and women during the Middle Ages, so that the historical record is generally much fuller when dealing with men than with women.

Therefore, to provide some balance to *Key Figures in Medieval Europe* and to ensure that it represents the wide range of cultural practices, as well as political events and religious thought, the selection privileges secular and artistic figures by including several individuals whose entries in the source volumes are relatively short. Since these individuals often worked outside the corridors of power and left few biographical records, there is little biographical detail to explore, yet their accomplishments are significant.

The selection of entries, in other words, is ultimately driven by the editorial sense of long-term importance and influence, as well as by what the reader may find interesting about the Middle Ages.

HOW TO USE THIS BOOK

Key Figures in Medieval Europe: An Encyclopedia is arranged in an easy-to-use A-to-Z reference format that contains 587 entries. **See also** end-references and **Further Reading** suggestions direct the reader to explore the topics further. To enhance the ease of use, readers will find an **alphabetical list of entries** and a **thematic list of entries** that organizes entries under such categories as artists and architects, authors, merchants and businessmen, musicians, political leaders, religious figures, scientists, travelers, as well as notable women. Also, a **list by region** organizes the entries by geographic areas, such as England, France, Germany, Iberia, Italy, Low Countries, and Scandinavia. Readers will also find a detailed index at the end of the book to help them further navigate the work.

THE ROUTLEDGE ENCYCLOPEDIAS OF THE MIDDLE AGES

Formerly the Garland Encyclopedias of the Middle Ages, this comprehensive series began in 1993 with the publication of *Medieval Scandinavia*. A major enterprise in medieval scholarship, the series brings the expertise of scholars specializing in myriad aspects of the medieval world together in a reference source accessible to students and the general public as well as to historians and scholars in related fields. Each volume focuses on a geographical area or theme important to medieval studies and is edited by a specialist in that field, who has called upon a board of consulting editors to establish the article list and review the articles. Each article is contributed by a scholar and followed by a bibliography and cross-references to guide further research.

Routledge is proud to carry on the tradition established by the first volumes in this important series. As the series continues to grow, we hope that it will provide the most comprehensive and detailed view of the medieval world in all its aspects ever presented in encyclopedia form.

Vol. 1   *Medieval Scandinavia: An Encyclopedia*. Edited by Phillip Pulsiano.

Vol. 2   *Medieval France: An Encyclopedia*. Edited by William W. Kibler, Grover A. Zinn, John Bell Henneman, Jr., and Lawrence Earp.

Vol. 3   *Medieval England: An Encyclopedia*. Edited by Paul E. Szarmach, M. Teresa Tavormina, and Joel T. Rosenthal.

Vol. 4   *Medieval Archaeology: An Encyclopedia*. Edited by Pamela Crabtree.

Vol. 5   *Trade, Travel, and Exploration in the Middle Ages: An Encyclopedia*. Edited by John Block Friedman and Kristen Mossler Figg.

Vol. 6   *Medieval Germany: An Encyclopedia*. Edited by John M. Jeep.

Vol. 7   *Medieval Jewish Civilization: An Encyclopedia*. Edited by Norman Roth.

Vol. 8   *Medieval Iberia: An Encyclopedia*. Edited by E. Michael Gerli.

Vol. 9   *Medieval Italy: An Encyclopedia*. Edited by Christopher Kleinhenz.

Vol. 10 *Medieval Ireland: An Encyclopedia*. Edited by Seán Duffy.

Vol. 11 *Medieval Science, Technology, and Medicine: An Encyclopedia*. Edited by Thomas Glick, Stephen J. Livesey, and Faith Wallis.

Vol. 12 *Medieval Islamic Civilization: An Encyclopedia*. Edited by Josef W. Meri.

The present volume, *Key Figures in Medieval Europe: An Encyclopedia*, edited by Richard K. Emmerson, reprises contents from volumes 1, 2, 3, 5, 6, 7, 8, and 9 and is Volume 13 in the series.

Contributors

Omeima Abou-Bakr
Cairo University

Emily Albu
University of California, Davis

James W. Alexander
University of Georgia

Gloria Allaire
Gettysburg College

J. Michael Allsen
University of Wisconsin, Madison

Martin Arbagi
Wright State University

Amanda Athey
University of Georgia

Martí Aurell I Cardona
Paris, France

Ellen L. Babinsky
Austin Presbyterian Theological Seminary

Lola Badia
Universitat de Girona

Peter S. Baker
University of Virginia

Søren Balle
Aarhus Universitet, Aarhus, Denmark

John W. Barker
University of Wisconsin, Madison

Frank Barlow
University of Exeter

Carl F. Barnes, Jr.
Oakland College

Peter Barnet
Metropolitan Museum of Art

Christopher C. Baswell
Barnard College

Janet M. Bately
King's College, London

Emmanuèle Baumgartner
Paris III, La Sorbonne Nouvelle

Priscilla Bawcutt
University of Liverpool

Thomas Bein
Universität Bonn

Rafael Beltrán
Universitat de Barcelona

Ingrid Bennewitz
Universität Bamberg

C. David Benson
University of Connecticut

Joseph R. Berrigan
University of Georgia

Robert E. Bjork
Arizona State University

CONTRIBUTORS

Renate Blumenfeld-Kosinski
University of Pittsburgh

Uta-Renate Blumenthal
Catholic University of America

Flavio Boggi
University College, Cork

H. Lawrence Bond
Appalachian State University

Anthony Bonner
Palma de Mallorca

Daniel E. Bornstein
Texas A&M University

Steven N. Botterill
University of California, Berkeley

Constance B. Bouchard
University of Akron

Maureen B. M. Boulton
University of Notre Dame

Ritamary Bradley
St. Ambrose University

Ross Brann
Cornell University

Annette Brasseur
Université Charles de Gaulle, Lille

Derek S. Brewer
Emmanuel College, Cambridge

George Hardin Brown
Stanford University

Elizabeth A. R. Brown
Brooklyn College, City University of New York

Matilda T. Bruckner
Boston College

James A. Brundage
University of Kansas

Charles Burnett
Warburg Institute, London

Robert I. Burns, S. J.
University of California, Los Angeles

Keith Busby
University of Oklahoma

Joseph P. Byrne
Belmont University

William C. Calin
University of Florida

Robert G. Calkins
Cornell University

Daniel F. Callahan
University of Delaware

C. Jean Campbell
Emory University

Miles Campbell
New Mexico State University

Vicente Cantarino
Ohio State University

Stephen M. Carey
Washington University, St. Louis

Brendan Cassidy
University of St. Andrews

Gary P. Cestaro
DePaul University

Martin Chase, S.J.
John Carroll University

Robert Chazan
New York University

Celia Chazelle
Trenton State College

Stephanie Christelow
Idaho State University

Eric Christiansen
New College, Oxford

Marlene Ciklamini
Rutgers University

Geert H. M. Claassens
Katholieke Universiteit Leuven

Albrecht Classen
University of Arizona

Margaret Clunies Ross
University of Sydney

Roger Collins
St. George's School, Edinburgh

Eleanor A. Congdon
Youngstown State University

Jane E. Connolly
University of Miami

Leo A. Connolly
University of Memphis

John J. Contreni
Purdue University

William R. Cook
State University of New York, Geneseo

Helen Cooper
University College, Oxford

Brigitte Corley
London, England

Rebecca M. Corrie
Bates College

Dustin Cowell
University of Wisconsin

Giuseppe Cremascoli
University of Bologna

Roger J. Crum
University of Dayton

Amanda Curry
Washington, D.C.

Gareth Curtis
Manchester, England

Daphne L. Davidson
New York, New York

Charles T. Davis

Guido O.E.J. De Baere
University of Antwerp

Dario Del Puppo
Trinity College, Hartford, Connecticut

Bradley J. Delaney
La Mesa, California

Peter F. Dembowski
University of Chicago

Ernst S. Dick
Atkinson College, York University, Toronto

Madelyn Bergen Dick
Atkinson College, York University, Toronto

John B. Dillon
University of Wisconsin, Madison

Peter Dinzelbache
Salzburg, Austria

Maria Dobozy
University of Utah

Keith R. Dockray
University of Huddersfield

Micheal R. Dodds
Southern Methodist University

Claire M. Donovan
Winchester, England

Joanna H. Drell
University of Richmond

Katherine F. Drew
Rice University

Graeme Dunphy
Universität Regensburg

André Duplat
Vesoul, France

Francis A. Dutra
University of California, Santa Barbara

Steven N. Dworkin
University of Michigan

CONTRIBUTORS

Theresa Earenfight
Seattle University

Lawrence Earp
University of Wisconsin, Madison

Sten Ebbesen
Københavns Universitet, Denmark

Bradford Lee Eden
University of Nevada, Las Vegas

A. S. G. Edwards
University of Victoria

Mary Douglas Edwards
Pratt Institute

Robert R. Edwards
Pennsylvania State University

Ólafía Einarsdóttir
Københavns Universitet, Denmark

Clara Estow
University of Massachusetts, Boston

An Faems
Katholieke Universiteit Leuven

David Fallows
University of Manchester

Richard C. Famiglietti
Providence, Rhode Island

Steven Fanning
University of Illinois, Chicago

Seymour Feldman
Rutgers University

Felipe Fernández-Armesto
Hakluyt Society

George Ferzoco
University of Leicester

Bjarne Fidjestøl
Universitetet i Bergen, Norway

Robert C. Figueira
Lander University, Greenwood, South Carolina

Charles Fraker
University of Michigan

Michael Frassetto
Encyclopedia Britannica

Peter Frenzel
Wesleyan University

Donald K. Fry
St. Petersburg, Florida

Richard Gameson
University of Kent, Canterbury

Gail L. Geiger
University of Wisconsin, Madison

Francis G. Gentry
Pennsylvania State University

Richard A. Gerberding
University of Alabama, Huntsville

Philip O. Gericke
University of California, Riverside

E. Michael Gerli
University of Virginia

Faye Marie Getz
Wellcome Institute, London

James L. Gillespie
Amman, Jordan

Jutta Goheen
Carleton University, Ottawa

Cristina González
University of California, Davis

Anthony E. Goodman
University of Edinburgh

Janice Gordon-Kelter
University of St. Thomas, Houston

T. J. Gorton
Paris, France

Karen Gould
University of Texas, Austin

Aryeh Grabois
University of Haifa

Angus Graham
Sultan Qaboos University

Timothy Graham
Western Michigan University

Theresa Gross-Diaz
Loyola University, Chicago

Steven Grossvogel
University of Georgia

Anna A. Grotans
Ohio State University

Joseph J. Gwara
United States Naval Academy

Cynthia Hahn
Florida State University

Rosemary Drage Hale
Concordia University, Montreal

E. Kay Harris
University of Southern Mississippi

Warren Zev Harvey
King's College, University of London

Herbert Heinen
University of Texas, Austin

Ingeborg Henderson
University of California, Davis

John Bell Henneman, Jr.
Princeton University

Jan W. Herlinger
Louisiana State University

Ernst Ralf Hintz
Fort Hays State University, Hays, Kansas

Maarten J. F. M. Hoenen
Katholieke Universiteit Nijmegen

Hanns Hohmann
San Jose State University

Joan A. Holladay
University of Texas, Austin

David Hook
University of Bristol

Gert Hübner
Universität Bamberg

Caroline Huey
University of Texas, Austin

Joseph P. Huffman
Messiah College, Grantham, Pennsylvania

Lois L. Huneycutt
University of Missouri, Columbia

Sylvia Huot
Northern Illinois University

Thomas M. Izbicki
Eisenhower Library, Johns Hopkins University

Sybille Jefferis
University of Pennsylvania

Frede Jensen
University of Colorado, Boulder

Phyllis G. Jestice
California State University, Hayward

Sidney M. Johnson
Indiana University

Michael Jones
University of London

William Chester Jordan
Princeton University

Donald J. Kagay
Albany State University

Henry Kamen
Consejo Superior de Investigaciones Científicas, Barcelona

Ruth Mazo Karras
University of Pennsylvania

V. Louise Katainen
Auburn University

CONTRIBUTORS

Richard Kay
University of Kansas

Hans-Erich Keller
Ohio State University

F. Douglas Kelly
University of Wisconsin, Madison

William W. Kibler
University of Texas, Austin

John L. Kirby
Streatham, London

Christopher Kleinhenz
University of Wisconsin, Madison

Alan E. Knight
Pennsylvania State University

C. H. Knowles
University of Wales, Cardiff

Jeanne E. Krochalis
Pennsylvania State University

Steven F. Kruger
City University of New York

Kelly Kubaca
University of Kentucky

Sigurd Kværndrup
Skælskør Folkehøjskole, Denmark

Maria Jesús Lacarra
Universidad de Zaragoza

Norris J. Lacy
Washington University, St. Louis

Miguel Angel Ladero Quesada
Universidad Complutense de Madrid

Maura K. Lafferty
Villanova University

Richard Landes
Boston University

Michelle I. Lapine
University of Texas, Austin

Jeremy Lawrance
University of Manchester

Peter M. Lefferts
University of Nebraska, Lincoln

Theodore Leinbaugh
University of North Carolina, Chapel Hill

Jessica Levenstein
New York, New York

Joan H. Levin
Philadelphia, Pennsylvania

Daniel M. Levine
Savannah College of Art and Design

Gertrud Jaron Lewis
Laurentian University, Sudbury, Canada

Karen E. Loaiza
State University of New York, Plattsburgh

Karma Lochrie
Loyola University, Chicago

John Lomax
Ohio Northern University

Graham A. Loud
University of Leeds

Sieglinde Lug
University of Denver

Niels Lund
Københavns Universitet, Denmark

Malcolm C. Lyons
Cambridge University

Angus MacKay
Edinburgh University

Giulio Maffii
Milan, Italy

John Margetts
University of Liverpool

Edith Marold
Christian-Albrechts-Universität, Kiel

William Marvin

Lister M. Matheson
Michigan State University

E. Ann Matter
University of Pennsylvania

R. Thomas McDonald
Fairleigh Dickinson University

William C. McDonald
University of Virginia

Michael R. McVaugh
University of North Carolina, Chapel Hill

Gustav Medicus
Kent State University

Thom Mertens
Antwerp, Belgium

Emmanuel J. Mickel
Indiana University

Clyde Lee Miller
State University of New York, Stony Brook

Maureen C. Miller
George Mason University

Scott B. Montgomery
University of North Texas

Jesús Montoya Martínez
Universidad de Granada

Bridget Morris
University of Hull, England

Karl F. Morrison
Rutgers University

Anita F. Moskowitz
State University of New York, Stony Brook

Deborah H. Nelson
Rice University

Janet L. Nelson
King's College, London

Colbert I. Nepaulsingh
State University of New York, Albany

James Noble
University of New Brunswick

Suzanne Noffke
Philadelphia, Pennsylvania

William North
Carleton College, Northfield, Minnesota

Tore Nyberg
Odense Universitet, Denmark

Robert Oakley
University of Birmingham

Joseph F. O'Callaghan
Fordham University

Eva Odelman
Riksarkivet, Stockholm

Jim Ogier
Roanoke College, Salem, Virginia

Willemien Otten
Boston College

William D. Paden
Northwestern University

Brian A. Pavlac
King's College, Wilkes-Barre, Pennsylvania

David A. E. Pelteret
University of Toronto

Rupert T. Pickens
University of Kentucky

Martin Picker
Rutgers University

Sandra Pinegar
Ohio State University

Paul B. Pixton
Brigham Young University

Russell Poole
Massey University, Palmerston North, New Zealand

Burcht Pranger
University of Amsterdam

Michael Prestwich
University of Durham

Ricardo J. Quinones
Claremont McKenna College

Matthew B. Raden
Tulane University

Sherry Reames
University of Wisconsin, Madison

Luis Rebelo
King's College, University of London

Susanne Reece
Ohio State University

Nancy F. Regalado
New York University

Bernard F. Reilly
Villanova University

Marta O. Renger
Rheinische Friedrich-Wilhelms Universität Bonn

Mary P. Richards
University of Delaware

Phyllis B. Roberts
City University of New York

Philipp W. Rosemann
University of Dallas

Samuel N. Rosenberg
Indiana University

Roy S. Rosenstein
American College in Paris

Norman Roth
University of Wisconsin, Madison

Jonathan Rotondo-McCord
Xavier University of Louisiana

Lara Ruffolo
Auckland, New Zealand

Alan Ryder
University of Bristol

Julio Samsó
Universidad de Barcelona

Michael G. Sargent
Queens College, City University of New York

Barbara N. Sargent-Baur
University of Pittsburgh

Helene Scheck
Rensselaer, New York

Brigitte Schliewen
Vaterstetten, Germany

Gary D. Schmidt
Calvin College

Simon Schwarzfuchs
Jerusalem, Israel

Laurie Shepard
Boston College

Leah Shopkow
Indiana University

Michael A. Signer
University of Notre Dame

James Simpson
Girton College, Cambridge

Patricia Skinner
University of Southampton

Carola M. Small
University of Edinburgh

Janet Levarie Smarr
University of California, San Diego

Lesley J. Smith
Linacre College, Oxford University

William Bradford Smith
Oglethorpe University, Atlanta

Jeffrey Chipps Smith
University of Texas, Austin

Kristine K. Sneeringer
Washington University, St. Louis

Paul D. Solon
Macalester College

Mary B. Speer
Rutgers University

Paolo Squatriti
University of Michigan

Ruggero Stefanini
University of California, Berkeley

Alexandra Sterling-Hellenbrand
Goshen College, Goshen, Indiana

Steven A. Stofferahn
Purdue University

H. Wayne Storey
Indiana University, Bloomington

Debra L. Stoudt
University of Toledo

Folke Ström
Göteborg Universitet, Sweden

Richard E. Sullivan
Michigan State University

Israel Ta-Shma
Hebrew University, Jerusalem

Laurie Taylor-Mitchell
Hood College

Lynn D. Thelen
Ursinus College, Collegeville, Pennsylvania

Timothy M. Thibodeau
Nazareth College of Rochester

J. A. F. Thomson
University of Glasgow

Frank Tobin
University of Nevada, Reno

Thomas Turley
Santa Clara University

Julio Valdeón Baruque
Universidad de Valladolid

Alfons M. J. van Buuren
Amersfort, The Netherlands

Stephanie Cain Van D'Elden
University of Minnesota

Dieuwke van der Poel
Rijksuniversiteit te Utrecht

Paul J. J. van Geest
Titus Brandsma Instituut

Amelia E. Van Vleck
University of Texas, Austin

Sally N. Vaughn
University of Houston

Alessandro Vettori
Rutgers University

Jón Viðar Sigurðsson
Universitetet i Oslo, Norway

Kim Vivian
Augustana College, Rock Island, Illinois

Thomas G. Waldman
University of Pennsylvania

David Wallace
University of Pennsylvania

Susan L. Ward
Rhode Island School of Design

David A. Warner
Rhode Island School of Design

W. L. Warren
Queen's University, Belfast

Scott L. Waugh
University of California, Los Angeles

Jill R. Webster
University of Toronto

Barbara F. Weissberger
University of Minnesota

Nicolas Wey-Gómez
Massachusetts Institute of Technology

CONTRIBUTORS

Diana Edwards Whaley
University of Newcastle upon Tyne

Ulrike Wiethaus
Wake Forest University

Constance L. Wilkins
Miami University

Charity Cannon Willard
Cornwall-on-Hudson, New York

Joan B. Williamson
Long Island University

Katharina M. Wilson
University of Georgia

James I. Wimsatt
University of Texas, Austin

George D. Winius
College of Charleston

Anders Winroth
Yale University

Anne Winston-Allen
Southern Illinois University, Carbondale

Ronald G. Witt
Duke University

Kenneth B. Wolf
Pomona College

Roger Wright
University of Liverpool

R. F. Yeager
University of North Carolina, Asheville

John Zemke
University of Missouri, Columbia

Mark Zier
University of the Pacific

Grover A. Zinn
Oberlin College

Janice C. Zinser
Oberlin College

Jan Ziolkowski
Harvard University

Alphabetical List of Entries

ALPHABETICAL LIST OF ENTRIES

Thematic List of Entries

ARTISTS AND ARCHITECTS
Altichiero da Zevio
Arnolfo di Cambio
Bonaventura Berlinghieri
Brailes, William de
Campin, Robert
Cimabue
Conrad von Soest
Daddi, Bernardo
Duccio di Buoninsegna
Erhart, Michel
Fouquet, Jean
Francke, Master
Frueauf, Rueland, the Elder
Gaddi, Taddeo
Gerthener, Madern
Giotto di Bondone
Giusto dé Menabuoi
Grasser, Erasmus
Koerbecke, Johann
Limbourg Brothers
Lochner, Stefan
Lorenzetti, Pietro and Ambrogio
Martini, Simone
Matthew Paris
Moser, Lucas
Multscher, Hans
Nardo di Cione
Nicholas of Verdun
Nicolaus Gerhaert von Leyden
Orcagna, Andrea di Cione
Pacher, Michael
Pisano, Andrea
Pisano, Giovanni
Pisano, Nicola
Pleydenwurff, Hans
Pucelle, Jean
Riemenschneider, Tillmann
Schongauer, Martin

Sluter, Claus
Spinello Aretino
Stoss, Veit
Traini, Francesco
Van der Weyden, Rogier
Van Eyck, Jan
Veneziano , Paolo
Villard de Honnecourt
Wiligelmus
Witz, Konrad
Wolgemut, Michael

AUTHORS
Abélard, Peter
Abraham Bar Ḥiyya (Ḥayya)
Abravanel, Isaac
Adam de la Halle
Adam of Bremen
Ælfric
Alain de Lille
Albertanus of Brescia
Albertino Mussato
Albertus Magnus
Alcuin
Aldhelm
Alexander of Hales
Alfonso X, El Sabio, King of Castile and León
Alfred the Great
Alvarus, Paulus
Andreas Capellanus
Andrew of Saint-Victor
Angelo Clareno
Antonio Pucci
Aquinas, Thomas
Archpoet
Aristippus, Henry
Arnórr Þórðarson jarlaskáld
Asher b. Yeḥiel

THEMATIC LIST OF ENTRIES

THEMATIC LIST OF ENTRIES

MERCHANTS AND BUSINESSMEN

RELIGIOUS FIGURES

THEMATIC LIST OF ENTRIES

SCIENTISTS

Abraham Bar Ḥiyya (Ḥayya)
Albertus Magnus
Alfonso X, El Sabio, King of Castile and León
Aristippus, Henry
Averroës, Abu 'L-Walīd Muḥammad B. Aḥmad B. Rushd
Byrhtferth
Cecco d'Ascoli
Eugenius of Palermo
Fulbert of Chartres
Harpestreng, Henrik
Ibn Zuhr, Abū Marwān 'Abd Al-Mālik
John of Seville
Laufenberg, Heinrich
Levi Ben Gershom (Gersonides)
Llull, Ramón
Martianus Capella
Maslama de Madrid
Michael Scot
Oresme, Nicole
Pedro Alfonso, or Petrus Alfonsi
Philipupe de Thaün
Pietro Abano
Prosdocimus de Beldemandis
Toscanelli, Paolo dal Pozzo
Trotula of Salerno
Vilanova, Arnau de
William of Conches

TRAVELERS

Angelo Clareno
Benjamin of Tudela
Burchard of Mount Sion
Cão, Diogo
Columbus, Christopher
Daniel the Abbot
Dias, Bartolomeu
Egeria
Gama, Vasco da
Giovanni di Piano Carpini
Guzmán, Nuño de
Ibn Sa'īd, Abū 'L-Ḥasan 'Alī B. Mūsā B. Muḥammad B. 'Abd al-Malik B. Sa'īd
Martí, Ramón
Valera, Diego de

NOTABLE WOMEN

Angela da Foligno, Saint
Beatrijs van Nazareth
Birgitta, Saint
Blanche of Castile
Cartagena, Teresa de
Catherine of Siena, Saint
Christine de Pizan
Clare, Saint
Constance
Dhuoda
Ebner, Margaretha
Egeria
Eleanor of Aquitaine
Elisabeth von Schönau
Elizabeth of Hungary
Frau Ava
Gertrud von Helfta
Hadewijch
Ḥafṣa Bint Al-Hayy Ar-Rakuniyya
Héloïse
Herrad von Hohenburg
Hild
Hildegard von Bingen
Hrosvit of Gandersheim
Humility of Faenza
Isabeau of Bavaria
Jeanne d'Arc
Jeanne of Navarre
Joanna I of Naples
Judith, Empress
Julian of Norwich
Kempe, Margery
Langmann, Adelheid
Leodegundia
López de Córdoba, Leonor
Luitgard of Aywières
Margaret of Cortona, Saint
Margrethe I
Marguerite d'Oingt
Marguerite of Provence
Marguerite Porete
Marie de France
Marie d'Oignies
Matilda, Empress
Mechthild von Hackeborn
Mechthild von Magdeburg
Molina, María de
Padilla, María de
Qasmūna Bint Ismā'īl
Theodora
Trotula of Salerno
Wallādah Bint Al-Mustafki

Entries by Region

Martí, Ramón
Maslama de Madrid
Mena, Juan de
Molina, María de
Moses Ben Naḥman
Nebrija, Elio Antonio de
Padilla, María de
Pedro Alfonso, or Petrus Alfonsi
Pedro I the Cruel, King of Castile
Pedro III, King of Aragón
Peñafort, Ramón de
Qasmūna Bint Ismā'īl
Ramón Berenguer IV, Count of Barcelona
Sancho III, King of Navarre
Sancho IV, King of Castile
Shem Tov of Carrión
Shushtarī, Al-, Abū Al-Ḥasan
Torquemada, Tomás de
Torre, Alfonso de la
Valera, Diego de
Vilanova, Arnau de
Wallādah Bint Al-Mustafki

ITALY
Albertanus of Brescia
Albertino Mussato
Altichiero da Zevio
Amadeo VI, Count of Savoy
Angela da Foligno, Saint
Angelo Clareno
Anthony of Padua, Saint
Antonio Pucci
Aquinas, Thomas
Aristippus, Henry
Arnold of Brescia
Arnolfo di Cambio
Avicenna
Benedict of Nursia, Saint
Boccaccio, Giovanni
Bohemond of Taranto
Bonagiunta Orbicciani degli Averardi
Bonaventura Berlinghieri
Bonaventure, Saint
Boniface VIII, Pope
Brunetto Latini
Buoncompagno da Signa
Cangrande della Scala
Cassiodorus
Catherine of Siena, Saint
Cavalcanti, Guido
Cavallini, Pietro
Cecco Angiolieri
Cecco d'Ascoli
Celestine V, Pope

Ciconia, Johannes
Cimabue
Cino da Pistoia
Clare, Saint
Clement V, Pope
Compagni, Dino
Constance
Daddi, Bernardo
Damian, Peter
Dante Alighieri
Dolcino, Fra
Dominic, Saint
Duccio di Buoninsegna
Eugenius of Palermo
Fazio degli Uberti
Francesco d'Accorso
Francis of Assisi, Saint
Frederick II
Gaddi, Taddeo
Giacomino da Verona
Giacomo da Lentini
Giotto di Bondone
Giovanni del Virgilio
Giovanni di Piano Carpini
Giusto de' Menabuoi
Godfrey of Viterbo
Gratian
Gregory I, Pope
Gregory VII, Pope
Guido d'Arezzo
Guido delle Colonne
Guinizzelli, Guido
Guittone d'Arezzo
Hadrian I, Pope
Hadrian IV, Pope
Humility of Faenza
Immanuel Romano
Innocent III, Pope
Innocent IV, Pope
Jacobus da Voragine
Jacopo da Milano
Jacopo de Cessolis
Jacopone da Todi
Joachim of Fiore
Joanna I of Naples
Justinian I
Landini, Francesco
Leo III, Emperor
Leo IX, Pope
Liudprand of Cremona
Lorenzetti, Pietro and Ambrogio
Macrobius
Malispini, Ricordano
Manfred
Marchetto da Padova

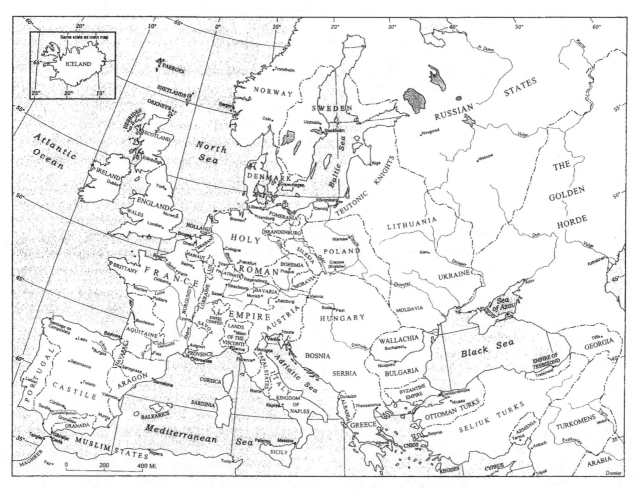

Regions and Peoples of Europe, Mid-Fourteenth Century

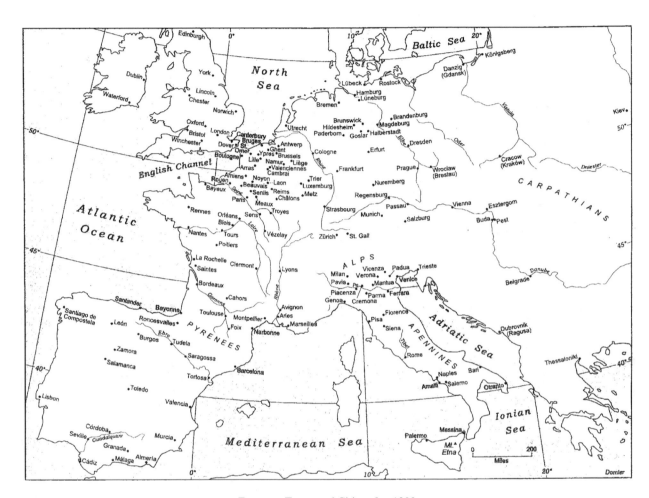

European Towns and Cities after 1200

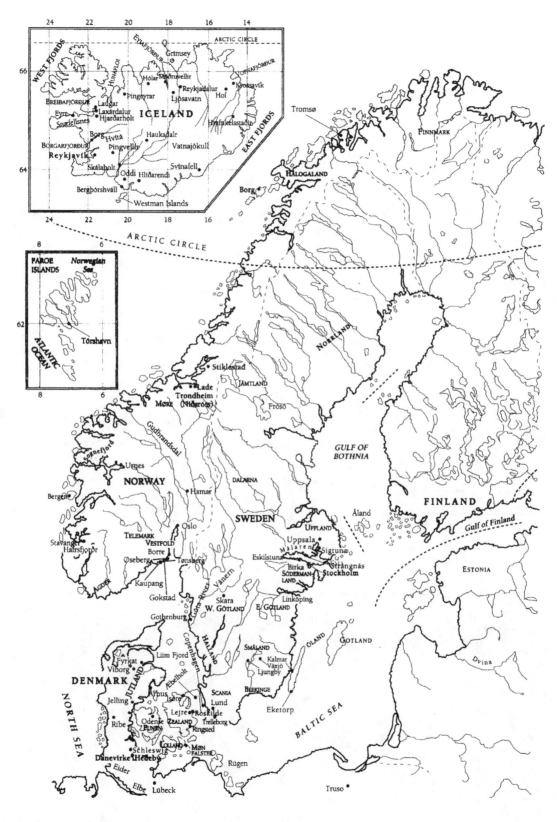

Scandinavia

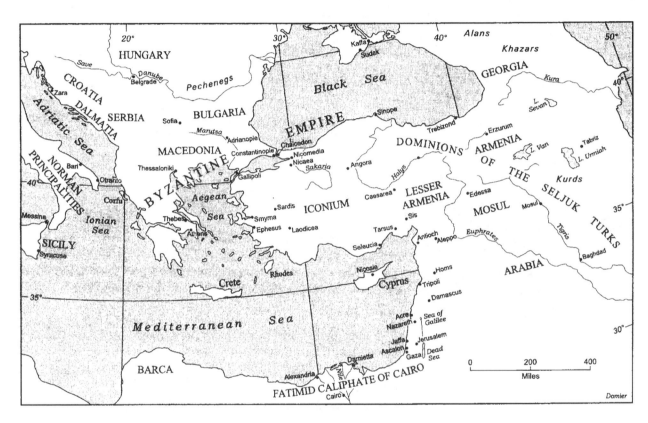

Mediterranean Regions, Early Twelfth Century

A

ABÉLARD, PETER (1079–1142)

Much of the life of Abélard, one of the most renowned 12th-century thinkers, is known from his *Historia calamitatum*, written ca. 1133. Born into a minor noble family in Le Pallet, Brittany, in 1079, Abélard embarked on a career as student, then master, in various French schools. He studied with leading masters at three cathedral schools: Roscelin (Loches), William of Champeaux (Paris), and Anselm of Laon (Laon). He himself taught at Paris (Mont-Sainte-Geneviève, Saint-Denis [while a monk there], and the cathedral school at Notre-Dame), Melun, Corbeil, Laon, and the Paraclete (near Troyes). An intellectual combatant, at Paris he challenged William of Champeaux on the existence of universals and at Laon criticized Anselm as lacking theological insight and dialectical skills. Abélard himself was harshly criticized and rebuked. In 1121, a council at Soissons found him guilty of heresy concerning the Trinity and required him to burn his treatise *On the Trinity and Unity of God* (or *Theologia "Summi Boni"*). In the late 1130s, William of Saint-Thierry, deeply troubled by Abélard's *Theologia Christiana*, wrote to Bernard of Clairvaux, who had Abélard summoned to a council at Sens in June 1140, where he was charged with heresy. The council condemned nineteen points in Abélard's theology; the pope soon thereafter also condemned Abélard. Following the condemnation at Sens, the Cluniac abbot Peter the Venerable offered Abélard a refuge at Cluny. According to Peter, Bernard and Abélard were reconciled before Abélard died in April 1142 at Saint-Marcel, a Cluniac priory near Chalons-sur-Saône.

While teaching in the schools of Paris, Abélard became involved in a passionate love affair with Héloïse, possibly the niece and certainly the ward of Fulbert, canon of the cathedral of Notre-Dame in Paris. Fulbert engaged Abélard to tutor the brilliant Héloïse, but the two were soon making love, not studying philosophy.

Héloïse became pregnant; Fulbert, unsatisfied by the secret marriage of Abélard and Héloïse, had Abélard castrated. Abélard and Héloïse entered the monastic life in 1119, she at the convent of Argenteuil, near Paris; he at the monastery of Saint-Denis, also near Paris. At Saint-Denis, Abélard began teaching again, at the request of students. He earned the monks' enmity by suggesting that the St. Denis to whom their abbey was dedicated was not the same as the mystical author Pseudo-Dionysius the Areopagite, an identification generally accepted in the 12th century.

Abélard's *Historia calamitatum* chronicles the love affair and its aftermath, particularly Abélard's career. A subsequent series of letters exchanged between Abélard and Héloïse reveals her deep attachment to him, his growing concern for her and her sister nuns, and his efforts to provide them with sermons, hymns, and a monastic rule. The authenticity of the correspondence has been challenged in recent years, but the consensus is that the letters represent a genuine exchange between Abélard and Héloïse.

Abélard finally left Saint-Denis and built a hermitage dedicated to the Paraclete at a remote spot near Troyes, where he taught students who sought him out. He later gave the land and buildings to Héloïse and her sister nuns for a convent after they were ejected from Argenteuil by Suger of Saint-Denis. In 1126, Abélard became abbot of Saint-Gildas de Rhuys in Brittany; after an abortive attempt to reform this lax monastic establishment, he fled, probably to Paris and the schools.

An accomplished master of dialectic (logic), Abélard pushed vigorously for questioning in the field of theology, with the goal of arriving at truth through a rigorous examination of conflicting opinions drawn from Scripture and authoritative writings (Augustine, Gregory the Great and other popes, church councils). This approach received classic expression in *Sic et non*.

Here, Abélard posed 158 theological questions, gathered statements from the tradition favoring each side of the question, but offered no solution (*sententia*) of the differences in position.

In ethics, Abélard taught a doctrine of intentionality and disinterested love. In *Scito te ipsum*, Abélard argues that the actual deed is morally indifferent; the key to ethical behavior is the intention with which the deed is carried out.

Concerning the doctrine of Christ's atonement, Abélard set forth in his commentary on the Epistle to the Romans a distinctive teaching, often called a "subjective" theory. Abélard argued that the effect of Christ's death was not an "objective" change in the relation of God and humanity (in light of human sin) as presented in Anselm of Bee's *Cur Deus homo*. Rather, Christ's death reveals self-sacrifice and absolute self-giving love, which evokes in the believer a response of total sacrifice and love and effects not a cosmic transaction involving divine justice but a personal and individual transformation of love and intention.

Among Abélard's other writings are an unfinished *Dialogus inter Philosophum, Judaeum, et Christianum*, the *Confessio fidei universalis*, letters, poems, forty-three sermons for use at the Paraclete, an *Apologia*, and *Hexaemeron* (a commentary on the six days of creation in Genesis). Abélard left disciples but no established school. Though he influenced the development of the scholastic method, especially the *quaestio*, in general his contributions to theology were topical and not systematic.

Abélard's poetry reveals exceptional emotional power in lyrics on biblical and religious themes, such as the lament (*planctus*) of David on the death of Jonathan, which he invests with a notable sensibility of personal pain and loss. He wrote other laments, liturgical poems, and a collection of hymns for Héloïse and the nuns at the Paraclete. In a letter, Héloïse remarks that Abélard wrote popular love poems that were the talk of Paris when he and Héloïse were lovers; none survives.

Peter the Venerable transferred Abélard's body to the Paraclete, where it was buried in the church. When Héloïse died in 1163/64, she was buried beside him. Their remains were taken to Paris when the Paraclete was destroyed after the Revolution, and they now rest in a tomb in the cemetery of Pere-La chaise.

See also **Anselm of Bec; Anselm of Laon; Bernard of Clairvaux**

Further Reading

Abélard, Peter. *Opera omnia. PL* 178.
——. *Petri Abélardi opera*, ed. Victor Cousin. 2 vols. Paris: Durand, 1849–59.
——. *Opera theologica*, ed. Eloi M. Buytaert. 3 vols. CCCM, 11, 12, 13. Turnhout: Brepols, 1969.
——. *Sic et non: A Critical Edition*, ed. Blanche B. Boyer and Richard P. McKeon. Chicago: University of Chicago Press, 1976–77.
——. *Philosophische Schriften*, ed. Bernhard Geyer. 1 vol. in 4 parts. Münster: Aschendorff, 1919–33.
——. *Ethics*, ed. and trans. David E, Luscombe. Oxford: Clarendon, 1971.
——. *Historia calamitatum: texte critique avec introduction*, ed. Jacques Monfrin. 2nd ed. Paris: Vrin, 1962.
——. *The Story of Abélard's Adversities*, trans. Joseph T. Muckle. Toronto: Pontifical Institute of Mediaeval Studies, 1964.
——. *A Dialogue of a Philosopher with a Jew and a Christian*, trans. Pierre J. Payer. Toronto: Pontifical Institute of Mediaeval Studies, 1979.
——. *The Hymns of Abélard in English Verse,* trans. Sister Joseph Patricia. Lanham: University Press of America, 1986.
——. *Dialogus inter Philosophum, Judaeum et, Christianum*, ed. Rudolf Thomas. Stuttgart: Fromann, 1970.
Radice, Betty, trans. *The Letters of Abélard and Heloise*. Harmondsworth: Penguin, 1974.
Luscombe, David E. *The School of Peter Abélard: The Influence of Abelard's Thought in the Early Scholastic Period*. Cambridge: Cambridge University Press, 1969.
Weingart, Richard E. *The Logic of Divine Love: A Critical Analysis of the Soteriology of Peter Abailard*. Oxford: Clarendon, 1970.

GROVER A. ZINN

ABRAHAM BARḤIYYA (ḤAYYA) (ca. 1070–1136)

Mathematician, astronomer, surveyor, philosopher, astrologer and translator Abraham bar Ḥiyya lived in Barcelona. He was known by the honorific titles Ha-Nasi (Hebrew: "the prince") and Savasorda (Latin corruption of the Arabic: ṣāḥib al-shurṭa ("master of the guard"), which indicate that he held high offices in both the Jewish and the Catalonian communities.

Nine works by him are known, all written in Hebrew. He was the first medieval author to write major philosophic and scientific works in Hebrew, and many of his termina technica are still used in modern Hebrew (e.g., *qeshet* = arc, *ma'alah* = degree, *merkaz* = center, *shoq* = side of an isoceles triangle). His works:

(1) *Ḥibbur ha-meshiḥah ve-ha-tishboret* (*On Measuring*), a comprehensive introduction to surveying. Translated into Latin (1145?) by Plato of Tivoli, it played an important role in transmitting Arabic geometry and trigonometry to the West. Hebrew text, ed. M. Guttmann, 1912–13, Catalan translation, J. M. Millás Vallicrosa, 1931.

(2) *Yesode ha-tebunah u-migdal ha-emunah* (*The Foundations of Reason and the Tower of Faith*), an encyclopedia of science; parts are lost.

Hebrew text and Spanish translation, J. M. Millás Vallicrosa, 1952.

(3) *Sod ha-'ibbur* (*The Secret of Intercalation*), a study of the Hebrew calendar, written in 1123. Maimonides praised it as by far the best book on the subject (Commentary on Mishnah, *'Arakhin* 2:2). Hebrew text, ed. H. Filipowski, 1851.

(4) *Megillat ha-megalleh* (*Scroll of the Revealer*), an eschatological and astrological work, written during the 1120s. According to it, the messianic era might begin by 1136, and the resurrection would take place in 1448 or 1493. Hebrew text, ed. A. Poznanski, 1924; Catalan translation, J. M. Millás Vallicrosa, 1929.

(5) *Epistle to Rabbi Judah ben Barzillai,* a defense of astrology, written ca. 1120. Abraham barHiyya had advised a student to delay his wedding for one hour in order to avoid the unpropitious influence of Mars. Judah ben Barzillai, the eminent talmudist, protested that such deference to astrology would amount to sorcery and idolatry. The wedding was not delayed, but Abraham wrote this epistle in defense of his view, arguing that astrological considerations are analogous to medical ones. Hebrew text, ed. A. Z. Schwarz, 1917.

(6) *Hegyon ha-nefesh ha-'aṣubah* (*The Meditation of the Sad Soul*), a philosophic study of human nature, discussing the place of human beings in the creation, the good life, repentance (including an analysis of *Jonah*), and the future world. While often described as neo-Platonic, it also reflects Aristotelian, Kalamic, and other influences. Hebrew text, ed. E. Freimann, 1860; G. Wigoder, 1971. English translation, G. Wigoder, 1969.

(7) *Ṣurat ha-areṣ ve-tabnit ha-shamavim* (*The Form of the Earth and the Figure of the Heavens*), a work on cosmography, written in 1132; part 1 of*Hokhmat ha-hizzavon* (*Science of Astronomy*). Hebrew text, Basel 1546 (abridged), Offenbach 1720; Spanish translation, J. M. Millás Vallicrosa, 1956.

(8) *Ḥeshbon mahalekhot ha-kokhabim* (*The Calculation of Astral Motions*), a textbook on Ptolemaic astronomy, written in 1136; part 2 of *Hokhmat ha-hizzayon*. Hebrew text and Spanish translation, J. M. Millás Vallirosa, 1959; this edition includes Abraham bar Ḥiyya's astronomical tables, *Luḥot ha-Nasi* (*The Prince's Tables*).

In addition, Abraham barḤiyya was active in translating scientific works from Arabic into Latin, mostly in collaboration with Plato of Tivoli.

WARREN ZEV HARVEY

Bibliography

Abraham barḤayya. *The Meditation of the Sad Soul*. Trans. and with an intro. by G. Wigoder. London, 1969.

Millás Vallicrosa, J. M. *Estudios sobre historia de la ciencia española*. Barcelona, 1949. 219–62.

——. *Nuevos estudios sobre historia de la ciencia española*. Barcelona, 1969. 183–90.

Sarfatti, G. B. *Mathematical Terminology in Hebrew Scientific Literature of the Middle Ages* (Hebrew). Jerusalem, 1968. 61–129.

Sirat, C. A *History of Jewish Philosophy in the Middle Ages*. Cambridge, 1985. 94–104, 425.

ABRAVANEL, ISAAC (1437–1508)

Isaac Abravanel was one of the most important Jewish writers and statesmen of his age. His grandfather Samuel was already prominent in the reign of Juan I, and was *contador mayor* of Enrique III and treasurer of the queen. He converted to Christianity, however (long before the pogroms of 1491), before attaining these high posts, and took the name Juan Sánchez de Sevilla. Eventually, he determined to return to Judaism, and in order to accomplish this had to flee to Portugal with some of his sons, while others remained as Christians in Castile. Isaac Abravanel thus grew up in Portugal, where he eventually became a wealthy merchant in Lisbon (together with his father), at least from 1463 on. Ultimately he became a confidant and financier of the Duke of Braganza (ca. 1480) and banker to the king of Portugal, Afonso V. The death of that king brought a change in attitude toward the Jews under his successor, and in 1483 Abravanel fled to Castile.

He was able to obtain a minor role as tax farmer, but in 1485 his position and influence increased greatly when he was placed in charge of all the taxes of Cardinal Pedro González de Mendoza, prelate of Spain and *canciller mayor* of the kingdom. Later, Abravanel became contador mayor of the powerful Iñigo López de Mendoza (it should be mentioned that the Mendoza family, many of whom were themselves of *converso* origin, were always intimately involved with Jews). He was able to make substantial loans to the Catholic Monarchs, and on one occasion (1491) acted as financial agent for the queen.

When the edict of expulsion of the Jews came in 1492, Abravanel apparently used his influence to annul or at least delay it, but to no avail. He chose to be among the minority of Jews who left the land, and like all the other exiles, he was permitted to collect outstanding debts and take with him money and personal property.

From Spain he went to Italy, where he again attained important political prominence, and where he did most of his writing. His son Judah (known as León Hebreo) was the author of the famous *Dialoghi d'amore*.

Never a rabbi, Abravanel was a deeply religious person, with a "fundamentalist" zeal for Jewish tradition. He wrote various treatises, including important commentaries on the Bible, all in Hebrew. In these, and even more in what may be called his "theological" treatises, he displayed his opposition to Aristotelian and Muslim philosophy, more than to Maimonides, whom he greatly revered while still disagreeing cautiously with some of his views. Contrary to the teachings, rather, of the more rationalist followers of Maimonides (Gerson and others), Abravanel believed literally in creation ex nihilo, and in a literal understanding of miracles. Though he showed himself ultimately opposed to any attempt to establish "fundamental principles" of faith in the Bible, since all of it is divine, these two ideas were bound up with his understanding of God as omnipotent. Unlike Maimonides, he believed that man is the "final cause," or purpose, of the Creation, and that man's purpose is the contemplation of God (perhaps under scholastic influence). Again unlike Maimonides, he was also a believer in astrology.

His political attitudes, while not systematic enough to be called (as they have been) a "political philosophy," are of interest.

Abravanel played an important role in the messianic expectations of the generation of the exiles, and had a lasting influence on Jewish thought, and no less on later Christian thinkers.

It is believed that the *Panels of St. Vincent* of the Portuguese artist Nuño Gonçalves (ca. 1481) present an actual portrait of Abravanel, one of only two known portraits of a medieval Spanish Jew.

See also **Maimonides**

Further Reading

Netanyahu, B. *Don Isaac Abravanel.* Philadelphia, 1972.
Kellner, M. *Gersonides and his Cultural Despisers: Arama and Abravanel.* Charlottesville, Va. 1976.
Gomes, P. A. *Filosofia hebraico-portuguesa.* Porto, 1981.

NORMAN ROTH

ADAM DE LA HALLE
(ca. 1240–ca. 1285)

Dramatist and poet. Also called "Adam le Bossu" or "le Bossu d'Arras" (*bossu* 'awkward' or 'crippled'), Adam de la Halle lived and wrote in Arras during the last third of the 13th century. His modern reputation is based primarily on two plays: a satiric drama, the *Jeu de la feuillée* (1,099 octosyllabic lines), and a work often referred to as a comic opera, the *Jeu de Robin et Marion.* Since *feuillée* has been interpreted to mean the shelter of branches built to house the reliquary of Notre Dame at Pentecost, the *Jeu de la feuillée* is thought to have been composed for performance in the town of Arras for this festival. This first extant secular drama in French contains little plot, presenting mostly a succession of scenes that tease and ridicule forty-nine named male and female citizens of Arras. The humor of the play depends on exploiting character traits known to the audience, as well as proverbs and puns whose full meaning could be appreciated only by those familiar with the citizenry of Arras. Contemporary documents that contain the names of the characters in the play allow us to date the work to 1276 or 1277. It provides the earliest example on the French stage of the ridicule of the medical profession, which reached its height with Molièere. The extant manuscripts preserve some of the music for the songs included in the play.

Closely related to the pastourelle, the *Jeu de Robin et Marion* (780 octosyllabic lines) dramatizes the encounter of a shepherdess and a knight on a spring morning. When his advances are rebuffed, the knight kidnaps the young girl and carries her away on his horse after beating her friend Robin. However, Marion is soon released unharmed, and friends arrive to sing, dance, eat, and play games. Spoken dialogue alternates with singing. When first presented in Arras, the play was preceded by a short dramatic prologue, in which a pilgrim tells of his travels in Italy and says that everywhere he went he heard about a talented, gracious, and noble clerk, native of Arras, loved and honored by the count of Artois because of his poetic and musical talent. The pilgrim states that he visited Adam's tomb the year before and sings two of Adam's songs as examples of his talent.

In addition to the plays, Adam wrote thirty-six chansons, seventeen *jeux-partis*, sixteen rondeaux, five motets, a *congé*, and the first nineteen laisses of an epic poem, the *Roi de Sicile*. Fifteen of the seventeen *jeux-partis* by Adam were composed with Jehan Bretel, who alludes to Adam's superior education, his youth, and his loves. Before 1271, the date of Bretel's death, Adam was already well enough known to write *jeux-partis* with the prince of the Puy. While his chansons written in the tradition of the Provençal love lyric dwell on the suffering endured patiently by a lover whose lady appears indifferent to him, there is no reason to believe that they were based on true feelings.

Although Adam lived and wrote in Picardy for much of his life, the language of his songs reflects relatively few traits of the Picard dialect, whereas the speech of the characters in his plays relies more heavily on dialect and probably resembles the language used in Arras in the 13th century.

In 1276 or 1277, Adam wrote his *Congé* (farewell poem), one of three such poems composed by trouvères (the others are by Jehan Bodel d'Arras and Baude Fastoul). In 156 lines divided into strophes of twelve octosyllabic verses, Adam takes leave for Paris to continue his studies; he expresses his gratitude, good wishes, and regrets to the people of Arras. His departure is by choice and not due to disease, as with the other two *congés*. In *Feuillée*, he also mentions his imminent departure for Paris, though it is not possible to know if he ever actually went.

During his lifetime, Adam's fame stemmed equally from his musical and poetic skills. Many of his melodies and lyrics have been preserved in versions that often resemble each other more closely than is normally the case with trouvère compositions, implying perhaps that they may have been copied from one model even though such a model has not survived. In addition to the typical songs for one voice, Adam also wrote music for five motets for three voices, fourteen rondeaux, and two other refrain songs, suggesting that he probably knew how to read and write music, a rare phenomenon among the trouvères.

Even though he must be considered one of the most versatile poets and composers of his time, no document survives that dates any event in the life of this prolific artist. However, Baude Fastoul, another trouvère of Arras, mentions him in a work dated 1272. Adam died between January 7, 1285, the date of the death of Charles of Anjou, for whom Adam began to compose *Le Roi de Sicile*, and before February 2, 1289, the date on which the copyist Jean Madot, upon finishing a transcription of the *Roman de Troie*, boasts of being the nephew of Adam le Bossu, who had died recently far from Arras.

Further Reading

Adam de la Halle. *CEuvres complètes du trouvère Adam de la Halle: poésies et musique*, ed. Edmond de Coussemaker. Paris: A. Durand et Pedone-Lauriel, 1872.
——. *Le jeu de la feuillée*, ed. Ernest Langlois. Paris: Champion, 1965.
——. *Le jeu de Robin et Marion suivi du jeu du Pélerin*, ed. Ernest Langlois. Paris: Champion, 1965.
——. *Le jeu de la feuillée* and *Le jeu de Robin et de Marion*, in *Medieval French Plays*, trans. Richard Axton and John Stevens. New York: Barnes and Noble, 1971, pp. 205–302.
——. *The Chansons of Adam de la Halle*, ed. John Henry Marshall. Manchester: Manchester University Press, 1971.
——. *The Lyrics and Melodies of Adam de la Halle*, ed. and trans. Deborah H. Nelson; music ed. Hendrik van der Werf. New York: Garland, 1985.

DEBORAH H. NELSON

ADAM OF BREMEN
(fl. 2nd half of the 11th c.)

Author of the *Gesta Hammaburgensis ecclesiae Pontificum* (History of the Archbishops of Hamburg-Bremen), Adam of Bremen is widely regarded as one of the finest historians of the Early Middle Ages, yet little is known about the man himself beyond the hints and allusions embedded in his history and its extensive marginalia. These suggest that Adam was born in Franconia and was probably trained in the cathedral school of either Bamberg or Würzburg. In 1066/1067 he joined the church of Bremen, having been recruited by the mercurial and ambitious Archbishop Adalbert (1043–1072), who probably saw in him a means to improve the literary reputation of his see. By 1069, Adam was in charge of the cathedral school at Bremen, appearing in a document as *magister scolarum* (master of learning). Soon thereafter, Adam began working on his *Gesta*. In his search for information on the history of his church and its privileges, he drew upon—often quite critically—a wide range of sources including Carolingian hagiography, diplomata, papal letters, and the accounts of eyewitnesses such as King Sven II Estridsen of Denmark, one of Adam's principal informants on the peoples of and Christian missions to Scandinavia. Completed just after Adalbert's death (1072), the first "edition" of the history (1075/1076) was dedicated to Adalbert's successor Liemar (1072–1101). Adam continued to revise and augment his history in marginalia until his death in the early 1080s.

In the first two of the four books comprising his work, Adam traced the history of the church of Hamburg-Bremen from its foundation in the eighth century until 1043, attentively documenting the vicissitudes of its wealth and power in the region and the role played by its bishops in the politics of the German Reich. In book 3, Adam turned to the pontificate of Bishop Adalbert and rendered a portrait of his late patron that is remarkable for its subtle portrayal of this tragic, complex man; indeed, it is recognized as a milestone in medieval biography. Having repeatedly highlighted his church's leading role in the conversion of the northern peoples to Christianity, Adam devoted the whole of book 4 to detailed descriptions of the geography, people, and customs of the Scandinavian lands as well as the progress of missionary efforts in those areas. Although perhaps intended to aid and inspire later missionaries, Adam's relatively balanced account of these non-Christian peoples makes his work a monument of medieval geographical writing and one of the most important sources of information concerning pre-Christian Scandinavia.

Further Reading

Adam of Bremen. *History of the Archbishops of Hamburg-Bremen*, trans. F. J. Tschan. New York: Columbia University Press, 1959.
——. *Magistri Adam Bremensis Gesta Hammaburgensis Ecclesiae Pontificum*, ed. B. Schmeidler. Monumenta Germaniae istorica. Scriptores Rerum Germanicarum 2. Hannover: Hahn, 1917.
Misch, Georg. *Geschichte der Autobiographie*, vol. 3, pt. 1. Frankfurt am Main: G. Schulte-Bulmke, 1959, pp. 168–214.

Theuerkauf, G. "Die Hamburgische Kirchengeschichte Adams von Bremen. Gesellschaftsformen und Weltbilder im elften Jahrhundert." In *Historiographia Mediaevalis . . . Festschrift für Franz-Josef Schmale*, ed. Dieter Berg and Hans-Werner Goetz. Darmstadt: Wissenschaftliche Buchgesellschaft, 1988, pp. 118–137.

WILLIAM NORTH

ÆLFRIC (ca. 945–ca. 1015)

Abbot of Eynsham, sometimes called "Grammaticus" ("the grammarian"), the greatest writer of English prose before the Norman Conquest and the leading scholar of his day. His contributions to the literary and religious life of 10th-century England mirror the achievements of his more illustrious predecessors from the 8th and 9th centuries, Bede and King Alfred the Great. Like Bede, whom he often consulted as a source, Ælfric produced a substantial body of homiletic and hagiographic writings. But following the example of King Alfred, Ælfric broke away from Latin, the traditional language of the church, and wrote primarily in English in order to reach a wider audience.

There seems little reason to doubt Ælfric's largely unnoticed autobiographical statement in his *Grammar* that he studied under and was ordained by Dunstan, a key figure in the Benedictine Reform who became archbishop of Canterbury in 960 and who is widely credited with restoring monastic life after its virtual demise by the middle of the 10th century ("If you were to say, 'Who taught you?' I would say 'Dunstan.' 'Who ordained you?' 'He ordained me.'"). If this statement is true, Ælfric's date of birth would almost certainly have to be placed some ten years earlier than the date of 955 given in virtually all other standard biographical references. No doubt surrounds Ælfric's later studies with another leading figure of monastic reform, Æthelwold, at the Benedictine monastery at Winchester. In 987, three years after Æthelwold's death, Ælfric obtained a position as monk and masspriest at Cernel Abbey in what is now Cerne Abbas, Dorset. Within a few years he had achieved a reputation as the preeminent literary figure of the Benedictine revival.

At Cernel Ælfric developed a remarkable and innovative "rhythmical prose" style, admirably suited for oral delivery, that resembles OE verse in its use of paired phrases linked by alliteration but differs from it in matters of tone, style, diction, and metrical constraints. Ælfric avoids, for example, the use of the kenning, *kend heiti*, *ókend heiti*, and other metaphoric statements commonly associated with OE heroic poetry and strives instead for "ordinary English speech" (*usitatam Anglicam sermocinationem*). Hickes praised Ælfric's prose as *purus*, *suavis*, *et regularis* ("pure, smooth, and orderly"), and W.P. Ker hailed Ælfric as "the great master of prose in all its forms." Yet his considerable skills as a prose stylist were undoubtedly of secondary importance to Ælfric, whose central and abiding literary concern (as John Pope has noted) was the instruction of the adult laity, most of whom knew no Latin, in the Christian faith.

Ælfric's seven chief works—two volumes of *Catholic Homilies* or *Sermones catholici*, two additional sets of homilies based in part on his previous writings, *De temporibus anni*, the *Grammar*, and the *lives of Saints*—form a reasonably complete educational program aimed at providing the spiritual instruction Ælfric deemed necessary for salvation. His literary canon builds upon the program of learning instituted by King Alfred a century earlier but differs from that program by virtue of its more tightly focused spiritual emphasis, its greater comprehensiveness, and its stricter accuracy in rendering Latin texts.

Ælfric reveals the impetus for his literary career by quoting in the preface to his first major work Christ's great commission to his disciples "to instruct and teach all people the things that he himself had taught them" (Matt. 28:19–20); Ælfric apparently patterned his life and writings not only upon this injunction but also upon the more dire scriptural text he cites in the same breath, namely that the Lord's servants must themselves face perdition if they fail to warn and exhort the unrighteous (Ezek. 33:8). This divine mandate lends to Ælfric's literary activities a spirit of personal mission and urgency, and this same spirit informs the inchoate program of instruction promulgated by King Alfred, which Ælfric both emulates and augments in his own writings. Ælfric borrows from King Alfred the revolutionary idea of using the vernacular to broaden the reach of instruction to "all people," which in practice meant reaching out to the uneducated majority of his countrymen who knew no Latin.

Yet Ælfric—traditional, conservative, and orthodox by temperament—proved a somewhat reluctant revolutionary. He persistently worried about the appropriateness of making Latin texts generally available to the laity, who might, for example, misconstrue scripture and believe that they might have four wives just as the patriarch Jacob did. Ælfric vowed on several occasions that he would cease from translating lest the pearls of Christ fall into disrespect, yet at the end of his career he apparently accepted the usefulness of his writings and, far from retracting them, conveniently enumerated them and in effect canonized them in the *Letter to Sigeweard*.

In addition to following Alfred's lead in translating, Ælfric turned to other sources of inspiration, such as Augustine's *De catechizandis rudibus* and *De doctrina christiana*, for more detailed guidance in establishing the range of texts and the survey of doctrine needed to fulfill the catechetical dimensions of Christ's commission to his disciples. Evangelical doctrine, therefore, forms the cornerstone of Ælfric's instructional mission, and, to that end, Ælfric composed his first major work, the *Catholic Homilies* (also known as the *Sermones catholici*), which appeared in two separate volumes, issued respectively in 989 and 992. Each set of the *Catholic Homilies* contains a series of 40 sermons arranged according to the calendar of the church year (beginning with Christmas and ending with the second Sunday in Advent) and designed for distribution among the priests of England as preaching texts for alternate years of the liturgical calendar. The texts provide instruction not only in such fundamental topics as the Creed, the Lord's Prayer, the Ten Commandments, the plan for salvation, the story of Christ, and other matters appropriate to the catechumenate, but also in more theologically advanced matters involving patristic exegesis and allied forms of allegorical and typological interpretation of scriptural texts.

Viking attacks, political tumult, the approach of the year 1000, and the disastrous reign of King Æthelred II doubtless contributed to the millenarian concerns voiced in Ælfric's preface to the first series of the *Catholic Homilies*. Yet his writings show less alarm for death at the hands of the Vikings or the coming end of the world (which, Ælfric points out, though soon, might still be distant by human measures of time) than for *gedwyld*, "error." *Gedwyld* for Ælfric meant more particularly religious error, especially the kind spread in unorthodox, apocryphal, or misleading religious writings, such as the popular *Vision of St. Paul* or works prohibited by the Gelasian Decretals, including narratives about the Virgin's birth or a certain *Passio sancti Georgii* that featured fantastic accounts of St. George's seven years of torture, the fragmentation of his body, and his several preliminary deaths and resuscitations.

The *Catholic Homilies* and later writings attempt to provide sound spiritual instruction, free from error and heresy, as weapons for the salvation of the English nation. Ælfric marshals the best patristic authorities available to him, and his corpus of writings offers an epitome of ecclesiastical thought as transmitted through the channels of Carolingian learning and the Benedictine Reform. His translations include the works of Augustine, Gregory the Great, Bede, Jerome, Smaragdus, Isidore, Ambrose, Leo the Great, Cassiodorus, Sulpicius Severus, a version of the *Vitae patrum*, Hilduin of St. Denis, Abbo of Fleury, Donatus, Priscian, a treatise on liturgy by Amalarius, and a host of other sources. Ælfric turns to his patristic authorities, particularly Augustine, Gregory, and Bede, for his exegetical homilies, which compose the great bulk of his *Catholic Homilies*, some 55 or so homilies out of 80, and he uses these and other sources for his other sermons, which include about seventeen saints' lives, expositions of the liturgy, and more thematically diverse works that encompass such general topics as creation and eschatological concerns.

Ælfric refers to the *Catholic Homilies* as a translation from Latin books, sometimes rendered literally but sometimes paraphrased to capture the sense rather than the wording of his source. Recent scholarship confirms Ælfric's enormous debt to the homiliary of Paul the Deacon, who edited and composed nearly 250 homilies at the request of Charlemagne for use throughout the Carolingian Empire. Yet those who closely scrutinize Ælfric's Latin sources now realize that he frequently consults other authorities, evaluates differences, selectively edits, conflates, and condenses to avoid tedium, amplifies to explicate an obscurity, and sometimes so deviates from his sources that his work approaches originality. As Pope has observed, the "thought is scrupulously traditional yet fully digested and feelingly his own" (1967: 150).

Nowhere is this more apparent than in Ælfric's famous *Sermon on the Sacrifice on Easter Day* (*Sermo de sacrificio in die Pascae*, item xv in *Catholic Homilies* II), the first and most controversial text ever printed in OE. Published in 1566 or 1567, Ælfric's sermon arguably marks the beginning of English studies, securing for the study of the English language an importance that had previously been accorded only to the classical languages. Printed by Archbishop Matthew Parker as ancient testimony of the continuity between the religious beliefs of the Protestant reformers and the Anglo-Saxons, particularly with regard to eucharistic teaching, Ælfric's sermon seemingly offered early evidence against the "bodely presence" of Christ in the eucharist or, as later Protestant theologians argued, against the doctrine of transubstantiation.

Although Ælfric's Easter homily raises a number of doctrinal questions, the second set of *Catholic Homilies* does not typically differ from the first by showing a keener interest in these matters of theological controversy. Ælfric instead seems to shift emphasis away from exegesis toward narrative. The second set of *Catholic Homilies*, for example, contains far more narratives of saints' lives, the Bible is more often treated as a story rather than as a text for analysis, and the narrative form itself receives sharper dramatic emphasis through Ælfric's initial and sporadic experiments with rhythmical prose.

Ælfric sustains and strengthens these narrative and stylistic impulses in his third major set of original translations, his *Lives of Saints*, which also contains 40 sermons ordered according to the church calendar, now predominantly cast in rhythmical prose. The set recounts the lives and passions of those saints honored by monks in their Latin services, but Ælfric's English translations make these lives available to a wider, presumably lay audience, including his patron, Æthelweard, who commissioned the work. Ælfric treats Old Testament saints by translating and paraphrasing sections of the book of Kings and Maccabees; he traces the passions of Roman martyrs, such as Julian, Sebastian, and George; and he honors the English saints Alban, Æthelthryth, Swithun, Oswald, and Edmund.

Even if his numerous patristic and hagiographic translations had not survived, Ælfric's reputation would have been secured for posterity solely by the survival of his brilliant biblical translations. He translated or adapted sections of Genesis, Numbers, Joshua, Judges, Kings, Esther, Judith, and Maccabees; his articulate and graceful translations of the pericopes (scriptural readings) that precede many of the *Catholic Homilies* contrast with the more awkward and mundane renderings found in the nearly contemporary West Saxon Gospels. The same ease and clarity of expression also mark Ælfric's other writings, particularly his letters and even his scientific writings, such as the *De temporibus anni*, which deals with astronomy, measures of time, the computation of Easter, and atmospheric phenomena.

Apart from his religious writings directed largely toward the educational needs of the laity, Ælfric's educational program also provided basic instructional texts for the study of Latin, presumably for future clerics, though here too the importance of the vernacular makes itself felt: Ælfric's is the first Latin grammar written in English, and his short conversation piece for boys to practice their Latin, the *Colloquy*, survives in one manuscript with a continuous interlinear English gloss. In his *Grammar* Ælfric translates and simplifies the *Excerptiones de Prisciano* (an intermediate grammar) and augments it with excerpts from Isidore's *Etymologiae*, biblical quotations, and a collection of paradigms in order to make grammar accessible to younger pupils.

In 1005 Ælfric was chosen to be the first abbot at Eynsham Monastery, about fifteen miles outside of Oxford. There he remembered his former teacher by composing a life of Æthelwold in Latin, and he also wrote a guide for his monks by abridging Æthelwold's *De consuetudine monachorum*. Other writings from this period include letters and homilies, such as *De creatore et creatura* and *De sex aetatibus mundi*, as well as reworkings of individual homilies and earlier collections of homilies. None of his works can be securely dated after about 1010, and he may have died between 1010 and 1020. The success of Ælfric's educational mission can be partially measured by the large number of surviving Anglo-Saxon manuscripts that preserve his writings; these manuscripts bear witness to the esteem of his contemporaries and to those scribes and scholars who continued to copy his writings for the next 150 years.

See also **Æthelwold of Winchester; Alfred the Great; Bede the Venerable; Dunstan of Canterbury; Paul the Deacon**

Further Reading

Primary Sources

Belfour, Algernon O., ed. and trans. *Twelfth-Century Homilies in MS. Bodley 343*. EETS o.s. 137. London: Kegan Paul, Trench, Trübner, 1909

Crawford, S.J., ed. *The Old English Version of the Heptateuch, Ælfric's Treatise on the Old and New Testament and His Preface to Genesis*. EETS o.s. 160. London: Oxford University Press, 1922

Godden, Malcolm, ed. *Ælfric's Catholic Homilies: The Second Series*. EETS s.s. 5. London: Oxford University Press, 1979

Pope, John C., ed. *Homilies of Ælfric: A Supplementary Collection*. EETS o.s. 259, 260. London: Oxford University Press, 1967–68

Skeat, Walter W., ed. *Ælfric's lives of Saints*. EETS o.s. 76, 82, 94, 114. London: Trübner, 1881–1900. Repr. in 2 vols. London: Oxford University Press, 1966

Thorpe, Benjamin, ed. *The Homilies of the Anglo-Saxon Church: The First Part, Containing the Sermones Catholici, or Homilies of Ælfric, in the Original Anglo-Saxon, with an English Version*. 2 vols. London: Richard & John E. Taylor, 1844–46. Repr. New York: Johnson Reprint, 1971.

Secondary Sources

Clemoes, Peter A.M. "The Chronology of Ælfric's Works." In *The Anglo-Saxons: Studies in Some Aspects of Their History and Culture Presented to Bruce Dickins*, ed. Peter A.M. Clemoes. London: Bowes & Bowes, 1959, pp. 212–47

Corrected repr. *The Chronology of Ælfric's Works*. OEN Subsidia 5. Binghamton: CEMERS, 1980

Clemoes, Peter A.M. "Ælfric." In *Continuations and Beginnings: Studies in Old English literature*, ed. E. Stanley. London: Nelson, 1966, pp. 176–209

Cross, J.E. "Ælfric—Mainly on Memory and Creative Method in Two Catholic Homilies." *SN* 41 (1969): 135–55

Hill, Joyce. "Ælfric and Smaragdus." *ASE* 21 (1992): 203–37

Hurt, James. *Ælfric*. New York: Twayne, 1972

Law, Vivien. "Anglo-Saxon England: Ælfric's *Excerptiones de arte grammatica anglice*." *Histoire épistémologie langage* 9 (1987): 47–71

Leinbaugh, Theodore H. "Ælfric's *Sermo de sacrificio in die Pascae*: Anglican Polemic in the Sixteenth and Seventeenth Centuries." In *Anglo-Saxon Scholarship: The First Three Centuries*, ed. Carl Berkhout and Milton McC. Gatch. Boston: Hall, 1982, pp. 51–68

Leinbaugh, Theodore H. "The Sources for Ælfric's Easter Sermon: The History of the Controversy and a New Source." *N&Q* n.s. 33 (1986): 294–311

Reinsma, Luke M. *Ælfric: An Annotated Bibliography*. New York: Garland, 1987 [excellent bibliographic study]

Smetana, Cyril L. "Ælfric and the Early Medieval Homiliary." *Traditio* 15 (1959): 163–204

Szarmach, Paul E. "Ælfric As Exegete: Approaches and Examples in the Study of the *Sermones catholici*." In *Hermeneutics and Medieval Culture*, ed. Patrick J. Gallacher and Helen Damico. Albany: SUNY Press, 1989, pp. 237–47

Wilcox, Jonathan, ed. *Ælfric's Prefaces*. Durham Medieval Texts 9. Durham: Jasprint, 1994

Zettel, Patrick H. "Saints' Lives in Old English: Latin Manuscripts and Vernacular Accounts: Ælfric." *Peritia* 1 (1982): 17–37.

THEODORE LEINBAUGH

ÆTHELWOLD OF WINCHESTER
(ca. 904/09–984)

Influential monastic teacher and administrator, and a principal initiator of the English Benedictine revival of the second half of the 10th century. Born at Winchester perhaps between 904 and 909, Æthelwold passed several years, probably the late 920ls and much of the 930s, at the court of King Æthelstan (924–39), enjoying the royal favor that was to characterize his career. Sometime between 934 and 939, in company with Dunstan, he was ordained priest by Ælfheah, bishop of Winchester. Æthelwold subsequently studied with Dunstan at Glastonbury Abbey, where he became a monk and was later appointed *decanus* (a position of authority over other monks). Desiring to experience reformed continental Benedictine practice at first hand, Æthelwold was prevented from traveling overseas by King Eadred (946–55), who instead appointed him (ca. 954) abbot of the derelict monastery of Abingdon, which Æthelwold restored energetically: he personally participated in the building work, sustaining serious bodily injury in the process. From Abingdon he sent the monk Osgar to observe Benedictinism as practiced at Fleury, and he summoned to Abingdon monks from Corbie who provided instruction in liturgical chant. Attention to continental models continued to mark Æthelwold's later career.

In 963 Æthelwold became bishop of Winchester, an office he held until his death and in which he made a profound impact upon contemporary religious life. More severe than his fellow reformers Dunstan and Oswald, he swiftly (in 964) expelled the secular clergy resident at his cathedral and at New Minster, Winchester, and replaced them with monks. Subsequently he founded or refounded monasteries at several locations, notably Peterborough (966), Ely (970), and Thorney (972). He worked in close harmony with King Edgar (957–75), whose tutor he had been and whose royal palace stood close to Æthelwold's cathedral. At the request of Edgar and his queen, Ælfthryth, Æthelwold translated the Rule of St. Benedict into OE. He was chiefly responsible for compiling the Latin document known as the *Regularis concordia*, aimed at standardizing religious observance in the English monasteries and prompted by a council convened by King Edgar at Winchester sometime between ca. 970 and ca. 973. Æthelwold is justifiably believed to have been the author of a vernacular account of the monastic revival known as "King Edgar's Establishment of Monasteries," which he probably intended to serve as the preface to his translation of the Benedictine Rule.

Æthelwold's work at Winchester included the rebuilding of the cathedral, which was equipped with a large organ remarkable for its time. He was responsible for reform of the liturgy and may have composed offices and prayers that survive in service books of his own time and later. Under Æthelwold Winchester became a major center of manuscript production, its most sumptuous accomplishment being the Benedictional made for Æthelwold himself by the scribe Godenan. A deeply learned man, Æthelwold presided over a monastic school at Winchester whose most distinguished students included his biographers, the prolific writers Wulfstan of Winchester and Ælfric. His students' work ensured the continuation of Æthelwold's influence beyond his death on 1 August 984. He was buried in the crypt of Winchester Cathedral and translated to the choir in 996.

See also **Ælfric; Dunstan of Canterbury**

Further Reading

Primary Sources

Winterbottom, Michael, ed. *Three Lives of English Saints*. Toronto: Pontifical Institute, 1972 [includes the lives of Æthelwold by Wulfstan and Ælfric]

Wulfstan of Winchester. *The Life of St Æthelwold*. Ed. Michael Lapidge and Michael Winterbottom. Oxford: Clarendon, 1991.

Secondary Sources

Gneuss, Helmut. "The Origin of Standard Old English and Æthelwold's School at Winchester." *ASE* 1 (1972): 63–83

Gretsch, Mechthild. "Æthelwold's Translation of the *Regula Sancti Benedicti* and Its Latin Exemplar." *ASE* 3 (1974): 125–51

Lapidge, Michael. "Three Latin Poems from Æthelwold's School at Winchester." *ASE* 1 (1972): 85–137

Lapidge, Michael. "The Hermeneutic Style in Tenth-Century Anglo-Latin Literature." *ASE* 4 (1975): 67–111, esp. 85–90

Whitelock, Dorothy. "The Authorship of the Account of King Edgar's Establishment of Monasteries." In *Philological Essays: Studies in Old and Middle English Literature in Honour of Herbert Dean Merits*, ed. James L. Rosier. The Hague: Mouton, 1970, pp. 125–36

Yorke, Barbara, ed. *Bishop Æthelwold: His Career and Influence*. Woodbridge: Boydell, 1988.

TIMOTHY GRAHAM

AFONSO III, KING OF PORTUGAL
(1210–1279)

The second son of Afonso II and Uracca of Castile, Afonso III was born in Coimbra on 5 May 1210. The fifth king of Portugal, he succeeded his brother Sancho II and reigned from early in 1248 to his death on 16 February 1279.

Before becoming king, Afonso lived first in Denmark and then in France, where in 1238 or 1239 he married the wealthy widow Matilda, heiress of the Count of Boulogne. Afonso was influential at the court of his maternal aunt, Queen Blanche, widow of Louis VIII and mother of Louis IX. While in France he became involved in Portuguese internal affairs, where his older brother was under attack by clergy and nobles. Pope Innocent IV, in a bull of 24 July 1245, effectively deposed Sancho II by reducing him to king in name only and by turning over the government to his younger brother, Afonso, Count of Boulogne. Innocent IV instructed the Portuguese to receive and obey Afonso as soon as he arrived in Portugal and to ignore the orders of Sancho II. After the pope issued his bull, a delegation of Portuguese—a number of whom had testified against Sancho II at the Council of Lyons—visited Paris, where they swore obedience to Afonso. They also exacted a series of promises from the future monarch to respect the Church, to honor the privileges and customs of Portugal, and to promote justice.

Arriving in Portugal in early 1246, Afonso took part in the civil war against supporters of the king. After Sancho II died in Toledo in January 1248, Afonso III was crowned king. The new monarch renewed the policies of Portugal's earlier monarchs by asserting authority wherever possible and by taking a hard line with the privileged classes when their immunities and prerogatives interfered with the royal treasury or administration. Early in his reign, Afonso III took up the task of driving the Muslims from their isolated strongholds in southwestern Portugal. The time was propitious for such a move. Fernando III of Castile, with the aid of the Portuguese military orders and some Portuguese nobles, had been campaigning successfully against the Muslim kingdoms in Andalucía. Seville would fall to Christian forces in November 1248. Afonso II personally led the drive to oust the Muslims from the Algarve. In March 1249 he captured Faro. Soon, Albufeira and Silves, along with a number of lesser towns and fortresses, fell to the Portuguese. This completed the ouster of Muslim military forces from what was to be the limits of modern Portugal. In 1251 Afonso II continued his campaign—this time to the east of the Guadiana River in territory that the Castilians regarded as their preserve. Castile, in the mean time, claimed parts of the Algarve. Armed conflict soon broke out between Portugal and Castile over these disputed territories.

In 1252 Alfonso X "el Sabio" (the Wise) ascended the Castilian throne. A year later, a truce was arranged between the two kings. It was resolved that Afonso III would marry Beatriz of Castile, the illegitimate daughter of Alfonso X. The marriage took place in 1253. In addition, it was decided that the administration of the newly conquered kingdom of the Algarve and the lands east of the Guadiana would be Portugal's but the usufruct of these territories would remain in the hands of Alfonso X until the firstborn son of the marriage between Afonso III and Beatriz reached the age of seven.

Unfortunately, there were a number of difficulties in implementing this marriage arrangement. Beatriz was very young and was related to Afonso III within the fourth degree of consanguinity. But most importantly, Afonso III was already married to Matilda, Countess of Boulogne, who was living in France. Soon Matilda was complaining to the pope about her husband's bigamous marriage. Although Pope Alexander IV placed under interdict those parts of Portugal where the king was residing, he was unable to persuade Afonso III to leave his young bride.

Matilda's death in 1258 helped resolve some of the Portuguese monarch's difficulties. But papal opposition to the marriage continued, as did the interdict. The bishops and cathedral chapters of Portugal came to the king's defense. In 1260—by which time Beatriz had already borne two children to Afonso—they pleaded with Pope Urban IV to lift the interdict and legitimize the children. They argued that the abandonment of Beatriz by Afonso would lead to war with Castile, and they claimed that ecclesiastical penalties were causing spiritual harm and scandal in Portugal. Finally, in 1263, after a visit to Rome by a delegation of Portuguese bishops, and after much lobbying by European leaders such as Louis IX of France and the Duke of Anjou, the request for the necessary dispensations and legitimizations was granted.

The birth in 1261 of Dinis, Afonso III's third child by Beatriz (the first was a girl, the second a boy who died in infancy), provided the necessary ingredient for the resolution of the controversy between Castile and Portugal. By the Treaty of Badajoz in 1267 Alfonso X of Castile renounced his rights to the kingdom of the Algarve, while Afonso III gave up Portuguese claims to the territories between the Guadiana and Guadalquivir Rivers. Portugal, however, would have authority over the territory to the west of the mouth of the Guadiana and its confluence with the Caia River.

In addition to the reconquest of the Algarve and the resolution of Portugal's boundaries with Castile, several other major accomplishments marked Afonso III's reign. Afonso promoted greater participation by towns and their officials in Portuguese national life. At Leiria in 1254, for the first time in the nation's history, representatives of the cities participated in the *cortes* (parliament) along with the nobility and the higher clergy. Laws were also enacted to protect commoners from abuse at the hands of the privileged classes. Furthermore, Afonso III restructured the country's monetary system. Charters issued during his reign show that a moneyed economy was replacing barter. Fixed monetary taxes replaced the custom of paying in kind. At the *cortes* of Coimbra in 1261, Afonso III agreed to devalue the currency only once during a reign instead of every seven years, as was becoming the practice. The monarch favored Lisbon over Coimbra as the kingdom's chief commercial and administrative center, and he increased the royal treasury by promoting the country's economy.

Afonso III continued his predecessors' policy of strengthening royal prerogatives. This was accomplished chiefly through the use of the *inquiricões gerais* (general inquiries) and *confirmacões* (confirmations). In 1258, in response to complaints from royal officials as well as commoners, the crown sent investigative teams into the *comarcas* (districts) of Entre Douro e Minho, Trás-os-Montes, and Beira Alta to examine titles to lands claimed by nobility and clergy. Sworn testimony was taken to determine if the rights of the crown were being respected. Afonso III was anxious to curb the power of the old nobility and the higher clergy, especially those in the comarca of Entre Douro e Minho, the oldest and most populous region of Portugal. These investigations revealed a wide range of violations, including the usurpation of the royal patrimony, evasion of taxes, and abuses of commoners by the privileged estates, both secular and clerical. Laws were promulgated to deal with these infractions and they soon sparked fresh opposition from clergy and nobility.

In 1267 a number of Portuguese prelates traveled to Rome and presented Pope Clement IV with an extensive list of grievances. They accused Afonso III of condoning, even encouraging, violence in civil administration, of using unfair practices in his business dealings, and of infringing on ecclesiastical liberties. The Portuguese monarch answered these charges with testimonials from the towns of the kingdom that defended his actions and praised his administration. In addition, in 1273, during the meeting of the cortes at Santarém, Afonso III established a commission to investigate his acts and those of his officials. But the papacy was not impressed by the results of this investigation, which maintained that there had been little wrongdoing. In 1275 Pope Gregory X ordered that the king correct abuses and promise not to repeat them under pain of a series of penalties. These penalties would be invoked in stages, beginning in 1277, and would progress from local interdict, to excommunication, to a general interdict for the kingdom, to freeing the Portuguese from obedience to their king. And, indeed, by the end of 1277, Afonso III had been excommunicated and the kingdom placed under interdict. Soon, minor revolts broke out against the king in which Afonso III's son and successor, Dinis, took part. In January 1279, a month before his death, Afonso III made his peace with the Church and with his son.

See also **Alfonso X, El Sabio, King of Castile and León; Blanche of Castile**

Further Reading

Livermore, H. V. *A History of Portugal.* Cambridge, U.K., 1977.
Serrão, J. V. *História de Portugal.* Lisbon, vol. 1 1977.
Mattoso, J. (ed.) *História de Portugal,* Lisbon, vol. 2 1993.

FRANCIS A. DUTRA

ALAIN DE LILLE (ca. 1115/20–1203)

Known throughout the later Middle Ages as *Doctor universalis*, Alain was probably born in the city of Lille (Nord), though the Île-de-la-Cité in Paris has also been proposed. He became a Cistercian shortly before his death; when his body at Cîteaux was exhumed in 1960, his age was put in the eighties, and his height at about 5 feet.

An anecdotal life sometimes appended to commentaries and frequently found in early printed editions of the *Parabolae* is late and untrustworthy. We have no contemporary record of where Alain studied, or of any ecclesiastical benefits he enjoyed. His early literary and theological works, however, imply a Paris training, and reliable 13th-century sources list him among the masters there. Study before 1150 at the Benedictine abbey of Bec has been suggested, but there is no proof.

Alain seems to have been based in the southwest by the 1160s and to have written extensively against the Cathars in that region. Manuscripts of his works often call him Alainus de Podio, implying a connection with Le Puy, and two 13th-century manuscripts call him Alain of Montpellier. His *De fide catholica contra haereticos* was dedicated to Guilhem VIII, count of Montpellier (r. 1172–1202); in four books, it argues successively against Cathars, Waldensians, Jews, and Muslims. His *Distinctiones dictionum theologicarum* was dedicated to Abbot Ermengaud of Saint-Gilles (r. 1179–95). The *Liber poenitentialis* is dedicated to Archbishop Henry Sully of Bourges (r. 1183–93), and his brief commentary on the Song of Songs was written for the prior of Cluny.

With a few exceptions, the dates and chronology of Alain's works are far from certain, but the earliest are generally thought to be the *Regulae caelestis iuris* (ca. 1160), also known as *De maximis theologicis*, which treated theology as an exact science, with scientific rules based on geometry, and the summa *Quoniam homines* (1160–65), an incomplete work discussing God and the Trinity, angels and humanity, according to the rules of logic. Some themes are repeated in the brief *De virtutibus et vitiis et de donis Spiritus Sancti*. His shorter theological works include numerous *Sermones diversi*, commentaries on the Lord's Prayer and the Apostles' and Nicene creeds, several short pieces on angels, including *De sex alis cherubim* (sometimes accompanied by a drawing), and the rules of celestial law, which made use of geometrical principles in its discussion of the heavens. A few hymns are also ascribed to Alain of which the best known is *Omnis mundi creatura*.

The Latin *Parabolae* are a collection of maxims in elegiac verse, similar in approach to the *Distichs* of Cato and also designed for use in Latin classes in the schools. They were frequently copied from the 12th through the 15th century, and early printed editions are common.

All of Alain's major works enjoyed wide European circulation throughout the Middle Ages. Many were innovative tools for clergy. His *Liber poenitentialis* built on the tradition of pentitential canons to present the first known manual for confessors. The *Ars praedicandi*, which applied rhetorical methods and techniques to the construction of forty-eight sample sermons, is the earliest known preaching manual. And the *Distinctiones dictionum theologicarum* was an alphabetical index of biblical words covering scriptural and theological topics, with appropriate quotations.

The earliest of Alain's literary works is usually considered to be the *De planctu Naturae*, written probably before 1171. Like Boethius's De *consolatione Philosophiae*, it is written in the mixture of verse and prose known as Menippean satire. The Goddess Nature, God's vicar, appears to the dreaming poet, robed in all creation, with signs of the zodiac in her crown and a flowery meadow at her feet. Only her heart, where man resides, is muddied and torn. She explains to him the ways in which he has violated the natural order, in thoughts and in deeds. The vividness of the condemnation of "unnatural" sex in the fifth prose and metrum led some medieval commentators to describe the work as *Contra sodomitam*, but all vices, including the ultimate corruption, of language and thought, are described at length and condemned. Good love is the offshoot of Venus and Hymenaeus, god of marriage. Evil love, Jocus, was begotten when Venus abandoned Hymenaeus for Anti-Genius. The remedy is provided at the end of the work, when Hymenaeus appears with a train of virtues. Nature's vicar, Genius, then appears, order is restored, and the poet awakens. An epilogue, *Vix nodosum valeo*, on the superiority of virgins to matrons, has traditionally been ascribed to Alain but seems more of a parody than a conclusion to the work.

In the epic Latin poem *Anticlaudianus*, usually dated ca. 1179–83, Nature is viewed more philosophically, and the allegory is more clearly and consistently developed. Nature, assisted by Nous, explains the making of the physical universe, with much material on astronomy and cosmology drawn from Bernard Silvestris. The Seven Liberal Arts build her a chariot in which to explore the universe.

The *Anticlaudianus* and the *De planctu* survive in over 150 manuscripts each and were read throughout medieval Europe as part of the advanced rhetoric curriculum in schools and universities. The *Anticlaudianus* was translated into German by Henry of Mursbach and received a detailed commentary by Raoul de Longchamp ca. 1212–25. Several commentaries on the *Anticlaudianus* and the *De planctu Naturae* remain in manuscript.

The figures of Nature and Genius in the *De planctu*, and Nature in the *Anticlaudianus*, had great influence on allegorical dream visions in the later Middle Ages.

Guillaume de Lorris and Jean de Meun used them in the *Roman de la Rose*. It was to Genius that the lover made his confession in Gower's 14th-century *Confessio Amantis*. Alain is also frequently cited in later medieval treaties on dictamen and rhetoric as a model of modern poetic style.

See also **Bernard Silvestris; Gower, John**

Further Reading

Alain de Lille. *Opera omnia. PL* 210.
——. *Anticlaudianus: texte critique, avec une introduction et des tables*, ed. Robert Bossuat. Paris: Vrin, 1955.
——. *Alain de Lille: textes inédits avec une introduction sur sa vie et ses ceuvres*, ed. Marie-Thérése d'Alverny. Paris: Vrin, 1965.
——. *Anticlaudianus, or the Good and Perfect Man*, trans. James J. Sheridan. Toronto: Pontifical Institute of Mediaeval Studies, 1973.
——. *The Art of Preaching*, trans. Gillian R.Evans. Kalamazoo: Cistercian, 1981.
——. *Plaint of Nature*, trans. James J. Sheridan. Toronto: Pontifical Institute of Mediaeval Studies, 1980.
Evans, Gillian R. *Alan of Lille: The Frontiers of Theology in the Later Twelfth Century*. Cambridge: Cambridge University Press, 1983.
Haring, Nikolaus. "Alan of Lille, De *Planctu Natural.*" *Studi Medievali* ser. 3, 19 (1978): 797–879.
Jauss, Hans-Robert. "La transformation de la forme allégorique entre 1180 et 1240: d'Alain de Lille à Guillaume de Lorris." In *L'humanisme médiéval dans les litératures romanes du XIIe au XlVe siècle, colloque de Strasbourg, 1962*, ed. Anthime Fourrier. Paris: Klincksieck, 1964, pp. 107–46.
Raynaud de Lage, Guy. *Alain de Lille, poète du XIIe siècle*. Montreal: Institut d'Études MédiéVales, 1951.
Roussel, Henri, and François Suard, eds. *Alain de Lille, Gautier de Chtillon, Jakemart Gielée et leur temps: actes du Colloque de Lille, octobre 1978*. Lille, 1980.
Wetherbee, Winthrop P. *Platonism and Poetry in the Twelfth Century: The Literary Influence of the School of Chartres*. Princeton: Princeton University Press, 1972.
Ziolkowski, Jan. *Alan of Lille's Grammar of Sex: The Meaning of Grammar to a Twelfth-Century Intellectual*. Cambridge: Medieval Academy of America, 1985.

JEANNE E. KROCHALIS

ALBERTANUS OF BRESCIA
(c. 1190–1251 or after)

Albertanus, an author of legal treatises and addresses, was active in the political and professional life of the commune of Brescia in the first half of the thirteenth century. We know quite a lot about him from his appearances in official records (e.g., as a witness to a treaty or to a legal document) and from what he reveals in his own writings. A *causidicus*, or legal intermediary, perhaps with judicial powers (the precise function of this role is now unclear), he was regarded highly enough to be called on to serve his commune politically. On at least one occasion he was an aide to his fellow-Brescian

Emmanuel de Madiis when the latter went to Genoa as *podestà*. In 1238, he was entrusted with the captaincy of the fortress of Gavardo, to defend it against the forces of Emperor Frederick II in the struggle of the Lombard League against the imperial campaign in northern Italy. He lost, but only after a vigorous defense against an especially vicious siege.

Albertanus was the author of three Latin didactic treatises and five "sermons"—spoken addresses delivered before his fellow *causidici* at meetings of their lay confraternity. These works became widely—in fact, explosively—available immediately after their creation and are to be found all across Europe; Albertanus's works were read and copied until the eve of Reformation. His first (and longest) work is *De amore et dilectione Dei et proximi et aliarum return et de forma vitae*, completed while he was imprisoned at Cremona in 1238. Here he first set out his notion that social transformation is to be achieved through voluntary personal commitment to a "rule," an idea which would permeate all his subsequent writing. A sermon he delivered in Genoa in 1243 provides a prototype for his *De doctrina dicendi et tacendi* of 1245. Structured according to the rhetorical "circumstances" of classical tradition, this treatise examines the use of spoken discourse, especially among the legal profession, as a means of social empowerment. A third treatise, *Liber consolationis et consilii* (1246), denounces the threat to order afforded by the urban vendetta—the northern cities of Italy were frequently riven by lobbyists, and street fights between politically partisan groups were far from unknown. In this work, he sees social change as to be achieved through personal moral development. His final works comprise four more sermons, delivered to his legal confraternity in Brescia in or about 1250. In these short sermons, Albertanus develops and reiterates themes of his major works, and they may be seen as reflecting the maturity of his thought. The last sermon, with its topic of fear of the Lord (and perhaps also its lack of clear structure), suggests that these sermons were his swan song. There is no reason to believe that he wrote anything after them, and further attributions of authorship are undoubtedly false.

Albertano drew on familiar sources for his works, among them Seneca, Cicero, Justinian, Cato, Godfrey of Winchester, and the Bible. But he appears also to be the first writer to make use of the work of the Spanish convert from Judaism, Peter Alfonsi, and may well be the first scholar to have assembled all twelve books of Cassiodorus's *Variae*. In this sense we can regard Albertanus as a precursor of the Renaissance book collector. The focus and synthesis of his writing, however, make it wrong to dismiss him as a mere compiler. His remedies for the social problems he met with professionally mark him as an early and insightful social theorist. His views

on the consensual adoption of a secular rule (*propositum*) as a way of life and its potential as an engine of social change make him unique for the period. That he wrote as a layman is also remarkable. His beliefs about the role of the legal profession as a body with responsibility for social stability and development reveal an early understanding of the significance of the rise of an urban professional class. His sermons are among the earliest evidence we have of lay preaching and oratory.

More than 320 surviving Latin manuscripts, across Europe, indicate that Albertanus was one of the most widely read authors in the latter medieval period. *De doctrina* in particular is well represented in manuscript, and it also went through at least thirty-five printed editions by 1500. Among the subsequent writers who knew and utilized these works are Brunetto Latini, Chaucer, John Gower, the author of the *Fiore di virtù*, Christine de Pizan, and (arguably) Dante. Except for his sermons, Albertanus's work was translated into every major western European language, though sometimes at quite a distance from the original context. More than 130 manuscripts and numerous early printed editions are known of vernacular versions of his treatises; these include English, German, Italian, French, Catalan, Castilian, Czech, and Dutch versions. More research on his influence is needed.

Powell (1992) supplies a recent and authoritative discussion of Albertanus and his works and provides a starting point for contemporary scholars working in English. Some discussion, especially of vernacular versions, is added by Angus Graham (1996), who extends Powell's bibliography. Both supply further reading. Further literature in English is concerned largely with Chaucer's use of Albertanus. Details of Latin manuscripts are given by Navone (1994, 1998), though she lists only 243, and supplemented by Graham (2000a,b). The currently published Latin editions do not reflect the best critical edition, but adequate ones are provided by Sundby (1884, *De doctrina*, app., 475–509), Romino (1980), Fè d'Ostiani (1874), Ferrari (1955), and more recently by Navone. Ahlquist offers a welcome fresh edition of the four Brescian sermons (with English translation); and Marx has translated, from Sundby, a portion of the *Liber consolationis* (in Blamires et al. 1992, 237–242). All but two of the published vernacular versions are cited by Graham (1996), and there are further discussions and vernacular manuscript listings in Graham (2000a,b).

Further Reading

Ahlquist, Gregory W. "The Four Sermons of Albertanus of Brescia: An Edition." M.A. thesis, Syracuse University, 1997.

Blamires, Alcuin, Karen Pratt, and C. W. Marx. *Woman Defamed and Woman Defended: An Anthology of Medieval Texts*. Oxford: Clarendon, 1992.

Fè d'Ostiani, Luigi F. *Sermone inedito di Albertano, giudice di Brescia.* Brescia: Pavoni, 1874.

Ferrari, Marta. *Sermones quattuor: Edizione curata sui codici bresciani.* Lonato: Fondazione Ugo da Como, 1955.

Graham, Angus. "Who Read Albertanus? Insights from the Manuscript Transmission." In *Albertano da Brescia: Alle origini del razionalismo economico, dell' umanesimo civile, della grande Europa,* ed. Franco Spinelli. Brescia: Grafo, 1996, pp. 69–82.

——. "Albertanus of Brescia: A Preliminary Census of Vernacular Manuscripts." *Studi Medievali,* 41, 2000a, pp. 891–924.

——. "Albertanus of Brescia: A Supplementary Census of Latin Manuscripts." *Studi Medievali,* 41, 2000b, pp. 429–445.

——. "The Anonymity of Albertano: A Case Study from the French." *Journal of the Early Book Society,* 3, 2000, pp. 198–203.

Navone, Paola. "La *Doctrtna loquendi et tacendi* di Albertano da Brescia: Censimento dei manoscritti." *Studi Medievali,* 35, 1994, pp. 895–930.

——. *Liber de doctrina dicendi et tacendi: La parola del cittadino nell' Italia del Duecento / Albertano da Brescia.* Per Verba, Testi Mediolatini con Traduzioni, 11. Tavarnuzze: SISMEL, 1998.

Powell, James M. *Albertanus of Brescia: The Pursuit of Happiness in the Early Thirteenth Century.* Philadelphia: University of Pennsylvania Press, 1992.

Romino, Sharon Hiltz. "De amore et dilectione Dei et proximi et aliarum rerum et de forma vitae: An Edition." Ph.D. dissertation, University of Pennsylvania, 1980.

Spinelli, Franco, ed. *Albertano da Brescia: Alle origini del razionalismo economico, dell' umanesimo civile, della grande Europa.* Brescia: Grafo, 1996.

Sundby, [Johannes] Thor. *Albertani Brixiensis Liber Consolationis et Consilii.* London: Chaucer Society and N. Trübner, 1873.

——. *Della vita e delle opere di Brunetto Latini,* 2nd ed. Florence: Le Monnier, 1884.

ANGUS GRAHAM

ALBERTINO MUSSATO (1261–1329)

Albertino, the greatest Latin poet of his age, was born in Padua of lowly parentage. Orphaned at a young age, he had the responsibility of caring for three younger siblings—two brothers and a sister. (One of the brothers would eventually become the abbot of Santa Giustina, the great Benedictine monastery of Padua.) Early in his life, Albertino earned money by copying books for students at the university; later he became a notary and the son-in-law of the powerful Guglielmo Lemici, a very successful Paduan usurer. With the backing of the Lemici clan and his own natural abilities, he played a prominent role in Paduan public life, at home and abroad, in peace and war, from around 1310 to his final exile in 1325, when the Carrara family finally broke the influence of the Lemici. He died in exile in Chioggia four years later.

But it was not Albertino's successes as orator, statesman, warrior, or diplomat of Padua that make his name illustrious today. It is, rather, his remarkable achieve-ments as a man of letters in the context of a late medieval Italian commune. Even before his emergence as a figure in Paduan political life, Albertino had become a member of a small group of scholars gathered around Lovato de' Lovati, an older Paduan judge. These men studied the Latin poets as an avocation. The existence of Carolingian manuscripts at the Capitular Library in Verona, and in the Benedictine abbey of Pomposa near Ravenna, made possible this learned diversion of the *cenacolo padovano* ("Paduan circle"). The members of the *cenacolo* were already familiar with the traditional set of Latin poets, established earlier in the thirteenth century—Virgil, Horace, Ovid, Lucan, and Statius—and Lovato was the first to take the next logical step, composing original Latin poetry himself. Indeed, Petrarch recalled his achievement.

Albertino, following in Lovato's wake, composed poems that helped to rehabilitate some forms of Latin poetry. One example is his defense of such poetry against the strictures of a Dominican, Fra Giovannino. Another is his birthday elegy, in which he reviews his life and the highlights of his career, including his laureation. This may have been the first work since antiquity in which an author focused on his own day of birth for reflection and celebration.

In the 1320s, Albertino went to Siena in his capacity as a diplomat and on the way, near Florence, fell ill. The literary result of this illness was his poem *Somnium* ("A Dream"), recounting his concept of the afterworld, with particular attention to the nether regions. (Dante's *Inferno* was already in circulation at this time.)

Albertino also left us a bountiful harvest of Latin prose works, especially contemporary histories of Italy—*De gestis Henrici VII Cesaris* (*The Deeds of the Emperor Henry VII*) and *De gestis italicorum post Henricum VII Cesarem* (*Italian Events after the Death of Emperor Henry VII*). However, for all his learning and experience, his histories were no match for his poetry, or for the historical text that was at the root of Padua's self-understanding: Rolandino's *Chronicles of the Trevisan March.*

Albertino also studied the tragedies of Seneca with Lovato and composed introductions to the plays, as well as an explanation of tragic meters for the younger Marsilius of Padua, the author of *Defensor pacis.* In 1315, in imitation of Seneca and in connection with local history. Albertino wrote his finest and most lasting work, *Ecerinis* (*The Tragedy of Ecerinus*), about the tyrant Ezzelino III da Romano (1194–1259), the ruler of Verona. Like some of his contemporaries, Albertino saw an analogy between Ezzelino and the current lord of Verona, Cangrande della Scala. Albertino was familiar with the details of Ezzelino's career from Rolandino's *Chronicles,* which stressed the heroic, united, Catholic character of Paduan resistance. This was the story

Albertino found ready to hand as he attempted to awaken his fellow citizens to the danger of renewed aggression by the Veronese. He was inspired to cast this tale in the form of a Senecan tragedy, *Thyestes*, and thus wrote the first tragedy since antiquity. It was for *Ecerinis* that Albertino was crowned with laurels, just as Rolandino had been crowned for the *Chronicles*. However, Albertino failed in his goal of awakening Padua, and Cangrande conquered the city in 1328. Because of his staunch political opposition to Cangrande, Albertino went into exile; he died at Chioggia on 31 May 1329.

Further Reading

Editions

Albertino Mussato. *Thesaurus antiquitatum et historiarum italiae*, ed. Graevius. Leyden, 1722, Vol. 6(2). (Poems.)

——. *Rerum italicarum scriptores*, ed. L. A. Muratori. Milan, 1727, Vol. 10. (Histories.)

——. *Ecerinide*, ed. L. Padrin. Bologna, 1900.

——. *Mussato's "Ecerinis" and Loschi's "Achilles,"* trans. Joseph R. Berrigan. Munich: Wilhelm Fink, 1975.

Critical Studies

Berrigan, Joseph R. "The Ecerinis: A Prehumanist View of Tyranny." *Delta Epsilon Sigma Bulletin*, 12, 1967, pp. 71–86.

——. "Early Neo-Latin Tragedy in Italy." In *Acta Conventus Neo-Latini Lovaniensis*. Leuven: Leuven University Press, 1973, pp. 85–93.

——. "A Tale of Two Cities: Verona and Padua in the Late Middle Ages." In *Art and Politics in Late Medieval and Early Renaissance Italy, 1250–1500*, ed. Charles M. Rosenberg. Notre Dame, Ind.: University of Notre Dame Press, 1990, pp. 67–80.

Billanovich, Giuseppe. *I primi umanisti e le tradizioni dei classici latini*. Fribourg: Edizioni Universitarie, 1953.

Billanovich, Guido. "*Veterum vestigia vatum* nei carmi dei preumanisti padovani." *Italia Medioevale e Umanistica*, 1, 1958, pp. 155–243.

Cosenza, Mario. *Biographical and Bibliographical Dictionary of Italian Humanists*. Boston, Mass., 1962, Vol. 3, pp. 2396–2398; Vol. 5, pp. 1223–1224.

Dazzi, Manlio Torquato. *Il Mussato preumanista (1261–1329): L'ambiente e l'opera*. Vicenza: Neri Pozza, 1964.

Hyde, J. K. *Padua in the Age of Dante*. Manchester: Manchester University Press, 1966.

Martellotti, Guido. "Mussato, Albertino." In *Enciclopedia Dantesca*. Rome: Istituto della Enciclopedia Italiana, 1984, Vol. 3, pp. 1066–1068.

Raimondi, Ezio. "L'*Ecerinis* di Albertino Mussato." In *Studi Ezzeliniani*, Fasc. 45–47 of *Studi storici*. Rome: Istituto Storico Italiano per il Medio Evo, 1963, pp. 189–203.

Weiss, Roberto. *The Dawn of Humanism in Italy*. London: Lewis, 1947.

JOSEPH R. BERRIGAN

ALBERTUS MAGNUS (ca. 1200–1280)

Also known as "Albert the Great" and "Universal Doctor," Albertus Magnus was a Dominican theologian, philosopher, scientist, and saint. One of the most famous

Fra Angelico (1387–1455); Saint Albertus Magnus, roundel. Detail from the Crucifixion. © Scala/Art Resource, New York.

medieval precursors of modern science and best known today as the teacher of Thomas Aquinas, Albert was renowned in his own day for his encyclopedic knowledge, his voluminous writings, and his interpretive rendering of Arabic Aristotelian sources into Latin. In part due to spurious works given his name, he gained further repute after his death and into the Renaissance as a magician and alchemist. Albert introduced his own sort of Aristotelian scholasticism to the Dominican houses of study he founded in Germany, and Albertist Aristotelianism became one strain of the scholastic *via antique* (old path) that endured in German universities.

Born in Lauingen, Bavaria, Albert first studied at Padua, joined the Dominicans in 1223, and went to Cologne to study theology. He moved to Paris (1241) to complete his master in theology (1245), and was the first German to hold a chair of theology there. He lectured at Paris until returning to Cologne (1248) to found the Dominican precursor to the university, *studium generale*. Thomas Aquinas, Ulrich of Strassburg, and Giles of Lessines were among his students during these years. Made provincial of German Dominicans (1254), Albert acted as arbiter in many difficult ecclesial and political disputes, one of which led to his being made bishop of Regensburg briefly in the 1260s. Sent to all Germany by Pope Urban IV to preach the Crusade in 1263–1264, he thereafter resided mostly in Cologne, although he traveled on foot continuously throughout Germany, as well as to France and to Italy. Albert preached, taught theology, and wrote continuously from the 1230s until just before his death in 1280.

In Paris in the 1240s he wrote his *Summa de creaturis* (Book of the Creatures) and commented on Peter Lombard's *Sentences.* Already making extensive use of Arabic and Greek Aristotelianism, Albert greeted the newly available Aristotle materials with enthusiasm. He decided to present the whole of human knowledge as found in Aristotle and his Arabic commentators to the Latin West and to correct or add to Aristotelian thinking by means of knowledge that had not been available to Aristotle. This monumental project of paraphrase and explanation took two decades and included mathematics, logic, natural philosophy and science—including botany, mineralogy, biology, and zoology—as well as ethics, politics, and metaphysics. Because of the suspicion cast on Aristotle by theological traditionalists, Albert's project amounted to a defense of philosophy and reason in its own right.

These commentaries, because of the nature of his sources, manifest the modified view of Aristotle in Neoplatonic commentators that was also adopted by Arabic Aristotelians such as Avicenna (Ibn Sīnā) and Averroës (Ibn Rushd). Albert generally adopted Aristotle's views of the physical world and repudiated what he believed were mistaken interpretations of Aristotle on such matters, while indicating where he himself thought the Stagirite incorrect. But Albert's view of what transcends the physical universe reflects the Christian Neoplatonic (and Augustinian) Aristotelianism that was the dominant view among later scholastics. In contrast, Aquinas's ideas, while arguably closer to Aristotle himself, were a minority view in the late Middle Ages.

A careful observer of natural phenomena, Albert often incorporated his own experience to correct and supplement his sources in his writings about the natural world. His discussion of place and time follows that of Avicenna, but with his own emphases: only two dimensions, length and width, are essential to place, while time's matter is the uninterrupted flow of indivisible nows, and its form is number. In logic Albert gave classic expression to the medieval doctrine of three types or modes of being of universals (*ante rem*: in divine thought; *in re*: in natural things; *post rem*: in human thought); this doctrine subordinated logic to metaphysics.

Albert elaborated on his own metaphysical ideas in *De causis et processu universitatis* (The Causes and Development of the Universe) during the 1260s when he was completing his commentary on Aristotle's *Metaphysics.* In this original synthesis he adopts Aristotle's cosmology and accepts the system of Intelligences governing the spheres (while denying that they are angels). But Albert modifies Avicenna's emanation doctrine so that it becomes primarily a causality of higher *attracting* lower rather than overflowing or emanating into lower. Within this concept, the first principle's goodness calls and brings together all the forms found inchoate in matter, calling them to resemble the first. This Neoplatonism thus completes a metaphysics of being with a natural theology of the cause of being—the one or good found in *The Book of Causes* (by the Greek philosopher Proclus, ca. 410–485) and Pseudo-Dionysius, an early theologian. Linking the physical universe with the spiritual is the function of intellect. Albert's psychology criticized the view that there was only one intellect for all human beings. Yet he also attempted to harmonize Averroës's ideas about the intellect with his own commitment to the nobility and immortality of the human soul, leaving the unity of soul and body at best ambiguous. For Albert the process of abstraction is not merely from experienced particulars, but the result of a complex illumination (and use) of the human soul by the Intelligences en route to making everything one in God.

That divine first cause thereby provides the object of his ethical ideal of the contemplative or speculative life as surpassing all others. This ideal entails what Albert calls the acquisition of intellect (*intellectus adeptus*), where the separate agent intellect becomes the form of the soul, producing a state of happiness or contemplative wisdom that consists in contemplation of the separated beings. It rewards philosophical effort that progressively detaches the soul from the world of perceptual experience and aims at acquisition of intellect, thus dovetailing nicely with Albert's religious beliefs and mystical leanings. For him theology based on religious faith is not merely speculative but also affective, however intellectual. All of his theological writings and commentaries concentrate on the reality of God, not just on ideas about him. For Albert there is no knowledge of the ultimate mystery that is not at once transformative of the knower's mind and heart and life.

See also **Aquinas, Thomas; Averroës, Abu 'L-Walīd Muḥammad B. Aḥmad B. Rushd; Avicenna**

Further Reading

Albertus Magnus. *Alberti Magni Opera omnia*, ed. Auguste Borgnet and E. Borgnet. 38 vols. Paris: Vives, 1890–1899.
——. *Alberti Magni Opera omnia edenda curavit Institutum Alberti Magni Coloniense Bernhardo Geyer praeside.* Muenster: Aschendorff, 1951–.
——. *Book of Minerals*, trans. Dorothy Wyckoff. Oxford: Clarendon, 1967.
Albertus Magnus and Thomas Aquinas. *Albert and Thomas: Selected Writings*, trans. Simon Tugwell, New York: Paulist, 1988.
Hoenen, Maarten J. F. M., and Alain de Libera, eds. *Albertus Magnus und der Albertismus: Deutsche philosophische Kultur des Mittelalters.* Leiden: Brill, 1995.
Kovach, Francis J., and Robert W. Shahan, eds. *Albert the Great: Commemorative Essays.* Norman: University of Oklahoma Press, 1980.
Libera, Alain de. *Albert le Grand et la Philosophie.* Paris: Vrin, 1990.

Wallace, William A., ed. *American Catholic Philosophical Quarterly* 70, no. 1 (1996). [Special Albertus Magnus issue.]

Weisheipl, J. A. ed. *Albertus Magnus and the Sciences: Commemorative Essays 1980*, Toronto: Pontifical Institute of Medieval Studies, 1980.

CLYDE LEE MILLER

ALBORNOZ, GIL ALVAREZ CARRILLO DE (1295–1367)

Gil de Albornoz was one of the most eminent Spanish churchmen of the fourteenth century. He was born at Cuenca (ca. 1295) and was the son of García de Albornoz and Teresa de Luna. Albornoz was educated in Zaragoza under the watchful eye of his influential uncle, Jimeno, who at the time was archbishop there, and under the tutelage of Pedro Egidio, who would later become a deacon at Cuenca and come to administer Albornoz's household. In 1316 to 1317, Gil de Albornoz enrolled at the University of Toulouse, where he remained for a decade and from where before 1325 he was awarded a doctorate in decretals and canon law. While at Toulouse, he doubtless came into contact with Stephan Aubert.

Gil de Albornoz's life can be divided into two phases, an early Iberian one and a later Italian period following the accession of Pedro I to the crown of Castile and Albornoz's voluntary departure from the Iberian Peninsula. Since Albornoz's exploits in Italy are more amply known and readily accessible in many sources, greater attention will be given here to his achievements in Spain.

Upon returning to Castile from Toulouse in 1327, Gil de Albornoz joined the circle of Alfonso XI and, in addition to his ecclesiastical benefices at Cuenca, held the title of counselor to the king and archdeacon of Calatrava. By 1335 he had participated in an embassy to the king of Aragón and was actively engaged in the political life of Castile. In 1338, he was named archbishop of Toledo to succeed his uncle Jimeno, who held that position when he died. Albornoz was subsequently given the secular title of canciller de Castilla. It is at this point that he began to intervene vigorously in reforming the kingdom's judicial administration and in the organization of the armed forces. His active participation in the *cortes* (parliament) of Castile show him to be a dynamic force in all manner of affairs concerning the governance of the realm. Although Albornoz's influence in the adoption of the Ordenamiento de Alcalá in 1348 has not been carefully studied, he was doubtless a major participant in drafting and promulgating the new legal code. At the same time, Albornoz is known to have been energetically engaged in Alfonso XI's military exploits against the Muslims in the south and was named comisario de la cruzada for his efforts. Albornoz was at Alfonso's side at the Battle of the Salado River (1340), at the siege and capture of Algeciras (1342–1344), and

at the siege of Gibraltar until the king's untimely death from the plague in 1350.

Albornoz's activity in the Spanish Church was no less forceful than his involvement in secular government. The synods and councils of Toledo in 1339 and 1345 show him to have been especially preoccupied with the moral life of his diocese, attempting to impose order upon the disposition of ecclesiastical property and benefices, the *cura pastoralis* and administration of the sacraments by the rectors of churches and parishes, and the general reform of the clergy, which was deemed to be in a lamentable state of decadence. Clerical simony and concubinage were two lapses that especially caught Albornoz's attention, and orders against these practices went out under his name. It is because of this that Albornoz is often associated with Juan Ruiz, the putative author of the *Libro de buen amor,* whom the Salamanca manuscript of the latter attests was jailed by the bishop for his carnal failings. Quite aside from reputedly policing the celibacy of the clergy in the diocese of Toledo, Albornoz was deeply concerned with the level of their culture, learning, and education. He began his reign as archbishop by ensuring that the edicts of the Council of Valladolid (1322) be strictly observed and that one out of every ten clergymen in every deaconry be commissioned to study theology and canon law, prohibiting the ordination of all who could not demonstrate an adequate level of clerical education, "ut nullus nisi litteratus ad clericatum promovetur" (unless literate, do not make him a cleric), according to the Council of Toledo of 1339. Albornoz's own fidelity to his vows and the requirements of ordination were said by all to have been exemplary.

The death of Alfonso XI led Albornoz to fear disgrace at the hands of Pedro I, the king's successor. As a result, he withdrew to the papal court at Avignon, where he was made a cardinal in December 1350. His career in the curia was as successful as it had been at the Court of Castile. He was made papal legate and vicar general of the Papal States, helping Pope Innocent VI to control firmly their administration and dominate central Italy politically. Between 1353 and 1360 Albornoz attempted to revive the Angevin-Guelph alliance of the 1320s to counter the power of the lords of Lombardy but, after great sacrifice and expenditure, he failed to pacify the Italian peninsula because of French inability to provide continued support.

Throughout his life Albornoz remained firmly committed to the education of the clergy. He was especially concerned with their preparation in canon law and ecclesiastical administration. As a result, he founded the Collegio di San Clemente, known as the Spanish College, at the University of Bologna. In the will he signed in 1364, he created the foundation to establish the college as the universal heir to his fortune and, in a codicil added in 1368, again made provisions for the disposition of his inheritance, which was to go in its entirety to support twenty-four Spanish students in the course of their studies at the university. By 1369, two years after Albornoz's death at Viterbo, the College of San Clemente received its first group of students, many of whom went on to become distinguished jurists upon completion of their studies and their return to the Iberian Peninsula. Albornoz's foundation of the Spanish College at Bologna served as a model for the subsequent development of the *colegios mayores* in Spanish universities.

See also **Pedro I the Cruel; King of Castile**

Further Reading

Beneyto Pérez, J. *El cardenal Albornoz, canciller de Castilla y caudillo de Italia.* Madrid, 1950.

——. *El cardenal Albornoz: Hombre de iglesia y de estado en Castilla y en Italia.* Madrid, 1986.

Colliva, P. *Il cardinale Albornoz, lo Stato della Chiesa, le Constitutiones Aegidianae (1353-1357).* Bologna, 1977.

Martí, B. M. *The Spanish College at Bologna in the Fourteenth Century.* New York, 1966.

Verdera y Tuells, E. *El cardenal Albornoz y el Colegio de España.* Bologna, 1972.

E. MICHAEL GERLI

ALCUIN (ca. 730/35–804)

The foremost educational leader of the 8th century, known in Latin as Albinus and in Charlemagne's court circle often as Flaccus (after Horace). After living nearly 50 years in York, he spent some twenty years working in the Frankish kingdom as adviser and teacher of Charlemagne and his court, architect of the Carolingian political, religious, and cultural reform, poet and voluminous author of letters and treatises, rectifier of the biblical text and liturgy, and in his last years abbot of Tours.

The brief *Vita Alcuini*, anonymously composed around 829, probably at Ferrières, at the direction of Alcuin's disciple Sigulf, contains amid its reminiscences and anecdotes disappointingly few facts. Little is known of Alcuin's life at York; however, with respect to his later career on the Continent, no intellectual of the period is more amply documented. Alcuin's own letters (more than 300) and poems (more than 220), supplemented by Carolingian correspondence, chronicles, and histories, furnish us with considerable information about him. Born of noble family in Northumbria, he was educated at the cathedral school of York in its epoch as western Christendom's center of learning. His teacher and patron was Ælberht, whom Alcuin succeeded in 767 as master of the school, when Ælberht was raised to the episcopacy. Ordained as deacon, Alcuin never advanced to the priesthood and may not have taken monastic vows, even though in old age he expressed a wish to become a Benedictine monk at Fulda. Alcuin accompanied Ælberht on his travels and book-acquiring forays on the Continent, and by 778–80 he had already established a reputation among cognoscenti.

Alcuin would never have attained his subsequent renown if it were not for a momentous (though not his first) encounter with Charlemagne. In March 781, while bearing the pallium of archiepiscopal authority from Pope Hadrian I for Eanbald, Ælberht's successor to the see of York, Alcuin en route met Charlemagne at Parma. Charlemagne urgently requested him to join the Frankish court, with its prestigious group of scholars (Peter of Pisa, Paul the Deacon, Paulinus of Aquileia, soon joined by others), and to assist him in his educational and religious reforms. Alcuin forsook England to remain on the Continent for the rest of his life. He returned to England only twice, once in 786 to accompany papal legates to the synods at York and at the court of King Offa of Mercia, and once in 790–93 for a stay at York, during which time he was in correspondence with Charlemagne about the decrees of the Second Council of Nicaea (787), which the Carolingians mistakenly believed upheld the worship of images (iconolatry). However, the resulting doctrinal declarations, called the *Libri Carolini*, were made in his absence and therefore not by Alcuin. They are, judging from the script and biblical citations, probably by Theodulf.

His erudition, administrative qualities, pragmatism, and responsibility gave Alcuin immense influence with Charlemagne. In addition to his own works Alcuin more than any other in the royal entourage wrote documents, correspondence, capitularies, texts, and poems under the king's name. This is not to say that he functioned only as the king's *persona*; despite his service and extreme deference to the king Alcuin expressed himself to Charlemagne freely and sometimes reprovingly. Although he honored the king as divinely appointed defender, protector, and spreader of the church and guardian of the people's mores as well as conqueror of nations, he insisted the king was not above the law. He protested strongly against the forced baptism and tithing of the constantly resurgent Saxons and urged that the same error not be repeated among the defeated Avars, whom he chose to call Huns. In old age he excused himself from journeying to the king or accompanying him in battle or at the papal court. As abbot of St. Martin's he granted sanctuary to a condemned cleric, much to the chagrin of the culprit's bishop, Theodulf of Orléans, and of the king himself.

Traveling with Charlemagne's itinerant court until 794, when the palace of Aachen became a capital, Alcuin was the central figure of a brilliant corps of scholar-poets creating the Carolingian renaissance. This academy was responsible for mythologizing the Germanic kingdom into a new Athens, a new Rome, and a new Jerusalem. Even though Theodulf of Orléans has been judged a better poet, Alcuin's own activity as a contributor to the myth and to the body of Carolingian Latin poetry is remarkable. He composed verse epistles, inscriptions, epigrams, hymns. To his pupils he wrote lighter, more lyrical verse. The artifice of his acrostic poems addressed to Charlemagne and to the Cross demonstrates his knowledge and control of late-antique Latin prosody. His elegies are particularly notable. "O mea cella" and "The Nightingale" have been often anthologized. The elegy on the Viking destruction of Lindisfarne in 793 is one of three longer poems; the others are his metrical life of St. Willbrord and the often-cited poem *The Bishops, Kings, and Saints of York*, which contains much valuable information about the school of York, its library (probably the best in Europe), and its personalities.

As master of the court school Alcuin wrote a number of educational texts. He resurrected Cassiodorus's system of the seven liberal arts but in his treatises concentrated on the disciplines of the trivium: grammar (including a work on orthography), rhetoric, and dialectic. His *De orthographia*, his instruction in computus (calendrical reckoning), and some of his exegetical works (e.g., on John's Gospel) are revisions of Bede's works. He probably authored the little educational piece of mathematical conundrums, *Propositiones ad acuendos iuvenes*. He is responsible for spreading the *Categoriae decem*, a version of the Latin Aristotle. He compiled biblical commentaries on Genesis (questions and responses), some Psalms, the Song of Songs and Ecclesiastes, John's Gospel, Revelation, and the letters of Paul to Titus, Philemon, and Hebrews. His hagiographic works consist mainly of reediting lives of saints important to Francia: he reworked the biographies of Martin of Tours, Richarius, Vedast, and Willibrord. Alcuin also produced three moral tracts: one on the virtues and vices (a popular work), another on the nature of the soul, and the third, for the boys at St. Martin's, on confession of sins.

In the area of liturgy Alcuin made major contributions. He took charge of removing errors of transcription from scriptural and liturgical texts and bringing them into conformity with Roman usage. He assembled a *comes*, a lectionary of epistles for the mass. He produced a revision of the Hadrian (so-called Gregorian) mass book, but the supplement and its preface, long attributed to him, are probably the work of Benedict of Aniane (ca. 750–821). Alcuin composed a set of beautiful votive masses, eventually incorporated into the Roman Missal, which drew upon the Irish-English tradition of intense personal piety put to the service of public prayer. He also introduced Hiberno-English customs, such as the recitation of the Creed at mass (newly formulated with

the *Filioque* clause by Paulinus of Aquileia) and the celebration of the Feast of All Saints.

The western christological doctrine called adoptionism propounded by Elipand of Toledo and Felix of Urgel, namely, that Jesus Christ in his human nature was not the natural Son of God but an adopted one, was vigorously rebutted as heretical by Charles's theologians, Paulinus and Alcuin. It was condemned at the synods of Regensburg (790), Rome (798), and Aachen (800). Although in the controversy Paulinus proved the better theologian, Alcuin participated energetically, writing three hasty apologetic treatises in response to the heresy. A more successful foray into theology is Alcuin's later tract on the Trinity, heavily indebted to Augustine's *De Trinitate* but demonstrating Alcuin's own sophisticated reasoning.

In 796 Alcuin had asked to retire as a monk at Fulda, sacred to the memory of Boniface; but Charlemagne in granting him leave made him abbot of Tours, where he remained until his death on 19 May 804. From Tours he wrote some of his most famous letters to kings, bishops, and monks in England, especially Northumbria. While lamenting the depredations of the Vikings, he exhorted his countrymen to courage and virtue. In keeping with Charlemagne's campaign to reform and publish sacred texts Alcuin resolved to correct the textual corruptions in the Vulgate Old and New Testaments, and the resultant (now lost) Bible was presented to Charlemagne in Rome on the day of his coronation as emperor, Christmas, 800. Alcuin's role in arranging for the coronation itself was like so much of his activity for the king—both behind the scene and effectual. Alcuin's leadership in creating better Latin texts led to increased care and production in Frankish scriptoria; his name is therefore associated with the creation of the Carolingian minuscule handwriting developed during the period (even though he himself continued to use insular script), and with the superb Bibles produced at Tours, which actually postdate him.

There were in the court of Charlemagne others who may have been better as grammarians or poets or diplomats or exegetes or theologians or liturgists, but Alcuin, confidant and friend of the king, not only practiced all these professions, he also taught, guided, and served as a model for each of them.

See also **Aldhelm; Bede the Venerable; Charlemagne; Paul the Deacon; Theodulf of Orléans**

Further Reading

Primary Sources

PL 90:667–76 and *PL* 100–01 [includes most of Alcuin's works, but in unreliable editions]

Arndt, Wilhelm, ed. *Vita Alcuini. MGH: Scriptores* 15/1 (1887): 182–97

Daly, L.W., and W. Suchier, eds. *Altercatio Hadriani Augusti et Epicteti Philosophi.* Illinois Studies in Language and Literature 24 (1939), nos. 1 & 2

Godman, Peter, ed. and trans. *Alcuin: The Bishops, Kings, and Saints of York.* Oxford: Clarendon, 1982

Godman, Peter, ed. and trans. *Poetry of the Carolingian Renaissance.* Norman: University of Oklahoma Press, 1985, pp. 118–49

Howell, Wilbur S., ed. *The Rhetoric of Alcuin and Charlemagne.* Princeton: Princeton University Press, 1941.

Secondary Sources

Bullough, Donald. "A Court of Scholars and the Revival of Learning." *The Age of Charlemagne.* London: Elek, 1965, pp. 99–128

Bullough, Donald. "Alcuin and the Kingdom of Heaven: Liturgy, Theology, and the Carolingian Age." In *Carolingian Essays,* ed. Ute-Renate Blumenthal. Washington, D.C.: Catholic University of America, 1983, pp. 1–69. Repr. in *Carolingian Renewal: Sources and Heritage.* Manchester: Manchester University Press, 1991, pp. 161–240

Duckett, Eleanor S. *Alcuin, Friend of Charlemagne.* New York: Macmillan, 1951

Ellard, Gerald. *Master Alcuin, Liturgist.* Chicago: Loyola University, 1956

Ganshof, François L. *The Carolingians and the Frankish Monarchy.* Trans. Janet Sondheimer. Ithaca: Cornell University Press, 1971, pp. 28–54

Godman, Peter. "The Anglo-Latin *Opus geminatum*: From Aldhelm to Alcuin." *MÆ*50 (1981): 215–29

Godman, Peter. "New Athens and Renascent Rome." In *Poets and Emperors.* Oxford: Oxford University Press, 1987, pp. 38–92

Levison, Wilhelm. *England and the Continent in the Eighth Century.* Oxford: Clarendon, 1946, pp. 148–70, 314–23

Marenbon, John. *From the Circle of Alcuin to the School of Auxerre.* Cambridge: Cambridge University Press, 1981

McKitterick, Rosamond. *The Frankish Church and the Carolingian Reforms, 789–895.* London: Royal Historical Society, 1977

Meyvaert, Paul. "The Authorship of the 'Libri Carolina': Observations Prompted by a Recent Book." *Revue bénédictine* 89 (1979): 29–57

Wallach, Luitpold. *Alcuin and Charlemagne.* Ithaca: Cornell University Press, 1959

Willis, G.G. "From Bede to Alcuin." In *Further Essays in Early Roman Liturgy.* Alcuin Club 50. London: SPCK, 1968, pp. 227–42

GEORGE HARDIN BROWN

ALDHELM (640?–709/10)

The learned founder and first major figure of Anglo-Latin letters. Aldhelm was born of noble family with royal connections in Wessex about the time of the district's conversion to Christianity. We have few details of his life. Of his education William of Malmesbury relates, without citing the source of his information, that Aldhelm received his early training from one Máelduib at the ancient Celtic foundation of Malmesbury. Later he studied under the abbot Hadrian in the renowned school of Canterbury but left after as little as two years, for health and other reasons. In one letter from Canterbury

written between 670 and 673 Aldhelm lists the subjects he was then pursuing, including Roman law, 100 types of meter and poetic devices, the principles of mathematical calculation (especially fractions), and astrology (the interpretation of the zodiacal signs).

Earlier scholars hypothesized that Aldhelm learned his showy latinity from Irish tutors like Máelduib, but recent specialists have established a convincing link between Aldhelm's writings and the work of continental grammarians and poets, who gloried in the same pompous style. Aldhelm somehow acquired an astonishing command of sacred and profane literature as he developed his extraordinary skill in writing ornate Latin.

He became involved in ecclesiastical affairs, attending a synod at Hertford in 672 and becoming abbot of Malmesbury ca. 673. He was very active, traveling to Rome and to sites in southern England; he labored to establish the church in Wessex physically (he built or rebuilt several churches) and spiritually (Bede speaks of his energy and zeal). When Bishop Hæddi died in 705, the vast diocese of Wessex was split into two, with sees at Winchester and Sherborne. In 705/06 Aldhelm, well acquainted with neighboring Devon and Cornwall, was unsurprisingly chosen and consecrated bishop of the western portion, Sherborne. He presided over his bishopric for four years until his death in 709/10.

For Aldhelm Latin was not only the language of Christian culture; it was also the language of the clerical elite. He therefore fostered a hermeneutic style of the initiate, whose most striking feature is the ostentatious parade of unusual, arcane, and learned vocabulary. Both his prose and poetry exhibit florid ornament, especially alliteration and rhyme. Aldhelm's extant prose writings include a dozen letters. In epistles to his students Heahfrith and Wihtfrith he tries to convince them of the advantages of English over Irish education and demonstrates his point by outdoing the rhetorical excesses of Celtic Latin (e.g., every one of the first fifteen words of his letter to Heahfrith begins with *p*). In his letter to Geraint, king of Dumnonia (Devon), he discusses the reckoning for Easter, a much-debated topic in the 8th century among Irish and continental clerics; and in a letter to the bishop of Wessex he addresses computistical matters in addition to metrics.

His weightiest letter is the *Epistola ad Acircium,* addressed to the well-educated King Aldfrith of Northumbria (686–705). The preface of this massive tract includes the longest recorded disquisition on the allegorical significance of the number seven; the main body of the letter contains two complementary treatises on Latin metrics. To illustrate the properties of the hexameter he inserts 100 *Aenigmata,* following the example of the late Latin poet Symphosius. These *Aenigmata,* or *Riddles,* which express the mysterious nature of things, proved popular in early-medieval Europe but especially in Anglo-Saxon circles, where they were imitated in Latin (by Tatwine, archbishop of Canterbury 731–34, Eusebius, and Boniface) and OE (in the Exeter Book Riddles).

Aldhelm's longest and most notable work was a treatise on chastity, *De virginitate*, composed for Abbess Hildelith and her nuns at Barking Abbey. The topic was a favorite patristic subject, and the method of composition was also traditional, with one version in prose and another in verse, a procedure (termed *opus geminatum* or *stilus geminus*, "twinned work" or "twin style") practiced by late Latin writers like Juvencus and Caelius Sedulius and subsequently by Bede, Alcuin, and Hrabanus Maurus. But Aldhelm's texts are most unusual, for, unlike other authors whose poetic versions were much more ornate than the prose counterparts, Aldhelm's dazzling prose is if anything more obscurantist, recherché, and artificial than the poetic version, which is also highly embellished. After an elaborate introduction on the nature, value, and difficulties of virginity the prose text presents a catalogue of male virgins from the Old Testament to the Church Fathers; this is followed by a catalogue of female virgins similarly ordered, with some further considerations of Old Testament patriarchs; before ending, Aldhelm denounces showy dress worn by ecclesiastics.

The poetic twin shares the general structure of the prose version, with the sequence of male and female exemplars, but it ends quite differently, with a long allegorical confrontation between the virtues and vices. Although the poem's hexameters are metrically limited and tiresomely repetitious, his vocabulary is formidably extensive. This 2,904-line *carmen* is the first full-scale Latin poem to be composed in the British Isles; Aldhelm, who compared himself to Virgil, was aware of its significance and his achievement.

The influence of Aldhelm's writings on his contemporaries and on the following generation can be measured by their imitation of his style. His student Æthilwald produced four poems in continuous octosyllables, clearly modeled on Aldhelm's *Carmen rhythmicum*. Alcuin, whose soberer style reflects the writing of Bede, also owes something to Aldhelm. Many short Latin poems from the Anglo-Saxon period are nothing more than centos woven from Aldhelm's poetry. Aldhelm's dense prose had even more imitators. Felix of Crowland is surely indebted to him for the elaborate and verbose prose style of his *Life of St. Guthlac* (ca. 740). The great missionary Boniface and his coterie of English correspondents write Aldhelmian prose, as does Boniface's biographer, Willibald, and the biographer of Sts. Willibald and Wynnebald, the nun Hygeburg. Later Latin writings of the time of King Alfred and especially of the time of the Benedictine Reform (late 10th and early 11th centuries) likewise reveal Aldhelm's influence, diminished finally only after the Norman Conquest.

See also **Alcuin; Boniface VIII, Pope**

Further Reading

Primary Sources
Ehwald, Rudolf, ed. *Aldhelmi opera omnia. MGH: Auctores antiquissimi* 15. Berlin: Weidmann, 1919
Lapidge, Michael, and Michael Herren, trans. *Aldhelm: The Prose Works.* Cambridge: Brewer, 1970
Lapidge, Michael, and James Rosier, trans. *Aldhelm: The Poetic Works.* Cambridge: Brewer, 1985
Pitman, J.H., trans. *The Riddles of Aldhelm.* New Haven: Yale University Press, 1925. Repr. Hamden: Archon, 1970 [based on Ehwald's text of the *Aenigmata*].

Secondary Sources
Browne, G.F. *St. Aldhelm.* London: SPCK, 1903
Godman, Peter. "The Anglo-Latin *Opus geminatum*: From Aldhelm to Alcuin." *MÆ* 50 (1981): 215–29
Lapidge, Michael. "The Hermeneutic Style in Tenth-Century Anglo-Latin Literature." *ASE* 4 (1975): 67–111
Lapidge, Michael. "Aldhelm's Latin Poetry and Old English Verse." *Comparative Literature* 31 (1979): 209–31
Wieland, Gernot R. "*Feminus stilus*: Studies in Anglo-Latin Hagiography." In *Insular Latin Studies*, ed. Michael W. Herren. Toronto: Pontifical Institute, 1981, pp. 113–33
Winterbottom, Michael. "Aldhelm's Prose Style and Its Origins." *ASE* 6 (1977): 39–76.

GEORGE HARDIN BROWN

ALEXANDER OF HALES (ca. 1185–1245)

Theologian. Alexander's early life is conjectural: born probably in Hales (now Hales Owen), in the English Midlands, he studied arts, then theology, in Paris, from around the turn of the century. From 1226 to 1229, he was a canon of Saint Paul's, London, although he remained in Paris. He was one of four masters sent to Rome by the University of Paris in 1230 to represent its case in the famous dispute (which led to strike and dissolution) with the French king. Gregory IX's bull *Parens scientiarum* (1231), arising out of the dispute, was partly Alexander's work. In 1231, he was made canon of Lichfield and archdeacon of Coventry. At the height of his career, in 1235, he joined the fledgling Franciscan order (apparently breaking off a sermon he was preaching, taking the habit, and returning to finish the sermon), thus giving the Franciscans their first holder of a magisterial chair in the University of Paris. He was active in teaching for the Franciscans and as an adjudicator of disputes until his sudden death, probably of an epidemic disease, in Paris in 1245.

The catalogue of Alexander's works is unclear. He is best remembered today for introducing commentary on Peter Lombard's *Sententiae* into the Paris theology syllabus. His own *Sententiae* gloss, the earliest we possess, survives in more than one version, apparently being student *reportationes* of his lectures. A set of *Quaestiones disputatae* "antequam esset frater" belongs to him, but a *Summa theologiae* begun by Alexander was finished by William of Melitona, John of La Rochelle, and other members of the "Franciscan school" that Alexander headed. It is thus a useful summary of 13th-century Franciscan ideas. The same group of friars was responsible for an exposition of the Franciscan *Rule*, in 1242.

With William of Auvergne, Alexander (known as *Doctor irrefragibilis*), was the first Paris master to use Aristotle in the service of theology; and, like William, he used Aristotle's ideas in a framework of traditional Augustinian orthodoxy. Alexander's main sources are Augustine, Pseudo-Dionysius, Boethius, and the "moderns" of the 12th century: Bernard of Clairvaux, Gilbert of Poitiers, Anselm, and others.

Alexander's prosaic style makes it difficult for us today to appreciate his enormous contemporary success, although his structured and ordered approach remains a key feature of his work. Bonaventure was of one of the succeeding generation who revered Alexander, suggesting that his teaching in person may have been more gripping than the remnant left to us.

See also **Bonaventure, Saint; Peter Lombard; William of Auvergne**

Further Reading

Alexander of Hales. *Glossa in Sententias*, ed. P. Doucet. 4 vols. Florence: Ex Typographia Collegii S. Bonaventurae, 1951–57.
——. *Questiones disputatae* "antequam esset frater." 3 vols. Florence: Ex Typographia Collegii S. Bonaventurae, 1960.
——. *Summa theologica*, ed. Bernardini Klumper. 4 vols. Florence: Ex Typographia Collegii S. Bonaventurae, 1924.
——. *Summa theologica. Indices in tom. I–IV*, ed. Constantini Koser. Grottaferrata (Rome): Editiones Collegii S. Bonaventurae ad Claras Aquas, 1979.
Catania, F.J. *Knowledge of God in Alexander of Hales and John Duns Scotus.* Kalamazoo: Medieval Institute, 1966.
Herscher, I. "A Bibliography of Alexander of Hales." *Franciscan Studies* 5 (1945): 434–54.
Huber, Raphael M. "Alexander of Hales O.F.M. (ca. 1170–1245): His Life and Influence on Medieval Scholasticism." *Franciscan Studies* 26 (1945): 353–65.
Principe, Walter H. *The Theology of the Hypostatic Union in the Early Thirteenth Century.* 4 vols. Toronto: Pontifical Institute of Mediaeval Studies, 1963–75, Vol. 2: *Alexander of Hales's Theology of the Hypostatic Union.*

LESLEY J. SMITH

ALFONSO V, KING OF ARAGÓN, THE MAGNANIMOUS (1396–1458)

Born 1396, the eldest son of Fernando of Antequera and Leonor de Alburquerque, Alfonso V passed much of his childhood in the court of his uncle, Enrique III of Castile. Fernando, Victor of Antequera (1410), coregent of Castile from 1406, and from 1412 (Compromise of Caspe) King of Aragón, became the boy's hero, a model of knightly prowess and kingly virtue. An abiding thirst for adventure, deep piety, and a passion for hunting all derived from that paternal source.

Fernando's brief reign in Aragón (1412–1416), besides grounding Alfonso in the arts of government, introduced him to the constitutional pretensions and Mediterranean concerns of his future subjects. Castile remained nonetheless a vital element in the family's dynastic and political calculations, as evidenced by his marriage to María of Castile (1415), a match that proved loveless and barren. Thrust by his father's fatal illness (1415–1416) into the center of affairs, Alfonso found himself confronting the antipope Benedict XIII and Sigismund, King of the Romans, in a meeting called at Perpignan to end the Schism. In this, his first great test of political judgment, he opted for the Council of Constance, yet took care to keep Benedict in reserve as a bargaining counter in dealings with the restored authority of Rome.

On 2 April 1416 Alfonso became King of Aragón. Looking around for warlike ventures that had hitherto eluded him, he saw Sicily and Sardinia restive under Aragonese domination, Genoa challenging Catalan aspirations in Corsica, and Castile chafing at the overweening Antequera presence. His subjects, however, especially the Catalans and Valencians, opposed all foreign projects for they mistrusted their new Castilian dynasty and were resolved to bind it in constitutional fetters. In the succeeding four-year contest of wills he won the upper hand thanks largely to clerical and Castilian subventions, then sailed in high spirits for Italian shores.

Touching first at Sardinia, he subdued that island without difficulty, but in his next objective—Corsica—encountered a desperate Genovese defense. Frustrated there, he moved on to Naples in the guise of champion and adopted heir of Giovanna II against Louis III of Anjou whom Pope Martin V, suzerain of the kingdom, planned to install as successor to the childless queen. Enthusiasm greeted his arrival (July 1421), but the war against Louis soon embroiled him in intrigues that within two years left him totally isolated. Rescued by a Catalan fleet, he embarked for Spain in October 1423, having first sacked Naples; on the homeward voyage he paused to burn Angevin Marseilles.

Spain presented its own problems: Catalan demands for curbs on royal authority, the consequences of a breach with Rome over the Neapolitan investiture, and turmoil in Castile provoked by blind rivalry between his brothers and Álvaro de Luna for control of that kingdom. Against his better judgment he allowed Juan and a party of Castilian nobles to maneuver him into an intervention (1425) that freed another brother, Enrique, from captivity and briefly restored Antequera dominance. Within two years the brothers were again at odds, and Alfonso found himself once more driven to invade Castile. Álvaro Luna countered devastatingly by throwing the Antequera estates to his wavering adherents; a mere handful stirred to support Alfonso, Catalonia denounced the operation, and rebellion threatened in Aragón. His frontiers menaced by vastly superior Castilian forces, Alfonso was compelled to seek a truce that left the Antequera hold upon Castile broken and his own reputation battered. Small wonder that he developed an aversion to further involvement in Castile and seized upon an invitation from the anti-Angevin faction in Naples to prepare another Italian expedition. It cost many substantial concessions to the ruling classes of Catalonia before he could sail again in 1432, leaving his wife and Juan as regents in that province and Aragón, respectively.

Uncertain how matters stood in Naples, he alighted first in Sicily, then essayed a punitive raid against Tunisia that demonstrated his naval power and crusading credentials but deepened the hostility of that Muslim state. An attempt to force the issue in Naples by a show of strength at Ischia (1435) having come to nothing, he had to retire once again to Sicily and wait for the unfolding of events. At this juncture pressure from his brothers threatened to draw him back to Spa, where renewed war loomed with Castile. Orders for return had already been given when news that first Louis of Anjou, then Giovanna, had died transformed his prospects. Supported by all his brothers, he made for the mainland to claim his inheritance.

Yet again, Genoa's fear of a Catalan stranglehold on the western Mediterranean snatched away apparently certain victory. In a battle off Ponza (5 August 1435) its fleet not only destroyed an overconfident enemy but took Alfonso, two brothers, and a host of nobles as prisoners. Hauled, albeit courteously, to Milan—Genoa's overlord—Alfonso looked to all the world a beaten man. Yet by a veritable coup de theatre he transformed his captor, the volatile Visconti duke, into a devoted ally. Together they plotted a condominium over Italy, and early in 1436 Alfonso was once more pursuing his conquest of Naples. Dogged opposition from the papacy, Genoa, and René of Anjou delayed victory for another six years until with the fall of the capital on 2 June 1442 all resistance crumbled. A great triumph had crowned decades of unremitting persistence.

Alfonso now faced a choice between exploiting his Italian victory and returning to Spain, where domestic problems and Castilian complications continued to fester. While always proclaiming his intention to return, he chose instead to spend the rest of his life in Italy, where he enjoyed more unfettered authority, alluring

international opportunities, and a stimulating cultural environment. Already he had gathered there his three children—all illegitimate—and proclaimed his only son, Ferdinando, heir to Naples. Wholeheartedly he threw himself into the strife of Italy, seeking to establish a virtual protectorate over the papal states, reduce Genoa to subservience, make good his claim upon Corsica, and secure, despite Venice, a hold upon the eastern shores of the Adriatic. Failure to find a dependable ally frustrated all these ambitions in some measure. Most galling of all was the about-face of his former chancellor, Alfonso Borja, who, once planted on the papal throne as Calixtus III (1455), tamed from servitor into implacable foe.

More successfully, Alfonso exploited the commercial potential of his conquest, encouraging Catalans and Valencians to follow royal example. From Flanders to Alexandria royal vessels plied their trade as he wove schemes to integrate his states into an economic community.

Art and learning also fascinated him. From early youth he developed a taste for music and books; later he cultivated interests in architecture, painting, and sculpture. In his maturity these resulted in a library, a musical establishment, and a royal palace (Castelnuovo, Naples) to rival any in Europe. Under his patronage Italian and Spanish men of arts and letters brought the Renaissance to life in southern Italy and sowed its seed in Spain.

Ambitious, inscrutable, politically shrewd, and an indefatigable administrator, Alfonso V devoted himself conscientiously to his duty in the conviction that royal authority divinely ordained better served the common good than did the play of private interest. In war he displayed tenacity, courage, and a sense of mission rather than brilliant generalship. Sobriety marked his behavior as man and king, save for the occasional display of magnificence, and his autumnal passion for Lucrezia d'Alagno, a young Neapolitan.

He died on 27 June 1458, leaving Naples to his son and his other dominions to his brother Juan.

Further Reading

Ametller y Vinyas, J. *Alfonso V de Aragón en Italia y la crisis religiosa del siglo XV.* 3 vols. Gerona, 1903–1928.

Beccadelli, A. *De dictis et factis Alphonsi regis Aragonum et Neapolis.* Basel, 1538.

Pontieri, E. *Alfonso il Magnanimo: Re di Napoli 1435–1458.* Naples, 1975.

Ryder, A. *Alfonso the Magnanimous, King of Aragón, Naples and Sicily, 1396–1458.* Oxford, 1990.

ALAN RYDER

ALFONSO VI, KING OF LEÓN-CASTILE (1037–1109)

The second son of Fernando I, King of León-Castile (1037–1065), he was born about 1037. On the death of

Fernando I the kingdom was divided between Alfonso and his two brothers. Sancho, the eldest, received the kingdom of Castile and the overlordship of the tributary Christian kingdom of Navarre as well as that of the Muslim *tā'ifa* (party kingdom) of Zaragoza. García, the youngest, was awarded Galicia-Portugal and the tributary Muslim kingdom of Badajoz. To Alfonso went Asturias, León, parts of the Bierzo and the Sorian highlands, and the tributary tā'ifa of Toledo. The division did not last long. In 1071 Alfonso took control of the lands of García and in 1072 was himself defeated in battle and dispossessed briefly by his brother Sancho in 1072. After a short term of exile in Toledo, Alfonso returned after the assassination of Sancho, outside the walls of Zamora in September 1072, and now became the ruler of the reconstituted kingdom of his father. When García returned from exile in Badajoz in 1073, Alfonso had him imprisoned until the former's death in March 1090.

The kingdom of León-Castile grew under Alfonso VI to be the greatest realm of the peninsula, Christian or Muslim. The major step in this process was the conquest of the tā'ifa of Toledo, which formally surrendered on 25 May 1085. With that success, the southern boundary of the kingdom was carried from the north bank of the Duero River to the north bank of the Tajo River. It enabled Alfonso to carry out the repopulation of the northern *meseta* (plateau) between the Duero and the Guadarrama Mountains unhindered and to begin that of the southern meseta between the Guadarrama and the Tajo. For a brief time the kingdom even included the old Toledan lands south of the Tajo and north of the Sierra Morena. Moreover, on the assassination of the king of Navarre, his cousin Sancho García IV (1054–1076), Alfonso participated with the King of Aragón, his cousin Sancho Ramírez I (1063–1094), in the partition of Navarre. León-Castile's share was most of the upper Rioja along the Ebro River.

The surrender of Toledo to Alfonso VI in 1085 was followed by his installation of the former Muslim ruler there, Al-Qādir, in the tā'ifa of Valencia in the east as his tributary. Since the other Muslim kings in Iberia, from Zaragoza through Granada, Seville, and Badajoz, were also his tributaries, the Leonese was virtually master of the entire peninsula. Under the circumstances, the Muslim rulers of the south appealed to the Murābit emir, Yūsuf Ibn Tāshfīn of Morocco, for protection. The Murābit were a Berber fundamentalist sect who from midcentury had been gradually overrunning Morocco and by this date controlled an empire stretching from the southern Sahara to the Mediterranean with its capital at the newly built Marrakesh.

In 1086 in response to the appeal of the Muslims of Andalusia, the Murābit crossed the Strait of Gibraltar. They advanced to the neighborhood of Badajoz where, with their Andalusian allies, they defeated the army of Alfonso VI at Zallāqah on 23 October 1086. Although Alfonso and much of his army escaped, he was to spend the remainder of his life battling to defend his realm against the Murābit.

In the aftermath of Zallāqah, the fundamentalist Murābit were to depose, one by one, the rulers of the Iberian tā'ifas whom they considered unfaithful to the Qur'ān because of their imposition of illegal taxes on the faithful; their use of alcohol, music, and poetry; and their payment of tribute to Alfonso VI, an infidel, above all. Gradually Muslim Iberia became the province of a North African empire. Yūsuf annexed Granada in 1090, Seville in 1091, and Badajoz in 1094. Valencia eluded him until 1102 when it was conquered by the Castilian adventurer Rodrigo Díaz de Vivar, usually called El Cid, who held it until his death in 1099. Zaragoza remained independent until 1110, by which time both Alfonso VI and Yūsuf Ibn Tāshfīn were dead. The Leonese monarch was the major Murābit opponent in all of this and defended the independence of the tā'ifas as best he could. Yet by his death in 1109, he had been forced back to the line of the Tajo and it was unclear if even the north bank of that river and the city of Toledo itself could be held.

At the same time, León-Castile was entering into a much closer relationship with Europe north of the Pyrenees. Fernando I had sealed a pact of friendship with the great Burgundian monastery of Cluny and agreed to subsidize that house in the amount of 1,000 gold *dinars* per annum. Alfonso VI would double that census and, in addition, begin the process of granting possession and authority over Leonese royal monasteries to the French house. By the end of his reign the Cluniac province in his kingdom counted better than a half-dozen houses. This cooperation with Cluny was joined to a similar policy of close ties with the Roman church. At the urging of Pope Gregory VII, Alfonso agreed to see that the Roman liturgical ritual replaced the Mozarabic one. In return he received the support of Rome for the restoration of the metropolitan sees of Braga and Toledo, the bishoprics of Salamanca, Segovia, Osma, Burgos, and Coimbra, and the recognition of the older royal creation at Oviedo. The former Cluniac monk Bernard was recognized by Pope Urban II as archbishop of Toledo in 1088, and that archbishop and his king and patron would fill up most of the new sees created with reforming French Cluniac monks.

These processes were accompanied by a rapid growth of the pilgrimage to the shrine of St. James at Santiago de Compostela by the peoples of western Europe. This also meant the infusion of the new Romanesque art, the Carolingian script, a more rigorous Latin, and a variety of other French manners into León-Castile. The great Romanesque cathedral at Santiago de Compostela, begun in 1076, is the most monumental example of this phenomenon. Most larger towns, even Toledo in the extreme south, would come to have their *barrio* (quarter) of French artisans and merchants as a side effect of the pilgrimage but there was no significant immigration of French nobles such as would shortly take place in Aragón.

In that respect, the most significant development was the marriage by Alfonso VI to a succession of foreign brides for his queens as he sought both a male heir and the prestige of an international match for its effect in the peninsula. Inés of Aquitaine (1074–1077), Constance of Burgundy (1078–1093), Berta of Lombardy (1095–1100), Elizabeth of France (1100–1106), and Béatrice of France (1108–1109) were such brides. On the other hand, Alfonso's only known son, Sancho Alfónsez (1094?–1108), was the son of the Muslim concubine Zaida, who became his wife in 1106 and died shortly thereafter.

The Burgundian alliance was also to be reflected in the marriage of Alfonso's daughter by Constance, Urraca, to Count Raymond of Burgundy who became Count of Galicia-Portugal and probably heir apparent in 1088. That match was followed by a similar marriage of a daughter by the Asturian noblewoman Jimena Muñoz, Teresa, to Raymond's cousin, Count Henri of Burgundy in 1096. Henri thus became Count of Portugal. The son of Raymond and Urraca was to become Alfonso VII of León-Castile (1126–1157). The son of Henri and Teresa was to become Afonso I of Portugal (1128–1185). In the lifetime of Alfonso VI the two counts were to become chief figures at his court and administrators and defenders of the west during the campaigning season. Another daughter, Elvira, born of Jimena Muñoz, was married to Count Raymond of Toulouse by 1094 and subsequently bore him a son in the Holy Land, Alfonso Jordán, who himself later became count of Toulouse.

In the spring of 1108 Alfonso VI was still engrossed in defending his realm from the attacks of the Murābit emirs of Morocco. On 29 May 1108 at the fortress of Uclés, about thirty kilometers south of the Tajo, one of his armies was routed by the enemy and his only son, Sancho Alfónsez, was killed. To solve the succession crisis the king turned to his daughter, Urraca (1109–1126), whose husband Raymond of Burgundy had died in November 1107. But he also provided for her future marriage to her cousin, Alfonso I, el Batallador, of Aragón (1104–1134), so as to provide for the military safety of the kingdom. Alfonso VI himself was seeing to those defenses at Toledo when he died on 1 July 1109, at the age of seventy-two. He was buried at the royal monastery of Sahagún on 21 July 1109.

See also **Díaz de Vivar, Rodrigo**

Further Reading

Fletcher, R. A. *The Quest for El Cid.* New York, 1990.
González, J. *Repoblación de Castilla la Nueva.* 2 vols. Madrid, 1975–76.
Lomax, D. W. *The Reconquest of Spain.* New York, 1978.
Reilly, B. F. *The Kingdom of León-Castilla under King Alfonso VI, 1065-1109.* Princeton, N.J., 1988.

BERNARD F. REILLY

ALFONSO X, EL SABIO, KING OF CASTILE AND LEÓN (1221–1284)

Alfonso X, king of León-Castile (1252–1284), the son of Fernando III and Beatrice of Swabia, was born on 23 November 1221 in Toledo and is known as El Sabio, the wise or the learned. His first task was to complete the colonization of Seville and the recently reconquered territory in Andalusia. An ambitious ruler, he also tried to assert his supremacy over neighboring Christian territories. He quarreled with Afonso III of Portugal over lands east of the Guadiana River and the Algarve, but reached a preliminary settlement in 1253 by arranging the marriage of his illegitimate daughter, Beatriz, to the Portuguese ruler. When Alfonso X demanded that Thibault II, the new king of Navarre, become his vassal, the Navarrese appealed for help to Jaime I of Aragón. As a consequence, Alfonso X had to give up his attempt to subjugate Navarre in 1256. He also had alleged rights to Gascony, but yielded them in 1254 to his sister Leonor and her husband Edward, the son and heir of Henry III of England.

Advancing claims to the Holy Roman Empire derived from his mother Beatrice, daughter of Emperor Philip of Swabia, Alfonso X was elected in 1257 in opposition to Richard of Cornwall. He incurred great expenses in a vain effort to win recognition, but he was unable to persuade the majority of the Germans and several popes to acknowledge him.

Alfonso X also planned an invasion of Morocco to deprive the Moors of easy access to the peninsula, but his African crusade accomplished nothing more than the plundering of Sale, a town on the Atlantic coast, in 1260. In order to broaden Castilian access to the sea, he developed Cádiz and the nearby Puerto de Santa María and conquered Niebla in 1262. When he demanded the surrender of Gibraltar and Tarifa, his vassal, Ibn al-Aḥmar, King of Granada, refused, because he realized that this would make it difficult for Morocco to aid Granada against Castile.

Threatened by Castilian expansion, Ibn al-Aḥmar in the spring of 1264 stirred up rebellion among the Mudejars or Muslims subject to Castilian rule in Andalusia and Murcia. Alfonso X took steps to contain the revolt in Andalusia, while appealing for help to his father-in-law, Jaime I of Aragón, who subdued Murcia by early 1266.

Jerez, the last rebel stronghold in Andalusia, capitulated in October. As a result of the rebellion, the king expelled the Muslims from the recaptured towns and brought in Christian settlers. The suppression of the revolt was completed when Ibn al-Aḥmar resumed payment of a yearly tribute to Castile in 1267. In that same year, Alfonso X, in return for Afonso III's assistance in crushing the revolt, yielded all rights in the Algarve and agreed to a delimitation of the frontier with Portugal along the Guadiana River to the Atlantic Ocean.

Although tranquility was restored, Alfonso X soon encountered strong domestic opposition because of his innovations in law and taxation. Intent on achieving greater juridical uniformity, he drew upon Roman law in preparing the *Espéculo de las Leyes* (known in its later redaction as the *Siete Partidas*), intended as the law of the royal court, and the *Fuero Real,* a code of municipal law. The nobles accused him of denying them the right to be judged by their peers in accordance with their customs, and the townsmen were distressed by frequent imposition of extraordinary taxes.

Under the leadership of the king's brother Felipe, the nobles confronted the king during the *cortes* (parliament) of Burgos in 1272. By confirming traditional customs, he modified his plan for a uniform body of law, but as compensation, the towns granted him a tax levy every year for "the affair of the empire." Despite his efforts at accommodation many of the nobles went into exile to Granada, but were finally persuaded to return to royal service in 1274. With his realm at peace, Alfonso X then journeyed to Beaucaire in southern France, where in May 1275 he vainly tried to convince Pope Gregory X to recognize him as Holy Roman Emperor. Thereafter Alfonso X could not realistically expect to satisfy his imperial ambitions.

During his absence, Abū Yūsuf, the Marīnid emir of Morocco, invaded Castile. The king's son and heir, Fernando de la Cerda, died suddenly en route to the frontier in 1275, and Abū Yūsuf routed the Castilian forces. At that point, Alfonso X's second son, Sancho, reorganized the defense, cutting Marīnid communications with Morocco. A truce was arrived at, but Abū Yūsuf invaded again in 1277. Avoiding a battlefield encounter, Alfonso X blockaded Algeciras in 1278, but had to give it up early in 1279. In spite of the Moroccan threat, Castile emerged from this crisis without a loss of territory.

Meanwhile, the death of his oldest son in 1275 presented Alfonso X with a serious juridical problem. Fernando de la Cerda's oldest child, Alfonso, could claim recognition as heir to the throne, but Sancho appealed to the older custom that gave preference to a king's surviving sons. After much debate, the king in the cortes of Burgos in 1276 acknowledged Sancho. Fearing for the safety of her two sons, Fernando de la Cerda's widow,

Blanche, accompanied by Queen Violante, took them in 1278 to the court of Violante's brother, Pedro III of Aragón, who kept them in protective custody.

Philip III of France, the uncle of the two boys, pressured Alfonso X to partition his realm and to establish a vassal kingdom for Alfonso de la Cerda. During the cortes of Seville in 1281, while the people complained that they were being impoverished by the heavy taxes, Sancho, angered by the possibility of losing any portion of the kingdom broke with his father. A public assembly held at Valladolid in April 1282 transferred royal power to Sancho, leaving Alfonso X only the royal title. Abandoned by his family and many of his subjects, the king turned to Abū Yūsuf, the Marīnid emir, who invaded Castile again. As many of Sancho's supporters renewed their allegiance to the king, a vain attempt at reconciliation was made, but in his last will Alfonso X disinherited his son. The king died at Seville on 4 April 1284 and was buried in the cathedral.

Despite the unhappy end to his reign Alfonso X was one of the greatest medieval kings of Castile, and his impact on the development of Spanish law and institutions was lasting.

Further Reading

Ballesteros, A. *Alfonso X.* Barcelona and Madrid, 1963; reprt. Barcelona, 1984.

O'Callaghan, J. F. "Image and Reality: The King Creates his Kingdom." In *Emperor of Culture. Alfonso X the Learned of Castile and his Thirteenth-Century Renaissance.* Ed. R. I. Burns. Philadelphia, 1990. 14–32.

JOSEPH F. O'CALLAGHAN

ALFRED THE GREAT
(849–899; r. 871–99)

History

Youngest son of Æthelwulf, king of Wessex, Alfred was born at Wantage, Berkshire, in 849. This is recorded in Asser's *Life of King Alfred*, written during Alfred's lifetime and dedicated to him. In 853 Æthelwulf sent Alfred to Rome, where he received a special investiture from Pope Leo IV (844–55). Though this ritual is depicted by the Anglo-Saxon Chronicle and Asser as an anointing to kingship, in 853 Alfred had three elder brothers living. Asser also claims to have from Alfred the story of how his mother, Osburh, promised a book of "Saxon songs" to whichever son could learn it first; the winner was Alfred.

When Æthelwulf married the Carolingian princess Judith in 856, Alfred's eldest brother, Æthelbald, revolted and assumed rule of Wessex, while Æthelwulf retained Kent, Surrey, and Sussex until his own death in 858, when Æthelbald succeeded to the whole kingdom.

After his death in 860 his brothers Æthelberht (860–65), then Æthelred (865–71), ruled in turn. No further partition occurred. Though Alfred was depicted by Asser as heir-apparent in the late 860ls, his chances of succession were slim, since Æthelred had two sons.

In 865 a large army of Danes landed in East Anglia and in 866–67 gained control of Northumbria. In 868 Danes attacked Mercia, and Alfred joined King Burgred (his brother-in-law) in a campaign of limited success. Alfred now married Ealhswith, a Mercian noblewoman of royal descent. Asser reports that Alfred was struck down by a mysterious illness at his wedding and interprets this as divinely sent preventive medicine against pride.

In 869–70 Danes took control of East Anglia, killing King Edmund. Raids against Wessex began. When Æthelred died in 871, Alfred succeeded, excluding Æthelred's sons; their supporters were overruled. Wessex came under attack from several Danish warbands. Under 871 the Anglo-Saxon Chronicle records nine battles, most of which Alfred lost. He probably bought off attackers with tribute; his coinage became increasingly debased. In 874 Burgred departed for Rome, leaving Mercia to be partitioned between a coalition of Danish warlords and a new Mercian king, Ceolwulf. Though the written record is silent, joint coinage suggests that Alfred and Ceolwulf sometimes allied. In 876 and 877 Danes raided far into Wessex. At Wareham and Exeter Alfred pursued Danish warbands, paying tribute to induce their withdrawal. Protests from the archbishop of Canterbury imply that he extracted substantial contributions from churches, as did Carolingian contemporaries.

In January 878 a Danish force under Guthrum surprised Alfred at Chippenham, Wiltshire, and obliged him to withdraw to Athelney, Somerset, whence with his "vassals" he "harried Danes and Christians who had accepted Danish lordship" (Asser, ch. 53). In May 878 Alfred defeated Guthrum at Edington, Wiltshire. Guthrum made peace, accepting baptism and agreeing to leave Alfred's kingdom. In 879 some Danes withdrew to Mercia and then to East Anglia, while others went to Francia (the "French" or western portion of the Carolingian Empire). Victory at Edington enabled Alfred to recruit further support. It was probably now that a defector, the ealdorman of Wiltshire, was punished by loss of office and lands. Also at this time the coinage was reformed.

During the 880s, with Danes active in the Thames estuary and in Francia, Wessex was unscathed. By 883 Ceolwulf was dead and Alfred established overlordship of western Mercia, with a Mercian noble, Æthelræd, as his ealdorman. Leading Mercians joined Alfred's court; some West Saxons probably gained Mercian lands. A formal peace was made with Guthrum, leaving Alfred in control of Mercia west of Watling Street, the old Roman route that divided the southwest and the northwest. In 886 London, "restored" by Alfred, was handed over to Æthelræd, who married Alfred's daughter Æthelflæd.

Alfred used both preexisting and new fortified settlements to organize a system of burhs covering his kingdom. A few, like Winchester, were intended as political and fiscal centers. Basically the burhs' function was military; garrisoned by mounted warriors (thegns), they could act as refuges and launchpads for counteroffensives. The followers of Alfred and his magnates (ealdormen and probably bishops) were coordinated with the *burh-thegns* (Anglo-Saxon Chronicle, 893). Alfred thus imposed heavy burdens on his nobility.

To secure cooperation Alfred wanted to retrain nobles to think of themselves as an aristocracy of service. Books purveying the service ideal and enhancing royal authority were translated into OE, and bishops were mobilized to ensure their distribution; nobles were told to learn to read and threatened, if they failed, with loss of office. Since Alfred personally participated in the translation project, it offers a unique window on the mind of a medieval king. Royal patronage attracted scholars from Mercia, Wales, and Francia and inspired the production of the Anglo-Saxon Chronicle and Asser's *Life*.

Danish attacks on Wessex resumed in 892 after their defeat in Francia. Alfred was better prepared. The Anglo-Saxon Chronicle for the years 893 to 896 is essentially a record of success, including a minor naval encounter. Alfred suffered less from Danish onslaughts than from "high mortality among his best thegns."

Alfred's law code probably belongs to this decade. It was to apply in Mercia as in Wessex. Some clauses were monuments to Alfred's talents as judge; others asserted the claims of lordship, especially royal lordship. Perhaps following Carolingian models, he imposed the death penalty for treason and probably demanded a generalized oath of fidelity. He secured acknowledgment of his overlordship from Welsh princes, weaning Anarawd of Gwynedd from alliance with the Danes at York. The marriage of Alfred's daughter Ælfthryth with Count Baldwin of Flanders signaled a new West Saxon involvement, on Alfred's terms, in Carolingian politics. Alfred sould to avert dynastic disputes by arranging for sole succession of his elder son, Edward, to his expanded kingdom, acknowledging Edward's infant son, Æthelstan, as a future king. Alfred died in October 899.

Though claims have been made for Alfred as a innovator in law, military organization, and economic planning, his essential success was political. He enhanced West Saxon royal power both practically, extending his control over part of Mercia and dealing ruthlessly with opponents, and ideologically, by publicizing Bede's construct of the unity of English-kind and by winning aristocratic consensus. His posthumous reputation grew, helped by such legends as the 11th-century tale of how he allowed a peasant woman's cakes to burn as he mused on the fate of Wessex and the apocryphal 13th-century *Proverbs of Alfred.* It reached an apogee in his Victorian representation as father of the navy and founder of liberties and national unity. At least in proclaiming Alfred's greatness these myths have a grain of truth.

Alfred's Influence on Learning

In spite of what he described as the "various and manifold preoccupations" of his kingdom, King Alfred not only achieved considerable political success but also instigated and made a major contribution toward the revival of learning in Anglo-Saxon England. In a letter prefaced to his *Pastoral Care* he relates, not without some rhetorical exaggeration, how greatly education had declined by the time that he came to the throne, with few people able to understand Latin, the language of learning. For Alfred learning and the wisdom that could be acquired as a result of it were essential to the spiritual as well as to the economic health of his kingdom: loss of wisdom, he believed, brought with it calamity. Aware that many who did not know Latin could yet read English, he resolved to provide essential texts in the vernacular and called on his scholars to join him in translating those books that were "most necessary for all men to know."

Alfred himself produced three major works—the *Pastoral Care*, the *Consolation of Philosophy*, and the *Soliloquies*—writing mainly in prose but partly in verse; he was apparently also the translator of the first 50 prose psalms of the Paris Psalter. In addition he incorporated translation from the Bible into an important preface to his collection of laws, which set out his concepts of law and lawgiving. How far his colleagues responded to his request for translation is not known. Only one other attributable vernacular work has survived from the late 9th century, Wærferth's translation of Gregory's *Dialogues*, and Alfred's preface to this work tells us that it was commissioned for his personal use, that he "might occasionally reflect in his mind on heavenly things amid these earthly tribulations." However, he acknowledges the help of four people in his *Pastoral Care*, while the anonymous translations of Orosius's *Seven Books of History against the Pagans* and Bede's *Ecclesiastical History*, both of which were once wrongly attributed to him, probably date from this period and may also have been undertaken as part of his plan.

Alfred is sometimes described as father of English prose. His patronage and personal involvement in translation must have contributed to the acceptance of the vernacular as an appropriate medium for serious subjects. His works were still being copied in the 12th century. At the same time there seems to have been a flowering of prose literature in the last part of the 9th century. Works apparently composed in this period include not only the OE Orosius, the OE Bede, Wærferth's translation of the *Dialogues*, and Alfred's own compositions but also the first sections of the Anglo-Saxon Chronicle and the OE *Martyrology*. The Bede and the *Dialogues* follow their sources faithfully. Alfred's translations and the OE Orosius, in contrast, are rarely word-for-word. The *Pastoral Care* is essentially a paraphrase of Gregory's *Regula pastoralis* with explanations and expansions, including a metrical epilogue, based on John 7:38. Gregory was writing for those in authority in spiritual matters, advising "rulers" both how to order their own lives and how to advise the different types of people in their charge, but many of his injunctions applied to the exercise of authority in general and had come to be seen as applicable to secular rulers. In Alfred's hands it becomes virtually a treatise about power and authority.

Liberties are also taken with the text in the prose psalms: Alfred demonstrates a surprising willingness to modify scripture here and elsewhere, with explanation and comment freely inserted. So, for instance, the scribe's quill of Psalm 44:2 is "Christ, the word and tongue of God the Father"; the king's daughters of verse 10 are the souls of righteous men, while the queen is the Christian church. To all the psalms except the first are prefixed brief introductions, giving their meaning at several levels, including their significance for every human being. Indeed, what makes Alfred's writings of peculiar interest and importance is the way the king has modified and added to the substance of his (often learned) Latin originals, in order to render them intelligible to Anglo-Saxons, familiar only with a limited amount of writing in the vernacular, and, where appropriate, even to change the arguments, to bring them into line with his own thinking.

The texts in which Alfred demonstrates the most independence are the renderings of Boethius and Augustine. In the *Consolation of Philosophy* Boethius, writing in the Platonic tradition, sought to demonstrate the divine ordering of the universe without appeal to Christian revelation. Alfred, reading the work in the light of the Christian perspective of his day and as a ruler, accepting the doctrine of merit and the forgiveness of sins, rejects a number of Boethius's ideas and recasts his source. He makes substantial changes to passages involving the Platonic doctrine of Forms, the conception of a World-Soul, and a belief in the preexistence of the soul. The personifications Natura and Fortuna are removed; Lady Philosophy becomes *se heofoncund wisdom* (masc. "divine Wisdom") or *gesceadwisnes* (fem. "Discrimination, Reason"), while her interlocutor "Boethius" is frequently replaced by *Mod* ("Mind"), with the effect of making the speaker appear less of an individual and more of a representative of humanity.

Many references to Boethius that are of a personal nature are removed, and attitudes reflecting the circumstances in which the original was written are softened. Boethius, the philosopher-politician, imprisoned and about to be executed by the king he had served, attacks the pursuit of wealth, position, power, and fame, all of which come under Fortune's jurisdiction and fall in abundance on the most wicked people. Alfred, the ruler, sees power and wealth as both necessary and potentially good, having been bestowed on men by God so that they may do his will. Honor and fame are not to be rejected, and it is right that a man's reputation should live after him as an encouragement and example to others. In transforming his Latin original in this way Alfred resembles the translator of Orosius, who also takes great liberties with his text and moves from an exercise in polemic, showing how evils have ever occurred in cycles, to a demonstration of God's mercy as manifested through and after Christ's birth. However, both Alfred and the Orosius translator preserve the structural divisions of their sources.

A different kind of freedom is exercised in the work known as the *Soliloquies*. A lengthy allegorical preface is followed by an adaptation of Augustine's *Soliloquies* reflecting the king's major concerns; subsequently Alfred draws on Augustine's *De videndo Deo*, the Bible, and works by Gregory the Great. The text, organized in three books, for much of its length follows Augustine in using dialogue form: the speakers are *Mod* ("Mind") and *Gesceadwisnes* ("Discrimination" or "Reason," Augustine's *Ratio*), and the subjects explored include the nature of God and of the soul, the eternal qualities of knowing, what constitutes Truth, and the many roads to Wisdom, that is, to God. Much space is devoted to the subject of the immortality of the soul, in an attempt to reply to a question asked by Augustine at the end of his *Soliloquies* but not answered there.

The interest of Alfred's works for the modern reader does not, however, lie solely in the modifications of substance that he makes to his primary sources. The perceived need for clarification has resulted in many minor additions and modifications, a need met also in the Orosius, where the Latin author's assumption of classical and historical knowledge in his audience has led the OE translator to make an extraordinary number of expansions—telling the story of Regulus, for instance, or the Rape of the Sabines, or Cato's suicide. Alfred similarly fills in a number of details, such as the fate of Busiris, and relates at some length the stories of Orpheus and Eurydice and of Ulysses and Circe. Like the translator of the Orosius he has drawn his material from an impressive range of classical and patristic sources, though whether directly or via an intermediary cannot be determined. In the case of the *Pastoral Care* we know, from Alfred's own preface, that the king had the work explained to him by the group of English, Welsh, and continental scholars he had gathered round him. The introductions to the Psalms and some of the explanations within them appear to be derived from written commentaries. Boethius's *Consolation*, according to William of Malmesbury, was explained to Alfred by Asser, though whether orally or in writing is not stated. Attempts to identify a written form of Asser's explanation have so far failed. The use of a commentary or glossed manuscripts might account for a number of the additions in Alfredian texts (as, for instance, the many identifications of biblical quotations in the *Pastoral Care*) but cannot be proven for these or indeed for the new information in the OE Orosius.

Another important and interesting group of changes reflects attempts by the king to modify the severity of some of the harsher pronouncements of his sources. So, for instance, when Gregory's *Regula pastoralis* states that all sins will be punished on Doomsday, the *Pastoral Care* refers to all sins that are unatoned for; when Gregory condemns those who abandon a good work unfinished, Alfred inserts the words "willingly and deliberately"; when Gregory quotes the statement from James 4:4 that one must not become a friend of the world, Alfred supplies the important qualification, "too immoderately." Gregory's list of sins for which God will make exception is extended to include not only sins committed out of ignorance or folly but also those committed from the instincts of the flesh or from weakness of character or from infirmity of mind or body. Similarly, in the Boethius translation, Alfred regularly reminds his reader that punishment can be avoided by repentance and constantly stresses God's mercy: God judges by the good will and not by the performance. In the Psalms the statement that God hates all who work iniquity is modified to apply only to those who do not abandon it or repent of it, and a similar qualification is added to the claim that "those who do evil shall be exterminated." In the *Soliloquies* as in the Boethius, the king refuses to agree that wealth is necessarily bad and that honor should be abandoned unless it is excessive. Perhaps the most interesting "minor" changes, however, are those that involve making potentially difficult points more accessible through simple and familiar analogues.

Alfred's love of expanded metaphor and simile manifests itself in his preface to the *Soliloquies* as well as in the body of his works. Favorite themes include flowing water and ships; others reflect the preoccupations of a ruler and the everyday concerns of his people: the ways to a king's court, for instance, or the relationship between a man and his lord, or the building of a dwelling. A Boethian simile comparing the universe to a number of spheres turning on a center, is replaced by an elaborate and carefully sustained image, explaining the relationship between various sorts and conditions of men and God in terms of a wheel set on an axle.

The chronology of Alfred's works is not known. The only vernacular text mentioned by Asser in 893 is the *Dialogues*. However, this may be because the *Life of King Alfred* was never completed. Equally inconclusive is William of Malmesbury's claim that Alfred was working on the Psalms at the time of his death: he may have drawn his conclusion from the fact that only the first 50 psalms had been translated, even though the practice of subdividing the Psalter into units of 50 seems to have been a common one. It is probable, however, that the *Pastoral Care* (circulated ca. 890–95) was the first of Alfred's translations, while verbal echoes may (less certainly) suggest that the *Soliloquies* followed the Boethius, which in its turn may have been later than the anonymous Orosius, a text possibly completed as early as 890 or 891.

See also **Bede the Venerable; Gregory I, Pope**

Further Reading

Primary Sources

Bately, Janet M., ed. *The Old English Orosius.* EETS s.s. 6. London: Oxford University Press, 1980

Bright, James W., and Robert L. Ramsay, eds. *Liber Psalmorum: The West-Saxon Psalms, Being the Prose Portion, or the "First Fifty," of the So-Called Paris Psalter.* Boston: Heath, 1907

Carnicelli, Thomas A., ed. *King Alfred's Version of St. Augustine's Soliloquies.* Cambridge: Harvard University Press, 1969

Hargrove, Henry Lee, trans. *King Alfred's Old English Version of St. Augustine's Soliloquies Turned into Modern English.* New York: Holt, 1904

Hecht, Hans, ed. *Bischof Warferths von Worcester Übersetzung der Dialogue Gregors des Grossen.* 2 vols. Bibliothek der angelsächsischen Prosa 5. Leipzig: Wigand, 1900–07

Keynes, Simon, and Michael Lapidge, trans. *Alfred the Great: Asser's Life of King Alfred and Other Contemporary Sources.* Harmondsworth: Penguin, 1983

Kotzor, G., ed. *Das altenglische Martyrologium.* Bayerische Akademie der Wissenschaften, Phil.-Hist. Klasse 88/1–2. Munich: Bayerische Akademie der Wissenschaften, 1981

Miller, Thomas, ed. and trans. *The Old English Version of Bede's Ecclesiastical History of the English People.* EETS o.s. 95, 96, 110, 111. London: Trübner, 1890–98

Sedgefield, Walter John, ed. *King Alfred's Old English Version of Boethius De consolatione Philosophiae.* Oxford: Clarendon, 1899

Sedgefield, Walter John, trans. *King Alfred's Version of the Consolations of Boethius.* Oxford: Clarendon, 1900

Stevenson, William Henry, ed. *Asser's Life of King Alfred.* Oxford: Clarendon, 1904. Repr. Oxford: Clarendon, 1959

Sweet, Henry, ed. and trans. *King Alfred's West-Saxon Version of Gregory's "Pastoral Care."* EETS o.s. 45, 50. London: Trübner, 1871–72. Repr. with corrections by N.R. Ker. London: Oxford University Press, 1958.

History

Abels, Richard P. *Lordship and Military Obligation in Anglo-Saxon England.* Berkeley: University of California Press, 1988

Brooks, Nicholas P. "England in the Ninth Century: The Crucible of Defeat." *TRHS*, 5th ser. 29 (1979): 1–20

Campbell, James. "Asser's Life of Alfred." In *The Inheritance of Historiography, 350–900*, ed. C. Holdsworth and T.P Wiseman. Exeter: University of Exeter, 1986, pp. 115–35

Hinton, David A. *Alfred's Kingdom: Wessex and the South, 800–1500.* London: Dent, 1977

Hodges, Richard. *The Anglo-Saxon Achievement: Archaeology and the Beginnings of English Society.* London: Duckworth, 1989

Keynes, Simon. "A Tale of Two Kings: Alfred the Great and Æthelred the Unready." *TRHS*, 5th ser. 36 (1986): 195–217

Maddicott, J.R. "Trade, Industry and the Wealth of King Alfred." *Past and Present* 123 (May 1989): 3–51

Nelson, JX. "'A King across the Sea': Alfred in Continental Perspective." *TRHS*, 5th ser. 36 (1986): 45–68

Nelson, J.L. "Reconstructing a Royal Family: Reflections on Alfred, from Asser, Chapter 2." In *People and Places in Northern Europe, 500–1600: Essays in Honour of Peter Sawyer*, ed. Ian Wood and Niels Lund. Woodbridge: Boydell, 1990, pp. 47–66

Nelson, J.L. "The Political Ideas of Alfred of Wessex." In *Kings and Kingship in Medieval Europe.* London: King's College London, 1993, pp. 125–58

Smyth, A.P. *King Alfred the Great.* Oxford: Oxford University Press, 1995 [idiosyncratic but in parts thought-provoking study]

Sturdy, D.J. *Alfred the Great.* London: Constable, 1995

Wormald, Patrick. "The Ninth Century." In *The Anglo-Saxons*, ed. James Campbell. Oxford: Phaidon, 1982, pp. 132–59 [excellent short account, in the absence of a full-scale modern scholarly study].

Alfred and Learning

Bately, Janet. *The Literary Prose of King Alfred's Reign: Translation or Transformation?* London: King's College London, 1980. Repr. *OEN Subsidia* 10. Binghamton: CEMERS, 1984

Frantzen, Allen J. *King Alfred.* Boston: Twayne, 1986

Liggins, Elizabeth M. "The Authorship of the Old English Orosius." *Anglia* 88 (1970): 289–322

O'Neill, Patrick. "Old English Introductions to the Prose Psalms of the Paris Psalter: Sources, Structure and Composition." *SP78* (1981): 20–38

Payne, F. Anne. *King Alfred and Boethius: An Analysts of the OE Version of the "Consolation of Philosophy."* Madison: University of Wisconsin Press, 1968

Potter, Simeon. *On the Relation of the Old English Bede to Werferth's Gregory and to Alfred's Translations.* Prague: Nákladem Král, 1931

Szarmach, Paul E. "The Meaning of Alfred's *Preface* to the Pastoral Care." *Mediaevalia* 6 (1982 for 1980): 57–86

Szarmach, Paul E., ed. *Studies in Earlier Old English Prose.* Albany: SUNY Press, 1986 [many relevant articles]

Whitelock, Dorothy. "The Old English Bede." *PBA* 48 (1962): 57–90. Repr. in *British Academy Papers on Anglo-Saxon England*, ed. E.G. Stanley. Oxford: Oxford University Press, 1990, pp. 227–60

Whitelock, Dorothy. "The Prose of Alfred's Reign.'" In *Continuations and Beginnings: Studies in Old English Literature*, ed. E.G. Stanley. London: Nelson, 1966, pp. 67–103

Wittig, Joseph S. "King Alfred's Boethius and Its Latin Sources: A Reconsideration." *ASE* 11 (1983): 157–98

Wormald, Patrick. "The Uses of Literacy in Anglo-Saxon England and Its Neighbours." *TRHS*, 5th ser. 27 (1977): 95–114.

JANET L NELSON
JANET M. BATELY

ALTICHIERO DA ZEVIO
(c. 1330–after 1390)

Altichiero was already an established painter in March 1369, when he is first documented in his native Verona. All subsequent documents relating to Altichiero refer to his activities in Padua. The earliest of these documents—dated April 1376—has to do with an altarpiece in a church at Polverara, near Padua. That altarpiece and another one paid for in 1382 are lost or untraceable, and no other altarpiece panels currently attributed to Altichiero are actually by him.

Works

The earliest surviving documented works by Altichiero are some frescoes in the chapel of San Giacomo (now San Felice) in the basilica di Sant'Antonio in Padua; this was the mortuary chapel of Lupi, a soldier and diplomat serving the ruling house of Carrara. The contract for the architecture and sculpture in the chapel was signed in February 1372 by Bonifacio Lupi and the Venetian Andriolo de Santi. The original ledger survives and records work in the chapel from 1372 to 1379. The painting appears to have been done during the last two or three years. Altichiero, the only painter recorded by name, was paid for his work in the chapel (and for the decoration of the sacristy, now lost) in 1379. It is clear from stylistic evidence that another artist, working independently and not from Altichiero's designs, executed some of the lunettes—the first four and the sixth—depicting the legend of Saint James the Greater. Except for some marginal figures, the remainder of the decoration is by Altichiero: the other scenes of Saint James, the panoramic three-bay Crucifixion, the votive fresco, and the Annunciation, Resurrection, and Man of Sorrows.

The identity of the other artist is a subject of controversy. He was probably the Bolognese painter Jacopo d'Avanzo (or Avanzi), who is mentioned by some of the early sources—including the earliest, Michele Savonarola (c. 1446)—as having worked in the chapel. This seems to be the artist who is cited in Bolognese archival documents from 1375 to 1384, but it could instead be a Jacopo di Pietro Avanzi, who was already dead in 1378. The artist Avanzo (or Avanzi) who represented the brotherhood of painters in Padua in March 1405 appears to have been a different person; this is also certainly true of a homonymous painter recorded in Vicenza in 1379, 1380, and 1389. The Bolognese Avanzo signed a Crucifixion (now in the Colonna Gallery in Rome)—the basis for the attribution of the Massacre of the Hebrews, detached from the church of Sant'A-pollonia di Mezzarata in Bologna and now in the Pinacoteca there. Twelve miniatures now in Dublin, illuminating Statius's *Thebaid*, have also been ascribed to Avanzo, but they may be by a close follower. (In either case, they cannot be a clear reflection of the lost frescoes by Guariento in the Carrara Palace in Padua, as is sometimes claimed.)

After completing the chapel of San Giacomo, Altichiero decorated the nearby oratorio of San Giorgio, a barrel-vaulted structure modeled on the Arena Chapel. It became the resting place of Raimondino Lupi, who was Bonifacio's relative and, like Bonifacio, a soldier of Francesco da Carrara, lord of the city. The elaborate freestanding tomb has been much reduced. Documents show that the oratory was constructed by December 1379, possibly by May 1378, and that Altichiero finished his painting by May 1384. Other documents attest to his presence in Padua from July 1381 to 1384. The frescoes depict the legends of saints George, Catherine, and Lucy, with some scenes from the lives of Christ and Mary, and a votive image. Although it has been damaged by moisture, this is one of the most magnificent picture cycles of its century. The hand of Avanzo is not visible—we see only the hands of Altichiero and the expected assistants—nor is Avanzo mentioned in the documents. Yet it is sometimes claimed, on the basis of some of the early sources and an illegible inscription, that Avanzo's work is present.

The last record of Altichiero is a Paduan archival document of September 1384. At that time he was either in Verona or about to go there. The Florentine art historian Giorgio Vasari (1568) is the source of the tradition that Altichiero returned to Verona after working in Padua.

Vasari is the authority who tells us that Altichiero painted frescoes illustrating Flavius Josephus's *Jewish War* in the palace of the Scaligeri lords of Verona. Vasari writes that Avanzo also worked in the room, which he discusses before Altichiero's and Avanzo's Paduan works. This has given rise to the belief that the frescoes, for which there are no relevant documents, were done before Altichiero moved to Padua, for Cansignorio (1359–1375). Some portraits of Roman emperors and empresses survive and may be attributed to Altichiero, although these are not the subjects of the border medallions described by Vasari. They reflect a study of Roman coins, directly or indirectly through the illustrations of the *Historia imperialis* by the Veronese protohumanist Giovanni de Matociis (Mansionario). The rest of the decoration is lost, though some drawings may reflect it.

The early sources mention the undocumented *Sala virorum illustrium* (Room of Famous Men) in the Carrara Palace at Padua. The sources give conflicting attributions: Guariento; Altichiero; Avanzo; and an artist by whom no documented works survive, Ottaviano (Prandino) da Brescia. The decoration was destroyed by fire and repainted with an altered scheme. The portion of the portrait of Petrarch which alone survives of the original decoration suggests that Altichiero worked in the room. Historical and literary evidence shows that the frescoes could not have been begun before 1367 and had been completed, or nearly completed, by January 1379. The decoration was based on *De viris illustribus* (*On Famous Men*), begun by Petrarch, finished after his death by Lombardo della Seta, and dedicated by both to Francesco da Carrara the Elder. The original program must have consisted of thirty-six figures of famous generals and statesmen from Romulus to Trajan, all but three of them Roman, with narrative scenes and inscriptions beneath; portraits of Petrarch and Lombardo in their studies; and a Triumph of Fame. Assisting with this reconstruction are illuminations from two manuscripts of *De viris illustribus* in the Bibliothèque Nationale in Paris (Lat. 6069F and I) and one in Darmstadt (ms. 101). The Triumphs of Fame in the first two and an allegory of Padua and Venice in a third manuscript in Paris (Lat. 6069G) are often attributed to Altichiero, though it seems more likely that they were painted by his followers.

No sources or documents exist for the votive fresco of the Coronation of the Virgin on the tomb of Diamante Dotto, which was in the church of the Eremitani in Padua before it was destroyed during World War II, or for the votive fresco in the Cavalli Chapel in the church of Sant'Anastasia in Verona. Scholars unanimously attribute both to Altichiero, although they disagree on the dates. The first was probably painted around 1371, when Dotto died. The other was done before September 1390, when it was broken by another monument. It must have been painted after the chapel of San Giacomo in Padua, which its architectural background presupposes, and it may have been done after 1384, when Altichiero presumably returned to his native city.

Style and Influence

By about mid-century, the painters of Verona had absorbed the style of Giotto from nearby Padua, along with more recent Florentine and Sienese influences that seem to have been transmitted primarily through Riminese and Lombard intermediaries. With the exception of a polyptych signed by Turone and dated 1360, in the Castelvecchio, and some attributions based on it, the surviving works of this school are all anonymous.

Altichiero built on the local school, which had already naturalized the art of Giotto. Although he also knew the work of Maso di Banco and probably other Florentine followers of Giotto, he turned directly to the great example of Giotto's frescoes in Padua for the essentials of his own style. However, whereas Giotto's forms are abstract and timeless, Altichiero's figures are dressed in the costume of his time. Also, their features are more individualized than Giotto's, and the flesh tones are more softly graduated. Altichiero was more sensitive to nuances of light, color, and surface texture. His figures are smaller in scale than Giotto's, relative to their surroundings and to the picture field; they are more numerous; and their distribution is more random and lifelike. Despite these differences, Altichiero retains Giotto's sense of monumentality and-human dignity. His architectural settings, which were inspired by the Carrara court painter, Guariento, are more spacious and complex than Giotto's. But unlike these artists and others of their century, Altichiero generally avoided showing a structure with its front wall arbitrarily removed to reveal the interior; he preferred views more truthful to optical experience.

Altichiero, like Giusto de' Menabuoi, was probably called to Padua to fill the vacancy left by the death of Guariento. Altichiero, Giusto, and Avanzo (whose frescoes in Sant'Antonio are close to Altichiero and were influenced by him) were the leaders of a Giottoesque revival in Padua at a time when painting in Florence had stagnated, owing to a relaxation of Giotto's principles. Altichiero and, to a lesser extent, Avanzo had a dominant influence on painting and manuscript illumination in Padua and Verona that lasted to the beginning of the fifteenth century. This influence extended chronologically as far as Pisanello, Jacopo Bellini, and the Renaissance. Geographically, it extended beyond the Veneto as far as Austria and France, where the Limbourg brothers worked.

See also **Giotto di Bondone; Guisto de' Menabuoi**

Further Reading

Benati, Daniele. *Jacopo Avanzi nel rinnovamento della pittura padana del secondo '300*. Bologna: Grafis Edizioni d'Arte, 1992.

Cuppini, Maria Teresa. "La pittura a Verona e nel territorio veronese dal principio del sec. XIV alia metà del Quattrocento." In *Verona e il suo territorio*. Verona: Istituto per gli Studi Storici Veronesi, 1969, Vol. 3, pt. 2, pp. 286–383.

Gnudi, Cesare. "Introduzione." In *Pittura bolognese del '300: Scritti di Francesco Arcangeli*, ed. Pier Giovanni Castagnoli, Alessandro Conti, and Massimo Ferretti. Bologna: Grafis Edizioni d'Arte, 1978, pp. 234–239.

Kruft, Hanno-Walter. *Altichiero und Avanzo: Untersuchungen zur oberitalienischen Malerei des ausgehenden Trecento*. Bonn: Rheinishche Friedrich-Wilhelms-Universität, 1966.

Mellini, Gian Lorenzo. *Altichiero e Jacopo Avanzi* Milan: Edizioni di Comunità, 1965.

Mommsen, Theodor E. "Petrarch and the Decoration of the Sala Virorum Illustrium in Padua." *Art Bulletin*, 34, 1952, pp. 95–116. (Reprinted in his *Medieval and Renaissance Studies*. Ithaca, N.Y.: Cornell University Press, 1959, pp. 130–174.)

Pettenella, Plinia. *Altichiero e la pittura veronese del Trecento*. Verona: Edizioni di Vita Veronese, 1961.

Sartori, Antonio. "La cappella di S. Giacomo al Santo di Padova." *Il Santo*, 6, 1966, pp. 267–359.

——. "Nota su Altichiero." *Il Santo*, 3, 1963, pp. 291–326.

Simon, Robin. "Altichiero versus Avanzo." *Papers of the British School at Rome*, 45, 1977, pp. 252–271.

Vavalà, Evelyn Sandberg. *La pittura veronese del Trecento e del primo Quattrocento.* Verona: Tipografica Veronese, 1926.

BRADLEY J. DELANEY

ALVARUS, PAULUS
(mid-9th century)

Córdoban laymen, author. Very little is known about his life. A reference in one of his letters hints at Jewish ancestry; another suggests Gothic blood. Either or both could, however, have been intended metaphorically given their contexts. His family owned enough land to allow them to use part of it to endow a monastery. Alvarus studied under Abbot Speraindeo at the church of St. Zoylus in Córdoba, where he met and befriended Eulogius. There, among other things, the two developed an interest in poetry, which Alvarus would pursue later in life, composing a number of poems that have survived. The preface to his *Vita Eulogii* suggests that Alvarus did not follow his friend into the priesthood. He appears to have married and to have lost three of his daughters, though the circumstances are unknown.

Letters to and from a variety of correspondents constitute the bulk of his extant writing. The earliest of these are the four directed to Bodo, a deacon in the Carolingian court who converted to Judaism, adopted the name Eleazar, and moved to Spain. Alvarus's letters to Bodo-Eleazar predictably attempt to prove that Jesus was the Messiah. Three responses survive, though in fragmentary form. Alvarus also wrote to his former teacher Speraindeo asking him to respond to an outbreak of some unnamed heresy. Alvarus directed another four letters to his friend (and perhaps brother-in-law) John of Seville, another layman, in which he explored the role of rhetoric in Christian education and delved into Christology.

Alvarus's role in the Córdoban Martyrs' Movement of the 850s was an auxiliary one. From his cell in the autumn of 851, Eulogius sent drafts of the *Memoriale sanctorum* and the *Documentum martyriale* to Alvarus for his comments. The letters that Alvarus wrote in response were subsequently appended to the treatises. We know from Eulogius that Alvarus advised at least one of the would-be martyrs who sought him out for advice. In 854 Alvarus wrote his *Indiculus luminosus,* the first half of which is a defense of the martyrs, and the second half a novel attempt to portray Muiammad as a precursor of Antichrist by interpreting passages from Daniel, Job, and the Apocalypse in light of Alvarus's knowledge of Islam. Toward the end of the treatise, which seems not to have been completed, is the frequently quoted passage lamenting the fact that Christian youths of the day were more interested in studying Arabic than Latin literature. Finally, sometime after Eulogius's execution in 859, Alvarus wrote the *Vita Eulogii.*

The last of Alvarus's letters indicate that he had suffered from a serious illness and had received penance in anticipation of his death, only to recover. He solicited Bishop Saul of Córdoba to release him from his penitential obligation to refrain from participation in communion, a request that was denied. Alvarus's *Confessio,* a lengthy formal prayer for forgiveness of sins, probably also dates from this period. The fact that he is not mentioned in Samson's *Apologeticus* (864) and that Alvarus never referred to the controversies that elicited its composition suggests that he died in the early 860s.

See also **Eulogius of Córdoba**

Further Reading

Gil, J. (ed.) *Corpus scriptorum muzarabicorum.* 2 vols. Madrid, 1973. 1:143–361.

Sage, C. "Paul Albar of Córdoba: Studies on his Life and Writings." Washington, D.C., 1943.

KENNETH B. WOLF

AMADEO VI, COUNT OF SAVOY
(1334–1383)

Amadeus VI (Amadeo), the son of Count Aymon of Savoy and Violante de Montferrat, was born at the family seat of Chambéry. Through earlier and subsequent genealogical and matrimonial ties, he was related to numerous royal and princely families of western Europe, and even Byzantium; but he belonged to a dynasty—the house of Savoy—that was, in the midst of terrible divisions, struggling to create the beginnings of a state in the rough, disconnected rural and mountainous territories in the western Alpine regions. Amadeo's grandfather, Amadeo V "the Great" (1285–1323), had begun drawing together territories in areas long disputed between the French crown and the German empire and caught in a tangle of conflicting feudal claims by local ruling families. The house of Savoy itself was divided between the main branch of Amadeo V's line and the rival Savoyard line of the titular princes of Achaea.

Amadeo was only nine in 1343 when his rather died and he succeeded to the still rickety titles. Under a responsible regency of feudal relatives, he continued to receive a solid education in both military skills and intellectual disciplines, which developed in him a genuine religious bent shaped by the highest ideals of chivalry. In his early years, both under the regency and after his majority was proclaimed (in 1348, when he was fourteen), Amadeo gained experience in balancing the pressures of the French crown, the independence of his Swiss subjects, and the disloyalty of separatist vassals.

In 1352, he won his first military victory. At a tournament held during the following Christmas season, his elaborate use of green robes and trappings earned him the sobriquet "Green Count"—a name that would last and an identity that he would continue to cultivate deliberately. By 1360, through both military and diplomatic assertion, Amadeo had expanded his territories in the western Alps, including significant areas of present-day France and Switzerland, and thus consolidated the western regions of the nascent Savoyard state. In many of these regions, he remained a vassal of the French king, whose cousin he took as his first wife in 1355; it was only by a turn of circumstances that Amadeo did not participate in the battle of Poitiers the following year and thus escaped being captured there with his overlord.

Amadeo was drawn meanwhile to protect the interests of his southern holdings in the Piedmont. Through the marriage in 1350 of his sister Bianca to Galeazzo II Visconti of Milan (Bianca and Galeazzo II became the parents of the great Gian Galeazzo), Amadeo developed cordial relations with the powerful Visconti family, eventually consolidating power over territories he had held in vassalage to them. He accomplished an uneasy subjection of his cousin of the Achaea branch, Giacomo, whose territories he annexed and with whom he developed a long and bitter rivalry. This rivalry was extended to Giacomo's son Filippo, whom Amadeo was finally to destroy in 1368. In a campaign in 1363, Amadeo subjected his rebellious vassal the marquis of Saluzzo. Two years later, Amadeo entertained the Holy Roman emperor Charles IV, who confirmed Amadeo's title of imperial vicar over areas that corresponded to much of the old kingdom of Aries. This status was more symbolic than real, but it allowed Amadeo to play off his dependency on the French crown against his vassalage to the empire.

In 1364, Amadeo was caught up in schemes for a crusade being fostered by Pierre de Lusignan, the king of Cyprus. Amadeo formally "took the cross" and organized a crusading Order of the Collar, signaling his new ambition to distinguish himself in this sphere. However, he was drawn away from Lusignan's project by an idea of collaborating with Louis the Great of Hungary against the Turks, who were progressing in the Balkans. He was also distracted by the needs of the Byzantine emperor John V Palaiologos (Palaeologus), his first cousin through their shared Montferrat links; Amadeo might have seen himself as a distant pretender to John's title. Leaving his wife as regent, Amadeo set forth in the spring of 1366, sailing from Venice with a substantial military force. John was himself visiting the Hungarian court when Amadeo set out for Constantinople. The Green Count undertook some immediate military operations on his way, compelling the Turks to surrender the crucial port city of Gallipoli, and then

making a demonstration against the Bulgarian king, who was preventing John's return to his capital.

Amadeo's limited resources prevented anything more than token local military operations. Nevertheless, on the basis of discussions held during the winter, Amadeo persuaded John to appeal directly to Pope Urban V for more aid against the Turks. John achieved few practical results from this, but Amadeo established his own stature as an international diplomat and a valiant crusader. Following his triumphant return to Italy in the summer of 1367, Amadeo personally attended Urban V on his arrival in Rome from Avignon.

In the following years, Amadeo was caught up in the tangle of northern Italian politics, which were strained by the bold new ambitions of the Visconti, directed especially against the lands of Montferrat. By July 1372, Amadeo joined a broad alliance against the Visconti—the coalition included Pope Gregory XI; the princes of Montferrat, Este, and Carrara; the queen of Naples; and the republics of Genoa and Florence. Accepting the command of the allies' forces, Amadeo broke the Visconti's siege of Asti and, in concert with the league's other commander, John Hawkwood, discomfited the enemy forces. In the spring of 1374, satisfied with his record, Amadeo withdrew from the league and became reconciled with the Visconti; but relations between the house of Savoy and the Visconti continued to be precarious. Through complex manipulations, Amadeo was able to annex considerable areas of Montferrat lands, although Gian Galeazzo Visconti, who was in power by 1378, retained Asti.

As he consolidated the Savoy lands, Amadeo began to develop orderly institutions for his nascent state. The Great Schism of 1378 brought the election of the French counterpope Clement VII, a cousin of Amadeo. Clement was naturally recognized gladly by Savoy, which benefited from his resolutions of some jurisdictional disputes. By 1380, Amadeo became concerned about the expansion of the latest war between Genoa and Venice; initially, this was a conflict over the Greek island of Tenedos, but it expanded into the "Chiogga war," with a scrambling of alliances that threatened the balance of power in northern Italy and encouraged the Visconti's aggression. Amadeo's offer of mediation was accepted, and his negotiation of the Peace of Turin (April 1381) established him even more firmly as a statesman of international stature. One faction in strife-ridden Genoa even offered Amadeo the protectorship of the city, with the title of doge. Meanwhile, with the Visconti momentarily checked again, Amadeo established his theoretical rights over Asti (though not actual control of it) and, more tangibly, secured possession of the important border city of Cuneo.

Amadeo is said to have dreamed of a new crusade, directly to the Holy Land. But his final adventure instead involved him in a scheme by Louis of Anjou to claim the throne of Naples, in collaboration with the efforts of Pope Clement VII to establish himself in Rome. In the spring of 1382, Amadeo set forth, marching through Italy into a badly mismanaged campaign that was foiled in part by John Hawkwood, who was now a Florentine captain in support of the Roman pope Urban VI, and Hawkwood's Neapolitan ally Charles of Durazzo. Over the winter, Amadeo's forces were ravaged by disease, which finally took his own life (on 27 February 1383). His remains were lovingly transported back to Savoy for burial.

Though he was an occasional patron of Guillaume de Machaut and Francesco Petrarca (Petrarch), Amadeo VI was a man of war and statecraft rather than of culture. Shaped at first by the traditions of chivalry, Amadeo learned to blend them with the newer impulses of pragmatic realism. From his grandfather he inherited bare feudal elements which he began to fuse into a viable entity, balanced between the neighboring powers of France and Italy and acquiring prestige from his personal reputation. His grandson, Amadeo VIII, would further consolidate Savoy as a duchy, established in the natural capital of Turin and securely set on a course that would turn the once peripheral house of Savoy into a monarchy which would eventually unite Italy.

See also **Hawkwood, sir John; Machaut, Guillaume de**

Further Reading

Cognasso, Francesco. *Il conte verde.* Turin, 1926.
Cox, Eugene L. *The Green Count of Savoy: Amadeus VI and Transalpine Savoy in the Fourteenth Century.* Princeton, N.J.: Princeton University Press, 1967.

JOHN W. BARKER

ANDREAS CAPELLANUS
(André le Chapelain; fl. late 12th c.)

Author of a treatise on the art of love, *De amore* (or *De arte honeste amandi*), composed for a certain Gautier. Andreas's identity remains enigmatic. He has most frequently been identified with a chaplain of the same name in the service of Marie de Champagne, the daughter of Louis VII and Eleanor of Aquitaine and the patroness of Chrétien de Troyes.

De amore, preserved in over thirty manuscripts and collections, is composed of three books. The first expounds the nature of love; the second, in a series of twenty-one judgments attributed to some of the noblest ladies of France (Eleanor of Aquitaine, Marie de Champagne, Elizabeth of Vermandois, and others), tells how to maintain love; and the third condemns love. The entire treatise shows the influence of Ovid's *Ars amatoris* and

Remedia amoris, as well as an intimate knowledge of the casuistry and rhetorical traditions of the medieval Latin school system. Its interpretation, however, like that of Chrétien's *Chevalier de la charrette*, remains problematic. Modern critics are divided as to whether to take the work seriously or read it ironically. If Andreas's intention was to produce a treatise on the practice of (courtly) love, then how can one explain the aritifeminism of the final book? Was this true remorse or an ironic stance to avoid ecclesiastical condemnation?

The work was translated into Franco-Italian prose in the second half of the 13th century and into Old French by Drouart la Vache in 1290. It also made its way into Catalan, Italian, and German.

See also **Chrétien de Troyes; Eleanor of Aquitane; Jean de Meun**

Further Reading

Andreas Capellanus. *Andreae Capellani regii Francorum De amore libri tres*, ed. E. Trojel. Copenhagen: Libraria Gandiana, 1892.
——. *The Art of Courtly Love*, trans. John J. Parry. New York: Columbia University Press, 1941.
——. *Traité de l'amour courtois*, trans. Claude Buridant. Paris: Champion, 1974.
Karnein, Alfred. "La réception d'André le Chapelain au XIIIe siècle." *Romania* 12 (1981): 324–51, 501–42.
Kelly, F. Douglas. "Courtly Love in Perspective: The Hierarchy of Love in Andreas Capellanus." *Traditio* 24 (1968): 119–47.
Monson, Don A. "Andreas Capellanus and the Problem of Ironly." *Speculum* 63 (1988): 539–72.

WILLIAM W. KIBLER

ANDREW OF SAINT-VICTOR (d. 1175)

Biblical exegete who provided the most sustained treatment of the Hebrew Bible according to the literal sense since the time of St. Jerome (4th–5th c). Born probably in England, Andrew entered the abbey of Saint-Victor in Paris and studied under Hugh of Saint-Victor. He later returned to England as abbot of Wigmore, a house of regular canons in Herefordshire.

Andrew was influenced by Hugh's emphasis on the importance of the literal sense of Scripture as the foundation for understanding the allegorical and moral senses. In contrast to Hugh's interest in the threefold interpretation of Scripture, Andrew wrote exegetical treatises only on the Hebrew Bible, with the literal sense his only focus. His commentaries on the Octateuch, Historical Books, Wisdom Books, Minor Prophets, and Isaiah, Jeremiah, Ezekiel, and Daniel have been preserved. These commentaries indicate that Andrew consulted with Jews in the vernacular and then translated their interpretations into Latin. It is not likely that he had extensive knowledge of biblical or postbiblical Hebrew. From Andrew's commentaries, however, we learn about Jewish liturgical practices and mourning customs. Richard of Saint-Victor wrote *De Emmanuele* condemning Andrew's acceptance of Jewish teachings about Isaiah 7:14, an important messianic prophecy for Christians. But Andrew did not accept all Jewish explications in uncritical fashion. He considered Jewish claims about messianic deliverance and restoration of the sacrificial cult in Jerusalem to be "fables." Andrew's writings influenced Peter Comestor, Peter the Chanter, Stephen Langton, and Herbert of Bosham.

See also **Hugh of Saint-Victor; Peter Comestor; Peter the Chanter**

Further Reading

Andreas de Sancto Victore. *Expositio in Ezechielem*, ed. Michael A. Signer. *CCCM* 53E. Turnhout: Brepols, 1991.

——. *Expositio super Danielem*, ed. Mark Zier. *CCCM* 53F. Turnhout: Brepols, 1990.

——. *Expositio super heptateuchum,* ed. Charles Lohr and Ranier Berndt. *CCCM* 53. Turnhout: Brepols, 1986.

——. *Expositiones historicae in Libros Salomonis,* ed. Ranier Berndt. *CCCM* 53B. Turnhout: Brepols, 1991.

Berndt, Ranier. *André de Saint-Victor (+1175). Exégète et théologien.* Turnhout: Brepols, 1992.

Signer, Michael A. "*Peshat, Sensus Litteralis* and Sequential Narrative: Jewish Exegesis and the School of St. Victor in the 12th Century." In *The Frank Talmage Memorial Volume*, ed. Barry Walfish. 2 vols. Haifa: Haifa University Press, 1993, vol. 1, pp. 203–16.

Smalley, Beryl. *The Study of the Bible in the Middle Ages.* 3rd ed. Oxford: Blackwell, 1983, chap. 4.

Zweiten, Jan W.M. "Jewish Exegesis Within Christian Bounds: Richard of St. Victor's *De Emmanuele* and Victorine Hermeneutics." *Bijdragen* 48 (1987): 327–35.

MICHAEL A. SIGNER

ANGELA DA FOLIGNO, SAINT (1248 or 1249–1309)

Angela was born into a wealthy family in Foligno. She underwent a conversion after her mother, husband, and children died c. 1288, and her renunciation of worldly goods and increasing devotion thereafter to a life of penitence and good works eventually led her to become a tertiary in the Franciscan order (1290–1291). From this time on she experienced numerous visions, especially of the suffering and death of Christ; one very public *raptus* during a pilgrimage to Assist, in which she had a vision of the Trinity, caused some controversy. She dictated these visions (presumably in the vernacular of Foligno) to her confessor, Arnaldo, whose written version (in Latin), *Memoriale*, prepared between 1292 and 1296, became widely popular and influential in late medieval Italy. It was approved in 1296 by a Franciscan theological commission headed by Cardinal Colonna. As her reputation grew, Angela attracted many follow-

ers, and she was visited in 1298 by the leading Spiritual Franciscan Ubertino da Casale, who mentions her with gratitude in his *Arbor vite crucifixe Jesu*; among her surviving texts is a letter to Ubertino, dating from 1302. She continued to have visions, including a famous experience at the Portiuncola in 1300. She was beatified in 1693.

Angela's dictated writings were collected in *Liber sororis Lelle de Fulgineo* (*Book of Sister Leila* [*Angela*] *of Foligno*), also known as *Liber de vera fidelium experientia* (*Book of the True Experience of the Faithful*). This consists of the *Memoriale*, various sayings, moral precepts, advice, letters, and some shorter accounts of visions. Vernacular works, including the *Via della salute* (*Way of Salvation*) have been attributed to Angela but appear to be a product of her admirers.

Angela's mysticism owes much to the Victorine tradition and to Bonaventure but has a force and originality of its own, centered on Angela's concept of Christ's encouragement to the believer to ascend through various levels of mystical experience to the point of identification with Christ himself.

See also **Ubertino da Casale**

Further Reading

Angela of Foligno. *Il libra della Beata Angela da Foligno*, ed. Ludger Thier and Abele Calufetti. Grottaferrata; Editiones Collegii S. Bonaventurae ad Claras Aquas, 1985.

——. *Complete Works*, ed. and trans. Paul Lachance. New York: Paulist, 1993. Schmitt, C., ed. *Vita e spiritualità della Beata Angela da Foligno: Atti del convegno per il VII centenario della conversione della Beata Angela da Foligno.* Perugia, 1985.

STEVEN N. BOTTERILL

ANGELO CLARENO (c. 1247/55–1337)

Angelo Clareno (or Chiareno) was born at Fossombrone between 1247 and 1255 and died in 1337. He led an extraordinary life and was at the heart of a bitter dispute between the Spiritual Franciscans and the Official or Conventual wing of the order. Angelo became a Franciscan as Pietro da Fossombrone in 1270 and immediately allied himself with the Spirituals; he was persecuted, imprisoned, and finally sent, apparently for disciplinary reasons, on a mission to Armenia (1290). In Armenia, he encountered opposition from the Conventuals already working there, and he was driven back to Italy in 1294. He attempted to found a community of his own in Italy, to perpetuate the strict observance of the Franciscan rule, and at this time took the name Angelo Clareno ("angelic trumpet"). He was initially encouraged by Pope Celestine V, but after Celestine's brief reign he was firmly discouraged and then again subjected to persecution by the succeeding pope, Boniface VIII. Further travels and tribulations followed: Angelo went on a pilgrimage to Greece in the early 1300s; was back in Italy in 1304–1305; and in 1311, having been named leader of the Spirituals in 1307–1308, went to the Council of Vienne to advocate their cause, with some success. He was persecuted yet again under Pope John XXII after 1316 and was imprisoned in Avignon, but he soon obtained his release, at the cost of surrendering his membership of the Franciscan order. He returned to Italy in 1318 and continued to work on behalf of the Spiritual Franciscans under the protection of the sympathetic abbot of Subiaco. But die church remained hostile, and eventually Angelo took refuge in Basilicata, where he lived in poverty and sickness until his death.

Angelo's writings, all in Latin, include several translations from the Greek fathers, a rule for the Spiritual Franciscans, spiritual treatises, letters, and *Historia septem tribulationum Ordinis Minorum* (*History of the Seven Tribulations of the Order of Friars Minor*). Many of these were quickly turned into vernacular versions and circulated widely during the *Trecento*.

See also **Celestine V, Pope**

Further Reading

Angeli Clareni opera, Vol. 1, *Epistole*, ed. Lydia von Auw. Rome: Istituto storico italiano per il Medio Evo, 1980.

Potestà, Gian Luca. *Angelo Clareno: Dai poveri eremiti ai fraticelli*. Rome: Istituto storico italiano per il Medio Evo, 1990.

von Auw, Lydia. *Angelo Clareno et les spirituels italiens*. Rome: Edizioni di Storia e Letteratura, 1979.

STEVEN N. BOTTERILL

ANNO (r. 1056–1075)

Born to a minor noble family in Swabia, Anno II, archbishop of Cologne, became one of medieval Germany's most powerful ecclesiastics. Driven by the ambition to advance the see of Cologne during his tenure as archbishop from 1056 to 1075, Anno left a controversial legacy as saint on the one hand and manipulative power player on the other.

Anno built or renovated several of Cologne's churches, including St. Mary's ad gradus ("on the steps"), St. George, St. Mary-in-the-Capitol, St. Gereon, and Great St. Martin. He also took on political rivals, especially the aristocratic Ezzonid family. In the late 1050s, Anno persuaded Ezzo's daughter Richeza to assign a number of important family properties to Cologne. In 1060, a bitter conflict between Anno and Richeza's cousin, Count Palatine Henry, resulted in Henry's loss of the Siegberg (Southeast of Cologne), where Anno founded a monastic community. With Ezzonid power broken, Anno focused his political acumen on the affairs of the realm. The death of Emperor Henry III in 1056 quickly led to instability in the Reich. The young Henry IV was barely six years old, and the regency exercised by the empress Agnes was unpopular with the German aristocracy. In 1062, Anno took matters into his own hands by kidnapping the boy-king at Kaiserswerth on the Rhine. Temporarily, Anno, as new regent, was the most powerful person in Germany. In 1064, however, Anno was called to Italy in the wake of a papal schism. Upon his return, Anno found that his rival Adalbert, archbishop of Hamburg-Bremen, had ingratiated himself with the young king. In 1065, Henry IV celebrated his coming of age, and promptly shook off whatever was left of the authority Anno had once exercised over him.

Despite his role as archchancellor of Italy and the Roman church, Anno distanced himself in the 1070s from papal reform developments south of the Alps. More important for Anno was monastic reform as a means of furthering the influence of Cologne. Monks from Anno's Siegberg foundation reformed a number of important communities in Germany. Other storms were brewing in the twilight years of Anno's pontificate. Cologne was a wealthy city with a substantial middle class, and early yearnings for urban liberty clashed with the archbishop's grip as lord of the city. In 1074, after Anno's servants impounded a merchant boat, the city rebelled. Anno locked himself in the cathedral to escape rioting burghers, and in disguise that evening fled through a hole in the city wall. The rebellion was brutally suppressed by Anno a few days later, but left a bitter memory for both city and bishop. When Anno died in 1075, he was buried in his beloved monastery on the Siegberg, where he was soon honored for his personal sanctity. His career, on the eve of the Investiture Controversy, cannot be stereotyped as either proimperial or propapal. Anno fought for the rights not of the Roman church as much as for those of his own see.

See also **Henry III; Henry IV, Emperor**

Further Reading

Arnold, Benjamin. "From Warfare on Earth to Eternal Paradise: Archbishop Anno II of Cologne, the History of the Western Empire in the Annolied, and the Salvation of Mankind." *Viator 25* (1992): 95–113.

Jenal, Georg. *Erzbischof Anno II. von Köln (1056–75) und sein politisches Wirken: Ein Beitrag zur Geschichte der Reichs—und Territorialpolitik im 11. Jahrhundert*. Stuttgart: Hiersemann, 1974/1975.

Oediger, Frederick Wilhelm. *Die Regesten der Erzbischöfe von Köln im Mittelalter*, vol. 1. Düsseldorf: Droste, 1978, pp. 313–1099.

Rotondo-McCord, Jonathan. "Body Snatching and Episcopal Power: Archbishop Anno II of Cologne, Burials in St. Mary's ad gradus, and the Minority of Henry IV." *Journal of Medieval History* 22 (1996): 297–312.

JONATHAN ROTONDO-MCCORD

ANSELM OF BEC
(or Canterbury, or Aosta; 1033–1109)

Anselm of Bec was born in Aosta, Italy. After the death of his mother, he left for Burgundy and France, where he was attracted to the monastic life and entered the remote monastery of Bec in Normandy in 1059. His countryman Lanfranc of Pavia (d. 1089) was prior at Bec and taught grammar and logic. Anselm became Lanfranc's student, then his assistant, and finally a fellow teacher. When in 1063 Lanfranc became abbot of Saint-Étienne, Caen (before becoming archbishop of Canterbury in 1070), Anselm succeeded him as prior at Bec and became abbot after the death of the monastery's founder, Herluin, in 1078. As abbot, he paid frequent visits to England to inspect the lands owned by Bec. While at Bec, Anselm wrote works of a mixed devotional and philosophical nature: *De grammatico* (1060–63), a linguistico-philosophical treatise about the term "*grammarian*"; Monologion, a soliloquy on proving the existence of God by reason alone; *Proslogion*, an improved version of the *Monologion*; and three treatises, *De veritate*, *De libertáte arbitrii*, and *De casu diaboli*. During this period, he also wrote his *Orationes sive meditationes*.

Anselm succeeded Lanfranc as archbishop of Canterbury in 1093. Before long, he clashed with King William II Rufus over such issues as church property, the right of appointment to ecclesiastical offices, and the recognition of Urban II as pope. Another contentious issue was Anselm's wish to travel to Rome to receive the token of his episcopal dignity, the *pallium*, directly from the pope. In the end, Anselm did not go, yet he did succeed in preventing the king from usurping the right of investiture. There followed a period of relative calm during which Anselm published his *Epistola de incarnatione verbi* in 1094 and started work on his *magnum opus, Cur Deus homo*. In the meantime, Anselm's relations with the king had once more become strained; in 1098, he went in exile to Rome, where he completed *Cur Deus homo*. He also attended the Council of Bari, at which he defended the "double procession" of the Holy Spirit (from the Father and the Son) against the Greeks (later published as *De processione Spiritus Sanctus*).

Following William Rufus's death in 1100, Anselm returned to England. After a peaceful interval, he collided with the new king, Henry I, over old issues, such as homage and investiture. From 1103 until 1106, he lived in exile, mainly in France, and returned to England only after a compromise had been reached with the king. He died in 1109 at Canterbury, having completed in 1108 his *De concordia* (on the concordance of foreknowledge and predestination and the grace of God with free will).

Anselm's writings are marked by a balance between rational argumentation and contemplative intensity. Claiming in his *Proslogion* to prove the existence of God by one single argument and by reason alone, he takes his starting point in a negation of that existence. This negation has to be seen as a dialectical-intellectual game within the monastic context in which it serves the aim of bringing out the presence of the divine. The fool who denies the existence of God is met with the argument that God is that than which no greater can be thought. The logical implications of this formula are such as to exclude the possibility of God's nonexistence. As a consequence, God's presence, which in the beginning of the treatise had been phrased in terms of monastic desperation, frustrated by an inaccessible light, gains clarity and offers joy to the meditating mind. *Cur Deus homo* follows the same pattern. The accusation by the infidels that the Christian concept of incarnation is primitive is met by an analysis of the beauty of God's order. God is bound by intrinsic necessity to keep his order intact and save humanity, which for its part is bound to make satisfaction for its sin. The two elements come together in the necessary appearance of a God-man, who is no other than Christ.

Anselm's dense style of argumentation is further developed in his treatises on truth, on the will, and on the fall of the Devil. In conformity with his monastic way of life, it is the real truth and the real existence of justice that count most. As a result, the freedom of will is the freedom to do the right thing. By the same token, the freedom to sin turns out to lack a real object—injustice having no subsistence of its own—and therefore to be illusory.

Although Anselm has always been held in high esteem, his philosophical and theological influence has been limited mainly to the so-called ontological proof of God's existence and the argument of *Cur Deus* homo. The *Orationes sive mediationes*, on the other hand, were widely read all through the Middle Ages.

See also **Lanfranc of Bec; Henry I; Urban II, Pope**

Further Reading

Anselm of Bec. S. *Anselmi Cantuariensis archiepiscopi opera omnia*, ed. Franciscus S. Schmitt. 6 vol. Stuttgart: Fromann, 1968.

——. *Anselm of Canterbury*, ed. and trans. jasper Hopkins and Herbert Richardson. 4 vols. 2nd ed. New York: Mellen, 1975–76.

——. *The Prayers and Meditations of St. Anselm*, trans. Benedicta Ward. Harmondsworth: Penguin, 1973.

Eadmer. *The Life of St. Anselm, Archbishop of Canterbury by Eadmer*, ed. and trans. Richard W. Southern. Oxford: Clarendon, 1972.

Campbell, Richard. *From Belief to Understanding: A Study of Anselm's* Proslogion *Argument on the Existence of God*. Canberra: Faculty of Arts, Australian National University, 1976.

Hopkins, Jasper. *A Companion to the Study of St. Anselm*. Minneapolis: University of Minneapolis Press, 1972.

Evans, Gillian R. *Anselm and Talking About God*. Oxford: Clarendon, 1978.

Southern, Richard W. *Saint Anselm: A Portrait in a Landscape*. Cambridge: Cambridge University Press, 1990.

Vaughn, Sally N. *Anselm of Bec and Robert of Meulan: The Innocence of the Dove and the Wisdom of the Serpent.* Berkeley: University of California Press, 1987.

BURCHT PRANGER

ANSELM OF LAON (ca. 1050–1117)

As schoolmaster at the cathedral of Laon, Anselm stands at the beginning of an era that saw the expansion of literacy and intellectual training beyond the cloister walls, reaching out to a burgeoning urban population. Through a curriculum that focused on the study of the Bible and basic Christian principles of belief and daily living, Anselm helped to channel both the spiritual awakening that was sweeping Europe and the ecclesiastical reform that was an important focus of the Gregorian papacy.

Anselm composed commentaries on several books of the Bible, including Isaiah, Matthew, the Psalms, the Song of Songs, the opening chapters of Genesis, and Revelation. With his brother Ralph and a younger contemporary, Gilbert the Universal (later schoolmaster at Auxerre and then bishop of London), Anselm began to compile a commentary that was to become the standard (*Glossa ordinaria*) for the Bible by the end of the 12th century. Anselm and his associates digested, abbreviated, supplemented, and otherwise edited the vast deposit of commentaries produced by the Christian authors of late antiquity and the Carolingian era, placing the longer comments in the broad margins of Bibles designed for this purpose and the shorter comments between the lines of the biblical text itself. Anselm was responsible for the *Glossa ordinaria* for the Psalms, for the epistles of Paul, and perhaps for the Fourth Gospel as well.

Equally important were Anselm's collections of theological opinions (*sententiae*). They ranged over the whole spectrum of Christian teaching, from God and Creation to redemption and the sacraments, but focused on such current issues as the nature of marriage and relations with Jews, who had been severely persecuted in the wake of the First Crusade.

Anselm was one of the more successful scholars in addressing the need for a trained and competent clergy, able to deal with the needs of the newly emerging society. Some of the most distinguished theologians of the 12th century studied with him, including Gilbert of Poitiers and William of Champeaux. However influential Anselm was as the central figure of a school for teaching, he did not establish a school of thought characterized by a common set of assumptions.

See also **Gilbert of Poitiers**

Further Reading

Anselm of Laon. *Sententie divine pagine* and *Sententie Anselmi*, ed. Franz P. Bliemetzrieder. In *Anselms von Laon system-atische Sentenzen.* Münster: Aschendorff, 1919.
Bliemetzrieder, Franz P., ed. "Trente-trois piéces inédites des ceuvres théologiques d'Anselme de Laon." *Recherches de théologie ancienne et médiévale* 2 (1930): 54–79.
Lottin, Odon, ed. "Nouveaux fragments théologiques de l'école d'Anselme de Laon." *Recherches de théologie ancienne et médiévale* 11 (1939): 305–23; 12(1940): 49–77; 13(1946): 202–21, 261–81; 14 (1947): 5–31.
Bertola, Ermenegildo. "Le critiche di Abélardo ad Anselmo di Laon ed a Guglielmo di Champeaux." *Rivista di filosofia neoscolastica* 52 (1960): 495–522.
Cavallera, Ferdinand. "D'Anselme de Laon à Pierre Lombard." *Bulletin de literature ecclésiastique* 2 (1940): 40–54,102–14.
Colish, Marcia. "Another Look at the School of Laon." *Archives d'histoire doctrinale et littéraire du moyen âge* 53 (1986): 7–22.
Flint, Valerie I.J. "The 'School of Laon': A Reconsideration." *Recherches de téologie ancienne et médiévale* 43 (1976): 89–110.
Ghellinck, Joseph de. Le *mouvement théologique du XIIe siècle.* 2nd ed. Bruges: De Tempel, 1948.
Landgraf, Artur Michael. *Introduction à l'histoire de la litérature théologique de la scolastique naissante*, ed. Albert-Marie Landry, trans. Louis-B. Geiger. Montreal: Institut d'Études Médiévales, 1979.
Smalley, Beryl. *The Study of the Bible in the Middle Ages.* 3rd ed. Oxford: Blackwell, 1983.
Weisweiler, Heinrich. "Le recueil de sentences 'Deus de cuius principio et fine tacetur' et son remaniement." *Recherches de théologie ancienne et médiévale* 5 (1933): 245–74.

MARK ZIER

ANSGAR, SAINT (c. 801-865)

Also known as the "Apostle of the North," St. Ansgar was born in Picardy around 801 and died in Bremen on February 3, 865, the date of his feast day. He was educated at the Benedictine monastery at Corbie, and in 822 was sent as a teacher to the monastery of Corvey in Westphalia. When King Harald Klak of Denmark converted to Christianity in 826 at the court of Emperor Louis the Pious, Ansgar was recommended by Archbishop Ebo of Reims and Abbot Wala of Corvey to undertake missionary activity in Denmark. After the expulsion of Harald from the country, Ansgar traveled to Sweden, where King Björn permitted him to found the first church in Scandinavia at Björkö. In 831, Ansgar was consecrated first bishop of Hamburg, and in 832 was named by Pope Gregory IV as papal legate for the Scandiavian and Slavonic mission. Ansgar entrusted the mission of Sweden to Gausbert, and focused his attention on converting Denmark. In 834, through the patronage of Emperor Louis, the monastery of Turnhout, Flanders, was assigned to Ansgar as a training center and source of revenue for the Scandinavian mission. But in 845, the Christian mission suffered a severe setback when the Vikings plundered Hamburg. In 847, Ansgar was appointed to the see of Bremen, which was united with Hamburg in 847/8, and he began his missionary efforts anew. He succeeded in founding churches in Schleswig, Ribe, and Sigtuna.

Ansgar probably wrote many volumes, including extracts from devotional texts and perhaps also a booklet on his visions by which the whole of his life was guided. But only one letter, some prayers (*pigmentum*), and a life of St. Willehad are preserved. The main source about Ansgar's life is Rimbert's *Vita Anskarii*, which contains much valuable information on the history of the Catholic mission in early-medieval Scandinavia.

See also **Louis the Pious**

Further Reading

Rimbert. *Vita Anskarii. Scriptores rerum Germanicarum* 55. Ed. G. Waitz. Hannover: Bibliopoli Hahniani, 1884

Robinson, Charles H., trans. *Anskar, the Apostle of the North, 801–865: Translated from the Vita Anskarii by Bishop Rimbert, His Fellow Missionary and Successor.* London: Society for the Propagation of the Gospel in Foreign Parts, 1921; Allmang, G. "Anschaire." In *Dictionnaire d'histoire et de géographie ecclésiastiques*3. Ed. Mgr. Alfred Baudrillart. Paris: Letouzey et Ané, 1924, cols. 435–41

Oppenheim, Philippus. *Der heilige Ansgar und die Anfánge des Christentums in den nordischen Lndern: Ein Lebens- und Zeitbild.* Munich: Heuber, 1931

Oppermann, C J. A. *The English Missionaries in Sweden and Finland.* London: Society for Promoting Christian Knowledge; New York: Macmillan, 1937

Weibull, L. "Ansgarius." *Scandia* l4 (1941), 186–99

"St.Anskar." In *Butler's Lives of the Saints* 1. Rev. ed. Herbert Thurston, S.J., and Donald Attwater. New York: Kenedy, 1956, pp. 242–3

Hilpisch, St. "Ansgar." In *Lexikon für Theologie und Kirche* 1. Ed. Josef Höfler and Karl Rahner. Freiburg im Breisgau: Herder, 1957, cols. 597–8

Maarschallkerweerd, Pancrazi. "Anscario." In *Bibliotheca Sanctorum* l. Rome: Città Nuova, 1961, cols. 1337–9

Mehnert, Gottfried. *Ansgar, Apostel des Nordens.* Kiel: Lutherische Verlagsgesellschaft, 1964

Dörres, Hermann, and Georg Kretschmar. *Ansgar: Seine Bedeutung für die Mission.* Hamburg: Velmede, 1965

Schultz, S. A. "Ansgar, St." In *New Catholic Encyclopedia* 1. New York *etc.*: McGraw-Hill, 1967, p. 586

Lammers, W. "Ansgar." In *Lexikon des Mittelalters* 1. Munich and Zurich: Artemis, 1980, cols. 690–1

Hallencreutz, Carl. F. "Missionary Spirituality—the Case of Ansgar." *Studia Theologica* 36 (1982), 105–18.

PETER DINZELBACHER

ANTHONY OF PADUA, SAINT
(c. 1195–1231)

Saint Anthony of Padua (Fernando de Bulhoes) was a Franciscan preacher and theologian. As one of the first generation of Franciscans, he helped determine the theological orientation of the order. He also achieved great fame as a preacher. After his death, his reputation as a miracle worker made him an extremely popular saint.

Anthony was a member of the lesser Portuguese

Alvise Vivarini (c. 1445–1505); Saint Anthony of Padua. Distemper on wood. Inv. I, 22. ©Erich Lessing/Art Resource, New York.

nobility; he was educated at the cathedral school of Lisbon and entered the order of Augustinian canons regular at age fifteen. After two years at the monastery of São Vicente in Lisbon, he was transferred to the order's study house in Coimbra, where he received instruction in scripture and theology and was ordained a priest.

Devoted to an austere and studious life, Anthony was apparently disappointed by the level of religious observance in his order. Thus he was drawn to a group of Franciscans who frequently begged for food there; he found their emphasis on absolute poverty, mendicancy, popular preaching, and conversion of the Muslims closer to his concept of the apostolic life than what was becoming the more conventual monastic rule of his own order. When the relics of Franciscan missionaries recently killed in North Africa were displayed in Coimbra, Anthony was seized with a desire to continue their work. He joined the Franciscan order soon afterward, at the friary of San Antonio, probably changing his name when he professed. He then set off for Morocco. But a serious illness halted his missionary journey just after he arrived in North Africa, and he was forced to return to Portugal. When a storm drove his ship to Sicily, Anthony decided to travel to Assisi in search of direction. After meeting Saint Francis and taking part in the order's general chapter of May 1221, he was sent to a hermitage near Forlì, where he spent a considerable period in contemplation and penance.

Anthony found a new focus for his Franciscan vocation by accident, when he was called to preach at an ordination. His learning and skill as a speaker astounded his hearers, and he was soon commissioned to preach against Cathar and Waldensian heretics in northern Italy. He preached in the north from 1222 to 1224, then in southern France in late 1224. From 1227 to 1231, he was back in northern Italy, keeping an exhausting schedule. By 1228, he had achieved sufficient fame to be asked to preach before the papal curia.

Anthony also served his order in other capacities. In 1223, Saint Francis himself seems to have commissioned Anthony to be the first Franciscan lector in theology. Over the next few years Anthony taught at Franciscan houses of study in Bologna, Arles, Montpellier, Toulouse, Le Puy-en-Velay, and Padua and introduced the theology of Saint Augustine to the order. In 1224, Anthony helped found Franciscan houses at Limoges and Brive in Aquitaine. In 1225, he was chosen as guardian of the house at Le Puy; then he was chosen as *custos* at Limoges; and in 1227, he was chosen as provincial of Lombardy and Emilia. He held the last post until 1230, when he asked to be relieved so that he could pursue his preaching without hindrance. At about this time Anthony's health began to fail, apparently as a result of his intense schedule. In 1231, he developed what was described as dropsy; he died in Arcello, outside Padua, on 13 June. Eleven months later, on 30 May 1232, he was canonized.

Anthony's preaching made him a tremendously popular figure in Padua during the late 1220s. His sermons survive in four major collections: *Sermones in festivitatibus sanctorum per anni circulum, Sermones per annum dominicales, Sermones in Psalmos,* and *Sermones in laudem et honorem beatae Mariae Virginis.* The published versions are rather academic, but it is likely that these sermons were much livelier when he preached them. Anthony's themes are typically Franciscan: he urges evangelical virtue, reception of the eucharist, devotion to Christ's humanity and to the Virgin Mary, civic harmony, and just treatment of the poor. There was a trend in Franciscan preaching toward vivid examples taken from popular stories and romances, but Anthony resisted this, preferring to drive home his message with constant references to scriptural texts and examples. He urged other Franciscans to use this conservative technique but had little success in persuading them. In two other areas, however, he influenced Franciscan preaching profoundly. The first Franciscan preachers had focused only on repentance and moral reform. Anthony and other educated men added a new emphasis when they began to instruct the faithful in dogma in order to combat heresy. In addition,

Anthony's academic training led him to construct his sermons systematically and analytically. This approach was much admired and widely imitated.

Anthony's reputation during his lifetime rested on his preaching; his popularity after his death was based on his miracles. Wonders were reported at his tomb almost immediately after his burial. Belief in his miraculous powers was reinforced by several biographies written shortly after his death, and later hagiographers continued to develop his fame as a miracle worker. His reputation for miracles led to his inclusion in the collection of Franciscan stories known as the *Fioretti* (*Little Flowers*). Eventually Anthony's popularity outstripped that of all the other Franciscan saints except, of course, Francis himself. Anthony came to be venerated as a patron of charity and marriage who cured fevers and diseases in animals, recovered lost articles, and protected lovers, women in labor, and miners.

Anthony was one of the best-educated of the early Franciscans, and so his authority as a theologian was quickly established in the order. After his death the order treated him as a doctor of the church, although he did not have that tide officially until 1946, when it was granted by Pius XII. Anthony's theological views are fairly conventional for his time and training as an Augustinian canon; they derive from a biblical theology rooted in the church fathers, particularly Augustine. His scriptural exegesis focuses on the moral sense of the text, which he uses primarily to call his audience to moral reform and avoidance of heresy. Like many early Franciscans, he was very much interested in the humanity of Christ and in the theological role of Mary, and he was among the first to articulate a variety of characteristic Franciscan Christological and Mariological doctrines.

The main biographies of Anthony are *Legenda prima* commonly called *Assidua*; and *Legenda secunda*, also called *Anonyma*. Both were written in the 1230s. Several other biographies were published during the thirteenth century, all based generally on the material in *Assidua* and *Anonyna*. At the end of the century another biography appeared that may contain some authentic material not included in the first two; this is known as *Benignitas*. The authorship of all three works is uncertain.

See also **Francis of Assisi, Saint**

Further Reading

Editions

Costa, Beniamino, et al., eds. *Sancti Antonii Patavini sermons dominicales et festivi ad fidem codicum recogniti.* Padua: Centro Studi Antoniani, Edizioni Messaggero, 1979.

de Kerval, Léon, ed. *Sancti Antonii de Padua vitae duae.* Paris: Fischbacher, 1904.

Palandrini, Eletto, ed. "La legenda fiorentina." *Studi Francescani,* 4, 1932, pp. 454–496.

Critical Studies

Clasen, Sophronius. *Saint Anthony, Doctor of the Gospel*, trans. Ignatius Brady. Chicago, Ill.: Franciscan Herald, 1961.

Felder, Hilarin. *Die Antoniuswunder nach den älteren Quellen.* Paderborn: Schöningh, 1933.

Giiliat-Smith, Ernest. *Saint Anthony of Padua According to His Contemporaries.* New York: Dutton, 1926.

Kleinschmidt, Beda. *Antonius von Padua in Leben und Kunst, Kult und Volkstum.* Düsseldorf: Schwann, 1931.

McHam, Sarah Blake. "The Cult of Saint Anthony of Padua." In *Saints: Studies in Hagiography*, ed. Sandro Sticco. Medieval and Renaissance Texts and Studies, 141. Binghamton, N.Y., Medieval and Renaissance Texts and Studies, 1996, pp. 216–232.

Toussaert, Jacques. *Antonius von Padua: Versuch einer kritischen Biographic.* Cologne: Bachem, 1967.

THOMAS TURLEY

ANTONIO PUCCI (c. 1310–1388)

The Florentine poet Antonio Pucci is known for sonnets in the medieval Italian comic tradition; poems on historical events involving Florence; *cantari* on popular legends; and *Centiloquio*, a poetic transcription of Giovanni Villani's *Cronica* (*Chronicles*) in terza rima. The son of a bronze caster whose specialty was church bells, Pucci was appointed the official bell ringer of Florence in 1334. In 1349 he became the *banditore* (town crier), a position he held for the next twenty years. During his tenure as *banditore*, he had occasion to spread the news concerning many events of Florentine history, and some of them became subjects of his *serventesi*: the flood of the Arno in 1333, the famine of 1346, the plague of 1348, the victory of the Florentine militia over Padua in 1337, and the overthrow of Gualtieri di Brienne, the duke of Athens, in 1343.

The great variety of themes found in Pucci's poetry gives the reader a broad picture of life in Florence during the mid-fourteenth century. In addition to historical events, Pucci delighted in portraying quotidian life: for example, an invective against a chicken vendor who sold the poet a desiccated old hen (*Andrea, tu mi vendesti per pollastra*), an ode to a sloppy barber (*Amico mio barbier, quando tu meni*), and the poet's lament at being forced to churn out his art for inadequate compensation or none (*Deh fammi una canzon, fammi un sonetto*). Many sonnets are didactic, offering advice on how to be a good husband or wife (*Amico mio, da poi ch'hai tolto moglie* and *Figliuola mia, poi che se' maritata*), or how to raise children (*Quando 'l fanciul da piccolo scioccheggia* and *Il giovane cbe vuol avere onore*). *Ternario sulle noie* lists numerous annoyances of daily life in the form of the traditional Provençal *enueg*, beloved of many medieval Italian comic poets.

Pucci was a great admirer of Dante. He wrote a sonnet (*Questi che veste di color sanguigno*) commemorating the portrait of Dante that Giotto painted in 1335; and in *Centiloquio*, Canto LV is dedicated to praise of Dante, a description of his works, and the story of his life. In *Libro di varie storie*, also known as *Zibaldone*, which Pucci intended for his private use, there are frequent citations from Dante's *Commedia*.

Another painting by Giotto, the allegory of the *comune rubato* ("robbed city"), was the probable model for two of Pucci's sonnets: *Ohmè, Comun, come conciar ti veggio*, a lament on the suffering of Florence due to bad government; and *Se nel mio ben ciascun fosse leale*, in which Florence, personified, addresses those who maltreat her.

One of Pucci's recurring themes is his defense and praise of women. In response to a misogynistic sonnet by Buto Giovan-nini, *Antonio mio, di femma pavento*, Pucci wrote *La femmina fa l'uom viver contento*, extolling the virtues of feminine companionship and lamenting the abuse without provocation that many women receive at the hands of men. This theme is more amply developed in *Il contrasto delle donne*, a poem of seventy-five stanzas cast as a debate between an unnamed misogynist and a defender of women. Using *exempla* from the Bible and classical literature, each interlocutor presents a case, but the poem is structured so that the defender of women can refute all the arguments advanced by the detractor.

Exemplary women are the protagonists of three of Pucci's five *cantari* on popular legends: *Gismirante*, *Bruto di Brettagna*, *Madonna Leonessa*, *La reina d'Oriente*, and *Apollonio di Tiro*. Other *cantari* were written to commemorate political events; the seven *cantari* of *Guerra di Pisa* (*War with Pisa*) are examples. These short poems in *ottave*, written in a formulaic style, were composed for recital in the *piazze* of Florence. The virtuous behavior of the heroes and heroines of the *cantari* and other *canzoni* written by Pucci to illustrate a moral point are indicative of the didactic bent of much of his poetry.

Pucci enjoyed writing sonnets in the tradition of courtly love, adding a note of overt sensuality to an allusive but circumspect genre. *Corona del messaggio d'amore*, a cycle of nineteen sonnets depicting the ritual of courtship, concludes with a description of lovemaking. The *serventese* on the beauties of his lady, *Quella di cui i' son veracemente*, is also markedly sensual.

As a man whose work involved riding around Florence on horseback blowing a trumpet and making official proclamations, Pucci knew the streets of the city well. In *Ternario delle proprietà di Mercato Vecchio*, Pucci describes the colorful bustle of the market piazza at various seasons of the year, giving the reader a rich and vivid document of Florentine life in the poet's time.

See also **Dante Alighieri; Giotto di Bondone; Villani, Giovanni**

Further Reading

Editions

Corsi, Giuseppe. *Rimatori del Trecento*. Turin: UTET, 1969, pp. 870–880.

D'Ancona, Alessandro. "L'arte del dire in rima: Sonetti di Antonio Pucci." In *Miscellanea di filologia e linguistica in memoria di Napoleone Caix e Ugo Angelo Canello*. Florence: Le Monnier, 1886, pp. 293–303.

Levi, Ezio. *Fiore di leggende*: *Cantari antichi*. Bari: Laterza, 1914. (*Gismirante*, *Bruto di Brettagna*, *Madonna Lionessa*, and *La reina d'Oriente*.)

McKenzie, Kenneth. "Antonio Pucci on Old Age." *Speculum*, 15, 1940, pp. 160–185. (*Delia vecchiezza*.)

Pucci, Antonio. *Le noie*, ed. Kenneth McKenzie. Princeton, N.J.: Princeton University Press, 1931.

———. *Il contrasto delle donne*: *A Critical Edition with Introduction and Notes*, ed. Antonio Pace. Menasha, Wis.: George Banta, 1944.

Sapegno, Natalino, ed. *Poeti minori del Trecento*. Milan: Ricciardi, 1952, pp. 349–420.

Critical Studies

Brambilla Ageno, Franca. "Per l'interpretazione delle Proprietà di Mercato Vecchio di Antonio Pucci." *Lingua Nostra*, 37, 1976, pp. 9–10.

Fasani, Remo. "*Il Fiore* e la poesia del Pucci." *Deutsches Dante jahrbuch*, 49–50, (1974–1975), pp. 82–141.

Kleinhenz, Christopher. "The Other Face of the Late Thirteenth-Century Lyric: Realism, Comedy, and the Bourgeoisie." In *The Early Italian Sonnet*: *The First Century (1220–1321)*, Lecce: Milella, 1986, pp. 157–200.

Messina, Michele. "Pucci, Antonio." In *Enciclopedia Dantesca*. Rome: Istituto della Enciclopedia Italiana, 1970–1978.

Petrocchi, Giorgio. "Cultura e poesia del Trecento." In *Il Trecento*. Milan: Garzanti, 1965; rpt. 1979.

Rabboni, Renzo. "La tradizione manoscritta dell'Apollonio di Tiro di Antonio Pucci." In *Studi in onore di Raffaele Spongano*, ed. Emilio Pasquini. Bologna: Boni, 1980, pp. 29–47.

JOAN LEVIN

AQUINAS, THOMAS (ca. 1224–1274)

The only medieval philosopher whose ideas command an active following in the 20th century. The symmetry of Thomas's methodical synthesis of traditional Christian (Augustinian and Platonist) theology with Aristotelian methods and categories may be thought of at once as the zenith of medieval scholastic thought and its downfall. Thomas's apparently comprehensive, even-tempered certainties, the product of method and reason, continue to attract those seeking answers to the problems of faith.

Thomas was born in Roccasecca, near Monte Cassino, Italy, the youngest son of Count Landulf of Aquino, a relative of the emperor and the king of France. He was schooled at Monte Cassino, where his family hoped he would become abbot, and later (1240) studied arts at Naples. Thomas's love of Christian learning urged him to join the Dominican order. His family opposed his becoming a mendicant, when the wealth of the Benedictines beckoned, and kept him prisoner, fruitlessly, in Roccasecca for fifteen months. In April 1244, he joined the Dominicans and was sent to Paris (1245–48) to study theology with Albert the Great. In 1248, he accompanied Albert to the new Dominican *studium* at Cologne, but by 1252 he was back in Paris as lecturer at Saint-Jacques, the Dominican convent. Here he defended mendicant poverty against the attacks of William of Saint-Amour and his followers, writing *Contra impugnantes Dei cultum*. He became master of theology (his formal degree having been delayed by the dispute) in 1256. From 1259 to 1269, he taught at Dominican houses in Italy: Anagni, Orvieto, Santa Sabina and the *studium generale* in Rome, and Viterbo. In 1269, just before the condemnation of Aristotelian errors by Étienne Tempier, he returned to Paris but was moved once more, to establish a Dominican *studium* in Naples, in 1272. He was traveling again, to the Second Council of Lyon, when he died at Fossanuova, on March 7, 1274.

Thomas, known as *Doctor angelicus* and *Doctor communis*, is renowned for his massive output, which was remarked upon in the evidence for his canonization. He was said to dictate seamlessly to several secretaries at once, each writing a different work. He wrote biblical commentaries, at least one commentary on the *Sententiae* of Peter Lombard, commentaries on much of Aristotle and the *liber de causis*, disputed and quodlibetal questions, and other works common to a Paris master, as well as short tracts in answer to specific questions, whether in opposition to the Averroists or Avicebron, for instance, or in reply to the duchess of Brabant on government. Aware of the inadequacy of western knowledge of Aristotle, he had William of Moerbecke (1215–1286) translate or retranslate many of his works, leaving a valuable legacy for later scholars. But Thomas's name is almost synonymous with his *Summa theologica* (or *Summa theologiae*), which, together with the earlier *Summa contra Gentiles*, is a massive statement of the whole of Christian theology. The *Summa* is in three parts, the first (*prima*) dealing with God *in se*, the second dealing first (*prima secundae*) with God's relations with humanity and second (*secunda secundae*) with humanity's relations with God, and the third (*tertia*) with Christ and the sacraments as the path for the human return to God. (The plan is similar to Peter Lombard's *Sententiae* but in three unequal books rather than four.)

Although Thomas's place in the hierarchy of medieval philosopher-theologians is secure, he is perhaps recognized today more for his system and clarity than for his originality of thought. As we learn more about earlier 13th-century scholastics, we see Thomistic ideas in prototype or isolation. His gift was in a synthesis of what had previously tended to the imposition of Aristotelian categories of thought within a Platonist Christian worldview. He brought the so-called scholastic method of argument and truth seeking to its finest honing.

Although Thomas is not generally remembered for his spirituality and is not a mystical theologian in the style of Bonaventure, he was nevertheless revered in his lifetime for his holiness, simplicity, and devotion. Quiet (he was nicknamed "the dumb ox") and unassuming, he had powers of concentration that took on a semimiraculous quality for the secretaries who worked with him. He was canonized in 1323.

Thomas was not without his critics. Some of his positions were condemned by Bishop Étienne Tempier in 1270 and 1277, by Robert Kilwardby in the latter year, and by John Peckham in 1284; but his opinions were officially imposed on the Dominican order in 1278. The Roman Catholic church considers his teaching an authentic expression of doctrine, and canon law makes study of his works the accepted basis for theology.

See also **Albert the Great; Hugues de Saint-Cher; Peter Lombard**

Further Reading

Thomas Aquinas. *Summa theologiae*, ed. Dominican Fathers of the English Province. 60 vols. Cambridge: Blackfriar's, 1964–76. [Latin text and English translation, introductions, notes, appendices, and glossaries.]
——. *Somme théologique (Summa theologiae)*. 61 vols. Paris, 1925–72. [Latin-French with commentaries.]
——. *Quaestiones quodlibetales 1–2: English Quodlibetal Questions 1–2*, trans. Sandra Edwards. Toronto: Pontifical Institute of Mediaeval Studies, 1983.
——. *Basic Writings of Saint Thomas Aquinas*, trans. Anton Pegis. 2 vols. New York: Random House, 1945.
——. *On the Truth of the Catholic Faith (Summa Contra Gentiles)*, trans. Anton C. Pegis, James Anderson, Vernon J. Bourke, and Charles J. O'Neil. 5 vols. Garden City: Hanover House, 1955–57.
Chenu, Marie-Dominique. *Toward Understanding Saint Thomas*, trans. Albert M. Landry and Dominic Hughes. Chicago: Regnery, 1964.
Farrell, Walter. *A Companion to the Summa.* 4 vols. New York: Sheed and Ward, 1941–42.
Glorieux, Palémon. *Répertoire des maîtres en théologie de Paris au XIIIe siécle.* 2 vols. Paris: Vrin, 1933, Vol. 1, pp. 85–104. [Complete listing of works.]

LESLEY J. SMITH

ARCHPOET

The so-called Archpoet (the Latin form *Archipoeta* is followed in German), whose real name is unknown, was probably born around 1130 in Germany or eastern France. Nothing is known of him except what he reveals in ten surviving poems. Despite a knightly background, he disliked martial arts and preferred poetry. His nickname, which is found as a subscription in the main manuscript of his poems, may have been given to him because of the esteem in which his audience held him,

or it may play upon the "arch-" elements in the titles of his chief patron, Reinald of Dassel (d. 1167), who was the archbishop of Cologne and the archchancellor of Frederick I Barbarossa (ca. 1122–1190). Because Frederick was king of Germany and Holy Roman Emperor, Reinald's court moved frequently in Germany, Burgundy, and northern Italy.

The Archpoet's poems date from the early and mid-1160s, and all of them can be classed as occasional poems, relating to the chief concerns and events of Reinald's court. In them the Archpoet gives signs of knowing the trivium of grammar, rhetoric, and dialectic as well as the basics of theology, whereas his short-lived study of medicine leaves almost no marks. He alludes with apparent ease to the Vulgate Bible and Roman poets, and he incorporates parody of confessions, sermons, and liturgy. Although his poems often constitute petitions for food, drink (especially wine), money, and clothing, and although they seem always to have been meant for public recitation at the court, the Archpoet differentiates himself sharply from professional entertainers of a humbler sort.

Two of the poems are in leonine hexameters, but the rest are based on accentual rhythms. The most famous of the poems is the Archpoet's confession to the archchancellor (incipit, or first line, "Aestuans intrinsecus"). Whereas the other nine poems survive mostly in only a single manuscript, this one is extant in more than thirty, most famously in the *Carmina burana*; Carl Orff set its first five strophes to musk in his oratorio (1937). The confession is one of four in the *Vagantenstrophe*, with dissyllabic rhyme.

One remarkable aspect of the Archpoet—or of his persona as a poet, if his name does not in itself indicate such distancing—is his candor about his shortcomings. He discusses his proclivity for love affairs, drinking, gambling, and keeping bad company. Nor is his physical condition much better than his moral, to judge by his complaints about his cough and his proximity to death. The former failings may be little more than a stance struck by the poet to entertain his audience; the persona could be as far from the reality as that of Chaucer the character was from Chaucer the poet or man. Unfortunately the latter defects may well have taken the life of the Archpoet at a young age, since he disappears from our view in 1167 at the latest.

See also **Frederick I. Barbarossa**

Further Reading

Adcock, Fleur, ed. and trans. *Hugh Primas and the Archpoet.* Cambridge: Cambridge University Press, 1994.
Krefeld, Heinrich, ed. and trans. *Der Archipoeta*, Berlin: Akademie, 1992.
Dronke, Peter. "The Archpoet and the Classics." In *Latin Poetry and the Classical Tradition. Essays in Medieval and Renais-*

sance Literature, ed. Peter Godman and Oswyn Murray. Oxford: Clarendon Press, 1990, pp. 57–72.

Pucci, Joseph, "Job and Ovid in the Archpoet's *Confession.*" *Classica et mediaevalia* 40 (1989): 235–250.

Shurtleff, Steven. "The Archpoet as Poet, Persona, and Self: The Problem of Individuality in the Confession." *Philological Quarterly* 73 (1994): 373–384.

JAN ZIOLKOWSKI

ARISTIPPUS, HENRY (d. 1162)

Henry or Henricus Aristippus, a prominent Latin cleric and court figure in the kingdom of Sicily during the reign of William I, brought important Greek philosophical and scientific writings into the intellectual orbit of the medieval Latin west. How he acquired his knowledge of Greek is unknown. His translation of Plato's *Meno* was finished sometime between early 1154 and 10 November 1160. His translation of Plato's *Phaedo* was begun in the spring of 1156 while Aristippus, now archdeacon of Catania, was in camp during William's siege of Benevento. It was completed in Palermo shortly thereafter and was later revised; two forms are known, both thought to be auctorial. The *Phaedo* and the *Meno* are the only Platonic dialogues that refer by name to an Aristippus; this fact may have some bearing either on Henry Aristippus's adopted byname or, if he was already so called (probably after the ancient Greek philosopher Aristippus, also a Sicilian court figure), on his decision to translate these works. Though they were not the only sources for a knowledge of Plato, these versions in Latin, made from the original Greek, are the only complete translations of any of his dialogues known to have circulated outside the Arab world during the Middle Ages. Henry Aristippus's designedly literal efforts are now and probably always were preserved in relatively few manuscripts, but they were sought out and read by early humanists for whom their content must have been more appealing than their style.

In 1158 Aristippus returned from a diplomatic mission to Constantinople with gifts to the kingdom from the emperor Manuel I Comnenus that included a copy of the Greek text of Ptolemy's *Almagest* and, in all likelihood, the Greek *Prophecy of the Erythrean Sibyl* later translated into Latin by Eugenius of Palermo. The anonymous early translator of the *Almagest* (who had come to Sicily from Salerno in 1158 or 1159) tells us that he found Aristippus investigating, at some personal risk, the wonders of Mount Etna, the volcano whose lava flows have often threatened Catania and its vicinity. Apparently connected with this interest is Aristippus's undated and still only partly edited translation, from the original Greek, of Book 4 of Aristotle's *Meteorology*, a text dealing in part with the liquefying and congealing of matter. Known to Gerard of Cremona (d. 1187), who translated *Meteorology* from the Arabic, this remained the standard Latin version of Book 4 until it was super-seded in the thirteenth century by William of Moerbeke's new translation of the entire work. Even so, much of it lived on, as William s version here is largely a revision of Aristippus's. Probably Aristippus's as well, and also known to Gerard, is a translation of the Greek *scholia* (annotations) for this book.

Preserved with the earlier form of Aristippus's translation of the *Phaedo* is a preface praising the king's intellectual curiosity and providing valuable information about secular Greek texts available in Sicily. In the prologue to his translation of the *Meno*, Aristippus parades his connections with the powerful while proclaiming their interest in this sort of cultural acquisition: the admiral Maio (King William's chief minister) and Hugh, the archbishop of Palermo, have asked him, he says, to translate the ancient Greek Diogenes Laertius's *Lives of the Philosophers*; and the king himself has commanded him to translate some writings of the Greek church father Gregory of Nazianzus. It is not absolutely certain that these announced versions were completed, but if they were, they may have been the source of quotations from both authors by Aristippus's contemporary John of Salisbury. A lost partial translation of Diogenes Laertius is usually supposed to have been Aristippus's: excerpts from it showing characteristics of his style, which allowed more lexical variation than that of most medieval western word-for-word translators, occur in the widely read *De vita et moribus philosophorum* (*Lives of the Philosophers*), formerly attributed to Walter Burley but now believed to have originated in northern Italy early in the fourteenth century. According to a recent argument, this translation was only of Books 1 and 2 of the Laertian original (plus, perhaps, the *Life of Aristotle* from Book 5), rather than, as commonly thought, of the entire first five books. If so, and if Henry Aristippus really was the translator, then he left it unfinished: the earlier Aristippus and Plato are both in Book 3.

Henry Aristippus's scholarly activity is often said to have ended in November 1160, when, after Maio's assassination, William I chose Aristippus to be his interim chief minister and also head of the royal chancery. Thereafter Aristippus was involved, deeply but ultimately unsuccessfully, in the tumultuous affairs of the kingdom. Suspected by William of complicity in a coup of 1161 that failed but had almost cost the king his life, Aristippus was imprisoned in the spring of 1162 and died soon afterward.

Further Reading

Editions

Fobes, F. H. "Mediaeval Versions of Aristotle's *Meteorology.*" *Classical Philology*, 10, 1915, pp. 297–314. (See pp. 310–311, ch. 1 of Henry Aristippus's translation.)

Kordeuter, Victor, and Cariotta Labowsky, eds. *Meno interprete Henrico Aristippo.* Plato Latinus, 1. London: Inaedibus Instituti Warburgiani, 1940.

Minio-Paluello, Lorenzo. *Aristoteles Latinus: Codices. Supplementa altera.* Bruges: Desclée de Brouwer, 1961, pp. 23, 38–39. (Specimens of the translation of *scholia* to *Meteorology*, Book 4.)

——, ed. *Phaedo interprete Henrico Aristippo.* Plato Latinus, 2. London: Inaedibus Instituti Warburgiani, 1950.

Manuscripts

Lacombe, Georges, et al. *Aristoteles Latinus: Codices.* Rome: Libreria dello Stato, 1939 (Vol. 1); Cambridge: Cambridge University Press, 1955 (Vol. 2, suppl.); Bruges: Desclée de Brouwer, 1961 (suppl. altera).

Critical Studies

Bluck, R. S., ed. *Plato's Meno.* Cambridge: Cambridge University Press, 1961, pp. 142–145.

Dorandi, Tiziano. "La *versio latina antiqua* di Diogene Laerzio e la sua recezione nel Medioevo occidentale: Il *Compendium moralium notabilium* di Geremia da Montagnone e il *Liber de vita et moribus philosophorum* dello ps. Burleo." *Documenti e Studi sulla Tradizione Filosofica Medievale*, 10, 1999, pp. 371–396.

Grant, Edward. "Henricus Aristippus, William of Moerbeke, and Two Alleged Medieval Translations of Hero's *Pneumatica*." *Speculum*, 46, 1971, pp. 656–669.

Hankins, James. *Plato in the Italian Renaissance.* Leiden: Brill, 1990, Vol. 1, pp. 40–48.

Jamison, Evelyn. *Admiral Eugenius of Sicily: His Life and Work and the Authorship of the Epistola ad Petrum and the Historia Hugonis Falcandi Siculi.* London: Oxford University Press for the British Academy, 1957. (See especially pp. xvii–xxi.)

Minio-Paluello, Lorenzo. *Opuscula: The Latin Aristotle.* Amsterdam: Adolf M. Hakkert, 1972. (See especially pp. 57–86, 87–93, 94–97.)

Round, Nicholas G., ed. *Libro llamado Fedrón: Plato's Phaedo Translated by Pero Díaz de Toledo (MS Madrid, Biblioteca Nacional Vitr. 17,4).* London: Tamesis, 1993, pp. 18–36. (And elsewhere as noted in index, p. 381.)

Takayama, Hiroshi. *The Administration of the Norman Kingdom of Sicily.* The Medieval Mediterranean: Peoples, Economies and Cultures, 400–1453, 3 Leiden: Brill, 1993. (See especially pp. 98–102.)

JOHN B. DILLON

ARNOLD OF BRESCIA (c. 1100–1155)

The blurriness of the line separating radical reformers from heretics is dramatically evident in the career of the cleric and ecclesiastical critic Arnold of Brescia. The backdrop for this drama was Patarine error, Hildebrandine reform, Italian communalism, and the struggle between pope and emperor. However, at many points the record is silent, sketchy, or contradictory. Of Arnold's origins and youth we know nothing, and the idea that he studied with Peter Abelard in Paris c. 1115–1119 is speculation based on Arnold's later defense of Abelard. Whether or not Arnold was ordained, he became a canon of the Augustinian friary in Brescia c. 1120 and served as prior. His moral life remained free from criticism, even by his enemies. Saint Bernard of Clairvaux, who heartily opposed both Arnold and Abelard, nevertheless described Arnold as "a man who comes neither eating nor drinking . . . whose life is as sweet as honey." John of Salisbury, who served in the papal court, said that Arnold was "a priest by office, a canon regular by profession, and one who had mortified his flesh with fasting and coarse raiment: of keen intelligence, persevering in the study of the scriptures, eloquent of speech and a vehement preacher against the vanities of the world."

In the mid-1130s, Prior Arnold became involved in a movement against Bishop Manfred of Brescia, whose efforts at reform had angered the local clergy and had, among the populace, added to the impetus for communalism. Arnold probably admired the bishop's efforts to end simony and clerical marriage, but he stood against the clerical hierarchy and sympathized with the people's defense of their political "liberties." Whatever his actual activity may have been, he was condemned as schismatic by the Second Lateran Council, was exiled from Brescia, and apparently wandered as an itinerant preacher in Lombardy in 1139–1140. In the spring of 1140, he traveled to Sens, where he accompanied Abelard in the latter's defense against the accusations of Bernard of Clairvaux. Abelard's failure to sway the council resulted in the condemnation and burning of books containing his errors and those of Arnold, a sentence confirmed by the pope. No works by Arnold survive, nor do contemporary references to any of his works, so it is unclear which books were meant in this sentence; it is also unclear whether Arnold's ideas were spreading through written sources as well as by his preaching.

Arnold immediately set himself up in Abelard's old school on Mont-Sainte-Geneviève in Paris, where he railed against Bernard and against the church's unholy wealth and temporal power. Reflecting Patarine ideas, and anticipating those of later groups, he fervently believed that preaching the gospel could not be accompanied by the accumulation and use of wealth and political authority, and that the church must divest itself of these things in order to adhere to the gospels. The clergy had rights to no funds other than ecclesiastical tithes, first fruits, and freewill offerings and should have no hierarchical organization. The laity should be free to organize their communal life as they saw fit. These concepts were not heretical, but neither were they ideas with which any authorities of the period were comfortable. Bernard persuaded Louis VII to exile Arnold from French territory, and Arnold went to Zurich, where he continued to preach church reform and to be hounded by Bernard's missives. Moving to Passau in 1142 or 1143, he befriended the local bishop and papal legate, Guido. Arnold was subsequently reconciled with Pope Eugenius III at Viterbo in 1145 or 1146.

A penance imposed by the papacy, and possibly Guido's patronage, took Arnold to Rome shortly thereafter. Here he gathered a following because of his public sermons and disputations and his reputation for piety and asceticism. He continued to attack the vices and wealth of the clergy and the nature of the ecclesiastical hierarchy, gradually developing from a critic to a radical demagogue. His support came initially from the lower clergy and devout women and later, more broadly, from the lower classes in Rome, where antipapal communalism had been active since 1143. This pressure forced Pope Eugenius to flee in 1147, and from Brescia the pope issued an ineffective bull branding Arnold as a schismatic (though not a heretic) and forbidding the clergy to have contact with him.

The Roman aristocracy, dueling with the pope for political control of Rome, found the newly demagogic Arnold a useful ally who could deliver and control the support of the lower classes. The Roman senate and Arnold exchanged oaths of loyalty, in regard of which the senators refused to hand Arnold over to the pope, who had returned and made his peace with the new Roman republic in 1149. With this settlement between Eugenius and the republic, Arnold's influence began to wane, although in mid-1152 he nonetheless attempted a coup, supported only by the lower classes. According to Eugenius's agreement with the republic, his followers were to be made senators, and a new emperor would be elected in Rome but would remain only a symbolic figure in the self-governing commune. Despite its failure, this move led the pope to arrange the Treaty of Constance (1153) for mutual support with the newly elected but uncrowned Frederick I Barbaxossa.

When Nicholas Breakspeare became Pope Hadrian IV in 1155, he demanded Arnold's expulsion and the dismantling of the republic and put the city under interdict during Holy Week to enforce his will. Both the mob and the senate quickly abandoned their republic and Arnold for the eucharist, and Arnold fled north toward Tuscany. At Bricole he was captured by Cardinal Odo, but he was soon rescued by the counts of Campagnatico. When Frederick, advancing on Rome for his coronation, captured one of the counts, Arnold was exchanged for the hostage. In Rome, there was armed resistance to the return of the pope and to the imperial coronation (18 June 1155); and the subsequent flight of emperor and pope from Rome convinced Frederick that he should put Arnold before a canonical tribunal The tribunal condemned Arnold, and the Roman prefect, or chief criminal magistrate, carried out the civil sentence of hanging and burning. Arnold's ashes were dumped into the Tiber.

Arnold's legacy is twofold, lending subsequent support to Roman republican communalism and to radical ecclesiastical reform: the poor and pure church. One strand leads to Brancaleone and Cola di Rienzo and the other to the Waldensians and Spiritual Franciscans. His most immediate effect may have been the establishment of the Arnoldist sect, whose members shared many of Arnold's ideas but in addition heretically denied the efficacy of the sacraments.

See also **Abélard, Peter; Bernard of Clairvaux; Boniface VIII, Pope**

Further Reading

Bernard of Clairvaux. *The Letters of Saint Bernard of Clairvaux*, ed. and trans. Bruno Scott James. Kalamazoo: Cistercian Publications, 1998.
De Stefano, Antonino. *Riformatori ed eretici del Medio Evo.* Palermo: Società Siciliana per la Storia Patria, 1990.
Frugoni, Arsenio. *Arnaldo da Brescia nelle fonti del secolo XII.* Turin: Einaudi, 1989.
Giesebrecht, Wilhelm von. *Arnold von Brescia: Ein akademischer Vortrag.* Munich: Veriag der Könighiche Akademie, 1873.
Greenaway, G. W. *Arnold of Brescia.* Cambridge: Cambridge University Press, 1931; New York: AMS, 1978.
John of Salisbury. *Htstoria pontificalis,* ed. and trans. Marjorie Chibnall. New York: Oxford University Press, 1986.
Merlo, Grado. *Eretici e eresie medievali.* Bologna: II Mulino, 1989.
Moore, R. I. *The Origins of European Dissent.* London: Penguin, 1977.
Otto of Freising. *The Deeds of Frederick Barbawssa,* trans. C. C. Mierow with R. Emery. New York: Norton, 1966.

JOSEPH P. BYRNE

ARNOLFO DI CAMBIO
(c. 1245 or 1250–1302 or 1305)

Arnolfo was one of the more prolific and innovative Italian sculptors and architects of the late thirteenth century. He was born near Florence, in the town of Colle Val d'Elsa, and was trained in the workshop of Nicola Pisano together with his contemporaries Giovanni Pisano and Tino da Camaino. Arnolfo, Giovanni, and Tino developed into strikingly different masters. While Giovanni's art became increasingly "expressionistic" and leaned more toward French Gothic, Arnolfo's and Tino's sculpture continued Nicola Pisano's more classical, reserved manner. During his later years, Arnolfo also distinguished himself as an architect in Florence.

Arnolfo is first documented in 1265 as one of Nicola Pisano's assistants on the Area of San Domenico in Bologna (1264–1267); he then worked on the pulpit for Siena Cathedral (1265–1268); and the Fontana Maggiore in Perugia (1277–1281). It is clear that by the time of the commission in Perugia, Arnolfo was already in the service of King Charles of Anjou. This is confirmed in a letter that Charles sent to the Perugian authorities in 1277, releasing the mason "Magister Arnulfus de Florentia" to work on a fountain. For Charles himself, who was resident in Rome as the senator of that city, Arnoifo served as a court mason, becoming conversant with ancient Roman art and architecture and the decorative manner of the contemporary Cosmati workshops. Arnolfo's appointment at the court put him into position to receive royal commissions, such as a seated portrait of Charles dated before 1278 (now in the Museo Capitolino in Rome); it also led to important commissions from high-ranking curial patrons, including two altar canopies in Roman basilicas and a small though highly influential series of sepulchral monuments in Rome and Orvieto. Inscriptions of 1285 and 1293 establish that "Arnolfus" was responsible for the altar canopies in two Roman churches: San Paolo fuori le Mura and Santa Cecilia. These canopies, both of marble with rich Cosmati-style ornamentation, seem to have been part of larger redecorating projects at the two churches, projects in which the fresco painter Pietro Cavallini was also involved. For these commissions, or at least for the canopy in San Paolo, Arnolfo may have collaborated with Piero Oderisi.

Arnolfo's best-documented sepulchral works include tombs erected for Cardinal Guillaume de Bray (San Domenico, Orvieto, after 1282); Pope Honorius IV (Santa Maria in Aracoeli, Rome, after 1287); Cardinal Riccardo Annibaldi (San Giovanni in Laterano, Rome, after 1289); and Pope Boniface VIII (old Saint Peter's, Rome, after 1303). Boniface's tomb, now destroyed, was part of an entire chapel; a recorded inscription on it mentioned "Arnolfus Architectus," indicating that Arnolfo had been responsible for both the architecture of the chapel and its sculpture. Finally, a statue of a deacon with a part of a curtain (now in the Walker Art Gallery in Liverpool) is believed to be a fragment from a fifth sepulchral monument. Of these tombs, de Bray's was perhaps the most influential, and today—despite a problematic reconstruction—it is the best preserved. This monument is a large wall construction with an elaborate base; an effigy and accompanying acolytes who draw back curtains in the middle register; and a kneeling resurrected de Bray, patron saints, a dedicatory inscription, and a Madonna and Child at the summit. Every surface that is not a figure is embellished with mosaic inlay in the Cosmati style.

The multiple figures in de Bray's tomb and the other tombs were also a feature of Arnolfo's unfinished (and now dismantled) facade for the cathedral of Florence (c. 1300); its original appearance is known from a sixteenth-century drawing in the Opera del Duomo in Florence. Many parts of this facade, both statuettes and relief carvings, are also preserved in the Opera del Duomo. Arnolfo certainly received the commission for the facade in conjunction with his control of the architecture of the cathedral itself. He is widely believed to have been the architect of the cathedral, for which he was appointed *capomaestro* (foreman) in 1300.

Architectural historians also attribute to Arnolfo the designs of other building projects in Florence that were begun during a boom in the last decade of the thirteenth century. These buildings include the Benedictine church of the Badia, the Franciscan church of Santa Croce, and the civic Palazzo della Signoria. They are clearly indebted to his knowledge of late Roman and early Christian buildings and are characterized by bold powerful massing, large unencumbered spatial volumes, and—unlike the facade of the cathedral—a minimum of ornamentation. Today, only the Badia, which was substantially remodeled by Giorgio Vasari in the sixteenth century, gives little evidence of its original appearance. The Palazzo della Signoria strongly influenced the design of other civic *palazzi* in Tuscany as well as the development of private *palazzo* architecture in the fourteenth and fifteenth centuries.

Arnolfo died sometime in the first decade of the fourteenth century.

See also **Boniface VIII, Pope; Pisano, Giovanni; Pisano, Nicola**

Further Reading

Gardner, Julian. *The Tomb and the Tiara: Curial Tomb Sculpture in Rome and Avignon in the Later Middle Ages.* Oxford: Oxford University Press, 1992.

White, John. *Art and Architecture in Italy 1250–1400*, 2nd ed. Harmondsworth: Penguin, 1987.

ROGER CRUM

ARNÓRR ÞÓRÐARSON JARLASKÁLD (after 1010–after 1073)

The son of the skald Þórðr Kolbeinsson, Arnórr grew up at Hítarnes, West Iceland. In early adulthood, he sailed to Norway (and possibly Denmark) as a merchant and skald, making an exuberant appearance before Magnús Óláfsson góði ("good") and Haraldr Sigurðarson (later harðráði, "hard ruler"). His nickname, "earls' skald," celebrates his service of the earls of Orkney, Rgnvaldr Brúsason (d. *ca.* 1045), to whom he was related by marriage, and Þorfinnr Sigurðarson (d. *ca.* 1065). His (now vestigial) memorial poems for Icelanders who died around 1055 and around 1073 might suggest that he resettled in Iceland in later life.

Arnórr's verse survives in 581 and one-half lines of fragmentary quotations in vellum MSS of the late 13th to 15th centuries and in 17th- or 18th-century paper copies. The chief sources are *Flateyjarbók* (108 half-strophes), *Hrokkinskinna* (83), *Hulda* (68), *Morkinskinna* (33), and MSS of *Heimskringla* (41), *Orkneyinga saga* (38), *Snorra Edda* (18 and 3 couplets), *Fagrskinna* (16), and Snorri Sturluson's separate *Óláfs saga helga* (15).

Arnórr's poetry richly exploits skaldic tradition with motifs of weapons flying, carríon beasts scavenging, or ships being launched; a great variety of *heiti*, including nine for "sword"; and some 150 kennings, from the obvious *Áleifs sonr* to the esoteric *erfiði Austra* ("burden of [the dwarf] Austri" = "sky"). He also employs more unusual items, including images of sparks flying from weapons and horns sounding, and several rare and unique words. Fleeting allusions to the gods Óðinn, Njrðr, or Baldr, to valkyries, or to pagan creation myths, belong, like those to such legendary heroes as the Burgundian Gjúki, purely to the level of diction. The numerous Christian references, including one to God and St. Michael judging mankind, seem by contrast substantial and sincere. The poetry is by skaldic standards moderately ornate in diction and word order, rather than extremely artificial. There are verbal resemblances to lines by the 11th-century skalds Hallfreðr vandræðaskáld ("the troublesome skald"), Sighvatr Þórðarson, and Þjóðólfr Arnórsson. The *hrynhent* poems by Markús Skeggjason (*ca.* 1104) and Sturla Þórðarson (*ca.* 1262) echo Arnórr.

Four main poems can be reconstructed from the fragments, all panegyrics on contemporary Norse rulers and all in the *dróttkvætt* meter except *Hrynhenda*, which is the first surviving panegyric in *hrynhent*. *Hrynhenda* (*ca.* 1045) begins with fleeting references to Arnórr's own trading voyages, but mainly concerns Magnús Óláfsson: his boyhood journey out of exile in Russia, conquest of Norway, triumphant voyage to Denmark, suppression of Wends at Jóm (Jomne) and Hlýrskógsheiðr (Lyrskovsheden), and ousting of Sven Estridsen from Denmark, especially at Helganes (Helgenæs). The only major poem by Arnórr to address directly a living hero, *Hrynhenda* is distinguished by extravagant praise (in apostrophes and second-person verbs) and seafaring descriptions both precise and imaginative. Named for its novel meter, *Hrynhenda* has a strongly trochaic pulse and relatively straightforward word order.

Magnússdrápa (*ca.* 1046/7) covers much the same events, but offers more factual detail and close-up battle description, including macabre images of the wolf scavenging on the battlefield.

Þorfinnsdrápa (*ca.* 1065) commemorates Þorfinnr Sigurðarson's victories against the Scots at Dýrnes (Deerness) and Torfnes (Tarbatness), defeat of his nephew Rgnvaldr off Rauðabjrg (Roberry), and raiding at Vatnsfjrðr (Loch Vatten) in the Hebrides and in England. It has an unusually personal tone of lament, and Arnórr recalls winter drinking scenes and his own presence at Vatnsfjrðr and (reluctantly) at Rauðabjrg. Battle descriptions are enlivened by short clauses focusing on graphic details and sharpened by specification of place, time, and numbers of ships. The general praise includes the *impossibilia* topos, "the sun will turn black, the earth sink in the sea, and the sky be rent before a ruler finer than Þorfinnr will be born in the isles," which echoes *Vluspá* or a common source.

Haraldsdrápa (*ca.* 1066, called simply an *erfidrápa* 'memorial poem' for Haraldr in the MSS) covers Haraldr Sigurðarson's later career: his struggle for Denmark against Sven Estridsen (especially a raid on Fjón [Funen] and victory at the Niz [Nis/Nissan] estuary), home policy (suppression of an Upland rebellion), and attempted conquest of England (victory near York, defeat and death in the unnamed battle of Stamfórd Bridge). There is one personal prayer for Haraldr, but otherwise the treatment is distant and vague, padded out by generalized praise and heroic clichés. Here, Arnórr uses interesting compound adjectives, but fewer and plainer kennings than elsewhere.

See also **Sighvatr Þórðarson**

Further Reading

Editions
Finnur Jónsson, ed. *Dennorsk-islandske skjaldedigtning.* Vols. 1A–2A (tekst efter håndskrifterne) and 1B–2B (rettet tekst). Copenhagen and Christiania [Oslo]: Gyldendal, 1912–15; rpt. Rosenkilde & Bagger, 1967 (A) and 1973 (B), vol. 1A, pp. 332–54 [diplomatic text]; vol. 1B, pp. 305–27 [edited text]

Turville-Perre, E. O. G. *Scaldic Poetry.* Oxford: Clarendon, 1976, pp. 93–7

Edwards, Diana. "The Poetry of Arnórr jarlaskáld: An Edition and Study." Diss. Oxford University, 1980 [published version forthcoming].

Bibliographies
Hollander, Lee M. *A Bibliography of Skaldic Studies.* Copenhagen: Munksgaard, 1958, pp. 65–6 [supplement forthcoming by Paul Bibire *et al.*].

Literature
Hollander, Lee M. "Anórr Thórdarson jarlaskáld and His Poem *Hrynhent.*" *Scandinavian Studies* 17 (1942), 99–109

Edwards, Diana. "Christian and Pagan References in Eleventh-century Norse Poetry: The Case of Arnórr jarlaskáld." *Saga-Book of the Viking Society* 21.1–2 (1982–83), 34–53

Edwards, Diana C. "Clause Arrangement in Skaldic Poetry." *Arkiv för nordisk filologi* 98 (1983), 123–75, esp. 149–75

Fidjestøl Bjarne. "Arnórr Þórðarson: Skald of the Orkney Jarls." In *The Northern and Western Isles in the Viking World: Survival, Continuity and Change.* Ed. Alexander Fenton and Hermann Pálsson. Edinburgh: Donald, 1984, pp.239–57.

DIANA EDWARDS WHALEY

ASHER B. YEHIEL (1250–1327)

Rabbi Asher b. Yehiel, known by the Hebrew acronym "*Rosh*" (not only the initial letters of *R*abbi *Ash*er, but not coincidentally also meaning "head; chief in importance" in Hebrew) was born ca. 1250 in Germany and died in 1327 in Spain. He was born into an elite rabbinic family, fourth generation in direct descent from Rabbi Eli'ezer b. Natan (the famous *Ra'avan*). His father Yehiel was descended also from the renowned *Rabbenu* Gershom b. Judah, as well as from Natan of Rome, author of the famous dictionary *'Arukh.* Asher studied in France when he was very young, and continued his studies in Germany, where he ultimately became second in importance only to his principal teacher, Rabbi Meir b. Barukh of

Rothenburg, the leading figure of the Ashkenazic communities in the thirteenth century. After his teacher was imprisoned in 1286 (he was captured while trying to emigrate following a pogrom), and particularly following his death in 1293, Asher was recognized as the chief rabbinical authority in Germany. He and his family also fled Germany because of the difficult conditions under Rudolf I, and, passing through France and Provence, he finally reached Spain in 1305.

There were already many Jewish refugees from Germany in Spain, including one of Asher's own sons who had been sent ahead to prepare a place for the family. He may have spent some time in Barcelona, with the renowned sage Solomon Ibn Adret; but in any case he soon made his way to Toledo at the request of community leaders there. He became the leading rabbi of the community, opening also his own yeshivah. While in Germany he had taught at the yeshivah of his own teacher, Meir b. Barukh, and may also have had his own yeshivah later. His yeshivah in Toledo, however, was to become internationally famous.

Asher was a prolific writer, and his literary output belongs to the great classics of medieval rabbinic literature. Primarily, he is famous for his three main works: novellae on the Talmud (titled *Tosafot ha-Rosh* on many tractates, written in the classical style of the French *Tosafot*); *Pisqey ha-Rosh*, a running commentary on the *Halakhot* of Isaac al-Fāsī; and a collection of some thousand responsa covering a multitude of aspects of daily life and Jewish law. Most of this work was done, or at least brought to its final phase, in Spain, including his responsa, most of which were written in answer to Spanish questioners. An astonishing fact is the disappearance of most of his responsa written in Germany, a small number of which survive in the collections of his teacher Meir of Rothenburg. The collection of his Spanish responsa was made by his son Jacob, for reasons to be explained below, and in itself bears witness to the successful acclimatization of the family to Spain. His compilation of *Tosafot*, based on the French prototype, incorporated also many sources from Spain. This work greatly facilitated the acceptance of the French *Tosafot* in Spain, where they soon became an integral part of talmudic study, thus providing a central vehicle for the important historical process of cultural integration between Spain and Franco-Germany. The *Pisqey ha-Rosh*, or "decisions," is dedicated mainly to a detailed comparison between the legal interpretations of al-Fāsī and the parallel Franco-German tradition of the *Tosafot*, with the important addition of later Spanish traditions such as those of Jonah Gerundi, Meir Abulafia, and Moses b. Naḥman.

The chief distinction between the *Pisqey ha-Rosh* and his *Tosafot* is that the former deal with practical application of law rather than mere commentary upon the talmudic text. Spanish Jewish legal tradition often differed from that in France or Germany, and Asher followed generally the positions taken by his teacher Meir b. Barukh, who accepted al-Fāsī and Maimonides except where they were contradicted by the *Tosafot*. Asher nevertheless made concessions to Spanish Jewish law and custom, while always maintaining the superiority of Ashkenazic positions with regard to liturgical, festival, and dietary customs. These "decisions," together with many of the responsa, were later adapted and processed by his eldest son and successor, Jacob, into a formal code of law, *Arba'ah ṭuriym* ("Four rows"), which together with the codes of Maimonides and al-Fāsī became one of the three pillars upon which Joseph Karo in the sixteenth century erected the final work of codification of Jewish law, the *Shulḥ-an 'arukh* ("Prepared table"). Asher's responsa, alongside those of his friend and colleague Ibn Adret, are the choicest of their kind in medieval rabbinic literature. Asher's responsa are organized in a unique method, according to topics (*Kelaliym*), but this was not the original arrangement and was probably instituted by his son Jacob to expedite locating specific laws. However, in the process, and with additional errors made in copying and printing, completely wrong attributions of historical data have been made. Urbach was the first to call attention to this fact, and a new and much better organized edition, on the basis of manuscript material, was published in 1994.

Asher was asked his opinion on many problems arising from accepted local practices in. Spain that were often foreign to his native, German, way of life, and to which he had to habituate himself or ruthlessly resist if he wished to be obeyed. One of the secrets of his great success in winning his way in Castile was his insight and judgment as to when a struggle was important and worth the effort and when to yield or keep quiet and adopt a neutral stand. As an example, in Spain *shemiṭat kesafim*, the remission of debts every seventh year, was not practiced. Asher tried hard to change this but had to admit failure, and he therefore refused to handle problems arising from such debts. Another example is the law of *yiybbum*, levirate marriage (Deut. 25.5-10). This was practically annulled in Germany, and the *yavam* was forced to give *ḥaliyṣah* to his sister-in-law. Spain followed Maimonides' ruling that *yiybbum* was always preferable, even when it was clear that the woman was justified in refusing to cooperate. In this case, Asher was far less tolerant. More important than these specific cases of divergence in legal tradition was the essential problem of whether it was permissible, and at all possible, to mix philosophic, abstract logical, linguistic, and general juristic considerations in the process of deciding Jewish law. The procedure was quite acceptable within the Spanish tradition, but extremely foreign to German rabbis, and Asher took an extreme stand on the issue, totally negating the option and deeming it sacrilegious and contrary to the nature of the halakhic procedure. This bitter argument went on for many years, and it finally brought about a breach between Asher and Rabbi Israel of Toledo, who for many years had been a friend and colleague of his.

A similar ambivalence existed in his relations with Ibn Adret, whom he admired and to whom he wrote with extreme respect. But the striking fact is that throughout Asher's responsa Ibn Adret is not quoted more than once or twice, and only a few more times in his monumental *Pisqey ha-Rosh.* Similarly, Asher is scarcely ever mentioned in Ibn Adret's work or that of his pupils [nevertheless, the *Tosafot ha-Rosh* were cited by Ibn Adrets pupil Zeraḥyah b. Isaac ha-Levy of Zaragoza, prior to 1411]. The two rabbis admired each other deeply, but when dealing with halakhic issues they stuck to their native traditions, thus creating in Spain two distinct "camps" whose strong influence can be detected up to the time of the Expulsion. Asher was the final link in the long chain of Franco-German inroads into Spanish rabbinic literature and culture, the origins of which can be traced to Jonah Gerundi.

[*Ed. note:* Asher, as noted above, achieved great renown through his yeshivah in Toledo, which was maintained after his death by his eldest son, Jacob. Students came from ail over Europe—Germany, France, Bohemia, and other lands—to study under Asher. Since these students obviously did not know Spanish, and it is indeed doubtful that Asher himself knew that language, it is probable that the language of instruction was Hebrew. Illustrious students of Asher included Yeruḥam b. Meshullam of Provence, who later wrote the halakhic work *Toldot Adam ve-Ḥava;* Estoriy ha-Farḥiy, author of a noted work that is still a valuable source of the geography of Palestine, *Kaftor ve-peraḥ* (which contains important references to his teacher); Isaac b. Joseph Israeli, who as noted composed at Asher's request an important work on astronomy; Abba Mari b. Moses of Lunel, who later lived in Montpellier and was a central figure in the "Maimonidean controversy"; Yissakhar b. Yequtiel, whose sister married Asher's son Solomon, and who wrote an abridgment of the important halakhic work *Sefer ha-teru-mot* of Samuel b. Isaac ha-Sardi; and many others. Asher had eight (not seven, as sometimes stated) sons. In order of their birth they were Yeḥiel, who died while Asher was still alive; Solomon (known as "the pious"); Jacob; Judah (who took his father's place as rabbi in Toledo; author also of several responsa); Eliakim; Moses; Eli'ezer; and Simon. The tombstones of many of the family, including sons, grandsons, and their wives, were extant in Toledo in the last century, and the inscriptions have been published.]

See also **Maimonides**

Further Reading

Baer, Yitzhak. *A History of the Jews in Christian Spain* (Philadelphia, 1966), vol. 1.

Freimann, Alfred. "Ascher ben Jechiel." *Jahrbuch der jüdisch-literarischen Gesselschaft* 12 (1918):237–317. Hebrew version, *ha-Rosh ve-ṣeṣa'av* (Jerusalem, 1986).

Galinsky, Yehuda D. "*Arba'ah m-urim ve-ha-sifrut ha-halakhtit shel Sefarad be-meah ha-14.*" (Bar-Ilan University, 1999; dissertation).

Greene, Wallace. "Life and Times of Judah b. Asher." (New York, Yeshiva University, 1919; dissertation).

Ta-Shma, I. "Shiqulim filosofi'im be-hakhra'at ha-halakhah [Heb.]," *Sefunot* 16 (1985): 99–110.

——. "Rabbenu Asher u-veno Rabbi Ya'aqov—bein Ashkenaz le-Sefarad [Heb.]," *Pe'amim* 46–47 (1991): 75–91.

——. "Rashi-Rif-and Rashi-Rosh." In *Rashi, 'iyyunim be-yeṣirato,* ed Z. A. Steinfeld. (Bar Ilan University, 1993), pp. 209–20.

Urbach, E[phraim] E. "She'elot u-teshuvo ha-Rosh be-kitvey yad u-ve-defusim." *Shanaton ha-mishpaṭ ha-'ivriy* 2 (1975):1–153.

——. *Ba'aley ha-tosafot* (Jerusalem, 1980), pp. 586–99, and index, *passim*

ISRAEL TA-SHMA

AUGUSTINE OF CANTERBURY
(d. by 609)

First archbishop of Canterbury. Little is known about Augustine's early life beyond the fact that he was a pupil of Felix, bishop of Messana in Italy, and subsequently a monk and then prior of St. Andrew's Monastery on the Caelian Hill, Rome.

In 596 Pope Gregory I selected Augustine to lead a mission of monks to convert the English. The political climate in England was favorable for the venture, since Kent enjoyed close contact with the Christian Franks; in particular Æthelberht of Kent, overlord of the English kings south of the Humber, had married a Frankish princess, Bertha, who practiced the faith with her own chaplain. Nevertheless, Æthelberht was initially wary of the missionaries, and he insisted on meeting them outdoors, where hostile magic could less easily harm him. Augustine and his companions met him on the Isle of Thanet, approaching (as Bede records) with a silver cross and an icon of Christ.

At first Augustine operated from the old Roman church of St. Martin, where Bertha had practiced her devotions, but by ca. 602–03 he had repaired another Roman church, which he dedicated to Christ (Christ Church, Canterbury). Nearby he began to construct a monastery (known initially as St. Peter's, subsequently as St. Augustine's), to become a necropolis for Kentish kings and archbishops. Augustine presumably founded a school at Canterbury to provide converts with the learning they needed as clerics. The books and materials he had brought were augmented by further dispatches from Rome. The impact of writing was rapidly felt in the political sphere also, for under Æthelberht the earliest written collection of Anglo-Saxon laws was produced.

Augustine is recorded as having astonishing success in winning converts; by Christmas 597, shortly after he had received episcopal consecration, 10,000 are reputed to have been baptized. Surviving correspondence reveals that he sought and received guidance from Gregory on the organization, rites, and practices of the infant church. Particularly notable is Gregory's advice that pagan temples not be destroyed but purified and rededicated to Christian service. Augustine did not manage to realize Gregory's ideals for the organization of an English church in northern and southern provinces, each with an archbishop and twelve bishops. He also failed to obtain the British (Celtic) church's recognition of his authority and their help in converting the English. Augustine's mission affected only the southeast of England, and the difficulties that beset the new church following the death of Æthelberht (in 616?) underline the extent to which the early successes had depended on the king's favor. But then Augustine did not have many years in which to work; he died somewhere between 604 and 609.

See also **Bede the Venerable; Gregory I, Pope; Grosseteste, Robert; Joachim of Fiore**

Further Reading

Attenborough, F.L., ed. and trans. *The Laws of the Earliest English Kings.* Cambridge: Cambridge University Press, 1922

Brooks, Nicholas. *The Early History of the Church of Canterbury: Christ Church from 597 to 1066.* Leicester: Leicester University Press, 1984

Chaplais, Pierre. "Who Introduced Charters into England? The Case for Augustine." In *Prisca Munimenta: Studies in Archival and Administrative History Presented to A.E.J. Hollaender,* ed. Felicity Ranger. London: University of London Press, 1973, pp. 88–107

Mayr-Harting, Henry. *The Coming of Christianity to Anglo-Saxon England.* 3d ed. University Park: Pennsylvania State University Press, 1991

Wood, Ian. "The Mission of Augustine of Canterbury to the English." *Speculum* 69 (1994): 1–17

Wormald, Francis. *The Miniatures in the Gospels of St. Augustine: Corpus Christi College, MS. 286.* Cambridge: Cambridge University Press, 1948.

RICHARD GAMESON

AVERROËS, ABU ʼL-WALĪD MUḤAMMAD B. AḤMAD B. RUSHD (1126-1198)

Commentator on Aristotle, philosopher, physician and jurist; the greatest intellectual figure of Islamic Iberia. Averroës (the name is a corrupt Judaeo-Latin transcription of the Arabic name Ibn Rushd) was born in Córdoba in 1126, into a family of eminent judges. Little is known for certain about his early career, but he undoubtedly received the traditional Islamic education in Arabic literature and linguistics, jurisprudence and theology, together with instruction in medicine and philosophy. Of the great Muslim sages of medieval Iberia, Ibn Rushd can personally only have known Ibn Ṭufayl, who became his mentor at the court of the Almohad caliph Abū Yaʼqūb Yūsuf. In an incident that Gauthier has described as being "of capital importance not only in the biography of Averroës, but in the development of European philosophy" Ibn Ṭufayl introduced Averroës to the learned sovereign, who was deeply impressed by his subject's thorough knowledge of the opinions of the "philosophers" (that is to say, the Arabic *falasifa* working in the tradition of Aristotle and the Neoplatonists). Abū Yaʼqūb subsequently called upon Averroës to make Aristotle's hitherto all-too-obscure writings more perspicuous by means of commentaries. As a result of the caliph's favors, he was appointed qāḍī of Seville in 1169, chief qāḍī of Córdoba in 1171, and physician to the court of Marrakesh in 1182. The accession to the caliphate, in 1184, of Abū Yaqʼūb's son, Al-Mansūr, did not at first change Ibn Rushd's fortunes. However, around 1194/5, Al-Mancūr found himself obliged to dissociate himself from him, yielding to the growing pressures of popular fundamentalism; Averroës' s philosophical writings were burned, and the philosopher himself exiled to Lucena, southeast of Córdoba. This sentence, so obviously out of tune with the caliph's own intellectual leanings, was soon revoked, however and Averroës was allowed to return to Marrakesh, where he died on 10 December 1198. Averroës's cardinal legacy are his commentaries on Aristotle; they earned him the antonomastic title "the Commentator" among the Latin schoolmen, who kept relying on his translated commentaries after St. Thomas Aquinas had tried to supplant them with his own work and even after the great Averroistic crisis of the 1270s. Significantly, Aristotle's works continued to be accompanied by the elucidations of his commentator in the printed editions of the fifteenth and sixteenth centuries. Averroës composed two kinds of commentaries, "short" and "middle," on most of the writings of the Aristotelian corpus accessible to him; in addition, we have "long" commentaries" on the *Posterior Analytics, Physics, De Caelo, De Anima* and *Metaphysics.* The short commentaries or *epitomai* (in Arabic *jawmi'*) are manuals of Aristotelian philosophy, paraphrases written early in Averroës's career, and show the commentator under the influence of the Neoplatonizing Aristotelianism of his predecessors Al-Fārābī and Ibn Sīnā (Avicenna). In the later middle commentaries (Arabic, *talkhīs*), more detailed expositions of the philosopher's thought, we already witness a gradual emancipation from this older tradition of interpretation and see Averroës working toward an ideal of recovering Aristotle's thought in its original purity. Ibn Rushd's exegetical endeavors culminated in the long commentaries (Arabic *tafsīr*), scrupulous word-for-word commentaries of a rigorous literary form resembling that used in traditional Qur'ānic exegesis: and appropriately so, for the words of Aristotle had by that time gained almost divine authority for Averroës.

The long commentary on *De Anima,* fruit of a lifelong exploration of Aristotelian psychology, contains Averroës's final and most mature solution to the problems posed by Aristotle's notoriously difficult remarks on the nature of the "agent intellect." According to Aristotle, there is an active and a passive aspect to the human mind: the intellect, which is passive insofar as it receives the immaterial forms of sense percepts, is seen as active inasmuch as it must, prior to their reception, abstract these forms from the material conditions of sense perception. Averroës believed that both the active (or "agent") and the passive ("material," "possible") powers of the intellect were one for all human beings. The possible intellect, being the receptacle for the forms of material things, could not itself possess such a form; otherwise it would interfere with and distort the forms it received. But if it was immaterial, it had to be unique, for it is matter that causes plurality. The unicity of the agent intellect, on the other hand, safeguards the universal validity of human cognition in that the individuals' data of sense perception are abstracted and universalized by one faculty common to all. The activity of thought can on this interpretation only be ascribed to the individual inasmuch as his or her material organs of sense are necessary to furnish the transpersonal intellect with data to abstract. The thoughts themselves are no single person's possession; rather, the intellect is envisaged as a common pool of knowledge participated in by the individual according to each person's abilities. Full "conjunction" with the transcendent intellect, the possession of all possible knowledge, is the end and rare fulfillment of intellectual activity. Despite the denial of personal immortality that it implies, this theory of "monopsychism" exercised a deep and lasting influence on the development of philosophy in the Latin west. Its adoption by some Parisian masters in the latter half of the thirteenth century provoked the most profound intellectual crisis in the as yet young history of medieval Aristotelianism, but even the condemnations of 1270 and 1277 could not, in the long run, thwart its attraction. As Philip Merlan has brilliantly argued, the structures of Averroean psychology continue to be discernible in contemporary philosophy, especially in the Kantian tradition (compare with Kant's transcendental unity of apperception/*Bewußtsein überhaupt*).

Averroës never held the theory of "double truth" often falsely attributed to him: in his view, the truths of philosophy and religion were in perfect agreement. As he wrote in chapter 2 of the *Faṣl al-maqāl,* "truth does not oppose truth but accords with it and bears witness to it." Hence, contradictions between religious and demonstrative truth can only be apparent, caused by the fact that the Qur'ān frequently uses symbols and rhetorical or dialectical arguments in order to reach the majority of the people. The superficial oppositions thus arising must be resolved by an allegorical interpretation (*ta'wīl*) of Scripture that penetrates from the level of its apparent (*ẓāhir*) to that of its hidden (*bāṭin*) meanings. But ta'wīl is only for the philosophers and should be taught esoterically, as it would endanger the faith of those untrained in demonstrative reasoning. With philosophy thus becoming the ultimate judge of the meaning of revealed truth, Averroës takes a rationalist stance toward religion: it has nothing to offer that reason cannot reach autonomously and without the veil of symbols. This attitude, while replacing faith with intellectual conviction, does not overtly challenge the truth of Islam (which does not contain any supernatural mystery in the Christan sense); however, it relegates it to the pragmatic role of teaching the "simple people" through symbols what the philosophers know with the clarity of reason.

As in the speculative branches of philosophy, Averroës also championed a resolute return to the principles of pure Aristotelianism in the natural sciences. In what has been called the "Andalusian revolt against Ptolemaic astronomy," (A.I. Sabra) Averroës and his contemporary Al-Biṭrūjī (Alpetragius) censured Ptolemy for departing from Aristotelian physics by postulating epicycles and eccentrics; but unlike Al-Biṭrūjī, Averroës's grasp of the Aristotelian alternative to epicycles and eccentrics remained unsatisfactory and vague. Averroës was not prepared to meet Ptolemy on the level of empirical observation; indeed he dismissed his computational evidence as "arrived at by the use of instruments" and "based on the senses," opposing to the empirical method "the true theories based on rational precepts" (especially in the *Long Commentary* on the *Metaphysics*). According to Averroës, Ptolemaic astronomy was in outright contradiction to these rational principles, mainly because it assumed circular movement not around the center of the universe and two contrary motions for one planet (nature would not employ two movements for what it could possibly achieve with one, Averroës claimed, for "nature does nothing in vain"). He hoped to account for the movement of the planets by positing, in Aristotelian fashion, simple homocentric spiral motions in one direction—without, however, checking the empirical viability of this proposition. It is interesting that Averroës's criticisms of Ptolemy, although almost exclusively negative in their failure to provide an alternative theory, later influenced Copernicus by convincing him of the shortcomings of traditional astronomy.

Similarly, the *Kullīyat fī-l-ṭibb* (*Generalities in Medicine in Seven Books*), or *Colliget,* imparted impulses toward a reform of medical science to Renaissance physicians, who appreciated Averroës's detached and apparently disinterested attitude vis-à-vis Galen without seeing the rather reactionary Aristotelianism underlying it. In a detailed analysis of the *Colliget* chapter on respiration, Bürgel has discovered general tendencies comparable to those also present in Averroës's astronomy: a preponderantly (albeit not exclusively) speculative approach rooted in Aristotelian natural philosophy, a preparedness to sacrifice scientific progress to defend the teachings of the master, and, to a lesser extent than in astronomy, resignation in the face of technical difficulties. In the *Colliget,* health is defined in the traditional manner as an equilibrium of the four humors; accordingly, the task of the physician consists in preserving this harmony or in restoring it when it has become disturbed through illness. The physician fights the cause of an illness with its opposite: an excess of moisture with dryness, a superabundance of heat with cold, amd so forth. In spite of interesting medical details, the *Colliget* is intended as a compilation of received medical wisdom rather than as an original work; but it has certainly not yet received the scholarly attention that it deserves.

The same could be said a fortiori of Averroës's handbook of Islamic law, the *Bidāyat al-mujtahid wa nihāyat al-muqtaṣid* (*Beginning for Him Who Works Toward an Independent Judgment and End for Him who Contents Himself with Received Opinion*), a book that became a standard work of reference in the Islamic world (unlike Averroës's philosophical writings, which remained virtually unread by his fellow Muslims). The *Bidāya* aims at furnishing the reader with an exposition of the differences of opinion between the various juridico-religious schools concerning the main points of the law. The objective is to enable the user of the *Bidāya* to come to an *ijtihād,* an independent legal judgment based on free choice among the orthodox traditions. The opinions taken into consideration are almost exclusively Sunnite, Averroës's acquaintance with the Malikite tradition (in which he was brought up) being most profound, but he is careful to be scrupulously objective and impartial in his presentation. Brunschvig has described the *Bidāya* as the "most accomplished example of the methical application of the principles of Islamic law to the entirety of Sunnite jurisprudence." Together with Averroës's other writings, it testifies to the versatility and greatness of an encyclopedic mind.

See also **Aquinas, Thomas**

Further Reading

Aristotelis Opera cum Averrois Commentariis. 9 vols. and 3 suppl. Venice, 1562; reprt, Frankfurt am Main, 1962.

Brunschvig, R. "Averroès juriste." In *Études d'Islamologie.* Vol. 2. Paris, 1976. 167–200.

Bürgel, J. C. "Averroes 'contra Galenum': Das Kapitel von der Atmung im Colliget des Averroes (...) eingeleitet, arabisch herausgegeben und übersetzt," *Nachrichten der Akademie der Wissenschaften in Göttingen* (1967). Philologisch-historische Klasse no. 9, 263–340.

Corpus Commentariorum Averrois in Aristotelem (in progress). Series Arabica: 9 vols.; Series Hebraica: 3 vols.; Series Latina: 3 vols.; Series Anglica: 3 vols. Published since 1949, variously in Cairo, Madrid, and Cambridge, Mass. More recently, several important editions have appeared in other series.

Gauthier, L. *Ibn Rochd (Averroès).* Paris, 1948.

Rosemann, P. W. "Averroes: A Catalogue of Editions and Scholarly Writings from 1821 Onwards," *Bulletin de Philosophie Médiévale* 30 (1988), 153–221.

Urvoy, D. *Ibn Rushd (Averroes).* Trans. O. Stewart. London, 1991.

PHILIPP W. ROSEMANN

AVICENNA (980–1037)

The Persian philosopher, poet, and physician Ibn Sina (Abu Ali al-Husayn ibn Abdallah ibn Sina) is known in the west as Avicenna. He was born in Bukhara and died m Hamadan, Persia.

Avicenna was famous in Italy during the Middle Ages as the author of the *Canon of Medicine* (*al-Qanun fi 'l tibb*), a gigantic medical encyclopedia that remains one of the most remarkable achievements of medieval philosophical thought. The *Canon* was first translated from Arabic into Latin by Gerard of Cremona and his pupils in Spain during the twelfth century, and thereafter it formed the basis of the medical curriculum at every university in the medieval west. Avicenna's great work is so comprehensive, well-constructed, and detailed that today it is still the foundation for medical teaching in some parts of the Middle East.

The life of Avicenna resembles that of many celebrated sages from the east. He was born into an educated family and displayed remarkable precocity at an early age, learning the Qur'an (Koran) from memory and then studying texts of natural philosophy and medicine; by the time he was sixteen, he was already a famous physician. He spent most of his life wandering throughout Persia, often following a wealthy patron, and serving as a physician, teacher, and government official. In the Islamic world, he is famous as a natural philosopher whose melding and reconciliation of Aristotelian, Neoplatonic, and Muslim thought was universally admired in Arabic-and Persian-speaking cultures.

From the standpoint of medieval Christian culture, Avicenna's achievement was twofold. Not only did he return Aristotle's and Galen's medical thought to the west after it had been lost for many centuries, but he also helped establish the physician as a gentleman, whose decorous behavior admitted him to the most intimate circles of the wealthy and powerful. In the Islamic world of Avicenna's time, medicine was much more than mere cures for sundry diseases: it was the dispensing of learned advice about the welfare of the body. The medieval Muslim physician, like Galen in the second century, applied an intimate knowledge of nature, combined with astrology, pharmacy, and not a few merry tales and bits of gossip, to teach his patrons how to live well. It is not surprising, then, that men like Avicenna, who wrote numerous medical and philosophical treatises, also took up poetry as a mark of their gentility.

Avicenna's cultured, philosophical medicine had an immediate appeal to Latin-speaking physicians.

Aristotle had said that where natural philosophy ended, there medicine began (*De sensu.* Book 1,436a), but, to the constant frustration of medieval physicians, he did not elaborate on this point. Avicenna was the first philosopher to demonstrate how medicine might indeed be a development from natural philosophy and therefore a subject worthy of advanced study.

Further Reading

Avicenna (Ibn Sina). *Liber canonis.* Hildesheim, 1964. (Facsimile of the Latin edition of the *Carton*, Venice, 1507.)

Grant, Edward, ed. *A Source Book in Medieval Science.* Cambridge, Mass.: Harvard University Press, 1974, pp. 715–720. (Includes part of the *Canon*, trans. into English, O. Cameron Gruner; annot. and corrections, Michael McVaugh.)

Siraisi, Nancy. *Avicenna in Renaissance Italy: The Canon and Medical Teaching in Italian Universities after 1500.* Princeton, N.J.: Princeton University Press, 1987. (The best study of the reputation of Avicenna in medieval and Renaissance Italy.)

FAYE. M. GETZ

B

BACON, ROGER (ca. 1213/19–1292)

Little is known of the origins of Roger Bacon, Franciscan philosopher and scientific thinker. He was born ca. 1213–19. His writings reveal his English origins: his birthplace is unknown. His family was well-off and scholarly, able to assist him in the buying of books and scientific instruments. Educated at Oxford and Paris, he received the degree of master of arts around 1240 and lectured on Aristotle's natural philosophy for many years.

Under the influence of the works of Grosseteste and Arab authors, Bacon devoted himself to the study of mathematics, and languages, including Greek and Hebrew. He also conducted observational experiments, especially in optics. He entered the Franciscan order in 1257 but found Franciscan attempts to censor his writings disturbing. He appealed to the future Pope Clement IV for assistance in the compilation of a great encyclopedia of the sciences. As a result of papal encouragement Bacon composed the *Opus maius*, *Opus minus*, and *Opus tertium*—works that described his proposed reform of education and society, criticized magic, suggested calendar reform, and emphasized the importance of scientific knowledge for Christianity.

For reasons not entirely clear to us his works were again condemned in 1278 by the head of his order, owing to "certain suspect novelties." It is possible that his interest in alchemy, astrology, and the teachings of Joachim of Fiore, the Italian mystical preacher, led to his condemnation. As a result Bacon may have been imprisoned for several years, although he continued to study and write. His last work, *Compendium studii theologiae* (1292), still assailed the corruption of his day.

Although many of his works were forgotten after his death, Bacon was rediscovered in the Elizabethan period as a prototype of the modern "scientist." Bacon's modernity now appears exaggerated; his experimentalism was very much in the medieval tradition, and his ultimate aim was the advancement of the new learning as a useful tool for religion. At the same time his enthusiastic support for and synthesis of the new science helped introduce it into European intellectual life.

Further Reading

Primary Sources

Burke, Robert B., trans. *The Opus Maius of Roger Bacon*. 2 vols. Philadelphia: University of Pennsylvania Press, 1928.

Lindberg, David C., ed. and trans. *Roger Bacon's Philosophy of Nature: A Critical Edition*. Oxford: Clarendon, 1983.

Secondary Sources

Crowley, Theodore. *Roger Bacon: The Problem of the Soul in His Philosophical Commentaries*. Louvain: Éditions de l'Institut Supérieur de Philosophie, 1950.

Easton, Stewart C. *Roger Bacon and His Search for a Universal Science*. Oxford: Blackwell, 1950.

JANICE GORDON-KELTER

BEATRIJS VAN NAZARETH (1200–1268)

The Brabantine mystic Beatrijs van Nazareth was born in 1200, the youngest child of a burgher family in Tienen (in the present-day Belgian province of Flemish-Brabant); for that reason she is also known as Beatrijs van Tienen. She evidently was trained in the medieval liberal arts (*artes liberales*), showing a good knowledge of Latin. In 1215 she took the solemn vows as a Cistercian nun. In 1236 she moved to the convent in Nazareth (near the town of Lier), where she was prioress until her death in 1268.

Quite a lot is known about the life of this mystic thanks to the Latin text *Vita Beatricis*, written in the last quarter of the thirteenth century by an anonymous Cistercian monk. Allegedly this *vita* was based on a diary that Beatrijs kept in Middle Dutch, but which is now lost. The only surviving work by her is entitled *Van seven manieren van heileger minne* (The Seven Steps of Holy Love), a short treatise in prose, dealing with seven aspects of the love for God. This work dates back to 1250 and is therefore one of the oldest Middle Dutch texts in prose (together with some works by the other Brabantine mystic, Hadewijch). *Van seuen manieren van heileger minne* has come down to us in three manuscripts from the fourteenth and fifteenth centuries, always in combination with other texts.

Beatrijs van Nazareth is, alongside Hadewijch, one of the most prominent representatives of female mysticism in the medieval Low Countries. Her treatise was probably meant for people within her own circle, possibly as an introduction into the spiritual life for the novices of her own convent. Beatrijs considers the love of man for God to be a gift of God and describes in seven steps the experience of joy and longing as well as tension and agony caused by this spiritual *minne*. The ultimate goal of mystical ascent, according to Beatrijs, is the fulfillment of love and the union of the soul with its heavenly bridegroom.

Beatrijs's treatise reveals influences of the *amor* (love of God) concept as was current in twelfth-century Northern French spirituality, prominently expressed in texts of Cistercian origin. In the *minne*, then, God reveals Himself and man is free to comply with that love; in love, man can meet God.

The works of Beatrijs and Hadewijch are of the utmost importance for the development of Middle Dutch as a written language. Both mystics tried to express the role of the divine and the experiencing of God in their lives, while realizing that their vernacular falls short vis-à-vis such an endeavor. Thus they frequently made use of neologisms, using the language in a creative way. They laid the foundations of a Middle Dutch mystical language, which made itself felt in the oeuvre of Jan van Ruusbroec and, through him, in the writings of the Modern Devotion, a later religious movement.

See also **Hadewijch; Jan van Ruusbroec**

Further Reading

Carton, M. J., trans. "Beatrice of Nazareth. The Seven Steps of Love." *Cistercian Studies* 19 (1984): 31–42.

Vekeman, Herman W. J. "Beatrijs van Nazareth. Die Mystik einer Zisterzienserin," In Peter Dinzelbacher and Dieter R. Bauer, ed. *Frauenmystik im Mittelalter.* Ostfildern: Schwabenverlag, 1985, pp. 78–98.

——. *Hoezeer heeft God mij bemind. Beatrijs van Nazareth (1200–1268).* Vertaling van de Latijnse *Vita* met inleiding en commentaar. Kampen/Averbode: Kok/Altiora, 1993.

Vekeman, Herman W. J., and Jacques J. Th. M. Tersteeg, ed. *Beatrijs van Nazareth. Van seuen manieren van heileger minnen.* Zutphen: Thieme, 1971.

AN FAEMS

BEATUS OF LIÉBANA (8th century)

Participant in the adoptionist controversy, commentator on the Apocalypse; very little is known about his life beyond his participation in the former. He appears to have been a priest or a monk in Liébana (Cantabria). In 785 he coauthored (with Eterius, who would later become bishop of Osma) a letter to Elipandus, the metropolitan of Toledo, that denounced the latter's belief that Christ had adopted his human nature at the time of the Incarnation. This letter was prompted by one written a short time before by Elipandus to an abbot Fidelis, asking him to reprimand Beatus and Eterius for an earlier challenge to his views on the Incarnation. At stake, at least from Elipandus' perspective, was not only doctrinal accuracy but the continued authority of the metropolitan see of Toledo over the greater Spanish church. Beatus was also attacked in two subsequent letters from the bishops of Spain to the bishops of Gaul and to Charlemagne, respectively, expressing their support for the adoptionist position. Charlemagne responded by convening the Council of Frankfurt in 794, at which the assembled bishops condemned adoptionism as heresy.

Beatus is better known today as the author of a commentary on the Apocalypse, though the evidence supporting this attribution is circumstantial. The first version of the commentary was finished in 776, with subsequent editions in 784 and 786. The commentary is little more than a compilation of the opinions of previous authorities on the subject, though the names of the sources from which the author drew reveal something of the range of materials available to a scholar in the early period of the Asturian monarchy. The conservatism of the author is interesting in light of the fact that he was writing more than fifty years after the Muslim invasion and thus was in a position to cast the invaders in an apocalyptic role, if he had been so inclined. The primary significance of the commentary lies not in the text but in the illuminations that accompany it in the many manuscripts of the work that have survived from the tenth through the twelfth centuries. These so-called "Beatos" contain some of the most impressive examples of the so-called Mozarabic artistic style.

See also **Charlemagne**

Further Reading

"Beati et Eterii Adversus Elipandum." *Corpus Christianorum* 59 (1984), 320–22.

Colbert, E. "The Martyrs of Córdoba (850–859): A Study of the Sources." Ph.D. diss., Catholic University of America. Washington, D.C., 1962.

Collins, R. *The Arab Conquest of Spain, 710–797.* Oxford, 1989.

Saunders, H. (ed.) *Beati in Apocalypsim libri duodecim.* Rome, 1930.

KENNETH B. WOLF

BEAUMANOIR, PHILIPPE DE REMI, SIRE DE (ca. 1250–1296)

Jurist, author, and royal official, Beaumanoir came from the village of Remy, near Compiègne, where his family held a fief from the abbey of Saint-Denis. He was the second son of Philippe de Remi (ca. 1205–ca. 1265), who served as *bailli* of Gâtinais for Robert, count of Artois, from 1237 to 1250. By 1255, the father had apparently built a manor house on the property, for he then styled himself "lord of Beaumanoir," a title that passed to his heir, Girard, then to the younger Philippe at Girard's death. Beaumanoir *fils* began his administrative career in 1279 as *bailli* of Clermont-en-Beauvaisis for Robert, count of Clermont. In 1283, he completed the *Coutumes de Beauvaisis*, a systematic treatise on customary law composed in Francien prose with strong traces of Picard. Beaumanoir declares in his prologue that it is essential to write down the legal customs of the region so that they can be maintained without change "because, since memories are fleeting and human lives are short, what is not written is soon forgotten." His book was widely copied in the Middle Ages (thirteen manuscripts extant, ten or eleven other copies known to be lost) and is today considered the most significant work on French customary law of the 13th century. In 1284, Beaumanoir was knighted and entered royal administration; he served as seneschal of Poitou (1284–87) and Saintonge (1287–89), then as *bailli* of Vermandois (1289–91), Touraine (1291–92), and Senlis until his death (1292–96).

Since the 1870s, a substantial body of narrative and lyric poetry has been attributed to the author of the Coutumes: two romances in octosyllabic verse, *La Manekine* (8,590 lines) and *Jehan et Blonde* (6,262 lines), both signed Phelippe de Remi; at least three *chansons courtoises*, two naming the poet Phelippe de Remi; a moralistic fabliau, *Fole Larguece*; and several shorter poems, including a *Salu d'amours* signed Phelippe de Beaumanoir, two *fatrasies*, and an *Ave Maria*. Traditional scholarship holds that Beaumanoir composed most of these works as Philippe de Remi while in his twenties, between 1270 and 1280, and assumed the name Philippe de Beaumanoir only in 1279, when he turned his energies to law and administration. Some recent scholars, troubled by the unusual productivity of such a young man and by the disparity between courtly and legal subjects, prefer to attribute all the poetry to the father and date it between 1237 and 1262. A major factor underlying the revisionist attribution is the revival of a turn-of-the-century Germanist argument that Rudolf von Ems used both romances as sources for his *Willehalm von Orlens*, completed before 1243. Attribution and dating of the poetry remain open questions.

La Manekine is a pious adventure romance based on the folklore motif of "The Maiden Without Hands," also treated in the somewhat later *Belle Helaine de Constantinople* and *Lion de Bourges*. A Hungarian princess who cuts off her right hand rather than marry her father incestuously is set adrift and lands in Scotland, where she marries the king, only to be betrayed by his mother; set adrift again, she lands in Rome, where she is miraculously healed, reunited with her husband, and reconciled with her father. *Jehan et Blonde*, perhaps based in part on the Roman de Horn and deeply influenced by the romances of Chrétien de Troyes, tells the story of an impecunious French knight, Jehan, who rises in the world by serving as squire to the Count of Oxford and winning the love of Blonde, the count's daughter; it can be read as a how-to manual for success at court and for moral behavior by lordly vassals. The 15th-century prose romance *Jehan de Paris* is a free adaptation of *Jehan et Blonde*.

Further Reading

Philippe de Remi, sire de Beaumanoir. *Œuvres poétiques*, ed. Hermann Suchier. 2 vols. Paris: SATF, 1884–85, Vol. 1: La Manekine, Vol. 2: *Jehan et Blonde; poésies diverses*. [Based on the unique MS (B.N. fr. 1588).]

——. *La Manekine: roman du XIIIe siécle*, trans. Christiane Marcello-Nizia. Paris: Stock, 1980. [Modern French.]

——. Philippe de Remi's *"La Manekine,"* ed. and trans. Irene Gnarra. New York: Garland, 1990.

——. *Jehan et Blonde de Philippe de Rémi: roman du XIIIe siècle*, ed. Sylvie Lécuyer. Paris: Champion, 1984. [Modern French trans., 1987.]

——. "Les chansons de Philippe de Beaumanoir," ed. Alfred Jeanroy. Romania 26 (1897): 517–36. [From B.N. fr. 24406.]

——. *Coutumes de Beauvaisis*, Vol. 1 and 2: ed. Amédée Salmon. Paris: Picard, 1899–1900 [English trans. by F.R.P. Akehurst. Philadelphia: University of Pennsylvania Press, 1992]. Vol. 3: Commentaire historique et juridique par Georges Hubrecht. Paris: Picard, 1974.

Dufournet, Jean, ed. *Un roman à découvrir: "Jean et Blonde" de Philippe de Remy (XIIIe siècle)*. Paris: Champion, 1991.

Gicquel, Bernard. "Le Jehan et Blonde de Philippe de Rémi peutil être une source du Willehalm von Orlens?" *Romania* 102 (1981); 306–22.

Shepherd, M. *Tradition and Re-Creation in Thirteenth-Century Romance: "La Manekine" and "Jehan et Blonde" by Philippe de Rémi*. Amsterdam: Rodopi, 1990.

MARY B. SPEER

BECKET, THOMAS (1120–1170)

England's best-known saint and martyr. Archbishop Thomas was murdered in Canterbury Cathedral on 29 December 1170 by four household knights of Henry II. He subsequently became one of the greatest medieval cult figures and Canterbury one of Europe's greatest pilgrimage centers.

Thomas, son of a respectable, moderately wealthy London merchant, was educated in an Augustinian priory, a London grammar school, and Paris in its preuniversity days. From 1143 to 1145 he was apprenticed to a London banker, enjoying a wild, frivolous life; he supported the Angevin side in the civil war of Stephen's reign. Thereafter he joined the household of Archbishop Theobald of Canterbury, where his companions included John of Salisbury, Gilbert Foliot, Roger of Pont l'Évêque, John of Pagham, and John of Canterbury—scholars and future bishops who together suggested a protouniversity. He learned superb administrative skills, derived from Theobald's training at the hands of his own predecessors, Lanfranc and Anselm. Theobald supported the Angevins against Stephen and went into exile; Thomas accompanied him to Rome, learning international diplomacy. As papal legate after 1150 Theobald arranged Henry of Anjou's succession as Henry II.

When Henry acceded in 1154 at age 22, his English backers, seeking to control, counsel, and educate him, chose Thomas as the chancellor (1155–62). Becket became almost Henry's alter ego and best friend, raising the office of chancellor to new heights of power and responsibility. His magnificent lifestyle—the grandeur and ostentation befitting the king's constant companion in hunting, gaming, feasting, and joking—would haunt him later. But he counseled Henry to rule justly for the welfare of kingdom and church, and Henry obeyed. Theobald is said to have designated Thomas as his successor.

Henry chose Thomas for Canterbury, primate of the English church, on Theobald's death (1162). Immediately Thomas underwent a surprising transformation; from model courtier he became model archbishop. His lavish extravagance became lavish charity, his household of courtiers became one of scholars and learned lawyers. Days of hunting and feasting became days of study, devotion, and prayer. Scholars still cannot explain this metamorphosis.

Becket, now a fanatic reformer, clashed with Henry over royal and ecclesiastical rights. Thomas claimed his duty was to rule the church according to "law and right"—by which he may have meant the canon law just then being systematized by the papal court. Henry insisted on his duty to preserve England's "ancestral customs"—later the "precedents" of English common law—as crystallized in the Constitutions of Clarendon (1163). Thomas protested violently, fleeing into exile (1164). During the next six years both men sent secret missions to Pope Alexander III, the French king, the German emperor, and counts, abbots, bishops, and archbishops throughout Europe to gain allies. Reams of propagandistic letters flew from court to court, replete with deceptions, half-truths, and manipulations of public and private opinion. Neither man displayed statesmanlike talents in this contest, both remaining

volatile and inflexible on minor points. Thus repeated attempts to compromise failed over obscure sometimes silly demands.

While Henry grudgingly yielded on specific issues —at last virtually acceding to Thomas's demands—he underhandedly resurrected Becket's worldly reputation as chancellor and torpedoed one settlement by refusing the Kiss of Peace. While Thomas was admired for his immovable, righteous stance, he so offended nearly everyone that he was hated almost universally in his victory. When compromise came (at Freteval, 1170), Thomas ruined it, returning to England and promptly excommunicating all Henry's supporters—including most of the bishops. This further enraged the four already-infuriated knights who took Henry's exasperated statement that none of his household were helping him against Thomas as a signal for murder.

Becket's supporters declared him a martyr. But no modern historian has yet explained satisfactorily his motivations and actions. He claimed, following his predecessor Anselm, to fight for God and Right. Indeed he succeeded in forcing Henry to submit to papal formulations of canon law and partial papal control, yet only at the near-destruction of the English church, of which Thomas was shepherd and guardian. Thus Thomas still remains a mystery, a mass of contradictions and controversies—as his companions suggested, a "sacred monster,"

See also **Henry II; Lanfranc of Bec**

Further Reading

Barlow, Frank. *Thomas Becket*. London: Weidenfield & Nicolson, 1986.
Knowles, David. *The Episcopal colleagues of Archbishop Thomas Becket*. Cambridge: Cambridge University Press, 1970.
Knowles, David. *Thomas Becket*. Cambridge: Cambridge University Press, 1970.
Radford, Lewis B. *Thomas of London before His Consecration*. Cambridge: Cambridge University Press, 1894.
Saltman, Avram. *Theobald, Archbishop of Canterbury*. London: Athlone, 1956.
Smalley, Beryl, *The Becket Conflict and the Schools: A Study of Intellectuals in Politics*. Oxford: Blackwell, 1973.
Wilks, Michael, ed. *The World of John of Salisbury*. Oxford: Blackwell, for the Ecclesiastical History Society, 1984.

SALLY N. VAUGHN

BEDE THE VENERABLE (CA. 673–735)

Honored as "the Venerable" even in his own day, Bede (Baeda Beda in earliest sources) was the foremost educator, exegete and historian of his epoch, the Northumbrian Golden Age. Of his life Bede himself provides nearly all we know, in the short autobiographical note he appended to the last chapter of his *Ecclesiastical History of the English People*, with a list of his numerous writings. He occasionally gives a personal detail in one of his other works. Bede was born on land that a year or two later (674) was given by King Oswiu (Oswy) to Benedict Biscop to build the very monastery Bede would enter at age seven, St. Peter's, Wearmouth. In 681, two years after Bede's initiation into the community, Benedict established at nearby Jarrow the twin foundation of St. Paul's, formed as an integral part of a single monastery with St. Peter's. At some point Bede was transferred to this new foundation under the strict and learned Ceolfrith, whose place was later filled by Hwætberht. With the exception of a few short trips to Lindisfarne and York Bede spent his entire life as a monk-scholar at St. Paul's.

Ordained a deacon at the age of nineteen (six years before the usual canonical age), Bede then proceeded to the priesthood at age 30 (703). He became the "beloved father and master," as his disciple Cuthbert called him, of the thriving intellectual and spiritual center of learning. Bede taught the basic disciplines of grammar and computus: grammar, the science of the Latin language and its interpretation; computus, the science of determining time, especially the ensemble of rules by which the date of Easter is reckoned. Since the master in many early monasteries was also responsible for teaching psalmody, Bede also may have taught chant.

Bede wrote several educational treatises to complement the texts available from late antiquity. He wrote "a book on the art of meter," the *De arte metrica*, a systematic exposition of Latin versification by means of a judicious compilation of late-antique commentaries on the grammarian Donatus, demonstrated by examples from Virgil and Christian poets. The book makes evident Bede's qualities as a textbook writer: apt selection, concentration on essentials, simplicity, and precision. His own contribution to metrical history is his description in chapter 24 of isosyllabic stress rhythm, accentual meter, which eventually superseded quantitative Latin verse in medieval poetry. Bede appended to this work his *De schematibus et tropis*, "a small book on figures of speech or tropes, that is, concerning the figures and modes of speech with which the holy scriptures are adorned." Bede adds considerably to Donatus's section on the trope of allegory, with a section on symbol in deeds and in words. Bede's *De orthographia*, "a book about orthography," consists of short alphabetized entries about the meaning and correct usage or spelling of words likely to cause difficulties for a medieval Latinist.

For the basic curriculum Bede composed another little educational piece, *De natura rerum*, "a separate book on the nature of things," serving as an introduction to cosmology in 51 chapters on the earth, the heavens, stars, and planets. The text, a reworking and betterment of Isidore's *Liber rotarum* and Pseudo-Isidore's *De ordine creaturarum*, incorporates much from Pliny's *Natural History*. Near the beginning and near the end of his distinguished writing career Bede composed works on time and its calculation. The first, *De temporibus*, a radical revision of material in Isidore's *Etymologies* and Irish supplements, consists of 22 brief chapters on measurement of time, the six ages of the world, and a short chronicle of the most important events in salvation history. His recalculation of the time spans of each age according to Jerome's translation of the Hebrew Bible instead of Jerome's earlier figures from Eusebius led to a charge of heresy being leveled against Bede in Bishop Wilfrid's court at Hexham, on the grounds that he placed Christ in the fifth instead of the sixth age—a charge he vigorously denied in a formal and ferocious letter to Plegwin, a monk of Hexham.

Bede's students found the first book on time to be too dense for easy learning, so Bede remedied this by producing a new, expanded version, *De temporum ratione*. After initial chapters on finger calculation, Greek and Roman letters symbolizing numbers, various aspects of time and historical modes of measurement he proceeds, as he did in the *De temporibus* but in much greater detail, from the smallest to the largest units of time. He includes a chapter on English months, with precious information for students of Germanic and Anglo-Saxon culture. He concludes the work with an extended discussion of the ages of the world.

Bede considered all his educational treatises, grammatical and scientific, as preparatory instruction for the study of scripture. Although Bede is known today mainly as an historian, in his own time and throughout the Middle Ages he was known primarily as an exegete. The books of the Bible he chose to interpret are of two kinds: those that were already favorites of the Fathers, such as the commentaries on Genesis and on Luke, and those that were largely ignored by earlier exegetes, such as the commentaries on Ezra and Nehemiah and on the New Testament Catholic Epistles. Both filled pedagogical needs: the former, selected and simplified for his English pupils, display Bede's talents as an adapter and synthesizer; and the latter, supplementing the Fathers, demonstrate his originality within the exegetical tradition.

Bede's usual method of commentary is the early-medieval one of phrase-by-phrase exegesis of a biblical text, from beginning to end; it is a process of rumination, fostered in the monastic tradition. Bede relies heavily on Augustine for doctrine and much of his exposition, but in interpretive spirit he favors Gregory the Great, with whom he shares a kind of spiritual affinity. Like Gregory and many of the Fathers he interprets the Bible both literally (according to the basic, obvious, surface meaning) and allegorically (according to the deeper, hidden, spiritual, symbolic meaning). Bede's exegetical practice is eclectic and literary. If appropriate, he will point out the typology (an Old Testament event as prefiguration of the New). Often he presents a twofold relationship in a text, with a single allegorical interpretation superimposed upon the literal meaning, At other times he spreads out a threefold meaning, either historical, allegorical, and moral (applying to one's own life) or historical, allegorical, and anagogic (applying to the final Judgment), or he follows the fourfold method of historical, allegorical, tropological (moral), and anagogic interpretations. Though he derived this schema from Cassian, Bede became the definitive authority in the Middle Ages for it. In addition to his biblical commentaries he compiled two biblical aids, a compendium on the places of the Holy Land, derived primarily from the itinerarium of Adomnán, and a gazetteer explaining and locating places mentioned in the Bible.

For Bede preaching was a priest's primary function and had a special, even sacramental, significance: preachers are the successors of the prophets and apostles. For the liturgical year he composed two books of 25 homilies each. In hagiography Bede revised the lives of various saints, including Felix, Athanasius, and Cuthbert; he also composed an historical martyrology, 114 brief accounts of martyrs' lives and deaths, which played an important role in the development of the Roman martyrology. Although Bede wrote "a book of hymns in various meters and rhythms" and "a book of epigrams in heroic and elegiac meter," we now possess only a few of each, about two dozen poems in all. These include a poetic tour de force in honor of St. Æthelthryth, the famous *Hymnos canamus gloriae*, and the even more famous *De die iudicii*, on Judgment Day. Although well versed in OE poetry, he may not have composed the five-line OE poem called "Bede's Death Song," which he recited on his deathbed.

Bedes fame today derives mainly from his work as an historian. His histories not only provide us with information now known only because of him; as products of his mature scholarship and long writing career they also mark momentous advances in the science of historiography. His *History of the Abbots of Wearmouth and Jarrow* first describes the life and career of the great founder of the monastery, Benedict Biscop, then incorporates and edits the anonymous life of Abbot Ceolfrith, fused with descriptions of the abbots Eostorwine and Sigefrith, and ending with Bede's coeval Hwætberht. Although he attributes no miracles to any of the five remarkable abbots, he represents them in this monastic chronicle as splendid characters. Unlike the two world chronicles he appended to his treatises on time his *Ecclesiastical History of the English Peoples* is history in the grand and full scale, which has gained Bede the well-deserved title of "father of English history."

The first Englishman to write history with a full sense of historical responsibility and with control by his use, arrangement, and omission of materials, Bede was also the first to relate the history of England. He is the first literary authority for a structured history stretching from Roman Britain, the invasions of the Angles, Saxons, and Jutes, some events in Scotland and Ireland, to the mission of Augustine to Kent, Paulinus to Northumbria, the doings of Theodore, Chad, and Acca, the power and glory of Northumbria, and events in the recent past. Each division contains memorable events told with extraordinary but restrained artistry: Gregory the Great's apostolic love for the English, the conversion of King Edwin and his people, King Oswald and St. Aidan, Abbess Hild and the poet Cædmon.

Bede's title tells us that his work belongs to the genre and tradition of ecclesiastical history, based on biblical rather than classical concepts of time and event, presupposing a theocentric universe in which the secular is understood in terms of the sacred, tracing the progress of the church as it advances in time and geography. Furthermore it is "of the *English* people," treating the Anglo-Saxons as one nation, God's chosen, even though divided into kingdoms and privileging Northumbria in the later books. The first three books of the *History* deal primarily with the christianization of the English; the last two describe the way in which the Christian life developed among them, especially in Northumbria. The first book sweeps through 650 years, whereas each of the remaining four covers about a generation. Dedicated to Ceolwulf, king of Northumbria (729–37), the *History* emphasizes the good and bad influence of various Anglo-Saxon kings; it also stresses the influence of the clergy and their activity, offering as models John of Hexham (Beverley), Aidan, and especially Cuthbert, with whom the *History* comes to a climax in book 4.27–32. In contrast to Stephens admiring *Life of Wilfrid*, Bede adroitly diminishes the worth and importance of Bishop Wilfrid by downplaying his role in the Northumbrian church and passing over in silence some major facts in Wilfrid's career, such as the Council of Austerfield, even while giving Wilfrid credit for gaining the victory of the Roman practice of Easter-dating and tonsure over the Irish faction under Colmán at the Synod of Whitby in 664.

The *History* is written in a soberly elegant Latin. It was translated into OE during the period of King Alfred. Over 150 manuscripts from the Middle Ages and many editions and translations of the *History* attest to its perduring importance and interest. No one was comparable to Bede as an historian until the 12th century, and his work still provides medieval English historians with endless topics for research and discussion.

Bede wrote a number of formal instructional letters, one of which has great historical importance, his late *Letter to Ecgbert*, a disciple who was to become the first archbishop of York (735) and whose brother Eadberht would become king of Northumbria (737). Whereas the *Ecclesiastical History* ends on an optimistic note of Christian progress, the letter paints a bleak picture of greed, subterfuge, and fraud. Outspoken and condemnatory of pseudo-monasteries and ecclesiastical and secular abuses, Bede details a program of reform. To meet the needs of far-flung and hard-to-reach communities, he proposes that new bishoprics be founded, based, and financed at prosperous monasteries.

Bede became an author in great demand after his death. By the 9th century the admiration for Bede was so extensive that he was considered a Father of the Church. Venerated now by Anglicans and Catholics alike, he bears the title of saint and doctor of the Catholic church.

See also **Alfred the Great; Augustine of Canterbury; Cædmon**

Further Reading

Primary Sources

The collected works of Bede (*Bedae venerabilis opera*) are being reliably edited by various hands in the Corpus Christianorum Series Latina (CCSL). Turnhout: Brepols, 1955–[vols. 118A–22 so far].

Colgrave, Bertram, ed. and trans. *Two Lives of St. Cuthbert*, Cambridge: Cambridge University Press, 1940.

Colgrave, Bertram, and R.A.B. Mynors, eds. and trans. *Bede's Ecclesiastical History of the English People*. Oxford: Clarendon, 1969.

Connolly, Seán, trans. *Bede: On the Temple*. Liverpool: Liverpool University Press, 1995.

Holder, Arthur G., trans. *Bede: On the Tabernacle*. Liverpool: Liverpool University Press, 1994.

Hurst, David, trans. *The Commentary on the Seven Catholic Epistles*. Cistercian Studies 82. Kalamazoo: Cistercian Publications, 1985.

Jaager, Werner, ed. *Bedas metrische Vita sancti Cuthberti*. Palaestra 198. Leipzig: Mayer & Müller, 1935 [verse life of Cuthbert].

Martin, Lawrence T., and David Hurst, trans. *Homilies on the Gospels*. 2 vols. Kalamazoo: Cistercian Publications, 1991.

Miller, Thomas, ed. and trans. *The Old English Version of Bede's Ecclesiastical History of the English People*. EETS o.s. 95, 96, 110, 111. London: Trübner, 1890–98.

Plummer, Charles, ed. *Venerabilis Baedae opera historica*. 2 vols. Oxford: Clarendon, 1896. Repr. in 1 vol. Oxford: Clarendon, 1946 [introduction and notes still valuable].

Sherley-Price, Leo, trans. *The Ecclesiastical History of the English People*. Rev, R.E. Latham. Harmondsworth: Penguin, 1968.

Tanenhaus, Gussie Hecht, trans. "Bede's *De Schematibus et Tropis*—A Translation." *Quarterly Journal of Speech* 48 (1962): 237–53. Repr. in *Readings in Medieval Rhetoric*, ed. Joseph M. Miller et al. Bloomington: Indiana University Press, 1973, pp. 76–80.

Secondary Sources

For recent Bedan research see "The Year's Work in Old English Studies." *Old English Newsletter*, Winter issues, and the annual bibliography in *Anglo-Saxon England*.

Brown, George Hardin. *Bede the Venerable*. Boston: Twayne, 1987 [with bibliography of editions and studies until 1986]

Goffart, Walter. *The Narrators of Barbarian History* (A.D. *550–800*). Ch. 4, "Bede and the Ghost of Bishop Wilfrid," Princeton: Princeton University Press, 1988, pp. 235–328 [extensive, speculative investigation of Bede's motives as an historian].

Lapidge, Michael. "Bede's Metrical *Vita S, Cuthberti*." In *St. Cuthbert, His Cult and His Community to AD 1200*, ed. Gerald Bonner, David Rollason, and Clare Stancliffe. Woodbridge: Boydell, 1989, pp. 77–93.

Lapidge, Michael, ed. *Bede and His World*: *The Jarrow Lectures 1958–1993*. 2 vols. Aldershot: Variorum, 1994.

McCready, William D. *Miracles and the Venerable Bede*. Toronto: Pontifical Institute, 1994.

Wallace-Hadrill, J.M. *Bede's Ecclesiastical History of the English People*: *A Historical Commentary*. Oxford: Clarendon, 1988.

Webb, J.F. *The Age of Bede*, Harmondsworth: Penguin, 1983 [with translations of selected works].

GEORGE HARDIN BROWN

BEDFORD, JOHN DUKE OF (1389–1435)

Third son of Henry IV; created duke of Bedford in 1414, he was a courageous soldier and gifted administrator. He served with distinction during the reign of his brother, Henry V, safeguarding the Scottish border and defeating a Franco-Genoese fleet at the Battle of the Seine (1416). After Henry's death in 1422 he became Regent of France. His determined efforts to protect the rights of Henry VI, the young heir of Henry and Katherine of Valois, were a remarkable accomplishment upon which his fame and political reputation deservedly rest.

In the first years of regency Bedford was able to extend Henry V's conquests. His emphatic victory at Verneuil (1424), where he fought with "the strength of a lion," led to the subjugation of Maine and northern Anjou. But the advent of Joan of Arc in 1429 transformed the situation. The English were forced onto the defensive, and Bedford, conservative in religious outlook, saw Joan as a witch whose enchantments and sorcery punished the English for a lack of sound faith. The constant campaigning of Bedford's last year wore away his strength; his death in September 1435, combined with the defection of the Burgundians as allies, dealt Lancastrian France a blow from which it never recovered.

Bedford earned high praise from English and French chroniclers alike. A great landowner and possessor of rich manuscripts, vestments, and plate, he cleverly exploited the media of painting, pageantry, and poetry to promote the cause of the dual monarchy of Henry VI over England and France. His strong sense of justice, whether disciplining his troops or punishing brigands, won him universal respect. His encouragement of trade and commerce led to a revival of Normandy's economic fortunes; his willingness to employ French administrators and his use of native institutions gave his regime considerable authority.

Less of a diplomat than Henry V, Bedford sometimes allowed pride and quick temper to get the better of him. His relations with the Burgundians were not always easy, and he never fully gained the confidence of the English aristocracy. His regency nevertheless was a superb political and military accomplishment.

See also **Henry V**

Further Reading

Stevenson, Joseph, ed. *Letters...of the Wars of the English in France*. Rolls Series 22. 2 vols. in 3. London: Longmans, 1861–64.

Stratford, Jenny. "The Manuscripts of John Duke of Bedford: Library and Chapel." In *England in the Fifteenth Century: Proceedings of the 1986 Harlaxton Symposium*, ed. Daniel Williams. Woodbridge: Boydell, 1987, pp. 329–50.

Williams, Ethel Carleton. *My Lord of Bedford, 1389–1435*. London: Longmans, 1963 [not critical, but a useful narrative].

MICHAEL JONES

BEHEIM, MICHAEL (1416/1421–1472/1479)

A prolific author and composer of almost five hundred song-poems, Michael (or Michel) Beheim (also Behaim; Beham) was until the late twentieth century dismissed as a *Vielschreiber* (scribbler) and mere cultural-historical curiosity. He is now recognized as one of the most important singers, composers, and publishers (*Liedpublizisten*) of the fifteenth century. Beheim's reevaluation, facilitated by the appearance of a critical edition of his poems (*Gedichte*, published 1968–1972), coincided with the reassessment of fifteenth-century aesthetics in general. Beheim is an important figure because of his poetic range and the range of his ambition. A manuscript scribe, poet, and composer, he produced a virtual summa of medieval themes and poetic forms, creating religious songs, moral and ethical poetry, political and historical writings, autobiographical verse, love songs, fables, and songs on the nature and status of the singer's art. (He even writes on Dracula, Vlad the Impaler.) As a poetic musician (*musicus poeticus*) and lay theologian, Beheim championed *rechte kunst* (proper art) and artistic individuality, the latter grounded in the composition of original songs, or *Töne* (occasion pieces with titles such as *Zugweise, Kurze Weise, Verkehrte Weise, Osterweise, Trummetenweise, Gekrönte Weise, Slecht guldin Weise, Hohe guldin Weise, Hofweise, Slegweise, Lange Weise, Angstweise*). Beheim also fashioned lengthy chronicles in verse: *Pfälzische Reimchronik* (Palatine Rhyme Chronicle), *Buck von der statt Triest* (The Book of the City Treist), and *Buch von den Wienern* (The Book of the Viennese). Since the poet set these chronicles to music, thus making them sung epics (*Sangvers-Epen*), they hold the distinction of being the final specimens of Middle High German epic material that was sung. All of Beheim's oeuvre can in fact be performed to music, and he perhaps surprisingly leaves to his audience a choice of modes of reception. In the foreword to the *Buch von der statt Triest* he states, for example, that "you can read it like a rhymed book or sing it like a song" (*man es lesen mag als ein gereimptes puch oder singen als ain lied*). By presenting an alternative to traditional, communal, oral song performance, Beheim makes one of the first appeals in German literature to silent readers.

Literary criticism on Michael Beheim is devoted to taxonomy; for example, whether he was a medieval or modern poet, whether he was a Meistersinger, and if the term "professional poet" (*Berufsdichter*), frequently applied to him in research, helps us to understand him any better. That his work is difficult to pigeonhole arises from Beheim's status as a transition poet par excellence; as such, he embodies clashing and contradictory, but not mutually exclusive, tendencies: For instance, although he was a conservative author who cataloged and recapitulated the entire repertoire of fourteenth- and fifteenth-century German political writers, or *Spruchdichter*, Beheim sanctioned, and made a specific appeal to, a modern reading audience, recognizing the power and place of the book. Similarly, his great concern for the accurate textual transmission of his "collected works" on the manuscript page marks him as both a conservator and a protohumanistic student of the word. Although Beheim esteemed tradition, imitating and paraphrasing revered masters (Johann von Neumarkt, Heinrich von Mügeln, Heinrich Seuse, Heinrich von Langenstein, Thomas Peuntner, the Nicholas von Dinkelsbühl redactor, Muskatblüt), he reanimated not only poetry but theology, promulgating an Augustinian renewal in the vernacular that deserves the name of pre-Lutheran biblical humanism. Using song-poetry as a medium for proselytism among the laity, Beheim stylized himself as a poet-theologian and transmitter of patristic theology, who translated, versified, and set to music Scripture, sacred tractates, and sermons.

It is uncertain whether Michael Beheim was born in 1416 or 1421, or if he died before 1472 or after 1479, but it is possible to reconstruct his life in otherwise remarkable detail from rich autobiographical verses, for example, Song 24, "On Michael Peham's [sic] birth and his travels to this country" (*Von Michel Pehams gepurt und seinem her chomen in dis lannd*). In strophes bearing the traces of emendation as authorial intervention, Beheim alludes to his humble origins as a weaver's son, and sketches a career path that leads to no less than the imperial court of Frederick III of Habsburg. Among his prominent patrons were King Christian I of Denmark, Konrad von Weinsberg (the imperial archchamberlain),

Count Ulrich II von Cilli, and Margrave Albrecht III, ("Achilles") von Brandenburg-Ansbach. For another noble sponsor, Frederick I of Wittelsbach, elector and Count Palatine, the poet reformulates the centuries-old adage concerning medieval German literary patronage, "Whose bread I eat, their song I sing" (*Wes' Brot ich eß, des Lied ich sing*). These words have had an extraordinarily negative resonance in Beheim scholarship because they are deemed an expression of personal ethics rather than a rhetorical formula. A master of the rhetorical art, he was a loquacious, self-conscious artist with a sharp eye for accuracy of textual transmission and a strong belief that poetry should serve a moral purpose. His melodies and strophic structures, his wide-ranging and varied themes, his ecumenical impulses and his promotion of sacred subject matter as appropriate to secular audiences, all make him the architect of a rich compendium of songs and song types.

See also **Seuse, Heinrich**

Further Reading

Gille, Hans, and Ingeborg Spriewald, ed. *Die Gedichte des Michel Beheim.* 3 vols. Berlin: Akademie-Verlag, 1968–1972.

McDonald, William C. *"Whose Bread I Eat": The Song-Poetry of Michel Beheim.* Göppingen: Kümmerle, 1981.

Müller, Ulrich. "Autobiographische Tendenzen im deutschsprachigen Mittelalter: Probleme und Perspektiven der Edition. Vorgeführt am exemplarischen Fall der Sangvers-Lyrik und Sangvers-Epik des Michel Beheim." *Editio* 9 (1995): 63–79.

Schanze, Frieder. *Meisterliche Liedkunst zwischen Heinrich von Mügeln und Hans Sachs.* 2 vols. Munich: Artemis, 1983–1984.

Scholz, Manfred Günter. *Zum Verhältnis von Mäzen, Autor und Publikum im 14. und 15. Jahrhundert: "Wilhelm von Österreich" "Rappoltsteiner Parzifal," Michel Beheim.* Darmstadt: Wissenschaftliche Buchgesellschaft, 1987.

WILLIAM C. MCDONALD

BENEDICT OF NURSIA, SAINT
(ca. 480–ca. 560)

A south Italian abbot and, like many other monastic leaders of his day, author of a monastic rule for his small community. By virtue of the wide adoption of that slender manual, the Benedictine Rule, Benedict became the most famous monk in the world and the patriarch of western monasticism, designated by Pope Paul VI (1963–78) "the patron of Europe." For some centuries the first and only life of Benedict was the hagiographic account by Pope Gregory the Great in the second book of his edifying *Dialogues.* Writing in 593–94, Gregory composed this melange of fact and legend at least a generation after Benedict's death; but historians accept as factual the bit of biographical data Gregory said he received from four of Benedict's disciples.

After education in Rome Benedict turned to religious life, first with a small community at Enfide and then as an anchorite near Subiaco. Attracting disciples because of his holiness, and sometimes alienating them because of his severity, Benedict eventually returned to communal religious life, organizing monasteries first in the Subiaco region and later (ca. 529) on Monte Cassino, in Campania halfway between Rome and Naples.

Benedict's real claim to fame is the rule he composed ca. 526. "This little rule for beginners" is based in part on the nearly contemporaneous *Rule of the Master,* but a comparison of the two reveals why Benedicts has been awarded the crown by history and the monastic movement. Gregory designates it well as a rule "remarkable for its discernment." The Rule is a relatively short document, consisting of a prologue, 72 brief chapters, and an epilogue. The chapters, laying down the principles of monastic life and practical directives for living it, are not logically ordered; chapters 67–72 are an appendix attached to 66.8, and the liturgical and penitential codes (8–18, 20–23) may have been inserted later. But for all its lack of order and elegant language it judiciously presents the basic principles of cenobitic life. It advocates a spirit of charity for the whole monastic family and an egalitarianism (e.g., priests have no special rank); its concern is not for the heroic achievers but for the weaker, more needful members of the group: "In drawing up its regulations, we hope to set down nothing harsh, nothing burdensome" (Prologue, 46).

During the 7th and 8th centuries the Rule was only one among many in use. In England Celtic monasticism had propagated over the north from the Irish foundation of Iona, whereas in the Midlands several foundations seemed to follow composite rules. Wilfrid was the first to introduce the Benedictine Rule in England for his Northumbrian monasteries at Ripon (ca. 661) and Hexham (674); Wilfrid also served as director of other monasteries of men and women. Benedict Biscop, founder of the joint monastery of Wearmouth (674) and Jarrow (681), whose most illustrious monk was the historian, exegete, and educator Bede, introduced a rule heavily influenced by the Benedictine but assembled from six different models. In the southwest near Winchester, Nursling, the home community of Boniface (Wynfrith), followed the Benedictine Rule.

Regular monastic life was greatly disrupted and in places disappeared during the troubled 9th century. Despite the attempts of King Alfred (871–99) to restore monastic life by founding the convent of Shaftesbury (which succeeded) and the monastery at Athelney (which did not), religious life languished. In the 10th century, under the close support of King Edgar (957–75), three dynamic monks, Dunstan (abbot of Glastonbury and later archbishop of Canterbury), the authoritarian Æthelwold (abbot of Abingdon, later bishop of Winchester), and Oswald (who became bishop of Worcester and later archbishop of York), imported the Benedictine Reform from the Continent and reinvigorated monastic life. To enforce the Benedictine Rule buttressed by effective continental and native regulations, they promulgated a code of approved practice, the *Regularis concordia* (ca. 970). The monasteries, some 40 in number with none in the north, were declared free of dependency on local nobles and became powerful supporters of the West Saxon monarchy.

Thanks to the renewed energies that resulted from the Reform, the monasteries again became centers of learning and art, providing education and culture. Æhelwold's school at Winchester developed a highly refined Latin style and produced the two finest OE prose stylists and preachers, Ælfric and Wulfstan. It was during this period that much Anglo-Latin and most extant OE texts were written, created for the most part in Benedictine scriptoria. Canterbury was especially active as a writing center, and Winchester gained particular renown for manuscript illustration, identifiable as "the Winchester School."

As the guide for traditional Benedictines (Black Monks and Nuns), augmented for Cluniacs, and reformed by the Cistercians (White Monks), the Rule of Benedict continued to dominate life in religious orders until the advent of the friars (Franciscans and Dominicans) in the 13th century. Benedictine abbeys, priories, and cells became ubiquitous throughout the realm, sometimes enormously wealthy and politically and economically powerful under forceful leaders, such as Abbot Samson of Bury St. Edmunds (ca. 1135–1212). The order also continued to foster scholars and especially historians, such as William of Malmesbury (ca. 1095–ca. 1143), and at St. Albans Roger of Wendover (d. 1236) and Matthew Paris (ca. 1199–1259).

Further Reading

Primary Sources

Fry, Timothy, ed. and trans. *RB 1980: The Rule of St. Benedict.* Collegeville: Liturgical Press, 1981.

Gregory the Great. *Life and Miracles of St. Benedict* (*Books Two of the Dialogues*). Trans. Odo J. Zimmermann and Benedict R. Avery. Collegeville: St. John's Abbey Press, 1949.

Kornexl, Lucia, ed. *Die* Regularis Concordia *und Ihre Altenglische Interlinearversion.* Texte und Untersuchungen zur Englischen Philologie 17. Munich: Wilhelm Fink Verlag, 1993.

Secondary Sources

Burton, Janet. *Monastic and Religious Orders in Britain 1000–1300.* Cambridge: Cambridge University Press, 1994.

Farmer, David Hugh, ed. *Benedict's Disciples.* Leominster: Fowler Wright, 1980.

Knowles, David. *The Monastic Order in England: A History of Its Development from the Times of St Dunstan to the Fourth Lateran Council 940–1216.* 2d ed. Cambridge: Cambridge University Press, 1963.

Platt, C.P.S. *The Abbeys and Priories of Medieval England.* London: Secker & Warburg, 1984.

Turner, D.H.,ed. *The Benedictines in Britain.* London: British Library, 1980.

GEORGE HARDIN BROWN

BENJAMIN OF TUDELA (fl. 1160–1172)

Benjamin of Tudela was a Jewish merchant renowned for his travels through various countries from about 1160 to about 1172, when he returned to Spain, dying shortly thereafter. He left a book in Hebrew (or more correctly his notes, which were turned into a book by an anonymous hand) concerning his travels, which became famous and in translation was one of the most widely read travel accounts of all time.

Muslim and Jewish travelers in the Mediterranean, and particularly from Spain, were numerous, and we have accounts of such voyages from many (among Jews, the most famous, besides Benjamin, were Ibrāhīm ibn Yaqūb of the tenth century and Judah al-Harīzī of the thirteenth). Benjamin's account is particularly valuable because of its details on commerce, agriculture, manufacture, and so on, and for the information it gives concerning remote and exotic areas of the world (including China). True, he did not personally reach these lands, but at least some of the information he received from secondhand reports is of value. His own personal travels were limited to the coast of Provence; Italy; the Greek isles; Constantinople and Asia Minor; Syria and Mesopotamia (nearly to India); Palestine, and Egypt.

His primary goals were to investigate and report on commerce and agriculture and to report on the presence and condition of Jews in various parts of the world, as well as to visit "holy sites." His estimates of Jewish populations in various regions and towns are generally substantiated by other sources, and his work is an important source for Jewish history. For general history there is also much of great value, including his listing of some thirty Christian nations which had merchants in Alexandria, and certainly his information on agriculture and technology.

The first Hebrew edition appeared in 1543, based on a faulty manuscript, and was copied in subsequent editions and Latin and early English translations, in spite of the more accurate edition of 1556, which subsequently appeared. The edition, with English translation, of Asher is based on a much better manuscript reading. Most important are the extensive notes (English) in the second volume. Adler's edition, finally, is based on the most accurate extant manuscript. The Spanish Hebraist Benito Arias Montano made the first translation, in Latin (1575), from which Purchas's *Pilgrims* English translation and others in French were made. A second Latin translation by Constantin l'Empereur appeared in

1633. Among more modern translations, that in Spanish by the Hebraist Igancio González Llubera, *Viajes de Benjamín de Tudela* (Madrid, 1918), is of importance for its erudite notes and critical apparatus. The modern Spanish translation by Magdalena is generally excellent, but unfortunately he did not utilize the notes in Asher and thus there are several errors.

Further Reading

The Itinerary of Benjamin of Tudela. Ed. and trans. M. N. Adler. London, 1907; reprt. 1964.
The Itinerary of Benjamin of Tudela. Trans. A. Asher. 2 vols. London and Berlin, 1840.
Libro de Viajes de Benjamín de Tudela. Trans. J. R. Magdalena Nom de Déu. Barcelona, 1982.

NORMAN ROTH

BENOÎT DE SAINTE-MAURE (fl. 1160–70)

Little is known about Benoît de Sainte-Maure that does not emerge directly from his texts. The author of the *Roman de Troie* names himself in line 132 as Beneeit de Sainte-More, and as Beneit in lines 2065, 5093, and 19,207. He praises Eleanor of Aquitaine in the *Roman de Troie* and flatters Henry II in the other text of which he is believed to be the author, the *Chronique des ducs de Normandie*. Here, the author is identified simply as Beneit from Touraine (albeit in summary passages that may not be by the author himself), who, it is presumed, took over for the aged Wace when the latter abandoned his *Roman de Rou*, also a history of the dukes of Normandy. Benoît's *Chronique* has 44,542 lines in octosyllabic rhymed couplets. It begins with the creation and division of the world and ends with the death of Henry I of England. The Latin chronicles of Dudo de Saint-Quentin and Guillaume de Jumièges provided much of the material. But Benoît also invented long discourses for his historical characters and inserted countless proverbs into his narrative. As in the Romances of Antiquity, anachronism and medievalization are rampant. The romance form of the *Chronique* suggests that it was part of the repertoire of texts recited in a courtly milieu. The *Chronique*, together with Wace's *Rou*, is an excellent example of the desire of a new dynasty (as the Angevins with Henry II were in England) to celebrate their roots and their history in vernacular texts that would be accessible not only to a learned clerical audience but also to the aristocracy.

See also **Eleanor of Aquitaine; Henry II; Wace**

Further Reading

Benoît de Sainte-Maure. *Chronique des ducs de Normandie*, ed. Carin Fahlin. 3 vols. Uppsala: Almqvist and Wiksell, 1951–67.

[A fourth volume of notes was published by Sven Sandqvist in 1979 with the same publisher.]
——. *Le roman de Troie*, ed. Léopold Constans. 6 vols. Paris: Didot, 1904–12.

RENATE BLUMEOFELD-KOSINSKI

BERCEO, GONZALO DE (1196?–1264?)

The first Castilian poet to identify himself by name, Gonzalo de Berceo is considered by many to be the master of *cuaderna vía*. He was educated at the Benedictine monastery in San Millán (he reminds us of this in *Vida de San Millán*, is listed as a deacon in a document dating from 1221, and registered as a secular priest in Berceo and notary to Abbot Juan Sánchez in later manuscripts. Dutton suggests that, given his profession and his literary background, he was probably trained at the Estudio General at Palencia between 1221 and 1228.

Dutton and Kurlat de Weber have established the following chronology for Berceo's works:

1. *Vida de San Millán*
2. Vida de Santo Domingo de Silos
3. *Sacrificio de la Misa*
4. *Duelo que fizo la Virgen*
5. *Himnos*
6. *Loores de Nuestra Señora*
7. *Signos del Juicio Final*
8. *Milagros de Nuestra Señora*
9. *Vida de Santa Oria*
10. *Martirio de San Lorenzo*

Additionally, two lost works (*Historia de Valvanera*, *Traslación de los Mártires de Arlanza*) have been attributed to him. Berceo's poetry may be divided into three categories: hagiography (*San Millán*, *Santo Domingo*, *Santa Oria*, *San Lorenzo*), Marian works (*Loores*, *Duelo*, *Milagros*), and liturgical/doctrinal works (*Sacrificio*, *Himnos*, *Signos*)

Dutton argues convincingly that, in addition to the two purposes traditionally ascribed to Berceo's works (instruction and entertainment), the hagiographic materials were designed to propagate the legends of saints related to San Millán in order to bolster the prosperity of the monastery, which had declined due to the rise of new pilgrimage centers. This goal is clearly reflected in Berceo's first work, dedicated to the patron saint of his monastery. *San Millán* derives from various sources (the *Vita Beati Emiliani* of Braulio, the writings of the monk Fernandus including the forged *Votos de San Millán*) and it follows the tripartite structure of a saint's life (biography, miracles performed in life, posthumous miracles). Berceo introduces the propagandistic element at the outset, promising his public that it will be happy to pay the tribute due to the monastery after hearing the life of San Millán (st. 2 cd). The climax of the poem (st. 362–481) recounts the origin of the tithe, justifies its continuance, and instructs the debtor towns (many of which he names) to pay the tribute owed to the saint for his miraculous intervention in battle.

Santo Domingo, based on the late eleventh-century *Vita Beati Dominici* by Grimaldus, narrates the life of another local saint. Once a hermit in San Millán de Suso as well as a monk and prior of its monastery, the saint became abbot of the monastery at Silos, which later (1190) signed a pact of mutual help and cooperation with San Millán; the renewal of this agreement in 1236 may have been the occasion for the composition of *Santo Domingo*. While there is no request for tributes such as that in *San Millán*, Berceo nonetheless reveals his desire to attract pilgrims to Silos by urging those who wish to know more of the saint's miracles to go to that monastery (st. 385–386).

Santa Oria, composed in his old age (st. 2 c), deals with a recluse unknown outside La Rioja but closely associated with San Millán de Suso; indeed, the poet gives directions to the saint's tomb near the monastery (st. 180–182). The most lyrical and allegorical of the hagiographic works, *Santa Oria* relates not the saint's miracles but three heavenly visions. "While Berceo indicates that his poem is based on a narrative by Oria's confessor Muño, no source has yet been identified. Although most critics accept the theory of a lost eleventh-century *Vita Beatae Aureae*, Walsh, noting differences from the other hagiographic works, argues that *Santa Oria* draws heavily on otherworld literature as well as saints' legends and that it is primarily Berceo's own creation.

San Lorenzo, Berceo's only incomplete work, follows the structure of a *passio* rather than a *vita*. The poem breaks off in the middle of St. Lawrence's prayer during his martyrdom, suggesting that it was interrupted by the poet's own death. Dutton contends that there was a cult to the saint at San Millán related to a hermitage on nearby Pico de San Lorenzo, and he proposes that the missing portion would have made clear the connection between the monastery and the hermitage. Although the source is unknown, Pompilio Tesauro identifies the *Passio Polychroni* as the closest model.

Dutton believes that the Marian poems, like the saints' lives, are part of Berceo's propagandistic work, arguing that they do not reflect devotion to a universal figure of the Virgin but to the cult of Our Lady of March established in the tenth century at San Millán de Yuso. Dutton thinks that the Marian works, unlike the hagiographic poems, were not meant to attract pilgrims but to instruct and entertain them once they had arrived.

Some scholars have suggested that *Duelo*, because of its dramatic nature, is based on a lost French mystery or a Latin liturgical drama. Nonetheless, the most probable source of *Duelo* (a narrative of the Easter vigil of the Virgin as she tells her sorrows to St. Bernard of Clairvaux) is an apocryphal sermon of St. Bernard similar to the one found in Migne's *Patrologia latina*. The poem contains a song (*¡Eya velar!*) of the Jewish sentries ordered to guard the sepulchre. This early example of Castilian lyric, which is not composed in *cuaderna vía*, has been the subject of some debate: convinced that the verses are misordered, several scholars have tried to reconstruct the song based on parallel structure; others have rejected this reordering, arguing that the canticle is an imitation of a liturgical chant and that confusion may be eliminated if the stanzas are divided into antiphonal parts.

The content of *Loores* is diverse: lyrical exaltations of the Virgin at the beginning and end of the poem enclose a brief narrative of the life of Jesus as well as of various events from the Old and New Testaments. No source has been identified for the poem, and it seems likely that it is based on Berceo's knowledge of the Bible.

The source of *Milagros* is a lost collection of *miracula* similar to Royal Library of Copenhagen MS Thott 128. Berceo uses twenty four of the twenty eight miracles found there, adding one ("La iglesia robada") which occurs in Spain and may derive from oral traditions. The miracles fall into three categories (reward and punishment, forgiveness, conversion or spiritual crisis), and have as their premise devotion to the Virgin. The allegorical introduction, apparently an original composition based on common motifs, ties together the twenty-five miracles. As Michael Gerli confirms, the introduction traces the fall and salvation of mankind, while the miracles narrate the fall and salvation of individuals. Thus the introduction and miracles illustrate the redemptive role of the Virgin: through Her, original sin (introduction) and actual sin (miracles) are forgiven.

The first of the liturgical-doctrinal works, *Sacrificio*, is, with the exception of *Milagros*, Berceo's most allegorical poem. Dutton identifies the source of this poem as National Library of Madrid manuscript 298, which is a commentary on the mass solidly within the exegetic tradition. The three *Himnos*, each seven strophes long, are vernacular translations of *Veni Creator Spiritus*, *Ave Maris Stella*, and *Christe, qui lux est et dies*. *Signos*, a sermon in verse, treats the common medieval theme of the fifteen signs of the Apocalypse. The first twenty two strophes derive from a Latin poem in *cuaderna vía* by St. Jerónimo; the source of the remaining fifty five strophes is unknown, but Dutton suggests that they may be attributed to an extended version of the Latin poem used by Berceo.

Once portrayed in literary histories as a simple country priest, Berceo is now viewed as an educated and complex individual who, desiring to promote his monastery, skillfully transforms Latin texts (most of these of special interest to San Millán) into vernacular poetry intended for oral presentation. In order to reach a rural public accustomed to the *cantares*, Berceo uses rustic imagery and appropriates many techniques of the *juglar*'s (minstrel's) art. This strategy may be seen clearly in *San Millán* where he not only uses juglaresque formulae and epithets but portrays the saint as both a divine peasant and an epic hero; and, although Berceo occasionally criticizes juglares, he refers to himself in *Santo Domingo* as God's juglar and to his poem as a *gesta* (compilation of deeds).

See also **Bernard of Clairvaux**

Further Reading

Artiles, J. *Los recursos literarios de Berceo.* Madrid, 1964.

Dutton, B. (ed.) *Gonzalo de Berceo: Obras Completas I–V.* London, 1967–1981.

Gariano, C. *Análisis estilístico de los "Milagros de Nuestra Señora" de Berceo.* Madrid, 1965.

Gerli, E. M. "La tipología bíblica y la introducción a los *Milagros de Nuestra Señora.*" *Bulletin of Hispanic Studies* 62 (1985), 7–14.

Tesauro, P. (ed.) *Gonzalo de Berceo: "Martirio de San Lorenzo."* Romanica Neapolitana VI. Naples, 1971.

Walsh, J. K. "The Other World in Berceo's *Vida de Santa Oria.*" In *Hispanic Studies in Honor of Alan D. Deyermond: A North American Tribute.* Ed. J. S. Miletich. Madison, Wisc., 1986. 291–307.

Kurlat de Weber, F. "Notas para la cronología y composición de las vidas de santos de Berceo." *Nueva Revista de Filología Hispánica* 15 (1961), 113–30.

JANE E. CONNOLLY

BERNARD GUI
(Bernardus Guidonis; ca. 1261–1331)

Historian, inquisitor, and bishop, Bernard was a Dominican who rose through the ecclesiastical ranks in southern France, in Limoges, Castres, Albi, and Carcassonne. He was inquisitor at Toulouse from 1307 to 1323. Between 1317 and 1321, he also served Pope John XXII on diplomatic missions in Italy and Flanders. All of Bernard's writings were in Latin. Though most were of a historical nature, he also produced several works of theology (*De articulis fidei, De peccato originali*), liturgy (*De ordinatione officii missae*), and hagiography (*Legenda sancti Thome de Aquino, Speculum sanctorale*). The *Speculum*, a collection of a number of saints' lives in four parts, was extremely popular in its day. His most important work is the still unpublished *Flores chronicorum* (ca. 1316), a history of the papacy from the birth of Christ to Clement V. This work, known in over fifty manuscripts (some now lost), went through ten revisions, the latest of which continues the history to 1331 (John XXII). Already in the 14th century, it was translated into Occitan (B.N. fr. 24940) and twice into French (four manuscripts). Other historical works by Bernard include treatises on the Roman emperors (*Imperatores Romani*, over forty manuscripts), on the kings of France (*Reges Francorum*, which exists in four revisions and two French translations), and on the Dominican order (catalogues of provincial priors, monographs on individual houses, acts of General Chapters, etc.).

Especially noteworthy is Bernard's history of the Inquisition (*Practica officii Inquisitionis*; ca. 1314–16; four manuscripts), which includes an important section on such heretical groups as Manichaeans, Vaudois, Pseudo-Apostles, béguines, relapsed Jews, and sorcerers. He also composed local histories of the cities in which, he lived: Limoges, Toulouse, and Lodève. In spite of the great popularity of his work in the late Middle Ages, as evidenced by the numerous manuscripts and the translation of much of his œuvre into French by Jean Golem for Charles V, few of Bernard's works have found modern editors. He was a diligent compiler and accurate researcher, keen to tease the truth from contradictory sources. Traveling from monastery to monastery, Bernard assembled evidence, interviewed witnesses, and verified his sources at every step. As information accumulated, he prepared copious lists, edited, revised, and expanded. Faced with mountains of material, he regularly composed abridged versions of his most important works. Bernard's lack of literary skill is compensated for by his careful preservation of significant documents and information whose original sources have been lost.

Further Reading

Bernard Gui. *Practica Inquisitionis heretice pravitatis*, ed. C. Douais. Paris: Picard, 1886.

——. *Manuel de l'inquisiteur*, ed. and trans. G. Mollat. 2 vols. Paris: Champion, 1926–27.

Delisle, Léopold. "Notice sur les manuscrits de Bernard Gui." *Notices et extraits des manuscrits de la Bibliothèque Nationale* 27 (1885): 169–455.

Thomas, Antoine. "Bernard Gui, frère prêcheur." *Histoire littéraire de la France* 35 (1921): 139–232.

Vernet, A. "La diffusion de l'œuvre de Bernard Gui d'après la tradition manuscrite." *Cahiers de Fanjeaux* 16 (1981): 221–42.

GROVER A. ZINN

BERNARD OF CHARTRES (d. 1124–30)

Most of our knowledge of Bernard comes through John of Salisbury's *Metalogicon*. John studied with Gilbert of Poitiers, William of Conches, and Richard the Bishop, who were all Bernard's pupils at Chartres when he was chancellor of the schools. Not only was John's knowledge secondhand, but his *Metalogicon* has an ulterior motive: he is not merely describing Bernard for archival reasons but wishes to contrast his good, old teaching methods with the newfangled approach of the Cornificians. It is difficult, then, to be certain how far to trust John's encomium.

John counted Bernard the best Platonist of his time, although to us he seems less interesting than Gilbert of Poitiers or Thierry of Chartres (who is unlikely to have been his younger brother, as is sometimes asserted). He seems to have had no academic contact with the great scholars of his day, William of Champeaux, Roscelin, or Anselm of Laon. Like all the Chartrians, he got his Plato through Neoplatonist sources, chiefly Chalcidius, Boethius, and Eriugena. His work survives only in fragments quoted by John of Salisbury, though a possible set of glosses on the *Timaeus* by Bernard is now in print. Famous for his cultivation of faith and goodness, as well as simple academic brilliance, Bernard is perhaps best remembered today for reporting the aphorism that compared scholars of the modern age to dwarfs standing on giants' shoulders—their further vision was the result of their elevated viewpoint, not their greater acumen (*Metalogicon* 3.4).

See also **Eriugena, Johannes Scottus; Gilbert of Poitiers; John of Salisbury**

Further Reading

Bernard of Chartres. *Glosae super Platonem*, ed. Paul Edward Dutton. Toronto: Pontifical Institute of Mediaeval Studies, 1991.
Dutton, Paul Edward. "The Uncovering of the 'Glosae super Platonem' of Bernard of Chartres." *Mediaeval Studies* 46 (1984): 192–221.
Gilson, Ètienne. "Le platonisme de Bernard de Chartres." *Revue néo-scholastique de philosophie* 25 (1923): 5–19.

LESLEY J. SMITH

BERNARD OF CLAIRVAUX (1090/91–1153)

Born in Fontaines near Dijon and educated with the canons of Saint-Vorles in Châtillon-sur-Seine, Bernard entered the Cistercian monastery of Cîteaux, together with thirty companions, in 1112. In 1115, he founded the monastery of Clairvaux. From this remote corner of the civilized world, he intervened in matters both political and ecclesiastical. In 1128, at the Synod of Troyes, he obtained recognition for the *Rule* of the new order of Knights Templar. In 1130, he supported Innocent II against Anacletus II in the dispute over papal succession, and a few years later he supported Innocent in the conflict with Arnold of Brescia. In 1145, a pupil of his became Pope Eugenius III. Besides continuing to mediate in all kinds of conflicts, Bernard energetically preached the Second Crusade and lived to witness its utter failure in 1148.

Bernard presided over the enormous expansion of the Cistercian order. The first houses founded from Cîteaux—La Ferté, Pontigny, Morimond, and Clairvaux—became centers from which hundreds of monasteries spread over all of western Europe. As abbot of Clairvaux, an obscure Cistercian settlement on the border of Burgundy and the Champagne, Bernard traveled widely, not only advising bishops and princes but also raising his voice on delicate doctrinal isssues. Lacking the modern dialectical skills of his opponents, he focused his criticism on their alleged deviations from traditional theological methods. At the Council of Sens (1141), his intervention decided the fate of Abélard, and a few years later, at the Council of Reims, he spoke out against Gilbert of Poitiers. Bernard was canonized in 1174 and created a doctor of the church in 1830.

Bernard's *œuvre* consists of treatises, many sermons, and letters. His most famous work is the series of sermons on the Song of Songs (*Sermones super Cantica canticorum*), left unfinished at his death. In it, he deals with a variety of themes from the behavior of monks to the mystical union between the Bridegroom from the Canticle (Christ) and the Bride (Bernard, or the church). The method applied to the Canticle text is based on the medieval exegetical scheme of the fourfold meaning of Scripture: literal, allegorical, moral, and mystical. However, unlike earlier medieval commentators on the Canticle, such as Bede, Bernard never loses sight of the literal, dramatic power of the Canticle text. Isolating one textual fragment or even a single word, he then creates clusters of associations with other biblical and patristic writings. The result is a rich and a meticulously organized text that could be used both by the monks as an amplification of their ritual form of life and by a wider literate public, both clergy and lay, for literary enjoyment and religious insight.

Many of Bernard's other sermons follow the cycle of the liturgical feast days (*Sermones per annum*), such as the Annunciation, Christmas, Epiphany, Easter, the Assumption. Noteworthy for their poetic quality and intensity, Bernard's sermons on the Virgin Mary contributed to the development of mariological devotion in the later Middle Ages.

In his treatises, Bernard deals in a more thematic way with the issues of monastic life and of religion in general. A treatise on the steps of humility, *De gradibus humilitatis et superbiae*, is a commentary on a passage from the Benedictine *Rule*. A treatise on love, *De diligendo Deo*, describes the journey toward God, who is to be loved because of himself with a love that is "measure without measure" (*modus sine modo*). Bernard combines the relentless desire for God characteristic of the monastic life with the stability of its goal. The long treatise on consideration, *De consideratione*, dedicated to Pope Eugenius III, outlines the ideal portrait of a pope while offering theological and mystical reflections on the knowledge of God.

In his many letters, Bernard often takes circumstantial matters as a point of departure for reflection. His first letter is, like his *Apologia*, a fierce attack on the luxuriousness of the Cluniac (or, more widely, Benedictine) way of life. This critical attitude was based on Bernard's own Cistercian predilection for simplicity and austerity in art. The lengthy Letter 190, to Innocent II, is directed against Abélard on the occasion of the latter's condemnation at the Council of Sens, depicting him as a dangerous innovator whose application of reason to matters of faith threatens religious stability. In fact, it is Bernard's concern about the legitimacy of his own monastic way of life in the light of the Christian tradition and culture, rather than the motives of his opponent, that comes to the fore. Yet in spite of his claim that he, unlike Abélard, is staying within the bounds of the Christian tradition, Bernard is to be seen as part of the general renaissance of the 12th century. In defending the quality of his own ascetic life, he cherished a sophistication that many of his contemporaries sought in the further refinement of reasoning and art.

See also **Abélard, Peter; Gilbert of Poitiers; William of Saint-Thierry**

Further Reading

Bernard of Clairvaux. *Sancti Bernardi opera omnia*, ed. Jean Leclercq, Charles H. Talbot, and Henri Rochais. 8 vols. Rome: Editiones Cistercienses, 1957–78.
——. *Selected Works*, trans. Gillian R. Evans. New York: Paulist, 1987.
Bredero, A.H. *Études sur la Vita prima de S. Bernard*. Rome, 1960.
Casey, M. *Athirst for God: Spiritual Desire in Bernard of Clairvaux's Sermons on the Song of Songs*. Kalamazoo: Cistercian, 1988.
Duby, Georges. *Bernard de Clairvaux et l'art cistercien*. Paris: Arts et Métiers Graphiques, 1976.
Evans, Gillian R. *The Mind of Bernard of Clairvaux*. Oxford: Clarendon, 1983.
Gilson, Étienne. *The Mystical Theology of St. Bernard*, trans. A.H.C. Downes. London: Sheed and Ward, 1940.
Leclercq, Jean. *Recueil d'études sur saint Bernard et ses écrits*. 3 vols. Rome: Edizioni di Storia e Letteratura, 1966–92.
——. *Monks and Love in Twelfth-Century France: Psycho-Historical Essays*. Oxford: Clarendon, 1979.
Pranger, M. Burcht. *Bernard of Clairvaux and the Shape of Monastic Thought: Broken Dreams*. Leiden: Brill, 1994.

BURCHT PRANGER

BERNARD SILVESTRIS (d. ca. 1159)

Bernard probably taught in the cathedral school at Tours in the second third of the 12th century, where one of his students was Matthieu de Vendôme. The dedication of his longest and most important work, the *Cosmographia*, to Thierry of Chartres, has led some scholars to confuse him with John of Salisbury's beloved teacher Bernard of Chartres, who would have been a generation older than Silvestris. If, as seems likely, Bernard was also trained at Tours, he would have studied under Hildebert of Lavardin.

Bernard's earliest works are a commentary on the first six books of Virgil's *Aeneid* and another, incomplete, on Martianus Capella. The commentary on Plato's *Timæus* mentioned in the Martianus commentary has not been identified. In his elegiac poem *Mathematicus*, Bernard discusses destiny and necessity in mathematical terms. Also at least partly his is the Experimentarius, a work taken from Arabic sources on cosmography. Two short opuscules derived from problems in Quintilian and Seneca are also usually attributed to him: respectively, *De gemellis* and *De paupere ingrato*.

The *Cosmographia* (ca. 1147–48) has two parts, *Megacosmos* and *Microcosmos*. In the first part, Nature approaches Nous, the personification of the divine eternal mind of God, whom she begs to improve the physical universe. Nous separates the four elements, gives matter form from divine ideas, and shapes the world soul. The new universe is described in detail. *Microcosmos* depicts the formation of humankind. Nature encounters Genius, and they set out to seek Urania and Physis, who will guide them through the heavens to find man's soul and bring it back to earth. The title is explained: man is the world in little.

Though the work has multiple sources, including Boethius, Martianus Capella, and ancient and Arabic scientific sources, the basic concept is apparently original with Bernard. His poem circulated widely—over fifty copies survive in European libraries—and influenced the two most widely read 12th-century allegorical visions of nature, the world, and humanity: Alain de Lille's *De planctu Naturae* and *Anticlaudianus*. In the rhetorical work of Matthieu de Vendôme, he is frequently cited for his excellence of style.

See also **Alain de Lille; Martianus Capella**

Further Reading

Bernard Silvestris. *Cosmographia*, ed. Peter Dronke. Leiden: Brill, 1978.
——. *The Commentary on the First Six Books of the Aeneid of Vergil Commonly Attributed to Bernardus Silvestris*, ed. Julian Ward Jones and Elizabeth Francis Jones. Lincoln: University of Nebraska Press, 1977.
——. "Il 'Dictamen' di Bernardo Silvestre," ed. M. Brini Savorelli. Rivista critica di storia della filosofia 20 (1965): 182–230.
——. "Un manuale de geomanzia presentato da Bernardo Silvestre de Tours (XII secolo): l'Experimentarius," ed. M. Brini Savorelli. Rivista critica di storia della filosofia 14 (1959): 283–341.
——. *The Cosmographia*, trans. Winthrop P. Wetherbee. New York: Columbia University Press, 1973.
Stock, Brian. *Myth and Science in the Twelfth Century: A Study of Bernard Silvester*. Princeton: Princeton University Press, 1972.

JEANNE E. KROCHALIS

BERNART DE VENTADORN
(fl. ca. 1145–1180)

With Jaufre Rudel, Bemart de Ventadorn was one of the most popular and most imitated of the 12th-century troubadours. His romanticized biography, or *vida*, says that he was of humble origins but rose to sing his love for the wife of the lord of Ventadorn. Aside from links to the Ventadorn castle and school, which are clear from his name and style, Bernart sang at the court of Count Raymond V of Toulouse and probably also visited England, perhaps in the entourage of Eleanor of Aquitaine. The *vida* further tells us that he retired to the Cistercian abbey of Dalon, but this, like the reports of his early years, has not been documented.

Of his lyric production, some forty-one songs survive, all but three of which are love songs, or *cansos*. (Two of the three *tensos*, or debate poems, are of less than certain attribution.) Eighteen of Bernart's songs are preserved with their music. Bernart sang in the clear style called *trobar leu*. His *cansos* are characterized by the melodious language, nostalgic tone, vivid imagery, and musical virtuosity that won him imitators among medieval poets. But it is their lyrical intensity and emotional span that have especially earned him admirers in our own time.

See also **Eleanor of Aquitane; Jaufre Rudel**

Further Reading

Bernard de Ventadour. *Chansons d'amour,* ed. Moshé Lazar. Paris: Klincksieck, 1966.
——. *The Songs of Bernart de Ventadom*, ed. Stephen G. Nichols, Jr., et al. Chapel Hill: University of North Carolina Press, 1962.
Kaehne, Michael. *Studien zur Dichtung Bernarts von Ventadom.* Munich: Fink, 1983.
Schemer-Van Ortmerssen, Gisela. *Die Text-Mehdiestruktur in den Liedern des Bernart de Ventadorn.* Münster: Aschendorff, 1973.

ROY S. ROSENSTEIN

BERNO VON REICHENAU
(d. June 7, 1048)

The abbot of one of southern Germany's leading monasteries, Berno von Reichenau (also Bern, Bernardus, Berno Augiensis) contributed richly to medieval German culture. His writings encompass treatises on music theory, liturgy, and theology, as well as saints' lives, sermons, letters, and musical compositions. His most famous pupil was the music theorist, composer, and historian Hermann von Reichenau (also Hermannus Contractus), whose historical writings provide essential information concerning Berno's biography.

The circumstances of Berno's birth are unknown, although he was probably born to a German family of some prominence. He is first associated with the monastery of Prüm. In 1008 Emperor Henry II appointed him abbot of the island monastery of Reichenau. In 1014 Berno traveled to Rome for Henry's coronation, a measure of his high political standing. In 1022 he again accompanied Henry to Rome, this time also visiting Monte Cassino. These journeys, as well as a third trip in 1027 to attend the coronation of Emperor Conrad II, doubtless gave him access to sources important for his musical and liturgical research. Upon the accession of the unsympathetic Conrad, Berno was embroiled in disputes over encroachments upon previously granted ecclesiastical privileges. Emperor Henry III, son of Conrad II, proved to be a more supportive sovereign than his predecessor, and visited Berno at Reichenau on February 4, 1040. Berno died there on June 7, 1048, having in his forty years as abbot guided the monastery to new levels of artistic and scholarly achievement. He was buried in the newly consecrated choir of the abbey church. Berno's tomb was rediscovered in 1929; measurements of his remains show that he stood an imposing six feet three inches tall.

As a music theorist, Berno struck a balance between practical application and abstract theory. His most significant contributions are three tonaries (lists of chants ordered by mode). Most important of these is the *Prologus in tonarium*, a tonary with explanatory prologue that was widely distributed during the eleventh and twelfth centuries, sometimes with later interpolations. By Berno's own admission it is mainly a compendium from earlier sources. Another, abridged, tonary, *De consona tonorum diversitate*, was apparently intended for teaching novices at Reichenau. In addition to the tonaries, a treatise entitled *De mensurando monochordo* (On measuring monochords) has been tentatively attributed to Berno. Berno's views on mode appear to have been relatively conservative, and do not reflect the growing influence of the Italian music theorist Guido of Arezzo. Berno's treatment of transposition and modal affinity forms an important background to Hermann's highly original work. In the area of rhythm, Berno warns against the failure to distinguish between long and short notes.

Berno's musical compositions include three hymns, an Epiphany trope, three sequences, and an office for Saint Ulrich; an office for Saint Meinrad is also tentatively ascribed to him.

As hagiographer, liturgist, and theologian, Berno's contributions are also rich. His *Vita sancti Udalrici* (Life of Saint Ulrich) is noteworthy for its fine literary style. Also ascribed to Berno are treatises on religious topics including Advent, prayer (in hexameter), fasting, and heresy, as well as on the Mass (*De quibusdam rebus ad missae officium pertinentibus*, On Certain Things Pertaining to the Office of the Mass) and on differences between the Gallic and Roman Psalters (*De varia psalmorum*); Berno's authorship of these latter two treatises has been questioned by modern scholars, however. More than a dozen sermons and sermon fragments are preserved, many of them on Marian topics, as well as about twenty letters to emperors, bishops, abbots, and other leaders. That numerous other works of music theory, history, and poetry came to be attributed to Berno, often on weak grounds, testifies to the esteem in which he was held by later generations of medieval scribes.

See also **Conrad II; Guido d'Arezzo; Henry III**

Further Reading

Gerbert, Martin. *Scriptores ecclesiastici de musica sacra potissimum.* Sankt-Blasien, 1784; Graecii, Styria, 1905; rpt. Hildesheim: Olms, 1963, 1990.

Hiley, David. *Western Plainchant: A Handbook.* Oxford: Oxford University Press, 1993.

Migne, Jacques-Paul. *Patrologiae cursus completus.* Series Latina. Paris, 1844–1864; on CD-ROM: Arlington, Va: Chadwyck-Healey, 1995.

Oesch, Hans. *Berno und Hermann von Reichenau als Musiktheoretiker.* Publikationen der Schweizerischen Musikforschenden Gesellschaft, ser. II, vol. 9. Bern: Haupt, 1961.

Rausch, Andreas. "Die Musiktraktate des Abtes Bern von Reichenau." Ph.D diss., Universität Wien, 1996.

Waesberghe, J. Smits van. *Bernonis Augiensis Abbatis: De arte musica disputationes traditae. Pars A. Bernonis Augiensis de Mensurando Monochordo. Pars B. Quae ratio est inter tria opera de arte musica Bernonis Augiensis.* Divitiae Musicae Artis ser. A, lib. VI. 2 vols. Buren: Knuf, 1979 [includes facsimiles].

MICHAEL R. DODDS

BERNWARD OF HILDESHEIM
(960–1022)

Bishop of Hildesheim and abbot of St. Michael's, Hildesheim (1007–1022), Bernward was a pivotal member of the Ottonian court, and his patronage stimulated the arts at Hildesheim. He was born in 960 into a noble Saxon family that enjoyed the friendship of the Ottonian emperors. By 977 he had joined the imperial chancellery as a notary. He subsequently became court chaplain and tutor to Otto III. As bishop of Hildesheim, Bernward continued to advise and represent Otto III and Henry II. His imperial service entailed considerable travel. Under Otto II, during the regency, and under Otto III, he was frequently in Italy, especially Rome. As Henry II's diplomatic representative to Robert II of France in 1007, he visited Paris, Saint-Denis, and Tours. The various cultural sources to which Bernward was exposed on these occasions were fundamental with respect to his patronage of the arts at Hildesheim.

As bishop of Hildesheim, Bernward was responsible for several major commissions. In addition to the Bene-dictine monastery church of St. Michael's, his patronage is represented by a series of illuminated manuscripts and several important works in metal, especially the hollow-cast bronze column and doors now in the cathedral at Hildesheim. The complex program of the doors, which relates to the fall of man and his redemption through Christ, depends on a typological reading of paired Old and New Testament scenes and indicates the erudition of the patron. Formally and iconographically, the doors and the column derive from Carolingian sources from Tours, Reims, and Metz, but the general concept as well as the hollow-cast technique reflect Bernward's acquaintance with classical and early Christian Roman monuments.

See also **Otto II, Otto III**

Further Reading

Brandt, Michael, and Arne Eggebrecht, ed. *Bernward von Hildesheim und as Zeitalter der Ottonen.* Hildesheim: Dom-und Diözesanmuseum, 1993.

KAREN W. LOAIZA

BÉROUL (fl. late 12th c)

Nothing is known of Béroul other than that he was the author of a late 12th-century Tristan verse romance. He twice names himself in his surviving text. Owing to certain stylistic inconsistencies and even factual contradictions within the poem, some scholars have concluded that his *Tristan* is the work of two authors, or even more. Such suggestions remain unproved, however, and a good many scholars have argued the case for single authorship.

Béroul clearly composed the poem during the second half of the 12th century, but the date or even decade remains in question; some have contended that it was as early as 1165, while others, concluding that line 3,849 of the poem refers to an epidemic that attacked the Crusaders at Acre in 1190–91, assign the poem to the last decade of the century. The *Tristan* is preserved in fragmentary form in a single manuscript (B.N. fr. 2171) that was copied during the second half of the 13th century. The beginning and end of the poem are both missing, leaving a single long fragment of nearly 4,500 lines of octosyllabic narrative verse; in addition, the manuscript contains a number of lacunae, and the text is obviously defective in many passages.

The poem belongs to what is generally called the primitive or common version (as opposed to the courtly version) of the Tristan legend. That is, it is presumed that this text derives from an earlier, noncourtly stage of the legend, whereas that of Thomas d'Angleterre integrates the work thoroughly into the current of courtly love.

Béroul's extensive fragment begins with the famous

encounter of Tristan with Iseut under the tree in which her husband, Marc, is hiding to trap them; they see his reflection in the water and speak in such a way as to allay his suspicions. The poem continues with the episode in which the dwarf spreads flour on Iseut's floor in order to detect Tristan's footprints (should he visit her at night); the scene in which Tristan, having been taken prisoner, asks permission to enter a chapel and pray, whereupon he leaps to freedom from a window; Marc's delivering Iseut to a colony of lepers (for their pleasure and her punishment) and Tristan's rescue of her; the lovers' miserable life in the forest (including Marc's discovery of them, as they sleep with a bare sword between them, and his erroneous conclusion that they are guiltless); their eventual repentance, caused by the waning of the love potion (which, in this tradition, had been made to be effective for three years); and the long episode in which Iseut, tested in the presence of Arthur and his knights, succeeds in exonerating herself by swearing an equivocal oath. At the end, Tristan ambushes and kills one of the lovers' enemies and brings his hair to show Iseut; when he arrives, they discover another of their enemies spying on them, Tristan immediately kills him, and the text breaks off in mid-sentence.

As in the Tristan tradition in general, Beroul's narrative presents a cyclical form: whether physically separated, threatened by Marc or their enemies, or resolved to reform, the young lovers repeatedly fall back into their sinful ways; Marc becomes suspicious, initially refuses to believe he is being betrayed, and is finally convinced; after a period of separation or abstinence on their part, the cycle repeats itself. Most often, the lovers have in fact no great desire to reform, and when they do they are motivated by less than noble impulses. Yet despite their sin and despite the fact that they both betray Marc (Iseut is his wife, while Tristan is both his vassal and his nephew), the sympathies of the author and of the reader remain with the couple, both because their enemies are presented as despicable and jealous characters and because Béroul frequently insists that God favors the lovers and will punish those who oppose them.

The *Tristan* is a highly ironic and ambiguous text. Appearances are always deceiving: when the lovers appear most innocent, they are consistently the most guilty. When Marc thinks them innocent, he is being deceived or else, as in the episode where they sleep with a naked sword between them, he is misinterpreting the evidence. Tristan is a trickster who clearly takes pleasure in deception, as, for example, when, disguised as a leper, he explains to Marc that he was infected by his unnamed lady, who resembled Iseut and whose husband was a leper.

Despite the potential tragedy of the lovers' passion, Béroul's poem is characterized by humor and, in many passages, by a tone far more reminiscent of the fabliau than of the courtly romance. His style is lively and engaging, bearing many of the marks (such as frequent addresses to *Seigneurs*) of both public presentation and authorial personality. Despite numerous textual problems, the poem as we have it holds considerable charm and appeal.

Although Béroul's composition is incompletely preserved, the *Tristrant* of Eilhart von Oberge, written before 1190, presents the common version of the Tristan story in the form of a complete romance. Although Eilhart's German text abridges or omits some episodes found in Béroul's, the two works appear to have at very least a common source, and it has sometimes been suggested that Eilhart adapted the story directly from Béroul's account of the lovers.

See also **Eilhart von Oberg; Thomas D'Angleterre**

Further Reading

Béroul. *Le roman de Tristan*, ed. Ernest Muret. Paris: Didot, 1913, 4th rev. ed. L.M. Defourques. Paris: Champion, 1962.
——. *The Romance of Tristran*, ed. and trans. Norris J. Lacy. New York: Garland, 1989.
Walter, Philippe and D. Lacroix, trans. *Tristan et Iseut: les poèmes français, la saga norroise*. Paris: Livre de Poche, 1989.
Raynaud de Lage, Guy. "Faut-il attribuer a Béroul tout le Tristan?" *Moyen âge* 64 (1958): 249–70; 67 (1961): 167–68; 70 (1964): 33–38.
Reid, Thomas Bertram Wallace. *The "Tristan" of Béroul: A Textual Commentary*. New York: Barnes and Noble, 1972.

NORRIS J. LACY

BERSUIRE, PIERRE (ca. 1290–1362)

Encyclopedist, moralist, and translator born probably in the Vendée region, Bersuire entered the Franciscan order before joining the Benedictines. His early career (ca. 1320–ca. 1350) was spent amid the fervent intellectual climate of the papal court at Avignon, where he enjoyed the protection and extensive library of Cardinal Pierre des Prés of Quercy, and it was here that he produced his major Latin works. Bersuire came ca. 1350 to Paris, where he seems to have studied theology late in life. He was accused of heresy, imprisoned, and eventually released through the intervention of the new king, John II the Good. In 1354, he was made prior of the Benedictine abbey of Saint-Éloy in Paris, a benefice he held until his death. Both in Avignon and Paris, Bersuire frequented the leading intellectuals and scientists of his day, among them the Italian humanist Petrarch, the surgeon Gui de Chauliac, the English Dominican Thomas Waleys, the musician Philippe de Vitry, and the poet Guillaume de Machaut.

Bersuire's works comprise voluminous original treatises in Latin on moral theology and translations into French. None of his works has been preserved complete or in an autograph manuscript. Of his Latin works, the *Reductorium morale* and Repertorium morale have survived fairly intact, while the *Breviarium morale* and *Cosmographia* (or *Descriptio mundi*) have not been positively identified. The encyclopedic *Reductorium* and *Repertorium* are extensive biblical commentaries designed to organize and locate material for preaching. The *Reductorium* is so named because its purpose was to "reduce" to its moral interpretation all that was known or could be known about God, nature, and the world, both visible and invisible. The first-thirteen books (ca. 1340), which survive in only one complete exemplar, were based largely on Bartholomew the Englishman's *Liber de proprietatibus* and cite hundreds of classical and medieval *auctores*. The final three books were composed later and circulated independently: *De natura mirabilibus* (1343–45) is a moralization of the marvels of the natural world, drawing especially upon the legends of the Poitou region and the *Otia imperialia* of Gervais of Tilbury; *Ovidius moralizatus* (or *De fabulis poetarum*) is a moralizing commentary on Ovid's *Metamorphoses*, for which Bersuire drew upon, among other sources, the French *Ovide moralisé*; and *Super totam Bibliam* offers moral interpretations of the best-known Old and New Testament episodes.

The *Repertorium morale* is an alphabetical listing of several thousand biblical words of all sorts (proper and common nouns, verbs, adverbs, etc.), each of which is accorded a moralizing interpretation. This work, if printed today, would run to over twenty octavo volumes. Bersuire's usual procedure is to list all the different meanings the word has in Scripture, which are followed by a series of short rhymed statements, each expounded by reference to the Bible, the fathers, theological commentators, or even pagan authors. The lost *Breviarium morale* was perhaps a general introduction to the *Reductorium* and *Repertorium*.

Between 1354 and 1356, Bersuire undertook at the behest of King John a translation into French of the three decades (1, 3, 4) of Livy's *Ab urbe condita* then known. The principal source for late-medieval knowledge of Roman history, the translation survives in some eighty manuscripts and was possibly reworked by Laurent de Premierfait. An important glossary of technical words, many forged by Bersuire, precedes the translation proper.

An important compiler of received knowledge rather than an original thinker, Bersuire was a significant moralist and polemicist, who frequently castigated abuses of ecclesiastical and political offices. With his translation of Livy, his friendship with Petrarch, and his frequent citations of classical authorities, he can be seen as a precursor of humanistic thinking in France.

See also **Machaut, Guillaume de**

Further Reading

Bersuire, Pierre. *Opera omnia*. Cologne: Friessem and Fromart, 1712.

——. *Reductorium morale: Liber XV, cap. 11–XV, "Ovidius moralizatus,"* ed. Joseph Engels. Utrecht, 1962. [Based on the Paris printed edition of 1509.]

Samaran, Charles. "Pierre Bersuire." *Histoire littéraire de la France* 39 (1962): 259–450.

GROVER A. ZINN

BERTHOLD VON REGENSBURG (ca. 1210–1272)

The most well-known and effectual preacher in the vernacular in the German Middle Ages was the Franciscan priest Berthold von Regensburg. Neither Berthold's birthdate nor birthplace has been established, but he is identified with the Minorite order in Regensburg, of which he became a member, possibly after years of study in Magdeburg. While Berthold acted as confessor to the women of nearby Obermünster and Niedermünster, his fellow Franciscan David von Augsburg probably served as his assistant. Beginning in 1240 and continuing until his death, Berthold preached to religious and lay audiences first in southern Germany, then Bohemia, Switzerland, Styria, and France. In 1263 Pope Urban IV requested that Berthold assist Albertus Magnus in preaching the Crusades. Berthold's preaching to the masses took place outside the church and in the vernacular; embellished descriptions of his sermonizing assert that the lay crowds sometimes numbered forty thousand to two hundred thousand. Such exaggerated estimates substantiate Berthold's popularity and the respect in which he was held. Because of his notoriety he also was called upon to settle disputes in the political and religious spheres.

The only extant works by and attributed to Berthold are Latin and German sermons. Five collections of sermons comprise the Latin corpus. Of these only the first three collections—*Rusticanus de Dominicis* (Rural Sunday Sermons), *Rusticanus de Sanctis* (Holy Day), and *Commune Sanctorum Rusticani* (Rural Saints' Day Sermons)—numbering 254 works, are indisputably by Berthold; they were prepared between 1250 and 1255 for his fellow preachers. The authenticity of the remaining 135 Latin sermons is uncertain. In the preface to the sermons Berthold states that he undertook the editing of the works to counter the error-ridden versions being produced by enthusiastic but unskilled clerics.

The authorship of the German sermons cannot be ascertained with any degree of certainty. More than two hundred pieces have at one time or another been attributed to Berthold, but today fewer than one hundred are identified as works based on the sermons of the Franciscan. It is presumed that the vernacular sermons were copied and edited by Franciscan monks in or around Augsburg beginning in the 1260s, before Berthold's death, until approximately 1275; nonetheless, it is unlikely that Berthold read or approved of many of the works. The editor's hand is clearly discernible; thus these sermons should not be viewed as mere transcriptions of the sermons as preached by Berthold. The German sermons reveal a dependence on the earlier Latin homiletic works, but none is a translation from the Latin.

More than three hundred manuscripts containing Berthold's Latin sermons have been identified; in contrast only eight principal manuscripts that include the vernacular sermons are extant. The Latin homiletic works follow the tradition of the thematic or university-style sermon of the Scholastics, whereas the vernacular sermons emphasize *exempla* (examples) as opposed to a rigid structure or an interpretation of Scripture. In general Berthold would have preached the Latin sermons to a learned, religious audience and the vernacular sermons to the laity; the notable exceptions are the German *Sermones ad Religiosas* (*Klosterpredigten*, Sermons for the Religious), which were preached to women in Berthold's spiritual care.

The frequency of Berthold's name in medieval chronicles, the wealth of extant sermons by and attributed to him, and the esteem in which his contemporaries held him and successors attest to his influence and importance.

See also **Albertus Magnus, David von Augsburg**

Further Reading

Banta, Frank G. "Berthold von Regensburg: Investigations Past and Present." *Traditio* 25 (1969): 472–479.

De Alcantara Hoetzl, Petrus, ed. *Sermones ad religiosos XX ex Erlangensi codice Unacum sermone in honorem S. Francisci e duobus codicibus monacensibus in centenarium septimum familiae franciscanae.* Munich: Huttler, 1882 [Latin works].

Pfeiffer, Franz, and Joseph Strobl, eds. *Berthold von Regensburg. Vollständige Ausgabe seiner deutschen Predigten.* Vienna: Braumüller, 1862 and 1880; rpt. ed. Kurt Ruh [with supplementary material]. Deutsche Neudrucke, Texte des Mittelalters. Berlin: de Gruyter, 1965 [German works].

Richter, Dieter. *Die deutsche Überlieferung der Predigten Bertholds von Regensburg.* Munich: Beck, 1969.

Schönbach, Anton. "Studien zur Geschichte der altdeutschen Predigt, I–VIII." *Sitzungsberichte der Kaiserlichen Akademie der Wissenschaften in Wien, Philosophisch-historische Klasse* 142 (1900), 147 (1904), and 151–155 (1905–1907); rpt. Hildesheim: Olms, 1968.

DEBRA L. STOUDT

BIRGITTA, SAINT (1302 [1303?]–1373)

St. Bridget of Sweden was a Swedish saint and mystic and founder of the Brigettine Order. Born in Finsta, Uppland, she was the daughter of *lagman* ("lawman")

Birger Persson, and, on her mother's side, was related to the royal house of Sweden. At age fourteen, she married Ulf Gudmarsson, who became a knight and *lagman* in the province of Närke. There were eight children of the marriage; the best known was the second-eldest daughter, St. Katarina, who became the first abbess (although never consecrated) of the monastic foundation at Vadstena in Östergötland. Ulf died in 1344, and shortly afterward Birgitta received her "vision of calling." She renounced her worldly possessions, and took up residence near the Cistercian monastery of Alvastra in Östergötland.

Here, she received some of her most important visions, including the revelation of the Rule for a new monastic order. She was supported by spiritual counselors and confessors, including Mathias, canon of Linköping, Sweden's foremost theologian of the time, and two clerics with the name Petrus Olofsson, who were authors of the *Vita*, the earliest biography of the saint. In 1349, Birgitta was instructed in a vision to go to Rome, and she arrived there in time for the holy year of Jubilee in 1350. She remained in Rome, with a small following of Swedes for the rest of her life, and never returned to her native country. In Rome, she was involved in seeking papal authorization for her new order, which was granted in 1370. But it was not until 1419 that the order was formally constituted by Pope Martin V. Birgitta made occasional visits abroad, to Cyprus and Sicily. In 1372, she traveled to the Holy Land, where she received an important cycle of visions relating to the nativity and life of Christ. Toward the end of her life, she made the acquaintance of Alphonso of Pecha, formerly bishop of Jaen; he edited and published her collected revelations and promoted her case for canonization. After her death on July 23, 1373, her relics were translated to Vadstena. She was canonized in 1391, and her official feast day today is July 23.

Altogether, Birgitta received some 700 visions, many of which were extremely influential long after her death. They vary considerably in length, and cover an enormous range of material, from questions of theology, to descriptions of heaven and hell, to judgment scenes of church and political magnates, to highly personalized messages intended for her intimate circle of followers, and to a monastic rule and instructions for life. Nearly all of the recorded visions are occasional pieces, and rarely do they contain circumstantial details. Birgitta's revelations came to her in different ways: she would appear as one half-dead, or she would experience God through her senses, or feel Him as a palpable movement in her breast; or she would simply become rapt in ecstatic prayer. When she was roused from a vision, she wrote it down immediately in her native tongue, and her confessors translated it into Latin. During her lifetime, her revelations remained as private documents. The canonization edition consists of eight books, the last of which contains revelations concerning kings and church leaders that are of political interest and relevance, and other works, such as the *Regula salvatoris* and the *Sermo angelicus,* which is a collection of daily readings to be used during the night office at the monastery.

St. Birgitta's spirituality is characterized by a strong interest in the humanity of Christ, who is perceived as a crusading knight impatiently waiting to do justice. She also identifies closely with the Virgin, who is the central devotional figure in the Brigettine Order. Her Marian revelations were popular throughout Europe during the 15th century. Her legal background is reflected in another cycle of visions that involve judgment scenes of the souls of the departed. Another characteristic is the practical interest she takes in temporal matters. Hers is a missionary mysticism, and she is intent upon regeneration and reform. Like the Old Testament prophets, she puts special emphasis on God's severe judgment of the wicked, and she strives to save human souls, to renovate the Church militant, and to raise the degenerate moral standards she observes all around her, among clergy and laypeople alike. The monastic order she founded is a testimony to her lasting influence not only in Sweden, but also throughout Europe.

Further Reading

Editions

Revelationes S. Birgitte. Lübeck: Ghotan, 1492 [*editio princeps*].

Collijn, Isak, ed. *Acta et processus canonizacionis beate Birgitte, efter cod. A14 Holm.,cod. Onob. lat 90, o. cod. Harl. 612, med inledning, person- och ortregister.* Samlingar utgivna av Svenska fornskrift–sällskapet, ser. 2. Latinska skrifter, 1. Uppsala: Almqvist & Wiksell, 1924–31.

Collijn, Isak, ed. *Birgerus Gregorii. Legenda sancte Birgitte.* Samlingar utgivna av Svenska fornskrift–sällskapet, ser. 2, Latinska skrifter, 4. Uppsala: Almqvist & Wiksell, 1946.

Undhagen, Carl-Gustaf, ed. *Birger Gregerssons Birgitta-officium.* Samlingar utgivna av Svenska fornskrift–sällskapet, ser 2, Latinska skrifter, 6. Uppsala: Almqvist & Wiksell, 1960.

Bergh, Birger, ed. *Den heliga Birgittas Revelaciones: Book VII.* Samlingar utgivna av Svenska fornskrift–sällskapet, ser. 2, Latinska skrifter, 7.7. Uppsala: Almqvist & Wiksell, 1967.

Bergh, Birger, ed. *Sancta Birgitta. Revelaciones: Book V: Liber questionum.* Samlingar utgivna av Svenska fornskrift–sällskapet, ser. 2, Latinska skrifter, 7.5. Uppsala: Almqvist & Wiksell, 1971.

Eklund, Sten, ed. *Sancta. Birgitta, Opera minora. II. Sermo Angelicus.* Samlingar utgivna av Svenska fornskrift–sällskapet, ser. 2, Latinska skrifter 8.2. Uppsala: Almqvist & Wiksell, 1972.

Eklund, Sten, ed. *Sancta Birgitta. Opera minora. I. Regula Salvatoris.* Samlingar uigivna av Svenska fornskrift–sällskapet, ser. 2, Latinska skrifter, 8.1. Uppsala: Almqvist & Wiksell, 1975.

Undhagen, Carl-Gustaf, ed. *Sancta Birgitta. Revelaciones. Book I, with Magister Mathias' Prologue.* Samlingar utgivna av Svenska fornskrift–sällskapet, ser. 2, Latinska skrifter, 7.1. Uppsala: Almqvist & Wiksell, 1978.

Morris, Bridget, ed. *Book VofSt. Birgitta's Uppenbarelser. Edited from MS Cod. Ups. C61.* Samlingar utgivna av Svenska fornskrift–sällskapet, 80. Lund: Blom, 1991.

Literature

Westman, K. B. *Birgitta-studier.* Uppsala: Akademiska boktryckeriet Berling, 1911 [published also as *Uppsala universitets årsskrift* 1 (1911)].

Kraft, Salomon. *Textstudier till Birgittas revelationer.* Kyrkohistorisk årsskrift, 29. Uppsala: Almqvist & Wiksell, 1929.

Vernet, F. "Brigitte de Suède." In *Dictionnaire de spiritualité ascétique et mystique.* Ed. Marcel Viller, S. J. Paris: Beauchesne, 1937, vol. 1, cols. 1943–58.

Brilioth, Yngve. *Svenska kyrkans historia. Den senare medeltiden 1274–1521.* Uppsala: Almqvist & Wiksell, 1941.

Jørgensen, Johannes. *St Bridget of Sweden.* 2 vols. Trans. Ingeborg Lund. London: Longmans, 1954.

Colledge, Eric. "*Epistola solitarii ad reges:* Alphonse of Pecha as Organizer of Brigittine and Urbanist Propaganda." *Mediaeval Studies* 18 (1956), 19–49.

Nyberg, Tore. *Birgittinische Klostergründungen des Mittelalters.* Bibliotheca historica Lundensis, 15. Lund: Gleerup, 1965.

Ekwall, Sara. *Våräldsta Birgittabiografi och dennas viktigaste varianter.* Kungl. vitterhets historie och antikitets akademiens handlingar, hist. ser., 12. Stockholm: Kungl. vitterhets historie och antikvitets akademien, 1965.

Montag, Ulrich. *Das Werk der heiligen Birgitta von Schweden in oberdeutscher Überlieferung Texte und Untersuchungen.* Münchener Texte und Untersuchungen zur deutschen Literatur des Mittelalters, 18. Munich: Beck, 1968.

Klockars, Birgit. *Birgitta och böckerna. En undersökning av den heliga Birgittas källor.* Kungl. vitterhets historie och antikvitets akademiens handlingar, hist. ser., 11. Stockholm: Kungl. vitterhets historie och antikvitets akademien, 1966.

Kilström, Bengt Ingmar. *Bibliographia Birgittina. Skrifter av och om den heliga Birgitta samt om birgittinska kloster och birgittinskt fromhetsliv, i urval.* Strängnäs: Societatis Sanctae Birgittae, 1973.

Stolpe, Sven. *Birgitta i Sverige.* Stockholm: Askild & Karnekull, 1973.

Stolpe, Sven. *Birgitta i Rom.* Stockholm: Askild & Karnekull, 1973.

Rossing, Anna. *Studier i den heliga Birgittas spiritualitet.* Akademisk avhandling för filosofie, doktorsexamen, Litteraturvetenskapliga institutionen. Stockholm: Stockholms Universitet, 1986.

BRIDGET MORRIS

BJARNI KOLBEINSSON (d. 1223)

Bjarni Kolbeinsson was the son of the well-known Norwegian Orkneyian chief Kolbeinn hrúga ("heap") and a great-granddaughter of Páll Þorsteinsson, earl of the Orkneys. Bjarni thus came of a mighty family in the Isles, as *Orkneyinga saga,* states, and he was a close friend of Earl Haraldr Maddaðarson (*Orkneyinga saga,* ch. 109). From 1188 until his death (September 15, 1223), he was bishop of the Orkneys. As such, he initiated the canonization of Earl Rǫgnvaldr Kali Kolsson, and while he was in office an important part of the St. Magnus cathedral in Kirkwall was erected. Bjarni is mentioned five times as a participant in diplomatic missions or political assemblies in Norway (1194, 1208,

1210, 1218, 1223). He is also known to have had friends among the Icelandic aristocrats of his day (Hrafn Sveinbjarnarson, Sæmundr Jónsson).

At the end of the *Snorra Edda* in GkS 2367 4to are preserved forty stanzas of a poem called *Jómsvíkingadrápa,* together with thirty stanzas of an unnamed poem, most commonly called *Málsháttakvæði.* The *stef* ("refrain") stanza of this last poem is also quoted anonymously in *Flateyjarbók.* In *Snorra Edda,* no author is given for either poem, but in *Óláfs saga Tryggvasonar en mesta,* where eighteen stanzas *of Jómsvíkingadrápa* are preserved (five of which are not in the *Snorra Edda*), they are assigned to "Bjarni byskup." *Jómsvíkingasaga* in MS AM 510 4to also contains an allusion to the *drápa* that "Bjarni biskup...orti um Jómsvíkinga." Möbius conjectured that both *Jómsvíkingadrápa* and *Málshattakvæði,* quoted in GkS 2367 4to, are by the same skald.

Jómsvíkingadrápa is a regularly built *drápa* with *stef* in stanzas 15, 19, 23, 27, 31, and 35. Untypically, the *stef* occupies lines 1, 4, 5, and 8 of each *stef* stanza. If the *slæmr* ("slim end"; the last subdivision of a poem) originally had the same length as the *inngangr* ("introduction"), as was generally the case, the poem would have been fifty stanzas long, five stanzas now being lost. The *drápa* is composed in the meter *munnvǫrp,* which is a simplified *dróttkvætt* meter, without *hendingar* in the odd lines and with *skothendingar* instead of *aðalhendingar* in the even lines.

The poem tells part of the story of the Jomsvikings, and seems to refer to oral tradition in numerous phrases such as *frák* ("I heard"), *frágum vér* ("we heard"), and *segja menn* ("men say"). The poem probably was composed in the same period as the written sagas about the Jomvikings, and it seems to have been influenced by them or by traditions used by them, e.g., in the mention of the skalds Vigfúss and Hǫvarðr (st. 34). On the other hand, the poem differs from the prose tradition, e.g., in the prominence given to the Norwegian chieftain Ármóðr, forefather of the well-known Arnmœðlingar (sts. 21, 29). The main subject of the poem is the Jomsvikings' attack on Norway and the battle against Earl Hákon in Hjǫrungavágr (Sunnmøre). In particular, it concentrates on Vagn Ákason, who, despite the Jomsvikings' military defeat, succeeded in realizing his vow to marry Ingibjǫrg, the daughter of the Norwegian chief Þorkell leira ("loam-field").

The *stef in* this poem on Viking warfare and love contains a complaint in which the poet gives vent to his grief that the wife of a nobleman causes him sorrow. This *stef* seems to be a model for the stereotypical introductory stanzas with an erotic content called *mansǫngr,* found in the later Icelandic *rímur,* a word that occurs nowhere in skaldic poetry, except in *Jómsvíkingadrápa,* where it is said that Vagn Ákason "spoke *mansǫngr* on"

Ingibjǫrg, and in *Málsháttakvæði.* *Jómsvíkingadrápa* probably marks a turning point in the history of skaldic verse, as it is the first poem by a historically well-known poet, who chooses as his subject old lore, hence the skald's own denomination *sǫgukvæði,* and treats it in a light-hearted, ironic manner. In his introduction to the poem, the skald alludes to his unhappy love, and he parodies common skaldic introductions: "I call nobody to listen to my poem.... I have not learned poetry under hanged men.... I present a *sǫgukvæði* to people who are not listening." It may be significant that the skald is a compatriot of Rǫgnvaldr Kali, who half a century earlier had introduced troubadour influences into skaldic poetry after his visit to Narbonne, where he was accompanied by Bjarni's predecessor as bishop, Vilhjálmr. Moreover, Rǫgnvaldr was a coauthor of *Háttalykill,* which also tells *forn fræði* ("old lore"). The Orkney islands seem to have been a center for the flourishing of *sǫgukvæði* around 1200.

Although Bjarni's authorship of *Málsháttakvæði* cannot be proven, some similarities between this proverb poem and *Jómsvíkingadrápa* are worth mentioning: a light tone of irony, numerous allusions to real and heroic history, and a concentration on erotic motives (Möbius 1874, Holtsmark 1937). Several scholars remain skeptical about Bjarni's authorship, however, and take *Málsháttakvæði* to be an imitation of Bjarni's poem (de Vries 1941–42), which may be considerably later (Hermann Pálsson 1984). Bjarni has also been mentioned, with little real evidence, as the possible author of some *Þulur* preserved in the *Snorra Edda* (Bugge).

Further Reading

Editions

Möbius, Theodor, "Malshatta-kvædi." *Zeitschrift für deutsche Philologie. Ergänzungsband* (1874), 3–74, 615–6 [edition and commentary].

Petersens, Carl af, ed. *Jómsvikinga saga (efter Cod. AM. 510, 4: to) samt Jómsvíkingadrápa.* Lund: Gleerup, 1879 [diplomatic and critical editions of *Jómsvíkingadrápa* with commentary, pp. 104–33].

Finnur Jónsson, ed. *Den norsk-islandske skjaldedigtning.* Vols. 1A–2A (tekst efter håndskrifterne) and 1B–2B (rettet tekst). Copenhagen and Christiania [Oslo]: Gyldendal, 1912–15; rpt. Copenhagen: Rosenkilde & Bagger, 1967 (A) and 1973 (B), Vol. 2A, pp. 1–10, 129–36; vol. 2B, pp. 1–10, 138–45 [standard edition].

Literature

Bugge, Sophus. "Biskop Bjarne Kolbeinssøn og Snorres Edda." *Annaler for nordisk Oldkyndighed og Historic* (1875), 209–46 [on *Þulur*].

Jón Stefànsson. "Bjarne Kolbeinsson, the Skald, Bishop of Orkney, 1188–1223." *Orkney and Shetland Miscellany* 1 (1907), 43–7.

Holtsmark, Anne. "Bjarne Kolbeinsson og hans forfatterskap." *Edda* 37 (1937), 1–17.

Vries, Jan de. *Altnordische Literaturgeschichte*. 2 vols. Grundriss der germanischen Philologie, 15–6. Berlin: de Gruyter, 1941–42; rpt. 1964–67

Lindow, John. "Narrative and the Nature of Skaldic Poetry." *Arkiv för nordisk filologi* 92 (1981), 94–121

Hermann Pálsson. "A Florilegium in Norse from Medieval Orkney." In *The Northern and* Western *Isles in the Viking World: Survival, Continuity and Change*. Ed. Alexander Fenton and Hermann Pálsson. Edinburgh: Donald, 1984, pp. 258–64.

BJARNE FIDJESTØL

BLANCHE OF CASTILE (1188–1252)

At the age of twelve, Blanche of Castile, the daughter of Alfonso VIII of Castile, was married to Prince Louis of France, who would reign briefly as Louis VIII (1223–26). Louis's early death while on the Albigensian Crusade left the throne to their young son, Louis IX. The regency was entrusted not to a male relative or a council of barons but to Blanche.

In the first years of her regency, Blanche was confronted with armed rebellions intended to displace her and with the serious possibility of a reversal of French successes in the southern lands that had been conquered in the Albigensian Crusade. She triumphed in both cases. Gifted with an iron will and clever in her ability to cultivate allies but careful not to link her fortunes too closely to any baronial house, such as the house of Champagne, through a hasty remarriage, she pursued a policy of divide-and-conquer against the rebellious barons. Their uprisings and shows of force never achieved a decision in their favor. Blanche's success against the baronial opposition in the north was both cause and effect of her maintenance of French dominance in the south. The swiftness and decisiveness of her actions against the northerners induced the southern nobles to negotiate their grievances; and the army that had been left in the south at her husband's death remained, despite some difficulties, loyally commanded and in firm control. By 1229 and the Treaty of Meaux-Paris, the opposition in Languedoc acknowledged its defeat. The prestige of victory in the south encouraged loyalty and support in the north when the crown had to respond to new baronial demonstrations against it in the 1230s led by, among others, the titular count of Brittany, Pierre Mauclerc.

Blanche's regency was distinguished by a balanced foreign policy. On the one hand, the traditional enemy, the English, never effectively made inroads into those provinces, like Normandy, that they had lost in 1204. On the other hand, she made no concerted effort to eject the English from their remaining territories in Aquitaine. In the war of words and sometimes of men between the emperor Frederick II and the papacy, she kept to a neutral path.

In the later 1230s down to 1244, Blanche's role in government gradually diminished. Her son reached adulthood, married, and became more active, especially in military affairs. This translation of power was not entirely easy. There was mutual dislike between Blanche and her son's wife, Marguerite of Provence; Blanche also vigorously opposed Louis's decision in 1244 to take the crusader's vow. Nonetheless, she remained a close political adviser to the king, far closer than his wife, and Louis entrusted the reins of government to Blanche when he embarked on crusade in 1248.

As a deeply devout and morally strict woman, an enthusiastic patroness of the church, especially the Cistercian order, and a Castilian who grew up in an environment of fierce commitment to the holy war of reconquest in Spain, Blanche's opposition to her son's crusade remains something of a puzzle. But however she felt about his enterprise in the abstract, she devoted her full energies to making certain that he was well supplied and that he need not trouble himself about governance at home while he fought in the East. She managed to negotiate a two-year extension of the clerical income tax of one-tenth in order both to finance the war effort and to replenish the king's coffers after the disastrous early phase of the crusade that saw Louis captured and ransomed in Egypt. She acted with her characteristic firmness in 1249, on the death of the count of Toulouse, when a movement took shape to turn aside the settlement of 1229 that designated her son Alphonse to be the new count of Toulouse. She thought well of the so-called Pastoureaux (1251), Flemish and northern French rustics who proclaimed themselves crusaders determined to rescue and otherwise aid the king. But when bands of these forces rioted in Paris and pillaged other towns, it was she who authorized and oversaw their destruction. Blanche died in November 1252. When her son, still in the Holy Land, received the news some months later, he succumbed to a grief so profound that it troubled all who knew and loved him.

See also **Louis IX**

Further Reading

Sivéry, Gerard. *Blanche de Castille*. Paris: Fayard, 1990.

WILLIAM CHESTER JORDAN

BOCCACCIO, GIOVANNI (1313–1375)

Boccaccio is now best known as the author of the *Decameron*; but he wrote many works very different in kind, and in the century following his death he was most famous as a humanist and a herald of the Renaissance. He was the illegitimate son of a businessman, Boccaccino di Chelino, and a mother whose name is unknown to us, and he spent his earliest years in or near Florence. Boccaccino encouraged his son's education, but not along the lines of Boccaccio's own interests. In *Genealogie deorum gentilium* (*Genealogy of the Pagan Gods*), Boccaccio says:

> Even in my boyhood [my father] directed all my endeavors towards business. As a mere child, he put me in the charge of a great business man for instruction in arithmetic. For six years I did nothing but waste irrevocable time. Then, as there seemed to be some indication that I was more disposed to literary pursuits, this same father decided that I should study for holy orders, as a good way to get rich. My teacher was famous, but I wasted under him almost as much time as before....I turned out neither a business man, nor a canon-lawyer, and missed being a good poet besides. (*Boccaccio on Poetry*, trans. Osgood, 1930, 131–132).

Around 1327, when Boccaccio was fourteen, he moved to Naples, where his father worked as an agent of the Bardi bank at the royal court. The French court and the busy port of Naples offered Boccaccio a wide new range of educational experiences to complement the hours he spent in unwanted studies. Cino da Pistoia, who taught him law, may well have encouraged Boccaccio's interest in poetry, showing him writings by Dante and other recent poets. (One of Cino's lyrics appears as a song in Boccaccio's *Filostrato*.) Boccaccio was also befriended by a circle of Petrarch's acquaintances, including Barbato, Giovanni Barrili, and the Augustinian father Dionigi di Borgo San Sepolcro. Paolo da Perugia, the king's librarian, contributed a more classical education; Paolo, with the help of Barlaam's knowledge of Greek, was collecting materials on ancient mythology that later became the basis for Boccaccio's *Genealogie*.

Boccaccio began to try his hand at literature while still pursuing other studies. His apprenticeship in the classics is shown in his earliest endeavors, preserved in his notebooks: *Elegia di Costanza* (in verse), paraphrasing a classical epitaph; and *Allegoria mitologica* (*Mythological Allegory*, in prose), a brief and highly artificial string of mythical references from Ovid used to prefigure Christian history. He turned to Dante's *sirventese* as the model for *Caccia di Diana* (1334?)—an ambiguous title which can mean either Diana's hunt or the chasing away of Diana. Here, the verses describe a hunt for various beasts by fifty-nine beautiful women of Naples and their leader, Diana; the women then transfer their allegiance ro Venus, who turns the beasts into men. The problem of how to understand Boccaccio's work begins with the start of his career: *Caccia* has been read as an elegant compliment, as Christian allegory, and as ironic satire.

Il Filocolo (1335–1336?), a long, ambitious romance about separated lovers, reveals that many influences were working on Boccaccio. It is filled with idyllic descriptions of Neapolitan gatherings and with plots popular at the French court, but he also includes classical gods, metamorphoses, significant Greek names, and numerous echoes of Dante. Boccaccio presents *Filocolo* as a written version of an oral tale, and *cantari* on Florio's search for Biancifiore do exist; however, Boccaccio frames that story in a broader history of the conversion of Florio, and Europe, to Christianity. The most famous scene is a debate on questions of love in a Neapolitan garden (4.14–72); two of the questions reappear in the *Decameron* as tales 4 and 5 of the tenth day.

Il Filostrato seems to have been written at about the same time as *Il Filocolo*, perhaps in 1335; however, the language of *Filostrato* is much more fluent and humorous than the artificially elaborate prose of *Filocolo*, and one scholar has therefore suggested a later date. *Filostrato* became the model for Chaucer's *Troilus and Criseyde*. Its nine books of *ottava rima* stanzas tell of the Trojan prince Troiolo's love for Criseida; the seduction, aided by her uncle, Pandaro; her betrayal of Troiolo for the Greek Diomedes; and Troiolo's despairing death. Boccaccio seems to have associated the number nine with tragedy: he also uses nine books in *Elegia di madonna Fiammetta* and in *De casibus virorum illustrorum* (*Fall of Illustrious Men*).

For *Teseida delle nozze di Emilia* (1340–1341), twelve-book romance-epic, Boccaccio again drew on classical history, this time continuing Statius's *Thebaid*. He described *Teseida* as the first martial poem in Italian. It begins with Theseus's conquest of the Amazons and tells of two Theban knights' rivalry for the love of the Amazon Emilia, whom they first see from their prison window. Theseus arranges a tournament to decide which one is to marry her. Boccaccio appended notes to educate his readers about Greek myths and customs, and he tried to base his description of the games and the arena on classical accounts. His famous glosses to the temples of Venus and Mars in Book 7 suggest that the work may be read allegorically, since these two deities represent concupiscence and irascibility. The work became a basis for Chaucer's "Knight's Tale."

By the time he finished *Teseida*, Boccaccio had been forced by business troubles to return with his father to Florence (1341). The move back to Florence is described in depressing terms at the end of *Comedia delle ninfe fiorentine* (*Comedy of the Florentine Nymphs*, 1341–1342); Boccaccio remained nostalgic for the cultural brilliance of Naples, and he tried several times to return there to live, but disappointing circumstances repeatedly forced him to abandon this aim. However, the return to Florence did not interrupt his writing. Within a year he had produced two pastoral works. One, a pair of Latin eclogues, would become the first two poems of *Buccolicum carmen*, written over many years and completed shortly before his death. The other was *Comedia delle ninfe fiorentine*. In this allegory, the shepherd Ameto overhears seven nymphs (virtues) tell, each in turn, how they won over their lovers (vices). Then Ameto is stripped of his animal skins and baptized, and he realizes that the nymphs he lusted for are even more desirable as moral virtues. Venus descends, announcing herself as the triune god, while the nymphs sing, in veiled terms, of the mysteries of Christian belief. The title and plot of *Comedia delle ninfe fiorentine*, the use of *terza rima*, and the usual borrowings of phrases show Boccaccio's indebtedness to Dante. Yet Boccaccio's work is radically new in kind, and it was to be a major influence on the uses of the pastoral mode during the Renaissance. Its alternation of prose narrative with verse provided a model for Sannazaro's *Arcadia*.

Boethius's *Consolation of Philosophy* and the *Roman de la Rose* as well as Dante were the major sources for *Amorosa visione* (*Amorous Vision*, 1342). In this dream vision, the narrator must choose between a narrow flight of ascending stairs and a broad doorway into a palace. A heavenly guide follows the narrator into the palace, commenting on the murals he sees painted there—triumphs of wisdom, glory, wealth, love, and fortune. The notion of a series of triumphs and the catalogs of figures in them inspired Petrarch's *Trionfi* and many Renaissance paintings. In *Amorosa visione* three poems run as an acrostic down the entire length of the work, spelled out by the first letter of each tercet; Boccaccio's own name appears in the acrostic at the point where he sees his beloved painted in love's triumph. Boccaccio circulated a manuscript into which he had copied *Caccia di Diana*, the lyric *Contento quasi*, and *Amorosa visione*, all in *terza rima*.

Meanwhile Petrarch, recently made the laureate at Naples (1341), was stirring the enthusiasm of literary circles. Boccaccio composed a brief Latin life, *De vita et moribus domini Francisci Petracchi* (1341–1342), noting that no poet had been crowned at Rome since late antiquity but praising Petrarch's Italian lyrics as well as his Latin endeavors. Boccaccio wrote that if souls were reincarnated, people would think of Petrarch as the reincarnation of Virgil. Clearly, excitement over a revival of ancient culture had much to do with Boccaccio's own enthusiasm.

In 1343–1344, Boccaccio was once again experimenting with a new kind of work; the result—*Elegia di madonna Fiammetta* (*Elegy of Lady Fiammetta*)—has been considered one of the first novels. *Elegia* is narrated by Fiammetta, a young married woman of Naples; she tells of her falling in love, the departure of her beloved, and his failure to return despite his promises. Small events evoke long psychological reactions as Fiammetta's alternating hope and depression lead her ever deeper into despair. Her attempted suicide is foiled,

and she writes her book both to warn other women and to glory in her own tragedy. As in the earlier works, descriptions of real life are mingled with mythical references; and psychological realism coexists with hints of a moral allegory about passion and reason. Venus is associated with the Fury Tesiphone, and in a sense we witness Fiammetta's descent into hell (there are echoes of Dante's *Inferno*)—a hell of misery, violence, hypocrisy, and stubborn pride. Ovid's *Heroides* and Seneca's tragedies, especially *Phaedra* and *Hippolytus*, were important sources for this work.

Boccaccio had used the name Fiammetta for his beloved in earlier books (*Filocolo, Teseida, Comedia delle ninfe*, and *Amorosa visione*); however, her identity changed from work to work—she was a daughter of the king of Naples from before or after his coronation, a nymph, and a descendant of Aquinas. In *Elegia* she is a middle-class Neapolitan, and her unhappy love mirrors the unhappiness of her lover in the earlier works. His is the pain of unrequited desire; hers the pain of having been seduced and abandoned. Her name will appear once more, in the *Decameron*—where, as a Florentine, she is one of the narrators, ruling the day of love stories with happy endings. It is worth noting that most of these happy endings consist in marriage.

Marriage is also celebrated in *Ninfale fiesolano* (1344–1346?), an Ovidian pastoral narrative about the love of the country boy Africo and one of Diana's nymphs, Mensola. Diana turns the pregnant Mensola into a stream in the Tuscan countryside; and Africo, who commits suicide, gives his name to another stream nearby. Both Venus's advocacy of rape and Diana's insistence on chastity yield before social marriage, however, as Africo and Mensola's son grows up, marries, and sires citizens of the new community, Fiesole. The work ends with a rapid history of the origins of and relations between Fiesole and Florence. As in *Filostrato*, clarity and lightness of language go hand in hand with the use of stanzas of *ottava rima*; if Boccaccio did not invent this form, he established it as a graceful and effective mode of narrative, taken up by poets of the Renaissance. The adoption of Ovidian metamorphoses to mythicize features of the local landscape is another feature that became immensely popular.

The mid-1340s saw political turmoil and violence in Florence, along with the failure of Florentine banks. Perhaps to escape all this, Boccaccio lived for a while (1345–1346?) in Ravenna; he dedicated his translation of Livy's fourth decade to its ruler, Ostasio da Polenta. He next spent a short time (1347–1348?) in Forlì. Naples was then undergoing a period of chaos: the king of Hungary invaded it to avenge the death of his brother Andrew, who had been the husband of the queen of Naples and had been mysteriously murdered. Francesco Ordelaffi, lord of Forlì, wanted to join the Hungarian expedition and nearly took Boccaccio along. Boccaccio wrote several Latin eclogues on the situation in Naples; he was at first critical of the Neapolitans but was later outraged by the brutality of the king of Hungary.

Boccaccio was back in Florence when the dreadful plague of 1348 struck. Both his father and his stepmother died, leaving Boccaccio responsible for the remaining family and its property. The death of between one-third and half of the population of Florence, and the survivors' fear of contagion, caused a temporary breakdown of Florentine society. Out of this terrible experience came the *Decameron* (1349–1351), whose ten narrators flee the plague, take refuge in their villas in the hills, and tell each other stories for ten days, ending each day with a song. (Activities such as singing and telling comic tales were actually recommended by doctors to preserve the balance of humors and thus prevent disease.) The hundred tales are "retold" by Boccaccio for women who are obsessed by love and unable to distract themselves as men can. (There are echoes here of Ovid's *Remedia amoris*.) By chasing away their melancholy, Boccaccio hopes to restore their mental health. The Dantean journey from the pestilential city to a garden which resembles an earthly paradise suggests a moral as well as a physical meaning. Yet the layering of narrative voices (the real Boccaccio, the inscribed "I", the narrators, and often characters telling tales within tales) complicates the possible interpretations. As with Boccaccio's earlier writings, critics have disagreed about how to read this work. Some have seen it as championing the rights of "nature" against social morality; others as teaching Christian morals; others as rejecting any moral function of literature in favor of aesthetic pleasure; others as intentionally thwarting any possibility of fixed meaning. The *Decameron* has been considered feminist and misogynist, radical and conservative, conducive to the reordering of society after its breakdown and subversive of established order.

In writing the *Decameron* Boccaccio drew on a complex mixture of popular and literary sources. Proverbs and tales from the oral tradition; recent events and anecdotes; evocations of Dante; and classical narratives by Ovid, Apuleius, and Valerius Maximus all merge in a rich work that has been called the "human comedy." Although many of the tales take place in Italian towns in Boccaccio's own time or the recent past, there are also other settings, including the Orient and ancient Athens. Branca (1976) has suggested that the wandering knights of romance have been replaced here by wandering merchants who encounter everything from prostitutes to disguised princesses.

Each day (except days 1 and 9) is assigned a topic, so that the tales interact as variations on a theme, while Dioneo's final tale on each day often parodies the preceding stories. The topics are also linked: the power of fortune is followed by the achievement of one's desires; unhappy love stories are followed by happy ones; tricks by women against men are followed by the deceits of humans generally against each other; and the final topic, magnanimous behavior, is introduced as a corrective to all that has gone before.

This collection had an enormous influence on prose fiction throughout Europe for the next several centuries. The major themes of the *Decameron*—fortune, love, trickery, the deceits of women, the hypocrisy of clergymen—became those of a genre called the *novella*. Another feature, the framing tale, was also copied, with variations. Dramatists found the *Decameron* a wonderful source of plots. Boccaccio's prose—combining formal Latinate syntax with lively, realistic dialogue—established a standard for Italian prose, just as Petrarch became the model for Italian poetry. However, unlike Petrarch, who denigrated Italian and encouraged writing in Latin, Boccaccio defended Italian as a literary language. His admiration for Dante, whose *Commedia* he sent to Petrarch with exhortations not to scorn it, undoubtedly persuaded him of the potential power and range of the vernacular.

In October 1350, Petrarch came to Florence, and Boccaccio went outside the gates of town to meet him and invite him home. This was the beginning of a deep friendship that lasted to the end of their lives, and many of their letters to each other are still extant.

From 1350 on, Boccaccio became more and more involved in public life. He was given responsible offices within the city and was sent on sensitive embassies abroad, including one to the pope in Avignon in 1354. In 1355, he made one of his disappointing trips to Naples; during this journey, the best beloved of his five illegitimate children died—the little girl whom he affectionately memorialized in his eclogue *Olympia*. (All five children seem to have died very young.) At the rich library of Monte Cassino, he copied a number of classical texts, because he was beginning to work on his own historical volumes: *Genealogy of the Pagan Gods, The Fall of Illustrious Men*, and the geographical dictionary *Of Mountains, Forests, . . . and Seas* (*De montibus . . .*). All these works took many years to complete. They reflect Boccaccio's more humanistic, scholarly side, which was encouraged by Petrarch and was highly valued by the humanists of the following century.

In the early 1350s, Boccaccio wrote, in Italian, *Trattatello in laude di Dante* (*Little Treatise in Praise of Dante*) for a manuscript in which he copied all the known poetry of Dante; this collection became a major source for the transmission of Dante's verse. *Tratatello*, which was revised several times (c. 1360 and before 1372), was a celebration as well as a biography, offered in lieu of the ancients' physical monuments to great men. Boccaccio praises Dante as a poet-theologian and discusses poetic theory but also passes on popular anecdotes about Dante and describes his appearance and manners.

Boccaccio's last work of Italian fiction, *Corbaccio* (*Old Crow*, 1355 or perhaps 1365), is a dream vision in which a mocked lover, the narrator, encounters the ghost of his lady's husband. The ghost reveals the wife as evil, turning the narrator's love into hatred, and urges him to compose a work that will bring the woman shame instead of glory. This misogynistic tirade has left readers perplexed. Some see it as angry, but others see it as humorous—as a work meant to show us the narrator's double error, first in falling in love and then in swerving to the opposite extreme. Still others see it as a moral lesson. On the one hand, the husband has been taken as Boccaccio's mouthpiece; on the other hand, the husband has been seen as an infernal ghost who seeks to bring his rival to harm. The title has been seen as referring to the widow, to the husband, to lust, and to the harsh-voiced book as a whole. The form of the book, a dream vision, is reminiscent of *Amorosa visione*, which Boccaccio was simultaneously revising.

Genealogie deorum gentilium (*Genealogy of the Pagan Gods*), first circulated c. 1360 but revised in 1372, contains further reflections on poetry. In its fifteen books, classical myths are organized according to major gods and their descendants. The myths are then glossed; but although they are given natural, historical, or moral meanings, they are not Christianized. Boccaccio had frequently used classical myths in order to formulate Christian meanings, but here he was concerned to discover what the ancients themselves might have meant by these tales. The final two books contain a defense of literature and of the study of pagan writings. The work remained a basic source about mythology for writers and artists of the Renaissance.

De casibus virorum illustrium (*The Fates of Illustrious Men*) was finished c. 1360 but was enlarged later (1373–1374). It offers a series of examples of the instability of worldly glory, running all the way from Adam through King Arthur to contemporary cases but mainly emphasizing classical history. Inserted among these examples are famous chapters on the praise of poverty, the combat between Poverty and Fortune, the defense of literature, the nature of dreams, and other topics. The work became known in England through Lydgate's *Fall of Princes*.

Boccaccio also took up the case of women, protesting against their neglect by other historians, including Petrarch. *De mulieribus claris* (*On Famous Women*), written and revised several times between 1361 and 1375, presents biographies from Eve to Queen Giovanna of Naples, i.e., it covers the same span of time as *De casibus*. In *Genealogie*, Boccaccio had given historical readings of some myths; similarly, in *De mulieribus claris* he assumes that classical goddesses were human women deified for their contributions to human life; thus Ceres, for example, is considered an early teacher of agriculture. Boccaccio finds far fewer women to praise in his own time than in the past. He celebrates ancient women writers for their intellectual pursuits, exhorting his contemporaries not to let their minds lie idle. Christine de Pizan reworked these histories into her feminist *Book of the City of Ladies*.

During the political crisis in Florence in 1360, several of Boccaccio's friends were exiled or killed. He himself withdrew from Florence to Certaldo c. 1365. In a letter of consolation (1361–1362) to his exiled friend Pino de' Rossi, Boccaccio declares the advent of a new era: the path of the ancients, long overgrown, has been cleared by Petrarch, and others may now follow in his steps. This sense of a new opening also appears in Boccaccio's praise of Giotto (*Decameron*, 6.5) for reviving an art long dead. Boccaccio himself also participated in launching this new era, reviving classical forms, themes, and histories. In contrast to his usual humility, *Genealogie* contains his one boast—that he had revived Greek studies (15.7):

> Was it not I who intercepted Leontius Pilatus on his way from Venice to the western Babylon [Avignon]...? Did I not make the utmost effort personally that he should be appointed professor [of Greek] in Florence, and his salary paid out of the city's funds [1360–1362]? Indeed I did; and I too was the first who, at my own expense, called back to Tuscany the writings of Homer and of other Greek authors, whence they had departed many centuries before, never meanwhile to return....I, too, was the first to hear Leontius privately render the *Iliad* in Latin [1359–1360]; and I it was who tried to arrange public readings from Homer.

Devotion to the classics, as Boccaccio argued in *Genealogie*, was in no way anti-Christian. In 1360–1361, the pope gave Boccaccio a full dispensation for his illegitimate birth, enabling him to hold some church office or benefice that probably provided him with an income. Nonetheless, a message in 1362 from the holy man Pietro Petroni, warning Petrarch and Boccaccio to turn from literature to God or risk damnation, caused Boccaccio serious misgivings. His fears were calmed by Petrarch, who argued that although intellectual pursuits are not necessary to salvation, they offer a higher way than simple faith. Petrarch even invited Boccaccio to live with him, but Boccaccio preferred to remain independent.

In 1363, Boccaccio did accept an invitation to live at the court of Naples, bringing *De mulieribus* and probably *De casibus* with him as a gift. His illusion of ending his days comfortably as a great man at the court were quickly shattered, however. In an angry letter, he complained of having been lodged and fed with lowly servants and forced to follow the seneschal, Niccolò Acciaiuoli, around in his constant travels, making study impossible; as a final insult, he had even been left behind by the entourage. After a consoling visit with Petrarch in Venice, Boccaccio returned to Certaldo bitterly confirmed in his preference for impoverished independence. His public duties for Florence resumed in 1365.

Besides Boccaccio's prose and verse narratives, 126 of his securely attributed lyric poems remain. They were written throughout his life on such topics as love, religion, and poetry and were never assembled into any fixed collection. (Nearly fifty poems less surely attributed to him have also been published.) The influence of Ovid, the *stilnovisti*, and Petrarch is recognizable in many of Boccaccio's verses. Around 1370, Boccaccio circulated his completed *Carmen buccolicum*: sixteen diverse Latin eclogues on amatory, political, moral, literary, and religious matters. Three of the later eclogues present a hell, paradise, and purgatory clearly inspired by Dante's. Boccaccio also copied together into one manuscript the eclogues of Virgil, Petrarch, Dante, Giovanni del Virgilio, Checco di Meletto de' Rossi, and his own; this anthology of pastoral verse contributed to the subsequent popularity of the genre.

In 1373, Boccaccio was invited to give the first public lectures in Florence on Dante's *Commedia*. These lectures were interrupted by his illness during the following year; moreover, Boccaccio expressed his concern, in several sonnets (122–125), that he might be prostituting the muses by exposing Dante's poetry to the crowds. His written *Esposizioni* (*Commentaries*), divided into literal and allegorical explanations, break off at *Inferno* 17. In the midst of his own illness, Boccaccio received news of Petrarch's death (July 1374), and he mourned Petrarch in Italian verse. Near the end of Boccaccio's life, one of his most devoted friends was Coluccio Salutari, who was to be important to the next generation of humanists. On 21 December 1375, Boccaccio died at Certaldo, leaving his books to the Augustinians of Santo Spirito. He had composed his own epitaph:

> Beneath this stone lie the ashes and bones of Giovanni;
> His spirit sits before God adorned with the merits of the labors
> Of his mortal life. His father was Boccaccio,
> His home Certaldo, his eager study was nourishing poetry.

See also Chaucer, Geoffrey; Cino da Pistoia; Dante Alighieri; Petrarca, Francesco

Further Reading

Editions of Boccacio's Works

Amorosa visione, ed. Vittore Branca. *Tutte le opere*, Vol. 3. Verona: Mondadori, 1974.

Caccia di Diana, ed. Vittore Branca. *Tutte le Opere,* Vol. 1. Verona: Mondadori, 1967.

Carmina, ed. Giuseppe Velli. *Tutte le opere*, Vol. 5, t. 1. Milan: Mondadori, 1992.

Comedia delle ninfe Fiorentine, ed. Antonio Enzo Quaglio. *Tutte le opere*, Vol. 2. Verona: Mondadori, 1964.

Corbaccio, ed. Tauno Nurmela. Suomalaisen Tiedeakatemian Toimituksia: Annales Academiae Scientiarum Fennicae, Series B, 146. Helsinki, 1968.

Decameron, ed. Vittore Branca. *Tutte le opere*, Vol. 4. Verona: Mondadori, 1976.

De Canaria, ed. Manlio Pastore Stocchi. *Tutte le opere*, Vol. 5, t. 1. Milan: Mondadori, 1992.

De mulieribus Claris, ed. Vittorio Zaccaria. *Tutte le opere*, Vol. 10. Verona: Mondadori, 1970. *Elegia di madonna Fiammetta*, ed. Cesare Segre. In *Opere di Giovanni Boccaccio*. Milan: Mursia, 1963.

Epistole e lettere, ed. Ginetta Auzzas. *Tutte le opere*, Vol. 5, t. 1. Milan: Mondadori, 1992.

Esposizioni sopra la Comedia di Dante, ed. Giorgio Padoan. *Tutte le opere*, Vol. 6. Verona: Mondadori, 1965.

Filocolo, ed. Antonio Enzo Quaglio. *Tutte le opere*, Vol. 1. Verona: Mondadori, 1967.

Filostrato, ed. Vittore Branca. *Tutte le opere*, Vol. 2. Verona: Mondadori, 1964.

Genealogie deorum gentilium libri, 2 vols., ed. Vincenzo Romano. Bari: Laterza, 1951.

Lettere edite e inedite, ed. Francesco Corazzini. Florence, 1877.

Ninfale fiesolano, ed. Armando Balduino. *Tutte le opere*, Vol. 3. Verona: Mondadori, 1974.

Opere Latine minori, ed. Aldo Francesco Massèra. Bari: Laterza, 1928.

Rime, ed. Vittore Branca. *Tutte le opere*, Vol. 5, t. 1. Milan: Mondadori, 1992.

Teseida delle nozze di Emilia, ed. Alberto Limentani. *Tutte le opere*, Vol. 2. Verona: Mondadori, 1964.

Trattatello in laude di Dante, ed. Pier Giorgio Ricci. *Tutte le opere*, Vol. 3. Verona: Mondadori, 1974.

Vite, ed. Renata Fabbri. *Tutte le opere*, Vol. 5, t. 1. Milan: Mondadori, 1992.

Translations of Boccaccio's Works (by Work)

L'Ameto, trans. Judith Serafini-Sauli. New York: Garland, 1985.

Amorosa visione, trans. Robert Hollander, Timothy Hampton, and Margherita Frankel. Hanover, N.H., and London: University Press of New England, 1986.

Amorous Fiammetta (*Elegia di madonna Fiammetta*), trans. Bartholomew Young. London, 1587. (Rev. ed., Edward Hutton, London, 1926. Reprint, Westport, Conn.: Greenwood, 1970.)

Boccaccio on Poetry, trans. Charles Osgood. Indianapolis, Ind.: Bobbs-Merrill, 1930. (*Genealogie*, books 14 and 15.)

The Book of Theseus (*Teseida*), trans. Bernadette McCoy. New York: Medieval Text Association, 1974.

Concerning Famous Women, trans. Guido Guarino. New Brunswick, N.J.: Rutgers University Press, 1963.

The Corbaccio, trans. Anthony K. Cassell. Urbana: University of Illinois Press, 1975. (2nd ed. rev., Binghamton: Medieval and Renaissance Texts and Studies, 1993.)

Decameron, trans. G. H. McWilliam. Harmondsworth: Penguin, 1972. (2nd ed., 1995.)

Decameron, trans. Mark Musa and Peter Bondanella. New York: Norton, 1982.

Diana's Hunt: Caccia di Diana—Boccaccio's First Fiction, ed. and trans. Anthony K. Cassell and Victoria Kirkham. Philadelphia: University of Pennsylvania Press, 1991.

Eclogues, trans. Janet Levarie Smarr. New York: Garland, 1987.

The Elegia di Lady Fiammetta, trans. Mariangela Causa Steindler and Thomas Mauch. Chicago, Ill.: University of Chicago Press, 1990.

The Fates of Illustrious Men, trans. and abridged Louis Brewer Hall. New York: Ungar, 1965.

Il Filocolo, trans. Donald Cheney with the collaboration of Thomas G. Bergin. New York: Garland, 1985.

[*Il Fibcolo*, extract.] *Thirteen Most Pleasant and Delectable Questions of Love*, trans. H. G. London, 1566. (Rev. ed., Harry Carter, New York: Potter, 1974. ("H. G." may be Henry Grantham.)

Il Fibstrato, ed. Vincenzo Pernicone, trans. Robert P. ap Roberts and Anna Bruni Seldis. New York: Garland, 1986.

The Fibstrato, trans. Nathaniel Edward Griffin and Arthur Beckwith Myrick. Philadelphia: University of Pennsylvania Press, 1929. (Reprint, New York: Octagon, 1970.)

[*Il Filostrato.*] *The Story of Troilus* (*Filostrato*), trans. Robert Kay Gordon. London: Dent, 1934. (Reprint, Toronto: University of Toronto Press, 1978.)

Life of Dante, trans. James Robinson Smith. In *The Earliest Lives of Dante*. New York: Holt, 1902. (Reprint, Norwood, Pa.: Norwood Editions, 1976.)

The Life of Dante (*Trattatello in laude di Dante*), trans. Vincenzo Zin Bollettino. New York: Garland, 1990.

The Nymph of Fiesole, trans. Daniel J. Donno. New York: Columbia University Press, 1960.

Nymphs of Fiesole (*Ninfale fiesolano*), trans. Joseph Tusiani. Rutherford, N.J.: Fairleigh Dickinson University Press, 1971.

Theseid of the Nuptials of Emilia, trans. Vincenzo Traversa. New York: Peter Lang, 2002.

Boccaccio Bibliographies

Consoli, Joseph P. *Giovanni Boccaccio: An Annotated Bibliography.* New York: Garland, 1992.

Esposito, Enzo, with the collaboration of Christopher Kleinhenz. *Boccacciana: Bibliografia delle edizioni e degli scritti critici 1939–1974.* Ravenna: Longo, 1976.

Studi sul Boccaccio. 1963– . (Contains bibliographic updates.)

Traversari, Guido. *Bibliografia boccaccesca.* Città di Castello: S. Lapi, 1907.

Criticism: General

Barolini, Teodolinda. "Giovanni Boccaccio." In *European Writers: The Middle Ages and the Renaissance*, ed. William T. Jackson. New York: Scribner, 1983, Vol. 2, pp. 509–534.

Bergin, Thomas G. *Boccaccio.* New York: Viking, 1981.

Boccaccio 1975: Secoli di vita—Atti del Congresso Internazionale, Boccaccio 1975, ed. Marga Cottino-Jones and Edward Tuttle. Ravenna: Longo, 1978.

Branca, Vittore. *Boccaccio: The Man and His Works*, trans. Richard Monges. New York: New York University Press, 1976.

de' Negri, Enrico. "The Legendary Style of the *Decameron*." *Romanic Review*, 43, 1952, pp. 166–189.

Hollander, Robert. *Boccaccio's Two Venuses.* New York: Columbia University Press, 1977.

Lee, A. Collingwood. *The Decameron: Its Sources and Analogues.* London: David Nutt, 1909.

Serafini-Sauli, Judith Powers. *Giovanni Boccaccio.* Boston, Mass.: Twayne, 1982.

Smarr Janet L. *Boccaccio and Fiammetta: The Narrator as Lover.* Urbana: University of Illinois Press, 1986.

Criticism: Decameron

Almansi, Guido. *The Writer as Liar: Narrative Technique in the Decameron.* London: Routledge and Kegan Paul, 1975.

Cottino-Jones, Marga. *Order from Chaos.* Washington, D.C.: University Press of America, 1982.

Dombroski, Robert, ed. *Critical Perspectives on the Decameron.* London: Hodder and Stoughton, 1976.

Fido, Franco. "Boccaccio's *Ars Narrandi* in the Sixth Day of the *Decameron*." In *Roots and Branches: Essays in Honor of Thomas G. Bergin*, ed. Giose Rimanelli and Kenneth John Atchity. New Haven, Conn.: Yale University Press, 1976, pp. 225–242.

Forni, Pier Massimo. *Forme complesse nel Decameron.* Florence: Olschki, 1992.

———. *Adventures in Speech: Rhetoric and Narration in Boccaccio's Decameron.* Philadelphia: University of Pennsylvania Press, 1996.

Greene, Thomas. "Forms of Accommodation in the *Decameron*." *Italica*, 45, 1968, pp. 297–313.

Hollander, Robert. "Utilità in Boccaccio's *Decameron*." *Studi sul Boccaccio*, 15, 1985–1986, pp. 215–233.

———. *Boccaccio's Dante and the Shaping Force of Fiction.* Ann Arbor: University of Michigan Press, 1997.

Kirkham, Victoria. "Love's Labors Rewarded and Paradise Lost." *Romanic Review*, 72, 1981, 79–93. (Day 3.)

———. "An Allegorically Tempered *Decameron*." *Italica*, 62, 1985a, pp. 1–23.

———. "Boccaccio's Dedication to Women in Love." In *Renaissance Studies in Honor of Craig Hugh Smyth*, ed. Andrew Morrogh et al. Florence: Giunti Barbera, 1985b, Vol. I, pp. 333–343.

Lessico critico decameroniano, ed. Renzo Bragantini and Pier Massimo Froni. Turin: Bollati Boringhieri, 1995.

Marcus, Millicent. *An Allegory of Form: Literary Self-Consciousness in the Decameron.* Stanford French and Italian Studies, 18. Saratoga, Calif., 1979.

Mazzotta, Giuseppe. *The World at Play in Boccaccio's Decameron.* Princeton, N.J.: Princeton University Press, 1986.

Musa, Mark, and Peter Bondanella, eds. *The Decameron: 21 Novelle, Contemporary Reactions, Modern Criticism.* New York: Norton, 1977.

Olson, Glending. *Literature as Recreation in the Later Middle Ages.* Ithaca, N.Y.: Cornell University Press, 1982.

Scaglione, Aldo D. *Nature and Love in the Late Middle Ages: An Essay on the Cultural Context of the Decameron.* Berkeley: University of California Press, 1963.

Smarr, Janet. "Symmetry and Balance in the *Decameron*." *Medievalia*, 2, 1976, pp. 159–186.

Wallace, David. *Giovanni Boccaccio: Decameron.* Cambridge: Cambridge University Press, 1991.

JANET LEVARIE SMARR

BOETHIUS DE DACIA (13th century)

Boethius de Dacia was a Danish philosopher active at the University of Paris in the 1270s. "Boethius" is a latinization of the Nordic name "Bo." Because of a misinterpretation of the epithet "de Dacia/Dacus" = "from Denmark," some scholars have called him "Boethius of Sweden." Nothing is known about Boethius's life except that he was a master of arts, the author of some thirty learned works (ten preserved), and with Siger of Brabant became one of the main targets of the condemnation issued by the bishop of Paris in 1277. He may at some later time have become a Dominican. Boethius was an important linguistic theoretician who contributed to the development of the theory of "modi significandi." The theory distinguishes between a word's lexical meaning (the thing it signifies) and its secondary semantic components (the ways in which it signifies the thing, "modi significandi"). Grammaticality depends exclusively on concord of "modi significandi." The "modi significandi" were supposed to be linguistic universals, although not having the same sort of morphological expression in all languages. The "modi significandi" reflect ways of understanding ("modi intelligendi") common to all humankind, and they in turn are based on real features of things ("modi essendi"). Boethius is best known for his theory of knowledge and science, which makes each science an autonomous system into which it is impossible to incorporate nonscientific facts known only through revelation. Thus, Christian beliefs about a temporal beginning of the world, about the existence of a first pair of human beings, or about the resurrection and the ultimate good of the individual are true, but it would be an error to try to assign them a place in scientific theories.

See also **Siger of Brabant**

Further Reading

Editions

Boethii Daci Opera = Corpus Philosophorum Danicorum Medii Aevi [CPhD], 4–9. The Danish Society of Language and Literature. Copenhagen: Gad, 1969–; contents of individual volumes: Pinborg, Joannes, and Henricus Roos, eds. *Modi significandi sive Quaestiones super Priscianum minorem.* CPhD, 4.1–2, 1969.

Sajó, Gèza, ed. *Quaestiones de generatione et corruptione—Quaestiones super libros Physicorum.* CPhD, 5.1–2, 1972–74.

Green-Pedersen, N.J., *et al.*, eds. *Topica—Opuscula.* CPhD, 6.1–2, 1976 [*Opuscula* = *De aeternitate mundi, De summo bono, De somniis*].

Fioravanti, Gianfranco, ed. *Quaestiones super IVm Meteorlogicorum.* CPhD, 8, 1979.

Ebbesen, S. *Sophismata.* CPhD, 9.

Translations

McDermott, A. Charlene Senape, trans. *Godfrey of Fontaine's Abridgement of Boethius of Dacia's Modi significandi sive Quaestiones super Priscianum maiorem.* History of Linguistic Science, ser. 3; Studies in the History of Linguistics, 22. Amsterdam: Benjamin, 1980.

Wippel, John F., trans. *Boethius of Dacia: On the Supreme Good, On the Eternity of the World, On Dreams.* Mediaeval Sources in Translation, 30. Toronto: Pontifical Institute of Mediaeval Studies; Leiden: Brill, 1987.

Bibliographies

Pinborg, Jan. "Zur Philosophie des Boethius de Dacia. Ein Ueberblick." *Studia Mediewistyczne* 15 (1974), 165–85; rpt. in Pinborg, Jan. *Medieval Semantics, Selected Studies on Medieval Logic and Grammar.* Ed. Sten Ebbesen, London: Variorum, 1984.

Green-Pedersen, N. J., in CPhD, 6.2, 1976 [see above].

Wippel, J. F. *Boethius de Dacia* [see above].

Literature

Jensen, Søren Skovgaard. "On the National Origin of the Philosopher Boetius de Dacia." "*Classica et Mediaevalia* 24 (1963), 232–41.

Pinborg, Jan. *Die Entwicklung der Sprachtheorie im Mittelalter.* Beiträge zur Geschichte der Philosophie und Theologie des Mittelalters, Texte und Untersuchungen, 42.2. Münster: Aschendorff; Copenhagen: Frost-Hansen, 1967; Pinborg, Jan. "Zur Philosophie" [see above].

STEN EBBESEN

BOHEMOND OF TARANTO (c. 1050 or 1058–1111)

Bohemond (or Bohemund; Bohemond I, prince of Antioch) was the eldest son of Robert Guiscard by Robert's first wife, Alberada. He developed in the shadow of his father's transformation from a Norman brigand-mercenary to the founder, as duke of Apulia, of a powerful new state in southern Italy. Bohemond emerged early as his father's chief lieutenant, notably during Robert Guiscard's daring invasion of the Byzantine empire in the early 1080s.

Bohemond was bypassed in the succession to his father's Apulian realm in favor of Roger Borsa, Robert's eldest son by his second wife. However, Bohemond forcibly extorted from his half-brother a territorial enclave that included Bari. Beyond that, he had inherited his father's grandiose dream of carving out a realm in the east at the expense of Byzantium. The great project that was to become the First Crusade was clearly a perfect opportunity for Bohemond. When Pope Urban II called for crusaders to champion Christendom against Islam, Bohemond was among the western barons who responded. He was an archetype of the self-seeking opportunist, hungry for a principality of his own in the east.

Bohemond set out in the autumn of 1096 for Constantinople, where the crusaders had agreed to meet. The Byzantines, who knew him all too well, inevitably suspected that he had ulterior motives; but Bohemond went out of his way to be deferential to Emperor Alexius I Comnenus (Alexios Komnenos). Pledging loyalty, he sought for himself the Byzantine post of *domestikos* of the east, and he became a leading negotiator between the crusaders and Alexius. He accepted Alexius's terms—an oath of fealty and a promise to surrender to the emperor any conquered cities or lands that had previously belonged to the empire—but Alexius had no illusions about Bohemond's sincerity or goals. As the expedition proceeded beyond the taking of Nicaea, Bohemond's self-interest became increasingly evident, and at a very early point he seems to have set his sights on the important Syrian city of Antioch, one particularly desired by Alexius. Bohemond was a leader in the prolonged, brutal siege of Antioch (1097–1098), and by clever manipulation he was able to secure its surrender to himself. He refused to share it with the other leaders, and—by now outspoken in his hostility to Alexius—he made it the center of his own principality. Bohemond remained in Antioch while the rest of the crusaders' forces went on to storm Jerusalem (1099).

Bohemond soon found himself beleaguered by both Byzantines and Turks; he was even briefly taken prisoner by the Turks, and he felt that his hold on Antioch was precarious. Convinced that Alexius was his supreme obstacle, Bohemond developed a characteristically daring scheme of attacking Byzantium directly, in his father's pattern. In 1104, he left behind his nephew and longtime deputy, Tancred, to hold Antioch, and secretly had himself conveyed back to Europe. (A story is told that, to avoid interception by Byzantine squadrons, Bohemond gave out the report that he was dead and then spent much of the voyage in a coffin, along with a dead chicken to add olfactory verisimilitude.) In Rome he convinced the gullible Pope Paschal II of Alexius's treachery and animosity to the crusade and was given a blessing to organize a force to attack Byzantine lands, disseminating vicious propaganda against Alexius in the process. Bohemond made a landing at Avlona in October 1107 but was quickly contained by Alexius at Dyracchium. Compelled to surrender, Bohemond signed a humiliating treaty with Alexius in September 1108, once again accepting Byzantine suzerainty over Antioch. Bohemond never returned to his hard-won principality; shortly after making this treaty, he died, perhaps in Bari. Tancred refused to recognize the treaty of 1108 and thus initiated an independent Norman rule in Antioch that would last for the next few generations.

Bohemond was buried in a curious tomb, of either Muslim or crusader design, still to be seen outside the *duomo* in the town of Canosa di Puglia. On its bronze door there is an inscription of fulsome praise to this restless but ultimately futile Norman prince.

See also **Urban II, Pope**

Further Reading

Anna Comnena. *Alexiad*, trans. Elizabeth A. S. Dawes. London, 1928.
——. *Alexiad*, trans. E. R. A. Sewter. London, 1969; Harmondsworth: Penguin, 1979.
Douglas, David C. *The Norman Achievement, 1050–1100*. Berkeley: University of California Press, 1969.
——. *The Norman Fate, 1100–1154*. Berkeley: University of California Press, 1976.
Rowe, J. G. "Paschal II, Bohemund of Antioch, and the Byzantine Empire." *Bulletin of the John Rylands Library*, 49, 1966–1967, pp. 165–202.
Runciman, Steven. *The First Crusade*. Cambridge: Cambridge University Press, 1980. (Abridged from Vol. 1 of his *History of the Crusades*, 1951.)
Yewdale, Ralph Bailey. *Bohemond I, Prince of Antioch*. Princeton, N.J.: Princeton University Press, 1924. (Reprint, Amsterdam, 1970.)

JOHN W. BARKER

BONAGIUNTA ORBICCIANI DEGLI AVERARDI (c. 1220–before 1300)

Bonagiunta, a poet from Lucca who preceded the *stil novo*, is a character in Dante's *Divine Comedy* (*Purgatorio*, 24). Bonagiunta was a judge and a notary; accordingly, in two authoritative manuscripts (Vatican 3793 and 3214) the poet is given the honorific *ser,* and his name is preserved in deeds drawn up between 1242 and 1257. Fewer than forty of his poems have survived: eleven *canzoni*, two "discords" (*descorts*, or disputes), five ballads, and some twenty sonnets. Three of the sonnets are addressed to other poets: one to Guinizzelli (d. 1276) and two to unidentified correspondents. Another two or three sonnets belong to a *tenzone*—a cycle of verses by several authors—initiated by the judge Gonnella Antelminelli with Bonagiunta and a certain Bonodico, all from Lucca. Bonagiunta's themes include, as might be expected, his changing moods (sorrow, hope, joy, disappointment) as an apprehensive lover, and praise of his lady. In some poems, as is also true of Guittone d'Arezzo (c. 1235–1294) and other Tuscan poets of the time, Bonagiunta touches on or develops moral topics: honor versus pleasure; wisdom and integrity versus foolishness; boasters; corrupt judges; how to deal with fortune; and so on.

To ascertain Bonagiunta's place in poetry, and to give him his due in the development of the Italian lyric, three crucial connections must be explored. How can we relate him to (1) the Sicilian school, (2) Guittone d'Arezzo, and (3) the *stil novo*? An adjunct to the third question is this: Why did Dante, in seeking a narrative catalyst to give himself an opportunity to proclaim and define his *dolce stil nuovo* (*Purgatorio*, 24:57), select Bonagiunta and not, as Contini (1960) wonders, Giacomo da Lentini or Guittone?

With regard to question 1, it is easy to reach agreement. Between the Sicilian school and Bonagiunta there is, in fact, a clear path of transfer and continuity; thus we have no trouble in granting, with Contini, that "apart from the very members of the School, Bonagiunta was the real transplanter of the Sicilian poetry to Tuscany."

However, as regards questions 2 and 3, Contini seems to go too far by loosening the connection between Bonagiunta and Guittone in an attempt to establish, instead, a more direct link between Bonagiunta and the poets of the *stil novo*; according to Contini, beneath the cumbersome superstructure of Guittone's *trobar clus* (hermetic style), Bonagiunta elaborated the Sicilian tradition and channeled it toward the results finally achieved by the Florentine *stil novo*. Marti (1973) has toned down this interpretation. *Bonagiuntismo* may have been the state of affairs to which Guittone was reacting in developing his own innovative, pithy writing; but Bonagiunta was no doubt attracted by the younger, more authoritative, and more charismatic Giuttone. Although Bonagiunta's own tendency was comparatively archaic and *leu* (free, open), he considered himself a staunch supporter of Guittone. This is revealed in the sonnet directed to Guinizzelli (*Voi, ch'avete mutata la mainera*, "You who have changed the manner"), where he harshly chides Guinizzelli for changing the style then gloriously in force: that is, Guittone's. In addition, Dante perceived—and condemned—Bonagiunta as a Guittonian, in *De vulgari eloquentia* (l.xiii.l) and also in a famous episode in *Purgatory*, 24 (although, we should note, *lato sensu*, i.e., without the benefit of a detailed stylistic analysis).

An even thornier question is whether Bonagiunta might be considered a forerunner or incubator of the *stil novo* (a problem which also arises, for instance, in trying to place Chiaro Davanzati). This question is especially difficult because we do not know when Bonagiunta died or, more important, when he stopped writing. He probably outlived Guinizzelli, but we have no idea how long he remained active as a poet in the last twenty years of the century. However, it is not very likely, given his advanced age, that the features of the *stil novo* which some readers discern in his verses were due to any influence exerted on him by the new school (especially Cavalcanti), as Francesco Novati was inclined to believe. Considering the continuity and the constraints of the lyrical tradition, one should be cautious in retrospectively applying the term *stil novo*, or even "stilnovistic," to lexical and metric combinations in the work of earlier poets. In such cases the real significance is to be found in the context, both literal and cultural.

For the episode in *Purgatory* 24, then, Dante would have thought of Bonagiunta for several reasons. For one thing, only through Bonagiunta could the lyrical reminiscence of Gentucca be introduced; for another, Dante certainly held Bonagiunta responsible for having blindly exalted Guittone's reputation (*Purgatory*, 26.124–126) over that of Guinizzelli, whom Dante considered his own poetic father. Bonagiunta had resented and objected to the novelty of Guinizzelli's "sweet style"; let him now joyfully acknowledge, in the unescapable dialectics of *contrappasso*, the messianic renewal that Dante was bringing about.

See also **Dante Alighieri; Guinizzelli, Guido**

Further Reading

Barolini, Teodolinda. *Dante's Poets: Textuality and Truth in the "Comedy."* Princeton, N.J.: Princeton University Press, 1984.

Contini, Gianfranco, ed. *Poeti del Duecento*, 2 vols. Milan-Naples: Ricciardi, 1960, Vol. 1, pp. 257–282; Vol. 2, p. 825.

De Sanctis, Francesco, and Gerolamo Lazzeri, eds. *Storia della letteratura italiana dai primi secoli agli albori del Trecento.* Milan: Hoepli, 1950, pp. 376, 396, 520–529.

Marti, Mario. "Orbicciani, Bonagiunta." In *Enciclopedia dantesca*. Rome: Istituto della Enciclopedia Italiana, 1973, Vol. 4, pp. 181–182.

Quaglio, Antonio Enzo. "I poeti siculo-toscani." In *La letteratura italiana: Storia e testi*, ed. Carlo Muscetta. Bari: Laterza, 1970, pp. 241–258.

Tartaro, Achille. "Guittone e i rimatori siculo-toscani." In *Storia della letteratura italiana*, ed. Emilio Cecchi and Natalino Sapegno. Milan: Garzanti, 1965, Vol. 1, pp. 381–389.

Zaccagnini, Guido, and Amos Parducci, eds. *Rimatori siculo-toscani del Dugento*. Series 1a: Pistoiesi, Lucchesi, Pisani. Bari: Laterza, 1915, pp. 47–93, 112–118.

RUGGERO STEFANINI

BONAVENTURA BERLINGHIERI
(fl. 1235–1244)

Bonaventura Berlinghieri painted a gabled altarpiece at Pescia depicting Saint Francis flanked by six scenes of Francis's life and miracles. This work, unusual because it is both signed and dated (1235), is a linchpin in the chronology of Italian painting: it clarifies developments in style as well as in Franciscan iconography; and current analyses have been aided by its restoration in 1982.

The format and style of this work suggest that Bonaventura was the most innovative of the three sons of the Lucchese painter Berlinghiero di Milanese. Documents place the activity of Berlinghiero and his sons—Bonaventura, Barone, and Marco—between 1228 and 1282, primarily at Lucca; a relatively recent attempt by Caleca (1981) to associate the Berlinghieri of Lucca with Volterra has not changed that localization. Although Marco was commissioned to illuminate manuscripts and both Marco and Bonaventura received commissions for frescoes, most of the extant works associated with the Berlinghieri are images of the Virgin and Child and the Passion painted on wooden panels. These works are in a distinctive style, in which the linear Italian Romanesque tradition is transformed by a new and intense familiarity with Byzantine images produced shortly before 1200. On the basis of the resulting angular, expressive facial types and the architectural and landscape settings, a large number of works have been associated with the Berlinghieri family. Several of these have been attributed to Bonaventura Berlinghieri and his followers, including a diptych originally from Lucca but now in the Uffizi in Florence, portions of a Crucifixion in Tereglio, and a group of works sometimes attributed to a separate "Oblate Cross Master." Together, these Lucchese painters had a profound impact on the style of painters in other Tuscan centers, especially Florence, such as the Bardi Saint Francis Master, the Bigallo Master, the Master of the Uffizi Crucifix 434, and Coppo di Marcovaldo.

See also **Francis of Assisi, Saint**

Further Reading

Angiola, Eloise M. "Nuovi documenti su Bonaventura e Marco di Berlinghiero." *Prospettiva*, 21, 1980, pp. 82–84.

Ayer, Elizabeth. "Thirteenth-Century Imagery in Transition: The Berlighiero Family in Lucca." Dissertation, Rutgers the State University, 1991.

Belting, Hans. *Likeness and Presence: A History of the Image before the Era of Art*, trans. Edmund Jephcott. Chicago, Ill.: University of Chicago Press, 1994.

Boskovits, Miklós. *The Origins of Florentine Painting 1100–1270*, trans. Robert Erich Wolf. A Critical and Historical Corpus of Florentine Painting, 1, Vol. 1, 1993.

Caleca, Antonino, and Mariagiulia Burresi. *Momenti dell'arte a Volterra: Volterra, Palazzo Minucci Solaini, Agosto-Settembre 1981*. Pisa: Pacini, 1981.

Capohvori e Restauri, Firenze, Palazzo Vecchio, 14 Dicembre 1986–26 Aprile 1987. Florence: Cantini Edizioni d'Arte, 1986.

Garrison, Edward B., Jr. "A Berlinghieresque Fresco in S. Stefano, Bologna." *Art Bulletin*, 28, 1946, pp. 211–225.

——. "Post-War Discoveries—III: The Madonna 'di sotto gli Organi.' " *Burlington Magazine*, 89, 1947, pp. 274–279.

——. *Italian Romanesque Panel Painting*. Florence: Olschki, 1949.

——. "Toward a New History of Early Lucchese Painting." *Art Bulletin*, 33, 1951, pp. 11–31.

——. *Studies in the History of Medieval Italian Painting*, 4 vols. Florence: L'Impronta, 1953–1963.

Gombrich, Ernst H. "Bonaventura Berlinghiero's Palmettes." *Journal of the Warburg and Courtauld Institutes*, 39, 1976, pp. 234–236.

Krüger, Klaus. *Der frühe Bildkunst des Franziskus in Italien: Gestaltund Funktionswandel des Tafelbildes im 13. und 14. Jahrhundert*. Berlin: Gebr. Mann Verlag, 1992.

Marcucci, Luisa. *Gallerie Nazionali di Firenze, I Dipinti toscani del secolo XIII, scuole bizantine e russe dal secolo XII al secolo XVIII*. Rome: Istituto Poligrafico dello Stato, 1959.

La pittura in Italia: Il Duecento e il Trecento. Milan: Edizioni Electa, 1985, Vol. 2, pp. 557–558.

Sandberg-Vavalà, Evelyn. *La croce dipinta italiana e l'iconografia della passione*. Verona: Casa Editrice Apollo, 1929.

Sinabaldi, Giulia, and Giulia Brunetti. *Pittura italiana del Duecento e Trecento, catalogo della Mostra Giottesca di Firenze del 1937*. Florence: Sansoni, 1943.

REBECCA W. CORRIE

BONAVENTURE, SAINT
(John of Fidanza; ca. 1217–74)

Bonaventure was born in Bagnoregio, near Viterbo, and sources say that he fought his well-to-do family to enter the Franciscan order; this he did in Paris, probably in 1243. Legend has it that as a child he was miraculously cured by St. Francis's intervention. He was educated in the Franciscan friary in Bagnoregio and moved to Paris for the arts course ca. 1234. He studied theology in the Franciscan school under Alexander of Hales, John of La Rochelle, William of Melitona, and Odo Rigaldus; his wide use of the Dominican Hugues de Saint-Cher suggests that he may have been Hugues's pupil as well. He was made regent master, probably in 1253, but formal acceptance for him and for Thomas Aquinas was delayed until October 1257 by the dispute between secular masters and the mendicants.

In February 1257, Bonaventure was made minister-general of the Franciscans, on the suggestion of John of Parma, who had resigned under pressure from Pope Alexander IV. His nomination suggests that the divide between the two wings of the order (Conventual and Spiritual) was not yet unbridgeable, since John was later characterized as a Spiritual and Bonaventure a Conventual. As a master, he composed a commentary on Peter Lombard's *Sententiae* (by far his longest and most systematic work) and biblical commentaries, as well as various theological "questions."

Bonaventure's accession to the minister-generalate effectively ended his academic career, but he continued to write devotional works. His writing is marked by a lucid latinity and deep devotion, qualities that he could also bring to academic argument. He combined academic discipline with fervent piety: for Bonaventure, more clearly than for any other scholastic theologian, the point of any theology was the building up of the life of faith and prayer. After a visit to La Verna, in Italy, in 1259, he began to write mystical texts of great influence; he had, in the Franciscan tradition, a particular devotion to the Passion.

During the 1260–70s, he worked to defend the order, which did not practice the absolute poverty of its founder, against charges of hypocrisy, especially by his *Apologia pauperum* (1270). His aim was to reinterpret Francis's Testament for subsequent generations. He was called the "second father of the order," because of his attempt to produce a theology of the Franciscan life. On the publication of his new *Life of Francis* (1266), all previous Lives were ordered to be destroyed, as had happened similarly when Humbert of Romans had produced his new *Life of Dominic* (1260). Bonaventure was made Cardinal-Bishop of Albano in 1273; he died unexpectedly at the Second Council of Lyon in 1274.

Bonaventure's theology is traditionally Augustinian. He is willing to make use of whatever tools come to hand, and to this end he was prepared to use Aristotle, but he held no specifically "Aristotelian" opinions. As well as Aristotle, his sources include Pseudo-Dionysius the Areopagite's *Celestial Hierarchy*, John Damascene, Boethius, and mystical "moderns" like Richard of Saint-Victor. For Bonaventure, theology was so far above philosophy in purpose that there could be no difficulty deciding between faith and reason. This is not to say that faith is irrational; in cases of apparent disagreement, faith is clearly acting out of a different rationality. He made careful distinction among the object of faith *per se*, which is God, who can be known directly (the "believable" or "credible" thing); the object of faith as known through the authority of Scripture; and the object of faith as investigated in theological inquiry. Theology's task is not superior to either revelation or Scripture, or undermining of it, but is intended to cast a new light—that of intelligibility—on the search for God.

Bonaventure, known as *Doctor devotus* and *Doctor seraphicus*, saw the Son of God as the pattern for life on earth, and his theology is particularly Trinitarian—indeed, he described many things in threes. For instance, he developed a theology-spirituality of the triple way: the purgative way, moved by the prick of conscience; the illuminative way, moved by the light of the intellect; and the unitive way, moved by the flame of wisdom.

The obviously devotional stance of Bonaventure's work has sometimes led to his being unfavorably compared with Thomas Aquinas; the two are better seen as complementary than as comparable.

See also **Alexander of Hales; Francis of Assisi; Hugues de Saint-Cher**

Further Reading

Bonaventure. *Opera omnia*, ed. PP. Collegii a S. Bonaventura. 11 vols. in 28. Ad claras Aquas (Quaracchi): Typographia Colegii S. Bonaventurae, 1882–1902.

——. *Sermones dominicales*, ed. Jacques-Guy Bougerol. Grottaferrata (Rome): Collegio S. Bonaventura, Padri Editori di Quaracchi, 1977.

——. *Saint Bonaventure's Disputed Questions on the Mystery of the Trinity*, trans. Zachary Hayes. St. Bonaventure: Franciscan Institute, St. Bonaventure University, 1979.

——. *The Works of St. Bonaventure*, trans. José de Vinck. 5 vols. Paterson: St. Anthony Guild, 1960–70.

——. *What Manner of Man? Sermons on Christ by St. Bonaventure*, trans. Zachary Hayes. Chicago: Franciscan Herald, 1974.

Bougerol, Jacques-Guy. *Introduction à Saint Bonaventure*. Paris: Vrin. 1988.

——. *Introduction to the Works of Bonaventure*, trans. José de Vinck. Paterson: St. Anthony Guild, 1964.

——. *St. Bonaventure et la sagesse chrétienne*. Paris: Seuil, 1963.

——. *Lexique saint Bona venture*. Paris: Éditions Franciscaines, 1969.

Chavero Blanco, Francisco de Asis, ed. *Bonaventuriana: miscellanea in onore di Jacques-Guy Bougerol*. 2 vols. Rome: Antonianum, 1988.

Cousins, Ewert H. *Bonaventure and the Coincidence of Opposites*. Chicago: Franciscan Herald, 1978.

S. Bonaventura 1274–1974. 5 vols. Grottaferrata (Rome): Collegio S. Bonaventura, 1973–74.

Hayes, Zachary. *The Hidden Center: Spirituality and Speculative Christology in St. Bonaventure*. New York: Paulist, 1981.

LESLEY J. SMITH

BONIFACE VIII, POPE
(c. 1235 or 1240–1303)

Pope Boniface VIII (Benedetto Caetani, sometimes Gaetani, r. 1294–1303) was born in Anagni, a hill town southeast of Rome that was his family's ancestral home. He is remembered as the last great monarch-pope, an ambitious amasser of power and wealth. He asserted the supremacy of papal authority in the power struggles attending the advent of the European nation-states—struggles in which he was an able player. However, he was defeated in his clash with the French king Philip IV (the Fair) and was tried posthumously. Often, it is from the record of these posthumous proceedings that historians and Boniface's biographers have gleaned details of his personal character; thus it is difficult to know how seriously to take the charge that Boniface was a heretic who openly denied the immortality of the soul and the sanctity of the eucharist. He did surely use his office to increase the wealth of the church and did openly declare that it was a logical impossibility for the pope to be guilty of simony. Dante, for one, begged to differ and proclaimed Boniface's imminent arrival among the simoniacs in *Inferno* 19.

The young Benedetto (Benedict) Caetani began his legal education and his ecclesiastical career at Todi and Spoleto in the 1260s; he gained valuable diplomatic experience as a papal legate in France and England. He was made a cardinal by Pope Martin IV in 1281. The following year, the uprising known as the Sicilian Vespers transferred control of Sicily from Charles I of Anjou, king of Naples (a papal fief), to Pedro III of Aragon. The struggle between Anjou and Aragon for the control of Sicily was to plague Boniface's entire tenure as pope.

The precise circumstances that led to Cardinal Benedict's accession to the papacy as Boniface VIII remain somewhat mysterious. After the death of Nicholas IV in 1292, the Colonna and Orsini factions in the College of Cardinals could not come to terms, and the conclave, removed to Perugia from malarial Rome, dragged on into the hot summer months of 1294. Benedict, who was now in his sixties and was intermittently unwell, with gout and kidney stones, rested in Viterbo and Sismano. He spent time in the company of a certain Parisian doctor with whom he discussed, rather casually, questions of faith and sexual morality. One witness reported having overheard Benedict say, "Sleeping with women or boys is no more a sin than rubbing your hands together." Meanwhile, the weary conclave finally agreed on an unlikely outsider, Pietro Morrone, a devout eremite of the Abruzzi who was an exponent of the fanatical asceticism that had been sweeping central Italy for a century. Pietro became Pope Celestine V and spent his entire his five-month papacy in Naples under the watch of Charles of Anjou, frustrating the Franciscan Spirituals who hoped to make Celestine their longawaited reformer, and overwhelmed by political demands he could not fathom. Celestine wanted to escape, and although it was unclear whether a pope could legally abdicate, Benedict assured him that abdication was both legal and appropriate. (One of the more wild-eyed chronicles has Benedict haunting Celestine at night, casting his voice into Celestine's cell through a tube and urging him to resign.) Celestine resigned on 13 December, and Benedict became Boniface VIII on the day before Christmas.

Boniface acted at once to reimpose papal authority by invalidating Celestine's appointments, which in any case had been rather arbitrary. During the first few years of his papacy, he intervened deftly in European affairs. By 1296, however, his tense relations with Philip the Fair and with Edward I of England had reached a crisis over the issue of taxation: did secular monarchs have the authority to tax the clergy? In the bull *Clericis laicos*, Boniface soundly forbade taxation of the clergy without the pope's approval. Philip responded by expelling Italian trading agents from France and outlawing the export of gold bullion. The scene was set for their final conflict.

In 1297, however, mere was a commotion closer to home. The Colonna, who were alarmed by the loss of their lands to the Caetani and Orsini under Boniface, at last openly challenged the legitimacy of his election. Boniface declared war, indeed a holy war, against the Colonna and their property, and by late 1298 he had the Colonna at his mercy: they had taken refuge in their mountaintop fortress at Palestrina. These events inform Dante's encounter in *Inferno* 27 with Guido da Montefeltro, a soldier turned Franciscan, an encounter in which the apparently penitent friar provides treacherous advice. In the end, Palestrina was razed, and the Colonna fled to France to bide their time.

Also in 1298, Boniface published an important compilation of canon law. In 1300, he declared the first jubilee. In 1301, he invited Philip's landless brother Charles of Valois to Italy, ostensibly to help him restore peace in Sicily—and in upstart Florence, where dangerous experiments in republican democracy had been under

way since the early 1290s and the aristocratic Black Guelfs had been banished from power. By November 1301, Charles had entered Florence, reinstalled the Black Guelfs, and taken what he could for himself; but no peace came of his efforts. The Black Guelfs immediately exiled the leading Whites, including Dante, whose disdain for Boniface as an emblem of ecclesiastical corruption marks the entire *Comedy*.

In the meantime, the tension with Philip had led to open conflict and defiance on both sides. In 1301, Boniface issued the letter *Ausculta fili* (*Listen Here, Son*), an unbridled indictment of Philip; and in November 1302 he issued the famous bull *Unam sanctam*. According to *Unam sanctam*, it is true that the world is ruled by two swords, temporal and spiritual, but the spiritual must forever guide and judge the temporal; and this must be taken on faith as divine revelation. In April 1303, Boniface recognized Albert of Hapsburg as Holy Roman emperor while reaffirming the absolute supremacy of the papacy in the bull *Patris aeterni*, in which the earlier military metaphors are replaced by astronomy: pope and emperor are, respectively, like the sun and moon, a greater source and a lesser, reflected light. Dante would redefine this traditional imagery in Book 3 of *Monarchia*, where both lights are declared to be equally dependent on God. In the same month that he issued *Patris aeterni*, Boniface founded the University of Rome.

Through the spring and summer of 1303, Philip the Fair held council with his ministers and the alienated Colonna and drew up formal charges against Boniface, denying the legitimacy of Boniface's rule and demanding that he stand trial. Boniface moved to excommunicate Philip. A contingent of men led by Sciarra Colonna and Philip's minister Guillaume de Nogaret laid siege to Boniface at Anagni and seized the pope during the first week of September. Boniface managed to escape after three days, but he was utterly undone by the episode. He died in Rome on 12 October.

See also **Celestine V, Pope; Dante Alighieri; Edward I, Philip IV the Fair**

Further Reading

Boase, T. S. R. *Boniface VIII*. London: Constable, 1933.

Bonifacio VIII e il suo tempo: Anno 1300 *il primo giubileo,* ed. Marina Righetti Tosti-Croce. Milan: Electa, 2000. (Catalog of exhibit in Palazzo Venezia, Rome, 12 April–16 July 2000.)

Chamberlin, E. R. "The Lord of Europe: Benedict Gaetani/Pope Boniface VIII (1294–1303)." In *The Bad Popes*. New York: Barnes and Noble, 1969, pp. 75–103.

DuPuy, Pierre. *Histoire du diffirend d'entre le pape Boniface VIII et Philippes le Bel, roy de France*. Paris: Cramoisy, 1655. (Reissue, Tucson, Ariz.: Audax, 1963.)

Ferrante, Joan M. "Boniface VIII, Pope." In *The Dante Encyclopedia*, ed. Richard Lansing. New York and London: Garland, 2000, pp. 122–124.

Kessler, Herbert L., and Johanna Zacharias. *Rome 1300: On the Path of the Pilgrim.* New Haven, Conn.: Yale University Press, 2000.

Oestreich, Thomas. "Pope Boniface VIII." *The Catholic Encyclopedia,* 1999. (Online edition: http://www.newadvent.org/cathen/02662a.htm.)

Tosti, Luigi. *Pope Boniface VIII and His Times,* trans. Eugene J. Donnelly. New York: Samuel R. Leland, 1933.

GARY P. CESTARO

BOPPE, MEISTER (fl. end of the 13th c.)

Boppe was a poet and composer best known for didactic lyrics. References to fellow poet Konrad von Würzburg (d. 1287) in an obituary prayer to King Rudolf of Habsburg (1273–1291) and to the margraves of Baden indicate that Boppe had composed his verses and music in southern Germany by the end of the thirteenth century. As for most of the didactic lyrical poets (*Sangspruchdichter*), however, there is no external documentary evidence of this. The famous Heidelberg University *Codex Manesse* attributes forty stanzas in eight different metrical and melodical forms (*Töne*) to him, but other manuscripts ascribe six of these *Töne* and seven of the strophes to other poets. The Jena manuscript, which gives Boppe the title *Meister* (master) preserves only the first *Ton,* later named *Hofton* (court verse form), with eighteen stanzas. A nine-strophical *Ave Maria* in the *Hofton* survives in a fourteenth-century Heidelberg manuscript. As Boppe ranks with a group of twelve famous old *Sangspruch* masters, more than two hundred further stanzas in the *Hofton* are recorded in *Meistersang* manuscripts of the fifteenth and sixteenth centuries. Boppe is commonly regarded as the composer of the *Hofton* and the author of the *Hofton* stanzas in the older manuscripts, with the exception of the religious *Ave Maria.* The stanzas of the other *Töne* not attributed to other poets may be his. The number of the *Meistersang* texts that are his work—and to what extent they are his work—remains uncertain.

Boppe's poems treat the common themes of the thirteenth-century didactic lyric (*Sangspruchdichtung*) in conventional ways. In the role of teacher and counselor, the poet gives instruction and advice to his courtly audience, praising secular chivalric ideals and female virtues as well as God and the Virgin Mary. While divine grace is the highest value in one stanza, earthly love's rewards outrank everything else in another, and in a satirical strophe money is the ultimate ideal. The poet laments his own poverty and extols decency, charity, and princely generosity, a merit particularly important for the wandering artists; he decries miserliness, self-praise, and unjustified eulogy. He has knowledge of the mysteries of Redemption, the dignity of the priesthood and of mankind, the preexistence of the Virgin and her identity as God's mercy, the contrasts between outer appearance and inner worth, good advice and false counsel. In the role of the minnesinger, he gives a satirical catalog of the lady's preposterous demands. Boppe's technical devices indicate considerable rhetorical skill. He repeatedly uses the traditional bestiary imagery to exemplify good and false behavior and has a special preference for cumulative enumerations, displayed by catalogs of countries and peoples, values and virtues, biblical *exempla* (examples), and series of parallel statements and rhetorical questions, often combined with anaphora.

See also **Konrad von Würzburg**

Further Reading

Alex, Heidrun. *Der Spruchdichter Boppe*: Edition, Übersetzung, -Kommentar. Tübingen: Niemeyer, 1998.

Brunner, Horst, and Burghart Wachinger, eds. *Repertorium der Sangsprüche und Meisterlieder des 12. bis 18. Jahrhunderts.* Vol. 3. Tübingen: Niemeyer, 1986, pp. 209–245.

Tolle, Georg. *Der Spruchdichter Boppe. Versuch einer kritischen Ausgabe seiner Dichtungen.* Sondershausen: Programm der fürstlichen Realschule, 1894.

GERT HÜBNER

BRAGI BODDASON (9th century)

Braggi Boddason (the Old), a Norwegian poet probably of the second half of the 9th century, is generally reckoned to be the earliest skald whose compositions have been preserved, although in fragmentary form. Details of his life are tentative, and several semimythological stories exist, linking him in one case with ancestors of settlers in Iceland (*Landnämabók,* S112, H86, M30; *Hálfs saga ok Hälfsrekka,* ch. 11; *Geirmundar Þattr heljarskinns,* ch. 2). *Skáldatal,* an Icelandic catalogue of poets and their patrons, names him as a court poet of Ragnarr loðbrók ("hairy-breeches"), Eysteinn beli ("belly"), and Bjǫrn at Haugi (*Edda Snorra Sturlusonar,* ch. 3, pp. 251–69). Snorri Sturluson also connected Bragi with Ragnarr loðbrók and attributed two groups of stanzas to a *Ragnarsdrápa,* a *drápa* or sequence of stanzas with a refrain, in honor of Ragnarr. Snorri quotes these stanzas in chs. 52 and 62 of *Skáldskaparmál* (Finnur Jónsson 1931: 134, 155; Faulkes 1987: 106, 123–4). Although Ragnarr was a hero of the Danes, recent scholarship indicates the probability of a Norwegian origin for this legendary Viking (Smyth 1977).

Bragi's *Ragnarsdrápa* is thought to have been a shield poem, which gave verbal representation to a set of pictures and mythological subjects painted on a leather-covered shield that the poet had received from his patron. The resulting poem was the skald's countergift to his lord. A similar context underlies Þjóðólfr of Hvin's *Haustlǫng.* In 1860, Gísli Brynjúlfsson proposed that such shields were divided into four fields and hence had four poetic subjects. Subsequent editorial arrangement of the hypothetical *Ragnarsdrápa* has followed this view, even though Snorri clearly admits only the stanzas mentioned above (3–7 and 8–12 in Finnur Jónsson's *Skjaldedigtning)* as part of this *drápa*. Following Finnur Jónsson's arrangement, *Ragnarsdrápa's* four subjects were the encounter between the heroes Hamðir and Sǫrli and the Gothic tyrant Jǫrmunrekkr (Ermanaric), also subject of the eddic poem *Hamðismál* (sts. 3–7); Hildr's incitement to battle of her father, Hǫgni, and her abductor, Heðinn (8–12); how Gefjon and her giant oxen won land from the Swedish king Gylfi (13); and a version of the god Þórr's fishing expedition to catch the World Serpent (14–19). Convention has also allocated to the *drápa* two half-stanza introductory verses, in the second of which the poet thanks the "son of Sigurðr" (Ragnarr's father is said to have been Sigurðr hringr ["ring"]) for the shield (1–2), and finishes off the *drápa* with a half-stanza (20) on the metamorphosis of the giant Þjazi's eyes into a pair of stars. Hence the *Ragnarsdrápa* we read in the standard editions is a scholarly reconstruction for which there is only partial authority in the work in which its component verses are to be found, Snorri Sturluson's *Edda* (*ca.* 1225).

Other medieval texts in which stanzas attributed to Bragi occur are MSS F (*Codex Frisianus*, AM 45 fol.), J (*Jöfraskinna*, AM 38 fol.), and K (AM 35 fol.) of *Heimskringla* (*Ynglinga saga*, ch. 5) for *Ragnarsdrápa* 13; the *Fourth Grammatical Treatise* (Ólsen 1884: 129) for *Ragnarsdrápa* 3; MSS of *Landnámabók, Hálfs saga* and *Geirmundar Þáttr* (for details see paragraph 1) for a *lausavísa* on the twins Geirmundr and Hámundr heljarskinn.

See also **Snorri Sturluson**

Further Reading

Editions

Björn Magnússon Ólsen, ed. *Den Tredje og Fjærde Grammatiske Afhandling i Snorres Edda Tilligemed de Grammatiske Afhandlingers Prolog og To Andre Tillæg.* Samfund til udgivelse af gammel nordisk litteratur, 12. Islands grammatiske litteratur i middelalderen 2. Copenhagen: Knudtzon, 1884 [for *Ragnarsdrápa* 3].

Finnur Jónsson, ed. *Den norsk-islandske skjaldedigtning.* Vols. 1A–2A (tekst efter håndskrifteme) and 1B–2B (rettet tekst). Copenhagen and Christiania [Oslo]: Gyldendal, 1912–15; rpt. Copenhagen: Rosenkilde & Bagger, 1967 (A) and 1973 (B)

Finnur Jónsson, ed. *Edda Snorra Sturlusonar.* Copenhagen: Gyldendal, 1931.

Jón Jóhannesson *et al.,* eds. *Sturlunga saga.* 2 vols. Reykjavik: Sturlunguútgafan, 1946 [for *Geirmundar Þáttr heljarskinns,*vol. 1, pp.5–11].

Bjarni Aðalbjamarson, ed. *Heimskringla.* 3 vols. Íslenzk fornrit, 26–8. Reykjavik: Hið íslenzka fornritafélag, 1941–51 [*Ragnarsdrápa* 13, vol. 1, p. 21].

Jakob Benediktsson, ed. *Íslendingabók. Landnámabók.* Íslenzk fornrit, 1. Reykjavik: Hið íslenzka fornritafélag, 1968 [for *lausavísa* on Geirmundr and Hámundr heljarskinn, p. 151].

Dronke, Ursula, ed. and trans. *The Poetic Edda. 1. Heroic Poems.* Oxford: Clarendon, 1969 [for *Ragnaradrápa* 3–6 and *Hamðismál,* pp. 204–14].

Clunies Ross, Margaret. "An Edition of the *Ragnarsdràpa* of Bragi Boddason." Diss. Oxford University, 1973

Turville-Petre, E. O. G. *Scaldic Poetry.* Oxford: Clarendon, 1976.

Frank, Roberta. *Old Norse Court Poetry*: The Dróttkvætt *Stanza.* Islandica, 42. Ithaca and London: Cornell University Press, 1978.

Seelow, Hubert, ed. *Hálfs saga ok Hálfsrekka.* Reykjavik: Stofnun Árna Magnússonar, 1981 [for *lausavísa* on Geirmundr and Hámundr heljarskinn].

Translations

Hollander, Lee M. *The Skalds: A Selection of Their Poems, With Introductions and Notes.* New York: American-Scandinavian Foundation, 1945; rpt. Ann Arbor: University of Michigan Press, 1968 [Bragi Boddason, pp. 25–37].

Faulkes, Anthony, trans. *SnorriSturluson. Edda.* Everyman Classics. London and Melbourne: Dent, 1987 [Bragi's verses pp. 7, 69, 72–4, 89, 95, 99, 105–6, 120, 123–4, 132, 142; see also Index of Names, p. 224].

Bibliographies

Hollander, Lee M. *A Bibliography of Skaldic Studies.* Copenhagen: Munksgaard, 1958.

Bekker-Nielsen, Hans. *Old Norse–Icelandic Studies: A Select Bibliography.* Toronto Medieval Bibliographies, 1. Toronto: University of Toronto Press, 1967.

Literature

Gísli Brynjúlfsson. "Brage den Gamles Kvad om Ragnar Lodbrogs Skjold." *Aarbøger for nordisk Oldkyndighed og Historie* (1860), 3–13.

Reichhardt, Konstantin. *Studien zu den Skalden des 9. und 10. Jahrhunderts.* Palaestra, 159. Leipzig: Mayer & Müller, 1928.

Finnur Jónsson. "Brage skjald." *Acta Philologica Scandinavica* 5 (1930–31), 237–86.

Vogt, W. H. "Bragis schild." *Acta Philologica Scandinavica* 5 (1930–31), 1–28.

Jón Jóhannesson. *Gerðir Landnámabókar.* Reykjavik: Félagsprentsmiðjan, 1941, pp. 165–70.

Lie, Hallvard. "Skaldestil-studier." *Maal og minne* (1952), 1–92; rpt. *Om Sagakunst og Skaldskap. Utvalgte Avhandlinger.* Øvre Ervik: Alvheim & Eide, 1982, pp. 109–200

Lie, Hallvard. "Billedbeskrivende dikt." *KLNM* 1 (1956), 542–5.

Lie, Hallvard. *"Natur"* og *"unatur"* i skaldekunsten. Avhandlinger utg. av Det norske Videnskaps-Akademie i Oslo, 2. Hist.-filos. Kl. No. 1. Oslo: Aschehoug, 1957; rpt. *Om Sagakunst og Skaldskap,* pp. 201–315.

Almqvist, Bo. *Norrön niddiktning. Traditionshistoriska studier i versmagi. 1. Nid mot furstar.* Nordiska texter och undersökningar, 21. Uppsala: Almqvist & Wiksell, 1965, pp. 28–34 [for analysis of exchange between Bragi and a troll-woman, as reported in *Snorra Edda,* in tradition of Icelandic *ákvæðaskáld* to whom supernatural powers were attributed].

Lie, Hallvard. *"Ragnarsdrápa."* *KLNM* 13 (1968), 647–9

Clunies Ross, Margaret. "Hildr's Ring: A Problem in the *Ragnarsdrápa,* Strophes 8–12." *Mediaeval Scandinavia* 6 (1973), 75–92.

Lindow, John. "The Two Skaldic Stanzas in Gylfaginning: Notes on Sources and Text History." *Arkiv för nordisk filologi* 92 (1977), 106–24 [on Bragi's Gefjon stanza].

Smyth, Alfred P. *Scandinavian Kings in the British Isles, 850–80.* Oxford: Oxford University Press, 1977.

Clunies Ross, Margaret. "The Myth of Gefjon and Gylfi and Its Function in *Snorra Edda* and *Heimskringla*." *Arkiv för nordisk filologi* 93 (1978), 149–65.

Clunies Ross, Margaret. "Style and Authorial Presence in Skaldic Mythological Poetry." *Saga-Book of the Viking Society* 20 (1981), 276–304; Lindow, John. "Narrative and the Nature of Skaldic Poetry." *Arkiv för nordisk filologi* 97 (1982), 94–121.

Kuhn, Hans. *Das Dróttkvætt.* Heidelberg: Winter, 1983 [esp. pp. 275–9].

Marold, Edith. *Kenningkunst. Ein Beitrag zu einer Poetik der Skaldendichtung.* Berlin and New York: de Gruyter, 1983 [esp. pp. 67–114].

Sørensen, Preben Meulengracht. "Thor's Fishing Expedition." In *Words and Objects: Towards a Dialogue Between Archaeology and History of Religion.* Ed. Gro Steinsland. The Institute for Comparative Research in Human Culture, B.71. Oslo: Norwegian University Press; Oxford and New York: Oxford University Press, 1986, pp. 257–78.

MARGARET CLUNIES ROSS

BRAILES, WILLIAM DE (fl.1230–60)

A 13th-century illuminator recorded in Oxford ca. 1230–60, de Brailes secured his memory—among many hundreds of unnamed illuminators—through his self-portraits, three of which survive in two manuscripts. From these, accompanied by the name "*w de brail*," his hand and his style are established. His style is found in a considerable corpus of manuscripts, some of which were evidently produced in Oxford. Documents show that in 13th-century Oxford there was an active community of book producers living in the streets surrounding St. Mary the Virgin. Among them, ca. 1230–60, was one William de Brailes. He achieved a certain prosperity, had a wife, Celena, and probably came from Brailes in Warwickshire. His identity is near certain.

Oxford in William's time was dominated by the developing university, creating a demand for books. The variety of manuscripts illuminated by William, or by the large number of hands associated with him, would have satisfied the demands of scholars, churchmen, and laity. Characteristically his manuscripts, often pocket-sized, are illustrated with many small historiated initials, creating a visual narrative to accompany the text. Even large manuscripts or full-page images are fragmented with foliage decoration to create multiple small spaces for illustration.

Filling, even spilling over, their restricted frames, William's figures convey the narrative with emphatic gesture, dynamic poses, and firmly focused eyes. Although he may use established iconography, it is filtered through his imagination and retold with new immediacy. Rarely does he use elaborate settings, although the essentials are clear—a mountain for Christ's temptation, steps for the child Mary to climb to the Temple—and costume is equally important in identifying his characters, as in the case of crowned kings, mitered bishops (or high priests), round-hatted Jews, or heavy-homed devils. De Brailes's style is not one of courtly elegance. It is a "literary" one, appropriate to the books of a university town.

Further Reading

Cockerell, Sydney Carlyle. *The Work of W. de Brailes.* Oxford: Roxburghe Club, 1930.

Donovan, Claire. *The de Brailes Hours: Shaping the Book of Hours in Thirteenth-Century Oxford.* London: British Library, 1991.

Morgan, Nigel. *Early Gothic Manuscripts (1) 1190–1250.* A Survey of Manuscripts Illuminated in the British Isles 4:1, ed. J.J.G. Alexander. London: Harvey Miller, 1982, p. 14 and nos. 68–74.

Pollard, G. "William de Brailes." *Bodleian Library Record* 5/4 (1955): 202–09.

Swarzenski, Hanns. "Unknown Bible Pictures by W. de Brailes and Some Notes on Early English Bible Illustrations." *Journal of the Walters Art Gallery* 1 (1938): 55–69.

CLAIRE M. DONOVAN

BRUNETTO LATINI (c. 1220–1294)

Brunetto was active in Florentine public life as a *notaio* (notary) or lawyer by 1254. In 1260, he was sent as ambassador by the Florentine commune to King Alfonso X el Sabio (the Wise) of Castile, with the aim of enlisting Alfonso—a Guelf—in the struggle against Manfred and the Ghibellines. Brunetto was returning from this embassy, according to his *Tesoretto* (verses 123–162), when he met at the Pass of Roncesvalles a student from Bologna who told him of the Guelfs' defeat at Montaperti (4 September 1260). Brunetto then spent six years of exile in France until the defeat and death of Manfred at Benevento (28 February 1266). During his exile Brunetto visited friars at Montpellier (*Tesoretto*, 2539–2545); wrote notarial letters at Paris (September 1263) and Bar-sur-Aube (April 1264); and composed his two most important didactical works: the prose *Livres dou trésor* (*Book of the Treasure*) in the Picardian dialect, and the verse *Tesoretto* (*Little Treasure*) in his native Tuscan. In France Brunetto also wrote his *Rettorica*, an Italian translation of and commentary on the first seventeen chapters of Cicero's *De inventione*. After returning to Florence, Brunetto held a series of important public offices and was frequently consulted by the Florentine government. He introduced the *stilus altus* (high style) of the imperial chancery into Florentine letters; he also continued his efforts toward public education by translating a number of Ciceronian orations into Italian and composing his *Sommetta*, a collection of letters for teaching *ars dictaminis*. Brunetto was married and was the father of a daughter and two sons. He was buried at Santa Maria Maggiore, Florence.

In both *Trésor* and *Tesoretto*, Brunetto strove for a compendium of diverse technical information, but any closer association that he may have intended for these works remains unclear. Since he decided to write in the vernacular, both works are aimed at a secular readership, although in different ways: in *Trésor* he transposes Latin learning into a flourishing Romance koine for popular use, whereas *Tesoretto* fosters Italian as a *vulgaris illustris* (refined vernacular). Brunetto followed the example of the *Roman de la Rose* (c. 1225–1230) of Guillaume de Lorris—predating the continuation of the *Roman* by Jean de Meun (Jean Chopinel, Jean de Meung, c. 1269–1278) and beginning an interest in this great allegory of love that would absorb four or five generations of Italian poets. This early italianization of the *Roman de la Rose* proved to be rough going: the narrator of *Tesoretto* repeatedly interrupts himself to lament that its heptasyllabic couplets impose constrictions on his burgeoning material.

Tesoretto opens with an adulatory dedication to an anonymous *valente segnore* (skillful lord), a man peerless in all the arts of peace and war, surpassing even the respective virtues of such figures as Solomon, Alexander, and Cicero. The narrative introduces the political turmoil that occasioned Brunetto's embassy to Alfonso the Wise; but then the student's calamitous news and his own exile cause his thoughts to turn inward, he loses his way in a forest, and the historic-biographical scene modulates into a visionary landscape. There his thoughts revive, and he observes the vast spectacle of Nature, a personification closely akin to figures in two other influential models for *Tesoretto*: Boethius's *Consolatio philosophiae* (*Consolation of Philosophy*) and Alanus de Insulis's *De planctu naturae* (*Lament of Nature*). Nature instructs Brunetto in the history and metaphysics of creation, in human psychology and physiognomy, and in astronomy and geography. Carrying Nature's *insegna* (banner) to guard against evil, Brunetto moves from cosmology to ethics: he proceeds to the court of the empress Virtue, who, with her four daughter-queens, is encircled by magnates and scholars. He overhears the practical advice—mostly concerning interrelations of honor and finance—given to a knight by Larghezza (Largesse), Cortesia (Courtesy), and Prodeçça (Prowess, who counsels the knight to hire a lawyer before opting to avenge a tort bodily). The narrator then decides to seek Fortune, parting from the knight and going to the right along a forking road to arrive at a fair meadow, the Kingdom of Love. There follows an excursus on the psychology of pleasure until the narrator, exasperatingly, falls subject to Cupid's power; suddenly, however, he sees Ovid, who teaches him self-mastery in matters of love. He next journeys to the friars at Montpellier, where

Tesoretto closes on a note of penitent introspection and reopens (verse 2427) in the *modus dicendi* (style) of a personal letter. Now acutely conscious of the ambiguity of this world, and of its characteristically slippery language, Brunetto is disposed to ask his *fino amico caro* (dear friend): *Non sai tu ke lo mondo/Si dovria dir "non mondo"?* (2457–2458, "Don't you know that the world/Itself should be called impure?"). The glorious personages invoked in the dedication are now seen to have been vanquished by death, and Brunetto's previous investment in fame is retracted through an exposition of the seven deadly sins, with pride foremost. Brunetto is then sufficiently penitent to take up his journey to the seven liberal arts, forgoing his search for Fortune. Finally he finds himself on Mount Olympus, where he meets Ptolemy; the poem breaks off (2944) just as Ptolemy is about to respond to a question on the interlinking of the four elements.

Tesoretto has recently been characterized as an Ovidian "art and remedy of fame"; be that as it may, Dante Alighieri evidently found Brunetto himself in need of therapy. The hunger for knowledge that inspired *Trésor* and impels Brunetto through *Tesoretto* informs—more or less directly—the controversial depiction in Canto 15 in Dante's *Inferno*, where Brunetto appears among the sodomites, bitterly cursing the Florentines for not overcoming their savage origins. Dante's Brunetto believes that the published treasure of his learning (*mio Tesoro*) can effect a kind of worldly immortality, and Dante honors him for teaching *come l'uom s'etterna* ("how man makes himself immortal," 85). However, it remains to be answered why Dante damned his Brunetto, his former teacher, to this part of hell. The grammar teacher as pederast was, often, little more than a common trope; thus critics have been skeptical about the idea that Dante was imputing homosexuality to Brunetto—either they deny the notion (for which, in fact, there is no evidence) or they contextualize it, correctly identifying the medieval use of "sodomy" as connoting various forms of behavior, sexual or not, that signify violence done to nature. In this sense, Dante could also be implying that Brunetto betrayed his heritage by seeking renown through his French writings and thereby committing an unnatural act against his mother tongue (cf. *Convivio*, 1:10–13).

Tesoretto survives in sixteen manuscripts. Its influence, though considerable, was confined mostly to *Trecento* Italy. Boccaccio was sufficiently inspired by it to extend its general enterprise in his *Amorosa visione*, adapting French narrative models to Italian conditions for expressly didactic purposes.

See also **Alain de Lille; Alfonso X, El Sabio, King of Castile and León; Dante Alighieri; Guillaume de Lorris**

Further Reading

Armour, Peter. "Inferno XV." *Lectura Dantis*, 6 (suppl.), 1990, pp. 189–208.

Brunetto Latini. *Il tesoretto*, ed. and trans. Julia Bolton Holloway. New York: Garland, 1981.

———. *The Book of the Treasure (Li livres dou trésor)*, trans. Paul Barrette and Spurgeon Baldwin. New York: Garland, 1993.

Carmody, Francis J., ed. *Li Livres dou Trésor de Brunetto Latini.* Berkeley: University of California Press, 1947.

Ceva, Bianca. *Brunetto Latini: L'uomo e l'opera.* Milan: Ricciardi, 1965.

Holloway, Julia Bolton. ed. *Brunetto Latini: An Analytic Bibliography.* London: Grant and Cutler, 1986.

Jauss, Hans Robert. "Brunetto Latini als allegorischer Dichter." In *Formenwandel: Festschrift zum 65. Geburtstag von Paul Böckmann.* Hamburg: Hoffmann und Campe, 1964, pp. 47–92.

Kay, Richard. *Dante's Swift and Strong: Essays on Inferno XV.* Lawrence: Regents Press of Kansas, 1978.

Wallace, David. "Chaucer and the European Rose." *Studies in the Age of Chaucer, Proceedings*, 1, 1984, pp. 61–67.

———. "Brunetto Latini." In *Medieval France: An Encyclopedia*, ed. William W. Kibler and Grover A. Zinn. New York: Garland, 1995, pp. 151–152.

WILLIAM MARVIN AND DAVID WALLACE

BUONCOMPAGNO DA SIGNA
(c. 1165–c. 1240)

Together with Bene da Firenze and Guido Faba, Buoncompagno (or Boncompagno) was among the leading representatives of the Bolognese school of the rhetorical *ars dictaminis* (art of prose composition) during its heyday in the thirteenth century, and of these three he was by far the most versatile and colorful. He was born in Signa, near Florence, sometime between 1165 and 1175. He began his studies in Florence and probably completed them in Bologna. By 1194, he had begun his career in Bologna as a teacher (*magister*) of rhetoric; eventually he became the preeminent doctor of that discipline, which served largely as a propaedeutic to the study of law. (At the time, law predominated in the university at Bologna.) After 1215, he worked in Venice, Reggio, and Padua; he returned to Bologna by 1235, but in 1240 we find him in Florence. The chronicler Salimbene of Parma also reports that Buoncompagno tried, unsuccessfully, to obtain an appointment at the papal curia in Rome in 1240. Buoncompagno died, apparently in poverty, in the hospital of San Giovanni Evangelista in Florence.

Buoncompagno's writings centered on *ars dictaminis*, and his most influential work in this genre is the *Rhetorica antiqua*, or *Ancient Rhetoric*, also known as *Boncompagnus* (1215, revised 1226). This is primarily a vast collection of sample letters, arranged according to the social positions of writers and recipients, and covering a wide variety of situations from students' requests for money from home to correspondence with popes and emperors. It had been preceded by smaller works in the genre. *V tabule salutationum (Five Catalogs of Salutations,* c. 1194) gave a systematic overview of epistolary greetings, to which *X tabule (Ten Catalogs)* added instructions, now lost, for composing letters, privileges, orations, and wills. *Tractatus virtutum (Treatise on Virtues,* c. 1197) discussed virtues and vices of style. *Notule auree (Golden Notes,* c. 1197) provided suggestions for openings of letters, a subject revisited in *Breviloquium (Summary,* c. 1203). *Palma* (c. 1198) gave general rules for the main parts of a letter—salutation, narration, and petition—as well as for some secondary parts, such as the introduction (*exordium*), appeal for goodwill (*captatio benevolentiae*), and conclusion; it also discussed prose style. *Ysagoge* (1204) provided systematic instruction on salutations, the parts of the letter, and introductions. *Rota veneris* (before 1215) was a collection of sample exchanges of love letters, i.e., letters for initiating, maintaining, and ending amorous relationships; it thus was part of a tradition of *ars amatoria* exemplified by Ovid and Andreas Capellanus. In *Rota veneris*, Buoncompagno in effect constructed satirical (epistolary) *novellae*, anticipating aspects of the narrative art of Giovanni Boccaccio.

Buoncompagno's interest in prose composition extended beyond letters to various types of legal documents; thus he included within *ars dictaminis* elements of *ars notaria*, which received particular attention in the legally-oriented professional climate of Bologna. He published brief works on the writing of privileges and confirmations (*Oliva,* 1199), statutes (*Cedrus,* 1201), and wills (*Mirra,* after 1201).

While Buoncompagno's work reflects a general shift toward written composition in medieval rhetorical studies, he did not entirely neglect the traditional focus of the discipline: oratory. His historical work on the siege of Ancona (c. 1172), *Liber de obsidione Ancone* (written between 1198 and 1200), echoes the rhetorical traditions of classical historiography both in its emphasis on the moral lessons of history (in this case the encouragement of the heroic defense of Italian liberties against a foreign oppressor) and in its inclusion of several orations during the course of the narrative. Moreover, Buoncompagno's second major treatise, *Rhetorica novissima* (1235), was devoted to training advocates in rhetoric for their oral pleadings; it represented an attempt (unsuccessful) to replace classical works such as Cicero's *De inventione* and *Rhetorica ad Herennium*, which continued to be used for such instruction in the Middle Ages. *Rhetorica novissima* also includes brief remarks on the conduct of negotiations and popular assemblies.

Rivalry with Cicero is also a theme of Buoncompagno's two philosophical tracts: *Liber de amicitia (Book of Friendship,* c. 1204) and *Libellus de malo senectutis et senii (Little Book on the Evils of Old Age and Decline,* c. 1240). In *Liber de amicitia*, Buoncompagno distinguishes twenty-six types of friends; since many of them are less than admirable, he is here undercutting more uplifting works such as Cicero's *De amicitia. Libellus de malo senectutis et senii,* Buoncompagno's pessimistic last work, is based on his sad experience of his own decline; here, then, he is undermining Cicero's paean to the blessings of old age, *De senectute.*

Many of the characteristics of Buoncompagno's writing that make it interesting to the modern reader—such as his lively flights of narrative fancy, his pervasive sense of irony and satire, his fondness for quirky digressions into obscure erudition, and his quarrelsome insistence on his originality—allow a strong individuality to emerge from his work. However, these same traits limited its practical impact in his own time, compared with the more mundane efforts of his less colorful contemporaries. Nevertheless, Buoncompagno's advocacy of a more direct and less artificial style of letter writing, in contrast to the classicizing and ornate approach favored by the Orléans school of *dictamen,* ultimately carried the day.

See also **Boccaccio, Giovanni**

Further Reading

Editions and Translations

"Boncompagnus." In *Testi riguardanti la vita degli studenti a Bologna nel sec. XIII (dal Boncompagnus, lib. 1),* ed. Virgilio Pini. Testi per Esercitazioni Accademiche, 6. Bologna: Biblioteca di Quadrivium, 1968. (Excerpts.)

Breviloquium, ed. Giuseppe Vecchi. Bologna, 1954.

"Cedrus" and "Boncompagnus (or Bonconpagnus or Rhetorica antiqua)." In *Briefsteller und formelbücher des eilften bis vierzehnten jahrhunderts,* ed. Ludwig, Rockinger. New York: Burt Franklin, 1961, Vol. 1, pp. 121–127, 128–174. (Reprint of 1863–1864 ed.; *Cedrus,* complete; *Boncompagnus,* excerpts.)

Libellus de malo senectutis et senii, ed. F. Novati. Rendiconti della Regia Accademia dei Lincei, Classe di Science Morale, Series 5(1), 1892, pp. 50–59.

Liber de amicitia, ed. S. Nathan. Miscellanea di Letteratura del Medio Evo. Rome, 1909, Vol. 3, pp. 46–88.

Liber de obsidione Ancone, ed. Giosuè Carducci et al. In *Rerum Italicarum Scriptores,* 2nd ed., Giulio C. Zimolo. Bologna: Zanichelli, 1937, Vol. 6, part 3, pp. 3–55.

"Palma." In Carl Sutter, *Aus Leben und Schriften des Magisters Boncompagno: Ein Beitrag zur italienischen Kulturgeschichte im dreizehnten Jahrhundert.* Freiburg im Breisgau: Mohr, 1894, pp. 105–127.

"Rhetorica novissvma." In *Bibliotheca iuridica medii aevi: Script anecdota glossatorum,* ed. Augusto Gaudenzi. Bononiae (Bologna): P. Virano, 1892, Vol. 2, pp. 249–297.

Rota veneris, ed. Friedrich Baethgen. Rome, 1927.

Rota veneris, ed. Paolo Garbini. Rome: Salerno, 1996.

Rota veneris: A facsimile Reproduction of the Strassburg Incunabulum, ed. and trans. Josef Purkart. Delmar, N.Y.: Scholars' Facsimiles and Reprints, 1975.

V tabule salutationum. In Giulietta Voltolina, "Lo scambio epistolare nella società medioevale attraverso l'opera inedita di un *magister* dell'Universita di Bologna: Boncompagno da

Signa." *Rivista di Cultura Classics e Medioevale,* 30, 1988, pp. 49–55.

Critical Studies

Gaudenzi, Augusto. "Sulla cronologia delle opere dei dettatori da Buoncompagno a Bene di Lucca." *Bulletino dell'Istituto Storico Italiano,* 14, 1895, pp. 85–174. (For Buoncompagno, see pp. 86–118.)

Purkart, Josef. "Boncompagno of Signa and the Rhetoric of Love." In *Medieval Eloquence: Studies in the Theory and Practice of Medieval Rhetoric,* ed. James J. Murphy. Berkeley: University of California Press, 1978, pp. 319–331.

Sutter, Carl. *Aus Leben und Schriften des Magisters Boncompagno: Ein Beitrag zur italienischen Kulturgeschichte im dreizehnten Jahrhundert.* Freiburg im Breisgau: Mohr, 1894.

Tunberg, Terence O. "What Is Boncompagno's 'Newest Rhetoric'?" *Traditio,* 42, 1986, pp. 299–334.

Voltolina, Giulietta. "Lo scambio epistolare nella società medioevale attraverso l'opera inedita di un *magister* dell'Università di Bologna: Boncompagno da Signa." *Rivista di Cultura Classica e Medioevale,* 30, 1988, pp. 45–55.

Witt, Ronald G. "Boncompagno and the Defense of Rhetoric." *Journal of Medieval and Renaissance Studies,* 16(1), 1986, pp. 1–31.

HANNS HOHMANN

BURCHARD OF MOUNT SION (fl. 1280)

German Dominican, pilgrim to the Holy Land and author of a travel narrative, *Descriptio Terrae Sanctae,* the first systematic description of the portion of Palestine west of the Jordan.

Nothing is known about Burchard's origins or life except that he joined the Dominican convent at Magdeburg and by 1280 had undertaken his pilgrimage. Burchard stayed in Acre for some time and was connected with the Dominican convent of Mount Sion, from which his name is derived.

In 1283, Burchard wrote his travelogue, entitled *Descriptio Terrae Sanctae,* based on his recollections of the Christian holy sites he visited, of the topography, flora, and fauna, and of the sociopolitical conditions of the Holy Land, with a particular emphasis on Jerusalem.

He was an excellent observer, critical and empirical by nature; he often challenged statements made by previous authors no matter how authoritative, if their accounts were contradicted by his own observations. For example, during his visit on Mount Gilboa, he experienced a heavy rain, despite the account of King David's curse "neither let there be rain upon you" given in the magnificent passage in II Samuel 1:21; thus he challenged the interpretation of the biblical text. He also showed a very early interest in biblical archaeology. Having been aware of the historical evolution that had caused the destruction of many early Christian sites in Palestine, he recommended digging through the strata of ruins in order to reach the original holy places.

Burchard's description of Palestinian society is an important record of the ethno-social conditions of the region in the last generation of the Crusader presence. Among the Eastern Christian communities there, he praised the Armenians for their piety and vehemently criticized the Crusaders for their behavior, prophesying the loss of the Holy Land to Christendom "due to their sins."

Further Reading

Burchard of Mount Sion. *Descriptio Terrae Sanctae.* Ed. C.J.J. Laurent. Leipzig: Akademie Verlag, 1864.

Grabois, Aryeh. "Christian Pilgrims in the Thirteenth Century and the Latin Kingdom of Jerusalem: Burchard of Mount Sion." In *Outremer: Studies in the History of the Crusading Kingdom of Jerusalem Presented to Joshua Prawer.* Ed. B.Z. Kedar et al. Jerusalem: Yad Izhak Ben-Zvi, 1982, pp. 285–296.

ARYEH GRABOIS

BUSNOYS, ANTOINE
(Busnois; ca. 1430–1492)

French composer in the service of the Burgundian court. His works, of which three-voice chansons are most numerous, typify the Franco-Burgundian style in the third quarter of the 15th century.

Busnoys's name indicates that he or his family came from Busne (Pas-de-Calais), a town in northeastern France. Nothing is known of his early life and education, but in 1461 he was recorded as a chaplain at Saint-Gatien in Tours, at which time he was involved in an attack on a priest and was excommunicated. He did not remain in disgrace for long, since he soon became a singer and minor cleric at the royal abbey of Saint-Martin in Tours and in April 1465 was promoted from the position of choir clerk to subdeacon there. At Tours, he was a colleague and perhaps a student of the famous composer Johannes Ockeghem, master of the French royal chapel and treasurer of the abbey of Saint-Martin. In September 1465, Busnoys sought and received the post of master of the choirboys at Saint-Hilaire-le-Grand, Poitiers, which he held until July 1466.

In his motet *In hydraulis*, which pays homage to Ockeghem, Busnoys describes himself as "unworthy musician of the illustrious count of Charolais," referring to Charles the Bold, son of Philip the Good, duke in June 1467, Busnoys was listed as a singer in Charles's private service in March 1467, and he continued in that position when Charles succeeded his father as duke in June 1467. Busnoys was officially admitted to the ducal chapel in 1471 and, with other members of the chapel, followed Charles on most of his military campaigns, but probably not the last, the disastrous battle at Nancy in 1477, at which Charles was killed.

After Charles's death, Busnoys served his daughter,

Marie de Bourgogne, and her consort, Maximilian of Austria, whom she married in 1478. He remained a member of the Habsburg-Burgundian chapel in the Netherlands until it was temporarily disbanded in 1483 after Marie's death. He is listed in court documents of that time as a "priest-chaplain."

Busnoys's subsequent activities are uncertain, but they may have included a visit to Italy, since some works with Italian texts are attributed to him and his music was widely disseminated there. At the time of his death in 1492, he was choirmaster at Saint-Sauveur in Bruges.

Busnoys's reputation as a composer during his later years and after his death was exceeded among his contemporaries only by that of Ockeghem. The theorist Johannes Tinctoris dedicated his treatise on the modes (1476) jointly to Ockeghem and Busnoys, and as late as 1529 Pietro Aron called him "a great man and an excellent musician."

Busnoys was also an outstanding poet. A friend of Jean Molinet, with whom he exchanged poems, he undoubtedly wrote many of the texts he set to music, in the tradition of such earlier poet-musicians as Adam de la Halle and Guillaume de Machaut. His works include two Masses for four voices (*L'homme armé, O crux lignum*), a Credo, a Magnificat, eight motets (mostly four-voice), two hymns, and some seventy-five secular pieces, almost all French rondeaux and virelais. His music is characterized by its triadic sonority, strong harmonic progressions, clear structure, and extensive use of imitation, securing for him a central position in the evolution of musical style from Dufay to Josquin.

See also **Adam de la Halle; Machaut, Guillaume de; Ockeghem, Johannes**

Further Reading

Busnoys, Antoine. *Collected Works.* New York: Broude Trust, 1990. Parts 2 and 3: The Latin-Texted Works, ed. Richard Taruskin.

Higgins, Paula M. "Antoine Busnois and Musical Culture in Late Fifteenth-Century France and Burgundy." Diss. Princeton University, 1987.

——. "*In hydraulis* Revisited: New Light on the Career of Antoine Busnois." *Journal of the American Musicological Society* 39 (1986): 36–86.

Perkins, Leeman L. "The *L'homme armé* Masses of Busnoys and Ockeghem: A Comparison." *Journal of Musicology* 3 (1984): 363–96.

Taruskin, Richard. "Antoine Busnoys and the *L'homme armé* Tradition." *Journal of the American Musicological Society* 39 (1986): 255–93.

MARTIN PICKER

BYRHTFERTH (fl. 985–1011)

Priest and monk of the Abbey of Ramsey, one of the most learned Englishmen of his time, and a student of Abbo of Fleury during Abbo's visit to England in 985–87. Byrhtferth's varied literary career appears to have begun shortly after the departure of that great scholar. His works fall into three genres: computistical, hagiographical, and historical.

Computus

Computus (OE *gerim*, *gerimcræft*) is the science of computation as it relates to the ecclesiastical calendar. The word can also be used of any collection of short texts on that science; these generally contained a calendar accompanied by tables and instructions for performing such tasks as finding the moon's age and calculating the dates of movable feasts.

The earliest of the datable works associated with Byrhtferth is a compilation of materials on computus. Of the three copies of this compilation all are incomplete, and two were evidently revised or augmented at later periods. The version that seems closest to Byrhtferth's is in Oxford, St. John's College 17, a large and elegant manuscript written around 1110–11 at the nearby Abbey of Thorney. This manuscript contains, among other items, several computistical works by Bede and Helperic and a computus, all accompanied by extensive marginal glosses and introduced by a Latin *Epilogus* ("preface") by Byrhtferth. Several passages in the computus and glosses date the compilation (leaving aside those items that postdate Byrhtferth) to the years 988–96. Apart from the *Epilogus* the only item in the compilation attributed to Byrhtferth is a full-page diagram illustrating the harmony of the universe, and suggesting correspondences among cosmological, numerological, and physiological aspects of the world. Though other, minor items in St. John's 17 may well be by Byrhtferth, their authorship cannot be proved; nor can it be proved beyond doubt that he was responsible for the compilation as a whole. But the date of the compilation, the presence in it of the *Epilogus* and diagram, and its close association with the *Enchiridion*, discussed below, make it likely that Byrhtferth built it up from a smaller compilation left behind at Ramsey by his teacher Abbo.

Byrhtferth's *Enchiridion* (also called his *Manual*), preserved in a single manuscript, Bodl. Ashmole 328, can be dated from internal evidence to the year 1011. Written in Latin and OE, it treats a variety of subjects; however, the largest part of it is a guide to the use of the computus. The first three of the four books of the *Enchiridion* take the student step by step through a computus evidently similar to the one in St. John's 17, introducing its tables and the calendar with explanations drawn largely from Helperic, Hrabanus Maurus, and Bede. Byrhtferth frequently digresses from the computus to touch on matters as diverse as the organization of the universe, elision of syllables in Latin verse, and rhetorical figures and diacritics. Book Four of the *Enchiridion* is a clearly presented Latin treatise on number symbolism, the fullest statement anywhere in Byrhtferth's writings of his belief that the divine order of the universe can be perceived through the study of numbers; it is also an excellent general source for the modern student interested in medieval number symbolism.

The last of Byrhtferth's works on computus is an unsigned fragment of an OE text preserved in BL Cotton Caligula A.xv, fols. 142v–143r; his authorship of the fragment is suggested by its stylistic similarity to the OE of the *Enchiridion*.

Hagiography

Two Latin saints' lives have been attributed to Byrhtferth on the basis of their stylistic affinity with the Latin of his signed works, the *Epilogus* and *Enchiridion*. These works, the *Life of St. Oswald* and the *Life of St. Ecgwine*, are preserved together in a single manuscript, BL Cotton Nero E.i, a large passional to which they were added in the last half of the 11th century. Both the original passional and the additions were written at Worcester.

The *Life of St. Oswald*, written between 996 and 1005, details the career of the bishop of Worcester and archbishop of York who, with Dunstan and Æthelwold, was one of the leaders of the Benedictine Reform of the 10th century; Byrhtferth's work is considered the most important source for his life. The *Life* is also cited as a historical source for the murder of King Edward in 978 and, more famously, for the Battle of Maldon in 991. However, the *Life* tells us little about the latter two incidents that we cannot learn from other sources, and historians have at times shown impatience with its lack of circumstantial detail—forgetting, perhaps, that hagiographers, unlike chroniclers, were interested less in events themselves than in their theological significance.

The danger of using saints' lives as historical sources is perhaps nowhere better illustrated than in Byrhtferth's *Life of St. Ecgwine*, written after the year 1000, evidently at the request of the monks of Evesham, the monastery that Ecgwine, as bishop of Worcester, had founded around the beginning of the 8th century. While Byrhtferth could draw on a wealth of documentary evidence, eyewitness report, and personal recollection in writing about St. Oswald, with Ecgwine he had no documents beyond a spurious charter and an irrelevant letter; all other evidence was filtered through some two centuries of oral tradition. It is no surprise, then, that Ecgwine emerges as an utterly conventional saint and that parallels for the incidents of his life can generally be found in the lives of other, equally conventional saints.

History

That Byrhtferth was responsible for the early sections (up to 887) of the *Historia regum* (*History of the Kings*) attributed to the 12th-century writer Simeon of Durham is suggested by the stylistic affinity of those sections with Byrhtferth's other works. Byrhtferth's work is diverse and might be better characterized as a "historical miscellany" than as a history. It contains the following sections: 1) legends of Kentish saints; 2) lists of Northumbrian kings; 3) material based mainly on Bede's *Historia abbatum*; 4) a chronicle covering the years 732–802; 5) a chronicle covering the years 849–87, based mainly on Asser's *Life of King Alfred*.

Like Byrhtferth's other Latin works the *Historia regum* is written in bombastic style, much loved in the 10th century, that modern critics call "hermeneutic." Like all of his works it betrays his unusual interest in computus, in numerology, and in the figural interpretation of biblical history and the material world—sometimes introducing such topics in places that seem to us inappropriate. Indeed one of the most prominent characteristics of Byrhtferth's style is his tendency to digress suddenly, for reasons that are not always apparent at first glance.

The student should be aware that some older scholars attributed to Byrhtferth an extensive set of glosses on Bede's scientific works, a life of St. Dunstan, and two works entitled *De principiis mathematicis* and *De institutione monachorum*. More recent scholarship has shown that Byrhtferth had nothing to do with the saint's life or the glosses on Bede, and it is likely that the other two works never existed.

See also **Bede the Venerable; Dunstan of Canterbury; Isidore of Seville, Saint**

Further Reading

Primary Sources

Many of the older editions below are unreliable; new editions are in progress: Arnold, T, ed. *Symeonis monachi opera omnia*. Rolls Series 75. 2 vols. London: Longmans, 1882–85, 2:3–91, except for interpolations at pp. 32–38 and 47–50 [*Historia regum*].

Baker, Peter S., and Michael Lapidge, eds. *Byrhtferth's Enchiridion*. EETS s.s. 15. London: Oxford University Press, 1995

Forsey, G.F., ed. and trans. "Byrhtferth's Preface." *Speculum* 3 (1928): 505–22.

Giles, J.A, ed. *Vita quorundam Anglo-Saxonum*. London: Caxton Society, 1854, pp. 349–96. Repr. New York: Burt Franklin, 1967 [*Life of St. Ecgwine*].

Raine, J., ed. *Historians of the Church of York*. Rolls Series 71.3 vols. London: Eyre & Spottiswoode, 1879, 1:399–475 [*Life of St. Oswald*].

Secondary Sources

Baker, Peter S. "The Old English Canon of Byrhtferth of Ramsey." *Speculum* 55 (1980): 22–37.

Baker, Peter S. "Byrhtferth's *Enchiridion* and the Computus in Oxford, St John's College 17." *ASE* 10 (1981): 123–42.

Hart, C.R. "Byrhtferth's Northumbrian Chronicle." *EHR* 97 (1982): 558–82.

Lapidge, Michael. "Byrhtferth and the Vita S. Ecgwini." *MS* 41 (1979): 331–53. Repr. in *Anglo-Latin Literature, 900–1066*. London: Hambledon, 1993, pp. 293–315.

Lapidge, Michael. "Byrhtferth of Ramsey and the Early Sections of the *Historia regum* Attributed to Symeon of Durham." *ASE* 10 (1981): 97–122. Repr. in *Anglo-Latin Literature, 900–1066*. London: Hambledon, 1993, pp. 317–42.

PETER S. BAKER

C

CÆDMON (fl. 657–80)

The first English poet with any vernacular work surviving ("Cædmon's Hymn"), who invented English religious poetry by combining secular verse techniques with Christian subject matter.

Bede tells the story in his *Ecclesiastical History* 4.24, the only source. Cædmon was a cowherd at the monastery of Abbess Hild at Whitby. One night, after leaving a feast at the monastery in order to avoid performing with the harp, he had a dream in which a man commanded him to sing. Although he demurred, the man insisted that he do so and gave him the subject matter for his song: the Creation. At this Cædmon began to sing the poem that has come to be called Cædmon's Hymn, the first recorded English poem. Upon waking Cædmon reported his dream to the steward and then to Hild and her advisers, who recited another biblical narrative to him and asked him to turn it into song as well. When he had done so, he was invited and chose to become a monk and devoted his life to composing vernacular poetry based on religious subjects.

Bede lists Cædmon's works, which included poems on Genesis and Exodus, the life of Christ, the apostles' teachings, the Last Judgment, and heaven and hell. None survive, but the list resembles the contents of Bodl. Junius 11, which has thus been called the "Cædmon Manuscript," though its contents are not now attributed to Cædmon.

Cædmon's Hymn survives in Northumbrian and West Saxon versions; the latter follows:

> Nu sculon herigean heofonrices weard,
> metodes meahte and his modgeþanc,
> weorc wuldorfæder, swa he wundra gehwæs,
> ece drihten, or onstealde.

He ærest sceop eorðan bearnum
heofon to hrofb, halig scyppend;
þa middangeard moncynnes weard,
ece drihten, æfter teode
firum foldan, frea ælmihtig

[Now should we praise the guardian of the heavenly kingdom, the power of the Creator and the counsel of his mind, the works of the Father of glory, how he, the eternal Lord, originated every marvel. He, the holy Creator, first created the heaven, as a roof for the children of the earth; then the eternal Lord, guardian of the human race, the almighty ruler, afterward fashioned the world as a soil for men.]

Cædmon composed in the repetitious style associated with formulaic, memorized verse. The three-part poem turns on the favorite subjects of the Anglo-Saxons: praise, mind, power, time, and God, who creates the earth as a metaphorical hall ("heaven as a roof") for human beings to live in. In verse 6b the brand-new poet calls God "scyppend" (Shaper), punning on "scop" (Shaper, poet).

Some cynics dismiss the whole story as another miracle tale, but Bede, fond of miracles, never uses the term "miracle" about Cædmon. Hild's scholars saw Cædmon's accomplishment as a heavenly gift, while modern critics debate how an illiterate cowherd suddenly learned to compose sophisticated verse. Theories include overcoming stage fright, practicing secretly, and modifying formulas heard in secular verse.

Cædmon's style and subject matter dominated Anglo-Saxon verse for 400 years and probably reinforced the native tendency toward stressed meter. In that sense Cædmon, encouraged by Abbess Hild, "invented" English verse as we know it.

See also **Bede the Venerable; Hild**

Further Reading

Primary Sources

ASPR 6:105–06; Colgrave, Bertram, and R.A.B. Mynors, eds. and trans. *Bede's Ecclesiastical History of the English People.* Oxford: Clarendon, 1969, pp. 414–21.

Secondary Sources

Dobbie, E.V.K. *The Manuscripts of Cædmon's Hymn and Bede's Death Song: With a Critical Text of the Epistola Cuthberti de obitu Bedae.* New York: Columbia University Press, 1937.

Fritz, Donald W. "Cædmon: A Monastic Exegete." *American Benedictine Review* 25 (1974): 351–63.

Fry, Donald K. "Cædmon as a Formulaic Poet." *Forum for Modern Language Studies* 10 (1974): 227–47.

Fry, Donald K. "The Memory of Cædmon." In *Oral Traditional Literature: A Festschrift far Albert Bates Lord*, ed. John Miles Foley. Columbus: Slavica, 1981, pp. 282–93.

Howlett, D.R. "The Theology of Cædmon's Hymn." *Leeds Studies in English*, n.s. 7 (1973–74): 1–12.

Lester, GA. "The Cædmon Story and Its Analogues." *Neophilologus* 58 (1974): 225–37.

Magoun, Francis P., Jr. "Bedes Story of Cædmon: The Case History of an Anglo-Saxon Oral Singer." *Speculum* 30 (1955): 49–63.

O'Keeffe, Katherine O'Brien. "Orality and the Developing Text of Cædmon's Hymn." *Speculum* 62 (1987): 1–20.

Wrenn, Charles Leslie. "The Poetry of Cædmon." *PBA* 33 (1946): 277–95.

DONALD K. FRY

CAESARIUS OF HEISTERBACH (1180–ca. 1240)

A Cistercian monk educated in Cologne, Caesarius became the prior and master of novices at the monastery of Heisterbach. His extant writings include a number of sermons and a few saints' lives, but Caesarius is most noted for his *Dialogus miraculorum* (Dialogue on Miracles), compiled and written in Latin between 1219 and 1223. As novice master, he gathered the material together in a collection of stories intended to illustrate Christian doctrine for the monks in his charge and aid in the development and preparation of sermons on particular topics. Hence, the stories are divided into a variety of thematic units, with subject headings such as conversion, contrition, confession, temptation, demons, the Eucharist, and the Miracles of the Virgin Mary. The collection is framed by a dialogue between a novice monk (*novicius interrogans*) and the master (*monacbus respondent*). The content, owing as much to an oral tradition as to religious sources, straddles the border between official canonical doctrine and that of folk legend. Many of the stories depict scenes drawn from the everyday life of the region and time period, including that of emperors, peasants, townspeople, beggars, and clergy. Because the stories are meant to serve as examples to live by, they are called *exempla*, and while they are shaped as miracle tales, weaving religious doctrine with popular material, each has a particular moral point. While the primary audience for the *Dialogus miraculorum* was that of male Cistercian monasteries, there is evidence that the works of Caesarius are important in the history of medieval women's spirituality in Germany. There are over two hundred references to women's cloisters in Caesarius's works and evidence that he personally knew six Cistercian women's monasteries in the Lower Rhineland.

Further Reading

Caesarius of Heisterbach. *Caesari Heisterbacensis Monachi Ordinis Cisterciensis Dialogus miraculorum*, ed. Joseph Strange. 2 vols. Bonn: Colonia, 1871.

——. *The Dialogue on Miracles*, trans. H. von E. Scott and C. C. Swinton Bland. London: Routledge, 1929.

Moolenbroek, J. J. van. "Caesarius von Heisterbach über Zisterzienserinnes." *Citeaux* 41 (1990): 45–65.

ROSEMARY DRAGE HALE

CAMPIN, ROBERT (ca. 1376–1444)

Late-medieval painter whose career is shrouded in mystery because of limited archival information and few attributed works. He is known principally for his famous pupil Rogier van der Weyden. Campin's reputation in Tournai as a master is substantiated by the positions he held: subdeacon of the goldsmith's guild, head of the painter's guild, and one of the stewards to the city in charge of finances and accounts. Tournai's relationship with the Burgundian court ultimately affected Campin's production. In one of his earlier works, the *Entombment Triptych* (1415–20), Campin displays a knowledge of the italianate painters of the court, such as Malouel and Bellechose, in his use of gold background and treatment of the angels. Court patronage, however, did not provide the artists of Tournai with a steady source of income. Instead, they belonged to guilds and served the city and local clients. Campin's most famous work and the one that epitomizes his style is the *Merode Altarpiece* (ca. 1425), now at the Cloisters in New York. Commissioned by the Ingebrecht family, who appear at the left of the panel, the triptych demonstrates Campin's skill with disguised symbolism. The composition teems with mundane objects that acquire meaning in the presence of the divine. Sadly, Campin's career suffered greatly in the 1430s, when the pro-Burgundian faction in Tournai snatched power away from the guilds. In the midst of the conflict, Campin was arrested and, though he was eventually set free, his career never recovered.

See also **Van der Weyden, Rogier**

Further Reading

Frinta, Mojmír S. *The Genius of Robert Campin*. Paris: Mouton, 1966.

Snyder, James. *Northern Renaissance Art*. New York: Abrams, 1985.

MICHELLE I. LAPINE

CANGRANDE DELLA SCALA (1291–1329)

Cangrande I della Scala (Canfrancesco) was the third son of Alberto I della Scala, lord of Verona. He was probably born on 8 or 9 May 1291 and was christened Canfrancesco, but from his childhood he was called Canis Magnus, or Cangrande (also Can Grande, "great dog"). Little is known of his youth. In 1294, at the age of three, he was made a knight during a courtly celebration of his father's victory over the d'Este family. Upon his father's death in 1301, he was entrusted to the care of his elder brother Bartolomeo.

In 1306, Cangrande was invested with a fief by the bishop of Vicenza and began to take part in his brother Alboino's military campaigns. The brothers collaborated as rulers of Verona from 1308 on, and in 1308 Cangrande was married to Giovanna of Svevia, daughter of Conrad of Antioch. Both Alboino and Cangrande were made imperial *vicarii* of the city in 1311, during the Italian expedition of Emperor Henry VII. When Alboino died later that year, Cangrande became the sole ruler of Verona.

Cangrande was clearly the most militarily gifted of the Scaliger lords (Scaliger was a name adopted by descendants of the della Scala). He expanded his rule over the entire mark of Verona-Treviso. He was granted the imperial vicariate of Vicenza early in 1312 and quickly established himself as personal ruler of the city. After Emperor Henry VII died in 1313, Cangrande remained loyal to the imperial party. He did homage to Frederick of Austria in 1317 and received a confirmation of his vicariate of Verona; when he refused to renounce the imperial vicariate, Pope John XXII excommunicated him the following year. Allied with Duke Henry of Gorizia and Henry of Carinthia, Cangrande conquered much of the countryside south of Padua in the winter of 1317–1318, and most of the castles in the territory of Treviso the following September. His participation in the siege of Genoa (in the autumn of 1318) increased his stature among other Ghibelline leaders, but Cangrande's ambitions were focused on the Veneto. In 1319 he laid siege to Padua, but a defeat in August 1320 led to the lifting of the blockade. The following year, however, he conquered Feltre (June 1321) and then Belluno (October 1322). After a brief flirtation with the papal party in the early 1320s (he was negotiating with the curia to rescind his excommunication), Cangrande reaffirmed his Ghibelline connection and helped to lift the siege of Milan in 1323. He entered a league with Mantua, Ferrara, and the emperor in 1324–1325 and brought his forces to various sieges in the countryside around Modena. In 1327, Cangrande finally gained control of Padua with the help of exiled malcontents, entering the city on 11 September. Early in July 1329 he began a war against Treviso, conquering the city on 17 September. Cangrande fell ill after entering Treviso and died there on 22 July 1329. He left no legitimate heir.

While he is chiefly known for his military exploits, Cangrande also sheltered the poet Dante during Dante's long exile (1312–1318). Dante eulogized him in *Paradiso* 17 (76–93), describing him as so magnificent "that his enemies will not repress/Their tongues from telling what things he hath done" (*Le sue magnificenze conosciute/saranno ancora, si che' suoi nemici/non ne potran tener le lingue mute*).

The essential work on Cangrande is still Spangenberg (1892–1895), a derailed narrative political biography organized chronologically; the auditor's annotations are an invaluable guide to primary sources, and the work includes a few key documents (2:151–163). None of the sources for Cangrande's career, however, is available in translation. The sources most central to an analysis of his rule are *Antiche cronache Veronesi* and *Statuti di Verona del 1327*.

See also **Dante Alighieri; Henry VII of Luxembourg**

Further Reading

Primary Sources

Antiche cronache Veronesi, ed. Carlo Cipolla. Monumenti Storici Pubblicati dalla R. Deputazione Veneta di Storia Patria, Series 3, Vol. 2. Venice: R. Deputazione Veneta di Storia Patria, 1890.

Statuti di Verona del 1327, ed. Silvana Anna Bianchi and Rosalba Granuzzo, 2 vols. Rome: Jouvence, 1992.

Studies

Allen, A. M. *A History of Verona*. London: Methuen, 1910.

Bowsky, William M. *Henry VII in Italy: The Conflict of Empire and City-State (1310–1313)*. Lincoln: University of Nebraska Press, 1960.

Dante e Verona: Studi, ed. Antonio Avena and Pieraluise di Serego-Alighleri. Verona: Tip. Cooperativa, 1921.

Hyde, John Kenneth. *Padua in the Age of Dante: The Social Life of an Italian City State*. Manchester: University of Manchester Press; and New York: Barnes and Noble, 1966.

Rossini, Egidio. *Verona Scaligera*. Vol. 3, part 1 of *Verona e il suo territorio*. Verona: Istituto per gli Studi Storici Veronesi, 1975.

Gli Scaligeri 1277–1387: Saggi e schede pubblicati in occasione della mostra storico-documentaria allestita dal Museo di Castelvecchio di Verona (giugno-novembre 1988), ed. Gian Maria Varanini. Verona: Arnoldo Mondadori, 1988.

Spangenberg, Hans. *Cangrande I. della Scala (1291–1329)*, 2 vols. Berlin: R. Gaertner, 1892–1895. (Vol. 1 covers 1291–1320; Vol. 2 covers 1321–1329.)

Varanini, Gian Maria. "Delia Scala, Cangrande." In *Dizionario biografico degli Italiani*. Rome: Istituto della Enciclopedia Italiana, 1960–.

MAUREEN C. MILLER

CÃO, DIOGO (fl. 1482-1486)

Portuguese navigator in the service of João II who explored the African coast as far south as Cape Saint Catherine; his most memorable discovery was the Congo River. His itineraries and other accomplishments are unclear, as are the dates of his birth and death. He was descended from a Trasmontane family that had fought for Portuguese independence in the 1380s and, according to tradition, was born in Vila Real. The first mention of him is from 1480, as already being in the service of João II as a navigator; it is recorded that he returned from Africa with captured Spanish vessels.

In 1482 his career as an explorer seems to have begun on an expedition that stopped at San Jorge da Mina (Elmina) before proceeding south into the unknown seas beyond Cape Saint Catherine. It was on this voyage that he discovered the Congo (Zaire) River and planted the stone pillar known as the Padraõ de San Jorge. He then proceeded south to Cape Santa Maria, where he erected another *padrão* before returning to Lisbon.

He brought with him four Sonyo nobles taken as hostages in return for the safety of Portuguese crew members, who had been sent on an embassy to the Manicongo but had not returned before the ship sailed. The nobles were treated well; according to the chronicler Barros, the intent was to teach them the Portuguese language for future communication with natives of the region. João II was highly pleased with the results of the expedition and ennobled Cão, apparently believing, that his navigator had approached "the Arabian Gulf."

The outlines of Cão's second voyage of 1485 are much hazier, but it is known from Barros that he returned the hostages to their homeland; he then, planted a padrão at Cape Negro, Morocco, according to Martin Behaim's globe of 1492, and another at Cape Cross, before reaching Walvis Bay. During this voyage he seems to have visited the Manicongo, at least according to the chroniclers Rui de Pina and João de Barros. And, given the authenticity of inscriptions on the cliff at Ielala, he sailed his ships a hundred miles up the Congo River. Otherwise, reports on this second voyage are contradictory. A legend on the famous globe by the German cartographer Martin Behaim, *hic moritur*, has been taken to indicate Cão's death, probably in 1486, though Barros does not mention it in his *Decades*, (I, book 3, chapter 3) and speaks as if Cão returned safely home. Whether or not Cão actually returned from this second voyage, he fell into complete obscurity. The late Damião Peres suggests (based on the Soligo map) that Cão may have incurred the displeasure of João II (and subsequently fallen into obscurity) by asserting that he had found the terminal cape of Africa—which turned out to be only a deep, but blind, bay.

Two other confusions render even the briefest biography of Cão uncertain: the fact that one or more other voyages of Portuguese discovery somewhat overlap his and easily become confused with them, and the question of whether Martin Behaim accompanied Cão and labeled his maps in accordance with the explorer's discoveries.

See also **Beheim, Michael**

Further Reading

Barros, João de. *Décadas da Ásia*. Decade I, books 2 and 3. Lisbon, 1778.

Peres, D. *Descobrimentos portugueses*. 2d ed. Coimbra, 1960.

GEORGE D. WINIUS

CARTAGENA, ALFONSO DE (1385/6–1456)

Alfonso García de Santa Maria (*Alphonsus Burgensis*) was the second son of Shlomo ha-Levi, *rab de la corte* of the Jewish *aljama* of Burgos, who on 21 July 1390, before Alfonso had been taught Hebrew, converted to Christianity under the name Pablo de Santa María and was subsequently elected bishop of Cartagena (1402) and Burgos (1415). The Santa María became leading members of the Burgos patriciate, intermarrying with the noble houses of Manrique, Mendoza, Rojas, and others; on being granted a royal patent of nobility in 1440, the family changed its surname to Cartagena. Alfonso García read canon law at Salamanca (ca. 1400–1406) before entering the church and court bureaucracy. By 1415 he was dean of Santiago de Compostela (dean of Segovia and canon of Burgos, 1420) and judge in the royal *audiencia* of Castile; in 1419, on the majority of Juan II of Castile (1406–1454), he was appointed to the king's council. In 1421–1423 he was sent on the first of several diplomatic missions to the Portuguese court of João I, where in the summer of 1422, at the behest of Prince Duarte, he wrote the "first-born of all my writings," *Memoriale uirtutum*, a scholastic *compilatio* of Aristotle's *Nicomachean Ethics* with glosses from Aquinas written in rhythmical Latin prose; the prologue to Book II extols the delights of studious solitude, adducing the parallels of Scipio Africanus (Cicero, *De officiis*, III, 1) and Count Fernán González in Pelayo's cave on the banks of the Arlanza, while the *ultilogus* illustrates the effects of vice in public life with Tarquin's rape of Lucretia and King Roderick's of La Cava, while virtue is represented by the heroes of the Reconquest.

These *exempla* foreshadow a civic humanist ideal, based on the model of classical Roman culture and virtue but with a significant admixture of native elements, which it became Cartagena's life-long project to preach to the aristocracy. Within months he penned his first Castilian work, a completion of Pero López de Ayala's unfinished translation of Boccaccio, *De casibus illustrium uirorum* (*Caída de príncipes de Juan Bocaçio*, 30 September 1422); this was followed by versions of Cicero's *De senectute* and *De officiis* (*Quatro libros de Tulio*, Montemór o Novo, 10 January 1422 o.s./1423 n.s.), *Pro Marcello* (*Oración de Tulio a Julio Çesar*), and *De inuentione*, I (*Rethórica de Marco Tulio Çicerón*, 1425–27), whose prologues make explicit the program for educating knights in "lengua clara vulgar e maternal," steering a *via media* between the competing claims of classical rhetoric and scholastic philosophy.

Cartagena's next project was a cycle of vernacular translations from the Córdoban Stoic Seneca the Younger which, under the patronage of Juan II, was designed to show the antiquity and worth of Hispanic classical culture in defiance of the Italians (*Gran copilaçión del alphabeto de algunos dichos de Séneca*, from Fra Luca Manelli's fourteenth-century *Tabulatio et expositio Senecae*, 1428/9–30; *Cinco libros de Séneca*, from *De uita beata*, *Ep. Ad Lucilium* 88, *Deprov-identia*, the apocryphal *De institutis legalĩbus*, and Seneca the Elder's *Controuersiae*, 1431; *De constantia; De clementia*).

It was on a third Portuguese legation in 1427 that Cartagena experienced a first direct contact with Italian humanism through a pair of Leonardo Bruni's Latin translations from the Greek brought back from Bologna by some Portuguese jurists. The result was his *Declinationes super noua quadam Ethicorum Aristotelis translatione*, dedicated to Fernán Díaz de Toledo in 1431, a pamphlet criticizing Bruni's humanist version of Aristotle's *Ethics* as too rhetorical and unphilosophical. The *Declinationes* aroused European controversy when, in 1434, Cartagena took a copy to the General Council of Basel as a member of the Castilian delegation. There he also pronounced a number of public speeches, notably a disputation on *Lex Gallus de postumis instituendis uel exheredandis* (Avignon, 18 July 1434), sermons on the feasts of St. Thomas Aquinas (Juan II's birthday) and All Saints, and political briefs on the powers of the Council and the papal *plenitudo postestatis*, on the preeminence of the crown of Castile over that of England (*Propositio super altercatione preeminentie sedium inter reges Castelle et Anglie*, 14 September 1434), and on the Castilian right to the conquest of the Canaries (*Allegationes super conquesta insularum Canarie contra Portugalenses*, 27 August 1437). The latter are no less interesting for their Ciceronian rhetorical schemes than for their political ideology.

Aeneas Sylvius Piccolomini informs us that Cartagena's oratory so deeply impressed everyone that, when Pablo de Santa María died in 1435, Pope Eugenius IV immediately provided him to the vacant see; his election as bishop of Burgos was confirmed by Juan II's nomination. A further outcome of his stay in Basel was his Latin correspondence with Leonardo Bruni and Pier Candido Decembrio, in which he successfully requested translations from Greek (Porphyry, Homer, and Plato's *Republic*). In March 1438 Cartagena attended the imperial coronation of Albrecht III of Austria in Breslau, where he met Diego de Valera and Pero Tafur. He returned via Prague, Nuremburg, and Mainz, reaching Spain in December 1439, where his first act was to grant a canonry in Burgos to his protégé Rodrigo Sánchez de Arévalo; at the same time the young Alfonso de Palencia entered his retinue. In 1440 he was the chief negotiator in the marriage of Juan II's son Prince Enrique to Blanca of Navarre; it was during the princess's stay in his brother Pedro's palace in Burgos that the Bohemian traveler Rozmital met Cartagena, and it was probably also at this time that the latter formed his close friendships with Pedro Fernández de Velasco (*Epistola ad comitem de Haro*, ca. 1441, a Latin treatise on noble education which again propounds Cartagena's ideal of educated chivalry), with Íñigo López de Mendoza (*Respuesta a la questión fecha por el marqués de Santillana*, 1444, on Leonardo Bruni's *De militia*, a discussion of the classical origins of chivalry), and with Diego Gómez de Sandoval, Count of Castrojeriz (*Doctrinal de cavalleros*, ca. 1445, a compendium of laws and commentaries on chivalry). Cartagena formed a deeper friendship with Fernán Pérez de Guzmán, to whom he dedicated his *Duodenarium*, a set of Latin essays on political, moral, and linguistic questions sent to its addressee (unfinished) soon after 1442.

In the 1440s Cartagena wrote a number of juridical briefs on the rights and constitutions of his bishopric against the pretensions of Alfonso Carrillo, archbishop of Toledo (*Liber Mauricianus*, *Conflatorium*), and reorganized the cathedral archive; he was also responsible for major building works, including the cathedral's two famous openwork stone spires, designed by Johann von Köln, and the Chapel of the Visitation, which houses his own tomb, and the plaza and episcopal palace of El Sarmental. To these years belong his gloss on a devotional sermon of St. John Chrysostom and *Apologia super psalmum Judica me Deus*, a "*contemplación mezclada con oratión*" on the Penitential Psalm 26, both written in Latin and subsequently translated by the author into Castilian; and the massive *Defensorium unitatis Christianae*, a reasoned impugnation of the anti-*converso* libels of Pero Sarmiento in the Rebellion of Toledo, addressed to Juan II in 1449, in which, once again, Cartagena brought his vast knowledge of history, theology, and oratory to bear on a subject which other writers had treated only in legal terms. The political situation in the wake of Sarmiento's rebellion was volatile, however, and, after Álvaro de Luna's arrest and imprisonment in his brother Pedro's Burgos palace in March 1453, Cartagena found himself in the invidious position of having to draw up the charges for the execution of the *privado* whose policy he had so loyally supported for twenty years.

Cartagena's last works were the *Oracional* (ca. 1455), a layman's treatise on prayer written in Castilian for Fernán Pérez de Guzmán, which lays stress on the inwardness of spiritual life in ways which point to the *Devotio moderna* and Illuminism rather than Italian humanism, while the Latin *Anacephaleosis regum Hispanie*, on which he was working in the months before his death and which he dedicated to Burgos cathedral chapter, develops the Neo-Gothic myth expounded in his father's *Coplas de las siete edades del mundo* on the Messianic imperial and crusading destiny of Hispania. In the summer 1456 Cartagena undertook a pilgrimage to Santiago for the jubilee, but he was already ill, and had to return before the feast of St. James, dying at Villasandino on 22 July. His decease is recounted in touching terms, with the obligatory deathbed miracle, in the contemporary *De actibus domini Alfonsi de Cartagena* (BNM 7432, fols. 89–92ᵛ, attributed to his amanuensis Juan S*f*nchez de Nebreda). Other tributes were penned by Fernando de la Torre in a letter to Pedro de Cartagena; by Fernán Pérez de Guzmán in his *Coplas sobre el transitu del reverendo padre don Alfonso de Cartajena* ("Aquel Séneca espiró l a quien yo era Luçilo"); and by his pupil and *camarero* Diego Rodríguez de Almela in a *semblanza* included in a work undertaken at Cartagena's behest, *Valerio de las estorias escolásticas e de España*, VIII, 6, 9 (completed March 1462, printed Murcia 1487). The most vivid portraits, however, are those by his fellow *conversos* (Catholic converts) Juan de Lucena (*Diálogo moral de vita felici*, 1463) and Fernando del Pulgar, whose *semblanza* shows Cartagena as a man of deep intelligence, pious modesty, and complete integrity (*Claros varones de Castilla*, ca. 1483–1486, published 1486).

See also **Aquinas, Thomas**

Further Reading

Birkenmajer, A. "Der Streit des Alonso von Cartagena mit Leonardo Bruni Aretino," *Beiträge zur Geschichte der Philosophie des Mittelalters* 20 (1917–22), Heft 5 (1922), 128–210, 226–35.

Cartagena, A. de *Defensorium unitatis Christianae*. Ed. M. Alonso. Madrid, 1943.

Espinosa Fernandez, Y. (ed.) *La Anacephaleosis de Alonso de Cartagena*. 3 vols. Madrid, 1989.

Gómez Moreno, A. "La *Qüestión* del Marqués de Santillana a don Alfonso de Cartagena," *El Crotalón: Ánuario de Filología Española* 2 (1985), 335–63.

González-Quevedo Alonso, S. (ed.) *El Oracional de Alonso de Cartagena*. Chapel Hill, N.C., 1983.

Lawrance, J. (ed.) *Un tratado de Alonso de Cartagena sobre la educación y los estudios literarios*. Bellaterra, 1979.

Morrás, M. (ed). *Texto y concordancias del De officiis de Cicerón, traducción castellana por Alfonso de Cartagena*. Madison, Wisc., 1989.

JEREMY LAWRANCE

CARTAGENA, TERESA DE (1420/25–?)

Born between 1420 and 1425, Teresa de Cartagena was the author of two important pious prose works, the *Arboleda de los enfermos* (ca. 1450) and the *Admiración operum Dey* (of uncertain date but written out of self-justification to counter the surprise caused by the reception of the *Arboleda*). She was a member of the most illustrious *converso* family of fifteenth-century Castile, the Santa María-Cartagenas, whose members achieved great distinction in literature and the church. She was the grandaughter of Pablo de Santa María, successively the chief rabbi and bishop of Burgos as well as the author of an historical work, *Siete edades del mundo*, the niece of the humanist, statesman, and polemicist Alfonso de Cartagena, also bishop of Burgos, as well as his brother, the intellectual and chronicler Alvar García de Santa María. Teresa also corresponded with Gómez Manrique, one of the principal literary figures of the realm, and was urged by Manrique to continue her literary endeavors. Teresa lost her hearing at an early age and, educated at Salamanca, she became a Franciscan nun. Her deafness appears to have been instrumental in the development of both her spiritual sensibilities and her literary enterprise.

The *Arboleda de los enfermos* is a consolatory work couched in terms of an allegorical exposition and meditation on the spiritual benefits of illness, specifically her deafness, as a means of isolation from worldly distractions. In it, Teresa distinguishes between the physical and the spiritual ability to hear, concluding that deafness can be a defense against metaphysical blindness. Her aim in writing it was to teach others to cope with adversity. The work is rich with images and demonstrates an intimate spirituality that also places great value on human relationships, especially family. Its sources are complex, largely biblical and Patristic (Augustine, Boethius, Jerome, Gregory the Great, and St. Bernard, among them), and stand as a testimonial to Teresa's learning and erudition. At the same time, the *Arboleda* is notable for its authenticity and as a record of an intimate religious experience tempered by personal hardship.

The *Admiración*, although derived from largely the same sources as the *Arboleda*, was composed in response to her critics, whom she says disbelieved she could have written the *Arboleda* and chastised her for the audacity of pretending that a woman could have composed such a work. Although the *Admiración* is crafted in a tone framed by obligatory rhetorical modesty, there are at times murmurs of irony in Teresa's voice as she defends the *Arboleda*'s divine inspiration and fails to give ground on the fact that God may endow women with both strength and intelligence. The *Admiración* is notable because it constitutes an apology for female authorship as well as a series of reflections by Teresa on her own writing and its place in society and in the church.

Although there is no hint of heterodoxy in her works, Teresa's *converso* origins may have complicated her existence and helped shape the nature of her writing. Both her works were composed shortly after the anti-*converso* riots of 1449 in Toledo and appear to incorporate that experience into her choice of imagery. The traditional Augustinian allegory of the City of God is transformed by Teresa from a secure and ordered place into one of fear, suspicion, and isolation.

The date of her death is unknown.

See also **Cartagena, Alfonso de**

Further Reading

Cartagena, T. de. *The Writings of Teresa de Cartagena.* Trans. Dayle Seidenspinner-Núñez. Cambridge, U.K., 1998.
Deyermond, A. "Spain's First Women Writers." In *Women in Hispanic Literature.* Ed. Beth Miller. Berkeley, 1983.

E. MICHAEL GERLI

CASSIAN, JOHN (d. 435)

Essentially nothing is known of the early life of this important figure in the development of Christian monasticism in southern France. Born probably in the Roman province of Scythia Minor (present-day Romania), Cassian appears ca. 385 as a member of a monastic community in Bethlehem; in 385, or shortly thereafter, he and a friend named Germanus left for a "tour" of the monastic settlements in Egypt, where they discussed such matters as ascetic discipline and prayer with desert monks. By 399 or 400, Cassian and Germanus had left Egypt, probably because of controversy over the theology of Origen. In Constantinople, Cassian was ordained deacon by John Chrysostom and then, in 405, went on to Rome. By 410–15, Cassian was at Marseille in southern Gaul, where he founded two monasteries, one for women, the other for men.

Cassian's fame rests on two books that he wrote after settling at Marseille: the *Institutes* and the *Conferences.* The *Institutes* was composed at the request of Castor, bishop of Apt, who had decided to found a monastery.

In Books 1–4, Cassian deals with the dress, prayer, and rules for monks in community and draws extensively on his Egyptian experience. Books 5–12 are each devoted to one of the eight capital sins (gluttony, lust, covetousness, anger, melancholy, accedia, vanity, and pride), their symptoms, and their remedies; in this, as in many other aspects of his spirituality, he follows the Greek monastic author Evagrius. In the *Conferences,* Cassian claims to be recounting conversations held several decades earlier with Egyptian desert ascetics. The twenty-four conferences are concerned primarily with the techniques of bodily and spiritual discipline that lead to effective prayer, and thus contemplation. Within the monastic life, Cassian distinguishes an "active life," which he understands as the pursuit of virtue and flight from sin, from the "contemplative life," the life of quietness, prayer, and contemplation. Drawing again upon Evagrius, Cassian sees the goal of the active life as *apatheia* (Evagrius's Greek term for a state of passionlessness or detachment) or "purity of heart" (Cassian's usual term for the same state; cf. Matthew 5:8, "Blessed are the pure in heart for they shall see God"). This state of tranquillity, purity, and freedom from distraction is the starting point for concentration, interiorization, and advancement in prayer leading toward the experience of divine presence.

Cassian also wrote an anti-Nestorian christological treatise (*De incarnatione*) and in his thirteenth *Conference* opposed Augustine's ideas about grace by suggesting that the human will has some independent role in salvation (a position later known as Semi-Pelagianism).

Cassian's influence on western monasticism and spirituality was profound and lasting. His monastic regulations and spirituality influenced Benedict of Nursia and many later monastic writers. His transmission of the ideas of Evagrius, especially on *apatheia* or purity of heart, was crucial for western spirituality. The *Rule of St. Benedict*'s requirement that the *Conferences* be read to the monks during meals ensured that generations of monks would be shaped by the ideals of asceticism and prayer that Cassian had gleaned from the desert ascetics.

See also **Benedict of Nursia, Saint**

Further Reading

Cassian, John. *Opera. PL* 49–50.
——. *Opera,* ed. Michael Petschenig. *CSEL* 13, 17. Vindobonae: apud C. Geroldi filium, 1886–88.
——. *John Cassian*: *Conferences,* trans. Colin Luibheid. New York: Paulist, 1985.
Chadwick, Owen. *John Cassian*: *A Study in Primitive Monasticism.* 2nd ed. London: Cambridge University Press, 1968.
——. *Western Asceticism.* Philadelphia: Westminster, 1958. [Translation of selected *Conferences.*]

Rousseau, Philip. *Ascetics, Authority and the Church in the Age of Jerome and Cassian.* Oxford: Oxford University Press, 1978.

GROVER A. ZINN

CASSIODORUS
(c. 490-c. 583 or 585)

Flavius Magnus Aurelius Cassiodorus Senator, a statesman, ecclesiastical writer, and educator, was born to a senatorial family from southern Italy. His life can be divided into a political period from 507 to c. 540 and a scholarly and monastic period from 540 to his death.

Cassiodorus served the Ostrogothic rulers in various positions: he was quaestor in 507, ordinary counsel in 514, master of offices from 523 to 527, and praetorian prefect from 533 to 537. He also applied his literary talents to glorify the Ostrogoth regime. During his political career, he produced *Chronica,* a chronological account of the Italian rulers up to 519; *Historia Gothorum,* a history of the Goths (now lost); and *Variae,* a collection of state papers and diplomatic correspondence that became popular for its artful rhetoric.

Cassiodorus retired from public service c. 540 and moved to Constantinople, where he devoted himself to ecclesiastical writing. He added to *Variae* a philosophical thirteenth book on the nature of the soul, *De anima;* and he embarked on *Expositio Psalmarum,* a complete commentary on the Psalms that was to occupy him until 548. In *Expositio Psalmarum* he attempts to rework Augustine's *Enarrationes in Psalmorum* into a more accessible form; Cassiodorus's orderly method, didactic approach, and reliance on allegorical and numerical symbolism provided a model for medieval scriptural exegesis.

Probably sometime before he moved to Constantinople, Cassiodorus founded the monastery of Vivarium on his family's property in Squillace, on the southern coast of Italy. In 554, he himself settled at the monastery. He was a strong believer in institutionalized classical and Christian education, and he fashioned Vivarium as a theological school and scriptorium. Cassiodorus believed that the monastic ideal should emphasize study above all. To that end, he arranged for the extensive recopying of manuscripts, commissioned the translation of theological writings from Greek into Latin, and produced his most important later work, *Institutiones divinarum et saecularum litterarum* (*Institutes Concerning Divine and Human Readings,* c. 562).

Institutiones provides a manual for monastic scholars and copyists and explains the motivations behind Cassiodorus's library and school. In the first book Cassiodorus describes the manuscript collection at Vivarium, indicates the methods copyists should adopt, instructs his readers in the study of scripture, and identifies heretical works to be avoided. In the second book, Cassiodorus sets forth his views on the seven liberal arts, which he deemed necessary for the proper education of Christian students. *Institutiones* included a detailed bibliography on theology and the liberal arts that would benefit manuscript collectors for years to come; and Cassiodorus's concise examination of the liberal arts influenced writers such as Isidore of Seville (Saint Isidore, c, 560–636) and Rabanus Maurus (Hrabanus, Rhabanus; c. 780–856).

Late in his life, Cassiodorus composed *De orthographia,* a spelling handbook to be used as a reference by manuscript copyists.

With Cassiodorus's death came the demise of the monastery at Vivarium, but the manuscripts his scriptorium had produced circulated for years throughout medieval Europe. His legacy, moreover, reaches beyond these manuscripts. By founding his school within the monastery itself, Cassiodorus helped to shape monasticism as an educational movement. Monasteries like the one at Vivarium became indispensable agents of the transmission of classical and Christian thought in early Christian Europe.

See also **Isidore of Seville, Saint; Rabanus Maurus**

Further Reading

Editions of Cassiodorus

Chronica, ed. Theodor Mommsen. Monumenta Germaniae Historica, Auctores Antichissimi, 11. Berlin: Weidmann, 1894. *De anima,* ed. James W. Halporn. Corpus Christianorum, Series Latina, 96. Turnholt: Brepols, 1973.

De orthographia, ed. Heinrich Keil. Grammatici Latini, 7 Leipzig: Teubner, 1880.

Expositio Psalmarum, ed. M. Adriaen. Corpus Christianorum, Series Latina, 97–98. Turnholt: Brepols, 1958.

Institutiones, ed. Roger A. B. Mynors. Oxford: Clarendon, 1937. *Omnia opera,* 2 vols. In *Patrolgia Latina,* 69–70. *Variae,* ed. Theodor Mommsen and Ludwig Traube. Monumenta Germaniae Historica, Autores Antichissimi, 12. Berlin: Weidmann, 1894.

Variae, ed. Åke J. Fridh. Corpus Christianorum, Series Latina, 96. Turnholt: Brepols, 1973.

Translations

Expositio Psalmarum, trans. Patrick G. Walsh. New York: Paulist, 1990–1991.

An Introduction to Divine and Human Reasoning, trans. Leslie Webber Jones. New York: Columbia University Press, 1946. *Variae,* trans. S. J. B. Barnish. Liverpool: Liverpool University Press, 1992.

Critical Study

O' Donnell, James J. *Cassiodorus.* Berkeley: University of California Press, 1979.

JESSICA LEVENSTEIN

CATHERINE OF SIENA, SAINT
(1347–1380)

Saint Catherine of Siena (Caterina di Iacopo di Benincasa) was a significant force in the Italian church and Italian society of the late fourteenth century. Catherine was the twenty-fourth of twenty-five children of a Sienese wool-dyer. She adopted a fierce asceticism in early childhood, determined never to marry so that she might belong entirely to God. In her late teens she was admitted into the lay third order of Saint Dominic, which until then had been composed only of widows. Thereafter she lived in almost total seclusion in her parents' home until, when she was about twenty years old, she experienced a dramatic conversion: her prayers led her to the realization that her love for God could no longer be detached from service of others.

Catherine then began to work with the poor and sick of Siena, but her influence soon extended to the civic and ecclesiastical spheres as her powerful personality and her gift for conciliation were recognized. She attracted disciples, many of whom were her seniors in age and her superiors in education and status. She found an ideal mentor—intellectually, spiritually, and politically—in the Dominican Raymond of Capua, who in 1374 was appointed by the Dominican order (an appointment later confirmed by the pope) to be her confessor and the director of her public activities. In partnership with Raymond, she became deeply involved in attempts to mediate and resolve the growing tension and rifts between the republics of the Italian peninsula and the Avignonese papacy. This conflict was basically political, but because it threatened the unity of the church, it represented for Catherine a religious crisis in which she repeatedly felt compelled to intervene. Her efforts took her to Pisa, Lucca, and Florence and eventually to Avignon, where in 1376 she persuaded the hesitant Pope Gregory XI to return with his curia to Rome. However, her own political naïvete, when Raymond was not actually at her side, often complicated matters, and her realization of this fact was a heavy psychological burden to her.

Catherine passionately promoted Gregory's projected crusade against the Turks, convinced that the venture would not only unite the rebellious republics with the pope in a common defense of Christian lands but would also bring converted Muslims into the church as a leaven of needed reform.

After Gregory's death on 27 March 1378, a tumultuous election brought to the papal throne Urban VI. Urban's violent ways soon caused the majority of the cardinals to disavow him and elect an antipope, Clement VII, thus bringing about the Great Schism. Catherine, however, considered Urban the legitimate pope and supported him vehemently, even while urging him to moderation. At his invitation she moved with a number of her disciples to Rome in November 1378, to support

Domenico Beccafumi (1486–1551). Saint Catherine of Sienna receiving the stigmata. © Scala/Art Resources, New York.

his cause. By this time, however, her health was failing as a result of her extreme asceticism. (Her early patterns of fasting had led to an inability to eat normally, which she regretted but was unable to reverse.) In addition, the apparent failure of her dearest causes became a crushing load that she actually felt as a physical weight. Still, she continued to preach, write, pray, and fast in defense of the church's unity until she became totally disabled early in 1380. She died on 29 April of that year.

Though unschooled, Catherine had learned to read during her years of solitude. At some later time, she probably learned to write, but she usually found dictation a more efficient vehicle for her prolific mind. Several of her disciples served as her secretaries, and to them we owe the preservation of her letters, a book, and a collection of her prayers.

From the early 1370s on, nearly until she died, Catherine wrote a vast number of letters to counsel others and to influence them in favor of her causes. To date, 382 of her letters have been discovered and published. They are addressed to a remarkably wide variety of her contemporaries: two popes, several cardinals and bishops, two kings, two queens, numerous lesser public officials, her religious and lay associates, her family and friends, her disciples, and an assortment of others, including allies and opponents, a mercenary captain, a prostitute, a homosexual, and the prisoners of Siena. Unfortunately, the early compilers of these letters were intent on edification and sometimes on maintaining confidentiality, and so they deleted much of the personal content. But even abridged, the letters provide a window onto Catherine's evolving thought and personality and onto the history and culture of her age. They are particularly interesting because her activities extended so far beyond the normal bounds for a woman of her time and of her status in church and society.

During an eleven-month period in 1377 and 1378, in addition to her missions of mediation, Catherine composed a book that came to be known as *The Dialogue* (*Il dialogo*) because she cast it as a conversation with God. Her purpose in writing it was to share with her disciples and others the insights into Christian life that she had gained from her own prayer and experience. Also, during the last few years of Catherine's life, her secretaries often recorded her words as she spoke aloud in ecstasy. Twenty-six such prayers have been preserved.

The volume by Dupré Theseider (1940) is the only truly critical edition of Catherine's letters. At the time of the present writing, his work was being continued by Antonio Volpato, but further volumes had not yet been published. Letters and fragments of letters discovered more recently can be found in Dupré Theseider (1931), Fawtier (1914), Gardner (1907), and Motzo (1911). Critical editions of Catherine's other works are those by Cavallini (1968, 1978).

Catherine's works were among the earliest disseminated (and printed) in the Italian vernacular, and she was the first woman to produce extensive work in that vernacular. Because she used the Sienese dialect, her writings became important (through the works of Girolamo Gigli) in the eighteenth century, when various Italian dialects were contending for supremacy.

Critics have offered varying assessments of Catherine's genius and her importance in the history of Italian literature. Most of their analyses have concentrated nearly exclusively on her letters in preference to her other works. Her style is oratorical but spontaneous and unstudied; probably, she never proofread most of her letters. Her thinking drew heavily, on the Bible and on preaching, conversation, and her own reading. There are clear strains in her thought of the ideas of, among others, Augustine, Gregory the Great, Bernard de Clairvaux, Thomas Aquinas, and especially her near contemporary Domenico Cavalca. While she does not add any really new link to the content of theological tradition, she does bring a refreshing new synthesis that is markedly pastoral and strongly based on experience. For clarification, she resorts less often to conceptual argumentation than to everyday images, which, over the years, she develops individually and interweaves.

Catherine was canonized in 1461. In 1939 she was proclaimed patron of Italy, with Saint Francis of Assisi. In 1970 Pope Paul VI named her a doctor of the church, a title that she and Teresa of Avila are so far the only women to bear.

Further Reading

Editions

Cavallini, Giuliana, ed. *Il dialogo* (1968). Rome: Edizioni Cateriniane, 1968.

——, ed. *Le orazioni.* Rome: Edizioni Cateriniane, 1978; Siena: Cantagalli, 1993.

Dupré Theseider, Eugenio. "Un codice inedito dell' epistolario di santa Caterina da Siena." *Bullettino dell'Istituto Storico Italiano e Archivio Muratoriano* (47), 1931.

——, ed. *Epistolario di Santa Caterina da Siena.* Rome: Istituto Storico Italiano per il Medio Evo, 1940.

Fawtier, Robert. "Catheriniana." *Mélanges d'Archéologie e d'Histoire,* 34, 1914, pp. 3–95.

Gardner, Edmund G. *Saint Catherine of Siena: A Study in the Religion, Literature, and History of the Fourteenth Century in Italy.* London: Dent; New York: Dutton, 1907.

Le lettere di S. Caterina da Siena, 4 vols., ed. Niccolò Tommaseo, rev. Piero Misciattelli. Florence: C/E Giunti-G. Barbèra, 1940. (Originally published 1860.)

Motzo, Bacchisio. "Alcune lettere di santa Caterina da Siena in parte inedita." *Bullettino Senese di Storia Patria,* 18, 1911, pp. 369–395.

Translations

Catherine of Siena: The Dialogue, trans. Suzanne Noffke, O.P. New York: Paulist, 1980.

Foster, Kenelm, and Mary John Ronayne, eds. *I, Catherine: Selected Writings of Catherine of Siena.* London: Collins, 1980. (Includes translations of selected letters.)

The Letters of Saint Catherine of Siena, trans. Suzanne Noffke, O.P., 2 vols. Tempe: Arizona Center for Medieval and Renaissance Studies, 2000–2001.

The Prayers of Catherine of Siena, trans. Suzanne Noffke, O.P. New York: Paulist, 1983.

Scudder, Vida, ed. *Selected Letters of Catherine Benincasa: Saint Catherine of Siena as Seen in Her Letters.* London: Dent; New York: Dutton, 1927. (Includes translations of selected letters.)

Studies

Bell, Rudolph M. *Holy Anorexia.* Chicago, Ill., and London: University of Chicago Press, 1985.

Cavallini, Giuliana. *Catherine of Siena.* London: Geoffrey Chapman, 1998.

——. *Things Visible and Invisible: Images in the Spirituality of Saint Catherine of Siena,* trans. Sister Mary Jeremiah. New York: Alba House, 1996.

Dupré Theseider, Eugenio. "Il problema critico delle lettere di santa Caterina da Siena." *Bullettino dell'Istituto Storico Italiano e Archivio Muratoriano* (49), 1933, pp. 117–278.

Fawtier, Robert. *Sainte Catherine de Sienne: Essai de critique des sources,* 1, *Sources hagiographiques.* Paris: De Boccard, 1921.

——, *Sainte Catherine di Sienne: Essai de critique des sources,* 2, *Les oeuvres de Sainte Catherine de Sienne.* Paris: De Boccard, 1930. Noffke, Suzanne. *Catherine of Siena: Vision through a Distant Eye.* Collegeville, Minn.: Liturgical, 1996.

Zanini, Lina. *Bibliografia analitica di s. Caterina da Siena: 1901–1950.* Rome: Edizioni Cateriniane, 1971.

SUZANNE NOFFKE, O.P.

CAVALCANTI, GUIDO (c. 1255–1300)

The significant events in the life of the poet Guido Cavalcanti were inextricably bound up with the political tumult in Florence. Cavalcanti was born into a Guelf family that had established itself as one of the wealthiest and most powerful clans in Florence. In 1267 he married a daughter of Farinata degli Uberti, head of the Florentine Ghibellines, a political arrangement intended to promote peace between Guelf and Ghibelline factions. A force in Florentine politics, Guido Cavalcanti served as a public guarantor for the Guelf party in a peace accord brokered in 1280, and as a member of the *consiglio generate* of Florence in 1284 and 1290. His political role in Florence ended abruptly in 1295, when the *ordinamento di giustizia,* an ordinance against magnates, was adopted. However, he remained engaged in the power struggle between factions of the Guelf party, and he was held responsible for the assassination attempt of a rival, Corso Donati. In June 1300, Guido Cavalcanti was exiled from Florence for the sake of public tranquillity, but he was recalled shortly thereafter because of ill health, and he died in August of the same year.

During his lifetime, Cavalcanti was reputed to be a parsimonious, impetuous, and irascible; in the decades following his death, he became an icon of the aloof, intellectual urban aristocrat. Boccaccio, in the *Decameron* (6.9), describes Cavalcanti as one of the best logicians in the world and an outstanding natural philosopher, adding that Cavalcanti was a perfect nobleman: wealthy, eloquent, and accomplished. The *Decameron* introduced the notion that Cavalcanti was widely held to be an Epicurean who denied the immortality of the soul, although there is no historical evidence for this. Cavalcanti's interest in philosophy is borne out, however, in a philosophical tract dedicated to him in 1280 by Iacopo da Pistoia, a professor at the University of Bologna.

Cavalcanti was a pivotal figure in the development of thirteenth-century lyric poetry, and he is regarded by many modern readers as the finest lyric poet of the Italian *Duecento.* He firmly rejected, in terms more disdainful than Dante's, the heavily ornamented, conceptually curtailed poetry of Guittone d'Arezzo (c. 1235–1294). Cavalcanti's language combines intensity of expression with intellectual clarity, defining what Dante dubbed the *dolce stil nuovo;* his corpus of fifty-two poems is characterized by a highly subjective and intimate exploration of the experience of love. Cavalcanti's probing poetic voice became the inspiration for Dante's own youthful writing of love poetry in *Vita Nuova,* and in fact Dante dedicated this book to Cavalcanti. Later, though, there is ample evidence of rancor and ideological discord between the two poets.

The Bolognese Guido Guinizzelli (fl. mid-thirteenth century) influenced Cavalcanti's early sonnets written in praise of his lady. In the marvelous sonnet *Chi è questa che vèn ch 'ogn' om la mira* ("Who is this who comes, upon whom every man gazes?"), Cavalcanti repeats the two rhyme words and four rhymes of Guiniz-zelli's *Io voglio del ver la mia donna laudare* ("I truly wish to praise my lady"). Yet even this early sonnet reveals significant deviations from its model. In the quatrains, Guinizzelli's poem describes a lady by using hyperbolic comparisons to natural beauty; in the tercets, her spiritually salutary effects on those in her presence are recounted. Cavalcanti's poem turns on its own inadequacy: the impossibility of giving voice to the commotion he feels in the lady's presence, the ineffable quality of her beauty, and the incapacity of the mind to ascend to and comprehend the lady's splendor. The sonnet also differs from its model in the poet's detachment as he contemplates his lady, and in the universality of the effects ascribed to her beatitude. *Chi è questa che vèn* is characterized by many of the features that defined Cavalcanti's poetry throughout his career: a marriage of form and content; phonic lightness; rhythmic grace; supple syntax; subtle allusions to the Old and New Testaments (the opening line echoes the Song of Songs) and to other vernacular poets; and references to logic and science (the visible trembling of the air that creates a halo of light around the lady in line 2 is a phenomenon appropriated from the physics of sound). Personification, the most prominent characteristic of Cavalcanti's poetry, is present in the figure of Love, (Amor), who is charged with telling of the lady's gaze when the poet cannot. In other works, personification is accompanied by frequent apostrophes, as the poet appeals to his denatured heart or soul or spirits and begs that they, in turn, appeal to his lady.

Other poems develop the implications of Cavalcanti's paradoxical understanding of love poetry: since he is unable to sing of his lady, whom his mind cannot conceive or his words convey, his poems explore the fear, despair, anguish, and disorientation that result from the experience of love. Guittone d'Arezzo had equated love with a loss of reason and virtue, and even with death; Cavalcanti dramatizes the psychological disintegration and internal commotion caused by love, in sonnets like *Deh, spiriti miei, quando mi vedete* ("My spirits, when you see me"), *L'anima mia vilment' è sbigotita* ("My soul is so cruelly aggrieved"), and *Voi che per li occhi mi passsste 'l core* ("You who pass through my eyes to my heart"). In these poems the poet's heart, mind, eyes, sighs, soul, and spirits—vital vapors, according to the physiology of the time—are engaged in his plea for survival: some are sent to the lady to beg for mercy;

others are described as helpless witnesses to the poet's crisis. *Noi siàn le tristepenne isbigotite* ("We are the sad and mournful pens") takes the process a step further: the languishing poet's writing tools are all that is left to plead to the lady.

Guido Cavalcanti sought to understand his experience of love in terms that transcended the literary and purely subjective.

Gianni Alfani, his follower, jokingly refers to Cavalcanti as the only man who actually *sees* Love (*Ballatetta dolente,* 19), and lexical studies bear this out: *vedere* occurs fifty-five times in Cavalcanti's corpus; *guardare* fifteen times; *mimare* thirteen times; *sguardare* twice; *riguardare* once; *guatare* once; *occhi* thirty-one times; *sguardo* four times; *veduta* once, and *vista* once, according to Calenda (1976, 82–83). The eyes are, of course, the conduit for love; but perhaps more important for Cavalcanti was the fact that visibility represented the most concrete form of demonstration in Aristotelian natural philosophy. As the young Dante pursued the understanding and appropriation of the experience of love, he was profoundly influenced by Cavalcanti's poetic "research." In Chapter 26 of *Vita Nuova,* when Dante is finally able to define his poetry of praise as beatitude, and his *credo che* ("I believe that") becomes the more objective *pare che* ("it seems that," as in *Tanto gentile e tanto onesta pare* and the surrounding prose), Dante borrows essential elements from two of Cavalcanti's ballatas: *Posso degli occhi miei novella dire* and *Veggio negli occhi de la donna mia* (De Robertis 1961, 142–145).

The *ballata* was Cavalcanti's preferred form, and eleven of his *ballate* are extant. In contrast to the Italian *canzone,* which in the course of the *Duecento* became the form of choice for doctrinal poetry, the *ballata* was associated with music, dance, and—given its codification at the court of Charles of Anjou (Asperti 1995, 107–112)—perhaps a certain spirit of aristocratic hedonism. Cavalcanti may have preferred the asymmetrical musicality of the *ballata* or, as Calenda has suggested (115–117), may have consciously refused to engage in writing *canzoni,* which were becoming, with Guido Gunizzelli and Dante, ideological "manifestos" for the emerging bourgeoisie. In one of most famous *ballate, Perch'io no spero di tornar giammai* ("Because I do not hope ever to return"), Cavalcanti expands the expressive potential of the recurring rhyme, engaging it in conversation with the stanzas, as the writer Ugo Foscolo (1778–1827) pointed out. This poem was long thought to be an autobiographical final appeal to his lady from afar, by a poet fearing his imminent death; but Calenda (33–52) has shown that the work actually represents a *summa* of the poet's themes and stylistic elements.

An important achievement in Cavalcanti's hendecasyllabic *ballate* is his fluid, natural elaboration of ideas within the stanza. This presents a marked contrast to the more "scholastic" use of conjunctions of coordination and subordination to develop ideas, in *canzoni* like Guinizzelli's *Al cor gentil rempaira sempre amore* ("Love makes its home in the noble heart"). De Robertis points to this as a major accomplishment of the *dolce stil nuovo,* and an essential lesson that Dante learned from one of his first friends (134–135).

Of the two extant *canzoni* by Guido Cavalcanti, one, *Donna me prega,* is regarded as the most difficult in the Italian language. It has been interpreted from numerous perspectives, although a strictly neo-Aristotelian interpretation in line with contemporary teaching at the universities of Bologna and Paris now seems to prevail. *Donna me prega* represents a significant departure from the dramatic form of Cavalcanti's other poems. The work offers a philosophical and scientific presentation of the essence of love, how love manifests itself, and what its effects are; the questions are divided into eight topics, two of which are treated in each of the four remaining stanzas. The structure of the poem is tightly controlled, and internal rhymes enhance the rigor of the *canzone.*

See also **Dante Alighieri; Guinizzelli, Guido; Guittoni d'Arezzo**

Further Reading

Asperti, Stefano. *Carlo d'Angiò e i trovatori.* Ravenna: Longo, 1995.

Barolini, Teodolina. *Dante's Poets: Textuality and Truth in the Comedy.* Princeton, N.J.: Princeton University Press, 1984.

Calenda, Corrado. *Per altezza d'ingegno: Saggi su Guido Cavalcanti.* Naples: Liguori, 1976.

Cavalcanti, Guido. *Rime: Con le rime di Iacopo Cavalcanti,* ed. Domenico De Robertis. Turin:-Einaudi, 1986.

Contini, Gianfranco, ed. *Poeti del Duecento,* 2 vols. Milan and Naples: Ricciardi, 1960.

Corri, Maria. "La fisionomia stilistica di Guido Cavalcanti." *Rendiconti dell'Accademia Nazionale dei Lincei,* 8(5), 1950, pp. 530–552.

——. *La felicità mentale: Nuove prospettive per Cavalcanti e Dante.* Turin: Einaudi, 1983.

De Robertis, Domenico. *Il libro della Vita Nuova.* Florence: Sansoni, 1961.

Favati, Guido. *Inchiesta sul dolce stil nuovo.* Florence: Le Monnier, 1975.

Gorni, Guglielmo. "Lippo contro Lapo (sul Canone del Dolce Stil Nuovo)." In *Il nodo della lingua e il verbo d'Amore.* Florence: Olschki, 1981, pp. 99–124.

Kleinhenz, Christopher. *The Early Italian Sonnet: The First Century (1220–1321),* Lecce: Milella, 1986.

Marti, Mario. *Storia dello stil nuovo.* Lecce: Miieila, 1974.

Nelson, Lowry, Jr., ed. *The Poetry of Guido Cavalcanti.* New York: Garland, 1986.

Russell, Rinaldina. *Tre versanti della poesia stilnovistics: Guinizzelli, Cavalcanti, Dante.* Bari: Adriatica, 1973.

LAURIE SHEPARD

CAVALLINI, PIETRO (fl. c. 1270–c. 1330)

The painter and mosaicist, Pietro Cavallini is generally considered the most important Roman artist of his day and one of the protagonists in the revival of the visual arts in Italy during the late *Duecento*. His art, which is characterized by vivid naturalism, is a masterful synthesis of contemporary Byzantine and northern European styles and iconography with the artistic traditions of classical and early Christian Rome. Evidently much admired and sought after, Cavallini worked for most of his life in Rome. There, beginning with the papacy of Nicholas III (r. 1277–1280), the recently consolidated power base of the popes offered him significant opportunities for employment. He was also active in Naples, where he worked for the Angevin king Charles II; and, as is sometimes argued, possibly in Assisi. Some scholars (though they are in the minority) maintain that Cavallini was the principal master of the fresco cycle *The Legend of Saint Francis,* traditionally attributed to Giotto, in Assisi. Whatever the truth may be regarding Cavallini's supposed links with Assisi, Giotto—who was younger than Cavallini and whose known career began when Cavallini had already reached artistic maturity—was probably inspired by and indebted to Cavallini's innovative work.

Cavallini's known career in Rome and Naples: c. 1273–1325. Cavallini's career is sparsely documented, but some details about his life and work were included in Lorenzo Ghiberti's *Commentarii* (mid-1400s) and Giorgio Vasari's *Vite* (1550, revised 1568). Cavallini was a member of the noble de' Cerroni family (if the notarial act of 1273 is in fact a reference to him). He is believed to have been active from the 1270s to the 1280s as a fresco painter in the venerated Roman basilica San Paolo fuori le Mura. This work, his earliest known commission, was destroyed in a fire in 1823. The general appearance of the paintings, however, can be seen in surviving copies, most notably in watercolors executed for Cardinal Francesco Barberini in 1634. The subjects were episodes from the Old Testament (on the south wall of the nave); and scenes from the New Testament, with particular emphasis on Saint Paul, patron of the basilica (on the north wall). It would appear that Cavallini largely restored or at most reworked a vast fifth-century fresco cycle. This experience, however, would have given him a valuable opportunity to study early Christian iconographic traditions and principles of design, and possibly to study techniques of late antique painting as well.

Cavallini's skill as an artist is manifest in somewhat later fresco work that is extant: fragments in the Roman church of Santa Cecilia in Trastevere. This cycle was partially destroyed in the eighteenth century and rediscovered in the early twentieth century; it is generally dated to c. 1293, the year the Tuscan sculptor Arnolfo di Cambio signed and dated the *ciborium,* which apparently formed part of a wider scheme of redecoration in which Cavallini was intensely involved. According to Ghiberti, the frescoes once filled the whole interior. The surviving frescoes depict the Last Judgment on the entrance wall and episodes from the Old and New Testaments on the side walls. Cavallini's style, especially evident in the solemnly enthroned apostles in the Last Judgment, is characterized by a remarkable sensitivity to the properties of light, which are fully exploited in order to define the volumetric forms of figures wrapped in weighty but soft expanses of fabric. Another aspect of this sensitivity is an expressive play of color, made possible by the artist's ability to create subtle transitions in tone; these transitions are particularly striking in the seraphim in the Last Judgment. The iconography of the frescoes in Santa Cecilia would have been considered innovative by Cavallini's contemporaries: these frescoes blend Byzantine iconographic traditions—highly structured and symmetrical Last Judgment schemes—with a recent French practice of depicting the apostles with the symbols of their martyrdom.

Cavallini's work in Santa Maria in Trastevere is also extant. Both Ghiberti and Vasari recorded Cavallini's activity in this church, where a mosaic cycle depicting six episodes from the life of the Virgin and a central donor panel survive. The work, generally dated to the 1290s, once bore the artist's signature in the dedicatory panel, which could still be read in the seventeenth century. Each framed scene carries Latin verses that were composed by Cardinal Giacomo Gaetano Stefaneschi, brother of Bertoldo Stefaneschi, the patron of the project. Although Cavallini was working in a different medium he managed in these mosaics to evoke the refined effects in lighting that he had produced in the frescoes in Santa Cecilia. Furthermore, the design of each episode in the mosaics is informed by monumental clarity. In the Presentation in the Temple, for example, human figures that express great tactile power are rhythmically positioned in front of and around architectural features that define and create space.

According to Vasari, Cavallini's masterpiece in Rome was a fresco cycle in the apse of Santa Maria in Aracoeli (c. 1298). These frescoes were destroyed in the second half of the sixteenth century. However, Cavallini executed another fresco cycle for the same church; it included a Virgin and Child between Saints, surviving fragments of which were discovered in 2000 in the the chapel of San Pasquale Baylon. The fragments are imbued with a classical monumentality and, through skillful handling of chiaroscuro, also convey a pronounced plasticity. Other Roman works convincingly attributed to Cavallini on the basis of style and technique include a fresco over the tomb of Cardinal Matteo d'Acquasparta in Santa Maria Aracoeli (c. 1302) and a fresco in the apse of San Giorgio in Velabro {possibly late 1290s).

In 1308 Cavallini was lured to Naples by King Charles II, who offered him a yearly salary of thirty ounces of gold with a further two ounces to maintain a house. Fresco fragments associated with Cavallini, his workshop, or his immediate followers that survive there exhibit the monumental design principles and atmospheric subtlety of his Roman works. The frescoes in Santa Maria Donna Regina (c. 1320), for example, manifest a rigorous understanding of form, a profound characterization of the figures, and continued experimentation with lighting effects.

Critical reception and posthumous reputation. A marked decline in Cavallini's reputation began in the sixteenth century, when Vasari claimed that Cavallini had been a pupil of Giotto; this notion, reflecting the general line of argument in Vasari's *Vite,* supported the idea of the superiority of Tuscan art. The falling-off of Cavallini's stature was exacerbated by the gradual destruction of his work, especially in the wake of the Counter-Reformation, when many churches in Rome were remodeled or refurbished.

The discovery of the frescoes in Santa Cecilia in 1900 revived interest in Cavallini, since Vasari's chronology was no longer considered tenable. Through the twentieth century, scholars restored Cavallini's reputation and emphasized his role as a the pioneering figure in the history of early Italian art. The discovery of the frescoes in Santa Maria Aracoeli in 2000 brought about another new wave of interest in and debate about Cavallini, late *Duecento* Roman art, and the attribution of the frescoes in the upper church at Assisi.

See also **Giotto di Bondone**

Further Reading

Barbero, Alessandro. "Un documento inedito su Pietro Cavallini." *Pamgone,* 40, 1989, pp. 84–88.
Gardner, Julian. "Copies of Roman Mosaics in Edinburgh." *Burlington Magazine,* 115, 1973, pp. 583–591.
——."Gian Paolo Panini, San Paolo fuori le Mura, and Pietro Cavallini: Some Notes on Colour and Setting." In *Mosaics of Friendship: Studies in Art and History for Eve Borsook,* ed. Omella Francisci Osti. Florence: Centro Di, 1999, pp. 245–254.
Ghiberti, Lorenzo. *I commentarii,* ed. Lorenzo Bartoli. Florence: Giunti, 1998, pp. 86–87.
Hetherington, Paul. "Pietro Cavallini: Artistic Style and Patronage in Late Medieval Rome." *Burlington Magazine,* 114, 1972, pp. 4–10.
——, *Pietro Cavallini: A Study in the Art of Late Medieval Rome.* London: Sagittarius, 1979.
Pestelli, Livio. "'Ficus latine a fecunditate vocatur': On a Unique Iconographic Detail in Cavallini's Annunciation in Santa Maria in Trastevere." *Source,* 20, 2001, pp. 5–14.
Tiberia, Vitaliano. *I mosaici del XII secolo e di Pietro Cavallini in Santa Maria in Trastevere: Restauri e nuove ipotesi.* Todi:

Ediart, 1996. Tomei, Alessandro. "Bonifacio VIII e il Giubileo del 1300: La Roma di Cavallini e di Giotto." In *Bonifacio VIII e il suo tempo: Anno 1300 il primo Giubileo,* ed. Marina Righetti Tosti-Croce. Milan: Electa, 2000a, pp. 93–98.
——. *Pietro Cavallini.* Cinisello Balsamo (Milan): Silvana Editoriale, 2000b.
Vasari, Giorgio. *Le vite de'più eccellenti pittori, scultori, e architettori,* ed. Gaetano Milanesi, Florence: G. C. Sansoni, 1878–1885, Vol. l, pp. 537–543.
Zanardi, Bruno. *Giotto e Pietro Cavallini: La questione di Assisi e il cantiere medievale di pittura a fresco.* Milan: Skira, 2001.

FLAVIO BOGGI

CAXTON, WILLIAM (1415/24–1491/92)

Printer, publisher, translator, and merchant. Caxton was born in Kent, though probably not at Strood, which has been suggested as his birthplace. After (or perhaps toward the end of) his apprenticeship as a mercer Caxton engaged in trade between England and the Low Countries, where he may have moved in the 1440s. Eventually he was appointed Governor of the English Nation at Bruges, a major commercial town. As part of his official functions he took part in foreign trade negotiations for the English government. In 1471, presumably after resigning his office, Caxton traveled to Cologne. In the course of a stay of some eighteen months he learned the technique of printing, possibly participating in the production of an edition of Bartholomaeus Anglicus's *De proprietatibus rerum.* After returning to Bruges Caxton established a press and produced the first printed English book, *The Recuyell of the Historyes of Troye,* his own translation from the French, begun in 1469 and encouraged by Margaret, duchess of Burgundy.

In 1476 Caxton returned to England and set up his business in the precincts of Westminster Abbey (i.e., in premises belonging to and near the abbey). The first major work printed there was probably his first edition of Chaucer's *Canterbury Tales.* In the next fifteen years he published some 100 or mote works. Caxton died in late 1491 or early 1492, bequeathing his business to his long-time assistant, Wynkyn de Worde.

Caxton's choice of texts to print was both a response to and an influence in shaping fashionable demand and taste. Besides two editions of the *Canterbury Tales,* one of *Troilus,* and other collections of Chaucerian verse he published Gower's *Confessio Amantis,* several works by Lydgate, and Burgh's *Cato.* In 1485 he printed Malory's *Morte Darthur,* and this edition and its reprints remained the sole witness to the *Morte* until the Winchester Manuscript was discovered in 1934. Influenced by Burgundian or French taste, he translated and published prose works in the courtly mode, including *Jason, Godefroy of Boulogne, Aesop, The Order of Chivalry, Charles the Great, Blanchardin and Eglantine,* and *Eneydos.*

Moral and religious works published by Caxton include Chaucer's *Boethius,* Mirk's *Festial,* and *The*

Mirror of the Blessed Life of Christ, as well as translations by Earl Rivers (*The Cordial*, *The Dicts and Saying of the Philosophers*, and *Moral Proverbs*) and by Caxton himself, such as *The Mirror of the World*, *The Golden Legend*, *The Book of the Knight of the Tower*, and *The Art of Dying*.

Caxton produced editions of the two most popular historical works of his day, Trevisa's translation of Higden's *Polychronicon* and the prose *Brut* (under the title *Chronicles of England*), both of which he brought up to date with material compiled by himself. He also published a number of practical works: *The Governal of Health*, a French-English vocabulary, statutes, devotional works, and a few Latin works on rhetoric that may have been used as university textbooks.

Of considerable importance are the prologues and epilogues to many of Caxton's publications, in which he comments on his choice and treatment of texts and on matters of style, language, and the function of literature. His own prose style is prolix and shows a predilection for elevated foreign words. As an editor he sometimes updated old-fashioned vocabulary, as in the *Polychronicon*, or revised sections of the test, as in book 5 of the *Morte Darthur* (though some scholars suggest the revisions are by Malory himself).

Caxton's translations and other publications are representative of late-medieval practices and tastes; his primary importance lies in his highly successful introduction of the revolutionary technique of printing to England.

See also **Chaucer, Geoffrey; Gower, John; Malory, Thomas**

Further Reading

Primary Sources
Blake, N.F. *Caxton's Own Prose*. London: Deutsch, 1973 [for a full listing of other editions through the early 1980s].

Secondary Sources
New *CBEL* 1:667–74 *Manual* 3:771–807, 924–51
Blake, N.F. *Caxton and His World*. London: Deutsch, 1969.
Blake, N.F. "William Caxton." In *Middle English Prose: A Critical Guide to Major Authors and Genres*, ed. A.S.G. Edwards. New Brunswick: Rutgers University Press, 1984, pp. 389–412.
Blake, N.F. *William Caxton: A Bibliographical Guide*. New York: Garland, 1985.
Painter, George D. *William Caxton: A Quincentenary Biography of England's First Printer*, London: Chatto & Windus, 1976.

LISTER M. MATHESON

CECCO ANGIOLIERI (c. 1260–1312)

Cecco is the most prolific and best-known of the medieval comic poets. His father, Messer Angioliero, was the banker of Pope Gregory IX from 1230 to 1233, a member of the Frati Gaudenti, and a prominent Guelf who participated in the political life of Siena. Cecco belonged to the Arte del Cambio, i.e., the money changers' or money brokers' guild. He served as a soldier in the Sienese militia in 1281, in a siege of the castle of Turri in Maremma (during which he was fined for arbitrary absences while the fighting was going on); and in 1288, in a campaign against Arezzo (during which he was fined for violating a curfew). It appears that Cecco was plagued with financial problems throughout his lifetime. In 1302 he sold a vineyard. After his death, his five children were made to renounce their inheritance and to pay additional monies to the commune in order to satisfy his debts.

Cecco's *canzoniere* are the largest body of work by a thirteenth-century comic poet, consisting of 112 sonnets of undoubted authorship and fourteen sonnets whose attribution is dubious. Questions of authenticity of authorship preoccupied many scholars in the past, especially because Cecco's style had set a tone for many subsequent comic poets. Until 1914, the entire corpus of poetry by Meo dei Tolomei (c. 1260–c. 1310) was attributed to Cecco, as were two sonnets by Nicola Muscia (late thirteenth century). Many of Cecco's poems are found in MS Chigiano L.VIII.305 of the Vatican Library; smaller groups are found in Escorialense e.III.23 and Vaticano Barberino Latino 3953. Many other codices contain one or two sonnets by Cecco, attesting to the widespread popularity of his poetry during his lifetime. However, the manuscript tradition also indicates that his popularity did not extend much beyond his own generation.

Cecco's best-known and most frequently anthologized sonnets— *Tre cose solamente mi so' in grado* and *S'i 'fosse foco, ardere' il mondo*—are in the Goliardic tradition (the Goliards were wandering entertainers) of odes to wine, women, and gambling; however, these sonnets are not indicative of the bulk of his *canzoniere*. A significant number of Cecco's sonnets recount a stormy relationship with a woman named Becchina, characterized by some scholars as an "anti-Beatrice" because her earthy language and behavior contrast sharply with the type of idealized, an-gelicized woman portrayed by Dante and other poets of the *dolce stil nuovo*. Of particular interest are the sonnets in dialogue between the poet-lover and Becchina, such as *"Becchin' amor!" "Che vuo, falso tradito?"* and *"Becchina mia!" "Cecco, nol ti confesso."* In these compositions Cecco raises the traditional *sonetto a dialogo* to a new level of artistry. By having both figures speak in each line, he accelerates the pace, thus heightening the theatrical and comic effect. Most of the love sonnets that revolve around Becchina have as their theme two moments in the relationship: the poet's initial frustration in getting her to accept him as a lover; and, after the relationship has ended, his despair at losing her.

One reason cited by the poet for his inability to win Becchina back is his constant lack of money. The cause of the poet's poverty is his avaricious father, the subject of many of Cecco's sonnets written in the vituperative tradition of medieval comic poetry. In *Sed i' credesse vìvar un dì solo, V ho un padre sì compressionato, Sed i'avesse mille lingue in bocca,* and other sonnets, the poet describes his father's stinginess in hyperbolic terms and fears that the old man will live forever, thus preventing his son from ever inheriting his money.

The anti-paternal theme, unique to Cecco, gives rise to a series of sonnets about the power of money and the misery of the poor. According to sonnets such as *Così è l'uomo che non ha denari* and *Quando non ho denar, ogn' om mi schiva,* those who find themselves thrust into poverty discover that their friends desert them and that people point to them as objects of derision. Cecco's ingenious use of hyperbole results in a sonnet in which the poet is so poor that he has pawned his smiles (*Per sì gran somma ho 'impegnate le risa*).

From the sonnets on poverty it is a short jump to sonnets written in the gnomic-moralizing tradition, in which the values and institutions of society are viewed as corrupt. Typical of this group are *Senno non val a cui fortuna è cònta* and *Egli è sì poco di fede e d'amore.*

Although many scholars have interpreted Cecco's poetry as autobiographical, it is important to keep in mind that his themes are deeply rooted in medieval literary tradition, and that his style attests to a thorough knowledge of the medieval arts of composition, *artes dictandi.*

See also **Dante Alighieri; Rustico Filippi**

Further Reading

Editions

Angiolieri, Cecco. *Rime,* ed. Gigi Cavalli. Milan: Biblioteca Universale Rizzoli, 1959. (3rd ed., 1984.)
——. *Le rime,* ed. Antonio Lanza. Rome: Archivio Guido Izzi, 1990.
Contini, Gianfranco, ed. *Poeti del Duecento,* 2 vols. Milan and Naples: Ricciardi, 1960, Vol. 2, pp. 367–401.
Marti, Mario, ed. *Poeti giocosi del tempo di Dante.* Milan: Rizzoii, 1956, pp. 113–250.
Massèra, Aldo Francesco, ed. *Sonetti burleschi e realistici dei primi due secoli,* 2 vols. Bari: Laterza, 1920; rev. Luigi Russo, 1940, Vol. 2, pp. 63–138.
Vitale, Maurizio, ed. *Rimatori comico-realistici.* Turin: UTET, 1956, pp. 257–453. (Reprint, 1976.)

Translations

Angiolieri, Cecco. *The Sonnets of a Handsome and Well-Mannered Rogue,* trans. Thomas Caldecot Chubb. Hamden, Conn.: Archon, 1970.
——.*Cecco As I Am and Was: The Poems of Cecco Angiolieri,*
trans. Tracy Barrett. Boston, Mass.: International Pocket Library, 1994.
Dante and His Circle, with the Italian Poets Preceding Him (1100–1200–1300), trans. Dante Gabriel Rossetti. London: Ellis and Elvey, 1892, pp. 183–205.
Tusiani, Joseph, trans. *The Age of Dante: An Anthology of Early Italian Poetry.* New York: Baroque, 1974, pp. 123–128.

Studies

Alfie, Fabian. *Comedy and Culture: Cecco Angiolieri's Poetry and Late Medieval Society.* Leeds: Northern Universities Press, 2001.
——."'I son sì magro che quasi traiuco': Inspiration and Indebtedness among Cecco Angiolieri, Meo Dei Tolomei, and Il Burchiello." *Italian Quarterly,* 135–136, 1998, pp. 5–28.
Angiolillo, Paul F. "Cecco Angiolieri, Scamp and Poet of Medieval Siena." *Forum Italicum,* 1, 1967, pp. 156–170.
Figurelli, Fernando. *La musa bizzarra di Cecco Angiolieri.* Naples: Pironti, 1950.
Kleinhenz, Christopher. *The Early Italian Sonnet: The First Century (1220–1321).* Lecce: Milella, 1986, pp. 157–200.
Levin, Joan H. *Rustico di Filippo and the Florentine Lyric Tradition.* New York: Peter Lang, 1986, pp. 99–111.
Maier, Bruno. *La personalità e la poesia di Cecco Angiolieri: Studio critico.* Bologna: Cappelli, 1947.
Marti, Mario. "Cecco Angiolieri." In *Cultura e stile nei poeti giocosi del tempo di Dante.* Pisa: Nistri-Lischi, 1953, pp. 83–129.
——."Angiolieri, Cecco." In *Encicbpedia Dantesca,* 6 vols. Rome: Istituto della Enciclopedia Italiana, 1970–1978.
——, *Con Dante fra i poeti del suo tempo.* Lecce: Milella, 1971.
Nannetti, Elvira. *Cecco Angiolieri: La sua patria, i suoi tempi, e la sua poesia.* Siena: Libreria Editrice Senese, 1929.
Orwen, Gifford P. "Cecco Angiolieri: The Sonnets of Dubious Attribution." *Italica,* 51, 1974, pp. 409–422.
——. *Cecco Angiolieri: A Study.* Chapel Hill: University of North Carolina Department of Romance Languages, 1979.
Petrocchi, Giorgio. "I poeti realisti." In *Le origini e il Duecento.* Milan: Garzanti, 1965, pp. 575–607. (Reprint, 1979.)
Quaglio, Antonio Enzo. "La poesia realistica." In *Il Duecento: Dalle origini a Dante.* Bari: Laterza, 1970, pp. 183–253.

JOAN H. LEVIN

CECCO D'ASCOLI (1269–1327)

The physician, poet, and astrologer, Francesco Stabili, known as Cecco d'Ascoli, was born in Ancarano, near Ascoli Piceno in the Marches. At age fifteen he attended medical school in Salerno. He continued his training in Paris and later became a lecturer in medicine at the University of Bologna. In 1324, he was suspended from teaching after having been accused of heresy by the inquisitor Lamberto da Cingoli. In 1326, he was in Florence in the service of Charles, duke of Calabria, and became Charles's personal physician and astrologer. Cecco's troubles in Bologna, however, followed him to Florence, where he made some powerful enemies. Dino del Garbo, a renowned Florentine physician, conspired to ruin him. The pretext for Dino's animosity was Cecco's belief that the birth of Christ had been foreshadowed by the stars, but historians have speculated about the actual reasons for the conspiracy. Were the Florentine doctors envious of Cecco's professional success, or were they truly opposed to his scientific beliefs, which he promoted in his widely read commentaries on important astrological treatises? At the same time that Dino was conspiring against him, Cecco fell out of favor with his patron, Charles; according to a contemporary, the Florentine chronicler Giovanni Villani, Cecco had predicted that Charles's daughter Giovanna would lead a lascivious life. Undermined by envious intellectuals and doctors, abandoned by his protector, and faced with a prejudicial case against him, Cecco was convicted of heresy and sentenced to death; he was burned at the stake on 16 September 1327.

Cecco d'Ascoli was renowned for his Latin commentaries on John of Holywood's *Spera mundi* and on the *Deprincipiis astrologie* of the Arab astronomer Alcabizio, as well as for his tract *Prelectiones ordinarie astrologie habite Bononie.* Today, he is best remembered for his doctrinal or didactic poem *Acerba,* with its polemic against Dante. The title *Acerba* may be derived from *cerva* (a doe) and thus may be an allegorical allusion to love, in this case a love of science and knowledge. However, a more plausible etymology is that *Acerba* derives from the Latin *acervus,* meaning a compendium of various topics.

Acerba consists of five books, the last of which was left unfinished at the poet's death. Each book is divided into short chapters containing strophes of six hendecasyllables. The first book (9 chapters) is a disquisition on astronomy and cosmology. The second (19 chapters) deals with the relationship between ethics and astrology. Whereas Dante sees Fortune as an angelic intelligence who distributes her gifts unpredictably, Cecco believes that human beings can alter their own fate through the proper exercise of free will. In the third book (18 chapters), the poet describes his moral bestiary: each animal or gem corresponds to a spiritual inclination and a moral belief. In the fourth book (12 chapters), the author uses the dialogue form to underscore the relationship between the natural world and the moral life of human beings. In a famous passage (4.13, 1–6), Cecco criticizes Dante for having used fiction to speak about divine matters:

> Qui non si canta al modo delle rane
> qui non si canta al modo del poeta
> che finge imaginando cose vane;
> ma qui resplende e luce onne natura
> che a chi entende fa la menta leta.
> Qui non si gira per la selva oscura.

("Here one does not sing like the frogs, here one does not sing like the poet who imagines false things and sets them forth, but here all nature shines and sheds light such that the minds of those who hear are gladdened. Here one does not go through the dark wood.") At first

glance, Cecco's position against fiction appears similar to that of orthodox clerics who opposed popular fictional representations of theological issues. In reality, Cecco argues with Dante from a completely different perspective. The mysteries of the universe can be explained by a profound understanding of nature. The moral life, moreover, does not require belief in a transcendental figure. Cecco denies neither the existence of God nor the importance of divinity in the universe. He simply asserts that knowledge about the world humans inhabit can help them lead an ethical life.

With the exception of few passages, *Acerba* is aesthetically uninspiring and prosaic. Scholars read it primarily as an example of *Trecento* didactic poetry and for the polemic concerning Dante. They would do better, however, to give greater consideration to this poet's life and work. For one thing, even his adversaries respected his intellectual courage and conviction. He was, moreover, an unorthodox and profound thinker whose secular views represent an Important strand in the intellectual history of the early *Trecento.*

See also **Dante Alighieri**

Further Reading

Camuffo, Maria Luisa, and Aldo Costantini. "Il lapidario dell'*Acerba.*" *Lettere Italiane,* 51, 1988, pp. 526–535.
Castelli, Giuseppe. *La vita e le opere di Cecco d'Ascoli.* Bologna: Zanichelli, 1892.
Cecco d'Ascoli. *"L'Acerba, "secondo la lezione del codice Eugubino del 1376,* ed. Basilio Censori and Emidio Vittori. Verona: Stamperia Valdonega, 1971.
Censori, Basilio, ed. *Atti del I convegno di studi su Cecco d'Ascoli: Ascoli Piceno, Palazzo dei Congressi, 23–24 novembre 1969.* Florence: Giunti Barbera, 1976.
Stabili, Francesco. *L'Acerba,* ed. Achille Crespi. Ascoli Piceno: Giuseppe Cesari, 1927.
Thorndike, Lynn. *The "Sphere" of Sacrobosco and Its Commentators.* Chicago, Ill.: University of Chicago Press, 1949. (See p. 53 for an assessment of Cecco's commentaries and pp. 343–411 for Cecco's commentary on the *Sphere.*)

DARIO DEL PUPPO

CELESTINE V, POPE
(c. 1209 or 1210–1296, r. 1294)

Pope Celestine V (Pietro da Morrone) was born in the region of Molise in central Italy; the precise place is probably Sant' Angelo Limosano, a small rural community. After being introduced to monastic life, Pietro (or Peter) became a hermit in the early 1230s, living in the Apennines of Abraazzo, notably on Mount Maiella and Mount Morrone. His fame as a miracle worker attracted a constant stream of visitors, and his holiness drew many followers to him. He needed to obtain ecclesiastical approbation for his community of followers, and this was granted in 1263 or 1264 by Pope Urban IV, who incorporated the Celestines into the order of Saint Benedict. To ensure the stability of the new congregation, Pietro went to Lyon and obtained a confirmation from Pope Gregory X in 1275.

By the 1290s, Pietro had founded or effectively controlled dozens of monasteries, mainly in the central part of the Italian peninsula. In 1293 he established the seat of the order at the new abbey of Santo Spirito del Morrone, near Sulmona; he himself lived in a hermitage on a mountainside overlooking the monastery.

This move occurred during an interregnum following the death of Pope Nicholas IV (4 April 1292) when the cardinals, divided between the Orsini and Colonna factions, could not agree on a new pope. Charles II of Anjou and others exerted pressure to help break the impasse, and on 5 July 1294, in Perugia, Pietro—by then an octogenarian—was unexpectedly and unanimously elected pope. Although Pietro was known to some important clerics and secular leaders, he was probably selected not for his qualities or potential qualities as a leader but rather as a compromise candidate whose reign was not expected to be long.

Pietro was crowned Pope Celestine V in L'Aquila, the main city of Abruzzo, on 29 August 1294; he established an unusual indulgence that granted complete absolution to those who visited, under certain conditions, the church where he was crowned. Celestine appointed twelve new cardinals, gave the Franciscan Spirituals protection within the Pauperes Eremite Domini Celestini, and granted many favors to his monastic congregation; but it soon became apparent that he had little talent or inclination for his new tasks. When the Curia moved to Naples in November, Celestine considered renouncing the papacy and returning to his life as a hermit; he did so on 13 December 1294, after consultations with Cardinal Benedetto Caetani—who was elected Pope Boniface VIII eleven days later. Boniface, fearing that Pietro (as Celestine was now called again) might retract the abdication, sent emissaries to bring Pietro to him. Pietro was arrested trying to flee to Greece and was brought to Fumone, where he was confined until he died on 19 May 1296. Under pressure from the French king Philip the Fair, Pope Clement V canonized Pietro on 5 May 1313 in Avignon.

Celestine has been identified with Dante's *colui che fece per viltade il gran rifiuto,* "the one who made through cowardice the great refusal" (*Inferno* 3.59–60), but it is not certain that this was Dante's intention.

See also Boniface VIII, Pope; Clement V, Pope; Dante Alighieri

Further Reading

Analecta Bollandiana, 16, 1897, pp. 365–487.

Frugoni, Arsenio. *Celestiniana.* Studi Storici, 6–7. Rome: Istituto Storico Italiano per il Medio Evo, 1954. (Reprint, 1991.)

Herde, Peter. *Cölestin V. (1294) (Peter vom Morrone), der Engelpapst.* Päpste und Papsttum, 16. Stuttgart: Anton Hiersemann, 1981.

———. "Celestine V." In *The Papacy: An Encyclopedia,* ed. Philippe Levallain. New York: Routledge, 2002, Vol. 1, pp. 279–283.

Seppelt, Franz Xaver. *Monumenta Coelestiniana: Quellen zur Geschichte des Papstes Coelestin V.* Quellen und Forschungen aus dem Gebiete der Geschichte. Paderborn: Ferdinand Schoningh, 1921.

GEORGE FERZOCO

CHARLEMAGNE (747–814)

Charles the Great (*magnus,* whence the French "Charlemagne"), King of the Franks (768–814) and emperor of the West (800–814) was born in 747 to Pippin (Pépin) III and his wife, Bertha, daughter of the powerful Count Caribert of Laon. Pippin, mayor of the palace of the Franks, named his son after his own father, the redoubtable Charles Martel (d. 742). In 751 when Charles was still a boy, Pippin became king after deposing Childeric III (743–751), the last member of the Merovingian dynasty established by Clovis (481–511). The legitimacy of the new dynasty was bolstered when Pope Stephen II (also III, 752–757) came to Francia to bless Bertrada (Bertha) and in the name of Saint Peter anoint Pippin and his sons Charles and Carloman as "patricians of the Romans." The pope forbade the Franks from choosing anyone as king other than a Carolingian (from the Latin Carolus, Charles). This dynastic change and the relationship binding the political and military power of the Carolingian family to the spiritual power of the papacy were revolutionary events. Pippin III proved to be a resourceful and energetic king whose conquest of Aquitaine, two successful expeditions against the Lombards, and promotion of religious reform demonstrated the potential and direction of the new dynasty.

During his long reign Charles more fully realized and amplified Pippin's initiatives. So spectacular was his achievement that his posthumous reputation assumed legendary proportions. Einhard (ca. 770–840), who grew up at Charles's court, in his valuable *Life of Charles* borrowed language from Suetonius's *Lives of the Caesars* (second-century C.E.) to add rhetorical luster appropriate to his subject. In later centuries crusading and romance legends inspired by Charles's memory enriched medieval vernacular literature. In the twentieth century his memory served to advance the prospects of a united Europe. Since 1949, the citizens of Aachen, Germany, have annually awarded the International Charlemagne Prize (*Karl-pries*) to individuals whose activities further "the creation of a United States of Europe." In his own time, Charles grappled with the implications of a new style of kingship, faced the challenges of conquest, revolt, and the future of the dynasty, and attempted to unify and reform a society embracing a welter of different peoples within a community that eventually stretched over one million square kilometers.

The kingdom Charles inherited from his father in 768 was much smaller, essentially modern France, Belgium, the Netherlands, Luxembourg, and western Germany. At first Charles shared the kingdom with his younger brother Carloman. Corulership set the stage for rivalry within the family, especially when Carloman refused to aid in suppressing rebellions in Aquitaine, but Carloman's death in December 771 averted serious dynastic tension. As sole king, Charles turned his attention to solidifying control of political and military resources and to crises outside his realm. A successful king in the early Middle Ages was a successful warlord. Charles, as had Pippin III and Charles Martel before him, succeeded as a leader because he succeeded as a warrior. Charles drew the warrior class, some 250 to 300 counts and their followers, to his cause by sharing with them the spoils of war and political authority. Aristocratic loyalty and support provided the mainstay of Charles's war machine. Charles's detailed orders to his warriors stipulating when and where to mobilize and what equipment and manpower to bring offer an unparalleled insight to his command and control structure. His ability to make war almost continually and most often successfully for more than thirty years on many fronts attests to Charles's success as a military commander.

After Carloman's death Charles's armies began to campaign outside Francia. In 772, rejecting his mother's efforts to ally with the Lombard kingdom (Charles had even married a soon to be repudiated Lombard princess), Charles responded to calls of Pope Hadrian I (772–795) for help against the "pestiferous" Lombards. After a siege of nine months the Lombard capital of Pavia fell in 774 and Desiderius, the last Lombard king of the two-century-old kingdom, was captured and confined to the monastery of Corbie in northern Francia. Charles became the king of the Lombards. During the siege of Pavia, he made the first ever visit by a Frankish king to Rome. Charles's political relationship to the pope was ambiguous and Hadrian soon chafed under the growing presence and influence of Frankish counts and ecclesiastics in Italy. Although linked to Desiderius by family ties, Duke Tassilo III of Bavaria did not intervene in the Lombard war. Tassilo earlier had agreed to become a vassal of Pippin. When Charles required Tassilo to renew his pledges in 781, the semi-independent duke balked. After military threats and a decade of diplomatic intrigue, Tassilo was confined to a monastery and in 794 "abdicated." The annexation of Lombardy and Bavaria is all the more impressive when viewed together with the continuous conflict in Saxony. One of the last centers of vibrant Germanic paganism, the Saxon homeland east of

Bronze equestrian statue of Charlemagne (horse probably later). Carolingian, 9th CE. © Erich Lessing/Art Resource, New York.

the Rhine was a hotbed of political resistance to Carolingian aggression fueled by devotion to Saxon culture and skillful exploitation of Frankish preoccupation in other regions. Earlier in the eighth century Charles Martel fought against the Saxons, a struggle his grandson continued in 772. Saxony was finally subdued in 804, but not until after several uprisings led by the spirited Widukind (also Wittekind), the massacre of forty-five hundred Saxon prisoners, and the forced deportation of Saxons to Francia. The conquest and eventual Christianization of Saxony extended Carolingian power into a region never controlled by the Roman Empire.

In 777 the emir of Barcelona, no doubt encouraged by the success of Frankish arms, persuaded Charles to invade Spain, which had been under Muslim control since 711. This bold venture ended in 778 in a disaster immortalized in the *Song of Roland*, the attack on Charles's rear guard by Basques in the Pyrenees. Operations in the 790s in the Danube basin where the Avars had been settled from the sixth century, met greater success. As the partisans of the Lombards and of Tassilo, these "new Huns" defined themselves as enemies of the Carolingians. In 791 Charles initiated an eastern campaign that Einhard described as second only to the Saxon wars in its intensity and significance. By 796 Charles had crushed Avar power. Significantly, Einhard seemed most impressed by the fifteen wagons, each drawn by four oxen, that were required to haul Avar treasure back to Francia. Three years later in 799 the Bretons in Brittany, who had long been foes of the Franks, surrendered to Charles's armies.

Charles's ceaseless campaigns enriched and transformed his kingdom. As the lands under his control expanded to cover most of western Europe, the Carolingians established contact with peoples on their periphery including Scandinavians, Slavs, Byzantines, Muslims, and Anglo-Saxons. The patriarch of Jerusalem as well as Hārkūn ar-Rashīd, the caliph of Baghdad, and the imperial court at Constantinople exchanged embassies and correspondence with Charles's court. But Charles's primary focus lay in controlling the heterogeneous lands and peoples of his vast domain measuring some six hundred miles along each axis from Scandinavia to the Mediterranean and from the Atlantic to the Danube. Charles's administrative and political structure was multilayered. Although master of all, Charles delegated power and authority to trusted followers. His sons Louis and Pippin were appointed sub-kings of Aquitaine and Italy, respectively, while his brother-in-law Gerold was put in charge of Bavaria. Charles established marches in dangerous border regions whose governors controlled the local counts. Elsewhere counts exercised military, judicial, and fiscal authority. Charles tried to hold this centrifugal system of shared authority together by several means. Royal capitularies, documents organized by topics (*capitula*), established and broadcast policy. The subjects of these—including farm management, minting, heresy, religious reform, justice, famine, warfare, education, feuds, homicide, rape, widows, and orphans—suggests the range of his concept of governance. Several capitularies addressed specifically to the *missi*, the king's personal representatives dispatched throughout the kingdom to carry out his wishes and to investigate local problems, point to another level of administrative and political control. *Missi* (from the Latin *missus*, "one who is sent out") had been used by Merovingian kings, but Charles extended and regularized their use as agents of government, who linked a highly fragmented political system to the king's household.

When he was not campaigning Charles settled in favorite palaces at Frankfurt, Herstal, Ingelheim, Mainz, Worms, and Thionville, in the heartlands of the Frankish kingdom. After 794 he resided semipermanently at the new palace complex at Aachen. The king's household, with its feasts, rituals, comings and goings, hunting expeditions, and, in Aachen's warm springs, group bathing, formed a dynamic community. Carolingian poets memorialized the conviviality of the royal entourage. Charles's household consisted of the seneschal who maintained provisions, butlers, cupbearers, chamberlains, who took care of the living quarters, the constable, who attended the stable, a host of domestics, and family members. By the end of his long life, Charles presided over a large, three-generation family. Einhard mentions five wives as well as four concubines who were a part of Charles's household and bore at least sixteen children who survived infancy. His wives, especially Hildegard, Fastrada, and Liutgard played important political and public roles, as did his sons and daughters, some of whom became bishops, abbots, and abbesses. Ironically, the religious reform that Charles encouraged would shortly after his death lead to condemnation of his Germanic warlord lifestyle. In a widely reported dream, the monk Wetti related in 824 that he had observed in the afterlife a wild beast gnawing at Charles's genitals as punishment for his sexual sins.

The system of governance and administration that Charles gradually built up depended on loyalty and commitment to his policies. In practice the system was often compromised by the personal and family interests of officials who used their positions to enrich themselves. Charges of corruption and abuse of power by rapacious counts, judges, and even *missi* who succumbed to bribery occur commonly in the sources, especially during the last decade of Charles's reign. Important family connections made it difficult to bring corrupt officials to justice. In addition to periodic rebellions of conquered peoples, Charles also faced serious challenges to his regime. In 785–786, a rebellion led by Count Hadrad of Thuringia had to be brutally suppressed. A few years later in 792 one of Charles's sons was discovered at the center of a plot against the king's life involving Frankish aristocrats. After dealing swiftly with the rebels, Charles attempted to enforce loyalty by legal and religious means. In 786, 789, 792, and again in 802 after he became emperor, he required an ever widening group, which eventually embraced all freemen, lay and clerical, over the age of twelve, to swear personal loyalty to him. The 802 oath was especially significant, since it bound oath takers not only to obey the emperor and protect his life, but also to live Christian lives.

The nexus between politics and religion had long been a feature of Frankish life and culture. Charles

Martel and Pippin III enjoyed close relations with clergy and identified with religious reform. The prologue to the mid-eighth-century revision of the Salic Law unabashedly depicted the Franks as God's new Chosen People. Within this tradition Charles enacted religious reforms and promoted Christianity as vigorously as he waged war and managed his kingdom. He drew talented churchmen to his court as advisers, many of whom he was able to place strategically in bishoprics and monasteries throughout his realm. These churchmen often performed important political duties as well. Court scholars honored Charles's patronage of their work by calling him David after the biblical king. In religious matters, however, Charles modeled himself on Johiah, the Hebrew king who undertook a root and branch reform of Israel based on biblical precepts. His great reform capitulary, the *Admonitio Generalis* of 789, outlines the king's blueprint for a biblically based society. With the biblical kings of old, Charles confidently determined religious policy and used his court to define religious orthodoxy in the West, especially opposing Spanish views on the nature of Christ and Byzantine views of images in worship.

The centrality of the Bible in Carolingian political culture sparked reform in education and stimulated literary culture. During Charles's reign political authority in a massive, sustained, and visible way promoted intellectual culture as essential to the well-being of society. Charles's patronage attracted the leading scholars of Europe to his court, often non-Franks such as the Anglo-Saxon Alcuin, the Visigoth Theodulf, the Italian Peter of Pisa, and the Irishman Dungal. Alcuin, who enjoyed a close personal relationship with Charles, played an especially significant role in establishing a new pedagogy and in training Frankish students to serve as "soldiers of Christ" in the parishes, cathedrals, and monasteries of Carolingian Europe. Charles interacted comfortably with his court scholars, admired Augustine's *City of God*, spoke Latin fluently, and was particularly interested in astronomy and time reckoning. In their pursuit of biblical wisdom as a guide for the reform of their society, Carolingian scholars produced a more legible form of Latin script, Carolingian minuscule. In their efforts to improve learning in Latin and the liberal arts as a stepping-stone to more profound comprehension of sacred wisdom, they copied Roman texts that might otherwise have perished. Carolingian masters and students composed the first audience to systematically read and interpret the works of the Christian church fathers. In their numerous commentaries, technical schoolbooks, theological, philosophical, and political treatises, histories, poetry, and letters, they attempted to integrate secular learning and sacred wisdom in the services of Carolingian society. The emergence of controversy and debate on fundamental theological, philosophical, political, and legal issues testifies to the sophistication and originality of the new culture. Charles's patronage and the wealth flowing into the hands of aristocrats and ecclesiastics also stimulated artistic production in the form of metalwork, elaborate book covers, jewelry, crystal, ivory carving, painting, and manuscript illumination. Some six hundred new buildings went up in the Carolingian realms, including cathedrals, monasteries, and palace complexes at Aachen and Paderborn.

On December 25, 800, Pope Leo III (795–816) crowned Charles emperor in Rome. Charles's continent-wide conquests and strong leadership certainly justified the title, but contemporary sources are unclear about the meaning of the coronation and modern scholars continue to debate its significance. Not even the participants seemed fully aware of the implication of the revival of the imperial title in the West. Certainly the coronation was not a surprise, as Einhard reported, since Charles's circle in the late 790s had already begun to describe him in imperial terms. Charles had come to Rome to rescue the city from his political enemies. The pope no doubt saw conferral of the imperial title as a means to draw Charles even closer to the see of St. Peter and to forge new links with a Western emperor to replace the fractured links with the emperor in Constantinople. "David" was to become Constantine. Again, Rome was disappointed in the new arrangement since Charles dominated the Roman church as he had the church to the north of the Alps. The great programmatic Capitulary of 802 defining an imperial Christian political culture for Europe was crafted in Aachen, not Rome. What the imperial office meant to the relationship between pope and emperor, religion and politics, would be debated for centuries to come. For Charles the emperorship was a personal honor. When in 806 he outlined the future division of the empire among his legitimate sons, Charles, Pippin, and Louis, the question of the imperial title was ignored. In 813, with two of his three heirs dead, Charles bestowed the title on Louis without benefit of papal consultation or approval.

The division of 806 and Louis's coronation in 813 were the actions of a man contemplating his last years. Charles died on January 28, 814 at Aachen and was buried there. His long reign strengthened the power of his family in Europe, entrenched warrior-aristocrats as partners with kings in governing, promoted a distinctly European Christian religion and culture, defined a new sacral kingship, and revived the ambiguous ideology of empire. More than anything, Charles consolidated the fundamental elements of an emerging European identity that late generations would refine and burnish.

See also **Charles Martel; Einhard; Hadrian I, Pope; Louis the Pious; Pepin**

Further Reading

Bullough, Donald. *The Age of Charlemagne*, 2d ed. London: Paul Elek, 1973.

Collins, Roger. *Charlemagne*. Toronto: University of Toronto Press, 1998.

Contreni, John J. "The Carolingian Renaissance: Education and Literary Culture." In *The New Cambridge Medieval History*, ed. Rosamond McKitterick. *Vol. 2, c. 700—c. 900*. Cambridge: Cambridge University Press, 1997, pp. 709–757.

——. "Carolingian Biblical Culture." In *Iohannes Scottus Eriugena: The Bible and Hermeneutics*, ed. Gerd Van Riel, Carlos Steel, and James McEvoy. Ancient and Medieval Philosophy, De-Wulf-Mansion Centre, Series 1, XX. Louvain: Louvain University Press, 1996, pp. 1–23.

Dutton, Paul Edward. *The Politics of Dreaming in the Carolingian Empire*. Lincoln: University of Nebraska Press, 1994.

——, ed. *Carolingian Civilization: A Reader*. Peterborough, Ont.: Broadview Press, 1993.

Fichtenau, Heinrich. *The Carolingian Empire: The Age of Charlemagne*, trans. Peter Munz. Oxford: Basil Blackwell, 1957.

Ganshof, François Louis. *Frankish Institutions Under Charlemagne*, rrans. Bryce and Mary Lyon. Providence, R.I.: Brown University Press, 1968.

Godman, Peter. *Poets and Emperors: Frankish Politics and Carolingian Poetry*. Oxford: Clarendon Press, 1987.

——. trans. *Poetry of the Carolingian Empire*. Norman: University of Oklahoma Press, 1985.

King, P. D., trans. *Charlemagne: Translated Sources*. Lambrigg, England: P. D. King, 1987.

Loyn, H. R., and John Percival, trans. *The Reign of Charlemagne: Documents on Carolingian Government and Administration*. London: Edward Arnold, 1975.

McKitterick, Rosamond. *The Frankish Kingdoms Under the Carolingians, 751–987*. London and New York: Longman, 1983.

Nees, Lawrence. *A Tainted Mantle: Hercules and the Classical Tradition at the Carolingian Court*. Philadelphia: University of Pennsylvania Press, 1991.

Nelson, Janet. "Women at the Court of Charlemagne: A Case of Monstrous Regiment?" In Janet Nelson, *The Frankish World, 750–900*. London: Hambledon Press, 1996, pp. 223–242.

Riché, Pierre. *The Carolingians: A Family Who Forged Europe*, trans. Michael Idomir Allen. Philadelphia: University of Pennsylvania Press, 1993.

Sullivan, Richard E. *Aix-la-Chapelle in the Age of Charlemagne*. Norman: University of Oklahoma Press, 1963.

JOHN J. CONTRENI

CHARLES D'ORLÉANS (1394–1465)

Son of Valentina, daughter of the duke of Milan, and Louis, duke of Orléans and brother of King Charles VI. In 1407, Louis was murdered by John the Fearless, duke of Burgundy, and Valentine died at Blois the following year. In 1406, Charles had married Isabelle, widow of Richard II of England and daughter of Charles VI. The year after her death in 1409, he married Bonne d'Armagnac. Captured by the English at the Battle of Agincourt in 1415, Charles spent the next twenty-five years in England in the custody of several noblemen. Bonne died in France during this period. Released in 1440, Charles returned joyfully to France and soon afterward married fourteen-year-old Marie de Clèves,

niece of Philip of Burgundy, who had helped to arrange his release. After a period of political involvement, he spent most of his remaining years at Blois, where two daughters and a son who was to become King Louis XII were born.

During the last fifteen years of his life at Blois, Charles received many visitors, who joined with members of his household to participate in poetry contests. Samples of this literary activity have survived in a manuscript (B.N. fr. 25458) that served as Charles's personal album, in which he recorded in his own hand his own poems, had some entered by scribes, and also invited members of his entourage and visitors to make contributions. Included in this collection are poems by important political figures of the day, by writers with established reputations, and even by the itinerant poet and sometime criminal François Villon, who may have received a small allowance while living at the court. Charles often proposed the first line of a rondeau or ballade and asked his entourage to write a poem following the restrictions of the prescribed form. It was under these circumstances that Villon wrote *Je meurs de suef auprés de la fontaine*, probably in 1457 or 1458. Villon's other poem in the collection, *Épître à Marie d'Orléans*, was probably composed to celebrate the birth of Charles's daughter in December 1457. The wit and good-natured bantering found in the poems written at the court of Blois serve as evidence of an unusually pleasant and relaxed atmosphere, in which poetry writing was an agreeable pastime.

Charles and his two younger brothers, Philippe and Jean, received a traditional medieval education under the direction of a private tutor. Writing in verse seems to have come naturally, since the first work attributed to Charles, *Le livre contre tout péché*, was written at the age of ten. His numerous poetic works include the *Complainte de France*, written in 1433 after he had been in England for many years; *Retenue d'amours*, composed prior to his capture; the *Songe en complainte* (1437), a 550-line sequel to *Retenue d'amours*; eighty-nine chansons and five complaintes written in England, perhaps after Bonne's death; 123 ballades written mostly during but also after his captivity; four *caroles*; and 435 rondeaux written mostly at Blois. In addition to the poems in French, about 125 in English, many with French counterparts, are attributed to him with increasing confidence.

Charles d'Orléans is known particularly for his use of allegory and the introspective nature of his poetry. Recurring themes in his ballades and rondeaux include exile, the passage of time, the flight of love, life as a prison, old age, the decomposition of the human body, and melancholy. He may be one of the best known and least appreciated French poets. Nearly every anthology of French poetry includes a few of his ballades and rondeaux, especially the ubiquitous *Le temps a laissié son manteau*. Many literary historians refer patronizingly to the charm and superficiality of his poetry and the seeming ineffectiveness of his life, echoing Gaston Paris's assessment that Charles was merely a child with a gift for polished verse, who never understood his role in life. Scholars long considered Charles the last courtly poet, using outmoded medieval conventions to express traditional clichés, while they lionized Villon as a fresh and original forerunner of modern poetry. In addition, because so much biographical information is available, scholarship has often been stifled by the attempt to tie Charles's creative work to his life. Recently, however, scholars have taken a closer look at his poetry, have become aware of the libraries to which he had access in both England and France, and consequently have begun to discover in many of his poems a new depth and complexity never before suspected. He is now often classed as a precursor of some of the 19th-century romantic and symbolist poets, especially Baudelaire. His *nonchaloir* has been likened to the "spleen" of later times.

Charles's poems have been translated into English, Dutch, Italian, and Romanian. In addition, scholarly books about his life and works have been published in Japanese, Polish, and Russian.

See also **Charles VI; Chartier, Alain; Villon, François**

Further Reading

Charles d'Orléans. *Charles d'Orléans, Poésies*, ed. Pierre Champion. 2 vols. Paris: Champion, 1923–27, Vol. 1: *La retenue d'amours, ballades, chansons, complaintes et caroles*; Vol. 2: *Rondeaux*.

——. *Le manuscrit autographe des poésies de Charles d'Orléans*, ed. Pierre Champion. Paris: Champion, 1907.

——. *The French Chansons of Charles d'Orléans with the Corresponding Middle English Chansons*, ed. and trans. Sarah Spence. New York: Garland, 1986.

Champion, Pierre. *La vie de Charles d'Orléans*. Paris: Champion, 1911.

Fox, John. *The Lyric Poetry of Charles d'Orléans*. Oxford: Clarendon, 1969.

Nelson, Deborah H. *Charles d'Orléans: An Analytical Bibliography*. London: Grant and Cutler, 1990.

Planche, Alice. *Charles d'Orléans, ou la recherche d'un langage*. Paris: Champion, 1975.

Steele, Robert, and Mabel Day. *The English Poems of Charles d'Orléans*. London: Oxford University Press, 1941.

Yenal, Edith. *Charles d'Orléans: A Bibliography of Primary and Secondary Sources*. New York: AMS, 1984.

DEBORAH H. NELSON

CHARLES II THE BAD (1332–1387)

King of Navarre. The son of Philippe d'Évreux and Jeanne, daughter of Louis X of France, Charles succeeded his father as count of Évreux in 1343 and became king of Navarre (as Charles II) when his mother died in October 1349. Although he became a bitter enemy of the royal house of Valois, whose propagandists accused him of many nefarious deeds and plots, Charles was a popular young man who commanded a considerable political following in the 1350s. Not until the 16th century did he appear as "El Malo" in Navarrese historiography, but this sobriquet gained wide acceptance among subsequent generations of royalist or nationalist historians in France.

The Évreux family had serious grievances against the Valois monarchy, which kept possession of Jeanne's inheritance of Champagne and Brie, never relinquished to her the promised compensation, Angoulême, and remained dilatory in providing the revenues that were to have replaced these territories. The northwestern nobles, disaffected for much of Philip VI's reign, had many connections to the house of Évreux, which had cultivated clients among them. Other critics of the monarchy were genuine reformers whose intellectual wing was based in the Collège de Navarre in Paris, a longtime recipient of Évreux patronage.

The Valois rulers made efforts to cultivate their Évreux cousins. Philip VI, as an aging widower, married Charles's teenaged sister Blanche in 1349, and Charles himself married Jeanne, the eldest daughter of John II, a few years later. These overtures, however, did not defuse the grievances, and the delays in paying his wife's large dowry embittered Charles further. John II aggravated the bad royal relations with the northwestern nobility by summarily executing the constable Raoul de Brienne in 1350. The new constable, John's inexperienced young favorite Charles of Spain, received lavish royal gifts, including the county of Angoulême, which Charles the Bad considered to be rightfully his own. With considerable sympathy from critics of the regime, Charles had the constable murdered in January 1354, thus beginning a decade of rebellion against his father-in-law.

To shield himself from royal wrath, Charles called on the English for aid, and John II had to conclude the Treaty of Mantes (February 1354), which pardoned Charles and his followers and granted him substantial new lands in lower Normandy in return for his definitive renunciation of Champagne and Brie. Charles then proceeded to disrupt Anglo-French negotiations at Avignon and bring troops to Normandy, where he hoped to cooperate with an English invasion. When contrary winds kept Edward III from coming, Charles had to conclude a less advantageous treaty with John II at Valognes (September 10, 1355). The king of Navarre remained a magnet for discontented elements in northwestern France and apparently tried to subvert the dauphin, John's eldest son, into rebelling against his father.

Increasingly bitter toward his son-in-law, John II suddenly arrested Charles at Rouen in April 1356, executing several of his followers and placing him in prison. Normandy was swept by civil war, and in September John and his supporters suffered devastating defeat by the Prince of Wales near Poitiers. With John II now a captive, the dauphin's weakened government faced a large array of critics, some of whom demanded the release of Charles the Bad.

Released by his friends in November 1357, Charles resumed his role as a leader of forces opposed to the crown, yet within a year his position had eroded. Nobles in particular and reformers generally became attracted to the dauphin's camp after the hostility of the Parisians toward nobles drove a wedge between noble and bourgeois reformers. Charles the Bad became suspect because he cooperated with the Parisians and because his negotiations with the English indicated an interest in partitioning France. He and his supporters failed to prevent the release of John II via the Treaty of Brétigny. An uneasy peace with John ended when the king bestowed Burgundy on his son Philip the Bold in 1363. Charles asserted a claim to Burgundy, and with the new hostilities thousands of unemployed soldiers (*routiers*) claimed to be fighting in his name.

At the end of 1363, the Estates General of northern France established a tax to support a regular salaried army. In the spring of 1364, as Charles V was succeeding John II on the French throne, this new army, commanded by Bertrand du Guesclin, won a crushing victory over the forces of Charles the Bad at Cocherel in Normandy. This campaign broke the power of the Navarrese party in Normandy and around Paris. Charles was forced to accept the southern barony of Montpellier and relinquish some of his family's Norman strongholds.

After this time, Charles played a diminished role in French politics, although a scandal came to light in 1378 that implicated him in plots against the crown. With the dissidents who formerly supported him now firmly in the royal camp, Charles was restricted to his role as ruler of a minor Spanish kingdom.

See also **Charles V the Wise; Guesclin, Bertrand du; John II the Good**

Further Reading

Bessen, David M. *Charles of Navarre and John II: Disloyalty in Northern France 1350–1360*. Diss. University of Toronto, 1983.

Cazelles, Raymond. *Société politique, noblesse et couronne sous Jean le Bon et Charles V*. Geneva: Droz, 1982.

Henneman, John Bell. *Royal Taxation in Fourteenth Century France: The Captivity and Ransom of John II 1356–1370*. Philadelphia: American Philosophical Society, 1976.

Secousse, Denis F. *Recueil de pièces servant de preuves aux Mémoires sur les troubles excités en France par Charles II dit le Mauvais, roi de Navarre et comte d'Évreux*. Paris: Durand, 1755.

JOHN BELL HENNEMAN, JR.

CHARLES IV (1316–1378)

Emperor Charles IV (r. 1346–1378) was born in Prague, May 14, 1316, the eldest son of John of Luxembourg and Elizabeth of Bohemia. He was baptized under the name of Wenceslas, following the tradition of the Premyslid (Bohemian) dynasty. At the age of seven he was sent to Paris to be educated at the court of Charles IV of France. At his confirmation Wenceslas was given the name of Charles. In Paris he met the Benedictine abbot Pierre Roger de Fécamp, later Pope Clement VI, whose sermons made a major impact on young Charles's spiritual development. He also studied briefly at the University of Paris.

Following campaigns in Italy to secure Luxembourg interests (1331–1333), Charles administered the kingdom of Bohemia during his father's absence. During his stay in Bohemia (1334–1336) Charles retrieved mortgaged crown lands and negotiated two very important treaties with Poland (Trencin and Visegrád). These treaties established one of the basic aspects of Charles's foreign policy: the abandonment of military expansion in favor of a policy based on treaties and alliances. Charles consistently aimed to maintain the balance of power between Poland, Hungary, the Teutonic Knights, the Habsburg dominions, and his own Bohemian crown lands.

In 1340, when his father became blind, Charles assumed control over the Luxembourg domains, opening the way for his eventual acquisition of the imperial throne. Emperor Louis the Bavarian's policies, particularly his attempts to obtain Tyrol and his renewed conflicts with the papacy, had aroused the enmity of the other German princes. In 1344 an assembly of princes demanded that Louis do sufficient penance to lift the ban of excommunication within two years or face deposition. When Louis failed to do so, the electors met, declared Louis deposed, and elected Charles as emperor on July 1, 1346. Charles's uncle, Archbishop Baldwin of Trier, played a leading role in the negotiations with the princes and the papacy that led to the election.

Initially, Charles's position was rather weak. Because of his support from Clement VI, he was identified by some as yet another "clergy king" (*Pfaffenkönig*). Many bishops and nearly all the imperial cities remained loyal to Louis. Worse for Charles, shortly after his election, he lost a good number of supporters, including his father blind King John, who died fighting for the French at Crècy (August 26, 1346). Civil war was prevented when Louis the Bavarian died bear hunting in October 1347. Although supporters of the Wittelsbach dynasty elected Günther of Schwarzburg king of Germany in January 1349, he was dead by the end of summer.

Prague served as the political, cultural, and spiritual center of Charles's domain. The city had already risen to prominence under the Premyslid rulers, but had suffered serious neglect under King John. Charles began reconstruction of the Hradschin castle during his first long stay in Bohemia in the 1330s. In 1344 he arranged for the bishop of Prague to be elevated to the rank of archbishop. After his coronation as King of Bohemia in 1347, Charles initiated a number of projects that substantially reshaped the city. A new cathedral dedicated to St. Veit was begun on the Hradschin. Within the cathedral, Chatles had built a special chapel to hold the relics of St. Wenceslas. He also founded a university in 1348, the first in the empire. With the foundation of the New Town (*Nové Mesto*) in Prague, Charles nearly tripled the size of the city.

Charles's political views and his religious ideas were closely connected. From his early years in Paris and Italy, he had developed a sense of his own divine mission. This ideal was represented in the new coronation *ordo*, or rites, devised for Bohemia in 1347. The coronation *ordo*, like his mania for collecting religious relics, reflected the conservative side of Charles's religiosity. But, although his personal religious views connected him most strongly with the *Devotio Antiqua*, he was not without sympathy for the *Devotio Moderna*. He was acquainted with Johannes Tauler and Christina Ebner among the German mystics. In 1363 Charles brought the fiery preacher Conrad Waldhauser to Prague and later supported and defended Waldhauser's student Jan Milic, albeit after Milic stopped identifying the emperor as the Antichrist.

Charles's Italian policies reflected a realization that it would be nearly impossible to restore imperial authority in that region. He made two trips to Rome after his election as emperor. In the winter of 1354–1355 Charles traveled to Rome for his imperial coronation (January 6, 1355) and to settle affairs in the Holy City following the revolt and death of the tribunal official Cola de Rienzo the previous fall. During his trip, Charles met the poet Petrarch in Mantua on December 15, 1354. Two years later Petrarch traveled to Prague as part of a diplomatic mission from the Visconti, a Lombard noble family. During that visit, Charles failed ro convince the poet to remain at his court. He likewise refused Petrarch's invitation to intervene more forcibly in Italian affairs.

In Bohemia, Charles sought to establish a more centralized administration. Much of his effort was aimed at increasing the size and scope of the area that compromised the Bohemian crown lands. He transferred the Silesian duchies from their status as fiefs of the empire to the Bohemian crown. Charles also undertook to create "New Bohemia," a string of possessions in the Upper Palatinate and Franconia that would link Bohemia with the Rhineland. The Bohemian nobles were not wholly supportive of these ventures, however, and sharply resisted Charles's attempts to codify Bohemian law in the *Majestas Carolina* of 1355.

Charles was much more successful in dealing with the states of the empire. Three general trends typify his German policy. First, he devoted his dynastic policy (*Hausmachtpolitik*), to maintaining and increasing the power of the Luxembourg dynasty within and without the empire. Second, Charles sought to fill vacant bishoprics with his supporters, reviviling the imperial church as a political tool for the emperors. Finally, he made alliances with leading states and cities in the empire and sponsored leagues, in particular, city leagues, to help maintain the public peace. The cities of Nuremberg and Lübeck, as well as the Hohenzollern burggraves (districts) of Nurembert and the margraves of Miessen, benefited from Charles's patronage. In general, Charles's German policy focused on maintaining a balance of power within the empire.

One of the main achievements of Charles's reign was the promulgation of the Golden Bull on January 10, 1356. The Golden Bull regulated the conduct of imperial elections, fixing the number of electors at seven: the archbishops of Mainz, Trier, and Cologne, the king of Bohemia, the margraves of Miessen and Brandenburg, and the counts Palatine of the Rhine. Succession in the secular electoral principalities was to follow primogeniture. The Golden Bull gave the electoral princes extensive rights, including the *jus de non appellando et de non evo-cando*, or privilege of nomination and selection, and elevated the position of the king of Bohemia over that of the other electors. Charles sought to create unity among the electoral princes, and ultimately, to ensure hereditary succession through the regulated process of election.

Charles leaned heavily on the imperial cities, particularly those in Swabia, as executors of the public peace (*Landfriede*). Although the Golden Bull forbade leagues in principle, city leagues and princely leagues created by the emperor in order to secure the peace became a fixed part of Charles's *Landfrieden* policy. The Swabian *Landfriede* of 1370, comprised almost entirely of imperial cities, was clearly directed against a growing alliance of the Habsburgs and the counts of Württemberg.

In 1377 Charles returned to France, accompanied by his son Wenceslas, to gain French support for his plans to put his younger son, Sigismund, on the Polish throne. During the negotiations, Charles agreed to recognize the French dauphin as imperial vicar in the kingdom of Arles, effectively ceding the Arelat to France in perpetuity.

In the last years of his reign, Charles occupied himself largely with the succession and with returning the papacy to Rome. The emperor needed to acquire the mark (territory) of Brandenburg in order to secure the election to emperor of his eldest son Wenceslas (June 10, 1376). To raise money, Charles opted to mortgage a number of imperial cities. On July 4, 1376, in opposition to this decision, a group of Swabian cities formed a league. War broke out the following spring, by which time twenty-eight cities had joined the Swabian city league, with the aim of achieving the status of free imperial cities.

Conflict also ensured from Charles's determination to return the papacy to Rome. He was able to convince Pope Gregory XI and the curia to return to Rome in September 1377, but after Gregory's death (March 26, 1378), a series of disputes between the newly elected Pope Urban VI and Charles ultimately resulted in the Great Schism.

Charles IV died in Prague on November 29, 1378. He was married four times: to Blanche of Valois (1316–1348), Anna of Wittelsbach (1329–1353), Anna von Schweidnitz (1339–1362), and Elizabeth of Pomerania (1347–1393). At his death the Luxembourg lands were divided between his sons, Wenceslas IV (Bohemia and Silesia), Sigismund (Brandenburg), and Johann (Görlitz), and his brothers Johann Heinrich (Moravia) and Wenceslas (Luxembourg and Brabant).

See also **Wenceslas**

Further Reading

Seibt, Ferdinand. *Karl IV. und Sein Kreis.*, Munich: Oldenbourg, 1978.
——. ed. *Karl IV Staatsmann und Mäzen.* Munich: Prezel, 1978.
Spevacek, Jirí. *Karel IV. Zivot a dílo.* Prague: Svoboda (Rudé právo), 1979.
——. *Karl IV. Sein Leben und seine staatsmänische Leistung.* Prague: Academie nakladatelstri Ceskoslovenské akademi ved, 1978.
Werunsky, E. *Geschishte Kaiser Karls IV. und seiner Zeit.* Innsbruck: Wagner, 1880–1892.
Zeumer, Karl. *Die Goldene Bulle Kaiser Karls IV.* Weimar: Hermann Böhlaus Nachfolger, 1908.

WILLIAM BRADFORD SMITH

CHARLES MARTEL (ca. 688/9–741)

The founder of the Carolingian dynasty, Charles Martel was the dominant figure of western Europe in the first half of the 8th century. As sole mayor of the palace, he ruled the Frankish kingdom as a virtual monarch, and in his active career he reestablished Frankish unity and restored Frankish authority over most of the surrounding regions. His most celebrated victory was over a Muslim raiding expedition, near Poitiers in 732, the first serious check on the advance of Islam in Europe. His activities paved the way for the even greater careers of his son Pepin the Short and his grandson Charlemagne.

Charles was the illegitimate son of Pepin II of Heristal, the last of the Pippinid, or Arnulfing, mayors of the palace. Pepin II's death in 714, with the only legitimate heirs his young grandchildren, led to an intense power struggle within the Frankish kingdom and invasions by

Frisians and Aquitanians. Aided by the powerful Australian relatives of his mother, Alpaide, Charles was able to defeat his opponents and by 723 had established himself as the sole mayor of the palace under the nominal kingship of the Merovingian Theuderic IV.

Charles, now usually styled *princeps*, then extended his rule over the neighboring regions, waging successful campaigns against the Frisians, Saxons, and Alemanni. As part of his effort to dominate the Germanic territories, he supported Anglo-Saxon missionaries, especially the disciples of Willibrord in Frisia and Boniface in Thuringia and Hesse. Boniface's close ties to the papacy led to warm relations between Charles and popes Gregory II and Gregory III.

The advance of the Muslims into southern France after the fall of the Visigothic kingdom threatened the Aquitanians, whose duke, Eudes, appealed to Charles for military assistance. The victory won by Charles at Moussais, near Poitiers, on October 25, 732, was not the battle that saved Europe from Islam, but it did lead to his being given the sobriquet Martel—from the Latin *martellus* "hammer"—in the 9th century. His campaigns in the south for the rest of the 730s did halt Muslim advances and led to his conquest of Provence, which realized the old Frankish dream of gaining direct access to the Mediterranean. Charles, however, was not able to bring Aquitaine fully under his authority. He paid for manpower for his many wars in the 730s in part by appropriating church lands and giving them to his military followers, supposedly to be held from the church. Historians consider these grants the beginning of feudal institutions in the Frankish kingdom.

King Theuderic IV died in 737. Charles did not allow a Merovingian successor to be recognized, and he ruled the last four years of his life without a nominal king. In 739, Pope Gregory III recognized Charles's position as the most powerful Christian ruler of western Europe by appealing to him for assistance against the Lombard king Liutprand. But Charles and Liutprand were close allies, and this initial effort to bring in the Franks as papal allies against the Lombards failed.

Charles's death in 741 temporarily broke the unity of the Frankish kingdom. His elder son, Carloman, was made mayor over Austrasia, Alemannia, and Thuringia, while the younger, Pepin the Short, received Neustria, Burgundy, and Provence. Charles was buried in Merovingian royal style at Saint-Denis.

See also **Pepin III the Short**

Further Reading

Wallace-Hadrill, J.M., ed. and trans. *The Fourth Book of the Chronicle of Fredegar with Its Continuations.* London: Nelson, 1960.

Gerberding, Richard A. *The Rise of the Carolingians and the "Liber Historiæ Francorum."* Oxford: Clarendon, 1987.

McKitterick, Rosamond. *The Frankish Kingdoms Under the Carolingians, 751–987.* London: Longman, 1983.

Riché, Pierre. *The Carolingians: A Family Who Forged Europe,* trans. Michael I. Allen. Philadelphia: University of Pennsylvania Press, 1993.

Roi, Jean-Henri, and Jean Devoisse. *La bataille de Poitiers.* Paris: Gallimard, 1966.

STEVEN FANNING

CHARLES V THE WISE (1338–1380)

The third French king of the Valois line, Charles V was born on January 21, 1338, the oldest son of John II and Bonne de Luxembourg. He was the first heir of a French king to be styled dauphin of Viennois. Charles owes much of his reputation to Christine de Pizan, who depicted him as a prudent and skillful ruler despite chronic poor health. His reign as king (1364–80) was a time of success for France, in contrast to those of his predecessor and successor, but some recent scholars have questioned how much of the success can be attributed to his abilities.

Charles had an eventful political career before becoming king. In 1355, he was implicated in conspiracies against his father fomented by Charles the Bad, king of Navarre. In 1356, after the defeat and capture of John II at Poitiers, Charles was left to face attacks on the government from partisans of Charles the Bad, genuine political reformers, and ambitious men who hoped to oust unpopular royal financial officers and take their place. Nonnobles were increasingly hostile to nobles, while much of the nobility of northern and western France had been hostile to the Valois monarchy for years.

As royal lieutenant and later regent in the name of his captive father, Charles had to deal with a serious crisis in the years 1356–58. Riot and rebellion in Paris, independent military action by the forces of Charles the Bad, and the savage uprising against nobles known as the Jacquerie all contributed to this crisis, as did a seriously unstable currency and the ravages of unemployed companies of soldiers (*routiers*). Throughout the period, the Estates General convened repeatedly, but the militance of the urban representatives soon alienated the nobles, who slowly gravitated into the royalist camp.

After Charles regained Paris in 1358, the royal government began to recover its authority and institute reforms. A new English invasion in 1359–60 failed to capture any major towns, and the Treaty of Brétigny in 1360 secured John II's release. To pay his ransom, stabilize the currency, and deal with the brigandage of *routiers*, the crown was able to establish substantial regular taxes in 1360 and 1363, and these financed the troops that won a major victory over the Navarrese at Cocherel on May 6, 1364. Charles V, who had just succeeded his father as king, inherited a favorable situation and a reform-minded royal council led by Guillaume de Melun, archbishop of Sens. Charles continued to cultivate the newly royalist nobility of the north and west, who began to provide the bulk of his military leaders. His brother Louis I of Anjou became royal lieutenant in Languedoc, providing energetic leadership there for most of the reign.

As king, Charles profited from two important international developments, both of them in 1369. His brother Philip the Bold married the heiress of Flanders and Artois, thus denying these strategic lands to a potential English suitor. In Spain, Bertrand du Guesclin, the victor of Cocherel, helped establish a pro-French candidate on the throne of Castile, giving Charles an ally with an important fleet. At home, Charles lured into the French camp Olivier de Clisson, who brought with him a host of Breton knights who played a vital role in the French army. The king also cultivated discontented Gascon magnates, accepting their appeal against the English regime in Aquitaine, thus reopening the Hundred Years' War in 1369, when France was able to win quick victories. Aided by a Castilian naval victory off La Rochelle in 1372 and the policy, promoted by Clisson, of avoiding pitched battles, France reduced the English possessions in France to a few coastal enclaves by the end of the reign.

Charles V made his two great mistakes in 1378. One was the attempted confiscation of Brittany, which cost him the valuable military services of the Breton magnates. The other was his quick recognition of the questionable papal election of Clement VII, which brought about the Great Schism. A pious ruler with a strong sense of royal majesty and duty, Charles had profited greatly from the taxes enacted toward the end of his father's reign, but he felt uneasy about their rightness. An important intellectual in his circle, Nicole Oresme, had written a French version of Aristotle's *Politics* in which he strongly criticized taxation. In this climate of opinion, Charles, on his deathbed, canceled the *fouage* (hearth tax), which had financed his victorious armies.

Although clearly not as able a leader as traditionally portrayed, Charles V was a successful ruler who picked effective subordinates, encouraged needed reforms, and had the skill to use rather than antagonize the politically most influential groups in his kingdom.

See also **Charles II the Bad; Guesclin, Bertrand du; Marcel, Étienne; Oresme, Nicole**

Further Reading

Babbitt, Susan M. *Oresme's "Livre de politiques" and the France of Charles V.* Philadelphia: American Philosophical Society, 1985.

Cazelles, Raymond. *Société politique, noblesse et couronne sous Jean le Bon et Charles V*. Geneva: Droz, 1982.

Delachenal, Roland. *Histoire de Charles V*. 5 vols. Paris: Picard, 1909–31.

Dodu, Gaston. "Les idées de Charles V en matière de gouvernement." *Revue des questions historiques* 110 (1929): 5–46.

Henneman, John Bell. *Royal Taxation in Fourteenth Century France: The Captivity and Ransom of John II, 1356–1370*. Philadelphia: American Philosophical Society, 1976.

JOHN BELL HENNEMAN, JR.

CHARLES VI (1368–1422)

Charles VI (r. 1380–1422) was born in Paris on December 3, 1368, to Charles V and Jeanne de Bourbon. He was crowned king on November 4, 1380. His father had stipulated that during his minority the oldest of his paternal uncles, Louis I of Anjou, was to be regent, but Anjou agreed under pressure, on October 2, 1380, that Charles VI be declared of age and the kingdom ruled in his name according to the advice of all four royal uncles. In 1388, influenced by a plan set in motion by Olivier de Clisson, Charles VI took control of the government himself. The counselors he then favored, scornfully called Marmousets by the dukes, initiated a program of reform that was cut short by the onset of his mental illness on August 5, 1392.

This crisis enabled the dukes to regain their power. The king considered himself recovered within five weeks, but other psychotic episodes followed. Charles VI suffered from recurring persecutory delusions and exhibited forms of behavior commonly observed today in schizophrenics. There was often no clearly visible line of demarcation to distinguish his schizophrenic thought patterns from "sane" ones. Since he often seemed able to function, he was allowed to continue to rule with full power, his royal prerogative protected by the sacred character of French kingship. Despite a manifest desire to be a good king, Charles VI made many important decisions while his thinking was disordered, and this soon upset the equilibrium of his government.

His mental illness caused him to deal in an inconsistent and questionable manner with the assassination of his brother, Louis of Orléans, in 1407. The consequence was almost constant civil war that exacerbated the persecutory delusions suffered by the king, for suspicion of treason was everywhere. This atmosphere also had the effect of making the king's schizophrenic thinking often seem sane.

In an attempt to protect the monarchy from control by either the Burgundians or the Armagnacs (the Orléanist party), the king's eldest son, Duke Louis of Guyenne, sought to form a separate royalist party. These efforts, spoiled by the invasion of Henry V of England and by Louis's own death in December, were not continued by the dauphin Charles (later Charles VII), who fled Paris as it fell to the Burgundians on May 29, 1418. He did not return until 1437.

The dauphin Charles and the Armagnacs found support in each other for their demands. The government was anxious for the dauphin to return to the royal court, but reconciliation became impossible after he sanctioned the assassination of John the Fearless, duke of Burgundy, at Montereau in September 1419 and then committed treason by usurping royal authority to call himself regent of France. As a result, Charles VI accepted the Anglo-French-Burgundian Treaty of Troyes in May 1420 and married his daughter Catherine to Henry V. The treaty declared Henry heir to the French throne with the powers of regent, but preserved Charles VI's rights and authority. Charles VI survived Henry and died at the Hôtel de Saint-Pol on October 21, 1422.

See also **Henry V**

Further Reading

Autrand, Françoise. *Charles VI*. Paris: Fayard, 1986.

Famiglietti, R. C. *Royal Intrigue: Crisis at the Court of Charles VI 1392–1420*. New York: AMS, 1986.

Grandeau, Yann. "La mort et les obsèques de Charles VI." *Bulletin philologique et historique du Comité des Travaux Historiques et Scientifiques* (1970): 133–86.

Hindman, Sandra L. *Christine de Pizan's "Epistre Othea": Painting and Politics at the Court of Charles VI*. Toronto: Pontifical Institute of Mediaeval Studies, 1986.

Rey, Maurice. *Les finances royales sous Charles VI: les causes du déficit (1388–1413)*. Paris: SEVPEN, 1965.

RICHARD C. FAMIGLIETTI

CHARLES VII (1403–1461)

One of the best known but least understood of the medieval kings of France, Charles VII was the eleventh child of Charles VI and Isabeau of Bavaria. That he would become king or be immortalized by his association with Jeanne d'Arc and the reconquest of France was unimagined during his youth. Becoming dauphin in 1417 after the unexpected deaths of older brothers, he entered the political scene in one of the darkest periods of French history. In 1418, upon escaping a Burgundian coup in Paris, he became head of a government in exile dominated by the Armagnac faction. His ill-advised role in the assassination of the duke of Burgundy in 1419 united the English and Burgundians, and they sought to disinherit him in the 1420 Treaty of Troyes. When Charles did become king in October 1422, he controlled only the third of the realm south of the Loire. He indiscriminately accepted a wide range of supporters and advisers, whom he only slowly learned to control.

Denied access to Paris and derisively called "king of Bourges," Charles courted provincial estates and the *bonnes villes*. His actions foreshadowed the administrative decentralization of his later reign.

After years of catastrophic defeats, the appearance of Jeanne d'Arc marked a turning point in Charles's fortunes. Her victories at Orléans and Patay brought Charles to Reims for a coronation in July 1429. By 1435, he brought Burgundy to a separate peace in the Treaty of Arras, which allowed the Valois reentry into Paris in 1436. A contentious decade of reform passed before Charles could complete the reconquest of France. The Pragmatic Sanction of Bourges in 1438 affirmed royal control of the French episcopacy and ecclesiastical revenues, and, at the Estates of 1439, Charles increased taxation and attempted to outlaw unauthorized armed forces. The military anarchy of the brigandage (*écorcherie*) and the revolt of his son, the future Louis XI, and many peers in the Praguerie posed a new crisis that took all of Charles's tactical and diplomatic skills to overcome. Influenced by his mistress Agnès Sorel, he settled on his two reliable advisers: Pierre de Brézé and the constable Richemont, and by 1445 he was able to implement his program. In 1449, the revitalized Valois army renewed the war, and by 1453 the English had been driven from Normandy and Guyenne.

Consolidating his authority for the rest of his years, Charles easily disciplined such restive princes as the count of Armagnac and the duke of Alençon, used the courts to reconcile a nation embittered by civil war, and perfected the administrative structures that had brought him victory. Only his son, the future Louis XI, impatiently waiting in Burgundian exile, celebrated his death. Sometimes called "the Victorious," Charles was a man who preferred negotiations to war and judiciously waited to exploit his enemies' divisions. He is better remembered as "The Well-Served" king, skilled in the selection and management of advisers who helped him construct a new monarchy out of the cruel necessities of a lifelong struggle to reunite France.

See also **Jeanne d'Arc**

Further Reading

Beaucourt, Gaston du Fresne de. *Histoire de Charles VII*. 4 vols. Paris: Librairie de la Société Bibliographique, 1881–91.

Lewis, Peter S. *Later Medieval France: The Polity*. London: Macmillan, 1968.

Perroy, Edouard. *The Hundred Years War*. Bloomington: Indiana University Press, 1951.

Vale, Malcolm G.A. *Charles VII*. Berkeley: University of California Press, 1974.

Vallet de Viriville, Auguste. *Histoire de Charles VII, roi de France, et de son époque: 1403–1461*. 3 vols. Paris: Renouard, 1862–65.

PAUL D. SOLON

CHARTIER, ALAIN (ca. 1385–ca. 1430)

Author and diplomat, known chiefly for his controversial poem, the *Belle dame sans merci*, and for his talent as an orator. A native of Bayeux, Alain Chartier studied at the University of Paris, earning the title of "maistre." Early in his career, in the period between 1409 and 1414, Chartier worked in the household of Yolande d'Anjou, mother of King René and of Marie d'Anjou, who was betrothed to the future Charles VII in 1413. Charles's presence at the Angevin court gave him occasion to acquaint himself with Chartier's talents. By 1417, Chartier was in the service of the dauphin as notary and secretary, serving also for a time King Charles VI.

For a decade beginning in 1418, Chartier's life followed the wandering of the exiled dauphin through Berry and Touraine, areas withstanding the Anglo-Burgundian onslaught. In addition to routine duties as secretary and notary, Chartier's later service to Charles included ambassadorial functions on missions during 1425 to the emperor Sigismund's court in Hungary and to the Venetian senate in an effort to convince Sigismund to side with the French against the English. In 1428, at the court of James I of Scotland, Chartier helped to renew relations between France and Scotland and to negotiate the marriage between James's daughter Margaret and the dauphin Louis. During these missions, Chartier provided eloquent introductory discourses opening the diplomatic exchanges.

From 1420 on, Chartier held various ecclesiastical offices. In 1420, he was named canon of Notre-Dame of Paris, although he was unable to assume the responsibilities of the office because of the Burgundian occupation of the city. In 1425, he was named curate of Saint-Lambert-des-Levées near Angers; in 1426, he was granted the pre-bendal canonry of Tours; and in 1428, he was appointed chancellor of Bayeux. An epitaph engraved in 1458 mentions that he was archdeacon of Paris.

It is generally assumed that Chartier died ca. 1430, since his signature does not appear on any royal document after 1428; *L'esperance*, begun in 1428, was never finished; and shortly after July 17, 1429, he sent a letter to Sigismund recounting Jeanne d'Arc's achievements and the consecration of Charles VII in Reims. By 1432, Chartier's brother had succeeded him as curate of Saint-Lambert-des-Levées. Record of a tombal inscription suggests that he was buried in the church of Saint-Antoine in Avignon, although the reason for his presence in Avignon at the time of his death is unknown.

An active and valued royal servant who held important ecclesiastical positions, Chartier was also a master of prose both in Latin and French and an accomplished poet. The range of style, form, and subject matter in Chartier's work is impressive.

His most controversial, celebrated, and imitated work, the *Belle dame sans merci* (1424), begins with a conventional situation: the wandering, mournful narrator overhears an exchange between a disconsolate lover and his lady. The language the lover uses to persuade the lady of his love and to ask for hers in return reveals that he has been cast in the old mold, in which the lady either granted such requests or maintained a neutral distance. Chartier's *belle dame* reserves her right to refuse and to disabuse the lover of his belief in the power of his own courtly rhetoric. To the lover, who says he will die if she does not take pity on him, she suggests that he is succumbing to a metaphor, since she has seen no one actually die of unrequited love. To his persistent and sometimes accusatory pleas, she affirms that her indifference is neither cruel nor harmful. She counsels him to be reasonable and to take her refusal in stride. The narrator suggests at the close of the work that the lover did in fact die as a consequence. He asks lovers to shun meddlers and braggarts who have done harm to the cause of love; and he asks women not to be as cruel as the *belle dame sans merci*.

The reaction in courtly circles to the *Belle dame sans merci* attests both to the continuing hold that convention had at court in determining codes of amorous conduct and to Chartier's innovative view of these codes. By the following year, while on his mission to Hungary, Chartier was summoned to appear before a "Court of Love" because of objections women at the French court had made to his work. Chartier defended himself from a distance, composing *L'excusacion aux dames* (1425), in which the God of Love accuses the author of wrongs against love's rights. The author responds that, while in some women pity is so deeply hidden as to be invisible, he maintains confidence in love itself. He also claims that he had merely recorded the exchange between lover and lady. It is not known to what extent his *Excusacion* won him forgiveness at court.

The *Lay de Plaisance* (1414) and numerous short lyrics composed throughout his career show Chartier's mastery of poetic conventions in portraying states of love. Two amusing debate works, the *Débat des deux fortunés d'Amour* (1425) and the *Débat du réveille-matin* (uncertain date), present divergent and unreconciled views on the value and nature of love. More frequently, Chartier's poems rely heavily on convention, while introducing new vantages or combining other concerns with the subject of love. Just as the *Belle dame sans merci* moves outside of convention to challenge it, the *Livre des quatre dames* (1416), composed in the wake of the French disaster at Agincourt, intertwines love stories with the moral and political elements of a national tragedy. The traditional springtime *locus amoenus* in this work, replete with the amorous diversions of a shepherd and shepherdess, provides the backdrop for the sorrowful tales of four women whom the narrator encounters. Each woman describes the fate of her beloved at Agincourt: the lover of the first has been killed, the second lady's lover has been taken prisoner, the fate of the third lady's lover is unknown, and the fourth lady's lover has disgraced himself by fleeing the battlefield. They ask the narrator to say which of them is to be pitied the most. He confesses inability to judge and refers debate to his own lady in writing.

Chartier rarely supplies resolutions to the debates related in many of his works. The *Débat du hérauk, du vassault et du villain* (ca. 1421–26) explores but does not resolve the conflict between generations and between social classes. His best-known prose work, the *Quadrilogue invectif* (1422), is also cast in the form of a debate. Lady France, disheveled and tattered, eloquently inveighs against her three "children," asking them to account for their role in the lamentable state of the nation. The Knight, the Cleric, and the Peasant present in turn excuses, accusations, and expressions of despair. No single estate is to bear the burden of blame at the end of the *Quadrilogue*, yet it is clear that each must assume a share of responsibility and that the divisive forces that cause them to rail against one another need to be eliminated through concern for the common good. Chartier seems to have borrowed from his Latin to provide the first known occurrence of the word *patrie* in this work, as well as the concept of a socially and politically unified France.

While the *Quadrilogue* remains Chartier's best-known prose work in French, the complexity of his concern for the political and spiritual welfare of his compatriots is best seen in the *Livre de l'esperance ou Le livre des trois vertus*, a work begun in 1428 and left unfinished. Interspersing with lyric interludes extensive prose dialogue between the author's personified faculty of Understanding and personifications representing Hope and Faith, Chartier explores many seemingly unanswerable questions about the turmoil and moral decline in France. Having chased away the specters of Melancholy, Indignation, Mistrust, and Despair, whose cumulative influence had brought Understanding to the brink of suicide, Faith and Hope, chiefly the latter, provide extensive lessons to aid in Understanding's recovery. His memory is reawakened to allow him to apply the lessons of secular and biblical history, recounted through numerous exempla, to the current state of affairs in France and to his own spiritual state. Even in its unfinished form, *L'esperance* is a summa of Chartier's own erudition, put to the task of resolving the political turmoil of his time or, at least, of finding an appropriate spiritual context in which to understand it.

Numerous other works, in Latin and French, also bear witness to Chartier's versatility as a writer. Life as a courtier is criticized in the Curial (*De vita curiale*), written after 1422. The *Epistola ad regem* (1418), *Epistola ad Universitatem Parisiensem* (1420), and *Epistola ad detestacionem belli gallici et suasione pacis* (ca. 1422–24) display strongly held political convictions. A number of his diplomatic orations survive, no doubt because of their eloquence: *Oratio ad imperatorem* (1425), *Oratio ad regem Romanorum* (1425), *Persuasio ad Pragenses in fide deviantes* (1425), and the *Discours au roi d'Ecosse* (1428). A number of shorter, more personal Latin prose works bear the clear influence of Cicero: *Invectiva contra ingratum amicum* (ca. 1425), *Invectiva contra invidium et detractorem* (ca. 1425), and *Epistola ad fratrem suum iuvenem* (uncertain date).

The large number of manuscripts, early printed editions, and imitations of Chartier's works attests to his continuing popularity as an author well into the 16th century and beyond.

See also **Charles d'Orléans**

Further Reading

Chartier, Alain. *Les œuvres latines d'Alain Chartier*, ed. Pascale Bourgain-Hemeryck. Paris: CNRS, 1977.

——. *Le quadrilogue invectif*, ed. Eugénie Droz. 2nd ed. Paris: Champion, 1950.

——. *The Poetical Works of Alain Chartier*, ed. J. C. Laidlaw. Cambridge: Cambridge University Press, 1974.

——. *Poèmes par Alain Chartier*, ed. J.C. Laidlaw. Paris: Union Générale d'Éditions, 1988.

——. *Le livre de l'esperance*, ed. François Rouy. Diss. Université de Paris, 1967.

Champion, Pierre. *Histoire poétique du XVe siècle*. 2 vols. Paris: Champion, 1923, Vol. l, pp. 1–165.

Hoffman, E. J. *Alain Chartier: His Work and Reputation.* New York: Wittes, 1942.

Rouy, François, ed. *L'esthétique du traité moral d'après les œuvres d'Alain Chartier*. Geneva: Droz, 1980.

Walravens, C. J. H. *Alain Chartier: études biographiques, suivies de pièces justificatives, d'une description des éditions et d'une édition des ouvrages inédits*. Amsterdam: Meulenhoff-Didier, 1971.

JANICE C. ZINSER

CHAUCER, GEOFFREY (ca. 1342–1400)

England's greatest nondramatic poet, whose superb poetry—often moving, sometimes disturbing, always immensely readable—gave a new direction to English literature.

Life

Chaucer was born into a London merchant family; by 1357 he was connected with the court, initially in the household of Elizabeth countess of Ulster, later in the service of successive kings. His wife, Philippa, was herself connected with the royal households of Elizabeth of Ulster, Queen Philippa, and Constanza of Castile, second wife of John of Gaunt; Philippa's sister, Katherine Swynford, was for many years Gaunt's mistress and eventually his third wife.

Chaucer made a number of journeys abroad on the king's business: to France on several occasions, apparently to Spain in 1366, and to Italy in 1372–73 and 1378, where he discovered the great literature of the Trecento. He held a number of senior "civil service" posts, including a controllership of customs (1374–85), the clerkship of the king's works (1389–91), and a deputy forestership in Somerset (1390s). He was a justice of the peace for Kent and represented the county in the parliament of 1386. Although there are numerous records of payments to him in both money and kind (clothing and wine) by Edward III, Richard II, and Henry IV, and to both himself and his wife by John of Gaunt, these are always in return for work or services; there is no mention of patronage specifically for his poetry.

Linguistic and Literary Backgrounds

Chaucer's life coincided with a turning point in the history of the English language. Under Edward III the dominant language spoken and written within the royal household was French, in its Anglo-Norman form; parliamentary proceedings were conducted in the same language. By the end of the century English predominated in court and parliament, and schoolboys were translating their Latin into English instead of French. Chaucer's poetry reflects, and encouraged, the new self-confidence of the language and contributed to the standing of the London dialect. His style combines specifically English features, such as alliterating phrases, with French flexibility of sentence structure and, increasingly, a spaciousness of syntax similar to that seen in the long complex found in Latin.

Chaucer was familiar with English literary forms, including alliterative verse (cf. the sea fight in the Legend of Cleopatra, *Legend of Good Women* 635–48, and the tournaments in the *Knight's Tale* 2602–16) and rail rhyme (parodied in *Sir Thopas*); he probably knew Langland's work, and certainly Gower's. His earnest identifiable poetic models, however, were French. Most important was the 13th-century *Roman de la Rose* of Guillaume de Lorris and Jean de Meun, an allegorical love vision that Chaucer claims to have translated; of the three fragments of an ME translation that survive, only the first is likely to be his. It may be the earliest surviving example of his work. The *Roman* remained a key influence throughout his career, but his career, but his use of it changed significantly: his earlier poems draw most on Guillaume's account of falling in love in an idyllic courtly garden, while Jeans more cynical writing was an inspiration behind such characters as the Pardoner and the Wife of Bath. From the 1370s onward

Chaucer was deeply influenced by Dante, Petrarch, and above all Boccaccio, and his poetry becomes increasingly cosmopolitan as he consciously participates in the highest Western tradition of poetry. Like Dante and Boccaccio he presents himself following in the great classical line of Homer, Virgil, Ovid, Lucan, and Statius (*Troilus* 5.1792); of these Ovid was the most important to him. Other cultural traditions are represented in his work by his use of the 6th-century *Consolation of Philosophy* of Boethius, which he translated in the early 1380s, and supremely, by his constant allusions to the Bible, the liturgy, and Christian doctrine.

Works

Chaucer's earliest known original poem, *The Book of the Duchess* (ca. 1368–72), was a response to the death of Blanche, duchess of Lancaster, first wife of John of Gaunt. It draws largely on French models and is written in a four-stress couplet form similar to French octosyllabics. Its narrator dreams of meeting a man in black who is mourning the death of his lady, named "White": the characters bear some relationship to Chaucer, the duke, and Blanche, but Chaucer's use of the dream form enables him to transcend historical circumstance to explore the contraries of love and loss, joy and grief. Three characteristics of the poem are notable as precursors of his later work. First is his exploitation of convention in unconventional ways: most strikingly in death's invasion of the idyllic garden where the lover falls in love. Second is the sophistication of Chaucer's use of a first-person narrator. Despite his overtly muted role within the dream he is a figure for the poet; and since the dream takes place within his own mind, he is also the originator of the encomium and lament spoken by the man in black. Chaucer thus becomes the spokesman for the duke both in fact and within the structure of the poem. Third is its secular focus—a focus exceptional for elegy, but typical of the great majority of Chaucer's works: Christianity is not denied, but the field of poetic "interest is this world, not the next.

Chaucer's poetry of the 1370s and early 1380s continues to use French models—the *Roman*, Guillaume de Machaut, Jean Froissart—but Ovidian and Italian influences also appear. His major works of those years, whose order of composition is uncertain, are *The Parliament of Fowls*, *The Home of Fame*, and possibly the *Knight's Tale* under the title of "Palamon and Arcite." *The Parliament* is probably Chaucer's earliest poem in the seven-line rime royal stanza, which he would later use in the *Troilus* and the tales of pathos in the *Canterbury Tales*. It may have been written for some particular occasion, possibly to do with Richard II's future wife, Anne. It is a dream poem that analyzes the various forms that earthly love can take, as illustrated by the claustrophobic temple of Priapus, inhabited by Venus, and by the hill of Nature, God's "vicaire" or deputy, before whom all the birds from the eagle to the goose have assembled on St. Valentine's Day to choose their mates. The poem suggests a series of contraries that it in fact refuses to endorse: both temple and hill are contained within the same walled park; inscriptions over the entrance promise bliss and threaten sterility and death, but the entrance is single; the birds that are given their mates and the three eagles that endure suffering and long service in love are alike under the aegis of Nature; the broader context for the dream is Scipio's vision, from Cicero, of the great cycle of the universe, with its injunction to serve the common good, while the dream itself shows the processes of natural regeneration within a single year—processes explicitly invoked in the concluding roundel celebrating the return of summer after winter.

The House of Fame is again a dream poem, told by a narrator-dreamer named "Geffrey" and written, like *The Book of the Duchess*, in octosyllabic couplets. The subject here is the nature of poetry, specifically the problem of recording the great deeds of the past—the function of narrative poetry—when the authorities who record those deeds are fallible. The problem is epitomized in the first section by setting the *Aeneid* against Ovid's account of Dido from the *Heroides*. In the third part it arises again in the form of quarrels among the various authorities for the story of Troy and in the description of Fame herself, whose apportionment of good or bad reputation or oblivion is shown as utterly arbitrary. The dreamer ends up in the house of Rumor, where truth and lies are inextricably jumbled and where there are no authoritative histories but only "tidynges" told by shipmen and pilgrims. The poem breaks off unfinished; the occasion for its composition is unknown, but in some ways it might be seen as foreshadowing the *Canterbury Tales*, with its substitution of fallible pilgrim narrators for an authoritative poet.

Troilus and Criseyde, of the mid-1380s, tells a story regarded in the Middle Ages as historical, but Chaucer constantly stresses the impossibility of establishing truth. His main source, Boccaccio's *Filostrato*, is never mentioned (it is conceivable that he did not know who wrote it); instead he invents an authority named Lollius, to whom he appeals when he is in fact making up the story. The spare plot—of how Criseyde abandons her Trojan lover Troilus for the Greek Diomede—becomes in Chaucer's hands an elaborate work of over 8,000 lines, in poetry of an order unparalleled in earlier English, from its magnificent hymns to Love through the easy colloquialisms of conversation to the eroticism of the central book. The depth of thought in the poem results from Chaucer's setting this story from the unalterable past in counterpoint to arguments from Boethius's

Consolation on destiny and free will and juxtaposing its theme of faithlessness against the providential ordering of the universe through "Love, that of erthe and se hath governaunce" (*Tr* 3.1744, *Consolation* 2.met.8).

The interpretations of *Troilus* over the centuries form an index to the varying responses to Chaucer: to his contemporaries it was most notable for its philosophy, the 15th and 16th centuries took it as a model of rhetorical eloquence; to the age of naturalism it was the first psychological novel; the search for values of the 1960s read it as a condemnation of inadequate secular goals; our own text-centered age stresses Chaucer's refusal to commit himself to motive, meaning, or fact. The God of the closing stanzas is the one fixed point, the unwritten author (Dante's "uncircumscript, and at maist circumscrive," *Tr* 5.1865), but the protagonists, as pagans, cannot have access to him, and the questions they raise remain unanswered.

The reason, or excuse, that Chaucer gives for writing his *Legend of Good Women*, is that his portrayal of Criseyde provoked objections; in its dream prologue (extant in two versions) he describes how the God of Love and Alcestis, model of the faithful wife, commanded him to do penance by telling the stories of good women—in practice, wronged women. Nine stories follow, mostly drawn from Ovid's *Heroides*—of Cleopatra, Thisbe, Dido, Hypsipyle and Medea, Lucretia, Ariadne, Philomela, Phyllis, and Hypermnestra; the last breaks off in mid-sentence. It has generally been assumed that Chaucer found such writing to formula restrictive; his only similar assemblage of single-subject stories forms the *Monk's Tale*, which is interrupted by the restless pilgrim audience.

The *Canterbury Tales* (ca. 1387–1400) is a story collection that achieves the maximum variety within a unifying frame. The tales are told by a group of pilgrims journeying to St. Thomas Becket's shrine at Canterbury, and both the pilgrims and their tales are selected to give a cross-section of human and literary possibility. Each pilgrim represents a different profession or social estate, on the model of the satiric social analyses offered by medieval estates literature. Chaucer's ideal figures, the Knight, Parson, and Plowman, mirror the basic tripartite division of society into those who fight, pray, and labor; the Clerk represents a fourth ideal, of those who learn and teach. The other portraits are more equivocal; Chaucer's persistent mode is superlative praise, but often aimed at the "wrong" attributes—the Friar's skill in begging, the Physician's financial success, the Prioress's social accomplishments. Women were often treated as an estate to themselves, and the one laywoman among the pilgrims, the Wife of Bath, is well capable of counterbalancing some 27 men.

The Host of the Tabard Inn, who accompanies the pilgrims as master of ceremonies, suggests that each pilgrim should tell four tales, competing with each other to tell "tales of best sentence and moost solaas"; the winning teller is to be given a dinner on their return to the Tabard. Whether or not Chaucer ever intended to write such an extensive work is unknown; he wrote only 24 tales within an incomplete framework. These stories are linked to form seven to twelve distinct fragments (the number is arguable); most editors opt for ten. There is some variation in the manuscript order of these fragments, but the most widely accepted order is that of the Ellesmere manuscript of the *Tales*, copied shortly after Chaucer's death:

I. *General Prologue*; *Knight's Tale* (a high-style romance based on Boccaccio's *Teseida*, of the love of Palamon and Arcite for Emily); *Miller's Tale* and *Reeve's Tale* (rival fabliaux in which one Oxford student seduces one woman, and two Cambridge students have sex with two); the fragmentary *Cook's Tale* (of a London reveler condemned by a battery of proverbs).

II. *Man of Law's Tale* (the trials and miraculous preservation of Custance, taken from Nicholas Trevet's *Cronicles* but treated as a pious romance).

III. *Wife of Bath's Prologue* (a defense of marriage against the hostile clerical establishment, especially St. Jerome, in the guise of her autobiography); her *Tale* (the folktale romance of the knight who has to discover what women most desire); *Friar's Tale* (an elaboration of a preaching exemplum, of a rapacious summoner carried off by the Devil); *Summoner's Tale* (a fabliau of a scatological bequest to the friars).

IV. *Clerk's Tale* (from Petrarch's version of Boccaccio's story of Patient Griselda); *Merchant's Tale* (a fabliau given high-style treatment, of the blind old knight January, whose sight is restored as his wife commits adultery in a pear tree).

V. *Squire's Tale* (an unfinished romance of magic gifts and an abandoned falcon); *Franklin's Tale* (described as a Breton lay though actually adapted from Boccaccio, of a suitor who fulfills his lady's supposedly impossible condition to remove the rocks that threaten her husband).

VI. *Physician's Tale* (Livy's story of Virginia and the unjust judge, taken from the *Roman de la Rose*); *Pardoner's Prologue* (on his methods of extorting money) and *Tale* (presented as a sample homily and including the widely disseminated tale of three rioters who find death in the form of gold).

VII. *Shipman's Tale* (a fabliau apparently once assigned to the Wife of Bath, of an adulterous wife and a monk); *Prioress's Tale* (a miracle of the Virgin concerning a boy murdered by the Jews); two tales told by the pilgrim Chaucer that effectively write him out of the competition, *Sir Thopas* (a parody of popular romance) and the prose *Melibee* (Prudence's discourse on the need for reconciliation, translated from a French version of Albertanus of Brescia); *Monk's Tale* (the falls of great men from biblical, secular, and contemporary history); *Nun's Priest's Tale* (the beast fable of the cock and the fox).

VIII. *Second Nun's Tale* (the life of St. Cecilia, written earlier and incorporated into the *Tales*); *Canon's Yeoman's Tale* (the autobiography of an alchemist's assistant and an account of alchemical frauds).

IX. *Manciple's Tale* (of Phoebus and the crow, from Ovid's *Metamorphoses*).

X. *Parson's Tale* (a prose penitential tract epitomized from Latin treatises); Chaucer's *Retractions* (which combines recording the canon of his works with revoking "worldly vanities").

The various tales cover most possible source areas (prose and verse, classical and contemporary, English and continental, sacred and secular), five prosodic forms besides prose itself (couplets, rime royal, tail rhyme, the eight-line *Monk's Tale* stanza, and the virtuoso rhyme scheme of the *Clerk's Tale* "Envoy"), most available genres, and a wide range of rhetoric and style. Each tale also gives a distinct moral and linguistic reading of the world and humankind's goals within it, often appropriate to its teller, in a way that makes the whole work resistant to univocal interpretation.

Chaucer's shorter poems and *balades* are a mixture of serious and playful love poems, addresses to friends, patrons, and a scribe, and moral and religious pieces. Together with the Dantesque prologues to the *Prioress's Tale* and the *Second Nun's Tale*, his strongest expressions of Christian devotion are *An ABC to the Virgin* (adapted from Guillaume de Deguilevilles' *Pèlerinage de vie humaine*) and the *Balade de Bon Conseyl*, also called "Truth." A longer fragmentary poem, *Anelida and Arcite*, is notable for its technical experimentation. Chaucer also wrote what is possibly the first English vernacular textbook, the *Treatise on the Astrolabe*; a second, *The Equatorie of the Planetis*, may also be his. Further works were falsely attributed to him in the 15th and 16th centuries, among them some antiecclesiastical works that gave him a reputation as a proto-Protestant.

Dissemination and Influence

No manuscripts of Chaucer's works survive from his lifetime, but they were widely copied throughout the 15th century. The *Tales* survives in some eighty manuscripts, *Troilus* in sixteen, *The Parliament* in fourteen, *Anelida* in thirteen, *The Book of the Duchess* and *The House of Fame* in three. The *Tales* was among the first books printed by Caxton, and everexpanding editions of the complete works appeared from 1483, notably Thynne's (1532), Stow's (1561), and Speght's (1598, the first to contain a glossary). Chaucerian scholarship effectively began with Tyrwhitt's edition of the *Tales* (1775–78).

Chaucer's influence made itself felt from his own lifetime. It may show in works by his contemporaries Froissart, Oton de Grandson, and Gower, though the direction of the influence is unclear. Lydgate and the "aureate" poets of the 15th century owed an explicit debt to him, usually phrased in terms of his mastery of rhetoric. Some of the major works of early Scottish literature, such as *The Kingis Quair* and Henryson's *Testament of Cresseid*, would have been impossible without him. Numerous poets, including Bokenham, Hawes, and Skelton, praised the poetic trinity of Chaucer, Gower, and Lydgate. He was the leading model for poetry throughout the 16th century, not least for Spenser, until the Elizabethan poets established their own standards of excellence. His preeminence has never been in question; he is the only ME author to have been read and praised in an unbroken tradition. There have been many adaptations and modernizations of his work, including samples by Dryden, Pope, and Wordsworth. His unique combination of accessibility and depth is indicated by has being the only poet to figure frequently both in British primary school teaching and as a key example in modern critical theory, and, in Pasolini's *Canterbury Tales*, as a box-office hit.

See also **Boccaccio, Giovanni; Dante Alighieri; Gower, John; Guillaume de Lorris; Henryson, Robert**

Further Reading

Primary Sources

Benson, tarry D., gen. ed. *The Riverside Chaucer*. 3d ed. Boston: Houghton Mifflin, 1987 [based on *The Works of Geoffrey Chaucer*, ed. RN. Robinson].

Coghill, Nevill, trans. *Troilus and Criseyde*. Harmondsworth: Penguin, 1971.

Ruggiers, Paul G., and Donald C. Baker, gen. eds. *A Variorum Edition of the Works of Geoffrey Chaucer*. Norman: University of Oklahoma Press, 1979–.

Windeatt, Barry A., ed. *Troilus and CriseydeA New Edition of "The Book of Troilus."* London: Longman, 1984.

Wright, David, trans. *The Canterbury Tales*. Oxford: Oxford University Press, 1985.

Secondary Sources

New *CBEL* 1: 557–628

Allen, Mark, and John H. Fisher. *The Essential Chaucer: An*

Annotated Bibliography of Major Modern Studies. London: Mansell, 1987 [for criticism].

The Chaucer Bibliographies. Toronto: University of Toronto Press, 1983–[ongoing series].

Leyerle, John, and Anne Quick. *Chaucer: A Bibliographical Introduction*. Toronto Medieval Bibliographies 10. Toronto: University of Toronto Press, 1986 [for scholarship].

Studies in the Age of Chaucer. 1979–[annual annotated bibliographies for 1975 on].

General Criticism

Boitani, Piero, and Jill Mann, eds. *The Cambridge Chaucer Companion*. Cambridge: Cambridge University Press, 1986.

Burnley, David. *A Guide to Chaucer's Language*. London; Macmillan, 1983. Repr. as *The Language of Chaucer*; London: Macmillan, 1989.

Crow, Martin M., and Clair C. Olson, eds. *Chaucer Life-Records*. Austin: University of Texas Press, 1966.

David, Alfred. *The Strumpet Muse: Art and Morals in Chaucer's Poetry*. Bloomington: Indiana University Press, 1976.

Jordan, Robert M. *Chaucer's Poetics and the Modern Reader*. Berkeley. University of California Press, 1987.

Kean, P.M. *Chaucer and the Making of English Poetry*. 2 vols. London: Routledge & Kegan Paul, 1972.

Mann, Jill. *Geoffrey Chaucer*. Feminist Readings. London: Harvester Wheatsheaf, 1991.

Muscatine, Charles. *Chaucer and the French Tradition: A Study in Style ami Meaning*. Berkeley. University of California Press, 1957.

The Oxford Guides to Chaucer: Helen Cooper, *The Canterbury Tales*.

Alastair J. Minnis, *The Shorter Poems*.

Barry A. Windeatt, *Troilus and Criseyde*. Oxford: Clarendon, 1989–95.

Pearsall, Derek. *The Life of Geoffrey Chaucer*. Oxford: Blackwell, 1992.

Robertson, D.W., Jr. *A Preface to Chaucer: Studies in Medieval Perspectives*. Princeton: Princeton University Press, 1962.

Schoeck, Richard J., and Jerome Taylor, eds. *Chaucer Criticism*. 2 vols. Notre Dame: University of Notre Dame Press, I960 [reprints of classic essays].

Shorter Poems and Troilus

Wetherbee, Winthrop. *Chaucer and the Poets: An Essay on Troilus and Criseyde*. Ithaca: Cornell University Press, 1984.

Windeatt, Barry A., ed. and trans. *Chaucer's Dream Poetry: Sources and Analogues*. Cambridge: Brewer, 1982.

Canterbury Tales

Bryan, William F., and Germaine Dempster, eds. *Sources and Analogues of Chaucer's Canterbury Tales*. Chicago: University of Chicago Press, 1941.

Cooper, Helen. *The Structure of the Canterbury Tales*. London: Duckworth, 1983.

Howard, Donald R. *The Idea of the Canterbury Tales*. Berkeley: University of California Press, 1976.

Mann, Jill. *Chaucer and Medieval Estates Satire: The Literature of Social Classes and the General Prologue to the Canterbury Tales*. Cambridge: Cambridge University Press, 1973.

Pearsall, Derek. *The Canterbury Tales*. London: Allen & Unwin, 1985.

HELEN COOPER

CHRÉTIEN DE TROYES (fl. 1165–91)

Although Chrétien wrote lyric poetry in the troubadour and trouvère traditions, he is known principally for his Arthurian romances, where he appears to have treated for the first time, in French at least, the chivalric quest, the love of Lancelot and Guenevere, and the Grail as a sacred object. He also emphasized the problematic side of the love of Tristan and Iseut and may have contributed to the spread of this legend in French in an early work that is lost today.

Although the chronology of his writings is uncertain, the order of composition of his major romances seems to be as follows: *Erec et Enide*, *Cligés*, *Le chevalier de la charrette* (*Lancelot*), *Yvain* (*Le chevalier au lion*), and *Le conte du graal* (*Perceval*). He may also have written *Philomena*, an adaptation of the Ovidian story of Philomela (*Metamorphoses* 6.426–74), and *Guillaume d'Angleterre*, a saint's life told like an adventure romance. The prologue to *Cligés* refers to works Chrétien wrote in his early years: *Philomena* ("de la hupe et de l'aronde") and another, lost, on the tale of Pelops ("de la mors de l'espaule"), as well as French versions of Ovid's *Ars amatoria* and *Remedia amoris*, and a Tristan story, concerning which, curiously, Chrétien does not mention Tristan himself: "del roi Marc et d'Iseut la blonde." He is also the author of two courtly chansons in the trouvère tradition.

Chrétien names as patrons Marie de Champagne, the first daughter of Eleanor of Aquitaine and Louis VII of France, who, he writes, gave him the *matiere* and *san* for the *Charrette*, and Philippe d'Alsace, count of Flanders, who gave him "the book" for the *Conte du graal*. Philippe died in the Holy Land in 1191, which may explain why the romance is incomplete. But there is also evidence that Chrétien died before completing it. The last 1,000 lines of the *Charrette* were written by the otherwise unknown Godefroi de Leigni, who names himself in the epilogue and says that he is following Chrétien's plan for the romance. The *Charrette* plot is referred to three times in *Yvain*, and it is likely that Chrétien worked on the two romances at about the same time; this may explain why he left the completion of the *Charrette* to another, whose work he supervised while himself completing *Yvain*.

Erec treats the love of Erec and Enide. In the first part, Erec successfully completes the combat for the sparrow-hawk and brings Enide to Arthur's court, where they marry. A dispute between husband and wife breaks out in the second part because Erec abandons deeds of prowess, notably in tournaments, to dally with his wife. Erec and Enide set out in quest of reconciliation, after which they return to Arthur's court and are crowned king and queen there upon the death of Erec's father.

Cligés also has two parts. The first relates how Alixandre, the first son of the Emperor of Constantinople, goes to Arthur's court to test his mettle, falls in love with Gauvain's sister, Soredamors, and helps put down an insurrection by one of Arthur's vassals. Alixandre and Soredamors then marry. The second part recounts the career of their son, Cligés. Alixandre's younger brother, Alis, had been crowned emperor during his older brother's absence. The latter relinquished the throne after Alis had promised not to marry so as to allow Cligés to succeed him. But Alis breaks his word by marrying Fenice. Fenice and Cligés fall in love. At the end of a complicated plot, including a magic potion, a false death, and a secret hideaway, Alis dies and Cligés and Fenice are united in matrimony.

The *Charrette* tells the first known version of the love of Lancelot and Guenevere. The queen is abducted by Meleagant to the land of Gorre. Lancelot, known as the Knight of the Cart after riding in that infamous conveyance, succeeds in saving her from her captors while liberating Arthur's subjects held captive with her.

Yvain tells how the hero knight wins the hand of Laudine, the lady of the magic fountain, by defeating and mortally wounding her husband. After this courtly variant of the Widow of Ephesus tale, Yvain neglects to return to her after more than a year of following tournaments, then goes mad when she repudiates his love. A quest ends with their reconciliation. During the quest, Yvain aids, befriends, and is accompanied by a lion—whence his sobriquet: the Knight with the Lion. *Yvain* offers interesting parallels and contrasts in plot, structure, and theme with *Erec*.

Chrétien's last major work, the incomplete *Conte du graal*, or *Perceval*, relates how a young, naive squire rises to prominence through combat and love, then fails in the adventure at the Grail Castle because an earlier wrong or "sin" committed against his mother ties his tongue, preventing him from asking the questions he should. The Grail Castle is closed to him, and, as he later learns, great misfortune spreads through the land because of his fault, affecting orphans, widows, and others whom the knight should protect. Perceval sets out to right the wrong. After five years of wandering, during which time he forgets God, Perceval finds himself and God again at his uncle's hermitage, where he also learns of his fault. Interlaced with Perceval's quest are the adventures of Gauvain, accused of murder, and later obliged to seek the Bleeding Lance, which was also found in the Grail Castle during Perceval's visit there. The romance breaks off while relating his remarkable adventures.

Chrétien's romances each average about 7,000 lines and comprise two parts, with the exception of the *Conte du graal*, which extends to somewhat more than 10,000 lines, an apparently more complex variant of the two-part narrative structure. All are written in octosyllabic rhymed couplets, but without the regular alternation between masculine and feminine rhymes that came to characterize classical Alexandrine couplets. Of more importance for the evolution of French romance from verse to prose was Chrétien's extensive use of the "broken" couplet. Before Chrétien, rhymed couplets in French tended to be taken as wholes, so that no sense or breath arrest took place other than on the even-numbered line. Chrétien favored "breaking," whereby the arrest occurred on the odd-numbered line. This reduced the formality of verse enunciation and, besides the freedom it allowed the writer, was a step toward the transition to prose romance in the 13th century.

Chrétien is remarkable for his self-conscious artistry. He seems to have been proud of his achievement, judging by the evidence of the prologues written to almost all his works, as well as by interventions wherein the narrator comments on his art, ideas, and narratives. He knew that his works contributed to fostering French civilization, especially its chivalric and intellectual features. The *Cligés* prologue in particular stresses and conjoins aristocratic *chevalerie* and learned *clergie*. Whatever he may have understood specifically by these ideals, it is clear that they vouchsafed a civilization that came to France from Greece and Rome. However, the prologues to *Erec* and the *Charrette* are most explicit regarding the art of romance, which Chrétien helped define and illustrate. They identify three major features of Chrétien's art: *matiere*, *san*, and *conjointure*.

The question of Chrétien's putative sources is complex. He refers to written sources in the prologues to *Cligés* and the *Conte du graal*; his Ovidian tales also illustrate his use of traditional written sources. However, the Arthurian *matiere* is explained by its origins in Celtic legend. Chrétien mined oral traditions for his tales. The prologue to *Erec* mentions the jongleurs who had related the story before him, and other sources refer to itinerant storytellers who told marvelous stories about Arthur, Tristan and Iseut, and other Celtic heroes and heroines. We know little about these stories. None has survived in its original state. It is generally believed that they provided the Round Table, as well as most of the names of knights and ladies; the motif of the quest as a passage into the otherworld—the world of the dead, of adventure, of marvelous love between a man and a woman who is not mortal—was probably drawn from Celtic traditions circulating in Chrétien's time. Earlier versions probably had a mythological basis, but Chrétien most likely knew or understood little about it. One clear example of the "Celticity" of Chrétien's sources is the quest in *Erec*. Erec and his wife have a misunderstanding about his love for her. They both set out on a quest and encounter many adventures that test Erec's prowess and Enide's love. The final adventure in the quest is with the count Limors, readily understandable to French ears as "the Dead." During the couple's return, they encounter the adventure known as the Joy of the Court. A huge knight does battle in a magic garden of eternal spring. Whenever he defeats an opponent, the latter loses his head, which is then fixed on a stake in the garden. Erec's victory ends the custom and releases joy in the garden and the outside world. Rituals of combat and death, following prescribed custom, were known in Celtic tradition as *geis*. In Chrétien's romances, they become the more or less euhemerized adventures of questing knights. The inexplicability of such adventures accounts for their marvelous quality.

The *san* that Chrétien says he received for the *Charrette* from Marie de Champagne seems to imply context, significance, an informing idea that is drawn out of the *matiere* to explain it in a manner comprehensible to Chrétien's audiences. In the *Charrette*, for example, the bringing together of Lancelot and Guenevere as lovers has generally been taken to imply that Marie's *san* was what is today called courtly love—an ennobling love shared by the queen and her lover. That Chrétien makes a mystery of Lancelot's name until near the midpoint of the romance suggests that his audiences did not know who Lancelot was until Guenevere names him for the first time while he is fighting for her liberation.

The *Charrette* begins with a quest for Guenevere after her abduction. The knight who liberates her and others entrapped in the kingdom of Gorre makes it obvious early in the narrative that he loves the queen in a most extraordinary way. He is willing to compromise his honor in the eyes of all if it serves her liberation by mounting the shameful cart in order to find her again. Although Lancelot is subject to fits of despair and self-forgetfulness, nothing prevents him from carrying out his service and liberating the queen. In fact, his love seems rather to make it possible for him alone to accomplish the quest. He meets numerous adventures along the way, including a damsel who offers her love if he will protect her from a would-be rapist; the lifting of a mysterious tomb that only the knight able to liberate the queen can open; and the crossing of a sword-bridge on bare hands and knees. Lancelot's return to Arthur involves his own abduction and a great tournament that demonstrates anew his service for the queen.

Much ink has flowed in efforts to determine whether Chrétien approved or disapproved of the adulterous liaison between Lancelot and Guenevere. Basic to the dispute is the presumed adulterous character of courtly love. Courtly love, as a term, is a modern invention. In the Middle Ages, writers spoke of *fin' amors*, stressing the adaptability of love to different contexts, environments, and social circumstances. The basic features seem to have been the joy it produced and the resulting good that accrued to the lovers and the world in which

they lived. Chrétien affirms Lancelot's joy, as well as his accomplishments, despite the difficulties the love causes him.

A striking feature of Chrétien's romances is the close relation obtaining between love and prowess. Prowess is not only prowess in arms but the sum of those qualities that represent worth in the knight or lady—the *chevalerie* of the *Cligés* prologue. Arms may demonstrate worth, but so may the quality of love the knight and lady share. Chrétien's courtly chansons evince an effort to overcome the constraints of human passion and make it enhance individual worth and serve noble ends, most notably by the rejection of the irrational features of Tristan and Iseut's love. The rejection also occurs in the romances, especially *Cligés*. It is important to note that, in both the broader medieval context and in Chrétien's own romances, adultery is not predominant, despite the example of Lancelot and Guenevere. More striking, in a medieval context, is the emphasis on conjugal love. The notion must have seemed much more original in the 12th century than it may appear today, after centuries of love stories. That marriage could be more than a social or family obligation is obvious in Chrétien. Erec chooses his bride without consulting his family, and so does Yvain. And there is no sense of forced marriage except for Fenice in *Cligés*, and that marriage does not succeed precisely because it is forced and because the husband, Alis, in marrying, violates an oath made to his brother and thus threatens the succession of his brother's son, Cligés, to the throne.

Marital problems do arise, but they are also solved. Chrétien insists on a certain equality between the spouses. Not that he meant a contractual equality in any modern legal sense but rather a natural, noble equality that was tried and tested in conflict with the outside world and in the resolution of disputes that occur in the marriage.

The word *conjointure* occurs only once, at least in the sense used to describe romance narrative—in the prologue to *Erec*. Chrétien distinguishes his "very beautiful" *conjointure* from the stories about *Erec* told by storytellers, who were wont, he says, to take apart and leave out material (*depecier et corronpre*) that belonged in the tale. This seems to mean that Chrétien's romance puts the story together as it should be, omitting nothing essential. That "putting together" would include both *matiere* and *san*. This appears to be the case in *Erec*, whose first part combines two stories, the sparrowhawk episode and the hunt for the white stag, to each of which Enide, because of the qualities that make her desirable as a spouse, provides a denouement. In the sparrowhawk contest, Erec proves that Enide is the most beautiful woman, and Arthur bestows the "kiss of the white stag" on her for the same reason.

Enide's beauty comprehends qualities of body,

vestment, and, most importantly, mind and mentality that make her exemplary of perfect womanhood. In the aristocratic world of medieval romance, where everyone of worth is "naturally" on a pedestal, Erec and Enide come together out of admiration and a kind of noble affinity. By the identification of the qualities of persons—the invention of those qualities in source material and their elucidation in romance narrative—Chrétien brings together the disparate elements of the storytellers' versions and fills out the missing features in his new romance. The *molt bele conjointure* depends on the disparate elements of romance marvels, reveals the ideal truth perceived in them by 12th-century civilization, and articulates a new, marvelous narrative. Once the exceptional quality of that narrative was recognized—apparently as early as *Cligés*—a new genre had emerged. The word *roman*, which first meant "in the French language," came to mean "romance" as a narrative recounting marvelous adventures that express an aristocratic ethos. That achievement was Chrétien's.

Chrétien's popularity in his own day is attested both by the unusually large number of surviving manuscripts of his romances—an average of seven for the first four, and as many as fifteen for the *Conte du Graal*—and the enduring influence he had on the romancers who succeeded him. While such writers as Jean Renart and Gautier d'Arras deliberately set out to rival him, others more wisely welcomed his influence in their work. His most influential romances were the two he left unfinished: the *Chevalier de la charrette* and the *Conte du Graal*. The latter spawned a series of verse continuations in the early 13th century, while both provided inspiration for the immensely successful *Lancelot-Grail* or *Vulgate Cycle* of the second quarter of the same century. The Grail story was also reworked independently by the anonymous author of the *Perlesvaus*.

See also **Gautier D'Arras; Raoul de Houdenc; Wace**

Further Reading

Chrétien de Troyes. *Christian von Troyes, Smtliche Werke*, ed. Wendelin Foerster. 4 vols. Halle: Niemeyer, 1884–99.

——. *Œuvres complètes*, ed. Daniel Poirion, et al. Paris: Gallimard, 1994.

——. *Romans*, ed. Michel Zink, et al. Paris: Librarie Générale Française, 1994.

——. *Les chansons courtoises de Chrétien de Troyes*, ed. Marie-Claire Zai. Bern: Lang & Lang, 1974.

——. *Arthurian Romances*, trans. D. D. R. Owen. London: Dent, 1987.

——. *The Complete Romances of Chrétien de Troyes*, trans. David Staines. Bloomington: Indiana University Press, 1990.

——. *Arthurian Romances*, trans. William W. Kibler. Harmondsworth: Penguin, 1991.

Busby, Keith, Terry Nixon, Alison Stones, Lori Walters, eds. *Les manuscrits de Chrétien de Troyes/The Manuscripts of Chrétien de Troyes*. 2 vols. Amsterdam: Rodopi, 1993.

Kelly, F. Douglas. *Chrétien de Troyes: An Analytic Bibliography*. London: Grant and Cutler, 1976.

Reiss, Edmund, Louise Horner Reiss, and Beverly Taylor. *Arthurian Legend and Literature: An Annotated Bibliography*. Vol. 1: *The Middle Ages*, New York, London: Garland, 1984.

Frappier, Jean, *Chrétien de Troyes: l'homme et l'œuvre*. Paris: Hatier, 1968 (English trans. by Raymond J. Cormier, Athens: University of Ohio Press, 1982).

Lacy, Norris J. *The Craft of Chrétien de Troyes: An Essay on Narrative Art*. Leiden: Brill, 1980.

Topsfield, Leslie T. *Chrétien de Troyes: A Study of the Arthurian Romances*. Cambridge: Cambridge University Press, 1981.

Kelly, Douglas, ed. *The Romances of Chrétien de Troyes: A Symposium*. Lexington: French Forum, 1985.

Lacy, Norris J., Douglas Kelly, and Keith Busby, eds. *The Legacy of Chrétien de Troyes*. 2 vols. Amsterdam: Rodopi, 1987–88.

F. DOUGLAS KELLY

CHRISTINE DE PIZAN (ca. 1364–ca. 1430)

France's first woman of letters was in fact born in Italy, where her father, Tommaso de Pizzano of Bologna, was employed by the Venetian Republic. Soon after Christine's birth, her father was appointed astrologer and scientific adviser to the French king Charles V, so the family established itself in Paris in the shadow of the French court. Christine's early taste for study was interrupted by marriage at sixteen to Etienne du Castel, a young notary from Picardy, who was soon given a promising appointment to the royal chancellery. This happy marriage was interrupted ten years later by the husband's unexpected death, leaving Christine to support three children and a widowed mother. She found herself in a world that had little respect for women, where she was cheated at every turn. She found comfort in study and in writing poetry to express her grief and she soon discovered a talent for writing verse in the fixed forms popular in her day.

Her writing brought her into contact with the court of Louis of Orléans, to whom she dedicated several works, beginning with a narrative poem, the *Épistre au Dieu d'Amour* (1399), which makes fun of fashionable young men who pretend to *fin'amor* while reading Ovid and Jean de Meun. This work was followed by other narrative poems: the *Dit de Poissy* (1401), *Le Débat des deux amams*, *Livre des trois jugemens*, and *Dit de la pastoure* (1403). These eventually led to even more ambitious allegorical poems, the semiautobiographical *Chemin de long estude* (1402–03), which also commented on society's current troubles and proposed an international monarchy, and a lengthy account of the role of Fortune in universal history, the *Mutacion de Fortune* (finished at the end of 1403).

It was also to Louis of Orléans that Christine dedicated an equally ambitious work in poetry and prose, the *Épistre Othea* (ca. 1400) combining a commentary on classical mythology with advice to a young knight.

It was one of her most popular works. As the duke was unwilling to find a place in his household for Christine's son, Jean du Castel, after 1404 no further works were dedicated to him. At about this same time, Christine was commissioned by the duke of Burgundy, Philip the Bold, to write a biography of the late king, the *Faits et bonnes meurs du sage roy Charles V* (1404), her first work entirely in prose.

Slightly earlier, her views on Jean de Meun and the *Roman de la Rose* had involved Christine in a debate with members of the royal chancellery, Jean de Montreuil and Gontier and Pierre Col, who admired Jean de Meun's erudition, whereas she saw his unfortunate influence on society's attitudes toward women. Christine did not start the debate, as was formerly thought, but she moved it from a private theoretical discussion to a wider audience by giving copies of the letters it inspired to the queen and the provost of Paris (1402), a gesture that added to her literary reputation and marked her first important defense of her sex against traditional misogynistic literature. It also inspired her to compose three later works: the *Dit de la Rose*, a long poem written in the midst of the debate; the *Cité des dames*, inspired largely by Boccaccio's *De claris mulieribus*, in a certain sense a rewriting of it from a feminine point of view; and the *Livre des trois vertus* (1405), offering advice to women of all classes in an interesting commentary on contemporary French society.

The year 1405 marked a turning point in France's affairs, an open break between the political ambitions of the dukes of Orléans and Burgundy, inspiring Christine to write a letter to the French queen, Isabeau of Bavaria (October 5), begging her to act as savior of the country. The letter had little effect on the queen, but it focused Christine's attention on matters of public interest, inspiring the *Livre du corps de policie* (1407), on the ideal of the perfect prince, the first of several works directed to the dauphin Louis of Guyenne. These also included the *Livre des fais d'armes et de chevalerie* (ca. 1410), based on Vegetius and on Honoré Bouvet, outlining the essentials of military leadership and stressing international laws to govern warfare. With affairs in France steadily worsening, in 1410 she addressed a letter to the elderly duke of Berry, King Charles VI's uncle, begging him to act to save the country. A civil uprising, the Cabochien revolt, led her to appeal once more to Louis of Guyenne in the *Livre de la paix* (1412–14). This prince appeared to be developing qualities of leadership, but his untimely death (December 1415) added to France's chaos following the defeat at Agincourt. This disaster inspired Christine's *Épistre de la prison de vie humaine*, addressed to Marie de Berry, duchess of Bourbon, but speaking to all women who had suffered losses at Agincourt and indeed to widows and bereaved women of all wars.

As violence in Paris increased, Christine sought refuge in a convent, probably the abbey of Poissy, where her daughter had been a nun for many years. There, she wrote the *Heures de contemplation de Notre Dame*, possibly at the time of her son's death in 1425. Her hopes for France were unexpectedly renewed by the appearance of Jeanne d'Arc, who inspired her final poem, the *Ditié de Jehanne d'Arc*, written shortly after the coronation of Charles VII at Reims in July 1429.

The date of Christine's death is unknown, but Guillebert de Mets, writing memories of Paris in 1434, refers to her in the past tense.

Although not French by birth, Christine wrote many pages inspired by her concern for France; as the mother of three children, her views on education of the young were considerably in advance of her times; as a woman obliged to make her own way in an unfriendly society, she courageously raised her voice in protest against traditional misogyny. She is an unusually interesting witness of her times. Her works were printed and read well into the 16th century, providing for her the earthly fame she, like other early Renaissance writers, so greatly desired.

See also **Boccaccio, Giovanni; Charles V the Wise; Jeanne d'arc; Jean de Meun**

Further Reading

Christine de Pizan. *Œuvres poétiques*, ed. Maurice Roy. 3 vols. Paris: Didot, 1886–96.

Bomstein, Diane, ed. *Ideals For Women in the Works of Christine de Pizan*. Detroit: Michigan Consortium for Medieval and Early Modern Studies, 1981.

Kennedy, Angus J. *Christine de Pizan: A Bibliographical Guide*. London: Grant and Cutler, 1984.

Richards, J. E. *Reinterpreting Christine de Pizan*. Athens: University of Georgia Press, 1991.

Solente, Suzanne. "Christine de Pizan." In *Histoire littéraire de la France*. Paris: Imprimerie Nationale, 1974, Vol. 40.

Willard, Charity C. *Christine de Pizan: Her Life and Works*. New York: Persea, 1984.

CHARITY CANNON WILLARD

CICONIA, JOHANNES (c. 1370–1412)

Johannes Ciconia, a musician of northern origins, became perhaps the most important figure connecting the *ars nova* of the *Trecento* and the Renaissance or proto-Renaissance styles that emerged in the *Quattrocento*. His biography has been a battleground for scholars. In her exhaustive study of his life and work, Clercx (1960) constructed an extended chronology according to which he was born in Liège c. 1335, served the papal court at Avignon from 1350 on, traveled in Italy during 1358–1363, returned to Liège in 1372, and then finally setded in Padua in 1403, where he remained until his death in 1412. Later discoveries and reinterpretations by other scholars, however, indicate that this chronology confused the lives of two or three different people of the same name. It is now accepted that the composer Ciconia was born c. 1370 (apparently he was the illegitimate son of a priest), and he is documented as a choirboy in Liège in 1385. By 1390, Ciconia was a musician in Rome, during the reign of Pope Boniface IX. In 1401, he went to Padua, where he served at its cathedral and university until his death in 1412; one of his chief patrons there was the great Paduan scholar and prelate Francesco Zabarella.

Ciconia was not only a musician but also a poet and theorist; he wrote several theoretical treatises. As a composer, he left a substantial and significant legacy of surviving works: twelve movements of the mass, fourteen polytextual Latin motets, two French *virelais,* four Italian madrigals, and seven Italian *ballate,* plus several miscellaneous and uncertainly attributed pieces. He was trained in the French *ars nova* style but obviously also encountered distinctly Italian *ars nova* practices, and as a result he developed a progressive synthesis of his own. In his French music, as well as in some of his Latin polyphonic pieces, Ciconia demonstrates a commitment to the intricate techniques of French *ars subtilior,* and in his settings of Italian texts he assimilates the Italianate lyricism of the Tuscan school but also infuses it subtly with French structural procedures.

By contrast, Ciconia built his complex polyphonic motets, with their multiple texts and their very northern isorhythmic counterpoint, around individual melodic lines, some of which were first conceived as Italianate songs. Through such compositions; Ciconia helped to introduce the motet style in the Italian musical scene. In his movements for the mass, he gave the upper parts remarkable melodic freedom; and he was one of the earliest composers to draw a clear distinction between passages for solo singers and those for the full choral ensemble. In all, both in his technique and in his Franco-Italian fusion of idioms, Ciconia is recognized as the founder of what can be called a new "international Gothic" style that would take shape during the fifteenth century. The elegant intricacy and beauty of his music can still appeal to us. Ciconia's career also prefigures a pattern of the following 150 years, during which Italian courts and cultural centers were eager to import and patronize "Netherlandish" Franco-Flemish northerners (beginning with Guillaume Dufay), in preference to native Italian musicians, as musical stars and pacesetters.

A number of Ciconia's compositions were written as occasional pieces for specific patrons and situations. An early canonic composition with a French text may have been dedicated to Gian Galeazzo Visconti. One madrigal was written in honor of the city of Lucca; another madrigal and one of the motets praise members of the Carrara family, then reigning in Padua; one *ballata.* may mourn the death (1406) in prison of the last Carrara lord. Among Ciconia's motets, two are dedicated to Francesco Zabarella; a third commemorates the submission of Padua to the Venetian republic, negotiated by Zabarella after the overthrow of the Carrara (1406). Another motet praises Doge Michele Steno, architect of the Venetian takeover, and two others apparently commemorate the installation of two Venetians as successive bishops of Padua—Albano Michiel (1406) and Pietro Marcello (1409). Still another motet may also be in honor of Pietro Marcello or, alternatively, of the antipope Benedict XIII.

Further Reading

Clercx, Suzanne. "Johannes Ciconia théoricien." *Annales Musicologiques*, 3, 1955, pp. 39–75.
——. *Johannes Ciconia: Un musicien liégeois et son temps,* 2 vols. Brussels: Palais des Académies, 1960.
Fallows, David. "Ciconia padre e figlio." *Rivista Italiana di Musicologia,* 11, 1976, pp. 171ff.
Fischer, Kurt von. *Studien zur italienischen Musik des Trecento und frühen Quattrocento.* Bern: P. Haupt, 1956.
Krohn, Ernst C. *"Nova musica* of Johannes Ciconia." *Manuscripta,* 5, 1961, pp. 3–16.
Reese, Gustav. *Music of the Middle Ages.* New York: Norton, 1940.

JOHN W. BARKER

CIMABUE (c. 1240–c. 1302)

The Florentine painter Cenni di Pepe (or Bencivieni di Pepo) is commonly known by his nickname, Cimabue connoting bullheadedness. He is generally said to have marked the division between the art of the Middle Ages and the Renaissance by recalling painting to the task of imitating nature. Cimabue was Florentine by birth, but his activity stretched from Bologna southward to Rome and Assisi, and west to Pisa. Biographical information on Cimabue (the *Ottimo commento* on the *Divine Comedy*; Villani, 1381–1382; and Vasari, 1550–1564) is scanty and unreliable, and specific documentation of his work is almost non existent. The earliest archival mention of Cimabue is from June 1272, when *Cimabove, picture de Florencia* was witness to the signing of a legal contract in Rome. Besides this, the only other documentation of the artist comes from Pisa, thirty years later. Between September 1301 and February 1302, Cimabue was commissioned to complete the apse mosaic of Christ Enthroned in the cathedral of Pisa (begun by Maestro Francesco) with a figure of Saint John the Evangelist. Also in 1302, Cimabue and a Giovanni di Apparecchiato were commissioned to paint a panel (now lost) for the hospital church of Santa Chiara in Pisa. The Saint John in the cathedral of Pisa is Cimabue's single surviving documented work; it provides such a frail scaffold on which to hang an artistic career that German scholars in the early twentieth century thought Cimabue to have been a legendary figure. A number of works survive, however, which correlate stylistically with the figure of Saint John; and most recent scholars agree that these constitute a core body of works definitely attributable to Cimabue.

Cimabue's greatest surviving cycle of works is the series of frescoes (at one point badly disfigured by chemical corrosion over much of the surface) in the transept and presbytery of the upper basilica of San Francesco of Assisi. These frescoes were most likely executed, with considerable participation by workshop assistants, during the papacy of either of two Franciscans: Nicholas III Orsini (1277–1280) or Nicholas IV Masci (1288–1292).

Despite their variety of narratives and decorative elements, Cimabue took great pains to give the frescoes in San Francesco overall unity as a program. This work—one of the first and most ambitious of such efforts—successfully conveys the impression that the east end of the church is, in terms of its decoration, a single cohesive entity.

Other works often attributed to Cimabue and his workshop include some of the mosaics in the Baptistery in Florence, a fresco of the *Maestà and Saint Francis* in the lower basilica of San Francesco at Assisi, a *Maestà* from San Francesco in Pisa (now at the Louvre in Paris), and a *Maestà* from Santa Maria dei Servi in Bologna.

See also **Dante Alighieri; Francis of Assisi, Saint; Nicholas III, Pope**

Further Reading

Battisti, Eugenio. *Cimabue,* trans. R. Enggass and C. Enggass. University Park: Pennsylvania Stare University Press, 1966.
Bellosi, Luciano. *La pecora di Giotto.* Turin: Einaudi, 1985.
Chiellini, Monica. *Cimabue,* trans. Lisa Pelletti. Florence: Scala, 1988. Nicholson, Alfred. *Cimabue: A Critical Study.* Princeton, N.J: Princeton University Press, 1932.
Sindona, Enio. *L'opera completa di Cimabue e il momenta figurativo pregiottesco.* Milan: Rizzoli, 1975.
White, John, and B. Zanardi. "Cimabue and the Decorative Sequence in the Upper Church of San Francesco, Assisi." In *Roma Anno 1300: Atti del Convegno (1980).* Rome: L'Erma di Bretschneider, 1983.

GUSTAV MEDICUS

CINO DA PISTOIA
(c. 1270-c. 1336 or 1337)

The jurist and poet Cino, or Guittoncino, da Pistoia (Cino dei Sighibuldi) was born in the properous city of Pistoia, some 20 miles (32 kilometers) northwest of Florence. His father, Francesco dei Sighibuldi (Sinib-

uldi, Sigisbuldi), was a notary who belonged to one of the older and powerful families of Pistoia, adherents of the Black faction. Cino's mother, Diamante, was the daughter of the well-known physician Bona-ventura di Tonello. We know very little about Cino's early life except that for five years he was the pupil of Francesco da Colle, who provided excellent instruction in grammar and the classics. Cino may have begun his legal studies in Pistoia in 1279–1284, under Dino dei Rossoni of Mugello; he then went to Bologna to continue his studies and remained there, in all probability, from 1284 to 1292, because the normal course for a law degree required eight years. The period in Bologna was critical for Cino's development both as a jurist and as a poet. He benefited from the lectures of Francesco d'Accursio and Lambertino Ramponi. In Bologna, Cino felt the lingering poetic influence of Guido Guinizzelli and Guittone d'Arezzo, as well as that of Onesto degli Onesti, with whom he exchanged several sonnets. Perhaps during these years in Bologna Cino met Dante, who visited there in 1287. The first textual evidence we have of their friendship is Cino's *canzone Avegna che io aggia più per tempo,* written to console Dante on the death of Beatrice (1290).

In 1292–1294, Cino may have traveled to France (in particular, to Orléans and Paris), for in his major juridical work, *Lectura in codicem,* he makes specific references to the legal writings of Frenchmen such as Pierre de Belleperche and Jacob da Revigni. Cino and Dante united in their fervent support of Henry VII of Luxumbourg. The solemn *canzone Da poi che la natura ha fine posto,* written to commemorate the death of Henry, conveys Cino's sense of loss and desolation. Cino also wrote the moving *canzone Su per la costa, Amor, de l'alto monte* to commemorate the death of Dante.

While Henry's death marked the end of Cino's active involvement in partisan politics, it did not diminish his firm adherence to Ghibelline ideals, and this may be clearly seen in his legal writings. On 11 June 1314, probably in Pistoia, Cino completed *Lectura in codicem,* his great commentary on the first nine books of the Justinian code of laws. He had been working on this commentary desultorily since the last decade of the thirteenth century and had finally succeeded in assembling it in final form in two years. On 9 December 1314, he successfully completed a public examination (the *conventus*) and was awarded, in Bologna, a doctoral degree in legal studies. In the diploma, Cino is called *sapientissimus et eloquentissimus vir* ("a very wise and eloquent man").

As a lawyer and teacher, Cino was active in Florence, Macerata, Siena, Bologna, and Perugia. In 1324 in Bologna, Cino probably met Petrarch, who was a student in the *studium.* Cino, having earned a great reputation through his legal writings and lectures, was much sought after to add luster to the *studia* in other Italian cities. On 15 August 1330, Robert of Anjou invited Cino to teach civil law at the university in Naples, but Cino remained there for only one year. Some reasons for his brief stay may be found in the satirical poem *Deh, quando rivedrò il dolce paese,* in which he rails against the vile untutored citizenry, the enviousness of his legal colleagues, and the generally disreputable nature of the city. Robert—although he may have considered Cino, and Cino's political beliefs, distasteful—held *Lectura in codicem in* high esteem, acquiring a personal copy in 1332.

During the last four years of his life Cino was in Florence, Perugia, and Pistoia. In Pistoia on 13 July 1334, he was elected *gonfaloniere* (standard-bearer) for August and September. Perhaps because of ill health, he resigned that post, but on 31 March 1336 his fellow citizens elected him to the *consiglio del popolo* ("council of the people") for a six-month term. After the first signs of his final illness began on 12 December 1336, Cino made his will on 23 December. He died shortly thereafter, either in late December 1336 or in early January 1337. Because Cino's son Mino had died earlier, Mino's son Francesco—Cino's grandson—was named an heir, with Cino's four daughters (Diamante, Giovanna, Lornbarduccia, and Beatrice) as *legatarie.* Cino was buried with honor in the cathedral of San Jacopo of Pistoia, and a funereal monument was erected near the altar of the Porrine in 1337. In the sculptural relief Cino is remembered as a teacher (twice), but not as a politician, jurist, or poet.

Nevertheless, it is for his poetry that Cino is most often remembered. In addition to his synthesis of various stilnovistic elements, Cino's basic contribution to the lyric tradition was his objective psychological realism, which manifested itself in the intensely personal, almost confessional tone of his poems; and in this regard he serves as a bridge between the *dolce stil nuovo* and Petrarch. Because of his extreme versatility as a poet, Cino was able to mediate among various "schools" and individual poets, compose lyrics in a number of modes and styles, and ultimately profit from and contribute directly to the several major literary currents of his time. Cino enjoyed literary and personal friendships with the greatest contemporary Italian poets, all of whom regarded him with much admiration: in addition to Dante's praise in *De vulgari eloquentia,* Boccaccio paid him tribute by incorporating almost all of his canzone *La dolce vista e 'l bel guardo soave* in *Filostrato* (5.62–65), and Petrarch lamented his death in the sonnet *Piangete, donne, et con voi pianga Amore.*

See also **Dante Alighieri; Henry VII of Luxembourg; Petrarca, Francesco**

Further Reading

Editions

Cino da Pistoia. *Le rime di Cino da Pistoia,* ed. Guido Zaccagnini. Biblioteca dell' Archivum Romanicum, Series 1, Vol. 4. Geneva: Olschki, 1925.

Poeti del dolce stil nuovo, ed. Mario Marti. Florence: Le Monnier, 1969. *Rimatori del dolce stil novo,* ed. Luigi di Benedetto. Scrittori d'Italia, 172. Bari: Laterza, 1939.

Critical Studies

Chiappelli, Luigi. *Vita e opere giuridiche di Cino da Pistoia con molti documenti inediti.* Pistoia: Tip. Cino dei Fratelli Bracali, 1881.

——. *Nuove ricerche su Cino da Pistoia.* Pistoia: Officina Tipografica Cooperativa, 1911.

Colloquio Cino da Pistoia (Roma, 25 ottobre 1975). Rome: Accademia Nazionale dei Lincei, 1976.

Corti, Maria. "Il linguaggio poetico di Cino da Pistoia." *Cultura Neolatina,* 12, 1952, pp. 185–223.

De Robertis, Domenico. "Cino e le 'imitazioni' dalle rime di Dante." *Studi Danteschi,* 29, 1950, pp. 103–177.

——. "Cino e i poeti bolognesi." *Giornale Storico della Letteratura Italiana,* 128, 1951, pp. 273–312.

——. "Cino da Pistoia e la crisi del linguaggio poetico." *Convivium,* 1952, pp. 1–35.

——. "Cino da Pistoia." In *I Minori.* Milan: Marzorati, 1961, pp. 285–306.

Hollander, Robert. "Dante and Cino da Pistoia." *Dante Studies,* 110, 1992, pp. 201–231.

Kleinhenz, Christopher. *The Early Italian Sonnet: The First Century (1220–1321).* Lecce: Milella, 1986.

——. "Cino da Pistoia and the Italian Lyric Tradition." In *L'imaginaire courtois et son double,* ed. Giovanna Angeli and Luciano Formisano. Naples: Edizioni Scientifiche Italiane, 1992, pp. 147–163.

Monti, Gennaro Maria. *Cino da Pistoia giurista.* Città di Casrello: Il Solco, 1924.

Treves, E. "La satira di Cino da Pistoia contro Napoli." *Giornale Storico della Letteratura Italiana,* 58, 1911, pp. 122–139.

Zaccagnini, Guido. *Cino da Pistoia: Studio biografico.* Pistoia: Pagnini, 1918.

CHRISTOPHER KLEINHENZ

CLARE, SAINT (1193 or 1194–1253)

Clare (in Italian, Chiara) was among the earliest followers of Saint Francis, and founder with him of the second order of Franciscans, better known as the Poor Clares. Clare renounced her worldly possessions to follow Francis c. 1212. Before long, she was joined by a number of other women devoted to Franciscan ideals, and c. 1215 Francis himself named her the abbess of a new foundation for women at San Damiano, near Assisi. The second order grew from this community, of which Clare remained head until her death; its first rule was granted in 1219 by Cardinal Ugolino (later Pope Gregory IX). Thereafter, numerous daughter houses were founded in Italy and eventually throughout Europe. The austerity of the Poor Clares went far beyond anything previously practiced by religious women, especially after modifications in the rule granted by Pope Innocent IV in 1247 and 1253. After Clare's death, a milder rule was granted by Pope Urban IV in 1263 and was adopted by the majority of the houses. Clare's own foundation at San Damiano, however, had insisted, from its earliest days and at her personal urging, on the strict observance of *the privilegium paupertatis* or privilege of poverty, as originally granted, and it never accepted any relaxation of the rule. Clare was canonized in 1255.

Various writings attributed to Clare survive in the corpus of material associated with the early development of the Franciscan order. At least four letters are generally accepted as genuine; another letter and two devotional texts known as the *Testament* and the *Blessing* are disputed. A contemporary biography of Clare, attributed to Thomas of Celano, Francis's first biographer, is preserved in *Acta sanctorum.*

See also **Francis of Assisi, Saint; Innocent IV, Pope; Thomas of Celano**

Further Reading

Brooke, R. B., and C. N. L. Brooke. "Saint Clare." In *Medieval Women,* ed. Derek Baker. Oxford: Blackwell, 1978, pp. 275–287.
Clare of Assisi: Early Documents, 2nd ed., ed. and trans. Regis Armstrong. Saint Bonaventure, N.Y.: Franciscan Institute, 1993.
Francis and Clare: The Complete Works, ed. and trans. Regis J. Armstrong and Ignatius C. Brady. New York; Paulist, 1982.

STEVEN N. BOTTERILL

CLEMENT V, POPE
(c. 1260 or 1264–1314,
r. 5 June 1305–20 April 1314)

Clement V (Bertrand de Got) was the first of the Avignonese popes. He was born in Gascony to a noble family, studied the arts at Toulouse, and then studied law at Orléans and Bologna. Through family connections he rose rapidly in the church, holding several canonries before becoming vicar-general to his brother, the bishop of Lyon. After serving as a papal chaplain, he was made bishop of Comminges in 1295 and archbishop of Bordeaux in 1299.

When Benedict XI died in 1304, the college of cardinals was deadlocked for almost a year over a successor, primarily because they were divided over papal policy toward the French king Philip the Fair. They settled on Clement because he had good relations with Philip but had also been a favorite of Philip's enemy Boniface VIII and had braved the king's wrath to attend a council called by Boniface during his struggle with Philip.

Disturbances at Rome and in the papal states prevented Clement's coronation there, so he was crowned instead at Lyon, on 14 November 1305. He spent the rest of his pontificate in France, in what he considered temporary residences. During the first four years of his reign he moved frequenly, never spending more than a year in one place, but after 1309 he favored Avignon, a city subject not to the French king but to the king of Naples, a papal vassal. His intended to stay in Avignon only briefly, but his successors were to remain there until 1376.

Within weeks of his coronation, Clement initiated policies which convinced some contemporaries that he was a creature of King Philip. He annulled Boniface VIII's bull *Clericis laicos,* which had been directed at Philip, and declared that Boniface's *Unam sanctam* had not claimed any new papal authority over France or its king. He confirmed Benedict XI's absolution of Philip and restored Philip's deposed allies Giacomo and Pietro Colonna to the cardinalate. Also, within a month of his election he made the first of a series of appointments to the college of cardinals that gave a clear advantage to the faction which favored the French. Of ten cardinals appointed in 1305, nine were French. In 1307, Clement ordered an investigation of the Templars, again at Philip's prompting. Philip seems to have had political motives for attacking the Templars; he coveted their wealth. Moreover, the evidence Philip submitted to Clement of sexual misconduct and witchcraft by the Templars had been extracted under torture. Nevertheless, Clement carried the investigation forward for several years, uncomfortable with the evidence but unwilling to drop the matter. He referred the case to the Council of Vienne for review, then decided not to wait for its decision. Rendering no decision on the evidence, he simply suppressed the Templars, citing the good of the church, on 22 March 1312. He then turned their enormous wealth over to the Hospitallers and to other military orders fighting the Muslims in Iberia, much to King Philip's chagrin. Some see this move as an example of indecision; others consider it a clever resolution of a complicated and embarrassing crisis.

In his relations with the empire, Clement was more decisive. He backed the election of Henry VII in 1308 and Henry's coronation as emperor in 1312, although he had been pressured by King Philip to support Charles of Valois, Philip's brother. In 1313 Clement prevented a war between Henry and Robert of Naples, the leader of Clement's forces in Italy, by threatening Henry with excommunication. On Henry's death a few months later, Clement claimed authority to supervise the empire during the vacancy.

In Italy, Clement and his Guelf allies struggled, though desultorily, to regain control of the papal states. Throughout Clement's reign, Rome remained too unstable to be occupied safely. Clement also did his own cause considerable harm by appointing rapacious Gascon favorites to govern the Italian lands he did control.

Perhaps Clement's most important achievement was the Council of Vienne (1311–1312). It was originally called to consider the case of the Templars, but it accomplished much more, taking measures to ease the tension between the Spiritual and Conventual factions in the Franciscan order and to arbitrate disputes between secular and mendicant clergy. It also addressed the tension between papal delegates and bishops. The council's work was preserved in *Constitutiones Clementinae,* a collection of decretals redacted by Clement; this collection was promulgated by Clement's successor, John XXII, and became the seventh book of the *Decretales* in the church's Corpus iuris canonici. Clement also founded the universities of Perugia and Orléans and established the statutes of the medical faculty at Montpellier. At the urging of Ramon Llull, he commanded that chairs in Syriac, Arabic, and Hebrew be established at Oxford, Paris, Salamanca, and Bologna, in order to aid mission work in Asia.

During much of his reign Clement was seriously ill, perhaps with stomach cancer. This may account for his seeming malleability and his lack of stamina in dealing with Philip the Fair. His illness also left him incapable of supervising the papal court for long periods; as a result, serious corruption developed. Clement had hopes of returning to Rome after the Council of Vienne, but his bad health prevented it. He died at Rocquemaure on a final journey to Gascony.

See also **Boniface VIII, Pope; Henry VII of Luxembourg; Philip IV the Fair**

Further Reading

Baluze, Étienne. *Vitae paparum Avenionensium,* 4 vols., ed. Guillaume Mollat. Paris: Letouzey et Ane, 1914–1927, Vol. 1, pp. 1–106.

Barber, Malcolm. *The Trial of the Templars.* Cambridge: Cambridge University Press, 1993.

Delorme, Ferdinand M., and Aloysius L. Tautù, eds. *Acta Clementis PP. V.* Vatican City: Typis Polyglottis Vaticanis, 1955.

Finke, Heinrich. *Papsttum und Untergang des Templerordens,* 2 vols. Münster-in-Westfalen: Aschendorff, 1907.

Gaignard, Romain. "Le gouvernement pontifical au travail: L'exemple des dernières années du règne de Clèment V, ler août 1311–20 avril 1314." *Annales du Midi,* 72, 1960, pp, 169–214.

Housley, Norman. "Pope Clement V and the Crusades of 1309–1310." *Journal of Medieval History,* 8, 1982, pp. 29–43.

Lizerand, Georges. *Clement V et Philippe le Bel.* Paris: Hachette, 1911. Menache, Sophia. *Clement V.* Cambridge: Cambridge University Press, 1998.

Mollat, Guillaume. *The Popes at Avignon, 1305–1378,* trans. Janet Love. New York: Harper and Row, 1963.

Müller, Ewald. *Das Konzil von Vienne, 1311–1312: Seine Quellen und seine Geschichte.* Münster-in-Westfalen: Aschendorff, 1934.

Renoard, Yves. *The Avignon Papacy, 1305–1403,* trans. Denis Bethell. Hamden, Conn.: Archon, 1970.

Wenck, Carl. *Clemens V. und Heinrich VII.* Halle: Niemeyer, 1882.

THOMAS TURLEY

CLOVIS I (ca. 466–511)

The most important of the Merovingian kings, Clovis I was the unifier of the Franks, the conqueror of most of Gaul, and the real founder of the kingdom of the Franks under Merovingian rule. He was also the first Christian king of the Franks. He is the possessor of a reputation for astonishing ruthlessness, brutality, and unscrupulousness.

Upon the death of his father, Childeric I, in 482, Clovis succeeded as chieftain over the group of Salian Franks settled around Tournai, in modern Belgium. He began his conquests in 486 by defeating Syagrius, an independent ruler over northern Gaul. This victory made Clovis the master of Gaul north of the Loire, the later Neustria, and he transferred his capital to Soissons, accompanied by his Frankish entourage.

The chronology and sequence of events of most of the rest of Clovis's reign are unclear and highly debated. Essentially, he became the sole Frankish king by eliminating the kings of other bands of Salian Franks through attack, treachery, and deceit. By similar means, he also rose to mastery over the Ripuarian, or Rhineland, Franks. Through a series of bitter and closely contested battles, he brought the Alemanni and Thuringians under his authority as well.

In the course of one of his battles against the Alemanni, at Zülpich (Tolbiac) in the mid-490s, Clovis converted to orthodox Christianity. This was not a sudden move, however. Like his father, Childeric, Clovis had been careful to maintain good relations with Christian authorities in his lands, and he had also married an orthodox Christian, the Burgundian princess Clotilde. The conversion of Clovis and some of his followers had little immediate effect on their pagan and polygamous habits, nor did it immediately christianize the Frankish people, but it did make Clovis the hero of orthodox Christians in Gaul.

Clovis exploited this position to gain his greatest victory. He attacked the Arian Visigoths, who controlled Gaul south of the Loire as well as Spain. In 507, Clovis defeated their army at Vouillé, near Poitiers, and in the ensuing campaigns his forces swept over most of southern Gaul. Only the military intervention of Theodoric the Ostrogoth preserved Septimania for the Visigoths and prevented the Franks from gaining the Mediterranean. Nonetheless, Clovis was the master of almost all of Gaul. For a time, he even exacted tribute from the Burgundians.

After the victory over the Visigoths, Clovis was given some sort of official recognition by the Byzantine Empire, which began a century-long tradition of Frankish-Byzantine cooperation, and he moved his capital to Paris. The years after 507 saw two of his most notable achievements. It was he who probably issued the Salic Law for his Salian Franks and all those living north of the Loire, and in 511, at Orléans, he presided over the first great church council of the Frankish kingdom.

Clovis was the master of a heterogeneous population. Franks and other Germanic peoples were in the northeast, northern Gaul was Gallo-Roman but relatively barbarized and included Franks as well, and the south was thoroughly romanized. His administration continued Roman practices; Clovis worked closely with the Gallo-Roman aristocrats, while his military was primarily Frankish. Upon his death in 511, in proper Frankish fashion his kingdom was divided equally among his four sons. The Frankish kingdom was not united again until 558, by his youngest son, Clotar I.

Most of our knowledge of Clovis comes from the writings of Gregory of Tours, three-quarters of a century after the king's death. Despite the obvious greed and treachery of his hero, Gregory was impressed by Clovis's promotion of orthodox Christianity, especially in the face of the detested Arians. Gregory hailed Clovis as a new Constantine and praised him in terms borrowed from biblical laud for King David. The name "Clovis," which evolved into the French name "Louis," was itself a French form of his correct Frankish name, Chlodovech (Chlodwig in German).

See also **Gregory of Tours**

Further Reading

Gregory of Tours. *History of the Franks*, trans. Lewis Thorpe. Harmondsworth: Penguin, 1974.
James, Edward. *The Franks*. Oxford: Blackwell, 1988.
Martindale, J.R. "Chlodovechus (Clovis)." In *Prosopography of the Later Roman Empire*. 3 vols. in 4. London: Cambridge University Press, 1980, Vol. 2: *A.D. 395–527*, pp. 288–90.
Tessier, Georges. *Le baptême de Clovis*. Paris: Gallimard, 1964.
Wood, Ian N. "Gregory of Tours and Clovis." *Revue belge de philologie et d'histoire* 63 (1985): 249–72.
——. *The Merovingian Kingdoms, 450–751*. London: Longman, 1994.

STEVEN FANNING

CNUT (d. 1035; r. 1016–35)

Danish and English king, best known in English legend as the king whose command to the waves to stop was ignored by the incoming tide. The story, first recounted by Henry of Huntingdon in his *Historia Anglorum*, shows Cnut's posthumous fame as a man of power.

From his youth Cnut certainly understood power and wielded it ruthlessly. On the death of his father, Swein, in 1014 the Scandinavian army tried to make him king of England, but the Anglo-Saxon leadership negotiated instead for Æthelred II's return from Normandy. In Denmark Cnut's brother, Harald, had become king, so in August 1015 he again sought the throne of England, joined now by Thorkell the Tall, a former supporter of

Æthelred. Cnut gained control of Wessex but foiled to capture the southeast. When Æthelred died in 1016, the Londoners recognized his son, Edmund Ironside, as king, while Cnut retained his support in Wessex. After Edmund's defeat at Ashingdon in Essex he and Cnut agreed to divide the country between them.

The death of Edmund on 30 November 1016 enabled Cnut to become ruler of England. Three strategies ensured his hold on power. In July 1017 Emma, sister of Duke Richard II of Normandy and widow of Æthelred II, became his queen, thereby neutralizing any threat from Normandy, where Æthelred's two sons, Edward and Alfred, were residing. The young sons of Edmund Ironside were moved to Hungary, well beyond Cnut's grasp, unlike Edmund's brother Eadwig, who was murdered by agents of Cnut.

Cnut's second step was to eliminate several of Æthelred's supporters, most notably the duplicitous Eadric Streona; he initially depended on Thorkell the Tall and Edward the Norwegian, whom he recognized as earls of East Anglia and Northumbria, respectively. His third policy was to acknowledge the power of the church by founding monastic houses and becoming, with Emma, a lavish ecclesiastical benefactor. His generosity was doubtless assisted by the mammoth geld payment of £72,000 levied in 1017 on his new kingdom, supplemented by a further £10,500 extracted from London's citizenry.

In the first of four trips he made to Scandinavia between 1019 and 1028 Cnut obtained the throne of Denmark following his brother Harald's death. Our knowledge of his rule in the early 1020s is sketchy. In England Thorkell became an outlaw in 1021 but must have retained a substantial band of supporters, as Cnut was persuaded to accept him as his vicegerent in Denmark in 1023.

In 1027 Cnut attended the coronation of Conrad as Holy Roman Emperor in Rome, presumably in part as a diplomatic move to protect his southern Danish flank against German encroachments. The following year he conquered Norway, driving out Olaf Haraldsson and he made Ælfgifu of Northampton regent there for their young son, Swein. He had contracted a union with Ælfgifu before his marriage with Emma, and he never repudiated the English woman. In the same year Cnut received the submission of three Scottish kings, including Malcolm and (probably) Macbeth of later Shakespearean fame, possibly to ensure that the Norse settlers in northern Britain would not return to Norway to assist in rebellion against his rule there. His Norwegian conquest was nevertheless unsuccessful, and in 1035, just before his death, Ælfgifu and her son had to withdraw to Denmark.

The administrative structures in England were strong enough to continue through his reign, though few of

Cnut's charters survive. Two law codes, one of them substantial and revealing the influence of Archbishop Wulfstan, were published in his name, and he issued letters to the English people in 1020 and 1027. In the latter he claims to have negotiated, during his visit to Rome, for the abolition of the tolls exacted from merchants traveling to Italy and the large sums required from archbishops for papal recognition.

In 1017 Cnut had replaced the ealdormen by four earls, though other earldoms were later created. This was to be less significant than the fact that such new men as Earl Godwin displaced the cadre of ealdormen and thegns who had formerly been tied to the Anglo-Saxon kings through a complex network of relationships. Godwin's power base in Wessex, the heartland of the English kingdom, later weakened Edward the Confessor and enabled Godwin's son, Harold, to gain the throne that he held through most of the year 1066.

Cnut did not found a lasting dynasty. After his death in 1035 Harold Harefoot, his son by Ælfgifu, eventually succeeded him in England, and in 1040 his and Emma's son, Harthacnut, became king for two years. Unlike his predecessor Æthelred II, Cnut died in time to leave his reputation intact. He gave England 20 years' respite from invasion, though he left a native dynasty fatally weakened and the country with strengthened ties to Normandy. When he died, the young William the Bastard had just inherited the Norman duchy; as "the Conqueror," William was to accomplish a far more successful *coup d'état* than Cnut and bring the Anglo-Saxon era to a close.

See also **Edward the Confessor; Harold Godwinson; Wulfstan of York**

Further Reading

Primary Sources

Arnold, Thomas, ed. *Henrici archidiaconi Huntendunensis historia Anglorum: The History of the English, by Henry of Huntingdon, from* A.D. *55 to* A.D. *1154.* Rolls Series 74. London: Longman, 1879.

Greenway, Diana E. ed. and trans. *Henry, Archdeacon of Huntington: History of the English People.* Oxford: Oxford University Press, 1996.

Palsson, Hermann, and Paul Edwards, trans. *Knytlinga Saga: The History of the Kings of Denmark.* Odense: City of Odense, 1986.

Whitelock, Dorothy, ed. *English Historical Documents.* Vol. 1: *c. 500–1042.* 2d ed. London: Eyre Methuen, 1979 [documents 47–50 pertain to Cnut's reign].

Secondary Sources

Fleming, Robin. *Kings and Lords in Conquest England.* Cambridge: Cambridge University Press, 1991.

Hudson, Benjamin T. "Cnut and the Scottish Kings." *HER* 107 (1992): 350–60.

Lawson, M.X. *Cnut: The Danes in England in the Early Eleventh Century.* London: Longman, 1993.

Raraty, David G.J. "Earl Godwine and Wessex: The Origins of His Power and His Political Loyalties." *History* 74 (1989): 3–19.

Rumble, Alexander R., ed. *The Reign of Cnut: King of England, Denmark, and Norway.* London: Leicester University Press, 1994.

DAVID A.E. PELTERET

CŒUR, JACQUES (ca. 1395–1456)

The most important businessman of medieval France, Jacques Cœur was born into a wealthy family in Bourges. By 1430, he was established as a financier, merchant, and master of France's Levantine trade, and he soon became a favorite of Charles VII. Royal *argentier* after 1438 and ennobled after 1441, he reorganized Valois coinage and finances and served as royal commissioner in financial and commercial negotiations. His vast financial, commercial, and industrial empire eventually made him the wealthiest man in Europe. During this period, he built a house in Bourges that symbolized his magnificence and remains a monument of Gothic architecture. His most significant public action was to finance the reconquest of Normandy and Guyenne, but by 1451 his wealth and pride had won him the envy and resentment of both crown and nobility. Charles VII found it easier to ruin than repay his greatest creditor. Arrested on the absurd charge of having poisoned the king's mistress, Agnès Sorel, Jacques Cœur was condemned for irregularities in fact typical of contemporary public finance. His holdings were confiscated by the crown, and he was imprisoned until 1454, when he escaped to Rome, where Calixtus III gave him command of a papal fleet. He died on campaign against the Turks at Chios in November 1456.

See also **Charles VII**

Further Reading

Dauvet, Jean. *Les affaires de Jacques Cœur: journal du Procureur Dauvet, procès-verbaux de séquestre et d'adjudication,* ed. Michel Mollat, Anne-Marie Yvon-Briand, Yvonne Lanhers, Constantin Marinesco. 2 vols. Paris: Colin, 1952–53.

Kerr, Albert Boardman. *Jacques Cœur: Merchant Prince of the Middle Ages.* New York: Scribner, 1927.

Mollat, Michel, *Jacques Cœur.* Paris: Aubier, 1988.

PAUL D. SOLON

COLUMBUS, CHRISTOPHER (1451–1506)

Christopher Columbus is seldom associated with late medieval European thought. Yet his written work and other written sources suggest that he was informed by an intellectual tradition resting more heavily on ancient, medieval, and scholastic authors than on the authority of experience one associates with the Modern

Age. Columbus is in the company of scholastics who, between the twelfth and seventeenth centuries, strove to systematize knowledge by reconciling Aristotle and other pagan authors with Christian doctrine. If this literary influence is not explicit in his *Diario* or much of his early writing, it would become so in response to protests voiced by his enemies in the Spanish court for his administrative tactics in Hispaniola and for his failure to meet the expectations fueled by the enterprise of the Indies. The list of authors directly or indirectly cited, or alluded to, by Columbus is too extensive to mention here, but striking examples of his reliance on the *auctores* sanctioned by scholastics may be found in his *Letter of the Third Voyage* (1498) and his *Libro de las profecías* (1501–1502), a compilation and commentary of mostly scriptural passages that he thought signified his discovery as the final stage in completing God's apocalyptic scheme. Columbus was strongly influenced by Franciscan eschatology, particularly by the ideas of the Calabrian Joachim of Fiore friar.

No record exists of Columbus's formal schooling except for the assertion, forwarded by the bibliophile Hernando Colón (Fernando Columbus) in the apologetic biography of his father, that Columbus had attended the university in Pavia. Columbus was probably an astute autodidact who absorbed the theology and philosophy of his time from the ecclesiastic and scientific communities in the courts of Portugal and Spain, and, particularly, from the important monastic learning centers of Santa María de la Rábida and Nuestra Señora Santa María de las Cuevas in Spain.

The earliest and most influential accounts of the admiral's learning are provided by Hernando and by the Dominican friar Bartolomé de las Casas, Columbus's most devoted early biographer, in his *Historia de las Indias* (completed in 1559). Both biographers—the latter follows Hernando's lead almost to the letter—offer a list of authors who appear to have kindled the admiral's wish to cross the ocean. According to Hernando and las Casas, Columbus' s belief that the greater part of the globe had been circumnavigated and that only the space between Asia's eastern end and the Azores and Cape Verde Islands remained to be discovered comes from the Alexandrine astronomer Ptolemy, the Greek geographers Marinus of Tyre, and Strabo, the Greek physician and historian Ctesias, Onesicritus and Nearchus, respectively captain and admiral to Alexander the Great during the Macedonian campaign in India, the Roman historian Pliny the Elder, and the Arabic astronomer Alfraganus. Likewise, his belief that the distance between continents was small rests, in their view, on the works of Aristotle, the Córdoban astronomer Averröes, the Roman philosopher Lucius Annaeus Seneca, the Roman poet and grammarian Gaius Julius Solinus, the Venetian Marco Polo, the fictional author Sir John

of Mandeville, the French theologian and natural philosopher Cardinal Peter Aliacus, and the Roman writer Julius Capitolinus. Las Casas, clearly more schooled than the discoverer, adds a list of Christian and pagan auctores from whom Columbus might have persuaded himself of the plausibility of his project. Whether Columbus was as learned as Hernando and las Casas claim is still the subject of debate. Columbus probably owes his acquaintance with many auctores in the scholastic tradition to encyclopedic works such as Peter Aliacus's widely read *Ymago mundi* (1410–1414) and Pliny the Elder's *Historia naturalis.*

The most concrete evidence of Columbus's learning are the incunabula he is known to have possessed. A few of these volumes, held in the Biblioteca Colombina of Seville, contain abundant postilles by his hand, a number of which betray firsthand knowledge of numerous other works. The following volumes have long been identified as his: an extensive geographical treatise by the humanist Aeneas Sylvius Piccolomini (Pope Pius II), *Historia rerum ubique gestarum* (1477); Peter Aliacus's *Ymago mundi* (1483); Francesco Pipino's Latin translation of Marco Polo's *Il milione: De consuetudinibus et conditionibus orientalium regionum* (1485); and the manuscript of the *Libro de las pro fecías* (dated 1504). Others identified in 1891 as Columbus's are the following: Christophoro Landino's Italian translation of Pliny the elder's work: *Historia naturale* (1489); Abraham Zacut's *Almanach perpetuum* (1496), which contained a tabulation of planetary aspects and may have helped Columbus predict an eclipse on Jamaica (1504); Alfonso de Palencia's Spanish translation of Plutarch's *Parallel Lives* (*Vidas de los ilustres varones*, 1491); a manuscript of the anonymous fifteenth-century *Concordiae Bibliae Cardinalis*, which may have furnished Columbus with quotes for his *Libro.* Albertus Magnus's *Philosophia naturalis* (Venice 1496), also known as *Philosophia pauperum*, containing the saint's commentaries to the works of Aristotle's cosmology: *Physics, On the Heavens, Metereology, On Generation and Corruption*, and *On the Soul*, St. Antoninus of Florence's confessional guide, the *Sumula confessionis* (1476); and a fifteenth-century palimpsest of Seneca's tragedies containing the *Medea*, from which Columbus extracted a passage foretelling the discovery of a new orb.

Las Casas judged the *Ymago mundi* to be the primary source for the enterprise of the Indies. Peter Aliacus wrote this series of treatises in preparation for the Council at Constance, which ended the Western Schism (1414). The *Ymago mundi*, essentially an astrological work, includes a systematic account of the geocentric world, incorporating ancient geoethnography into the theoretical frames of Aristotle's physics and Ptolemy's scientia stellarum. Although this work's influence on Columbus has been discussed primarily on the basis of its place in late medieval geoethnography, its central purpose was to describe the mechanics of the natural world and to chart out the motion of the *machina mundi* over time. (The "machine of the world" in motion represented apocalyptic time unfolding.) By this method, Peter Aliacus hoped to discern the historical status of the religious crisis at hand in relation to the rise of the Antichrist and the dawning of the end of time. This eschatological work illustrates the union of Christian theology and Aristotelian science, that characterized intellectual production in the Latin West between the twelfth and seventeenth centuries. Columbus owes much of his thought to this tradition.

See also **Joachim of Fiore**

Further Reading

Casas, B. de las. *Historia de las Indias.* 3 vols. Ed. C. Agustín Millares. México, 1992.

Columbus, C. *The "Libro de las Profecías" of Christopher Columbus: An 'en face' Edition.* Ed. and trans. D. C. West. Gainesville, Fla., 1992.

Columbus, F. *The Life of the Admiral Christopher Columbus by his Son Fernando.* Ed. and trans. B. Keen. New Brunswick, N. J., 1959.

Flint, V.J. *The Imaginative Landscape of Christopher Columbus.* Princeton, N. J., 1992.

Milhou, A. *Cristóbal Colón y su mentalidad mesiánica en el ambiente franciscanista español.* Valladolid, 1983.

Rosa y López, S. de la. *Libros y autógrafos de Cristóbal Colón.* Sevilla, 1891.

NICOLÁS WEY-GÓMEZ

COMMYNES, PHILIPPE DE
(ca. 1447–1511)

A member of the Flemish nobility, Commynes was first an important official of Charles the Bold of Burgundy and then afterward served as chamberlain, counselor, and confidant of Louis XI of France. His experiences in both capacities are the subject of his *Mémoires*, written between 1489 and 1498. Commynes's memoirs are one of the first examples of the memoir-as-history, a genre that was to be highly popular in the Renaissance.

Commynes was the son of Colard van den Clyte, a functionary of the dukes of Burgundy. Commynes took his name from Comines near Lille, the holding of his uncle, who raised him from the age of seven. From 1464, he was an intimate adviser of the future Duke Charles the Bold. In July 1472, Commynes defected from the Burgundian side, perhaps for mercenary motives, and entered the service of the king of France, who compensated him with new titles and the holding of Talmont (a territory with 1,700 dependent fiefs), a pension, and, upon his marriage in 1473, the territory of Argenton. The relationship between Louis and Commynes was close; contemporaries noted that he was like the king's alter ego, and as Louis lay paralyzed on his deathbed, Commynes was the only person able to interpret his gestures and noises.

After the death of Louis in 1483, however, Commynes's position deteriorated; he was driven from the court and, between 1487 and 1489, imprisoned. He lost both Talmont and Argenton. In prison, Commynes underwent the religious conversion that explains the moralist tone of his memoirs. Commynes began composing them while still in exile, completing the first five books by 1490. After his rehabilitation, he continued working, completing Book 6 in 1493. Between 1494 and 1495, he accompanied Charles VIII on his disastrous Italian campaign, which became the subject of Book 7. The last book was completed shortly after the death of Charles VIII in 1498.

The *Mémoires* are an eyewitness account of a turbulent and crucial period of French and Flemish history, when the Burgundian dukes were attempting to establish their independence of the kings of France, and the kings were struggling to consolidate and centralize their political control. Commynes's intent was to present events as moral lessons about proper governance; his work is a mirror for princes. He wanted to see rational government and, to that end, to have diplomacy replace reliance on military might. No ruler in this violent age, therefore, was wholly admirable, not even Louis, whom Commynes loved. Commynes deliberately altered events to suit his didactic purposes; the *Mémoires* are factually treacherous. But they do shed light on rapidly changing 15th-century politics and political ideas.

Both the frank and factual quality of the *Mémoires* and its larger philosophical concerns have ensured the popularity of the work. Six manuscripts survive (only one of which contains Book 8), while the first printed edition was published in 1524, only twenty-six years after Commynes laid down his pen. This has been followed by more than a hundred editions and translations.

Further Reading

Commynes, Philippe de. *Mémoires,* ed. Joseph Calmette and Georges Durville. 3 vols. Paris: Champion, 1924–25.

——. *Philippe de Commynes: Mémoires,* ed. Bernard de Mandrot. 2 vols. Paris: Picard, 1901–03.

——. *The Memoirs of Philippe de Commynes,* ed. Samuel Kinser, trans. Isabelle Cazeaux. 2 vols. Columbia: University of South Carolina Press, 1969–73.

Dufournet, Jean. *La destruction des mythes dans les "Mémoires" de Philippe de Commynes.* Geneva: Droz, 1966.

——. *La vie de Philippe de Commynes.* Paris: Société d'Édition d'Enseignement Supérieur, 1969.

——. *Études sur Philippe de Commynes.* Paris: Champion, 1975.

LEAH SHOPKOW

COMPAGNI, DINO (c. 1246–1324)

Dino Compagni was a Florentine merchant, political figure, and chronicler. He was born into a well-established Florentine family, embarked on a career in the cloth industry, was inscribed in the guild of Por Santa Maria (manufacturers of silk cloth and retail cloth dealers) in 1269, and served repeatedly as consul of his guild between 1282 and 1299. This was the period during which a government based on guilds and headed by priors and a standard-bearer of justice was established in Florence; and Compagni, as a prominent and respected member of a major guild, was deeply involved in these developments. In 1282, he was one of a group of six citizens that took the lead in establishing the guild regime; he himself served as one of the priors in 1289 and as standard-bearer of justice in 1293. When he was not himself in office, he served regularly in a consultative capacity, advising the officeholders as they tried to preserve peace and order in an increasingly turbulent political climate. Compagni was again one of the priors in October 1301, when factional conflict between the Black and White Guelfs erupted into open warfare in the streets of Florence. Compagni and his fellow priors were forced to resign; the Black Guelfs seized and plundered the city; and many of the White Guelfs, including Dante Alighieri, were forced into exile. Compagni was spared that fate because of a law barring judicial proceedings against certain important officials for a year after they left office; nevertheless, the defeat of his party meant the end of his public career. He spent the rest of his life as if he were an exile in his own city, tending to his business and mulling over the events that had led to the defeat of the White Guelfs.

The fruit of Compagni's reflections was a chronicle that has ensured his fame ever since its rediscovery in the seventeenth century. In contrast to most medieval chronicles, which tend to be formless compilations of miscellaneous information, Compagni's is a tightly focused, dramatic account of the factional strife that tore at Florence between 1280 and 1312. Rather than a daily chronicle of events, Compagni produced a retrospective history. He wrote it between 1310, when an expedition of Emperor Henry VII to Italy aroused the hope that the White Guelfs would soon be restored to power in Florence, and 1313, when that hope was dashed by Henry's death. Freed from the obligation to record events as they occurred, Compagni was able to seek causes and connections. His detailed and exact information, incisive analysis of political motivations and alignments, and vivid portraits of such leading figures as Giano della Bella and Corso Donati—and the fact that this information comes from someone who was himself a participant in the events—make Compagni's chronicle an unsurpassed narrative source for the political life of Florence in the age of Dante.

See also **Dante Alighieri; Henry VII of Luxembourg; Villani, Giovanni**

Further Reading

Editions and Translations

Compagni, Dino. *Cronica delle cose occorrenti ne' tempi suoi.* ed. Isidoro Del Lungo. In *Rerum Italicarum Scriptores,* new ed., Vol. 9, part 2. Città di Castello: S. Lapi, 1913.
——. *Cronica,* ed. Gino Luzzatto. Turin: Einaudi, 1968.
——. *Cronica,* ed. Bruna Cordati, Turin: Loescher, 1969.
Dino Compagni's Chronicle of Florence, trans. Daniel E. Bornstein. Philadelphia: University of Pennsylvania Press, 1986.

Critical Studies

Arnaldi, Girolamo. "Dino Compagni cronista e militante 'popolano.'" *Cultura,* 21, 1983, pp. 37–82.
Cochrane, Eric. *History and Historians in the Italian Renaissance.* Chicago, Ill: University of Chicago Press, 1981.
Green, Louis. *Chronicle into History: An Essay on the Interpretation of History in Florentine Fourteenth-Century Chronicles.* Cambridge: Cambridge University Press, 1972.
Lansing, Carol. *The Florentine Magnates: Lineage and Faction in a Medieval Commune.* Princeton, N.J.: Princeton University Press, 1991.
Raveggi, Sergio, Massimo Tarassi, Daniela Medici, and Patrizia Parenti. *Ghibellini, Guelfi, e Popolo grasso: I detentori del potere politico a Firenze nella seconda metà del Dugento.* Florence: La Nuova Italia, 1978.

DANIEL. E. BORNSTEIN

CONRAD II (CA. 990–JUNE 4, 1039)

The first monarch of the new royal dynasty of the Salians, Conrad (Konrad) II was born circa 990 to Heinrich, son of Duke Otto of Carinthia and grandson of Duke Conrad of Lotharingia (d. 955). After his father's death, he was raised by his grandfather and uncle Conrad until he was taken into the episcopal household of Bishop Burchard of Worms (1000–d. 1025), supposedly because of ill-treatment at the hands of his relatives. In 1016, he married Gisela (d. 1043), daughter of Hermann II of Bavaria, thereby allying himself with one of the noblest families in the *Reich* (empire). The future king Henry III was born to the couple one year later in 1017.

When King Henry II died childless early in 1024, the nobility of the *Reich* was presented with the opportunity to elect a new monarch and ruling house. The royal election, recounted in unusual detail by the royal biographer and chaplain Wipo, was held at Kamba on the Rhine on September 4, 1024. Chosen over his rival and cousin Conrad the Younger (d. 1039), Conrad II was consecrated and crowned king by Archbishop Aribo of Mainz on September 8.

Once crowned king, Conrad had to make his kingship, his royal *presentia*, felt throughout his realm by establishing the personal bonds with local ecclesiastics, monasteries, and nobles that were the true guarantees of his kingship's power and stability. Furthermore, he had to gain the support of the Saxons and the members of the Lotharingian nobility who had not consented to his election. Therefore, following the tradition of his Ottonian predecessors, he devoted the next fifteen months to a royal *iter* (journey) that enabled him to meet and negotiate with nobles from Lotharingia to Saxony as well as those in Alemannia, Bavaria, Franconia, and Swabia.

With his rule thus consolidated by late 1025, Conrad embarked upon an expedition to Italy that lasted from the spring of 1026 until early summer of 1027. There he reestablished his authority over such rebellious cities of northern Italy as Pavia and Ravenna and broke down the opposition to royal rule within the Italian nobility through a combination of diplomacy and military might. Crowned Roman emperor by Pope John XIX (1024–1032) on Easter (March 26) of 1027 with King Cnut of England and Denmark and King Rudolf III of Burgundy in attendance, Conrad then headed south into Apulia, where he reestablished nominal German sovereignty over the Lombard princes and attempted to secure the frontier with Byzantine southern Italy.

Back in Germany, Conrad pondered the future of the dynasty. At Regensburg in June of 1027, he elevated his son Henry as duke of Bavaria and, on Easter of 1028, had him crowned king at Aachen with the consent of the princes of the *Reich*. The death in 1033 of King Rudolf III enabled the Salan monarch to expand his hegemony by incorporating the kingdom of Burgundy into the *Reich*. Around 1034, after his earlier bid for a marriage alliance with Byzantium had failed, Conrad turned to Denmark for a bride for his son; Henry III married King Cnut's (1017–1035) daughter Kunigunde in 1036. With the deaths of the reigning dukes of Swabia and Carinthia in 1038 and 1039 respectively, Conrad invested Henry III with those duchies, thereby giving him a unique position of power in the three southernmost duchies of the German *Reich*.

Despite the extent of his power, Conrad II faced several internal rebellions and significant foreign challenges during his reign. Just two years after Conrad's election, a group of conspirators led by his rival Conrad the Younger rebelled during the king's first expedition to Italy. After an initial show of loyalty, the king's stepson Duke Ernst II of Swabia later joined this rebellion; he persisted in his opposition to Conrad, despite brief returns to grace and appointments to office, until he was killed in August of 1030.

In 1036 Conrad journeyed again to Lombardy to settle widespread disputes between subvassals and their lay and ecclesiastical overlords over the security of the subvassals' legal status and rights. After overcoming the resistance of the Italian episcopate and their attempt to introduce Count Odo of Champagne (995–1037) as king, Conrad finally settled the dispute in favor of the subvassals with his decree *Constitutio de feudis* of 1037, which represented a major departure from the earlier, proepiscopal policies of his Ottonian predecessors.

On his eastern frontiers, Conrad responded to the repeated political challenges posed by Poland, Bohemia, and Hungary through a combination of military might, alliances with neighboring princes, territorial exchanges, and diplomacy, designed essentially to maintain the status quo rather than expand German hegemony.

Perhaps the most debated aspect today of Conrad's kingship is his ecclesiastical policy. Earlier scholarship stressed the secularity of Conrad II's reign and the king's calculated development and exploitation of the *Reichskirche* (imperial church) to achieve secular political aims. More recent studies, however, while not ignoring Conrad's political and economic reliance on ecclesiastical and monastic structures, have offered a more balanced assessment that highlights Conrad's personal association with leading monastic reformers of his time, including Odilo of Cluny, William of Dijon, and Poppo of Stablo; his efforts to further their reforms; his swift change in policy after a unique case of simony reported by Wipo; and his support of reformers such as Bruno of Egisheim, the future Pope Leo IX. Finally, they argue that, although Conrad undoubtedly saw himself as the head of the imperial Church, this position of leadership remained, in his mind, a religious as well as a secular office, an attitude certainly manifested by his son Henry III.

Dying on June 4, 1039, Conrad II was laid to rest by Empress Gisela and King Henry III in the cathedral of Speyer.

See also **Henry III; Leo IX, Pope**

Further Reading

Boshof, Egon. *Die Salier*, 3rd ed. Stuttgart and Berlin: Kohlhammer, 1995, pp. 33–91.

Die Urkunden Conrads II., ed. Harry Bresslau and P. Kehr. Munich: Mortumenta Germaniae Historica, 1909; rpt. 1980.

Hoffmann, Hartmut. *Monchskönig und "rex idiota". Studien zur Kirchenpolitik Heinrichs II. und Conrads II.* Hannover: Hahn, 1995.

Morrison, K. F. "The Deeds of Conrad II." In *Imperial Lives and Letters of the Eleventh Century*, ed. Theodor E. Mommsen and Karl F. Morrison. New York: Columbia University Press, 1962.

Trillmich, Werner. *Kaiser Conrad II. und seine Zeit*, ed. Otto Bardong. Bonn: Europa Union Verlag, 1991.

Wipo. *Gesta Chuonradi*, ed. Harry Bresslau. Hannover: Hahn, 1878; rpt. 1993.

W.L. NORTH

CONRAD OF MARBURG (ca. 1180–1233)

One of medieval Germany's most fascinating personalities was born about 1180, probably near Marburg, in

Hesse. Eventually he became a Premonstratensian priest. In 1214 he was commissioned by Pope Innocent III to press the crusade against the Albigensians, a mandate which resulted in a series of bloody massacres. Two years later he appeared as a different type of crusade preacher, this time as a recruiter of men to participate in the Fifth Crusade which had been called into being in 1213 by Pope Innocent. According to the chronicler Burchard of Ursberg, most recruiting activity slowed down following the death of Innocent in July 1216, but Conrad of Marburg and Conrad of Krosigk were two who apparently continued their efforts without ceasing.

By 1226 Conrad of Marburg had acquired an influential position at the court of Ludwig IV, landgrave of Thuringia; a year earlier he became the confessor of Ludwig's wife, Elizabeth, whom he disciplined with physical brutality. The prolonged fasts which he prescribed for her eventually wore down her health and ultimately may have caused her early death, but in the process she developed a reputation for piety which served to promote her beatification almost immediately. Here too, Conrad of Marburg was influential, just as he had been in determining her place of burial at Marburg where St. Elizabeth's church soon arose as a fitting shrine for her relics.

Conrad had meanwhile obtained another papal assignment: Pope Gregory IX made him the chief inquisitor in Germany, with the mandate to exterminate heresy, denounce clerical marriages, and reform the monasteries. His methods were so severe that a plea went out from the German bishops to have the pope remove him. Their plea was ignored, however.

In 1233 he took his maniacal inquisition to the final extreme by accusing one of the highest members of German society—Count Henry of Sayn—of various forms of heretical activity, including such bizarre behavior as riding on turtles. Henry in turn appealed to a court of his peers, an assembly of princes. Such a diet, held at Mainz under the presidency of King Henry VII declared him innocent. Speaking for the others, Archbishop Dietrich II of Trier declared that Count Henry was departing from the session "a free man and a Christian." Conrad of Marburg is said to have muttered that, had he been found guilty, things would have been very different.

The hatred toward Conrad was by now difficult to control. As he and his companions rode away from Mainz toward Marburg, he was brutally murdered on July 30, 1233. When news of this event reached Rome, the pope merely accepted it; no effort was made to punish the perpetrators. The contemporary chronicles report that, with the death of Conrad, peace and quiet returned to Germany once again.

See also **Innocent III, Pope**

Further Reading

Förg, Ludwig. *Die Ketzerverfolgung in Deutschland unter Gregor IX*. Historische Studien 218. Berlin: Ebering, 1932.

Kaltner, Balthasar, *Konrad von Marburg und die Inquisition in Deutschland*. Prague: F.Tempsky, A. Haase, 1882.

Maurer, Wilhelm. "Zum Verständnis der heiligen Elisabeth von Thüringen." *Zeitschrift der Geschichte und Kunst* 65 (1953/1954).

Shannon, Albert Clement. *The Popes and Heresy in the Thirteenth Century*. Villanova, Pa: Augustinian, 1949.

PAUL B. PIXTON

CONRAD OF URACH (fl. late 12th c.)

Conrad of Urach was the son of Count Egino the Bearded of Urach; his mother came from the family of the dukes of Zähringen. His birth fell before 1170. Apparently determined for a clerical career early on, he received his training at the cathedral school of Liège (St. Lambert's), where his maternal great-uncle, Rudolf of Zähringen, sat as bishop 1167–1191. At some point (probably while his uncle was still bishop), Conrad acquired a canonate in the cathedral; in 1196 he appears as cathedral dean, charged with maintaining order among the community. That the canons were in need of reform can be seen from the statutes issued in 1202 by Cardinal legate Guy Poré. By that time, however, Conrad had left the chapter.

Conrad's uncle, Duke Berthold V of Zähringen, was a candidate for the throne of Germany in the disputed election which followed the untimely death of Henry VI in 1197. As guarantees that he would produce the money needed to secure his election, Berthold offered his nephews—Conrad and Berthold of Urach—to the archbishops of Cologne and Trier; meanwhile, most other German princes had elected Philip of Swabia, brother of the deceased king. Hearing this, the duke renounced his claims, but the two archbishops retained their hostages for some time longer. This use of them as pawns in the political game of chess apparently had a profound effect upon both hostages: should they be released, they vowed to become monks, and, in fact, both became Cistercians. In 1199, Conrad entered the Cistercian house at Villers-on-the-Dyle in Brabant.

Meanwhile, on February 1, 1200, Albert of Cuyck, the successor to Rudolf of Zähringen as bishop of Liège, died, and the see was left vacant. Part of the cathedral chapter elected Conrad of Urach, who had not yet made his final profession at Villers, as bishop; another faction elected an archdeacon who was studying at Paris at the time. Conrad renounced any claim to the office, however, apparently preferring the *vita contemplativa* (contemplative life) to the *vita activa* (active life) required of a German prince bishop. He made his final vows at Villers. His family ties, as well as his obvious abilities, led to his becoming prior at Villers by ca. 1204, and in

1208/1209 he was elected abbot. His reputation as an ardent reformer and as a rigorous administrator led to his elevation as abbot of Clairvaux in 1214, and, as such, he attended the Fourth Lateran Council.

Despite his having become a monk, Conrad could not escape the responsibilities placed on him as one of the most influential individuals in the Latin Christendom of his day. In December 1216, he was sent with Abbot Arnald of Citeaux to Philip II and Louis of France to negotiate peace with England. In 1217 Conrad became abbot of Citeaux and general of the Cistercian Order; he probably assumed office at the general meeting of the chapter of the order held at the end of the year.

In January 1219, Pope Honorius III consecrated Conrad as cardinal bishop of Porto and San Rufina. At the time, there were twenty members of the College of Cardinals: four cardinal bishops, eight cardinal priests, and eight cardinal deacons. Of these, sixteen were from Italian provinces, two from Iberia, one from England, and one from Languedoc. Conrad thus joined the college as its only German member and remained so thus until 1225. During Lent 1220, he was appointed as the successor of Cardinal Bertrand as legate to the Albigensian lands, and given a mandate to support Amalrich de Montfort against Count Raymond of Toulouse. His fame spread, to the extent that soon thereafter, he was nominated to the archbishopric of Besançon. Honorius III would not allow this, however, claiming that Conrad's talents were needed throughout the Church.

In 1224 Conrad was given the legation as crusade preacher in Germany, but he also participated in various other activities, such as the condemnation of the accused renegade prior Henry Minneke at Hildesheim in October 1224, the national synod held at Mainz in November and December 1225, and the burial of Archbishop Engelbert of Cologne in December 1225. By May 1226 he was back in Rome, and he was present on March 18, 1227, when Honorius III died. According to tradition, Conrad was the first to be offered the tiara, but, again, he rejected an episcopal office. Only then was Gregory IX chosen. Even had Conrad accepted, however, his pontificate might well have been a brief one: he died on September 29, 1227, and was buried at Clairvaux, at the side of the smaller altar.

See also **Henry VI**

Further Reading

Neiningen, Fulk. *Konrad von Urach (†1227): Zähringer, Zisterzienser, Kardinallegat.* Paderborn: Schöningh, 1994.

Pixton, Paul B. "Cardinal Bishop Conrad of Porto and S. Rufina and the Implementation of Innocent III's Conciliar Decrees in Germany, 1224–1226." In *Proceedings of the Tenth International Congress of Medieval Canon Law* [. . .] 1996.

Schreckenstein, Karl Heinrich Freiherr Roth von. "Konrad von Urach, Bischof von Porto und S. Rufina, als Cardinallegat in Deutschland 1224–1226." *Forschungen zur deutschen Geschichte,* 7 (1867):319–393.

Winter, F. "Ergänzungen der Regesten zur Geschichte des Cardinallegaten Conrad von Urach, Bischof von Porto und St. Rufina." *Forschungen zur deutschen Geschichte* 11 (1871):631–632.

PAUL B. PIXTON

CONRAD VON SOEST (ca. 1360–ca. 1422)

One of the most significant German painters of the late Middle Ages, Conrad von Soest played a pivotal role in the diffusion of the International Courtly Style in northern Europe. His name is known through signatures on two altarpieces. A marriage contract, dated February 11, 1394, can plausibly be connected with the painter. It was signed by six of the most prominent patricians of Dortmund and attests to the painter's considerable wealth and high social standing. He was a member of the confraternities of the Marienkirche (1396—?) and of the Nikolaikirche (1412–1422).

Iconographic and stylistic evidence suggests that, following his apprenticeship in Dortmund, Conrad joined the workshop of the Parement Master in Paris in the 1380s. There he seems to have had access also to designs by Jacquemart de Hesdin. The creative and vigorous style of Conrad's underdrawing, consistent in the two signed altarpieces, refutes any notion of an imitative artist dependent on Burgundian patterns. Instead, Conrad achieved a synthesis of the style and technique learned in the royal workshops in Paris with this Westphalian inheritance, without forsaking originality.

His earliest surviving work, the signed Niederwildungen Altarpiece from 1403 (Stadtkirche, Bad Wildungen), was painted under the patronage of the Order of St. John. The Closed altarpiece depicts four saints venerated in the church. When open, twelve painted scenes, arranged in two rows around a central full-height Crucifixion, describe the life of Christ from the Annunciation to the Last Judgment. In the multifigured Crucifixion, the courtly elegance of some attendants contrasts with the realism of bucolic figures. The noted art historian Erwin Panofsky (1953, p. 71) spoke of precocious naturalism when he extolled the sharp characterization and powerful modeling of the thieves, and he compared the linear description of the noble figures to work by the universally esteemed Limbourg brothers. Conrad was a gifted and observant storyteller. The tender humanity of his elegant protagonists combined with selective naturalistic description, together with the outstanding craftsmanship, decorative surface pattern created by sinuous line, and a sophisticated iconography, place the altarpiece in the forefront of artistic development around 1400.

By around 1420, when Conrad painted his other signed work, the altarpiece for the church of the Virgin (*Marienkirche*) in Dortmund, he concentrated on the dramatic potential of his now monumental figures and the emotional power of color. The altarpiece was commissioned by his own confraternity. The panels were cut in 1720 to fit into a (lost) baroque framework. They originally showed a central Death of the Virgin, surmounted by a lunette, flanked by the Nativity and Adoration on the obverse, and the Annunciation and Coronation on the reverse sides of the wings. Conrad's subtle and varied palette was now supported by a sensitive awareness of the effect of light and shade in the modeling of forms. His courtly figures, careful characterization, costly pigments, and exquisite punchwork would have gratified the taste and chivalric ideals of his cosmopolitan patrons.

The patrician members of the confraternity belonged to an exclusive, well-educated, and prosperous group who played a leading part in the influential international trading association, the Hanseatic League. Their lifestyle eased the diffusion of Conrad's last perpetuated style abroad. Conrad's influence was most profoundly felt in Cologne; his style was introduced there by the immigrant Veronica Master and still reflected in the work of Stefan Lochner.

See also **Lochner, Stefan**

Further Reading

Corley, Brigitte. *Conrad von Soest: Painter among Merchant Princes.* London: Harvey Miller, 1996.
—— "A Plausible Provenance for Stefan Lochner?" *Zeitschrift für Kunstgeschicte* 59 (1996): 78–96.
——. "A Nineteenth Century Photograph and the Reconstruction of the Dortmund Altarpiece." *Visual Resources: An International Journal of Documentation* 13 (1997): 169–188.
——. "Historical Links and Artistic Reflections: England and Northern Germany in the Late Middle Ages," in *Harlaxton Medieval Studies,* ed. John Mitchell [forthcoming].
——. "Meister Konrad von Soest, ein geborener Dortmunder Bürger, und andere Dortmunder Maler." *Beiträge zur Geschichte Dortumnds und der Grafschaft Mark* 32 (1925): 141–145.
Fritz, Rolf. "Conrad von Soest als Zeichner." *Westfalen* 28 (1953): 10–19.
Panofsky, Erwin. *Early Netherlandish Painting: Its Origins and Character.* Cambridge, Mass.: Harvard University press, 1953, pp. 71, 93–94, 129.
Steinbart, Kurt. *Konrad von Soest.* Vienna: Schroll, 1946.
Winterfeld, Luise von. *Geschichte der freien Reichs- und Hansestadt Dortumnd,* 7th ed. Dortmund: F. W. Ruhfus, 1981.

BRIGITTE CORLEY

CONSTANCE (1154–1198)

Constance of Sicily was the posthumous daughter of Roger II Hauteville and his third wife, Beatrice of Rethel. She was probably born in Palermo, where she died.

Constance lived in obscurity until her betrothal to Henry VI, the son of Frederick I Barbarossa, on 29 October 1184. Their marriage in Milan on 27 January 1186 signaled a diplomatic realignment in Italy. The peace of Venice of 1177 had ended the conflict between the emperor and his Italian enemies: the papacy, Venice, the Lombard League, and the kingdom of Sicily. Under the conditions of the marriage, Frederick was required to relinquish the long-standing imperial claim to southern Italy, but he wanted to detach Sicily from the alliance that had led to his defeat in northern Italy. For his part, William II of Sicily sought to neutralize the Hohenstaufen threat so that he could freely attack the Byzantine empire. Neither Frederick nor William anticipated that Constance would succeed to the Sicilian throne, although at the curia of Troia in 1185 the Norman barons agreed to accept her as queen if William died without an heir.

When he departed on a crusade in 1187, Frederick Barbarossa named Henry imperial regent; but after William II died on 18 November 1189, Henry directed his attention to Sicily. A faction of Norman barons elected Tancred of Lecce, the illegitimate grandson of Roger II, as king and crowned him on 18 January 1190. Meanwhile, Frederick had died on his crusade, in 1189. Pope Celestine III crowned Henry VI emperor on 15 April 1191. Henry attacked Naples in May 1191, but disease drove the imperial forces out by August. At that time Constance was captured and sent to Tancred. Celestine negotiated her release, but pro-imperial forces rescued her and sent her to Germany before she could be delivered to the pope. Henry financed his return to southern Italy in 1194 with the ransom that he had extracted from the English king, Richard Lionheart, but effective opposition to the emperor collapsed with the death of Tancred on 20 February 1194. Henry quickly disposed of Tancred's nephew and successor, the child king William III, and was himself crowned king of Sicily in Palermo on 25 December 1194.

Constance, who was then forty years old, gave birth to a son at Jesi on 26 December 1194. She named him Constantine, but he was subsequently renamed Frederick Roger. A rumor later circulated that Frederick was not Constance's son, and a legend arose—which was unfounded—that she gave birth publicly to dispel such doubts. Constance left the infant Frederick in Foligno, where he lived until age three.

Henry ruled Sicily with a heavy hand. At the curia of Bari in 1195, he clarified the nature of the union between the empire and the kingdom, thereby reducing the tension between the Norman barons and his German followers. Constance was crowned queen at Bari. Henry returned to Germany in 1195. Constance ruled the Sicilian kingdom day to day and issued diplomas in her own name. In Germany, Henry pursued a scheme to make the imperial title hereditary. He failed in this, but he did manage to have Frederick elected king of the Romans in December 1196. In 1197, Henry returned to Sicily. Constance spent Easter with him in Palermo, where he renewed a far-reaching revocation of privileges. A revolt against Henry ensued, but the emperor crushed it by July. Some German sources suggest that Constance played a role in the conspiracy against Henry, but he apparently did not act on reports of her complicity. Henry and Constance continued to live together and to issue diplomas jointly.

Henry died in Messina on 28 September 1197. Constance quickly secured the kingdom. She hastened to Palermo, where she deposed the chancellor and recovered the royal seals; she recalled Frederick from Foligno; and she expelled from the kingdom the German barons who had been most closely associated with Henry. Constance negotiated an accord with the Roman curia for the coronation of Frederick and the burial of Henry, who had been excommunicate when he died. To obtain the cooperation of Pope Innocent III, she conceded Frederick's imperial title. Henry's funeral took place in Palermo in early May 1198, and Frederick was crowned on 17 May. Constance continued to use her imperial title but issued diplomas jointly with Frederick after his coronation.

Constance was an active ruler, and her position was secure, but she negotiated with Innocent to define the feudal status of the kingdom and later to obtain papal protection for Frederick after her death. Innocent forced her to relinquish traditional royal rights over church councils, legates, appeals, and elections.

She retained only the right to approve a bishop-elect before he could occupy his see. The pope sent a cardinal to receive her homage and confer vassalage, but she died before he arrived. Frederick does not seem to have felt bound by her concessions to the papacy until he renewed them in 1212.

On 25 November 1198, Constance wrote her last testament. She commended Frederick to the protection of the pope as regent and guardian and directed her subjects to swear fidelity to the pope. She died on 27 ot 28 November and was buried in the cathedral of Palermo, next to Henry VI, on 29 November. The papal regency notwithstanding, her death initiated a period of violence and chaos in the kingdom of Sicily that persisted until Frederick reached his majority in 1208.

The legend that Constance had once been a nun developed in the thirteenth century and was used by papal polemicists in anti-Hohenstaufen propaganda. Constance was said to have been raised in monastic solitude and to have taken religious vows, only to be torn from the contemplative life to marry Henry. Dante immortalized her legend in *Paradiso* (3.113). Later, several religious communities claimed her, some as ab-

bess. By the fifteenth century, San Salvatore in Palermo seems to have won the competition to claim Constance as a member.

See also **Frederick I Barbarossa; Frederick II, Henry VI; Innocent III, Pope**

Further Reading

Kölzer, Theo. "Costanza d'Altavilla." In *Dizionario biografico degli Italiani.* Rome: Istituto della Enciclopedia Italiana, 1960–.

———. *Die Staufer im Süden: Sizilien und das Reich.* Sigmaringem: J. Thorbecke, 1996.

Matthew, Donald. *The Norman Kingdom of Sicily.* Cambridge: Cambridge University Press, 1992.

Die Urkunden der deutschen Könige und Kaiser: Die Urkunden der Kaiserin Konstanze, ed. Theo Kölzer. Monumenta Germaniae Historica, 11(3). Hannover: Hahn, 1990.

JOHN LOMAX

CYNEWULF
(fl. early 9th–late 10th century?)

One of the two named Anglo-Saxon poets (the other is Cædmon). His identity is unknown, although he wove his name into the epilogues of four poems; his dates are undetermined, although he probably did not write before 750 nor after the late 10th century, his provenance is uncertain, although dialect features of his poems indicate that he was either Mercian or Northumbrian; and his corpus has been limited in the last half-century to the four poems that bear his signature and appear in the Exeter Book (*Christ II, Juliana*) and the Vercelli Book (*The Fates of the Apostles, Elene*).

Identity and Language

Cynewulf uses runic letters to incorporate his name into his poems, spelling it CYNWULF in *The Fates of the Apostles* and *Christ II*, CYNEWULF in *Juliana* and *Elene*, and making it an integral part of his message as he asks for his audience's prayers. In three epilogues he exploits the fact that runes stand both for letters and for things or concepts such as "need" (the N rune is named *nyd*, "need, necessity") and "joy" (the W rune stands for *wynn*, "joy"). Only in *Juliana*, where he groups the letters CYN, EWU, and LF, does Cynewulf seem to use runes solely as letters. Scholars are uncertain about how to interpret the signatures just as they are about how to assess their historical significance. It has been argued that Cynewulf's signing his work merely conforms with an ancient Germanic practice of signing art objects in runes, that it reflects a vogue among contemporary Latin writers for using acrostics, and that it may signal a shift in Anglo-Saxon society from orality to literacy. It may also indicate a move away from the traditional view of both poet and poetry as communal and therefore necessarily anonymous.

Scholars in the 19th and early 20th centuries favored four candidates for being the poet: Cynewulf, bishop of Lindisfarne in Northumbria (d. ca. 783); Cynulf, a priest of Dunwich in East Anglia (fl. 803); Cynewulf, the father of Bishop Cyneweard of Wells in Wessex (d. ca. 975); and Cenwulf or Kenulf, abbot of Peterborough in Mercia (d. 1006). Historical and linguistic evidence is far too meager to support any of these identifications. Furthermore nonliterary sources make clear that a large number of ecclesiastics named Cynewulf and theoretically capable of writing poetry lived during the period when the poet may have flourished. His identity remains a mystery.

Lacking historical data, scholars depend primarily on Cynewulf s name for determining when he may have lived. The form "Cynewulf" derives from an earlier form, "Cyniwulf." The spelling change from -i- to -e- reflects a sound change that took place because of the weak stress on the syllable in which the vowel appears, and philologists have shown that that change could have occurred as early as 750. Scholars have also found that the particular order of apostles in *The Fates of the Apostles* does not appear in comparable texts until after the early 9th century. Cynewulf was thought most probably active, therefore, around the late 8th and early 9th centuries. Recent research on a later source for *The Fates of the Apostles*, however, strongly supports the possibility that he flourished between the late 9th century and the late 10th, when the Exeter and Vercelli books were composed.

Scholars know that Cynewulf wrote in the Anglian dialect, although they still dispute whether it was Northumbrian or Mercian within that broad category. The scribes of the Exeter and Vercelli books both wrote in West Saxon, and the two imperfect leonine (internal) rhymes in *Christ II* and the four in the epilogue to *Elene* can be corrected by translating those rhymes into Anglian. Compare, for example, West Saxon *hienþu I mærþu* of *Christ II*, line 591, with Anglian *hænþu I mærþu*, or West Saxon *riht I geþeaht* of *Elene*, line 1240, with Anglian *reht l geþeht*.

Works

When Cynewulf was first discovered in 1840, one editor attributed all poems in the Exeter and Vercelli books to him. Other scholars subsequently asserted that Cynewulf wrote every OE poem that Cædmon did not and was perhaps even the final redactor of *Beowulf*. Later 19th-century scholars argued more conservatively, eventually claiming that in addition to his four signed poems Cynewulf wrote just eight others that resemble them in subject matter or style: *Guthlac A*, *Guthlac B*,

Christ I, *Christ III*, *Physiologus* (or *The Panther*, *The Whale*, and *The Partridge*), and *The Phoenix* from the Exeter Book; *Andreas* and *The Dream of the Rood* from the Vercelli Book. These twelve poems constitute "the Cynewulf Group." Largely because of studies by Das, Schaar, and Diamond in the 1940s and 1950s, however, scholars now recognize only the four signed poems as Cynewulf's own. The question of the order in which Cynewulf composed his poems remains vexed, but most scholars currently feel that he wrote *Elene* last.

The Fates of the Apostles, a 122-line poem, follows *Andreas* in the Vercelli Book and was therefore once counted part of that poem; it is perhaps the least appreciated of Cynewulf's works. Deriving from the martyrology with no single Latin source and classified primarily as a catalogue poem, it offers the barest detail about the missions and deaths of the twelve apostles. It consequently has been placed either first or last in Cynewulf's canon, the product of a clumsy novice or a feeble old man. Recent critics have treated the poem more sympathetically, arguing, for example, for a sophisticated numerical structure or for Cynewulf's establishing an implicit comparison between himself and the apostles, between their work and his, while simultaneously creating an ironic distance between himself as a fallible human being and them as transcendent followers of Christ. Notable in this poem is the unique arrangement of Cynewulf's signature: F, W, U, L, C, Y, N. The letters' dislocation and placement of the last first may reflect both the poet's sense of personal dislocation at being a sinner and personal joy in the biblical promise that the last shall be first.

Cynewulf's 426-line, meditative poem about Christ's Ascension into heaven is known as *Christ II* or *The Ascension*. It is the second of three poems in the Exeter Book about Christ. The poem's source is the final three sections of Gregory the Greats 29th homily on the Gospels, in which Gregory asks why angels did not wear white robes at the Incarnation while they did at the Ascension. Cynewulf draws mainly on that homily but mines passages of scripture as well, including the 23rd Psalm, and seems indebted to Bede's hymn on the Ascension, some patristic texts, and iconographic items. In the course of this loosely structured, reiterative poem Cynewulf describes the Ascension and human beings' and angels' reaction to it; admonishes his audience to be grateful for all God's gifts, especially salvation granted to humankind through the Ascension; likens Christ's mission on earth to the flight of a bird; praises Christ for his dignifying both angels and humankind by his actions and for granting intellectual gifts to men; thanks Christ for his six "leaps" (the Incarnation, Nativity, Crucifixion, Burial, Descent into Hell, and Ascension); encourages his audience to prepare for the Last Judgment; and concludes with a conventional but extended simile comparing human life to a sea voyage. Whereas Gregory answers the question about the angels' white robes directly, Cynewulf does not. They were appropriate at the Ascension, he implies, because Christ, angels, and human beings are all exalted through Christ's gifts and leaps.

Juliana, a 731-line poem about the early-4th-century St. Juliana of Nicomedia, vies with *The Fates of the Apostles* for being deemed Cynewulf's worst—and therefore either his first or last—work. Whatever early scholars' estimation of its quality, the poem has the distinction of being the earliest extant vernacular version of this saint's life, and recent studies show that it does have artistic merit. Cynewulf's source for the poem is probably a Latin prose life close to one contained in the *Acta sanctorum* for 16 February, in which is told the simple story of Juliana, daughter of the pagan Africanus, who promises her in marriage to the pagan prefect Heliseus. She refuses to marry Heliseus unless he converts to Christianity. He refuses, and she is imprisoned, tortured, tempted at length by a demon, and ultimately beheaded. Cynewulf polarizes the saint and her persecutors much more emphatically than does his source, and he amplifies dialogue considerably to emphasize Juliana's verbal power and spiritual resilience. Cynewulf's dislocated signature (CYN, EWU, LF), like that in *The Fates of the Apostles*, probably reflects the dislocation he feels, this time at the separation his soul must experience from his body in death.

Elene, Cynewulf's 1321-line poem about the discovery of the Cross by St. Helena, mother of Constantine, is uniformly considered his best. Its source probably closely resembles the *Acta Cyriaci* (*Acta sanctorum*, 4 May). After defeating the Goths by the sign of the Cross, which was revealed to him in a dream, Constantine is converted to Christianity and sends his mother to Jerusalem to locate the actual Cross. Elene confronts the Jews about its location through their chosen representative, Judas, who refuses to help her and whom she confines to a pit without food. Judas quickly relents and is himself converted. His prayer brings a sign indicating where the Cross lies buried, and a church, by order of Constantine, is later erected there. After being baptized, Judas becomes Cyriacus, bishop of Jerusalem, and prays for another sign to show where the nails of the Cross might be. He receives that sign, and the nails are made into a bit for Constantine's horse. The poem ends with Cynewulf's signature and a passage on the Last Judgment. The poet's major themes concern revelation and conversion (of Constantine, Judas, and Cynewulf), and he skillfully manipulates style and structure to develop those themes. The speeches in the narrative—considerable elaborations, as in *Juliana*, of their Latin source—play a crucial role in Cynewulf's affirming the Cross's transforming power.

See also **Cædmon**

Further Reading

Primary Sources
ASPR 2:51–54 [*Fates*], 66–102 [*Elene*]; 3:15–27 [*Christ II*], 113–33 [*Juliana*].
Brooks, Kenneth R., ed. *Andreas and The Fates of the Apostles*. Oxford: Clarendon, 1961.
Gradon, P.O.E., ed. *Elene*. London: Methuen, 1958. Repr. Exeter: University of Exeter, 1977.
Woolf, Rosemary, ed. *Juliana*. London: Methuen, 1955. Repr. Exeter: University of Exeter, 1977.

Secondary Sources
Anderson, Earl R. *Cynewulf: Structure, Style, and Theme in His Poetry*. London: Associated University Presses, 1983.
Bjork, Robert E. *The Old English Verse Saints' Lives: A Study in Direct Discourse and the Iconography of Style*. Toronto: University of Toronto Press, 1985 [chapters on *Elene*, *Juliana*].
Bjork, Robert E,, ed. *Cynewulf Basic Headings*. New York: Garland, 1996 [with reprints of Brown, Clemoes, Diamond, and Frese articles cited below].
Bridges, Margaret Enid. *Generic Contrast in Old English Hagiogmphical Poetry*. Copenhagen: Rosenkilde & Bagger, 1984 [chapters on *Elene*, *Juliana*].
Brown, George H. "The Descent-Ascent Motif in *Christ II* of Cynewulf." *JEGP* 73 (1974): 1–12.
Butler, S.E. "The Cynewulf Question Revived." *NM* 83 (1982): 15–23.
Calder, Daniel G. *Cynewulf*. Boston: Twayne, 1981.
Clemoes, Peter. "Cynewulf's Image of the Ascension." In *England before the Conquest*, ed. Peter Clemoes and Kathleen Hughes. Cambridge: Cambridge University Press, 1971, pp. 293–304.
Das, S.K. *Cynewulf and the Cynewulf Canon*. Calcutta: University of Calcutta Press, 1942.
Diamond, Robert E. "The Diction of the Signed Poems of Cynewulf." *PQ* 38 (1959): 228–41.
Frese, Dolores Warwick. "The Art of Cynewulf's Runic Signatures." In *Anglo-Saxon Poetry: Essays in Appreciation*, ed. Lewis E. Nicholson and Dolores Warwick Frese. Notre Dame: University of Notre Dame Press, 1975, pp. 312–34.
Hermann, John P. *Allegories of War: Language and Violence in Old English Poetry*. Ann Arbor: University of Michigan Press, 1989 [chapters on *Elene*, *Juliana*].
Olsen, Alexandra Hennessey. *Speech, Song, and Poetic Craft: The Artistry of the Cynewulf Canon*. New York: Lang, 1984.
Rice, Robert C. "The Penitential Motif in Cynewulf's *Fates of the Apostles* and in His Epilogues." *ASE* 6 (1977): 105–20.
Schaar, Claes. *Critical Studies in the Cynewulf Group*. Lund: Gleerup, 1949. Repr. New York: Haskell House, 1967.

ROBERT E. BJORK

D

DADDI, BERNARDO
(fl. c. 1320–1348)

The Florentine Bernardo Daddi, "an artist of rare and exquisite gifts" (Offner and Steinweg, 1930–1947), may have been trained in Giotto's workshop. Daddi's early panels, such as the triptych from the church of Ognissanti in Florence (signed and dated 1328), are strongly influenced by Giotto; but as Daddi matured, he began to diverge from Giotto's weighty forms and developed a style that united the Florentine heritage with the Sienese affinity for graceful figures, decorative settings, and more spontaneous interactions between the Madonna and child. The large number of panels executed in a Daddesque idiom indicates that Daddi himself had a large and productive workshop in Florence.

In his best works—such as the San Pancrazio Polyptych (c. 1340), now thought to have been commissioned for the cathedral of Florence; and the Madonna and Child of the Berenson Collection (Florence, I Tatti, c. 1340)—Daddi's figures are imbued with emotional tenderness and grace, in contrast to Giotto's more massive and somber mode of expression. The intimacy between the Madonna and child is characteristic of Daddi and his school; often, the Madonna holds up an index finger to present the child with a bird or a flower, or in some examples to admonish him.

Daddi appears to have been partly responsible for the popularization of the triptych in Florence. The portable hinged triptych, derived from Byzantine prototypes, could be closed to protect the image and opened for times of private devotion. During the 1320s and 1330s, painters including Daddi and Taddeo Gaddi developed a Gothic format for the panel type. Daddi's Bigallo Triptych (dated 1333, although the last digits have been repainted), a relatively large and richly decorated example that is closely related to a similar triptych by Taddeo Gaddi (1334, now in Berlin), may have been intended as a votive offering.

Daddi had close stylistic affinities to painters of the "miniaturist tendency" such as the Saint Cecilia Master, and his intimate, lyrical style was best suited to works on a small scale. The only frescoes attributed to him are those depicting the martyrdom of saints Lawrence and Stephen in the Pulci-Berardi Chapel of Santa Croce in Florence (c. 1330). A Madonna and Child with Angels painted for the confraternity of Or San Michele in 1347 was meant to recall a miracle-working image of the *Duecento* that had previously been in Or San Michele. Daddi's panel, which was eventually set into Andrea Orcagna's imposing marble tabernacle (1357), attracted many survivors of the plague and accelerated the transformation of Or San Michele from a granary into a church. The Gambier-Parry Polyptych (signed and dated 1348), with its pronounced compression of space and form, provides further evidence that by midcentury Daddi had moved away from the spacious monumentality of the Giottesque tradition.

Like many other artists of his time, Daddi died during the black death of 1348.

See also **Gaddi, Taddeo; Giotto di Bondone; Orcagna, Andrea di Cione**

Further Reading

Cole, Bruce. *Giotto and Florentine Painting, 1280–1375.* New York: Harper and Row, 1976.

Fabri, N., and Nina Rutenberg. "The Tabernacle of Orsanmichele in Context." *Art Bulletin*, 53, 1981, pp. 385–405.

Lusanna, E. "Daddi, Bernardo." In *The Dictionary of Art*, Vol. 8. New York, 1996, pp. 441–444. Offner, Richard, and Klara Steinweg. *A Critical and Historical Corpus of Florentine Painting*, Section 3, Vols. 3–5, *Daddi and His School.* New York, 1930–1947. (See also: *Corpus*, Section 3, Vol. 3, ed.

Miklós Boskovits and E. N. Lusanna. Florence, 1989. Section 3, Vol. 4, ed. Miklós Boskovits. Florence, 1991.)

Wilkins, D. G. "Bernardo Daddi's Triptych in the Bigallo and Changing Patterns in the History of the Devotional Image in Italy." *Italian Culture*, 6, 1987, pp. 31–41.

LAURIE TAYLOR-MITCHELL

D'AILLY, PIERRE (1350–1420)

D'Ailly studied at the Collège de Navarre in Paris and received the master of arts degree in 1368. He lectured at the Sorbonne on Peter Lombard's *Sententiae* in 1375 and promoted Ockham's teaching. In 1381, he became doctor of theology and canon in Noyon. He was rector of the college from 1384 to 1389 and befriended Jean Gerson, his most celebrated pupil. In 1389, he was made chancellor of the University of Paris. From 1389 to 1395, he became influential in Charles VI's court as the king's confessor and almoner. Appointed bishop of Le Puy in 1395, he never entered the see; in 1397, he was made archbishop of Cambrai. He attended the Council of Pisa in 1409 but supported the newly elected Alexander V unenthusiastically. Alexander's successor, the antipope John XXIII, utilized D'Ailly at the Council of Rome in 1411 and named him cardinal in 1412. The following year, he was appointed papal legate to Emperor Sigismund, subsequently playing a prominent role in the Council of Constance (1414–17). He presided over the first session without a pope in residence and supported the primacy of the general council over the pope. As president of the commission of faith, he examined John Hus and witnessed his condemnation in 1415. Martin V, elected by the council as the sole legitimate pope, appointed D'Ailly as legate to Avignon. He died there in 1420.

D'Ailly devoted most of his public life to ecclesiastical reform and to healing the Great Schism by means of a general council. Nevertheless, his writings covered a wide range of topics, including *Quaestiones* on Lombard's *Sententiae* (1390); a large collection of sermons; numerous ecclesiological and legal tracts (many of them later included with Jean Gerson's works), such as *De materia concilii generalis*, *Tractatus super reformatione ecclesiae*, and *Tractatus de ecclesiae autoritate*; treatises on the soul and the sacraments; a concordance of astronomy; and his famous *Imago mundi*, later owned and annotated by Columbus, who found it to confirm a western passage to India.

See also **Gerson, Jean; Ockham, William of; Peter Lombard**

Further Reading

D'Ailly, Pierre. *De materia concilii generalis*, *Tractatus super reformatione ecclesiae*, and *Tractatus de ecclesiae autoritate.*

In Jean Gerson. *Opera omnia*, ed. Louis E. Dupin. 5 vols. Antwerp: Sumptibus Societatis, 1706, Vol. 2.

——. *Ymago mundi de Pierre d'Ailly*, ed. and trans. Edmond Buron. 3 vols. Paris: Maisonneuve, 1930.

Glorieux, Palémon. "L'œuvre littéraire de Pierre d'Ailly: remarques et précisions." *Mélanges de science religieuse* 22 (1965).

Oakley, Francis. *The Political Thought of Pierre d'Ailly: The Voluntarist Tradition.* New Haven: Yale University Press, 1964.

Salembier, Louis. Le *cardinal Pierre d'Ailly.* Tourcoing: Georges Frère, 1932.

H. LAWRENCE BOND

DAMIAN, PETER (1007–1072)

Peter Damian was a leading advocate of church reform. According to his biographer, John of Lodi, he was born in Ravenna to a family which was respectable but had many mouths to feed. Fearing that one more heir would deplete the inheritance of all, his mother refused to suckle him. When he was black and nearly dead with hunger and cold, a priest's concubine took him and restored him to health. Other adversities followed, though. Orphaned early in childhood, Peter was left to the care of a married brother; the brother and his wife subjected the boy to extreme privation, lodging him with the swine. From this wretchedness he was rescued by a second brother, Damian, who cared for him with fatherly affection and saw that he was carefully educated in the liberal arts. Peter took this brother's name, Damian, in gratitude.

Peter Damian's studies took him to Faenza and Parma. For a short time, he taught rhetoric in Ravenna. But when celebrity and wealth seemed within his grasp, a disposition to austerity, acquired through the harsh experiences of his childhood, asserted itself. He took monastic vows in the eremitic community of the Holy Cross, at Fonte Avellana, later the nucleus of the order of Camaldoli.

For Damian, the term "spiritual militia" was not metaphorical. He practiced asceticism militantly, always fighting against unseen evils by voluntarily subjecting himself to mortifications, by zealously expanding the physical resources of the community when he became prior of Fonte Avellana (after 1043), by encouraging the foundation of daughter houses, and by preaching. His earliest treatises, which date from this period, express a combination of intellectual and rhetorical brilliance with merciless zeal that remained his signature: these were *Counterblast against the Jews* and a *Life of Saint Romuald,* the founder of Fonte Avellana.

As a deeply learned, resourceful, and tireless advocate of reform, Peter Damian was taken into the circles of the Emperor Henry III and of others who wished to bring about the reform of the whole church from the head down, beginning with the papacy. He attended the synod of Sutri (1046), at which three papal claimants were removed and a new pope was installed; he also attended reform synods held by popes Clement II and Leo IX. For Leo IX, Damian wrote his first major treatise, the *Book of Gomorrah*, against forbidden sexual practices among the clergy, including homosexuality.

Although Damian was always reluctant to leave the rigors of monastic life, he was forced by Pope Stephen IX to enter the college of cardinals, as bishop of Ostia (perhaps in 1057). He then became a fervent advocate of papal primacy, which he enforced in an important legation that he undertook to settle disputes in the church of Milan (1059), subordinating the alleged privileges of that church to Roman norms. In support of the pope's universal powers, he encouraged the making of an early collection of canonistic texts. Yet among reformers he was a moderate, as he showed in his conciliatory attitude toward the imperial court and in his treatise *Liber gratissimus*, in which—contrary to the opinion of Cardinal Humbert of Silva Candida—he defended the validity of sacraments performed by clergy who had committed simony or lived in concubinage.

In 1067, after making several requests, Damian was allowed to abdicate his bishopric and return to Fonte Avellana. Throughout his career, he had continued to practice spiritual devotions, instituting liturgies in honor of Christ's passion and of the Virgin Mary, attending to the needs of the poor, and inflicting on himself every rigor of spiritual warfare, including hairshirts and flagellation.

In the last years of his life, the papacy called him from monastic retirement for other diplomatic missions: to Florence (1066–1067), to adjudge charges of simony against the archbishop; to Frankfurt (1069), to persuade King Henry IV to abandon an intended divorce; and to Ravenna (1072), to release the city and its bishop from an excommunication they had incurred through adherence to the antipope Honorius II (Cadalus of Parma). Returning from Ravenna, Damian died in the monastery of Santa Maria foris Portam in Faenza.

The exceptional range of Peter Damian's learning and achievement is plain in the large body of his extant writings. These include 180 letters (some of which are actually treatises on ascetic and mystical theology) and about fifty sermons, as well as legal briefs and devotional works such as prayers, hymns, and accounts of the deeds of saints.

Miracles had been ascribed to Peter Damian during his lifetime, and from the moment of his death he was venerated as a saint. In 1828, he was proclaimed a doctor of the church.

See also **Leo IX, Pope**

Further Reading

Editions

Die Briefe des Petrus Damiani, 4 vols., ed. Kurt Reindel. Die Briefe der Deutschen Kaiserzeit, 4(1–4). Munich: Monumenta Germaniae Historica, 1983–1993.

Lettre sur la Toute-Puissance divine, ed. André Cantin. Sources Chrétiennes, 191. Paris: Éditions du Cerf, 1972.

Sancti Petri Damiani sermones, ed. Giovanni Lucchesi. Corpus Christianorum, Continuatio Medievalis, 57. Turnhout: Brepols, 1983.

Translations

Book of Gomorrah: An Eleventh-Century Treatise against Clerical Homosexual Practices, trans. Pierre J. Payer. Waterloo, Ont.: Wilfrid Laurier University Press, 1982.

The Letters of Peter Damian, 4 vols., trans. Owen J. Blum. Fathers of the Church, Mediaeval Continuation. Washington, D.C.: Catholic University of America Press, 1989– . (Letters 1–120.)

Selected Writings on the Spiritual Life, trans. Patricia McNulty. London: Faber and Faber, 1959.

Critical Studies

Blum, Owen J. *Saint Peter Damian: His Teaching on the Spiritual Life*. Studies in Mediaeval History, n.s. 10. Washington, D.C.: Catholic University of America, 1947.

Cantin, André. *Les sciences séculières et la foi: Les deux voies de la science au jugement de Saint Pierre Damien, 1007–1072*. Pubblicazioni, Centro Italiano di Studi sull' Alto Medioevo, 5. Spoleto: Centro Italiano di Studi sull' Alto Medioevo, 1975.

Fornasari, Giuseppe. *Medioevo riformato del secolo XI: Pier Damiani e Gregorio VII*. Naples: Liguori, 1996.

Freund, Stephan. *Studien zur literarischen Wirksamkeit des Petrus Damiani*. Hannover: Hahnsche Buchhandlung, 1995.

Resnick, Irven Michael. *Divine Power and Possibility in Saint Peter Damian's "De Divina Omnipotentia."* Leiden: Brill, 1992.

Ryan, John Joseph [Jack Lord]. *Saint Peter Damian and His Canonical Sources: A Preliminary Study in the Antecedents of the Gregorian Reform.* Studies and Texts, Pontifical Institute of Medieval Studies, 2. Toronto: Pontificium Institutum Studiorum Mediae Aetatis, 1956.

KARL F. MORRISON

DANIEL THE ABBOT (fl. 1106–1118)

The earliest Russian travel writer, known for his journeys to the Levant (*c.* 1106 and 1107), and for his visit to Palestine during the reign of Baldwin I, the Latin king of Jerusalem (1100–1118). The abbot of a Russian monastery, Daniel began the account of his journey at Constantinople. He crossed the Bosporus, sailed through the Dardanelles and into the Mediterranean, and headed to Ephesus, Patmos, and Rhodes. From there he traveled to Jaffa and Jerusalem, entering that city through the western Gate of Benjamin.

His account of the sea journey is an itinerary of the marvelous: the sacred oil that rose from the sea in honor of martyrs near Heraclea, the Tomb of St. John and the Seven Sleepers, the miraculous cross of St.

Helena that dangled in space above a Cyrian mountain. But his most vivid pictures are of his time in the Holy Land. He made three excursions while in Palestine: to the Jordan (which he compares to a Russian river, the Snov) and the Dead Sea, to Bethlehem and Hebron, and to Damascus. On this last expedition he accompanied Baldwin, whose armed escort gave him access to places no Christian pilgrim would normally visit. Toward the end of his stay he remained in the Jerusalem House, a Christian hostel, for sixteen months, recording minute observations about Jerusalem from this vantage point near the Tower of David. On his return voyage to Constantinople, his ship was plundered by four pirate galleys; narrowly escaping with his life, he thanked God for his good fortune.

Daniel's depiction of the Holy Land is invaluable as a record of conditions at the beginning of the twelfth century. He writes of the unsettled world of Palestine: Muslim raiders approached the walls of Christian Jerusalem and constantly attacked Christian travelers on the road from Jaffa to Jerusalem; armed escorts were needed for Christians on roads leading out of Jerusalem toward the Sea of Galilee or Nazareth; panthers and wild asses lurked on the west side of the Dead Sea, and lions hunted below the Jordan valley. But he also includes happier details—the date palms by Jericho, the genial relations between the Greek and Latin monasteries—as well as the conventional connections between geography and sacred story—the Sea of Sodom that oozes a vile and stinking breath, the stone column of Lot's wife near Segor. Daniels is a sharp and observant eye, if at times also credulous and inaccurate. Along with blunders in topography come detailed records of ritual and liturgy; along with errors in distance and confusion of names come accounts of life under the crusader government of Jerusalem.

Further Reading

Beazley, C. Raymond. *The Life and Journey of Daniel, Abbot of the Russian Land.* Trans. John Wilkinson. In *Jerusalem Pilgrimage 1099–1185.* Ed. John Wilkinson. Hakluyt Society, 2nd series, 167. London: Hakluyt Society, 1988, pp. 120–171.

Wright, Thomas, ed. *Early Travels in Palestine.* London, 1848; rpt. Hew York: AMS, 1969.

GARY D. SCHMIDT

DANTE ALIGHIERI (1265–1321)

The *Divine Comedy* or *Divina commedia* of Dante (Dante Alighieri) is a classic of western literature. Generations of readers have valued it as much for continuing and transforming the epic tradition of Homer's *Iliad* and *Odyssey* and Virgil's *Aeneid* as for initiating the Renaissance tradition of the long poem. From Dante's poem to Milton's *Paradise Lost* unrolled a single cycle of European literature that fused the forms and structures of the classical epic, the theology and religious passion of Christian belief, and the forces of contemporary experience in stunning poetic achievements.

Because Dante's great poem became recognized a classic, it continued to enter into the lives of readers even when the epic cycle that it had helped initiate lost impetus and was replaced by other forms of literary expression. In fact, Dante's *Divine Comedy* has the kind of power and appeal unique to a classic: successive eras have found reflected in it their own intellectual concerns; and just as a river takes on the coloration of the many terrains through which it passes, so Dante's poem has accumulated the tones of many successive readings.

Yet although Dante has become, as Ben Jonson said of Shakespeare, a figure for all time, he was still of a time. The *Divine Comedy* may have taken on the attributes of a living, growing organism, but it was nevertheless a product of medieval Italian culture. This masterpiece needs to be considered in light of the evolution of Dante's own poetic practice and theory, his attitude toward the newly emergent Italian language, his own acquisition of scholastic philosophy, the new mediating role of the lay philosopher, the vicissitudes of Dante's own political career both within and outside his native Florence, and the crucial changes in the large public forces that fashioned Dante's own life and times and the Italian culture of his day.

One factor that makes this larger frame so necessary is Dante's own nature and temperament—his willing engagement with the most powerful forces of his time. Although in the *Divine Comedy* he chastises himself for heedlessness, he makes the dominant historical events of his day and the major elements of his culture not the background but the foreground of his poem: in fact, its very substance. Like many of the poets who would follow him over the next three centuries, Dante himself was a considerable public figure.

Dante was born, as he tells us, under the sign of Gemini (21 May–20 June). He passed his youth in an ascendant, triumphant Guelf Florence, which, in league with the papacy and France, had finally, after nearly fifty years of intermittent strife, succeeded in defeating and permanently banishing the Guelfs' adversaries, the Ghibellines. As a young man Dante was a loyal son of the commune, imbued with the civic humanism of Brunetto Latini, who after his return from exile in 1266 became the spiritual mentor of an entire generation of young Florentines. In two instances in the *Commedia*, Dante personally recalls battles fought by the Florentine commune at Campaldino and Caprona, indicating that he himself was present. In many respects Dante belonged to a jeunesse dorée, a group of golden youths—as he indicates, for example, in *Paradiso* 8, when he records the favor shown to him by Charles Martel when Charles made a princely entrance into Florence. At age eighteen, already possessed of remarkable self-confidence, Dante sent his first poem to the most famous writers of the day, including Guido Cavalcanti.

Early in the 1290s, Dante collected the poems, mostly sonnets, that he had been writing over the preceding decade and brought them out as a little book (*libello*) that was to become famous: *Vita nuova* (*The New Life*). Here he made his first gesture toward a lifelong endeavor that itself would undergo some twists and turns, praise of the lady Beatrice. *Vita nuova* contains forty-two brief chapters with commentaries on twenty-five sonnets, one *ballata*, and four *canzoni*; a fifth *canzone* is left dramatically interrupted by Beattice's death. The prose commentary provides the flaming story, which does not emerge from the poems themselves. The story is simple enough: Dante's first sight of Beatrice when they both are nine years old; her salutation when they are eighteen; Dante's subterfuges to conceal his love for her; the crisis he experiences when Beatrice withholds her greeting; his anguish at the thought that she is making light of him; his determination to rise above anguish and sing only of his lady's virtues; his experiences that anticipate her death (a young friend dies, Beatrice's father dies, and Dante has a premonitory dream); and finally the death of Beatrice, Dante's mourning, his temptation by a sympathetic *donna gentile* (a young woman who temporarily replaces Beatrice), Beatrice's final triumph and apotheosis, and in the last chapter Dante's determination to write at some later time about her "that which has never been written of any woman." Beatrice thus became one of the most famous unknowns in history.

It was in accordance with the opinion of Guido Cavalcanti that Dante had decided to write *Vita nuova* in Italian; therefore, he dedicates it to his "first friend," whose brilliant and haughty spirit he memorializes most adroitly in *Inferno* 10. A second contemporary figure who influenced Dante was Guido Guinizzelli, the poet most responsible for altering the prevailing local, or "municipal," poetry. Guido's poems were written in praise of his lady and of *gentilezza* (nobility), the virtue that she brought out in her admirer. The concept of love that Guido extolled was part of a refined and noble sense of life; and his influence was responsible for the poetic and spiritual turning point of *Vita nuova*. In chapters 17–21, Dante experiences a change of heart, and rather than write poems of anguish he determines to write poems in praise of his own lady, especially the *canzone Donne ch'avete intelletto d'amore* ("Ladies who have understanding of love"). This *canzone* is followed immediately by the sonnet *Amore e 'l cor gentil sono una cosa* ("Love and the noble heart are the same thing"), in which the first line is clearly an adaptation of Guinizzelli's *Al cor gentil ripara sempre amore* ("In every noble heart love finds its home"). This was the beginning of Dante's association with a new poetic style, the *dolce stil nuovo* ("sweet new style"). He dramatically explains the significance of this style—the simple means by which it transcended the narrow range of more regional poetry—in Canto 24 of the *Purgatorio*.

Another significant change was Dante's more active involvement in the political affairs of the commune. As a philosopher, Dante was eligible to join one of the guilds that constituted the main entry into Florentine political life, and in 1295 he became a member of the

Domenico di Michelino (1417–1491).
Dante and the *Divine Comedy*.
© Nicolo Orsi Battaglini/Art Resource,
New York.

guild of physicians and apothecaries. This was a perilous time, as the triumphant Guelfs had fallen into vehement strife among themselves; thus in *Inferno* 6, Dante refers to the *città partita*, the divided city. Later, Dante was forced to recognize, bitterly, that the antagonism between Guelfs and Ghibellines had been replicated in the division within the Guelfs. This factionalism gave birth to the Black Guelf party, which was more or less intent on imposing severe restrictions on the defeated aristocrats; and the White Guelfs, who were more conciliatory. Dante was elected prior in the fateful bimester (two-month period) of 1300, and he became an active opponent of intrusions by the papacy in communal matters. These political activities heralded a significant change: Dante was gradually becoming opposed to the basis of Florentine hegemony, the alliance among the Guelf party, the papacy, and France. In time, he would oppose all three; in fact, in his later political prose work and in the *Commedia* his voice expresses a lofty, if qualified, Ghibelline—that is, imperial—idealism.

The alliance of the Black Guelfs with the papacy and France, the alliance that had been responsible for the defeat of the Ghibellines a generation earlier, effectively became a deceitful conspiracy responsible for the ejection of the White Guelfs from Florence. Thus in 1302, Dante himself became an exile. The course of his peregrinations remains somewhat obscure. At first, he may have made temporary league with remnants of the exiled Ghibellines in Tuscany, who had never relinquished their strong though illusory hope of staging a military return to Florence; but if so, he soon wearied of these false allies and became a party unto himself. For the remainder of his life he moved from court to court, mainly in the principalities of northern Italy.

Of one thing we can be relatively sure: Dante would not have written his *Commedia* without the bitter experience of exile. This is one reason why the poem is fictionally dated as taking place in 1300—that is, at the time of Dante's most active political involvement, which led to his exile—and why its central plotline is his growing awareness, through a series of cryptic prophecies, of an impending disastrous blow. It also helps to explain the values of divine comedy itself: along his way, Dante the pilgrim acquires the spiritual strength and courage he needs to cope with the tragedy of history. As a result, when he receives the clearest indication of his fate (*Paradiso*, 17), he already possesses the means to surmount it. Exile is the pivotal event and the central spiritual struggle of the poem. It becomes in fact a fortunate fall, without which Dante would not have been moved to appropriate the actual meaning of the philosophy of Christ. This explains why, beyond the classical prototypes of a visit to the underworld, the grander background of Dante's journey is Christ's passion and, particularly in the *Inferno*, Christ's descent into hell.

Early in his exile, however, in order to clear his name of whatever slander may have been spread about him as a fugitive, Dante set about composing *Convivio* (*The Banquet*), a work of high seriousness that was intended to restore his reputation not only as a poet but as a moral philosopher. There is every indication that when he began writing *Convivio*, he was committing himself to a major undertaking. He projected a work of considerable length: fifteen books, fourteen of which would be extended commentaries showing the philosophical arguments of his poems. *Convivio* is, like *Vita nuova*, largely a collection of the poems he had written during the preceding decade, but in this work the poems are held together by more elaborate commentary. Apparently, Dante was never content with the experience of a single poem; rather, he was ever ready to place the poetic experience in a frame of larger coherence and meaning. Dante completed only four of the books he had projected for *Convivio*, but they are valuable by themselves, detailing his ideas about philosophy, allegory, and nobility (*gentilezza*). His arguments about *gentilezza* appear in Book 4, which is his greatest work before the *Commedia*; he interrupts Book 4 to insert his first extended argument for the necessity and legitimacy of the empire.

Dante's career took another crucial turn while he was in exile. The hopes of all the Florentine exiles were revitalized in 1308 by the emergence of a new emperor, Henry VII. Stirred by new possibilities, Dante began addressing epistles in Latin to the nobles of Italy, urging them to support this great hope. These epistles are evidence of the high esteem in which Dante was held throughout Italy, and of his personal authority. But Henry delayed unaccountably, as Dante saw it, and also fell victim to deceit on the part of the papacy; shortly after the emperor arrived in Italy in 1310, his appeal began to fade and the French pope, Clement V, turned against him. It was in the midst of this activity and controversy that Dante wrote one of the important polemical works of the late Middle Ages in Italy: *Monarchia* (*Monarchy*, c. 1313). Here, particularly in the third book, Dante uses his philosophical training to good advantage. Formerly, he had argued that there was a need for imperial rule but had avoided alienating the papacy. In *Monarchia* he disputes the papacy's various arguments that imperial power is derivative and hence subordinate. Dante's arguments—clear, incisive, and logical—show that his philosophical training in making rational distinctions had become a very powerful tool. The arguments he makes here are those he would also make throughout the *Commedia*: that secular authority itself has a concern with justice and a power derived from the deity independently. Dante's position is actually more complex than this, however, because he tries to steer a course between secularism and theocracy. On the one hand, he is well aware of the disadvantages of theocracy, and he feels confident in attributing the origins of Italy's troubles to intrusions by the papacy in the affairs of the empire. The result, which he deplores again and again, is that the empire is frustrated, and also that the papacy is tainted by its own worldly interests. The victims of this confusion of roles are the people of Italy, who have no social order, since the arm of the state is unable to impose such order and the church cannot inspire them to follow the teachings of Christ. On the other hand, neither is secularism the answer. Dante argues that somehow there is a connection between the vision of the earthly city and that of the heavenly city, and an emperor must have some vision of the heavenly city. Dante's problem is, of course, that he is trying to present a theoretical solution for what is a highly nuanced and delicate relationship. He is at his best when he cites historical examples of what cannot be theoretically ascertained; thus he refers to Charlemagne's goodwill toward the church, and to the fact that Justinian could not codify Roman law until he had been disabused by Pope Agapetus of a theological error. It was a sore disappointment for Dante when young Henry VII died before being able to complete what had seemed to be a divinely appointed mission. In the lofty circles of paradise, however, Dante reveals his own philosophical vision: he sees a seat reserved for the "great Harry" (*alto Arrigo*) who, tragically, came to save Italy before Italy itself was ready to be saved. In all of his divine comedy, Dante sadly and judiciously records such historical tragedies.

As we try to locate Dante in relation to late medieval Italian culture, we can see that he led the way to creativity in several critical areas. A fundamental area is his lifelong defense of the Italian vernacular as an effective language for literary and philosophical expression. This concern first appears in *Vita nuova*, where Dante informs the reader that what drew him and Guido Cavalcanti together was their agreement that this work would be written entirely in the vernacular. Dante's interest in the vernacular grew into one of its first great defenses—in *Convivio*, which was also written in Italian; and in *De vulgari eloquentia*. He also developed a corollary: that the poetic powers of the vernacular needed to be enhanced through imitation of the ancients. These motives and arguments would be echoed in the literary renascence of France and England.

Dante's defense of the vernacular is a confident and forthright defense of the validity of his own culture and experience. In particular, Dante disputes the poetasters who try to excuse their own deficiencies by denigrating their native language and holding up the Provencal *langue d'oc* as its poetic superior. Dante invokes a parallel situation, Latin versus Greek literature, arguing that if the Romans had acquiesced in the purported natural superiority of Greek, there would never have

been a Latin literature. The analysis is remarkable, as is its conclusion—Dante's quite accurate prophecy of an entirely new literary culture. Dante predicts that the Italian vernacular:

> …shall be the new light, the new sun, which shall arise when the worn-out one shall set, and shall give light to them who are in darkness because of the old sun, which does not enlighten them.

The sociological implications of this statement are no less astonishing than its literary implications. The Italian language will be used to bring learning and lessons in virtue to people who have until now enjoyed no such benefits. Dante is describing a revolution: the twilight of Latin culture and the emergence of an uban lay culture. Through Dante's promotion of the vernacular, and his own example, Italian was soon to become the leading literary language of Europe, a position it would continue to hold for more than 300 years.

Still, this defense of the Italian vernacular did not satisfy Dante's purposes: his real, abiding aim was to enhance it. Thus *De vulgari eloquentia* is a natural complement to the arguments in Book 1 of *Convivio*, the one defending the vernacular and the other showing how the vernacular can become a vehicle for superior literary expression. Although the formulations here are quite specific, it should be remembered that this impulse to elevate poetic practice beyond the local and the municipal had already been present in *Vita nuova*. Dante's own ambitions aspired to the level of the classics. The lesson he devises in *De vulgari eloquentia* is clear, and it would be repeated by all the ambitious writers of the Renaissance. To become true poets, Dante insists, those who write in the vernacular must abandon chance and acquire doctrine: that is, they must themselves adopt a conscious poetics. The best way to achieve this higher skill is by imitating the ancients; the more closely we imitate them, the better poets we will become (*quantum illos proximius imitemur, tantum rectius poetemur*). Thus when Virgil returns in *Inferno* 1, he brings with him the larger poetic vision and practice of the classical world as well as its moral wisdom. In an even more memorable reunion in *Inferno* 4, Dante himself joins the circle of five classical poets, bridging the gap between them and becoming the sixth of their company (*sesto tra cotanto senno*, 102).

These astonishing changes in society, in language, and in poetics that Dante announces require a new personage: the philosopher as mediator, the lay philosopher—someone who might today be called an intellectual. This person moves with skill and understanding between the technical philosophers in the schools and the newly enfranchised lay readership. Dante casts a new role for himself, a role he has inherited by adhering to the civic humanism of Brunetto Latini. But Dante went one step farther. In 1292, as he tells us in *Convivio*, to console himself for the death of Beatrice, he began attending lectures in philosophy. His concept of poetry thus came to include a notion of the poet as teacher and even as seer, a figure combining art and learning. Separating him even farther from his Florentine teachers and his compeers was his later insistence on Italy's need for a single ruler—an emperor. In all these ways, Dante separated himself from much of contemporary Florentine opinion. Indeed, we can see that Dante's evolving attitude toward politics, philosophy, and poetics was setting the stage for the *Commedia*. At the same time, though, we can also see that little in Dante's earlier career prepares us for the scope and poetic reality of the *Commedia*; it has the sheer unpredictability that is a prime quality of any work of genius.

The *Commedia* uses a relatively simple storytelling device: an extraordinary visit by a living human being to the three realms of the afterlife. There is much that is fantastic in this conception, and much that shows Dante's extensive powers of invention as he works out its details. But what is even more important is that this fiction allows an extraordinarily rich panorama, the fullest imaginable account of the people, manners, ways, issues, and thought of his time. One of the earliest critics of the *Commedia*, Leonardo Bruni (c. 1370–1444), who had himself inherited and shaped Florentine civic humanism, praised the freedom and range that Dante's structure permitted. Bruni doubted that anyone else ever "took a larger and more fertile subject by which to deliver the mind of all its conceptions through the different spirits who discourse on diverse causes of things, on the different countries, and on the various chances of fortune."

Within this larger structure, the primary unit of the poem is the canto—itself a major poetic device and one of Dante's most important inventions. The cantos are powerfully condensed segments varying in length from about 115 to 150 lines, and they allow Dante to do two things: vary his landscapes and engage a remarkable array of different individuals in discourse. In fact, the meaning of a canto derives partly from an interaction between landscape and personal exchange. The canto has scope and yet compactness, so that it is a dense, complex dramatic unit in which simple or sometimes elliptical phrases can have extraordinary powers of reference. In modern times, the study of individual cantos—*letture dantesche*—has become a favored and rewarding approach to the poem.

In fact, the study of individual cantos has become so valuable that it has had the unfortunate side effect of hindering fuller study of another quality of Dante's imagination: his network of imaginative-cross references. There are larger connections between cantos, startling juxtapositions, suites of cantos, and parallel placements of individuals in the various canticles, all of which invite comparison. Appreciating Dante's architectonics is one of the genuine pleasures of reading his text. The superabundance of Dante's imagination gives his enormous poem some of the qualities of a medieval cathedral; but we can also see that the *Commedia* reveals the higher function of literature—its coherent power—that Dante had tried to make his own as early as *Vita nuova*.

All great poets discover their own forms, and another important invention in the *Commedia* is the canticle, a set of cantos. *Inferno*, *Purgatorio*, and *Paradiso* are surprisingly similar in structure. Each has a prologue (in *Inferno*, introducing the entire poem, there are two such cantos), followed by preliminary cantos: in *Inferno* the cantos preceding the city of Dis; in the second canticle, the *ante-Purgatorio*; and in *Paradiso*, those under the shadow of the earth. Approximately one-third of the way through, the purpose of the canticle is intensified. In these long middle sections, the heavy work is done. The canticle culminates in the fuller meaning of its experience in the nadir of hell or at the heights of Purgatory and paradise. In *Inferno*, after the Malebolge, this climax is the Cocytus, beginning in Canto 31; in *Purgatorio*, the climax is the Earthly Paradise, beginning in Canto 27; in *Paradiso*, a new tone and intensity of experience are gained beginning with the address to Mary in Canto 23.

In the mysterious and miraculous circumstances of *Inferno* 1, the long-absent spirit of Virgil returns to prevent Dante from backsliding and to redirect his energies. The specific itinerary involving this change of direction brings back to western literature a central theme of classical epics, the visit to the underworld. However, this itinerary is itself revised: Dante quite consciously alters the pattern of the classical epic. In classic examples such as *The Odyssey* and *The Aeneid*, the visit to the underworld occupies the middle books (Book 11 in *The Odyssey* and Book 6 in *The Aeneid*); and these episodes are central not only in placement but also because they communicate essential wisdom. Dante's Christian itinerary is different. Hell is not the pivot but rather a preliminary episode, in which Dante encounters not the true values of his culture but rather the gods that failed. Dante's motive is not to take on the wisdom of the place but rather to unlearn the values that failed to serve him in his travail. He must be disabused of false notions, and consequently hell is a place of disaffection. For this reason, hell is the initial experience, not the median (in this schedule, Dante and another Christian poet, Milton, are perfectly in stride).

To be sure, we encounter in hell imposing and memorable characters such as Francesca, Farinata, Brunetto Latini, Ulysses, and Ugolino. Their stories, their fates, and their agonies are so inventive and so powerful that it was almost natural for the Romantics of the nineteenth century—the post-Napoleonic age—to identify with these doomed characters, to see them as icons of dismay, and to take them as the significant heroes of Dante's poem. In the twentieth century, a time when readers cast a more ironic eye on such projections of the self, these characters lost some of their allure. Indeed, some twentieth-century counter-Romantics called Francesca a Madame Bovary and regarded Ulysses merely as a footloose adventurer. Twentieth-century critics tended to be more conscious of the totality of the poem and considered it appropriate to put some distance between the reader and the characters of the *Inferno*. They also discerned a distance between the author, with his full understanding, and the naive narrator—the pilgrim who is only on the way toward gaining the fuller comprehension that has been in the author's possession from the beginning.

The intermediate but central and pivotal poem in Dante's trilogy is *Purgatorio*. Here the painful process of reconstruction begins. In *Inferno*, the characters have distinct identities, but in *Purgatorio* they adhere to the central motif of pilgrimage. In this sense, *Purgatorio* is dominated not by individualism but by spiritual brotherhood. Poetically, the cantos are not devoted to grand individuals but consist of a medley of forces and figures.

Purgatorio includes abundant discussions of art, poetry, philosophy, which are notably absent from *Inferno*. Nevertheless, *Purgatorio* is a canticle of stringent exclusions: any forces that do not contribute directly to salvation must be abandoned. For this reason, the summary plot of *Purgatorio* involves a rejection of Virgil. Virgil, the father to whom Dante gave himself for his salvation, the embodiment of the poetry and wisdom of the classical world, is now himself found to be deficient. Because he did not present in his own poetic works the kind of fullness that Dante discovered in the philosophy of Christ, Virgil must now succumb to the historical vision that was his own. Virgil must give place to Beatrice, who will now be Dante's mentor and his guide to the possibilities of the Christian vision.

Dante was heir to a heroic Roman culture and was convinced of the rightness of the creative design for the universe; therefore, it would not have been fitting for him to rest his poem on the straitened consolations of the purgatorial way. The purpose of the original divine creation was not restraint but fulfillment. Appropriately, then, Dante's trilogy is capped by *Paradiso*, where the original human instinct to return to God finds its rightful, heroic fulfillment in the lives of the saints. *Paradiso* brings to completion the triptychs of the poem. But while the vision of *Paradiso* is transcendent, it does not obscure the preceding books; rather, it asks us to look back, to consider its exemplars in relation to their

antecedents. In this sense, although the *Commedia* is a poem in process, its vision is retrospective. The meeting with Piccarda Donati in *Paradiso* 3, which creates a powerful impression, is intended to recall the meetings with Francesca in *Inferno* and La Pia in *Purgatorio*; these meetings are an ensemble of cross-references and mutual commentary. We cannot fully assess Francesca until we have experienced La Pia, and each of these two is incomplete until we have known Piccarda. This method implies freedom as well as divine trust. We are not confined to Francesca's powerful appeal; the essential life-force and motives of love that are misdirected by Francesca are redirected by La Pia and find their fulfillment in Piccarda's sublime faith: "In his will is our peace" (*E 'n la sua volontade è nostra pace*, 3.85).

These motives—freedom and fulfillment—are realized in an even greater triptych controlling the central cantos of each canticle. Imitating and transforming the pivotal episode in Book 6 of *The Aeneid*, where Aeneas receives the message of his life from his own father, Anchises, Dante constructs the central encounter of each of his books around a father figure: Brunetto Latini in Canto 15 of *Inferno*; a composite of Guido del Duca and Marco Lombardo in Cantos 14–16 of *Purgatorio*; and his own great-great-grandfather in *Paradiso* 15–17. Each meeting addresses the central topic of the *Commedia*, Dante's preparation for the coming blow: for exile. Although each provides essential information, it is from Cacciaguida that Dante acquires the clearest idea of the impending tragedy; and as we have noted, at the same time he receives (as he has been receiving all along) the resources to cope with that catastrophe. Christian realism encompasses the tragedy of history and also provides the means for transcending history; this is why, in its fullest meaning, the poem may be regarded as a divine comedy. Brunetto Latini is a worthy man but a marred exemplar; Guido del Duca and Marco Lombardo are sustaining figures along the way; but it is in the presence of Cacciaguida, Dante's biological as well as spiritual source, that he discovers the intimate meaning of his life. He transcends the need for consolation: "You are my father, you give me all boldness to speak, you uplift me so that I am more than myself" (*Paradiso*, 16.16–18). These lines manifest the purpose of the poem, heroic paideia (or ultimate education). In *Inferno*, paideia is dysfunctional: the exemplars are false figures, parts of the mind of hell and aspects of the problem rather than of the solution. In *Purgatorio* there are no heroic figures at all; all the figures partake of a penitential discipline and a spiritual brotherhood. In *Paradiso*, heroic paideia functions rightly as Dante finds his own true nature and expression in the models of Christian history. Not even Virgil offered these intimate, personal, and yet transcendent possibilities for redemption.

Dante's poem is the fullest and most imaginative appropriation of Christian salvation. Within the confines of the Christian scheme, the *Commedia* stretches from the first day to the last night, from the creation to the crucifixion and the resurrection. Its greatest distinction is that it embodies this scheme in significant, distinctive historical types. In fact, these lively, realistic individuals rescue the Christian sense of history from certain monochromatism. Dante is an incarnationist, imbued with the sense that the Christian calendar is always being relived, relearned, and reengaged. When it vividly realizes religious passion, Dante's poem is part of its own age and a prelude to another age. It stretches from heaven to hell, which are points or coordinates in Dante's fundamental faith that humankind has an innate purpose to return to God, to redeem itself from nothingness. When it is realized, this innate drive leads to the fullness of the saint, whose life bespeaks an absolute dedication to a worthy ideal; but when it is misdirected or defeated by poor educational models, it leads to frustration and obsessive attachments, which are the primary evidence of hell. In this passionate world of manic extremes, such misdirection must result in the terrible thought that it is better not to have been born. A long line of modern western literature, originating in the late Middle Ages in Italy and realized in the Renaissance, rests on these principles: the grand scheme of Christian salvation, expressed by individuals and presented aesthetically in imaginative fiction; and religious passion that stretches humankind between the poles of salvation and damnation. Dante was the first master of this great cycle of literature.

Dante's exile was a difficult time of wandering from one place to another. Throughout these years he was sustained by work on his great poem, which he may have begun before 1308 and completed just before his death in 1321. In his final years, Dante was received honorably in many noble houses in northern Italy, most notably by Cangrande della Scala in Verona and by Guido Novello da Polenta, the nephew of the remarkable Francesca, in Ravenna. Dante died in Ravenna; his burial was attended by the leading men of letters, and the funeral oration was delivered by Guido himself.

Dante's *Commedia* did not have to wait long for recognition and honors. By the year 1400, no fewer than fourteen commentaries devoted to detailed expositions of its meaning had appeared. Giovanni Boccaccio wrote a life of Dante and in 1373–1374 delivered the first public lectures on the *Commedia*. Dante became known as the *divino poeta*, and in a splendid edition of the *Commedia* published in 1555 the adjective *divina* was applied to the poem itself; thus the simple *Commedia* became *La divina commedia*.

See also **Boccaccio, Giovanni; Boniface VIII, Pope; Brunetto Latini; Cavalcanti, Guido**

Further Reading

Editions, Translations, and Commentaries: General

Le opere di Dante: Testo critico della società dantesca italiana, ed. Michele Barbi et al., 2nd ed. Florence: Società Dantesca Italiana, 1960.

Le opere di Dante Alighieri, ed. Edward Moore and Paget Toynbee, 5th ed. Oxford: Oxford University Press, 1963.

Opere minori, Vol. 2., ed. Pier Vincenzo Mengaldo, Bruno Nardi, Arsenio Frugoni, Giorgio Brugnoli, Enzo Cecchini, and Francesco Mazzoni. Milan and Naples: Ricciardi, 1979.

Editions, Translations, and Commentaries: Commedia

La commedia secondo l'antica vulgata, 4 vols., ed. Giorgio Petrocchi. Milan: Mondadori, 1966–1967.

La Divina Commedia, 3 vols., ed. Natalino Sapegno. 3rd ed. Florence: La Nuova Italia, 1985.

La Divina Commedia di Dante Alighieri, ed. C. H. Grandgent. Boston, Mass.: Heath, 1933. (Rev. ed., Charles S. Singleton. Cambridge, Mass.: Harvard University Press, 1972.)

The Divine Comedy, 6 vols., trans. and commentary Charles S. Singleton. Princeton, N.J.: Princeton University Press, 1970–1975.

The Divine Comedy of Dante Alighieri, 3 vols., trans. John D. Sinclair. New York: Oxford University Press, 1958.

Editions, Translations, and Commentaries: Other Works

The Banquet, trans. Christopher Ryan. Saratoga, Calif.: Anma Libri, 1989.

Il Convivio, 2nd ed., 2 vols., ed. Giovanni Busnelli and Giuseppe Vandelli. Florence: Le Monnier, 1968. (With appendixes by Antonio Enzo Quaglio.)

Convivio, ed. Cesare Vasoli. Dante Alighieri: Opere Minori, 1 (part 2). Milan and Naples: Ricciardi, 1988.

Convivio, 3 vols., ed. Franca Brambilla Ageno. Florence: Casa Editrice Le Lettere, 1995.

Dante and Giovanni del Virgilio, Including a Critical Edition of the Text of Dante's "Eclogae Latinae" and of the Poetic Remains of Giovanni del Virgilio, ed. Philip H. Wicksteed and Edmund G. Gardner. Westminster: Constable, 1902.

Dante's Il Convivio (The Banquet), trans. Richard H. Lansing. New York: Garland, 1990.

Dante's Lyric Poetry, 2 vols., ed. and trans. Kenelm Foster and Patrick Boyde. Oxford: Clarendon, 1967.

Dante's Monarchia, trans. with commentary Richard Kay. Toronto: Pontifical Institute of Mediaeval Studies, 1998.

Dante's Treatise De Vulgari Eloquentia, trans. A. G. Ferrers Howell. Temple Classics. London: Dent, 1890.

Dante's Vita Nuova, trans. Mark Musa. Bloomington: Indiana University Press, 1973.

De vulgari eloquentia, ed. Aristide Marigo. Florence: Le Monnier, 1957.

De vulgari eloquentia, ed. and trans. Steven Botterill. Cambridge: Cambridge University Press, 1996.

The Flore and the Detto d'Amore: A Late 13th-Century Italian Translation of the Roman de la Rose, trans. Santa Casciani and Christopher Kleinhenz. Notre Dame, Ind.: University of Notre Dame Press, 2000.

Literary Criticism of Dante Alighieri, trans. and ed. Robert S. Haller. Lincoln: University of Nebraska Press, 1973.

Monarchia, ed. Pier Giorgio Ricci. Milan: Mondadori, 1965.

Monarchia, trans. and ed. Prue Shaw. Cambridge: Cambridge University Press, 1995.

On World Government, or, De Monarchia, trans. Herbert W. Schneider, 2nd rev. ed. New York: Liberal Arts, 1957.

Rime, ed. Gianfranco Contini. Turin: Einaudi, 1965.

Rime della maturità e dell' esilio, ed. Michele Barbi and Vincenzo Pernicone. Florence: Le Monnier, 1969.

Rime della "Vita nuova" e della giovinezza, ed. Michele Barbi and Francesco Maggini. Florence: Le Monnier, 1956.

La vita nuova, ed. Michele Barbi. Florence: Bemporad, 1932.

Concordances, Dictionaries, and Encyclopedias

Cosmo, Umberto. *A Handbook to Dante Studies*, trans. David Moore. New York: Barnes and Noble, 1947. (Reprint, 1978; originally published in Italian, 1947.)

The Dante Encyclopedia, ed. Richard Lansing. New York and London: Garland, 2000.

Enciclopedia dantesca, 6 vols., 2nd ed. Rome: Istituto della Enciclopedia Italiana, 1984.

Rand, Edward Kennard, and Ernest Hatch Wilkins. *Dantis Alagherii Operum Latinorum Concordantiae*. Oxford: Clarendon, 1912 (Reprint, 1970).

Sheldon, Edward S., and Alain C. White. *Concordanza delle opere italiane in prosa e del Canzoniere di Dante Alighieri*. Oxford: Stamperia dell'Università, 1905. (Reprint, New York: Russel and Russell, 1969, with *Supplementary Concordance to the Minor Italian Works of Dante*, comp. Lewis H. Gordon.)

Toynbee, Paget. *A Dictionary of Proper Names and Notable Matters in the Works of Dante*, rev. ed. Charles S. Singleton. Oxford: Oxford University Press, 1968.

Wilkins, Ernest Hatch, and Thomas Goddard Bergin. *A Concordance to the Divine Comedy of Dante Alighieri*. Cambridge, Mass.: Belknap Press of Harvard University Press, 1965.

Studies: Life and Works

Anderson, William. *Dante the Maker*. London: Routledge and Kegan Paul, 1980.

Barbi, Michele. *Life of Dante*, trans. Paul G. Ruggiers. Berkeley: University of California Press, 1954. (Reprint, 1966; originally published in Italian, 1933.)

Bergin, Thomas G. *Dante*. Boston, Mass.: Houghton Mifflin, 1965. (Reprint, 1976.)

Codice diplomatico dantesco, ed. Renato Piattoli, 2nd ed. Florence: Gonnelli, 1950.

Holmes, George. *Dante*, Oxford: Clarendon, 1980.

Quinones, Ricardo J. *Dante Alighieri*. Boston, Mass.: Twayne, 1979. (Reprint, 1985.)

Vallone, Aldo. *Dante*, 2nd ed. Milan: Vallardi, 1981.

Zingarelli, Nicola. *La vita, i tempi, e le opere di Dante*, 3rd ed., 2 vols. Milan: Vallardi, 1931.

Studies: General

Biagi, Guido, ed. *La Divina Commedia nella figurazione artistica e nel secolare commento*. Turin: UTET, 1924–1939.

Boyde, Patrick. *Dante Philomythes and Philosopher: Man in the Cosmos*. Cambridge: Cambridge University Press, 1981.

Croce, Benedetto. *The Poetry of Dante*, trans. Douglas Ainslie. New York: Holt, 1922. (Reissued 1971; originally published in Italian, 1920.)

Dante e la "bella scola" della poesia: Autorita e sfida poetica, ed. Amilcare A. Iannucci. Ravenna: Longo, 1993.

Dante Now: Current Trends in Dante Studies, ed. Theodore J. Cachey, Jr. Notre Dame, Ind.: University of Notre Dame Press, 1995.

Dante and Ovid: Essays in Intertextuality, ed. Madison U. Sowell. Binghamton, N.Y.: Medieval and Renaissane Texts and Studies, 1991.

De Sua, William J., and Gino Rizzo, eds. *A Dante Symposium in Commemoration of the 700th Anniversary of the Poet's Birth (1265–1965)*. Chapel Hill: University of North Carolina Press, 1965.

Durling, Robert M., and Ronald L. Martinez. *Time and the Crystal: Studies in Dante's "Rime Petrose."* Berkeley: University of California Press, 1990.

Eliot, T. S. *Dante*. London: Faber and Faber, 1929. (Reprint, 1974.)

Freccero, John, ed. *Dante: A Collection of Critical Essays*. Englewood Cliffs, N.J.: Prentice Hall, 1965.

Grayson, Cecil, ed. *The World of Dante: Essays on Dante and His Times*. Oxford: Clarendon, 1980.

Jacoff, Rachel, ed. *The Cambridge Companion to Dante*. Cambridge: Cambridge University Press, 1993.

Limentani, Uberto, ed. *The Mind of Dante*. Cambridge: Cambridge University Press, 1965.

Mazzoni, Francesco. *Saggio di un nuovo commento alla Divina Commedia: Inferno, canti I–III*. Florence: Sansoni, 1967.

Moore, Edward. *Studies in Dante*, 4 vols. Oxford: Clarendon, 1896–1917. (Reprint, with new introductory material by Colin Hardie, 1968.)

Morgan, Alison. *Dante and the Medieval Other World*. Cambridge: Cambridge University Press, 1990.

Musa, Mark. *Advent at the Gates: Dante's Comedy*. Bloomington: Indiana University Press, 1974.

Nolan, David, ed. *Dante Commentaries: Eight Studies of the Divine Comedy*. Totowa, N.J.: Rowman and Littlefield, 1977.

——. *Dante Soundings: Eight Literary and Historical Essays*. Totowa, N.J.: Rowman and Littiefield, 1981.

Oxford Dante Society. *Centenary Essays on Dante*. Oxford: Clarendon, 1965.

The Poetry of Allusion: Virgil and Ovid in Dante's Commedia, ed. Rachel Jacoff and Jeffrey T. Schnapp. Stanford, Calif.: Stanford University Press, 1991.

Toynbee, Paget. *Dante Studies*. Oxford: Clarendon, 1921.

Studies: Specialized

Armour, Peter. *The Door of Purgatory: A Study of Multiple Symbolism in Dante's Purgatorio*. Oxford: Clarendon, 1983.

——. *Dante's Griffin and the History of the World*. Oxford: Oxford University Press, 1990.

Barolini, Teodolinda. *Dante's Poets: Textuality and Truth in the Comedy*. Princeton, N.J.: Princeton University Press, 1984.

——. *The Undivine Comedy: Detheologizing Dante*. Princeton, N.J.: Princeton University Press, 1992.

Bergin, Thomas G. *Perspectives on the Divine Comedy*. New Brunswick, N.J.: Rutgers University Press, 1967.

——. *A Diversity of Dante*. New Brunswick, N.J.: Rutgers University Press, 1969.

Boyde, Patrick. *Dante's Style in His Lyric Poetry*. Cambridge: Cambridge University Press, 1971.

Brandeis, Irma. *The Ladder of Vision: A Study of Dante's Comedy*. London: Chatto and Windus, 1960.

Curtius, Ernst Robert. *European Literature and the Latin Middle Ages*, trans. Willard R. Trask. New York: Pantheon, 1953. (Reissued 1973; originally published in German, 1948.)

Davis, Charles T. *Dante and the Idea of Rome*. Oxford: Clarendon, 1957.

——. *Dante's Italy and Other Essays*. Philadelphia: University of Pennsylvania Press, 1984.

Dunbar, Helen Flanders. *Symbolism in Medieval Thought and Its Consummation in the Divine Comedy*. New Haven, Conn.: Yale University Press, 1929. (Reissued 1961.)

Fergusson, Francis. *Dante's Drama of the Mind: A Modern Reading of the Purgatorio*. Princeton, N.J.: Princeton University Press, 1953 (Reissued 1981.)

Ferrante, Joan. *The Political Vision of the Divine Comedy*. Princeton, N.J.: Princeton University Press, 1984.

Ferrucci, Franco. *Il poema del desiderio: Poetica e passione in Dante*. Milan: Leonardo, 1990.

Freccero, John. *Dante: The Poetics of Conversion*, ed. Rachel Jacoff. Cambridge, Mass.: Harvard University Press, 1986.

Gilson, Etienne. *Dante and Philosophy*, trans. David Moore. New York: Harper and Row, 1973. (Originally published in French, 1939; trans, originally published 1948.)

Hollander, Robert. *Allegory in Dante's "Commedia."* Princeton, N.J.: Princeton University Press, 1969.

——. *Studies in Dante*. Ravenna: Longo, 1980.

——. *Il Virgilio dantesco: Tragedia nella Commedia*. Florence: Olschki, 1983.

Lewis, Ewart K. *Medieval Political Ideas*, 2 vols. New York: Knopf, 1954. (Reprint, 1974.) Mazzeo, Joseph Anthony. *Medieval Cultural Tradition in Dante's "Comedy."* Ithaca, N.Y.: Cornell University Press, 1960. (Reprint, 1968.)

——. *Structure and Thought in the Paradiso*. Ithaca, N.Y.: Cornell University Press, 1958. (Reissued 1968.)

Mazzotta, Giuseppe. *Dante, Poet of the Desert: History and Allegory in the Divine Comedy*. Princeton, N.J.: Princeton University Press, 1979.

——. *Dante's Vision and the Circle of Knowledge*. Princeton, N.J.: Princeton University Press, 1993

Passerin D'Entreves, Alessandro. *Dante as a Political Thinker*. Oxford: Clarendon, 1952. (Reprint, 1965.)

Reade, William H. V. *The Moral System of Dante's Inferno*. Oxford: Clarendon, 1909. (Reprint, 1969.)

Scott, John A. *Dante's Political Purgatory*. Philadelphia: University of Pennsylvania Press, 1996.

Shapiro, Marianne. *De Vulgari Eloquentia: Dante's Book of Exile*. Lincoln: University of Nebraska Press, 1990.

Singleton, Charles S. *An Essay on the Vita Nuova*. Cambridge, Mass.: Harvard University Press, 1949. (Reprint, 1977.)

——. *Dante Studies, I, Commedia: Elements of Structure*. Cambridge, Mass.: Harvard University Press, 1954. (Reprint, 1977.)

——. *Dante Studies, 2, Journey to Beatrice*. Cambridge, Mass.: Harvard University Press, 1957.

Took, J. F. *Dante Lyric Poet and Philosopher: An Introduction to the Minor Works*. Oxford: Clarendon, 1990.

Vossler, Karl. *Medieval Culture: An Introduction to Dante and His Times*, 2 vols., trans. William Cranston Lawton. New York: Harcourt, Brace, 1929. (Reissued 1970; originally published in German, 1907–1910.)

Bibliographic Studies

Esposito, Enzo. *Bibliografia analitica degli scritti su Dante, 1950–1970*, 4 vols. Florence: Olschki, 1990.

Giovannetti, Luciana. *Dante in America: Bibliografia 1965–1980*. Ravenna: Longo, 1987.

RICARDO J. QUINONES

DAVID VON AUGSBURG (1200/1210–1272)

The Franciscan teacher and preacher David von Augsburg profoundly influenced his contemporaries and successors through his vernacular and Latin tracts on the ascetic and mystical nature of religious life. Around 1240 David became the novice master at the Franciscan monastery in Regensburg, which along with Augsburg was the spiritual center of the Franciscans in the thirteenth century. In 1246 he was appointed papal visitator of two abbeys in the vicinity, a position he shared with Berthold von Regensburg and several other Minorites. As Berthold's assistant, David accompanied the renowned preacher on homiletic and mission tours.

David's extant works consist solely of his Latin and German tracts and letters; in many instances the authenticity is still disputed. His *De exterioris et interioris hominis compositione secundum triplicem statum incipientium, proficientium et perfectorum* is one of the most significant works on the spiritual life in the Middle Ages and survives in some four hundred manuscripts, including many German and Dutch translations. The work consists of three treatises, each devoted to one aspect of the threefold way. The first part focuses on the life of the spiritual neophyte and how the novice must free himself of the world and its enticements and be educated. In part two the inner person is called to reform in light of the image of the trinity. The third part enumerates seven steps to be followed by a religious person seeking perfection, i.e., divine knowledge. Speculative mystical theology predominates as well in the *Sieben Staffeln des Gebetes* (The Seven Steps of Prayer), which survives in three German versions as well as a Latin source; only the German version "B" is unquestionably by David. David's tracts proved particularly influential in the Netherlands among the Windesheimer and the adherents of the *Devotio moderna* (New Piety).

Further Reading

De exterioris et interioris hominis compositione secundum triplicem statum: incipientium, proficientium et perfectorum, ed. PP. Collegii S. Bonaventurae. Ad Claras Aquas (Quaracchi): Ex Typographia Eiusdem Collegii, 1899 [Latin works].

Pfeiffer, Franz, ed. *Deutsche Mystiker des 14. Jahrhunderts*. Vol. 1. 1845; rpt. Aalen: Scientia, 1962, pp. 309–397 [German works].

Schwab, Francis Mary. *David of Augsburg's "Paternoster" and the Authenticity of his German Works*. Munich: Beck, 1971.

Spiritual Life and Progress, trans. Dominic Devas. London: Burns, Oates, and Washbourne, 1937.

DEBRA L. STOUDT

DESCHAMPS, EUSTACHE (ca.1346–ca.1406)

Born near Reims at Vertus, in the family home burned in 1380 by the English, Deschamps says that he long applied himself to grammar and logic. He later studied law, probably at Orléans. From 1360, Deschamps was in the service of high nobility, and in 1367 he joined the king's retinue. For most of his life thereafter, he was attached in various capacities to Charles V, and to Charles VI and his brother Louis d'Orléans, as well as to other great personages. From 1375, his name appears in the records as *bailli* of Valois; he became *bailli* of Senlis in 1389. Married ca. 1373, he had two sons and a daughter, his wife dying in childbirth, probably in 1376. He did not remarry.

Until his final years, Deschamps associated with a wide circle of nobility and important figures, and much of his poetry deals with current political and social events. His works also show that he knew many poets of the time: he writes of a joke that Oton de Granson played on him, composes a ballade in praise of Chaucer and another poem praising Christine de Pizan (in response to a poem of praise from her), and in other works speaks of Philippe de Vitry, Jean de Garencières, and most of the poets of the *Cent ballades*. But his most important literary association was with his fellow Champenois Guillaume de Machaut, who figures prominently in several of his works and whose death he laments in a double ballade with the refrain, *La mort Machaut, le noble rethouryque*. He may have been a nephew of Machaut, whom he credits with "nurturing" (educating?) him. Accordingly, his poetry is mostly in the fixed forms that Machaut popularized. But Deschamps writes more on moral and topical subjects than on his mentor's predominating subject, love, and he did not write long *dits amoureux* comparable with Machaut's.

Deschamps's bulky *œuvre* is almost all preserved in a single thick manuscript compiled a few years after his death (B.N. fr. 840). Ballades predominate, 1,017 surviving. In addition, there are 171 rondeaux, eighty-four virelais, 139 *chansons royales*, fourteen *lais*, and fifty-nine other pieces, including twelve poems in Latin. His one important prose piece is the *Art de dictier et de fere chançons* (1392), probably written to instruct one of his "great lords" in the composition of lyrics; it is the only extant treatise on the art of poetry from 14th-century France. Notable is Deschamps's classification and discussion of poetry without music as "natural music"; musical notation is for him "artificial music." The treatise otherwise concentrates on illustrating the ballade, virelai, rondeau, and *lai*.

Neither of Deschamps's two extant long poems was completed, and in both cases rubrics state that death prevented the author from finishing them. The *Fiction du lyon* is a beast-fable on political events in France, with Charles VI presented as Noble the Lion, Charles the Bad of Navarre as Renard the Fox, and Richard II of England as the Leopard. Deschamps's *Miroir de mariage* is his longest poem by far, 12,004 lines in octosyllabic couplets. Drawing on standard writings against matrimony like St. Jerome's *Adversus Jovinianum*, it opens with a discussion of friendship, which leads to the main question, whether a young man named Franc Vouloir (Free Will) should marry. While such friends as Desir and Folie advise him to take a wife,

Repertoire de Science (Wisdom) counsels against it in a long enumeration of the dangers and ills of carnal marriage. He contrasts spiritual marriage, which Franc Vouloir eventually chooses. The work ends with a poorly integrated review of history, interrupted at the Treaty of Brétigny (1360). The *Miroir* has been thought an important source for Chaucer's *Canterbury Tales*, but this is questionable.

The great bulk of poetry preserved in the major Deschamps manuscript, edited in eleven impressive volumes, his ballade to Chaucer, his wit, and his interest in current affairs have made Deschamps seem a more important poet than he was. Had it not been for a literary friend who gathered his works together after his death and had them copied, there would remain little evidence of his versifying. Much of the work is journalistic, and virtually none of the alleged influence on Chaucer is sure. Nevertheless, Deschamps was undoubtedly a master of the ballade, and his reports of quotidian incident, dialogues, petitions to his patrons, observances of ceremonial events, and a great variety of other discourses in ballade form are often amusing and well done. Without his work, we would certainly know much less about public life and literature in late 14th-century France.

See also **Charles II the Bad; Charles V the Wise; Chaucer, Geoffrey**

Further Reading

Deschamps, Eustache. *Œuvres complètes d'Eustache Deschamps*, ed. Auguste Queux de Saint-Hilaire and Gaston Raynaud. 11 vols. Paris: Didot, 1878–1903. [Vol. 11 includes biographical study and survey of sources.]

Hoepffner, Ernest. *Eustache Deschamps: Leben und Werke*. Strassburg: Trübner, 1904.

Thundy, Zacharias. "Matheolus, Chaucer, and the Wife of Bath." In *Chaucer Problems and Perspectives*, ed. Edward Vasta and Zacharias Thundy. Notre Dame: Notre Dame University Press, 1979, pp. 24–58.

JAMES I. WIMSATT

DHUODA (ca. 800–ca. 845)

Few biographical details remain on Dhuoda, the only known female author of the Carolingian Renaissance. This well-educated noblewoman from a powerful Austrasian family married Bernard, duke of Septimania, at the royal palace at Aachen on June 29, 824. Bernard, a powerful imperial magnate, played an important but unpredictable role in the turbulent 830s and 840s. During the duke's extended absences between the births of their two sons, William (826) and Bernard (841), Dhuoda played a key role administering the province. To counter Bernard's emerging disloyalty, King Charles the Bald summoned William to court as a royal hostage in 841. In response, Dhuoda crafted her *Liber manualis*

(Handbook) to guide her teenage son through his perilous stay at the palace. Tragically, she may have witnessed her husband's execution for treason in 844, and perhaps also that of William in 849 after his failed attempts to avenge his father's death. The younger Bernard (d. 886) lived long enough to carry on the family line, for it was his son, William the Pious of Aquitaine, who founded the monastery Cluny in 910. Dhuoda's own death date is unknown, but the *Liber's* references to her recurring sickness, as well as its detailed instructions for her funeral, indicate that she may have died shortly after finishing her book in 843.

Although much of what is known of Dhuoda centers around the men in her life, her own work has commanded far greater scholarly interest. Written in the genre of the "mirror for princes," the *Liber manualis* endeavored to help William fulfill his complementary and sometimes contradictory roles of son, vassal, and Christian. Despite the author's protestations of ignorance, her advice exhibits an intimate and wide-ranging familiarity with scripture and patristics well situated within the broader literary and theological currents of the Carolingian era. Recent studies of Dhuoda's book have uncovered veiled critiques of Bernard's political inconstancy, as well as several inherent assertions of matriarchal authority. Once dismissed as artless and incoherent, the *Liber manualis* is a monument of medieval women's literature.

Further Reading

Dhuoda. *Manuel pour mon fils*, ed. Pierre Riché, trans. Bernard de Vregille and Claude Mondésert. Sources chrétiennes 225. Paris: Les Éditions du Cerf, 1975.
——. *Handbook for William: A Carolingian Woman's Counsel for Her Son*, ed. and trans. Carol Neel. Lincoln: University of Nebraska Press, 1991.
Dronke, Peter. *Women Writers of the Middle Ages: A Critical Study of Texts from Perpetua (d. 203) to Marguerite Porete († 1310)*. Cambridge: Cambridge University Press, 1984.
Claussen, Martin A. "Fathers of Power and Mothers of Authority: Dhuoda and the *Liber manualis*." *French Historical Studies*. 19 (1996): 785–809.
Nelson, Janet. *Charles the Bald*. London: Longman, 1992.
Riché, Pierre. *The Carolinians: A Family Who Forged Europe*, trans. Michael Idomir Allen. Philadelphia: University of Pennsylvania Press, 1993.

STEVEN A. STOFFERAHN

DIAS, BARTOLOMEU (fl. 1440s)

It is not known when or where this Portuguese navigator was born. Certainly he came from a family with some maritime tradition, for an ancestor was Dinis Dias e Fernandes who explored the North African shore in the 1440s and discovered Cape Verde in 1444.

Ptolemaic and medieval Italian conceptions of the disposition and shape of the Euro-African landmass had led cartographers to grossly underestimate the extent of the African continent. It was probably in the wake of the frustration felt by the Portuguese king João II, when the second expedition of Diogo Cão (1485–1486) revealed a seemingly unending coastline southward, that another expedition was immediately ordered, with Dias as its commander. His fleet consisted of two caravels and a supply ship captained by his brother Diogo.

The fleet left Lisbon in August 1487 and reached the farthest point attained by Diogo Cão (Cape Cross in modern Namibia) in early December. According to some accounts prolonged stormy weather then drove the fleet out of sight of land. In the event, Dias ran, heavily reefed, before the southeast trade winds and, then, at approximately forty degrees south latitude, encountered the Antarctic westerlies, which enabled him to turn to the northeast and make his first landfall, probably in Mossel Bay. He continued eastward as far as the Great Fish River, although his main stop was in Algoa Bay. Here, mindful of serious discontent among the half-starved crew, his fellow officers may have forced a reluctant Dias to turn for home.

On the return journey he discovered the southernmost tip of Africa, Cabo das Agulhas, where he experienced very bad weather. Thus, that when he reached False Bay, he named its promontory Cabo Tormentoso (Cape of Storms); he, or possibly King João, subsequently renamed it Cabo da Boa Esperança (Cape of Good Hope). He reached Lisbon in December 1488 but was received with none of the pomp and munificence enjoyed by his predecessor Diogo Cão or his successor Vasco da Gama. He later took part in Gama's voyage in 1497 and that of Pedro Alvares Cabral in 1500. He died on Cabral's expedition when his ship sank in heavy seas off the Cape of Good Hope.

Dias was the first European navigator to sail entirely out of sight of land in the southern hemisphere, discovering in the process the southeast trades winds and the westerlies; he confirmed that all existing maps of Africa were erroneous, and effectively opened up the sea route from Europe to Asia.

Further Reading

Barros, João de. *Décadas*. 4 vols. 6th ed. Lisbon, 1945.
Peres, Damião. *História dos descobrimentos portugueses*. Oporto, 1943.

ROBERT OAKLEY

DÍAZ DE GAMES, GUTIERRE (EL VICTORIAL)

Only one other fifteenth-century Castilian biography, that of Alvaro de Luna, is comparable in extension and importance to *El Victorial*, the only known work of Gutierre Díaz de Games. Written in an elegant, lively style, the work's lucid prose is enriched by rich nautical vocabulary, painting an expressive tableau composed of both real and imaginary scenes of chivalric life. This biography of Pero Niño, Count of Buelna, is historically authentic; but as a panegyric that exalts its subject to heroic levels, it also becomes a literary narration synthesizing the fifteenth-century European chivalric ideal of victory.

The author makes his presence known at the end of the *proemio*, manifesting not only his close, dependent relationship with Pero Niño but also his privileged position as a reliable witness of the "todas las más de las cavallerías" (*all the other forms of chivalry*) that will be narrated in the text. His position as naval lieutenant would not be incompatible with his career as notary; it seems probable, therefore, that he is the same Gutierre Díaz, notary to the king, who acted as diplomatic ambassador on various occasions during the regency of Fernando de Antequera and the reign of Juan II. The environment of the royal chancellery would have been favorable for the production of what Juan Marichal has called Gutierre Díaz's "voluntad de estilo."

It is commonly believed that Díaz started *El Victorial* in 1435, the year of Pero Niño's last will and testament, which contains a note about the work's commission and destination. However, the author may have begun the biography as early as 1431, when Pero Niño was named Count of Buelna. The work would likely have been finished (save perhaps some of the supplementary material) no later than 1436.

An extensive doctrinal and historical *proemio* opens the text as a means of justifying the novelty of the biographical story. Pero Niño's life will serve as a specific noble and Christian *exemplum* in a chivalric treatise ("tratado de caballería") that had universal appeal. The *tratado* itself, dedicated to narrating the count's life, is divided into three parts. The first relates Pero Niño's lineage, birth, childhood, education, the initiation of his career, and his first marriage.

Díaz shrouds Pero Niño's birth with an aura of legend facilitated by the fact that Enrique III was born around the same time and that Pero Niño's own mother served as the king's wet nurse. In this way the author infers a sort of "blood brotherhood" that is later ratified as the two boys are brought up together at court. To emphasize the count's education, the author incorporates a fragment of the *castigos* used by an anonymous master to indoctrinate the boy. The chapters dedicated to Pero Niño's initiation into knighthood continue incomplete scenes or add details that are absent from Ayala's chronicles; they also add new motifs to the chivalric biography genre, such as the precocity of the hero, the appearance of good omens, fights against animals, the petition of the king's weapons during first battle, or the comic challenge made to a foreign giant. The protagonist's

physical and moral portrait precedes his marriage to his first wife, Constanza de Guevara, which is embellished with a curious discourse on the degrees of love.

The second part relates the expeditions that Pero Niño made to the Mediterranean and the Atlantic as captain of the Castilian fleet between 1404 and 1406. The essentially truthful nature of the historical events narrated in these sections is confirmed through the detail of some of the diary like episodes, that mark the passing of time day by day. Gutierre Díaz takes advantage of Pero Niño's arrival in England to introduce the fictitious "History of Bruto and Dorotea," pushing the chronicle once more into novelistic territory and seasoning the Pero Niño's already notable exoticism with shades of legend. The second part ends with a summary of the knight's participation in the first year of the War of Granada (1407).

The third part tells of the travails of the count's life up to his death. Of particular interest is the chapter on Pero Niño's "conquest" of Beatriz de Portugal, who would become his second wife. The author also includes an exonerative version of Pero Niño's participation in the sacking of Tordesillas, in which Juan II was retained by the *infante* Enrique and his men. The biography ends with a brief description of Pero Niño's exile to Aragón, a result of his support of Enrique's faction; his return and recuperation of the king's trust; a summary of the life of his ill-fated firstborn son, Juan; and passing references to the count's interventions in other military affairs.

Even though it is a fifteenth-century biography, the first representative of a genre associated with the dawn of the Renaissance, *El Victorial* does not display even the slightest humanist influence in its treatment of fame and the biographical subject, nor a trace of knowledge of or curiosity for the classics. Díaz constructs a perfect chivalric world, without fissures, that seems destined to ward off the political and ethical disorder of the real world. He makes use of the basic procedures of the chronicle narrative and the compositional organization of chivalric fiction. The unique characteristics of *El Victorial* arise precisely from the way in which the author attempts to assimilate the aristocratic conceptualization of life. Therefore, the work is as contradictory as it is harmonic, as disconcerting for the collector of objective past facts as it is attractive for the cultural and literary histórian.

Further Reading

Beltrán, R. (ed.) *Gutierre Díaz de Games, "El Victoria."* Salamanca, 1996.

Carriazo, J. M. (ed.) *El Victorial. Crónica de Pero Niño, conde de Buelna. Por su alférez Gutierre Díaz de Games.* Madrid, 1940.

Circourt Puymaigre, C. E. (trans.) *Le Victorial. Chronique de Don Pedro Niño, comte de Buelna. par Gutierre Díaz de Gamez son alferez* (1379–1449). París, 1987.

Evans, J. (selec. and trans.) *The Unconquered Knight. A Chronicle of Deeds of Don Pero Niño, Count of Buelna, by his Standard-bearer Gutierre Díaz de Games* (1431–1449). London, 1928.

Ferrer Mallol, M. T. "Els corsaris castellans i la campanya de Pero Niño al Mediterrani (1404). Documents sobre *El Victorial*," *Anuario de Estudios Medievales* 5 (1968), 265–338.

Marichal, J. "Gutierre Díaz de Games y su *Victorial* " en *La voluntad de estilo. Teoría e história del ensayismo hispánico*. Madrid, 1971, 51–67. Pardo, M. "Un épisode du *mania Victorial*: biographie et élaboration romanesque," *Romania*, 85 (1964), 269–92.

——. "Pero Niño visto por Bernat Metge." In *Studia Philologica. Homenaje ofrecido a Dámaso Alonso.* Vol. III. Madrid, 1963. 215–23. Riquer, M. de. "Las armas en *El Victorial*." In *Serta Philologica F. Lázaro Carrater.* Vol. I. Madrid, 1983. 159–78.

Scholberg, K. R. "Ingenuidad y escepticismo: nota sobre *El Victorial* de Gutierre Díaz de Games," *Hispania* 72 (1989), 890–94.

Surtz, R. E. "Díaz de Games' Deforming Mirror of Chivalry: the Prologue to the *Victorial*," *N* 65 (1981), 214–18.

Tate, Robert B. "The Literary *Persona* from Díaz de Games to Santa Teresa," *Romance Philology* 13 (1960), 298–304.

RAFAEL BELTRÁN

DÍAZ DE VIVAR, RODRIGO (1043–1099)

Rodrigo Díaz was born at Vivar, near Burgos, in 1043, the son of the *infanzón* Diego Laínez. Because of his noble status and the protection of his maternal uncle, Nuño Alvarez, he was reared in the household of Infante Sancho, the son of Fernando I. He accompanied Sancho on his expeditions to protect the petty Muslim king (*tā'ifa*) of Zaragoza against the attacks of Ramiro I of Aragón, whom they defeated at Graus (1063). When Sancho II ascended the throne of Castile (1066), he named Rodrigo royal *alférez* (*armiger regis*, or standard bearer). As such he participated in quarrels with the neighboring kingdoms: a dispute with Navarre over the castle of Pazuengos, in which he gained the nickname *Campi doctor* or *Campeador;* an expedition against the *tā'ifa* of Zaragoza, who had stopped paying tributes (*parias*) to Castile (1067); the battles or "judgments of God" at Llantada (1068) and Golpejera (1072), fought by Sancho II and his brother, Alfonso VI of León, to determine to whom the thrones of Castile and León belonged. Sancho won both battles. Rodrigo's deeds during the siege of Zamora, which supported Alfonso, were extolled in legend. The assassination of Sancho II during the siege (October 1072) forced the Castilians to accept Alfonso as king, although Rodrigo and his followers required him first to swear an oath of purgation, in the Germanic fashion, that he had had no part in Sancho's death and had not plotted it. Rodrigo Díaz became a vassal of Alfonso but lost his important position at court.

In 1074 the king arranged a very advantageous marriage for him to Jimena Díaz, daughter of the Count of Oviedo and great-granddaughter of Alfonso V. At the end of 1079 he went to Seville to collect tribute owed by that *tā'ifa* to Alfonso VI. In 1081, as a consequence of an incursion that he made into the *tā'ifa* kingdom of Toledo, under Leónese protection, and the accusations made against him by Count García Ordóñez and other courtiers, Alfonso VI declared him subject to the *ira regia* (royal wrath), compelling him to go into exile.

Rodrigo's exile with his retinue interrupted his courtly career and launched him on enterprises in which he showed his capabilities and gained fame as well as the nickname El Cid (lord). He rendered military services to the *tā'ifa* of Zaragoza against King Sancho Ramírez of Aragón and Navarre (whom he routed in 1084) and against the Count of Barcelona and the *tā'ifa* of Lérida. After the African Almoravids' first invasion of al-Andalus and their rout of Alfonso VI at Zallāqah (1086), the king received Rodrigo again (in the spring of 1087) and entrusted him with the mission of protecting the *tā'ifa* of Valencia, al-Qādir, formerly king of Toledo. In 1089, when the *tā'ifa* of Zaragoza and the Count of Barcelona besieged Valencia, El Cid received from Alfonso VI all the lands that he might conquer in the eastern part of the peninsula, to be held by hereditary right. He lifted the siege of Valencia, using as a base of operations Albarracín, whose *tā'ifa* resumed payment of tribute to Castile.

The second Almoravid invasion (autumn of 1089) resulted in Rodrigo's disgrace once again because he was unable to relieve the advanced Castilian position at Aledo in the southeast. At the beginning of 1090 he consolidated his protectorate over Valencia when he routed and captured the count of Barcelona near Morella (Battle of the Pines of Tévar), dissolving his coalition with the *tā'ifa* of Lérída, Albarracín, and Zaragoza. The Almoravid conquest of al-Andalus after 1090 required Rodrigo, again in royal favor on various occasions, to strengthen his dominion in the east, thereby covering one of the flanks of the kingdom of Toledo and of all Castile, and blocking the coastal road to the Ebro valley. In the face of this danger, the *tā'ifa* of Zaragoza and Sancho Ramírez of Aragón allied against him. Alfonso VI, who tried to take Valencia in 1092, entrusted the defense of Christian interests in that zone to Rodrigo. Al-Qādir of Valencia was deposed and killed by the Valencian *qādī* Ibn Jahhaf, with Almoravid help. El Cid, with the aid of anti-African Muslims and of the Mozarabs, occupied Valencia and repelled the Almoravid relieving army (Battle of Cuarte, October 1094).

The Cid established himself as "lord of Valencia" and supreme judge, by hereditary right, maintaining his fidelity to Alfonso VI; he coined money and resided with his troops in the citadel of the city. He established a regime of coexistence, allowing the Muslims to keep their property, their system of taxation, and religious liberty, although they surrendered their arms. Former rebels were relocated to the suburb of Alcudia. After the Almoravid attack in January 1097, their defeat in the Battle of Bairén, and the capture of Murviedro (modern Sagunto) in 1098, Rodrigo converted the mosque into a cathedral (the first bishop was a Frenchman, Jerome of Perigord). To consolidate alliances he arranged the marriage of his daughters Cristina and María to Infante Ramiro of Navarre and Ramón Berenger III, Count of Barcelona, respectively. He died 10 July 1099 without a male heir, and Valencia fell to the Almoravids in 1102. Thus the route to the northeast was opened, and Castile's effort to consolidate its dominion in the east was nullified.

Rodrigo quickly became an epic personality, although the memory of his historical existence was not lost. He was a military genius, a hero formed by exile and adventure during the difficult years of the Almoravid invasion; he represented to perfection the values of chivalry and vassalage, the spirit of the frontier, and coexistence between Christians and Muslims, under the aegis of the king-emperor of León and Castile.

Further Reading

Fletcher, R. *The Quest for El Cid.* Oxford, 1989.
Menéndez Pidal, R. *La España del Cid.* 7th ed. Madrid, 1969.
Lacarra, M. E. "*El poema de mío Cid. Realidad histórica e ideología.*" Madrid, 1980.

MIGUEL ANGEL LADERO QUESADA

DIGULLEVILLE, GUILLAUME DE (1295–1358)

Guillaume, son of Thomas of Digulleville (Degulleville or Deguileville), Normandy, lived as a monk in the Cistercian abbey of Chaalis, Île-de-France, from 1326 until his death. He is known for his dream-allegory moral poems. Inspired by Jean de Meun's *Roman de la Rose* and perhaps by other allegories, he created a trilogy on the Piligrimage of Life theme, in which divine grace, nature, and the virtues and vices are personified. He composed the *Pèlerinage de vie humaine* in a first version in 1330–31, with a recension in 1355, and the *Pèlerinage de l'âme* between 1355 and 1358. He wrote a summary of both the second version of the *Pèlerinage de vie humaine* and the *Pèlerinage de l'âme* that survives in its entirety in only one manuscript. In 1358, he wrote the third part, the *Pèlerinage Jhesucrist*. He also composed a series of Latin poems intended for inclusion at the end of the *Pèlerinage de l'âme*, but these remain unpublished, as does the 1355 recension of the *Pèlerinage de vie humaine*. He wrote a further allegorical poem in French, the *Roman de la Fleur de lys*. This last work, which survives in two manuscripts, explains the origins

and symbolism of the arms of France as a defense of the French royal dynasty against the claims of Edward III. Digulleville's popular pilgrimage trilogy, surviving in more than seventy-five manuscripts, inspired Chaucer, Lydgate, and Bunyan. The poems show the way to salvation through obedience to the church, its sacraments, and its principles. The first work takes a Pilgrim-monk from a prenatal vision of the New Jerusalem to his death, with authorial digressions of an encyclopedic nature along the way. In the second pilgrimage, the Pilgrim's soul visits the places on earth where he had sinned, the cemetery where his body rots, and Hell with its torments of the damned, ending in Purgatory. The third part is a life of Christ.

See also **Chaucer, Geoffrey; Jean de Meun; Lydgate, John**

Further Reading

Digulleville, Guillaume de. Le *pèlerinage de vie humaine,* Le *pèlerinage de l'âme,* Le *pèlerinage Jhesucrist,* ed. Jacob Stürzinger. 3 vols. London: Roxburghe Club, 1893, 1895, 1897.
Faral, Edmond. "Guillaume de Digulleville, moine de Chaalis." *Histoire littéraire de la France.* Paris: Imprimerie Nationale, 1962, Vol. 39, pp. 1–132.
Huot, Sylvia. *The* Romance of the Rose *and Its Medieval Readers: Interpretation, Reception, Manuscript Transmission,* Cambridge: Cambridge University Press, 1993, pp. 207–38.
Piaget, Arthur. "Un poème inédit de Guillaume de Digulleville: *Le roman de la Fleur de lys.*" *Romania* 63 (1936): 317–58.

JOAN B. WILLIAMSON

DINIS, KING OF PORTUGAL (1261–1325)

King Dinis, son of King Afonso III and Queen Beatriz of Castile, was born 9 October 1261 and died on 7 January 1325. The sixth king of Portugal, he ascended the throne on 16 February 1279.

During the long reign of Dinis, Portugal reached in many respects its high-water mark in the Middle Ages. The monarch's actions generated significant internal growth within his kingdom and also did much to ensure the viability of Portugal as an independent entity in the Iberian Peninsula. With the Muslim threat largely neutralized, Dinis was free to turn his attention to Portugal's boundaries with Castile. Towns, castles, and strongholds in three areas were of particular concern: (1) those on the east bank of the Guadiana River, (2) those of the Ribacoa district in the region of Boira Baixa, and (3) those near the Castilian border which were under the control of Dinis's younger brother Afonso.

Through shrewd alliances and the judicious use of military force, Dinis took advantage of the dynastic problems in Castile following the death of Sancho IV in 1295. The Portuguese monarch first gained undisputed authority over the towns of Moura, Serpa, and Mourão.

Then, in the Treaty of Alcañices (1297), which definitively fixed Portugal's borders with Castile, Portugal gained the towns and fortresses it desired in the Ribacoa district. The treaty was sealed by marriage alliances between Fernando IV of Castile and Constança, Dinis' daughter, and between Fernando's sister Beatriz and Dinis' heir, the future Afonso IV.

Dinis also resolved the problems inherent in his younger brother's control of a number of towns on the Castilian border, which Prince Afonso used as staging points to intervene in Castilian affairs. Dinis was determined to bring Afonso's towns under royal authority and surrounded his brother's fortresses. In 1299 an accord was reached in which Afonso received privileges over Sintra, Ourém, and other places closer to Lisbon in exchange for his rights over the towns near Castile's borders. This action not only helped secure Dinis' borders, but also removed an irritant to Portugal's relations with Castile.

To further strengthen his kingdom's borders, Dinis undertook a large-scale program of renovation and repair, constructing forty-four new strongholds and castles and repairing many old ones. Also, because many of the border towns were underpopulated, Dinis promoted resettlement. The Ribacoa district and the east bank of the Guadiana River received the greatest attention. But the region north of the Duero River was not neglected. Walls were built to strengthen Guimarães and Braga, as well as several smaller towns. In addition, Dinis had a wall constructed along the banks of the Tagus River to protect Lisbon from attacks by sea.

Related to these activities were Dinis's efforts to separate from Castilian influence and authority the four clericomilitary orders active in Portugal: the Templars, the Hospitalers, Santiago, and Avis. The first two were international orders with headquarters in the Holy Land and branches throughout Europe; the latter two had their origins in the Iberian Peninsula. All four had played important roles in driving out the Muslims, holding the frontiers, and reclaiming the newly won lands. For these activities, the orders had been given extensive spiritual and temporal privileges.

Portugal's conflicts with Castile, especially during the reigns of Sancho IV (1284–1295) and his son Fernando IV (1295–1312), convinced Dinis that his kingdom's security was threatened by the fact that the clericomilitary orders in Portugal were under the jurisdiction of non-Portuguese leaders. Castilian interference in the political and military life of the monk-knights living in Portugal was an ever-present danger, especially in the Order of Santiago. During the Portuguese Reconquest much land and many strongholds had been given to the order. As boundary disputes became more intense during the reign of Sancho IV, Dinis sought to obtain from the papacy a measure of independence for the order. But it was a long, drawn out struggle. However, by the time of Dinis' death, the Portuguese Order of Santiago was for all practical purposes under Portuguese control.

In the meantime the Templars had fallen on hard times. The loss of the Holy Land in 1291 was one of two main factors that led to the demise of the order. The other was the ultimately successful personal campaign of Philip IV the Fair of France and his advisers to destroy the order and gain control of its valuable and extensive holdings. In 1312 Pope Clement V suppressed the Templars and shortly afterward ordered their holdings to be distributed to their archrivals, the Knights Hospitalers. Dinis of Portugal, like a number of the other European monarchs, had sequestered all the Templar properties in his kingdom and put its knights under his protection. The Portuguese monarch's agents at the papal court argued that the annexation of the Templars' properties in Portugal by the Knights Hospitalers would be prejudicial to the Portuguese crown and the Portuguese people. As an alternative, they proposed the foundation of a new order of monk-knights that would incorporate the property of the Templars and, with headquarters in the Algarve, would protect the Portuguese frontier from the Muslims. Clement V's successor, John XXII, agreed with this proposal and on 14 March 1319 by the bull *Ad ca ex quibus* established the Military Order of Our Lord Jesus Christ, which would eventually, by the second half of the sixteenth century, become the premier order in Portugal.

During the reign of Dinis the economic foundations of Portugal were greatly strengthened. So energetic were the monarch's agricultural reforms that he was given the epithet "O Lavrador" (the farmer). Dinis cut back on large landholdings by the church and the higher nobility. He improved landholding patterns on a regional basis and affirmed the nobility of farming one's own land. He promoted the reclamation of marshes and swamps and ordered the planting of pine forests near Leiria to prevent the encroachment of coastal sand and salt as well as to provide needed timber. Dinis's agricultural reforms ranged from the division of uncultivated lands into groups of ten, twenty, or thirty *casais* with lifetime leases in Entre Douro e Minho; to cooperatives in Trás-os-Montes; to an emphasis on repopulating the Alentejo by founding towns, hampering the wealthy from unproductively monopolizing large tracts of property, and granting land to those who would cultivate it. In this way, Dinis increased the number of small proprietors and rural workers who paid rent to the crown. During the thirteenth century, Portugal's population probably numbered between 800,000 and 1,000,000 inhabitants.

Dinis also took note of Portugal's foreign trade. He encouraged the export of agricultural produce, salt, and salted fish to Flanders, England, and France in exchange for textiles and metals. He increased Portugal's foreign contacts as well and encouraged maritime development in the Algarve. In 1293 he supported the creation of a *bolsa de comércio* (commercial fund) by Portuguese merchants for their legal defense in foreign ports. The monarch promoted trade fairs and gave the towns that held them privileges and exemptions. Dinis also reformed the kingdom's coinage. Further, he promoted the mining industry by encouraging the extraction of silver, tin, sulphur, and iron.

Although Portuguese shipping had played a role in the kingdom's defense, as well as in the offensive against the Muslims, it was not until the reign of Dinis that a Portuguese navy was officially established. In 1317 the Portuguese monarch signed a contract with the Genoese Manuele Pessagno (Manuel Peçanha) that made him and his heirs admirals of Portugal and gave him many important rights and privileges. Pessagno was to provide twenty Genoese captains and build up the king's fleet. He was obliged to defend Portugal's coast, but at the same time was free to engage in commerce between his native Italy and England and Flanders.

Dinis ordered the exclusive use of Portuguese as the nation's language. Works of history and law were translated into Portuguese, including the *Siete Partidas* of Dinis's grandfather, Alfonso X of Castile and León. In 1290 papal approval was received for the University of Lisbon, which Dinis had founded several years earlier. In 1308 the university was transferred to Coimbra, where it remained until 1338. Between 1354 and 1377 it was again at Coimbra; then it returned to Lisbon and remained there until 1537.

By promoting royal justice and cracking down on the usurpation of royal prerogatives, Dinis also greatly increased royal authority. He reinstituted the *inquiricMes* (general inquiries) of his predecessors, especially in the regions of Beira Baixa and Entre Douro e Minho. Further, he gradually resolved the kingdom's problems with the papacy, ending the twenty-two years struggle with Rome that had left his father and him excommunicates and Portugal under interdict. In 1289 a compromise, the Concordat of the Forty Articles, was signed. Although the church did not give up any of its ideas regarding the immunity of its holdings and its jurisdiction, it did agree to obey royal authority.

An important figure in Portugal during Dinis's reign was his wife, Isabel—the future St. Isabel—whom he married in 1288. The daughter of Pedro III of Aragón, the Portuguese queen played an important role as a mediator in the feuds between her husband and his brother Afonso, and between the king and his son, the future Afonso IV. In addition, her skill as a conciliator was of major significance in the negotiations leading to the Treaty of Alcañices, which fixed the definitive boundaries between Portugal and Castile.

See also **Clement V, Pope; Philip IV the Fair; Sancho IV, King of Castile**

Further Reading

Livermore, H. V. A. *History of Portugal.* Cambridge, 1947.
Serrão, J. V. *História de Portugal.* Vol. 1. Lisbon, 1977.
Mattoso, J. (ed.) *História de Portugal.* Vol. 2. Lisbon, 1993.

FRANCIS A. DUTRA

DIRC VAN DELF (ca. 1365–ca. 1404)

Dirc van Delf, author of Dutch religious texts, was one of the most learned men of his time. He was probably born in Delft (county of Holland) around 1365. At an early age he entered the Dominican convent at Utrecht. After many years of study he became doctor of theology. From December 1399 onward we find him at the court of Duke Albrecht of Bavaria, count of Holland, in The Hague. There he had the function of court chaplain, but he also lectured at German universities, such as Cologne and Erfurt. We lose all trace of Dirc van Delf after the death of his patron Albrecht in the year 1404.

In 1401, a book presumably written by Dirc for countess Margaret of Cleves, wife of Albrecht, is mentioned in the accounts of the court in The Hague, but unfortunately it has not survived. For Duke Albrecht he started writing around 1403 the *Tafel van den Kersten Ghelove* (*Handbook of the Christian Faith*), a scholastic summa, or compendium, in the vernacular. Stylistically, it is one of the best Middle Dutch prose works, and is indeed one of the most learned encyclopedias of all European vernacular languages. The text consists of two large parts: the Winterstuc (Winter Piece) and the Somerstuc (Summer Piece). The main source of the *Tafel van den Kersten Ghelove* is the *Compendium of Religious Truths* (*Compendium theologicae veritatis*) by Hugh Ripelin of Strasbourg (also known as Hugo Argentinensis, ca. 1210–ca. 1270), but Dirc made use of many other Latin sources as well. Dirc's personal achievement consists in his regrouping and reformulating of this large amount of knowledge. He always takes into account the intellectual level of his audience, and his use of images often corresponds with the experiences of the members of the court. His work deals with the whole creation: there are, among others, chapters about God, the creation of the world, the creation of humankind, the angels, more scientific subjects like the planets, the four elements, physiognomy, and also virtues and vices, God's mercy, the life of Christ, the acts of the apostles, the ecclesiastical hierarchy, works of mercy, liturgy, the sacraments, social order, the Antichrist, and the Last Judgment. Using the Aristotelian system of dialectical reasoning, Dirc expounds God's perfect plan for the laity: nothing is without sense or reason. Finally, he significantly enriched the Middle Dutch vocabulary with neologisms from scholasticism.

His dedication manuscript that has come down to us is illuminated with superb miniatures with an aesthetic as well as a didactic function. They form a concrete support of the text. Besides richly illuminated manuscripts for the aristocracy, less luxuriously executed manuscripts have survived as well. The latter were used by the clergy and especially in nunneries and Beguine communities. In an environment where knowledge of Latin could be problematic, the vernacular *Tafel van den Kersten Ghelove* filled a need for religious reading material. In addition, many miscellanies with religious texts contain excerpts from the *Tafel van den Kersten Ghelove*. A Middle Low German adaptation exists as well.

Further Reading

Daniëls, F. A. M. *Meester Dirc van Delf. Zijn persoon en zijn werk*. Utrecht: N. V. Dekker and Van de Vegt en J. W. van Leeuwen, 1932.
——. ed. *Meester Dirc van Delf, Tafel van den Kersten Ghelove*. 4 vols. Utrecht: N. V. Dekker and Van de Vegt en J. W. van Leeuwen, 1937–1939.
van Oostrom, Frits P. *Court and Culture: Dutch Literature, 1350–1450*. Berkeley: University of California Press, 1992.

AN FAEMS

DOLCINO, FRA (D. 1307)

Fra Dolcino was the leader of the Apostolic Brotherhood, a heretical sect centered in Parma. Under Dolcino the brotherhood became increasingly violent, and it was eventually suppressed by a crusade.

Dolcino was born in the diocese of Novara, the son of a priest. He seems to have received a good education before joining the Apostolic Brotherhood in 1291. The brotherhood had been founded c. 1260 by Gerardo Segarelli; through preaching and apostolic poverty, it sought to usher in a new age of Christian perfection, which the disciples of Joachim of Fiore had predicted would begin in that year. The brotherhood was tolerated at first, but after 1290 it became a target of the Inquisition.

Segarelli was executed in 1300, and soon afterward Dolcino became the leader of the sect. Dolcino proposed a radical form of Joachism that condemned all his opponents, especially the clergy, as ministers of the devil and declared them worthy of death because they were oppressing the true church. He also claimed that he and Segarelli had been sent by God to restore the apostolic life in preparation for Christ's second coming, and that he spoke with the authority of God.

Dolcino and a band of followers fled to the mountains shortly after he took control of the Apostolic Brother-

hood, and soon they were plundering the countryside from a stronghold in the Alps. Pope Clement V called a crusade against them in 1305; two years later an expedition led by the bishop of Vercelli defeated them and captured Dolcino. He was executed on 23 March 1307.

See also **Clement V, Pope; Joachim of Fiore**

Further Reading

Edition
Bernard Gui. *Practica inquisitionis haereticae pravitatis*, ed. Célestin Douais. Paris: Picard, 1886, pp. 340–353.

Critical Studies
Anagnine, Eugenio. *Dolcino e il movimento ereticale all'inizio del Trecento*. Florence: La Nuova Italia, 1964.
Bossi, Alberto. *Fra Dolcino, gli apostolici e la Valdesia*. Borgosesia: Corradini, 1973.
Duprè Theseider, Eugenio. "Fra Dolcino, storia e mito." *Bollettino di Società di Studi Valdesi*, 104, 1958, pp. 5–25.
Miccoli, Giovanni. "Note sulla fortuna di Fra Dolcino." *Annali della Scuola Normale Superiore di Pisa*, Series 2(25), 1956, pp. 245–259.
Orioli, Raniero, ed. *Fra Dolcino: Nascita, vita, e morte di un'eresia medievale*, 3rd ed. Novara: Europia, 1988.

THOMAS TURLEY

DOMINIC, SAINT (C. 1170–1221)

Saint Dominic (Domingo de Guzmàn), the founder of the Dominican order, was born in Castile. He did not come to Italy until he was already the father of the fledgling Order of Preachers, but he spent much of his later life in Italy, and he died in Bologna. His remains rest in the church of San Domenico in Bologna, where they are housed in a great stone monument designed by Nicola Pisano and decorated with scenes from the saint's life and the early years of the order.

As with many saints, Dominic's early life is almost undocumented, but portents were written into it later. His mother was said to have dreamed that she gave birth to a dog holding a torch in its mouth: the dog symbolized Dominic's order, which saw itself as God's watchdogs (*domini canes*) protecting the flock from the wolves of heresy; the torch symbolized Dominic's work of rekindling the fire of charity in a world grown cold. The reality was less dramatic: Dominic became a cleric at an early age and was educated by an uncle. He later studied in Palencia, where he acquired a reputation for devotion and zeal. This led to his appointment as subprior of the cathedral chapter in Osma.

In 1203, Dominic accompanied Bishop Diego d'Acebes of Osma (d. 1207) on a diplomatic mission to Denmark. While the two were returning to Castile, they stopped in Montpellier, where they encountered Cistercians who were discouraged by their failure to win the heretical Cathars back to orthodoxy. Diego and Dominic decided to undertake the challenge of answering error by preaching the truth. So as not to look like worldly prelates, they abandoned all their property and went about unattended by pomp. Here, too, legend would provide miracles befitting the zeal of the saint and his mentor. According to one such legend, there was an ordeal by fire, in which orthodox and Cathar alike committed their writings to the flames; the heretical texts were consumed, but those of the orthodox were spared. The initial results of this apostolate were less spectacular; but when Diego returned to his diocese, Dominic remained to carry on with a few brothers. A house for devout women also was founded at Prouille.

Dominic's young family of preachers continued their work despite the upheavals of the Albigensian crusade. On the invitation of Bishop Fulk of Toulouse, Dominic made that city the seat of his operation. In 1215, he went with Folk to Pope Innocent III's Fourth Lateran Council in Rome. (Another established Dominican legend, often depicted in art, was that at this council Dominic met Saint Francis of Assisi. Still another is that saints Peter and Paul appeared to Dominic and presented him, respectively, with a staff and a gospel book.) While Dominic was in Rome, he sought the pope's approval of his order, but since the council had forbidden the establishment of new orders, the pope required him to adopt the rule of an existing community. Dominic and his followers chose the Augustinian rule, which was by far the most flexible of the models available. Innocent's successor, Honorius III, was quick to extend his approval to Dominic's family once their choice had been made. In 1217, Honorius also approved the name Order of Preachers, which supposedly had first been suggested by Innocent III.

On returning to Toulouse in 1217, Dominic announced a decision to scatter his brothers throughout western Europe. He was helped in this effort by someone he had recruited in Rome, Reginald of Orléans. Reginald, a trained canonist, was in turn able to recruit university-trained clerics. This facilitated not just the work of preaching but the establishment of Dominican convents in Paris and Bologna, Europe's greatest seats of learning. One of Reginald's important recruits was Moneta of Cremona, a master of the arts. Moneta, with the theologian Roland of Cremona, later founded the friars' house in Cremona; he also wrote *Summa against the Cathars and Waldensians*, one of the earliest Dominican polemical works.

Dominic now decided that he needed a base in Rome itself. As in France, he founded houses of both men and women. In Rome, he took over an abandoned Gilbertine house for the friary he founded at San Sisto; later, he entrusted this site to a community of nuns, and the friars,

except for a few chaplains, eventually went to Santa Sabina. The Dominicans would also establish a friary at Santa Maria sopra Minerva in Rome. In Bologna, Dominic made an enthusiastic convert, Diana d'Andalò; but her noble kin refused to allow her to become a nun. Dominic continued to encourage her through his remaining years; but it was left to his successor, Jordan of Saxony, to house Diana and her sister in the monastery of Sant' Agnese.

There was a good reason why Dominic wanted a presence for his friars near the papal court. The diocesan clergy raised considerable objections to having religious do pastoral tasks like hearing confessions, and tradition reserved preaching for bishops. Dominic did discourage his friars from meddling in the affairs of parishes; but he also sought commendations from the papacy for the work of preaching, and Honorius III gave him warm letters of commendation. Honorius's successors would go even farther, granting the friars privileges and often exempting them from episcopal authority. Dominic also made a friend of the papal vice-chancellor, William of Piedmont, whose clerks drafted these papal letters; he himself reciprocated by traveling from Viterbo to Rome to represent the pope in dealings with the Roman populace.

Though he was frequently in Italy, Dominic continued traveling to visit the outposts of his young order. A tour in 1218–1219 included parts of Italy, France, and Spain. One of Dominic's principal efforts was to encourage mendicancy; thus he required the houses in southern France to abandon such fixed revenues as they had obtained. Poverty was fused with preaching, and preaching became tied to a network of houses of study. This allowed the Friars Preachers to avoid, for the most part, a drift into radical opinions that could have threatened the survival of the order. Dominic's emphasis on education can be discerned as early as 1215–1216, when he encouraged theologians to settle in Toulouse. By 1217, friars were being sent to study in Paris. In 1218, Dominic took the first steps toward founding a house of study in Bologna. The Dominicans' educational program focused at first on the Bible, but other subjects were added to the curriculum later. Moreover, instruction of nuns in the rudiments of sound doctrine was encouraged.

This emphasis on education helped make the university cities of Paris and Bologna the two poles of the order. For a time, Dominic concentrated on Italy, while Reginald, until his death, worked from Paris. The first general chapter of the Dominicans was held in Bologna in 1220. At this meeting, it was decided to alternate chapters annually between Bologna and Paris, beginning in Bologna in 1221. Provinces were established to group the friars' convents. It is a mark of the order's youth that Jordan of Saxony, who had been a member of the order for less than a year, became the first provincial of Lombardy. All convents within a province were to have teachers of theology. Other constitutions were adopted to supplement the Augustinian rule; some were adapted from the constitutions of the Praemonstratensian canons, who had been involved in public ministry early in their history.

Dominic had suffered from occasional bouts of dysentery, but they had not discouraged him from traveling extensively to preach and to visit his brethren. In 1221, shortly after the second general chapter of the order, he was overtaken by his final illness, near Santa Maria dei Monti outside Bologna. He was housed in the cell of Moneta of Cremona and had to use Moneta's spare gown. On his deathbed, warning against the temptations of the flesh, Dominic admitted that he had always preferred speaking with young women rather than older ones. According to Jordan's account, Dominic also promised to be of more use to the order after his death than he had been in life. Later, the story was told that at the moment of Dominic's death, Guala, the prior of Brescia, saw a friar being drawn up into heaven on a ladder of gold. Dominic's burial service was conducted by Cardinal Hugolino (later Pope Gregory IX), who was then visiting Bologna.

Shortly after Dominic's death, stories of miraculous cures began to circulate. The friars of Bologna soon had to move the body to a more convenient place; they reported that when the tomb was opened, a sweet odor arose from the body. Early on, efforts were made to secure Dominic's canonization. Testimony was taken in Bologna and then in France, and the results of the inquiry were reported to Pope Gregory IX. After the evidence had been winnowed, in July 1234, the pope declared Dominic a saint. His feast day was fixed as 5 August, the day before the anniversary of his death. Throughout the later Middle Ages, Dominic would be especially venerated by his order, together with Peter Martyr and Thomas Aquinas.

Aside from the legends already mentioned, Dominic left behind few colorful stories. In this regard he differed from Francis; however, Dominic's memory would soon be paired with that of Francis, beginning with the story of their meeting in Rome. In *Paradiso*, Dante, responding to tension between the adherents of the two saints, has Thomas Aquinas praise Francis while Bonaventure, the great Franciscan theologian, praises Dominic. In art, Dominic was depicted with a light, on his forehead, frequently as he clings to the foot of the cross. Panels depicting Dominic's life include scenes such as the trial of theological writings by fire. Not until much later, in the paintings of Pedro Berruguete (d. 1504), would Dominic be shown presiding at an auto-da-fé.

Dominic wrote little that has survived. There is one authentic letter to the nuns in Madrid. *The Nine Ways of Prayer of Saint Dominic* is a considerably later text that probably attained its present form c. 1300; however, it achieved a certain popularity. Recently, art historians have discerned its influence in the paintings done by Fra Angelico for the convent of Observant Dominicans at San Marco in Florence.

See also **Innocent III, Pope**

Further Reading

Early Dominicans: Selected Writings, ed. Simon Tugwell. New York: Paulist, 1982

Galbraith, G. R. *The Constitution of the Dominican Order 1216 to 1360*. Manchester: University Press, 1925.

Georges, Norbert. *Blessed Diana and Blessed Jordan of the Order of Preachers: The Story of a Holy Friendship and a Successful Spiritual Direction*. Somerset, Ohio: Rosary, 1933.

Hinnebusch, William A. *The Dominicans: A Short History*. Dublin: Dominican Publications, 1985.

Hood, William. *Fra Angelico at San Marco*. New Haven, Conn.: Yale University Press, 1993.

Jordan of Saxony. *On the Beginnings of the Order of Preachers*, ed. Simon Tugwell. Dublin: Dominican Publications, 1982.

Koudelka, Vladimir. *Dominic*, trans. Consuelo Fissler and Simon Tugwell, London: Darton, Longman, and Todd, 1997.

Moskowitz, Anita Fiderer. *Nicola Pisano's Arca di San Domenico and Its Legacy*. University Park: Pennsylvania State University Press, 1964.

THOMAS M. IZBICKI

DOUGLAS, GAVIN (CA. 1475–1522)

Scottish poet, churchman, and courtier best known for his translation of Virgil's *Aeneid* (*Eneados*, 1513). Other works include a dream vision, *The Palice of Honour* (1501), and possibly a brief poem on church corruption, "Conscience" (after 1513). The allegory *King Hart*, despite later attribution, is probably not by Douglas. The *Eneados* survives in several manuscripts, of which the early-16th-century Cambridge, Trinity College 1184, is the basis for the most recent scholarly edition (Coldwell); no manuscript of *The Palice of Honour* is extant, but it can be found in three 16th-century printed editions.

A younger son of an earl of Angus, Douglas was drawn to ambition and conflict, both at church and court. His poetic efforts were at least partly intended to attract patronage. Educated at St. Andrews and possibly Paris, he became bishop of Dunkeld in 1516, but the family fortunes declined soon afterward. Douglas ended his life in exile in England.

Douglas's literary output reflects his wide reading in Scots and English vernacular writers, continental poets, and Italian humanists. In both his major works he is deeply proud of his Scottish language yet equally aware of his ambition in introducing classical and continental forms into "rurell termes rude" (*Palice* 126).

Indeed much of *The Palice*'s stylistic power lies in its leaps between highly rhetorical "aureate" language and colloquial diction. *The Palice* shows an encyclopedic command of the conventional motifs of courdy allegory, but it also has descriptive flair and vivid, often comic, dramatic settings. Its narrative centers on the various approaches to honor, through chastity, faithful love, and especially through poetry itself. This looks forward to the *Eneados,* in which lay Douglas's greatest hope for honor and worldly immortality.

The ambitious task of gathering a whole prior tradition into a new language and culture also characterizes the *Eneados.* Douglas seeks to bring not merely the text of Virgil but also the whole medieval and Renaissance Latin tradition surrounding that text to a noble Scots vernacular readership. In addition to the justly famous Prologues to the books of the poem Douglas provides a framework of prose commentary, chapter division, and verse summaries that closely imitates the structure of Latin Virgil manuscripts and early printed editions.

The Prologues are simultaneously apologetic and boastful. They regret the "difference betwix my blunt endyte / And thy scharp sugarate sang Virgiliane" (I Pro. 28–29), and they defuse attacks on Virgil's pagan content by proposing euhemerist, astronomical, and christianizing interpretations of the gods. Yet they criticize Caxton's and Chaucer's earlier English versions of the story. Despite Douglass modesty about his native tradition the Prologues display formal and stylistic variety as great as that which he praises in Virgil: heroic couplets, rime royal, alliterative stanzas, and other forms.

Douglas's translation itself, which replaces Virgil's hexameters with heroic couplets, is remarkably faithful to Virgil, in both spirit and detail. If Douglas rarely captures Virgil's quieter metrical nuances, he consistently succeeds with scenes of action and the more emotional speeches. He expands on Virgil at various points, sometimes adding brief explanations of Virgilian terms (usually derived from Latin glosses on the poem) and sometimes putting additional emphasis on Aeneas's political role. But even more, Douglas's expansions reflect his own readerly enthusiasms: naval technology, storms, hunts, landscapes, and battles. Here, even more than in the artificial structure of the Prologues, Virgil and his Scots translator coalesce into a single, if extended, voice.

Further Reading

Primary Sources

Bawcutt, Priscilla J., ed. *The Shorter Poems of Gavin Douglas.* STS, 4th ser. 3. Edinburgh: Blackwood, 1967.

Coldwell, David F.C., ed. *Virgil's "Aeneid" Translated into Scottish Verse by Gavin Douglas, Bishop of Dunkeld.* STS, 3d ser. 25, 27, 28, 30. Edinburgh: Blackwood, 1957–64.

Secondary Sources

New *CBEL* 1:662–64.

Manual 4:988–1005, 1180–1204.

Bawcutt, Priscilla J. *Gavin Douglas: A Critical Study.* Edinburgh: Edinburgh University Press, 1976.

Blyth, Charles R. *"The Knychtlyke Stile": A Study of Gavin Douglas'Aeneid.* New York: Garland, 1987.

Scheps, Walter, and J. Anna Looney. *Middle Scots Poets: A Reference Guide.* Boston: Hall, 1986, pp. 195–246.

CHRISTOPHER C. BASWELL

DUCCIO DI BUONINSEGNA
(c. 1255 or 1260–1319)

The painter Duccio di Buoninsegna was born in Siena. He was active largely in Tuscany—and especially in Siena—from the 1270s until he died. Along with a few other artists, including Cimabue, Giotto, and the Pisano family of sculptors, Duccio must be recognized as responsible for taking the arts in a new direction and thereby helping to usher in a new cultural era. Ducdo's art has a quality very different from Giotto's but displays the same earnest exploration and experimentation in the depiction of pictorial space and human psychology. Duccio would serve as the touchstone for the Sienese approach to painting for the next 250 years, because he originated a distinctively Sienese type of color, line, composition, and narrative.

The earliest documentary mention of Duccio comes from 1278, when he was paid by the commune of Siena for painting twelve storage chests for official documents. The commune of Siena employed Duccio on numerous occasions. In 1279, 1286, 1291, 1292, 1294, and 1295 he was commissioned by the office of the *biccherna*, the fiscal branch of the government, to paint the wooden panels (known as *biccherna covers*) that bound the communal registers kept in this office. Duccio's panels (now lost) mark the inception of the commune's practice of commissioning such panels from its leading painters, a tradition that was maintained through the fourteenth and fifteenth centuries. Also in 1295, the commune called on Duccio, along with the sculptor Giovanni Pisano, to be part of a commission to decide where to locate the city's new fountain, the Fonte Ovile.

Duccio's frequent employment by the commune of Siena in what appears to have been the early part of his career must indicate that people had confidence in his ability. However, another side of the artist emerges in some of the documents bound in Duccio's *biccherna* covers: his name appears regularly in the register of penalties levied for offenses against the commune. The first of these, from 1280, does not specify Duccio's crime, but the considerable sum of 100 *lire* suggests that it was serious. (To put this in perspective, Duccio was paid only forty-eight *lire* for one of his largest commissions, a now lost *Maestà* painted twenty-two years later for the Palazzo Pubblico in Siena.) Subsequently, fines were imposed on Duccio for refusing to join a citizens' militia raised to do battle in the Maremma, for being absent from meetings of the town council, for refusing to swear an oath to the ruling *podestà*, and possibly for practicing witchcraft, since one fine originated from the office that was in charge of controlling sorcery. Still, these charges cannot have been taken too seriously, for Duccio continued to be employed by the state and ultimately received the most exalted commission the city could confer on an artist—an enormous *Maestà* for the high altar of the cathedral (*duomo*) of Siena.

Only two of Duccio's documented works survive, but fortunately they are two of the most important. The first is the *Rucellai Madonna and Child Enthroned*, commissioned in 1285 by the Confraternity of the Compagnia dei Laudesi for its chapel in Santa Maria Novella in Florence. (This work was transferred to the Rucellai Chapel in the 1500s, and after 1937 it was removed to the Uffizi in Florence.) The other is the *Maestà* for the cathedral of Siena, commissioned by the administrator of the cathedral in October 1308 and brought to the high altar there in June 1311. (Today most of the *Maestà* is in the Museo dell'Opera del Duomo, Siena; but fragments are scattered in many other collections worldwide). Separated by some twenty-six years, these two works set the standard for any additional attributions to Duccio and give a clear idea of his stylistic development.

Because his *biccherna* covers are lost, Duccio's artistic training and activity before the *Rucellai Madonna* are shrouded in mystery. The very fact that early in his career Duccio received such an important commission for a monumental and luxurious altarpiece in one of the largest churches in Florence—which was then Siena's archrival—has led to speculation. Some scholars suggest that the Florentines, who were jealously protective of their own civic accomplishments, would commission only artists with connections to Florence, and therefore that Duccio must at one time been have been a pupil of or collaborator with the Florentine artist Cimabue. This hypothesis is strengthened by the fact that until the twentieth century the *Rucellai Madonna* was believed to have been painted by Cimabue. However, the one surviving work by Duccio that critics are unanimous in placing before the *Rucellai Madonna*, the *Crevole Madonna* (Siena, Museo dell'Opera del Duomo, possibly 1280), shows little relationship to Cimabue, at a time when any such resemblance should have been strongest had Duccio truly been apprenticed to Cimabue. The *Crevole Madonna* demonstrates Duccio's familiarity with the work of later *Duecento* Sienese artists, such as Guido da Siena, and his fundamental indebtedness to the art of Byzantium. The format of the Madonna pointing to the child as the pathway to salvation and the schematization of the Madonna's nose, eyes, and hands are derived from these sources. But this apparently youthful work already shows a refined, elegant, taut line; polished modeling; and a warm humanity that herald a fresh interpretation of an old tradition.

Duccio's refinement is seen again in the *Rucellai Madonna*, perhaps the most opulent altarpiece of the *Duecento*. Since it was recently restored, we can fully appreciate the splendid effect of the fields of precious lapis lazuli blue forming the Virgin's gown, set like a gem against a rich variety of tooled gold patterns and delicate hues forming the throne and the shimmering cloth of honor behind her. Everything about the panel conveys ethereal grace and airiness. The gold hem of the Madonna's cloak trickles slowly down in a wandering, sinuous line. Although the angels are kneeling, they seem weightless, hovering one above another, and grasping the throne as if they might otherwise float away into space. The gold itself plays a role in creating this sense of lightness, for every figure and form, including the throne, is enveloped by gold as if in a bubble. Despite its celestial airiness, the *Rucellai Madonna* is full of details drawn from close analysis of nature. Duccio has abandoned the schematic pattern of gold striation in the Madonna's cloak, which was still in use in Cimabue's *Santa Trinita Maestà*, and has taken great pains to model the form of her body beneath her cloak. The Christ child likewise sits believably on the Madonna's lap and, while giving his blessing, turns his gaze to something at the side that has caught his attention. The accordion folds of the cloth of honor are so carefully modeled that they truly seem three-dimensional. This is an image of exquisite, rarefied elegance, and it must have perfectly fulfilled its function, receiving the hymns of praise sung to the Madonna by the Laudesi before their altar.

Although documents mention a *Maestà*, now lost, painted for the chapel in the Palazzo Pubblico in Siena in 1302, we have no sure example of Duccio's activity after the *Rucellai Madonna* until we reach his greatest masterpiece, the *Maestà* of 1308–1311. Commissioned for the holiest location in the city, the high altar of the cathedral of Siena, the *Maestà* replaced a much venerated image of the Madonna—the *Madonna dagli Occhi Grossi* (Museo dell'Opera del Duomo, Siena)—that was believed to have produced the miraculous victory of the Sienese over the Florentines at the famous battle of Montaperti in 1260. Such an important location required a new altarpiece of suitable grandeur; and while it was still intact the *Maestà* was the largest and most complex polyptych up to its day: 15 feet (4.5 meters) high by 16 feet (4.8 meters) long. The *Maestà* was painted on both sides, the rear panel providing an extensive series of narratives for the devotional meditation of the monks seated in the choir during the mass; the polyptych also had narratives in a series of predella panels below the central scene and an upper tier of pinnacles. Duccio's *Maestà* coincided with Siena's hope of achieving economic and political hegemony in Tuscany, and it was an expression of civic ambition and pride as much as of sacred devotion. This is underscored by Duccio's signature at the base of the Virgin's throne, which invokes the special protection of the Virgin for her city: *Mater Sancta DeiSis Causa Senis Requiei-Sis Ducio Vita-Te Quia Pinxit Ita* ("Holy Mother of God, bring peace to Siena, and life to Duccio, as he painted you this way").

The Madonna is shown enthroned in a gold empyrean as queen of heaven, surrounded by a court of saints and angels; Siena's four patron saints, Ansanus, Savinus, Crescentius, and Victor kneel prominently in the foreground, in supplication for their city. Despite the glittering opulence of this celestial panorama, a new degree of realism pervades the scene, derived from a knowledge of Giotto and Giovanni Pisano. The Madonna is firmly described in terms of full round volumes, and her throne is not the spindly wooden design of the *Rucellai* panel but a solidly anchored marble structure with arms opening outward as in Giotto's *Ognissanti Madonna* (1306–1310, Florence, Uffizi). The narrative scenes framing the enthroned Virgin and covering the back of the altarpiece contain some the most remarkable pictorial advances of the *Trecento*. Beginning with seven scenes of the life of Mary in the front predella, the narrative continued with nine scenes of Christ's earthly ministry in the rear predella, moving on to twenty-six scenes of Christ's passion and resurrection, topped by eight scenes of Christ's life after the resurrection, and, returning to the front, completed by eight episodes from the last events of Mary's life. In their delicacy of line and subtle harmonies of color, these scenes are utterly different from Giotto's narratives in the Arena Chapel; nevertheless, they parallel Giotto's work in their unprecedented exploration of spatial and psychological realism. For example, the *Entry into Jerusalem*, which initiates the cycle of Christ's passion, describes four carefully defined zones of space moving sequentially back into the distance. The skyline of Jerusalem at the top is the most convincing cityscape up to its time (specifically, Siena, with a recognizable cathedral), and it must have provoked Giotto to create his complex cityscapes in the Peruzzi Chapel. Different episodes having the same location in the gospels, such as the events surrounding the Last Supper, or the agony in the garden and the betrayal, are pointedly given the same setting from one scene to the next in Duccio's depictions, establishing a logical continuity which makes the complex structure of the polyptych astonishingly easy to follow. Certain architectural constructions, such as the *Temptation of Christ in the Temple* or the *Feast at Cana*, hint at intricate perspective vistas anticipating the sense of space that would be developed by the Lorenzetti brothers.

On 9 June 1311, after thirty-two months of work on the panel (though there is some speculation that such a large polyptych must have taken longer and thus was begun earlier), the *Maestà* was ready for installation. The day of its transport was declared a civil and religious holiday; all shops were closed, and contemporary documents describe a magnificent procession, amid the ringing of all the bells in the city, of church, dignitaries, government magistrates, drummers and trumpeters, and the general populace of Siena, leading the altarpiece from Duccio's studio down to and around the town square, and up the hill to the cathedral. Nowhere else can the medieval fusion of the civic and the sacred be observed so clearly.

Until 1506 the *Maestà* remained on the high altar of the cathedral; from 1506 onward, it stood in a side chapel, remaining a continuous sourcebook of inspiration for Sienese artists through the sixteenth century. In 1771, it was removed to the small church of Sant' Ansano. Shortly thereafter the polyptych was sawn apart: the front and back were separated, and small panels were removed; these have since been dispersed to various collections, but the bulk of the polyptych has been reassembled and has been exhibited in Museo dell'Opera del Duomo since 1878.

Little is known for certain about Duccio's activity after the completion of the *Maestà* until his death (by 1319). The main work attributed to him during this period is a polyptych of the *Madonna and Saints* (number 47, after 131, Siena, Pinacoteca). Other important works attributed to Duccio include a glass oculus of the *Dormition*, *Assumption*, and *Coronation of the Virgin* and *Saints* in the choir wall of the cathedral of Siena (1288); a *Maestà* (1288–1300, now in the Kunstmuseum, Bern); a tiny panel of the *Madonna and Child with Three Kneeling Franciscans* (c. 1300, Siena, Pinacoteca); a *Madonna and Child* (c. 1300, Stoclet Collection, Brussels); a portable triptych of the *Madonna and Saints* (c. 1305, London, National Gallery); a *Madonna and Child with Six Angels* (c. 1305, Perugia, Galleria Nazionale dell'Umbria); and a dossal of the *Madonna Flanked by Four Saints* (c. 1305, Siena, Pinacoteca). A fresco discovered in 1980 in the Sala del Mappamondo in the Palazzo Pubblico of Siena, *Submission of a Castle to Siena*, has also been attributed to Duccio (c. 1314).

Immediate followers of Duccio included his nephew, Segna da Bonaventura, the Badia a Isola Master, and Ugolino da Siena; and it seems extremely likely that major *Trecento* Sienese artists such as Simone Martini and Pietro and Ambrogio Lorenzetti were also Duccio's apprentices.

See also **Cimabue; Giotta; Lorenzetti; Martini, Simone; Pisano, Giovanni**

Further Reading

Cattaneo, G., and E. Baccheschi. *L'opera completa di Duccio*. Milan: Rizzoli, 1972.

Cole, Bruce. *Sienese Painting from Its Origins to the Fifteenth Century*. New York: Harper and Row, 1980.

Deuchler, Florens. *Duccio*. Milan: Electa, 1983.

Jannella, Cecilia. *Duccio*. Florence: Scala, 1991.

La pittura in Italia: Il Duecento e il Trecento, 2 vols. Milan: Electa, 1986.

Ragionieri, Giovanna. *Duccio: Catalogo completo dei dipinti*. Florence: Cantini, 1989.

Santi, Bruno, et al. *La Maestà di Duccio restaurata*. Florence: Centro Di, 1990.

Stubblebine, James H. "Duccio and His Collaborators in the Cathedral Maestà." *Art Bulletin*, 55, 1973, pp. 185–204.

———. *Duccio di Buoninsegna and His School*. Princeton, N.J.: Princeton University Press, 1979.

White, John. "Measurement, Design, and Carpentry in Duccio's Maestà." *Art Bulletin*, 55, 1973, pp. 334–366; 547–569.

———. *Duccio: Tuscan Art and the Medieval Workshop*. London: Thames and Hudson, 1979.

GUSTAV MEDICUS

DUFAY, GUILLAUME
(Du Fay, Du Fayt; 1397–1474)

Composer, musician, and cleric. During a career that spanned over fifty years, Dufay produced some of the finest music of the late Middle Ages. Contemporary esteem for Dufay and his music was matched only by the reputation of his contemporary Gilles Binchois.

Dufay's life and peripatetic musical career have been outlined to an extent matched by no other 15th-century composer. There are hundreds of surviving documents relating to his career, and gaps in the documentary record are often filled by evidence from the occasional works he composed. According to recent discoveries by Planchart, Dufay was born near Brussels, the illegitimate son of a priest, on August 5, 1397. The earliest documents regarding his musical career date from 1409, when he is listed as a *puer altaris* at Cambrai cathedral. By 1414, he had risen to the rank of *clericus altaris* and had been granted a chaplaincy at Cambrai. His precise whereabouts are unknown over the next few years, but it is likely that he was at the Council of Constance, possibly in the entourage of Pierre d'Ailly, bishop of Cambrai.

During the early 1420s, Dufay was in northern Italy. Two of his earliest datable works were written for the Malatesta family. He returned to France for a time, from 1423 or 1424 until 1426, probably with an eye toward securing prebends in the area of Laon. His rondeau *Adieu ces bons vins de Lannoys* (1426) bade fond farewell to Laon, as he returned once more to Italy. Dufay was in Bologna by early 1426, serving as secretary to Cardinal Louis Aleman, under whom he was ordained in 1427 or 1428. From 1428 until 1433 or 1434, Dufay served popes Martin V (d.1431) and Eugenius IV in the papal chapel, where he was associated with some of the best composers of the day, among them Arnold de Lantins and Johannes Brassart. His output included occasional motets in celebration of Eugenius IV.

Dufay traveled extensively over the next few years. During 1434–35, he was in the employ of the court of Savoy and made at least one extended visit to Cambrai. At Savoy, Dufay met Gilles Binchois for the first time; it was probably this meeting that is documented in Martin Le Franc's *Champion des dames*. He returned to Italy in 1435, rejoining the entourage of Eugenius IV in Florence. Dufay composed the motet *Nuper rosarum flores* in 1436 for the consecration of Florence cathedral by Eugenius. By 1437, he had returned once again to the court of Savoy, composing one of his last isorhythmic motets, *Magnanimae gentis* (1438), in celebration of a peace treaty between Louis, duke of Savoy, and Louis's brother, Philippe, count of Geneva.

By 1439, Dufay had settled once more in Cambrai, although he was frequently absent throughout the rest of his life, both on cathedral business and on a few freelance excursions. Dufay's activities at Cambrai included a wide variety of musical and clerical duties: supervising choirboys and *petits vicaires* and overseeing the revision and editing of the cathedral's choirbooks. Throughout the 1440s, Dufay maintained an unofficial though familiar relationship with Philip the Good, duke of Burgundy, and some of Dufay's liturgical music of this period, including a sizable number of Mass Proper settings, was composed for the Burgundian chape. Louis, duke of Savoy, continued to woo the composer as well, and during an extended absence from Cambrai, in 1452–58, Dufay was employed by the Savoy court. It was probably during this last Savoy sojourn that Dufay composed most of his late songs. By 1458, Dufay had returned to Cambrai and remained there for the rest of his life, although he maintained contact with several important patrons, including the dukes of Burgundy and Savoy and, indirectly, with young Lorenzo de' Medici of Florence.

When Dufay died on November 27, 1474, he left explicit instructions regarding the music to be sung at his funeral, which was to include his large four-voice setting of the Marian antiphon *Ave regina celorum*. His will attests to a man of considerable means—books, furnishings, property, and money garnered from a lifetime of patronage and shrewd trading in canonical benefices. There is evidence that both Johannes Ockeghem and Antoine Busnoys composed *déplorations* on Dufay's death, although these works are now lost.

Dufay composed in virtually every polyphonic form of the 15th century, and it has recently been discovered that he composed plainchant as well. His works show an impressive command of every compositional technique available to a 15th-century musician: *faux-bourdon*, isorhythmic writing, *cantus firmus* technique, and imitation.

Dufay's thirteen, possibly fourteen or fifteen, surviving isorhythmic motets are among the latest and finest examples of this longstanding compositional tradition. In nearly all cases, they are works written for a specific event or patron, or may be tied to a period in Dufay's career. His earliest isorhythmic motet, *Vasilissa ergo gaude*, continues the tradition of Royllart's *Rex Karole* (written some forty-five years earlier for Charles V). The brilliant *Ecclesie militantis*, a motet written between 1431 and 1433 for Eugenius IV, is Dufay's most complex essay in isorhythm, in six sections, with two tenors based on different chants and three texted upper voices. With *Supremum est mortalibus* (1433) and his later isorhythmic motets, Dufay turned toward a simpler style, based upon English practices, with long upper-voice duets delineating the *talea* structure.

The majority of Dufay's surviving works are sacred: perhaps thirty or more settings of the complete Mass Ordinary, combined Ordinary and Proper, or Proper; nearly forty additional Mass movements; and nearly fifty settings of hymns, Magnificats, and antiphons for the Office and Marian antiphons. During the 1440s, Dufay conceived at least two large cycles of Proper settings, a series of Masses to various martyrs for Cambrai, and a cycle of votive Masses, probably for the Burgundian Order of the Golden Fleece. In the *Missa Se la face ay pale* and *Missa L'homme armé*, possibly written in the 1450s for the Savoy court, Dufay used secular tenors as a unifying device. His latest Mass, the *Missa Ave regina celorum*, was written in 1472 for the dedication of Cambrai cathedral. Dufay foreshadows later practices in Mass composition by quoting and reworking polyphonic material from his own motet *Ave regina celorum* and his *Missa Ecce ancilla*.

In his Office music and nonliturgical Latin works, Dufay sets the chant usually in the uppermost voice, often paraphrased, transforming it into a flowing melody similar to that of his secular songs. The simplest settings are his Office hymns, set in *fauxbourdon*. Some of Dufay's most expressive writing appears in his settings of Marian antiphons. His four-voice *Ave regina celorum* (ca. 1464), sung at Dufay's funeral and reworked in his *Missa Ave regina*, uses the chant melody as a *cantus firmus* and includes emotional prayers on behalf of the composer himself.

There are over eighty surviving songs by Dufay, composed from ca. 1420 to ca. 1465. His earliest songs exhibit a great variety of styles, from the virtuosity and notational complexity of *Resvelliés vous* (1423) to relatively simple works, such as the rondeau *J'atendray tant*. His late songs, such as *Adieu m'amour* or *Par le regart*, products of a composer in his fifties and sixties,

are more sedate than the vivacious songs of the 1420s and exhibit careful attention to text expression and formal balance.

Dufay and Binchois were acknowledged by their contemporaries as the best song composers of their generation, but there are striking differences between them. Binchois's nearly sixty songs are more or less unified in style, while Dufay's song style evolved substantially over his career. As in Binchois's songs, Dufay's most frequent subject is courtly love, but his works exhibit great variety, with texts celebrating May Day or New Year's Day (*Ce jour le doibt* and others), honoring patrons (*Resvelliés vous* for Carlo Malatesta), and other subjects. Like those of Binchois, the bulk of Dufay's texts are in fixed forms—rondeau, ballade, and (in later works) *bergerette*—but his songs also include settings of Latin or Italian poetry, including Petrarch's *Vergene bella*.

See also **Philip the Good**

Further Reading

Dufay, Guillaume. *Guillelmi Dufay: opera omnia*, 6 vols. (Vol. 1 in two parts), ed. Heinrich Besseler. Rome: American Institute of Musicology, 1951–66.

Adas, Allan, ed. *Papers Read at the Dufay Quincentenary Conference, Brooklyn College, December 6–7, 1974.* New York: Department of Music, School of Performing Arts, Brooklyn College, 1976.

Fallows, David. *Dufay.* London: Dent, 1982.

Planchart, Alejandro Enrique. "Guillaume Du Fay's Benefices and His Relationship to the Court of Burgundy." *Early Music History* 8 (1988): 117–71.

——. "The Early Career of Guillaume Du Fay." *Journal of the American Musicological Society* 46 (1993): 341–68.

Wright, Craig. "Dufay at Cambrai: Discoveries and Revisions." *Journal of the American Musicological Society* 28 (1975): 175–229.

J. Michael Allsen

DUNBAR, WILLIAM (ca. 1460-ca. 1513)

The most brilliant of the late-medieval Scottish poets. Dunbar graduated from St. Andrews University in 1479. For the next twenty years biographical evidence is lacking, but he may have been abroad; in 1500–01 he was in England. The most fully documented period in Dunbar's life is from 1500 to 1513; he then received a generous "pensioun," or annual salary, as a "servitour" in the household of James IV. Yet the details of Dunbar's court career remain mysterious. This is one reason why it is difficult to establish the chronology of the 80 or so poems attributed to him. Although a chaplain, Dunbar never obtained high office in the church. Several poems voice hopes for a benefice, yet there is no evidence that he obtained even the humble "kirk scant coverit with hadder [heather]" mentioned in one of them. It is likely that Dunbar had some role in the royal secretariat, perhaps as a scribe or envoy. He is last mentioned on 14 May 1513, but there is a gap in the records following the Battle of Flodden (September 1513), in which James IV died; Dunbar possibly survived into James V's reign, but there is no evidence that he did so.

The court provided Dunbar not only with a livelihood but also with his primary audience and much of his subject matter. Many of his poems are located "heir at hame" in Scotland; he writes of actual people, sometimes explicitly, sometimes obliquely, through the medium of dream, table, and fantasy. He celebrates some of the great festive occasions in James IV's reign—*The Thrissill and the Rois* treats of the king's marriage to Margaret Tudor in 1503, and another poem describes the queen's visit to Aberdeen in 1511. He employs two favorite courtly modes, eulogy and elegy: greeting the distinguished knight Bernard Stewart in one piece and lamenting his death in another. But Dunbar also writes, more informally, about trivial events—what he sees, in his own words, "Daylie in court befoir myn e [eye]." He devises comic squibs about fellow servitors, including fools and alchemists. Many poems were written, in the first instance, for a small group of people—king, queen, and courtiers, several of whom were, like Dunbar, both "clerkis" and poets. These poems are playful and recreative, intimate in tone and often colloquial.

Scholars have sought, with little success, to establish Dunbar's indebtedness to earlier writers. It is often easier to indicate the genres to which his poems belong than to pinpoint sources. Yet "Timor Morris Conturbat Me" reveals keen interest in other Scottish poets, from the 14th century to his own time; and he was also familiar with alliterative works, such as Richard Holland's *Buke of the Howlat*. Dunbar seems aware of the Gaelic literary tradition but humorously dissociates himself from it in *The Flyting of Dunbar and Kennedy*. Ignoring the political boundaries between England and Scotland, Dunbar embraces their shared language and poetic traditions. At the close of The *Goldyn Targe* he speaks of "oure Inglisch," and pays homage to the high style of poetry associated with Chaucer and Lydgate; he himself writes in this tradition effectively.

Yet Dunbar was also familiar with less sophisticated literary forms—drinking songs, bawdy love poems, and the ballads he mentions in "Schir Thomas Norny." Casual, throw away remarks in this and other poems provide our chief clues both to Dunbar's literary tastes and his view of himself as a poet. He calls himself a "makar" and his poetry "making." Such terms lay stress on the poet as craftsman and the poem as artifact; most critics see Dunbar in this light, praising him less for the originality of his ideas than for his verbal "energy" and metrical virtuosity.

Dunbar's finest poems almost all contain some strain of comedy. His range of tone is wide: occasionally flippant and bantering but more often sardonic and derisive. He does not merely mock deviants and outsiders, traditional comic butts like the friars, or those low in the social hierarchy; he makes fun of himself and can be disrespectful to the king. Dunbar delights in exploiting areas of social tension, between Lowlanders and Highlanders, clerics and laypeople, or men and women. Certain modes seem particularly congenial. He is a master of invective and grotesque portraiture and also excels at parody and burlesque. Several poems are mock-chivalric, and two, "The Dregy" and "The Testament of Andro Kennedy," draw upon the tradition of medieval Latin parody. Dunbar is a witty poet, but his wit is contextual, displayed less in neat epigrams than in topical allusions, puns, and a pervasive irony, particularly evident in his ambitious poem the *Tretis of the Tua Mariit Wemen and the Wedo*. A cluster of dream poems displays a strikingly black "eldritch" comedy.

Dunbar also wrote fine hymnlike religious poems and other wholly serious verse, some of which is didactic in a manner uncongenial to modern readers; yet such pieces were popular with contemporaries. Their style is plain, and their tone impersonal and hortatory. Many could have been written by any competent poet of the time; indeed several attributed to Dunbar in one manuscript are elsewhere assigned to another poet or anonymous. This uncertainty as to authorship is symptomatic of their extreme conventionality. Yet some of Dunbar's moral poems, which undoubtedly spring from this same tradition, have far greater individuality. Two of the finest, "Timor Mortis Conturbat Me" and "In to thir Dirk and Drublie Dayis" (by later editors called "The Lament for the Makaris" and "Meditatioun in Wyntir"), give poignant expression to ancient commonplaces about death and mutability.

Dunbar's poems are so varied that critics find it difficult to form a coherent image of their protean author. Some seek to reconcile the disparate elements in his poetry through an underlying "morality"; others stress rather the generic nature of his poems. The exact degree of self-expression in Dunbar remains difficult to assess but seems to fluctuate. The "I"-figure of some poems is largely a narrative persona, and in others a spokesman for orthodox morality; but in some, particularly the petitionary poems, we hear an intimate and private-sounding voice.

See also **Chaucer, Geoffrey; Douglas, Gavin; Henryson, Robert**

Further Reading

Primary Sources

Bawcutt, Priscilla, ed. *William Dunbar: Selected Poems*. London: Longman, 1996.

Kinsley, James, ed. *The Poems of William Dunbar*. Oxford: Clarendon, 1979.

Secondary Sources

New *CBEL* 1:660–62.

Manual 4:1005–60,1204–84.

Bawcutt, Priscilla. "Aspects of Dunbar's Imagery." In *Chaucer and Middle English Studies*, ed. Beryl Rowland. London: Allen & Unwin, 1974, pp. 190–200.

Bawcutt, Priscilla. "William Dunbar and Gavin Douglas." In *The History of Scottish Literature*. Vol. 1, ed. R.D.S. Jack. Aberdeen: Aberdeen University Press, 1988, pp. 73–89.

Bawcutt, Priscilla. *Dunbar the Makar*. Oxford: Clarendon, 1992.

Baxter, J.W. *William Dunbar: A Biographical Study*. Edinburgh: Oliver & Boyd, 1952.

Fox, Denton. "Dunbar's *The Golden Targe*." *ELH 26* (1959): 311–34.

Morgan, Edwin. "Dunbar and the Language of Poetry." *EIC 2* (1952): 138–58.

Reiss, Edmund. *William Dunbar*. Boston: Twayne, 1979.

Ross, Ian. *William Dunbar*. Leiden: Brill, 1981.

Roth, Elizabeth. "Criticism and Taste: Readings of Dunbar's *Tretis*." *Scottish Literary Journal* Supplement 15 (1981): 57–90.

Scheps, Walter, and J. Anna Looney. *Middle Scots Poets: A Reference Guide*. Boston: Hall, 1986, pp. 119–94.

PRISCILLA BAWCUTT

DUNS SCOTUS, JOHN
(ca. 1266–1308)

Born in Scotland, Duns Scotus probably obtained his early education at the Franciscan convent in Dumfries, where he entered the order by 1280. He was sent to Oxford no later than 1290 to begin his studies and may have received his baccalaureate there. He lectured on the *Sententiae* of Peter Lombard at both Cambridge and Oxford. Ordained at Northampton in 1291, he went to the University of Paris in 1293 to study for the master's degree in theology, but before completing the degree he returned in 1296 to Oxford, where he commented again on the *Sententiae*. Duns Scotus went once more to Paris in 1302 and continued to lecture on the *Sententiae*. He was exiled in 1303, when he opposed Philip IV the Fair's appeal to a general council against Pope Boniface VIII. He returned in 1304, received the master's degree in 1305, and became regent master in the Franciscan chair for the next two years. In 1307, he was sent to teach at the Franciscan house in Cologne, where he died on November 8, 1308.

Possibly nicknamed "the Scot" early on at Oxford, he engaged in theological disputes with such skill and subtlety that he posthumously received the scholastic titles *Doctor subtilis* and *Doctor maximus*. Duns Scotus extended the moderate realism of Albert the Great and Thomas Aquinas but was intent less on constructing a system than on pursuing, often relentlessly, solutions to philosophical and theological problems that he considered to blemish the systems of his predecessors, such as the issues of contingency, individuation, distinctions and univocity of being, the primary object of the intellect, and the relation of love and will to intellect. He took immense pains to distinguish and then properly to reconnect the tasks and provinces of "philosophy" and "theology." He reacted to the efforts of Henry of Ghent and others to reestablish Augustinianism at the University of Paris. Although influenced by Avicenna, he rejected both Augustinian and Aristotelian epistemologies and argued that being, not God or material things or their essences, is the primary object of knowledge. He saw theology as a science whose knowledge provides the "practical" means to reach the soul's supernatural end. He emphasized the special uniqueness, or *haecceitas*, of the individual, because each is the product of God's thoroughly free creative and loving election. He distinguished between nature and will and argued that the will alone possesses fundamental freedom and is the primary rational power. He analyzed the human capacity to love and to experience God. He distinguished the will's inclination to choose what is advantageous from its "affection" toward justice for its own sake, which enables the will to love God for God's sake and not for the soul's advantage alone. Scotus's concept of intellectual intuition explained the capacity of beatific and unique temporal visions of God in contrast with the ordinary process of knowledge through sensory experience. He promoted the doctrine of the Immaculate Conception and maintained that the Incarnation would have occurred regardless of the Fall.

Duns Scotus's principal composition was his commentary on the *Sententiae*. The two chief extant versions are included in the collections *Opus Oxoniense*, especially the *Ordinatio*, and in the *Opus Parisiense*, also known as the *Reporta Parisiensia*, containing notes from students and scribes. The *Tractatus de Primo Principio* and the quodlibetal questions represent his mature theological constructions. He also composed a series of logical commentaries, in the genre of "questions," on Porphyry's *Isogoge* and Aristotle's *Categories*. Especially interesting are his *Collationes*, composed of disputations held at Oxford and Paris. His writings not only influenced later Franciscan theologians, known as the Scotists, but also such diverse figures as Galileo, C.S. Peirce, and Gerard Manley Hopkins.

See also **Albert the Great; Aquinas, Thomas; Boniface VIII, Pope; Peter Lombard**

Further Reading

Duns Scotus, John, *Opera omnia*, ed. Luke Wadding. Lyon: Sumptibus Laurentii Durand, 1639.

——. *Opera omnia*. Vatican City: Typis Polyglottis Vaticanis, 1950–.

——. *Philosophical Writings*, trans. Allan B. Wolter. Indianapolis: Bobbs-Merrill, 1962.

——. *A Treatise on God as First Principle: A Latin Text and English Translation of the De Primo Principio*, ed. and trans. Allan B. Wolter. 2nd ed. Chicago: Franciscan Herald, 1983.

——. *Duns Scotus on the Will and Morality*, ed. and trans. Allan B. Wolter. Washington, D.C: Catholic University of America Press, 1986.

——. *God and Creatures*: *The Quodlibetal Questions*, ed. and trans. Allan B. Wolter and Felix Alluntis. Princeton: Princeton University Press, 1975.

Schäfer, Odulfus. *Bibliographia de vita, operibus et doctrina I. D. Scoti saecula XIX–XX*. Rome: Orbis Catholicus, 1955.

Wolter, Allan B. *The Transcendentals and Their Function in the Metaphysics of Duns Scotus*. St. Bonaventure: Franciscan Institute, 1946.

H. LAWRENCE BOND

DUNSTABLE, JOHN (ca. 1395–1453)

Composer, mathematician, and astronomer. He is the author of over 70 surviving works, including music for masses, offices, Marian devotions, isorhythmic motets, and secular songs. Dunstable (or Dunstaple) stands at the head of an influential group of English composers whose music, beginning in the later 1420s and 1430s, circulated on the Continent, where it had an immense stylistic impact. Fifteenth-century musical commentators recognized Dunstable's importance, and he held a high posthumous reputation for many subsequent generations.

Of Dunstable's biography we know little. The paucity of documentation seems to be due to a career that kept him out of the records of the court, and there is no evidence of a direct association with any cathedral or monastic establishment or the Chapel Royal. He seems to have begun composing around 1415, but he is not represented in the first layer of the Old Hall Manuscript, which was copied by 1421. A few long-known pieces of evidence, along with important recent archival discoveries, suggest that Dunstable was in service to John duke of Bedford before 1427; moved into the household of the duke's stepmother, the dowager Queen Joan, from 1427 until her death in 1437; and at that point entered the *familia* (household) of her stepson and John's brother, Humphrey duke of Gloucester. Dunstable's relationship with Gloucester is described as that of "serviteur et familier domestique," an appellation that probably can be extended to his previous relationships with John and Joan, suggesting a high-ranking role in administrative service while not, significantly, a member of the household chapel. Though Dunstable's music is preserved mainly in continental sources, it now appears that his personal presence in France was limited and intermittent. Thus he is not likely to be the central agent in the transmission of English music across the Channel that he was once thought to be.

The scale and nature of the rewards Dunstable received from his patrons indicate the high regard they held for him. He enjoyed lavish gifts, landed income at a high level, and a large annuity from Queen Joan; and he held a lordship, estates, and fiefs in Normandy under the patronage of Gloucester in the years 1437–41. In England Dunstable owned property in Cambridgeshire, Essex, and London. Documents style him esquire or armiger, suggesting he was a wealthy landholder of an order of society just below the knightly class. In London he held rents in the parish of St. Stephen Walbroke, in which church he was buried, outlived by his wife and other descendants. The church and his monument do not survive, but his epitaph there was recorded. A second epitaph, by John of Wheathampstead, abbot of St. Albans, is also known. Dunstable's further ties to St. Albans include two motets, one on St. Alban (the text is possibly by Wheathampstead) and another on St. Germanus. The composer's link to the abbey undoubtedly came through two of his employers, Queen Joan and Gloucester, who were among its principal aristocratic benefactors (Gloucester was buried there).

Dunstable's music is the preeminent exemplification of the influential "nouvelle practique" that one continental observer of around 1440 called "la contenance Angloise." Chief features of this style include the predominance of triple meter in flowing rhythms of quarter notes and eighth notes with gentle syncopations and hemiola, smooth triadic melodies with distinctive cadential turns of phrase, and a uniformly consonant harmonic-contrapuntal language rich with the warm sound of imperfect consonances—thirds, sixths, and tenths.

Dunstable's eleven isorhythmic motets are among the last in an English and continental tradition stretching back to the middle of the 14th century. Polytextual, based on plainsong tenors, and written for three or four voices, they are almost all variations upon a "classical" pattern with tripartite proportional diminution. Sustaining a particularly English tradition, their texts are all sacred, with six dedicated to saints (John the Baptist, Catherine, Alban, Germanus, Michael, Anne), three to the Virgin Mary, and two for Whitsunday. Their origins are likely to have been ceremonial rather than strictly liturgical. From the testimony of a chronicler it appears that Dunstable's motet on John the Baptist, *Preco preheminencie Precursor premittitur* with tenor *Inter natos* (perhaps one of his earliest compositions), was sung before Henry V and Emperor Sigismund in Canterbury Cathedral on 21 August 1416 to celebrate victory at the siege of Harfleur and the Battle of the Seine.

For settings of liturgical texts outside the mass Ordinary Dunstable principally draws upon processional and office antiphons for Mary, constructing compositions of roughly the same dimensions as an isorhythmic motet or mass movement that are destined for performance at Marian devotions. These pieces are nearly all for three voices, occasionally reducing to two, with a songlike top part over a supporting tenor and contratenor; some are based on chant but the majority are freely composed. Though neither polytextual nor isorhythmtc, they were apparently regarded as a species of motet by some continental scribes, and they are called motets by many modern authorities. It has been shown recently that careful mathematical planning governs their proportions.

Most of Dunstable's compositions for the Ordinary of the mass (Kyrie, Gloria, Credo, Sanctus, Agnus) are single isolated movements; all but three of these pieces are freely composed, without reference to plainsong. In the 1420s and 1430s, however, Dunstable and his English contemporaries, including Leonel Power and John Benet, pioneered the musical integration of a complete five-movement mass cycle, achieving unification by using the same "alien" *cantus firmus* as the tenor in all movements. These early English cyclic tenor masses were based on sacred plainsongs (antiphons and responds); Dunstable's cycles include *Jesu Christi filli Dei*, *Da gaudiorum premia*, *Rex seculorum* (also ascribed to Leonel), and a *Missa "sine nomitte"*(also ascribed to Leonel and Benet). It may be the case that a number of anonymous cycles of the 1440s are also of Dunstable's authorship. Continental composers, such as Guillaume Dufay, began to imitate these English cycles around 1450.

Few secular songs survive by members of Dunstable's generation. Sources credit him with just three, two of which are plausibly attributed elsewhere to a younger contemporary, John Bedingham, leaving only a French-texted rondeau, *Puisque m'amour*, to represent the courtly side of his output. However, Dunstable's lifetime saw the great flowering of the polyphonic carol, and amid this anonymous repertoire are likely to be works by the great English master.

See also **Power, Leonel**

Further Reading

Primary Sources

Bukofzer, Manfred, ed. *John Dunstable: Complete Works*. 2d rev. ed., prepared by Margaret Bent, Ian Bent, and Brian Trowell. Musica Britannica 8. London: Stainer & Bell, 1970.

Secondary Sources

Bent, Margaret. *Dunstaple*. London: Oxford University Press, 1981.

Bent, Margaret. "Dunstable." *NGD* 5:720–25.
Stell, Judith, and Andrew Wathey. "New Light on the Biography of John Dunstable?" *Music and Letters* 62 (1981): 60–63.
Trowell, Brian. "Proportion in the Music of Dunstable." *Proceedings of the Royal Musical Association* 105 (1978–79): 100–41.
Wathey, Andrew. "Dunstable in France." *Music and Letters* 67 (1986): 1–36.

PETER M. LEFFERTS

DUNSTAN OF CANTERBURY
(ca. 910–988)

Monk and archbishop of Canterbury. The son of a Somerset noble, he was educated at Glastonbury Abbey, probably by Irish monks. Related to the royal line with several kinsmen who held episcopal sees, in his youth he was often at the court of King Æthelstan. The enmity of other young nobles, however, led to his expulsion. He stayed for a period with his uncle Ælfheah, bishop of Winchester, under whose influence and in the wake of a serious illness he committed himself to the monastic life. Retiring to a hermitage near Glastonbury, he studied sctiptures and served as a scribe, illuminator, composer, and metalworker.

Recalled to court by Æthelstan's brother and successor Edmund (939–46), he became one of his counselors, only to be again banished. Soon afterward Edmund, nearly killed in a riding accident, concluded that he had wronged Dunstan; he named him abbot of Glastonbury and promised to endow that institution as a regular monastery. Under Dunstan's guidance a monastery was built with an organized community of monks adhering to the Benedictine Rule. Its foundation is seen as marking a long-enduring revival of English monasticism after several generations of decay.

Under Edmund's successor Eadred (946–55) Dunstan and his monastery were the recipients of even greater favors, but his fortunes waned with the accession of Eadwig (955–59). In 956, having angered an influential woman at court, he was forced into exile in Flanders. Restored by Edgar (957–75), he became the king's chief adviser and treasurer. Named bishop of Worcester (957) and London (959), in 960 he became archbishop of Canterbury. On Edgar's death he supported the royal claim of Edward the Martyr and, after Edward's murder in 979, the claim of Æthelred II. Dunstan's final years were spent at Canterbury, devoted to prayer, study, and teaching. He died on 19 May 988, the "patron and father of the monks of medieval England."

Further Reading

Knowles, David. *The Monastic Order in England: A History of Its Development from the Times of St. Dunstan to the Fourth Lateran Council, 940–1216*. 2d ed. Cambridge: Cambridge University Press, 1963.

Robinson, Joseph Armitage. *The Times of Saint Dunstan.* Oxford: Clarendon, 1923.

Stubbs, William, ed. *Memorials of Saint Dunstan, Archbishop of Canterbury.* Rolls Series 63. London: Longman, 1874.

Symons, Thomas. "The English Monastic Reform of the Tenth Century." *DownR 60* (1942): 1–22,196–222, 268–79.

MILES CAMPBELL

E

EBNER, MARGARETHA (1291–1351)

Born in 1291 in Donauwörth, near Regensburg, to a patrician family, Margaretha Ebner entered the Dominican cloister of Maria-Mödingen at an early age and was buried there in 1351. In 1332, Heinrich von Nördlingen, her Dominican confessor, convinced her to write a record of her spiritual journey. Without the aid of an amanuensis, she wrote her *Offenbarungen* (Revelations) herself in Alemannic, a dialect of Middle High German. A lengthy manuscript for the Middle Ages (over 100 folio pages) Margaretha's *Revelations* follows a chronological description of her spiritual life from 1312 to 1348, the experiences arranged according to the liturgical calendar. The text belongs to a medieval religious genre referred to as autohagiography. In 1312 Margaretha became seriously ill and for three years endured a variety of afflictions described in the opening chapters of her book. Suffering a severe illness for an extended period of time is a feature commonly reported in medieval hagiography or autohagiography and figures prominently in the religious experiences of medieval women. Recovered, Margaretha undertook a rigorous program of asceticism, self-mortification, fasting, and flagellation. At one point she begged Mary to ask God that she be granted the miracle of stigmata. Quite in keeping with fourteenth-century piety, her devotions center on the humanity of Christ, primarily on his birth and death. Material images of both cradle and cross are, therefore, conspicuous in her devotional exercises. The religious experiences that Margaretha narrates in her writings typify those of ecstatic mystics described in a variety of texts in late medieval Europe, particularly prominent in late medieval Germany. It is also noteworthy that fifty-four letters from Heinrich von Nördlingen and other contemporaries are included in the nineteenth-century Strauch edition.

Further Reading

Hale, Drage Rosemary. "Rocking the Cradle: Margaretha Ebner (Be)Holds the Divine," in *Performance and Transformation: New Approaches to Late Medieval Spirituality*, ed. Mary A. Suydam and Joanna E. Ziegler. New York: St. Martin's Press, 1999, pp. 210–241.

Margaretha Ebner und Heinrich von Nördlingen, ed. Philipp Strauch. Frieburg im Breisgau: Mohr, 1882; rpt. Amsterdam: P. Shippers N. V., 1966.

Margaretha Ebner: Major Works, trans. Leonard P. Hindsley. New York: Paulist, 1993.

ROSEMARY DRAGE HALE

EDWARD I (1239–1307; r. 1272–1307)

Usually rated as one of the great kings of medieval England. His reign witnessed military triumphs against the Welsh and considerable successes against Scotland, apparently conquered by 1304. A magnificent chain of castles in north Wales is testament to the confidence of the age, and a succession of statutes bears witness to Edward's efforts to reform the legal system. In constitutional terms this reign was of fundamental importance in the development of parliament. Yet there are shadows in this picture. The later years of the reign lacked the constructive qualities of the earlier. War imposed an increasing strain upon political society and the economy. Law and order were not maintained with the expected vigor.

Edward is not an easy character to assess. Son of Henry III, he served a hard apprenticeship in his youth, displaying energy and ambition, with a reputation for false dealing in the civil wars of the early 1260s. He went on St. Louis's crusade in 1270 and was the only one of the leaders who did not abandon the expedition, He went on to the Holy Land, where he achieved little but greatly improved his public image.

On his return to England in 1274 major reforms were instituted. A massive inquiry that yielded the Hundred Rolls demonstrated that the king was committed to at least some of the concepts that had inspired the baronial reform movement of 1258. Yet there was no single principle providing consistency to the new statutes. Individual measures were devised to deal with particular problems; some favored the magnates, some their tenants, and some the merchants. A concerted campaign of *quo warranto* inquiries ("by what warrant") into baronial rights over jurisdiction lacked proper direction from above and became bogged down in technicalities, until a compromise was eventually worked out in 1290. The extent to which Edward was himself responsible for the legal measures is hard to assess; it seems probable that he left the details of drafting to his experts. In his personal conduct he was certainly not above manipulating the law in a cynical fashion. His desire to acquire sufficient lands with which to endow his children led him into some highly suspect dealing, such as defrauding the rightful heir to the Forz inheritance.

Edward was jealous of his own rights and privileges, and insensitive to those of others. He took an exalted view of his feudal rights of suzerainty in Wales and Scotland, and in both cases this led him into war. An autocratic determination to enforce his interpretation of his rights drove both Welsh and Scots to take up arms against him. Failure to reward his allies, such as the Welsh prince Dafydd and the Scottish magnate Robert Bruce, led to serious rebellions. He met his match, however, in Philip IV of France, and in 1294 English diplomacy suffered a serious reverse when the king's brother, Edmund of Lancaster, was duped into handing over the duchy of Gascony to the French without receiving adequate guarantees that it would be returned.

Edward's successes in war were not achieved by any brilliant strokes of generalship. Rather, efficient administration mustered the resources of the realm, in terms of men, money, and materials, on an unprecedented scale. This had severe political consequences; successive years of heavy taxation, after 1294, led to the major political crisis in 1297. The determination of Archbishop Winchelsey to follow the papal line, set out in the bull *Clericis laicos*, of not paying taxes to the lay power, added to the problems. Though civil war threatened, Edward persisted in his plans for a campaign in the Low Countries, for which he did not have an adequate army. He was fortunate in that the French king failed to appreciate the weakness of the English position, while a defeat in Scotland at Stirling Bridge brought the English baronage back to a sense of patriotic duty. The political crisis was settled with the issue of the *Confirmatio cartarum* (Confirmation of the Charters).

Edward's reign was important for the evolution of parliament. The hearing of petitions and determination of cases have been stressed by some historians, but parliament was also the occasion for the discussion of great affairs of state. Representatives of shire and borough, and of lower clergy, attended only a minority of parliaments, but the concept that they should come with full power (*plena potestas*) to consent on behalf of their communities was established. How far the king considered himself bound by such ideas as "What touches all should be approved by all" (*quod omnes tangit*) is open to doubt; that phrase was used only once in a parliamentary summons and is likely to have been inserted by a clerk, not the king himself. Examination of the limited nature of royal patronage does not suggest that Edward was a man who believed in the subtle arts of political management; his style was brusque, autocratic, and effective.

Edward was a conventionally religious man who founded the Abbey of Vale Royal in fulfillment of a vow taken when he thought he was about to be shipwrecked. The work on the abbey, however, was abruptly terminated in 1290. His piety did not lead him into any subservience to the church. He faced considerable difficulties from archbishops Pecham and "Winchelsey, two of the few able to stand up to the masterful king. He was clearly fond of his first queen, Eleanor of Castile, in whose honor he had a fine series of commemorative crosses built. He also seems to have been fond of his daughters, but his relationship with his heir, the unsatisfactory Edward II, was a stormy one.

The final years of the reign were difficult. There were financial problems, with a debt increasing to about £200,000. Public order was poorly maintained as a result of the government's singleminded concentration on war. English forces proved incapable of dealing with the Scots under Robert Bruce. The legacy Edward left his son was an impossible one.

See also **Philip IV the Fair**

Further Reading

Gransden, Antonia. *Historical Writing in England*. Vol. 1: *c. 550 to c. 1307*. London: Routledge & Kegan Paul, 1974, pp. 439–86 [on the contemporary chronicles].

Parsons, John Carmi. *Eleanor of Castile Queen and Society in Thirteenth-Century England* New York: St. Martins, 1995.

Powicke, EM. *The Thirteenth Century, 1216–1307*. 2d ed. Oxford: Clarendon, 1962 [this study; originally published in 1953, dominated thinking on the period for many years].

Prestwich, Michael. *Edward I*. London: Methuen, 1988 [the most recent full study].

Rothwell, Harry, ed. *English Historical Documents*. Vol. 3: *1189–1327*. London: Eyre & Spottiswoode, 1975 [translated texts].

MICHAEL PRESTWICH

EDWARD III (1312–1377; r. 1327–77)

Edward achieved stunning military success against Scotland and France while maintaining domestic harmony for most of the 50 years he ruled. His early years were overshadowed by the political storms that had engulfed Edward II. When he was sent to France in 1325 to do homage for Gascony, he joined his mother, Isabella, who engineered Edward II's overthrow the following year. The young Edward was crowned on 25 January 1327, only fourteen years old, after parliament had deposed his father. A year later he married Philippa of Hainault, whose father had contributed heavily to Isabella's invasion.

Edward was tightly controlled by his mother and her lover, Roger Mortimer, sparking new conflict. Henry of Lancaster led an abortive rebellion in 1329, and Edward's uncle the earl of Kent was summarily executed in 1330 for plotting against them. Finally Edward and a group of young courtiers seized Mortimer in October 1330. He was tried in parliament and executed. Isabella received a generous estate, where she lived until her death in 1358.

Edward then turned his attention to Scotland. After co-vertly aiding Edward Balliol, a claimant to the Scottish throne, and the "Disinherited" (Balliol's followers) in their attempt to recover power he marched northward in 1333, defeated the Scots at Halidon Hill on 19 July, and captured Berwick. It was the first English victory in years, but it did not subdue the Scots. Subsequent campaigns likewise failed to deliver a decisive blow.

France also demanded Edward's attention. The last Capetian king, Charles IV, had died in 1328 without descendants, and his cousin Philip of Valois had taken the throne. Edward had a claim through his mother, Charles's sister, even though he had twice performed homage for Gascony. When Philip moved to seize Gascony as well as aid the Scots, Edward won parliamentary approval in 1337 to pursue his claim. The enterprise was a disaster. He spent lavishly but achieved little. Despite a victory over the French fleet at Sluys on 24 June, by the end of 1340 he was broke and forced to conclude an ignominious truce.

This fiasco precipitated a political crisis in 1341. Unjustly blaming his officials for the failure, Edward stormed back to England, fired them, and launched an investigation into their misconduct. His anger focused in particular on his chancellor, the archbishop of Canterbury, John Stratford. In reality the wartime demands had been excessive. A restive population spurred Commons to demand reforms. Edward was forced to concede a statute limiting his power, though he overturned it later in the year.

The disputed inheritance of Brittany in 1342 gave Edward an opportunity to return to campaigning, and when the truce with France expired in 1345 he was ready for war. Armies under the earls of Lancaster and Northampton were successful in Gascony and Brittany. The greatest victory came in 1346, when Edward defeated the much larger French army at Crecy on 24 August. Then, on 17 October, the English defeated the Scots and captured King David at the Battle of Neville's Cross, The following year Calais fell to Edward.

Despite these brilliant victories Scottish resistance continued and the French refused to accede to Edward's demands, especially after Philip died in 1350 and John II (1350–64) came to the throne. Though Edward's prestige had risen tremendously, throughout the 1340s Commons still complained about taxation and purveyance. The complaints did not provoke conflict, but Edward had to negotiate carefully. Furthermore the Black Death struck in 1348–49, causing widespread death and havoc.

The war with France resumed in 1355, when Edward dispatched two armies under his son Edward the Black Prince and his cousin Henry of Lancaster. They were smaller than earlier ones but more destructive. The campaigns, called *chevauchées*, were intended to disrupt the enemy, rather than engage in set battle. The French army under King John, however, on 19 September managed to catch the Black Prince at Poitiers, where the English again prevailed over superior forces and even took John prisoner. Despite the triumph the French refused to give in to Edward's demands. He led another army to France in 1359 with the aim of being crowned at Reims, but the mission failed. In 1360 he concluded the Treaty of Brétigny, which gave him some of the territory and authority he sought.

Despite these disappointments Edward was at the peak of his career. His fame spread throughout Europe, and he was popular at home. Through his military triumphs, his participation in tournaments, and his founding of the Order of the Garter in 1346–47 he had become a chivalric hero. During the 1350s and 1360s revenues from customs and the ransoms of David of Scotland and John of France allowed him to reduce the level of direct taxation, producing greater harmony with parliament. His family was large and illustrious.

The end of his reign was less glorious. Queen Philippas death in 1369 seems to have affected him deeply, though he took a mistress, Alice Perrers. When war resumed with France in 1369, the English position disintegrated. Edward's son John of Gaunt, who took over leadership, was less capable than his ailing elder brother, the Black Prince, and expeditions in 1369 and 1373 produced little. England was forced to give ground. Moreover discontent at home increased as high taxation resumed. Plague struck again in 1360–61 and 1374. The court was dominated by a small group of courtiers around the grasping Alice, enriching themselves at public expense. In the Good Parliament of 1376 Commons impeached the courtiers and called for sweeping reforms, Edward, who did not participate, was forced to grant its demands. He died less than a year later, on 21 June 1377, and was succeeded by his grandson Richard II, whose father, the Black Prince, had died in 1376.

Edward's character is difficult to reconstruct, because chroniclers tended to treat him heroically without offering personal insights. He clearly inspired great *esprit de corps* among the nobility and soldiers. He loved display and indulged in tournaments, ceremonies, and pageants. He was also quick-tempered and tended to blame others for his misfortunes. He was conventionally pious, making pilgrimages to holy sites in England before and after campaigns and giving to the church; he also distrusted clergymen and for the first time appointed laymen as chancellor and treasurer in 1341 and 1371. Finally, despite their immediate glory, his victories in France did not bring lasting success nor were they universally popular in England, where peasants and townsfolk had to shoulder the burden of paying for war.

See also **Froissart, Jean; Richard III**

Further Reading

Allmand, C.T. *The Hundred Years War: England and France at War, c. 1300–c. 1450.* Cambridge: Cambridge University Press, 1988.

Given-Wilson, Chris. *The English Nobility in the Late Middle Ages: The Fourteenth-Century Political Community.* London: Routledge & Kegan Paul, 1987.

McKisack, May. *The Fourteenth Century, 1307–1399.* Oxford History of England 5. Oxford: Clarendon, 1959.

Ormrod, W.M. *The Reign of Edward III: Crown and Political Society in England, 1327–1377.* New Haven: Yale University Press, 1990.

Prestwich, Michael. *The Three Edwards: War and State in England, 1272–1377.* London: Weidenfeld & Nicolson, 1980.

Tout, T.F. *Chapters in the Administrative History of Mediaeval England: The Wardrobe, the Chamber and the Small Seals.* Vol. 3. Manchester: Manchester University Press, 1928.

Waugh, Scott L. *England in the Reign of Edward III.* Cambridge: Cambridge University Press, 1991.

SCOTT L. WAUGH

EDWARD THE CONFESSOR
(1002/05–1066; r. 1042–66)

Edward owes his tide of Confessor to his canonization in 1161 by Pope Alexander III at the request of Henry II and the church and at the instigation of the monks of Westminster Abbey, where he was buried. Although the historical figure and the image of the Confessor have little in common, the title serves to distinguish him from such Anglo-Saxon kings as Edward the Elder and Edward the Martyr.

Edward was born at Islip, near Oxford, between 1002 and 1005, the seventh son of Æthelred II, "the Unready," and the first from his second marriage, to Emma, sister of Duke Richard II of Normandy, an alliance designed to protect the king from Viking attacks. Edwards "miraculous" acquisition of the throne in 1042, after 24 years of obscure exile in Normandy and its environs (1017–4l), was made possible by the deaths of the Danish usurpers Cnut and his sons, Harold Harefoot and Harthacnut, and of most other potential pretenders, his younger brother, Alfred, and his six senior half-brothers, represented only by Edmund Ironside's son, Edward "the Exile," in Hungary.

But to gain and hold the throne Edward had to accept the protection of Godwin, earl of Wessex, marry Godwin's daughter, Edith (Eadgyth), and raise his sons to earldoms. Edward found it hard to break free. Because of Cnut's division of the kingdom into great provincial earldoms and the erosion of the royal demesne Edward could provide only small estates for his French followers. Although he had more scope in the church and appointed some interesting continentals to bishoprics, his best hope of independence lay in the suspicion of Godwin felt by the other great earls, the English Leofric of Mercia and the Danish Siward of Northumbria.

Like his father, Æthelred II, Edward has an undeserved reputation as a weak king, Healthy, a keen hunter and soldier, a great survivor, and—although occasionally rash and ill advised—determined not to go on his travels again, he warded off his external enemies by warlike gestures and shrewd diplomacy. He exploited his childlessness—explained by later legend as due to an unconsummated marriage—as a diplomatic asset, making empty promises of the succession to Earl Godwin's nephew, King Swein of Denmark, in the 1040s; his cousin-once-removed William duke of Normandy, at the end of the decade; his half-nephew, Edward the Exile, in 1054–57. He may also have aroused the hopes of other relatives of his parents and wife.

In 1051, under the influence of Robert of Jumièges, a Norman abbot whom he made bishop of London and then archbishop of Canterbury, Edward fell foul of his father-in-law and provoked a showdown. Godwin's half-hearted rebellion collapsed when earls Leofric and Siward supported the king; the rebel and his sons were outlawed and fled abroad. In the following year, however, they returned by force and, as Leofric and Siward, alienated by Edward's willfulness, now stood aloof, secured their restoration. This time it was Robert of Jumièges and other Frenchmen who fled.

After Godwin's death in 1053 Edward and the Godwinsons reached a *modus vivendi*, and a period of prosperity set in. According to the *Vita Aedwardi regis*, an early account of the reign, the dominance of Godwin's children made England great. Harold, earl of

Wessex after 1053, ruled the south; Tostig, after 1055 earl of Northumbria, ruled the north; Queen Edith ruled the court. The Welsh and the Scots were dominated, good laws prevailed, and the king and queen refounded monasteries as their mausoleums. But in 1065 some of Tostig's vassals rebelled against his harsh rule, Harold would not save his brother from exile, and Edward's mortification was such that he suffered a fatal stroke.

He died on 5 January 1066, just after the dedication of his new church at Westminster (pictured on the Bayeux Tapestry). His achievement was to have held his unstable kingdom together for 24 years and bequeath it intact to his brother-in-law Harold. No wonder that in the following centuries the "Laws of King Edward" became the symbol of a Golden Age.

See also **Cnut; Harold Godwinson; William I**

Further Reading

Primary Sources

Barlow, Frank, ed. and trans. *The Life of King Edward Who Rests at Westminster* [*Vita Aedwardi regis*]. 2d ed. Oxford: Clarendon, 1992.

Whitelock, Dorothy, ed., with David C. Douglas and Susie I. Tucker. *The Anglo-Saxon Chronicle: A Revised Translation.* London: Eyre & Spottiswoode, 1961.

Secondary Sources

Barlow, Frank. *Edward the Confessor.* Berkeley: University of California Press, 1970 [the only modern biography].

Loyn, H.R. *Anglo-Saxon England and the Norman Conquest.* London: Longmans, 1962.

FRANK BARLOW

EGERIA

Egeria, whose *Peregrinatio* is the first travel book produced in the Christian West, is the most famous medieval woman writer from the Iberian Peninsula. Curiously, she is much better known beyond the borders of the peninsula, perhaps because for many years scholars believed her to be from France (and some still do).

Very little is known about her. Most scholars think that her name was Egeria, not Aetheria or Sylvia, and that she was a rich woman from Gallaecia (Gallcia) province who traveled to the Holy Land and wrote her work overseas in the late fourth century. However, some favor a French origin and an early fifth-century date. The name Egeria is unusual, but it has been found in a document from Oviedo, so the author of the *Peregrinatio* was not the only one with that name. Theories that she was a member of the nobility or an abbess have not been substantiated, nor has the theory that she was a middle-class laywoman. The consensus at present seems to be that, whatever her origin, Egeria was a nun or at least a member of a religious community. Her work obviously is addressed to a congregation of pious women to which she has strong emotional ties.

The *Peregrinatio* is a long letter to Egeria's fellow nuns that relates her activities and travel, over more than three years, in and around the Holy Land. Although Egeria based her work primarily on her own observations, she also used literary sources. Most of her quotations appear to be from the Bible and the *Onomasticon* of Eusebius of Caesarea. The text, which survives in one manuscript found in the nineteenth century in the library of the Brotherhood of St. Mary at Arezzo by Giovanni Gamurrini, is missing both the beginning and the end.

Through later references to her work by other authors, it is possible tentatively to reconstruct Egeria's trip. It apparently included an initial exploration of Jerusalem, and visits to Alexandria, the Thebaid, and Galilee, before her journey to Mount Sinai, as well as a visit to St. John of Ephesus after her arrival in Constantinople. The first twenty-three chapters narrate Egeria's ascent of Mount Sinai and her retracing of the route of the Exodus, a visit to the tomb of Job at Carneas, and the return trip to Constantinople, including a detour to the tomb of St. Thomas the Apostle at Edessa (modern Urfa) and the house of Abraham in Carrhae (modern Harrae), and another to the shrines of St. Thecla in Seleucia and St. Euphemia in Chalcedon. The last twenty-six chapters describe daily and weekly ceremonies, and the ceremonies of the major holidays from Epiphany through Pentecost and the feast of the dedication of the Basilica of the Holy Sepulchre.

Although there is a very extensive bibliography about Egeria's *Peregrinatio* (over three hundred titles), most studies deal with linguistic and liturgical issues. She is well known among students of Romance philology and church history because her work is an interesting example of Vulgar Latin and contains detailed information about Jerusalem rituals not found elsewhere. Her work has been studied as literature by only a few critics, who think the *Peregrinatio* is impersonal because it limits itself to describing the places visited from the point of view of whether or not they match the places in the Bible. These critics believe Egeria behaves like a Christian speaking to all Christians. Such a view has been questioned by critics who see Egeria's *Peregrinatio* as the work of a woman who writes for other women.

Egeria was not the first person to write about the Holy Land. Many others, before and after her, wrote itineraries (lists of places visited) giving the distance between places and describing each one in greater or lesser detail. The purpose of these itineraries was primarily to serve as guides for future pilgrims. They are written in the third person and contain little or no information about their authors or their experiences. Egeria's *Peregrinatio*, written in the first person, is a chronicle of her trip. Egeria could not write an itinerary because she was a woman, and women did not write guides addressed to the entire world. Women did not write very much at all. When they did, they wrote mainly things of a private nature, such as letters, often addressed to other women, and that is what Egeria did. Since her fellow nuns were not in a position to emulate her adventure, it was appropriate to justify and share such an uncommon deed by writing a letter. Had Egeria been a man, perhaps she and her peers would not have found her experience so remarkable, and she would not have written her work. Her overwhelming curiosity, scholarly abilities, social skills, and tremendous vitality come through clearly in the *Peregrinatio*, which was truly a woman's adventure.

Further Reading

Campbell, M. B. *The Witness and the Other World: Exotic European Travel Writing, 400–1600*. Ithaca, N.Y., 1988.

Franceschini, E., and R. Weber, eds. *Itinerarium Egeriae.* Corpus Christianarum, Series Latina, 175. Turhout, 1965.

Gingras, G. E., ed. *Egeria: Diary of a Pilgrimage.* New York, 1970. Snyder, J. M. *The Woman and the Lyre: Women Writers in Classical Greece and Rome.* Carbondale: Ill., 1989.

CRISTINA GONZÁLEZ

EIKE VON REPGOW (fl. 1210–1235)

Beginning about 1150 we have records of a family living in Saxony between the rivers Saale and Mulde who called itself after the village of Reppichau near the city of Dessau. Eike von Repgow (also Eike von Reppichowe) probably belonged to this family of ministerials eligible to serve in the judiciary as *Schöffe*, that is, one of a group who determines judgments in a lawsuit. He is probably the person who appears as a witness in charters from 1209 to 1233. Although these charters place him in contact with Count Heinrich of Anhalt, Margrave Dietrich of Meißen, and Landgrave Ludwig of Thuringia and it is certain that he was liegeman to Count Hoyer of Falkenstein in Quedlinburg, we know little of the events in his life and cannot even be sure he was a *Schöffe*. What we do know is that he wrote arguably the most significant text of the German Middle Ages: the *Sachsenspiegel* (The Saxon Mirror, ca. 1225–1235). This is a compendium of the customary laws of thirteenth-century Saxony. Eike's text reveals an education in the seven liberal arts (possibly Halberstadt or Magdeburg), for he had learned Latin and was highly familiar with the Bible and canon law.

The reception of Eike's book was vast. Not only was it appropriated by the rest of Germany within forty years, including High German translations—*Deutschenspiegel* (Germans' Mirror), *Schwabenspiegel* (Swabians' Mirror), but as the four hundred extant manuscript versions demonstrate, it was frequently consulted and much of it remained in force for over three hundred years, thus confirming his contribution to German jurisprudence and culture. Authorship of the *Sächsische Weltchronik* (Saxon World Chronicle, 1260–1275), a lengthy summary of world history and catalog of Roman kings up to Eike's own age, is no longer attributed to Eike.

Further Reading

Dobozy, Maria, trans. *The Saxon Mirror: A Sachsenspiegel of the Fourteenth Century*. Philadelphia: University of Pennsylvania Press, 1999.

Eckhardt, Karl August. *Sachsenspiegel Landrecht*. Monumenta Germaniae historica. Fontes juris Germanici antiqui, n.s. 1/1. Göttingen: Musterschmidt, 1955, rpt. 1973.

———. *Sachsenspiegel Lehnrecht*. Monumenta Germaniae historica. Fontes juris Germanici antiqui, n.s. 1/2. Göttingen: Musterschmidt, 1956, rpt. 1973.

Herkommer, Hubert. "Eike von Repgows *Sachsenspiegel und die Sächsische Weltchronik*." *Niederdeutsches Jahrbuch* 100 (1977): 7–42.

Schmidt-Wiegand, Ruth, and Dagmar Hüpper, eds. *Der Sachsenspiegel als Buch*. New York: Lang, 1991.

Schmidt-Wiegand, Ruth, "Eike von Repgow," in *Die deutsche Literatur des Mittelalters: Verfasserlexikon*, ed. Kurt Ruh et al. Berlin: de Gruyter, 1980, vol. 2, cols. 400–409.

Schott, Clausdieter, ed. *Der Sachsenspiegel Eikes von Repgow*, trans. Ruth Schmidt-Wiegand [*Landrecht*] and Clausdieter Schott [*Lehnrecht*]. Zürich: Manesse, 1984.

Weiland, L. *Sächsische Weltchronik*. Monumenta Germaniae historica. Deutsche Chroniken 2. Hannover: Hahn, 1877, rpt. 1971, pp. 1–384.

MARIA DOBOZY

EILHART VON OBERG (fl. 1170–1190)

The history of Middle High German *Tristan* versions begins with Eilhart von Oberg's *Tristrant*, composed sometime between 1170 and 1190. In contrast to Gottfried von Straßburg's *Tristan* (ca. 1210), the older poem seems to have borrowed directly from a Celtic source, although a French intermediary story (*estoire*) is also possible. Hardly anything is known about the author except that he was a member of the noble family of Oberg who lived in the vicinity of Brunswick and were in the service of the bishops of Hildesheim and the Welf family. It seems highly likely that Eilhart created his *Tristrant* at the Brunswick court of his patroness, duchess Mechthild of England, who was married to Henry the Lion. Mechthild had been raised in London in a highly literate Anglo-Norman world where the Old French *Chanson de Roland* (Song of Roland) enjoyed considerable popularity. It can be assumed that she commissioned the translation of the latter into Middle High German (*Rolandslied*), and also promoted the creation of the goliardic epic *Herzog Ernst*, based on the *Chanson d'Aspremont*, and finally the composition of the *Tristrant* romance. Eilhart's text has been preserved in three fragmentary twelfth- and thirteenth-century manuscripts that contain altogether more than a thousand verses.

The complete text is extant in three fifteenth-century paper manuscripts and was first printed by Anton Sorg in Augsburg as a prose version (chapbook) in 1484. This chapbook experienced a long-lasting popularity far into the eighteenth century. Eilhart's *Tristrant* was extensively used as an inspirational source for thirteenth-and fourteenth-century tapestry (e.g., Wienhausen).

In contrast to Gottfried's later version, Eilhart relies on simpler motivational elements to explain how Tristrant and the Irish princess Isalde meet and fall in love. The couple is eventually forced to leave the court and spends two miserable years in the woods until the effects of a love potion fade and each of them can return to his or her life. Tristrant marries Kehenis's sister, also named Isalde, but continues to love fair Isalde, his King's, Marke's, wife, whom he meets several times in secret. The lovers are caught flagrants delicto and are supposed to be executed. But a leper suggests that Isalde be turned over to his band to be raped by all of them, which then provides the opportunity for Tristrant to free himself and rescue his beloved mistress. Later Tristrant returns home from another adventure, mortally wounded, and calls his mistress for his rescue. When she arrives, however, he has already died, and so she also succumbs to death. Now King Marke learns about the love potion, forgives the lovers, and buries them together. Because Eilhart included more comical elements, gave a time limit to the power of the potion, and hence described love as a dangerous power undermining both King Marke's and Tristrant's marriage, this courtly romance had a more mundane and entertaining character than Gottfried's *Tristan*. Here the figure of King Arthur and his court also play a significant role.

See also **Gottfried von Straßburg**

Further Reading

Bertau, Karl. *Deutsche Literatur im europäischen Mittelalter*, vol. 1, 800–1197. Munich: Beck, 1972.

Eilhart von Oberg. *Tristrant*, ed. Hadumond Bußmann. Tübingen: Niemeyer, 1969.

Eilhart von Oberg. *Tristrant und Isalde*, ed. Danielle Buschinger and Wolfgang Spiewok. Greifswald: Reineke, 1993.

——. *Tristrant*, trans. J.W. Thomas. Lincoln: University of Nebraska Press, 1978.

McDonald, William C. "King Mark, the Holy Penitent: On a Neglected Motif in the Eilhart Literary Tradition." *Zeitschrift für deutsches Altertum und deutsche Literatur* 120 (1991): 393–441.

Mertens, Volker. "Eilhart, der Herzog und der Truchseß. Der 'Tristrant' am Welfenhof." in *Tristan et Iseut, mythe européen et mondial*, ed. Danielle Buschinger. Göppingen: Kümmerle, 1987, pp. 262–281.

Strohschneider, Peter. "Herrschaft und Liebe: Strukturprobleme des Tristanromans bei Eilhart von Oberg." *Zeitschrift für deutsches Altertum und deutsche Literatur* 122 (1993): 36–61.

ALBRECHT CLAASEN

EINARR HELGASON SKÁLAGLAMM (10th century)

Einarr Helgason skálaglamm was one of the most notable poets of the 10th century. He was of a distinguished family of western Iceland, the brother of Ósvífr, father of Guðrún, whose life is depicted in *Laxdæla saga*. Little is known about Einarr's life, except some episodes connecting him with Egill Skalla-Grímsson, whose influence is apparent in Einarr's poetry. Presumably, he spent a great part of his life at the court of Earl Hákon (d. 995). According to *Jómsvíkinga saga*, Einarr was first known as "skjaldmeyjar" ("shield-maiden") Einarr, but was later called "skálaglamm" ("scale-tinkle"), because Earl Hákon gave him a pair of scales that gave a tinkling sound and foretold the future. Apart from *Vellekla*, a panegyric on the Norwegian sovereign Earl Hákon, some other stanzas by Einarr have been preserved: two stanzas of a panegyric on the Danish king Harald Blåtand (BB uetooth), a stanza of another panegyric on Earl Hákon, and some *lausavísur*. *Vellekla* is one of the most important skaldic poems of the 10th century. Unfortunately, the poem has not been preserved as a whole; yet, many of the stanzas are quoted in the biographies of the Norwegian kings Haraldr gräfeldr ("grey-cloak") Eiríksson and Óláfr Tryggvason in *Heimskringla* and in that of Earl Hákon in *Fagrskinna*. The introductory stanzas and those that deal with the battle of the Jómsvíkingar are preserved in *Snorra Edda*. Certainly, the poem in its present state is not complete; for example, the "stef"-stanza, which is essential for a *drápa*, is lacking.

Although the original structure of *Vellekla* is uncertain because of the poem's state of preservation, it is possible to offer a synopsis of its contents. After a comparatively long introduction (six stanzas) containing the customary elements, such as the request for silence, the praise of the sovereign, and the announcement of the theme, the *drápa* depicts the events that mark Earl Hákon's advance to power over the whole of Norway: the wars with Haraldr gräfeldr and his brothers, the sons of Eiríkr blóðøx ("blood-axe") Haraldsson, during which he took vengeance on his uncle Grjotgarðr and Haraldr for his father's, Earl Sigurðr's, death; the battles with Ragnfrøðr, another of Eiríkr's sons, who tried to reconquer Norway; the victorious battle at the Danevirke against the German emperor Otto II, which he fought in the service of the Danish king; the long expedition through the unknown Gautland back to Trondheim. It is doubtful whether the stanzas relating to the battle of the Jómsvíkingar under Earl Sigvaldi belong to this poem, since they are cited neither in *Heimskringla* nor in *Fagrskinna*; some of these stanzas describe the beneficial consequences of the earl's government. He restored the old pagan cults that had been abolished under Eiríkr's sons, which returned good harvests to the country. Usually, these stanzas are placed after the successful war against Haraldr in accordance with the historical accounts of *Heimskringla* and *Fagrskinna*. However, considering the present tense used in these stanzas, they could also be regarded as a praise of the earl's rule at the moment when the *drápa* was written, and therefore placed just before the concluding praise of the sovereign.

Thus far, no satisfactory explanations of the title of the poem, *Vellekla*, meaning "shortage of gold," have been found. Either it expresses the poet's hopes for a reward from the sovereign (but in the preserved stanzas this theme takes no more space than is usual in panegyrics), or it could be an ironic allusion to some unknown situation. There is a third possibilty: *Vellekla* could be part of a kenning for the sovereign (*e.g.*, "remover of shortage of gold").

It is also somewhat difficult to date the poem. Supposing that the stanzas about the battle of the Jómsvíkingar were part of the original poem, it must be dated in the years after 985. In this case, chronological problems arise concerning the episodes related in *Egils saga*, but this objection may not prove serious, because these episodes are partly typical skaldic anecdotes whose content is historically doubtful. If the contested stanzas do not belong to the poem, it must be dated to the years after 975.

In *Vellekla,* Einarr skálaglamm proves to be a remarkable artist. He creates a brilliant poem by the sophistication of his language and metrics, especially by extensive and ingenious kennings, which he intended to equal the glory of his sovereign.

Vellekla is also important as evidence of the late Old Norse pagan religion. It shows the connection between political power and religion in the concept of the sovereign who is guided by the god, and who reintroduces the old cults that are the fundamental condition of the prosperity of the country. A literary allusion to *Vǫluspá* suggests that the poet wanted to praise Earl Hákon's rule as comparable to that of the god Baldr, who returns after Ragnarǫk.

Further Reading

Editions

Finnur Jónsson, ed. *Den norsk-islandske skjaldedigtning.* Vols. 1A–2A (tekst efter håndskrifterne) and lB–2B(rettet tekst). Copenhagen and Christiania [Oslo]: Gyldendal, 1912–15; rpt. Copenhagen: Rosenkilde & Bagger, 1967(A) and 1973(B), vol. lA, pp. 122–31, 1B, pp. 117–24.

Lindquist, lvar, ed. *Norröna lovkväden från 800– och 900– talen. 1. Förslag till restituerad täxt jämte översättning.* Lund: Gleerup, 1929, pp. 44–55.

Kock, Ernst A., ed. *Den norsk-isländska skaldediktningen. 2 vols.* Lund: Gleerup, 1946–50, vol. 1, pp. 66–9.

Translations

Hollander, Lee M., trans. *The Skalds: A Selection of Their Poems.* New York: American-Scandinavian Foundation; Princeton: Princeton University Press, 1945.

Literature

Björn M. Ólsen. "Skýring." *Árbók hins Íslenzka fornleifafélags* (1882), 154–6.

Konráð Gíslason. *Forelæsninger over oldnorske Skjaldekvad.* Efterladte Skrifter, 1. Copenhagen: Gyldendal, 1895.

Patzig, H. "Die Abfassung von Einars Vellekla." *Zeitschrift für deutsches Altertum und deutsche Literatur* 67 (1930), 55–65.

Indrebø, Gustav. "Fylke og fylkesnamn." *Bergens Museums Årbok,* Hist. -ant. rekke nr. 1 (1931), 43–4.

Finnur Jónsson. *Tekstkritiske Bemærkninger til Skjaldekvad.* Danske Videnskabernes Selskab. Historisk-filologiske Meddelelser, 20.2. Copenhagen: Levin & Munksgaard, 1934.

Oben, Magnus. "Eldste Forekomst av Navnet Hlaðir (Velleka 14)." *Maal og minne* (1941), 154–6.

Turville-Petre, E. O. G. *Scaldic Poetry.* Oxford: Clarendon, 1976, pp. 59–63.

EDITH MAROLD

EINARR SKÚLASON (12th century)

Einarr Skúlason was the most prolific skald of the 12th century. He was a favorite of Snorri Sturluson, who in his *Snorra Edda* and *Heimskringla* quotes twice as many verses from Einarr as from any other skald. In the surviving corpus of skaldic poetry, Einarr's verses are outnumbered only by those of Sighvatr Þórðarson.

Little is known of Einarr's life. He was a member of the Kveld-Úlfr family and, as a descendant of Skalla-Grímr, was a kinsman of Egill Skalla-Grímsson, Snorri, and Óláfr Þórðarson. The date and place of his birth are obscure, but he was probably born in the last decade of the 11th century in the area around the Borgarfjörður. By 1114, he was in Norway with King Sigurðr Jórsalafari ("crusader") Magnússon; *Þinga saga* reports that he was used as a messenger in a series of disputes between the king and Sigurðr Hranason that occurred between 1112 and 1114. *Morkinskinna* tells another anecdote concerning Einarr and Sigurðr Jórsalafari that took place when Sigurðr was awaiting the arrival of King Haraldr Gilli Magnússon in Norway, around 1124, although this passage may be an unreliable interpolation. We know that Einarr was with Haraldr Magnússon sometime during his reign (1130–1136), because he composed two poems in honor of Haraldr, and *Skáldatal* reports that he composed a poem (now lost) for Magnús blindi ("blind") Sigurðarson, who shared the rule with Haraldr from 1130 to 1135. By 1143, he was back in Iceland; his name appears in a list of priests in the west country compiled in that year. The position of his name in the list suggests that he lived in the Borgarfjörður district, probably at Borg. It is not clear where Einarr received his clerical education. The schools at Skálholt, Haukadalr, and Oddi were well established by this time, but he may have followed the example of the many learned Icelanders who studied in Germany and France.

Sometime during the joint reign of the Haraldssons, Einarr returned to Norway. He composed poems for all three, as well as a "Haraldssonakvæði." But his principal patron and great friend was Eysteinn, who, according to *Morkinskinna*, made Einarr his *stallari* ("marshall"). Einarr probably remained with King Eysteinn until Eysteinn's death in 1157, and then he may have left Norway to travel through Denmark and Sweden. *Skáldatal* reports that he composed poems for King Sørkvir of Sweden and his son Jón, and for King Sven of Denmark, although none of these poems survives. At some time, he returned to Norway and was with King Ingi and Grégórius Dagsson: his poem *Elfarvísur* was composed for Grégórius sometime between the battle of Elfr (1159) and the fall of Ingi and Grégórius in 1161. It is not known whether Einarr then went home to Iceland or remained in Norway, but he would have been an old man and cannot have lived long after.

Einarr's masterpiece is *Geisli,* the long *drápa* on St. Óláfr Haraldsson, which he composed for a meeting in Trondheim in 1152 or 1153. The poem emphasizes Óláfr's sanctity by comparing him to Christ in an elaborately wrought typological parallel. *Geisli* may be the earliest of the Christian *drápur*; its influence can be seen in all the others. In addition to *Geisli,* a number of the poems Einarr made in praise of his patrons survive: fragments of the two *drápur* on Sigurðr and of two on Haraldr Gilli Magnússon (one in *tøglag* meter); the fragmentary *Haraldssonakvæði*; fragments of a poem in *runhent* meter on an unknown prince; the *Elfarvísur*; and the fragments of an *Eysteinsdrápa* and an *Ingadrápa*. His most difficult poem is the *Øxarflokkr*, containing extremely complex kennings, many in the metonymic style that Snorri calls *ofljóst* ("unclear"). Although the content of Einarr's poetry (apart from *Geisli)* is mundane, his verses show a remarkable facility with skaldic diction, rhyme, and meter.

Further Reading

Editions

Finnur Jónsson, ed. *Den norsk-islandske skjaldedigtning.* Vols. 1A–2A (tekst eftir håndskrifterne) and 1B–2B (rettet tekst). Copenhagen and Christiania [Oslo]: Gyldendal, 1912–15; rpt. Copenhagen: Rosenkilde & Bagger, 1967 (A) and 1973 (B), vols. 1A, pp. 455–55, 1B, pp. 423–57.

Finnur Jónsson, ed. *Morkinskinna.* Samfund til udgivelse af gammel nordisk litteratur, 53. Copenhagen: Jørgensen, 1932.

Sigurður Nordal and Guðni Jónsson, eds. *Borgfirðinga sgur.* Íslenzk fornrit. 3. Reykjavik: Hið íslenzka fornritafélag, 1938.

Bjarni Aðalbjamarson, ed. *Heimskringla.* 3 vols. Íslenzk fornrit, 26–8. Reykjavik: Hið íslenzka fornritafélag, 1941–51.

Chase, Martin. "Einar Skúlason's *Geisli*: A Critical Edition." Diss. University of Toronto, 1981.

Literature

Finnur Jónsson. *Den oldnorske og oldislandske Littersturs Historie.* 2 vols. Copenhagen: Gad, 1894–1901, vol. 2, pp. 62–73

Paasche, Fredrik. *Kristendom og Kvad: En studie i norrøn middelalder.* Kristiania [Oslo]: Aschehoug, 1914, pp. 72–84.

Paasche, Fredrik. *Norges og Islands Litteratur.* Kristiania [Oslo]: Aschehoug, 1924, pp. 288–90.

Vries, Jan de. *Altnordische Literaturgeschichte.* 2 vols. Grundriss der germanischen Philologie, 15–6. Berlin: de Gruyter, 1941–42; rpt. 1964–67, vol. 2, pp. 15–23.

Fidjestøl, Bjarne. *Det norrøne fyrstediktet.* Øvre Ervik: Alvheim & Eide, 1982, pp. 153–6.

Tate, George S. "Einarr Skúlason." In *Dictionary of the Middle Ages.* Ed. Joseph R. Strayer. New York: Scribner, 1982–89, vol. 4, pp. 411–2.

MARTIN CHASE, S.J.

EINHARD (ca. 770–840)

Frankish scholar and biographer. The author of the 9th-century *Vita Caroli,* the first known western biography of a secular leader since late antiquity, was born to noble parents in the Main Valley. As a boy, Einhard was educated at the monastery of Fulda and soon after 791 went to the palace school at Aix-la-Chapelle, headed by Alcuin. He became a close friend of Charlemagne (r. 768–814) as well as his adviser, official representative, and probably the supervisor of the building program at Aix.

After Charlemagne's death in 814, Einhard remained at the court of Louis the Pious (r. 814–840), as adviser to Louis's eldest son, Lothair I (d. 855). In 830, he retired with his wife, Imma, to a monastery founded by him on lands granted by Louis. The area became known as Seligenstadt (City of the Saints) after the church there that Einhard had dedicated to SS. Marcellinus and Peter and in which he placed relics of the two saints acquired by nefarious means. He died March 14, 840.

Einhard's extant writings include seventy letters, the treatise *Historia translationis BB. Christi martyrum Marcellini et Petri,* the short *Quaestio de adoranda cruce,* and the *Vita Caroli* (ca. 829–36). The biography is based on Einhard's personal knowledge of Charlemagne and events at Aix between his arrival there and 814, as well as on written sources and likely the eyewitness accounts of older members of the court for the years before ca. 791. Composed in an excellent Latin, the *Vita* shows the influence of various classical writers, above all of Suetonius's *De vita Caesarum,* particularly the life of Augustus. Like many Carolingian authors, however, Einhard did not borrow mindlessly from his sources but selected and manipulated his material to accord with what he wanted to say.

See also **Alcuin; Charlemagne; Lothair I; Louis the Pious**

Further Reading

Einhard. *Einhard: Vita Caroli Magni. The Life of Charlemagne*, ed. and trans. Evelyn Scherabon Firchow and Edwin H. Zeydel. Coral Gables: University of Miami Press, 1972.

Thorpe, Lewis, trans. *Einhard and Notker the Stammerer: Two Lives of Charlemagne*. Harmondsworth: Penguin, 1969.

Beumann, Helmut. *Ideengeschichtliche Studien zu Einhard und anderen Geschichtsschreibern des friheren Mittelalters*. Darmstadt: Wissenschaftliche Buchgesellschaft, 1969.

Fleckenstein, Josef. "Einhard, seine Grindung und sein Vermächtnis in Seligenstadt." In *Das Einhardkreuz: Vortraege und Studien der Muensteraner Diskussion zum arcus Einhardi*, ed. Karl Hauck. Göttingen: Vandenhoeck and Ruprecht, 1974, pp. 96–121.

CELIA CHAZELLE

EIXIMENIS, FRANCESC (1330/35–1409)

A Catalan religious writer, Eiximenis, was born at Girona between 1330 and 1335. He entered the Franciscan order in his youth and studied in Italy, France, and England. In 1374, with the support of the king of Aragón, he obtained the *licentia docendi* at Toulouse University. He was highly esteemed by king Pedro III, while in whose entourage Eiximenis planned the *Crestià*, his ambitious Christian vernacular encyclopedia in thirteen large volumes. The first volume, *Primer del Crestià* (1381), was written in Barcelona and deals with the foundations of Christian dogma. The second, *Segon del Crestià*, which discusses temptation and divine grace, was finished in Valencia, "where Eiximenis spent his mature years. In 1383 Eiximenis offered the citizens of Valencia a compendium of moral and political advice, the *Regiment de la cosa pública*, a vast treatise on the nature of human society and its government that was later included in the *Dotzè*. Meanwhile he finished another volume of the encyclopedia, the *Terç* (1384), an extensive description of the seven deadly sins, with theological explanations as well as all sorts of exempla and practical digressions. The *Dotzè* (1386, with an interpolation of 1391) is the twelfth, and the most popular, book of Eiximenis's encyclopedia. Titled *Regiment de prínceps i comunitats*, it is addressed to princes and kings, as well as to administrative officers with civil responsibilities. The two huge volumes of the *Dotzè* were kept in the city hall of Valencia for public consultation. Presumably Eiximenis did not complete the *Crestià* as planned. In 1392 he finished a very successful treatise on heavenly creatures, the *Llibre dels àngels*, and probably in 1396 a monograph on morals for women: the *Llibre de les dones*. Eiximenis also produced a *Vida de Jesucrist* (ca. 1400), which enjoyed great success and was designed to teach a personal approach to the human and divine figure of the Son of God, in the manner of Ludolph of Saxony and Ubertino of Casale's Latin *Vitae Christi*. Eiximenis's Latin works include an *Ars praedicandi*, a *Pastorale* giving advice to the bishop of Valencia, and a *Psalterium alias Laudatorium papae Benedicto XIII dedicatum*. The prayers of the latter were translated into Catalan in 1416.

Eiximenis supported Pope Benedict XIII, who in 1408 designated him patriarch of Jerusalem and bishop of Elna. He died at Perpignan, France, in April 1409. His books enjoyed a great success: There are many extant manuscripts of some of them; others were translated into Spanish and even into French; and some were printed in the fifteenth century. Eiximenis was a compiler deeply indebted to his sources (the great Franciscan writers of the thirteenth century, the treatises on vices and virtues), but he was also an extraordinarily talented vernacular prose writer and an acute observer of his times. His writings provided a fruitful bridge between the learned church traditions and the cultural needs of the inhabitants of the Catalan towns of the late Middle Ages.

See also **Pedro III, King of Aragón**

Further Reading

Eiximenis, F. *Lo crestià*. Ed. by A. Hauf. In *Les millors obres de la literatura catalana*. Vol. 98. Barcelona, 1983.

Viera, D. *Bibliografia anotada de la vida i obra de Francesc Eiximenis*. Barcelona, 1980.

LOLA BADÍA

ELEANOR OF AQUITAINE (ca. 1122–1204)

The duchy of Aquitaine was the largest, most populous region of France in the 12th and 13th centuries. Its proximity to the Mediterranean and its cultural and commercial contacts with the Greek and Byzantine worlds attracted wealth and immigrants. It was openly coveted by French kings, who, in the 13th century, would rely on the pretext of eradicating heresy to invade it. Earlier, in the 10th and 11th centuries, it had been controlled, for the most part with generosity and flexibility, by dukes whose creativity and precocity are legendary. William III founded the Abbey of Cluny in 910; William IX offered his irreverent troubadour poems to the courts of Europe.

In 1137 the only child of William X, Eleanor, who possessed the spirited character of her forebears, inherited the duchy and was immediately married to the French king, Louis VII. Later, after befriending Geoffrey, count of Anjou, she became wife to his son, the future Henry II of England. The marriage not only transferred the richness of Aquitaine from the French to the English monarchy, where it remained until 1214, but it united two formerly competing provinces.

Thus it might be supposed that Eleanor was a key

Eleanor of Aquitane. Died 1204 in Fontevrault, France. Tombs of the Plantagenet Kings. 13th c. © Erich Lessing/Art Resources, New York.

individual in the government of the Angevin Empire, but the evidence for her influence is slight. Narrative sources deal mainly with the kings, and she appears fleetingly in them. Few charters are extant from Poitou, which Eleanor governed in the 1160s and 1180s. In other areas of the Angevin Empire, where more charters survive, she attested infrequently—a reflection, perhaps, of the time spent early on bearing children and her long interval of imprisonment.

Eleanor supported Henry II's early endeavors to expand and control Angevin lands and, later, her sons' revolts against their father to obtain portions of those lands; her independent policies are difficult to trace. Her cultural influence may have been pervasive, however. The movement of her court from southern to northern France and England helped convey the ideals of courtly love to the European nobility. Romantic themes found full literary expression at the court of her daughter, Marie countess of Champagne, who sponsored the work of Chrétien de Troyes, and in her son Richard the Lionheart, whose love songs were sung throughout France.

Thus Eleanor is often viewed as a mirror of her husbands' and sons' achievements. It is perhaps more instructive to view her condition as fairly typical of women of the upper nobility in the high Middle Ages. Despite her talent and strength of character her key roles involved bearing children and the transfer of land.

Married at fifteen, she lost her first child when he was three years old, and she bore her last, John, in what was likely to have been a difficult pregnancy, at 44. Her willful nature embarrassed Louis VII, incurred the censure of his clerical friends, and may have brought about their divorce after fifteen years of marriage (1137–52), although there is some suggestion that Eleanor herself engineered the split.

She protested the infidelity of her second husband, Henry, whom she married at 30 (when he was only 19) and to whom she would be wife for 37 years (1152–89). This audacity, together with her power over her children and her influence in Aquitaine and at the English and Angevin courts, resulted in imprisonment at Winchester for sixteen years (1173–89, when Henry died). After regaining her freedom she acted as regent for both Richard and John, realizing her potential only in widowhood.

Eleanor's acts involved a reversal of Henrys oppression—amnesty for those awaiting judicial trial and a relaxing of obligations imposed on abbeys—as well as patronage. She protected Richard's interests against the ambitions of France's Philip Augustus and Prince John. Then, when Richard died in 1199, Eleanor undertook goodwill visits on John's behalf. Toward the end of her life, dispirited and worn, she took up residence at the Angevin abbey of Fontevrault, where she is buried.

See also **Guilhem IX; Henry II; John; Richard I**

Further Reading

Duby, Georges. *Medieval Marriage: Two Models from Twelfth-Century France.* Trans. Elborg Forster. Baltimore: Johns Hopkins University Press, 1978.

Kelly, Amy. *Eleanor of Aquitaine and the Four Kings.* Cambridge: Harvard University Press, 1950.

Warren, W.L. *Henry II.* Rev. ed. London: Methuen, 1991.

STEPHANIE CHRISTELOW

ELISABETH VON SCHÖNAU (1129–1164)

A Benedictine nun, visionary, mystic, and women's *magistra* (teacher) in the double monastery of Schönau near St. Goarshausen, Elisabeth was strongly influenced by Hildegard von Bingen and yet her accomplishments were very different in scope and originality from the renowned contemporary visionary. Elisabeth's ecstasies, visions, and auditions started in 1152. In her visions, which were always accompanied by physical and mental suffering, Elisabeth sees herself guided by an angel.

Although she had begun to set down her own spiritual experiences in writing, in 1155 Elisabeth asked her brother, Ekbert (the author of *Sermones contra Catharos,* "Sermons against the Cathars," and later the abbot of Schönau), to join her at Schönau as her personal adviser and scribe. Much of her text, including some of her less orthodox visions (such as Christ as a woman), was reinterpreted by Ekbert. Similar to Hildegard, Elisabeth was deeply concerned with the corruption in the church of her time and pleaded for reform. Elisabeth faced strong clerical criticism throughout her life.

While never canonized, Elisabeth enjoyed a widespread saintly reputation among her contemporaries. Her work, less complicated than that of Hildegard von Bingen, was uniquely successful (becoming known as far away as twelfth-century Iceland); more than 150 medieval manuscripts are extant. The twelfth-century codex 3 of the Landesbibliothek at Wiesbaden, which contains her complete work, was compiled under Ekbert's supervision.

Besides over twenty letters (most of them written between 1154 and 1164), Elisabeth's work comprises the *Liber visionum*, a collection of her visions in three parts (1152–1160), which contains topical themes of interest today for the history of religion; the *Liber viarum dei* (Book of the Ways of God), 1156–1157, patterned after Hildegard von Bingen's *Scivias* (Know the Ways); and the *Liber revelationum de sacro exercitu virginum Coloniensium*, an imaginative embellishment of the then very popular Ursula legend, which had an enormous influence on medieval hagiography and iconography. While the Latin text of Elisabeth's work was edited (by F.W.E. Roth) in 1884, a critical edition is still outstanding.

See also **Hildegard von Bingen**

Further Reading

Clark, Anne L. *Elisabeth of Schönau: A Twelfth-Century Visionary*. Philadelphia: University of Pennsylvania Press, 1992.

Lewis, Gertrud Jaron. *Bibliographie zur deutschen Frauenmystik des Mittelalters*. Berlin: Erich Schmidt Verlag, 1989 [comprehensive list of primary texts and secondary sources up to 1988, pp. 146–158].

Ruh, Kurt. *Geschichte der abendländischen Mystik*, vol. 2, *Frauenmystik und Franziskanische Mystik der Frühzeit*. Munich: Beck, 1993, pp. 64–85.

GERTRUD JARON LEWIS

ELIZABETH OF HUNGARY (1207–1231)

Saint Elizabeth (of Hungary, also of Thuringia) was born in 1207 to Andreas II, king of Hungary, and his wife, Gertrude of Andechs-Meranien. At the age of four she was betrothed to the eldest son of Hermann, landgrave of Thuringia, and was taken to be raised at his court. The marriage took place in 1221, four years after Hermann's death and his son's succession as Landgrave Ludwig IV. Elizabeth bore two children, a son Hermann and a daughter Sophie, before her husband's departure on Crusade with Frederick II in 1227. A third child, Gertrude, was born three weeks after Ludwig's death

on board ship off the coast of Italy. After her husband's death, Elizabeth left the court and moved to Marburg in the western part of Thuringia, where she established a hospital and spent the last four years of her life nursing the sick with her own hands. She was canonized in 1235, only four years after her death. The cornerstone for a new, Gothic church over her burial site was laid at that time. The testimony collected in support of Elizabeth's canonization soon augmented the bare facts of her life. She is said to have been unusually pious as a child, when she preferred praying to playing with other children and stole bread from the court kitchens to feed the poor. She was reputed to have tended the sick in her marriage bed and to have organized large-scale donations of grain from the landgraves' stores in time of famine. Popular legend too augmented the saint's image. An early story that she was chased from the Wartburg by her brothers-in-law alter her husband's death is now thought to be apocryphal; it seems more likely that she left of her own volition to lead a life of piety and charity that was not possible at court. From the time of her death, she was venerated as a saint; the director of her ascetic spiritual practice during the last years of her life, Konrad of Marburg, quickly built a stone basilica over her burial site and began assembling testimony, particularly evidence of miracles, in support of her canonization. After Konrad's death in 1233, Elizabeth's powerful brothers-in-law actively supported the canonization; additional documentation accumulated at this time, including the *Libellus de dictis quatuor ancillarum*, (a brief treatise on her works) placed more emphasis on Elizabeth's earthly deeds. The pope's interest in Elizabeth's sainthood is clearly stated in the canonization documents: a new and popular saint was perceived to be a useful tool in the fight against heresy. Elizabeth's popularity in the eyes of the people seems to have relied not only on her generosity but, more specifically, on her adherence to the tenets of the new Franciscan order, which preached an ascetic lifestyle in which devotion to God was reflected in service to the less fortunate.

Two of the earliest works of art commemorating the new saint record scenes from her life. The roof panels from the great gilt shrine, probably underway by 1248, portray Ludwig's decision to take the cross, his departure from Elizabeth, the return of his bones to his wife, and Elizabeth clothing a beggar, taking the simple gray robes of a hospital worker as a sign of her poverty and devotion to others, distributing alms to the poor, feeding the hungry, and giving drink to the thirsty and washing the feet of a beggar. The nearly contemporary stained glass window, also in her church at Marburg, strengthens the emphasis on her charitable deeds by increasing their number to six, to correspond to the canonical Acts of Charity according to Matthew 25: 34–36, and organizing them together in the window's left lancet. Since a

Master Theoderich, Saint Elizabeth. © Erich Lessing/Art Resource, New York.

restoration in 1977–1979, they have been juxtaposed to single, unrepeated events from her life in the right lancet. All the scenes from the roof of the shrine also appear in the window in closely related compositions. In the roundel at the top of the window, Christ and the Virgin crown Francis and Elizabeth, respectively.

While later altarpieces both at St. Elizabeth's and elsewhere repeat scenes from her life (see *700 Jahre*, 1983: E, nos. 10 and 20, and II, nos. 2–4, 50–51), the preference in later works, both paintings and sculptures, is for single figures of the saint (see *700 Jahre*: II, nos. 3, 7–11, 14–15, 17–33, 40, 43–48). This type too derives from an early work, a window from the first stained glass campaign at St. Elizabeth's, circa 1240, which portrays the standing saint crowned and elegantly dressed. The single figures typically amplify this model with an attribute referring to Elizabeth's charity: a loaf of bread or a roll, a pitcher, or a garment. Frequently a beggar in smaller scale kneels at her feet awaiting her gift. Although the church dedicated to her at Marburg was not started until the day after her canonization, from the middle of the fourteenth century Elizabeth was also portrayed bearing a church model, the attribute typical of church founders and patrons (see *700 Jahre* 1983:

II, nos. 57, 61–62, 64–66). Sometimes, especially in late medieval works produced in Hesse, the church is clearly identifiable as St. Elizabeth's, with its distinctive tri-conch (arched) apse and two tall facade towers.

Further Reading

Bierschenk, Monika. *Glasmalereien der Elisabethkirche in Marburg*: *Die figürlichen Fenster um 1240*. Berlin: Deutscher Verlag für Kunstwissenschaft, 1991.

Demandt, Karl. "Verfremdung und Wiederkehr der heiligen Elisabeth." *Hessisches Jahrbuch für Landesgeschichte* 22(1972): 112–161.

Der sog. Libellus de dictis quatuor ancillarum S. Elisabeth confectus, ed. Albert Huyskens. Kempten: Joseph Kosel, 1911.

Dinkler-von Schubert, Erika. *Der Schrein der hl. Elisabeth zu Marburg*: *Studien zur Schrein-Ikonographie*. Marburg: Verlag des Kunstgeschichtlichen Seminars der Universität, 1964.

Sankt Elisabeth: *Fürstin, Dienerin, Heilige*. Sigmaringen: Thorbecke, 1981.

Schmoll, Friedrich. *Die hl. Elisabeth in der bildenden Kunst des 13. bis 16. Jahrhunderts*. Marburg: Elwert, 1918.

700 Jahre Elisabethkirche in Marburg 1283–1983. 8 vols. Marburg: Elwert, 1983.

Werner, Matthias. "Die Heilige Elisabeth und die Anfänge des Deutschen Ordens in Marburg," in *Marburger Geschichte*: *Rückblick auf die Stadtgeschichte in Einzelbeiträgen*, ed. Erhart Dettmering and Rudolf Grenz. Marburg: Der Magistral, 1980, pp. 121–164.

JOAN A. HOLLADAY

ENCINA, JUAN DEL (1468–ca.1530)

A man of prodigious talent and driving ambition, Juan del Encina was born, in 1468, into the musically gifted family of a prosperous Salamancan cobbler. Under the tutelage of his older brothers, one a professor of music at the University of Salamanca and the other a chorister of the cathedral, Encina soon became an accomplished musician. His skill is evidenced by an extant corpus of sixty-two original works, the largest of any musician of the period. Several of his compositions are dedicated to Prince Juan, suggesting that he enjoyed favor at the Aragónese court of Fernando II.

As a student of the humanities at the University of Salamanca, Encina met two distinguished figures who would significantly influence his literary career: Antonio de Nebrija, who taught him Latin and rhetoric, and Gutierre de Toledo, chancellor of the university and brother of the second duke of Alba. In 1492 Encina became part of the duke's household, as creator of musical and theatrical entertainments. It was in this sumptuous, aristocratic milieu that Encina began his remarkable dramatic output and aggressive bid for professional advancement.

Encina's reputation rests primarily on the *Cancionero* of 1496, a collection of lyrics, long poems, original and translated prose works, and dramatic eclogues that he carefully prepared for publication. The volume contains a remarkable number of firsts in Spanish literary history: the first treatise on poetic theory (*Arte de poesía castellana*); the earliest rendering of Latin verse in Castilian meter (a paraphrase of Virgil's *Bucolics*); and the eight pastoral eclogues that have earned him the title "father of the Castilian theater."

The playlets that Encina produced and acted in at the ducal court were to have a lasting influence on Iberian drama throughout the sixteenth century. Their single greatest contribution was the character of the shepherd (*pastor*), the uncouth, unkempt, and ignorant rustic whose highly expressive stage language of *sayagués* Encina modeled on the rural dialect of his region. On one level the *pastor* was simply a comic figure intended to elicit laughter from a noble audience. In Encina's hands, however, he also gave voice to a variety of serious issues, such as social conflict, religious disharmony between Old and New Christians, and the difficulties of the artist-patron relationship. Last but not least, and aided by the fact that Encina often played the role himself, the shpherd became a vehicle for blatant self-promotion.

A notable lack of dramatic illusion often complements the multifarious role of the shepherd. In eclogues 1 and 2, for example, the shepherds are alternately contemporary Salamancan rustics guarding the duke of Alba's flocks, the four Evangelists, and biblical witnesses of the Nativity; one of them also represents the playwright and his anxieties about receiving adequate recognition from his patrons.

Another important influence on Encina's theater is clearly evinced in the final eclogues of the 1496 collection: the vast body of fifteenth-century love lyrics. In order to dramatize the power of love to transform lives and equalize social differences, eclogues 7 and 8 in particular draw heavily on the language and concepts of this amatory verse.

Social harmony becomes more elusive and love less benevolent in Encina's six remaining plays, probably written between 1493 and 1499. Eclogue 9, a Christmas play, deals only marginally with the Nativity, dwelling instead on the desolation wrought on town and country by the great rains of 1498 and the squabbling of four shepherds seeking shelter from the storm. The work seems to reflect a growing disillusionment, common to Encina's generation, with the possibility of peaceful coexistence between Old and New Christians in Spain.

It is believed that Encina's failure to secure ecclesiastical advancement and his continuing dissatisfaction with the Duke of Alba's patronage caused him to leave the latter's employ sometime around 1498. Shortly thereafter he left Spain for the first of three extended stays in Rome.

Encina's best-known works, eclogues 11–14, reflect his experience of the cultural wealth of Renaissance Rome, where his musical talents gained him the protection of three successive popes. The plays are noteworthy for their greater structural complexity, their borrowings from classical and Italian literature, and their increasing secularization, culminating in the sacrilegious suicide for love that occurs in eclogue 14, *Égloga de Plácida y Victoriano*. Eclogue 11, *Égloga de Cristino y Febea*, is generally regarded to be Encina's most accomplished. Although he had previously dramatized its theme of love's power to resolve conflicting values and lifestyles, here he achieves a more highly developed scenic structure.

Égloga de Plácida y Victoriano was performed in 1513. Some six years later Encina was ordained a priest and went on pilgrimage to Jerusalem. He spent the last ten years of his life (ca. 1520–ca. 1530) as prior of the cathedral of León. He had written the plays that determined the shape of Spain's secular theater before the age of thirty.

Further Reading

Andrews, J. R. *Juan del Encina: Prometheus in Search of Prestige.* Berkeley, 1959.
Encina, J. del. *Obras dramáticas.* Vol. 1. *Cancionero de 1496.* Ed. R. Gimeno. Madrid, 1975.
———. *Teatro (Segunda producción dramática).* Ed. R. Gimeno. Madrid, 1977.
Sullivan, H. *Juan del Encina.* Boston, 1976.

BARBARA F. WEISSBERGER

ENGELBERT OF BERG (d. 1225)

A member of the noble family of the counts of Berg and Altena, Engelbert of Berg became a member of the cathedral chapter at Cologne during the episcopate of his cousin Adolf of Altena, who sat as archbishop 1193–1205. Over time he acquired the provostships of the collegiate churches of St. George, St. Severin, St. Mary in Aachen, Deventer, and Züften. In 1203, he was even elected bishop of Münster but declined, claiming he was too young for such an honor. In reality, he had his eye on the Cologne archiepiscopal chair. Adolf's political position in 1205 led to his being deposed, but the support of many of the prominent cathedral canons and other dignitaries of the archdiocese precipitated a schism that lasted until the Fourth Lateran Council in 1215. During the schism, Engelbert continued to support Adolf, and in 1216 the priors of Cologne elected Engelbert, who by now was cathedral provost as well as archdeacon, to be archbishop.

In 1220, just before returning to Sicily, Emperor Frederick II appointed Engelbert as regent for young Henry (VII), the not yet ten-year-old heir to the Staufen thrones. As regent, Engelbert displayed great administrative ability, though he did not always pursue policies in harmony with the emperor's intentions. He tried to create some stability in the political situation by instituting regional public peace agreements. But in his attempts to bring about closer relations with the English royal court, in line with Cologne tradition, and to bolster them by marriage projects between the Staufen king and the English royal family, he seems to have been more influenced by what was good for Cologne than by what was pleasing to Frederick II. Once war broke out anew between the English and French kings in 1224, Frederick sought to conclude a peace agreement with the Capetians. And instead of being wedded to one of the daughters of the English king, as urged by the archbishop, young Henry (VII), who was still a minor, was married to the daughter of the Babenberg Duke Leopold of Austria in November 1225.

There were also differences between the emperor in Sicily and the archiepiscopal regent concerning the treatment of King Valdemar of Denmark, who had been taken prisoner. Frederick endeavored to force Valdemar to give back former imperial areas between the Elbe and the Baltic that Otto IV and also he himself (in 1214) had granted to the Danish king.

Ultimately, Archbishop Engelbert fell victim to his own extensive family and territorial politics. He was ambushed and fatally wounded on the evening of November 7, 1225, while en route from Soest to Schwelm in Westfalia. The leader of the assailants was his cousin's son, Frederick of Isenberg, who himself had influential comrades-in-arms in his brothers, the bishops of Osnabrück and Münster. The immediate cause of the attack was the archbishop's efforts to remove a canoness foundation at Essen from the repressive actions of its lay advocates, the counts of Isenberg, but it was part of a larger policy aimed at placing as many ecclesiastical establishments as possible under the direct protection of Cologne's archbishop himself.

Engelbert's remains were buried in Cologne Cathedral on December 27, 1225, but they were ceremoniously transferred to a new grave in the cathedral during Lent 1226 in a ceremony presided over by Cardinal-bishop Conrad of Urach, then active in Germany as a papal legate. The legate also presided over a diet, during which a full investigation of the assassination was carried out. Both Walter von der Vogelweide and Caesarius of Heisterbach wrote pieces in honor of the slain prelate; the latter in fact began to collect anecdotal information that he eventually turned into a panegyric aimed at securing Engelbert's canonization as a martyr. Efforts to secure for Engelbert the martyr's crown similar to that of Thomas of Canterbury ultimately failed, however.

It is noteworthy that Frederick II did not appoint another prelate to the position of regent and guardian for his son; in place of the murdered archbishop he

nominated Duke Ludwig of Bavaria. The move can be seen as an effort on Frederick's part to keep the German nobility from becoming totally alienated following Engelbert's ecclesiastical regime.

See also **Caesarius of Heisterbach; Frederick II; Otto IV**

Further Reading

Ficker, Julius. *Engelbert der Heilige, Erzbischof von Köln und Reichsverweser*. Cologne: Heberle, 1853.

Foerster, Hans. "Engelbert von Berg der Heilige." *Bergische Forschungen* 1 (1925): 108–123.

Greven, Joseph. "Die Entstehung der Vita Engelberti des Caesarius von Heisterbach." *Annalen des historischen Vereins für den Niederrhein* 102 (1918): 2ff.

Kleist, Wolfgang. "Der Tod des Erzbischofs Engelbert von Köln: eine kritische Studie." *Zeitschrift für vaterländische Geschichte und Altertumskunde Westfalens* 75 (1917): 182–249.

Lothmann, Josef. *Erzbischof Engelbert I. von Köln (1216–1225): Graf von Berg, Erzbischof und Herzog, Reichsverweser*. Cologne: Kölnischer Geschichtsverein, 1993.

Ribbeck, Walter. "Die Kölner Erzbischöfe und die Vogtei des Suites Essen 1221–1228." *Korrespondenzblatt des Gesamtvereins der deutschen Geschichte und Altertumsvereine*. 2 (1903): 35ff.

PAUL B. PIXTON

ENRIQUE II, KING OF CASTILE (1333–1379)

Son of Alfonso XI, king of Castile, and his mistress, Leónor de Guzmán, Enrique II was born in Seville in 1333. He was adopted by the magnate Rodrigo Alvarez de las Asturias, from whom he received the *condado* of Trastámara, which provided the name of the dynasty initiated by Enrique. In 1350, he married Juana Manuel, daughter of the author and aristocrat, Juan Manuel. He died in Santo Domingo de la Calzada in May 1379 and was buried in the cathedral of Toledo.

From a very young age, Enrique opposed the kingship of his stepbrother, Pedro I of Castile, who had been accused of cruelty and of favoring the Jews. After the failure of the first uprisings against Pedro I in 1356 and 1360, Enrique, aspiring to crown himself king of Castile, sought strong military and diplomatic support before renewing the attacks. He found this support in two places: in the *Compañías Blancas* led by Beltrán Du Guesclin of Brittany in Aragón, who signed the Treaty of Monzón with Enrique in 1363, and in the pope, who consecrated the projected campaign as a crusade. In March 1366, Enrique invaded Castile, crowning himself king in Burgos the next month. As the illegitimate prince was waging his offensive, which reached as far as Seville, his stepbrother Pedro fled, seeking help from the English. But the defeat that Enrique suffered in Nájera (April 1367) at the hands of Pedro I and the English temporarily crippled his plans. He had to seek refuge in France, although he was able to return to Castile at the end of 1367. At that point a corrosive war between the brothers began, with Enrique increasingly gaining the upper hand, due to the economic travails of the time as well as the growing unpopularity of his rival. The assassination of Pedro I in Montiel (March, 1369) cleared Enrique's path to the Castilian throne.

The political outlook Enrique faced in the spring of 1369 was far from promising. In the Castilian interior, several regions maintained loyalty to Pedro I, including Carmona, Zamora, and a large part of Galicia, but an anti-Castilian coalition composed of the remaining Spanish kingdoms was forming. In 1371 the pockets of *petrista* support were crushed; at the same time, due to the signing of the treaty of Santarem with the Portuguese, its defensive strongholds along the frontiers of Aragón, Portugal, and Navarre crumbled. In 1375 the Treaty of Almazán made peace between Enrique II and Pedro IV of Aragón, who agreed to yield Molina to Castile, abandon his claims to Murcia, and consent to marriage between his daughter Leónor and Juan, the heir to the Castilian throne. Only the conflict with Navarre remained, though with the Treaty of Santo Domingo de la Calzada in 1379, this too was resolved. Clearly, between 1371 and 1379 the foundations were established for Castile's future hegemony in the Iberian Peninsula.

On the international front, Enrique II's rise to power produced a period of close alliance between Castile and France, beginning with the Treaty of Toledo, signed in 1368 by the illegitimate prince and delegates sent by the king of France. As a result of this accord, Castile aided France in the Hundred Years War: its participation was particularly notable in the naval victory at La Rochelle (1372) and in the sacking of the Isle of Wight (1373). Accompanying the French alliance was Castile's hostility toward England; their economic rivalry acquired political motives as the duke of Lancaster laid claim to the Castilian throne due to his marriage to Constanza, daughter of Pedro I.

The generosity Enrique II displayed to the noblemen that helped him acquire the throne explains why he received the nickname "*el de las mercedes*" (he of the favors, or mercies). For the high Castilian nobility, Enrique II's ascent to the throne provided a prime solution for the problems created by the deep economic crisis of the time. For the crown, on the other hand, the *mercedes enriqueñas* produced a considerable decrease of royal property. Enrique's donations to his supporters consisted largely in seigneurial territories whose beneficiaries received revenues and possessed jurisdictional rights. Enrique II gave territories to captains of foreign troops such as Du Guesclin, who received but never occupied

Soria and Molina, and Bernal de Béarne, who was awarded Medinaceli. The king's brothers, Sancho and Tello, were also beneficiaries of royal *mercedes*, as was his illegitimate son Alfonso Enríquez. But the majority of the donations were made to nobles, both from time-honored, traditionally powerful lineages (the Guzmán family, for example) and from social-climbing, newly powerful groups (like the Mendoza or Velasco families). Despite everything, Enrique II managed to slow down the negative impact these concessions had on the royal estates, establishing restrictive norms regulating their primogeniture succession.

In the political realm Enrique II strengthened the crown's power. In 1371 the seven-member *Audiencia* was established, serving as the kingdom's high court of justice. Also notable was the development of a system of estate administration, which by the end of the monarch's reign had taken the form of a *casa de cuentas* (billing house). Enrique II also called for frequent meetings of the *cortes* (parliament), which served as an essential instrument of dialogue with the kingdom and its cities. The principal sessions of the cortes occurred in Toro in 1369, when important legislation regarding price and salary regulation was approved, and in 1371. In conclusion, Enrique II lay the groundwork for the modern state in Castile.

In Enrique II's times, the tolerance that until then had prevailed between Christians and Jews began to crumble. Anti-Semitic propaganda, supported by the monarch during the war with his brother, led to violent attacks against numerous Jewish groups in Castile. Also supporting this trend were the intense criticisms made by the third estate of the cortes against the Jews. Once he had assured his place on the throne, Enrique II clearly changed his attitude, attempting to protect the Jews, even naming some to governmental positions, such as Yuçaf Pichon, *almojarife mayor* (chief tax collector) of the king's estate. But the anti-Semitic sentiments of the popular Christian sectors of Castile were already unstoppable.

Further Reading

Suárez, L. "Política internacional de Enrique II," *Hispania*, 16 (1956), 16–129.

Valdeón, J. *Enrique II de Castilla: la guerra civil y la consolidación del régimen (1366–1371)*. Valladolid, 1966.

Suárez, L. "Castilla (1350–1406)." In *Historia de España*. Vol. 14. Ed. R. Menéndez Pidal. Madrid, 1966. 3–378.

Valdeón, J. *Los judíos de Castilla y la revolución Trastámara*. Valladolid, 1968.

——. "La victoria de Enrique II: Los Trastámaras en el poder." In *Génesis medieval del Estado Moderno: Castilla y Navarra (1250–1370)*. Ed. A. Rucquoi. Valladolid, 1988. 245–58.

JULIO VALDEÓN BARUQUE

ERHART, MICHEL
(ca. 1440/1450–ca. 1520/1530)

Only a few concrete dates are known in the biography of Michel Erhart, who is always called *bildhower* (stone sculptor) in the documents. He is assumed to have been born between 1440 and 1450. Documented as a master in Ulm from 1469, he must have married the daughter of Vinzenz Ensinger, a masterbuilder in Constance, about this time; this familial relationship supports the thesis that Erhart probably served as a stone sculptor's apprentice in southern Germany. Repeated appearances as a sponsor for applicants for citizenship in the city of Ulm suggest that he possessed a position of considerable trust before the city council. He seems to have died at about eighty years of age. His son Gregor and at least one other son followed in their father's profession.

Of Erhart's nine works documented in archives between 1474 and 1516, which include the high altar for Ulm Cathedral finished in 1479, only two are preserved: a sandstone epitaph for the Abbot Konrad Mîrlin dated 1497 (now Augsburg, Städtische Kunstsammlungen) and five prophets created between 1517 and 1520 for a stone Mount of Olives group that originally comprised thirteen figures (Ulm, Ulmer Museum).

These works, together with an over-life-size Crucifix at St. Michael's in Schwäbisch-Hall, which is signed and dated 1494, serve as the point of departure for numerous attributions. With five further crucifixes, including one over five meters tall at St. Martin's in Landshut from 1495, a Madonna of Mercy dated about 1480 (Berlin, Bodemuseum) and an over-life-size standing Virgin from Kaufbeuren from about 1475–1480 (Munich, Bayerisches Nationalmuseum) number among the seventy major works attributed to the master by Anja Broschek. "The tightly composed figural forms" (Miller 1971:51), the radiant beauty of the virgins' faces, and the lively representation of details reveal the influence of Hans Multscher as well as Netherlandish sculptors on Erhart's aristocratic art.

The authorship of the busts on the end panels of the choir stalls in Ulm Cathedral between about 1469 and 1474 remains disputed. The high altar of Blaubeuren, however, is now considered as a joint work of Michel and his son Gregor, made while the son was active in the father's shop.

See also **Multscher, Hans**

Further Reading

Broschek, Anja. *Michel Erhart: Ein Beitrag zur schwäbischen Plastik der Spätgotik.* Berlin: de Gruyter, 1973.

Deutsch, Wolfgang. "Der ehemalige Hochaltar und das Chorgestühl: Zur Syrlin- und zur Bildhauerfrage," in *600 Jahre Ulmer Münster: Festschrift,* ed. Hans Eugen Specker and Reinhard Wortmann. Ulm: Kohlhammer, 1977, pp. 242–322.

Miller, Albrecht. "Der Kaufbeurer Altar des Michel Erhart." *Münchner Jahrbuch der Bildenden Kunst* 22 (1971): 46–62.

Müller, Hannelore. "Michel und Gregor Erhart," in *Lebensbilder aus dem bayerischen Schwaben,* ed. Götz Freiherr von Pölnitz. Veröffentlichungen der Schwäbischen Forschungsgemeinschaft bei der Kommission für Bayerische Landesgeschichte, 3d series, vol. 5. Munich: Max Hueber, 1956, pp. 16–44.

Roth, Michael, and Hanns Westhoff. "Beobachtungen zu Malerei und Fassung des Blaubeurer Hochaltars," in *Flügelaltäre des späten Mittelalters,* ed. Hartmut Krohm and Eike Oellermann. Berlin: Dietrich Reimer, 1992, pp. 167–188.

Schahl, Adolf. "Michel Erhart: Der Meister des Haller Kruzifixes." *Württembergisch-Franken* 47 (1963): 37–58.

BRIGITTE SCHLIEWEN

ERIK, SAINT (12 century)

Erik was king of Sweden, and son of an unknown Jedvard (Edward). He was venerated as a saint in Uppsala from at least 1198 (the Vallentuna Calendar). In his legend, the oldest version of which is now dated to the 1180s (Sjögren 1983), he is said to have been killed by a Danish pretender to the Swedish throne, Magnus, son of Henrik Skadelår, an offspring of the Danish royal family, on Ascension Day, May 18, 1160, at the Mountain of the Holy Trinity in Uppsala after having heard mass. The legend characterizes his ten-year reign as model years of royal justice. But the chronology is erroneous. Ascension Day fell on the 5th of May in 1160, but on the 18th of May in 1167, one month after Erik's son Knut had slain his competitor for the Swedish throne, Karl Sverkerson. Thus, the legendary date is rather to be explained as the day of glorification of Knut's father as a saint in 1167. Numismatic evidence from the reign of Knut (1167–1196) proves that he promoted Erik's cult (Sjögren 1983). It must have received episcopal approbation by Stephen, archbishop 1164–1185. The saint's name was used as a symbol by aristocratic insurrections against later dynasties in the 13th century (Sjögren 1986). A rhymed liturgical office was created shortly before 1300 under Dominican influence, and from this period most of the miracles derive. The full version of his legend dates from 1344; new parts were composed for his office by Bishop Nils Hermansson (d. 1391).

St. Erik became a symbol of the Church in Sweden from the 14th century, and patron saint of Sweden and Stockholm in the 15th century. *Erik konungs lag* ("King Erik's Law") became a symbol for "old, good law." His relics are still kept in Uppsala cathedral. The feast of *translatio* of his relics was celebrated on January 24th, probably in memory of their transfer to the new cathedral in 1273 (Carlsson 1944). St. Erik was connected with a crusade for the propagation of faith to Finland. A Bishop Henrik, later venerated as a saint in Nousis and the patron saint of Finland, is supposed to have accompanied him and been killed at the campaign dated by historians to 1155/9. But there is no evidence outside the legend to support the crusade, and Henrik is not found among the bishops of Uppsala.

There is better evidence for Erik's origin in the province of Västergötland, where his son Knut probably supervised the building of Eriksberg church in memory of his father. Erik and his queen, Christina, tried to prevent the Cistercian foundation in Västergötland from moving from Lurö/Lugnås to Vamhem around 1158 (*Scriptores Minores Historiae Danicae Medii Aevi* 2:138, 141). Since Uppsala cathedral chapter followed *ordo monasticus* 1188/97, and since Erik's reign is the most probable period for the establishment of such a monastic chapter in Uppsala (Gallén 1976), we may see the reason for Erik's aversion to the Cistercians in his support for the Black Benedictines. Such a monastic chapter existed only in Odense, Denmark, so it cannot be ruled out that Erik had connections with Denmark, where we find *Ericus dux et eius filii Karolus et Kanutus* (*jarl* Erik and his sons Karl and Knut) in Lund 1145 (*Diplomatarium Danicum* 1:2, no. 88) and *Ericus* [lord of] *Falster* at Haraldsted 1131 (*Vita Sanctorum Danorum* 239; Gallén 1985). Erik's crusade may then tentatively be identified with the campaign mentioned under 1142 in the Novgorod chronicle.

Further Reading

Editions

Fant, Eric Michael, ed. *Scriptores rerum svecicarum medii ævi* 2.1. Uppsala: Zeipel & Palmblad, 1828, 270–320.

Nelson, Axel, ed. *Vita et miracula Sancti Erici regis Sueciae. Latine et Suecice. Codex Vat. reg. lat. 525 Suecice et Britannice praefatus.* Corpus Codicum Suecicorum Medii Aevi, 3. Copenhagen: Munksgaard, 1944.

Schmid. Toni, ed. "Erik den heliges legend på latin, fornsvenska och modern svenska." In *Erik den Helige. Historia, Kult, Reliker.* Ed. Bengt Thordeman. Stockholm: Nordiska rotogravyr, 1954, xi–xx.

Lundén, Tryggve, ed. "Eriksofficiet och Eriksmässen." In *Sankt Erik Konung.* Ed. Jarl Gallén and Tryggve Lundén. Svenska Katolska Akademiens Handlingar, 2. Stockholm: Niketryck. 1960, 19–47.

Bibliographies

Bohrn, Harald, and Percy Elfstrand. *Svensk historisk bibliografi 1936–1950.* Skrifter utgivna av Historiska Föreningen, 5. Stockholm: Norstedt, 1964, 495–6.

Rydbeck, Jan, ed. *Svensk historisk bibliografi 1951–1960.* Skrifter utgivna av Historiska Föreningen, 6. Stockholm: Norstedt, 1968, 455–6.

Bachman, Marie-Louise, and Yvonne Hirdman, eds. *Svensk historisk bibliografi 1961–1970.* Skrifter utgivna av Historiska Föreningen, 8. Stockholm: Almqvist & Wiksell, 1978, 485–6.

Literature

Carlsson, Einar. *Translacio archiepiscoporum. Erikslegendens historicitet i belysning av ärkebiskopssätets förflyttning från Upsala till Östra Åros.* Uppsala Universitets Årsskrift, 1944:2. Uppsala: Lundequistska Bokhandeln, 1944.

Bolin, Sture. "Erik den helige." *Svenskt biografiskt lexikon.* Ed. Bengt Hildebrand. Stockholm: Bonnier, 1953, vol. 14, pp. 248–57.

Thordeman, Bengt, ed. *Erik den Helige: Historia, Kult, Reliker.* Stockholm: Nordiska rotogravyr, 1954.

Schmid, Toni. "Erik den helige." *KLNM* 4 (1959), 13–16.

Gallén, Jarl. "Erik den helige, Sveriges helgonkonung." In *Sankt Erik Konung,* pp. 1–15.

Andersson, Ingvar. "Uppsala ärkestifts tillkomst." *Historisk tidskrift* (Sweden), 84 (1964), 389–410.

Sibilia, Anna Lisa. "Erico (Erik) IX." *Bibliotheca Sanctorum* 4. Rome: Pontificia Università Lateranense, 1955, cols. 1322–6.

Nyberg, Tore. "Eskil av Lund och Erik den helige." In *Historia och samhälle. Studier tillägnade Jerker Rosén.* Malmö: Studentlitteratur, 1975, pp. 5–21.

Gallén, Jarl. "De engelska munkama i Uppsala—ett katedralkloster på 1100–talet." *Historisk Tidskrift för Finland* 61 (1976), 1–21.

Sjöberg, Rolf. "Via regia incedens. Ett bidrag till frågan om Erikslegendens ålder." *Fornvännen* 78 (1983), 252–60.

Gallén, Jarl "Knut den helige och Adela av Flandern. Europeiska kontakter och genealogiska konsekvenser." In *Studier i äldre historia tillägnade Herman Schück.* Stockholm: Gotab, 1985, pp. 49–66.

Sjöberg, Rolf. "Rex Upsalie och vicarius—Erik den helige och hans ställföreträdare." *Fornvännen* 81 (1986), 1–13.

TORE NYBERG

ERIUGENA, JOHANNES SCOTTUS (810–877)

Little is known about the life of this Irish scholar who taught the liberal arts at the court of Charles the Bald in and around Laon in northern France. Although the earlier view of Eriugena as a lonely genius in a barren period has recently been modified, the wealth of his erudition and his remarkable knowledge of Greek make him stand out among his Carolingian contemporaries.

Eriugena first emerges as a participant in the controversy surrounding predestination in 850–51. In his campaign against the monk Gottschalk of Orbais, archbishop Hincmar of Reims asked Eriugena to refute Gottschalk's doctrine of double predestination (to eternal life and to eternal death), which the latter claimed to be the true Augustinian teaching. Eriugena, who is not known to have been a monk or priest, wrote *De divina praedestinatione* in compliance with Hincmar's request. Instead of advocating Hincmar's view of a single predestination, however, Eriugena argues that predestination is nothing more than God's eternal knowledge, and that humans have freedom of choice even after the Fall. After the condemnation of his views at the councils of Valence (855) and Langres (859), Eriugena never returned to the arena of ecclesiastical politics.

For Eriugena's next assignment, Charles the Bald ordered a new translation be made of the works of Pseudo-Dionysius the Areopagite. The Greek texts of this 6th-century Syrian mystic, who was identified with

St. Denis, patron of the Franks, had become available through a codex donated by the Byzantine emperor Michael the Stammerer to Louis the Pious in 827. Through his reading and translation of Pseudo-Dionysius, Eriugena was introduced to certain features of Greek theology, such as the unfolding of the universe according to procession and return and the methods of negative and affirmative theology, which he subsequently incorporated into his own thinking. He also translated Maximus the Confessor's *Quaestiones ad Thalassium* and Gregory of Nyssa's *De hominis opificio*.

Eriugena's major intellectual achievement was the *Periphyseon*, or *On the Division of Nature*. This work, written ca. 864–66, is the mature product of his reflections on Greek theology as well as on the western tradition of Augustine and Boethius. Its most impressive feature is its scope: an inclusive treatment of all of nature, under which he classifies both God and creation. Structuring the universe along the lines of procession and return, Eriugena discusses all major theological and philosophical issues of his time in a dialectical fashion. The discussion of nature ranges from God (nature that creates but is not created) through a treatment of the divine ideas (nature that is created and creates) and of spatiotemporal creations (nature that is created and does not create) back to God (nature that does not create and is not created). In addition, his *Expositiones in ierarchiam coelestem* (on Pseudo-Dionysius's *Celestial Hierarchy*) and his homily *Vox spiritualis aquilae* have become famous.

Due to the later association of Eriugena with the heresy of Amalric of Bène, Pope Honorius III in 1225 ordered that all extant copies of the *Periphyseon* be burned. Yet, through direct and indirect influence, Eriugena's voice continued to be heard in the medieval Christian-Platonic tradition. In connection with idealist philosophy and process theology, Eriugena's ideas also stimulate modern thinking.

See also **Gottschalk**

Further Reading

Eriugena, Johannes Scottus. *Commentaire sur l'évangile de Jean*, ed. and trans. Édouard Jeauneau. Paris: Cerf, 1972.
——. *De divina praedestinatione liber*, ed. Goulven Madec. CCCM 50. Turnhout: Brepols, 1978.
——. *Expositiones in ierarchiam coelestem*, ed. Jeanne Barbet. CCCM 31. Turnhout: Brepols, 1975.
——. *Periphyseon (De divisione naturae)*, ed. I.P. Sheldon-Williams and Ludwig Bieler. 3 vols. Dublin: Dublin Institute for Advanced Studies, 1968–81.
——. *Periphyseon = On the Division of Nature*, trans. Myra I. Uhlfelder with summaries by Jean A. Potter. Indianapolis: Bobbs-Merrill, 1976.
Marenbon, John. *From the Circle of Alcuin to the School of Auxerre: Logic, Theology and Philosophy in the Early Middle Ages*. Cambridge: Cambridge University Press, 1982.
Moran, Dermot. *The Philosophy of John Scottus Eriugena: A Study of Idealism in the Middle Ages*. Cambridge: Cambridge University Press, 1990.
O'Meara, John J., and Ludwig Bieler, eds. *The Mind of Eriugena*. Dublin; Irish University Press, 1973.
Otten, Willemien. *The Anthropology of Johannes Scottus Eriugena*. Leiden: Brill, 1991.

WILLEMIEN OTTEN

EUGENIUS OF PALERMO
(c. 1130-c. 1202)

Eugenius of Palermo was a highly placed official, an accomplished poet, and a translator of scientific and literary works. He facilitated east-west cultural transmission in the kingdom of Sicily when it was still significantly polyglot.

Eugenius was a member of the Italian-Greek nobility that had filled important positions since the early days of Norman rule; he was the son, nephew, and grandson of officials who had attained the rank of admiral, or *emir*—a title that was not exclusively naval—and whose work must have required a knowledge of Arabic. From 1174 to 1190, Eugenius served as master of the *duana baronum*, a royal financial office, then based in Salerno, for the mainland part of the kingdom. Eugenius himself was made an admiral in 1190 by the newly crowned king, Tancred; he was a major figure at the court in Palermo during the reigns of Tancred and Tancred's immediate successor, William III. Along with others close to William, Eugenius was arrested at the end of 1194; he was charged with conspiracy against Henry VI and was imprisoned in southern Germany. By July 1196, however, he was back in the kingdom and was serving, in Apulia and without the title of admiral, as a senior subordinate of the imperial legate Conrad of Querfurt. He may also have been the Eugenius who was master chamberlain for Apulia and Terra di Lavoro from 1198 to at least 1202; this is less certain but is usually accepted. The date of his death is unknown.

Eugenius's multilingualism bore considerable fruit. He is assumed to be the Eugenius who assisted the author of the first Latin translation (c. 1159) of Ptolemy's *Almagest*, an astronomical text transmitted in Greek and Arabic manuscripts; his fluency in all three tongues is noted in the translator's acknowledgment. His own Latin translation of Ptolemy's *Optics* from its Arabic version (the original Greek is lost), which seems to have been contemporary with the translation of the *Almagest*, was used by Roger Bacon in the thirteenth century and survives in more than a dozen manuscripts. Eugenius's Latin translation of the cryptic *Prophecy of the Erythrean Sibyl* from Greek is now known only through its very popular thirteenth-century Joachite reworking by John of Parma or an associate, but significant portions of this apocalyptic text are believed to belong to Eugenius's original. Eugenius also prepared or at least commissioned, probably during his later years at court, an edition of the Greek "mirror of princes" *Stephanites and Ichnelates*, itself a translation of the Arabic *Kalila wa-Dimna* (selections from the Indian *Panchatantra* or *Fables of Bidpai*).

Eugenius is the front rank of the Greek poets of medieval Italy. From his larger production, twenty-four poems survive, preserved in a single fourteenth-century manuscript written at the famous monastery of San Nicola at Casole near Otranto. These poems are in metrically careful twelve-syllable iambics; some are epigrams, but most are longer reflections on ethics and other aspects of the human condition. The two longest and best-known are the first and last: *When he was in prison* (number 1, in 207 lines) and *To the most renowned and trophy-holding king William* (number 24, in 102 lines, a panegyric probably addressed to William I). Other noteworthy pieces include an elegant description of a locally common water lily (number 10); a derogatory rejoinder to the ancient satirist Lucian's *Praise of the Fly* (number 15); and the mildly didactic *On kingship*, perhaps written for the young William III (number 21).

In the unique copy of Peter of Eboli's *Liber ad honorem Augusti*, the caption to a group portrait of the alleged conspirators of December 1194 names Eugenius, among others. But more names are listed than there are faces in the illustration, and it is not clear which if any of those depicted is meant to be Eugenius. Specimens of his signature survive in official documents. A modern scholarly attribution to Eugenius of the writings of his now anonymous contemporary, called Hugo Falcandus, has found little favor.

Further Reading

Editions and Translations

Gigante, Marcello, ed. and trans. *Eugenii Panormitani Versus iambici*. Istituto Siciliano di Studi Bizantini e Neoellenici, Testi, 10. Palermo: Istituto Siciliano di Studi Bizantini e Neoellenici, 1964.

Holder-Egger, O., ed. "Italienische Prophetieen des 13 Jahrhunderts, 1." *Neues Archiv der Gesellschaft für ältere deutsche Geschichtskunde*, 15, 1890, pp. 141–178. (Critical edition of *Vaticinium Sibillae Eritheae* [sic] and similar texts.)

Lejeune, Albert, ed. and trans. *L'Optique de Claude Ptolémée dans la version latine d'après l'arabe de l'émir Eugène de Sicile*, augmented ed. Collection de Travaux de l'Académie Internationale d'Histoire des Sciences, 31. Leiden: Brill, 1989.

McGinn, Bernard, trans. "The Erythraean Sibyl." In *Visions of the End: Apocalyptic Traditions in the Middle Ages*. New York: Columbia University Press, 1979, pp. 122–125, 312–313. (Annotated selections from the Eugenian portions of this text.)

Critical Studies

Billerbeck, Margarethe, and Christian Zubler, eds. and trans. *Das Lob der Fliege von Lukian bis L. B. Alberti: Gattungsgeschichte, Texte, Übersetzungen, und Kommentar*. Sapheneia: Beiträge zur Klassischen Philologie, 5. Bern: Peter Lang, 2000. (See especially pp. 39–41, 173–179.)

Falkenhausen, V. von. "Eugenio da Palermo." In *Dizionario biografico degli Italiani*, Vol. 43. Rome: Istituto della Enciclopedia Italiana, 1993, pp. 502–505.

Gigante, Marcello. "Il tema dell'instabilità della vita nel primo carme di Eugenic di Palermo." *Byzantion*, 33, 1963, pp. 325–356.

——. "La civiltà letteraria." In *I bizantini in Italia*, ed. Guglielmo Cavallo et al. Antica Madre, 5. Milan: Scheiwiller, 1982, pp. 613–651. (See especially pp. 628–630.)

Jamison, Evelyn. *Admiral Eugenius of Sicily: His Life and Work and the Authorship of the Epistola ad Petrum and the Historia Hugonis Falcandi Siculi*. London: Oxford University Press for the British Academy, 1957.

Loud, Graham A. "The Authorship of the History." In *The History of the Tyrants of Sicily by "Hugo Falcandus" 1154–1169*, trans. Graham A. Loud and Thomas Wiedemann. Manchester: Manchester University Press, 1998, pp. 28–42.

McGinn, Bernard. "*Teste David cum Sibylla*: The Significance of the Sibylline Tradition in the Middle Ages." In *Women of the Medieval World: Essays in Honor of John H. Mundy*, ed. Julius Kirshner and Suzanne F. Wemple. Oxford: Blackwell, 1985, pp. 7–35. (Reprint, *Apocalypticism in the Western Tradition*. Aldershot: Variorum, 1994, article 4.)

Ménager, Léon-Robert. *Amiratus—'Aîâl: L'émirat et les origines de l'amirauté*. Paris: SEVPEN, 1960. (See especially pp. 75–78.)

Sjöberg, Lars-Olof. *Stephanites und Ichnelates: Überlieferungsgeschichte und Text*. Acta Universitatis Upsaliensis, Studia Graeca Upsaliensia, 2. Stockholm: Almqvist and Wiksell, 1962. (See especially pp. 103–111.)

JOHN B. DILLON

EULOGIUS OF CÓRDOBA
(c. 800–859)

Priest and apologist for the Martyrs of Córdoba who died in 859 Eulogius was born (c. 800) into a noble Christian family in Córdoba. His parents dedicated him as a child to the Church of St. Zoylus, where he was educated and trained for the priesthood by the abbot Speraindeo. There he met and befriended Paulus Alvarus, later the author of the *Vita Eulogii*, upon which much modern knowledge of Eulogius is based. After his ordination Eulogius seems to have replaced Speraindeo as the *magister* responsible for training future priests. Around 849 or 850 Eulogius traveled north, visiting Navarrese monasteries and acquiring books.

Shortly after Eulogius's return, a monk named Isaac was arrested by the Muslim authorities for blaspheming Islam and was executed on 3 June 851. Within two months ten more Christians followed Isaac's example, launching what has come to be known as the Córdoban Martyrs' Movement. Sometime during that summer Eulogius took it upon himself to begin composing the

Memoriale sanctorum, a martyrology containing brief accounts of the passions of the executed Christians. Shortly thereafter the Muslim authorities, looking for a way to stem the growing tide of dissent, ordered the arrest of the Córdoban clergy. Among those incarcerated was Eulogius. During his detention he continued to work on the *Memoriale sanctorum*, to which he added a preface designed to convince skeptical members of the Córdoban Christian community that the executed Christians were indeed legitimate martyrs who had suffered as the result of actual persecution. He also wrote the *Documentum martyriale*, a hortative treatise designed to encourage Flora and Maria, who had been arrested for apostasy and blasphemy, respectively, to maintain their resolve to become martyrs.

Eulogius was released in late November 851, but his relations with the local authorities, both Muslim and Christian, became increasingly strained. At one point he contemplated suspending himself from celebrating Mass in order to dramatize his dissatisfaction with the Church authorities who seemed intent on working with the emir to bring the martyrdoms to an end. The unpopularity of Eulogius's position seems to have prevented him from accepting his nomination to succeed Wistremirus as metropolitan of Toledo in early 852. That summer he had to hide to avoid being arrested a second time and was subsequently denounced at an episcopal council that had been convened by the emir to deal with the problem of the martyrs. Little is known about Eulogius's life over the next five years except that he continued to add to the *Memoriale sanctorum* as the executions continued. Sometime after March 857 he wrote another martyrology, the *Liber apologeticus martyrum*, dedicated to Rudericus and Salomon, who were put to death as apostate Muslims at that time. It also is known, from an independent source, that in 858 Eulogius met with the monks Usuard and Odilard, who had come from Paris to Zaragoza in search of relics and had been referred to Córdoba. In the late winter of 859 Eulogius was arrested for harboring a fugitive apostate named Leocritia. He defended himself by claiming that as a priest he was bound to instruct anyone seeking knowledge of the faith. When the judge ordered him whipped, Eulogius responded by denouncing Islam and was executed for blasphemy on 11 March 859.

Most assume that Eulogius's role vis-à-vis the martyrdoms was that of an orchestrator of a martyrs' movement. Yet a close look at the sources reveals that he had personal contact with only a few of the martyrs. His self-appointed function seems instead to have been one of promoting their cult when many of the Córdoban Christians seemed inclined to reject the wouldbe martyrs as suicides whose actions jeopardized their day-to-day relations with the Muslims. To this end Eulogius struggled in his writings to cast the Muslims as perse- cutors of the ancient Roman type and to portray Islam as a diabolically inspired false prophecy. Eulogius's apologetic treatises are important, then, not only as evidence of the wide spectrum of Christian responses to life under Muslim rule—from outright rejection to almost complete assimilation—but also as one of the earliest extant sources for Western views of Islam.

See also **Alvarus, Paulus**

Further Reading

Colbert, E. "The Martyrs of Córdoba (850–859): A Study of the Sources." Ph.D. diss., Catholic University of America, 1962.

Gil, J. (ed.) *Corpus scriptorum muzarabicorum*. Vol. 2. Madrid, 1973. 363–503.

Wolf, K. *Christian Martyrs in Muslim Spain*. Cambridge, 1988.

KENNETH B. WOLF

EYVINDR FINNSSON SKÁLDASPILLIR (10th century)

Eyvindr Finnsson skáldaspillir ("the plagiarist"?) was a Norwegian poet of the 10th century, a man of noble descent from Hålogaland, whose mother was a descendant of Haraldr hárfagri ("fair-hair") Hálfdanarson. He was a skald at the court of Hákon góði ("the good") Haraldsson, and closely connected with the party of the earls of Hlaðir, who supported Hákon against the sons of Eiríkr, who were allied with the Danes. According to *Heimskringla*, Eyvindr seems to have been in a position of trust at the king's court. After Hákon's death, he was probably among the enemies of the new king, Haraldr gráfeldr ("grey-cloak") Eiríksson. Nevertheless, in the end, he became a skald at Haraldr's court, but the peaceful relations between them seem not to have lasted long, as his *lausavísur* make plain. The poem *Háleygjatal* shows him at the end of his life at the court of the victorious and powerful Earl Hákon Sigurðarson of the Hlaðir family.

Two poems by Eyvindr, *Hákonarmál* and *Háleyg-jatal,* and fourteen *lausavísur* (single stanzas) have been preserved. Nothing remains of a third poem, **Íslendingadrápa,* mentioned in *Heimskringla*.

The poem *Hákonarmál* is a panegyric on the dead Norwegian king Hákon góði (935–961), who was killed in the battle of Storð against the sons of Eiríkr blóðøx ("blood-axe") Haraldsson, his brother and adversary. The poem is contained in the MSS of *Heimskringla* (J, K, F) and some stanzas of it also appear in *Fagrskinna* (A, B) and in *Snorra Edda*.

The poem consists of three parts: the battle; the king's ensuing dialogue with the valkyries who have decided that he is to go to Óðinn, and the king's welcome in Valhǫll and among the gods; and the concluding praise of the greatness and uniqueness of the late king, followed by words of grief over the situation of the country now enslaved. This three-part structure is also underlined by the meter. The traditional epic meter *fornyrðislag* is used for the battle section; the parts in which mythical persons are protagonists and the concluding praise use *ljóðaháttr* meter. For that reason, some scholars have assumed that two different poems have been combined in *Hákonarmál* (Sahlgren 1927). But this change of meter is characteristic of the genre of "eddic panegyrics," as well as the epic presentation and the use of mythical scenes and motifs for the purpose of praise. In the battle scenes, however, the poem is influenced to a greater extent by skaldic metaphors and kennings used to create impressive imagery.

As to the themes, the poem is cognate with *Eiríksmál*, although there are considerable differences. Whereas *Eiríksmál* is confined to a single scene, the entry of the king into Valhǫll, *Hákonarmál* also contains the battle and the praise of the king. There are also differences in religious attitudes, Valhǫll and Óðinn are presented very unfavorably. The valkyries, not Óðinn, choose the hero, and they also determine victory or defeat. Whether because of his Christian faith or his fear, the king does not want to go to Óðinn. Moreover, the king's welcome in Valhǫll is surpassed by his reception among the gods, for whom the poet uses the collective terms characteristic of the late-pagan religion of the environment of the earls of Hlaðir (*bnd, regin, rǫð, heiðin goð*). Unlike *Eiríksmál*, the poem reveals intense national feelings. The king is shown as a sovereign defending his kingdom, protecting the sanctuaries. His character is praised; there is no better king to some after him. And the gods who have invited him to join them are the gods worshiped in the environment of the earls of Hlaðir.

Taking into account the last stanza, where the poet speaks of the enslaved people, we have to assume that the poem was composed for the earls of Hlaðir after Hákon's death, when Haraldr gráfeldr's rule had become increasingly oppressive.

Most scholars accept the statement in *Fagrskinna* that *Eiríksmál* was the model for *Hákonarmál*. There are some very obvious parallels between the two poems. But there have also been voices in favor of the priority of *Hákonarmál* (Wadstein 1895, von See 1963); they argue that the poem's conception of Valhǫll is more archaic, and its poetic quality greater. Yet, both lines of argument are unconvincing, and it seems more correct to assume that the author of the *Hákonarmál* deliberately made his poem different from *Eiríksmál*, and had political motives for surpassing his model (Wolf 1969, Marold 1972).

Eyvindr's *Háleygjatal* was composed for Earl Hákon after his victory over the Jómsvíkingar in 985. This poem, as the opening stanza announces, traces the earl's ancestors to the gods. Only fragments are left: nine complete stanzas and seven half-stanzas are contained in *Heimskringla, Snorra Edda, Fagrskinna*, and *Flateyjarbók*. A 13th-century Icelandic MS (*cf.* Storm 1899: 111, Anm. 4), whose author probably used *Háleygjatal* to enumerate twenty-seven earls of Hlaðir, permits the conjecture that the poem also enumerated twenty-seven ancestors of Earl Hákon, just as *Ynglingatal,* which was presumably the model for *Háleygjatal*, does for the Ynglingar. The *kviðuháttr* meter also follows *Ynglingatal* (*cf.* Storm). The stanzas preserved show that *Háleygjatal* also relates how each of the princes met his death. The burial place of a prince is mentioned in only one case. The first of Hákon's ancestors is Sæmingr, the son of Óðinn and the giantess Skaði. The opening stanzas contain two traditional elements: the request for silence and the paraphrasing of "poem" by the myth of Óðinn's mead, the drink of poetical inspiration; this pattern shows clearly that the poem was composed as a panegyric.

The poem is connected with *Ynglingatal* by the meter, the genealogical content, and the concentration on the deaths of the princes. There are also certain similarities between the kennings and other metaphorical phrases in the two poems. Therefore, it has been generally supposed that *Háleygjatal* was composed for political reasons, following the model of *Ynglingatal*, in order to prove that the family of the earls of Hlaðir was just as old as the Ynglingar's, their rivals for the power in Norway, and that the earls were also descended from the gods. However, it has sometimes been argued that *Ynglingatal* is later than *Háleygjatal* (Wadstein 1895).

The fact that Eyvindr was called "skáldaspillir" plays a certain role in this discussion. The term was interpreted as "destroyer of skalds," and it was thought that this name implied that the poet had imitated older poems, especially their kennings. But since the style of skaldic poetry was highly traditional, we must beware of regarding these analogies from a modern point of view and dismissing them as lacking originality. It would be better to interpret the name of "skáldaspillir" as "who puts the other skalds in the shade" (Wadstein 1895, M. Olsen 1916).

Eyvindr's *lausavísur* are composed in *dróttkvætt* meter, the ceremonial, courtly style. The first six of them have to do with the battle of Fitjar: the first announces the arrival of the enemies' army to the king, the second calls the warriors to the battle. Stanzas 3–5 focus on one episode of the battle, the encounter of Hákon góði and Eyvindr skreyja ("bragger"). Stanza 6 is an answer to a well-known poem by Glúmr Geirason, skald of Haraldr gráfeldr, which praised his victory over Hákon. Eyvindr answered with a stanza recalling a previous victory of Hákon over the sons of Eiríkr.

Stanza 7 is a conventional praise of Haraldr gráfeldr. In stanza 10, the cool relation between king and skald is obvious. The remaining stanzas could be regarded as reflecting the author's critical attitude toward Haraldr's rule. In stanzas 8 and 9, he complains about the greed of the king, to whom he must even give his own gold (st. 10). Stanza 12 complains about the bad weather, for which in the contemporary view the king was responsible (*cf.* the fact that in *Vellekla* Earl Hákon was praised for bringing back good harvests). Stanzas 13 and 14 may also be read in this light: they deal with fishing and buying herring, partly in humorous paraphrases. In exchange for herring, the poet is forced to give a needle, which he had received as a present from the Icelanders. Seen in connection with the preceding stanzas, stanzas 13 and 14 could imply that the poet has lost his fortune as a consequence of his conflict with the king, and is forced in bad years to live by fishing for herring and selling his last possessions.

See also **Hákon góði (the good) Haraldsson**

Further Reading

Editions

Finnur Jónsson, ed. *Den norsk-islandske skjaldedigtning.* Vols. 1A–2A (tekst efter håndskrifterne) and 1B–2B(rettet tekst). Copenhagen and Christiania [Oslo]: Gyldendal, 1912–15; rpt. Copenhagen: Rosenkilde & Bagger, 1967 (A) and 1973 (B), vol. 1A, pp. 64–74, vol. 1B, pp. 57–65 [*Hákonarmal, Háleygjatal, lausavísur*].

Lindquist, Ivar, ed. *Norröna lovkväden från 800– och 900–talen.* 1. *Förslag till restituerad täxt jämte översättning.* Lund: Gleerup, 1929, pp. 10–7 [*Hákonarmál*], pp. 74–5 [*Háleygjatal 1–4*].

Kock, Ernst A., ed. *Den noss-isländska skaldediktningen.* 2 vols. Lund: Gleerup, 1946–49, vol. 1, pp. 35–40 [*Hákonarmál, Háleygjatal, lausavísur*].

Translations

Hollander, Lee M., trans. *Old Norse Poems: The Most Important Non-Skaldic Verse Not Included* in *the Poetic Edda.* New York: Columbia University Press, 1936; rpt. Millwood: Kraus, 1973.

Leach, Howard G. *A Pageant of Old Scandinavia.* Princeton: Princeton University Press; New York: American-Scandinavian Foundation, 1946.

Literature

Wadstein, Elis. "Bidrag till tolkning och belysning av skalde- och Eddadikter." *Arkiv förnordisk filologi* 11 (1895), 64–92.

Storm, Gustav. "Ynglingatal, dels Forfatter og Forfattelsestid." *Arkiv för nordisk filologi* 15 (1899), 107–41.

Olsen, Magnus. "Fortjener Hákonarmáls digter tilnavnet 'skaldaspillir?" In *Til Gerhard Gran, 9. des. 1916.* Kristiania [Oslo]: Aschehoug, 1916, pp. 1–9.

Paasche, Frederik. "Hákonarmál." In *Til Gerhard Gran, 9. des. 1916,* pp. 10–6.

Genzmer, Felix. "Das eddische Preislied." *Beitrge zur Geschichte der deutschen Sprache und Literatur* 44 (1919), 138–68.

Noreen, Erik. "Anmärkninger till Eyvinds dikter." *Studier i fornvästnordisk diktning* (1921), 45–62.

Noreen, Erik. "Eiríksmál och Hákonarmál." *Nordisk Tidskrift för vetenskap konst och industri, udg. av. Letterstedska Föreningen* (1922), 535–42.

Sahlgren, Jöran. *Eddica et Scaldica. Fornvästnordiska studier* 1. Nordisk Filologi, 1. Lund: Gleerup, 1927, pp. 40–109.

Flornes, H.M, "'Spåteme.' Merknader til ei lausavise av Eyvind Finsson." *Maal og minne* (1939), 15–16.

Midtun, S. D. "En lausavísa av Øyvind Finsson." *Maal og minne* (1940), 143–4.

Olsen, Magnus. "Skaldevers om nøds-år nordenfjells." *Festskrift til Konrad Nielsen på 70-årsdagen 28.8.1945.* Studia Septentrionalia, 2. Oslo: Brøgger, 1945, pp. 176–92.

Lie, Hallvard. "Et upåaktet gammelnorsk ord: *hausi* og Hákonarmál 6." *Arkiv för nordisk filologi* 63 (1948), 200–3.

Wolff, Ludvig. "Eddische-skaldische Blütenlese." In *Edda, Skalden, Saga: Festschrift zum 70. Geburtstag von Felix Genzmer.* Ed. Hermann Schneider. Heidelberg: Winter, 1952, pp. 92–107.

Holm-Olsen, Ludvig. "Øyvind *Skaldaspillir*" *Edda* 53 (1953), 145–65; See, Klaus von. "Zwei eddische Preislieder: Eiríksmál und Hákonarmál." In *Festgabe für Ulrich Pretzel zum 65. Geburtstag dargebracht von seinen Freunden und Schülern.* Ed. Wemer Simon *et al.* Berlin: Schmidt, 1963, pp. 107–17.

Schier, Kurt. "Freys und Fróðis Bestattung." In *Festschrift für Otto Höfler zum 65. Geburtstag.* Ed. Helmut Birkhan *et al.* Vienna: Notring, 1968, pp. 389–409.

Wolf, Alois. "Zitat und Polemik in den *Hákonarmál* Eyvinds." In *Germanische Studien.* Ed. J. Erben and E. Thurnher. Innsbrucker Beiträge zur Kulturwissenschaft, 15. Innsbruck: Institut für Vergleichende Sprachwissenschaft der Universität Innsbruck, 1969, pp. 9–32.

Marold, Edith. "Das Walhallbild in den *Eiríksmál* und den *Hákonarmál.*" *Mediaeval Scandinavia* 5 (1972), 19–33.

Schier, Kurt. "Háleygjatal." *Kindlers Literatur Lexikon* 5. Zurich: Kindler, 1970, pp. 1396–7; See, Klaus von. *Edda, Saga, Skaldendichtung.* Heidelberg: Winter, 1981, pp. 522–5.

EDITH MAROLD

EZZO (d. after 1065)

Presumed author of the *Cantilena de miraculis Christi* (Song on Christ's Miracles), more commonly known as the *Ezzolied* (Ezzo's Song), the first vernacular German work of mature literary quality since the Old High German *Christus und die Samariterin* (Christ and the Samaritin Woman, ca. 900). The earliest connection between the name Ezzo and a hymn composed around the middle of the eleventh century is found in the *Vita altmanni.* The *Vita* (ca. 1130) describes, among other events from the life of Altmann (d. 1091), a pilgrimage to the Holy Land in which the Passau bishop took part in 1064/1065. Also participating in this pilgrimage, according to the *Vita,* was a cleric named Ezzo who wrote a *Cantilena de miraculis Christi* in German. That the *cantilena* in the vernacular by someone named Ezzo and the *Ezzolied* are one and the same thing is a virtual certainty.

The work exists in two redactions, the *Strasbourg* (Bibliothèque Nationale et Universitaire, manuscript no. germ. 278, fol. 74v. "S"), and the *Vorau* (no. 276,

Chorherrenstift, parchment, fol. 128r-129v "V"). The Strasbourg manuscript contains the older and without doubt more authentic, even if fragmentary version of the two (only seven strophes are preserved), whereas the Vorau redaction contains thirty-four strophes and is clearly a revision intended for a monastic audience. Both are probably revisions of a lost "Bamberg Ezzolied" original.

The hymn presents the immutable lessons of Christianity beginning with Creation ("S" 2–4; "V" 5–8), proceeding to the Fall ("S" 5–6; "V" 9–10), moving through the Old Testament period, culminating in the mission of John the Baptist ("S" 7; "V" 11–13), concentrating on the birth of Christ and his baptism ("V" 14–17), the miracles done during Christ's public ministry ("V" 18–19), the crucifixion and its significance, including the Harrowing of Hell ("V" 20–30), and concluding with a paean to the Cross ("V" 31–34).

The *Ezzolied* is a joyous celebration of the triumph of Christ over death and Satan. Emphasized is not the suffering Christ of later Gothic centuries but, rather, the victorious Christ the King of the Romanesque.

Further Reading

Barack, K. A., ed. *Ezzos Gesang von den Wundern Christi und Nokers "Memento mori" in phototypischen Faksimile der Straßburger Handschrift*. Strasbourg: Trubner, 1879.

Barack, K. A. "Althochdeutsche Funde." *Zeitschrift für deutsches Altertum* 23 (1879): 210–212 ["S"].

Diemer, Joseph. "Beiträge zur älteren deutschen Sprache und Literatur, 22–23. Ezzo's Lied von dem Anegenge aus dem Jahr 1065." *Sitzungsberichte der philosophischhistorischen Klasse der österreichischen Akademie der Wissenschaften in Wien* 52 (1866): 183–202; 427–469 [notes; first complete edition of the Vorau version].

Freytag, Hartmut. "Ezzos Gesang. Text und Funktion." in *Geistliche Denkformen in der Literatur des Mittelalters*. Munich: Fink, 1984, pp. 154–170.

Gentry, Francis G. *Bibliographie zur frühmittelhochdeutschen geistlichen Dichtung*. Berlin: Schmidt, 1992, pp. 184–191.

Maurer, Friedrich, ed. *Die religiösen Dichtungen des 11. und 12. Jahrhunderts. Nach ihren Formen besprochen und herausgegeben*, vol. 1. Tübingen: Niemeyer, 1964, pp. 284–303 ["V," "S"].

Polheim, Karl Konrad, ed. *Die deutschen Gedichte der Vorauer Handschrift (Kodex 276/2)*. Graz: Akademischer Verlagsanstalt, 1958.

Rupp, Heinz. *Deutsche Religiöse Dichtungen des 11. und 12. Jahrhunderts. Untersuchungen und Interpretationen*, 2d ed. Bern: Francke, 1971, pp. 33–83.

Schmidt-Wiegand, Ruth. "Die Weltalter in Ezzos Gesang," in *Zeiten und Formen in Sprache und Dichtung: Festschrift für Fritz Tschirch zum 70. Geburtstag*, ed. Karl-Heinz Schirmer and Bernhard Sowinski. Cologne: Böhlau, 1972, pp. 42–51.

Schröder, Werner, ed. *Kleinere deutsche Gedichte des 11. und 12. Jahrhunderts*. Tubingen: Niemeyer, 1972, pp. 10–26 ["V," "S"].

Vollmann-Profe, Gisela. *Geschichte der deutschen Literatur von den Anfängen bis zum Beginn der Neuzeit, vol. 1, 2: Wiederbeginn volkssprachiger Schriftlichkeit im hohen Mittelalter*, 2d ed. Tübingen: Niemeyer, 1994, passim.

FRANCIS G. GENTRY

F

FAZIO DEGLI UBERTI
(c. 1301 or 1305–c. 1367)

Bonifazio, or Fazio, degli Uberti was a member of a Ghibelline family expelled from Florence in 1267. He was born in Pisa and never lived in Florence, the city of his ancestors, from which he considered himself an exile. Fazio was a court intellectual and a poet; his most important work is an encyclopedic poem called *Il dittamondo*. In 1336, he was in the service of Mastino II della Scala of Verona; in 1346, he was at the court of Luchino Visconti; and in 1358, he was in Bologna at the court of Giovanni Visconti d'Oleggio. Fazio's adopted city was Verona, a bastion of Ghibelline and imperial ideals, where he probably died.

Fazio's thirty-five poems include *canzoni*, sonnets, and *frottole* dealing with love, religion, politics, and ethics. He composed seven *canzoni* and one sonnet for his mistress, Ghidola (or Ghida), the daughter of Spinetto Malaspina, lord of Lunigiana. Among these, three *canzoni*—*Nel tempo che s'infiora e cuopre d'erba, Io guardo i crespi e i biondi capelli,* and *I' guardo in fra l'erbette per li prati*—are picturesque representations of love and nature in the springtime that recall the Provençal poets and Dante. In all his poems to Ghida, Fazio underscores the emotional and physical effects of love rather than its spiritual or symbolic meaning. There is a "fresh sensuality" (Corsi 1969, 226, 238) in his love poems that is mirrored in his joyous celebration of the beauty and pleasures of nature. Contrary to the observations of many critics, therefore, Fazio was not a follower of Dante or of Petrarch.

Fazio's poetry shows that he never wavered from his political and cultural ideals. The political *rime* are characterized by aristocratic dignity. When Fazio praises Ludwig of Bavaria's Italian campaign of 1327–1329 (in *Tanto son void i ciel di parte in parte*), criticizes Florentine politics (in the *frottola O tu che leggi*), inveighs against Emperor Charles IV of Bohemia (in *Di quel possi tu her che bevve Crasso*), or laments the demise of Florence (in *O sommo bene, o glorioso Iddio*), he is an ardent supporter of the empire and of the cultural primacy of Florence.

Fazio's greatest achievement was *Il dittamondo* (*Dicta mundi*), which recounts the poet's fictional journey around the world. This poem is divided into six books and is written, in *terza rima*. In Book 1, Fazio states his wish to acquire fame by reporting the marvels he will see on his journey. Yet the poet-pilgrim loses his way shortly after setting out. The first night he dreams that Dame Virtue invites him to follow the path of salvation. He then meets the ancient astronomer Ptolemy and, later, the third-century geographer Solinus, who becomes his guide. Together, Fazio and Solinus visit Rome, which appears to them as a weeping, disheveled woman. In Books 1 and 2, Rome narrates her history, from the time of Julius Caesar to that of Charles of Bohemia. In Book 3, the pilgrims' quest for knowledge takes them to Greece, where Fazio reflects on the Hellenistic legacy of Italy. In Book 4, the poet and Solinus visit Asia Minor, Scandinavia, England, France, and Spain. In Book 5, they travel by ship to Africa; there they meet Pliny, who speaks to them of astrology and the heavens. After visiting several regions of Africa, they travel to Egypt; from there, Fazio and Solinus go to Palestine—in Book 6—in order to see the Holy Sepulcher. There they meet another pilgrim, who narrates important episodes from the Bible.

Dittamondo is often compared to Dante's *Divine Comedy*, but these two works are very different from each other. For Dante, knowledge of the real world is an important means of spiritual salvation, whereas for Fazio knowledge is the aim of his quest. *Dittamondo* is based on contemporary chronicles and medieval encyclopedias, including Brunetto Latini's *Tresor* and

Giovanni De Matociis's *Historiae imperiales*. Fazio often revised his poem in order to reflect developments in science; this would explain the gaps in the poem and the fact that it was unfinished at the time of the author's death. Although it is aesthetically uneven, *Dittamondo* is an accomplished poem in the passages that evoke the passion and spirit of Fazio's lyric poetry; an example is the representation of the Florentine and Italian landscape in Book 3.

Having come of age in the second quarter of the *Trecento*, Fazio saw the rise of humanism, and he shared the humanists' enthusiasm for the classical world. At the same time, however, he typified the Ghibelline intellectual during the downward spiral of imperial politics.

See also **Brunetto Latini; Dante Alighieri**

Further Reading

Editions

Corsi, Giuseppe, ed. *Il Dittamondo e le rime*, 2 vols. Bari: Laterza, 1952.

——, ed. "Fazio degli Uberti." In *Rimatori del Trecento*. Turin: UTET, 1969, pp. 224–318.

Renier, Rodolfo, ed. *Liriche edite ed inedite di Fazio degli Uberti*. Florence: Sansoni, 1883.

Critical Studies

Berisso, Marco. "Testo e contesto della frottola *O tu che leggi* di Fazio degli Uberti." *Studi di Filologia Italians*, 51, 1993, pp. 53–88.

Casali, Marino. *La lirica di Fazio degli Uberti*. Domodossola: Antonioli, 1949.

Croce, Benedetto. *Poesia popolare e poesia d'arte: Studi sulla poesia italiana dal Tre al Cinquecento*. Bari: Laterza, 1933, pp. 107–132.

Pellizzari, Achille. *Il Dittamondo e la Divina commedia: Saggio sulle fonti del "Dittamondo" e sulla imitazione dantesca nel secolo XIV*. Pisa: Mariotti, 1905.

Tartaro, Achille. "L'esperienza poetica di Fazio degli Uberti." In *Il Trecento*, Vol. 2(1). Bari: Laterza, 1971, pp. 487–511.

DARIO DEL PUPPO

FERNANDO I, KING OF LEÓN (1016/8-1065)

The second son of Sancho III Garcés (el Mayor), king of Navarre (r. 1000–1035), and the sister of Count García Sánchez of Castile, Fernando was installed as the count of Castile when García Sánchez was murdered in 1029. Subsequently he was married to Sancha, sister of Vermudo III of León. After his father's death Fernando defeated and killed his father-in-law at Tamarón on 4 September 1037. Vermudo had no direct heirs, so Fernando and Sancha were recognized as the monarchs of León-Castile.

The royal couple seems to have faced no serious internal challenge to their rule. They began the reform of the church of the realm with a council held at Coyanza (modern Valencia de Don Juan) in 1055, although the acts of that meeting show that reform was largely limited to a new policy of enforcing the traditional canon law. However, at some point in the ten years following, Fernando and Sancha entered into a close relationship with the great Burgundian reform monastery of Cluny, which would endure and grow under their heirs and successors. In return for Cluny's prayers for the well-being of their persons and dynasty, the Leonese monarchs began an annual subsidy of 1,000 gold dinars, which would do much to support the construction of a new, third monastic church structure at Cluny.

The royal couple also exerted themselves to enrich and endow the cathedrals and monasteries of their own realm. In 1063 an expedition to the Muslim *ṭā'ifa* (kingdom) of Seville secured the surrender of the relics of St. Isidore of Seville. These were transported to León and installed there in what would later become a major shrine. At the same time other relics were reclaimed from the ruins of Ávila and redistributed among the churches of the north. From what can be determined, Fernando and Sancha were comparatively modest in their patronage of Santiago de Compostela, even though the devotion and pilgrimage to the shrine of St. James was growing substantially during their reign. They were also generous to one of the favorite royal residences, the monastery of Sahagún, which was more central to the kingdom as it was then developing than was Santiago de Compostela. Despite all of this religious activity, relations between the churches of León-Castile and the papacy at Rome were minimal.

In the Christian north of the peninsula, Fernando asserted the hegemony of the new León-Castile that his victory in 1037 had established. During the reign of his father, lands in the Castilian northeast had been detached from that county and added to the kingdom of Navarre. That kingdom had been the portion of his older brother, García IV Sánchez (r. 1035–1054). Following the death of their father, relations between the brothers gradually worsened. On 15 September 1054, the two met in battle at Atapuerca, and García Sánchez was defeated and killed. The district of the Bureba, northeast of Burgos, was reclaimed for León-Castile, and the kingdom of Navarre became a tributary under Fernando's nephew, Sancho García IV (r. 1054–1076).

With the leadership of León-Castille secure in the Christian north, Fernando embarked on an ambitious series of campaigns against the Muslim *ṭā'ifa* kingdoms of the Iberian Peninsula. Perhaps as early as 1055 he launched his offensive against the Portuguese territories of Muslim Badajoz. On 29 November 1057 his forces took the town of Lamego, one hundred kilometers upriver from Christian Oporto. With that victory the valley of the Douro (Duero) River was secured for León. The next objective was the hill city of Viseu, on the

Mondego River to the south. It fell to Fernando's troops on 25 July 1058. Nevertheless, clearing the Mondego valley and plain of Muslims proved to be arduous. The key position was occupied by the hilltop fortress city of Coimbra, seventy kilometers southwest of Viseu. Not until 25 July 1064, after a six-month siege, did that city surrender to the Leonese. When it did, the northern two-fifths of modern Portugal had been reclaimed from the Muslims and could be reorganized as a possession of León-Castile.

More directly to the south of Fernando and Sancho's realm lay the ṭā'ifa of Toledo. It may have been a tributary as early as 1058, for in that year the last known Mozarabic bishop of Toledo was consecrated in León, presumably because of León's tributary status. Nevertheless, in 1062 Fernando's army invaded that ṭā'ifa took Talamanca, north of Madrid; and laid siege to Alcalá. The Muslim king, Al-Ma'mūn, agreed to annual *parias* (tribute payments) to secure Fernando's withdrawal. During the following year Fernando struck deep into Muslim Andalucia, ravaging the lands of the ṭā'ifa of Seville and Badajoz. If those two realms had not already pledged the payment *of parias*, they certainly began to do so at this time.

Prior to his southern campaigns Fernando had moved against the great ṭā'ifa of Zaragoza on the Middle Ebro River. The chronology is not clear, but probably in about 1060 he seized the territories on the upper Duero with their strongholds at San Esteban de Gormaz, Berlanga, and Vadorrey. He also took control of the rolling country to the south of the river about Santiuste, Huermeces, and Santamara. Most likely Zaragoza paid *parias* from this time, but in 1064 that kingdom broke off payments. The Leonese response involved a victorious campaign that carried all the way to the plains around Valencia on the Mediterranean. That Muslim kingdom had joined with Zaragoza in the attack on the Leonese positions on the upper Duero. It seems to have been turned over to Fernando's ally and tributary, Al-Ma'mūn of Toledo, but Zaragoza itself once again came under Leonese suzerainty.

Fernando now had reached both the apogee of his reign and the end of it. He died on 27 December, 1065, and was buried in the Church of St. Isidore in León. His wife, Sancha, lived until 27 November 1067. On the death of Fernando, the kingdom was divided among his three sons. The oldest, Sancho II (r. 1065—1072), received Castile and the tribute payments of Navarre and Seville.

See also **Isidore of Seville, Saint**

Further Reading

O'Callaghan, J.F. *A History of Medieval Spain.* Ithaca, NY, 1975.
Jackson, G. *The Making of Medieval Spain.* New York, 1972.
Mackay, A. *Spain in the Middle Ages.* New York, 1977.
Reilly, B.F. *The Kingdom of León-Castilla under King Alfonso VI.* Princeton, 1988.
——. *The Kingdom of León-Castilla under Queen Urraca.* Princeton, 1982.

BERNARD F. REILLY

FERNANDO III, KING OF CASTILE (1201–1252)

Fernando, king of Castile (1217–1252) and León (1230–1252), was the son of Alfonso IX of León and Berenguela, the daughter of Alfonso VII of Castile. He was born in June or July 1201. After his parents separated in 1204, because of consanguity, he was reared in his father's court. His mother, summoned him to Castile following the sudden death of her brother, Enrique I (r. 1214–1217). Though she was acknowledged as queen of Castile, she bowed to the wishes of the Castilians assembled at Valladolid and transferred her rights to the throne to her son, and Fernando III was then proclaimed king. When Alfonso IX discovered what had happened, he invaded Castile with the intention of uniting it to the Leonese crown, thereby restoring the unity of the two realms, separated since 1157. Finding little support for his cause, he retreated to León at the end of the summer and recognized Fernando as king of Castile in August 1218. Father and son pledged to live peacefully with one another and to act in concert against the Moors. Following his mother's counsel, Fernando III married Beatrice, daughter of the Holy Roman Emperor, Philip of Swabia and granddaughter of Frederick Barbarossa, at Burgos in 1219. As a consequence, their firstborn child, Alfonso X, was later able to put forward claims to the imperial throne.

As the Almohad empire that dominated Morocco and Muslim Spain began to disintegrate, Fernando directed his energy to the Reconquest. Seizing Quesada in 1224, he also accepted the vassalage of al-Bayasi, the ruler of Baeza, and his brother, Abú Zayd of Valencia, who hoped, with Castilian help, to secure their independence of the Almohads. Al-Bayasi collaborated with Fernando in his campaigns against Jaén and Granada in the summer of 1225, and his fellow Muslims, disgusted by his submissive attitude, murdered him the next year. Soon afterward the Moors of Spain threw off the last vestiges of Almohad authority, but as a result Muslim unity dissolved, thereby giving advantage to the Christian rulers.

While Fernando vainly attempted to besiege Jaén, his father captured Mérida and Badajoz. His death soon afterward, in September 1230, radically altered Fernando's fortunes. Although Alfonso IX had never formally determined the succession to the Leonese throne, Fernando claimed it at once and moved swiftly to take possession. In order to secure an undisputed title, he had to persuade Alfonso IX's two surviving daughters by his first wife, Teresa of Portugal, to renounce their rights. The two former queens of León, Teresa and Berenguela, negotiated the settlement at Benavente on 11 December 1230, which compensated the infantas for their renunciation. Thus the kingdoms of León and Castile, separated since 1157, were reunited under Fernando, who was able to use their combined resources to prosecute the Reconquest.

Meanwhile, rivalry between Ibn Hkd of Murcia and Ibn al-Aḥmar (1232–1273), founder of the Nasrid dynasty and the kingdom of Granada, benefited Fernando, who launched a major offensive that resulted in the capture of Úbeda in 1232. Elsewhere he laid waste the land around Arjona and Jaén, and threatened Córdoba and Seville. As 1235 drew to a close, a small band of Castilians, after invading the suburbs of Córdoba, quickly summoned Fernando to come to their aid. Receiving their message at Benavente in the middle of January 1236, he rapidly marched south and reached Córdoba on 7 February. In the weeks that followed, the bulk of his army tightened the siege of the city. When it became apparent that they could expect no help from their correligionists, the defenders surrendered on 29 June 1236. Those who wished to do so were permitted to leave, taking whatever they could carry, those who chose to remain were assured of religious liberty. The mosque of Córdoba was consecrated as a cathedral for the newly established Christian bishopric. The bells of Santiago de Compostela, which the Moorish ruler Al-Manṣūr, had carried off in 997 and hung in the mosque, were returned to the Christian shrine in Galicia.

In the years immediately following the conquest of Córdoba, many dependent towns and fortresses in the Guadalquivir valley submitted to Fernando. A few years later Murcia, in the southeast, also acknowledged his sovereignty. The assassination in 1238 of Ibn Hūd, who ruled Murcia, opened the possibility that the area might fall under the domination of Ibn al-Aḥmar, the emir of Tunis. To avert that, Ibn Hūd's family proposed to submit to Fernando as their suzerain and protector. Because he was ill, he sent his oldest son, Alfonso, to receive the homage of the Murcian towns. The Banū Hūd received him at Murcia in April 1243, and Lorca, Cartagena, and other towns, after a show of resistance, also submitted. As vassals of Fernando, the Murcian lords pledged an annual tribute of half their revenues, but otherwise they continued to rule as before. When Alfonso tried to seize Alcira and Játiva, towns reserved for Aragón (according to the Treaty of Cazola, 1179), he encountered opposition from Jaime I of Aragón. After negotiations they concluded the Treaty of Almizra on 26 March 1244, establishing the boundaries between Castilian and Aragónese conquests in that part of the peninsula.

Once he had recovered from his illness, Fernando resumed the offensive, taking Arjona and several neighboring towns in 1244. His next objective was Jaén, a seemingly impregnable fortress. After systematically destroying the crops, the king blockaded the city in August 1245. Ibn al-Aḥmar, now the undisputed master in Granada, Jaén, Málaga, and Almería, was unable to offer any support to the defenders, who faced the real prospect of starvation. Because his hands were tied, Ibn al-Aḥmar authorized them to surrender in March 1246. As the Moors departed, Fernando introduced Christian settlers and converted the mosque into a cathedral. In the hope of preserving himself and his dynasty, Ibn al-Aḥmar pledged homage and fealty to Fernando, promising to serve him as a loyal vassal, both in battle and in his court, and to pay a tribute of 150,000 *maravedis* over a term of twenty years.

Seville, the wealthiest city in all of Spain, a port on the lower Guadalquivir River with access to both the Mediterranean and the Atlantic, next attracted Fernando's attention. Preliminary operations disrupted the outer defenses of the city and severed supply lines. Alcalá de Guadaira, Carmona, Constantina, Reina, Lora, Cantillana, Guillena, Gerena, Alcalá del Río, and other adjacent towns capitulated in 1246–1247. A formal siege of Seville was established in July 1247.

The blockade of Seville was completed when Ramón Bonifaz of Burgos, acting on the king's orders, organized a fleet in the ports on the Bay of Cádiz and entered the mouth of the Guadalquivir. Repelling enemy ships, he made his way upriver and broke the bridge of boats connecting Seville and Triana. Their supplies steadily dwindling, the defenders appealed to the Almohads in North Africa for help, but in vain.

Isolated, with no expectation of relief, the defenders of Seville surrendered on 23 November 1248. Fernando III permitted them to leave, carrying their movable property, with safe conduct to Jerez or on Castilian ships to Ceuta, in Morocco. The Moors were given a month to settle their affairs before departure, and a Castilian garrison immediately occupied the *alcázar* fortress Fernando entered the city in triumph on 22 December 1248. An archbishopric was established in Seville, and the king dedicated the remaining years of his reign to the colonization of Seville and the surrounding region, distributing houses and lands to those who had participated in the conquest or who were willing to settle there.

Fernando achieved the greatest success of all the Castilian kings in the Reconquest because the collapse of the Almohad Empire disrupted the unity of Muslim Spain. Taking advantage of the jealousies of rival Moorish leaders, he gained control of the valley of the Guadalquivir from Úbeda to Seville and reduced the Moors of Murcia and Granada to the tributary status of vassals.

Aside from his efforts to eradicate Muslim rule in

Spain, Fernando gave impetus to the development of the institutions and culture of his realm. He tried to reinvigorate the universities of Salamanca and Palencia, and welcomed scholars to his court. In the course of his reign, Castilian supplanted Latin as the official language of government and administration. His son, Alfonso X, eventually brought to fruition Fernando's plan to develop a uniform code of law for the kingdom. The *cortes*, in process of growth for a half-century, appeared as a fully constituted assembly of prelates, magnates, and townsmen representing the estates of the realm at Seville in 1250.

In the expectation of protecting his kingdom against any future Almohad intrusion into the peninsula, Fernando III was planning an invasion of North Africa, but death intervened on 30 May 1252. Buried in the cathedral at Seville, he was declared a saint by Pope Clement X in 1671. By his first wife, Beatrice of Swabia, he had had ten children including Alfonso X who succeed him. Two years after Beatrice's death in 1235, he had married Jeanne de Ponthieu, by whom he had three children.

See also **Alfonso X, El Sabio, King of Castile and León**

Further Reading

González, J. *Reinado y diplomas de Fernando III.* 3 vols. Córdoba, 1980–1986.
Mansilla, D. *Iglesia castellano-leonesa y curia romana en los tiempos del Rey San Fernando.* Madrid, 1945.

JOSEPH F. O'CALLAGHAN

FERRER, VICENTE, SAINT
(1350–1419)

Son of a Girona notary, St. Vicente Ferrer entered the Order of Preachers, studied theology, philosophy, and logic in Barcelona, Lérida, and Tortosa, having obtained the degree of master of theology by 1389.

After his ordination in 1378 he took up residence in Valencia, where he remained for some years and was known for his preaching and rivalry with his Franciscan contemporary, Francesc Eiximenis.

A lector in theology in the cathedral of Valencia protected by the royal family and confessor to the heir to the throne Juan and his French wife, Violante, he was a strong supporter of Pope Clement VII in Avignon and later confessor to Benedict XIII. Called upon to form part of the *junta* to settle the question of the papal schism, he was also among those who supported Fernando de Antequera in the Compromise of Caspe in 1412, subsequently enjoying good relations with him and acting as his constant adviser.

Between 1399 and 1412 Vicente traveled extensively throughout the Crown of Aragón, Castile, and even reached Flanders; after this date his missionary endeavors were intensified and his attention seemed to be directed primarily at the conversion of the Jews and Moors who were obliged to listen to his sermons. These occasions, like others from over a century earlier, frequently provoked the people to fervent expressions of faith and violent vituperations against the non-Christians.

Some of the sermons that he preached during the latter years of the fourteenth and beginning of the fifteenth centuries have been preserved, including some forty-three on the subject of Lent, which he preached in Valencia, and others he preached on ceremonial occasions, including one on Palm Sunday 1416 in Toulouse, where he had studied some years earlier. As was his custom he entered the town triumphantly, riding his mule, and preached indefatigably, but bystanders noted his sickly countenance, suggesting that by that date Vicente was no longer in good health. It is for his sermons on a wide variety of topics, many of which have survived in part if not in their entirety, that he is regarded as one of the great Catalan and Latin writers of the late Middle Ages. Studies have been made of his use of the *artes praedicandi*, a use reminiscent of the structure advocated in the treatise of Francesc Eiximenis known as the *Ars praedicandi populo*—a tripartite division consisting of introduction, theme, and exposition of the theme. The text was usually in Catalan and was chosen from the Bible, frequently from the Gospel for the day, but Vicente would frequently append its Latin equivalent. He then proceeded to enunciate the theme and explain its significance in contemporary language, often punctuating his exposé with exclamations and illustrative stories, miracles, lives of the saints, current events, and the occasional personal anecdote, at times dramatizing the stories or adding a touch of humor. His sources were those of any medieval friar—the Bible, patristic literature, lives of the saints, books of *exempla* and other similar compendia of useful material for preachers—but in his hands they took on a new significance, for they became a means of commentary on life around him.

He was a scholar, able to speak to his contemporaries using vocabulary and images they could understand and indicating to them the corruption he saw in all aspects of life. He criticized many of the daily customs and popular beliefs, bewailed the moral depravity seen in the behavior of his contemporaries—lay and clerical alike—regarding the disintegration of society and the confusion that beset the church, characteristic of the late fourteenth and early fifteenth centuries, as signs that the end of the world was near. He is remembered for the sermons he preached in an attempt to make society aware of the problems and redress them before it was too late, and for the active role he played in resolving the questions of the Papal Schism and the royal succession to the Crown of Aragón, but most of all, perhaps, it is his contribution to Catalan language and literature that have ensured him a place in history.

Now regarded as patron of the city of Valencia and revered as a worker of miracles, his canonization process was begun under the Valencian pope, Calixtus III, in 1455, and completed three years later under his successor, Pius II.

See also **Eiximenis, Francesc**

Further Reading

Cátdera, Pedro M. *Sermón, sociedad y literatura en la Edad Media: San Vicente Ferrer en Castilla (1411–1414).* Salamanca, 1994.

Sanchisi Sivera, J. (ed.) *Quaresma de Sant Vicente Ferrer, Predicada a València l'any 1413.* Barcelona 1927.

Schib, G. "Els Sermons de Saut Vicent Ferrer." In *Actes del Tercer Col·loqui Internacional de Llengua i Literatures catalanes celebrat a Cambridge des gal 14 d'abril de 1973.* Oxford, 1976. 325–36.

JILL R. WEBSTER

FLORES, JUAN DE
(c. 1455–c. 1525)

A courtier, writer, knight, royal administrator, and diplomat, Flores was associated with the court of Garci Álvarez de Toledo, First Duke of Alba and, eventually, with that of the Catholic Monarchs. Extant documentation suggests that he was the nephew of Pedro Álvarez Osorio, third señor of Cabrera y Ribera and the first count of Lemos, and politically allied with the Enríquez, Osorio, Álvarez de Toledo, and Quiñones families. His formative years were probably spent at the ducal palace of Alba (Alba de Tormes), where he enjoyed considerable educational and political advantages, and in Salamanca, where he appears to have been active in local politics. On 20 May 1476 he was appointed official chronicler to Fernando and Isabel, and subsequently joined the royal entourage. During the civil war of the 1470s, he is known to have participated in attacks against the Portuguese and their *juanista* allies; there is evidence that he later joined Fernando in the Granada campaign. Documentation also suggests that he received various judicial assignments in Castile after 1477, and may have held the title of *protonotario de Lucena*. The dates of his birth and death are uncertain, but early genealogical sources suggest a long life, from about 1455 to 1525. He appears to have married Beatriz de Quiñones, a distant relative of Suero de Quiñones, and a son named Gaspar was apparently appointed chaplain to Isabel in 1503.

The extant works bearing Flores's name belong to a large body of courtly prose that examines the tragic nature of human passion, devotion, and intimacy. They include two sentimental romances, *Grisel y Mirabella* and *Grimalte y Gradisa*, and an allegorical vision narrative, *Triunfo de Amor*, recovered in 1976. All probably were written between 1470 and 1477, the period of Flores's affiliation with the first duke of Alba. Of the three works, *Grisel* experienced the greatest commercial success, especially in the sixteenth century, when it was translated into numerous European languages as (*Historia de*) *Aurelio et Isabel*. It constitutes an ambiguous response to Pere Torroellas's *Coplas de las calidades de las donas* (before 1458), a superficially virulent, but arguably only playful, misogynistic poem. Although *Grisel* implicitly promotes the cause of women by condemning the egocentric nature of male passion and the political abuses of men, there are ironic indications that women lack the virtues they self-righteously claim for themselves. The romance ends with the ritualistic slaughter of Torrellas—a fictional persona of the real-life poet—by the queen of Scotland and her retinue. Flores may have intended to point out the equal contribution of both sexes to illicit love, while underscoring the inherently self-destructive nature of passion.

Owing to its emotional intensity and narrative sophistication, *Grimalte* is now generally recognized as Flores's masterpiece. A continuation and implicit interpretation of the *Elegia di Madonna Fiammetta* of Boccaccio (1313–1375), it seeks to reconcile the contradictory notions of sexual freedom, devotion, and social responsibility as perceived by Fiometa (Fiammetta), her lover Pánfilo, and their counterparts Gradisa and Grimalte. Grimalte's vain attempts to reunite the Italian couple ultimately result in Fiometa's suicide, Pánfilo's self-imposed exile, and the breakup of his own unstable relationship with Gradisa. Philosophically complex and engaging, *Grimalte* explores the selfish motivations for love and the tragedies that ensue from a one-sided passion. *Grimalte* became a favorite source of sentimental material for later chivalric romances, including *Tristán de Leonis* (1501) and the *Quarta parte de don Clarián de Landanís* (1528), which contain substantial plagiarisms.

Though largely addressing the same erotic themes as the romances, *Triunfo* is more lighthearted. A felicitous combination of courtly romance, political allegory, and fictionalized chronicle, it tells the story of Cupid's capture by disgruntled dead lovers seeking redress for their amorous suffering. Following a trial and death sentence, the god of love is rescued, and his supporters receive as a reward the reversal of the customary courting ritual: men replace women as the custodians of virtue and women importune them for sexual favors. In response to the social turmoil of the period, political issues receive prominent attention, but Flores tends to exploit them as a vehicle for exploring the inevitable tension between joyous and tragic love.

Three other texts have been attributed to Flores with reasonable certainty: (1) *La coronación de la señora Gracisla*, (2) a short epistolary exchange between Tristan and Isolde, and (3) a fragmentary royal chronicle, the *Crónica incompleta de los Reyes Católicos*. Once thought to be artistically flawed, *Gracisla* is in fact a subtle *consolatio* written for Leonor de Acuña, the eldest daughter of Juan de Acuña, the second count of Valencia de don Juan, after the failure of her engagement to Pedro Álvarez Osorio, the third marquis of Astorga (April 1475). The work's plot, which relates the experiences of Gracisla, a Castilian maiden, at a beauty contest sponsored by the king of France, closely follows that of *Grisel*, and incorporates a number of allusions to actual events and individuals from the 1470s.

The *Crónica incompleta* represents Flores's official production as chronicler to the Catholic Monarchs. It is the most important source of information on his life and personal attitudes, since it contains circumstantial evidence of his activities in support of Isabel, most of which take place around Salamanca between 1475 and 1476. The extant text of the chronicle is evidently the copy of a working draft and has numerous gaps and inconsistencies. Nonetheless, it contains detailed information found in no other contemporary sources and has attracted the attention of historians. As a literary document it has hardly been studied.

Flores's works are known for their imagination, vividness of expression, and narrative complexity. He is a representative of a class of humanist knights dedicated to the ideals of the chivalric lifestyle, including the pursuit of literature as entertainment for the social elite. He is indisputably one of late medieval Spain's most prolific and versatile writers.

Further Reading

Gwara, J.J. "A Study of the Works of Juan de Flores, with a Critical Edition of *La historia de Grisel y Mirabella*." Ph.D. diss., Westfield College, University of London, 1988.

Matulka, B. *The Novels of Juan de Flores and Their European Diffusion: A Study in Comparative Literature*. New York, 1931. Repr. Geneva, 1974.

JOSEPH J. GWARA

FOLZ, HANS (ca. 1450–1515)

Hans Folz is generally known in literary history as a master craftsman, Meistersinger, and carnival playwright, and as Hans Sachs's predecessor in the Nuremberg *Meistersang* and carnival play tradition.

Folz's first recorded residence was Worms. His profession as a barber/wound dresser, or *barbierer*, is apparent from the signature, or *impressum* (*hans von wurms bar-wirer*), that typically appears in his writings. In 1459 Folz applied for citizenship in the city of Nuremberg, and in a Nuremberg council document of i486 he is referred to as a *Meister*, a master artisan or craftsman. In his works, Folz demonstrates an unusual amount of formal knowledge for an artisan. He shows a relatively developed understanding of Latin and also reveals knowledge of academic medicine, alchemy, and theology in his written work. Folz was one of the most multifaceted writers of his time. Scholars identify as his extant work approximately one hundred *Meisterlieder*, from twelve to thirty-five carnival plays, forty-eight fabliaux (poems), and two prose works.

Folz published almost all his work on his own printing press between 1479 and 1488. Most of the surviving prints are accompanied by woodcuts. He was probably the earliest Meistersinger to print his own songs, although only ten survive in print; the others exist in manuscript. It is possible that Folz intended his press as a means to a second income.

Folz's work varies widely in genre and theme, but was consistently popular at several levels of Nuremberg society. Records of personal libraries and Folz's own dedications reveal that he aspired to, and achieved, an elite readership in certain works. He addressed other works directly to lower levels of Nuremberg society.

Folz was one of the earliest authors in the Nuremberg carnival play tradition, writing plays and participating in their performance. Scholars have described his uniquely vehement use of carnival obscenity and scatological themes, and have described how Folz used the carnival play medium for an anti-Jewish agenda, revealing a strategic and political mindset that is apparent in much of his work.

Folz may have chosen the simple fabliau form (a rhyme-pair poem of varying length) to express himself most easily politically, humorously, or didactically. As his fabliaux are so varied thematically—they include religious, worldly, political, and traditional themes—one may deduce that Folz was giving free range to his every interest in this particular form.

The *Meisterlieder* (songs created within a guildlike group, for which Nuremberg was particularly well known) are primarily on spiritual-religious themes, especially the Virgin Mary, the Trinity, and the Incarnation. Also noteworthy is a series of songs in which Folz criticizes his fellow Meistersingers. Early scholarship identifies Folz as the author of a far-reaching *Meistersangsreform* "reform" through these songs, but later scholars deny this and convincingly characterize them simply as complaints against overregulation by the Nuremberg Meistersinger society. Other songs form thematic series as well.

Folz wrote six texts in his capacity as a wound dresser. The existence of subsequent editions shows that Folz succeeded in finding a popular audience for these instructional works.

No comprehensive edition of Folz's works exists at present. Separate German edition this *Meisterlieder*, fabliaux, and carnival plays vary in reliability.

Further Reading

Folz, Hans, in *Fastnachtspiele aus dem fünfzehnten Jahr-hundert*, ed. Adelbert Keller. 3 vols. Stuttgart: Literarischer Verein, 1853.
——. *Die Meisterlieder des Hans Folz aus der Münchener Onginalhandschrift und der Weimarer Handsckrift Q. 566*, ed. August L. Mayer. Berlin: Weidmannsche Buchhandlung, 1908.
——. *Die Reimpaarsprüche*, ed. Hanns Fischer. Munich: Beck, 1961.
Janota, Johannes. "Hans Folz in Nürnberg: ein Autor etabliert sich in einer stadtbürgerlichen Gesellschaft," in *Philologie und Geschichtswissenschaft: Demonstrationen literarischer Texte des Mittelalters*, ed. Heinz Rupp. Heidelberg: Quelle and Meyer, 1977, pp. 74–91.
Price, David. "Hans Folz's Anti-Jewish Carnival Plays." *Fifteenth-Century Studies* 19 (1992): 209–228.

CAROLINE HUEY

FOUQUET, JEAN (ca. 1420–1481)

The most influential painter of the mid-15th century in France, Jean Fouquet infused elements of Italian Renaissance art with his own native French style. He painted a portrait of Pope Eugenius IV (now lost) in Rome before 1447. By 1448, he was working for Charles VII at Tours, and he was appointed as court painter to Louis XI in 1475. He is best known for a book of hours that he illuminated for Étienne Chevalier ca. 1452, fragments of which survive in the Musée Condé at Chantilly. Among the panel paintings that have been attributed to Fouquet are portraits of Charles VII (ca. 1445) and Juvenal des Ursins (ca. 1455), both in the Louvre. Recently, it has been shown that Fouquet was probably not the head of a large, prolific atelier but worked as an independent artist who contributed sporadically to manuscripts from a variety of sources.

See also **Charles VII**

Further Reading

Clancy, Stephen. *Books of Hours in the* Fouquet *Style: The Relationship of Jean Fouquet and the* Hours of Étienne Chevalier *to French Manuscript Illumination of the Fifteenth Century*. Diss. Cornell University, 1988. [With bibliography.]
Reynaud, Nicole. *Jean Fouquet*. Paris: Éditions de la Reunion des Museés Nationaux, 1981.
Sterling, Charles, and Claude Schaeffer. *The Hours of Étienne Chevalier: Miniatures by Jean Fouquet*. New York: Braziller, 1971.
Wescher, Paul. *Jean Fouquet and His Time*. Basel: Pleiades, 1947.

ROBERT G. CALKINS

Jean Fouquet, Saint Bernard, Abbot of Clairvaux, preaching to the monks (above), Saint Bernard tempted by Satan (below). Heures d'Etienne Chevalier, Suffrage des saints. Ms. 71, fol. 36. Ca 1445. © Réunion des Musées Nationaux/Art Resource, New York.

FRANCESCO D'ACCORSO (1225–1293)

Francesco d'Accorso was the eldest son of Accursius and, like Accursius, was a professor of Roman law. In fact, Francesco studied under his famous father, the author of the ordinary gloss on the *Corpus iuris civilis*. Francesco taught at the university in his native city of Bologna from at least 1270 on. In 1274, he was recruited as a legal adviser by Edward I of England, who was then returning home from a pilgrimage to the Holy Land. According to one authority (Panzirolo 1968), the Bolognese threatened to confiscate Francesco's property if he left the city, and so he attempted—unsuccessfully—to transfer his possessions to a friend who was in collusion with him. Francesco's eagerness to enter the king's employ and leave Bologna was probably due partly to a desire to avoid the factional struggles between the Bolognese Guelfs and Ghibellines. He was present at legal proceedings before the king at Limoges in May 1274, and reportedly participated in a disputation at the law faculty in Orléans the same year. A report that he also taught at the university of Toulouse probably pertains to this period, and it may represent merely a repetition of the event at Orléans, attributed to a different city. In any case, Francesco supposedly had to defend some argument against another professor, Jacques de Revigny, who was disguised as a student.

In England, Francesco was described as the king's *consiliarius*, *familiaris*, *secretarius*, and *clericus*. He served Edward in various diplomatic and legal capacities and attended meetings of the royal council, presumably to advise the councillors on legal matters. In 1274–1275, Francesco was one of the king's proctors at a *parlement* of Philip III of France in litigation against a rebel viscount, Gaston VII of Béarn. In 1276, Edward commissioned Francesco to adjudicate a complaint of extortion brought by Jews in Oxford against the local sheriff. Also in 1276, he attended the Michaelmas parliament. In 1278, Francesco acted as one of Edward's proctorial emissaries to the papal curia, where he petitioned unsuccessfully for the postulation of Robert Burnell (royal chancellor and bishop of Bath and Wells) to the archbishopric of Canterbury.

Francesco received considerable rewards from the king: an annual salary of 200 marks, the custody of the manor and castle of Dunster (May 1280), the manor of Martleigh (June 1280), a lifetime pension of forty marks per year (1281), and ultimately a severance payment of 400 marks. The grant of the message of Badelkyng by Andrew de Scaccario (May 1275) was perhaps another mark of royal favor. Perhaps Francesco taught civil law at Oxford, but there is no evidence of this. His only connections with Oxford were the royal commission regarding the Jews' complaint, and Edward's offer of the use of Beaumont Manor (the *aula regis*, or king's hall); it is uncertain for what purpose this offer was made. On one occasion Francesco petitioned for the king's favor; he asked Edward to pardon a fellow countryman, Simone Spinelli, for the commission of a homicide.

While Francesco was absent in England, he and his brothers—all associated with the Ghibellines—were condemned to banishment by a new government which had come to power in Bologna in June 1274 and which supported the papacy. In 1282, however, Francesco returned to Bologna, where he was allowed to resume his teaching post and to reclaim his confiscated property after swearing loyalty to Pope Martin IV and to the city's government. Shortly thereafter the Bolognese government passed an edict against the Ghibellines wherein Francesco was specifically exempted from any penalty. In 1286, his full return to public life was signaled by a formal repetition of his oath of loyalty before Bologna's ruling council.

At some point in his career Francesco taught law to Cino da Pistoia. There is an anecdote that Dino da Mugello once substituted for Francesco and had the temerity to criticize some detail in Accursius's ordinary gloss. On his return, Francesco, ever "the true and pious defender of his father's glosses" (according to Diplovatatius), learned of this and insisted on repeating the entire lecture in order to defend his father's teaching. Francesco's reputation as a legal scholar must rest for the most part on his teaching, since few of his written works survive. Von Savigny (1834—1851) held that most of the writings attributed to Francesco were in fact by other authors. Francesco's most important scholarly work was a *Casus* or epitome of the *New Digest* which begins *Vlpianus iurisconsultus expositururs*; it is available in an early edition (Freiburg im Breisgau, c. 1494) and was included in the Paris edition of 1536 of the *Corpus iuris civilis*. Two *disputationes* by Francesco are still extant, and some *consilia* are attributed to him. Cino noted some of Francesco's opinions in his own works, but he was probably referring to matters heard in lectures, not to separate publications. The extant portion of Francesco's oration before Nicholas III (delivered in autumn 1278) has been edited by Haskins and Kantorowicz (1943).

A story in *Cento novelle antiche* tells of Francesco's proverbial avarice. On his return to Bologna, he was said to have claimed a share of the profits that his former students—now masters themselves—had earned during his absence, and to have supported his request by citing a right accorded in Roman law to absent fathers regarding their sons' property! Although this tale, if even partly genuine, probably recalls some jest, Francesco did find it necessary in 1291 to petition Nicholas IV for absolution from the sin of usury. It seems that both Francesco and his father had lent money to students at interest and had received bribes from students.

Francesco had two wives, Aichina Guezzi and Remgarda di Papazzone Aldighieri. Aichina Guezzi probably joined him for some part of his sojourn in England, because Edward sent her an invitation to do so at royal expense. Nonetheless, Dante immortalized Francesco in the *Commedia* (*Inferno*, 15.110) by placing him in the seventh circle of hell among the sodomites. No other text suggesting this character trait exists. Kay (1978) suggests that Dante did not mean this charge in a literal sense but rather was holding Francesco guilty of "unnatural" opinions: a denial of world rule by the Roman emperor and an exaltation—as evidenced by Francesco's oration—of papal jurisdiction independent of the emperor.

When Francesco died, he was buried next to his father in Bologna. It is said that the two shared an epitaph: *Sepvlchrvm Acvrsi Glosatoris Legvm Francisci Eivs Filii*, "The tomb of Accursius, glossator of the law, and Francis his son."

See also Cino da Pistoia; Dante Alighieri; Edward I; Philip III the Bold

Further Reading

Clarence Smith, J. A. *Medieval Law Teachers and Writers, Civilian and Canonist*. Ottawa: University of Ottawa Press, 1975, p. 53.

Diplovatatius, Thomas. *De claris iuris consultis: Pars posterior*, ed. Fritz Schulz, Hermann Kantorowicz, and Giuseppe Rabotti. Studia Gratiana, 10. Bologna: Institutum Gratianum, 1968, pp. 158–161.

Emden, A. B. "Accorso, Francesco." In *A Biographical Register of the University of Oxford to 1500*, 3 vols. Oxford: Clarendon, 1957, Vol. 1, pp. 9–10.

Haskins, George L. "Francis Accursius: A New Document." *Speculum*, 13, 1938a, pp. 76–77.

——. "Three English Documents relating to Francis Accursius." *Law Quarterly Review*, 54, 1938b, pp. 87–94.

Haskins, George L, and Ernst H. Kantorowicz. "A Diplomatic Mission of Francis Accursius and His Oration before Pope Nicholas III." *English Historical Review*, 58, 1943, pp. 424–447.

Kay, Richard. "Francesco d'Accorso the Unnatural Lawyer." In *Dante's Swift and Strong. Essays on "Inferno" XV*. Lawrence: The Regents Press of Kansas, 1978, pp. 39–66, 319–332.

Panzirolo, Guido. *De claris legum interpretibus*. Leipzig: J. F. Gleditsch, 1721, pp. 120–121. (Reprint, Farnborough: Gregg, 1968.)

Sarti, Mauro, and Mauro Fattorini. *De claris Archigymnasii Bononiensis professoribus a saeculo XI usque ad saeculum XIV*, 2 vols., ed. C. Albicini and C. Malagola. Bologna: Ex Officina Regia Fratrum Merlani, 1888–1896, Vol. 1, pp. 193–203.

Senior, W. "Accursius and His Son Franciscus." *Law Quarterly Review*, 51, 1935, pp. 513–516.

von Savigny, Friedrich Karl. *Geschichte des romischen Rechts im Mittelaker*, 7 vols. Heidelberg: J. C. B. Mohr, 1834–1851, Vol. 5, pp. 306–322.

Weimar, Peter. "Die legistische Literarur der Glossatorenzeit." In *Handbuch der Quellen und Literatur der neueren europäischen Privatrechtsgeschichte*, ed. Helmut Coing. Munich: Beck, 1973, Vol. 1, p. 220.

ROBERT C. FIGUEIRA

FRANCIS OF ASSISI, SAINT
(1181 or 1182—1226)

Saint Francis of Assisi (Francesco di Pietro di Bernardone) was a religious reformer and the founder of the Franciscan order and the Poor Clares.

By some estimates, more books have been written about Francis of Assisi than about any other person who ever lived. In the twentieth century, for instance, he was the subject not only of historical and religious works but also of literary fiction, movies, songs, and comic books. Nikos Kazantzakis wrote a novel about Francis, and W. E. B. DuBois once gave a commencement speech in which he urged the graduates to make Francis their model. Hermann Hesse and G. K. Chesterton wrote essays on Francis. Adolf Holl called Francis "the last Christian," and the theologian Leonardo Boff described him as the "model for human liberation." In the nineteenth century, to take just one example, Henry Thode (during the 1880s) described Francis as the initiator of the Renaissance.

There was nothing new in the attention given to Francis during the nineteenth and twentieth centuries. The artists who were called to Assisi in the century after his death to decorate his burial church are a who's who of Italian painting: they included, among many others, Giunta Pisano, Cimabue, Pietro Cavallini, Giotto, Simone Martini, and Pietro Lorenzetti. The name Francis was often given to boys, in Italy and beyond, during the fourteenth century. Dante devoted a canto of *Paradiso* to praising Francis. In short, Francis was an extraordinary man who has inspired people of very different ways of life and beliefs ever since he walked the roads of Italy in the early thirteenth century.

Francis was born in the small Umbrian town of Assisi, the son of a prosperous cloth merchant. Almost nothing is known for certain about his youth. Apparently, Francis was renowned for generosity, even for prodigality; and he clearly had an interest in chivalry and military affairs. When he was about twenty years old, he fought in a war between Assisi and its hated neighbor, Perugia. Assisi was defeated, and Francis spent some time as a prisoner of war. Later, he planned to enter the service of Walter of Brienne in Apulia against the Hohenstaufen king and to make a name for himself as a knight. Francis also worked in his father's cloth business, of which he was to be the heir. Literally, Francis did not get very far in his military career—he turned around and returned to Assisi after traveling only a few miles—but he was learning the cloth business, and he enjoyed the social life of wealthy, popular youth.

When Francis was in his early twenties, he began to find solace in solitary prayer in the countryside around Assisi. Soon, he came to believe that God wanted him to rebuild churches, both by providing supplies and by helping with the reconstruction. Thus far, Francis's father had indulged him, but a crisis came when Francis sold some of his father's cloth and offered the money to the priest of San Damiano, a church in need of repair. The family conflict became a public matter when the bishop was called on to decide between Francis and his father, and this was also the moment when Francis's life crystallized. Francis stripped himself naked before the bishop and returned every stitch of clothing to his father. He had chosen a new path in life, and there was no going back to his father; even after Francis came to be famous and revered, he and his father were never reconciled. Francis was to find a different kind of family and rely on a different kind of wealth.

Francis's dramatic conversion is often represented as a complete repudiation of everything he had been taught, and as a metamorphosis of his own personality and character. However, Saint Bonaventure (d. 1274), who may have been Francis's most sophisticated biographer, did not understand Francis's conversion in this way. According to Bonaventure, Francis remained as impetuous as always, and other elements of his character were altered rather than rooted out. Bonaventure describes Francis after his conversion as a great merchant because, like the merchant of the gospel, Francis had found the pearl of great price and single-mindedly sold everything to obtain it; and as a man seeking knighthood as a loyal soldier in the army of the great king, Christ, Bonaventure describes Francis's stigmata as the coat of arms of his new lord; in feudal terms, everyone could see, from the stigmata, exactly whose man Francis was.

After breaking with his family, Francis lived for a while as a hermit and continued to help rebuild churches. One of these churches, the Portiuncula (or Saint Mary of the Angels), later became his headquarters when he was in Assisi; this church remained his favorite place, and he insisted that he be allowed to return there to die. It was during a mass at the Portiuncula that Francis had the experience which changed the focus of his religious vocation: he heard the Gospel in which Jesus tells the apostles to take nothing with them on their journey. In cities like Assisi, possessions were taking an ever larger role in shaping people's lives and values; and Francis was struck by Jesus's call to the apostles to do without them—even to do without necessities. This deeper poverty would become a cornerstone of Francis's way of life.

In Francis's unlikely story, perhaps nothing is more surprising than the fact that he was soon joined by other young men from Assisi and its environs. Within about three years after he broke with his father, Francis had a new family of some dozen "brothers" who shared his work, his prayer, and his poverty; went begging with him; and with him exhorted all they met to repent.

Bishop Guido of Assisi, among others, was supportive of Francis and his brothers; but certain people were suspicious about these young laymen, who seemed to them very like the Cathars of Umbria and Tuscany—enemies of the Roman church. Therefore, probably at the urging of the bishop, Francis and his brothers went to Rome in 1209 or 1210 to seek the support of Pope Innocent III for their way of life. Another surprising part of Francis's story is that he was able to see the pope; even more surprising, or shocking, is that Innocent agreed to allow the brothers to live by a simple rule, consisting largely of scriptural passages, and to preach. But Innocent knew what he was doing. The Cathars and other heretical groups were attractive partly because, unlike most of the leaders of the Roman church, they tried to live as Jesus and the apostles had lived. Francis and his band were, then, a potential counterforce; Innocent no doubt perceived that Francis combined a zeal for the apostolic life with a passionate loyalty to the church. Innocent must also have been affected by those qualities

in Francis that made it difficult to say no to him. For example, Francis was incapable of duplicity; what he said was what he meant, and how he looked reflected what he really was.

Thus the Franciscan order was established and was given the task of preaching penance. In the next decade, the order grew from a small group of Umbrians into an international brother hood. Just as Francis had attracted followers in and around Assisi, he now—personally or by repute—brought thousands to embrace a hard life of preaching, working, and begging. His words and his example spoke to many who found themselves conflicted and unfulfilled in a world where trade and personal wealth were growing alongside desperate poverty. With Francis as their model and guide, the Franciscans became a great new army of the church.

Not long after the meeting with Innocent III, an event as extraordinary as Francis's own conversion took place; as a result, the Franciscan order came to have sisters as well as brothers. A young aristocratic woman of Assisi named Clare left her family and joined Francis and his brothers at the Portiuncula, where Francis tonsured her and welcomed her into the band of poor people for Christ. It is worth noting that Clare was hardly a *tabula rasa* on which Francis wrote. She had an extraordinary mother who traveled as a pilgrim to Jerusalem, and the household in which Clare had been raised was devoted to prayer and apostolic work. Still, Francis gave Clare a focus for her religious concerns and desires. Clare soon went to San Damiano, one of the churches Francis had repaired, where she lived in a cloistered environment with other sisters; and she developed a spirituality and a way of life that constitute one of the grandest statements ever made about the Christian life. However, she always remained devoted to Francis and always turned to him for guidance and support.

When Francis first returned from Rome, he had no clear idea about exactly what he and his brothers would do—whether they would be essentially a contemplative order or would live "in the world." They decided on an active life supported by both prayer and work; later, if not at this moment, they based their decision on the fact that Jesus had lived in the world. Thus Christ and the apostles were the models for the Franciscan order.

The Franciscan friars were poor not only as individuals but as an institution. In this regard, their order was quite different from traditional monasticism, in which the individual brothers owned nothing but the monastery itself was often quite rich. Francis had originally envisioned the friars as working for their food and other necessities, perhaps as transient laborers or farm workers. They would beg only if they were unable to provide necessities for themselves by manual labor. In no circumstances were they to accept money, because Francis was aware of the problems associated with it.

First, money often made people act irrationally; they took a sensuous pleasure in counting coins and running their fingers through coins. Second, some people made the acquisition of money their goal in life. Third, saving money conduced to laziness: if a brother earned enough money for several days' worth of food, he might decide not to work during those days. More philosophically, when Francis stripped himself naked before the bishop, he had decided to forgo all security but God's; and it would be impossible to depend only on God if there was a possibility of accumulating wealth. Ultimately, Francis decided to reject in its entirety the money economy that was then developing in Italy.

Francis and his band covered great distances, working to support themselves and preaching to anyone who would listen (although unfortunately we do not have a single sermon of his). Since Francis and most of the brothers were not trained in theology, they focused on calling people to penance and on trying to reconcile people who were odds with one another. As regards penance, this early ministry was a difficult one, because many of the people to whom it was directed felt that they were already followers of Jesus: they had been baptized; they went to mass; they crossed themselves and prayed. But Francis felt that such people often took Christianity for granted, as a routine, whereas he wanted them to experience Christ and seek forgiveness more intensely. Francis was on fire with the love of Christ and wanted to spread the fire throughout the world. As regards reconciliation, Francis's profound desire may have arisen because he had seen so much divisiveness—in his family, in his town, in the church, and between secular and ecclesiastical authorities. There is evidence that he helped bring peace in several divided cities, including Arezzo, Siena, Bologna, and Assisi itself. There is a popular story, probably apocryphal, that he worked out a peace agreement between the people of Gubbio and a wolf which had eaten several of their fellow citizens.

The story of the wolf of Gubbio is, of course, only one of many stories about Saint Francis and animals. One of the most famous concerns a sermon he preached to the birds at Bevagna, near Assisi. Francis did indeed love animals; he also loved plants and even rocks, regarding all of creation as his brothers and sisters. He reasoned that God created not just humans but every thing that exists, and that therefore all things had a common parent and were all part of the same family, with God as the father. Francis tried to live that belief by treating everything with respect and reverence. He is the author of a great song, *Canticle of the Creatures*, in which he sings the praises of Brother Sun, Sister Moon, and his other siblings, including Sister Death.

It is easy to romanticize Francis's love of creation and think of him as a precursor of modern conservationists and people who hug trees. However, for Francis the love of creatures was always a consequence of the love of God and of a desire to experience God through God's creation. Bonaventure writes that "in beautiful things Francis saw beauty itself," and that for Francis God's works were like footprints one could follow in order to get closer to God. In theological terms, Francis had a sacramental understanding of creation.

In the years after Innocent III approved the "primitive rule," the Franciscan brotherhood underwent tremendous growth. Eventually, the order had to change because it was no longer simply a small band of brothers wandering the roads of Italy, working in the fields, sleeping in barns, and preaching on street corners. Francis himself had no real plans for this new order. He was intuitive rather than analytical, and his charismatic personality was not very well suited for the head of a large group of men, most of whom he did not know. Thus he asked the pope for a cardinal protector to be a guide and a liaison with the hierarchy, and he was fortunate in the appointment of Cardinal Ugolino (later Pope Gregory IX), an astute churchman who was deeply moved by and devoted to Francis.

However, even with Cardinal Ugolino to help him, Francis was not equipped to handle the tasks of the reader of an order. Not only was he frustrated; so were many of the newer friars who did not know him personally and had not experiencd his powerful attraction. There were a number of legitimate concerns. For example, could the friars build permanent places to live? Could they have books?—and if so, would they not need money to buy books and places to keep them? As more priests joined the order, where were they to say the mass? How were they to obtain and keep the vestments and vessels necessary for celebrating the sacraments? What was to happen to friars who had grown too old to live as transients? These were not the sort of questions with which Francis had much patience, and he became perplexed and deeply troubled by the growing complexity of his order. Toward the end of his life, there was already a distance between friars who saw a need for the order to evolve and change and those who regarded any change from the way Francis lived as a betrayal of their founder. Many of these problems were not resolved in Francis's lifetime or, for that matter, for long afterward.

The "primitive rule" that Innocent III approved was little more than a collection of passages from scripture, and we have no copy of it today. By 1221, Francis had composed a longer and more complex rule; but many friars did not approve of it, and it was never made the official rule of the order. Finally, in 1223, Pope Honorius III approved a rule, the *Regula bullata*, that remains to this day the rule for the Friars Minor (the actual name of the Franciscan order). Francis no doubt had help from

Cardinal Ugolino in its composition, and Francis was always uncomfortable with some of the compromises it contained.

Early on, Francis had wanted to do missionary work outside the regions where Christianity was dominant; and in 1219 he went to the Holy Land and preached to the sultan, after having seen the army of the fifth crusade and predicted its failure. Apparently Francis impressed the sultan, though without converting him to Christianity. Francis's journey established missionary activities as a part of the work of the order; for several centuries, Francis's followers would be missionaries in Africa, Asia, and the Americas. (The city of Los Angeles, for example, is named for Saint Mary of the Angels—the Portiuncola—because Franciscan friars established a mission of that name there in the eighteenth century.)

As Francis became ill, and increasingly discouraged about the development of an order that already looked very different from the one he had founded, he spent more time in prayer and contemplation. But he never lost his zeal for bringing people to closer to Christ. For instance, for a special Christmas mass at Greccio, he placed a manger with an ox and an ass in the church. Francis wanted people not just to commemorate the birth of Christ but in some real way to experience it. As his first biographer said, "Out of Greccio he made a new Bethlehem."

In 1224, while he was on an extended retreat at La Verna, a mountain in southern Tuscany, Francis had a vision and received the stigmata, the five wounds of Christ. During the last two years of his life, he tried, with some success, to keep these wounds hidden, but news of them spread quickly after his death. People interpreted this "new and unheard-of miracle" in various ways. First, it was taken as evidence that Francis was a mystic, one who experienced union with God in some significant, albeit temporary, way while on earth. Second, God's "seal"—the stigmata—were said to signify that Francis's way of life, and by extension the life of the friars, was authentic and worthy of respect and imitation. Third, the stigmata were said to mean that Francis was more than just another holy man: he was a saint among saints and uniquely Christlike.

A little more than two years after receiving the stigmata, Francis died at the Portiuncula. He was buried in his former parish church, San Giorgio (which was later incorporated into Santa Chiara); and immediately people began to report that miracles of healing were taking place at his tomb. In July 1228, his old friend Cardinal Ugolino, now Pope Gregory IX, came to Assisi for the official proclamation of Francis's sainthood. Gregory also laid the cornerstone for a new burial church; by 1230, this new church was complete enough for the translation of Francis's body to it. From then to the present, millions of pilgrims have come there to venerate Saint Francis.

Francis was the founder of a new order and a man whose personal life became widely known. For many people, his spirituality, although rooted in tradition, nevertheless revolutionized the practice of Christianity. Francis focused on the humanity of Christ, teaching that to know Christ one must be with him both at the incarnation in Bethlehem (Greccio) and at the atonement on Calvary (La Verna). Whereas much of Christian practice in Francis's day had its origins in monasteries and the feudal aristocracy, Francis and his followers were active in cities, seeking to explain and practice the great truths of the faith in ways that would make sense to urban people. Francis, who started by rebuilding churches around Assisi, ultimately rebuilt the Roman Catholic church itself.

Francis wrote several works, the most famous being *Canticle of the Creatures* (or *Canticle of Brother Sun*). The most recent edition in English of Francis's writings is *Francis of Assisi: The Saint* (1999), the first volume of *Francis of Assisi: Early Documents*; as of 2002, two more volumes were projected, to include virtually all the thirteenth-century sources for the life of Francis. Until this work is completed, readers will still need to consult *Saint Francis of Assisi: Writings* (1973).

See also **Bonaventure, Saint; Clare, Saint; Dante Alighieri, Innocent III, Pope**

Further Reading

Writings by Francis

Francis of Assisi: The Saint, ed. Regis Armstrong, A. Wayne Hellmann, and William Short. New York: New City, 1999. (Vol. 1 of *Francis of Assisi: Early Documents*.)

Saint Francis of Assisi: Writings and Early Biographies—English Omnibus of the Sources for the Life of Saint Francis, ed. Marion Habig. Chicago, Ill.: Franciscan Herald, 1973. (Later Quincy, Ill.: Franciscan Press.)

Biographies

Bonaventure. *Writings*, ed. and trans. Ewert Cousins. Classics of Western Spirituality. New York: Paulist, 1978. (Includes a translation of Bonaventure's life of Saint Francis, *Legenda maior*.)

Chesterton, G. K. *Saint Francis of Assisi*. Garden City, N.Y.: Doubleday, 1957. (Originally published 1924.)

Cook, William R. *Francis of Assisi: The Way of Poverty and Humility*. Vol. 8 of *The Way of the Christian Mystics*. Wilmington, Del.: Michael Glazier, 1989. (Later Collegeville, Minn.: Liturgical Press.)

Englebert, Omer. *Saint Francis of Assisi: A Biography*, trans. Eva Marie Cooper. Chicago, Ill.: Franciscan Herald, 1965. (Later Quincy, Ill.: Franciscan Press.)

Fortini, Arnaldo. *Francis of Assisi*, trans. Helen Moak. New York: Crossroad, 1981. (Edited translation of Fortini's 2,000-page biography of Francis; includes information about Assisi.)

Frugoni, Chiara. *Francis of Assisi*, trans. John Bowden. New York: Continuum, 1998.

Green, Julien. *God's Fool: The Life and Times of Francis of Assisi*, trans. Peter Heinegg. London: Hodder and Stoughton, 1986.

Holl, Adolf. *The Last Christian: A Biography of Francis of Assisi*, trans. Peter Heinegg. Garden City, N.Y.: Doubleday, 1980.

Jörgensen, Johannes. *Saint Francis of Assisi, a Biography*, trans. T. O'Conor Sloane. Garden City, N.Y.: Doubleday, 1955. (Originally published 1932; remains one of the best accounts.)

Robson, Michael. *Saint Francis of Assisi: The Legend and the Life*. London: Geoffrey Chapman, 1997.

Sabatier, Paul. *Life of Saint Francis of Assisi*, trans. Louise Seymour Houghton. New York: Charles Scribner, 1894. (Marks the beginning of modern scholarship on Saint Francis.)

Smith, John Holland. *Francis of Assisi*. New York: Scribner, 1972.

Critical Studies

Allen, Paul M., and Joan deRis Allen. *Francis of Assisi's "Canticle of the Creatures": A Modern Spiritual Path*. New York: Continuum, 1996.

Armstrong, Edward A. *Saint Francis: Nature Mystic—The Derivation and Significance of the Nature Stories in the Franciscan Legend*. Berkeley: University of California Press, 1973. (Addresses both hagiographical literature and the natural world.)

Boff, Leonardo. *Saint Francis: A Model for Human Liberation*, trans. John Diercksmeier. New York: Crossroad, 1982.

Cook, William R. *Images of Saint Francis of Assisi in Painting, Stone, and Glass from the Earliest to c 1320 in Italy: A Catalogue*. Florence: Leo S. Olschki, 1999.

Doyle, Eric. *Saint Francis and the Song of Brotherhood*. New York: Seabury, 1981. (Reinterpretation of Francis's "Canticle of the Creatures" for modern times, by a friar.)

DuBois, W. E. B. "Saint Francis of Assisi." In *W. E. B. DuBois: A Reader*, ed. Andrew Paschal. New York: Macmillan, 1971, pp. 290–302.

Frugoni, Chiara. *Francesco e l'invenzione delle Stimmate: Una storia per parole e immagini fino a Bonaventura e Giotto*. Turin: Einaudi, 1993.

Hesse, Hermann. *Francesco d'Assisi*, trans. Barbara Griffini. Parma: Ugo Guanda, 1989.

Kazantzakis, Nikos. *Saint Francis*, trans. P. A. Bien. New York: Simon and Schuster, 1962.

McMichaels, Susan W. *Journey out of the Garden: Saint Francis of Assisi and the Process of Individuation*. New York: Paulist, 1997.

Peterson, Ingrid J. *Clare of Assisi: A Biographical Study*. Quincy, Ill.: Franciscan Press, 1993.

Sorrell, Roger D. *Saint Francis of Assisi and Nature: Tradition and Innovation in Western Christian Attitudes toward the Environment*. New York: Oxford University Press, 1988. (Perhaps the best scholarly treatment of Francis and nature.)

Thode, Henry. *Franz von Assisi und die Anfänge der Kunst der Renaissance in Italien*, 2nd ed. Berlin: G. Grote, 1904.

Trexler, Richard C. *Naked Before the Father: The Renunciation of Francis of Assisi*. New York: Peter Lang, 1989.

WILLIAM R. COOK

FRANCKE, MASTER (ca. 1380–ca. 1440)

A commission from the confraternity of "England-Travellers," dated 1424, names Master Francke. It has been suggested that, although working in a Hamburg monastery, he was a Dominican monk from Zutphen in Holland. This is the more plausible, as his intensely spiritual work differs profoundly from that of Bertram, the leading master in Hamburg. Francke's expressive linear style, figure canon, and iconography could derive from the Netherlands and certainly indicate an acquaintance, around 1415, with French work from the Boucicaut and Rohan workshops.

Netherlandish influences dominate his double-winged St. Barbara Altarpiece (ca. 1420–1425; Kansallismuseo, Helsinki), especially in the realism and dramatic force of the male protagonists. The often friezelike arrangement of the figures in the painted martyrdom scenes is sculptural in character, and the designs in the carved shrine section have therefore also, controversially, been attributed to Francke.

The commission of 1424 is thought to relate to the St. Thomas Altarpiece, completed in 1436, of which only fragments survive (Kunsthalle, Hamburg). In the closed state, the altarpiece originally showed scenes from the childhood of Christ and the martyrdom of Saint Thomas; when opened, the drama of the passion of Christ was revealed. Francke employed steep hillside settings, silhouetted against a starred red ground for the outside scenes, and a gold ground on the festive side. In this altarpiece, certain motives, such as the women under the cross in the Crucifixion, suggest direct knowledge of the courtly art of Conrad von Soest. However, Francke favored poignant drama in contrast to Conrad's more lyrical mood.

Francke's work found numerous followers in Germany, but only in paintings by Rogier van der Weyden do we find a similar emotive use of line.

Further Reading

Corley, Brigitte. *Conrad von Soest: Painter among Merchant Princes*. London: Harvey Miller, 1997, pp. 152–156.

Martens, Bella. *Meister Francke*, 2 vols. Hamburg: Friederichsen, de Gruyter, 1929.

Meister Francke und die Kunst um 1400. Hamburg: Kunsthalle, 1969.

Pylkkänen, Riitta. *Pyhän Barbaran legenda*. Helsinki: n. p., 1966.

BRIGITTE CORLEY

FRAU AVA (fl. first half the 12th c.)

Author ("Lady Ava") of a series of four religious Middle High German poems, written circa 1120 to 1125, transmitted in two versions known as the *Vorauer Handschrift* (manuscript "V") from the latter half of the twelfth century, and the missing fourteenth-century *Görlitzer Handschrift* (manuscript "G"). Frau Ava's work, viewed as a whole, provides a poetic rendering of the history of salvation. *Johannis*, the first poem of the series ("G" version only), begins with John the Baptist's future parents, Zacharias and his barren wife, Elizabeth, and Zacharias's failure to believe in the annunciation of the approaching birth of their son. Zacharias's lack of faith in the angelic message is punished by muteness. The poem next recounts the annunciation of Jesus to Mary, who in contrast to the doubting Zacharias, acknowledges her absolute faith in God. After the Baptists birth and circumcision, and the restoration of speech to Zacharias through the intercession of the Holy Spirit, the exemplary character of Johannis highlights the need for repentance and vigilance. Johannis's ascetic discipline stands in opposition to Harod's lasciviousness. While the king enslaves himself to erotic passion, Johannis struggles to uphold the rule of reason and to bridle the desires of the flesh. The poem underscores the Baptist's role as a helper to all Christians. His spiritual orientation enables him to serve God and humankind, to bear witness as a martyr, and to merit the praise of Christendom. The major poem in the series, *Das Leben Jesu* (Life of Jesus), recapitulates the annunciation to Zacharias, the mission of John the Baptist, and the machinations of Herod. After the account of Jesus' baptism in the Jordan, Ava tells of his fast in the desert and encounter with Satan, his tempter. The defeat of the devil as tempter culminates in his actual subjection during Christ's triumphal Harrowing of Hell. Following the scenes of Jesus' temptations in the desert, the narrative recounts his miracles or healing. The capture, trial, and crucifixion of Jesus place charity—the central commandment to his disciples—in the context of giving one's own life for a friend. After depicting the Resurrection and the Ascension, the poem focuses on the arrival of the Holy Spirit in the upper room and the recipients' use of the divine gifts to teach others. The main body of *Das Leben Jesu* ends with Peter winning many converts as bishop in Antioch and Rome. The transitional verses that follow constitute *Die Sieben Gaben des Heiligen Geistes* (The Seven Gifts of the Holy Spirit) and offer a catalogue of virtues given by Jesus to his disciples. The third work in the series is *Der Antichrist*. This short poem of twelve strophes relates how the Antichrist will take possession of the world and overthrow the existing social order. Ava shows that his qualities are antithetical to the seven gifts of the Holy Spirit. Those who lack the correct orientation to God will succumb to the impostor's deception. Although the Antichrists reign will last for four and one-half years and inflict great suffering on all Christians, the sin of pride will eventually lead to his fall and destruction. *Das jüngste Gericht*, the final poem in the series, previews the fifteen days that precede the Last Judgment and the purification of the world by fire. The second half of the poem describes the *Parousia*, the glorious second coming of Christ. Preceded by the four evangelists, he awakens the dead to reward the good and punish those who caused him suffering. As the requirements for salvation can no longer be fulfilled once Christ has returned, Ava advocates repentance and the immediate practice of redeeming virtues, particularly applicable to an aristocratic audience: protecting the poor, ransoming prisoners, holding court without bribe taking, showing mercy to those of lesser power, and generous giving of alms. After the account of the Last Judgment, the poem commemorates the beginning of the liturgical year at Easter as an appropriate time for spiritual reorientation.

Ava's poems are the earliest extent work of an identifiable woman author written in German. Little is known about the author apart from some autobiographical disclosures in her work and from records of her death. Only in the final poem of the series does Ava tell something about her life. Her sons are likely to have been clerics who advised her on interpreting Scripture and other religious sources. The record of Ava's death in the necrology of the Austrian monastery of Melk notes the year 1127 and her vocation as religious recluse.

Further Reading

de Boor, Helmut. *Frühmittelhochdeutsche Studien. Zwei Untersuchungen.* Halle/Saale: Niemeyer, 1926.

Domitrovic, Martin. "Die Sprache in den Gedichten der Frau Ava, Vokalismus und Konsonantismus." Ph.D. diss., University of Graz, 1950.

Freytag, Wiebke. "Geistliches Leben und christliche Bildung. Hrotsvit und andere Autorinnen des frühen Mittelalters." *Deutsche Literatur von Frauen*, vol. 1. Munich: Beck, 1988, pp. 65–76.

Greinemann, S. Eoliba, OSB. "Die Gedichte der Frau Ava Untersuchungen zur Quellenfrage." Ph.D. diss., University of Freiburg im Breisgau, 1967.

Heer, Friedrich. *Aufgang Europas. Eine Studie zu den Zusammenhängen zwischen politischer Religiosität, Fröm-migkeitsstil und dem Westen Europas im 12. Jahrhundert.* Vienna: Europa, 1949.

Helm, Karl. "Untersuchungen über Heinrich Heslers Evangelium Nicodemi." *Beiträge zur Geschichte der deutschen Sprache und Literatur* 24 (1899): 85–187.

Henschel, Erich. "Zu Ava 'Leben Jesu'." *Beiträge zur Geschichte der deutschen Sprache und Literatur* (Halle) 78 (1956): 479–484.

Hintz, Ernst Ralf. "Frau Ava," in *Semper idem et novus. Festschrift for Frank Banta*, ed. Ftancis G. Gentry. Göppingen: Kümmerle, 1988, pp. 209–230.

———. "Frau Ava (?–1127)." In *German Writers and Works of the Early Middle Ages: 800–1170*, ed. Will Hasty and James Hardin. Detroit: Gale, 1995, pp. 39–44.

———. *Learning and Persuasion in the German Middle Ages.* New Yotk: Garland, 1997, pp. 103–137.

Hoffmann von Fallersleben, Heinrich. *Fundgruben für Geschichte deutscher Sprache und Literatur.* Breslau: Grass, Barth, 1830. [part 1, ("G") only, *Johannis* omitted].

Kienast, Richard. "Ava-Studien. 1–3" *Zeitschrift für deutsches Altertum und deutsche Literatur* 74 (1937): 1–36; 74 (1937): 277–308: 77 (1940): 45–104.

Mauter, Friedrich. *Die Dichtungen der Frau Ava.* Tübingen: Niemeyer, 1966.

Menhardt, Hermann. "Ein früher Teildruck der Görlitzer Ava-

FRA AVA

Handschrift." *Beiträge zur Geschichte der deutschen Sprache und Literatur* 81 (1959): 111–115.

Piper, Paul. "Die Gedichte der Ava." *Zeitschrift für deutsche Philologie* 19 (1887): 129–196, 275–321 [("V" and "G")].

Schacks, Kurt. *Die Dichtungen der Frau Ava*. Graz: Wiener Neudrucke, 1986.

Schröder, Edward. "Frau Ava und die Osterfeier." *Zeitschrift für deutsches Altertum und deutsche Literatur* 50 (1908): 312–313.

——. "Ava und Bettina." *Anzeiger für deutsches Altertum und deutsche Literatur* 42 (1923): 90–91.

——. "Aus der Gelehrsamkeit der Frau Ava." *Zeitschrift für deutsches Altertum und deutsche Literatur* 66 (1929): 171–172.

——. "Spiel und Spielmann." *Zeitschrift für deutsches Altertum und deutsche Literatur* 74 (1937): 45–46.

Stein, Peter K. "Stil, Struktur, historischer Ort und Funktion. Literarhistorische Beobachtungen und methodologische Überlegungen zu den Dichtungen Frau Avas," in *Festschrift für Adalbert Schmidt zum 70. Geburtstag*. Stuttgart: Heinz, 1976.

Wesenick, Gertrude. "Frühmittelhochdeutsche Dichtung des 12. Jahrhunderts aus der Wachau. Frau Avas Gedichte." Ph.D. diss., University of Tübingen, 1963.

Woelfert, Rosemarie. "Wandel der religiösen Epik zwischen 1100 und 1200 dargestellt an Frau Avas Leben Jesu und der Kindheit Jesu des Konrad von Fusses-brunnen." Ph.D. diss., University of Tübingen, 1963.

ERNST RALF HINTZ

FRAUENLOB (d. November 29, 1318)

Heinrich von Meißen, called *Frauenlob* (literally, Praise of Women), wrote Middle High German poetry in the late thirteenth and early fourteenth centuries. He died on November 29, 1318, and lies buried in Mainz. There being practically no nonliterary traces of his life, nearly all we know of him derives from his literary production. In later political poems (*Sangspruchdichtung*), Frauenlob names a series of historical personalities who provide dates for certain texts and may indicate a degree of mobility (e.g., Duke Heinrich von Breslau, King Eric of Denmark, among others); living and deceased poets of his time are named (e.g., Walther von der Vogelweide, Konrad von Würzburg, and many others) who offer hints of a relative chronology.

Frauenlob's literary production is broad, but many of the texts are extant in only one copy, thus making editing difficult. For example, numerous poems have been distorted by scribal misunderstandings and errors, and present a daunting philological challenge. Equally problematic is the question of authenticity. Owing to questionable reasoning on the part of the scholar Helmuth Thomas, the standard edition of Frauenlob's poems, edited by Stackmann and Bertau, contains an incomplete catalogue. To attain the broadest possible picture of Frauenlob's oeuvre, one must consult Ettmullter's edition of 1843.

Frauenlob was comfortable composing in all genres: songs, political lyrics, disputes, and narrative poetry.

Often his songs represent traditions common in the first half of the thirteenth century, employing topics such as courtly love (*minne*), nature, and religion. His series of songs, especially those on the Virgin Mary and the Trinity, are thematically and formally more ambitious. Frauenlob combines and refines traditional motives, often in a particular fashion: cryptic, encoded, aimed at a knowledgeable, elite audience. Within his *Spruchdichtung*, Frauenlob also expressed his own thoughts on poetry and his own role as a poet. Thus, on the one hand, he sees himself as a grateful successor to the great poets of the past (he especially honors Konrad von Würzburg), while, on the other hand, he presents himself as their superior: once he remarks, *ûz kezzels grunde gât mîn kunst* (from the depth of the caldron emerges my art), thereby setting himself apart from other poets.

A noteworthy composition is Frauenlob's "Dispute between Minne and the World," in which both allegorical partners—*minne* as courtly love personified—argue in learned fashion for their respective relative rank.

Frauenlob's *Leiche* are undoubtedly achievements of the highest order. He composed praises of the Crucifix, of *minne*, and of the Virgin Mary, and the melodies for each. It is because of the song to Mary, in praise of the heavenly woman, that Frauenlob received his nickname, Praise of Women, although his praise of worldly women may have also played a role. This song is Frauenlob's masterpiece: his theology, pious praise of Mary, and natural philosophy are combined in an immense concept and present a dimension of popular language praise of Mary hitherto unseen in this genre, a dimension that still today presents critical challenges. The love poem provides an unconventional concept of courtly love: *minne* is now founded in natural philosophy as a productive force of nature that unites opposites to create nature anew and to perpetuate the process of nature. The crucifix poem, finally, deals with the theological concepts of trinity, incarnation, salvation, and crucifix worship, at one unique linguistically and from the point of view of the motif.

Frauenlob marks a literary transition; he looks back on some one hundred years of tradition he knows well; intellectually he is well trained in many areas; he attempts to reapproach the great poetical topics aesthetically and substantively.

See also **Konrad von Würzburg; Walther von der Vogelweide**

Further Reading

Bein, Thomas. *Studien zu Frauenlobs Minneleich*. Frankfurt am Main: Lang, 1988.

Cambridger "Frauenlob"-Kolloquium 1986. Wolfram-Studien 10, ed. Werner Schröder. Berlin: Schmidt, 1988 [collection of papers from conference].

Ettmüller, Ludwig, ed. *Heinrich von Meißen, des Frauenlobs*

Leiche, Sprüche, Streitgedichte und Lieder. Quedlinburg: Basse, 1843.

Huber, Christoph. *Die Aufnahme und Verbreitung des Alanus ab Insulis in mhd. Dichtungen.* Zurich: Artemis and Winkler, 1988.

März, Christoph. *Frauenlobs Marienliech Untersuchungen zur spätmittelalterlichen Monodie.* Erlangen: Palm and Enke, 1987.

Stackmann, Karle and Karl Bertau, eds. *Frauenlob (Heinrich von Meißen): Leichs, Sangsprüche, Lieder,* 2 vols. Gottingen: Vandenhoeck and Ruprecht, 1981.

Steinmetz, Ralf-Henning. *Liebe als universales Prinzip bei Frauenlob.* Tübingen: Niemeyer, 1994.

THOMAS BEIN

FREDERICK I BARBAROSSA (d. 1190)

Perhaps the greatest figure of the twelfth century, Frederick I Barbarossa ruled the empire from 1152 until his untimely death while on crusade in 1190. Barbarossa was an effective and sometimes brutal ruler whose reign was marked by his efforts to establish his authority in Italy, often stormy relations with the papacy, and equally stormy relations with the princes in Germany. His efforts in one area often influenced the course of events in another, and his reign strengthened the place of his family in the empire and laid the foundation for both subsequent successes and defeats.

According to his biographer Rahewin, Barbarossa had golden hair, a reddish beard, piercing eyes, and a cheerful face. He was also a devout son of the church who honored the clergy and was a great builder of palaces and other public buildings. A "lover of warfare, but only that peace may be secured thereby," Barbarossa, Rahewin tells us further, possessed the virtues of an emperor. Indeed, his military prowess and imperial bearing would be of value for Barbarossa when his uncle, Conrad III, chose him as his successor. Barbarossa was chosen because Conrad's son was still a minor and because of Barbarossa's relations to two of the greatest families in the empire, the Staufen and the Welfs (Guelfs).

Although he was chosen for his important family connections in the German lands of the empire, one of Barbarossa's primary concerns was the establishment of his authority in Italy. Relations with Italy, and especially with Rome, formed the core of his conception of the imperial authority because without formal coronation by the pope, Barbarossa could not claim the imperial title. As a consequence he spent much time in Italy, and shortly after the death of Conrad, Barbarossa made his first trip there. His relations began on a promising note as he and Pope Eugenius III (1145–1153) agreed to respect each other's interests in the Treaty of Constance (March 23, 1153). In 1155, Frederick was crowned emperor by the English pope, Hadrian IV (1154–1159), and restored Hadrian to the throne in Rome by suppressing a revolt led by Arnold of Brescia. But cordial relations would not last as both sides railed to adhere to the terms of the treaty, and advisers for both sides, including Rainald of Dassel and Roland Bandinelli, stressed principle over compromise. In 1157, the first great conflict erupted at the imperial court in Besançon over Hadrians declaration that Barbarossa had received the empire as a *beneficium*, or fief, from the pope. Hadrian would apologize for the use of the term, explaining it meant "favor," but too late as relations had begun to sour.

An even greater breach would emerge during the reign of Alexander III (1159–1181), the former Roland Bandinelli. A disputed election in 1159 led to a schism and the emergence of two popes, Alexander III and Victor IV (1159–1164). The prolonged schism made Barbarossa's already complex dealings with Italy more difficult. The northern Italian cities that had opposed the expansion of the emperor's authority into Italy found a natural ally in Alexander, who, in turn, found much support from the king of France. Barbarossa's activities during the schism had mixed success. In the 1160s he managed to raze the northern Italian power of Milan and force Alexander out of Italy. He witnessed the succession of a series of imperial antipopes, including Paschal III (1164–1168), who crowned Barbarossa's wife, Beatrix, empress and who was enthroned in Rome by the emperor. Frederick's invasions of Italy witnessed victories over his rivals in northern Italy and Rome, and his efforts to establish a universal power to rival Rome that had begun in 1157 with the use of the term *sacrum imperium* (holy empire) were continued with his canonization of Charlemagne in 1165. But Frederick had been excommunicated by Alexander, and support for the pope was too strong throughout western Christendom and especially in Italy. The northern Italian cities formed a league at Verona that built a castle at Alessandria that would be a key stronghold and then rallied around the rebuilt city of Milan in the Lombard League. Moreover, although the emperor managed to take the city of Rome in 1166, he did so at great cost because many of his troops and key advisers, especially Rainald of Dassel, died from malaria. He never managed to take Alessandria and was defeated by the league in 1176 at the battle of Legnano. A peace conference followed the defeat and led to the peace of Venice in 1177. The settlement lifted the excommunication and recognized the imperial bishops appointed by Barbarossa. It also established a permanent peace between emperor and pope and a fifteen-year truce between emperor and the Lombard cities. Finally, it granted Barbarossa extensive rights in the much coveted Mathildine lands of Tuscany.

Much of the conflict with Rome involved the broader concerns of imperial rights in Italy, and relations with Rome were greatly complicated by Barbarossa's Italian policies. As emperor, Barbarossa saw control of Italy as essential to his authority, and, consequently, the emperor spent much time on the peninsula, undertaking a number of campaigns there. His efforts to establish his authority in Italy were shaped by his appreciation of Roman law and the teachings of the masters at Bologna. The clearest example of the influence of Roman law on Barbarossa and the desire to establish his rights in Italy can be found in the so-called Roncaglia decrees of 1158. The decrees were pronounced during the emperor's second Italian expedition and while tensions between Frederick and Pope Hadrian remained high. The decrees, the result of a council that included a number of jurists from Bologna, listed and defined royal rights, (regalia) in Italy. The regalia included, as Rahewin notes, "dukedoms, marches, counties, consulates, mines, market tolls, forage tax, wagons tolls, transit tolls, mills, fisheries, bridges," and an annual tax on land arid persons. The decrees also asserted Frederick's rights to nominate and confirm the various magistrates and judges of the cities of northern Italy. Finally, the decrees instituted the newly developing law of fiefs in Italy, limiting the rights of alienation of fiefs and defining more precisely the nature of a fief. The promulgation of the Roncaglian decrees was an effort by Frederick to establish himself as the governing authority in Italy, a legal pronouncement followed by ruthless enforcement. Although an important step for Barbarossa, the proclamation of the decrees was greatly resented by the northern Italian cities and led to much conflict between them and the emperor. In fact, the animosity generated by the decrees would complicate Barbarossa's efforts in Italy, a controversy that, in some ways, would not be resolved until the peace of Venice.

Frederick's other great concern was, of course, Germany and his relations with the German princes, especially with the Welf family and its greatest scion, Henry the Lion. To avoid the conflicts of his predecessor, Barbarossa needed to work at reconciliation with the major families of the realm from the very beginning of his reign. To satisfy the Staufen line he made his displaced cousin and son of Conrad III, the eight-year-old Frederick of Rothenburg, duke of Swabia. He granted the Babenberger Henry Jasomirgott the duchy of Austria after earlier depriving him of his Bavarian title. But the greatest grants were made to the Welf, Henry, who was granted the duchy of Bavaria and Saxony. And as duke of Saxony, Henry was allowed to expand his authority in the north by Frederick as a means of maintaining Henry's support for the emperor. Having placated the great families, Barbarossa sought to strengthen his position and that of his family. A first step was taken when Barbarossa married Beatrix, the heiress to the county of Burgundy and parts of Province. Barbarossa sought to expand familial and imperial lands throughout the realm, attaching Staufen territory to himself and also laying claim to possessions of other nobles when pos-

sible. Moreover, his willingness to allow Henry the Lion to fall for failure to attend imperial courts and for abuse of power as duke enabled Barbarossa to restructure the duchies of the realm, break up the larger duchies of the Lion, raise lesser noble families to higher authority, and establish feudal law in Germany. Finally, Barbarossa intervened in disputed episcopal elections and made greater use of *ministeriales* (clerics) during his reign to make his authority more effective.

Barbarossa's last great act was his participation in the Third Crusade. Long a supporter of these holy wars and a participant in the Second Crusade, Frederick took the cross at an assembly at Mainz in 1188. With great hope, Barbarossa led a large force toward the Holy Lands and enjoyed early success along the way. Unfortunately, while crossing the river Saleph on June 10, 1190, Barbarossa drowned. His army fragmented, with part returning home and part continuing on. The death of the emperor weakened the crusader army and, perhaps, undermined chances for success. Despite his unfortunate end, Barbarossa had made a lasting impact on the empire and left it at peace and in the relatively capable hands of his son, Henry VI (d. 1197).

See also **Gerhoh of Reichersberg; Hadrian IV, Pope; Henry IV, Emperor**

Further Reading

Benson, Robert L. "Political *Renovatio:* Two Models from Roman Antiquity," in *Renaissance and Renewal in the Twelfth Century*, ed. Robert L. Benson and Giles Constable with Carol D. Lanham. Toronto: University of Toronto Press, 1982, pp. 339–386.

Die Urkunden Friedrichs I, ed. Heinrich Appelt. Monumenta Germaniae historica. Die Urkunden der deut-schen Konige und Kaiser 10, 1–3. Hannover: Hahn, 1975–1979.

Fuhrmann, Horst. *Germany in the High Middle Ages*, trans. Timothy Reuter. Cambridge: Cambridge University Press, 1986.

Gillingham, J. B. *The Kingdom of Germany in the High Middle Ages (900–1200)*. London: Historical Association, 1971.

Leyser, Karl. "Frederick Barbarossa and the Hohen-staufen Polity," in *Communications and Power in Medieval Europe: The Gregorian Revolution and Beyond,* ed. Timothy Reuter. London: Hambledon Press, 1994, pp. 115–142.

———. "Frederick Barbarossa: Court and Country," in *Communications and Power in Medieval Europe: The Gregorian Revolution and Beyond,* ed. Timothy Reuter. London: Hambledon Press, 1994, pp. 143–155.

Morena, Otto. *Historia Frederici I*, ed. Ferdinand Güterbock. Monumenta Germaniae historica. Scriptores rerum germanicarum. Nova series 7. Berlin: Weidmann, 1930.

Munz, Peter. *Frederick Barbarossa: A Study in Medieval Politics*. Ithaca, N.Y.: Cornell University Press, 1969.

Otto of Freising and Rahewin. *Gesta Friderici Imperatoris*, ed. G. Waitz. Monumenta Germaniae historica. Scriptores rerum germanicarum 46. Hannover: Hahn, 1912.

———, and his Continuator, Rahewin. *The Deeds of Frederick Barbarossa*, trans. Charles Chrisopher Mierow. Toronto: University of Toronto Press, 1994.

MICHAEL FRASSETTO

FREDERICK II
(December 26, 1194–December 13, 1250)

King of Sicily, Roman emperor, king of Jerusalem, Frederick was born on December 26, 1194, in Jesi (Ancona), the eldest child of Emperor Henry VI Hohenstaufen and Constance (daughter of Roger II and heiress to Sicily). Baptized Frederick Roger (after his grandfathers), his name signaled his two heritages, namely, rule over the empire and the Italian *regno* (reign) and their fateful fusion. The German princes elected him king of the Romans (1196), and he was crowned king of Sicily (1198) after his father's death. North of the Alps, the competing royal elections of Otto (IV) of Brunswick and Frederick's uncle, Philip of Swabia, plunged Germany into dynastic civil war. Before her own death, Constance named Pope Innocent III guardian over the four year old and regent of the kingdom.

As the young orphan grew into manhood, political disorder engulfed the *regno*. The child-king became a pawn of feuding native and German aristocratic factions while other outside parties pursued their own interest at the expense of the royal power. Childhood in cosmopolitan Palermo—scene of an intermingling of Arab, Norman, Italian, and Greek cultural impulses—favored Frederick's intellectual alertness, mental and emotional precocity, and polygon talents. His cheerfulness, amiability, and calculation were balanced by the capacity for mistrust, coldness, cruelty, misanthropy, a demonic temperament, and a general lack of scruples.

In June 1208, the murder of Frederick's uncle Philip paved the way for Otto's accession to royal power in Germany. Six months later Frederick attained his majority according to Sicilian law. A marriage was arranged by the pope to Constance of Aragon, sister of King Peter II; it brought Frederick the Aragonese military support that enabled him to bolster his political position in the kingdom before new danger arose. In return for various promises, including an undertaking not to interfere in Sicilian affairs, Otto IV secured imperial coronation at Pope Innocents hands in 1209. But the new emperor's repudiation of his promise and his invasion of the kingdom triggered excommunication by the pope and papal support for a Hohenstaufen candidacy for the German and imperial crowns. In 1211 a group of German princes opposed to Otto met in Nuremberg and elected Frederick king of the Romans. In early 1212 Frederick decided to accept this election. Now he solidified the pope's support by confirming his mother's concessions regarding the Sicilian church; he also protected the dynasty's future by having his infant son, Henry, crowned co-king of Sicily.

During Autumn 1212 Frederick embarked on an unexpected and adventurous trip over the Alps to southwest Germany. Pro-Hohenstaufen princes, bishops, and towns now rallied to the support of the seemingly wondrous "boy of Apulia"; money and diplomatic support also came from Philip of France. Next Frederick moved north, where he was elected king of the Romans (for the third time) in Frankfurt and crowned in Mainz. During 1213 Frederick solidified his political and military position against Otto and confirmed various concessions to the papacy and the German ecclesiastical princes. Otto now staked his future chances on an invasion of northern France, but Philip II won a decisive victory over him at Bouvines (1214). The chastened Welf withdrew to his Saxon strongholds, where he died in May 1218.

Now crowned king of the Romans a second time at Aachen (1215), an enthusiastic Frederick made a fateful vow to go on crusade to recover the Holy Places. A year later he renewed another commitment by formally promising Pope Innocent that he would turn the government of Sicily over to his young son Henry by right after he himself received the imperial crown. Innocent's death in 1216 was followed by the election of Honorius III, a decidedly less stern pope. In 1220 Frederick engineered Henry VIII's election as co-king of the Romans, thus assuring the union of Sicily and the empire that Innocent had feared. Frederick disingenuously informed Honorius that the election had occurred at the wish of the princes; in fact, the purchase price was not inconsiderable: to secure electoral support from the ecclesiastical princes Frederick promulgated the *Confoederatio* or *Privilegium cum principibus ecclesiasticis*, which contained the renunciation (at least in theory) of many royal rights in ecclesiastical territories. That same year Honorius crowned Frederick emperor in St. Peter's basilica.

For much of the next decade Frederick maintained his strong political position; despite his prior promises, the union of the imperial and Sicilian crowns meant a potential encirclement of the papacy. And now his attention could be turned to the *regno* for a five-year period of consolidation: the strengthening of fortifications and harbor facilities, establishment of a large war fleet and merchant navy, and restriction of the trading and extraterritorial privileges hitherto held by Pisan and Genoese merchants. In 1220 at Capua he promulgated assizes that included a requirement that all royal privileges granted since 1189 must be reviewed before given any further credence. In this manner, Frederick could recoup some royal rights and properties lost through usurpation or ill-advised concession. He also suppressed a Muslim revolt in Sicily and resettled many defeated Saracens in Lucera, where they established a Muslim enclave that in time became a center of royal support. To further the training of civil servants for a burgeoning royal bureaucracy, Frederick also founded the University of Naples.

His commitment to depart on crusade was postponed repeatedly as Frederick consolidated control over the *regno*. But it was never forgotten by Honorius and the papal curia. The pope even helped to arrange Frederick's marriage in 1225 to the heiress of the kingdom of Jerusalem, Isabella Yolande of Brienne. Frederick reiterated his crusade obligations: under pain of excommunication he would depart for the East before August 1227. In a related matter, Frederick promulgated, in 1226, for the Teutonic Knights the Golden Bull of Rimini, establishing the foundations of their autonomous state in Prussia. That same year the emperor attempted to convoke a diet to restore imperial rights in northern Italy, but his intentions were thwarted by the resistance of the reconstituted Lombard League under the leadership of Milan. The death of Honorius III in 1227 led to the election of Gregory IX, who as cardinal had been friendly to the emperor. But when plague struck the gathering crusaders in Brindisi during late summer 1227, the embarkation became a debacle; the emperor himself sailed but immediately became ill, returning three days later and postponing further departure to spring 1228. Yet Gregory, long impatient with the emperor's past excuses, held him strictly to the terms of his promises and excommunicated the emperor despite the latters protestations.

Frederick nonetheless continued preparations for the voyage east despite the spiritual ban and Empress Yolande's death shortly after giving birth to Conrad (IV). In June 1228 the emperor reembarked with a small army and arrived in Acre, where he found little support from the local Syrian-Frankish baronage, the ecclesiastical hierarchy, or the military orders. Despite such handicaps, Frederick drew on his knowledge of Arabic and Muslim culture to negotiate a favorable treaty with the Egyptian sultan al-Kamil. The emperor next entered the Holy City and crowned himself king of Jerusalem, basing his title on his deceased wife's claim and on their son Conrad's minor status.

The pope's enmity did not slacken, however. War had already broken out in Italy. Since any further actions in Outremer were doomed to failure, the emperor set sail and returned to Brindisi. Frederick quickly assembled troops and swept the papal invaders back northward, taking care to halt his victorious advance at the border. Negotiations during the next year, 1230, culminated in the treaties of San Germano and Ceprano. Gregory absolved Frederick from excommunication, the territorial status quo was restored, and the emperor promised the Sicilian church freedom of prelatial elections and other privileges. But otherwise nothing was decided regarding the threatened encirclement of papal territory, papal doubts regarding the emperor's stance toward ecclesiastical liberty, and the Lombard's autonomy.

A fragile peace now restored, Frederick embarked on his most memorable legal project—the codification of royal laws for the *regno* in *Liber Augustalis,* or Constitu-

tions of Melfi (1231). This work of synthesis organized royal enactments with a view to centralize authority, bureaucratize royal government, and weaken all other non-royal intermediate jurisdictions.

But trouble now loomed in Germany, where young King Henry's weakly executed and unsteady policy of alliance with imperial ministerials, towns, and lesser aristocrats provoked opposition and demands from the greater princes. Henry was compelled to issue *Statutum in favorem principum* (1231), and his father had no choice but to confirm the same document a year later. In constitutional terms the autonomy of the princes was thereby somewhat strengthened, while restrictions on imperial cities were somewhat tightened. In 1232, Frederick imposed on his son an oath not to pursue in the future his former policies, but Henry nonetheless rebelled in 1234, and even allied himself with the Lombard League. When Frederick himself journeyed north in 1235, however, all resistance collapsed. Henry submitted unconditionally to his father, was stripped of his title and crown, and imprisoned for the rest of his life in various castles. He died by suicide in 1242.

Frederick now married again, this time to Isabella Plantagenet, sister of Henry III of England. The emperor proceeded to celebrate his triumphs at an imperial diet in Mainz, where he promulgated a peace edict that created the post of high court judge and proclaimed that all rights of governance originated in the monarchy. Frederick also staged a reconciliation with the Welfs by creating the feudal principality of Brunswick-Lüneburg for Otto, nephew of Otto IV.

Frederick returned to Italy, where he waged a military campaign during 1236 against the Lombards. Winter brought the emperor north again, this time to depose the outlawed rebel Frederick II of Austria and Styria. The emperor also arranged that his son Conrad was elected king of the Romans in Vienna (1237). He journeyed back to Italy, where his political fortunes now reached their zenith; Frederick led his army to victory over the League of Cortenuova, an alliance between Maitland and Lombard. The vanquished Lombards became eager to negotiate peace, but the emperor's intransigence encouraged instead a spirit of desperate resistance among a hard core of league members. Six cities chose to fight on. His relations with Pope Gregory also worsened. Frederick's illegitimate son Enzio married at his father's urging the heiress to a large portion of Sardinia and, in a calculated affront, immediately styled himself king of that island, thereby ignoring papal claims to overlordship. In 1239, the pope excommunicated Frederick a second time, charging that the emperor had oppressed the Sicilian church, impeded crusades, and assisted rebellious Romans. The real reasons for conflict, namely, the emperor's ongoing struggle with the Lombards and his perceived threat to papal autonomy, received no explicit mention.

The struggle quickly developed its apocalyptic as well as military aspects. Detractors called Frederick Antichrist; supporters hailed him as the expected messianic ruler of the Last Day. Crucial to Frederick's propaganda was his minister Petrus de Vinea, the architect of a new high rhetorical style that rivaled the fulminations of the papal chancery. On the military front the emperor and his subordinate commanders went from strength to strength. The disputed territories of Spoleto and the March were seized, and Frederick himself conducted an invasion of papal territories farther north. After a long siege Faenze surrendered. The emperor even managed to ruin the pope's impending Easter 1241 council in Rome, where Frederick expected further condemnations: his Pisan allies won a complete naval victory near the island of Montecristo over the Genoese fleet carrying many prelates to Rome. More than a hundred prospective council participants were captured and imprisoned under harsh conditions. But this triumph soon boomeranged to Frederick's discredit, for it confirmed the popes characterization of him as an oppressor of the church.

The struggle consumed the emperor's political and military energies to such an extent that he played no role in confronting the Mongol storm that since 1273 had swept irresistibly through the Russian principalities, Poland, Hungary, and into Germany. At Liegnitz in Silesia in 1241, the Mongols annihilated a German-Polish army, but news of the death of their Great Khan Ogotai and the expectation of a succession struggle led to their withdrawal eastward. Nonetheless, Frederick was still castigated by many German subjects for his inactivity.

When Gregory IX died in August 1241, the emperor prudently awaited further developments. The election and short pontificate of Celestine IV led to a nineteen-month interregnum until a sufficient number of cardinals elected Innocent IV in 1243. Negotiations began immediately between Frederick and the new pope. The emperor offered several concessions, but Innocent continued to distrust his commitments and to fear his ultimate intentions. For their part, both papal and imperial partisans occasionally broke the truce. Eventually, the pope's unwillingness to abandon the Lombards convinced Frederick to break off negotiations and secure his own safety through flight across the Alps to Lyon in 1244.

To that city Innocent summoned a general council to meet the following summer in order to deal with the many accusations leveled against Frederick. When the synod met, the verdict was a foregone conclusion: the pope solemnly excommunicated the emperor again and deposed him from his imperial and royal offices.

Under papal pressure in 1246 and 1247, several German princes elected in succession antikings Henry Raspe of Thuringia and William of Holland, but neither ultimately had much effect on Frederick's position in Germany.

More serious, however, were the conspiracies and revolts in Italy. A plot by some Apulian officials and aristocrats was discovered and crushed in 1246. Parma unexpectedly revolted in 1247 against Frederick and stymied his impending trip to Lyon and to Germany. To retake Parma the emperor now ordered construction of a new wooden siege town named Vittoria. But a sally by the besieged while Frederick was absent hunting scattered imperial forces, destroyed the siege town, and inflicted heavy casualties in 1248. The emperor had to discontinue the siege and withdraw. His misfortunes continued during 1249. First Frederick narrowly escaped an attempted poisoning by his personal physician. Next he had his close associate, Petrus de Vinea, arrested under mysterious circumstances as a traitor. Perhaps Petrus's actual crime was official corruption; in any event, he died shortly afterward, probably by suicide. Finally, the emperor's beloved son Enzio was captured by the Bolognese, never to be released until his death two decades later.

Despite these setbacks, Frederick's position in Germany, where Conrad IV defended his interests, was still strong. And while the emperors political and military fortunes in northern and central Italy swung back and forth, he was still a force to be reckoned with. But a decisive reckoning would not occur. While in Apulia at the end of November 1250 Frederick became seriously ill, probably with dysentery. He managed to reach Castel Fiorentino; there he made his last testament, disposing of titles and territories, received absolution and extreme unction at the hands of a loyal bishop, and died on December 13. Frederick was buried in the cathedral of Palermo.

Frederick was an object of wonderment and fear during his life, but his death marked the beginning of the end for the Hohenstaufen dynasty; his sons and grandson were overwhelmed by premature and often violent deaths. The chronicler Matthew Paris called the emperor "wonder and marvelous transformer of the world" (*stupor mundi et immutator mirabilis*). Frederick's three major constitutional documents for Germany—the *Confoederatio cum principibus ecclesiasticis,* the *Constitutio in favorem principum,* and the Mainz *Landfriede*—represented not the surrender of his political position there but, instead, the salvaging of royal prerogatives and a sober recognition of what the princes had already achieved. It was Frederick's death and the disappearance of his dynasty that created the interregnum that weakened forever the German monarchy's ability to imitate the piecemeal consolidations of English and French royal power. In Sicily, on the other hand, Frederick and his associates built on the strong royal traditions of the Norman kings and fashioned a government that rivaled other strong contemporary monarchies. Yet even there the time was not ripe for a thoroughly bureaucratic centralized state without autonomous communal, feudal, or ecclesiastical authorities. And whatever skepticism he may have possessed regarding the Catholic faith or religion in general, Frederick took great pains to stress his position as an orthodox Christian monarch.

When assessing Frederick's importance for the culture of his time, one must again note the mixed nature of his Sicilian milieu. Himself conversant in several languages, the emperor had a cosmopolitan outlook, eclectic tastes, and diverse interests in mathematics, the natural sciences, and philosophy. Frederick adopted startling Arab habits such as the harem and the traveling menagerie. He surrounded himself with intellectuals such as Petrus de Vinea, Michael Scot, and Leonardo Fibonacci. His Sicilian court witnessed the beginnings of literature in Italian *volgare* (popular tongue as opposed to Latin) as Frederick himself and his courtiers participated in a sudden flowering of lyric poetry. Architectural projects such as the stark Castel del Monte and the (now lost) Triumphal Gate in Capua expressed an originality that derived from both classical and nonclassical sources. His gold coinage—the *augustalis*—represented both a pioneering achievement of medieval European government as well as an enduring numismatic event. Finally, Frederick himself was a scientific author. His ornithological treatise on hunting with birds—the emperor's favorite sport—stressed the value of observation to correct received authority.

See also **Henry VI; Matthew Paris; Michael Scot; Otto IV**

Further Reading

Abulafia, David. *Frederick II: A Medieval Emperor.* London: Pimlico, 1988.

Fleckenstein, Josef, ed: *Probleme um Friedrich II.* Vorträge und Forschungen 16. Sigmaringen: Thorbecke, 1974.

Kantorowicz, Ernst. *Frederick the Second, 1194–1250,* trans. E. O. Lorimer. New York: Ungar, 1957.

Schaller, Hans Martin. *Kaiser Friedrich II. Verwandler der Welt.* Persönlichkeit un Geschichte 35. Göttingen: Musterschmidr, 1964.

Van Cleve, Thomas Curtis. *The Emperor Frederick II of Hohenstaufen. "Immutator Mundi."* Oxford: Clarendon Press, 1972.

Willemsen, C. A. *Bibliographie zur Geschichte Kaiser Friedrichs II. und der letzten Staufer.* Munich: Monumenta Germaniae Historica, 1986.

Wolf, Gunter G., ed. *Stupor mundi. Zur Geschichte Friedrichs II. von Hohenstaufen.* Darmstadt: Wissenschaftliche Buchgesellschaft, 1966.

ROBERT C. FIGUEIRA

FREDERICK III (1415–1493)

Because of the early death of his parents, Duke Ernst of Austria and Cimburgis of Masovia, Frederic III Habsburg (1415–1493) became the ward of his uncle Duke Frederick IV "with the Empty Pockets" of the Tyrol. He was able to free himself from the guardianship only in 1435 at the late age of twenty, becoming in his own right duke of Styria, Carinthia, and Carniola. His first independent act was a pilgrimage to Jerusalem the next year, where he was knighted at the Holy Sepulchre.

The unexpected deaths of his uncle Frederick and cousin King Albrecht II in 1439 improved Frederick's situation, since he became the head of the House of Habsburg. As leader of the dynasty, he assumed the guardianship for younger relatives, reversing the situation of his own youth. First, he supervised the Tyrol for his nephew Sigismund for several years. But the Tyrolean and Alsatian possessions drew him into wasteful, inconclusive wars with the Swiss Confederation. Second, he controlled King Albrecht's son Ladislaus, born after his father's death, hence the sobriquet "Posthumous." Ladislaus was not only heir to lands in lower Austria but also the crowns of Hungary and Bohemia.

Frederick's preeminent position led the electoral princes unanimously to elevate the young duke to king of the Romans on February 2, 1440. Early in his reign, in August 1441, he issued a reform proposal for the empire, indicating the new king's intention to be an active monarch. A bad sign, however, was the long delay of more than two and a half years until his coronation in Aachen. Indeed, from 1444 to 1471 Frederick did not leave his hereditary lands. Hence royal influence, especially through the royal court of justice, wasted away while the power of the cities and princes grew correspondingly. Confined to Austria, Frederick's court nonetheless attracted some of the most important lawyers of the day, like Gregory Heimburg and Martin Mair. Frederick also tried to build a court promoting the newest arts and humanistic ideas, for a time attracting the support of the famous humanist Aeneus Silvius Piccolomini, the later Pope Pius II. Frederick's own interest in numerology, alchemy, and astrology may have prompted his frequent use of the mystical motto AEIOU, which centuries later was interpreted as "All the world is subject to Austria" *(Alles Erdreich Ist Oesterrekh Untertan)*.

Meanwhile, as leader of the Holy Roman Empire, Frederick did have some success with the church. At first neutral in the schism caused by the Council of Basel, he soon leaned toward supporting Rome. He gained lasting success by signing the Concordat of Vienna with Rome in 1448. Although not quite as advantageous to the monarchy as contemporary agreements in France or Hungary, it allowed Frederick control of seventeen episcopal sees. That agreement regulated papal-imperial relations for the rest of the empire's duration, leading to the continuing decline of papal influence on episcopal elections. Partially financed with money provided by the pope, Frederick went to Rome, where he was crowned emperor on March 19, 1452. He was the last emperor to undergo this traditional ceremony there. On a later trip to Rome in 1468, he gained the foundation of the diocese of Vienna.

Most important for Frederick was his position in his hereditary lands. He promoted its interests, for example, by accepting as genuine the forged *Privilegium Maius* (May Privilege), which claimed broad prerogatives for the Habsburgs and Austria. Yet dynastic quarrels with his relatives and rebellions by the estates continued to squander his resources. On his return from his imperial coronation in 1452, he found Austria in rebellion. Soon besieged in Wiener Neustadt, he had to release Ladislaus from his guardianship. Again in 1462 the citizens of Vienna and then his brother Albrecht VI besieged Frederick. While Albrecht VI's unexpected death in 1463 quieted the situation, Frederick's territories remained exhausted.

And new, more energetic rivals appeared after the death of his nephew Ladislaus Posthumous in 1457. In Hungary Matthias Corvinus (r. 1458–1490) and in Bohemia George von Podiebrady (r. 1458–1471) became kings at the head of nationalistic movements. While George's influence was limited by his closeness to the Hussite heresy, Matthias of Hungary became a major force in Central Europe. Frederick at first tried to come to terms with Matthias, selling him back the famed Hungarian national Crown of St. Stephen in 1463. Matthias soon drove George from power in Bohemia. Then in 1477 Matthias went to war with Frederick by 1485 conquering Vienna itself. In 1487 Matthias took Wiener Neustadt and lower Austria, forcing the emperor to retreat to Linz in Upper Austria.

Meanwhile in the west of the empire the dukes of Burgundy had been expanding what was once a French royal appanage into a vast territorial complex between France and Germany. Duke Charles the Rash, who hoped to transform his possessions into a kingdom, undertook negotiations with. Frederick in Trier during 1473. Although the negotiations at first failed, Fredericks son Maximilian eventually gained the promise of marriage to Charles's daughter, Mary (although she had already been engaged six times). After Charles's death at the Battle of Nancy, Maximilian had to defend Mary's inheritance largely without any help from his father. Only when Maximilian was captured and held prisoner in Bruges in 1488 did Frederick arrive at the head of an imperial army and intimidate the city into freeing his son.

Slowly Frederick's position began to improve as Maximilian asserted his own authority. In 1490, Matthias Corvinus's death provided the opportunity for Maximilian to drive the Hungarian forces out of Austria. Maximilian seemed to be achieving success after success when his father, Frederick, died in Linz on August 19, 1493. He was finally interred in a magnificent tomb in St. Stephan's Cathedral in Vienna years later.

Although Frederick III had the longest reign of any German monarch, many historians have complained that he accomplished little. He has long been mocked as the *Heiliges Römisches Reiches Erzschlafmütze* (Holy Roman Empire's Arch-sleepingcap). Some say his greatest accomplishment was merely to outlive his enemies. Others maintain that while such an attitude may apply to the empire at large, in his own dynastic lands Frederick III was able to build for the future. By patiently insisting on his rights, helping to arrange his son's marriage, and insisting on his imperial prestige, Frederick helped to establish the future success of the Habsburgs.

Further Reading

Hödl, Günther. "Habsburg und Österreich," in *Gestalten und Gestalt des österreichischen Spatmittelalters*. Vienna: Böhlau Verlag, 1988, pp. 173–193.

Nehring, Karl. *Matthias Corvinus, Kaiser Friedrich III., und das Reich: zum hunyadisch-habsburgischen Gegensatz im Donauraum*. Südosteuropäische Arbeiten 72. Munich: R. Oldenbourg, 1975.

Rill, Bernd. *Friedrich III.: Habsburgs europäischer Durchbruch*. Graz: Verlag Styria, 1987.

Thomas, Heinz. *Deutsche Geschichte des Spätmittelalters*. Stuttgart: Kohlhammer, 1983.

BRIAN A. PAVLAC

FRIEDRICH VON HAUSEN
(fl. late 12th c.)

By adopting and adapting the forms and motifs of Occitan lyrics, melding them with German ones, Friedrich von Hausen (present-day Rheinhausen, now a part of Mannheim) expanded and modernized German minnesong. Better documented as an historical figure, a *ministeriale* (court clerk) of Emperor Friedrich Barbarossa, than most minnesingers, he witnessed documents from 1171 to shortly before his death as a crusader in Anatolia in 1190 and was mentioned in many contemporary chronicles. His importance as a minnesinger can be seen in many apparent borrowings from his songs by others. The death of the minnesinger qua singer is lamented, a generation or so after the fact, in several songs and in Heinrich von dem Türlin's *Crône*. However, his contemporary fame, as attested, was as a political figure. From the twelfth to the fifteenth century, whenever singers are documented historical figures, their singing is never mentioned in official historical documents, and Hausen is no exception to this rule.

Hausens love laments exalt the lady as desirable but unattainable; his general lack of concrete imagery and hypotactic style (employing subordinate clauses) adumbrate Reinmar. However, situational references such as those detailing a love reverie while riding, set him apart from the later singer. Though his songs of love from afar parallel similar songs by, for instance, the troubadour Jaufré Rudel, they also fit what we know about his history (he was often absent from home in the service of his liege lord). Though his praise of a lady and of ladies was part of a broader courtly fiction, there are definite parallels between the love at court he discusses and the life at court he led. He wrote several crusading songs in which, in contrast, for example, to Albrecht von Johansdorf, the service of God trumps service of his lady. In his scorn for the slackers who remained at home (*Des Minnesangs Frühling* [MF], song no. 53,21), he both echoes Romance lyric motifs and touches on a topic that doubtless resonated with the actual courtiers of his day. He is the first singer for whom a song (MF no. 42,1) is transmitted in three distinct versions, which examplifies minnesong's inherent mutability. His extended monologue in the woman's voice (MF no. 54,1, three strophes in C) presents a lady as skilled in lamenting the dilemma her intense love for her worthy suitor causes her as Reinmar's persona is in stating his (MF no. 165,10). This has led various scholars (probably incorrectly) to consider as spurious the song's ascription to Hausen.

See also **Frederick I Barbarossa; Heinrich von dem Türlin**

Further Reading

Bekker, Hugo. *Friedrich von Hausen: Inquiries into His Poetry*. Chapel Hill: University of North Carolina Press, 1977.

Moser, Hugo, and Helmut Tervooren, eds. *Des Minnesangs Frühling*. 2 vols., 36th ed. Stuttgart: Hirzel, 1977.

Mowatt, D.G. *Friederich von Hûsen: Introduction, Text, Commentary and Glossary*. Cambridge: Cambridge University Press, 1971.

Schweikle, Günther, ed. *Friedrich von Hausen: Lieder*. Stuttgart: Reclam, 1984.

HERBERT HEINEN

FROISSART, JEAN (1337–after 1404)

The greatest French chronicler, as well as an outstanding poet and romancer, Jean Froissart was born the year the Hundred Years' War began, to a humble bourgeois family of Valenciennes, which lay then outside the French kingdom. After a clerical education, he entered the service of the counts of Hainaut. All his life, Froissart was a servant of powerful nobles. His ability to please his aristocratic patrons and protectors is his chief characteristic as a man and writer. In 1361, he went to England to become one of the *clercs de la chambre* of Philippa of Hainaut, wife of Edward III. He remained in that service until her death in 1369. His stay in England was interrupted by extensive travels to Scotland, to southern France in the suite of the Black Prince, and later, in the retinue of Edward's second son, Lionel, duke of Clarence (patron and protector of Chaucer), to northern Italy, where Lionel married the daughter of the duke of Milan. After the wedding, Froissart traveled to Rome and returned to England via Hainaut and Brabant. These travels doubtless furnished him with the "pan-European" outlook informing much of his *Chronicles*. The youthful service at the very French court of Philippa imprinted in him a permanent, idealized image of a chivalric "paradise lost" so evident in his romance *Meliador*. After the death of Philippa, Froissart returned to his native Hainaut in search of new patrons. His chief benefactors were Robert de Namur (d. 1392); more importantly, Gui II, count of Blois (d. 1397), who in all probability urged him to work on the *Chroniques*; and Wenceslas, duke of Luxembourg and Brabant (d. 1383), who certainly encouraged his poetry, for he was a poet in his own right. We know that Froissart took holy orders and that, in 1373, he received a benefice in Les Estiennes near Mons. In 1384, he became a canon at Chimay. Sometime later, he received another canonry at Lille. He spent the winter of 1388–89 in Orthez, at the splendid court of another aristocratic man of letters, Gaston Phoebus, count of Foix (d. 1391). He traveled to the Low Countries, and in 1394 he briefly revisited England. Little is known about Froissart's declining years. He died some time after 1404.

Froissart's main achievement is *Les chroniques de France, d'Angleterre et de païs voisins…*, a history of almost all of western Europe spanning the years 1327 (the accession of Edward III) and ca. 1400 (the death of Richard II). This history, although providing us with an enormous wealth of realistic detail, is written from a distinctive point of view. Like so much of Froissart's poetry, it embodies a frank glorification of an aristocratic, idealized, "international," chivalric life. Up to 1361, his work is a recasting of Jean le Bel's (ca. 1290–1370) *Vrayes chroniques*, which present the first years of the reign of Edward III and the beginnings of the Hundred Years' War. After this date, Froissart follows his own observations, hearsay, and, occasionally, documents. He was certainly conscious of partisan points of view in history and took some pains to ascertain the facts, interviewing eyewitnesses and participants in the events described. He traveled widely to seek out sources and constantly recast the first two books of his *Chroniques* to suit changing political circumstances and the tastes and views of his patrons.

Froissart's *Chroniques* are divided into four books. Book 1 was recast by the chronicler into four redactions.

It relates events up to 1369, 1372, or 1377 depending on redactions. After this book, Froissart wrote the independent *Chronique de Flandre*, which relates the disorders occurring in that country between 1378 and 1387. This chronicle was later incorporated into Book 2, which ends with events in 1387; there are two redactions of Book 2. The last two books exist in only one redaction. The third relates events to ca. 1390 and the fourth to ca. 1400.

Froissart's *Chroniques*, an important monument of an elegant and efficient French prose, enjoyed an instant, wide, and lasting success. They were particularly appreciated in England, not only for their pro-English stance (inherited, so to speak, from Jean le Bel), but also for their archaizing, chivalric outlook. The *Chroniques* are a priceless source for the history of the 14th century, especially for the reader who understands the aristocratic vantage point from which Froissart viewed it. One should not expect to find either penetrating explanations of political history or subtle social commentary. Froissart's views were limited by those of his patrons: he never understood the aspirations and growing power of the bourgeoisie. He had nothing but contempt for the peasant revolt of the French Jacquerie of 1358, or for its English counterpart led by Wat Tyler in 1381. His *Chroniques* give us a vivid mirror of the epoch, the distortions of which can be more easily understood through the ideology informing his poetry.

Froissart wrote lyric verse, narrative-didactic poetry, and a long, rhymed Arthurian romance. His lyrical output is considerable: thirteen *lais*, *six chansons royaux*, forty ballades, thirteen virelais, 107 rondeaux, and twenty *pastourelles*. They come to us in the two manuscripts carefully copied under his supervision (B.N. fr. 830 and 831), which also contain his narrative-didactic poetry. He also wrote several *serventois* in honor of the Virgin. Otherwise, all his lyrical poems, most of which were composed before 1372, celebrate courtly love. In lyrical as well as narrative-didactic poems, his unavowed model was Guillaume de Machaut (ca. 1300–77), but Froissart, as far as we know, composed no music.

Of special historical interest because of their historical *realia* are Froissart's *pastourelles*. The lovestruck shepherds sometimes make historical allusions, and under the easily penetrated fictional cover, six of these *pastourelles* celebrate public events, such as the arrival in Paris of Queen Isabeau (1385), or the marriage of the elderly John, duke of Berry, to the very young Jeanne de Boulogne (1389). The *pastourelles* present real affinities between Froissart's lyric poetry and his *Chroniques*.

Much of Froissart's lyric poetry exists in two "redactions," for many of the poems were not only grouped according to their genre, but also inserted (sometimes slightly modified) in narrative *dits* (called also *dittiés* or *trettiés*). The oldest of them is the *Paradis d'Amour* (1,724 lines with five lyric insertions), an allegorical dream vision (in the manner of the first part of the *Roman de la Rose*) in which the poet-lover encounters in the Garden (Paradise) of Love such traditional figures of the God of Love, Plaisance, Hope, Pity, and Sweet Looks. The protagonist tells the story of his love to the God of Love, recites his poems, and meets his ladylove, who makes him a wreath of daisies. To reward her, the poet recites his ballade *Sur toutes flours j'aimme la margerite*. Her touch wakes him from his delightful dream. What is important in this *dit* is Froissart's explicit connection between the love-dream and the ability and capacity for composing lyric poetry.

The *Orloge amoureus* is the only *dit* written in decasyllabic couplets (unlike the others composed in octosyllables). Its 1,174 verses describe the workings of the clock, then a relatively new invention. In all probability, it was the real Parisian clock in the tower of the Palais Royal on the Île de la Cité that Froissart examined in 1368 during his return trip from Italy. The poet systematically compares his love-filled heart with the "subtlety" of the workings of the clock. Thus, the foliot or bar-balance is Fear, the main weight is Beauty, the mother wheel is Desire, the 'scape wheel is Moderation, the striking wheel is Sweet Talk, and so on. Each part of the mechanism corresponds thus to a "well-working," allegorical system of courtly love. The presentation of the workings of the clock is so detailed and exact that the *Orloge amoureus* was cited and partially translated by an English historian of horology. This *dit* is, like the *Chroniques*, a monument to Froissart's unquenchable curiosity concerning the things of this world.

The *Espinette amoureuse* (4,198 verses with fourteen lyric insertions) offers first a long pseudo-autobiographical introduction describing his childhood and stressing the precocity of his love inclination. Then the poet presents a dream vision in which he encounters Juno, Pallas Athene, Mercury, and Venus. Venus makes him a gift of a "[c]œur gai, joli et amoureus" (l. 547). The rest of the *dit* is quite similar to the *Paradis*. The poet-lover encounters his ladylove, they exchange poems, they dance, but after a while the lady must leave because she is to marry someone else. The poet becomes ill and alternates between hope and despair.

The *Prison amoureuse* (3,895 lines with sixteen inserted poems and twelve letters in prose) tells, under the usual allegorical cover, the real story of Wenceslas of Luxemburg, captured in the Battle of Baesweiler in 1371 and awaiting the ransom money to be paid by his brother, the emperor Charles IV. The seven letters written by Rose (=Wenceslas) and five by Flos (=Froissart) present the backbone of the *dit*. They discuss the subtleties of courtly love. We know that the combination of letters and verse-narration was made popular by Machaut in his *Voir dit* (ca. 1362), but whereas Machaut presents a real plot, in Froissart the plot is replaced by two *exempla*: a pseudomythological love story told by Flos and an allegorical vision experienced by Rose, in which we can made out the real story of the imprisoned Wenceslas.

The *Joli buisson de Jonece* is the longest and most ambitious of Froissart's *dits* (5,442 lines, with twenty-seven inserted poems). It is a dream vision that Froissart, aged thirty-five, had on November 30, 1373. In his dream, populated by mythological and allegorical figures, Youth leads him to an allegorical Bush. Awakened, the poet realizes the real danger and turns his thoughts toward the Virgin, whom he praises in a *lai*. She becomes "li Buissons resplendissans" (I. 5,402) and her Son" [e]st li feus plaisans,/Non ardans,/Mais enluminans" (ll. 5,407–10).

Like the *Orloge*, the *Temple d'honneur* (1,076 lines) does not contain any inserted lyrics. In this allegorical dream, Honor marries his son, Desire, to Lady Plaisance. Froissart calls this poem not a *dit amoureus*, but *trettié de moralité*. Indeed, most of the *trettié* consists of Honor's long moral sermon on love and marriage. It is quite possible that the *Temple* is indeed an egithalamium celebrating a real couple.

Besides these five *dits*, Froissart composed six shorter lyrico-narrative poems. The *Dit dou bleu chevalier* (504 lines) tells, in a complicated metric scheme, the efforts of the poet to console a lovesick knight dressed in blue (the color of fidelity). The *Joli mois de mai* (464 lines with three lyric insertions) is a purely lyrical composition in which the poet, addressing a nightingale, extolls the beauty of his ladylove. Purely lyrical also is the *Dit de la margueritte* (192 lines): the poet sings the praise of his flower-ladylove. The *Plaidoirie de la rose et de la violette* (342 lines) is a perfect example of Froissart's ability to flatter: these two flowers ask the court of France to decide which of them is more worthy of praise. The court, presided over by "noble et haulte Flour de Lys" (l. 308) and seconded not only by the usual allegorical figures of Prowess, Youth, Sense, Gemerosity, and others, but also by the dukes of Berry, Burgundy, Eu, and La Marche, will some day pronounce a judgment on all flowers, even on Froissart's flower, the daisy.

More apparently autobiographical are the last two *dits* presented without inserted lyrics or mythological allusions. The *Debat dou cheval et dou levrier* (92 lines) shows Froissart returning from Scotland and overhearing a discussion between his horse and his greyhound on the joys and sorrows of their respective existences. The *Dit dou florin* (490 lines) is a debate between Froissart and the last of his coins left from a dissipated fortune. The poet tells us about the eighty *florins* that he received from the count of Foix and, more importantly, informs us that during his stay in Orthez, Froissart read each night, for eleven weeks, a passage of his *Méliador* to the count.

If in his lyric and lyrico-narrative poetry Froissart adheres closely to the literary canons established by Machaut, his verse romance *Méliador* is perhaps more "original," for it is a conscious return to a much earlier tradition. Its other claim to originality lies in Froissart's insertion of seventy-nine lyric poems from the pen of his patron Wenceslas of Luxembourg. While most 14th-century romances are recastings or continuations, usually in prose, *Méliador's* subject is new, though it is composed in the traditional octosyllabic couplets. The romance of more than 30,000 lines (unfinished and with two lacunae) is set in a youthful Arthurian court and could be called the "enfances de la Table Ronde." It depicts the innumerable adventures, chiefly jousting and chance armed encounters, of innumerable knights-errant, but the main plot is easily discernible: Hermione, princess of Scotland, is promised to the knight who proves himself most valiant in a series of tournaments organized by the ladies. Méliador, son of the duke of Cornwell, is an ideal knight-errant. At the end, he wins not only Hermione but also the Scottish kingdom, while his companions win lesser princesses. *Méliador*, begun in the early 1360s and completed only after the death of Wenceslas in 1383, reflects the geography and ideology of Froissart's early service in Great Britain. As a frank glorification of chivalry, with its implied desire to revive it in Froissart's own time, *Méliador* is a powerful link between his poetry and the greatest accomplishment of his life, his idealizing, and "restoratory" *Chroniques*.

See also **Charles IV; Chaucer, Geoffrey; Edward III; John, Duke of Berry**

Further Reading

Froissart, Jean. *Les œuvres de Froissart—Chroniques*, ed. Joseph M.B.C. Kervyn de Lettenhove. 25 vols. in 26. Vols. 1–17, Brussels: Devaux, 1867–73; Vols. 18–25, Brussels: Closson, 1874–77. [The only complete, but idiosyncratic, edition of the chronicles.]

——. *Chroniques de Jean Froissart.* 15 vols. Vols. 1–8, part 1, ed. Siméon Luce. Vol. 8, parts 2–11, ed. Gaston Raynaud. Vol. 12, ed. Léon Mirot. Vol. 13, ed. Léon Mirot and Albert Mirot. Vols. 14 and 15, ed. Albert Mirot. Vols. 1–4, Paris: Renouard, 1869–73. Vols. 5–7, Paris: Renouard, H. Loones, successeur, 1874–78. Vols. 8–11, Paris: Renouard, H. Laurens, successeur, 1888–99. Vol. 12, Paris: Champion, 1931. Vols. 13–15. Paris: Klincksieck, 1957–75. [Vols. 1–8 contain Book 1 with variants; Vols. 9–11, Book 2 with variants; Vols. 12–15, most of Book 3 (up to 1389). This "national edition," begun in 1869, is still "in progress."]

——. *Ballades et rondeaux*, ed. Rae S. Baudoin. Geneva: Droz, 1978.

——. *Le paradis d'amour; L'orloge amoureus*, ed. Peter F. Dembowski. Geneva: Droz, 1986.

——. *L'espinette amoreuse*, ed. Anthime Fourrier. Paris: Klincksieck, 1972.

——. *La prison amoureuse*, ed. Anthime Fourrier. Paris: Klincksieck, 1974.

——. *Le joli buisson de Jonece*, ed. Anthime Fourrier. Geneva: Droz, 1975.

——. *"Dits" et "Débats" avec en appendice quelques poèmes de Guillame de Machaut*, ed. Anthime Fourrier. Geneva: Droz, 1979. [Edited here are: *Le temple d'honneur, Le joli mois de may, Le dit de la margueritte, Le dit dou bleu chevalier, Le debat dou cheval et dou levrier, Le dit dou florin, La plaidoirie de la rose et de la violette.*]

——. *Chroniques: début du premier livre: édition du manuscrit de Rome Reg. lat. 869*, ed. George T. Diller. Geneva: Droz, 1972.

——. *Méliador. roman comprenant les poésies lyriques de Wenceslas de Bohême, due de Luxembourg et de Brabant*, ed. Auguste Longnon. 3 vols. Paris: Didot, 1895–99.

——. *The Lyric Poems of Jean Froissart*, ed. Rob Roy McGregor, Jr. Chapel Hill: University of North Carolina Press, 1975.

——. *Chronicles*, trans. Geoffrey Brereton. Harmondsworth: Penguin, 1968.

Dembowski, Peter F. *Jean Froissart and His* Méliador: *Context, Craft, and Sense*. Lexington: French Forum, 1983.

Shears, Frederic Sidney. *Froissart: Chronicler and Poet*. London: Routledge, 1930.

PETER F. DEMBOWSKI

FRUEAUF, RUELAND, THE ELDER (ca. 1440/1450–1507)

Both documents and signed paintings allow us to trace the career of Rueland Frueauf, who divided his time between Passau and Salzburg. In the earliest records, in the 1470s, he is working for St. Peter's in Salzburg. The modern scholar Alfred Stange assumes that he received his training in Salzburg, perhaps with Conrad Laib, but also notes the influence of the anonymous Bavarian painters known as the Master of 1467 and the Master of the Tegernsee Tabula Magna. In 1480, Freauf acquired citizenship in Passau, where in the next four years he completed the frescoes in the Rathaus (town hall), now lost, that a Master Ruprecht had begun a decade earlier.

In May 1484, Frueauf was called back to Salzburg to discuss the altar planned for the Franciscan church, but in August two donors, offering substantial sums for the altar's execution, managed to direct the commission to Michael Pacher. How these events are to be interpreted is a matter of debate. Stange sees the loss of the commission as a hard blow for Frueauf and the reason for his disappearance from the written records for three years, and proposes that he spent this time on a study trip, trying to update his style. Another scholar, Grere Ring, by contrast, thinks it unlikely that Frueauf was ever a candidate for the commission and that being asked to deliver an expertise on such an important project was an honor.

In any case, we next encounter Frueauf in Nuremberg, where, in 1487, he dated and signed a panel with his initials. Stange sees the influence of the Dutch painter known as the Master of Flémalle in Frueauf's work after this date, without proposing that his travels took him all the way to the Low Countries. By 1490, Frueauf was back in Salzburg, working on a major commission. In this year and the following he initialed and dated two of eight scenes intended to serve in the wings of an altarpiece. Scenes from the Passion—Christ in the Garden of Gethsemane, the Flagellation, the Road to Calvary, and the Crucifixion—were visible at the sides of the sculptured shrine when the altarpiece was open, while scenes from the life if the Virgin—Annunciation, Nativity, Adoration of the Magi, and Assumption—occupied the out-sides of the wings (Vienna, Kunsthistorisches Museum, nos. 1397–1400).

In 1497 Frueauf is mentioned again as citizen of Passau, as is his son, the painter Rueland Frueauf the Younger. A year later the father's citizenship was revoked for failure to pay his debts, but it was soon reinstated on the recommendation of well-placed friends. From the last decade of Frueauf's life comes the initialed but undated portrait of Jobst Seyfried (Vienna, Kunsthistorisches Museum), the only preserved evidence of Frueauf's work in this genre.

This group of autograph works allows a clear definition of Frueauf's innovative style. Painted in bright colors with hard outlines, his figures are tall and slim. Individualized facial types convey a variety of expressions, which are heightened by dramatic gestures and lively drapery patterns. His figures tend to fill the foreground, prohibiting a view into the background, another device for concentrating the emotional impact of the works. On the basis of similarities to Frueauf's known paintings, a number of other works have been attributed to him; most common among these are twelve Passion scenes from an altarpiece, probably from circa 1480 (Regensburg, Historisches Verein), and a large, late panel representing Christ as Man of Sorrows (*Schmerzensmann*) (Munich, Alte Pinakothek, no. 10681).

See also **Pacher, Michael**

Further Reading

Baldass, Ludwig von. *Conrad Laib und die beiden Rueland Frueauf*. Vienna: Schroll, 1946.

Buchner, Ernst. "Ein Schmerzensmann von Rueiand Frueauf d. é." *Pantheon* 16 (1943): 73–76.

Ring, Grete. "Frueauf, Rueland d. é." *Allgemeines Lexikon der bildenden Künstler von der Antike bis zur Gegenwart*, ed. Ulrich Thieme. Leipzig: Seemann, 1916, vol. 12, pp. 532–534.

Stange, Alfred. *Deutsche Malerei der Gotik. vol. 10: Salzburg, Bayern und Tirol in der Zeit von 1400 bis 1500*. Munich: Deutscher Kunstverlag, 1960, pp. 38–42.

JOAN A. HOLLADAY

FULBERT OF CHARTRES
(ca. 960–1028)

Born of humble parents probably in Aquitaine, perhaps Poitou, Fulbert studied at Reims under Gerbert of Aurillac (later Pope Sylvester II), the outstanding master of the day. Fulbert became master of the cathedral school at Chartres in the 990s and served as master and chancellor before becoming bishop of Chartres in 1006. He had a close association with King Robert II the Pious of France, a schoolmate of Fulbert's at Reims. Fulbert was particularly well versed in law and medicine and was familiar with the astronomical works that had been recently translated from the Arabic. Although intellectually conservative (he avoided the new discipline of dialectics), his teaching attracted one of the most dialectical thinkers of the time: Berengar of Tours, condemned for his novel eucharistic opinions.

After the cathedral burned in 1020, Fulbert began a campaign to rebuild it, a project made possible by the generosity of King Canute of England and Denmark, as well as King Robert of France. The new, spacious crypt constructed by Fulbert remains the largest crypt in France and became the basis for all further construction at the site. The new crypt was meant to accommodate the pilgrims who came to venerate the holy relic of the *sancta camisia*, a garment reputed to have been worn by Mary when she gave birth to Jesus; it was enshrined at Chartres from the 9th century forward and is still possessed by the cathedral. Fulbert was an avid promoter of devotion to the Virgin.

Fulbert was also a reformer who campaigned against simony (buying and selling church office's) and clerical marriage. Like most bishops of his day, Fulbert was both a churchman and a feudal lord, and he knew first-hand the tension of dual allegiances. In a well-known letter to Duke William V of Aquitaine, his long-time benefactor, Fulbert explains the meaning of the feudal oath. But in another, he is highly critical of ecclesiastics who are intent on bearing arms rather than on keeping the peace of the church. In several letters, he rebukes Foulques III Nerra, count of Anjou, for his depredations.

Of Fulbert's sermons, the best known is that composed for the feast of the Nativity of the Virgin Mary, in which he recounts the history of Théophile, a Christian who after selling his soul to the Devil was rescued by the Virgin. Fulbert's legend of Théophile is the subject of Rutebeuf's *Miracle de Théophile*. An excellent latinist and one of the best writers of his day, Fulbert left behind a substantial body of correspondence, some 140 letters, with leading churchmen, including abbots Abbo of Fleury, Richard of Saint-Vannes, and Odilo of Cluny. He also wrote several poems and a few other miscellaneous works.

See also **Cnut**

Further Reading

Fulbert of Chartres. *Opera omnia. PL* 141.185–368.
——. *The Letters and Poems of Fulbert of Chartres*, ed. and trans. Frederick Behrends. Oxford: Clarendon, 1976.
MacKinney, Loren Carey. *Bishop Fulbert and Education at the School of Chartres*. Notre Dame: Mediaeval Institute, University of Notre Dame, 1957.

MARK ZIER

G

GADDI, TADDEO
(fl. mid-1320s, d. 1366)

Taddeo Gaddi was the leading painter of the Florentine school after the death of Giotto in 1337, as early sources and documents confirm. In the general literature, Giotto continues to overshadow this very capable artist, but specialists have long recognized not only Taddeo's continuation of Giotto's monumental style but also his innovative, earthy wit; his subtle understanding of light and color; and his extensive and varied work in fresco, panel painting, and window design.

About 1330, Taddeo matriculated in the Arte dei Medici e Speziali. Between 1331 and 1337, the account books of the Bardi banking company (Ser Miniato di Ser Biagio Boccadibue, 1322–1343, Archivio di Stato, Notarile antecosimiano B 1951) note that Taddeo decorated Gualterotto di Jacopo de' Bardi's chapel of Saint Louis of Toulouse and Saint Louis of France at Santa Croce in Florence. Nothing of this project remains. The first documented extant painting by Taddeo is from 1334: a signed and dated beautiful small, portable triptych (now in Berlin, Gemaeldeg. 1079–1081). This work is in the tradition of Bernardo Daddi and suggests Taddeo's interest in the less monumental form that was then gaining popularity.

The major extant fresco cycle attributed to Taddeo from these early years is in the Baroncelli Chapel at Santa Croce. Its chronology is debated by scholars. The earlier suggested date, February 1328, is based on a tomb inscription in the chapel, for members of the Vanni and Baroncelli families. The later possible date, the 1330s, is based on a series of documents associated with the Augustinian friar Simone Fidati, believed by some scholars to have inspired the iconography of the cycle. These frescoes—which are devoted to the life of the Virgin—exemplify Taddeo's early style. Although

Taddeo was influenced by Giotto's cycle in the Peruzzi Chapel in Santa Croce, he is more fascinated with pictorial space, lighting, and lively anecdotal episodes than Giotto, who favored greater psychological subtlety. As Ladis (1982) has noted, Taddeo's *Marriage of the Virgin* seems to refer considerably to the *mattinata*, the shivaree that satirized widowers' marriages and other unlikely marriages. The imagery is in the spirit of Boccaccio rather than the heavy morality of an Augustinian preacher. Taddeo's innovative use of light to convey miraculous revelation is exemplified in the *Annunciation to the Shepherds*, where natural light from a window is transformed into a divine light emitted by an angel and falling on the awakened shepherds.

An equally important commission in these earlier years was a collection of panels (now in the Accademia in Florence) devoted to the parallel lives of Christ and Saint Francis of Assisi. These panels were broken apart in 1810, and scholars have debated both their original configuration and their attribution. Taddeo is now the undisputed creator of the small quatrefoil images, probably dating from before the frescoes in the Baroncelli Chapel; but their arrangement as part of a reliquary cabinet remains disputed. The saturated color of the sacristy panels in tempera, combined with the miraculous expressive light, represents an alternative to the monumental figures more typical of fresco as a medium and is an important element of Taddeo's powerful compositions.

In the period from Giotto's death (1337) until the onslaught of the Black Plague (1348), Taddeo and his shop had many commissions, although the evidence has been poorly preserved for the best-documented frescoes, done between 1341 and 1342 in the crypt of San Miniato al Monte in Florence. Taddeo's works for the Gambacorti family in Pisa and subsequently for the

Strozzi in Florence do not survive, nor does the documenting letter itself, apparently the first written by an Italian artist to have been recorded.

Following Meiss's groundbreaking study (1951) of the effect of the plague on the arts of central Italy, critics argued for a significant stylistic change among the new generation of artists, such as the Clone brothers, Andrea (known as Orcagna) and Nardo. For many critics, Taddeo's own reputation after 1348 is captured in *Il libro delle trecentonovelle* (c. 1390) of Franco Sacchetti. In the pertinent story, Orcagna asks a group of friends gathered at San Miniato al Monte to name the best painter after Giotto, but they cannot agree. Taddeo observes that art is in decline, a remark that stops the conversation until someone suggests that the cosmetics used by the women of Florence qualify them as the best artists. Taddeo's bleak view has, according to some scholars, obscured his own genuine accomplishment in coming to terms with the aesthetics of the new generation. Certainly, he continued to receive considerable commissions that allowed him to live comfortably in the Santa Croce quarter, as his tax records indicate.

The Florentines respected Taddeo's judgment, however somber, as is indicated by the fact that he served as an adviser to the Opera del Duomo (cathedral works) between 1355 and 1366. His presence, which is documented—and for which the documentation is augmented by accounts from Antonio Billi, the Anonimo Gaddiano, and Giorgio Vasari—led to the idea that Taddeo was also an architect and that in this capacity he finished Giotto's campanile, worked on Or San Michele, and created the model and design for the Ponte Vecchio after the flood of 1333. Architectural historians remain skeptical about this; but it is clear that in any case, as Ghiberti noted in *I commentarii*, Taddeo was very learned.

In 1348, Taddeo appeared on a list of painters who were being considered for the completion of Alesso di Andrea's unfinished polyptych of the Virgin and Child and Saints for San Giovanni Fuorcivitas in Pistoia. In 1353, he was paid for this work, portions of which remain in the church. On 3 April 1353, Taddeo returned ten florins and paid restitution for breaking his contract with the Commune of Florence by failing to paint the tribunal of the *mercanzia*, the high court of the merchants. That year he also signed a Virgin and Child for Giovanni di Ser Segna for the church of Sail Lucchese, Poggibonsi (it was recorded as being there in seventeenth century but is now in the Uffizi in Florence).

In this last period Taddeo completed one of this most memorable fresco projects, for the refectory of Santa Croce. Vasari claimed that Giotto had created this fresco, but scholars now accept Taddeo as the artist. Although the date is still debated, it is increasingly thought to be c. 1360. This unusual composition includes the a Tree of Life, inspired by Saint Bonaventure's *Lignum vitae*, flanked by four pictorially framed scenes devoted to saints important to the Franciscan order. Beneath these paintings, spanning the entire width of the wall at the end of the refectory, Taddeo did a fresco of the Last Supper. He depicts a table that gives the illusion of projecting outward, at which sit Christ and the apostles, with Judas relegated to the side nearest the friars at their own tables in the refectory. This decidedly Franciscan iconography concluded Taddeo's long devotion to artistic projects for the priory and private quarters of the Franciscans in Florence, and it was one of the first of many depictions of the Last Supper in refectories of religious houses over the next two centuries. It also reflects Taddeo's lifelong commitment to—and success in handling—problems of pictorial illusionism.

In 1366, Taddeo Gaddi was recorded in the register of the Compagnia di San Luca, and that same year his wife was identified as a widow. Taddeo was buried, as Vasari notes, by his sons Angnolo and Giovanni at Santa Croce in the tomb he had made for his father, Gaddo.

See also **Bonaventure, Saint; Giotto di Bondone; Orcagna, Andrea di Cione**

Further Reading

Anonimo Gaddiano. *Il codice Magliabechiano*, CL.XVII.17, ed. C. Frey. Berlin: G. Grotesche Verlagsbuchhandlung, 1892.

Billi, Antonio. *Il libro di Antonio Billi*, ed. Fabio Benedettucci. Anzio (Rome): De Rubeis, 1991.

Borsook, Eve. *The Mural Painters of Tuscany from Cimabue to Andrea del Sarto*. London: Phaidon, 1960. (Rev. ed., Oxford: Clarendon, 1980.)

Cennini, Cennino. *Il libro dell'arte*, ed. Franco Brunello and Licisco Magagnato. Vicenza: Neri Pozza, 1971. (Work of c. 1390.)

Cennino d'Andrea Cennini. *The Craftsman's Handbook: The Italian Il Libro dell'arte*, ed. and trans. David V. Thompson. New Haven, Conn.: Yale University Press, 1933; New York: Dover, 1960.

Gardner, Julian. "The Decoration of the Baroncelli Chapel." *Zeitschrift für Kunstgeschichte*, 34, 1971, pp. 89–113.

Ghiberti, Lorenzo, c. 1450. *Lorenzo Ghibertis Denkwürdigkeiten (I commentarii)*, 2 vols., ed. Julius von Schlosser. Berlin: J. Bard, 1912.

Hueck, I. "Stifter und Patronatsrecht: Dokumente zu zwei Kapellen der Bardi." *Mitteilungen des Kunsthistorischen Institutes in Florenz*, 20, 1976, pp. 263–270.

Ladis, Andrew. *Taddeo Gaddi*. Columbia: University of Missouri Press, 1982.

Longhi, R. "Qualità e industria in Taddeo Gaddi ed altri." *Paragone*, 1959, 10(109), pp. 31–40; 10(111), pp. 3–12.

Meiss, Millard. *Painting in Florence and Siena after the Black Death: The Arts, Religion, and Society in the Mid-Fourteenth Century*. Princeton, N.J.: Princeton University Press, 1951.

Offner, Richard, and Klara Steinweg. *A Critical and Historical Corpus of Florentine Painting*. New York: College of Fine Arts, New York University, 1930–. (See suppl., ed. H. B. J. Maginnis, 1981, pp. 67–71.)

Rave, August. *Christiformitas: Studien zur franziskanischen Ikonographie des florentiner Trecento am Beispiel des ehe-*

maligen Sakristeischrankzyklus von Taddeo Gaddi in Santa Croce. Worms: Wernersche Verlagsgesellschaft, 1984.

Trachtenberg, Marvin. *The Campanile of Florence Cathedral "Giotto's Tower."* New York: New York University Press, 1971.

Vasari, Giorgio. *Le vite de' più eccellenti pittori, scultori, e architettori nelle redazioni del 1550 e 1568,* 2 vols., ed. R. Bettarini and P. Barocchi. Florence: Sansoni, 1966.

GAIL L. GEIGER

GAMA, VASCO DA (1460–1524)

Vasco da Gama was born about 1460 in Sines. He was the son of Estevão da Gama, a minor noble who had fought in North Africa and later became admiral of Portugal and governor of Sines.

The rounding of the Cape of Good Hope by Bartolomeu Dias in 1488 had confirmed the existence of a sea route from western Europe to Asia; consequently King Manuel I of Portugal ordered another, larger expedition and put the young Vasco de Gama in command of it. His fleet consisted of four ships: two *naus,* the *São Gabriel,* captained by Gama himself, and the *São Rafael,* captained by his brother Paulo; the *Bérrio,* a smaller ship, probably a caravel, captained by Nicolau Coelho; and a large supply ship captained by Gonçalo Nunes. The number of sailors and soldiers who took ship on Gama's first voyage was between 150 and 200 men.

Gama sailed out of the Tagus on 8 July 1497. He reprovisioned in the Cape Verde Islands, leaving there on 3 August and heading southwest to avoid the doldrums. Like Dias he picked up the westerlies and, turning east, made his first South African landfall at Saint Helena Bay on 7 or 8 November. He rounded the Cape of Good Hope on 22 November and anchored in Mossel Bay. Having abandoned his supply ship and redistributed its remaining provisions, he sailed on, reaching the Great Fish River on 16 December. Soon thereafter he was at present-day Natal Point, so named by Gama because it was sighted on Christmas Day. He reached Quelimane on 24 January 1498, Mozambique Island on 2 March, Mombasa on 7 April, and Malindi on 13 April. Favorably received there by the sultan, who liberally resupplied him, Gama set out to cross the Indian Ocean on 24 April. He was able to profit from the southwest summer monsoon wind, which took him to India in under a month. By 20 May he was anchored off the Malabar coast just above Calicut. The *samorin* of Calicut received him coldly, and at one point held Gama and his retinue prisoner. By a judicious mixture of threats and astuteness, Gama extricated his fleet and left India at the end of August 1498.

The return journey was disastrous: he was obliged to burn Paulo's ship for lack of men to sail her, for many had died of scurvy and dysentery; Paulo died on Ilha Terceira in the Azores. Gama arrived in Lisbon at the beginning of September and was rewarded magnificently by Manuel I with three pensions, the admiralty of India, and, much later, the countship of Vidigueira.

In 1502 Gama made his second exploratory expedition with a fleet of twenty ships that bombarded Calicut and left a five-warship guard at the entrance of the Red Sea to thwart Muslim trading competition. He also cemented an alliance with the more friendly Malabar state of Cochin. He returned briefly to India as viceroy of Portuguese India in 1524, dying there at the close of that year.

Vasco da Gama's achievement cannot be overestimated: he circumnavigated the African continent, directly linking the Indian Ocean with Europe, and he effectively sent into economic and political decline the powers of the eastern Mediterranean (Venice, Genoa, Egypt, and Turkey) so that economic power would shift permanently to the Atlantic. The consequent European dominance of western Asiatic waters was to continue until 1941–1942, when the Japanese overthrew British, French, and Dutch power; thus some Indian historians still call the period 1497–1941 "the Vasco de Gama era" of Indian history.

See also **Dias, Bartolomeu**

Further Reading

Jayne, K.G. *Vasco da Gama and His Successors: 1460–1580.* London, 1910.

Velho, A., *Roteiro da viagem que em descobrimento da India pelo Cabo da Boa Esperança fez dom Vasco da Gama em 1497–1499.* 2 vols. Oporto, 1945.

ROBERT OAKLEY

GAUTIER D'ARRAS

A contemporary and rival of Chrétien de Troyes, Gautier d'Arras identifies himself in two romances as a writer linked to important political and literary courts: *Eracle* was begun for Thibaut V of Blois and his sister-in-law, Countess Marie de Champagne, then completed and dedicated to Baudouin de Hainaut (if Baudouin IV, probable dates are 1164–71; if Baudouin V, somewhat later), *Ille et Galeron,* begun after *Eracle* but possibly finished before it (ca. 1167–70), praises the empress Béatrice de Bourgogne (d. 1184), for whom he started the romance (Chrétien may allude ironically to Gautier's praise in his prologue to the *Charrette*). The romance was completed for Count Thibaut. The poet may be the same man as the Gautier d'Arras who was an officer at the court of Philippe d'Alsace and signed many documents between 1160 and 1185.

Eracle is a hagiographical romance in octosyllabic rhymed couplets that offers a biography of Heraclius, the Roman emperor who recovered from King Cosdroes of Persia and placed in Jerusalem a piece of the Holy Cross. The first half, probably based on oral legends and popular tales, which Gautier weaves together with as much coherence and *vraisemblance* as possible, tells how Eracle uses his miraculous gifts in the service of the Emperor of Rome: Eracle is a perfect judge of jewels, horses, and women. When the emperor must go away, he places his young and beautiful wife, Athanaïs, in a tower under close surveillance. The inevitable happens when she falls in love and manages to start a liaison with Paridés. Eracle informs the emperor and convinces him to unite the two lovers. The second half, based on written sources and more historical in orientation, retells the legend of the cross and St. Cyriacus, to whom is dedicated the main church at Provins in Champagne, and Eracle's expedition, after he himself had become emperor, to return the holy relic to Jerusalem. Gautier thus makes available to a courtly public Latin texts and religious legends worked into a narrative whose use of adventure and the marvelous clearly locates it within the domain of romance, as does the importance given to love in the Athenaïs episode (4,319 lines out of 6,593).

Though apparently part of the *matière de Bretagne*, *Ille et Galeron* retains the Roman and Byzantine orientation of *Eracle*, as it retells and transforms the familiar tale of a man with two wives. Chased out of Brittany, the young llle takes refuge in France. Knighted, he returns and reconquers his family lands, for which he pays homage to Conain, count of Brittany. Ille falls in love with Galeron, Conain's sister. Their love is mutual, but the difference in their social rank poses an obstacle, until Ille's military service elevates him to the post of seneschal and marriage with Galeron. When Ille subsequently loses an eye (in a tournament according to one manuscript, a battle in another), he fears the loss of Galeron's love, steals away, and fights as mercenary for the Emperor of Rome. Given his prowess, Ille quickly becomes seneschal of Rome and inspires love in Ganor, the emperor's daughter. Galeron, who has searched fruitlessly for her husband, now lives secretly in Rome in the greatest misery. When offered Ganor's hand in marriage, Ille reveals that he is married; only if Galeron cannot be found will he marry Ganor. Just as that ceremony is about to be celebrated, Galeron recognizes her husband. When Galeron assures Ille of her continuing love, they return to Brittany. Their happy life is interrupted when Galeron makes a vow to become a nun, if she survives the difficult birth of a third child. Ille grieves, but is called to fulfill his promise to aid Ganor, now empress and under attack by the Emperor of Constantinople. Ille triumphs, he and Ganor are married in Rome and live happily with their own children and those of the first marriage.

Comparison with Marie de France's *Eliduc*, a *lai* that either furnishes Gautier's model or has a common source, reveals how Gautier has significantly reworked a short tale into an episodic romance whose two parts are clearly related through the key event: Ille's loss of an eye furnishes a crisis that resembles one of the love judgments reported in Andreas Capellanus's *De amore*: can love survive disfigurement? This event and the exploration of Ille's psychology before and after the crisis keep the romance plot squarely situated within the realm of the possible. The marvelous death and rebirth described in *Eliduc* are eliminated, as Gautier d'Arras places his art in the service of mimetic realism. Gautier thus appears as a kind of link between Chrétien and Jean Renart, as Fourrier has suggested. In elaborating the episodes that fill in Ille's story, Gautier demonstrates his ability to reuse materials from a variety of literary traditions (chansons de geste, saints' lives, *Énéas*). A narrator clearly able to please his audience, Gautier d'Arras plays an important role in the development of a romance tradition oriented toward realism, psychological interest, and contemporary life.

See also **Andreas Capellanus; Chrétien de Troyes; Marie de France**

Further Reading

Gautier d'Arras. *Eracle*, ed. Guy Raynaud de Lage. Paris: Champion, 1976.
——. *Ille et Galeron*, ed. Yves Lefèvre. Paris: Champion, 1988.
Calin, William. "Structure and Meaning in Eracle by Gautier d'Arras." *Symposium* 16 (1962): 275–87.
Fourrier, Antoine. *Le courant réaliste dans le roman courtois en France au moyen âge.* Paris: Nizet, 1960, Vol. 1: *Les débuts (XIIe siècle)*.
Haidu, Peter. "Narrativity and Language in Some Twelfth Century Romances." *Yale French Studies* 51 (1974): 133–46.
Nykrog, Per. "Two Creators of Narrative Form in Twelfth Century France: Gautier d'Arras and Chrétien de Troyes." *Speculum* 48 (1973): 258–76.
Zumthor, Paul. "L'écriture et la voix: *Le roman d'Eracle*." In *The Craft of Fiction: Essays on Medieval Poetics*, ed. Leigh Arrathoon. Rochester: Solaris, 1984, pp. 161–209.

MATILDA T. BRUCKNER

GAUTIER DE COINCI
(1177/78–1236)

Gautier entered the Benedictine monastery of Saint-Médard in Soissons in 1193, was appointed prior of Vic-sur-Aisne in 1214, and returned to Soissons in 1233 as prior of Saint-Médard. He was a prolific writer, whose works include religious songs, two sermons, and four saints' lives, as well as the *Miracles de Nostre Dame*, for which he is most famous. A series of narrative poems on the birth of Mary, the childhood of Jesus, and the Assumption, and a paraphrase of the Psalm *Eructavit*, appear in some manuscripts of the *Miracles* and are sometimes credited to him. The attribution of the *Saint dent Nostre Seigneur*, a poem about a relic discovered at Soissons, which appears in only two manuscripts, is even less certain.

The *Miracles* (ca. 30,000 lines) are divided into two books organized symmetrically. Each begins with a prologue and a series of seven songs in honor of the Virgin. The first book, begun in 1218 and revised four years later, contains thirty-five miracles and ends with three songs in honor of St. Leocadia. The second book, with twenty-three miracles, was perhaps written between 1223 and 1227. Gautier, who sought to convert the lapsed and strengthen the faith of the believer, intended his collection for an unlearned but aristocratic audience, as he expresses contempt for the *vileins*.

Gautier found his stories in a collection of Latin Marian legends in his monastery at Soissons. Although this manuscript has been lost, enough of its character has been established to determine the way Gautier treated his sources. He did not follow his model slavishly but sometimes expanded it by resorting to other sources and even drew on events of his own life. In most stories, a sinner is saved by a single redeeming virtue, usually devotion to the Virgin. The final sections of the stories, often satirical attacks on all classes of society, are original and of great interest to modern readers. Gautier was a skilled versifier who made frequent use of rich and equivocal rhymes. The reactions of modern critics to this material range from enthusiasm to hostility but depend largely on their appreciation of the genre rather than Gautier's treatment of it.

The songs that begin each book are important in their own right, for they are the best examples of religious lyric poetry from the 13th century. Despite his antipathy to secular literature, Gautier's lyric poetry was strongly influenced by the secular tradition. If his musical compositions were not of the first rank, he was nevertheless a musician of considerable skill and refinement.

Further Reading

Gautier de Coinci. *Les miracles de Nostre Dame*, ed. V. Frederic Koenig. 4 vols. Geneva: Droz, 1955–70.

——. *Miracles de Gautier de Coinci: extraits du manuscrit de l'Ermitage*, ed. Arthur Långfors. Helsinki, 1937.

Drzewicka, A. "La fonction des emprunts à la poésie profane dans les chansons mariates de Gautier de Coinci." *Moyen âge* 91 (1985): 33–51, 179–200.

Ducrot-Granderye, Arlette. *Études sur les Miracles Nostre Dame de Gautier de Coinci*. Helsinki, 1932.

Långfors, Arthur. "Mélanges de poésie lyrique, II, III." *Romania* 53 (1927): 474–538; 56 (1930): 33–79.

Lommatzsch, Ernst. *Gautier de Coincy als Satiriker*. Halle: Niemeyer, 1913.

Verrier, Paul. "La 'Chanson de Notre Dame' de Gautier de Coinci." *Romania* 59 (1933): 497–519; 61 (1935): 97.

MAUREEN B.M. BOULTON

GELMÍREZ, DIEGO, ARCHBISHOP OF COMPOSTELA
(c. 1070-1140)

This most famous and most powerful ordinary of the shrine of Santiago de Compostela was a native of Galicia, born about 1070 into a family of the minor nobility of that province. He probably was educated in part at the court of Alfonso VI (1065–1109) of León-Castile and in part within the clerical community of the cathedral. In 1090, and again in 1096, Gelmírez was the royal administrator for the possessions of the then vacant see of Compostela. In 1094 he had become the notary of Count Raymond of Galicia (1090–1107), originally from Burgundy, who held the province by virtue of his marriage to Urraca, daughter of King Alfonso. The choice of both king and count, Gelmírez was elected bishop of Compostela perhaps as early as 1098, and certainly by 1100. He was consecrated on 21 April 1101. The see to which he succeeded had been famous since the ninth century as the shrine-church purportedly housing the relics of the apostle St. James the Great. As the only site of apostolic remains in the Western world except Rome, it had long been the destination of pilgrims. In 1095 Pope Urban II had approved the exemption of the see from its traditional metropolitan, Portuguese Braga, and made it directly dependent on Rome.

Gelmírez's major triumph was to secure the transfer of the former metropolitanate of Visigothic Mérida to Compostela by Pope Calixtus II in 1120. As a result Compostela immediately became the metropolitan see for Ávila, Salamanca, and Coimbra, and Gelmírez, an archbishop. The suffragan see of Coimbra finally could not be retained, but in the long rivalry for power that ensued, Compostela ultimately wrested the Galician sees of Túy, Lugo, Mondoñedo, and Orense away from Braga.

In addition Gelmírez had been named papal legate for the ecclesiastical provinces of both Braga and Mérida by Calixtus II, and used his power for the aggrandizement of his own church. He also hoped to have Compostela replace Toledo as the primatial see of Iberia, but fell short of his goal. He was also an energetic reformer of the church and cathedral chapter of Santiago de Compostela, and carried out much of the construction of a major new Romanesque cathedral there, begun a quarter of a century earlier.

Gelmírez was also a major political figure of the realm of León–Castile. He was guardian, along with the Galician magnate Count Pedro of Traba, of the only son of Count Raymond and Alfonso VI's daughter, Urraca. When Urraca succeeded to her father's realm in 1109 and married King Alfonso I of Aragón (r. 1105–1134), Gelmírez and Pedro raised a revolt against the royal couple in the name of the rights of the future Alfonso VII. The Galician prelate was sometimes the soul of the opposition to Queen Urraca and sometimes, particularly after her separation from Alfonso in 1112, her close collaborator. With the death of Urraca in 1126 and the succession of her son as Alfonso VII (r. 1126–1157), Gelmírez initially shared the glory of his former protégé. At the Council of León in 1130 he was able to place canons of his church in the bishoprics of the royal city of León and of Salamanca. Three years later another canon of Compostela became bishop of Orense.

But royal favor was inconstant, and as early as 1127 Gelmírez found himself the subject of extortion at the hands of a needy Alfonso VII. After 1134 the archbishop was increasingly eclipsed by the rising influence of the archbishop of Toledo, who placed his own canons as royal chancellor and then in Compostela's suffragan see of Salamanca in 1135. The following year the king collaborated in an attempt to have Gelmírez removed from his ecclesiastical dignity. At the Council of Burgos in 1136 the Galician prelate was rescued only by the support of the papacy and the ineptitude of the conspirators. Nevertheless, the cost of maintaining his office again came at the price of substantial future subsidies to the king.

The troubles of the archbishop of Santiago de Compostela were, in good part, due to his position as one of the great magnates of Galicia as well as a prelate there. His office made him the administrator of widespread royal lands, and these, combined with the lands of the shrine–church itself, automatically established him as the most powerful figure of central Galica. There he was caught between the ambitions of the Trastámara counts of Traba in the north and of the monarchs Teresa (r. 1112–1128) and Afonso I Enriques (r. 1139–1185) of Portugal in the south.

By royal grant and policy Gelmírez was also the lessee of the royal mint in Compostela and the city's civil administrator. In the latter capacity he resisted the ambitions of a nascent citizen commune to a share in the goverment of the town, although he did grant a measure of participation to it. The communal movement had allies even within the cathedral chapter. When his troubles in the larger political arena became acute, he faced outright revolt in 1117 and again in 1135. Both began with unsuccessful attempts on his life that failed only by the narrowest of margins. In each case the crown had initially encouraged Gelmírez's enemies, and repudiated them only when their attempt at assassination had failed.

After 1136 Gelmírez played only a small part in the life of the realm, and his activities in the church seem to have tapered down as well. From 1138 he was probably intermittently ill, and he died on 31 March 1140.

See also **Alfonso VI, King of León-Castile; Urban II, Pope**

Further Reading

Briggs, A. G. *Diego Gelmírez, First Archbishop of Compostela.* Washington, D. C., 1949.
Falque Rey, E. (ed.) *Historia compostelana.* Turnhout, 1988.
Fletcher, R. A. *Saint James's Catapult: The Life and Times of Diego Gelmírez of Santiago de Compostela.* Oxford, 1984.

BERNARD F. REILLY

GEOFFREY OF MONMOUTH (ca. 1100–1155)

Author of the highly influential *Historia regum Britanniae* (*History of the Kings of Britain*). Probably born in Wales and possibly of Breton descent, Geoffrey lived in Oxford from 1129 to 1151, presumably as a secular canon at the College of St. George, where he was engaged in teaching. By 1151 or 1152 he had been elected bishop of St. Asaph in northeast Wales, although there is no evidence to suggest that he ever visited his Welsh see.

Geoffrey's first book, the *Prophetiae Merlini*, or *Prophecies of Merlin* (ca. 1135), purports to be a series of prophecies delivered by Merlin to the 5th-century king Vortigern and translated from British verse into Latin. The prophecies are retrospective, anticipatory, or apocalyptic: that is, some allude to events before Geoffrey's time; others to events that in 1135 seemed relatively imminent (e.g., the Norman conquest of Ireland); and still others to events that might be anticipated at the end of the world. Although the *Prophecies stems* mainly from Geoffrey's vivid imagination, parts of it betray a debt to native prophetic traditions and to such written sources as Lucan's *Pharsalia* and the Bible. Having circulated independently in a manuscript or manuscripts no longer extant, the prophecies were ultimately incorporated into the enormously popular *History of the Kings of Britain*, a Latin work that was probably completed in 1138 and survives in over 200 manuscripts.

Geoffrey claims that he translated his history of the Britons from the time of Brutus to the reign of Cadwalader from an ancient book in the Breton (or Welsh) tongue. That which Geoffrey did not simply invent for the purposes of his history, however, seems to be derived from not one but several sources. Much of his account of the founding of the British nation, for example, derives from Virgil and from Nennius's *Historia Brittonum*. The history of Britain from its founding by Brutus to the reigns of Uther Pendragon and Arthur would seem to derive largely from Welsh genealogies and legends. Geoffrey concludes his history with an account of the Saxon conquest that owes much to these same sources and to accounts of the conquest found in Gildas and Bede.

The impact of the *History of the Kings of Britain* on later literature has been considerable, for to this work we owe not only the vernacular *Bruts* of Wace, Laȝamon, and several Welsh poets but also some of the works of such distinguished writers as Chrétien de Troyes, Malory, Spenser, Tennyson, Morris, Twain, Swinburne, and E.A. Robinson. Much less influential was Geoffrey's last work, the *Vita Merlini*, or *Life of Merlin* (ca. 1150), a Latin poem recounting the story of Merlin's going mad after a battle and retreating to the forest of Calidon. He is visited there by his sister Ganieda, the learned bard Taliesin, and the latter's friend Maeldinus. Merlin eventually regains his sanity, whereupon he and his three visitors decide to end their days in the forest, engaging themselves in the pursuit of esoteric knowledge.

Because the central character of the *Life* is not the Merlin Ambrosius of the *History* but the Celtic Merlin Calidonius (or Silvester), Geoffrey's tale of Merlin is thought to have originated in the Welsh prophetic and poetic traditions. Sources for the work, which contains numerous contemporary political allusions and extensive passages of learned or prophetic discourse, include Bede, Isidore of Seville, and material from Geoffrey's own *Prophecies of Merlin*.

See also **Bede the Venerable; Chrétien de Troyes; Laȝamon or Layamon; Malory, Thomas**

Further Reading

Primary Sources

Thorpe, Lewis, trans. *The History of the Kings of Britain*. Harmondsworth: Penguin, 1966

Clarke, Basil, ed. and trans. *Life of Merlin: Vita Merlini*. Cardiff: University of Wales Press, 1973.

Secondary Sources

New *CBEL* 1:393–96, 478

Manual 1:41–42, 231–32; 46, 234–35

Curley, Michael J. *Geoffrey of Monmouth*. New York: Twayne, 1994

Leckie, R. William, Jr. *The Passage of Dominion: Geoffrey of Monmouth and the Periodization of Insular History in the Twelfth Century*. Toronto: University of Toronto Press, 1981

Parry, John J., and Robert A. Caldwell. "Geoffrey of Monmouth." In *Arthurian Literature in the Middle Ages: A Collaborative History*, ed, Roger Sherman Loomis. Oxford: Clarendon, 1959, pp. 72–93

Reiss, Edmund, et al. *Arthurian Legend and Literature: An Annotated Bibliography*. Vol. 1. New York, Garland, 1984, pp. 66–68

Tatlock, John S.P. *The Legendary History of Britain: Geoffrey of Monmouth's "Historia Regum Britanniae" and Its Early Vernacular Versions*. Berkeley: University of California Press, 1950.

JAMES NOBLE

GERHOH OF REICHERSBERG (1093–1169)

Bavarian canon, controversialist reformer, and correspondent with emperors and popes, Gerhoh, provost of Reichersberg, was a prolific writer and an important figure in twelfth-century literature and religion. Gerhoh was a strong advocate of continued reform of the church and was a vocal critic of the worldliness and wealth of the ecclesiastical hierarchy. Although critical of ecclesiastical abuses, Gerhoh was equally critical of secular abuses of power and was an important supporter of Innocent II in the papal schism of 1130 and a supporter, after initial neutrality, of Alexander III during the schism of that pope's reign. Gerhoh was also a representative of the new apostolic spirituality and the new urban milieu emerging in twelfth-century Europe. A canon and active preacher, Gerhoh's teaching offered an ideal of radical reform rooted in Gregorian ideals of the world. His definition of simony, the selling of indulgences, threatened the prebendary (grant-giving) system of the church and opened him to accusations of heresy in the autumn of 1130. He was saved from a heretic's fate only by the protection of powerful reform-minded members of the ecclesiastical hierarchy. But Gerhoh's criticism was not limited to the secular and religious elite; it extended to the representatives of the "new learning" including Peter Abelard, Gilbert de la Porée, and Peter Lombard. Finally, Gerhoh was a theologian of some note and author of a number of important treatises including *Liber de aedificio Dei* (On God's House) and *Libellus de ordine donorum Spiritus sancti* (On the Order of the Gifts of the Holy Spirit). His most interesting theological work, however, can be found in his apocalyptic treatises, *De investigatione Antichristi* (The Investigation of Antichrist) and *De quarta vigilia noctis* (The Fourth Watch of the Night). In these works he develops a theology of history that posits the imminent end of time in his own day. He provides an outline of history based on the church's successful struggle against various antichrists culminating in the age of Pope Gregory VII. It was in the years following the reign of Gregory that the times of trouble and turmoil—evident for Gerhoh in the rampant simony and worldliness of many clerics and in the struggles between the pope and the emperor, Frederick Barbarossa—preceding the appearance of Antichrist occurred. Indeed, Gerhoh's work suggests that the biblical prophecies forewarning of Antichrist had been fulfilled and that his coming was imminent.

See also **Abélard, Peter; Gregory VII, Pope; Peter Lombard**

Further Reading

Classen, Peter. "*Res Gestae,* Universal History, Apocalypse: Visions of Past and Future," in *Renaissance and Renewal in the*

Twelfth Century, ed. Robert L. Benson and Giles Constable. Toronto: University of Toronto Press, 1991, pp. 387–417.

Meuthen, Erich. *Kirche und Heilsgeschichte bei Gerhoh von Reichersberg.* Leiden: Brill, 1959.

Morrison, Karl F. "The Exercise of Thoughtful Minds: The Apocalypse in Some German Historical Writings," in *The Apocalypse in the Middle Ages,* ed. Richard K. Emmerson and Bernard McGinn. Ithaca, N.Y.: Cornell University Press, 1992, pp. 352–373.

MICHAEL FRASSETTO

GERSHOM B. JUDAH (c. 960–1028)

Gershom b. Judah, better known as *Rabbenu* ("our rabbi") Gershom, *Me'or ha-golah* ("the light of the exile"), is generally recognized as the founding father of rabbinic studies in northern Europe. [In his responsum dealing with the first ordinance, "*Rashi*" made the statement that Gershom "enlightened the eyes of the exile, and all of us live by his words; and all the children of the exile of Germany and Rome [*Kiyttiym;* cf. "*Rashi*" on Isa. 23.1] are the students of his students" (*Teshuvot ḥokhmey Ṣarfat ve-Lotir,* Vienna, 1881; No. 21)—*ed.*]. He was born ca. 960, probably in Metz (Germany), but spent most of his active life in Mainz, which was then the most important Jewish community of the Rhineland. His greatness was acknowledged at an early stage, and many students, including the future teachers of "*Rashi*," gathered around him and spread his teachings. Thus, Mainz soon became the center of Jewish learning. It is not very clear where he himself had studied, but it would seem that he was near scholars who originated in Italy. There is very little information about his life. He is reported to have died in 1028.

His activities were numerous. His teaching of the Talmud resulted in talmudic commentary, inasmuch as his students very probably summarized his teachings in their notes. Some of these commentaries have been published in modern times under his name, but it is very doubtful that they originated from him in their present form. Successive generations of students very probably completed, amplified, and occasionally summarized his commentary, while applying their own additions, but it can be admitted that this commentary, probably called the Mainz commentary, ultimately was the pathfinder of European talmudic commentaries, later superseded by that of "*Rashi.*" Gershom was also active as a liturgical poet; ten of his *seliyḥot* (penitential poems) have been preserved [legend has it that his son and possibly his wife were forcibly baptized—*ed.*]. However, his reputation today rests more on his public activities than his teachings.

His name is connected with a number of bans or *taqqanot* (ordinances) that exerted enormous influence on the evolution of European Jewry. Most important are those dealing with family life. These include the interdiction of polygamy, and against divorce without consent of the wife. These decisions were intended to bar other possibilities [without seeming to create new law, not found in the Talmud]. It has been remarked that during the following generations these decrees were not attributed to him but were designated as community ordinances. Some have deduced from this that he was not their author, but that his name was connected with them later in order to enhance their authority. Such an explanation does not seem necessary; the fact that such measures required the decision of a community does not preclude the fact that Gershom suggested the ordinances and was active in having them accepted. There is therefore no reason to deny him his part in their authorship. It should nevertheless be kept in mind that these ordinances were not accepted right away in all communities; the Spanish communities, for example, did not recognize them. It also took some time until they were generally enacted in northern Europe. Their acceptance was facilitated by the Christian doctrine on monogamy. It would also seem that very soon the rather extreme nature of these ordinances was recognized—that they did not take into account some unusual situations that made divorce very difficult, such as mental illness, or disappearance of the wife—and therefore sometimes these ordinances were deferred. Many other ordinances have been attributed to Gershom. The only one that can be so attributed with certainty—it is already quoted in his name by "*Rashi*"—is the one that forbids reminding an apostate who has made penance and returned to Judaism of his former condition. The ordinance forbidding the reading of a letter sent to someone else without his permission is much later and cannot be attributed to Gershom.

Further Reading

Enṣiqlopediah talmudit (Hebrew) (Jerusalem, 1987), Vol. 21, 378–454, 757–70.

Germania Judaica (Tübingen, 1963), Vol. 2, 189–91.

Grossman, Abraham. *Ḥokhmei Ashkenaz ha-rishonim* (Jerusalem, 1981).

SIMON SCHWARZFUCHS

GERSON, JEAN
(Jean Charlier; 1363–1429)

Theologian, scholar, teacher, translator, poet, mystic, and humanist, Gerson was one of the most illustrious and prolific writers of the late Middle Ages. One of twelve children, he grew up in a pious household in Champagne, the son of an educated artisan. Three of his brothers became monks and another a priest. Although his sisters did not enter religious orders, they formed among themselves an informal religious group devoted to prayer and spiritual exercises. Gerson entered the University of Paris in 1377 and received an arts degree in 1381 from the Collège de Navarre. Subsequently, he studied theology and obtained the doctorate in 1392.

Tailoring his sermons to his audience, Gerson gained fame as an orator who could preach with eloquence to both kings and the laity at large. He succeeded his friend and mentor Pierre d'Ailly as chancellor of the university in 1395, taking over the duties in the midst of the Great Schism (1378–1417). Although Gerson opposed the withdrawal of French obedience from the Avignon pope, Benedict XIII, and worked to restore it in 1403, he nevertheless sought a reconciliation between the two contending popes by suggesting that both claimants resign. In 1407, the Roman pope, Gregory XII, indicated a willingness to meet with Benedict and discuss mutual resignation. Gerson was chosen to head the French delegation and facilitate the meeting, which was, however, a failure. With the aim of restoring church unity, Gerson supported a move to resolve the conflict through a church council. The Council of Pisa, held in 1409, was not successful. Although it elected a new pope, Alexander V, this strategy served only to introduce a third contender. The Council of Constance (1415–18) finally put an end to the Schism with the election of Martin V. Writing numerous treatises to justify the work of the council, Gerson was an outspoken proponent of conciliarism, setting out the limitations of papal authority.

Gerson was also strenuous in efforts to eradicate heresy. Critical of the writings of Wyclif and Hus, Gerson was an adviser to Pierre d'Ailly, who served on the commission that condemned Hus to death. Also interested in secular affairs, Gerson openly opposed the Burgundian assassination of the duke of Orléans in 1407, attacking and condemning Jean Petit's *Apologia* for favoring tyrannicide in justification of the Burgundian deed. His position so angered the duke of Burgundy, who had previously been one of Gerson's strongest protectors, that he was prevented from returning to Paris after the Council of Constance. Gerson retired to Lyon, living first at a Celestine monastery where his youngest brother, also named Jean, who became his copyist and editor, was prior, and then at the church of Saint-Paul. During his exile, however, Gerson continued to write as he had before on such subjects as spiritual renewal, church reform, Christian education, and the integration of mystical and speculative theology. His writings have not received extensive attention from historians, although they offer insights into the culture of the late Middle Ages. His work, for example, on the Christian education of the young provides important information on medieval attitudes on children and childhood.

Gerson was also a Latin poet of notable talent and skill. Influenced by Petrarch, his eclogue on the Schism is perhaps the first humanist work produced in France. Other works include *De vita spirituali animae*, in which he locates ecclesiastical authority in church councils rather than in the pope; *De unitate ecclesiae*, one of twenty-seven extant treatises on the church; *Mémoire*

sur la réforme de la faculté de théologie, which outlines his pedagogy; and informal writings on the spiritual life, such as the *Montague de contemplation*. Although it is often attributed to him, Gerson did not write the *Imitatio Christi*. Among his last writings is a defense of Jeanne d'Arc, *Puella Aurelianensi* (1429).

See also **D'ailly, Pierre; Eriugena, Johannes Scottus; Jeanne d'Arc; Petrarca, Francesco; Wyclif, John**

Further Reading

Gerson, Jean. *Œuvres complètes de Jean Gerson*, ed. Palémon Glorieux. 10 vols. Paris: Desclée, 1960–73.

Combes, André. *La théologie mystique de Gerson*. 2 vols. Rome: Editores Pontificii, 1965.

Delaruelle, Étienne, L.R. Labande, and Papul Ourliac. *L'église au temps du Grand Schisme et de la crise conciliaire (1378–1449)*. 2 vols. Paris: Blond et Gay, 1962.

Morrall, John B. *Gerson and the Great Schism*. Manchester: Manchester University Press, 1960.

E. KAY HARRIS

GERTHENER, MADERN
(1360/1370–1430)

Named with his father, Johann, among the stone masons of Frankfurt in 1387, Gerthener had taken over his father's shop by 1391. In 1395 he was taken onto the city payroll. In 1415 he calls himself *"der stadt frankenfurd werkmeister"* (master of the works of the city of Frankfurt), a position he had probably already held for some time. Most of his documented career was spent working on the church of St. Bartholomew: he was appointed head of the works in 1408. After finishing the transept here, he designed and, in 1415, began building the single tower that stood as a symbol of the city's independence. An octagonal story topped by a dome and an elaborate lantern surmounts the two lower stories on a square plan. The tracery decoration and especially the corner buttresses become increasingly ornate with each succeeding story. On the two portals we see the innovative uses of tracery forms, specifically hanging tracery and tracery vaults, that would become hallmarks of Gerthener's style.

In addition to his work on St. Bartholomew's, Gerthener was also involved in other projects in and around Frankfurt. In 1399 he guaranteed his work on the Alte Brücke (Old Bridge) across the Main, and in 1411 his work on the city wall is documented. Gerthener's mastery of the forms of late Gothic architecture, plus his visibility as head of the works on the coronation cathedral, drew his work to the attention of other patrons, and by the 1410s his reputation reached outside the city. Payments to Gerthener in 1407 from the funds of the so-called Gelnhausen tax, to which only King Ruprecht von der Pfalz (1400–1410) had access, may have been in compensation for the so-called Ruprechts-bau (Ruprecht building) at Heidelberg castle and/or the sacristy at Speyer Cathedral, begun in 1409. Gerthener's name appears in 1414–1415 in the financial records of the church of St. Katherine in Oppenheim, where he designed the west choir. The variety of the unusually fanciful tracery patterns in the tall windows and other details recall Gerthener's work in Frankfurt. In 1419 he was called to Strasbourg, where, with other masters, he advised on the continuation of the cathedral facade.

Other works sometimes associated with Gerthener fall into two groups: those on which his participation is assumed on the basis of his city positions and attributions on the basis of stylistic affinities with his secured works. Into the former category fall work on the town hall (the Römer), adapted from two patrician houses beginning in 1405, and the trade hall for linen, flax, and hemp products, the Leinwandhaus. Work on the city fortification system underway circa 1400 would also have been expected of the city's *Werkmeister*. This variety in the production of the medieval builder/architect—repair or rebuilding of existing structures, design and erection of both functional buildings, like bridges and fortification towers, and what we might today think of as "high" architecture, seen especially in churches—is typical of the era. The career of Peter Parler, for example, with whom Gerthener may have worked in Prague during his travels as a journeyman, also exhibits this diversity.

The high quality and use of architectural forms similar to those at Frankfurt produce general agreement that Gerthener was also at work on the so-called Memoreinpforte (portal to the memorial chapel) at Mainz Cathedral about 1425. At Frankfurt, work on the church of the Virgin (Liebfrauenkirche), that of the Carmelites, and St. Leonhard's, all dated between 1415 and circa 1430, is sometimes associated with Gerthener on the basis of stylistic similarities to his documented works.

Three payment records indicate that Gerthener was also active as a sculptor. The sweet expressions and smoothed volumes of both the faces and the draperies of the two male saints on the cathedral side of the Memorienpforte are typically considered to exemplify his style. Other works sometimes assigned to Gerthener on stylistic grounds include the tympanum with the elaborate, multifigured scene of the Adoration of the Magi above the south portal of the Liebfrauenkirche in Frankfurt (ca. 1425), and the tomb of Anna von Dalberg (d. 1410) in the church of St. Katherine in Oppenheim. The art historian Knifner argues that the epitaph of Siegfried xum Paradies, now in St. Nikolaus in Frankfurt (ca. 1420), and that of Johann II von Nassau (d. 1419), archbishop of Mainz, are more likely to be the master's own work.

Somewhat more problematic attributions are a print with the depiction of the Holy Grave (Berlin, Staatliche Museen Preussischer Kulturbesitz, Kupferstichkabinett), whose figures are close in style to those of the Memorienpforte, and a large-scale drawing with the design for Gerthener's tower at St. Bartholomew's (Frankfurt, Historisches Museum). Whether these are works by the master himself or by those who worked with him closely, Gerthener was an inventive artist of unusual energy and breadth.

Further Reading

Beck, Herbert, Wolfgang Beeh, and Horst Bredekamp. *Kunst um 1400 am Mittelrhein: Ein Teil der Wirklichkeit.* Frankfurt am Main: Liebieghaus Museum alter Piastik, 1975, pp. 49–56.

Haberland, Ernst-Dietrich, and Hans-Otto Schrembs. *Madern Gerthener "der Stadt Franckenfurd Werkmeister": Baumeister und Bildbauer der Spätgotik,* Frankfurt am Main: Knecht, 1992.

Kniffler, Gisela. *Die Grabdenkmäler der Mainzer Erzbischöfi vow. 13. bis zum früben 16. Jahrhundert.* Ph.D. diss., University of Mainz, Dissertationen zur Kunstgeschichte 7. Cologne: Böhlau, 1978, pp. 51–109.

Ringshausen, Gerhard Johannes. "Madern Gerthener: Leben und Werk nach den Urkunden," Ph.D. diss., University of Gottingen, 1968.

JOAN A. HOLLADAY

GERTRUD VON HELFTA (1256–1301/1302)

A monastic, mystic author, Gertrud the Great *(die Größe)* entered the monastery of Helfta (near Eisleben) at the age of almost five. Her *Vita* (Life) presents her as a precocious child keenly interested in studying and eventually acquiring a comprehensive liberal arts education in Helfta. Under its abbess Gertrud von Hackeborn, the Helfta monastery had developed at that time into a center of culture and learning. Together with her older sisters in community, Mechthild von Hackeborn (the abbess's sister) and the Beguine Mechthild von Magdeburg, Gertrud was instrumental in making Helfta into the focal point of thirteenth-century mysticism.

Gertrud's mystical conversion experience happened when she was twenty-five (on January 27, 1281). From a lukewarm monastic, avid in the pursuit of secular literature, she was turned into an ardent lover who dedicated herself wholeheartedly to a Christ-centered spirituality. Some eight years later, during Holy Week of 1289, Gertrud suddenly felt "violently compelled" by the Spirit to write the memorial of this pivotal experience (to be found in Book II of the *Legatus,* "Herald").

Gertrud never held an important office in her monastery. She spent her life studying theology (influences of Bernard of Clairvaux, William of St. Thierry, Hugh of St. Victor, and others are noticeable) and writing exegetical and spiritual texts in which scriptural and liturgical references abound, and where even nature plays a role. She also collaborated on Mechthild von Hackeborn's work, the *Liber specialis gratiae* (Book of Special Grace). Moreover, Gertrud functioned as a much sought-after pastoral counselor both of her sisters and of lay people. Gertrud died on November 17 at the age of forty-five or forty-six, but details of her death are not known. Gertrud von Helfta has been venerated as a saint first by the Benedictine Order (since 1674) and since 1734 officially by the entire Roman Catholic Church. She was also made the patron saint of the West Indies.

Presumably only a portion of Gertrud's writings has been preserved. Numerous prayer books that were published in many languages since the sixteenth century under the names of St. Gertrud and Mechthild (latest English edition, Philadelphia 1955) are not authentic. The *Legatus divinae pietatis* and her brief *Exercitia spiritualia*, consisting of prayerful meditations based on Scripture and the liturgy, are commonly listed as Gertrud von Helfta's works. *The Legatus* (The Herald of God's Loving-Kindness) consists of five parts: Books 3–5, roughly based on material provided by Gertrud, were composed by a sister in the Helfta community; Book 1 constitutes Gertrud's *vita* written after her death. Only Book 2 was written by Gertrud's own hand. Together with the equally authentic *Spiritual* Exercises, these two texts are unique jewels of medieval mysticism.

Gertrud's work was composed in Latin. An early fifteenth-century Middle High German translation, *ein botte der götlichen miltekeit* (its oldest mansucript is dated 1448) is a deliberately shortened version of Books 3–5 of the *Legatus*. The manuscript tradition of Gertrud von Helfta's work is meager. Of the *Legatus*, eight complete or partial fifteenth-century manuscripts are known. No manuscript is extant of the *Spiritual Exercises*. Its survival was made possible by the first publication of Gertrud von Helfta's Latin work in 1536 by the Carthusian Johannes Lanspergius of Cologne. Since then, most early editors and translators found it necessary to attach to Gertrud's work an initial *apologia* attesting to the orthodoxy of her writings.

To separate Gertrud von Helfta's specific way of thinking from the general mystical and intellectual atmosphere of Helfta, interpretation must focus on the Exercitia and her own Book 2 of the *Legatus*. Gertrud's "confessions" show her as profoundly humble. Yet simultaneously she sees all human beings invested with regal dignity through Christ's incarnation. Invisibly stigmatized and mystically united to Christ through an exchange of hearts, Gertrud encounters the divine as a self-confident woman. Her distinctive characteristic is her inner freedom *(libertas cordis),* which leaves her little patience with petty ecclesiastical regulations. The dominant tone of Gertrud von Helfta's work is that of intense joy, as best expressed in her mystical *jubilus (Exercitia)*. Her God-language is notable for its imagi-

native indusiveness. The theology of the Sacred Heart is to be credited more to the general Helfta community than to Gertrud.

See also **Bernard of Clairvaux; Hugh of Saint-Victor**

Further Reading

Barratt, Alexandra. *The Herald of God's Loving-Kindness by Gertrud the Great of Helfta, Books One and Two.* Kalamazoo, Mich.: Cistercian Publications, 1991.

Bynum, Caroline Walker. *Jesus as Mother: Studies in the Spirituality of the High Middle Ages.* Berkeley: University of California Press, 1982, pp. 170–262.

Finnegan, Mary Jeremy. *The Women of Helfta: Scholars and Mystics.* Athens: University of Georgia Press, 1991.

Hart, Mother Columba, trans. *The Exercises of St. Gertrude.* Westminster, Md.: Newman Press, 1956.

Hourlier, Jacques, et al. eds. *Gertrude d'Helfta. Oeuvres spirituelles.* Sources chrétiennes 127, 139, 143, 255, 331. Paris: du Cerf, 1967–1986 [bilingual, Latin-French].

Lewis, Gertrud Jaron. *Bibliographic zur deutschen Frauenmystik des Mittelalters.* Berlin: Erich Schmidt Verlag, 1989, pp.196–223 [comprehensive list of primary and secondary sources].

Lewis, Gertrud Jaron, and Jack Lewis, trans. *Gertrud the Great of Helfta: Spiritual Exercises.* Kalamazoo, Mich.: Cistercian Publications, 1989.

Shank, Lillian Thomas, and John A. Nichols. *Medieval Religious Women,* 2. Kalamazoo, Mich.: Cistercian Publications, 1987, pp. 239–273.

Winkworth, Margaret, trans. *Gertrude of Helfta: The Herald of Divine Love.* New York and Mahwah, N.J.: Paulist Press, 1993 [Books 1 and 2, and partially Book 3].

GERTRUD JARON LEWIS

GIACOMINO DA VERONA
(13th century)

Giacomino da Verona was a notable figure in both Lombard (northern Italian) and Franciscan literature. He is known for two vernacular poems: one about paradise (in 1,108 verses) and the other about hell (in 1,348 verses). The verse form is caesured alexandrine (7 + 7 syllables), arranged in a sequence of monorhymed quatrains; however, the presence of shorter hemistichs often brings the lines near the epic decasyllable of the jongleurs. There are four manuscripts. The one in Venice (V, Marciana Library) and the one in Seville (S, Colombina Library) are closely related and provide the best reading of the poems. They also feature, before each poem, a long title (Latin in V and vernacular in S) in which paradise is called a "heavenly Jerusalem" (*De Jerusalem celesti*) and hell a "hellish Babylon" (*De Babilonia infernali*). The other two manuscripts are found in Udine (U, Arcivescovile Library) and Oxford (O, Bodleian); the latter, O, contains only the first poem (*Jerusalem*). The two poems were initially published only from V by *Ozanam* (1850) and, more competently, by Mussafia (1864) but were finally edited from the four extant manuscripts (with critical apparatus) by Barana (1921) and again by May (1930). May's edition includes an ample commentary on Giacomino's culture and sources. The text established by Contini (1960) and R. Broggini was the first edition based on a genealogical presentation of tile manuscripts and is therefore, strictly speaking, the only critical edition available as of the present writing.

In *De Babilonia infernali* (335), the poet clearly identifies himself as "Iacomino da Verona—de l'Orden de Minori." This poem and *De Jerusalem celesti* are followed, in V and S, by five other religious poems. Mussafia was inclined to attribute these five to Giacomino as well, on the basis of linguistic (Old Veronese) and cultural (Franciscan), though not metrical, affinities. The most relevant of these poems is the one titled *Dela caducità della vita umana*, "On the transience of human life" (Contini 1960, Vol. 1, *653–666*). The question whether the selection was made to include works of the same author or simply of the same genre cannot be decided.

There has been much speculation about Giacomino's life, but little is known for sure. He was a Franciscan friar from Verona who lived in the Veneto, in a city other than his own (possibly Venice) during the mid-thirteenth century. Judging from the musical expertise he shows in *Jerusalem*, he might have been a *magister cantus* in his convent.

Giacomino represents heaven and hell as two cities; this was a quite common view during the Middle Ages, and it also turns up in the topography of Dante's *Inferno* (the city of Dis) and, at feast figuratively (as metaphors and similes), in his *Paradiso*. In this instance, however, the reference may well be to imperial Rome rather than to Jerusalem. Drawing mainly on biblical sources, Franciscan visions, and the repertoire of preachers, Giacomino produces a vivid, if naive, picture of the Christian after life; he also resorts to fictitious examples and comparisons in order to evoke a sense of marvel in his readers (*Jerusalem*, 165–168; *Babilonia*, 35–36). *Jerusalem* is, as one might expect, more descriptive; *Babilonia* tends to be more dramatic. In *Jerusalem*, crystal, silver, gold, and precious stones are combined with the vernal delights of the *locus amoenus* (pleasant place) in order to build up the heavenly city, from which all earthly miseries and dangers are banned. The angels and the blessed, in splendid attire, gather around the throne of God (unpretentiously visualized as Jesus Christ) and sing his praise in the most melodious way, while being directed by Jesus himself (170). At the end of the poem, particular attention is given to the glory of Mary: in a courtly vein, she is introduced as a dignified *chatelaine* surrounded by her champion knights, to whom she graciously offers fragrant wreaths, dazzling palfreys, and well-deserved coats of arms (285–316).

As an urban landscape, Giacomino's hell in *Babilonia* is the terrifying opposite of his paradise. Bronze, iron, and steel are the metals that make up its walls and even its sky. The fire is blazing, the stench unbearable. The watchmen perched on the main gate do not let any inmate escape but are eager to lay hands on newcomers. The reader discovers many of these horrors through the experience of a newly arrived sinner, and both reader and sinner are bound to be appalled by the rigor of divine justice. Swarms of hyperactive, sadistic, raving devils torture the damned with great inventiveness while making sarcastic comments about the futile laments of their victims. Two unforgettable highlights are a sinner roasted on a spit by chef Balzabù and then presented in spicy sauce to the king of hell, who predictably finds the meat only half-cooked and sends it back to the fire (117–136); and a shocking debate between a father and son who fiercely blame each other for their damnation.

Further Reading

Barana, E. *La "Gerusalemme celeste" e la "Babilonia infernale" di Giacomino da Verona, secondo la lezione dei quattro codici conosciuti*. Verona, 1921.

Contini, Gianfranco, ed. *Poeti del Duecento*. Milan: Ricciardi, 1960, Vol. 1, pp. 625–652; Vol. 2, pp. 842–843.

De Sanctis, Francesco, and Gerolamo Lazzeri, eds. *Storia della letteratura italiana dai primi secoli agli albori del Trecento*. Milan: Hoepli, 1950, pp. 132–136 and 219–237.

Dionisotti, Carlo, and Cecil Grayson, eds. *Early Italian Texts*, 2nd ed. Oxford: Blackwell, 1965, pp. 153–161. (Originally published 1949.)

May, Esther Isopel. *The "De Jerusalem Celesti" and the "De Babilonia Infernali" of Fra Giacomino da Verona*. Florence: Le Monnier, 1930.

Mussafia, A. "Monumenti antichi di dialetti italiani." *Sitzungsberichte der k. k. Akademie der Wissenschaften in Wien, Philologisch-historische Klasse*, 46, 1864, pp. 113–235.

Ozanam, Antoine-Frédéric. *Documents inédits pour servir à l'histoire littéraire de l'Italie depuis le VIIIe siècle jusqu'au XIIIe*. Paris: Lecoffre, 1850, pp. 291ff.

Rossi, Aldo. "Poesia didattica e poesia popolare del Nord." In *Storia della letteratura italiana*. Vol. 1, *Le origini e il Duecento*, ed. Emilio Cecchi and Natalino Sapegno. Milan: Garzanti, 1981, pp. 377–383.

Schrage, Mark. "Giacomino da Verona: eine Übersicht zur forschungslage." *Letteratura Italiana Antica*, 3, 2002, pp. 278–298.

RUGGERO STEFANINI

GIACOMO DA LENTINI
(13th century)

Little is known about the life of the thirteenth-century poet Giacomo da Lentini. His fame as one of the most important notaries at the court of Frederick II was so firmly established that Dante refers to him simply as the *Notaro*, and in the codices Giacomo's name is usually preceded by this title; but there are surprisingly few documents testifying to his professional career. The year of his birth is unknown; but there is no room for doubt about his birthplace, since in two or three of his poems he describes himself as having been born in Lentino (*nato da Lentino*), a small locality on the eastern coast of Sicily. The documents bearing witness to his juridical activities date from 1233 and 1240. In 1233, two privileges were drawn up by the hand of Giacomo da Lentini—*per manus Iacobi de Lentino* (or *Lintin*)—the first one in March at Policoro on the Basilicata coast, and the second in June in Catania. The formula *per manus Iacobi notarii* is encountered in a document from Palermo and in a letter from Castrogiovanni (modern-day Enna) that same year; thus we have enough evidence to show that the *Notaro* must have accompanied the emperor on a journey in March–August 1233 from Policoro via Messina and Catania to Palermo. A document issued in Messina on 5 May 1240 bears the signature *Iacobus de Lentino domini Imperatoris notarius* (Giacomo da Lentini, notary of the emperor). Nothing else is known of the biography of the founder and most famous poet of the Sicilian school, and his end is veiled in mystery.

Internal evidence is of little help in establishing a chronology for Giacomo's life. In the canzone *Ben m'è venuto prima al cor doglienza*, he compares his lady's arrogance to the pride of Milan over its *carroccio* and makes a brief reference to a feud between Florence and Pisa. Sanesi (1899) and Gaspary (1882) assumed that Giacomo must have written this passage before the battle of Cortenuova in 1237, a battle at which the Milanese suffered a humiliating defeat. Torraca (1902), however, opted for 1246–1248 as the period when these lines were composed. In 1246, the Guelf Florentines voiced their dissatisfaction with the *podestà* appointed by the emperor, and in 1248 they were defeated by the Ghibellines. Zenatti (1896) dated the war between Florence and Pisa to 1233 and Santangelo (1959) suggested the summer of 1234, but Langley (1915) considered these references too vague to be of much use in dating the poem. A reference in *La 'namoranza disiosa* to a naval encounter near Syracuse, tentatively dated to 1205 by Cesareo (1924), offers no proof of the composition date, and it remains highly unlikely that this poem could have been written during the decade 1200–1210. The period of Giacomo's most intense poetic activity probably coincided with the years of his documented professional duties at the imperial court. The episode involving Bonagiunta da Lucca in Canto 24 of Dante's *Purgatorio* (verses 55–57) confirms Giacomo's role as the chief representative of the Sicilian school, and Dante praises the poem *Madonna dir vi voglio*, though without mentioning the poet by name. Giacomo's prestige may also be inferred from the poem *Di penne di paone e d'altre assai*, in which Chiaro Davanzati accuses Bonagiunta

of plagiarizing the *Notaro*. In the Vatican Codex (Vat. Lat. 3793), Giacomo is given more prominence than any of his contemporaries: his poems are listed first in each genre section; and with some forty pieces definitively attributed to him, he far outdistances all other Sicilian poets in sheer numbers.

We have little reason to doubt that Giacomo was instrumental in choosing an Italian dialect for poetry composed in the Provençal mode in Sicily. He may also have played a decisive role in imposing a very narrow thematic orientation on the school, and he is usually credited with being the inventor of the sonnet form. Except for a single sonnet on friendship, Giacomo wrote solely on amorous themes. Most of his *canzoni* are conventional in theme and style; and his sonnets, twenty-one in all, with four more of uncertain attribution, show the same adherence to the Provençal mode. Even at this early stage in its evolution, however, the sonnet tends to become more philosophically oriented, serving as a forum for discussions of the nature and power of love. In the poem *Amor non vole ch'io clami*, Giacomo ridicules the abuse of lovers' laments, but this satirical approach is itself purely conventional and does not reveal any beginnings of disenchantment with a stereotyped motif. This poem, therefore, is not to be considered a literary manifesto. Giacomo wrote many *canzoni* or *canzonette* of great technical simplicity, but other poems of his testify to his mastery of some of the most complex metrical schemes inherited from the troubadours.

See also **Bonagiunta Orbicciani degli Averardi; Frederick II**

Further Reading

Antonelli, Roberto, ed. *Giacomo da Lentini: Poesie*. Rome: Bulzoni, 1979.

Apollonio, Mario. *Uomini e forme nella cultura italiana delle origini*. Florence: Sansoni, 1943, pp. 208–217.

Cesareo, G. A. *Le origini delta poesia lirica e lapoesia siciliana sotto gli Svevi*, 2nd ed. Palermo: Sandron, 1924, pp. 124–131, 332–354.

Contini, Gianfranco, ed. *Poeti del Duecento*. Milan and Naples: Ricciardi, 1960, Vol. 1, pp. 49–90.

De Lollis, Cesare. "G. A. Cesareo, *La poesia siciliana sotto gli Svevi* (Catania, 1894)." In *Giornale Storico delta Letteratura Italiana*, 27, 1896, pp. 112ff. (Review of 1st ed.)

Gaspary, Adolfo. *La scuola poetica siciliana del secolo XIII*, trans. S. Friedmann. Livorno: Vigo, 1882.

Langley, Ernest F., ed. *The Poetry of Giacomo da Lentini, Sicilian Poet of the Thirteenth Century*. Cambridge, Mass.: Harvard University Press, 1915.

Pasquini, Emilio, and Antonio Enzo Quaglio. *Il Duecento dalle origini a Dante*. Bari: Laterza, 1970, pp. 189–203.

Sanesi, I. "Il toscaneggiamento della poesia siciliana." *Giornale Storico della Letteratum Italiana*, 34, 1899, pp. 354–367.

Santangelo, Salvatore. "La canzone *Ben m'è venuto* e la politica remissiva di Federico II." In *Saggi Critici*. Modena: Società Tipografica Editrice Modenese, 1959, pp. 191–209.

Torraca, Francesco. "Il notaro Giacomo da Lentino." In *Studi su la lirica italiana del Duecento*, pp. 1–88. Bologna: Zanichelli, 1902.

Zenatti, Albino. *Arrigo Testa e i primordi della lirica italiana.* Florence: Sansoni, 1896.

FREDE JENSEN

GILBERT OF POITIERS
(Gilbertus, Gislebertus, or Gillibertus Porreta or Porretanus; also, less correctly, de la Porrée, 1075/80–1154)

Gilbert was born in Poitiers and returned there as bishop in 1141 or 1142. After studying the liberal arts and philosophy with Hilary in Poitiers and Bernard in Chartres, he immersed himself in the study of the Bible in Laon. As Anselm of Laon's disciple, Gilbert participated in the great exegetical undertaking that was to culminate in the formation of the *Glossa ordinaria* in Paris during the middle decades of the century. Gilbert's commentaries on the Psalms (before 1117) and on the Epistles of Paul (perhaps a decade later) owed much to Anselm's glosses and to his use of *quaestiones* and *sententiae* to explore theological and pastoral topics. In addition, Gilbert introduced to scriptural exegesis pedagogical techniques, such as the *accessus ad auctores*, used by grammarians to teach works of profane literature. These methods influenced subsequent exegetes: Peter Lombard's biblical commentaries, for example, rely heavily on Gilbert's work.

Gilbert returned to Chartres as a canon and by 1126 was chancellor of the cathedral. (There is no evidence to support the claim that he taught in Poitiers.) Though he certainly taught in Chartres, most contemporary testimony associates Gilbert with Paris, where he is reported teaching grammar, logic, and theology and where he helped promote the biblical glosses that were developing into the *Glossa ordinaria.*

In his commentaries (ca. 1140) on the *Opuscula sacra* of Boethius, Gilbert distinguishes between different aspects of a being: that which a thing is (*id, quod est*) and that by which a thing is what it is (*id, quo est*). The resulting attempt to differentiate among persons, natures, attributes, and essences, when applied to Trinitarian issues, led Gilbert to the brink of disaster. In March 1148, after the Council of Reims, Gilbert's orthodoxy was examined on four counts: that God is not "divinity" or divine nature; that the Persons of the Trinity are not "divinity"; that God's properties are not God and are not eternal; that the divine nature is not incarnate. The theologians present at the consistory never got a chance to debate these propositions fully: when it became clear that the curia sided with Gilbert, Bernard of Clairvaux (appointed to the prosecution) drew up a "confession of faith" of sound spiritual instinct (but loose terminology)

that he presented to Eugenius III, in effect pressuring the pope to declare either Gilbert or Bernard a heretic. Eugenius sidestepped the maneuver and made some token pronouncements regarding theological language; Gilbert, acquitted of heresy, declared that he "believed whatever Eugenius believed" and promised to correct any offending passages in his writings. No such, "corrections" were ever made, to Bernard's chagrin.

See also **Anselm of Laon; Bernard of Chartres; Bernard of Clairvaux**

Further Reading

Gilbert of Poitiers. *The Commentaries on Boethius*, ed. Nikolaus M. Häring. Toronto: Pontifical Institute of Mediaeval Studies, 1966.

Colish, Marcia L. "Early Porretan Theology." *Recherches de théologie ancienne et médiévale* 56 (1989): 59–79.

Gross-Diaz, Theresa. *The Psalms Commentary of Gilbert of Poitiers: From lectio divina to the Lecture Room.* Leiden: Brill.

Häring, Nikolaus M. "Handschriftliches zu den Werken Gilberts, Bishof von Poitiers." *Revue d'histoire des textes* 8 (1978): 133–94.

Maioli, Bruno. *Gilberto Porretano: dalla grammatics speculative alla metafisica del concreto.* Rome: Bulzoni, 1979.

Nielsen, Lauge Olaf. *Theology and Philosophy in the Twelfth Century: A Study of Gilbert of Porreta's Thinking and the Theological Expositions of the Doctrine of the Incarnation During the Period 1130–1180.* Leiden: Brill, 1982.

van Elswijk, H.C. *Gilbert Poneta: sa vie, son œuvre, sa pensée.* Louvain: Spicilegium Sacrum Lovaniense, 1966.

THERESA GROSS-DIAZ

GILES OF ROME
(Aegidius Colonna; ca. 1243–1316)

One of the most outstanding students of Thomas Aquinas, Giles was born at Rome, perhaps of the Colonna family. Contrary to his family's wishes, Giles embraced the religious life ca. 1258 at the convent of Santa Maria del Populo of the Hermits of St. Augustine. Arriving at Paris ca. 1260, he studied and taught there until 1278. He heard the lectures of Thomas during the latter's second period of teaching at Paris (1269–71) and strenuously defended Thomistic teachings against Bishop Étienne Tempier's condemnation in 1277. This dispute with the bishop occasioned Giles's departure from Paris; the bishop's death helped smooth the way for Giles's return in 1285 as master of theology and the first Augustinian friar to hold a chair in theology at Paris (1285–91).

King Philip III of France had charged Giles with the education of his son, the future Philip IV the Fair, for whom Giles composed perhaps his best-known work, *De regimine principum* (1280). By 1282, the work had been translated into French and in the 14th century was translated into Castilian, Portuguese, Catalan, English,

German, and Hebrew. The work was an admirable combination of Aristotelian ethics and Christian moral and spiritual teaching.

Giles maintained good relations with Philip, and in the year following his election to the post of prior-general of the Augustinians (1292) Philip granted the order the Grand Convent of the Augustinians in Paris. In 1295, Pope Boniface VIII, with Philip's consent, elevated Giles to the archiepiscopal see of Bourges. But in the ensuing controversy between Philip and Boniface, Giles sided with Boniface, composing the treatise *De ecclesiastica potestate* (1301)—one of the principal sources for the papal bull *Unam sanctam* (1302) and one of the broadest expressions of papal supremacy in the entire controversy.

Following the death of Boniface, Giles returned to his duties in Bourges. He was active in several controversies at the time, among them the disputes with the Templars and with Peter Olivi. He was active at the Council of Vienne (1311–12) and died a few years later in Avignon.

As a teacher, Giles lectured according to the prescribed course of study, commenting first on the Bible and on the *Sententiae* of Peter Lombard; but his greatest love was philosophy. He left commentaries on many of Aristotle's works on logic, physics, and metaphysics, including the Pseudo-Aristotelian *Liber de causis*. His works were held in such high esteem that the general chapter of his order meeting at Florence in 1287 declared that his "opinions, positions, and conclusions [*sententiae*] both written and yet to be written" were to receive the unqualified assent of all Augustinian teachers and students. The Franciscan philosopher William of Ockham went so far as to speak of Giles as the "Expositor" of Aristotle's *Physics*.

Giles was an independent thinker, and though he shared many ideas with Aquinas he disagreed markedly with him on the relationship between essence and existence. For Giles, these are two separate things, the latter not necessarily implied in the former. In this way, he stressed the contingency of all things on the will of God and enunciated a theme that would become one of the hallmarks of later nominalism.

See also **Aquinas, Thomas; Boniface VIII, Pope; Ockham, William of; Peter Lombard**

Further Reading

Giles of Rome. *De ecclesiastica potestate*, ed. Richard Scholz. Weimar: Böhlaus, 1929.
——. *Errores philosophorum*, ed. Josef Koch, trans. John Riedl. Milwaukee: Marquette University Press, 1944.
——. Sermons. In *Repertorium der lateinischen Sermones des Mittelalters von 1150–1350*, ed. Johannes-Baptist Schneyer. 6 vols. Münster: Aschendorff, 1969–74, Vol. 1, p. 57.
Hocediz, E. "La condemnation de Gilles de Rome." *Recherches de théologie ancienne et médiévale* 4 (1932): 34–58.
Luna, C. "La lecture de Gilles de Rome sur le quatrième livre des sentences: les extraits du Clm 8005." *Recherches de théologie ancienne et médiévale* 57 (1992): 183–255.
Nash, P.W. "Giles of Rome: Auditor and Critic of St Thomas." *Modern Schoolman* 28 (1950): 1–20.
——. "Giles of Rome on Boethius' *Diversum est esse et id quod est*." *Medieval Studies* 12 (1950): 57–91.
——. "The Accidentally of *Esse* According to Giles of Rome." *Gregorianum* 38 (1957): 103–15.

MARK ZIER

GIOTTO DI BONDONE
(c. 1266–1337)

Giotto (Giotto di Bondone), a Florentine painter from Colle di Vespignano, near Florence, was the single most important figure in the redirection of the arts away from medieval stylization to Renaissance naturalism. During his lifetime, Giotto received a level of acclaim accorded to no other medieval artist. The revolutionary aspect of his accomplishment was already understood by his contemporaries. By 1316, Dante proclaimed Giotto the most famous painter of the day in a passage (*Purgatorio*, 11.94–96) decrying the folly of pride:

> Credette Cimabue ne la pittura
> tener lo campo, e ora ha Giotto il grido,
> si che la fama di colui è scura.

("Once, Cimabue thought to hold the field / in painting; Giotto's all the rage today; / The other's fame lies in the dust concealed.") Boccaccio, in the *Decameron* (c. 1350), credited Giotto with bringing back to light a true, intellectual art, which had lain in neglect for centuries. Giotto's work continued to serve as a model for Florentine artists from the *Quattrocento* to the high Renaissance, when the young Michelangelo copied motifs from the Peruzzi Chapel in Santa Croce in Florence.

Administrative, legal, and literary documents attest to Giotto's long, prolific, and far-ranging career. Despite this, little is certainly known or agreed on about the artistic career of this master. Only a select core of work is today ascribed to Giotto with any consensus. Among these works, the Arena Chapel in Padua, decorated with frescoes as a family chapel or oratory for Enrico Scrovegni between 1302 and 1306, serves as the most secure anchor for an understanding of Giotto's style. The interior of the Arena Chapel is covered from floor to vault with an epic cycle of frescoes illustrating the redemption of humankind, leading from the lives of Joachim and Anna, Mary, and Christ to an enormous Last Judgment covering the west entrance wall.

The other major series of undisputed works are the fresco cycles for two adjacent chapels—those of the Bardi and the Peruzzi—in the Franciscan church of Santa Croce in Florence. The Bardi Chapel, immediately to the right of the high altar, features seven scenes from the life of Saint Francis; the Peruzzi Chapel, painted in *fresco secco* and now in poor condition, depicts three scenes each of the lives of saints John the Evangelist and John the Baptist, themes probably suggested by the patron's name, Giovanni Peruzzi. These two cycles are key works in any reconstruction of Giotto's career, but both lack any documentation whatsoever. The only certainty is that they postdate the cycle in the Arena Chapel and give us our best indication of Giotto's later activity. Most of Giotto's documented works— such as his frescoes for the Lateran Palace in Rome, painted for the jubilee year of 1300; and the Navicella mosaic for the facade of old Saint Peter's in Rome (possibly 1310), Giotto's most celebrated composition in his own day—survive only in much altered fragments. His signed works, such as the Baroncelli Altar-piece (in Santa Croce, Florence; possibly 1328) and the Bologna Polyptych (in the Pinacoteca, Bologna; possibly 1332), are manifestly not products of his own hand but rather workshop assemblages probably following his designs.

Giotto's great success and fortune in his day is attested to by numerous known circumstances: the large workshop under his training, including such subsequently successful artists as Bernardo Daddi, Maso di Banco, and Taddeo Gaddi; his numerous land purchases and business transactions, recorded in various archives, including guarantees of loans and the lease of a loom for a considerable sum; and his extensive sojourns in the Italian peninsula and beyond. He went to Rome, Rimini, Padua, Naples (from 1328 to 1334; there, he was made first painter to King Robert of Anjou), Milan (where he was sent by the commune of Florence to work in the service of Duke Azzone Sforza in 1336), and possibly Avignon. Late in life Giotto was honored with appointments as head of works at Santa Reparata, the cathedral of Florence; and as chief engineer to the city of Florence, in which capacity he designed the campanile, or bell tower, of the cathedral.

The magnitude of Giotto's accomplishment is still breathtaking. His works have a physical and psychological naturalism that seems thoroughly removed from medieval conventions of stylization and abstraction. When one compares Cimabue's Santa Croce Crucifix (1280s, Museo dell'Opera di Santa Croce, Florence), which was already quite innovative for the suppleness of its forms, with Giotto's Santa Maria Novella Cross (1301–1302, Santa Maria Novella, Florence), executed only some twenty years later, a vast gulf seems to separate the two. Cimabue's gracefully abstracted symbolic presence of Christ on the cross contrasts with the corpse depicted by Giotto—the body extended forward in space, the legs buckled under its weight, the head hanging down, and the face in a death grimace. Giotto's brutal rendering is, in fact, the first thoroughly realistic portrayal of

Christ crucified in the history of Christian imagery. His *Madonna and Child Enthroned*, painted for the church of the Ognissanti in Florence (1306–1310; now in the Uffizi, Florence), advances this insistent realism even further. Through sheer volume, the Madonna conveys a commanding physical presence. Great pleats of cloth clearly articulate the massive form of the body beneath the drapery, and the angels and saints overlap one another in space as they attentively turn their gaze on the mother and child. No longer a miniature adult as in Cimabue's Santa Trinita Maestà (c. 1280, Uffizi, Florence), Giotto's Christ child has the chubby constitution of a real infanr. Perhaps most compelling for the viewer's sense of communion with the divine, especially in comparison with the slightly earlier maestàs of Cimabue or Duccio, the throne in Giotto's *Madonna and Child Enthroned* truly seems to surround and sustain the great bulk of the Madonna, and to project forward believably into space. A series of steps leads logically up to the Madonna and child; the viewer is given the impression of implicit accessibility to the divine by this clear path of approach. In fact, the Ognissanti *Madonna and Child Enthroned* is ingeniously designed as a participatory work of art, for the Christ child's blessing is actuated only when viewers stand before the altarpiece, completing the circle of adoration that has been left open in order to include them. No earlier *maestà* had made the presence of the divine so persuasive, and subsequent treatments such as Duccio's great *Maestà* (1309–1311) for the high altar of the cathedral in Siena were perhaps influenced by Giotto's spatially convincing design.

Besides his volumetric and spatial constructions, Giotto man ifested a genius for narrative drama; his scenes of the *Life of the Virgin and Christ* in the Arena Chapel or the *Life of Saint Francis* in the Bardi Chapel in Santa Croce display some of the canniest understanding of human nature ever set down in paint. This physical and psychological realism is perfectly congruent with the evangelical designs of a contemporary movement: the mendicant orders, such as the Dominicans and above all the Franciscans, that earnestly sought to educate the public in the message of the faith through empathic meditation on the lives of the central protagonists of the Christian saga of salvation, especially Mary and Christ. Giotto's sponsorship chiefly by Franciscan patronage throughout his career was certainly no coincidence, for his lifelike rendering of biblical narratives was precisely the kind of physical cue the Franciscans sought to effect a union between layman and creed.

One of the most intractable problems in art history has been unraveling the mystery of Giotto's beginnings. To develop his revolution, Giotto clearly had to draw on extant sources and ideas. Most obvious is his debt to the sculptors Arnolfo di Cambio, Nicola Pisano, and Nicola's son Giovanni Pisano, whose works of the later

Duecento are infused with a similar pursuit of monumentality, a natural outcome in the medium of sculpture. But the works of Nicola Pisano and, especially, Giovanni Pisano also indicate an interest in narrative legibility, dramatic focus, and distinct psychological states that presage Giotto's narrative studies. Certain painters of the Roman school, particularly Pietro Cavallini, point toward the volumetric buildup of forms in Giotto's painting. In addition, Giotto was influenced by artists who had previously absorbed his lessons. The complex architectural skyline that serves as the backdrop for the *Raising of Drusiana* in the Peruzzi Chapel, for example, is preceded by the intricate cityscape of the *Entry into Jerusalem* from the rear of Duccio's *Maestà*. The legend of Giotto's tutelage under Cimabue, first set down in a late *Trecento* commentary on the *Divine Comedy* and picked up by Lorenzo Ghiberti (*Commentarii*, c. 1450), is difficult to comprehend as a logical stylistic progression. Especially controversial is Giotto's presumed authorship as a young master of a great portion of the frescoes in the nave of the upper basilica at Assisi, particularly two well-preserved Old Testament scenes—*Isaac Blessing Jacob and Isaac Rejecting Esau*—and the bulk of *Scenes of the Life of Saints Francis*, probably painted in the 1280s–1290s. Through the nineteenth century, these frescoes were considered Giotto's, virtually without question; but later a growing coterie of scholars, including Richard Offner and Millard Meiss, found it difficult to see them as congruent with the body of Giotto's work—although it should be noted that other scholars (such as Cesare Gnudi and Luciano Bellosi) believe that no comprehension of Giotto's style is possible without them. The frescoes in Assisi serve as a fascinating test case for paradigms of artistic formation and development, since different attributions and chronologies lead naturally to wholly different conclusions about the artist.

Giotto's style was so persuasive that, once it had been introduced, it spread like wildfire in any center which was exposed to his idiom. Thus Padua, Rimini, Rome, Naples, and especially Florence had successive generations of Giottesque painters. Despite the popularity of his approach, however, only a few artists, including Maso di Banco and the Lorenzetti brothers, understood the profound implications of his spatial narratives. Partly as a result of a change in outlook and patronage brought about by the black death, it took the greater part of a century for another artist to appear who comprehended the real potential of Giotto's vision. It was Masaccio, in the 1420s in Florence, who effected a return once and for all to the grave and monumental sobriety of Giotto's approach in painting.

See also **Arnolfo di Cambio; Cimabue; Dante Alighieri; Duccio di Buoninsegna**

Further Reading

Baccheschi, Edi, and Andrew Martindale. *The Complete Paintings of Giotto*. New York: Abrams, 1966.
Basile, Giuseppe, ed. *Giotto: La cappella degli Scrovegni*. Milan: Electa, 1992.
Battisti, Eugenio. *Giotto: Biographical and Critical Study*, trans. J. Emmons. Lausanne: Skira, 1966.
Bellosi, Luciano. *La pecora di Giotto*. Turin: Giulio Enaudi, 1985.
——. *Giotto at Assisi*. Assisi: DACA, 1989.
Bistoletti, Sandrina Bandera. *Giotto: Catalogo completo dei dipinti*. Florence: Cantini, 1989.
Brandi, Cesare. *Giotto*. Milan: Mondadori, 1983.
Cole, Bruce. *Giotto and Florentine Painting, 1280–1375*. New York: Harper and Row, 1976.
Gnudi, Cesare. *Giotto*. Milan: Martello, 1959.
Ladis, Andrew, ed. *Franciscanism, the Papacy, and Art in the Age of Giotto: Assisi and Rome*. Giotto and the World of Early Italian Art, 4. New York: Garland, 1998a.
——. *Giotto as a Historical and Literary Figure: Miscellaneous Specialized Studies*. Giotto and the World of Early Italian Art, 1. New York: Garland, 1998b.
——. *Giotto, Master Painter and Architect: Florence*. Giotto and the World of Early Italian Art, 3. New York: Garland, 1998c.
——. ed. *The Arena Chapel and the Genius of Giotto: Padua*. Giotto and the World of Early Italian Art, 2. New York: Garland, 1998.
Offner, Richard. "Giotto, Non-Giotto." *Burlington Magazine*, 74, 1939, pp. 259–268; 75, 1939, pp. 96–113.
Previtali, Giovanni. *Giotto e la sua bottega*. Milan: Fabbri, 1967.
Salvini, Roberto. *Giotto: Bibliografia*. Rome: Palombi, 1938.
Sirén, Osvald. *Giotto and Some of His Followers*, trans. F. Schenck. Cambridge, Mass.: Harvard University Press, 1917.
Smart, Alastair. *The Assisi Problem and the Art of Giotto*. New York: Hacker Art, 1983.
Stubblebine, James. *Assisi and the Rise of Vernacular Art*. New York: Harper and Row, 1985.

GUSTAV MEDICUS

GIOVANNI DEL VIRGILIO
(fourteenth century)

Giovanni del Virgilio became famous as a professor of classical poetry at Bologna in the 1320s. His life and career were connected with those of two of his contemporaries, the Paduan protohumanist Albertino Mussato (1261–1329) and the Florentine poet Dante Alighieri (1265–1321). Giovanni was given the name Virgilio in reference to his pedagogical and scholarly devotion to the Roman poet Virgil. He was formally hired by the University of Bologna in 1321 to lecture on Virgil, Statius, Ovid, and Lucan, but he had already been teaching there in some capacity before that date. He appears to have spent the years 1324–1325 in Cesena, where he probably composed an eclogue to Mussato. After 1327 we lose all record of him.

Giovanni's fame rests primarily on his correspondence in Latin hexameters with Dante in 1319–1320 and the epitaph he composed for Dante's tomb that was recorded by Boccaccio in his life of Dante. The correspondence has come down to us in the Laurentian Library manuscript 29.8, which was owned and possibly copied by Boccaccio. This manuscript also contains the longer eclogue to Mussato, two other verse epistles, and part of an epic poem about a besieged city and the conquered queen's pleas for mercy. This last fragment reflects Giovanni's protohumanist Virgilian mind-set, which rather pedantically deemed great literature the eloquent account in Latin hexameters of a contemporary political or military event. This is the source of Giovanni's dismay at Dante's choice of argument and vernacular expression—a dismay that prompted Giovanni to initiate the Latin correspondence. In the first epistle, Giovanni suggests worthy matter from contemporary Italian history for a proper Latin opus: the tragic drama of the late Holy Roman emperor Henry VII in his struggles in Italy; the recent aggression by Uguccione della Faggiuola in Tuscany; the victories of the imperial vicar Cangrande della Scala (Dante's esteemed patron and the dedicatee of *Paradiso*, and Mussato's nemesis) against Padua. Giovanni chastises Dante for wasting his talent by trying to bring serious themes to the vulgar herd (*seria vulgo*). Ever the professor, Giovanni begs of Dante something worthy of academic study. He offers to place the coveted laurel crown, the ancient sign of literary glory, on Dante's brow in triumphant celebration amid the scholars of Bologna.

Dante satisfies his request, though not without some degree of ironic—perhaps even affectionately mocking—play. Dante had already been resident for some years in Ravenna at the court of Guido Novello da Polenta when he received the missive from Bologna. He takes up Giovanni's classical challenge by reviving the highly stylized conventions of the eclogue or pastoral poem, usually a dialogue among shepherds in a prelapsarian fantasy land. Virgil had written ten. Thus Dante casts himself as Tityrus, his friend and fellow exile Dino Parini as Meliboeus, and Giovanni as Mopsus. Within this elaborate code, Dante explains that he should defer the poetic coronation until he has completed *Paradiso* and hopes even then to be celebrated in his native Florence. Hoping to improve Giovanni's opinion of his vernacular verse, Dante announces that he will send along "ten bottles" (*decem vascula*) of milk from a segregated, much-loved sheep of his flock (*ovis gratissima*), as yet unmilked and on the verge of bursting (*ubera vix quae ferre potest, tam lactis abundans*). Some critics take this as a reference to ten cantos of *Paradiso*, a significant confirmation that the poem was circulating in part before its completion.

In response, Giovanni delights in taking up the pastoral fiction and returns a work strongly dependent on Virgil's second eclogue, in which the shepherd Corydon sings his love for the beautiful young boy Alexis. At the end of Virgil's poem, Corydon threatens to find himself "another Alexis" (*alienum Alexim*) should his affections continue to be scorned. Giovanni's eclogue professes his admiration and love for Dante, sympathizes with Dante's desire to be celebrated in Florence, but implores him nonetheless to visit Bologna, where an alluring pastoral idyll awaits ("Alexis shall spread wild thyme to be thy couch..."). Finally, Giovanni warns that should Dante scorn him, he will "quench his thirst at the Phrygian Musone," a reference to Padua's river and to Mussato, Dante's poetic rival. Curiously (for us), Giovanni appears to have considered Mussato the greater poet: Mussato had, after all, composed his epic *Ecerinis* on the cruel tyranny of Ezzelino in Padua and had accordingly been crowned poet laureate in 1315, a distinction which neither Dante nor Giovanni had achieved and which inspired awe in Giovanni at least.

The response from Dante apparently reached Giovanni in Bologna only after Dante's death. In this enigmatic final eclogue, Dante relates that he would visit Bologna were it not for his fear of a certain "Polyphemus," whose precise identity remains a mystery. In his (never inscribed) epitaph for Dante's tomb, Giovanni lauds him as theologian, philosopher, and "glory of the muses, most-loved author of the common people" (*gloria musarum, vulgo gratissitnus auctor*), who wrote in both Latin and the vernacular (*laicis rhetoricisque modis*). Of Dante's works, Giovanni singles out for mention the *Comedy*, *Monarchia*, and, appropriately, the series of eclogues interrupted by his death.

Giovanni was also the author of a verse epistle known as *Diaffonus* and several pedagogical works: commentaries on Virgil's *Georgics* and Ovid and a brief *ars dictaminis*.

See also **Albertino Mussato; Dante Alighieri**

Further Reading

Alessio, Gian Carlo. "I trattati grammaticali di Giovanni del Virgilio." *Italia Medioevale e Umanistica*, 24, 1981, pp. 159–212.

Cestaro, Gary P. "Virgilio, Giovanni del." In *The Dante Encyclopedia*, ed. Richard Lansing. New York and London: Garland, 2000, pp. 865–866.

"Egloge." In *Dante Alighieri, Opere Minori*, Vol. 2, ed. Enzo Cecchini. Milan and Naples: Ricciardi, 1979, pp. 645–689.

Kristeller, Paul Oskar. "Un' *Ars dictaminis* di Giovanni del Virgilio." *Italia Medioevale e Umanistica*, 4, 1961, pp. 181–200.

Martellotti, Guido. "Egloghe. In *Enciclopedia dantesca*, Vol. 2. Rome: Istituto della Enciclopedia Italiana, 1970a, pp. 644–646.

——. "Giovanni del Virgilio." In *Enciclopedia dantesca*, Vol. 3. Rome: Istituto della Enciclopedia Italiana, 1970b, pp. 193–194.

Raffit, Guy P. "Dante's Mocking Pastoral Muse." *Dante Studies*, 114, 1996, pp. 271–291.

Wicksteed, Philip H., and Edmund G. Gardner. *Dante and Giovanni del Virgilio*. Westminster: A. Constable, 1902. (Reprint, New York: Haskell House, 1970.)

GARY P. CESTARO

GIOVANNI DI PIANO CARPINI
(c. 1180–1252)

Giovanni was born at Pian di Carpini (Piano delia Magione) in Umbria and was a first-generation Franciscan, from c. 1220. He served as a provincial official in Germany, Spain, and possibly Barbary. His fame, however, rests on his mission to the court of the Mongol khan.

Pope Innocent IV chose Giovanni and two other friars to act as emissaries to protest against the Mongols' expansion into Christian Europe, perhaps to gain aid against militant Islam, and to observe the Mongols closely. The party departed from Lyon in April 1245 and arrived at Karakorum on 22 July 1246. The new khan, Kuyuk (enthroned on 24 August) promised nothing and made no concessions, dismissing the envoys in November. After a hard winter's journey they arrived in Kiev in June 1247, and they were with the pope in Lyon seventeen months later. The pope made Giovanni bishop of Antivari (Dalmatia) in 1248; but after a dispute over the see Giovanni returned to Italy, where he died, near Perugia, on 1 August 1252.

Giovanni's *Historic Mongolorum* (*Mongol History*), or *Liber Tatarorum* (*Book of the Tartars*), constitutes his official report on the mission. It is a generally reliable discussion of the territories traversed and the peoples encountered. Although it was not published in full until the nineteenth century, it circulated in Europe and was used by, among others, Vincent of Beauvais (*Speculum Historiale*, c. 1260) and Roger Bacon (*Opus mains*, c. 1266).

Further Reading

Dawson, Christopher, ed. *The Mission to Asia*. Toronto: University of Toronto Press, 1986.

Saunders, J. J. "John of Plan Carpini: The Papal Envoy to the Mongol Conquerors Who Traveled through Russia to Eastern Asia in 1245–1247." *History Today*, 22, 1972, pp. 547–555.

Spuler, Benold. *History of the Mongols, Based on Eastern and Western Accounts of the Thirteenth and Fourteenth Centuries*, trans. Helga and Stuart Drummond. Berkeley: University of California Press, 1972.

JOSEPH P. BYRNE

GIUSTO DE' MENABUOI
(fl. 14th century)

Giusto de' Menabuoi was a northern Italian painter. The earliest secure record of him is a dismembered polyptych signed and dated March 1363, of Milanese provenance (parts of this polyptych are now in the Kress Collection at the University of Georgia at Athens). A signed and dated tabernacle of 1367 (now in the National Gallery, London) was also painted in Milan, according to its inscription. Some frescoes in and near Milan may be attributed to Giusto on the basis of their style. The most significant of these are in the tribune of the Abbazia di San Pietro at Viboldone. A Madonna and Child with saints and donor bears the date 1349; if the attribution is correct, this would be the artist's earliest surviving work. The Last Judgment on the three other walls of the tribune was done by Giusto after an interval of at least five years. No documents mentioning Giusto have been found in the Milanese archives, and none dealing with his origins in Florence has yet come to light.

That Giusto was born and trained in Florence is evident from his style and from documents in the Paduan archives. He is first documented in Padua in September 1373, but some frescoes in the church of the Eremitani in that city may be attributed to him and dated c. 1370. Sometime after 1367, when he painted the tabernacle that is now in London, Giusto transferred his activities to Padua. From the time of his arrival there until the end of his career, he worked for the powerful and ambitious lord of Padua, Francesco da Carrara the Elder, and Francesco's court. Giusto was probably called to fill the vacancy left by the death of the most important earlier local painter, Guariento di Arpo, who had enjoyed the patronage of the house of Carrara. From 1373 to 1382, Giusto is mentioned in Paduan documents at regular intervals. He became a citizen of Padua in April 1375. After 1382, there is no mention of Giusto in the Paduan archives until July 1387. He died in Padua sometime between then and May 1391. His name is inscribed in 1387 in the register of the painters' guild in Florence, but there is no evidence that he was there at the time.

The most important works by Giusto in Padua are not strictly documented, but they are strongly supported by local tradition and by comparison with signed paintings from his Lombard period. They are the votive fresco of the Coronation of the Virgin in the basilica of Saint Anthony (c.1380); the heavily repainted frescoes in the Belludi (or Conti) Chapel of the same church, depicting scenes from the legends of the Blessed Luca Belludi, Saint James the Less, and Saint Philip, probably newly completed for the consecration of the chapel in September 1382; and the decoration of the cathedral baptistery.

The Romanesque baptistery was redecorated by Giusto to serve as the mausoleum of Francesco da Carrara the Elder and his wife, Fina Buzzacarina. Work probably had been completed by October 1378, when Fina was buried in her wall tomb (later destroyed). Francesco, who died in a Visconti prison at Monza, was interred in November 1393 in a freestanding sepulchre (also later destroyed). The fresco decoration covers every available surface and is encyclopedic in scope. It reflects the dual nature of the building as baptistery and mausoleum—functions that were closely linked since early times. In the principal dome is a representation of Paradise; the Pantocrator and Virgin Orante are Byzantine elements explicable by the proximity of Venice. On the drum is an extensive series from Genesis; and stories of the Virgin, Christ, and John the Baptist cover the walls. The exhaustive Apocalypse cycle in the apse seems to depend, either directly or indirectly, on an illuminated manuscript of the twelfth or thirteenth century. The polyptych is also richly embellished with narrative scenes from the legend of John the Baptist.

The identity of Giusto's master is a subject of debate. Giusto's early works suggest that he was trained in Florence in the work shop of Bernardo Daddi. Giusto turned to Daddi's master, Giotto, for the fundamentals of his style. Direct borrowings from Giotto's work in the Arena Chapel may be seen as early as Giusto's Viboldone Last Judgment and in the London tabernacle. Giusto's Lombard work also reflects Giovanni da Milano; and throughout his career Giusto utilized recent Florentine sources. Giusto influenced Lombard fresco painting in its most advanced Tuscan phase of the 1360s and slightly later manuscript illumination in the region, although Giovanni da Milano, a native, had a more profound impact. Similarly, Giusto's presence helped invigorate Paduan painting at a time when art in Florence had stagnated through a relaxation of Giottesque principles. Again, although Giusto influenced monumental painting and manuscript illumination in Padua until about the turn of the century, the style of a local artist, Altichiero, was dominant. Despite some concessions to indigenous naturalism, particularly an expansion of the number of figures and their spatial setting, Giusto's art was fundamentally Florentine and hence less accessible to local taste.

See also **Daddi, Bernardo; Giotto di Bondone**

Further Reading

Bettini, Sergio. *Giusto de' Menabuoi e l'arte del Trecento*. Padua: Le Tre Venezie, 1944.
——. *Le pitture di Giusto de' Menabuoi nel Battistero del Duomo di Padova*. Venice: Neri Pozza, 1960.
Delaney, Bradley Joseph. *Giusto de' Menabuoi: Iconography and Style*. Ann Arbor, Mich.: University Microfilms, 1972.
——. "Giusto de' Menabuoi in Lombardy." *Art Bulletin*, 58, 1976, pp. 19–35.

BRADLEY J. DELANEY

GODEFROI DE BOUILLON
(ca. 1061–1100)

Duke of Lower Lorraine, leader of the First Crusade, and first Latin ruler of Jerusalem, Godefroi was the second son of Count Eustache II of Boulogne and of Ide, daughter of Duke Godefroi II of Lower Lorraine. In 1076, the emperor Henry IV refused him the succession to his grandfather's duchy, but Godefroi finally acceded in 1089.

He participated in the First Crusade in 1096 along with his brothers Eustache III of Boulogne and Baudouin, choosing the land route via Hungary. On arriving at Constantinople, he at first refused the requested oath to the emperor Alexios I Comnenos but consented finally after an attack on the suburbs of the city when the emperor cut off provisions for his forces. Though he did not figure as prominently as the other crusading leaders prior to their arrival at Jerusalem, his forces were the first to break in, and he became the compromise candidate for ruler of the Holy City. Refusing the title king, he became the Advocate of the Holy Sepulcher and secured the Latin position in Palestine by defeating an invading relief army from Fatimid Egypt at Ascalon.

Godefroi's rule was brief and made difficult by the ambitions of the other crusading leaders, He also had to deal with the pretensions to rule of Daimbert of Pisa, the first Latin patriarch of Jerusalem. On his death (July 18, 1100), he was succeeded by his younger brother, Baudouin, who had founded the first of the Crusading States at Edessa and who took the title king of Jerusalem.

Godefroi's life almost immediately became the stuff of legends. He was one of the three medieval members, with Charlemagne and Arthur, of the Nine Worthies and is the principal hero of the Crusade epics, including the 35,000-line *Chevalier au cygne et Godefroid de Bouillon* (1356), the final reworking of the cycle.

See also **Henry IV, Emperor**

Further Reading

Andressohn, John Carl. *The Ancestry and Life of Godfrey of Bouillon*. Bloomington: Indiana University Press, 1947.

R. THOMAS MCDONALD

GODFREY OF VITERBO
(c. 1125–after 1202)

The poet-historian Godfrey of Viterbo was Italian by birth but of recent German ancestry. He was taken to Germany at an early age and was educated in the cathedral school of Bamberg. Returning to Italy, probably shortly after 1140, he entered the papal chancery; but within a decade he was back in Germany as a member of the royal chapel under Conrad III (d. 1151). Godfrey served the emperors Frederick I Barbarossa and Henry VI as court chaplain and notary, taking part in their Italian expeditions until at least 1186, when he witnessed a document for Henry during the siege of Orvieto. His official travels also took him to France many times and less often to Provence, Sicily, and Spain. After he had retired to his native Viterbo, he revised and in 1191 completed his selective world history in Latin verse and prose, *Pantheon*. A note at the end of a later poem, *Gesta Henrici sexti* (*Deeds of Henry VI*), mentions the death in Sicily of the imperial steward Markward of Anweiler (September 1202). The aged Godfrey is unlikely to have long survived Markward.

Pantheon, Godfrey's major literary accomplishment, is in concept a pro-Staufen imperial chronicle from biblical and early pagan times to his own day. Its title—a Greek compound meaning "all-divine"—suggests the universality of its scope and the divine origin of the political and theological wisdom it expounds. This work took shape in several stages, of which the first was the largely verse *Speculum regum* (*Mirror of Kings*), dedicated to Henry VI and completed in 1183. *Speculum regum* was replaced in 1185 by *Memoria seculorum* (*Memory of the Ages*), subsequently renamed *Liber memorialis* (*Book of Memory*). That in turn was expanded into the more encyclopedic *Liber universalis* (*Book of All*), itself the basis for three successive versions of the final Pantheon. Supplementary writings include *Gesta Friderici* (*Deeds of Frederick*), in verse; and the aforementioned *Gesta Henrid sexti*. Godfrey's *Pantheon* entertains as well as instructs and presents as fact, or at least neutrally, a significant amount of popular, legendary, or otherwise fictional material in fulfilment of its political objectives. Especially notable are an influential account of the Trojan origins of various European peoples and versions of the medieval *Prophecy of the Tiburtine Sibyl* and of the Latin romance of Apollonius of Tyre. Godfrey's preferred verse form, an uncommon strophe consisting of two rhyming hexameters followed by a single pentameter, may be thought of as an ennobled elegiac distich.

Godfrey's history, ostensibly aimed at young people but well suited for many adults, was widely read in the later Middle Ages. It survives in at least thirty-three more or less complete manuscripts (including the author's original for most of *Liber universalis*) and in fragments of many others. Resonances can be discerned in the writings of Brunetto Latini, Giovanni Villani, Quilichino of Spoleto, Orfino of Lodi, Riccobaldo of Ferrara, Tolomeo ("Ptolemy") of Lucca, Benzo of Alessandria, James of Acqui, Galvano Fiamma, and William of Pastrengo, to say nothing of the very considerable reception of *Pantheon* among non-Italians. The one modern attempt at a critical edition is incomplete and otherwise unsatisfactory.

Godfrey is also the apparent author of a 186-line political-geographical poem with autobiographical content, *Denumeratio regnorum imperio subiectorum* ("List of Kingdoms Subject to the Empire"), whose focus shifts toward the end to German-speaking cities.

Other minor writings have, with varying degrees of probability, also been assigned to him.

See also **Frederick I Barbarossa; Henry VI**

Further Reading

Editions

Delisle, Léopold, ed. *Denumeratio regnorum imperio subiectorum*. In *Littérature latine et histoire du moyen âge*. Paris: Ernest Leroux, 1890, pp. 41–50.

Waltz, Georg, ed. *Gotofridi Viterbiensis opera*. Monumenta Germaniae Historica, Scriptores, 22. Hannover: Hahn, 1872, pp. 1–376.

Critical Studies

Archibald, Elizabeth. *Apolionius of Tyre: Medieval and Renaissance Themes and Variations, Including the Text of the* Historia Apollonii Regis Tyri *with an English Translation*. Cambridge: Brewer, 1991.

Dorninger, Maria E. *Gottfried von Viterbo: Ein Autor in der Umgebung der frühen Staufer*. Stuttgarter Arbeiten zur Germanistik, 345. Stuttgart: Hans-Dieter Heinz, 1997.

Hausmann, Friedrich. "Gottfried von Viterbo: Kapellan und Notar, Magister, Geschichtsschreiber, und Dichter." In *Friedrich Barbarossa: Handlungsspielraume und Wirkungsiveise des staufischen Kaisers*, ed. Alfred Haverkamp. Vorträge und Forschungen Herausgegeben vom Konstanzer Arbeitskreis für Mittelalterliche Geschichte, 40. Sigmaringen: Jan Thorbecke, 1992, pp. 603–621.

Meyer, Lucienne. *Les légendes des matières de Rome, de France, et de Bretagne dans le "Panthéon" de Godefroi de Viterbe*. Paris: E. de Boccard, 1933. (Reprint, Geneva: Slatkine, 1981.)

Mulder-Bakker, A. M. "A Pantheon Full of Examples: The World Chronicle of Godfrey of Viterbo." In *Exemplum et Similitudo: Alexander the Great and Other Heroes as Points of Reference in Medieval Literature*. Mediaevalia Groningana, fasc. 8, ed. W. J. Aerts and M. Gosman. Groningen: Egbert Forsten, 1988, pp. 85–98.

JOHN B. DILLON

GOTTFRIED VON STRASSBURG (fl. 1210)

The greatest poet of the German Middle Ages, Gottfried is known for his Middle High German *Tristan* romance, a fragment of just under twenty thousand lines composed in rhymed couplets. Gottfried may also be the author of two poems in the famous Manesse manuscript (University of Heidelberg library) under Ulrich von Liechtenstein's name. Falsely attributed to him are three other poems that are found in various manuscripts. The contours of his biography remain vague owing to lack of historical evidence. Ulrich von Türheim and Heinrich von Freiberg, two thirteenth-century writers of continuations of his fragment, name Gottfried explicitly as its author. That the majority of the earliest manuscripts were probably produced in Alsace or even directly in Strasbourg (he is known by the German form Straßburg) locates Gottfried in this medieval cultural center.

Our clearest picture of him is provided by the romance itself. Its date of composition—generally put at around 1210—is based mainly on mention in its so-called literary excursus of the poets Heinrich von Veldeke and Reinmar von Hagenau as being deceased, and of Hartmann von Aue, Bligger von Steinach, and Walther von der Vogelweide as still living. Gottfried's remarkable erudition—so evident throughout the romance—in French, German, and classical Latin literature; rhetoric and poetics; theology; law; and music as well as the elegance and artistry of his language and style are a sure indication of a humanist cathedral school education.

Though familiar with several versions of the Tristan story, Gottfried claims allegiance to only one: Thomas of Britain, of whose work only the latter part, which Gottfried did not get to, has survived. Until recently, only two small fragments overlapped with Gottfried's version, thus hampering a precise determination of Gottfried's reliance on Thomas. In 1995, however, a new fragment of Thomas's work surfaced that coincides with key-scenes in Gottfried, namely, Tristan's and Isolde's reactions to the love potion, their arrival in Cornwall, and the wedding night. Initial assessments have led scholars to revise the prevalent (though not unanimous) assumption of Gottfried's fairly high degree of faithfulness to Thomas. For one thing, Gottfried innovated more than was previously thought; for another, it is now supposed that Gottfried drew on a greater number of sources. Among these, Eilhart von Oberge has gained particular significance because of common elements not found in the new Thomas fragment.

Though it shares numerous features with chivalric Arthurian romance, Gottfried's *Tristan* has more accurately been termed a courtier romance, since its hero acts more often in the capacity of courtier and artist than of knight, and since the narrative action tends to occur in the worldly, political arena of the court, rather than to depict knights on marvelous quests for adventure. Not only is Gottfried thoroughly acquainted with, he also details and explores various facets of the decorum, mores, and material culture of the court.

What follows is a highly condensed summary of the romance. It begins with a prologue in which Gottfried's narrator persona sets a discriminating tone by describing the audience of "noble hearts" to whom he specifically addresses his work. This elite group distinguishes itself by seeking not merely joy but by accepting both joy and sorrow, sweetness and bitterness into their lives. Gottfried offers them his love story as a palliative for the pain they suffer from love, and introduces his hero and heroine as the epitome of true lovers. The first strophes of the prologue create the acrostic *GDIETÊRICHTI. Dietêrich* is assumed to be Gottfried's patron (an otherwise unknown Dietrich), the *G* may be short for "Gottfried,"

and the *TI* stands for Tristan and Isolde.

The plot opens with an account of Tristan's parents, Riwalin and Blancheflur. Riwalin of Parmenie journeys to Cornwall, where he intends to refine his manners and his knightly skills at the court of the highly reputable King Marke. He and Marke's sister Blancheflur fall in love and conceive a child. Blancheflur steals away with Riwalin to Parmenie, where they marry. Riwalin's death in battle at the hand of his overlord Morgan causes Blancheflur to die of grief on giving birth to Tristan. To protect Tristan from Morgan, Riwalin's loyal marshal Rual has Tristan grow up as his child, though he sees to it that Tristan receives an education befitting a future ruler.

At age fourteen Tristan is kidnapped by Norwegian ship merchants but is later released on the shores of Cornwall. He meets King Marke, who takes Tristan into close favor on the basis of his dazzling accomplishments in hunting, musical performance, and foreign languages. Not until Rual arrives after a three-and-a-half-year search are Marke and Tristan enlightened as to their relationship as uncle and nephew.

Tristan is knighted in a ceremony whose portrayal is extraordinary for its literary value and its contravention of reader expectations. Initially dispensing with literal depiction, Gottfried cloaks events in allegory instead. From here he shifts to a metapoetic level, where his narrator persona expresses (ironically) an inability to prepare Tristan appropriately for the ceremony. A eulogistic critique of style follows of the five contemporary German poets and minnesingers mentioned above; one unnamed poet (in all likelihood Wolfram von Eschenbach) receives scathing criticism. Now thoroughly "tongue-tied," however, the poet requests inspiration to complete his task in a two-part invocation: first to Apollo and the Muses, then to the supernal Christian God. Only after distinguishing Tristan from his compatriots by delineating his special inborn virtues does Gottfried descend to the literal level and describe the presentation of sword, spurs, and shield. In disdaining to tell of the tournament that concludes the ceremony, Gottfried both distances himself from and gets in a sly dig at contemporaries who go on and on about such spectacles in great detail. The literary excursus is significant for its unique vernacular contribution to literary criticism.

The next episodes involve Tristan in trials of battle, in politics, and at court. His journey to Parmenie includes an attempt to legitimize his right to hold his fathers fief. The encounter between Tristan and his would-be overlord, Morgan, goes awry, however, and Tristan ends up killing Morgan and acquiring his lands by force.

Upon Tristan's return to Cornwall, he learns that Marke is not an autonomous ruler but has been obliged since childhood to pay tribute to King Gurmun of Ireland. Taking up their cause, Tristan delivers Marke's kingdoms from further subjection by killing Gurmuns envoy, Morolt. During their judicial duel, one of Tristan's blows leaves a piece of his sword lodged in Morolt's skull. By his turn, Morolt has wounded Tristan with his poisoned sword, informing him that only his sister, Queen Isolde of Ireland, can cure him of its fatal effect. Tristan sets off for Ireland disguised as the minstrel/merchant "Tantris," and gains access to the queen by means of his sweetly compelling musical performance. She cures him in exchange for tutoring her daughter, the princess Isolde, whom he educates in letters, music, and courteous manners. After his return to Cornwall, intrigues brew against him by barons envious of his position as Marke's heir. To appease them, Marke reluctantly agrees to marry Princess Isolde, hoping this venture will fail because of the hostility between the two countries. But Tristan, who heads the bridal quest, succeeds. First he kills the dragon who has been terrorizing the Irish countryside, a prerequisite to winning Isolde's hand. The dragon's tongue, however, which Tristan has cut out as proof, is poisonous, and causes Tristan to sink, unconscious, into a bog. Meanwhile, the cowardly Irish steward, having found and appropriated the carcass of the dragon, has claimed Isolde as his reward, much to the dismay of the royal family. Through concerted efforts, the queen and her daughter find "Tantris," and the queen cures him anew.

A combination of events leads to Princess Isolde's discovery of Tristan's identity, and she almost slays him in revenge for Morolt. Spared, Tristan conveys Marke's offer of marriage and, after assisting the queen in thwarting the steward with his testimony, Tristan sails for Cornwall with Princess Isolde and Brangaene, her maid, in tow. Brangaene is in possession of a love potion given her by the queen, who wishes to ensure her daughter's happiness with her new husband, King Marke. But Tristan and Isolde inadvertently drink the potion together on their voyage, sealing their eternal love for each other. Though they consummate their love on the ship, loyalty forces Tristan to deliver Isolde to Marke, whom she weds. On the wedding night, Brangaene stands in for Isolde in order to conceal Isolde's loss of virginity. Fearing treason, Isolde attempts to have Brangaene murdered, but Brangaene demonstrates her discretion and trustworthiness, and continues to help the lovers carry on their clandestine affair.

When the Cornish steward Marjodo chances to discover their adulterous relationship, he relates "rumors" of it to Marke, who embarks on a series of attempts designed to catch the lovers out. Finally, the growing threat to the king's reputation and authority by the rumors induces Marke to force Isolde to undergo an ordeal of the hot iron. In this famous episode, the king desires the queen to destroy the rumors. She performs this feat with such calculating ingenuity and winning courtesy that the iron does not burn her when she carries it. Thus she restores both her own and the king's honor.

At court the lovers, unable to restrain their display of mutual affection, provoke Marke to banish them. They take refuge in a cave of lovers whose qualities bear mention. Each of the architectural elements of the cave is allegorically appropriate to a true lover's environment: the white, smooth wall means love's integrity, the cave's width is love's strength, its green floor love's constancy, and the crystal bed love's purity. Moreover, the door to the cave is constructed so as to admit only true lovers. Miraculously, the lovers need not eat, but subsist solely on love and love's gazes. One day, Marke happens upon the cave while hunting. Anticipating detection, Tristan places a sword between Isolde and himself before they fall asleep together. The sword's position convinces Marke of their innocence, and he has them fetched back to court.

There Isolde plans a rendezvous with Tristan in the garden in the face of increased surveillance by her husband. Marke discovers them while they are sleeping, but Tristan awakens in time to see him depart. Realizing that they must part company, Tristan and Isolde say a tender farewell, and Tristan flees Cornwall before Marke returns with his councillors.

Tristan seeks combat in an attempt to divert himself (albeit unsuccessfully) from the pain of separation from Isolde. He travels to Arundel, a coastal duchy, where he assists the inhabitants to a victory. On meeting its ruler's daughter, Isolde of the White Hands, Tristan spirals into confusion; her beauty and her name remind him of his Isolde. Isolde of the White Hands meanwhile falls in love with Tristan. Their proximity to each other at court causes Tristan to waver in his original love, and the romance breaks off as he laments the unfairness of his situation.

The dialectic and the nature of Gottfried's concept of love, his unorthodox relationship to Christianity, his attitude toward courtliness, and the interplay between narrator excursuses and narrative action are only some of the many aspects of the romance that have served both to stimulate and to vex scholarly attempts at interpretation. And yet, despite the obstacles caused by the abundant ambivalences and ironies and, quite simply, the alterity (uniqueness) of the work, Gottfried continues to delight and seduce his readership, leaving the impression of a brilliant poet, an aesthete of aloof yet discerning eye, and a superb master in absolute control of his art.

See also **Hartmann von Aue;
Ulrich von Liechtenstein**

Further Reading

Batts, Michael. *Gottfried von Strassburg*. New York: Twayne, 1971.

Chinca, Mark. *Gottfried von Strassburg: Tristan*. Cambridge: Cambridge University Press, 1997.

Dietz, Reiner. *Der "Tristan" Gottfrieds von Strassburg. Probleme der Forschung (1902–1970)*. Göppingen: Kümmerle, 1974.

Draesner, Ulrike. "Zeichen—Körper—Gesang. Das Lied in der Isolde-Weiss-Hand Episode des "Tristans" Got-frits von Strassburg," in *Wechselspiele: Kommunikations-formen und Gattungsinterferenzen mittelhochdeutscher Lyrik*, ed. Michael Schilling and Peter Strohschneider. Heidelberg: Winter, 1996, pp. 77–101.

Gottfried von Straßburg. *Tristan*, ed. Peter Ganz. Wiesbaden: Brockhaus, 1978 [text of Reinhold Bechstein's edition 1890–1891].

——. *Tristan*, ed. and trans. Rüdiger Krohn, 3 vols. Stuttgart: Reclam, 1984–1995 [text of Friedrich Ranke's edition 1930].

——. *Tristan*, ed. Karl Marold and Werner Schröder. Berlin: de Gruyter, 1906, rpt. 1969.

——. *"Tristan" with the "Tristan" of Thomas*, trans. A. T. Hatto. Harmondsworth: Penguin, 1967.

Haug, Walter. "Reinterpreting the Tristan Romances of Thomas and Gotfrid: Implications of a Recent Discovery." *Arthuriana* 7 (1997): 45–59.

Jackson, W. T. H. *The Anatomy of Love: The "Tristan" of Gottfried von Strassburg*. New York: Columbia University Press, 1971.

Jaeger, C. Stephen. *Medieval Humanism in Gottfried von Strassburg's "Tristan und Isolde."* Heidelberg: Carl Winter, 1977.

Kucaba, Kelley. "Höfisch inszenierte Wahrheiten. Zu Isolds Gottesurteil bei Gottfried von Strassburg," in *Fremdes wahrnehmen—fremdes Wahrnehmen*, ed. Wolfgang Harms and C. Stephen Jaeger in connection with Alexandra Stein. Stuttgart: Hirzel, 1997, pp. 73–93.

Picozzi, Rosemary. *A History of Tristan Scholarship*. Bern: Lang, 1971.

Steinhoff, Hans-Hugo. *Bibliographic zu Gottfriedvon Srassburg*, 2 vols. Berlin: Schmidt, 1971–1986.

Stevens, Adrian, and Roy Wisbey, eds. *Gottfried von Strassburg and the Medieval Tristan Legend*. Papers from an Anglo–North American Symposium. Cambridge: Brewer, 1990.

Wenzel, Horst. "Öffentlichkeit und Heimlichkeit in Gottfrieds *Tristan*" *Zeitschrift für deutsche Philologie* 107 (1988): 335–361.

KELLEY KUCABA

GOTTSCHALK (ca. 803–ca. 867/69)

Saxon theologian and poet, author of works on predestination that aroused controversy in 9th-century France. Gottschalk was presented by his father, Berno, as an oblate to the Benedictine monastery of Fulda. His boyhood was spent at Fulda, where Rabanus Maurus was abbot, and at Reichenau. In 829, Gottschalk petitioned a church synod at Mainz to be released from his monastic vows, claiming that his profession had not been voluntary and was not binding since there had been no Saxon witnesses present. The synod agreed that Gottschalk could return to secular life but did not agree to return the inheritance given by his father to Fulda. Rabanus Maurus won a reversal of that decision at a synod at Worms. Gottschalk spent the next ten years at Orbais and Corbie, where he dedicated himself to a study of the writings of Augustine. He was ordained a priest in the late 830s, apparently without the approval of the bishop of Soissons, in whose jurisdiction such ordination rested.

During a pilgrimage to Rome in the 840s, Gottschalk taught and preached about predestination in Italy and the Balkans and made visits to Count Eberhard of Friuli and Bishop Noting of Brescia. News of Gottschalk's teachings provoked Rabanus Maurus, who compelled him to return to Francia. In 848, Gottschalk was condemned twice, at synods at Mainz and Quierzy-sur-Oise. The second synod ordered him whipped and imprisoned at the monastery of Hautvillers. His writings were burned, and his ordination to the priesthood was revoked. Gottschalk continued to write, principally on predestination, until his death. A number of influential theologians, including Florus of Lyon, Prudentius of Troyes, and Ratramnus of Corbie wrote in support of Gottschalk's ideas on predestination, although these views were condemned by such important ecclesiastical figures as Amalarius of Metz, Hincmar of Reims, Johannes Scottus Eriugena, and of course Rabanus Maurus. On an official level, Gottschalk's teachings were repeatedly condemned: at the synod of Quierzy-sur-Oise in 853 and at numerous other synods and national councils in the 850s and 860s. An appeal to Rome on Gottschalk's behalf made by Guntbert of Hautvillers in 866 was cut short by the death of Pope Nicholas I.

The theological position that led to this drama is difficult to reconstruct because of the fragmentary nature of Gottschalk's extant writings. It seems to have been a logical derivation from the late writings of Augustine, stressing the point that God had, from eternity, not only foreseen but also predestined either the salvation and damnation of every human being. What was absolutely unacceptable to his contemporaries was the conclusion that Jesus therefore died only for the saved, and that the sacraments, even baptism, were not efficacious for all.

In spite of the condemnation of his contemporaries and the increasingly harsh treatment he received, Gottschalk never renounced his position but continued to write, with increasing complexity, until his death. His later works include speculation on the eucharist, supporting the position of Ratramnus of Corbie over that of Paschasius Radbertus; two works on the Trinity, apparently aimed against Hincmar of Reims, and lyrical poems that were especially innovative in their use of rhyme.

See also **Eriugena, Johannes Scottus; Rabanus Maurus**

Further Reading

Gottschalk. *Œuvres théologiques et grammaticales de Godescalc d'Orbais*, ed. Cyril Lambot. Louvain: Spicilegium Sacrum Lovaniense, 1945.

——. "Lettre inédite de Godescalc d'Orbais," ed. Cyril Lambot. *Revue bénédictine* (1958).

Duckett, Eleanor Shipley. *Carolingian Portraits: A Study in the Ninth Century.* Ann Arbor: University of Michigan Press, 1962.

Van Moos, Peter. "Gottschalks Gedicht *O mi custos—eine confessio.*" *Frühmittelalterliche Studien* 4–5 (1970–71).

Vielhaber, Klaus. *Gottschalk der Sachse.* Bonn: Rohrscheid, 1956.

E. Ann Matter

GOWER, JOHN (1330?–1408)

Poet and friend of Chaucer. Gower was probably born of a Kentish family during the third decade of the 14th century. He may have attended the Inns of Court, perhaps with Chaucer, acquiring legal training possibly put to use in land dealings recorded of a "John Gower" in the Close Rolls ca. 1365–74. We have better evidence that Gower the poet owned lands in Norfolk, Suffolk, and Kent by 1382 and that he was familiar enough with the Lancastrian house to be awarded a collar of silver "SS" links upon the ascension of Henry IV in 1399.

In his later years Gower took an interest in the monastery of St. Mary Overeys in Southwark, apparently restoring several of its buildings with his own and friends' money. Sometime after 1377 he took his residence there, probably as a lay brother, for he did not join the order. On 23 January 1398 Gower received a license from the see of Winchester to marry one Agnes Groundolf (probably his nurse) at his house on the priory grounds. Gower's will, dated 15 August 1408, divides substantial property among several religious houses and his wife. It gives no evidence of an earlier marriage or of children. An elaborate tomb, surmounted by a near-life-sized effigy wearing the "SS" collar, representations of his three major works, and protective angels, rests in the north aisle of St. Saviour's Church, Southwark.

A prolific and versatile writer, Gower composed nearly 80,000 lines of poetry in French, Latin, and English. Although the chronology of individual works remains imprecise, it is generally thought that his earliest compositions were in Anglo-Norman and that his English poems were the product of the last two decades of his life. He continued to write in Latin and French until the end, however, making him a truly trilingual poet—an achievement unique among English literary figures.

French Works

Of the French poems the earliest and longest is commonly known by the title *Mirour de l'Omme.* (Alternative names are *Speculum Hominis* or *Speculum Meditantis,* but these are used infrequently.) The *Mirour* exists in one manuscript only, copied by a single hand: CUL Add. 3035, presently containing 28,603 lines, but missing at least a dozen leaves. It seems likely that the complete poem consisted of approximately 31,000 lines. The *Mirour* is written in twelve-line stanzas of octosyllabic verse, rhyming aab aab bba bba.

The subject of the *Mirour de l'Omme* is the complete moral life of man. To describe this Gower created a poem in three parts, unequal in length but seemingly equivalent in import. The first section—about two-thirds of the work— presents a complex but familiar allegory: the begetting of Death by the Devil on Sin, his own daughter; the subsequent coupling of Sin and Death to produce seven "daughters," the deadly sins or Vices; the marriage of the World to the seven Vices, as a strategy to beget helpers to seduce Man; their mutual assault on Man; the prayer of Conscience and Reason to God for assistance; the divinely arranged marriage of the seven Virtues to Reason, and the description of their daughters; the oppositional pairing of the Virtues and their offspring against the Vices and their offspring. The second section considers how the battle of good and evil is going in the world. The Three Estates—clergy, knights or lords, and peasants— are subdivided and examined, from pope to parish priest, emperor to laborer; all are found thoroughly corrupt and incapable of reforming themselves without merciful grace. The poem concludes with a third section describing the source of this extraordinary succor—the Virgin Mary, whose life, joys, and sorrows are related in some detail. The final lines of the *Mirour* as we have them are the poet's prayer to the Virgin for mercy and a list of her names and titles, cut short by the missing manuscript leaves.

Gower's remaining French poetry consists of two sequences of ballades, one generally known as the *Cinkante Balades,* the other as the *Traitié pour Essampler les Amantz Marietz,* or simply the *Traitié.* Although an early date was once assumed for the *Cinkante Balades* and a late one for the *Traitié,* in fact no firm evidence exists to establish when, or in what context or order, Gower composed these poems. Theories connecting the former sequence with a still-flourishing merchant *puy* (a bourgeois literary and social organization) in London, or the latter with Gower's marriage (whatever might be true of individual ballades), are without firm foundation. The *Cinkante Balades* (*Fifty Ballades*), despite the title found in its unique manuscript, actually contains 54 poems, each in seven- or eight-line stanzas and almost all with standard four-line envois (short dosing stanzas). The poems trace the correspondence of two lovers during an affair, with both a male and female voice represented. The collection is overtly critical of amoral dalliance and seems created to offer alternative images of love and love poetry compatible with Christian marriage.

The eighteen ballades known as the *Traitié* repeat the same firm directives concerning the unique propriety of lawful affection and (by extension) poetics. These poems, each consisting of three seven-line stanzas without envoi, exist in ten manuscripts, never alone. On eight occasions they follow Gower's major English work, the *Confessio Amantis*, and would seem, if the French prose introduction and the Latin prose sidenotes are authorial, to have been intended as a sort of a coda or conclusion to the *Confessio*. Because the *Traitié* ends with a Latin poem in which Gower speaks of his own impending marriage, the sequence has sometimes been considered a late work, possibly composed in 1398, though some of its ballades may have actually been written earlier, without relation to the marriage.

Latin Works

Gower's independent extant Latin poetry amounts to somewhat fewer than 13,000 lines, mostly in unrhymed elegiac couplets. By far his most significant Latin poem is the *Vox Clamantis*, the title of which derives from the "vox clamantis in deserto" ("a voice of one crying in the desert") of John 1:23. Spanning 10,265 lines, it is known in ten manuscripts, of which four are contemporary with the author and probably show signs of personal revision. Although dating is uncertain, the *Vox* seems motivated by the social unrest resulting in the Peasants' Revolt of 1381.

The *Vox* resembles classical models in form, being arranged in seven books. This structural neoclassicism is supported by Gower's incorporation of many lines borrowed intact from Roman authors, primarily Ovid, and such medieval authorities as Alexander Neckham (in particular his *De vita monachorum*) and Peter Riga (author of the *Aurora*, a versified Bible).

The contents of the *Vox* may be summarized briefly as follows. Book 1 ("Visio") relates a horrific dream of the author, who witnesses the destruction of "New Troy" by anthropomorphic animals. In fear for his life the dreamer flees, first on foot and then by ship; after storms and attacks by monsters the ship eventually regains port, on the island of "Brute," from which the journey began. The dream is usually read as a thinly disguised allegory of major figures and events in the Peasants' Revolt. Book 2 describes human misery, condemns Fortune and her misperceived power, and concludes by reaffirming the Christian view of the order of things and urging its readers to hold fast to their Christian faith.

In the next three books the degeneracies of the Three Estates are enumerated (somewhat in the manner of the *Mirour*), beginning with the clergy (books 3 and 4), then treating the knights and peasants (5). Book 6 addresses the failures of the "ministers of law"; it concludes with extensive advice to the king, as chief guardian of the nation and its legal tradition. Finally, in book 7, the statue of Nebuchadnezzar's dream from the second chapter of Daniel (one of Gower's favorite metaphors) is used

to focus discussion on the sinfullness of man and his precarious mortal circumstances. The *Vox* ends with a pointed (and poignant) appeal to the English to follow the advice of the dream and make their country a place of peace and decency.

Of next importance after the *Vox* is the *Cronica Tripertita*, written in leonine hexameters (hexameter lines with internal rhyme). It treats the failed government of Richard II, brought down by treachery and weakness, and celebrates the new order to come under his successor, Henry IV. Besides these two longer poems Gower's Latin poetry includes about twenty short pieces on political, moral, and personal themes, and the Latin verses interposed throughout the *Confessio Amantis*.

English Works

Gower's ME verse consists of two poems, the *Confessio Amantis*, his best-known and most admired work, and "To King Henry IV, In Praise of Peace." Comprising some 33,000 lines, the *Confessio* was frequently copied (over 40 manuscripts survive) and later was among the earliest books printed in England, with blackletter editions by Caxton (1483) and Berthelette (1532 and 1554). The text exists in a variety of versions, the exact relationship of which is presently under fresh study. The best manuscript of the poem seems to be Bodl. Fairfax 3, on which the best scholarly edition (Macaulay's) is based.

With the *Confessio* Gower helps establish his native language as a medium for poetry while displaying extraordinary erudition and reaching new levels of fiction making and characterization in English poetry. The poem consists of a prologue and eight books, all in tetrameter couplets except for some twelve rime royal stanzas in book 8 and occasional Latin verses highlighting the themes of the poem. The framing fiction is, as the title indicates, the confession of a lover ("Amans") to Genius, the priest of Venus. Each of the books is concerned with one of the seven cardinal sins and its branches, except book 7, which rehearses the education given Prince Alexander by Aristotle. In the process of the lover's confession Amans and Genius grow as characters, becoming multidimensional by the end; in addition many stories are told, primarily by Genius, who uses them to illustrate his moral points to Amans.

While the sources of the *Confessio Amantis* are understandably too numerous to list completely, its broad outline suggests major debts to the *Roman de la Rose*, manuals of the penitential tradition, such as the *Somme le roi*, Lucretius's *De rerum natura*, and Boethius's *Consolation of Philosophy*. To these may be added a thorough acquaintance with the works of Ovid, Statius, the *Aeneid*, the *Ovide moralisé*, the *Legenda aurea*, and Brunetto Latini's *Trésor*.

The *Confessio Amantis* opens with a prologue in which the author attributes the anarchy of his times to corrupt leadership and division within society. Central to the opening is Nebuchadnezzar's dream from the book of Daniel (2:31–45), concerning the giant statue of gold, silver, brass, steel, and clay, symbolizing the decline of civilization. The prologue concludes with a prayer that a new Arion (a legendary harper of classical mythology) might be found to bring back the golden age of peace and harmony with his musicianship. Book 1 sets the frame for the poem itself. The poet, lovesick and seeking solace, goes one May morning into the woods. He prays to Cupid and Venus, the king and queen of love, who then appear to him; Cupid pierces his heart with a fiery dart, and Venus commands him to confess his sins to Genius, the priest of love. Genius presents his method: he will question Amans concerning his sins, after the manner of a confessor; but since he is a priest only of love, he will speak of sin only as it affects love. The remainder of book 1 is devoted to describing several "branches" of Pride (Hypocrisy, Disobedience, Presumption, Boasting, and Vain Glory), each made memorable by one or more illustrative stories, or exempla, of varied length and complexity. The last section of book 1 offers a description of Humility, Pride's opposing virtue, and an exemplum of humble behavior.

This pattern—the subdivision of a sin into its branches, the use of exempla to illustrate these branch sins, and (usually) the presentation and illustration of a major opposing virtue— recurs in books 2 through 6, which cover Envy, Wrath, Sloth, Avarice, and Gluttony. Book 3 also includes a digression in which Amans inquires about the morality of war, a question of great importance to Gower. Book 7, on the education of Alexander, devotes most of its space to a *speculum principum*, or "mirror for princes," in which five "points of policy" (Truth, Largesse, Justice, Pity, and Chastity) are identified as the central elements of good kingship. Again exempla of varying length illustrate the points under discussion. Book 8 turns to Lechery, the remaining cardinal sin, focusing almost entirely on a single branch sin, Incest. For most of the book Genius tells the tale of Apollonius of tyre, which illustrates not merely the commission and avoidance of incest and lechery but also the other six sins and their opposing virtues. Book 8 thus simultaneously explores the worst kind of lechery and effectively recapitulates the themes of the first seven books.

Following his confession Amans again meets the Queen of Love and identifies himself at last as "John Gower." Surprisingly Venus now holds up a mirror so that the lover can see that he is old, and unfit for the kind of dalliance he pursues. She also removes the fiery dart from Amans's heart, releasing him from his passion. Finally Genius absolves Amans and Venus gives the cured lover a set of beads and the admonition to "pray for the peace." In the poem's closing lines we are returned to the universal themes of the prologue, including the evils of division and the hope for good kingship and loving harmony in society.

"To King Henry IV, In Praise of Peace" is Gower's only other extant English poem. Containing 55 rime royal stanzas, it occurs in one manuscript version (BL Add. 59495, the Trentham Manuscript) and was printed by Thynne in his 1532 edition of Chaucer's *Works*. As in the *Confessio* Gower's pacifistic concern for an end to domestic and international strife receives a prominent place.

Although Gower has been slighted by modern critical opinion (usually, indeed, dismissed as "moral Gower," as Chaucer calls him, albeit with no denigrating intent, at the conclusion of *Troilus*), recent scholarship is returning his work to its earlier prominence. Clearly Chaucer's most significant poetic confidant, Gower appears to have influenced his friend at least in the tales they tell in common, notably those of "Constance" (*MLT*), "Florent" (*WBT*), "Phebus and Cornide" (*MancT*), and "Tereus" ("Philomela" in *LGW*). For "Constance" and the *Man of Law's Tale* it is thought that the two friends exchanged drafts of their work, with Gower's assumed to be the earlier version.

Gowers reputation remained high during the 15th century, his name appearing in paeans by Lydgate, Hoccleve, Henryson, Dunbar, and others as a cofounder, with Chaucer, of the national poetic language. In the 16th and 17th centuries his work was praised and plundered by Spenser, Milton, and Shakespeare (whose *Pericles* adapts the "Apollonius of Tyre" story and brings "Ancient Gower" onto the stage as chorus). A moralist and scholar, Gower is often lauded for the spare, no-nonsense approach he takes to narration—a quality especially visible in the *Confessio Amantis*—and he is increasingly perceived as an independent literary theorist with strong views as to the role poetry might play in making a just, peaceful society.

See also **Brunetto Latini; Caxton, William; Chaucer, Geoffrey; Henry IV; Richard II**

Further Reading

Primary Sources

Echard, Siân, and Claire Fanger, trans. *The Latin Verses in the Confessio Amantis: An Annotated Translation*. East Lansing: Colleagues, 1991.

Macaulay, G.C., ed. *The Complete Works of John Gower*. 4 vols. Oxford: Clarendon, 1899-1902. Vols. 2 and 3 repr. as *The English Works of John Gower*, EETS e.s. 81–82. London: Kegan Paul, Trench, Trübner, 1900–01.

Peck, Russell A., ed, *Confessio Amantis*. New York: Holt, Rinehart & Winston, 1968.

Stockton, Eric W., trans. *The Major Latin Works of John Gower*. Seattle: University of Washington Press, 1962.

Wilson, William B., trans. *John Gower's Mirour de l'Omme*. East Lansing: Colleagues, 1992.

Secondary Sources

New *CBEL* 1:553–56, 804.

Manual 7:2195–2210, 2399–2418.

Beidler, Peter G., ed. *John Gower's Literary Transformations in the Confessio Amantis: Original Articles and Translations.* Washington, D.C.: University Press of America, 1982.

Bennett, J.A.W. "Gower's 'Honeste Love.'" In *Patterns of Love and Courtesy: Essays in Memory of C.S. Lewis,* ed. John Lawlor. London: Arnold, 1966, pp. 107–21.

Burrow, John A. *Ricardian Poetry: Chaucer, Gower, Langland and the Gawain-Poet.* London: Routledge & Kegan Paul, 1971.

Burrow, John A. "The Poet As Petitioner." *SAC* 3 (1981): 61–75.

Fisher, John H. *John Gower: Moral Philosopher and Friend of Chaucer.* New York: New York University Press, 1964.

Middleton, Anne. "The Idea of Public Poetry in the Reign of Richard II." *Speculum* 53 (1978): 94–114.

Minnis, Alastair J. "The Influence of Academic Prologues on the Prologues and Literary Attitudes of Late Medieval English Writers." *MS* 43 (1981): 342–83.

Minnis, Alastair J.,ed. *Gower's Confessio Amantis: Responses and Reassessments.* Cambridge: Brewer, 1983.

Nicholson, Peter, *An Annotated Index to the Commentary on Gower's Confessio Amantis.* MRTS 62. Binghamton: MRTS, 1989.

Olsson, Kurt. "Natural Law and John Gower's *Confessio Amantis:*" *M&H* n.s. 11 (1982): 229–61.

Pearsall, Derek. "Gower's Narrative Art." *PMLA* 81 (1966): 475–84.

Peck, Russell A. *Kingship and Common Profit in Gower's Confessio Amantis,* Carbondale: Southern Illinois University Press, 1978.

Pickles, J.D., and J.L. Dawson, eds. *A Concordance to John Gower's Confessio Amantis.* Cambridge: Brewer, 1987.

Scanlon, Larry. *Narrative, Authority and Power: The Medieval Exemplum and the Chaucerian Tradition.* Cambridge: Cambridge University Press, 1993.

Schueler, Donald G. "Gower's Characterization of Genius in the *Confessio Amantis.*" *MLQ* 33 (1972): 240–56.

Simpson, James. *Sciences and the Self in Medieval Poetry: Alan of Lille's Anticlaudianus and John Gower's Confessio Amantis.* Cambridge: Cambridge University Press, 1995.

Strohm, Paul. "Form and Social Statement in *Confessio Amantis* and *The Canterbury Tales.*" *SAC* 1 (1979): 17–40.

Wickert, Maria. *Studies in John Gower.* Trans. Robert J. Meindl. Washington, D.C.: University Press of America, 1981 [only book-length study of *Vox Clamantis*].

Yeager, R.F. *John Gower Materials: A Bibliography through 1979.* New York: Garland, 1981.

Yeager, R.F. "*Pax Poetica:* On the Pacifism of Chaucer and Gower." *SAC* 9 (1987): 97–121.

Yeager, R.F., ed. *John Goiver: Recent Readings.* Kalamazoo: Medieval Institute, 1989.

Yeager, R.F. *John Gower's Poetic: The Search for a New Arion.* Cambridge: Brewer, 1990.

R.F. YEAGER

GRASSER, ERASMUS (1445/1450–1518)

Born between 1445 and 1450 in Schmidmühlen near Regensburg, this master builder and sculptor in both stone and wood spent his career in Munich. Here he acquired the status of master in 1477, repeatedly held the office of head of the painter's guild, and occupied an especially privileged position at the court of the dukes of Bavaria. The strength of his sensual temperament is apparent in the peculiar style of his early wood sculpture, suggesting almost grotesque movements, which gives way to calmer forms only in his late works. The series of preserved architectural and sculptural works, of which only the epitaph of Ulrich Aresinger from 1482 (Munich, St. Peter's) is signed and dated, allows the conclusion that Grasser completed at least a six-year apprenticeship as a builder and stonecutter before the "quarrelsome, confused, and deceitful" journeyman appeared unexpectedly in Munich about 1474 (Frankl 1942: 257).

Only one of Grasser's architectural projects still stands—the ingenious extension added to the church of the Virgin in Schwaz in Tyrol between 1490 and 1502. Three other monuments are known through documents: the cloister Mariaberg near Rorschach from 1487, the tabernacle for the host at Freising Cathedral from 1489, and the well-room with accompanying chapel at the salt works at Reichenhall. Likewise four sculptures or groups are documented from the oeuvre of *maister Erasem schnitzer* (Master Erasmus wood-carver). Of the original sixteen Morris Dancers carved for the Altes Rathaus (old town hall) in Munich about 1480, ten are preserved today in the city museum. Seven mourners from a Lamentation group in limestone dated 1492 are preserved in Freising Cathedral. Wood figures of the Virgin and Saints Leonhard and Eligius, carved between 1502 and 1505, and the altar of St. Achatius (1503–1506) are to be found in the church at Reichersdorf in Upper Bavaria (Otto 1988:31–37).

The attributed works are more numerous. A multi-figured altar of the Holy Cross from about 1482 at the church of the Assumption at Ramersdorf and a similar small-scale monstrance altar from about 1483, now in the Bavarian National Museum in Munich, reveal a knowledge of Netherlandish carved altarpieces. The often-cited influence of Nicolaus Gerhaert von Leyden on Grasser's style is visible in three groups representing the Virgin and John the Evangelist under the cross: at the church of St. Leonhard at Traidendorf in the Oberpfalz (after 1470), from the church of St. Wolfgang in Munich (now Bavarian National Museum, 1485–1490), and at St. Arsatius in Ilmmünster (about 1500). The high-quality wood figure of a Throne of Grace (*Gnadenstuhl*) in Schliersee, from about 1480, depends closely on an engraving of the same subject by the anonymous Master E. S.

See also **Nicolaus Gerhaert von Leyden**

Further Reading

Frankl, Paul. "Early Works of Erasmus Grasser." *Art Quarterly* 5 (1942): 242–258.

Fuhrmann, Franz. "Die Stadtpfarrkirche zu Unserer Lieben Frau in Schwaz," in *Festschrift Heinz Mackowitz*, ed. Sybille-Karin Moser and Christoph Bertsch. Lustenau: Neufeld-Verlag, 1985, pp. 87–94.

Halm, Philipp Maria. *Erasmus Grasser.* Augsburg: Benno Filser Verlag, 1928.

Müller-Meiningen, Johanna. *Die Moriskentänzer und andere Arbeiten des Erasmus Grasser für das Alte Rathaus in München.* Munich: Schnell und Steiner, 1984.

Otto, Komelius. *Erasmus Grasser und der Meister des Blutenburger Apostelzyklus.* Miscellanea Bavarica Monacensia 150; Neue Schriftenreihe des Stadtarchivs München. Munich: UNI-Druck, 1988.

Ramisch, Hans. "Funde und Bemerkungen zu Erasmus Grasser und seinem Umkreis." *Bayerische Landesamt fürDenkmalpflege, Berichte* 26 (1968): 83–95.

Rorimer, James J. "Three Kings from Lichtenthal." *The Metropolitan Museum of Art Bulletin* 12 (1953): 81–91.

BRIGITTE SCHLIEWEN

GRATIAN (mid-12th century)

The Bolognese jurist Gratian is famous as the author of *Concordia discordantium canonum,* better-known as the *Decretum.* This collection of church laws remained in use in law schools and courts for the rest of the Middle Ages and beyond, until 1917.

Very little is known about Gratian's life. He was perhaps the Gratian who in 1143 in Venice, together with two other Bolognese jurists, advised a papal legate on a legal issue. Assertions that he was a monk or a bishop rest on precarious evidence. From the form and contents of the *Decretum,* it seems clear that he was a teacher of canon law.

The *Decretum* first circulated in a short version preserved in four manuscripts and a fragment (not edited, but for lists of its contents see Winroth 2000). This first recension was finished in 1139 or somewhat later; the second recension was completed by the early 1150s (see Friedberg 1879). It has been argued that Gratian was the author of only the first recension and that a student of his who had also studied Roman law was responsible for the second recension; for convenience, the two supposed authors are called, respectively, Gratian 1 and Gratian 2.

The first recension contained approximately 1,900 excerpts of ecclesiastical law, or canons. The canons were accompanied by brief comments (*dicta*) in which Gratian interpreted the legal texts and attempted to harmonize contradictions among them. The first recension was included, practically complete, in the second recension, which added further canons so that the total amounted to some 3,800. Only a few new *dicta* were composed for this recension. The second recension became accepted as the definitive collection of earlier legislation (the *ius antiquum),* and later canonists only rarely went back to earlier sources.

The legal texts quoted in the *Decretum* derive from many kinds of sources, including general and provincial councils, papal decretals, the writings of the church fathers, the Pseudo-Isidorian decretals, penitentials, and secular law. In most cases, the authors of the *Decretum* took these texts not from the original sources but from earlier canonical collections.

Gratian 1 used a larger set of sources than his successor; these sources included, notably, Ivo of Chartres's *Panormia,* Anselm of Lucca's collection, Gregory of Saint Grisogono's *Polycarpus,* Alger of Liège's *De misericordia et iustitia,* and *Collectio tripartite.* Gratian 2 based much of his work on only three sources: *Tripartita, Collection in Three Books,* and Justinian's *Corpus iuris civilis.*

The third part of the *Decretum, De consecrathne,* was added, complete, in the second recension. The structure of the work is otherwise similar in both recensions. In the first recension, the first part was a long treatise without any internal divisions; in the second recension it was divided into 101 *distinctiones.* The second part was divided into thirty-six *causae,* outlining thirty-six more or less complicated legal cases. In each case, Gratian isolated two to eleven questions and treated them separately in *questiones.* The subjects treated include the nature of law, the hierarchy of the church, clerical ordination, legal procedure, the power and duties of bishops and the clergy, ecclesiastical censure, monasticism, heresy, marriage, and penance. The only major subject added in the second recension was law concerning the remaining sacraments (in *De consecratione*).

In collecting a mass of law, Gratians 1 and 2 followed in the footsteps of earlier canonists. Gratian 1's innovation was to apply the dialectic methods of early scholasticism to the body of law that he had collected. Foremost among his methods of reconciling seemingly contradictory statements is the distinction between different meanings of the same word. Elsewhere, he points out that a specific law concerns a special case, place, or time. The methods were probably inspired by Ivo of Chartres's *Prologue* and Alger of Liège's *De misericordia et iustitia.* There is no evidence that Gratian 1's methods were influenced by Aristotle, Peter Abelard, or Roman law.

Gratian 1 shows very little knowledge of Roman law from Justinian's codifications; instead he made use of pre-Justinian Roman law transmitted, for example, through *Lex Romdna Visigothorum* and the Pseudo-Isidorian decretals. His reliance on so-called vulgar Roman law meant that his concept of many legal issues appeared disturbingly primitive to Gratian 2, who in such cases supplemented the first recension with skillful compilations of excerpts from *Corpus iuris civilis.*

Also, in purely canonical matters the work of Gratian 2 is characterized by more sophisticated jurisprudential thinking than the work of Gratian 1. For example,

Gratian 2 introduced the important distinction between "excommunication" and "anathema" as technical terms. Gratian 1 had used the two terms interchangeably for rhetorical variation. Since Gratian 2 seldom changed or deleted the original text of Gratian 1, the resulting text often seems confused.

An enormous number of glosses and commentaries on Gratian's *Decretum* are preserved. Important commentaries were composed by Johannes Faventinus, Huguccio, and Johannes Teutonicus, who c. 1215 published what would become the standard gloss, called the *Glossa ordinaria*. Gratian's enduring fame is endorsed by Dante, who places him among philosophers in Canto 10 of *Paradiso*.

Further Reading

Friedberg, Emil, ed. *Decretum magistri Gratiani*. Corpus Iuris Canonici, 1. Leipzig: Bernhardi Tauchnitz, 1879.

Kuttner, Stephan. *Gratian and the Schools of Law, 1140–1234*. London: Variorum Reprints, 1983.

Landau, Peter. *Kanones und Dekretalen: Beiträge zur Geschichte der Quellen des kanonischen Rechts*. Goldbach, 1997.

Noonan, John T. "Gratian Slept Here: The Changing Identity of the Father of the Systematic Study of Canon Law." *Traditio*, 35, 1979, pp. 145–172.

Rambaud, Jacqueline. "Le legs du droit ancien: Gratien." In *L'âge classique, 1140—1378: Sources et théorie du droit*. Histoire du Droit et des Institutions de l'Église en Occident, 7. Paris: Sirey, 1965, pp. 52–119.

Southern, R. W. *Scholastic Humanism and the Unification of Europe*. Oxford: Blackwell, 1995.

Vemlani, Adam. *Sur Gratien et les décrétales*. Aldershot, Hampshire: Variorum, 1990.

Weigand, Rudolf. *Die Glossen zum Dekret Gratians: Studien zu den frühen Glossen und Glossenkompositionen*. Rome: n.p., 1991.

Winroth, Anders. "The Two Recensions of Gratian's Decretum." *Zeitschrift der Savigny-Stiftung für Rechtsgeschichte, Kanonistische Abteilung,* 83, 1996, pp. 22–31.

——. *The Making of Gratian's Decretum*. Cambridge Studies in Medieval Life and Thought, Series 4(49). Cambridge: Cambridge University Press, 2000.

ANDERS WINROTH

GREBAN, ARNOUL
(d. before 1473)

Author of a well-known *Mystère de la Passion*, Greban was born in Le Mans and studied theology at the University of Paris. From 1450 to 1455, he lived in the cloister of the cathedral of Notre-Dame in Paris, where he was organist and master of the choirboys. It was here that he wrote his Passion play, probably in 1450–52. This work is set in the framework of the *Procès de Paradis*, first introduced by Eustache Marcadé, and its 35,000 lines are divided into four playing days. Despite its variety of styles (sermons, debates, lamentations) and moods (solemn in Heaven, comic in Hell, pathetic in torture

scenes), the play exhibits a strong unity. Greban employs many poetic forms and punctuates the action throughout with music. The life of Jesus is presented against the background of a cosmic struggle between the forces of good and evil. This conflict is introduced in the first scenes, where Lucifer rebels against God then out of envy tempts Adam and Eve to fall from grace. Greban's *Passion* was played three times in Paris before 1473. It served as the basis for Jean Michel's Passion play and was adapted for production in a number of other cities.

Further Reading

Greban, Amoul. *Le mystère de la Passion*, ed. Omer Jodogne. 2 vols. Brussels: Palais des Académies, 1965–83.

Champion, Pierre. *Histoire poétique du quinzième siècle*. 2 vols. Paris: Champion, 1923, Vol. 2, pp. 133–88.

ALAN E. KNIGHT

GREGORY I, POPE (c. 540–604)

Pope Gregory I (Gregory the Great) is one of the most notable personalities in the early church. The defining characteristics and organization of the medieval papacy, and indeed of modern Catholicism, owe their foundations to Gregory. His legacy includes associations with major liturgical and musical developments, so much so that the music of the Catholic church is named for him—Gregorian chant. He is also remembered, among numerous other accomplishments, for sending Saint Augustine of Canterbury to evangelize the British Isles.

Early Life

Gregory was descended from the senatorial nobility in Rome. His father, Gordianus, was a wealthy patrician of the famous *gens* Amicia and owned large estates in Sicily and a mansion on the Caelian Hill in Rome. Gregory's mother, Silvia, also was of good family; she is celebrated as a saint on 3 November, and her two sisters were canonized as well. Little is known of Gregory's early education, but he was, according to Gregory of Tours (538–594), unsurpassed in Rome in grammar, dialectic, and rhetoric. The religious atmosphere of his childhood—a time when, John the Deacon tells us, he was like a saint among saints—gave him an solid grounding in the scriptures. His rank and position certainly indicated that he should embark on a public career. Our first record of him is in 573, when he became prefect of Rome at age thirty. Though this office was not then as prestigious as it had formerly been, it was still the highest civil dignity in the city. Soon after achieving this honor, however, Gregory gave up his office and the tenor of life and became a monk, c. 574. His estates were donated to the church, and his mansion on the Caelian Hill became a monastery devoted to Saint Andrew.

Monastic Life

From 574 to 578, Gregory lived as a monk in Saint Andrew's, probably following the rule of Saint Benedict. In his own writings he describes this as the happiest time of his life. In 578, Gregory—against his will—was ordained by the pope and was sent as the pope's ambassador to the court of Byzantium. Since the Lombards were advancing toward Rome, the pope needed the help of Emperor Tiberius, and this crisis required Gregory's political acumen. For six years, Gregory endured the worldly court at Byzantium, adhering as much as possible to his monastic regimen. It was during this time that he wrote his *Morals* on the book of Job, after meeting Saint Leander of Seville. A dispute arose between Gregory and Eutychius, the patriarch of Constantinople, on certain aspects of the resurrection. Gregory's mission was a failure, and he learned from it that Rome could no longer count on help from the eastern church. Gregory's subsequent course of action as pope would determine the policy of the western papacy toward Constantinople throughout the Middle Ages.

Around 585–586, Gregory returned to Rome and Saint Andrew's monastery, where he was elected abbot soon afterward. During this time, his *Morals* was published and distributed. Gregory's famous encounter with English slaves in the Roman Forum also happened during this period. As a result of his renown, he advanced to become chief adviser, assistant, and secretary to Pope Pelagius II. A letter by Gregory to the schismatic bishops of Istria still survives from this time; as a treatise, it gives hints of his skill as a writer and theologian.

The year 589 brought disasters throughout Italy. The Tiber overflowed its banks, and indeed there were floods in the entire peninsula. A plague swept through Rome, leaving the city full of corpses and virtually deserted by the living. When Pope Pelagius II died in February 590, the clergy and people of Rome were unanimous in their choice of Gregory as his successor; but Gregory, who did not want to be pope, wrote to Emperor Maurice asking him not to confirm the election. While waiting for a reply, Gregory was called on to lead a sevenfold procession through Rome, praying to God to end the plague. The legend that the archangel Michael himself was seen stopping the plague reinforced the belief among the Romans that Gregory was God's elect, and when the emperor confirmed their choice Gregory was consecrated pope on 3 September 590, despite his protests.

Gregory's Pontificate (590–604)

The papacy proved to be a considerable strain on Gregory's health; he suffered constantly from indigestion, fever, and also from gout during the later years of his life. It is remarkable how much he accomplished despite his infirmities. The short work *Liber pastoralis curae* (*Book on the Office of a Bishop*) was published by Gregory at the beginning of his pontificate, and he adhered to it closely. One of his first acts was to replace the laypeople in the Lateran palace with clerics; and since no *magister militum* lived in Rome, he also assumed command of all military matters in the city. He instituted the "stations" still observed today and recorded in the missal.

There is some disagreement on the extent of Gregory's reforms of the Roman liturgy, but he did make the following modifications:

1. He ordered the paternoster (Lord's prayer) to be recited in the canon before the breaking of the host.
2. He prohibited the use of the chasuble by subdeacons assisting at mass.
3. He inserted the words *diesque nostros in tua pace disponas, atque ab aeterna damnatione nos eripi, et in electorum tuorum jubras grege numerari* in the canon of the mass.
4. He provided that the alleluia should be chanted after the gradual except during paschaltide (the period following Easter).
5. He forbade deacons to perform any of the musical portions of the mass other than singing the gospel.

Gregory was a peerless manager of the vast estates owned by the church: the yearly income from its landholdings in Africa, Sicily, and Campania—well over 1,300 square miles (3,380 square kilometers) all together—has been estimated at more than $1.5 million by today's standards. He appointed clerics as his rectors, teaching them how to provide detailed accounts and reports concerning their districts.

Even though much of Italian territory was in the hands of the Lombards and their Arian clergy, Gregory tried to care for the needs of the faithful in these dioceses whenever an opportunity arose. On the islands near Italy, of which Sicily was the largest and most important, he maintained and strengthened the existing church structure. Local synods on a regular basis were strictly enforced, and Gregory's many letters attest to his concern for this practice. He approached the filling of bishoprics in a disciplined way, enforced the celibacy of the clergy, maintained the exemption of clerics from lay tribunals, and did not hesitate to deprive clerics of their holdings and offices if they were guilty of criminal or scandalous offenses.

It is well documented that Gregory maintained, strengthened, and extended the powers, privileges, and jurisdiction of the head of the Roman see over all other Christian churches. In fact, Gregory's claim that the Roman see had supreme authority over the church universal was the basis for the primacy of the papacy in the medieval period and in modern times. The title of ecumenical bishop assumed by the patriarch of Constantinople was brought up for debate by Gregory at a synod held in 588. His manner toward all bishops and patriarchs, western or eastern, was cordial, despite his differences with the eastern church.

In his relations with the Lombards, Gregory worked hard to achieve a lasting peace. Authari, king of the Lombards, died a few days after Gregory's consecration as pope and was succeeded by Agilulf, duke of Turin. Gregory attempted to negotiate a separate peace for Rome with the Lombards, using Queen Theodolinda, who was a Catholic and a close friend, as an intermediary with King Agilulf and other Lombard chiefs. He exercised his temporal authority in response to the Lombard threat by appointing governors to cities, providing munitions, counseling generals, sending ambassadors, and negotiating, often without imperial authorization from Constantinople.

Gregory's connections with the Franks were perhaps the most important legacy of his papacy, because they resulted directly in his major diplomatic and spiritual accomplishment—the missionary effort in the British Isles. The Kentish queen, Bertha, was a Catholic Frank who wrote to Gregory often and at length, asking him to send spiritual ambassadors to the Kentish court and eventually to the entire island. The story of the mission to England of Saint Augustine of Canterbury in 597 was recorded in Gregory's letters and was also recounted by an anonymous monk of the English abbey at Whitby in the early eighth century. The English mission eventually brought together the Celtic and the Roman churches that had been torn apart by the breakup of the Roman empire two centuries earlier. After settling ecclesiastical and liturgical practices, English monasticism would reach its full flowering in the early ninth century, when Alcuin, a monk of York, became chief spiritual adviser to Charlemagne. Gregory's accomplishment earned him the title "apostle to the English."

In his relations with the imperial government, Gregory again trod new ground. He believed that church and state should form a united whole, yet be as distinct and independent from each other as possible in their respective spheres, the ecclesiastical and the secular. The records of the imperial government centered in Constantinople under Emperor Maurice and eventually Emperor Phocus are a source for the interaction between it and the Roman church, as is Gregory's immense correspondence.

Besides his missionary effort to the Angles, Gregory also made efforts to root out paganism in Gaul, Africa, northern Italy, and Istria. His policy toward schismatics, pagans, and heretics was to use persuasion first and force only as a last resort. His contribution to monasticism followed naturally from his own background as a monk.

Gregory's firm opinions on discipline, order, austerity, and obedience among monks, abbots, and bishops are extensively recorded in his numerous letters and were applied by many monastic orders during the Middle Ages.

The last years of Gregory's life were filled with suffering, both mental and physical. He died on 12 March 604, and his body was displayed in the portico of Saint Peter's basilica. His relics were moved several times during the medieval period and later, most recently by Pope Paul V in 1606. He was canonized immediately by popular acclaim. In art, the dove is his special emblem, because of a story, recorded by Peter the Deacon, that a dove placed the word of God on Gregory's lips while he was dictating his homilies on Ezekiel to his secretary.

Gregory the Great was not a philosopher or a man of profound learning; but he was a trained Roman lawyer, a monk and missionary, a highly regarded preacher, and a leader of men. His two major contributions to the papacy were his intense focus on convincing the world that the see of Peter was the one supreme, decisive, authority in the Catholic church, and his mission to the British Isles. He enabled the papacy, eventually, to become a power stronger than king, emperor, or patriarch. In his writings, Gregory summed up the teachings of the early fathers in a harmonious whole, so that they became a textbook for laymen and clerics alike throughout the medieval period. Writings confidently attributed to Gregory are *Moralium libri XXXV, Regulae pastoralis liber, Dialogorum libri IV, Homiliarum in evangelia libri II, Homiliarum in eqechielem prophetam libri II,* and *Epistolarum libri XIV.* Gregory's extensive contributions to the standardization of the liturgy and liturgical music include several hymns, the Gregorian sacramentary, and the antiphonary.

See also **Augustine of Canterbury**

Further Reading

Editions

Epistolae, ed. P. Ewald and L. M. Hartmann. Monumenta Germaniae Historica, Epist., 1, 2. Berlin, 1891–1899.
Opera Sancti Gregorii Magni. Editio princeps, Paris, 1518; ed. P. Tossianensis, 6 vols., Rome, 1588–1603; ed. P. Goussainville, 3 vols., Paris, 1675; ed. Cong. S. Mauri (Saint-Marthe, 4 vols., Paris, 1705; reedited with additions by J. B. Gallicioli, 17 vols., Venice, 1768–1776, reprinted in Jacques-Paul Migne, *Patrologia Latina,* 75–79.

Translations

The Book of Pastoral Care, trans. J. Barmby. In Nicene and Post-Nicene Fathers, Series 2(12). Oxford and New York, 1895.
King Alfred's West Saxon Version of Gregory's Pastoral Care, ed. H. Sweet. London, 1871.

Studies

Barmby, J. *Gregory the Great.* London, 1879. (Reissue, 1892.)

Dudden, F. *Gregory the Great: His Place in History and in Thought,* 2 vols. London, 1905.

Marcus, R. *Gregory the Great and His World.* Cambridge, 1997.

Snow, T. *Saint Gregory the Great: His Work and His Spirit.* London, 1892.

Straw, C. *Gregory the Great.* Aldershot, 1996.

——. *Gregory the Great: Perfection in Imperfection.* Berkeley: University of California Press, 1988.

BRADFORD LEE EDEN

GREGORY OF TOURS (ca. 538–594)

Born Georgius Florentius, the man known as Gregory pursued many careers during his fifty-five years of life: monk, author, builder, administrator, ambassador, propagandist, politician, and bishop of Tours. He was descended from rich and influential families on both his father's and his mother's side. Senators and bishops, especially the bishops of Langres and Tours, hung thick on the branches of his family tree. Destined for the episcopacy, he spent his youth in the care of uncles and cousins, all of whom were important churchmen. In 573, he was elected bishop of Tours, one of the most powerful of all the Frankish sees, holding its episcopal throne until his death in 594.

Gregory vigorously performed his ecclesiastical duties and played an active role in both local and national politics, as he himself tells us. His position often demanded that he stand up for Tours against the Frankish kings, especially Chilperic I (r. 561–84) of Neustria. He seems to have found ample time to write. At one point, he grouped his massive literary output into five major works: ten books of *Histories,* seven books of *Miracles* (which include four books on the miracles of St. Martin), one on the *Life of the Fathers,* a *Commentary on the Psalms,* and a tract *On the Office of the Church.*

Most famous for his *Histories,* often improperly called *History of the Franks* (though now scholars are gaining a great deal from his other works as well), Gregory is certainly the first writer in medieval France worthy to be called a historian. The *Histories* were not conceived specifically as a "History of the Franks," but within 200 years of their completion this became their most common name. They are by far our most valuable source for Merovingian Gaul; the Frankish Dark Ages would be even darker without them.

Drawing on the Bible, Eusebius, Jerome, Orosius, Sulpicius Severus, Renatus Profuturus Frigeridus, Sulpicius Alexander, and others, Gregory's first four books cover world history from Adam to his own age. Book 5 begins with an elaborate preface and completes the work with accounts of Gregory's own times. The overall result is, especially in the later books, frequently confusing. While perceptive and analytical, Gregory often skips from episode to episode without obvious order or structure. Scholars have tried to present Gregory as a beguiling storyteller, or as an advocate for the earlier and sterner rule the Franks had enjoyed under Clovis, or as a provider of a cure for the disorder of his times, or as the sincere author of an artless reflection of the chaos of Merovingian society in general. A more charitable assessment sees Gregory as intentionally presenting history as chaotic: the very nature of secular history, that is, the story of fallen humanity, is chaos; true order and structure are divine.

Gregory's other works treat the divine. Here, critics have viewed him as a credulous hagiographer, devoid of the analytical intellect obvious in the *Histories.* For Gregory, however, there could be nothing more concrete than God's power evidenced in a miracle. Particularly revealing of Gregory, and of the 6th-century Gallic episcopacy generally, is his attitude toward St. Martin. Martin had been bishop of Tours two centuries before, and that city guarded his relics. Gregory saw himself as Martin's successor; Martin was his present guide. Gregory protected Martin's interests and Martin protected Gregory's city. His relationship to the saint is a poignant reminder that, though remembered largely for having been a historian, Gregory was first and foremost a Christian bishop.

See also **Clovis I**

Further Reading

Gregory of Tours. *Monumenta Germaniae Historica, Scriptores Rerum Merovingicarum,* ed. Bruno Krusch and Wilhelm Levison. Hanover: Hahn, 1951; and II–2, Hanover: Hahn, 1885.

——. *The History of the Franks,* trans. Lewis Thorpe. Harmondsworth: Penguin, 1974.

Goffart, Walter. "Gregory of Tours and 'The Triumph of Superstition.'" In *The Narrators of Barbarian History.* Princeton: Princeton University Press, 1988, pp. 112–234.

Hellmann, Siegmund. "Studien zur mittelalterliche Geschichtsschreibung, I, Gregor von Tours." *Historische Zeitschrift* 107 (1911): 1–43.

Wallace-Hadrill, J. M. *The Long-Haired Kings.* Toronto: University of Toronto Press, 1982, pp. 49–70.

RICHARD A. GERBERDING

GREGORY VII, POPE
(c. 1020–1085, r. 1073–1085)

Pope Gregory VII (Hildebrand) was the only Italian among the eleventh-century reforming popes involved in the investiture controversy, apart from Paschal II (r. 1099–1118). Gregory VII was born in southern Tuscany (possibly in Soana) into a well-to-do family and came to Rome as a young child. In his letters, Gregory mentions that he grew up in the bosom of the Roman church, and he refers to the special guardianship of the apostle Peter, as well as to a Roman palace (perhaps the

Lateran) where he attended school with other upper-class Romans. He spent some time at the monastery of Saint Mary on the Aventine Hill, where his uncle was abbot. Saint Mary's had once been reformed by Abbot Odo of Cluny and had connections with certain local reformers of the church.

The first secure date for Gregory VII—then Hildebrand—is January 1047. He accompanied Pope Gregory VI (r. 1045–1046) into exile in Germany after the latter's deposition by Emperor Henry III at the synod of Sutri (20 December 1046). In early 1049, Hildebrand returned to Rome in the entourage of Pope Leo IX (r. 1049–1054). He had probably become a monk by then, although it remains unclear where and when he made his vows. Certainly, however, this did not occur at Cluny. In Rome, he became subdeacon and then rector of the Abbey of Saint Paul's Outside the Walls. He was sent as papal legate in 1054 to the synod of Tours and in 1056 to the synod of Chalon-sur-Saône. The synod at Tours was concerned with the teachings of Berengar of Tours on the eucharist (a topic that Hildebrand would have to deal with again later, as pope); the synod at Chalon dealt with simony and led to the deposition of six simoniac bishops by Hildebrand. At least once during these years, Hildebrand must have been at the court of Emperor Henry III (d. 5 October 1056); later, as pope, he would note that Henry III honored him more than other Italians. Moreover, Hildebrand participated in a court ceremony in which the boy Henry IV (r. 1056–1105) was either elected or acclaimed king. In 1057, Pope Stephen IX (r. 1057–1058) once again sent Hildebrand to Germany, together with Anselm of Lucca (later Pope Alexander II, r. 1061–1073). Stephen IX demanded a solemn oath from the cardinal bishops and the clergy and laity of Rome that if he died they would await Hildebrand's return from Germany before electing a successor; this is an indication of Hildebrand's standing in Rome. It is very likely that Hildebrand collaborated actively with Stephen's successor, Pope Nicholas II (r. 1059–1061) and helped shape Nicholas's policies toward the Normans and the Patarenes; but it is difficult to identify Hildebrand's influence precisely or to determine whether he differed from other reformers. Apparently, he did not sign the election decree of the Lateran synod of April—May 1059, but in a speech at this council he severely condemned the Aachen rule of 816 for regular canons, which had permitted the holding of private property. In the autumn of 1059, Nicholas II named Hildebrand archdeacon of the Roman church, entrusted with financial, judicial, and military tasks. Hildebrand would also have been responsible for the papal states, would have acted as vicar during the pope's absence, and would have administered the see of Rome during a vacancy. These were heavy responsibilities, but it would be an exaggeration to claim that Hildebrand was the power behind the papal throne during his more than twenty years at the curia.

Pontificate

During the funeral of Alexander II on 22 April 1073, Hildebrand was proclaimed Pope Gregory VII in a tumultuous election by the Roman people—an election that was subsequently formalized by the cardinals, the clergy, and the Roman laity in San Pietro in Vincoli. Gregory's pontificate is relatively well known. His invaluable register, the official papal record containing chiefly his letters but also some synodal protocols, feudal oaths, etc., is still preserved in the Vatican's Archivio Segreto. It provides a solid basis for an evaluation of Gregory's policies, but it is limited because only a certain number of letters were registered (the selection criteria are unknown), because many important letters were originally supplemented with oral messages, and not least because many of Gregory's declarations are ambiguous and often impenetrable for modern readers.

Gregory interpreted his election as a call by God to continue unhesitatingly, not to say ruthlessly, the fight for what he considered the proper world order and to restore the church to its original splendor, as envisioned by the eleventh-century reformers. He linked the battle against simony and for celibacy—the chief characteristics of the Gregorian reform (which took its name from him)—with a marked emphasis on the primacy of the papacy. This primacy did indeed include the subordination of all temporal Christian governments to the pope's authority, but it applied first of all to the ecclesiastical hierarchy. In Gregory's view, all Christians, including kings and emperors, owed the papacy unquestioned obedience because the pope alone, by virtue of his mystic connection with Saint Peter, would never deviate from the Christian faith. According to Gregory, Saint Peter himself, through the pope, directed the church. Obedience to God became obedience to the papacy.

Gregory's attitude had profound political consequences. He emphasized the territorial claims of the papacy and tried to bring several areas of Europe under the overlordship of Saint Peter, i.e., the pope. The conditions varied; they included the simple oath of fealty by William of Burgundy and clearly feudal relationships involving homage and investiture as well as fealty. The popes thus became feudal lords. The vassals' obligations corresponded to those customary in the secular sphere and included military and financial aid. Examples are the alliances with the Normans (1059), Aragon (1068), Denmark, Hungary, Kiev, Croatia, and Dalmatia. Like his predecessor, Gregory supported the *reconquista* in Spain by French knights, provided that they were willing to take over the conquered lands as vassals of Saint Peter—since, Gregory argued, Spain had belonged to Peter from ancient times. Some princes of Poland and Bohemia had asked Gregory for support of their claims, and it is not surprising that he expected special links to the papacy in return. He saw the relationship with England similarly. In 1080, he wrote to William the Conqueror, reminding William of his assistance in 1066. As we can gather from William's negative reply, the messengers who delivered the letter had asked him to do homage for England to the pope. The legal premises for the largely unsuccessful papal claims are still disputed, but evidently the Donation of Constantine played only a subordinate role. These feudal relationships—which were an innovation as far as the papacy was concerned—were intended to further church reform and to gain financial and military support for papal policies. Episcopal oaths also included the promise of troops. Since Gregory also planned to lead an army to assist Constantinople against the Muslims, it is not surprising that he has the reputation of being a particularly warlike pope.

Gregory never had occasion to intervene in England; and Spain largely accommodated the claims of the papacy. In France and Germany, however, direct intervention by the papacy in the appointment of bishops and the prohibition of their investiture with ring and staff (possibly 1077–1078) created severe tension. Especially serious were Gregory's clashes with Germany, although, despite some initial problems, there was no hint of this at the outset of Gregory's pontificate. Gregory, who saw in Henry the future emperor, suggested in a letter of December 1074 that Henry was to protect Rome and the Roman church during the papal crusade. It was the German episcopacy rather than the king that appeared to hinder church reform in Germany. Gregory counted on Henry's support. But events taught him otherwise, and in a letter of December 1075 to Henry, Gregory can barely contain his anger. It is possible that the oral message accompanying the missive was a threat of excommunication. In harsh language, Gregory blamed Henry especially on account of the customary royal appointments to the Italian bishoprics of Milan, Fermo, and Spoleto. A second issue was Henry's continued contact with his excommunicated advisers. On 24 January 1076, at the Diet of Worms, Henry IV and the vast majority of the German bishops replied in even harsher terms. In a letter addressed to "Brother Hildebrand," they renounced their obedience to Gregory. The king asked Gregory to abdicate and the Romans to elect a new pope. Northern Italian bishops immediately joined in this renunciation of obedience. The letters reached Gregory during the Lenten synod (14–20 February 1076), and he replied at once, declaring Henry deposed and absolving all of Henry's Christian subjects from their oath of fealty. Henceforth no one was to serve Henry as king, and Henry was anathematized.

The effect of the excommunication was tremendous. Gregory assumed that he had historical precedents on his side, but never before had a pope deposed a king. Gregory's deposition of Henry was then, and has remained, his most hotly debated action. Gregory had pursued to its logical conclusion his conviction that papal primacy was secular as well as spiritual. Church reform now became a struggle over dominance between priestly power and royal power. To save his crown, Henry submitted to Gregory at Canossa (28 January 1077), implicitly recognizing the papal claim to universal lordship.

The encounter at Canossa interrupted Gregory's journey to Augsburg, where the German princes had intended to elect a new king. After the reconciliation of Henry with the church, Gregory returned to Rome, but the German princes nevertheless proceeded to elect Rudolf of Swabia (15 March 1077). Gregory waited until the Lenten synod of 1080 to grant Rudolf full recognition as king; at that time he repeated the excommunication and deposition of Henry IV. However, Henry had reasserted himself after his absolution at Canossa; the new excommunication had little effect; and the king was victorious in a civil war. A royal synod at Brixen formally deposed Gregory (25 June 1080) and elected Wibert (Guibert, Guiberto) of Ravenna pope, or antipope; he was eventually enthroned in 1084 as Clement III. Henry's Italian campaign of 1081 was successfully concluded when he entered Rome on 21 March 1084; the gates of the city were opened to him by many members of the Roman clergy who condemned Gregory's inflexible attitude, and by the Roman populace. Clement III crowned Henry emperor on 31 March 1084. Gregory VII had fled to Castel Sant'Angelo. He was freed by his Norman vassal Robert Guiscard in May and accompanied Robert to Salerno; there, in exile, Gregory died on 25 May 1085. Pope Paul V canonized Gregory in 1606, and his feast day (25 May) was expanded from Salerno to the entire church in 1728.

Gregory VII was certainly one of the great medieval popes. The history of papal primacy—especially but not only with regard to secular power—cannot be imagined without him. Gregory attempted to translate his own religious experience, with its mystical core, into historical reality. Concepts that he grasped intuitively were legally and theoretically elaborated in the twelfth and thirteenth centuries, resulting in what is known as the papal monarchy.

See also **Henry IV, Emperor; Robert Guiscard; William I**

Further Reading

Sources
Cowdrey, H. E. J. *The Epistolae vagantes of Pope Gregory VII.* Oxford: Clarendon, 1972.

Epistolae selectae. Monumenta Germaniae Historica, 2(1–2).

Das Register Gregors VII, ed. Erich Caspar. Berlin: Weidmannsche Buchhandlung, 1920–1923.

Santifaller, Leo. *Quellen u.Forsckungen zum Urkunden-und Kanzleiwesen Papst Gregors VII.* Studi e Testi 190. Vatican City: Biblioteca Apostolica Vaticana, 1957.

Viae Gregorii VII, ed. I. M. Waiterich. In *Pontificum romanorum vitae,* Vol. 1. Leipzig: Engelmann, 1862.

Studies

Benson, Robert L. *The Bishop-Elect.* Princeton, N.J., Princeton University Press, 1968.

Blumenthal, Uta-Renate. "Gregor VII., Papst." In *Theologische Realenzyklopaedie,* 14, pp.145–152.

——. *The Investiture Controversy.* Philadelphia: University of Pennsylvania Press, 1988. (Translation by the author of *Der Investiturstreit.* Stuttgart: Kohlhammer, 1982.)

Brooke, Zachary Nugent. *The English Church and the Papacy.* Cambridge: Cambridge University Press, 1931. (Reprints, 1952, 1968.)

Robinson, Ian S. "Pope Gregory VII and Episcopal Authority." *Viator,* 9, 1978, pp. 103–131.

——. *The Papacy.* Cambridge: Cambridge University Press, 1990.

UTA-RENATE BLUMENTHAL

GROCHEIO, JOHANNES DE
(fl. ca. 1300)

French music theorist, whose treatise *De musica* is our most important source of information on genre distinctions between medieval French secular music with vernacular texts and instrumental music. Grocheio focuses on the musical practice of Paris, distinguishing broadly between monophonic vernacular music (*musica vulgaris*), measured, or polyphonic, music (*musica mensurata*), and sacred music (*musica ecclesiastica*).

Grocheio divides *musica vulgaris* into *cantus* (vocal music without refrain) and *cantilena* (popular dance music with refrain). There are three categories of *cantus: gestualis, versualis,* and *coronatus. Cantus gestualis* refers to French medieval epic, the chanson de geste. Grocheio provides more information than any other source about the performance practice of the epic. *Cantus versicularis* refers to French chansons organized by syllable count and rhyme scheme, that is, the songs of the troubadours and trouveres. *Cantus coronatus* refers to particularly distinguished and elevated examples of *cantus versualis,* the *grands chants courtois.*

Under the term *cantilena,* Grocheio provides us with our best descriptions of popular dance forms, distinguishing *rotundellus* (rondeau), *stantipes* (estampie), and *ductia* (carole), the latter two with both vocal and instrumental forms. He provides a useful distinction between dance forms in which all parts of the song are dependent on the refrain (i.e., rondeau) from those that have additional music not dependent on the refrain (i.e., virelai and ballade). The instrumental *ductia* and

stantipes are articulated by alternating phrases called *puncta* (each with first and second endings) with the refrain and are best played on the vielle.

For polyphonic music, Grocheio discusses the motet, organum, conductus, and hocket, describing a successive compositional process in which first the tenor voice is organized and then upper voices are built one at a time over the tenor.

Grocheio peppers his treatise with fascinating comments on the social functions of musical forms; for instance, girls and youths in Normandy sing rondeaux at festivals and banquets, *stantipes* turn the souls of the rich from depraved thinking, motets are not suitable for common people, who do not understand their subtleties, but should be performed for the learned.

Further Reading

Grocheio, Johannes de. *Die Quellenhandschriften zum Musiktraktat des Johannes de Grocheio,* ed. Ernst Rohloff. Leipzig: Deutscher Verlag für Musik, 1972.

——. *Johannes de Grocheo: Concerning Music (De musica),* trans. Albert Seay. 2nd ed. Colorado Springs: Colorado College Music Press, 1973.

Page, Christopher. "Johannes de Grocheio on Secular Music: A Corrected Text and a New Translation." *Plainsong and Medieval Music* 2 (1993): 17–41.

—— *Discarding Images: Reflections on Music and Culture in Medieval France.* Oxford: Clarendon, 1993, pp. 65–111.

Stevens, John. *Words and Music in the Middle Ages: Song, Narrative, Dance and Drama, 1050–1350.* Cambridge: Cambridge University Press, 1986, pp. 429–34.

LAWRENCE EARP

GROSSETESTE, ROBERT
(ca. 1170–1253)

The great English scholar and bishop of Lincoln (1235–53). Born in Suffolk of humble parentage, he probably spent his early years as clerk in the episcopal households at Lincoln and Hereford. While his education in Oxford or Paris is a matter of conjecture, he was master of theology in Oxford by the early 1220s and was subsequently elected chancellor of the university. In 1229–30 he was the first Oxford lecturer to the newly arrived Franciscans.

As a scholar Grosseteste was among the early-13th-century theologians who contributed to the development of the western scientific tradition. A scientific observer of causes and predictor of consequences, he urged the use of experiments in natural sciences. In his methodology he began with individual cases and worked to formulate general rules. His study of optics, for example, led him to ascribe to light a central role in the production and constitution of the physical world.

Grosseteste's works, written in Latin, French, and

English, included scientific, philosophical, theological, and pastoral treatises. His theological works included the *Hexaemeron* (1230s) and numerous biblical commentaries and sermons. He wrote important commentaries on Aristotle's *Posterior Analytics* and *Physics* and translated the *Nicomocheon Ethics* from Greek into Latin. His scientific interests were reflected in books on astronomy, comets, the tides, mathematics, and the rainbow.

As a bishop with a strong sense of pastoral responsibilities Grosseteste was an important figure in the reform movement in the 13th-century church; his devotional treatises were influential and widely read. While he supported the doctrine of papal plenitude of power, he clashed with the papacy over the growing practice of papal provisions (direct papal appointment of ecclesiastical personnel) and attacked corrupt papal politics at Rome in 1250.

Robert Grosseteste died on 9 October 1253. His books and notes were bequeathed to the Franciscan library at Oxford, ensuring his continuing scholarly influence on later generations of Oxford scholars.

See also **Bacon, Roger**

Further Reading

Callus, Daniel A., ed. *Robert Grosseteste: Scholar and Bishop.* Oxford: Clarendon, 1955

Crombie, A.C. *Robert Grosseteste and the Origins of Experimental Science, 1100-1700.* Oxford: Clarendon, 1953

Southern, R.W. *Robert Grosseteste: The Growth of an English Mind in Medieval Europe,* Oxford: Clarendon, 1986.

GUESCLIN, BERTRAND DU
(ca. 1320–1380)

Constable of France. Bertrand du Guesclin, perhaps the most famous French warrior of the Hundred Years' War, was the first of three distinguished Breton noblemen to serve as constable of France during this conflict. Du Guesclin was born into an old but not very wealthy family. In 1353, he succeeded his father as lord of Broons and a year later was knighted. He began serving the French crown at Pontorson as early as 1351, and for the next thirteen years his military career was confined to Normandy, where he fought for the king against the supporters of Charles the Bad, king of Navarre, and Brittany, where he fought for Charles de Blois against Jean de Montfort, the English-backed claimant to the duchy. In 1357, he led the forces that supplied the besieged city of Rennes. In May 1364, he won a great victory over the Navarrese forces at Cocherel in Normandy after feigning a withdrawal that induced his foes to abandon a superior position. In the same period, he also suffered defeats, as the English captured him at Pas d'Évran in

1359, at the bridge of Juigne in 1360, and at Auray in 1364. In this last battle, Charles de Blois was killed and Montfort became duke of Brittany.

With Normandy and Brittany now pacified, Du Guesclin devoted the rest of the 1360s to service in southern France and Spain. Louis of Anjou, brother of Charles V, was royal lieutenant in Languedoc and needed him to lead numerous *routiers* (unemployed soldiers) outside the realm on campaigns in Provence and Castile. His successful expedition to Spain in 1365 was followed by his defeat and capture at Nájera in 1367. In 1369, however, he returned to Spain and reinstalled a pro-French king on the Castilian throne.

Rarely successful at pitched battles, Du Guesclin was adept at handling bands of *routiers* and fighting with their tactics. In 1370, when a *routier* chieftain, Robert Knolles, was leading an English raid into northwestern France, Charles V summoned Du Guesclin and made him constable. The latter then made a private alliance with Olivier de Clisson, a wealthy Breton lord who had fought against him at Auray and Nájera. Clisson brought powerful contingents of Bretons into the French army, and he and Du Guesclin conquered Poitou and Saintonge in 1371–72. In 1373, they secured Brittany, whose duke had gone over to the English.

For the next five years, the constable led French forces against the English in various parts of France. At the end of 1378, Charles V made the political error of trying to confiscate Brittany. Du Guesclin, one of those charged with implementing this unpopular decision, was reluctant to do so, since many of his old comrades had rallied to the duke. Never popular with the king's nonmilitary advisers, he was nearly removed from office but instead was sent to fight against *routiers* in Auvergne, where he died from an unknown illness (perhaps dysentery) in the summer of 1380 while besieging the town of Châteauneuf-de-Randon.

Admired by his contemporaries for his military prowess, Du Guesclin earned the titles count of Longueville and duke of Molina. He was buried at Saint-Denis.

See also **Charles II the Bad; Charles V the Wise**

Further Reading

Cazelles, Raymond. "Du Guesclin avant Cocherel." *Actes du Colloque International de Cocherel* (1964): 33–40.

Dupuy, Micheline. *Bertrand du Guesclin: capitaine d'aventure, connétable de France.* Paris: Perrin, 1977.

Hay du Chastelet, Paul. *Histoire de Bertrand du Guesclin, connétable de France.* Paris: Billaine, 1666.

Jacob, Yves. *Bertrand du Guesclin, connétable de France.* Paris: Tallandier, 1992.

Luce, Siméon. *Histoire de Bertrand du Guesclin et de son époque.* Paris: Hachette, 1876.

JOHN BELL HENNEMAN, JR.

GUIBERT DE NOGENT
(ca. 1064–ca. 1125)

Perhaps best known for his autobiography, *De vita sua sive monodiarum suarum libri tres*, and a treatise concerning the veneration of relics, *De pignoribus sanctorum*, this Benedictine monk also wrote a popular history of the First Crusade (*Gesta Dei per Francos*), a moral commentary on Genesis, a handbook for preachers (*Liber quo ordine sermo fieri debeat*), and lesser works.

Born at Clermont-en-Beauvaisis in northern France, Guibert was dedicated by his parents to the monastic life. His father died soon after his birth, and he was raised by his mother, who isolated him from other children. As a young adolescent, he entered the monastery of Saint-Germer-de-Fly, where he studied not only the Bible and theology but also classical authors, especially Ovid and Virgil. In 1104, he became abbot of a small Benedictine house at Nogent-sous-Coucy. There, he wrote his history of the First Crusade and, in 1115, his autobiography. Guibert's attitudes toward his mother, sexuality and sexual sins, cleanliness, and his (and others') visionary experiences are important aspects of the autobiography, which also offers numerous insights into daily life, education, and social and political history. Guibert's treatise on relics attacks the veneration of a supposed tooth of Christ at the abbey of Saint-Médard, Soissons, but it is not a total rejection of either the cult of the saints or the veneration of relics.

Further Reading

Guibert de Nogent. *Opera*. PL 166.

——. *Autobiographie*, ed. and trans. Edmond-René Labande. Paris: Les Belles Lettres, 1981.

——. *How to Make a Sermon*, trans. George E. McCracken. In *Early Medieval Theology*, ed. George E. McCracken with Allen Cabaniss. Philadelphia: Westminster, 1957.

——. *Gesta Dei per Francos*, ed. M. Thurot. In *Recueil des historiens des croisades*. 16 vols. Paris: Imprimerie Royale, 1879, Vol. 4: *Historiens occidentaux*, pp. 115–263.

——. *Self and Society in Medieval France: The Memoirs of Abbot Guibert of Nogent*, trans. John F. Benton. New York: Harper Torchbooks, 1970. [Excellent introduction and bibliography.]

——. *De vita sua sive monodiarum suarum libri tres*, ed. Georges Bourgin as *Histoire de sa vie*. Paris: Picard, 1907.

GROVER A. ZINN

GUIDO D'AREZZO (c. 991–1050)

Guido d'Arezzo (Guido Aretinus) was an important Italian music theorist. The circumstances Guido describes in the prefaces to his treatises place his activity in Arezzo, Pomposa, and Rome c. 1025–1032. Four treatises can be attributed to him: *Micrologus* (between 1023 and 1032, perhaps 1025–1026); *Prologus in antiphonarium* (later than *Micrologus*); *Regule rhythmice* (later than *Micrologus*); and *Epistola de ignoto cantu* (later than *Prologus* and *Regulae rhythmicae*).

In *Micrologus,* Guido surveyed, principally, the music theory that would be of use to a practicing musician. He described a scale extending from G at the bottom of the modern bass-clef staff to C in the third space of the treble, including all natural notes plus B-flat below middle C, and presented them in a tuning with all perfect fifths pure. With the addition of B-flat above middle C and of the high D and E, this scale and this tuning (the latter since called Pythagorean) became the standard of the Middle Ages. Guido enumerated and described the six intervals most typically used in plainchant and early medieval polyphony (major and minor seconds and thirds, perfect fourths and fifths). He presented the basics of the theory of melodic modes, first explaining the classification of four modal types on the basis of the location of a central tone within the context of a series of major and minor seconds above and below that central tone, and then describing the division of each into a pair differentiated by relatively high or low register. Similar classifications and differentiations persisted in theories of mode throughout the Middle Ages and beyond. He described a procedure for composing a melody by deriving its pitches from the vowels of the text to be sung. He described the traditional practice of polyphonic composition with parallel fourths and fifths as "harsh" (*durus*) and appended a set of rudimentary counterpoint rules for using other intervals, particularly at the ends of phrases, which produce a result he characterized as "soft" (*mollis*). To all this he added a speculative chapter recounting how Pythagoras discovered the nature of musical harmony by studying the weights of hammers striking an anvil; this story, in one version or another, has since been recounted in dozens of music treatises. *Micrologus* became one of the most widely copied music treatises of the Middle Ages (almost eighty manuscript sources survive), and one of the most influential.

Two of Guido's innovations, however, must be reckoned even more influential than anything he described in *Micrologus*. He seems to have been the first (in *Prologus*) to describe the use of the staff in music notation: the placement, that is, of notes on or between any of a set of parallel lines, with the positions of C's and F's indicated first by the placement of these letters in the appropriate positions at the beginning of the staff (like modern clef signs); and second by the use of the colors yellow and red, respectively, to highlight the positions of the two letters (much as the C and F strings of a harp are colored today). He also seems to have been the first (in *Epistola*) to name the ascending degrees of the C scale *ut re mi fa sol la*, syllables derived from the openings of lines of the hymn *Ut queant laxis/Resonare fibris*....

In *Regulae rhythmicae* Guido reworked in poetic form material he had covered for the most part in *Micrologus*; he also included one example in staff notation.

Writers of a much later date transposed the series *ut re mi fa sol la* to pitches other than C and constructed an interlocking array of such series spanning the entire musical gamut. Although the "Guidonian hand"—a representation of the left hand with the notes of the musical gamut depicted on the various joints of the fingers—was during the Middle Ages and later often attributed to Guido of Arezzo, it is documented only from the twelfth century.

Further Reading

Editions

Amelli, Ambrosio M., ed. *Guidonis Monachi Aretini Micrologus ad praestantiores codices mss. exactus.* Rome: Desclèe, Lefebvre, 1904.

Gerbert, Martin, ed. *Scriptores ecclesiastici de musica sacra potissimum,* Vol. 2. Includes *Micrologus,* 2–24; *Prologus in antiphonarium* (*Alie Guidonis regulae de ignoto cantu identidem in antiphonarii sui prologum prolatae*), 34–37; *Regule rhythmice* (*Musicae Guidonis regulae rhythmicae,* 25–33 (34?); *Epistota de ignoto cantu ,* 43–50. Saint Blasien, 1784. (Reprint, Hildesheim: Olms, 1963.)

——, and Schola Palaeographica Amstelodamensis, eds. *Tres tractatuli Guidonis Aretini: Guidonis Prologus in antiphonarium.* Divitiae Musicae Artis, A(3). Buren: Knuf, 1975.

——, and Eddie Vetter, eds. *Guidonis Aretini Regulae rhythmicae.* Divitiae Musicae Artis, A(4). Buren: Knuf, 1985.

Pesce, Dolores, ed. *Guido d'Arezzo's Regulae rhythmicae, Prologus antiphonarii, and Epistola ad Michahelem.* Ottawa: Institute of Mediaeval Music, 1999. (With translation.)

Smits van Waesberghe, Joseph, ed. *Guidonis Aretini Micrologus.* Corpus Scriptorum de Musica, 4. N.p.: American Institute of Musicology, 1955.

Translations

Babb, Warren, trans. *Hucbald, Guido, and John on Music: Three Medieval Treatises,* ed. Claude V. Palisca. Music Theory Translation Series, 3. New Haven, Conn., and London: Yale University Press, 1978.

Strunk, Oliver, ed. and trans. *Source Readings in Music History from Classical Antiquity through the Romantic Era.* New York: Norton, 1950. (See pp. 117–120 for *Prologus in antiphonarium* and 121–125 for *Epistola de ignoto cantu*; the latter is incomplete.)

Critical Studies

Brockett, Clyde W. "A Comparison of the Five Monochords of Guido d'Arezzo." *Current Musicology,* 32, 1981, pp. 29–42.

Kartsovnik, Viarcheslav. "Institutiones grammaticae and Mensura monochordi: A New Source of Guido of Arezzo's *Micrologus.*" *Musica Disciplina,* 42, 1988, pp. 7–22.

Kiesewetter, Raphael Georg. *Guido von Arezzo: Sein Leben und Wirken.* Leipzig: Breitkopf and Hartel, 1840.

Oesch, Hans. *Guido von Arezzo: Biographisches und Theoretisches unter besonderer Beücksichtigung der sogenannten odonischen Traktate.* Publikationen der Schweizerischen Musikforschenden Gesellschaft. Bern: Haupt, 1954.

Smits van Waesberghe, Joseph. "Guido of Arezzo and Musical Improvisation." *Musica Disciplina,* 5, 1951a, pp. 55–63.

——. "The Musical Notation of Guido of Arezzo." *Musica Disciplina,* 5, 1951b, pp. 15–53.

——. *De musico-paedagogico et theoretico Guidone Aretino eiusque vita et moribus.* Florence: Olschki, 1953.

——. *Musikerziehung: Lehre und Theorie der Musik im Mittelalter.* Musikgeschichte in Bildern, 3(3). Leipzig: VEB Deutscher Verlag für Musik, 1969.

JAN HERLINGER

GUIDO DELLE COLONNE (13th century)

The thirteenth-century judge Guido de (or da) le Colonne di Messina is referred to by Dante in *De vulgari eloquentia* as *Iudex de Columpnis de Messana* or simply as *Iudex de Messana.* Guido's name appears in a total of fifteen documents, some of them bearing his signature, issued in Messina between 1243 and 1280. This documentary evidence testifies to his activity as a judge in that city. Since he was acting in a professional capacity as early as 1243, he must have been born c. 1210; this date makes it rather unlikely he could be identical with a Guido de Columna who was the author of a Latin version of *Historia destructionis Troiae,* a prose rendition of Benoît de Sainte-Maure's *Roman de Troie,* begun in 1272 but not finished until 1287. Bertoni (1947) accepts this identity, however, thereby placing Guido's poetic activity during the Manfred era. Guido's birthplace is unknown; there is nothing to support Monaci's claim (1955) that Guido was descended from the Colonna family in Rome, nor do we have any firm proof that he was related to the other poet of the same name in Messina, Odo delle Colonne. Nothing is known about Guido's personal life. His poetic legacy consists of only five *canzoni,* of which one—*La mia vit' è si fort' e dura e fera* ("My life is so harsh and fierce")—is of uncertain attribution: it is described as anonymous in the Vatican Codex (Vat. Lat. 3793) but is given to Guido in the Palatine Codex (Florence, Biblioteca Nazionale Centrale, Banco Rari 217, formerly Palatino 418). Included in this count is the poem *Gioiosamente canto* ("Joyously I sing"), which scholars almost unanimously assign to Guido on the strength of the attributions proposed by the most reliable manuscripts (Vatican 3793 and Laurentian Rediano 9); but many other codices, among them the Palatine, Chigiano L.VIII.308, and Vatican 3214, concur in giving it to Mazzeo di Ricco, who may simply have been the recipient rather than the author of the poem.

Although Guido delle Colonne's lyrical production is thus very modest in scope, his poems rank among the most technically elaborate of the Sicilian school. Guido treats the traditional amorous themes with exceptional rhetorical skill and has at his disposal an impressive fund of abstract imagery that enables him to bring variety to even the most conventional motifs. His rhetorical resources and his technical virtuosity drew high praise from Dante, who, in *De vulgari eloquentia,* cites two of Guido's poems as particularly elegant: *Amor che lungiamente m'hai menato* ("Love who has driven me for a long time") and *Ancor che l'aigua per lo foco lassi* ("Although water, because of fire, loses"). The second of these *canzoni* is quoted as an example of *suprema constructio* because of its structural complexity and its difficult rhyme scheme. Whereas the Sicilians treat the motifs of atmospheric and other natural phenomena merely as part of a comprehensive repertoire designed to offer an illustration of the prevailing cultural-philosophical climate, Guido delle Colonne is able to move beyond loosely connected encyclopedic detail to express subtle analogies between a variety of natural phenomena, and he skillfully applies these images to the nature of love. A prime example of his virtuosity in dealing with these motifs is the poem *Ancor che l'aigua per lo foco lassi,* with its intricate associations of fire and snow. It is from this *canzone* that Guido Guinizzelli drew the inspiration for his poem *Al cor gentil ripara sempre amore* ("Love always dwells in the noble heart").

See also **Benoît de Sainte-Maure; Dante Alighieri**

Further Reading

Bertoni, Giulio. *Il Duecento.* Milan: Vallardi, 1947, pp. 117–118.

Cesareo, G. A. "La patria di Guido dalle Colonne." *Giornale Dantesco, 9,* 1901, pp. 81ff.

Chiantèra, Raffaele. *Guido delle Colonne, poeta e storico latino del secolo XIII.* Naples, 1956.

Contini, Gianfranco. "Le rime di Guido delle Colonne." *Bollettino del Centro di Studi Filologici e Linguistici Siciliani,* 2, 1954, pp. 178–200.

——, ed. *Poeti del Duecento.* Milan-Naples: Ricciardi, 1960, Vol. 1, pp. 95–110.

Dionisotti, Carlo. "Proposta per Guido Giudice." *Rivista di Cultura Classica e Medioevale,* 7, 1965, pp. 452–466.

Marti, Mario. "Il giudizio di Dante su Guido delle Colonne." In *Con Dante fra i poeti del suo tempo.* Lecce: Milella, 1966, pp. 29–42.

Monaci, Ernesto. *Crestomazia italiana dei primi secoli,* rev. ed., ed. Felice Arese. Rome, Naples, and Città di Castello: Società Ed. Dante Alighieri, 1955, pp. 258–263.

Pasquini, Emilio, and Antonio Enzo Quaglio. *Il Duecento dale origini a Dante.* Bari: Laterza, 1970, pp. 203–210.

Torraca, Francesco. "Il giudice Guido delle Colonne di Messina." In *Studi su la lirica italiana del Duecento.* Bologna: Zanichelli, 1902, pp. 379–468.

Zacca, E. *Vita e opere di Guido delle Colonne,* Palermo, 1908.

FREDE JENSEN

GUILHEM IX (William IX, 1071–1126)

The first troubadour was also the seventh count of Poitiers, ninth duke of Aquitaine, and grandfather of Eleanor of Aquitaine. One of the few who returned to France after the First Crusade (1096–99), he successfully led a crusading army to Spain in 1120. Contemporary anecdotes recall him entertaining crowds with jokes, verses, and stories; some sources style him a reckless, violent, sarcastic infidel who earned his excommunication.

Eleven songs survive, one of doubtful attribution. Though often seeming to parody or recast a preexisting tradition, Guilhem's work lays the foundation for later troubadour song, including the love lyric, satire, and *pastorela;* the figures of warrior and lover, boasting and humility, ribaldry and nascent courtliness are all represented. Three songs addressed to his "companions" jocularly compare women to property (horses, fishing holes, woodlands), subject to legal disputes; in three more, the poet, disguised as a fool or madman, claims prowess in both word games and sexual games. Four meditate more soberly on love, using feudal and natural metaphors; these inaugurate in Occitan the vocabulary and topoi of *fin'amors,* among them the nature introduction, with woods and birdsongs inspiring the poet and the paradoxical joy that cures the sick and drives wise men insane. Natural imagery is not confined to the *exordium:* in a middle strophe, Guilhem compares fragile love to a hawthorn branch that trembles at night in the freezing rain, then gleams with sunlight the next day. The same poem includes indoor, domestic scenes. Recalling a "battle" with his lady that ended in mutual desire, he concludes that words are cheap: "Let others brag of love; we have the bread and the knife." A final farewell song recants his youthful frivolity and impiety; throwing off his furs, he relinquishes Poitiers to the care of his old enemy Foulques of Anjou.

Researches into Guilhem's sources of inspiration involve the origins of troubadour poetry itself. In the *pastorela*-like "poem of the red cat" (*Farai un vers, pos mi sonelh*), whose hero feigns muteness (or foreignness) to fool two ladies who abduct him for an eight-day orgy, the words *babariol, babarian* have suggested to some a possible Andalusian-Arabic influence. Guilhem's range of registers is interpreted sometimes as schizophrenia (was he two poets?), sometimes as a progression that invents courtliness in moving from bawdy to idealistic views of love. If his *Farai un vers de dreit nien* mocks distant love:

> Anc non la vi ez am la fort; ...
> Quan no la vei, be m'en deport,
> Noøm prez un jau: ... /
> No sai lo luec ves on s'esta

("I've never seen her and 1 love her a lot. / ...When I don't see her, I'm quite happy; / 1 don't care a rooster. / ...I don't know where she lives"), then what was its antecedent? This and the "red cat" song were, he claims, composed while sleeping; the two poems thus suggest dream visions. Guilhem's verse often uses long lines of eleven, twelve, or fourteen syllables (with internal rhyme)—lines seldom used by later troubadours. Studies of his verse forms suggest connections with Latin poetry, the liturgy, the popular round dance, and even epic measures. A fragment of his music is preserved as a *contrafactum* in the 14th-century *Jeu de sainte Agnès*; though doubtless adapted, it shows the melody's filiation with monastic music.

See also **Eleanor of Aquitaine**

Further Reading

Guilhem IX. *The Poetry of William VII, Count of Poitiers, IX Duke of Aquitaine*, ed. and trans. Gerald A. Bond. New York: Garland, 1982.

——. *Guglielmo IX: poesie*, ed. Nicolo Pasero. Modena: Mucchi, 1973.

Bezzola, Reto R. "Guillaume IX et les origines de l'amour courtois." *Romania* 66 (1940): 145–237.

AMELIA E. VAN VLECK

GUILLAUME DE LORRIS (fl. 1220–40)

The *Roman de la Rose* of Guillaume de Lorris, a poem of 4,028 lines thought to have been written ca. 1225–40, has always been linked to jean de Meun's *Roman de la Rose*, a poem more than four times the length of Guillaume's and written as its continuation. It is in Jean's poem that the reader learns the names of the authors of the two works and the fact that Guillaume died before completing his *roman*, which he had written some forty years earlier.

Although jean de Meun's *roman* became one of the most popular works of the Middle Ages, read and cited extensively through the Renaissance and existing in more than 250 manuscripts, Guillaume de Lorris's unfinished poem has captured the imagination of the post-18th-century reading public and remains a source of lively critical debate.

In a prologue of twenty lines, the author discusses the importance of dreams (with a reference to Macrobius) and establishes the dream narrative of the text itself. In the narrative proper, set in. springtime, the dreamer discovers an enclosed garden. On the wall of the garden are portrayed Hate, Felony, Baseness, Covetousness, Avarice, Envy, Sadness, Old Age, Hypocrisy, and Poverty—all characters excluded from the inside of the garden. The Dreamer enters through the only gate, guarded by Idleness, a beautiful lady whose day is spent fixing her hair and face. Inside the garden, the Dreamer meets Merriment and his friends Beauty, Wealth, Generosity, Nobility, Courtesy, and Youth. As the Dreamer makes a tour of the garden, he is stalked by the God of Love and overcome at the Fountain of Narcissus, a spring at the center of the garden whose two brilliant crystals allow one to see all things in the garden. While looking into the crystals, the Dreamer sees a rose, falls in love, and becomes the Lover. The God of Love now takes his new vassal in charge and instructs him carefully in the art of love. The Lover makes an attempt to approach the Rose but is repulsed by Resistance, the figure in charge of the Rose and the precincts within the hedge around her. Dejected by his failure and miserable from the pains of love, the rejected Lover is approached by Reason, described in Boethian terms as a lady of such lineage that she must have come from Paradise, as Nature would not have been able to make a work of such dimension. Reason reproaches the Lover for his foolishness in becoming acquainted with Idleness and explains that the evil he calls love is really madness. Is it wise or foolish to follow what causes you to live in grief, she asks? The Lover reacts angrily to Reason's advice, arguing that it would not be right for him to betray his lord, Love.

The Lover then seeks consolation from a Friend, who advises him that, though Resistance is angry at the moment, he can be overcome by flattery. With the aid of Openness and Pity, who plead for mercy on the Lover's behalf, the Lover once again gains access to Fair Welcome, who is persuaded to allow him to draw ever nearer the Rose, finally bestowing a kiss. Outraged, Slander arouses Jealousy; Shame, and Fear go to awaken the sleeping Resistance. Angry that he has been duped, Resistance chases the Lover from the Rose, and Jealousy builds a prison to keep Fair Welcome locked up. The Lover laments his misery and stresses that he is worse off now than he was before. The poet returns to the contrasting theme of the brevity of love's pleasures and the eternity of grief that follows. The Lover evokes the Wheel of Fortune, comparing Love's treatment of him to Fortune's own behavior. In the midst of further lamenting, the poem breaks off.

From the beginning, the reader of the *Roman de la Rose* is faced with difficulties in understanding Guillaume's poem. The dream-allegory setting implies multiple levels of meaning, in the medieval sense of allegory as saying one thing and meaning another. Macrobius's *Commentary on the Dream of Scipio* demonstrates the medieval concern for the dream and its relationship to other orders of reality. Moreover, the narrator is not merely the author but also the Dreamer and Lover, who operates in an objective world of personifications. Or are the personifications merely devices for the psychological description of the Lover and the Rose? In this question lies one of the most difficult medieval problems concerning the understanding of character and personality. But beyond these questions of form and meaning lie questions raised by the narrative itself. What is this garden the Lover enters—a kind of paradise involving a beautiful, elite society and a new form of love that transcends ordinary morality? Or is it a society obsessed with its own youth and the pleasures of self-gratification, careful to exclude images of Old Age and Poverty from the inner precincts of its own self-interest? Is this a love beyond Reason's comprehension, or is it the self-delusion of youth calling something *amor* that is really *folie*? Is this the meaning of the Fountain of Narcissus for the Lover? Is it really a dangerous fountain that might lead ultimately to death, or are the crystals a gateway to a higher form of love?

Because the poem breaks off with no hint of how it will end, or even how near the end the reader is, scholars have often turned to Jean de Meun's continuation and other texts for help in interpreting Guillaume's formidable *roman*. It is a poem shrouded in mystery and tantalizingly inconclusive.

See also **Jean de Meun, Macrobius**

Further Reading

Guillaume de Lorris and Jean de Meun. *Le roman de la Rose*, ed. and trans. Armand Strubel. Paris: Livre de Poche, 1992.

———. *Le roman de la Rose*, ed. Félix Lecoy. 3 vols. Paris: Champion, 1965–70.

———. *The Romance of the Rose*, trans. Charles Dahlberg. Princeton: Princeton University Press, 1971.

Arden, Heather. *The Romance of the Rose*. Boston: Twayne, 1987.

———. *The Roman de la Rose: An Annotated Bibliography*. New York: Garland, 1993.

Batany, Jean. *Approches du "Roman de la Rose."* Paris: Bordas, 1974.

Brownlee, Kevin, and Sylvia Huot. *Rethinking the "Romance of the Rose": Text, Image, Reception*. Philadelphia: University of Pennsylvania Press, 1992.

Fleming, John V. *"The Roman de la Rose": A Study in Allegory and Iconography*. Princeton: Princeton University Press, 1969.

Gunn, Alan M.F. *The Mirror of Love: A Reinterpretation of the Romance of the Rose*. Lubbock: Texas Tech Press, 1952.

Lewis, C.S. *The Allegory of Love*. London: Oxford University Press, 1936.

Muscatine, Charles. "The Emergence of Psychological Allegory in Old French Romance," *PMLA* 68 (1953): 1160–82.

Poirion, Daniel. *Le roman de la Rose*. Paris: Hatier, 1973.

Robertson, D.W. *A Preface to Chaucer*. Princeton: Princeton University Press, 1962.

Spearing, Anthony. *Medieval Dream-Poetry*. Cambridge: Cambridge University Press, 1976.

EMANUEL J. MICKEL

GUINIZZELLI, GUIDO (c. 1230–1276)

The Bolognese poet and jurist Guido Guinizzelli is the first great poetic figure associated with the *dolce stil nuovo*. Although he was once thought to have been from the de' Principi family, his family was most likely the Magnani. His grandfather, Magnano, was a prosecutor for the Bolognese commune; his father, Guinizello di Magnano, was appointed to the council of the people and served as a judge and later as *podestà* at Narni. Guido Guinizzelli was evidently the eldest of six children. He married Beatrice della Fratta in 1272, and their son Guiduccio was born the following year. Guinizzelli led an active professional and political life. He was a member of the Ghibelline Lambertazzi party and was banished, with his brothers Giacomo and Uberto and his son Guiduccio, by the victorious Guelf Geremei party in 1274. He chose Monselice near Padua as his place of exile and died there.

Guinizzelli's poetry comprises five *canzoni* and fifteen sonnets confidently ascribed to him, two fragmentary poems, and four *canzoni* whose authenticity is disputed. Most of the authentic poems appear in one or more of three great early (late thirteenth- or early fourteenth-century) manuscript anthologies of Italian lyric poetry. Two of these anthologies are in Florence: Rediano 9 (Laurentian Library) and Banco Rari 217 (Biblioteca Nazionale Centrale). The third is in the Vatican Library (Latino 3793) and in later collections—for example, Chigi L.VIII.305 (Vatican Library) and the Raccolta Bartoliniana (Accademia della Crusca, Florence). Each poem has a separate, often complex, textual history, and no reliable chronology can be established. Guinizzelli's verse techniques are generally conservative, and his language incorporates forms from Sicilian, Provençal, Tuscan, Latin, and French sources. All the poems aim at musical effects, but they vary greatly in style. The opening *sententia* and moralizing tone of the *canzone Tegno di folle 'mpres', a lo ver dire* ("I think a man foolish, to tell the truth") echo contemporary Tuscan poets, especially Guittone d'Arezzo. The themes, diction, and syntactic complexity of *Madonna, il fino amor ched eo vo porto* ("My lady, the perfect love I offer you") recall the tradition of Sicilian-Provençal poetry. Sonnets like *Pur a pensar mi par gran meraviglia* ("It seems a great wonder to me merely to think") and *Fra l'altre pene maggio credo sia* ("Among all evils I believe the worst") are examples of didactic lyrics in the middle style, whose subject matter Dante *(De vulgari eloquentia,* 2.2.6–10) identifies as virtue. *Volvol te levi, vecchia rabbiosa* ("May a whirlwind strike you, you vicious old woman") is lively, satiric, and vituperative.

The poems associated with the *dolce stil nuovo* represent a quarter of Guinizzelli's extant verse, but on the strength of them Guinizzelli has been regarded variously as a founder or precursor of the changes that occurred in Florentine poetry between 1280 and 1310. His most influential piece is the *canzone Al cor gentil rempaira sempre amore* ("Love returns always to a noble heart"), which announces two important concepts—the coexistence of love and the noble heart and the figure of the *donna angelicata* (angelic beloved). The first concept associates love with nobility and nobility with character. It consequently addresses a question, much debated by classical and medieval writers—whether nobility is determined by one's lineage or one's innate qualities. Unlike his predecessors, who describe a process in which the soul is made noble by love, Guinizzelli argues for a simultaneous appearance: *né fe' amor anti che gentil core,/ne gentil core anti ch'amor, natura* ("Nature did not make love before the noble heart,/Nor the noble heart before love"). The second concept redefines the rhetoric of praise. Earlier poets had spoken of the angelic beloved by approximation, addressing her as if she were an angel. Guinizzelli objectifies her as the embodiment of spiritual values who stands between human experience and the abstract truth of divine creation. In contrast to Dante's later formulation of Beatrice, however, Guinizzelli's beloved finally remains secular and earthbound; she has, he says, the likeness of an angel.

To express these concepts, Guinizzelli draws on medieval science and philosophy, giving the poem a richly allusive texture; and he adopts a style of closely reasoned philosophical argumentation. Love's existence in the noble heart is explained through the Aristotelian-scholastic analysis of potency and act and through the imagery of astral influences imbuing a precious stone with its properties. Love, the poet says, is like fire on the tip of a candle or a diamond in a vein of ore, while the proud man's boast of his heritage is like mud unchanged by the sun's power. The lover's wish to serve his beautiful lady duplicates the movement of the Neoplatonic angelic intelligences who contemplate divine perfection directly and instantly understand its wishes. Guinizzelli also brings to the poem a Franciscan-Augustinian metaphysics of light, which also influences the stilnovist sonnets *Vedut' ho la lucente Stella diana* ("I have seen the bright morning star") and *Io vogl' del ver la mia donna laudare* ("I want to praise my lady truly").

Guinizzelli's innovations in theme and style drew criticism from conservative poets like Guittone and Bonagiunta of Lucca; but Dante admired these innovations, and Guinizzelli's poetic craftsmanship in general. Dante echoes *Al cor gentil* in *Vita nuova* (19 and 20) and cites it in his discussion of nobility in *Convivio* (4.20). Francesca's apology for her adulterous love in *Inferno* 5 ironically echoes it, too. But Guinizzelli's position in literary history was established by Dante's historical representation of him at several points in the *Comedy*. In *Purgatorio* 11 Oderisi proposes a literary succession from Guinizzelli to Cavalcanti to perhaps a greater poet, presumably Dante. In *Purgatorio* 24 Bonagiunta concedes that he and other Sicilian-Tuscan poets fell short of Dante's *dolce stil novo*. In *Purgatorio* 26 Dante greets Guinizzelli as "the father of me and of others my betters who ever used sweet and gracious

rhymes of love." Dante's portrayal consciously makes Guinizzelli the originating figure in the thirteenth-century polemic over the Italian love lyric, and it amplifies the break from tradition that Guittone and Bonagiunta saw. Yet Guinizzelli's actual position is somewhat different from either view. A precursor of the new style, he was at once connected to traditional poetic practice and committed to experiment and innovation. Unlike the Florentine poets he influenced, Guinizzelli did sharply distinguish the stilnovist elements of his work from the influence of his Sicilian predecessors or his Tuscan contemporaries. Most scholars emphasize the shifting dimensions of his work—sometimes prestilnovist, sometimes protostilnovist.

See also **Cavalcanti, Guido; Dante Alighieri; Guittone d'Arezzo**

Further Reading

Editions

Contini, Gianfranco, ed. *Poeti del Duecento,* 2 vols. Milan and Naples: Ricciardi, 1960, Vol. 2, pp. 447–485.

Edwards, Robert R., ed. and trans. *The Poetry of Guido Guinizelli.* New York: Garland, 1987.

Marti, Mario, ed. *Poeti del dolce stil nuovo.* Florence: Le Monnier, 1969, pp. 35–114.

Translations

Goldin, Frederick, trans. *German and Italian Lyrics of the Middle Ages.* Garden City, N.Y.: Anchor/Doubleday, 1973.

Rossetti, Dante Gabriel, trans. *The Early Italian Poets.* In *The Collected Works of Dante Gabriel Rossetti,* ed. William M. Rossetti, 2 vols. London: Ellis and Elvey, 1888, Vol. 2, pp. 263–270.

Wilhelm, James J. *Lyrics of the Middle Ages.* New York: Garland, 1990.

Critical Studies

Barolini, Teodolinda. *Dante's Poets: Textuality and Truth in the Comedy.* Princeton, N.J.: Princeton University Press, 1984.

Bertelli, Italo. *Poeti del dolce stil nuovo: Guido Guinizelli e Lapo Gianni.* Pisa: Nistri-Lischi, 1963.

——. *La poesia di Guido Guinizelli e la poetica del dolce stil nuovo.* Florence: Le Monnier, 1983.

Folena, Gianfranco, ed. *Per Guido Guinizelli: Il comune de Monselice (1276–1976).* Padua: Antenore, 1980.

Ker, W. P. "Dante, Guido Guinizelli, and Arnaut Daniel." *Modern Language Review,* 4, 1909, pp. 145–152. (Reprinted in *Form and Style in Poetry.* London: Macmillan, 1929, pp. 319–328.)

Marti, Mario. *Storia dello stil nuovo,* 2 vols. Lecce: Milella, 1973.

Moleta, Vincent. *Guinizzelli in Dante.* Rome: Edizioni di Storia e Letteratura, 1980.

Valency, Maurice. *In Praise of Love.* New York: Macmillan, 1961.

Wilkins, Ernest Hatch. "A Note on Guinizelli's 'Al cor gentil' " *Modern Philology,* 12, 1914, pp. 325–330.

——. "Guinizelli Praised and Corrected." In *The Invention of the Sonnet and other Studies in Italian Literature,* pp. 111–113. Rome: Edizioni di Storia e Letteratura, 1959.

ROBERT R. EDWARDS

GUITTONE D'AREZZO
(c. 1235–21 August 1294)

Guittone d'Arezzo was the master of thirteenth-century literary culture in Tuscany and Emilia. Guido Guinizzelli deferred to his command of style; and Dante, like other poets, experimented with Guittone's formal techniques and elevated tone, striving to surpass his poetic fame and expressivity. In spite of the anti-Guittonean polemic set in motion by the stilnovists, Guittone's corpus of fifty Italian epistles, fifty *canzoni,* and some 250 sonnets—evincing a vast range of formal experimentation, political-moral discourse, and public correspondence—profoundly influenced and altered the course of vernacular literature in Italy.

Guittone probably joined the order of the Knights of Saint Mary (the so-called Frati Gaudenti, "jovial friars") in 1265. This was a turning point in his life and writing; and it is impossible to ignore the other, albeit sparse, biographical data available to us, for in few poets of Guittone's era was the connection between life and literature more keenly developed. Before his took up his literary career in the 1250s, Guittone had an inside view of municipal politics—perhaps beginning in 1249, when he helped his father in the Aretine treasury. By the late 1250s, Guittone's conservative Guelf values and his dissatisfaction with Arezzo's Ghibelline government led him to seek voluntary exile in places such as Pisa, Bologna, and Florence. Pisa is the provenance of the most authoritative manuscripts of his works: Rediano 9 (Laurentian Library, Florence) and its lateral Riccardiano 2533 (Riccardian Library, Florence). The wide circulation of Guittone's literary work during his lifetime probably contributed to his stature as the head of an entire poetic movement.

There is no doubt that Guittone was a powerful literary model for thirteenth-century Tuscan poets. He succeeded in converting the detached courtly traditions of the Sicilians and Occitans into a poetry that reflected the political and ethical concerns of the municipal citizen, the pivot of a new Tuscan power structure founded on the sometimes contradictory worlds of Christian morality and the new commercial order. In his writing, Guittone established a delicate balance between wisdom and wealth by emphasizing the ethics of their acquisition and use: *Saver.... vale in ben condurlo....[N]on peccato in ricchezze e, ma in male aquistarle e male usarle* ("Wisdom is good in that it leads one to happiness.... There is no sin in riches, but in acquiring and using them evilly," Letter 25). The two polysemous foundations of these ethics, often repeated in Guittone's poetry and letters as *onor e pro* ("honor and profit"), are in fact the classical concepts of *honor* and *utilitas* overlaid with the Christian ideals of goodness and service and adapted to contemporary mercantile notions of family honor and useful efficiency. To this groundwork of a

poetics of moral virtue Guittone added a dimension of political philosophy, moving from a defense of collective culture in his early invectives against the Aretines (*Gente noiosa e villana*—"Bothersome and uncourtly people") and the Ghibelline Florentines after the rout of the Guelfs at Montaperti *(Ahi lasso, or è stagion de doler tanto*—"Alas, now is the time of great sorrow") to his later concentration on individual peace as an integral part of the Christian collective (*Magni baroni certo e rep quasi*— "Great barons certainly and kings almost"). Guittone's fusion of rhetorical skill and civil morality solidified, in Italian letters, the perspective of the involved civic poet writing in the vernacular.

Guittone's poetics was equally influential among his contemporaries. It was based on the highly elaborated rhetorical devices of *ars dictandi* and the complicated formalism of the Occitan *trobar clus* (hermetic style). In his poetry and letters, which had a common language and syntax, Guittone's style reflects more than studied and refurbished borrowings of these two earlier traditions. In both cases, Guittone not only reexamines these two sources of knowledge and self-reflection but also tailors them to the cultural needs of the vernacular of his day. Guittone's vernacular exploitation of conventionally Latin-bound rhetoric and his revision of *scuro parlare* (obscure speech) or *trobar clus*, taken in part form his extensive knowledge of Occitan poets (including Raimbaut d'Aurenga and Arnaut Daniel), represents a commitment to link the honored traditions of the past with the language and values of the new power base of the commune. Guittone's discursive investment in literary Tuscan inspired two generations of Tuscan and Emilian literary circles bent on imitating this new, even overextended, attention to the development of a highly articulated poetic language.

Guittone also led the way in challenging other aspects of literary convention. He helped transform the vernacular poem from something composed for performance by singers to a text of writers and correspondents. His refinement of the songbook, or song cycle (conjectured to have been five separate collections), and even its illustration (in *Trattato d'amore,* "Treatise on Love"), and his experimentation with expanded verse forms reveal his involvement in literature not simply as a vehicle for his formal talents but as a committed redefinition of the relationship of literature to its public. This new sense of a public, and of a public sphere, runs throughout Guittone's works, reshaping the narcissistic "I" of courdy lyrics into a self-reflective individual linked to his fellow citizens not through a political faction but through *thepolis* or city itself (see Letter 14). In his *canzone Ora parrà s'eo saverò cantare* ("Now it will be evident if I know how to write poetry," written after his conversion), Guittone spells out the four essential elements of human existence: *Natura, Dio, ragion scritta, e comune*

("Nature, God, philosophy, and common sense"). The cohesion of civilization depends on trust and the application of reason. The most basic transgression of that trust, self-deception, corrupts the entire fabric of civilization: *che mal l'averebbe d'altrui/chi se medesimo decede* ("for those who deceive themselves would certainly not have mercy from others," in *O dolce terra aretina*). Thus when Guittone adddresses Finfo del Buono (Letter 20), or an infirm brother (Letter 21), or any of his numerous verse and epistolary correspondents (his *societas amicorum*), he also addresses the citizenry at large, embracing the universal within the individual.

However, Guittone was not exclusively a moralist. His early poems treat primarily the theme of love. Three of his five song cycles examine loyalty, joy, and unhappiness in love; the third cycle, partially, takes the form of a feigned debate between a woman and her lover. The sonnet sequence theorized to have been his fourth amounts to an *ars amandi*, dubbed by Avalle a manual of seduction, which is retracted in the fifth cycle (*Trattato d'amore*). Yet even Guittone's love lyrics have a rhetorical cast; their intellectual ardor overwhelms the conventional necessities of tolerance and torment with almost legalistic analyses of the process of love. Sentimental passion seems to be replaced by what Quaglio (1975) calls Guittone's "casuistry of love," in which system dominates the lyric's focus on the moment. Consequently, Guittone's theory of love sometimes reflects moralistic symmetry and a strong sense of reciprocity in a process that helps refine the lover's spirit and nobility. Nobility is no longer defined as a matter of aristocratic lineage; it is now the education of the heart: *Non ver lignaggio fa sangue, ma core,* "The heart, not the blood, makes for true lineage" (in *Comune perta fa comun dolore,* "A common loss makes for a common sorrow").

Perhaps the most significant feature of Guittone's production is its high level of contrast. Guittone startles his reader with unexpected technical and structural revelations to support his repeated messages of peace or—earlier in his career—conventional courtly themes, now adapted to the municipal reader. Guittone's strategy seems to be based on enigmas of faith, echoed in his advice that spiritual richness can be found in only poverty (Letter 3) and happiness only in strife: *solamente apresso travaglio è poso* ("tranquillity is achieved only after strife," Letter 25). Guittone's opus is itself divided between his early verses, described in a sonnet to Monte Andrea (*A te, Montuccio*—"To you, Montuccio") as "poisonous fruits," and his "conversion poems," which are assigned in the manuscripts to "Fra (Brother) Guittone." This distinction reflects mostly Guittone's entry into the Gaudenti, a lay order known for its religious dedication to pacification and antifactionalism. Yet even Guittone's preconversion works declare the common humanity of all citizens, regardless of faction.

Guittone's poetic trademark is severe rhetorical artifice. In his early poems, this artifice is penetrable only by "those who love": *Scuro saccio che par lo/mio detto, ma/che parlo/a chi s'entend' ed ame,* "I know my writing may seem obscure, except that I speak to those who have understanding and love" (in *Tuttor, s'eo veglio o dormo,* "Always if I lie awake or sleep"). In his later poems it is penetrable by those who have forgone the constraints of love ("where... madness reigns," in *Ora parrà*). This distinction seems to have been born naturally from a vital contrast in all his poetry between the past and the present. His remembrance of Arezzo's past glories (*O dolce term aretina/... membrando ch'eri.../arca d'onni divizia*—"O sweet city of Arezzo... when I recall that you contained all wealth") is bitterly countered, in a bold display of rhetorical antithesis, by the city's present "abundance of moral dearth" (in *Or è di cavo piena l'arca*). Yet the symbolism of these temporal terms is not static. In the collective conscience, the past—the *benedetto tempo*—recognized the concepts of value and love as distinct from wealth and self-indulgent solitude. But in the progress of the soul, the individual's past represents a worse state of moral ignorance.

Guittone's poetics of formal obscurity is, by contrast, the vehicle for themes often linked by the absolute moral maxims of his political Christianity and the concrete pragmatism of his traditional Guelf and mercantile ethos. However, his political-moral writing forges not so much municipal realism, more germane to Monte's poetry, as civic idealism. Nevertheless, he is prone to express these ideals with stormy sarcasm and subtle irony reinforced by a syntax designed to persuade by its brilliantly articulated complexity.

The artistic refutation of Guittone was first voiced by Guido Cavalcanti and Dante. Cavalcanti, in *Da più a uno face un sollegismo* ("From the many to the one makes a syllogism"), condemned Guittone's literary language, excessively difficult rhymes, and lack of imagination. Dante (who was, like Guittone, an exile) undertook his own stylistic ventures—especially in his *rime petrose* and *tenzoni* with Dante da Maiano. Afterward, in his assessment of the new courtly-literary language of Italy (*De vulgari eloquentia,* l.xiii.l), Dante dismissed the "municipal" elements in the poetic language of Guittone and Guittone's followers. Dante recognized Guittone's historical stature in *Purgatorio* 24, while deriding his notoriety in *Purgatorio* 26. In spite of these early negative judgments, imprints of Guittone's harsh style, polemical and sarcastic logic, and moralistic themes appear throughout the *Commedia* and are ingrained in the poetry of rectitude of the Italian Middle Ages.

See also **Bonagiunta Orbicciani degli Averardi; Dante Alighieri; Guinizzelli, Guido**

Further Reading

Texts

Contini, Gianfranco, ed. *Poeti del Duecento* Milan and Naples: Ricciardi, 1960, Vol. 1, pp. 189–255.

Egidi, Francesco, ed. *Rime* Bari: Laterza, 1940. (See also review by Gianfranco Contini. *Giornale Storico della Letteratura Italiana,* 117, 1941, pp. 55–82.)

Leonardi, Lino, ed. *Canzoniere: I sonetti d'amore del Coicke Laurenziano.* Turin: Einaudi, 1994.

Margueron, Claude, ed. *Lettere.* Bologna: Commissione per i Testi di Lingua, 1990.

Meriano, Francesco, ed. *Le lettere di Fra Guittone d'Arezzo* Bologna: Commissione per i Testi di Lingua, 1923.

Segre, Cesare, and Mario Marti, eds. *La prosa del Duecento* Milan-Naples: Ricciardi, 1959, 25–93.

Studies

Avalle, D'Arco Silvio. *Ai luoghi di delizia pieni.* Milan and Naples: Ricciardi, 1977, pp. 17–68.

Baehr, Rudolf. "Studien zur Rhetorik in den Rime Guittones von Arezzo." *Zeitschrift für romanische Philologie,* 73, 1957, pp. 193–258; and 74, 1958, pp. 163–211.

Kleinhenz, Christopher. *The Early Italian Sonnet: The First Century (1220–1321)* Lecce: Milella, 1986, pp. 93–109.

Leonardi, Lino. "Guictone cortese?" *Medioevo Romanzo,* 13, 1988, pp. 421–455.

Margueron, Claude. *Recherches sur Guittone d'Arezzo: Sa vie, son époque, sa culture.* Paris: Presses Universitaires de France, 1966.

Minetti, Francesco F. *Sondaggi guittoniani.* Turin: Giappichelli, 1974.

Moleta, Vincent. *The Early Poetry of Guittone d'Arezzo.* London: Modern Humanities Research Association, 1976.

Picone, Michelangelo. "Lettura guittoniana: La canzone 'Ora che la freddore.'" *Yearbook of Italian Studies,* 5, 1983, pp. 102–116.

Quaglio, Antonio Enzo. "L'esperimento di Guittone d'Arezzo." In *Le origini e la scuola siciliana,* 2nd ed. Bari: Laterza, 1975, pp. 259–300.

Segre, Cesare. *Lingua, stile, e società: Studi sulla storia della prosa italiana.* Milan: Feltrinelli, 1963.

Storey, H. Wayne. "The Missing Picture in the Text of Escorial e.III.23: Guittone's *Trattato d'amore.*" In *Italiana: Selected Papers from the Proceedings of the Third Annual Conference of the American Association of Teachers of Italian, December 27–28, 1986,* ed. Albert Mancini and Paolo Giordano, River Forest, Ill.: Rosary College, 1988, pp. 59–75.

Tartaro, Achille. *Il manifesto di Guittone e altri studi fra Due e Quattrocento.* Rome: Bulzoni, 1974.

——. "Cronologia guittoniana." In *Letteratura e critica: Studi in onore di Natalino Sapegno.* Rome: Bulzoni, 1975. pp. 34–48.

H. WAYNE STOREY

GUTENBERG, JOHANN
(ca. 1400–February 3, 1468)

Credited with the invention of printing with movable metal type, Johann Gutenberg probably learned metalworking from his father's family who worked for the archbishop's mint. Gutenberg lived in Strasbourg from about 1428 to 1448, when he returned to Mainz where he had been born. There, he produced the Gutenberg Bible, the first major printed book. He died in Mainz on February 3, 1468.

Gutenberg's historical significance arises from his role in the development of printing. Records of lawsuits during his residence in Strasbourg point to his early experiments with the craft. The heirs of one of his partners, for example, sued to be included in the partnership.

The printing press invented by Johann Gutenberg. © Erich Lessing/Art Resource, New York.

Testimony mentions "materials pertaining to printing," including a press, *Formen* (a word for type), and a purchase of metal. These items suggest that Gutenberg was working out the printing process, but no printed material has survived to support this theory.

After Gutenberg returned to Mainz, his efforts at printing continued. Another lawsuit, the so-called Helmasperger Instrument of 1455, connects Gutenberg with the Gutenberg Bible. Johann Fust, a Mainz businessman, sued Gutenberg to recover loans made in 1450 and 1452 for expenses incurred in making equipment, paying wages, and purchasing parchment paper and ink for "the work of the books." This document combined with analysis of the paper and its watermarks, the ink, and typography in the Gutenberg Bible lead to the conclusion that Gutenberg, aided by several assistants, including future printers Peter Schoeffer, Berthold Ruppel, and Heinrich Kefer, printed this Bible between 1450 and 1455.

Attribution of other printed books to Gutenberg is more problematic. He probably continued printing in Mainz. He has been connected with several works in the so-called "B36" group that used a larger and less refined Gothic font than the Gutenberg Bible. He has also been associated with a Mainz press that produced a Latin dictionary known as the *Catholicon* in 1460. However, the aesthetic and technical quality of the Gutenberg Bible makes this book the high point of his achievement.

Further Reading

Fuhrmann, Otto W. *Gutenberg and the Strasbourg Documents of 1439*. New York: Press of the Wooly Whale, 1940.

Gutenberg, Aventur und Kunst: Vom Geheimunternehmen zur ersten Medienrevolution. Das offizielle Buch der Stadt Mainz zum Gutenbergjahr. Mainz: Schmidt, 2000.

Ing, Janet Thompson. *Johann Gutenberg and His Bible: A Historical Study*. New York: Typophiles, 1988.

Kapr, Albert. *Johann Gutenberg: The Man and his Invention*. trans. Douglas Martin. Aldershot, England: Scolar Press, 1996.

McMurtrie, Douglas C., ed. and trans. *The Gutenberg Documents: With translations of the texts into English, based with authority on the compilation by Dr. Karl Schorbach*. New York: Oxford University Press, 1941.

Ruppel, Aloys. *Johannes Gutenberg: Sein Leben und sein Werk*. 3d ed. Nieuwkoop: B. de Graaf, 1967.

Scholderer, Victor. *Johann Gutenberg: The Inventor of Printing*. 2d ed. London: British Museum, 1970.

KAREN GOULD

GUZMÁN, DOMINGO DE
(c. 1170-1221)

Domingo's birth at Calaruega, Castile, about 1170 and his infancy were said to have been attended by marvels forecasting his sanctity and great achievements. From the ages of seven to fourteen he studied under the tutelage of his uncle, the archpriest Gumiel de Izán. In 1184 Domingo entered the University of Palencia, where he remained as a student for ten years. On one occasion he sold his books to help the poor and homeless of Palencia. His biographer, Bartholomew of Trent, says that he twice tried to sell himself into slavery to raise money to free captives held by the Moors.

The date of Domingo's ordination to the priesthood is unknown. He was a student at Palencia when Martín de Bazán, bishop of Osma, called him to be a member of the cathedral chapter and to assist in its reform. In recognition of his success, Domingo was appointed subprior of the reformed chapter. On the accession of Diego de Azevedo to the bishopric of Osma in 1201, Domingo became prior of the chapter. As a canon of Osma, he spent nine years in contemplation, scarcely ever leaving the chapter house. In 1203 King Alfonso IX of Castile deputized the bishop of Osma to ask for the hand of a Danish princess on behalf of his son, Prince Fernando. The bishop chose Domingo to accompany him. Passing through Toulouse, they witnessed with consternation the effects of the Albigensian heresy. As a result Domingo conceived the idea of founding an order for combating heresy and spreading the Gospel by preaching throughout the world. After completing their mission in 1204, Diego and Domingo went to Rome, and from there they were sent by Pope Innocent III to join forces with the Cistercians, who had been entrusted with the crusade against the Albigensians. The pair quickly saw that the failure of the Cistercians was due to the monks' indulgent habits, and prevailed upon them to adopt a more austere life. The result was a greatly increased number of converts. Theological disputations played a prominent part in the preaching to the heretics, and Domingo and his companion lost no time in engaging in them. Unable to refute his arguments or counteract the influence of his preaching, the heretics often made Domingo the target of insults and threats.

Domingo realized the need for an institution that would protect women from the influence of the heretics. Many of them had already embraced Albigensianism and were among its most active advocates. With the permission of Foulque, bishop of Toulouse, he established a convent for women at Prouille in 1206. To this community he gave the rule and constitution that to the present day guide the nuns of the Second Order of Saint Dominic. On 15 January 1208 Pierre de Castelnau, a Cistercian legate, was assassinated, an event that precipitated the Albigensian Crusade under Simon de Montfort and led to the temporary subjugation of the heretics. During the crusade Domingo followed the Catholic army, seeking to revive religion and reconcile heretics in the cities that capitulated to Montfort. In September 1209 he came into direct contact with Montfort and formed a close friendship that would last until Montfort's death at Toulouse in 1218. Montfort regarded his victory at Muret as a miracle attributable to Domingo's prayers. Domingo's reputation for sanctity, apostolic zeal, and learning made him a much sought-after candidate for various bishoprics, all of which he refused, preferring to preach. The foundation of the Inquisition, and his appointment as the first inquisitor, is ascribed to Domingo during this period, although there is evidence to indicate that the Inquisition was functioning as early as 1198.

By 1214 the influence of Domingo's preaching and his reputation for holiness had drawn a group of disciples around him. The time was right for the realization of his desire to found a religious order to propagate the faith and combat heresy. With the approval of Bishop Foulque of Toulouse, who made him chaplain of Fanjeaux in July 1215, he organized and canonically established a community of followers as a religious congregation whose mission was the propagation of true doctrine and good morals, and the eradication of heresy. Pierre Seilan, a wealthy citizen of Toulouse, placed himself under Domingo's direction and put his large house at Domingo's disposal. There the first convent of the future Order of Preachers (now known as the Dominicans) was established on 25 April 1215.

In November 1215 an ecumenical council convened in Rome to deliberate on the improvement of morals, the extinction of heresy, and the strengthening of the faith, an agenda identical to the mission of Domingo's new order. Along with the bishop of Toulouse, Domingo went to Rome to petition that his new order carry out the mandates of the council. His request, however, was not granted. Returning to Languedoc in December 1215, he informed his followers of the council's mandate that there be no new rules for religious orders. As a result the community adopted the rule of St. Augustine, which, because of its generality, easily lent itself to any form they might wish. In August 1216 Domingo returned to Rome and appeared before Pope Honorius III to solicit confirmation for his order. The bull of confirmation was issued on 22 December 1216.

In 1218, to facilitate the spread of the order, Pope Honorius III addressed a bull to all archbishops, bishops, abbots, and priors, requesting them to show favor toward the Order of Preachers. Later Honorius bestowed the Church of Saint Sixtus in Rome upon the order. In February 1219 Domingo founded the first monastery of the order in Spain at Segovia, followed by a convent for women at Madrid. It is probable that on this journey he also presided over the establishment of a convent in connection with the University of Palencia and, at the invitation of the bishop of Barcelona, a house of the order was founded in that city. Shortly before his death on 6 August 1221, Domingo returned to Rome for the last time and received many new, valuable concessions

for his order. He was canonized on 13 July 1234 by Pope Gregory IX, who declared him to be as saintly as Peter and Paul.

See also **Innocent III, Pope; Simon de Montfort, Earl of Leicester**

Further Reading

Galmés, L., and V.T. Gómez. (eds.) *Santo Domingo de Guzmán. Fuentes para su conocimiento.* Madrid, 1987.
Vicaire, M.-H. *Saint Dominic and His Times.* Trans. Kathleen Pond. New York, 1964.

E. Michael Gerli

GUZMÁN, NUÑO DE
(d. ca. 1467/90)

The youngest of the illegitimate children of Luis González de Guzmán, master of the military order of Calatrava (1406–1407 and 1414–1443), by Inés de Torres, a wealthy heiress from Zamora, Nuño de Guzmán was educated by private tutor in the maternal home in Córdoba during a period of estrangement between his parents (1416–1430). Under his mother's guidance he became deeply interested in literature, "so that a day spent without reading seemed to me utterly wasted" (*Apologia Nunnii*), but he did not learn Latin. In 1430 he undertook a pilgrimage to Jerusalem and Sinai, returning via Cairo, the Aegean islands, Venice, Rome, Siena, Bologna, Genoa, Milan, Bohemia, Basle, Cologne, Lyon, and Tours before arriving at the court of Duke Philip the Good of Burgundy in Bruges (autumn 1432), where by his own account he was given an important office (*magistratus*), probably in the household of the duke's wife, Isabel of Portugal. On his return to Spain (ca. 1435) Guzmán found himself in the bad graces of his father, despite the personal intervention of Juan II and the support of his mother; consequently he set out for Burgundy again in 1439, but decided to visit Florence first, where the ecumenical council called by Pope Eugenius IV for reunion with the Eastern Church was just beginning. Guzmán was instantly dazzled by the intellectual ferment he encountered in Florence and, abandoning his Burgundian trip in favor of a vocation as literary patron and book collector, he befriended the celebrated *libralo* Vespasiano da Bisticci, Leonardo Bruni, Pier Candido Decembrio, and other humanists. He had Bruni's apologetic life of Cicero (*Cicero Nouus*) and his humanist version of Aristotle's *Ethics* translated into Tuscan, and received the dedications of Decembrio's Italian translations of Seneca's *Apocolocyntosis diui Claudii* and Quintus Curtius's *Life of Alexander*, while commissioning many superb *lettera antica* manuscripts from Vespasiano's *bottega*. In later years, Vespasiano tells us, Guzmán continued to commission Tuscan translations of classical and humanistic works, among which we know of Quintilian's *Declamationes maiores* (1456), Cicero's *Disputationes Tusculanae* (1456) and *De oratore* (date unknown), and Macrobius's *Sanumalia* (1463 or later). The most important fruit of his Florentine visit, however, was his personal friendship with the humanist Giannozzo Manetti (1396–1459), who dedicated his *De illustribus longaeuis* (1439) to Guzmán's father and his pathfinding Plutarchan parallel lives of Socrates and Seneca to Guzmán himself (1440, with notes on Seneca's Córdoban connections supplied by the addressee). In addition, Manetti cast two works into humanist Latin from notes prepared by Guzmán (1439); *Apologia Nunnii*, an autobiographical selfjustification addressed to his father, and *Laudatio Agnetis Numantinae*, an extended eulogy of his mother supposedly replacing a lost *alabanza* (works of praise) by Enrique de Villena. After returning to Seville in early 1440 Guzmán corresponded on literary matters with Alfonso de Cartagena, Alfonso de Palencia, and the Marquis of Santillana. The only works definitely attributable to Guzmán's own hand are his translation of Manetti's epideictic Tuscan oration on the qualities of the military commander, *Orazione a Gismondo Pandolfo de' Malatesia* (1453), made for the Marquis of Santillana (c. 1455); a revision of the Alfonsine translation of Seneca's *De ira* made (probably) for his mother (1445); and a highly popular vernacular compendium of Aristotle's *Ethics* made for his brother Juan de Guzmán, *señor* of La Algaba, (1467) and subsequently copied and printed a number of times either without attribution, or under false ascriptions to Alfonso de Cartagena and Alfonso de la Torre. It is highly probable, however, that Guzmán was instrumental in the Castilian translations of Bruni's *Vita di Marco Tulio Cicerone* and of Decembrio's versions of the works by Seneca and Quintus Curtius mentioned above, as well as the dissemination of other classical texts. When Guzmán died in Seville at some date between 1467 and 1490, Vespasiano tells us in his curious *Vita di messer Nugno di casa reale di Gusmano* (our fullest contemporary source) that Guzmán's splendid library came to a bad end. Nevertheless, Schiff's judgment that he was one of those to whom early Spanish humanism owed the most is fully justified.

See also **Philip the Good**

Further Reading

Bisticci, V. da. *Le vite.* Vol. 1. Ed. A. Greco. Florence, 1970. 435–41.

Lawrance, J. *Un episodio del proto-humanismo español*: *tres opúsculos de Nuño de Guzmán y Giannozzo Manetti.* Salamanca, 1989.

Morel-Fatio, A. "Notice au trois manuscrits de la bibliothèque d'Osuna," *Romania* 14 (1885), 94–108.

Russell, P.E., and A.R.D. Pagden. "Nueva luz sobre una versión de la *Ética a Nicómaco*: Bodleian Library MS Span. D. 1." In *Homenaje a Guillenno Guastavino.* Madrid, 1974. 125–46.

Schiff M. *La Bibliothèque du Marquis de Santillane. Paris, 1905. 449–59.*

JEREMY LAWRANCE

H

HADEWIJCH (fl. mid-13th c.)

In the final line of her twelfth vision, the thirteenth-century Brabant mystic Hadewijch writes: "By that abyss I saw myself swallowed. And there I received certainty about my being received, in this form, in my beloved, and my beloved also in me." The line not only provides a glimpse into the ecstatic experience of the author, but also suggests the aesthetic sense which imbues all of Hadewijch's writings. Indeed, her letters, visions, and poems have recently been praised as eminent in the literature of the *minnemystiek* (love mystic) tradition for their description of an unmediated experience of the divine, which is perfected in *minne*, or love, and not in ecclesiastical worship. During her lifetime as a Beguine, however, Hadewijch was forced into exile and her literary reputation into obscurity.

Although there is a paucity of biographical information about Hadewijch, her writings in the vernacular Middle Dutch convey the imaginative force with which she appropriated the courtly love tradition to reveal her desire for union with love. Addressed variously as a persona and as an abstraction, love represents for Hadewijch both the experience of the divine and the achievement of perfection offered by that experience. Her letters and poems encourage her readers to devote themselves to love as a principle of engagement in both spiritual and mundane matters, while the visions record the account of her progression into love as a sublime experience. The three manuscripts of her writings illustrate the skill with which Hadewijch crafted enthralling examples of the language of love.

Further Reading

Fraeters, Veerle, "Hadewijch." In *Women Writing in Dutch*, ed. Kristiaan Aercke. (New York, 1994), pp. 18–60.
Vanderauwera, Ria. "The Brabant Mystic: Hadewijch." In *Medieval Women Writers*. Athens: University of Georgia Press, 1984 [English trans.].

AMANDA ATHEY

HADRIAN I, POPE
(d. 795, r. 772–795)

The pontificate of Hadrian I (Adrian I) was notable for the establishment of the long-hallowed contours of the papal patrimony, for the development of relations between the papacy and the Franks, and for the final emancipation of the papacy from Byzantine authority. Hadrian was born into a noble Roman family and was raised by an uncle who was influential in papal government. Before 767, at the behest of Pope Paul I, Hadrian entered an ecclesiastical career. He was an impressive figure, and his effective preaching, wide learning, and diligence as a papal notary made him popular in Rome. His election to the pontificate in February 772 began an anti-Lombard reaction in the city; exiles were recalled, and the pro-Lombard leader Afiarta was prosecuted for murder, though Hadrian was apparently disappointed when Afiarta was summarily executed in Ravenna.

Hadrian was involved in a dispute with the Lombard king Desiderius over the application of treaties of 754 and 756, by which the Lombards ceded much territory to the papacy; consequently, the pope appealed to Charlemagne (in the spring of 773). After that, Hadrian became embroiled in an extended, courteous debate with the Frankish king over the *promissio donationis,* an oath Charlemagne took at Rome, shortly after Easter 774, by which he granted most of Italy south of the Luni-Monselice line to Saint Peter. After Charlemagne became king of the Lombards (in June 774), he was disinclined to dissolve his kingdom, and in the end Hadrian obtained only a fraction of what had been promised. However,

Charlemagne did lead an army south of Rome against Hadrian's hostile Lombard neighbors.

Hadrian's relations with Charlemagne were strained by their different understanding of the privileges and duties of bishops in important Italian sees and were further complicated by Hadrian's involvement in Byzantine affairs. Although his papal documents were the first to abandon Byzantine dating systems, Hadrian did not neglect the Byzantine world. He participated vigorously in the dispute over icons in the Byzantine empire; he corresponded with the Byzantine emperor and empress; and papal envoys were prominent at the second Nicaean council, which discussed the worship of icons. This openness to Byzantium irritated Charlemagne, who was scandalized by the Nicaean canons; the Latin translation of these canons, prepared in Rome, was garbled (exchanging *proskinesis* for *adoratio)* and elicited a strong response from Charlemagne's court in the form of the *Libri Carolini.* Though Hadrian defended the second Nicaean Council in a letter to Charlemagne, he was unable to avert the condemnation of its decrees by the Council of Frankfurt (794).

Hadrian was a lover of churches, and he built extensively in Rome. His building program included not only churches but also refurbished aqueducts, restored walls, and a portico joining Saint Peter's to the Tiber. He also founded four new *domuscultae,* partly on his family's property north of Rome, to furnish the church with victuals and to nourish the poor. Hadrian was the first pope to mint coins and one of very few popes to put a portrait bust on his coinage.

Hadrian died on Christmas day, or the day after, in 795. Charlemagne, whose ascendancy had influenced Hadrian's pontificate deeply, is reported to have wept on learning of his death. The metrical epitaph the king sent to Rome for the tomb of his "father" can be seen today in the portico of Saint Peter's.

Some of Hadrian's letters (forty-eight) are in *Codex Carolinus;* two other letters are in Monumenta Germaniae Historica Epistularum, 5; still others (some spurious) are in Migne. A poem by Hadrian is in Monumenta Germaniae Historica Poetarum Latinorum, 1. For synods and councils held during Hadrian's pontificate, see Mansi. A translation of his epitaph is in Gregorovius (1903).

See also **Charlemagne**

Further Reading

Primary Sources

Codex Carolinus, ed. W. Gundlach. Monumenta Germaniae Historica Epistularum, 3. Berlin, 1892, pp. 469–657.

Gregorovius, F. *The Tombs of the Popes,* trans. R. Seton-Watson. Westminster, 1903. pp. 20–23. *Liber Pontificate,* ed. L. Duchesne. Paris, 1886, Vol. I, pp. 486–514.

Mansi, J. *Concilia,* 12, cols. 850–1153.

Migne, J. *Patrologia Latina,* 96, cols. 1203–1242.

Monumenta Germaniae Historica Epistularum, 5, ed. K. Hampe. Berlin, 1889, pp. 3–57. Monumenta Germaniea Historica Poetarum Latinorum, 1. Berlin 1880, pp. 90–91.

Studies

Bertolini, O. *Roma di fronte a Bisanzio e ai Longobardi.* Rome, 1941.

Classen, P. *Karl der Grosse, das Papstum, und Byzanz.* Düsseldorf, 1968.

Drabeck, A. *Die Vertrage der frankischen und deutschen Herrscher mit dem Papstum von 754 bis 1020.* Vienna, 1974.

Engels, O. "Zum Papstlich-frankischen Bundnis im VIII. Jahrhundert: *Ecclesia* und *Regnum.*" In *Festschrift F. Schmale,* ed. D. Bergu. Bochum, 1989, pp. 21–38.

Gero, S. "The *Libri Carolini* and the Image Controversy." *Greek Orthodox Theological Review,* 18, 1973, pp. 7–34.

Hallenbeck, J. "The Election of Pope Hadrian I." *Church History,* 37, 1968, pp. 261–270.

Herrin, J. *The Formation of Christendom.* Princeton, N.J.: Princeton University Press, 1988.

Hodgkin, T. *Italy and Her Invaders,* Vol. 7. Oxford 1899.

Mann, H. *Lives of the Popes of the Early Middle Ages,* Vol. 1, part 2. London, 1903, pp. 394–497.

Noble, Thomas F. X. *The Republic of Saint Peter.* Philadelphia: University of Pennsylvania Press, 1984.

Stevens Sefton, D. "Pope Hadrian I and the Fall of the Kingdom of the Lombards." *Catholic Historical Review,* 65, 1979, pp. 206–220.

PAOLO SQUATRITI

HADRIAN IV, POPE
(c. 1100–1159, r. 1154–1159)

Almost nothing is known about the birth, parentage, or childhood of Pope Hadrian IV (Adrian IV; Nicholas Breakspear or Brekespear). Most of our information derives from two sources: Cardinal Boso and John of Salisbury.

Boso wrote a *vita* (life) of Hadrian, which is in the collection of Nicolas Roselli, cardinal of Aragon, in 1356. According Boso, Hadrian was born in England near Saint Albans and went to Aries in France to study early in his boyhood. At the monastery of Saint Rufus near Avignon, it is recorded that he took the vows and habit of an Augustinian. After a short time, he was elected abbot of Saint Rufus. On a trip to Rome on business for the monastery, he endeared himself to Pope Eugenius III, who made him cardinal bishop of Albano in 1146.

John of Salisbury adds to our knowledge of Hadrian's life at this point, and mentions that Hadrian's father was Robert Brekespear and that Hadrian's original name was Nicholas Brekespear. Another source corroborating this information is in Norway, where Hadrian established an independent archiepiscopal see at Trondheim and made Saint Olaf its patron saint. As a papal legate in 1152, Hadrian also tried to establish an archiepiscopal see in Sweden, but Gothland opposed Sweden regarding where it should be located. Hadrian did, however, reform abuses and establish Peter's pence in Sweden before returning to Rome. In Rome, Hadrian was apparently at the right place at the right time: he was hailed as the apostle of the north; and when Pope Anastasius IV died on 2 December 1154, Hadrian was elected pope on the very next day. He is the only English pope.

Hadrian IV's tenure as pope was fraught with political intrigue and conflict. King William of Sicily and Hadrian were openly hostile to each other; Frederick Barbarossa merely professed friendship; the barons of Campania raided and robbed each other and also robbed pilgrims on their way to Rome; and the populace of Rome, under the leadership of Arnold of Brescia, was in open revolt against Hadrian. Hadrian, after determining his situation in Rome, placed the city under interdict and retired to Viterbo. The Roman populace, unable to observe any sacred services until after Lent, eventually made its submission to Hadrian and banished Arnold of Brescia, who was ultimately executed. As Hadrian returned to Rome, Frederick Barbarossa was advancing through Lombardy. Frederick, having received the Iron Crown in Pavia, was intent on receiving the imperial crown in Rome from the hands of Hadrian. A famous meeting between the two rulers, temporal and spiritual, took place north of Rome at Sutri on 9 June 1155. Frederick, omitting a part of the customary ceremony of homage, did not hold Hadrian's stirrup when the pope dismounted. Because of this insolence, Hadrian withheld his kiss of peace and refused to crown Frederick until full homage was performed. Frederick submitted, performing the necessary act of homage on 11 June 1155 at Nepi; he was subsequently crowned in Saint Peter's on 18 June. Immediately afterward, fighting broke out between the imperial army and the Roman army; during this fighting, more than 1,000 Romans were killed. Without so much as an acknowledgment of the deaths, Frederick left Rome and went northward; on his way, he proceeded to burn the city of Spoleto to the ground.

William I of Sicily and Hadrian IV never established cordial relations. Hadrian called William lord rather than king; William took offense, ravaging and ransacking southern Campania, whereupon Hadrian excommunicated him. John of Salisbury spent three months with Hadrian in Benevento during this period and obtained from him the famous Donation of Ireland. The authenticity of the *Laudabiliter*, the document containing this grant, is in doubt; but in any case the basic assumption that the pope was overlord of Ireland and could therefore grant the entire island itself to whomever he pleased—in this case King Henry II of England—was an interesting legal labyrinth. For more than four centuries the popes maintained their right as overlords of Ireland.

By 1154, William I had captured important Italian cities and had even confiscated 5,000 pounds of gold meant for the pope from his ally Manuel I. Eventually, Hadrian IV sued for peace. Under the peace agreement, William was invested with the territories of Naples, Amalfi, Salerno, and the March of Ancona; for his part, he pledged to be the pope's liegeman and pay a yearly tribute. Soon after this, Hadrian made peace with the Romans and returned to Rome. However, continued tension between the emperor, William I, and the papacy challenged Hadrian until his death on 1 September 1159.

See also **Arnold of Brescia; Frederick I Barbarossa**

Further Reading

"Pope Adrian IV." *Catholic Encyclopedia.* Internet ed., 1998.
Tarleton, Alfred. *Nicholas Breakspear (Hadrian IV), Englishman and Pope.* London, 1906.

BRADFORD LEE EDEN

HAFSA BINT AL-HAYY AR-RAKUNIYYA (12th c.)

A poet who lived in Granada in the twelfth century, Hafsa belonged to a noble family and received a superior education, which enabled her to become a teacher later in life. Like Wallādah, she was the lover of a poet, Abū Yafar, and many of her poems take the form of a dialogue with him. For example:

> Shall I go to your house, or will you come to mine?
> My heart always goes where you desire.
> You may be sure you will not be thirsty or hot when
>   you meet me.
> A fountain fresh and sweet are my lips, and the
>   branches of my braids cast a thick shadow.
> Answer me quickly, for it would be wrong to make
>   your Butaynah wait, oh, my Yamil.

No less loving than the famous poet Yamil to his beloved Butaynah, Abū Yafar replied to Hafsa:

> If I can find a way, I will go to you.
> You are too important to come to me.
> The garden does not move, but receives the soft puff of
>   the breeze.

Hafsa also was being courted by the governor, Abû Sa'īd, whose great passion for her she did not dare reject, and probably enjoyed to some extent. Mutual jealousy caused the relationship between Abū Sa'īd and Abū Yafar, who was his secretary, to deteriorate. Eventually the former had the latter killed. Despite the danger, Hafsa did not hide her grief, and wrote the following lines:

They threaten me for mourning a lover they killed by
  sword.
May God be merciful to one generous with her tears
or to her who cries for one killed by his rivals,
and may the afternoon clouds so generously drench the
  land wherever she may go.

After Abū Yafar's death Ḥafṣa went to Marrakech,
where she became tutor to the princesses.

All seventeen of Ḥafṣa known poems were written in
the earlier part of her life. Although she produced some
satirical and panegyrical poems, most of her works are
love poems, at which she excelled. Of the almost forty
women poets of al-Andalus, Ḥafṣa is the most representative and the best known.

See also **Wallādah Bint Al-Mustafki**

Further Reading

Garulo, T. *Diwan de las poetisas de al-Andalus.* Madrid, 1986.
Sobh, M. (comp.) *Poetisas arábigo-andaluzas.* Granada, 1985.
                                        CRISTINA GONZÁLEZ

HÁKON GÓÐI ("THE GOOD") HARALDSSON (ca. 920–960)

Hákon góði Haraldsson was a younger son and successor of Haraldr hárfagri ("fair-hair") Hálfdanarson, who
first brought Norway under a single kingship. Hákon
was also called "Æthelstan's foster-son," because he
was fostered in England at the Christian court of King
Æthelstan of Wessex. Around 935, Hákon learned in
England of his father's death, and returned to Norway
to regain the throne from his haif-brother, Eirikr blóðøx
("blood-axe") Haraldsson. Hákon sought the support of
Earl Sigurðr Hákonarson in Trondheim, and was named
king in Trøndelag after promising the farmers that he
would restore their patrimonial rights (óðal). When
Hákon moved south and seized power in Oppland and
Vík, Eiríkr, without further resistance, fled from Norway
to York. Hákon became king over Norway, but in reality
his power lay in the southwest; he allowed Earl Sigurðr
to retain sovereignty in Trøndelag, and he gave his nephews, Tryggvi Óláfsson and Guðrøðr Bjarnarson, virtual
autonomy over parts of southeastern Norway.

Hákon's popularity has been traditionally ascribed to
his achievements as a lawgiver and organizer of military
defense. The poet Sighvatr Þóðarson's *Bersǫglisvísur*
("Plain-speaking Verses," ca. 1038) extol Hákon for his
justice and his laws. The histories *Ágrip*, *Fagrskinna*,
and *Heimskringla* variously credit him with establishing
the Gulaþing Law for the *fylkir* ("districts") of Rogaland,
Hordaland, Sogn, and the Fjords, and the Frostuþing
Law for the *fylkir* of Trøndelag together with Nordmøre,
Namdal, and later Romsdal. But these histories are not
wholly accurate, for the Guiaþing, at least, had probably
been established in the 930s. It is more likely that Hákon
reorganized existing law federations (the Gulaþing in
western Norway, Frostaþing in northern Norway, and
Eiðsivaþing around the southeastern Lake Mjøsa area)
by extending their reach into neighboring districts and
changing them into representative and consultive bodies.
Each district was required to send a certain number of
delegates (*nefndarmenn*) to the þing. The integration of
fylkir into larger regions and the reorganization of the
law federations on a more representative basis enabled
the monarchy to consult more easily with the several
regions and thereby seek both legal and popular approval
for national as well as local matters. Thus, Hákon can
probably be credited with introducing the principle of
representation into the Norwegian social order.

According to *Heimskringla* and *Fagrskinna*, Hákon
also reorganized the military defense set up by his father,
Haraldr Hálfdanarson, into a levy system (*leiðangr*), by
which the king could summon on a proportional basis a
levy of ships, warriors, weapons, and equipment. Hákon
divided all the coastal lands into *skipreiður* ("ship-pro-
viding [districts]") and stipulated by law the number of
warships and men to be supplied by each district. He
also instituted a system of war signal fires along the
mountaintops to warn of approaching enemies.

Although Hákon had been raised a Christian, his
attempts to introduce Christianity into Norway did not
succeed. According to *Heimskringla*, Hákon invited
priests from England and built churches in western
Norway. Further evidence of English mission activity in
mid-10th-century Norway may be provided by the listing of a "Sigefridus norwegensis" among the names of
Glastonbury monks who were bishops during the reign
of King Edgar (d. 975). When Hákon proposed at the
Frostaþing that the people accept Christianity, however,
he reportedly met with great resistance and was forced
to abandon his attempt. Hákon presumably left the faith
himself, for the memorial poem *Hákonarmál* (*ca.* 961)
commemorates him as a staunch upholder of pagan
sanctuaries, although this poem may reflect the poet's
sentiment more than the historical accuracy of Hákon's
return to paganism.

Around 955, Hákon repelled the first of many attacks
on Norway by his nephews, the Eiríkssons, who had
taken refuge in Denmark with their uncle, King Harald
Gormsson. Hákon retaliated with raids on Denmark, but
when the Eiríkssons (ca. 960) renewed attacks at Fitje
(Fitjar) on the island of Stord (Storð) off western Norway, Hákon was mortally wounded. *Heimskringla* reports that he was given a pagan burial, and lauds Hákon
as a king who brought peace and good seasons. His
famous eulogy *Hákonarmál* states: "Unbound against
the dwellings of men/the Fenris-wolf shall go/before a
king as good as he / walks on that empty path."

See also **Eyvindr Finsson skáldaspillir; Sighvatr Þorðarson**

Further Reading

Literature

Andersen, Per Sveaas. *Samlingen av Norge og kristningen av landet* 800–1130. Handbok i Norges historie 2. Bergen: Universiteisforlaget, 1977, pp. 84–99, 247–73.

Birkeli, Fridtjov. "Hadde Hákon Adalsteinsfostre likevel en Biskop Sigfrid hos seg?" *Historisk tidsskrift* (Norway) 40 (1960–61), 113–36.

Birkeli, Fridtjov. "The Earliest Missionary Activity from England to Norway." *Nottingham Mediaeval Studies* 15 (1971), 27–37; Holmsen, Andreas. *Norges historie fra de eldste tider* til 1660.3rd ed. Oslo: Universitetsforlaget, 1971, pp. 141–51.

Foote, Peter G., and David M. Wilson. *The Viking Achievement: The Society and Culture of Early Medieval Scandinavia.* London: Sidgwick & Jackson, 1970, pp. 36–42, 46–7, 280–2.

Jones, Gwyn. *A History of the Vikings.* 2nd ed. Oxford and New York: Oxford University Press, 1984, pp. 92–6, 118–23.

Koht, Halvdan. "Haakon Adalsteinsfostre." *Norsk biografisk leksikon* 5. Oslo: Aschehoug, 1931, pp. 152–7.

DAPHNE L. DAVIDSON

HÁKON HÁKONARSON (1204-1263)

Hákon Hákonarson, king of Norway 1217–1263, was born in 1204, the son of King Hákon Sverrisson, and grandson of Sverrir Sigurðarson.

After King Ingi Bárðarson's death in 1217, the Birkibeinar ("birch-legs") disagreed on his successor. The choice was among Hákon Hákonarson, Ingi's son Guttormr, and Ingi's brother Earl Skúli. Hákon was elected king but Skúli continued as earl and adviser to the young king, responsible for the rule of a third of Norway. In 1219, Hákon was engaged to Earl Skúli's daughter Margrét, and they were married in 1225.

During the 1220s, Hákon and Skúli had to fight a group of rebels, the Ribbungar from Viken. The fight lasted until 1227 and became a major reason why the king and Skúli supported each other. But gradually Hákon began to act increasingly independently, and during the 1230s open conflict broke out between Hákon and Skúli over the administration of the kingdom. In 1239, Skúli rebelled against Hákon, and assumed the title of king at Eyraþing in Niðaróss (Trondheim). Hákon crushed the resistance, and in 1240 Skúli was killed by the Birkibeinar. After that, Hákon was the uncontested king of Norway.

Practical cooperation between the archbishop and the kingdom characterized the greater part of Hákon Hákonarson's reign. In collaboration with the Church, hereditary succession to the throne was established. Hákon was recognized as the lawful successor to the kingdom of Norway at a meeting in Bergen in 1223. The archbishop confirmed the decision, and this act

validated the principles concerning ecclesiastical influence on the succession; this influence had its roots in the Law of Succession to the Throne from 1163. In 1240, allegiance was sworn to Hákon's eldest legitimate son, Hákon, which proved a clear victory for the hereditary throne. At the same time, the principle of legitimacy was strengthened, since the son Hákon was preferred to an older, illegitimate half-brother. Papal assent that Hákon Hákonarson's successors were to rule Norway came in 1247, when Hákon was crowned by Cardinal William of Sabina.

In Hákon Hákonarson's time, European chivalric literature began its influence in Norway. Hákon Hákonarson, and later his son Magnús, wanted the Norwegian court to be comparable with those in Europe. Hákon had a number of European Latin works translated into Old Norse. The oldest of these translations is *Tristrams saga* from 1226. Five MSS containing *riddarasögur* expressly state that the works were translated at Hákon's request, and it is likely that Hákon also had *Konungs skuggsjá* written, modeled on the European *specula.* These translations were significant for the Norse cultural milieu, and among other things influenced a number of *Íslendingasögur,* among them *Laxdoela saga.* The *riddarasögur* became popular especially in Iceland, where as early as 1300 people began composing their own.

During Hákon's reign, the people of Lübeck began trading with Norway. The importance of this trade increased, and in 1250, Hákon signed a treaty with the city. The following year, an agreement was entered into with Novgorod concerning peace in the northern tributary countries. Hákon was also active in Scandinavian politics after 1248, when trouble arose in Denmark and Sweden. He married his son Hákon to Earl Birgir's daughter in Sweden, and his other son, Magnús, to King Erik's daughter in Denmark.

From 1220, Hákon Hákonarson had tried to subjugate the Norse islands in the west, but this conquest was impossible as long as there were conflicts in Norway. After Skúli's death, however, Hákon attempted to secure control over Iceland. Through the chieftains in Iceland, who were also his retainers, he succeeded in gaining control of the *goðorð* little by little. Thereafter, he could distribute the *goðorð* among the chieftains he found best suited to advancing his policies. In addition, he received support from the Norwegian bishops in Iceland; and in 1262–1264, he subjected Iceland and Greenland to the kingdom of Norway.

In the Hebrides and on the Isle of Man, there had been trouble throughout Hákon's reign, and in 1262 the Scots attacked the islands. Hákon gathered a mercenary army and attacked Scotland in 1263. The result was meager, and he did not secure Norwegian control over the islands. Hákon then went to the Orkney Islands, where he died in the winter of 1263.

Further Reading

Literature

Bagge, Sverre. "Kirkens jurisdiksjon i kristenrettssaker før 1277." *Historisk tidsskrift* (Norway) 60 (1981), 133–59.

Bagge, Sverre. "The Formation of the State and Concepts of Society in 13th Century Norway." In *Continuity and Change: Political Institutions and Literary Monuments in the Middle Ages. A Symposium.* Ed. Elisabeth Vestergard. Odense: Odense University Press, 1986, pp. 43–61.

Bagge, Sverre. "Borgerkrig og statsutvikling i Norge i middelalderen." *Historisk tidsskrift* (Norway) 65 (1986), 145–97.

Bagge, Sverre. *The Political Thought of the King's Mirror.* Mediaeval Scandinavia Supplements, 3. Odense: Odense University Press, 1987.

Bjørgo, Narve. "Om skriftlege kjelder for Hákonar saga." *Historisk tidsskrift* (Norway) 46 (1967), 185–229.

Crawford, Barbara E "The Earls of Orkney-Caithness and Their Relations with the Kings of Norway and Scotland: 1150–1470." Diss. Si. Andrews University, 1971.

Crawford, Barbara E. "Weland of Stiklaw: A Scottish Royal Servant at the Norwegian Court." *Historiskodsskrift* (Norway) 52 (1973), 329–39.

Gunnes, Erik. "Kirkelig jurisdiksjon i Norge 1153–1277." *Historisk tidsskrift* (Norway) 49 (1970), 109–60.

Helle, Knut. "Tendenser i nyere norsk høymiddelalderforskning." *Historisk tidsskrift* (Norway) 40 (1960–61), 337–70.

Helle, Knut. "Trade and Shipping Between Norway and England in the Reign of Hákon Hákonsson (1217–1263)." *Sjøfartshistorisk årbok* (Bergen) (1967), 7–33.

Helle, Knut. "Anglo-Norwegian Relations in the Reign of Håkon Håkonsson (1217–63)." *Mediaeval Scandinavia* 1 (1968), 101–14.

Helle, Knut. *Konge og gode menn i norsk riksstyring ca. 1150–1319.* Bergen: Universitetsforlaget, 1972.

Helle, Knut. *Norge blir en stat, 1130–1319.* Handbok i Norges historie, 3. 2nd ed. Bergen: Universitetsforlaget, 1974.

Helle, Knut. "Norway in the High Middle Ages: Recent Views on the Structure of Society." *Scandinavian Journal of History* 6 (1981), 161–89.

Koht, Halvdan. "The Scandinavian Kingdoms Until the End of the Thirteenth Century." In *The Cambridge Medieval History* 6. Ed. J. R. Tanner *et al.* Cambridge: Cambridge University Press, 1929, pp. 362–92.

Lunden, Kårå. *Norge under Sverreætten 1177–1319.* Norges Historie, 3. Oslo: Cappelen, 1976.

JÓN VIÐAR SIGURÐSSON

HARALDR HARÐRÁÐI ("HARD-RULER") SIGURÐARSON (1046–1066)

Haraldr harðraði ("hard-ruler") was the half-brother of St. Óláfr, the son of Óláfr's mother, Ásta, and her husband, Sigurðr sýr ("sow") Hálfdanarson. His hereditary claim to the Norwegian throne was thus dubious, but he lived in an age when hereditary rights were not paramount. According to *Heimskringla*, Haraldr "excelled other men in shrewdness and resourcefulness.... He was exceedingly skilled in arms, and victorious in his undertakings...a handsome man of stately, appearance. He was light blond, with a blond beard and long mustaches, with one eyebrow higher than the other...ruthless with his enemies, and given to harsh punishment of all who opposed him...inordinately covetous of power and of valuable possessions of all kinds" (ch. 99). He succeeded to sole possession of the Norwegian throne in 1047.

Haraldr's career is recounted mainly in his saga in Snorri Sturluson's *Heimskringla*. At the age of fifteen, he fought alongside his half-brother in the battle of Stiklastaðir (Stiklestad), where Óláfr was killed. He then spent fifteen years away from Norway in the service of the Kievan prince Jaroslav, whose daughter he later married, and in the imperial service in Byzantium. The saga describes his years as leader of the Varangian Guard there in exaggerated terms: the empress Zóe falls in love with him; he captures cities using stratagems that are common folktale motifs. A Greek work written in the 1070s, *Logos nuthetikos,* also refers to his campaigns. Haraldr was also imprisoned in Byzantium for a time.

In 1045, Haraldr returned to Norway and made a treaty to share the rule with Óláfr's son Magnús inn góði ("the good") until the tetter's death without male issue, when Haraldr became sole ruler. The years of Haraldr's rule in Norway are characterized by his repeated campaigns against Sven Estridsen in Denmark, including the burning of Hedeby in 1049. The two finally reached a treaty in 1064. Haraldr's mobilization against Denmark was made possible by his consolidation of control over Norway itself, in what Icelandic authors, at least, perceived as a harsh and overbearing manner. He was also known for his influence over the Norwegian Church, building churches and handpicking bishops and other officials. According to the sources, he founded Oslo and introduced coins as a common means of payment, although other rulers had struck coins previously. His reputation, which has come down to us mainly through Icelandic literature, is generally favorable, since he is credited with saving Iceland from famine. But some of the *þættir* included in the *Morkinskinna* version of his saga depict his personality rather unsympathetically. His nickname reflects the harshness many authors attributed to him.

Haraldr had a claim to the English throne by virtue of a treaty between his nephew Magnús and Hardacnut, son of Knud (Cnut) the Great. Upon the death of Edward the Confessor in January 1066, Haraldr saw an opportunity to make that claim. He landed in Yorkshire, and was eventually defeated by Harold Godwinsson at the battle of Stamford Bridge. But the English army's desperate ride north, losses sustained at Stamford Bridge, and rapid return south weakened it greatly just before Harold Godwinsson had to meet William the Conquerer at the battle of Hastings. Haraldr harðráði's invasion was thus the determining factor in Harald Godwinsson's loss to William, which changed the political face of Europe.

Haraldr's death at Stamford Bridge is often taken as

symbolizing the end of the Viking Age in Scandinavia. His was not the last major overseas Viking campaign but it was the last, perhaps, with some chance of success, and the sagas of subsequent kings do not paint the same sort of pictures of Viking heroes.

See also **Cnut; Harold Godwinson; William I**

Further Reading

Editions

Bjami Aðalbjarnarson, ed. "Haralds saga Sigurðarsonar." In *Heimskringla*. 3 vols. Íslenzk fomrit, 26–8. Reykjavik: Hið íslenzka fomritafélag, 1941–51, vol. 3, pp. 68–202.

Finnur Jonsson, ed. *Fagrskinna: Nóregs konunga tal.* Samfund til udgiveke af gammd nordisk litteratur, 30. Copenhagen: [s.n.], 1902–03.

Finnur Jónsson, ed. *Morkinskinna.* Samfund til udgivelse af gammel nordisk litteratur, 80. Copenhagen: [s.n.], 1932.

Translations

Hollander, Lee M., trans. *Heimskringla: History of the Kings of Norway.* Austin: University of Texas Press, 1964, pp. 577–663.

Magnus Magnusson and Hermann Pálsson, trans. *King Harald's Saga: Harald Hardradi of Norway.* Hammondsworth: Penguin, 1966.

Literature

Andersen, Per Sveaas. *Samlingen av Norge og kristningen av landet 800–1130.* Handbok i Norges historie, 2. Bergen: Universitetsforlaget, 1977.

Andersson, Theodore M. "Kings' Sagas (*Konungasögur*)." In *Old Norse-Icelandic Literature: A Critical Guide.* Ed, Carol J. Clover and John Lindow. Islandica, 45. Ithaca and London: Cornell University Press, 1985, pp. 197–238.

Blóndal, Sigfús. "The Last Exploits of Harald Sigurdsson in Greek Service: A Chapter from the History of the Varangians." *Classica et Mediaevalia* 1.2 (1939), 1–26.

Ellis Davidson, H. R. *The Viking Road to Byzantium.* London: Allen & Unwin, 1976.

Bjarni Aðalbjamarson. "Formáli." *Heimskringla,* vol. 3, pp. v–cxv.

Indrebø, Gustav. "Harald haardraade i Morkinskinna." In *Festskrift til FinnurJónsson 29. maj 1928.* Ed. Johs. Brøndum-Nielsen *et al.* Copenhagen: Levin & Munksgaard, 1928, pp. 173–80.

Jones, Gwyn. *A History of the Vikings.* 2nd ed. Oxford and New York: Oxford University Press, 1984.

Turville-Petre, G. *Haraldr the Hard-Ruler and His Poets.* Dorothea Coke Memorial Lecture in Northern Studies. London: University College; Lewis, 1968.

RUTH MAZO KARRAS

HARALDR HÁRFAGRI ("FAIR-HAIR") HÁLFDANARSON
(d. ca. 930/40)

Haraldr hárfagri Hálfdanarson is the king credited with unifying Norway. According to his saga in Snorri Sturluson's *Heimskringla,* the fullest account of Haraldr's life although not to be taken as accurate in historical detail, he descended from the Yngling dynasty and came to the throne of his father's kingdom of Vestfold at the age of ten (scholars estimate the date of this accession at *ca.* 860–880). Haraldr desired to become king over all of Norway, and swore a vow not to cut or comb his hair until he had achieved this goal, hence his nickname. The story is legendary, and it is doubtful anyone had a concept of Norway as a unity before his conquest of the different regions.

The *Heimskringla* version is based on a lost * *Haralds saga,* as is a *þáttr* about him in *Flateyjarbók.* Haraldr's saga recounts a series of campaigns against various petty kings and his alliance with the powerful northern Earl Hákon Grjótgarðarson, as well as his conflicts with the Swedish king who was his rival for the eastern districts of Norway. At the battle of Hafrsfjrðr (Havsfjord), now dated between 885 and 890, Haraldr defeated a coalition of kings and earls and established his hegemony.

The political significance of Haraldr's unification of Norway was not as great as the Icelandic saga literature implies. Haraldr's hold upon northern and eastern Norway was never firm. Traditionally, the settlement of Iceland by Ingólfr Arnarson and others around 870 was attributed to their desire to escape from Haraldr's tyranny. However, the battle of Hafrsfjrðr cannot have been fought that early, and the settlers must have had motives other than fleeing the unified kingdom. Many leading Norwegians did flee after Hafrsfjrðr, to Shetland, Orkney, and the Hebrides, if not Iceland. According to Snorri, they continued to conduct raids upon Norway from there until Haraldr strengthened his navy and put a stop to this Viking activity. But scholars now doubt whether Haraldr actually made any expedition to Britain. Many of the original settlers of Iceland came not from Norway directly, but from the British Isles. To support the myth of Haraldr's tyranny as the cause of settlement, Icelanders probably invented an extension of Haraldr's power over the islands.

Snorri's account of Haraldr's establishment of a Norwegian state is most likely anachronistic. Haraldr was accused of having appropriated the óðal land of all the farmers, making them his tenants, and of imposing heavy taxation. The system of taxation and military organization Snorri describes, however, is probably a reflection of Snorri's own time. The accusations of tyranny may be due to an Icelandic tradition of hostility toward Haraldr, which allowed Icelanders to hearken back to a Golden Age of freedom. But society before Haraldr was dominated by chieftains, earls, or petty kings, and was not as egalitarian as Snorri indicates.

Haraldr's unified Norway did not survive his death (between 930 and 940), largely because he left so many sons, as many as twenty according to some sources. Snorri recounts his division of the realm among his sons and the sharing of his revenue with them before his death, assigning Eiríkr blóðøx ("blood-axe") to be high king. While this account is not likely to be accurate, the sons certainly all believed themselves entitled to the dignity of king. Upon Haraldr's death, his sons sought power in various of the petty kingdoms their father had controlled. Any governmental reforms he made collapsed with the end of his personal rule.

Further Reading

Editions

Bjarni Aðalbjamarson, ed. "Haralds saga inshárfagra." In *Heimskringla*. 3 vols. Íslenzk fornrit, 26–8. Reykjavik: Hið íslenzka fornritafélag, 1941–51, vol. 1, pp. 94–149.

Guðbrandr Vigfússon and C.R. Unger, eds. "Haralds Þáttr hárfagra." In *Flatelyarbok. En Samling af norske Konge-Sagaer med indskudte mindre Fortællinger om Begivenheder i og undenfor Norge samt Annaler*. 3 vols. Christiania [Oslo]: Malling, 1860–68, vol. 1. pp. 567–76.

Sigurður Nordal, ed. *Egils saga Skalla-Grímssonar*. Íslenzk fornrit, 2. Reykavik: Hið íslenzka fornritafélag, 1933.

Storm, Gustav, ed. *Monumenta historiae norvegiae: latinske kildeskrifter til Noregs historie i middelalderen*. Christiania [Oslo]: Brögger, 1880.

Translations

Hermann Palsson and Paul Edwards, trans. *Egil's Saga*. Harmondsworth: Penguin, 1976.

Hollander, Lee M., trans., *Heimskringla: History of the Kings of Norway*. Austin: University of Texas Press, 1964, pp. 59–95.

Literature

Andersen, Per Sveaas. *Samlingen av Norge og kristningen av landet 800–1130*. Handbok i Norges historie, 2. Bergen: Universitetsforlaget, 1977.

Andersson, Theodore M. "Kings' Sagas (*Konungasögur*)." In *Old Norse–Icelandic Literature: A Critical Guide*. Ed. Carol J. Clover and John Lindow. Islandica, 45. Ithaca and London: Cornell University Press, 1985.

Berman, Melissa A. "*Egils saga* and *Heimskringla*." *Scandinavian Studies* 54 (1982), 21–50.

Bjami Aðalbjarnarson. "Formáli." In *Heimskringla*, vol. 1

Campbell, Alistair. "The Opponents of Haraldr Hárfagri at Hafrsfjrøðr." *Saga-Book of the Viking Socacy* 12.4(1942), 232–7.

Gunnes, Erik. *Rikssamling og kristning 800–1177*. Oslo: Cappelen, 1976.

Holmsen, Andreas. *Nye studier i gammel historie* Oslo: Universitetsforlaget, 1976.

Jones, Gwyn. *A History of the Vikings*. 2nd ed. Oxford and New York: Oxford University Press, 1984.

Ólafía Einarsdóttir. "Dateringen af Harald hårfagers død." *Historisk tidsskrift* (Norway) 47 (1968). 15–34.

Sawyer, P. H. "Harald Fairhair and the British Isles." In *Les Vikings et leur civilisation: problèmes actuels*. Ed. Régis Boyer. École des hautes études en sciences sociales, Bibliothèque Arctique et Antarctique, 5. Paris and La Haye: Mouton, 1976, pp. 105–9.

RUTH MAZO KARRAS

HAROLD GODWINSON (ca. 1020–1066)

On 14 October 1066 Harold Godwinson, the last Saxon king of England, lay dead on the field of Battle, near Hastings in Kent. The hopes of his family to create a royal dynasty were dashed, the fortunes and lives of his supporters wasted in what may have been as audacious a bid for royal power as that of William the Conqueror.

Harold had been opposed by several contenders for the throne after the death of Edward the Confessor in January 1066 and had defeated them all, including his brother Tostig and Tostig's ally, King Harald of Norway, at the Battle of Stamford Bridge in late September 1066. The decision to undertake a forced march from Stamford, near York, to Hastings, where William waited with his continental army, is often seen as a move made in desperation; it is likely that Harold was confident of victory or, at the very least, of a temporary repulse of William.

William's success has dominated the history of late Anglo-Saxon times. It is often forgotten that Harold, formerly earl of Wessex, had been king for nearly a year. The short duration of his reign means that little was written about it, or about Harold's character, by the historians of the day. William of Poitiers, who wrote his *Gesta Guillelmi ducis Normannorum et regis Anglorum* in the 1070s, describes Harold as brave, ambitious, and clever, but an unwise dispenser of patronage. The English author of the *Vita Aedwardi regis* is more enthusiastic; Harold "was a true friend of his race and country, he wielded his father's powers even more actively, and walked in his ways, that is, in patience and mercy, and with kindness to men of good will." It is not entirely surprising that legends of Harold's survival after Hastings circulated for some years after the battle.

Harold was 27 when he inherited the earldom of Wessex on Godwin's death in 1053. Harold and his brothers Leofwine, Gyrth, and Tostig controlled, as earls, all of southern England, including East Anglia and even a part of Northumbria. Harold and Tostig were successful in England's defense against Welsh and Scottish forces, and both won Edward's gratitude. But it was to Harold that the dying king commended his wife (Harold's sister Edith) and kingdom in January 1066.

Harold had held a special position at court, referred to as Edward's governor by the *Vita Aedwardi regis,* and in 1064 or 1065 royal ambassador to Normandy. This visit, at which Harold presumably promised to support William's claim to the English throne, is recorded mainly in pro-Norman sources; the story is difficult to reconcile with the silence of Anglo-Saxon writers on the subject. The *Vita Aedwardi* hints of the visit, but the Anglo-Saxon Chronicle does not refer to it. Harold clearly believed, at Stamford Bridge and Hastings, that he was defending England from its enemies, not that he was asserting a doubtful claim.

It is possible that the Confessor may have fed the hopes of several contenders with hints of a future bequest. Such a ploy would have been useful in preventing invasions from Scandinavia and France during his lifetime. As a prominent royal adviser, Harold may have been cognizant of the double dealing and thus unlikely to take seriously foreign claims to the throne.

It is impossible to know what kind of king Harold would have made or what tone he would have established had he repelled the Normans. The combination of lands inherited from Edward and his own earldom made him extraordinarily powerful, and the successful exploitation of these resources gave him the means to finance important projects. His founding of a college of canons at Waltham suggests that patronage of religious houses would have been one aspect of his policies. His efforts to extend English influence in Wales would no doubt have continued after 1066, and he might have built his own retinue of loyal, powerful nobles.

See also **Edward the Confessor; Haraldr harðraði ("hard-ruler") Sigurðarson; Henry I**

Further Reading

Primary Sources

Barlow, Frank, ed. and trans. *The Life of King Edward Who Rests at Westminster* [*Vita Aedwardi Regis*]. 2d ed. Oxford: Clarendon, 1992.

Secondary Sources

Barlow, Frank. *Edward the Confessor*. Berkeley: University of California Press, 1970.
Williams, Ann. "Land and Power in the Eleventh Century: The Estates of Harold Godwineson." *Anglo-Norman Studies* 3 (1981): 171–87, 230–34.

STEPHANIE CHRISTELOW

HARPESTRENG, HENRIK (d. 1244)

A large body of medical work has been preserved from the Danish doctor Master Henrik Harpestreng, who died April 2, 1244, as a canon in Rosktlde and physician-in-ordinary of King Erik Plovpenning ("plow-penny"). Two Latin works by a certain Henricus Dacus, presumably the same man, are known: a book about laxatives, *De simplicibus medicinis laxativis,* and a book about herbs, *Liber herbarum,* extant in several MSS from the 15th century.

His other works are written in older Middle Danish, according to the late MS Thott 710 4to (A, 1450), by the author's own efforts: "Here a medical book in Danish is begun, the one that Master Henrik Harpestreng composed from his great mastership." This is the prologue to Harpestreng's best-known work, *Urtebogen* ("The Book of Herbs"), which is known from late MSS and two MSS from around 1300. In one of these MSS (NkS 66 8vo by Brother Khud Juul, attorney of the monastery of Sorø), two books about herbs are followed by a *Stenbog* ("Book of Stones") about the curative properties of gem-stones, and by a *Kogebog* ("Cookbook"), the oldest one with "French cuisine." The *Urtebog* is translated from a Latin poem in hexameters written under the French pseudonym Macer, *De viribus herbarum (ca.* 1090), and from Constantinus Africanus's *De gradibus liber,* a major work from the Salerno school (1050).

An astrological-prognostic work, which also contains the doctor's instructions for the bloodletting of King Erik Plovpenning, is still unedited (GkS 3656 8vo, from *ca.* 1500). Harpestreng also wrote about hygiene, bloodletting, and cupping, and may have collected his comprehensive knowledge in a leechbook. A Swedish leechbook (AM 45 4to, from *ca.* 1450) names Harpestreng as author, but his name had such a reputation in all of Scandinavia that it recommended any work. The provenance is thus uncertain, and more detailed examination of the authorship is lacking.

Harpestreng's works reveal him as a pupil of the international medical school in Salerno, Italy, which pursued Greek traditions (*e.g.,* Galen, 2nd century A.D.) and Arabic ones (*e.g.,* Avicenna's *Canon,* 1030). This antique system was based on a theory that the body was influenced by four cardinal liquids or humors, corresponding to the four elements and temperaments: air corresponding to blood (*sanguis*); fire to red or yellow gall (*cholera rubea*); soil to black gall (*melancholia*); and water to phlegm (*flegma*). Illnesses were caused by a lack of balance among these liquids, and medicine prescribed natural plants and minerals to restore the balance by a contrasting principle. Phlegm has, for example, the attributes of cold and moistness, and one gets pains if there is too much of it in the stomach, Harpestreng therefore suggests peas against stomach pains, because the attributes of peas are dryness and warmth like the yellow gall: "Pea is dry and warm; boiled and eaten it causes a good digestion and warms the stomach, but be careful not to eat it if you have an ulcer or abcess, because it increases the pain, and do not eat it during bloodletting nor when you suffer from pains in your eyes, because it brings about and increases warmth and infection and causes bad stitches and does not allow the unclean liquid to flow from one's eyes" (from *Liber herbarum*).

Further Reading

Editions

Konráðr Gíslason, ed. *Fire og fyrretyve for en stor deel forhen utrykte prøver af oldnordisk sprog og literatur.* Copenhagen: Gyldendal, 1860.
Klemming, G. E., ed. *Läke- och örteböker från Sveriges Medeltid.* Samlingar utgivna av Svenska fomskrift-sällskapet, 82, 84, 90. Stockholm: Norstedt, 1883–86.
Hægstad, M. *Gamalnorsk fragment av Henrik Harpestreng.* Videnskabs-selskabets skrifter. II, Hist.-filos. Klasse 1906. Christiania [Oslo]: Dybwad, 1906.

Harpestreng, H. *Gamle danske Urtebøger, Stenbøger og Koge-bøger.* Ed. Marius Kristensen. Copenhagen: Thiele, 1908–20 [originally issued in 7 parts as Universitets-Jubilæets danske Samfund, Skrifter Nr. 182, 192, 200, 215,226,236, and 253 edits Stock. K 48 (S, *ca.* 1300), Knud Juul MS, NkS 66,8 (K, *ca.* 1300), a fragment of Linköping T67 (L, *ca.* 1350), NkS 7OR, 8vo (Q, after 1350), *Stenbogh* from Stockholm K4 (S,*ca.* 1450)]

Henricus Dacus. *De simplicibus medicinis laxativis.* Ed. J. W. S. Johnson. Copenhagen: Hofboghandel, 1914.

Hauberg, P., ed. *"En middelalderlig dansk lægebog."* Copenhagen: Koppel, 1927.

Harpestreng, Henrik, *Liber Herbarum.* Ed. Poul Hauberg. Copenhagen: Kretzschmer, 1936.

Literature

Hauberg, Poul. "Lidt om Henrik Harpestrængs Lægebog." *Danske Studier* 19 (1919), 111–28.

Otto, Alfred. *Liber Daticus Roskildensis.* Tillæg 4. Copenhagen: Levin & Munksgaard, 1933.

Møller-Christensen, Vilhelm. *Middelalderens Lægekunst i Danmark* Copenhagen: Munksgaard, 1944 [English summary]

Skov, Sigv. "Henrik Harpestreng og middelalderens medicin." *Danske Studier* 45 (1945), 125–39.

Gotfredsen, Edvard. *Medicinens historie.* 3rd ed. Copenhagen: Nyt Nordisk Forlag, 1973.

SIGURD KVÆRNDRUP

HARTMANN VON AUE
(ca. 1160–after 1210)

Of the four major writers of the High Middle Ages during the Hohenstaufen dynasty—Hartmann von Aue, Walther von der Vogelweide, Wolfram von Eschenbach, and Gottfried von Straßburg—Hartmann von Aue stands out as the most prolific and diverse. His works include a verse treatise on love, *Diu Klage* (The Lament, ca. 1180), two Arthurian epics, *Erec* (ca. 1180) and *Iwen* (ca. 1200), two verse tales, *Gregorius* (ca. 1190) and *Armer Heinrich* (Poor Heinrich, ca. 1195), and eighteen poems—some spurious—spread out over much of his writing career.

Both Gottfried von Strasbourg, author of *Tristan*, and Wolfram von Eschenbach, author of *Parzival*, mention Hartmann in their works, and their comments reveal the esteem in which he was held by contemporary writers. As the poet who introduced the Arthurian romance into German-language literature, Hartmann influenced not only his literary generation but those who followed, well into the thirteenth century.

Like all of the major writers of the period, very little is known about Hartmann's life, and what is known must be gleaned from comments in his works, as nothing has come down to us in contemporary documents. Setting aside the question of whether Hartmann speaks in his works in an autobiographical or a literary voice, current thinking generally agrees on a rough sketch of Hartmann's life. In *Poor Heinrich* Hartmann calls himself a *dienstman*, consigning himself in an unembar-rassed way to the class of *ministeriales*, an important, emerging, diverse class of court functionaries dependent for their living on the largesse of the nobility. Whether Hartmann came from a family that was in the ascendant or one that had fallen from free indentured status, is uncertain. By designating himself a *rîter* (knight) in the prologues to *Poor Heinrich* and *Iwein*, Hartmann reveals his knowledge of country life, the backdrop nor only of his Arthurian romances, but also his verse tales and poetry.

Where Hartmann obtained the education he speaks of in *Poor Heinrich*, and whose traces are evident throughout his writings, is not known. Such an education could only have been obtained at a cathedral school or in a monastery; the setting of the monastery in *Gregorius* and discussions of the life and education there would favor the latter supposition. It appears that, in addition to Latin, Hartmann knew Old French, the language of Chrétien de Troyes and the influential French courtly culture. His allusions to classical works and to church philosophers confirm that Hartmann was one of the most learned poets of the age.

Hartmann must have had a wealthy, and thus powerful, patron, for writers of Hartmann's *ministerial*-knightly class were dependent on the court not only for the expensive outfitting of a knight, but also for costly writing resources, access to a courtly audience, and the availability of precious manuscripts of the French sources that Hartmann must have read. Numerous attempts made to pinpoint Hartmann's homeland have been inconclusive. His Alemannic language—a dialect covering a swath from northern Switzerland, southwestern Germany, and southeastern France, that is, modern Alsace—and a few scant descriptions in his works point to modern southern or southwestern Germany as his home. Two powerful families, the Zähringer and the Hohenstaufen, have been posited as Hartmann's patrons, and the Zähringer, with their seat near Freiburg at the crossroads of French and German culture, seem more likely. Finally, it should be no surprise that even the dates of Hartmann's life are disputed, but the period from around 1160 to shortly after 1210 would seem to have encompassed most of his years.

The chronology of Hartmann's writings is also disputed. However, some consensus has been reached: the *Lament* and some of the lyric poetry belong to an early phase, followed by the Arthurian romance *Erec*. Most critics agree that a dramatic metamorphosis then took place in Hartmann's life, something that shaped the themes of his next two works, *Gregorius* and *Poor Heinrich*, and some of his later poetry. Finally, toward the end of his life, Hartmann again turned to the Arthurian epic, this time to *Iwein*. (The beginning of *Iwein* may, however, have been written earlier and set aside, possibly during the presumed upheaval in the poet's life.)

The *Lament* may trace its heritage to the contemporary scholastic *disputatio*, a learned argument between two university professors, or to legal cases or classical models of disputation. The stichomythic (rapid dialogue exchange) give-and-take between the heart and body in the third part of the work points ahead to the debate between the abbot and the young knight-to-be in *Gregorius*, and to alternating dialogue in *Erec* and *Iwein*. Whatever the origin of the work, this early writing bears the imprint of Hartmann's education, whether in a monastery or a church school.

After the body and the heart exchange reproaches and offer their defenses in the *Lament*, and after the stichomythic exchange between the two, the body, having seen the wisdom of the heart's arguments, redirects its attention in the final exchange to the courtly lady in question. A striking feature of the *Lament* is the heart's paradigmatic explanation of what makes up courtly love. Ethical attributes that form the underpinnings of *Minnesang* find echoes in some of Hartmann's poetry, and, coupled with a Christian ethic, resonate throughout Hartmann's works in the striving of the heroes toward betterment and self-fulfillment.

Of all of Hartmann's writings, his lyric poetry has raised the most contention among critics. The nineteenth-century Romantic/positivist viewpoint held that the lyrics mirrored Hartmann's life and could thus be grouped in chronological fashion, tracing first Hartmann's obeisance to the concepts of *minne* (courtly love), then, his disillusionment with and subsequent rejection of it in poetry praising common women, and, finally, to an ethical-spiritual substitution for *minne*, as represented in his *Kreuzlieder* (crusading songs).

What can be said is that Hartmann's poems—eighteen in the canon, but some of these are spurious—can be divided thematically: (1) traditional *Minnesang*; (2) complaints, whether by a man or a woman—the latter being called a *Frauenklage*; (3) songs of anti-*minne*, comprising a rejection of the high ideals of *minne* and a turn to more worldly love for fulfillment; and (4) crusading songs. Taken as a whole, much of Hartmann's lyrical poetry reads like the poetry of his age, and influences from earlier *Minnesänger* are apparent. At times he uses some stunning imagery, and his anti-*minne* songs and crusading songs strike the reader as honest and bold; they certainly must have influenced his contemporaries, including Walther von der Vogelweide. But Hartmann is a more conventional, conservative poet than others of his time, disdaining the erotic and the comical.

Hartmann most likely composed his *Erec* sometime in the 1180s, when he was in his twenties, shortly after the *Lament*, and contemporaneously with some of his lyric poetry. Although the legend of King Arthur had nationalistic overtones in England and France, mirroring the court of Henry II Plantagenet, king of England and of large parts of western France through his marriage to Eleanor of Aquitaine, this nationalism gave way to the trappings of courtly society and chivalry when Hartmann introduced the large-scale Arthurian romance in Germany.

Though he may have also used other sources, written and oral, Hartmann based *Erec* largely on Chrétien de Troye's *Erec et Enide* and acknowledged that fact in line 4629. It would be more appropriate to call *Erec* a reworking, or an adaptation, rather than a translation, however, for Hartmann took great liberties with his French model and expanded Chrétien's version by over 3,000 lines: 10,192 versus 6,958.

The differences between the two *Erecs* illuminate the disparate intentions of the two authors and highlight the similarities and dissimilarities of the two courtly societies. What strikes the reader of both works is Hartmann's focus on courtly society, and its concomitant etiquette of chivalry, and on the relationship between Erec and Enite. One can justifiably call Hartmann didactic, moralistic, and possibly even preachy, for, behind the Arthurian façade, he had a point to make. Both Erec and Enite are guilty of failing to understand their roles in a courtly society. It is their perilous journey that leads them to the awareness that courtly love is more than just physical attraction; it entails a mutually supportive relationship integrated into and supportive of a courtly society. While *Erec* is not a *Fürstenspiegel* (a sort of primer for the education of a prince), Hartmann would probably not have been disappointed had all knights turned out like his hero.

Hartmann also modeled *Gregorius* after a French prototype, the popular *La Vie du Pape Saint Grégoire*. *Gregorius* shows similarities with varying versions, leading to the conjecture that an *Ur-Gregorius* existed at some point. Whatever the exemplar of *Gregorius*, Hartmann's use of it, as with *Erec* and *Iwein*, amounts more to a reworking or adaptation than a strict translation. Compared to the extant Old French versions, *Gregorius* is between one-third and one-half again as long, showing once more that, for Hartmann, the French original served mainly as a foundation on which he could use his poetic skill to erect a vastly different structure.

Gregorius followed *Erec* and the *Lament*, perhaps toward the end of the 1180s, and this positioning of the work has led to one aspect of its interpretation, i.e., that *Gregorius* is "anti-*Erec*," or anti-chivalric, a rejection by a more mature author of his earlier work, namely *Erec*. The thread of individual self-realization, a kind of *rite de passage*, ties Hartmann's major works together. Gregorius, moving from infancy through boyhood to manhood and finally to a precocious middle age of insight and wisdom, comes closest among Hartmann's characters to the *Bildungsfigur* (character undergoing formative changes) of Wolfram von Eschenbach's *Parzival*.

Perhaps the interpretive focus should not, as some scholarship suggests, rest so heavily on the incest of Gregorius' parents, and on his own incest with his mother—for these acts, due to mitigating circumstances, seem pardonable to both medieval and modern thinking—or even on his own *superbia* (pride) at leaving the monastic world, but rather on the journey that Gregorius undertakes, both physically and spiritually, on the path that is mentioned both in the prologue and toward the end of the tale, when Gregorius seeks to do penance in the wilderness. This path may be seen as the path we all take in life.

(Like Erec early on,) the knightly Gregorius leads an exemplary life, an indication that *Gregorius* is not an anti-chivalric work. He falls, as Erec does, but differently, and, like Erec, he must come to an understanding of what has happened to him. He takes the initiative, directs his mother's actions, and sets out to do penance, for, after all, as the prologue and ending make clear, none is so stricken with sin that he cannot rise again, cleansed, and attain grace.

Heinrich von Aue, the protagonist in *Poor Heinrich*, like Erec and Gregorius, has reached what appears to be the pinnacle of success and happiness, only to fall. In his case, leprosy, which must be seen as a curse from God, strikes him down. Unlike Erec and Gregorius, Heinrich, at the beginning of the story, does not have to set out on a path to attain his goal; he has already reached it. Because of the narrator's praise of Heinrich, readers may wonder initially what brought about the knight's fall, but the narrator's comparison of Heinrich with Absalom and the many repetitions of the adjective "worldly" reveal that hubris and the pursuit of worldly things bring about Heinrich's predicament. From the onset of Heinrich's leprosy till the change "in his old way of thinking," he takes a number of positive steps, but he also missteps, and readers must determine if or why Heinrich deserves the salvation granted to him at the end of the story.

When Heinrich disposes of much of his wordly goods and moves in with the family of one of his tenants, Hartmann introduces his most controversial character, a girl of eight who, for three years, rarely departs from her afflicted master's side. Heinrich ends up calling her his "bride," and she ultimately agrees to sacrifice herself for him, for she has learned that only the blood of a willing virgin can save him. The controversy revolves around her motivations: is she selfless or selfish? Is her willingness to sacrifice herself only an arrogant pursuit of salvation? Or is she motivated out of love for her parents and for Heinrich? After all, since the pursuit of salvation recurs in Hartmann's works, and, since salvation was a teaching of the Church, can she be faulted for pursuing what appears to her, a girl without means, as the only road to salvation?

The fairy-tale ending of the story (his healing), in addition to the girl's virtual disappearance from the action, and the couple's ultimate salvation leave some readers dissatisfied. Has Heinrich actually earned his happiness? Do his actions at the end reveal a real change of heart? Not for this reason alone does *Poor Heinrich* remain the most controversial of Hartmann's major works. Where it fits in the chronology of Hartmann's work is also uncertain. It seems to mitigate, with its happy ending, the somberness of *Gregorius*, and point ahead to *Iwein*, Hartmann's return to the Arthurian theme.

The large number of manuscripts and fragments of *Iwein*, its being most often mentioned among Hartmann's work by contemporary writers, and the many depictions of scenes from it in frescoes and tapestries, all point to its popularity. As with *Erec*, Hartmann based *Iwein* on a work by Chrétien de Troyes, *Yvain: Le Chevalier au lion*, and, as in *Erec*, Hartmann greatly expanded upon the French original, by about twenty percent; 8,166 lines versus 6,818. Nevertheless, in *Iwein*, Hartmann followed Chrétien's plot line more closely adding mainly dialogue and authorial reflection.

The theme in *Iwein*, as in *Erec*, is the reconciliation of individual actions and individual love with chivalric ideals and a higher, ethical love. Like Erec, Iwein undergoes a series of adventures before and after his marriage to Laudine. Some critics have questioned Iwein's behavior when he kills Ascalon, Laudine's husband; others have criticized the later adventures as being too inconsequential to fit in the overall structure of the epic. But even more than with *Erec*, Hartmann juxtaposes courtly society with one man's actions, and what is a more requisite component of chivalric society than adventures and quests?

Hartmann treats the court of King Arthur in *Iwein* differently than he presented it in *Erec*. In the earlier work he toned down or eliminated much of Chrétien's criticism of the court, but in *Iwein* the court not only plays a more essential role, but the reader gets glimpses of a courtly society where all is not well. This change in tone could be due to an older Hartmann's lifelong experience at court, but whatever the reason, the court's flaws underline the ethical and moral perfectibility of the individual. From Erec via Gregorius and Heinrich and finally to Iwein, this is the thread that connects Hartmann's major works, for, as with many great writers, Hartmann had an ethical ideal and set out to show how it might be attained.

See also **Chrétien de Troyes; Gottfried von Straßburg**

Further Reading

Bühne, Sheema Zeeban, trans. *Gregorius.* New York: Ungar, 1966.

Clark, Susan L. *Hartmann von Aue: Landscapes of Mind*. Houston: Rice University Press, 1989.

Fisher, R. W., trans. *Narrative Works of Hartmann von Aue*. Göppingen: Kümmerle, 1983.

Gibbs, Marion E., and Sidney M. Johnson. *Medieval German Literature: A Companion*. New York and London: Garland, 1997, pp. 132–156.

Hasty, Will. *Adventures in Interpretation: The Works of Hartmann von Aue and Their Critical Reception*. Columbia, S.C.: Camden House, 1996.

——. *Adventure as Social Performance. A Study of the German Court Epic*. Tübingen: Niemeyer, 1990.

Jackson, William Henry. *Chivalry in Twelfth-Century Germany: The Works of Hartmann von Aue*. Cambridge: Brewer, 1994.

Keller, Thomas L., trans. *Hartmann von Aue. Erec*. New York & London: Garland, 1987.

——. *Hartmann von Aue. Klagebüchlein*. Göppingen: Kümmerle, 1986.

McConeghy, Patrick M., trans. *Iwein*. New York: Garland, 1984.

McFarland, Timothy, and Silvia Ranawake, ed. *Hartmann von Aue. Changing Perspectives: London Hartmann Symposium*. Göppingen: Kümmerle, 1988.

Resler, Michael, trans. *Erec by Hartmann von Aue*. Philadelphia: University of Pennsylvania Press, 1987.

Thomas, John Wesley, trans. *Erec*. Lincoln: University of Nebraska Press, 1982.

——. *Iwein*. Lincoln: University of Nebraska Press, 1979.

——. *Medieval German Lyric Verse in English Translation*. Chapel Hill: University of North Carolina Press, 1968.

——. *Poor Heinrich*. In: *The Best Novellas of Medieval Germany*. Columbia, S.C.: Camden House, 1984.

Tobin, Frank, trans. *Der arme Heinrich* [Medieval text with facing literal English translation]. In: *McGraw-Hill Anthology of German Literature*, vol. I: *Early Middle Ages to Storm and Stress*, ed. Kim Vivian, Frank Tobin, and Richard H. Lawson. New York: McGraw-Hill, 1993; rpt. *Anthology of German Literature: Vom frühen Mittelalter bis zum Sturm und Drang*. Chicago: Waveland, 1998, pp. 69–104.

——. *The Unfortunate Lord Henry*. In: *German Medieval Tales*, ed. Francis G. Gentry. New York: Continuum, 1983, pp. 1–21.

Tobin, Frank, Kim Vivian, and Richard H. Lawson. *Hartmann von Aue. The Complete Arthurian Romances, Tales, and Lyric Poetry*. University Park: Pennsylvania State University Press, 2000.

Tobin, Frank. "High Middle Ages." *In A Concise History of German Literature*, ed. Kim Vivian. Columbia, S.C.: Camden House, 1992, pp. 30–34, 45–48.

Zeydel, Edwin H., trans. (with Bayard Quincy Morgan). *Gregorius: A Medieval Oedipus Legend by Hartmann von Aue*. Chapel Hill: University of North Carolina Press, 1955.

KIM VIVIAN

HAWKWOOD, SIR JOHN (c. 1320–1394)

Sir John Hawkwood (Sir John de Hawkwood, Giovanni Acuto) was born in Sible Hedingham, Essex, the second son of a landowner and tanner named Gilbert Hawkwood, and died in Florence. John Hawkwood, a soldier and leader of mercenary troops, started his military career m France at the beginning of the Hundred Years' War and then became chief of mercenary bands for more then thirty years in Italy, where he was known as Giovanni Acuto.

John Hawkwood served in the army of Edward III, in France, and is said to have fought in the famous battles of Crécy (1346) and Poitiers (1356), gaining a knighthood. After the peace of Bretigny (1360), a great number of the troops were dismissed and many soldiers formed companies of free lances. Hawkwood became the chief of one such band. In 1362, he crossed the Alps and went south, into the service of the republic of Pisa, which was then at war with Florence. In 1364, he was elected captain general of a company of Englishmen called the White Company because of their shining arms and their splendid armor. With other mercenaries at the service of Pisa, Hawkwood attacked Florence and came near enough to the city to burn some suburbs. But the gold of Florence produced its effect, and all the other mercenaries, as well as a number of soldiers of the White Company itself, deserted him. He retired to Pisa with only 800 men.

In 1368, Hawkwood went north to Milan, where he was hired by Barnabò Visconti to fight against the pope and Florence. Hawkwood was sent again to central Italy to support Perugia in its revolt against the pope; there, he was surprised near Arezzo by German mercenaries who had been hired by the pope, was defeated, and was taken prisoner. However, he was ransomed by the Visconti, and he enjoyed such fame and prestige that he was able, in a short time, to put together another company, consisting of his formerly scattered forces and hundreds of other mercenaries willing to serve under him. His army was so strong that it menaced the pope in Montefiascone and in Viterbo. Then, at Cascina, Hawkwood intercepted and defeated a force of Florentines with more then 4,000 men. Back in northern Italy, he defeated the forces of the marquis of Montferrat at Rubiera, in 1372, and laid siege to Asti. But he then left the service of Barnabò Visconti when Barnabò decided to reduce his pay.

Within a few weeks, Hawkwood entered the service of the most determined of the current enemies of the Visconti, Pope Gregorius XI, who also had other leaders of mercenary troops at his service. One of the other leaders, the French mercenary de Coucy, used a strategy that was based on attacking enemies at any cost, whereas Hawkwood thought that intimidation and threats could be more efficient and immensely less costly then open attack. For this reason, Hawkwood's contemporaries called him *cautissimus*. De Coucy caused Hawkwood to suffer an unmerited defeat at Montechiaro; but a few days after this, Hawkwood was able to turn on the pursuing Milanese and rout them.

In 1375, Hawkwood had to move against the free cities of Tuscany as commander of the papal army, which was strong enough to devastate the country but not to conquer the city-states of the region. When the

Florentines offered a large sum of money in exchange for a solemn promise not to damage Florence and the other allied cities, Hawkwood persuaded the papal representative to accept the offer.

The pope was a bad paymaster and habitually answered Hawkwood's requests with vague promises and apostolic blessings. However, as payment for his services Hawkwood obtained the papal territories of Bagnacavallo, Cotignola, and Conselice in Romagna in 1376. In Italy, most of the cities in the papal territories were in rebellion against tyrannical exploitation by the papal legates, and Hawkwood was often asked to fight not against other armies but against the rebels—and to slaughter civilians, as he did in Cesena early in 1377. Chronicles report that 4,000 people were killed at Cesena. To avoid being used for the punishment of innocent people, Hawkwood decided to abandon the service of the pope in 1377 and joined the antipapal league, where he found his earlier enemies Barnabò Visconti and the Florentines.

Hawkwood, who was apparently a widower, married an illegitimate daughter of Barnabò, Donnina, in 1377. He moved to Romagna in order to establish himself in his possessions there, but soon the small dimensions of his land and the unfriendliness of his neighbors led him to change his mind. He decided instead to accept an offer from the republic of Florence, thus beginning a period of almost permanent service to the Florentine *signoria*. During the following fifteen years he fought against the pope and then against Gian Galeazzo Visconti, Barnabò's nephew, who had risen to power in Milan after ousting Barnabò. Hawkwood guided an army against Gian Galeazzo Visconti in northern Italy, with some success, and was able to retreat without losses when a disagreement with the allied forces made the course of the campaign unfavorable. Contemporary sources regarded this retreat as a victory. When Hawkwood went again to northern Italy to fight against Verona, which was allied with the Visconti, he achieved a significant victory over the Milanese and Veronese forces at Castagnaro on 11 March 1387. In 1391, he bravely and efficaciously defended Florentine positions in Tuscany against the army of the Visconti, which eventually retreated.

Hawkwood received honors and consideration from the Florentine *signoria* and had a palace neat Florence. He lived at this palace until his death, which occurred during the night of 16–17 March 1394. Solemn funerals were provided by the *signoria*, and his widow received a life pension. In 1430, the republic commissioned the famous artist Paolo Uccello to paint an equestrian portrait of John Hawkwood in the cathedral of Florence. The large fresco is still there, as well as the inscription, which begins: *Ioannis Acutus Eques Britannicus, Dux Aetatis suae Cautis-simus et Rei Militaris Peritissimus.*

John Hawkwood was a typical *condottiere* and one of the best-known leaders of mercenary troops of his time. He served the most important and mightiest states of Italy—Florence, Milan, and the pope. His military ability was universally recognized. He is said to have introduced into Italy a strategy of the English army that involved dismounted knights wielding long lances and mobile archery squads with longbows. As a *condottiere* employed by different states, he could rarely develop autonomous strategies, but whenever possible he avoided the risk of fighting for targets that could be obtained by other means.

See also **Edward III**

Further Reading

Chalmers, Alexander. *The General Biographical Dictionary.* London: J. Nichols, 1812–1817. (See "John Hawkwood.")

Gaupp, Fritz. "The Condottiere John Hawkwood." *History*, 23, 1938–1939, pp. 305–321.

Machiavelli, Niccolò. *Istorie fiorentine*, ed. Franco Gaeta. Milan: Feltrinelli, 1962.

R[igg], J[ames] M[cMullen]. "Hawkwood, Sir John." *The Dictionary of National Biography.* Oxford: Oxford University Press, 1886–1887, Vol. 9, pp. 236–242.

Tabanelli, Mario. *Giovanni Acuto, capitano di ventura.* Faenza: Stab. Grafico Fratelli Lega, 1975.

Temple-Leader, John, and Giuseppe Marcotti. *Sir John Hawkwood (L'Acuto): Story of a Condottiere.* London: T. F. Unwin, 1889.

Winstanley, William. "The Life of Sir J. Hawkwood." In *England's Worthies.* London: Printed for Nath. Brooke, at the Sign of the Angel in Cornhill, 1660.

GIULIO MAFFII

HEINRIC (fl. ca. 1300)

This Middle Dutch poet, also known as Hein van Aken, is mentioned as an author in a number of Middle Dutch texts.

One, *Van den coninc Saladijn ende van Tabaryen* (Of King Saladijn and of Tabaryen), is an adaptation of the French courtesy book *l'Ordene de chevalerie* (The Chivalric Order). The text has been shortened by over two hundred verses and its metrical form has been altered as well. The Old French source is continuous text in paired rhyme, but the Middle Dutch adaptation is stanzaic, with the rhyme scheme *ABABABAB.* The contents of the two are similar. Hughe van Tabaryen, who is a prisoner of war, makes Sultan Saladijn a knight and talks to him about the essence of knighthood. In the final line of the poem, the author's name is revealed: Hein van Aken. This text is the only one to mention Heinric's surname.

In the past, scholars have attributed other works to this author, but their evidence is weak. The translator of *Die Rose* ("The Rose"), for example, calls himself *van Brusele Henrecke* (Henrecke from Brussels, 1. 9901). In

Der leken spieghel, Jan van Boendale mentions a certain "Van Bruesele Heyne van Aken" (Book III, cap. 17, 1. 91). This line has been used to argue that the translator of *Die Rose* is Hein van Aken, but the argument is not convincing.

Two other Middle Dutch texts have wrongly been attributed to Hein van Aken: the second part of an adaptation of *Li miserere* by the Renclus de Moiliens (in which the Christian name *Heinrec* is mentioned), and the *Vierde Martijn*, a stanzaic poem following the *Martijns* by Jacob van Maerlant, which a modern editor supposed contained a reference to Saladijn.

The *Roman van Heinric ende Margriete van Limborch* (Tale of Heinric and Margriete of Limborch) is very colorful and long epic text (ca. 22,000 lines in twelve books). The entire text has come down to us in two codices, presently in Brussels and Leyden. The latter codex contains an epilogue in which the poet calls himself Heinric. The notion that Heinric is identical with the translator of *Die Rose*, is a proposition that has never been proven. *Margriete van Limborch* was probably written between 1291 and 1318 and was meant for the Brabantine court. The work is an original Middle Dutch composition into which a large number of well-known medieval literary motifs have been incorporated. Margriete, the daughter of Duke van Limburg, gets lost during a hunt and eventually finds herself at the court in Athens where the count's son, Echites, falls in love with her. After many adventures, the couple marries. A number of subplots are interwoven into this basic story, including one which deals with Margriete's brother Heinric, who travels around from place to place looking for his sister. A tale about Evax, who seeks Echites, and descriptions of entire sieges and wars are also included in the epic.

See also **Jacob van Maerlant; Jan van Boendale**

Further Reading

Asselbergs, Willem J. A. "Het landschap van de Vierde Martijn," in Asselbergs, Willem J. A. *Nijmeegse colleges.* Zwolle: Tjeenk Willink, 1967, pp. 43–91.

de Keyser, P., ed. *Hein van Aken, Van den coninc Saladijn ende van Hughen van Tabaryen.* Leyden: Brill, 1950.

De Wachter, Lieve, "Een literair-historisch onderzoek naar de effecten van ontleningen op de compositie en de zingeving van de Roman van Heinric en Margriete van Limborch." Dissertation University of Brussels, 1998.

Hegman, Willy A., ed. *Hein van Aken, Vierde Martijn.* Zwolle: Tjeenk-Willink, 1958.

Janssens, Jozef D. 'Brabantse knipoogjes' in de Roman van Heinric ende Margriete van Limborch, *Eigen schoon en de Brabander* 60 (1977): 1–16.

Leendertz, Pieter, ed. *Het Middelnederlandsche leerdicht Rinclus.* Amsterdam: Jan Leendertz en Zoon, 1893.

Lievens, Robrecht. "De dichter Hein van Aken." *Spiegel der Letteren* 4 (1960): 57–74.

Meesters, Rob, ed. *Roman van Heinric ende Margriete van Limborch.* Amsterdam/Antwerpen: Wereldbibliotheek, 1951.

van Uytven, Raymond. "Historische knipoogjes naar 'Heinric ende Margriete van Limborch.'" *Bijdragen tot de geschiedenis* 66 (1983): 3–11.

Verwijs, Eelco, ed. *Heinric van Aken, Die Rose.* 1868; rpt. Utrecht: HES, 1976.

DIEUWKE VAN DER POEL

HEINRICH DER GLÎCHEZÂRE
(fl. late 12th c.)

Heinrich, the Alsatian author of *Reinhart Fuchs* (*Reynard the Fox*, last decade of the twelfth century), was the first to utilize myriad tales about the adventures of the clever fox and his opponents already treated satirically in the Latin poem *Ysengrimus* and the various branches of the French episodic narrative *Roman de Renart*, several of which were his principal sources, to form an extended animal epic. The appellation often attached to his name in scholarship, *Glîchezâre* (hypocrite), was surely intended by him to refer to Reinhart, as a fragment of the work from the beginning of the thirteenth century makes clear, but in the two very similar manuscripts, both written between 1320 and 1330, that preserve the whole work (with a small lacuna, or gap) it seems to be part of his own name. Several brief German didactic poems witness that Heinrich's version continued to be read to some extent in later centuries, but the French branches were independently shaped into a longer narrative in French and in Dutch, and the Dutch version(s) became the basis for the Low German *Reynke de Vos* and the Middle English *Reynard the Fox.*

The lacuna in *Reinhart Fuchs* is intentional; the narrative breaks off (in one manuscript with the words *et cetera*) just before Ysengrin the wolf is castrated, and picks up again with his laments. Heinrich, however, was not as prudish as a later medieval editor. His explicit account can be reconstructed from a didactic song attacking false oaths by Der Marner that clearly utilizes it. In a way, such explicitness is unusual; such details are generally hinted at rather than stated. Nevertheless, it was apparently his own invention—his known sources do not contain the episode, though *Reynke de Vos* has a distant parallel, as does its source.

All versions of the material utilize beasts in two ways: essentially, in that animals behave according to their nature (as understood in the Middle Ages), and allegorically, in that the animals portray human vices. Even where allusions to human institutions and actions are clear, the animals are never totally anthropomorphized. But, they all can speak, and they interact as if their differences were less consequential than their similarities. Almost all the versions, although perhaps not all branches of the *Roman de Renart*, criticize the misuse of office, be it secular or clerical. Heinrich demonstrates, through the implications of the episodes he adds to those he adapts from his sources, an intimate knowledge of local politics in the late twelfth century; the position discernible in his work is opposed to the Hohenstaufen, imperial one. He also is knowledgeable in the intricacies of Germanic law, adjusting his French sources where necessary to make the trial scene at the end of the work accord with audience's understanding of legal procedure.

Further Reading

Düwel, Klaus, ed. *Der Reinhart Fuchs des Elsässers Heinrich.* Tübingen: Niemeyer, 1984.
Göttert, Karl-Heinz, ed. and trans. *Heinrich der Glîchezâre*: *Reinhart Fuchs.* Stuttgart: Reclam: 1978.

HUBERT HEINEN

HEINRICH VON DEM TÜRLIN
(fl. first half of the 13th c.)

The author of *Diu Crône* (The Crown), a 30,000-line Middle High German Arthurian romance in rhymed couplets, with triplets marking the end of each section, may also have written *Der Mantel* (The Cloak), a fragment of 994 lines, the authorship of which is rather uncertain.

Heinrich lived in the first half of the 13th century. The *Crône* must have been completed by ca. 1230. The date is linked to Rudolf von Ems's *Alexander*, where Heinrich's work receives favorable mention as *Allr Aventiure Krône* ("Crown of all Adventures"). Of Heinrich's biographical background, virtually nothing is known with certainty. The previously accepted connection with the family name *von dem Türlin* (meaning "of the doorway") in the Carinthian town of St. Veit seems untenable. From his work we can identify only his name, his language (Bavarian-Austrian), the degree of his education (extensive knowledge of French and Latin, and some Italian), and possibly his social status (hardly a knight). Internal evidence also suggests strong ties with the area of the Eastern Alps. Since his work has been shown to be uniquely syncretistic and thus dependent on numerous French and German literary sources, only a major court with strong dynastic connections to France could have enabled him to embark on a project of such scope. As potential patrons, recent research has considered the Counts of Görz and Otto of Andechs-Meran.

Diu Crône belongs to a later group of Arthurian romances often referred to as "postclassical." Apart from recasting much of the *matière de Bretagne* (Breton, i.e., French, material), it takes a new and innovative approach to the aesthetics of romance: in its form, as an

unprecedented venture into the medium of the fantastic; in its theme, because of its new emphasis on *Fortuna* (fortune); and in its structure, by departing from the standard two-part scheme of Chrétien's classic form of romance.

The work is also unique in making Gawein the central hero. In a plot that synthesizes the exploits of a great many Arthurian heroes, Gawein turns into an almost operatic superhero and savior figure who makes their adventures part of his own mission. In essentially three narrative sequences, he rescues Arthur's court from the threat of losing Ginover, undergoes a sequence of adventures structured around his own role in the Grail romance, and finally–like a second Parzival–reaches a somewhat anticlimactic zenith in delivering the living dead at the Grail castle.

As a protégé of Lady Fortune (*Salde*), Gawein's *raison d'être* is the preservation of Arthur's court. Instead of pursuing a search for spiritual perfection, Heinrich's new type of hero operates in the secular context of a model court. Arthurian romance, as redefined by Heinrich, turns into a romance of society, stressing the stability of a central court as an indispensable basis of chivalrous existence. Heinrich's view of Arthur's court, no longer Utopian, rather aims at a mythic model whose basis is fragile and ultimately doomed.

See also **Rudolph von Ems**

Further Reading

Cormeau, Christoph. '*Wigalois*' *und* '*Diu Crône*': *Zwei Kapitel zur Gattungsgeschichte des nachklassischen Aventiureromans.* Munich: Artemis, 1977.
Dick, Ernst S. "Tradition and Emancipation: The Generic Aspect of Heinrich's *Crône*." In *Genres in Medieval German Literature*, ed. Hubert Heinen and Ingeborg Henderson. Göppingen: Kümmerle, 1986, pp. 74–92.
Jillings, Lewis. *Diu Crone of Heinrich von dem Türlein*: *The Attempted Emancipation of Secular Narrative.* Göppingen: Kümmerle, 1980.
Kratz, Bernd. "Zur Biographie Heinrichs von dem Türlin." *Amsterdamer Beiträge zur älteren Germanistik* 11 (1976): 123–167.
Scholl, G. H. F. *Diu Crône von Heinrîch von dem Türlîn*, 1852; rpt. Amsterdam: Rodopi, 1966.
Thomas, J. W. *The Crown: A Tale of Sir Gawein and King Arthur's Court by Heinrich von dem Türlin.* Lincoln, Neb.: University of Neberaska Press, 1989.

ERNST S. DICK

HEINRICH VON MELK (d. after 1150)

Heinrich is believed to be the author of *Vom Priesterleben* (On the Life of Priests) and *Von des todes gehugde* (On the Remembrance of Death), both written after 1150. Although the virtual identity of lines 397–402 in *Vom Priesterleben* with lines 181–186 in *Von des todes*

Gehugde, as well as the closely related subject matter, suggest that the two poems were written by the same individual, the matter of common authorship continues to be the subject of lively speculation.

At the end of *Von des Todes gehugde*, in the midst of a description of Paradise, the following verses appear: "Lord God, bring to that place [i.e. Paradise] for the glory of your mother and for the sake of all your saints Heinrich, your humble servant, and the abbot Erkenfried" (1029–1033). These few lines represent a biographical hint, and from them a most ingenious biography has been constructed for Heinrich. He has been identified as a *conversus*, a lay brother associated with a monastery. The monastery in question was assumed to be the Benedictine monastery of Melk in Austria, since an abbot Erkenfried governed that monastery 1122–1163. Because of the sharpness of the poet's attacks and the depth of his acquaintanceship with courtly life, Heinrich was thought to be a noble who, becoming progressively repelled by the world and rejected by ungrateful children, withdrew to a monastery as an older man. There, he seemed to have immersed himself in studies and found it as his duty to admonish all classes of society, particularly disreputable priests, regarding their duties as Christians.

Unfortunately, this biography is not accurate. Abbot Erkenfried of Melk could scarcely be Heinrich's patron since the two poems exhibit verse and rhyme techniques that reflect a period later than 1163 (e.g., a very high percentage of pure rhymes and a minimum of overlong lines of twelve to fourteen syllables). In addition, the contents of the poems underscore concerns such as the validity of sacraments administered by unworthy priests, and display conventions regarding court customs and the secular love lyric of a time more accurately located within the last quarter of the twelfth century. In the final analysis, there is only reasonable certainty that the author of both works was a layman, possibly a *conversus*, who demonstrated in his writings many manifestations of the popular piety movement of the twelfth century. These included his diatribes against dishonorable priests, criticisms of violations of sumptuary laws, invectives against the pride of the nobility, and general hostility toward worldly affairs when they interfered with performing one's Christian duty.

The Heinrich of *Von des todes Gehugde* and *Vom Priesterleben* is a layman who speaks about theological matters on an equal level with members of the clergy. He not only addresses a noble lay audience in the one work, he represents the interests of this group to a clerical audience in the other. His writing affirms the worth of the lay nobility and its view of the vital role it plays within the Christian order, a role that is becoming a dominant one in relation to the clergy. This confidence and positive self-image finds its quintessential expression in the secular tales of the courtly period, in which society is improved by the actions of members of the nobility and not by representatives of the institutionalized Church. The path to salvation begins to lead not solely through priests, but, primarily, through the good works of each individual.

Further Reading

Freytag, Wiebke. "Das Priesterleben des sogenannten Heinrich von Melk. Redeformen, Rezeptionsmo dus und Gattung." *Deutsche Vierteljahresschrift* 52 (1978): 558–580.

Gentry, Francis G. *Bibliographie zur frühmittelhochdeutschen geistlichen Dichtung.* Berlin: Schmidt, 1992, pp. 233–239.

——. "*Owe armiu phaffheite*: Heinrich von Melk's Views on Clerical Life." In *Medieval Purity and Piety*: *Essays on Medieval Clerical Celibacy and Religious Reform*, ed. Michael Frassetto. New York and London: Garland, 1998, pp. 337–352.

Kienast, Richard. *Der sogenannte Heinrich von Melk. Nach R. Heinzels Ausgabe von 1867.* Heidelberg: Winter, 1946.

Maurer, Friedrich, ed. *Die religiösen Dichtungen des 11. und 12. Jahrhunderts. Nach ihren Formen Besprochen*, Vol. 3. Tübingen: Niemeyer, 1970, pp. 258–359.

Neuser, Peter-Erich. "Der sogenannte Heinrich von Melk." In *Die deutsche Literatur des Mittelalters: Verfasserlexikon*, ed. Kurt Ruh, et al, vol. 3. Berlin and New York: de Gruyter, 1981, cols. 787–797.

——. *Zum sogenannten Heinrich von Melk. Überlieferung, Forschungsgeschichte und Verfasserfrage der Dichtungen Vom Priesterleben und Von des todes gehugede.* Vienna and Cologne: Böhlau, 1973.

Scholz Williams, Gerhild. "Against Court and School. Heinrich of Melk and Hlinant of Froidmont as Critics of Twelfth-Century Society." *Neophilologus* 62 (1978): 513–526.

——. *The Vision of Death*: *A Study of the "Memento mori" Expressions in some Latin, German and French Didactic Texts of the 11th and 12th Centuries.* Göppingen: Kümmerle, 1976.

Vollmann-Profe, Gisela. *Geschichte der deutschen Literatur von den Anfängen bis zum Beginn der Neuzeit*, vol. 1, pt. 2: *Wiederbeginn volkssprachiger Schriftlichkeit im hohen Mittelalter.* 2nd ed. Tübingen: Niemeyer, 1994, pp. 93–97; 130–137.

FRANCIS G. GENTRY

HEINRICH VON MORUNGEN (D. 1220)

A contemporary of Albrecht von Johansdorf and Hartmann von Aue, Heinrich von Morungen represents the pinnacle of "classical" *Minnesang* around 1200. He is considered to be one of the most important lyric poets writing in German during the courtly period, and perhaps the most important Minnesänger after Reinmar and Walther von der Vogelweide.

Traces of dialect in Morungen's poems show him to be from central eastern Germany. Morungen's family probably came from a manor near Sangershausen in Thuringia. The poet named as *Her Heinrich von Morunge* in the famous Heidelberg *Minnesang* manuscript is commonly identified with a certain *Hendricus/Henricus de Morungen*, who is mentioned in two documents from between 1213 and 1218 that bear the seal of the margrave Dietrich of Meissen. In one of the documents, Morungen is described as a retired soldier (*miles emeritus*), who has received for his good service a yearly pension of ten marks. He apparently gave this pension to the cloister of St. Thomas in Leipzig. According to later sources, Morungen died in the monastery in 1222. Since Dietrich of Meissen was the son-in-law of Hermann of Thuringia, patron of Wolfram von Eschenbach and others, the records thus place Morungen at a court that was a center of literary activity in the German-speaking area in the early thirteenth century. Since Morungen hailed from an area controlled by the Hohenstaufen family, it is quite possible that Heinrich could have learned his craft at the court of Frederick I Barbarossa. As a poet, then, Morungen could possibly have appeared and/or performed at the court of Meissen contemporaneously with poets such as Walther von der Vogelweide.

While it is not known whether Morungen was a professional poet, he was one of the first Latin-educated secular poets (*Minnesänger*) in Germany; probably there was no other poet of the time who owed so much to the Latin poet Ovid. Morungen's adaptations of classical Ovidian themes influenced such younger contemporaries, as Herbort von Fritzlar. Morungen's poems are dated approximately twenty years before the documents that show his name. Characteristic is his formal style, artistically advanced, yet owing much to the style of the earlier French troubadors. Formal stylistic connections to the school of Friedrich von Hausen (such as rhymed strophes and dactyls) and Morungen's later influence on Walther von der Vogelweide suggest that Morungen wrote before 1200. Although a definitive chronology has not been established, 115 strophes, arranged in 35 poems, are attributed to Morungen.

Morungen is known primarily, not for his style, but for his use of images and symbols. The images grow out of the senses; foremost among these is sight: mirrors, windows, dreams, colors, dawn and twilight. As a visual person (*Augenmensch*), Morungen describes love that centers around vision and the contemplation of the beloved. It is a woman's beauty, not her virtue, that awakens in men the desire for love. Morungen does not, however, focus on physical sensuality; rather it is the act of seeing, or of beholding physical beauty, that enables the looker to perceive actual or true love, a perfect happiness, an absolute love. The looker, like Narcissus, loses and forgets himself as he beholds the beauty before him; moreover, this experience also enables him to create his own identity as a subject. This act of creating the subject is epitomized in the poem *Mir ist geschehen als einem kindelîne* ("It happened to me like a child," no. 145, 1), known as the "Narcissus Song" (*Narzissuslied*) for its allusions to this myth. Here the speaker/lover/subject overcomes his narcissism by distinguishing himself from the object of his affections, and by speaking about his desire in the language of the text. Through the poem and through language, the act of looking transcends a purely erotic level of reflection, approaching a more existential one. Thus, looking also functions as a metaphor for the poetic process, for the search for truth and its representation through language. In this way, Morungen raises *Minnesang* from a purely social purpose to an art form, thereby creating an aesthetic of service to women (*Frauendienst*).

Motifs that previously played a relatively minor role in *Minnesang*, particularly those that show love as enchantment or a magic force that pulls human beings into its sphere, take on a central role. Classical in origin (Ovid), such motifs closely connect Morungen's lyric to the concept of love portrayed in the early courtly epic of the late twelfth century. In Veldeke's *Eneit* and in Gottfried's *Tristan*, for example, courtly love (*minne*) is a magical and sometimes deadly power. As the lyric subject, Morungen experiences the same fate as the epic heroes—submission through the magic of love despite the threat of sickness, madness, or death. This magic arises from the beauty of the beloved; she is the moon, the stars, the sun, who sends down her light from afar. In the poem known as the *Venus-Lied*, the lady is a noble Venus ("*ein Venus hêre*," no. 138, 33), whose beauty shines like the sun from a window. This beauty can inspire pure joy, and the word *wunne* (joy) appears often in Morungen's poems. (A notable example is *In sô hôher swebender wunne* ["In joy floating so high," no. 125, 19].) The beloved can also be a sweet murderess in the poem *Vil süeziu, senftiu tôterinne* ("Very sweet, soft murderess," no. 147, 4), who inspires a love that will last into the next world beyond death. The intimate connection between love, death, and sorrow brings this love very close to a mystical experience; there is an obvious link to Gottfried here as well. But in the conflict it reveals between reality and dream or fantasy, the experience of the lover also harkens back to the metaphor of Narcissus, whose fascination with his own projection has deadly results.

Although Morungen cannot be said to have a school of his own like that of Friedrch von Hausen, one can find thematic and stylistic evidence of his influence on Walther von der Vogelweide. Interestingly, Morungen himself is the hero of a ballad, "On the Honorable Morunger" (*Vom Edlen Möringer*), that dates from the middle of the fifteenth century.

See also **Friedrich von Hausen; Gottfried von Straßburg**

Further Reading

Bertau, Karl. *Deutsche Literatur im europäischen Mittelalter*, vol. 1: 800–1197. Munich: Beck, 1972, pp. 676–677.

Bumke, Joachim. *Geschichte der deutschen Literatur im hohen Mittelalter*, vol. 2. Munich: Deutscher Taschenbuchverlag, 1990.

de Boor, Helmut. *Geschichte der deutschen Literatur von den Anfängen bis zur Gegenwart*, vol. 2. 11th ed. *Die höfische Literatur. Vorbereitung, Blüte, Ausklang*. 1170–1250. Munich: Beck, 1991.

Glaser, Horst Albert, ed. *Mündlichkeit in die Schriftlichkeit*. Hamburg: Rowohlt, 1988, pp. 164–185.

Hayes, Nancy Karl. "Negativizing Narcissus: Heinrich von Morungen at Julia Kristeva's Court." *The Journal of the Midwest Modern Language Association* 22 (1989): 43–60.

"Heinrich von Morungen." In *Lexikon des Mittelalters*, vol. 4. Munich and Zurich: Artemis, 1977, cols. 2101–2102.

Kasten, Ingrid. "Klassischer Minnesang." In: *Deutsche Literatur. Eine Sozialgeschichte. Bd. 1*.

Moser, Hugo and Helmut Tervooren, ed. *Des Minnesangs Frühling*, 37th rev. ed. Stuttgart: Hirzel, 1981 [poems cited above by no.].

Schnell, Rüdiger. "Andreas Capellanus, Heinrich von Morungen und Herbort von Fritzlar." *Zeitschriji für Deutsches Altertum und Deutsche Literatur* 104 (1975): 131–151.

ALEXANDRA STERLING-HELLENBRAND

HEINRICH VON VELDEKE
(ca. 1150–1200)

Uncertainty surrounds the poet Heinrich von Veldeke, known primarily for his *Eneasroman* (The Story of Aeneas), but known also as the composer of *St. Servatius* and several love lyrics. Heinrich finished only about four-fifths of his *Eneide* between 1170 and 1175, because someone purportedly stole his manuscript from a wedding celebration at Cleve. Through the intervention of Hermann, count of Thuringia, he regained access to it and completed it about 1185. Heinrich's works remain elusive due to a dearth of adequate critical research; and the literature that attempts to outline the circumstances of his life and his creative activity is also inconclusive. Nevertheless, he is considered the father of German vernacular literature of the Middle Ages, a model for immediate contemporaries and later imitators alike.

Heinrich must have been born in the first half of the twelfth century, perhaps in a place called *Veldeke* or *Velker Mole* near Hasselt and Maastricht in what was, at the time, Limburgian Belgium. Early witnesses recorded his identity variously as *Heinrich, Heynrijck, Hainrich*, or *Heinric*, from (van or von) *Veltkilche(n), Veldeckh, Veldeg*, and *Veldig*, as well as *Veldeke*. Some poets referred to him as "Lord" and "Master," indicating that he was a noble and educated. There was, in fact, a Veldeke family of the lesser nobility in the Maastricht region. Heinrich may have been related to and served the counts of Loon. Reminiscences of other authors and texts in his own work are evidence of his familiarity with ancient and contemporary literature, suggesting that he might have studied in a cathedral or monastery school.

He was knowledgeable in the literatures and languages of Germany, of France, and of antiquity, employing the *Straßburg Alexander*, the Old French *Roman d'Eneas* and Virgil's *Aeneid* as models for his own version of the epic. He was also acquainted with Dictys and Dares, Ovid, and Servius. Both German and Dutch scholars claim him as their own.

Whether or not the original language of Veldeke's major work was Old Limburgian or a more universal German literary language has occupied a great deal of time and effort among Veldeke scholars. Ludwig Ettmüller published the first edition of the *Eneasroman* in 1882 based upon the larger number of Upper German manuscripts. Ettmüller believed the original to have been transcribed in a lowland dialect, but he did not think it was possible to reconstruct the original text. Some thirty years later, Otto Behaghel attempted a *Rückübersetzung* (a translation back to the older language), as did Gabriele Schieb and Theodor Frings in the 1960s. All existing versions of the epic, however, are Middle German, Upper German, or High German (*Ober-deutscb and Hochdeutsch*).

Whatever the original language, the work's influence reached exclusively to Upper German regions rather than to Veldeke's supposed home in Limburg. Gottfried von Straßburg acknowledges Heinrich as the first graft upon the stem of German literature, and his influence can be traced in a number of later German authors. In addition, one of his sources seems to have been the *Straßburg Alexander*, composed in an Alemannic dialect (and thus Upper German). The *Eneide* also bears a close, but problematic, relationship to the German *Tristrant* of Eilhart von Oberge. The question of language is known in Veldeke studies as "The Veldeke Problem." Though no one has unequivocally settled the question, the interpolation of a Limburg dialect seems to be the invention of Ettmüller rather than an actual fact. Veldeke apparently sought the widest possible German-speaking audience for his work.

Among scholars, the most widely-discussed critical topics concerning the *Eneasroman*, include the romances of Eneas with Dido and Lavinia, and the comparison of these to the Old French versions and to Virgil. For instance, for pursuing his fate and the will of the gods, Virgil does not blame Aeneas for abandoning Dido. The Old French and Middle High German authors portray her love as undisciplined, unsanctioned by society, and unrequited by Eneas, but do so more sympathetically than does Virgil. Veldeke demonstrates even more compassion for Dido than does the French poet. In both vernacular versions, the poets expand upon the relationship of Virgil's Aeneas and Lavinia, providing a commentary on ideal love, Lavinia's "legitimate" love, overcoming the "illicit" love of Dido and Eneas. According to the critical literature, the love theme then blends with the notion of governing (*Herrschaft und Liebe*), and finally modulates until notions of peace and of rulership prevail.

Commentators have related various portions of the text, especially those known as the *Stauferpartien*, to the rule of Frederick I Barbarossa. These include references to the great *Hoffest* at Mainz in 1184 and the finding of Pallas's grave by the emperor. At least one scholar, however, believes the work may have been written, at least initially, on behalf of Henry the Lion. Although critics debate many details of this work, they agree that Veldeke refined and expanded upon his model, and in general created an important work of art. Finally, Veldeke was the first to imitate French models in composing love songs in the German vernacular.

Of less interest and importance is Heinrich's *St. Servatius*, a work that exists in total in a manuscript of the fifteenth century in a New Limburgian dialect. A fragment remains of an Old Limburg version, though there is also an Upper German *Servatius*. As with the *Eneasroman*, text and critical problems have significantly hampered understanding of this work. Like the *Eneide*, the transcription of Heinrich's lyric poetry is entirely Upper German, though the impurity of his rhymes in these poems and songs points to less care and perhaps a greater affinity for his mother tongue than does his romance.

See also **Eilhart von Oberge;
Frederick I Barbarossa**

Further Reading

Bathgate, R. H. "Hendrik van Veldeke's *The Legend of St. Servaes* Translated." *Dutch Crossing* 40 (1990): 3–22.

Behaghel, Otto, ed. *Heinrichs von Veldeke Eneide*, Heilbronn: Gebr. Henninger, 1882.

Dittrich, Marie-Luise. *Die 'Eneide' Heinrichs von Veldeke*. Part 1. Wiesbaden: Steiner, 1966.

Fromm, Hans. *Arbeiten zur deutschen Literatur des Mittelalters*. Tübingen: Niemeyer, 1989.

Kasten, Ingrid. "Herrschaft und Liebe. Zur Rolle und Darstellung des 'Helden' im Roman d'Eneas und in Veldeke's Eneasroman." *Deutsche Vierteljahrsschrift für deutsche Literaturwissenschaft und Geistesgeschichte* 62 (1988): 227–245.

Kistler, Renate. *Heinrich von Veldeke und Ovid*. Tübingen: Niemeyer, 1993.

Klein, Thomas. "Heinrich von Veldeke und die mitteldeutschen Literatursprachen. Untersuchungen zum Veldeke-Problem." *Zwei Studien zu Veldeke und zum Strassburger Alexander*. Amsterdam: Rodopi, 1985.

von Veldeke, Heinrich. *Eneasroman. Mittelhochdeutsch / Neuhochdeutsch*, trans. Dieter Kartschoke. Stuttgart: Reclam, 1986.

——. *Eneide*, ed. Theodor Frings and Gabriele Schieb. 3 vols. Berlin: Akademie, 1964–1970.

——. *Eneit*, trans. J. W. Thomas. New York: Garland, 1985.

——. *Sente Servos, Sanctus Servatius*, ed. Theodor Frings and Gabriele Schieb. Die epischen Werke des Henric van Veldeken, vol. 1. Halle (Saale): Niemeyer, 1956.

KRISTINE K. SNEERINGER

HÉLOÏSE (1100/01–1163/64)

Héloïse, abbess of the famous monastery of the Paraclete and its six daughter houses, was raised as a possibly illegitimate child in the Benedictine convent of Sainte-Marie of Argenteuil. At the age of seventeen, she continued her studies at her uncle Fulbert's house in Paris, where she was tutored by the theologian Peter Abélard (1079–1142). After a stormy love affair with Héloïse, Abélard offered the Paraclete and its lands as a refuge to Héloïse and her fellow nuns. Pope Innocent II confirmed the donation in 1131. Héloïse left us three letters to Abélard and one letter to Peter the Venerable (ca. 1092–1156). She is mentioned frequently in the cartulary of the Paraclete as a competent and efficient abbess who turned her religious house into one of the most prestigious women's monasteries in France. Its rule stressed the importance of education for all nuns, the unusual relaxation of strict enclosure, and the authority of the abbess over both male and female members of the monastic community.

In Peter Abélard's biographical *Historia calamitatum* and his moving correspondence with her, Héloïse emerges as an articulate and heroic person who equals Abélard in rhetorical sophistication and surpasses him in personal integrity. Her letters reveal a woman of deep love and devotion who remained attached to Abélard with both the bond of friendship and the memory of their earlier passion. Moreover, in her own mind, she was convinced that she had acted throughout the entire affair with disinterested love, devoted only to Abélard, while he had begun with lust only and never achieved her level of disinterested love, even though it was he who had taught her the true understanding of love and friendship.

See also **Abélard, Peter; Peter the Venerable**

Further Reading

Abélard, Peter. *Historia calamitatum: texte critique avec introduction*, ed. Jacques Monfrin. 2nd ed. Paris: Vrin, 1962.

Charrier, Charlotte. *Héloïse dans l'histoire et la légende*. Paris: Champion, 1933.

Newman, Barbara. "Authority, Authenticity, and the Repression of Heloise." *Journal of Medieval and Renaissance Studies* 22 (1992): 121–57.

Pernoud, Régine. *Héloïse and Abélard*, trans. Peter Wiles. London: Collins, 1973.

Peter the Venerable. *The Letters of Peter the Venerable*, ed. Giles Constable. 2 vols. Cambridge: Harvard University Press, 1967.

Radice, Betty, trans. *The Letters of Abelard and Heloise*. Harmondsworth: Penguin, 1974.

ULRIKE WIETHAUS

HENRIQUE, PRINCE OF PORTUGAL (1394-1460)

Conventionally known as "the Navigator," Henrique was born in Oporto (Portuguese: Porto) on 4 March 1394. His father, João I, was a bastard who had fought his way to the throne. The chivalric culture of the court in which Henrique grew up cloaked the imperfections of the new dynasty's credentials.

As the fourth of the king's sons, Henrique had no prospect of the crown. He had, however, the example of his grandfather, John of Gaunt, who maintained an affinity of kingly proportions and sought a crown of his own in Spain through wars, conducted to resemble knightly cavalcades. Though little direct evidence survives of Henrique's life up to 1415, the priorities of an upbringing dominated by knightly exercises are conveyed in the treatise on chivalry attributed to his eldest brother. The chivalric ideal informed his whole career. Though he was later obliged to become involved in commerce and industry in an effort to maintain his estate, he always projected the self-perception of a perfect knight, espousing celibacy, practicing asceticism, and professing religious motives for slave raids and attempted conquests.

After contemplating a tournament of unprecedented magnificence to celebrate the knighting of his sons, the king decided in 1415 to launch instead a real *chevauchée* (chivalric attack) against a traditional enemy, the Muslims of Ceuta. The princes themselves were said to have urged this change of plan. The chronicle tradition assigns Henrique a prominent part in the conquest and in the next few years he earned offices of honor and profit comparable to those of his brothers. By 1423 he was the duke of Viseu, the governor of Ceuta and the Algarve, and the administrator of the Order of Christ. He remained, however, a cadet prince with an ill-defined role who chose to reside away from court, chiefly in the Algarve, and to surround himself with a retinue of "knights" and "squires" whom he maintained at great cost and no small trouble: documents concerning crimes by members of his household cover murder, rape, and piracy. This entourage was not only evidence of Henrique's pretensions; it also committed him to a quest for patronage with which to reward his followers.

His ambitions are suggested in a memorandum addressed to his father in April 1432: the Count of Arraiolos, who knew Henrique well, observed that he might acquire a kingdom in Morocco, Granada, Castile, or the Canary Islands, "and have the affairs of this kingdom [Portugal] in the palm of his hand." Little survives of any writing of Henriques's own, but the two probably authentic memoranda from his pen recommend crusades against Tangier and Málaga. His attempt to conquer Tangier in 1437, however, was a costly failure, and thereafter he concentrated on alternative fields of endeavor in which he had already dabbled: maritime deeds and, in particular, his effort to acquire a realm in the Canary Islands.

Many chivalric romances of the period had a seaborne setting, and a common denouement placed the hero in an island-kingdom. Portuguese ports had played a part in the exploration of the eastern Atlantic since the 1340s and there is evidence in chronicles and maps that Portuguese navigation intensified in that arena in the 1420s. That Henrique was already involved is an assertion of a chronicle he later commissioned. In the following decade, however, independent documents confirmed his interest. In 1432 his claims to the Canaries led the pope to solicit opinions from jurists on the question of the legitimacy of war against the pagan inhabitants. It is evident from friars' protests that Henrique's career as a slaver, to be continued in the next decade on the African coast, began in the Canaries by 1434. His efforts to secure a base in the archipelago continued with few interruptions almost until his death but were rewarded with no permanent success: some islands remained in the natives' hands, others in those of Castilian adventures or settlers.

After his father's death in 1433, the sense of vocation attributed to him by contemporaries seems to have deepened. He felt destined for great deeds by his horoscope—his chronicler tells us—and endowed, by inheritance from King João, with a "talent" that had to "shine forth." Portuguese ambassadors in 1437 told the pope that Henrique's aim was "expressly to fulfil the image and likeness of King João." Between 1438 and 1449, all his surviving brothers died. The death of the Infante Fernando, in captivity in Fez in 1443, was a heavy charge on his conscience, for Fernando was a victim of the debacle at Tangier and Henrique had opposed the possible surrender of Ceuta in ransom. In adopting a homonymous nephew as his heir, he shouldered a fatherly responsibility. In 1449 he became the senior surviving prince of his line when his elder brother, Pedro, fell in rebellion against the crown.

Meanwhile, he had accumulated resources to invest in his offshore activities. As well as the income from the Order of Christ and the revenues of his many fiefs, he controlled extensive fishing rights, including the monopoly of the tuna-curing industry of the Algarve; the monopoly of soap manufacture throughout the kingdom was his, as was that of coral gathering off Ceuta. His maritime activities were exempt from the royal tax on booty and he had the sole right to license voyages to Madeira, the Azores, and the Atlantic coast of Africa.

These arenas occupied an increasing amount of his attention as his prospects in Morocco and the Canaries waned. He expressed interest in settling a colony on Madeira as early as 1433; in June and July 1439, seed and sheep were shipped to Madeira and at least one of the Azores; thereafter, colonization was farmed out to enterprising intermediate lords, who were normally Henrique's dependents (though his brother and nephew were the superior lords in some cases). Henrique was a partner in the building of the first recorded sugar-mill in Madeira in 1452: this made him a founding patron of an important new industry of the late Middle Ages.

Meanwhile, navigation under Henrique's patronage, or with his license, extended along the African coast. The chronicle he commissioned established the belief, which historians continued to uphold until very recently, that African exploration was the primary focus of the prince's endeavours. The much-vaunted rounding of Cape Bojador in 1434 was a minor byproduct of the effort to seize the Canaries; to judge from surviving maps and sailing directions, "Cape Bojador" probably signified nothing more remote than the modern Cape Juby. The great series of African voyages began in earnest only in 1441. From the mid-1440s, this enterprise began to yield appreciable amounts of gold and slaves. Around the middle of the next decade, when Henrique employed Genoese technicians to supplement his household personnel, significant progress in navigation was made when the Senegal and Gambia Rivers were investigated and the Cape Verde Islands discovered. The big advances, however, both in the reach of exploration and the yield of exploitable resources, came in the generation after Henrique's death, as Portuguese navigators worked their way around Africa's bulge. Meanwhile, in 1458, Portugal's crusading vocation in the Maghrib was briefly revived and Henrique accompanied the royal expedition that seized Al-Qasr Kebir, near Ceuta.

Henrique died in Sagres on 13 November 1460. The Canaries still eluded him; no crown adorned his head; of the gold of Africa only a few threads had come within his grasp; and he was heavily in debt. He had, however, invested wisely in posthumous fame and has enjoyed an enduring reputation as Portugal's culture hero, credited anachronistically with the foundation of the Portuguese Empire and with the inauguration of a tradition of scientific exploration. Modern scholarship disavows these claims, but as a patron of the colonization of Madeira and the Azores he can genuinely be counted among the creators of Atlantic colonial societies.

See also **João I, King of Portugal**

Further Reading

Dias Dinis, A.J. *Estudos henriquinos*. Coimbra, 1960.
Monumenta Henricina. 15 vols. Coimbra, 1960–75.
Russell, P. E. *Henry the Navigator*. New Haven, Conn. 2001.
——. *Prince Henry the Navigator: The Rise and Fall of a Culture-Hero*. Oxford, 1984.
Zurara, G.E. de. *Cronica dos feitos notáveis que se passaram na conquista da Guiné*. Ed. T. de Sousa Soares. Lisbon, 1978.

FELIPE FERNÁNDEZ–ARMESTO

HENRY I (1067/68–1135; r. 1100–35)

Youngest son of William the Conqueror and Matilda of Flanders, he was left rich but landless on William's death in 1087. He used part of his inheritance to purchase the Cotentin and Avranchin from his eldest brother, the perpetually penniless Robert Curthose, duke of Normandy. In 1091 he lost these provinces to the combined military forces of his brothers Robert and William Rufus, king of England, but he later came to terms with Rufus. In 1096 Robert pawned Normandy to William and set off upon crusade. As Robert was returning in 1100, William was killed in a hunting accident and Henry seized the throne. Because of the timing of the death Henry has been suspected of being in a murder plot, but the evidence supports the view that Rufus was accidentally shot.

Upon his accession Henry issued a coronation charter, denouncing the abuses of his brother's reign and agreeing to rule England by the laws of Edward the Confessor. He set about filling some of the vacant bishoprics and recalled Anselm, archbishop of Canterbury, from continental exile. He then married the Scottish princess Matilda, who carried the blood of the line of Alfred the Great. The marriage produced two children, Matilda (b. 1102) and William (b. 1103). Matilda was betrothed to the German emperor Henry V and left England in 1110.

The first years of Henry's reign were spent consolidating his rule and fighting against Robert Curthose, who invaded in 1101 to claim the throne. In the Treaty of Alton Robert renounced his claim to the throne in return for an annual pension. However, he continued to be troublesome, and because he could not keep peace in the duchy of Normandy Henry was asked to intervene. In July 1106 Henry launched an invasion that culminated in the pitched battle at Tinchebrai on 28 September. Robert was captured and remained in captivity until he died in 1134. Even then Henry could not be secure in his possession of Normandy, because Robert's son, William Clito, also had a claim to the duchy, and Henry had to put down several revolts.

A major challenge to Henry came in 1111, when Louis VI of France joined with the counts of Anjou and Flanders. Henry emerged the victor by negotiating a separate peace with the count of Anjou; Louis was forced to recognize English overlordship in Maine and Brittany. Hostilities resumed in 1116, when some Norman barons joined a rebellion in favor of Clito. When the count of Flanders was killed in 1118, Henry again used his diplomatic skills, marrying his son William to the daughter of the Angevin count. At this point Louis complained to the pope about Henry's action, but Calixtus II remained friendly to both sides and Normandy was at peace by 1120.

Tragedy struck in 1120, with the death of Henry's only legitimate son, William, drowned when his ship struck a rock in the Channel. With this death the succession was thrown into doubt. Henry's queen had died in 1118, and after William's death Henry quickly married Adeliza (or Alice) of Louvain in 1121. But as time passed, it became clear that they were not going to produce children, and Henry was forced to make plans for a successor.

The years 1123–24 were marked by Norman insurrection. When Henry V of Germany died in 1125, Henry recalled his daughter and began to concentrate on making her a viable candidate for the throne. After obtaining a promise from his barons to support Matilda, Henry married her to Geoffrey of Anjou. This marriage was not popular with the barons, and Matilda herself did not command their loyalty. After Henry's death in 1135 the throne was seized by his nephew Stephen of Blois. After years of civil war Matilda renounced her own claim, and Stephen agreed to recognize her eldest son, Henry, as his heir.

Henry I's reign occurred during the European investiture controversy, in which the reform papacy struggled with secular powers for control of the bishoprics. In England this crisis came to a head when Archbishop Anselm refused to do homage to Henry for his fiefs and to consecrate bishops whom Henry had already invested with the ring and staff, the symbols of episcopal office. When the pope refused to condone the English customs concerning lay investiture of clerics, Anselm returned to the Continent. A compromise, giving the church the right to invest the ring and staff but permitting the king to take oaths of homage from the prelates, was effected in 1106.

In addition to unprecedented peace and prosperity Henry I's reign also saw the development of important institutions of government. One of his accomplishments was the reform of the *curia regis* (king's court). He organized royal offices and instituted regular payments to his officials. This eliminated the need to plunder the countryside as they moved about with the itinerant king. Henry also systematized the treasury, and his reign saw the development of the exchequer's twice-yearly meetings for collecting the taxes due the king. These sessions were recorded onto the "pipe rolls." One pipe roll (from 1130) survives for Henry's reign, and its completeness

and sophistication argue that it is one of a series of such documents. It is a rich source, showing among other things that many legal reforms once credited to Henry II were operative by the reign of his grandfather.

Although some historians have characterized Henry's rule over England and Normandy as harsh, others have shown that contemporaries considered the reign to be successful; it provided England with 33 years of peace and prosperity. Even in Normandy, which traditionally suffered from a fractious barony, Henry's peace was seriously broken only twice after 1106. His accomplishments in war and diplomacy, law, and administration combine to show him as one of England's most able and effective rulers.

See also **Anselm of Bec; William I**

Further Reading

Green, Judith A. *The Government of England under Henry I.* Cambridge: Cambridge University Press, 1986
Hollister, C. Warren. *Monarchy, Magnates, and Institutions in the Anglo-Norman World.* London: Hambledon, 1986 [valuable collected papers, mainly on political and administrative topics]
Hollister, C. Warren. "Courtly Culture and Courtly Style in the Anglo-Norman World." *Albion* 20 (1988): 1–17
Mooers, Stephanie I. "A Reevaluation of Royal Justice under Henry I of England." *American Historical Review* 93 (1988): 340–58
Newman, Charlotte A. *The Anglo-Norman Nobility in the Reign of Henry I: The Second Generation.* Philadelphia: University of Pennsylvania Press, 1988.

LOIS L. HONEYCUTT

HENRY I OF SAXONY
(ca. 876–July 2, 936)

King of East Francia/Germany (*König von Ostfranken*), Henry I (Heinrich I.) was born in ca. 876, the third son of Otto, duke of Saxony (ca. 830/40–912), a Liudolfing, and Hadwig (d. ca. 903), daughter of Henry of *Ostfranken*, a Babenberger. Henry was named after his maternal grandfather. (The name Henry was rare in the ninth century; its oldest form is *Haimeric* [lord of the house].)

About 900 Henry married Hatheburg (ca. 876–ca. 909) in order to gain her inheritance of Merseburg and other lands in East Saxony. Hatheburg was a widow; the local clergy objected to the marriage as she was said to have planned to become a nun. Their opposition did not deter Henry, however. They had one son, Thankmar (906–937). The marriage was dissolved in 909. Not long after, Henry married Mathilde (born ca. 894/897) of the family of Widukind of Saxony, Charlemagne's adversary. Though hardly love at first sight, contemporary sources noted a powerful attraction between the couple. Mathilde would become an influential wife and a formidable dowager before she died in March 968. Their eldest son Otto was born on November 23, 912, seven days before the death of the grandfather whose name he bore. There were four more children; Gerberga (919–968), Henry (922–955), Hadwig (923–958), and Brun (925–965).

Upon the death of his father in 912, Henry became duke of Saxony; there was immediate trouble with Conrad I (*Konrad I*), king of East Francia since 911. Conrad distrusted Henry's power in Saxony. In addition, a long-standing feud existed between them over the execution in 906 of the Babenberger Adalbert, Henry's maternal uncle. Conrad's success in consolidating control over Saxony was minimal, however. When he died in late December 918, he requested his brother Eberhard to offer the crown to his former rival. Following several months of negotiations, Henry was chosen king at Fritzlar on May 5, 919. He was forty-three years old.

Henry declined to be crowned by the Church, as was the Carolingian custom, for reasons that ate not altogether clear and have been debated by historians ever since. His first actions were designed to extend his rule beyond the Carolingian kingdom of the Saxons and the Franks into the southern areas of East Francia. In Bavaria Duke Arnulf had declared himself king but eventually abandoned his ambitions. Henry wisely left Arnulf in control of Bavaria, demanding only that Arnulf acknowledge Henry's status as king. In Swabia the situation was more complicated. Burchard II, who had only recently become duke, acknowledged Henry as king in 919 and promptly defeated his Burgundian rival Rudolph II in battle. In 922 the two made peace, and Rudolph married Burchard's daughter, persuading his father-in-law to help him gain the crown of Italy. This adventure ended in Burchard's death in 926. Henry was now in a position to impose a settlement in Swabia, and he appointed Hermann (a Conradiner) as duke. Henry also made a pact of friendship with Rudolph II. In return for the Holy Lance, a valuable relic which the German king coveted, Rudolph was allowed to keep the area of Basel which he already controlled.

Diplomacy, military pressure, and waiting patiently for the right moment to put his plans into action characterized Henry's dealings with the West Frankish king Charles the Simple (d. 929) and his opponents, Robert (d. 923) and Raoul (d. 936). Henry also secured the submission of the volatile area of Lotharingia and its duke Gilbert (Giselbert), who married Henry's daughter Gerberga in 928.

Now in his fifties, Henry issued a charter in 929 detailing the dower rights of his wife, the clerical education of his youngest son, Brun, and the marriage of his son Otto. The chosen bride was an Anglo-Saxon princess called Edith (ca. 912–946), a daughter of Edward the Elder, who arrived in Saxony with a younger sister, Adiva. The marriage between Otto and Edith took place sometime early in 930, when Henry undertook a lengthy circuit of his kingdom.

Henry's greatest accomplishment, however, was his decisive action against the Magyars who had been attacking East and West Francia since about 900. In 924 Henry's soldiers captured a Magyar chief, and, for his safe return, Henry demanded a nine-year truce, also securing a yearly tribute. During this truce, Henry created a mounted troop of soldiers to fight the Magyars and tested his new model army against the Slavs. He may also have built fortifications (*Burgen*) on the Elbe frontier. In March 933 Henry met with the invading Magyar forces at the battle of Riade, which ended in victory for Henry's new cavalry. There was to be peace on the Elbe frontier for a number of years.

By 935 Henry had achieved many of his goals: his relations with the dukes were based on contracts of friendship; he had defeated the Magyars, and his diplomacy had secured a modicum of peace on his Western frontier. After a long illness, Henry held a diet at Erfurt where he designated his eldest son by Mathilde as his successor. The future Otto I was then 24, married with two children, and a well-trained soldier. Henry I died on July 2, 936, at Memleben. He was buried in the Abbey Church of Quedlinburg where his tomb can still be found.

Modern historians have given Henry an important place in the history of early medieval Germany, crediting him with laying the foundations upon which his son Otto the Great created his empire. Tenth century writers noted his prowess as a warrior and his physical beauty and charm. In the twelfth century, Henry and Mathilde were perceived as the ancestors of the kings of Europe. Henry was also surrounded by legends and stories. Perhaps the most enduring of these is the tale about his receiving the crown while hunting birds. Thus, Henry I would enter the popular imagination under the name "the Fowler" (*der Vogler*).

See also **Otto I**

Further Reading

Althoff, Gerd and Hagen Keller. *Heinrich I. und Otto der Grosse. Neubeginn auf karolingischem Erbe*. Göttingen: Musterschmidt, 1985.

Büttner, Heinrich. *Heinrichs I. Südwest- und Westpolitik*. Constance: Thorbecke, 1964.

Diwalt, Helmut. *Heinrich der Erste*. Bergisch Gladbach: Lübbe, 1987.

Leyser, Karl. *Medieval Germany and its Neighbours, 900–1250*. London: Hambledon, 1982.

Reuter, Timothy. *Germany in the Early Middle Ages 800–1056*. London: Longman, 1991.

MADELYN BERGEN DICK

HENRY II (1133–1189; r. 1154–89)

The eldest son of Count Geoffrey of Anjou and Matilda of England (heiress of Henry I), born 5 March 1133. He became duke of Normandy in 1150 and count of Anjou in 1151. In May 1152 he married Eleanor, duchess of Aquitaine and disowned wife of Louis VII of France. On the death of Stephen he became king of England, at age 21, and was crowned on 19 December 1154. His children included Henry (d. 1183), Matilda, Richard the Lionheart, Geoffrey, duke of Brittany, Eleanor, Joan, and John, as well as the illegitimate Geoffrey archbishop of York and William Longsword, earl of Salisbury. He died on 6 July 1189.

Tireless, well educated, and dismissive of conventional wisdom, Henry was also a man of seemingly contradictory qualities: willful but calculating, obstinate but open-minded, volatile but purposeful, both magnanimous and vindictive, jealous of his rights but indifferent to pomp and personal dignity. He was an enigma to contemporaries and has elicited varying judgments from historians. Few students have denied that he exercised a major influence on the course of western European history.

The wide dominions under his direct rule, covering more than half of France as well as England, may have seemed largely ungovernable, but Henry's achievement was to oblige all over whom he claimed jurisdiction to respect his authority and to overcome resistance swiftly and decisively. It was achieved largely by a daring use of mercenary forces skilled in siege techniques, thus devaluing the castle as the traditional base of defense. His dominance aroused not only the resentment of the greater barons but also the apprehensions of his neighbors.

The most publicized but by no means the only example of Henry challenging special interest groups was his conflict with the church. Though not opposed in principle to the church extending and refining its jurisdiction, Henry insisted that it should neither encroach on the crown's jurisdiction nor threaten crown interests. His tactic for ensuring smooth relations by installing an ally, his chancellor and friend Thomas Becket, as archbishop of Canterbury, backfired when Becket, showing a dedication to the church's power and independence that surprised many who had been lukewarm about his nomination, vigorously defended his own authority.

Henry tried to settle the issue by fiat, by issuing his Constitutions of Clarendon (1166), based largely but selectively on customary practice. His demand for an unprecedented oath of observance from the bishops united them in resistance. It did not, however, unite them in support of Becket; some believed him to be mistakenly provocative and tactically inept. Henry's not unreasonable stance was undermined by his vindictive harrying of the archbishop, and it culminated, after a purported reconciliation, in intemperate words that prompted some

King Henry II arguing with St. Thomas Becket, c1300–c1325. Illustrated page of Latin text from "Chronical of England" by Peter of Langtoft. © Scala/Art Resource, New York.

members of the royal household to murder Becket in December 1170. Henry was obliged to retreat publicly. Eventually he salvaged much of what he had originally sought, though in a less provocative form. There are parallels to this in other aspects of his career.

All who resented his dominance sought to profit from the setback to his reputation in the wake of Becket's martyrdom. In 1173—74 Louis VII of France organized a coalition of Henry's opponents, both internal and external, in a determined attempt to unseat him by insurrection and invasion. Henry, sustained by the loyalty of his servants and by popular support, survived triumphantly. He exacted no revenge, save upon his headstrong wife, who remained in close confinement for the rest of his life, for having conspired with her former husband Louis to replace Henry with their malleable eldest son, the young king Henry. His victory persuaded most barons that their future lay in cooperating with the king to secure his patronage instead of striving for autonomy.

Whether Henry intended the formation of an "Angevin Empire" is debatable. His initial aggressiveness suggested expansionist aims, but there are clear signs that he came to detest the wasteful futility of warfare and limited his objectives to internal order. His intervention in Ireland (1171) seems to have been a reluctant response to the need to control Anglo-Norman adventurers. He was content to secure amicable relations with the Irish, as with the Welsh and the Scots. He intended to partition his dominions among his sons; it was his successors who sought to consolidate a unitary control that collapsed before a resurgent French monarchy. Henry's rule had, however, demonstrated how to make authority respected and how to harness it to effective government.

In the kingdom of England there was, in Henry's reign, a transformation in the processes of government and in the methods of administering justice. It rested essentially on three linked developments. First, the decision to rest responsibility for bringing criminal prosecutions not on official prosecutors but on local communities through "juries of presentment" (the origins of the grand jury). Second, the supervision of the operations of local government by investigative teams of justices, who carried royal government into the shires, empowered but also limited by the terms of a carefully framed commission. Third, the offer of the new and much swifter methods of righting civil wrongs by means of common-form writs that set in motion standardized procedures and rested decisions on questions of fact put to juries under the supervision of royal justices who could put the power of the crown behind enforcement.

The flood of business that ensued prompted the development of central courts of justice and a quest for more rational and swifter methods in all aspects of administration. In essence Henry and his advisers had found a solution to the age-old problem of how to deploy royal authority effectively without putting too much discretionary power into the hands of subordinates. A less welcome consequence was the enhanced power of the crown to discriminate against individuals who were out of favor. A necessary corrective to overweening royal government was eventually to be found in Magna Carta, but it is significant that there was no attempt in the Great Charter to reverse the trends that Henry II had fostered, that the closer integration of central and local government was accepted and the development of the common law welcomed.

See also **Eleanor of Aquitaine; John; Richard I; Becket, Thomas**

Further Reading

Gillingham, John. *The Angevin Empire.* London: Arnold, 1984; Turner, Ralph V. "The Problem of Survival for the Angevin 'Empire': Henry II's and His Sons' Visions versus Late Twelfth-Century Realities." *American Historical Renew* 100 (1995): 78–96.

Warren, W.L. *The Governance of Norman and Angevin England, 1086–1272.* London: Arnold, 1987 [differs in interpretation from Gillingham's study].

Warren, W.L. *Henry II.* Rev. ed. London: Methuen, 1991.

W.L. WARREN

HENRY III (1028/1046–1056)

Henry III, son of the Emperor Conrad II (d. 1039) and Queen Gisela, daughter of Duke Hermann II of Swabia, was born on October 28, 1017 and died at age 39 on October 5, 1056. Made duke of Bavaria at age ten, Henry was elevated by his father and the German magnates to the kingship of Germany in the following year (1028). He shared the throne with his father until Conrad's death in 1039. In 1036, as part of a move to secure the northern frontiers of the empire and perhaps control the Saxon nobility, Henry married his first wife, Kunigunde, daughter of King Cnut of Denmark. Their daughter Beatrix (d. 1060) later became abbess of the Ottonian foundation of Quedlinburg. Kunigunde died in 1038.

The year before his father's death, Henry had also obtained the kingship of Burgundy and duchy of Swabia, the latter of which he held until 1045.

In 1043, after assuming sole kingship of Germany in 1039, he married his second wife, Agnes of Poitou (d. 1077), daughter of Duke William V of Aquitaine, with whom he had three daughters and a son. One daughter, Adelheid (d. 1095), became another abbess of Quedlinburg; the other two, Mathilda (d. 1060) and Judith (Sophia, d. 1092/1096), were married, respectively, to Rudolf of Rheinfelden and King Salamo of Hungary and later King Wladyslaw of Poland. Crowned Holy Roman

Emperor in 1046, Henry ruled as king and emperor until his death in 1056, when he was succeeded by his young son Henry IV (1050–1106).

Henry III's assumption of full royal powers in 1039 was a smooth one, since the transition had been prepared over a decade before by Henry's elevation to cokingship during his father's lifetime and by his direct control of the duchies of Bavaria and Swabia and the kingdom of Burgundy. The addition of the southeastern duchy of Carinthia to the regions under his direct rule in 1039 only enhanced his already strong political hold on the southern portion of the German realm. He had also arrived at the pinnacle of royal power after a careful process of practical political and military training which rendered him familiar with both the protocols of royal justice and court business and the demands of military campaigns and the battlefield: in short, with the business of medieval rule. These experiences also prepared him to begin building the vital networks of personal connections with other magnates that enabled so much of royal rule in medieval Germany.

Ecclesiastics, such as the historian Wipo and the polymath Berno of Reichenau, ensured that Henry not only received a basic literary education but also absorbed the ideals of theocratic kingship and participated, to a degree, in contemporary currents of religious revival and reform.

Honored with the epithets *spes imperii* (hope of the empire) and *amicus pacis* (friend of peace), Henry III showed his commitment to the ideals of peace and justice early in his reign with his proclamation of public peace and forgiveness of his opponents. At gatherings in Constance (1043), Trier (Christmas 1043), Menfö in Hungary (1044), and Rome (1046), Henry exhorted, begged, and ordered his audiences to keep the peace and to forsake revenge upon enemies by following their king's example. Despite Henry's emphasis on and general success in establishing peace within his kingdom—a success which has led historians to consider his reign the "high-point of early medieval imperial rule" —his reign was not without both internal and external political crises.

Internally, Henry's aggressive assertion of royal prerogatives and control met with particularly stiff local resistance in Lotharingia and Saxony. In Saxony, Henry exploited royal and imperial domains more intensively than had his predecessors, established a new palace at Goslar, and exercised tighter control over ecclesiastical affairs in the region, all of which set him at odds with the regional nobility and, especially, the noble family of the Billungs. In contrast to the opposition of the Saxon nobility, which simmered until the reign of Henry's son and only erupted in the Saxon War (1073–1089), the nobility of Lotharingia presented Henry with a formidable rival in the person of Godfried the Bearded,

Duke of Upper Lotharingia. After Henry had ignored the duke's legitimate claim to the duchy of Lower Lotharingia, deprived Godfried of his rule, and engaged in a program of ecclesiastical appointments designed to contain or weaken Godfried's power, the duke and his allies revolted in 1044. Defeated in 1049, the duke took refuge in Italy, where, in 1054, he married, without the king's approval, the heir to the margraviate of Tuscany, Beatrix, the former wife of the most powerful ruler in Italy, margrave Boniface. Fearing Godfried's potential control of both Lotharingia and northern Italy, Henry entered Italy in 1055 and captured Beatrix and her daughter Mathilda, while Godfried escaped north to Lotharingia. He submitted to Henry in the following year.

Externally, Henry III was occupied by a series of wars against the kings of Bohemia and Hungary. Taking advantage of political disorder in Poland, King Vratislav I of Bohemia (1034–1058) invaded Poland, thus challenging Henry's overlordship of the German kingdom. After a disastrous initial campaign in August of 1040, Henry emerged victorious over the Bohemians in 1041 and compelled their king to pay tribute and recognize German hegemony. Henry then responded to Hungarian attacks upon the southern frontier with a series of expeditions in 1042, 1043, and 1044, which resulted in victory and the submission of Hungary to Germany at Menfö. According to one scholar (Egon Boshof), Henry's aim was simple: the reduction of Germany's eastern neighbors from independent states to kingdoms subordinate to German rule. Relations with Capetian France in the West, though generally amicable, suffered a setback in 1043–1046, when Henry's marriage to Agnes of Poitou increased anxieties about an alliance between the German kingdom and Aquitaine and provoked an abortive French invasion of Lotharingia.

Known for his largely successful attempts to expand and enforce royal and imperial prerogatives within the German kingdom, Henry III is perhaps most famous for his zealous support of efforts to purify the clergy and for his decisive action in reforming the Roman papacy. Like his predecessors, Henry had used clerics extensively both as administrative functionaries in his *Hofkapelle* and as loyal agents who, once established in bishoprics throughout Germany and Italy, enabled him to strengthen the network of allies used to control the empire's territories. But, touched by the contemporary ideals of a clergy free from the heretical taint of simony (which came to be defined as the acquisition of ecclesiastical office through any form of recompense) and sexual impurity, Henry vigorously forbade simoniacal elections, granted free elections to abbeys and churches, and took measures to raise the moral caliber of the clergy, efforts which brought him praise from monastic reformers like Peter Damian.

His most famous acts, however, came in 1046 when

he entered Italy, deposed the three competing popes, Gregory VI, Benedict DC, and Sylvester III, at synods in Sutri and Rome, and appointed a succession of German bishops as popes: Clement II and Damasus II, both of whom died soon after their elections. Although his bold action at Sutri was criticized by some as an inappropriate invasion of the ecclesiastical sphere by a secular ruler, Henry was nonetheless widely recognized for his efforts to rid the papacy of corruption. His selection in 1048 of Bishop Bruno of Toul, who would become Pope Leo IX (1049–1054), ushered in a new era of the papacy and of ecclesiastical reform.

See also **Conrad II; Henry IV, Emperor; Leo IX, Pope**

Further Reading

Boshof, Egon, *Die Salier*, 3rd ed. Stuttgart and Cologne: Kohlhammer, 1995, pp. 143–166.

Henry III. *Monumenta Germaniae Historica Diplomata Heinrichs III*, ed. H. Breßlau and P. Kehr. Berlin 1926–1931; rpt. Munich: Monumenta Germaniae Historica, 1993.

Prinz, Friedrich. "Kaiser Heinrich III. Seine widersprüchliche Beurteilung und deren Gründe." *Historische Zeitschrift* 246 (1988): 529–548.

Schnith, K. "Recht und Friede. Zum Königsgedanken im Umkreis Heinrichs III." *Historisches Jahrbuch* 81 (1962): 22–57.

Weinfurter, Stefan, et al., ed. *Die Salier und das Reich*. 3 vols. Sigmaringen: Thorbecke, 1992, *passim.*

Wipo. *The Deeds of Conrad II*, trans. K. F. Morrison and T. Mommsen, in *Imperial Lives and Letters.* New York: Columbia University Press, 1962.

WILLIAM NORTH

HENRY IV (1366–1413; r. 1399–1413)

The only legitimate son of John of Gaunt, duke of Lancaster, a younger son of Edward III. Henry was born at Bolingbroke, Lincolnshire, probably in April 1366. Although a king's grandson, he could never have had any real expectations of becoming king and received no training for kingship.

England was overrun without a fight. Richard was captured and induced to abdicate by the guile of Arundel and Northumberland. The oath that Henry swore at Doncaster—that he had come to claim his own inheritance, not the crown—was conveniently forgotten. On 30 September 1399 in the parliament at Westminster, without specifying the exact nature of his title, Henry claimed the throne. Twelve days later he was crowned king. Holding the crown was to prove more difficult than winning it.

Among the nobility and gentry Henry found little support, and he was afraid to offend them by asking his parliaments for the taxes he needed. In the early part of the reign the great officers of state, the chancellor and treasurer and other counselors, were drawn from the humbler ranks of clerks and squires. Lack of money and financial inexperience were his greatest handicaps. Lavish grants from the royal revenues were made in the hope of winning friends and loyal support; they only added to the problem. Plots to depose Henry and restore Richard helped ensure the latter's death but did not end opposition to the new king.

Moreover in 1403 he married, as his second wife, Joan of Navarre, widowed duchess of Brittany, whom he may have met while in exile. A foreign queen, generously endowed with estates and a household that was, like Henry's, regarded by the Commons as extravagant, provided a further target for critics. Though earlier rebellions had been easily suppressed, the Welsh rising led by Owen Glendower proved a serious harassment for most of the reign. The Percys, entrusted to defend the northern border and to govern north Wales, defeated the Scots at Homildon Hill in 1402 but soon became discontented with the role Henry permitted them and with the payments he was able to afford them.

The Percys' first rebellion was defeated at Shrewsbury in 1403, owing to Henry's swift reaction. Hotspur was killed in battle and his uncle Worcester captured and beheaded, but the old earl of Northumberland lived to rebel again and finally to menace Henry from exile in Scotland. With his parliaments Henry had a constant struggle to secure money and to prevent them taking control of his council, from which his humbler friends were slowly excluded. After the Long Parliament of 1406 Arundel, his ablest counselor, became chancellor and controlled the government for several years but had to face new rivals: the emerging Beaufort family, the children of Gaunt's mistress and then wife, Katherine Swynford, and thus the king's half-brothers.

Meanwhile Henry had been stricken with the mysterious illness that disfigured, disabled, and eventually killed him. After several years of campaigning in Wales the king's eldest son, Henry, succeeded in defeating the rebels and now joined the Beauforts to control the council. Thomas Beaufort replaced Arundel as chancellor. At some point the Beauforts tried to force Henry to abdicate in favor of the prince, but as the plot failed evidence is almost entirely lacking. After some disputes, mainly over the question of war with France, a formal reconciliation between father and son was effected, and Henry the usurper was able to leave his son an undisputed succession when he died in 1413.

See also **Edward III; Henry V; Richard II**

Further Reading

Brown, Alfred L. "The Commons and the Council in the Reign of Henry IV." *EHR* 79 (1964): 125–56.

Davies, Richard G. "Thomas Arundel as Archbishop of Canterbury, 1396–1414." *Journal of Ecclesiastical History* 19 (1973): 9–21.

Harriss, G.L. *Cardinal Beaufort: A Study of the Lancastrian Ascendancy and Decline.* Oxford: Clarendon, 1988 [especially valuable for the later part of the reign].

Kirby, John L. *Henry IV of England.* London: Constable, 1970 [modern and concise compared with Wylie].

McNiven, Peter. "Prince Henry and the English Political Crisis of 1412." *History* 65 (1980): 1–16.

McNiven, Peter. *Heresy and Politics in the Reign of Henry IV: The Burning of John Badby.* Woodbridge: Boydell, 1987 [a broader study than the title suggests].

Wylie, James H. *History of England under Henry the Fourth.* 4 vols. London: Longmans Green, 1884–98 [still valuable, though mostly an uncritical collection of facts].

JOHN L. KIRBY

HENRY IV, EMPEROR (r. 1056–1106)

Born on November 11, 1050, the future Emperor Henry IV was the much longed-for son and heir of Emperor Henry III and Agnes of Poitou. He was baptized by Archbishop Hermann of Cologne at Easter 1051. Abbot Hugh of Cluny, who had come specially from Burgundy at the invitation of the emperor, lifted the baby from the font, thus becoming his godfather and, apparently, also naming him. Elected king at Tribur in November 1053, Henry was crowned July 17, 1054, at Aachen and betrothed the next year to Bertha, a girl of his own age and daughter of the count of Turin. He was not even six years old when his father died on October 5, 1056, at the palace of Bodfeld in the Harz mountains.

On his deathbed, Henry III had entrusted his heir to Pope Victor II (1055–1057), the former bishop of Eichstätt and imperial chancellor. Victor managed to obtain recognition of little Henry's succession to the throne. Nominally, Henry IV began his reign in 1056. The guardianship lay in the hands of his pious mother, the Empress Agnes, until April 1063, however, when a faction of conspirators, led by Archbishop Anno II of Cologne, abducted the young king, who tried to save himself by jumping overboard into the Rhine. Anno now became the leading influence at court, replacing another bishop, Adalbert of Bremen. Anno had good relations with ecclesiastical reformers in Rome and reversed an earlier imperial policy which had supported the election of Bishop Cadalus of Parma as (anti)pope Honorius III. In collaboration with Peter Damian a papal legate, Anno and the German court recognized, instead, Pope Alexander II (1061–1073), who had been elected by Hildebrand (the fixture Gregory VII) and other reformers.

Henry IV began to govern in his own name at age six in March 1056. In July 1066 he married Bertha of Turin but tried to divorce her three years later. He desisted in face of the remonstrations of Peter Damian, who had been sent to Germany by the pope as a legate.

Henry's relationship with several German nobles was tense from the beginning of the reign. His troubles increased from about 1068, when he began to try to recover the crown lands, originally in the hands of the Ottonian rulers, in eastern Saxony and Thuringia. Essentially continuing his father's policies, Henry strengthened and expanded them, forcing the Saxons to build and maintain fortifications that were garrisoned with southern German *ministeriales.* This policy provoked Saxon resistance, playing into the hands of Otto of Northeim. Otto had forfeited the duchy of Bavaria in 1070 and formed an alliance with Magnus Billung, the duke of Saxony, and other magnates who had made their fortunes under Ottonian emperors during their eastward expansion. Together with the region's bishops, and with massive support from the Saxons in general, the magnates confronted Henry IV in the summer of 1073 at Goslar. They demanded that the castles he had recently built should be razed, that lands unjustly confiscated should be restored by the council of princes, and that the king should stay in Saxony and dismiss his low-born advisers and instead follow the princes' advice. Henry, who had also lost the support of the south German dukes, was besieged by the Saxon army and barely escaped from his fortress, the Harzburg, to find protection in the town of Worms. The Harzburg was stormed by the Saxons, but their army was defeated in September 1075. By the end of the year, however, Henry seemed to have mastered the situation. At Christmas the nobles elected his son Conrad their king.

At the request of the higher clergy of Milan, who had defeated the Pataria reform movement in the spring of 1075, Henry nominated the imperial chaplain Tedald as archbishop of Milan instead of Atto, who had the support of Pope Gregory VII and the Pararia. Gregory expressed his furious opposition in a letter (December 8, 1075) and in a verbal message, perhaps threatening the king with excommunication. From Worms, where nobles and ecclesiastics met jointly in a diet on January 24, 1076, came the reply. The German bishops, who resented papal claims of hierocracy and centralization, renounced their obedience to the pontiff, whom they called "Brother Hildebrand," and claimed his election had been illegal; Henry IV called upon Gregory to resign, and the Romans were asked to elect a new pope. The north Italian episcopate supported these measures immediately.

From the Lenten synod he was holding in Rome from February 14–20, 1076, Gregory deposed Henry, absolved his subjects from the oath of fealty, and excommunicated the king. Many of the bishops then deserted Henry, joining forces with the Bavarian and Saxon opposition. By October 1076, at the meeting of Tribur, the king had to accept their terms and to declare his submission to the pontiff. Unless Henry was absolved from his excommunication by February 1077, the assembly of Tribur threatened, they would proceed with the election of a new king. The German princes invited Gregory to come as an arbitrator to a diet that was to be held at Augsburg in February 1077. With no way out, Henry decided in mid-December 1076 to meet Gregory, who had already left Rome on his way to Augsburg in northern Italy. With his wife Bertha and his two-year-old son Conrad, Henry managed to cross Mount Cernis in severe winter weather. When he learned of the king's arrival, Gregory withdrew to the fortress of Canossa, owned by Countess Matilda of Tuscany. Thanks to the mediation of Henry's godfather, Abbot Hugh of Cluny, of Matilda, and of Adelheid of Turin (mother of the queen), Gregory reconciled Henry IV with the Church on January 28, 1077. Henry was forced to appear barefoot and dressed in a penitent's hair shirt for three days in a row in the inner courtyard of the castle requesting permission to enter before he was absolved by the pope.

In fact, though not in theory, when he reconciled Henry with the church, Gregory again recognized Henry as king. At the Lenten synod of 1080, however, the pontiff recognized Rudolf of Rheinfelden, whom the German opposition had elected in March 1077 despite the absolution of Canossa, as king. Henry was once again excommunicated, but, this time, ineffectively. At the synod of Brixen, June 1080, Henry and the princes nominated Archbishop Wibert of Ravenna to replace Gregory, whom the synod then deposed. The death of Rudolf, and military as well as political successes, enabled Henry to enter Rome in March 1084 when Wibert was consecrated Pope Clement III. On Easter Sunday, Henry IV was crowned emperor. Meanwhile, Gregory, freed by his vassals from his place of refuge, the Castello S. Angelo in Rome, withdrew to Salerno, where he died in May 1085.

After his return to Germany, Henry at first was able to consolidate his position. With the death of Clement III in 1100 the end of the schism in the Church seemed possible. However, the negotiations between Henry IV and Pope Paschal II (1099–1118) always ended in failure, since Henry refused to give up his right to invest bishops with the ring and staff, the one demand on which Paschal insisted.

The collapse of these negotiations with the papacy lay behind the rebellion of Henry V against his rather in late 1104. Through a ruse, the younger Henry captured Henry IV in late 1105. At Ingelheim on December 31, 1105, Henry IV was forced to abdicate. He managed to flee, however, and attempted to regain power. He died at Liège on August 7, 1106, eventually to be buried in the cathedral of Speyer.

A contemporary, albeit anonymous, biographer most movingly bemoaned the death of the emperor, the protector of the poor, opening with the words of Jeremiah 9.1: "Oh that my head were waters, and mine eyes a fountain of tears, that I might weep day and night for the slain daughter of my people."

See also **Anno; Gregory VII, Pope; Henry III**

Further Reading

Benson, Robert L. ed. *Imperial Lives and Letters of the Eleventh Century*, trans. Theodor E. Mommsen and Karl F. Morrison. New York: Columbia University Press, 1962.
Freed, John B. "Henry IV of Germany." In *Dictionary of the Middle Ages*, vol. 6. New York: Scribner, 1985, p. 163.
Fuhrman, Horst. *Germany in the High Middle Ages*, trans. Timothy Reuter. Cambridge: Cambridge University Press, 1986.
Leyser, Karl. "The Crisis in Medieval Germany." In Karl Leyser, *Communications and Power in Medieval Europe*, trans. Timothy Reuter. London: Hambledon, 1994, pp. 21–49.
Lynch, J. H. "Hugh I of Cluny's Sponsorship of Henry IV: Its Context and Consequences." *Speculum* 60 (1985): 800–826.
Struve, Tilman. "Heinrich IV." In *Lexikon des Mittelalters*, vol. 4. Munich: Artemis, 1989, pp. 2041–2043.
von Gladiss, Dietrich, et al., ed. *Die Urkunden Heinrichs IV*, pts. 1–3. Monumenta Germaniae Historica. Diplomata 6/1–3. Hanover: Hahn, 1977, 1959, 1978.
Wies, Erbst W. *Kaiser Heinrich IV*: *Canossa und der Kampf um die Weltherrshaft*. Munich and Esslingen: Bechtle, 1996.

UTA-RENATE BLUMENTHAL

HENRY THE LION
(1129/1131–August 6, 1195)

Duke of Saxony and Bavaria (*Heinrich der Lowe, Herzog von Sachsen und Bayern*), Henry the Lion was born 1129/1131, the son of the Welf Henry the Proud (*Heinrich der Stolze*) and Gertrude, daughter of Lothar III. His father died in 1139, dispossessed of all his titles in his feud with Conrad III, but the Empress Richenza, Henry's grandmother, and Count Adolf of Holstein secured the boy's northern inheritance. Henry was enfeoffed with Saxony in 1142. (Bavaria had already been granted to Conrad Ill's half-brother Henry of Babenberg [Heinrich Jasomirgott]). Henry became a tough soldier and a ruthless politician, particularly in his Saxon lands and in his relationship to the Archbishopric of Bremen, and participated in the Wendish Crusade in 1147.

Frederick I Barbarossa of Swabia, Henry's cousin, became king in 1152. Henry accompanied Frederick to Italy in 1154–1155, and, during the coronation riots in Rome, saved his cousin's life. In 1156 Frederick returned Bavaria to Henry, but without the East Mark, which became Austria. Frederick granted that fiefdom to his uncle Henry Babenberg in the *Privilegium minus* (Lesser Privilege).

Over the next twenty years Henry supported Frederick but also expanded his own power. He founded Munich in 1157 and Lübeck in 1159, and married Mathilda of England (daughter of Henry II and Eleanor of Aquitaine) in 1165. Henry also built the cathedral and the castle in Brunswick (Braunschweig), was in Italy twice, and went on a pilgrimage to Jerusalem in 1172.

In 1176, at Chiavenna, Frederick demanded Henry's

support for his war with the papacy and the Italian communes, but the Saxon duke refused to help without a substantial reward. Frederick's war ended in defeat, and he had to make peace with the pope in 1177. Upon his return to Germany, Frederick began legal proceedings against his cousin. For non-appearance at his trial, Henry was outlawed at the diet of Würzburg in 1180. He had few allies, and an imperial army defeated him in Saxony. In 1181 Henry was deposed from all his possessions and exiled; he and his family fled to his father-in-law, Henry II, in England, where he remained until 1185. Saxony was split between the Archbishop of Cologne and the Ascanian counts of Brandenburg. Bavaria went to a member of the Wittelsbach family.

When Frederick went on crusade in 1189, he exiled his cousin again; but Mathilda stayed in Brunswick, where she died that year. Henry returned to Germany upon the news of his cousin's death. He was finally pardoned by Henry VI and spent his remaining years in Saxony. Henry the Lion died on August 6, 1195 and was buried in the cathedral at Brunswick beside his wife.

A man who fascinated his contemporaries, Henry the Lion was one of the most controversial German princes of the twelfth century. Italian historian Acerbus Morena, who met him in 1163, described him as of medium height, but strong and agile, with dark eyes and hair. Henry was arrogant and ruthless, but his dealings with Frederick in the 1180s show that he could seriously overplay his hand.

Some historians have celebrated him as the champion of nationalism and the expansion eastward, while others have chided him for deserting Frederick I at a crucial time in the empire's history. It is perhaps time to lay the old controversies to rest.

See also **Frederick I Barbarossa; Matilda, Empress**

Further Reading

Jordan, Karl. *Henry the Lion*, trans. P. S. Falla. Oxford: Clarendon, 1986.
Luckhardt, Jochen, and Franz Niehoff, ed. *Heinrich der Löwe und seine Zeit*: *Herrschaft und Repräsentation der Welfen* 1125–1235. 3 vols. Munich: Hirmer, 1995.
Mohrmann, Wolf-Dieter, ed. *Heinrich der Löwe*. Göttingen: Vandenhoek & Ruprecht, 1980.

MADELYN BERGEN DICK

HENRY V (1387–1422; r. 1413–22)

The popular and Shakespearean hero-king *par excellence*, although liberal historians have been less impressed with his militarism and religious intolerance. Born in 1387 to the future Henry IV and Mary de Bohun, he was too young to be involved in the political intrigues of Richard II's reign. Richard took him to Ireland in 1399 and knighted him during this expedition, which opened England to the invasion and usurpation of Henry IV. Henry V would later rebury Richard among the kings at Westminster Abbey.

Young Henry was made Prince of Wales; from 1400 to 1408 he earned his spurs combating the Welsh revolt of Owen Glendower and the Percys. The prince played a major role at the Battle of Shrewsbury in 1403. During his father's illness (1410–11) Henry and his supporters dominated the royal council, but Henry IV feared his ambition and differed with the prince over which faction to support as France fell into turmoil. The king removed his son from the council. The final two years of Henry IV's reign were a period of tension and frustration for the Prince, which may explain the later stories of his dissipated lifestyle.

Henry succeeded on 20 March 1413. He was faced with both religious and political plots that threatened the tranquility of his realm. His erstwhile friend Sir John Oldcastle, perhaps the model for Shakespeare's Falstaff, led a Lollard conspiracy in 1414 to kill the king and seize London. The conspiracy was discovered and put down, but Oldcastle remained at large until 1417, when he was taken and executed. The king remained a vigorous persecutor of Lollards. Henry, self-righteously pious, supported the efforts of the Council of Constance to end the Great Schism of the papacy, and he was a supporter of elaborate public liturgy. The king joined public worship and private devotion in his monastic foundations, a form of piety long out of fashion with monarchs. The palace at Sheen was to be restored, almost in anticipation of the Escorial (in Spain, by Charles V), with a Carthusian house and a house of Brigettine nuns.

On the political front Henry V was faced in 1415 with a plot led by the earl of Cambridge, Lord Scrope, and Sir Thomas Grey to eliminate the Lancastrian dynasty and declare the earl of March as the legitimate heir of Richard II. March revealed the plot to the king as Henry was preparing to invade France. The leaders were executed, and Henry, his domestic enemies all in flight, was free to pursue foreign ambitions.

Ignoring his questionable title to the English throne and sure of his right, Henry V revived Edward III's claim to the French crown, and it is with his French conquests that Henry is forever identified. France was torn by strife between the aristocratic factions of Armagnacs and Burgundians under the mentally ill Charles VI. Henry led a plundering expedition to Normandy in August 1415. The English captured Harfleur and then marched toward Calais. On 15 October they were overtaken by a vastly superior French army at Agincourt. Henry proved an inspirational leader who skillfully deployed his archers to win a stunning victory that encouraged English ambition and a desire for French wealth and ransoms.

Henry returned to Normandy with a second expedition in 1417, bent now upon a genuine conquest. When the Armagnacs murdered the duke of Burgundy in 1419, the new duke, Philip the Good, allied with Henry. Careful diplomacy and continued military pressure forced Charles VI to agree to the Treaty of Troyes, 21 May 1420. Under its terms Charles disinherited his son (the future Charles VII) in favor of Henry V, who became regent of France and married Charles's daughter, Catherine of Valois.

France south of the Loire remained defiant and unconquered. With the vital support of his Burgundian allies Henry pursued his conquests against the disinherited dauphin and his Armagnac allies. During the course of the campaign Henry contracted dysentery; he died at Bois de Vincennes on 31 August 1422, not yet 35 years of age. Charles VI outlived him by two months. Under the terms of the Treaty of Troyes the crowns of England and France passed to Henry V's infant son, Henry VI, who grew up to be an incompetent and hopeless weakling.

Henry V's dream of a French conquest was lost by 1453, and he has been condemned by historians for squandering England's resources in an unattainable quest for foreign glory. Yet to contemporaries he was an heroic figure. A cunning propagandist and diplomat, a skillful and ruthless general, and—as historians are discovering—a just and careful administrator, he can be faulted for dying inopportunely.

See also **Henry IV; Philip the Good; Richard II**

Further Reading

Allmand, C.T. *Henry V.* Berkeley: University of California Press, 1992.

Harriss, G.L., ed. *Henry V: The Practice of Kingship.* Oxford: Oxford University Press, 1985.

Kingsford, Charles L., ed. *The First English Life of King Henry the Fifth.* Oxford: Clarendon, 1911.

Labarge, Margaret Wade. *Henry V: The Cautious Conqueror.* London: Seeker & Warburg, 1975.

McFarlane, K.B. *Lancastrian Kings and Lollard Knights.* Oxford: Clarendon, 1972 [for the view of Henry as the "greatest man that ever ruled England"].

Taylor, Frank, and John S. Roskell, eds. and trans. *Gesta Henrici Quinti: The Deeds of Henry the Fifth.* Oxford: Clarendon, 1975.

Wylie, James H., and W.T. Waugh. *The Reign of Henry the Fifth.* 3 vols. Cambridge: Cambridge University Press, 1914–29.

JAMES L. GILLESPIE

HENRY VI (1165–1197)

At the tender age of three, Henry VI Staufen was already an elected and crowned king. His father, Emperor Frederick I Barbarossa, not only had him participate in the imperial government, but even tried to get him elected co-emperor. Scholars, such as Godfrey of Viterbo, provided the young king's education, according to several songs that appear in medieval collections of *Minnesang* (courtly love poetry). His father granted Henry the belt of knighthood at the famous tournament at Mainz during Pentecost 1184. By that autumn, Henry had become betrothed to Constance, eleven years his senior and the aunt of King William II of Sicily. During Barbarossa's disputes with Pope Urban III, Henry successfully conducted military campaigns against the papal states; but Urban's successor, Clement III, promised to crown him emperor. Henry took over the regency while Barbarossa went off upon the third Crusade in the spring of 1189.

When Barbarossa died in July 1190, Henry should have quietly succeeded to his father's inheritance. But several obstacles soon arose. For example, the Welf Henry the Lion, Duke of Saxony, had returned from exile in England and defied the royal armies by reclaiming his old power in the north. The sudden death of King William II of Sicily in November had, in Henry's view, left his wife Constance as the heir to that rich kingdom. When the Sicilians, with papal cooperation, elected William's illegitimate cousin, Count Tancred of Lecce, as king, Henry resolved to attack that kingdom after being crowned emperor in Rome. Finally, after coming to a truce with the Welfs and turning to Italy, Henry found that Pope Celestine III had replaced Clement.

Meanwhile, the city leaders of Rome had been pressuring the pope to destroy Tusculum, a city which had been loyal to and garrisoned by the Staufen, but which the Romans considered a rival. The aged pope-elect demanded that the king abandon Tusculum before any imperial coronation. With Tusculum torn down stone by stone, the Romans gladly cheered the papal consecration of Celestine on Easter Sunday, April 14, and the imperial coronation of Henry on Easter Monday. The new emperor then turned to the conquest of Southern Italy and Sicily. But, after a few successes, he failed at a siege of Naples, largely because of the summer heat and the effects of diseases like dysentery, cholera, and malaria on his troops. Although Henry survived a bout with sickness, many others died, and the army retreated northward. Meanwhile, the Empress Constance briefly became a prisoner of Tancred, king of Sicily.

Back in Germany, Henry faced new problems, especially as he tried to solve a quarrel over the see of Liège by naming his own candidate. Another candidate, Albert of Louvain, brother of the Duke of Brabant, had the backing of Pope Celestine, however, and was consecrated bishop. Five days later, German knights murdered him, and many blamed Henry for instigating the deed. Encouraged by the Welfs and the papacy, widespread opposition to Henry began to organize itself into open rebellion.

At this juncture, Henry was rescued by the capture of the English king, Richard the Lionhearted, who was returning from a Crusade in December 1192. Henry forced Richard's captor, Duke Leopold V of Austria, to turn the king over to imperial control; he then demanded a huge ransom for Richard's freedom. By the time Richard was released in February 1194, Henry had extorted 150,000 marks, which he divided with Leopold, as well as Richard's pledge of England as a fief of the empire with a yearly tribute of five thousand marks. Although the promised payments were never entirely realized, Henry used the large ransom to finance his invasion of Sicily.

His efforts were aided by the death of Tancred in February 1194, leaving only an infant son as heir, and Henry and his armies quickly conquered Sicily. On Christmas day 1194 he celebrated his kingship in the cathedral in Palermo. The next day, in Jesi on the mainland, Henry's wife gave birth to his own son and heir, the future Frederick II.

Through ruthless policies, Henry quickly secured his rule in Sicily. An alleged plot against him gave the emperor an excuse to banish the usurper's family to Germany, and, allegedly, in Byzantine fashion, to blind the infant former king as well as some officials. The Sicilian treasury was carried to Henry's castle, Trifels, in Swabia by more than 150 pack animals. By Easter 1195 the emperor had proclaimed his wife as regent for the Sicilian lands and set one of his powerful ministerials in place as viceroy; arranged the betrothal of his brother, Philip of Swabia, to Tancred's widow, Irene, a Byzantine princess; installed Philip as margrave of Tuscany (including the oft-disputed Mathildine lands); and begun to proclaim and organize a Crusade to the Holy Land.

Returning to Germany, Henry convinced many other princes to participate in the Crusade. He also nearly managed to get his young son recognized as king of the Romans by right of inheritance instead of by election. Henry suggested what is known as the *Erbreichsplan*, a, proposal to ensure that the royal, and hence imperial, title would be inherited in the Staufen dynasty. In return, for secular princes, Henry promised to make fiefs held by the crown inheritable in the female line; for spiritual princes, he promised not to practice the *spolia*, a king's exploitation of the temporal powers and royal rights during a vacancy. At first, most of the princes accepted the plan, but, when Henry returned to Italy, they began to express their dissatisfaction. Even more, the Roman Curia opposed both the idea of uniting the crown of the Holy Roman Empire with that of Sicily and of giving up papal prerogatives in the imperial coronation process. By November 1196 Henry offered the pope what he claimed was more than any other emperor had ever done, the so-called *höchstes Angebot* (highest offer). But by the end of the year, Henry had given up on the inheritance plan, and the princes elected his son as king the old-fashioned way.

Back in Sicily during the spring of 1197, Henry barely escaped an attempted assassination, plotted probably with the tacit knowledge of the pope and Henry's own wife. Henry crushed the rebellion, executing some of the rebels in a brutal fashion. At the beginning of September, the main Crusader fleet set off for the Holy Land, where they gained promising victories. Later that month however, the emperor was taken seriously ill. He died at the age of only thirty-one on September 28, 1197, in Palermo. Revolts in Sicily and Italy and civil war in Germany over control of the crown soon gravely weakened the monarchy.

Both contemporary and historical opinion on Henry has been severely divided between those who viewed his death as a blessing or as a curse. His critics worry he might have established world dominion had he lived long enough; his advocates note the breakdown of German imperial authority after his death. Certainly, his death provided the opportunity for Innocent III to seize the leadership of Christendom. Overshadowed by the reputations of his father and son, Henry VI's short reign is nonetheless remarkable both for it successes and its flaws.

See also **Frederick I Barbarossa; Frederick II; Godfrey of Viterbo**

Further Reading

Csendes, Peter. *Heinrich VI.* Darmstadt: Wissenschafttiche Buchgesellschaft, 1993.
Naumann, Claudia. *Der Kreuzzug Kaiser Heinrichs VI.* Frankfurt am Main: Lang, 1994.
Pavlac, Brian A. "Emperor Henry VI (1191–97) and the Papacy: Influences on Innocent III's Staufen Policies." In *Pope Innocent III and His World*, ed. John C. Moore. London: Ashgate, 1998.
Seltmann, Ingeborg. *Heinrich VI: Herrschaftspraxis und Umgebung.* Erlangen: Palm & Enke, 1983.
Toeche, Theodor. *Heinrich VI.* Jahrbücher der deutschen Geschichte 18. Leipzig, 1867; rpt. Darmstadt: Wissenschaftliche Buchgesellschaft, 1965.

BRIAN A. PAVLAC

HENRY VII OF LUXEMBOURG (c. 1275–1313)

Henry of Luxembourg was the son and heir of Count Henry III of Luxembourg (d. 1288). Young Henry was raised at the French court and spoke French as his native tongue. In 1292, he married Margaret, daughter of the duke of Brabant. As count, Henry he was noted for his effective rule, especially as peacekeeper in local feudal disputes. After Albert, king of the Romans, was assassinated on 1 May 1308, Henry was elected unanimously in Frankfurt on 27 November 1308. He was crowned on 6 January 1309 in Aachen.

Within weeks of his coronation Henry began preparations for his *Romzug*, the journey to Rome for coronation as emperor. Although several of his predecessors had avoided it, Henry felt a need to gain the prestige that the Germans associated with the imperial title, given his own dynastic obscurity and the concessions he had made to be elected. He also wanted to reassert the imperial presence in Italy, which, although practically semi-autonomous, was legally subject to the emperor.

In July 1309, Henry assured Pope Clement V, who was resident in Avignon, that he would observe and defend the rights and privileges of the cities of the papal states and would embark, as emperor, on a crusade. In return, the pope formally supported Henry's journey. During the spring of 1310, royal emissaries traveled through Lombardy and Tuscany to prepare the cities for Henry's arrival. In early November 1310, Henry arrived in Turin accompanied by some 5,000 men, including 500 cavalry. Henry would never cross the Alps again.

Northern Italy was fragmented into nearly independent city-states that often suffered from deep social and political divisions. Guelfs and Ghibellines fought openly in cities, often making bitter, potent exiles of the losers. Urban nobles had long clashed with the non-noble classes over interests and political power bases, and in many cities strong leaders emerged as one-man rulers, or *signori*. For decades, cities had created and followed their own laws and policies, controlled their hinterlands, and maintained delicate intercity relations by custom and compromise without reference to imperial interests. Although Henry had been a successful politician and lord north of the Alps, his ignorance of Italian institutions, politics, and recent history would prove fatal to him in Italy. With the best intentions—he wanted to be an impartial conciliator and peacemaker—he would upset these complicated relationships by consciously supporting Ghibellines and nobles, deposing old *signori* and imposing new ones, pressing imperial claims to what had become communal lands and rights, and replacing communal statutes with imperial laws.

As early as March 1310, Tuscan cities led by Florence and Bologna created a Guelf defensive league, nominally under the patronage of the pope and the Angevin King Robert of Naples. The league wanted guarantees against imperial interference in communal affairs; in return, the league would support Henry with cash and troops. Early in his campaign, Henry confirmed the Guelfs' fears. Between 11 November and 11 December he radically interfered in the affairs of the town of Asti—reorganizing political offices, releasing officials, and retrying criminals. As Henry marched toward Milan, the Guelf *signore* Guido della Torre refused to give up his palace or his personal mercenary guard. Guido's defiance remained peaceful, however, and on 23 December Henry entered Milan. He soon replaced Guido

with the Ghibelline Matteo Visconti. On 6 January 1311, Henry was crowned king of the Lombards; the dismayed Tuscan Guelfs avoided attending the ceremony. The Milanese offered Henry a "gift" of 100,000 florins; and Henry, taking 100 young noblemen as a bodyguard (and hostages), left Milan on 14 February.

On 10 January, Henry had made his brother-in-law, Amadeus of Savoy, vicar-general of Lombardy, to act as fiscal, judicial, and military agent of the king. This arrangement would cost the cities some 300,000 florins per year. By February, Guelf forces reacted. On 12 February, the della Torre faction revolted in Milan and were put down with moderation. Later in the month Brescia, Crema, Cremona, and Reggio expelled both their Ghibellines and their imperial vicars. Again, Henry responded moderately, but the rebels resisted and holed up in Cremona. Many of them submitted to Henry on 26 April, but he took revenge by destroying the city gates and walls and the rebels' houses, imposing fines, and withdrawing civic rights and privileges. Resistance stiffened, and by 19 May Henry's army was besieging Brescia. Despite plague and desertion, it remained in place for four months and broke the resistance. Harsh reprisals, but no death penalties, followed.

Henry moved on to Genoa, arriving on 21 October. Town leaders and the king carried out long negotiations over regalian rights in the countryside, most of which Henry retained or regained. Between October 1311 and mid-February 1312, when Henry left for Pisa, Guelfs in Lodi, Reggio, Cremona, Piacenza, Parma, Pavia, Padua, and Brescia rebelled against their imperial governments. Since Florence was the key supporter of the revolts, Henry declared all Florentines rebels and released their debtors of their debts. Revolts in Brescia, Lodi, and Piacenza were quelled, but in April both Asti and Treviso rebelled. Pisa welcomed Henry on 6 March, and while he waited for reinforcements he wisely refrained from interfering in Pisan affairs.

By 7 May, Henry's force was outside Rome, now controlled by Angevin Guelfs from Naples. Henry's long-delayed coronation was delayed further by military resistance in Rome. Despite a major victory on 26 May, Henry could not capture Saint Peter's, so the pope's reluctant representatives crowned Henry in Saint John Lateran (29 June 1312). The new emperor now turned against Tuscany to punish Florence. In mid-September Henry's siege began, with 15,000 men and 2,000 cavalry against the Florentines' 60,000 men and 4,000 knights. The operation was unsuccessful, though it lasted six weeks.

On 10 March 1313, Henry reentered faithful Pisa. His patience long since exhausted, the emperor condemned all inhabitants of rebellious cities to be captured, stripped, and hanged. Papal interests were also threatened as Henry condemned Bologna, for example, and declared the papal vassal Robert of Naples guilty of lèse-majesté for having opposed the coronation and having interfered in Rome. Publicists revived papal and imperial claims to universal authority, and a lively scholarly debate—which involved Dante (in *Monarchia*)—ensued. Henry also prepared to invade Naples, and on 8 August 1313 he left Pisa for Siena and points south. He died of malaria while besieging Guelf Siena on 24 August, and was buried in the baptistery of Pisa.

See also **Clement V, Pope; Dante Alighieri; Robert of Anjou**

Further Reading

Bowsky, William. *Henry VII in Italy.* Lincoln: University of Nebraska Press, 1960.

JOSEPH P. BYRNE

HENRYSON, ROBERT (ca. 1425/35–1505)

Scottish poet. Although Robert Henryson was perhaps the greatest poet writing in English during the 15th century (his dialect was Middle Scots), little is known about his life. The only sure information is Dunbar's brief reference in "Timor Mortis Conturbat Me," amid mention of other dead Scots writers, to a "Maister Robert Henrisoun" of Dunfermline. The name is a common one, but a Master Robert Henryson, who may be the poet, is listed at the University of Glasgow in 1462 and as a witness to three deeds in Dunfermline during 1477–78. Many early manuscripts and prints refer to him as school-master at Dunfermline, an important royal and monastic town. In unpublished notes to his 17th-century Latin translation of Henryson's *Testament* (and Chaucer's *Troilus*) Sir Francis Kynaston tells a humorous if dubious anecdote about the poet's death, though he also perceptively notes his wit, learning, and literary skill. It seems likely that Henryson was born about 1425, though some would say a decade later; from Dunbar's poem we know he must have been dead by 1505. Perhaps a notary as well as a schoolmaster, Henryson does not seem to have held ecclesiastical office.

The three major works in the canon—the *Fables, Testament of Cresseid*, and *Orpheus and Eurydice*—are undoubtedly by Henryson, though we have no sure idea of their dates or order of composition. Some of the dozen or so short poems usually attributed to him are more doubtful. The textual tradition of Henryson's poetry is almost as uncertain as his biography. Most of the works are found in witnesses that date from at least 75 years after the presumed time of his death. Moreover the printed editions of his works (many of which have been lost or exist only in unique copies) are generally more authoritative than the surviving manuscripts, which were often copied from prints. Henryson's influence on later Scots literature was not great, and he was so obscure to English readers that his *Testament* was included in editions of Chaucer throughout the 16th century as the conclusion to *Troilus and Criseyde.* Its true authorship was not recognized in print until Urry's edition of Chaucer in 1721.

As is also true for Dunbar, Henryson's short poems are written in various genres and meters, which he handles with skill. They range from "Sum Practysis of Medecyne," an extravagant, and often gross, rhymed alliterative burlesque of quack prescriptions (supporting the belief of some that Henryson had studied medicine), to the devout lyricism of "The Annunciation." Most of the short poems deal with serious Christian themes, especially the uncertainties of this world. "The Ressoning betuix Aige and Yowth" and "The Ressoning betuix Deth and Man" are vigorous *memento mori* debates about the inevitable passing of earthly joy, which is also the subject of three powerful meditations: "The Praise of Age," "The Thre Deid Pollis," and "The Abbey Walk." A more humorous treatment of temporality is found in the superb and original *pastourelle* "Robene and Makyne," in which a shepherd returns a maidens love too late. "The Bludy Serk" and "The Garmont of Gud Ladeis" are chivalric moral allegories in ballad stanzas, more vividly told than their probable sources. The metrically complex "Ane Prayer for the Pest" is a more topical poem whose sense of human powerlessness before the divine is also found in the poet's longer works. Like "Sum Pracrysis of Medecyne" "Against Hasty Credence" is fierce social satire (against flatterers) that may derive from Lydgate. Another secular satire, "The Want of Wyse Men," is probably not by Henryson.

The least well regarded of Henryson's major works is *Orpheus and Eurydice*, a 414-line narrative in rime royal (with Orpheus's complaint in ten-line stanzas) followed by a 218-line *moralitas*, or moral, in heroic couplets. The poem tells the familiar story of how Orpheus's beloved wife, Eurydice, fleeing the attempted rape by Aristaeus, was bitten by a serpent and taken to Hades, where she was finally discovered by her grief-stricken husband. By his harp playing Orpheus made the infernal gods promise that she could leave with him, on condition that he not look back. Moved by affection, he did so look on the return journey and so lost her forever. The *moralitas* identifies Orpheus as the intellectual part of the soul, Eurydice as the affectionate part, and Aristaeus as virtue.

The narrative in *Orpheus and Eurydice* is based on Boethius's *Consolation of Philosophy* (book 3, meter 12), whereas the *moralitas* and some of the narrative details are based on Nicholas Trevet's commentary on the *Consolation*, itself derived from the commentary of William of Conches. The poem reveals Henryson's interest in human limitation, his poetic skill (especially in Orpheus's complaint), and perhaps even his allegorical audacity (as in his not unprecedented identification of the rapist with virtue). Very different from the ME romance *Sir Orfeo*, Henryson's poem is a learned, rhetorically sophisticated allegory that is also a defense of poetry. Like Boethius Henryson allows no explicitly Christian reference in this deeply Christian work.

The *Testament of Cresseid*, 79 rime royal stanzas plus Cresseid's complaint in seven nine-line stanzas, is Henryson's acknowledged masterpiece. On a cold night in Lent the poet reads Chaucer's account of Cresseid before turning to another book about her wretched end. Having become a prostitute after her rejection by Diomede, Cresseid is then punished with leprosy by the planetary gods for her blasphemy in blaming her misfortune on Venus and Cupid. As she is begging one day with other lepers, Cresseid encounters Troilus. Though neither recognizes the other, Troilus gives her alms in memory of his lost love. After learning the identity of her benefactor Cresseid praises Troilus, blames only herself for what happened, makes her final testament, and dies.

Although the *Testament* is strikingly original, it obviously draws on *Troilus and Criseyde*, as well as on other Chaucerian poems. The formal descriptions of the planetary gods are based on traditional information, though the specific influence of Chaucer, Lydgate, Boccaccio, and the mythography of Pseudo-Albricus has been claimed. The relationship of the *Testament* to the somewhat similar story in the *Spektakle of Luf* (1492) is unclear. The poem reveals a detailed knowledge of medicine (in the account of Cresseid's leprosy), law, and meteorology. Henryson brilliantly adapts a number of literary topoi to his own purposes, including a seasonal opening, citation of a famous source, trial scene, complaint, and testament.

In part because its tone and structure are so deliberately different the *Testament* is the worthiest successor to *Troilus and Criseyde*. Henryson not only understands but is also able to reproduce such diverse Chaucerian achievements as consistent but developing characterization, a believable pagan setting, deliberately obtuse narration, and rime royal (in contrast to the metrical ineptness of the English Chaucerians). Henryson is also virtually alone with Chaucer in his sympathy for Cresseid. Although some modern critics judge the *Testament* to be pessimistic or unforgiving, Henryson's Cresseid, for all her physical suffering, grows throughout the poem until, though still a pagan, she fully accepts responsibility for her own actions. Because the *Testament* was printed as the conclusion to *Troilus* beginning with Thynne's 1532 edition of Chaucer, most English Renaissance portraits of Cresseid (including Shakespeare's) depend as much on Henryson as on Chaucer.

Henryson's most complex work is the *Fables*, which consists of a prologue and thirteen beast fables, each with a narrative followed by a *moralitas*, for a total of 2,975 lines, mostly in rime royal stanzas. Beast fables in the Middle Ages were not only elementary school texts but also an important literary genre. The source for Henryson's prologue and seven of the fables is the popular 12th-century Latin *Romulus* collection now attributed to Walter the Englishman. Henryson also drew on Chaucer's *Nun's Priest's Tale* for "The Cock and the Fox" and, directly or indirectly, on Petrus Alfonsi for "The Fox, the Wolf, and the Husbandman." For some of the other tales he may have used other Latin fable collections, some version of the *Roman de Renart*, Lydgate's fables, Caxton's *Reynard* and *Aesop,* and the French Isopets, though specific borrowings are much debated.

Older critics saw the *Fables* as examples of social realism or rustic humor, but, without denying the political seriousness of these works or their insight into Scottish life, critics have increasingly appreciated their strictly literary achievement in recent years. The order of the fables seems carefully designed, and the wit of "The Cock and the Fox" at moments surpasses even its Chaucerian model. The prologue is a sophisticated discussion of the complex relationship between story and lesson, which is then demonstrated in the fables themselves. Henryson's moralities are not dull or dutiful but have an intricate, often ironic, connection with the preceding narratives and constantly challenge the reader. The pessimism with which the natural world is portrayed in the fables is less a questioning of divine justice than a passionate statement of our need for God's mercy. Henryson the man remains a mysterious figure, but his poetry, which is still too often treated as primarily regional, is the most substantial work in English verse between Chaucer and Spenser.

See also **Boccaccio, Giovanni; Chaucer, Geoffrey; Douglas, Gavin; Dunbar, William; Lydgate, John**

Further Reading

Primary Sources
Bawcutt, P., and Felicity Riddy, eds. *Selected Poems of Henryson and Dunbar.* Edinburgh: Scottish Academic Press, 1992.

Fox, Denton, ed. *The Poems of Robert Henryson.* Oxford: Clarendon, 1981.

Secondary Sources
New *CBEL* 1:658–60.

Manual 4:965–88, 1137–80.

Gray, Douglas. *Robert Henryson.* Leiden: Brill, 1979.

Gros Louis, Kenneth R.R. "Robert Henryson's *Orpheus and Eurydice* and the Orpheus Traditions of the Middle Ages." *Speculum* 41 (1966): 643–55.

Jamieson, I.W.A. "The Minor Poems of Robert Henryson." *Studies in Scottish Literature* 9 (1971): 125–47.

Kindrick, Robert. *Robert Henryson.* Boston: Twayne, 1979.

Scheps, Walter, and J. Anna Looney. *Middle Scots Poets: A Reference Guide.* Boston: Hall, 1986, pp. 53–117.

Spearing, A.C. "The *Testament of Cresseid and* the 'High Concise Style.'" *Speculum* 37 (1962): 208–25. Repr. in *Criticism and Medieval Poetry,.* 2d ed. New York: Barnes & Noble, 1972, pp. 157–92.

Yeager, R.F., ed. *Fifteenth-Century Studies: Recent Essays.* Hamden: Archon, 1984, pp. 65–92, 215–35, 275–81 [bibliographic and interpretive essays on Henryson].

C. DAVID BENSON

HERMANN VON FRITZLAR
(ca. 1275–ca. 1350)

Hermann von Fritzlar is known as a hagiologist (chronicler of saints), who wrote the first prose legendary in German, the *Heiligenleben* (Lives of the Saints), in 1443/1449. He is also the author of mystical sermons, tractates, and similar pieces, which he composed before the *Heiligenleben* and partially integrated into the legendary.

The *Heiligenleben* also includes the *Bartholomäus* sermon by Eckhart Rube from the anonymous Dominican collection of sermons *Paradisus anime intelligentis* (in two manuscripts from Erfurt) with the saint's life added at the end. From the *Postille* of the Dominican Heinrich von Erfurt (in six manuscripts) the legendary incorporated ten sermons from the Christmas cycle. Two other sermons were borrowed: from Gerhard von Sterngassen, a Dominican, *Antonius*; and from Hermann von Schildesche, an Augustinian, the *Heiligkreuzauffindung* (Finding the Holy Cross). Besides these thirteen sermons by master preachers, which all fit into the church calendar of the *Heiligenleben*, starting with Advent, the remaining seventy-five feast days are devoted to saints' legends, which Hermann von Fritzlar composed using collections such as the *Legenda aurea*, the *Passional*, the *Väterbuch*, and the *Märtyrerbuch* as sources.

In the prologue to the *Heiligenleben*, Hermann von Fritzlar writes an exemplum about a secret "friend of God" (*Gottesfreund*), achieving a *Unto mystica* (mystical union). At the center of his philosophy (and religion) is the belief that "God is born in the soul." He expands on this theme in the *Annunciation of Mary*, noting that he purposely started the legendary in the last week of March, when the *Annunciation of Mary*, was celebrated, as if to be in the right spirit to write this mystical work. In the sermon on the *Annunciation* (*Maria Verkündigung*), he mentions his other work, the tractate *Die Blume der Schauung* (The Blossom of the Vision), which he had published anonymously, and in which he had written more about this topic than on all other central Christian teachings. Three later manuscripts exist of *Die Blume der Schauung*, in Nürnberg, Köln and Gent.

Another treatise on the same topic of *Geburt des Wortes* (*Gottes*) *in der Seele* (The Birth of the Word [of God] in the Soul), as a *Programmschrift* (treatise) of Meister Eckhart and mysticism, exists in two Swabian manuscripts in Augsburg and is integrated into the *Heiligenleben*, in three parts after *Barbara*, *Lucia*, and *Thomas*.

Of the ten manuscripts of the *Heiligenleben*, only the Heidelberg codex is complete. The illustrated Salem codex is in fragments, the *Darmstädter Legendar* is a reworking, and the others are selections of one of three legendary, either very early (manuscripts in Trier and Halberstadt) or later (Berlin, Göttingen, and Dessau). In the *Darmstädter Legendar* of 1420, seventy-one legends are the same as in the *Heiligenleben*, but only thirteen are exact copies. Of the learned sermons, only *Antonius* was retained. The saints' legends were sorted into four thematic groups: male, female (mostly martyrs), and the rest following the church calendar in two groups. The *Heiligenleben* of Hermann von Fritzlar also served as a partial source for new verse legends of the fifteenth century: *Katharina* (manuscript in Bielefeld), *Dorothea* (Brussels, originally from Braunschweig), and the so-called *Alexius K.*

Further Reading

Jefferis, Sibylle. "Die Überlieferung und Rezeption des *Heiligenlebens* Hermanns von Fritzlar, einschließlich des niederdeutschen Alexius." In *Mittelalterliche Literatur im niederdeutschen Raum (Tagung Braunschweig 1996)*, ed. Hans-Joachim Behr. *Jahrbuch der Oswald-von-Wolkenstein-Gesellschaft* 10 (1998): 191–209.

Morvay, Karin and Dagmar Grube. *Bibliographie der deutschen Predigt des Mittelalters: Veröffentlichte Predigten*, ed. Kurt Ruh. Munich: Beck, 1974, pp. 102–110, 119–123, 123–125.

Steer, Georg. "Geistliche Prosa." In *Die deutsche Literatur im späten Mittelalter 1250–1370*, ed. Ingeborg Glier. Munich: Beck, 1987, pt. 2, pp. 306–307.

Wagner, Bettina. "Die Darmstädter Handschrift 1886: Ein deutsches Prosalegendar des späten Mittelalters." *Bibliothek und Wissenschaft* 21. (1987): 1–37.

Werner, Wilfried and Kurt Ruh. "Hermann von Fritzlar." In *Die deutsche Literatur des Mittelalters: Verfasserlexikon*, ed. Kurt Ruh, et al., vol. 3, coll. 1055–1059. Berlin and New York: de Gruyter, 1981.

SIBYLLE JEFFERIS

HERRAD VON HOHENBURG
(fl. late 12th c.)

The abbess Herrad of the Augustinian convent Hohenburg (Landsberg), today, Sainte-Odile, near Strasbourg, whose name appears in documents between 1178 and 1196, is famous for her monumental compilation *Hortus deliciarum* (Garden of Delights). This encyclopedic work of 324 folio pages contains some sixty poems by various medieval Latin poets, such as Hildebert of Lavardin, Petrus Pictor, and Walther of Châtillon, a number of songs with their musical notations, various prose texts excerpted from the Bible, biblical commentaries, historical chronicles, church laws, the liturgy, and scholarly studies. Philosophical and legal statements by Peter Lombard and scientific observations by Isidor of Seville are also extensively copied in the *Hortus*, often accompanied by German glosses.

The manuscript was richly illuminated and is nearly unparalleled in medieval book production. The 153 miniatures, often taking up a whole page, illustrate the meanings of biblical texts, aspects of Christian belief, and the arts. In many respects the *Hortus* served as an encyclopedia, structured by the principles of the divine plan for the salvation of mankind.

Although the original manuscript burned in a fire in the Strasbourg library in 1870, older copies and descriptions provide a good idea of the splendor and learnedness of the *Hortus*. The abbess Herrad initiated and supervised the production of the manuscript, which was to instruct the women in the convent on how to reach paradise through a virtuous life on earth. Many leading twelfth-century scholars, such as Honorius Augustodunensis, Rupert of Deutz, and Peter Comestor, are well represented in the *Hortus*.

Apart from her considerable editorial work, Herrad also contributed to the significant expansion of her convent in political and economic terms.

Further Reading

Bertau, Karl. *Deutsche Literatur im europäischen Mittelalter*, vol. 1. Munich: Beck, 1972, pp. 585–590.

Curschmann, Michael. "Texte — Bilder — Strukturen: Der *hortus deliciarum*, und die frühmittelhoch-deutsche Geistlichendichtung." *Deutsche Vierteljahrsschrift für Literaturwissenschaft und Geistesgeschichte* 55 (1981): 379–418.

Green, Rosalie, et al. *Herrad of Hohenburg, Hortus deliciarum.* 2 vols. London and Leiden: 1979.

Saxl, F. "Illustrated Medieval Encyclopaedias." In Saxl, Fritz. *Lectures*. London: Warburg, 1957, vol. 1, pp. 228–254; vol. 2, figures 169–174.

ALBRECHT CLASSEN

HERRAND VON WILDONIE
(ca. 1230–1278/1282)

A Middle High German author of songs and narratives, Herrand II of Wildonie was descended from an important Styrian family holding the hereditary office of high steward of Styria. The family seat was the now ruined castle of Alt Wildon, near Graz, Austria, on the River Mur. He was born circa 1230 and died about 1278/1282. Herrand was married to Perhta, daughter of Ulrich von Lichtenstein. He was active politically in the Interregnum years, first for Bela of Hungary, then Ottokar of Bohemia, and finally for Rudolf of Habsburg.

His literary oeuvre comprises three extant courtly love songs and four short narratives (*maere*). The songs are contained in the famous Heidelberg manuscript named for the family which commissioned the collection of love songs, or *minnesang* (University Library, no. cpg 848, the "Manesse Codex"). On fol. 201rv, is a miniature of the poet with an incorrect coat of arms. The narratives are also contained in another famous manuscript in Vienna (National Library, no. Ser. Nov. 2663), the *Ambraser Heldenbuch* (Book of heroes from Ambras [Castle]), fol. 217ra–220va.

Herrand's songs are considered largely conventional in nature, but his short narratives show him to be a leading writer in this genre's "post-Stricker" phase. The texts all seem to deal with constancy and loyalty, arranged in contrasting pairs. The first pair, *Die treue Gattin* (The Faithful Wife) and *Der betrogene Gatte* (The Betrayed Husband), present, respectively, a wife moved by such intense love and devotion that she disfigures her face to match her old and injured ugly husband and a young wife who tries to deceive her old husband with a younger lover.

The second pair of stories, *Der nackte Kaiser* (The Naked Emperor) and *Die Katze* (The Cat), deals with, first, the obligation of the ruler to carry out his duties conscientiously—the negligent Emperor Gornäus, cast down in a lowly position and replaced by an angel, must witness the latter's exemplary success until he acknowledges his former errors and be reinstated by his Doppelganger—and, then, the vassal's obligation to remain faithful to his overlord—a dissatisfied tom cat does the rounds among a series of incongruous partners only to return in the end to his cat queen. In a time of great political upheaval, after the deaths of the last Babenberg Duke of Austria (1246) and the last Staufen Emperor (1250), these apparently generalized political admonitions must have been particularly pointed. These four distinct narratives document their author's literary modernity, whereas the content of these narratives points to a conservative stance by the author and a dialectic possibly aimed at the "classless" didacticism of Der Stricker. There is evidence that Herrand's work was known outside Styrian aristocratic circles.

See also **Stricker, Der; Ulrich von Liechtenstein**

Further Reading

Curschmann, Michael. "Herrand von Wildonie (Wildon)." In *Die deutsche Literatur des Mittelalters. Verfasserlexikon*, ed. Kurt Ruh, et al., vol. 3. Berlin and New York: de Gruyter, 1981, cols. 1144–1147.

Deighton, Alan. "Die 'nichtpolitischen' Erzählungen Herrands von Wildonie." In *Kleinere Erzählformen im Mittelalter. Paderborner Colloquium 1987*, ed. Klaus Grubmüller, et al. Paderborn: Schöningh, 1988, pp. 111–120.

Fischer, Hanns. *Herrand von Wildonie. Vier Erzählungen.* Tübingen: Niemeyer, 1959. 2nd ed. 1969 [narratives].

Hofmeister, Wernfried. *Die steierischen Minnesänger. Edition, Übersetzung, Kommentar.* Göppingen: Kümmerle, 1987.

Margetts, John. "Herrand von Wildonie: The Political Intentions of *Der blöze keiser* and *Diu katze.*" In *Court and Poet. Selected Proceedings of the Third Congress of the International Courtly Literature Society* (*Liverpool 1980*), ed. Glyn S. Burgess. Trowbridge: Francis Cairns, 1981, pp. 249–266.

Ottmann, Christa and Hedda Ragotzky. "Zur Funktion exemplarischer *triuwe*-Beweise in Minne-Mären: "Die treue Gattin" Herrands von Wildone, "Das Herzemäre" Konrads von Würzburg und die "Frauentreue." In *Kleinere Erzählformen im Mittelalter. Paderborner Colloquium 1987*, ed. Klaus Grubmüller, et al. Paderborn: Schöningh, 1988, pp. 89–109.

Thomas, J. W., trans. *The Tales and Songs of Herrand von Wildonie.* Kentucky: University Press of Kentucky, 1972.

von Kraus, Carl. *Deutsche Liederdichter des 13. Jahrhunderts,* Vol. 1. *Text.* Tübingen: Niemeyer, 1952, pp. 588–589 [songs]. Vol. 2. *Kommentar* ed. Hugo Kuhn. 1958, pp. 635–638 [commentary].

JOHN MARGETTS

HILD (ca. 614–680)

Hild (or Hilda) lived a dual life: 33 years as a princess, then 33 years as an abbess and teacher. Bede's *Ecclesiastical History* tells most of what we know about her. She was born ca. 614, posthumously and in exile, to Princess Breguswith and Hereric, a nephew of King Edwin (616–33). As a child she shared exile in East Anglia at the court of King Rædwald with her great-uncle Edwin. After Edwin regained his kingdom in 617, Hild returned with him to Northumbria. She may have observed his famous council in 627, after which she received baptism with him and 12,000 of his subjects on 12 April after religious instruction from Bishop Paulinus (*Ecclesiastical History* 2.13–14). When Edwin died in 633, Hild returned to exile in East Anglia with her mother, Breguswith, and her sister, Hereswith, who later married King Æthelhere there. In 647 Hild, probably a widow, became a nun and the following year founded the nunnery at Wear. In 649 she became abbess of Hartlepool and in 657 abbess of the double monastery at Whitby (OE *Streones-healch*).

In 664 she hosted the Synod of Whitby, where King Oswiu of Northumbria decided that the English church would follow Roman practice rather than Irish (*Ecclesiastical History* 3.25). Her side lost, and she observed Roman rules thereafter. During her reign at Whitby she promoted the training of missionaries and scholars. Five of her students became bishops: Ætla, of Dorchester; Bosa, of Deira and York; John, of Hexham and York; Oftfor, of Worcester; and Wilfrid II, of York. Hearing Cædmon sing his inspired Hymn, she recruited him into religious life and sponsored his career as a composer of religious verse, probably used for conversion and strengthening faith (*Ecclesiastical History* 4.24).

Hild suffered a long illness beginning in 674, dying on 17 November 680. One of the nuns of her monastery, Ælfflæd, King Oswiu's daughter, succeeded her as abbess, ruling with her mother, Eanfæd. Several nuns saw visions of Hild's death and ascent into heaven (*Ecclesiastical History* 4.23). Her remains were translated to Glastonbury in the 10th century.

See also **Bede the Venerable; Cædmon**

Further Reading

Colgrave, Bertram, and R.A.B. Mynors, eds. and trans. *Bede's Ecclesiastical History of the English People.* Oxford: Clarendon, 1969, pp. 404–21 and passim.

Cross, J.E. "A Lost Life of Hilda of Whitby: The Evidence of the Old English Martyrology." *Acta* 5 (1979): 21–43.

Fell, Christine E. "Hild, Abbess of Streoneshalch." In *Hagiography and Medieval Literature: A Symposium,* ed. Hans Bekker-Nielsen et al. Odense: Odense University Press, 1981, pp. 76–99.

Hession, Ætheldreda. "St Hilda and St Etheldreda." In *Benedict's Disciples,* ed. D.H. Farmer. Leominster: Fowler Wright, 1980, pp. 70–85.

DONALD K. FRY

HILDEGARD VON BINGEN (1098–1179)

Benedictine, visionary, author, composer, and Germany's first female physician, Hildegard was the tenth child of Hildebert and Mechthild von Bermersheim. She was raised by the recluse Jutta von Spanheim at the Benedictine monastery of Disibodenberg (near Bingen) and made her monastic profession between 1112–1115. In 1136 she was elected *magistra* (mistress) of the Disibodenberg women's community which had by then become quite large.

While aware of a "shadow of the living light" (*umbra viventis lucis*) from childhood on, Hildegard had her first clear vision in 1141 at the age of 43. She understood her insights as divine revelations concerning the meaning of Scripture and obeyed the command to write. The Cistercian Pope Eugene III officially recognized her visionary gift at the Trier Synod in 1147/1148.

That same year, Hildegard founded her own Benedictine women's monastery, St. Rupertsberg (opposite Bingen), whose abbess she became, and in 1165, a second monastery in Eibingen (today, the Abbey St. Hildegard).

Between 1160–1170, Hildegard undertook four public preaching tours to German cities and monasteries, as far away as Bamberg and Swabia. Known as the *prophetissa teutonica* (German, female prophet), she was consulted by and corresponded with popes, kings, including Frederick I Barbarossa, abbots and abbesses, and many other renowned contemporaries, among them, Bernard of Clairvaux. In composing her complex visionary, exegetical, speculative, and scientific works,

Saint Hildegard of Bingen (1098–1179) and the Four Seasons. From "De Operatione Dei." Rupertsburg, Germany, 1200 CE. Codex Latiunm 1942. f.38r. © Scala/Art Resource, New York.

Hildegard was at first assisted by her former teacher, the monk Volmar of Disibodenberg, and from 1177 on, by Guibert of Gembloux, who is also the author of a partial *vita* of the Benedictine nun. Her complete *vita* was written by the monks Gottfried and Theoderich between 1177–1181. Listed in the *Martyrologium romanum* (list of martyrs) since the fifteenth century, Hildegard is venerated as a saint in Germany.

Hildegard von Bingen's most famous work *Scivias* (Know the Ways) (1141–1151) constitutes the first part of her trilogy of visions whose second and third parts are the *Liber vitae meritorum* (Book of Meritorious Life) (1158–1163) and the *Liber divinorum operum* (Book of Divine Works), the latter also entitled *Liber de operatione del* (Book of the Works of God, [1163–1173]). In these works she speaks both of what she was given to see and of a divine voice interpreting these visions to her. Hildegard also conducted comprehensive studies of natural science and medicine, which she described in *Physica* (*Subtilitatum diversarum naturarum creaturarum libri novem*). Nine books on the nature of various creatures and *Causae et curae* (Afflictions and cures, between 1150–1160). Several hundred letters of her correspondence have been preserved as well as many musical compositions including some seventy-seven liturgical songs, and a drama, the *Ordo virtutum* (The

Order of Virtue). Hildegard also wrote two *vitae*, a treatise against the contemporary Cathars, and a linguistic essay on a *lingua ignota* (unknown language).

Hildegard's visionary and prophetic work deals with complex theological, anthropological, and ecclesiological issues. Her idea of the church and society was a strictly hierarchical one. Anchored in the Benedictine liturgical tradition, and the Bible, Hildegard was familiar with the church fathers as well as with the writings of her contemporaries, Honorius Augustodunensis, Rupert von Deutz, and Bernard of Clairvaux.

Hildegard von Bingen was well known in her own century. Manuscripts of her works, especially some containing resplendent illuminations made under her own supervision, stem from the twelfth century. Thereafter, forgotten for centuries, her work was finally published in the extensive series of medieval Latin works, *Patrologia latina* (Vol. 197, 1855) and by Joannes Baptista Pitra (*Analecta*, Vol. 8, 1882). The twentieth century gave rise to a revival of Hildegard's work through studies and translations initiated by the Benedictine nuns of Eibingen, notably by the meticulous manuscript study of Marianne Schrader and Adelgundis Führkötter: *Die Echtheit des Schrifttums der heiligen Hildegard von Bingen. Quellenkritische Untersuchungen*, 1956 (On the Authenticity of the Writing of St. Hildegard von Bingen: Source Studies). Extended concentrated research in Hildegard von Bingen's voluminous work began in Germany around 1979 in the context of the 800-year celebration of her death. Since then, she has become probably the most studied and the best known of all medieval women writers, not only among literary and feminist scholars, but also among theologians, historians, and musicologists. Unfortunately, her literary and musical works have sometimes been popularized and misinterpreted beyond recognition.

See also **Bernard of Clairvaux; Frederick I Barbarossa**

Further Reading

Hildegard of Bingen. *The Book of the Rewards of Life—Liber vitae meritorum*, trans. Bruce W. Hozeski. New York: Garland, 1994.

Hildegard of Bingen. *Scivias*, trans. Mother Columba Hart and Jane Bishop. New York: Paulist Press, 1990.

Klaes, Monica. *Vita Sanctae Hildegardis*. CCCM 126. Turnhout: Brepols, 1993 [Latin "Life"].

Lewis, Gertrud Jaron. *Bibliographie zur deutschen Frauenmystik des Mittelalters*. Berlin: Erich Schmidt Verlag, 1989 [primary texts, pp. 70–84; secondary sources, pp. 66–70 and 84–145].

Newman, Barbara. *From Virile Woman to Woman Christ: Studies in Medieval Religion and Literature*. Philadelphia: University of Pennsylvania Press, 1995.

van Acker, L. *Hildegardis Bingensis Epistolarium*. 2 vols. Turnhout: Brepols, 1991–1993 [Latin letters].

GERTRUD JARON LEWIS

HILTON, WALTER (d. 1396)

Mystical writer; a hermit probably until the mid-1380s, then an Augustinian canon at Thurgarton in Nottinghamshire. Probably to be identified with the bachelor of civil law recorded in Lincoln and Ely in the early 1370s; *inceptor* in canon law in the early 1380s. If he was an M.A. before proceeding to the study of law (which is not necessary), he would have been born in the early 1340s.

The chronology of Hilton's works is uncertain. Clark and Taylor have suggested that the Latin tract *De imagine peccati* was Hilton's earliest extant work, written soon after 1381–82. The letter *De utilitate et prerogativis religionis* (or *Epistola aurea*), written to encourage Adam Horsley in his decision to lay down civil office and enter the Carthusian order, was probably written shortly before 1387. The idea of the perversion of the human soul from an image of the divine Trinity into an image of sin is important particularly in the first of these pieces and in the first book of Hilton's most important work, the English *Scale of Perfection*; there are also similarities between *Scale* I and the *De utilitate* and his English letter *On the Mixed Life* that suggest that all four of these works were written in the mid-1380s. Hilton probably wrote his *De adoracione imaginum*, an anti-Wycliffite defense of the use of images (painting, sculpture, etc.) in worship, in the late 1380s.

The dating of Hilton's other writings is even less certain. These works include the English translations of *Eight Chapters on Perfection* by Lluis de Font, an Aragonese Franciscan contemporary of Hilton's at Cambridge, and the Pseudo-Bonaventuran *Stimulus amoris (The Pricking of Love* or *Goad of Love); com*mentaries on the texts "Qui Habitat" (Ps. 90:1) and "BonumEst" (Ps. 91:1); and *On Angels' Song*, a work on the dangers of seeking physical expression of mystical experience. The attribution to Hilton of a further English commentary on the "Benedictus" is unsure. Three other Latin treatises survive: the *Epistola de leccione, intencione, oracione, meditacione et aliis*, the *Epistola ad quemdam seculo renunciare volentem*, and *Quantum ad futura* (also known as "Firmissima crede"). Finally we should note that the second book of Hilton's *Scale of Perfection* probably marks the culmination of his thought and experience.

Because the two books of *The Scale of Perfection* were written as many as ten years apart, their relationship to each other has been a major focus of the discussion of Hilton's works. Prospective editors of the *Scale* have noted the presence of a long expository passage on the devotion to the name of Jesus (and two other similar passages) apparently added to the text of *Scale* I after it was already in circulation, as well as a number of smaller additions and rewordings, many of which appear to focus on devotion to the person of Christ, rather than the Trinity or the Godhead itself. All of these christocentric additions and alterations were added in the margins and on inserted scraps of paper in BL Harley 6579, on which all modern editions of the *Scale* to date have been based. Despite this widespread editorial practice the current consensus of scholars and textual critics is that the "Holy Name" passage and the passages similar to it were probably added by Hilton himself, whereas the "christocentric" additions were made by later scribes. The forthcoming EETS edition of the *Scale* will therefore base *Scale* I on a manuscript whose text predates both the "Holy Name" and the "christocentric" additions, as well as the writing of *Scale* II. The importance of this textual decision is that it renders invalid a good deal of earlier discussion of the "christocentricity" of Hilton's mysticism.

Probably the most important idea in Hilton's works is that of the human soul as an image of the divine Trinity, perverted into an image of sin: an idea that originates in Augustine's *De Trinitate* and is expanded upon by the Victorines and the early Franciscan writers. According to this trinitarian psychology the soul comprises the faculties of Memory (or Mind, as it was usually translated into ME), corresponding to the Father; Understanding (or Reason), corresponding to the Son; and Will, corresponding to the Holy Spirit. Through original sin, however, the soul has been perverted into the image of the seven deadly sins. Because the recently enclosed anchoress for whom Hilton wrote *Scale* I could not read and meditate on the Latin text of scripture, Hilton proposes for her an exercise of introspection aimed at discovering and extirpating each of these sins in herself.

Hilton's contemplative exercises for his anchoress correspondent go significantly beyond the meditation on the Passion of Christ that was normally enjoined upon women at that time, though he does briefly discuss such Passion meditations, immediately before proposing his more introspective exercises. This same concern with providing alternative modes of contemplation for nonmonastic or nonclerical audiences also informs his letter *On the Mixed Life*, whose opening sections echo those *of Scale* I. In this innovative treatise Hilton proposes a life of both action and contemplation to a man whose worldly activities and responsibilities do not allow him to retire from the world as a monk or hermit but who feels the same stirrings of devotion that they do.

In *Scale* II Hilton covers much of the same ground as in *Scale* I, with greater psychological and theological precision. Clark has suggested that at one point, at least, his intention was to express more carefully an idea for which he had been criticized (anonymously) in *The Cloud of Unknowing*. *Scale* II describes particularly the progress from "reformation in faith" to "reformation in faith and feeling" (i.e., the point where one actually feels as true what one had previously known only by faith), culminating with the allegory of the journey to the heavenly Jerusalem and a discussion of contemplative prayer and the special gifts of God.

Hilton's works were influential in the century immediately preceding the Reformation, surviving in numerous manuscripts, transmitted in Latin to continental Europe, and printed several times at the end of the 15th century and the beginning of the 16th.

See alo **Rolle, Richard, of Hampole**

Further Reading

Primary Sources

There is no critical edition of *The Scale of Perfection,* but an EETS edition is in preparation.

Clark, John P.H., and Rosemary Dorward, trans. *The Scale of Perfection.* New York: Paulist Press, 1991.

Clark, J.P.H., and Cheryl Taylor, eds. *Walter Hilton's Latin Writings.* Salzburg: Institut fur Anglistik und Amerikanistik, 1987.

Jones, Dorothy, ed. *Minor Works of Walter Hilton,* London: Burns, Oates, & Washbourne, 1929 [modernized text].

Kane, Harold, ed. *The Prickynge of Love.* Salzburg: Institut für Anglistik und Amerikanistik, 1983.

Ogilvie-Thomson, S.J., ed. *Walter Hilton's Mixed Life.* Salzburg: Institut für Anglistik und Amerikanistik, 1986.

Wallner, Björn, ed. *An Exposition Of "Qui Habitat" and "Bonum Est" in English.* Lund: Gleerup, 1954.

Secondary Sources

Manual 9:3074–82, 3430–38.

Clark, J.P.H. "Walter Hilton in Defense of the Religious Life and of the Veneration of Images." *DownR* 102 (1985): 1–25 [the latest in an important series of studies of Hilton's works].

Milosh, Joseph E. *The Scale of Perfection and the English Mystical Tradition.* Madison: University of Wisconsin Press, 1966.

Minnis, Alastair. "The *Cloud of Unknowing* and Walter Hilton's *Scale of Perfection.*" In *Middle English Prose*: *A Critical Guide to Major Authors and Genres, ed.* A.S.G. Edwards. New Brunswick: Rutgers University Press, 1984, pp. 61–81.

Sargent, Michael G. "Walter Hilton's *Scale of Perfection:* The London Manuscript Group Reconsidered." *MÆ* 52 (1983): 189–216.

MICHAEL G. SARGENT

HOCCLEVE, THOMAS (ca. 1366–1426)

Poet, scribe, and minor bureaucrat; author of *The Letter of Cupid* (1402), *La Male Regle* (1405–06), *The Regement of Princes* (1411), a compilation in verse and prose now known as the *Series* (including the *Complaint,* the *Dialogue with a Friend,* and *Learn to Die;* 1419–21), and many shorter religious and political poems.

Hoccleve's biography looms large in any account of him as a poet, since his supposedly autobiographical passages constitute the main attraction for modern readers, treating as they do Hoccleve's poverty and mental breakdown in an often subtly comic or moving manner. At the same time caution must be exercised in accepting these passages as historical. What is certain is that from 1387 Hoccleve was a clerk at the office of the privy seal in London, where he remained for the rest of his working life. The last payment to him is made in 1426, where he is described as "lately" a clerk of the privy seal. In his *Complaint* he describes the result of a mental breakdown he had five years earlier; his payment for 1416 was paid to him through friends. Most of his poetry is addressed to powerful patrons, often in the explicit hope of reward.

The Letter of Cupid, a translation of Christine de Pizan's *Epistre au dieu d'amours,* praises the virtues of women. It survives in ten manuscripts, two of which are autographs (Durham University Cosin V.ii.13 and Huntington HM 744). *La Male Regle,* written in the form of a confession for a misspent youth, is really a well-shaped begging poem; it is found in Huntington HM 111, another autograph, which contains many other short occasional and religious pieces by Hoccleve. Hoccleve's largest work, *The Regement of Princes,* is in the "mirror for princes" genre and is largely indebted to Latin works in the genre; 45 manuscripts contain the text, of which BL Arundel 38 and Harley 4866 are the most authoritative. The complete *Series* appears in five manuscripts, of which Durham University Cosin V.iii.9 is an autograph, except for the *Complaint.*

Hoccleve claims Chaucer as his master and friend (e.g., *Regement* 2077–2107, 4982–98). From Chaucer Hoccleve certainly learns much, in particular, perhaps, the presentation of the author's own persona in his work as a self-deprecating and naive character. But in Hoccleve's case this topos dominates the poetry (see especially *La Male Regle,* the Prologue to the *Regement,* and the *Series*), and discussion of it has dominated recent critical studies. Some critics take Hoccleve's self-presentation as purely conventional, whereas others have tried to define the ways in which Hoccleve draws on conventional topoi to negotiate his way out of the crises of poverty and mental instability.

See also **Chaucer, Geoffrey; Christine de Pizan**

Further Reading

Primary Sources

Furnivall, Frederick J., ed. *Hoccleve's Regement of Princes and Fourteen Minor Poems.* EETS e.s. 72. London: Humphrey Milford, 1897.

Furnivall, Frederick J., and Israel Gollancz, eds. *Hoccleve's Works*: *The Minor Poems.* Rev. Jerome Mitchell and A.I. Doyle. 2 vols. in 1. EETS e.s. 61, 73. London: Oxford University Press, 1970.

Secondary Sources

New *CBEL* 1:646–47.

Manual 3:746–56, 903-08.

Burrow, J.A. "Hoccleve's *Series*: Experience and Books." In *Fifteenth-Century Studies*: *Recent Essays*, ed. R.F. Yeager. Hamden: Archon, 1984, pp. 259–73.

Burrow, J.A. *Thomas Hoccleve*. Aldershot: Variorum, 1994.

Greetham, D.C. "Self-Referential Artifacts: Hoccleve's Persona As a Literary Device." *MP* 86 (1989): 242–51.

Mitchell, Jerome. "Hoccleve Studies, 1965–81." In *Fifteenth-Century Studies*: *Recent Essays*, ed. R.F. Yeager. Hamden: Archon, 1984, pp. 49–63.

JAMES SIMPSON

HRABANUS MAURUS
(ca. 780–February 4, 856)

The name Hrabanus derives from the Old High German word for "raven"; Maurus is a nickname he acquired later, perhaps from his teacher Alcuin, and it pays tribute to his dutiful piety as a disciple: Saint Maurus was Saint Benedict's favorite pupil. For his encyclopedic learning and the energy he manifested in administration and teaching, Hrabanus Maurus was dubbed in early modern times *praeceptor Germaniae* (the teacher of Germany).

Born at Mainz around 780 of noble Frankish parents, Hrabanus was given as a child to the monastery of Fulda. There, he was ordained deacon (801) before being sent for further education under Alcuin at Tours. He returned to Fulda, first as head of the cloister school and later as abbot (822–842). Upon resigning as abbot, he went into seclusion near Fulda at Petersberg. Later, he was named archbishop of Mainz (847), an office he held until his death on February 4, 856.

Hrabanus made a major contribution in educating young men, such as Otfrid von Weißenburg, Lupus of Ferrières, and Walahfrid Strabo, who became the foremost churchmen, scholars, and poets of the next generation. Unfortunately, he is also remembered for one major failure in mentoring: he first forced Gottschalk of Orbais, a monk at Fulda, to take the tonsure against his will and later persecuted him, with severe beatings and imprisonment, for his beliefs on predestination.

Many of Hrabanus' numerous writings are derivative compilations. He sought to make available the scholarship of earlier eras by taking extracts from original works and knitting them together into a coherent whole, so that students and churchmen who did not have extensive libraries at their disposal could find in his works the essentials they needed for building their faith and extending their intellectual training.

De institutione clericorum (On the education of the clergy) is typical of Hrabanus' oeuvre in being replete with excerpted material. The first book sets forth the various ecclesiastical grades, liturgical vestments, and instruction to be given to catechumens; the second deals with liturgy; and the third focuses on liberal education, especially with the goal of training preachers.

Hrabanus wrote biblical commentaries on the historical books of the Old Testament (Pentateuch), some prophets (Jeremiah and Ezekiel), one of the Gospels (Matthew), and the epistles of Paul. In his exegeses, Hrabanus consistently excerpts patristic writers, such as Isidore's and Bede, and supplies little of his own writing apart from allegorical and mystical interpretations.

Hrabanus's erudition and writing ability perhaps culminated in his encyclopedic *De rerum naturis* (later called *De universo*), in which he relies on Isidore's *Etymologies* as both source and inspiration. As in his exegeses, Hrabanus distinguishes himself from his predecessor by supplying allegorical explications.

Among his poems, the most successful was the *De laudibus sanctae crucis*, the first book of which contains a collection of twenty-eight *carmina figurata* (pattern or figure poems) that are arranged to form intricate designs. The second book offers a prose paraphrase.

Most of his other poems are conventional compositions in distichs and hexameters, but he also wrote rhythmic poetry and hymns.

Hrabanus, although not original, was an erudite and prolific scholar, whose efforts in extracting and synthesizing the writings of earlier interpreters served well the needs of his contemporaries and successors.

See also **Charlemagne; Otfrid, Walafrid Strabo**

Further Reading

Brunhölzl, Franz. *Histoire de la littérature latine du moyen âge*, vol. 1 "De Cassiodore à la fin de la renaissance carolingienne"; vol. 2 "L'époque carolingienne," trans. Henri Rochais, with bibliographic supplements by Jean-Paul Bouhot. Turnhout: Brepols, 1991, pp. 84–98, 282–286.

Dümmler, Ernst, ed. *Hrabani Mauri carmina*. In: *Monumenta Germaniae Historica Poetae Latini Aevi Carolini* 2. Berlin: Weidmann, 1884, pp. 154–258.

Knöpfler, Alois, ed. *Rabani Mauri de institutione clericorum libri tres*. Veröffentlichungen aus dem Kirchenhistorischen Seminar München. Munich: Verlag der J. J. Lentner'schen Buchhandlung, 1900.

Kottje, Raymund. "Hrabanus Maurus." In *Die deutsche Literatur des Mittelalters*: *Verfasserlexikon*, ed. Kurt Ruh, et al. 2nd ed. Berlin and New York: de Gruyter, 1988, vol. 4, cols. 166–196.

Migne, J.-P., ed. *Patrologiae cursus completus*; *series latina*, 221 vols. Paris: J.-P. Migne, 1844–1864, vols. 107–112.

JAN M. ZIOLKOWSKI

HROSVIT OF GANDERSHEIM (10th c.)

Born in the fourth decade of the tenth century, Hrosvit lived and wrote in the Gandersheim Abbey in Saxony, during the abbey's "Golden Age" under Gerberga II's rule. Her name, "Strong Voice (or Testimony)," expresses her poetic mission; the glorification of Christian heroes, both secular and religious. The subject of her poems are the Ottonians and the whole Liudolf dynasty as well as the saints and martyrs of the Christian church. Writing in Latin, mostly in leonine hexameters and rhymed, rhythmic prose, Hrosvit chose hagiographic plots for her legends and plays and contemporary and near-contemporary events for her secular epics.

Her works are arranged in three books, organized generically and chronologically, and delineated as such by prefatory and dedicatory materials. Book One contains eight legends (*Marian, Ascencio, Gongolf, Pelagius, Basilius, Theolphilus, Dionysius, and Agnes*); all but *Pelagius*, which she claims to have composed based on an eyewitness report, are based on biblical, apocryphal, and hagiographic texts.

Book Two, Hrosvit's best-known and most controversial work, contains six dramas, based, she claimed, on the comedies of Terence. For his alluring, but morally perilous, mimetic powers, she said she wished to substitute the glorious and morally beneficial ideals of militantly chaste Christianity. She chose the dramatic form, she argued, because the sweetness of Terence's style attracted many readers who, in turn, became corrupted by the wickedness of his subject matter. Of her six plays, two (*Dulcitius* and Sapientia) deal with the martyrdom of three allegorical virgins during the persecution of Christians under Diocletian and Hadrian; two concern the salvation of repentant harlots (*Abraham* and *Paphnutius*); and two (*Gallicanus* and *Calimachus*) are conversion plays.

Her two extant epics in Book 3, narrate the rise of the Ottonian dynasty (*Gesta Ottonis*, or Deeds of the Ottonians) and the foundation of the Gandersheim Abbey (*Primordia*). Throughout all her works, Hrosvit extols the ideals of monastic Christianity and exhorts her audience and readers to imitate and emulate her saintly models.

Further Reading

Wilson, Katharina, trans, and ed. *Hrotsvit of Gandersheim: a florilegium of her works.* Woodbridge (Suffolk) and Rochester, N.Y.: Brewer, 1998.

——. trans. *The plays of Hrotsvit of Gandersheim.* New York: Garland, 1989.

KATHARINA M. WILSON

HUGH CAPET (ca. 940–996)

The son of Hugues le Grand, duke of Francia, Hugh Capet is traditionally considered the founder of the third dynasty of French kings, the Capetians, who ruled, through collateral lines, up to and after the French Revolution. Hugh became duke of Francia and Aquitaine in 961, five years after his father's death. Like his ancestors, the Robertians, Hugh had landholdings and an influence over the Neustrian aristocracy that effectively made him more powerful than the king, Lothair I (r. 954–86). From ca. 980 on, the two were in constant conflict. With the deaths of Lothair (986) and Louis V (987), Hugh rose to the throne (June–July 987) and had his son Robert crowned soon after in Orléans (December 987).

Once king, however, Hugh proved as weak as he had been strong as duke: the last Carolingian claimant, Charles of Lorraine, rebelled against him, and only the treachery of Bishop Adalbero of Laon resolved the conflict (991). The treachery of Arnulf, archbishop of Reims, and the papal deposition of his replacement, Gerbert of Aurillac, set in motion a conflict that marred the remainder of Hugh's reign. Although it had started before he took the throne, the castellan revolution reached a peak in many regions of the kingdom at this point, and the impotence of both royal power and local Carolingian political structures (the *pagus*) drove some areas of his kingdom to seek their own solutions to disorder and violence. Among the most famous and consequential of these efforts was the Peace of God. In October 996, Hugh died on campaign near Tours.

Unable to assert the kind of royal authority at least theoretically available to Carolingians, Hugh sought legitimacy in an alliance with the church, both the episcopacy and the reforming monastic movement, and with some of his most powerful neighbors, such as William V of Aquitaine and Richard II of Normandy, who gave support in exchange for still greater levels of autonomy. As a result, the monarchy underwent a shift in the basis of its authority, from the essentially aristocratic Carolingian model to one more dependent on ecclesiastical legitimation and popular support.

See also **Lothair I**

Further Reading

Lemarignier, Jean-François. *Le gouvernement royal aux premiers temps capétiens (987–1108).* Paris: Picard, 1964.

Lewis, Andrew. *Royal Succession in Capetian France: Studies on Familial Order and the State.* Cambridge: Harvard University Press, 1981.

Lot, Ferdinand. *Études sur le règne d'Hugues Capet.* Paris: Bouillon, 1903.

Sassier, Yves. *Hugues Capet.* Paris: Fayard, 1987.

Theis, Laurent. *L'avènement d'Hugues Capet.* Paris: Gallimard, 1984.

RICHARD LANDES

HUGH OF SAINT-VICTOR (d. 1141)

A leading theologian, biblical interpreter, and mystic of the first half of the 12th century, Hugh was the effective founder of the important school of the abbey of Saint-

Victor at Paris. Hugh's place of birth is uncertain—evidence supports both Saxony and the Low Countries, with birth in one and early life in the other area a possibility. He came to the new community of regular canons at Saint-Victor, probably in the early 1120s; by 1125, he was writing and teaching and beginning to gain a wide following among students and peers. Hugh was instrumental in asserting the fundamental need to understand the literal, historical sense of the biblical text before undertaking allegorical and moral interpretation. Indeed, his whole exegetical and theological project was founded on the premise that one must understand history, the unfolding of events in time, as the fundamental category for God's revelation in the history of the Jewish and Christian peoples. Hugh sought contemporary Jewish interpretations for understanding the literal sense of the Hebrew Scriptures, and he inspired others, especially Andrew of Saint-Victor and Herbert of Bosham, to pursue more thoroughly the understanding of Scripture through knowledge of the Hebrew language and consultation with Jewish rabbis. In theology, Hugh composed the first *summa* of theology in the Parisian schools, *De sacramentis christianae fidei*, thus paving the way for the long series of *summae* that would characterize much of medieval scholastic theology. His mystical writings, especially the two treatises on the symbolic meaning of Isaiah's vision of the seraphim and the structure of Noah's Ark (*De arca Noe morali* and *De arca Noe mystica*) are some of the first attempts to systematize in treatises teaching on the ascetic-contemplative life. *De arca Noe mystica* describes a complex drawing (meant to be used as a focus for meditation) that presented a visualization of the cosmos, the unfolding of the history of salvation, and the stages of the interior spiritual journey of the individual to contemplative ecstasy. His commentary on the *Celestial Hierarchy* of Pseudo-Dionysius the Areopagite (*In hierarchiam coelestem*) was a major moment in bringing the thought of Pseudo-Dionysius into the mainstream of western theology and mysticism. Hugh based his work upon the 9th-century translation and commentary by "Johannes Scottus Eriugena, but the interpretation was stamped with his own distinctive understanding of Dionysius's thought, an understanding deeply influenced by Hugh's Augustinian theology and his own view of the function of symbols in the mediation of divine truth to human beings living in a material world. Hugh's encyclopedic learning is reflected in his *Didascalicon: de studio legendi*, that provides a guide for the student of philosophy (Books 1–3) and the Bible (Books 4–6). In this work, Hugh presents the liberal arts as the remedy for the loss of knowledge and goodness in the Fall, while the mechanical arts (e.g., weaving) provide for the resulting weakness of the human body. The section on reading Scripture outlines Hugh's understanding of a sequence of disciplines of study (history, allegory, and tropology), and gives for each discipline the proper order in which to read the biblical books appropriate for that approach to the interpretation of the text. For the student pursuing the discipline of history, Hugh compiled a *Chronicon* with numerous chronological tables and historical aids; for the student of allegory, his theological masterwork, *De sacramentis christianae fidei*, was intended to serve as an introduction. *De scripturis et scriptoribus sacris*, the preface to Hugh's collection of literal comments on the Pentateuch and other Old Testament books (these comments are printed as *Notulae* in Migne), is modeled on the form of the *accessus ad auctores* then being used by the arts faculty to introduce classical authors and by biblical interpreters to introduce their commentaries. The introduction to Hugh's *Chronicon* contains a treatise on the "art of memory," an important contribution to the memory tradition. Hugh's other works include an unfinished series of sermons on Ecclesiastes; short pieces, extracts, and fragments collected into several books of *miscellania*; short contemplative and theological treatises; several letters; and numerous sermons scattered throughout medieval collections and only recently fully identified.

See also **Andrew of Saint Victor; Eriugena, Johannes Scottus**

Further Reading

Hugh of Saint-Victor. *Opera. PL* 175–77.
——. *Hugonis de Sancto Victore, Didascalicon: de studio legendi. A Critical Text*, ed. Charles Henry Buttimer. Washington, D.C.: Catholic University Press, 1939.
——. *The "Didascalicon" of Hugh of St. Victor: A Medieval Guide to the Arts*, trans. Jerome Taylor. New York: Columbia University Press, 1961.
——. *Hugh of Saint Victor on the Sacraments of the Christian Faith (De sacramentis)*, trans. Roy J. Deferrari. Cambridge: Mediaeval Academy of America, 1951.
Baron, Roger. *Science et sagesse chez Hugues de Saint-Victor.* Paris: Lethielleux, 1957.
Ehlers, Joachim. *Hugo von St. Viktor: Studien zum Geschichtsdenken und zur Geschichtsschreibung des 12. Jahrhunderts.* Wiesbaden: Steiner, 1973.
Goy, Rudolf. *Die Überlieferung der Werke Hugos von St. Viktor: Ein Beitrag zur Kommunikationsgeschichte des Mittelalters.* Stuttgart: Hiersemann, 1976.
Sicard, Patrice. *Hugues de Saint-Victor et son école.* Turnhout: Brepols, 1991.
Van den Eynde, Damien. *Essai sur la succession et la date des écrits de Hugues de Saint-Victor.* Rome: Apud Pontificium Athenaeum Antonianum, 1960.
Zinn, Grover A. "Mandala Symbolism and Use in the Mysticism of Hugh of St. Victor." *History of Religions* 12 (1972–73): 317–41.
——. "Hugh of St. Victor, Isaiah's Vision, and *De arca Noe.*" In *The Church and the Arts*, ed. Diana Wood. Oxford: Blackwell, 1992.

GROVER A. ZINN

HUGO VON TRIMBERG
(1230/1240–ca. 1313)

Documented (1290) as teacher (*magister/rector scolarum*) of St. Gangolfstift in Teuerstadt near Bamberg, Hugo composed twelve works, seven of which survive. Among his four Latin texts, aids for teaching and preaching, the *Registrum Multorum Auctorum*, listing some eighty authors from classical antiquity to the Middle Ages, established a canon of Latin literary learning which was still observed as late as the seventeenth century.

The surviving work in Middle High German, *Der Renner*, about 24,600 verses, lives on in seventy manuscripts, and was printed at Frankfurt am Main in 1549. This gnomic text rivalled Wolfram von Eschenbach's *Parzival* in popularity for some time. Its thematic scope made the *Renner* a forerunner of the *Narrenliteratur* of Heinrich Wittenweiler and Sebastian Brant. The schema of the seven cardinal sins (medieval German, *hôchvart*/Latin, *superbia*, *gîtikeit/avaritia*, *frâz/gula*, *zorn/ira*, *nît/invidia*, *unkiusche/luxuria*, *lazheit/accedia*) structured a vision of late medieval *societas Christiana* (Christian society) ruled by greed, as demonstrated in commerce and usury. The *Renner* documents an anxious view of early capitalism, a system seen to be deriving its impetus from Satan. Striving for money in this text separates the foolish rich from the wise and willing poor.

The *Renner*'s stylistic diversity exemplifies the art of gnomic writing in the vernacular. Biblical examples, folk narrative, well worn fables, and quotations from classical and medieval authorities are used to support the author's attempt to lead fellow Christians from sin to virtue. For the literary and social historian, this extensive gnomic text provides a rich source for research into (late) medieval mentality, It portrays a deep ambivalence in Christian morality in relation to social roles of women, in the relationship of Christians to Jews, and in the view of *litterati* (the educated) regarding *illitterati* (the uneducated), and peasants (*rustici*) in particular. The *Renner* is an important representative of a popular literary genre which has left deep traces in the cultural memory.

See also **Wittenweiler, Heinrich;
Wolfram von Eschenbach**

Further Reading

Ehrismann, Gustav, ed. *Der Renner von Hugo von Trimberg.* 4 vols. 1980–1911; rpt. ed. Günther Schweikle. Berlin: de Gruyter, 1970–1971.

Goheen, Jutta. *Mensch und Moral im Mittelalter.* Darmstadt: Wissenschaftliche Buchgesellschaft, 1990.

Rosenplenter, Lutz. *Zitat und Autoritätenberufung im "Renner" Hugos von Trimberg.* Frankfurt am Main: Lang, 1982.

Sprandel, Rolf. "Der Adel des 13. Jahrhunderts im Spiegel des Renner von Hugo von Trimberg." In *Otto von Botenlauben: Minnesänger, Kreuzfahrer, Klostergründer.* Würzburg: Schöningh, 1994, pp. 296–308.

JUTTA GOHEEN

HUGUES DE SAINT-CHER
(ca. 1195–1263)

Nothing is known of Hugues's origins, except that he was born, in Saint-Cher, not far from Vienne in the south of France. He had become a doctor of canon law and a bachelor of theology even before he joined the Dominicans at Paris in 1225, where he studied under Roland of Cremona, the first Dominican to hold a chair in theology at the University of Paris. Hugues soon set upon a vocation that would make him one of the most prominent churchmen of his day. He first served in an administrative capacity as provincial of the Order for France from 1227 to 1229. Subsequently, he took up the posts of master of theology (1230–36) at the university and prior of the Dominican convent of Saint-Jacques (1233–36). After leaving his posts at the university and the convent, he resumed his duties for the next eight years as provincial-general of the Order of Preachers for the French province, while continuing to maintain a lively interest in the scholarly activities of his order in Paris. He became vicar-general of his order in 1240 and attained his highest administrative post with his selection as the first Dominican cardinal on May 28, 1244.

Hugues played a central role in the study of the Bible and theology in the 13th century. At Saint-Jacques, he assembled a team that produced three works that served as essential starting points for the theologians and preachers of his day: an expanded commentary on the Bible; a version of the Latin Vulgate incorporating a vast series of linguistic notes "correcting" the contemporary version of the text; and the first alphabetical concordance to the Bible. His set of commentaries, known as *Postillae*, use as their starting point the *Glossa ordinaria*, itself a digest of patristic and Carolingian exegesis, and add to it the fruits of the study of the Bible produced from the middle of the 12th century to his own time. His "corrected" Vulgate, the *Correctoria*, gives as full a sense of the literal meaning of the text as was possible for the 13th century, and his *Concordantia* greatly facilitated the task of preaching, allowing a relative novice to find his way around in the Bible without having to commit the entire text to memory.

Hugues began his work on the *Correctoria* as early as 1227, although the latest versions of this work date from his years as cardinal (1244–63). The *Postillae* date from his years as master (1230–36), and his *Concordantia* from 1238–40—a work to which some 500 friars contributed. Although the Bible had been given standard chapter divisions by Stephen Langton at the end of the 12th century, Hugues was the first to introduce subdivisions (a,b,c,d,e,f,g), an essential element for his correctoria and concordance.

His *Commentary* on the *Sententiae* of Peter Lombard, dating from his early years as master of theology, was among the first to employ the form of the *quaestio* in preference to a running commentary. In effect, this form signaled a shift away from simply commenting on Lombard's text to rewriting it, a process that was to reach its perfected form a generation later in the *Summa theologica* of Thomas Aquinas.

Among Hugues's more original contributions to theology was his teaching of the "treasury of merits" that held that the superabundance of the merits and good works of Christ, the Virgin, and the saints are at the disposal of the church, in the office of the pope, to distribute to the faithful. With the articulation of the treasury of merits, the theology of indulgences became integral to the practice of private penance.

As cardinal, Hugues worked closely with three popes and served on papal commissions that heard the controversies over Joachim of Fiore, the posthumous champion of the Spiritual Franciscans, in 1255 and William of Saint-Amour, the most vocal critic of the mendicant orders, in 1256. Hugues's eucharistic devotion is epitomized in the feast of Corpus Christi, which he authorized in Liège while legate there between 1251 and 1253 and which was placed in the calendar of the universal church in 1264 by Pope Urban IV, whom Hugues had served.

See also **Aquinas, Thomas; Joachim of Fiore; Peter Lombard**

Further Reading

Kaeppeli, Thomas. *Scriptores ordinis praedicatorum medii aevi.* 3 vols. Rome: Ad S. Sabinae, 1975–80, Vol. 2, pp. 269–81.

Lerner, Robert E. "Poverty, Preaching, and Eschatology in the Revelation Commentaries of Hugh of Saint-Cher." In *The Bible in the Medieval World: Essays in Memory of Beryl Smalley*, ed. Catharine Walsh and Diana Wood. Oxford: Blackwell, 1985.

Principe, Walter. *The Theology of the Hypostatic Union in the Early Thirteenth Century.* 4 vols. Toronto: Pontifical Institute of Mediaeval Studies, 1970, Vol. 3: *Hugh of Saint-Cher's Theology of the Hypostatic Union.*

Smalley, Beryl. *The Study of the Bible in the Middle Ages.* 3rd ed. Oxford: Blackwell, 1983.

MARK ZIER

HUMILITY OF FAENZA
(c. 1226–1310)

Humility of Faenza (Umiltà, Humilitas de Faventia, Rosanese) was an abbess and mystic and was said to be a miracle worker. She is perhaps unique in medieval Italy as a known woman author of a substantial body of Latin texts that are unlikely to have been ghostwritten or significantly redacted by a male secretary or confessor. These are her fifteen so-called *Sermons*, of which some are sermons in the general medieval and modern sense and the remainder—for which she accurately uses the term *oratio* ("prayer")—are formal addresses of devo-

tion to Christ, the Virgin Mary, and others. The writing is forceful, expressive, prone to grammatical errors of case and gender, and replete with resonances of biblical and other widely known Latin Christian texts. Rhetorical artifice is present but not overwhelming. A linear syntax reminiscent of ordinary speech patterns and the occasional inappropriate substitution of one similarly-sounding word for another suggest the oral environment in which these pieces were delivered and taken down by dictation. The present Sermon 9 (the division and arrangement of Humility's work has varied according to the judgment of her editors) consists largely of rhythmic poems of the sort called *laude* ("songs of praise"). Much matter in the higher-numbered *Sermons* can be analyzed somewhat similarly, even if it is not printed similarly; and there is evidence from the early modern period that several passages were sung in Vallombrosian monasteries and transcribed as separate *laude* in Latin or in Italian translations, or both.

Apart from the testimony of the *Sermons* themselves, almost all that we know of Humility comes from two early fourteenth-century lives, one in Latin and one in Italian. She was a talented and determined individual, with little if any formal education, who had been born into a noble family at Faenza. Humility was her name in religion; Rosanese was her original name. She went from married life to the life of a conventual, then became an ascetic solitary, and subsequently founded a community of Vallombrosian nuns. In 1282, together with a few companions, she traveled to Florence, where she established the Vallombrosian convent of Saint John the Evangelist and spent the remaining years of her life. Humility was recognized as a living saint both in Faenza and in Florence; shortly after her death she was the subject of a statue by Andrea di Cione (Orcagna) and of a polyptych altarpiece whose paintings have often been attributed to Pietro Lorenzetti. Her cult was authorized by the papacy in 1720 for the Vallombrosians and in 1721 for the dioceses of Florence and Faenza. She was canonized in 1948.

Further Reading

Editions

Simonetti, Adele, ed. *I sermoni di Umiltà da Faenza.* Biblioteca di Medioevo Latino, 14. Spoleto: Centro Italiano di Studi sull' Alto Medioevo, 1995.

——. *Le vite di Umiltà da Faenza: Agiografia trecentesca dal latino al volgare.* Per Verba: Testi Mediolatini con Traduzione, 8. Florence: SISMEL-Edizioni del Galluzzo, 1997.

Translations

"Life of Saint Umiltà, Abbess of the Vallombrosan Order in Florence," trans. Elizabeth Petroff. In *Consolation of the Blessed.* New York: Alta Gaia Society, 1979. pp. 121–150. (See introductory material, pp. 7–10. Includes translations of the Latin life, pp. 121–137; and of much later *Analects* written on the basis of the Italian version, pp. 137–150. The latter is revised, with new introductory material, in Elizabeth Petroff, trans. "The Analects of Saint Umiltà." *Vox Benedictina*, 7, 1990, pp. 31–52.)

"Sermons," trans. Richard J. Pioli. In *Medieval Women's Visionary Literature,* ed. Elizabeth Alvilda Petroff. New York: Oxford University Press, 1986, pp. 247–253. (Partial translations of three texts as differentiated and numbered in a now superseded edition of Torello Sala, Florence, 1884. See also corresponding material in Simonetti, sermons 4, 10, and 11.)

Critical Studies

Baccetti, E. "Vallombrosans." In *New Catholic Encyclopedia*, Vol. 15. New York: McGraw-Hill, 1967, p. 526. (See also later supplements.)

Benvenuti Papi, Anna. "Mendicant Friars and Female Pinzochere in Tuscany: From Social Marginality to Models of Sanctity." In *Religion in Medieval and Renaissance Italy,* ed. Daniel Bornstein and Roberto Rusconi. Chicago, Ill: University of Chicago Press, 1996, pp. 84–103.

Cantagalli, Gaspare, and Maria Chiara Celletti. "Umiltà." In *Bibliotheca Sanctorum,* ed. Filippo Caraffa et al., Vol. 12. Rome: Città Nuova Editrice for Istituto Giovanni XXIII della Pontificia Università Lateranense, 1969, cols. 818–822. (See Celletti for "Iconografia" only.)

Fumagalli Beonio-Brocchieri, Mariateresa. "The Feminine Mind in Medieval Mysticism." In *Creative Women in Medieval and Early Modern Italy: A Religious and Artistic Renaissance,* ed. E. Ann Matter and John Coakley. Philadelphia: University of Pennsylvania Press, 1994, pp. 19–33.

Mooney, Catherine M. "Authority and Inspiration in the *Vitae* and Sermons of Humility of Faenza." In *Medieval Monastic Preaching,* ed. Carolyn Muessig. Brill's Studies in Intellectual History, 90. Leiden: Brill, 1998, pp. 123–144.

Petroff, Elizabeth Alvilda. "Introduction: The Visionary Tradition in Women's Writings—Dialogue and Autobiography." In *Medieval Women's Visionary Literature,* ed. Elizabeth Alvilda Petroff. New York: Oxford University Press, 1986, pp. 3–59. (See especially pp. 23–30, on qualities of style and expression.)

———. *Body and Soul: Essays on Medieval Women and Mysticism.* New York: Oxford University Press, 1994, pp. 110–136, 161–181, 204–224.

Vasaturo, R. N. "Umiltà" and "Vallombrosa, Vallombrosane, Vallombrosani." In Dizionario degli istituti di perfezione, ed. Guerrino Pelliccia and Giancarlo Rocca, Vol. 9. Rome: Edizioni Paoline, 1997, cols. 1509–1510, 1692–1702. (See especially cols. 1695–1697.)

JOHN B. DILLON

I

IBN ADRET, SOLOMON
(ca. 1233–ca. 1310)

Solomon ibn Adret was the most important rabbinical authority in Spain in his period, and one of the most important of all time. We possess from his pen several volumes of commentaries on most of the tractates of the Talmud and several more volumes of legal responsa numbering in the thousands. All of these are a major source of information on the history of the period, of both Jews and non-Jews. He was the student of two great masters, both of Barcelona—Rabbi Jonah Gerundi and Moses ben Naḥman (Naḥmanides; not a rabbi)—and succeeded them as chief authority of the Aragón-Catalonia Jewish community. He had many famous students, almost all of whom became outstanding legal authorities and rabbis of the next generation in Aragón-Catalonia, Tudela, and Castile. Aside from Moses ben Maimon (Maimonides), who left Muslim Spain in his youth, no other Spanish Jewish scholar had as lasting an influence as Ibn Adret. (Nevertheless, scholars have made incredible errors in naming his students, and Scholem attributed to him the founding of a "school" of *qabbalah* based on his confusion of two sources with similar names, one written by a student of Ibn Adret but having nothing to do with *qabbalah* and the other written centuries later.)

However, Ibn Adret was strongly influenced by *qabbalah* in ways unknown to Scholem. He sometimes borrowed whole sections verbatim from the *qabbalist* ʿAzriel of Girona in his commentaries on the *aggadot* (homilies) of the Talmud; indeed, the order of the commentaries is based on that of ʿAzriel. Additional *qabbalistic* interpretations of Ibn Adret are cited in his student Meir Ibn Sahulah's (attributed) commentary on Naḥmanides on the Torah.

Ibn Adret joined in the controversy against the allegorical interpretation of the Bible and commandments fostered by those who misunderstood Maimonides, and even signed his name to the ban against the study of philosophy. Nevertheless, while he frequently wrote harsh criticisms of philosophy, he was deeply indebted to it, and matter-of-factly accepted certain of Maimonides' most "extreme" interpretations. He was the first anywhere to cite Maimonides' commentary on the Mishnah, and in fact arranged for its translation from Judeo-Arabic into Hebrew. He had, indeed, the greatest respect for Maimonides, whom he frequently cited.

His importance as communal leader and representative of the Catalan Jews cannot be overemphasized. Ibn Adret served as adviser to three rulers: Jaime I, Pedro III, and Jaime II (the last addressed a letter to him as "faithful" servant). He frequently was appointed by the kings as executor of important estates, and also served at various times as tax collector and secretary of the Jewish community of Barcelona.

Late in his life Ibn Adret composed other legal works, such as the *Torat ha-bayit ha-arokh* and a commentary on his own earlier abridged version of that work, which also serve as important source material for certain issues of the time. He left two, or possibly three, sons who were also scholars but never attained to their father's importance.

See also **Jaime (Jaume) I of Aragón-Catalonia; Maimonides; Moses ben Naham**

Further Reading

Epstein, I. *The "Responsa" of Rabbi Solomon Ben Adreth* [sic] *of Barcelona as a Source of the History of Spain.* New York, 1968. (First published 1925.) (Of limited value.)

R. Salomo b. Abraham b. Adereth [sic]. Breslau, 1863. (In German; of limited value, but better than Epstein.)

Scholem, G. *Kabbalah.* New York, 1974.

NORMAN ROTH

IBN DAŪD, ABRAHAM
(ca. 1110 – 1180?)

Abraham ibn Daūd, who was born in al-Andalus about 1110 or later and died (supposedly a martyr's death) possibly in 1180 at Toledo, is an important if neglected figure in the cultural history of the Jews of al-Andalus.

He was apparently the first to introduce Aristotelian philosophy to the Jews of Spain; his work is extant only in the medieval Hebrew translation, *ha-Emunah ha-ramah* (edited with German translation, 1853; there is a very poor modern English translation). In particular he utilized the philosophy of Ibn Sīnā (Avicenna), and was the first to argue for the agreement between Judaism and rational philosophical thought. Neither Jewish nor Muslim philosophers, of course, had any "double faith" or "reason versus revelation" conflict, which later plagued the Scholastics, so one should not view Ibn Daūd's effort as an attempt to convince readers that it was unnecessary to choose between religion and philosophy. Rather, somewhat like Maimonides after him, he was concerned with demonstrating the harmony between religion and reason in achieving the same truth. It was left to the far greater capacity of Maimonides to make this demonstration (which explains the lack of influence of Ibn Daūd's work on later thought).

More significantly, Ibn Daūd was first in another area: he was the first (and, in fact, the only) Jewish writer of al-Andalus to compose historical chronicles. He composed two such treatises, one of minor importance, on the history of the Second Temple and the Roman Empire, with an abridged version of the medieval Hebrew *Yossifon*, and the much more interesting and significant *Sefer ha-qabbalah* (*Book of Tradition*). Both of these works, like his philosophical work (in part), were written with a certain degree of polemical propaganda. While it is true that they were produced during the period of Almoravid dominance of al-Andalus, a time of some persecution (it is, however, scarcely true that "thousands" of Christians were "wiped out," or that "thousands" of Jews converted, as has been claimed), these works show no evidence of anti-Muslim hostility.

On the contrary, the latter book in particular seems to have been directed primarily against the Qaraite sectarians of Judaism. It purports to be a history of the Jews from the biblical period to Ibn Daūd's day. Much of the work is of interest only to the specialist in Jewish historiography, therefore, but the relatively small portion on Jews in medieval al-Andalus is obviously of great value, chiefly for biographical information on important scholars and other persons. Some light is also shed on historical events and on the general culture of Jews at the time.

Thus, *Sefer ha-qabbalah* served as a major source for the few later medieval Hebrew chronicles composed in Spain, and entire sections were utilized by Abraham Zacut; for example. Aside from these three or four chronicles, however, neither the author nor his work seems to have left any lasting impression on the Jews of Spain.

There is yet another aspect of Ibn Daūd's career to mention. It has frequently been claimed (even by the editor-translator of *Sefer ha-qabbalah*) that he was the famous "Avendauth" who, with the archdeacon Domingo Gundisalvo, translated numerous Arabic philosophical and scientific treatises into Latin. In fact, this is a confusion with a Jewish philosopher (virtually unknown) by the name of Solomon ibn Daūd, who converted to Christianity and was known as Juan Hispano (*not* Johannes Hispalensis, which has caused further confusion between him and a supposed John of Seville and even a Juan who was archbishop of Toledo in 1166). In Latin this converted Jew was known as Johannes Avendaut or Avendehut. Only Albertus Magnus calls him "archbishop of Toledo," undoubtedly confusing him with the previously mentioned Juan. Who this David Iudaeus, whom Albert says included "dicta" of several Muslim philosophers in his writing, may be is unclear; there is the possibility that this reference is to Abraham ibn Daūd.

Finally, when the fourteenth-century Jewish astronomer of Toledo, Isaac Israeli, stated that Ibn Daūd wrote a treatise on astronomy, otherwise unknown, he may very well have confused it with one of the translations done by Avendaut. More research on all of this is still needed.

See also Avicenna; Maimonides

Further Reading

Guttmann, J. *Philosophies of Judaism.* New York, 1964. pp. 143–52.

Ibn Daūd, A. *Sefer ha-Qabbalah: The Book of Tradition.* Ed. and Trans. G. Cohen. Philadelphia, 1967.

NORMAN ROTH

IBN EZRA, MOSES (ca. 1055–1138)

Moses ibn Ezra was the second of four sons in an influential family of Granadan Jewish patricians, and the first important Hebrew poet born during the politically turbulent but culturally productive period of the *muluk at-tawā'if* (*los reyes de taifas*, the party kings). Civil disturbances connected with the 1066 murder of Yehosef ibn Naghrila forced the family to flee to nearby Lucena, where Moses studied with Isaac ibn Ghiyath, the master rabbi associated with the famous Talmudic academy of that town. When the clan returned to Granada, Moses enjoyed the material culture and stimulating intellectual and social life characteristic of the Jewish nobility. During the years prior to 1090 he came into his own as a courtier-rabbi and won acclaim as a poet's poet.

In 1090 the Almoravid invasion broke the sociopoliti-cal stability of Granada, whose Jewish community was devastated for the second time in twenty-five years. For reasons that are unclear, Moses did not join his brothers' exodus to Córdoba and Toledo. He remained alone in Granada, "a resident alien" in his desolate native land. Subsequently, sometime between 1090 and 1095, Ibn Ezra was mysteriously compelled to abandon his wife and children, and leave Granada for exile in Christian Spain. So began the poet's forty-year odyssey though the towns of Castile, Navarre, and, it appears, Aragón. This tragic event proved to be the turning point in Ibn Ezra's personal, intellectual, and artistic life because he was never able to reconcile himself to an environment that he believed was socially, culturally, and intellectually inferior to that of his native Muslim Spain.

Ibn Ezra was, arguably, the most conservative of the Andalusian school of Hebrew poets. He initiated no major genres; his classicizing language and style are manifest in both his secular and his liturgical verse; he revived, in Hebrew form, the traditional structure of the neoclassical Arabic ode (*qaṣida*); and he was the first Hebrew poet to compose an Arabic-style book of man-neristic homonym poems. Even Ibn Ezra's most identifi-ably personal occasional poems, the lyrical complaints in which the poet laments his exile from Granada, are stylized in form and conventional in content. It would be incorrect to conclude, however, that his poetry is lacking in either originality or self-expression. On the contrary, he achieved distinction as a poet through his creative reworking of poetic tradition and his artistic mastery of rhetorical style.

Apart from his literary conservatism, what imme-diately distinguishes Ibn Ezra from other poets of the school are his Judeo-Arabic prose writings on Hebrew poetry and Andalusian Jewish culture. *The Book of Discussion and Conversation*, the most complete and comprehensive work on Hebrew poetics to come down from the Middle Ages, is a prescriptive and probing treatment of the legitimacy of Arabic-style Hebrew poetry. *The Treatise of the Garden on Metaphorical and Literal Language* is a theoretical study of the nature of poetic diction as manifested in the Hebrew Bible. Along with his substantial corpus of secular and devotional He-brew poetry, these works serve to identify Ibn Ezra as the embodiment of the traditions and ideals of Andalusian Jewish literary intellectuals of the period.

Further Reading

Pagis, D. *Secular Poetry and Poetic Theory: Moses Ibn Ezra and His Contemporaries.* Jerusalem, 1970. (In Hebrew.)

Scheindlin, R. P. "Rabbi Moshe ibn Ezra on the Legitimacy of Poetry." In *Medievalia et Humanistica*, new series, Vol. 7. Ed. by Paul M. Clogan. Cambridge, 1976. 101–15.

ROSS BRANN

IBN ḤAZM (994 – 1063)

Abū Muhammad 'Alī ibn Ḥazm was born in 994 at Munyat al-Mughīra, a suburb of Córdoba, and died on Mont Lishan, near Huelva, in 1063. He enjoyed the luxury and the education of the wealthy during the last years of the last Córdoban caliph, 'Abd al-Raḥmān IV, at whose court his father was a high-ranking official. His first attempts to follow in his father's steps in political life proved unsuccessful. After the fall of Córdoba, and some years of residence in various places, in 1016 he sought refuge in Játiva, near Valencia. Between 1016 and 1023 he was minister during the short reign of the Ummayyad caliph, and after the latter's assasination Ibn Ḥazm was thrown into prison. Between 1027 and 1031 he seems to have been active again in political life, from which he withdrew to turn to scholarship.

Ibn Ḥazm's education, with the best-known teach-ers of his time, encompassed the Qur'ān and religious sciences, theology, literature, medicine, history, and logic. He was a prolific author, with some four hundred titles attributed to him, of which only fourteen(?) are extant.

Ibn Ḥazm is especially well known in the West for his book *Tawq al-hamāma (The Dove's Necklace)*, written during his exile in Játiva and thus a work of his youth. It is in the strictest sense a literary epistle (*risāla*), a mixture of prose and his own poetry. It offers, in thirty chapters, a rather nostalgic contemplation of the na-ture and experience of love, which he treats with some autobiographical references, a considerable amount of sensuality, and a great deal of sensitivity. A book on love of enduring appeal, it has been incongruently compared to Ovid's and Andreas Capellanus's somewhat similar works.

Of greater importance, yet lesser known, are his other books, works in which the image of the playful and sensitive youth dissipates, replaced by that of the pious, often rigid Muslim scholar that he was. In his *Maratib al-'ulum (Categories of Sciences)* he encour-ages the study of all sciences, but with an objective that is clearly religious, for in his opinion religion should be the aim of all learning. Less important in his view is the study of poetry, especially the lyrical (*ghazal*), which may lead to temptation, and the panegyrical (*madḥ*), which tends toward deceitful exaggerations. His moral concerns are the topic of another book, the *Kitāb al-akhlāq wa'lñ-siyar (Book of Conduct)* consist-ing of twelve chapters in the form of admonishments and reflections on virtuous life.

The most important of all Ibn Ḥazm's extant works is his voluminous *Kitāb al-fisal fī' l-milal (Decision Among Religions)*. Aiming at demonstrating the truth of Islam in comparison with all other religions, Ibn Ḥazm writes what has been considered a treatise on comparative religion. Beginning with the religious and philosophical doctrines farthest removed from the truth of Islam, such as the cynics for their rejection of any truth, and atheists, for their repudiation of the existence of a God, he progresses to discuss the polytheists, as such Zoroastrians and Manichaeans, who recognize God but not his uniqueness. Christianity is included here because of the Trinitarian doctrine, which he understands to be a form of polytheism. Judaism is, in his view, the religion closest to Islam, except for its adulteration of the divine revelation, which he proves with reference to such Jewish sects as the Samaritans, Sadducees, and Talmudites. His analysis of the various religious doctrines is solidly based on textual references that show his vast erudition.

Dealing with Islam, Ibn Ḥazm refers to its various sects, from the Mu'tazilites to the Kharigites, which he sees to have in common their esoteric and allegorical interpretations of the Revelation. To avoid this, the true Muslim must follow the obvious (zahīr) and the literal meaning of the Qur'ān. In this way he justifies the school of the literalist Thahimites that for a time became popular in al-Andalus.

Points of great importance in Ibn Ḥazm's theology are harmony between faith and reason, divine predetermination, and free will. Possibly the most important is his effort to demonstrate the existence of God and the temporality of the world, and the necessity of divine revelation. Because of them, Ibn Ḥazm is considered a precursor of Christian scholasticism.

Ibn Ḥazm exerted a great influence, and his doctrine of literal interpretation became mainstream among the Zahīrites, and was continued by his followers, known as Hazmites. Of his direct students many are known in their own right. Well known also in the Orient, Ibn Ḥazm was praised by Al-Ghazālī, and his influence extended to the end of the sixteenth century, when it disappeared under bloody persecution. In the Maghrib the favor shown to his doctrines by the Almohad reformer Muhammad ibn Tūmart al-Mahdī helped to enhance the political influence of his followers in North Africa and al-Andalus. Among the most famous scholars that totally or partially followed Ibn Ḥazm's doctrines are the philosopher Averroës and the mystic Ibn al-'Arabī.

Further Reading

Asín Palacios, M. *Abenházam de Córdoba y su historia crítica de las ideas religiosas.* 5 vols. Madrid, 1927–32.
García Gómez, E. *El collar de la paloma, tratado sobre el amor y los amantes, de Ibn Hazm de Córdoba.* Madrid, 1952.
Ibn Ḥazm. *A Book Containing the Risāla Known as The Dove's Neckring.* Translated by A. R. Nykl. Paris, 1931.
——. *The Ring of the Dove.* Translated by A. J. Arberry. London, 1953.

VICENTE CANTARINO

IBN KHALDŪN (1332-1406)

Born 27 May 1332 and died 16 March 1406, he is regarded as one of the greatest of all historians, but especially of the Muslim world. He developed a theory, method, and philosophy of history he called '*umrān al-basharī*, or the social study of human civilization. As a result, many credit Ibn Khaldūn with the invention of sociology. Born into a distinguished family of Andalusí origins in Tunisia (they had emigrated from Seville), Ibn Khaldūn received a thorough education at home, in the mosque, and among the many Iberian Muslim intellectuals who were refugees in North Africa. In 1345, his parents died of the plague, and he found employment at the court of the Hafsids. For almost thirty years thereafter, he was deeply involved in the turbulent politics of North Africa and Spain. At one point, he was imprisoned for his political activities. In 1362 he went to Granada, where he was well received by the vizier, Ibn al-Khatīb. There he was enlisted to serve on a diplomatic mission to Seville and the court of Pedro I of Castile. Disillusioned by what he found in Iberia, he returned to Tunisia, where he became *hājib*, or chamberlain to the ruler. Soon embroiled again in political intrigue, he decided on voluntary retirement to the oasis of Baskarah in what today is Algeria. Circumstances, however, compelled him to return to politics, even though he foresaw dangerous consequences. In 1375 he withdrew again from court life to a castle in Oran, where during the course of the next five years he wrote *Al-Muqaddimah*, his greatest work. Drawn back into politics in 1380, his experience proved nearly fatal and, in 1382, he left Tunis never to return. He went to Egypt, where he became a Malikite *qāḍi*, or judge, and a prominent teacher of Islamic law at Al-Azhar University.

Ibn Khaldūn's *Muqaddimah* serves as an introduction to his *Universal History. Kitāb al-'Ibar Kitāb al-'Ibar* is a valuable source for the history of North Africa and Iberia, but the *Muqaddimah* is a brilliant exposition of the methodological and cultural knowledge necessary to produce a scientific understanding of the past. Ibn Khaldūn was interested primarily in the reasons for the rise and fall of human civilizations; he contended that the basic causes of historical evolution are to be sought in the economic and social structure of society. In his work, he emphasizes environment, politics, economics, and religion as the determining factors in the development of societies. He surveys the sciences, refuting some like alchemy and astrology, and reflects on the manner of acquiring and using them. History, like science, involves more than a description of events, it calls for speculation, discrimination, and an attempt to identify the true causes and origins of existing things. The historian needs to possess a clear knowledge of customs, social organization, and beliefs and use critical judgment in dealing always with all the versions of the past. As such, history merits a place in the rearm of philosophy. While *Al-Muqaddimah* serves as the introduction to *Kitāb al-'Ibar*, in the six parts that follow *Al-Muqaddimah* he goes on to apply his ideas to the entire history of humankind. The work is, for the most part, a political history and is arranged around individuals, dynasties, rulers, and important events, but also includes striking reflections on human association as a dynamic interaction of many motives. Ibn Khaldūn's work stands as a monument to the history of history itself and remains an extremely important source of scholarship for the late medieval Maghrib and Iberia in particular.

Further Reading

Al-Azmeh, Aziz, *Ibn Khaldūn: A Reinterpretation.* London, 1990.
Ibn Khaldūn. *The Muquaddimah.* 2 vols. Trans. Franz Rosenthal. Princeton, N.J., 1967.
Mahdi, Muhsin. *Ibn Khaldun's Philosophy of History: A Study in the Philosophic Foundation of the Science of Culture.* London, 1957.

E. MICHAEL GERLI

IBN QUZMĀN (ca. 1086-1160)

Abū Bakr Muhammad ibn 'Isā ibn 'Abd al-Malik ibn Quzmān al-Asghar al-Zajjāl was born in Córdoba, probably just after the battle of Zallāqah (Sagrajas) in 1086, and died in 1160. He called himself *wazīr* (vizir), and his family had produced several such, as well as other minor dignitaries, so the title may have been authentic, though it was a debased coinage by his time. Little else of his biography is certain, even his legendary ugliness, there being much confusion in the minds of later medieval as well as modern literary historians between him and at least one of his eponymous relatives. Much of what is commonly said to be descriptive of him and his life is gained from the internal evidence of his poetry, which by definition is subject to poetic license.

What we do know with certainly is that he had as patrons some of the more important political figures of Córdoba, Seville, and Granada during the turbulent years of his lifetime, which more or less coincided with the first seventy years of Almoravid domination. He was considered to be an important literary figure shortly after his death, and even gained some renown in the Arab East, despite the fact that his poetry was written principally in the dialect of southern al-Andalus and in a form outside the normal canon of Arabic poetry.

Our sources for Ibn Quzmān's work consist primarily of one manuscript of his *Dīwān* (collected poems), copied in Safad (Palestine) a century or so after the poet's death. This is known as the "lesser" *Dīwān* because the existence of a more complete one may be inferred from citations by anthologists and historians, who provide a number of fragmentary, and a few complete, *zajals* as well as Ibn Quzmān's surviving poems in classical Arabic, including one *muwashsahaha.*

Ibn Quzmān considered himself to be the master of an Andalusian poetic form he did not invent, but perfected, as he immodestly claims in the prologue to the St. Petersburg manuscript of his *Dīwān*, though he does express admiration for one predecessor (Ibn Numāra, about whom next to nothing is known). The *zajal* is a strophic poem apparently derived from the *muwashshah*: the rhyme scheme is similar (mostly ABcccAB or AA cccAA or AA cccA, the latter differing slightly from the standard muwashshah scheme AA(or AB) cccAA(or AB), but whereas the muwashshah is not meant to exceed five to seven strophes, the zajal may do so. The muwasshah is in classical Arabic, with only the final refrain (*kharja*) in colloquial Arabic, Romance, or a mixture of both, whereas the zajal is entirely in the Arabic dialect of Córdoba, with an occasional sprinkling of pithy Romance words and phrases. The Arabic shows occasional lapses from the colloquial, probably for metrical reasons, possibly playing on different registers or levels of style.

The meter of the zajal, like that of the muwashshah, has been the subject of virulent controversy. Most scholars who have studied Ibn Quzmān since he came to light in the late nineteenth century have concluded that the materical basis of his songs is closely related to the quantitative rhythmic patterns of classical Arabic prosody. Another group, composed mostly of Spanish scholars, argues that the zajal is governed by syllable count and accent, like old Spanish poetry. Given the uncertainties involved, it is doubtful that the issue will ever be proved ole way or the other, certainly not to the satisfaction of all.

The literary quality of Ibn Quzmān's zajals has not been questioned, and if his is not a "voice in the street," it is an original and vivid one. Even the long odes to the talent, good looks, and generosity of his benefactors are not devoid of local color and vividly expressed feeling; the occasional poems can be sublime, especially the love poems such as the famous

> Now do I love you, Laleima, little star (zajal 10, I. 1)
> or
> Strangeness and solitude and violent passion—
> Such is my lot: I am the lonely stranger! (zajal 124, II. 1–2)

Ibn Quzmān's emotional palette ranges from pathetic, unrequited love to graphic description of love-making with a Berber girl. Wine, food, companionship in revelry, music, and money or (more often) the lack thereof, as of other refinements such as elegant clothes, are favorite themes. His poems, even at their most conventional (the long panegyrics), are well crafted, often playfully evoking the conventional loci of Arabic verse for the dramatic or lyrical purposes of his piece. He paints an irreplaceably vivid picture of twelfth-century Córdoba, a city, a civilization conscious that its glory days were past:

Where is Ibn . . .'s Lane, with its bustle?
Where is the Mosque Quarter, and its beauty?
Laden it is with more spite than it can bear—
Come close! you'll see a
Field to plough and seed;
The rest infested
Head-high with weed. (zajal 147, strophe 3 and refrain)

Further Reading

An-Nawājī, Shams ad-Dīn Muhammad ibh Hasan. *ʿUqūd al-la'l fi 'l-muwashshah.at wa'l-azjāl*. Ms. Escorial 434.

Colin, G. S. "Ibn Kuzmān." In *Encyclopaedia of Islam*. New ed. Vol. 3. Leiden, 1960. 849–52.

Corriente, F. *Gramática, métrica, y texto del cancionero hispanoárabe de Abén Quzmán*. Madrid, 1980. 69ff.

García Gómez, E. *Todo Ben Guzman*. Madrid, 1933.

Gorton, T. J. "The Metre of Ibn Quzmān: A 'Classical' Approach." *Journal of Arabic Literature* 6 (1975), 1–29.

——. "Back to Ibn Quzmān." In *Cultures in Contact in Medieval Spain: Historical and Literary Essays Presented to L. P. Harvey*. Eds. D. Hook and B. Taylor. London, 1990. 103–09.

Gunzburg, D. de. *Le Divan d'Ibn Guzman: Texte, traduction, commentaire*. Fasc. 1, *Le Texte d'après le manuscrit unique du Musée impérial de St-Pétersbourg*. Berlin, 1896.

Monroe, J. T. "Romance Prosody in the Poetry of Ibn Quzmān." In *Perspectives on Arabic Linguistics*. Vol. 6, *Papers from the Sixth Annual Symposium on Arabic Linguistics*. Ed. Mushira Eid et al. Amsterdam, 1994, 63–87.

Nykl, A. R. (ed.) *El cancionero de Abén Guzmán*. Madrid, 1933.

Stern, S. M. *Hispano-Arabic Strophic Poetry*. Ed. L. P. Harvey. Oxford, 1974. Ch. 4.

T. J. GORTON

IBN SAʿĪD, ABŪ 'L-ḤASAN ʿALĪ B. MŪSĀ B. MUḤAMMAD B. ʿABD AL-MALIK B. SAʿĪD (1208/13–1286)

Poet, traveler and adventurer, geographer, literary historian and anthologist, Ibn Saʿī is recognized as a leading exponent of Andalusian culture of the thirteenth century. He was bora into a noble family of Yemeni ancestry that, during the period of the Ṭā'ifas, came to govern a fortress at the present site of Alcalá la Real to the northwest of Granada. Ibn Saʿīd's grandfather had served as *wālī* (governor) of both Seville and Granada, and his father apparently left the family fortress definitively in 1224 to become *wālī* of Algeciras. Ibn Saʿīd spent much of his youth at Seville, the leading intellectual center of al-Andalus at the time, where he studied under the tutelage of many of the outstanding scholars of his day. His father, who loved learning and scholarship more than politics, instilled in his son the same zest for learning and inquiry, and the two traveled about al-Andalus and Morocco to seek out rare books for their literary research. Father and son left al-Andalus in 1241 at a time when their political fortunes had been reversed, declaring their intention to perform the pilgrimage, though neither ever returned to his native land. The father fell ill and died in Alexandria in 1242, and Ibn Saʿīd then proceeded to Cairo, where he found an enthusiastic reception and was admired for his scholarship and literary talents. In an age of political uncertainty, Ibn Saʿīd's scholarship coincided with the fervent desire of many scholars to preserve the legacy of Arab civilization. Ibn Saʿīd traveled extensively, and his travels took him to Arabia, Syria, Iraq, Iran, and Armenia.

Much of Ibn Saʿīd's fame rests on a multivolume work entitled *Al-Mughrib fi Ḥulā 'l-Maghrib*, a work to which he put on the finishing touches, but which in actuality took shape gradually over a period of about eleven decades. In 1135–1136, a man of letters by the name of Al-Ḥidjārī visited the family fortress, and the great-grandfather of Ibn Saʿīd encouraged the visitor to compile an anthology of Andalusian poets. In this anthology the author arranged all the poets according to the town or district to which they belonged. Then, for over a century, the original patron, his son, his grandson, and finally his great-grandson (our Ibn Saʿīd) sought to improve upon the work and to make numerous additions. In its final form it came to deal with the literary history and geography of not only al-Andalus, but of North Africa, Sicily, and Egypt, as well. The section devoted to al-Andalus, conserved in almost its entirety, gives brief geographical descriptions of each area as well as biographical notes of important personages, seasoned with anecdotes and poetical excerpts. Aside from its literary value, this work tells us much about the intellectual and social life of al-Andalus up until the time of the work's completion. Drawing principally on materials from this anthology, Ibn Saʿīd composed short works for patrons on given topics or themes. There have come down to us several volumes of a companion work to *Al-Mughrib* identical in format, dealing with the literary history of the Arab East, and originally conceived of by Ibn Saʿīd's father.

Though Ibn Saʿīd's *dīwān* has been lost, a number of his poems have come down to us. His poetry is conventional in many ways; nevertheless, his verses of nostalgia recalling the days of his youth in al-Andalus speak of a heartfelt yearning to return and are rich in many imaginative images often succeeding one another in an almost dizzying kaleidoscopic fashion.

Even though Ibn Saʿīd's contributions to literary history are remarkable, no less so is the geographical information he either recorded from personal observation or culled from the sources he consulted in libraries throughout the many countries he visited. Among works attributed to him are travel accounts and a number of geographical and historical treatises.

Further Reading

Arberry, A. J. *Moorish Poetry: A Translation of the Pennants, an Anthology Compiled in 1243 by the Andalusian Ibn Saʿīd.* Cambridge, 1953.

Arié, R. "Un lettré andalou en Ifriqiya et en Orient au XIIIᵉ siècle: Ibn Saʿīd." In *L'occident musulman au bas Moyen Age.* Ed. R. Arié. Paris, 1992.

DUSTIN COWELL

IBN ZAYDŪN (1003-1071)

Abu' l-Walid Ahmad ibn 'Abdullah ibn Ahmad ibn Ghalib al-Makhzumi ibn Zaydūn was born in Córdoba in 1003, and died in Seville in 1071. He became famous as one of the best neoclassical poets in al-Andalus, and more specifically for his love poetry to the Umayyad princess Wallāda. The fact that three editions of his *Dīwān,* two of them also containing his letters, are available attests to his popularity among his contemporaries as well as twentieth-century Arabs who edited them.

Ibn Zaydūn was born into an illustrious family of Arab origin during a period of great cultural splendor in Muslim Spain that was also the beginning of an era of political instability. He was in a position to acquire an extensive education in literary culture, specifically classical Arabic literature, and he started writing his own verse when he was very young. He was first publicly recognized at the age of nineteen for a long elegy upon the death of one of his teachers, Ibn Dhāqwan, whom he admired very much.

After Caliph Al-Mustakfi was killed in 1025, his unconventional daughter Wallāda, herself a poet, became the center of Córdoba's literary circles, in which Ibn Zaydūn played an active part. Poems tracing the stages of his love for Wallāda dominate the greatest part of Ibn Zaydūn's ensuing literary work and also show its most original poetic aspects, though he also drew on his extensive literary training to produce erudite, beautifully crafted poems in a more traditional style, such as one *qaṣīda* against his rival Ibn Abdūs.

In his love poetry Ibn Zaydūn uses many stock themes of courtly love poetry as well as the poetic code of classical Arabic poetry, but he excels in endowing them with new suggestive power and poetic intensity. His first poems give expression to happy union, the elevation of the beloved, and the submission of the lover to the point where a glance is enough and he is even ready to die for her. Their union is threatened only by "the envious" and "slanderers." Soon, however, his poems deal with themes of separation because of her rejection and with his imprisonment, which probably had to do with his political aspirations. He fled from prison and then tried to entice Wallāda to join him.

Ibn Zaydūn's most famous poems spring from this era: the *Nūnīya* and his memories in the garden of Medīnat al-Zahrā. In the *Nūnīya,* he tries to induce his beloved to go with him. With the repeated rhyme *na,* meaning "us," in addition to the frequent use of the sixth verbal form, suggesting mutuality, he endows language forms and the accepted poetic code (monorhyme) with the suggestive power to express his hope. Numerous other acoustic and structural patterns that are derived from the tradition of classical Arabic literature are creatively employed to support the poetic message in subtle ways. In his famous poem from *Al-Zahrā,* he uses the acoustic effects of the rhyme *aqa,* which together with frequent other guttural sounds reflects the melancholy, dark mood of yearning in a way that could not be achieved through rational verbalization alone.

Ibn Zaydūn's use of concepts goes far beyond a beautiful reworking of well-known images. Traditionally parts of nature were often compared to the beloved's beauty. Ibn Zaydūn, however, humanizes and spiritualizes nature by describing it as capable of feelings and their manifestations. For instance, the breeze becomes a friendly spirit sympathizing with the lover's sickness, and the flowers drooping under the morning dew are weeping with him.

Ibn Zaydūn also incorporates many Neoplatonic spiritual ideas into his love poetry, including love as the upsurge of the soul, love having its seat in the soul, and the purity of love, which—in its mixture with sensuality—is quite different from central European courtly love poetry.

After an extended exile Ibn Zaydūn was granted permission to return to Córdoba, where he became court poet at the age of thirty-eight. He left Córdoba again, however, and spent his last years at the court of Seville, as court adviser and poet of panegyrics. In the last year of his life, he was able to return to Córdoba in triumph because his patron, Al-Mutʿamid, took over the city.

Ibn Zaydūn enriched the tradition of classical Arabic poetry with his conceptual innovativeness and his creative use of accepted acoustic and structural elements.

See also **Wallādah Bint Al-Mustafki**

Further Reading

Cour, A. *Un Poète arabe d'Andalousie: Ibn Zaidoun.* Constantine, Algeria, 1920.

Lug, S. *Poetic Techniques and Conceptual Elements in Ibn Zaydūn's Love Poetry.* Washington, D.C., 1982.

SIEGINDE LUG

IBN ZUHR, ABŪ MARWĀN 'ABD AL-MĀLIK (1092?–1161?)

Called Avenzoar in Latin translations, he was one of the most important physicians in the history of al-Andalus. Born circa 1092 into an important family of physicians: his grandfather, 'Abd Al-Mālik ibn Zuhr (d. ca. 1078) studied medicine in Cairo and, when he returned, became personal doctor to al-Mujāhid, king of the *ṭā'ifa* (free kingdom) of Denia (ca. 1010–1045). His father, Abū-l-'Alā' Zuhr, served as a physician to King al-Mu'tamid of Seville (1069–1091) and, later, to the Almoravids Yūsuf ibn Tashfīn (d. 1106) and 'Ali ibn Yūsuf (d. 1143). Abū Marwān was born and died in Seville but after 1120 spent a good part of his life in Marrākesh, where he inherited his father's post as royal physician to 'Ali ibn Yūsuf. Difficulties with this emir, due to obscure reasons, took him into prison (ca. 1131–ca. 1140). With the arrival of the Almohads he became, once more and until his death, personal physician to Caliph 'Abd al-Mu'min (1130–1163). His son, Abū Bakr (1113–1199), served in the same way to Caliph Ya'qūb al-Manṣūr (1184–1199).

Unlike his friend, the famous philosopher and physician Ibn Rushd (Averroë's), and following his family tradition, his attitude toward medicine is essentially practical and his works always contain case records and other observations drawn from his own personal experience or from that of other members of his family. Among his extant works, a few merit special attention. *Kitāb al-iqtiṣad fī iṣlāḥ. al-anfus wa-l-ajsād* (On the Adequate Way to Treat Souls and Bodies) is a collection of texts of approximately equal length, written when the author was about thirty years old, to be read to prince Ibrāhīm Ibn Yūsuf Ibn Tashf'īn, Almoravid governor of Seville, to whom Abū Marwān was introduced in 1031. It deals with (*zina*) (cosmetics), i.e., the different ways to preserve and embellish the external parts of the human body, including plastic surgery and sexual hygiene, to which Abū Marwān adds a handbook on pathology that deals with the description and treatment of all known diseases classified "from head to toe." *Kitāb al-taysīr fī' l-mudāwā wa-l-tadbīr* (Simplification of Medical Treatment with Drugs and Diet), written after 1147 as an attempt by a cultivated, mature physician to improve the quality of the purely practical therapeutical treatises known as *kunnāsh*, is an excellent handbook of pathology and therapeutics for the daily use of the practicing physician written by a man with both a long medical experience and an excellent knowledge of medical theory. *Kitāb al-jāmi' fī'l-ashriba wa-l-ma'ājin* (A Comprehensive List of Syrups and Electuaries), written—like his *Kitāb al-aghdhiya* (On Food)—for Caliph 'Abd al-Mu'min, it is usually considered a kind of appendix to the *Taysīr*, and both appear together in the edition by *M. Khūri* (Damascus, 1983). It proves the interest Abū Marwān had in practical pharmacology: it consists of a collection of recipes for the preparation of compounded drugs (syrups, electuaries, pills, ointments, and so on). To this list one should, perhaps, add the *Al-Tadhkira fī-l-adwa' al-mushila wa ghayri-hā* (Memento on Laxative and Nonlaxative Drugs), a short treatise ascribed by G. S. Colin to Abū-l-'Alā Zuhr, though Khaṭṭābī has given, recently, arguments in favor of Abū Marwān's authorship. It is a work that shows that its author had a solid knowledge in pharmaceutical theory and a very cautious attitude toward the administration of drugs to patients.

See also **Averroës, Abu 'L-Walid Muhammad B. Ahmad B. Rushd**

Further Reading

Arnáldez, R. "Ibn Zuhr." In *Encyclopédie de l'Islam.* Vol. 3. Leyden-Paris, 1971, 1001–03.

Colin, G. S., *La Tedhkira d'Aboul 'Alā'.* Paris, 1911.

Khaṭṭābi, M. A. *al-Ṭibb wa-l-aṭibba' fī'-l-Andalus,* Vol. 1. Beirut, 1988. 277–317.

Ibn Zuhr, A. *Taysīr*, Ed. M. Khūri. Damascus, 1983.

JULIO SAMSÓ

IMMANUEL ROMANO (c. 1265 to 1331)

Immanuel Roman (Immanuele Giudeo; in Hebrew Immanu'el ha-Romî) was a Jewish philosopher and comic poet. He was the son of Rabbi Salomone of the Sifronide (Zi-fronî) family and was raised in the Jewish community of Rome. Immanuel lived in Ancona, Gubbio, and Verona; worked as a tutor for wealthy Jewish families in Fabriano and Fermo; and was a member of a group of Jewish philosophers centered in Rome and headed by Jehudà Romano (Lionello).

Immanuel's philosophical writings take the form of biblical commentaries in Hebrew. He also wrote, again in Hebrew, a treatise on hermeneutics and a collection of poetry, *Mekhabbérôth*, inspired by Dante's *Divine Comedy*. In *Mekhabbérôth*, Immanuel narrates a journey to the inferno and to paradise under the guidance of the prophet Daniel. Immanuel also wrote, in the Italian vernacular, three sonnets, a *tenzone*, and a *frottola* he called *Bisbidis*. In his first sonnet, *Amor non lesse mai l'avemaria* ("Love never read the Ave Maria"), he declares that love observes no particular faith or religion; he thus takes issue with poets such as the stilnovists who depict love in Christian terms. The other two sonnets reiterate Immanuel's pragmatic view of life: he vows to support whatever political faction or religion happens to be in power. In the *tenzone*, Bosone da Gubbio invites Immanuel to mourn the deaths of Dante and of his lady: *Duo lumi son di novo spenti al mondo* ("Two lights are again extinguished on earth"). Immanuel responds *per le rime* (with matching rhymes) in *Io, che trassi le lagrime del fondo* ("I who draw up tears from the depths"). *Bisbidis*, in a kinetic, onomatopoeic style, depicts life at the court of Cangrande della Scala of Verona.

See also **Dante Alighieris**

Further Reading

Editions

Jarden, D., ed. *The Cantos of Immanuel of Rome*, 2 vols. Jerusalem, 1957. (In Hebrew.)

Marti, Mario. *Poeti giocosi del tempo di Dante*. Milan: Rizzoli, 1956, pp. 315–327.

Massèra, Aldo Francesco, ed. *Sonetti burleschi e realistici dei primi due secoli*. Bari: Laterza, 1920. (Rev. Luigi Russo, 1940. See Vol. l, pp. 145–147.)

Vitale, Maurizio, ed. *Rimatori comico-realistici*. Turin: UTET, 1956, pp. 539–560. (Reprint, 1976.)

Studies

Bruni, Francesco. "Bene comune, spirito di parte, indifferentismo nella cultura toscana medievale e in Immanuel Romano." In *Studi di italianistica in onore di Giovanni Cecchetti*, ed. Paolo Cherchi and Michelangelo Picone. Ravenna: Longo, 1988, pp. 39–55.

Mandelbaum, Allen. "A Millennium of Hebrew Poetry in Italy." In *Gardens and Ghettos: The Art of Jewish Life in Italy*, ed. Vivian B. Mann. Berkeley: University of California Press, 1989, pp. 191–207. (Exhibition catalog, Jewish Museum, New York.)

Rinaldi, Giovanni, and Fabrizio Beggiato. "Immanuele Giudeo." In *Enciclopedia dantesca*, 6 vols. Rome: Istituto della Enciclopedia Italiana, 1970–1978.

JOAN H. LEVIN

INNOCENT III, POPE
(1160 or 1161–16 July 1216)

Innocent III (Lothario dei Conti di Segni, Lothar of Segni) is often described as the most powerful of the medieval popes; he was certainly one of the most ambitious of all the Roman popes in his assertion of papal authority. He was born into the noble house of the counts of Segni; his parents were Count Trasimund and Clarissa, the daughter of a powerful Roman family. From an early age, the boy was destined for a clerical career. He began his formal education at Rome, where he studied under Abbot Peter Ismael in the monastery of Saint Andrew in Celio. He continued his studies in the liberal arts and theology at Paris, where he was a pupil of Peter of Corbeil and perhaps also of Peter the Chanter. Later, for a time, he was a student at Bologna, although it is unclear what he studied there. Innocent has often been called a lawyer-pope. There is little in his known writing to support this description; but if he was trained in law, as tradition has it, he almost certainly received that training at Bologna, perhaps from the great decretalist Huguccio (Uguccione da Pisa), whom he treated with deference even after becoming pope.

Innocent (then Lotharo) completed his formal education when he was in his mid-twenties and soon thereafter appeared at Rome, where he became a member of the papal curia. He was ordained a subdeacon by Pope Gregory VIII in 1187; and in 1190, at about age thirty, he was named cardinal deacon of Saints Sergius and Bacchus by Pope Clement III.

During his years in the curia he wrote three treatises on moral questions. The best-known of these is *On the Misery of the Human Condition* (*De miseria humanae conditionis*), an extended reflection on the sinfulness of humankind, our utter unworthiness of salvation, and our dependence on the undeserved mercy that God bestows on us. This became a medieval best-seller; it was by far the most widely read of Innocent's writings and survives in some 600 manuscripts. In addition, before his pontificate he completed two other spiritual treatises: *On the Mysteries of the Mass* and *On the Four Kinds of Marriage*.

Pope Celestine III died on 8 January 1198; before that day was over Cardinal Lotharo dei Segni had been elected to succeed him. At his coronation six weeks later the new pope took the name Innocent III. During the weeks between his election and his coronation, he had been busy reorganizing the curia and dealing with the political opportunities that the death of Emperor Henry VI had created in the papal states.

During the nineteen years of his pontificate Innocent III was to remain deeply involved in political affairs in Europe and throughout the Mediterranean world. His active pursuit of political goals was consistent with his exalted view of the papacy as the supreme representative of divine authority in the world and of himself as God's principal agent in human affairs. The pope, he declared, was God's chief minister, "set between God and man, lower than God but higher than man, who judges all and is judged by no one." Innocent believed that as pope he had not merely a right but an obligation to intervene wherever God's interests were violated or God's plans, as the pope saw them, were in danger of being thwarted.

It was entirely consistent with these beliefs that Innocent should pursue active political goals in every part of the world he knew. As the guardian of Frederick of Hohenstaufen, the son and putative successor of Henry VI, Innocent intervened repeatedly and actively in the political maelstrom that swept through the empire in the early thirteenth century. When the German electors failed to agree on the successor to Henry VI, Innocent at first supported the Guelf candidate, Otto IV; then, when Otto failed to observe the commitments he had made about the management of the empire's Italian territories, Innocent switched allegiance and actively promoted the claims of his ward, young Frederick II, who ultimately secured the imperial title, in part as a consequence of Innocent's support. The new emperor's gratitude was deeply (and understandably) tinged with suspicion, however, and his relations with the pope deteriorated perceptibly during the latter years of Innocent's life.

Innocent III was also intensely involved in French and English politics. In France Innocent had to deal with the intricate problems raised by the desire of King Philip Augustus to annul his marriage with his second wife, Ingeborg of Denmark, and marry Agnes of Meran. The case not only raised complex questions of canon law but was also fraught with touchy diplomatic issues. Ultimately Innocent prevented Philip from divorcing Ingeborg, but he compromised with the king on the essential question of the succession to the throne by legitimizing Philip and Agnes's two children. Innocent was simultaneously engaged in a struggle with King John of England over royal control of English bishoprics and, in particular, the succession of Stephen Langton to the archbishopric of Canterbury. The pope placed England under an interdict and forced John to back down, surrender his crown to Innocent, and then receive it back as a papal fief.

Innocent's concept of papal power led him to sponsor military campaigns on many fronts against the foes of Christendom. He strongly encouraged German colonization and the forcible conversion of pagans in the eastern Baltic, and he endowed these colonizing expeditions with the privileges of a crusade. He proclaimed other crusades in the Middle East. One of these, called the Fourth Crusade, made war on the Byzantine Empire—instead of attacking Egypt as Innocent had expected—and, to Innocent's dismay, captured and looted Constantinople, the capital of the largest Christian power of the eastern Mediterranean. Undeterred by this, the pope set in motion a further crusade against Egypt, often called the Fifth Crusade; it achieved a short-lived success when the crusaders briefly captured Damietta, although Innocent himself did not live to see this. Innocent also used the mechanism of the crusade in Europe when he launched the first of a series of attacks that came to be known as the Albigensian Crusade against Cathar heretics in the south of France.

Innocent was also busy with the internal affairs of the church establishment. He spent many hours each day sitting as judge in disputes that had been referred to the papal court from every part of the Christian world. He actively promoted and encouraged new orders of religious men and women, most notably the Dominican and Franciscan friars, as well as numerous smaller groups.

The climax of Innocent's pontificate, in many ways, was the Fourth Lateran Council, a great meeting of bishops, abbots, and other prelates from throughout the Christian world. This council met in Rome from 11 to 30 November 1215, after more than two years of energetic preparations. Its agenda included a wide array of measures designed to reform the church and to meet the challenges that the pope and his advisers saw facing it. Among these were repressing heresy (the council authorized vigorous new measures against heretics), reforming the clergy and enforcing clerical discipline more strictly, establishing a minimum wage for the clergy, restructuring judicial procedure by abolishing ordeals as a means of proof, improving the morals of the laity by requiring every Christian to make an annual confession of sins and receive communion, instituting a sweeping reform of the church's marriage law, and numerous other measures, seventy in all, that the council formally adopted at its solemn closing session. The Fourth Lateran Council was thus a major effort to reshape the Christian west, the culmination of Innocent III's grand design to place a newly reinvigorated church at the center of European life and power.

See also **Frederick II; Henry VI; Peter the Chanter**

Further Reading

Editions
Migne, J.-P. *Patrologia Latina*, Vols. 214–217.
Regestum Innocentii III papae super negatio Romani imperii, ed. Friedrich Kempf. Rome: Pontificia Università Gregoriana, 1947.
Die Register Innocenz III, ed. Othmar Hageneder and Anton Haidacher. Graz and Cologne: Böhlaus, 1964–.

Studies
Imkamp, Wilhelm. *Das Kirchenbild Innocenz' III. (1198–1216).* Stuttgart: A. Hiersemann, 1983.
Kuttner, Stephan, and António García y García. "A New Eyewitness Account of the Fourth Lateran Council." *Traditio,* 20, 1964, pp. 115–178.
Laufs, Manfred. *Politik und Recht bei Innozenz III.: Kaiserprivilegien, Thronstreitregister, und Egerer Goldbulle in der Reichs- und Rekuperationspolitik Papst Innozenz' III.* Cologne: Böhlau, 1980.
Luchaire, Achille. *Innocent III,* 6 vols. Paris: Hachette, 1905–1908.
Maccarrone, Michele. *Chiesa e stato nella dottrina di Innocenzo III.* Rome: Facultas Theologica Pontificii Athenaei Lateranensis, 1940.
Pennington, Kenneth. "The Legal Education of Pope Innocent III." *Bulletin of Medieval Canon Law,* 4, 1974, pp. 70–77.
Roscher, Helmut. *Papst Innocenz III. und die Kreuzzüge.* Göttingen: Vandenhoeck u. Ruprecht, 1969.
Tillmann, Héiène. *Papst Innocenz II.* Bonn: L. Rohrscheid, 1954.

JAMES A. BRUNDAGE

INNOCENT IV, POPE (c. 1190–1254, r. 25 June 1243–7 December 1254)

Pope Innocent IV (Sinibaldo Fieschi) was born in Genoa. He was a descendant of the counts of Lavagna, who had traditionally supported the emperor rather than the pope, even though they themselves produced two popes (Innocent IV and later Adrian V) and several cardinals. After studying canon law at Bologna, he became a notable canonist. He joined the Roman curia under Pope Honorius III in 1226; and under Pope Gregory IX he was appointed vice-chancellor of the Roman church, cardinal priest of Saint Lawrence in Lucina, and rector of the March of Ancona. He succeeded Celestine IV (whose papacy had lasted less than a month) following a two-year vacancy during which Emperor Frederick II Hohenstuafen had prevented the election of a new pope. Innocent IV's choice of his papal name reflected a desire to continue in the wake of his great predecessor, Innocent III.

The struggle between the papacy and the empire reached a climax during the pontificate of Innocent IV. In order to escape imperial domination, the pope was forced in 1244 to flee to Lyon, where he came under the protection of the French king Louis IX and where he remained until 1251. Innocent called the first general council of Lyon (the thirteenth general council of the church) in 1245, to consider and solve several pressing problems. The sentence of excommunication against Frederick II was renewed: the charges against Frederick included perjury, suspicion of heresy, and failure to heed his excommunication. Innocent pressed the princes of the empire to elect a new king and emperor. Henry Raspe, landgrave of Thuringia, was elected to replace the deposed Frederick in May 1246. After Henry Raspe died in 1247, William, count of Holland, was elected. Frederick then threatened to capture the pope. Evidence to implicate Innocent in an attempted assassination of Frederick in 1246 is inconclusive; but since Frederick was deemed a tyrant and a heretic, medieval law and thought would have justified his elimination. His excommunication was renewed again in 1248. This struggle continued after Frederick died (of natural causes) in 1250 and his illegitimate son Manfred became regent of Sicily.

Innocent IV took an unwavering stand concerning the temporal political power of the papacy. He affirmed that secular power was not ordained by God and was therefore tyrannical. Pontifical power, on the other hand, represented a culmination not only of religious sacerdotal government but also of secular imperial government. These claims did not, in their full extent, become a generally accepted part of the teaching of the Catholic church.

Innocent IV was a patron of legal studies and was himself a canonist. He added several decretals to those of Gregory IX, and his legal reputation rests for the most part on his *Commentaria in quinque libros decretalium*, a subtle and sophisticated, although sometimes obscure, commentary on the *Decretales*. The unique feature of this work is that Innocent included some of his own decretal letters, accompanied by his commentary as a canonist. Because of its intrinsic worth and its authoritativeness, Innocent was called "father of law" by later generations of canonists. Innocent strove to promote learning by protecting students in every way. He also helped establish schools and universities, such as the University of Valencia; instituted schools of theology and of canon and civil law at Lyon and at Naples; founded the University of Piacenza; and granted special privileges to the University of Toulouse.

During his pontificate Innocent had to resolve important issues between factions concerning the internal life of the church. He favored the secular clergy at the University of Paris during their struggle with the mendicants. In a divisive conflict between Conventuals and Spirituals in the Franciscan order, he sided with the Conventuals: in 1254 he issued the papal bull *Ordinem veterem*, according to which Franciscans were allowed to use money and possessions because the pope himself assumed ownership of such property.

Contemporary evidence makes it certain that it was Innocent IV who bestowed on the cardinals their distinctive red hat, a symbol they have maintained for centuries. Innocent sent missionaries to the far east to convert the Mongols, and the Franciscan John of Pian dei Carpini paid a visit to the court of the great khan in 1246. Innocent's favors to his family, and particularly to his nephews, made him famous (or notorious) for introducing nepotism into church matters. The eventual victory of the papacy over the empire ended the ambitions of the Hohenstaufen to create a centralized state by uniting Sicily and northern Italy.

See also **Frederick II**

Further Reading

Berger, Elie. *Saint Louis et Innocent IV: Étude sur les rapports de la France et du saint-siège.* Paris: Thorin, 1893.
Enciclopedia Cattolica. Florence: Sansoni, 1950.
Mann, Horace K. *The Lives of the Popes in the Middle Ages.* London: Kegan Paul, Trench, Trubner; Saint Louis, Mo., Herder, 1925.
Melloni, Alberto. *Innocenzo IV: La concezione e l'esperienza della cristianità come regimen unius personae.* Prefazione di Brian Tierney. Genoa: Marietti, 1990.
The New Catholic Encyclopedia, 2nd ed. Detroit, Mich.: Thomson-Gale, 2003.
Strayer, Joseph R., ed. *Dictionary of the Middle Ages.* New York: Scribner, 1983.

ALESSANDRO VETTORI

ISABEAU OF BAVARIA
(ca. 1370–1435)

Queen of France. Born to Stephen, duke of Bavaria, and Taddea Visconti, Isabeau married Charles VI of France on July 17, 1385. Charles VI had fallen in love with her at their first meeting on July 14 and married her without a marriage contract or dowry. Their relationship was troubled by his schizophrenia, which caused him to have an ambivalent attitude toward her. Isabeau was adept at politics, and on July 1, 1402, Charles empowered her to deal with government business in his absence, aided by the dukes and whichever counselors she wished, but her prerogative was tempered in April 1403, when a group of royal ordinances attempted to achieve a balance of power among the royal relatives.

In 1405, Isabeau's court was accused of moral corruption and the queen herself was rebuked for instigating extravagant fashions by Jacques Legrand, an Augustinian friar. Until recently, historians have considered her frivolous and, more significantly, involved in an adulterous relationship with her brother-in-law, Louis of Orléans. The accusation of adultery first appeared in the anti-dauphin Paris of 1422–29, as part of an effort to throw doubts on the paternity of Charles VII. The myth found expression in the *Pastoralet*, a poem composed at that time to glorify John the Fearless of Burgundy, recently murdered at the dauphin's command.

Politically, Isabeau was quite unsupportive of Louis of Orléans until late 1404 or 1405, and she opposed John the Fearless until he rescued her from the exile imposed by the Armagnacs (Orléanist party) in 1417. Her objective from 1409 until that time had been to set up her eldest son as a replacement for the king during his periods of illness and thus keep the power to govern within the immediate royal family and away from the warring dukes. In January 1418, viewing the king and dauphin as prisoners of the Armagnacs in Paris, Isabeau formed a rival government with John the Fearless in Troyes. The Burgundian invasion of Paris in May 1418 produced a rapprochement between the king and queen but caused the departure of the dauphin, breaking the familial link that was essential to save the independence of the monarchy. Isabeau played an important role in the negotiations that led to the Treaty of Troyes (1420), and her policy of this period, aimed at protecting the monarchy, was long misinterpreted by historians as anti-French. Isabeau died at the Hôtel Saint-Pol in Paris in 1435.

See also **Charles VI**

Further Reading

Famiglietti, R.C. *Royal Intrigue: Crisis at the Court of Charles VI 1392–1420.* New York: AMS, 1986.

Grandeau, Yann. "Les dernières années d'Isabeau de Bavière." *Cercle Archéologique et Historique de Valenciennes* 9 (1976): 411–28.

———. "Isabeau de Bavière, ou l'amour conjugal." *Actes du 102e Congrès National des Sociétés Savantes, Limoges 1977,*

Section de Philologie et d'Histoire jusqu'à 1610 (1979): 117–48.

Kimm, Heidrun. *Isabeau de Bavière, reine de France, 1370–1435.* Munich: Stadtarchiv München, 1969.

Thibault, Marcel. *Isabeau de Bavière, reine de France: la jeunesse 1370–1405.* Paris: Perrin, 1903.

Richard C. Famiglietti

ISIDORE OF SEVILLE, SAINT (ca. 560-636)

Isidore, born in the 560s, was the younger brother of Leander, bishop of Seville from 576, who met Pope Gregory I the Great at Constantinople about 580 and subsequently played a central part in the official conversion of the Visigothic state from Arianism to Catholicism (589). The southern fringe of the Iberian Peninsula was under Byzantine influence after 552, and Isidore's family, from Cartagena, may have been of Greek descent. He was probably born in Seville. There was a sister, Florentina, and an intermediate brother, Fulgentius. The Catholic conversion offered a potent prospect of achieving religious and political unity, in which Isidore was the single most influential intellectual figure. He succeeded to the bishopric about 601, and presided over the influential Second Council of Seville (619) and the seminal Fourth Council of Toledo (633), which, among other things, threatened excommunication for opponents of the king, at a time when kings had come to feel the need for episcopal legitimization.

Isidore died on 4 April 636. His main professional aim had been to consolidate the doctrinal, political, and intellectual triumphs of Catholicism, and he succeeded in inspiring what is sometimes called the "Visigothic Renaissance"; the realm was not as united, educated, and Catholic as subsequent myth came to suggest, but it was the most educated part of western Europe, and Isidore deserves large credit for that. His personality is largely indecipherable, although Díaz y Díaz decided that he was shy, lacking in confidence, eager to please, and obsessively hardworking. Braulio of Zaragoza, his biographer, said that his eloquence would move any kind of hearer.

Isidore's intellectual education was largely in the hands of Leander, who built up the episcopal library (with the works of Augustine, Gregory, African grammarians, etc.). Isidore's 633 council required all bishops to run schools, and he felt a didactic need to raise educational levels; part of his success was that Spanish Christian education and culture remained in his tradition for another five centuries. After his death he slowly metamorphosed from intellectual into saint; his body was translated to León in 1063 as part of Fernando I's affirmation of links with the glorious Gothic past, 4 April was given a special office bearing his name, and, as "Esidre," he was invoked as a national patron (e.g., three times by Alfonso VI in the *Poema de Mío Cid*). He was named doctor of the church in 1722.

Outside the peninsula, Isidore's historical and institutional importance was rarely understood, and he became a mere name appended to influential texts. Surviving early manuscripts are from Irish, English, and Gaulish, rather than Iberian, centers. The works are listed here in tentative chronological order (the precise titles are often later inventions). The *De differentiis verborum*, on semantic distinctions, may precede his episcopacy. The *De differentiis rerum* was prepared independently. The *In libros veteris ac novi testamenti proemia* and the *De ortu et obitu patrum* are biblical and doctrinal; the *De ecclesiasticis officiis* is still a vital source of evidence on the history of the liturgy and the different roles of contemporary clerics. The *Synonyma*, an ascetic confession of and repentance for sins (ca. 610), developed the eventually fashionable style for piling up synonyms. The *De natura rerum*, commissioned by the Visigothic king Sisebut about 613, combines pagan (Lucretian) and Christian views on cosmography (and related allegory).

The *De numeris* considers the symbolism of numbers found in biblical texts. The *Allegoriae quaedam sacrae scripturae* comments on nearly three hundred biblical characters; the *De haeresibus*, on eighty-four sects. The *Sententiae* is Isidore's main spiritual work, combining knowledge and personal experience into a practical guide to Christian life. The *Chronica* is a history of the world from the beginning to A.D. 615. The *De fide catholica contra Judaeos* is polemical. The *De viris illustribus* contains brief summaries of the works (rather than the lives) of thirty-three churchmen, mostly African and Spanish, of the previous two centuries. The *Historia Gothorum, Vandalorum et Sueborum* (625–626) begins with the famous *Laus Hispaniae* and suggests that the Goths, rather than the Byzantines, are the genuine inheritors of Roman culture. The *Quaestiones in vetus testamentum* consists of commentaries.

Various minor works also survive, plus the conciliar and liturgical texts Isidore helped draft, monastic rules, and brief letters (mostly to Braulio); others are forgeries or apocryphally attributed; but his fame came to rest on his main work, still unfinished at his death, which subsumed much previous study and developed from his increasing appreciation of pagan learning: the *Etymologiae*.

The *Etymologiae* is an enormous encyclopedia, of both objectively erudite and pastorally didactic intent, meant to preserve and convey an all-inclusive synthesis of all fields of knowledge available in respectably ancient texts, with added comments from Isidore's own experience to make it relevant to his readers; it is mostly, therefore, written in the present tense, referring to fifty-two classical authors and only twenty Christian ones (plus the Bible). Braulio advised readers to read it through entire, often and carefully, and then they would know everything; thus it is prepared in a simpler style than many Visigothic works. The title is explained by Isidore's persistent attempts to explain why words have the written form they do; in modern terms, this is "popular etymology" (largely accidental word association given unconvincingly mystical explanatory force), not philology.

The *Etymologiae* was probably begun about 615, and a preliminary version of probably ten books (titled *Origines*) was circulating by 621. It is much more than a traditional glossary since, in essence, it presents an accumulation of compartmentalized detail rather than overviews, it is possible to deduce that Isidore worked with a kind of index-card system, preparing lemmas first and adding details as he found them later; this would explain both why several subheadings are left unexplained (particularly in the more technical chapters), and why the latest manuscript versions (from Spain) have additional material at the end of sections not attested in earlier versions. Even though the task covered twenty years, the amount of material is such that Isidore may have had collaborators. If we can overcome the modern scholarly obsession with sources, we can see that the didactic intention (looking to the future) often overrides the scientific (recording the ancient); to this extent the *Etymologiae* was astonishingly successful, being read, studied, and copied in European intellectual centers for another eight hundred years. Modern editions of all Isidore's texts, however, unhelpfully overclassicize the language of the early manuscripts.

Further Reading

Díaz y Díaz, M. C. "Introducción." In *San Isidoro de Sevilla. Etimologías (edición bilingüe)*. Ed. J. Oroz Reta. Madrid, 1982. 1–257.
——, ed. *Isidoriana*. León, 1961.
Fontaine, J. *Isidore de Séville et la culture classique dans l'Espagne wisigothique*. 2d ed. 3 vols. Paris, 1983.

ROGER WRIGHT

J

JACOB VAN MAERLANT
(ca. 1230–ca. 1290)

A Flemish poet, Maerlant came from Bruxambacht, or, the "Freedom of Bruges" (*het Brugse Vrije*). His oeuvre, which shows strong didactic tendencies, clearly indicates that he was well educated, even though his exact place in society is unclear. He probably received minor orders and held several positions as a clerk (*clerc*). In the late 1350s, Maerlant moved northward to the island of Voorne (in the estuary of the River Maas in the southern part of the county of Holland), taking his name from the village Maerlant (near Brielle) on that island. He became sexton (*coster, custos*) of the local church of St. Peter (if *Coster* is not his family name), a profession that agreed perfectly with his activities as an author. During his stay in Maerlant he was possibly a tutor to young Floris V (d. 1296), count of Holland. Around 1270 he returned to Flanders, to Damme, near Bruges, earning his livelihood as a civil servant (in toll regulations) and continuing his writing. Tradition (unproved) has it that he was buried after his death ca. 1290 "under the bells" of the church of Our Lady in Damme.

Some of Maerlant's works are only known from references in his other works, such as the *Sompniarijs* (a book on dream interpretation), the *Lapidarijs* (a book on the mineral qualities of stones), and a *vita* (life) of St. Clare of Assisi. Maerlant's authorship of some works is still a matter of dispute, but his oeuvre amounted to at least 225,000 lines in coupled rhyme.

The oldest surviving work is *Alexanders Geesten* [Deeds of Alexander (ca. 1260, 14,277 verses)]. Maerlant wrote this history of Alexander the Great on a commission from Aleide van Avesnes, to whom he gives the pseudonym *Gheile* in an acrostichon (series of first letters in lines of a poem which spell words). The text is a translation and adaptation of the *Alexandreïs* of Walter of Châtillon, which Maerlant took from a manuscript with glosses. But the poet used a broad range of additional sources, including the *Historia Scholastica* (Scholastic History) of Petrus Comestor, Lucanus's *De Bello Civile* (Civil War), Ovid's *Metamorphoses*, Virgil's *Aeneid*, the *Disciplina Clericalis* (Clerical Discipline) of Pedro Alfonso, the *Secreta Secretorum* (Secret of Secrets), and Honorius of Autun's *Imago Mundi* (Image of the World).

For Albrecht of Voorne, Maerlant wrote *Merlijn* in 1261. The text encompasses two separate tales: the *Historic van den Grale* (History of the Grail, 1607 verses) and *Boek van Merline* (Book of Merlin, 8485 verses), which were adaptations of Robert de Boron's *Joseph d'Arimathie* (Joseph of Arimathia) and *Roman de Merlin* (Tale of Merlin). The *Torec* (ca. 1262) is Maerlant's second Arthurian romance. This text (about 3,800 verses) has only been handed down to us in an abridged form, included in the vast *Lancelot Compilation* of The Hague.

Maerlant's *Historie van Troyen* (ca. 1264, 40,880 verses) renders the history of the Trojan War, from its preparatory stages to its aftermath. Among the sources he used were the *Roman de Troie* of Benoît of St. Maure, the *Achilleid* of Statius, the *Aeneid* of Virgil, Ovid's *Metamorphoses* and his own *Alexanders Geesten*. In addition, he incorporated the complete *Trojeroman* of Segher Diengotgaf into his text. The patron behind this work is not yet known, but it is likely the *Historie van Troyen* was intended for a noble audience.

The "Mirror of Princes," the *Heimelijkheid der Heimelijkheden* (ca. 1266, 2,158 verses), was possibly written for the young count of Holland, Floris V, and is a translation of the *Secreta Secretorum* of Pseudo-Aristoteles. (Maerlant's authorship of this text is sometimes disputed.) *Der naturen bloeme* [Flower of Nature (ca. 1266, 16,670 verses)], the first bestiary in the vernacular, assimilated Aristotle's books on biology. Maerlant derived his text from his immediate source, the *Liber de Natura Rerum* (Book of Natural Things) by Thomas of Cantimpré. The bestiary was commissioned by the nobleman Nicolaas of Cats (d. 1283).

In 1271 Maerlant finished his *Scolastica*, an abridged adaptation of Petrus Comestor's *Historia Scolastica*. To this book, of some 27,000 verses, he added an adaptation of Flavius Josephus' *De Bello Iudaïco* (On the Jewish War). Maerlant considered the total text of almost 35,000 verses as a single work. Probably commissioned by a noble patron, it was intended to serve an audience of noble laymen (*illiterati*). Even though it was not a translation of the Bible, the *Scolastica* marked the beginning of the popularization of the Bible in the Dutch language.

In the early seventies Maerlant wrote *Sente Franciscus Leven* (10,545 verses). This fairly literal translation of the *Legenda Maior* of St. Bonaventure is perhaps the first *vita* of Saint Francis in the vernacular. Maerlant wrote it at the request of the *fratres minores* (Order of the Lesser Brothers) in Utrecht. During his career as a poet, Maerlant composed several shorter stanzaic poems. These lyrical texts with a didactic aim show a fervent devotion to the Virgin Mary and a strong critical attitude towards society.

Maerlant's *magnum opus* is undoubtedly his *Spiegel Historiael*. He worked from 1283 until 1288 on this world chronicle, dedicated to Count Floris V of Holland. The major source by this text is Vincent of Beauvais's *Speculum Historiale* but Maerlant consulted and absorbed many more sources, among them the Vulgate, the *Secreta Secretorum*, *De Hormesta Mundi* of Orosius, *De Origine et Rebus Gestis Getarum* of Jordanes, two works by Martin of Braga (the *Liber de Moribus* and the *Formulae vitae honestae*), Paulus Diaconus's *Historia Miscella*, the *Historia Regum Brittanniae* by Geoffrey of Monmouth, as well as the Crusade chronicles by Albert of Aken and (probably) William of Tyre. As it has come down to us, the *Spiegel Historiael* (ca. 91,000 verses), is not solely from the hand of Maerlant. He had planned a work in four parts (which he called *partieën*), and he wrote the first, the third, and three "books" of the fourth part. He had postponed work on the second part, containing the years 54–367 C.E., and never was able to complete it. Apart from the lacuna of the second part and the remaining "books" of part four, Maerlant wrote a history from the Creation to the year 1113. The *Spiegel Historiael* was completed by two of his younger contemporaries, Philip Utenbroeke and Lodewijc van Velthem. The latter added a fifth part, bringing the history to the year 1316.

The extent and diversity of his oeuvre, and his exceptionally erudite and critical style, marks Jacob van Maerlant as a leading author of his time whose stature extended beyond his Dutch homeland.

See also **Benoît de Sainte-Maure; Pedro Alfonso, or Petrus Alfonsi; Peter Comester**

Further Readng

Berendrecht, Petra. *Proeven van bekwaamheid. Jacob van Maerlant en de omgang met zijn Latijnse bronnen*. Amsterdam: Prometheus, 1996.

Claassens, Geert H. M. "Maerlant on Muhammad and Islam." In *Medieval Christian Perceptions of Islam. A Book of Essays*, ed. John V. Tolan. New York & London: Garland, 1996, pp. 211–242 and 361–393.

de Pauw, Napoleon, and Edward Gaillard, ed. *Die Istory van Troyen*. 4 vols. Ghent: Siffer, 1889–1892.

de Vries, Matthijs, and Eelco Verwijs, ed. *Jacob van Maerlant's Spiegel Historiael, met de fragmenten der later toegevoegde gedeelten, bewerkt door Philip Utenbroeke and Lodewijc van Velthem*. 3 vols. Leyden: Brill, 1863–1879.

Franck, Johannes, ed. *Alexanders Geesten, van Jacob van Maerlant*, Groningen: Wolters, 1882.

Franck, Johannes, and Jakob Verdam, ed. *Jacob van Maerlants Strophische Gedichten*. Leyden: Sijthoff, 1898.

Gysseling, Maurits, ed. *Corpus van Middelnederlandse teksten. Reeks II: Literaire handschriften*, Vol. 3, *Rijmbijbel/tekst*, Leyden: Nijhoff, 1983.

Maximilianus, O. F. M., ed. *Sinte Franciscus Leven van Jacob van Maerlant*. 2 vols. Zwolle: Tjeenk-Willink, 1954.

Sodmann, Timothy, ed. *Jacob van Maerlant, Historie van den Grale und Boek van Merline*. Cologne/Vienna: Böhlau, 1980.

te Winkel, Jan. *Maerlant's werken beschouwd als spiegel van de 13de eeuw*. Ghent 1892; rpt. Utrecht: HES, 1979.

van Oostrom, Frits P. *Maerlants werteld*. Amsterdam: Prometheus, 1996.

Verdenius, Andries A., ed. *Jacob van Maerlant's Heimelijkheid der Heimelijkheden*. Amsterdam: Kruyt, 1917.

Verwijs, Eelco, ed. *Jacob van Maerlant's Naturen Bloem*. 2 vols. Groningen: Wolters, 1872–1878.

GEERT H. M. CLAASSENS

JACOBUS DA VORAGINE
(c. 1228-1298)

Jacobus da Voragine (Jacopo da Varazze) was a Dominican writer, administrator, and archbishop; his name suggests that he or his forbears came from Varazze, a town near Genoa. He entered the Order of Preachers—i.e., the Dominican order—as a youth, in 1244. After completing his education, he is reputed to have distinguished himself both as a public preacher and as a teacher of preachers in training, and also to have been prior (local head) of the Dominican community in Genoa. From 1267 on, his career is more clearly documented. His fellow Dominicans repeatedly elected him prior of the entire province of Lombardy, a post he held from 1267 to 1277 and again from 1281 to 1286. Both the order and the papacy entrusted him with sensitive diplomatic missions. From 1292 until his death, he was archbishop of Genoa, and he had such an exemplary reputation in this office that he was eventually beatified (in 1816).

Among the literary works Joacobus wrote or compiled, the earliest and most famous is a *Legenda sanctorum aurea (Golden Legend)*. After the *Legenda*, Jacobus composed four large sets of Latin sermons, which evidently circulated as models for other preachers to use: *Sermones de sanctis*, on major saints and festivals of the church year; *Sermones de tempore*, on the Sunday gospels for the year; *Sermones quadragesimales*, on the weekday gospels for Lent; and *Mariade*, or *Laudes deiparae virginis*, sermons in praise of the Virgin Mary. Jacobus's sermons survive in numerous manuscripts and early printed editions and thus must have enjoyed a wide and long-lasting popularity. His last major work, *Chronicle of Genoa*, which he wrote as archbishop, is noteworthy for the local history and hagiography it preserves and for some autobiographical passages that shed light on his own life.

Further Reading

Kaeppeli, Thomas. *Scriptores Ordini Praedicatorum medii aevi*, Vol. 2. Rome: Ad S. Sabinae, 1975, pp. 348-369.

Monleone, Giovanni. *Iacopo da Varagine e la sua Cronaca di Genova dale origini al MCCXCVII*, 3 vols. Rome: Tipografia del Senato, 1941.

Sermones aurei . . ., 2 vols. Ed. Rudolph Clutius. Augsburg and Cracow: Apud Christophorum Bartl, 1760. (Latin edition: includes all four sermons).

SHERRY REAMES

JACOPO DA MILANO
(13th century)

The Franciscan lector Jacopo da Milano (Jacob of Milan, James of Milan, Jacobus Mediolanensis, Giacomo da Milano) was the author of the original version of a spiritual classic in Latin, *Stimulus amoris (Prick of Love)*. Much has been surmised but little is known for certain about Jacopo. From the date of the earliest evidence for the *Stimulus amoris*, and from the acquaintance it shows with the writings of Saint Bonaventure, Jacopo must have composed it in the second half of the thirteenth century. Jacopo has been plausibly but not conclusively identified with a Brother James of Milan recorded as a lector at the Franciscan convent at Domodossola in 1305. Some scholars have thought him identical or possibly identical with a mid-thirteenth-century Milanese theologian who was known until 1979—incorrectly—as Giacomo Capelli or de Capellis; but this person is no longer credibly a Jacopo. Jacopo could well have been the renowned Franciscan, formerly a lector in Milan, who sometime after 1296 read and approved Arnaldo of Foligno's *Memorial* on the mystic and visionary Angela of Foligno. One modern scholar has ascribed to Jacopo a meditation on the hymn *Salve Regina*, transmitted in some of his manuscripts and at times attributed to Bernard of Clairvaux (among others), but this idea has not found widespread acceptance.

Recent investigation has revealed *Stimulus amoris* in its Jacopean form to be an unstable "open text" whose very title is uncertain. As now edited, it consists of a prologue and twenty-three brief chapters; the first nine chapters guide the reader toward divine rapture, and the rest deal with other aspects of the contemplative life. The writing style is often intense and rhetorically effective; it combines direct address, exclamation, and figures of repetition with an intentionally simple vocabulary. Chapter 14, an especially vivid meditation on Christ's passion, is thought by some to have furnished the theological basis for the imagery in the window of the Glorification of Saint Francis in the upper church of Francis's basilica at Assisi. However, the ideas in question were common in later thirteenth-century Franciscan contexts, and the dating of both the window and the earliest version or versions of the text is uncertain.

Jacopo's *Stimulus* circulated with Bonaventure's works, was soon mistakenly attributed to Bonaventure, and was expanded twice in the fourteenth century by persons unknown. Modern scholars differentiate these texts by calling the original *Stimulus (amoris) minor* and the expansions (treated as a single version) *Stimulus (amoris) maior*. The *maior* was more widely read: there are more than 130 manuscripts of it, as opposed to some ninety manuscripts of the *minor*. A recent suggestion that the *maior* was actually the original seems unpersuasive. Starting in the later fourteenth century, this very different larger version was translated into other European languages, including English. A fourteenth-century translation (now lost) of *Stimulus minor* into Tuscan dialect is thought to underlie its first printing in Italian (Venice, 1521).

See also **Angela da Foligno, Saint; Bonaventure, Saint**

Further Reading

Edition

Fathers of the College of Saint Bonaventure, eds. *Stimulus amoris fr. Iacobi Mediolanensis—Canticum pauperis fr. Ioannis Peckam*. Bibliotheca Franciscans Ascetica Medii Aevi, 4. Quaracchi: Collegium S. Bonaventurae, 1905, pp. vi–xvii, 1–132. (Reprint, 1949).

Critical Studies

Alberzoni, Maria Pia.' "L'*approbatio*': Curia Romana, ordine minoritico e *Liber*." In *Angèle de Foligno: Le dossier*, ed. Giulia Barone and Jacques Dalarun. Collection de l'École Française de Rome, 255. Rome: École Française de Rome, 1999, pp. 293–318. (See especially pp. 311–114.)

Canal, Jose M., "El *Stimulus amoris* de Santiago de Milán y la *Meditatio in Salve regina*." *Franciscan Studies*, 26, 1966, pp. 174–188.

Cremaschi, Chiara Giovanna, trans. "Introduzione" and *Stimulus*

(Giacomo da Milano, *Il pungolo dell'amore*). In *I mistici: Scritti dei mistici francescani*. Assisi: Editrici Francescane, 1995– , Vol. 1, pp. 795–881.

Eisermann, Falk. "*Diversae et plurimae materiae in diversis capitulis*: Der 'Stimulus amoris' als literarisches Dokument der normativen Zentrierung." *Frühmittelalterliche Studien*, 31, 1997, pp. 214–232.

———. *Stimulus amoris: Inhalt, lateinische Überlieferung, deutsche Übersetzungen, Rezeption*. Münchener Texte und Untersuchungen zur Deutschen Literatur des Mittelalters, 118. Tübingen: Max Niemeyer Verlag, 2001.

Mostaccio, S. "Giacomo da Milano." In *Dizionario biografico degli Italiani*, Vol. 54. Rome: Istituto della Enciclopedia Italiana, 2000, pp. 221–223.

Piana, Celestino. "Il 'fr. Iacobus de Mediolano lector' autore dello pseudo-Bonaventuriano *Stimulus amoris* ed un convento del suo insegnamento." *Antonianum*, 61, 1986, pp. 329–339.

Poulenc, Jerôme. "Saint François dans le 'vitrail des anges' de l'église supérieure de la basilique d'Assise." *Archivum Franciscanum Historicum*, 76, 1983, pp. 701–713.

Wessley, Stephen E., "James of Milan and the Guglielmites: Franciscan Spirituality and Popular Heresy in Late Thirteenth-Century Milan." *Collectanea Franciscana*, 54, 1984, pp. 5–20.

JOHN B. DILLON

JACOPO DE CESSOLIS
(fl. 1275–1322)

Jacopo Jacobus was born in the small town of Cessole, near Asti, in Piedmont. He entered the Dominican order, probably at the convent of Santa Maddalena near Asti. From 1317 to 1322, he lived in Genoa, where he became vicar of the Inquisition attached to the convent of San Domenico. At the request of fellow Dominicans and several laypeople, he wrote his only extant work, *De moribus hominum ed de officiis nobilum super ludo scaccorum* (*On the Customs of Men and Their Noble Actions with Regard to the Game of Chess*), known simply as *Ludus scaccorum*.

Ludus scaccorum is a moralized explanation of chess based on the medieval estates, whereby each chess piece represents a different social class. It consists of twenty-four chapters divided into four sections (*tractatus*). The first section consists of three chapters that narrate when, how, and by whom chess was invented. The narrative, in the form of a medieval *exemplum*, recounts how a Greek philosopher named Xerxes or Perses invented the game to show his cruel king Evilmerodach "the maners and conditicions of a kynge of the nobles and of the comun people and of theyr offices and how they shold be touchid and drawen. And how he shold amende hymself & become vertuous." Xerxes explains that he invented the game to keep the king from "ydlenesse," which can induce men to sin, and to satisfy man's desire for "noueltees & tydynges," which in turn sharpen the mind. The *exemplum* ends with Evilmerodach's eventual conversion, thus setting a precedent for using chess to teach people how to behave.

The second section is divided into five chapters describing, respectively, the five different chess pieces in the first row: (1) king, (2) queen, (3) alphinus (judge), (4) knight, and (5) rook (legate). Each piece is described in terms of its clothing, its symbols of power, the moral significance of those symbols, and—most important—the way a represented by the piece must behave in society. Jacopo narrates several *exempla* to illustrate the kind of behavior he has in mind for each person.

The third section deals with the pawns and is divided into eight chapters, each taking up a particular group of commoners (one pawn representing one group): (1) laborers (farmers), (2) smiths, (3) notaries, (4) merchants, (5) physicians, (6) innkeepers, (7) city watchmen and guards, and (8) ribalds and town couriers. Each pawn is described in terms of the tools of its trade, its relationship to the chess piece behind it, and how the person represented should behave. For each group of commoners, Jacopo narrates one or more *exempla*, illustrating either appropriate or inappropriate behavior of that group.

The fourth section is also divided into eight chapters. The first chapter describes the chessboard as an allegorical representation of Babylon, where the game was presumably invented. The next six chapters deal with the actual moves of each chess piece on the chessboard. These moves reflect the rules of chess that were then in effect in Lombardy and are allegorized to illustrate a moral. For example, when a pawn becomes a queen, the fact that many great rulers had humble origins is illustrated. In the eighth chapter in this section—the final chapter—Jacopo reiterates the history of the origins of chess, reminding his readers that chess is a social allegory of the various classes of medieval society working together for the common good.

As Kaeppeli (1960) noted, the convent of San Domenico in Genoa produced a considerable amount of popular religious literature. It is not surprising, therefore, that *Ludus scaccorum* spread rapidly throughout western and eastern Europe; there were even a Scottish translation and a Czech translation. When *Ludus scaccorum* was translated from Latin into a vernacular, or from one vernacular into another, the content was sometimes modified to reflect a country's particular ways of representing its own social classes (Buuren 1997).

The diffusion and popularity of *Ludus scaccorum* during the fourteenth and fifteenrh centuries are reflected in the numerous manuscripts and early printed editions of the work. It was the second book to be printed in the English language: William Caxton printed an English translation of Jehan de Vignay's French translation (c. 1350) of *Ludus scaccorum* in 1474. Despite the popularity of *Ludus scaccorum* in the late Middle Ages and the early Renaissance, there are no critical editions in print of the Latin original, nor are there any modern translarions in either English or Italian. There are, however, modern critical editions of Jean Ferron's French translation of 1347 (the best of the medieval French translations), and of the Middle Scots translation of c. 1515.

Further Reading

Editions

Burt, Marie Anita. "Jacobus de Cessolis: *Libellus de moribus hominum et officiis nobilium ac popularium super ludo scachorum.*" Dissertation, University of Texas, Austin, 1957.

Jacobus de Cessolis. *Libellus de ludo scachorum*, ed. Ernst Köpke. Mittheilungen aus den Handschriften der Ritter-Akademie zu Brandenburg a. H., 2. Brandenburg a. d. Havel: G. Matthes, 1879.

Das Schachbuch des Jacobus de Cessolis: Codex Palatinus Latinus 961, 2 vols. Belser Faksimile Editionen aus der Biblioteca Apostolica Vaticana, 74. Zürich: Belser Verlag, 1988.

Vetter, Ferdinand, ed. *Das Schachzabelbuch Kunrats von Ammenhausen, Mönchs, und Leutpriesters zu Stein am Rhein, nebst den Schachbüchern des Jakob von Cessole und des Jakob Mannel.* Frauenfeld: Huber, 1892.

Translations

Caxton, William. *The Game and Play of Chesse (1474),* intro. N. F. Blake. London: Scolar, 1976.

Caxton's Game and Playe of the Cheese, 1474: A Verbatim Reprint of the First Edition with an Introduction by William E. A. Axon. London: Elliot Stock, 1883.

The Game of the Cheese by William Caxton: Reproduction in Facsimile with Remarks by Vincent Figgins. London: John Russell Smith, 1860.

Volgarizzamento del libro de' costumi e degli offizi de' nobili sopra il giuoco degli scacchi di frate Jacopo da Cessole: Tratto nuovamente da un codice Magliabechiano, ed. Pietro Marocco. Milan: Dalla Tipografia del Dott. Giulio Ferrario, 1829.

Critical Studies

Buuren, Catherine van, ed. *The Buke of the Chess: Edited from the Asloan Manuscript (NLS MS 16500).* Edinburgh: Scottish Text Society, 1997.

Collet, Alain, ed. *Le Jeu des Eschaz Moralisé: Traduction de Jean Ferron (1347).* Paris: Honoré Champion, 1999.

Di Lorenzo, Robert D. "The Collection Form and the Art of Memory in the *Libellus super Ludo Scaccorum* of Jacobus de Cessolis." *Mediaeval Studies,* 35, 1973, pp. 205–221.

Kaeppeli, Thomas, O.P. "Pour la biographie de Jacques de Cessole." *Archivum Fratrum Praedicatorum,* 30, 1960, pp. 149–162.

Mann, Jill. *Chaucer and Medieval Estates Satire.* Cambridge: Cambridge University Press, 1973. Murray, Harold James R. *A History of Chess.* Oxford: Clarendon, 1913, pp. 537–549. (Reprints, 1961, 1987.)

STEVEN GROSSVOGEL

JACOPONE DA TODI
(c. 1230 or 1236–1306)

The Franciscan friar and mystic Jacopone da Todi (Jacobus de Benedictis, Jacopus de Tuderto, Jacopo de' Benedetti, Giacopone de' Benedetti) is considered by some to be Italy's greatest poet before Dante. The principal type of verse that Jacopone used is the *lauda*, a nonliturgical song of praise in vernacular ballad form, although some works in Latin are also attributed to him.

Details about Jacopone's life before his religious conversion are sketchy, but it is generally accepted that he was born (as his name implies) in Todi, Umbria, to a family of the lesser nobility. He received an education typical of his time and social class (he may have studied at the University of Bologna) and then is believed to have practiced the profession of notary in Todi and, in his mid-thirties, to have married Vanna di Bernardino di Guidone, of the counts of Collemedio (or Coldimezzo). According to early *vitae* (lives) of Jacopone, Vanna's accidental death at a party devastated him, provoked a profound psychological crisis, and led to his religious conversion in 1268. The precipitating factor in this rapid chain of events appears to have been his discovery that Vanna, like many others during this tumultuous period of Italian history, had practiced self-mortification as a form of religious penance—in her case, by wearing a hairshirt under her beautiful and costly outer garb. To the consternation of his family and the disbelief of his fellow citizens, Jacopo divested himself of all his worldly goods and habits and became a *bezocone*, or mendicant Franciscan tertiary (*Laude*, ed. Mancini, 1974, 151). For the next ten years, he traveled the highways of Umbria, singing God's praise and preaching salvation, not in the Latin of the church but in the language of the people, as was the custom of the Franciscans. In 1278, on his second request, he was finally admitted to the order of Friars Minor (i.e., the Franciscan order; Casolini 1966, 620). He thus became Fra Jacopone—a name that can be translated as Big Jim or Big Jake.

In the years following the death of Saint Francis (1226), the Franciscans split into two opposing camps. The Spirituals believed in the strict interpretation of Francis's rule, which called for complete poverty; the Community, sometimes referred to as the Conventuals, supported a more relaxed interpretation that permitted ownership of property and other material comforts. Jacopone sided with the more extreme Spirituals and, as a consequence, found himself locked in the bitter and sometimes dangerous struggle between the two factions. When Boniface VIII became pope, Jacopone allied himself with the Colonna family, Boniface's enemies. Jacopone's open and virulent opposition to the powerful new pope earned him excommunication and five years of solitary confinement.

While he was in prison, Jacopone wrote many *laude*. In one of them—*Que farai, fra Iacovone?* ("What will you do, Brother Jacopone?" number 55 in Ageno's edition, 53 in Mancini's)—he comments with mordant irony on the dire conditions of his imprisonment. We know from two *laude*—*O papa Bonifazio/io porto el tuo prefazio* ("O Pope Boniface, I bring your sentence," number 56 in Ageno and 55 in Mancini) and *Lo pastor per mio peccato/posto m'à for de l'ovile* ("Because of my sin the shepherd has cast me out of the sheepfold," number 57 in Ageno and 67 in Mancini)—that Jacopone twice begged the pope for absolution. Although the pope granted absolution to many in the jubilee year of 1300, Jacopone was not among them. In 1303, however, Jacopone received personal liberty and release from religious censure from Boniface's more compassionate successor as pope, Benedict XI.

The elderly Jacopone then retired to the convent of San Lorenzo in Collazzone, where he died on Christmas eve, 1306. In 1433, his remains were discovered in the convent of Santa Maria di Montecristo, and in 1596 his tomb in the crypt of the Franciscan church of San Fortunato in Todi was dedicated. Although he has not been beatified or canonized by the church, Jacopone is inscribed in the Franciscan martyrology and is popularly referred to and venerated as "blessed" or "saint."

Jacopone wrote approximately 100 *laude* in the Umbrian vernacular that express the mystic's innermost sentiments about the state of his soul and seek to instruct others who are seeking greater closeness to God. Unlike many *laude* composed by others at this time (which was the form's most fertile period), Jacopone's hymns were written not for the general lay public but for his own personal use, and possibly for his Franciscan brothers. Jacopone's *laude* treat a wide range of subjects and present a variety of tones and moods. His important themes include the following (for each example, the number in Ageno is followed by the number in Mancini): praise of God (e.g., *La bontade enfinita*, "The infinite goodness," 79, 21), Christ (*Ad l'amor ch'è venuto*, "To the Love that came," 65, 86), and the Virgin Mary (*O Vergen più che femina*, "O Virgin more than woman," 2, 32); Saint Francis and the Franciscan ideal of poverty (*Povertade enamorata*, "Beloved poverty," 59, 47); the condemnation of all types of secular temptation (*Guarda che non caggi, amico*, "Be careful not to fall, my friend," 6, 20); detailed descriptions of disease, death, and dying (*Quando t'alegri*, "When you are glad," 25, 61); soul-searching self-criticism (*Que farai, fra Iacovone?* "What will you do, Brother Jacopone?" 55, 53); extreme self-abnegation (*O Signor, per cortesia,/mandame la malsanìa*, "O Lord, please infect me with disease," 48, 81); biting political satire (*Que farai, Pier da Morrone?* "What will you do, Pier da Morrone?" 54, 74); laments on the state of the church (*Piange la Ecclesia*, "The church weeps," 53, 35); descriptions of the mystical stare of ecstasy, akin to madness, that the poet entered during his spiritual meditation (*Senno me pare e cortesia*, "It seems to be wise and courteous," 84, 87); and the passionate praise of divine love (*O iubilo del core*, "O heartfelt joy," 76, 9; and *Sopr'onne lengua amore*, "Ineffable love," 91, 92). Misogyny is patently evident in some of his *laude* (e.g., *O femene, guardate*, "Women, beware," 8, 45), revealing Jacopone to be a man of his time. However, there is also evidence that he gave some thought to the difficult living conditions of many women in the late thirteenth century (e.g., *O vita penosa*, "O sorrowful life," 24, 58). One simple yet supremely elegant *lauda—Donna del paradiso* ("Lady of Paradise," 93, 70)—is important because it represents the pinnacle of Jacopone's poetic art and also because it constitutes a crucial step in the evolution of Italian religious theater: it has four speakers, and many scholars consider it the first religious drama in Italy.

Although critics are not in complete agreement regarding Jacopone's authorship of a number of works in Latin, the following have variously been attributed to him: the famous sequence *Stabat mater dolorosa*, now a part of the Roman Catholic liturgy; pithy moral sayings known as the *Detti*; and *Trattato* (*Treatise*), whose subject is mystical union with God.

See also **Boniface VIII, Pope; Celestine V, Pope**

Further Reading

Editions

Contini, Gianfranco, ed. *Poeti del Duecento*, 2 vols. Milan and Naples: Ricciardi, 1960, Vol. 2, pp. 61–166.

Jacopone da Todi. *Le laude, ristampa integrale della prima edizione (1490)*, ed. Giovanni Papini. Florence: Libreria Editrice Fiorentina, 1923.

——. *Le laude secondo la stampa riorentina del 1490*, ed. Giovanni Ferri. Bari: Laterza, 1930.

——. *Laudi, Trattato, e Detti*, ed. Franca Ageno. Florence: Le Monnier, 1953.

——. *Le laude*, ed. Luigi Fallacara. Florence: Liberia Editrice Fiorentina, 1955.

——. *Laude*, ed. Franco Mancini. Bari: Laterza, 1974.

Menestò, Enrico, ed. *Le vite antiche di Iacopone da Todi*. Florence: La Nuova Italia, 1977.

——, ed. *Le prose latine attribuite a Jacopone da Todi*. Bologna: Pàtron, 1979.

Ugolini, Francesco A., ed. *Laude di Jacopone da Todi tratte da due manoscritti umbri*. Turin: Istituto Editrice Gheroni, 1947.

Translations

Jacopone da Todi. *The Lauds*, trans. Serge Hughes and Elizabeth Hughes. New York: Paulist, 1982.

Underhill, Evelyn. *Jacopone da Todi: Poet and Mystic 1228–1306: A Spiritual Biography*. London: Dent; and New York: Dutton, 1919. (Reprint, Freeport, N.Y.: Books for Libraries, 1972.)

Studies

Ageno, Franca. "Modi stilistici delle laudi di Iacopone da Todi." *La Rassegna d'Italia*, 5, 1946, pp. 20–29.

——. "Motivi francescani nelle laudi di Iacopone da Todi." *Lettere Italiane*, 2, 1960, pp. 180–184.

Apollonio, Mario. *Jacopone da Todi e la poetica delle confraternite religiose nella cultura preumanistica*. Milan: Vita e Pensiero, 1946.

Bettarini, Rosanna. *Jacopone e il Laudario Urbinate*. Florence: Sansoni, 1969.

Casolini, Fausta. "Iacopone da Todi." *Biblioteca Sanctorum*, 7, 1966, pp. 617–628.

Convegni del Centro di studi sulla spiritualità medievale: Jacopone e il suo tempo (13–15 ottobre 1957). Todi: Accademia Tudertina, 1959.

D'Ascoli, Emidio. *Il misticismo nei canti spirituali di fra Iacopone da Todi*. Recanati: n.p., 1925.

Dick, Bradley B. "Jacopone da Todi and the Poetics of Franciscan Spirituality." Ph.D. dissertation, New York University, 1993.

Furia, Paola. "Sulla lingua delle 'laude' di Iacopone da Todi." *Cultura e Scuola*, 28(110), 1989, pp. 44–49.

Katainen, V. Louise. "Jacopone da Todi, Poet and Mystic: A Review of the History of the Criticism." *Mystics Quarterly*, 22, 1996, pp. 46–57.

Lograsso, A. H. "Jacopone da Todi." In *New Catholic Encyclopedia*. New York: McGraw Hill, 1967.

McGinn, Bernard. *The Flowering of Mysticism: Men and Women in the New Mysticism (1200–1350)*. The Presence of God: A History of Western Mysticism, 3. New York: Crossroad, 1998.

Menestò, Enrico, ed. *Atti del convegno storico iacoponico in occasione del 750 anniversario della nascita di Iacopone da Todi: Todi, 29–30 novembre 1980*. Florence: La Nuova Italia, 1981.

Neri, Ferdinando. "La pazzia e la poesia di Jacopone da Todi." In *Saggi di Letteratura Italiana, Francese, Inglese*. Naples: n.p., 1936.

Parodi, Ernesto Giacomo. "II Giullare di Dio." *Il Marzocco*, 19(26), 1915. (Reprinted in *Poeti antichi e moderni: Studi critici*. Florence: Sansoni, 1923, pp. 129–141.)

Peck, George T. *The Fool of God: Jacopone da Todi*. Tuscaloosa: University of Alabama Press, 1980.

Petrocchi, Giorgio. *Scrittori religiosi del Duecento*. Florence: Sansoni, 1974.

Russo, Luigi. "Jacopone da Todi mistico-poeta." In *Studi sul Due e Trecento*. Rome: Edizioni Italiane, 1946, pp. 31–57.

Sapegno, Natalino. *Frate Jacopone*. Turin: Baretti, 1926.

Toschi, Paolo. *Il valore attuale ed eterno della poesia di Jacopone*. Todi: Res Tudertinae, 1964. Triplo, Gary. "Mysticism and the Elements of the Spiritual Life in Jacopone da Todi." Ph.D. dissertation, Rutgers University, 1994.

Ungaretti, Giuseppe. "Sulla vita di Iacopone da Todi e la poesia di Iacopone da Todi." In *Invenzione della poesia moderna: Lezioni brasiliane di letteratura*, ed. Paola Montefoschi. Naples: Edizioni Scientifiche Italiane, 1984, pp. 41–68.

V. LOUISE KATAINEN

JACQUES DE VITRY
ca. 1160/70–1240)

The son of a wealthy bourgeois family in Vitry-en-Perthios near Reims, Jacques studied in Paris at a time when Peter the Chanter, one of the most celebrated preachers of his day, was master of the cathedral school. In 1211, he entered the monastery of Augustinian regular canons dedicated to St. Nicolas in Oignies, not far from Cambrai. Over the next five years, he was close to the lay religious group known as the béguines, whose leader was Marie d'Oignies. During this same period, he became a preacher of crusades, first against the Albigensians in 1213 and then against the infidels in the Holy Land in 1214. His preaching won him the see of Acre on the coast of Palestine. Jacques arrived in Palestine in 1216 and accompanied the armies of the Fifth Crusade at Damietta, 1218–21. Weary of constant strife, Jacques left Acre in 1225 and served Pope Gregory IX in Italy and in the Low Countries over the next three years. In 1228, Gregory appointed him cardinal bishop of Tusculum, and he remained in Rome until his death. Jacques was buried at the monastery in Oignies, where he had begun his ecclesiastical vocation.

Jacques's most significant contribution to the history of the church comprised his collections of sermons intended to serve as models for preachers. One collection, *Sermones dominicales* (*de tempore*), gives three sermons for each of the Sundays of the ecclesiastical calendar; *Sermones de sanctis* gives 115 sermons for saints' days and special feasts; *Sermones communes et feriales* gives twenty-seven sermons for daily use; *Sermones vulgares* (or *ad status*) gives seventy-four sermons addressing social classes and religious groups. The first small collection of such model sermons was compiled only the generation before by Alain de Lille, and Jacques went far beyond them with his collections, particularly in their homiletic illustrations, or exempla, which provide a wealth of amusing and instructive anecdotes.

Jacques also composed a biography of Marie d'Oignies (1213) that helped gain papal approval for the béguine movement and has since become a valuable historical source for the early days of that controversial movement. Several of his letters date from his sojourn in Palestine (up to 1221), and his *Historia Hierosolymitana abbreviata* in three books recounts not only the history of Jerusalem during the Crusades but also, and perhaps more importantly, the new and often controversial religious movements of the day, such as the béguines, the Humiliati, and even the Franciscans (at least in their more colorful manifestations), as they relate to the renewal of the church and to the success of its mission.

Although Jacques's religious vocation took the more traditional form of an Augustinian canon, both his sympathies for the spiritual revival of his day and his talents as an extraordinary preacher place him firmly in the mainstream of the life of the church in the 13th century.

See also **Alain de Lille; Marie d'Oignies**

Further Reading

Jacques de Vitry. *The Historia occidentalis of Jacques de Vitry*, ed. John F. Hinnebusch. Fribourg: University Press, 1972.

——. *Lettres de Jacques de Vitry, 1160/70–1240, évêque de Saint-Jean d'Acre*, ed. R.B.C. Huygens. Leiden: Brill, 1960.

——. *Sermones vulgares*. In *Analecta nouissima spicilegii Solesmensis, altera continuatio*, ed. Jean Baptiste Pitra. 2 vols. Paris: Typis Tusculanis, 1885–88, Vol. 2.

Funk, Philipp. *Jakob von Vitry: Leben und Werke*. Leipzig: Teubner, 1909.

MARK ZIER

JAIME (JAUME) I OF ARAGÓN-CATALONIA (1208–1276)

Jaime (Jaume) I "the Conqueror," count-king of the realms (*regnes*) of Aragón-Catalonia, was the leading figure of the Reconquest in eastern Spain, founder of his realms' greatness in the western Mediterranean, and an innovative contributor to Europe's administrative, educational, legal, and literary evolution. The only son of Pedro II (Pere I of Catalonia), "the Catholic," he was born in a townsman's home at Montpellier, the principality inherited by his half-Byzantine mother, Marie. His father, hero of the battle of Las Navas (1212), which opened Almohad Islam to Jaime's later conquests, died at Muret (1213) at battle in the Albigensian crusade in Occitania. Simon de Montfort, leader of the Albigensian crusade, kidnapped Jaime and held him at Carcassonne. Jaime was rescued by Pope Innocent III, who then placed his realms under Templar protection. The orphan Jaime—his mother had died at Rome—was brought up from his sixth to his ninth years at the Templar headquarters castle of Monzón in Aragón. By the time he was almost ten, he had begun his personal rule (1217), and had captained armies in a league for order—the beginning of his intermittent domestic wars with refractory nobles (particularly in 1227 and 1273–1275).

In 1225 Jaime led an abortive crusade against Peñíscola in Islamic Valencia. Four years later he mounted a successful amphibious invasion of Mallorca, adding Minorca in 1232 and Ibiza in 1235 as tributaries. Organizing his Balearic conquests as a separate kingdom of Mallorca, Jaime embarked on a nearly fifteen-year campaign to conquer Almohad Valencia piecemeal (1232–1245). Only three major cities fell to siege (Burriana, Valencia, Biar), with consequent expulsion of Muslims, and Játiva succumbed to a combination of siege, feint, and negotiated arrangements from 1239 to 1248 and on to 1252. One set-piece battle was fought in 1237 at Puig; and Valencia surrendered in 1238. Flanking naval power supplied Jaime's war and fended off Tunisian help. Alfonso X of Castile was conquering northward out of Murcia, and the two kings narrowly averted war over southernmost Valencia by the treaty of Almizra in 1244.

Historians have followed Jaime's own account in ending this crusade (actually a series of papal crusades) in 1245, followed by Mudéjar revolts in the 1250s, 1260s, and 1270s. It now seems clear that he patched up a truce with Al-Azraq, the last leader in the field, to take advantage of his last opportunity to recover Provence. He rushed north, personally led a raid to kidnap the heiress of Provence at Marseilles, was foiled by a counterraid by Charles of Anjou, protested noisily to the pope, and withdrew. Hailed as a hero of Christendom for his conquest of Valencia at this lowest point of Europe's crusading movement, in 1246 Jaime rashly announced a crusade to help Latin Byzantium. However, Al-Azraq plunged Valencia into a decade of countercrusade (1247–1258), put down piecemeal again by Jaime in a new papal crusade. Jaime continually organized his Valencian realm as his original invasion progressed, down to his last years of life. Some of his massive land distribution is recorded in his detailed *Repartiment*. His Mudéjar treaties set up semi-autonomous Muslim enclaves throughout Valencia, on a scale unmatched elsewhere in Spain, forming a colonialist society with a thin grid of Christians dominating until the following century. He brought in more Muslims, and also attracted Jewish settlers from Occitania and North Africa, as part of a planned program. He set up Valencia as a separate kingdom with its own law code, money, parliament, and administration.

Meanwhile, Jaime signed away all but his coastal rights in Occitania to Louis IX of France in the treaty of Corbeil (1258). His peninsular politics, notably with Alfonso X of Castile, are only beginning to be explored in depth. Both kings were ambitious to absorb Navarre; they confronted one another as champions, respectively, of the Guelph and Ghibelline movements in the Mediterranean, especially after Jaime married his heir, Pedro, to the Hohenstaufen heiress, Constance of Sicily. In 1265–1266 Jaime helped Alfonso recover the Murcian kingdom from Mudéjar rebellion, an adventure counted as Jaime's third conquest of an Islamic power. From that time on, the confrontational character of their mutual policies turned to friendship.

Jaime also negotiated with the Mongols, who wanted allies against Islam, in 1267. In 1269 he finally mounted his long-awaited crusade to the Holy Land, but abandoned his fleet due to storms (his own excuse) or to reluctance to leave his mistress (the charge by his enemies). After a brief estrangement from his heir, Pedro, and a bitter baronial revolt led by Jaime's bastard son Ferran Sanxis, the conqueror had a moment of triumph again on the world stage. Pope Gregory X summoned him to the Second Ecumenical Council of Lyons in 1274, particularly for his expertise in crusading; Jaime devoted twenty chapters of his autobiography to recounting his reception and activities there. In 1276 the worst of Valencia's Mudéjar revolts erupted, a sustained effort with North African and Granadan help, to recover the land. Jaime fell ill while fighting at Alcira (20 July 1276) and died at Valencia (27 July).

He abdicated on his deathbed, to take the vows and habit of a Cistercian monk, a not uncommon deathbed piety then. The Mudéjar war required his burial at Valencia; only in May 1278 could his successor inter him properly at Poblet monastery near Tarragona. When mobs sacked his tomb during the nineteenth-century Carlist wars, his body was removed to Tarragona cathedral, and only recently has been returned to Poblet.

At his death the troubadour Matieu de Carsin hailed him as exalter of the cross "beyond all kings here or overseas," another Arthur of Camelot. His younger contemporary Ramón Muntaner records that people called him "the Good King"; another chronicler records his title as "James the Fortunate," founder of two thousand churches. A myth grew that he had co-founded the Mercedarian ransomer order. A later movement to canonize him did not receive ecclesiastical encouragement.

Jaime had his dark side, however. He could be cruel in warfare after the manner of the times. He cut out the tongue of the bishop of Girona in 1246, for which he suffered papal thunders and public penance. And he was notoriously a womanizer. His guardians had married him in 1221 to an older woman, Leónor, the sister of Fernando III of Castile, for reasons of state. When he was able to consummate the union, Jaime produced his son and first heir, Alfonso (who died in 1260). Rome annulled the marriage in 1229, and in 1235 he married the true love of his life, Violante, the daughter of King Bela IV of Hungary, by whom he had two sons and two daughters. She died in 1251, and in 1255 Jaime married Teresa Gil de Vidaure, by whom he had two sons. Historians often count Teresa as a mistress, but Pope Gregory X regarded the marriage as firm in his thunders against Jaime's efforts to divorce her (1274) after he had relegated her to a nunnery in Valencia. Jaime also had seven formal or contract mistresses and at least five illegitimate children. This led some moderns to dub him "the Henry VIII of Spain."

Jaime promulgated the first Romanized law code of general application, *the furs* of Valencia (1261), as well as the *fueros* of Aragón (1247), the Lérida *Costums* (1258), and the *Costums de la mar* (ca. 1240). Besides founding the papal University of Valencia (1245), he reorganized the statutes of the University of Montpellier to make it the first effective royal university in Europe. He fully supported the mendicant movement and its Arabic/Hebrew language schools, including the Dominicans' 1263 Disputation of Barcelona with the Jews. By his prodigal use of Játiva paper he elaborated the first substantial archives in Europe after the papacy's, leaving a remarkable record of life and administration in his registers. He promoted commerce in many ways, particularly by his trade monopoly at Alexandria, his tributary control of Ḥafṣid Tunis, the North Africa–Valencia–Mallorca–Occitania trade, and his monetary policy. He presided over a literary court (Bernat Desclot and the troubadour Cerverí de Girona stand out) and contributed his *Llibre dels feyts*, the only autobiography by a medieval king except for his great-great-grandson's imitation, to European letters. Done by collaborators at Játiva in 1244 (the first three hundred chapters) and at Barcelona in 1274, it is a lively personal account of himself as a military Roland or Cid. Desclot

describes him as taller than most, with athletic frame and reddish-blond hair, a man cordial to everyone and adventurously bold. His skeletal remains confirm the physical details, and a portrait in Alfonso X's *Cantigas de Santa María* shows him at around sixty, majestic, with his short beard gone white.

See also **Alfonso X, El Sabio, King of Castile and León; Louis IX**

Further Reading

Belenguer Cebrià, E. *Jaume I a través de la història.* 2 vols. Valencia, 1984.

Burns, R. I. *Society and Documentation in Crusader Valencia.* Princeton, N.J., 1985.

——, ed. *The Worlds of Alfonso the Learned and James the Conqueror: Intellect and Force in the Middle Ages.* Princeton, N.J., 1985.

Jaime I y su época: X Congrés d'història de la Corona d'Aragó. 5 vols. in 2. Zaragoza, 1979–82.

Tourtoulon, C. de. *Études sur la maison de Barcelone: Jacme ler le Conquérant, roi d'Aragón.* 2 vols. Montpellier, 1863–67. Rev. in trans, by Teodoro L'orente. *Don Jaime I el Conquistador.* 2 vols. Valencia, 1874.

ROBERT I. BURNS, S. J.

JAIME II (1267–1327)

Second son of Pedro III (r. 1276–1285) and Constanza de Hohenstaufen, Jaime II was an amalgam of the stubborn courage of his grandfather Jaime I (1213–1276) and a keen and crafty mind that provided a clear ruling template for his grandson Pedro IV (1336–1387). With his father's acquisition of Sicily in 1283, Jaime as a teenager became a pivotal figure in central Mediterranean affairs, serving as king of Sicily from 1285 to 1291. In this post, he developed a ruling style which combined unbridled force with patient diplomacy. Holding at bay his family's archenemy, Charles of Anjou, by the development of a strong fleet, Jaime established such an efficient Sicihan government that, according to one chronicler, the island population "grew prosperous in a very short time."

With the death of his brother, the ineffectual Alfonso III (1285–1291), Jaime quickly realized that far greater power was open to him on the Iberian mainland than as Sicilian ruler. Shamefully deserting his island vassals, the new Aragónese sovereign began transforming old enemies into new friends. Making peace with Charles of Anjou and sealing the new relationship by marrying his old foe's daughter in 1295, Jaime then rapidly mended fences with Pope Boniface VIII (papacy 1294–1303), becoming the standard bearer and protector of the papacy in exchange for conquest rights to Sardinia and Corsica. The changed reality of this *realpolitik* was especially dramatic in regard to Sicily, which chose Jaime's younger brother, Fadrique, as its sovereign and then supported their new lord in a war of survival with his sibling (1296–1298) that guaranteed at least temporarily Sicilian independence.

The combination of specifically applied force and wide-ranging diplomatic activity marked all of Jaime's subsequent forays into foreign affairs. Maintaining generally peaceful relations with Castile, he used the death of his cousin, Sancho IV of Castile (1284–1296) to block the accession of the young heir, Fernando IV (1296–1312), in favor of another contender for the Castilian crown, hoping to gain the pivotal district of Murcia in the process. Though this conspiracy proved unsuccessful, Jaime persistently pressed his claim to Murcia. By 1304, the Castilians relented partially and granted Jaime the right to conquer Almería and its surroundings. Since the region was still under Muslim control, an Aragónese attack of the city brought overwhelming response from the Granada emir, Muḥammad III (1302–1309) and this effectively ended Aragónese military operations in Andalusia until the era of the Catholic kings.

Despite these aftershocks of the great Reconquest, events soon convinced Jaime that much greater geopolitical prizes awaited him in the Mediterranean than on the Iberian Peninsula. When the Sicilian war ended in 1302, mercenary forces (*almogávares*) who had served Fadrique were out of a job. Accepting an offer for employment from the Byzantine emperor Michael IX (1295–1320), the company was soon thrown out of work again by a premature peace with the Ottoman Turks and then went into business for itself by ravaging much of the central Mediterranean and establishing a loose colonial structure, the Duchy of Athens, which remained in Catalan hands until 1388. Indirectly thrust into Mediterranean affairs by this "Catalan Vengeance," Jaime bided time until 1322 when he attempted to make good his claim to Sardinia with extensive military operations that, however, never brought the island under his control and ultimately consumed the very Barcelona dynasty itself when in 1410 the last heir to the dynasty died putting down yet another Sardinian uprising. Despite this lingering Sardinian debacle, Jaime's reign had ushered in a new economic era in the Mediterranean that made the Catalans, with bases in Athens, Sardinia, the North African litoral, and the Balearics, a strong rival to Pisa and Genoa for market dominance.

Jaime also played a significant role in domestic affairs. Trained in Sicilian politics, which gave much greater power to the sovereign, Jaime brought to eastern Spain not a revolution, but a steady manipulation of legal and constitutional norms. Under his tutelage, royal government became steadily more efficient and productive. Quickly realizing the disparate nature of his realms, the king soon moved to set up structures that firmly tied the ruling center to its many peripheries. His most far-reaching action in this regard was the Privilege of Union (1319), which affirmed "whoever was the king of Aragón would also be the king of Valencia and the count of Barcelona." To further this unity, Jaime completely reformed royal government, dividing it into such departments as the chancellery and the treasury, and staffing these with university educated specialists such as the chancellor, treasurer, and master of accounts. From this pool of curial talent, he chose advisers who, along with trusted nobles and clergy, constituted the royal council.

The wholesale administrative changes that accompanied Jaime's accession enraged his conservative realms of Aragón and Valencia, which had spent the last three decades in stamping out royal "innovations" and in legally subordinating the crown to baronial control. Rather than using military means to confront this insurgency (occasionally bound together as the *Unión*), the king, in August 1301, used the very laws forced on his ancestors to charge his rebellious barons with treason and did so before the unionist functionary, the *Justicia de Aragón*. Despite this temporary triumph, Jaime knew he could not fully defeat the barons and admitted as much in the *Declaration of the General Privilege* (1325), in which he formally accepted many of the legal restrictions the *Unión* had previously imposed on the crown.

Jaime II died on 2 November 1327. He married four times: to Isabel of Castile (1291), Blanche of Anjou (1295), Maria de Lusignan (1317), and Elisenda de Montcada (1322). The most fecund of these unions was the second, which produced ten children, including the princes Jaime, Alfonso (the eventual successor), and Juan (late archbishop of Tarragona). To later historians, Jaime was known as "the Just" or "the Justiciar" because he would allow no one but himself to "render verdicts for disputes." Despite these judicial sobriquets, his greatest accomplishment was the transformation of the Crown of Aragón from a solely Iberian to a strong Mediterranean power.

See also **Pedro III, King of Aragón; Sancho IV, King of Castile**

Further Reading

Abulafia D., *A Mediterranean Emporium: The Catalan Kingdom of Majorca.* Cambridge, 1994.

Archivo de la Corona de Aragón, Cancillería real, Regs. 90–350; Pergaminos, Carp. 128–214.

Kagay D. J. "Rebellion on Trial: The Aragónese *Union* and Its Uneasy Connection to Royal Law, 1265–1301," *Journal of Legal History* 18, no. 3(1997): 30–43.

Martínez Ferrando, J. E. "Jaime II," in *Els Descendants de Pere el Gran.* Barcelona, 1980.

Salavert, V. *Cerdena y la expansion mediterránea de la Corona de Aragón, 1297–1314.* Madrid, 1956.

DONALD J. KAGAY

JAN VAN BOENDALE (ca. 1280–1351)

A Brabantine poet and a native of Tervuren, a small town between Leuven and Brussels, Jan van Boendale spent most of his working life as secretary to the aldermen of the city of Antwerp. In this position he dealt with all levels of society, an experience that affected his writing. His oeuvre consists of some seven works, although some of those texts cannot definitively be attributed to him. Boendale wrote several versions of some of his works, mainly updates of his historiography texts, which were then dedicated to other patrons.

His first work, the *Brabantsche yeesten* (Brabantine Deeds), is a chronicle in coupled rhyme, dealing with the history of the Brabantine ducal house in the period from ca. 600 to ca. 1350. This chronicle is divided in five parts ("books"), of which the first four describe the history of Brabant before Boendale's own lifetime, and the fifth is devoted to the three dukes contemporaneous with him: Jan I (d. 1294), Jan II (d. 1312), and Jan III (d. 1355). This voluminous work of some 16,000 lines was not written in one effort; the first version dates from ca. 1316, the fifth from 1347, and a sixth version may have been written around 1351, each one providing an updated version of the history of the duchy. This does not imply that Boendale was completely original in his chronicle. Large parts of his text were copied from the *Spiegel historiael* (Mirror of History) by Jacob van Maerlant—whom Boendale elsewhere called "the father of all Dutch poets"—and the anonymous *Chronica de origine ducum Brabantiae* (Chronicle of the Origins of the Duchy of Brabant); only when writing about his own lifetime is Boendale original.

After completing a second version of the *Brabantsche yeesten* in 1318 he used the text in 1322 as the source for a very short rhyme-chronicle, the so-called *Korte kroniek van Brabant* (374 lines). He later wrote a second version of this text too, in the years 1332–1333.

But between 1325–1330, he composed an extensive didactic poem of more than 20,000 lines, called *Der leken spiegel* (The Layman's Mirror). In using this title, Boendale explicitly addresses an audience of non-readers (*illiterati*), offering them an encyclopedic text, dealing with cosmology, the nature of human body and soul, the history of the Old and New Testaments, church history, devotional practice, etc. The poem is structured according to the *Heilsgeschichte* (divine plan) and divided into four books. Books one and two deal with God's Creation, the structure of the universe, and the course of history; book three is concerned with the present, and book four with the future. *Der leken spiegel* contains the oldest poetical treatise in Dutch: in book three, chapter fifteen, Boendale presents, under the title *Hoe dichters dichten sullen ende wat si hantieren sullen* (How writers should write and what they should pay attention to), his views on literature. This is not a treatise on technical aspects of poetry, but a declaration by a self-conscious author concerning the cultural responsibilities inherent in authorship. Here, Boendale presents his ideas on, among other topics, the prerequisites of true authorship, the value of literary tradition, and the relationship between genre and fictionality.

Between 1330–1334 Boendale wrote his *Jans teesteye* (Jans testimony), a dialogue in some 4100 lines of coupled rhyme. In this polemic-didactic dialogue the participants are "Jan," Boendale's *alter ego*, and "Wouter," probably a fictitious person, playing the role of the pupil. The topic of discussion is *grosso modo*, the quality of life in their time. Jan takes a positive, but not uncritical position; Wouter's position is negative: he is the "praiser of times past" (*laudator temporis acti*).

Shortly after 1340 Boendale wrote *Van den derden Eduwaert*, describing in 2,018 lines the role of the English king Edward III (d. 1377) in continental European politics. The poem was not only a tribute to this king, whom Boendale probably had met in person; it was first and foremost a panegyric to Duke Jan III of Brabant, an ally of the English king at the outbreak of the Hundred Year's War in 1337.

Boendale's authorship of two poems is disputed. The first is the very short *Hoemen ene stat regeren sal* (18 lines, before ca. 1350), a poem advising officials on "how to rule a town." The poem is known in several versions, some written on the tie-beams of city halls, including those in Brussels and Emmerich. The oldest known version is incorporated in a manuscript of *Der leken spiegel* (Brussels, Koninklijke Bibliotheek, manuscript no. 15.658, fol. 122r).

The second disputed poem is called the *Boec van der wraken* [The book of punishment (5,870 lines, ca. 1346)]. Reacting to the conflict between Pope Clemens VI and the German emperor Louis of Bavaria, in which he chose the imperial side, Boendale has written a pamphlet-like poem around the theme of God's punishment for human sinfulness, with strong eschatological overtones. A second, updated version was written in 1351.

Typical of Boendale's historiographic works is his orientation on Brabantine history, apparent in the recurrent *origo*-motive (the tracing back of the origin of the ducal house to the Trojans) and the *reditus*-motive (the dukes of Brabant as the true inheritors of Charlemagne). Boendale's didactic perspective revolves around the theme of the *ghemeyn oirbaer* ("the common good"), which is the basis for his social criticism. Boendale criticizes clergy, aristocracy, and commoners alike, but evidently tends to identify himself with his urban environment. This somewhat intermediate position shows itself clearly in the dedications of his poems. Though often explicitly intended for a broad audience of laymen, many of the manuscripts contain dedications to members of the aristocracy, including Willem van Bornecolve, alderman of Antwerp, Rogier van Leefdale, viscount of Brussels, and Duke Jan III of Brabant.

Jan van Boendale is an example of what is called the Antwerp School, a designation for the explosive literary output of Antwerp in the first half of the fourteenth century. When cities began to emerge as centers of literary activity in the late thirteenth century, Antwerp was the third most culturally important town of Brabant (after Brussels and Leuven). In Antwerp this increased literary activity resulted in a rather homogeneous group of texts, which included, besides Boendale's works, the *Sidrac*, the *Melibeus*, and the *Dietsche doctrinale*. The *Sidrac* is an extensive encyclopedic and didactic dialogue in prose, translated from French in 1318. The *Melibeus* (1342) is a translation of the *Liber consolationis et consilii* (Book of Consolation and Counsel) by Albertanus of Brescia (d. after 1246). In 3,771 lines, a moralizing dialogue between allegorical characters is presented.

The *Dietsche doctrinale* (German Doctrine 1345) is another translation of a misogynistic didactic text by Albertanus of Brescia, *De amore et dilectione Dei et proximi et aliorum rerum et de forma vitae* (On God's love...). This work of some 6,650 lines, divided in three "books," deals with love and friendship, virtues and vices, and closes with an interesting section on the nature of God. It thus presents a compendium of laymen's ethics. The thematic similarities between the *Melibeus*, the *Dietsche doctrinale*, and Boendale's oeuvre—that history is a framework for laymen's ethics as well as the central concept of the "common good"—has sometimes led to the attribution of these two texts to Jan van Boendale.

See also **Jacob van Maerlant**

Further Reading

Avonds, Piet. "*Ghemeyn Oirbaer*. Volkssoevereiniteit en politieke ethiek in Brabant in de veertiende eeuw." In Reynaert, Joris et al. *Wat is wijsheid? Lekenethiek in de Middelnederlandse letterkunde*. Amsterdam: Prometheus, 1994, pp, 164–180 and 405–411.

Gerritsen, Willem P., et al. "A fourteenth-century vernacular poetics: Jan van Boendale's 'How Writers Should Write'." In Erik Kooper, ed. *Medieval Dutch Literature in its European Context*. Cambridge, Cambridge University Press, 1994, pp. 245–260.

De Vries, Matthijs, ed. *Der leken spieghel, leerdicht van den jare 1330, door Jan Boendale, gezegd Jan de Clerc, schepenklerk te Antwerpen*. 3 vols. Leyden, Du Mortier, 1844–1848.

Heymans, Jo, ed. *Van den derden Eduwaert*. Nijmegen, Alfa, 1983.

Heymans, Jo. "Geschiedenis in *Der Leken Spiegel*." In Geert R. W. Dibbets and Paul W. M. Wackers, ed. *Wat duikers van is dit! Opstellen voor W.M.H. Hummelen*. Wijhe: Quarto, 1989, pp. 25–40.

Jonckbloet, Willem J. A., ed. *Die Dietsche Doctrinale, leerdicht van den jare 1345, toegekend aan Jan Deckers*. The Hague, 1842.

Kinable, Dirk, *Facetten van Boendale. Literair-historische*

verkenningen van Jans teesteye en de Lekenspiegel. Leyden: Dimensie, 1998.

Lucas, H.S. "Edward III and the poet chronicler John Boendale." *Speculum* 12 (1937): 367–369.

Reynaert, Joris. "Ethiek en 'filosofie' voor leken: de *Dietsche doctrinale*." In Joris Reynaert, et al. *Wat is wijsheid? Lekenethiek in de Middelnederlandse letterkunde*. Amsterdam: Prometheus, 1994, pp. 199–214 and 415–419.

Snellaert, Ferdinand A., ed. *Nederlandsche gedichten uit de veertiende eeuw van Jan Boendale, Hein van Aken en anderen naar het Oxfordsch handschrift*. Brussels, Hayez, 1869 [*Jans teesteye; Boec van der Wraken; Melibeus*].

Van Anrooij, Wim, ed. "Hoemen ene stat regeren sal. Een vroege stadstekst uit de Zuidelijke Nederlanden." *Spiegel der Lettern* 34 (1992): 139–157.

Van Anrooij, Wim. "Recht en rechtvaardigheid binnen de Antwerpse School." In Reynaert, Joris et al. *Wat is wijsheid? Lekenethiek in de Middelnederlandse letterkunde*. Amsterdam: Prometheus, 1994, pp. 149–163 and 399–405.

Van Eerden, Peter C. "*Eschatology in the Boec van der wraken*." In Werner Verbeke, Daniel Verhelst, and Andries Welkenhuysen, ed. *The Use and Abuse of Eschatology in the Middle Ages*. Leuven: Leuven University Press, 1988, pp. 425–440.

Van Tol, J. F. J., ed. *Het boek van Sidrac in de Nederlanden*. Amsterdam: H. J. Paris, 1936.

Willems, Jan Frans, ed. *De Brabantsche yeesten of rymkronyk van Braband*. 2 vols. Brussels: Hayez, 1839, 1843 and J. H. Bormans, *De Brabantsche yeesten, of rijmkronijk van Braband*, vol. 3. Brussel, Hayez, 1869 [with the *Korte kronike van Brabant*].

GEERT H. M. CLAASSENS

JAN VAN RUUSBROEC (1293–1381)

Jan van Ruusbroec, a Brabantine mystic, was born in 1293 in the village of Ruisbroek southeast of Brussels. When he was eleven, he went to live in the city with a relative, John (Jan) Hinckaert (d. 1350/1358), who was a canon of the collegiate church of St. Gudula. The boy attended the school attached to the church, and after the required studies, he was ordained a priest in 1317 and became a chaplain there. In Brussels he began to compose his first treatises on mystical life, among which were some of his most important writings: *Die geestelike brulocht* (The Spiritual Espousals) and *Vanden blinkenden steen* (The Sparkling Stone).

The *Spiritual Espousals* is the most famous and most translated of his works. It describes the entire path to a mystic life from a humble beginning to complete development and indicates the risks and possible deviations at each stage. According to Ruusbroec, the essence of mystical life is the direct and passive experience of God. To describe the different stages, he uses three terms in the *Espousals* which recur in all his treatises: *dat werkende leven* (the active life), *dat innighe leven* (the interior life), *and dat schouwende leven* (the contemplative life). Each is a way to live one's relation with God. In the active life, love manifests itself in the exercise of virtue; in the interior life, a new dimension of love is discovered: to adhere intimately to the Beloved; finally, in the contemplative life, the loving person is elevated above him- or herself and introduced into the most intimate life of God, the love of the Father, Son and Spirit in one divine being. Ruusbroec strongly emphasizes the point that, at each level, the higher life does not neglect, let alone reject, the lower life. A person who has discovered the interior life should not despise the active life. And, one who has been introduced into the contemplative life should not disdain God nor active service to his neighbor. Just as the interior life does not replace the need for an active life, but inspires and purifies it, the contemplative life enhances and elevates both.

Whereas the *Espousals* is famous for its all-encompassing view, Ruusbroec's small treatise, *The Sparkling Stone*, is a masterpiece of conciseness. It briefly describes the three lives of the *Espousals* and then concentrates on the highest of the three, the contemplative life.

In 1343 Ruusbroec, together with John Hinckaert and Frank of Coudenberg (d. 1386), another Canon of St. Gudula, left Brussels to live a contemplative life in Groenendaal (Green Valley), a site in the Wood of Soignes about ten kilometers south of Brussels. To cope with the juridical problems, resulting from their living together as a religious community without belonging to an established order or following a recognized rule, the group, which had meanwhile increased, became a provostry of canons regular of St. Augustine. Ruusbroec was the first prior of the newly founded monastery.

In Groenendaal he continued his work as a writer. There, he finished his largest work, *Van den geesteliken tabernakel* (The Spiritual Tabernacle). As the number of the manuscripts still preserved indicates, this treatise must have been very popular in its time. For the modern reader, access is difficult because the *Tabernacle* is a continuous allegory on some passages from the biblical books, Exodus and Leviticus, which describe the construction of the tabernacle and give ritual prescriptions during Israel's stay in the desert. The link between material image and spiritual reality may seem somewhat farfetched today, but the way in which Ruusbroec masters the complex whole of image and reality is astonishing.

In Groenendaal Ruusbroec not only wrote books, but also met people who came to him with their questions about a life of prayer. Among the most famous was Geert Grote (1340–1384), the founder of the religious movement, the Modern Devotion. Very rarely, Ruusbroec left Groenendaal to visit those who were not allowed to leave their monasteries. At an advanced age, he traveled on foot to a monastery of Carthusians to help them with some difficulties concerning his description of the highest stages of mystical life. This visit gave rise to one of his last works, *Boecksen der verclaringhe* (Little Book of Enlightenment). By means of another tripartition, *enecheit met middel* (unity with intermediary), *sonder middel* (without intermediary), and *sonder differencie* (without difference), he tries to explain to his friends that—though the distinction between Creator and creature is eternal—there is a moment in mystical life when nothing of the opposition between the beloved "you" and the loving "I" is left.

In 1381 Ruusbroec died in Groenendaal at the age of eighty-eight, but his works have survived him. During his lifetime, some were translated from the Brabantine Middle Dutch into High German for the *Gottesfreunde* (Friends of God) in Strasbourg and Basle, and into Latin. About the middle of the sixteenth century his *Opera Omnia* (entire works) were translated into Latin by a Carthusian in Cologne, Laurentius Surius (1523–1578). This was the basis for many later translations into modern languages, including German and Spanish. Ruusbroec's influence is evident in the first generations of the Modern Devotion: the canons regular of the Windesheim Chapter, Gerlach Peters (d. 1411), Hendrik Mande (d. 1431), and Thomas à Kempis (1379/1380–1471). Another member of the Modern Devotion, Hendrik Herp (d. 1477), was so deeply influenced by Ruusbroec that he earned the name of "Herold of Ruusbroec." Through him, Ruusbroec's influence reached France through Benedict of Canneld (1562–1610) and John of Saint Samson (1571–1636). Born in England, Benedict passed much of his life in France, where he became a Capuchin. There, he introduced Ruusbroec to mystical circles, for example, to one Madame Acarie (1566–1618). John, blind from his early youth, joined the Carmelites and became one of the most outstanding mystical writers of his order.

See also **Thomas à Kempis**

Further Reading

Dupré, Louis. *The Common Life: The Origins of Trinitarian Mysticism and its Development by Jan van Ruusbroec.* New York: Crossroad, 1984.

Mommaers, Paul and Norbert de Paepe, ed. *Jan van Ruusbroec: the sources, content and sequels of his mysticism.* Mediaevalia Lovaniensia ser. 1. Studia 12. Leuven: Leuven University Press, 1984.

Underhill, Evelyn. *Ruysbroeck.* London: Bell, 1915.

van Ruusbroec, Jan. *Werken.* Naar het standaardhandschrift van Groenendaal uitgegeven door het Ruusbroec-genootschap te Antwerpen. 4 vols. Mechelen/Amsterdam: Kompas, 1932–1934; 2nd ed. Tielt: Lannoo, 1944–1948.

———. *Opera Omnia.* Studiën en tekstuitgaven van Ons Geestelijk Erf, XX. Leiden: Brill; Tielt: Lannoo; Turn-hour: Brepols, 1981ff. [Middle Dutch text, English and Latin trans.; Dutch and Latin introd.; 10 vols. planned, 4 published].

———. *The Spiritual Espousals and Other Works,* Trans. James A. Wiseman. New York/Mahwah/Toronto: Paulist, 1985.

Wiseman, James A. *"Minne in Die gheestelike brulocht* of Jan van Ruusbroec." S.T.D. Thesis. Catholic University of America, 1979.

GUIDO O. E. J. DE BAERE

JAUFRE RUDEL (fl. 1120–48)

The troubadour Jaufre Rudel, lord of Blaye in the Gironde, sang of earthly love infused by a mystical quest expressed also through his participation in the Second Crusade. Of his six surviving songs of certain authenticity, Jaufre's most successful *canso* is directed to his love from afar, or *amor de loing*, which gives this lyric its leitmotif and keyword. In this song and in *Qan lo rius*, he voices his yearning for a distant love, diversely interpreted by critics as a woman, the Virgin Mary, God, or the Holy Land. Recent scholarship underlines instead the deliberate ambiguity in jaufre's fusion of linguistic registers and love objects drawn from both profane and sacred traditions. The legend of his love for the Countess of Tripoli dates from the pseudobiographical *vida* and earlier. It has been echoed in every century since the 13th by authors as varied as Petrarch, Stendhal, Rostand, Browning, Heine, Carducci, Pound, and Döblin.

See also **Petrarca, Francesco**

Further Reading

Jaufre Rudel. *The Songs of Jaufre Rudel*, ed. Rupert T. Pickens. Toronto: Pontifical Institute of Mediaeval Studies, 1978.
——. *The Poetry of Cercamon and Jaufre Rudel*, ed. and trans. George Wolf and Roy Rosenstein. New York: Garland, 1983.
——. *Il canzoniere di Jaufre Rudel*, ed. Giorgio Chiarini. Rome: Japadre, 1985.
Rosenstein, Roy. "New Perspectives on Distant Love: Jaufre Rudel, Uc Bru, and Sarrazina." *Modern Philology* 87 (1990): 225–38.

ROY S. ROSENSTEIN

JEAN DE GARLANDE
(Johannes de Garlandia; ca. 1195–ca. 1272)

Born in England, Jean first studied at Oxford shortly after 1200 and went to Paris in 1217 or 1218, first to complete his studies and then to teach. At Paris, he lived in the Clos de Garlande, from which he derives his name. At the close of the Albigensian Crusade, the papal legate Romain Frangipani commissioned him to teach at the newly formed University of Toulouse (April 2, 1229), together with the Dominican master Roland of Cremona. Jean remained at Toulouse for only a few years. He may have returned to England during the 1230s but in any case was again teaching in Paris by 1241.

Jean's interests ranged primarily over the field of literary studies: etymology, rhetoric, grammar, and poetics. One of his earliest and best-known works, the *Parisiana poetria* (ca. 1220; revised a decade later), was a treatise on the art of poetry in the tradition of Matthieu de Vendôme and Geoffroi de Vinsauf. In this work, he stresses the place of both verse and prose composition in the arts curriculum. From this same period comes his *Dictionarius*, perhaps the first word book to be so entitled. Jean also wrote a brief verse commentary to Ovid's *Metamorphoses*, the *Integumenta Ovidii*, giving interpretations sometimes moral, sometimes scientific or historical, to the fables. Like many of his works, the *Integumenta* presupposes a vast general knowledge of the subject and is not intended for the novice.

Jean was also concerned about the moral formation of his students and wrote several works with that aim, among them the *Morale scolarium* (1241), an admonition on the values and habits of the ideal scholar, and the *Stella maris* (ca. 1249), in praise of the Virgin Mary as a paragon of Christian virtue and action. A later work, *De triumphis ecclesiae* (ca. 1252), is a polemic against pagans and heretics, based on his earlier experiences in Toulouse.

Jean had a prominent reputation in the 13th century. But though his promotion of lay piety was in keeping with the contemporary mission of the Dominicans and Franciscans, his resistance to Aristotelian studies and to the new emphasis on logic in the curriculum bespeak a conservatism more in keeping with the schools of the 12th century than with the universities of the 13th.

Jean must not be confused with the musician of the same name.

Further Reading

Jean de Garlande. *Morale scolarium of John of Garland (Johannes de Garlandia), a Professor in the Universities of Paris and Toulouse in the Thirteenth Century*, ed. Louis J. Paetow. Berkeley: University of California Press, 1927.
Wilson, Evelyn Faye. *The Stella maris of John of Garland*. Cambridge: Mediaeval Academy of America, 1946.

MARK ZIER

JEAN DE MEUN
(Jehan de Meung; 1235/40–1305)

Born at Meung-sur-Loire, Jean Chopinel (or Clopinel) obtained the Master of Arts, most likely in Paris. He dwelt for much of his adult life in the capital, where from at least 1292 to his death he was housed in the Hôtel de la Tourelle in the Faubourg Saint-Jacques. Jean's works exhibit a rich classical and scholastic culture. Among the works he translated into French are Vegetius, *De re militari*, dedicated to Jean de Brienne, count of Eu; Boethius, *De consolatione Philosophiae*, dedicated to Philip the Fair; and the correspondence of Abélard and Héloïse. He also claims two additional translations, which are not extant, versions of Giraldus Cambrensis, *De mirabilibus Hiberniae*, and of Aelred of Rievaulx, *De spirituali amicitia*. More likely than not, Jean was also the author of the satirical *Testament maistre Jehan de Meun* and *Codicile maistre Jehan de Meun*.

But Jean is best remembered as the second author of

the *Roman de la Rose*, an allegorical narrative begun by Guillaume de Lorris. This masterwork has survived in over 250 manuscripts. It also had twenty-one printed editions from 1481 to 1538. The *Rose* was translated partially or *in toto* during the medieval period once into Dutch, twice into Italian, and three times into English—the first English fragment is attributed to Chaucer. Jean de Meun influenced Dante, Boccaccio, Machaut, and Froissart; he played a crucial role in the formation of both Chaucer and Gower. Jean's section of the *Rose* became the subject of the first great literary quarrel, at the beginning of the 15th century. Jean de Meun was the first recognized *auctor* and *auctoritas* in French literary history, and his book the first true French classic, glossed, explicated, quoted, indexed, anthologized, and fought over—treated as if it were a masterpiece from antiquity.

Guillaume de Lorris wrote his *Roman de la Rose*, 4,028 lines left unfinished, in the early 1220s. In the decade 1264–74 Jean de Meun brought Guillaume's text to a conclusion. Jean's *Rose*, some 17,722 lines, does not merely complete the earlier poem: he grafts a totally original sequel onto it.

The God of Love comes with his army to succor Guillaume's forlorn Lover. First, False Seeming and Constrained Abstinence slay Foul Mouth, permitting the Lover to speak with Fair Welcome. A pitched battle occurs between the attackers and the defenders of the castle, ending in a truce. Finally, Venus leads a victorious assault, flinging her torch into the sanctuary: the castle bursts into flames, and the Lover wins the Rose.

The action and the allegory no longer play a primary role, as they did for Guillaume de Lorris. They serve as supports, and pretexts, for discourse: exhortations from Reason and Friend to the Lover, False Seeming's confession of his true nature to the God of Love before he is admitted into the army, the Old Woman's exhortation to Fair Welcome, Nature's confession to her priest, Genius, and Genius's exhortation to the army before the final battle.

The God of Love refers to Jean's book as a *miroër aus amoreus* (1. 10,621). It is, in one sense, a *speculum* or anatomy, a medieval encyclopedia, treating all knowledge, including ethics, economics, cosmology, astronomy, optics, alchemy, and the university. The knowledge in the *speculum*, however, is granted unity and coherence by means of its inclusion under the category of love, which Jean expounds in all facets, both good (sex and reproduction, friendship, justice, the love of reason, one's neighbor, and God) and bad (lust for money, enslavement to Fortune, clerical celibacy, and the hypocrisy and deceit that exist between false lovers and false friends).

That the *Roman de la Rose* is didactic no one denies, but the precise nature of the message, the world vision that Jean de Meun wishes to instill, is subject to controversy. Most scholars believe that Jean transforms and refutes Guillaume de Lorris's *Rose*, that he derides, undermines, and destroys the ideal of *fin'amors* at every turn. One school of thought argues that Jean counters *fin'amors* with a call to procreation, to free love in the service of cosmic plenitude. Another school proposes that Jean treats all his characters, with the exception of Lady Reason, with irony and that his philosophy conforms to orthodox, Augustinian Christianity. The reason scholarly opinion differs so strikingly, why it is so difficult to pin down the author's personal doctrine, lies in the fact that Jean de Meun has chosen to exploit a unique version of narrative technique, quite different from that of his predecessors. Jean distinguishes himself as author from the dreamer-protagonist of his story, proclaimed to be Guillaume de Lorris, thus creating a first level of irony and distance. Second, the dreamer-protagonist, Fair Welcome, and Genius listen to and approve or disapprove of the lengthy discourses listed above, all of which are also presented with comedy and irony. Speakers have a proclivity to contradict themselves, and to cite texts from antiquity that refute rather than support their position. There is no foolproof method for determining which, if any, of the discourses are to be given greater weight than the others; which, if any, carry Jean's own conviction. Readers must judge each of these delegated voices in turn, analyzing the facts and rhetoric, to come to their own conclusions. The result, perhaps intended by Jean de Meun, is a state of doctrinal indeterminacy, in which the Lover and the audience are offered a sequence of philosophies and worldviews. The Lover, in the end, decides—he opens the sanctuary with joy—but the reader-audience is not obliged to applaud his decision. The indeterminacy remains, part and parcel of Jean's text and of a certain late Gothic mentality of which he is the first outstanding master.

Less controversial are the texture and ambience of Jean's imaginative world, a domain in which he is as great an innovator as in narrative technique. Compared with Guillaume de Lorris, Jean is a master of truculent vulgar speech, material detail, and picaresque naturalism. He shifts the audience's perspective from top to bottom, from rose petals to what they hide. A generation before Dante, three generations before Chaucer, Jean juxtaposes lofty and humble registers of style. Scenes, images, and speech once reserved to the fabliaux or excluded from polite letters altogether are now included in a serious work of art, alongside the sublime.

Jean's demystification of courtly love assumes several forms. His characters underscore the role of money in the erotic life, that so often the opposite sex is an object to be purchased, bartered, or exchanged for money or other commodities. The process of reification, and perhaps of antifeminism, is crowned by Jean de

Meun's transformation of the woman-rose into a piece of lifeless architecture, a sanctuary, which the Lover pries open with his pilgrim's staff.

Still more striking is the role the author applies to manipulation and duplicity. Speech serves two purposes: to instruct and to trick. All people can be divided into knaves and fools, masters and slaves, deceivers and deceived. The deceivers create illusion by hiding behind masks; it is not easy for the Lover, Fair Welcome, or anyone else to distinguish appearance from reality, the mask from the flesh, the literal bark from an allegorical kernel. The author tells us that, since the end of the Golden Age, dissimulation, violence, and evil are part of the human condition and that we must learn to cope with them. Throughout the *Rose*, he implicitly urges the Lover and the audience to go beyond appearances and seek the truth, to open our eyes and rip aside the mask of falsehood. Knowledge can then lead to action. Some of Jean's characters remain passive, blind, impotent. Others, including the Lover, attain a measure of freedom, becoming masters not slaves, adults not children.

Jean's is a world of comedy. Several of his characters embody comic archetypes derived from the classics of ancient Rome. They are rigid, mechanical, obsessed with their narrow concerns. Furthermore, the narrative line, such as it is, constitutes the triumph of young love over old constraint. In spite of the blocking figures, Venus's torch burns and the story ends, as comedies must, with the couple packed off to bed. Whatever Jean's doctrine, whether for good or ill, the victory of our animal nature is achieved in a denouement of erotic explosion and the exaltation of life. It is for this reason that many scholars, especially in France, associate Jean de Meun with the awakening of humanism, the rebirth of reverence for antiquity, lust for life, and the revaluation of art that are hallmarks of the 12th- and 13th-century renaissance.

See also **Abélard, Peter; Boccaccio, Giovanni; Chaucer, Geoffrey; Dante Alighieri; Guillaume de Lorris**

Further Reading

Guillaume de Lorris and Jean de Meun. *Le roman de la Rose*, ed. and trans. Armand Strubel. Paris: Livre de Poche, 1992.

——. *Le roman de la Rose*, ed. Félix Lecoy. 3 vols. Paris: Champion, 1965–70.

——. *The Romance of the Rose*, trans. Charles Dahlberg. Princeton: Princeton University Press, 1971.

Arden, Heather M. *The Romance of the Rose*. Boston: Twayne, 1987.

——. *The Roman de la Rose*: *An Annotated Bibliography*. New York: Garland, 1993.

Badel, Pierre-Yves. *Le roman de la Rose au XIVe siècle*: *étude de la réception de l'œuvre*. Geneva: Droz, 1980.

Brownlee, Kevin, and Sylvia Huot. *Rethinking the Romance of the Rose*: *Text, Image, Reception*. Philadelphia: University of Pennsylvania Press, 1992.

Calin, William. *A Muse for Heroes*: *Nine Centuries of the Epic in France*. Toronto: University of Toronto Press, 1983, chap. 5.

Fleming, John V. *The Roman de la Rose*: *A Study in Allegory and Iconography*. Princeton: Princeton University Press, 1969.

Gunn, Alan M. F. *The Mirror of Love*: *A Reinterpretation of the Romance of the Rose*. Lubbock: Texas Tech Press, 1952.

Payen, Jean-Charles. *La Rose et l'utopie*: *révolution sexuelle et communisme nostalgique chez Jean de Meung*. Paris: Éditions Sociales, 1976.

WILLIAM C. CALIN

JEANNE D'ARC (ca. 1412–1431)

The most heroic of France's saints, Jeanne d'Arc was born to a peasant family in Lorraine. At thirteen, Jeanne began hearing the "voices" (of SS. Michael, Catherine, and Margaret) that inspired her. In February 1429, she persuaded a Valois captain to provide an escort for her dangerous journey to the court of Charles VII. At Chinon, Jeanne convinced the king of her divine mission to defeat the English and to assist at his overdue coronation. After formal inquiry into her orthodoxy and chastity, she was given a commanding role in a relief force for Orléans and led reinforcements into the besieged city on April 29. She inspired counterattacks that compelled the English to abandon the siege on May 8. A month later, her army's decisive victory at Patay ensured Valois control over the Loire Valley and destroyed the myth of English invincibility. The subsequent campaign that brought Charles to Reims for a triumphant coronation on July 17 was the high point of Jeanne's meteoric career.

Now a political force, Jeanne became a recognized leader of the court faction favoring renewed war over negotiations with the Anglo-Burgundians. Failure in war soon destroyed her influence. When, she was defeated and wounded in an ill-considered assault on Paris in September, Charles arranged a truce and disbanded his army. Though her family had been ennobled, Jeanne was politically isolated and left the court in the spring to bolster Compiègne's resistance to a Burgundian siege. She was captured there on May 24, 1430, and, to his eternal discredit, abandoned by Charles. Jeanne's cross-dressing, claims to divine guidance, and success had aroused suspicions of sorcery, but her subsequent trial and execution for heresy were acts intended primarily to discredit the Valois cause. In response to an accusation by representatives of the University of Paris, her Burgundian captors delivered her for trial at Rouen under the direction of Bishop Pierre Cauchon. Eloquent in testimony and steadfast when threatened with torture, Jeanne submitted only when weakened by illness and faced with execution. Sentenced to a life of imprisonment and penance, she relapsed and was condemned. Courageous to the end, she insisted on her innocence and asked the executioner to hold the cross high so

Arrival of Joan of Arc at Chinon. German tapestry (called Azeghio tapestry), 15th c. Photo: Bulloz. © Réunion des Musées Nationaux/Art Resource, New York.

she could see it through the flames. Jeanne remained a controversial figure, and in 1456 Charles VII arranged the annulment of her conviction mainly to clear himself of a suspect association.

Shrouded in myth and exalted by unceasing artistic glorification, Jeanne endures as a figure inspiring even the most skeptical. Her historical importance could be narrowly construed: she was essentially a military figure whose inspirational leadership and ephemeral battlefield success helped restore the prestige of the Valois dynasty, ensuring its survival but not its eventual triumph. Few, however, would restrict themselves to such a reductive assessment. Jeanne's courageous example and her martyrdom assure her an enduring role in modern life, not unlike that played by Roland in the Middle Ages. She has become a symbolic figure emblematic of many and varied hopes. Above all, she is the symbol of 20th-century France at war with both itself and its German invaders. In the late 19th century, the "Maid of Orléans" become a popular heroine who inspired generations of French conservatives in the struggle against the secularism of the Third Republic and reminded all Frenchmen of the need to regain the lost provinces of Alsace and Lorraine seized by Germany in 1870. This popular devotion led to her canonization in the aftermath of the First World War and final confirmation that her greatness transcends if not defies historical analysis.

See also **Charles VII, Christine de Pizan**

Further Reading

Doncoeur, Paul, and Yvonne Lanhers, eds. Documents et recherches relatifs à Jeanne la Pucelle. *5 vols. Vols. 1–4, Melun:* Librairie d'Argences, *1921–58; Vol. 5, Paris: De Brouwer, 1961.*

Tisset, Pierre, and Yvonne Lanhers, eds. Procès de condamnation de Jeanne d'Arc. *3 vols. Paris: Klincksieck, 1960–71.*

Gies, Frances. Joan of Arc: The Legend and the Reality. *New York: Harper and Row, 1981.*

Margolis, Nadia. Joan of Arc in History, Literature, and Film: A Select, Annotated Bibliography. *New York: Garland, 1990.*

Vale, Malcolm G.A. Charles VII. *Berkeley: University of California Press, 1974.*

Warner, Marina. Joan of Arc: The Image of Female Heroism. *New York: Knopf, 1981.*

PAUL D. SOLON

JEANNE OF NAVARRE (1273–1305)

Queen of France. The daughter of Henri III of Champagne and Navarre and Blanche of Artois, granddaughter of Louis VIII, Jeanne inherited her father's lands in 1274. Plans for her to marry the heirs, first of Edward I of England and then the king of Aragon, failed after problems in Spain led Blanche and Jeanne to seek asylum with Philip III. In May 1275, Blanche put Navarre under Philip's protection and affianced Jeanne to one of his sons. Raised at the French court, Jeanne was declared of age on May 17, 1284, and on August 16 married Philip IV the Fair, who on October 6, 1285, succeeded his father as king. Jeanne was closely involved with the administration of Champagne and Navarre, but Philip effectively controlled them.

Jeanne was a popular queen, and Philip was devoted to her. In 1288, he deferred until after her death collection of money owed for the defense of Navarre. In October 1294, he appointed her regent of France if he died before their eldest son came of age. Her name was associated with Philip's in important acts, and she accompanied him on his grand tour of the Midi in 1303–04. She showed independence in supporting the Franciscan Bernard Délicieux and accepting gifts from citizens of Béziers, whose orthodoxy and loyalty were suspect. She pressed the prosecution of Guichard, bishop of Troyes, accused of cheating her and her mother (and later charged with killing Jeanne by sorcery). A woman of considerable culture, she commissioned Joinville's *Vie de saint Louis*; Ramon Lull and her confessor Durand de Champagne dedicated works to her, and Raymond of Béziers began for her his translation of *Kalila et Dimna*. She was godmother of Enguerran de Marigny's wife, and Enguerran was the officer in charge of Jeanne's pantry before joining Philip's service in 1302.

Jeanne bore Philip four sons and a daughter before dying on April 2, 1305. In her lavish testament, she used 40,000 *livres parisis* and three years' revenues of Champagne, assigned her by Philip, to endow a hospital at Château-Thierry and the Collége de Navarre in Paris. Having rejected burial at Saint-Denis, the royal mausoleum, she was interred at the Franciscan church in Paris.

See also **Llull, Ramón; Philip IV the Fair**

Further Reading

Arbois de Jubainville, Henry d'. *Histoire des ducs et des comtes de Champagne*. 7 vols. Paris: Durand et Lauriel, 1859–69.

Brown, Elizabeth A.R. *The Monarchy of Capetain France and Royal Ceremonial*. London: Variorum, 1991.

Favier, Jean. *Un conseiller de Philippe le Bel: Enguerran de Marigny*. Paris: Presses Universitaires de France, 1963.

Lalou, Elisabeth. "Le gouvernement de la reine Jeanne, 1285–1304." *Cahiers Haut-Marnais* 167 (1986): 16–30.

ELIZABETH A.R. BROWN

JEHAN BODEL (d. 1210)

A trouvère from Arras in the second half of the 12th century and one of the most prominent writers of his time. Jehan Bodel's life is only sketchily known—neither the date nor the place of his birth has been established with accuracy.

Jehan Bodel had strong links with the city of Arras and its surroundings. He introduces himself as a minstrel in his *Congés*: he was a member of the Arras minstrel and burgher brotherhood and contributed to the rapid expansion of this society. Stanza 40 of the *Congés* suggests that he was a familiar of the Arras *échevinage*, or town council, to which he was presumably attached. Elated by Foulque de Neuilly's preaching, he was about to follow Baudouin of Flanders, the future conqueror of Constantinople, to the Holy Land, when he began to suffer from the first signs of leprosy. In 1202, he withdrew to a leprosarium in the Arras region, most likely at Grant Val near Beaurains, where he died, according

to the death-roll of the brotherhood, between February 2 and June 16, 1210.

Jehan's work has only gradually unveiled its secrets. Long underestimated, it now appears as one of the richest, most original *œuvres* in medieval literature. Because he tackled various genres simultaneously, the chronology of his works is difficult to establish. He is one of the earliest writers of *pastourelles* in *langue d'oïl*; five have been ascribed to him. Such narrative lyrics had already been composed by troubadours, but the Arragese minstrel left his mark upon the genre. Within a conventional framework, he proved original in his skilled composition in a wide range of prosodic structures and in the impression of truthfulness he gives due to subtle characterization and concrete details taken from peasant life.

Slightly different in inspiration were his one fable and eight fabliaux, those merry tales that give full scope to the imagination of an artist aiming at entertaining a noble audience at the expense of the middle class, peasants, women, and churchmen. If not as incisive as Gautier le Leu's, Jehan's fabliaux evince acute observation and a rich experience of the life of Picard peasants and merchants. The genre, free enough to encompass risqué tales and cautionary fables, appealed to this storyteller keen on Gallic mirth: *Jehan Bodiax, un rimoieres de flabiax*, as he called himself.

His versatility led him to widen the scope of his writings. A connoisseur of chansons de geste, he soon realized that the Saxon wars, a landmark in Charlemagne's reign, were a fit subject for a vast epic, and by 1180 he undertook the composition of the *Chanson des Saisnes*, which his disease prevented him from completing. Four drafts of this work are extant, the shortest one known as *A* (4,337 lines) and the longest as *T* (8,019 lines). Analysis shows that later writers tried to bring the unfinished poem to completion after the 12th century. The first 3,307 lines of *A* provide us with a text as close as possible to what Jehan's original work may have been. Here, we can recognize the innovator at once by his art and literary theories as well as his idea of history. In keeping with the Roland tradition of the chanson de geste, he foregrounds Charlemagne but also humanizes the God-chosen emperor, whose character underwent further transformation with the continuators. Nor is Jehan's inspiration purely epic: with the amours of Baudouin, the young Frenchman, romance is woven into the martial narrative, while the comedy peculiar to fabliaux creeps into the episode of Saint-Herbert du Rhin. The poem synthesizes all the components of the author's craftsmanship: a scholarly minstrel, fascinated by history and committed to his times, both an observer of reality and a visionary, but first and foremost a poet capable of breathing life into whatever he portrayed.

Jehan dealt once more with an epic subject in the *Jeu*

de saint Nicolas, a semiliturgical drama produced during the *grand siège*, or convention, of the Arras brotherhood, between 1194 and 1202. As in the *Chanson des Saisnes*, the background is the war of Christians and heathens. After an initial victory by the king of Africa's Saracens, the only survivor of the Christian host eventually ensures the triumph of his party, thanks to the protection of the saint; the king and his men convert to Christianity. The *Jeu* is a chanson de geste in miniature. Yet once more, the narrow frame of the genre, the dramatized miracle play, bursts under the poet's creative power. "Throughout the play," Albert Henry writes, "sacred and profane, sublime and comic, marvelous ... and realistic elements are to be found side by side." In this powerful and original work, a masterpiece of medieval dramatic literature, is reflected the multifarious personality of an author who showed as much sincerity in praising Auxerre wine as in extolling the crusade.

Disease turned Jehan into one of our great lyric poets. When obliged to withdraw from the society of his contemporaries, he wrote a long supplication to his friends and benefactors in his farewell poems (*Congés*), composed in 1202. Taking up the stanzaic form of Hélinant de Froid-mont's *Vers de la Mort*, he bade a pathetic farewell to the world in forty-five octosyllabic stanzas. The regret of bygone joys, rebellion against and resignation to his misfortune, faith in God, gratitude to those who harbored him "half sound and half rotten"—all the themes of a new genre are to be found here. A work of harrowing sincerity, the *Congés* stand, in the early 13th century, as the first example of "ordeal lyricism" to be found in so many poets from Rutebeuf to Verlaine.

A teller of spicy stories, the author of a chanson de geste, a skillful dramatist, a lyric poet, and a critic (in the prologue to the *Chanson des Saisnes*, he puts forward a classification of the three principal poetic genres), Jehan Bodel tackled most contemporary forms and achieved creativity in each.

Further Reading

Bartsch, Karl, ed. *Altfranzösische Romanzen und Pastourellen.* Leipzig: Vogel, 1870, pp. 287–91. [Based on MS *F* (B.N. fr. 12645).]

Berger, Roger, ed. *La nécrologie de la confrérie des jongleurs et des bourgeois d'Arras (1194–1361): texte et tables.* Arras: Imprimerie Centrale de l'Artois, 1963.

Bodel, Jehan. *La chanson des Saisnes*, ed. Annette Brasseur. 2 vols. Geneva: Droz, 1989.

——. *La chanson des Saxons*, trans. Annette Brasseur. Paris: Champion, 1992.

——. *Le jeu de saint Nicolas de Jehan Bodel*, ed. Albert Henry. Brussels: Palais des Académies, 1980. [Based on MS *V* (B.N. fr. 25566).]

——. *Les fabliaux de Jean Bodel*, ed. Pierre Nardin. Paris: Nizet, 1965. [Based on MS *A* (B.N. fr. 837).]

——. *Les congés d'Arras (Jean Bodel, Baude Fastoul, Adam de la Halle)*, ed. Pierre Ruelle. Paris: Presses Universitaires de France, 1965, pp. 83–104. [Based on MS. *A* (Arsenal 3142).]

Brasseur, Annette. *Étude linguistique et littéraire de la "Chanson des Saisnes" de Jehan Bodel.* Geneva: Droz, 1990.

——. "Index des rimes de Jehan Bodel." *Olifant* 15 (1990): 211–336.

Foulon, Charles. *L'œuvre de Jehan Bodel.* Paris: Presses Universitaires de France, 1958.

ANNETTE BRASSEUR

JIMÉNEZ DE RADA, RODRIGO (ca. 1170 – 1247)

Jiménez was born about 1170 in Puente la Reina in Navarre, to a family of the minor nobility. His father was Jimeno Pérez de Rada, and his mother, Eva de Finojosa. His uncle, Martín, was abbot of the monastery of Santa María ais de la Huerta. Family connections probably led to a stay at the royal court of Navarre before his departure to secure a higher education at the Universities of Bologna and of Paris. The dates of his stay at those institutions are unknown, although it appears that he was in Paris in 1201. He had returned to Navarre and the court of Sancho VII well before 1207. In that year he participated in the negotiation of a peace between Sancho and Alfonso VIII of Castile. His ambition and talent must have recommended Rodrigo instantly to the latter, to whom he became a major adviser and confidant for the rest of his reign.

Their relationship had become so strong by 1208 that Jiménez, not yet an ordained a priest, was nominated by Alfonso to the see of Osma, although he was never consecrated to it. Instead, further royal favor propelled him in that same year into the primatial see of Toledo. In that capacity he toured western Europe in 1211, soliciting aid for a crusade against Muslim Andalusia. In July 1212 he was present in the army of Alfonso VIII when the great victory over Muslim forces from North Africa was won at Las Navas de Tolosa.

During the next few years the debility of the king and realm prevented any immediate exploitation of that victory, but Jiménez was active in consolidating the resultant territorial gains of the kingdom and of his see in La Mancha. He was a major political figure in the brief reign of Enrique I (1214–1217) and again during the minority of Fernando III. When the latter reached his majority, Jiménez became a royal confidant and one of the chief royal advisers as Fernando ruled Castile (1217–1252) and then León (1230–1252) after the reunion of the two realms, In those capacities he assisted the king in the campaigns that saw the definitive conquest of eastern and central Andalusia—Baeza (1225), Úbeda (1233), and Córdoba (1236)—although he did not live to see the conquest of Seville (1248).

Jiménez's tenure as archbishop also saw the territorial

and juridical consolidation of the see of Toledo, whose aggrandizement was one of the great passions of his life. The other peninsular archiepiscopates—Braga, Santiago de Compostela, and Tarragona—were forced to recognize the primacy of Toledo. Bishoprics for the newly conquered cities of Baeza and Córdoba in Andalusia were made suffragans of Toledo. However, claims to Zamora and Plasencia, where sees had been created during the earlier re-conquest period, were lost to Santiago de Compostela. Also, despite much acrimony, newly conquered Valencia was assigned by Rome to Tarragona rather than Toledo, and the ancient see of Oviedo in the north continued to be exempt from all metropolitan jurisdiction.

Given the conditions of the age, none of this could be carried through without the cooperation of the papacy, and Jiménez was well known at Rome. He had gone there first in 1211 to secure backing for the campaign of Alfonso VIII against the Almohads in 1212. He returned there to attend the Fourth Lateran Council in 1215. And in 1236 and 1241 he visited the pope. In 1218 he was named papal legate in the peninsula, and from 1224 was entrusted by the papacy with a contemplated creation of a diocese for North Africa in Morocco. Nevertheless, Jiménez had his problems with Rome. Often they flowed from the collection and utilization of ecclesiastical revenues for the reconquest of the south. Jiménez had helped to persuade Rome of their necessity, and was involved in their application to the benefit of the crown. Inevitably he was caught between the necessities of the crown, the reluctance of the Spanish clergy, and the suspicions of Rome.

Some of the moneys from this source certainly contributed, directly or indirectly, to the glorification of the church at Toledo and of its archbishop. Jiménez had hardly been consecrated when he began the construction of a new archiepiscopal palace in Alcalá de Henares (ca. 1209). The present Gothic cathedral at Toledo was begun under his aegis (ca. 1221) to replace the mosque that had served as a cathedral since 1085.

Without question Jiménez was the dominant figure in the Iberian Church during the first half of the thirteenth century, and a major political and court figure as well. Even so, he found time to produce six historical works, and so became the major historian of that period. The most important of these is his *De rebus Hispaniae,* in which he carried on the tradition of the Latin chronicle from Genesis down to the recent conquest of Córdoba. In large measure he continued the work of his older contemporary, Lucas of Túy, and supplied the materials that would underpin the new vernacular history of the *Primera crónica general,* begun in the second half of the century. His *Historia Arabum,* on the other hand, had no known precursor in Christian Iberia, and few in western Europe. Beginning with the biography of Muḥammad,

the work deals primarily with the Muslim conquest of Iberia down through the arrival in the peninsula of the North African Murābit (Almoravids). It demonstrates his acquaintance with both the Arabic language and some of the Muslim historians, as well as the breadth of his interests. A *Historia Romanorum* displays his classical interests, and a *Historia Ostrogothorum* and a *Historia Hunnorum, Vandalorum, Suevorum, Alanorum, et Silingorum* demonstrate his debt to the school of Iberian historians of Visigothic times, especially Isidore of Seville.

During the spring of 1247 Jiménez traveled to France to visit Pope Innocent IV at Lyons. On his return journey to Iberia he drowned in the Rhone on 10 June. His body was embalmed and returned to the monastery of Santa María de la Huerta, where it was entombed. His tomb was opened for examination as recently as 1907.

See also **Fernando III, King of Castile**

Further Reading

Ballesteros Gaibros, M. *Don Rodrigo Jiménez de Rada.* Madrid, 1943. (A highly laudatory and semipopular introduction.)

Gorosterratzu, J. *Don Rodrigo Jiménez de Rada: Gran estadista, escritor y prelado.* Pamplona, 1925. (The only modern biography; old-fashioned, but thorough.)

Jimémez de Rada, Rodrigo. *Rodericus Ximenius de Rada. Opera.* Ed. María Desamparades Cabanes Pecourt. Valencia, 1968. (Reprint of the 1793 complete edition of his work.)

——. *Historia Arabum.* Ed. J. Lozano Sánchez. Anales de la Universidad Hispalense, serie Filosofía y Letras. Vol. 21. Seville, 1974.

——. *Historia de rebus Hispaniae sive Historia gothica.* Ed. J. Hernández Valverde. Corpus Christianorum, Continuatio Medievalia, Vol. 72. Tumhout, 1987.

BERNARD F. REILLY

JOACHIM OF FIORE
(c. 1135–30 March 1202)

Joachim of Fiore (Flora, Floris) was a biblical exegete and the founder of the order of San Giovanni in Fiore, commonly known as the Florensians. Joachim's attempts to explain the patterns of Christian history gained him a reputation as a prophet in the thirteenth century, as well as a following among the Spiritual faction of the Franciscan order. His reputation as a prophet made his thought very influential in the later Middle Ages, but some people considered him a heretic because of his Trinitarian doctrine and his adoption by the Spirituals.

Joachim was born in Celico, near Cosenza in Calabria. As a young man, he trained to be a notary like his father, and for some years he served in this capacity at the Corte del Giustiziere in Calabria and later at the court of King William II of Sicily in Salerno. Around 1167, a serious illness led Joachim to make a pilgrimage to the Holy Land, where he decided to become a monk. On his return to Calabria, Joachim retired first to the Cistercian monastery of Sambucina and then to the monastery of Corazzo, near Catanzaro. There he professed and was ordained in 1168. Sometime before 1177, he was elected abbot. Joachim found administration arduous; and when negotiations to have Corazzo officially accepted by the Cistercian order led to a two-year residence at the Cistercian monastery of Casamari (1182–1184), he took advantage of the respite to begin two major works of biblical exegesis. These were *Liber de concordia Novi ac Veteris Testamenti* (*Book on the Concordance between the Old and the New Testaments*) and *Expositio in Apocalypsim* (*Exposition of the Apocalypse*). Now convinced that exegesis was his real calling, Joachim turned to the papacy to obtain a release from administration. When Pope Lucius III took up residence in nearby Veroli during 1184, Joachim obtained Lucius's permission to devote himself to writing for a year and a half. He received a renewal of this permission from Pope Urban III in 1186, and another from Pope Clement III in 1188. Clement also seems to have approved Joachim's resignation as abbot of Corazzo, which was now fully incorporated into the Cistercian order.

In the mid-1180s, Joachim became dissatisfied with the Cistercian life. He moved to a hermitage at Petralata, and then to San Giovanni in Fiore, in the Sila mountains. Meanwhile, his reputation as a prophet was growing. In 1191, he was summoned to an interview with Richard I Coeur de Lion (Lion-Heart) at Messina; later that year he was summoned to another, with Emperor Henry VI near Naples. The Cistercian leadership did not approve of Joachim's activities, however. In 1192, the order's chapter general declared that if Joachim and his companion Ranier of Ponza did not return to Corazzo by the feast of John the Baptist in 1193, they would be considered fugitives. Joachim ignored the deadline and instead founded his own order at Fiore. Again he turned to the papacy to legitimize his actions. The rule of Joachim's new order, based on that of the Cistercians but more austere, was approved by Pope Celestine III in 1196. Joachim also received a charter for his monastery and an annual stipend from Emperor Henry VI. The new order spread rapidly, establishing thirty-eight houses in Calabria and twenty-two elsewhere within the first few decades of its existence. But its growth stopped in the mid-thirteenth century, apparently because of competition from the Mendicant orders. It was united with the Cistercian order in 1570.

Joachim died at the Florensian monastery of San Martino di Giove near Canale. In 1240, his body was translated to San Giovanni, where it became the center of a local cult.

Joachim's fame rests on his novel method of scriptural exegesis. He sought understanding of what he called *concordia*—harmony between the Old Testament and the New Testament, manifested in parallel events. Joachim described this as "a similarity of equal proportion between the Old and the New Testaments, equal, I say, as to number, not as to dignity." The idea of *concordia* had no real precedent in earlier Christian exegesis. Typology had been used to argue that certain Old Testament events and figures foreshadowed Christ and that Christ was therefore the fulfillment of Old Testament prophecies, but Joachim's *concordia* presumed a steady parallel between Old Testament and Christian history. Moreover, Joachim treated Christ as one of many parallel figures and events in scriptural *concordia*, whereas previous exegetes had seen Christ as the only figure foreshadowed in the Old Testament. It has been suggested that Joachim's *concordia* derived from a desire, common in the twelfth century, to find meaning and pattern in human history. In this sense, Joachim's exegesis was very much in the spirit of his time.

Joachim believed that three visions had given him the spiritual insight to perceive scriptural *concordia*. His study of *concordia* revealed, in turn, the patterns of history. These were overlapping numerical sequences of events, arranged mainly in twos, threes, and sevens. The two most important were the synchronous *diffinitio alpha* and *diffinitio omega*. *Diffinitio alpha* divided history into three *status* or states, corresponding to the persons of the Trinity and symbolizing the spiritual progress of humanity. *Diffinitio omega* was arranged in two stages corresponding to the Old Testament on the one hand, and the New Testament, the Christian era, and a final period of special spiritual understanding on the other. This final period would be the completion of the Christian era. The first *status* of *diffinitio alpha* was marked by an order of married people and the second by an order of clerics; the third would be characterized by an order of monks. This third *status* would be a time of joyous contemplation and understanding of the scriptures, in which the church would become truly spiritual. Joachim thought that the second *status* was gradually giving way to the third in his own rime. On the basis of the pattern of twos that he saw throughout the Old and New Testaments, he predicted that the church would be led into the new *status* by two new orders of spiritual men: one an order of hermits, the other of preachers. These orders would not end the Roman church but would, rather, lead its transition to a higher quality of spiritual life. There would be a period of peace before the last great persecution preceding the last judgment.

Joachim subdivided the stages of historical *diffinitiones* into lesser overlapping patterns, also numerically based. For example, the first *status* featured twelve patriarchs who founded twelve tribes, the second had twelve apostles who founded twelve churches, and the third had twelve great religious who founded twelve monasteries. Although each set of twelve dominated its own *status*, it also had roots in the previous *status*, thus producing the overlap. By far the most important of these lesser sequences was a pattern of sevens arranging the Old and New Testament stages of history. There was some precedent for this among previous exegetes, who had often divided history into seven periods. But whereas traditional commentators such as Augustine envisioned the seventh period as a time of peace beyond the end of history, Joachim placed his seventh age before the last judgment. He considered this seventh age to be concomitant with the third *status*. Joachim was also original in imposing a pattern of concordant double sevens subdividing the seven ages: one a sequence of seven seals that appeared during the second and third ages, the other a sequence of seven openings of the seals that occurred in the sixth age. Joachim believed that he was living at the end of the sixth age and near the end of the fifth seal-opening, so he speculated a good deal on the identity of contemporaries who might figure in the transition to the next age. This established an important precedent for his followers.

Joachim's Trinitarian concerns led him to question Peter Lombard's commonly accepted description of the unity of the Trinity, *vera et propria*, suggesting instead *collectiva et similitudi-naria*. This formulation was condemned as tritheistic at the Fourth Lateran Council in 1215. The council's failure to comment on the rest of Joachim's doctrines created uncertainty about his orthodoxy, and this uncertainty was never really resolved. While many were drawn to Joachim's vision of a coming spiritual age, others remained suspicious of his doctrine. In the mid-thirteenth century and the early fourteenth, Joachim's reputation suffered further blows. His predictions regarding the two orders of spiritual men who would herald the new *status* attracted the interest of the newly founded Dominicans and Franciscans. Soon radical Franciscans had woven their own apocalyptic notions around Joachim's thought. Gerard of Borgo San Donnino's *Eternal Evangel* was condemned as heretical in 1255. The doctrines of the Spiritual Franciscans met a similar fate in the 1310s. Both were deeply rooted in Joachim's teachings, and their censure increased doubts about his orthodoxy.

Joachim's double reputation as a prophet and a heretic continued into modern times. Thomas Aquinas, Duns Scotus, and the sixteenth-century historian Cesare Baronius all considered him heterodox; Dante, Boccaccio, and the usually skeptical Bollandist Daniel Papebroch considered him a prophet. Early Protestant writers were similarly divided. During the Enlightenment, attacks on the notion of prophecy drastically diminished Joachim's influence, but in the nineteenth and twentieth centuries it could still be found in figures as diverse as Auguste Comte and Carl Jung.

See also **Dante Alighieri; Henry VI; Richard I**

Further Reading

Editions

Joachim of Fiore. *Liber de concordia Novi ac Veteris Testamenti*, ed. E. Randolph Daniel. Transactions of the American Philosophical Society, 73(8). Philadelphia, Pa.: American Philosophical Society, 1983.

———. *Enchiridion super Apocalypsim*, ed. Edward Kilian Burger. Studies and Tests, 78. Toronto: Pontifical Institute of Mediaeval Studies, 1986.

Studies

Bloomfield, Morton. "Recent Scholarship on Joachim of Flora and His Influence." In *Prophecy and Millenarianism: Essays in Honour of Marjorie Reeves*, ed. Ann Williams. Essex: Longman, 1980, pp. 23–52.

Daniel, E. Randolph. "The Double Procession of the Holy Spirit in Joachim of Fiore's Understanding of History." *Speculum*, 55, 1980, pp. 469–483.

Emmerson, Richard K., and Bernard McGinn, eds. *The Apocalypse in the Middle Ages*. Ithaca, N.Y.: Cornell University Press, 1992.

Lee, Harold, Marjorie Reeves, and Giulio Silano. *Western Mediterranean Prophecy: The School of Joachim of Fiore and the Fourteenth-Century Breviloquium*. Studies and Texts, 88. Toronto: Pontifical Institute of Mediaeval Studies, 1989.

McGinn, Bernard. *The Calabrian Abbot: Joachim of Fiore in the History of Western Thought*. New York: Macmillan, 1985.

Potestà, Gian Luca, ed. *Il profetismo gioachimita tra Quattrocento e Cinquecento: Atti del III Congresso Internazionale di Studi Gioachimiti, S. Giovanni in Fiore, 17–21 settembre 1989*. Genoa: Marietti, 1991.

Reeves, Marjorie. *The Influence of Prophecy in the Later Middle Ages: A Study in Joachimism*. Oxford: Clarendon, 1969.

———. *Joachim of Fiore and the Prophetic Future*. London: SPCK, 1976.

———. "The Originality and Influence of Joachim of Fiore." *Traditio*, 36, 1980, pp. 269–316. Reeves, Marjorie, and Beatrice Hirsch-Reich. *The Figurae of Joachim of Fiore*. Oxford-Warburg Studies. Oxford: Clarendon, 1972.

West, Delno C., ed. *Joachim of Fiore in Christian Thought: Essays on the Influence of the Calabrian Abbot*, 2 vols. New York: Burt Franklin, 1974.

West, Delno C., and Sandra Zimdars-Swartz. *Joachim of Fiore: A Study in Spiritual Perception and History*. Bloomington: Indiana University Press, 1983.

THOMAS TURLEY

JOANNA I OF NAPLES
(1326–1382, r. 1343–1382)

Joanna (Joan, Joanne, Giovanna) was queen regnant of Naples. She was the elder daughter of Robert the Wise, king of Naples, and was married four times: to Andrew of Hungary (in 1340), Louis of Taranto (1347), James of Majorca (1362), and Otto of Brunswick (1375). She had no surviving issue.

In 1345, Andrew was assassinated. His death provoked an invasion by his brother, Louis the Great of Hungary, who accused Joanna of complicity in Andrew's murder and claimed the throne for himself (as the grandson of Charles Martel, firstborn son of Charles I of Anjou). Louis entered Naples in 1348. Few Italians opposed him, and some, including Cola di Rienzo, were actively supportive. (Cola, however, fell before the Hungarian triumph, his defeat having been partly engineered by Joanna's supporters.) Joanna, seeking allies, married one cousin, Louis of Taranto, secretly and without papal sanction (she and Louis were related closely enough to require a dispensation in order to marry); and appointed another cousin, Charles of Durazzo (d. 1348), guardian of her son, though Charles played an equivocal role in the invasion. As the Hungarians approached, Joanna and Louis fled to their overlord, Pope Clement VI, at Avignon. To recover his support after their marriage and the murder of Andrew and to obtain money with which to renew the fight against Hungary, Joanna sold Avignon to Clement for 80,000 florins, considerably less than its worth. Meanwhile, the black death broke out, and the Hungarians, much reduced in number, returned home, taking as hostage Joanna's son (who died in Hungary) but leaving Joanna and Louis of Taranto in possession of the Regno. The Hungarians returned later, but never successfully. By 1352, Louis of Taranto, with help from the papacy, was recognized in Naples and had also established his rights against his wife's claims to sovereignty. Organized by the grand seneschal, Niccolò Acciaiuoli, the Regno experienced a brief period of recovery before war was renewed. The war was undertaken again partly in an unsuccessful attempt to reunite Sicily (which had been under Aragonese rule since 1285) with the Regno, and pardy because of renewed rebellion by the Durazzo branch of the Angevins, who resented the dominance of Louis of Taranto.

Louis died in 1362. Joanna's third husband, James of Majorca, was given no authority in government. James—who had recently escaped from fourteen years' imprisonment in an iron cage by his uncle, Peter IV of Aragon—was half mad and periodically violent. He soon returned to Spain, and from 1362 to 1375 Joanna ruled alone. Despite minor rebellions initiated by her sister Maria, who was the widow of Charles of Durazzo, and by Maria's sons, the realm achieved a measure of peace. In 1368—1370, Urban V briefly returned to Italy from Avignon, with Joanna's protection.

In 1378, Urban VI, formerly archbishop of Bari and Joanna's subject, became pope and quickly indicated his intention to revive and support the Hungarian claim to Naples. Accordingly, when a rival pope, Clement VII, was elected, Joanna took Clement's part; and her next husband, Otto of Brunswick, proved entirely willing to persecute Urban's followers. Urban reacted by excommunicating Joanna and conceding her throne to Louis of Hungary. Charles III of Durazzo (nephew of Maria and the late elder Charles) encouraged Louis, so, although Charles III was her nearest relative, Joanna excluded him from the succession. Instead, with Clement VII's approval, she bequeathed all her rights to Louis of Anjou, eldest brother of Charles V of France (in January 1380). In 1381, Urban, despairing of the Hungarians, crowned Charles III of Durazzo king of Naples. In the ensuing civil war, Charles was successful: in August Otto was taken prisoner and Joanna surrendered. She died in prison, probably stifled to death on Charles's orders, in July 1382, while her adopted heir, Louis of Anjou, was coming over the Alps to her rescue.

Joanna's lament "I regret only one thing, that the Almighty did not make me a man" has some justification. Urban VI's main complaint against her was apparently that he disliked queens regnant. She had some devotees, notably Giovanni Boccaccio, but she was more usually scorned as immoral and incompetent. Still, she did her best work when she ruled alone: although her reign was a disaster, the problems were not all of her making.

See also **Boccaccio, Giovanni; Charles V the Wise**

Further Reading

Editions

Caracciolo, Tristan. *Vita Joannae primae Neapolis regina*, ed. Giuseppe Paladino. Rerum Italicarum Scriptores, 22. Bologna: Zanichelli, 1933, pp. 1–18.

Dominicus de Gravina. *Cronicon de rebus in Apulia gestis, 1333–1350*, ed. Albano Sorbelli. Rerum Italicarum Scriptores, 12. Città di Castello: Tipi dell'Editore S. Lapi, 1903.

Villani, Mattreo. *Cronica*, 5 vols., ed. Ignazio Moutier. Florence: Magheri, 1926.

Studies

De Feo, Italo. *Giovanna d'Angiò, regina di Napoli*. Naples: F. Fiorentino, 1968.

Léonard, Émile G. *Histoire de Jeanne Ire, reine de Naples, comtesse de Provence (1343–1382)*, 3 vols. Paris: Picard, 1932–1936.

——. *Les Angevins de Naples*. Paris: Presses Universitaires de France, 1954.

Louis the Great, King of Hungary and Poland, ed. S. B. Vardy, Geza Grosschmid, and Leslie. S. Domonkos. New York: Columbia University Press, 1986.

CAROLA M. SMALL

JOÃO I, KING OF PORTUGAL (1357?–1433)

João, the illegitimate son of Pedro I and Teresa Lourenço, was born probably in Lisbon on 14 August 1357 and died there on 14 August 1433. In 1363, when he was still a child, he became the master of the Order of Avis.

In normal circumstances, he would never have acceded to the throne, but the situation created in the latter years of Fernando I's reign (1367–1383) opened a crisis of succession. By his marriage to Leonor Teles in 1372, Fernando had a daughter, Beatriz (1372–ca. 1409), who married Juan I of Castile in 1383. Under Fernando, Portugal had three wars with Castile, and this marriage was intended to settle the conflict between the two countries. The marriage contract laid down that Portugal would be ruled by the first heir born to Beatriz, and until the child reached fourteen, Queen Leonor would govern the country as regent. This marriage gave Juan I the possibility of one day sitting on the Portuguese throne. However, Queen Leonor, in collusion with her lover, João Fernandes Andeiro, kept an oligarchic rule that excluded the merchants from the privy council. These, fearing the regency by the queen, persuaded João to kill Andeiro in order to force an accommodation with her. But, following the death of Andeiro and the rising of the people against her, the queen appealed to Juan I, who invaded Portugal.

João immediately organized the defense of Lisbon, relying on the military support of Nuno' Alvares Pereira (Nun' Alvares), a knight who proved to be a supreme strategist. The peasants, artisans, and merchants rallied to Dom João's cause, and the younger sons of noble families with no land of their own joined his forces. While João held Lisbon against the Castilian army, Nun' Alvares fought in the south and eventually neared Almada, close to Lisbon, wreaking havoc upon the Castilians. On 3 September 1384, Juan I, fearing the plague that had smitten his camp, lifted the siege of the city, which had lasted four months, and withdrew to Castile. *Cortes* (parliament) were convened at Coimbra to solve the problem of succession. And while João besieged the castles loyal to Beatriz, Nun' Alvares harassed the Castilian loyalists.

João and Nun' Alvares arrived in Coimbra on 3 March 1385. At the *cartes*, the lawyer João Afonso das Regras argued João's case, showing that the other pretenders, the sons of Pedro I and Inês de Castro, were illegitimate in view of the irregular relationship between their parents. As for Juan I, his invasion of Portugal had disqualified him, because it was a breach of the treaty. Having disposed of the argument of rights by birth, João das Regras claimed that since João was the one who had taken up arms to defend the realm from the Castilian invader, he deserved to be king. By acclamation he became João I on 6 April 1385.

Yet the war with Castile was not over. Following Fernando's previous policy of getting military support from England, João I gained some assistance from the duke of Lancaster. An English contingent fought alongside the Portuguese in the battle of Aljubarrota (14 August 1385), which was a decisive victory for the Portuguese. Portugal's ties with England were strengthened by the Treaty of Windsor (9 May 1386), a military alliance between the two countries. This was followed by the marriage of João I to Philippa of Lancaster (1359–1415), daughter of John of Gaunt, duke of Lancaster, on 2 February 1387. From this marriage

were born Duarte (1391), Pedro (1392), Henrique (1394, known as Prince Henry the Navigator), João (1400), and Fernando (1402). In 1415, four years after the peace treaty with Castile had been signed, João I, encouraged by his minister of the treasury, complied with the wishes of his sons and led an expedition to Ceuta in Morocco, taking the city. This initiated the period of Portuguese expansion in which all the princes were deeply involved. Between 1418 and 1427, Prince Henrique promoted the discovery of the islands of Madeira and the Azores.

João I was a popular king who listened to his subjects and tried to satisfy their demands. The dynastic crisis of 1383–1385 gave Portugal its independence and enabled the productive classes—traders, merchants, and artisans—to take a leading role in the development of the country. By relieving the people of Lisbon and Oporto from the payment of tithes and seigniorial rights, João I paved the way for a new age. He was a cultivated man and wrote a remarkable treatise on hunting (*Livro da montaria*) that reflects his views on court life and a pre-Renaissance awareness of the value of the human body.

Further Reading

Bernardino, T. *A revolução portuguesa de 1383–1385.* Lisbon, 1984.

Eannes de Zurara, G. C*rónica da tomada de Ceuta por el rei dom João I.* Lisbon, 1915.

Lopes, F. *Crónica de dom Pedro.* Rome, 1966.

——. *Crónica del rei dom Johan I.* 2 vols. Lisbon, 1968–73.

——. *Crónica de dom Fernando.* Lisbon, 1975. Peres, D. *Dom João I.* Oporto, 1983.

Suárez Fernández, L. *Historia del reinado de Juan I de Castilla.* 2 vols. Madrid, 1977.

LUIS REBELO

JOHANN VON WÜRZBURG (fl. ca. 1300)

As in most cases of medieval German literature, hardly anything is known about the author, except for some self-references in his courtly romance, *Wilhelm von Österreich.* He mentions that he was born in Würzburg and worked as a scribe, perhaps for the counts of Hohenberg and Haigerloch, especially Count Albrecht von Haigerloch (d. 1298). He also expresses his thanks to a citizen of Esslingen, Dieprecht, for helping him with his work. *Wilhelm von Österreich* was completed in May of 1314 and was dedicated to the Dukes Leopold and Frederick of Austria. It appears to have been rather popular, since it has come down to us in a large number of manuscripts (in Gießen, Gotha, The Hague, Heidelberg, etc.). In total, there are ten complete manuscripts and ten fragments extant.

Wilhelm von Österreich is a biographical romance combining chivalrous with amorous adventutes providing a mythical-historical background for the ruling House of Hapsburg. Duke Leopold of Austria and the heathen king Agrant of Zyzia make a pilgrimage to the holy site of John of Ephesus to pray for an heir. They meet by chance and make their sacrifices together. Leopold's wife delivers a son, Wilhelm, and Agrant's wife has a daughter, Aglye. The goddess Venus awakens love in both children through dreams and instigates Wilhelm to leave home on a search for Aglye. After exotic travels he meets Aglye, and the children fall in love. Her father, Agrant, separates them, however, because he wants to marry his daughter to a heathen prince. The lovers exchange an extensive correspondence that documents the high level of literacy that members of the higher aristocracy could acquire in the later Middle Ages. Aglye is twice promised as wife to heathen princes, but Wilhelm kills them both in battles and jousts. Only after he has liberated Queen Crispin of Belgalgan's kingdom of monsters are the lovers able to meet again. Soon afterwards a massive battle involves the heathen and Christian forces, which concludes with the Christians' victory and the heathens' baptism. Finally, King Agrant agrees with the marriage of Aglye and Wilhelm, to whom a son is born called Friedrich. Wilhelm dies thereafter when he is ambushed by an envious brother-in-law. Aglye's heart breaks when she hears the news and dies as well.

Wilhelm experiences a large number of allegorical adventures throughout his quest for his beloved. These, and other aspects, are often commented on by the narrator, who fully enjoyed the use of the so-called *geblümter Stil* (flowery style). Johann von Würzburg refers to Gottfried von Straßburg, Wolfram von Eschenbach, and Rudolf von Ems as his literary models. He also knows Albrecht's *Jüngeren Titurel* and other thirteenth century romances.

Wilhelm von Österreich displays a surprising openness toward the heathen culture, although the paradigm of Christianity as the only true religion is not abandoned in favor of global tolerance. Johann von Würzburg enjoyed considerable success with his work, which glorifies the House of Austria and combines the exotic world of the Orient with the world of Arthurian romance. The text was copied far into the fifteenth century and discussed by other writers such as Püterich of Reichertshausen and Ulrich Fuetrer. Anton Sorg printed a prose version in 1481 and 1491 in Augsburg, which was also reprinted, probably in Wittenberg in 1530–1540. Wilhelm and Aglye, the main characters in the romance, are portrayed in the fifteenth-century frescoes on Castle Runkelstein as ideal lovers, next to Tristan and Isolde, and Wilhelm of Orleans and Amelie.

See also **Gottfried von Straßburg; Wolfram von Eschenbach**

Further Reading

Brackert, Helmut: "*Da stuont daz minne wol gezam*," *Zeitschrift fur deutsche Philologie, Sonderheft*, 93 (1974): 1–18.

Juergens, Albrecht: '*Wilhelm von Österreich*'. *Johanns von Würzburg 'Historia Poetica von 1314 und Aufgabenstellung einer narrativen Fürstenlehre*. Frankfurt am Main: Lang, 1990.

Johanns von Würzburg "*Wilhelm von Österreich*. "*Aus der Gothaer Hs.*, ed. Ernst Regel. Berlin: Weidmann, 1906; rpt. Zurich: Weidmann, 1970.

Mayser, Eugen. *Studien zur Dichtung Johanns von Würzburg*. Berlin: Ebering, 1931.

Ridder, Klaus. *Mittelhochdeutsche Minne- und Aventiure-romane: Fiktion, Geschichte und literarische Tradition im späthöfischen Roman: Reinfried von Braunschweig, Wilhelm von Österreich, Friedrich von Schwaben*. Berlin: de Gruyter, 1998.

Straub, Veronika: *Entstehung und Entwicklung des frühneuhochdeutschen Prosaromans. Studien zur Prosaauflösung 'Wilhelm von Österreich'*. Amsterdam: Rodopi, 1974.

Wentzlaff-Eggebert, Friedrich-Wilhelm: *Kreuzzugsdichtung des Mittelalters*. Berlin: Walter de Gruyter, 1960, pp. 290–293.

ALBRECHT CLASSEN

JOHANNES VON TEPL
(ca. 1350–early 15th c.)

Born in German and Czech-speaking Bohemia, Tepl (also known as Johannes von Saaz or Johannes Henslini de Sitbor) has been identified as the author of the *Ackermann aus Böhmen* (The Bohemian Plowman) by means of the acrostic IOHANNES, and by the signature de Tepla ("of Tepl") in a letter accompanying the work sent to friend Peter Rothirsch of Prague. Appointments as rector of the Latin school and notary of the cities of Saaz and later Prague-Neustadt show Tepl to have been literate in both Czech and Latin as well as German. Besides the *Ackermann aus Böhmen*, only a few German and Latin verses, plus parts of a Latin votive office (1404), have been identified as Tepl's work. It is unclear whether the *Czech Tkadlecek* (ca. 1407), a text similar to the *Ackermann* in which a weaver laments the loss of his unfaithful sweetheart, might also have been composed by him. *The Ackermann* is preserved whole or in part in sixteen manuscript editions, mostly of upper German provenance, as well as in seventeen early printed editions. The Pfister edition of 1460 is one of the two earliest printed books in German.

The work, an audacious debate with death, is framed as a legal proceeding in which a grief-stricken widower, a "plowman of the pen" (i.e., a scribe) brings a complaint against the justice and justification of death in God's world order. The plowman bewails the loss of his virtuous young wife, Margaretha, and rails at Death's cruelty and unfairness. In sixteen rounds of spirited debate, the plowman condemns Death while defending life, love, and man, God's finest creation. Death, in his turn, denies any dignity of man and any right to life, vaunting, instead, his own power and arbitrariness. Only in chapter 33 is the argument silenced when God is called on to deliver a verdict in the case. Because the plaintiff has fought well, God awards him honor, but gives the victory to Death by affirming the status quo. The work ends with an impassioned prayer for the soul of Margaretha.

The emotional verisimilitude of the argumentation and the correspondence of biographical data in the text to certain facts of Tepl's life have raised the question whether the work might not have been precipitated by an actual bereavement of the author, perhaps his first wife, the mother of his two oldest children. Records show Tepl to have been survived by a widow, Clara (possibly a second wife), and five children. The autobiographical thesis seems to be at odds, however, with the tone of the author's letter to Rothirsch, which emphasizes the stylistic devices and rhetorical strategies deployed in the work.

More significant than the unresolved autobiographical issue is the controversy over whether the arguments and style place the work further within the realm of late medieval or of early humanist thought. Although thematically and formally the *Ackermann* remains largely indebted to earlier medieval traditions, stylistically its language echos that of Johann von Neumarkt's chancellery German, which shows the strong influence of the Latin rhetorical forms of Italian humanists.

Further Reading

Hahn, Gerhard. *Der Ackermann aus Böhmen des Johannes von Tepl*. Erträge der Forschung 215. Darmstadt: Wissenschaftliche Buchgesellschaft, 1984.

Hruby, Antonín. *Der Ackermann und seine Vorlage*. Munich: Beck, 1971.

Hübner, Arthur. "Deutsches Mittelalter und italienische Renaissance im *Ackermann aus Böhmen*." *Zeitschrift für Deutschkunde* 51 (1937): 225–239.

Jafre, Samuel. "Des Witwers Verlangen nach Rat: Ironie und Struktureinheit im *Ackermann aus Böhmen*." *Daphnis* 7 (1978): 1–53.

Johannes von Saaz. *Der Ackermann aus Böhmen*, ed. Günther Jungbluth. 2 vols. Heidelberg: Winter, 1969–1983.

Johannes von Tepl. *Death and the Plowman; or, The Bohemian Plowman*, trans. Ernst N. Kirrmann from the Modern German version of Alois Bernt. Chapel Hill: University of North Carolina Press, 1958.

Schwarz, Ernst, ed. *Der Ackermann aus Böhmen des Johannes von Tepl und seine Zeit*. Wege der Forschung 143. Darmstadt: Wissenschaftliche Buchgesellschaft, 1968.

ANNE WINSTON-ALLEN

JOHN (1167–1216; r. 1199–1216)

Born on December 24, 1167, he was the youngest of the four sons of Henry II and Eleanor of Aquitaine to reach manhood. His father intended him to be the ruler of an autonomous kingdom of Ireland (and from 1185 he bore the title Lord of Ireland), but with the deaths of his elder brothers he aspired to wider ambitions. After the death of the childless Richard (1199) he became king of England, duke of Normandy, duke of Aquitaine, and count of Anjou, and he prevailed against the claims of his nephew Arthur of Brittany, son of his brother Geoffrey.

It was a difficult inheritance. The financial burdens of Richard's reign had been extraordinarily heavy, for his crusade and ransom, and for the defense of the continental dominions against persistent attacks and subversion by Philip II (Philip Augustus) of France. The revenues of England, vital for survival, were devalued by inflation. The balance of advantage in resources and influence had tipped decisively in favor of the French crown. Normandy was war-weary, weakened, and demoralized; when Philip renewed his attack in 1204, the will to resist suddenly collapsed and John retired to England without putting up a fight.

John never reconciled himself to the loss of Normandy. His efforts to accumulate a war chest were remarkably successful, but achieved by a relentless and ruthless exploitation of royal rights over subjects that exposed the arbitrary nature of many of his royal powers and called their legitimacy into question. His barons, seeking to rebuild family fortunes after the loss of their Norman estates, had to bid expensively for royal favors granted, or withheld, capriciously.

Disaffection was for a time deflected by John's resistance to Pope Innocent III, who set aside a royal nominee for the archbishopric of Canterbury and instead appointed Stephen Langton, whom the king rejected. John's stand was generally supported by the laity, who patiently endured an interdict for six years. John confidently disregarded a sentence of excommunication while his coffers were augmented by the appropriated revenues of the clergy. That the English clergy should be so completely at his mercy was, however, a chilling demonstration of royal power to override established rights, and there was a growing feeling among some of the barons that their own safety and their families' fortunes depended on getting rid of him.

Faced by incipient rebellions and an invasion fleet mustered by Philip of France, John could not ignore the ultimate papal weapon, a sentence of deposition. He accepted the pope's terms for lifting the sanctions and in addition offered his kingdoms of England and Ireland as fiefs of the papacy, in effect putting them under the protection of the Holy See.

John's carefully nurtured grand strategy for the defeat of the French king collapsed when his allies, the count of Flanders and his nephew Emperor Otto IV of Germany, were decisively defeated by Philip at the Battle of Bouvines, May 1214. Open rebellion erupted in

JOHN II THE GOOD

England. At a moment when neither side could be sure of winning, an attempt at a negotiated peace produced Magna Carta (June 1215), by which the crown's claims to executive privilege were brought within the bounds of agreed law. As a peace formula it failed, and John had it annulled by the pope. He was winning the civil war when he died (October 1216). Loyalists reissued Magna Carta to rally support for his infant son, Henry III.

While curtailing the possibility of tyranny Magna Carta also recognized the advantages of efficient royal government, which John had done much to foster. He understood administration and did much in a short reign to refine and rationalize it. He created a precedent (in the Thirteenth of 1207) for a proper taxation system. He created the navy that thwarted Philip's projected invasion. He failed, however, at the crucial arts of government in the management of men and what was currently recognized as "good lordship."

John has been portrayed as a monster of depravity. This is a fanciful elaboration of a distorting half-truth. He was no more domineering than his father and brother, and hardly more morally reprehensible, but he lacked their redeeming qualities. He was crafty and vindictive and instead of charismatic leadership could offer only dogged determination. Failing to inspire loyalty, he tried to dominate by menace and—constantly fearing disloyalty—he fed his fears by a corrosive suspicion. He is a classic case of a ruler undone not merely by adverse circumstances but by defects of personality.

See also **Eleanor of Aquitaine; Henry II; Innocent III, Pope; Philip II Augustus**

Further Reading

Hollister, C. Warren. "King John and the Historians." *Journal of British Studies* 1 (1961): 1–29

Holt, J.C. *The Northerners: A Study in the Reign of King John.* London: Oxford University Press, 1961

Holt, J.C. *Magna Carta and Medieval Government.* London: Hambledon, 1985 [collected papers especially valuable are "King John," first published in 1963, and "The End of the Anglo-Norman Realm," from 1975]

Turner, Ralph V. *King John.* New York: Longman, 1994

Warren, W.L. *King John.* 2d ed. London: Eyre Methuen, 1978

Warren, W.L. "Painters King John Forty Years On." *Haskins Society Journal I* (1989): 1–9.

W.L. WARREN

JOHN II THE GOOD (1319–1364)

King of France, 1350–64. The elder son of Philip VI and Jeanne of Burgundy, John became heir to the throne when his father succeeded to it in 1328. In 1332, John married Bonne de Luxembourg, daughter of the king of Bohemia. Before she died of plague in 1349, Bonne bore him nine children, among whom were the future Charles V and Jeanne, who married Charles the Bad of Navarre.

In the early campaigns of the Hundred Years' War, John's first important command was at the abortive siege of Aiguillon in 1345. He was much attached to his mother and to the strong Burgundian faction in French politics, with which she was aligned. When Philip VI finally tried to mollify the dissident northwestern nobility in the 1340s and reduce the role of Burgundians, John remained linked to the latter in opposition to his father.

John's accession to the throne in 1350, soon followed by the summary execution of the constable Raoul de Brienne, revived the old tension between the Valois monarchy and the northwestern nobles. Leadership of the opposition passed to the Évreux branch of the royal family, headed by Charles of Navarre, who engineered the murder of the new constable, Charles of Spain, in 1354. After two provisional settlements with his dangerous son-in-law, John finally lost patience and arrested Charles in April 1356, executing several of his Norman allies and plunging northwestern France into civil war.

John also attracted criticism for his style of government, which gave great responsibility to the heads of administrative bodies, who tended to be men of modest social origins. Their continuity in office contrasted with that of the royal council, which frequently changed in composition as John had to appoint representatives of political factions rather than trusted men of his own choosing. Reformers on this council resented their lack of control over the administrative bodies. Bourgeois reformers, led by Parisians, harbored personal and political resentments against these royal officials. Noble reformers had an agenda based on class and geography as well as governmental philosophy, while clergy were found in both camps.

These opposition groups both played a role in the Estates General of 1355, but their failure to generate needed revenues provoked the king into policies that alienated both groups during 1356. In September, with an army consisting of his own noble supporters, John II met defeat and capture at the hands of an Anglo-Gascon army at Poitiers. For the next four years, he was a prisoner in England, trying to negotiate a treaty that would secure his release, while his son Charles struggled to preserve some authority for the monarchy in Paris.

As the bourgeois reformers showed increasing hostility to the nobles, and as the nobles became disillusioned with their erratic leader Charles the Bad, the crown managed to recruit important dissident nobles and rebuilt its power around a new coalition. This realignment occurred during the last six years of John's reign, but historians differ as to whether he or his son deserves credit for the royal recovery. Released for a large ransom under the terms of the Treaty of Brétigny in 1360, John had to contend with the violence of thousands of unemployed soldiers. After considering a crusade to lure them away, he secured from the Estates in December 1363 an important new tax, the *fouage*, to finance an army to restore order. Continuing unresolved problems with England were complicated when the king's son Louis, a hostage for his father's ransom, broke parole and fled. John returned to captivity in England and died there in the spring of 1364.

See also **Charles II the Bad; Charles V the Wise**

Further Reading

Bordonove, Georges. *Jean le Bon et son temps.* Paris: Ramsay, 1980.

Cazelles, Raymond. "Jean II le Bon: quel homme? quel roi?" *Revue historique* 509 (1974): 5–26.

——. *Société politique, noblesse et couronne sous Jean le Bon et Charles V.* Geneva: Droz, 1982.

Deviosse, Jean. *Jean le Bon.* Paris: Fayard, 1985.

Henneman, John Bell. *Royal Taxation in Fourteenth Century France: The Captivity and Ransom of John II, 1356–70.* Philadelphia: American Philosophical Society, 1976.

JOHN BELL HENNEMAN, JR.

JOHN OF SALISBURY
(ca. 1115–1180)

John was born in Old Sarum, England, and entered a clerical career as a young man, studying in the schools of Paris from 1136 until the mid-1140s. There, he heard lectures by Peter Abélard, Robert of Melun, William of Conches, Thierry of Chartres, Gilbert of Poitiers, and other masters of the day. He then traveled to Rome, where he entered the service of the pope. In 1148, he attended the synod at Reims where Gilbert of Poitiers was tried for heresy, a trial that John recounts in his *Historia pontificalis*. In 1153–54, he returned to England, where he served as secretary to Theobald, archbishop of Canterbury, and to his successor, Thomas Becket. John was part of one of the most striking public conflicts of royal and ecclesiastical power in the 12th century, that between Becket and King Henry II Plantagenêt of England. Becket's exile to France took John of Salisbury there as well. John was present in Christ Church cathedral, Canterbury, when Becket was attacked, but he fled the scene before the actual murder. In 1176, John was consecrated bishop of Chartres and died there in 1180. He knew well the worlds of episcopal patronage, education in the schools of Paris, the papal and royal courts, and the web of personal and professional friendships woven by the exchange of letters. Each of these circles influenced his life and writings.

The *Metalogicon*, a spirited defense of the Trivium, with emphasis upon the discipline of logic, is a valuable resource for understanding the world of the 12th-century schools and lists the masters with whom John studied. His *Policraticus* combines political theory, a handbook for government, criticism of court life, and a program of education for courtiers. In the *Historia pontificalis*, John offers a history focused on the papal court from the Synod of Reims (1148) through the year 1152. Among his other writings are a *vita* of Anselm of Bec and a brief *vita* of Becket, probably meant to serve as preface to a collection of the murdered archbishop's letters. Some 325 of John's letters survive.

See also **Abélard, Peter; Becket, Thomas; Gilbert of Poitiers; Henry II**

Further Reading

John of Salisbury. *Memoirs of the Papal Court*, ed. and trans. Marjorie Chibnall. London: Nelson, 1956.

——. *The Metalogicon of John of Salisbury: A Twelfth-Century Defense of the Verbal and Logical Arts of the Trivium*, trans. D.D. McGarry. Berkeley: University of California Press, 1955.

——. *The Letters of John of Salisbury, 1: The Early Letters (1153–1161)*, ed. W.J. Millor and H.E. Butler, rev. Christopher N.L. Brooke. London: Nelson, 1955.

——. *The Letters of John of Salisbury, 2: The Later Letters (1163–1180)*, ed. W.J. Millor and Christopher N. L. Brooke. Oxford: Oxford University Press, 1979.

Smalley, Beryl. *The Beckett Conflict and the Schools: A Study of Intellectuals in Politics.* Oxford: Blackwell, 1973, pp. 87–108.

Webb, C.C.J. *John of Salisbury.* London: Methuen, 1932.

Wilkes, Michael, ed. *The World of John of Salisbury.* Oxford: Blackwell, 1984.

GROVER A. ZINN

JOHN OF SEVILLE (fl. 1133–1135)

John of Seville was an astrologer and translator of scientific works from Arabic into Latin. His full name appears to have been Iohannes His-palensis et Lunensis (or Limiensis). Attempts to identify him with Avendauth, the collaborator of Dominigo Gundisalvo, John David of Toledo, and other Johns are not convincing. He is known only through his translations, which include Abū Ma'shar's *Greater Introduction to Astrology* (1133), Al-Farghānī's *Rudiments of Astronomy* (1135), 'Urnar ibn al-Farrukhān's *Universal Book* (on astrology), Al-Qabīsī's *Introduction to Astrology,* Thābit ibn Qurra's *On Talismans* (*De imaginibus*) and astrological works by Māshā'allāh and Sahl ibn Bishr. These were the most important texts on astrology in the Arabic world, and established Latin astrology on a firm scientific footing. To them, John added his own *Epitome of Astrology* or *Liber quadripartitus* (1135), which covered all the main aspects of astrology and, having four books, was clearly meant to be analogous to, and perhaps to replace, the best-known text on astrology from classical antiquity, Ptolemy's *Quadripartitum.*

John appears to have ventured also into the field of medicine, for he is credited with a translation of the medical portion of Pseudo-Aristotle's *Secret of Secrets, On the Regimen of Health,* and Qusta ibn Lāqā's *On the Difference between the Spirit and the Soul.* These medical texts are the only works that put their author into a historical context, since the first is dedicated to a queen of Spain with the initial T.—often identified with Tharasia, daughter of Alfonso VI of Castile and León, who married Henry of Burgundy, count of Portugal (1057–1114), and the second is dedicated to Raymond, archbishop of Toledo (1125–1152), and thereby is the earliest text to have some connection with the cathedral.

John's astrological translations are pedantically literal, suggesting that Arabic may have been his first language. The medical translations are more fluent, and the excerpt from the *Secret of Secrets* is preceded by a preface in which the translator justifies departing from the literal sense of the original. Both the astrological and the medical texts remained popular throughout the Middle Ages and several of the astrological texts, including the *Epitome,* were printed in the Renaissance.

Further Reading

Lemay, R. *Abū Mashar and Latin Aristotelianism in the Twelfth Century.* Beirut, 1962.

Thorndike, L. "John of Seville." *Speculum* 34 (1959): 20–38.

CHARLES BURNETT

JOHN, DUKE OF BERRY
(1340–1416)

The son of John II the Good of France and Bonne de Luxembourg, John was born in the castle of Vincennes on November 30, 1340. His father named him count of Poitou in 1356, but when this territory was ceded to England by the treaty of 1360 John became duke of Berry and Auvergne. During the years 1360–64, he was one of the hostages sent to England after the release of his father from captivity.

In 1369, John was charged with guarding the western frontier to keep the English contained within Poitou, and his brother Charles V reassigned him this county as an incentive to recover it from the English. His ineptitude at military strategy soon became clear. In 1374, Charles V's attitude toward John changed, perhaps because of a distaste for his private life. In October, when arranging for the succession, Charles V ordered that John not be one of his son's guardians if the dauphin, the future Charles VI, should succeed to the throne as a minor. Despite some rapprochement between the brothers in 1375

Jean de Cambrai (fl. 1397–1438). John, Duke of Berry, life-size statue. © Erich Lessing/Art Resource, New York.

and 1376, John never regained Charles's full confidence. With the accession of Charles VI in 1380, however, John was officially accorded a place in the government and began to act as mediator between his two surviving brothers, the dukes of Anjou and Burgundy.

In November 1380, John was named royal lieutenant-general in Languedoc, where his officers and his policies soon made him unpopular. He rarely visited the Midi personally, and his lack of direct involvement produced near-anarchy in the province. When the king resolved to go to the south in person in 1389, John resigned his lieutenancy. The details of John's political behavior, especially in the years following the assassination of his nephew Louis of Orléans in 1407, show him to have been unethical, unreliable, and selfish. Despite this evidence, contemporaries viewed him as gregarious, eloquent, and philanthropic. He did show both consistency and determination in his ecclesiastical policy, being the French prince most committed to ending the papal Schism.

After April 1404, as the king's sole surviving paternal uncle, John enjoyed a prestigious position and important role at court, serving as mediator between the Burgundian and Armagnac parties, particularly after the murder of the duke of Orléans. He was married twice: in 1360 to Jeanne d'Armagnac and, after her death, in

1389 to Jeanne de Boulogne. He died in Paris on June 15, 1416, leaving no male heirs.

One of the greatest patrons in the history of art, John was an inveterate collector—of books, dogs, castles, tapestries, jewels, and *objets d'art*, whether antique or contemporary. If he overtaxed his people, as has been claimed, it was to transform his immense wealth into works of art. Probably the best-known work commissioned by him is the unfinished *Très Riches Heures* (Chantilly, Musée Condé), illuminated by the limbourg brothers and Jean Colombe. The famous calendar illuminations in this manuscript picture some of the duke's seventeen castles: Lusignan, Dourdan, Hôtel de Nesle, Clain, Étampes, Saumur, the Louvre, and Vincennes. Another favorite castle, Mehun-sur-Yèvre, dominates the Temptation of Christ scene. Other works illuminated by the brothers include the *Très Belles Heures de Notre Dame* (B.N. lat. 3093) and the *Belles Heures* (New York, The Cloisters). They also contributed a miniature of the duke setting off on a journey in the *Petites Heures* (B.N. lat. 18014) and some scenes in *grisaille* for a *Bible historiale* (B.N. fr. 166). Another famous book of hours associated with the duke is the *Grandes Heures* (B.N. lat. 919), commissioned in 1407 and completed in 1409. Unfortunately, its original sixteen large miniatures, possibly by Jacquemart de Hesdin, who had illuminated the *Heures de Bruxelles* (before 1402) for the duke, have been lost. The list of artists contributing small miniatures reads like a who's who of the day, including the Boucicaut and Bedford Masters, as well as the Pseudo-Jacquemart. Other artists in the duke's employ were his master architect Gui de Dammartin, André Beauneveu, and Jean de Cambrai, who sculpted the duke's tomb.

John's extensive library included thirty-eight chivalric romances, forty-one histories, as well as works by Aristotle, Nicole Oresme, and Marco Polo. His secular books were outnumbered by religious works, especially prayer books: fourteen Bibles, sixteen psalters, eighteen breviaries, six missals, and fifteen books of hours. Of the over 300 illuminated manuscripts in the duke's library, some one hundred are extant today. Most of the other objects in his collections are known to us only through the extensive registers he caused to be kept after 1401.

See also **Charles VI; John II the Good; Limbourg Brothers**

Further Reading

Guiffrey, J. *Inventaires de Jean, duc de Berry (1401–1416)*. 2 vols. Paris, 1894–96.

Lacour, René. *Le gouvernement de l'apanage de Jean, duc de Berry 1360–1416*. Paris: Picard, 1934.

Lehoux, Francoise. *Jean de France, duc de Berri: sa vie, son action politique*. 4 vols. Paris: Picard, 1966–68.

Longnon, Jean, and Raymond Cazelles. *The Très Riches Heures of Jean, Duke of Berry*. New York: Braziller, 1969.

Meiss, Millard. *French Painting the Time of Jean de Berry: The Late Fourteenth Century and the Patronage of the Duke*. 2nd ed. 2 vols. London: Phaidon, 1969.

——, and Elizabeth H. Beatson. *The Belles Heures of Jean, Duke of Berry*. New York: Braziller, 1974.

Thomas, Marcel. *The Grandes Heures of Jean, Duke of Berry*. New York: Braziller, 1971.

RICHARD C. FAMIGLIETTI
WILLIAM W. KIBLER

JOINVILLE, JEAN DE (1225–1317)

Joinville's *Vie de saint Louis*, a French prose memoir by a powerful aristocrat, is one of our most valuable accounts of noble society in the 13th century. Joinville's father was seneschal of Champagne, an office he inherited. In 1248, he decided to take part in the Seventh Crusade and thus met St. Louis, becoming a close friend. The two endured captivity together, then Joinville served as royal steward at Acre (1250–54) before returning to France. Joinville began his memoirs of the king in 1272, just after Louis's death, but undertook the second part (composed 1298–1309) when Jeanne of Navarre, wife of Philip IV, requested it.

Joinville's narrative has many virtues. As an important noble, he advised the king during the crusade; as a warrior, he fought in it. Although a close friend, Joinville, unlike other biographers of Louis, respected but was not overawed by the king and sometimes disapproved of his actions, particularly when Louis's saintliness conflicted with what Joinville perceived to be his duties as king, aristocrat, and layman. Louis's decision to go on crusade in 1270 was one such occasion, but there were others. Joinville felt free at the time to speak his mind and records a number of salty interchanges between himself and his ruler. He was also candid about his own prejudices; he defended aristocratic privileges and was contemptuous of bourgeois upstarts. His observations are vivid, and his frankness makes the *Vie* delightful reading.

Joinville's work was overshadowed in his own day by Guillaume de Nangis's biography of Louis; of the three extant manuscripts, only one is medieval, a copy of the presentation manuscript of 1309.

See also **Louis IX**

Further Reading

Joinville, Jean de. *La vie de saint Louis*, ed. Noel L. Corbett. Sherbrooke: Naaman, 1977.

—— and Villehardouin. *Chronicles of the Crusades*, trans. Margaret R.B. Shaw. Harmondsworth: Penguin, 1963.

Billson, Marcus K. "Joinville's *Histoire de Saint-Louis*: Hagiography, History and Memoir." *American Benedictine Review* 31 (1980): 418–42.

Perret, Michèle. "'À la fin de sa vie ne fuz-je mie': Joinville's *Vie de Saint-Louis.*" *Revue des sciences humaines* 183 (1981): 16–37.

LEAH SHOPKOW

JUAN MANUEL (1282–1348)

Son of Alfonso X's younger brother, Manuel, and grandson of Fernando III; born in Escalona (Toledo) in 1282. From a very young age, he participated both in war (particularly in the advances on Murcia, which lasted from 1284 to 1339) and in politics, though not without differences with his council.

Along with his hectic political life during the reigns of Fernando IV (1295–1312) and Alfonso XI (1312–1350), which was largely motivated, as he himself says, by questions of *onra* [honor/reputation] and *facienda* [property/wealth], Juan Manuel displayed an encyclopedic knowledge that was indicative of his desire to emulate his uncle, Alfonso X, whom he admired from an exclusively cultural (and not political) perspective. He was also a devout man, influenced by the Dominican tradition, which he followed throughout the various didactic works of his career. After retiring from active political life, Juan Manuel died in 1348; he is buried in the monastery at Peñafiel, which he founded.

In the general prologue to his works, the author expresses the philological/critical anxiety that his texts might be poorly copied, declaring that the authentic, original books, against which any potentially confusing transcripts can be compared, are in the convent at Peñafiel. Although this is essentially nothing more than a repetition of what Nicolás de Lira had already said, this disclaimer serves as a mark of authenticity for Juan Manuel's work. With this notice, the author participates in the medieval concept of an ethics of language opposing the lie, and is thus able to forestall any willful error on his part. For those inevitable involuntary errors, he resorts to the *topos* of modesty—already in use since antiquity—attributing such lapses to his lack of intelligence. Juan Manuel manipulates the vernacular language in a fresh, renewed manner, and with a wider vocabulary and a more purified syntax than Alfonso X. He is partial to concision and clarity, qualities he praises in his uncle's writing, although he does experiment with a more hermetic, obtuse style. The discovery of a skillful use of dialogue is frequently attributed to Juan Manuel, who arguably anticipates certain subtleties of the Renaissance.

A list of Juan Manuel's works appears both in the *Prólogo general* and in the prologue to *El conde Lucanor,* although there are discrepancies between the two prologues with regard to the order and number of works listed. Without the lost Peñafiel codex, what remains of the author's writings is found in various fourteenth-century manuscripts, among them Manuscript 6376 in the Biblioteca Nacional in Madrid. This manuscript lacks the *Crónic abreviada,* which in turn was found by Sánchez Alonso (in MS. F. 81 [now 1356]), also in the Biblioteca Nacional. Both have served as the basis for the edition of Juan Manuel's *Obras completas.*

Of the preserved texts one must first cite the *Libro del cavallero et del escudero.* Written before 1330, the work is one of many encyclopedic treatises of the time. Similar to Ramón Llull's *Llibre de l'ordre de cavalleria,* to which Juan Manuel seems to allude, the plot consists of the encounter between a young squire on his way to the court, and a former knight—now a hermit—who answers the young man's numerous questions. The hermit upholds knighthood as the most honorable estate in this world and indoctrinates the squire through a brief discourse on chivalry; later, the former knight gives the young man, now a novice *caballero,* a treatise on theology, another on astrology, and several expositions on the animal, vegetable, and mineral kingdoms; finally he tells the young man about the sea and the land, ending with an exaltation of creation as "manifestación de la gloria de Dios" (manifestation of God's glory).

Libro de los estados, finished in 1330, consists of two books distributed in three parts: the first book's hundred chapters, which address different religions and the estates of the lay population; the first fifty chapters of the second book, concerning the different laws (among which only the Christian law is true) as well as the mysteries of Christ and the estates of the secular clergy; and the fifty-first chapter of the second book, dedicated to religious orders and their regulations, especially the orders of preaching friars and of lesser friars. The structure is that of a work within a work, all written using dialogue as a technique supported by the main characters: the pagan king Morobán, the *infante* Johas and his tutor/teacher Turín, and a Christian preacher named Julio. The basic framework is similar to that of *Barlaam y Josafat.* Turín, committed to avoid having to address the concept of mortality, ends his phase of the prince's education by explaining the meaning of death in front of a fortuitously discovered cadaver. Chapter 22 introduces the Castilian preacher Julio, "omne muy letrado et muy entendido" [a very educated and intelligent man] in matters of Christian doctrine. Julio claims to be tutor to Prince Juan, son of the *infante* Don Manuel, and from that moment on he will carry the burden of Prince Johas's education. The work teaches that, in order to be saved, he who did not keep the law of nature should follow Christian law, which fulfilled Old Testament designs. This law is contained in the Holy Scriptures and is preached by the church, whose accepted hierarchy, divided into "legos" [the lay population] and "eclesiásticos" [the clergy], is described in detail.

Crónic abreviada, written during the tutelage of Alfonso XI (around 1320), was thought lost until Sánchez Alonso found it in 1941. It is a summary of Alfonso X's *Estoria de España,* and though Juan Manuel claims to follow his uncle's work step by step, it is actually much more than just a faithful copy.

Libro de la caza, thought by some to be written late in the author's life, is a treatise on the art of falconry, addressing the care, training, and medication of falcons and hawks. Juan Manuel relates not only his knowledge of the hunt, but also his own personal experience, to which he alludes in the text.

Libro infinido, or *Castigos y consejos a su hijo don Fernando* (1337), is inscribed within the tradition of the education of princes, although it also contains a strong dose of personal and autobiographical content. It refers frequently to *Libro de los estados.*

Libro de las armas, or *Libro de las tres razones,* written after 1335, addresses three issues: the meaning of the coat of arms given to Juan Manuel's father; the reason a person may knight others without having been knighted himself; and the content of Juan Manuel's conversation with King Sancho at his deathbed (1295). The author explains the symbolism of the coat of arms (especially the angelic *ala* [wing]) that appeared in his grandfather's prophetic vision while his father, Don Manuel, was in the womb. He relates various anecdotes told both to his father and to himself, among them the legend of Doña Sancha de Aragón, similar to the legend of Saint Alexis. He concludes that both his uncle, Alfonso X, and his father had wanted him to knight others during their lifetime. Finally, the author describes Ring Sancho's deathbed speech, in which he tells Juan Manuel of the anguish caused by his parents' misfortune, and entrusts the young man to the king's wife María and their son Fernando. This work, which has been praised by Américo Castro as "la primera página, íntima y palpitante de una confesión escrita en castellano" [the first intimate, true life confession written in the Spanish language], has recently been analyzed from a literary perspective.

Tratado de la Asunción de la Virgen María was likely the last work to leave Juan Manuel's pen. A brief theological treatise on the Christian miracle of the Virgin's Assumption, the work gives several reasons why "omne del mundo no deve dubdar que sancta María no sea en cielo" [men in this world should not doubt that Saint Mary is in heaven].

Finally, *Libro del conde Lucanor,* (or *Libro de los Enxiemplos del conde Lucanor et de Patronio*), finished in 1335, has come down to the modern reader in a rather contaminated state. The preservation of five manuscripts, all from the fifteenth century, attest to its wide diffusion. The work is divided into five parts, of which the first is the most extensive, consisting of fifty-one known *exempla.* In the second part the style changes, and in its prologue the author praises the use of subtlety as a way of making the merit of his work known. Books 2, 3, and 4 are essentially one book of proverbs, and the fifth and final book is a general reflection on Christian doctrine. It is difficult to separate the didactic from the narrative; the work's rhetoric manages to overcome the dichotomy of the two elements.

The sources—especially of the *exiemplos*—can be found in stories of Oriental origin that, like the *Disciplina clericalis,* were well known in the Western world through their Latin versions. It is important to remember that in Alfonso X's day *Calila e Dinna* and *Sendebar* had already been translated into Castilian. Other works also circulated in medieval translations, including Aesop's fables, *Barlaan e Josafat, Sintipas,* the *Gesta romanorum,* the *Legenda aurea,* which was used by preachers who collected exempla, and contemporary works such as chronicles and bestiaries.

Some of the exempla may come from oral sources later recorded in some textual form selected by the author. Others are indications of Juan Manuel's own originality as a creator, as well as his artistic manner of reelaborating extant texts.

The purpose of the majority of Juan Manuel's writings is to teach through pleasure (*docere delectando*); in several occasions, the author expresses his goal of morally attending to his readers, orienting their conduct—including the increase of *onras* and *faciendas*—according to their estate. Consequently, and especially in *El conde Lucanor,* the author filled his exiemplos with the most useful and entertaining stories he knew, hoping that his readers would benefit from the work's *palabras falagueras et apuestas* (delightful and elegant words), while at the same time taking in the *cosas aprovechosas* (useful things) mixed in.

Starting in the thirteenth century, the exemplum played a didactic role, offering models of behavior for its readers. With Juan Manuel, however, the exemplum becomes something much more: it is an explicitly structural, well-determined genre chosen consciously by the author. Furthermore, it allows Juan Manuel to establish a perfect accord between the duelling narrative and didactic elements, a desire already implicit in the prologue's affirmations.

See also **Llull, Ramón**

Further Reading

Caldera, E. "Retórica narrativa e didáttica nel "Conde Lucanor," *Miscellanea di studi ispanici,* 14 (1966–67), 5–120.

Catalán, D. "Don Juan Manuel ante el modelo alfonsí. El testimonio de la *Crónica abreviada*" In *Juan Manuel Studies.* Ed. I. Macpherson. London, 1977, 17–51.

Don Juan Manuel. VII Centenario. Murcia, 1982.

Giménez Soler, A. *Don Juan Manuel. Biografía y estudio crítico.* Zaragoza, 1932.
Juan Manuel, *Obras Compietas.* Ed., prologue, and notes by J. M. Blecua. Vols. 1–2. Madrid, 1983.
Rico, F., "Crítica del texto y modelos de cultura en el *Prólogo General* de Don Juan Manuel." In *Studia in honorem prof. M. de Riquer.* Vol. 1. Barcelona, 1990, 409–423.

JESÚS MONTOYA MARTÍNEZ

JUDITH, EMPRESS (ca. 800–843)

Adulated as a Rachel, vilified as a Jezebel, Empress Judith (r. 819–840) has likely suffered more than any other Carolingian from a polarized historiography. Primarily known as the second wife of Emperor Louis the Pious (r. 814–840) and mother of King Charles the Bald (r. 840–877), she assumed a commanding role in the volatile world of ninth-century Frankish politics, earning the respect of many, and the enmity of many more.

Presented at the February, 819, Aachen assembly by her parents (Welf, count of Alemannia, and the Saxon noblewoman Heilwig), a beautiful Judith caught the recently-widowed emperor's eye; they were married immediately. Judith gave birth in 821 to a daughter, Gisela, but did not pose a real threat to her three stepsons until producing a rival male heir, Charles, on June 13, 823. From that day forth she strove to procure a stable future for her son (and herself) by arranging advantageous marriage alliances, installing relatives in key imperial offices, and using her proximity to her husband on behalf of several influential courtiers. She achieved her greatest successes in Louis's territorial grants to Charles in 829 (Alemannia), 832 (Aquitaine), and 837 (Neustria), followed by the actual crowning of Charles as "king" in August, 838. Among such auspicious occasions, however, lay a series of rebellions in 830 and 833–834, each led by Louis's eldest son, Lothar, in an attempt to assert his own imperial authority. He and his followers focused much of their hostility on Judith, accusing her in 830 of adultery and sorcery (charges later cleared by her oath of innocence at Aachen on February 2, 831), and banishing her to Poitiers. They exiled her again in the later revolt to a convent in Tortona, Lombardy. Lothar's overconfidence and the ephemeral help of his brothers (Louis and Pepin) assured his failure in both instances, however, leaving Judith and Charles several years to consolidate their position (and according to some accounts, to wreak revenge) before Louis died on June 20, 840.

Civil war ensued, despite Louis's revised division of the empire in 839 between Lothar and Charles. In the end, it was the help of Louis the Bavarian (who had married Judith's sister, Emma, in 827) that made possible Charles's and Judith's victory over Lothar at Fontenoy on June 25, 841. Afterward, Charles further shored up his powerbase, benefiting particularly from his mother's activities in Aquitaine from her base in Bourges. On December 13, 842, Judith witnessed the strategic marriage of her son to Ermentrude (niece of Adalard, count of Tours). Charles soon enhanced this declaration of independence by dispossessing his mother of her lands and placing her in "retirement" at Tours, probably in February, 843. She died there two months later, on April 19, 843, comforted, perhaps, that her consistent efforts on behalf of her son had changed the course of Carolingian history.

Acclaimed by several contemporary writers for both her beauty and erudition, Judith also fostered Carolingian learning. She arranged for Walahfrid Strabo to tutor Charles from 829 to 838, and commissioned the second book of Freculf of Lisieux's important *Chronicle.* Hrabanus Maurus's dedication of a commentary on the biblical books of Judith and Esther, as well as a figure poem to Judith also testifies to her literary patronage, and has supported the contention that she may have personally supervised the creation and expansion of Louis the Pious's court library.

See also **Lothair I; Rabanus Maurus; Walafrid Strabo**

Further Reading

Bischoff, Bernhard. "Benedictine Monasteries and the Survival of Classical Literature." In *Manuscripts and Libraries in the Age of Charlemagne,* trans. Michael Gorman. Cambridge, England: Cambridge University Press, 1994, pp. 134–160.
Boshof, Egon. *Ludwig der Fromme.* Darmstadt: Primus, 1996.
Cabaniss, Allen. "Judith Augusta and Her Time." *Studies in English* 10 (1969): 67–109.
Konecny, Silvia. *Die Frauen des karolingischen Königshauses.* Vienna: VWGÖ, 1976.
McKitterick, Rosamond. *The Frankish Kingdoms under the Carolingians, 751–987.* London: Longman, 1983.
Nelson, Janet L. *Charles the Bald.* London: Longman, 1992.
Ward, Elizabeth. "Caesar's Wife: The Career of the Empress Judith, 819–829." In *Charlemagne's Heir: New Perspectives on the Reign of Louis the Pious (814–840),* eds. Peter Godman and Roger Collins. Oxford: Clarendon, 1990, pp. 205–227.

STEVEN A. STOFFERAHN

JULIAN OF NORWICH (1342/43–after 1416)

Mystical writer and the first known woman author in English literature. Her book of *Showings,* or *Revelations of Divine Love,* ranks with the best medieval English prose and is a primary text in the literature of mysticism. It is extant in a short version, probably written first, and in an extended form, completed 20 years later.

Biographical information about Julian is sparse. It is limited to tacts in her own text, mention in a few wills, and a passage in the *Book of Margery Kempe.* Julian's birthplace is unknown. The dialect in the oldest extant copy of her book shows northern features, leading to the conjecture that she may have come from Yorkshire. Sometime between 1413 and 1416 Margery Kempe visited Julian and received counsel from her. As late as 1416 Julian was living in Norwich in Norfolk as an anchoress, enclosed in a cell attached to the Church of St. Julian. She may have received the name Julian upon her entrance into the anchorhold.

On 8 May (or possibly 13 May) 1373, at the age of 30 and a half, she fell seriously ill, most likely while still at home. She then recalled having prayed in her youth for a bodily sickness, to prepare her for death, and for the wounds of true contrition, natural compassion, and resolute longing for God. Surrounded by her mother and friends, and attended by a priest, she believed, with them, that she was about to die. Suddenly, however, while she was looking at a crucifix, her health returned. Then followed a series of fifteen visions, mostly of the crucified Christ. These were interrupted by attacks from the Devil, and then confirmed in a sixteenth and final showing. This experience gives the content to the short version of her book, in which she explains that the visions were threefold in character—visual, intellectual, and spiritual or intuitive. The long version of the text is enriched with 20 years of theological reflection, pastoral counseling, and spiritual growth. Her teachings are oriented to the instruction of other believers, her "even-Christians."

The shorter version of Julian's book is extant in one manuscript copy—the 15th-century Amherst Manuscript (BL Add. 37790). The longer text is complete in three manuscripts: the Paris Manuscript (BN Fonds angl. 40), copied around 1650; and two Sloane manuscripts (Sloane 1—BL Sloane 2499, early 17th century; Sloane 2—BL Sloane 3705, an 18th-century modernization of Sloane 1). Excerpts from the longer version exist in Westminster Treasury 4 (W), written in the early 16th century; and in a 17th-century manuscript from Upholland Northern Institute (formerly St. Joseph's College). The Upholland manuscript was written by English Benedictine nuns, living at Cambrai, after the Dissolution of the monasteries. The earliest printed edition (1670) is by Serenus Cressy, an English Benedictine, chaplain for the Paris house of the nuns.

T.S. Eliot, in the *Four Quartets*, familiarized the literary world with Julian's key phrase, "All shall be well," and with some of her mystical symbolism. Thomas Merton cited her as "one of the greatest English theologians" (1967). An observance at Norwich (1973) commemorated the sixth centenary of her showings. Since then Julian has become the focus of extensive study by literary scholars and theologians and has a growing following as a spiritual guide.

Textual critics disagree on the choice of a preferred copy text for a Julian edition. Colledge and Walsh (1978) opted for Paris, favoring its more conventionally correct rhetorical structures. Marion Glasscoe selected Sloane 1 for a student edition (2d ed. 1986). Glasscoe notes the pitfalls of following, in disputed readings, either Sloane 1 or Paris, or creating an eclectic text; nonetheless, she finds special qualities to recommend reliance on Sloane 1, which, she says, often reflects "a greater sense of theology as a live issue at the heart of human creativity" (1989: 119) thereby coming closer to Julian's central concern.

Theological approaches diverge widely. A plethora of devotional books have been based on a surface reading of the *Revelations*, stressing Julian's optimism and oversimplifying her doctrine of love. Her terms "substance" and "sensuality" are often misunderstood. A misreading, sometimes abetted by inaccurate translations, assumes that by "substance" Julian means the human soul and by "sensuality" the body or the five senses. Substance designates, rather, "the truth of our being, body and soul: the way we are meant to be, as whole persons" (Pelphrey, 1982: 90): "Where the blessed soul of Christ is, there is the substance of all souls that will be saved by Christ....Our soul is made to be God's dwelling place, and the dwelling place of the soul is God....It is a high understanding inwardly to see and to know that God our creator dwells in our soul; and a higher understanding it is inwardly to see and to know that our soul which is created dwells in God's substance, of which substance, through God, we are what we are" (Long Text, ch. 54).

Usually "sensuality" refers to that human existence which becomes God's in the Incarnation: it is the "place" of the city of God, the glory of the Trinity abiding in collective humanity. Human beings are called to be helpers or partners in the unfolding of what humanity is meant to become—a city fit for God to reign and find rest in. These difficult concepts are carefully explored by Pelphrey, who succinctly summarizes Julian's teaching about divine love: "The reflection of divine love into humanity is...seen to take place in three ways: in the creation of humanity (our capacity for God); in the maturing or 'increasing' of humanity (to which she also refers as our 'remaking' in Christ); and in the perfecting or fulfilling of human beings through the indwelling Christ" (1982: 90).

Julian presents this theology principally through the parable of the Lord and the Servant: "This story conveys Julian's insights about the first Adam, the cosmic Christ, the Trinity, and the unity of all who are to be saved. The one great reality in the parable is the person of Christ, in whom are mysterious compenetrations of other realities—the Adam of Genesis; the total Adam (all humanity); Christ as the second Adam (and in one sense the first Adam, since to his eternal image all things were made);

and Christ, meaning all humanity to be saved. The basic parable weaves into other metaphors: for example, the sinful Adam fell in misery to the earth, but likewise the divine Adam falls on the earth—into human nature in Mary's womb—and makes the garden of the earth spring forth with food and drink for which the Father thirsts and longs, in his unending love for the treasure which was hidden in the earth" (Bradley, 1984: 209). The Trinity is revealed in Christ. God is active as "maker, preserver, and lover," an insight Julian experienced when she saw creation in the likeness of a hazelnut. Since God is the ground of the soul, the desire for God is natural, and sin (all chat is not good) is unnatural. Prayer unites the soul to God, the foundation from which the prayer arises. In the depths or core of the believer, the being of God intersects with the being of the creature and is the root of a "godly will" that always inclines toward the good. Nonetheless, humanity continues to sin, for evil was permitted to arise contrary to goodness, which will triumph in the end in the form of a good greater than what would otherwise have been. How "all things shall be well," as Christ promised Julian, will remain hidden until a great deed is accomplished on the Last Day (Long Text, ch. 32).

Literary and linguistic critics contribute to the explication of this mystical core, Reynolds explores the key images of Christ as courteous and "homely," in its medieval sense. Courtesy signifies that Christ possesses without limit the largesse and fidelity attributed to the medieval knight. Courtesy fuses with "homeliness," the familiar manner used at home, among equals, and implies nearness, so that "we are clothed and enclosed in the goodness of God" (Long Text, ch. 6). In his familiar aspect Christ is mother, an image rooted in scripture and in biblical exegesis but developed with originality by Julian. As the archetypal mother Christ bears his children not to pain and dying but to joy and endless living. His Passion is a birthing, which entailed the sharpest throes that ever were, and was undertaken to satisfy his love. The maternal image further signifies that humanity dwells in Christ, as in a mother's womb, and is also fed, nurtured, chastised, and tenderly cared for, as a child. The sensual nature of humanity (that which is born into time) is in the second person, Jesus Christ, and is knit—as in fabric making—to its ground in God. This motherhood metaphor has attracted the attention of feminist criticism, adding to Julian's popularity today. The overall lesson of the revelations is love in three meanings: uncreated love, or God; created love—the human soul in God; and a love that is bestowed as virtue, enabling believers to love God, themselves, and all creation, especially their "even-Christians."

See also **Kempe, Margery**

Further Reading

Primary Sources

Colledge, Edmund, and James Walsh, eds. *A Book of Showings to the Anchoress Julian of Norwich.* 2 vols. Toronto: Pontifical Institute, 1978

Colledge, Edmund, and James Walsh, trans. *Showings.* New York: Paulist Press, 1978

del Mastro, M.L., trans. *Revelation of Divine Love in Sixteen Showings.* Liguori, Mo.: Triumph Books, 1994

Glasscoe, Marion, ed. *A Revelation of Love.* 2d ed. Exeter: University of Exeter, 1986.

Secondary Sources

New *CBEL* 1:522–24

Manual 9:3082–84, 3438–44

Bradley, Ritamary. "Julian of Norwich: Writer and Mystic." In *An Introduction to the Medieval Mystics of Europe,* ed. Paul E. Szarmach. Albany: SUNY Press, 1984, pp. 195–216

Bradley, Ritamary. *Julian's Way: A Practical Commentary on Julian of Norwich.* London: HarperCollins, 1992

Glasscoe, Marion. "Visions and Revisions: A Further Look at the Manuscripts of Julian of Norwich." *SB* 42 (1989): 103–20

Lagorio, Valerie Marie, and Ritamary Bradley. "Julian of Norwich." In *The 14th-Century English Mystics: A Comprehensive Annotated Bibliography.* New York: Garland, 1981, pp. 105–26

Llewelyn, Robert, ed. *Julian: Woman of Our Day.* Mystic: Twenty-Third Publications, 1987

Molinari, Paolo. *Julian of Norwich: The Teaching of a 14th Century English Mystic.* London: Longmans, Green, 1958

Nuth, Joan. *Wisdom's Daughter.* New York: Crossroad, 1991

Pelphrey, Brant. *Love Was His Meaning: The Theology and Mysticism of Julian of Norwich.* Salzburg: Institut fur Anglistik und Amerikanistik, 1982

Reynolds, Anna Maria. "'Courtesy' and 'Homeliness' in the Revelations of Julian of Norwich." *14th-Century English Mystics Newsletter* (*Mystics Quarterly*) 5/2 (1979): 12–20

von Nolcken, Christina. "Julian of Norwich." In *Middle English Prose: A Critical Guide to Major Genres and Authors,* ed. A.S.G. Edwards. New Brunswick: Rutgers University Press, 1984, pp. 97–108.

RITAMARY BRADLEY

JULIAN OF TOLEDO (b. ca. 640)

Born around 640, Julian was of partly Jewish descent. Knowledge of his career comes primarily from the brief "Eulogy" of him written by Bishop Felix of Toledo (693–ca. 700). He was a pupil of Bishop Eugenius 11 (647–657), and subsequently became a member of the clergy of the church in Toledo while following a rigorous ascetic regime. Following the death of Bishop Quiricus (667–680) he was chosen by King Wamba to take over the see. The choice may have been influenced by Julian's eulogistic *Historia Wambae,* an account of the opening events of that king's reign. However, before the end of 680 Julian had been caught up in, or even had initiated, the chain of events leading to Wamba's enforced abdication and retirement to a monastery. With the new king, Ervig (680–687), to whom he had previously dedicated a now lost work on divine judgment, Julian seems to have cooperated closely. In 686 he dedicated to the king his most significant surviving book, *On the Proof of the Sixth Age,* a polemical reply to Jewish denials of Christ's messiahship. This work redefined the chronological framework of human history within an apocalyptic context, and was to be highly influential in Spain and western Europe throughout the Middle Ages. He died in Gao.

Other extant writings by Julian include the *Antikeimenon* and *the Prognosticum futuri saeculi.* In these, as in lost collections referred to in the "Eulogy," Julian is revealed as an assiduous reader of the works of Augustine. Like Ildefonsus, Julian is credited by Felix with the composition of verse and also of a substantial body of liturgy. The latter cannot be disentangled from the vast corpus of Mozarafaic liturgical texts.

During his episcopate Julianus presided over four Councils of Toledo: the twelfth (680–681), thirteenth (683), fourteenth (684), and fifteenth (688). The first of these formalized the primacy of Toledo over all the other churches of the Visigothic kingdom. Julian himself contributed to this by his emphasis on the role of the anointing of the king in the "royal city" as a precondition for a new ruler's legitimacy.

Further Reading

Collins, R. "Julian of Toledo and the Royal Succession in Late Seventh-Century Spain." In *Early Medieval King-ship.* Eds. P. Sawyer and I. Wood. Leeds, 1977. 30–49.

Hillgarth, J. N. "St. Julian of Toledo in the Middle Ages." *Journal of the Warburg and Courtauld Institutes* 21 (1958), 7–26.

Murphy, F. X. "Julian of Toledo and the Fall of the Visigothic Kingdom in Spain." *Speculum* 27 (1952), 1–21.

ROGER COLLINS

JUSTINIAN I
(c. 482 or 483–565, r. 527–565)

Justinian I (Flavius Sabbatius) was the sovereign of the eastern Roman, or Byzantine, empire during an age of vast transition and was a figure of both glory and paradox. Born a peasant, he appreciated the awesome Roman heritage as few others could appreciate it; but in seeking to be its steward and restorer, he also opened the way to its transformation. His reign—one of the longest in the Byzantine empire—saw achievements that were substantial and enduring but brought ruin and disaster as their price. In his very quest to restore the territorial and doctrinal unity of the Roman world, Justinian guaranteed its further fragmentation.

Justinian was of Thracian-Illyrian stock and was born in a Latin-speaking district of the Macedonian Balkans. His uncle, Justin, having achieved success as a member of the new imperial guards in Constantinople, sent for the boy and several other nephews in order to give them an education, and opportunities, in the capital. Adopting a new name in tribute to his uncle, Justinian learned Greek, took a liking to intellectual pursuits such as theology, and learned the workings of the military and the court. In 518, by a quirk of fortune, Justin seized the throne, and Justinian quickly emerged as his right-hand man, becoming heir-designate in 525 and full successor two years later.

By that time, Justinian had met and married Theodora, the remarkable woman who was to be his invaluable partner in rule. He had also identified administrators and commanders on whom he could rely and had formulated the main lines of his policies. During the first four years of his reign, he was trapped in an unwanted war with his powerful eastern neighbor, Persia; and just as he was winning peace and freedom there, the devastating Nika riots of January 532 nearly swept him off the throne. He recovered quickly, however, thanks partly to the advice of Theodora and to the soldiers of the young general Belisarius, and was then in a stronger position that allowed him to initiate an array of projects. These included a codification of the Roman legal tradition as *Corpus juris civilis,* schemes to end the religious and political dissent of the Monophysites and other heterodox movements, and a large-scale building program that was to culminate in the triumphant cathedral of Hagia Sophia in the capital.

Justinian's chief project, though, was his program of reconquest, aimed at recovering the western provinces that had been detached by various Germanic tribes during the previous century. He was inspired in this by his duty to rescue the orthodox provincials in those districts from their Arian Christian rulers, and he was also prodded by dispossessed landowners who sought the restitution of their property; more broadly, he was motivated by his broad perception that the barbarian "successor states" in the west were only a temporary aberration, and by a sense that he was responsible for restoring the Roman empire to its former scope, encompassing the entire Mediterranean.

Exploiting diplomatic opportunities, Justinian dispatched the brilliant Belisarius to North Africa, where the destruction of the Vandal kingdom was effected with lightning speed (533–534). Meanwhile, given the deterioration of relations with the Ostrogoths in Italy during the last years of their king, Theoderic, and the dynastic crisis attending the succession of Theodoric's daughter Amalasuntha, Justinian was next able to address the conquest of the Ostrogoth kingdom. While another general was sent to seize the Ostrogoths' holdings in the Balkans, Belisarius landed in Sicily in the summer of 535, beginning the long episode of the Gothic wars in Italy.

Uneasy about Belisarius's popularity and military prowess, Justinian vacillated in his support for his general and was then furious when Belisarius dared to entertain an offer from the Goths to take the imperial title in the west. When the settlement of 540 with the Goths broke down and a counter-offensive by Totila began undoing Belisarius's work, Justinian sent Belisarius back to Italy, though grudgingly and without adequate support or resources. Only when Belisarius asked to be recalled and the outlook in Italy seemed hopeless did Justinian commission Narses to organize a new army and complete the conquest of Italy.

When Justinian's commitment to the reconquest was most intense and the reconquest itself was in full tide and was proving more prolonged than he had intended, the rapacious Persian king reopened war with the empire on a wide range of fronts. This drained the emperor's manpower and resources, which were further reduced by a plague that ravaged the Mediterranean world in 542–543. Justinian, increasingly pressed, was forced to impose oppressive taxes and to skimp on expenditures wherever he could. His economies and his withdrawals of troops particularly weakened the Balkan regions, which were exposed to raids by various peoples, notably the Huns, who menaced Constantinople several times. This weakening allowed even more disastrous penetrations of the Balkans by Avars and Slavs in the decades following Justinian's death.

Throughout his reign, Justinian strove to achieve religious unity in the face of intractable dissent and regional resistance. His continually shirting responses included persecution, conciliation, schemes for compromise, and the bullying of Pope Vigilius to win the accord of Rome. Justinian's increasing obsession with religious coercion poisoned his last years, during which the ruinous effects of his overstrained finances darkened his reputation and made his death in November 565 a relief to his subjects.

Among Justinian's achievements, for good or ill, must be reckoned his lasting impact on Italy. Although his wars of reconquest left the peninsula devastated and exhausted, he nevertheless set the pattern for its restored government through his Pragmatic Sanction of 554; and the extraordinarily comprehensive powers that he granted to Belisarius and Narses laid the foundation for the governmental agency of the exarchate, through which the Byzantine empire was to rule its Italian holdings in the face of invasions by the Lombards. The exarchs' capital, Ravenna, provided a model for imperial style and imagery for centuries and had an important influence on Charlemagne. This model was conveyed most notably through the wondrous mosaic decorations carried out under Justinian, which include the famous portraits of him and Theodora in San Vitale. As the sponsor of the great *Corpus juris civilis*—whose rediscovery in Italy in the eleventh century was influential in reviving Roman law and legal studies in later medieval Italy and the west in general—Justinian himself became a symbol of the traditions of Roman sovereignty. Dante was to celebrate Justinian as a paradigm of imperial majesty in Canto 6 of *Paradiso*.

See also **Theodora**

Further Reading

Barker, John W. Justinian and the Later Roman Empire. Madison: University of Wisconsin Press, 1966. (General account setting the reign in the context of the fourth-seventh centuries.)

Browning, Robert. Justinian and Theodora, rev. ed. London: Thames and Hudson, 1987. (Vivid and insightful.)

Bury, J. B. A History of the Later Roman Empire from the Death of Theodosius I to the Death of Justinian I (A.D. 395–565), Vol. 2. London: Macmillan, 1923. (Reprint, New York: Dover, 1958. Fullest modern scholarly study in English.)

Downey, Glanville W. Constantinople in the Age of Justinian. Norman: University of Oklahoma Press, 1960. (Lively evocation of the era.)

Holmes, W. G. The Age of Justinian and Theodora: A History of the Sixth Century, 2 vols. London: G. Bell and Sons, 1905–1907. (2nd ed., 1912. Extended and detailed but somewhat uninspired and dated.)

Procopius of Caesarea. History of the Wars, Secret History, and Buildings. Loeb Classical Library Series, 7 vols. London and Cambridge, Mass.: Heinemann and Harvard University Press, 1914–1940. (With reprints. Full English translation of the complete works of the most important contemporaneous historian of Justinian.)

Ure, Percy N. Justinian and His Age. Harmondsworth and Baltimore, Md.: Penguin, 1951. (Stimulating and perceptive study.)

JOHN W. BARKER

K

KEMPE, MARGERY (ca. 1373–after 1438)

Controversial mystic and author of the first extant autobiography in English. *The Book of Margery Kempe* is both a mystical treatise consisting of the author's visions and conversations with Christ and a narrative of her life, including her conversion, pilgrimages, and arguments with church authorities. Kempe, who was illiterate, dictated her autobiography to two different scribes. The original manuscript has been lost, but a 15th-century copy was discovered in 1934.

Born in the East Anglian town of King's Lynn ca. 1373, Margery was the daughter of John Brunham, mayor of the town. At the age of twenty she married John Kempe. After the difficult birth of their first child Kempe suffered a breakdown. This experience, followed by business failures in brewing and milling, led eventually to her mystical conversion. Her first ordeal as a mystic was to convince her husband to be celibate, but only after twenty years of marriage and fourteen children did he agree, on the condition that she pay off all his debts. With the consent of her husband and the church Kempe was finally free to pursue her vocation as a mystic.

The "way to high perfection," however, was fraught with difficulties. Kempe encountered hostility from people who doubted her holiness and questioned her orthodoxy. She traveled around England seeking support and verification of her visions from many holy people, including the anchoress Julian of Norwich. Nevertheless, she continued to arouse suspicion and persecution for her behavior, including her bold speech and her "boisterous weeping." She was arrested as a Lollard, threatened with burning at the stake by her English detractors, and deserted by her fellow pilgrims on her travels abroad. Kempe's weeping in particular inspired her contemporaries to revile her and modern readers to label her "hysterical."

Kempe's travels took her to the Holy Land, Italy, Santiago de Compostela, and finally, near the end of her life, to Danzig, Prussia. The *Book* ends with her return to King's Lynn, where she still inspires both hostility and marvel as a woman in her sixties.

The Book of Margery Kempe departs from the medieval saint's life and mystical treatise. Unlike the saint's life, which is biographical, Kempe's book is autobiographical. As author and narrator of her own life Kempe develops some hagiographic conventions, such as the themes of her suffering, patience, and charity, while ignoring others. Her book is also unusual as a mystical treatise. Kempe's visions and revelations are grounded in everyday, autobiographical details, including her struggles for acceptance, her fears for her own safety, and her travels.

Kempe's work is divided into two sections, or books. The first book ends with the death of her scribe. Kempe spent four years trying to convince the second scribe to recopy and finish her book. He hesitated because of her notoriety and the illegibility of the first scribe's writing but finally agreed. The 15th-century manuscript that survives may be a copy of the original dictated by Kempe to the second scribe. This copy belonged to Mount Grace, a Carthusian monastery in Yorkshire, but was later lost. William Butler-Bowdon discovered it in 1934 in his family library, and Hope Emily Allen identified it as *The Book of Margery Kempe*. (It is now BL Add. 61823.) Until 1934 only brief extracts of Kempe's book had been known; these extracts, printed by Wynkyn de Worde (ca. 1501) and Henry Pepwell (1521), misleadingly omit Kempe's autobiographical passages, and one incorrectly labels her a "devout anchoress."

As a mystical treatise Kempe's *Book* is often compared with the work of her contemporary Julian of Norwich. Kempe's mysticism, like Julian's, belongs to the tradition called affective piety, characterized by personal devotion to Christ's humanity, particularly in the Nativity and Passion. The emotions, or affections, play a crucial role in this devotion. By identifying with the suffering humanity of Christ the mystic is transported through her emotions to spiritual love.

Kempe's life and mysticism, however, differ considerably from Julian's. Her boisterous weeping, her insistent identification with Christ, her self-preoccupation, and her refusal to live the more orthodox life of a nun or recluse distinguish her from Julian of Norwich. Critics in her own time as well as today fault her for the excessive emotionalism and literalness of her visions. Yet Kempe's mysticism was not unique. She found models for it in the lives and mystical works of other female mystics, such as Marie d'Oignies, Birgitta (Bridget) of Sweden, and Elizabeth of Hungary, and in the writings of the English mystic Richard Rolle.

The core of the controversy about Margery Kempe is her version of imitating Christ. Although the practice of imitating Christ's suffering was common in medieval spirituality, Kempe is preoccupied with this suffering. Her meditations on the Passion elicit this suffering and her roaring draws attention to it, disrupting sermons and disturbing the people around her. In addition Kempe's use of erotic language to describe mystical union—words like ravishment, dalliance, and even homeliness—is boldly literal. She translates the mystical concept of marriage to Christ into an alarmingly worldly one, as Christ instructs Kempe to take him to bed with her as her husband (ch. 36). Although Rolle before her had used sensual imagery to describe mystical union, Kempe's usage startles with its emphasis on the literal rather than the figurative or symbolic.

Kempe's book poses problems for literary analysis as well. Her narrative is not strictly chronological, and with its digressions and repetitions it seems unconstructed. How much Kempe's scribes contributed to the shape of the narrative is a further problem facing literary analysis. Finally Kempe s illiteracy makes the question of influence an interesting one. She exhibits some knowledge of both Latin and vernacular religious texts in spite of her inability to read or write.

Like her book Margery Kempe is an interesting and problematic subject. As a woman charting her own "way to high perfection" she challenged the religious, social, and gender expectations of her time. Her book offers valuable insight into the struggles of an extraordinary medieval woman who refused to conform to those expectations in her pursuit of a "singular grace."

See also **Julian of Norwich; Rolle, Richard, of Hampole**

Further Reading

Primary Sources

Butler-Bowdon, William, ed. and trans. *The Book of Margery Kempe,* New York: Devin-Adair, 1944.

Meech, Sanford Brown, and Hope Emily Allen, eds. *The Book of Margery Kempe.* EETS o.s. 212. London: Oxford University Press, 1940.

Windeatt, B.A., trans. *The Book of Margery Kempe.* New York: Penguin, 1985.

Secondary Sources

New *CBEL* 1:524.

Manual 9:3084–86, 3444–45.

Atkinson, Clarissa W. *Mystic and Pilgrim*: *The Book and the World of Margery Kempe.* Ithaca: Cornell University Press, 1983.

Beckwith, Sarah. "A Very Material Mysticism: The Medieval Mysticism of Margery Kempe." In *Medieval Literature*: *Criticism, Ideology & History*, ed. David Aers. New York: St. Martin, 1986, pp. 34–57.

Fries, Maureen. "Margery Kempe." In *An Introduction to the Medieval Mystics of Europe*, ed. Paul E. Szarmach. Albany: SUNY Press, 1984, pp. 217–35.

Goodman, Anthony E. "The Piety of John Brunham's Daughter, of Lynn." In *Medieval Women*, ed. Derek Baker. Oxford: Blackwell, 1978, pp. 347–58.

Hirsh, John C. "Margery Kempe." In *Middle English Prose*: *A Critical Guide to Major Authors and Genres*, ed. A.S.G. Edwards. New Brunswick: Rutgers University Press, 1984, pp. 109–19.

Lochrie, Karma. *Margery Kempe and Translations of the Flesh.* Philadelphia: University of Pennsylvania Press, 1991.

McEntire, Sandra J., ed. *Margery Kempe*: *A Book of Essays.* New York: Garland, 1992.

KARMA LOCHRIE

KOERBECKE, JOHANN (ca. 1420–1491)

A contemporary of Stefan Lochner and Konrad Witz, this painter contributed to the transition from the international Gothic style to a more realistic one, inspired by Netherlandish art. Koerbecke was probably born circa 1420 in Coesfeld (Northrhine Westphalia). He is first recorded in Münster in 1443, when he purchased a house. He led an important workshop there until his death on June 13, 1491.

Koerbecke's sole documented work is the Marienfeld Altarpiece, for which he received payment in 1456. Installed on the high altar of the Marienfeld monastery church in 1457, it originally consisted of a carved shrine and painted wings with scenes from the life of the Virgin and the Passion. In the seventeenth century, the wings were sawn into sixteen panels, now located in several collections (Avignon, Musée Calvet; Berlin, Gemäldegalerie; Chicago, Art Institute; Cracow, National Museum; Madrid, Thyssen Collection; Moscow, Pushkin Museum; Münster, Westfälisches Landesmuseum; Nuremberg, Germanisches Nationalmuseum;

Washington, National Gallery). They reveal knowledge of works by important painters of the preceding generation in Westphalia and Cologne. Koerbecke's Crucifixion is inspired by Conrad von Soest's paintings of that subject, his Presentation is an interpretation of Stephan Lochner's 1447 version (Darmstadt, Hessisches Landesmuseum), and his Resurrection is based on Master Francke's 1424 *Englandfahrer Altarpiece* (Hamburg, Kunsthalle). Koerbecke's volumetric figures and detailed, naturalistic treatment of interiors and landscapes derive from Netherlandish art.

Other attributed works are the wings of the Langenhorst Altarpiece with eight scenes from the Passion (Münster, Westfälisches Landesmuseum), ca. 1445, and three panels from an altarpiece with scenes from the life of Saint John the Baptist: the baptism of Christ and Christ with Saint John (Münster, Westfälisches Landesmuseum), and the beheading of the Baptist (The Hague, Meermanno-Westreenianum Museum), ca. 1470. A wing with Saints John the Baptist and George, and a fragment with Saint Christopher, survive from the Freckenhorst Altarpiece of ca. 1470–1480 (Munster, Westfalisches Landesmuseum).

See also **Francke, Master; Lochner, Stefan**

Further Reading

Kirchhoff, Karl-Heinz. "Maler und Malerfamilien in Münster." *Westfalen* 4 (1977): 98–110.

Luckhardt, Jochen. *Der Hochaltar der Zisterzienserklosterkirche Marienfeld.* Münster: Westfälisches Landesmuseum für Kunst und Kulturgeschichte, 1987.

Pieper, Paul, *Die deutschen, niederländischen und italienischen Tafelbilder bis um 1530.* Bestandskataloge des Westfälischen Landesmuseum für Kunst und Kulturgeschichte. Münster: Aschendorff, 1986, pp. 140–200.

Sommer, Johannes. *Johann Koerbecke: Der Meister des Marienfelder Altars von 1457.* Dissertation, Universtität Bonn, 1937. Münster: Westfälische Vereinsdruckerei, 1937.

SUSANNE REECE

KONRAD VON WÜRZBURG
(ca. 1230–1287)

Included among the "twelve old masters" revered by Meistersingers, Konrad produced one of the largest and most varied oeuvres in all of Middle High German literature. Initially neglected by modern scholars as an epigone and mannerist, critics are now examining Konrad's work in its own context. Konrad embodies a turn in German literature, he was neither noble (Song 32, line 189: *waere ich edel*, if I were noble) nor a part of the court. Konrad plied his trade in the cities and wrote for the wealthy bourgeoisie and the urban nobility. Archives, official documents, and Konrad's works themselves provide us with an extraordinary amount of information about his life and patronage. Born in Würzburg, Konrad began as a wandering poet, spent time in Strasbourg and eventually settled in Basle. Konrad wrote two lays. *Got gewaltec waz du schickest* (Powerful God, what you send) is a religious lay in praise of the Virgin and the Trinity. *Vênus diu feine diust entslâfen* (Elegant Venus has fallen asleep) is a secular lay treating courtly love. Unfortunately, the melodies to both of these have been lost. Konrad's shorter love lyric consists primarily of nine summer songs and eleven winter songs characterized by floral metaphors and the *jârlanc* introduction (nos. 5, 6, 10, 13, 17, 21, 23, 27). Konrad also produced three dawn songs (nos. 14, 15, 30), as well as exempla (nos. 18, 24, 25), maxims, and religious poetry. In Konrad's short lyric, one finds all the qualities of literary mannerism. For example, in song 26, every single word is part of a rhyming pair: *Gar bar lît wît walt, kalt snê wê tuot: gluot sî bî mir*. The excessive, albeit impressive rhyme schemes, especially in songs 26, 27, 28 and 30, ultimately obscure the meaning and emotion of the poetry and Konrad's use of traditional imagery often undermines the originality of his stylistic innovations. Konrad's allegory, *Die Klage der Kunst* (Art's Complaint), appeals for patronage and support of "true art" (*rehte kunst*). His hymn in praise of the Virgin Mary, *Die goldene Schmiede* (The Golden Smith), draws on and synthesizes an extraordinary range of medieval images and symbols. This work may have been commissioned by the Strasbourg Bishop Konrad von Lichtenberg. Other religious-oriented works include Konrad's verse legends. *Silvester* (1260) was commissioned by Liutold von Roeteln, the legend of Alexius (1265), by Johannes von Bermeswil and Heinrich Iselin, and Konrad composed the story of Pantaleon (1258) for Johannes von Arguel. The patronage of Konrad's earliest narrative work, *Das Turnier von Nantes* (The Tournament of Nantes, 1257–1258) is unknown, but critics suspect that it was written for someone affiliated with the Lower Rhine region. The tournament takes place at the Arthurian capital of Nantes and pits the German princes under the leadership of Richard of England against the French princes, under the leadership of the king of France. This poem was probably intended to win the support of the lower German princes for the recently crowned king of the Romans, Richard, earl of Cornwall (May 17, 1257). Konrad's fragment, *Schwannritter* (Swan Knight), also seems to have been written during this period. The tale is related to the French *Chevalier au Cygne* (1200) and the Lohengrin story found at the end of Wolfram von Eschenbach's *Parzival* (1210). Undoubtedly, Konrad's *Mären* (lyric novellas) are the most impressive and well-known works in his oeuvre. *Das Herzemaere* relates the popular tale of the jealous lord who feeds his wife the heart of her beloved knight. Konrad's introduction to this story recalls the work of Gottfried von Straßburg. This reference serves to underscore Gottfried's conspicuous influence on Konrad's style. In *Der Welt Lohn* (Worldly Reward), Konrad describes Wirnt von Grafenberg's (the poet of the courtly verse novel *Wigalois*) encounter with *Frau Welt* (Lady World). Although no certain source has been identified for this tale, it belongs to the *contemptus mundi* (contempt of the world) tradition. After gazing upon the infested backside of *Frau Welt*, Wirnt rejects the world, takes up the cross, and achieves martyrdom in the Holy Land. The dark comedy *Heinrich von Kempten* (also called *Otte mit dem Bart*, Otto with the Beard, 1261), illustrates the benefits of loyalty. Composed for the dean of Strasbourg Cathedral, Berthold von Tiersberg, the story plays on the traditions of the ill-tempered Emperor Otte (probably Emperor Otto II), Critics dispute the authorship of other Maren attributed to Konrad (*Die halbe Birne*, Half of the Pear, *Der Mvnch ah Liebesbote*, The Monk as Go-between, etc.).

Konrad composed three romances. *Engelhard*, set in the time of Charlemagne, tells a tale of fidelity (*triuwe*) in friendship. Engelhard and Dietrich resemble one another almost exactly and develop a close friendship at court in Denmark. Dietrich leaves the court to assume his position as the duke of Brabant but returns to Denmark to help Engelhard win the hand of Engeltrud, the daughter of the king of Denmark. Later, Dietrich is stricken with leprosy. Reminiscent of Hartmann von Aue's tale, *Der Arme Heinrich*, the poem culminates after Dietrich reveals that the blood of Engelhard's children is the only remedy for his illness. In *Partonopier und Meliur* (1277), Konrad draws on the extremely popular French romance *Partonopeus de Blois* (1200). While out hunting, Partonopier chances on a boat that takes him to the invisible island castle of the heiress of the Byzantine imperial throne, an enchantress named Meliur. At the castle, invisible hands tend to the youth. Partonopier lies with the invisible Meliur each night. Meliur plans to marry him when he comes of age under the condition that he does not look upon her before the appointed time. After a year has passed, Partonopier, plagued by doubts, chances to look upon Meliur and she rejects him. A year later, the pair is reconciled. Partonopier wins Meliur's hand through knightly prowess and becomes the Byzantine emperor. The romance comprises a mix of several different traditions, including: fairy tales, antique epics, *matère de Bretange* (tales of Bretange), and the *chansons de geste* (songs of heroic deeds). Similar motifs appear in *Die Königen von Brennenden See* (The Queen of the Burning Lake, 1220–1240), Egenolf von Staufenberg's courtly tale, *Ritter Peter* (1310), and in Thüring von Ringoltingen's verse tale *Melusine* (1456).

Konrad's last and greatest endeavor, *Trojanerkrieg* (The Trojan War, 1281) surpasses, with its 40,424 verses, Herbert von Fritzlar's Middle High German rendition of the fall of Troy, *Liet von Troye* (1190–1217) in both length and quality. Benoît de Sainte-Maure's *Estoire de Troie* is the main source for both German works. Konrad's narrative includes the birth of Paris and Achilles, relates the tale of Jason and Medea, the kidnapping of Helen and the preparation for war. Konrad's tale breaks off in the middle of the siege of Troy. The poem, concluded by a lesser, anonymous poet, was well received. The exact nature of the relationship of Konrad's *Trojanerkrieg* to the *Göttweiger Trojanerkrieg* (1270–1300) has not yet been determined. However, at the very least, Konrad's Schwannritter seems to have influenced the anonymous poet of *Göttweiger Trojanerkrieg*, erroneously attributed to Wolfram von Eschenbach. Konrad died in Basle either on August 31 or between October 8–22, 1287. He and his wife, Bertcha, had two daughters Gerina and Agnese. He was buried in Basle. Konrad von Würzburg was highly esteemed by contemporaries and successors. He is depicted dictating his work in the Codex Manesse. Hugo von Timberg praises Konrad in *Der Renner* (II. 1202–1220), and Frauenlob (Heinrich von Meißen) mourns him with the lament that art itself had died with the passing of Konrad: *ach kunst ist tôt!* (313, 15–21).

See also **Frauenlob; Gottfried von Straßburg; Hartmann von Aue**

Further Reading

Brandt, Rüdiger. *Konrad von Würzburg*. Darmstadt: Wissenschaftliche Buchgesellschaft, 1989.

Kokott, Hartmut. *Konrad von Würzburg: Ein Autor zwischen Auftrag und Autonomie*. Stuttgart: Hirzel, 1989.

Konrad von Würzburg. *Der Trojanische Krieg*, ed. Adelbert von Keller. Amsterdam: Rodopi, 1965.

——. *Die goldene Schmiede*, ed. Edward Schröder. Göttingen: Vandenhoeck & Ruprecht, 1969.

——. *Die Legenden: Silvester, Alexius, Pantaleon*, ed. Paul Gereke. Halle: Niemeyer, 1925–1927.

——. *Engelhard*, ed. Paul Gereke. Tübingen: Niemeyer, 1982.

——. *Kleinere Dichtungen*, ed. Edward Schröder. 3 vols. Berlin: Weidmann, 1959–1963 [*Der Welt Lohn, Das Herzmaere, Heinrich von Kempten, Der Schwanritter. Das Turnier von Nantes, Die Klage der Kunst*, songs].

——. *Partonopier und Meliur*, eds. Karl Bartsch and Franz Pfeiffer. Berlin: de Gruyter, 1871; rpt. 1970.

——. *Trojanerkrieg: Staatsbibliothek Preussischer Kulturbesitz, Ms. germ. fol. 1*. Munich: Lengenfelder, 1989 [color microfiche].

Musica practica. *Minnesänger und Meistersinger Lieder um Konrad von Würzburg*. Freiburg: Christophorus, 1988 [audio recording].

STEPHEN M. CAREY

KORMÁKR QGMUMDARSON
(ca. 930–970)

Kormákr Qgmumdarson was an Icelandic poet, the chief character of *Kormáks saga*. The name (Irish *Cormac*) suggests Celtic family connections. According to Haukr Valdísarson's *Íslendingadrápa,* Kormákr was of high birth (*kynstórr*). The saga belongs to the category of *skáldasögur,* and is particularly remarkable for the large number of verses (*lausavísur*) it contains scattered throughout. Sixty-four of the eighty-five verses are spoken by the hero. Of the remaining ones, fifteen are attributed to his chief rival, Bersi. A few verses are faked, corrupt, or of doubtful origin (in particular 6, 24, 61, 73, and 79). The prose story of the saga, the biography of the poet, is unusually short and constitutes little more than a connecting framework around the many verses. There are linguistic indications that it was composed at the beginning of the 13th century, the earliest period of saga writing.

Its all-dominating theme is the hero's unhappy love story, a love that is never consummated. Right from the start, it contains bizarre elements. A glimpse of a young girl's beautiful ankles is enough to make the poet fall in love and causes a flow of poetic inspiration. He realizes that love for the young Steingerðr is to be his fate for the rest of his life. But although his feelings are reciprocated, and, after incidents in which blood is shed, her father's resistance is overcome, the planned marriage falls through. Paradoxically enough, the direct cause of the failure is Kormákr himself: when the time comes, he does not turn up at the wedding that has already been prepared. According to the saga, the real reason is the harmful spell put upon him by a woman whose sons the poet had killed. Against her will, Steingerðr is married to the scarred warrior Bersi. With the arrogance that always characterizes him, Kormákr insists on his first right to the girl and challenges Bersi to single combat, but after a slight wound has to admit defeat. Scornful verses, challenges, and single combats follow. Steingerðr leaves Bersi and later marries again, this time a peaceful man whom Kormákr deeply despises and mocks.

Off on his Viking journeys, the poet dreams of his beloved and sings the praises of her beauty. What seems to be a promising meeting between the two occurs when Kormákr visits his country, but a night spent with Steingerðr ends in a frustrating anticlimax: the physical role of a lover seems to have been something denied to Kormákr.

One thing is certain: no Icelandic skald can compete with Kormákr as the master of love poetry, which is not, however, his only genre. *Skáldatal* informs us that Kormákr had sung the praises of both Earl Sigurðr in Hlaðir and Haraldr gráfeldr ("grey-cloak") Eiríksson. Only a part of the former's poem has survived; there are seven half-strophes from *Sigurðardrápa,* cited in *Skáldskaparmál* in Snorri's *Edda,* and one complete strophe in *Heimskringla.* An original artistic device of the poet is his way of replacing the *drápa's* refrain (*stef*) by varying mythological allusions that do not seem to have any connection with the content of the rest of the poem. In Snorri's *Háttatal,* this variety of *dróttkvætt* is called *hjástælt.*

A much-discussed theory would have us believe that *Kormáks saga* is an entirely literary product, with prose and poetry as equally authentic literary components. The author, it is suggested, was a 13th-century writer who had been influenced by continental European troubadour poetry and the medieval love poetry of which Tristan is the hero (Bjarni Einarsson 1976). This theory has been contested on both linguistic and literary-historical grounds (Einar Ól. Sveinsson 1966–69, Andersson 1969, Hallberg 1975).

Further Reading

Editions

Einar Ól. Sveinsson, ed. *Vatnsdcela saga.* Íslenzk fornrit, 8. Reykjavik: Hið íslenzka fornritafélag, 1939.

Literature

Wood, Cecil. "Kormak's Stanzas Called the *Sigurðardrápa.*" *Neophilologus* 43 (1959), 305–19.

Hallberg, Peter. *The Icelandic Saga.* Trans. Paul Schach. Lincoln: University of Nebraska Press,' 1962.

Einar Ól. Sveinsson. "Kormákr the Poet and His Verses." *Saga-Book of the Viking* Society 17 (1966–69), 18–60.

Andersson, Theodore M. "Skalds and Troubadours." *Mediaeval Scandinavia* 2 (1969), 7–41.

Frank, Roberta. "Onomastic Play in Kormákr's Verse: The Name Steingerðr." *Mediaeval Scandinavia* 3 (1970), 7–34.

Bjarni Einarsson. "The Lovesick Skald: A Reply to Theodore M. Andersson (*Mediaeval Scandinavia* 1969)." *Mediaeval Scandinavia* 4 (1971) 21–41.

Hallberg, Peter. Old *Icelandic Poetry: Eddie Lay and Skaldic Verse.* Trans. Paul Schach and Sonja Lindgrenson. Lincoln: University of Nebraska Press, 1975.

Turville-Petre, E. O. G. *Scaldic Poetry.* Oxford: Clarendon, 1976.

Bjarni Einarsson. *To skjaldesagaer. En analyse af Kormáks saga og Hallfreðar saga.* Bergen, Oslo, and Tromsø: Universitetsforlaget, 1976.

See, Klaus von. "Skaldenstrophe und Sagaprosa. Ein Beitrag zum Problem der mündlichen Überlieferung in der altnordischen Literatur." *Mediaeval Scandinavia* 10 (1977), 58–82.

Frank, Roberta. *Old Norse Court Poetry: The Dróttkvætt Stanza.* Islandica, 42. Ithaca and London: Cornell University Press, 1978.

See, Klaus von. "Mündliche Prosa und Skaldendichtung. Mit einem Exkurs über Skaldensagas und Trobadorbiographien." *Mediaeval Scandinavia* 11 (1978–79), 82–91.

Schottmann, Hans. "Der Bau der Kormáks saga." *Skandinavistik* 12 (1982) 22–36.

Lie, Hallvard. *Om sagakunst og skaldskap. Utvalgte avhandlinger.* Øvre Ervik: Alvheim & Eide, 1982.

Clover, Carol J., and John lindow, eds. *Old Norse–Icelandic Literature: A Critical Guide.* Islandica, 45. Ithaca and London: Cornell University Press, 1985.

FOLKE STRÖM

KÜRENBERC, DER VON (fl. late 12th c.)

Der von Kürenberc is the earliest named German lyric poet. His poems are preserved only in the famous Heidelberg University library *Minnesang* manuscript "C," where he is grouped among the barons. He is possibly a member of the Kürenberg family who had a castle near Linz, Austria, during the mid-twelfth century. He is part of what is known as the Danube or indigenous school, showing very little French influence.

Fifteen stanzas have been preserved. The basic metrical unit is the four-beat half-line; the long lines formed of two such halves are combined in rhyming couplets. There are two stanza patterns: the predominant one of four long lines, which is the basis of the so-called Nibelung stanza, or *Nibelungenstrophe*, and that where a rhymeless line is inserted as the odd fifth half-line. Several are so-called "Women's stanzas," or *Frauenstrophen*, written from the woman's point of view. In one poem, a lady stands at night on battlements, listening to a knight singing from among the crowd, in *kürenberges wîse* (*Minnesangs Frühling [MF]*, no. 8,1). In another poem, the lady is compared with a falcon: women and falcons are easily tamed, if one entices them rightly, they will seek the man (*MF* 10, 17).

Kürenberc makes dramatic and effective use of the *Wechsel*, or lyrical dialogue, alternating speeches of identical length. Frequently the speeches do not make contact; the man and woman talk past each other. In a *Wechsel*, he parodies the figure of the lover who so idealizes the lady that he stands beside her bed and does not dare wake her up, much less think of enjoying her favors (*MF* 8, 9–15). He has a dramatic sense of situations; his lyrics often tell little stories. His best known song has the falcon as its subject, *Ich zôch mir einen valken*, for which many widely differing interpretations have been proposed (*MF* 8, 33). A person rears a falcon for more than a year, trains and adorns it with gold wire and silken jesses. The falcon flies away "into other lands." Later, the person sees the falcon, still with the gold and the silk, and says: *Got sende si zesamene, die geliep wellen gerne sîn* (God bring those together who wish to be lovers!). The poem might be the literal story of the loss of a falcon or the falcon might be a symbol for a messenger of love, or for the yearning of lovers, or for an unfaithful lover. If the woman is speaking, the poem may be identified as *Frauenstrophen*, if a man, as a *Botenlied*. If it is first the man and then the lady, it is a *Wechsel*.

Der von Kürenberc introduces several elements that appear in later *minnesang*: the message and messenger taken from medieval Latin epistle form; the need for secrecy and fear of spies, *merkære* (slanderers) and *lügenære* (liars); the submissive role of the man.

Further Reading

Agler-Beck, Gayle. *Der von Kürenberg: Edition, Notes, and Commentary*. German Language and Literature Monographs 4. Amsterdam: John Benjamins, 1978.

Heffner, R.-M.S, and Kathe Peterson. *A Word-Index to Des Minnesangs Frühling*. Madison: University of Wisconsin Press, 1942.

Koschorreck, Walter, and Wilfried Werner, eds. *Codex Manesse. Die Große* Heidelberger Liederhandschrift. Faksimile-Ausgage des Cod. Pal. Germ. 848 der Universitdts-Bibliothek Heidelberg. Kassel: Ganymed, 1981 [facsimile].

Moser, Hugo, and Helmut Tervooren. *Des Minnesangs Frühling unter Benutzung der Ausgdben von Karl Lachmann und Moriz Haupt, Friedrich Vogt und Carl von Kraus*. Stuttgart: Hirzel, 1982.

Rakel, Hans-Herbert S. *Der deutsche Minnesang. Eine Einfrührung mit Texten und Materialien*. Munich: Beck, 1986.

Sayce, Olive. *Poets of the Minnesang. Introduction, Notes and Glossary*. Oxford: University Press, 1967.

Schweikle, Günther. *Die mittelhochdeutsche Minnelyrik*, vol. 1. *Die frühe Minnelyrik. Texte und Übertragungen, Einführung und Kommentar*. Darmstadt: Wissenschaftliche Buchgesellschaft, 1977.

———. *Minnesang*. Stuttgart: Metzler, 1989.

Tervooren, Helmut. *Bibliographie zum Minnesang und zuden Dichtern aus "Des Minnesangs Frühling."* Berlin: Schmidt, 1969, pp. 55–58.

Wapnewski, Peter. "Des Kürenberger's Falkenlied." *Euphorion* 53 (1959): 1–19.

STEPHANIE CAIN VAN D'ELDEN

L

LA VIGNE, ANDRÉ DE
(ca. 1457–ca. 1515)

Late-medieval poet and playwright. Born between 1457 and 1470 in the port city of La Rochelle, La Vigne was in the service of Marie d'Orléans from ca. 1488 until her death in 1493, when he became secretary to the duke of Savoy. In 1494, in an effort to attract a more powerful protector, he presented a work to King Charles VIII, the *Ressource de la Crestienté*. This poem is a dream allegory in which the king, in the personage of Magesté Royalle, is shown as the protector of Dame Crestienté, who is in peril. Impressed with La Vigne's talents, Charles appointed him historiographer of his military expedition into Italy to conquer the kingdom of Naples (1494–95). The resulting chronicle, the *Voyage de Naples*, is an eyewitness record of the events of the Italian campaign. Like the *Ressource*, it is written in alternating verse and prose.

In May 1496, La Vigne was invited to the town of Seurre in Burgundy, where he was commissioned to write a play on the life of St. Martin, patron of the town. Within five weeks, he had completed not only the *Mystère de saint Martin*, comprising more than 10,000 lines of verse, but also a comic morality play, the *Aveugle et le boiteux*, and a farce, the *Meunier de qui le diable emporte l'âme en enfer*. The mystery play was written to edify the people with scenes from the holy and devout life of their patron saint. To this end, there are sermons, miracles, and conversions, as well as scenes set in Heaven and Hell. The play is also a rich tapestry of daily life, showing people of all sorts and conditions engaged in their daily tasks. La Vigne portrays this milieu from a variety of stylistic perspectives. He sympathetically treats family difficulties and explores the psychology of suffering; he satirizes the abuses of the powerful, the faults of the clergy, and the venality of the merchant class; he depicts the bombast of braggart soldiers and the antics of drunken messengers. All these strands are woven together in a seamless dramatic action in which the playwright deftly alternates affective and comic scenes for maximum effect.

Toward the end of the century, La Vigne collected a number of his early works in the *Vergier d'honneur*. In 1504, he brought suit against Michel Le Noir, a Parisian printer, to stop an unauthorized edition of this work; the Parlement de Paris issued the injunction. Before the death of Charles VIII in 1498, La Vigne had been appointed secretary to the queen, Anne of Brittany. He remained in this capacity until her death in 1514. His later works included epitaphs for his patrons and other panegyric poems. He wrote two other plays, the *Sotise à huit personnages*, attacking the abuses of his day, and the *Moralité du nouveau monde* against the abolition of the Pragmatic Sanction, as well as political poems. In the *Louenge des roys de France*, for example, he supported Louis XII in his quarrel with the pope. Francis I in the year of his accession (1515) named La Vigne his historiographer and charged him with writing the history of his reign. Since only a few pages of the chronicle were completed, La Vigne is thought to have died shortly after.

Further Reading

La Vigne, André de. *Le mystère de saint Martin, 1496*, ed. André Duplat. Geneva: Droz, 1979.

——. *Le voyage de Naples*, ed. Anna Slerca. Milan: Pubblicazioni della Università Cattolica del Sacro Cuore, 1981.

Brown, Cynthia Jane. *The Shaping of History and Poetry in Late Medieval France: Propaganda and Artistic Expression in the Works of the Rhétoriqueurs*. Birmingham: Summa, 1985.

Duplat, André. "La *Moralité de l'aveugle et du boiteux* d'Andrieu de la Vigne: étude littéraire et édition." *Travaux de linguistique et de littérature* 21 (1983): 41–79.

ANDRÉ DUPLAT

LANDINI, FRANCESCO
(c. 1325–2 September 1397)

Francesco Landini was a composer, organist, singer, instrument maker, and poet of the second generation of the Italian *Trecento*. He may have been born in Fiesole or Florence and was the son of the painter Jacopo Del Casentino (d. 1349), a cofounder of the Florentine guild of painters. Landini lost his sight after having smallpox as a child; as a result, he turned to music with a passion. He mastered several instruments, including the organ; worked as an organ builder, organ tuner, and instrument maker; and played, sang, and wrote poetry. As a scholar, he is recorded as following the teachings of William of Ockham, and he was knowledgeable in many areas of astrology, philosophy, and ethics. Landini was very active in religious and political events. His musical works indicate that he spent some time in northern Italy before 1370, probably in Venice. He was organist at the monastery of Santa Trinita in 1361; and from 1365 until his death he was *capellanus* at the church of San Lorenzo. His acquaintances included the Florentine chancellor of state and humanist Coluccio Salutati and the composer Andreas de Florentia. In 1379 and 1387, Landini was involved in building organs at the church of Santa Annunziata and at the cathedral of Florence. Giovanni da Prato, in *Il paradiso degli Alberti* (1389), a narrative poetic account of Florence, portrays Landini as an active musician and humanist, taking part in extensive philosophical and political conversations as well as singing and playing the organ. Landini died in Florence, in the church of San Lorenzo; his tombstone was discovered in Prato in the nineteenth century. A picture of Landini can be seen on folio 121v of the Squarcialupi Codex (I-Fl 87). His fame continued well into the fifteenth century. The French musicologist Fetis rediscovered Landini's music in 1827.

Not only was Landini a very prolific composer, but the survival of his musical works attests to his popularity and importance. His extant works represent almost a quarter of the entire known repertoire of secular *Trecento* music. One hundred fifty-four works can be definitely attributed to Landini: ninety *ballate* for two voices, forty-two *ballate* for three voices, eight *ballate* that survive in two-part and three-part versions, one French *virelai*, nine madrigals for two or three voices, one three-voice canonic madrigal, and one *caccia*. Works of doubtful authenticity include two or three *ballate* for two voices, and four motets with fragmentary single voices. More than 145 works by Landini are contained in the Squarcialupi Codex.

Landini's musical style is multifaceted; he wrote works ranging from simple dances to complex isorhythmic and canonic pieces. His compositional technique is often described as a synthesis of French and Italian musical influences. The melodic inventiveness of Landini's music is readily apparent. A special musical cadence—which musicologists call the Landini cadence—appears frequently in his music; it is recognizable at the end of phrases as a leaping upward by an interval of a third. Landini's music points toward the polyphonic imitation in fifteenth-century early Renaissance music.

Further Reading

Editions
The Works of Francesco Landini, ed. Leonard Ellinwood. Cambridge, Mass.: Medieval Academy of America, 1939. (2nd ed., 1945; reprint, New York: Kraus Reprint, 1970.)
The Works of Francesco Landini, ed. Leo Schrade. Polyphonic Music of the Fourteenth Century, 4. Monaco: Éditions de l'Oiseau-Lyre, 1958.

Studies
Ellinwood, Leonard. "Francesco Landini and His Music." *Musical Quarterly*, 22, 1936, pp. 190ff. Fischer, Kurt von. "On the Technique, Origin, and Evolution of Italian Trecento Music." *Musical Quarterly*, 47, 1963, pp. 41ff.
"Landini, Francesco." In *New Grove Dictionary of Music and Musicians*, Vol. 10, pp. 428–434.

BRADFORD LEE EDEN

LANFRANC OF BEC
(ca. 1010–1089)

Born into a good family in Pavia, Lanfranc was educated in that city and more generally in northern Italy. He left Italy for France while still a young man and made his reputation as an itinerant teacher in the area around Avranches. In 1042, he entered the new monastery at Bec (founded 1041); he was abbot of Saint-Étienne, Caen, in 1063; in 1070, he was made archbishop of Canterbury. He had a dual reputation, first as a teacher and scholar and later as a brilliant administrator and leader.

His scholarship falls into two periods, before and after his entry into Bec. The earlier works, no longer extant, are on the Trivium; after 1042, he devoted himself to theology, writing commentaries on the Psalms and Pauline epistles that circulated widely. About 1063, he wrote a treatise *De sacramento corporis et sanguinis Christi*, against the opinions of Berengar of Tours's *De eucharistia*, and to which Berengar replied in *De sacra coena*. Berengar's ideas caused widespread antagonism and were finally condemned by Pope Gregory VII in 1079. The issue centers on the changes taking place in the bread and wine of the eucharist in order for them to become the body and blood of Christ. Both Berengar and Lanfranc believed in the Real Presence, but they differed on the necessity and type of any change in the elements, Berengar insisting that no material alteration was needed and Lanfranc arguing for outward identity concealing inner grace. The question was compounded by difficulties of language: no clearer statement of the central issue was to be possible until the introduction of Aristotelian notions of substance and accident in the 13th century.

Lanfranc's leadership of the school at Bec made it into one of the most famous of its day, and pupils included Anselm of Bec, Ivo of Chartres, and Guitmund of Aversa (later Pope Alexander II). He was a valued counselor to Duke William of Normandy (the Conqueror) despite having declared William's marriage invalid.

Lanfranc was a great holder of synods (in 1075, 1076, 1078, 1081), which he used to promulgate canon law, and he was the first to create separate courts of ecclesiastical jurisdiction. His legal turn of mind (he seems to have practiced or at least studied civil law in Pavia) was coupled with a traditionalist viewpoint, so that his outlook reminds us of Carolingian attitudes and practices rather than any innovation. The collection of canon law, the so-called *Collectio Lanfranci*, which Lanfranc brought to Canterbury from Bec, has an old-fashioned cast, in contrast to the *Collection in Seventy-Four Titles* (*Diversorum patrum sententiae*) or Ivo of Chartres's *Panormia* and other legal works, the new breed of legal collections that it seems Lanfranc preferred to ignore.

As archbishop of Canterbury, Lanfranc replaced many Saxon bishops with Normans, to the displeasure of some in the English church, but in doing so he increased ties with the Continent and with Gregory VII's reforms, with which, at least in the area of the moral reform of the church, he was largely in sympathy. Lanfranc rebuilt the church at Canterbury and established its library. He reestablished many of the old monastic privileges and lands.

See also **Anselm of Bec; Gregory VII, Pope; William I**

Further Reading

Lanfranc of Bec. *Opera. PL* 150. 1–782.
———. *The Letters of Lanfranc, Archbishop of Canterbury*, ed. Helen Clover and Margaret T. Gibson. Oxford: Clarendon, 1979.
Gibson, Margaret T. *Lanfranc of Bec*. Oxford: Clarendon, 1978.
Huygens, R.B.C. "Bérenger de Tours, Lanfranc et Bernold de Constance." *Sacris Euridiri* 16 (1965): 355–403.
Southern, Richard W., ed. *Essays in Medieval History*. London: Macmillan, 1948.

LESLEY J. SMITH

LANGMANN, ADELHEID
(ca. 1312–1375)

Born to a politically and socially powerful family in Nuremberg around 1312, at the age of thirteen, Adel-

heid Langmann was betrothed to Gottfried Teufel, who died shortly afterward. Following what she describes as a lengthy spiritual struggle, around 1330, Adelheid entered the Franconian Dominican cloister of Engelthal. Regarded as a particularly prosperous and renowned cloister, Engelthal housed the daughters of many of the prominent burghers of the area. Among them was Christina Ebner, whose widespread praise included bishops and kings. Adelheid was cloistered at Engelthal in 1350 when King Charles IV (later Emperor Charles) visited the monastery for spiritual advice. She was educated in Latin and learned to read and write in her vernacular German dialect. Shortly after Christina wrote her spiritual autobiography, Adelheid recorded her visions and revelations along with a lengthy prayer dedicated to the Trinity. Her *Revelations*, extant in three manuscript variations, were written in a Bavarian dialect and chronicle her spiritual life from 1330 to 1344. While the content is essentially autohagiographical, representing the religious experiences of its author, there are stylistic similarities and thematic parallels with the mystical lives narrated in the convent chronicles of Helfta, Toss, Unterlinden, Diessenhoven, and Adlehausen. Influenced by biblical sources, especially the Song of Songs, Adelheid's ecstatic mysticism reflects the bride mysticism of the Middle Ages. Her texts, as well as several other manuscripts written by Dominican cloistered women in Southern Germany, were rediscovered and edited by nineteenth-century scholars interested in the linguistic history of German.

See also **Charles IV; Ebner, Margaretha**

Further Reading

Die Offenbarungen der Adelheid Langmann: Klosterfrau zu Englethal, ed. Phillip Strauch. Strasbourg: Trübner, 1878.
Hale, Rosemary Drage. "*Imitatio Mariae*: Motherhood Motifs in Devotional Memoirs." *Mystics Quarterly* 16 (1990): 193–214.
Hindsley, Leonard P. *The Mystics of Engelthal: Writings from a Medieval Monastery*. New York: St. Martin's Press, 1998.

ROSEMARY DRAGE HALE

LAUFENBERG, HEINRICH
(ca. 1390–1460)

Laufenberg, a cleric active in Freiburg im Breisgau and Zofingen, composed the bulk of his verses between 1413 and 1445. In the latter year he entered a cloister in Strasbourg that had been founded by Rulman Merswin (d. 1382), the lay mystic and guiding spirit for the so-called Friends of God. Laufenberg is best known as the author of some 120 sacred songs written in the German vernacular, among them Christmas and New Year's verses. His Christmas song *Jn einem krippfly lag ein kind* (In a little crib lay a child) is representative in its straightforward narration, plain diction, and heartfelt religious devotion. Especially pronounced is Laufenberg's veneration of the Virgin Mary; few medieval poets command his breadth of Mariological symbols and tropes. The culmination of his Mariology is the *Buck der Figuren* (1441), a massive versified catalogue and interpretative commentary on more than 100 prefigurations of the Virgin in the Old Testament. Another lengthy work from his pen is the *Regimen sanitatis* (1429), a combination cosmology and medical reference tool of more than 6,000 German verses based on many source texts, Avicenna among them. The *Regimen*, besides treating health concerns, pregnancy, and child-care, examines the solar system, the elements, and natural phenomena—including pestilence. Very popular, Laufenberg's *Regimen* was an early printed book. Rounding out his longer works is a 1437 translation, in 15,000 verses, of a fourteenth-century discourse on salvation, *Speculum humanae salvationis*.

The prolific author, who had regular ecclesiastical duties as pastor, curate, and dean, evinces broad learning, theological sophistication, and mastery of a wide range of vernacular and Latin literary forms. At home in verse and prose, Laufenberg translated Latin church hymns and sequences and composed "mixed" poetry, that is, songs in alternating Latin and German verses. Musical composer and self-aware author in one person (Laufenberg liked to sign and date his compositions), he influenced hymn writing in the Reformation and beyond. As Martin Luther was to do, Heinrich Laufenberg penned many pointed *contrafactura*, appropriating secular texts and melodies for the Christian sphere. His most famous example—and his most famous song—is *Ich wölt, daz ich doheime wer* (I wished I were at home). The "home" of which the singer speaks is heaven; he longs for a home far from earth where he can gaze eternally upon God. In like vein, Laufenberg wrote Christian dawn songs and adapted secular love songs for worship of the Virgin Mary. She appears typically in his verse as the *mülnerin* (the miller's wife/female operator of a mill), a figure who threshes, grinds, and bakes the biblical "corn of wheat" (John 12:24) that is Jesus Christ. Evident everywhere in Laufenberg's work is the desire to increase piety in his broad audience, be these nuns, religious societies, or laymen. That his texts were read silently by individual readers for meditation and private devotion is very probable.

Scholarly research on Heinrich Laufenberg has labored under the loss of unique versions of most of his creations, the result of destruction of manuscripts in Strasbourg during the Franco-Prussian War in 1870. A critical edition of his works has not yet appeared and would necessarily contain presumed transcriptions.

Further Reading

Schiendorfer, Max. "Der Wächter und die Müllerin 'verkert,' 'geistlich.' Fußnoten zur Liedkontrafaktur bei Heinrich Laufenberg." In *Contemplata aliis tradere, Studien zum Verhältnis von Literatur und Spiritualität. Festschrift für Alois Haas zum 60. Geburtstag*, eds. Claudia Brinker, et al. Bern: Lang, 1995, pp. 273–316.

Wachinger, Burghart. "Notizen zu den Liedern Heinrich Laufenbergs." In *Medium aevum deutsch, Beiträge zur deutschen Literatur des hohen und späten Mittelalters. Festschrift für Kurt Ruh zum 65. Geburtstag*, eds. Dietrich Huschenbett, et al. Tübingen; Niemeyer, 1979, pp. 349–385.

WILLIAM C. McDONALD

LAƷAMON OR LAYAMON (fl. ca. 1200-25?)

Author of the *Brut*, a major poem of the early ME period that contains, among other items of interest, the first account in English of the Arthurian legend. Laʒamon identifies himself in the opening lines of his poem as a priest residing in Ernleʒe (Areley Kings, Worcestershire). Having resolved to write a history of England, he says, he consulted as source material Bede's *Ecclesiastical History*, a Latin book written by Sts. Albin and Augustine, and Wace's *Roman de Brut*. In fact Laʒamon appears to have made little use of Bede's history (tentatively identified by scholars as the OE translation of Bede) or the untitled Latin text (identified still more tentatively as a book containing selections by Albin and Augustine of Canterbury, the Latin text of Bede, or a mere fiction invented by the poet to display his erudition). Thus, with some significant modifications and additions, Laʒamon's poem is essentially an English paraphrase of Wace's *Brut* rendered into alliterative long lines, some 16,000 in number. Because of an allusion in the opening lines of the poem to Eleanor, "who was Henry's queen," it is generally accepted that the *Brut* was written some time after the death of Henry II in 1189 and possibly even after the death of Eleanor herself in 1204; but scholarly opinion relating to the precise date of composition ranges from the late 12th century to the second half of the 13th.

The *Brut* survives in two manuscripts dating from 1250–1350. Although both are thought to derive from a common archetype, BL Cotton Caligula A.ix is commonly held to be closer to its exemplar—and hence to Laʒamon's original text—than is BL Cotton Otho C.xiii. The latter is considered an inferior text because its scribe apparently attempted to modernize his original by eliminating many of the rhetorical embellishments intended to give it what has been called an "antique colouring" (Stanley). These embellishments include lengthy repetitions of detail and incident and archaisms of the type that survive in and characterize the Caligula text—that is, the many coinages and poetic compounds with a distinctly Anglo-Saxon ring about them and the marked preference for words of Anglo-Saxon origin (many of which have been replaced in the Otho text by French loanwords).

In subject matter and method Laȝamon imitates Wace so as to be able to afford his readers a history of the Britons from the time of Brutus, great-grandson of Aeneas, to the ascendancy of the Saxons over the Britons during the reign of Cadwalader in the 7th century. Lazamon's additions to and modifications of his Anglo-Norman source have much to tell us, however, about his purpose in adapting Wace's poem into English: as scholars have been quick to notice, Lazamon's numerous accounts of feasts, sea voyages, and battles, many of which have no counterparts in Wace's poem, evoke the ethos of OE poetic accounts of such events and seem to have been intended to do so. Similarly Wace's interest in love, courtesy, and the ideals of chivalry is not one that Laȝamon shares: indeed, in his adaptation of many of the events described in Wace's poem, we find Laȝamon attempting to recreate the ethos of the heroic, as opposed to the chivalric, world. His Arthur, for example, is not a Norman king presiding over a chivalric court as in Wace, but a Saxon chieftain as disposed to committing acts of brutality and violence as to rewarding his faithful retainers, after a battle, with rings, garments, and horses. As in the meadhalls of OE poetry, there are *scops* in Arthur's court and *dream* (joy) when a victory is being celebrated; by the same token here and elsewhere in the poem there prevails, as in OE verse, an overwhelming sense of the role played by Fate in the human lives, but especially in the lives of those destined to enter the field of battle.

Further evidence of Laȝamon's familiarity with and desire to imitate the verse of OE poets can be discerned in his use of formulas, not simply as tags and line fillers but also to advance his narrative in a manner in keeping with the formulaic practices of OE poetry. Not surprisingly, perhaps, the *Brut* is most noticeably formulaic in passages tliat have no counterpart in Wace and in which Laȝamon seems to have been particularly eager to recreate the ethos of the past, such as his accounts of feasts, sea voyages, and battles. Equally indicative of Laȝamon's admiration for the verse of the OE poets is his use of certain rhetorical tropes and patterns found in their poetry. With an unmistakable sense of what he is about Laȝamon employs, with varying degrees of frequency, the kenning, the descriptive epithet, the simile, litotes, variation, chiasmus, and more complex structural repetitions, such as the envelope pattern, repetition parallels, and balance parallels.

Laȝamon's unmistakable nostalgia for the pre-Conquest period is reflected not only in the poem's style and content but also in its verse form. He patterns his verse, like his language and themes, after that of the OE poets. Laȝamon's basic metrical unit is the alliterative long line consisting of two two-stress hemistichs linked by alliteration, rhyme, or both. His use of rhyme as well as alliteration, of a longer line (to accommodate the hypotactic constructions of ME), and of some metrical patterns that do not conform to the metrical patterns of OE verse suggest that Laȝamon was working within a much more flexible prosody than that governing the composition of OE poetry; however, his verse should not be relegated, as some of his critics have suggested, to the ranks of "popular" poetry. Rather it is an evolutionary form of the "classical" alliterative verse of the English Middle Ages.

See also **Geoffrey of Monmouth; Wace**

Further Reading

Primary Sources
Brook, G.L., and R.F. Leslie, eds. *Laȝamon: Brut*. 2 vols. EETS o.s. 250, 277. London: Oxford University Press, 1963–78.
Bzdyl, Donald G., trans. *Layamon's Brut: A History of the Britons*. Binghamton: MRTS, 1989.

Secondary Sources
New *CBEL* 1:460–63
Le Saux, Françoise H.M. *Laȝamon's Brut: The Poem and Its Sources*. Cambridge: Brewer, 1989.
Le Saux, Françoise H.M. *The Text and Tradition of Laȝamon's Brut*. Cambridge: Brewer, 1994.
Reiss, Edmund, et al. *Arthurian Legend and Literature: An Annotated Bibliography*. Vol. 1. New York: Garland, 1984, pp. 79–80.
Stanley, E.G. "Layamon's Antiquarian Sentiments." *MÆ* 38 (1969): 23–37.

JAMES NOBLE

LEO III, EMPEROR
(c. 680–741, r. 717–741)

Leo III (Conon) was a Byzantine—i.e., eastern Roman—emperor. In older works he was mistakenly called "the Isaurian," but research has now established that he was from Germanicea (modern Marash or Maraš in southeastern Turkey). His native tongue was Syriac or Arabic, and as regards religion he was most likely a Jacobite (Syrian Monophysite).

Conon probably changed his original name to the more "Roman" Leo and became religiously orthodox when he joined the Byzantine army. As a young man he became a protégé of Emperor Justinian II during Justinian's second reign (705–711), and he continued to rise during the short reigns of emperors Philippicus (711–713) and Anastasius II (713–715). When Theodosius III (715–717) deposed the latter, Leo marched on Constantinople to avenge Anastasius. With a large Arab land and naval force also approaching Constantinople,

Theodosius voluntarily handed Leo the throne.

Leo's greatest achievement was to thwart the Arab siege of Constantinople in 717–718. Although the Arabs continued to be a threat, they never again endangered the existence of the empire. Also important was his promulgation of the *Ecloga*, the first Byzantine legal collection since the *Corpus iuris civilis* of Justinian I.

Leo's espousal of Iconoclasm, which condemned religious art, in 726 caused a revolt in those portions of Italy still under imperial control (Sicily had already shown signs of resistance early in Leo's reign). Tax increases imposed by Leo may also have been a factor in this revolt. Pope Gregory II—who lacked sufficient resources to withstand the Lombards and thus was still dependent on the Byzantines' military power—urged the Italians to exercise moderation, even though Leo (probably at about this time) removed parts of Illyricum from papal jurisdiction. Pope Gregory III, who was less conciliatory, also continued a limited cooperation with the empire; but by this time the popes were allies of the empire rather than its subjects. Leo may have caused some immigration to Italy from the empire's heartland, though this mainly occurred during the reign of his son. Refugees, many of them monks, augmented the existing Italo-Greek population—especially monastic communities—in Rome and central and southern Italy. Iconoclasm seems to have been little enforced in Byzantine Italy.

Further Reading

Editions and Translations

Gouilland, Jean. "Aux origines de l'iconoclasme: Le témoinage de Grègoire II." *Travaux et Mémoires*, 3, 1968, pp. 243–367. (Greek text and French translation of two letters of Pope Gtegory II to Leo III protesting Leo's Iconoclastic policies.)

Le liber pontificalis, ed. Louis Duchesne. Bibliothèque des Écoles Françaises d'Athènes et de Rome. Paris, 1955. (Not a new edition, but incorporates the editor's corrections, deletions, and emendations up to his death and thus supersedes earlier printings. The life of Gregory II in *Liber pontificalis* is the most important source for the effects of Leo III's policies in Italy. As of the present writing there was no English translation of Gregory II's biography or of any other from the Iconoclastic period.)

Nicephorus, Saint, Patriarch of Constantinople. *Breviarium historicum (Short History)*, trans., with commentary, Cyril Mango. Dumbarton Oaks Texts, 10; Corpus Fontium Historiae Byzantinae, 13. Washington, D.C.: Dumbarton Oaks, 1990. (Short chronicle covering some of the same rime as Theophanes. Nicephorus was an Iconophile patriarch of Constantinople, dismissed by Emperor Leo V.)

Santoro, Anthony, trans. *Theophanes' Chronographia: A Chronicle of Eighth-Century Byzantium*. Gorham, Me.: Heathersfield, 1982. (With maps; translates only the notices from 717 to 803, but these years included most of the Iconoclastic epoch.)

Theophanes. *Chronographia*, ed. Charles de Boor. Leipzig: Teubner, 1883–1885. (Reprint, 1963. Principal Greek source for Leo's reign, but badly informed and often confused on Italian affairs.)

———. *Chronographia: The Chronicle of Theophanes Confessor—Byzantine and Near Eastern History*, A.D. 284–813, trans., with introduction and commentary, Cyril Mango and Roger Scott, with Geoffrey Greatrex. Oxford and New York: Oxford University Press, 1997.

Turtledove, Harry, trans. *The Chronicle of Theophanes: An English Translation of Annus Mundi 6095–6305 (a.d. 602–813), with Introduction and Notes*. Philadelphia: University of Pennsylvania Press, 1982.

Critical Studies

Anastos, Milton V. "The Transfer of Illyricum, Calabria, and Sicily to the Jurisdiction of the Patriarchate of Constantinople in 732–733." In *Silloge Bizantina in Onore di Silvio Giuseppe Mercati*. Rome, 1957, pp. 14–31.

———. "Leo III's Edict against the Images in the Year 726–727 and Italo-Byzantine Relations between 726 and 730." *Byzantinischen Forschungen*, 3, 1968, pp. 281–327.

Barnard, Leslie W. *The Graeco-Roman and Oriental Background of the Iconoclastic Controversy*. Byzantina Neerlandica, 5. Leiden: Brill, 1974.

Gero, Stephen. *Byzantine Iconoclasm during the Reign of Leo III, with Particular Attention to the Oriental Sources*. Corpus Scriptorum Christianorum Orientorum, 384, Subsidia, 52. Louvain: Corpussco, 1977. (Source for Leo's early years, though occasionally mistaken on western matters.)

Hodgkin, Thomas. *Italy and Her Invaders*, Vol. 6, *The Lombard Kingdom*. Oxford: Oxford University Press, 1916. (Classic account.)

Noble, Thomas F. X. *The Republic of Saint Peter: The Birth of the Papal State, 680–825*. Philadelphia: University of Pennsylvania Press, 1984. (Full bibliography through the early 1980s.)

Richards, Jeffrey. *The Popes and the Papacy in the Early Middle Ages, 476–752*. London: Routledge and Kegan Paul, 1979.

MARTIN ARBAGI

LEO IX, POPE (1002–1054)

Pope Leo IX was born as Bruno of Egisheim in 1002 into a noble Alsatian family. His early studies were at the regional center in Lorraine of Toul, where, in 1017, he became a canon at the cathedral. Related to the German ruler Conrad II, he served prominently in the royal army in Lombardy in 1026. Conrad appointed him the bishop of Toul in 1027. Inspired by the monastic reform efforts of the tenth and eleventh centuries, Bruno sought to bring the fruits of these movements to such monasteries in his diocese as St. Aper, St. Dié, Moyenmourier, and Remiremont. Reform of the diocesan clergy also was the order of a number of the synods he held. His efforts to reinvigorate his diocese as the bishop of Toul would prepare him for extending these activities to the whole Western Church when he became pope.

The emperor Henry III, his cousin, selected him to be pope in 1048, after the brief reigns of Henry's previous two appointees, and he was crowned at St. Peters with the acclamation of the Roman people. From Lorraine he would summon such like-minded reformers as Humbert, abbot of Moyenmoutiers; Frederick of Liege, the future

Pope Stephen IX, and Hugh of Remiremont. Joining the men of the north would be such Italian churchmen as Peter Damian and Hildebrand, the future Pope Gregory VII, to become the nucleus of what became the college of cardinals. Aided by the efforts of these and other reforming churchmen, the new pope sought through the holding of numerous regional synods in Italy, Germany, and the kingdom of the French to curb the problems of simony, nicolaitism (opposition to celibacy), and violence against churchmen and the poor and to deal with numerous other problems facing the church in this period. Pope Leo presided over these gatherings and exhibited the presence of the papacy to a substantial portion of Western Christendom, quite unlike that of his predecessors. He extended papal protection to monasteries in a series of charters and in 1050 issued a canonical collection that drew on earlier rulings to support his papal activities. His aggressive attempt to deal with the problems faced by the church is also apparent in his personally leading an army into southern Italy in 1053, with the approval of Henry III, to oppose the Normans, a major preoccupation in the latter part of his papacy, because they were such a threat to the ecclesiastical and papal political holdings in the region. The Normans defeated the army of the pope in June of that year and held Leo captive. Incensed by this invasion into a region where the Byzantines had claims, Patriarch Michael Cerularius of Constantinople closed the Latin churches in his city. Humbert was dispatched from Rome to lead a papal embassy to try to solve the problem. The result was not the desired rapprochement but a mutual excommunication by Humbert and the patriarch and the beginning, in July of 1054, of the great schism between Rome and Constantinople, between the Western Church and the Eastern Church that continues to the present. Pope Leo, however, was not alive to witness the separation. He died in April of that year in Rome shortly after his release from Norman captivity.

John of Fécamp called Pope Leo "the marvelous pope" (*papa mirabilis*), a title that in many ways he well deserved. His papacy marks an important moment in the history of the church. His achievements provided the foundation for the Gregorian reform and the future papal monarchy. He brought the presence of the bishop of Rome to many parts of Western Christendom, in a manner comparable to the papal global travels in the late twentieth century. At the Council of Rheims, he used the title of universal to emphasize the scope of the power of the vicar of Peter. His very name demonstrates his awareness of the singular importance of his position, so clearly delineated in the Petrine doctrine of Leo the Great. But he also utilized the Donation of Constantine to justify his actions in southern Italy where he aggressively displayed his leadership in a new papal militarism that looked forward to the summons of the First Crusade

by Urban II in 1095. This aggressive leadership, however, also led to the great schism of 1054, a separation that has had a profound importance in the history of the church and of Europe as a whole. Few papacies, if any, have marked such a major change in the direction of the church.

See also **Conrad II; Gregory VII, Pope; Henry III; Damian, Peter; Urban II, Pope**

Further Reading

Analecta Bollandiana 25 (1906): 258–297 [Brussels, 1892ff.; continues *Acta Sanctorum*].

Brucker, P. P. *L'Alsace et l'Eglise au temps du pape saint Léon IX (Bruno d'Egisheim) 1002–1054*, 2 vols. Strasbourg: F. X. Le Roux, 1889.

Fliche, A. *La réforme grégorienne*, vol. 1 Louvain: Spicilegium sacrum louvaniense, 1924.

Leo IX, in *Acta Sanctorum*. London: Snowden, 164lff. April 11, pp. 641–673 [lives of saints by calendar].

Migne, Jaques-Paul, ed. *Patrologia Latina*, vol. 143. Paris: Migne, 1882, cols. 457–800.

Nicol, D. M. "Byzantium and the Papacy in the Eleventh Century." *Journal of Ecclesiastical History* 13 (1962): 1–20.

Tellenbach, Gerd. *The Church in Western Europe from the Tenth to the Early Twelfth Century*, trans. T. Reuter. Cambridge, England: Cambridge University Press, 1993.

DANIEL F. CALLAHAN

LEODEGUNDIA

In addition to Egeria, other Iberian women were involved in literary activities in the early Middle Ages. Some wrote letters of a more or less artistic nature. Some participated, in various ways, in producing texts. Such is the case with Leodegundia of Bobadilla, a Galician nun who wrote a *Codex regularum,* a Visigothic compendium that was widely read for centuries. Her manuscript is one of the oldest versions of this work, which typically contains the teachings and lives of the holy fathers of the church.

The manuscript, which was moved from Oviedo to the Escorial (a.I.13) in the sixteenth century, includes the following colophon: "O vos omnes qui legeritis hunc codicem mementote/clientula et exigua Leodigundia qui hunc scripsi in monasterio Bobatelle regnante Adefonso principe in era 950 quisquis pro alium oraver it semetipsum deum commendat." The manuscript appears to refer to King Alfonso II and presumably was written in 850 rather than 950.

Leodegundia's calligraphy has been highly praised. However, it is logical to assume she did more than copy the manuscript. In addition to the usual teachings and lives of the holy fathers, her version of the *Codex regularum* contains St. Jerome's letters to women friends, St. Augustine's letter to his sister Marceline, St. Leander's letters to his sister Florentina, and the lives of a number of women saints. That the additions have to do with women would seem not to be a coincidence. Neither would the fact that some of the women saints are of Spanish origin, and one, St. Melanie, is believed to have made her living by writing. Rather, this collection appears to be a mirror in which its author and her audience, the nuns of her convent, recognize themselves, a feminine adaptation of a masculine work.

Further Reading

Antolín, G. "Historia y descriptión de un *Codex regularum* del siglo LX (Eiblioteca del Escorial: a.1.13)." *Ciudad de Dios* 75 (1908), 23–33, 304–16, 460–71, 637–49.

Benedictines of Bouvert. *Colophons de manuscrits occidentaux des origines au XVIᵉ sie"le.* Fribourg, 1976, 36.

Pérez de Urbel, J. *Los monjes españoles en la Edad Media.* 2 vols. Madrid, 1934.

CRISTINA GONZÁLEZ

LEÓN, MOSÉS DE (1250–1305)

Spanish cabalist. *Cabala* means "receiving," referring to that which has been handed down by tradition. By the time of Mosés de León, the term was used to denote the mystic and esoteric teachings and practices of a growing body of mystical literature.

Little is known about his life; he settled in Guadalajara sometime between 1275 and 1280 and relocated to Avila sometime after 1291. Best known for his revelation of the *Zohar* (*The Book of Splendor or Enlightenment*) to fellow cabalists, he also composed twenty cabalistic works, only two of which have been printed: *Ha-Nephesh ha Hakhamah* (*The Wise Soul*) and *Shekel ha-Kodesh.* (*The Holy Shekel, or Weight*). By 1264 he undertook the study of Maimonides' Neoplatonic philosophy, a belief system that rejected a literal interpretation of Torah and sought to spiritualize its teachings.

While in Guadalajara, Mosés de León composed a mystical midrash, which he titled *Midrash ha-Ne'elam* (*Concealed, Esoteric Midrash*). A midrash is an analytical text that seeks to uncover the meaning of biblical passages, words and phrases and often employs philology, etymology, hermeneutics, homiletics, and imagination. This work represents the earliest stratum of the *Zohar* and contains commentary on parts of the Torah and the Book of Ruth. Between 1280 and 1286, he produced the main body of the *Zohar,* a mystical commentary on the Torah written in Aramaic, which is spoken by Rabbi Shim'on ben Yohai and his disciples as they ruminate over distinct passages of the Torah.

The text upon which the *Zohar* was purportedly based was said to have been sent from Israel to Catalonia, where it fell into the hands of Mosés de León of Guadalajara, who assumed the task of copying and disseminating different portions of it from the original manuscript. After the Mamluk conquest of the city of Acre (Israel) in 1291, Isaac, son of Samuel, was one of the few to escape to Spain. When he arrived in Toledo in 1305, he heard reports about the existence of a newly discovered midrash of Rabbi Shim'on ben Yohai. Ostensibly written in Israel, the manuscript was unfamiliar to Isaac. He sought out Mosés de León, who assured him that he owned the original ancient manuscript upon which the *Zohar* was based and offered to show it to him if he came to his residence in Avila. After their separation, Moses became ill and died in Arévalo on his way home. When Isaac learned of the news, he traveled to Avila, where he was told that the wife of provincial tax-collector Joseph of Avila was living. After Mosés de León's death, Joseph de Avila's wife had made a deal in which she would offer her son's hand in marriage to the daughter of Mosés de León's widow in exchange for the ancient manuscript. During Isaac's visit, Joseph de Avila's wife denied that her late husband had ever possessed such a book, insisting instead that Mosés de León had composed it himself.

Mosés de León attributed the work to Shim'on ben Yohai, a famous teacher of the second century A.D. known for his piety and mysticism. Ben Yohai lived in Israel, where he reportedly spent twelve years in seclusion in a cave. After his death, his book was either hidden away or secretly transmitted from master to disciple. When Mosés de León began circulating booklets among his friends containing previously unknown teachings and tales, he claimed to be a mere scribe copying from an ancient book of wisdom. In addition, he distributed portions of the book rather than entire copies. No complete manuscript of the work has ever been found. When the *Zohar* was first printed in Italy in the fifteenth century, the editors combined several manuscripts to produce a complete text. Other manuscripts located later were added to an additional volume which was printed later. Today, most standard editions comprise some 1,100 leaves consisting of at least two dozen separate compositions.

The *Zohar* consists of a mystical commentary on the Pentateuch, describing how God—referred to by the cabalists as *Ein Sof* (the infinite, endless)—rules the universe through the Ten *Sefirot* (Ten Spheres). In other cabalistic texts, the sefirot are often organized in the form of a hierarchy of divine emanations from the apex of the Godhead with *Keter* or *Da'at* (the highest aspect of God) being followed by *Hokhmah* and *Binah* (divine wisdom and understanding respectively). Ein Sof is rarely emphasized in the *Zohar.* Instead, the work focuses on the sefirot as the manifestations of Ein Sof, its mystical attributes in which God thinks, feels, and responds to the human realm. The characters include Rabbi Shim'on and his comrades, biblical figures and the sefirot. At times the distinction between the latter two is ambiguous. Throughout the work, the *Zohar* never loses sight of its goal: to create a mystical commentary on the Torah in which God is simultaneously revealed and concealed. To study Torah is to meditate on the name of God. As Daniel C. Matt explains, "*Zohar* is an adventure, a challenge to the normal workings of consciousness. It dares you to examine your usual ways of making sense, your assumptions about tradition, God, and self. Textual analysis is essential, but you must engage *Zohar* and cultivate a taste for its multiple layers of meaning. It is tempting and safe to reduce the symbols to a familiar scheme: psychological, historical, literary, or religious. But do not forfeit wonder."

The authorship of the text, its method of composition and its use of sources (contemporary or ancient) have remained polemical among scholars. Among the most representative opinions in this controversy are Jellinek, Graetz, Scholem, and Giller. Jellinek concluded that many of the passages in the *Zohar* were derived from ancient sources and that Mosés de León was at least one of the authors of the work. Graetz concurred with Jellinek on the nature of its sources, but believed that the text represented a forgery executed entirely by Mosés de León. Scholem argued that the text was purely a product of the thirteenth century and was based on medieval Jewish Neoplatonism and Gnosticism. For him, the author and the translator were one and the same. More recent scholarship in the tradition of Giller and Liebes tends to view the *Zohar* as the product of a group collaboration among thinkers who grappled with cabalistic doctrine. Mosés de León was a main figure in this group but is not the sole author.

Regarding the overall structure of the *Zohar*, there is some consensus among scholars. The work is divided into distinct sections or strata, each of which has its own literary nature and mystical doctrines which are unique to it. The *Midrash ha-Ne'elam* is the earliest and is followed by the long midrash on the Torah and another group of compositions resembling it; the *Tiqqunei ha-Zohar* (*Embellishments on the Zohar*) and the *Ra'aya Meheimna* (*The Faithful Shepherd*) constitute another stratum. The *Midrash ha-Ne'elam* establishes an organizing fulcrum for the entire work in creating a protagonist Shim'on bar Yohai who does not appear until later. Until his subsequent appearance in the text, the teachings are conveyed by other rabbis from the second century with no single dominant figure. Further, there is a pattern of development in which certain ideas and themes are developed and reach their culmination over the course of the work's composition.

The *Zohar* was not accepted immediately as an ancient work. Students of Rabbi Solomon ibn Adret of Barcelona treated it with restraint. In 1340, the philosopher and cabalist Joseph ibn Waqqar warned about the preponderance of errors in the book. Slowly,

its antiquity became accepted by cabalists, but as late as the mid-fifteenth century was not read or circulated except in small circles. It did not become the Bible of the Cabalah movement until after the Jewish expulsion from Spain in 1492. After 1530, Safed (Israel) gained importance as a meeting place for cabalists. Among them was Mosés Cordovero who wrote two systematic books based on the *Zohar*, along with an extensive commentary. Isaac Luria developed a new system based on Cabalah that relied heavily on portions of the *Zohar*. The trend of mystical-ethical literature emerging from this circle helped popularize the *Zohar*'s teachings as did the messianic fervor that encouraged the dissemination of its enigmas. If early qabbalists had drawn an analogy between spread of Cabalah and the redemption of Israel, in the sixteenth century, studying the *Zohar* became elevated to the level of a divine command, equal in importance to studying the Bible and the Talmud. Today, the *Zohar* retains its distinction as the fundamental text of cabalistic thought.

See also **Ibn Adret, Solomon; Maimonides**

Further Reading

Fine, L. *Essential Papers on Kabbalah.* New York, 1995.
Giller, P. *Reading the Zohar: The Sacred Text of the Kabbalah.* Oxford, 2001.
Holtz, B. (ed.) *Back to the Sources: Reading the Classic Jewish Texts.* New York, 1984.
Liebes, Y. *Studies in the Zohar.* Trans. A. Schwartz, St. Nakache, and P. Peli. Albany, N.Y., 1993.
Matt, D. C. (ed.) *Zoliar: Book of Enlightenment.* New York, 1983. 38.

MATTHEW B. RADEN

LÉONIN (Leoninus; fl. 1154–ca. 1201)

Anonymous 4's epithet *optimus organista* ("the best singer/improviser/composer/compiler/notator of organum") assured Léonin a significant place in music history long before any convincing identification of the person was suggested. Since he was responsible for the new polyphonic repertory of the cathedral of Notre-Dame in Paris in the decades after its founding in the 1160s, his place was evidently among the dignitaries of its ecclesiastical hierarchy, but the familiar use of the Latin diminutive of his name, as "Magister Leoninus," in the theoretical treatise of Anonymous 4—the only source for information on his considerable musical achievement—long seemed to belie this. Anonymous 4 credited Léonin with the *Magnus liber organi de gradali et antifonario* some one hundred years after its compilation, a fact that recommends cautious use of his testimony and the need for independent verification. Three major manuscript sources (*W1*, *F*, and *W2*) confirm a repertory of organum that fits Anonymous 4's description of a *Magnus liber organi*, and the melodies of the plainchant that form the basis of that organum match notated plainchant sources used at Notre-Dame. Still, this does not clarify what Léonin's role may have been in making such a book. *Optimus organista* suggests a youthful man in full voice, while the diminutive implies a beloved elder whose practical contributions may have been overshadowed by his administrative usefulness—two very different "portraits" of the individual. It may not have been so much by his initiative as by his approval that modal rhythm became the primary innovation of the Notre-Dame School, and there is no certain evidence that such rhythm was subject to systematic theoretical or notational principles during his lifetime.

Archival evidence only recently brought to light establishes a probable identity for Anonymous 4's Magister Leoninus as Magister Leoninus presbyter, a canon active in the affairs of the cathedral during the late 12th century and a Latin poet whose hexametric Old Testament commentary, *Hystorie sacre gestas ab origine mundi*, was long praised after his death. There is, however, no document, except possibly the treatise of Anonymous 4, to substantiate the involvement of Leoninus presbyter with music at all, a striking omission given the significance of the *Magnus liber organi* and the stature of the poet. Thus, while the search for independent, corroborating evidence continues, the hypothesis that Leonin, known also as Magister Leoninus presbyter, was responsible for the vanguard of virtually a new era in music with the *Magnus liber organi* should remain compelling.

See also **Pérotin**

Further Reading

Reckow, Fritz. *Der Musiktraktat des Anonymus 4.* Wiesbaden: Steiner, 1967.
Wright, Craig. "Leoninus, Poet and Musician," *Journal of the American Musicological Society* 39 (1986): 1–35.

SANDRA PINEGAR

LEOVIGILD (d. 586)

The brother of Liuva I (r. 568–72/3), who made him coruler in 569, with responsibility for the south and center of the Iberian Peninsula, Leovigild proved to be perhaps the greatest of the kings of Visigothic Spain. Even those who opposed his religious policies, such as Isidore of Seville and John of Biclaro, admired his military capacity and achievements. At the time of his accession the kingdom was threatened by Frankish aggression from the north and Byzantine aggression in the southeast. Much of the north of the peninsula and various areas in the south, including the city of Córdoba, had broken free of royal control. An independent Suevic kingdom survived in the northwest. Leo-vigild's initial campaigns were directed against the Byzantine enclave, and he regained Sidonia and Málaga. In 572, he reimposed Visigothic rule on Córdoba. Following the death of his brother Liuva I, Leovigild turned his attention northward, and in a series of campaigns between 573 and 577 made himself master of most of the north of the peninsula, from the Rioja to the frontiers of the Suevic kingdom, whose ruler Miro became tributary to him. In the peaceful years of 578 and 579, the king established the new town of Recco-polis, named after his younger son, and also set up his elder son Hermenegild in Seville as coruler with responsibility for the south. This failed when Hermenegild rebelled, at the instigation of Leovigild's second wife, Goisuintha, widow of the former Visigothic king Athanagild (r. 554–568). Initially Leovigild made no move to curtail his son's independence, and in 581 launched a campaign northward to contain the Basques. There he founded another new town, called Victoriacum (probably Olite in Navarre). Only when an alliance between Hermenegild and the Byzantines developed, symbolized by the former's conversion to Catholicism, did Leovigild act. In 583 he took Mérida and Seville, and in 584 Córdoba, where Hermenegild was captured. After the suppression of the revolt in the south, Leovigild overran the Suevic kingdom in the northwest, where the son of his former ally Miro had recently been overthrown by a usurper. With this achieved, the Basques temporarily pacified, and a Frankish invasion of the province of Narbonensis repelled in 585, Leovigild had achieved a military reunification of the Visigothic kingdom in the peninsula and Septimania. To turn this into a genuine political and cultural unification required the solution of the theological division between Arians and Catholics, which had provided a context for factionalism and local power struggles. This problem Leovigild hoped to tackle by holding a council in Toledo in 580 with the aim of modifying the theological tenets of Arianism, to make this view of the Trinity more acceptable. In the outcome, the polarization of religious and political opinion following the conversion of Hermenegild in 582 made such a compromise unworkable. The only solution was the acceptance by all of the uncompromising doctrinal stand of the Catholics. It is reported in Gregory of Tours's *histories* that Leovigild himself secretly converted prior to his death in 586, but the public resolution of the issue was left to his heir Reccared.

Further Reading

Collins, R. "Mérida and Toledo, 550–585." In Visigothic Spain: New Approaches. Ed. E. James: Oxford, 1980. 189–219.
Stroheker, K. F. "Leovigild. Aus einer Wendezeit westgotischer Geschichte," Die Welt als Geschichte 5 (1939), 446–485.
Thompson, E. A. The Goths in Spain. Oxford, 1969, 57–91.

ROGER COLLINS

LEVI BEN GERSHOM (GERSONIDES) (1288–1344)

Although he was born and lived his entire life in then French Provence, Gersonides was the heir of the Spanish Hebrew-Arabic medieval culture. Deeply influenced by Averroës and Maimonides in philosophy and by Abraham ibn Ezra in biblical exegesis, Gersonides not only excelled in both these areas but also made important contributions to astronomy and mathematics. Besides inventing or improving upon several astronomical observational instruments, he compiled his own astronomical tables, made many of his own observations, and engaged in a critical analysis of several of Ptolemy's hypotheses. In mathematics he wrote a commentary on parts of Euclid's *Elements* and a treatise on trigonometry.

But it was in philosophy and biblical exegesis that Gersonides was most influential. Continuing the tradition of the Córdoban philosopher Averroës, Gersonides wrote many supercommentaries on Averroës's commentaries on Aristotle, in which he exhibited a critical and independent approach to both his predecessors. But it is *The Wars of the Lord* that is his most important philosophical work. In this long treatise most of the topics of medieval philosophy and science are discussed in detail and with acuity. Some of his more novel or radical conclusions were (1) the individual human intellect is immortal (contrary to Averroës); (2) God does not have knowledge of particular future contingent events (contrary to Maimonides); (3) yet there is divine providence over deserving individuals; (4) the universe was divinely created out of an eternal shapeless body (contrary to Averroës and Maimonides); (5) although it has a beginning, the universe is indestructible (contrary to Aristotle).

Whereas *The Wars of the Lord* elicited considerable criticism from his coreligionists, Gersonides' commentaries upon the Bible were widely studied, even among nonphilosophical Jews; his *Commentary on Job* was particularly popular. This is remarkable because in these commentaries Gersonides pulls no punches: the ideas of *The Wars of the Lord* are repeated or assumed, and there is no effort to mute their impact. He did not obey Averroës's and Maimonides' rule that the teaching of philosophy ought to be reserved for the philosophers alone. In his *Commentary on Job*, for example, he has each character represent a distinct philosophical position on the question of divine providence. These various positions are philosophically analyzed, and eventually one emerges as the true solution to Job's predicament. Thus, the Book of Job is transformed into a Platonic dialogue.

See also **Averroës, Abu 'L-Walīd Muhammad B. Ahmad B. Rushd; Gregory of Tours; Isidore of Seville, Saint**

Further Reading

Levi ben Gershom. *The Wars of the Lord.* 2 vols. Trans. Seymour Feldman. Phildelphia, 1984–87. Touati, C. *La Pensée philosophique et théologique de Gersonide.* Paris, 1974.

SEYMOUR FELDMAN

LIMBOURG BROTHERS (fl. late 14th–early 15th c.)

Three brothers (Paul, Jean, and Herman), nephews of the painter Jean Malouel, came to Paris from Nijmegen in the Low Countries as youths to serve as apprentices under a goldsmith but had to leave because of the plague. Imprisoned on their way home in 1399, they were ransomed by Philip the Bold, duke of Burgundy, for whom they illuminated a Bible, now lost, between 1400 and 1404. They may have been in the service of John, duke of Berry, by 1405; for him, they produced their most notable works: miniatures in the *Très Belles Heures de*

Limbourg Brothers. January: The Feast of the Duke of Berry. Illustrated manuscript page from *Les Très Riches Heures de Duc de Berry*, 1416. Ms. 65; fol. 1V. Photo: R.G. Ojeda. © Réunion des Musées Nationaux/Art Resource, New York.

Notre Dame (B.N. n.a. lat. 3093), a miniature of the duke of Berry embarking on a journey in the *Petites Heures* (B.N. lat. 18014), some scenes in *grisaille* for a *Bible historiale* (B.N. fr. 166), the illuminations of the *Belles Heures* (New York, The Cloisters), and, most notably, miniatures in the *Très Riches Heures* (Chantilly, Musée Condé), which remained unfinished in 1416, when all three brothers and their patron appear to have died in an epidemic.

Their miniatures, particularly in the *Très Riches Heures*, are representative of the height of the International Gothic style in France, combining courtly elegance, sumptuous coloration, and a mixture of fanciful and remarkably naturalistic landscape settings. Although attempts have been made to define the style of each of the brothers, these have not always been successful, and they are generally regarded to have participated collectively on their productions.

See also **John, Duke of Berry; Philip the Bold**

Further Reading

Longnon, Jean, and Raymond Cazelles. *The Très Riches Heures of Jean, Duke of Berry*. New York: Braziller, 1969.
Meiss, Millard. *French Painting in the Time of Jean de Berry: The Limbourgs and Their Contemporaries*. 2 vols. New York: Braziller, 1974.
——, and Elizabeth H. Beatson. *The Belles Heures of Jean, Duke of Berry*. New York: Braziller, 1974.

ROBERT G. CALKINS

LIUDPRAND OF CREMONA
(c. 920–972)

Liudprand (Liutprand, Liuzo) was bishop of Cremona (961–972) and also a historian and diplomat. He was born in Pavia in northern Italy into a wealthy family who may have been either merchants or urban aristocrats. His father (who died young) and stepfather had served Hugh of Aries, king of Italy, as diplomats. Liudprand himself went to Constantinople, capital of the Byzantine (eastern Roman) empire, in 949 during the reign of Constantine VII (called Porphyrogenitus) on a mission for Hugh's successor, Berengar of Ivrea. Liudprand fell out with Berengar and went into exile at the court of Otto I, duke of Saxony. There, Liudprand met Recemund, bishop of Elvira in Muslim Spain, who suggested that Liudprand write a history of their time. The result was *Antapodosis*. Liudprand rose in Otto's favor, was granted the see of Cremona, and accompanied Otto on an expedition to Italy that resulted in Otto's coronation as emperor in February 962. Liudprand went on at least two missions to Constantinople on behalf of Otto: in 960 (when he seems not to have reached Constantinople); and in 968–969, during the reign of Nicephorus II Phocas, to arrange a marriage with a Byzantine princess for Otto's son, Otto II. The second embassy was a miserable failure, but later Nicephorus's successor, John I Tzimisces, did consent to a match between Otto II and Theophano. Liudprand probably went to Constantinople a fourth time in 972 (though he seems to have been reluctant to do so, possibly because of ill health) to help escort Theophano to the west; and apparently he died at some point during that trip.

Liudprand's principal works are *Antapodosis* (translated into English as *Tit for Tat* or *The Book of Retribution*); *Relatio de legatio Constantinopolitana* (*Report on the Embassy to Constantinople*), i.e., the embassy of 968–969; and *Liber de rebus gestibus Ottonis* (*The Deeds of Otto*), i.e., Otto I. Recent scholarship (Bischoff 1984) has also identified Liudprand as author of a sermon given at Easter c. 960.

Antapodosis is a gossipy history running from 887 to 949. It forms our principal guide to northern and central Italy during that confused period and contains much information on other areas: Germany, Burgundy, southern Italy, and the Byzantine empire—especially Constantinople. *Antapodosis* was written to show that the major figures in Italian politics of the first half of the tenth century whom Liudprand disliked—notably Berengar of Ivrea and his wife, Willa—eventually met bad ends. Though an excellent storyteller, Liudprand obviously does not pretend to be impartial.

Relatio is bitterly anti-Byzantine. It is often cited to show the growing estrangement of the Latin west from Byzantium but in fact demonstrates no such thing. Liudprand's tirades against the "Greeks" are a result of the hostile and demeaning treatment he received at the hands of Emperor Nicephorus. There is no trace of anti-Greek sentiment in *Antapodosis*, which gives a good-natured account of Liudprand's mission of 949. The fascinating narrative and Liudprand's caustic humor compensate for the whining tone of *Relatio*.

The Deeds of Otto is a record not of the great Saxon ruler's entire reign (Liudprand died a year before Otto), but of one incident: the deposition of Pope John XII by Otto in 963.

Despite his admiration for and devotion to Otto and the Saxons, Liudprand is a figure essentially centered on the Mediterranean. He claimed to know Greek and interlarded his work with Greek words (followed by their Latin translations). Although some scholars consider this merely a display of pedantry, most now believe that Liudprand did know the spoken Byzantine tongue of his day (which was closer to modern than to classical Greek), and perhaps some classical or *koiné* Greek as well. Although Liudprand had the requisite education and social background for a diplomat, his effectiveness was vitiated by his explosive temper (amply demonstrated in *Legatio*) and his acerbic disposition (of which *Antapodosis* is a prime example). His urbane, witty, sarcastic, and occasionally ribald style makes him sound curiously modern, especially if one reads him in a good translation.

See also **Otto I; Otto II**

Further Reading

Editions

Bischoff, Bernard. "Einer Osterpredigt Liudprands von Cremona (um 960)." In *Anecdota novissima: Texte des vierten bis sechzehnten Jahrhunderts—Quellen und Untersuchungen zur lateinischen Philologie des Mittelalters*, Vol. 7. Stuttgart, 1984, pp. 93–100. (First publication of the text of an Easter sermon by Liudprand, previously anonymous, c. 960.)

Liudprand of Cremona. *Opera omnia Liudprandi Cremonensis*, ed. Paolo Chiesa. Corpus Christianorum. Continuatio Mediaevalis. Turnholti: Brepois, 1998.

Translatio Sanctae Hymeri, ed. Ferdinand Ughelli. Itala Sacra, 4. Rome: Vitale Mascardi, 1592, cols. 797–798. (Includes a notice of Liudprand's death. Reprinted in Monumenta Germaniae Historica, Scriptorum, 3. Hannover and Leipzig: Hanische Buchhandlung, 1839, pp. 266–267, note 23.)

Translations

Relatio de Legatio Constantinopolitana, ed., trans., intro., and commentary by Brian Scott. Reading Medieval and Renaissance Texts. Bristol: Bristol Classical Press, 1993. (With textual notes.)

The Works of Liudprand of Cremona, trans. and intro. F. A. Wright. Broadway Medieval Library. London: Routledge, 1930. (Classic English translation. Includes *Translatio Hymeri* but not the Easter Sermon. Wright substitutes French for the Greek words in the original, creating much the same effect.)

Critical Studies

Halphen, Louis. "The Kingdom of Burgundy." In *The Cambridge Medieval History*, Vol. 3, *Germany and the Western Empire*. Cambridge: Cambridge University Press, 1922, ch. 6.

Hiestand, Rudolf. *Byzanz und das Regnum italicum im 10. Jahrhundert*. Geist und Werke zu Zeit. Zurich: Fretz and Wasmuth, 1964.

Koder, Johannes, and Thomas Weber. *Liutprand von Cremona in Konstantinopel*. Herausgegeben von der Kommission für Fühchristliche und Östkirchliche Kunst der Österreichischen Akademie der Wissenschaften und vom Institut für Byzantinistik und Neograzistik der Universität Wien, 13. Vienna: Verlag der Österreichischen Akademie der Wissenschaften, 1980. (Two brief monographs: one is on Liudprand's knowledge of Greek, with a glossary of all Greek words in his works; the second essay uses Liudprand as a source for the diet of the period in Byzantium and the west.)

Kreutz, Barbara. *Before the Normans: Southern Italy in the Ninth and Tenth Centuries*. Philadelphia: University of Pennsylvania Press, 1991.

Leyser, Karl. "Ends and Means in Liudprand of Cremona." In *Byzantium and the West, c. 850–c. 1200: Proceedings of the XVIII Spring Symposium of Byzantine Studies, Oxford, 30th March–1st April 1984*, ed. J. D. Howard-Johnston. Amsterdam: Adolf Hakkert, 1988, pp. 119–143. (Survey in English of Liudprand's work that also summarizes scholarship.)

Lintzel, M. *Studien über Liudprand von Cremona*. Historische Studien, 3. 1933. (A standard monograph.)

Previté-Orton, Charles. "Italy in the Tenth Century." In *The Cambridge Medieval History,* Vol. 3, *Germany and the Western Empire.* Cambridge: Cambridge University Press, 1922, ch. 7.

Rentschler, Michael. *Liudprand von Cremona: Eine Studie zum öst-westlichen Kulturgefälle im Mittelalter.* Frankfurter Wissenschaftliche Beiträge, 14. Frankfurt: Vittorio Klosrermann, 1981.

Sutherland, J. N. "The Idea of Revenge in Lombard Society in the Eighth and Tenth Centuries: The Cases of Paul the Deacon and Liudprand of Cremona." *Speculum*, 50, 1975, pp. 391–410 (Revenge is a major theme in *Antapodosis*.)

Martin Arbagi

LLULL, RAMÓN (1232/3–1316)

Catalan lay missionary, philosopher, mystic, poet, and novelist, Ramón Llull was one of the creators of literary Catalan; the first European to write philosophy and theology in a vernacular tongue; the first to write prose novels on contemporary themes; and the founder of a combinatory "art" that was a distant forerunner of computer science. He wrote some 265 works in Catalan, Latin, Arabic (none of these last have been preserved), and perhaps Provençal. In addition we have medieval translations of his works into Spanish, French, and Italian.

Life

Born on the island of Mallorca (modern-day Majorca), which had only recently been reconquered (at the end of 1229), and brought up in a wealthy family in a colonial situation, amid a still considerable Muslim population (perhaps a third of the entire population of the island), Llull's youth was that of a courtier who dabbled in troubadour verse. He married, had two children, and was appointed seneschal to the future Jaume II of Mallorca. Then, in 1263, repeated visions of the Crucifixion made him decide to dedicate his life to the service of Christ, and specifically to carrying out three aims: to try to convert Muslims even if it meant risking his life; to "write a book, the best in the world, against the errors of unbelievers"; and to found monasteries for the teaching of languages to missionaries. Llull bought a Muslim slave in order to learn Arabic and began nine years of study not only of that language, but also of Latin, philosophy, theology, and logic, as well as a certain amount of law, medicine (surely in Montpellier), and astronomy. At the end of this period he wrote a compendium of Al-Ghazālī's logic and the *Llibre de contemplació en Déu* (Book of Contemplation), a vast work combining semi-mystic effusions with the germs of most of his later thought. The changing methodological tactics of the work, however, were finally resolved on Mount Randa in Mallorca, where, after a week's meditation, "The Lord suddenly illuminated his mind, giving him the form and method for writing the aforementioned book against the errors of the unbelievers." (See below for *Contemporary Life* from which this and other passages are quoted.) This "form and method" was the art, of which he now wrote the first work (*Ars compendiosa inveniendi veritatem*, c. 1274), thereby fulfilling the second of his three aims. The third was soon (1276) to be fulfilled with the founding of the monastery of Miramar on the northwest coast of Mallorca for the teaching of Arabic to thirteen Franciscan missionaries.

From this point on, apart from his feverish literary activity, Llull's life became one of ceaseless travel in an attempt to interest the world in his missionary projects. Using Montpellier as a base (it then formed part of the kingdom of Mallorca), he visited Paris four times, where he lectured at the university and had audiences with the king (Philippe IV the Fair, nephew of his patron, Jaume II of Mallorca); he traveled to Italy some six times (to Genoa, where he was in contact with rich merchants, to Pisa, to Rome, where he had audiences with at least three popes, to Naples, and near the end of his life to Sicily); he went three times to North Africa (Tunis and Bougie [modern-day Bejaïa]), thereby fulfilling the first of his three proseltyzing aims; and once to Cyprus (from where he visited the Turkish port of Ayas, and perhaps Jerusalem). Llull's lack of success was typical for an idealist approaching practical politicians with schemes for the betterment of mankind. As he himself admitted in a work of the same title, he was everywhere treated as a *phantasticus*, or as he put it in earlier works, "Ramon lo Foll." And in a touching passage from the poem *Desconhort* (1295), he complained that people read his art "like a cat passing rapidly over hot coals." But these epithets and complaints must not make us forget that he did manage to have the ear of kings and popes, that he presented them with political tracts that recent research has shown to have been far more realistic than was formerly believed. Nor must we forget that on his last trip to Paris, overcoming at last the incomprehensions attendant on his former attempts to teach his peculiar system there, Llull received (1310–1311) letters of commendation from Philippe IV and the chancellor of the university, as well as a document in which forty masters and bachelors in arts and medicine approved of Llull's lectures in *Ars brevis*. The Council of Vienne (1311–1312) subsequently endorsed his proposal for the founding of schools of Oriental languages.

After Llull's discovery of the methodology of the art, his literary and philosophical production can be divided into three periods.

The Quaternary Phase (ca. 1274–1289). This was so called because the basic components of the art (divine attributes, relative principles, and elements) appear in multiples of four. The first work of the art, *Ars compen-diosa inveniendi veritatem*, was rapidly accompanied by a series of satellite works explaining it and showing the other fields to which it could be applied. Among these, the most important was *Llibre del gentil e dels tres savis* (Book of the Gentile and the Three Wise Men), Llull's principal apologetic work. It was also around this same time that Llull wrote a pedagogical tract for his son, *Doctrina pueril*, and a manual of knighthood, the *Llibre de l'orde de cavalleria* (*Book of the Order of Chivalry*), destined to become popular in its French translation, and later translated into English by William Caxton. It was also during this time (1283) that he wrote his first didactic novel, *Blaquerna* (this seems to have been the original form of the name, and not the later *Blanquerna*), which included his most famous mystic work, the *Llibre d'amic e amat* (*Book of the Lover and the Beloved*).

In the same year of 1283, Llull decided to refashion many minor aspects of his system in a new version called *Ars demonstrativa*, around which he wrote a new cycle of explicative and satellite works. It was during this period that he wrote his second didactic novel, *Félix o El libre de meravelles* (Felix, or the Book of Wonders), which includes the political animal fable, *Llibre de les baèsties* (*Book of the Beasts*).

The Ternary Phase (1290–1308). In this phase the principles of the art appear in multiples of three (and the four elements disappear as one of its foundations). Because of "the weakness of human intellect" that Llull encountered on his first trip to Paris, he reduced the number of figures with which his system invariably began from twelve (or sixteen) to four, and he removed all algebraic notation from the actual discourse of the art. This phase begins not with a single work surrounded by satellites, but with twin works: *Ars inventiva verïtatis* which, as Llull says, treats *ciència* or knowledge, and *Ars amativa* which treats *amància* or love of God; it ends with the final formulation of his system in *Ars generalis ultima* (1305–1308), and in shorter form in *Ars brevis* (1308). This period is rich in important works, among which one might mention the immense encyclopedia, *Arbre de ciència* (Tree of Science, 1295–1296), as well as his principal work on logic, epistemology, and politics, *Logica nova* (1303), *Liber de ascensu et descensu intellectus* (1305), and *Liber de fine* (also 1305).

The Postart Phase (1308–1315). With the definitive formulation of his system now out of the way, Llull is free to concentrate on specific logical and epistemological topics, many directed toward his campaign against the Parisian "Averröists" while on his last trip there (1309–1311). It was at the end of this stay that he dictated what has come to be known in its English translation as *Contemporary Life*. He also became more and more involved in the art of preaching, writing a vast *Summa sermonum* in Mallorca (1312–1313).

Llull's last works are dated from Tunis, December 1315, after which he disappears from history. He probably died early the following year, either there on the ship returning to his native Mallorca, or on the island itself, where he is buried. The story of his martyrdom (he was stoned to death) is a legend bolstered by pious falsifications in the early seventeenth century, in which an earlier (1307) stoning in Bejaï'a was transposed and made into the cause of his death.

Thought and Influence

The unusual nature of Llull's system and of his thought in general is due to his insistence that any apologetic system that hoped to persuade Muslims and Jews would have to abandon the use of Scripture, which only caused endless discussions over validity and interpretation, and try to prove the articles of the Christian faith, above all those of the Trinity and Incarnation that Muslims and Jews found most difficult to accept. The first consideration forced Llull to forge an abstract system that could stand completely by itself. This was the art, each work of which begins with a series of concepts distributed amid geometric figures, and then proceeds to describe the correct method of combining these concepts. The point was to display the basic structure of reality, which, noted Llull, begins with the attributes of God, goodness, greatness, eternity, and so forth, which are not static but unfold into three correlatives of action. Thus *bonitas* (goodness) unfolds into an agent (*bonificativum*) and a patient (*bonificabile*), and the act joining them (*bonificare*). Their necessary activity *ad intra* produces the Trinity, and their: contingent activity *ad extra* the act of creation. Moreover, this triad of action is then reproduced at every level of creation, so that, for instance, man's intellect is composed of *intellectivum*, *intelligibile*, and *intelligere*, and fire of *ignificativum*, *ignificabile*, and *ignificare*.

This metaphysics of action exerted a strong influence on Nicholas of Cusa, as did the combinatorial art on Giordano Bruno and Gottfried Wilhelm Leibniz. But at the same time, Llull's system was taken over by alchemists, and eventually over one hundred such works were falsely attributed to him. This, plus his self-image as a *phantasticus*, the unusual nature of his system, and the fact that his attempts to prove the articles of the faith made him suspect to the Inquisition, helped propagate the image of a peculiar, countercultural figure.

Llull's influence in the Iberian Peninsula was less hetorodox and countercultural than in the rest of Europe. Aside from the fifteenth-century Llullist schools of Mallorca and Barcelona, there were a certain number of Castilian translations of his works done in the later

Middle Ages, although interest in him seems to have been of a dispersed, sporadic nature, at least until the beginning of the sixteenth century. Then we find a Lullist school at Valencia (where some of his works were published), the chief figure of which was the humanist Alonso de Proaza. He in turn was in contact with Cardinal Francisco Jiménez de Cisneros, who in his foundation in 1508 of the University of Alcalá de Henares, instituted a chair of Lullian philosophy and theology. Later in the century, Felipe II was an admirer of Llull, as was his chief architect, Juan de Herrera, who not only wrote a *Tratado del cuerpo cúbico* based on Llull's art, but in 1582 founded a mathematical-philosophical academy in Madrid in whose program the art was to have a prominent place.

Literary Works

Llull's most unusual literary feature is that he dared to modify the conventional genres of contemporary romance tradition to fit his own didactic needs. Llull first attempted the novel, in the *Libre de Evast e Blaquerna* (Book of Evast and Blaquerna, 1283), and *Félix o El libre de meravelles* (Felix, or the Book of Wonders, 1288) he recounted stories morally useful to his readers. He similarly adjusted the narrative wrapping of an early apologetical work, the *Llibre del gentil e dels tres savis* (Book of the Gentile and the Three Wise Men), in which an unbeliever struggles to find the truth and finally embraces the faith.

The plot of *Blaquerna* follows the outline of a hero's biography; the main character is endowed with the mental strength permitting him to overcome the obstacles in the way of his becoming a contemplative hermit. These "obstacles" are the ties that link a man to society: a family, a religious order, a diocese, and the whole of Christianity ruled by the pope. Blaquerna abandons his parents, Evast and Aloma, and convinces his bride, Natana, to become an exemplary nun, whereupon he enters a monastery and becomes a reforming abbot who is then elected bishop. Blaquerna improves the spiritual life of his diocese and as a result is elected pope; from Rome Blaquerna manages to reorganize the world and to change the moral attitudes of people. Finally he renounces the papacy and becomes the perfect hermit, which permits him to write *Llibre d'amic e amat* (*Book of the Lover and the Beloved*), a collection of short mystical proverbs lyrically embellished and artistically constructed.

The *Book of Wonders* follows the spiritual journey of Felix through events that cause him "wonder" because they seem to be contrary to God's will, and that allow various hermits and philosophers to explain the fundamental points of Christian knowledge about God, angels, the heavens, the elements, plants, minerals, animals, man, paradise, and hell. Like *Blaquerna,* this novel offers plenty of morally meaningful exempla, but unlike the earlier work, it betrays considerable pessimism about the capacity of mankind to better its moral behavior. One chapter of *Félix* has become particularly famous: *Llibre de les baèsties* (*Book of the Beasts*), a Llullian adaptation of the old Iranian *Book of Kalila and Dimna* with some references to the French *Roman de Renard.*

In search of a literary vehicle for his message, Llull attempted autobiography, so *Desconhort* (1295) and *Cant de Ramon* (1300), two splendid lyric poems, explain from a personal point of view the disappointments and failures of his career. In the process Llull himself becomes a new literary character: a poor, old, and despised man who has devoted his life to revealing a treasury of knowledge, an art given to him by God. A short late prose work, *Phantasticus* (1311), offers the most complete picture of this personage, whom, as was noted above, he sometimes called "Ramon lo Foll."

Plant de la Verge and *Llibre de Santa Maria,* both probably written between 1290 and 1293, are two pieces of devotional literature: the former, in verse, is a moving description of Christ's Passion, the latter, in prose, an unusual application of the Llullian art to a prayer to the Virgin Mary. Another treatise with rich literary contents is the *Arbre de filosofia d'amor* (*Tree of Philosophy of Love,* 1289), which encloses a short, touching mystical novel.

In his immense encyclopedia of 1295–1296, the (*Arbre de ciència*) (Tree of Science) Llull included a little *Arbre exemplifical* (Tree of Examples), in which a preacher could find the way to "translate science into exemplary literature." This work is the first of Llull's contributions to homiletics, a trend that later developed both into theoretical treatises—*Rhetorica nova* (1302), *Liber de praedicatione* (1304), *Ars brevis pradicationis* (1313)—and sermon writing. Llull in later years, in fact, put aside romance literary genres and devoted himself to sermon collections; the most important being *Summa sermonum* of 1312–1313, which offers an unusual model for preaching, since Llull wanted to persuade lay audiences intellectually rather than to touch their hearts with moving anecdotes.

See also **Caxton, William; Nicholas of Cusa; Philip IV the Fair**

Further Reading

Bonner, A., and Badia, L. *Ramon Llull: Vida, pensament i obra literària.* Barcelona, 1988.
Carreras y Artau, T., and J. *Historia de la filosofía espaſola: Filosofía cristiana de los siglo XIII al XV.* 2 vols. Madrid, 1939–43.
Hillgarth, J. N. *Ramon Lull and Lullism in Fourteenth-Century France.* Oxford, 1971.
Llull, R. *Obres essencials.* 2 vols. Barcelona, 1957–60.
——. *Selected Works of Ramon Llull* (*1232–1316*). 2 vols. Ed. A. Bonner. Princeton, N.J., 1985. Catalan version in *Obres selectes de Ramon Llull* (*1232–1316*). 2 vols. Majorca, 1989.

ANTHONY BONNER AND LOLA BADÍA

LOCHNER, STEFAN (1400/1410–1451)

The most important painter of the early Cologne school of painting, Lochner is the only artist whose name can be associated with individual works. However, the entire attribution of his body of works is based on Albrecht Dürer's 1530 diary entry, in which he mentions the altarpiece in Cologne he saw painted by a "Master Stefan." The work in question is presumed to be the altarpiece representing the patron saints of the city in attendance at the Adoration of the Magi (now in Cologne cathedral), the most significant altarpiece produced in Cologne. All other works associated with Lochner are attributed through stylistic affinity to this piece. As a result of the meager documentation, some scholarship has cast doubt on the identity of the creator of these works. The historical Stefan Lochner, the only Stefan in the Cologne guilds, was active ca. 1435–1451, and is presumed to have been born between 1400 and 1410 in Meersburg, on Lake Constance. Little is known of his life, but he was first documented as a master in Cologne in June, 1442, and died, probably of the plague, in September, 1451. His life was probably short, as he died within a year of his parents. Two works are dated: the 1445 Presentation in the Temple (Lisbon, Gulbenkian Collection), and the 1447 work of the same subject (Darmstadt, Hessisches Landesmuseum).

Lochner's work often shows traces of Flemish realism, causing some to question the nature of his training. His paintings show little stylistic relationship to works from Lochner's homeland near Constance. Also, Lochner introduced numerous innovations to the essentially conservative Cologne school of painting. Lochner's figures inhabited landscapes and architectural settings full of specific details that clearly reflect a familiarity with Flemish works. His work shows figures that have somewhat more volume than previously seen, and these figures exist in space far more effectively than those of his Cologne predecessors.

Several of his works, such as the Nativity (Munich, Alte Pinakothek), the Gulbenkian Presentation in the Temple, and the St. Jerome in his Cell (Raleigh, North Carolina Museum of Art), all bear numerous similarities to the works of Robert Campin and his followers, particularly in the representation of interior spaces. Lochner's largest extant work, and the best known, is the previously noted City Patrons' Altarpiece or *Dombild.* This work seems to reflect both the knowledge of the Ghent Altarpiece, particularly on the exterior Annunciation, and Lochner's characteristic sweetness, grace, and delicacy. The figures in this altarpiece are the first life-size figures painted in Cologne.

Nevertheless, Lochner's paintings maintained links to the past and are noted for a tension between their fully modeled forms and linear patterns. He also often used gold backgrounds and, like earlier Cologne painters, outlined figures in red. Lochner's paintings are also characterized by a distinctly personal quality of calm and sweetness, creating a sense of quiet mysticism. These qualities are created through idealization of features, particularly those of women, and rich, glowing colors, often created with oil glazes. All these qualities are perhaps best seen in his Madonna of the Rosebower (Cologne, Wallraf-Richartz-Museum).

Further Reading

Corley, Brigitte. "A Plausible Provenance for Stefan Lochner?" *Zeitschrift für Kunstgeschichte* 59 (1996): 78–96.

Förstesr, Otto H. *Stefan Lochner: Ein Maler zu Köln*. Frankfurt am Main: Prestel, 1938.

Goldberg, Gisela, and Gisela Scheffler. *Altdeutsche Gemälde, Köln und Nordwestdeutschland. Alte Pinakotek, München*. 2 vols. Bayerische Staatsgemäldesammlung Gemäldekataloge 14. Munich: Bayerische Staatsgemäldesammlung, 1972, vol. 1, pp. 190–210.

Stefan Lochner, Meister zu Köln: Herkunft, Werke, Wirkung, ed. Frank Günter Zehnder. Cologne: Wallraf-Richartz-Museum, 1993.

Zehnder, Frank Günter. *Katalog der Altkölner Malerei*. Kataloge des "Wallraf-Richartz-Museums 11. Cologne: Stadt Köln, 1990, pp. 212–244.

DANIEL M. LEVINE

LÓPEZ DE AYALA, PERO
(1332–1407)

Pero López de Ayala was a chronicler, poet, and statesman who lived in a period that spanned the reigns of five Castilian kings. He was born into a wealthy, noble family in the northern province of Alava. Although not a great deal is known of his youth, Ayala's knowledge of Latin and French, plus his interest in the Bible and other religious writings may have come from early ecclesiastical training by his uncle, Cardinal Pedro Gómez Barroso, who raised and educated him. Much of what is known of Ayala's activities is derived from the chronicles he wrote describing the reigns of Pedro I (1350–1369), Enrique II (1369–1379), Juan I (1379–1390), and Enrique III (1390–1406). Beginning with his first appearance in the *Crónicas des los reyes de Castilla: don Pedro* (Chronicle of the Kings of Castile: Peter I) in 1353 as a page selected to carry the king's banner, Ayala served Pedro in various capacities for over a dozen years. By 1367, however, he had joined Enrique of Trastámara, Pedro's illegitimate half-brother and rival for the throne. Shortly

afterward, Ayala was taken prisoner by the English at the battle of Nájera.

During the reign of Enrique II, Ayala received many royal favors, including territorial possessions and political posts. His political activity greatly increased during the reign of Juan I, when he served as royal counselor and as ambassador to France. Although he opposed the plan of Juan I to assume the Portuguese throne and thereby unite the two kingdoms, Ayala participated in the disastrous battle of Aljubarrota, where he was captured by the Portuguese and imprisoned for two years. It is probable that some of his writings were done during this period, especially the *Libro de la caza de las aves* and some poetic works. Ayala's importance and influence continued to grow during the reign of Enrique III. He was a member of the Council of Regents during the king's minority and served as a negotiator in the peace talks with Portugal. In the mid-1390s, Ayala spent several years in semiretirement at his estate in Álava and at the adjacent Hieronymite monastery. It is believed that he wrote his chronicles and *Libro del linaje de Ayala* during this time. In 1399, he was appointed grand chancellor of Castile.

In addition to being an impressive political and military leader who was personally acquainted with popes and kings, Ayala must also be acknowledged as one of the three major literary figures of his century. Juan Ruiz, Juan Manuel, and Pero López de Ayala all in their own way reflect the social, economic, and political milieu in which they lived as well as their own personal reactions to their circumstances. Although a self-consciousness as literary creators is apparent in the work of each of these authors, their primary purpose remains didactic—ranging from the jocular tongue-in-cheek admonitions of Ruiz to the chivalric preoccupations and moralizing of Manuel to the almost ascetic severity of Ayala. As the most important writer of the last half of the fourteenth century, Ayala's prose and poetic works are significant for a number of reasons. Linguistically, they comprise an extensive and reliable source of late-fourteenth- and early fifteenth-century Spanish. His chronicles are of great historical value as they are a major source of information concerning events in Spain from 1350 to 1396. The epoch that Ayala chronicles is a period of crisis and of such peninsular and international conflicts as civil and religious wars in Spain, the Hundred Years' War, the Black Death, and the schism in the Catholic Church. An eyewitness to many of these events, Ayala identifies himself with the purpose and norms of ancient chroniclers, explaining in his preface that the purpose of knowing about events in the past is to serve as a guide for present actions. He further comments that his sole intention is to tell the truth based on what he himself observed and from testimony of trustworthy persons. Nevertheless, the chronicler's impartiality, and at times even his veracity, has been questioned because he reports so many barbarous acts, and because he views Pedro I primarily as a negative example. Ayala's support of the Trastámaran pretender and his later involvement in the royal court further clouds the picture. The two manuscript traditions *abreviada* and *vulgar* suggest a process of revision that served to soften the condemnation of Pedro I after the reconciliation of the two dynastic lines, with the marriage of the grandchildren of the two contenders.

The literary nature of these narratives and the chronicler's acute awareness of literary style must also be taken into account. Among the variety of literary devices used in the chronicles, Ayala includes the skillful arrangement of all the contributing elements to form an organic unity: tense choice, paired words or doublets, alternation, contrast, parallelism, repetition, and portraiture. The author's skill in the use of direct address such as dialogues, one-liners, discourses, letters, and sayings enliven narrative passages and reveal the dramatic nature of the events. The dramatic structure of the death scenes is also evident in other episodes; for example, the farewell scene between Leónor de Guzmán and her son Fadrique, the confrontation with the Queen Mother at Toro, the departure of Pedro I from Burgos, and the papal election that began the schism. Ayala must be recognized as a talented prose stylist as he relates events more varied and fascinating than many fictional sagas, consisting of wars, fratricides, marriages, mistresses, international intrigues, and power struggles at the highest levels of government.

Ayala's long poetic work *Rimado de Palacio*, completed in 1404, is a highly personal and creative expression of the author's moral and philosophical preoccupations. Most of its 2,168 stanzas (totalling more than 8,000 lines) are written in the verse form *cuaderna via*, characterized by four-line stanzas, each fourteen-syllable line divided by a caesura after the seventh syllable and ending in uniform consonantal rhyme. In spite of being the last of the *cuaderna via* poets, Ayala demonstrates poetic innovations that include increased use of the eight-syllable line and the introduction of *arte mayor*, both most apparent in the *Cancionero* portion, stanzas 732–919. At the center of *Cancionero*, the poet again reveals his concern for the Church in a long allegory in which the ship of St. Peter is being torn apart by the destructive storm of the Great Schism.

The *Rimado* consists of a large number of poems of varied content and structure whose composition undoubtedly spans decades and whose impetus springs from the experiences of a long, adventurous life as well as from periods of reading and meditation. To say that it is a didactic-moral work or a long confessional poem is true. Nonetheless, this would slight the literary value and variety of Ayala's forcefully sober verse. Ayala's

fine, satirically traced pictures of medieval society have, above all else, attracted readers to *Rimado*. These vigorous scenes of contemporary society and court life are found in the first part of the book, along with other poems that arise from the chancellor's personal experiences and his reflections. The poet's description of personages in the royal courts, the almost caricaturelike presentation of merchants and lawyers, prefigure later satirical works that culminate in the mordant sarcasm and ridicule of Francisco Quevedo, as well as in subsequent vignettes of manners and customs.

The more extensive final part of the work provides a focus on doctrine rather than experience. Ayala demonstrates originality in combining confessional and doctrinal themes and materials based on the Bible and the *Morals* of St. Gregory in order to produce a didactic exposition in verse. Many of the themes of the fifteenth-century rhymmed confessions undoubtedly received some impetus from the meditations on life, death, original sin, and the brief duration of worldly gains portrayed in *Rimado*. In addition to influencing the verse forms, topics, and themes of later poets, Ayala's devout and moving poems dedicated to the Virgin had an impact on religious lyrical poetry of the fifteenth century. Ayala also made an important contribution to Castilian intellectual life through his translations of works of Livy, Gregory, Isidore, and Boethius.

See also **Enrique II, King of Castile; Juan Manuel**

Further Reading

García, M. *Obra y personalidad del Canciller Ayala*. Madrid, 1983.

López de Ayala, P. *Libra Rimado de Palacio*. 2 vols. Ed. J. Joset. Madrid, 1978.

Strong, E. B. "The *Rimado de Palacio*: López de Ayala's Rimed Confession." *Hispanic Review* 37 (1969), 439–51.

Tate, R. B. "López de Ayala, Humanist Historian?" *Hispanic Review* 25 (1957), 157–74.

Wilkins, C. *Pern López de Ayala*. Boston, 1989.

CONSTANCE L. WILKINS

LÓPEZ DE CÓRDOBA, LEONOR (b. 1362)

Born in 1362, Leonor López de Córdoba composed one of the most singular chronicles of the late Middle Ages in Castile. Her *Memorias*, which were dictated to a scribe around the beginning of the fifteenth century, are a personal testimony of a society ravaged by civil war, pestilence, and class upheaval.

Due to the dramatic circumstances of the narrator's life, the *Memorias* present a point of view that is rare in the historiography of this period. Leonor López was the sole survivor of a family destroyed because of its allegiance to Pedro I, the legitimate king of Castile, during the dynastic struggle he waged against his half-brother, Enrique de Trastámara. The social climate of the decades following this civil war was dominated by the usurper's followers, who spread propaganda alluding to the brutality of Pedro "the Cruel," and the low social class of his supporters, as a means of justifying their overthrow of the rightful monarch. In an effort to repudiate such rumors in her *Memorias*, Leonor López described in detail the nobility of her lineage, the bravery of her father in defense of the loyalist cause, and the atrocities that Enrique de Trastámara himself inflicted upon her family. Her work is a historical curiosity, both as a document of a dispossessed class, and as a feat of honor performed verbally by a woman.

Memorias also merits attention for its literary significance as one of the earliest examples of autobiographical expression produced in medieval Spain. In order to exonerate herself, Leonor López elaborated a self-portrait that exemplified the conduct deemed appropriate for a noble lady. Her persuasive manipulation of language is particularly evident in her use of motifs derived from pious literature to associate herself with a popular ideal of Christian virtue.

Despite their limitations as a historical record and artistic work, the *Memorias* of Leonor López are notable as a re-creation of the past that preserves a uniquely feminine interpretation of the values of medieval Castilian society.

See also **Pedro I the Cruel, King of Castile**

Further Reading

Ayerbe-Chaux, R. "Las memorias de Leonor López de Córdoba." *Journal of Hispanic Philology* 2 (1977–78), 11–33.

Deyennond, A. "Spain's First Women Writers." In *Women in Hispanic Literature: Icons and Fallen Idols.* Ed. B. Miller, Berkeley, Calif., 1983. 26–52.

AMANDA CURRY

LÓPEZ DE MENDOZA, IÑIGO
(1398–1458)

Born in 1398, Iñigo López de Mendoza (first marqués de Santillana, and señor de Hita and Buitrago) was the son of Diego Hurtado de Mendoza, the influential admiral of Castile. His uncle was Pero López de Ayala, poet, statesman, military figure, and the commanding chancellor of Castile during the last quarter of the fourteenth century. During the reign of Juan II of Castile, López de Mendoza was head of the powerful Mendoza clan, which was connected through marriage to many of the most influential families of the kingdom.

López de Mendoza is one of the major cultural and political figures of the fifteenth century. He spent a part of his youth in Aragón, where he became friends and shared intellectual pursuits with Enrique de Villena, one of the great learned men of his time. López de Mendoza distinguished himself both militarily and literarily on the Granadan frontier, at Ágreda in 1429 and again at Jaén in 1438. Although he fought alongside Juan II and his confidant Álvaro de Luna, Constable of Castile, at the battle of Olmedo in 1445 defending the interests of the monarchy against the challenges of the Infantes de Aragón, López de Mendoza quickly became don Álvaro's sworn enemy. Along with other powerful nobles, López de Mendoza then conspired to topple Luna from power and went on to write admonitory poetry about the example of Luna's life and execution in 1453.

The Marqués, as López de Mendoza was referred to simply in his time, surrounded himself in Guadalajara with artists, writers, and thinkers like Nuño de Guzmán, Pero Díaz de Toledo, and Martín González de Lucena, and was perhaps the greatest single cultural and artistic force of his time. As both intellectual and patron, López de Mendoza was the single most important figure in the propagation of humanistic knowledge in Castile during the first half of the fifteenth century. In addition to having gathered in Guadalajara the most significant library of humanistic works in lay hands and patronized the translation of Homer's *Iliad*, Plato, Ovid, Cicero, Seneca, Dante, and Boccaccio into Castilian, López de Mendoza was in his own right a celebrated poet, literary critic, and theoretician. Although he collected Latin manuscripts, he could not read Latin, but he read several vernaculars fluently and was aware of contemporary developments in European poetry, especially in France and Italy. His *Carta e prohemio al Condestable de Portugal*, which draws heavily on classical and patristic writers as well as Boccaccio's *De genealogia deorum*, is considered the first concerted work of literary theory and criticism in Castilian. Its novelty lies in its historical descriptions of different genres and the catalogue of works that it contains, just as it offers an evaluation of the qualities and defects of the poets he mentions. In addition, his *Sonetos fechos al itálico modo* (1438), which follow the example of Dante and Petrarch, mark the first coherent attempt to cultivate the sonnet form in Castilian. Besides these two works and his patronage, López de Mendoza was a prolific writer responsible for a vast body of work in both prose and verse that deals with moral, religious, political, and sentimental themes, all of which contributed to his vast fame during his lifetime. Among the best known of his lyrical works are his *serranillas,* or pastourelles, that tell of rural love encounters between knights and rustic shepherdesses. His ambitious narrative and allegorical poems, known as *decires* (*Bías contra Fortuna, Doctrinal de Privados, Comedieta de Ponza*), are replete with mythological, biblical, and other learned themes that attest to his humanistic knowledge and intellectual aspirations. The *Comedieta* (1436), a patriotic composition that exalts the Aragónese in their Italian campaign at the naval battle of Ponza, represents the culmination of López de Mendoza's allegorical works. It is built upon a complicated image pattern developed through the use of highly learned language and allusion. *Bías contra Fortuna*, written in 1448 as a consolation to mark the political imprisonment of a cousin by don Álvaro de Luna, marks the climax of the theme of Fortune in his work. In contradistinction to the difficult allegory of the *Comedieta*, Bías, the Greek philosopher who is the spokesperson for Santillana, makes his views on Fortune and the world clearly known. The *Doctrinal* reveals a final vindictive side of López de Mendoza's character, in which he employs Fortune and confession to make Álvaro de Luna, his dead enemy, denounce his own transgressions.

When López de Mendoza died in 1458, the event inspired his contemporaries to write a number of elegies and other literary compositions to mourn his passing.

See also **Boccaccio, Giovanni; Dante Alighieri; Guzmán, Domingo de; Petrarca, Francesco**

Further Reading

Lapesa, R. *La obra literaria del Marqués de Santillana.* Madrid, 1959.
Nader, H. *The Mendoza Family in the Spanish Renaissance, 1350–1550.* Rutgers, N.J., 1979.
Schiff, M. *La bibliothèque du marquis de Santillane.* Paris, 1905.

E. MICHAEL GERLI

LORENZETTI, PIETRO (c. 1280–1348) AND AMBROGIO (c. 1290–1348)

The brothers Pietro Lorenzetti and Ambrogio Lorenzetti were Sienese painters; they represent two of the most radical and innovative forces in *Trecento* art. Pietro and Lorenzetti were probably pupils of Duccio, and they both enlarged on the study of narrative and pictorial realism common to Sienese and Florentine art at this time. Their art manifests an interesting admixture of the styles of both schools, combining Sienese sensitivity to color and line with Florentine monumentality.

Relatively few documents regarding the life or artistic activity of either Pietro or Ambrogio have come down to us. Although Lorenzo Ghiberti, in the first written account of Ambrogio, provides a long and enthusiastic discussion of his work (*Commentarii,* c. 1450), he never mentions Pietro in his survey of Sienese artists. Vasari (*Lives,* 1568) did not even realize that the two artists were brothers; he misidentifed one of them as Pietro Laurati. Reconstruction of their careers has understandably proved to be difficult, especially because some

of their most celebrated compositions have been lost. Although the brothers worked quite independently of each another, some commissions appear to have been joint undertakings, and the intensity of each brother's exploration of pictorial realism suggests a greater degree of contact and collaboration between the two than we now suppose.

Pietro, traditionally considered the elder brother, has usually been overlooked in comparison with Ambrogio, who has a greater reputation for invention. However, Pietro's own brilliant technical innovation is shown as early as his first documented work, a polyptych painted for the high altar of rhe parish church of Santa Maria in Arezzo (1320). In one portion of the *Arezzo Polyptych,* the frame is treated as if it were contiguous with the architecture of the painted narrative, so that the pilasters and arches framing the *Annunciation* are seen as supporting elements for the front wall of Mary's chamber. The space of this room is seen logically as extending back from the supporting columns and arches on the surface, creating an illusion of a box of space extending beyond the frame. This was an advance in a direct line with the development of one-point perspective a century later, and it was an idea to which Pietro would subsequently return even more daringly. Analysis of Pietro's forms in the *Arezzo Polyptych* reveals a mélange of stylistic sources influencing his art. In the central panel of the *Madonna and Child* especially, the Madonna exhibits a graceful sway and pattern indebted to Duccio; the pronounced twist of her neck recalls Giovanni Pisano's sculptures for the facade of the cathedral in Siena; and her firm support of the child's solidly rounded body echoes Giotto's massive forms.

Important pictorial features are found in Pietro's most extensive surviving work, the frescoes in the left transept of the lower basilica of San Francesco in Assisi. These narrate the *Passion and Resurrection of Christ* and the *Stigmatization of Saint Francis*; and there is an unusual section of trompe l'oeil depictions of chapel furnishings, including an unoccupied pew, a fictive altarpiece, and a niche containing liturgical objects. These frescoes are undocumented, and their dating has provoked controversy, but most scholars place them c. 1320. Many scenes, such as the *Entry into Jerusalem* and the epic *Crucifixion,* continue the Sienese tradition of sensitivity to color and love of profusion, but they are characterized by an unprecedented wealth of observation. The *Last Supper,* for example, deftly juxtaposes three distinct types of light in a confrontation of the mundane and the divine. A remarkably detailed night sky, the first portrayal of its kind, meticulously differentiates the light of the moon, stars, and meteors streaking across the heavens above the structure containing the main scene. This natural light is contrasted with the artificial light of the hearth fire in the kitchen, which casts the first shadows in western art since antiquity. Both of these lights pale in relation to the floodlit interior of the supper chamber, which seems to be illuminated by the supernatural glory of Christ and his disciples. In another astonishing step toward realism, Pietro makes it clear that the narratives are to be understood as a sequence of stories unfolding over time; the moon, high over the pavilion in the *Last Supper*, is shown to be setting behind the Mount of Olives in the adjacent *Arrest of Christ*. Other frescoes in the left transept, such as the *Deposition from the Cross* and the *Entombment*, do away with all anecdotal detail to approach the monumental grandeur and dramatic tension of Giotto's narratives. The *Deposition*, in which Christ's broken body is ingeniously interlaced with the living, forms one of the most sustained images of grief in western art.

Three securely dated works succeeded the Assisi frescoes: the *Carmine Altarpiece* of 1327–1329 (Siena, Pinacoteca; New Haven, Yale Museum; Princeton, Princeton Museum), a polyptych made to celebrate the final approval of the Carmelite order by Pope John XXIII in 1326 for its Sienese church of San Niccolò; the *Uffizi Madonna and Child* (Florence, Uffizi; signed and dated 1340); and the *Birth of the Virgin* (Siena, Museo dell'Opera Metropolitana; commissioned 1335, signed and dated 1342). This last altarpiece, made as part of a cycle of Marian altarpieces celebrating feasts of the Virgin surrounding Duccio's *Maestà* in the cathedral of Siena, returns to the integration of frame and painting seen in the *Arezzo Polyptych* of twenty-two years earlier. Here the illusion of continuity is much more thorough. We seem to be peering into a miniature Gothic palace which is structurally supported by the columns and arches of the frame and from which the exterior walls have been removed (as in a dollhouse) to allow us to witness the events within. And although this work is technically a polyptych (the two lateral panels of saints originally flanking the *Birth* are now lost), there is none of compartmentalization traditionally seen in separate panels. The space of one panel is treated as continuous with that of the next; thus, the two panels on the right convey information concerning the same time and place, Mary's birthing chamber. To emphasize this, the figure of the woman bearing a fly whisk continues on either side of the vertical pier of the frame. Also gone is the traditional flattening backdrop of gold leaf signifying a sacred event. Instead, an opulently appointed interior, described in rich patterns from the vault to the floor tiles, defines a remarkably convincing illusion of spatial recession. In the left panel depicting Joachim and the herald, the setting suggests a vast structure beyond the two visible chambers, indicating Pietro's concern to construct a completely plausible world for his figures to inhabit.

Pietro worked, together with Ambrogio and Simone Martini, on a cycle of frescoes illustrating the life of the Virgin for the facade of the hospital of Santa Maria della Scala in Siena. (These frescoes are now lost, but a recorded inscription bore the date 1335.) Pietro also worked alongside Ambrogio on a fresco cycle for the chapter hall of the monastery of San Francesco in Siena, of which a *Crucifixion* and a *Resurrected Christ* survive (possibly 1336). A *Massacre of the Innocents* from a fresco cycle in San Clemente ai Servi in Siena and an altarpiece depicting stories of the *Life of the Blessed Humilitas* (Florence, Uffizi) are two other works frequently attributed to Pietro.

Lorenzo Ghiberti considered Ambrogio Lorenzetti the greatest Sienese painter of the 1300s, surpassing even Simone Martini in ability and sophistication. A *Madonna and Child* from Vico L'Abate (signed and dated 1319; Florence, Museo Arcivescovile del Cestello) is the earliest of only three dated works by Ambrogio. It shows the originality of the artist's concepts from the beginning of his career. Ambrogio's panel is based on a Byzantine type of the Virgin as the throne of God, and the rigidly frontal, iconic pose of the Madonna adheres closely to the archaic format. The sovereign detachment between mother and God, typically upright in front of the Madonna, has, however, here been replaced by a restless, squirming Christ child seeking his mother's attention. Both figures have the solidity and roundness of Giotto's paintings, and the throne is also presented as a spatially receding three-dimensional structure. This modernization of an ancient type in the latest Giottoesque idiom reveals Ambrogio's special understanding of the Florentines' achievement. In fact, Ambrogio worked periodically in Florence between 1318 and 1332, and he is listed in the registry of the Florentine painters' guild in 1327. The Vico L'Abate panel is a prime example of the astonishing variety and inventiveness that both Pietro and Ambrogio brought to the theme of the Madonna and child. Both artists composed ceaseless variations on this popular devotional subject, but Ambrogio's Madonnas, especially, attained a level of iconographic and aesthetic sophistication that seems to belong more to the Renaissance, or even to the Baroque, than to the *Trecento*. A few of Ambrogio's groupings of the Madonna and child are shown as if responding to the viewer's presence, as in the *Madonna del Latte* (Siena, Palazzo Arcivescovile), in which the suckling child looks out at the viewer with intense curiosity; or the *Rapolano Madonna* (Siena, Pinacoteca), which portrays a Christ child so surprised and frightened by the attention coming from our direction that he crushes his pet goldfinch. This psychologizing of the mother's and the child's response to their surroundings reaches a climax in the Sant'Agostino *Maestà* in Siena (possibly 1339), the last surviving fragment of a fresco cycle illustrating episodes of the life of Saint Catherine of

Alexandria for an Augustinian chapter house formerly adjacent to the church. The *Maestà* depicts Mary and Christ adored by saints who bear the attributes of their faith; these include some who were brutally martyred: Saint Bartholemew with his flayed skin, Saint Agatha with her breasts, and Saint Catherine with her severed head all kneel and present their tokens of faith to the child. This grisly spectacle strikes terror into the child, who staggers unsteadily backward in an attempt to escape—the most natural response a child could have.

Some of Ambrogio's patrons apparently felt that his daringly human interpretation of the divine breached the limits of decorum. The chapel of Monte Siepi in the rural abbey of San Galgano near Siena was built to honor this Sienese saint and to commemorate a vision of the Madonna that Galgano had on this site. The surviving frescoes are fragmentary; but Ambrogio's original program for the chapel, c. 1336, included a depiction of Galgano's vision, portraying a procession of saints and angels on the side walls converging, along with the visitors inside the chapel, toward the Madonna enthroned as queen of heaven on the wall behind the altar. By portraying saints on the walls flanking the enthroned Madonna, Ambrogio involved the entire space of the chapel, surrounding the viewer with Galgano's vision—a bold experiment that anticipates the carefully coordinated chapel interiors of the seventeenth century. The complex iconographic program for the wall portrayed the Virgin's central role in the mystery of human redemption: she was shown both as the exalted queen of heaven at the top of the fresco and as the humble *Virgin Annunciate* at the bottom. As the discovery (in 1996) of the *sinopie* underlying the frescoes revealed, Ambrogio originally portrayed the Virgin of the annunciation cowering in utter terror before the angel, while the *Maestà* above showed her enthroned without the child, wearing a crown, and bearing worldly symbols of power—the orb and scepter—in her hands. Both of these unique images were suppressed shortly after completion of the frescoes: the trembling annunciate was painted over by another artist, who replaced her with a typical meekly accepting Madonna; and the empress was transformed into the more usual image of motherhood by placing the Christ child on her lap. Presumably, the patrons had been disturbed by Ambrogio's provocative interpretations and had subsequently commissioned something more conventional.

From 1337 to 1340, under commission from Siena's ruling Council of Nine, Ambrogio worked on the most important surviving cycle of medieval secular decorations, the *Allegory and Effects of Good and Bad Government*, painted on three walls of the Sala della Pace (or Sala dei Nove), one of the ruling council's meeting rooms in the Palazzo Pubblico in Siena. This cycle is almost completely devoid of religious content; its complex philosophical underpinnings—along the lines of antique Aristotelian, Ciceronian, or more strictly medieval tracts—are still disputed. We may take comfort in the fact that even during the *Trecento*, visitors to the *sala* needed the learned interpretation of a guide in order to understand the extremely intricate allegorical message of the cycle. The fresco juxtaposes the elements of just and harmonious rule with the evil elements of tyranny, contrasting the effects of each form of rule on city and country. The mural is filled with visual puns (Harmony, for instance, is shown with a wood plane, smoothing out any unevenness) and references to the antique (the figure of Peace is derived from an antique Roman coin). In his depiction of the prosperous city, Ambrogio created an unparalleled catalog of the myriad activities of town life. Nothing else in medieval art prepares us for the panoramic landscape adjacent to the well-governed city, which is the first landscape since antiquity, and really the first "portrait" of a particular terrain—a glance out the window of this hall reveals the close affinity between the fresco and the Tuscan countryside surrounding Siena.

As noted above, Ambrogio collaborated with Pietro on (lost) frescoes for a hospital in Siena, and on frescoes for a Franciscan chapter house (the latter included a painting of a typhoon, since lost, that Ghiberti praised highly). Ambrogio also painted an altarpiece of the *Presentation at the Temple and Purification of Mary* (1342; Florence, Uffizi) for the same cycle in the cathedral at Siena for which Pietro executed his *Birth of the Virgin*. Like Pietro's work, Ambrogio's *Presentation* is startling for its sophisticated suggestion of space and light. Ambrogio's last signed and dated work is from 1344: an *Annunciation* (Siena, Pinacoteca) painted for the chamber of the tax magistrate in the Palazzo Pubblico in Siena. The moment of incarnation depicted here presents an interpretation of great theological subtlety, and the spatial construction of the panel shows the tile floor converging to a single vanishing point; this is the closest any *Trecento* painting comes to true one-point perspective.

Ambrogio and Pietro both evidently died of the plague in 1348; with their deaths, Siena's period of cultural ascendancy came to an end.

See also **Duccio di Buoninsegna; Martini, Simone**

Further Reading

Borsook, Eve. *Ambrogio Lorenzetti.* Florence: Sadea Sansoni, 1966.

Brandi, Cesare. *Pietro Lorenzetti: Affreschi nella basilica inferiore di Assisi.* Rome: Pirelli, 1957.

——. *Pietro Lorenzetti.* Rome: Edizioni Mediteranee, 1958.

Carli, Enzo. *Pietro Lorenzetti.* Milan: A. Martello, 1956.

——. *I Lorenzetti.* Milan: Fabbri, 1965.

——. *La pittura senese del Trecento.* Milan: Electa, 1981.

Cole, Bruce. *Sienese Painting from Its Origins to the Fifteenth Century.* New York: Harper and Row, 1980.

DeWald, Ernest T. *Pietro Lorenzetti.* Cambridge, Mass.: Harvard University Press, 1930.

Frugoni, Chiara. *Pietro and Ambrogio Lorenzetti*, trans. L. Pelletti. Florence: Scala, 1988. Maginnis, Hayden B. J. "Pietro Lorenzetti: A Chronology." *Art Bulletin*, 66, 1984, pp. 183–211.

——. *Painting in the Age of Giotto: A Historical Reevaluation.* University Park: Pennsylvania State University, 1997.

Norman, Diana. "'Love Justice, You Who Judge the Earth': The Paintings of the Sala dei Nove in the Palazzo Pubblico, Siena." In *Siena, Florence, and Padua: Art, Society, and Religion 1280–1400*, Vol. 2, *Case Studies*, ed. Diana Norman. New Haven, Conn.: Yale University Press, 1995, pp. 145–167.

Offner, Richard. "Reflections on Ambrogio Lorenzetti." *Gazette des Beaux Arts*, 56, 1960, pp. 235–238.

Rowley, George. *Ambrogio Lorenzetti*, 2 vols. Princeton, N.J.: Princeton University Press, 1958. Rubinstein, Nicolai. "Political Ideas in Sienese Art: The Frescoes by Ambrogio Lorenzetti and Taddeo di Bartolo in the Palazzo Pubblico." *Journal of the Warburg and Courtauld Institutes*, 21, 1958, pp. 179–207.

Southard, Edna. *The Frescoes in Siena's Palazzo Pubblico, 1289–1359: Studies in Imagery and Relations to Other Communal Palaces in Tuscany.* New York: Garland, 1979.

——. "Ambrogio Lorenzetti's Frescoes in the Sala della Pace: A Change of Names." *Mitteilungen des Kunsthistorischen Institutes in Florenz*, 24, 1980, pp. 361–365.

Starn, Randolph, and Loren Partridge. "The Republican Regime of the *Sala dei Nove* in Siena, 1338–1340." In *Arts of Power: Three Halls of State in Italy, 1300–1600.* Berkeley: University of California Press, 1992, pp. 11–59.

Volpe, Carlo. *Pietro Lorenzetti.* Milan: Electa, 1989.

GUSTAV MEDICUS

LOTHAIR I (795–855)

King of Lotharingia and emperor. The eldest son of Emperor Louis the Pious (778–840) and Irmengarde, Lothair I is remembered chiefly for his role in dismembering the empire constructed by Charlemagne. In 817, Louis the Pious sought to ensure the empire's unity after his death by promulgating the *Ordinatio imperii*. This divided the Carolingian territories into kingdoms for Lothair I and his brothers, Pepin of Aquitaine (800–838) and Louis the German (804–876), while leaving Italy under their father's nephew, Bernard. Lothair, who was made co-emperor, was granted the largest, central realm, including Aix-la-Chapelle and Rome. After his father's death, he was to exercise supremacy over his brothers and Bernard.

Difficulties emerged in 817 with the revolt of Bernard, who died after being blinded as punishment. Italy was transferred to Lothair. In 823, the birth of another son, Charles the Bald, to Louis the Pious (by his second wife, Judith) forced the emperor to modify his plans for the inheritance by allotting to Charles lands earlier assigned to his half-brothers. Lothair revolted in 830, and again in 833 with the help of his brothers Louis the German and Pepin. While their father emerged victorious and in 834 confined Lothair to Italy, the remaining years of Louis's reign saw continued political unrest.

Upon Louis's death in 840, Lothair I proclaimed again the *Ordinatio imperii* and turned against his surviving brothers, Louis the German and Charles. The power struggle among those rulers led to the Treaty of Verdun (843), dividing the Carolingian territories into separate kingdoms for Louis, Charles, and Lothair. This testified to the end of the ideal of a united empire, though Lothair retained the imperial title.

Lothair was in conflict with one or both brothers most of the rest of his life. Upon his death in 855, his lands were divided among his sons, Louis II (d. 875), Lothair II (d. 869), and Charles of Provence (d. 863). Louis II alone was left the imperial crown, which he had received in 850.

See also **Louis the Pious**

Further Reading

Ganshof, François L. *The Carolingians and the Frankish Monarchy: Studies in Carolingian History*, trans. Janet Sondheimer. London: Longman, 1971, pp. 289–302.

McKitterick, Rosamond. *The Frankish Kingdoms Under the Carolingians, 751–987.* London: Longman, 1983.

Nelson, Janet L. *Charles the Bald.* London: Longman, 1992.

Riché, Pierre. *The Carolingians: A Family Who Forged Europe*, trans. Michael I. Allen. Philadelphia: University of Pennsylvania Press, 1993.

CELIA CHAZELLE

LOTHAR III (1075–1137)

Lothar III of Supplinburg was born shortly after his father, Count Gebhard of Supplinburg, died in battle against King Henry IV. Historians know little about his youth, his rise to prominence, or exactly why King Henry V named Lothar as successor to the late Magnus Billung, duke of Saxony, on August 25, 1106. Soon after, having grown still more powerful through other inheritances and his own political and military ability, Lothar became the leader of the opposition to Henry V.

With the death of Emperor Henry V in 1125 without a son, German princes reasserted their traditional right to elect a new king. Representative magnates of the four ethnic divisions of Swabia, Bavaria, Saxony, and Franconia were delegated to the election at Mainz under the leadership of the archbishop. Although Duke Frederick II of Swabia, Henry V's nephew and heir, and Margrave Leopold III of Austria found a great deal of support, the archbishop promoted the case of the duke of Saxony, Lothar von Supplinburg. Lothar's party probably gained the support of the main holdout, the Welf duke of Bavaria, Henry the Black, with a promised marriage alliance between Henry's son, Henry the Proud, and Lothar's only child and heir, Gertrude. Elected on August 30 as king of the Romans, Lothar was crowned in Aachen about two weeks later.

The succession did not go smoothly, however. Between the Staufen Frederick II of Swabia and Lothar a new rivalry developed. The new king needed to assert his control over royal and imperial rights and properties. But royal prerogatives were mixed together with the personal inheritance of Henry V and the Salian dynasty inherited by the Staufen. Because Frederick was reluctant to turn over certain possessions, Lothar outlawed him at Christmas, 1125. Distracted by the defiance of Sobeslav of Bohemia, Lothar could not begin a military campaign against the Staufen until summer 1127, when he began to besiege Nuremburg. There the Staufen party elected Frederick's younger brother Conrad as anti-king in December, 1127. This conflict disturbed the peace of the empire until Conrad's capitulation in 1135. Nineteenth-century historians inflated these disagreements into a grand vendetta between two dynasties, the Welf (or in Italian, Guelph) versus the Staufen (or in Italian, Ghibelline after the castle Waiblingen). While such a view oversimplified the issues involved, the competing interests of these powerful families would recurrently affect imperial affairs for decades.

Meanwhile, Lothar was capably handling the affairs of his kingdom. His exploitation of extinct noble dynasties changed the political landscape. Lothar helped establish the Zähringens in Burgundy as rivals to the Staufen. Lothar's intervention of the succession of the duchy of Lower Lotharingia led to its breakup into the duchies of Brabant and Limburg. In Saxony, his home territory, he enfeoffed the Askaniens with the Nordmark and the Wettins with the Marches of Meissen and Lausitz, dynasties that would, however, later become rivals of the Welfs. Lothar made his will felt beyond his kingdom's borders. He carried out several campaigns against the Slavs, collecting tribute from Poland and granting Pomerania as a fief. And a quick military demonstration against the Danish, where rivalry for the throne had caused disorder, encouraged the various candidates to acknowledge his over-lordship almost without bloodshed.

Most importantly, Lothar became entangled in the papal schism between Innocent II and Anacletus II. Since both sides had respectable claims to the papacy, Lothar faced a real dilemma about whom to recognize as legitimate pope. Under the influence of the important Cistercian Abbot Bernard of Clairvaux and Norbert of Xanten (the founder of the Premonstratentian order, whom Lothar had made archbishop of Magdeburg), Lothar decided at a synod at Würzburg in 1130 to give allegiance to Innocent. Greeting the pope in Liège in

March, 1131, Lothar acted as a groom and horse-marshal (*Strator- und Marschaldienst*), leading the pope's horse by the bridle and holding his stirrup during dismounting. The memorialization of this act with a fresco in the Vatican, implying that Lothar served as a vassal of the pope, later caused tension between imperial and papal ideologues.

In return for offering to conquer Rome for Innocent, Lothar tried to get back the old rights of investiture of bishops that had been lost for the monarchy in the Concordat of Worms. But Innocent only gave a promise of the imperial election. In late summer 1132, Lothar began an expedition to Italy with a small army. His attack on Rome brought one success: Innocent crowned Lothar and his wife, Richenza, emperor and empress on June 4, 1133, although in the Lateran Palace, since Anacletus's forces still held the Vatican. Again Lothar tried to reclaim investiture, but only received confirmation that his rights would be the same as his predecessors. In negotiations about the Mathildine lands, he gained more success. Lothar recognized the claims of overlordship by the church, but he gained use of the lands in exchange for an annual payment of 100 pounds silver. Although the emperor immediately enfeoffed his son-in-law Henry the Proud with the lands, the papacy tried to portray him as a vassal of the church.

Within months Lothar returned to Germany, unable to defeat Anacletus's main ally, King Roger II of Sicily. Soon, Innocent was forced to flee Rome. Once the Staufen had reconciled with Lothar, however, the worsening plight of Innocent prompted Lothar to lead a second, much larger, Italian expedition in 1136. In northern Italy Lothar was triumphant; by the beginning of 1137 he invaded the kingdom of Roger of Sicily. But the quarrels between pope and emperor over the disposition of conquests and leadership, as well as the heat of summer, led to the breakup of the campaign before lasting success could be won. On the return northward Lothar sickened, finally dying in Breitenwang near Reutte in Tyrol on December 4, 1137.

Both his contemporaries and later historians have tended to judge Lothar harshly, especially those who resented his rather friendly relations with leaders of the church. Other modern historians reject his image as *Pfaffenkönig* (parson's king): his quarrels with the pope and his wars with local territorial bishops belie that charge. The conflicts after his death that ruined his legacy were largely caused by the change in dynasty, which Lothar had tried to forestall by giving the imperial insignia to Henry the Proud. In many ways Lothar successfully expanded political authority in Saxony, Germany, and the empire.

See also **Henry IV, Emperor; Roger II**

Further Reading

Bernhardi, Wilhelm. *Lothar von Supplinburg (1125–1127).* Jahrbücher der deutschen Geschichte 15. 1879; repr., Berlin: Duncker und Humblot, 1975.

Crone, Marie-Luise. *Untersuchungen zur Reichskirchenpolitik Lothars III. (1125–1137) zwischen reichskirchlicher Tradition und Reformkurie.* Frankfurt am Main: Lang, 1982.

Wadle, Elmar. *Reichsgut und Königsherrschaft unter Lothar III. (1125–1137): Ein Beitrag zur Verfassungsgeschichte des 12. Jahrhunderts.* Berlin: Duncker & Humblot, 1969.

BRIAN A. PAVLAC

LOUIS IX (1214–1270)

King of France and saint. The son of Louis VIII, Louis IX came to the throne as a child in 1226. He spent his early years as king under the tutelage of his mother, Blanche of Castile. Many northern barons resented the assignment of the regency to a woman, let alone a foreigner. Others resented the growing authoritarianism of the crown during the preceding fifty years, the reigns of Philip II Augustus and Louis VIII. Many baronial families in the west nursed grievances from the period of the conquest of the Plantagenêt fiefs in the early years of the century. And in the south, local notables remained unreconciled to the French regime established in the wake of the Albigensian Crusade. These resentments periodically broke into rebellion: the late 1220s and early 1230s saw the crown confronting shifting alliances of northern barons (including the count of Brittany, Pierre Mauclerc) in defense of aristocratic interests. In the opening years of the 1240s, nobles and townsmen in the southwest and Languedoc banded together with the support of the Plantagenêt king of England to undo the conquests of the previous half-century. The crown defeated all these movements. The credit for the early successes goes largely to Blanche of Castile, but gradually in the 1230s her son became the effective ruler of the kingdom.

Married in 1234 to Marguerite of Provence, who came to dislike his mother, Louis remained devoted to Blanche and responsive to her political advice. Only in one matter is there evidence of political disagreement between mother and son: Louis's decision in late 1244 to take the crusader's vow. Despite Blanche's objections, Louis fulfilled the vow after almost four years of preparation that included commissioning *enquêteurs*, or special investigators, to identify the perpetrators of injustices in his government. In addition to the goodwill that these investigations produced, the information allowed Louis to improve the machinery of government by retiring or reassigning certain of his administrators. At the same time, he worked hard to encourage national and international support for his venture and to build a port, Aigues-Mortes, in the south of France for the embarkation of his army, estimated at 15,000–25,000 men.

Louis departed for the Seventh Crusade in 1248, leaving his mother as regent; his wife accompanied him on the expedition. After wintering in Cyprus, he began the invasion of Egypt in May 1249. The crusaders captured the coastal city of Damietta, and then, after a considerable respite, they began the invasion of the Egyptian interior late in the year, continuing into the early months of 1250. Daily running up against fiercer opposition, they were decisively defeated in April at Al-Mansura; Louis and the remnants of his army were captured. After difficult negotiations, the king and his men were ransomed, and many, including the king's two surviving brothers, Alphonse of Poitiers and Charles of Anjou, took ship for Europe. The king and a small group of crusaders, spent the next several years in the Christian states of the Holy Land helping to rebuild fortifications and to formulate effective strategies against the enemy.

The queen-mother died in November 1252. Although he learned of her death in the spring of 1253, it was not until a year later that Louis was persuaded by the steady stream of information that reached him from France that conditions there necessitated his return. Landing at Hyères, not far from Marseille, in July 1254, he began immediately to transform the governance of his realm. Convinced that his failure on crusade was the result of his own sinfulness, and translating this conviction into a decision to live up to his notion of the ideal Christian ruler, he set about restraining the excesses of the Inquisition, reintroducing the *enquêteurs*, reforming the administration of the city of Paris, and, most far-reaching, undertaking a thorough overhaul of royal administrators in the provinces. Louis ceaselessly traversed the realm to hear petitions and do justice personally. Traditional institutions of rule, like Parlement, were improved in their organization and were leavened by his commitment to equity. He worked hard, too, to execute a severely restrictive policy toward the Jews that was in part intended to encourage them to convert.

In the late 1260s, Louis committed himself to another crusade. After considerable preparations, he departed in 1270. His wife remained in France. Following a brief stopover in Sardinia, the army, perhaps 5,000–10,000 strong, launched its attack on Tunis. Before the city could be taken—and in the event it never was—the king died (August 25, 1270). He was succeeded by his son, Philip III. As his bones were being transported to their final rest at Saint-Denis, miracles began to be reported. A few years later, the canonization process began in earnest. In 1297, the former king was raised to the catalogue of saints as St. Louis Confessor.

See also **Blanche of Castile; Joinville, Jean de; Philip II Augustus**

Further Reading

Jordan, William C. *Louis IX and the Challenge of the Crusade: A Study in Rulership*. Princeton: Princeton University Press, 1979.

Richard, Jean. *Saint Louis: Crusader King of France*, trans. by Jean Birrell. Cambridge: Cambridge University Press, 1992.

Sivéry, Gérard. *Saint Louis et son siècle*. Paris: Tallandier, 1983.

WILLIAM CHESTER JORDAN

LOUIS THE PIOUS
(April 16, 778–June 20, 840)

Louis (*Hludowicus*) and Lothar, a twin who soon died, were born on April 16, 778, in the palace of Chasseneuil near Poitiers to Hildegard, the wife of Charles the Great (Charlemagne). "Pious," not a contemporary epithet, was applied to Louis only at the end of the ninth century. In 781, Charles appointed Louis king of Aquitaine, an office he would grow into and hold for the next thirty-three years. In 794, sixteen-year-old Louis, already the father of two children by concubines, married Irmingard (d. 818), the daughter of Count Ingram. The royal couple produced five children within the decade.

Louis, as Charles's only surviving legitimate son, was crowned co-emperor at Aachen on September 11, 813. The implications of the imperial title Charles received in 800 remained ambiguous during his last years. The increasing involvement of churchmen in the administration of his realm suggests that Charles's concept of empire embraced religious as well as political leadership. A capitulary from this period wonders, "Are we indeed Christians?" One of Louis's great tasks after his father's death in January, 814, was to continue to define a Christian empire. Under Louis, Aachen became a beehive of activity. Charles had issued twenty diplomas during his last thirteen years; Louis nearly doubled that in his first year as emperor. Louis regarded his empire as a divine gift for whose welfare and improvement he was chiefly responsible. Much of his early legislation focused on monastic and ecclesiastical reform. With the help of Benedict of Aniane, a monk who had joined his inner circle back in Aquitaine and whom he installed at Inden nearby Aachen, Louis crafted a vision of empire in which religion, society, and politics coalesced. Concern for the unity of the Christian people animated the *Ordinatio imperii* of 817, his attempt to establish the imperial succession in a manner that would preserve the integrity of the empire. Lothar (b. 795) became co-emperor with Louis while his other sons, Pippin (b. 797) and Louis the Younger (b. 806), were assigned subordinate roles. In placing the unity of the empire before division among his heirs, Louis proposed a transpersonal vision of empire that emulated the unity of the church.

Louis saw himself as emperor of the Christian people, not of various ethnic groups. His reforms and concept of empire owed nothing to papal guidance or initiative. The historic *Pactum Hludowicianum* agreement of 817 for the first time outlined specifically the nature of the papal-imperial relationship, a relationship that Louis dominated. Elsewhere he referred to the pope as his helper (*adiutor*) in caring for God's people.

Louis was equally forceful in the political realm. When his nephew, King Bernard of Italy, challenged his authority in 817 he acted swiftly to quash the rebellion, blinding Bernard and exiling the conspirators. (When Bernard died of his injuries, Louis demonstrated the depth of his commitment to Christian kingship by performing public penance.) To preempt further dynastic challenges, he had his half-brothers Drogo, Hugo, and Theodoric tonsured and placed in monasteries. After the death of Irmingard (October 3, 818), Louis married Judith, daughter of Count Welf and his wife, Eigilwi, who bore him two children, Gisela (821) and Charles (June 13, 823). The birth of Louis's fourth son later triggered searing conflicts within the family and Carolingian society at large. Other problems also challenged his reign during its second decade. Churchmen such as Bishop Agobard of Lyon began to complain about rampant corruption in Carolingian society, including exploitation of church lands and oppression of the poor by the warrior class. With the expansion of Carolingian hegemony at an end, powerful nobles who little understood the ideals of Louis's empire ransacked the Christian people and churches for material gain. The many groups ranged along the empire's extensive borders required continual attention. In the southeast, the Slovenians proved troublesome, while in the northeast Louis was able to effectively manage the Danish threat, which was defused when the Danish king Harald was baptized and adopted by Louis in 826. In the west, Louis campaigned personally in Brittany where he established nominal authority. In Gascony and the Pyrenees borderlands chronic instability reigned, partly because counts Hugo and Matfrid failed to support Louis's military efforts, a dereliction for which the emperor stripped them of their positions. Count Bernard of Barcelona was much more effective and for his efforts was appointed in 829 as the emperor's chamberlain, an office that brought him into intimate contact with the imperial family. Judith saw Bernard as a protector while Louis regarded him as the second man in the empire. Louis's forceful handling of counts Hugo and Matfrid and the empowerment of Bernard and Judith combined with the fear that any provision made for the young Charles would come at the expense of his half-brothers provoked a palace revolt in 830. Pippin and the younger Louis, aided by Hugo and Matfrid, sought to "free" the emperor from the tyrant Bernard and the Jezebel Judith, but Louis's supporters, sowing discord among his older sons, restored him to authority in October, 830. Although abortive, the coup claimed a victim when the vision of empire outlined in the 817 *Ordinatio imperii* was annulled. The new *Divisio regnum* of 831 restored traditional Frankish practice when it partitioned the empire into four approximately equal kingdoms on Louis's death. The new status quo, however, was only temporary. Adherents of a unified empire agitated against the *Divisio*, while conflict among the brothers continued and was exacerbated when enterprising nobles took sides. On June 30, 833, Louis met with Lothar near Colmar in Alsace to compose their differences, but instead the emperor found himself on the "Field of Lies" facing a coalition of his older sons, their supporters, Pope Gregory IV, and several leading clergy, who took him and Judith into custody. Judith was sent to a monastery in Italy while Louis was confined to the monastery of Saint-Medard in Soissons. Leading clerics, including Agobard of Lyon and Ebbo of Reims, argued that Louis failed as a king and must abdicate the throne. In a humiliating ceremony, he acknowledged his crimes, removed his imperial regalia, and was condemned to perpetual penance. This mistreatment of a father by his sons, another round of conflict among the older brothers and their supporters, and increasing violence soon swung sympathy and support back to Louis who, from his confinement, was orchestrating his return. Freed from captivity, his weapons, his wife, and his youngest son were restored to him.

Emperor once again, Louis continued to rule energetically, bestowing key appointments on his supporters and punishing those such as Agobard and Ebbo who had betrayed him. He continued successfully to provide for Charles against the resistance of the younger Louis. When Pippin died in 838, Louis ignored the complaints of Pippin's son and granted the kingdom of Aquitaine to Charles. Lothar dedicated himself to his Italian lands and never challenged his father again. Louis rebuilt his own political network by holding frequent assemblies after 835 and by presiding at ceremonial and ritual activities, especially hunting, his favorite pastime. He continued to see to the collection of public revenue and directed successful military campaigns. In 839, an embassy from the Byzantine Empire arrived to congratulate him for his stout defense of Christendom.

On June 20, 840, Louis died on Petersaue, an island in the Rhine near his palace at Ingelehim. His last words reportedly were *Hutz, hutz* (German for "Away, away"), shouted as his mourners imagined to circling evil spirits. He was laid to rest in the monastery of Saint-Arnulf of Metz beside his mother and his sisters, Rotrud and Hilde-gard. Bishop Drogo, his half-brother, chose a late antique sarcophagus for him that depicted the flight of the Israelites across the Red Sea before the pursuing Egyptians. The motif symbolized baptism and triumph.

Bitter civil war broke out among his sons, resulting in 843 in the formal division of the empire recorded in the Treaty of Verdun.

See also **Charlemagne; Judith, Empress; Lothair I**

Further Reading

Boshof, Egon. *Ludwig der Fromme*. Darmstadt: Primus, 1996.
De Jong, Mayke. "Power and Humility in Carolingian Society: The Public Penance of Louis the Pious." *Early Medieval Europe* 1 (1992): 29–52.
Godman, Peter, and Roger Collins, eds. *Charlemagne's Heir: New Perspectives on the Reign of Louis the Pious*. Oxford: Clarendon Press, 1992.

JOHN J. CONTRENI

LOUIS XI (1423–1483)

The eldest son of Charles VII, Louis XI was raised in isolation from his father, and their subsequent animosity made Louis XI a political force long before he ascended the throne. Charged with the defense of Languedoc in 1439, he fell under the influence of rebellious nobles and joined the Praguerie. He was soon forgiven, but the continuing animosity between Louis and Charles seems to have increased after the death of Louis's wife, Margaret of Scotland, in 1445 and Louis retired to his apanage of the Dauphiné in 1447. There he began an apprenticeship for the throne by reforming provincial government. A disobedient remarriage to Charlotte of Savoy completed the family breach, and Louis fled the realm in 1456.

Louis began his reign in 1461 by ambitiously seeking to expand his authority both abroad, through the invasion of Catalonia, and at home, with his vengeful dismissal of his father's advisers and foolish rejection of previous allies. He barely survived the subsequent *Guerre du Bien Publique* and the indecisive Battle of Montlhéry in July 1465, but the rest of the reign was marked by a remarkable ability to learn from his mistakes. Henceforth, Louis handled his domestic adversaries by isolating and destroying each in turn and sought international success through diplomacy rather than war.

By judicious gifts and appointments, Louis reconciled himself to his father's advisers, Dunois and Chabannes and such dangerous peers as the duke of Bourbon. He isolated his brother Charles of France by the award of the apanage of Guyenne. Louis supported first the Lancastrians and then the Yorkists to prevent English intervention in France, subsidized Swiss resistance to Burgundy, and supported Angevin ventures in Italy to secure the southwest. The birth of a son in 1470 (the future Charles VIII), the death of his brother Charles in 1472, the destruction of remaining Armagnac strongholds in 1473, the execution of the count of Saint-Pol in 1475—all these combined to secure Louis's domestic authority.

Thereafter, Louis concentrated on Charles the Bold, duke of Burgundy, who, at Péronne in 1468, had humiliated him by extorting a guarantee of the independence of Flanders. Charles's death in 1477 was Louis's greatest stroke of good fortune. The remaining years of the reign were devoted to the acquisition of Burgundian territories. In these same years, Louis's annexation of Anjou and inheritance of Maine and Provence virtually completed the territorial unification of modern France before his death.

Louis's successes came as a fulfillment of his predecessors' policies. Ugly and socially isolated from his peers, Louis's rejection of medieval courtly behavior, dress, and ritual later endeared him to 19th-century romantics but in his own day alienated many whose help he needed. Louis was not some sort of "New Monarch" but rather an idiosyncratic medieval king whose breaches with convention often proved self-defeating and whose greatest successes came through the traditional means of diplomacy and warfare made possible by the military and fiscal reforms of his less colorful father.

See also **Charles VII**

Further Reading

Bittmann, Karl. *Ludwig XI. und Karl der Kuhne: Die Memoiren des Phillipe des Commynes als historische Quelle.* Göttingen: Vandenhoeck und Ruprecht, 1964.

Champion, Pierre. *Louis XI.* New York: Dodd, Mead, 1929.

Kendall, Paul M. *Louis XI: The Universal Spider.* New York: Norton, 1970.

Lewis, Peter S. *Later Medieval France: The Polity.* New York: St. Martin, 1968.

Tyrell, Joseph M. *Louis XI.* Boston: Twayne, 1980.

PAUL D. SOLON

LUITGARD OF AYWIÈRES
(Luitgard of Tongres; 1182–1246)

Born into a wealthy family, Luitgard entered the monastery of Sainte-Catherine at Saint-Trond at the age of twelve. Twelve years later, she was elected prioress but chose instead to leave for the Cistercian monastery at Aywières. After a long life of exemplary holiness, Luitgard died among her fellow sisters on July 16, 1246. She eventually became the patron saint of Flanders. Several *vitae* of Luitgard exist, the most notable being composed by Thomas de Cantimpré three years after her death. Luitgard's life was filled with an extravagant array of visions and miracles. The visions include highly abstract apparitions of light, concrete personal admonitions by Christ and by angelic messengers, political and ecclesiastical messages (e.g., asking her to fast for seven years because of the Albigensians), and contacts with souls in Purgatory. Among her miracles are such physical phenomena as levitation, profuse sweating and crying, ecstasies, healing with spittle and the laying on of hands, prophecy, and raptures.

Illiterate and unable to speak French, Luitgard nonetheless contributed powerful images to the growing movement of christocentric mysticism: Christ urges her repeatedly to drink directly from his bleeding wound and receives her heart in his own. Luitgard's *vita* offers remarkable insight into the flourishing communities of spiritual women and their mutual influence on each other. Marie d'Oignies, for example, is present at her deathbed and predicts Luitgard's miraculous activities from beyond the grave. A Cistercian nun, Sybille de Gages, composes a poem in her honor; Luitgard's spirit frequently appears to other nuns in visions.

See also **Marie d'Oignies**

Further Reading

Thomas de Cantimpré. *Vita Lutgardis,* ed. Pinius. *Acta Sanctorum* (1867) 3.187–209.

———. *The Life of Lutgard of Aywières,* trans. Margot H. King. Saskatoon: Peregrina, 1987.

Deboutte, A. "S. Lutgarde et sa spiritualité." *Collectanea cisterciensa* 44 (1982): 73–87.

Dinzelbacher, Peter. "Das Christusbild der heiligen Luitgard von Tongeren im Rahmen der Passionsmystik und Bildkunst des 12. und 13. Jahrhunderts." *Ons geestelijk erf* 56 (1982): 217–77.

ULRIKE WIETHAUS

LUNA, ÁLVARO DE (1388–1453)

Don Álvaro, as he is commonly referred to, was the illegitimate son of a minor noble of Aragónese origin by the same name. He was born in Castile at Cañete in 1388, and his mother was from that village. When his father died in 1395, Álvaro was taken in by his uncle, Juan Martínez de Luna. In 1408 Álvaro de Luna was sent to court to further his education. There he was known for his elegance and wit, and quickly became the friend, companion, and favorite of Prince Juan, the considerably younger boy who had inherited the throne during infancy and would become Juan II, king of Castile. From their earliest days together, Luna and the king were constant companions and confidantes. Fearing the worst of the association, the young prince's mother, the Queen Regent Catalina de Lancaster, arranged to have Luna removed from court in 1415. Juan was miserable without his friend's company, and Luna was quickly recalled. By 1418, when Catalina had died, Luna and the king's relationship had grown to the point that it inspired both public gossip and private envy among many of the nobles, who sought influence to augment their power at the expense of the crown. (In later years the king would be confronted by the nobles with rumors of their homosexual relationship). Luna, however, remained confident of the king's support and relied heavily on the backing of others who associated the crown's interests with their-own, namely the lower and middle layers of society. Luna brilliantly exploited the concerns and aspirations of the non-noble sectors of society and, at the same time, sought to increase his own influence as well as centralize the power of the monarchy. As a result, he undermined the power of the *cortes* (parliament) and the local municipalities, as he gathered more and more power for the crown and for himself. The king, who remained largely disinterested in affairs of state, became a virtual pawn of the ambitious Luna.

In 1420 Luna, who had been elevated to count and been given large estates, rescued the king from the Infantes de Aragón, who had seized the monarch and taken him to Talavera de la Reina. The Infantes, brothers of Alfonso V of Aragón, were closely allied with the Castilian nobles who sought to curb the power of the monarchy in the kingdom. Both had regal ambitions themselves and looked to protect their family's enormous interests in Castile. Luna was made the constable of Castile in 1423, a step which greatly increased his power and influence by making them official. The move provoked the nobles and the Infantes to multiply their efforts against him, which met with success in 1427, when they and the other nobles forced the king to exile Luna. Neither the king nor the nobles, however, were capable of governing Castile without Luna, whose talents had ensured his indispensability. As a result, he was quickly recalled and fully reinstated. The Castilian victory in the war against Aragón (1429) not only restored but amplified Luna's power and influence.

Luna seemed unstoppable. At one point, the mastery of the military Order of Santiago was conferred upon him after it had been stripped from the Infante Enrique, heir to the throne. With this new power in hand, Luna began to campaign against the Muslim south and led the Castilians to an important victory at the battle of La Higueruela in 1431. The nobles, presided over by the Manrique and Enríquez clans, continued to resist Luna and plot against him at court. Although their efforts led to a second exile in 1438, by 1445 Luna had been restored to favor and had handed the nobles a resounding defeat at the battle of Olmedo. Only King Juan's second wife, Isabel of Portugal, managed to rid the kingdom of Luna. With the collaboration of the nobles, especially the conde de Haro and the marqués de Santillana, she persuaded the king to arrest Luna and condemn him to death. He was taken prisoner at Easter, 1453, and publically beheaded at Valladolid on 22 June of that year.

As he went to his death, Luna, whose bravery was legendary, calmly requested that his executioner not tie his hands with the customary rope but with the silk cord he had brought for that purpose. Luna's spectacular rise and dramatic fall would continue to haunt the Castilian imagination for the next several centuries as an example of the whims of Fortune, inspiring many literary works that commemorated it. He is buried in the cathedral at Toledo. Juan II died the year after Luna's execution, overcome by personal grief and remorse.

Álvaro de Luna's diplomatic and military skills rank him among the most influential Iberian political leaders of the fifteenth century. Committed to a powerful monarchy and centralized authority based on broad popular support, his vision was only betrayed by an indecisive king and his own venality.

See also **Alfonso V, King of Aragón, The Magnanimous**

Further Reading

Round, N. G. *The Greatest Man Uncrowned: A Study of the Fall of Don Alvaro de Luna.* London, 1986.

E. MICHAEL GERLI

LYDGATE, JOHN (ca. 1370–1449)

The most prolific versifier of the 15th century. Lydgate was probably born in the village of Lydgate in Suffolk and apparently educated at the Benedictine monastery at Bury St. Edmunds, at which he was professed at the age of fifteen. He later studied at Oxford, probably at Gloucester Hall. He was ordained priest in the Benedictine order in 1397. In 1406 Prince Henry supported his return to study at Oxford. It was possibly while at Oxford that he wrote his translation of Aesop's *Fables*. His subsequent career suggests that he enjoyed Henry V's patronage. In 1423, after Henry's death, Lydgate became prior of Hatfield Broadoak in Essex. But from 1426 to 1429 he was in Paris as part of the entourage of John duke of Bedford, regent of France. By 1433 he had returned to Bury. Most of his later works seem to have been written there. He received a royal annuity in 1439 and died ten years later.

Lydgate's earliest major work was probably his *Troy Book*, a translation of Guido delle Colonne's *Historia destruccionis Troiae* (30,117 lines in couplets), which was begun at the behest of Henry V in 1412 and completed in 1420. Its composition appears to have been interrupted by the writing of *The Life of Our Lady*, ca. 1415–16 (5,932 lines, mostly in rime royal stanzas), written, he says, at Henry's "excitacioun." *The Siege of Thebes*, a history of the Theban legend, apparently based on a French source, was probably composed ca. 1420–21, as a continuation of Chaucer's *Canterbury Tales*. While in France in the late 1420s Lydgate probably wrote his translation of Deguileville's *Pilgrimage of the Life of Man* (24,832 lines in couplets) for Thomas Montacute, earl of Salisbury. Some of his shorter poems, including the *Danse Machabre*, also date from this time.

After his return to England in 1429 Lydgate wrote a number of celebratory verses for Henry VI's coronation. His *Lives of Sts. Edmund and Fremund* (3,508 lines in rime royal) was presented to the king in the 1430s, probably after the king's visit to Bury St. Edmunds in 1433–34. For the king's brother, Humphrey, duke of Gloucester, Lydgate wrote his longest work, *The Fall of Princes* (36,365 lines in rime royal), between ca. 1431 and 1438. It is a rendering of Laurent de Premierfait's French prose translation of Boccaccio's *De casibus virorum illustrium*. His last major works seem to have been his *Lives of Sts. Albon and Amphibel* (4,724 lines in rime royal), commissioned in 1439 by John Whethamstede, abbot of St. Albans, and a rime royal translation of the Pseudo-Aristotelian *Secreta secretorum*, left incomplete on his death and finished by Benedict Burgh. Other substantial poems attributed to Lydgate include a lengthy allegory, *Reason and Sensuality* (7,042 lines in couplets), and many shorter poems of doubtful canonicity.

In addition to these long poems there are numerous shorter ones on a variety of subjects. These include a popular dream vision, *The Temple of Glass*, and short verse narratives, such as his *Debate of the Horse Sheep and Goose* and *The Churl and the Bird*, several mummings, and a number of devotional lyrics. But the variety of Lydgate's poetic output resists concise summary: it ranges from his translation of Aesop to a treatise for laundresses and a dietary (instructions on healthy diet and behavior). By the most capacious estimates it runs to about 150,000 lines of verse. His sole prose work, *The Serpent of Division*, is a brief history of Rome.

This range of subject matter is reflected in the range of his patrons, which extended from royalty and nobility through a broad spectrum of English society, both religious and lay, male and female, individual and institutional. He was at the call of those who wished him to entertain, instruct, admonish, and propagandize on their behalf.

Lydgate stands crucially between Chaucer and the later evolution of English poetry. He wrote in the generation immediately after Chaucer's death and acknowledges Chaucer as his "master" in frequent lavish tributes. A number of his works are self-consciously conceived within a tradition of Chaucer's works that is reflected in imitation at conceptual, stylistic, and verbal levels. Thus his *Troy Book* sets itself in relation to the subject matter of *Troilus and Criseyde; The Siege of Thebes* contains an imitation of the beginning of the General Prologue and extensive verbal borrowings from the *Knight's Tale; The Complaint of the Black Knight* and *The Temple of Glass* imitate Chaucer's dream visions, *The Book of the Duchess* and *The House of Fame*, respectively. Lydgate was to play an important role in the creation and dissemination of the Chaucer tradition, particularly through his own popularizing of Chaucerian style and subjects.

Lydgate's Chaucerian imitation is related to the most distinctive tendency in his art, its rhetorical amplification. His instinct was to elaborate his materials, often on a massive scale. The most striking—or notorious—example of this tendency is the opening sentence of his *Siege of Thebes,* which imitates the opening sentence of Chaucer's General Prologue, Lydgate's sentence extends Chaucer's from eighteen to 65 lines. Indeed much of Lydgate's amplification comes from a natural tendency nurtured by a careful reading of Chaucer, through which poetic hints of his "master" could be vastly expanded. Thus, out of suggestions in Chaucer's language, he created a distinctive aureate diction, a Latin-derived, polysyllabic language that often characterizes his "high style," particularly in his religious verse. At its least successful, in conjunction with elaboration of allusion and syntax, it could lead to the obscurity that has earned him the condemnation of many modern critics.

Lydgate's meter systematizes Chaucer's versification through a regular use of five types of iambic pentameter line. One particularly striking feature of this systematization is the frequent use of the "headless" line (one that lacks an initial stressed syllable). Lydgate's own development of Chaucer's metrics was the "broken-backed" line, in which stressed syllables clash across the caesura.

It was probably through his amplification and systematization of Chaucer's art that Lydgate gained his considerable reputation in the 15th and 16th centuries. Allusions in that period acclaim him as part of a great triumvirate of ME poets, together with Chaucer and Gower. And in simple quantitative terms, in numbers of surviving manuscripts, Lydgate was the most popular of all ME poets. His *Fall of Princes* survives in complete or selected forms in over 80 manuscripts, his *Life of Our Lady* in nearly 50, *The Siege of Thebes* in 30. Among Lydgate's shorter poems both his *Verses on the Kings of England* and his *Dietary* exist in over 50 copies. In addition many of his works were issued by the early printers, Caxton, Pynson, and de Worde, often more than once.

This massive dissemination of Lydgate's works during the later Middle Ages led to his wide-ranging influence on later writers and forms. *The Fall of Princes* shaped literary conceptions of tragedy in the early Renaissance. His mummings are important texts in the evolution of English drama. And the works of (among others) Dunbar, Henryson, Douglas, Hawes, and Skelton, as well as many lesser figures, show the influence of his work in their writings, an influence that extended into the 17th century.

See also **Boccaccio, Giovanni; Chaucer, Geoffrey; Digulleville, Guillaume de; Gower, John; Henry** *V*

Further Reading

Primary Sources

Bergen, Henry, ed. *Lydgate's Troy Book.* 4 vols. EETS e.s. 97, 103, 106, 126. London: Humphrey Milford, 1906–35.

Bergen, Henry, ed. *Lydgate's Fall of Princes.* 4 vols. EETS e.s. 121–24. London: Humphrey Milford, 1924–27.

Erdmann, Axel, and Eilert Ekwall, eds. *Lydgate's Siege of Thebes,* 2 vols. EETS e.s. 108, 125. London: Kegan Paul, Trench, Trübner, 1911–30.

Furnivall, Frederick J., and Katherine B. Locock, eds. *The Pilgrimage of the Life of Man.* 3 vols. EETS e.s. 77, 83, 92. London: Kegan Paul, Trench, Trübner, 1899–1904.

Lauritis, Joseph A., R.A. Klinefelter, and V.F. Gallagher, eds. *A Critical Edition of John Lydgate's Life of Our Lady.* Pittsburgh: Duquesne University, 1961.

MacCracken, Henry Noble, ed. *The Minor Poems of John Lydgate.* 2 vols. EETS e.s. 107, o.s. 192. London: Kegan Paul, Trench, Trübner, 1911.

Humphrey Milford, 1934.

Norton-Smith, John, ed. *John Lydgate: Poems.* Oxford: Clarendon, 1966.

Reinecke, George F., ed. *Saint Albon and Saint Amphibalus.* New York: Garland, 1985.

Steele, Robert, ed. *Lydgate and Burgh's Secrees of Old Philisoffres.* EETS e.s. 66. London: Kegan Paul, Trench, Trübner, 1894.

Secondary Sources

New *CBEL* 1:639–46, 740.

Manual 6:1809–1920, 2071–2175.

Edwards, A.S.G. "Lydgate Scholarship: Progress and Prospects." In *Fifteenth Century Studies: Recent Essays,* ed. Robert F. Yeager. Hamden: Archon, 1984, pp. 29–47.

Pearsall, Derek. *John Lydgate.* London: Routledge & Kegan Paul, 1970.

Schirmer, Walter F. *John Lydgate: A Study in the Culture of the XVth Century.* Trans. Ann E. Keep. Berkeley: University of California Press, 1961.

A.S.G. EDWARDS

M

MACHAUT, GUILLAUME DE
(ca. 1300–1377)

The greatest French poet and composer of the 14th century. Machaut's narrative *dits* set a style in poetry that would predominate in France and England through the 15th century; his lyrics, many set to music, established and popularized the *formes fixes*; his *Messe de Nostre Dame* is the earliest surviving polyphonic setting of all movements of the Mass Ordinary by one composer; his strong interest in manuscript production made him a prime force in creating an awareness of the artist as a professional figure.

Born near Reims, Machaut probably received a university education in Paris. After his studies, he served from ca. 1323 to the late 1330s as personal secretary and clerk to Jean l'Aveugle of Luxembourg, king of Bohemia. In 1333, Jean procured a canonry at Reims for Machaut, whose name appears regularly in the records of Reims after 1340. With Jean's death in 1346 at the Battle of Crécy, Machaut did not lack for patrons. He composed his *Remede de Fortune* for Jean's daughter, Bonne of Luxembourg, who was also the mother of two of his most important patrons, Charles, duke of Normandy (later Charles V), and John, duke of Berry. Machaut praises Charles in his *Voir dit* (1363–65) and probably composed his last major poem, the verse chronicle *Prise d'Alexandrie* (ca. 1369–71), at his instigation. Machaut dedicated his *Fonteinne amoureuse* to the duke of Berry, and one of the most elaborate manuscripts of Machaut's collected works bears the duke's signature. In the early 1350s, Machaut established an important association with Charles the Bad, king of Navarre, whose family had hereditary connections with Champagne and who had married a daughter of Bonne and King John II. Although he apparently continued to cultivate royal patrons, no major works by Machaut are known after

the *Prise*, and public records do not speak of him again until his death in April 1377.

Most of Machaut's poetic and musical production can be dated to the period after he settled at Reims in the late 1330s until ca. 1370. He composed some 420 lyric poems, most in the *formes fixes* of *chant royal* (eight extant), ballade (239), rondeau (seventy-seven), virelai (forty), and *lai* (twenty-three). He also wrote twenty-three motets, nine *complaintes*, eight long and four shorter *dits amoureux*, a poem of comfort and counsel (*Confort d'ami*), the *Prise d'Alexandrie*, as well as a *Prologue* that introduced his late complete-works manuscripts. In total, Machaut produced some 60,000 lines of verse. He set about 140 of his lyrics to music, providing polyphonic settings of forty ballades, twenty-one rondeaux, four *lais*, one virelai, and twenty-three motets and monophonic settings for one ballade, sixteen *lais*, thirty virelais, one *complainte*, one chant *royal*, and two miscellaneous lyrics. The manuscripts also include music for his famous *Messe de Nostre Dame* and a text-less three-voice hocket.

Machaut's earliest narrative poem, the *Dit du vergier* (late 1330s; 1,293 lines), is an allegorical dream vision in the tradition of the *Roman de la Rose*. It is a first-person account of an encounter with the God of Love, who together with six youths and six maidens appears to the narrator in a grove. In three lengthy speeches, the god discourses on love and promises to help the narrator in his own amours, if he proves worthy.

The *Jugement du roy de Behaigne* (late 1330s; 2,079 lines) narrates a love debate and its resolution by Jean l'Aveugle. The allusions to this poem and the large number of extant manuscripts (twenty) are evidence that this was the most popular of Machaut's works. The question debated is who suffers more, the knight whose lady has taken a new lover or the lady whose beloved has died.

Jean decides in favor of the knight, then entertains both parties at his castle of Durbuy for a week. Elements of verisimilitude and the participation of a historical king bring a new air of realism to the *dit amoureux*.

Remede de Fortune (ca. 1340; 4,300 lines) is arguably the best and most influential French love poem of the 14th century. The Lover/Narrator tells of his long but silent love service to his lady. To pass time, he writes poems in the *formes fixes* about his love and circulates them anonymously, until one day a *lai* comes into his lady's hands. When she asks him who had written it, he is unable to speak and retreats in despondency to the Park of Hesdin, where he delivers a lengthy *complainte* against Love and Fortune. In response, Lady Hope appears and tells him that both Fortune and Love had treated him as well as could be expected. Encouraged by Hope, the Lover finally goes to his Lady's chateau and declares his love. Although they exchange rings, the Lady, prompted by the need for discretion and secrecy in love, later ignores him, and the poem ends on an ambiguous note. *Remede de Fortune* is an important didactic poem, serving as a manual for courtiers and providing a poetic and musical model for each of the *formes fixes*. Among the last and best of a line of French love poems that integrated lyrics with narrative, it also provided a model for the nonmusical narratives of such poets as Froissart, Granson, and especially Chaucer.

The *Dit du lyon* (2,204 lines), with the action set on April 2, 1342, is sometimes thought to be the original of Chaucer's lost *Book of the Lion*. The narrator comes onto an island, where he encounters a friendly lion; the lion leads him through a wasteland into a grove, where they are received by a noble lady and her retainers. Here, the narrator observes the love experience of the lion, who is harassed by the persecution of hostile beasts whenever his lady takes her gaze from him. The narrator intercedes on behalf of the lion before returning to his manor.

In the *Jugement du roy de Navarre* (1349; 4,212 lines), Machaut returns to the love debate of *Behaigne* and this time pronounces, through the person of Charles the Bad, king of Navarre, in favor of the Lady. Much more than a simple love debate, the poem is a complex commentary on the role of a poet and poetry in society. An important prologue evokes the Black Death.

The *Dit de l'alerion* (1350s; 4,814 lines) is a bird allegory that presents extensive analogies between birds of prey and women, between hawking and *fin'amors*. The Narrator/Lover tells of four raptors he has acquired, loved, and lost: a sparrowhawk, an alerion (a type of large eagle), an eagle, and a gerfalcon. Like the *Remede*, it is a didactic treatise on love; unlike that poem, it incorporates exempla drawn from historical and literary sources to make its points.

The *Fonteinne amoureuse* (1360–62; 2,848 lines) is a dream vision in which Machaut offers advice to his patron, Duke John of Berry. One night, the Narrator overhears a Lover bemoaning the fact he must go into exile (in actuality, John went to England in 1360 as a hostage after the Treaty of Brétigny) and be separated from his Lady. The next day in a garden, the Narrator and the Lover fall asleep near a fountain and are visited by Venus, who brings the Lady to comfort her suitor and assure him of her fidelity. The two men awaken and return to the castle; several days later, the Lover crosses the sea, but with joy in his heart.

In his last and lengthiest *dit amoureux*, the *Voir dit* (1363–65; 9,009 lines with intercalated prose letters), Machaut gives a pseudoautobiographical account of an affair with a young admirer, Toute-Belle. A sort of epistolary novel in verse, the work is more likely a fiction than an account of a real affair, though many early scholars sought to see in it a *roman à clef*. It is notable for its verisimilitude and for its apparently parodic depiction of *fin'amors*.

The shorter *dits* include the *Dit de la Marguerite*, the *Dit de la Fleur de Lis et de la Marguerite*, the *Dit de la Harpe*, and the *Dit de la Rose*.

In addition to his *dits amoureux*, Machaut composed two other long poems: *Confort d'ami* (1356–57; 4,004 lines) and *Prise d'Alexandrie* (1369–71; 8,886 lines and three prose letters). The *Confort*, incorporating many exempla, was written to console Charles the Bad, who had been taken prisoner by John II in April 1356. The *Prise* is a verse account of the career of Pierre de Lusignan, king of Cyprus, which culminated with the capture of Alexandria in 1365.

Machaut's musical works fall into three genres: motets, settings of fixed-form lyrics, and Mass. Fifteen of Machaut's motets set French texts, six set Latin texts, and two mix French and Latin. The earliest date we have for a work by Machaut is the Latin motet *Bone pastor Guillerme/Bone pastor qui/Bone pastor*, written for the occasion of the election of Guillaume de Trie as archbishop of Reims in 1324. Most of the remaining motets, dated before ca. 1350, celebrate *fin'amors*. The invective against Fortune in Machaut's most popular motet, *Qui es promesses/Ha Fortune/Et non est*, was known to Chaucer. The last three of Machaut's motets appear to relate to political events of the late 1350s. Formally, the motets use isorhythmic designs based on chant tenors and are evenly divided among bipartite designs with diminution and unipartite designs. Three motets are based on secular tenors in virelai or rondeau form, one of which, *Lasse comment oublieray/Se j'aim mon loyal/Pour quoy me bat mes maris*, sets a 13th-century dance song, the complaint of a *malmariée*.

Machaut is unique among 14th-century composers in his cultivation of the difficult *lai* with music. Although most of the musical *lais* are monophonic, their great length, demanding a half-hour or more in performance, requires an attention to formal balance and development unprecedented in medieval music.

The composition of polyphonic songs based on the *formes fixes* of ballade, rondeau, and virelai, began probably in the 1340s. Several experimental early works give the impression that Machaut was decisive in the development of this new musical style. The mature works, with a highly melismatic text carrying voice accompanied by textless tenor and contratenor, remained standard through most of the 15th century. A small core of works, mostly ballades, circulated widely, reaching Languedoc, Italy, and the empire, especially the popular *De petit po*, *De Fortune me day plaindre*, and *De toutes fleurs*. The learned enumeration of mythological characters in the *Voir dit* double ballade *Quant Theseus/Ne quier veoir* and the clear musical setting-off of the refrain are characteristics imitated in later 14th-century ballades.

Machaut's Mass, formerly thought to have been composed for the coronation of Charles V at Reims on May 19, 1364, is now considered to have been composed for a foundation made by Guillaume and his brother Jean for services to commemorate their deaths. The Mass appears to have been performed regularly at these services at the cathedral of Reims until after 1411.

Machaut stands at the culmination of a movement in French literature marked by a growing interest in the manuscript presentation of an author's works. Several manuscripts, prepared at various stages of Machaut's career, collect his complete works, carefully organized into sections by genre, most usually retaining the same order from manuscript to manuscript, with new works added at the end of each series. In general, it appears that each genre is arranged in chronological order. Such complete-works manuscripts had an influence on later poets, such as Froissart and Christine de Pizan; the transmission of musical works after Machaut, however, was confined largely to mixed anthologies.

The Machaut manuscripts are often elaborately illuminated, and the series of illustrations for a given narrative poem was in many cases doubtless determined by the author. The several artists who illustrated Machaut's manuscripts include figures known for their work on manuscripts of kings John II and Charles V. Unfortunately, the original owners of these volumes, except for a posthumous collection belonging to the duke of Berry, have not been conclusively identified.

See also **Charles II the Bad; Charles V the Wise; Christine de Pizan**

Further Reading

Machaut, Guillaume de. *Œuvres de Guillaume de Machaut*, ed. Ernest Hoepffner. 3 vols. Paris: Didot, 1908–21.
——. *Guillaume de Machaut: poésies lyriques*, ed. Vladimir Chichmaref. 2 vols. Paris: Champion, 1909.
——. *Guillaume de Machaut: Musikalische Werke*, ed. Friedrich Ludwig. 4 vols. Leipzig: Breitkopf and Härtel, 1926–54.
——. *Polyphonic Music of the Fourteenth Century*, ed. Leo Schrade. Monaco: L'Oiseau-Lyre, 1956, Vols. 2–3: *The Works of Guillaume de Machaut*.
——. *Guillaume de Machaut*: *Le jugement du roy de Behaigne and Remede de Fortune*, ed. and trans. James I. Wimsatt, William W. Kibler, and Rebecca A. Baltzer. Athens: University of Georgia Press, 1988.
——. *The Judgment of the King of Navarre*, ed. and trans. R. Barton Palmer. New York: Garland, 1988.
——. *Le confort d'ami*, ed. and trans. R. Barton Palmer. New York: Garland, 1992.
Avril, François. *Manuscript Painting at the Court of France*: *The Fourteenth Century*. New York: Braziller, 1978.
Brownlee, Kevin. *Poetic Identity in Guillaume de Machaut*. Madison: University of Wisconsin Press, 1984.
Calin, William. *A Poet at the Fountain: Essays on the Narrative Verse of Guillaume de Machaut*. Lexington: University of Kentucky Press, 1974.
Cerquiglini, Jacqueline. "*Un engin si soutil*": *Guillaume de Machaut et l'écriture au XIVe siècle*. Paris: Champion, 1985.
Earp, Lawrence. *Guillaume de Machaut: A Guide to Research*. Forthcoming.
Guillaume de Machaut: poète et compositeur. Paris: Klincksieck, 1982.
Huot, Silvia. *From Song to Book: The Poetics of Writing in Old French Lyric and Lyrical Narrative Poetry*. Ithaca: Cornell University Press, 1987.
Imbs, Paul. *Le Voir-dit de Guillaume de Machaut: étude littéraire*. Paris: Klincksieck, 1991.
Leech-Wilkinson, Daniel. *Machaut's Mass*: *An Introduction*. Oxford: Clarendon, 1990.
Machabey, Armand. *Guillaume de Machaut: La vie et l'œuvre musicale*. 2 vols. Paris: Richard-Masse, 1955.
Poirion, Daniel. *Le poète et le prince*: *l'évolution du lyrisme courtois de Guillaume de Machaut à Charles d'Orléans*. Paris: Presses Universitaires de France, 1965.

WILLIAM W. KIBLER/LAWRENCE EARP

MACROBIUS (fl. 400-425)

The identity of Macrobius is disputed. Although not a Roman by birthplace, he lived in Rome and received a good education by the standards of his time. His two major works—written for the education of his son, Eustathius—were *Saturnalia* and *Commentary on the Dream of Scipio*. These had the greatest influence in the Middle Ages and Renaissance, although one or two other writings have also been attributed to Macrobius. Macrobius's thought is based on Platonic philosophy and cosmology; he also was recognized as an authority on the virtues.

The *Saturnalia* has not survived in its entirety. All extant manuscripts derive from a single codex of the late eighth or early ninth century. Today the work is divided into seven books that constitute a symposium or banquet; that is, the *Saturnalia* purports to relate how a gathering of learned men celebrated in seemly fashion the three-day feast of the Saturnalia by discussing learned or entertaining features of Virgil's life, knowledge, and poetry. Virgil is esteemed by almost every celebrant as a master of all knowledge; his *Aeneid* is itself viewed as a kind of sacred poem deserving admiration and understanding. Various topics are chosen for discussion and debate during the gathering. On the first day, the men take up different Roman institutions such as the Saturnalian feast itself, the calendar, and religion; these subjects are followed, in the afternoon, by striking sayings from antiquity and, later, topics such as wine and pleasure (Books 1 and 2). On the second day, they take up philosophical and astronomical topics and legal institutions, then commentary on civilization, and finally the quality of different fruits (Book 3). On the third and last day, there is discussion of Virgil as an artist, and especially as a rhetorician and a consummate imitator of Homer and other Greek and Latin antecedents; this section includes extensive quotations from, and cross-references to, Virgil's three masterpieces: *the Aeneid, Bucolics,* and *Georgics* (Books 4, 5, and 6). The last book treats scientific and medical matters. The *Saturnalia* therefore illustrates what was of interest to educated, civilized Romans in Macrobius's time.

The *Commentary on the Dream of Scipio* survives complete. Its two books contain extensive commentary on scientific and philosophical topics suggested by Cicero's account of Scipio's dream of his elevation to the heavens after death. The most influential part of the *Commentary* is found at the beginning. Here Macrobius discusses the uses of fables *(narratio fabulosa)* in philosophical discourse and the distinction between true and false dreams. Philosophical fables are allegories in which the myth covers a truth about divinity, science, or morality. Among the allegories are dreams, which Macrobius classifies as true or false prophecies (he categorizes them according to mode). The most important are enigmatic dreams that may be true *(somnium)* or false *(insomnium),* as in wish-fulfillment dreams or nightmares. The *visum* shows the dreamer what will actually happen, and the *oraculum* has someone tell him or her of future events. However, if what is seen or foretold in the dream is false, it is termed a *visio.* These definitions serve as an introduction to Cicero's text, the fictional account of a dream. The commentary that follows draws its abundant philosophical and scientific information from Platonic cosmology.

The *Saturnalia* and the *Commentary* were widely disseminated during the Middle Ages, although their relative influence varied, if we can judge by the dates and numbers of manuscripts that survive from different periods. Both served as encyclopedic sources in Platonic and Neoplatonic philosophy and cosmogony. The influence of the *Commentary* reached a high point in the twelfth and thirteenth centuries, whereas the *Saturnalia* came into its own in the late medieval period and the Renaissance. This is not to say, however, that both were not widely known and used in all periods. In Italy, Macrobius influenced Boccacio, Petrarch, and probably Dante, among others. Moreover, the discussion in *Saturnalia* concerning Virgil's art fit medieval ideas on literary composition and interpretation, especially in the art of invention and rewriting of antecedent sources. Such rewriting could be original. The way Virgil is said to imitate and allude to his Greek and Latin antecedents might well have influenced Dante's rewriting of his master Virgil in the *Divine Comedy.* The representation of his universe might well have been influenced by cosmogonies like that in Macrobius's *Commentary.*

See also **Boccaccio, Giovanni; Dante Alighieri; Petrarca, Francesco**

Further Reading

Editions and Translations

Macrobius. *Commentary on the Dream of Scipio,* trans. William Harris Stahl. Records of Civilization: Sources and Studies, 48. New York: Columbia University Press, 1952.

——. *Commentarii in somnium Scipionis,* ed. Jacob Willis. Leipzig: Teubner, 1963a.

——. *Saturnalia,* ed. Jacob Willis. Leipzig: Teubner, 1963b.

——. *I saturnali,* ed. and trans. Nino Marinone. Classici Latini. Turin: Unione Tipografico-Edkrice Torinese, 1967.

——. *The Saturnalia,* trans. Percival Vaughan Davies. Records of Civilization: Sources and Studies, 79. New York: Columbia University Press, 1969.

Studies

Barker-Benfield, B. C., and P. K. Marshall. "Macrobius." In *Texts and Transmission: A Survey of the Latin Classics,* ed. L. D. Reynolds. Oxford: Clarendon, 1983, pp. 222–235.

De Paolis, Paolo. "Macrobio 1934–1984." *Lustrum,* 28–29, 1986, pp. 107–254.

——. "Addendum." *Lustrum,* 30, 1988, pp. 7–9.

Dronke, Peter. *Fabula: Explorations into the Uses of Myth in Medieval Platonism.* Mittellateinische Studien und Texte, 9. Leiden, Cologne: Brill, 1974.

Hüttig, Albrecht. *Macrobius im Mittelaker: Ein Beitrag zur Rezeptionsgeschichte der Commentarii in Somnium Scipionis.* Freiburger Beiträge zur Mittelaiterlichen Geschichte: Studien und Texte, 2. Frankfurt, Bern, New York, and Paris: Peter Lang, 1990.

Kelly, Douglas. *The Conspiracy of Allusion: Description, Rewriting, and Authorship from Macrobius to Medieval Romance.* Studies in Christian Thought, 20. Leiden: Brill, 1999.

Maronine, Nino. "Macrobio." *Enciclopedia virgiliana,* Vol. 3. Rome: Istituto della Enciclopedia Italians, 1987, pp. 299–304.

Rabuse, Georg. "Macrobio, Ambrosio Teodosio." *Enciclopedia dantesca.* Vol. 3. Rome: Istituto della Enciclopedia Italiana, 1984, pp. 757–759.

DOUGLAS KELLY

MAGNÚS HÁKONARSON
(r. 1263-1280)

Magnús Hákonarson son of Hákon Hákonarson, ruled Norway 1263–1280; he became king in 1257, and ruled together with his father until Hákon died in 1263.

Magnús Hákonarson and his closest advisers, the "good men," concentrated on the domestic conditions of Norway. Legislative and organizational work characterized Magnús Hákonarson's reign, and secured him the name *lagabætir* ("law-mender"). During his reign, the State Council was more firmly structured than before. Furthermore, he saw to it that a staff of civil servants was educated at the royal chapel, the Apostolic Church in Bergen. We are able to distinguish a group of diplomats employed in his service during his reign.

The object of his legislation was a comprehensive revision of the old law books. The legal revision was a continuation of the State Laws dating from the time of Magnús Erlingsson (1161–1184) and Hákon Hákonarson (1217–1263). The latter had initiated the revision of the Frostuþing Law. The revision of the law went through two stages. The first one included a revision of the law books for Gulaþing in 1267, and Eiðsifa- and Borgarþing in 1268. The latter consisted of the working out of the National Law in 1274 (which also came to apply to the Faroe Islands), a Town Law in 1276, and two law codes for Iceland, *Járnsíða* in 1271 and *Jónsbók* in 1281. An older court law was expanded and revised, and became the *Hirðskrá* (1273–1277).

The object of this legislative work was to create uniform laws for the entire country. The legislation increased the authority of the king with regard to the administration and execution of the laws, as well as the public regulation of society. At the same time, it entailed important reforms, regulation of the tax system and of the institutions for the poor. There is no actual Christian Law in the National Law. The reason for this exclusion was a major conflict between the monarchy and the Church concerning Christian legislation, dating from the end of the 1260s. Magnús Hákonarson claimed that the king and the Church should administer the Christian legislation in unison. On the basis of this claim, Christian legislative decisions were publicized in a statute dating from the middle of the 1260s. The revision of the Gulaþing Law and the Eiðsifa-and Borgarþing law in 1267 and 1268 included the Christian Law. During the revision of the Frostubing Law, the king was strongly opposed by the new archbishop, Jón rauði ("the red"), who independently started to make a Trondic Christian Law in accordance with purely ecclesiastical principles. The conflict between the king and the archbishop was difficult, but an agreement was reached in Tønsberg in 1277.

Magnús Hákonarson's first task as absolute monarch was to conclude a peace treaty with Scotland. Thus, he abandoned his father's expansive foreign policy. The negotiations with the Scottish king began in 1264, and an agreement was reached two years later, the Treaty of Perth. Magnús Hákonarson gave up his claim to the contested islands, the Hebrides and the Isle of Man, in return for a one-time compensation of 4,000 pounds sterling and 100 pounds sterling annually in perpetuity; at the same time, Norwegian control over the Orkney Islands and the Shetland Islands was secured. Magnús Hákonarson preserved the contact his father had established with neighboring countries and with Europe. His relations with Sweden and Denmark were peaceful, even though he became involved in the dispute over the throne in Sweden in the 1270s and in inheritance claims in Denmark. He also extended legal rights of all German-speaking merchants in Norway, surpassing the rights of native and other foreign merchants. This was the first step in the development of special privileges for the Germans in Norway, based upon their special role in the economy of the country.

See also **Hákon Hákonarson**

Further Reading

Literature

Koht, Halvdan. "The Scandinavian Kingdoms Until the End of the Thirteenth Century." In *The Cambridge Medieval History 6*. Ed. J. R. Tanner *et al.* Cambridge: Cambridge University Press, 1929, pp. 362–92.

Seip, Jens Arup. *Sættargjerden i Tunsberg og kirkens jurisdiksjon.* Oslo: Det Norske Videnskaps-akademi i Oslo, 1942.

Helle, Knui. "Tendenser i nyere norsk høymiddelalderforskning." *Historisk tidsskrift* (Norway) 40 (1960–61), 337–70.

Helle, Knut. "Trade and Shipping Between Norway and England in the Reign of Håkon Håkonsson (1217–1263)." *Sjøfartshistorisk årbok* (Bergen) (1967), 7–33.

Helle, Knut. "Anglo-Norwegian Relations in the Reign of Håkon Håkonsson 1217–63." *Mediaeval Scandinavia* 1 (1968), 101–14.

Gunnes, Erik. "Kirkeligjurisdiksjon i Norge 1153–1277." *Historisk tidsskrift* (Norway) 49 (1970), 121–60.

Crawford, Barbara E. "The Earls of Orkney-Caithness and Their Relations with the Kings of Norway and Scotland: 1150–1470." Diss. St. Andrews University, 1971.

Helle, Knut. *Konge og gode menn i norsk riksstyring ca. 1150–1319.* Bergern Universitetsforlaget, 1972.

Crawford, Barbara E. "Weland of Stiklaw: A Scottish Royal Servant at the Norwegian Court." *Historisk tidsskrift* (Norway) 52 (1973), 329–39.

Helle, Knut. *Norge blir en stat 1130–1319.* 2nd ed. Handbok i Norges historie, 3. Bergen: Universitetsforiaget, 1974.

Lunden, Kåre. *Norge under Sverreætten 1177–1319.* Norges historie, 3. Oslo: Cappelen, 1976.

Bagge, Sverre. "Kirkens jurisdiksjon i kristenrettssaker før 1277." *Historisk tidsskrift* (Norway) 60 (1981), 133–59.

Helle, Knut. "Norway in the High Middle Ages: Recent Views

on the Structure of Society." *Scandinavian Journal of History* 6 (1981), 161–89.

Bagge, Sverre. "The Formation of the State and Concepts of Society in 13th Century Norway." In *Continuity and Change: Political Institutions and Literary Monuments in the Middle Ages. A Symposium.* Ed. Elisabeth Vestergaard. Odense: Odense University Press, 1986, pp. 43–61.

Bagge, Sverre. "Borgerkrig og statsutvikling i Norge i middelalderen." *Historisk tidsskrift* (Norway) 65 (1986), 145–97.

Sandvik, Gudmund. "Sættargjerda i Tunsberg og kongens jurisdiksjon." In *Samfunn. Rett. Rettferdighet. Festskrift til Torstein Eckhoffs 70-årsdag.* Ed. A. Bratholm *et al.* Oslo: Tano, 1986, pp. 563–85.

Bagge, Sverre. *The Political Thought of the King's Mirror.* Mediaeval Scandinavia Supplements, 3. Odense: Odense University Press, 1987.

JÓN VIÐAR SIGURÐSSON

MAIMONIDES (1138–1204)

Likened by more than one medieval Jewish writer to the prophet Moses ("From Moses to Moses there was none like Moses"), Moses ben Maimon (correctly, Maimūn) was born in Córdoba not in 1135, as is usually assumed (and so the 850th anniversary was universally celebrated in 1985) but in 1138, where he was educated and began writing his first works.

His father, Maimkn, was a *dayan* (religious judge) of the Jewish community of Córdoba, and a student of the great Joseph ibn Megash, and himself author of some responsa and "Letters of Consolation" meant to strengthen the Jews in the face of the Almohad persecution. It was due to this that the family left Spain around 1160, settling first in Fez, Morocco, and then briefly in Palestine. From there they went to Egypt and settled at Fustat, a suburb of Cairo, where Jews were allowed to live. The twin tragedies of the death of his father and then his brother David devasted the young scholar, who had to support himself and his family by becoming a doctor and court physician to the *wazīr* (prime minister) and his son. Never did he convert, or even appear outwardly to do so, to Islam, as a long-discredited legend maintains.

Within a few years he had become by reputation the most famous physician of the Muslim world. At the same time, his reputation in Jewish learning, established already by his brilliant commentary on the Mishnah, was growing. Questions poured in from all parts of the world. Working almost entirely from memory, and under the most difficult conditions imposed upon him by the demands of his medical practice, he composed in clear and simple Hebrew the *Mishneh Torah*, a work in fourteen volumes that encompasses the whole of Jewish law. This work quickly became the accepted authority for Jewish law, the only such composition ever written by someone who was not a rabbi.

Nevertheless, there were critics. First, he had not cited his sources, and although sources have been found for virtually every statement, lesser scholars had difficulty in accepting some of his rulings. Second, there were disagreements in some cases as to the rulings themselves. Finally, certain religious zealots who lacked training in philosophy objected strenuously to his philosophical notions, contained both in his commentary on the Mishnah and in the legal code. The situation worsened when he wrote his great philosophical work, *Dalālat al-bā'irīn* (*Guide for the Perplexed*). Clearly intended only for those with the necessary preliminary background of rigorous study, the book was translated twice from Judeo-Arabic into Hebrew and thus soon fell into the hands of those without such background. Its clear denial of such fundamental popular beliefs as miracles, creation in time, resurrection, and so forth combined with allegorizing of many biblical and rabbinic statements, gave rise to charges of heresy. The result was a controversy that lasted in Spain and Provence for hundreds of years, and actually led to Jewish-inspired condemnation and burning of the book at Montpellier around 1232.

In spite of the philosophical controversy, Maimonides continued to be revered as a legal authority throughout the Middle Ages in Spain and elsewhere. Even those who disagreed with him, such as Nahmanides and Ibn Adret, cite him constantly and respectfully. Communities, such as Tudela, enacted decrees according to which only his rulings were to be followed; similar decisions were made throughout North Africa and Yemen.

No less important was his impact on Christians in Spain. In Aragón-Catalonia, various kings ordered translations of the *Guide* and even of the *Mishneh Torah*. Philosophers in Spain (and, of course, the scholastics in general) who were influenced by him include Poncio Carbonell (fourteenth century) and, more important, Alfonso de la Torre (fifteenth century). Sancho, son of Jaime I, archbishop of Toledo (1266–1275), and Archbishop Gonzalo García Gudiel (1280–1299) both possessed copies of his work. In the fifteenth century, Pedro Díaz de Toledo, possibly a *converso* (Jewish convert to Christianity), made a Spanish translation of the *Guide*.

Maimonides died in 1204, and tradition maintains that his grave is near Tiberias.

Further Reading

Maimonides. *Guide for the Perplexed.* Trans. P. Díaz de Toledo. Ed. Moshé Lazar. Madison, Wisc., 1989.

Ormsby, E. (ed.) *Moses Maimonides and His Time.* Washington, D.C., 1989.

Roth, N. *Maimonides: Essays and Texts.* Madison, Wisc., 1985 (also with bibliographies, including Spanish).

NORMAN ROTH

MALISPINI, RICORDANO
(probably 14th century)

Ricordano Malispini was allegedly the thirteenth-century author of a history of Florence from its legendary origins to 1282; a continuation down to 1286 was ascribed to a nephew, Giacotto. Some scholars consider this chronicle an important source for Giovanni Villani and Dante. Documentary evidence has been found for Giacotto's existence, though not for Ricordano's. However, the chronicle itself contains anachronisms, some of which were first noted by Scheffer-Boichorst (1870), and these make a fourteenth-century date very probable. A chief purpose of the chronicle appears to have been to celebrate the exploits of members of the Bonaguisi family, and to link the Bonaguisi with the aristocratic and once-powerful Malispini family. Malispini writes that he derived his information from chronicles he found in the house of his Capocci kinsmen in Rome, and also in the Badia of Florence. The Capocci records seem identifiable with the *Libro fiesolano,* which is a translation and adaptation of the *Liber de origine civitatis,* the first surviving account of the founding of Florence. The Badia records seem identifiable with an anonymous compendium of Giovanni Villani. The only known text of this compendium, discovered by Lami (1890), is manuscript 2.1.252, held in the Biblioteca Nazionale Centrale in Florence. Malispini also includes information about some families that are not mentioned either in the *Libro fiesolano* or in the compendium of Villani.

The *Libro fiesolano* covers the period from the legendary origins of Florence to its rebuilding after Totila's sack (which is fictitious) and the final capture of Fiesole. The anonymous compendium abridges and paraphrases Villani's chronicle from chapter 30 of the first book (Catiline's conspiracy) until 1336. Malispini copies his account of early Florentine history from the *Libro fiesolano,* rather than from the anonymous compendium, but he includes Charlemagne's supposed participation in the rebuilding of Florence, which is mentioned in the compendium but omitted in *Libro fiesolano.* Malispini then follows the anonymous compendium to 1282, and Giacotto's coda follows it to 1286.

One manuscript, often considered the oldest and most reliable copy of Malispini, has a distinctive relationship to the anonymous compendium. This is manuscript 2.4.27, in the Biblioteca Nazionale Centrale in Florence. It corresponds almost exactly to the anonymous compendium not only for the period from Charlemagne to 1286, but also for 1286–1317. The only novelty in this concluding post-Malispinian portion of the manuscript is its interpolated passages praising the Bonaguisi and other related families. These passages are very similar to others praising the same families in this and other manuscripts of the Malispinian chronicle. The presence of such passages in both the Malispinian and the post-Malispinian portions of this manuscript points to the genealogical purpose and the fourteenth-century date of the Malispinian compilation. A further confirmation of its late date is furnished by Porta (1986, 1994), who discovered links between the texts of the anonymous compendium of Villani and Malispini on the one hand, and a revised version, made after 1333, of Giovanni Villani's chronicle on the other. If Villani had copied Malispini, diese links would be present in the first version of Villani's chronicle as well.

Such evidence should lay to rest the old theory that Malispini was the thirteenth-century father of Florentine historiography. Malispini was, rather, a late fourteenth-century compiler, whose originality was limited to celebrating the nobility and antiquity of certain Florentine families and to furnishing information about himself and his sources designed to validate such genealogical lore.

Further Reading

Editions

Libro fiesolano, ed. Otio Hartwig. In *Quellen und Forschungen zur ältesten Geschichte der Stadt Florenz,* Vol. 1. Marburg: N. G. Elwert'sche Verlagsbuch, 1875, pp. 37–65.

Malispini, Ricordano. *Storia fiorentina, col seguito di Giacotto Malispini, dalla edificazione di Firenze sino all'anno 1286,* ed.Vincenzio Follini. Florence: G. Ricri, 1816.

Villani, Giovanni. *Nuova cronica,* 3 vols., ed. Giuseppe Porta. Parma: Ugo Guanda Editore, 1990–1991.

Critical Studies

Aquilecchia, Giovanni. "Malispini, Ricordano." In *Encyclopedia dantesca,* Vol. 3. Rome: Istituto della Encyclopedia Italiana, 1971, pp. 791–792.

Barnes, John C. "Un problems in via di chiusura: La 'Cronica' malispiniana." *Studi e Problemi di Critica Testuale,* 27, 1983, pp. 15–32.

Davis, Charles T. *Dante and the Idea of Rome.* Oxford: Clarendon, 1957, pp. 244–263.

——. "The Malispini Question." *Studi Medievali,* Series 3(10), 1970, pp. 215–254. (Reprinted in *Dante's Italy and Other Essays.* Philadelphia: University of Pennsylvania Press, 1984, pp. 94–136.)

De Matteis, Maria C. "Ancora su Malispini, Villani, e Dante: Per un riesame dei rapporti tra cultura storica e profezia Erica nell'Alighieri." *Bullettino dell'Istituto Storico Italiano per il Medio Evo e Archivio Muratoriano,* 82, 1970, pp. 329–390. (Published 1973.)

——. "Malispini da Villani o Villani da Malispini? Una ipotesi sui rapporti tra Ricordano Malispini, il 'Compendiatore,' e Giovanni Villani." *Bullettino dell'Istituto Storico Italiano per il Media Evo e Archivio Muratoriano,* 84, 1973, pp. 145–221. (Published 1978.)

Lami, Vittorio. "Di un compendio inedito della cronica di Giovanni Villani nelle sue relazioni con la storia fiorentina malispiniana." *Archivio Storico Italiano,* Series 5(5), 1890, pp. 369–416.

Maissen, Thomas. "Actila, Totila, e Cario Magno." *Archivio Storico Italiano,* 152 (fasc. 561), 1994, pp. 586–639.

Morghen, Raffaello. "Note malispiniane." *Bullettino dell'Istituto Storico Italiano per il Media Evo e Archivio Muratoriano,* 40, 1920, pp. 105–126.

——. "Dante, il Villani, e Ricordano Malispini." *Bullettino dell'Istituto Storico Italiano per il Media Evo e Archivio Muratoriano,* 41, 1921, pp. 171–194.

——. "Ancora sulla questione malispiniana." *Bullettino dell'Istituto Storico Italiano per il Media Evo e Archivio Muratoriano,* 46, 1931, pp. 41–92.

Porta, Giuseppe. "Sul testo e la lingua di Giovanni Villani." *Lingua Nostra,* 47, 1986, pp. 37–40.

——. "Le varianti redazionali come strumento di verifica dell'autenticità dei testi: Villani e Malispini." *Convegno della società italiana di filologia romanza, Università di Messina, December 19–22, 1991.* Messina, 1994, pp. 481–529.

Scheffer–Boichorst, Paul. "Die florentinische Geschichte der Malespini, eine Fälschung." *Historische Zeitschrift,* 24, 1870, pp. 274–313. (Reprinted in *Florentiner Studien.* Leipzig: S. Hirzel, 1874, pp. 1–44.)

CHARLES T. DAVIS

MALORY, THOMAS (1414/18–1471)

One of the latest and most effective of the many medieval writers about King Arthur and his knights of the Round Table. In his book traditionally called *Le Morte Darthur (The Death of Arthur)* Malory gathers together the results of centuries of storytelling, mainly by medieval French authors. He synthesizes the narratives into one massive, varied book of the life, acts, and death of Arthur and his company. The wealth of incident, rich implications, and laconic style make his the only version of the huge number of medieval Arthurian tales in European languages that continues to be read directly and simply for pleasure by the modern reader. The main characters—King Arthur himself; Sir Lancelot, his best knight, but also lover of his queen, Guinevere; his sister's son the violent Sir Gawain; his incestuously begotten son and nephew Sir Mordred, who kills him; Merlin the magician—are at the center of a set of tales of wonders, bravery, love, joy, and tragedy. But Malory tells romance as history—the history of England said to be in the 5th century, but actually represented in terms of the feelings, strivings, ideals, betrayals, even the armor and the geography (e.g., Camelot is identified with Winchester) of Malory's own troubled 15th-century England. Malory's achievement is the source of many of the retellings of Arthurian story so common today in the United States and Britain.

Life

Identification of the Sir Thomas Malory who names himself as author of *Le Morte Darthur* has been controversial, but thanks to the work of P.J.C. Field and others it seems once more to be probable that he was the Sir Thomas Malory of Newbold Revel in Warwickshire. He was the son of a country gentleman, inherited his lands in 1433 or 1434, was knighted, and perhaps served as a soldier in France. In 1445 he became a member of parliament—a sign of gentry status, not of democratic election. He also became embroiled in the factional disturbances of the times and was on numerous occasions in the next ten years accused of such violent crimes as ambush, rape, extortion, cattle stealing, theft of money, and prison breaking. He underwent a series of imprisonments and despite his escapes spent much time in jail. Some of the accusations, perhaps some of the violence, may have been politically motivated, for Malory supported various noblemen (including Warwick the "Kingmaker") who contended for power during the Wars of the Roses, following now one king, the Lancastrian Henry VI, and now another, the Yorkist Edward IV.

After a period of freedom Malory spent the years 1468–70 in prison, where he wrote *Le Morte Darthur.* The book is full of violent adventure and concludes in civil war and Arthur's death. But it is also deeply concerned with the high ideals of chivalry, with honor, loyalty, and goodness. It may seem that the book's inherent nobility contrasts strangely with the apparent criminality of the author. But perhaps Malory saw himself in imagination as a modern Sir Lancelot fighting for and asserting his own and his lord's rights against other "false recreant knights," as he might have called them.

Text

Two versions of *Le Morte Darthur* survive, neither originating immediately from Malory's hand. One is the edition printed by Caxton in 1485, reprinted 1498, 1529, 1557, circa 1578, again (somewhat changed) in 1634, then not again till 1816, In the later 19th century began the modern series of editions based on Caxton, including that notoriously illustrated by Aubrey Beardsley (1893–94). But in 1934 a manuscript of *Le Morte Darthur* now in the British Library (Add. 59678) was discovered in Winchester College; it was first edited in 1947 by Eugène Vinaver.

The Winchester manuscript contains a text slightly different from Caxton's, including fuller versions of eight addresses by Malory to the reader, varying in length from a few sentences to the paragraph at the end of the whole book. They come at the end of substantial sections and are known as *explicits* (*explicit,* "it is finished"). From these *explicits* Vinaver deduced that, instead of one book, Malory wrote eight entirely separate romances. Their apparent separateness is enhanced in his edition by such typographical devices as capitals at the end of the sections for which there is no manuscript justification. Vinaver's edition is thus confusingly entitled *The Works of Sir Thomas Malory*. Virtually all scholars and critics now reject this concept of totally separate works but do accept the episodic nature of the work even within the eight main sections and the existence of a number of inevitable inconsistencies both between and within the main sections.

The Winchester manuscript is separated from Malory's own writing by at least one intermediate copy and lacks a few leaves at beginning and end. Although Caxton had the Winchester manuscript in his shop for a period of time, his own edition differs from it significantly. He edited the text by cutting it into 21 books comptising 507 chapters, adding a fine Prologue and chapter headings, reducing some of the *explicits*, shortening (to its advantage) the episode of the Roman War by almost half, and making some other minor verbal changes. By comparing the two versions we can reconstruct Malory's authentic text, which is now most nearly approached by Vinaver's edition.

The language of the Winchester manuscript and Caxton's edition is mainly standard mid-15th-century London English, with occasional northernisms. Being prose, it is easily modernized; the original, though old-fashioned and containing a few unfamiliar words, offers no difficulty apart from idiosyncratic spelling. As a narrative the story is engrossing, but it is not at all like a modern novel, and to read it as such is to court disappointment and misunderstanding.

Summary

Malory plunges straight into his story, telling of the begetting of Arthur by Uther Pendragon, king of all England, on the beautiful widow (as she has just unwittingly become) of the duke of Cornwall, Uther being magically transformed by Merlin into the duke's likeness so as to enter her bedroom. The laconic matter-of-fact style, concentrating on essentials, contrasts piquantly with the drama of passionate feeling and the magic. This contrast, much developed, is part of Malory's unending fascination. As his great story progresses, he makes less use of magic, though it is always an element of mystery in the background, suggesting a dimension beyond the material world and becoming prominent again near the end, with the return of Excalibur to the lake and the queens who carry off the dying Arthur.

We learn of Arthur's fostering, his acceptance as king by the miracle that he alone can draw a sword from a stone, and the gradual establishment of his power over dissident barons and neighboring kings. Merlin's magic helps. Arthur lusts after King Lot of Orkney's wife, Morgause, mother of Gawain and other heroic knights and, unknown to him, his own half-sister. On her he begets Mordred, who will ultimately be his death. Arthur loves and marries Guinevere, though Merlin warns him that she and Lancelot will love each other. She brings with her the Round Table, which henceforth will denote the elite company of knights in Arthur's court.

This first section thus sets the scene and establishes Arthur's supremacy, though with its account of wars it is a little less typical of Malory's mature style, which concentrates more on individual adventures. Malory is attempting to summarize his complex sources of French prose romance, turning them into a kind of history, and minor inconsistencies inevitably arise. This section also contains the tragic tale of the brothers Balin and Balan; with its concentration on individuals, its fated accidents, nobility of temper, deceit, dissension, and tragedy it is as stark and moving a story as any Icelandic saga.

But there are also stories of mystery, magic, adventure, betrayal, and mishap that end in triumph. Arthur gains the magic sword Excalibur from the Lady of the Lake. The noble concept of the High Order of Knighthood is affirmed, reinforced as it is by the oath, sworn by knights of the Round Table at the annual feast of Pentecost, never to do wrong, always to honor ladies, and so on.

Malory's *explicit* to the first main section refers to himself as a "knight-prisoner" and appears to suggest that he may not be able to continue to write. But the opening words of the second section echo this *explicit so* clearly as to make continuity certain. This next section is based mainly on a 14th-century English alliterative poem, the *Morte Arthure*, which makes Malory's own style more alliterative. It tells how Arthur rejects the obligation to pay tribute to the emperor of Rome and how he wages successful war right into Italy. Here Lancelot makes his first appearance as a brave young warrior.

The third main section moves into the area Malory has made his own for ever—the feats of individual knights wandering in search of adventure in strange forests and castles. The hero of this book is Lancelot himself, Malory's favorite knight, killing wicked knights, rescuing ladies, resisting seduction. He is rumored to be the lover of Queen Guinevere, which he denies, and Malory does not describe their love. It is a relatively short section, delightfully varied and vividly interesting in event, created from a cunning selection of incidents widely spaced in Malory's voluminous source, the French prose *Lancelot*.

Having now established both Arthur with his Round Table and Lancelot, the supreme example of chivalry, Malory turns in his fourth section to the story of another knight, significant to the whole history, exemplary in himself, and an adornment to the Round Table—Sir Gareth of Orkney, brother to Sir Gawain. The source is unknown. The story is based on the familiar general pattern of the Fair Unknown, who is a young hero, handsome, brave, and clever but unrecognized. He achieves success by defeating foes older and more experienced than he, winning his beloved, and establishing his identity and his place in society. This has been termed a version of the "family drama," common in fairy tale and romance. It also illustrates the Malorian themes of bravery, noble bearing, and courtesy.

There follows the long section, over a third of the whole work, centered on the story of Tristram and Isolde, with so many other knights and adventures intermingled that it is impossible to summarize adequately. The ancient tragedy of Tristram's and Isoldes obsessive mutual infatuation had already been diluted by Malory's French sources, and at the end of Malory's version the lovers retire to adulterous bliss in Lancelot's castle of Joyous Gard. Tristram is here an adventurous knight similar and almost equal to Lancelot. He has a jesting companion, Sir Dinadan, who brings commonsensical skepticism to the craziness of knight-errantry but is a good knight of his hands for all that. King Mark, husband of Isolde, is portrayed as a treacherous villain. Only incidentally, in a later section, is Mark's murder of Tristram noted. This Tristram section, full of adventures, disguises, unexpected meetings, unexplained departures, and arbitrary battles, has all the mystery and excitement of romance. It is the part of Malory's work least like the world of plausible appearances of the novel.

A digression toward the end of the Tristram section tells how Lancelot was tricked into begetting Sir Galahad upon Elaine, daughter of Sir Pelles. This leads naturally to the sixth section, in which Sir Galahad, now a pure virginal young knight, comes to King Arthur's court. Miraculous events initiate the Quest of the Holy Grail. The Grail, according to Malory, is the dish from which Christ ate with the apostles on Easter, brought to England by Joseph of Arimathea and endowed with properties both holy and magical. Hermits exhort the knights in their quest, visions and allegories abound, though Malory greatly abbreviates the religious didacticism of his French source. Only Galahad, Percival, and Bors succeed in seeing the Grail; Galahad and Percival both die, passing beyond human ken, and Bors is the only successful Grail knight to return to Camelot. Lancelot is granted only a partial vision of the Grail. He is flawed by his love of Guinevere, but Malory changes the monastic spirit of the original, so that Lancelot remains in a sense the hero. Despite all the changes many beautiful and magical scenes remain, as in the appearance of the ship with Percival's sister.

The last two sections of *Le Morte Darthur*, the seventh and eighth, may be considered as one, for they tell of the supreme glory of the Round Table and its tragic end in a series of closely connected episodes. Malory's art is here at its greatest. He blends French and English sources, but what he makes, fleshed out with his own invention, is entirely his own and one of the great achievements of English literature. The core of the story is the continuing love between Lancelot and Guinevere, and the determination of some malcontents to trap them, so that King Arthur has to condemn them. Lancelot has to rescue the queen three times, and on one occasion he accidentally kills Sir Gareth, his beloved friend, whom he had himself knighted. This joins Gareth's brother Gawain to Lancelot's enemies, and eventually Arthur is forced by Gawain to declare war on Lancelot.

During Arthur's absence at the war Mordred claims the throne and attempts to marry Guinevere. Ultimately, after Gawain has repented of his vengeful feud against Lancelot and died from wounds, Mordred confronts Arthur in battle. The bastard son and noble father kill each other in the desolation of the corpse-strewn battlefield. Arthur dies slowly by a "water-side." Excalibur is thrown into a lake and a hand mysteriously grasps it. Queens come in a boat to take Arthur to Avalon. It is an unforgettably eerie scene, rich in the ancient potent symbolism of the separation, dissolution, and healing power of death. Guinevere enters a nunnery; after a final interview with her Lancelot withdraws to a hermitage, and they die without meeting again.

No mere summary can convey the power, beauty, and pathos of these two sections. Much of the action is conveyed through brilliant terse dialogue, occasionally with a touch of grim or sarcastic humor. There is a wealth of incident in such episodes as Lancelot's rescues of Guinevere, or in the beautiful account of the Fair Maid of Ascolat (later spelled Astolat), who dies for love of Lancelot, or the moving story of Lancelot's healing of Sir Urry. The best knight in the world weeps in humility as he performs the miraculous cure, yet he is the one who causes the destruction of Arthur's Round Table.

Malory's imaginative world is narrow. It is composed only of Arthur, of good or bad knights, and a few desirable or treacherous ladies who, with two or three exceptions, are hardly more than ciphers. No ordinary concerns of life appear. Simple themes are illustrated by simple actions, performed by characters with few traits and virtually no inner life. Yet Malory's earnest concentration on fundamental issues of loyalty, love, and combat, guided by a complex system of honor, is intensely alive. The encounters, friendly or hostile, the wanderings, the seemingly arbitrary events combined with the sense of destiny, the comradeship and the betrayals, create a profound symbol of life that we can easily relate to. Malory's prose creates a sense of the man as in his essence he would be: no mere "narrator" but writing directly to us in the colloquial yet dignified manner of a brave and courteous country gentleman, on a subject that deeply matters to him, the history of Arthur, of England, of all of us.

See also **Caxton, William**

Further Reading

Primary Sources

Brewer, Derek Stanley, ed. *The Morte Darthur, Parts Seven and Eight*. London: Arnold, 1968 [modernized text].

Cowen, Janet, ed. *Le Morte D'Arthur*. 2 vols. Harmondsworth: Penguin, 1969 [Caxton's edition in modernized spelling].

Le Morte D'Arthur Printed by William Caxton 1485. London: Scolar, 1976 [facsimile] .

Spisak, James W., ed. *Caxton's Malory*. 2 vols. Berkeley: University of California Press, 1983.

Vinaver, Eugène, ed. *The Works of Sir Thomas Malory*. 3d ed. Rev. P.J.C. Field. 3 vols. Oxford: Clarendon, 1990.

The Winchester Malory. EETS s.s. 4. London: Oxford University Press, 1976 [facsimile].

Secondary Sources

New *CBEL* 1:674–78.

Manual 3:757–71, 909–24.

Archibald, Elizabeth, and A.S.G. Edwards, eds. *A Companion to Malory*. Cambridge: Brewer, 1996.

Bennett, J.A.W., ed. *Essays on Malory*. Oxford: Clarendon, 1963.

Benson, Larry D. *Malory's Morte Darthur*. Cambridge: Harvard University Press, 1976.

Brewer, Derek Stanley. *Symbolic Stories: Traditional Narratives of the Family Drama in English Literature*. Cambridge: Brewer, 1980 [on the story of Sir Gareth].

Field, P.J.C. *The Life and Times of Sir Thomas Malory*. Cambridge: Brewer, 1993.

Gaines, Barry. *Sir Thomas Malory: An Anecdotal Bibliography of Editions 1485–1985*. New York: AMS, 1990.

Ihle, Sandra Ness. *Malory's Grail Quest: Invention and Adaptation in Medieval Prose Romance*. Madison: University of Wisconsin Press, 1983.

Kato, Tomomi, ed. *A Concordance to the Works of Sir Thomas Malory*. Tokyo: University of Tokyo Press, 1974.

Kennedy, Beverly. *Knighthood in the Morte Darthur*. Cambridge: Brewer, 1985.

Knight, Stephen. *Arthurian Literature and Society*. London: Macmillan, 1983.

Lambert, Mark. *Malory: Style and Vision in Le Morte Darthur*. New Haven: Yale University Press, 1975.

Life, Page West. *Sir Thomas Malory and the Morte Darthur: A Survey of Scholarship and Annotated Bibliography*. Charlottesville: University Press of Virginia, 1980.

McCarthy, Terence. *An Introduction to Malory*. Cambridge: Brewer, 1993.

Parins, Marylyn Jackson, ed. *Malory: The Critical Heritage*. London: Routledge, 1988.

Riddy, Felicity. *Sir Thomas Malory*. Leiden: Brill, 1987.

Sandved, Arthur O. *Studies in the Language of Caxton's Malory and That of the Winchester Manuscript*. Oslo: Norwegian Universities Press, 1968.

Spisak, James W., ed. *Studies in Malory*. Kalamazoo: Medieval Institute, 1985.

Takamiya, Toshiyuki, and Derek S. Brewer, eds. *Aspects of Malory*. Cambridge: Brewer, 1981. Repr. with updated bibliography, 1986.

Whitaker, Muriel. *Arthur's Kingdom of Adventure: The World of Malory's Morte Darthur*. Cambridge: Brewer, 1984.

DEREK S. BREWER

MANDEVILLE, JEAN DE
(d. 1372)

Composed at Liège ca. 1357 by an otherwise unidentifiable English knight-voyager, Mandeville's *Voyages d'outre-mer* was the most popular secular book of its day, surviving in over 250 manuscripts and some ninety incunabula, including translations into Latin, English, Danish, Dutch, German, Italian, Spanish, Czech, and Irish. Of the three distinct versions, the earliest was certainly composed in French on the Continent. An "insular" version, done ca. 1390 in England, is a Middle English classic, whose anonymous author is sometimes considered the "father" of English prose. The *Voyages* popularized the newly discovered wonders of the East, including much fabulous material, and gives a lengthy description of the Holy Land. Mandeville compiled the work at third hand from French translations by Jean Le Long of Saint-Omer (d. 1383) of genuine Latin travel accounts from the early 14th century. Le Long's translations of five Latin travel accounts are found together in several manuscripts, of which the best known is the *Livre des merveilles* (B.N. fr. 2810), copied ca. 1400 for the duke of Burgundy. Mandeville also drew liberally from Vincent de Beauvais's *Speculum naturale*, Marco Polo's *Devisement du monde*, Gossuin de Metz's *Image du monde*, and Brunetto Latini.

Though filled with fabulous accounts, the *Voyages* relates in a simple and unselfconscious prose the sum of medieval knowledge of the world. It explains, for example, why the world is round and incorporates many other accurate observations. Through the centuries, it has been alternately praised for its style and richness and damned for absurdities and plagiarism. The author has on occasion been confused with a Liège physician, Jean de Bourgogne, and with the writer and notary Jean d'Outremeuse. Mandeville is also credited with a French prose lapidary found in 15th-century manuscripts and early printed editions.

See also **Brunetto Latini; Polo, Marco; Vincent de Beauvais**

Further Reading

Mandeville, Jean de. *Mandeville's Travels, Texts and Translations*, ed. M. Letts. London: Hakluyt Society, 1953. [Edition of B.N. fr. 4515 and the English "Egerton" translation.]

——. *Mandeville's Travels*, ed. Michael C. Seymour. Oxford: Clarendon, 1967. [Edition of the English "Cotton" translation.]

——. *The Metrical Version of Mandeville's Travels*, ed. Michael C. Seymour. London: Early English Text Society, 1973.

——. *The Travels of Sir John Mandeville*, trans. C.W.R.D. Moseley. Harmondsworth: Penguin, 1983. [Modern English translation.]

De Poerck, Guy. "La tradition manuscrite des *Voyages* de Jean de Mandeville." *Romanica gandensia* 4 (1955): 125–58.

Goosse, A. "Les lapidaires attribués à Mandeville." *Dialectes belgo-romans* 17 (1960): 63–112.

WILLIAM W. KIBLER

MANFRED (1232–26 February 1266)

Manfred was the natural son of Emperor Frederick II Hohenstaufen and Bianca Lancia of Monferrato; he closely resembled his father physically and, to a considerable degree, temperamentally. Manfred was an astute politician and courageous soldier; he was the emperor's intellectual soulmate, but his own personality was less dynamic. Manfred's career was confined to Italy. His illegitimate birth limited his political effectiveness, and he ultimately lost his kingdom to the combined forces of the papacy, Charles of Anjou, Tuscan financiers, and Sicilian barons. The defeat of Manfred sent the *Mezzogiorno* (southern Italy) into a centuries-long decline, the effects of which linger to the present.

Manfred may have studied at Paris and Bologna, and he was active in the courtly culture of the kingdom of Sicily. When Frederick died in December 1250, Manfred became the regent of his half brother, Conrad IV (1250–1254), who was in Germany. Manfred was generally popular among the feudal nobles of the kingdom, but he faced persistent opposition from important barons and cities. In December 1251, he tried but failed to reach an accord with Pope Innocent IV (r. 1243–1254). Manfred may have offered to exchange recognition of papal overlordship for the Sicilian crown. In December 1251, Conrad went to the kingdom to establish his own royal authority. He revoked all of Manfred's fiefs except the principality of Taranto and forced the humiliated Manfred to remain at court.

Conrad died in May 1254. Guelf chroniclers insist that Manfred poisoned him, but other sources do not concur. Manfred then faced great difficulties. Conrad had named the church as guardian of his son, Conradin, and appointed the leader of the German barons, Berthold of Hohenburg, as his bailiff. Innocent IV invested Edmund, the second son of King Henry III of England, with the kingdom. Meanwhile, Pietro Ruffo, who controlled Calabria and Sicily, played Manfred against Innocent.

Most of the nobility of the kingdom rallied to Manfred, whom they considered the natural regent of young Conradin. The pope refused to recognize Conradin's rights and demanded possession of the kingdom. Open warfare ensued, and Innocent excommunicated Manfred and his adherents. Manfred was unprepared for war and quickly sued for peace. During the negotiations he killed a papal partisan and fled to Lucera, the imperial Muslim stronghold near Foggia. Manfred seized the treasury of Frederick II and Conrad IV and raised a powerful army. He defeated the papal army near Foggia. Almost all of Apulia had fallen into his hands by the time Innocent died (10 August 1254).

Manfred could not placate Innocent's successor, Pope Alexander IV (r. 1254–1261), but Alexander actually put little effort into the vendetta of the papacy against the Hohenstaufen. Manfred was thus free to put the kingdom in order. By 1257, he had imprisoned Berthold and banished Pietro Ruffo. On the false rumor that Conradin had died, the Sicilian barons proclaimed Manfred king. He was crowned at Palermo on 10 August 1258. Manfred soon became deeply involved in central and northern Italy. He attempted to create a federation of barons, cities, and factions under his leadership by providing military assistance, negotiating treaties and marriages, and courting urban factions. In 1258, he joined in a promising but unsuccessful alliance with the despot of Epirus, Michael II, against the Byzantine emperor, Michael VIII Palaeologus. In 1262, Manfred arranged a marriage between his daughter Constance and the *infante,* Peter of Aragon; this marriage would later justify Aragon's intervention in the Sicilian Vespers uprising of 1282.

Manfred reached the height of his power when he and the Ghibelline factions of Florence and Siena defeated the Guelfs of Tuscany at Montaperti on 4 September 1260. He subsequently posed as lord of Italy and sent vicars throughout the peninsula, but he did not have the force to sustain his ambitions. When the energetic Urban IV (r. 1261–1264) became pope, he renewed the assault on Manfred. Urban found a champion in Charles of Anjou, count of Provence and brother of Louis IX of France. Louis had previously blocked papal overtures to Charles, but Urban argued that Manfred had unlawfully dispossessed his nephew Conradin, and this reasoning apparently laid the scruples of the saintly king to rest. The pope also persuaded Florentine and Sienese bankers to finance an invasion of the kingdom of Sicily.

Late in 1262, Manfred attempted to make a deal with Urban, but the negotiations collapsed. The pope invested Charles with the kingdom in December 1262. War soon followed. Manfred's allies scored several early victories against papal and Guelf forces and almost captured the city of Rome in 1264. After Urban died, the new pope, Clement IV (r. 1265–1268), quickly confirmed the treaty with Charles, who left Provence for Rome in May 1265. Manfred dispatched a manifesto to Rome, in which he revived Frederick's argument that the Romans—not the pope—had the right to choose the emperor. There is no extant reply. Charles arrived in Rome on 28 June 1265 and took charge of the war against Manfred.

After an unsuccessful attack on Rome in August 1265, Manfred returned to his kingdom to find his domestic enemies ranged against him and his treasury empty. Many of his allies went over to Charles, made peace with the pope, or became neutral. In December

1265, Charles's army from Provence passed through Piedmont and Lombardy without opposition. Charles moved into Campania in January 1266 without a fight. Betrayed and deserted by the Sicilian barons, Manfred died bravely on the plain of Grandella near Benevento on 26 February 1266. He was buried outside Benevento, but the archbishop of Cosenza later had his remains disinterred and removed from the kingdom to an unmarked grave near Garigliano.

Manfred's fall may have been inevitable. The papacy was determined to extinguish the Hohenstaufen dynasty, and Charles of Anjou was a hard and relentless campaigner, whose talents and war chest were equal to his greed and ambition. The fickle Sicilian barons who betrayed Manfred did not prosper as a result. After slaughtering Manfred's adherents, Charles replaced the treasonous barons with his own French supporters. Charles exploited the efficient Sicilian fiscal apparatus to bleed the kingdom white, but he returned none of the good government that had accompanied the Normans' and the Hohenstaufen's exactions. Commerce fell into the hands of Venetian and Genoese merchants and Tuscan bankers, and wealth flowed to the Angevins or migrated from the *Mezzogiorno* altogether. The powerful, well-ordered, and prosperous kingdom of Sicily gave way to bad government and chronic poverty.

Manfred was an active patron of poets and scientists and a scholar in his own right. He sponsored and perhaps engaged in the translation of Greek and Arab treatises on philosophy. He revised and commented on the *De arte venandi cum avibus* of Frederick II, which the emperor had dedicated to him. In the *Commedia,* Dante depicts Manfred at the base of the mount of Purgatory with a band of souls who had repented their sins at the moment of death (*Purgatory,* 3.103–145). The legend of Manfred's heroic and pious end, which inspired Dante, was turned to nationalist purposes in the nineteenth century during the Risorgimento.

See also **Frederick II**

Further Reading

Edition

Capasso, Bartolommeo, ed. *Historia diplomatica regnt Siciliae inde ab anno 1250 ad annum 1266.* Naples: Typographia Regiae Universitacis, 1874.

Critical Studies

Abulafia, David. *Frederick II: A Medieval Emperor.* London: Allen Lane/Penguin, 1988. (See the final chapter.)

Housley, Norman. *The Italian Crusades: The Papal–Angevin Alliance and the Crusades against Christian Lay Powers, 1254–1343.* Oxford: Clarendon, 1982.

Leone, Gino. *La salvazione dell'anima di Manfredi in Dante ad opera di Dante nel III canto del Purgatorio.* Matera: Montemurro, 1969. (Reprinted as *Un re nel purgatorio: Manfredi di Svevia—Dalla vita terrena all'oltretomba dantesco.* Fasano: Schena, 1994.)

Morghen, Raffaello. *Il tramonto della potenza Sveva in Italia.* Rome: Tunninelli, 1936. (Reprinted as *L'età degli svevi in Italia.* Palermo: Paiumbo, 1974.)

Nardi, Bruno. *Il canto di Manfredi e il Liber de pomo sive De morte Aristotilis.* Turin: Società Editrice Internazionale, 1964.

Pispisa, Enrico. *Il regno di Manfredi: Proposte di interpretazione.* Messina: Sicania, 1991.

JOHN LOMAX

MANRIQUE, JORGE
(ca. 1440–1479)

The reputation of Jorge Manrique has long rested principally upon his *Coplas por la muerte de su padre*, most familiar to English-speaking readers through Longfellow's translation. His poetic range extends, however, beyond the serious mood of the *Coplas* to a wide variety of compositions found in the late medieval and fifteenth-century *cancioneros*, in which Manrique demonstrates a fluent handling of the current verbal and conceptual conventions of the genres and categories involved. These include personal satire and various approaches to conventional amorous themes, among them verses in which a lady's name is conveyed acrostically, and renderings of the traditional motif of love as a siege (*Escala de amor*), a castle (*Castillo de amor*), or membership of a religious order (*Profesion que hizo en la orden de amor*). Critical evaluation of Manrique's verse has concentrated primarily upon the *Coplas*, but the importance of his other writings is now generally recognized.

Jorge Manrique's life was marked by active involvement in the politics of his day and their military extension. His family was prominent in the turbulent events of the reign of Enrique IV; his father Rodrigo (1406–1476), count of Paredes and a master of the Order of Santiago, was involved in the abortive elevation of the puppet-king Alfonso against Enrique (an event alluded to in the *Coplas*). To Jorge fell the role of maintaining this involvement in the next phase of the succession dispute, and, having actively espoused the cause of Fernando and Isabel he was fatally wounded in a minor action.

The military aspect of Manrique's career fundamentally marked his poetry; his work stands comparison with that of any war poet of any period. Imagery drawn from the experience and equipment of medieval warfare abounds even in the amorous poems (it is, indeed, the very foundation of *Escala* and *Castillo*, while isolated images occur in other poems), and permeates the *Coplas*, where death is expressed in terms of an ambush and an arrow, against whose force the strongest fortifications and armies are powerless and ineffective. The tournament panoply of the warrior caste (among other dimensions of its courtly existence such as music and dancing) is richly evoked in the poet's examination of the meaning of life. For Manrique, war is a necessary element in existence: the noble's duty is to fight for his faith against its enemies (just as that of the priest is to pray), and by doing so he merits salvation. His father, Rodrigo, is praised for his effectiveness in this sphere, and his entry to paradise is, as a result, taken for granted in the idealized deathbed scene that closes the poem. But Rodrigo is also commended by the poet for his part in the civil wars in support of the legitimate candidate for the throne, and also for fighting fellow-Christians in the maintenance of his own status and domains. The political aspect of his career is thus an essential element in the poet's eulogy of his father Rodrigo's greatness. In this Jorge Manrique is merely reflecting the importance attached to *estado* (state) and to the behavior appropriate to one's rank, in contemporary thinking; beyond mere physical existence lies a further dimension of *fama*, the existence implied in one's reputation, which survives after death; this itself is, of course, a poor second to eternal life, though an essential prerequisite for it in so far as it indicates a worthy life. In addition to the doctrinal statements made and political points scored in the poem, various conscious statements of literary attitude are explicit, as in the rejection of traditional poetic invocations and classical examples in the *Ubi sunt?*, while others remain implicit. Although the *Coplas* have been widely praised, and is indubitably in many respects a masterpiece, problems have been noted in various aspects of the poem from the earliest commentators to the present. The *Coplas* make use of a wide range of traditional imagery drawn from the Bible and other sources in addition to the author's military experience, with the transience of earthly life and the inevitability of death being conveyed in a densely textured series of metaphors. The skillful updating of the topos of the *Ubi sunt?* by reference to politically prominent persons of recent memory is but one dimension of Manrique's artistry in handling traditional concepts and poetic commonplaces. The eulogy of his father (apparently controversial among early commentators, and ignored by most glossators) draws upon classical archetypes and established medieval concepts of hierarchy and makes effective use of the personification of death.

Despite the prominence traditionally assigned to the *Coplas* in Spanish literary studies, the first truly critical edition (which is likely to become the standard text) was not published until 1991; the many previous editions vary, because of problems in the complex transmission of the text, both in the number of stanzas (forty or forty-two) and in their order. The stanza that begins "Si fuesse en nuestro poder," in particular, has been variously placed as number seven or thirteen; the earlier location is undoubtedly the original. The additional two stanzas found in many early editions (and in Longfellow's

translation) are problematic; they do not form a natural part of the poem. Their attribution to Manrique remains questionable; even if ultimately proven to be by his hand, they are best viewed as originally independent stanzas that later became an accretion to the *Coplas*. During the sixteenth century, the *Coplas* were frequently printed, and private manuscript copies further attest their popularity. It is clear that the poem circulated in a wide variety of forms and contexts. Important among these are the early printed editions in which the text is accompanied by a poetic gloss; the *Coplas* soon attracted the attention of glossators, the earliest of whom was Alonso de Cervantes (first printed in 1501).

Further Reading

Editions
Beltrán, V. *Coplas que hizo Jorge Manrique a la muerte de su padre.* Barcelona, 1991.
Serrano de Haro, A. *Jorge Manrique; Obras.* Madrid, 1986.

Studies
Domínguez, F. A. *Love and Remembrance: The Poetry of Jorge Manrique.* Lexington, Ky., 1988.
Serrano de Haro, A. *Personalidad y destino de Jorge Manrique.* 2d ed. Madrid, 1975.

DAVID HOOK

MANṢŪR, AL- (fl. 976-1002)

Ibn ʿAbī Āmir, later known as Al-Manṣūr was the last of the great rulers during the caliphate period in al-Andalus. Initially he served as vizir, virtually assuming effective control of the caliphate after the death of Al-Ḥakam II, who appointed his young son Hishām to succeed him in 976. Allegedly acting on Hishām's behalf, Al-Manṣūr eliminated all who wished to compete for power, including his father-in-law Al-Ghālib, securing it all for himself. Al-Manṣūr remained in power from 976 to 1002 and was feared and noted for his decisive action, vigilance, and ruthlessness; it was in 981 that he assumed the sobriquet (*laqab*) Al-Manṣūr, "The Victorious."

The caliph Hishām, who was a virtual captive of Al-Manṣūr, was a weak individual who allowed his weaknesses to be exploited. A brilliant politician, Al-Manṣūr filled the political vacuum created by the death of Hishām's father, Al-Ḥakam II. He ruled with an iron hand, galvanizing the army and leading daring incursions into Christian territory that struck terror into the hearts of the northern populations. His name alone was enough to make them shudder with fear. As a response to the Christians who, sensing disunity among the Muslims in al-Andalus, had begun to make their first incursions into Muslim territories, Al-Manṣūr led some fifty expeditions against the Christians. In 997 he struck at their very heart, taking Santiago de Compostela, the alleged burial place of the apostle James. When he entered Santiago the town was all but deserted, except for a Christian monk whom Al-Manṣūr allowed to go free. Although Al-Manṣūr rode his horse into the cathedral to show his contempt for Christianity, the tomb of the apostle was not disturbed. He destroyed all the surrounding buildings and took the bells of the cathedral back to Córdoba both as booty and as a sign of humiliation. He converted the bells into lamps for the mosque, where they remained until the thirteenth century. Besides warrior and statesman, Al-Manṣūr was a poet and a builder, and he expanded the Great Mosque of Córdoba. A devout religious man, he publicly abjured philosophy and science by burning the books in Al-Ḥakam II's library that dealt with these subjects, and always carried with him a Qu'rān that was copied out in his own hand. Whenever the name of Allah was uttered in his presence, he never failed to repeat it. If tempted to act in an impious way, he was reputed always to have resisted temptation. Nevertheless, he was known to have enjoyed all pleasures—even wine, which he failed to renounce until two years before his death.

In 991, virtually ignoring Hishām, he made his eighteen-year-old son 'Abd al- Mālik chamberlain, and later designated 'Abd al- Mālik as his successor. Al-Manṣūr died in 1002 while on an expedition against the Christians. His other son, Al-Muzaffar, succeeded him, but died six years later. Al-Muzaffar was briefly succeeded by his brother, 'Abd al-Rahmān, known as Sanchuelo, who conspired to grasp the title of caliph for himself. The death of Al-Manṣūr was followed by a crisis of authority and struggles among his family; Hishām II, the grandson of 'Abd al-Rahmān III, who was incapable of ruling; and several other contenders, including Al-Mahdi, who eventually seized power. Al-Manṣūr's biography, al-Ma'āthir al-'Āmiriyyah was written by Husayn Ibn 'Āsim at the end of the eleventh century.

Further Reading

Chejne, A. G. *Muslim Spain: Its History and Culture.* Minneapolis, 1974.

E. MICHAEL GERLI

MARCABRU (fl. 1130–49)

Little can be said for certain about the origins of the troubadour Marcabru. Relying in part on the lyrics, his two *vidas* are probably right to describe him as an early Gascon singer of low birth. Evidence in the songs ties him to courts in southern France and Spain, where he was evidently a jongleur. In some forty-two surviving lyrics, Marcabru is preoccupied largely with social satire and moral allegory. He vehemently denounces a decline in societal mores. One *vida* also describes him as "maligning women and love." But it is still debated whether Marcabru's many pronouncements on love in society are entirely negative or rather idealize love along the lines of a Christian or courtly model. His voice is raw and bitter, his images original and forceful, his language aphoristic and difficult. He is sometimes read as a precursor of the *trobar clus* school. Aside from his thirty-two *sirventes*, his lyrics include the romance *A la fontana del vergier*, the crusade song *Pax in nomine domini*, and the *pastorela Autrier jost' una sebissa*. Marcabru's thematic and stylistic influence on subsequent troubadour song was massive and pervasive.

Further Reading

Marcabru. *Poésies complètes du troubadour Marcabru*, ed. Jean-Marie-Lucien Dejeanne. Toulouse: Privat, 1909.

Harvey, Ruth E. *The Troubadour Marcabru and Love*. London: Westfield College, 1989.

Pirot, François. "Bibliographie commentée du troubadour Marcabru." *Moyen âge* 73 (1967): 87–126. ["Mise à jour," by Ruth E. Harvey and Simon Gaunt. *Moyen âge* 94 (1988): 425–55.]

Thiolier-Méjean, Suzanne. *Les poésies satiriques et morales des troubadours du XIIe siècle à la fin du XIIIe siècle*. Paris: Nizet, 1978.

ROY S. ROSENSTEIN

MARCEL, ÉTIENNE (1310–1358)

A prosperous Parisian draper who, as *prévôt des marchands*, led a rebellion against the monarchy in 1357–58. Born into a less wealthy cadet branch of a large and influential family, Marcel was successful in business, a supplier for the royal household, and a respected figure in Paris by the late 1340s. He was elected *prévôt* in 1354. Connected by kinship or marriage to many Parisians who had gained wealth and sometimes ennoblement in royal service, risking disgrace and destitution for corrupt practices but often regaining royal favor, Marcel was perhaps too cautious or too honest to follow their example, and he increasingly resented these rich royal officers from his own circle.

In December 1355, the Estates General met in Paris, and Marcel became the spokesman for the towns of Languedoil, as the assembly worked out an ambitious plan to raise a large tax to support the army, in exchange for governmental reforms and a return to stable currency. Marcel and the Parisians were then staunch supporters of John II in his campaign against the kings of England and Navarre, who had claims to the French throne and sought to partition the realm. By May 1356, however, the tax plan was failing, and without adequate revenues for his troops John II resumed manipulating the currency and restored to power the officials he had agreed to dismiss.

These actions caused Marcel to break with the king, no longer providing him with Parisian troops. When John met defeat and capture at Poitiers in September, he had no bourgeois troops but relied solely on nobles.

In the last months of 1356, Marcel seems to have become a partisan of Charles the Bad, the rebellious king of Navarre. An inflammatory Navarrese partisan, Robert Le Coq, dominated the Estates that met after Poitiers, and the urban representatives, led by Marcel, lent at least tacit support to his demands. In December, Marcel organized his first large Parisian street demonstration against the government. He made frequent use of such intimidating tactics in subsequent months.

The Estates obtained a sweeping ordinance of reform in March 1357, but when they failed repeatedly to deliver the taxes needed to prosecute the war, the government ceased to feel bound by the reforms. Marcel and the Parisian crowd became increasingly intimidating, and in February 1358 they murdered two military commanders in the presence of the dauphin Charles, thereby alienating the nobles who had originally spearheaded the reform movement. Marcel and his followers became increasingly radical in their hostility to nobles and gave some support to the Jacquerie of late May. The dauphin, meanwhile, left Paris in March and began to rally noble support. Marcel failed in his effort to organize a league of towns to oppose them, and Paris became increasingly isolated. At the end of July, one of the citizens murdered Marcel, paving the way for the dauphin's triumphant return to the capital.

See also **Charles II the Bad**

Further Reading

Avout, Jacques d'. *Le meurtre d'Étienne Marcel.* Paris: Gallimard, 1960.
Cazelles, Raymond. *Étienne Marcel: champion de l'unité française.* Paris: Tallandier, 1984.

JOHN BELL HENNEMAN, JR.

MARCHETTO DA PADOVA
(early 14th century)

Marchetto da Padova (Marchetus de Padua) was the most important and most influential music theorist in Italy during his time. Documents at the cathedral of Padua attest to his presence as a teacher in 1305–1307. Three treatises of his survive: *Lucidarium in arte musice plane* (Cesena and Verona, 1317 or 1318), *Pomerium in arte musice mensurate* (Cesena, later than *Lucidarium* but no later than 1319), and *Brevis compilatio in arte musice mensurate pro rudibus et modernis* (later than *Pomerium*). An acrostic in the text of the motet *Ave regina celoruml Mater innocencie* identifies Marchetto as its author.

Marchetto made fundamental contributions to the theories of mode, chromaticism, and tuning in *Lucidarium,* and to the theory or mensuration in *Pomerium* and *Brevis compilatio.* The theory of mode involves the classification of plainchant melodies by final (a sort of keynote), range, scale structure, and melodic articulation. This classification is crucial for the correlation of (among other sorts of pieces) recitation tones for the psalms with the antiphons that frame them. Whereas traditional modal theory had stressed final and range as determinants of mode, Marchetto stressed scale structure and articulation; this change of perspective, along with his development of the concept of modal mixture, enabled the classification of melodies that had earlier been dismissed as anomalous. Marchetto's modal doctrine spread through Italy and beyond during the next 200 years and became the foundation of the modal theory of polyphonic music during the Renaissance.

Earlier theories of melody based on hexachords (six-note *ut-re-mi-fa-sol-la* prototypes) and their connection through a process called mutation allowed only for diatonic progressions; though they served plainchant melodies well, these theories failed the chromatic progressions (e.g., progressions directly from c-natural to c-sharp) favored by Italian composers of the early fourteenth century. Marchetto developed a theory to accommodate such progressions and coined the term "permutation" for the hexachord connections they entail; though the term gained a certain currency in music theory of the fourteenth century, it disappeared as fifteenth-century composers abandoned chromatic progressions.

Though he espoused the traditional so-called Pythagorean tuning system, in which all perfect fifths are pure, Marchetto modified the system by describing the slight raising of sharped notes in certain contrapuntal contexts, a process that increases the harmonic piquancy of some combinations of notes and makes them seem to drive toward notes of resolution; this procedure has important implications for the performance of fourteenth-century music. Marchetto's "fifths" of whole tones must surely be taken as rough approximations rather than precise measurements; nonetheless, the concept of fractional division of whole tones represents a crucial step in the abandonment of the arithmetic strictures of the Pythagorean system, in which equal division of the whole tone was conceptually impossible. This step was necessary for the eventual development of equal temperament.

The thirteenth century had seen far-reaching developments in the theory of mensural notation, a theory which Franco of Cologne codified late in the century. Franco based his system on a note value called the breve (corresponding roughly to a measure in modern notation) that was divisible only into thirds at primary and secondary levels; Franco worked out elaborate rules for notating rhythms within these limitations. A handful of theoretical and practical sources from around 1300 documents attempts to expand Franco's system, but the earliest comprehensive treatise to succeed in doing so was Marchetto's *Pomerium,* which describes primary and secondary divisions of the breve into two or three parts and tertiary division into two parts, resulting in divisions of the breve into two, three, four, six, eight, nine, or twelve parts, which can then be combined in various ways, even involving syncopation within and between breve units. *Pomerium* became the foundation of Italian mensural theory of the fourteenth century, and it sheds light as well on the early stage of French mensural notation, a system that coexisted with the Italian and eventually supplanted it.

Further Reading

Editions

Coussemaker, Edmond de, ed. *Scriptorum de musica medii aevi nova series,* Vol. 3. Paris: Durand, 1869. (Reprint, Hildesheim: Olms, 1963. Includes *Brevis compilatio,* 1–12.)

Gallo, F. Alberto, and Kurt von Fischer, eds. *Italian Sacred Music.* Polyphonic Music of the Fourteenth Century, 12. Monaco: Éditions de I'Oiseau-Lyre, 1972. (Includes *Ave regina celoruml Mater innocencie.)*

Gerbert, Martin, ed. *Scriptores ecclesiastici de musica sacra potissimum,* Vol. 3. Saint Blasien, 1784. (Reprint, Hildesheim: Olms, 1963. Includes *Lucidarium,* 64–121; and *Pomerium,* 121–188.)

Herlinger, Jan, ed. *The Lucidarium of Marchetto of Padua: A Critical Edition, Translation, and Commentary.* Chicago, Ill., and London: University of Chicago Press, 1985.

Vecchi, Giuseppe, ed. *Marcheti de Padua Pomerium,* Corpus Scriptorum de Musica, 6. Rome: American Institute of Musicology, 1961.

Critical Studies

Berger, Karol. *Musica Ficta: Theories of Accidental Inflections in Vocal Polyphony from Marchetto da Padova to Gioseffo Zarlino.* Cambridge: Cambridge University Press, 1987.

Gallo, F. Alberto. "Marchetus in Padua und die 'franco-venetische' Musik des frühen Trecento." *Archiv für Musikwissenschaft,* 31, 1974, pp. 42–56. (Includes *Ave regina celoruml Mater innocencie.)*

Herlinger, Jan. "Fractional Divisions of the Whole Tone." *Music Theory Spectrum,* 3, 1981a, pp. 74–83.

——. "Marchetto's Division of the Whole Tone." *Journal of the American Musicologkal Society,* 34, 1981b, pp. 193–216.

——. "What Trecento Music Theory Tells Us." In *Explorations in Music, the Arts, and Ideas: Essays in Honor of Leonard B. Meyer,* ed. Eugene Narmour and Ruth A. Solie. Festschrift Series, 7. Stuyvesant, N.Y.: Pendragon, 1988, pp. 177–197.

——. "Marchetto's Influence: The Manuscript Evidence." In *Music Theory and Its Sources: Antiquity and the Middle Ages,* ed. André Barbera. Notre Dame Conferences in Medieval Studies, 1. Notre Dame, Ind.: University of Notre Dame Press, 1990, pp. 235–258.

Martinez–Göllner, Marie Louise. "Marchettus of Padua and Chromaticism." *L'Ars Nova Italiana del Trecento,* 3, 1970, pp. 187–202.

Pirrotta, Nino. "Marchettus de Padua and the Italian Ars Nova." *Musica Disciplina,* 9, 1955, pp. 57–71.

Rahn, Jay. "Marchetto's Theory of Commixture and Interruptions." *Music Theory Spectrum,* 9, 1987, pp. 117–135.

Ristory, Heinz. *Post-franconische Theorie und Früh–Trecento: Die Petrus de Cruce–Neuerungen und ihre Bedeutung für die italienische Mensuralnotenschrift zu Beginn des 14. Jahrhunderts.* Europäische Hochschufschriften, Series 36; Musicology, 26. Frankfurt and New York: Peter Lang, 1988.

Strunk, Oliver. "Intorno a Marchetto da Padova." *Rassegna Musicale,* 20, 1950, pp. 312–315. (Trans., "On the Date of Marchetto da Padova." In Oliver Strunk. *Essays on Music in the Western World.* New York: Norton, 1974, pp. 39–43.)

Vecchi, Giuseppe. "Su la composizione del *Pomerium* di Marchetto da Padova e la *Brevis compilatio.*" *Quadrivium,* 1, 1956, pp. 153–205. (Includes *Brevis compilatio,* pp. 177–205.)

JAN HERLINGER

MARGARET OF CORTONA, SAINT (c. 1247–1297)

Margaret of Cortona was a penitent and mystic. Her *Legenda,* the most authoritative account of her life, begins like a tragic romance: Margaret, the beautiful daughter of a peasant farmer in Laviano, ran away at sixteen with a nobleman who promised to marry her but did not. They lived together for nine years and had a son, but then Margaret's lover was killed, and she was shocked into repentance. She left all her possessions and tried to return home, asking forgiveness. When her father and stepmother turned her away, she and her child found refuge in Cortona with two gentlewomen who were associated with the Franciscan community there. A few years later Margaret was admitted to the Franciscan-sponsored Order of Penitents (which later became the third order). She spent the rest of her life as a humble penitent in Cortona, enduring extreme deprivations to atone for her sins and devoting her time to charity, peacemaking, and intense periods of prayer and meditation. By the time she died, local belief in her sainthood was so strong that miraculous cures were spontaneously reported at her tomb. Despite repeated petitions to the papacy, however, annual celebration of her feast day (22 February) in Cortona was not officially authorized until 1515, and her actual canonization was delayed until 1728.

The early documents about Margaret raise tantalizing questions because they speak with multiple and sometimes clashing voices. Although her *Legenda* is attributed to the Franciscan friar Giunta Bevegnati, who served as one of her confessors and eventually compiled most of the text, in reality it has several layers of authorship: Margaret recounted her visions while Fra Giunta took notes; another priest filled this role during the last seven years of her life, when Fra Giunta was absent from Cortona; other witnesses supplied supplementary information; and the final text was reviewed and further edited by both civil and ecclesiastical officials. Recovering Margaret's authentic voice and experience from such a composite text may be impossible, although feminist scholars have begun to try. What does emerge clearly from the *Legenda* and other early sources is the struggle that went on after her death over the right to display her relics and claim the benefits of her patronage. Recent studies have identified three main parties in this struggle: Franciscan friars; civic leaders of Cortona; and adherents of San Basilio, the church that became Margaret's shrine.

In the *Legenda* itself, the strongest voice is Franciscan. Indeed, the text recounts numerous visions in which Christ expresses special favor toward the Franciscans, reminds Margaret that he has personally entrusted her to their keeping, and urges her always to obey them. The *Legenda* also holds Margaret up as an example for other Franciscan teftiaries to follow and portrays her, in effect, as a testimonial to the virtues that a lay penitent could acquire under Franciscan guidance: humility, self-discipline, reverence for the clergy and the eucharist, perfect orthodoxy (always a key question about uncloistered women), and even the restoration of virginity. As Schlager (1998) has suggested, these emphases may have been chosen partly to overcome the friars' own resistance to the papal mandates that made them responsible for potentially dangerous female penitents.

Other portions of the *Legenda*—*including* practically all the miracle stories, which were originally omitted from Fra Giunta's account and appended in the last chapter—link Margaret more closely with local needs and aspirations in Cortona. And Margaret's own reported words and actions sometimes support the local agendas too. In the decade before her death, she distanced herself somewhat from the Franciscan friars by moving to a solitary cell near San Basilio, which was then just a small secular church in poor condition, and choosing its priest, *ser* Badia, as her final confessor. She supported this church by obtaining an indulgence for those who helped with its rebuilding, and she founded a charitable confraternity whose first chaplain was *ser* Badia. When she died, it was San Basilio that received her body for burial, although the Franciscans insisted for decades that she had made a permanent commitment to them. Civic leaders asserted the town's own claim to her body, arguing that she had chosen to live in Cortona and had contributed significantly to the general welfare by founding a hospital for the poor, resolving conflicts between rival factions, and negotiating an agreement that persuaded the warlike bishop of Arezzo to cancel an impending attack.

As Bornstein (1993) has shown, using archival sources that survive in Cortona, the contest over Margaret's relics had economic and political ramifications. When the miracles began around her tomb, San Basilio reaped the most obvious benefits. In the next few decades, this church acquired an impressive new sanctuary, suitable for welcoming pilgrims, and a rich endowment based on bequests. Civic leaders invested generously in the expansion and adornment of San Basilio (eventually renamed Santa Margherita) and the promotion of Margaret's cult, and the investment evidently paid off in terms of Cortona's increasing prestige and political independence. The Franciscans were shut out until the end of the fourteenth century, when town leaders invited them to replace the secular clergy who had hitherto administered the new church and Margaret's shrine. But the town itself retained—and still retains—legal ownership of Margaret's body.

An ambitious study by Cannon and Vauchez (1999) enriches and complicates this picture by reminding us that the contest over Margaret's cult was partly about the right to define the religious and symbolic identity of Cortona's patron saint. This issue mattered greatly not only to the Franciscans, but also to the civic authorities of Cortona and certain subgroups within the town, including the local clergy and the next generation of male and female terriaries. The different ways in which these Cortonese groups reconstructed Margaret's identity, in the light of their own corporate traditions and priorities, are barely suggested in the *Legenda* and other written sources. But, as Cannon demonstrates, a great deal can still be learned about them by studying what remains of the paintings and sculpture that were added to the church of Santa Margherita in the fourteenth century to honor this not yet canonized saint. More work will surely be done with the wealth of fascinating detail that Cannon and Vauchez have brought to light.

Further Reading

Benvenuti Papi, Anna. "*In castro poenitentiae*": *Santità e società femminile nell'Italia medievale.* Italia Sacra, 45. Rome: Herder, 1990. (Collection of Benvenuti's articles that includes her most detailed and important pieces on Margaret of Cortona.)

——. "Mendicant Friars and Female *Pinzochere* in Tuscany: From Social Marginality to Models of Sanctity." In *Women and Religion in Medieval and Renaissance Italy,* ed. Daniel Bornstein and Roberto Rusconi, trans. Margery J. Schneider. Chicago, Ill.: University of Chicago Press, 1996, pp. 84–103. (Overview suggesting societal patterns; the original title of the edited collection was *Mistiche e devote nell'Italia tardomedievale.*)

Bevegnati, Giunta. *Leggenda delld vita e dei miracoli di Santa Margherita da Cortona,* trans. and ed. Eliodoro Mariani, Vicenza: LIEF, 1978. (With historical notes.)

——. *Legenda de vita et miraculis beatae Margaritae de Cortona,* ed. Fortunato Iozzelli. Bibliotheca Franciscans Ascetica Medii Aevi, 13. Grottaferrata: Ediciones Collegii S. Bonaventurae ad Claras Aquas, 1997. (Published in Rome. Critical edition of the Latin text, with detailed discussions of its structure, genre, sources, and major themes, plus extensive bibliography.)

——. *Life and Miracles of Saint Margaret of Cortona,* trans. Thomas Renna. (Forthcoming from Franciscan Institute.)

Bornstein, Daniel. "The Uses of the Body: The Church and the Cult of Santa Margherita da Cortona." *Church History, 62,* 1993, pp. 163–177.

Cannon, Joanna, and André Vauchez. *Margaret of Cortona and the Lorenzetti: Sienese Art and the Cult of a Holy Woman in Medieval Tuscany.* University Park: Pennsylvania State University Press, 1999. (See especially parts 1 and 5.)

"Margherita da Cortona." In *Bibliotheca sanctorum,* Vol. 8. Rome: Istituto Giovanni XXIII nella Pontificia Università Lateranense, 1961–1971, cols. 759–773.

Schlager, Bernard. "Foundresses of the Franciscan Life: Umiliana Cerchi and Margaret of Cortona." *Viator, 29,* 1998, pp. 141–166.

SHERRY REAMES

MARGRETHE I
(1353–October 27, 1412)

Queen of Norway, Sweden, and Denmark, Margrethe was the daughter of King Valdemar IV Atterdag ("everday") of Denmark and Queen Helvig. At the age of six, she was betrothed, and at the age of ten married, to King Hákon of Norway, son of King Magnus of Sweden of the Folkungs dynasty. Rebellion in Sweden brought Albrecht of Mecklenburg to the throne, but Hákon kept a firm grip on the western parts of the country. Thus, by marriage, Margrethe acquired the additional titles of queen of Norway and Sweden. The upbringing of the young queen was overseen by the Swedish noblewoman Merethe Ulfsdotter, together with that of Merethe's own daughter, and "both often tasted the same birch." Merethe herself was of notable birth; her father was a Swedish nobleman, and her mother St. Birgitta of Vadstena. The young Queen Margrethe was from the very beginning made familiar with current political themes, and was raised in an environment that doubtless shaped her opinion of the possibilities for women in society.

In 1370, around Christmas, she gave birth to her only child, Óláf (Óláfr), the legitimate heir to the crown of Norway and, more or less, Sweden. In Denmark, the problem of succession was deliberately kept undecided. Margrethe's rebellious brother, Christoffer, had died, and King Valdemar had made vague promises to the son of Margrethe's sister Ingeborg, Albrecht of Mecklenburg (not to be confused with King Albrecht of Sweden, his father's brother). When King Valdemar died on October 24, 1375, the Danish Council was faced with a difficult choice, since the Mecklenburg candidate was heavily supported by the German emperor, Charles IV. Margrethe acted swiftly, as if she were the recognized ruler of the realm. After many negotiations, the Danes elected Olaf king in May 1376. But under the military threat by Albrecht, an agreement was reached in September that opened the way for recognition of Albrecht's rights, without detracting from Olaf's, by submitting the issue to arbitration by a number of German princes. Margrethe thwarted this accord by claiming that all arbitration had to follow Danish rules of succession, of which there were none, since Danish kings were elected freely. The death of Emperor Charles in November 1378 and of Duke Albrecht in February 1379 left Margrethe to skirmish only with Albrecht of Sweden. King Hákon died in the late summer of 1380, only forty years old. The next summer, Olaf was acclaimed with all rights as hereditary king of Norway.

In 1386, diplomacy separated the Holsteinians from the Mecklenburg party, albeit at the cost of concessions regarding tile status of the duchy of Schleswig under the Crown, but, as usual, with an enfeoffment of doubtful character, supplemented with clauses that cried out for interpretation. In Sweden, Albrecht gradually lost control over the main fiefs to the councilors. Details of their contacts with Margrethe are not known. But Olaf's sudden death on August 3, 1387, for the moment upset all possible plans. Then, on August 10, Margrethe established herself as "authorized lady and husband and guardian of all of the realm of Denmark," until a new king could be elected according to her proposal. The following year, she performed a similar "coup d'état" in Norway, and managed to secure similar recognition from a number of Swedish magnates. The resulting war with King Albrecht was decided on February 24, 1389, by her victory at Axevall and Åsle, where Albrecht was captured while the German faction still kept Stockholm. The same year, Margrethe adopted her sister's maternal grandson, Bugislav of Pomerania, now renamed Erik, who would become king of all three kingdoms. Everything seemed settled, when a war of revenge with Mecklenburg broke out. The peace in 1395 secured the release of Albrecht, who put up Stockholm as a pledge for the release sum. As this sum was not paid, Stockholm finally fell into the hands of Margrethe by 1398. Margrethe had already instituted her famous Union of Kalmar the year before. The resulting document, when compared with the coronation document for Erik, suggests that the outcome was not fully in accord with her ideas of monarchial reign. This may explain why the document was written only as a semivalid paper draft, kept secret in Denmark. The stipulated parchment copies to be sent to all three countries were never made, but the document was later used to curb the government of Erik of Pomerania. The lack of a son and the varying rules of succession in the three kingdoms would eventually prove to be the ultimate obstacle for Erik and thus for the life work of Margrethe. Nevertheless, the union between Denmark and Norway lasted until 1814, and with Sweden until the 1520s, indirectly giving fuel to the wars of the 17th and 18th centuries, and playing a major role in the politics of Scandinavia from the 19th century to the present day.

Further Reading

Literature

Erslev, Kristian. *Danmarks Historie under Dronning Margrethe og hendes nærmeste Efterfølgere 1375–1448. 1. Dronning Margrethe og Kahmarunionens Grundlæsggelse.* Copenhagen: Erslev, 1882.

Lönnroth, Erik. *Sverige och Kalmarunionen 1397–1457.* Gothenburg: Elander, 1934; rpt.: Akademiförlaget, 1969.

Linton, Michael *Drottning Margareta. Fullmäktig fru och rätt husbonde. Studier i kalmarunionens förhistoria.* Studia Historica Gothoburgensia, 12. Gothenburg: Akademiförlaget, 1971.

Christensen, Aksel E. *Kalmarunionen ognordisk politik 1319–1439.* Copenhagen: Gyldendal, 1980 [with extensive references to scholarly literature].

Hørby, Kai. *Danmarks historie. 2.1: Tiden 1340–1648.* Copenhagen: Gyldendal, 1980 [with extensive bibliography in vols. 2.1 and 2.2].

Albrectsen, Esben. *Herredømmet over Sønderjylland 1375–1404. Studier over Hertugdømmets lensforhold og indre opbygning på dronning Margrethes tid.* Copenhagen: Den danske historiske forening, 1981.

Etting, Vivian. *Margrethe den Første.* Copenhagen: Fogtdal, 1986 [lavishly illustrated].

SØREN BALLE

MARGUERITE D'OINGT
(ca. 1240–1310)

Marguerite was born to noble parents in the French Beaujolais region. By 1288, she became prioress of the Carthusian monastery of Poletains at Lyon. Although she was never canonized, a popular cult in her honor flourished until the Revolution, and she was revered as blessed. Marguerite is the only medieval Carthusian woman writer known to us. The *Pagina meditationum*, a response in Latin to a visionary experience during Mass, interweaves liturgical sections with reflections on Christ's Passion and the Last Judgment. In a remarkable passage, Marguerite develops the image of Christ as a woman undergoing the suffering of labor. The *Speculum*, written in Franco-Provençal and dedicated to Hugo, prior of Vallebonne, describes three visions and their meaning. In the first, Christ shows her a book with white, black, red, and golden letters symbolizing his suffering. In the second, the book opens and reveals a vision of Paradise and the heavens, whence all goodness emanates. In the third, she is shown the glorified body of Christ and meditates on its meaning for Christian spirituality. Marguerite's final work is the biography of Béatrice of Ornacieux (ca. 1260–1303/09), a stigmatized nun at the charterhouse of Parmenie, whose cult was recognized by Pope Pius IX in 1869. Also written in the vernacular, the biography stresses Beatrice's intense mystical experiences, including frequent apparitions, the gift of tears, severe acts of penance to ward off the Devil, and eucharistic visions and miracles. Marguerite's christocentric mysticism includes not only Carthusian but also Franciscan and Cistercian elements. Some letters by Marguerite also survive.

Further Reading

Marguerite d'Oingt. *Les œuvres de Marguerite d'Oingt*, ed. Antonin Duraffour, Pierre Gardette, and Paulette Durdilly. Paris: Les Belles Lettres, 1965.

——. *The Writings of Margaret of Oingt, Medieval Prioress and Mystic*, trans. Renate Blumenfeld-Kosinski. Newbury-port: Focus Information Group, 1990.

Dinzelbacher, Peter. "Margarete von Oingt und ihre *Pagina meditationum*." *Analecta cartusiana* 16 (1988): 69–100.

Maisonneuve, Roland. "L'expérience mystique et visionnaire de Marguerite d'Oingt (d. 1310), moniale chartreuse." *Analecta cartusiana* 55 (1981): 81–102.

ULRIKE WIETHAUS

MARGUERITE OF PROVENCE
(ca. 1221–1295)

Marguerite was the eldest of four daughters of Count Raymond-Berenguer V of Provence. In 1234, at the age of twelve or thirteen, she became queen of France by her marriage to Louis IX. The wedding and her coronation as queen were celebrated at the cathedral of Sens. Eleven children were eventually born to the couple. The marriage was difficult in a number of respects. From the beginning, Marguerite resented and was resented by her mother-in-law, Blanche of Castile; yet she admired Blanche's influence with Louis. She tried to achieve the same position with her son, the future Philip III, but provoked her husband to intervene and have the young Philip's ill-considered oath to obey her until the age of thirty quashed. Though Marguerite by no means lacked in courage or ability (e.g., she successfully preserved order in Damietta in Egypt in 1250 at a particularly difficult moment in her husband's first crusade), Louis almost always ignored her political advice.

After the king's death in 1270, Marguerite became a more active political figure. She was particularly exigent—to the point of raising troops—in defending her rights in Provence, where her husband's brother, Charles of Anjou, maintained his political authority and control of property after his wife's (her sister's) death, contrary to the intentions of the old count, who had died in 1245. Philip III had his hands full in restraining her. Only his death in 1285 and Charles of Anjou's in the same year resolved the situation. At the behest of the new king, Philip IV, she accepted an assignment of income from Anjou as compensation for recognizing the preeminent rights of Charles of Anjou's heirs in Provence. Her last years were spent in doing pious work, including founding in 1289 the Franciscan nunnery of Lourcines, which eventually became a focal point of the cult of her late husband, Louis. Although she does not seem to have testified for her husband's canonization, Marguerite was active in the propagation of his memory: her confessor, Guillaume de Saint-Pathus, for example, wrote an important and reverential biography of the king. Marguerite died on December 30, 1295, nearly two years before the process of canonization was completed.

See also **Blanche of Castile**

Further Reading

Le mariage de saint Louis à Sens en 1234. Sens: Musées de Sens, 1984.

Sivéry, Gérard. *Marguerite de Provence: une reine au temps des cathédrales.* Paris: Fayard, 1987.

WILLIAM CHESTER JORDAN

MARGUERITE PORETE
(d. 1310)

Biographical information about Marguerite Porete comes from inquisitorial documents, which tell us that she was a béguine from Hainaut. Quite possibly, she was a solitary itinerant who expounded her teachings to interested listeners. She wrote the *Mirouer des simples ames anienties* in Old French sometime between 1296 and 1306. Since there is no indication that someone else wrote the text of the *Mirouer* from the author's dictation, we can surmise that the author wrote the treatise herself and that she was well educated.

The text received approvals from three Orthodox Church leaders, one of whom was Godfrey of Fontaines, a scholastic at Paris between 1285 and 1306, who also counseled the author to use caution in her expressions. Approval was not universal, however, and the text was condemned and burned in the author's presence with the orders not to spread her views under threat of being turned over to the secular authorities. Marguerite was arrested at the end of 1308 and remained in prison for a year and a half before being condemned to the flames as a relapsed heretic. Despite the condemnation, the *Mirouer* apparently enjoyed widespread popularity, for in addition to copies made of the text in Old French it was translated into Middle English, Italian, and Latin.

The *Mirouer* is a dialogue among allegorical figures who represent the nature of the relation between the soul and God. The fundamental structure of the discourse is grounded in traditional Neoplatonic philosophy, and courtly language is used to express theological abstractions. The *Mirouer* is a theological treatise that analyzes how love in human beings is related to divine love and how the human soul by means of this relation may experience a lasting union of indistinction with God in this life. The *Mirouer* is also a handbook, or "mirror," that aims to teach the "hearers of the book" about themselves and how to attain union with God.

Further Reading

Marguerite Porete. *Le mirouer des simple ames anienties*, ed. Romana Guarnieri and Paul Verdeyen. *CCCM* 69. Turnhout: Brepols, 1986.

——. *The Mirror of Simple Souls*, trans. Ellen L. Babinsky. New York: Paulist, 1993.

Lerner, Robert E. *The Heresy of the Free Spirit in the Later Middle Ages.* Los Angeles: University of California Press, 1972.

Verdeyen, Paul. "Le procès d'inquisition contre Marguerite Porete et Guiard de Cressonessart (1309–1310)." *Revue d'histoire ecclésiastique* 81 (1986): 47–94.

ELLEN L. BABINSKY

MARIE DE FRANCE
(fl. 1160–1210)

Recognized today among the major poets of the renaissance of the 12th century, Marie de France was equally admired by her contemporaries at court, according to the testimony of Denis Piramus in his *Vie seint Edmunt le rei*. Three works of the period are signed "Marie" and are usually attributed to the same author: the *Lais*, the *Fables*, and the *Espurgatoire saint Patrice*. In the epilogue to the *Fables*, the author adds to her name *si sui de France* (l. 4). This is probably an indication of continental birth, a fact to be remarked if, as seems likely, she was living in England. A number of identities have been proposed for Marie, none of which can be established with certainty: the natural daughter of Geoffroi Plantagenêt (and half-sister of Henry II), abbess of Shaftsbury (1181–1216); Marie de Meulan or Beaumont, widow of Hugues Talbot and daughter of Waleron de Beaumont; and the abbess of Reading (the abbey where the Harley 978 manuscript may have been copied). Identifying her literary patrons is equally problematic. The *Lais* are dedicated to *vus, nobles reis* (l. 43), who may be either Henry II (1133–1189), the most likely candidate, or his son, Henry the Young King (crowned 1170, d. 1183). The Count William named in the *Fables* has been linked to a number of prominent figures, including William Marshal, William Longsword (the natural son of Henry II), William of Mandeville, William of Warren, William of Gloucester, and Guillaume de Dampierre.

Marie's works can be dated only approximately with reference to possible patrons and literary influences. The works themselves suggest that Marie knew Wace's *Brut* (1155) and the *Roman d'Énéas* (1160), an undetermined Tristan romance, classical (notably Ovid) and Celtic sources, but not the romances of Chrétien de Troyes. The *Lais* are therefore dated between 1160 and 1170, the *Fables* between 1167 and 1189, and the *Espurgatoire* after 1189 and probably between 1209 and 1215, since its Latin source, the *Tractatus de purgatorio sancti Patricii* (in the version of Hugh or Henry of Saltrey), has been placed no earlier than 1208.

Five manuscripts contain one or more of Marie's *lais*; only Harley 978 contains a general prologue, which presents the twelve *lais* that follow as a collection specifically arranged by the author (the same manuscript also contains a complete collection of the *Fables*). Marie appears to be the initiator of a narrative genre that flourished between about 1170 and the late 13th century. About forty narrative *lais* are extant. The lyric *lai*, which flourished from the 12th to the 15th century, seems to be an unrelated form.

The prologues and epilogues that frame each of Marie's tales refer to the *lais* performed by Breton storytellers in commemoration of past adventures truly lived. Celtic and English place-names and personal names corroborate Marie's claimed sources: four *lais* take place in Brittany, three in Wales, two in both places, and one in an undetermined *Bretagne*. Marie did not simply write down orally circulating stories. Her artfully crafted compositions combine the written traditions of Latin and vernacular writings with the legendary materials of Celtic and popular tales. While it may be impossible to untangle historical reference and literary topos in Marie's repeated claim to retell well-known *lais bretons*, her indications suggest a process of transmission that begins with an adventure heard by Bretons, who then compose a *lai*, sung with harp accompaniment. Marie has heard the music and the adventure, the latter perhaps told as a prelude to the song. She then tells us the adventure in rhymed octosyllables, the form used also in the *Fables* and the *Espurgatoire*, elaborating simultaneously its truth, or *reisun* (cf. the *razos* in the Provençal lyric tradition). The title itself, carefully designated in each case and sometimes translated into several languages, guarantees the authenticity of the process.

The general prologue opens with a traditional exordium on the obligation of writers to share their talents and then cites the authority of Priscian to describe the relationship between ancient and modern writers: do philosopher-poets hide a *surplus* of meaning to be found later in the obscurities of their writing, or do later, more subtle poets add it to their predecessors' works? Scholars have variously interpreted these verses (9–22): we are drawn into the problem of interpretation at the very moment the subject of glossing is introduced by Marie's authorial persona. She then explains the nature of her project: not a translation from the Latin as many have done, but something new, demanding hard labor and sleepless nights, the writing down in rhyme of those adventures commemorated in *lais*. Hoping to receive great joy in return, Marie then offers her collection to an unnamed king. She names herself in the following verses, printed by modern editors as the prologue to *Guigemar* (ll. 3–4) but set off in the manuscript only by a large capital indicating a new section (*G*1).

The twelve *lais* that follow in Harley 978 are *Guige-mar* (886 lines), *Equitan* (314), *Fresne* (518), *Bisclavret* (318), *Lanval* (646), *Deus amanz* (254), *Yonec* (558), *Laüstic* (160), Milun (534), *Chaitivel* (240), *Chievrefoil* (118), and *Eliduc* (1184). As indicated by the considerable variations in length, the *lais* offer great diversity, but they also operate as a collection unified by the themes of love and adventure. Indeed, they seem to invite exploration as an open-ended set of theme and variations, in which Marie reveals the complexities and varieties of human experience, without trying to contain them within the confines of any single doctrine of love. Heroes and heroines, all noble, beautiful, and courteous, are individualized not by psychological development but by the situations in which they find themselves. Consider the two short anecdotes that constitute *Laüstic* and *Chievrefoil*. Both involve a love triangle: married couple plus lover. *Chievrefoil* relates an episode in the story of Tristan and Iseut, a secret reunion of the lovers vouchsafed during one of Tristan's returns from exile. Whereas Marc here remains ignorant of the tryst, the husband of *Laüstic* discovers his wife's nocturnal meetings with her lover. Although their affair remains innocent, limited to their mutual gaze across facing windows, the angry husband puts an end to their meetings by trapping and killing the nightingale the lady claims as reason for her nightly visits to the window. When the lady sends to her lover the nightingale's body wrapped in an embroidered cloth, along with a messenger to explain the events, he has a golden box made, adorned with precious stones. The nightingale's body is placed in it, and the reliquary accompanies him wherever he goes—hence the name of the *lai*: *laüstic* is the Breton word for *russignol* in French, *nihtegale* in English (ll. 3–6).

The emblem that thus closes the *lai* figures the end of the lovers' meetings, though it may also suggest the triumph of continued love, however impossible to realize: optimistic and pessimistic readings of the ending are both possible. The emblem of *Chievrefoil* also testifies to the enduring nature of Tristan and Iseut's love: just as the hazelwood dies (so it was thought) if the honeysuckle growing around it was cut away, so the two lovers would die if separated: "*Bele amie, si est de nus: ne vus sanz mei, ne jeo sanz vus*" (ll. 77–78). But while that phrasing is negative, what we see realized in this episode is the reunion of the lovers thanks to the piece of hazelwood that Tristan prepares as a signal to Iseut, so that the queen will know he must be hiding in the woods near the route of her cortege. Whereas the emblem of *Laüstic* ends the lovers' meetings, *Chievrefoil's* emblem initiates Tristan and Iseut's reunion, as it symbolizes their love. And just as the repetition of characters, scenes, and situations in *Laüstic* and *Chievrefoil* creates doubles, echoes, and contrasts in positive and negative variations at all levels of the text, so the tendency to present and explore different combinations of the same materials characterizes the links between the *lais* and invites readers to analyze their interactions. The arrangement of twelve *lais* in a collection considerably increases the potential for meaning, however elusive that meaning remains in the beautiful obscurities of Marie's text, and begins to give her *lais* the weight and proportion we normally associate with romance.

The brevity of most *lais* limits their plot development to a single anecdote or episode, although in the mid-length and longer *lais*, especially *Guigemar* and *Eliduc*, there may be a fuller elaboration as the characters' love develops through a series of episodes. The type of adventure that appears in the *lais* differs somewhat from that of romance: it does not involve a quest, even in the longer *récits*; the hero is more passive and his experience leads to private fulfillment and happiness; no special relationship exists between the hero's destiny and that of his society.

While some *lais* have marvelous and folktale elements that recall their Celtic sources (e.g., *Guigemar*, *Yonec*, *Lanval*), others remain realistically placed in the courtly world of the 12th century (*Equitan*, *Fresne*, *Milun*, *Chaitivel*). All explore the intersection of two planes of existence, where otherness may be magically encountered or simply introduced by the new experience of love. Although efforts to thus categorize the *lais* often remain problematic, leading to overlap, omissions, and the like, they do respond to the sense of intertextual play that links the *lais* across echoes and contrasts.

Marie's art is as carefully crafted as the precious reliquary she describes in *Laüstic*. The economy and brevity of her style are enriched by the subtlety of her narrating voice. Her use of free indirect discourse, in particular, allows her to merge her voice with that of her characters, while maintaining the distinctness of both. Marie's literary art, sustained throughout the collection of twelve *lais*, joins her work to that of the philosopher-poets, described in the general prologue as worthy of glossing and interpretation.

The twenty-three extant manuscripts of Marie's *Fables*, two of which are complete with prologue, epilogue, and 102 fables, attest their popularity. Marie claims to translate from the English of King Alfred's adaptation from Latin. No such translation is known, and Marie may have invented a fictitious source. Her fables derive from the Latin *Romulus* in combination with other traditions: some details bring her collection closer to the Greek fables than to the Latin; evidence of oral tradition is also apparent. Hers is the first known example of Old French *Isopets*. Each short narrative (eight–124 lines) leads to an explicit moral lesson. This framework of moral and social values provides an underlying unity for the diversity of the fables. The political stance is basically conservative, reflecting an aristocratic point of view, but also shows concern for justice available to all classes: social hierarchy should be maintained for the sake of harmony; people should accept their place, as well as their responsibilities. Marie's concern for justice in terms of feudal loyalty between lord and vassal is demonstrated in a number of fables; elsewhere appears a more specific regard for mistreatment of the poor, as in Fable 2, *De lupo* et *agno*, in which the wolf invents a series of false accusations to justify killing the lamb. Marie's moral targets the abuse of rich robber barons, viscounts, and judges who exploit those in their power with trumped-up charges.

Extant in a single manuscript, the *Espurgatoire* combines in its over 2,000 lines a variety of materials, romanesque, hagiographic, and homiletic. In addition to various anecdotes, the principle narrative concerns the proselytizing efforts of St. Patrick, thanks to whom an entrance to Purgatory for the still-living has been established in a churchyard, in order to strengthen belief in the afterlife. After suitable prayers and instructions, many have descended to witness the tortures of the damned and the delights of the saved. Not all have returned from the perilous journey. The greater part of the story follows in detail the preparation and descent of the knight Owein. Through a series of diabolical torments, Owein is saved each time when he invokes the name of Jesus. Upon his return, he is confirmed in his knightly career, now purified and dedicated to saintly pursuits. The *Espurgatoire* offers one of the earliest vernacular examples of the same visionary tradition that inspires Dante's *Commedia*.

See also **Dante Alighieri; Gautier d'Arras; Henry II; Wace**

Further Reading

Marie de France. *Les lais de Marie de France*, ed. Jean Rychner. Paris: Champion, 1969.

——. *Les fables*, ed. and trans. Charles Brucker. Louvain: Peeters, 1990.

——. *The Lais of Marie de France*, trans. Glyn S. Burgess and Keith Busby. Harmondsworth: Penguin, 1986.

——. *Marie de France: Fables*, ed. and trans. Harriet Spiegel. Toronto: University of Toronto Press, 1987.

——. *The Espurgatoire Saint Patriz of Marie de France, with a Text of the Latin Original*, ed. Thomas Atkinson Jenkins. Chicago: Chicago University Press, 1903.

——. *Das Buch vom Espurgatoire s. Patrice der Marie de France und seine Quelle*, ed. Karl Warnke. Halle: Niemeyer, 1938.

——. *The Lais of Marie de France*, trans. Robert W. Hanning and Joan Ferrante. New York: Dutton, 1978.

——. *The "Fables" of Marie de France: An English Translation*, trans. Mary Lou Martin. Birmingham: Summa, 1984.

Burgess, Glyn S. *Marie de France: An Analytic Bibliography*. London: Grant and Cutler, 1977; First Supplement, 1985.

Ménard, Philippe. *Les lais de Marie de France: contes d'amour et d'aventure au moyen âge*. Paris: Presses Universitaires de France, 1979.

Mickel, Emanuel J., Jr. *Marie de France*. New York: Twayne, 1974.

Sienaert, Edgar. *Les lais de Marie de France: du conte merveilleux à la nouvelle psychologique*. Paris: Champion, 1978.

MATILDA T. BRUCKNER

MARIE D'OIGNIES (1177–1213)

Mystic and one of the founding mothers of the béguine movement. Testimonies of her life were recorded by Jacques de Vitry (ca. 1215) and Thomas de Cantimpré (ca. 1230/31).

Born in Nijvel (Brabant), Marie was married at the age of fourteen but did not consummate her marriage. Together with her spouse, she practiced the *vita apostolica* and cared for the sick. At the age of thirty, she retired to a cell at the Augustinian monastery of Aiseau-sur-Sambre and gained in stature as a spiritual healer and holy woman. According to her pupil Jacques de Vitry, Marie's spirituality was characterized by eucharistic devotion and christocentrism. She lived a life of strict asceticism, abstained from sleep and food, and frequently experienced visions, ecstasies, and trances. Her death was an example of a saintly *ars moriendi*, surrounded by miracles; most noteworthy perhaps is her feat of three days of incessant chanting and scriptural exegesis performed during ecstasy. Jacques de Vitry stressed Marie's allegiance to the church by structuring her *vita* in two parts: Part 1 records the outline of her life's journey towards holiness and aspects of saintliness; Part 2 describes her interior life according to the seven gifts of the Holy Spirit. As with other texts of this genre, it is difficult to distinguish between Marie d'Oignies as a prototype (exemplum) and her individuality and original contributions to medieval spirituality.

See also **Jacques de Vitry**

Further Reading

Jacques de Vitry. *The Life of Marie d'Oignies*, trans. Margot H. King. Saskatoon: Peregrina, 1986.

Thomas de Cantimpré. *Supplement to the Life of Marie d'Oignies*, trans. Hugh Feiss. Saskatoon: Peregrina, 1987.

Kowalczewski, J. "Thirteenth Century Asceticism: Marie d'Oignies and Liutgard of Aywières as Active and Passive Ascetics." *Vox benedictina* 3 (1986): 20–50.

——. The Life of "Marie d'Oignies." In *Medieval Women's Visionary Literature*, ed. Elizabeth Petroff. Oxford: Oxford University Press, 1986, pp. 179–84.

ULRIKE WIETHAUS

MARSILIO OF PADUA
(c. 1275 or 1280–1342 or 1343)

Marsilio of Padua (Marsiglio, Marsilius de Mainardino) was an antipapal political theorist. He was the son of the notary of the University of Padua and studied Aristotelian philosophy there; later, he taught this philosophy at Paris, where he was rector in 1313 and eventually studied theology. His obscure career took many turns: he also was a priest, a physician, and a diplomat. In 1319, he went on an embassy for the Ghibelline leaders Matreo Visconti and Cangrande della Scala. Among Marsilio's associates were the astrologer Peter of Abano; the humanist Albertino Mussato; the Averroist John of Jandun; and, in later years, William of Ockham.

In 1324, in Paris, Marsilio completed his masterwork, *Defensor pads* (*The Defender of Peace*), which circulated anonymously until his authorship was discovered in 1326. Expecting to be condemned as a heretic for his antipapal opinions, he took refuge at the court of the pope's archenemy Lewis of Bavaria, whom he served for the rest of his life. Lewis was guided by Marsilio's theories when he went to Rome in 1327 and was crowned emperor in the name of the people. Likewise, Lewis claimed that the Roman church should be administered by the emperor, and, accordingly, he appointed Marsilio as his administrator, with the title of imperial vicar for spiritual affairs in Rome. The emperor could not maintain himself for long in Italy, however, and by 1330 he was back in Bavaria. In 1342, Marsilio was still with Lewis, serving as his physician and counselor. At this time Marsilio wrote *Defensor minor,* in which his earlier work was summarized and extended to prove that the emperor had jurisdiction over questions of marriage.

Marsilio's central concern was the political power of the papacy, which he, like Dante, saw as the principal cause of civil strife in Italy. To restore peace, Dante sought to revive the Roman empire; Marsilio was more realistic. He insisted that the state should control the church, but he devised a generalized theory of the state that could fit not only the empire but also national monarchies and even city-states. Thus, his proposals, far from threatening civil governments, offered them control over their several churches. *Defensor pacis* is accordingly divided into two principal parts: the first discourse (*dictio*) argues that political power belongs exclusively to the secular state; the second counters the papacy's claims to independent political status and makes the state the administrator of organized religion.

Marsilio's concept of the state is closely modeled on Aristotle's *Politics*. The state is a natural phenomenon, arising from man's nature as a political animal. Government exists so that all men may lead the "sufficient life," i.e., "live and live well." The form of government is not set by nature, however; instead, a community is formed by the mutual agreement of its members to live together under laws to which they have consented. Thus, for Marsilio, the foundation of all government is the "human legislator," i.e., the people of the community who make the laws. Marsilio is not a democrat; he realizes that not everyone is fit to participate in legislation, and he restricts the *legislator humanus* to the "prevailing part" (*valentior pars*) of the citizens, who are better or more numerous (or both) than the others. The Marsilian "legislator" is usually too numerous to do more than authorize the actual ruler (*the pars principans),* e.g., an elective emperor, a hereditary king, *apodestà,* or a council. In practice, all legislative, judicial, and executive functions are delegated to this ruler, who can, however, be deposed by the human legislator that appointed him. Thus, Marsilio's general theory of the state allows for diverse constitutions—monarchical, aristocratic, and even democratic. The main point, for his purpose, was that the ruler has a monopoly on political power within his state. A competing power independent of the ruler would be contrary to nature.

The second discourse of *Defensor pads* defines the proper place of the clergy, and especially the pope, within this political framework. In general, the job of the clergy is to preach the gospel and administer the sacraments. Clergymen are chosen and supported by the state, which administers all the worldly affairs of the church. In effect, the Franciscan ideal of poverty is extended to the whole clergy. Furthermore, Marsilio regards bishops as priests to whom the ruler has delegated certain executive duties, and the bishop of Rome is superior to the rest only insofar as he has been granted a few broader powers. Marsilio elaborately rebuts the papacy's position that the pope is Peter's successor as vicar of Christ and denounces its claim to "plenitude of power" (*plenitudo potestatis)* as the "singular cause of strife or civil discord." Thus, each state controls the church within it. When questions of faith arise that affect the church as a whole, the emperor can call an international council, consisting of laymen as well as clergy, to settle the matter. Enforcement of the council's decisions, however, is wholly up to the local rulers.

Marsilio completely reversed the dominant view that church and state exercise coordinate jurisdictions ("Gelasian dualism"). For more than three centuries, *Defensor pacis* was the arsenal of antipapalists, especially in the age of conciliarism and the Reformation. Many of its ideas were already current in university circles, but Marsilio gave them coherent, scholarly, and passionate expression. Moreover, his arguments appealed to a broad audience trained in Aristotle's logic and political philosophy; no special knowledge of law or theology was required. He moved beyond scholasticism in his use of history to explain institutional development.

Marsilio's theory of the state was not the main thrust of his work, but many readers have been unduly impressed by this theory because it appears to anticipate such modern doctrines as popular sovereignty and the social contract; they thus overlook the other, deeper medieval roots of these ideas.

See also **Albertino Mussato; Cangrande della Scala; Ockham, William of**

Further Reading

The Cambridge History of Medieval Political Thought, c. 350- c. 1450, ed. J. H. Bams. Cambridge: Cambridge University Press, 1988, p. 680. (Bibliography.)

Marsilius of Padua. *The Defender of Peace, 2* vols., crans. and intro. Alan Gewirth. Records of Civilization: Sources and Studies, 46. New York: Columbia University Press, 1951–1956.

Rubinstein, N. "Marsilius of Padua and Italian Political Thought of His Time." In *Europe in the Late Middle Ages,* ed. John Hale et al. London: Faber and Faber, 1965 pp. 44–75.

RICHARD KAY

MARTÍ, RAMÓN (b. ca 1210/15)

The most erudite and accomplished Arabist and Hebraist of his day, missionary to Muslims and fierce polemicist against Jews, Ramón Martí was born at Subirats near Barcelona (ca. 1210/15). He joined the Dominican mendicants at Barcelona's Santa Caterina priory by 1240, and studied at Saint-Jacques College of the University of Paris alongside Thomas Aquinas under Albert the Great (Albertus Magnus). The order sent him in 1250 to help found a missionary school of Arabic at Tunis. In 1264 King Jaime I commissioned him to censor rabbinic texts at Barcelona (but probably he had no role or presence at the Barcelona Disputations of 1263). Martí perhaps worked at the Murcia Arabicum in 1266; in 1268 he was again at Tunis. In 1269 he successfully visited Louis IX of France to urge a North African crusade; while there he probably commissioned Thomas Aquinas, for the order's master general, to write his masterwork the *Contra gentiles.* Martí spent the 1270s and 1280s at Barcelona, where he held the chair of Hebrew in 1281. His contemporary Marsili titled him "Philosophus in arabico," and "beloved intimate" not only of Jaime I and Louis IX but of "the good king of Tunis." Martí's friend Ramon Llull has an anecdote about his nearly converting that Muslim ruler. King Jaime mentions him as a friend in his own autobiography, noting his trip from Tunis to Montpellier. Arnau de Villanova was one of his students.

Martí's prolific writings are a key to the contemporary anti-Talmudism and growing animosity toward Jews. Until 1260 his main focus had been the conversion of Muslims, beginning with his *Explanatio symboli apostolorum* at Tunis in 1257. He is most probably the author of the *Vocabulista in arabico,* an Arabic word list of some 650 printed pages in Celestino Schiaparelli's edition, a missionarys' dictionary of unrivaled importance today for studying the Arabic of eastern Spain. His Islamic phase ended in 1260 with the now lost *Summa* against the Qu'rān. In 1267 came his *Capistrum iudeorum,* which Aquinas seems to have used for his own *Contra gentiles.* Martí's masterwork was *Pugio fidei contra Mauros et iudeos* (*Dagger of Faith),* finished in 1281, filling over a thousand pages in its printed version, of wide influence over the next three centuries. Recent redating of Aquinas's *Contra gentiles* suggests that the hundreds of parallels between these two works show a strong dependence on Martí. With a wealth of rabbinic materials from and in Hebrew, *Pugio* is the most thorough of all the medieval anti-Judaic polemical works. Martí's writings are currently being studied intensively.

See also **Aquinas, Thomas; Llull, Ramón; Vilanova, Arnau de**

Further Reading

Cohen, J. *The Friars and the Jews.* Ithaca, N.Y., 1982. Chap. 6.
Robles, L. *Escritores dominicos de la corona de Aragón, siglos XIII-XV.* Salamanca, 1972.

ROBERT I. BURNS, S. J.

MARTIANUS CAPELLA
(fl. first half of the 5th c)

Between 410 and 439, Martianus Capella wrote his *De nuptiis Philologiae et Mercurii*. This non-Christian allegorical treatise, an encyclopedic work on the Seven Liberal Arts, was to have a widespread influence in the Christian schools of the late Middle Ages, as a source for teaching the Trivium and Quadrivium. The *De nuptiis* is in nine books, the first two describing the allegorical marriage and each of the next seven dealing with one of the liberal arts. In time-honored tradition, Martianus drew his material from a variety of earlier sources, chiefly Apulaius, Varro, Pliny, and Euclid. This (to us) derivative method only heightened its status in the Middle Ages.

Martianus had three clear "vogues": the first was among the scholars of the Carolingian renaissance centered on Charles the Bald. Johannes Scottus Eriugena and Remigius of Auxerre wrote commentaries on Martianus, and it is through Remigius's commentary that the *De nuptiis* became so influential. The second group of admirers were 10th-century Italians, like Notker of Saint-Gall, Rather of Verona, and Luitprand of Cremona. Finally, Martianus was one of the cosmographical authors most admired by the 12th-century Chartrians, like Alexander Neckham (who wrote a commentary), John of Salisbury, and Thierry of Chartres.

Of Martianus himself, little is known, except that he was a Roman citizen who spent most of his life at Carthage. One Victorian scholar, D. Samuel, describing the *De nuptiis* as a "mixture of dry traditional school learning and tasteless and extravagant theological ornament, applied to the most incongruous material, with an absolutely bizarre effect," illustrates the extant to which Martianus's work, with its interweaving of fact and fiction, has become foreign to our sensibility, although some earlier Christian writers, such as Cassiodorus and Gregory of Tours, similarly disliked this hybrid style.

See also **Eriugena, Johannes Scottus**

Further Reading

Martianus Capella. *De nuptiis Philologiae et Mercurii*, ed. Adolfus Dick, rev. Jean Preaux. Stuttgart: Teubner, 1983.
——. *The Marriage of Philology and Mercury*, trans. William Harris Stahl and Richard Johnson with E.L. Burge. New York: Columbia University Press, 1977.
Shanzer, Danuta. *A Philosophical and Literary Commentary on Martianus Capella's* De nuptiis Philologiae et Mercurii, *Book 1.* Berkeley: University of California Press, 1986.

LESLEY J. SMITH

MARTINI, SIMONE (c. 1284–1344)

The birthplace of the painter Simone Martini is unknown, but he must have been a citizen of Siena, for he is referred to as *de Senis*. We find no mention of Martini (as he will be called here, though he is often called simply Simone) in archival records before 1315. However, the year of his birth may be deduced from Vasari, who saw a memorial inscription in the church of San Francesco in Siena, according to which Martini died at age sixty. Martini's training is undocumented. He may have been a pupil of Duccio and may even have been one of several collaborators working on Duccio's *Maestà;* or, as Vasari wrote, he may have been a pupil of Giotto in Rome. Many scholars see in Martini's work the influence of the French courtly style, to which he may have been exposed during visits to Naples and Rome, where French culture throve at the time. Martini married Giovanna, the sister of the Sienese artist Lippo Memmi, in 1324; he bought the house they lived in from Memmi. The couple had no children. After 1333, there is no mention of Martini in Siena. By 1336, at the latest, he was in Avignon, where he remained until his death. Only his brother Donato, also a painter, and his wife traveled with Martini to France. The move may have been prompted by competition in Siena from the Lorenzetti brothers, who had been on the rise since c. 1328, or by an unrealized hope for papal commissions.

Siena, Naples, and Assist (c. 1315–1320)

By consensus, the fresco of the *Maestà* (Palazzo Pubblico, Siena) is Martini's earliest dated work; it was probably completed for the commune in 1315–1316 and repaired in 1321. It shows the Virgin and Child enthroned beneath a canopy supported by some of the saints standing on either side. In the foreground, four saintly protectors of the commune kneel with two angels, who present bowls of flowers to the holy pair. A surrounding border contains images in roundels of God the father, prophets, evangelists, church doctors, and others. This fresco is a unique example of a dialogue between the Virgin and the kneeling saints. The Virgin's statements still remain inscribed on the step below her, but the prayers originally offered by the saints have disappeared from the scrolls that only two of them still hold. The sense of space, defined by the canopy, is noteworthy, as is the textured surface, which creates the impression of a tapestry and includes insertions into the plaster of colored glass and imitation gems, as well as the earliest examples of patterned halos.

The *Saint Louis Altarpiece,* tempera on panel (Naples, Capo-dimonte Museum) is signed. It was probably commissioned by Louis's brother, King Robert of Anjou, and shows angels crowning an enthroned Louis, while the saint himself deposits a second crown on a minuscule figure of Robert, kneeling at the right. It is datable between 1317, when Louis was canonized, and 1319, when his remains were translated to a new tomb in Marseilles in a ceremony attended by Robert, who returned to Naples with Louis's brain as a relic. Martini probably traveled to Naples to execute the picture. Louis's royal status is emphasized by the fleur-de-lis and other emblems on the frame and the saint's robe. The intricate tooling and use of glass, stones, silver, and gold lend the work opulence. The narrative predella, the earliest of this form to survive, illustrates five events from the life, death, and miracles of Louis. Though the scenes are set in different architectural interiors, the intuitive perspective is synchronized in all five, with orthogonals moving toward the vertical axis of the central scene.

The narrative frescoes in the chapel of Saint Martin of Tours (Assisi, basilica of San Francesco) have been attributed to Martini since the nineteenth century for stylistic reasons. The commission was funded by Gentile di Partino da Montefiore, a Franciscan cardinal from the Marches who died in 1312. The paintings include ten scenes from the legend of Martin and many separate pictures of saints and angels, as well as a portrait of the donor kneeling before Martin. The cycle was probably painted after the donor's death in 1312 but before 1319, when a period of political strife in Assisi would have prevented artistic activity in the basilica. The dedication of an Italian chapel to Martin, a patron saint of France who was born in Hungary, is surprising. Perhaps the donor's education in Paris and a later trip to Hungary on a diplomatic mission inspired his choice. The pictures treat Martin's secular life, reign as bishop, death, and funeral. Their narrative sequence is unusual, moving from the bottom of the wall to the top. Though the space is shallow in all the scenes, whether set in architectural interiors or outdoors, the pictorial drama is clearly articulated through the gestures and glances of the figures—for example, a pauper in the first scene who grasps Martin's cloak. Also impressive are the fa-

Simone Martini. Saints Clare and Elizabeth of Hungary. Fresco. © Scala/Art Resource, New York.

cial expressions of singers and details of costume such as the colorful peaked hats from Hungary, both seen in *The Knighting of Saint Martin.* Some scholars believe that the frescoes illustrating the life of Saint Francis elsewhere in the basilica influenced Martini's style, both in the Saint Martin cycle and in his later work. Martini may also have been responsible for the three stained-glass windows in the chapel. These windows (of uncertain date) show Saint Martin and other figures. According to Vasari, the *Virgin and Child with Saints* and *Five Saints,* frescoes in the chapel of Santa Elisabetta in the basilica, were begun by Martini and finished by Lippo Memmi.

Siena, Orvieto, San Gimignano, and Pisa (c. 1320–1335)

The *Grieving Saint John* (Barber Institute, Birmingham), in tempera on wood, is dated 1320 but undocumented before 1932. The saint's emotions are beautifully expressed. This work is small in scale and was probably part of a triptych painted for a private patron.

The frescoed *Equestrian Portrait of Guidoriccio da Fogliano* (Siena, Palazzo Pubblico) is controversial. Documents show that *Simone dipentore* painted at least four pictures of castles in the Palazzo Pubblico in 1330 and 1331; Since *Guidoriccio* shows castles in the background, some scholars assume that it is among the documented pictures. However, the fresco was not mentioned by Ghiberti or Vasari, and it is not signed. Moreover, there are errors in the treatment of military details that lead some to conclude not only that the painting is not by Martini, but that it is later than the fourteenth century. A relatively recent discovery of a fresco containing a castle lower down on the same wall as *Guidoriccio* allows us to attribute that work to Martini in lieu of die disputed picture. But if *Guidoriccio* is by Martini, and the inaccuracies are due to sloppy restorations in later times, the fresco demonstrates the painter's innovativeness. The warrior, identified as Guidoriccio by his heraldry, rides alone immediately behind the picture plane, a broad landscape stretching far beyond him—an image without precedent in medieval secular palaces.

The *Saint Ansanus Annunciation* (Florence, Uffizi) is signed by both Simone Martini and Lippo Memmi and dated 1333. It is painted in tempera on wood and is an early example of an altarpiece illustrated with a narrative scene. The work shows Saint Ansanus and an unidentified female saint (Margaret?) at either side and prophets in roundels. It was the first of four altarpieces for the cathedral of Siena, dedicated to the four saintly protectors of the city, one of whom was Ansanus. The frame was added in the late nineteenth century. The records of payment shed no light on the respective responsibilities of the two collaborators. Probably Martini painted the Annunciation and Memmi painted the two saints and the prophets. A fifth roundel most likely portrayed God the father. The Annunciation is noteworthy for its Immediacy: Gabriel has just alighted, his cape still flying, while the Virgin recoils in fear. Elegant details include Mary's intarsia throne; the marble floor; and Gabriel's brocaded robe, plaid cape, and rose-tinged wings. As in other Sienese Annunciations, Gabriel bears an olive branch instead of a lily. He also wears a crown of olive leaves. Symbolic of peace, these leaves perhaps allude to the coming of Jesus, the prince of peace. The words of Gabriel's announcement, *Ave Gratia Plena Dominus Tecum* (Luke 1:28), are in relief; they can thus be read metaphorically as the word that becomes flesh in Mary's womb at this instant. The *Altarpiece of the Blessed Agostino Novello* (Siena, Pinaco-teca Nazionale) is a tempera painting in an old-fashioned *pala* format. Though it is unsigned and undated, most scholars believe that Martini was the artist. It was painted for Saint' Agostino in Siena and was first documented in 1638, together with the sarcophagus of the Beatus (now lost) that it decorated. Agostino, a hermit monk who died in 1309 outside Siena, was venerated locally. The central panel of the altarpiece portrays him standing amid four trees, book in hand, an inspirational angel at his ear. The side panels illustrate four posthumous miracles—two drawn from Augustinian texts, two unrecorded. Each contains two episodes, a disaster followed by salvation. Three of the four stories show Agostino saving small children, an emphasis compatible with the protohumanism of the early *Trecento*.

Martini and his workshop painted other polyptychs, typically showing a half-length Virgin and child in the center flanked by panels containing busts of saints. At least two rested on a predella, and all apparently were crowned with gables filled with bust-length figures. The altarpiece painted for Santa Caterina in Pisa (Pisa, Museo Nazionale di San Matteo) and signed by Martini seems to have survived intact. The others, broken up and with many panels missing, apparently were painted as altar-pieces for churches in Orvieto and San Gimignano.

Avignon (c. 1335–1344)

The frescoes originally in the porch of the cathedral of Notre Dame des Doms, Avignon, were probably commissioned by Cardinal Jacopo Stefaneschi (d. 1341). When the badly damaged fragments that survive were transferred to the museum of the Palais des Papes, up to three layers of *sinopie* were revealed. Two works are completely lost: *Andrea Corsini Healing a Blind Man,* a portrayal of a miracle that took place in the porch itself; and *Saint George and the Dragon,* known through a seventeenth-century copy. The extant fragments and *sinopie* portray the earliest known Madonna of Humility and an adult Jesus with an orb flanked by six angels. In the former, the donor kneels before the Virgin, and the child holds a scroll inscribed "I am the light of the world"; in the latter, the unusual orb contains a landscape framed between rippling water and a starry sky. The changes in the skillfully drawn series of *sinopie* suggest that the patron played an active role in the artist's progress.

The *Holy Family* (Liverpool, Walker Art Gallery) is signed and dated 1342. This small picture in tempera is a unique portrayal of Jesus, Mary, and Joseph immediately after the disputation with the doctors in the temple. The codex in the Virgin's lap contains an abbreviated quotation from Luke 2:48—"Son, why hast thou dealt with us thus?"—and the gestures indicate a parental reprimand of the defiant Jesus. This work is an unusual example of the Holy Family as an ordinary family with ordinary problems; as such, it reflects the human values of the time.

The *Virgil Frontispiece* (Milan, Biblioteca Ambrosiana) was painted on vellum for Petrarch between 1338 and 1344. A couplet inscribed on it states that the artist was Simone Martini. This painting was made for Petrarch's volume of classical texts, which included most of Virgil; it originally faced the first work, a fourth-century commentary by Servius on the *Bucolics.* The image seems to be an allegory explained by two other couplets that refer to the "unveiling" of the "secrets" of Virgil by Servius. It depicts Servius pulling back a curtain to reveal a reclining Virgil; nearby are a knight (representing the *Aeneid)*, a farmer (*Georgics*), and a shepherd (*Eclogues)*.

Two lost portraits by Martini probably also date from the Avignon period. The first, made for Petrarch, depicted Laura; it is known only through two of the poet's sonnets that refer to it. The second was of Cardinal Napoleone Orsini, and to it Martini added verses by Petrarch, which appear to come from the sitter's mouth. It was mentioned in a fifteenth-century text. These were the first-known individual portraits in Italy.

The seven surviving tempera panels of the *Antwerp* (*Orsini*) *Polyptych* (Antwerp, Musées Royaux des Beaux-Arts; Berlin, Staatliche Museen, Preussischer Kulturbesitz; Paris, Musée du Louvre) are dated by most scholars to Martini's years in Avignon. Originally a double-sided work, the polyptych probably folded like a concertina. The panels portray Gabriel, the Virgin Annunciate, and the *Via Crucis* (backed by the Orsini arms), *Crucifixion, Deposition,* and *Entombment.* One narrative panel and a second set of the family arms are lost. The patron, shown in the *Deposition,* was one of the four Orsini brothers, all of whom became cardinals. Most remarkable is the *Via Crucis,* which includes perturbed children; a rare depiction of Simon of Cyrene bearing the cross behind Jesus (Matthew 27:32); and a compassionate Saint John already protecting the Virgin, before Jesus asks him to do so from the cross. The polyptych was signed by Martini.

Saint Ladislas (Altomonte, Santa Maria della Consolazione, Museo), a small devotional panel in tempera known only since 1929, is attributed to Martini on the basis of style. It probably was made at Avignon. The veneration of Ladislas was rare in Italy at this time, and the portrayal of a saint standing in isolation was also unusual.

Other Lost or Destroyed Works

Account books in Siena mention other works done in the city but no longer extant. In addition, Ghiberti cites an altarpiece for the cathedral of Siena, now lost, and frescoes on the facade of the Opera del Duomo and the Ospedale della Scala, both destroyed. Finally, Vasari refers to an untraced panel in Santa Maria Novella in Florence.

See also **Duccio di Buoninsegna; Giotto di Bondone; Petrarca, Francesco; Robert of Anjou**

Further Reading

Borsook, Eve. *The Mural Painters of Tuscany, from Cimabue to Andrea del Sarto.* London: Phaidon, l960. (Rev. ed. Oxford: Clarendon, 1980, pp. 19–27.)

Brink, Joel. "Francesco Petrarch and the Problem of Chronology in the Late Paintings of Simone Martini." *Paragone,* 28(331), 1977a, pp. 3–9.
——. "Simone Martini, Francesco Petrarch and the Humanistic Program of the Virgil Frontispiece." *Mediaevalia,* 3, 1977b, pp. 83–117.
Cannon, Joanna. "Simone Martini, the Dominicans, and the Early Sienese Polyptych." *Journal of the Warburg and Courtauld Institutes,* 45, 1982, pp. 69–93.
Carli, Enzo, ed. *Simone Martini: La Maestà.* Milan: Electa, 1996.
Contini, Gianfranco, and Maria Cristina Gozzoli. *L'opera completa di Simone Martini.* Milan: Rizzoli, 1970.
Denny, Don. "Simone Martini's *Holy Family.*" *Journal of the Warburg and Courtauld Institutes,* 30, 1967, pp. 138–149.
Enaud, François. "Les frèsques de Simone Martini en Avignon." In *Les Monuments Historiques de la France.* Paris, 1963, pp. 114–180.
Gardner, Julian. "Saint Louis of Toulouse, Robert of Anjou, and Simone Martini." *Zeitschrift für Kunstgeschichte,* 39, 1976, pp. 12–33.
Garzelli, Annarosa. "Peculiarità di Simone Martini ad Assisi: Gli affreschi della cappella di San Martino." In *Simone Martini: Atti del convegno: Siena, 27, 28, 29 marzo 1985,* ed. Luciano Bellosi. Florence: Centro Di, 1988, pp. 55–65.
Hoch, Adrian S. "A New Document for Simone Martini's Chapel of Saint Martin at Assisi." *Gesta,* 24, 1985, pp. 141–146.
Hueck, Irene. "Die Kapellen der Basilika San Francesco in Assisi: Die Auftraggeber und die Franziskaner." In *Patronage and Public in the Trecento*: *Proceedings of the Saint Lambrecht Symposium, Abtei Saint Lambrecht, Styria, 16–19 July 1984,* ed. Vincent Moleta. Florence: L. S. Olschki, 1986.
Mallory, Michael, and Gordon Moran. "New Evidence Concerning *Guidoriccio.*" *Burlington Magazine,* 128, 1986, pp. 250–256.
Martindale, Andrew. "The Problem of *Guidoriccio.*" *Burlington Magazine,* 128, 1986, pp. 259–273.
——. *Simone Martini.* Oxford: Phaidon, 1988.
Milanesi, Gaetano. *Documenti per la storia dell' arte senese.* Siena: O. Porri, 1854–1856.
Paccagnini, Giovanni. *Simone Martini.* Milan: A. Martello, 1955.
——. "Martini." In *Encyclopedia of World Art,* Vol. 9. New York: McGraw-Hill, 1964, cols. 502–508.
Stubblebine, James H. *Duccio di Buoninsegna and His School.* Princeton, N.J.: Princeton University Press, 1979.
Vasari, Giorgio. *Vite,* ed. Gaetano Milanesi. Florence: G. C. Sansoni, 1878–1885. (Originally 1550, rev. 1568.)

MARY D. EDWARDS

MASLAMA DE MADRID
(d. 1007)

Abū-l-Qāsim Maslama ibn Aḥmad al-Majrīṭī, Andalusian astronomer and mathematician, was born in Majrīṭ (Madrid). He studied in Córdoba and practiced astrology: interested by the Saturn-Jupiter conjunction that took place in 1007, he predicted a series of catastrophes usually associated with the fall of the caliphate and the period of civil wars (*fitna,* 1009–1031). He is the author of the first documented astronomical observation in al-Andalus (the longitude of *Qalb al-Asad,* Regulus, 135° 40' in 977 or 979). He wrote a set of notes on the only trigonometrical tool used in antiquity, Menelaos' theorem (*al-shakl al-qaṭṭā'*), as well as a commentary, with frequent original digressions, on Ptolemy's *Planisphaerium*, which is the first of the studies dedicated by Andalusian astronomers to the astrolabe: its influence is clear in the thirteen-century Latin compilation on the instrument ascribed to Messahalla (Māshā'allāh, fl. Baçra, 762–809) the echoes of which reach the treatises on the astrolabe written by the collaborators of Alfonso X and by Geoffrey Chaucer (ca. 1340–1400). He is the creator of an important school of mathematicians and astronomers, and two of his disciples (Aḥmad ibn al-Ṣaffār and Abū-1-Qāsim Aṣbag ibn al-Samḥ) collaborated with him in his revision of the *Sindhind zīj* (astronomical handbook with tables) of Al-Khwārizmī (fl. 800–847), a work having an Indian pre-Ptolemaic origin, probably known in Al-Andalus since ca. 850. This revision, extant in a Latin translation by Adelard of Bath (fl. 1116–1142), adapted certain tables to the geographical coordinates of Córdoba, changed the Persian calendar used in the original for the Hijra calendar, introduced Hispanic and, possibly, Ptolemaic materials and added a considerable amount of new astrological tables (about one-fifth of the extant set of numerical tables), which improve considerably the techniques used by Al-Khwārizmī himself. He also introduced Ptolemaic astronomy in al-Andalus: he studied the *Almagest* and wrote astrological additions for the Ptolemaic *zīj* of Al-Battānī (d. 929).

Further Reading

Burnett, C. (ed.) *Adelard of Bath: An English Scientist of the Early Twelfth Century.* London, 1987. 87–118.

Mercier, R. *Astronomical Tables in the Twelfth Century.* London, 1988.

Neugebauer, O. *The Astronomical Tables of Al-Khwārizmī.* Trans. with commentary by H. Suter. Copenhagen, 1962.

Samsó, J. *Las Ciencias de los Antiguos en al-Andalus.* Madrid, 1992. 84–98.

Suter, H. *Die Astonomischen Tafeln des Muḥammed ibn Mūsa al-Khwārizmī in der Bearbeitung des malama ibn Ahmed al-Madjrīṭī und der latein. Uebersetzung des Athelhard von Bath.* Copenhagen, 1914.

Vernet, J., and M. A. Catalá. "Las obras matematicas de Maslama de Madrid." In *Estudios sobre Historia de la Ciencia Medieval.* Ed. J. Vernet. Barcelona, 1979. 241–71.

JULIO SAMSÓ

MATILDA, EMPRESS (1102–1167)

The daughter of King Henry I of England and his wife, Matilda of Scotland, Matilda became the empress by virtue of her marriage to the Salian emperor, Henry V. Her father accepted the marriage proposal during Whitsuntide of 1109, at which time she was only eight years old. In the spring of 1110 she was sent to Germany under the care of Bishop Burchard of Cambrai, betrothed to Henry V at Utrecht, and crowned at Mainz by Archbishop Frederick of Cologne. Henry V then dismissed all her English attendants, and the child was taken under the guardianship of Archbishop Bruno of Trier to learn the German language and customs. The marriage finally took place in January 1114 at Worms, the new consort now being twelve years old and her husband some thirty years her elder. Henry V had used the years between the betrothal and marriage to spend Matilda's enormous dowry of ten thousand silver marks on a major Roman expedition, during which he extracted the short-lived treaty of Ponte Mammolo from Pope Paschal II in hopes of decisively ending the Investiture Conflict.

Matilda soon played the crucial roles of patron and intercessor at court; she appeared on charters in subsequent years as the sponsor of many royal grants, and acted as petitioner several times on behalf of nobles or prelates who sought reconciliation with the emperor. Her imperial role expanded when she joined her husband on a military campaign in Rome in 1117. The imperial army occupied the city, and Matilda was crowned with her husband on Pentecost in St. Peter's Basilica by the archbishop of Braga. Matilda would choose to retain the imperial dignity even after leaving Germany, at least as a courtesy title. When her husband's presence was required north of the Alps after the coronation, Matilda remained in Italy as imperial regent. She assisted in the administration of imperial territories and presided over courts such as the session at Rocca Capineta near Reggio. She appears to have continued in this capacity during the year 1118, and then rejoined the emperor in Lotharingia in 1119. This royal apprenticeship at such a tender age prepared her well for the tumultuous years ahead. She was with Henry V in Utrecht at his untimely death in 1125, which left her a childless widow in possession of the imperial insignia at the age of twenty-three.

Her husband's hopes that she would produce an heir for the Salian line were quickly replaced by her father's need for an heir to the Norman dynasty, since Henry I's only son died in 1120. He therefore recalled her to England, and Matilda handed over the imperial insignia to Archbishop Adalbert of Mainz before returning to her Anglo-Norman homeland in 1125. After a sixteen–year absence she began yet another new life, with the only tokens of her imperial childhood in Germany being a treasure of jewels and personal regalia (most of which she would give to religious houses) and the precious relic of the hand of St. James (which she gave to the family abbey at Reading). She was recognized as the legitimate heir of Henry I in England and Normandy, and in 1128 Henry I married her to the unpopular Angevin suitor, Geoffrey Plantagenet. Matilda was the child in her first marriage, but in this second union Geoffrey was the child, being ten years her junior and only fifteen years old. Her second marriage of political expediency was a rocky one, but it did produce the needed heir in 1133 (Henry II Plantagenet). After her father's death in 1135 Matilda spent some twenty years asserting her son's claim to the Anglo-Norman throne against her cousin, Stephen of Blois.

Once Henry II succeeded Stephen in 1154, Matilda lived the remainder of her life in Normandy, and was buried at the abbey of Bec upon her death in 1167. She proved to be a valuable and trusted adviser to her royal son. Although she recommended against the appointment of Thomas à Becker as the archbishop of Canterbury, Matilda was turned to repeatedly by all sides as a mediator (mediatrix) in the subsequent dispute between the king and cleric. This remarkable woman's Anglo-Norman-German life was summed up in the epitaph on her tomb: "Great by birth, greater by marriage, greatest by offspring. Here lies the daughter, wife, and mother of Henry." Yet surely the legacy of this indomitable woman reaches beyond the men whose political needs set the boundaries of her life.

See also **Henry I**

Further Reading

Chibnall, Marjorie. *The Empress Matilda: Queen, Consort, Queen Mother and Lady of the English*. Oxford: Basil Blackwell, 1991.

Geldner, Ferdinand. "Kaiserin Mathilde, die deutsche Königswahl von 1125 und das Gegenkönigtum Konrads III." *Zeitschrift für bayerische Landesgeschichte* 40 (1977): 3–22.

Leyser, Karl. "Frederick Barbarossa, Henry II and the hand of St. James." *English Historical Review* 90 (1975): 481–506; rpt. in *Medieval Germany and its Neighbors*. London: Hambledon, 1980, pp. 215–40.

Pain, Nesta. *Matilda: Uncrowned Queen of England*. London: Weidenfeld and Nicolson, 1978.

Rössler, Oskar. *Kaiserin Mathilde, Mutter Heinrichs von Anjou, und das Zeitalter der Anarchie in England*. Berlin: E. Ebering, 1897; rpt. Vaduz: Kraus Reprint, 1965.

Schnith, Karl. "*Domina Anglorum*, Zur Bedeuntungsstreite eines hochmittelalterlichen Herrscherinentitels." In *Grundwissenschaften und Geschichte: Festschrift für Peter Acht*, ed. Waldemar Schlogl and Peter Herde. Kallmunz: Lassleben, 1976, pp. 101–111.

JOSEPH P. HUFFMAN

MATTEO DA PERUGIA (d. by 1418)

Matteo da Perugia (Matheus de Perusia) was born in the latter fourteenth century and belongs, officially, to the third and last generation of Italian *ars nova* musicians; however, his curious career and his stylistic focus make him almost a French musician.

Except for his presumed Perugian origin, we know nothing of Matteo's early life, although it is apparent that he chose to become a professional musician rather than a priest. At some point, he became a singer at the cathedral of Milan (which was then still unfinished), and in 1402 he was appointed to be its first choirmaster (*magister capellae* or *maestro di cappella*). This appointment is thought to reflect the influence of the colorful man who became Matteo's chief patron, Pietro Filargo di Candia (Petros Philargos). Pietro Filargo was born a Greek; joined the Roman church; studied and then taught theology at the University of Paris; was an adviser to Gian Galeazzo Visconti; was made bishop, successively, of Piacenza (1386), Vicenza (1387), and Novara (1389); became archbishop of Milan in 1402; was made a cardinal in 1405; and became the antipope Alexander V in 1409.

Filargo took up his episcopal residence in nearby Pavia, where he could teach at its university and hold a lavish court. Matteo, loyally, came to this court to serve Filargo, so annoying his own employers in Milan that he felt compelled to give up his cathedral post in 1407 and devote himself fully to Filargo. In 1409, when Filargo was elected as antipope Alexander V by the Council of Pisa, Matteo presumably moved with his master to a new residence in Bologna. It was apparently then that Matteo participated in the preparation of one of the most important musical manuscript collections of the day (now in the Estense Library in Modena). When Alexander V died in 1410 (by poison), Matteo evidently stayed on with his successor, John XXIII, until John was assured of deposition by the Council of Constance. In May 1414, Matteo resumed his post at the cathedral in Milan, officially until October 1416. However, but not until January 1418—by which time Matteo himself seems to have died—was his successor given full status as *maestro di canto*.

There is no evidence that Matteo himself ever visited France, but French cultural influences had been present in northern Italy for decades, thanks partly to the proximity of the absentee papal court at Avignon. Filargo's Francophile tastes, in particular, probably caused Matteo to develop an identification with French rather than Italian musical styles—whether by imposition or voluntary affinity. Matteo's output of compositions must have been extensive, and what survives of it, though small by some standards, is the largest of any of the Italian *ars nova* composers. Aside from some six Latin liturgical pieces (two of them complex polytextual motets), the surviving works are secular. Only two *ballate* are in Italian. The remainder (four *ballades*, seven *virelais*, ten *rondeaux*, and one canon) are all in French, presumably to suit the Francophile tastes of his patrons. Most of Matteo's compositions are for three vocal parts, and in virtually all his work—sacred or secular—he applies the arcane techniques of isorhythmic integration, carrying them to elaborate extremes (disjunct lines, conflicting time signatures, etc.) in the style of the so-called *ars subtilior*, the "mannerist" school of exaggerated effects, which he seem to have embraced wholeheartedly. Indeed, Matteo, along with Antonello da Caserta, was a leader of this imported stylistic movement.

Beyond his own authenticated compositions, there survive a number of substitute contratenor parts written for music by other composers. If these parts are indeed by Matteo, as is generally believed, they show him attempting, through these substitute voices, to update or enhance the work of earlier or contemporaneous masters (such as Machaut, Bartolino da Padova, and Antonello). It has been proposed that Matteo's supposedly "modern" style made him an important shaper of new musical directions for the *Quattrocento*; but there is also an argument against this idea, buttressed by the fact that Matteo's music survives in only a few manuscripts and apparently did not circulate widely. For all his fascination as a bold compositional personality, Matteo seems to have played a less significant role than the more focused and disciplined Johannes Ciconia in the transition from the age of Machaut to the age of Dufay.

See also **Ciconia, Johannes**

Further Reading

Apel, Willi. *French Secular Vocal Music of the Late Fourteenth Century.* Cambridge, Mass.: Mediaeval Academy of America, 1950.

——, ed. *French Secular Compositions of the Fourteenth Century,* 3 vols. Corpus Mensurabilis Musicae, 53. Rome: American Institute of Musicology, 1970–1972.

Besseler, Heinrich. "Hat Matheus de Perusio Epoche gemacht?" *Die Musikforschung,* 8, 1955, 19–23.

Fano, Fabio. "Origini della cappella musicale del Duomo di Milano." *Rivista Musicale Italiana,* 55, 1953, pp. 1ff.

——. *La cappella musicale del Duomo di Milano,* Vol. 1, *Le origini e il primo maestro di cappelia: Matteo da Perugia.* Milan: Ricordi, 1956.

Gombosi, Otto. "French Secular Music of the Fourteenth Century." *Musical Quarterly,* 36, 1950, pp. 603–610.

Günther, Ursula. "Das Manuskript Modena, Biblioteca Estense, a M.5.24." *Musica Disciplina,* 24, 1970, pp. 17–67.

Korte, Werner. *Studien zur Geschichte der Musik in Italien im ersten Viertel des 15. Jahrhunderts.* Kassel: Bärenreiter, 1933.

Marrocco, William Thomas, ed. "Italian Secular Music". In *Polyphonic Music of the Fourteenth Century,* Vol. 10. Monaco: Éditions de Oiseau-Lyre, 1977.

Pirrotta, Nino. *Il Codice Estense lat. 568 e la musica francese in Italia al principio del 1400.* Palermo: Reale Accademia di Scienze, Lettere, e Arti, 1946.

Reese, Gustav. *Music in the Middle Ages.* New York: Norton, 1940.

Sartori, Claudio. "Matteo da Perugia e Bertrand Feragut." *Acta,* 28, 1956, pp. 12–27.

JOHN W. BARKER

MATTHEW PARIS (ca. 1199–1259)

A monk at St. Albans from 1217 until his death in 1259, Matthew inherited the duties of historian from his predecessor in that capacity, Roger of Wendover,

and continued work on Rogers *Chronica majora*, to some extent rewriting but primarily extending and illustrating the text (Cambridge, Corpus Christi College 26 and 16, and BL Royal 14.C.vii, fols. 157–218). He also produced other Latin historical texts generally associated with the Chronicles (*Historia Anglorum*, BL Royal l4.C.vii, fols. 1–156; *Liber additamentorum*, BL Cotton Nero D.i; *Abbreviatio chronicorum*, BL Cotton Claudius D.vi) among others, and four saints' lives in Anglo-Norman.

The great bulk of Matthew's illustrative work in the historical texts may be characterized as *signa*, abbreviated symbols that help readers find their way in the text and signal important events. In addition Matthew included itineraries, maps, illustrated genealogies, and the oldest preserved record of heraldic arms. Narrative illustrations are added to the histories but tend to take a minor part and assume a telegraphic, hurried, yet also vividly dramatic aspect. A few full-page iconic illustrations (the Virgin and Child, the Veronica head of Christ) appended to the Chronicles are the only miniatures that could be considered polished works of art.

It is in his illustrated saints' lives that Matthew fully explores the possibilities of narrative and, in the *Vie de seint Auban* in Dublin, produces his most artistically complex work. The Dublin manuscript has been dated in the 1240s as Matthew's first attempt to illustrate the life of a saint and contains Latin versions of the lives, liturgical offices, and charters in addition to Matthew's Anglo-Norman text. The romance text is illustrated by framed miniatures across the top of the three-column page, and these continue above the Latin texts, after the romance text has ended, to detail the foundation of the monastery through the efforts of King Offa. Matthew worked in an accomplished but late version of the "Style 1200." His illustrations for the Dublin manuscript are done in line with some touches of color, primarily green, but also vermilion, blue, and ocher. Notes at the bottom of the pages in Matthew's hand give evidence that the iconography of the miniatures was carefully planned.

It would seem that similar planning would explain Matthew's involvement in the illustration of two other manuscripts of lives of saints. The *Life of St. Thomas of Canterbury* in Anglo-Norman (BL Loan 88) and the *Estoire de seint Aedward le rei* (CUL Ee.3.59) are executed in a different style from the Dublin manuscript but retain many of the features associated with Matthew, even compositions and the drawing of such details as ships and horses. All three manuscripts show an involvement with contemporary political concerns and were intended for an aristocratic audience: the life of Edward is dedicated to Queen Eleanor, and notes on the flyleaf of the Dublin manuscript detail its loan and that of other manuscripts of the lives of saints to aristocratic ladies.

Although Matthew made important innovations in format and narrative in illustrated lives of the saints that in turn influenced the illustration of Apocalypses and other English manuscripts, in general his work must be characterized as eccentric and isolated. He apparently worked apart from the scriptorium at St. Albans and produced his manuscripts as virtually a one-man effort, even writing his own fair copy. If he did plan the London and Cambridge manuscripts, he probably sent them off to London or Westminster for execution.

Matthew received a special commission as historian from Henry III and harbored many courtly prejudices, yet he lived in a monastery away from court and voiced some remarkably strong antiroyal opinions. Similarly he was a religious man who had little patience with the papacy. The unique form and visual content of his Chronicles, which he surely counted as his greatest achievement, had no successor and, as a recent scholar has lamented, have been little studied.

Further Reading

Primary Sources

Lowe, W.R.L., and E.F. Jacob, eds. *Illustrations to the Life of St. Alban*. Intro. M.R. James. Oxford: Clarendon, 1924.

Paris, Matthew. *Chronica majora*. Ed. Henry R. Luard. 7 vols. Rolls Series. London: Longman, 1872–83.Paris, Matthew. *La estoire de seint Aedward le rei*. Ed. Montague Rhodes James. Oxford: Roxburghe Club, 1920 [facsimile].

Secondary Sources

Backhouse, Janet, and Christopher de Hamel. *The Becket Leaves*. London: British Library, 1988.

Hahn, Cynthia. "Absent No Longer: The Saint and the Sign in Late Medieval Pictorial Hagiography." In *Hagiogmphie und Kunst*, ed. G. Kerscher. Berlin: Dietrich Reimer, 1993, pp. 152–75.

Lewis, Suzanne. *The Art of Matthew Paris in the Chronica majora*. Berkeley: University of California Press, 1987 [extensive bibliography and analysis of Chronicle illustrations].

Morgan, Nigel. *Early Gothic Manuscripts 1190–1285*. 2 vols. A Survey of Manuscripts Illuminated in the British Isles 4, ed. J.J.G. Alexander. London: Harvey Miller, 1982–88.

Vaughan, Richard. *Matthew Paris*. Cambridge: Cambridge University Press, 1958.

CYNTHIA HABN

MAXIMILIAN (1459–1519)

Emperor, patron of the arts, "the last knight," Maximilian I Habsburg enjoys a popular modern reputation. As the son of Emperor Frederick III, Maximilian experienced a youth tarnished by the wars and defeats his father suffered. His first important step into politics came in 1473, when his father negotiated with Duke Charles the Rash of Burgundy for the hand of his daughter, Mary. Although Charles's original demand of a royal crown was too high, the negotiations continued over the next few years. Then when Charles died unexpectedly at the Battle of Nancy in 1477, the king of France moved to seize Mary, who was holding out in Ghent. Maximilian sealed their marriage first through procurators in April, and finally concluded it in person when he arrived at the head of a rescuing army in August. Their marriage became a true love match. The emperor enfeoffed his son with the lands of the late duke of Burgundy. Yet Maximilian only truly secured most of the lands in a series of wars with France. His victory at the battle of Guinegate in 1479 guaranteed his possession of the Lowlands and most of Burgundy, some of the richest lands in Europe.

These new lands were not so easy to hold onto, however, since the citizens of the prosperous towns disputed the power of the new dynasty. After Mary died from a riding accident in 1482, many in the Lowlands openly rebelled against Maximilian's authority. Allied with France, town forces managed to wring from Maximilian the supervision of his children, Philip and Margaret. Even worse, the city of Bruges took him prisoner for fourteen weeks in 1488. His rather, in a rare but certainly necessary act of support, actually gathered an army that marched on the city, frightening the town into freeing Maximilian. Returning at the head of his own army, Maximilian conquered Bruges and many other towns, completing their defeat by 1493 in the Treaty of Senlis.

In the midst of these conflicts Frederick had managed to get Maximilian elected king of the Romans in Frankfurt on February 16, 1486, and crowned in Aachen on April 9. For the first time in a century a son had followed as king an imperial father during the father's lifetime. In 1490 Maximilian replaced his incompetent cousin, Sigismund "the Rich in Coins," as duke of Tyrol. He made that province, located between Burgundy and Austria on the way to Italy, and its capital, Innsbruck, the center of his imperial organization. From there to Mecheln in the Netherlands he established the first regular postal route in Europe. The silver of Tyrol helped to finance the reconquest of Austria from Matthias Corvinus, while the growing business with the Fugger banking family helped to underwrite many more imperial schemes. But with interest rates of over 35 percent on loans, Maximilian rarely had enough cash to fund all his plans.

After Mary's death, Maximilian fathered several illegitimate children, but he knew the importance of political marriages. To gain both cash and leverage against France, in 1490 Maximilian arranged his marriage by proxy with the twelve-year-old Anne of Brittany, who had just inherited that important province on her father's death. The next year Charles VIII invaded Brittany, dissolved his (unconsummated) marriage to Maximilian's daughter Margaret, and, without returning Margaret or her dowry of Burgundy, married Anne. Maximilian tried to gather an army to oppose these actions but was hopelessly outnumbered by French forces and hampered by his daughter's hostage status. The Brittany affair gained France a strategic province, earned Maximilian frustration and humiliation, and helped engender a centuries-long rivalry between the Habsburg and Valois dynasties. In 1497 Maximilian found another marriage partner in Bianca Maria Sforza, sister of Ludovico il Moro Sforza, who had usurped control of Milan. She brought a dowry of four hundred thousand gulden (guilders), or about three times what Maximilian could draw annually from the Habsburg Austrian lands. That money quickly disappeared also.

Soon after his father's death in 1493, Maximilian responded to a call for an imperial reform proposed for the Reichstag (imperial council) of Worms in 1495. There the archbishop of Mainz, Berthold von Henneberg, tried to gain a reform suitable to the princes. At the Reichstag, Maximilian agreed to the "eternal territorial peace" *(Ewige Landfriede),* once and for all, legally forbidding the many private wars and feuds among nobles that had disturbed the empire. To keep the peace, the Reichstag also created the Imperial Chamber Court (Reichskammergericht) and established a general tax, the "common penny" *(gemeine Pfennig).* Afterward many princes wanted further reform and withheld the general tax to put pressure on Maximilian. After his defeat in a brief war against the Swiss, the princes temporarily were able to further restrict Maximilian's authority, imposing an imperial regime *(Reichsregiment)* at Augsburg in 1500. By 1504, however, he had largely defeated the fractious princes. The possibility of a unified, effective imperial government vanished in these quarrels.

Maximilian's involvement in wars on the empire's fringes brought mixed results. He encouraged new developments in military tactics, like cannon. Or he increasingly abandoned the cavalry charge of armored knights in favor of infantry on foot with sword and pike, his *Landsknechte.* Maximilian regularly participated in the shifting diplomatic alliances, and he managed to maintain a reputation as an able commander. But he lost many wars, often through lack of funds. He fought frequently in Italy, which had become an open battleground since the invasion in 1494 by Charles VII of France. In 1508 Pope Julius II, needing Maximilian's military support in the League of Cambrai against Venice, offered to crown him emperor. Yet Maximilian was unable to fight his way to Rome. So he proclaimed himself "elected emperor of the Romans" on February 4, 1508, in Trient. Thus, with Julius's belated acceptance, he became emperor without a papal coronation.

Maximilian gained lasting importance for both his dynasty and European history because of two important double marriages he arranged. First in 1496 he married his son Philip "the Handsome," and daughter Margaret from his marriage with Mary, to the heirs of Spain, Juana "the Mad" and Juan, the children of Ferdinand of Aragon and Isabella of Castille. Philip and Juana had several children. The elder son, Charles V, eventually inherited both the Spanish and Austrian possessions and had an empire "on which the sun never set." The second double marriage was arranged in 1515, when Maximilian married his grandson Ferdinand and granddaughter Mary to the children of King Ladislaus of Bohemia and Hungary. This arrangement provided the legal claims to reunite Hungary and Bohemia with the Habsburg lands in 1526.

But Maximilian's attempts at building stronger institutions of rule in his own inherited lands led to increasing opposition, including open rebellion in some territories. Even the citizens of Innsbruck resented the burden of debts run up by the often cash-poor Maximilian. At the beginning of 1519 they finally refused to accept his credit, or to find stalls for his horses. In disdain he left the city for Vienna but sickened along the way and died on January 12. As a result, his magnificent tomb in Innsbruck lies empty; his body is buried in Wiener Neustadt, while his heart lies in Bruges, next to the body of his first wife, Mary.

Maximilian enjoys lasting fame as a well-rounded Renaissance prince. He was a patron of the arts and new sciences at the summit of the German Renaissance. His portrait by Albrecht Dürer is the most famous image of the monarch. Skilled and literate in several languages, he himself helped to produce two autobiographical epic poems *(Theuerdank* and *Weisskunig),* a hunting manual, and other works, including the *Ambraser Heldenbuch (Ambray Book of Heroes,* a compilation manuscript of courtly literature named after Castle Ambras). Sometimes called "the last knight," he was a great promoter of tournaments, drawing on the chivalric traditions of the court of Burgundy and continuing the Order of the Golden Fleece. Maximilian's idea of the Holy Roman Empire of the German nation ended the Middle Ages and looked forward to the attempt at universal empire by his successor, his grandson Charles V.

See also **Frederick III; Hartmann von Aue**

Further Reading

Benecke, Gerhard. *Maximilian I (1459–1519): An Analytical Biography.* London: Routledge and Kegan Paul, 1982.
Wiesflecker, Hermann. *Kaiser Maximilian I.: Das Reich, Österreich und Europa an der Wende zur Neuzeit.* 5 vols. Vienna: Verlag für Geschichte und Politik, 1971–1986.

BRIAN A. PAVLAC

MECHTHILD VON HACKEBORN (1241–1298/1299)

A Cistercian sister of the Helfta community, Mechthild von Hackeborn's mystical visions were recorded in the

Liber specialis gratiae (Book of Special Grace). At age seven, Mechthild entered the Rodersdorf cloister, where her sister Gertrud already resided. After the community had relocated to Helfta, Mechthild served in the capacities of magistra and cantrix. In 1261 the five-year-old Gertrud von Helfta *(die Große)* was given into her charge. Bedridden the last eight years of her life, Mechthild revealed her visions at this time to Gertrud and at least one other sister at Helfta, who recorded them without her knowledge; however, Mechthild did approve portions of the account before her death.

The original German version of Mechthild's visions has not survived. There are more than 250 contemporaneous and subsequent Latin and vernacular manuscript versions of the *Liber specialis gratiae,* but only one manuscript contains all seven books. Rich in allegory, the seven parts chronicle Mechthild's life and death, her visions, the special graces she experienced, her teachings concerning the true devotion to God and the virtuous life, and fragments of a correspondence with a female friend. In contrast to the *Fließendes Licht der Gottheit (Flowing Light of the Godhead)* of Mechthild's somewhat older namesake at Helfta, Mechthild von Magdeburg, the descriptions and observations found in the *Liber specialis gratiae* are based on liturgy, scripture, and the writings of the church fathers; however, like the *Fließendes Licht,* the *Liber* exhibits originality in imagery, language, and style. Of special note is Mechthild's description of the devotion to the Sacred Heart of Christ *(Herz-Jesu-Verehrung),* which she and Gertrud die Große promoted at Helfta.

See also **Gertrud von Helfta; Mechthild von Magdeburg**

Further Reading

Bynum, Caroline Walker. "Women Mystics in the Thirteenth Century: The Case of the Nuns of Helfta." In *Jesus as Mother: Studies in the Spirituality of the High Middle Ages.* Berkeley: University of California Press, 1982, pp. 170–262.

Finnegan, Jeremy. "Saint Mechtild of Hackeborn: *Nemo Communior.*" In *Medieval Religious Women,* vol. 2. *Peace Weavers,* ed. Lillian Thomas Shank and John A. Nichols. Kalamazoo, Mich.: Cistercian Publications, 1987, pp. 213–221.

Finnegan, Mary Jeremy. *The Women of Helfta.* Athens: University of Georgia Press, 1991 [first published 1962 as *Scholars and Mystics*].

Haas, Alois Maria. "Mechthild von Hackeborn. Eine Form zisterziensischer Frauenfrömmigkeit." In *Die Zisterzienser. Ordensleben zwischen Ideal und Wirklichkeit.* Ergänzungsband, ed. Kaspar Elm. Cologne: Rheinland-Verlag, 1982, pp. 221–239; rpt. "Themen und Aspekte der Mystik Mechthilds von Hackeborn." In *Geistliches Mittelalter,* ed. Alois Maria Haas. Dokimion 8. Freiburg, Switzerland: Universitätsverlag, 1984), pp. 373–391.

Halligan, Theresa, ed. *The Booke of Gostlye Grace of Mechthild of Hackeborn.* Toronto: Pontifical Institute of Mediaeval Studies. 1979.

Lewis, Gertrud Jaron. *Bibliographie zur deutschen Frauenmystik des Mittelalters.* Berlin: Schmidt, 1989, pp. 184–195.

Paquelin, Ludwig, ed. "Sanctae Mechtildis Virginis Ordinis Sancti Benedicti Liber specialis gratiae." In *Revelationes Gertrudianae ac Mechthildianae,* vol. 2. Poitiers: Oudin, 1877, pp. 1–422.

Schmidt, Margot. "Mechthild von Hackeborn." In *Die deutsche Literatur des Mittelalters: Verfasserlexikon,* 2d ed., ed. Kurt Ruh. Berlin: de Gruyter, 1987, vol. 6, cols. 251–260.

DEBRA L. STOUDT

MECHTHILD VON MAGDEBURG (ca. 1207–ca. 1282)

Beguine, visionary, and mystic, known to us through her sole book, *Das fließende Licht der Gottheit (The Flowing Light of the Godhead).* Biographical information gleaned or inferred from her book and its introductory material written in Latin by others indicates that she was born to a family of lower nobility near Magdeburg. She experienced her first vision at age twelve and left home about 1230 to take up the life of a Beguine in Magdeburg, returning home occasionally perhaps because of sickness or troubles caused by her book. Just as she criticized the deportment of some Beguines, male and female religious, clergy, the pope, and others, she, too, was subjected to criticism and even threats. Equally evident, however, is the support she received, especially from the Dominicans, whose order she praised. Baldwin, her brother, was received into this order, became subprior of the Dominican house in Halle, and was esteemed for virtue and learning. Another Dominican, Heinrich von Halle, was her spiritual adviser for many years and helped her edit (and, no doubt, circulate) incomplete versions of her book. About 1270 she entered the Cistercian convent at Helfta, renowned, under the leadership of Gertrud von Hackeborn, for its thriving spiritual life and devotion to learning, as witnessed by the writings of Mechthild von Hackeborn and Gertrud (the Great) von Helfta. Here Mechthild was sheltered from the trials of the unprotected life of a Beguine but, if we can believe her, was more revered from a distance than accepted into the community. With her health weakening and her sight failing, she completed the seventh and final section of her book. Her death is described in Gertrud of Helfta's *Legatus divinae pietatis.*

The original text of her book, written in Middle Low German with some Middle German characteristics, has been lost. A Middle High German version of the complete work translated about 1345 under the direction of Heinrich von Nördlingen in Basel survives in a manuscript at Einsiedeln ("E") and provides the principal textual basis for the study of Mechthild. Parts and short fragments have been discovered in other manuscripts. A Latin translation of the first six books of the Middle Low German original, probably the work of Dominicans in Halle, has come down to us preceded by a lengthy prologue justifying the book and its author.

Das fließende Licht can be described as confessional, visionary-revelatory, mystical, poetic, and devotional. It was written, we are told, by divine command to bear witness to the unusual divine favors bestowed on its author. Mechthild describes her visions, some global and some personal in scope, as well as her ecstatic mystical experiences of union. She prophesies, exhorts, criticizes, and teaches, using a rich variety of literary and nonliterary forms of expression, from highly lyrical courtly modes with their concomitant conventions to didactic expositions of moral and ascetical truths. She avails herself of prose, verse, and, most distinctively, colon rhyme—a short, verselike unit ending in rhyme or, more frequently, assonance. Much of this colon rhyme has been lost in the Middle High German version.

Because she knew little or no Latin, Mechthild acquired her knowledge of theology and spiritual traditions secondhand through instruction and the liturgy. The theological content of her book gives striking evidence of the care given religious education by her spiritual teachers and advisers, but more especially to Mechthild's own intellectual gifts and intuitive spiritual receptivity. Among the influences perceptible in her book are the Song of Songs, Augustine, Bernard of Clairvaux, Hugh and Richard of St. Victor, and Joachim of Fiore. More important, however, Mechthild's book must be seen as unique in its conception, without discernible predecessors or successors.

See also **Bernard of Clairvaux; Gertrud von Helfta**

Further Reading

Bynum, Caroline Walker. "Women Mystics in the Thirteenth Century: The Case of the Nuns of Helfta." In Bynum. *Jesus as Mother—Studies in the Spirituality of the High Middle Ages.* Berkeley: University of California Press, 1982, pp. 170–262.

Franklin, James C. *Mystical Transformations: The Imagery of Liquids in the Work of Mechthild von Magdeburg.* Rutherford, N.J.: Fairleigh Dickinson University Press, 1978.

Galvani, Christiana Mesch, trans. *Flowing Light of the Divinity.* New York: Garland, 1991.

Haug, Walter. "Das Gespräch mit dem unvergleichlichen Partner: Der mystische Dialog bei Mechthild von Magdeburg als Paradigma für eine personale Gesprächsstrutkur." *Poetik und Hermeneutik* 11 (1984): 251–279.

Lewis, Gertrud Jaron. *Bibliographie zur deutschen Frauenmystik des Mittelalters.* Berlin: Schmidt, 1989, pp. 164–183 [bibliography].

Neumann, Hans. "Mechthild von Magdeburg." In *Die deutsche Literatur des Mittelalters: Verfasserlexikon.* 2d ed, vol. 6. Berlin: de Gruyter, 1987, cols. 260–270.

Neumann, Hans, ed. *Mechthild von Magdeburg. Das fließende Licht der Gottheit.* 2 vols. Munich: Artemis, 1990.

Schmidt, Margot. "*Minne du gewaltige Kellerin:* On the Nature of *minne* in Mechthild of Magdeburg's *fliessendes licht der gottheit.*" *Vox Benedictina* 4 (1987): 100–125.

Scholl, Edith. "To Be a Full Grown Bride: Mechthild of Magdeburg." In *Medieval Religious Women. vol. 2.: Peace Weavers,* ed. John A. Nichols and Lillian Thomas Shank. Kalamazoo, Mich.: Cistercian, 1987, pp. 223–238.

Tax, Petrus. "Die große Himmelsschau Mechthilds von Magdeburg und ihre Höllenvision." *Zeitschrift für deutsches Altertum* 108 (1979): 112–137.

Tobin, Frank. *Mechthild von Magdeburg—A Medieval Mystic in Modern Eyes.* Columbia, S.C.: Camden House, 1995.

von Balthasar, Hans Urs. "Mechthilds kirchlicher Auftrag." In *Das fließende Licht der Gottheit,* trans. Margot Schmidt. 1955. 2d ed. Stuttgart-Bad Canstatt: F. Frommann, 1995, pp. 19–45.

FRANK TOBIN

MEIR B. BARUKH OF ROTHENBURG (ca. 1220 – 1293)

Meir b. Barukh, known as "*MaHRaM*' (*moreinu ha-rav Meir,* "our teacher Rabbi Meir"), was born in Worms ca. 1220 (not 1215; see Urbach, pp. 407–8). His father was a rabbi in Worms and an important scholar, as were many other members of his family. Meir's teachers included his father, and in Würzburg the renowned Isaac b. Moses of Vienna, author of the halakhic work *Or zarua',* and others. He also learned in yeshivot in France, where he copied responsa and talmudic commentaries that he later used in his own work. If the lamentation Meir wrote about the burning of books refers to the burning of the Talmud in Paris in 1242, then he may have been an eyewitness to that event and returned to Germany shortly thereafter. It is uncertain when he went to Rothenburg, the city most connected with his name, but probably soon after his return from France. He served also as rabbi in several other communities. After the death of his father (1276 or 1281), Meir went to Worms to replace him there. He had a *beit midrash,* or yeshivah, attached to his house there, with a "winter house" (i.e., heated, apparently) and rooms for the students to sleep. According to the information he himself wrote about this, the number of students was not large, even though his yeshivah was certainly the most famous one in Germany. His main students were Asher b. Yeḥiel, Mordecai b. Hillel, Samson b. Ṣaddoq, Ḥayyim b. Eli'ezer (grandson of Isaac, author of *Or zarua'),* and others, all outstanding scholars in their own right.

Meir was not, as Graetz had assumed, appointed "chief rabbi" of Germany (indeed, no such position existed); however, he was widely regarded as the foremost talmudic and legal authority, to whom rabbis not only from Germany but also France and other lands turned for decisions. Because of the large number of requests received, he even had to write his answers on the eve of holidays and the eve of Yom Kippur (see Urbach, p. 421). He was independent in his views and did not refrain from strongly disagreeing with those whose position he considered to be wrong (the story told by Urbach, p. 412, bottom, is not entirely accurate, however; see the text of the respon-sum ed. Bloch, p. 188, No. 81; it is understandable that the author whom Urbach cites thought that the bride's father was French, since the Amsterdam manuscript in fact reads "Roda," probably Dreux in France, cf. Gross, *Gallia Judaica*, p. 184, for similar spellings).

He used his authority to forestall enactments (*taqqa-not*) that he thought would create a burden on people, such as the attempt by some communities to allot a portion of the taxes to property, something that Meir said had never been done in all the kingdom; rather, taxes were collected only on buying and selling, and were not collected at all from the poor (*She'elot u-teshuvot*, ed. Prague, No. 541, second part of the question; cf. ed. Bloch, p. 209, No. 141, where he advised more cautiously that they investigate the custom throughout Germany and act accordingly, but in general the opinion agrees with that of the previous question).

The rapidly deteriorating situation of the Jews in Germany in the latter half of the thirteenth century resulted in many Jews leaving to move to other towns under different overlords or leaving the empire altogether. Some followed earlier French rabbis to settle in Palestine. Meir himself finally decided upon this plan. Emperor Rudolph issued a decree in December of 1286 prohibiting any Jew from going across the sea without his permission or that of their overlord (text in Guido Kisch, *The Jews in Medieval Germany* [Chicago, 1949], p. 130, in which book, incidentally, Meir is not mentioned). Meir and his entire family also decided to leave for Palestine in spite of the royal decree, but on the way they encountered the bishop of Basel, who had with him an apostate Jew who recognized the rabbi and informed the bishop. Meir was arrested and turned over to the emperor, who imprisoned him in the castle at Ensisheim. According to Urbach (p. 424), the place where Meir was caught, in the mountains of Lombard, was a transition point for those going on to Palestine, and Meir was arrested not only for transgressing the decree but for leading others seeking to leave. By 1288 the German Jewish communities had raised a substantial ransom, which they offered for Meir's release. According to Solomon Luria (commentary *Yam shet Shelomoh on Gittin* ch. 4. 6), the rabbi refused the ransom, saying that a captive should not be redeemed for more than his worth (lest this encourage capturing other Jews). In his "ethical testament," Judah, the son of Asher b. Yehiel, relates that the emperor held Asher responsible for the collection of the ransom money, and when Meir died in prison before the ransom could be paid, Asher decided to flee Germany. From the prison at Ensisheim Meir was apparently moved to the castle at Wasserburg, where his students were able to visit him, and one of them, the aforementioned Samson b. Saddoq, regularly administered to his needs and recorded his customs in a book that he later wrote. Meir continued also to write responsa from prison, in spite of his lack of books and even sufficient paper. He died in captivity in 1293.

His works include more than a thousand responsa; aside from the volumes published under his name, many are found in the writings of his students and elsewhere, such as in the responsa of Ibn Adret (*She'elot u-teshu-vot* I, Nos. 829–78; possibly others there). In addition, he composed *tosafot* (additional commentaries) on several tractates; all of those on *Yoma* in standard editions of the Talmud are by him. He is known also to have written commentaries on the Talmud (on *Yevamot* was published in 1986), and his commentaries on the *mishnayot* of *Neg'im* and *Ohalot* have been published, as well as fragments from commentaries on parts of the order of *Tehorot*. His customs (*minhagiym*), chiefly on religious matters and holidays, are found in *Sefer ha-Tashbas* of his student Samson b. Saddoq; in a collection by his student Moses Sheneur, published as *'Al ha-kol* (Berditchev, 1908); in Moses "Parnas" of Rothenburg, *ha-Parnas* (Vilna, 1865); and in a modern edition, *Sefer minhagiym de-vei MaHaRaM*, ed. S. Elfenbein (New York, 1948). He also wrote some twenty eulogies and religious poems that have survived.

See also **Asher b. Yehiel; Ibn Adret, Solomon**

Further Reading

Works by Meir b. Barukh

She'elot u-teshuvot (Cremona, 1557/8).

She'elot u-teshuvot (Prague, 1608; revised ed. by Moses Bloch, Pressburg, 1895, Budapest, 1896).

She'elot u-teshuvot, ed. Raphael N. Rabbinovicz (Lvov, 1860).

Sefer sha'arei teshuvot, ed. Moses Bloch (Berlin, 1891); according to mss. (additional responsa were published by Y. Kahana in *Sinai* [1943] and later, and as offprint in a limited edition [Jerusalem, 1957]; also in Solomon Wertheimer, *Ginzei Yerushalayim*, part 3 [Jerusalem, 1902], and by M. Hirschler in *Sinai 55* [1965]: 317–22).

Work on Meir b. Barukh

Urbach, Ephraim E. *Ba'aley ha-tosafot* (Jerusalem, 1968), ch. 10.

NORMAN ROTH

MEISTER ECKHART
(ca. 1260–1327/1328)

Dominican theologian, preacher, administrator, and mystic. The title *meister,* a corruption of the Latin *magister* (teacher) refers both to his having received the highest academic degree then attainable and to his professional duties at the University of Paris. He was born in Thuringia, possibly in a village called Hochheim, of which there are two, one near Erfurt and one near Gotha. One document refers to him as *de* (from, of) Hochheim, but some scholars consider this a familial rather than a geographical designation and use it to bolster the claim that Eckhart was of noble origin. He most likely entered the Order of Preachers (Dominicans) at the priory in Erfurt at about the age of fifteen. Possibly he received his early training in the arts at Paris and was witness to Bishop Stephen Tempier's condemnation of 219 articles of theology including several taught by Thomas Aquinas (d. 1274), the Dominican order's most distinguished theologian. At any rate, Eckhart is documented in Paris lecturing on Peter Lombard's *Sentences* in 1293–1294. Prior to this he had absolved the various stages of Dominican formation: one year novitiate, two years studying the order's constitutions and the divine office, about five years studying philosophy, with three additional years devoted to theology. Eckhart was no doubt also among those chosen for further study, very likely at the order's *studium generale* (early form of university) in Cologne, where he might have had direct contact with Albert the Great. After lecturing in Paris Eckhart advances rapidly within the order. He is prior in Erfurt 1294–1298, professor in Paris 1302–1303, provincial of the newly formed German Dominican province of Saxony 1303–1311, and again professor in Paris 1312–1313. There followed several years of preaching in the vernacular, to Beguines and nuns among others, in Strasbourg and then later in Cologne, where he might also have had professorial duties at the *studium generale.*

In 1325 the first clouds appear when some of Eckhart's teachings are investigated as to their orthodoxy. Eckhart is cleared, but the following year Henry of Virneburg, archbishop of Cologne, begins inquisitorial proceedings against him. Eckhart responds to lists of suspect theses taken from a broad selection of his Latin and German works and, on January 24, 1327, citing delays and the public scandal the proceedings are causing, appeals to the pope. On February 13 he protests his innocence from the pulpit of the Dominican church in Cologne and soon thereafter travels to Avignon, where a papal commission begins an investigation. On March 27, 1329, some time after Eckhart's death, a papal bull, *In agro dominico,* definitively ends the investigation. In it seventeen articles are condemned as heretical, two of which Eckhart claimed never to have taught. Eleven others are judged to be evil sounding but capable of an orthodox interpretation. The bull states that Eckhart, before his death, recanted the articles and anything else that might have caused error in the minds of his audience *quoad illum sensum.* In other words, he recanted a heretical interpretation of his words, not the words themselves.

Eckhart's writings can be divided into Latin works (professional theological treatises, learned commentaries on scripture, and some sermons or sermon outlines) and German works (spiritual tracts and, especially, sermons). Because of Eckhart's sad fate, his Latin works were generally forgotten and only rediscovered in the late nineteenth century. His German works became mixed with those of other spiritual authors or were often passed on with false or no attribution. As a result, the task of creating a reliable critical edition of the German works begun by Josef Quint in 1936 is just now nearing completion. Disagreement still remains concerning the authenticity of many German sermons not yet included in the critical edition, and discussion of their chronology has just begun. Eckhart is admired both for the brilliance of his mystical thought and for his virtuosity in expressing it. The first admirers of Eckhart after his rediscovery in the nineteenth century, because of their unfamiliarity with medieval philosophy and theology, made uninformed judgments about his originality in thought and language. Although scholars still view him as an original thinker, he is now recognized as being original within the context of the already well-developed system of scholastic thought. His mysticism has been termed speculative to indicate both its imbeddedness in scholastic philosophy and theology as well as the fact that he does not talk about mystical union in terms of personal experience. Rather, he describes the metaphysical constitution of both the human soul and God's nature that makes union possible. For Eckhart mystical union between God and the soul rests on their metaphysical oneness. Eckhart sees creatures as differing from God, but they differ only through the nothingness limiting the being that they possess; and being is God. Eckhart distinguishes between two kinds of being in creatures: formal or limited being, which constitutes them in existence separate from God, and virtual being—the being of creatures in the mind of God existing from eternity. The virtual being of creatures at one with God's being is their more real and vital being. Their formal being is a mere shadow by comparison. This distinction between formal and virtual being in creatures provides the context for understanding most of Eckhart's characteristic doctrines. Thus, for example, he urges us to become as poor in spirit as we were (in the mind of God) before we were (formally existing). In other words, we are to "reduce" our existence to existence in God. So, too, in becoming the just man, we do so by uniting completely with justice, which is identical with God's being. Through our oneness with God's being the birth of the Son takes place in us, as it does in Bethlehem, and united with this divine action we become both the begotten (Son) and the "begetter" (Father). The human intellect, that faculty most essential in establishing our likeness with God, is in its purely spiritual activity the spark of the soul in which we most throw off the confines of our creatureliness and imitate divine activity. And through detachment, a key term in

Eckhart's mystical asceticism, the creature frees himself from his own specific self or formal being, which is in essence the limiting factor separating us from God, to become whole or one with him.

The startling vigor of Eckhart's thought is matched by the power and artfulness with which he expresses it. Though the Latin works show skillful manipulation of language, it is his German works, especially the sermons, that display a rich variety of linguistic artistry, some of it best termed rhetorical and some clearly poetic. Often he overcomes the limitations of the young vernacular's ability to express his rarefied mysticism by placing a key term in a variety of juxtaposed contexts in the manner of a leitmotif and thus gradually reveals to his audience the treasures it contains. He employs such figures as accumulation, antithesis, parallelism, hyperbole, chiasmus, and paradox to great advantage. Word games and original verbal strategies of other kinds abound.

Eckhart influenced most immediately John Tauler and Henry Suso, Dominican mystics of the next generation, and less clearly their Flemish contemporary John (Jan van) Ruusbroec. From the library of the Swiss cardinal Nicholas of Cusa (Cusanus), Latin works by Eckhart have come down to us with comments by the cardinal scribbled in the margins. Cusanus shows much affinity in thought with Eckhart and defended him against the attacks of the Heidelberg theologian Johannes Wenck. The baroque poet Johann Scheffler (Angelus Silesius) was certainly touched by Eckhartian ideas, but, as in the case of many other authors and works of the reformation period and beyond, whether the influence was direct or indirect is impossible to tell. In more modern times the philosophers Hegel, Schelling, and Baader all admired his thought, though until the mid–twentieth century much of this admiration was based on misunderstandings arising from ignorance about Eckhart's own intellectual context. The last forty years have seen great progress in understanding this exhilarating mystic, though much of his uncharted profundity remains to be explored.

See also **Jan van Ruusbroec; Nicholas of Cusa; Peter Lombard; Seuse, Heinrich**

Further Reading

Colledge, Edmund, and Bernard McGinn, trans. *Meister Eckhart: The Essential Sermons, Commentaries, Treatises, and Defense,* New York: Paulist, 1981.

Koch, Josef. "Zur Analogielehre Meister Eckharts." 1959; rpt. in Josef Koch. *Kleine Schriften,* vol. 1. Rome: [n.p.], 1973, pp. 367–409.

Largier, Niklaus. *Bibliographie zu Meister Eckhart.* Freiburg: Universitätsverlag, 1989 [bibliography].

McGinn, Bernard. "Eckhart's Condemnation Reconsidered." *Thomist* 44 (1980): 390–414.

——. "The God Beyond God: Theology and Mysticism in the Thought of Meister Eckhart." *Journal of Religion* 61 (1981): 1–19.

——. "Meister Eckhart on God as Absolute Unity." In *Neoplatonism and Christian Thought,* ed. Dominic J. O'Meara. Albany: State University of New York Press, 1982, pp. 128–139.

——, ed., *Meister Eckhart and the Beguine Mystics.* New York: Continuum, 1994.

McGinn, Bernard, Frank Tobin, and Elvira Borgstadt. *Meister Eckhart: Teacher and Preacher.* New York: Paulist, 1986.

Meister Eckhart. *Die deutschen und lateinischen Werke,* ed. Josef Quint. Stuttgart: Kohlhammer, 1936ff.

Ruh, Kurt. *Meister Eckhart: Theologe, Prediger, Mystiker.* Munich: Beck, 1985.

Schürmann, Reiner. *Meister Eckhart: Mystic and Philosopher.* Bloomington: University of Indiana Press, 1978.

Smith, Cyprian. *Meister Eckhart: The Way of Paradox.* London: Darton, Longman and Todd, 1987.

Tobin, Frank. *Meister Eckhart: Thought and Language.* Philadelphia: University of Pennsylvania Press, 1986.

Walshe, M. O'C. *Meister Eckhart: Sermons and Treatises.* Rockport, Me.: Element, 1992.

FRANK TOBIN

MENA, JUAN DE (1411–1456)

Secretary and chronicler of Juan II of Castile and one of the outstanding poets of his time. Author of two long narrative poems, *La coronación del marques de Santillana* (c.1438), and his masterpiece, *El laberinto de Fortuna* (1444); an allegorical debate, *Coplas de los pecados mortales* (also known as *Debate de la Razón contra la Voluntad*), left incomplete at his death; and some fifty shorter compositions typical of the courtly verse of his day: queries and responses to other poets, occasional pieces, riddles, love poems, and satiric verse. His prose works include a prologue and commentary to his *Coronación; La llíada en romance*, a translation of the *Ilias latina*, with prologue (c. 1442); *Tratado de amor* (c. 1444); *Tratado del título de duque* (1445); a prologue to Alvaro de Luna's *Libro de las virtuosos e claras mugeres* (c. 1446); and the fragmentary *Memorias de algunos linajes antiquas é nobles de Castilla* (1448).

Reliable data on Mena's life is sparse. He was born in late December 1411 in Córdoba, and was named alderman (*veinticuatro*) there possibly as early as 1435. In his *Memorias* he traces the Mena lineage to the valley of Mena in La Montaña. Vatican archival documents place him in Florence in 1442–1443 at the court of Pope Eugene IV, from whom he unsuccessfully sought ecclesiastical benefices in Córdoba. He was appointed secretary for Latin and royal chronicler by King Juan II of Castile probably in the mid-1440s, although the earliest extant document which refers to him with either of these titles is his own *Memorias* (1448). He married Marina Méndez, some twenty years his junior, around 1450. Upon the death of King Juan II in 1454 he remained in the service of King Enrique IV; he died in Torrelaguna in 1456, leaving no descendants.

The poet's first editor, Hernán Núñez, supplies additional biographical data that cannot be corroborated: that he was the son of Pedrarias and of a sister of Ruy Fernández de Peñalosa, lord of Almenara and *veinticuatro* of Córdoba; that both parents died when he was very young; that he began his studies in Córdoba and continued them in Salamanca; and that he was married in Córdoba to a sister of García de Vaca and Lope de Vaca. Other early biographical accounts derive from Núñez, although they differ in some particulars.

Throughout his adult life Mena divided his time between Córdoba and the royal court. He was a loyal supporter of King Juan II and an unabashed admirer of Alvaro de Luna; at the same time, his friendship with the Marquis of Santillana transcended the political turmoil of the time and survived the Marquis's disaffection with the crown and the *condestable.*

El laberinto de Fortuna (popularly called *Las trescientas*), a narrative poem of 297 *arte mayor* stanzas, was presented to King Juan II in February 1444. The poet inveighs against capricious Fortune, and is forthwith transported in a visionary journey to her palace. There he is met by Providence, who will serve as his guide. Providence shows him the three wheels of Fortune corresponding to the past, present, and future, each with seven circles governed by the seven planets. The wheel of the unknowable future remains veiled, but the poet will be permitted to see those of the past and the present.

The main body of the poem (stanzas 61–238) recounts the histories of exemplary figures (exalted and condemned) in each of the seven circles. The first four circles (Diana, Mercury, Venus, and Phoebus) stress figures from the past and ethical concerns, while the last three (Mars, Jupiter, and Saturn) emphasize the present (and, by extension, the recent past). Here Fortune holds sway; only Alvaro de Luna has been able to conquer her, and the king must emulate his example if he is to attain the greatness foretold for him.

The work concludes with Providence's prophecy of future glory for the king, whose fame will eclipse that of his ancestors; the vision fades, however, before the poet can inquire of his guide as to the particulars of the king's future accomplishments. His task is clear: he must put an end to civil strife ("las guerras que vimos de nuestra Castilla," 141b) and unite the warring factions in a final push to victory over the Muslims (the "virtuosa, magnífica guerra" of 152a).

Mena drew selectively and deftly from a wide variety of sources. His allegorical construct owes much to such works as *Anticlaudianus*, *Roman de la rose*, and Dante's *Divine Comedy*, though he appears to have made his own contribution to the symbology of Fortune in the concept of the three wheels. He knew and utilized Latin epic poets (Virgil, Lucan, Statius) and relied heavily on Ovid's *Metamorphoses* for Greco-Roman mythology.

The language of the *Laberinto* is a language of poetic innovation. It is characterized by an abundance of neologisms coined from Latin roots, a tendency toward Latinate morphology and syntax, and the extensive use of a wide variety of rhetorical devices. Yet the poet does not hesitate to juxtapose a vulgar, archaic vernacular word and an elegant Latinism: "*fondón* del çilénico çerco segundo" (at the deepest bottom of the second celaenic [i.e., Meraniel] circle) (92b) or "con *túrbido* velo su *mote* cubría" (with turbid veil covered their riddle 57d). The result is a compendium of tragic, satiric, and comedic styles consistent with principles enunciated earlier by the poet (*Coronación*, prologue).

La coronación del marqués de Santillana was composed to celebrate Santillana's victory over the Moors in the Battle of Huelma in 1438. It consists of fifty-one octosyllabic *coplas reales*, accompanied by the author's extensive prose commentary in which he explicates each stanza, clarifying classical allusions and glossing his neologisms. Mena coined the term *calamicleos* (from the Latin *calamitas* and Greek *cleos*) to describe the work, "a treatise on the misery of evildoers and the glory of the good." The poet describes his allegorical journey through the valleys of Thessaly, where he contemplates the fate of figures from antiquity such as Ninus of Babylon (armless in punishment for his failure to raise his arms in defense of his city) and Jason (afire in punishment for his lust). He then makes his way through a forest of knowledge and ascends Mt Parnassus, reaching a place reserved for those who have attained fame through their works: Solomon, David, Homer, Lucan, Virgil, Seneca, and others. Under a canopy, attended by the immortal authors and the Muses, is the Marquis of Santillana; the poet watches as he receives the laurel crown from four maidens who represent the cardinal virtues, and exhorts the goddess Fame to spread the news of the event worldwide.

Stanza 42 and its commentary reveal that Santillana is being recognized for his diligence, loyalty, and valor in the service of the king against the Muslims rather than for his accomplishments as a writer. By implication, the poet's condemnation of those being punished for cowardice or irresponsibility could be extended to some of his contemporaries; the example of Santillana (like that of Alvaro de Luna in *Laberinto*) is worthy of emulation.

In *Coplas de los pecados mortales*, the poet invokes the Christian muse, disavowing the "dulçura enponzoñada" of his earlier works and ruing time misspent in the study of pagan antiquity. Written in octosyllabic *arte menor* stanzas and structured as an allegorical debate between Reason and the Seven Deadly Sins, represented as seven faces of Will, the work leaves off at Stanza 106, during the debate between Reason and Anger. An indication of the work's reception in its own time are the continuations of it written by Gómez Manrique, Pero Guillén de Segovia, and Fray Jerónimo de Olivares.

Mena's earliest prose work is probably his commentary to the *Coronación*. There he cultivates several styles, ranging from elaborate Latinate through simpler narrative to direct didactic. The *Ilias latina* is his translation of an abridged version of the Homeric epic in 1,070 Latin hexameters. *Tratado de amor*, in relatively straightforward didactic style, reveals some of the author's subtle humor as he concentrates on "el amor no líçito e insano" and devotes almost equal attention to that which engenders it as to that which repels it. *Tratado sobre el título de duque* purports to trace the origins, rights, privileges, insignia, and prerogatives of dukes but serves as a vehicle for the poet's praise of the duke of Medina Sidonia and count of Niebla, Juan de Guzmàn, to whom it is dedicated. In his brief prologue to Alvaro de Luna's *Libro de las virtuosas e claras mugeres*, Mena renders thanks at the behest, he says, of many well-born ladies to Alvaro for his defense of their honor; finally, the fragmentary *Memorias de algunos linages antiguos é nobles de Castilla* are brief sketches of the historical and geographical origins of fourteen lineages, including his own.

Mena's works—particularly the *Laberinto*—were well known to his contemporaries and to posterity. He was cited extensively by Elio Antonio de Nebrija and Juan del Encina, annotated by Hernán Núñez and Francisco Sánchez de las Brozas, and his influence can be found throughout the sixteenth century (in Cristóbal de Castillejo and Fernando de Herrera, for example), and into the seventeenth (Luis de Góngora). The point of departure for modern Mena scholarship is Lida de Malkiel's monumental study (1950).

See also **Luna, Álvaro de**

Further Reading

Deyermond, A. D. "Structure and Style as Instruments of Propaganda in Juan de Mena's *Laberinto de Fortuna*," *Proceedings of the Patristic, Medieval, and Renaissance Conference* 5 (1980), 159–67.

Gericke, P. O. "The Narrative Structure of the *Laberinto de Fortuna*" *Romance Philology* 21 (1968), 512–22.

Lida de Malkiel, M. R. *Juan de Mena, poeta del prerrenacimiento español* 2d ed. Mexico City, 1984.

Mena, J. de. *Obras completas.* Ed. M. A. Pérez Priego. Barcelona, 1989.

——. *Tratado sobre el título de duque.* Ed. L. Vasvari Fainberg. London, 1976.

PHILIP O. GERICKE
COLBERT I. NEPAULSINGH

MÉZIÈRES, PHILIPPE DE (1327–1405)

Born in Mézières in Picardy, Philippe was a soldier of fortune, then an advocate on the diplomatic and political levels of a crusade to regain Jerusalem for Christendom. He founded the chivalric Order of the Passion of Jesus Christ, was chancellor of Cyprus under Peter I, was a citizen of Venice, knew popes Urban V and Gregory XI and was a friend of Petrarch, and served as counselor to Charles V of France from 1373 until 1380, when he withdrew to the convent of the Celestines in Paris. Here, he wrote the major part of his work, in both French and Latin prose, remaining at the convent until his death. His first known work is the Latin *vita* (1366) of his spiritual adviser, Peter Thomas. He wrote on the feast of Mary's Presentation at the Temple, achieving celebration in the West of this originally eastern feast. Three of his treatises depict the order he had founded: *Nova religio milicie Passionis Jhesu Christi pro acquisicione sancte civitatis Jherusalem et Terre Sancte*, extant in two versions written in 1368 and 1384, respectively, but copied together in the only surviving manuscript; the *Sustance de la chevalerie de la Passion de Jhesu Crist en françois* (ca. 1389–94); and the *Chevalerie de la Passion de Jhesu Crist*, written in 1396 shortly before the Battle of Nicopolis. The *Livre sur la vertu du sacrement de mariage* (1384–89) contemplates the mystical union of Christ with the church and the human soul and includes the famous exemplum of "patient Griselda," translated by Philippe from the Latin of his friend Petrarch. The *Songe du vieil pèlerin*, an allegorical pilgrimage finished in 1389, points out the evils of the world and suggests remedies. His 1395 letter to Richard II of England urges the king to wed Isabella of France as a means to European peace. All of Philippe de Mézières' major works urge the social and political stability of Europe necessary for his long-sought but never to be realized crusade.

See also **Charles V the Wise; Petrarca, Francesco; Richard II**

Further Reading

Mézières, Philippe de. *Campaign for the Feast of Mary's Presentation*, ed. William E. Coleman. Toronto: Pontifical Institute of Mediaeval Studies, 1981.

——. *Letter to King Richard II*, ed. and trans. G.W. Coopland. New York: Harper and Row, 1976.

——. *Le songe du vieil pèlerin*, ed. G.W. Coopland. 2 vols. Cambridge: Cambridge University Press, 1969.

——. *La sustance de la chevalerie de la Passion de Jhesu Crist en françois: Philippe de Mézières and the New Order of the Passion*, ed. Abdel Hamid Hamdy. 3 vols. Alexandria: Alexandria University Press, 1964–65. [Transcription of Ashmole 813.]

——. *Vita sancti Petri Thomae*, ed. Joachim Smet. Rome: Institutum Carmelitanum, 1954.

Iorga, Nicolae. *Philippe de Mézières (1327–1405) et la croisade au XIVe siècle*. Paris: Bouillon, 1896.

JOAN B. WILLIAMSON

MICHAEL SCOT
(c. 1175 or 1195–1235 or 1236)

Though famous as an astrologer and magician, Michael Scot (or Scott) is chiefly important as a scientific translator. He was born in Scotland but went to Spain, where he learned enough Arabic to make Latin translations of numerous scientific and philosophical works, sometimes with a collaborator. The earliest of these works was al-Bitruji's defense of the Aristotelian astronomical model (Toledo, 1217), to which Aristotle's *De caelo* was a natural sequel, together with Averroës's major commentary on it. Equally important were Scot's translations of Aristotle's *History of Animals* and several related biological works. In addition to these major translations, which undoubtedly are the work of Scot, many others have been attributed to him (Minio-Paluello 1974). Like other Latin translations of Aristotle from Arabic, Scot's were replaced within a century by better versions from the original Greek, but his were the ones from which thirteenth-century scholastics worked.

By 1220, Scot had moved to Italy, where he remained until his death. His success as a translator gained him the patronage of the papacy, through which he secured several ecclesiastical benefices in England and Scotland (1224–1227); the income from these sinecures, which he never visited, apparently supported him for the rest of his life. From the papal letters of recommendation we learn that Scot was a priest and held a university degree (*magister*). Although some scholars have supposed that he studied and taught at Paris, his association with Bologna is better documented, for he was living there in 1220–1221 and predicted the future of the Lombard League for officials of Bologna in 1231.

Scot's most famous patron was Emperor Frederick II. A later generation (e.g., Salimbene, c. 1221–1290) would remember Scot as "astrologer to the emperor," although it is not clear whether Frederick retained Scot at court or only consulted him occasionally. Certainty Frederick and Scot conversed from time to time, as Scot repeatedly recalled with pride. In 1232, Scot translated Avicenna's treatise on animals for Frederick, who used it in his own work on falconry.

Scot also dedicated his most ambitious work to Frederick. This was an untitled trilogy on astrology to which he devoted his last years. The first book, *Liber introductorius,* is a rambling introduction to astrology that is addressed to amateurs with little background in science. Scot fleshes out the dry bones of professional astrology with examples, digressions, and encyclopedic information that make this work more lively and engaging, though less useful, than its predecessors. The second book, *Liber particularis,* adds more advanced explanations, including some given in response to questions asked by Frederick. The third book, *Liber physionomiae,* deals with living creatures, notably mankind, and shows especially how human character can be deduced from physical signs. An abridged version of the last book was immensely popular (it was printed about forty times), but the rest remains unpublished except for excerpts. Unlike other scholastics, Scot wrote for nonspecialists; he was remarkable not so much for his learning as for his willingness to display and exaggerate it. His contemporaries were duly impressed and regarded him as a magician, but in the next generation, Roger Bacon and Albertus Magnus insisted that he was a charlatan, and Dante put Scot in hell as a diviner (*Inferno,* 20.115–117).

See also **Frederick II**

Further Reading

Haskins, Charles Homer. *Studies in the History of Mediaeval Science,* 2nd ed. Cambridge, Mass.: Harvard University Press, 1927, pp. 272–298.
Kay, Richard. "The Spare Ribs of Dante's Michael Scot." *Dante Studies,* 103, 1985, pp. 1–14.
Minio-Paluello, Lorenzo. "Michael Scot." In *Dictionary of Scientific Biography*, ed. Charles Coulston Gillespie. New York: Scribner, 1974, Vol. 9, 361–365.
Thorndike, Lynn. *Michael Scot.* London: Nelson, 1965.

RICHARD KAY

MOLINA, MARÍA DE
(c. 1270–1321)

Queen of Castile María (c. 1270–1321) was the wife of Sancho IV (r.1284–1295) and the mother of Fernando IV (c.1295–1312). As the daughter of Alfonso de Molina and Mayor Téllez de Meneses, she was a niece of Fernando III and a first cousin of Alfonso X. In June 1282 at Toledo she married Infante Sancho, the son and heir of Alfonso X, even though they were related within the prohibited degrees of kindred. Threatening them with excommunication and interdict, Pope Martin IV ordered them to separate in 1283, but they would not do so. Inasmuch as they lacked a papal dispensation, their enemies regarded the marriage as invalid and their children as illegitimate. María was crowned with Sancho IV at Toledo in April 1284. She seems to have been an active counselor to her husband, but her powerful presence in Castilian politics was particularly felt after his death in 1295.

As guardian of their firstborn, Fernando IV, her responsibility was to protect his person and to repel those who challenged his right to the throne. Her brother-in-law, Infante Juan, denied Fernando IV's claims on the grounds that he was illegitimate. Alfonso de la Cerda, as the son of Fernando de la Cerda, Alfonso X's eldest son, alleged that he had a better right to rule. She also had to contend with Sancho IV's uncle, Infante Enrique, who, after long years in exile in Italy, returned home and now demanded the right to act as regent for the boy king. María skillfully won over the towns of the realm, who formed their *hermandades* (military and religions fraternities) in defense of their liberties and the rights of Fernando IV. Through her impassioned appeal the *cortes* (parliament) of Valladolid in 1295 recognized him as king, giving María custody of his person and naming Enrique as guardian of the realm. In the turmoil of the next few years she succeeded in keeping her son's domestic enemies at bay and eventually made peace with his external enemies, Portugal and Aragón. She then arranged his betrothal to Constanza, daughter of King Dinis of Portugal. When Fernando came of age in 1302 he wished to be free of his mother's control and so there followed a period of estrangement. Though forced to withdraw into the background, she later endeavored to induce the nobles to abandon their hostility toward her son.

After the sudden death of Fernando IV in 1312 and of Queen Constanza in 1313, María de Molina emerged once more as a central figure in Castilian politics, championing the cause of her grandson, Alfonso XI (r. 1312–1350), then an infant. Summoned to determine who should be regent, the cortes of Palencia in 1313 were unfortunately divided, some acknowledging her brother-in-law, Infante Juan, while others accepted María and her son, Infante Pedro. After a year of diplomatic, political, and military maneuvering, María took the lead in persuading the infantes to collaborate. The cortes of Burgos in 1315 acknowledged the unified regency, entrusting María with custody of the king. She successfully maintained the unity of the regency, despite the tensions between Juan and Pedro, but after both men died on the plains of Granada in 1319, her skill was tried to the utmost. Her son Felipe, Juan's son Juan, and Infante Juan Manuel, the distinguished writer, now all demanded a share in the regency. Insisting that nothing could be done without the consent of the cortes, she summoned them to Valladolid in 1321, but she fell gravely ill. After making her will on 29 June, she died the next day and was buried in the Cistercian nunnery in Valladolid. By her marriage to Sancho IV she had several children: Fernando IV, Alfonso, Enrique, Pedro, Felipe, and Beatriz. A truly remarkable woman, she deserves to be ranked among those who most effectively governed medieval Castile. In many respects both Fernando IV and Alfonso XI owed their thrones to her.

See also **Alfonso X, El Sabio, King of Castile and León; Dinis, King of Portugal; Fernando III, King of Castile; Juan Manuel**

Further Reading

Gaibrois de Ballesteros, M. *Doña María de Molina*. Madrid, 1936.
JOSEPH F. O'CALLAGHAN

MÖNCH VON SALZBURG, DER
(fl. 2d half of the 14th c.)

Known variously as Hermann, Johanns, or Hans in the over one hundred manuscripts in which his songs are transmitted, the Monk of Salzburg was the most prolific and popular German singer of the fourteenth century. His six polyphonic pieces are the earliest surviving part-songs in German. His forty-nine secular and fifty-seven religious songs represent nearly every genre current in fourteenth-century German singing, including the hymn, the sequence, the new year's song, the alba, the drinking song, and the *Leich* (lay). Virtually nothing is known about his life except that he moved in the courtly circles of the archbishop of Salzburg, Pilgrim II von Puchheim (r. 1365–1396).

His melodies fall between those of two dominant medieval German genres, *Spruchdichtung* and *Meistergesang*. Some reflect the traditional German e-based modalities (phrygian), though many tend toward the modern major, beginning on E or B-natural and ending on C. The songs are frequently adorned with richly textured preludes, interludes, and postludes. He sometimes favors *melissmas* at the beginning and end of lines and makes frequent use of refrains. "Josef, liber neve min" (Joseph, My Dear Nephew), a German Christmas song still sung today, is attributed to him in one of the manuscripts.

The monk's secular poetry combines themes of the courtly lyric and folk songs, earthy but sometimes simple and affecting, with strong reminiscences of the rhetoric of *Minnesang* and of the Neidhart tradition. His religious songs, some translations of Latin hymns, are closely akin to and probably influenced the songs of the Meistersinger in the fifteenth century. The most gifted German-language lyric singer of the next generation, Oswald von Wolkenstein, was indebted to the monk in both text and melody.

See also **Neidhart; Oswald von Wolkenstein**

Further Reading

Meyer, Friedrich Arnold, and Heinrich Rietsch. *Die Mondsee-Wiener Liederhandschrift und der Mönch von Salzburg*. Berlin: Mayer and Müller, 1896 [texts and melodies of the secular songs].
Spechtler, Franz Viktor, ed. *Die geistlichen Lieder des Mönchs von Salzburg*. Berlin: de Gruyter, New York, 1972 [texts and melodies of his religious songs].
Wachinger, Burghart. *Der Mönch von Salzburg: Zur Überlieferung geistlicher Lieder im späten Mittelalter*. Tübingen: Niemeyer, 1989.
PETER FRENZEL

MORTON, ROBERT (1430?–1497?)

Composer documented as a "chappellain angloix" at the Burgundian court chapel choir from 1457 to June 1475, though until 1471 he occupied the relatively humble position of "clerc" within that institution. He was certainly a priest by 1460; and he was still alive in March 1479, when he resigned the parish of Goutswaard Koorndijk in the diocese of Utrecht. There seems a good case for identifying him with the Robert Morton who had studied at Oxford, later becoming master of the rolls (January 1479) and bishop of Worcester (1486–97), under the patronage of his brother, Cardinal John Morton. His Burgundian career coincides with the years when the family was in political difficulties; his disappearance from the continental records just precedes the real political career of Bishop Robert Morton, and it coincides with a diplomatic visit to Burgundy by the newly reestablished John Morton.

Twelve songs are ascribed to Morton. Four are of contested authorship. But the other eight, all setting French rondeau texts, include two of the most widely copied and quoted songs of their generation: *Le souvenir de vous me tue* (fourteen sources) and *N'aray je jamais mieulx quej'ay* (fifteen sources). His *Il sera pour vous combatu*, built over the famous *L'homme arm–* tune and perhaps one of the earliest known settings of it, pokes fun at a colleague in the Burgundian choir, Simon Le Breton, possibly on the occasion of his retirement in 1464. The anonymous rondeau *La plus grant chiere que jamais* describes a visit to Cambrai by Morton and another famous song composer, Hayne van Ghizeghem.

Morton's music appears in none of the few surviving English song sources, but it is in continental manuscripts copied as far afield as Florence, Naples, the Loire Valley, and Poland. The theorist Tinctoris praised Morton as one of the most famous composers of his day.

Further Reading

Primary Sources

Atlas, Allan, ed. *Robert Morton: The Collected Works*. Masters and Monuments of the Renaissance 2. New York: Broude, 1981.

Secondary Sources

Emden, Alfred B. *A Biographical Register of the University of Oxford to A.D. 1500*. 3 vols. Oxford: Clarendon, 1957
Fallows, David. "Morton, Robert." NGD 12:596–97.

DAVID FALLOWS

MOSER, LUCAS (fl. ca. 1431/1432)

The reputation of the painter Lucas Moser rests on a single work, the altarpiece with scenes from the life of Mary Magdalene in the former chapel of the Virgin (now the parish church) in Tiefenbroon, near Pforzheim in southwestern Germany. An inscription dates the work 1431 or 1432—the last digit is hard to read with clarity—and names "Lucas Moser, painter from Weil," a nearby town, as its author. Apart from this brief mention, nothing is known of the artist's life or career, and attempts to link him with documentary mentions of painters named Lucas in this area and with other works have not been widely accepted. Even the attribution of the Magdalene altar to Moser was disputed in a highly controversial book on the altarpiece published by Gerhard Piccard in 1969. Considering the inscription as a nineteenth-century forgery, Piccard assigned the work to a follower of the Sienese painter Simone Martini and argued that it had been made for the church of the Magdalene at Vézelay in Burgundy. Piccard's book, which received much publicity in advance of its publication, occasioned numerous rebuttals afterward, many of them based on new art historical or technical work. Current consensus holds that the inscription is not modern; that the altarpiece was made for its present position, where its unusual shape reflects that of the wall painting underneath, which it replaced; and that the coats-of-arms, which may have been added very slightly later, represent the patrons of the work, Bernhard von Stein and his wife, Agnes (Engelin) Maiser von Berg.

The central part of the altarpiece is occupied by episodes from the life of Mary Magdalene as told in the *Legenda aurea*. At the left, the saint and her companions, set adrift by pagans in a rudderless boat, approach the coast of Marseille, portrayed here in a recognizable view. In the center, the saint's companions are asleep below, while in the attic room above, the Magdalene appears to the ruler's wife in her sleep to ask her to intervene with her husband on behalf of the Christians. In the final scene, angels deliver the saint, clothed only in her hair after long years in the desert, to a church where the Bishop Maximinus administers her the last rites. In the unusual arched upper panel, the Magdalene washes the feet of Christ, while bust-length figures representing Christ as the Man of Sorrows in the midst of the Wise and Foolish Virgins fill the long, horizontal predella below. On feast days the unusually narrow wings would have been opened to reveal the siblings of the Magdalene, Saints Martha and Lazarus, painted on their insides, flanking a sculpted figure of the Magdalene (now replaced) at the center of the shrine.

Moser's style provides some clues to his early training. His individualized head types, exceptional interest in detail, and use of disguised symbolism indicate knowledge of Flemish painting. Charles Sterling sees Moser as "a close follower of Robert Campin" and notes particularly the use of a continuous background across the four scenes of the center of the altarpiece, a device the Fleming had used as early as about 1420 (1972: 19–22). Sterling also suggests the influence of

Flemish and Franco-Flemish manuscript illumination and the possibility of a trip to Provence. What is clear is that Moser's only known work is a masterpiece in both its style and its virtuoso handling of material and technique.

Further Reading

Haussherr, Rainer. "Der Magdalenenaltar in Tiefenbronn: Bericht über die wissenschaftliche Tagung am 9. und 10. März 1971 im Zentralinstitut für Kunstgeschichte in München." *Kunstchronik* 24 (1971): 177–212.

Köhler, Wilhelm. Review of Gerhard Piccard, *Der Magdalenenaltar des 'Lucas Moser' in Tiefenbronn. Zeitschrift für Kunstgeschichte* 35 (1972): 228–249.

Piccard, Gerhard, *Der Magdalenenaltar des 'Lucas Moser' in Tiefenbronn: Ein Beitrag zur europäischen Kunstgeschichte.* Wiesbaden: Harrossowitz, 1969.

Richter, Ernst-Ludwig. "Zur Rekonstruktion des Tiefenbronner Magdalenen-Altars." *Pantheon* 30 (1972): 33–38.

Sterling, Charles. "Observations on Moser's Tiefenbronn Altarpiece." *Pantheon* (1972): 19–32.

JOAN A. HOLLADAY

MOSES BEN NAḤMAN

Moses ben Naḥman (Naḥmanides), rabbi of the Jewish community of Girona during the middle decades of the thirteenth century, was a leader of Iberian Jewry during his lifetime, and one of the most distinguished intellectual and spiritual figures in all of medieval Jewry. Like so many Iberian Jewish luminaries, Naḥmanides is striking for the remarkable range of his intellectual abilities and achievements. He was a master of Jewish law, mentoring important students and composing important *novellae* to major Talmudic tractates. He was, at the same time, a keen student of the Bible, composing an extensive commentary on the Pentateuch that is rich in exegetical insight and is still widely studied. He was one of the leaders in the rapidly developing school of Spanish Jewish mysticism, rather conservative in his approach to the explosive issues associated with the new mystical speculation but extremely important for the more traditional prestige and acumen that he brought to bear on the development of mystical teachings. His remarkable command of the Hebrew language in all its styles linked him to earlier tendencies in Iberian Jewry. The account that he composed of his public disputation with a former Jew, Pablo Christiani, who had become a Dominican friar, is a masterpiece of narrative art and one of the most effective Jewish polemical treatises of the Middle Ages.

That famous disputation highlights the public career of Naḥmanides. Prior to this engagement the rabbi was already known to King Jaime I of Aragón. In the face of the missionizing assault of the Dominicans, Rabbi Moses ben Naḥman was chosen as the Jewish spokesman for the encounter. Essentially the carefully contrived disputation involved an effort by the Dominican spokesman to prove to the Jews, from materials including both commentary on the Bible and rabbinic dicta, the truth of key Christian doctrines, most importantly the Christian claim that the promised Messiah had already appeared.

The role of the Jewish spokesman was to be limited to rebuttal of the Christian use of rabbinic texts only, with no allowance for Jewish negation of Christian teachings. Whether or not the limited parameters of Jewish rebuttal were in fact rigidly maintained is not altogether certain. In his brilliant narrative account of the disputation, Naḥmanides portrays himself as ranging far and wide in direct attack on central tenets of Christianity and on fundamental characteristics of Christian society. While modern researchers have questioned the reliability of these aspects of Naḥmanides' narrative, it is clear that the rabbi of Girona composed a captivating account of his public encounter and, in the process, provided his Jewish readers with appealing argumentation for the superiority of the Jewish faith.

The publication of Naḥmanides' narrative aroused the ire of ecclesiastical leadership and produced calls for punishment of the aged rabbi of Girona. The king of Aragón, who is portrayed most sympathetically in Naḥmanides' narrative, proved an effective supporter, although by 1267 Naḥmanides had made his way to the Holy Land. It is by no means clear whether this move reflects the pressures brought to bear against him or whether it resulted from his personal religiosity. He exercised leadership briefly within the Jewish community of Jerusalem, and died shortly thereafter.

See also **Jaime (Jaume) I of Aragón-Catalonia**

Further Reading

Baer, Y. *A History of the Jews in Christian Spain.* 2 vols. Trans., by L. Schoffman et al. Philadelphia, 1961–66.

Chazan, R. *Barcelona and Beyond: The Disputation of 1263 and Its Aftermath.* Berkeley, 1992.

Twersky, I. (ed.) *Rabbi Moses ben Naḥman (Ramban): Explorations in His Religious and Literary Virtuosity.* Cambridge, Mass., 1983.

Wolfson, E. R. " 'By Way of Truth': Aspects of Nahmanides' Kabbalistic Hermeneutic." *Association for Jewish Studies Review* 14 (1989), 103–78.

——. "The Secret of the Garment in Naḥmanides." *Daat* 24 (1990), Eng. sec., xxv–xlix.

MULTSCHER, HANS
(ca. 1400–before March 13, 1467)

Working in stone, wood, and metal, Multscher was Ulm's foremost sculptor during the mid–fifteenth century. Originally from the countryside near Leutkirch in the Allgäu, he moved to Ulm by 1427, when he was accepted as a freeman, married Adelheid Kitzin, daughter of a local sculptor, and became a citizen. Since he already owned a house in Ulm, Multscher may have arrived a few years earlier. Where and with whom he trained are unknown. Artistic influences in his work suggest he traveled to the Rhineland, Burgundy, and the Low Countries during his *Wanderjahr* (year as a journeyman).

Multscher's large workshop produced both single figures and complex retables with painted panels. His name is inscribed on the Karg Altar of 1433 in the cathedral of Ulm, whose statues were destroyed during the Protestant iconoclasm of 1531. Multscher signed the painted wings of the large Wurzbach Altar from 1437, portions of which are in Berlin (Germäldegalerie). This altarpiece may have been executed for the Church of the Assumption of the Virgin (St. Maria Himmelfahrt) in Landsberg am Lech, where the large stone Madonna and Child remains. Between 1456 and 1459 Multscher and his workshop prepared the high altar of the parish church at Sterzing (Vipiteno) in South Tyrol; the remnants of this altar, which was dismantled in 1779, are divided among the church and the Museo Multscher in Sterzing, the Ferdinandeum in Innsbruck, the Bayerisches Nationalmuseum in Munich, and a private collection in Basel. These works form the basis for other attributions. Although Multscher is often cited as a painter, there is little evidence that his personal involvement extended beyond his roles as workshop head, master designer, and sculptor of some of the statues.

The artist introduced a greater sense of realism into southern German art. At a time when the lyrical Soft Style with its Beautiful Virgins, gracefully curved poses, and elongated proportions was popular, Multscher developed solid, more naturalistic figures that display the general influence of Netherlandish post-Sluterian sculpture. The Landsberg Madonna and Child from 1437 still includes hints of the Soft Style with its swaying stance, yet her inherent stability, the clear treatment of the deeply cut drapery folds, and the marvelously animated Christ Child who squirms in Mary's grasp reveal Multscher's new aesthetic sensibilities. Using this and related works, scholars have attributed to Multscher several slightly earlier projects. The most significant of these are the images of Charlemagne and other figures made circa 1427–1430 to adorn the eastern window of Ulm's city hall (the originals are now in the Ulmer Museum), the life-size Man of Sorrows from 1429 above the western entry to the cathedral of Ulm, and the alabaster Trinity group from circa 1430 in the Liebieghaus in Frankfurt. The half-nude Christ evocatively displays his wounds

to all who enter the cathedral. Its spirit recalls similar Christ figures by both Claus Sluter and the Master of Flémalle. Related to the Man of Sorrows is the slightly later model for the tomb of Duke Ludwig the Bearded of Bavaria (1435, now in the Bayerisches Nationalmuseum, Munich). Employing fine Solnhofen limestone rather than the coarser sandstone that he typically used, Multscher devised a highly detailed scene of Ludwig kneeling before the Holy Trinity. The tomb, intended for Ingolstadt, was never executed.

In the ensuing decades Multscher and his shop supplied numerous Madonnas, crucifixions, and other religious figures for churches near Ulm. His most notable creations include the tomb effigy of Countess Mechthild von Württemberg-Urach (1450–1455), now in the Stiftskirche in Tübingen; the bronze reliquary bust (ca. 1460) in the Frick Collection in New York; the life-size wooden *Palmesel* (palm donkey, 1456, Ulm Museum), which was made initially for the church of St. Ulrich and Afra in Augsburg, and the now divided Sterzing High Altar. The latter was made in Ulm and then transported to Sterzing, where Multscher and several assistants spent about seven months erecting the altarpiece in 1458 and early 1459.

See also **Sluter, Claus**

Further Reading

Baxandall, Michael. The Limewood Sculptors of Renaissance Germany. New Haven, Conn.: Yale University Press, 1980, pp. 12–13, 245–247.

Beck, Herbert, and Maraike Bückling. Hans Multscher: Das Frankfurter Trinitätsrelief, Ein Zeugnis spekulativer Künstlerindividualität. Frankfurt: Fischer Taschenbuch Verlag, 1988.

Grosshans, Rainald. "'Hans Multscher hat das werk gemacht': die Flugel des 'Wurzacht Altars' und ihre Restaurierung." Museums Journal (Berlin) 10 (1996): 78–80.

Reisner, Sabine, and Peter Steckhan. "Ein Beitrag zur Grabmalvisier Hans Multschers für Herzog Ludwig den Bärtigen." In Das geschnitzte und gemalte bild auf den altaren stehen ist nutzlich und christenlich: Aufsätze zur süddeutschen Skulptur und Malerei des 15. und 16. Jahrhunderts, ed. Rupert Schreiber. Messkirch: A. Gmeiner, 1988, pp. 9–74.

Schädler, Alfred. "Bronzebildwerke von Hans Multscher." In Intuition und Kunstwissenschaft: Festschrift Hanns Swarzenski zum 70. Geburtstag am 30. August 1973, ed. Peter Bloch. Berlin: Gebrüder Mann, 1973, pp. 391–408.

Theil, Edmund. Der Multscher-Altar in Sterzing. Bozen: Athesia, 1992.

Tripps, Manfred. "Hans Multscher: Seine Ulmer Schaffenszeit 1427–1467." Dissertatin, Heidelberg University, 1966–1967. Weissenhorn: A. H. Konrad, 1969.

———. Hans Multscher: Meister der Spätgotik, sein Werk, seine Schule, seine Zeit. Leutkirch: Heimatpflege Leutkirch, 1993.

JEFFREY CHIPPS SMITH

N

NARDO DI CIONE (died c. 1336)

The Florentine painter Nardo di Cione, with his brothers Andrea (called Orcagna) and Jacopo, dominated painting in Florence in the decades following the black death of 1348. Nardo's date of birth is not known. His name appears for the first time in 1346–1348 in a list of members of the guild of doctors and apothecaries, the guild to which the painters belonged. By then his reputation was already established, for c. 1348, when the authorities of Pistoia asked the Florentines for the names of their best painters to execute the high altarpiece for Pistoia's church of San Giovanni Fuorcivitas, Nardo was recommended along with Orcagna. At this time the brothers were living in the parish of San Michele Visdomini and may have shared a workshop. In the 1350s and the first half of the 1360s Nardo lived in the center of Florence, but not always in the same parish as Orcagna, although the two of them may have continued to work together. In 1356 Nardo signed a panel of the Madonna which hung in the offices of the Gabella dei Contratti but which no longer survives. And in 1363 he was paid for painting "the vault and other things" in the oratory of the confraternity of the Bigallo; only fragments of this work remain. These are the only two works to which his name can positively be attached. Nardo made his will in 1365, and by May 1366 he had died. Apart from a bequest to the Bigallo, he left his money and possessions to be divided equally among his three brothers—Andrea, Jacopo, and Matteo. Since no wife or children are mentioned, Nardo was probably a bachelor. These few facts are all we have for a working life that can be documented over some twenty years. Although most of Nardo's painting seems to have been for locations in Florence, he may also have worked elsewhere. At an unknown date the Pistoian painter Bartolommeo Cristiani entered into an agreement whereby whenever he worked outside Florence, Nardo would help him.

In an altarpiece now in Prague the presence of Saint Ranieri, a patron saint of Pisa, suggests that Nardo may have painted it for a church in that town.

Nardo is credited with about a dozen surviving works comprising frescoes, altarpieces, and small-scale devotional panels. In reconstructing an oeuvre for him, Offner (I960) relied on stylistic evidence provided by the frescoes in the Strozzi Chapel in Santa Maria Novella (Florence), which Ghiberti, writing in the mid-fifteenth century, ascribed to Nardo. Here, on three walls, Nardo represented the Last Judgment with a scene of heaven and a hell in which the imagery is derived from Dante's description in the *Inferno.* The frescoes are probably contemporary with the altarpiece in the same chapel that Orcagna painted between 1354 and 1357. The decoration of the Strozzi Chapel exemplifies the Florentine taste in art after mid-century, a taste that departed in some ways from the more naturalistic style pioneered by Giotto. Spatial illusionism is rejected in favor of more abstract two-dimensional effects. The saints of Nardo's *Paradise,* for example, are stacked up tier on tier, like, as one writer said, a football crowd. Medieval conventions of scale, in which a figure's place in the hierarchy of the holy is indicated by his size, are strictly followed. God's divinity and the otherworldly piety of the saints tend to be emphasized at the expense of their humanity. The holy figures appear self-absorbed, preserving their distance from each other and from the spectator. Some of these characteristics may be seen in Nardo's large-scale panel of the Virgin and saints belonging to the New York Historical Society and his altarpiece with three saints in the National Gallery, London.

This reversion to what have been seen as archaizing modes of representation that draw on late thirteenth-century formulas has been explained in terms of the unsophisticated and conservative taste of a new bourgeois class in Florentine society (Antal 1948) and the psychological effects of the black death (Meiss 1951). However, Nardo's art evinces less obviously than Orcagna's the somber, pessimistic mood that Meiss identified in the art of Florence and Siena after 1348. Nardo's style is more lyrical and less austere than that of his brother; his color combinations are more harmonious, and the facial expressions of his saints are less intimidatingly severe. His stylistic origins lie in the decorative taste of Florentine painters such as Bernardo Daddi and the Sienese school as exemplified in the sumptuous work of Simone Martini. Bright enamel colors are juxtaposed with opulent brocades and patterned floors, as in the polyptych in Prague and the two panels with saints in the Alte Pinakothek in Munich. Nardo's Madonnas in Prague, Washington, and Minneapolis have a distinctive beauty that led Offner to describe him as "the most romantic artist of his age." The delicate *sfumato* modeling of pale flesh tones enlivened with rose-pink on the cheeks and lips, and of blond hair draped with diaphanous veils, is achieved by a patient application of successive layers of semitransparent glazes. The consummate care that Nardo lavished on his paintings—in the preparation of the panel, the detailed underdrawing, the meticulous application of paint and the painstaking execution of *sgraffito* and gilded punchwork—make him possibly the finest craftsman among *Trecento* painters. As a result, his works are remarkably well-preserved.

Nardo's reputation has fared less well. History has been unfair to Nardo. He has suffered from standing in the shadow of his more famous brother, Orcagna. Vasari must share some of the responsibility for this: he got the artist's name wrong (calling him Bernardo), relegated Nardo to the role of assistant in Orcagna's workshop, and credited to Nardo inferior works that were actually by others. Even now, despite Offner's study, Nardo has yet to receive the attention that is his due.

See also **Daddi, Bernardo; Martini, Simone; Orcagna, Andrea di Cione**

Further Reading

Antal, Frederick. *Florentine Painting and Its Social Background: The Bourgeois Republic before Cosimo de' Medici's Advent to Power— XIV and Early XV Centuries.* London: K. Paul, 1948.

Meiss, Millard. *Painting in Florence and Siena after the Black Death.* Princeton, N.J.: Princeton University Press, 1951.

Offner, Richard. *A Critical and Historical Corpus of Florentine Painting*, Section 4, Vol. 2, Nardo di Cione. New York: College of Fine Arts, New York University, 1960.

Pitts, Frances Lee. "Nardo di Cione and the Strozzi Chapel Frescoes: Iconographic Problems in Mid-Trecento Florentine Painting." Dissertation, University of California, Berkeley, 1982.

BRENDAN CASSIDY

NEBRIJA, ELIO ANTONIO DE (c. 1441–1522),

Spain's leading pre-Renaissance humanist was born Antonio Martínez de Cala e Hinojosa in the Andalusian town of Lebrija. Opinion is divided concerning the year of his birth. In the prologue to his undated Latin-Spanish dictionary he gives his age as fifty-one and states that he was born in the year prior to the battle of Olmedo (1444). However, other observations in the same prologue concerning the age at which he went to Italy, the length of his stay there and of his subsequent service to Alonso de Fonseca, archbishop of Seville, have led some specialists to place Nebrija's date of birth in 1441.

At the age of nineteen Nebrija left for Italy to study in the Spanish College of San Clemente in the University of Bologna, where he was exposed to the writings of Lorenzo Valla and to his critiques of the medieval system of teaching Latin grammar. Nebrija was appalled at the state of Latin instruction in the University of Salamanca, by the teaching manuals employed (typified by the highly popular verse *Doctrinale* of Alexander de Villadei), which stressed rote memorization of paradigms, and by the lack of attention paid to classical authors. Nebrija returned to Spain determined to introduce the reforms advocated by Valla. In 1476 he took possession of the chair of Latin grammar at Salamanca, where he remained until 1487, when he entered the service of his former student Juan de Zúñiga, master of the Order of Alcántara and future cardinal archbishop of Seville. The years spent with Zúñiga were among Nebrija's most productive. At the beginning of the sixteenth century, Nebrija joined the group headed by Cardinal Cisneros, that was preparing the edition of the *Biblia Poliglota* at the newly created University of Alcalá. Nebrija's insistence on applying strict philological criteria to the text of the Latin Bible brought him into conflict with the group's theologians. After Cisneros lent them his support, Nebrija chose to withdraw from the project and returned to the University of Salamanca where he held various chairs. In 1513 Nebrija failed in his bid to win the chair of prima de gramática. Embittered, he left Salamanca. In 1514 Cisneros granted the ageing Nebrija the chair of rhetoric at Alcalá de Henares, which he occupied until his death on 2 July 1522.

Nebrija can be described as Spain's first linguist, perhaps best known today for his studies of Latin, Greek, Hebrew, and the Castilian vernacular. Despite his pioneering work on Castilian, Latin seems to have been Nebrija's primary concern as a linguist. His first major book was *Introductiones Latinae* (1481), a direct result of Nebrija's concern with the quality of Latin teaching at Salamanca and his belief that *grammatica*, the acquisition of Latin, was the key to all other scholarly disciplines. *Introductiones* was designed as a clear and systematic pedagogical manual for university students, with which Nebrija sought to reintroduce into Spain classical models and the premedieval grammatical theory of Donates and Priscian. This work was an instant success. It was revised and reedited several times during Nebrija's life and frequently reprinted (often under different titles) throughout the sixteenth century in Spain and elsewhere. At the insistence of Queen Isabel, Nebrija published around 1488 (apparently reluctantly) a bilingual Latin and Spanish version of this manual. *Introductiones* became the basic manual for university teaching of Latin in Spain and was one of the books most often exported to the New World during the colonial period. Throughout his career Nebrija published a series of *Repetitiones*, formal university lectures dealing with the pronunciation of Latin, Greek, and Hebrew.

Within the intellectual framework of late-fifteenth-century Spain, Nebrija's Latin-Spanish (1492) and Spanish-Latin dictionaries (c. 1495) as well as his *Gramática de la lengua castellana* (1492) represent major innovations. In all likelihood the two dictionaries were designed to provide access to Latin rather than to constitute repositories of contemporary Spanish. They may well represent the fruits of an announced larger "*obra de vocablos*," which was to include lexicons of civil law, medicine, and the Scriptures (his *Ius Civilis Lexicon* of 1506 and his *Lexicon illarum vocum quae ad medicamentariam artem pertinent* appended to a 1518 edition of a Latin translation of Dioscorides). The Spanish-Latin dictionary was the first systematic and comprehensive work in which Spanish was the source language. Both dictionaries, in many respects quite modern in their lexicographic principles, were revised by Nebrija and underwent several editions. The Latin materials served other early sixteenth-century lexicographers in the preparation of bilingual dictionaries involving Catalan, French, and Sicilian.

According to its prologue, Nebrija published his *Gramática de la lengua castellana* to fix and stabilize the Spanish language in order to prevent its further decay, to facilitate the acquisition of Latin grammar, and to provide a means of learning Spanish for those peoples over whom Spain would one day rule. Within a framework of Latin grammatical theory, Nebrija examines the linguistic facts of Spanish, with emphasis on form rather than on function. The *Gramática* treats orthography and pronunciation, prosody, etymology (that is, morphology), the syntax of the ten parts of speech, and closes with an overview of Spanish for the second-language learner. Motivated by the belief that standardized spelling would contribute to language stability, Nebrija published a second spelling treatise in 1517 under the title *Reglas de orthographía en la lengua castellana*, essentially a resume of book 1 of the *Gramática castellana*. Nebrija's *Gramática* was not reprinted until the eighteenth century and did not seem to have much impact on the work of other sixteenth- and seventeenth-century Spanish grammarians, many of whom may not even have known this work.

In addition to his activities in the realm of language studies, Nebrija composed Latin verse and prepared in that language commentaries on Scripture, rhetorical treatises, works of historiography, geography, and cosmography, as well as editions of and commentaries on the writings of other humanists. Unfortunately, hardly any of these works is available in a modern edition (for titles, see Odriozola).

Further Reading

Braselmann, P. *Humanistische Grammatik und Volkssprache. Zur "Gramática de la lengua castellana" von Antonio de Nebrija.* Düsseldorf, 1991.

García de la Concha, V., ed. *Nebrija y la introduction del Renacimiento en España.* Salamanca, 1983.

Nebrija, A. de A. *Gramática de la lengua castellana.* A. Quilis, 3d ed. Madrid, 1989. Odriozola, Antonio. "La caracola del bibliófilo nebrisense," *Revista de bibliografía nacional* 7 (1946) 3–114.

Rico, F. *Nebrija frente a los bárbaros.* Salamanca, 1978.

STEVEN N. DWORKIN

NEIDHART (fl. ca. 1215–1230)

A Middle High German poet of some renown, there is no documentary evidence of Neidhart's name or of his origins. Under the title "Lord" *(her) nithart,* the so-called large ("C") and the small ("A") *Minnesang*-manuscripts at Heidelberg University Library record the stanzas attributed to him. The singer is apostrophized as der *von Riuwental* (the one from the Riuew Valley) in the *Summer Songs (Sommerlieder)* and the defiantly stated "response-verses" *(Trutzstrophen)* of the *Winter Songs (Winterlieder).* This explains the name Neidhart von Reuental, a term especially used by earlier scholars. Both names can also be interpreted allegorically *(nith-art* is a medieval name for the devil); *riuwental* taken literally reads as "valley of grief"). The only indication for dating Neidhart's poems is through an allusion in "Wolfram von Eschenbach's courtly novel *Willehalm* (l. 312,12; written ca. 1215), as well as references to contemporary political events or personalities in his songs (Archbishop Eberhard II of Salzburg, Duke Friedrich II of Austria). These clues lead to the conclusion that Neidhart may possibly have lived from circa 1190 to 1240. The author's occupation and social rank are just as unknown, although, like Walter von der Vogelweide, he was probably a professional poet. It is almost certain that Neidhart spent part of his early literary career in the area of Bavaria/Salzburg, which he was forced to leave for some unknown reason—possibly due to losing his patron and/or audience, as can perhaps be discerned in changes in his literary style. There are no definite clues that Neidhart might have belonged to the Wittelsbach court of Ludwig I the Kelheimer. On the other hand, Winter Song No. 37 directly addresses Archbishop Eberhard II of Salzburg. Later on Neidhart sang in the vicinity of the Babenberg court of Friedrich II the Valiant (der Streitbare) in Vienna. This may also have been the setting for a literary argument with Walter von der Vogelweide and his concept of *Minnesang* (see Song L 64,31). The writers of subsequent generations (Rubin, Der Marner, Hermann Damen) regarded Neidhart as a good example and "master." The special form of his poetry developed into a separate lyrical genre in the late Middle Ages, while the content partly underwent strong changes. These later poems were passed on under the name *ain nithart* (a Neidhart) in the manuscripts (these songs, regarded largely as imitations following the nineteenth-century scholar Moritz Haupt, have come to be put under the term "pseudo-Neidhart" by researchers). During the last stage of this reception Neidhart became the hero of the *Schwankroman Neidhart Fuchs Schwankerzählungen und Lieder* (*Neidhart Fox's Comical Tales and Songs,* published 1491/1497, 1537, und 1566), and many Neidhart plays, which belong to the oldest existing secular plays written in German. Altogether the numerous manuscripts (from the end of the thirteenth to the fifteenth century) record about 140 songs under the name of Neidhart, of which, however, only 66 are considered to be authentic. In the field of *Minnesang,* well-preserved songs form the major exception, even though they were recorded mostly only at a later period (about 68 tunes in all).

As far as form and content are concerned, Neidhart's songs, often described as "rustic/rural poetry" *(dörperlich),* can be divided into Summer Songs and Winter Songs (according to the varying introductory natural settings) and *Schwanklieder* (comic songs). The Summer Songs, divided into scenes, render simple verse forms that have been worked out in detail *(raien),* while their content forms a clear contrast to traditional *Minnesang.* The plot is shifted from the courtly to the rural realm, the "Knight," or Ritter von Riuwental, is exposed to the unconcealed sexual desires of the farmer's daughters and wives. Whereas the mother, who is the representative of socially accepted moral conventions, warns her daughter of the consequences of having an affair with the impoverished knight—in the so-called *Songs of the Aged (Altenlieder)* the positions of mother and daughter are reverse—the girl struggles to participate in the summer dance and thus also to gain the opportunity of a rendezvous. In the Sommer Songs, thought by some to be later, there are frequently statements on

the unsatisfactory position of the singer and the loss of *vreude* (happiness) in courtly society (demonstrated via the theme of Engelmar's mirror theft). The Winter Songs, structured by stollen, require an intimate acquaintance with form and content of "classical" *Minnesang* to be understood, since the patterns of content and representation in *Minnesang* are constantly referred to in quotations and opposed to the so-called *dörper,* or farmer-stanzas. They portray the threat posed to the singer by rural upstarts, who arrogate aristocratic clothing and lifestyles to themselves, and, even though they adopt only the superficial forms of courtly culture, but not its actual contents, alienate the singer from his *vrouwe* "lady" (who turns out to be a "farmer's daughter" or, in the so-called *werlt-süeze,* or "wordly delight" songs, "Hure Welt"/Whore World). In the *Schwanklieder* the knight Neidhart is promoted to the role of ever-victorious enemy of the physically and intellectually inferior peasants. According to massive tradition as well as extraliterary evidence, the Neidhart-*Lieder* (songs) with their transformations of content enjoyed sustained popularity from the thirteenth to the sixteenth century. Only in recent times has research begun to refrain from continuing the debate about authenticity and to accept instead the genre of the "Neidharts" in the fullness of its tradition and history.

See also **Wolfram von Eschenbach**

Further Reading

Bennewitz, Ingrid. *Original und Rezeption. Funktionsund überlieferungsgeschichtliche Studien zur Neidhart-Sammlung R.* Göppingen: Kümmerle, 1987.

Beyschlag, Siegfried, ed. *Die Lieder Neidharts.* Darmstadt: Wissenschaftliche Buchgesellschaft, 1975.

Fritz, Gerd, ed. *Abbildungen zur Neidhart-Überlieferung I. Die Berliner Neidhart-Hs. R und die Pergament-Fragmente Cb, K, O und M.* Göppingen: Kümmerle, 1973.

Haupt, Moriz, ed. *Neidhart von Reuenthal.* Leipzig, 1864. 2d ed. Edmund Wießner. Leipzig 1923; rpt. ed. Ingrid Bennewitz, Ulrich Müller, and Franz V. Spechtler. Stuttgart: Hirzel, 1986.

Herr Neidhart diesen Reihen sang. Die Texte und Melodien der Neidhartlieder mit 'Ubersetzungen und Kommentaren, ed. Siegfried Beyschlag and Horst Brunner. Göppingen: Kümmerle, 1968.

Holznagel, Franz-Josef. *Wege in die Schriftlichkeit. Untersuchungen und Materialien zur Überlieferung der mittelhochdeutschen Lyrik.* Tübingen: Francke, 1995.

Jöst, Erhard, ed. *Die Historien des Neithart Fuchs. Nach dem Frankfurter Druck von 1566.* Göppingen: Kümmerle, 1980.

Margetts, John, ed. *Neidhartspiele.* Graz: Akademische Druck- und Verlagsanstalt, 1982.

Schweikle, Günther. *Neidhart.* Stuttgart: Metzler, 1990.

Simon, Eckehard. *Neidhart v. Reuental. Geschichte der Forschung und Bibliographie.* The Hague: Mouton, 1968.

Wenzel.Edith, ed. *Abbildungen zur Neidhart-Überlieferung II. Die Berliner Neidhart-Hs. c (mgf779).* Göppingen: Kümmerle, 1975.

INGRID BENNEWITZ

NICHOLAS III, POPE
(c. 1225–1280, r. 1277–1280)

Pope Nicholas III (Giovanni Gaetano Orsini) was the son of Matteo Rosso Orsini, senator in 1244 and 1246. Nicholas had been created cardinal priest of Saint Nicholas in Carcere Tulliano in 1244 and succeeded John XXI as pope in 1277 after a vacancy of seven months, in the face of strongly voiced opposition from Charles of Anjou, then senator of Rome. Charles's term as senator expired in September 1278. Nicholas prevented its renewal and, in the bull *Fundamenta militantis Ecclesie,* specified that any emperor, king, prince, marquis, duke, or baron could become senator only with express permission from the pope, and never for more than one year; Romans could become senator without problems. Nicholas (as an Orsini) was then elected senator himself, but he exercised power through deputies, all Roman nobles.

Rudolf of Hapsburg was negotiating to come to Italy for his coronation when Nicholas became pope. Nicholas agreed to receive Rudolf in return for the cession of the Romagna to the papal state (1278). The province, influenced by the Ghibelline leader Guido da Montefeltro, proved difficult to pacify, despite conciliatory measures including a temporary recall of the exiled Ghibelline faction to Bologna. Nicholas finally requested help from Charles of Anjou but died before order was restored in the Romagna.

Ptolemy of Lucca accused Nicholas of aspiring to establish an Orsini kingdom based on the Romagna. This has been seen as either an attempt to counterbalance the Angevin power, which was encircling the papacy, or an Angevin fiction designed to bring Nicholas into disrepute. Probably it was neither: Charles manifested no intention of attacking the papal state. The coolness between him and Nicholas shown in his opposition to Nicholas's election, in the ending of Charles's tenure of the senate, and subsequently in the termination of Charles's papal vicariate in Tuscany has been exaggerated, notably by Giovanni Villani. Although Charles probably distrusted the Orsini, he continued to receive support from the papacy in the south and sent support to the pope further north. Dante's story that Nicholas was persuaded by Byzantine gold, offered by John of Procida, to transfer Sicily from the Angevins to the Aragonese seems unfounded.

However, Dante justifiably denounced Nicholas for unprecedented nepotism. Nicholas created three Orsini cardinals. One nephew was papal vicar in the Romagna; another nephew was papal legate there; in Tuscany, a brother was senator twice; and so on.

Before his election Nicholas had been cardinal protector of the Franciscans. As pope, he issued the bull *Exiit qui seminat,* which was based on the *Apologia pauperum* of Saint Bonaventura and was intended as a definitive statement on the problem of Franciscan poverty—on which it (unsuccessfully) forbade further discussion.

Nicholas began an artistic revival in Rome that was carried on by his successors. He extended and embellished Innocent Ill's palace on the Vatican, rebuilt the Sancta Sanctorum chapel (the only part of the medieval Lateran palace now surviving), and started improvements at Saint Peter's and Santa Maria in Aracoeli.

See also **Dante Alighieri; Ptolemy of Lucca, Villani, Giovanni**

Further Reading

Editions
Nicholas III. *Les registres,* ed. Jules Gay. Paris: A. Fontemoing, 1898–1938.
Ptolemy of Lucca. *Historia ecclesiastica.* In *Return Italicarum Scriptores,* ed. L. A. Muratori, Vol. 3. Milan: Societatis Palatinae, 1723–1751.

Critical Studies
Davis, Charles T. "Roman Patriotism and Republican Propaganda: Ptolemy of Lucca and Pope Nicholas III." *Speculum,* 50, 1975, pp. 411–433.
Demski, Augustin. *Papst Nikolaus III: Eine monographie.* Münster: H. Schöningh, 1903.
Léonard, Émile G. *Les Angevins de Naples.* Paris: Presses Universitaires de France, 1954. (See especially pp. 124–128.)
Partner, Peter. *The Lands of Saint Peter: The Papal State in the Middle Ages and the Early Renaissance.* London: Eyre Methuen, 1972, pp. 268–277.
Sternfeld, Richard. *Der Kardinal Johann Gaetan Orsini* (*Papst Nikolaus III.) 1244–1277: Ein Beitrag zur Geschichte der römischen Kurie im 13. Jahrhundert.* Berlin: E. Ebering, 1905.

CAROLA M. SMALL

NICHOLAS OF CUSA (1401–1464)

Most important German thinker of the fifteenth century (Latin, Nicolaus Cusanus), ecclesiastical reformer, administrator, and cardinal. His lifelong effort, as canon law expert at church councils, as legate to Constantinople and later to German dioceses and houses of religion, in his own diocese, and even in the papal curia was to reform and unite the universal and Roman Church. This active life finds written expression in several hundred Latin sermons and more theoretical background in his writings on ecclesiology, ecumenism, mathematics, philosophy, and theology. Curious and open-minded, learned and steeped in the Neoplatonic tradition, well aware of both humanist and scholastic learning, yet self-taught in philosophy and theology, Nicholas anticipated many later ideas in mathematics, cosmology, astronomy, and experimental science while constructing his own original version of systematic Neoplatonism. A whole range of earlier medieval writers influenced Nicholas, but his important intellectual roots are in Proclus and Pseudo-Dionysius. In spite of his significance few later thinkers, apart from Giordano Bruno, understood or were influenced by him until the late nineteenth century.

Born in Kues (between Koblenz and Trier), Nicholas studied liberal arts (and perhaps some theology) at Heidelberg (1416–1417) and canon law at Padua, where he earned his *doctor decretorum* (1423) and made initial contacts with Italian humanists and mathematicians. He studied and taught canon law at Cologne (1425), where Heimericus de Campo introduced him to the ideas of Albertus Magnus, Ramon Llull, and Pseudo-Dionysius. He soon ended his formal schooling and became secretary, then chancellor, to the archbishop of Trier. He refused chairs of canon law at Louvain in 1428 and 1435, preferring administrative work in the church. As an expert at the Council of Basel (1432–1438), he wrote on the Hussites, papal authority, and reform of the calendar. His important conciliarist treatise, *De concordia catholica* (*On Catholic Harmony,* 1433), stressed the principles of representation and of consent of the governed and embodied his lifelong commitment to bring harmony and unity out of conflict and diversity.

In 1437 Nicholas changed his support from the conciliarists to the pope to better work for unity. He traveled in the delegation to Constantinople seeking to reunite Greek and Roman churches. Ordained a priest by 1440, he traveled as legate to Germany for the next ten years on behalf of the papal cause, and was named (1448) and made (1450) cardinal. He was appointed bishop of Brixen in Tyrol the same year, but traveled to Germany and the Low Countries to preach the jubilee year and issue edicts of reform. His efforts to reform his own diocese led to enmity with the local archduke; twice Nicholas had to flee to Rome. After 1458 he remained in the papal curia of Pius II at Rome. Nicholas died in 1464 en route to Ancona from Rome.

His important masterpiece of 1440, *On Learned Ignorance (De docta ignorantia),* was the foundation for his writings over the next quarter century. While fully engaged in practical ecclesiastical affairs, Nicholas also wrote some twenty philosophical/theological treatises and dialogues, plus ten works on mathematics, focusing on the problem of squaring the circle and on using mathematics in philosophical theology. The three books of *On Learned Ignorance* expound his central ideas about God, the universe, and Christ. Nicholas was to extend, expand, and modify these speculations in later writings.

"Learned ignorance" is so called because it involves acknowledging the limits of human knowledge when we seek to know what God is (or, indeed, what the exact essence of anything amounts to). Our rational knowledge is a kind of conceptual measuring designed for the finite realm of more and less, but unable to reach the absolute maximum and thus inadequate for measuring the infinite God. There is no humanly conceivable proportion between God and creatures. Yet for Nicholas, we are supposed to move in ignorance beyond reason's inadequacies in hopes of touching God (*incomprehensibiliter comprehendere*) through a kind of intellectual-mystical vision wherein all things are one. Since God's fullness comprises everything, Nicholas invokes the idea of the coincidence of opposites (*coincidentia oppositorum*) as the ontological correlative of learned ignorance. By limiting the principle of contradiction to the realm of finite creatures and their differences, we recognize that in divinity all opposites coincide in the transcendent infinite oneness. The lack of resemblance between God and creatures means that all our knowledge of God must be metaphorical.

Nicholas's later writings propose conjectural metaphors for exploring the limits of our knowledge and at the same time seeking the God beyond. Of particular import are *De coniecturis: On conjectures* (ca. 1442), where Nicholas proposes a hierarchical Neoplatonic ontology as a speculative conjecture (while pointing out that all our conceptual knowledge is provisional or conjectural) and *Idiota de mente: The Layman—About Mind* (1450), which parallels our minds' creation of a conceptual universe and the divine mind's creation of the actual world. In *De visione Dei: The Vision of God* (1453), Nicholas proposes an all-seeing icon to hold together for imagination and thought how our striving to see God is one with God's seeing us.

De possest: On Actualized Possibility (1460) and *De li non aliud: On the Not-other* (1461–1462) work out two descriptions, or "names," of God. The first stresses how in God all possibilities are real or actually exist; thus in God possibility and actuality coincide. The second is concerned to express how God is and is not present to created things—intimately connected ("not other than") yet never identical with (*not* "nothing else but") creatures in space and time. Each of these metaphors and, indeed, all of Nicholas's later writings are calculated to initiate dialectical thinking so that one may move from thinking of God and creatures as exclusive and exhaustive alternatives to seeing them as identified, yet not identical. God is to be seen as both all and nothing of created things; creatures are limited images of the divine infinite oneness that they cannot resemble yet for which they ceaselessly strive.

See also **Albertus Magnus; Llull, Ramón**

Further Reading

The Catholic Concordance, trans. Paul E. Sigmund. Cambridge: Cambridge University Press, 1991.
De ludo globi = The Game of Spheres, trans. Pauline Moffitt Watts. New York: Abaris, 1986.

Duclow, D. F. "Nicholas of Cusa." In *Dictionary of Literary Biography: Medieval Philosophers,* vol. 115, ed. J. Hackett. Detroit: Bruccoli Clark, 1992.

Flasch, K. *Nikolaus von Kues: Geschichte einer Entwicklung.* Frankfurt am Main: Klostermann, 1998.

Haubst, R. *Streifzuege in die cusanische Theologie.* Münster: Aschendorff, 1991.

—— et al., eds. *Mitteilungen und Forschungsbeiträge der Cusanus-Gesellschaft.* Mainz: Mattias-Grünewald, 1961 ff. [Cusanus journal, bibliographies in vols. 1, 3, 6, 10, 15].

Hopkins, Jasper, trans. *Nicholas of Cusa on Learned Ignorance.* Minneapolis: Banning, 1985.

Hopkins, J. *A Concise Introduction to the Philosophy of Nicholas of Cusa,* 3d ed. Minneapolis: Banning, 1986.

Idiota de mente = The Layman, about Mind, trans. Clyde Lee Miller. New York: Abaris, 1979.

Jacobi, K. ed. *Nikolaus von Kues: Einführung in sein philosophisches Denken.* Freiburg: Alber, 1979.

The Layman on Wisdom and the Mind, trans. M.L. Fuhrer. Ottawa: Dovehouse, 1989.

Li non aliud. English & Latin. Nicholas of Cusa on God as notother, trans. Jasper Hopkins. 2d ed. Minneapolis: Banning, 1983.

Nicola de Cusa Opera Omnia, Heidelberg Academy Edition. Lepzig/Hamburg: Miner, 1932 ff.

Nicholas of Cusa's Metaphysic of Contraction, trans. Jasper Hopkins. Minneapolis: Banning, 1983.

Nicholas of Cusa: Selected Spiritual Writings, trans. H. Lawrence Bond. New York: Paulist, 1997.

Opera. 3 vols., ed. Jacques LeFevre d'Etaples. Paris: J. Blade, 1514; rpt. Frankfurt: Minerva, 1962.

CLYDE LEE MILLER

NICHOLAS OF VERDUN
(ca. 1150–ca. 1210)

A goldsmith and enamelist active in the late twelfth and early thirteenth centuries, Nicholas is known for the stylistic originality of his work. Two dated works inscribed with his name exist: the ambo, or pulpit, dated 1181 (and remodeled into an altarpiece in 1330), from the Augustinian Abbey of Klosterneuburg near Vienna, and the shrine of the Virgin in Tournai Cathedral, dated to 1205. The shrine of the Three Kings in Cologne Cathedral, usually dated to the 1190s, is also partially attributed to Nicholas. This large reliquary was built to house the relics of the Three Magi, which Archbishop Rainald von Dassel had received from Emperor Frederick Barbarossa in 1164. After Nicholas's creation of the shrine, the Magi, as examples of both the first Christian pilgrims and the first Christian kings, became closely associated with theories of German kingship and also with the city of Cologne, their crowns appearing on its coat of arms by the end of the thirteenth century.

In technical details and certain stylistic features, Nicholas's work is related to the general tradition of metalwork in the Rhine and Meuse valleys, a region known in the twelfth century for its sophistication. His work is particularly closely related to the Heribert Shrine, considered the major achievement in metalwork

from this area in the second half of the century. As with other Mosan artists, Nicholas was accomplished in creating both champlevé (decorative enamel filling) plaques, such as those found on the Klosterneuburg ambo, and three-dimensional figures, which are found on the Three Kings' Shrine and that of the Virgin. In addition to reflecting Mosan traditions, Nicholas's work, both two- and three-dimensional, shows a new interest in the natural proportioning of the human body, the fall of cloth garments over it, and a type of soft drapery fold called *Muldenfaltenstil* (trough fold style), which is smoothly curved and unlike the angular, inorganic drapery found in Romanesque art. This drapery style, perhaps first appearing in Nicholas's work, becomes extremely popular in the years around 1200 in a variety of other works, including cathedral sculpture, such as that at Bamberg Cathedral, stained glass, and manuscripts. The sources for these components of Nicholas's art are a matter of controversy with contemporary Byzantine art, Ottonian art, early Christian art, and even Roman minor arts cited as possible works Nicholas may have studied to acquire classicizing elements.

In spite of great stylistic innovation, there is evidence that Nicholas had the help of theologians in designing the complex iconographies of his shrines. A plaque of the Mouth of Hell from the Klosterneuburg ambo features a sketch of the Three Marys at the Tomb on the back. This is believed to represent a trial composition whose subject was later modified by the theological advisers to better accommodate the typological meaning of the whole ambo. The complex relationships between the Three Magi and contemporary kings implied by the images of the Three Kings' Shrine are also thought to reflect the ideas of theologians, in this case persons associated with Cologne Cathedral.

Further Reading

Dahm, Frederick. *Studien zur Ikonographie des Klosterneuburger Emailwerkes des Nicholaus von Verdun.* Vienna: VWGO, 1989.

Ornamenta Ecclesiae: Kunst und Künstler der Romanik in Köln, ed. Anton Legner. 3 vols. Cologne: Schnütgen Museum, 1985, vol. 2, pp. 216–224, 447–455.

Swarzenski, Hans. "The Style of Nicholas of Verdun: Saint Armand and Reims," in *Gatherings in Honor of Dorothy R. Miner,* ed. U. E. McCracken et al. Baltimore: Walters Art Gallery, 1974, pp. 111–114.

SUSAN L. WARD

NICOLAUS GERHAERT VON LEYDEN
(d. 1473)

A sculptor whose few surviving documented works are dispersed from Trier and Strasbourg to Vienna, Nicolaus Gerhaert von Leyden remains relatively unknown today even though his style influenced late Gothic sculpture throughout Germany. Of the surviving stone carvings attributed to him or to his school, only five are authenticated by documents or signatures. The earliest to display his new inner dynamism and portrait realism is the signed tomb effigy of Archbishop Jacob von Sierck, dated 1462, now in the Diocesan Museum in Trier. Originally the upper half of a two-tiered tomb with his decaying corpse below, the deeply cut effigy was undoubtedly made by a mature artist. His stay in Strasbourg, where Nicolaus was mentioned frequently in documents from 1463 to 1467 and where he became a citizen in 1464, is the best-documented and most productive period of his life. Here he was commissioned in 1464 to create the portal of the Neue Kanzlei (New Chancellery), on which busts appeared as if looking down from a window; only two heads survive: the so-called Bärbel von Ottenheim in the Liebieghaus Museum in Frankfurt and Count Jacob von Hanau-Lichtenberg in the Musée de l'Oeuvre NotreDame in Strasbourg. The Epitaph of Conrad von Busnang in the Chapel of St. John in the cathedral at Strasbourg, signed and dated 1464, provides the only comparison for Madonna statues attributed to his circle. In 1465–1467 he worked on the carved wood high altar for the Constance Minster that was later destroyed. His best-known work, the signed Crucifix for the Old Cemetery in Baden-Baden, now in the Stiftskirche there, was dated 1467. In the same year, in response to the second invitation of Emperor Frederick III, Nicolaus went to Vienna and Wiener Neustadt, where he was responsible for the tomb lid of the Emperor in the Apostle's Choir of St. Stephen in Vienna. Nicolaus died in 1473 and was buried in Wiener Neustadt. There are fewer documents from these last years, and they provide less certitude in regard to the extent of his work.

In spite of the widespread destruction of Netherlandish sculpture of the fifteenth century and a lack of study of French work of the same time, the stylistic origins of Nicolaus are generally agreed to lie in the Flemish-Burgundian region. The individualism of his portrait heads derives from those of Claus Sluter at Dijon, and his knowledge of the late work of Jan van Eyck is also generally accepted. His busts from the Chancellery at Strasbourg are often compared to the earlier figures above the entrance to the house of Jacques Coeur in Bourges. The new dynamism he infused into his figures together with their physical expressiveness and the drapery expanding into the surrounding space characterize his contribution to the new style. These characteristics also appear in the works of the Masters E.S. and Martin Schongauer, both working in the Rhineland at approximately the same time as Nicolaus; the engravings of these artists are partly responsible for the rapid spread of his style in the late fifteenth century.

The most convincing unsigned and undocumented work attributed to Nicolaus is the bust of a Meditating Man in the Strasbourg museum, assumed to be a self-portrait, also from the New Chancellery. The Crucifixion Altar in Nördlingen and the Virgin of Dangolsheim in Berlin are frequently considered his early work or that of a sculptor close to him.

See also **Frederick III, Schongauer, Martin; Sluter, Claus**

Further Reading

Müller, Theodor. *Sculpture in the Netherlands, Germany, France and Spain 1400 to 1500*. Pelican History of Art 25. Harmondsworth: Penguin, 1966, pp. 79–87.
Recht, Roland. *"Nicolas de Leyde et la sculpture à Strasbourg (1460–1525)."* Ph.D. diss., Université des Sciences Humaines de Strasbourg, 1978. Strasbourg: Presses Universitaires de Strasbourg, 1987, pp. 115–151, 341–345.

MARTA O. RENGER

NILUS OF ROSSANO
(c. 910–1004)

Nilus of Rossano (Neilos) is perhaps the best-known representative of Greek monasticism in medieval Italy before the Great Schism. The chief source for his biography is an anonymous eleventh-century *Life of Saint Nilus the Younger,* an impressive document of Italo-Greek monastic ideals; despite the exemplary import of the incidents chosen for narration, it seems in outline to be factually accurate. According to this account, Nilus was born to an aristocratic family in Rossano, an important eastern Roman (Byzantine) administrative center in eastern Calabria, received a good religious education, and was orphaned at an early age. At the age of thirty, he abandoned the world (he had sired a daughter, perhaps out of wedlock) for an ascetic life in the mountainous border region of the Mercurion and there came under the influence of Fantinus the Younger and other holy fathers. To evade a gubernatorial ban on his becoming a monk, he took the habit at a Greek monastery in the Lombard principality of Salerno. Nilus then returned to Fantinus's lavra (colony of anchorites). Living first there and then in a nearby cave, he learned and later taught calligraphy. During this time he also traveled to Rome to visit the tombs of the apostles and to consult books whose identity, regrettably, is unknown.

Arab raids caused Nilus to retreat in the late 940s to one of his properties near Rossano, where together with some of his students he founded a monastery of his own. He resided here as a penitent for the next quarter-century, achieving more than local repute as a holy man and miracle worker. He is said to have declined being named bishop of Rossano and to have obtained from the emir of Palermo the liberation of three of his monks who had been captured and enslaved. Around 980, fleeing further Arab incursions and his own growing fame, Nilus and his comrades left the eastern empire for good and were welcomed in the Latin west by the Lombard prince of Capua, Pandulf Ironhead. At the behest of Pandulf's successor Landulf IV, Abbot Aligern of Monte Cassino installed them in 981 at the abbey's daughter house at Vallelucio (now Valleluce), where they participated to a limited extent in the life of the neighboring Benedictine community. Here Nilus composed an office for Saint Benedict and probably some of his other poetry.

After Aligern's death, relations between the two groups soured, and in 994 and 995 Nilus founded a new monastery at tiny Serperi (now Sèrapo) in the duchy of Gaeta. From here he made journeys to Rome, where he failed to persuade his fellow Rossanese, John Philagathus, to renounce the papacy he had assumed in 997 after the ouster from the city of the imperially selected incumbent, Gregory V; and where, too, after John had been deposed and later blinded, Nilus attempted in an interview with the emperor Otto III to have the former antipope released to his custody. In 1004, the aged Nilus left Serperi and, staying at a small Greek monastery in the Alban hills not far from Rome, obtained land for a new foundation from Gregory I, count of Tusculum. Nilus died there shortly after his monks had arrived at the nearby site and begun work on what would become the famous Greek abbey of Grottaferrata.

Nilus's surviving verse, all in his native Greek, is not a large body of work. Specimens of his scribal work and that of his students also survive, however. His correspondence does not survive, apart from brief summaries and extracts (mostly in the *Life,* a partly eyewitness account sometimes ascribed to his companion and successor Bartholomew of Grottaferrata). To Nilus himself has been ascribed, on very slender grounds, the commentary of Nilus the Monk on the *Perí stáseon* (*On Issues*) of the ancient Greek rhetorician Hermogenes.

Further Reading

Editions

Gassisi, Sofronio, ed. *Poesie di San Nilo Iuniore e di Paolo monaco, abbati di Grottaferrata, nuova edizione con ritocchi ed aggiunte.* Innografi Italo-Greci, Fasc. 1. Rome: Tipografia Poliglotta della S. C. de Prop. Fide, 1906.

Giovanelli, Germano, ed. *Bíos kaí politeia toû hosíou patròs hemôn Neílou toû Néou.* Grottaferrata: Badia di Grottaferrata, 1972. (Bartholomew, Saint, Abbot of Grottaferrata, ascribed author.)

Translations

Giovanelli, Germano, trans. *Vita di S. Nilo, fondatore e patrono di Grottaferrata.* Grottaferrata: Badia di Grottaferrata, 1966.

Romano, Roberto, trans. "S. Nilo di Rossano, *Kondakion per S. Nilo di Ancira*." *Italoellenika,* 5, 1994–1998, pp. 401–405.

Manuscripts

Caruso, Stefano. "Un tabù etico e filologico: La mutilazione *verecundiae gratia* del Cryptensis B.b II (Bìos di Nilo da Rossano)." *PAN: Studi dell'Istituto di filologia latina "Giusto Monaco,"* 15–16, 1998, pp. 169–193.

D'Oria, Filippo, "Attività scrittoria e cultura greca in ambito longobardo (note e spunti di riflessione)." In *Scrittura e produzione documentaria nel Mezzogiorno longobardo: Atti del convegno internazionale di studio (Badia di Cava, 3–5 ottobre 1990),* ed. Giovanni Vitolo and Francesco Mottola. Cava dei Tirreni: Badia di Cava, 1991, pp. 131–167. (See especially pp. 135–144.)

Gassisi, Sofronio, "I manoscritti autografi di S. Nilo Iuniore, fondatore del monastera di S. M. di Grottaferrata." *Oriens Christianus,* 4, 1904, pp. 308–370.

Critical Studies

Atti del Congresso Internazionale su s. Nilo di Rossano (28 settembre–1 ottobre 1986). Rossano and Grottaferrata: n.p., 1989.

Follieri, Enrica. "Per una nuova edizione della Vita di san Nilo da Rossano." *Bollettino della Badia Greca di Grottaferrata,* n.s., 51, 1997, pp. 71–92.

Luzzatti Laganà, Francesca. "Catechesi e spiritualità nella Vita di S. Nilo di Rossano: Donne, ebrei e `santa follia.' " *Quaderni Storici,* 93, 1996, pp. 709–737. (Year 31, number 3.)

Romano, Roberto. "Il commentario a Ermogne attribuito a S. Nilo di Rossano." *Epeterìs Hetaireías Byzantinôn Spoudôn,* 47, 1987–1989, pp. 253–269.

Rousseau, Olivier. "La visite de Nil de Rossano au Mont-Cassin." In *La chiesa greca in Italia dall'VII al XVI secolo: Atti del convegno storico interecclesiale (Bari, 30 apr.-4 magg. 1969),* Vol. 3. Italia Sacra, 20–22. Padua: Antenore, 1973, pp. 1111–1137.

Sansterre, Jean-Marie. "Les coryphées des apôtres, Rome et la papauté dans les *Vies* des saints Nil et Barthélemy de Grottaferrata." *Byzantion,* 55, 1985, pp. 516–543.

——. "Otton III et les saints ascètes de son temps." *Rivista di Storia della Chiesa in Italia,* 43, 1989, pp. 377–412. (See especially pp. 390–396.)

——. "Saint Nil de Rossano et le monachisme latin." *Bollettino della Badia Greca di Grottaferrata,* n.s., 45, 1991, pp. 339–386.

JOHN B. DILLON

NOTKER LABEO (ca. 950–1022)

Also known as Notker III and Notker Teutonicus (Notker the German), Notker Labeo (the lip) was a St. Gall monk and teacher best known for his Old High German translation-commentaries of Latin classroom texts. In a letter to Bishop Hugo of Sitten (ca. 1019–1020), Notker refers to the vernacular translation project on which he has embarked as something uncommon and revolutionary and notes that it may even shock his reader. He argues, however, that students can understand texts in their mother tongue much more easily than in Latin. Notker's translation method adopts contemporary glossing practices (syntactical, morphological, and lexical) and develops and integrates them into a continuous Latin/German text. First Notker often rearranges the word order of the original Latin into a variant of the so-called natural order, the *ordo naturalis,* a current pedagogic word order that roughly corresponds to a subject-verb-object typology. He then expands on the text with additional classroom commentary—either his own or culled from other sources—by providing synonyms, supplying any implied subjects or objects, expounding rhetorical figures and etymologies, and interpreting mythological figures. Finally Notker appends his Old High German translation, which is sprinkled with further explanation in the vernacular and occasional Latin terms, a kind of mixed prose (*Mischsprosa*).

In his letter to the bishop, Notker also includes a list of works he had finished, thereby providing us with a fairly accurate account of his corpus: Boethius, *De consolatione Philosophiae (On the Consolation of Philosophy)*; Martianus Capella, *De nuptiis Philologiae et Mercurii* (On the Marriage of Philology and Mercury); Boethius's Latin versions of Aristotle's, *De categoriis* (Categories) and *De interpretatione* (On Interpretation), and, his most popular work, the Psalter (together with the *Cantica* and three catechistic texts). He also refers to several of his own classroom compositions, which contain translations of technical terms and/or examples in Old High German; among these are thought to be *De arte rhetorica* (On the Art of Rhetoric), *Computus* (Calculating the Calendar), *De definitione* (On Definition), *De musica* (On Music), *Partibus logicae* (On the Parts of Logic), and *De syllogismis* (On Syllogisms). A few Latin treatises produced in the St. Gall school may also have been compiled by him: *De dialectica* (On Dialectics), *Distributio* (Logic), and *The St. Gall Tractate*. Other translations listed by Notker have not survived: *Principia arithmetica* (Arithmetic Principles, by Boethius?), *De trinitate* (On the Trinity, by Boethius or Remigius of Auxerre?), Gregory the Great's *Moralia in Iob* (Moral Deliberations on the Book of Job), and Cato's *Distichs*, Vergil's *Bucolica,* and Terence's *Andria.* Notker's work did not find great resonance, and only the Psalter and several of the minor treatises are preserved outside of St. Gall.

Notker's late-tenth-century Alemannic marks an important transition period in the history of the German language. The extant eleventh-century St. Gall copies of his texts are recorded with a fairly consistent spelling, which modern scholars have interpreted to reflect guidelines that Notker imposed on the St. Gall scribes. They include the *Anlautgesetz* (devoicing initial voiced stops /b d g/ following a voiceless consonant and/or a pause and in compounds) and the use of the acute and circumflex accents to mark word and/or sentence stress and vowel length. Notker's lexicon has also received considerable scholarly attention, owing to the many new words he coined to render into Old High German the highly complex Latin terminology he was translating.

See also **Gregory I, Pope; Martianus Capella**

Further Reading

Colemnan, Evelyn S. "Bibliographie zu Notker III. von St. Gallen," in *Germanic Studies in Honor of Edward H. Sehrt*. Coral Gables, Fl.: University of Miami Press, 1968, pp. 61–76.

——. "Bibliographie zu Notker III. von St. Gallen: Zweiter Teil," in *Spectrum medii aevi. Göppingen: Kümmerle, 1983, pp. 91–110.*

De nuptiis Philologiae et Mercurii: Konkordanzen, Wortlisten und Abdruck des Textes nach dem Codex Sangallensis 872, ed. Evelyn S. Firchow. Hildesheim: Olms, 1999.

Ehrismann, Gustav. *Geschichte der deutschen Literatur bis zum Ausgang des Mittelalters.* Munich: Beck, 1932, pp. 416–458.

Hellgardt, Ernst. "Notker des Deutschen Brief an Bischof Hugo von Sitten," in *Befund und Deutung.* Tübingen: Niemeyer, 1979, pp. 169–192.

——. "Notker Teutonicus: Überlegungen zum Stand der Forschung." *Beiträge zur Geschichte der deutschen Sprache und Literatur* 108 (1986): 190–205 and 109 (1987): 202–221.

King, James, and Petrus Tax, eds. *Die Werke Notkers des Deutschen, Altdeutsche Textbibliothek.* 10 vols. Tübingen: Niemeyer, 1972–1996.

Notker der Deutsche. *De interpretatione: Boethius' Bearbeitung von Aristoteles' Schrift Peri hermeneias: Konkordanzen, Wortlisten und Abdruck des Textes nach dem Codex Sangallensis 818,* ed. Evelyn S. Firchow. Berlin: de Gruyter, 1995.

Notker der Deutsche von St. Gallen. Categoriae: Boethius' Bearbeitung von Aristoteles' Schrift Kategoriai: Konkordanzen, Wortlisten und Abdruck der Texte nach den Codices Sangallensis 818 and 825, ed. Evelyn S. Firchow. Berlin: de Gruyter, 1996.

Notker-Wortschatz, eds. Edward H. Sehrt und Wolfram K. Legner. Halle (Saale): Niemeyer, 1955. Sehrt, Edward H. *Notker-Glossar.* Tübingen: Niemeyer, 1962.

The St. Gall Tractate: A Rhetorical Guide to Classroom Syntax, eds. and trans. Anna Grotans and David Porter. Columbia, S.C.: Camden House, 1995.

Schröbler, Ingeborg. *Notker III. von St. Gallen als Übersetzer und Kommentator von Boethius' De consolatione Philosophiae.* Tübingen: Niemeyer, 1953.

Sonderegger, Stefan. *Althochdeutsch in St. Gallen.* St. Gallen: Ostschweiz, 1970.

——. *Althochdeutsche Sprache und Literatur,* 2d ed. Berlin: de Gruyter, 1987.

——. "Notker III. von St. Gallen," in *Die deutsche Literatur des Mittelalters: Verfasserlexikon,* vol. 6., 2d ed. Berlin: de Gruyter, 1987, cols. 1212–1236.

Tax, Petrus W. "Notker Teutonicus," in *Dictionary of the Middle Ages,* vol. 9. New York: Scribner's, 1987, pp. 188–190.

ANNA A. GROTANS

O

OCKEGHEM, JOHANNES
(ca. 1420–1497)

Franco-Flemish composer, active mainly in France. According to recently discovered documents, he was born in Saint-Ghislain, a village near Mons in the Belgian province of Hainaut. His career is first traced in Antwerp, where he was a singer at the church of Notre-Dame in 1443/44. From 1446 to 1448, he was singer in the chapel of Charles I, duke of Bourbon, at Moulins. He became a member of the French royal chapel under Charles VII ca. 1450 and continued to serve that institution under Louis XI and Charles VIII. Named as first chaplain in 1454, he was subsequently cited as master of the chapel (1464) and counselor to the king (1477). In 1459, Charles VII, who was hereditary abbot of Saint-Martin of Tours, appointed Ockeghem to the important post of treasurer of Saint-Martin. Sometime before 1472, possibly in 1464, he was ordained a priest at Cambrai. The only journey he is known to have undertaken outside France and the Low Countries is one to Spain in 1470. In 1484, he revisited his native country when he and other members of the royal chapel traveled to Damme and Bruges in Flanders. He eventually retired to Tours, where he died on February 6, 1497.

Among his pupils may have been Antoine Busnoys, a cleric at Saint-Martin of Tours in 1465 and subsequently singer in the chapel of Charles the Bold, duke of Burgundy. Busnoys honored Ockeghem in his motet *In hydraulis*, calling him the "true image of Orpheus." At Cambrai, Ockeghem met Guillaume Dufay, his greatest musical contemporary, who in 1464 entertained him at his house. The Flemish music theorist Johannes Tinctoris dedicated his treatise on the modes (1476) jointly to Ockeghem and Busnoys, and in his treatises on proportions and counterpoint he cited Ockeghem as "the most excellent of all the composers I have ever heard." In his last treatise, *De inventione et usu musicae* (ca. 1481), Tinctoris describes him not only as a distinguished composer but as the finest bass singer known to him.

Ockeghem's personal appearance and manner, as well as his musicianship, were often praised by his contemporaries. Guillaume Crétin wrote a *Déploration surle trespas de feu Okergan*, praising his "subtlety" and calling on his mourning colleagues, led by Dufay and Busnoys, to sing his music, including his "exquisite and most perfect Requiem Mass." The poet Jean Molinet also wrote a *déploration* on his death, which was set to music by Josquin des Prez, the great master of the next generation of French composers. An *epitaphium* for Ockeghem by Erasmus of Rotterdam was set by Johannes Lupi in the 16th century.

Ockeghem composed in all genres, but his most important works are his fourteen Masses. A single Credo and only five motets by him are known, but they are each highly individual works. Twenty-two secular songs, all but one in French, come down to us. The exception is a Spanish song, probably a memento of his visit to Spain.

In his time and throughout subsequent centuries, Ockeghem was renowned for his contrapuntal skill, especially in canonic writing. His masterpiece in this technique is his *Missa prolationum*, consisting almost entirely of double canons at all intervals within the octave, and in four different "prolations" (meters) simultaneously. Almost legendary in his time was a thirty-six-voice canon mentioned by Crétin and others, the identity of which remains controversial. His Requiem Mass, which may have been written on the death of Charles VII (1461), is the earliest surviving example of its kind.

The most distinctive features of Ockeghem's music are its varied, unpredictable rhythms and long-breathed, overlapping phrases. Its texture of equally important though highly independent melodic lines and its exploration of the bass register are progressive features, but in many respects its unpredictable, "mystical" character, which virtually defies analysis, evokes a Late Gothic spirit rather than displaying the clarity of the emerging Renaissance style of his contemporaries.

See also **Busnoys, Antoine; Charles VII; Dufay, Guillaume; Louis XI**

Further Reading

Ockeghem, Johannes. *Collected Works*, ed. Dragan Plamenac and Richard Wexler. 3 vols. N.p.: American Musicological Society, 1947–92.

Goldberg, Clemens, *Die Chansons Johannes Ockeghems.* Laaber: Laaber, 1992.

Lindmayr, Andrea. *Quellenstudien zu den Motetten von Johannes Ockeghem*, Laaber: Laaber, 1992.

Perkins, Leeman L. "The *L'homme armé* Masses of Busnoys and Ockeghem: A Comparison. "*Journal of Musicology* 3 (1984): 363–96.

Picker, Martin. *Johannes Ockeghem and Jacob Obrecht: A Guide to Research.* New York: Garland, 1988.

Sparks, Edgar H. *Cantus Firmus in the Mass and Motet, 1420–1520.* Berkeley: University of California Press, 1963.

Thein, Wolfgang. *Musikalischer Satz und Textdarbetung im Werk von Johannes Ockeghem.* Tutzing: Schneider, 1992.

MARTIN PICKER

OCKHAM, WILLIAM OF
(William Occam; ca. 1285–1347)

Born in Ockham in Surrey, England, William entered a Franciscan convent at an early age. In 1306, he was ordained subdeacon at Southwark in London and began his education at Oxford, where he lectured on Peter Lombard's *Sententiae* from 1317 to 1319. John Luttrell, the chancellor at Oxford, opposed Ockham's views. Pope John XXII called him to Avignon in 1323/24. A committee investigated Ockham's works and censured fifty-one propositions but did not formally condemn him. In 1327, he met Michael of Cesena, the minister-general of the Franciscan order and leader of the Spiritual Franciscans. Cesena requested Ockham to examine John XXII's constitutions on Franciscan poverty. Ockham declared them full of error and the following year fled Avignon with Cesena and others. He was excommunicated in 1328. He joined the emperor Louis of Bavaria in his dispute with the pope and in 1330 settled at the Franciscan convent in Munich. In 1331, Ockham was expelled from the order and sentenced to imprisonment. He died in Munich in 1347, still under Louis's protective care.

Ockham's writings fall into three stages corresponding to his major residences: Oxford (1306/07–23), Avignon (1323–28), and Germany (1330–47). At Oxford and Avignon, his writings include his commentary on the *Sententiae*, later published in two parts: the *Ordi-*

natio, his lectures on the first book, and the *Reportatio*, comprising notes taken at his lectures. He also composed commentaries on Aristotle's *Organon*; *Summa logicae*, his major statement on logic; seven quodlibetals; and treatises on the Body of Christ, on the eucharist, and on predestination. After his departure from Avignon in 1328, he wrote works against the Avignon papacy, the chief ones being *Opus nonaginta dierum*, about papal errors regarding poverty; *Dialogus inter magistrum et discipulum* (1333–47); eight *quaestiones* on papal authority (1340); and a treatise on the respective powers of emperor and pope (ca. 1347).

Ockham was principally a theologian, vigorously exploring the philosophical limits of each epistemological, logical, or metaphysical issue, often to see more clearly the theological application. He rejected the older Platonic Realism and the *via antiqua* of the Aristotelians to pursue a *via moderna*, a path of demonstration and the near-autonomy of faith. He insisted upon a method of economy of explanation, later termed "Ockham's razor." With the nominalists, he contested the reality of universals and affirmed the fundamental reality of particulars for the human mind. His own solution to the relationship between universals and particulars is often called "conceptualist" instead of "nominalist," because he viewed concepts not merely as creatures of the mind but rather as entities identical with the abstractive cognition by which the mind considers individual objects in a certain way. With Duns Scotus, he asserted the utter transcendence and unique necessity and freedom of God in contrast with the contingency of all else, including so-called natural and moral laws. He argued the distinction between God's absolute power and that of his ordained power, manifest in his decrees, by which God limits himself to operate within ordinations he established. Ockham also contributed to medieval and early-modern political theory and ecclesiology. He influenced conciliarism, and his theological legacy reached to Pierre d'Ailly, Gabriel Biel, and Martin Luther. He attacked the wealth of the church, challenged the notions of papal infallibility and plenitude of power, upheld the right of imperial election apart from papal interference, and conceded to the emperor the responsibility to depose a heretical pope. He maintained that the papacy was not established by Christ, that the general council was superior to the papacy, but that the pope possessed an ordinary executive authority unless he were heretical.

See also **D'ailly, Pierre; Duns Scotus, John**

Further Reading

Ockham, William of. *Opera philosophica*, ed. Philotheus Boehner et al. 3 vols. St. Bonaventure: Editiones Instituti Franciscani Universitatis S. Bonaventurae, 1974–85.

——. *Opera theologica*, ed. Gedeon Gá et al. 10 vols. St. Bonaventure: Editiones Instituti Franciscani Universitatis S. Bonaventurae, 1967–86.

——. *Opera politica*, ed. Jeffrey G. Sikes et al 3 vols. Manchester: University of Manchester Press, 1940–.

——. *William of Ockham. Philosophical Writings: A Selection*, ed. and trans. Philotheus Boehner. rev. ed. Stephen F. Brown. Indianapolis: Hackett, 1990.

Adams, Marilyn McCord. *William Ockham. 2 vols.* Notre Dame: University of Notre Dame Press, 1987.

Baudry, León. *Guillaume d'Occam: sa vie, ses œuvres, ses idées sociales et politiques.* Paris: Vrin, 1949, Vol. 1: *L'homme et les œuvres.*

Boehner, Philotheus. *Collected Articles on Ockham*, ed. Eligii M. Buytaert. St. Bonaventure: Franciscan Institute, 1958.

McGrade, Arthur Stephen. *The Political Thought of William of Ockham: Personal and Institutional Principles.* London: Cambridge University Press, 1974.

Moody, Ernest A. *The Logic of William Ockham.* London: Sheed and Ward, 1935.

H. LAWRENCE BOND

OFFA (r. 757–96)

King of Mercia in 757, after ousting another claimant. By the time of his death on 28 July 796 Offa also held sway over Sussex, Kent, and East Anglia. His daughters married rulers of Wessex and Northumbria, thus extending his sphere of influence. He clashed with the Welsh, which probably led him to construct the dike that bears his name. Running along much of the nearly 150 miles of the Welsh frontier, from the Severn estuary to a few miles south of the Dee estuary, Offa's Dyke is the longest earthwork in Britain. It could have been planned in one season and completed in the next; if this was indeed so, it is testimony to the organizational and coercive power that made him the leading English ruler of his day.

Offa utilized the church to enhance his power. He persuaded Pope Hadrian to sanction the creation of a new archdiocese at Lichfield in 787, only a few miles from his palace at Tamworth, thus effectively neutralizing the hostile archbishop of Canterbury. Probably imitating Charlemagne, he had his son, Ecgfrith, consecrated as his successor in 787, the first royal anointing in English history.

Offa seems to have had extensive trade contacts with the Carolingian realm, which in turn appears to have made monetary reform possible. His silver penny, influenced by a Carolingian model, was the basis of the English coinage until the reign of Henry III. He appreciated the coin's potential for symbolism; many bear his name and a finely wrought effigy, and some even carry the likeness of his wife, Cynethryth, a practice drawn either from Byzantine Italy or even late-imperial Rome.

The poems *Beowulf* and *Widsith*, a tribute list known as "The Tribal Hidage"—even the origin of a system of burghal defense later associated with Alfred the Great of Wessex—have been associated with Offa. Much more research will be needed, however, before a balanced assessment of the cultural and social contributions of his reign can be made.

Though his achievements did not long survive him, he was regarded as a great figure in the Middle Ages. Alfred claimed to have adopted and modified his laws; a sword reputed to be his was still treasured two centuries after his death; a 14th-century *Life* was composed by the monks of St. Albans, who revered him as their founder. An imitator rather than an innovator; his image of greatness derived from his longevity, ruthlessness, and astute ability to exploit the imagery of rulership. Apart from the dike little evidence of his power survives; the Mercian archives are lost, as is his burial place. His palace at Tamworm probably lies under the parish churchyard and so cannot be excavated.

Further Reading

Blunt, Christopher E. "The Coinage of Offa." In *Anglo-Saxon Coins: Studies Presented to F.M. Stenton on the Occasion of His 80th Birthday*, ed. R.H.M. Dolley. London: Methuen, 1961, pp. 39–62.

Brooks, Nicholas. "The Development of Military Obligations in Eighth- and Ninth-Century England." In *England before the Conquest: Studies in Primary Sources Presented to Dorothy Whitelock*, ed. Peter Clemoes and Kathleen Hughes. Cambridge: Cambridge University Press, 1971, pp. 69–84.

Hart, Cyril. "The Kingdom of Mercia." In *Mercian Studies*, ed. Ann Dornier. Leicester: Leicester University Press, 1977, pp. 43–61.

Keynes, Simon. "Changing Faces: Offa, King of Mercia." *History Today* 40/11 (November 1990): 14–19.

Levison, Wilhelm. *England and the Continent in the Eighth Century.* Oxford: Clarendon, 1946.

Noble, Frank. *Offa's Dyke Reviewed.* Ed. Margaret Gelling. BAR Brit. Ser. 114. Oxford: BAR, 1983.

Stenton, F.M. "The Supremacy of the Mercian Kings." In *Preparatory to Anglo-Saxon England*, ed. Doris M. Stenton. Oxford: Clarendon, 1970, pp. 48–66.

Wormald, Patrick. "The Age of Offa and Alcuin." In *The Anglo-Saxons*, ed, James Campbell. Oxford: Phaidon, 1982, pp. 101–31.

Wormald, Patrick. "In Search of King Offa's "Law-Code." In *People and Places in Northern Europe 500—1600: Essays in Honour of Peter Hayes Sawyer*, ed. Ian Wood and Niels Lund. Woodbridge: Boydell, 1991, pp. 25–45.

DAVID A.E. PELTERET

ÓLÁFR TRYGGVASON (r. 995-999/1000)

Óláfr Tryggvason was king of Norway 995–999/1000. He was the son of Tryggvi Óláfsson, grandson of Haraldr hárfagri ("fair-hair") Hálfdanarson, a petty king of Viken or the Upplands.

Before Óláfr Tryggvason became king, he led great Viking raids to England, Scotland, and Ireland. The *Anglo-Saxon Chronicle* for the years 991 and 994 states that Óláfr led a large Viking fleet to attack the eastern and southern coast of England. In both cases, the English king paid large amounts of silver, "Danegeld," to buy off the Vikings.

Just before Óláfr Tryggvason went to Norway, controversy arose in Trøndelag between Earl Hákon, who was the actual ruler of the country, and the Tronds. According to *Heimskringla,* the earl constantly abused their wives and daughters, "and the farmers began to grumble just as the Tronds are wont to do over anything which goes against them" (*Heimskringla* 1:343). One of the rich peasants who had refused to give up his wife to the earl gathered the farmers and set out against Hákon. The earl fled and was killed by his own slave, Karkr, while escaping. Óláfr Tryggvason, who was on his way to Niðaróss (Trondheim), inadvertently encountered one of the earl's sons and killed him in battle; the two other sons fled. Óláfr was chosen king by the people of Trøndelag at the Eyraþing. After that, he traveled throughout the country and was made king of all Norway. In 996, Óláfr was in Vikin (Viken), and from there he carried out his plans to introduce Christianity in Norway and to secure complete control over the country.

With the help of his paternal relatives, he succeeded in making the farmers of Viken accept the new faith in 996/7. Those who refused or disagreed with him, "he dealt with hard; some he slew, some he maimed, and some he drove away from the land" (*Heimskringla* 1:362). Gradually, his actions led to a conflict between the king and the farmers. In the summer of 997, he went to the southwestern part of the country, made the Rogalenders embrace the new faith, and secured their support by marrying his sister to one of the chieftains there, Erlingr Skjálgsson, at Sóli (Sole). In the west, he introduced Christianity through the support of his maternal relatives while securing control over this province. The introduction of Christianity in these provinces, the west, and Viken, was facilitated by long-lasting contact with Christian western Europe, especially the British Isles.

In the fall of 997, Óláfr Tryggvason, went to Trøndelag. There and in the north, paganism was stronger than in the other provinces. Óláfr Tryggvason met with strong opposition from the farmers and was forced to acquiesce. He returned one year later, killed the leader of the farmers, Járn-Skeggi, and made the Tronds embrace the new faith. Some of the rich farmers refused to accept the new order. They fled and went to Sweden, joining Eiríkr, son of Earl Hákon. Óláfr Tryggvason tried to secure control over Trøndelag and the good-will of the Tronds by marrying Guðrún, Járn-Skeggi's daughter. He did not succeed; Guðrún attempted to murder him on their wedding night. In 999, he made the people of Háleygjaland (Hålogaland) accept Christianity. Thus, he had christianized the entire coastal area of Norway. Óláfr Haraldsson later christianized the interior.

But it was not only in Norway that Óláfr Tryggvason tried to spread Christianity. His pressure on the Icelandic chieftains was undoubtedly one of the main reasons why the Icelanders accepted the new faith at the *Alþingi* in 999/1000. He also made the Greenlanders accept Christianity.

Óláfr Tryggvason's strengthening of the power of the king involved not only an expansion of the king's territorial control over the country, but also an attempt to develop the internal organization of the kingdom. It was most likely Óláf Tryggvason who introduced the office of district governor, a service rendered by a chieftain who received royal land in return. He was also the first Norwegian king to mint coins.

Óláfr Tryggvason died in the battle of Svǫlðr (Svold) in 999/1000, where he fought the Danish king Sven Haraldsson (Forkbeard), who had been forced to give up Viken, the Swedish king who wanted control of Gautaland, and Eirikr, son of Earl Hákon.

Further Reading

Literature

Finnur Jónsson, ed. *Heimskringla.* 4 vols. Samfund til udgivelse af gammel nordisk litterarur, 23. Copenhagen: Møller, 1893–1901.

Koht, Halvdan. "The Scandinavian Kingdoms Until the End of the Thirteenth Century." In The *Cambridge Medieval History* 6. Ed. J. R. Turner *et al.* Cambridge: Cambridge University Press, 1929, pp. 362–92.

Baetke, Walter. *Christliches Lehngut in der Saga-religion. Das Svolder-Problem. Zwei Beiträge zur Saga-kritikk.* Berichte über die Verhandlungen der sächsischen Akademie der Wissenschaften zu Leipzig. Philol.-hist. Klasse, 98.6. Berlin: Akademie-Verlag, 1951.

Ellehøj, Svend. "The Location of the Fall of Olaf Tryggvason." *Arbók hins íslenzka fornleifafélags,* Fylgirit (1958), 63–73

Gunnes, Erik. *Rikssamlingogkristning 800–1177.* Norges historie, 2. Oslo: Cappelen, 1976.

Andersen, Per Sveaas. *Samlingen av Norge og kristningen av landet, 800–1130.* Handbok i Norges historie 2. Bergen: Universitetsforlaget, 1977.

Helle, Knut. "Norway in the High Middle Ages: Recent Views on the Structure of Society." *Scandinavian Journal of History* 6 (*1981*), 161–89.

Birkeli, Fridtjov. *Hva vet vi om kristningen av Norge?* Oslo: Universitetsforlaget, 1982.

Bagge, Sverre. *Society and Politics in Snorri Sturluson's* Heimskringla. Berkeley and Los Angeles: University of California Press, 1991.

JÓN VIÐAR SIGURÐSSON

OLIVER OF PADERBORN (d. 1224)

Oliver of Paderborn (North Rhine-Westphalia) appears as the scholastic at Paderborn in the waning years of the twelfth century. His reputation was such, however, that by 1202 he had been appointed scholastic at Cologne Cathedral. In 1207 we find him in Paris, where he acted as the mediator between a canon from Reims and the monastery of St. Remy. Presumably, he had been attending the schools of Paris at the time. The following year, he appears in southern France, apparently as a preacher against the Albigensians. At this time, he established his lifelong friendship with Jacques de Vitry and Robert de Courçon, both of whom became well-known preachers of the Fifth Crusade in France.

In the papal encyclical *Quia maior nunc* of May 1213, Oliver was named as one of several crusade-preachers for Germany, with specific duties in the ecclesiastical province of Cologne. Assisting him was *magister* (master) Hermann, dean of St. Cassius's Church in Bonn. Over the next four years, he and his colleagues crisscrossed Germany, convening assemblies of people and exploiting every opportunity to present their message and enlist support for the crusade. They were armed with letters of indulgence with which to entice and reward participants. Following the Fourth Lateran Council in Rome (at which Oliver was also present), he and the other preachers were also charged with collecting the half-tithe that Innocent III had imposed on the clergy as a means of providing financial support for the crusade.

In the summer of 1217 the first company of warriors departed by ship from the Lower Rhine. Among them was Oliver himself, who played a viral role in the campaign against Damietta in the Nile delta. His *Historia* of this event and his other writings and letters make him the best known of the German preachers. Only after the fall of Damietta to the Muslims on September 8, 1221, did Oliver return to Cologne, where he appears again in the spring of 1222.

In 1223 Oliver was elected bishop of Paderborn. He never really occupied the office, however, having first resumed his role as crusade-preacher in 1224, and shortly thereafter being elevated to the cardinal-bishopric of St. Sabina. One sees the influence of his fellow German, Conrad of Urach, and perhaps also of Cardinal Robert de Courçon, in this appointment. Like Conrad, however, Oliver lived but a short time after donning the cardinal's hat; he died the same year.

See also **Conrad of Urach**

Further Reading

Hoogeweg, Hermann. "Der Kölner Domscholaster Oliver als Kreuzprediger." *Westdeutsche Zeitschrift für Geschichte und Kunst* 7 (1888): 237ff.
——. *Die Schriften des Kölner Domscholasters, späteren Bischofs von Paderborn und Kardinalbischof von S. Sabina Oliverus.* Stuttgart: Litterarischer Verein, 1894.
——. "Die Kreuzpredigt des Jahres 1224 in Deutschland mit besonderer Rücksicht auf die Erzdiözese Köln." *Deutsche Zeitschrift für Geschichtswissenschaft* 4 (1890): 54ff.
Pixton, Paul B. "Die Anwerbung des Heeres Christi: Prediger des Fünften Kreuzzuges in Deutschland." *Deutsches Archiv* 34 (1978): 166–191.

PAUL B. PIXTON

ORCAGNA, ANDREA DI CIONE (d. 1368)

Andrea di Cione, known as Orcagna, belonged to an extended family of Florentine artists, among whom he and his brother Nardo are best-known to modern scholars. Both artists were also well-known in their own time. Indeed, in a list identifying the six most prominent painters of Florence, compiled in 1349 (near the midpoint of Andrea's career), Andrea and Nardo occupy the third and fourth positions, respectively.

Over the course of his career Orcagna worked as a painter, sculptor, and architect, but he was trained as a painter and identifies himself as such even on the great sculptured tabernacle in Or San Michele (Orsanmichele). Thanks to the efforts of Kreytenberg and others, who have pieced together the extant documents and the known works, we now have a relatively comprehensive picture of Orcagna's career. We know that he matriculated in the Florentine painters' guild (part of the larger Arte dei Medici e Speziali) sometime between 1343 and 1346. We also know that he joined the guild of builders and masons in 1352. Between 1343 and 1360 Orcagna executed paintings and sculptures for many important civic and ecclesiastical sites in Florence, including the city's prison, the city grain market of Or San Michele, and the great mendicant churches of Santa Croce and Santa Maria Novella. At Santa Maria Novella, he was involved in the decoration of the Cappella Maggiore, one of the most important commissions of the day. Beginning in 1357 Orcagna participated in the ongoing planning of the cathedral of Florence; and in 1358 he was appointed *capomaestro* of the masons' workshop for the cathedral in Orvieto.

Orcagna's presumed early works include the great fresco of the *Triumph of Death, the Last Judgment, and Hell* for the nave of the church of Santa Croce, which was attributed to him following Ghiberti's testimony and is now generally held to have been painted in 1344–1345. Another early work is a frescoed roundel depicting the *Expulsion of the Duke of Athens* (now in the Palazzo Vecchio), painted for the entry hall of Florence's prison, the *carcere delle Stinche*. This fresco, which has been attributed to Orcagna on stylistic grounds, was possibly commissioned as early as 1343–1344, immediately after the expulsion from Florence of the infamous duke of Athens, Walter of Brienne. It is a permanent version of the type of ephemeral defamatory images (*pitture infamate*) commonly commissioned by Italian cities to be painted on the facades of public buildings. In Orcagna's painting, realistic details, including a remarkably accurate portrait of the Palazzo Vecchio as it appeared during the rule of the duke of Athens, are unified in an abstract narrative structure to produce an effect of reality within a timeless image of the triumph of virtue over tyranny.

Until relatively recently, scholars of art history generally associated Orcagna with a retrogressive style of painting that supposedly took hold in Florence after the black death. In fact, Meiss (1951) considered Orcagna's great altarpiece *Christ with Saints Thomas and Peter*, made for the Strozzi Chapel in Santa Maria Novella, an example of this style. Although Meiss's study remains a powerfully persuasive piece of *eckphrasis*, his assessment of Orcagna's style as the repository of a general cultural psychology has been challenged by scholars who have looked less to the history of style and more to the circumstances of individual commissions to explain the formal characteristics of Orcagna's work. In this process, paintings like the Strozzi altarpiece have emerged as highly sophisticated visual structures. In his work for the Strozzi Chapel, Orcagna manipulated space and form to evoke a sacred vision, which appears in the midst of a panoramic view of the *Last Judgment* painted by his brother Nardo on the surrounding walls.

One of Orcagna's most important commissions was the richly decorated marble tabernacle for Or San Michele, designed and executed between 1352 and 1360. The site—on the main street leading from the Duomo to the Palazzo Vecchio—was not only the city's grain market but also a nexus of power. Or San Michele served as the center of devotion for the city's guilds, and Orcagna's tabernacle was commissioned by the Compagnia della Madonna di Orsanmichele to enshrine a miracle-working image of the Madonna that had made the site the center of a popular cult. Actually, the object enshrined in Andrea's tabernacle was a newly painted image commissioned in 1346 by the *compagnia* from Bernardo Daddi. The tabernacle itself is a freestanding marble structure, inlaid with stone and gold glass and covered with relief sculptures, including scenes from the *Life of the Virgin*. The structure is neatly tied, both thematically and visually, to the surrounding loggia, with a crowning figure of Saint Michael (San Michele), rising to nearly touch one of the bosses of the vaulting. As Cassidy (1992) has shown, the tabernacle was also engineered to meet the needs of the cult, with movable screens which normally shrouded the image of the Virgin but which could be raised to reveal the icon on Sundays, feast days, and other significant occasions. It was in connection with this commission that Orcagna, a painter, became a member of the guild of masons and stone workers; and it was presumably through this project, for which he must have assembled a workshop of skilled masons and sculptors, that he established his credentials as an orchestrator of architectural decoration.

See also **Daddi, Bernardo; Nardo di Cione**

Further Reading

Belting, Hans. "Das Bild als Text: Wandmalerei und Literatur im Zeitalter Dantes." In *Malerei und Stadtkultur in der Dantezeit: Die Argumentation der Bilder*, ed. Hans Belting and Dieter Blume. Munich: Hirmer, 1989.

Boskovitz, Miklós. "Orcagna in 1357—and in Other Times." *Burlington Magazine*, 113, 1971, pp. 239–251.

Cassidy, Brendan. "The Assumption of the Virgin on the Tabernacle of Orsanmichele." *Journal of the Warburg and Courtauld Institutes,* 51, 1988a, pp. 174–180.

——. "The Financing of the Tabernacle of Orsanmichele." *Source,* 8, 1988b, pp. 1–6.

——. "Orcagna's Tabernacle in Florence: Design and Function." *Zeitschrift für Kunstgeschichte,* 55, 1992, pp. 180–211.

Cole, Bruce. "Some Thoughts on Orcagna and the Black Death Style." *Antichità Viva,* 22(2), 1983, pp. 27–37.

Giles, Kathleen Alden. "The Strozzi Chapel in Santa Maria Novella: Florentine Paintings and Patronage, 1340–1355." Dissertation, New York University, 1977.

Kreytenberg, Gert. "L'enfer d'Orcagna: La première peinture monumentale d'après les chants de Dante." *Gazette des Beaux Arts,* 6(114), 1989, pp. 243–262.

——. "Bemerkungen zum Fresko der Vertreibung des Duca d'Atene aus Florenz." In *Musagetes: Festschrift für Wolfram Prinz zu seinem 60. Geburtstag am 5. February 1989*. Berlin: Gebr. Mann Verlag, 1991, pp. 151–165.

——. "Image and Frame: Remarks on Orcagna's Pala Strozzi." *Burlington Magazine,* 134, 1992, pp. 634–638.

——. *Orcagna's Tabernacle in Orsanmichele, Florence.* New York: Abrams, 1994.

——. "Orcagnas Fresken im Hauptchor von Santa Maria Novella und deren Fragmente." *Studi di Storia dell'Arte,* 5–6, 1994–1995, pp. 9–40.

Meiss, Millard. *Painting in Florence and Siena after the Black Death.* Princeton, N.J.: Princeton University Press, 1951.

Padoa Rizzo, Anna. "Per Andrea Orcagna pittore." *Annali della Scuola Normale Superiore di Pisa,* Series 3, 11(3), 1981, pp. 835–893.

Paoletti, John T. "The Strozzi Altarpiece Reconsidered." *Memorie Domenicane,* 20, 1989, pp. 279–300.

Rash Fabbri, Nancy, and Nina Rutenberg. "The Tabernacle of Orsanmichele in Context." *Art Bulletin, 63,* 1981, pp. 385–405.

Taylor-Mitchell, Laurie. "Images of Saint Matthew Commissioned by the Arte del Cambio for Orsanmichele in Florence: Some Observations on Conservatism in Form and Patronage." *Gesta,* 31, 1992, pp. 54–72.

C. Jean Campbell

ORESME, NICOLE
(ca. 1320/25–1382)

A writer known mainly for his mathematical, scientific, and economic treatises and for his vernacular translations of Aristotle. Educated in arts and theology at the Collège de Navarre in Paris, Oresme was in 1356 appointed its grand master. During this period, his long association with the royal family began; he may have been tutor of John II's son, the future Charles V. Partly because of his royal connections, Oresme obtained church offices, becoming canon at Rouen (1362), canon at the Sainte-Chapelle (1363), dean of the cathedral of Rouen (1364), and bishop of Lisieux (1377).

Oresme's writings demonstrate his wide learning. His mathematical and scientific works, such as *De proportionibus proportionum*, *De configurationibus qualitatum et motuum*, and *De commensurabilitate vel incommensurabilitate motuum celi*, are important for their treatment of fractional exponents, their graphic representation of mathematical functions, and their sophisticated discussions of mechanics and astronomy. Oresme also used his learning, in such treatises as *Contra judiciarios astronomos*, *Livre de divinacions*, and De *causis mirabilium*, to attack the "misuse" of science, especially by the astrologers.

Certain of Oresme's works were written explicitly for the royal family. His economic treatise, *De mutationibus monetarum*, was composed during the 1350s for John II. In the late 1360s, Charles V asked Oresme to translate the Latin versions of four Aristotelian texts, the *Ethics*, the *Politics*, the pseudo-Aristotelian *Economics*, and *De caelo et mundo*. Oresme's vernacular translations helped to create a flexible French prose and to expand the French vocabulary, introducing as many as 1,000 new words.

Oresme has often been seen as anticipating modernity: in certain ways, his astronomy foreshadows Copernicus, Galileo, and Kepler, and his mathematics Descartes; his economics may anticipate Gresham's Law. But Oresme is perhaps most impressive in his ability to summarize and synthesize logically and intelligently, all the while advancing the important theories of his age.

See also **Charles V the Wise**

Further Reading

Oresme, Nicole. De *proportionibus proportionum and Ad pauca respicientes*, ed. and trans. Edward Grant. Madison: University of Wisconsin Press, 1966.
——. *Le livre de politiques d'Aristote*, ed. Albert Douglas Menut. Philadelphia: American Philosophical Society, 1970.
——. *Nicole Oresme and the Medieval Geometry of Qualities and Motions: A Treatise on the Uniformity and Difformity of Intensities Known as Tractatus de configurationibus qualitatum et motuum*, ed. and trans. Marshall Clagett. Madison: University of Wisconsin Press, 1968.
Hansen, Bert, ed. and trans. *Nicole Oresme and the Marvels of Nature: A Study of His De causis mirabilium with Critical Edition, Translation, and Commentary*. Toronto: Pontifical Institute of Mediaeval Studies, 1985.
Menut, Albert Douglas. "A Provisional Bibliography of Oresme's Writings." *Mediaeval Studies* 28 (1966): 279–99; supplementary note, 31 (1969): 346–47.

STEVEN F. KRUGER

OSWALD VON WOLKENSTEIN (1376 or 1377–1445)

No other medieval German poet is better known to us today than the South Tyrolean Oswald von Wolkenstein. Apart from amazingly concrete autobiographical references contained in his large oeuvre of 133 songs, the poet also left a vast number of historical traces in more than one thousand still extant documents. Even though the poetic statements about his own life have often to be taken as tongue-in-cheek and as topical in nature, recent research by Anton Schwob and others who have studied the archival material has confirmed most of Oswald's claims in his songs regarding his personal experiences. Born as the second son of an aristocratic South Tyrolean family, Oswald had to struggle for many years to establish his own existence both on the local and the international level. In 1401 he participated in a military campaign in Italy of the German King Ruprecht of the Palatinate; in 1410 he went on a pilgrimage to the Holy Land; between 1413 and 1415 he served Bishop Ulrich of Brixen and subsequently joined the diplomatic service of King Sigis-mund, with whom he traveled through western Europe. In 1417 Oswald married Margaretha von Schwangau and thus gained the rank of an imperial knight. In 1420–1421 he participated in one of the several wars against the always victorious Hussites, but in one of his songs ("Kl[ein]. [no.] 27") Oswald ridiculed the opponents. In the following years the poet was involved in many struggles and military conflicts with his neighbors, both peasants and aristocrats, and so also with the duke of Tyrol, Frederick IV of Habsburg. A major bone of contention was the castle Hauenstein in Seis am Schlern, to which Oswald had only a partial claim but which he took in his total possession after his marriage. At one point he even ended up in the ducal prison (1421–1422) and had to pay a huge ransom to be released. Although Oswald's power position improved over the next years to some degree, he was imprisoned again in 1427 and then had finally to submit under the centralized government of Duke Frederick. In 1429 Oswald joined the secret but highly influential court of justice, Feme, which was active all over Germany, and he also managed to consolidate his power base back home through manifold political connections and public services. In recognition of his accomplishments as diplomat and imperial servant, Oswald was inducted into the Order of the Dragon in 1431. In 1432 King Sigismund, while he stayed in northern Italy, called him into his service again and soon after sent him as one of his representatives to the Council of Basel. In 1433 Oswald probably witnessed the coronation of Sigismund as emperor at the hand of Pope Eugene IV in Rome. In 1434 Oswald participated in the imperial diet of Ulm, where Sigismund commissioned him to collect fines and taxes in South Tyrol and also confirmed his rank as imperial knight. After the death of Duke Frederick, Oswald and his allies successfully organized opposition against the Habsburgians in South Tyrol, as they could influence and dominate the young successor, Duke Sigmund, at that time still under age, for several years. Ultimately, however, the landed gentry, and so the Wolkenstein family, increasingly lost ground and had to submit to the centralized government, the growing weight of the urban class, and even the economic power of the peasants.

Whereas Oswald's political career sheds significant light on the political and economic history of the early fifteenth century, his poetic production has earned him greatest respect among modern philologists and musicologists since the full rediscovery of this amazing literary personality as of the early 1960s. In contrast to most other medieval poets Oswald created his songs for personal reasons and commissioned his first personal collection of his works in 1425, manuscript A, to which he added songs until 1436, perhaps even 1441. In 1432 the second collection was completed, manuscript "B," in which Oswald also incorporated a stunning portrait of himself created by the Italian Renaissance painter Antonio Pisanello or one of his disciples while the poet was staying in Piacenza, Italy, in the entourage of King Sigismund. Both manuscripts were most likely produced in Neustift, near Brixen, and contain melodies for many of the songs. In 1450 Oswald's family had another copy of his songs made in a paper manuscript ("c"—by convention, paper manuscripts are listed by lowercase, parchment by uppercase letters), which is almost identical with manuscript "B" but lacks the notations.

Although twenty of Oswald's more traditional songs were also copied in a number of other song collections all over Germany throughout the fifteenth and sixteenth centuries (the last one in 1572), the poet was soon forgotten after his death, probably because his most important songs were too autobiographical and idiosyncratic, and also too innovative for his time. Some of the texts contain surprisingly erotic elements and seem to reflect Oswald's private experiences with his wife. His prison songs and his dawn songs are unique for his time, and so the various polyglot songs in which he combined a string of languages to present his own linguistic mastership. On the one hand Oswald demonstrated a thorough familiarity with conventional German courtly love song, or *Minnesang*; on the other he introduced melodies and poetic images from French, Flemish, and Italian contemporaries. Many of Oswald's songs are polyphonic and reflect an amazing variety of musical forms, such as the *caccia* (hunt, Kl. 52), or the *lauda* (praise, Kl. 109).

Hardly any other poet before him had such an excellent command of the broadest range of lyrical genres, as his oeuvre contains marriage songs, spring songs, prison songs, war songs, autobiographical songs, travel songs, dawn songs, Marian hymns, calendar songs, Shrovetide songs, songs about city life, songs in which he criticized both the rich merchants and the arrogant courtiers, various religious songs, and repentance songs.

Oswald was also a master of onomatopoetic expressions, such as in his Kl. 50, where the arrival of spring is vividly conveyed through the imitation of birdsongs. He seems to have learned much both from the Middle High German Neidhart tradition and from the Middle Latin tradition of boisterous and vivacious love songs as in the *Carmina Burana*. In addition, the Italian trecento (thirteenth-century) poets Cecco Angiolieri, Giannozzo, and Franco Sacchetti might have provided Oswald with important poetic models, but in his many old-age songs we also discover possible influences from the French poet Charles d'Orléans. Moreover, some scholars have suggested François Villon as a possible source for Oswald's autobiographical songs. Considering Oswald's extensive travels throughout western and southern Europe, Spanish and Flemish poetry also might have had a considerable impact on his work, as he adapted his models by way of *contrafacture* (use of secular melody in religious song). Recently we have also learned that contemporary folk poetry, proverbs, and perhaps specific legal formulas can be discerned in Oswald's language. Even narrative epics such as the Old Spanish *El Cid* and the Italian *Decamerone* by Boccaccio might have influenced him in his compositions. Finally, the poet also translated several Latin sequences that were usually performed during the liturgy.

Oswald's poetic genius transformed all these sources and models into highly individual poetic expressions. We will probably never reach a full understanding of which elements the poet borrowed from his predecessors and contemporaries, but we know for sure that Oswald had an extremely open mind for novel ideas and thoroughly enjoyed experimenting with a wide variety of poetic genres, styles, and images. He was one of the first medieval German poets to correlate closely text and melody and also created astoundingly polyphonic effects typical of *Ars nova* and the Italian trecento culture. Curiously, though, Oswald does not seem to have been in contact with humanists and Renaissance writers, even though he once refers to Petrarch (Kl. 10, 28), whose concept of man's sinfulness seems to have influenced Oswald's religious thinking. In this regard the poet is quite representative of his own time, as he still lived in the medieval tradition and yet also opened his mind to many new approaches to music (*Ars nova*) and poetry.

Oswald's oeuvre can be located at the crossroads between the late Middle Ages and the Renaissance, as the poet belonged to neither cultural period yet shared elements with both. His songs already reflect a strong sense of the modern individual with the emphasis on personal experiences, ideas, needs, and desires, but they are, at the same time, deeply drenched in the medieval concept of human sinfulness and of life as nothing but a transitional period here on earth.

See also **Charles d'Orléans; Neidhart**

Further Reading

Classen, Albrecht. "Oswald von Wolkenstein," in *German Writers of the Renaissance and Reformation 1280–1580*, ed. James Hardin and Max Reinhart. Detroit: Gale, 1997, pp. 198–205.

Die Lieder Oswalds von Wolkenstein, ed. Karl Kurt Klein et al., 3d. ed. Tübingen: Niemeyer, 1987.

Jahrbuch der Oswald von Wolkenstein Gesellschaft, 1ff. (1980/1981ff.).

Joschko, Dirk. *Oswald von Wolkenstein. Eine Monographie zu Person, Werk und Forschungsgeschichte.* Göppingen: Kümmerle, 1985.

Oswald von Wolkenstein. *Sämtliche Lieder und Gedichte*, trans. Wernfried Hofmeister. Göppingen: Kümmerle, 1989 [modern German trans.].

Schwob, Anton. *Oswald von Wolkenstein. Eine Biographie*, 3d ed. Bozen: Athesia, 1979.

——. *Die Lebenszeugnisse Oswalds von Wolkenstein. Edition und Kommentar. Bd. 1, 1382–1419, Nr. 1–92.* Vienna: Böhlau, 1999.

Spicker, Johannes. *Literarische Stilisierung und artistische Kompetenz bei Oswald von Wolkenstein.* Stuttgart: Hirzel, 1993.

ALBRECHT CLASSEN

OTFRID (ca. 800–ca. 875)

A monk of the abbey of Weißenburg (now Wissembourg in Alsace), Otfrid is the author of a remarkable poem based on the four gospels, completed by about 870 and preserved in four manuscripts, three of them complete or nearly so. The famous Vienna manuscript was carefully corrected, and perhaps written in part, by Otfrid himself.

Otfrid composed the poem in a new, stress-based strophic verse form with two long lines per strophe. Each long line contains two half lines joined by rhyme or at least assonance at the caesura (audible break at the middle of a line). Thus the Lord's Prayer begins:

> *Fáter unser gúato, bist drúhtin thu gim‡ato*
> *in hímilon io hóher, uuíh si námo thiner.*
> *Biquéme uns thinaz ríchi, thaz hoha hímilrichi,*
> *thára uuir zua io gíngen ioh émmizigen thíngen.*

> Our Father good, thou art a kindly king
> so high in the heavens, holy be thy name.
> Thy kingdom come to us, the high kingdom of heaven,
> toward which may we always strive and firmly
> believe. (2,22,27-30)

All four manuscripts show the caesura and use initials, indentation, and rhythmic accents to explicate and show off the new verse form. Otfrid describes the meter and his spelling innovations in a letter to archbishop Liutbert of Mainz (included in two manuscripts), where his pride of invention is everywhere apparent. Suggestions that Otfrid merely modified an existing German verse form are therefore unlikely. Neither did Otfrid slavishly imitate Latin hymnody of the period: though some contemporary Latin hymns also show assonance, rhyme, and/or alternating stress, the overall effect of his poem is quite different. Otfrid's verse form was quickly used in several other Old High German and early Middle High German poems and seems the likely basis for the couplets of the Middle High German courtly epics.

Otfrid portrays the life of Christ as described in the four gospels, but his work is not merely a verse translation. After many narrative sections, he includes passages for reflection, labeling them *mystice*, or in a mystical sense. As in Germanic alliterative verse, Otfrid constantly repeats and restates ideas and phrases, often for the sake of the rhyme or the rhythm. His writing seems prolix; in the passage above, he uses thirty words where the alliterating Old Saxon Heliand has twenty-one and the prose Weißenburg Catechism only thirteen.

Otfrid's attention to meter and orthography suggests that the poem was meant to be read aloud or even chanted (one manuscript has some neums, an early form of musical notation), but it could have had no place in the Latin liturgy of the time.

The dialect of the poem is Southern Rhenish Franconian, though in part because of Otfrid's orthographic innovations, it differs slightly from that of other Weißenburg documents.

Further Reading

Haubrichs, Wolfgang. "Otfrid von Weißenburg: Übersetzer, Erzähler, Interpret. . . ." in *Übersetzer im Mittelalter*, ed. Joachim Heinzle et al. Wolfram-Studien 14. Berlin: Schmidt, 1996, pp. 13–45.

Kleiber, Wolfgang. *Otfrid von Weißenburg: Untersuchungen zur handschriftlichen Überlieferung und Studien zum Aufbau des Evangelienbuches.* Bern: Francke, 1971.

Murdoch, Brian O. *Old High German Literature.* Boston: Twayne, 1983.

Patzlaff, Rainer. *Otfrid von Weißenburg und die mittelalterliche versus-Tradition.* Tübingen: Niemeyer, 1975.

Schweikle, Gunther. "Die Herkunft des althochdeutschen Reimes: Zu Otfried von Weißenburgs formgeschichtlicher Stellung." *Zeitschrift für deutsches Altertum und deutsche Literatur* 96 (1967): 166–212.

LEO A. CONNOLLY

OTTO I (912–973)

King of Germany 936–973 and emperor 962–973, Otto (the Great) was a member of the Liudolfing, or Saxon, dynasty, born in 912 to the future Henry I and his wife,

Mathilda. Little is known of his early years. In 930 Otto married Edith, the half sister of King Aethelstan of Wessex, beginning a policy of marriage to foreign princesses that became the norm in Germany. He was almost certainly designated at that time as the next king. After his father's death, Otto was acclaimed by the nobles and crowned in Aachen on August 7, 936, reviving the coronation ritual that Henry I had foregone. This is the first sign of Otto's new view of kingship, marked by a policy of systematically increasing the gap between king and dukes and rejecting the rule by personal pacts that had characterized his father's reign. Perhaps this attitude helped provoke the civil wars of 937–941, as nobles took advantage of an unestablished king to settle old feuds and reduce royal rights. The two most important rebels were Otto's elder half brother Thankmar (who deeply resented that Henry I had declared his first marriage to Thankmar's mother invalid) and his younger brother Henry, who was supported by their mother, Mathilda. This has been hailed as resistance against a new Ottonian principle that the realm could not be divided as it had been by Merovingians and Carolingians; the truth was that Henry I had not had enough control of the kingdom to make a division possible, although he did divide his personal lands and treasure among his sons. The period of rebellion concluded with Thankmar's death and the submission of the other important rebels. Henry was forgiven and, in 947, given the duchy of Bavaria.

Otto continued his father's vigorous eastern and northern policy. Margraves Hermann Billung and Gero, acting with Otto's support, won a series of victories against the Slavs, gaining territory that Otto strove to pacify with an active policy that included both the establishment of fortified garrison outposts and active royal activity in missionary enterprises. The latter included the erection of several bishoprics—Brandenburg and Havelberg in 948; Oldenburg, Merseburg, Meissen, and Zeitz later in 968—at which time Otto's beloved monastic foundation of Magdeburg was also elevated to an archbishopric with authority over much of the eastern frontier. The success of the Ottonian eastern policy culminated in a series of victories in 955. On August 10 of that year, Otto decisively defeated a Magyar coalition at the battle of Lechfeld near Augsburg, an event that marked the end of Magyar raiding in Germany. This was followed by a victory over the Slavs at Recknitz on October 16th. Further campaigns led to the subjection of the Slavs between the middle Elbe and the middle Oder by 960, as well as making Bohemia and Poland tributary to the German king.

From an early period Otto had imperial ambitions. He took advantage of the disorders caused by Bangor's seizure of power in Lombardy to establish a foothold in Italy in 951. Otto accepted Bangor's submission and reinstated him as subking. To strengthen his personal control of Lombardy, though, the widower Otto married Adelheid, the widowed queen of the Lombards. At that time, Otto requested that the pope crown him as emperor, but the pope refused, probably from fear of a strong German presence in Italy. Otto had to cut short his time in Italy, returning to Germany to deal with the revolt of his eldest son, Liudulf, who apparently felt threatened by Otto's new marriage alliance. In 961, though, Pope John XII appealed for Otto's help against his enemies. Otto responded swiftly with a second expedition to Italy. He prepared for a long campaign, taking the precaution of having the six-year-old Otto II, his eldest son by Adelheid, elected and crowned as king, and establishing a regency in Germany. The pope's enemies fled before Otto's army, and John XII crowned Otto I as emperor on February 2, 962, reviving the imperial title that had fallen in abeyance early in the century, and creating a link to the prestige of Charlemagne.

The imperial coronation led to a major shift in Otto's interests, leading him to spend ten of the last twelve years of his life in Italy. John XII soon realized that Otto was exerting much more direct domination over Italian affairs than he had bargained for. The pope therefore took part in a conspiracy aimed at ending Ottonian involvement in Italy, which led Otto to drive John from Rome and arrange his deposition. Otto then set up a new pope of his own choice, initiating almost a century of German control of the papacy. Imperial interests also led to campaigns in southern Italy from 966 on, especially with the goal of gaining Byzantine recognition of Otto's imperial title.

Otto I was an even more peripatetic ruler than most of his contemporaries, ruling largely through verbal orders during constant travels throughout his realm. He received little formal education, learning to read only in 946, while mourning for his first wife, Edith. Despite this, Otto established a particularly strong and secure kingdom, thanks especially to his military successes, the wealth acquired through exploitation of the newly found silver mines at Goslar, and his alliance with the church, particularly with German monasteries. Beginning in the 940s, Otto gradually replaced the dukes of Germany with members of the Ottonian family, who on the whole proved to be loyal supporters of the throne. His personal prestige and close kinship to the top families in western Europe allowed Otto to act as mediator in Burgundy and in France between the last Carolingians and the rising Capetian (French kings, tenth to fourteenth century) family. By the time of Otto's death at Memleben on May 7, 973, his German-based empire was the strongest state in Europe, a position it held for the next century. He is buried in the church he founded at Magdeburg, beside his wife, Edith.

See also **Charlemagne; Henry I of Saxony; Otto II**

Further Reading

Althoff, Gerd, and Hagen Keller. *Heinrich I. und Otto der Große: Neubeginn und karolingisches Erbe*. Göttingen: Muster-Schmidt, 1985.

Leyser, Karl. *Communications and Power in Medieval Europe: The Carolingian and Ottonian Centuries*, ed. Timothy Reuter. London: Hambledon Press, 1994.

Reuter, Timothy. *Germany in the Early Middle Ages, 800–1056*. London: Longman, 1991.

PHYLLIS G. JESTICE

OTTO II (955–983)

King 961–983, emperor 967–983, sole ruler of the German Empire from 973, Otto II was born in 955 to Otto I and his second wife, Adelheid. His father arranged for the six-year-old Otto's election and coronation as king of the Germans in May 961, before setting out on his second Italian expedition. To secure the imperial title to his dynasty, the elder Otto further arranged to have his son crowned co-emperor on Christmas Day 967; Otto II was the last western emperor to receive imperial coronation in his father's lifetime. Despite these honors, the future Otto II was not given an independent position even after he came of age, and has left only twenty-seven extant documents from the twelve years of his official shared rule with Otto I. At his father's death in 973, the eighteen-year-old Otto was accepted as ruler without opposition.

The early years of Otto II's reign were occupied by a series of rebellions in Bavaria and Lotharingia. These rebellions were provoked by an attempt Otto made in 974 to reduce the power of his overly mighty cousin, Henry II "the Quarrelsome" (the nickname is not contemporary), duke of the semiautonomous duchy of Bavaria. Henry's defeat in 976 gave Otto the opportunity to reorganize the southern duchies, weakening Bavaria by turning its province of Carinthia into a separate duchy. Henry, unsatisfied with his position, led a second uprising in 976–977, and Bavaria was pacified only with Henry's imprisonment in 978.

Otto II's early military campaigns were successful, as Otto continued the strong eastern and northern policies of his father and grandfather. A victory over the Danes in 974 led to an expansion of German efforts to evangelize in the north. He also invaded Bohemia several times, returning it to its earlier tributary status after its ruler had seceded by joining with Henry the Quarrelsome in the rebellions of 974–977. On the western front, though, Otto was unable to play as strong a role as his father had. An effort of the French King Lothar to gain control of Lotharingia in 978 caught Otto by surprise, forcing him to flee Aachen before the French army. Otto quickly retaliated with a raid that penetrated France to the gates of Paris, but that accomplished little besides salving Otto's pride.

Emperor Otto receives the homage of the nations. Gospels of Emperor Otto (II or III), also called "Registrum Gregorii." Ottoian art, 10th. © Erich Lessing/Art Resource, New York.

In 972, Otto II had married the Byzantine princess Theophanu, a marriage arranged by his father to enhance the prestige of the Ottonian dynasty. Contemporary sources suggest that Theophanu exerted a very strong influence on Otto, including the belief that the empress's "childish advice" led to Otto's disastrous campaign in southern Italy in 982. In reality, the southern campaign needs little explanation. Otto decided in 981 on the conquest of southern Italy, split at that time among Saracens, Greeks, and Lombards. He probably planned the campaign as an extension of imperial policies begun by Otto I, who had conducted several inconclusive campaigns in the region. Otto II's army was, however, decisively defeated by a Saracen force at the battle of Cotrone (Cap Colonne) on July 13, 982. Almost the entire German army was destroyed; Otto himself escaped only by swimming his horse out to a Greek ship in the bay, then disguising his identity until he reached safety. The Saracen army was too badly weakened to press its advantage, so the battle had little effect on the balance of power in Italy. This defeat, though, dealt a severe blow to Otto's prestige. The Slavs responded to news of the German defeat with an uprising in the summer of 983. A Slavic confederation devastated the

German border, destroyed the bishoprics of Havelberg and Brandenburg, and burned Hamburg, reversing most of Otto I's successes in Slavic territory. Perhaps the seriousness of the political situation can be seen in the feet that Otto II summoned an imperial diet at Verona on May 27, 983, where he had his three-year-old son Otto III elected to the German kingship, then sent the child on to Aachen to be crowned. Otto II remained in Italy, trying to subject Venice to imperial control. He died of malaria in Rome on December 7, 983, at the age of twenty-eight, and is the only emperor to be buried in St. Peter's Basilica.

Otto II appears to have been dominated and overshadowed throughout his life by people of stronger character, first his father, then his wife Theophanu, and also by his counselors, especially the loyal and talented Archbishop Willigis of Mainz. Physically Otto was not as impressive as his father; the exhumation of his body in 1609 revealed that he was a small man, and eleventh-century sources describe him as a redhead. Certainly his reputation has suffered by comparison to his great father and exotic son. In general, his reign is best seen as one of consolidation and growing sophistication. Unlike his predecessors, Otto II was well educated. His love of luxury and ostentation was notorious, although this perhaps should be taken more as a sign of the enormous wealth the Ottonians were able to command than of character weakness. His reign saw advances in the imperial chancery and greater cooperation between the German and Italian parts of the empire. It also saw a closer identification with the ancient Roman Empire and the city of Rome, setting aside the Byzantine emperor's claim to be the only true successor of the caesars. Otto's chancery in 982 adopted for the first time the title Roman empire (*imperator Romanorum augustus*) as the designation of a German emperor, a title that became standard to Otto's successors. Despite his reverses in Italy and on the Slavic frontier, Otto left a firmly established realm, increasingly self-assured and international, to his son.

See also **Otto I, Otto III**

Further Reading

Beumann, Helmut. *Die Ottonen*. Stuttgart: Kohlhammer, 1987.
Reuter, Timothy. *Germany in the Early Middle Ages, 800–1056*. London: Longman, 1991.

PHYLLIS G. JESTICE

OTTO III (980–1002)

King of the Germans, 983–1002, emperor 996–1002, Otto III was the most flamboyant and controversial of the German emperors. He was born in 980, the only son of Emperor Otto II and the Byzantine princess Theophanu.

Otto II continued his own father's policy of assuring Ottonian rule by having the young Otto elected king at Verona, May 27, 983. He then dispatched the three-year-old Otto to Aachen for coronation on Christmas 983. This was several weeks after Otto II's death in Italy but before the news had reached the north.

A series of informal regents governed the empire for most of Otto's short life. By German custom, the young king's proper guardian was his closest adult male relative, Duke Henry II the Quarrelsome of Bavaria. Henry, though, soon tried to supplant his charge, claiming the kingship in his own name. Archbishop Willigis of Mainz, though, threw his support behind Otto III, summoning the young king's mother, Theophanu, and grandmother Adelheid from Italy to help him preserve Otto's rights. After a period of intense political maneuvering, Henry surrendered Otto to the two empresses on June 29, 984. Theophanu assumed the regency for her son. After her death in 991, Adelheid directed affairs until Otto III formally came of age in September 994.

Otto's role during his childhood was strictly symbolic. In 986 he was sent on a campaign against the Slavs—not to fight but so Mieszko of Poland could join the host and do homage. For the most part, though, Otto was not very visible in German affairs until he came of age. He was very well educated. His main tutor was Bernward, the future bishop of Hildesheim, but he also received instruction in Greek from his mother's friend John Philagathos, a southern Italian. After coming of age, Otto continued his education with the most learned man of the age, Gerbert of Aurillac.

Rome during Otto's minority had fallen into the hands of the local noble Crescentius II. Pope John XV asked for Otto's help in 995, leading to Otto's first Italian expedition. John died before his arrival, so Otto forced the Roman Church to accept his own cousin Bruno of Carinthia as pope, who took the name Gregory V. Gregory then crowned Otto as emperor on May 21, 996. The imposition of a German pope shows Otto's early determination to control Rome. This marked a new departure, since Gregory was the first non-Roman pope since the Byzantine emperors had appointed Greeks to the office in the seventh century. Gregory was soon driven from the city, forcing Otto to return and reinstate him in 998. This time Otto secured Rome by having Crescentius executed, and had Crescentius's antipope (none other than Otto's former tutor, John Philagathos) blinded and imprisoned. Afterward, Otto stayed in Rome, having decided to make the city the capital of his empire. He had a palace built for himself on the Aventine. This has been taken as evidence of Otto III's grandiose plan to create a new Roman empire. Certainly Otto greatly developed the idea of a western empire, but it was not inextricably linked to Rome. At first he wanted to set up Aachen as a "new Rome," placing the focus of the empire in the north. It is probable that political instability in Italy made Otto decide to stay closer, where he could intervene effectively in affairs. Naturally enough, this made him very unpopular with the Romans, who revolted in early 1001, besieging Otto for a time in his own palace. Otto sent for more troops and was preparing an attack on Rome at the time of his death.

The earlier Ottonians had ruled almost entirely by means of continual travel throughout their realm. The decision to reside in a permanent capital thus marked another new departure. It forced Otto to develop a larger bureaucracy and enabled him to acquire a larger and more glittering court. For a time Otto's aunt, Abbess Mathilda of Quedlinburg, acted as regent in Germany, but after her death the emperor relied ever more on bishops to perform the work of government, laying the groundwork for the "imperial Church system" of the late Ottonians and Salians. In Rome itself, Otto created a hierarchy of court officials, elaborate by German standards, most of whom had Greek titles in emulation of the Byzantine court. Otto also insisted on a higher degree of ceremony than had been known to earlier German rulers, modeled on Byzantine practice.

Otto clearly saw his role as emperor in terms of leadership over the Christian world, assuming the titles "servant of Jesus Christ," and "servant of the apostles." This strong development of the imperial idea was already visible in 996 with Otto's appointment of the first German pope; after Gregory V's death in 999, the emperor continued his effort to control the papacy by appointing his former tutor Gerbert of Aurillac, who took the name Sylvester II. The two cooperated closely, even declaring the Donation of Constantine to be invalid, Otto appears to have been personally pious; he was close to both St. Nilus and St. Romuald of Ravenna; Bruno of Querfurt claims that the emperor even swore an oath to abdicate and retire to the wilds of Poland as a hermit. While this is unlikely, Otto did take very seriously his duty toward the church. In 1000 he made a pilgrimage to the tomb of the martyred Bishop Adalbert of Prague in Gniezno, arranging at that time for Gniezno to become the archbishopric of Poland. He went on from there to Aachen, where he had Charlemagne's grave opened, taking the pectoral cross from the body. Certainly this was in part the effort of an upstart Ottonian to associate himself with the prestige of the Carolingian dynasty. It is very likely that the tomb opening was also the first step in a project to canonize Charlemagne, perhaps the best example of Otto III's belief in the divine nature of the empire (*imperium*). He also planned to continue the family alliance with the Byzantine emperors, arranging to marry the porphyrogenita (female successor) Theodora, but she arrived in Italy only at about the time of Otto's death.

Otto III's history, though, is one of largely unrealized potential. He died unexpectedly on January 24, 1002, at the age of twenty-one.

See also **Charlemagne; Otto II; Romuald of Ravenna, Saint**

Further Reading

Althoff, Gerd. *Otto III.* Darmstadt: Wissenschaftliche Buchgesellschaft, 1996.
Beumann, Helmut. *Die Ottonen.* Stuttgart: Kohlhammer, 1987.
Leyser, Karl J. *Medieval Germany and Its Neighbours 900–1250.* London: Hambledon, 1982.

PHYLLIS G. JESTICE

OTTO IV (1175/1182–May 19, 1218)

Emperor and sometime ally of Pope Innocent III (1198–1216), Otto's reign was a time of chaos after the premature death of Henry VI. Leader of the Welf house and son of Henry the Lion, Otto was involved in a civil war for control of the empire with candidates of the rival Hohenstaufen house, Philip of Swabia and Frederick II. The struggle for control of the imperial crown had international implications and involved the princes of Germany, the kings of England and France, and the pope. Otto would ultimately lose the struggle to maintain control of the empire to Frederick.

The unexpected death of Henry in 1197 left the empire in a difficult situation because his heir, Frederick, was only three years old. It also offered the papacy the opportunity to break free from encirclement by the Hohenstaufen, an opportunity Innocent would exploit by playing one side against the other in the civil strife in Germany or by acting as referee between them. The situation was complicated by shifting alliances both inside and outside the empire. Frederick was first supported by the Staufen, including his uncle, Philip of Swabia. But Philip, motivated by the activities of forces opposed to his family, presented himself as king and was crowned at Mainz in September 1198. He also revived the alliance between his family and the Capetian dynasty, headed by Philip Augustus, to improve his position in Germany and Europe. The anti-Staufen forces inside Germany, supported by King Richard I of England, did not stand idly by but promoted a Welf candidate. The eldest son of Henry the Lion was still on crusade, and therefore the younger son, Otto, became the anti-Staufen candidate.

Otto, who had been raised at the court of his uncle, Richard I, and had been made count of Poitou and duke of Aquitaine in 1190 and 1196, respectively, made the most of his opportunity. He was crowned before Philip by the proper ecclesiastic, the archbishop of Cologne, and in the right place, Aachen. His election also carried great weight because he was elected by those traditionally empowered to choose the king. Indeed, the nature of his election was of great importance to Innocent, who would involve himself in the succession crisis because of the close ties of empire and papacy and because of papal claims to superior jurisdiction. Innocent, suspicious of the Hohenstaufen family and fearful of their territorial gains in northern and southern Italy, came to support Otto. This was critical to the king's success because his situation in Germany was weak despite having been elected by the right people and crowned in the right place, and because his greatest international ally, Richard, died in early 1199. To maintain papal support, Otto made important territorial concessions to the pope in Italy.

Otto's difficulties did not end, however, even though he had papal support, which was reinforced by Otto's concessions. Despite his excommunication, Philip managed to increase his power in Germany in the opening decade of the thirteenth century. He managed to increase support among the bishops of the empire, including the very important archbishop of Cologne, Adolf. Perhaps motivated by hostility to Rome, many princes also came to support Philip. By 1207 the papal curia had come to support Philip's claim to the imperial dignity and kingship in Germany, and in the following year the pope himself recognized Philip as king. Negotiations over territory in Italy and the imperial coronation were held between Philip and the pope, but they made little headway before Philip was murdered by Otto of Wittelsbach over Philip's broken engagement to Otto's daughter.

In 1208, fortunes once again turned for Otto, and he now received widespread support in Germany. He was elected king by the German princes a second time in November in Frankfurt and was victorious over French attempts to establish a rival king. To further strengthen his position in Germany, Otto was betrothed to Philip's daughter Beatrix. He was then crowned emperor by Innocent in Rome in October 1209, after renewing his promises to respect papal territory in Italy and also to refrain from intervening in Sicilian affairs.

Otto's success, however, seems to have gotten the better of him and, following the advice of his ministerials, he decided to extend his authority in Italy. He sought to expand his rights into papal lands, and thus alienated an important ally and created a dangerous opponent, Innocent. He further raised the ire of the pope by occupying Tuscany and invading the Hohenstaufen kingdom of Sicily. His invasion and conquest of Sicily in November 1210 led to the very encirclement by a German ruler that Innocent had struggled to prevent. Otto's actions also led Innocent to excommunicate the emperor in the autumn of 1210, and in the spring of 1211 Innocent released Otto's vassals from their oaths to the emperor.

Otto's difficulties were not limited to the opposition from the pope. To secure his position in Germany, Otto married Beatrix in 1212, but she died shortly after their marriage. He faced revolts in northern Italy, where opposition to German domination had existed for more than a generation, and in Germany, where the nobility had been released from their obligation of loyalty by the pope. He faced a rival king because Frederick followed him to Germany, where the princely opposition to Otto, with papal support, crowned Frederick king at Mainz. Frederick was able to gain a solid foothold in southern Germany, thus undermining Otto's authority and blocking his access to Italy. And both Frederick and Otto benefited from their alliances with the kings of France and England.

Otto's alliance with King John, however, would prove his undoing. Fearing that Philip Augustus would take English territory in France, John invaded with his nephew and ally Otto, who hoped to weaken French support for his Hohenstaufen rival. First John was defeated on the Loire and then, on July 27, 1214, Otto was disastrously defeated at the Battle of Bouvines. His supporters melted away after the defeat, and Frederick went on the offensive in the empire, imposing himself on Otto's remaining allies. Otto was formally deposed the following July and was confined to his personal lands in Brunswick until his death on May 19, 1218.

See also **Frederick II; Henry the Lion; Innocent III, Pope**

Further Reading

Abulafia, David. *Frederick II: A Medieval Emperor*. Oxford: Oxford University Press, 1988.

Duby, Georges. *The Legend of Bouvines: War, Religion and Culture in the Middle Ages*, trans. Catherine Tihanyi. Berkeley: University of California Press, 1990.

Haverkamp, Alfred. *Medieval Germany, 1056–1273*. 2d ed., trans. Helga Braun and Richard Mortimer. Oxford: Oxford University Press, 1992.

MICHAEL FRASSETTO

OTTO OF FREISING (ca. 1112–1158)

The most important historian of the twelfth century, Otto of Freising was well placed to write his works of history. He was born into the most prominent families in the empire and was related to the imperial Salian and Staufen lines. His father was Leopold III of Austria and his mother was Agnes, daughter of Henry IV and whose first husband was Frederick I, duke of Swabia. Otto was thus half brother of Conrad III and uncle of Frederick I Barbarossa. His ecclesiastical career began while he was still a child, when he became provost of the house of canons at Klosterneuburg (near Vienna). In 1127 or 1128, Otto journeyed to France to study with the great masters at Paris, including Hugo of St. Victor, Gilbert de la Porrée, and, probably, Peter Abelard. He left Paris in 1133 and on his way home joined the Cistercian abbey at Morimond. He was later elected bishop of Freising, before the canonical age and as the result of family influence. He participated in the Second Crusade (1147—1148) and, while en route to a Cistercian general chapter, died in Morimond in 1158.

Otto is best known for two historical works, *The Two Cities* and *The Deeds of Frederick Barbarossa*. The first of the two, is the more pessimistic but also the more philosophical work. Written between 1143 and 1146, *The Two Cities* is a world chronicle that tells the tale of salvation history that was heavily influenced by the work of St. Augustine. The first seven books outline the history of the world from creation to 1146. Otto's history describes the struggles of good and evil and praises the monks, the true representatives of the City of God on earth. *The Two Cities* also is a history of the *translatio imperii*, describing the transfer of universal power from the Greeks to the Romans to the Franks and ultimately to the Germans. It was in the Christian empire of the Germans that Otto saw the possibility of the existence of the City of God on earth, but the troubled times facing the empire from the time of Henry IV to Conrad III left him with little hope. The eighth, and final, book of *The Two Cities* is thoroughly eschatological and describes the coming of Antichrist, the Final judgment, and establishment of the heavenly Jerusalem. Otto's somber perspective is not continued, however, in his other great work, *The Deeds of Frederick Barbarossa*. Completing the first two books before his death in 1158, Otto followed the plan outlined in a letter requested by Otto from his sponsor, Barbarossa himself. The first book details the events of the tumultuous reigns of Barbarossa's predecessors, and the second describes the first four years of the reign of Barbarossa, a time of peace and glory for the empire. Although *Deeds* overlooks matters unfavorable to the Staufen line, misrepresents the state of the realm at Barbarossa's ascension, and overstates his successes in Italy, it remains the most important source for events in the early years of Barabarossa's reign.

See also **Frederick I Barbarossa; Henry IV Emperor**

Further Reading

Otto of Freising. *Chronica sive Historia de Duabus Civitatibus*, ed. A. Hofmeister. Monumenta Germaniae Historica Scriptores Rerum Germanicarum 40. Hannover: Hahn, 1912.

Otto of Freising and Rahewin. *Gesta Friderici Imperatoris*, ed. G. Waitz. Monumenta Germaniae Historica Scriptores Rerum Germanicarum 46. Hannover: Hahn, 1912.

Otto of Freising. *The Two Cities, by Otto, Bishop of Freising*, trans. Charles Christopher Mierow. New York: Columbia University Press, 1928.

Otto of Freising and his continuator, Rahewin. *The Deeds of Frederick Barbarossa*, trans. Charles Christopher Mierow with Richard Emery, 1953; rpt. Toronto: University of Toronto Press, 1994.

MICHAEL FRASSETTO

P

PACHER, MICHAEL
(ca. 1430/1435–1498)

Born in the Puster valley in south Tyrol, the painter and wood carver Michael Pacher was one of those rare double talents of the late Middle Ages whose reputation reached well beyond his native region. Contemporary documents reveal, however, that he was primarily a painter, like Friedrich Pacher, who is presumed to be a relative. Thus, in spite of his astounding professional activity as a sculptor, most of his religious works comprise panel paintings and frescoes, including the vault paintings in the old sacristy at the cloister Neustift from about 1470. By 1467 at the latest he directed a workshop in Bruneck.

Pacher's importance lies in his adaptation of new artistic forms from Italy, the Netherlands, and southern Germany, which, in combination with his Alpine piety, he transforms into a new pictorial language. A clear understanding of Mantegna's frescoes in Padua and Mantua with their bold foreshortening and deep spaces constructed in virtuoso perspective is already apparent in four early panel paintings preserved from an otherwise lost altar dedicated to Thomas Becket (about 1460; Graz, Joanneum). In the altarpiece of the church fathers from Neustift near Brixen (1482–1483; Munich, Alte Pinakothek), he developed these pictorial techniques fully, setting the monumental figures under diagonally arranged trompe l'oeil baldachins (realistic figures) that seem to spring out of the paintings. Realistic, portraitlike facial features characterize the four small panels with the apostles and the helpers in need that were located at Wilten after 1820 (about 1465; now divided among the Österreichische Galerie in Vienna, the Museum Ferdinandeum in Innsbruck, and a private collection in the United States). No trace remains of a documented altarpiece, probably dedicated to the Archangel Michael, made for the parish church in Bozen between 1481 and 1484.

Of four Virgin altarpieces, all with richly sculptured shrines, three are fragmentarily preserved. An enthroned Madonna from 1462–1465 in the parish church of St. Lorenz near Bruneck, probably accompanied by the figures of St. Michael (Munich, Bayerisches Landesmuseum) and St. Lawrence (Innsbruck, Museum Ferdinandeum), has lasted through the centuries, although without the original shrine structure. Single panels from the wings, which were painted on both sides, are now housed in Munich (Alte Pinakothek) and Vienna (Österreichische Galerie). Pacher set a Coronation of the Virgin, composed as a scene rather than a stiff row of saints, into the center of the polyptych at Gries near Bozen (1471–1475); polychromed and gilded reliefs occupy the wings of the chapel-like shrine. Pacher's representation of the coronation before a gold brocade curtain supported by angels is based on Hans Multscher's altar in Sterzing. The contract mentions guard figures, which would have flanked the shrine; these, along with the painted wing panels, have disappeared. The masterpiece among Pacher's altars is the double triptych in the choir of the pilgrimage church at St. Wolfgang in the Salzkammergut; the contract is dated 1471, the execution between 1475 and 1481. With this work Pacher set the artistic standards against which other paintings and sculptures of the last phase of the late Gothic are measured. Here this "genius among altar sculptors of south Tyrol" (Paatz 1963: 44, my trans.) developed his own artistic language in the shimmering gold coronation set onto a stage under a filigreed tracery superstructure that reaches up to the vaults, in the imposing figures of the church's patron and St. Benedict, in the militant knight-saints at the sides of the shrine, and in the accompanying painted cycles with scenes from the lives of Christ, the Virgin, and St. Wolfgang. Probably the largest of Pacher's Virgin altars was that commissioned for the Franciscan church in Salzburg in 1484 and finished in 1498. This structure, greater than seventeen meters, was dismantled in the baroque period; its enthroned Madonna, later inserted into an altar by Fischer von Erlach, and several panels are preserved (Vienna, Österreichische Galerie). The extraordinary sum of 3,300 Rhenish gold florins was likely the highest paid for an altarpiece of this period. Pacher died in 1498, shortly before its completion.

See also **Multscher, Hans**

Further Reading

Egg, Erich. *Gotik in Tirol*: *Die Flügelaltäre.* Innsbruck: Haymon-Verlag, 1985, pp. 177–189.

Evans, Mark. "Appropriation and Application: The Significance of the Sources of Michael Pacher's Altarpieces," in *The Altarpiece in the Renaissance*, ed. Peter Humphrey and Martin Kemp. Cambridge: Cambridge University Press, 1990, pp. 106–128.

Goldberg, Gisela. "Late Gothic Painting from South Tyrol: Michael Pacher and Marx Reichlich." *Apollo 116* (1982): 240–245.

Hempel, Erhard. *Michael Pacher.* Vienna: A. Schroll, 1931.

Koller, Manfred, and Norbert Wibiral. *Der Pacher-Altar von St. Wolfgang*: *Untersuchung, Konservierung, Restaurierung 1969–1976.* Studien zu Denkmalschutz und Denkmalpflege 11. Vienna: Hermann Böhlaus Nachfolger, 1981.

Michael Pacher und sein Kreis: Bin Tiroler Künstler der europäischen Spätgotik (1498–1998). Bozen: Südtiroler Landesregierung, 1998.

Paatz, Walter. "Süddeutsche Schnitzaltäre der Spätgotik." *Heidelberger kunstgeschichtliche Abhandlungen. Neue Folge 8* (1963): 44–54.

Rasmo, Nicolo. *Michael Pacher.* London: Phaidon, 1971.

BRIGITTE SCHLIEWEN

PADILLA, MARÍA DE (d. 1361)

The daughter of a Castilian family of the lesser aristocracy, María de Padilla became Pedro I's favorite in 1352, shortly after meeting through the Pedro's chief minister Juan Alfonso de Alburquerque. María was a member of the household staff of Alburquerque's wife, Isabel de Meneses. In spite of two subsequent marriages, Pedro's attachment to María was the most enduring relationship of his life. It lasted, with brief interruptions, until her death in 1361.

María's reputation has remained largely unscathed, in spite of Pedro's many excesses. Contemporary sources generally praise her for her beauty and charm, and for attempting to soften Pedro's harshness. A notable exception is the collection of anti-Pedro ballads, *Romancero del rey don Pedro,* in which she is portrayed as cruel and vengeful. In Romance 9, for example, she is held responsible for breaking up Pedro's marriage to Blanche de Bourbon in 1353. Jealousy leads María to hire a Jewish necromancer to put a spell on a gem-encrusted belt that Blanche gave the king to wear on their wedding night. As Pedro puts it on, the belt turns into a snake; the king, horrified, flees from his bride.

Pedro's refusal to live with his French wife, and his attachment to María, served as a political excuse for his enemies and resulted in the alienation of Albur querque. At the same time, María's relatives gained ascendancy at court and replaced Alburquerque and his circle. Juan Fernández de Henestrosa, an uncle, became *camarero mayor mayordomo mayor*, and *canciller mayor.* María's brother Diego García de Padilla owed his election as Master of the Order of Calatrava to Pedro's influence. He later became the king's *mayordomo mayor.* A half-brother of María received the *encomienda mayor* of the Order of Santiago, while another relative, Juan Tenorio, became *repostero mayor.*

María, with Pedro's financial support, founded the monastery of Santa Clara at Astudillo in 1354 which, together with an earlier cession of Huelva, constituted the only significant settlement the king made on her.

María died in July 1361. She bore Pedro four children: three daughters and a son. Immediately after her death Pedro proclaimed María queen of Castile and ordered a royal burial at the monastery at Astudillo. The following year, Pedro hastily assembled a meeting of the *cortes* at Seville to declare their son Alfonso, then two years old, heir to the Castilian throne. Upon the child's death the following year, Pedro designated his first daughter Beatriz his heir. He also insisted that he and María had been legally wed and had her remains transferred and buried in the royal chapel at Seville. The Trastamáran usurpation of the Castilian throne in 1369 made Pedro's succession arrangements moot. However, Pedro's line eventually returned to the throne when his granddaughter Catherine of Lancaster, daughter of his and María's second child Constanza and John of Gaunt, duke of Lancaster, wed Enrique III of Castile.

See also **Pedro I the Cruel, King of Castile**

Further Reading

Romancero del rey don Pedro, 1368–1800. Ed. Antonio Pérez de Gómez. Valencia, 1954.

CLARA ESTOW

PAOLO DA FIRENZE
(d. September 1419)

The composer Paolo da Firenze (Tenorista, Magister Dominus Paulus Abbas de Florentia) was born sometime in the latter half of the fourteenth century and became a Camaldolese monk; he died in the order's monastery of

San Viti (Arezzo). He was a member of the final generation of Italian *Trecento* composers and is a connecting figure between Francesco Landini of the earlier generation and Andrea da Firenze of his own, both of whom he seems to have known well. Paolo is supposed to have accompanied one patron, Cardinal Angelo Acciaiuoli, to Rome c. 1404; and one of his madrigals, *Godi, Firençe* (with a text from Dante's *Commedia: Inferno*, 26), was clearly composed to celebrate Florence's conquest of Pisa in 1406.

Paolo was not only an active and admired composer but a learned and distinguished music theorist. Though the issue is hotly contested, some scholars have argued that he played a crucial role in assembling the famous Squarcialupi Codex. If so, it is ironic that, although his supposed portrait appears in the codex, the place reserved for his own musical works was left as seventeen blank folios; his surviving works are preserved in other Tuscan manuscripts.

These works comprise, beyond two scant Latin liturgical pieces, a sizable body of Italian vocal music. Attributed with relative certainty are twenty-two *ballate*, variously for two or three voices; and eleven madrigals, all for two voices. There are also two more *ballate* that survive as fragments; and thirteen other *ballate*, variously for two or three voices, which are preserved in one manuscript where the attributions of his name have been erased, leaving us uncertain as to their authenticity.

On the one hand, Paolo impresses for his conservatism. He is unusual in clinging to the madrigal, an older form bypassed by most musicians of his generation. In both, of his vocal forms, Paolo generally seems to continue the traditions of his older colleague, Landini. On the other hand, Paolo's writing clearly shows an assimilation not only of more progressive Italian styles but also of some influence from French styles of the late *ars nova*. Though his vocal lines are simple and clearly Italianate in tradition, he attempts to go beyond earlier flexibility and construct compositions with an overall logic of motivic development. His two liturgical works also show him combining Italianate vocal lines with *cantus firmus* material after the French polyphonic manner. He seems to have known something of Johannes Ciconia and Ciconia's work. Paolo belongs to a trend that envisioned a fusion of French and Italian elements at the dawn of the *Quattrocento*.

See also **Ciconia, Johannes; Landini, Francesco**

Further Reading

Becherini, Bianca. "Antonio Squarcialupi e il codice Mediceo Palatino 87." In *L'Ars nova italiana del Trecento: Primo convegno internazionale 23–26 luglio 1959,* ed. Bianca Becherini. Certaldo: Centro di Srudi sull'Ars Nova Italiana del Trecento, 1962, pp. 140–180.

Corsi, Giuseppe. *Poesie musicali del Trecento.* Bologna: Commissione per i Testi di Lingua, 1970.

Fischer, Kurt von. *Studien zur italienischen Musik des Trecento und frühen Quattrocento.* Bern: P. Haupt, 1956.

——. "Paolo da Firenze und der Sqnarcialupi-Kodex (I-Fl 87)." *Quadrivium,* 9, 1968, pp. 5–29.

Fischer, Kurt von, and F. Alberto Gallo, eds. *Italian Sacred Music.* Polyphonic Music of the Fourteenth Century, 12. Monaco: Éditions de L'Oiseau-Lyre, 1976.

Königsglow, Annamarie von. *Die italienischen Madrigalisten des Trecento.* Würzburg: Triltsch, 1940.

Li Gotti, Ettore, and Nino Pirrotta. "Paolo Tenorista fiorentino, extra moenia." In *Estudios dedicados a Mendénez Piáal,* Vol. 3. Madrid, 1952, pp. 577–606.

Marrocco, William Thomas, ed. *Italian Secular Music.* Polyphonic Music of the Fourteenth Century, 9. Monaco: Éditions de L'Oiseau-Lyre, 1975.

Pirrotta, Nino. "Paolo da Firenze in un nuovo frammento dell'Ars Nova." *Musica Disciplina,* 10, 1956, pp. 61–66.

——. ed. *Paolo Tenorista in a New Fragment of the Italian Ars Nova.* Palm Springs, Calif.: Gottlieb, 1961.

Pirrotta, Nino, and Ursula Günther, eds. *The Music of Fourteenth-Century Italy,* Vol. 6. Corpus Mensurabilis Musicae, 8(6). Rome: American Institute of Musicology, n.d.

Seay, Albert, "Paolo da Firenze: A Trecento Theorist." In *L'Ars nova italiana del Trecento: Primo convegno internazionale 23–26 luglio 1959,* ed. Bianca Becherini. Certaldo: Centro di Studi sull'Ars Nova Italiana del Trecento, 1962, pp. 118–140.

Wolf, Johannes. "Florenz in der Musikgeschichte des 14. Jahrhunderts." *Sammelbände der Internationalen Musikgesellschaft,* 3, 1901–1902, 599–646. (Leipzig.)

JOHN W. BARKER

PASCHAL II, POPE (d. 1118, r. 13 August 1099–21 January 1118)

Pope Paschal II (Rainerius) was born of a noble family at Bieda, south of Faenza in central Italy; his parents were Crescentius and Alfatia. While still a young boy, he was put into a Benedictine monastery. A general belief that he entered the monastery at Cluny was dismissed by Odericus, who confirmed that the monastery was Vallombrosa, between Florence and Arezzo. Rainerius was highly esteemed by his superiors and at age twenty was sent to Rome, where he gained the trust and favor of Pope Gregory VII, who made him cardinal priest of San Clemente. Under Urban II, Rainerius served as legate to Spain. He later became abbot of San Lorenzo Fuori le Mura. His intellectual and spiritual qualities made him an excellent candidate for the papacy and helped secure his election to succeed Pope Urban II. He was highly educated, a promoter of learning and culture; he was also pious, merciful, and forgiving. It was reported that during the conclave, when he realized that the consensus was turning toward him, he attempted to avoid being elected by fleeing, deeming himself unworthy of such an important position.

His pontificate as Paschal II was to prove very difficult because of the struggle between church and the state over the right of investiture for major church offices, but it also saw the initial signs of emancipation of the church from the state, which Gregory VII had worked so hard to achieve. Throughout his reign, Paschal had to fight on many fronts: against the antipopes, the German kings, and the Roman nobles. Paschal also strenuously fostered the crusade movement.

During Paschal's reign, settlements were made between Saint Anselm and Henry I of England and with Philip I of France; but there was a constant struggle with the German king Henry IV, who persistently encouraged and supported the elections of antipopes, in order to undermine the authority of the legitimately elected pope. There was a whole succession of antipopes. At the death of the antipope Guibert of Ravenna (Clement III) in 1100, Theoderic became antipope after a mock election in Saint Peter's (1101–1102); then came the antipopes Albert (1102) and Sylvester IV (1105–1111). Henry IV was excommunicated by Paschal in 1302 but restored himself to the pope's favor by promising to lead a crusade, although he never fulfilled this promise. In 1104, Henry IV's young son, Henry V, spurred on by disappointed princes, rebelled against his father. Weary of the constant struggle with the king, Paschal made an agreement with his rebellious son. The elder Henry resigned his power at Ingelheim on 31 December 1105, and his son was solemnly crowned emperor at Mainz on 1 February 1106. While the dethroned monarch was getting ready to fight back, he fell ill and died in August 1106.

The struggle between papacy and empire found no resolution with Henry V. From the beginning of his reign, the younger Henry proved just as determined as his father not to give up the right of investiture. Paschal II and Henry V met at Sutri in 1110. Initially, Henry showed willingness to renounce the right to investiture, while the pope committed himself to giving back all lands and rights received from the German crown by the church. However, these conditions were rejected by the German bishops, who considered that they were being deprived of all temporal power. Henry V fled Rome and took the pope with him as a prisoner, until Paschal conceded the right of investiture to the king. Despite the strong opposition of the Roman curia, Paschal crowned Henry V emperor in Saint Peter's on 13 April 1111, as part of their agreement. In September 1112, the emperor was excommunicated by the French bishops because of his capture of the pope and his extortion of the concession regarding investiture. Paschal subsequently confirmed the emperor's excommunication.

While struggling to achieve peace with the empire, Paschal had to fend off revolts in Rome itself. The Corsi family supported the third antipope, and Paschal retaliated by destroying their stronghold on the Capitoline hill.

Soon after his election to the papacy, Paschal, following the lead of his predecessors, congratulated the crusaders for their successes in Palestine and then urged bishops and soldiers to hasten to their help.

Although the relationship between papacy and empire was exceedingly tumultuous during his reign, Paschal's diplomatic accomplishments were instrumental in bringing a conclusion to the investiture controversy; his pontificate opened the way to the concordat that Pope Calixtus II concluded at Worms in 1122.

See also **Gregory VII, Pope; Henry I; Henry IV, Emperor; Urban II, Pope**

Further Reading

Cantarella, Glauco Maria. *Pasquale II e il suo tempo.* Naples: Liguori, 1997. *Enciclopedia Cattolica.* Florence: Sansoni, 1950.

Mann, Horace K. *The Lives of the Popes in the Middle Ages.* London: Kegan Paul, Trench, Trubner; Saint Louis, Mo.: Herder, 1925.

Morrison, Karl F. *Tradition and Authority in the Western Church, 300–1140.* Princeton, N.J.: Princeton University Press, 1969.

The New Catholic Encyclopedia, 2nd ed. Detroit, Mich.: Thomson-Gale, 2003.

Strayer, Joseph R., ed. *Dictionary of the Middle Ages.* New York: Scribner, 1983.

ALESSANDRO VETTORI

PAUL THE DEACON
(c. 720–c. 799)

Paul the Deacon (Paulus Diaconis) was the son of Warnefrid and was probably born at Cividale in Friuli. Paul was educated by the grammarian Flavianus, joined the royal court at Pavia, and became tutor to Adelperga, a daughter of the last independent Lombard king, Desiderius (r. 756–774). When Adelperga's husband, Arichis, was made duke of Benevento in 758, Paul became a part of the literary circle that developed at Benevento. There, in 763, Paul wrote his first poetic work (dedicated to Adelperga), followed by a prose continuation (also dedicated to Adelperga) of Eutropius's *Historia Romanum.*

After Charlemagne's defeat of the Lombards and his assumption of the Lombard crown in 774, Paul retired to the Benedictine monastery at Monte Cassino, where he remained until 783. He then left to seek the court of Charlemagne, ostensibly to plead on behalf of a brother, Arichis, who had been taken prisoner after participating in an unsuccessful revolt in northern Italy in 776. Paul remained at Charlemagne's court for two or three years before returning to Monte Cassino, where he continued to live and write until his death.

Paul is an important figure both in Italian letters and in the early Carolingian renaissance. He wrote in verse and in prose on secular and religious subjects. While he was at Aachen, in addition to a number of literary efforts that were primarily liturgical and homiletic, he composed in honor of the Carolingians a *History of the Bishops of Metz* (*Historia episcoporum Metensium*); after returning to Monte Cassino he produced a number of other works including his last and most important, *History of the Lombards* (*Historia Langobardorum*). This last work, which was never finished, covers the story of the Lombards from their semilegendary beginnings through the reign of King Liutprand (712–744). Paul's history is a typical eighth-century product, relying heavily on the materials available to him: Pliny; Isidore; Gregory of Tours; a work on the Lombards (now lost) by Secundus of Nun from Trent, who was a member of the court circle of King Agilulf (r. 590–616); Bede; and several much shorter and less reliable Lombard chronicles—an interesting commentary on the literary materials available at Monte Cassino in the late eighth century.

See also **Charlemagne; Gregory of Tours; Isidore of Seville, Saint; Wyclif, John**

Further Reading

Belting, Hans. "Studien zum beneventanischen Hof im 8. Jahrhundert." *Dumbarton Oaks Papers,* 16, 1962.

Bethmann, L., and G. Waitz, eds. *Pauli Historia Langobardorum.* Monumenta Germaniae Historica, Scriptores Rerum Langobardicarum et Italicarum, Saec. VI–IX. Hannover: Hahn, 1878.

Goffart, Walter. *Narrators of Barbarian History: Jordanes, Gregory of Tours, Bede, and Paul the Deacon.* Princeton, N.J.: Princeton University Press, 1988.

Paul the Deacon. *History of the Lombards,* trans. William Dudley Foulke. Philadelphia: University of Pennsylvania Press, 1974.

KATHERINE FISCHER DREW

PECOCK, REGINALD
(early 1390s-ca. 1460)

Theologian, religious educator, and bishop tried for and convicted of heresy. Pecock was a fellow of Oriel College, Oxford (ca. 1414–24); rector of St. Michael's, Gloucester (1424–31); rector of St. Michael Royal (also called St. Michael in Riola) and master of Whittington College (1431–44); bishop of St. Asaph (1444–50); and bishop of Chichester (1450–58). He was unusual in that he tried to bring the Lollards out of error by means of logical persuasion in vernacular treatises, especially in his *Repressor of Over Much Blaming of the Clergy.* Ironically the legal ground for his trial may have been an ecclesiastical statute originally designed to suppress Lollardy, not only because he wrote in English but also because he stressed the authority of reason, and particu-

larly of syllogistic logic, over that of the church doctors, of the scriptures, and sometimes of the church itself.

Pecock's position on these issues was not as extreme as his accusers asserted, but enough evidence was found in his works (many of which, he pointed out, had circulated without his approval) to convict him of heresy in 1457. Upon conviction he was offered the choice of recanting or being burned at the stake. He publicly abjured and handed over fourteen of his books, which were consigned to flames. Although he was reinstated in his bishopric for one more year, his enemies were soon able to remove him from office and have him placed under restrictive house arrest at Thorney Abbey in 1459. Not long after, perhaps within a year or so, he died there.

Pecock wrote or planned to write some 30 to 50 books in Latin and English, but only a few have survived. We know of at least some of those that perished by their mention in the surviving works, which in probable chronological order are these: *The Rule of Christian Religion* (ca. 1443); *The Donet* (ca. 1443–49); *The Poor Men's Mirror* (an extract of part 1 *of The Donet*); the "Abbreviatio Reginaldi Pecok" (ca. 1447); *The Folewer to the Donet* (ca. 1453–54); *The Repressor of Over Much Blaming of the Clergy* (written ca. 1449, published ca. 1455); and *The Book of Faith* (ca. 1456).

Pecock's extant English treatises are notable for their prose style, which is strongly shaped by the attempt to render theological and philosophical concepts in a relatively nonlatinate English, leading to frequent neologisms (e.g., *un-away-fallable; folewer* for "sequel"; *eendal* and *meenal for* "pertaining to ends" and "pertaining to means"). His language is often abstract and syntactically complex, especially in his expositions of logical arguments. He thoroughly reorganized the standard religious instructional topics (vices and virtues, sacraments, articles of faith, etc.) into a nontraditional arrangement of 31 virtues. Not surprisingly, given the destruction of many of his books and the dense, complex style of those few that survived, Pecock's works had little influence on later writers. Nonetheless, they remain worthy of study for what they reveal about the capacities of late ME prose as a medium for philosophical discourse and the degree to which 15th-century English religious instruction could—and could not—diverge from institutionally approved form and content.

Further Reading

Primary Sources

Babington, Churchill, ed. *The Repressor of Over Much Blaming of the Clergy.* 2 vols. Rolls Series. London: Longman, Green, Longman, & Roberts, 1860.

Greet, William Cabell, ed. *The Reule of Crysten Religioun.* EETS o.s. 171. London: Humphrey Milford, 1927.

Hitchcock, Elsie Vaughan, ed. *The Donet* and *The Folewer to the Donet.* EETS o.s. 156, 164. London: Humphrey Milford, 1921–24.

Morison, John L., ed. *The Book of Faith*. Glasgow: Maclehose, 1909.

Secondary Sources

New *CBEL* 1:665–66, 805.

Brockwell, Charles W., Jr. "Answering the 'Known Men': Bishop Reginald Pecock and Mr. Richard Hooker." *Church History* 49 (1980): 133–46.

Patrouch, Joseph E, Jr. *Reginald Pecock*. New York: Twayne, 1970.

LARA RUFFOLO

PEDRO ALFONSO, OR PETRUS ALFONSI

Moisés Sefardí, a noted Jew from Huesca, adopted the name Pedro Alfonso when he was baptized on 29 June 1106, with King Alfonso I el Batallador serving as godfather. Pedro Alfonso probably left the Iberian Peninsula soon after his baptism; a few years later he was located in England as a *magister* of liberal arts, where he likely contributed to the diffusion of Arabic science, especially astronomy and calculus, around the monastery of Malvern. Whether he was the physician to both Alfonso I and Henry I of England, as is often claimed, is not certain.

The preserved literary production of Pedro Alfonso is in Latin, and can be separated into three fields of interest: apologetic, scientific, and didactic literature. As a response to the scandal caused by his conversion, he wrote *Diálogos contra los judíos,* in which two characters, Pedro and Moisés, represent the author before and after his baptism. Throughout the work's twelve chapters, Pedro turns to a wide variety of medical, cabbalistic, and theological arguments to show Moisés the error of his ways. At the latter's insistence, in the fifth chapter Pedro traces a broad critical panorama of Islam. If the *Diálogos* enjoyed especially wide distribution, as the more than seventy preserved manuscripts dispersed throughout European libraries prove, the repercussions of this chapter were even greater.

Very few of Pedro Alfonso's scientific works are preserved, and only some incomplete *Tablas astronómicas* can be attributed to him with surety. These tablas are preceded by a curious preliminary text titled "Carta a los estudiosos franceses", which seems to have been motivated by a stay in France, and which becomes an important document with regard to the author's position on the cultural renaissance of the twelfth century. In the letter, Pedro Alfonso criticizes European intellectuals for their bookish culture, far removed from the world of scientific practice. He also addresses the traditional division of the liberal arts, positioning himself among those partial to the quadrivium, which includes the study of medicine; in the trivium only the study of dialectics is saved from the author's condemnation, but is still only regarded as a supplementary subject.

Pedro Alfonso's name has become unquestionably most associated with the *Disciplina clericalis,* a combination of exempla (thirty-four total), comparisons, proverbs, and so on—all focusing on the indoctrination of students as the title indicates. For the subject's organization, the author likely found inspiration in the books of the Bible, Hebrew religious texts, and mixed genres of oriental origin. The dialogue between anonymous characters (father-son, teacher-disciple) creates a frame that reaches its maximum development between examples 9 and 17. The subject matter—knowledge of self and of neighbor, but always remembering the fear of God—corresponds to other similar works of oriental literature. The most popular stories, though, deal with misogynistic themes, and are closer to the *fabliaux* in their narrative scheme. Medieval preachers turned to the *Disciplina clericalis* frequently, explaining its wide diffusion and its importance in the origins of the novel. Because it was written in Latin, the *Disciplina clericalis* became the first pathway through which oriental narrative began to circulate in the West.

Further Reading

Alfonso, Pedro. *Disciplina clericalis.* Intr. M. J. Lacarra, tran. E. Ducay. Zaragoza, 1980.

Reinhardt, K., and H. Santiago-Otero, *Biblioteca bíblica ibérica medieval* Madrid, 1986, 250–58.

MARÍA JESÚS LACARRA

PEDRO I THE CRUEL, KING OF CASTILE (1334–1369)

Born 30 August 1334 in Burgos, Pedro was the only legitimate child and heir of Alfonso XI of Castile (1312–1350). His mother was María daughter of King Afonso IV of Portugal. One of the most controversial kings of the Castilian Middle Ages, he is the only one who came to be known by the sobriquet of "the Cruel" for the many acts of violence associated with the last stages of his rule. Aside from the personal excesses that inspired this reputation, Pedro's reign (1350–1369) is distinctive for a number of other reasons.

His subjects experienced the full economic and demographic effects of the first wave of the Black Death that hit Castile from 1348 to 1350. He led an aggressive war of expansion against Aragón that lasted, intermittently, from 1357 until the end of the reign. His policies and alliances contributed to the involvement of international troops in the peninsular conflict, making Spain, from 1366 to 1369, the main theater for the larger military conflict known as the Hundred Years' War. His treatment of the aristocracy and his poor relations with the Castilian Church and the Avignon papacy alienated a substantial portion of his most important subjects, causing many to side with his chief rival, his half-brother Enrique de Trastámara, during the Castilian civil war of 1366–1369. The reign ended violently with Pedro's death and the usurpation of the throne by Enrique.

Coming to the throne 28 March 1350 shortly before his sixteenth birthday, Pedro spent the first two years under the influence of Juan Alfonso de Alburquerque, a Portuguese nobleman who had been in the service of Queen María, and had become Pedro's first minister. Under the auspices of Alburquerque, Pedro convened the Cortes of Valladolid in 1351, the only such meeting for which we have any detailed records for the entire reign. Through a series of measures redacted during these proceedings, Pedro attempted to remedy some of the economic consequences of the plague such as the abandonment of arable lands, and the steep rise in the cost of living. At the same time, the *cuadernos de cortes* (records of the courts) reveal Pedro's interest in a healthy royal treasury and an effective system of tax-collection. This concern with sound finances remained a constant feature of his reign, and resulted in the unpopular appointment of Samuel Halevi, a Jew, as his chief treasurer and the extensive use of Jews as tax-farmers. These measures, for which Pedro was severely criticized, served as evidence to his detractors of the king's presumed philojudaism, a quality almost as objectionable as his cruelty.

From the early days of his reign, Pedro also had to contend with an endemic feature of Castilian medieval politics, a restless and rebellious aristocracy. In his particular case, the situation was aggravated by the existence of a rival group of wealthy and influential individuals composed of the bastard children of Alfonso XI and his mistress Leonor de Guzmán, their allies, and retainers who challenged Pedro's authority almost from the beginning of the reign. Pedro reacted to these challenges in an increasingly suspicious and retaliatory manner.

In 1353 Pedro married the French princess Blanche de Bourbon and abandoned her two days after the wedding. It is likely that Blanche's sponsor, the French crown, was not able to fulfill the financial obligations of the marriage contract, and that Pedro left her for that reason. The more popular yet unverifiable reason given to explain the king's actions states that he abandoned Blanche because he could not bear to be away from the woman he loved, María de Padilla, whom he had met in 1352.

Whatever his motives, Pedro's refusal to cohabit with Blanche served to alienate his mother and Alburquerque, the principal architects of the marriage contract with the French, and gave his half-brothers a pretext for rebellion. As the minister and the bastards became allies, they were joined by other prominent Castilians displeased with the king's behavior. Outnumbered, Pedro gave himself up to the rebels at Toro only to escape after a month to begin a slow but successful campaign against them. With the capitulation of Toledo in 1355 and Toro in 1356, the main centers of antiroyal activity, Pedro succeeded in defeating the first serious challenge to his authority.

Shortly after this victory, Pedro went to war against Aragón, seeking redress over several territorial and dynastic grievances. Pedro IV was soon joined by Enrique de Trastámara, who had escaped from Castile before Pedro's victory at Toro, and other Castilians who had fled fearing the king's justice while Pedro counted on the support of Pedro's hated half-brother Ferrán. Pedro experienced several successes at Tarazona (1357); Guardamar (1359); Calatayud (1362); Teruel; Segorbe and Murviedo (1363); Alicante, Elche, Denia (1363), and Orihuela (1365); but he was never able to win a decisive victory. Several truces and peace efforts mediated by papal legates did not succeed in bringing a lasting peace between the two kingdoms.

Meanwhile, from the conspiracy at Toro onward Pedro had turned increasingly against those he suspected of treason. He eliminated many of his former allies; several of his half-brothers, among them Fadrique; and his aunt Leonor and her son Juan, and he was believed responsible for the death of his wife Blanche in 1361.

Pedro's policies, Enrique de Trastámara's ambitions, Pedro's predicament, and even the politics of Navarre all contributed to the participation of the French in peninsular affairs, beginning in 1360. The French crown agreed to sponsor Enrique's ambitions by commissioning Bertrand du Guesclin and an army of mercenaries to fight in Castile. When they entered the kingdom in 1366, Pedro was forced to flee in search of outside help, which he finally secured from Edward the Black Prince in Bordeaux. The ensuing battle at Nájera on 13 April 1367 was a resounding, albeit shortlived, victory for Pedro. His alliance with the English collapsed when the Castilian would not meet the terms of their agreement and, as the Black Prince's troops withdrew from the peninsula, Enrique and Guesclin returned in 1368 and received the support of several important regions.

Pedro determined to meet his enemy in the vicinity of Toledo. At the Battle of Montiel on 14 March 1369 Enrique and the French soundly defeated Pedro's scattered army. Pedro, who had fled to a nearby fortress, tried to buy his freedom from Guesclin. Some days later, believing that the French captain had accepted his terms, Pedro went to Guesclin's tent where, within a few minutes, Enrique arrived. He killed Pedro with a dagger, after a short struggle on 23 March 1369. Through this fratricide Enrique became uncontested king of Castile, a title he began to use when he first entered the kingdom alongside the French in 1366.

In addition to his marriage to Blanche de Bourbon, Pedro is said to have married María de Padilla—at least he claimed this following her death in 1361 in order to declare their four children (three daughters and a son, the youngest) legitimate heirs to the throne. Shortly after his marriage to Blanche, he had also wed Juana de Castro, but this marriage was just as ephemeral as his first and left no children. Eventually Pedro's line returned to the Castilian throne when his granddaughter, Catherine of Lancaster, daughter of John of Gaunt and Pedro and María's second daughter Constanza, married the future Enrique III of Castile.

See also **Padilla, María de**

Further Reading

Díaz Martín, L. V. *Itinerario de Pedro I de Castilla.* Valladolid, 1975.

López de Ayala, P. *Crónica del rey don Pedro.* Biblioteca de Autores Españoles, vol. 66. Madrid, 1953.

Sitges, J. B. *Las mujeres del rey Don Pedro I de Castilla.* Madrid, 1910.

CLARA ESTOW

PEDRO III, KING OF ARAGÓN
(1240–1285)

Pedro III the Great, Pere III of Aragón, Pere II of Catalonia, Pere I of Valencia, and Pere I of Sicily, "was the troubadour-warrior ruler of the realms of Aragón (1276–1285) and liberator-conqueror of Sicily. He was born at Valencia, two years after that Islamic city fell to his father Jaime the Conqueror, of Jaime's second wife Violante of Hungary. Jaime named him heir to Catalonia in 1253, procurator or vice-regent there at seventeen in 1257, and—at the death of Jaime's son Alfonso by his first wife in 1260—procurator of the Catalonia, Aragón, and Valencia realms. (Pedro's brother Jaime became procurator of the Balearics, Roussillon, and Cerdanya.) In 1262 Pedro married Constance, the daughter and heiress of Manfred, the Hohenstaufen ruler of Sicily-Naples. Besides four sons and two daughters by his mistresses María and Agnés Zapata, he had four sons (Including his successors Alfonso II and Jaime II, and Frederico III of Sicily), and two daughters (Queen Vio lante of Naples and Isabel Queen of Portugal).

Although his formal reign lasted only nine years versus his famous father's sixty-three, the Infante Pedro enjoyed a fifteen-year public career as procuratorial co-ruler and soldier before his coronation. He restored feudal order as a teenager, plunged into Mediterranean Ghibelline politics during negotiations for his marriage, championed Occitan refugees after such troubles as the 1263 Marseilles revolt, captained the first phase of the Murcian Crusade in 1265–1266, replaced his father at home during Jaime's abortive Holy Land Crusade in 1269 (and intervened in the Urgell wars of 1268), and prepared an invasion army to seize Toulouse in 1271. Relations with his father deteriorated in 1272, with Pedro stripped of all offices and revenues; reconciliation came the following year. When the northern Catalan nobles revolted, Pedro captured and drowned their leader, his bastard brother Ferran Sanxis. During a diplomatic visit to Paris, he met Philippe the Bold. His greatest test came in 1275–1277, when the Mudéjars of Valencia with Maghribian support revolted and nearly recovered their land. Pedro had one thousand horsemen and five thousand foot soldiers at first, but soon had to assume the entire responsibility when his father died on the field (27 July 1276). Burying Jaime provisionally at Valencia and deferring his coronation at Zaragoza to 17 November, Pedro grimly set about conquering much of Valencia "a second time," as the contemporary memoirist Ramón Muntaner puts it. Meanwhile his brother Jaume II of Mallorca received the Balearics, Cerdanya, Montpellier, and Roussillon.

With the Mudéjar headquarters at Montesa castle fallen (September 1277), Pedro began a vigorous domestic and international program. He demanded tribute from Tunis, harrying it through his admiral Conrad Llanca, pressured Jaime II of Mallorca into accepting vassalage, and moved strongly against the still-rebellious northern barons, ending their six-year war by his siege of Balaguer (1281) and winning their support by his clemency. By holding as "guest hostages" the Infantes de la Cerda, he dominated the Castilian succession crisis. His negotiations with Philippe the Bold at Toulouse in 1281, and his treaties of Campillo and Ágreda with Alfonso X and the Infante Sancho of Castile that year, stabilized his peninsular situation. He established understandings with Byzantium, England, Genoa, Granada, Portugal, and the papacy, and was finally ready for his life's coup: to foil the Angevin power that had absorbed Occitania and taken over Sicily-Naples, and to assume the Hohenstaufens' Sicilian kingdom and Ghibelline leadership in the western Mediterranean.

Massing his naval and military strength, he simulated a crusade against Tunis, actually taking Collo there; the pope refused crusade title or aid. Previously in contact with the Sicilians, Pedro now supported the Sicilian Vespers revolt of 30 March 1282. He moved eight hundred knights and fifteen thousand foot soldiers by sea to Trapani, receiving the crown of Sicily-Naples at Palermo and starting a twenty-year war. A succession of naval victories by his admirals, especially Roger de Llúria, established the Catalans as the dominant maritime power of the western Mediterranean after Genoa.

Besides Sicily and much of the Italian mainland, Pedro also took Malta and Tunisian Djerba island.

Meanwhile Pope Martin IV, feudal lord of Sicily and proponent of its Angevin king Charles of Anjou, excommunicated Pedro in November 1282, deposed him in March 1283, and transferred all his realms to the son of Philippe the Bold of France, Charles of Valois, in February 1284. The Catalans supported their king, but the Aragónese had been ill-disposed toward the Sicilian adventure from the start. In that long and bloody war, one episode stands out—the Challenge (*desafiament*) of Bordeaux. Anjou offered to settle the war by personal combat with Pedro, but instead arranged a trap for his arrival at English Bordeaux; Pedro still appeared, met the challenge, and escaped, to the edification of Europe's chivalric classes (1283). More formidably, a papal crusade to set Valois during Pedro's reign saw an army of 118,000 foot and 7,000 horse under Philippe the Bold sweep into Catalonia. Pedro delayed this greatest army since ancient Rome at Girona until Llúia's fleet from Sicily could arrive to destroy the French naval flank and logistics, ending the invasion (September 1285). Pedro suppressed a plebeian revolt in Barcelona under Berenguer Oller that same year, negotiated a major commercial treaty with Tunis, and mounted a punitive amphibious expedition against his traitorous brother on Mallorca, but died on the road to join the fleet.

The contemporary memoirist Bernat Desclot calls Pedro "a second Alexander" for his generalship. Dante lauds him as "the heavy-sinewed one [who] bore in his life the seal of every merit"; and he appears both in Boccaccio's *Decameron* and Shakespeare's *Much Ado about Nothing*. Pedro was a troubadour (two of his poems survive) and their patron. He presided over a constitutional revolution (Aragón's Privilege of Union, Catalonia's *Recognoverunt proceres* annual parliament) in 1283–1284. He stabilized coinage with his silver croat, and maritime law with his restructured *Llibre del Consolat* (1283). He protected Jews and gave them important posts in his administration. As a politician and diplomat he is thought superior to his great father, and he presided over a commercial, literary, and architectural flowering in Catalonia.

See also **Jaime II; Philip III the Bold**

Further Reading

Soldevila, F. *Pere el Gran.* 2 parts in 4 vols. Institut d'Estudis Catalans, Memòries de la Secció Històrico-arqueològica. Vols. 11, 13, 16, 22. Barcelona, 1950–1962.

———. *Vida de Pere el Gran i d'Alfons el Liberal.* Barcelona, 1963. XI Congres de Història de la Corona d'Aragó. 3 vols. Palermo, 1983–84.

ROBERT I. BURNS, S. J.

PEGOLOTTI, FRANCESCO DI BALDUCCIO (born c. 1280s)

Francesco di Balduccio Pegolotti was a Florentine factor for the great Bardi banking house in the first half of the fourteenth century, until its failure in 1347. His name appears in 1310 in the firm's payroll for the branch in Florence, at a rate which suggests that he already had considerable experience. His work was rewarded with promotions to positions of greater importance. In 1315, he negotiated trade rights for Florentines in Antwerp. From 1318 to 1321, as director of the firm's English office, he had duties that included financial transactions to help finance the English king, private business, and transferral of the tithes collected in England to the papal curia. Pegolotti next moved to Cyprus, where he remained until 1329; again, his job involved diplomacy, handling papal monies, and handling monies for individual merchants. He returned to Florence in order to hold civic office but then moved back to the east by 1335. In 1340, he returned again to Florence, for the last time. The last known mention of him is in 1347, when he was one of the civic officials overseeing the liquidation of the assets of the bankrupt Bardi firm.

Pegolotti is best known not for his service to the Bardi but for the compilation of his observations on trade now known as *La practica della mercatura.* The oldest known manuscript, from 1472, is a copy made by Filippo di Niccolaio Frescobaldi in the Riccardian Library in Florence. The manuscript has evident inaccuracies, which can be attributed to the copyist; these include misreadings that arose when the copyist was trying to expand the original abbreviations, and chapters that are out of place. Internal evidence, such as the mention of current kings, helps to show that the material in the *Practica* was collected throughout Pegolotti's career with the Bardi, and also that it was not written down all at one time.

The *Practica* is one of a "genre" of documents called merchant manuals. It is by far the best-known because historians have used Pegolotti's discussion of the route to Cathay as proof that Europeans had knowledge of and easy access to the Silk Road. The data come from Pegolotti's experience and from documents he collected that had something to do with his work—such as a list of brokerage fees charged in Pisa, quoted from the *Breve dell' Ordine del Mare* of 1323. The section on Cathay is almost certainly based on information Pegolotti collected rather than on personal experience. The manual contains information on conversions for weights, measures, and currencies between various places, as well as discussions of other topics such as the steps involved in producing the most important commodities of a particular region and the expenses involved in producing coins. The *Practica* is among the earliest known merchant manuals, but it is possible that Pegolotti borrowed some of his material from still earlier manuals, just as later manuals would borrow from his. This type of book probably functioned as an exemplar to teach apprentices how international trade worked, not as a reference for absolute values or information.

Further Reading

Borlandi, Antonia, ed. *Il manuale di mercatura di Saminiato de' Ricci.* Genoa: Di Stefano, 1963.

Borlandi, Franco, ed. *El libro di mercatantie et usanze de' paesi.* Turin: S. Lattes, 1936.

Cessi, Roberto, and Antonio Orlandini, eds. *Tarifa zoè noticia dy pexi e mesure di luoghi e tere che s'adovra mercadantia per el mondo.* Venice, 1925.

Ciano, Cesare, ed. *La pratica di mercatura datiniana.* Milan: Giuffrè, 1964.

Dotson, John, trans. and ed. *Merchant Culture in Fourteenth-Century Venice: The Zibaldone da Canal.* Binghamton, N.Y.: Center for Medieval and Renaissance Studies, 1994.

Pagnini del Ventura, Giovanni Francesco. *Della decima e di varie altre gravezze imposte dal comune di Firenze: Della moneta e della mercatura de' fiorentini fino al secolo XVI,* Vol. 3, *La pratica della mercatura* (by Balducci Pegolotti); Vol. 4, *La pratica della mercatura* (by Giovanni di Antonio da Uzzano). Lisbon, 1765–1766. (Reprint, Bologna: Forni, 1967.)

Pegolotti, Francesco Balducci. *La pratica della mercatura,* ed. Allen Evans. Cambridge, Mass.: Medieval Academy of America, 1936.

Stussi, Alfredo, ed. *Zibaldone da Canal: Manoscritto mercantile del sec. XIV.* Venice: Comitato per la Pubblicazione delle Fonti Relative alla Storia di Venezia, 1967.

ELEANOR A. CONGDON

PEIRE CARDENAL
(ca. 1180–ca. 1272)

One of the most prolific troubadours and the longest-lived, Peire Cardenal composed *sirventes*, or satires, on moral and religious subjects. He left some ninety-six poems. Born in Le Puy, he was employed as a clerk by Raymond VI of Toulouse and frequented the courts of Les Baux, Rodez, Auvergne, and (according to his *vida*) of Aragon. He may have died in Montpellier.

As a satirist, Peire is distant from Marcabru but closer to Bertran de Born, whom he imitated in a number of compositions, sometimes equaling the sting of Bertran's invective, on other occasions echoing his technique of martial description the better to express his disapproval of Bertran's eagerness for combat. Peire imitated the metrical and musical form of preceding compositions in at least 80 percent of his own songs, exploring the possibilities of an increasingly strict sense of contrafacture with impressive technical inventiveness.

As a moralist, Peire praises good actions and blames the bad but laments that he is understood by no one, as though he spoke a foreign language. He tells a fable, *Una ciutatz fo,* in which rain falls on a city and drives everyone mad except one man who has been sheltered; when he goes out into the street, he sees that everyone else is crazy, but they think him mad and drive him away. Thus, worldly spirits reject the man who hears the voice of God. In a few poems, Peire criticizes the worldly love sung by other troubadours and anticipates the *dolce stil nuovo* with his claim that *fin'amors* is born in a *franc cor gentil,* "a noble, gentle heart."

During the extended period of the Albigensian Crusade (1209–29), Peire expressed vigorous anticlericalism at the expense of Dominican inquisitors and severely criticized the French army led by Simon de Montfort. He did not, however, defend the cause of the Albigensians, regarded as heretics by the church, but rather championed the political cause of the counts of Toulouse, whose lands were invaded by the crusaders. In his religious poems, he expresses an orthodox belief in Catholic doctrine.

See also **Marcabru; Simon de Montfort, Earl of Leicester**

Further Reading

Peire Cardenal. *Poésies complètes du troubadour Peire Cardenal,* ed. René Lavaud. Toulouse: Privat, 1957.

Marshall, John Henry. "Imitation of Metrical Form in Peire Cardenal." *Romance Philology* 32 (1978): 18–48.

Riquer, Martín de, ed. *Los trovadores: historia literaria y textos.* 3 vols. Barcelona: Planeta, 1975, Vol. 3, pp. 1478–518.

Wilhelm, James J. *Seven Troubadours: The Creators of Modern Verse.* University Park: Pennsylvania State University Press, 1970, pp.173–95.

WILLIAM D. PADEN

PEÑAFORT, RAMÓN DE
(c. 1180–1275)

Ramón de Peñafort was the greatest canon lawyer of his century, third master general of the Dominicans, and architect of the century's novel program for proselytizing Muslims and Jews. Born at his father's castle or seignorial residence of Peñafort at Santa Margarida del Penedes, Ramón presumably received his arts education at the cathedral of Barcelona, where he became a cleric and *scriptor* in 1204. A decade later he undertook legal studies at the University of Bologna and subsequently taught there. By 1223 he was back at Barcelona Cathedral as provost canon of its chapter. He soon left all to become a Dominican mendicant, presumably at Barcelona's Santa Caterina priory. He is thought to have assisted Cardinal Jean d'Abbeville, the papal legate, in his travels across Spain beginning in 1228 to reinforce the reforms of the Fourth Lateran Council; he was certainly at Zaragoza in 1229 to decide the annulment of the marriage between Jaime I and Leonor of Castile. In 1230 he was called to Rome as papal chaplain and confessor. Pope Gregory IX commissioned him there to construct the *Decretals,* promulgated in 1234; with Gratian's *Decretum,* this systematization of a century's laws in some two thousand sections remained the code of the church until the twentieth century. Ramón then refused the metropolitanate of Tarragona, and in 1236 returned to the Barcelona priory. Continuously involved in important canonical cases there, he was active at the parliament (*corts*) of Monzón in 1236, was delegated to lift the papal excommunication from Jaime I (whose friend and counselor he was), and became involved in the dismissal of Tortosa's bishop and the provision of Huesca's and Mallorca's bishops. The Dominican chapter general elected him head of the order in 1238. He left a lasting mark especially by his revision of their constitutions and his integration of the order's nuns before suddenly resigning in 1240.

Returning to Santa Caterina priory, he spent the next thirty-five years there on massive missionary projects and in most of the Crown of Aragón's religious crises. He was active against heresy, persuading King Jaime to allow the Inquisition; he was regularly counselor to the king; and he adjudicated important public quarrels. Ramón's main preoccupation was with the founding of language schools for intrusive missionary disputation with Muslims and Jews, and with devising a program of persuasive confrontation and handbooks of polemical argumentation. He opened an Arabic language and disputation center at Tunis in 1245 and at Murcia in 1266. He persuaded Thomas Aquinas to construct his masterwork, *Contra gentiles,* for these missions.

Through the school centers, compulsory sermons in mosques and synagogues, the public disputation of 1263 in Barcelona, censorship of rabbinic books, and the aggressive labors of Dominicans like Pau Cristià and Ramon Martí, Ramón helped turn Mediterranean Spain into a stormy laboratory for the new rationalist-confrontational missionary methods. This was part of the wider mendicant effort to convert India, China, and Islamic countries by polemical dialogue. Jeremy Cohen argues for an even more revolutionary orientation in Ramón's vision: a conviction that Talmudic Judaism was antibiblical, depriving Jews of their right by Christian teaching to practice their faith in Christian lands. Contemporary hagiographers stress instead Ramón's mission to the Muslims of Spain, and he himself reported euphorically on the successful conversion of many. The roots of these movements, and the inevitability of their ultimate failure, have been more recently discussed by authors such as Robert Burns, Jeremy Cohen, and Dominique Urvoy.

Throughout all his activity in public life, missionary disputation, or Dominican administration, Ramón remained a scholar on the cutting edge of Roman and canon law. His legal publications multiplied from the start of his career at Bologna to his last year of life in Barcelona. The writings circulated throughout Europe and had immense influence. The most important were his *Summa iuris canonici,* written at Bologna; his *Summa de casibus poenitentiae* (or *Summa de confessoribus*), written in 1222–1225 but redone in 1234–1236; his *Decretales,* written between 1230 and 1234; and the Dominican constitutions. Some sermons and letters, as well as legal responses (*dubitalia*) survive. The *Decretales* had as great an influence on national codes, like Alfonso el Sabio's *Siete Partidas,* as his confessors' handbook had on the ethical and behavioral life of Christendom. Though a Tarragona Council presented a special report and petition for his canonization in 1279, that honor came only in 1601.

See also **Gratian; Jaime (Jaume) I of Aragón-Catalonia; Martí, Ramón**

Further Reading

Burns, R. I. "Christian-Islamic Confrontation in the West: The Thirteenth-Century Drearn of Conversion." *Amer can Historical Review* 76 (1971), 1386–1434.
Rius Serra, J. *San Raimundo de Peñafort: diplomatario.* Barcelona, 1954.

ROBERT I. BURNS, S. J.

PEPIN

Frankish leaders of the Carolingian family. Among Charlemagne's ancestors, three named Pepin were especially distinguished by their political authority among the Franks. Pepin I of Landen (Pepin the Old or the Elder; d. ca. 640) founded the family of the Arnulfings or the Pippinids, later known as the Carolingians, through the arranged marriage of his daughter, Begga, to Ansegisel, the son of Arnulf of Metz (d. ca. 645). Pepin was named mayor of the palace (*major domus*) of Austrasia by the Merovingian king Clotar II of Neustria (r. 584–629), for having assisted the monarch to unite the kingdoms of Austrasia and Neustria. During his mayoralty, the office grew into the most powerful position in the Frankish territories, equaling or surpassing the royal throne in importance.

After the murder of Pepin's son and successor, Grimoald in 656, the Pippinids lost control of the Austrasian mayoralty; but in 687, Pepin II of Heristal, duke of Austrasia and Grimoald's nephew, led the Austrasian army to victory over the Neustrians and became mayor of the palace in both regions. From this post, he gradually strengthened his authority over all the Merovingian kingdoms, through his support of the church, manipulation of ecclesiastical posts, and military campaigns.

Pepin III (the Short; d. 768) and Carloman I (d. 754), grandsons of Pepin II, each inherited half the Frankish territories on the death in 741 of their father, Charles Martel, mayor in the united realm. The two brothers cooperated closely in governing their lands; in 743, they together placed another Merovingian, Childeric III, on the royal throne, empty since 737. In 747, however, Carloman felt called to a religious life and abdicated; Pepin became mayor of the entire kingdom. Having deposed Childeric, a move supported by Pope Zachary I, Pepin was acclaimed king in November 751. During a visit to Francia in 754, Pope Stephen II anointed the new monarch along with his wife and sons, Charles (later Charlemagne; 742–814) and Carloman II (d. 771). In recognition of the hope that the new monarchy would protect the Roman church, the pope used the occasion to name Pepin and his sons "patricians of the Romans."

As ruler of the Franks, Pepin III oversaw reform of the secular government and, with the aid of the Irish missionary Boniface, of the ecclesiastical organization. His efforts in the latter regard, especially, provided the foundation for the cultural and intellectual revival known as the Carolingian renaissance, under Pepin's son Charlemagne.

See also **Charlemagne; Charles Martel; Pepin III the Short**

Further Reading

Hlawitschka, Eduard. "Die Vorfahren Karls des Grossen." In *Karl der Grosse: Lebenswerk und Nachleben*, ed. W. Braunfels et al. 5 vols. Dusseldorf: Schwann, 1965, Vol. 1, pp. 51–82.

McKitterick, Rosamond. *The Frankish Kingdoms Under the Carolingians, 751–987*. London: Longman, 1983.

Miller, David Harry. "Sacral Kingship, Biblical Kingship, and the Elevation of Pepin the Short." In *Religion, Culture, and Society in the Early Middle Ages: Studies in Honor of Richard E. Sullivan*, ed. Thomas F.X. Noble and John J. Contreni. Kalamazoo: Medieval Institute, 1987.

Noble, Thomas F.X. *The Republic of St. Peter: The Birth of the Papal State, 680–825*. Philadelphia: University of Pennsylvania Press, 1984.

Riché, Pierre. *The Carolingians: A Family Who Forged Europe*, trans. Michael I. Allen. Philadelphia: University of Pennsylvania Press, 1993.

CELIA CHAZELLE

PEPIN III THE SHORT
(714–768),

Pepin III, called "the Short" by later historians, played a key role in establishing the Carolingian family as the predominant force in the west. In 741 Pepin and his brother Carloman succeeded their father, Charles Martel, as joint holders of the office of mayor of the palace, an office that had been successfully exploited by Charles Martel (in 714–741) and his father, Pepin II of Herstal (in 687–714), to the point where they exercised real power at the expense of the Merovingian kings of the Franks whom they supposedly served. From 741 to 747 Pepin III and Carloman acted jointly to withstand threats to their position, especially from the dukes of Bavaria, Aquitaine, and Alemannia who were seeking to escape Frankish overlordship. They strengthened their ties with the church by supporting the missionary and reforming efforts of the Anglo-Saxon monk Boniface, acting in Francia under papal auspices.

In 747 Carloman withdrew from his office to become a monk. Pepin assumed sole power and soon decided to assume the royal office. To legitimatize this bold act against the claims of the Merovingian dynasty, he sought and received the approval of Pope Zacharias I (r. 741–752). In 751 Pepin deposed the last Merovingian king and had himself elected king by the Frankish magnates and anointed by a bishop, an innovation in Frankish history that gave a sacramental character to the royal office.

Pepin's accession to the royal office soon led to his involvement in Italian affairs. By the mid-eighth century a crisis had developed in Italy as a result of the decline of Byzantine power. The papacy, which had established control over the territory around Rome, was challenged by the Lombards, who in 751 seized Byzantine territories around Ravenna (called the Exarchate) and threatened Rome. Pope Stephen II (r. 752–757) turned to Pepin for protection and in late 753 traveled to Francia to negotiate with him. The result was a promise by Pepin to protect the pope and his Roman subjects and to restore to the papacy territories that Stephen claimed the Lombard had illegally seized. In return, Stephen reanointed Pepin and his sons and invested them with the title *patricius Romanorum*, which implied a role as protector of the Romans. Pepin made good his promise by conducting successful military campaigns against the Lombards in 755 and 756. He forced the Lombards to surrender to the papacy considerable territories legally belonging to the Byzantine empire. This "Donation of Pepin," coupled with the territory around Rome that the papacy already controlled, formed the basis of an independent papal state stretching across the Italian peninsula from Rome to Ravenna. During the remainder of his reign Pepin honored his role as protector of the papacy and the "republic of Rome" by using diplomatic means to restrain the Lombards.

As king of the Franks, Pepin was mainly concerned with solidifying and expanding the power and prestige of the royal office. He effectively used force to increase the Franks' control over Bavaria and Aquitaine and to ward off attacks by the pagan Saxons. He took the lead in promoting reform of the church, a role that gave substance to his claim to rule as an agent of God promoting the true faith. The expanding influence of the Franks in Italy and southern Gaul led to diplomatic exchanges with the Byzantine empire and the Abbasid caliphs of the Muslim world. By the end of his reign, the first Carolingian king of the Franks had expanded the position of his people to the status of a major power.

See also **Charles Martel; Stephen II, Pope**

Further Reading

Editions and Translations

Capitularia regum Francorum, ed. Alfred Boretius and Victor Krause. Monumenta Germaniae Historica, Leges, 2(1–2). Hannover: Hansche Buchhandlung, 1883–1897, Vol. 1, pp. 24–43.

Carolingian Chronicles: Royal Frankish Annals and Nithard's Histories, trans. Bernhard Walter Scholz with Barbara Rogers. Ann Arbor: University of Michigan Press, 1970, pp. 37–47.

Codex Carolinus, ed. Wilhelm Gundlach: Monumenta Germaniae Historica, Epistolae Merowingici et Karolini, 1. Berlin: Weidemann, 1892, pp. 469–558, 649–653.

Concilia aevi karolini, ed. Albert Werminghoff. Monumenta Germaniae Historica, Concilia, 2(1–2). Hannover and Leipzig: Hahnsche Buchhandlung, 1896–1898, pp. 1–73.

The Fourth Book of the Chronicle of Fredegar; with its Continuation, trans. J. M. Wallace-Hadrill. Medieval Classics. London and New York: Nelson, 1960, pp. 96–122. (Latin text with English translation.)

Die Urkunden der Karolinger, Vol. 1, *Die Urkunden Pippins, Karlomanns und Karls des Grossen,* ed. Engelbert Mühlbacher. Monumenta Germaniae Historica, Diplomatum Karolinorum, 1. Hannover: Hahnsche Buchhandlung, 1906, pp. 1–60.

Critical Studies

Affeldt, Werner. "Untersuchungen zur Königshebung Pippins." *Frühmittelalterliche Studien,* 14, 1980, pp. 95–187.

Hahn, Heinrich. *Jahrbücher des fränkischen Reiches, 741–752.* Berlin: Duncker und Humblot, 1863.

Halphen, Louis. *Charlemagne and the Carolingian Empire,* trans. Giselle de Nie. Europe in the Middle Ages, 3. Amsterdam: North-Holland, 1977, pp. 3–39.

Kempf, Friedrich, et al. *Handbook of Church History,* Vol. 3, *The Church in the Age of Feudalism,* ed. Hubert Jedin and John Dolan, trans. Anselm Biggs. New York: Herder and Herder; London: Burns and Oates, 1969, pp. 3–25.

Noble, Thomas F. X. *The Republic of Saint Peter: The Birth of the Papal State, 680–825.* The Middle Ages. Philadelphia: University of Pennsylvania Press, 1984, pp. 1–122.

Oelsner, Ludwig. *Jahrbücher des fränkischen Reiches unter König Pippin.* Leipzig: Duncker und Humblot, 1871.

Riché, Pierre. *Les carolingiens: Une famille qui fit l'Europe.* Paris: Hachette, 1983, pp. 71–103.

RICHARD E. SULLIVAN

PÉROTIN (Pérotinus; fl. late 12th–early 13th c.)

Because he composed liturgical vocal polyphony at Notre-Dame for two, three, and four parts (each part sung by a soloist) and employed the rhythmic modes, sophisticated devices of repetition and voice exchange, unprecedented length, and important notational innovations, Pérotin was the most significant musical figure of the early 13th century. His achievements profoundly influenced the course of Western music. The music theorists Johannes de Garlandia and Anonymous 4 mention "Magister Pérotinus," but only the latter lists seven of his musical compositions and chronologically places him as "the best discantor" among other singers, composers, and notators working in Paris from the late 12th to late 13th century. Anonymous 4 credits Pérotin with the polyphony found today at the beginning of each of the three major extant Notre-Dame sources *(W1, F,* and *W2):* the Graduals *Viderunt omnes* and *Sederunt principes,* both for four voices, and adds to the list three-part polyphony for the Alleluia *Posui adiutorium* and Alleluia *Narivitas,* and three conductus, the three-part *Salvatoris hodie,* the two-part *Dum sigillum,* and the monophonic *Beam viscera.* On the basis of stylistic affinity with these works, several other works in the Notre-Dame sources have been credited to him. Anonymous 4's statement that Pérotin made many clausulae and edited, revised, or shortened Léonin's *Magnus liber organi* has led many to attribute to him one or more of the series of independent discant clausulae that survive in *W1* and *F.*

Petrus, succentor (subcantor) of the cathedral ca. 1207–38, has been proposed as the most probable identity for Anonymous 4's *"Pérotinus optimus discantor,"* partly because responsibility for the daily services at the cathedral would have fallen to the succentor rather than the cantor, whose post had become largely administrative. Petrus' dates seem to correlate with Anonymous 4's description of Léonin's *Magnus liber organi,* which he stated was in use until the time of Pérotin, while Pérotin's "book or books" were used in the cathedral of Notre-Dame in Paris up to Anonymous 4's own time, probably the 1280s. Hans Tischler and others have maintained, however, that Pérotin lived ca. 1155/60–1200/05, largely on the basis that ordinances issued in 1198 and 1199 by Odo de Sully, bishop of Paris, sanctioned performance of three- and four-part organum at Notre-Dame during Christmas Week. That Pérotin's composition of the four-part polyphony for *Viderunt omnes* and *Sederunt principes* might have elicited these decrees can only be conjectured. The dating of Pérotin's polyphony is particularly important to a history of the musical style of the period. If it dates generally before 1200, that would mean that the rhythmic modes and their notation as well as the discant clausula and consequently the early motet were well advanced at the very beginning of the 13th century.

See also **Léonin; Philip the Chancellor**

Further Reading

Pérotin. Works, ed. Ethel Thurston. New York: Kalmus, 1970.

Tischler, Hans. "Pérotinus Revisited." In *Aspects of Medieval and Renaissance Music: A Birthday Offering to Gustave Reese,* ed. Jan LaRue. New York: Norton, 1966, pp. 803–17.

Wright, Craig. *Music and Ceremony at Notre Dame of Paris, 500 –1550.* Cambridge: Cambridge University Press, 1989, pp. 288–94.

SANDRA PINEGAR

PETER COMESTOR (ca. 1000–1178)

Born in Troyes, Peter became in 1147 dean of the cathedral there. Sometime before 1159, he went to Paris, where he studied under Peter Lombard and later taught theology. He became chancellor of the cathedral of Notre-Dame between 1164 and 1168. He died in 1178 and was buried at the abbey of Saint-Victor. Although known primarily for the *Historia scholastica*, Peter wrote other works, including some 150 sermons, the *Summa de sacramentis* (based on Peter Lombard's *Sententiae*), some *quaestiones*, and commentaries on the Gospels, as well as glosses on the *Glossa ordinaria*, on the *Magna glossatura* of Peter Lombard, and perhaps on Lombard's *Sententiae*. The *Historia scholastica*, used in the schools and later in the university curriculum, was a narrative presentation of biblical history from Creation through the life of Jesus. Peter here sought to counteract what he saw as the destruction of the connected literal-historical sense of the text through the practice of a spiritual exegesis that tended to divide the text into brief "fragments" for symbolic interpretation. Peter not only drew upon traditional patristic authors for the historical sense; he also used Josephus's *Jewish Antiquities* and the commentaries on the *Octateuch* by Andrew of Saint-Victor. In a practical way, Peter continued the emphasis on reading Scripture according to the literal-historical sense that had been established at the abbey of Saint-Victor by Hugh of Saint-Victor.

See also **Andrew of Saint Victor; Hugh of Saint-Victor; Peter Lombard**

Further Reading

Peter Comestor. *Historia scholastica; Sermons.* PL 198.1045–844.

——. *Summa de sacramentis*, ed. Raymond M. Martin. In *Maître Simon et son groupe: De sacramentis*, ed. Heinrich Weisweiler. Louvain: "Spicilegium Sacrum Lovaniense," 1937, appendix.

Smalley, Beryl. *The Study of the Bible in the Middle Ages.* 3rd ed. Oxford: Blackwell, 1983.

GROVER A. ZINN

PETER LOMBARD (ca. 1100–1160)

The "Master of the *Sentences*" born and educated in Novara, Lombardy, arrived in Paris via Reims (ca. 1135) with a letter of recommendation from Bernard of Clairvaux to Abbot Gilduin of Saint-Victor. While he apparently never taught at the abbey, Peter did preach there, and he maintained close ties with Saint-Victor throughout his life.

The Lombard soon made himself a reputation as a formidable theologian. By 1142–43, he had the dubious distinction of being named by Gerhoch of Reichersberg as a dangerous innovator; in 1148, he was summoned by Pope Eugenius III to the Consistory of Reims to help judge the orthodoxy of another innovator, Gilbert of Poitiers, whose christology Peter found lacking. Teaching at Notre-Dame by 1143, he was a canon by 1145 and steadily rose in rank (subdeacon by 1147, deacon by 1150, archdeacon by 1157). In 1158, his years of service were crowned by his election as bishop of Paris; this honor was short-lived, as he died in 1160.

The earliest works of the Lombard are his commentaries on the Psalms (before 1138) and on the epistles of Paul (by 1142). Though Herbert of Bosham reports that Peter meant them for his personal edification only and that he never finished them, they were swiftly and widely circulated, often even replacing the marginal-interlinear glosses for the Psalms and epistles in the *Glossa ordinaria*. Known as the *Magna glossatura*, they became the most frequently cited works of Scripture exegesis in the Middle Ages. Peter based his two commentaries on a close reading of Anselm of Laon's glosses and Gilbert of Poitiers's biblical commentaries. He kept the *Glossa's* patristic and Carolingian base, took over Gilbert's organization scheme and hermeneutic principles, and consistently worked out doctrinal positions and current theological issues in connection with the scriptural text.

Even more central to the history of medieval theology and philosophy is the Lombard's *Quattuor libri sententiarum*, or the *Sententiae*. Sentence collections proliferated in the 12th century, as theologians strove to systematize and professionalize their field. Peter Lombard's *Sententiae* (1155–57) became an instant and enduring success throughout Europe (legislated into the theological curriculum of the University of Paris in 1215) and remained without serious competition until replaced by the *Summa* of Thomas Aquinas in the 16th century. It was second only to the Bible in importance in theological training; hundreds of theologians wrote commentaries on the *Sententiae*. The reasons for its success have recently been set forth in a effort to restore the luster to the Lombard's tired reputation. Its comprehensive coverage of topics, logical order, lack of dependence on or promotion of any elaborate philosophical system, sensitivity to the need for clarity and consistency in theological language, and readiness to address controversial issues while acknowledging contemporary consensus, all ensured the utility of the *Sententiae* to generations of theologians and philosophers. In addition, Peter's christology avoided many of the semantic pitfalls that plagued contemporary theologians; his Trinitarian views were solemnly ratified at the Fourth Lateran Council in 1215.

See also **Anselm of Laon; Aquinas, Thomas; Bernard of Clairvaux**

Further Reading

Peter Lombard. *Commentariu sin psalmos davidicos. PL* 191.55–169.
——. *Collectanea in omnes b. Pauli epistolas. PL* 191.1297–696 and *PL* 192.9–520.
——. *Sententiae in IV libris distinctae*, ed. Ignatius Brady. 3rd ed. rev. In *Spicilegium Bonaventurianum.* Grottaferrata: Editiones Collegii S. Bonaventurae ad Claras Aquas, 1971–81,Vols. 4–5.
——. *Sermons* (printed under the name of Hildebert of Lavardin). *PL* 171.339–964. [See list in J. de Ghellinck, "Pierre Lombard." In *Dictionnarie de théologie catholique.* Vol. 12 (1935), cols. 1961–62.] Bertola, Ermenegildo. "Pietro Lombardo nella storiografia filosofica medioevale." *Pier Lombardo* 4 (1960): 95–113.
Colish, Marcia L. *Peter Lombard.* Leiden: Brill, 1993.
——. "Systematic Theology and Theological Renewal in the Twelfth Century." *Journal of Medieval and Renaissance Studies* 18 (1988): 135–56.
——. "From *sacra pagina* to *theologia:* Peter Lombard as an Exegete of Romans." *Medieval Perspectives* 7 (1991): 1–19.
——. "*Psalterium Scholasticorum:* Peter Lombard and the Emergence of Scholastic Psalms Exegesis." *Speculum* 67 (1992): 531–48.
Delhaye, Philippe. *Pierre Lombard: sa vie, ses œuvres, sa morale.* Montreal: Institut d'Études Medievales, 1961.

THERESA GROSS-DIAZ

PETER OF POITIERS (d. 1205)

Master in theology at Paris from ca. 1167, successor (1169) to the chair in theology held by Peter Comestor, and chancellor of the schools of Paris from 1193. Peter of Poitiers (to be distinguished from another contemporary Peter of Poitiers, a regular canon of the abbey of Saint-Victor at Paris) was a leading figure in the Parisian schools in the last third of the 12th century. A student under Peter Lombard and a strong supporter of the Lombard's theology when it came under attack in the last decades of the 12th century, Peter of Poitiers was a determined advocate of the usefulness of dialectics in theology.

He was also influenced by the Victorine tradition, represented by Hugh and Richard of Saint-Victor, Peter Comestor, and Peter the Chanter, that emphasized both historical study and the importance of biblical allegory. Four of Peter's works reveal these influences and also Peter's distinctive contributions to theological, historical, and exegetical-homiletic studies in the schools of Paris.

Peter's *Sententiarum libri quinque* (probably before 1170) is modeled directly on the dialectical method as used by Peter Lombard in his *Quattuor libri sententiarum* and also draws upon its content. Peter's work is not, however, a commentary on the Lombard's but is his own formulation of a "compendium of theology" to instruct those who are beginning the study of Scripture. Peter's faithfulness to the Lombard's thought earned him the distinction of being included with the Lombard, Gilbert of Poitiers, and Abelard as one of the "four labyrinths of France" in Walter of Saint-Victor's antidialectical polemic.

Three of Peter's works on scriptural interpretation deserve mention. *Allegoriae super tabernaculum Moysis* explicates the four senses of scriptural interpretation (history, allegory, tropology, and anagogy) and presents a detailed allegorical interpretation of the materials, construction, associated objects, and other aspects of the Tabernacle of Moses. *Compendium historiae in genealogia Christi* is a work of historical explication in service of biblical exegesis. By means of a grand genealogical schematic, with accompanying text, extending from Adam and Eve to Jesus Christ, Peter sketched out the essentials of biblical history for beginning students. Tradition held that he was the first to draw genealogical "trees" on animal skins and hang them on classroom walls in order to instruct students. Finally, *Distinctiones super psalterium* is part of a move within the schools to make resources for biblically based preaching more accessible to students and preachers. The *Distinctiones* takes a word from a psalm and gives a set of meanings, the *distinctio*, all supported by references to other passages of Scripture. Thus, the reader had ready at hand a compendium of many symbolic interpretations of such words as "bed," "fire," or "stone." Some manuscripts present the work as a continuous prose text; others have a schematic structure, with the "key word" in the margin and a series of red lines connecting with the meanings. Such a handbook would be of great use to preachers searching for allegories, and Peter's book is similar in its intent to Peter the Chanter's *Summa Abel* and Praepositinus of Cremona's *Summa super psalterium.*

See also **Hugh of Saint-Victor; Peter Comestor; Peter Lombard**

Further Reading

Moore, Philip S. *The Works of Peter of Poitiers, Master in Theology and Chancellor of Paris (1193–1205).* Notre Dame: University of Notre Dame Press. 1936.
—— and James Corbett, eds. *Petri Pictaviensis Allegoriae super tabernaculum Moysis.* Notre Dame: University of Notre Dame Press, 1938.
—— and Mathe Dulong, eds. *Pern Pictaviensis Sententiarum libri quinque.* Notre Dame: University of Notre Dame Press, 1943, Vol. 1.

——, Joseph N. Garvin, and Marthe Dulong, eds. *Petri Pictaviensis Sententiarum libri quinque.* 2 vols. Notre Dame: University of Notre Dame Press, 1950.

GROVER A. ZINN

PETER THE CHANTER (d. 1197)

Born near Beauvais, Peter studied at Reims and by ca. 1173 was a master in theology in the schools of Paris. In 1183, he was named chanter of the cathedral of Notre-Dame in Paris. Peter was judge delegate for the pope on a number of occasions, including the divorce trial of Philip II Augustus (1196). He was elected dean of the cathedral of Reims in 1196, but he became ill and was unable to take the position. He entered the Cistercian abbey of Longpont as a monk and died there.

As a teacher in the schools, Peter exerted a remarkable influence on both students and peers. He was at the center, with Peter Comestor and Stephen Langton, of what Beryl Smalley (following Grabmann) called the "biblical moral school," a group of masters in the late 12th-century schools who followed the emphasis on biblical study developed at the abbey of Saint-Victor by Hugh, Richard, and Andrew of Saint-Victor.

While most masters of the day commented only on the Psalms and Gospels, Peter, like Stephen Langton, commented on all the books of the Old and New Testaments. Moreover, Peter was critical of those masters who devoted themselves to seeking out details of the text and its interpretation rather than focusing on the important matters of moral teaching and behavior.

In addition to his lectures on Scripture (which were taken down as *reportationes* by his students), the Chanter devoted much of his time to lecturing and disputing on moral questions; he found the 12th-century church desperately lacking when compared with gospel injunctions and Paul's teaching. Dedicated to testing present practice against the straightforward teaching of Scripture, he was, however, a realist who saw that seriously embracing scripturally based reform could lead to criticism of accepted practices in the church of his day. He raised and resolved hundreds of moral "questions," which were incorporated in his *Summa de sacramentis et animae consiliis.* The questions, with numerous exempla to illustrate situations and conclusions, were grouped according to the sacraments of the church (baptism, confirmation, extreme unction, consecration of churches, the eucharist, and penance). All systematization seems to have given way in the section on penance, for it is a vast collection of case after case for analysis and resolution. Peter's *Verbum abbreviation* is also directed toward moral concerns, this time with copious citations of passages from "authorities" (Scripture, Christian writers, classical authors) and exempla to discourage vice and promote virtue. Although Peter

was recognized as a preacher, no sermons have survived. He was tireless in his devotion to ecclesiastical duties and to the work of a master in lecturing on Scripture, posing questions for resolution through disputation, and providing in his writings the outcome, in a text, of his labors in the classroom.

See also **Peter Comestor; Stephen Langton**

Further Reading

Peter the Chanter. *Summa de sacramentis et animae consiliis*, ed. Jean-Albert Dugauquier. 3 vols. in 5. Louvain: Nauwelaerts, 1954–67.
——. *Verbum abbreviation.* PL 205.1–554. [Short version.]
Baldwin, John W. *Masters, Princes, and Merchants: The Social Views of Peter the Chanter and His Circle.* 2 vols. Princeton: Princeton University Press, 1970.
Smalley, Beryl. The *Gospels in the Schools* c. *1100–c. 1280.* London: Hambledon, 1985, pp. 101–18.
——. *The Study of the Bible in the Middle Ages.* 3rd ed. rev. Oxford: Blackwell, 1983, chap. 5.

GROVER A. ZINN

PETER THE VENERABLE (1092/94–1156)

Born into the noble Montbossier family in Auvergne, Peter was dedicated by his mother as a child oblate to the Cluniac monastery of Sauxillanges, where he was educated. He became a monk of Cluny not long before 1109. Four of his six brothers also entered ecclesiastical careers; one became archbishop of Lyon while the other three were abbots of Vézelay, La Chaise-Dieu, and Manglieu. Peter served as prior of Vézelay and of Domène before being elected abbot of Cluny in 1122. He proved to be a skillful administrator of a vast monastic organization comprising over 1,000 dependent monasteries and priories; he was also an influential ecclesiastical leader, had scholarly interests, and was a strong defender of Cluniac customs against Cistercian criticisms. His extensive correspondence with notables throughout the western church (193 extant letters) is a rich source of information about various matters, both ecclesiastical and secular, including the world of learning and spirituality. Although Peter and Bernard of Clairvaux were in opposition on matters of monastic discipline and practice, they remained friends throughout life, as their letters reveal. Peter's health was never good, and he probably suffered from malaria on several occasions and from chronic bronchitis.

Peter's election to the abbacy of Cluny came at a time when the order needed a firm hand, following the disastrous abbacy of Pons de Melgeuil and the brief four-month abbacy of Hugues II. Monastic discipline was lax; finances needed attention; the large sprawling Cluniac order needed an effective leader. Peter rose to the occasion. He began to enforce a more strict discipline, attended to finances, and traveled often to deal with problems within the order. He was moderate in demands, conservative in outlook, conciliatory in approach, and thoughtful in controversy. Peter became enmeshed in the controversy between Cistercians and Cluniacs, which was marked by heated exchanges on both sides. Peter's Letter 28, a response (if not directly, at least in effect) to Bernard of Clairvaux's *Apologia ad Guillelmum* as well as the general Cistercian attack on Cluniac laxity in discipline and departure from the *Rule of St. Benedict*, is a carefully reasoned defense of the Cluniac way of life and offers one of the best sources for understanding both the conflict and the Cluniac point of view. Peter was no idle defender of the *status quo*, however; he actively reformed and strengthened Cluniac discipline.

Peter wrote against both heresy (the Petrobrusians [*Tractatus adversos Petrobrusianos haereticos*]) and non-Christian religions (Judaism [*Adversos Judaeorum inveteratum duritiem*] and Islam [*Epistola de translatione sua; Summa totius haeresis Saracenorum*]). After a journey to Spain in 1142, he commissioned a translation of the Qur'an, the first into Latin, and other Arabic texts, so that he might better understand Islam in order to refute it with reason rather than force. In writing against Judaism, he respected the Hebrew version of Scripture and argued without special pleading from Christian Scripture, i.e. the New Testament.

In addition to his numerous journeys in France, Peter traveled to England (1130 and 1155), Spain (1142; perhaps 1124 and 1127), and Rome (1139 [Lateran Council], 1144,1145,1147,1151–52,1154). He extended the hospitality of Cluny to Peter Ab–lard after Ab–lard's condemnation at Sens in 1140. Peter the Venerable wrote to H–lo+se a sensitive letter giving a detailed account of Ab–lard's last days. In addition to the works mentioned above, his writings include sermons, liturgical texts (including an Office of the Transfiguration), hymns, and a treatise recounting holy lives (*De miraculis*). He was an exemplar of the best of the Benedictine tradition.

See also **Abélard, Peter; Bernard of Clairvaux; Héloïse**

Further Reading

Peter the Venerable. *Opera omnia. PL* 189.61–1054.
——. *The Letters of Peter the Venerable*, ed. Giles Constable. 2 vols. Cambridge: Harvard University Press, 1967.
Constable, Giles, ed. *Petrus Venerabilis, 1156–1956: Studies and Texts Commemorating the Eighth Centenary of His Death*. Rome: Herder, 1956.
Knowles, David. *The Historian and Character*. Cambridge: Cambridge University Press, 1963, pp. 50–75.

GROVER A. ZINN

PETRARCA, FRANCESCO
(20 July 1304–19 July 1374)

It is a critical commonplace to refer to Dante Alighieri as the "last medieval man" and to Petrarch (Francesco Petrarca) as the "first modern man," but this tends to obscure the many distinctly "medieval" aspects of Petrarch's works. To be sure, Petrarch does anticipate certain characteristics that are central to our (modern) understanding of the changeover in attitudes in the passage from the Middle Ages to the Renaissance: the emphasis on the individual and on secular matters; the minute investigation of the human psyche; the imitation of classical literary forms, style, and language; the understanding of discrete periods in history; and the interest in travel undertaken to see and experience the world. While all these characteristics suggest Petrarch's desire to escape the narrow frame of the religiously and morally proper medieval world, he repeatedly and simultaneously gives evidence of his longing to embrace that same world and its precepts. This constant state of tension is what defines Petarch's so-called modern sensitivity and allows us, his readers, to identify with him and his seemingly contradictory aspirations; and this sentiment is aptly presented, over and over, in the *Canzoniere*. We find it in the poems themselves, as in the final verses of *canzone 264 (I' vo pensando)*: *ché co la morte a latol cerco del viver mio novo consiglio, le veggio 'l meglio et al peggior m'appiglio* (verses 136–136), of which the final verse is a direct and sympathetic translation from Ovid (*Metamorphoses*, 7.20–21). Or we note how Petrarch has ordered the poetic universe of the *Canzoniere* by juxtaposing poems that praise, alternately, his love of earthly things and his profound repentance for such an attitude, as, for example, in the positioning of the two sonnets *Benedetto sia 'l giorno, e' l mese, e l'anno* (61) and *Padre del ciel, dopo i perduti giorni* (62).

In all of Petrarch's works, we recognize the acute eye of the intellectual who carefully observes himself and the world around him and attempts to make some sense of the fragile human condition and its immediate and ultimate purpose within the great order of the cosmos. It is in this unprecedented focus on his own personal situation that we may observe Petrarch's genius and the human drama played out on a small yet universal stage.

While most of his works are ultimately about himself and are thus full of interesting though stylized and carefully crafted bits of autobiographical information, Petrarch did write, late in his life, a *Letter to Posterity* (the Latin title is *Ad posteros* or *Posteritati*), to future generations who might be curious to learn more about him and his life. This fragmentary epistle was first composed in 1367 and was revised in 1370–1371, yet the latest event recounted is from 1351. In the letter,

Petrarch intends to speak about himself, his interests, his outlook—in short, about his personality. What strikes the modern reader is the egotism that pervades the letter, the dramatic departure from the more humble attitude generally adopted by medieval authors who were less likely to put themselves and their accomplishments on display in such a self-centered and self-serving way. Although idealized, conventional portraits are common in works of medieval literature and although the *vidas* of the troubadours and Dante's *Vita nuova* present so-called personal data as historical facts, the authorial "I" and the empirical "I" remain distinctly separate persons. With Petrarch, however, we see a dramatic change in the attitude toward autobiography, such that we know more about this fourteenth-century author than about virtually any other person of his age, precisely because the author himself decided that this would be the case. To make sure that we would know about him, Petrarch compiled large collections of letters, made copious annotations on his manuscripts, and left us other pieces of evidence that allow us see and understand his life as he wanted it to be recorded and remembered. Thus, in the *Letter to Posterity*, Petrarch fashions his own identity, creates his own historical persona, and delineates his role in the events of his time. From other, independent documents we are able to judge the accuracy of the *Letter to Posterity*, and we may conclude that he was a master of self-promotion, acutely aware of his particular place in history. For this reason, we may view him as a precursor of humanistic attitudes on the individual that would emerge in the next centuries.

In the *Letter to Posterity*, Petrarch describes himself as modest and even tempered, as one who prefers sacred literature to vernacular poetry, who is acutely aware of the greatness of antiquity to the impoverished state of his own age, who yearns for the tranquil life of the country and disparages the hectic pace of urban society. While he notes that in his youth he had been overwhelmed by a powerful love, he declares that this is a thing of the past. Despite his voluminous literary production in both Latin and Italian, Petrarch refers only to his works in Latin—his epic poem *Africa*, his treatise on the solitary life (*De vita solitaria*), and his pastoral poems (*Bucolicum carmen*)—for they are the reason for his coronation as poet laureate in Rome atop the Capitoline Hill. As Petrarch tells the story, on the same day (1 September 1340), he received invitations for coronations from the chancellor of the University of Paris and from the Roman senate; to have chosen Paris would have been to give precedence to scholastic culture, and thus his choice of Rome was intended to help restore the ancient glory of that city.

In the *Letter to Posterity*, Petrarch also speaks about his family and friends, his personal habits, his travels, the cities where he lived, and the benefits—for work

and mind—of his "transalpine solitude." The last few sentences of the letter speak of Petrarch's affection for Jacopo da Carrara the Younger, ruler of Padua; and while Petrarch would have liked to reside permanently in Padua, Jacopo's untimely death in December 1350 made that impossible. Petrarch notes: "I could stay no longer [in Padua], and I returned to France, not so much from a desire to see again what I had already seen a thousand times as, like a sick man, to be rid of distress by shifting position." This sentence represents perfectly Petrarch's carefully constructed *persona*: he is the restless traveler, the seeker of old manuscripts, the frequenter of ancient sites in an attempt to recapture something of their past glory. The image of the sick man who tries to assuage his pain by shifting position recalls Saint Augustine's image of the sick woman, who, in allegorical terms, represents the unquiet human soul that will find its peace only in God (*Confessions*, 6.16); however, here Petrarch's frame of reference is limited to earthly life. In this passage, we also observe the drama of his own internal conflict as one caught between earthly attractions and spiritual aspirations, one who, profoundly discontent with his own age, but powerless to change it, dreams of a past grandeur and of a better future time. His confessional work, the *Secretum*, in which Augustine is one of the interlocutors, is concerned with this same conflict.

Life and Works

Petrarch was born in Arezzo to Pietro di Parenzo and Eletta Canigiani. His father, usually called Ser Petracco, was a notary who had migrated to Florence from his hometown of Incisa in the Arno River valley. During the tumultuous early years of the fourteenth century, he made some political enemies in Florence and was exiled on false charges of corruption in public office in October 1302—some nine months after the expulsion of Dante Alighieri on similar grounds. Early in 1305, Petrarch and his mother moved to Incisa, where his brother Gherardo was born in 1307. After six years in Incisa, the family moved to Pisa (1311), where Francesco may have seen Dante among a group of fellow Florentine exiles. In 1312, Ser Petracco resettled his family in Carpentras in southern France, where he was associated with the papal court of Clement V in Avignon. In Carpentras, Francesco began his study of grammar and rhetoric with Convenevole da Prato and became friends with Guido Sette, a boy his own age whose family had moved to France from Genoa. In 1316, Ser Petracco decided that Petrarch should become a lawyer and sent him to the University of Montpellier. During this period his mother died, and to commemorate the sorrowful occasion Petrarch composed his earliest surviving work, an elegiac poem in thirty-eight Latin hexameters. In 1320, Francesco went, together with his brother and Guido Sette, to Bologna

Altichiero da Zevio (1330–1385). Francesco Petrarca, poet. Detail from the Burial of Saint Lucia. Fresco (1479–1381). © Erick Lessing/Art Resource, New York.

to continue his legal studies, and although he excelled academically, he came to realize that the legal profession was not for him. Nevertheless, the years in Bologna were important in his literary and cultural development, for he befriended a number of other Students and became familiar with the Italian lyric tradition. On the death of his father in April 1326, he returned to Avignon.

On Good Friday, 6 April 1327, in the Church of Saint Clare in Avignon, Petrarch first saw and immediately fell in love with the woman whom he would call Laura. This passion would provide inspiration for his poetic imagination for his entire life. Many poems contained in the evolving collection known as the *Rerum vulgarium fragmenta* or *Canzoniere* celebrate his love for her, as well as her symbolic meaning. Her name, Laura—like that of Dante's Beatrice ("one who gives blessedness or salvation")—was significant in that it suggested the evergreen laurel tree, sacred to Apollo, and thus the laurel crown of poetic glory. Throughout the *Canzoniere*, Petrarch engages in elaborate wordplay based on "Laura," using such puns as *l'aura* ("the breeze") and *aureola* ("golden") to reiterate her importance.

In 1330, Petrarch and his brother Gherardo had almost dissipated their inheritance. Refusing to follow law or medicine as a profession, Petrarch had to find other employment. Fortunately, he had befriended the bishop of Lombez, Giacomo Colonna, who recommended Petrarch to his brother Cardinal Giovanni Colonna, who in

turn offered Petrarch a position as personal chaplain in his household. At Giacomo Colonna's residence in the summer of 1330, Petrarch met and became friends with two other young men: Lello di Pietro Stefano dei Tosetti from Rome (whom Petrarch nicknamed "Lelius") and Ludwig van Kempen ("Socrates") from Flanders, who served as chanter in Cardinal Colonna's chapel. These and other close friends would be very important to Petrarch throughout the course of his life.

As a member of the cardinal's staff, Petrarch was able to travel and meet many people. In 1333, he traveled to Paris and, from there, to Ghent, Liège, Aix-la-Chapelle, Cologne, and Lyon. During these travels he began his lifelong pursuit of manuscripts containing works by classical authors, discovering at Liège, for example, some of Cicero's orations (*Pro Archia*). Also in 1333, in Avignon, Petrarch met the Augustinian monk Dionigi da Borgo San Sepolcro, who introduced him to the works of early Christian writers, especially Saint Augustine, and who gave Petrarch his copy of the *Confessions*. In a letter to Dionigi (*Familiares*, 4.1, dated 26 April 1336), Petrarch gives an account of his and his brother Gherardo's ascent of Mont Ventoux. In it he relates, in thinly veiled allegorical language, how rapidly Gherardo arrives at the summit (signifying the benefits of his monastic vocation) but how difficult his own climb is (signifying the attraction of earthly things). Finally, arriving at the summit and overwhelmed by the majesty of the view, Petrarch opens his copy of Augustine's *Confessions* and reads the following morally oriented monitory sentence: "And men go about wondering at mountain heights and the mighty waves of the sea and broad flowing streams and the circuit of the sea and the wheeling of the stars: and to themselves they give no heed" (10.8.15). The relevance of these words to Petrarch's own situation and their call to introspection are obvious: it is always more difficult to ascend the steep path to the good than it is to wander around in the valleys looking for an easy route to happiness. This intensely Augustinian moment demonstrates the great influence that the saint had on Petrarch, not only in literature but also in life.

In January 1335, thanks to a recommendation by Cardinal Colonna, Petrarch was named by Pope Benedict XII to a canonry in the cathedral of Lombez, an appointment that supported him financially but did not require his residence. Sometime before this appointment, Petrarch had written a long letter in Latin verse to Pope Benedict XII encouraging Benedict to return to Rome. This is the first indication we have of Petrarch's firm belief in the preeminence of Rome as the rightful seat of both the papacy and the empire. Petrarch first journeyed to Rome, as a guest of the Colonna family, late in 1336, and that visit determined his attitude toward the classical past. In a letter to Cardinal Giovanni Colonna, dated 15 March 1337 (*Familiares*, 2.14), he recounts his first impressions of Rome: "No doubt I have accumulated a lot of matter to write about later, but at present I am so overwhelmed and stunned by the abundant marvels that I shouldn't dare to begin.... Rome was greater than I thought, and so are its remains. Now I wonder not that the world was ruled by this city but that the rule came so late." Petrarch's enthusiasm for Rome is complemented by his patriotism for Italy in general; for example, in *canzone* 128 of the *Canzoniere, Italia mia, benché 'l parlar sia indarno,* he laments Italy's abject, strife-torn condition; issues a call to arms (verses 93–96); and concludes with an urgent plea for peace, *i' vo gridando: Pace, pace, pace* (verse 122).

Shortly after his return to Avignon in 1337, Petrarch purchased property and a house in Vaucluse along the Sorgue River, and this became his resort of peace and solitude: *transalpina solitudo mea jocundissima* ("My most delightful transalpine solitary refuge"). In this *locus amoenus* he found the time to read, meditate, write, and entertain close friends. Vaucluse represented for Petrarch the Ciceronian ideal of *ottum,* the leisure to pursue one's interests without having to attend to the concerns of everyday life. A new acquaintance of his in Vaucluse was Philippe de Cabassoles, bishop of Cavillon, to whom Petrarch would later dedicate his Latin treatise *De vita solitaria* (*On the Solitary Life*).

During this period of meditative leisure, Petrarch began several of his works, some of classical inspiration: the treatise on the lives of famous men, *De viris illustribus*; his epic poem on the deeds of Scipio Africanus, *Africa*; his collection of Italian poems, the *Canzoniere* or *Rerum vulgarium fragmenta*; and the *Triumph of Love*, the first of the *Trionfi*—six allegorical poems in *terza rima*, based on the descriptions of ancient triumphal pageants. Petrarch would continue to revise most of these works for the rest of his life. The evolution of the *Canzoniere* can be traced through extant manuscripts, some in Petrarch's own hand, that disclose the successive forms of the collection; this would culminate in the version in the Vatican Library, Codex Lat. 3195. Although he divided his time at Vaucluse between Latin and Italian works, Petrarch clearly indicated his preference for the former. On 1 September 1340 he received two invitations to be crowned poet laureate: one letter came from the chancellor of the University of Paris and the other from the Roman senate. Because we know that Petrarch carefully planned the sequence of events leading to these invitations, we can appreciate the coyness with which he reports his careful weighing of these offers, his asking advice from Cardinal Colonna, and his eventual (but foregone) decision to accept the invitation from Rome. Petrarch was familiar with the coronation of poets in antiquity and with a recent revival of that tradition (the coronation of Albertino Mussato in Padua in 1315). This signal honor would, he thought, ensure

his fame for posterity and, just as important, reestablish Rome as the locus for culture in the world. To ascertain his worthiness for this honor, he voluntarily underwent a rigorous examination by his sponsor, King Robert of Anjou of Naples. On 8 April 1341, in the palace of the senate on the Capitoline, Petrarch was crowned poet laureate and delivered an oration, in which he spoke of the poet's responsibility and rewards as well as the nature of the poet's profession. The *Coronation Oration* is a wonderful combination of medieval homily and classical rhetoric; in it Petrarch begins with a citation from Virgil's *Georgics* (3.291–292), interrupts it with a recitation of the *Ave Maria*, and then immediately returns to the Virgilian passage. The remainder of the oration contains numerous citations from Virgil, Ovid, Cicero, Horace, and other classical authors. The fame that Petrarch achieved in this single event was immeasurable; indeed, he was now a celebrity, one who was in demand as an honored guest in cities throughout Europe and was cheered wherever he went. This was, in many ways, the beginning of what we might call the cult of personality that Petrarch cultivated and shaped for himself. After leaving Rome, Petrarch spent time in Parma as a guest of the Correggio family and finished a draft of his *Africa*. When he returned to Provence, he began to study Greek with the Calabrian monk Barlaam, but without mastering much beyond a very elementary level.

The year 1343 was important for Petrarch. At the papal court in Avignon, he met Cola di Rienzo, who would later become the Roman "tribune of the people." In February, Robert of Anjou died. In April, Petrarch's brother Gherardo became a Carthusian monk, and this led Petrarch to reexamine his own life and goals. In 1343, his illegitimate daughter, Francesca, was born. From these troubling events emerged his soul-searching imaginary dialogue with (Saint) Augustine—the *Secretum*—as well as his *Seven Penitential Psalms* and his treatise on the cardinal virtues, the *Rerum memorandarum libri*. In form and content, the *Secretum* is based on classical and early Christian models, especially Augustine's *Confessions*. Whereas in his work the saint achieves a relative peace, Petrarch is constantly tormented by the unresolved conflict between spiritual aspirations and worldly concerns. Despite the sound Christian advice imparted by the character Augustinus to Franciscus and the insistent call to meditate on death in order to prepare one's soul for the afterlife, Franciscus cannot easily abandon his earthly pursuits, nor does he really wish to. The lack of resolution at the end of the three-day dialogue suggests not so much Petrarch's lack of faith as his very human reluctance to abandon immediate worldly pursuits in favor of distant eternal rewards.

During the next few years, Petrarch traveled frequently: to Naples (in 1343), Parma (1344–1345), and Verona (1345). In the Capitular Library in Verona, he found and transcribed the manuscript of Cicero's letters to Atticus, a discovery that encouraged him to begin his own series of letters addressed to classical authors. After returning to Vaucluse in 1346, Petrarch began work on his treatise on the solitary life, *De vita solitaria*, which he subsequently dedicated to Philippe de Cabassoles. In 1347, Petrarch was happy to receive news of a revolution in Rome and the nomination of Cola di Rienzo to the position of tribune (essentially, dictator), for in these events he saw some signs of the old Roman grandeur. In letters to Cola and the Roman people, Petrarch encouraged them in their battle for liberty. However, Cola's excesses and megalomania would gradually undermine his position and destroy Petrarch's faith in him. After imprisonment in Avignon on charges of heresy, Cola returned to Rome as a senator, only to meet his death at the hands of the Roman people in 1354.

In 1347–1348, the time of the black death, Petrarch was in Verona and in Parma, where news of Laura's death (6 April 1348) came to him in a letter from his old friend "Socrates." The date of Laura's death and that of his first meeting with her, exactly twenty-one years before in 1327, would provide the basic chronological structure for a series of "anniversary" poems in the *Canzoniere*. The disastrous effects of the plague, which resulted in the deaths of several friends (e.g., Cardinal Colonna and Franceschino degli Albizzi), led Petrarch to write the *Triumph of Death* (*Triumphus mortis*).

His discovery of Cicero's letters in Verona in 1345 gave Petrarch the idea of collecting his own letters, and by 1350 he was actively engaged in this project, which would lead to the formation of the *Familiares* (twenty-four books), *Seniles* (seventeen books), *Sine nomine* (nineteen letters), and *Epistolae metricae* (three books). For the jubilee year of 1350, Petrarch traveled to Rome, stopping on the way in Florence, where he met Giovanni Boccaccio for the first time. Among Petrarch's many admirers in Florence were Boccaccio, Zanobi da Strada, Francesco Nelli, and Lapo da Castiglionchio. Always searching for manuscripts, Petrarch found in Lapo's library a copy of Quintilian's *Institutes* and some of Cicero's orations. After his Roman pilgrimage, Petrarch spent time in Parma and Padua. The Florentine republic offered him a teaching post at the university there, and the pope summoned him to return to Avignon. In 1351–1352, Petrarch was once again working in Vaucluse on *De viris illustribus* and the *Canzoniere*. In 1353, during his last months in Vaucluse, Petrarch was involved in an extended and intense debate with one of the pope's doctors over the relative merits of medicine and poetry, and this discussion resulted in the *Invective contra medicum*, in which Petrarch defends the supremacy of the liberal arts over the lower mechanical arts and praises poetry as the highest form of wisdom.

During 1353–1361, Petrarch lived for the most part in Milan, as a guest of the Visconti family and with the special support of Archbishop Giovanni Visconti. Despite the criticism he received from his friends for living under a despot, Petrarch was pleased with his circumstances, for he was able to do virtually anything he wanted. One project he began there became his longest work, *De remediis utriusque fortune*, a moral treatise in two books, the first dealing with the perils of good fortune and the second with the dangers of its opposite, adverse fortune. The form of *De remediis* is a series of dialogues between personified qualities; for example, in Book I, Joy and Hope—the children of Prosperity—argue against Reason; and in Book II, Reason's opponents are Sorrow and Fear, the offspring of Adversity. It was in Milan that Petrarch met Emperor Charles IV, whom he encouraged to reestablish the empire with Rome as its capital. These dealings with Charles, undertaken on behalf of the Visconti, allowed Petrarch to travel to Basel and Prague. In 1361, the Visconti sent him to Paris, where he delivered an oration, in Latin, in the presence of King John of France and John's court. Petrarch's eight years in Milan marked the longest nearly continuous residency of his life. Moreover, they were productive years, allowing him to complete *De remediis* and to make great progress in his compilation of the *Canzoniere* and the *Familiares*.

After his move to Padua in the summer of 1361, Petrarch received the sad news of the deaths of his illegitimate son Giovanni (who died in the plague in Milan) and of his old friends "Socrates" and Philippe de Vitry. However, he enjoyed frequent correspondence and encounters with Boccaccio, who often supplied him with copies of rare manuscripts (e.g., Augustine's *Expositions on the Psalms*, Varro's *De lingua latina*, the life of Peter Damian). In May 1362, Petrarch had an opportunity to advise Boccaccio, who had been terrified by a visit from a fanatical monk representing the late Pietro Petroni of Siena. Informed that he did not have long to live and that he should renounce the study of poetry, Boccaccio thought first to dispose of all his books, but Petrarch dissuaded him and encouraged him to continue his studies. However, Petrarch said that he would gladly buy Boccaccio's books if Boccaccio had a change of heart. Petrarch's love of books, and his zeal in collecting them, enabled him to amass what was at the time perhaps the largest private library in Europe. Recognizing the value of his collection, Petrarch reached a formal agreement with the *maggior consiglio* of Venice whereby he would give his library to Venice in exchange for a suitable house there and the assurance that his books would not be dispersed. Petrarch's collection thus formed the basis for the Biblioteca Marciana in Venice. In Venice, Petrarch enjoyed visits from Boccaccio and numerous other friends; he also was gladdened by the birth of his grandchildren (Eletta and Francesco) and saddened by the death of his friends "Laelius" and Francesco Nelli.

Around 1366, Petrarch employed Giovanni Malpaghini as a scribe for the tedious task of copying the *Familiares* and the *Canzoniere*. In 1367, during a journey to Pavia by canal barge, Petrarch was able to respond to accusations lodged against him a year previously by four Aristotelian philosophers (Leonardo Dandolo, Tommaso Talenti, Zaccaria Contarini, and Guido da Bagnolo) who claimed that he was "a good man, but uneducated." In his response, the invective *De sui ipsius et multorum ignorantia* (*On His Own Ignorance and That of Many Others*), Petrarch gives clear evidence of the changeover from the outmoded ideas of scholastic philosophy to the new humanism; in particular, he argues that the source of knowledge lies not in pseudoscientific syllogistic arguments but rather in a profound intuitive awareness of the self.

In 1368, Petrarch, having been given some land near Arquà (some 10 miles, or about 16 kilometers, southwest of Padua)—initiated the construction of a house, which was finished in 1370. Among his possessions were a lute and a painting of the Madonna by Giotto, both of which have disappeared. Failing health prevented him from undertaking some highly desired trips to Rome and Avignon. His last works include a translation into Latin of Boccaccio's story of Griselda (*Decameron*, 10.10) and the *Invective against the Man Who Maligned Italy* (*Invectiva contra eum qui maledixit Italie*). The motivation for the *Invective* was an anonymous letter written by a Frenchman (Jean de Hesdin) that praised the French and spoke ill of Italy. As for the tale of patient Griselda, Petrarch was so taken by its value as a moral example that he wanted to make it available to readers who did not know Italian, and his translation was Chaucer's model for the Clerk's Tale in the *Canterbury Tales*. In his last years, Petrarch went on several diplomatic missions for Francesco da Carrara; he wrote letters and continued to work on the definitive versions of the *Canzoniere*, *Trionfi*, and *De viris illustribus* as well as on the compilations of his letters. During the night between 18 and 19 July 1374, Petrarch died. He was buried on 24 July in a marble tomb in the parish church at Arquà.

The Vernacular Works

Although the *Letter to Posterity* says virtually nothing about his Italian works, Petrarch obviously considered them of great importance, for he was continuously revising them up to the very end of his life. If what he says in the *Letter to Posterity* is truly indicative of the way he wanted to be remembered, then it is a great irony, for his fame today rests primarily on his Italian poetry, which proved so influential during the Renaissance, particularly in France, Spain, and England. The compo-

sition of the *Canzoniere* was attended to with great care: its 366 poems are divided into two major sections—*In vita di madonna Laura* and *In morte di madonna Laura*—beginning with the secular sonnet *Voi ch'ascoltate in rime sparse il suono* ("You who hear the sound in scattered rhymes") and ending with the religious ode to the Virgin *Vergina bella, che di sol vestita* ("Beautiful Virgin, clothed with the sun"). A large variety of subjects and themes—amorous, political, artistic, moral, and religious—are treated; nevertheless, the truly remarkable feature of the collection is Petrarch's obsessive attention to the presentation of his own poetic persona. Many poems in the *Canzoniere* are characterized by stylized, conventional attitudes toward love and by the presentation of a pensive, introspective lover, and these features were imitated widely in the Renaissance. This combination of psychological and poetic conceits would come to constitute what we generally refer to today as Petrarchism. Although Petrarch was not the inventor of the sonnet, he brought it to such perfection that this fourteen-line metrical form has become known as the Petrarchan sonnet. The six allegorical *Triumphs* (*Trionfi*), which relate the progress of the soul in relation to love, chastity, death, fame, time, and eternity, had a major impact on Renaissance literature, art, and pageantry.

The Latin Works

Petrarch's literary production in Latin encompasses a number of major themes that highlight his crucial place in the history of western civilization. On the one hand, his treatises on fortune (*De remediis utriusque fortune*) and on the monastic life (*De otio religioso*) are distinctly medieval in flavor and conception. On the other hand, there is a definite, forward-looking "Renaissance" cast to many of the Latin works. Petrarch consciously attempted to revive classical genres and patterns in the epic poem *Africa* and in the series of famous lives (*De viris illustribus*) and events (*Rerum memorandarum libri*). His treatise on the solitary life, *De vita solitaria*, is a well-reasoned defense of the Ciceronian ideal of studious leisure (*otium*), which he tried to follow in his own life. He took the cue from classical examples in his collections of letters, in his invectives, in his pastoral poems (*Bucolicum carmen*), and in his dialogue with Augustine (*Secretum*).

See also **Boccaccio, Giovanni; Chaucer, Geoffrey; Dante Alighieri; Robert of Anjou**

Further Reading

Editions and Translations of Petrarch

Il Bucolicum carmen e i suoi commenti inediti, ed. Antonio Avena. Padua: Società Cooperativa Tipografica, 1906. (Reprint, Bologna: Forni, 1969.)

Canzoniere, ed. Gianfranco Contini. Turin: Einaudi, 1968.

Canzoniere, 2 vols, ed. Ugo Dotti. Rome: Donzelli, 1996.

Canzoniere, ed. Marco Santagata. Milan: Mondadori, 1996.

Il "De otio religioso," ed. Giuseppe Rotondi. Vatican City: Biblioteca Apostolica Vaticana, 1958.

De viris illustribus, ed. Guido Martellotti. Florence: Sansoni, 1964.

De vita solitaria, Buch I: Kritische Textausgabe und Ideengeschichtlicher Kommentar, ed. K. A. E. Enenkel. Leiden: Brill, 1990.

Epistolae de rebus familiaribus et varie, 3 vols, ed. G. Fracassetti. Florence: Le Monnier, 1859.

Invective contra medicum, ed. P. G. Ricci. Rome: Edizioni di Storia e Letteratura, 1950.

Letters from Petrarch, trans. Morris Bishop. Bloomington: Indiana University Press, 1966.

Letters of Old Age: Rerum Senilium Libri XVIII, 2 vols., trans. Aldo S. Bernardo, Saul Levin, and Reta A. Bernardo. Baltimore, Md.: Johns Hopkins University Press, 1992.

Letters on Familiar Matters (Rerum familiarum libri) I—XVI, trans. Aldo S. Bernardo. Baltimore, Md.: Johns Hopkins University Press, 1982.

Letters on Familiar Matters (Rerum familiarum libri) XVII—XXIV, trans. Aldo S. Bernardo. Baltimore, Md.: Johns Hopkins University Press, 1985.

The Life of Solitude, trans. Jacob Zeitlin. Urbana: University of Illinois Press, 1924.

Lord Morley's "Tryumphes of Fraunces Petrarcke": The First English Translation of the "Trionfi," ed. D. D. Carnicelli. Cambridge, Mass.: Harvard University Press, 1971.

Petrarch: The Canzoniere or Rerum vulgarium fragmenta, trans. Mark Musa. Bloomington: Indiana University Press, 1996.

Petrarch's Africa, trans. Thomas G. Bergin and Alice S. Wilson. New Haven, Conn.: Yale University Press, 1977.

Petrarch's Book without a Name: A Translation of the Liber Sine Nomine, trans. Norman P. Zacour. Toronto: Pontifical Institute of Mediaeval Studies, 1973.

Petrarch's Bucolicum Carmen, trans. Thomas G. Bergin. New Haven, Conn.: Yale University Press, 1974.

Petrarch's Letters to Classical Authors, trans. Mario Cosenza. Chicago, Ill.: University of Chicago Press, 1910.

Petrarch's Lyric Poems: The "Rime Sparse" and Other Lyrics, ed. and trans. Robert M. Durling. Cambridge, Mass.: Harvard University Press, 1976.

Petrarch's Remedies for Fortune Fair and Foul, 5 vols., trans. Conrad H. Rawski. Bloomington: Indiana University Press, 1991.

Petrarch's "Secretum" with Introduction, Notes, and Critical Anthology, trans. Davy A. Carozza and H. James Shey. New York: Peter Lang, 1989.

Petrarch's "Songbook," "Rerum vulgarium fragmenta": A Verse Translation, trans. James Wyatt Cook. Binghamton, N.Y.: Medieval and Renaissance Texts and Studies, 1995.

Prose, ed. G. Martellotti, P. G. Ricci, E. Carrara, and E. Bianchi. Milan and Naples: Ricciardi, 1955.

The Renaissance Philosophy of Man, ed. Ernst Cassirer, Paul Oskar Kristeller, and John Herman Randall, Jr. Chicago, Ill.: University of Chicago Press, 1948. (Contains the following translations: *A Self-Portrait; The Ascent of Mont Ventoux; On His Own Ignorance and That of Many Others; A Disapproval of an Unreasonable Use of the Discipline of Dialectic; An Averroist Visits Petrarca. Petrarca's Aversion to Arab Science; A Request to Take Up the Fight against Averroes.*)

Rerum familiarium: Libri I—VIII, trans. Aldo S. Bernardo. Albany: State University of New York Press, 1975.

Rerum memorandarum libri, ed. Giuseppe Billanovich. Florence, 1945.

Rime disperse, ed. and trans. Joseph A. Barber. New York: Garland, 1991.

Rime disperse, ed. Angelo Solerti. Florence: Sansoni, 1909.

Rime, Trionfi, e Poesie Latine, ed. F. Neri, G. Martellotti, E. Bianchi, and N. Sapegno. Milan and Naples: Ricciardi, 1951.

Salmi penitenziali, ed. Roberto Gigliucci. Rome: Salerno Editrice, 1997.

Secretum, ed. Ugo Dotti. Rome: Archivio Guido Izzi, 1993.

Sine nomine: Lettere polemiche e politiche. Bari: Laterza, 1974.

Trionfi, Rime estravaganti, Codice degli abbozzi, ed. Vinicio Pacca and Laura Paolino. Milan: Mondadori, 1996.

The Triumphs of Petrarch, trans. Ernest Hatch Wilkins. Chicago, Ill.: University of Chicago Press, 1962.

Critical Studies

Amaturo, Raffaele. *Petrarca.* Bari: Laterza, 1971.

Baron, Hans. *Petrarch's "Secretum": Its Making and Its Meaning.* Cambridge, Mass.: Harvard University Press, 1985.

Bernardo, Aldo S. *Petrarch, Scipio, and the "Africa": The Birth of Humanism's Dream.* Baltimore, Md.: Johns Hopkins University Press, 1962.

——. *Petrarch, Laura, and the Triumphs.* Albany: State University of New York Press, 1974.

Bishop, Morris. *Petrarch and His World.* Bloomington: Indiana University Press, 1963.

Bosco, Umberto. *Francesco Petrarca.* Bari: Laterza, 1961.

Cosenza, Mario Emilio. *Francesco Petrarca and the Revolution of Cola di Rienzo,* 2nd ed. New York: Italica, 1986. (With new introduction and bibliography by Ronald G. Musto. Originally published 1913.)

Dotti, Ugo. *Vita di Petrarca.* Bari: Laterza, 1987.

Forster, Leonard. *The Icy Fire: Five Studies in European Petrarchism.* Cambridge: Cambridge University Press, 1969.

Foster, Kenelm. *Petrarch: Poet and Humanist.* Edinburgh: Edinburgh University Press, 1984.

Francesco Petrarca, Citizen of the World, ed. Aldo S. Bernardo. Padua and Albany: Antenore and State University of New York Press, 1980.

Francis Petrarch, Six Centuries Later: A Symposium, ed. Aldo Scaglione. Chapel Hill and Chicago, Ill.: University of North Carolina and Newberry Library, 1975.

Hainsworth, Peter. *Petrarch the Poet: An Introduction to the Rerum Vulgarium Fragmenta.* New York and London: Routledge, 1988.

Jones, Frederic J. *The Structure of Petrarch's "Canzoniere": A Chronological, Psychological, and Stylistic Analysis.* Cambridge: D. S. Brewer, 1995.

Kennedy, William J. *Authorizing Petrarch.* Ithaca, N.Y.: Cornell University Press, 1994.

Mann, Nicholas. *Petrarch.* Oxford: Oxford University Press, 1984.

Mazzotta, Giuseppe. *The Worlds of Petrarch.* Durham, N.C.: Duke University Press, 1993.

Nolhac, Pierre de. *Petrarque et l'humanisme,* 2 vols. Paris: Champion, 1907.

Petrarch's "Triumphs": Allegory and Spectacle, ed. Konrad Eisenbichler and Amilcare A. Iannucci. Ottawa: Dovehouse, 1990.

Rico, Francisco. *Vida u obra de Petrarca.* Chapel Hill: University of North Carolina Press, 1974.

Shapiro, Marianne. *Hieroglyph of Time: The Petrarchan Sestina.* Minneapolis: University of Minnesota Press, 1980.

Sturm-Maddox, Sara. *Petrarch's Metamorphoses.* Columbia: University of Missouri Press, 1985.

——. *Petrarch's Laurels.* University Park: Pennsylvania State University Press, 1992.

Trinkaus, Charles. *The Poet as Philosopher: Petrarch and the Formation of Renaissance Consciousness.* New Haven, Conn.: Yale University Press, 1979.

Whitfield, J. H. *Petrarch and the Renascence.* Oxford: Blackwell, 1943.

Wilkins, Ernest Hatch. *The Making of the Canzoniere and Other Petrarchan Studies.* Rome: Edizioni di Storia e Letteratura, 1951.

——. *Studies in the Life and Works of Petrarch.* Cambridge, Mass.: Medieval Academy of America, 1955.

——. *Petrarch's Eight Years in Milan.* Cambridge, Mass.: Medieval Academy of America, 1958.

——. *Petrarch's Later Years.* Cambridge, Mass.: Medieval Academy of America, 1959.

——. *Life of Petrarch.* Chicago, Ill.: University of Chicago Press, 1961.

——. *Studies on Petrarch and Boccaccio.* Padua: Antenore, 1978.

CHRISTOPHER KLEINHENZ

PETRUS DE DACIA (ca. 1230–1289)

Petrus de Dacia is called Sweden's first author. While studying at the *studium generale* of the Dominicans in Cologne (1267–1269), Petrus visited the nearby village of Stommeln, where he met the German beguine Christina of Stommeln in 1267. As Christina's confessor, he often witnessed her remarkable and even terrifying experiences: ecstasies, stigmatizations, and visions that convinced him that Christina was a saint capable of showing him the right way to God. In 1269–1270, when studying in Paris, Petrus began the correspondence with Christina that continued until his death. In 1270, he returned to Sweden, revisiting Stommeln on his way home, and in 1271 he was appointed lector of the Dominican convent of Skanninge. Not earlier than 1277, he was transferred to Västerås, where he became lector and then prior, until 1280, when he was made lector of the convent of Visby in his native island of Gotland. In 1279, while staying a month in Cologne, he again paid several visits to Christina. Having become prior in Visby, he was also appointed *socius* of the provincial for the General Chapter at Bordeaux in summer 1287. On his way home from Bordeaux, Petrus met Christina at Stommeln for the last time. In a letter of September 9, 1289, Christina was informed that Petrus had died during the Lent of that year.

Two literary works in Latin by Petrus are known, both in the *Codex Juliacensis* from about 1300, now in the Bischöfliches Diözesanarchiv in Aachen. In the *Vita Christinae Stumbelensis* ("Life of Christina of Stommeln"), Petrus describes his visits to Stommeln and his strong emotional reactions to Christina's mystical experiences. The book also contains their correspondence and a biography of Christina written by the parish priest of Stommeln, who used to read and translate Petrus's letters to Christina and write down her letters.

Although Petrus was deeply attached to Christina, he repeatedly emphasizes that their love is a spiritual one, having Christ for its true object.

Petrus's other known work is *De gratia naturam ditante sive De virtutibus Christinae Stumbelensis* ("On Grace Enriching Nature, or On the Virtues of Christina of Stommeln"). It consists of a poem of forty-three hexameters praising Christina's virtues and a long theological treatise commenting on each word of the poem. The greater part of this work is lost. Petrus exploits his philosophical and theological learning to find theoretical explanations of Christina's behavior. The work presents few original thoughts, being mainly a compilation of the ideas of Petrus's masters in Cologne and Paris, Albertus Magnus and Thomas Aquinas.

Further Reading

Editions

Petrus de Dacia. *Vita Christinae Stumbelensis.* Ed. Johannes Paulson. Scriptores Latini Medii Aeui Suecani, 1. fasc. 2. Gothenburg: Wettergren & Kerber, 1896.

Petrus de Dacia. *De gratianaturam ditante sive De virtutibus Christinae Stumbelensis.* Edition *critique avec une introduction par Monika Asztalos.* Acta Universitatis Stockholmiensis. Studia Latina Stockholmiensia, 28. Stockholm: Almqvist & Wiksell, 1982 [review by Eva Odelman in *Archivum Latinitatis Medii Aevi,* 43 (1984), 166–76]; [a new edition of Petrus's letters with a Swedish translation is being prepared by Monika Asztalos].

Literature

Schück, Henrik. *Vår förste författare. En själshistoria från medeltiden.* Stockholm: Geber, 1916.

Lehmann, Paul. *Skandinaviens Anteil an der lateinischen Literatur und Wissenschaft des Mittelalters.* 1. Stück. Sitzungsberichte der Bayerischen Akademie der Wissenschaften. Philosophisch-historische Abteilung, jahrgang 1936, Heft 2. Munich: Bayerische Akademie der Wissenschaften, 1936, pp. 44–47.

Gallén, jarl. *La province de Dacie de l'ordre des Frères Prêcheurs. 1: Histoire générale jusqu'au grand schisme.* Helsinki: Söderström, 1946.

Olsen, T. D. "Petrus de Dacia." *New Catholic Encyclopedia.* New York: McGraw-Hill, 1967, vol. 11, p. 247.

Lindroth. Sten. *Svensk lärdomshistoria.* 4 vols. Stockholm: Norstedt, 1975–81. vol. 1, pp. 64–71.

Nieveler, Peter. *Codex luliacensis. Christina von Stommeln und Petrus von Dacien, ihr Leben und Nachleben in Geschichte. Kunst und Literatur.* Veröffentlichungen des Bischöflichen Diözesanarchivs Aachen, 34. Mönchengladbach: Kühlen, 1975.

Asztalos, Monika. "Les lettres de direction et les sermons épistolaires de Pierre de Dacie." In *The Editing of Theological and Philosophical Texts from the Middle Ages: Acts of the Conference Arranged by the Department of Classical Languages, University of Stockholm, 29–31 August 1984.* Ada Universitatis Stockholmiensis. Studia Latina Stockholmiensia, 30. Stockholm: Almqvist & Wiksell, 1986, pp. 161–84.

Den Svenska Litteraturen. 1: Från fomüd till frihetsid 800–1718. Stockholm: Bonnier, 1987, pp. 66–71.

EVA ODELMAN

PHILAGATHUS OF CERAMI
(d. 1154 or later)

Greek prose in medieval Italy reaches a high point with the sermons of the twelfth-century Siculo-Calabrian monk Philagathus. He is conventionally called "of Cerami," although it is not clear whether the designation *Keramítes* refers to Cerami in Sicily or to some other place, or is instead a classicizing version of the demotic surname *Kerameüs* ("Potter"). Until fairly recently, he was known as Theophanes Cerameus, thanks to a misattribution in one branch of a later Byzantine redaction that converted his sermon collection into a homiliary organized according to the liturgical calendar, and his work was at times presented as that of a ninth- or eleventh-century writer into which more recent material had been inserted. In his Italo-Greek manuscripts he is styled "the philosopher" (and therefore is sometimes so identified in library catalogs) and is also often called Philippus (perhaps his baptismal name) rather than Philagathus. Of his approximately ninety surviving sermons, only thirty-eight have a modern critical edition; the remainder either must be read in texts descended from the very defective *editio princeps* of Francesco Scorso (1644) or are still unpublished. Even so, these cultured and rhetorically accomplished productions have earned a considerable reputation for artistic excellence.

To the extent that they can be localized with certainty, Philagathus's early associations are Calabrian. After entering religion at an unidentified church of Saint Andrew, he trained at the Nea Hodegetria monastery near Rossano, later known as the Patír or the Patirion, for whose founder, Bartholomew of Simeri (d. 1130), he gave a commemorative sermon. Philagathus preached in Rossano proper; in Reggio; and in Sicily, at Messina, Taormina, Troina, and especially Palermo, where at least one of his sermons was delivered before King Roger II in the predecessor of today's cathedral. His sermon in Roger's Palatine Chapel (seemingly after 1140 but sometimes assigned to the chapel's consecration in 1140) contains the earliest extended description of this renowned monument.

Although Philagathus has been called a court preacher, it might be more accurate to call him a preacher whose distinction led to appearances at court. The venues of most of his sermons are not fully known. He was still active during the reign of William I (1154–1166). An allegorical commentary on the *Aethiopica* of Heliodorus (an ancient Greek novel used by Philagathus in at least one sermon), recently thought to be his, has now been shown to be much older. The attributions to him of the anonymous *Life* of Bartholomew of Simeri, of a grammatical textbook now lost, and of a verse introduction to the fables of Symeon Seth (one form of the Greek "mirror of princes" *Stephanites and Ichnelates*) are all very dubious.

Further Reading

Editions

Caruso, Stefano, ed. "Le tre omilie inedite 'Per la domenica delle palme' di Filagato da Cerami." *Epeterìs Hetaireías Byzantinôn Spoudôn*, 41, 1974, pp. 109–127.

Patrologia Graeca, 132, cols. 9–1078. (Scorso's edition and Latin translation of sixty-two sermons.)

Rossi Taibbi, Giuseppe, ed. *Filagato da Cerami: Omelie per i vangeli domenicali e le feste di tutto l'anno*, Vol. 1, *Omelie per le feste fisse*, Istituto siciliano di studi bizantini e neoellenici. Testi, 11. Palermo: Istituto Siciliano di Studi Bizantini e Neoetenici, 1969.

Translations

Gaşpar, Cristian-Nicolae. "Praising the Stylite in Southern Italy: Philagathos of Cerami on Saint Symeon the Stylite." *Annuario dell'Istituto Romeno di Cultura e Ricerca Umanistica*, 4, 2002, pp. 93–108.

Lavagnini, Bruno. *Profilo di Filagato da Cerami: Con traduzione della Omelia XXVII pronunziata dal pulpito della Cappe Palatina in Palermo*. Palermo: Accademia Nazionale di Scienze, Lettere, e Arti già del Buongusto, 1992. (Reprinted in *Bollettino della Badia Greca di Grottaferrata*, n.s., 44, 1990, pp. 231–244, issued in 1993.)

Manuscript

Rossi Taibbi, Giuseppe. *Sulla tradizione manoscritta dell'omiliario di Filagato da Cerami*. Istituto Siciliano di Studi Bizantini e Neoellenici, Quaderni, 1. Palermo: Istituto Siciliano di Studi Bizantini e Neoellenici, 1965.

Critical Studies

Acconcia Longo, Augusta. "Filippo il filosofo a Costantinopoli." *Rivista di Studi Bizantini e Neoellenici*, n.s., 28, 1991, pp. 3–21.

Foti, Maria Bianca. "Culture e scrittura nelle chiese e nei monasteri italo-greci." In *Civiltà del Mezzogiorno d'Italia: Libro, scrittura, documento in età normanno-sveva—Atti del convegno dell'Associazione Italiana dei Paleografi e Diplomatisti (Napoli–Badia di Cava dei Tirreni, 14–18 ottobre 1991)*, ed. Filippo D'Oria. Cultura Scritta e Memoria Storica, 1. Salerno: Carlone, 1994, pp. 41–76. (See especially pp. 65–67.)

Garzya, Antonio. "Per la cultura politica nella Sicilia greconormanna." In *Percorsi e tramiti di cultura*. Naples: M. D'Auria, 1997, pp. 241–247.

Houben, Hubert. "La predicazione." In *Strumenti, tempi, e luoghi di communicazione nel Mezzogiorno normanno-svevo: Atti delle undecime Giornate normanno-sveve, Bari, 26–29 ottobre 1993*, ed. Giosuè Musca and Vito Sivo. Bari: Dedalo, 1995, pp. 253–273.

Kitzinger, Ernst. "The Date of Philagathos' Homily for the Feast of Saints Peter and Paul." In *Byzantino-Sicula*, Vol. 2, *Miscellanea di scritti in memoria di Giuseppe Rossi Taibbi*. Istituto Siciliano di Studi Bizantini e Neoellenici, Quaderni, 8. Palermo: Istituto Siciliano di Studi Bizantini e Neoellenici, 1975, pp. 301–306.

Lucà, Santo. "I Normanni e la 'ritmica' del sec. XII." *Archivio Storico per la Calabria e la Lucania*, 60, 1993, pp. 1–91. (See especially pp. 69–79, 86–87.)

Perria, Lidia. "La clausola ritmica nella prosa di Filagato da Cerami." *Jahrbuch der österreichischen Byzantinistik*, 32 (*Akten des XVI. Internationalen Byzantinistenkongress, Wien, 4.–9. Oktober 1981*), part 3, 1982, pp. 365–373.

JOHN B. DILLON

PHILIP II AUGUSTUS
(1165–1223)

King of France, 1180–1223. Philip II was the first great architect of the medieval French monarchy. Building upon the accomplishments of Louis VI and Louis VII, he began the process of converting feudal into national monarchy, expanding the crown's political and geographical influence, by his death in 1223, far beyond what they had been at his accession in 1180.

As was common in the case of kings ascending as children to the throne, Philip was initially dominated by powerful relatives, in his case the influential and wealthy ruling family of Champagne. His early struggle to assert royal influence was supported by his father's rival, Henry II of England, who denied himself the pleasure of taking advantage of the fifteen-year-old king's apparent weakness. A few years later, Henry probably wished that he had not been so honorable, since Philip utilized the traditional patricidal conflict traditional in the Angevin family against his former protector. This policy saw the French king triumphant over his father's ancient adversary and his sons by 1204, when the luckless King John saw the Angevin territories in France dissolve. By the end of his reign, Philip II had increased his territory nearly fourfold. The English loss of territory north of the Loire augmented the French ruler's lands, but he also added to his acquisitions by the forfeitures of contumacious vassals, by political duplicity, by cleverly arranged marriages, and by manipulation of the confusion over land possession arising from the Albigensian Crusade. Philip Augustus was not a great military leader; he was an astute politician.

Philip was the founder of the centralized bureaucratic state. He chose bourgeois administrators, as well as men from the lower nobility, to run his kingdom, men whose primary loyalty was to their king rather than to their class or to their families. Their offices were remunerated by salary rather than farmed. Philip used feudal rights to enhance his royal position; in his reign, the authority of the king began shifting slowly from his rights exercised as feudal suzerain to his rights exercised as sovereign; he was becoming less a private, feudal lord than a public figure of authority. This obviously contributed to a decline in the functional importance of the feudal structure (it was never a feudal *system*), as did the growing commutation of lord-vassal relationships from mutually exchanged personal obligations into money payments. The administrators of Philip's domains, *baillis* and *prévôts*, were essentially estate managers, men with wide-ranging fiscal, judicial, military, and other responsibilities. Philip's financial administration improved greatly, his policies based upon the model of his newly conquered province, Normandy. He also made Paris what we moderns would call the capital of France.

Philip Augustus was, then, the monarch under whom French monarchy became more a practical than a theoretical concept. His domain, larger than the fief of any vassal, was to remain the dominant power base in France in succeeding generations. As Luchaire wrote, at Philip's death "the [Capetian] dynasty was solidly established, and France founded."

See also **Henry II; John**

Further Reading

Baldwin, John W. *The Government of Philip Augustus.* Berkeley: University of California Press, 1986.

Bautier, Robert-Henri, ed. *La France de Philippe Auguste:le temps des mutations.* Paris: CNRS, 1982.

Bordonove, Georges. *Philippe Auguste.* Paris; Pygmalion, 1983.

Fawtier, Robert. *The Capetian Kings of France.* London: St. Martin, 1960.

Hallam, Elizabeth. *Capetian France, 987–1328.* London: Longman, 1980.

JAMES W. ALEXANDER

PHILIP III THE BOLD
(1245–1285)

King of France, 1270–85. As a boy, Philip appears to have been easygoing and easily influenced, especially by his mother, Marguerite of Provence. As a king, he was dominated at the outset by the counsels of Pierre de la Broce, a former adviser of his father, Louis IX. Later, he came under the influence of his uncle Charles, count of Anjou. Philip became king while on crusade to Tunis with his father, who died of illness during the siege of the city. Philip is the first king whose regnal years begin with the burial of his predecessor rather than the coronation of the new king, which in his case was delayed until 1271.

Although most scholars regard Philip's reign as a hiatus in the development of the monarchy, it was marked by important events. The death, childless, of his uncle and aunt, Alphonse of Poitiers and Jeanne de Toulouse, in 1271 on the way back from crusade brought their vast holdings in the south of France into the royal domain despite the importunities of Charles of Anjou, who coveted the fiefs. The acquisition of these lands by the crown sealed the ascendancy of the French in Languedoc. Philip carried on an active foreign policy. With the support of Charles of Anjou, he briefly put forward his candidacy to the imperial throne. He made efforts to draw neighboring German principalities under French influence. He aggressively defended Capetian family interests in Castile and Aragon. And he intervened with military success in Navarre when a succession crisis there in the mid-1270s threatened French interests.

Philip was drawn into war in Spain again toward

the end of his reign when the Aragonese supported the rebellion of the Sicilians against Charles of Anjou (the Sicilian Vespers, 1282). Charles's pleas for support and the blessing of the pope led to the French crusade against Aragon, an ill-fated expedition across the Pyrénées in 1285, in which the French were routed. During the retreat, Philip III himself died.

Philip was married twice: first (1262) to Isabella of Aragon, who died in 1271 on the return from the crusade to Tunis. She was the mother of Philip's son and successor, Philip IV the Fair. In 1274, Philip III married Marie de Brabant, whose party at court was responsible for bringing an end to the influence of Pierre de la Broce; charged with treason, he was executed in 1278. Philip the Fair seems always to have had a strong dislike of Marie, about whom Pierre had spread ugly rumors. These included allegations that she and her party wanted to displace the children of her husband's first marriage by her own in the line of succession and that she had even poisoned Philip IV's older brother as part of her plan. No such conspiracy was ever proved, however, and the succession proceeded smoothly even under the difficult circumstances of the crusade against Aragon.

See also **Louis IX**

Further Reading

Langlois, Charles-Victor. *Le régne de Philippe III le Hardi*. Paris: Hachette, 1887.

WILLIAM CHESTER JORDAN

PHILIP IV THE FAIR
(1268–314)

King of France, 1285–1314. Philip expanded royal power within the kingdom and dominated the ecclesiastical and secular affairs of western Europe. The grandson of St. Louis, whose canonization he achieved in 1297, he imitated and attempted to surpass Louis's achievements. Served devotedly by a series of powerful ministers, he imposed his own stamp on governmental policies, instituting widespread consultation of his subjects, issuing a host of reform charters, canceling and returning taxes when the causes that prompted them ceased, and subordinating to his authority the dukes of Aquitaine/Guyenne (also kings of England) and the counts of Flanders. Attentive to matters of conscience and believing in his role as God's minister, he upheld Christian orthodoxy against Pope Boniface VIII and the Knights Templar, appealing to a general council against the pope and destroying the Templars; he obtained papal bulls forgiving him for sins he feared he might commit; he magnified the importance of the royal power to cure; in 1306, he expelled the Jews from France. Anxious to establish the full legitimacy and the glory of the Capetian house, he encouraged the reinterpretation of the Capetians' history. Upholding the highest standards of morality and publicizing his own scrupulosity, in 1314 he presided over the trial and execution of two knights charged with adultery with his own daughters-in-law, thus casting doubt on the legitimacy of his grandchildren.

Born between April and June 1268, while Louis IX was still ruling, Philip, second son of Philip III the Bold and Isabella of Aragon (d. 1271), had a troubled childhood, dominated by the scandals that erupted at court after his father's marriage in 1274 to Marie de Brabant, suspected of poisoning Philip's elder brother, who died in 1276, shortly before the death of his third brother. In 1284, Philip was knighted and married to Jeanne, heiress of Champagne and Navarre; he became king in 1285 after his father's death on a crusade against Aragon. Having extricated himself from the ill-fated venture, Philip avoided conflict for nine years, but in 1294 he precipitated war against the mighty Edward I of England, duke of Aquitaine/Guyenne. Settled in 1303, the fruitless episode strained the kingdom's finances and led to manipulation of the currency. It resulted in the marriages of Philip's sister Marguerite to Edward in 1299 and of his daughter Isabella to Edward II in 1308; the latter union would give Edward III grounds for claiming the throne of France. The war also initiated a conflict with the Flemings, Edward I's allies and Philip's subjects, which, settled in 1305, broke out again in 1312 because of the harsh peace terms Philip imposed. Clerical taxation imposed for the war occasioned Boniface VIII's controversial bull *Clericis laicos* in 1296. From then until Boniface's death in 1303, Philip and the pope were locked in sporadic but bitter struggles involving the limits of secular jurisdiction over ecclesiastics. In the spring of 1303, Philip presided over assemblies in Paris that charged Boniface with heresy and immorality; in September 1303, the pope was violently attacked in Anagni when Philip's minister Guillaume de Nogaret summoned him to submit to the judgment of a council. Clement V, the Gascon-born cardinal who became pope in 1305, was more to the king's liking; he granted Philip many privileges and in 1311 accepted the suppression of the Knights Templar, the crusading order whose assets Philip had seized in 1307, again because he believed them guilty of heresy and immorality.

Philip failed to achieve some of his ambitions. He never succeeded in placing a relative on the imperial throne; his visionary scheme after his wife's death in 1305 to become ruler of the Holy Land was abortive. The power he exercised within the kingdom led, at the end of his reign, to the formation of leagues of disgruntled subjects protesting his fiscal and monetary policies and demanding the restoration of old customs; his eldest son and successor, Louis X (r. 1314–16), issued numerous charters to pacify them, and he sacrificed Philip's minister Enguerran de Marigny and other officials to their princely enemies at court. Philip used his three sons and his daughter to advance his own goals. Isabella married Edward II of England; Louis married Marguerite, daughter of the duke of Burgundy; Philip's wife, Jeanne, brought to the crown the county of Burgundy; Jeanne's mother, Mahaut of Artois, offered a dowry of 100,000 *livres* to persuade Philip to accept another daughter, Blanche, as the wife of his youngest son, the future Charles IV. The imprisonment of Marguerite and Blanche for adultery in 1314 was the first of a series of tragedies suffered by Philip's direct descendants. Because of the death of Louis X's posthumous son, John I, the product of a second marriage, the throne passed to Philip V (r. 1316–22); because he left no male heir, he was succeeded by Charles IV (r. 1322–28), at whose death without male heir the rule of the direct Capetians ended and the crown passed to the house of Valois.

See also **Boniface VIII, Pope; Clement V, Pope; Edward I; Jeanne of Navarre**

Further Reading

Bautier, Robert-Henri. "Diplomatique et histoire politique: ce que la critique diplomatique nous apprend sur la personnalité de Philippe le Bel." Revue *historique* 259 (1978): 3–27.

Brown, Elizabeth A.R. *The Monarchy of Capetian France and Royal Ceremonial.* London: Variorum, 1991.

———. *Politics and Institutions in Capetian France.* London: Variorum, 1991.

Favier, Jean. *Philippe le Bel* Paris: Fayard, 1978.

Strayer, Joseph R. *The Reign of Philip the Fair.* Princeton: Princeton University Press, 1980.

ELIZABETH A.R. BROWN

PHILIP VI (1293–1350)

First Valois king of France, 1328–50. The son of Charles of Valois (brother of King Philip IV the Fair) and Marguerite, daughter of Charles II of Naples, Philip did not become an important figure until he inherited the counties of Valois, Anjou, and Maine from his father in 1325. By that time, the reigning monarch was Philip's first cousin Charles IV, who had no son or surviving brother. When Charles died at the end of January 1328, he left a pregnant queen, and the French magnates named Philip of Valois regent, with the understanding that he would become king if the queen gave birth to a daughter.

When a daughter was indeed born on April 1, Philip VI became king. He was crowned at Reims late in May, and then, at the behest of an important supporter, Louis I of Flanders, he led a French army against Flemish rebels and won a resounding victory at Cassel in August.

Throughout his reign, Philip VI had to maneuver among conflicting political groupings whose ability to cause him trouble was enhanced by the existence of other descendants of St. Louis who might claim the French throne. Philip IV the Fair, Louis X, and Philip V all had grandsons who were disqualified by the decision to exclude princes whose claims were through their mothers. Two of these, Edward III of England and the future Charles II of Navarre (r. 1349–87), presented malcontents with attractive alternatives to whom to give allegiance. To avoid alienating the count of Flanders and duke of Burgundy, Philip had to rule against his friend and cousin Robert of Artois in the disputed succession to Artois, and Robert then gave his allegiance to Edward III. When Philip ruled in favor of his nephew Charles de Blois in the disputed Breton succession (1341), the opposing claimant, Jean de Montfort, also turned to Edward. Many nobles of the north and west felt more closely tied to England than to the Valois, and they disliked Philip's queen, Jeanne of Burgundy. Perhaps because of her influence, Philip tended to distrust this important regional aristocracy and to draw a disproportionately large number of his advisers from regions like Auvergne and Burgundy.

Amid growing discontent in the north and west, Philip's relations with England steadily deteriorated. The two monarchies could not resolve differences over Aquitaine, and Philip supported Scottish opposition to Edward, while the latter built up an anti-Valois coalition in the Low Countries. In 1337, the Hundred Years' War began, with the first years marked by expensive preparations and little military action. Edward then defeated the French fleet at Sluys in 1340 and gained a valuable new fighting front the next year with the disputed succession in Brittany. Always short of money, Philip gave great power to the leaders of the Chambre des Comptes, whose aggressive fiscal measures did not produce the military success needed to offset the antagonism they caused.

In 1345, the military situation began to deteriorate seriously. The English victory at Auberoche that autumn secured important gains in Aquitaine. The next year, Edward III invaded Normandy, threatened Paris, and then crushed Philip's army at Crécy. In 1347, the English in Brittany won a major victory at La Roche-Derrien, while Philip could not save Calais from capitulating to Edward III in August.

At the end of 1347, the Estates General convened in Paris and demanded governmental reforms before endorsing plans for each region to raise large taxes to pay for an effective army. Before this initiative could achieve results, France began to be ravaged by the Black Death, which eventually claimed the lives of Philip's queen and daughter-in-law and left government and society in disarray. The plague also produced a lull in the war, but when he died in August 1350, Philip left behind many problems for his son and successor, John II the Good.

See also **Edward III; Philip IV the Fair**

Further Reading

Cazelles, Raymond. *La société politique et la crise de la royauté sous Philippe de Valois.* Paris: Argences, 1958.

Henneman, John Bell. *Royal Taxation in Fourteenth Century France: The Development of War Financing, 1322–1356.* Princeton: Princeton University Press, 1971.

Viard, Jules. "La France sous Philippe VI de Valois." *Bibliothèque de l'école des Chartes* 59 (1896): 337–402.

——. "Itinéraire de Philippe de Valois." *Bibliothèque de l'école des* Chartes 74 (1913): 74–128,524–92; 84 (1923): 166–70.

JOHN BELL HENNEMAN, JR.

PHILIP THE BOLD (1342–1404)

The first of the Valois dukes of Burgundy, Philip the Bold was the fourth son of King John II of France and Bonne de Luxembourg. Born at Pontoise on January 17, 1342, he fought beside his father at the age of fourteen and was captured with him at the Battle of Poitiers (1356). After he and the king secured release in 1360, he became, duke of Touraine, but he surrendered this duchy in 1363 when John II made him duke of Burgundy and first peer of France. In May 1364, the new king, Philip's brother Charles V, confirmed these titles.

After complex diplomatic maneuvering, Philip became an international figure with his marriage, in 1369, to Marguerite, daughter of the count of Flanders and heiress to five counties in northern and eastern France. The deaths of her grandmother (1382) and father (1384) brought these lands to her and Philip, but they needed military force to secure the most important of them, Flanders, which had been in rebellion since 1379. Marguerite also had a claim to the duchy of Brabant, and in 1385 she and Philip arranged the marriage of their son and daughter to members of the Wittelsbach family that ruled the counties of Hainaut, Holland, and Zeeland, thereby laying the foundations for a Burgundian state that eventually included most of the Low Countries.

Despite his expanding role in the Netherlands, Philip was above all the most powerful French prince of his generation. At the death of Charles V in 1380, he led a coalition that ousted from the regency his older brother Louis of Anjou, and he dominated the French government for the next eight years. He played an active diplomatic role in the Anglo-French war, the papal Schism, and imperial politics, and he secured the services of the French royal army to crush the Flemish rebels at Roosebeke in 1382 and to intimidate his enemy the duke of Guelders in 1388.

Philip supported his projects with vast sums drawn from the receipts of the French crown, as did his brother, John, duke of Berry. In the fall of 1388, Charles VI dismissed his uncles from the royal council at the urging of a reforming coalition of royal officials and military commanders, known as the Marmousets. Four years later, Charles VI's first attack of mental illness enabled the duke of Burgundy to regain his dominant position, which he held for another decade before gradually losing power at court to his nephew Louis of Orléns. He died near Brussels on April 27, 1404.

Besides establishing Burgundian power in the Netherlands, Philip the Bold began the tradition of lavish support for the arts by the Burgundian dukes. He also was the primary organizer of the abortive crusade of 1396 led by his eldest son, John, count of Nevers. His great achievements were to a large degree accomplished at the expense of the French taxpayers, but he gave his native land nearly twenty years of statesmanlike, if sometimes self-serving, leadership.

See also **Charles V the Wise; Charles VI**

Further Reading

Nieuwenhuysen, Andrée van. *Les finances du duc deBourgogne Philippe le Hardi (1384–1404).* Brussels: Éditions de l'Université de Bruxelles, 1984.

Palmer, John J.N. *England, France and Christendom, 1377–99.* London: Routledge and Kegan Paul, 1972.

Petit, Ernest. *Ducs de Bourgogne de la maison de Valois, I: Philippe le Hardi.* Paris: Champion, 1909.

Richard, Jean. *Les ducs de Bourgogne et la formation du duché* Paris: Les Belles Lettres, 1954.

Vaughan, Richard. *Philip the Bold: The Formation of the Burgundian State.* Cambridge: Harvard University Press, 1962.

JOHN BELL HENNEMAN, JR.

PHILIP THE CHANCELLOR (ca. 1160/85–ca. 1236)

An influential theologian, a preacher of considerable stature, and an accomplished poet, Philip was born into ecclesiastical circles: he was the illegitimate son of Archdeacon Philip of Paris and was related through his father to Bishop Étienne of Noyon (d. 1211) and Bishop Pierre of Paris (d. 1218), both of whom favored Philip's career. After studying theology and law, he appears in the historical record no later than 1211 as archdeacon of Noyon.

As chancellor of the University of Paris, a position that he held from 1217, Philip had authority over the fledgling university. Philip's chancellorship came in an era of discontent and controversy, and in a combative move early in his tenure (1219) he excommunicated the masters and students—a move that Pope Honorius III ordered him to reverse. During the strike initiated in 1229, Philip sided with the pope and the university against William of Auvergne, bishop of Paris, and Blanche of Castile, regent during Louis IX's minority. The papal bull *Parens scientiarum* of Gregory IX ended the university strike in 1231. Not long after Philip's death, Henri d'Andeli wrote a *Dit du chancelier Philippe*, in which he is associated with jongleurs, chansons, and vielle playing.

As a master of theology, Philip composed a treatise on moral theology, the *Summa de bono*, that had considerable influence on the earliest generation of Franciscan masters. It was organized into two main parts, *De bono naturae* and *De bono gratiae*, with the latter subdivided into three: *gratia gratum faciens, gratia gratis data, gratia virtutum* (both theological and cardinal). Philip is also credited with 723 sermons, which reveal a preacher vigorously calling both the clergy and the laity to a just and holy way of life.

Of the fifty-eight monophonic conductus attributed to Philip, at least twenty-one texts are confirmed as his. *Angelus ad virginem* was made famous by Chaucer: in *The Miller's Tale*, the scholarly but impoverished cleric Nicholas sings it. Medieval sources ascribe nine polyphonic conductus to Philip, and among four possible textings of conductus caudae at least *Bullia fulminante* (and its contrafact *Veste nuptiali*) and *Minor natu filiu* definitely can be counted as his; *Anima lugi lacrima* and *Crucifigat omnes* (which has two contrafacts: *Mundum renovavit* and *Curritur ad vocem*) are suspected of also being his. He penned the four known tropes to Pérotin's two great organa quadrupla: *Vide prophecie, Homo cum mandato dato, De Stephani roseo sanguine,* and *Adesse festina*. Philip and Pérotin appear to have known one another and may have collaborated. Since so many of Philip's texts were tropes or contrafacts for music that already had been composed, it would seem that he was not a composer himself. Although his defense of accumulating benefices earned him the displeasure of the Dominicans, he remained a friend of the Franciscans throughout his life and was buried in their church.

See also **Blanche of Castile; Chaucer, Geoffrey; Pérotin**

Further Reading

Dreves, Guido Maria, ed. *Lateinische Hymnendichter des Mittelalters.* Leipzig: Reisland, 1907. *Analecta hymnica medii aevi.* Vol. 50, pp. 528–32.

Paine, Thomas. *Associa tecum in patria:* A Newly Identified Organum Trope by Philip the Chancellor." *Journal of the American Musicological Society* 39 (1986): 233–54.

Principe, Walter H. *The Theology of the Hypostatic Union in the Early Thirteenth Century, IV: Philip the Chancellor's Theology of the Hypostatic Union.* Toronto: Pontifical Institute of Mediaeval Studies, 1975.

Steiner, Ruth. "Some Monophonic Songs Composed Around 1200." *Musical Quarterly* 52 (1966): 56–70.

Wright, Craig. *Music and Ceremony at Notre Dame of Paris 500–1550.* Cambridge: Cambridge University Press, 1989, pp. 249–99.

Wicki, Nikolaus. "La *pecia* dans la tradition manuscrite de la *Summa de bono* de Philippe le Chancelier." In The *Editing of Theological and Philosophical Texts from the Middle Ages,* ed. Monika Asztalos. Stockholm: Almqvist and Wiksell, 1986, pp. 93–104.

MARK ZIER/SANDRA PINEGAR

PHILIP THE GOOD (1396–1467)

Duke of Burgundy, 1419–67. The son and successor of John the Fearless, duke of Burgundy and count of Flanders, Philip was twenty-three years old when the assassination of his father in 1419 made him the mightiest peer of France and the most important prince of the Low Countries. His reign of forty-seven years brought prosperity, prestige, and territorial expansion to his lands. He guided the ill-fated Burgundian state to the peak of its power, but its greatness, dependant on the weakness of the French monarchy, dissipated after the end of the Hundred Years' War.

An astute diplomat and judicious in the use of force, Philip sought to overcome ducal Burgundy's status as a French apanage by enmeshing it in an independent polity in the territories between France and Germany. The Treaty of Troyes (1420) allied him with Henry V of England, secured his French holdings, and allowed him to concentrate on the Low Countries. His second (1422) and third (1430) marriages secured political allies and territorial claims. Conquests of Holland (1425–33) and Luxembourg (1443), and the peaceful acquisitions of Namur (1420) and Brabant (1430) doubled the size of his lands. Philip eventually sought the crown of a restored Lotharingia from the emperor Frederick III in 1447. His failure to obtain a crown had no immediate political consequences, but it foreshadowed the doom of the Burgundian polity, which remained an overextended Franco-imperial principality in an age of emerging sovereign states. Within France, Philip provided minimal support for the government of Henry VI of England and later realigned himself with Charles VII in 1435 (Treaty of Arras). Fearing a revitalized monarchy, Philip abstained from the decisive campaigns of the Hundred Years' War and sheltered the fugitive dauphin after 1456. The failure of such efforts became manifest when his son, the future Charles the Bold, assumed control of Burgundy in 1464 and launched the *Guerre du bien publique* against Louis XI. Philip's rule thus ended as it began, with Valois France and Valois Burgundy inextricably locked in mortal conflict.

Philip's most celebrated achievement was to make chivalric culture an instrument of policy. The creation of the Order of the Golden Fleece in 1430 provided a diplomatic tool linking the nobility of his disparate territories and precluding their affiliation with any other prince. Even such ostentatious festivals as the Pheasant Banquet in 1454 had political value, for through such devices the prestige of the Valois dukes reached its zenith. Philip himself was a model of late-medieval chivalry: handsome, courageous, pious, self-indulgent, extravagant. He maintained mistresses and bastards throughout his lands yet made heartfelt, albeit unfulfilled, promises to go on crusade. He is remembered as "the Good" above all for the talented artists who gave him the accolade and immortalized Burgundy in tapestries, the paintings of van Eyck, and literature ranging from the *Cent nouvelles nouvelles* to the histories of Chastellain. He may seem less successful in retrospect than he did at the time, but Burgundy was a phantasm and Philip sustained it the best of all his line.

See also **Bedford, John Duke of; Charles VII; Charles the Bold**

Further Reading

Bonenfant, Paul. *Philippe le Bon*. Brussels: La Renaissance du Livre, 1955.

Cartellieri, Otto. *The Court of Burgundy: Studies in the History of Civilization*. New York: Askell House, 1970.

Huizinga, Johan. *The Waningofthe Middle Ages: A Study of the Forms of Life, Thought and Art in France and the Netherlands in the Dawn of the Renaissance*. London: Arnold, 1924.

Vaughn, Richard. *Philip the Good: The Apogee of Burgundy*. London: Longman, 1970.

——. Valois *Burgundy*. London: Lane, 1975.

PAUL D. SOLON

PHILIPPE DE THAÜN
(fl. late llth–early 12th c)

Author of the earliest surviving scientific works in French. Philippe's Anglo-Norman dialect, which he helped establish as a literary medium, probably indicates that he was born in England, but he was of continental parentage originating in Thaon in lower Normandy, 13 miles northwest of Caen. His *Cumpoz* (probably 1113) is dedicated to an uncle, Humphrey (Honfroi) of Thaon, chaplain to Eudo Fitz-Hubert, also known as Eudo Dapifer, steward of Henry I of England, whose royal court was a center of learned activity. Philippe's two signed works, the *Cumpoz* and the *Bestiaire*, are in hexasyllabic rhymed, occasionally assonanced, couplets, but the *Bestiaire* ends with an octosyllabic lapidary. Several anonymous works have also been attributed to him.

The *Cumpoz* ("computus") is a practical treatise on the calendar that tells how to predict the dates of Easter and the movable feasts governed by Easter. The problem is reconciliation of the lunar calendar, which determines the date of Easter by its association with Passover, with the Julian solar calendar. Along with accurately detailed computational material, Philippe gives free rein to an allegorical bent in discussions of the zodiac and the names of the days and the months. He twice uses the year 1113 as an example for computing, once implying that it is the current year; in any case, the *Cumpoz* was dedicated before Eudo's death in 1120, for he is referred to as though still alive.

The *Bestiaire* (ca. 1125) is a "Book of Nature" divided into three sections: land animals and sea creatures, birds, and precious gems; it draws on traditional bestiary material from ancient myth and biblical sources. An article on a creature or stone generally opens with a physical description, often incorporating drawings with the text, followed by discussion of specific properties or habits. Allegorical commentary derived from the descriptive material then demonstrates the revelation of God in the natural world. The articles in the first two sections are arranged hierarchically, from the "kings" of each species (the lion, the eagle), which signify Christ, to the "lower" (land-bound birds, and fish), which refer to Satan; precious gems, beginning with their "king," the diamond, are associated with the powers of good. The *Bestiaire* is dedicated to Adeliza (Aaliz de Louvain), whom Henry I married in 1121; she retained the title of queen four years after Henry's death in 1135. Scholars tend to date the *Bestiaire* from early in Adeliza's marriage because of the date of the *Cumpoz*. One manuscript of the *Bestiaire* bears a rededication to Eleanor of Aquitaine, Henry II's queen, written after 1154.

The anonymous *Livre de Sibile* (1135–54), dedicated to the empress Matilda, Henry I's daughter, is a book of prophecies. Authorship has been ascribed to Philippe primarily because the text bears striking linguistic and stylistic resemblances to the signed works; in addition, personal content in the dedication parallels information found in the rededication of the *Bestiaire* to Eleanor of Aquitaine. On the basis of less convincing evidence, two early Anglo-Norman lapidaries, the *Alphabetical* and the *Apocalyptic*, an Anglo-Norman allegorical *Desputeisun del cors e de l'arme*, and a geographical treatise, *Les Divisiuns del mund*, have also been attributed to Philippe.

See also **Eleanor of Aquitaine, Henry I**

Further Reading

Philippe de Thaün. *Le bestiaire de Philippe de Thaün*, ed. Emanuel Walberg. Paris: Plon, 1900.

——. *Li cumpoz*, ed. Émile Mall. Strasbourg, 1873.

——. *Le livre de Sibile by Philippe de Thaon*, ed. Hugh Shields. London: Anglo-Norman Text Society, 1979.

Legge, M. Dominica. *Anglo-Norman Literature and Its Background*. Oxford: Clarendon, 1963.

McCulloch, Florence. *Mediaeval Latin and French Bestiaries*. Chapel Hill: University of North Carolina Press, 1960.

Pickens, Rupert T. "The Literary Activity of Philippe de Thaün." *Romance Notes* 12 (1970–71): 208–12.

Shields, Hugh. "Philippe de Thaon, auteur du *Livre de Sibylle?*" *Romania* 85 (1964): 455–77.

——. "More Poems by Philippe de Thaon?" In *Anglo-Norman Anniversary Essays*, ed. Ian Short. London: Anglo-Norman Text Society, 1993, pp. 337–59.

Studer, Paul, and Joan Evans. *Anglo-Norman Lapidaries*. Paris: Champion, 1924.

RUPERT T. PICKENS

PIER DELLA VIGNA (c. 1190–1249)

Pier della Vigna (Petrus de Vinea) was born in Capua of obscure parentage and became a senior bureaucrat and officer of state under Emperor Frederick II. Pier had broad and enduring influence as a master of Latin documentary composition and Latin prose stylistics more generally.

Pier's education included the study of law and rhetoric, the former probably at the University of Bologna, and the latter probably at a notarial school in Capua or Bologna, since Bologna and Capua were centers for this sort of instruction. He entered Frederick's court chancery in the early 1220s, became a high-ranking judge, had major financial responsibilities, and wrote private letters for Frederick that did not go through the chancery. It is thought that his superior skill as a stylist and advocate was immediately recognized and that from the beginning of his lifelong employment in this milieu it fell to him to compose the most important and stylistically taxing documents. By 1243, he was protonotary of the imperial court and logothete—a high official with the functions of chancellor—of the kingdom of Sicily. In 1244, he and his colleague (and fellow Campanian) Thaddeus of Sessa were authorized to decide on all petitions presented to the emperor. Pier was a trusted counselor to Frederick, and Frederick's spokesman in many of the emperor's troubled dealings with the papacy and with the communes of northern Italy. Throughout Frederick's long dispute with Pope Gregory IX, Pier represented the emperor at the papal court and at the courts of foreign princes; shortly before Pope Innocent IV deposed the emperor in 1245, Pier attempted to intervene on his sovereign's behalf.

That Pier used his position to enrich himself and to advance his family is not surprising. But in this regard he does appear to have been excessively grasping and thus to have made many enemies. For reasons that are unclear, Frederick had him arrested in Cremona early in 1249, and blinded a few months later, probably in the fortress of San Miniato near Pisa. Pier's death not long afterward was believed in some quarters to have been a suicide, a view shared by Dante. Pier is one of the most memorable souls in the *Divine Comedy,* though he is identified only as "the man who held the double key to Frederick's heart" (*Inferno*, 13 58–59). It seems likely, as Stephany (1982) has argued, that the portrayal and punishment of Pier in the *Divine Comedy* were provoked by Dante's literal reading of Pier's widely admired *Eulogy* of Frederick, a composition that may have struck Dante as blasphemous and idolatrous.

One of a pair of busts of bearded males from Frederick's monumental gate at Capua (the gate was demolished in 1557 and the bust is now in the Museo Provinciale Campano) is sometimes considered a portrait of Pier. But it seems unlikely that the Hohenstaufen regime would have knowingly permitted this showpiece of imperial iconography to retain, in close proximity to the image of Frederick himself, the likeness of a man stigmatized in official documents of the early 1250s as *Petrus proditor* ("Pier the traitor"). Pier has also been identified as one of the figures in a portrait (now lost) at the emperor's palace at Naples, which supposedly showed him dispensing justice in Frederick's presence; but this too seems dubious.

Pier was famous in his lifetime as a person of high culture and as an artist in Latin prose. His production as a writer falls into several different categories. His early official letters match the style of the Roman curia at the time, a style characterized by elaborate patterns of verbal, phonic, and rhythmic ornaments and laden with biblical citations, all intended to convey honor and respect for the addressee and a solemn celebration of the status quo. The same verbal musicality and allusive citations of well-known biblical and classical texts are evident in letters of consolation, as well as occasional pieces such as the famous *Eulogy*, in which messianic proclamations about Frederick are amplified with biblical language. After 1225, when the emperor abandoned his posture of gratitude toward the papacy and began to focus on what he perceived as conflicts of interest between papacy and empire, the rhetoric of Pier's letters shifts, in certain cases, from persuasion rooted in praise and affection for the addressee to persuasion based on the points of contention between the parties. The historical circumstances of controversial events become an integral part of the persuasive strategy. For nearly thirty years, Pier would wage a polemical campaign in defense of Frederick II in an attempt to win the support of prelates and princes throughout Latin Europe. Ultimately, his choice of rhetorical approaches would always depend on his perception of the intended public and the subject matter discussed in the letter.

Although the extent of his personal contribution remains controversial, Pier was at least partly responsible for the drafting of *Liber Augustalis* (1231), the Latin version of Frederick's Constitutions of Melfi, a massive law code asserting the absolute authority of the prince in his kingdom. The language of its *Proemium* is richly ornamented and cadenced. Just as the *Eulogy* appropriates biblical language to glorify the emperor and his court, the *Proemium* invokes biblical, patristic, and Aristotelian phrases, as well as classical Roman legal phrases, to suggest the universality of imperial rule.

Collections of Pier's documents, to which were added some of his personal letters and various writings of his correspondents and others, began to be made as early as the 1270s and came to be known as the *Epistole* (*Letters*), *Dictamina* (*Formal Communications*), or *Summa* (*Treatise*) of Pier della Vigna. Circulating in several different redactions, they served into the fifteenth century and beyond as models in rhetorical instruction and were used pragmatically in many chanceries. At least 230 manuscripts are known; their quantity and quality attest to the importance that contemporaries and successive generations attached to these writings. The Florentine Guelf Brunetto Latini, writing several decades after Pier's death, commemorates this imperial official as an exemplary orator, and as such, master of Frederick and of the empire.

Pier's other surviving works and possible works include two Latin poems in rhythmical quatrains whose attribution to Pier, though early, is not certain: one on the months of the year and their properties, the other a satire on the mendicants. Most of Pier's Latin writings and the Latin texts associated with him still lack modern critical editions.

Pier is also a minor figure in early Italian literature. He was one of the court poets of the Sicilian school and is named in the manuscripts as the author of at least eight pieces. Two *canzoni* and a sonnet (the latter is part of a *tenzone* with Jacopo Mostacci and Giacomo da Lentini) are securely attributed to Pier; a third *canzone* (*Poi tanta caunoscenza*) is less certainly his. The modern editor of the Sicilian school corpus, Panvini (1962–1964, 1994), rejects, on a variety of grounds, Pier's authorship of the remainder.

See also **Dante Alighieri; Frederick II**

Further Reading

Editions: Latin Writings

Böhmer, Johann Friedrich, ed. "Die Regesten des Kaiserreichs unter Philipp, Otto IV, Friedrich II, Heinrich (VII), Conrad IV, Heinrich Raspe, Wilhelm und Richard, 1198–1272." In *Regesta imperii*, Vol. 5, ed. Julius Ficker and Eduard Winkelmann. Innsbruck: Wagner, 1881–1901. (Reprint, Hildesheim: Georg Olms, 1971.)

Casters, Louis. "Prose latine attribuée à Pierre de la Vigne." *Revue des Langues Romanes*, 32, 1888, pp. 430–452. (Critical edition of the satire against the mendicants.)

Conrad, Hermann, Thea von der Lieck-Buycken, and Wolfgang Wagner, eds. *Die Konstitutionen Friedrichs II. von Hohenstaufen für sein Königreich Sizilien.* Studien und Quellen zur Welt Kaiser Friedrichs II, 2. Cologne: Böhlau, 1973. (Edition and German translation of *Liber Augustalis*.)

Holder-Egger, O. "Bericht über eine Reise nach Italien im Jahre 1891." *Neues Archiv der Gesellschaft für Ältere Deutsche Geschichtskunde*, 17, 1892, pp. 461–524. (Poem on the months of the year, pp. 501–503.)

Huillard-Bréholles, J.-L.-A., ed. *Historia diplomatica Friderici Secundi*, 6 vols. Paris: Plon, 1852–1861. (Reprint, Turin: Bottega d'Erasmo, 1963. Official documents in chronological order.)

——, ed. *Vie et correspondance de Pierre de la Vigne, ministre de l'Empereur Frédéric II.* Paris: Plon, 1865. (Reprint, Aalen: Scientia, 1966. See Latin personal correspondence, pp. 289–404; and *Eulogy* of Frederick, pp. 425–426.)

Editions: Italian Writings

Macciocca, Gabriella, ed. *Poesie volgari di Pier della Vigna.* Tesi di Dottorato di Ricerca, Dip. di Studi Romanzi, Università degli Studi di Roma. Rome: La Sapienza, 1996.

Panvini, Bruno, ed. *Le rime della scuola siciliana.* Biblioteca dell' Archivum Romanicum, Series 1(65 and 72). Florence: L. S. Olschki, 1962–1964, Vol. 1, pp. xliii–xlix, 125–130, 412–414, 647.

——, ed. *Poeti italiani della corte di Federico II*, rev. ed. Naples: Liguori, 1994, pp. 185–192, 259.

Manuscript

Schaller, Hans Martin, with Bernhard Vogel. *Handschriftenverzeichnis zur Briefsammlung des Petrus de Vinea.* Monumenta Germaniae Historica, Hilfsmittel, 18. Hannover: Hahn, 2002.

Critical Studies

Cassell, Anthony K. "Pier della Vigna's Metamorphosis: Iconography and History." In *Dante, Petrarch, Boccaccio: Studies in the Italian Trecento in Honor of Charles S. Singleton*, ed. Aldo S. Bernardo and Anthony L. Pellegrini. Medieval and Renaissance Texts and Studies, 22. Binghamton, N.Y.: Medieval and Renaissance Texts and Studies, 1983, pp. 31–76.

Delle Donne, Fulvio. "Lo stile della cancelleria di Federico II ed i presunti influssi arabi." In *Atti dell'Accademia Pontaniana*, n.s., 41, 1992, pp. 153–164.

——. "Le 'Consolationes' del IV libro del epistolario di Pier della Vigna." *Vichiana*, 4, 1993, pp. 268–290.

——. "Una perduta raffigurazione federiciana descritta da Francesco Pipino e la sede della cancelleria imperiale." *Studi Medievali*, Series 3, 38, 1997, pp. 737–749. (Reprinted in Fulvio Delle Donne. *Politica e letteratura nel Mezzogiorno medievale: La cronachistica dei secoli XII-XV.* Immagini del Medioevo, 4. Salerno: Cadone, 2001, pp. 111–126.)

Di Capua, Francesco. "Lo stile della Curia romana e il 'cursus' nelle epistole di Pier della Vigna e nei documenti della Cancelleria sveva." *Giornale Italiano di Filologia*, 2, 1949, pp. 97–166. (Reprinted in Francesco Di Capua. *Scritti minori*, Vol 1. New York: Desclée, 1958, pp. 500–523.)

Dilcher, Hermann. *Die sizilianische Gesetzgebung Kaiser Friedrichs II: Quellen der Constitutionen von Melfi und ihrer Novellen.* Studien und Quellen zur Welt Kaiser Friedrichs II, 3. Cologne: Böhlau, 1975. (See especially pp. 21–22, 26–27.)

Haskins, Charles Homer. "Latin Literature under Frederick II." In *Studies in Mediaeval Culture.* Oxford: Clarendon, 1929, pp. 124–147. (Reprint, New York: Frederick Ungar, 1958.)

Kantorowicz, Ernst. *Frederick the Second, 1194–1250*, trans. E. O. Lorimer. London: Constable; New York: Smith, 1931. (Reprint, New York: Frederick Ungat, 1957. See especially pp. 293–307, 663–667.)

Martin, Janet. "Classicism and Style in Latin Literature." In *Renaissance and Renewal in the Twelfth Century*, ed. Robert L. Benson, Giles Constable, and Carol D. Lanham. Cambridge, Mass.: Harvard University Press, 1982, pp. 537–568.

Meredith, Jill. "The Arch at Capua: The Strategic Use of *Spolia* and References to the Antique." In *Intellectual Life at the*

Court of Frederick II Hohenstaufen, ed. William Tronzo. Studies in the History of Art, 44. "Washington, D.C.: National Gallery of Art, 1994, pp. 108–126.

Oldoni, Massimo. "Pier della Vigna e Federico." In *Federico II e le nuove culture: Atti del XXXI Convegno storico internazionale, Todi, 9–12 ottobre 1994*. Atti dei Convegni del Centra Italiano di Studi sul Basso Medioevo–Accademia Tudertina e del Centro di Studi sulla Spiritualità Medievale, n.s., 8. Spoleto: Centro Italiano di Studi sull'Alto Medioevo, 1995, pp. 347–362.

Paratore, Ettore. "Alcuni Caratteri dello stile della cancelleria federiciana." In *Atti del Convegno Internazionale di Studi Federiciani, 10–18 December, 1950: VII Centenario della morte di Federico II, Imperatore e re di Sicilia*. Palermo: A. Renna, 1952, pp. 283–313.

Schaller, Hans Martin. "Zur Entstehung der sogenannten Briefsammlung des Petrus de Vinea." *Deutsches Archiv für die Erforschung des Mittelalters*, 12, 1956, pp. 114–159.

——. "Die Kanzlei Kaiser Friedrichs II.: Ihr Personal und Sprachstil." *Archiv für Diplomatik*, 3, 1957, pp. 207–286; 4, 1958, pp. 264–327.

——. "L'epistolario di Pier delle Vigne." In *Politica e cultura nell'Italia di Federico II*, ed. Sergio Gensini. Collana di Studi e Ricerche, Centro di Studi sulla Civiltà del Tardo Medioevo, San Miniato, 1. Pisa: Pacini, 1986, pp. 95–111.

——. "Della Vigna, Pietro." In *Dizionario biografico degli Italiani*, Vol. 37. Rome: Istituto della Enciclopedia Italiana, 1989, pp. 776–784.

——. *Stauferzeit: Ausgewählte Aufsätze*. Monumenta Germaniae Historica, Schriften, 38. Hannover: Hahn, 1993. (See especially pp. 197–223, 225–270, 463–478.)

Shepard, Laurie. *Courting Power: Persuasion and Politics in the Early Thirteenth Century*. New York: Garland, 1999.

Stephany, William A. "Pier della Vigna's Self-Fulfilling Prophecies: The *Eulogy* of Frederick II and *Inferno* 13." *Traditio*, 38, 1982, pp. 193–212.

Wieruszowski, Helene. *Politics and Culture in Medieval Spain and Italy*. Storia e Letteratura, 121. Rome: Edizioni di Storia e Letteratura, 1971. (See especially pp. 432–435, 605–610.)

LAURIE SHEPARD AND JOHN B. DILLON

PIERRE MAUCLERC
(ca. 1189/90–1250)

Pierre de Dreux (or de Braine), better known as Pierre Mauclerc, was a member of the distinguished Dreux family, a cadet branch of the Capetian line. He was a younger son of Louis VII's nephew Robert II, count of the small fiefs of Dreux and Braine. Although not a landless baron, Pierre's original endowment of lands from his father was small, the villas and manors of Fère-en-Tardenois, Brie-Comte-Robert, Chilly, and Longjumeau. By his marriage in 1212 to Alix, the heiress of Brittany and claimant to the English honor of Richmond, however, he became titular earl of Richmond and titular duke of Brittany (or count, in the view of French authorities unwilling to acknowledge Brittany's ducal status).

Pierre immediately set about imposing his will on the fiercely independent Breton baronage, exacting reliefs and wardships contrary to custom, despoiling or seizing seigneuries whose lords resisted, and commencing a concerted attack against the privileges of the episcopate. This last action precipitated his excommunication and, in retaliation, his expulsion of six of the seven bishops of Brittany. Although his wife died in 1221, he continued as guard (*custos*) and effective ruler of Brittany until his son came of age in late 1237.

Knighted in 1209 by Philip II Augustus, Pierre was secure in his position as ruler of Brittany as long as Philip, with whom he got along well, continued to reign. But with the old king's death in 1223, Pierre became a less trustworthy ally of the new king, Louis VIII (r. 1223–26), although he did take part in crusading expeditions against the Albigensian heretics led by Louis as prince (1219) and king (1226). His emerging lack of devotion to royal policies originated partly from his claims to land in England, claims that made him always eager to cultivate the Capetians' traditional enemy, the Plantagenêts. His own overweening ambition to be the preeminent baron in northwest Europe fueled his political maneuvering. After the death of his first wife, he aspired to the hand of the countess of Flanders in 1226 and the queen of Cyprus (who had claims in the great fief of Champagne) in 1229, only to be thwarted by the king and the pope, who had their own interests to preserve in the disposition of the heiresses and their fiefs. He was reduced to marrying a minor baroness, Marguerite de Montaigu, in 1230; and his resentment was strong. He had already become an open rebel in 1227 because of the failure of the regent, Blanche of Castile, to submit to his influence or cede the regency of the young Louis IX. He was instrumental in 1229 in attacking the count of Champagne, a supporter of the regent whose fief Pierre coveted. He courted the favor of the English king, received military support and large subsidies from him, and rebelled against the French crown again in 1230–31 and still again briefly in 1234. In all of these efforts, his forces were soundly thrashed, though never completely eliminated, by the royal troops.

In November 1237, after his son reached majority and took over control of Brittany, Pierre succeeded in consolidating a small lordship around the nucleus of his wife's lands in the Breton-Poitevin march. His subsequent career saw him active as a crusader against the Muslims, an effort that achieved a reconciliation with the papacy (1235) if not with local clerics, whom he continued to harass whenever he was in a position to do so. He served with distinction on the crusade of Thibaut de Navarre (1239–40) and died of illness and wounds in 1250 on the return home from St. Louis's crusade.

See also **Blanche of Castile; Louis IX; Philip II Augustus**

Further Reading

Painter, Sidney. *The Scourge of the Clergy: Peter of Dreux, Duke of Brittany*. Baltimore: John Hopkins University Press, 1937.

WILLIAM CHESTER JORDAN

PIETRO ABANO (d. 1316)

Pietro Abano (Pietro d'Abano) was the most important medical teacher in early fourteenth-century Padua. He was a Lombard by birth, but little is known of his life. In spite of his fame, and the fame he brought his university, he seems never to have accumulated the wealth of such successful teachers and practitioners as Taddeo Alderotti. Pietro's most famous book, *Conciliator of the Differences of the Philosophers and Especially the Physicians*, remained in use in universities well into the early modern period.

Pietro received his medical training at the University of Paris, where he would have been indoctrinated into the highest levels of scholarly debate surrounding the natural philosophy of Aristotle and Aristotle's interpreters. He returned to Italy from Paris c. 1306 to teach medicine, philosophy, and astrology at Padua. The *Conciliator*, which was completed sometime after 1310, shows his Parisian training. The book presents more than 200 disputed questions on the subject of medical philosophy and attempts to reconcile conflicts between the physiological teachings of Aristotle and the medical teachings of Galen. Pietro apparently was deeply impressed by similar attempts by Averroës and Avicenna, who adopted the Neoplatonic scheme of the ultimate reconciliation of conflicting philosophical viewpoints.

Pietro also distinguished himself as one of the early translators of Galen's works from the original Greek into Latin. Much of his writing examines the importance of medical astrology. This interest in astrology, as well as his devotion to Averroist teaching, marred his reputation in some circles.

See also **Averroës, Abu 'L-Walīd Muhammad B. Ahmad B. Rushd; Avicenna**

Further Reading

Olivieri, Luigi. *Pietro d'Abano e il pensiero neolatino: Filosofia, scienza, e ricerca dell'Aristotele greco tra i secoli XIII e XIV*. Padua: Antenore, 1988.
Paschetto, Eugenia. *Pietro d'Abano, medico e filosofo*. Florence: Vallecchi, 1984.
Siraisi, Nancy G. *Arts and Sciences at Padua*. Toronto: Pontifical Institute of Mediaeval Studies, 1973.
———. *Taddeo Alderotti and His Pupils: Two Generations of Italian Medical Learning*. Princeton, N.J.: Princeton University Press, 1981.

FAYE MARIE GETZ

PISANO, ANDREA
(c. 1295–c. 1348 or 1349)

Andrea Pisano (Andrea di Ugolino di Nino da Pontedera) is recorded as a sculptor, goldsmith, and *capomaestro* (master of works) of the cathedrals of Florence and Orvieto. Andrea was the son of a notary and is presumed to have been born in Pontedera, near Pisa. His reputation rests principally on his designs for the doors of the Baptistery in Florence (signed and dated 1330), which are considered among the greatest achievements of Tuscan *Trecento* sculpture. In this project, Andrea demonstrated that the direct narrative style and effective compositional principles of Giotto's painting could be successfully translated into the art of relief sculpture.

Though nothing is known for certain about Andrea's formative years, it is thought that he trained as a goldsmith, since the reliefs for the bronze doors, his earliest securely documented commission, exhibit attention to miniature detail and ornament as well as a high degree of competence in working with metal. Given the characteristics of his securely identifiable oeuvre, it comes as no surprise that Andrea was referred to as *orefice* (goldsmith) in 1335.

Andrea's Reliefs for the Baptistery, Florence (1330–1336)

In 1322, the Arte di Calimala (guild of importers and exporters of cloth) of Florence, the institution in charge of the decorative program of the Baptistery, had made plans for wooden doors covered with gilded metal. By 1329, the project had been revised, and the officials of the Calimala favored a more costly and technically more challenging option: doors in solid bronze. Andrea is first recorded in connection with this project in 1330, but his appointment almost certainly dates from 1329, when the Calimala sent a Florentine goldsmith to Pisa and Venice, which had a tradition of bronze casting, to examine examples of bronze doors. Though Andrea's reliefs carry the date 1330, his work did not end until late 1335: in 1330–1331 he worked on the wax models, which were cast in bronze by Venetian craftsmen in the *cire perdu* method; in 1333 the left door valve was installed; and the right wing was not completed until late 1335, owing to problems in the casting. The doors were dedicated on the feast of John the Baptist (the patron saint of the building and of Florence) in 1336; they originally adorned the east portal but were subsequently removed to the south portal to make way for Lorenzo Ghiberti's work.

Each wing comprises ten reliefs on the life of John the Baptist and four reliefs of virtues; all are set in quatrefoil frames that are, in turn, contained in rectangular fields. The general configuration of Andrea's doors was inspired by the Romanesque scheme of Bonanno's Porta San Ranieri at the cathedral in Pisa and, possibly, the Porta Regia (now destroyed) from the same building. The remarkable unity of Andrea's design, however, depends on a variety of decorative motifs, which include lions' heads that are placed at the corners of each panel, bands of studs and rosettes that unite the lions' heads, and dentiled moldings that frame each of the quatrefoils.

The iconographic program of the figural reliefs is closely related to the mosaic scenes of the life of John the Baptist in the interior of the Baptistery and to frescoes on the same theme by Giotto in the Peruzzi Chapel in Santa Croce (also in Florence). Giotto's influence is also reflected in the harmonious balance of the compositions, in which reliefs are carefully structured into planes; and in the classical economy of the narratives, which rely on the purposeful movements of concentrated groups of figures. The technique of applying figures to a plain background, a feature of Sienese metalwork of the early *Trecento*, adds to the solemnity of the compositions. Concessions were, however, made for the occasional motif of a doorway, curtain, or canopy; and in five reliefs from the left door valve, landscape is incorporated into the designs with great subtlety. The influence of Giotto's measured style in Andrea's work is tempered by a debt to French and Sienese artistic traditions: activated, spirited drapery forms, which envelope the bodies of Andrea's dignified figures, introduce a note of grace and elegance to the otherwise restrained reliefs.

That Andrea was at the height of his creative powers when he worked on the doors is clear from the precision of the finely chased details of the fire-gilt surfaces. The Calimala had, evidently, awarded this difficult commission to a mature and proficient artist, and his work would remain a benchmark for artistic excellence into the *Quattrocento*. In fact, when the Calimala set up a competition in 1400–1401, the aim was to attract an artist who could work on a second set of bronze doors that would follow Andrea's model and maintain his high standards.

Andrea as *Capomaestro* at Florence and Orvieto (1337–1348)

Andrea's contribution to the decoration of the *campanile* in Florence probably dates from before Giotto's death in 1337. Thereafter, Andrea succeeded Giotto as *capomaestro*, supervising work on the tower until 1341. He proceeded according to his great predecessor's plans for the lower part of the structure, which included two rows of reliefs: the lower group, within hexagonal frames, shows scenes from Genesis and practitioners of the arts, sciences, and works of man; the upper set shows the seven sacraments, the seven planets, the seven virtues, and the seven liberal arts in rhomboid frames. However,

Andrea departed from Giotto's scheme in adding niches designed to include statuary above these relief cycles. Though the precise nature of Andrea's contribution is still a matter of scholarly debate, one work generally attributed to him is the marble relief *Sculpture*, which, like the style of the bronze reliefs, is characterized by plastic form, harmonious composition, and attention to detail.

Around 1341, Andrea returned to Pisa, where he maintained a workshop even after 1347, the year he was appointed *capomaestro* at the cathedral of Orvieto. By 1349, however, Andrea had been replaced, and it is frequently assumed either that he died of the plague in 1348 or 1349 or, less probably, that he moved to Florence. The family tradition was carried on by Andrea's sons Nino (fl. 1334–1360s) and Tommaso (fl. 1363–1372), especially Nino, who succeeded his rather at Orvieto. Andrea's sons were less interested in the classicizing aspects of his work, and both of them evolved a mainly Gothic formal vocabulary. In the early *Quattrocento* the suave, lyrical style of their sculpture was still a force to reckon with, as the early work of Jacopo della Quercia demonstrates.

See also **Giotto di Bondone**

Further Reading

Burresi, Mariagiulia, ed. *Andrea, Nino, e Tommaso scultori pisani*. Milan: Electa, 1983.

Castelnuovo, Enrico. "Andrea Pisano scultore in legno." In *Sacre passioni: Scultura lignea a Pisa dal XII al XV secolo*, ed. Mariagiulia Burresi. Milan: Morta, 2000, pp. 152–163.

Clark, Kenneth, and David Finn. *The Florentine Baptistery Doors*. Kampala: Uganda Publishing and Advertising Services, 1980.

Garzelli, Annarosa. "Andrea Pisano a Firenze e una 'Madonna con il cardellino.'" *Antichità Viva*, 36(5–6), 1997, pp. 49–62.

Kreytenberg, Gert. "Andrea Pisano's Earliest Works in Marble." *Burlington Magazine*, 122, 1980, pp. 3–8.

——. *Andrea Pisano und die toskanische Skulptur des 14. Jahrhunderts*. Munich: Bruckmann, 1984.

——. "Eine unbekannte Verkündigungsmadonna als 'Maria gravida' von Andrea Pisano." In *Opere e giorni: Studi su mille anni di arte europea dedicati a Max Seidel*, ed. Klaus Bergdolt and Giorgio Bonsanti. Venice: Marsilio, 2001, pp. 147–154.

Moskowitz, Anita Fiderer. *The Sculpture of Andrea and Nino Pisano*. Cambridge: Cambridge University Press, 1986.

——. *Italian Gothic Sculpture, c. 1250–c. 1400*. Cambridge: Cambridge University Press, 2001.

Paolucci, Antonio. *Le porte del Battistero di Firenze alle origini del Rinascimento*. Modena: Panini, 1996.

Pope-Hennessy, John. *Italian Gothic Sculpture*, 4th ed. London: Phaidon, 1996

FLAVIO BOGGI

PISANO, GIOVANNI (d. by 1319)

Giovanni Pisano was the son of Nicola Pisano. Nicola executed the pulpits in the baptistery of Pisa and the cathedral of Siena, and Giovanni is first documented as an assistant to his father in the contract of 1265 for the pulpit in Siena; Giovanni received periodic payments until October 1268, when the pulpit was completed (Bacci 1926; Carli 1943; Milanesi 1854). Nothing certain is known of Giovanni's activities between 1268 and 1278, when his name appears together with Nicola's on the Fontana Maggiore in Perugia. From c. 1285 to c. 1297, Giovanni was at work in Siena, where he is mentioned as *capomaestro* of the project for the cathedral facade in 1290. His name is recorded in Siena in 1314, but in 1319 he is referred to as having died. There is considerable uncertainty regarding the attribution of his early work or supposed early work on the pulpit in Siena, and elsewhere; passages that convey a greater degree of "spiritual tension" have tended to be ascribed to him, whereas those characterized by greater emotional restraint have suggested the hand of Nicola. One image on the Fontana Maggiore is almost certainly by Giovanni: a pair of eagles with enormous claws, powerful breasts, and twisting bodies that seem to anticipate the griffin on the central support of the pulpit in Pistoia.

The facade of the cathedral in Siena was left incomplete on Giovanni's departure c. 1297, and scholars disagree as to whether the present facade reflects his original plan (Kosegarten 1984) or the upper section is a much later design, c. 1370 (Carli 1977; Keller 1937). The program in Siena (unlike the encyclopedic programs of French Gothic cathedrals) is strictly Mariological, and the coherence of its iconography is strong argument for assigning the conception of the entire facade to a single initial project. From early sources we know that a (lost) Madonna and Child stood in the lunette of the central portal flanked by a representative of the commune swearing an oath of allegiance on behalf of Siena, and by a personification of Siena holding up a model of the cathedral. Scenes from the lives of Joachim and Anna and from Mary's childhood adorned the lintel of the central portal; the side lunettes and the gable fields contained mosaics representing further events from Mary's life. On platforms projecting from the towers and between the lunettes of the lower facade were placed prophets and kings of the Old Testament and sibyls and pagan philosophers, i.e., those who in remote times had foreseen the miraculous birth of the savior. Spread out along the upper facade were evangelists and apostles, whose teachings are confirmed by the prophets. Though these were executed in the fourteenth century, they too were probably part of the original plan, which envisioned the prophets standing like foundations for the New Testament figures above. Around the rose window appeared a seated Madonna and Child flanked by half figures representing the genealogy of Christ; scenes from the life of David, an ancestor of Christ, appeared on one of the tendril columns that originally flanked the portals. The pictorial

program of the facade thus revealed the place of Siena within the total redemptive plan of Christian theology. The initial visual impact of the facade comes from an interplay of its chromatic, plastic, and structural effects: the contrasts of color, light, and shadow created by the deep jambs, gables, and gallery; the rich tactile plasticity and rhythmic flow of concave-convex movements across the lower horizontal band of portals and lunettes; and the stepping back of the upper facade behind the gables. The fourteen prophets and sibyls (the originals are in the Museo dell'Opera del Duomo) are dynamic, plastic forms whose gestures and movements embody the excitement of their special enlightenment. The dramatic effect of these figures communicating across real space has no medieval or antique precedent. However, the facade abounds in classicizing motifs such as bead and reel patterns, dentils, masks, acanthus foliage, and *all'antica* "peopled columns" originally flanking the main portal (Seidel 1968–1969, 1975; Venturi 1927). The traceried *bifore* and *trifore* and aspects of the figure style are influenced by French precedents, whereas the alternation of dark and light marble revetment belongs to the Tuscan Romanesque tradition. The facade, then, shows a creative synthesis of antique traditions, local traditions, and northern Gothic influences—the last of these seen also in the undermining of solid surface in favor of perforated mass.

Perhaps as a result of professional difficulties, Giovanni left Siena c. 1297, when the facade was still incomplete (Ayrton 1969). Around this time, or possibly earlier, he executed a number of sculptures for the exterior of the baptistery in Pisa. The remaining fragments (installed in the Museo dell'Opera del Duomo in Pisa) are badly weathered, but these swelling, twisting figures burst with inner energy.

Around 1297, Giovanni received his first commission for a pulpit, from the parish of Sant'Andrea in Pistoia. Pistoia was unusually rich in Romanesque monumental sculptured pulpits, and the proposal for Sant'Andrea insisted that it must not be inferior to one made for San Giovanni Fuorcivitas by Guglielmo, a student of Nicola Pisano; this suggests that there was a strong sense of rivalry among churches. Giovanni's pulpit is signed and dated 1301 and has an inscription that boasts of a "mastery greater than any seen before" (Pope-Hennessy 1972). This richly carved and elegant structure—its parapet poised on Gothic trefoil arches above slender columns with alternating animal and figural supports—reveals Giovanni's debt to Nicola's two earlier pulpits, but it also reveals that Giovanni was completely independent in terms of technique, composition, and expressiveness. Like Nicola's pulpit in the baptistery in Pisa, Giovanni's pulpit in Pistoia is hexagonal and has great structural clarity. But here Giovanni adopts an invention from his father's pulpit in Siena: the narrative reliefs are flanked by figures. All the forms—capitals, figures, narratives—are more energetic than the corresponding elements in Nicola's pulpits. In particular, the lion, griffin, and eagle of the central support are dynamic opposing forces, revolving around the column as hub. Traces of polychromy on the figures as well as remains of the glazed colored background *tesserae* give a hint of the original chromatic effect. The most stunning aspect of this pulpit, however, is the heightened emotional content of the narratives. In the Annunciation, for instance, the awesome message simultaneously thrusts the Virgin away from Gabriel and magnetically draws the figures together. Expressiveness combines with naturalism to bring the sacred figures down to earth: the Christ child in the Nativity is neither the miniature adult of medieval tradition nor the Herculean child rendered by Nicola but is arguably the first realistic newborn infant in the history of art (Moskowitz 2001). Giovanni's compositional and expressive powers are nowhere more evident than in the Massacre of the Innocents. At first the composition appears chaotic, but closer examination reveals that the violent movements, deep pockets of shadow, and flashing highlights cohere as a series of zigzag vertical and horizontal rhythms generated by the forward motion and gesture of King Herod. In a cinematic sequence, every moment of response is portrayed: to the left of Herod, three women plead before the brutal slaughter; immediately below and at the lower left, several mothers clutch their infants in terror, shielding the babies with their own bodies; at the base, three grieving mothers bend over their dead children. Finally, bringing the eye upward toward Herod again, mother and murderer—like an angel and devil fighting for a soul in the Last Judgment—battle over the body of a screaming infant who has already received the death blow.

A quieter, more intimate side of Giovanni's artistic personality is revealed in a series of depictions of the Madonna and child executed throughout his career. In Giovanni's hands, the image is transformed from austerity and rigidity to an expression of intimacy, as can be seen in a half-length Madonna from a tympanum of the *duomo* in Pisa of the mid-1270s (Keller 1942, 13). In several later Madonnas, the child leans toward his mother, resting his arm on her shoulder. Finally, in the Prato Madonna, universally attributed to Giovanni (c. 1312), the relationship intensifies, as Mary, smiling, bends her head down to direct her gaze at her son. In contrast to the regular, planar features of Giovanni's figure on the tympanum in Pisa, the Prato Madonna is characterized by refined features and delicate transitions in the soft planes and contours.

Giovanni's mastery extended to wood and ivory. He executed a beautiful ivory Madonna and child (Ragghianti 1954; Seidel 1972, 1991) and a series of wood and ivory crucifixes—none documented or dated—which are so compellingly close to his images on the pulpits that the attributions seem valid (Seidei 1971). These, too, mark a turning point in the history of the theme in Italy: the relative quietude of Nicola's representations is now often replaced by an aching pathos reminiscent of some transalpine examples.

In 1302, Giovanni was commissioned to execute a pulpit for the grand Tuscan Romanesque cathedral of Pisa. Because of its location within the vast space of the *duomo*—beneath the cupola, near the south transept—it had to be much larger than the pulpit in Pistoia. Like Nicola's pulpit in Siena, it is octagonal rather than hexagonal. Since each parapet of the bridge leading from stairway to balustrade contains a narrative, there are nine relief fields (an unprecedented number), with the first and last narratives (those on the bridge) on flat panels and the rest on curved slabs. This expanded sequence includes scenes from the life of John the Baptist: the first relief shows the Annunciation to Mary, Mary and Elizabeth in the Visitation, and the Nativity of John the Baptist. Parallels and intersections between the life of Christ and that of John, his precursor, were emphasized in the popular apocryphal literature of this period; and here they are made eloquently clear because the two Nativity scenes are at an angle to each other and thus can be seen simultaneously.

An inscription on the pulpit alludes, in a surprisingly self-conscious way, to difficulties: "The more I have achieved the more hostile injuries have I experienced" (Pope-Hennessy 1972). Further along, there is a reference to the "envy" of others and the "sorrow" of the sculptor who lacks adequate "recognition." Vasari was quite critical of this pulpit, and later in the sixteenth century, when an excuse presented itself, the monument was dismantled (Bacci 1926; Moore et al. 1993). After various proposals for reconstruction in the late nineteenth century, the present version was executed by Peleo Bacci in 1926. Responses continue to be mixed. Documents record the names of dozens of individuals engaged on this pulpit, and certainly the quality of the carving is not as uniform as that on the pulpit in Pistoia. Nevertheless, there are passages of unsurpassed emotional power and inventiveness, such as a saint dragging a resurrected soul toward Christ; moreover, many of the reliefs reveal a continuing engagement with issues of spatial illusionism and naturalism in the treatment of figures and landscape.

Both artist and patron must have felt the challenge posed by the three earlier pulpits and must have sought to surpass them in size, iconographic and sculptural complexity, and decorative richness. The pulpit in Pisa is, then, a recapitulation, synthesis, and amplification not only of the three others but also of the major innovations in almost all the earlier monuments by Giovanni and his father. In addition to the animals and figures supporting the columns—a feature of the earlier pulpits—here there are unusually complex figural supports: in the center the three theological virtues, supported by personifications of the eight liberal arts; *Ecclesia* supported by the cardinal virtues; statue columns of Saint Michael and Hercules (or Samson); and finally a statue column of Christ supported by the evangelists. Not only do the curved narrative panels boldly flout visual expectations; below the parapet, where in earlier works we would see round-headed or pointed trefoil arcades, we now find, supporting the spandrel reliefs, exuberant classical volutes that seem to anticipate the Baroque and are impossible to enclose within the regular geometric contours of architectural norms. Here, as in the convex reliefs above, Giovanni must have relished his radical departure from the expected. In its sheer inventiveness of form, and in the range of emotions and the effectiveness of gestures in the narratives, the pulpit in Pisa represents a tremendous intellectual and artistic achievement.

The last major work by Giovanni is the tomb of Margaret of Luxembourg, wife of Emperor Henry VII. After her death in 1310, a cult grew up around her remains; and reports of miracles led to her beatification in 1313, when the tomb was probably commissioned (Seidel 1987). Much of the original complex is lost, but a major element is extant: an exceptionally fine carving of the empress being raised heavenward by two angels. There is scholarly debate as to whether the group represents the *elevatio animae*, the soul elevated to heaven, fervently desired in the prayers for the dead; or the bodily resurrection, which should occur only at the last judgment but might be granted earlier to a saint. The visual evidence suggests a bodily resurrection, since Margaret is sufficiently weighty to require the physical exertion of the two angels. Also disputed is whether the tomb was a wall monument or, like many later saints' shrines, freestanding (Pope-Hennessy 1987; Seidel 1987).

See also **Pisano, Nicola**

Further Reading

Ayrton, Michael. *Giovanni Pisano: Sculptor.* London: Thames and Hudson, 1969.
Bacci, Peleo. *La ricostruzione del pergamo di Giovanni Pisano nel Duomo di Pisa.* Milan and Rome: Bestetti e Tumminelli, 1926.
Beani, Gaetano. *La pieve di Sant' Andrea.* Pistoia, 1907, p. 28
Carli, Enzo. *Il pulpito di Siena.* Bergamo: Istituto Italiano d'Arti Grafiche, 1943, pp. 4lff.
——. *Giovanni Pisano.* Pisa: Pacini, 1977.
Jászai, Géza. *Die Pisaner Domkanzel: Neuer Versuch zur Wiederherstellung ihres ursprünglichen Zustandes.* Munich, 1968.
——. "Giovanni Pisano." In *Enciclopedia dell'arte medievale*, Vol. 6. Rome: Istituto della Enciclopedia Italiana, 1995, pp. 740–754.
Keller, Harald. "Die Bauplastik des Sienese Doms." *Kunstgesch. Jahrbuch der Biblioth. Hertziana*, 1, 1937.
——. *Giovanni Pisano, mit 152 Bildern.* Vienna: A. Schroll, 1942, p. 66.
Kosegarten, Antje. "Die Skulpturen der Pisani am Baptisterium von Pisa." *Jahrbuch der Berliner Museen*, 10, 1969, pp. 36–100.
Kosegarten, Antje Middeldorf. *Sienesische Bildhauer am Duomo Vecchio.* Munich, 1984.
Milanesi, Gaetano. *Documenti per la storia dell'arte senese*, Vol. 1, *Secoli XIII e XIV.* Siena: O. Porri, 1854.
Moore, Henry, Gert Kreytenberg, and Crispino Valenziano. *L'ambone del duomo di Pisa,* Milan: Franco Maria Ricci, 1993.
Moskowitz, Anita Fiderer. *Italian Gothic Sculpture c. 1250–c. 1400* Cambridge: Cambridge University Press, 2001.
Pope-Hennessy, John. *Italian Gothic Sculpture.* London: Phaidon, 1972.
——. "Giovanni Pisano's Tomb of Empress Margaret: A Critical Reconstruction." *Apollo*, September 1987, p. 223.
Ragghianti, Carlo Lodovico. "La Madonna eburnea di Giovanni Pisano." *Critica d'Arte*, n.s., 1, 1954, pp. 385–396.
Scultura dipinta—Maestri di legname e pittori a Siena, 1250–1450: Siena, Pinacoteca Nazionale, 16 luglio—31 dicembre 1987. Firenze: Centre Di, 1987.
Seidel, Max. "Die Rankensäulen der sieneser Domfassade." *Jahrbuch der Berliner Museen*, 11, 1968–1969, pp. 80–160. .
——. *La scultura lignea di Giovanni Pisano.* Florence: Edam, 1971.
——. "Die Elfenbeinmadonna im Domschatz zu Pisa: Studien zur Herkunft und Umbildung Französischer Formen im Werk Giovanni Pisanos in der Epoche der Pistoieser Kanzel." *Mitteilungen des Kunsthistorischen Institutes in Florenz*, 16, 1972, pp. 1–50.
——. "Studien zur Antikenrezeptionrezeption Nicola Pisanos." *Mitteilungen des Kunsthistorischen Institutes in Florenz*, 19, 1975, pp. 303–392.
——, ed. *Giovanni Pisano a Genova.* Genoa: SAGEP, 1987.
——. "Un 'Crocifisso' di Giovanni Pisano a Massa Marittima." *Prospettiva*, 62, 1991, pp. 67–77.
Venturi, Adolfo. *Giovanni Pisano: Sein Leben und sein Werk.* Florence: Pantheon, 1927.

ANITA F. MOSKOWITZ

PISANO, NICOLA (c. 1220–1278 or 1284)

Nicola Pisano is generally assumed to have come from southern Italy and thus from the cultural milieu of Emperor Frederick II von Hohenstaufen. Nicola may have arrived in Tuscany as early as c. 1245; a series of carvings in the upper reaches of the cathedral of Siena have been plausibly attributed to him (Bagnoli 1981).

In 1260, Nicola signed and dated the pulpit in the baptistery of Pisa. This pulpit has an unprecedented form; it is a hexagonal freestanding structure whose shape was eminently suited to the centralized plan of the baptistery and echoed Guido da Como's octagonal font occupying the center of the interior space. Its parapet and platform are sustained by seven columns; the central column is surrounded by crouching figures and animals, and the six outer columns alternately rest on lions and on the ground. The columns support trilobed archivolts flanked by representations of the virtues and John the Baptist. Above these rises a balustrade with historiated relief fields separated by triple colonettes. When the pulpit was in its original state, the creamy marble reliefs framed by reddish colonettes and moldings, the speckled and patterned supporting columns, the relief backgrounds filled with colored glazed tesserae (some of which remain), and the polychromy accenting some parts of the figures produced a richly chromatic effect.

The reliefs embellish five of the six sides (the sixth is the entrance to the platform) with scenes from the life of Christ. In a continuous narrative, the first panel shows the *Annunciation, Nativity, Bathing of the Christ Child*, and *Annunciation to the Shepherds*. This is followed by panels illustrating the *Adoration of the Magi, Presentation in the Temple, Crucifixion*, and *Last Judgment*. The figures are powerfully plastic and expressive and reveal the sculptor's study of ancient art and northern Gothic art, enabling him to combine the serene majesty of the former with the deeply felt human experience of the latter. Nicola was not content to present symbolic narratives of transcendental events; his goal was, rather, to tell a human story in a credible and empathic manner. The work is enriched by naturalistic details; the figures convey a sense of bulk and weight, and gestures and movements are rendered with convincing naturalism. This new mode of sculpture was the visual counterpart of the widely diffused apocryphal literature, in which the sparse accounts of the Gospels were enriched with domestic incidents, making the sacred figures human.

In 1265, Nicola signed a contract for a second pulpit, in this case for the cathedral of Siena. Several assistants, including Arnolfo di Cambio and Nicola's son Giovanni, are named in the contract. This pulpit, completed in 1268 and placed within the enormous space of the *duomo*, is octagonal and is larger and more complex than the one in the baptistery in Pisa. Here, the narrative program began at the stairway bridge leading to the pulpit casket, with a figure of Gabriel (now in Berlin) corresponding to Mary of the *Annunciation* seen at the left edge of the first relief (Seidel 1970). As at Pisa, there are three tiers—supporting columns, arcade, and parapet. The central support includes figures representing, for the first time, the liberal arts. The narratives now include the emotionally wrenching *Massacre of the Innocents* and a *Last Judgment* that spreads over two fields, with a full-length figure of Christ the judge between the reliefs. Furthermore, instead of column clusters (as at Pisa), there are corner figures framing the reliefs, resulting in a continuous visual and narrative flow. The classicizing forms of the earlier pulpit give way to more elegantly proportioned figures with softer draperies and refined features—an ideal influenced by French Gothic art. In the narratives, the figures are smaller and more densely packed, and the compositions are organized to suggest

movement into depth. Furthermore, Nicola has greatly enlarged his emotional range. The crucified Christ in Siena, for instance, conveys a pathos lacking in the earlier relief: hanging with arms stretched in two great diagonals, shoulders dislocated, abdomen sunken by the weight of the upper torso, and head bent into the chest, the figure conveys human pain and tragedy, intensifying the meaning of the crucifixion.

In 1267, Nicola completed the Arca di San Domenico (tomb of Saint Dominic) in the church of San Domenico in Bologna. The form and structure of the *arca* became the prototype for an entire class of tombs through the fifteenth century (Moskowitz 1994). Many changes have been made to this tomb, but originally it consisted of a freestanding sarcophagus resting atop a series of supporting statue columns representing friars, archangels, and virtues. The sarcophagus, the only part of the original monument that is still in San Domenico, is embellished on all sides with an extensive cycle of biographical reliefs rather than the traditional biblical or symbolic themes. The relief backgrounds show patterns of red and gold *verre églomisé* (much of it restored). The narrative fields are separated by full-length figures projecting in high relief, including the Madonna and child on one long side, the Redeemer on the other long side, and the four church fathers—Augustine, Ambrose, Jerome, and Gregory—at the corners of the sarcophagus. The corner figures, both on and supporting the sarcophagus, project out diagonally, encouraging the observer to move around the ensemble.

The bold and original design of the *arca* has sources as disparate as pulpits, bishops' thrones, holy water fonts, and ancient sarcophagi and was conceived as addressing both laypeople and the Dominican hierarchy. When the tomb was in its original location between the presbytery and south aisle, Dominic's most public and most spectacular miracles were on the side facing the lay congregation, thus serving to promote the cult; and the scenes of the founding and expansion of the Dominican order, which were of greater interest to the clergy, were on the side facing the choir area.

The last major work securely associated with Nicola's name is the Fontana Maggiore ("great fountain") in Perugia, completed in 1278. This is a remarkable secular and civic monument, as original in form and conception among fountains as Nicola's pulpits and the *arca* are, respectively, among pulpits and tombs. The Fontana Maggiore is polygonal and embellished with sculptures; it stands in Perugia's main civic and religious square, and it began not as an artistic project but rather as an engineering and hydraulic problem: it was intended to bring an adequate water supply to Perugia, a town poor in freshwater springs (Nicco Fasola 1951). Precedents for some elements of the fountain's formal structure are found in two- and three-basin liturgical furnishings, such as baptismal and cloister fonts; and also in illustrations of the *fons vitae*, copies of the Holy Tomb, pulpits, and altar *ciboria* (Hoffmann-Curtis 1968; Schulze 1994). However, there is no close prototype for the scale, the complexity of design, or the richness of the program of this indispensably functional urban monument. The sculpture on the basins is uniquely expansive, including scenes from Genesis, prophets, saints, "labors of the months," the liberal arts, various fables, allegorical figures, and even contemporary civic personages. A ring of steps serves as a foundation; on this rests a twenty-five-sided basin with low reliefs separated by colonettes. Above this rises a smaller basin of twelve plain concave sides with figures at the angles and at the center of each face. From here a thick bronze column emerges supporting a third, still smaller basin, also of bronze, which in turn contains three graceful bronze female caryatids. The facets of the superimposed lower basins do not line up, resulting in a syncopated rhythm that impels the viewer to move around the structure. Simultaneously, the vertical elements, together with the diminishing sizes of the basins and the increasing plasticity of the sculpture, draw the eye upward. The effect is of a spiral movement that culminates in, and is resolved by, the caryatid group. The fountain was designed to be seen not only from the ground but also from the balcony of the communal palace (altered at a later date), which was used for announcements to the *piazza* below and as an entrance to the audience hall within for government officials and citizens. Even today, the view from above has its own special effect, as the play of descending water contrasts with the ascending concentric superimposed basins.

Nicola's sculpture provided the source and impetus for the development of his two major assistants. His son Giovanni took up the emotional current of Nicola's style, transforming it into a very personal and highly charged idiom. Arnolfo di Cambio's temperament led him instead toward a starkly monumental and classicizing mode. Nicola's art profoundly influenced not only his immediate successors but also the painting of Giotto and, indeed, the entire naturalistic and classicizing tradition of the art of the following centuries.

See also **Arnolfo di Cambio; Pisano, Giovanni**

Further Reading

Bagnoli, Alessandro. "Novità su Nicola Pisano scultore nel Duomo di Siena." *Prospettiva*, 27, October 1981, pp. 27–46.
Caleca, Antonino. *La dotta mano: Il battistero di Pisa*. Bergamo: Bolis, 1991.
Carli, Enzo. *Il duomo di Siena*. Genoa: SAGEP, 1979.
Cristiani Testi, Maria Laura. *Nicola Pisano: Architetto scultore*. Pisa: Pacini, 1987.
Gnudi, Cesare. *Nicola, Arnolfo, Lapo: L'arca di San Domenico in Bologna*. Florence: Edizioni U, 1948.
Hoffmann-Curtis, Kathrin. *Das Programm der Fontana Maggiore in Perugia*. Düsseldorf: Rheinland-Verlag, 1968.
Kosegarten, Antje Middeldorf. "Die Skulpturen der Pisani am Baptisterium von Pisa." *Jahrbuch der Berliner Museen*, 10, 1968, pp. 14–100.
Moskowitz, Anita Fiderer. *Nicola Pisano's Arca di San Domenico and Its Legacy*. University Park: Pennsylvania State University Press, 1994.
——. *Italian Gothic Sculpture c. 1250–c. 1400*. Cambridge: Cambridge University Press, 2001.
Nicco Fasola, Giusta. *Nicola Pisano: Orientamenti sulla formazione del gusto italiano*. Rome: Fratelli Palombi, 1941.
——. *La fontana di Perugia*. Rome: Libreria dello Stato, 1951.
Schulze, Ulrich. *Brunnen im Mittelalter: Politische Ikonographie der Kommunen in Italien*. Frankfurt am Main: Lang, 1994.
Seidel, Max. "Die Verkündigungsgruppe der Siena Domkanzel." *Münchener Jahrbuch der Bildenden Kunst*, 21, 1970, pp. 18–72.

ANITA F. MOSKOWITZ

PLEYDENWURFF, HANS (ca. 1425–1472)

This panel and glass painter was active in Franconia from circa 1450 until about 1472. He established the first significant painting workshop in Nuremberg, which produced works inspired by Netherlandish art. Michel Wolgemut was his pupil and assistant.

Pleydenwurff was born circa 1425 in Bamberg. Nothing is known of his initial training, but he probably went to the Netherlands in the early 1450s. He worked in Bamberg then in Nuremberg, where he became a citizen in 1457. At his death there in 1472, Pleydenwurff was listed as a glass painter. That year, Michel Wolgemut married his widow, Barbara, and inherited the workshop.

Pleydenwurff's only documented work is the Breslau Altarpiece, of which only fragments survive. Installed in the church of St. Elizabeth in Breslau on June 30, 1462, this large double-winged retable with a carved shrine featured scenes from Christ's Infancy and Passion, and Saints Jerome and Vincent of Teate. The upper part of the Presentation survives (Warsaw, Nationalmuseum). An undamaged wing with the Descent from the Cross (Nuremberg, Germanisches Nationalmuseum) is based on Roger van der Weyden's Deposition Altarpiece of circa 1444 (Madrid, Prado).

Other works have been attributed to Pleydenwurff on the basis of style. Earliest is the half-length Löwenstein Diptych of about 1456. Based on a type popularized by Roger van der Weyden in the Netherlands, it consists of a Man of Sorrows (Basel, Kunstmuseum) and a portrait of the Bamberg canon and subdeacon, Count Georg von Löwenstein (Nuremberg, Germanisches Nationalmuseum). Also ascribed to Pleydenwurff are a large Crucifixion (Munich, Alte Pinakothek), circa 1470, an altarpiece wing with St. Lawrence (Raleigh, North Carolina Museum of Art), after 1462, and wings with Infancy and Passion scenes from the Hof Altarpiece

(Munich, Alte Pinakothek), dated 1465. This last was a workshop production, executed by assistants, including Michel Wolgemut.

See also **Wolgemut, Michael**

Further Reading

Kahsnitz, Rainer. "Stained Glass in Nuremberg." *Gothic and Renaissance Art in Nuremberg 1300–1550.* New York: Metropolitan Museum of Art, 1986, pp. 87–92.

Löcher, Kurt. "Panel Painting in Nuremberg: 1350–1550." In *Gothic and Renaissance Art in Nuremberg 1300–1550.* New York: Metropolitan Museum of Art, 1986, pp. 81–86.

Stange, Alfred *Deutsche Malerei der Gotik.* 10 vols. Berlin: Deutscher Kunstverlag, 1934–1960, vol. 9, pp. 41–44.

Strieder, Peter. *Tafelmalerei in Nürnberg 1350–1550.* Königstein im Taunus: Karl Robert Langewiesche Nachfolger, 1993, pp. 52–59.

Suckale, Robert. "Hans Pleydenwurff in Bamberg." *Berichte des historischen Vereins Bamberg* 120 (1984): 423–438.

SUSANNE REECE

POLO, MARCO (1254–1324)

What we know of Marco Polo is based largely on his *Divisament dou monde*, later known as *Libra delle meraviglie del mondo*, or simply as *Il Milione* (after the name Emilione, which Marco Polo and his relatives used to distinguish themselves from the many other Polos in Venice). Tradition has it that Marco dictated this work to Rustichello da Pisa while the two were held in a Genoese prison. Rustichello, a writer of Arthurian romances, transcribed Marco's account into Old French (the preeminent vernacular of the romance genre), and embellished it with narrative and stylistic features typical of a medieval romance. Since people in the Middle Ages regarded *Il Milione* as a book of marvels, it took a long time before cartographers and explorers (including Christopher Columbus) became aware of its importance as a work of geography.

Marco Polo's work is more than a medieval romance or a book of marvels; it was probably meant to be a straightforward account of two journeys to China: the first by his father Niccolò Polo and his uncle Matteo Polo, and the second by all three Polos. There are numerous discrepancies among the manuscripts and early editions of *Il Milione* which probably do not reflect Marco's original account or Rustichello's lost rendition of it. There is, however, sufficient information in the most important manuscripts to enable scholars to reconstruct the Polos' two expeditions to China.

In 1260, the two Venetian brothers departed from Constantinople, where they had done business for six years, and arrived in Bukhara (in the Uzbek republic). They were forced to stay there for three years because local wars had cut off the roads leading back to the west. During that time they accepted an invitation to join an envoy from Hulaku Khan to Kublai Khan (grandson of the Mongul conqueror Genghis Khan); and in 1266 they arrived at Kublai Khan's summer palace in Shangtu (near Tolun on the Shan-tien Ho, or Luan River, about 150 miles—240 kilometers—north of Beijing). The brothers stayed at Shangtu for several months before returning to Italy with a message for Pope Clement IV from Kublai Khan.

Not long after their return to Venice in 1269, the brothers decided to bring Marco with them on their second expedition to China. They left Venice in 1271, accompanied by two Dominican monks who were supposed to travel with them to Shangtu but who soon withdrew from the expedition. When the Polos arrived in Acre (Akko) on the Syrian coast, they received letters from the newly elected Pope Gregory X for Kublai Khan. From Acre they went to Ayas (Cilicia) on the southeastern coast of Turkey and presumably took the caravan route to the Turkish cities of Kayseri, Sivas, Erzincan, and Erzurum before arriving at Lake Van. From there the Polos passed through eastern Armenia, where Marco describes Mount Ararat (the traditional site of Noah's landing after the flood), and then south to the Persian cities of Tabriz, Yazd, and Kerman before reaching the ancient Persian port of Hormuz (Bandar Abbas). When they realized that it was unsafe to go to China by ship, the Polos retraced their steps back to Kerman and went north to Mashhad, in northeastern Iran. It is at this point in the narrative that Marco recounts the tale of the "Old Man of the Mountain," one of the best-known episodes in *Il Milione.* From there the Polos went to Balkh (in northern Afghanistan), where, according to Marco, Alexander the Great married the daughter of Darius, and then to the castle of Taican (present Talikan), known for its nearby salt mountains. They spent a year in the province of Badakhshan while Marco recovered from an illness.

On Marco's recovery, the Polos presumably followed the Oxus (Amu-Dar'ya) and Vakhsh rivers, crossed the Pamirs (known to Marco as the "roof of the world"), and reached the old silk route. The Polos followed the silk route through eastern Turkestan to the Chinese cities of Kashgar (K'a-shih), Yarkand (Soch'e), Khotan (Hotien), Keriya (Yütien), and Cherchen (Ch'iehmo) before arriving in the ancient city of Lop (either Charkhliq or Milan), where they made preparations to cross the desert and the salt-encrusted bed of dry Lop Nor. After thirty days of travel through the desert, they arrived at Sha-Chou (Tun Huang), the first Chinese city under the khan's rule. From there they went to Kan Chou (Zhangye or Chang-yeh) in Kansu province, where they spent a year waiting, presumably, for the khan to send them an escort. They resumed their journey by going south to Lanchou and then north along the Yellow River (and perhaps along the Great Wall) in the direction of Beijing, and arrived at Shangtu in 1275.

Marco spent the next seventeen years serving Kublai Khan on several diplomatic missions to the southern regions of the khan's vast empire, including Yünnan province, Burma (as far as the Irrawaddy River), Cochin China (Vietnam), and even parts of Tibet. Although Marco was impressed by most of these places, his greatest praise and most detailed descriptions are reserved for Hangchou in Chechiang province, the largest and most important city in China at this time. As scholars have pointed out, it was probably Marco's ability to describe in detail the people, customs, and geography of all these places (most of which the khan himself had never seen) that enabled him to remain in the emperor's good graces for seventeen years. Marco, in fact, claims that Kublai Khan rewarded him for his services by making him "governor" of the city of Yangchou, 50 miles (80 kilometers) northeast of Nanking (Nanching). Scholars, however, find it hard to believe that a foreigner could have held such an important position: it is more likely that Marco held a minor post, such as that of inspector.

In 1292, the Polos found an opportunity to return to Venice by joining an envoy escorting the princess Cocacin to her groom, Arghun Khan of Persia, the grandnephew of Kublai Khan. The envoy departed from the port of Zaiton (Chuanchou or Chinchiang in Fuchien province on the Formosa Strait) and sailed along the coasts of China and Vietnam to Sumatra, Ceylon, and the Malabar Coast of India before reaching Hormuz almost two years later. In Hormuz, the Polos learned of Arghun's death and delivered Cocacin to Arghun's brother Kaikhatu. They spent the next nine months in Tabriz before going to Trebizond (the Turkish town of Trabzon on the Black Sea). From there they sailed to Constantinople and Negroponte (a Venetian colony on the Greek island of Euboea) before finally arriving in Venice in 1295. Not long after his return to Venice, Marco was taken prisoner by the Genoese while sailing a galley (possibly in 1296). He remained in prison until 1299, during which time he dictated to Rustichello his adventures in the far east.

The Polos' two journeys to China were the farthest any European had traveled to the Orient since the time of Justinian. In 1246, Giovanni di Piano Carpini, who was a Franciscan emissary of Pope Innocent IV and the author of a history on the Mongols (*Historia mongolorum*), went as far as Karakorum (the ancient Mongolian capital, about 250 miles—400 kilometers—west of Ulaan Baatar). In 1253, William of Rubruck, also a Franciscan friar, went to Karakorum as an envoy of King Louis IX of France. Although both friars left written accounts of their trips to Mongolia, neither account captured the imagination of so many people for so many centuries as Marco's *Il Milione*.

Further Reading

Editions

Benedetto, Luigi Foscolo. *Il libro di Messer Marco Polo cittadino di Venezia detto Milione si raccontano le Meraviglie del mondo.* Milan and Rome: Trèves, Treccani, Tumminelli, 1932.

Marco Polo. *Il libro di Marco Polo detto Milione nella versione trecentesca dell'Ottimo*, ed. Daniele Ponchiroli with an introduction by Sergio Solmi. Turin: Einaudi, 1974.

——. *Il Milione*, ed. Luigi Foscolo Benedetto. Florence: Leo Olschki, 1928.

——. *Il Milione*, ed. Ranieri Allulli. Classici Mondadori. Milan and Verona: Mondadori, 1954.

——. *Milione*, ed. Lucia Battaglia Ricci. Firenze: Sansoni, 2001.

——. *Milione: Le divisament dou monde; il Milione nelle redazioni toscana e franco italiana*, ed. Gabriella Ronchi, intro. Cesare Segre. Milan: Mondadori, 1982.

——. *Il Milione: Introduzione, edizione del testo toscano ("Ottimo")*, ed. Ruggero M. Ruggieri. Bibliotheca dell'Archivum Romanicum, Series 1(200). Florence: Olschki, 1986.

——. *Il "Milione" veneto: Ms. CM 211 della Biblioteca Civica di Padova*, ed. Alvaro Barbieri and Alvise Andreose. Venice: Marsilio, 1999.

——. *Milione: Versione toscana del trecento*, ed. Valeria Bertolucci Pizzorusso. Milan: Adelphi, 1975. (With index and glossary by Giorgio R. Cardona.)

Marco Polo: Milione; Giovanni da Pian del Carpine: Viaggi a' Tartari. Novara: Istituto Geografico De Agostini, 1982. (Includes an Italian translation of *Historia mongolorum*.)

English Translations

Bellonci, Maria. *The Travels of Marco Polo*, trans. Teresa Waugh. New York: Facts on File, 1984.

The Book of Ser Marco Polo, the Venetian, Concerning the Kingdoms and Marvels of the East, trans. and ed. Henry Yule. New York: Scribner, 1929. (3rd ed., "revised throughout in the light of recent discoveries," but not based on Benedetto's critical edition.)

Marco Polo. *The Description of the World*, trans. A. C. Pelliot and P. Pelliot. London: Routledge, 1938.

——. *The Travels of Marco Polo*, trans. Ronald Latham. Harmondsworth, Middlesex: Penguin Books, 1958.

Critical Studies

Barozzi, Pietro. *Appunti per la lettura del Milione.* Genoa: Fratelli Bozzi, 1971.

Bellonci, Maria. *Marco Polo.* Milan: Rizzoli, 1989.

Benedetto, Luigi Foscolo. *La tradizione manoscritta del Milione di Marco Polo.* Turin: Bottega d'Erasmo, 1982.

Brunello, Franco. *Marco Polo e le merci dell'Oriente.* Vicenza: Neri Pozza, 1986.

Capusso, Maria Grazia. *La lingua del Divisament dou monde di Marco Polo.* Pisa: Pacini, 1980.

Hart, Henry Hersh. *Marco Polo: Venetian Adventurer.* Norman: University of Oklahoma Press, 1967.

Komroff, Manuel. *Contemporaries of Marco Polo: Consisting of the Travel Records to the Eastern Parts of the World of William of Rubruck.* New York: Boni and Liveright, 1928.

Marco Polo, Venezia, e l'oriente, ed. Alvise Zorzi. Milan: Electa, 1982.

Olschki, Leonardo. *L'Asia di Marco Polo: Introduzione alla lettura e allo studio del Milione.* Florence: Civelli, 1957.

——. *Marco Polo's Asia: An Introduction to His "Description of the World" Called Il Milione*, trans. John A Scott. Los Angeles and Berkeley: University of California Press, 1960.

POLO, MARCO

Pelliot, Paul. *Notes on Marco Polo*, 2 vols. Paris: Imprimerie Nationale, 1959.

Ross, E. Denison. *Marco Polo and His Book.* Annual Italian Lectures of the British Academy: 1934. Oxford: Oxford University Press, 1934.

Segre, Cesare, Gabriella Ronchi, and Marisa Miianesi. *Avventure del Milione.* Parma: Zara, 1986.

Watanabe, Hiroshi. *Marco Polo Bibliography: 1477–1983.* Tokyo: Toyo Bunko, 1986.

Zorzi, Alvise. *Vita di Marco Polo Veneziano.* Milan: Rusconi, 1982.

STEVEN GROSSVOGEL

POTTER, DIRC
(ca. 1368/1370–April 30, 1428)

Dutch poet and diplomat. After he finished high school (the "Latin School,") Potter entered the service of the count of Holland. Having started as a treasury clerk, he was, after 1400, promoted to clerk of the court of justice, bailiff of The Hague, and secretary of the count. As a diplomat he went on a number of journeys to Rome (1411–1412). In his spare time he wrote works of literature: two discourses in prose (after March 1415), *Blome der doechden* (*Flowers of Virtue*), which goes back to the Italian *Fiore di virtù*, and *Mellibeus*, translated from a French translation of Albertanus of Brescia's *Liber consolationis*; but his principal work is *Der minnen loep* (*The Course of Love*, 1411–1412), a treatise in verse about love, larded with stories largely taken from the Bible and from Ovid, in particular from the *Heroides*. The work consists of four books (over eleven thousand lines). Potter distinguishes "foolish," "good," "illicit," and "licit" love; one book is devoted to each of them. Potter derived the classification in Books I, III, and IV from medieval commentaries on *Heroides*, which discern in the *Heroides amor stultus*, *illicitus*, and *licitus*. The "good" love of Book II does not originate from the *Heroides* commentaries, but (at least from Potter's point of view) it forms a whole with "licit" love, which is the highest degree of "good" love. It turns out that Potter knew the complete "medieval Ovid": Ovid's works, the commentaries on these works, and the *accessus*, i.e., the medieval introductions to them. Within the tradition of the "pagan" *artes amandi* (treatises on the art of love), Potter created a Christianized *ars amatoria*. As such he is highly original: *Der minnen loep* is unique in the European context.

Further Reading

Leendertz, Pieter, ed. *Der minnen loep*, 2 vols. Leiden: du Mortier, 1845–1847.

Overmaat, Bernard G. L. "Mellibeus. Arnhem." Ph.d. diss., University of Nijmegen, 1950.

Schoutens, Stephanus. *Dat bouck der bloemen.* Hoogstraten: Van Hoof-Roelans, 1904 [*Blome der doechden*].

van Buuren, A. M. J. *Der minnen loep van Dirc Potter: studie over een Middelnederlandse ars amandi.* Utrecht: HES, 1979.

——. "Dire Potter, a Medieval Ovid," in Erik Kooper, ed. *Medieval Dutch Literature in Its European Context.* Cambridge: Cambridge University Press, 1994, pp. 151–167.

van Oostrom, Frits P. *Court and Culture*: *Dutch Literature, 1350–1450.* Berkeley: University of California Press, 1992.

ALFONS M. J. VAN BUUREN

POWER, LEONEL (ca. 1375/85–1445)

Composer and music theorist, one of the most prolific and influential in the first half of the 15th century. The first reference to Leonel occurs in 1418 in the records of the household chapel of Thomas duke of Clarence, where he was probably employed as a specialist musician rather than as a cleric. Since his name is given second in the accounts, he may have been one of its most senior members, recruited perhaps as early as 1411–13. After Clarence's death in 1421 Leonel's movements become uncertain, though he may have worked in one of the other English ducal chapels. In 1423 he became a member of the confraternity of the priory at Christ Church, Canterbury, but there is no evidence that this involved any professional duties. That he spent his last years in Canterbury is confirmed by a legal document of 1438 and by records suggesting that from 1439 until his death he acted as master of the Lady Chapel choir of the cathedral.

Most of Leonel's substantial surviving output (over 40 pieces, not counting those with conflicting attributions) is either for the Ordinary of the mass or for Marian services; secular music and isorhythmic motets are lacking. This narrow range of genres is, however, counterbalanced by an unusually wide variety of styles, much wider than that shown by his younger contemporary Dunstable, and his music accurately reflects the important technical changes that occurred during his long career.

Leonel's earliest surviving music comes mainly from the Old Hall Manuscript and bears the hallmark of a skilled and inventive composer fully conversant with the techniques available at the beginning of the 15th century; clearly he was proficient at all levels of elaboration, from austere discant through florid melodic writing to ingenious use of isorhythm. He seems, however, to have taken a particular delight in rhythmic intricacies expressed through notational tricks that are esoteric even by the standards of Old Hall. Some of Leonel's music seems to be contrived around numerical relationships; in this respect he is typical of composers of his time, though his usage is notably less involved than that of Dunstable.

About this time he and others began to group mass movements in pairs, an idea that eventually led to the establishment of the cyclic mass. Only one such cycle survives with an undisputed attribution to Leonel (built on the plainsong *Alma redemptoris mater*), but two more carry conflicting ascriptions. In this and later music he inclined toward the melodically, rhythmically, and harmonically smoother style cultivated from the 1430s onward; and what appear to be his last Marian antiphons are as forward-looking as anything of the period. Most of these more modern-sounding works are preserved only in continental sources, and doubtless there is further music by Leonel among the many anonymous pieces in the earlier Trent Codices and other mid-century continental manuscripts.

Leonel's short treatise in the vernacular "for hem that wilbe syngers or makers or techers" provides a lucid explanation of improvised counterpoint, especially as it involves boys' voices.

See also **Dunstable, John**

Further Reading

Primary Sources

Hamm, Charles, ed. *Leonel Power: Complete Works*. Corpus Mensurabilis Musicae 50. Rome: American Institute of Musicology, 1969

Hughes, Andrew, and Margaret Bent, eds. *The Old Hall Manuscript*. 3 vols. in 4. Corpus Mensurabilis Musicae 46, Rome: American Institute of Musicology, 1969–73

Meech, Sanford B. "Three Musical Treatises in English from a Fifteenth-Century Manuscript." *Speculum* 10 (1935): 235–69.

Secondary Sources

Bent, Margaret. "Power, Leonel." *NGD* 15:174–79

Bowers, Roger D. "Some Observations on the Life and Career of Lionel Power," *Proceedings of the Royal Musical Association* 102 (1975–76): 103–27.

GARETH CURTIS

PROSDOCIMUS DE BELDEMANDIS (d. 1428)

Prosdocimus de Beldemandis (Prosdocimo de' Beldomandi), was the author of treatises on arithmetic, geometry, astronomy, and music. After studying in Bologna, he took a doctorate in arts at Padua on 15 May 1409 and received a license in medicine there on 15 April 1411. He was a professor of arts and medicine at Padua from 1422, at the latest, until his death.

Prosdocimus wrote on all four of the quadrivial arts; the following treatises have survived. On arithmetic: *Canon in quo docetur modus componendi et operandi tabulam quandam* (Padua, 1409 or 1419) and *Algorismus de integris sive pratica arismetrice de integris* (Padua, 1410). On geometry: *De parallelogramo*. On astronomy: *Brevis tractatulus de electionibus secundum situm lune in suis 28 mansionibus* (Montagnana, 1413); *Scriptum super tractatu de spera Johannis de Sacrobosco* (Padua, 1418); *Canones de motibus corporum supercelestium* (Padua, 1424); *Tabule mediorum motuum, equationum, stationum et latitudinum planetarum, elevationis signo-*rum, diversitatis aspectus lune, mediarum coniunctionum et oppositionum lunarium, feriarum, latitudinum climatum, longitudinum et latitudinum civitatum; *Stelle fixe verificate tempore Alphonsi; Canon ad inveniendum tempus introitus solis in quodcumque 12 signorum in zodiaco; Canon ad inveniendum introitum lune in quodlibet signorum in zodiaco; Compositio astrolabii;* and *Astrolabium*. On music: *Expositiones tractatus pratice cantus mensurabilis Johannis de Muris* (Padua, possibly 1404); *Tractatus pratice cantus mensurabilis* (1408); *Brevis summula proportionum quantum ad musicam pertinet* (1409); *Contrapunctus* (Montagnana, 1412); *Tractatus pratice cantus mensurabilis ad modum Ytalicorum* (Montagnana, 1412); *Tractatus plane musice* (Montagnana, 1412); *Parvus tractatulus de modo monacordum dividendi* (Padua, 1413); and *Tractatus musice speculative* (1425).

Prosdocimus based his *Algorismus de integris* on a similarly titled work of the thirteenth-century polymath Johannes de Sacrobosco; his *Scriptum super tractatu de spera Johannis de Sacrobosco* is based on the same author's textbook of Ptolemaic astronomy, one of the most widely disseminated medieval astronomical works.

Prosdocimus's musical treatises represent an attempt to survey the entire discipline; no earlier music theorist had attempted such a comprehensive project through separate treatises on the subdisciplines, and Prosdocimus's musical writings are of great importance because of their scope and clarity. In *Parvus tractatulus de modo monacordum dividendi*, he described a scale that preserved the standard medieval "Pythagorean" tuning (i.e., with pure perfect fifths, slightly wider than those of present-day equal temperament) but with seventeen notes to the octave (seven naturals, five flats, and five sharps not quite in tune with the flats); this expanded scale may have been an important step toward the tempered tunings of the later fifteenth century. In *Contrapunctus*, he confirmed that medieval scribes did not write all the accidentals they necessarily expected to be performed, and he gave rules that clarify where accidentals are appropriate, even if unwritten. He surveyed the theory of rhythmic mensuration in three treatises, *Expositiones tractatus pratice cantus mensurabilis Johannis de Muris* (a commentary on the *Libellus cantus mensurabilis*, the most widely disseminated medieval treatise on mensuration, which laid the foundation for French fourteenth-century rhythmic notation); *Tractatus pratice cantus mensurabilis*, his own account of fourteenth-century French mensuration; and *Tractatus pratice cantus mensurabilis ad modum Ytalicorum*, an exposition of contemporaneous Italian mensuration (this is the most comprehensive treatment of Italian mensuration in its mature stage). *Tractatus musice speculative* is an attack on the division of the tone into fifths described a century earlier by Marchetto da Padova, based on what

Prosdocimus saw as the earlier theorist's abandonment of "Pythagorean" tuning and his faulty logic.

The manuscript Florence, Biblioteca Medicea-Laurenziana, Ashburnham 206, written by Prosdocimus in 1409, is an anthology of the curriculum of the Paduan college of arts and medicine at the time. It includes the *Algorismus de integris* of Johannes de Sacrobosco, the *Algorismus de integris* of Johannes de Lineriis, the *Canones supra tabulas Alphonsi* and the *Scriptum super Alkabicium* of Johannes de Saxonia, the *De septem planetis* of Messahala, the *Tractatus quadrantis novi* and the *Canones de almanach perpetuum* of Profatius Judaeus, and the *De prognosticatione mortis et vite secundum motum lune* of Pseudo-Hippocrates, among shorter works on arithmetic, astronomy, and astrology and several compilations of medical prescriptions.

Further Reading

Editions and Translations

Algorismus de integris magistri Prosdocimi Debeldamandis Patavi simul cum Algorismo de de [sic] *minutiis seu fractionibus magistri Ioannis de Lineriis.* Venice, 1540.

Algorismus Prosdocimi de Beldamandis una cum minuciis Johannes de Lineriis. Padua, 1483.

Coussemaker, Edmond de, ed. *Scriptorum de musica medii aevi nova series*, Vol. 3. Paris: Durand, 1869. (Reprint, Hildesheim: Olms, 1963. Includes *Tractatus de contrapuncto*, pp. 193–199; *Tractatus practice de musica mensurabili*, pp. 200–228; *Tractatus practice de musica mensurabili ad modum Italicorum*, pp. 228–248; *Libellus monocordi*, pp. 248–258; *Brevis summula proportionum*, pp. 258–261.)

Gallo, F. Alberto, ed. *Prosdocimi de Beldemandis "Expositiones tractatus practice cantus mensurabilis magistri Johannis de Muris."* Prosdocimi de Beldemandis Opera, 1. Bologna: Antiquae Musicae Italicae Studiosi, 1966.

Herlinger, Jan, ed. *Prosdocimo de' Beldomandi: Contrapunctus.* Greek and Latin Music Theory 1. Lincoln: University of Nebraska Press, 1984.

——, ed. *Prosdocimo de' Beldomandi: Brevis summula proportionum quantum ad musicam pertinet* and *Parvus tractatulus de modo monacordum dividendi.* Greek and Latin Music Theory 4. Lincoln: University of Nebraska Press, 1987.

——, ed. *Prosdocimo de' Beldomandi: Tractatus plane musice* and *Tractatus musice speculative.* (Forthcoming.)

Huff, Jay A., trans. *Prosdocimus de Beldemandis: A Treatise on the Practice of Mensural Music in the Italian Manner.* Musicological Studies and Documents, 29. American Institute of Musicology, 1972.

Spherae tractatus Ioannis de Sacro Busto Anglici..., Prosdocimi de beldomando patavini super tractatu sphaerico commentaria.... Venice, 1531.

Critical Studies

Baralli, D. Raffaello, and Luigi Torri. "Il *Trattato* di Prosdocimo de' Beldomandi contro il *Lucidario* di Marchetto da Padova per la prima volta trascritto e illustrato." *Rivista Musicale Italiana*, 20, 1913, pp. 707–762. (Includes *Tractatus musice speculative*, pp. 731–762.)

Berger, Karol. *Musica Ficta: Theories of Accidental Inflections in Vocal Polyphony from Marchetto da Padova to Gioseffo Zarlino.* Cambridge: Cambridge University Press, 1987.

Favaro, Antonio. "Intorno alia vita ed alle opere di Prosdocimo de Beldomandi matematico padovano del secolo XV." *Bullettino di Bibliografia e di Storia delle Scienze Matematiche e Fisiche*, 12, 1979, pp. 1–74, 115–251. (Includes *Canon in quo docetur modus componendi et operandi tabulam quondam*, pp. 143–145; and *De parallelogrammo*, p. 170.)

——. "Appendice agli studi intorno alla vita ed alle opere di Prosdocimo de Beldomandi matematico padovano del secolo XV." *Bullettino di Bibliografia e di Storia delle Scienze Matematiche e Fisiche*, 18, 1985, pp. 405–423.

Gallo, F. Alberto. "La tradizione dei trattati musicali di Prosdocimo de Beldemandis." *Quadrivium*, 6, 1964, pp. 57–84.

Herlinger, Jan. "What Trecento Music Theory Tells Us." In *Explorations in Music, the Arts, and Ideas: Essays in Honor of Leonard B. Meyer*, ed. Eugene Narmour and Ruth A. Solie. Festschrift Series, 7. Stuyvesant, N.Y.: Pendragon, 1988, pp. 177–197.

Lindley, Mark. "Pythagorean Intonation and the Rise of the Triad." *Royal Musical Association Research Chronicle*, 16, 1980, pp. 4–61.

Sartori, Claudio. *La notazione italiana del Trecento in una redazione inedita del "Tractatus practice cantus mensurabilis ad modum ytalicorum" di Prosdocimo de Beldemandis.* Florence: Olschki, 1938. (Includes *Tractatus pratice cantus mensurabilis ad modum Ytalicorum*, pp. 35–71.)

JAN HERLINGER

PTOLEMY OF LUCCA
(c. 1236–1327)

Ptolemy Fiadoni of Lucca (Tolomeo, Tholomeo, Ptolomeo, Bartolomeo) was a member of a family that belonged to the Lucchese commercial elite, though not the aristocracy. He entered the Dominican convent of San Romano at Lucca at an unknown date, but obviously before he accompanied Thomas Aquinas on a journey from Rome to Naples in 1272. He remained in Rome with Aquinas until 1274, probably helping him set up a *studium* of theology in the Neapolitan convent of San Domenico. Ptolemy included a long account of Aquinas's life and works in his *Historia ecclesiastica nova*. Ptolemy may also have visited or lived in Rome during the time of Pope Nicholas III (r. 1278–1280), since his *Historia ecclesiastica* contains interesting descriptions of Nicholas's building projects. *Libellus de iurisdictione imperii et auctoritate summi pontificis* (usually called *Determinatio compendiosa*), written at about this period, seems to breathe the spirit of Nicholas's pontificate. In 1283–1285 Ptolemy visited Provence. In 1285 he was made prior of San Romano in Lucca. In 1288 he was named preacher-general of his order and attended its general chapter in Lucca; he was a *diffinitor* at the general chapters of 1300 at Marseilles and of 1302 at Cologne. During the years 1287–1307 there are frequent documentary references to his presence in the Lucchese convent, often as prior; he was also (from 1300 to 1302) prior of Santa Maria Novella in Florence. During this period he made other trips outside Lucca; for example, Ptolemy witnessed the election of Celestine V at Perugia and his crowning at Aquila and was in Naples during his pontificate in 1294. Ptolemy was in Avignon by 1309 and spent most of the next two decades there, serving at least two cardinals. He was named bishop of Torcello in 1318. Because of a quarrel with the patriarch of Grado, Ptolemy's episcopate was stormy, and he even suffered excommunication and imprisonment. Pope John XXII restored Ptolemy to his see in 1323, probably while the pope was in Avignon attending the festivities for Aquinas's canonization. Ptolemy died in Torcello.

Though he wrote one "scientific" work, *De operibus sex dierum*, published under the title *Exaemeron*, Ptolemy's achievements as a historian and political thinker far outweighed those in philosophy or theology. Besides his *Historia ecclesiastica nova*, which is based not only on Martin of Troppau and other chroniclers but also on numerous canonistic texts, Ptolemy wrote *Gesta Tuscorum*, a volume of annals extending from 1061 to 1303 in which Tuscany and particularly Lucca figured prominently. Ptolemy refers also to a third historical work, *Historia tripartita*, of which no manuscript is known. His desire to exalt the temporal jurisdiction of the papacy found expression in his *Libellus de Iurisdictione imperii et auctoritate summi pontificis*, published as *Determinatio compendiosa de iurisdictione imperii*; and *Tractatus de iurisdictione ecclesie super regnum Apulie et Sicilie*. Krammer, who edited *Determinatio compendiosa* (1909), also edited *De origine ac translatione et statu romani imperii* as a work probably by Ptolemy, but its authorship is uncertain. In about 1302 Ptolemy wrote his continuation of Aquinas's *De regno*; this composite work has usually been referred to as *De regimine principum* and attributed solely to Aquinas. In Ptolemy's continuation, another dimension of his political thought came to the fore: his republicanism. He arranged governments under two main headings, political and despotic, classifying aristocracies and popular governments as political and all forms of absolute rule, including kingship, as despotic. Ptolemy depended heavily on Aristotle's *Politics*, but Artistotle had drawn a sharp distinction between despotic and royal government—a distinction of which Ptolemy shows himself to be well aware in his *De operibus*. Ptolemy's preference for political government was revealed in his claim that this was the regime best suited for inhabitants of Eden, northern Italy, and Rome. In *De operibus* he said that in the state of innocence government would have been, as it was today among the angels, not despotic but political, a prelacy based on service, not a dominion involving subjection—subjection having come about only as a result of the fall of man. In *De regimine principum* he said that this was also true of northern Italy and Rome, whose inhabitants took pride in their own rationality, though it was not true of the majority of other postlapsarian men, who usually profited more from royal rule.

Ptolemy tried to reconcile this view with the frequency of despotism in contemporary Italy by saying that northern Italians could be subjected only by coercion. As for the Roman empire, not it but the church was the legitimate heir of the Roman republic. The virtues of the heroes of the Roman republic, to which Ptolemy also alluded in *Determinatio compendiosa*, recalled, in fact, the pristine state of human nature before the fall of man. Ptolemy's attempt to justify and harmonize republican and hierocratic theories makes him one of the most original political thinkers of the Middle Ages.

See also **Aquinas, Thomas**

Further Reading

Editions

De operibus sex dierum, ed. P. T. Masetti (as *Exaemeron*). Siena, 1880.

De regimine principum, ed. Joseph Mathis, 2nd ed. Turin: Marietti, 1948.

De regno sive de regimine principum. In Thomas Aquinas, *Opuscula omnia*, Vol. 1, *Opuscula philosophica*, ed. Johannes Perrier. Paris: P. Lethielleux, 1949, pp. 220–426.

Gesta Tuscorum, ed. Bernhard Schmeidler (as *Die Annalen des Tholomeus von Lucca*). Monumenta Germaniae Historica, Scriptores Rerum Germanicarum, New Series 8. Berlin: Weidmann, 1930.

Historia ecclesiastica nova, ed. L. A. Muratori. Rerum Italicarum Scriptores, 11. Milan, 1727, pp. 740–1203.

Libellus de iurisdictione imperii et auctoritate summi pontificis, ed. Mario Krammer (as *Determinatio compendiosa de iurisdictione imperii*). Monumenta Germaniae Historica, Fontes Iuris Germanici Antiqui. Hannover and Leipzig: Hahn, 1909.

Tractatus de iurisdictione ecclesiae super regnum Apuliae et Siciliae, ed. Etienne Baluze and Domenico Mansi. In *Miscellanea*, Vol. 1, *Monumenta historica tum sacra tum profane*. Lucca: Riccomini, 1761, pp. 468–473.

Translation

Ptolemy of Lucca. *On the Government of Rulers: De regimine principum—Ptolemy of Lucca with portions attributed to Thomas Aquinas*, trans. James M. Blythe. Philadelphia: University of Pennsylvania Press, 1997.

Critical Studies

Blythe, James M. *Ideal Government and the Mixed Constitution in the Middle Ages*. Princeton, N.J.: Princeton University Press, 1992.

Davis, Charles. "Ptolemy of Lucca and the Roman Republic." *Proceedings of the American Philosophical Society*, 118, 1974, pp. 30–50. (Reprinted in Charles Davis. *Dante's Italy and Other Essays*. Philadelphia: University of Pennsylvania Press, 1984, pp. 254–289.) .

——. "Roman Patriotism and Republican Propaganda: Ptolemy of Lucca and Pope Nicholas III." *Speculum*, 50, 1975, pp. 411–33. (Reprinted in Charles Davis. *Dante's Italy and Other Essays*. Philadelphia: University of Pennsylvania Press, 1984, pp. 224–253.)

Dondaine, Antoine. "Les 'Opuscula fratris Thomae' chez Ptolemée de Lucques." *Archivum Fratrum Praedicatorum*, 31, 1961, pp. 142–203.

Grabmann, Martin. "La scuola tomistica italiana nel sec. XIII e principio del XIV sec." *Rivista di Filosofia Neoscolastica*, 5, 1923, pp. 120–127.

Laurenti, Maria Cristina. "Tommaso e Tolomeo da Lucca 'commentatori' di Aristotele." *Sandalion*, 8–9, 1985–1986, pp. 343–371.

Panella, Emilio. "Priori di Santa Maria Novella di Firenze 1221–1325." *Memorie Domenicane*, 17, 1986, pp. 256–266.

——. "Livio in Tolomeo da Lucca." *Studi Petrarcheschi*, 6, 1989, pp. 43–52.

——. "Rilettura del *De operibus sex dierum* di Tolomeo dei Fiadoni da Lucca." *Archivum Fratrum Praedicatorum*, 63, 1993, pp. 51–111.

Rubenstein, Nicolai. "Marsilius of Padua and Italian Political Thought of His Time." In *Europe in the Late Middle Ages*, ed. J. L. Hale, J. R. L. Highfield, and B. Smalley. London: Faber and Faber, 1965, pp. 44–75.

Schmeidler, Bernhard. "Studien zu Tholomeus von Lucca, 1, Die *Annalen* oder *Gesta Tuscorum* des Tholomeus." *Neues Archiv*, 33, 1908a, pp. 287–308. .

——. "Studien zu Tholomeus von Lucca, 2, *Gesta Lucanorum* des Tholomeus." *Neues Archiv*, 33, 1908b, pp. 308–343.

——. "Studien zu Tholomeus von Lucca, 3, Zur Wiederherstellung der *Gesta Florentinorum* des Tholomeus." *Neues Archiv*, 34, 1909, pp. 725–756.

Schmugge, Ludwig. "Zur Überlieferung der Historia Ecclesiastica nova des Tholomeus von Lucca." *Deutsches Archiv für Erforschung des Mittelalters*, 32, 1976, pp. 495–545.

——. "Kanonistik und Geschichtsschreibung." *Zeitschrift der Savigny-Stiftung für Rechtsgeschichte, Kanonistische Abteilung*, 99, 1982, pp. 219–276.

——. "Fiadoni, Bartholomeo." In *Dizionario biografico degli Italiani*, Vol. 47. Rome: Istituto della Enciclopedia Italiana, 1997, pp. 317–320.

Taurisano, Innocenzo M. *I domenicani in Lucca*. Lucca: Baroni, 1914, pp. 59–76.

Witt, Thomas. "König Rudolf von Habsburg und Papst Nikolaus III. 'Erbreichsplan' und 'Vierstaatenprojekt' insbesondere bei Tholomeus von Lucca, Humbert of Romans, und Bernard Gui." Dissertation, Göttingen, 1957.

CHARLES T. DAVIS

PUCELLE, JEAN (d. 1334)

An artist documented as producing the seal of the confraternity of Saint-Jacques-aux-Pèlerins in Paris between 1319 and 1324 and whose name appears in marginal notes along with two other illuminators in the *Belleville Breviary* (B.N. lat. 10483–84), dated 1323–26. His name is also mentioned with two other illuminators in the Bible written by Robert de Billyng (B.N. lat. 11935), and inventory entries of the collection of John, duke of Berry, have suggested that between 1325 and 1328 he made the book known as the *Heures de Jeanne d'Évreux* (New York, The Cloisters) with miniatures and marginalia in *grisaille*. The styles of the miniatures in these manuscripts, however, are all different, and their authorship is the subject of ongoing controversy. At best, one can speak of a "Pucelle style" that manifests a new sense of three-dimensionality in modeled figures and architectural space in manuscripts produced for the royal court in the second quarter of the 14th century.

See also **John, Duke of Berry**

Further Reading

The *Hours of Jeanne d'Évreux Queen of France*, intro. James J. Rorimer. 2nd ed. New York: Metropolitan Museum of Art, 1965.

Blum, Rudolf. "Jean Pucelle et la miniature Parisienne du XlVe siècle." *Scriptorium* 3 (1949): 211–17.

Deuchler, Florens. "Jean Pucelle—Facts and Fictions." *Metropolitan Museum of Art Bulletin* 29 (1971): 253–56.

Morand, Kathleen. Jean Pucelle. Oxford: Clarendon, 1962. [With bibliography.]

ROBERT G. CALKINS

Q

QASMŪNA BINT ISMĀ'ĪL

Qasmūna was the first known Jewish woman writer on the Iberian Peninsula. She is believed to have been the daughter of the famous eleventh-century poet, Samuel Ha-Nagid (Ibn Narīllah), the vizier of the king of Granada and the leader of the Jewish community. He apparently had four children, three sons and one daughter, Qasmūna, whom he instructed in the art of poetry. He reportedly often began a strophe and called on Qasmūna to finish it, a form of recreation common among medieval Arabic peoples. Indeed the first of the three extant poems by Qasmūna is a reply to a short poem by her father concerning someone who harms his benefactor. Qasmūna's clever response compares that person with the moon, which receives its light from the sun and yet sometimes eclipses it. Tradition has it that, upon hearing this, her father said she was a greater poet than he was.

However, Samuel Ha-Nagid wrote his poems in Hebrew, while Qasmūna wrote hers in Arabic. As a Jewish woman, she had no access to Hebrew poetry and certainly no audience for it, even if she had written it. On the other hand, as a member of the court in Granada, she did have access to Arabic poetry, as well as an audience of like-minded women poets. Indeed, although Jewish, she is considered one of the foremost Arabic women poets of Al-Andalus.

Critics have pointed out some Biblical resonances in Qasmūna's poems. They also have underscored the fact that her poems seem to alude to the importance of marriage for women, a very Jewish concept. In effect, her two other poems are laments about her loneliness. The first is about a garden which is going to waste without a gardener. Youth is passing by and the only thing that remains is something the poet does not dare name. In the second poem, she compares herself with a deer in a garden. Critics have commented that her father seems to have been too busy to select a son-in-law. However, one wonders if this is what Qasmūna was complaining about. Obviously, she felt alienated, but her alienation might have been of a more profound nature. Being the daughter of a powerful Jewish official in an Arab court must not have been easy. Being a talented woman with no outlet for her talent must have been even more difficult. Qasmūna could be talking about her spiritual isolation and the waste of her talent. The deer is a restless animal meant to be free, not confined in a garden, however pleasant. What Qasmūna does not dare name could be her frustration.

Further Reading

Garulo, T., *Diwan de las poetisas de al-Andalus.* Madrid, 1986.
Sobh, M., *Poetisas arábigo-andaluzas.* Granada, n.d.

CRISTINA GONZÁLEZ

R

RABANUS MAURUS (HRABANUS, RHABANUS, ALSO KNOWN AS MAGNENTIUS; ca. 780–856).

Born in Mainz of a noble family, Rabanus (which means "raven" in Old High German) received the best education available in his day. A favorite pupil of Alcuin, he was called "Maurus" after a disciple of St. Benedict. Rabanus moved in the highest circles of power of the Carolingian world. He became abbot of Fulda in 822 and solicited the patronage of Lothair I to make this one of the outstanding monastic foundations of the age. Rabanus supported Louis the Pious in the political turmoil of the 830s and 840s, and Lothair I on Louis's death. The victory of Louis the German in 840 forced him into exile for about a year; upon his return to German lands, he retired to the abbey of Petersburg until named archbishop of Mainz in 847.

Rabanus was a prolific author and the teacher of some of the most outstanding of the Carolingian scholars, among them Walafrid Strabo. Many of his works have a pedagogical intent. *De institutione clericorum* (before 819) covers ecclesiastical grades, liturgy, liturgical vestments, catechetical instruction, and the Liberal Arts. *De rerum naturis* (after 840; also known as *De universo*) is an encyclopedic work in the style of Isidore of Seville but with an allegorical level of interpretation. His extensive corpus of poetry includes a number of *carmina figurata*, in which the words of poems are arranged in designs to illustrate them. However, it is for his biblical interpretation that Rabanus was most famous in the Middle Ages and early-modern period, even though this material has not been widely studied by modern scholars.

Rabanus wrote commentaries on most books of the Bible: all of the historical books of the Old Testament, many of the books of wisdom literature (significantly, not the Song of Songs), the Major Prophets, Maccabees, the Gospel of Matthew, the Acts of the Apostles, and the Pauline epistles. These are composites of patristic sources, but the extracts from the various patristic works are carefully arranged so as to present allegorical interpretations, mostly having to do with Christ and the church, in a coherent and easily accessible form. These interpretations were widely read before the modern period; they survive in many manuscripts and in printed versions through the 16th century. For his role as a Christian educator, Rabanus earned the title *praeceptor Germaniae*.

See also **Alcuin; Isidore of Seville, Saint; Lothair I, Louis the Pious**

Further Reading

Rabanus Maurus. *Omnia opera. PL* 107–12.

——. *Liber de laudibus sanctae crucis.* In *Vollständige Faksimile-Ausgabe im Original-format des Codex Vindobonensis 652 der Österreichischen Nationalbibliothek,* commentary by Kurt Holter. 2 vols. Graz: Akademische Druck- und Verlagsanstalt, 1972–73.

——. *The Life of Saint Mary Magdalene and of Her Sister Saint Martha: A Twelfth-Century Biography,* trans. David Mycoff. Kalamazoo: Cistercian, 1989.

——. *Martyrologium,* ed. John McCulloh, and *Liber de computo,* ed. Wesley M. Stevens. *CCCM* 44. Turnhout: Brepols, 1979.

——. *Poems. MGH Poetae* 2.154–258.

Kottje, Raymund, and Harald Zimmermann. *Hrabanus Maurus: Lehrer, Abt und Bischof.* Mainz: Akademie der Wissenschaften und der Literatur, 1982.

Laistner, Max Ludwig Wolfram. *Thought and Letters in Western Europe, A.D. 500 to 900.* London: Methuen, 1957.

Müller, Hans-Georg. *Hrabanus Maurus: De laudibus sancta crucis. Studien zur Überlieferung und Geistesgeschichte mit dem Faksimile-Textabdruck aus Codex Reg. Lat 124 der vatikanischen Bibliothek.* Ratingen: Henn, 1973.

Szoverffy, Josef. *Weltliche Dichtungen des lateinsichen Mittelalters: Ein Handbuch.* Berlin: Schmidt, 1970, Vol. 1.

Turnau, Dietrich W. *Rabanus Maurus, der Praeceptor Germaniae.* Munich: Lindauer, 1900.

E. Ann Matter

RADEWIJNS, FLORENS (ca. 1350–1400)

Exponent of the Modern Devotion, founder of the Brethren of the Common Life, founder of the monastery of Windesheim. Radewijns was born circa 1350 at Leerdam or Gorinchem and died at Deventer in 1400. He studied at Prague (master of arts) and became a canon in Utrecht. After a sermon of Geert Grote, he converted and accepted the lower position of vicar at Deventer, where Grote lived. For this vicariat he had to be ordained priest. He became the first leader of a congregation of Brethren of the Common Life. These Brethren gave guidance to a convict of schoolboys.

Radewijns compiled two little treatises, which are important because they influenced the treatises of his housemate Gerard Zerbolt of Zutphen. These widely spread treatises gave the Modern Devotion its spiritual fundament. We also have some fragments of Radewijns's letters. He also wrote a (lost?) *propositum*, a set of personal intentions.

In Radewijns's spirituality, humility is a central theme. The idea of externals pulling along the inner man leads to a severe asceticism, as did the idea that a humble inner self has to reflect itself in humble and austere exteriors. By fasting and waking Radewijns had broken his weak nature and almost lost his sense of taste and his appetite. This severe asceticism is colored by the spirituality of the Desert Fathers, which also seems to have influenced his fear of the demon. In his young days Thomas à Kempis lived together with Radewijns. In his biography of Radewijns, Thomas portrays him as a man who incites both love and fear with his straightforwardness.

See also **Thomas à Kempis**

Further Reading

Goossens, Leonardus A. M., ed. *De meditatie in de eerste tijd van de Moderne Devotie.* Haarlem: Gottmer, 1952, pp. 213–254 [*Tractatulus devotus*].

Épiney-Burgard, Georgette. "Florent Radewijns," in *Die deutsche Literatur des Mittelalters*: *Verfasserlexikon*, ed. Kurt Ruh et al. Berlin: de Gruyter, 2d ed. vol. 7, coll. 968–972.

——. "La Vie et les écrits de Florent Radewijns en langue vernaculaire." *Ons Geestelijk Erf* 63 (1989): 370–384.

Pohl, Michael J., ed. *Thomae Hemerken a Kempis Opera Omnia.* Freiburg: Herder, 1902–1922, vol. 7, pp. 116–210 [with bibliography].

Post, Regnerus R. *The Modern Devotion.* Leyden: Brill, 1968, pp. 317–325.

van Woerkum, M. "Florentius Radewijns. Schets van zijn leven, geschriften, persoonlijkheid en ideeën." *Ons Geestelijk Erf* 24 (1950): 337–346.

——. "Het Libellus 'Omnes, inquit, artes': een rapiarium van Florentius Radewijns." *Ons Geestelijk Erf* 25 (1951): 113–158, 225–268.

——. "Florent Radewijns," in *Dictionnaire de Spiritualité*, ed. Marcel Viller, vol. 5. Paris: Beauchesne, 1964, pp. 427–434.

Thom Mertens

RAINALD OF DASSEL (ca. 1120–1167)

From 1156 until his death in 1167, Rainald of Dassel was Frederick Barbarossa's most loyal and powerful adviser. Born to a family of Lower Saxon lesser nobility circa 1120, Rainald was educated first at the Hildesheim cathedral school, then in France in the 1140s. He returned to Hildesheim by 1146. Rainald cultivated an interest in arts and letters and would become the chief patron of the "Archpoet" circa 1060.

In 1156, Barbarossa chose Rainald as imperial chancellor. Rainald straightway committed himself to the Hohenstaufen agenda of rejecting papal claims to primacy and establishing German imperial hegemony over northern Italy. Rainald's leadership led to innovations in the chancery almost immediately, including the use of the phrase *sacrum imperium* (Holy Empire) and its variants.

Rainald played a consistently dramatic role in international relations after his elevation to the chancellorship. In 1157, papal legatees met Barbarossa's court in Besançon to protest the imprisonment of Archbishop Eskil of Lund. The Latin text of Pope Adrian IV's letter suggested that the imperial crown numbered among many possible *beneficia* that could be given by the pope. Rainald's translation of the document deliberately rendered *beneficium* as "fief" (*lehen*) rather than "good work" or "favor," Adrian's intended meaning. The subsequent uproar led to a propaganda victory for Rainald and a clear formulation of the imperial position: empire derived from election by the princes and the grace of God, not papal coronation, which was simply a ceremonial act incumbent upon the pope.

Elected archbishop of Cologne at Barbarossa's instigation in 1159, Rainald did not actually take major orders until 1165. Rainald's uncompromising attitude toward the Roman curia led Barbarossa to reject conciliatory papal offers; the result was formal schism with the election of the antipope Victor IV in 1159. In 1162, Rainald oversaw the brutal destruction of Milan, upon whose unconditional surrender he had insisted. Within a few months, however, he had to preside over the failed synod of Saint Jean de Losne, convoked to resolve the papal crisis, but ending in a diplomatic victory for Pope Alexander III, who stubbornly refused to appear and be judged. In April 1164, in Lucca, Rainald orchestrated the election of another antipope, Paschal III. In July 1164, Rainald brought the relics of the Three Kings from Milan to Cologne, where they became the object of a major cult. Late in 1165, Rainald presided over the canonization of Charlemagne in Aachen, the most dramatic step taken in the programmatic sacralization of Barbarossa's imperial rule.

Rainald's uncompromising policy toward the papacy meant that only open conflict could decide the schism. In July 1167, the imperial army won a major victory at Tusculum. Rome was taken, and Alexander III fled in disguise. Triumph was short-lived, however: an epidemic, probably malaria, decimated the German host, killing Rainald and several other princes. Barbarossa returned to Germany with what was left of his army. The political approach of the rest of his reign was markedly more flexible than it had been during the era of Rainald of Dassel.

See also **Frederick I Barbarossa**

Further Reading

Engels, Odilo. *Die Staufer*, 4th ed. Stuttgart: Kohlhammer, 1989.
Ficker, Julius. *Reinald von Dassel*: *Reichskanzler und Erzbischof von Köln 1156–1167*. Cologne, 1850; rpt. Aalen: Scientia, 1966.
Grebe, Werner. "Studien zur geistigen Welt Rainalds von Dassel." *Annalen des Historischen Vereins für den Niederrhein* 171 (1969): 5–44.
Munz, Peter. *Frederick Barbarossa*: *A Study in Medieval Politics*. London: Eyre and Spottiswoode, 1969.

JONATHAN ROTONDO-MCCORD

RAMÓN BERENGUER IV, COUNT OF BARCELONA (c. 1114–1162)

On the death of his father in 1131, the young Ramón Berenguer IV became the count of Barcelona at the age of seventeen. The first major event of his reign was the union of the Catalan principalities with the neighboring Kingdom of Aragón. In 1134 Alfonso I the Batallador died childless, and this raised the problem of who was to succeed him. His will, leaving his goods to the military orders, could not be applied; and this, together with the marriage of Ramiro, the brother of Alfonso I, made Alfonso VII of Castile give up all hope of succeeding to the throne. In August 1137 Petronella, born of Ramiro's recent marriage, was immediately promised to Ramón Berenguer, who became prince of Aragon; the marriage took place in 1150. In 1140 the holy see and the military orders gave up their rights over Aragón. It was by diplomatic means that Ramón Berenguer IV ended his disagreement with the king of Castile, whom he met in 1137 and 1140; at these meetings, he swore allegiance to the city of Zaragoza, and prepared a joint expedition against Navarre. Thanks to the diplomatic activities of Oleguer, archbishop of Tarragona, and the seneschal Guillem Ramón de Montcada, the count of Barcelona symbolized the union of the counties inherited from his father with the kingdom of Alfonso I. The Catalano-Aragónese confederation depended on a reciprocal respect for the institutions belonging to each territory.

Ramón Berenguer IV concentrated henceforward on the struggle against Islam. With Alfonso VII he participated in the expeditions to Murcia (1144) and Almerí'a (1147). He later directed campaigns intended to extend his principalities. In 1148 he took Tortosa where the help of Guillem Ramón de Montcada, of the Genoese fleet, and of contingents from Languedoc was decisive for the success of this expedition, recognized by Pope Eugene III as a true crusade. Franchises accorded to the city attracted new inhabitants, while an arrangement with the qādī and the fuqahā' ensured the respect of the Muslim population. On 24 October 1149, the cities of Fraga and Lleida also fell before the troops of Ramón Berenguer IV and Ermengol VII of Urgell. Between 1152 and 1153 Miravet was conquered, and the surviving pockets of Islamic resistance destroyed. Ibn Mardānish, king of Valencia, then swore allegiance to the count of Barcelona, to whom he payed a large tribute. The Ebro River was reached; Ramón Berenguer IV considerably extended the territory of New Catalonia beyond Tarragona. The same thing happened in Aragón, where he annexed Huesca (1154) and Alcáñiz (1157).

His political activities were continued beyond the Pyrenees; the families of Béziers-Carcassonne, of Narbonne and of Montpellier paid homage to him. In 1154 he became the tutor of Gaston V of Béarn; he fought successfully at Toulouse, to which he laid siege with Henri Plantagenet II in 1156. But most of his activities took place in Provence. In 1144, his brother Berenguer Ramón, count of Provence was killed in his wars against the count of Toulouse and the family of Baux, as well as Genoa and Pisa. His son, Ramón Berenguer of Provence, was still a minor and was powerless against so many enemies. In February 1147 Ramón Berenguer IV came to his aid; the leading nobles swore that they would be faithful to him. He wiped out Ramon of Baux, and brought him back in captivity to Catalonia. Three more wars were necessary to put an end to the seditious revolt of Ramon's wife, Stephania of Baux, their children, and their associates. During the summer of 1155 he took their castle at Trinquetaille; at the beginning of 1162, he laid siege to the fortress of Baux and conquered it. He then ensured that Frederick Barbarossa recognized Catalan dominion in Provence, ordering the marriage of his niece Riquilda and his nephew Ramón Berenguer of

Provence. It was during the journey to Turin, where he was to meet the emperor, that Ramon Berenguer IV met his death in Borgo San Dalmazzo, on 6 August 1162.

The work of Ramón Berenguer IV was fundamental on institutional and administrative levels. During his youth, in order to oppose the revolt of the Catalan aristocracy, he convened the Assemblies of Peace and Truce. He organized the management of his domain in such a way as to increase his financial resources, which he needed for his expansionary policy. An inspection carried out by Bertran of Castellet in Old Catalonia in 1151 furnished him with a precise inventory of the revenues of his domains; these were administered by bailiffs (*batlles*) or by creditors who accepted them as payment. His vicars (*vicaris*) mainly brought him the fines imposed by tribunals, the tolls levied, and the *parias* (tributes) of the Muslim chiefs. Justice was henceforth carried out by specialists in law, who applied the *Usatges de Barcelona*, a Roman legal code that he had just promulgated. The *Usatges* established the monopoly of the count as regards certain royal rights; castles, mint, and organization of the peace were under his control. The ecclesiastical map was redrawn; the bishoprics of Tortosa and of Lérida (Lleida) were reestablished instead of Roda-Barbastro. In 1154, the metropolitan province of Tarragona, including all the Catalan and Aragónese bishoprics, was also reestablished. Cistercian monks from Grandselve and from Fontfroide founded Santes Creus and Poblet in New Catalonia; the Templars and Hospitalers, who had received indemnities for their renunciation of Alfonso I's will, were also given domains on the frontier. The count welcomed to his court the first Catalan troubadours, Berenguer of Palol and Guerau of Cabrera. In 1162 he was praised in the first version of the *Gesta comitum barchinonensium*, drawn up at Ripoll. In 1157, on the death of Alfonso VII of Castilla-León, Ramón Berenguer IV had become the most important of the Iberian kings, and the arbiter of their struggles; he had a preponderant role in Occitania. His reign laid the basis for the great Mediterranean expansion of the Catalano-Aragónese confederation.

Further Reading

Aurell, M. "L'expansion catalane en Provence au XIIe siècle." In *La formació i expansió del feudalisme català.* Ed. J. Portella. Girona, 1985. 175–197.

Bisson, T. N. *Fiscal Accounts of Catalonia under the Early Count-Kings (1151–1213).* Berkeley, 1984.

———. *The Medieval Crown of Aragón: A Short History.* Oxford, 1986.

Schramm, P. E., J. F. Cabestany, and E. Bagué. *Els primers comtesreis; Ramon Berenguer IV. Alfons el Cast, Pere el Catòlic.* Barcelona, 1963.

Soldevila, F. *Història de Catalunya. 2nd* ed. Barcelona, 1963.

MARTÍ AUKELL I CARDONA

RAOUL DE HOUDENC (fl. 1210–20)

Radulfus de Hosdenc, *miles,* of Hodenc-en-Bray (Beauvaisis), was the author of an Arthurian romance of 5,938 octosyllabic lines, *Meraugis de Portlesguez,* and three short didactic poems, the *Songe d'enfer,* the *Roman des eles,* and a *Dit.* A second Arthurian romance, the *Vengeance Raguidel* (6,182 lines), whose author names himself as "Raols" is probably also by Raoul de Houdenc. Raoul is one of the most talented of the Chrétien epigones, and *Meraugis de Portlesguez,* concerned with the rivalry of two friends for the love of the fair Lidoine, is one of the best examples of the genre. Both *Meraugis* and the *Vengeance Raguidel,* which is concerned with the avenging of a murdered knight called Raguidel, can best be seen as the work of an author coming to grips with the specter of Chrétien de Troyes. All kinds of humor abound in the two romances, as well as in the short didactic pieces. The *Songe d'enfer* is a vision of Hell notable for a particularly gruesome banquet and some allegorical heraldry; the *Roman des eles* is a guide to *courtoisie.* Raoul was acknowledged, along with Chrétien, to be one of the greatest French poets by Huon de Méry in the *Tournoiement Antécrist* (ca. 1230).

See also **Chrétien de Troyes**

Further Reading

Raoul de Houdenc. "Li dis Raoul Hosdaing," ed. Charles H. Livingston. *Romanic Review* 13 (1922): 292–304.

———. *The* Songe d'enfer *of Raoul de Houdenc,* ed. Madelyn Timmel Mihm. Tübingen: Niemeyer, 1984.

———. *"Le roman des eles": The Anonymous "Ordene de Chevalerie,"* ed. Keith Busby. Amsterdam: Benjamins, 1983.

———. *Sämtliche Werke,* ed. Mathias Friedwagner. 2 vols. Halle: Niemeyer, 1897–1909, Vol. 1: *Meraugis de Portlesguez;* Vol. 2: *La vengeance Raguidel.*

Schmolke-Hasselmann, Beate. *Der arthurische Versroman von Chrestien bis Froissart.* Tübingen: Niemeyer, 1980, pp. 106–15, 117–29.

KEITH BUSBY

RAOUL GLABER (ca. 985–ca. 1046)

Born in Burgundy, perhaps out of wedlock, Raoul entered the monastery of Saint-Germain of Auxerre when he was about twelve. By nature restive and averse to discipline, he wandered from monastery to monastery, where, thanks to his literary talents, he was welcomed. From ca. 1015 to 1031, he was the traveling companion of William of Volpiano, abbot of Saint-Bénigne of Dijon and one of the foremost monastic reformers of the day. At William's command, he began a history of the prodigies and wonders surrounding the advent of the year 1000, which he kept with him and added to for the rest of his life. After William's death, Raoul spent time at Cluny (ca. 1031–35), then briefly at Béze, finally returning to Auxerre.

In addition to his Latin *Five Books of Histories,* Glaber wrote a hagiographical *vita* of William and some epigraphy that, due to the jealousy of the monks, was destroyed. He seems to have had difficult relations with a number of people, including his mentor, William, and some of his independence of mind shows up in his writing. His history, dedicated in a later recension to Odilo of Cluny, began with the year 900 and presented the history of the German emperors and French kings, which, as it reached Raoul's own time (Books 3–4), included events from all over the known world and, in his old age (Book 5), included a brief autobiography and anecdotes about anonymous people. Several accounts of the same global material also appear in the independently composed but contemporary history of Adémar de Chabannes.

Often criticized for inaccuracy, gossip, disorganization, and prodigy mongering by modern political historians, Raoul has proven a rich source for social history and mentalities; his theology of history, though crude, prefigures such 12th-century historians as Hugh of Saint-Victor, Otto of Freising, and Joachim of Fiore. Raoul is best known for his apocalyptic interpretation of the two millennial dates 1000 (Incarnation) and 1033 (Passion), which he linked to mass manifestations of religious fervor—heresy, church building, pilgrimage (especially to Jerusalem), and the Peace of God movement. He has accordingly suffered from polemical treatment at the hands of modern historians opposed to the romantic notion of the "terrors of the year 1000."

See also **Hugh of Saint-Victor; Joachim of Fiore; Otto of Freising**

Further Reading

Raoul Glaber. *Les cinq livres de ses histoires (900–1044),* ed. Maurice Prou. Paris: Picard, 1886.
——. *Rodulfus Glaber opera,* ed. John France, Neithard Bulst, and Paul Reynolds. Oxford: Clarendon, 1989.
——. *Rodolfo il Glabro: Cronche dell'anno mille (storie),* ed. Guglielmo Cavallo and Giovanni Orlandi. Milan, 1989.
France, J. "Rodulfus Glaber and the Cluniacs." *Journal of Ecclesiastical History* 39 (1988): 497–507.
Iogna-Prat, D., and R. Ortigues. "Raoul Glaber et l'historiographie clunisienne." *Studi medievali* 3rd ser. 26 (1985): 437–72.

RICHARD LANDES

"RASHI" (SOLOMON B. ISAAC)
(c. 1040- 1105)

Solomon b. Isaac, known by the acronym "*Rashi*" Rabbi Shelomoh [b.] Yiṣḥaq), was born ca. 1040 in Troyes (in the county of Champagne in France) and died in 1105- He was wrongly referred to as "Solomon *ha-Yarḥiy*" (i.e., from Lunel) by the Dominican polemicist Ramón

Martí and by the Christian Hebraists Sebastian Münster and Johannes Buxtorf, and (less incorrectly) "*ha-Rav ha-Ṣarfatiy*" and "Shelomoh *ha-Ṣarfatiy*" by Asher b. Saul and by Abraham b. Moses b. Maimon (son of Maimonides), Abraham b. David of Posquières referred to him simply as "*ha-Ṣarfatiy*." He was the first to compose a detailed and complete commentary, almost line by line, on the Talmud (except for parts not finished before he died). He is also famous for his commentary on the Torah and on several other books of the Bible, although in fact these commentaries have been overpraised. In addition, he wrote some responsa, or legal decisions, which are of importance also as a reflection of historical conditions. The first known printed Hebrew book was the commentary of "*Rashi*" on the Torah, but contrary to what virtually every scholar who has written on "*Rashi*" says, this was not the Reggio (Italy) edition (1475), but Rome, ca. 1470–72 (printed by Ovadyah b. Moses and the brothers Menasseh and Benjamin). This was followed by the Reggio edition, and almost immediately by an edition in Spain (1476), both without the biblical text; the first edition of the text and commentary was in 1482 (additions to the commentary, found in the Spanish Guadalajara and Ixar [Híjar] editions, were reproduced in *Kiryat sefer* 61 [1986–7]: 533–35). "*Rashi*"'s commentaries were unknown to Maimonides, and generally in Spain until relatively late; however, in Germany he was highly regarded. Meir b. Barukh of Rothenburg wrote of him "from his waters [commentaries] we drink every day" (responsa, Cremona ed., No. 137). An old saying has it that "all the commentaries of France may be thrown in the trash except those of *Parshandata* and *ben Porata*" *Parshandata,* of course, is "*Rashi*" (for the saying, see Azulai, *Shem ha-gedoliym,* s.v. "Rashi," and other sources). As for *ben Porata* (Joseph), this has been thought to refer to Joseph Ṭov 'Elem of France (contemporary of Rashi, a rabbi in Limoges; however, he is not known to have written any commentaries), but S. D. Luzzatto (*Beit ha-oṣar* [1881], p. 100) was surely correct in his opinion that it refers rather to Joseph Qara, a student of "*Rashi*" and possibly the editor of his commentary on the Torah, who wrote commentaries on most of the Bible.

"*Rashi*" studied at Mayence (Mainz) in Germany, where the yeshivah was headed by Jacob b. Yaqar and Isaac b. Judah, pupils of *Rabbēnu* Gershom (Gershom b. judah). Another teacher of "*Rashi*" was Isaac ha-Levy, about whom little is known. Gershom's students had collected his oral comments on the Talmud as they studied with him, and this written collection was known as "*Qunṭres Magenza*" (or Collection of Mayence), and was used by Natan of Rome in his famous talmudic dictionary *'Arukh*. Later in Italy it was attributed to Gershom himself, and it was printed in the famous Vilna Talmud edition (and see A. Epstein's introduction to *Ma'aseh ha-geonim*, ed. J. Freimann [Berlin, 1909], p. xiii; and see there pp. xxi–ii for citations from *"Rashi"* in that work). *"Rashi"* returned to Troyes where he served as rabbi and head of an important yeshivah, which essentially replaced those of Mayence and worms (where he may also have studied), which were destroyed in the attack on Jews during the First Crusade (see Crusades) in 1096.

"Rashi" had only daughters (two or three), one of whom married Meir b. Samuel. All of their children were scholars, the most famous being Samuel (*"Rashbam"*) and Jacob (*"Rabbēnu Tam"*). Another daughter, Miriam, married Judah b. Natan, whose commentary on the last pages of the talmudic tractate *Makkot* is in the printed editions (the legend that one of Rashi's daughters wrote the commentary on *Nedarim* may perhaps be a confusion with Judah's commentary on that tractate). The commentary on chapter 10 of *Sanhedrin* ascribed to Rashi is also apparently by Judah (see J. N. Epstein's article on Judah's commentaries in *Tarbiz* 4 [1932], and Saul Lieberman, *Sheqiʿin [Shkiʿin* as cataloged by libraries; 1939, rpt. 1970], pp. 92–96; and Ch. Merḥaviah, "Rashi's commentary to 'Ḥeleq'" [Heb.], *Tarbiz* 33 [1964]: 259–86).

While *"Rashi"* is best known to the non-Jewish world for his biblical commentary, in fact his commentary on the Talmud is far more important and has earned him his place as one of the foremost scholars in Jewish history. In addition to these works, he also wrote many responsa, a *siddur*—not actually a prayer book but rather a running compendium of laws and customs relating to blessings, prayers, holidays, etc. in the manner of similar works by the Geonim Saʿadyah and Amram—and other legal rulings and customs, recorded actually by his students in *Sēfer ha-orah* and *Pardēs*. (It has been argued that *Sēfer ha-orah* was probably written in Provence, but this is unlikely since several statements indicate a French origin; it contains statements also found in the *Siddur*, but sometimes corrupted; Abraham Epstein earlier observed that it is first cited by fourteenth-century Spanish authorities, which is not true, and may even have been written in Spain, but this is even more unlikely. On *Pardēs*, see A. Ehrenreich's introduction to his edition, and V. Aptowitzer, "Zu *"Raschi"*'s Pardes," *Zeitschrift für hebraischen Bibliografie* 20 [1917]: 14–16. Much of this work, and the *Sēfer ha-orah*, was taken from the *Maʿaseh geoniym*, written shortly after the time of *"Rashi."* Another important source was the collection *Maʿaseh ha-Makhiyriy*, by the sons of Makhiyr, brothet of Gershom b. Judah, which recorded the customs of the sages of their time and was probably edited by Menaḥem b. Makhiyr (see Leopold Zunz, *Literaturgeschichte der synagogalen Poesie* [Berlin, 1865], pp. 158, 161; Raphael Straus, *Regensburg and Augsburg* [1939], p. 51). On the other hand, it is not possible that the editor Menaḥem whose name appears in *Pardēs*—see f. 13b and No. 166, also possibly No. 150—was that Menaḥem b. Makhiyr, since he mentions *"Rashi"* specifically.

There is no doubt that *"Rashi"*'s talmudic commentary, in addition to making sometimes obscure statements clear (or clearer, at least), helped establish a more accurate text. The text had become corrupted and interpolated over the centuries, and *"Rashi"* utilized *Rabbēnu* Gershom's autograph corrected copy, and also other manuscripts. Because of the great amount of contact between Italy and France, *"Rashi"* also knew of Italian Jewish scholarship, and cites Italian commentaries on the Talmud (still unpublished) as *peirush*, or *qunṭres, Romiy*. Contrary to what has sometimes been claimed, he did not know of Natan of Rome's *'Arukh*, although his students later did. Nevertheless, he was in frequent contact with Natan and he addressed inquiries to him, according to Isaac b. Moses of Vienna (thirteenth century, author of *Or zaruaʾ*) and others. Although *"Rashi"* did not, of course, know Arabic and relied on the often erroneous views of Menaḥem b. Saruq and, less frequently, Dunash Ibn Labraṭ, especially in his biblical commentaries, his own grammatical explanations are sometimes valuable (see, e.g., his lengthy discussion of the possible meanings of the conjunction *kiy*, in *Teshuvot*, ed. Elfenbein, No. 251).

The authentic commentary of *"Rashi"* is only on the following tractates: *Berakhot, Shabbat, 'Eruvin, Pesaḥ. im* (chs. 1–9), *Yoma, Sukkah, Beiṣah, Rosh ha-Shannah, Megillah, Ḥagigah, Yevamot, Ketuvot, Soṭah, Giṭṭin, Qidduskin, B.Q., B.M., B.B.* (to fol. 29a), *Sanhedrin* (chs. 1–9), *Makkot* (to fol. 19a), *Shevuʿot, 'A.Z., Zevaḥ. im, Menaḥot, Ḥullin, Bekhorot, 'Arakin, Temurah,* and *Niddah*. The commentary on *Ta'anit* is doubtful, while that on *Zevaḥim* is in fact only partly by him (variant readings are also recorded in the *Diqduqei sofrim*). On *Menaḥot* one should see the commentary attributed to Ibn Adret, and also the new text of *"Rashi"*'s commentary in the Vilna edition. *"Rashi"* is said to have written a commentary also on *Nedarim*, but it is lost (see above on the legend that his daughter wrote that commentary). In the printed text of *B.B.* 29a is written "here Rashi died," but in other manuscripts it is "to here Rashi commented": not that he died but that he did not complete the commentary beyond that point. However, it does appear that he died while writing the commentary on *Makkot* (f. 19b). The printed commentary on *Mo'ed qaṭan* is not by *"Rashi"* but by Gershom b. Judah; however, the actual commentary of Rashi on that tractate has been published (ed. E. Kupfer, Jerusalem, 1961). A commentary on *Mashkin* attributed to *"Rashi"* was published in 1939 (rpt. 1969).

"Rashi"'s talmudic commentaries, unlike those on the Bible, had an almost immediate and lasting impact on

Spanish Jewish scholarship as well as that of France and Germany. While talmudic scholarship in Spain soon far outstripped that of the northern European countries, such outstanding scholars as nah.manides, Ibn Adret, Asher b. Yeḥiel and others frequently cited his interpretations, even if sometimes disagreeing.

Bible Commentaries

He clearly intended to write a commentary on all of the books of the Bible, but did not complete it (Berliner stated that the printed commentary ends with Job 40.27; he later published the completion of Job from manuscript, see Bibliography). The commentary on Chronicles (*Divrey ha-yomiyrn*) is not by him but by a German (?) scholar who lived for a time in Narbonne in the twelfth century (Gross, *Gallia judaica*, p. 416, No. 16). It was particularly the commentary on the Torah which earned his fame among ordinary Jews throughout the ages. It became indispensable, especially for the vast majority who did not have a sufficient knowledge of Hebrew to understand all of the text even of the Torah, much less the more complex biblical books. Eventually the study of the weekly *parashah* (portion read in the synagogue service) included the requirement of the study also of "*Rashi*"'s commentary. Unfortunately, his other commentaries were, and are, neglected, just as the study of the other biblical books was neglected. There are critical editions of several of the commentaries (see bibliography), but only that on the Torah has been translated into English (reliable translation).

"*Rashi*" repeatedly emphasized his intention to give the "plain" meaning *(peshuṭo)* of the text, and yet he did not always adhere to that. Already Ibn 'Ezra criticized him for this, noting that there was much allegory or *derash* in his *peshaṭ* (books have been written discussing these topics, although they have overlooked Ibn 'Ezra's criticism).

"*Rashi*"'s commentaries show evidence of good relations with Christians and a generally favorable attitude toward them. So also in his own legal rulings, which detail, for example, common ownership of ovens for baking among Jews and Christians (*Sēfer ha-orah* II, 41); Jews employed Christian laborers (ibid., p. 53); had their horses shoed by Christian blacksmiths and their clothes washed and repaired by Christians (p. 54). Jews borrowed food for their animals from Christian neighbors (p. 56). However, at times there are also polemical statements, although some of these, such as references to "heretics," do not necessarily refer to Christians (on polemics in his biblical commentaries see Shereshevsky, p. 120 ff., and in more detail, in Hebrew, Judah Rosenthal in *Sēfer Rashi*, pp. 45–59, rpt. in his *Meḥqarim vemeqorot* (1967) I, 101–16; however, Rosenthal was inclined to find anti-Christian polemics

where none was intended). There are no statements at all about Christians or Christianity in his commentary on the Torah. On Gen. 1.1, he did *not* say, as some have misinterpreted, that *Christians* accuse Jews of having stolen the Land of Israel from the Canaanites; rather "if the *Gentiles* should say." Similarly, he wrote that every Jew has land, since all jews have a "portion" of the Land of Israel, and although the "Gentiles" have conquered it they have no possessive right in it (*Sēfer ha-orah*, pt. II, p. 229, No. 155; Buber correctly noted there that this is because of the law that land can never be stolen; there is a misprint there: *aizeh* should read *ainah*). "Gentiles" in both these statements may mean Muslims, Christians, or any other group.

Customs and Other Things

"*Rashi*" prohibited looking in mirrors of metal or copper on the Sabbath, unless they were attached to a wall, but a glass mirror was permitted (*Pardēs*, p. 42). The reason probably is because one might be tempted to polish a metal mirror in order to see better, but not one made of glass, which is generally clean. He was asked about a Jew who rents an apartment in a building from a Gentile and on the Sabbath he needs to go outside to bring water from the well, and whether this is permitted since there is no *ēruv* (legal "enclosure" to permit carrying). Rashi replied that it is allowed, based on a legal fiction that assumes he "acquires" the use of the well and courtyard with his rent money, so that in effect it is his private property (ibid., p. 46). Side locks (*pē'ot*) were probably not worn in his time (later medieval manuscript illuminations are ambiguous, some with and some without), for in his commentary to Lev. 19.27 he refers to "one who makes his temples exactly like the back of his ears and forehead" (i.e., hairless). He was firmly opposed to the custom of giving gifts on Purim to Gentile slaves, or to Gentiles in general; for instance, many poor Jews because of embarrassment sent their children with Gentile nurses to the homes of wealthy Jews to receive gifts, and those Jews gave gifts also to the Gentiles. "*Rashi*" complained that the rabbinical requirement of giving on Purim was intended only for Jewish poor (*Siddur*, p. 168, No. 346, and cf. *Pardēs*, No. 205).

"*Rashi*" described the highly unusual practice of Christians in Germany in washing clothes: two rectangular pits were dug and rain water was collected. In the first pit, the water was mixed with excrement (probably urine) of dogs and allowed to ferment to serve as a detergent in which community laundry was soaked, and then rinsed in the second pit. Clothes were first perfumed to remove the odor and then pressed between boards (commentary on *B.B.* 17a; cf. also *Ketuvot* 77a). Some scholars have claimed to have found references to the "investiture controversy" (debate between kings and popes over the authority to appoint bishops) in his commentaries, but in fact there are no such references.

He was completely opposed to "secular" learning. In his commentary to Lev.18.4 he wrote: "Do not depart [from study of the Torah], and do not say 'I have learned the wisdom of Israel, now I shall go and learn the wisdom of the nations.'"

There are some interesting observations concerning the dispersion of the Jews; e.g., on Lev. 36.31, he refers to the "caravans of Jews who *used to* sanctify themselves and go" to the site of the destroyed Temple (since the Christians who at the time occupied Jerusalem did not allow the Jews to go there), or v. 33 ("I will scatter you among the nations"): "this is a harsh measure, since when people of a town are exiled to another place they see each other and are consoled, but the Israelites were scattered as with a winnowing fork, as a man who scatters barley with a sieve and not one [grain] adheres to another" (cf. also on v. 38: "when you are scattered among the nations you will be lost from one another"). On v. 35 he gives an interesting lengthy chronological analogy of the "seventy years" of the Babylonian exile corresponding to the "seventy years" of the sabbatical and jubilee years which were not observed in Israel (see the important notes in the English translation).

"Rashi" also was the source for many proverbial statements which became commonplace in later generations. One of the most important of these was "an Israelite even though he transgresses remains an Israelite," which was used by rabbinical authorities to allow repentant Jews who had been forcibly converted during the attacks of 1096 to return to the Jewish fold. Others are: "with Laban I dwelt and [but] the 613 commandments I kept" (where there is a play on words: *gartiy*, "I dwelt," and *tiryag*, 613), applied to one who remains faithful among bad companions; "prepared for prayer or for war," ready for any circumstance; "mercy of truth" (*ḥesed shel emet*), attending to the preparation of a dead person for burial. He also related various stories in his talmudic commentaries, derived or adapted from talmudic and geonic sources (see on this the important article of Lewis Landau, "The stories of "Rashi" printed in the Babylonian Talmud" (Heb.) in *Eshel Be'er Sheva'3* [1986]: 101–17).

"Rashi" and his grandson "Rabbēnu Tam" disagreed over the arrangement of the sections of biblical passages in *tefillin*. To this day some very strict Jews put on two pairs of *tefillin*.

Language

Since the nineteenth century, scholars have been interested in the French glosses (explanations of words or concepts in French, written of course in Hebrew

characters) in "Rashi"'s commentaries. There are at least ten thousand such words in his commentaries. Elaborate theories of a "Judeo-French" dialect were even developed on the basis of these see also Shereshevsky, p. 14, notes 20–22). Important French glosses appear in other works, most notably the *Siddur*, where the editor has provided a detailed explanation and transcription into Romance. Some of these are of importance not only linguistically, but for customs of the time (note, for example, the use of *salse*, or *sauce*, a mixture of wine and salt in which cooked meat was dipped; *Siddur*, p. 58, No. 118).

A topic that needs further scholarly investigation is the so-called Rashi script. The cumbersome nature of square Hebrew letters, with strokes of varying widths, makes writing extremely burdensome. At an early period a method of nearly "cursive" script was employed, first among Jews in Muslim lands and then in Spain generally (so-called Sefardic script), and in France and Germany the style which has come to be known as "Rashi script," for no apparent reason other than it was modified and used in the first printed edition of his commentary on the Torah.

See also **Asher b. Yeḥiel; Ibn Adret, Solomon; Ibn Ezra, Moses; Maimonides**

Further Reading

Works by "Rashi"

Pentateuch with Targum Onkelos, Haphtaroth and Rashi's Commentary, tr. M. Rosenbaum and A. M. Silberman (New York, s.a.), 2 vols.; rpt. New York [1965?], 5 vols.

Solomon b. Isaac. *Pardēs ha-gadol* (Jerusalem, s.a.; photo rpt. of 1870 ed.).

——. *Parshan-data*, ed. Isaac Maarsen (Amsterdam, Jerusalem, 1930–35; photo rpt. Jerusalem, 1972), critical ed. of commentaries: vol. 1: "minor" prophets, vol. 2: Isaiah, vol. 3: Psalms; with English introductions.

——. *Peirushey Rashi 'al ha-Torah*, ed. Charles Chavel (Jerusalem, 1982), based on Berliner's editions, with same manuscripts, and "corrections."

——. *Rashi 'al ha-Torah*, critical ed. Abraham Berliner (Berlin, 1866); second, revised edition (Frankfurt, 1905), based on many more manuscripts.

——. *Rashi's Commentary on Ezekiel 40–48*, edited on the basis of eleven manuscripts by Abraham J. Levy (Philadelphia, 1931).

——. *Sēfer ha-orah* (Lemberg, 1905; photo rpt., 1966), ed. S. Buber.

——. *Siddur Rashi* (Berlin, 1911), ed. S. Buber.

——. *Teshuvot Rashi* ed. I. Elfenbein (New York, 1943; photo rpt. Benei Berak, 1980).

——. [Teshuvot Rashi. German] *Rechtsentscheide Raschis aus Troyes: 1040–1105) Quellen über die sozialen und wirtschaftlichen Beziehungen zwischen Juden und Christen*, tr. Hans-Georg von Mutius (Frankfurt; New York, 1986–87), 2 vols.

(responsa of Rashi also in *Teshuvot hokhmey Ṣarfat ve-Lotir*, ed. Joel Mueller [Vienna, 1881], Nos. 11–13, 15,16,18 (?), 21–32, 33(?), 34(?), 40–42, 73–84).

——. completion of commentary on Job; ed. A. Berliner in *Meliṣ* 14: 397 ff., 389 ff., rpt. in Harkavy, Abraham. *Me'assef nidaḥ iym* (Jerusalem, 1970), pp. 53–56, 69–75; cf. also I. Maarsen in *M.G.W.J.* 83 (1939): 442–56.

——. *Secundum Salomonem: a thirteenth century Latin commentary on the Song of Solomon* [according to "*Rashi*"], ed. Sarah Kamin, Avrom Saltman (Benei Berak, 1989).

Secondary Literature

Berliner, Abraham. *Ketaviym nivḥariym* (Jerusalem, 1945–49), Vol. 2.

Blumenfeld, Samuel. *Master of Troyes. A study of Rashi the educator* (New York, 1946); actually only p. 75 ff. is on "Rashi," including excerpts from commentaries.

Hailperin, H. *Rashi and the Christian Scholars* (Pittsburgh, 1963).

Rashi Anniversary Volume (New York, 1941); collected studies.

Rashi, torato ve-iyshato (New York, 1948); collected studies.

Sed-Rajna, G., ed. *Rashi 1040–1990: Hommage a Ephraim E. Urbach* (Paris, 1993); I have not been able to see this in time for this article.

Sēfer Rashi (Jerusalem, 1956/57); collected studies.

Shereshevsky, Esra. *Rashi the Man and His World* (New York, 1982); see critical review by Roth in *Hebrew Studies* 24 (1983): 221–23 with additional bibliography.

NORMAN ROTH

REINMAR DER ALTE
(fl. late 12th c.–early 13th c.)

Reinmar der Alte (the old) or, as he is often called by scholars, Reinmar von Hagenau, is the most prolific minnesinger of the twelfth century. He flourished (in the last fifteen or so years of the twelfth and the first years of the thirteenth) at the Babenberg court in Vienna, and probably also traveled widely, as did most courtiers and court retainers. He left no documentary record; we know him only as he presents himself and as other poets refer to him. He lacks the range of Walther von der Vogelweide; the only didactic lyrics he wrote were a few reflections on love, there is no *Leich* transmitted for him, and the only political songs ascribed to him are a widow's lament and two crusading songs. Yet the view of him as a singer of only one style of minnesong (courtly love song)—the lament of the hapless suitor—though influenced by his own stylization of his persona, is largely an artifact of scholarship during the past two centuries. Especially toward the end of the nineteenth and the first half of the twentieth century, scholars created an ever narrower image of Reinmar by claiming that songs and strophes ascribed to him were spurious, until the number of "pseudo-Reinmar" strophes exceeded those accepted as genuine. If we accept that he sang (and, in large part, created) most of the songs and strophes ascribed to him, it becomes clear that his oeuvre was rich and varied in addition to being extensive.

Even the narrow Reinmar canon is more nuanced than scholars were initially willing to perceive. For one

thing, Reinmar utilizes the woman's voice more often and in more different ways than any minnesinger save Neidhart, whose peasant women and girls reflect the pastourelle (bucolic) rather than the *Wechsel* (exchange) that was Reinmar's inspiration. One thing becomes clear in the multifaceted roles the woman's voices depict: Reinmar's women cannot be equated with his persona's lady. The lady as the suitor describes her is recalcitrant, haughty, distant; the noble woman's voices show someone who, if she spurns her suitor, does so unwillingly, constrained by fear of social sanctions. Often, she demonstrates a desire for her lover far more impassioned (and physical) than that expressed by "Reinmar" in his stereotypical role. Indeed, she exposes his maunderings as misguided at best, ludicrous at worst. Of course, the woman's voice is Reinmar's projection just as much as the man's voice, but he surely intends the incongruity between the stances portrayed to be noted and relished. Just as Don Quixote is Cervantes's knight of the woeful countenance, Reinmar's suitor is doleful. Both are (tragi-) comic fictions. In many of the songs in the man's voice, the lady is marginalized, referred to sparingly and obliquely, and the primary subjects of the song are an examination of the suitor's feelings, the singer's singing, and the audience's reaction to songs or singer. The syntax is typically complex; abstractions and legalisms (casuistries) abound. Imagery is rare; it may be that where Reinmar tried to introduce imagery (in part, perhaps, by appropriating strophes from other singers), his audience rejected it. Several songs containing a strophe with some striking image omit this strophe in most versions and others are transmitted only once. For many minnesingers songs are transmitted in multiple versions; for no singer is this transmission tendency more common than for Reinmar. Not only was he prolific, he was apparently also intent on extending and varying his repertoire by changing the order and number of strophes and even, on occasion, the basic tenor of songs. Changes in wording, form, and most strikingly voice enable him to make new songs of old ones. Some of the variants we have are due to later singers (such as Niune) appropriating songs or scribes adding strophes from other versions or deleting ones they consider inappropriate or corrupt. And some of the textual variants are due to faulty copying, flawed memory, or scribal "improvements." Nevertheless, though most scholars dispute or disregard it, the texts make it abundantly clear that an authorial intention is behind most of the variance we find in Reinmar's (and other minnesingers') songs.

Many minnesingers thematize singing about singing; but Reinmar, with his unusually introspective and reflective persona, does so more than most. While focusing on the theme and engaging that segment of the listeners most concerned with singing, other singers, directly, he reacts to and may even borrow and adapt strophes from them. Such an interchange of allusions and even strophes gave rise to the notion that he feuded with Walther von der Vogelweide, with the latter objecting to Reinmar's ideology of love. Actually, their views on love are quite similar (and similarly diverse, depending on which genre they echo); nevertheless, both singers vie over which of the two is the superior artist. The *Wartburgkrieg*, a fictional account of a contest between singers at the Wartburg in Thuringia, probably reflects their competition (at considerable remove; Reinmar der Alte may have been conflated with Reinmar von Zweter). The coupling of the two singers in the Würzburg Song Codex may be another reflex of their strife. Gottfried von Straßburg pairs both "nightingales" as masters of minnesong. Walther, in his eulogies to Reinmar, praises his art but declares an antipathy toward his person; perhaps the latter is intended to lend veracity to the former, but it is also possible the two simply did not like each other very much. Reinmar arguably caused one of the most egregious instances of multiple ascription by copying a collection of Heinrich von Rugge's songs, or acquiring such a collection, to serve as models. A series of songs by Rugge, to which he may have added songs and strophes of his own, subsequently was copied into codex C twice, once under Rugge's name and once under Reinmar's. The affinities between the two singers are not restricted, however, to one block of songs, so the parallel transmission cannot be explained away as a mere scribal blunder, as scholars have tended to assume. Allusions to or strophes shared with Hartmann von Aue and Heinrich von Morungen probably also reflect Reinmar's willingness to appropriate; he in turn serves as a major model for such singers as Walther von Metze and Rubin.

See also **Hartmann von Aue;
Heinrich von Merungen; Neidhart**

Further Reading

Heinen, Hubert, ed. *Mutabilität im Minnesang: mehrfach überlieferte Lieder des 12. und frühen 13. Jahrhunderts.* Göppingen: Kümmerle, 1989.

Jackson, William E. *Reinmar's Women: A Study of the Woman's Song ("Frauenlied" and "Frauenstrophe") of Reinmar der Alte.* Amsterdam: John Benjamin, 1981.

Obermaier, Sabine. *Von Nachtigallen und Handwerkern: 'Dichtung tiber Dichtung' in Minnesang und Sangspruchdichtung.* Tübingen: Niemeyer, 1995.

Schweikle, Günther. *Minnesang in neuer Sicht.* Stuttgart: Metzler, 1994.

Stange, Manfred. *Reinmars Lyrik: Forschungskritik und Überlegungen zu einem neuen Verstädnis Reinmars des Alten.* Amsterdam: Rodopi, 1977.

Tervooren, Helmut. *Reinmar Studien: Ein Kommentar zu den "unechten" Liedern Reinmars des Alten.* Stuttgart: Hirzel, 1991.

Willms, Eva. *Liebesleid und Sangeslust: Untersuchungen zur deutschen Liebeslyrik des späten 12. und frühen 13. Jahrhunderts.* Munich: Artemis, 1992.

Ziegler, Vickie L. *The Leitword in* Minnesang: *Stylistic Analysis and Textual Criticism.* University Park: Penn State University Press, 1975.

HUBERT HEINEN

REINMAR VON ZWETTER
(ca. 1200–ca. 1250)

We know this prolific singer of *Sangspruchdichtung* (political and religious thought) only from his songs. They suggest he was born in the Rhineland, grew up in Austria, and was employed as a courtly singer by King Wenzel I of Bohemia in the 1230s. Other internal evidence indicates he sang at the court of the archbishop of Mainz in the 1240s. Reinmar's last datable piece stems from the years 1246 to 1248. He left some 230 single twelve-line, one-stanza songs, all sung to the same tune (called *Frauenehrenton* in manuscript "D") and a *Leich* (lay) without melody. There is also a handful of songs, probably spurious, in other stanzaic forms with which his name is associated. Only a few of his one-stanza songs can be thematically linked together. Most of Reinmar's work is contained in two sources, 219 stanzas in manuscript "C," the famous Manesse Song Manuscript (Heidelberg, no. Cod. Pal. Germ. 848), and 193 stanzas in manuscript "D" (Heidelberg, no. Cod. Pal. Germ. 350). Other stanzas are scattered over some twenty additional manuscripts. The illustration in "C" depicts him as a blind singer dictating his songs, though there is no evidence in the body of his work that he was sight-impaired.

The *Frauenehrenton*, Reinmar's only known melody, is a utilitarian d-based construction, a solid structure for the delivery of all his content-laden stanzas. It is possible that it is not an original composition, since one of Reinmar's confreres in courtly singing accuses him of being a tune thief (*doenediep*).

Reinmar's singing encompasses many of the popular subgenres of *Spruchdichtung*, e.g., political songs, religious songs, cautionary songs, songs of praise, songs about the nature of love, and songs extolling knightly virtue. In this he is a disciple of Walther von der Vogelweide, though his poetry lacks the nuance and lyricism of Walther. Many of his songs have an elegiac quality, lamenting the passing of the heyday of love, honor, and courtly values. In these Reinmar provides a canon for knightly behavior in the first half of the thirteenth century.

His rhetorical style is direct and convincing, underscoring his belief in the old-fashioned values of knighthood (especially *Minne*—courtly love—and honor) and reflecting a natural piety in which he pleads for righteousness, though never in a self-righteous way. His stanzas, especially the political ones, also afford glimpses of his life as a courtly singer. Like Walther before him, Reinmar had to generate political propaganda to suit the occasion. Illustrative are two songs composed in the 1230s, the first issuing a dire warning to those conspiring against Emperor Fredrick II (Roethe: No. 137), the second (composed after a change of patrons) urging willful resistance to the same monarch (Roethe: No. 149).

Pursuing the tradition of Walther's political and religious songs, Reinmar is the link to later singers of *Spruchdichtung* in the second half of the thirteenth century such as Bruder Werner, Meister Alexander, Meister Stolle, der Marner, and Frauenlob. That such a rich assortment of stanzas was collected in more than twenty manuscripts attests to his popularity. For three hundred years he was venerated by the Meistersinger, who counted him among the twelve old masters.

See also **Frauenlob; Frederick II; Walther von der Vogelweide**

Further Reading

Bonjour, Edgar. *Reimar von Zweter als politischer Dichter.* Bern: Haupt, 1922.
Gerhardt, Christoph. "Reinmars von Zweters Idealer Mann." *Beiträge zur Geschichte der deutschen Sprache und Literatur* (Tübingen) 109 (1987): 51–84, 222–251.
Roethe, Gustav. *Die Gedichte Reinmars von Zweter.* Leipzig: Hirzel, 1887.
Schubert, Martin J. "Die Form von Reinmars Leich." *Amsterdamer Beiträge zur älteren Germanistik* 41 (1995): 85–142.
Schupp, Volker. "Reinmar von Zweter, Dichter Kaisers Friedrichs II." *Wirkendes Wort* 19 (1969): 231–244.

PETER FRENZEL

REMIGIO DEI GIROLAMI (d. 1319)

The Dominican Remigio dei Girolami was a well-known teacher and preacher in Florence. He was a member of a family prominent in the wool guild and in municipal civic life. For many years, he was lector of theology in the great Dominican convent of Santa Maria Novella. In addition to his fame as a preacher, he also gained renown as a welcomer of visiting kings, cardinals, and other dignitaries; as an exhorter of civic officials to promote the common good; and as an orator at funerals and commemorative occasions for local and foreign notables. There were few types of public ceremony in Florence or in his order in which he was not at least occasionally a conspicuous participant. Although some of his closest relatives were exiled after the triumph of the Black Guelf faction in 1302, Remigio's own popularity with those in power seems to have continued. In 1313, answering a query from Sienese officials about his political soundness, the Florentine government called him "a leading father to our corporation (*universitati*)."

Remigio also wrote treatises on a rich variety of theological, philosophical, and political subjects, but these

seem to have aroused little interest until the second half of the twentieth century, when a number of them were edited. Early in the century, G. Salvadori published some extracts from Remigio's public sermons and advanced the thesis that he must have been Dante's teacher at the time when Dante tells us he was frequenting the "schools of the religious." The theory remains unproved, but it has been widely accepted and is not improbable, for during this period Remigio was the principal lector of one of the two leading schools of the religious in Florence.

Whether he taught Dante or not, Remigio's teaching was important in the Florence of his own day, and it was most emphasized by the chronicle or necrology of his own convent. The entry about Remigio says that at the time of his death he had been a Dominican for fifty-one years and ten months, of which more than forty years had been spent as lector of Santa Maria Novella. Remigio was licensed in arts in Paris, entered the Dominican Order in the "first flower of his youth," and made such rapid progress, according to the necrology, that he became lector at Florence while still a deacon and before being ordained as a priest. He must have become a Dominican in Paris c. 1267–1268, since, as Panella (1982) has shown, he heard Saint Thomas Aquinas during Aquinas's last period of teaching there, from 1269 to 1272. Remigio served in many important positions in his order, and he was already preacher-general by 1281. He returned to Paris c. 1298 at the express wish of his convent to continue his theological studies and qualify for the *magisterium*. He had returned to Florence in August 1301 but soon went to Rome in the hope of receiving the *magisterium* from Pope Boniface VIII, but this ambition was frustrated by Boniface's sudden death. Remigio finally received the *magisterium* from a fellow Dominican, Pope Benedict XI, probably in 1304 at Perugia; we know that he preached and disputed there, and apparently he did not return to Florence again until 1306 or 1307. This seems to have been his last long absence from the city and the lectorate of Santa Maria Novella, though the necrology says that he gave up teaching and preaching a few years before his death (probably by 1316, when there was a new lector of theology at the convent) and devoted himself to composing and compiling religious books. This activity seems to have consisted in large part in the collecting and editing of his own works.

Remigio's works are contained in four early fourteenth-century double-columned folio volumes and a later collection of Lenten sermons in the *Conventi soppressi* manuscript collection of the National Library of Florence, plus two copies of a commentary on the Song of Songs in the Laurentian Library, also in Florence. The four *Conventi soppressi* volumes are C.4.940, Remigio's treatises; D.1.937, sermons *de sanctis et festis*; G.3.465, questions; and G.4.936, sermons *de tempore*, and those for special occasions. The last includes a section of prologues that Remigio preached at the beginning of his courses. Most are on books of Peter Lombard's *Sentences* or the Bible; but two deal with Aristotle, and one of these is devoted specifically to Aristotle's *Ethics*. Together they comprise some 2,700 folio sides. The four folio volumes, except for the first seventy-four leaves of C.4.940, are all written in the same highly abbreviated hand, with additions, annotations, and corrections by a second hand, evidently that of Remigio himself. Although a few copies of particular sermons have been found in manuscripts of non-Florentine provenance, Remigio's fame was mainly local, and knowledge of his writings was confined almost entirely to his own convent. But his writings must have been important there, for they furnished a rich repository of materials for preaching and for instruction in an important, if somewhat provincial, Dominican school. The purpose of the compilation of these volumes is confirmed by an elaborate web of cross-references, both in the text and in the margins, that connect works in the same volume and in different volumes. Many of the sermons, for example, are merely outlines but often contain references to allegorical and anecdotal material in other sermons and in treatises. As for the treatises (contained in Biblioteca Nazionale, Florence, MS Conventi Soppressi C.4.940), they do not cite the sermons, but they often cite and thereby reinforce each other.

Originality is not the most striking characteristic of Remigio's works. On the other hand, his concern with contemporary events and problems and his intense Florentine patriotism are often apparent. Although Remigio copied quantities of material from Aquinas in his treatise *De peccato usure*, its editor describes Remigio's analysis of the sin of usury as somewhat more flexible than Aquinas's. In a long digression in another treatise, *Contra falsos ecclesie professores*, Remigio tried valiantly, if with only partial success, to find a middle ground between those who exalted and those who decried the claim of the papacy to universal temporal authority. Perhaps the most interesting aspect of Remigio's thought was his effort to fuse the Augustinian concept of peace with the Aristotelian concept of the common good and apply them to the problem of faction in his own city, identifying them with the good of the commune. Several of his treatises and a number of his sermons are devoted to this theme. He also—like his fellow Dominican Ptolemy of Lucca—tried to inspire his fellow citizens through examples of civic virtue furnished by the heroes of the Roman republic, whose willingness to sacrifice themselves for their *patria* he (again like Ptolemy) did not hesitate to identify with the Christian virtue of *caritas*. Not to be a citizen, he affirmed with Aristotle, was not to be a man; and for Remigio, citizenship required the realization that the good of the part was subordinated to and included in the good of the whole. Of course, the common good of Christendom took precedence over the common good of Florence, and its head should be obeyed whenever possible; but if a command of the pope contravened the peace and well-being of the commune, even that command should be disregarded.

See also **Aquinas, Thomas; Dante Alighieri; Ptolemy of Lucca**

Further Reading

Treatises by Remigio

Contra falsos ecclesie professores (fols. 154v–196v), ed. Filippo Tamburini. Rome, 1981.

De bono comuni (fols. 97r–106r), ed. M. C. De Matteis. In *La "teologia politica comunale" de Remigio de' Girolami*. Bologna, 1977 (text: 1–51).

De bono comuni (fols. 97r–106r), ed. Emilio Panella. In "Dal bene comune al bene del comune: I trattati politici di Remigio dei Girolami nella Firenze dei Bianchi-Neri." *Memorie Domenicane*, 16, 1985, 1–198. (Text, pp. 123–168.)

De bono pacis (fols. 106v–109r), ed. Charles T. Davis. In "Remigio de' Girolami and Dante: A Comparison of Their Conceptions of Peace." *Studi Danteschi*, 36, 1959, pp. 105–136. (Text, pp. 123–136. See also editions by M. C. De Matteis, in *La teologia . . .*, text, pp. 53–71; and Emilio Panella, in "Dal bene comune . . . ," text, pp. 169–183.)

De contrarietate peccati (fols. 124v–130v).

De iustitia (fols. 206r–207r), ed. Ovidio Capitani. In "L'incompiuto 'Tractatus de iustitia' di fra Remigio de' Girolami." *Bullettino dell'Istituto Storico Italiano per il Medio Evo*, 72, 1960, pp. 91–134. (Text, pp. 125–128.)

De misericordia (fols. 197r–206r), ed. A. Samaritani, in "La misericordia in Remigio de' Girolami e in Dante nel passaggio tra la teologia patristico-monastica e la scolastica." *Analecta Pomposiana*, 2, 1966, pp. 169–207. (Text, pp. 181–207.)

De mixtione elementorum inmixto (fols. 11v–17r).

De modis rerum (fols. 17v–70v). (Earlier version with Remigio's corrections in MS Conventi Soppressi E.7.938.)

De mutabilitate et inmutabilitate (fols. 131r–135v).

De peccato usure (fols. 109r–124v), ed. Ovidio Capitani. In "Il 'De peccato usure' di Remigio de' Girolami." *Studi Medievali*, 6(2), 1965, pp. 537–662. (Text, pp. 611–660.)

Determinatio de uno esse in Christo (fols. 7r–11v), ed. Martin Grabmann. In *Miscellania Tomista*. Estudis Franciscans, 24. Barcelona, October–December 1924, pp. 257–277.

Determinatio utrum sit licitum vendere mercationes ad terminum (fols. 130v–131r), ed. O. Capitani. In "La 'venditio ad terminum' nella valutazione morale di S. Tommaso d'Aquino e di Remigio de' Girolami." *Bullettino dell'Istituto Storico Italiano per il Medio Evo*, 70, 1958, pp. 299–363. (Text, pp. 343–345.)

De via paradisi (fols. 207r–352v).

Divisio scientie (fols. 1r–7r), ed. Emilio Panella. In "Un'introduzione alla filosofia in uno 'studium' dei Frati Predicatori del XIII secolo. 'Divisio scientie' di Remigio dei Girolami." *Memorie Domenicane*, n.s., 12, 1981, pp. 27–126. (Text, pp. 81–119.)

Questio de subiecto theologie (fols. 91r–95v), ed. Emilio Panella. In *Il "De subiecto theologie" (1297—1299) di Remigio dei Girolami*. Rome, 1982. (Text, pp. 4–71.)

Quodlibetum primum (fols. 71r–81v) and *Ouodlibetum secundum* (fols. 81v–90v), ed. Emilio Panella. In "I quodlibeti di Remigio." *Memorie Domenicane*, 14, 1983, pp. 1–149. (Text, pp. 66–146.)

Speculum (fols. 135v–l54v).

Questions by Remigio

Extractio ordinata per alphabetum de questionibus tractatis. Biblioteca Nazionale, Florence, MS Conventi Soppressi G 3.465. (See *Questio de duratione monitionum capitulorum Generalium et Provincialium*, ed. Emilio Panella. In "Dibattito sulla durata legale delle 'Admonitiones,'" pp. 85–101; text, pp. 97–101. See also table of contents at the end of the manuscript, ed. J. D. Caviglioli and R. Imbach. In "Brève notice sur *Extractio ordinata per alphabetum* de Remi," *Archivum Fratrum Praedicatorum*, 49, 1979, pp. 105–131; text, pp. 115–131.)

Remigio's Postille

Postille super Cantica Canticorum. Biblioteca Laurenziana, Florence, MSS Conventi Soppressi 362 (fols. 88r–123r; 516, fols. 221r–266v). (The latter MS contains also *Distinctiones* for the letter A, fols. 266v–268v, ed. Emilio Panella. In "Per lo studio di fra' Remigio dei Girolami." *Memorie Domenicane*, n.s., 10, 1979, pp. 271–283.)

Sermons by Remigio

Sermones de diversis materiis. Biblioteca Nazionale, Florence, MS Conventi Soppressi G.4.936, fols. 247r–404v. (See scraps from these sermons, as well as *Versus* and *Rithmi* placed by Remigio at the end of the codex, ed. G. Salvadori and V. Federici. "I Sermoni d'occasione, le sequenze e i ritmi di Remigio Girolami fiorentino." In *Scritti vari di filologia a Ernesto Monaci*, 455–508. Rome: Forzani, 1901. See also the sermons *De pace*, ed. Emilio Panella. In "Dal bene comune . . . ," pp. 187–198. This section of MS Conv. Soppr. G.4.936 also contains prologues to courses on books of the Bible, *Sentences*, and Aristotle's *Ethics*, fols. 276v–345r. See Emilio Panella, ed. *Prologus in fine sententiarum.* In *Il "De subiecto theologie,"* pp. 73–75. See also Emilio Panella, ed. *Prologus super librum Ethicorum.* In "' *Un'introduzione alla filosofia*," pp. 122–124.)

Sermones de quadragesima. Biblioteca Nazionale, Florence, MS Conventi Soppressi G.7.939.

Sermones de sanctis et de festis. Biblioteca Nazionale, Florence, MS Conventi Soppressi D.1.937.

Sermones de tempore. Biblioteca Nazionale, Florence, MS Conventi Soppressi G.4.936, fols. 1r–246v.

Studies

Davis, Charles T. "An Early Florentine Political Theorist: Fra Remigio de' Girolami." *Proceedings of the American Philosophical Society*, 104, 1960, pp. 662–676. (Reprinted in *Dante's Italy and Other Essays*. Philadelphia: University of Pennsylvania Press, 1984, pp. 198–223.)

Egenter, R. "Gemeinnutz vor Eigennutz: Die soziale Leitidee im *Tractatus de bono communi* des Fr. Remigius von Flotenz." *Scholastik*, 9, 1934, pp. 79–92.

Grabmann, Martin. "Die Wege von Thomas von Aquin zu Dante." *Deutsches Dante Jahrbuch*, 9, 1925, pp. 1–35.

Maccarrone, Michele. " 'Potestas directa' e 'potestas indirecta' nei teologi del XII e XIII secolo." *Miscellanea historiae pontificiae*, 18, 1954, pp. 27–47.

Minio-Paluello, Lorenzo. "Remigio Girolami's *De bono communi.*" *Italian Studies*, 2, 1956, pp. 56–71.

Orlandi, Srefano. *Necrologio di S. Maria Novella*, 2 vols. Florence: Olschki, 1955, Vol. 1, pp. 35–36, 276–307.

Panella, Emilio. "Per lo studio di fra Remigio dei Girolami († 1319)." *Memorie Domenicane*, n.s., 10, 1979.

——. "Il repertorio dello Schneyer e i sermonari di Remigio dei Girolami." *Memorie Domenicane*, n.s., 11, 1980, pp. 632–650.

——. "Remigiana: note biografiche e filologiche." *Memorie Domenicane*, n.s., 13, 1982, pp. 366–421.

——. "Nuova Cronologia Remigiana." *Archivum Fratrum Praedicatorum*, 60, 1990, pp. 145–311.

Pugh Rupp, T. "Ordo caritatis: The Political Thought of Remigio dei Girolami." Dissertation, Cornell University, 1988. (Ann Arbor Microfilms.)

"Remigio Dei Girolami." *Dictionnaire de spiritualité*, 13, 1987, pp. 343–347.

Schneyer, Johannes Baptist. *Repertorium der lateinischen Sermones des Mittelalters für die Zeit von 1150–1350*, Vol. 5. Münster: Aschendorff, 1974, pp. 65–134.

CHARLES T. DAVIS

RENÉ D'ANJOU (1409–1480)

Son of Louis II, duke of Anjou, and Yolande of Aragon, the "Good King René" is known for his accomplishments in several areas. This second son of the politically ambitious Yolande was, for strategic reasons, adopted by the duke of Bar. He was married in 1420 to Isabelle of Lorraine. He became duke of Bar in 1430 and duke of Lorraine in 1431, but his claim to the latter title cost him five years in prison. At the death of his elder brother Louis in 1434, René inherited the duchy of Anjou and the family claim to the kingdom of Naples. Although he lost the latter throne to Alfonso of Aragon in 1442, René's prestige and influence nonetheless continued to grow at the court of his brother-in-law, Charles VII, and in France generally. After the death of Isabelle in 1453, he married Jeanne de Laval. René, whose titles derived from the circumstances of aristocratic inheritance, was one of the last obstacles to the unification of France by Louis XI. Deprived of Bar and Anjou by Louis, René retreated in his later years to Provence.

Despite his political reversals, René d'Anjou was known as a good strategist in battle and an expert in warfare. He wrote a treatise on tournaments, the *Traictié de la forme et devis d'un tornoy* (1445–50), and organized several celebrated tournaments on Charles VII's behalf. He was a generous patron of the arts and himself a painter and writer. He composed two richly illuminated allegorical works in verse and prose: the *Mortifiement de vaine plaisance* (1455) and the *Livre du cuer d'amours espris* (1457).

See also **Charles VII**

Further Reading

René d'Anjou. *Le livre du cuer d'amours espris,* ed. Susan Wharton. Paris: Union Générale des Éditions, 1980.

——. *King René's Book of Love (Le cueur d'amours espris,* intro. and commentary F. Unterkircher, trans. Sophie Wilkins.

New York: Braziller, 1975. [Reproduces sixteen illuminations attributed to René.]

Des Garets, Marie Louyse. *Un artisan de la Renaissance française du XVe siècle, le roi René, 1409–1480.* Paris: Éditions de la Table Ronde, 1946.

Lyna, Frédéric. *Le mortifiement de vaine plaisance de René d'Anjou: étude du texte et des manuscrits à peintures.* Brussels: Weckesser, 1926.

JANICE C. ZINSER

RICHARD DE FOURNIVAL
(1201–before 1260)

Poet, canon, and chancellor at Amiens cathedral and canon of Rouen, Richard de Fournival produced a rich and varied corpus, composing songs in the trouvère style, the prose *Bestiaire d'amours* and its fragmentary verse redaction, and the Latin *Biblionomia,* the catalogue of his remarkable library. Three other prose treatises, the *Commens d'amours,* the *Consaus d'amours,* and the *Poissance d'amours,* are of questionable attribution.

It is for the *Bestiaire d'amours* that Richard is chiefly known. In this adaptation of the bestiary format, birds and animals represent aspects of the love experience. The text, immediately popular, has been transmitted in numerous manuscripts, richly illuminated. It inspired several literary responses, all anonymous. The earliest is the *Response au bestiaire,* in which the lady to whom the *Bestiaire d'amours* was addressed supposedly replies, turning each of the bestiary examples into an illustration of her need to take care to protect herself against male sexual advances. A verse adaptation, different from the fragmentary verse redaction apparently by Richard himself, also survives; although the author gives his name, he does so in an anagram of such complexity that it remains unsolved. In two 14th-century manuscripts, the *Bestiaire d'amours* is given a narrative continuation, in which the lover captures the lady and receives from her a red rose. In another 14th-century manuscript, the *Bestiaire* and its *Response* are embedded in a sequence of prose texts that form a dialogue between lover and lady; although none is a bestiary, all refer to the *Bestiaire,* which clearly inspired the sequence.

We know from the *Biblionomia* that Richard owned some unusual books, including the only known complete copy of the poems of Tibullus. At his death, his library passed to Gérard d'Abbeville and then to the Sorbonne.

Further Reading

Fournival, Richard de. *Le bestiaire d'amour rimé,* ed. Arvid Thordstein. Lund: Ohlssons, 1941.[The anonymous verse adaptation of the *Bestiaire d'amours.*]

——. *Li bestiaires d'amours di maistre Richart de Fornival e Li response du bestiaire*, ed. Cesare Segre. Milan: Riccardi, 1957.

——. *Biblionomia,* ed. Léopold Delisle. *Cabinet des Manuscrits* 2 (1874): 520–35.

——. *Richard de Fournival. l'oeuvre lyrique de Richard de Fournival*, ed. Yvan G. Lepage. Ottawa: University of Ottawa Press, 1984.

SYLVIA HUOT

RICHARD I (1157–1199; r. 1189–99)

Son of Henry II and Eleanor of Aquitaine. Richard the Lionheart was already duke of Aquitaine in right of his mother and heir-apparent to the English throne upon the death of his elder brother, Henry "the Young King," in 1183. His nickname, "the Lionheart" (Fr. "Coeur de Lion"), can be traced back to Gerald of Wales (d. ca. 1223), who compared the king to a lion, and can already be found circulating in a 13th-century romance of Richard's life.

Just as his late brother would have been a disastrous king, Richard could have been a great one had he spent his reign in England rather than on crusade and in the Angevin lands across the Channel. Although a man of knightly prowess, a writer of courtly poetry, patron of culture, cunning politician, and diplomat, Richard exhibited qualities regarded today as repulsive. Even by contemporary standards he could be less than humane, vengeful and beastly; however, he was the ideal martial king and a masterful leader of men. A recent study (by Gillingham) has refuted the view that Richard was homosexual. His reign is most conveniently examined by looking at his role in Angevin politics on the Continent, at his conduct of the Third Crusade, and at the governance of England during his nine-and-a-half-year absence.

Filial piety was not a characteristic of Richard's personality. Henry II sought to maintain the territorial integrity of his lands in France, fighting a doomed struggle against Louis VII (1137–80) and Philip II (1180–1223), a struggle that, under Richard's youngest brother, John, would result in the loss of all English holdings north of the Loire. Richard, desiring effective control of his inheritance, revolted against his father in 1173–74 and again in 1188–89, both times in alliance with the king of France. The warfare was not only patricidal, but fratricidal as well—as John and his brother Geoffrey of Brittany fought against both Henry II and Richard.

Although the conflict was not resolved before the death of Henry, after his return from crusade the fighting decisively favored the Lionheart. The promising course of the wars ended with Richard's death, while fighting a contumacious vassal in Aquitaine: an engagement waged over political issues, not over treasure trove (as some romantic versions of the story have it). Perhaps the greatest tragedy of Richard's early death was not the coming frustration of English ambitions on the Continent but the opportunity denied him to demonstrate his potential greatness as king of England.

Richard was best known in his own day as a crusader, as he is in literature, owing to the once great popularity of Walter Scott's *The Talisman.* For European affairs the most important development of the Crusade was the Treaty of Messina, sealed in 1191. Philip II (Philip Augustus) of France granted territorial boons to Richard, but by this agreement Richard recognized Philip's suzerainty over the Angevin lands on the Continent. Shortly after the two kings arrived in the Holy Land, Philip, a reluctant crusader, fell conveniently ill and returned home, motivated largely by his hope of taking advantage of Richard's absence so as to meddle in the English lordships in France. Richard conducted himself brilliantly as soldier and general and entered into Scott's legend as a revered and worthy opponent and respected friend of Saladin.

After helping to settle the political problems of the Latin kingdom of Jerusalem Richard left for England in October 1192. However, nature and politics interrupted the journey; a victim of shipwreck, he then fell into the hands of the duke of Austria, who delivered him to Henry, the Holy Roman Emperor. Henry, with the active support of Philip of France, kept the Lionheart in captivity until April 1194, when he was released after paying a king's ransom.

Richard had made careful plans for the governance of England during his absence; his kingdom, of course, had been accustomed to an absent king ever since the Norman conquest, owing to the royal policy of ruling personally over their French lands as over their English ones. Richard had a smoothly functioning machinery of government, guided such by able and experienced administrators as William Longchamp, Hubert Walter, and Geoffrey Fitz Peter. Every source of revenue was efficiently exploited, though at Richard's death the treasury was empty—unremitting warfare being the most expensive activity in which a government engages.

Despite the continuing plots of Prince John the country remained loyal to its king and his ministers. In Richard's absence there was less initiation of new institutions than refinement in administration; the great inquest of 1194 checked up on the enforcement of royal judicial, feudal, and financial rights. The role of what would become known as the gentry expanded in the administration of justice; while the end was not foreseen by Richard's ministers, the ultimate result of this enlargement of nonnobles' participation in government gave those of less than noble birth a sense that the government was theirs as well as the king's.

Until recent decades historians have tended to deprecate Richard, as they have Henry V. And yet the popular opinion of his own day is worth something. Wars were not viewed from a modern perspective, nor were their aims to be construed in terms of the goals of modern war. Richard was highly regarded by his contemporaries; perhaps they knew better than we what it meant to be a chivalric hero.

See also **Eleanor of Aquitaine; John; Philip II Augustus; Richard II**

Further Reading

Appleby, John. *England without Richard, 1189–1199.* Ithaca: Cornell University Press, 1965.

Bridge, Antony. *Richard the Lionheart.* London: Grafton, 1989

Gillingham, John. *Richard the Lionheart.* 2d ed. London: Weidenfeld & Nicolson, 1989 [the "select bibliography" and the chapter notes provide a full bibliography].

Gillingham, John. *Richard Coeur de Lion: Kingship, Chivalry and War in the Twelfth Century.* London: Hambledon, 1994.

Landon, Lionel. *The Itinerary of King Richard I.* Pipe Roll Society 51. London: Pipe Roll Society, 1935.

Nelson, Janet L., ed. *Richard Coeur de Lion in History and Myth.* London: King's College London, 1992.

Painter, Sidney. "The Third Crusade: Richard Lionhearted and Philip Augustus." In *A History of the Crusades,* gen. ed. Kenneth M. Setton. 2d ed. Vol. 2: *The Later Crusades, 1189–1311,* ed. Robert Lee Wolff and Harry W. Hazard. Madison: University of Wisconsin Press, 1969, pp. 45–86.

JAMES W. ALEXANDER

RICHARD II (1367–1399; r. 1377–99)

Born at Bordeaux on 6 January 1367, the second son of Edward the Black Prince, Prince of Wales (d. 1376). After Richard succeeded his grandfather Edward III in 1377, government in his minority was conducted jointly by his three uncles (especially the eldest, John of Gaunt), the earls, and leading officials of his grandfather and father.

Richard displayed courage and leadership during the Peasant Rebellion of 1381 and in the next few years was encouraged by bosom companions and some officials to assert his will over patronage and policies. His prestige was enhanced by his childless marriage in 1382 to Anne of Bohemia (d. 1394), daughter of the late Emperor Charles IV, and by his first major expedition to Scotland (1385). But parliaments were concerned about royal finances, and there was growing disquiet, expressed by some magnates, over failures to check the French in war and over royal indulgence of court intrigues against Gaunt. In 1386 Richard, freed from Gaunt's shadow by the latters expedition to Castile, alienated public opinion by the evasion of financial restraints and the failure to prevent the buildup of an invasion threat from a French armada in Flanders.

In the autumn parliament of 1386 the Commons, abetted by the king's uncle Thomas of Woodstock, duke of Gloucester, and Thomas Arundel, bishop of Ely, secured the dismissal from the chancellorship and the impeachment of a royal favorite, Michael de la Pole, earl of Suffolk. A commission was appointed with wide powers to monitor administration for a year. Determined to evade its control, Richard toured the realm in 1387, seeking support. He prompted the judges to define recent political initiatives as treasonable encroachments on royal prerogative; he aroused suspicions of a sellout to the French by seeking a conference with King Charles VI. In November Gloucester and the earls of Arundel and Warwick rose in arms and launched an Appeal of Treason against five of the king's supporters. Richard conceded that the appeal would be heard in parliament.

The "Appellants" were joined by Gaunt's son Henry Bolingbroke and by Thomas Mowbray, earl of Nottingham. Richard's close friend Robert de Vere, duke of Ireland, raised an army at his instigation, only to be defeated by the Appellants at Radcot Bridge (in Oxfordshire). In parliament in 1388 the appellees were found guilty; the two in custody, the Londoner Nicholas Brembre and Chief Justice Robert Tresilian, were executed. The Commons impeached other judges and four household officers; the latter (notably Sir Simon Burley, who had tutored the king) were executed.

The Appellants soon lost common purpose and support. The schemes of Gloucester and Arundel for an invasion of France failed, and in August, at Otterburn in Northumberland, the English suffered the worst defeat by the Scots since Bannockburn (1314). In May 1389 Richard declared himself of age and took control of government; in the early 1390s his moderate exercise of authority was underpinned by the returned Gaunt, principal negotiator in attempts to make a final peace with the French.

Richard boosted his authority by suspending the liberties of London (1391–92) and leading an expedition to Ireland (1394–95); London citizens and Irish chieftains alike submitted to his mercy. Continuous truces with the French since 1389 culminated in 1396 in a truce for 28 years; Richard married Charles VI's daughter Isabella.

But the moves in the 1390s toward an Anglo-French rapprochement provoked widespread disquiet; the earl of Arundel was a leading critic, and from 1395 Gloucester emerged as one. In July 1397 Richard arrested Gloucester, Arundel, and Warwick; young nobles made an Appeal of Treason against them for their acts in 1386–88, and they were found guilty in the September parliament. It was announced then that Gloucester had died in custody; Arundel was executed, Warwick sentenced to life imprisonment. The condemnations of 1388 were reversed, and Richard rewarded his noble partisans, such as his half-brother John Holland, earl of Huntingdon, with exalted peerage titles and the forfeited estates of the traitors.

In 1397 Richard had a more solid base of noble support than in 1387 and could call on the many knights and esquires he had retained in recent years, as well as his bodyguard of Cheshire archers. But the general alarm caused by his policies was augmented by the exclusion from the general pardon of January 1398, of those who had ridden against him. Supporters of the Appellants in 1387–88 now had to seek the royal mercy and pay fines. Richard's daring restructuring of magnate power was threatened when, in this session, Bolingbroke accused Thomas Mowbray, his fellow Appellant of 1387–88 and 1397, of treason. In September Richard intervened when the parties were about to settle their quarrel by judicial duel and sentenced Mowbray to exile for life and Bolingbroke for ten years. On the death of Bolingbroke's father, Gaunt, in February 1399 Richard made his banishment perpetual and confiscated the Lancastrian inheritance.

In June, soon after Richard had gone on expedition to Ireland to salvage his 1395 setdement, Bolingbroke sailed widi a small company from France and landed in Yorkshire. He was soon joined by Lancastrian retainers and northern lords, including the earls of Northumberland and Westmorland, disgruntled by Richard's interference in their sphere of influence. Bolingbroke advanced through the Midlands to seize Bristol; Richard's uncle and regent, Edmund duke of York, along with other supporters, was unable to rally effective opposition. From Bristol Bolingbroke moved up through the Welsh marches to capture Chester, the main bastion of Ricardian sentiment.

In Ireland Richard failed to appreciate the urgent need to rally support in person in north Wales and Cheshire; he landed too late in south Wales, moving north to Conway after his forces had disintegrated. The mediating earl of Northumberland betrayed Richard into Bolingbroke's hands; he was conveyed as a prisoner from Flint to the Tower of London. There he was apparently forced to abdicate, and in September a version of this agreement was submitted to the parliament summoned in his name. His requests for a public hearing were refused; the estates accepted the charges made against him in parliament as ground for deposition and acknowledged Bolingbroke's claim to the throne.

The deposed Richard was moved to other prisons, eventually to Pontefract in Yorkshire, where he died (or was killed) after the rising in January 1400 by some of his former favorites—Huntingdon, Huntingdon's nephew Thomas Holland, earl of Kent, John Montague, earl of Salisbury, and Thomas, Lord Despenser. It was easily suppressed. In February Richard's body was brought from his prison for public view in London and buried obscurely in the Dominican friary at Langley, Hertfordshire. In 1416 Henry V moved it to the splendid tomb Richard had prepared for himself in Westminster Abbey.

Richard was 6 feet tall, well built, handsome, and light-haired. Willful, devious, vindictive, sharp-tempered but not bloodthirsty, he was capable of showing affection and inspiring loyalty. He wanted his majesty to awe his subjects but could exert the common touch. He shared the conventional tastes of the higher nobility: hunting, the tournament (mainly as a spectator), courtly poetry. Not notably pious, in maturity he shared with Charles VI an enthusiasm for peace among Christians, an end to the Great Schism of the papacy, and a crusade against the Turks.

His real passion was to stabilize the personal authority of kingship, raising respect for its holy nature by trying to procure the canonization of Edward II and adopting the supposed heraldic arms of Edward the Confessor. His regal ideals and some of the ways in which he tried to project them can be seen in his portrait in Westminster Abbey, in the Wilton Diptych (National Gallery, London), and in his rebuilding of Westminster Hall. Denunciations of his rule are to be found in the poem *Richard the Redeless* and in John Gower's *Tripartite Chronicle*.

See also **Edward III; Gower, John; Henry IV**

Further Reading

Primary Sources

Creton, Jean. *A Metrical History of the Deposition of Richard II.* Ed. J. Webb. *Archaeologia* 20 (1824): 295–423.

Given-Wilson, Chris, ed. and trans. *Chronicles of the Revolution, 1397–1400: The Reign of Richard II.* Manchester: Manchester University Press, 1993.

Hector, L.C., and Barbara F. Harvey, eds. and trans. *The Westminster Chronicle, 1381–1394.* Oxford: Clarendon, 1982.

de Mézières, Philippe de. *Letter to Richard II.* Trans. G.W. Coopland. Liverpool: Liverpool University Press, 1975.

Secondary Sources

Aston, Margaret. *Thomas Arundel: A Study of Church Life in the Reign of Richard II.* Oxford: Clarendon, 1967.

Barron, Caroline M. "The Tyranny of Richard II." *BIHR* 41 (1968): 1–18.

Clarke, Maude V. *Fourteenth Century Studies.* Oxford: Clarendon, 1937.

Du Boulay, F.R.H., and Caroline M. Barron, eds. *The Reign of Richard II: Essays in Honour of May McKisack.* London: University of London, Athlone, 1971.

Gillespie, James L. "Richard II's Archers of the Crown." *Journal of British Studies* 18 (1979): 14–29.

Given-Wilson, Chris. *The Royal Household and the King's Affinity: Service, Politics and Finance in England, 1360–1413.* New Haven: Yale University Press, 1986.

Goodman, Anthony. *The Loyal Conspiracy: The Lords Appellant under Richard II.* London: Routledge & Kegan Paul, 1971.

Harvey, John H. "The Wilton Diptych—A Reexamination," *Archaeologia* 98 (1961): 1–28.

Mathew, Gervase. *The Court of Richard II.* London: Murray, 1968.

Palmer, J.J.N. *England, France and Christendom, 1377–99.* London: Routledge & Kegan Paul, 1972.

Saul, Nigel. *Richard II.* New Haven and London: Yale University Press, 1997.

Scattergood, V. J., and J.W. Sherborne, eds. *English Court Culture in the Later Middle Ages.* London: Duckworth, 1983.

Tuck, Anthony. *Richard II and the English Nobility.* London: Arnold, 1973.

ANTHONY E. GOODMAN

RICHARD III (1452–1485; R. 1483–85)

No medieval English king has generated more controversy and emotion, not least as a result of Shakespeare's portrayal of him as the personification of evil. Shakespeare, moreover, clearly reflected images already well formed in early Tudor times. Polydore Vergil, for instance, considered Richard a man who "thought of nothing but tyranny and cruelty"; Sir Thomas More derided him as an ambitious and ruthless monstrosity "who spared no man's death whose life withstood his purpose." Even the king's contemporaries were frequently critical. Dominic Mancini, writing within a few months of his seizure of the throne in June 1483, remarked forcefully on his "ambition and lust for power," and the well-informed Crowland chronicler was scathing on the tyrannical northern-dominated regime that, he believed, Richard established in the south.

Yet the last Yorkist king has always had his admirers as well as critics. Thomas Langton, bishop of St. David's, declared in August 1483 that "he contents the people wherever he goes better than ever did any prince," and the York Civic Records reported "great heaviness" in the city when news arrived of his fete ("piteously slain and murdered") on Bosworth Field in 1485. Modern historians, too, have brought in notably contrasting verdicts, ranging from Charles Ross's conclusion that no one familiar with "the careers of King Louis XI of France, in Richard's own time, or Henry VIII of England… would wish to cast any special slur on Richard, still less to select him as the exemplar of a tyrant" to Desmond Seward's hostile biography of this "peculiarly grim young English precursor of Machiavelli's Prince."

The youngest son of Richard of York, Richard duke of Gloucester proved notably loyal to his brother Edward IV during the crisis of 1469–71 and in the 1470s showed himself as reliable and trustworthy as any of the king's servants (and was rewarded accordingly). His rule of the north during these years was singularly successful; he built a powerful affinity there. Mancini admitted mat he "acquired the favour of the people." No one will ever know for certain whether he set his sights on the throne as soon as he heard of Edward IV's sudden death on 9 April 1483, or if, at first, he merely intended to obtain control of his nephew Edward V so as to prevent the Wydevilles—the family of young Edward's mother—from securing power. What is clear is that the series of preemptive strikes by which he outmaneuvered the queen's family, seized Edward V, eliminated William, Lord Hastings, and rendered the Yorkist establishment impotent, enabled him to become king in his own right before the end of June 1483. The probable murder of his nephews in the Tower of London was the inevitable culmination of this ruthless pursuit of power.

Richard III may have been convinced that he was indeed serving the interest of the nation; such, through the ages, has been the politician's justification for arbitrary action. The critical turning point in his fortunes probably was the rebellion of the duke of Buckingham (hitherto his closest and most spectacularly rewarded supporter) in October 1483. Edward IV's men, who for the most part had accepted Richard's protectorate and even acquiesced in his usurpation, now deserted him in droves in the south and west. Even more ominously the exiled Henry Tudor, earl of Richmond, emerged at the same time as a potentially serious rival. The king responded vigorously to these threats; the rebellion was put down. In its aftermath, however, given the extent of southern defection and the numbers who now fled the country, he was forced more and more into dependence on his own affinity. This meant, in particular, men from the north. Their advancement in the royal household and appointments to office, not only in southern and western counties but in the Midlands, is amply documented.

Since he reigned for so short a time, it is difficult either to judge Richard's potential and qualities as a ruler or to draw meaningful conclusions about his government. The 15th-century antiquary John Rous, later one of his harshest critics, recorded that he ruled his subjects "full commendably, punishing offenders of his laws, especially extortioners and oppressors of his commons," and won the "love of all his subjects rich and poor." His only parliament—perhaps with his personal encouragement—passed measures dearly benefiting the people; and his establishment of the Council of the North in July 1484 was both popular and enduring.

Though he did make considerable efforts to widen the basis of his support, with the threat of Henry Tudor looming ever larger, his reliance on his own affinity, largely from the north, remained paramount. When he at last faced his rival on the battlefield of Bosworth on 22 August 1485, he was backed largely by the same men who had brought him to power; many, though by no means all, probably fought for him with vigor. However, his own death (in the midst of the action and, according to the Crowland continuator, striving to the end "like a spirited and most courageous prince") made the accession of Henry VII inevitable.

Further Reading

Primary Sources

Armstrong, C.A.J., ed. and trans. *Dominic Macnini: The Usurpation of Richard III*. 2d ed. Oxford: Clarendon, 1969

Pronay, Nicholas, and John Cox, eds. *The Crowland Chronicle Continuations, 1459–1486*. London: Sutton, for the Richard III and Yorkist History Trust, 1986.

Secondary Sources

Dockray, Keith. *Richard III: A Reader in History*. Gloucester: Sutton, 1988 [commentary plus a selection of documents]

Hicks, Michael. *Richard III: The Man behind the Myth*. London: Collins & Brown, 1991

Horrox, Rosemary. *Richard III: A Study of Service*. Cambridge: Cambridge University Press, 1989 [scholarly treatment of politics and government]

Markham, Clements R. *Richard III: His Life and Character, Reviewed in the Light of Recent Research*. London: Smith, Elder, 1906 [very sympathetic]

Pollard, A.J. *Richard III and the Princes in the Tower*. Stroud: Sutton, 1991

Ross, Charles. *Richard III*. London: Eyre Methuen, 1981 [major modern scholarly treatment]

Seward, Desmond. *Richard III: England's Black Legend*. London: Country Life, 1983 [the case against].

KEITH R. DOCKRAY

RICHARD OF SAINT-VICTOR
(d. 1173)

A major writer on mysticism in the second half of the 12th century, Richard joined the regular canons of the abbey of Saint-Victor at Paris sometime near the middle of the century (certainly by the early 1150s but perhaps before the death of Hugh of Saint-Victor in 1141). He may have been born in Scotland. He served as subprior and was elected prior in 1161. His writings on the contemplative life were widely known and influenced Bonaventure's treatise *Itinerarium mentis in Deum*.

Richard followed the tradition of Victorine spirituality established by Hugh, but he concentrated more on the stages of development in the mystical life and on what today would be called the psychological aspects of that development. Two of his major mystical writings are symbolic interpretations of biblical persons, objects, and narratives. *De duodecim patriarchiis* (also called *Benjamin minor*) interprets the births and lives of the twelve sons and one daughter of Jacob, recorded in Genesis, as representing the stages of ascetic practice, mental discipline, and spiritual guidance that lead to contemplative ecstasy. *De arca mystica* (also called *Benjamin major*) presents the Ark of the Covenant and the two cherubim that stood on either side of it, described in Exodus, as symbolic of the six kinds or levels of contemplation. Books 4 and 5 of *De arca* give a subtle and influential analysis of types of visionary and ecstatic experience. Richard's *De IV gradibus violentae caritatis* analyzes the stages of the love of God and the transformation of the self by love in the mystical quest. Richard also wrote a commentary on the Book of Revelation, a treatise on the Trinity, mystical comments on various Psalms, a handbook for the Liberal Arts and the study of history (*Liber exceptionum*; digested primarily from works by Hugh of Saint-Victor), a collection of allegorical sermons, and treatises on biblical and mystical topics.

See also **Bonaventure, Saint; Hugh of Saint-Victor**

Further Reading

Richard of Saint-Victor. *Opera omnia. PL* 196.
——. *De Trinitate,* ed. Jean Ribaillier. Paris: Vrin, 1958.
——. *Liber exceptionum,* ed. Jean Châtillon. Paris: Vrin, 1958.
——. *Selected Writings on Contemplation,* trans. Claire Kirchberger. London: Faber, 1957.
——. *The Twelve Patriarchs, The Mystical Ark, and Book Three on the Trinity,* trans. Grover A. Zinn. New York: Paulist, 1979.
——. *Les quatre degrés de la violente charité,* ed. Gervais Dumeige. Paris: Vrin, 1955.
Dumeige, Gervais. *Richard de Saint-Victor et l'idée chrétienne de l'amour.* Paris: Presses Universitaires de France, 1952.
Zinn, Grover A. "Personification Allegory and Visions of Light in Richard of St. Victor's Teaching on Contemplation." *University of Toronto Quarterly* 46 (1977): 190–214.

GROVER A. ZINN

RIEMENSCHNEIDER, TILLMANN
(ca. 1460–1531)

Tillmann Riemenschneider is, perhaps, the best known of all German sculptors active during the years around 1500. His father, also Tillmann, was the mint master in Osterode in Lower Saxony, but by 1483 the younger Riemenschneider was a journeyman carver in southern Germany. Documents place him in the guild of St. Luke in Würzburg, where he was a master by 1485. His workshop was large and successful, with twelve apprentices registered between 1501 and 1517.

Riemenschneider's two sons were also sculptors. From 1505 Riemenschneider served on the Würzburg Council, and he was burgomaster (mayor) in 1520–1521. In 1525 he was fined for refusing to support the bishop against a peasant revolt.

Riemenschneider's sculpture reveals familiarity with German and Netherlandish styles from a broad area. None of his travel is documented, however, and at least some of these regional styles could have been assimilated through the study of exported sculptures. In addition to his carefully worked surfaces, Riemenschneider is known for his excellence in wood, especially linden wood, as well as stone, primarily alabaster and sandstone. His training as a stone carver is usually attributed to his North German origins.

Tilmann Riemenschneider. The alter of the Holy Blood, St. Jacob's Church, Rothenburg ob der Tauber, Germay. © Erich Lessing/Art Resource, New York.

Riemenschneider was an innovative wood carver, experimenting with unpainted surfaces in such early works as the Münnerstadt altarpiece of 1490–1492, the artist's first dated work. This winged altarpiece, dedicated to Mary Magdalene, is currently divided between the Münnerstadt parish church and the museums in Munich (Bayersiches Nationalmuseum) and Berlin (Staatliche Museen Preussicher Kulturbesitz). Recent conservation has removed later gilding and polychromy (painting) to reveal Riemenschneider's extraordinarily careful attention to surface detail and nuance, akin to sculptures on a smaller scale, such as ivory carving. The success of Riemenschneider's unpolychromed sculpture is seen in such works as the great altarpiece of the Holy Blood (ca. 1499–1505) still in situ in the Jakobskirche in Rothenburg, and the lindenwood sculpture of Saints Christopher, Eustace, and Erasmus (1494), a fragment of a relief originally representing fourteen helper saints, now in the Metropolitan Museum of Art in New York City (The Cloisters). All these works reveal Riemenschneider's ability to carve refined drapery and flesh as well to reveal the underlying bone structure. Shortly after the completion of the Rothenburg altarpiece, Riemenschneider created the Creglingen altarpiece (Herrgottskirche, ca. 1505–1510) representing the Assumption of the Virgin in a more elaborate and complex style than the earlier works.

Riemenschneider's works in stone include the sandstone figures carved for the Marienkapelle in Würzburg, including the figures of Adam and Eve (1492–1493), and the nine apostle figures of 1500–1506 (all these now in the Mainfränkisches Museum, Würzburg). Among his most extraordinary achievements, however, are the few surviving works in alabaster such as the Angel and the Virgin Annunciate in Amsterdam of about 1480–1485 (Rijksmuseum), and the St. Jerome with the Lion in Cleveland (Museum of Art), which probably dates before circa 1495. Like some of the linden wood sculptures, these works are sparingly decorated with polychrome and gilt highlights, but they rely on the fineness of the carved surface for their impact.

In addition to altarpieces and architectural sculptures in wood and stone produced for churches in and around Franconia, Riemenschneider's career can be traced through several tomb monuments that attest to his prestige. As early as about 1488 Riemenschneider carved the monument of Eberhard von Grumbach (d. 1487) now in the parish church at Rimpar, depicting the knight in full Gothic armor in relief. The same format is repeated in the tomb monument of Konrad von Schaumberg (d. 1499) in the Marienkapelle in Würzburg. This work, however, of about 1502 is more mature in style, more portrait than effigy. Much grander in scale is the sandstone and marble monument of Archbishop Rudolf von Scherenberg (d. 1495) in the cathedral of Würzburg. Most impressive is the limestone and sandstone tomb of Emperor Heinrich II and Empress Kunigunde (1499–1513) in the cathedral of Bamberg. Below the relief of the imperial couple are a series of six relief panels illustrating scenes from their lives. Finally, around 1520 Riemenschneider carved the sandstone and marble monument of Archbishop Lorenz von Bibra in Würzburg Cathedral.

Further Reading

Bier, Justus. *Tilmann Riemenschneider.* 4 vols. Würzburg: Verlagsdruckerei, 1925–1978.

——. *Tilman Riemenschneider: Frühe Werke.* Regensburg: Pustet, 1981.

——. *Tilmann Riemenschneider: His Life and Work.* Lexington: University Press of Kentucky, 1982.

PETER BARNET

ROBERT DE BORON (fl. 1180s–1190s)

The few facts known about the most important early Grail poet after Chrétien de Troyes are inferred from the epilogue of Robert's *Joseph d'Arimathie,* also called the *Roman de l'estoire dou Graal,* where he names himself and the nobleman in whose company he was writing, Gautier de Montbéliard. Montbéliard is in northern Franche-Comté; Boron is a small village about 12 miles to the northeast. Robert's verse bears traces of his eastern dialect. Gautier left on crusade in 1201, to remain in Palestine until his death in 1212; Robert must have finished the *Joseph* at or before the turn of the century. Robert's incorporation of material from Chrétien's *Conte du Graal* indicates that he wrote after the early 1180s. Other evidence suggests that the *Joseph* might be dated after 1191: Joseph foretells that the Grail will be taken to the "vales of Avaron [Avalon]"— that is, Glastonbury in Somerset; association of the Grail and of Arthurian matter with the abbey was not widespread before 1190–91, when the discovery there of a grave marked as Arthur's was announced.

Joseph d'Arimathie is a verse romance (3,500 octosyllables) that recounts the history of the Grail from the Last Supper and the Descent from the Cross, when Joseph used it to collect Christ's blood, through the imprisonment of Joseph, whom Christ visits and comforts with the holy vessel, until the moment when Joseph's brother-in-law, Bron (or Hebron), the Rich Fisher, is poised to take the Grail from a place of exile outside Palestine to Great Britain. As the *Joseph* draws to a close, the narrator announces that he will relate stories of adventures that Joseph has foretold, including that of the Rich Fisher, if he has time and strength and if he can find them written down in Latin; meanwhile, he will continue with the matter he has at hand.

Robert thus seems to project a complex work consisting of the *Joseph/Estoire,* the narrative to which he will pass immediately, and the fulfillment of Joseph's prophecies. The only manuscript to transmit Robert's verse *Joseph* (B.N. fr. 20047) in fact continues with the fragment of a *Merlin* romance (504 octosyllables), apparently the beginning of the second part; no more of Robert's original work survives.

However, a prose adaptation of the *Joseph,* by an anonymous author referred to as the Pseudo-Robert de Boron, was executed within a few years, and this is linked to a *Merlin* in prose, conjoining the history of the Grail and the history of Britain, that is found complete in a large number of manuscripts (forty-six) and fragments. Two manuscripts also contain a third prose romance, which portrays the Rich Fisher: the Didot *Perceval* (so called because one of the manuscripts was in the Firmin Didot collection). Unlike the first two romances, the Didot *Perceval* is never ascribed to Robert de Boron, nor is there any proof that a verse original of this text existed, yet it is clear that the Didot *Perceval* logically concludes the trilogy. It resembles one of the works projected at the end of the *Joseph/Estoire* and recounts the fulfillment of God's prophecy in the *Joseph* that the Rich Fisher will not die until he is visited by his son's son; it is also closely linked to the prose *Merlin*: finally succeeding at the Grail castle with Merlin's help, Perceval replaces his uncle as Rich Fisher; the hero's triumph coincides with the downfall of the Arthurian kingdom, the founding of which the *Merlin* had recounted.

In the *Joseph/Estoire* and what must have been the original verse *Merlin,* Robert de Boron in effect rewrites the *Conte du Graal* of Chrétien de Troyes. He expands the religious content of the original to provide the Grail's "sacred history," identifying it for the first time with the cup of the Last Supper. In addition, he extends Chrétien's references to pre-Arthurian Britain, which echo Wace's *Brut,* to provide the Grail's "secular history."

Robert's most important contribution is the generative power that infuses his verse. Not only are the prose adaptations of the *Joseph/Estoire* and *Merlin* among the earliest examples of literary prose in French, they also stand at the head of a long tradition that promoted the "translation" of imaginative and historical works written in "unreliable" verse into the "more stable" and "more authoritative" medium of prose. The better-known, more highly respected, Pseudo-Robert de Boron who was thus created, the one to whose authorship the more widely transmitted prose works are attributed, became in the early 13th century an even stronger literary force. He inspired the "completion" of Chrétien de Troyes's unfinished *Conte du Graal* in the anonymous Didot *Perceval,* and he is ultimately responsible for the germination of the Vulgate Cycle.

See also **Chrétien de Troyes**

Further Reading

Robert de Boron. *Merlin, roman du XIIIe siècle,* ed. Alexandre Micha. Geneva: Droz, 1979.
——. *Le roman de l'estoire dou Graal,* ed. William A. Nitze. Paris: Champion, 1927.
——. *Le roman du Graal,* ed. Bernard Cerquiglini. Paris: Union Générale d'Éditions, 1981.
Roach, William, ed. *The Didot* Perceval *According to the Manuscripts of Paris and Modena.* Philadelphia: University of Pennsylvania Press, 1941.
Cerquiglini, Bernard. *La parole médiévale.* Paris: Minuit, 1981.
O'Gorman, Richard F. "The Prose Version of Robert de Boron's *Joseph d'Arimathie.*" *Romance Philology* 23 (1969–70): 449–61.
——. "La tradition manuscrite du *Joseph d'Arimathie* en prose de Robert de Boron." *Revue d'histoire des textes* 1 (1971): 145–81.
Pickens, Rupert T. "Histoire et commentaire chez Chrétien de Troyes et Robert de Boron: Robert de Boron et le livre de Philippe de Flandre." In *The Legacy of Chrétien de Troyes,* ed. Norris J. Lacy, Douglas Kelly, and Keith Busby. 2 vols. Amsterdam: Rodopi, 1988, Vol. 2, pp. 17–39.
——. "'Mais de ço ne parole pas Crestiens de Troies ¼': A Re-examination of the Didot *Perceval.*" *Romania* 105 (1984): 492–510.

RUPERT T. PICKENS

ROBERT GUISCARD (c. 1015–1085)

When Robert Guiscard (Robert de Hauteville) rode into southern Italy in 1047, Norman mercenaries had been playing Lombards against Byzantines there for at least thirty years. Robert's half brothers, older sons of Tancred of Hauteville, had already claimed lands around Aversa, where the eldest, William, had earned the name "Iron-Arm" and had become the first Norman Italian count. William did not welcome Robert's arrival. Eventually another brother, Drogo, gave Robert a miserable outpost in Calabria, which he could control only by ousting the Byzantines. Yet this offered him a base from which to launch ambitious conquests, achieved with prodigious energy. Robert used terror and bloodshed, but his signature strategy was the ruse, as when he allegedly feigned death and penetrated a monastic stronghold inside a coffin, lying on a bed of swords. So wily was this trickster that the name Guiscard ("the clever") was used in the eleventh-century histories featuring his exploits.

Robert also proved his mettle on the battlefield. In 1053, a formidable coalition of Germans from the Holy Roman Empire and their Italian allies, led by Pope Leo IX, engaged the Normans at Civitate, hoping to dislodge them from Italy. Robert distinguished himself in this Norman victory, and soon he was challenging his brother Humphrey for hegemony among the Normans of Italy. Before Humphrey died in 1057, he commended his son Abelard to Robert's care, but Robert promptly claimed his nephew's lands. The boy would grow up to foment insurrections against his uncle but eventually sought asylum in Byzantium after yet another unsuccessful resistance in 1080. Such rebellions punctuated Robert's reign, even as he expanded his domination, seizing Capua from the Lombards and finally—in 1071, after a three-year siege—taking Bari, the last Byzantine foothold in Italy.

Along Robert's path to power, two events of 1059 enhanced his prestige and legitimized his authority. First, having repudiated his wife (the mother of his son, Bohemond), Robert compelled Prince Gisulf II of Salerno to surrender his sister Sichelgaita in marriage. Now linked to a venerable Lombard princely family, Robert also allied himself with the papacy, which sought the support of the Normans in the investiture conflict against the Holy Roman emperor and the imperial antipope. Thus at the synod of Melfi, Robert—who had been thrice excommunicated—acquired a papal blessing and the title of duke of Apulia and Calabria and Sicily.

Before this, Robert had not even visited Muslim Sicily. Yet he now engineered a reconquest increasingly dominated by his younger brother, Roger. Messina fell in 1061, followed by Palermo in 1072. But rebellions in Italy forced Robert to return there, effectively leaving Sicily to Roger. Robert, meanwhile, trained his eye on Byzantium, made enticingly vulnerable by dynastic struggles and the advance of the Seljuk Turks. Emperor Michael VII, desperate for aid from the Normans, had even betrothed his son to Robert's daughter. After Michael was dethroned in a coup in 1078, Robert invoked kinship as a pretext for invading Byzantium. Yet once again Italy drew him back from the campaign, this time to rescue Pope Gregory VII from the Holy Roman emperor Henry IV, who had seized Rome and deposed Gregory. In a mission notorious for its violence and for the alleged burning of Rome, Robert retrieved the pope and took him to Salerno, where he died in May 1085. Robert resumed his Byzantine offensive, taking Corfu while his younger son Roger accompanied Norman forces to the mainland. But Robert died suddenly, on 17 July 1085, when an epidemic of typhoid fever swept through his army. Roger's army promptly deserted, while Sichelgaita took Robert's body to Venosa for burial next to his older brothers in the church of the Holy Trinity. In the twelfth century, his grave attracted a suitable epitaph, which began: "Here lies the terror of the world, Guiscard."

See also **Bohemond of Taranto; Gregory VII, Pope; Leo IX, Pope**

Further Reading

Editions

Amatus. *Storia de' Normanni di Amato di Montecassino*, ed. Vincenzo de Bartholomaeis. Fonti per la Storia d'Italia, Scrittori. Secolo, 11(76). Rome: Tipografia del Senato, 1935.

Geoffrey Malaterra. *De rebus gestis Rogerii Calabriae et Sicliae comitis et Roberti Guiscardi ducis fratris eius*, ed. Ernesto Pontieri. In *Rerum Italicarum Scriptores*, 2nd ed., Vol. 5(1). Bologna: Nicola Zanichelli, 1925–1928.

William of Apulia. *La geste de Robert Guiscard*, ed. Marguerite Mathieu. Palermo: Istituto Siciliano di Studi Bizantini e Neoellenici, 1961.

Critical Studies

Chalandon, Ferdinand. *Histoire de la domination normande en Italie et en Sicile*, 2 vols. Paris: A. Picard et Fils, 1907. (Reprint, New York: B. Franklin, 1960.)

Douglas, David C. *The Norman Achievement, 1050–1100*. Berkeley and Los Angeles: University of California Press, 1969.

Loud, G. A. *The Age of Robert Guiscard: Southern Italy and the Norman Conquest*. Essex: Pearson Education, 2000.

Norwich, John Julius. *The Other Conquest*. New York: Harper and Row, 1967. (Published in England as *The Normans in the South, 1016–1130*.)

Taviani-Carozzi, Huguette. *La terreur du monde: Robert Guiscard et la conquête normande en Italie—Mythe et histoire*. Paris: Fayard, 1996.

Wolf, Kenneth Baxter. *Making History: The Normans and Their Historians in Eleventh-Century Italy*. Philadelphia: University of Pennsylvania Press, 1995.

EMILY ALBU

ROBERT OF ANJOU
(1278–1343; r. 1309–1343)

Robert of Anjou, king of Naples ("the Wise") was the third son of Charles II of Anjou. Robert was held hostage by the Aragonese from 1285 to 1295. He was created duke of Calabria and vicar of the Regno for his father in 1297, and he became prince of Salerno in 1304. Robert succeeded as king of Sicily and count of Piedmont, Provence, and Forcalquier in 1309, despite the claims of his eldest brother's son, Carobert. Robert's two wives were Violante of Aragon, sister of James II; and Sancia of Aragon, daughter of James II. Robert was survived by two daughters, Joanna and Maria; the former succeeded him, becoming Queen Joanna I of Naples.

Robert became king as Emperor Henry VII was preparing an expedition to Italy to be crowned. The Guelf party, which opposed Henry's plans, looked to Robert for leadership, but initially he supported Pope Clement V, who hoped to form a partnership with Henry to bring peace to Italy. Clement, recognizing Robert's support, made him rector of the Romagna (excluding Bologna) in 1310 and supported a marriage alliance between Robert's heir and Henry's daughter. This alliance was never achieved, and relations worsened when Robert refused to do homage to Henry in person for Piedmont, Provence, and Forcalquier. Robert did not prevent Henry from reaching Rome and being crowned; but as the Guelfs' opposition to Henry grew, an army sent by Robert hastened the emperor's withdrawal. Robert became captain of the Guelf league in February 1313 and soon afterward accepted the lordship of numerous communes. In April 1313 he became lord of Florence for five years. Henry responded by condemning Robert, but Henry died in 1313 while marching on Florence, where an army sent by Robert was preparing to oppose him.

Meanwhile Frederick of Sicily, supporting Henry in this quarrel (which he had helped to precipitate), invaded Calabria, thereby breaking the peace of Caltabellotta. Robert repulsed him and thereafter made several unsuccessful attempts (in 1314, 1316, 1325–1326, 1335, and 1339–1342) to recover Sicily; these attempts further impoverished his already troubled realm, and despite his sincere efforts to impose good justice and administration, Robert perpetuated corruption and disorder. The degree of Robert's failure to impose his ideal of good government is disputed, but that he failed is not in question.

Robert continued throughout his reign to be involved in politics farther north. In 1317, the Florentines renewed his lordship for four years. In 1325, he sanctioned an offer to make his son Charles of Calabria lord of Florence. Both Charles and Robert opposed the expedition by Emperor Lewis of Bavaria, not least because an alliance between Lewis and Frederick of Sicily posed a threat to the Regno.

Robert was religious to the point of bigotry and was detested by the northern Ghibellines, but in his own kingdom he was the most popular of the Angevin kings—a reputation for which his public works, especially in Naples, and his patronage of the arts and literature may have been partly responsible. Among those whom he patronized were Petrarch and Boccaccio. Simone Martini's picture of Robert worshiping his brother Louis is reputedly the first painted portrait in European art.

See also **Boccaccio, Giovanni; Clement V, Pope; Henry VII of Luxembourg; Petrarca, Francesco**

Further Reading

Editions
Dominicus de Gravina. *Chronicon de rebus in Apulia gestis, 1333—1350*, ed. Albano Sorbelli. Rerum Italicarum Scriptores, 12(3). Città di Castello: Lapi, 1903.
Mussato, Albertino. *Historia Augusta: Liber IV, Henrici VII; Liber V, De Gestis Italicorum post Henricum Septimum Caesarem.* Rerum Italicarum Scriptores, 10. Città di Castello: Lapi.
Villani, Giovanni, and Matteo Villani. *Croniche*, 13 vols., ed. Ignazio Moutier. Florence: Magheri, 1823–1826.

Critical Studies
Baddeley, St. Clair. *Robert the Wise and His Heirs: 1278–1352.* London, 1897.
Bowsky, W. M. *Henry VII in Italy: The Conflict of Empire and City State, 1310–1313.* Lincoln: University of Nebraska Press, 1960.
Caggese, Romolo. *Roberto d'Angio e i suoi tempi*, 2 vols. Florence: Bemporad, 1922–1930.
Housley, N. "Angevin Naples and the Defence of the Latin East: Robert the Wise and the Naval League of 1334." *Byzantion*, 51, 1981, pp. 548–556.
Léonard, Emile. *Les Angevins de Naples.* Paris: Presses Universitaires de France, 1954.
Monti, Gennaro Maria. *Da Carlo primo a Roberto di Angio.* Trani, 1936.

CAROLA M. SMALL

ROBERT OF MOLESME (ca. 1027–1111)

The founder of the monasteries of both Molesme and Cîteaux, Robert had spent much of his life trying to find or to establish a house where he thought the Benedictine *Rule* was being practiced with sufficient rigor. He spent time in the abbey of Moutier-la-Celle, in the diocese of Troyes; was briefly abbot of Saint-Michel of Langres, then prior of Saint-Ayoul of Provins; and for a period lived as a hermit. In 1075, deciding to try an entirely new Benedictine house, he and a small group of monks founded Molesme, of which he became first abbot (r. 1075–1111). In 1098, believing that even this house was not sufficiently rigorous, he left with a few brothers to found the New Monastery of Cîteaux. Although the monks at Molesme, feeling destitute, had the pope order Robert back to their house in the following year, Cîteaux flourished even without him and became in the 12th century the head of a large and influential order. Molesme, meanwhile, although overshadowed by Cîteaux, also acquired numerous gifts of property, including many priories and cells.

Further Reading
Bouton, Jean de la Croix, and Jean Baptiste Van Damme, eds. *Les plus anciens textes de Cîteaux.* Achel: Commentarii Cistercienses, 1974.
Laurent, Jacques, ed. *Cartulaires de l'abbaye de Molesme.* 2 vols. Paris: Picard, 1907–11.
Lackner, Bede K. *The Eleventh-Century Background of Cîteaux.* Washington, D.C.: Cistercian, 1972.
Spahr, Kolumban. *Das Leben des hl. Robert von Molesme: Eine Quelle zur Vorgeschichte von Cîteaux.* Freiburg: Paulusdruckerei, 1944.

CONSTANCE B. BOUCHARD

ROGER I (1031–1101, r. 1085–1101)

Roger I, count of Sicily, was the brother of Robert Guiscard and was largely responsible for the Norman conquest of Sicily. Roger had been campaigning there since at least 1061, when Messina had fallen, and he took the last Muslim stronghold, Noto, in 1091. He is said to have had only a handful of soldiers (just 130 knights at the battle of Cerami in 1063), but he became the most powerful figure in the south after his brother's death in 1085. Most scholars agree that Roger I laid the foundations for the later cohesion and wealth of the kingdom of Sicily.

Roger's comital activities can be partially reconstructed from evidence in surviving charters, most of which is published. At a meeting at Mazara in 1093, Roger and his followers divided up the conquered Muslims among their new lords using long lists known as *jara'ida*. One such list in favor of the cathedral at Catania in 1095 is extant in its original form, containing 345 names including fifty-three widows. A grant of peasants made to Guiscard's son, Duke Roger, was confirmed by his uncle to the cathedral of Palermo in the same year. Another element of Roger's documented activity was granting the monks of Saint Philip at Fragalà judicial rights over their peasants, a technique of local government that would be taken up and repeated by Roger II. Roger I's activities were not confined to the island of Sicily: his foundation of the monastery of the Holy Trinity at Mileto in Calabria in 1080–1081, including endowing the house with property and churches in

Calabria and Sicily, is recorded in a surviving copy of the original charter. Some judicial rights also appear to have been granted to the abbot in 1093, and Roget confirmed further privileges in a surviving but undated charter. Indeed, Mileto remained his chief residence throughout his life. In 1093, he also clarified a grant and presided over a court case in the Calabrian town of Stilo, and he is recorded as the patron of Greek monks there in 1094 and 1097.

Roger had a mostly cordial relationship with Pope Urban II, and the two cooperated, though sometimes uneasily, regarding the reorganization of the church in Sicily, with the see of Troina transferred to Messina, and Syracuse and Catania given bishops. In an unusual concession, Roger was given responsibility for many of the duties that a papal legate would have undertaken on the island, after he had objected to Urban's appointment of the bishop of Messina to that dignity.

Roger married three times. His first wife, in 1061, was Judith (d. 1080), daughter of William d'Evreux, who is said to have commanded the defense of Troina. His second wife was Eremburga, daughter of William de Mortain. His third wife was Adelasia (d. 1118), daughter of the marquis Manfred of Savona; his and Adelasia's sons were Simon (d. 1105) and Roger II. In addition, Roger I had two illegitimate sons: Jordan, who predeceased his father in 1089; and Geoffrey, who suffered from leprosy. Roger died in 1101, and after a period of minority during which Adelasia governed, Simon and Roger II succeeded him as counts of Sicily.

See also **Robert Giscard; Roger II**

Further Reading

Gaufredus Malaterra. *De Rebus Gestis Rogerii Calabriae et Siciliae Comitis et Roberti Guiscardi ducis fratris eius*, ed. E. Pontieri. Rerum Italicarum Scriptores, 1. Bologna, 1928.

Loud, G. A. "Byzantine Italy and the Normans." In *Byzantium and the West, c. 850–c. 1200: Proceedings of the XVIII Spring Symposium of Byzantine Studies, Oxford, 30 March–lst April 1984*, ed. J. D. Howard-Johnston. Amsterdam: Adolf M. Hakkert, 1988. (Reprinted, with other important essays, in G. A. Loud. *Conquerors and Churchmen in Norman Italy*. Aldershot and Brookfield, Vt.: Variorum, 1999.)

Matthew, Donald. *The Norman Kingdom of Sicily*. Cambridge: Cambridge University Press, 1992.

Ménager, L.-R. *Hommes et institutions de l'Italie normande*. London; Variorum, 1981.

Takayama, Hiroshi. *The Administration of the Norman Kingdom of Sicily*. Leiden: Brill, 1993.

PATRICIA SKINNER

ROGER II (1095–1154)

Roger II created the twelfth-century kingdom of southern Italy and Sicily, known as the Regno. He was the son of Count Roger I of Sicily and his third wife, Adelaide (Adelasia) of Savona, later queen of Jerusalem. Roger I died in 1101, and Roger II succeeded his elder brother, Simon, in 1105. Once he reached his majority, Roger II pursued a clear objective—to accumulate mainland territories in southern Italy. He conquered Calabria in 1122; he succeeded his childless cousin William to the duchy of Apulia in 1127 and was formally recognized as duke of Apulia on 23 August 1128; he acquired the principality of Capua in 1129. Finally, in Palermo, on Christmas day 1130, Roger was crowned king of Sicily, Calabria, and Apulia. The title was conferred, however, by the antipope Anacletus II, following a papal schism. On 25 July 1139, Pope Innocent II made Roger's title official, crowning him king of Sicily, duke of Apulia, and prince of Capua.

According to one chronicler, the celebrations and ceremony for Roger's coronation in Palermo in 1130 were so spectacular that "it was as if the whole city were being crowned." Many scholars have considered Roger's reign equally extraordinary. He ruled over all of Italy south of the Garigliano River, down through Sicily. Although he did not inherit a unified kingdom, accustomed to monarchical rule, he created something resembling one. Roger's rule is impossible to describe easily, for it did not conform to contemporary models of medieval kingship. He bound together the disparate ethnic groups who populated the region. Their coexistence was a practical necessity. He constructed a central government in Palermo that borrowed from the economic, administrative, and legal traditions of his Arab, Norman, Greek, and Italian-Lombard subjects. Roger was the leading feudal lord among feudal lords. He laid the groundwork for *Catalogus baronum*, the list of financial and military obligations owed to the crown by many of his barons. Arab-inspired offices were created to manage finances. A French-inspired chancery, overseen by a chamberlain, issued official court documents in Greek, Arabic, and Latin. A permanent Greek-style bureaucracy or civil service, based in Palermo, helped to manage the vast kingdom. Finally, the king himself, no doubt drawing inspiration from the Byzantium of Justinian, presented himself as a divinely appointed ruler. (Like Justinian, Roger may also have been a lawgiver. A law code, erroneously called the *Assises of Ariano*, has been attributed to him, but more recent scholarship disputes this.)

However one chooses to characterize the kingship of Roger II, he was undeniably successful. Periodic opposition to his rule—in particular, vassal rebellions led by his brother-in-law Rainulf—never lasted long. His foreign policy revealed ambitions, perhaps to expand his kingdom but more likely to safeguard it against external attack. He added much of North Africa to his kingdom while holding off threats from the Greeks, the northern Italians, and the German empire. He maintained a considerable war chest to support his army and navy. Roger's accomplishments did not go unnoticed: a contemporary observed that Roger "did more asleep than others did awake."

Roger II's personality and lineage should not be ignored in assessing his reign. He was described as the fairly stereotypical "Viking" warrior: tall, loud, regal, ruthless, and skilled from childhood on. Roger's upbringing was anything but standard: he was probably raised in the royal court at Mileto in Calabria, where he was schooled in Greek and Arabic. When he was king, his court at Palermo was famous for its eclectic group of western and eastern intellectuals. This tradition continued in Sicily long after Roger's death.

When Roger died, at age fifty-eight, he was survived by his third wife, Beatrice of Rethel, and their new daughter, Constance. Constance would eventually marry the son of Frederick I Barbarossa, Henry VI, thereby uniting the Norman and Hohenstaufen lines. In 1151, before his death, Roger had ensured the succession by naming and crowning as his heir his fourth son (his oldest surviving son), William I. William's mother was Roger's first wife, Elvira, daughter of Alfonso VI of Castille. A modern historian summed up Roger's reign by noting, "From his father he had inherited a county; to his son he bequeathed a kingdom." This kingdom would endure, largely intact, under the guidance of his son and grandson, William I and William II. They inherited the tradition of a strong, centralized monarchical rule established by their illustrious forebear.

Older scholarship proclaimed that Roger II had created the "first modern state." More recent work has suggested that the kingdom was not so unified as had previously been thought, and that Roger's apparent acceptance of the different cultures over which he ruled was motivated more by political expediency than by laudable tolerance. Roger's reign was an "absolute" monarchy that recognized the weaknesses of this unique kingdom and harnessed its strengths: a large geographic territory, surrounded by ambitious and watchful neighbors, and populated by people of vastly different religious, cultural, and administrative backgrounds. Roger II encouraged tolerance in this multiethnic state when it was politically necessary; overall, he expected strict obedience to his rule.

Roger's last wish, to be buried in the cathedral of Cefalù, which he had founded in 1131 outside Palermo, was not granted; he rests in the cathedral at Palermo. Nevertheless, the fusion of eastern and western architectural and artistic elements at Cefalù reflects the character of Roger's reign: innovative and intimidating political authority set against a glittering backdrop of cultural assimilation and coexistence.

See also **Roger I**

Further Reading

Editions

Alexander of Telese. *Alexandri Telesini Abbatis Ystoria Rogerii Regis Sicilie Calabrie atque Apulie*, ed. Ludovica De Nava. Istituto Storico Italiano per il Medio Evo, Fonti per la Stroria d'Italia, 112. Rome: Nella Sede dell'Istituto, 1991.

Brühl, Carlrichard. *Rogerii II: Regis diplomata Latina*. Codex Diplomaticus Regni Siciliae, Series 1, Diplomata Regum et Principum e Gente Normannorum, 2(1). Cologne: Böhlau, 1987.

Catalogus Baronum, ed. Evelyn Jamison. Rome: Istituto Storico Italiano per il Medio Evo, 1972.

The Liber Augustalis or Constitutions of Melfi Promulgated by the Emperor Frederick II for the Kingdom of Sicily in 1231, trans. James Powell. Syracuse, N.Y.: Syracuse University Press, 1971.

Critical Studies

Abulafia, David. *The Two Italics: Economic Relations between the Norman Kingdom of Sicily and the Northern Communes*. Cambridge; Cambridge University Press, 1977.

——. *Italy, Sicily, and the Mediterranean, 1100–1400*. London: Variorum Reprints, 1987.

——. *The Western Mediterranean Kingdoms 1200–1500: The Struggle for Dominion*. London: Longman, 1997.

Amari, Michele. *Storia dei musulmani di sicilia*, 2nd ed., ed. G. Levi della Vida and C. A. Nallino, 3 vols. Catania, 1930–1939.

Capitani, Ovidio. "Specific Motivations and Continuing Themes in the Norman Chronicles of Southern Italy in the Eleventh and Twelfth Centuries." In *The Normans in Sicily and Southern Italy: The Lincei Lectures 1974*. Oxford; Oxford University Press, 1977, pp. 1–46.

Caspar, Erich. *Roger II (1101–1154) und die Gründung der normannisch-sicilischen Monarchie*. Innsbruck: Wagner, 1904. (See also Italian version: *Ruggero II (1101–1145) e la fondazione della monarchia normanna di Sicilia*, intro. Ortensio Zecchino. Rome, 1999.)

Chalandon, Ferdinand. *Histoire de la domination normande en Italie et en Sicile*, 2 vols. Paris: Librarie A. Picard et fils, 1907. (Reprint, 1991.)

——. "The Conquest of South Italy and Sicily by the Normans" and "The Norman Kingdom of Sicily." *Cambridge Medieval History*, 5, 1926, pp. 167–207.

Cuozzo, Errico. *Catalogus Baronum commentario*. Istituto Storico Italiano per il Medio Evo, 101. Rome: Nella Sede dell'Istituto, 1984.

——. *"Quei maledetti normanni": Cavalieri e organizzazione militare nel mezzogiorno normanno*. Naples: Guida, 1989.

Drell, Joanna. "Family Structure in the Principality of Salerno under Norman Rule." *Anglo-Norman Studies*, 18, 1996, pp. 79–103.

——. "Cultural Syncretism and Ethnic Identity: The Norman 'Conquest' of Southern Italy and Sicily." *Journal of Medieval History* 25(3), 1999, pp. 187–202.

Falkenhausen, V. von. "I gruppi etnici nel regno di Ruggero II e la loro partecipazione al potere." In *Società, potere, e popolo nell'età di Ruggero II: Atti delle terze Giornate normanno-sveve—Bari, 23–25 maggio 1977*. Bari: Dedalo Libri, 1979, pp. 133–156.

Jamison, Evelyn. "The Norman Administration of Apulia and Capua, More Especially under Roger II and William I." *Papers of the British School at Rome*, 6, 1913, pp. 211–481. (See also 2nd ed., ed. D. R. Clementi and T. Kolzer, 1987; published as a separate monograph.)

——. "The Sicilian Norman Kingdom in the Mind of Anglo-

Norman Contemporaries." *Proceedings of the British Academy*, *24*, 1938, pp. 237–285.

Kehr, Karl Andreas. *Die Urkunden der normannisch-sizilischen Könige*. Innsbruck, 1902. (Reprint, 1962.)

Loud, G. A. *Church and Society in the Norman Principality of Capua 1058–1197*. Oxford: Clarendon, 1985.

——. *Conquerors and Churchmen in Norman Italy*. Aldershot: Ashgate, 1999.

——. *The Age of Robert Guiscard: Southern Italy and the Norman Conquest*. Essex: Pearson Education, 2000.

Marongiu, Antonio. "A Model State in the Middle Ages: The Norman-Hohenstaufen Kingdom of Sicily." *Comparative Studies in Society and History*, 4, 1963–1964, pp. 307–321.

——. *Byzantine, Norman, Swabian, and Later Institutions in Southern Italy*. London: Variorum Reprints, 1972.

Martin, Jean-Marie. "Città e Campagna: Economia e Società (sec. VII–XIII)." In *Storia del Mezzogiorno*, Vol. 3, *Alto Medioevo*. Rome: Edizioni del Sole, 1990, pp. 259–381.

——. *La pouille du VIe au XIIe siècle*. Rome: École Française de Rome, 1993.

Matthew, Donald. *The Norman Kingdom of Sicily*. Cambridge: Cambridge University Press, 1992.

Ménager, L. R. *Hommes et institutions de l'Italie Normande*. London: Variorum Reprints, 1981.

Norwich, John Julius. *The Other Conquest*. New York: Harper and Row, 1967. (Also published as *The Normans in the South 1016–1130*. London: Longmans, 1967 and 1981.)

——. *The Kingdom in the Sun, 1130–1194*. London: Longman, 1970.

Takayama, Hiroshi. *The Administration of the Norman Kingdom of Sicily*. Leiden: Brill, 1993.

Wolf, Kenneth Baxter. *Making History: The Normans and Their Historians in Eleventh-Century Italy*. Philadelphia: University of Pennsylvania Press, 1995.

JOANNA H. DRELL

ROLLE, RICHARD, OF HAMPOLE
(d. 1349)

Hermit and mystical writer. Little is known of Rolle's life, although some facts can be gleaned from the readings of the liturgical office prepared for the possibility of his canonization, and some conjectures can be made based on his writings. According to the office he came from Thornton, near Pickering, in the diocese of York, and was sent to Oxford with the support of Thomas Neville, archdeacon of Durham. He left the university at nineteen, however, and returned home, where he retired to the forest to live as a hermit. Shortly thereafter he was taken in by John de Dalton, a local squire, and given an eremitic lodging within Dalton's household. This proved inadequate, and he removed to some other place—apparendy against Dalton's will. Rolle seems also at this rime to have been tempted to take a lover (possibly a real person was involved, or perhaps only a diabolical apparition) but resisted the temptation by invoking the precious blood of Jesus.

Rolle's writings contain a number of passages referring to criticism, particularly for irregularity in changing his place of hermitage. However, no record survives indicating either his formal enclosure as a hermit or formal proceedings against him. Records of his education and possible ordination are similarly lacking. We do not know when he took up residence at Hampole, Yorkshire, nor in what relation he stood to the Cistercian convent there, in whose cemetery (later church) he was buried.

Although we have only the vaguest knowledge of his worldly life, Rolle has left us some clear indications of the progress of his spiritual development. In the *Incendium amoris* he describes the reception of the gifts of "heat, sweetness, and song" that are characteristic of his spirituality. The first gift he received was that of actual physical heat warming his breast. At first, he says, he thought that what he felt was some form of temptation; but he came to recognize it as corresponding to a second gift, of sweetness in prayers. Finally, while at prayer in chapel one day, he heard "as it were a ringing of singers of psalms, or rather, of songs." Time and again Rolle writes of this threefold gift of heat, sweetness, and song (*calor, dulcon, canor*).

Works

Rolle's works can be divided into three classes: scriptural commentaries, original mystical treatises, and lyrical and poetic compositions.

The most important scriptural commentaries are the Latin and English commentaries on the Psalter; Rolle also composed Latin commentaries on the first few verses of the Song of Songs, the first six chapters of the book of Revelation, and the Lamentations of Jeremiah. Five other treatises (including, particularly, the *Judica me Deus*) also derive their name and form from their commentary on particular scriptural verses. Another four commentaries are based on biblical texts used in the liturgy or on ecclesiastical texts. All of these lesser commentaries are in Latin. Although the commentaries are based for the most pan on earlier works in the same genre (the Psalter commentaries, for example, derive largely from the "literal" explication in Peter Lombard's *Commentarium*), they also develop a number of themes characteristic of Rolle's interests and teaching, such as devotion to the name of Jesus, and the experience of heat, sweetness, and song. These works probably derive from the period of Rolle's spiritual maturity.

The most important works in Rolle's canon are his three great Latin treatises and his four Latin and English epistolary tracts. The first treatise, *De amore Dei contra amatores mundi*, compares the eternal joys of the lover of God with the passing pleasures of this world. In each of its seven chapters Rolle describes a different aspect of worldly love and shows how the lovers of this world, though they seem happier, will be betrayed in the end into eternal sorrow. The second major treatise, the *Incendium amoris*, deals more specifically than any of Rolle's other writings with his experience of spiritual heat, sweetness, and song and is more autobiographical as well. Although focused on these themes, the *Incendium* also treats discursively a number of theological topics—yet it always returns to Rolle's own spiritual experience and to the idea that God's contemplative gifts to those who love him alone far outweigh the worldly satisfaction of merely intellectual pursuits. The *Incendium* was translated into ME, along with the *Emendatio vitae*, by the Carmelite Richard Misyn. The third of Rolle's Latin treatises, the *Melos amoris*, is in some ways the most difficult of his works to describe: highly alliterative in style and allusive in form, it appears to represent and attempt to reproduce in writing the transformation of contemplative prayer into heavenly song that he describes as the culmination of his spiritual experience. The probable aim of the *Melos* is not so much persuasion as mystagogy—the re-creation in the reader's mind of the author's spiritual experience, which by grace the reader may also attain. The style of the *Melos* has led many to regard it as an immature work; but Arnould, its editor, has pointed out that it more probably manifests the latest stage of his spirituality.

Rolle's most important epistolary tract, and by far his most popular work, is the *Emendatio vitae*. This letter and the parallel English *Form of Living* are addressed in some manuscripts to two of Rolle's disciples—William (Stopes?) in the former case, Margaret Kirkby in the latter—and are probably the last things he wrote. Of particular importance in both is the treatment of the "three stages of love": insuperable, inseparable, and singular. The treatises also exhort Rolle's audience to an immediate rejection of the world's blandishments and conversion to God in the eremitic life. The *Form of Living* was translated into Latin, and the *Emendatio vitae* into English by Richard Misyn and no fewer than six other, independent translators. The themes of the stages of the love of God and the necessity of total conversion to him also occur in Rolle's two other English epistolary tracts, the *Commandment* and the *Ego dormio*. Rolle included a number of lyrics in the *Ego dormio* and the *Form of Living*; a further collection of eight to ten lyrics is attributed to him in two manuscripts. He also wrote the *Canticum amoris*, a Latin hymn of praise to the Virgin Mary.

Rolle's reputation, like that of many influential medieval writers, was so great that many works not written by him came to be associated with his name. Hope Emily Allen's *Writings Ascribed to Richard Rolle* has proven decisive in establishing his canon, although her conclu-sions regarding chronology and biographical references must still be viewed with some skepticism.

Teaching and Influence

The most distinctive feature of Richard Rolle's spirituality is the experience of the graces of heat, sweetness, and song that follows upon the total conversion from the world to God. He is not always consistent in the hierarchical and chronological ordering of these graces, however; nor despite important similarities, is their description entirely consistent with that of the diree degrees of love—insuperable, inseparable, and singular—found in the later epistles. These three degrees apparendy derive From Richard of St. Victor's *Quattuor gradus violentae charitatis*, minus the fourth (insatiable) degree.

For Rolle the rejection of the false pleasures of this world and a complete conversion to God are the *sine qua non* of the contemplative life, which he believes is most fully lived in the eremitic life. He considered the religious vocation to be comparatively worldly and grouped members of religious orders together with other lovers of this world.

The experience of heavenly song, with that of sensible heat and sweetness in prayer, is particularly characteristic of Rolle's spirituality and that of his followers. Certain sections of *The Cloud of Unknowing* and of Walter Hilton's *Scale of Perfection* and *Of Angels' Song* caution against using words like "heat," "sweetness," or "song" too literally in describing spiritual experience, a feet that suggests that this form of affective mysticism was popular in the later 14th century. These negative comments, together with more positive presentations of this kind of affective mysticism by Thomas Basset, Richard Methley, and John Norton, can be taken as evidence for an informal "school" of Richard Rolle.

Rolle achieved his greatest degree of popular influence with the spread of the devotion (particularly in lyric poetry) to the Passion of Christ and to the Holy Name of Jesus. According to Knowlton the cult of the Holy Name does not seem to have been prominent in England, despite imitations of the "Dulcis Jesu Memoria" and devotional pieces in the tradition of Anselm of Canterbury's *Meditations*, until after the time of Rolle. A number of late-14th- and 15th-century ME lyrics reflect not merely these devotional themes but also the phrasing of Rolle's devotional poems and descriptions of his own spiritual experiences. Rolle was not merely the first of the 14th-century English mystics; he also had the greatest influence on popular piety before the Reformation.

See also **Hilton, Walter**

Further Reading

Primary Sources

Allen, Hope Emily, ed. *English Writing of Richard Rolle Hermit of Hampole.* Oxford: Clarendon, 1931.

Allen, Rosamund S., trans. *The English Writings.* New York: Paulist Press, 1988.

Arnould, E.J.F., ed. *The Melos Amoris of Richard Rolle of Hampole.* Oxford: Blackwell, 1957.

Deanesly, Margaret, ed. *The Incendium amoris of Richard Rolle of Hampole.* Manchester, Manchester University Press, 1915

del Mastro, ML., trans. *The Fire of Love and the Mending of Life.* New York: Doubleday, 1981.

Harvey, Ralph, ed. *The Fire of Love and the Mending of Life, or The Rule of Living of Richard Rolle.* EETS o.s. 106. Oxford: Kegan Paul, Trench, Trübner, 1896.

Ogilvie-Thomson, Sarah J., ed. *Richard Rolle: Prose and Verse.* EETS o.s. 293. Oxford: Oxford University Press, 1988.

Theiner, Paul F., ed. *The Contra amatores mundi of Richard Rolle of Hampole.* Berkeley: University of California Press, 1968.

Secondary Sources

Manual 9:3051–68, 3411–25.

Alford, John A. "Richard Rolle and Related Works." In *Middle English Prose: A Critical Guide to Major Authors and Genres,* ed. A.S.G. Edwards. New Brunswick: Rutgers University Press, 1984, pp. 35–60.

Allen, Hope Emily. *Writings Ascribed to Richard Rolle, Hermit of Hampole, and Materials for His Biography.* New York: Heath, 1927.

Clark, J.P.H. "Richard Rolle: ATheological Re-Assessment." *DownR* 101 (1983): 108-39.

Clark, J.P.H. "Richard Rolle as a Biblical Commentator." *DownR* 104 (1986): 165–213.

Knowlton, Mary Arthur. *The Influence of Richard Rolle and of Julian of Norwich on the Middle English Lyrics.* The Hague: Mouton, 1973.

Watson, Nicholas. "Richard Rolle as Elitist and as Popularist: The Case *Judica me.*" In *De Cella in Seculum: Religious and Secular Life and Devotion in Late Medieval England,* ed. Michael G. Sargent. Cambridge: Brewer, 1989, pp. 123–43.

Watson, Nicholas. *Richard Rolle and the Invention of Authority.* Cambridge: Cambridge University Press, 1991.

MICHAEL G. SARGENT

ROMUALD OF RAVENNA, SAINT (c. 952–1027)

Saint Romuald of Ravenna was a monastic reformer and the founder of the Camaldolese order and is considered one of the founders of the Italian eremitical movement of the eleventh century.

Romuald was born into the ducal Onesti family at Ravenna. When he was twenty, his father killed a kinsman in a duel, and Romuald entered the Benedictine monastery of Sant'Apollinare in Classe to perform a forty-day penance for this act. The monastery had a profound effect on him. At the end of the penance he decided to stay, took monastic vows, and entered enthusiastically into a rigorous observance of the Benedictine rule. However, reading the lives of the desert fathers led Romuald to criticize what he con- sidered laxity at Sant'Apollinare, and he soon left the monastery to live as an anchorite in the marshes surrounding Ravenna. About 975, Romuald became the disciple of the hermit Marino and followed him to the vicinity of Venice.

Through Marino, Romuald was drawn into the circle of Venice's doge, Pietro Orseolo, who was then undergo- ing a religious conversion. When Orseolo abdicated to join the monastery at Cuxa in the Pyrenees, Romuald and Marino went with him. Romuald remained at Cuxa for ten years, studying the works in its library in order to refine his understanding of the monastic ideal. Although the final shape of his reform was the product of many years of experimentation, the basic notions seem to have been formulated at Cuxa. Romuald's foundations would be among the first expressions of an eleventh-century monastic reform movement that sought to revive the primitive rigor of early Egyptian eremitism.

Romuald returned to Italy on the death of Orseolo in 988. He spent the next ten years based in Pereum, a hermitage in Ravenna's marshes, while he wandered the Apennines seeking followers, founding monasteries, and experimenting with monastic organization. Like a number of other reformers of his time, Romuald was de- termined to develop a greater spirit of contemplation in monastic houses; accordingly, he established hermitages and cenobitic communities together. But unlike other reformers, Romuald did not believe that a cenobitic life was a necessary prerequisite for an eremitic life. At his foundations, promising candidates were immediately introduced to the life of the hermit. Moreover, he did not subordinate the hermitage to the abbot of the monastery but rather put the cenobites under the moral authority of an experienced hermit. The monastery and hermitage were supposed to complement each other in drawing all monks toward the eremitical ideal of fasting, silence, and solitude.

In 998 Emperor Otto III appointed Romuald abbot of Sant'Apollinare in Classe, but the monks' resistance to his austerity led to his resignation within a year. He then moved to the environs of Rome, near the imperial court, and soon attracted the patronage of several of the emperor's courtiers. When civil unrest at Rome drove the court to Ravenna in 1001, Romuald followed, again settling in Pereum. Romuald now had significant sup- port from the empire. Followers flocked to him. Many, including the imperial chaplain Bruno of Querfurt, went as missionaries to convert the Slavs, inspired by Romuald's insistence that preaching and conversion were the ultimate role of the monk and hermit.

After the death of Otto III in 1002, Romuald left Pereum to wander again in the Apennines. Sometime between 1010 and 1020, he founded a small monastery and hermitage at Camaldoli near Arezzo. This influential institution, famous for its rigor, proved to be his most lasting contribution to eremitical reform. Romuald died at Val di Castro in 1027. By then, his other foundations were already looking to Camaldoli for leadership, and other monastic reformers were drawing inspiration from it.

Romuald had not intended to establish an order separate from the Benedictines. However, after his death the thirty-odd monasteries he had founded drew together around Camaldoli, in part to protect the peculiar customs Romuald had established for them. By the late eleventh century, the Gregorian popes were treating them as an order. The most famous Camaldolese monk, Petet Damian, drew many of his reforming ideals from Romuald. Peter wrote a very influential biography of Romuald in 1042.

See also **Damian, Peter; Otto III**

Further Reading

Edition

Tabacco, Giovanni, ed. *Petri Damiani Vita beati Romualdi.* Fonti per la Storia d'Italia, 94. Rome: Istituto Storico Italiano per il Medio Evo, 1957.

Critical Studies

Belisle, Peter Damian. "Primitive Romauldian/Camaldolese Spirituality." *Cistercian Studies Quarterly*, 31, 1996, pp. 413–429.

Kurze, Wilhelm. "Campus Malduli: Die Frühgeschichte Camaldolis." *Quellen und Forschungen aus Italienischen Archiven und Bibliotheken*, 44, 1964, pp. 1–34.

Leclercq, Jean. "Saint Romuald et le monachisme missionaire." *Revue Bénédictine*, 77, 1962, pp. 307–322.

Phipps, Colin. "Romuald—Model Hermit: Eremitical Theory in Saint Peter Damian's *Vita Beati Romualdi*, Chapters 16–27." *Studies in Church History*, 22, 1985, pp. 65–77.

Schmidtmann, Christian. "Romuald von Camoldi: Modell einer eremitischen Existenz in 10./11. Jahrhundert." *Studia Monastica*, 39, 1997, pp. 329–338.

Tabacco, Giovanni. *Romualdo di Ravenna.* Turin: Bottega d'Erasmo, 1968.

THOMAS TURLEY

RUDOLF VON EMS (ca. 1190–ca. 1255)

The presumably Swiss author from Hohenems wrote five surviving quasi-historical epics in verse for important men close to the Staufer court (at first, during the reign of King Heinrich VII) and eventually for King Konrad IV himself, whom he might have accompanied on a campaign to Italy, where the king (and maybe the poet) died in 1254.

The works (based on French and Latin sources) in approximate chronological order are *Der gute Gerhard* (*Good Gerard*), commissioned by Rudolf von Steinach (ministerial of the bishop of Constance) circa 1220; *Barlaam und Josaphat*, after a literary model of abbot Wido von Cappel (near Zürich); *Alexander*, without a known commissioner; *Willehalm von Orlens*, commissioned by Konrad von Winterstetten at the Staufer court in Swabia, before 1243; the French source was provided by Johannes von Ravensburg's *Weltchronik*, dedicated to King Konrad IV Another theory is that Rudolf did not go to Italy and continued the *Weltchronik* beyond "Salomo," after which he added still two later excursus to *Alexander*. If Rudolf had also produced earlier courtly works, which he claimed in *Barlaam und Josaphat*, that is unproven. But an *Eustachius*-Legend, mentioned in *Alexander*, is lost.

Der gute Gerhard, after an unknown source, demonstrates courtly humanity toward a heathen (two manuscripts are extant). *Barlaam und Josaphat* describes the Indian Legend of Buddha after a Latin source of 1220–1223. (Extant in 47 manuscripts; the only illustrated manuscript, of 1469, was done by Diebold Lauber, with 138 drawings.) Alongside the *Laubacher Barlaam* of the Freisinger Bishop Otto II, Rudolf's is the second German version. In *Eustachius*, a high Roman general under Trajan converted to Christianity. *Willehalm von Orlens* is neither an *aventiure*, or courtly chivalric romance (Wolfram), nor a chanson de geste (heroic ballad, like Guillaume), but rather basically a courtly *Fürstenspiegel*, or guide for nobility. An ideal government, Staufer knighthood, exists also in France and England. (Of the twenty-nine extant manuscripts, seven are illustrated, mostly by Diebold Lauber.) A shorter narrative in rhymed couplets, *Wilham von Orlens*, was created in the fifteenth century, extant in four manuscripts and one print of Anton Sorg (Augsburg, 1491). Hans Sachs based his drama of 1559 on this print. In 1522, an anonymous Swabian writer reworked Rudolf's epic as stropbic form in the Herzog-Ernst-Tone, a thirteen-line pattern. The story is also recounted in pictures, on a tapestry in Frankfurt of the first quarter of the fifteenth century, in fifteen scenes. The couple Wilhelm and Amelie is also found as a fresco at Runkelstein castle near Bozen. In *Alexander*, Rudolf wanted to portray history, not a heroic or courtly romance. Ten volumes were planned, which were stopped in the middle of the sixth book, however (death of Darius and victory over his followers). The two main sources were the *Historia de preliis* and Curtius Rufus. Fairy-tale portions were left out. (Of the three extant manuscripts, the Munich State Library manuscript was illustrated by Diebold Lauber.) The *Weltchronik* ends, after thirty-six thousand verses, in the middle of the Jewish history of the kings. (Over one hundred manuscripts are extant, as well as reworkings and rhymed bibles.)

Further Reading

Green, Dennis. "On the Primary Reception of the Works of Rudolf von Ems." *Zeitschrift für deutsches Altertum* 115 (1986): 151–180.

Haug, Walter. "Wolframs 'Willehalm'—Prolog im Lichte seiner Bearbeitung durch Rudolf von Ems," in *Kritische Bewährung*: *Beiträge zur deutschen Philologie*: *Festschrift für Werner Schröder zum 60. Geburtstag*, ed. Ernst-Joachim Schmidt. Berlin: E. Schmidt, 1974, pp. 298–327.

Walliczek, Wolfgang. "Rudolf von Ems," in *Die deutsche Literatur des Mittelalters. Verfasserlexikon*, ed. Kurt Ruh et al. Berlin: de Gruyter, 1991, vol. 8, coll. 322–345.

Wenzel, Horst. "Höfische Geschichte." *Europäische Hochschulschriften* 1, 284 (1980): 71–87.

Wunderlich, Werner. *Der 'ritterliche' Kaufmann: literatursoziologische Studien zu Rudolf von Ems' "Der guote Gerhart."* Scriptor. Hochschulschriften. Literaturwissenschaft 7. Kronberg im Taunus: Scriptor, 1975.

Zaenker, Karl A. "The Manuscript Relationship of Rudolf von Ems' *Barlaam und Josaphat*." Ph.D. diss., University of British Columbia, 1974.

SIBYLLE JEFFERIES

RUSTICO FILIPPI
(c. 1230–c. 1280 or 1285)

The Florentine poet Rustico Filippi (Rustico di Filippo) is credited with initiating the comic style in the medieval Italian lyric. Rustico wrote fifty-seven sonnets transmitted by the Vaticano manuscript Latino 3793, and a *tenzone* with Bondie Dietaiuti found in three other codices. Half of his sonnets were written in the serious style of courtly love; the other half provide one of the earliest examples of the comic, or jocose, style in Italian literature. Brunetto Latini, who considered Rustico one of his closest friends and an accomplished poet, dedicated the *Favolello* to him. Rustico was also the acknowledged teacher of Jacopo da Lèona and is the protagonist of a comic sonnet by Jacopo. Rustico was an ardent Ghibelline.

Rustico's comic sonnets fall into two categories: personal invective, and caricature directed against Florentines of all ages and social conditions. Among the figures he caricatured are warriors who inspire laughter rather than awe, a miser, a cuckolded husband, a man who is the paradigm of laziness, people with offensive body odors, libertines on the prowl, and prostitutes. Rustico displays a great talent for euphemism and uses a plethora of creative metaphors, similes, paraphrases, and hyperbole to describe his characters, the sexual act, and certain parts of the human anatomy. Several of the comic sonnets are linked. For example, there is a three-sonnet group that begins with *Poi che guerito son de le mascelle*, recounting the implausible proposals made by a matchmaker to a poor father with two daughters; and there is a two-sonnet group beginning with *Su, donna Gemma, co la farinata*, which ponders the suspicious reasons behind the sudden loss of weight of a young girl named Mita. The best-known of Rustico's comic sonnets, *Quando Dio messer Messerin fece*, describes Albizzo de' Caponsacchi as a unique combination of bird, beast, and man—a miracle of God's creation.

In the sonnet describing "*messer* Messerin," and in other sonnets, Rustico frequently compares the targets of his caricatures to animals, at a time when such comparisons were in vogue in the serious courtly love lyric. Whereas in his comic poetry Rustico mocked the overuse of animal comparisons, he avoided them altogether in his twenty-eight sonnets and the *tenzone* in the traditional courtly style. In these compositions, he experimented with various rhetorical devices in order to achieve more drama and more narrative flexibility. Among his innovations, he broke the unity of address, extended personification from the conventional god of love to other items involved in the *psychomachia* of courtly love (the heart, the eyes), and abandoned the extended simile. One sonnet that illustrates all these elements is *Amor fa nel mio cor fermo soggiorno*. The integration of dramatic techniques into the lyric, and the cultivation of a kinetic rather than a descriptive style, reached a culmination in the poetry of the *dolce stil nuovo*. Thus Rustico was an innovator in introducing comic poetry to Italian literature and, to a lesser extent, in the development of the love lyric.

See also **Brunetto Latini**

Further Reading

Editions

Contini, Gianfranco. *Poeti del Duecento*, Vol. 2. Milan and Naples: Ricciardi, 1960, pp. 353–364.

Federici, Vincenzo. *Le rime di Rustico di Filippo, rimatore fiorentino del sec. XIII*. Bergamo: Istituto Italiano d'Arti Grafiche, 1899.

Figurelli, Fernando. *La poesia comico-giocosa dei primi due secoli*. Naples: Pironti, 1960, pp. 74–112.

Marti, Mario. *Poeti giocosi del tempo di Dante*. Milan: Rizzoli, 1956, pp. 29–91.

Massèra, Aldo Francesco. *Sonetti burleschi e realistici dei primi due secoli*. Bari: Laterza, 1920. (See also rev. ed, ed. Luigi Russo, 1940, Vol. 1, pp. 1–30.)

Rustico Filippi. *Sonetti*, ed. Pier Vincenzo Mengaldo. Turin: Einaudi, 1971.

Vitale, Maurizio. *Rimatori comico-realistici*. Turin: UTET, 1956, pp. 99–197. (Reprint, 1976.)

Translations

Dante and His Circle, with the Italian Poets Preceding Him (1100–1200–1300), trans. Dante Gabriel Rossetti. London: Ellis and Elvey, 1892, pp. 360–362.

Poems from Italy, ed. William Jay Smith and Dana Gioìa. Saint Paul, Minn.: New Rivers, 1985, pp. 32–33.

Tusiani, Joseph. *The Age of Dante: An Anthology of Early Italian Poetry Translated into English Verse and with an Introduction*. New York: Baroque, 1974, pp. 56–57.

Critical Studies

Baldelli, Ignazio. "Dante e i poeti fiorentini del Duecento." In *Lectura Dantis Scaligera*. Florence: Le Monnier, 1968.

Buzzetti Gallarati, Silvia. "Sull'organizzazione del discorso comico nella produzione giocosa di Rustico Filippi." *Medioevo Romanzo*, 9(2), 1984, pp. 189–213.

Casini, Tommaso. "Un poeta umorista del secolo decimoterzo (Rustico di Filippo)." In *Scritti danteschi*. Città di Casrello: Lapi, 1913, pp. 225–255.

Folena, Gianfranco. "Cultura poetica dei primi fiorentini." *Giornale Storico della Letteratura Italiana*, 147, 1970, pp. 1–42.

Kleinhenz, Christopher. *The Early Italian Sonnet: The First Century (1220–1321)*. Collezione di Studi e Testi, 2. Lecce: Milella, 1986.

Levin, Joan H. *Rustico di Filippo and the Florentine Lyric Tradition*. American University Studies, 2(16). New York: Peter Lang, 1986.

Marti, Mario. "La coscienza stilistica di Rustico di Filippo e la sua poesia." In *Cultura e stile net poeti giocosi del tempo di Dante*. Pisa: Nistri-Lischi, 1953.

Petrocchi, Giorgio. "I poeti realisti." In *Storia della letteratura italiana*, Vol. 1, *Le origini e il Duecento*, ed. Emilio Cecchi and Natalino Sapegno. Milan: Garzanti, 1965, pp. 575–607. (Reprint, 1979.)

Quaglio, Antonio Enzo. "La poesia realistica." In *La letteratura italiana: storia e testi*, Vol. 1(2), *Il Duecento: Dalle origini a Dante*. Bari: Laterza, 1970, pp. 183–253.

Russo, Vittorio. " 'Verba obscena' e comico: Rustico Filippi." *Filologia e Critica*, 5, 1980, pp. 169–182.

Savona, Eugenio. "Rustico di Filippo e la poesia comico-realistica." In *Cultura e ideologia nell'età comunale: Ricerche sulla letteratura italiana dell'età comunale*. Ii Portico, 57. Ravenna: Longo, 1975, pp. 57–70.

Suitner, Franco. *La poesia satirica e giocosa nell'età dei comuni*. Padua: Antenore, 1983.

JOAN H. LEVIN

RUTEBEUF (fl. 1248–85)

The Parisian Rutebeuf composed works in a greater variety of genres than any other medieval poet. Known from a dozen manuscripts, his fifty-five extant pieces illustrate the range of medieval urban poetry. Rutebeuf composed in every vernacular genre except those especially cultivated in the provincial courts of 13th-century France: chivalric epics, romances, and songs of courtly love. At a time when manuscript compilations grouped lyric, dramatic, and narrative pieces separately, Rutebeuf, like his contemporary Adam de la Halle, imposed such a vivid and coherent poetic identity on all his compositions that they were gathered as a corpus in three contemporary compilations. Unlike the vagabond Goliards or jongleurs who traveled from castle to court, Rutebeuf remained in Paris, where he wrote to please many patrons—the royal family, the university, the higher clergy, the papal legate—and to amuse a public in city streets and taverns. While the aristocratic provincial courts were attuned to the refined art of the chanson and the idealizing fantasies of Arthurian romance, Rutebeuf's heterogeneous urban public relished topical works that spoke to issues of the day, such as the Crusades and the proliferation of mendicant orders in Paris. Rutebeuf's political verse follows historical events closely and presupposes familiarity with Parisian topography, personalities, and issues. The notable variety of genres and the historical content that characterize Rutebeuf's poetry are inseparable from Paris, the city that was its essential and nurturing environment, and from the colorful figure of the poet himself.

Although no document preserves any record of Rutebeuf's life, his poems reveal much about his background, training, and relations with patrons. He may have come from the region of Champagne; his earliest polemical poem, the *Dit des Cordeliers* (1249), favors the rights of Franciscan monks in Troyes. Throughout his career, Rutebeuf composed eulogies of nobles from Champagne, although mostly in connection with his role as a Parisian propagandist of papal crusade policy, as in his *complaintes* for Count Eudes de Nevers (1266) and Count Thibaut V of Champagne (1279). Rutebeuf's *Vie de sainte Elysabel* (ca. 1271) was commissioned for Isabelle, daughter of King Louis IX and wife of Thibaut V. Rutebeuf's most prominent benefactors were members of the royal family, such as Alphonse of Poitiers, brother of Louis IX, whom he addresses in his request poem *Complainte Rutebeuf* and in his crusade piece *Dit de Pouille* (ca. 1265) and whom he eulogizes in 1271. The poet also appeals repeatedly to King Philip III the Bold to replace generous benefactors lost on the Crusades. Like the eulogies and commissioned devotional works, Rutebeuf's political poems and appeals for largesse mark his status as a skilled professional poet and his relations with patrons in the highest ecclesiastical and aristocratic circle.

Rutebeuf composed a number of comic pieces like those described in minstrel repertoires. His *Dit de l'herberie* is one of several examples of a dramatic monologue by a quack who amuses an audience with rapid enumerations of coins, exotic places, stones, and herbal remedies. All of Rutebeuf's fabliaux are known in other medieval versions: the story of the Franciscan who enrolls a girl in his monastic order (*Frère Denise*); the tale of the wife who pretends that her midnight rendezvous with the priest is a devotional exercise (*Dame qui fist trois tours autour du moutier*); the account of the bishop who gave Christian burial to a donkey who left him twenty pounds (*Testament de l'âne*). The theme of the obscene *Pet au vilain* is reused in André de la Vigne's farce, the *Meunier de qui le diable emporte l'âme en enfer* (1496).

Rutebeuf also had sufficient clerical training to read Latin and know the student's life. His *Dit de l'université* is a sympathetic account of a peasant boy come to study in Paris who soon squanders his hard-earned funds on pretty city girls. Though not a vulgarizer of philosophical and scientific concepts like his contemporary Jean de Meun, he draws on Latin sources for his saints' lives, miracles, polemical poems, and requests for largesse. In the *Dit d'Aristote,* he translates a passage from the epic *Alexandreis* by Walter of Châtillon; in *Sainte Elysabel,* he abridges a Latin *vita;* in his miracle of the *Sacristain et la femme au chevalier,* he expands an exemplum from the early 13th-century *Sermones vulgares* of the preacher Jacques de Vitry. Rutebeuf's lives of exemplary penitents combine French and Latin sources in the narrative *Sainte Marie l'Egyptienne* and the *Miracle de Théophile,* which dramatizes versions by Gautier de Coinci and Fulbert of Chartres. He even translates and glosses lines from Ovid's *Metamorphoses* in his allegorical *Voie de paradis.*

Rutebeuf's clerical training not only led him to rich literary sources, it also determined his subjects and his style. Rutebeuf's moral poems contribute to the ecclesiastical effort, inspired by the Fourth Lateran Council (1215), to instruct laypeople in religious doctrine: his *Voie de paradis* is an allegorical catechism of confession; three works, the *Etat, Vie,* and *Plaies du monde,* adapt the conventional estates satire of Latin preachers and moralists for a lay public. In contrast with the self-reflective mode of contemporary courtly lyric and moral verse, Rutebeuf's poetry often seeks to turn its hearers toward the outer world of history painted in dramatic moral colors.

Commissioned by supporters of the crusade policies of Louis IX and the pope, Rutebeuf's eleven crusade poems incorporate estates satire and rhetorical techniques of moral persuasion from the didactic tradition to rouse public opinion in favor of increasingly unpopular crusades against Charles of Anjou's Christian rival for the Sicilian throne (1265) and against the Muslims in Tunis (1270). As a professional pamphleteer, Rutebeuf does not express personal opinions in his poems. He advocates the differing views of the two causes he served in order to sway public opinion and encourage partisans to action; he is an ardent supporter of papal policies in his crusade verse, a fiery Gallican in his defense of university autonomy.

In his fourteen poems supporting the secular university masters against their Franciscan and Dominican rivals and the pope, Rutebeuf again recasts the motifs of didactic poetry to new, polemical ends. Dream allegories, battles of vices and virtues, animal satires, complaints attributed to the church personified—all the resources of the Latin and French satirical tradition are brought to bear on partisan concerns. Knowledge of historical circumstances is essential to the understanding of Rutebeuf's topical poems: the proliferation of mendicant orders in Paris (*Ordres de Paris, Chanson des ordres, Des béguines*); the struggle between mendicants and secular clergy for parish privileges and university chairs (*Discorde de l'université et des Jacobins, Des règles, Dit de sainte Église, Bataille des vices et des vertus, Des Jacobins*); the writings of William of Saint-Amour,

banished leader of the university masters (*Dit* and *Complainte de Guillaume*). Out of this factional literature rises a new allegorical figure, Hypocrisy, which comes to overshadow earlier concern with pride and avarice and dominate moral literature of the late 13th and 14th centuries. Personified in Rutebeuf's *Du Pharisien* and *Dit d'Hypocrisie,* hypocrisy is central to Jean de Meun's character False Seeming in the *Roman de la Rose* as well as in late animal satires, such as *Renart le contrefait* and the *Livres de Fauvel.*

Polemical, pious, or entertaining in topic and nonlyric in form, Rutebeuf's poems have a style and shape that owe little to prevailing courtly modes. His characteristic form is the first-person nonmusical *dit,* a rambling, open form, most often cast in octosyllabic couplets or tercets, that accommodates all the topical themes of contemporary history that found little place in courtly song, romance, or epic. In spite of their rhetorical embroidery and rich rhymes, Rutebeuf's poems give an overall impression of artless simplicity and directness. His verses are engaging and amusing: enlivened with frequent irony, animated with proverbs, touched with realistic details. Lively, colloquial direct discourse and dialogue characterize both Rutebeuf's poems and the tableaux of his *Miracle de Théophile.* Often shaped as *complaintes,* Rutebeuf's *dits* pass easily from one subject to another via apostrophes and exclamations that are united more by appeal to emotion than by rigorous logic.

The figure of the poet himself, however, is the element that unifies Rutebeuf's works. Identified by a signature pun as *Rustebeuf qui rudement cevre* ("Rutebeuf who works crudely"), the persona of the poet is protagonist in many of his moral, political, and comic pieces: "Rutebeuf" is the pilgrim in the allegorical *Voie de paradis;* he is the character who goes to Rome in a dream vision to hear news of the election of Pope Urban IV (*Dit d'Hypocrisie,* 1261). It is in his own name that Rutebeuf accuses church prelates of caring less for the Crusades than for "good wine, good meat, and that the pepper be strong" (*Complainte d'Outremer,* ll. 94–95). It is he who witnesses the chaste speech of Alphonse of Poitiers in his eulogy and who is called to judge the comic debate between Charlot and the barber.

Characterization of his poetic persona is most vividly developed in Rutebeuf's best-known works, his ten poems of personal misfortune. His poetic "I" is based on the conventional character type of the poor fool that figures in medieval request verse by Goliards and minstrels and later in the poetry of Eustache Deschamps and François Villon. Picturesquely personal rather than autobiographical in content, his poems of misfortune dramatize an exaggerated, grotesque self, deserted by friends, grimacing with cold and want, and martyred by marriage and a weakness for gambling. In the plaintive or ironic tones of the *Dit d'Aristote,* the

Paix de Rutebeuf, and *De Brichemer,* the poet reminds his patrons of the virtue of largesse and prompt payment. The *Repentance Rutebeuf* gives a solemn, subjective resonance to the conventional poetry of remorse found in his saints' lives and miracles. Furthermore, in his *Griesche d'hiver, Griesche d'été* and *Dit des ribauds de Grève,* Rutebeuf shows the reader a social world excluded from courtly song, romance, and epic, that of a homeless urban proletariat, stung by white snowflakes in winter and by black flies in summer.

Appreciatively collected by contemporaries, Rutebeuf's poetry was forgotten after his time. But in his works we discover a poetic voice that dramatizes and particularizes the subjective lyric while it speaks with satirical wit and ethical fervor about concerns of the urban world of medieval France.

See also **Adam de la Halle; Deschamps, Eustache; Fulbert of Chartres**

Further Reading

Rutebeuf. *Œuvres complètes de Rutebeuf,* ed. Edmond Faral and Julia Bastin. 2 vols. Paris: Picard, 1959.

——. *Œuvres complètes,* ed. and trans. Michel Zink. 2 vols. Paris: Bordas, 1989–90.

Cerquiglini, Jacqueline. "'Le clerc et le louche': Sociology of an Esthetic." *Poetics Today* 5 (1984): 479–91.

Huot, Sylvia. *From Song to Book: The Poetics of Writing in Old French Lyric and Lyrical Narrative Poetry.* Ithaca: Cornell University Press, 1987, pp. 213–19.

Regalado, Nancy Freeman. *Poetic Patterns in Rutebeuf: A Study in Noncourtly Poetic Modes of the Thirteenth Century.* New Haven: Yale University Press, 1970.

Rousse, Michel. "Le mariage Rutebeuf et la fête des fous." *Moyen âge* 88 (1982): 435–49.

Zink, Michel. "Time and Representation of the Self in Thirteenth-Century French Poetry." *Poetics Today* 5 (1984): 611–27.

——. "*La subjectivité littéraire autour du siècle de saint Louis.* Paris: Presses Universitaires de France, 1985, pp. 47–74.

NANCY F. REGALADO

S

SACCHETTI, FRANCO
(c. 1330–1400)

Franco Sacchetti was born to a noble Florentine Guelf family, perhaps in Ragusa, where his father did business. Sacchetti spent many years as a merchant. By 1352, he was also composing traditional love poems. In 1354, he married Felice di Nicolò Strozzi. In honor of the Strozzi women, he composed, probably shortly before his marriage, *The Battle of Women*, consisting of 272 mediocre octaves describing the victory of young, beautiful, virtuous ladies over old, ugly, vice-ridden hags. In the early 1360s, during the war between Florence and Pisa, Sacchetti began to be involved in the city's politics and as an administrator of Florentine territories. In 1376 he was sent as ambassador to Bologna; in 1383, when he married for the second time, he was a member of the *otto di balia*; in 1384 he became a prior for the San Giovanni area; during the wars with the Visconti in 1388–1392, he served as counselor to the Florentine government; and throughout the late 1380s and the 1390s he was governor over a series of Florentine territories outside the city.

The 1370s brought a series of sorrows, both personal and public. Sacchetti was in Florence during the plague of 1374. That year and the next saw the deaths of Petrarch and Boccaccio, whom he lamented in sonnets expressing his admiration and sense of loss. Two years later, his first wife died, mourned affectionately in his verse. Meanwhile Florence was threatened by the expansionism of the Milanese and by papal agents who sought to restrict Florentine trade routes across papal territories. To fend off the latter, Sacchetti became involved in the "war of the eight saints" (1375), but hard times and high wartime taxes contributed to the revolt of the *ciompi* (1378). Some of Sacchetti's poems express his views on current political events. "The world is full of false prophets," begins one; another starts, "Wherever

virtue is lacking, there all worldly power must soon fail and come to a painful end"; and one ends, "Tell the pope, where he is awaited, that all the limbs fare ill when the head is obstinate in evil."

At the same time, Sacchetti was composing song lyrics, combining a popular immediacy of content with a technical interest in various forms for music. One *cactia* describes how girls, gathering flowers and mushrooms in the woods, are scattered by a thunderstorm while the poet, watching them entranced, gets soaked by the rain. "Blessed be the summertime," begins another song. In 1389, during a moment when tension had relaxed, he took part in the garden conversations and entertainments described in *Il paradiso degli Alberti*. He married for a third time in 1396.

During his later years, Sacchetti began to write in prose. His unfinished *Commentary on the New Testament*, perhaps written in 1381, seeks to apply the evangelists' words to problems and issues of daily life. The use of contemporary moral examples in his biblical commentary led to his writing the *Trecentonovelle* (*Three Hundred Stories*, 1385–1397), accounts of recent events or jokes, unframed but surrounded by personal and moral reflections. The work includes serious issues, despite the frequent stories about pranks and witticisms. Although Sacchetti refers to himself in the preface as "unschooled," his life experiences had made him sensitive to the importance of peace and to the prevalence of injustice. A number of *novelle* comment on how degenerate nobles live by plunder taken from the less fortunate and get away with crimes while the poor, persecuted for minor offenses, have no recourse against the rich and powerful. On the other hand, Sacchetti opposed the presumption of ignorant folk, and several tales present Giotto or Dante wittily putting down ambitious fools. With a clear eye for details of food, dress, and behavior, and with a conversational style, Sacchetti delightfully captured aspects of contemporary life: the difficulty of enforcing dress codes, a chase after a runaway pig, a quarrel between husband and wife, the embarrassment of a youth who trips and falls while eyeing girls, a wet soldier's refuge from his own bare hovel in the warm and well-stocked kitchen of a neighboring ecclesiast. This period also saw the composition of some moral and political *canzoni*, with pleas for peace and moderation. Sacchetti himself collected his poetry over the years into one volume, of which the autograph is preserved in the Laurentian Library in Florence. He compiled his collection of tales in the 1380s and 1390s. Of the 300 stories, 223 survived, a few with gaps or in fragments. Besides these writings, we have sixteen of his letters and a notebook, never intended for publication.

Sachetti died at San Miniato, where he was governor. His tales went unappreciated by the humanists of the following century, but two sixteenth-century manuscripts survived. The first printed edition of a selection of tales appeared in 1724.

See also **Boccaccio, Giovanni**

Further Reading

Editions and Translation

La Battaglia delle belle donne, le Lettere, le Sposizioni di Vangeli, ed. Alberto Chiari. Bari: Laterza, 1938.

Il libro delle rime, ed. Alberto Chiari. Bari: Laterza, 1936.

Opere, ed. Aldo Borlenghi. Milan: Rizzoli, 1957. (*Trecentonovelle, Sposizioni di Vangeli, Libro delle rime, Lettere.*)

Tales from Sacchetti, trans. Mary Steegman. London: Dent, 1908. (Eighty-three prudishly selected tales.)

Trecentonovelle, ed. Vincenzo Pernicone. Florence: Sansoni, 1946.

Il Trecentonovelle, ed. Antonio Lanza. Florence: Sansoni, 1984.

Critical Studies

Barbi, Michele. "Per una nuova edizione delle *Novelle* del Sacchetti." *Studi di Filologia Italiana*, 1, 1927, pp. 87–131.

Caretti, Lanfranco. *Saggio sul Sacchetti*. Bari: Laterza, 1951.

Croce, Benedetto. *Poesia popolare e poesia d'arte*. Bari: Laterza, 1933, pp. 94–105.

Curato, Baldo. *Lettura del Sacchetti*. Cremona: Gianni Mangiarotti, 1966.

Francia, Letterio di. *Franco Sacchetti, novelliere*. Pisa: Tipografia Successori Fratelli Nistri, 1902.

———. *Novellistica*. Milan: Vallardi, 1924, pp. 260–300.

Li Gotti, Ettore. *Franco Sacchetti, uomo "discolo e grosso."* Florence: Sansoni, 1940.

Li Gotti, Ettore, and Nino Pirrotta. *Il Sacchetti e la tecnica musicale del Trecento italiano*. Florence: Sansoni, 1935.

Pernicone, Vincenzo. *Fra. rime e novelle del Sacchetti*. Florence: Sansoni, 1942.

Wilkins, Ernest Hatch. *A History of Italian Literature*, rev. ed., ed. Thomas G. Bergin. Cambridge, Mass.: Harvard University Press, 1974, 117–119.

JANET LEVARIE SMARR

SÆMUNDR SIGFÚSSON INN FRÓÐI
("the learned"; 1056–1133)

To his contemporaries, Sæmundr was known as a pre-eminent churchman and a man of great learning. To modern scholarship, he is known primarily as a founding father of historical writing in Iceland, and of the great dynasty of the Oddaverjar ("men of Oddi"). At various points in the intervening centuries, folklore accused him of sorcery, while scholarly speculation credited him with the *Eddas* and with sagas ranging from *Njáls saga* to *Jómsvíkinga saga*.

"Sæmundr (prestr) inn fróði" is mentioned several times in the *biskupa sögur* (especially *Hungrvaka, Kristni saga*, and the sagas of Jón Qmundarson), *Íslendingabók*, annals, genealogies, and in other historical writings. But there is no coherent medieval account of his life, and virtually nothing by him survives in writing, so that much remains unknown.

Sæmundr, the son of a priest, was born into a distinguished family that had lived at Oddi, South Iceland, since about 900. He studied for some years in "Frakkland." The *Oddaverja annáll* for 1077 specifies Paris, but this may be no more than a surmise, as is the suggestion by modern scholars that Sæmundr attended the cathedral school of Notre Dame in Paris. An entertaining account of his return to Iceland in Gunnlaugr Leifsson's *Jóns saga helga* (early 13th century) tells how Jón and Sæmundr outwitted the master astrologer who held Sæmundr in his power. This legend seems to contain the germ of later folktales in which Sæmundr, learned in the black art, uses his cleverness to foil the Devil.

After his return to Iceland in or after 1076, Sæmundr was ordained priest and became a "pillar of the church," building a new church at Oddi dedicated to St. Nicholas, increasing its endowments and clergy, and preaching and dispensing wise counsel in the neighborhood. He probably also had a school there, for he is said in *Sturlu saga* (ch. 1) to have fostered Oddi Þorgilsson, who, like Sæmundr himself, became *fróðr*, "learned (especially in native lore)." Of still greater national importance was Sæmundr's part, with the bishops, in establishing tithe laws (1096) and other ecclesiastical laws.

Little else is known of Sæmundr's life or activities as priest and secular chieftain, because the records are slight and the times relatively uneventful. However, it is known that he and his two brothers married the three daughters of Kolbeinn Flosason. With his wife, Guðrún, he had three sons and a daughter, and their descendants, who came to be known as the Oddaverjar, in many senses built on the foundations laid by Sæmundr at Oddi. Their power and wealth, augmented especially by the tithes and other revenues paid to family-owned churches, overtook those of other chieftainly families during the time of Sæmundr's distinguished grandson Jón Loptsson (1124–1197), and were maintained throughout the following decades without the viciousness found elsewhere. The intellectual tradition of Oddi also flourished. Sæmundr's son, the priest Eyjólfr, had a school there attended by the future St. Þorlákr; Jón Loptsson fostered and educated Snorri Sturluson there. Jón's son, the bishop Páll, compiled a miracle book of St. Þorlákr, and is himself the subject of one of the *biskupa sögur.* The poem *Nóregs konunga tal* was composed around 1190 to celebrate Jón Loptsson's descent through his mother from the Norwegian kings; other works, notably *Orkneyinga saga* and *Skjǫldunga saga,* may have links with Oddi.

Sæmundr is frequently named as an authority by medieval Icelandic historians, and these references provide the main clues about his learning and its transmission. That he composed a work, now lost, on the rulers of Norway from Haraldr hárfagri ("fair-hair") in the late 9th century down to Magnús góði ("the good," d. 1046/7) is suggested by *Nóregs konunga tal* (st. 40), which acknowledges Sæmundr inn fróði as its model for the lives (*ævi*) of these eleven rulers. The scraps of information attributed to Sæmundr elsewhere, however, especially concern the late 10th century: the length of Hákon jarl's reign (in Oddr Snorrason's *Óláfs saga Tryggvasonar*); the number of ships in the Jómsviking fleet at Hjǫrungavágr (Liavåg) (in AM 510 4to, a late MS of *Jómsvikinga saga*); details of Óláfr Tryggvason's christianization of Norway (in a fifty-word quotation from Sæmundr in Oddr Snorrason's saga); and the date of his death (in Ari Þorgilsson's *Íslendingabók*). Sæmundr is also named in certain versions of the Icelandic annals as authority for the ice-bound Scandinavian winter of 1047. It seems from all this evidence, and from the example of the near-contemporary *Íslendingabók,* that Sæmundr's legacy to later historiography must have been a chronological scheme, with brief narratives on each ruler, in a sober style but with Christian bias.

Sæmundr's presumed history was probably written rather than oral, especially since the long quotation from Sæmundr in Oddr Snorrason's saga (which survives only in Icelandic versions of a Latin original) is followed by "Svá hefir Sæmundr ritað um Óláf konung i sinni bók" ("Thus has Sæmundr written about King Óláfr in his book"). Storm (1873: 15) and Meissner (1902: 35ff.) nevertheless disputed that there was a written work by Sæmundr. The language seems to have been Latin, for Snorri Sturluson, in his prologue to *Óláfs saga helga* and *Heimskringla,* refers to Ari Þorgilsson as the first writer of history in Norse, although Sæmundr, an older contemporary whom Ari consulted over the writing of *Íslendingabók,* probably completed his history first. The nature of Sæmundr's writing and its influence on other histories of Norway, such as *Fagrskinna, Ágrip, Historia Norwegiae,* and even on *Knýtlinga saga,* have been much discussed by scholars such as Bjarni Aðalbjarnarson, Siegfried Beyschlag, Svend Ellehøj, and Bjarni Guðnason (see the summary in Andersson 1985).

Sæmundr is also acknowledged as an authority for certain facts about Iceland, including its discovery by the Viking Naddoddr (*Landnámabók, Sturlubók* text), but whether such matters were included in the history of Norwegian kings, whether there was a separate work on Iceland, and whether some of Sæmundr's more fragmentary pieces of learning were at first only transmitted orally cannot now be established. The "oral" theory is supported by the report in *Kristni saga,* that "in that year [1118–1119], there was such great loss of life, that the priest Sæmundr the learned said [*sagði*] at the þing that no fewer must have died of sickness than had come to the þing." It is also possible that Sæmundr simply became a model of learning, to whom miscellaneous facts could be attached. This tendency could apply to such patently clerical facts as the details about the creation of the sun and the moon (in AM 624 4to) or the body of Adam (in AM 764 4to).

The title *Sæmundar Edda* appeared on editions of the *Codex Regius* poems of the *Poetic Edda* until well into this century, and this attribution goes back to 16th- and 17th-century theories that credited Sæmundr first with the *Prose Edda* (now attributed to Snorri) and then with the *Codex Regius* poems. The connection may not be completely unfounded, for it is possible, as Halldór Hermannsson (1932) argued, that Snorri found the poetic materials for his *Edda* at Oddi, and that Sæmundr had a hand in collecting them.

See also **Snorri Sturluson**

Further Reading

Literature

Storm, Gustav. *Snorre SturlassMns Historieskrivning.* Copenhagen: Luno, 1873.

Meissner, Rudolf. *Die Strengleikar: Ein Beitrag zur Geschichte der almordischen Prosalitteratur.* Halle: Niemeyer, 1902.

Halldór Hermannsson. *Sæmund Sigfússon and the Oddaverjar.* Islandica, 22. Ithaca: Cornell University Library, 1932.

Buckhurst, Helen T. McM. "Sæmundr inn fróði in Icelandic Folklore." *Saga-Book of the Viking Society* 11 (1928–36), 84–92.

Einar Ól. Sveinsson. *Sagnaritun Oddaverja. Nokkrar athuganir.* Studia Islandica, 1. Reykjavik: Ísafold, 1937 [English summary, pp. 47–51].

Turville-Petre, G. *Origins of Icelandic Literature.* Oxford: Oxford University Press, 1953 rpt. 1975 [esp. pp. 81–7].

Andersson, Theodore M. "Kings' Sagas (*Konungasögur*)." In *Old Norse–Icelandic Literature: A Critical Guide.* Ed. Carol J. Clover and John Lindow. Islandica, 45. Ithaca and London: Cornell University Press, 1985 [esp. pp. 197–211].

DIANA EDWARDS WHALEY

SALADIN (SALĀH AL-DĪN YŪKSUF B. AYYŪB) (A.H. 564–589 / 1138–1193 C.E.)

Sultan of Egypt and Syria, Saladin led military ventures that won back for Islam much of the territory in the Holy Land occupied by Western crusaders. Saladin was born at Tekrit into a Kurdish family in service to 'Imād-al-Dīn Zangī of Mosul; Saladin served 'Imād-al-Dīn's son, Nūr al-Dīn Emir of Syria. At this time, political and moral authority was divided between, the Fātimid caliphate of Cairo and the Abbasid caliphate of Baghdad; regions and cities were held by independent warlords, and wide divisions separated the general population from the military men who wielded power. The crusader states, with their small populations, represented an additional irritating complication, a potential if not an actual threat.

After serving for ten years in Nūr al-Dīn's court at Damascus, Saladin accompanied his uncle Shīrkūh to Egypt on an expedition, during which Shīrkūh seized effective power in Cairo in 1169; Shīrkūh died almost immediately, and Saladin succeeded him in command. He played a dual role as Fātimid vizier and as Nūr al-Dīn's subordinate until the caliph's death in 1171 and Nūr al-Dīn's in 1174. Saladin proclaimed himself sultan of Egypt, with authority over Mesopotamia, and initiated the Ayyūbid dynasty. Part of the rest of his career was spent in a power struggle with the Zangids, in the course of which he successfully established his power in Syria, where he took Damascus and later Aleppo with the aid of his brother Tūrānshāh. He failed, however, to subdue the city of Mosul completely, or to win unqualified approval from the Abbasid caliphs.

Saladin represented himself as the champion of Islam against the crusaders, a role whose potentialities had been developed by Nūr al-Dīn, and his intermittent campaigns against the crusader states culminated in the battle of Hattin (near Tiberias) in 1187, in which he destroyed the field army of the Latin Kingdom of Jerusalem; he went on to capture Jerusalem and take most of the crusader strongholds. Tyre, however, provided the crusaders with a base, and Saladin's victories prompted the calling of the Third Crusade in 1189, during which the western armies were able only to capture Acre. Although the engagements between Christian and Muslim forces were to a degree politically indecisive, they greatly influenced cultural life in the West owing to the famous encounter between England's King Richard the Lionheart (r. 1189–1199) and Saladin. The sultan's ensuing reputation for generosity and chivalry earned him a place of honor in medieval romance, and even Dante located his soul in Limbo. The crusaders were not strong enough to recapture Jerusalem but neither could Saladin clear them from the coast. This stalemate led to a truce in 1192, the Peace of Ramleh [Ramla], shortly after which Saladin died.

Cristofano dell' Altissimo (c. 1525–1605). Portrait of Saladin, Sultan of Egypt. © SEF/Art Resource, New York.

During the late 1100s, trade was an important source of revenue, which Saladin needed for his military campaigns. The armament industry and the slave trade flourished, and anecdotal evidence indicates that trade routes remained open even while wars were being fought nearby, and that huge profits could be made from military supplies (although risks of loss were also high). During the Third Crusade (1189–1192) there was considerable interference with Mediterranean shipping, but Saladin enjoyed the benefits of an open trade route between Egypt and India (via the Red Sea, thanks to the extension of his control over Yemen).

Saladin unquestionably changed the pattern of Middle Eastern history, not so much because he established his own dynasty (the Ayyūbids were short-lived) but, immediately, because he gave the coup-de-grâce to the ailing Fātimid dynasty. He also made Europe aware that retaining crusader states would involve enormous effort and expense. As a corollary to this, he demonstrated the increasing importance of an efficient, if expensive, professional army, which later contributed to the refinement of the Mamluk system; this, arguably, led to a profound change in the economic and social resources of Egypt and Syria.

See also **Dante Alighieri; Richard I**

Further Reading

Ehrenkreutz, Andrew S. *Saladin.* Albany: State U of New York P, 1972.

Gibb, H.A.R. *The Life of Saladin: From the Works of Imad ad-Din and Baha ad-Din.* Oxford: Clarendon, 1973.

Lyons, Malcolm Cameron, and D.E.P. Jackson. *Saladin: The Politics of the Holy War.* Cambridge and New York: Cambridge UP, 1997.

MALCOLM C. LYONS

SALIMBENE DE ADAM
(1221–c. 1289)

What we know of Fra Salimbene de Adam of Parma is based entirely on the *Chronicle*, his only extant work. In it Salimbene tells us that he was born to Guido de Adam and Inmelda de Cassio, members of two well-established families in Parma. He was christened Balian of Sidon but was simply called Ognibene by his family. In 1238 he entered the Franciscan order and was given the name Salimbene by the last friar Saint Francis had admitted to the order. During his novitiate, Salimbene met Bernard of Quintavalle, the first friar Saint Francis had admitted to the order; and Elias of Cortona, the order's first minister general.

After completing his novitiate at Fano, Salimbene went to a convent in Lucca where he studied music and first saw the Holy Roman emperor Frederick II. From there he moved to Siena, where he continued his study of music and came into contact with the theories of Joachim of Fiore through the work of Hugo of Digne. From 1243 to 1247 Salimbene was in Pisa, where his education in Joachism continued under Rudolf of Saxony. Salimbene's acquaintance with some of the most distinguished people of his rime continued during his trips to France in 1247–1248. At Provins he met the Joachist Gerard of Borgo San Donnino. At Villefranche and at Sens he met Giovanni di Piano Carpini, the Franciscan provincial general of Germany and Spain, who had been an emissary for Pope Innocent IV at the court of the khan Guyuk at Karakoram in Mongolia. At Hyères Salimbene heard the lectures of Hugo of Digne, and at Auxerre he met Saint Louis of France. In 1248 he was ordained a priest at Genoa; later he was sent to Ferrara, where he remained for seven years. He probably spent the years 1279–1285 in Reggio Emilia and its province, where, in 1283, he began working on the *Chronicle*. In 1287 he moved to Montefalcone, where he died shortly after 1288.

Despite his close contact with several of the leading thinkers of his time, and despite the opportunities to study at several of the most important universities of his day (he spent a week studying at the University in Paris but left without the permission of his superiors), Salimbene's intellectual background is regarded by scholars as superficial. His knowledge of the Bible was thorough, as is shown by his extensive use of biblical quotations throughout the *Chronicle*; but as scholars have indicated, these quotations are used to support statements which often have little if anything to do with the Bible. Scholars concur that even when Salimbene discusses issues about which he was knowledgeable (such as the prophesies of Joachim of Fiore and the relative merits and shortcomings of Elias of Cortona), he is often subjective and biased.

Salimbene's numerous acquaintances and travels provided him with plenty of material for his *Chronicle*. Besides narrating famous and less-known events in Italy and France, the *Chronicle* also narrates personal moments in Salimbene's life and that of his family. The *Chronicle* is regarded by scholars as historically accurate for the most part, but its importance is not purely historical. As Baird (1986) has shown, it is the earliest account of the spread of Joachism within the Franciscan order, as well as an important document of Franciscan life in the thirteenth century and the extent to which the Franciscan order had deviated from Saint Francis's original rule. Salimbene does not hesitate to reveal his own worldly interests while narrating the worldliness of his age. His narrative, however, also includes *exempla* of spiritual piety; as seen in his characterizations of Saint Louis of France, John of Parma (minister general of the Francis can order), and even himself (Salimbene's visions of the holy family are narrated in great detail). In fact his extensive use of *exempla* gives the *Chronicle* a narrative style that anticipates Boccaccio's *Decameron*. The *exempla* are an integral part of the *Chronicle* and are used not only to illustrate a moral but also to produce comic effects. Moreover, these *exempla* are rich in detail making the characterizations both vivid and realistic (Auerbach 1957).

In addition to vivid portraits of well-known and lesser-known people of his time, Salimbene himself often appears in the *Chronicle*, giving the work an autobiographical dimension. He comes across as having a great interest in worldly matters, and (as Baird notes) he often expresses contempt for qualities he himself is guilty of, indicating a contradictory or ambiguous personality. Nevertheless, Salimbene's candid and uninhibited nature suggests that he is true to himself throughout the *Chronicle*, even when his evaluation of others (e.g., Elias of Cortona) is not as truthful.

The *Chronicle* has come down to us in a single manuscript: (Vatican Latin 7260) of which the first 277 folios are missing. The manuscript, written by Salimbene himself, narrates events from 1168 to 1287. The years 1168–1212 are based on Sicardo of Cremona's *Chronicle*; and the historic events occurring from 1212 to 1283 (the year Salimbene began writing the work) seem to have much in common with two chronicles attributed to Albert Milioli: *Liber de temporibus* and *Cronica imperatorm*. Not until the twentieth century did Salimbene's *Chronicle* receive the scholarly and critical attention it deserves.

See also **Frederick II; Giovanni di Piano Carpini; Joachim of Fiore**

Further Reading

Editions and Translation
The Chronicle of Salimbene de Adam, trans. Joseph L. Baird, Giuseppe Baglívi, and John Robert Kane. Medieval and Renaissance Texts and Studies, 40. Binghamton, N.Y.: Medieval and Renaissance Texts and Studies, 1986. (With bibliography.)
Cronica Fratris Salimbene de Adam, 2 vols., ed. Ferdinando Bernini Scrittori d'Italia, 187–188. Bari: Laterza, 1942.
Salimbene de Adam. *Cronica*, 2 vols., ed. Giuseppe Scalia. Scrittorl d'Italia, 232–233. Bari: Laterza, 1966.

Critical Studies
Auerbach, Erich. *Mimesis*. New York: Doubleday, 1957, pp. 187–188.
Auzzas, Ginetta. "Salimbene da Parma." In *Dizionario critico della letteratura italiana*, 3 vols. Turin: UTET, 1973, Vol. 3, pp. 293–294.
Carile, Antonio. *Salimbene e la sua opera storiografica*: *Delle lezioni tenute alla. Facoltà di Magistero dell'Università di Bologna nell'anno accademico 1970–1971*. Bologna: Pàtron, 1971.
Coulton, George Gordon. *From Saint Francis to Dante*. New York: Russell and Russell, 1968.
Crocco, Antonio. *Federico II nella Cronica di Salimbene*. Naples: Empireo, 1970.
D'Alatri, Mariano, and Jacques Paul. *Salimbene da Parma*: *Testimone e cronista*. Rome: Istituto Storico dei Cappuccini, 1992.
Sainati, Augusto. *Studi di letteratura latina medievale e umanistica*: *Raccolti in occasione del suo ottantacinquesimo compleanno*. Padua: Antenore, 1972.
Violante, Cinzio. *La cortesia chiericale e borghese nel Duecento*. Florence: Olschki, 1995.

STEVEN GROSSVOGEL

SALUTATI, COLUCCIO (1331–1406)

Coluccio Salutati was born at Stignano, on the frontier between Ghibelline Lucca and Guelf Florence, and was carried into exile when the Ghibellines seized power in the area shortly after his birth. He was raised and educated at Bologna, where he studied under Pietro da Moglio, a member of the third generation of Italian humanists. Salutati was trained as notary and in 1350–1351, after his father's death, he returned to Stignano with his family and began practicing his profession. Between 1351 and 1367 Salutati earned his living as a notary, but by 1356 he was already playing a major political role in the rural commune of Buggiano, of which Stignano formed one of four villages. He married a local woman, Caterina di Tomeo di Balducci, in 1366.

In 1367 he moved to Todi to become its chancellor; in 1368 he moved to Rome, where he worked in the papal chancery under Francesco Bruni. After being unable to find suitable employment with the papacy, Salutati became chancellor of Lucca with Bruni's help in 1370. Almost immediately, however, he became embroiled in a factional dispute, and in 1371 he lost his position and reluctantly returned to Stignano. He had lost his first wife while he was still in Lucca; sometime between 1372 and 1374, widowed with a small boy, he married Piera, the daughter of Simone Riccomi. He and Piera had at least eight children.

Salutati was called to Florence in 1374 to assume the newly created secretaryship of the *tratte*, the office supervising elections to Florentine offices; in 1375 he became chancellor. As the official responsible for conducting the Florentine government's correspondence with the provinces and with foreign powers, he almost immediately established his reputation as the greatest author of official letters in western Europe. He was able to demonstrate his virtuosity immediately, because 1375 marked the beginning of a three-year war between Florence and the papacy, a war whose major battles were propaganda campaigns designed to retain and attract allies. Perhaps his greatest epistolary triumphs came in 1390–1406, when he assumed responsibility for representing to western European powers the issues involved in Florence's bitter struggle with the Visconti of Milan. Florence's archenemy, Gian Galeazzo Visconti, is said to have stated that "a letter of Salutati's was worth a troop of horses." Having been chancellor for thirty-one years, during which time he navigated the troubled waters of Florentine political life with unerring tact, Salutati died in 1406.

Salutati was influenced, after 1367, by Petrarch's concern with integrating Christianity and pagan letters, but he never achieved the mature Petrarch's confidence in their harmoniousness. Salutati, who is less classicizing in style than Petrarch and more obviously intrigued by scholastic philosophy and theology, betrays, the weak welds in Christian humanism. Although he was a family man and a devout Florentine patriot, his *De seculo et religione* (1381), praising the superiority of the monastic life, represented a genuine ascetic element in his thought. His last private letters unambiguously affirm his allegiance to Christian truth over and against pagan culture. Nonetheless, up to the last year of his life his devotion to ancient literature remained strong. Under his influence, Florence brought the great Greek scholar Manuel Chrysoloras from Constantinople in 1397 to teach Greek at the university. Whereas a previous attempt in 1360–1362, with Leonzio Pilato, had failed to arouse the interest of the city's young people, the arrival of Chrysoloras marked the rebirth of Greek studies in western Europe.

Salutati made Florence the capital of this major movement in European cultural and intellectual life through his prestige as chancellor; the fame of his public letters; his eagerness to relate classical studies to moral and religious problems of his day; his effort to encompass within a continuous tradition the ancient Latin authors, the church fathers, and the medieval rhetoricians; and his successful introduction of Hellenic studies into the Latin west. That Florence was the center of humanistic studies down to the mid-fifteenth century testifies enduring intellectual legacy.

See also **Petrarca, Francesco**

Further Reading

Epistolario di Coluccio Salutati, ed. Francesco Novati. Fonti per la Storia d'Italia, 15–18. Rome. 1891–1916.

Ullman, Berthold L. *The Humanisum of Coluccio Salutati*. Medioevo e Umanesimo, 4 Padua: Antenore, 1983.

Witt, Ronald G. *Hercules at the Crossroads: The Life, Works, and Thought of Coluccio Salutati*. Durham, N.C.: Duke University Press, 1983.

RONALD G. WITT

SANCHO III, KING OF NAVARRE
(r. 1000–1035)

The reign of Sancho III Garcés, known as "el Mayor" (1000–1035) was a pivotal one, not only for Navarre but for all of Christian Spain. Possessed with prodigious political talents, he brought his small kingdom of Navarre to its apogee in the Middle Ages. Because the decline of Muslim influence in the region left him relatively free to focus his attentions elsewhere, he made no serious efforts to continue the Reconquest. Instead, he set about unifying all the Christian states except Castile under his rule. His cultural and political influences were French, and by his outlook and his actions he helped draw Spain out of its isolation and incorporate it into the rest of Western Christendom.

His inheritance was small—little more than a string of tiny counties in the foothills of the Pyrenees—but by skillful manipulation of marriage alliances, Sancho was able to widen his domains by acquiring adjacent territories. An important factor in his success was the marriage of his sister Urraca to King Alfonso V of León. Through Urraca, Sancho III continued to be a real power in that kingdom even after Alfonso's death. While Urraca served as regent for her son, Vermudo, Sancho gained control of Aragón and the old Marches counties of Sobrarbe and Ribagorza to the east of Aragón.

From his base in León, Sancho extended his influence to Castillian affairs through his brother-in-law García Sanchez, the count of Castile. When García Sanchez was murdered in 1029, Sancho took possession of Castile in

his sister's name and designated his own son, Fernando, as heir. The Navarrese dynasty was firmly established in Castile in 1032 when Fernando married his first cousin Sancha, sister of Vermudo III, whose dowry brought to Navarre the disputed lands between the Cea and Pisguerga rivers.

Not all of Sancho's attempts to bring the Pyrenean states under Navarrese hegemony were so fruitful. By holding out the prospect of a military alliance against the Muslims in the central Ebro basin, he forced the count of Barcelona, Ramón Berenguer I (1018–1035), to become his vassal, although neither party would benefit much from this coalition. He tried to press his rights to succession in the duchy of Gascony, but his attempt to link the two Basque-speaking regions under one banner ultimately failed.

His political strength remained in Spain, however, and the high point of his career took place in 1034 when he occupied of the city of León, unseating his nephew Vermudo. Finally, possessing a political authority that encompassed Navarre, León, Aragón, and Castile, he styled himself Emperor of Hispania ("rex Dei gratia Hispaniarum") and coined money in affirmation of his new imperial dignity, thereby laying claim to a peninsular supremacy that had previously been attributed to the king of León.

His imperial career was short-lived, however. He died suddenly the next year, and Vermudo III regained León, ruling it until 1037. Although he governed a unified kingdom, Sancho's adherence to the patrimonial concept of kingship, as was the custom in France, which declared royal domains heritable and divisible among his heirs, made any permanent union of these states impossible. In his will Sancho stipulated that his several realms be divided among his sons, all of whom eventually bore the title of king: Navarre was granted to García III Sánchez (1035–1054); Castile, to Fernando I (1035–1065); and Aragon, to Ramiro I (1035–1063). As a result, the new frontier kingdoms of Castile and Aragón attained the status of kingdoms, and ultimately would overshadow Navarre and León.

His permanent influence on medieval Spanish culture extended far beyond territorial expansion and royal inheritances, however. During his reign, feudal concepts of law and landholding current in France penetrated into the peninsula. Under his aegis, Romanesque artistic styles, especially in architecture, became well established in Spain. He encouraged the pilgrimage to Santiago de Compostela, a principle vehicle for transmission of French ideas. For the convenience of the pilgrims, he modified and improved the difficult route through Álava and the Cantabrian Mountains. And during his reign Cluniac reform was introduced into the monasteries of Oña, Lerie, and San Juan de la Peña.

See also **Alfonso V, King of Aragón,
The Magnanimous; Ramón Berenguer IV,
Count of Barcelona**

Further Reading

Lacarra, J. M. *Historia del reino de Navarra en la Edad Media.* Pamplona, 1975.
O'Callaghan, J. F. *A History of Medieval Spain.* Ithaca, N.Y., 1975.
Pérez de Urbel, J. *Sancho el Mayor de Navarra.* Madrid, 1950.
THERESA EARENFIGHT

SANCHO IV, KING OF CASTILE (1258–1295)

Sancho IV, the second son of Alfonso X and Queen Violante, was born on 12 May 1258 in Valladolid. His sobriquet, "el Bravo," referred to his strength of will and determination. After the sudden death of his older brother Fernando de la Cerda in 1275, Sancho, rejecting the claims of his nephew, Alfonso de la Cerda, and demanded recognition as heir to the throne. Although Alfonso X acknowledged him, continual pressure from France and the papacy led the king to propose giving a portion of his dominions to his grandsons, Alfonso and Fernando, known collectively as the Infantes de la Cerda. Breaking with his father, Sancho, with the consent of the estates of the realm assembled at Valladolid in 1282, assumed royal authority, though he did not take the crown. A desultory civil war followed until the death of Alfonso X on 4 April 1284. Unreconciled and disinherited by his father, Sancho IV, nevertheless, was acclaimed as king and crowned at Toledo.

His situation was exceedingly precarious. Not only did Alfonso de la Cerda, supported by France, dispute his claim to the throne, but the pope had excommunicated Sancho and placed an interdict on his kingdom. The pope also denied the legitimacy of his marriage to his cousin, María de Molina; thus, their children would be considered illegitimate and lack any claim to inherit the throne. By challenging his father and by making many promises that he was unable to carry out, Sancho IV also weakened the authority of the crown.

Throughout his reign he was engaged in an intense struggle to gain control of the straits of Gibraltar in order to prevent any Moroccan invasion in the future. Immediately after his accession he had to provide for the defense of the southern frontier against a new challenge by Abū Yūsuf, the Merinid emir, Alfonso X's last ally. Landing at Tarifa in April 1285, he besieged Jerez while his troops devastated a broad zone from Medina Sidonia to Carmona, Écija, and Seville. While Sancho IV sent his Genoese admiral, Benedetto Zaccaria, to protect the mouth of the Guadalquivir, a Castilian fleet of about one hundred ships waited in the straits to relieve Jerez or to disrupt the emir's communications with Morocco. When Sancho IV marched southward from Seville to Jerez, Abk Yksuf decided not to test his fortunes in battle, and retreated to the safety of Algeciras in August. Two months later Sancho IV made peace with the emir.

Meanwhile, after the failure of the French crusade against Aragón, Sancho IV, because of continuing concern over the claims of Alfonso de la Cerda, was under pressure to enter an alliance with either kingdom. On the one hand, Philippe IV of France was Alfonso's cousin while Alfonso III of Aragón had custody of the two Infantes de la Cerda. Lope Díaz de Haro, lord of Vizcaya, who had much to do with securing Sancho IV's recognition as heir to the Castilian throne, preferred the alliance with Aragón as a guarantee that Alfonso de la Cerda would not be free to press his claims. Lope was the most influential person in the realm because the king had given him control over the royal household and finances as well as custody of all royal strongholds. Other members of the royal council eventually convinced Sancho IV that he had entrusted Lope with far too much authority. Thus the king turned against him in 1288 and caused his death in a violent scene.

Now free to decide for himself, Sancho IV broke with Aragón and allied with France. He expected that the continual threat of French intervention on behalf of the Infantes de la Cerda and papal opposition to the legitimation of his marriage and his children would be eliminated. He also promised to give the Infantes joint rule over Murcia and Ciudad Real as an independent realm, provided they renounced all claims to Castile. At that, Alfonso III of Aragón liberated the Infantes and proclaimed Alfonso de la Cerda as king of Castile. Inconclusive border warfare followed until 1291, when the new king of Aragón, Jaime II, concerned about his capacity to retain the kingdom of Sicily against papal opposition, decided to make peace. Jaime II left the Infantes de la Cerda to fend for themselves and agreed with Sancho IV on zones of future exploitation and conquest in North Africa.

The conclusion of this treaty came at an opportune moment because the Merinids were preparing to resume hostilities as soon as the truce with Castile ran out. Although Benedetto Zaccaria, again in Castilian service, defeated the Moroccan fleet in August 1291, Abū Ya'qūb, the Merinid emir, invaded Spain soon after. In the spring of 1292, Sancho IV, aided by Muḥammad II of Granada (who feared the Merinids), besieged Tarifa, a port often used by Moroccan forces entering Spain. Sancho IV entered the town in triumph on 13 October 1292. The king of Granada, who had expected that Tarifa would be restored to him, now broke with Castile and joined the Moroccans in a new siege of Tarifa in 1294. Nevertheless, Alfonso Pérez de Guzmán, known thereafter as "el bueno," successfully defended Tarifa until a Castilian and Catalan fleet compelled the enemy to withdraw. The capture and subsequent defense of Tarifa was the first stage in closing the gates of the peninsula to future Moroccan invasions.

Not long after Sancho IV died on 25 April 1295, his wife María de Molina, whom he married at Toledo in July 1282, became regent for their son, Fernando IV. Sancho wrote a book of counsel titled *Castigos e documentos* for Fernando.

See also **Alfonso X, El Sabio, King of Castile and León; Molina, María de; Philip IV the Fair**

Further Reading

Gaibrois de Ballesteros, M. *Historia del reinado de Sancho IV.* 3 vols. Madrid, 1922.

JOSEPH F. O'CALLAGHAN

SAXO GRAMMATICUS (13th century)

Toward the end of the 12th century, the Danish historian Sven Aggesen wrote that his old associate Saxo was composing a full-length history of the Danish kings of the previous century. Four MS fragments of this work (one, from Angers, probably autograph), a compendium of around 1345, and an edition printed at Paris in 1514 from a lost MS provide the surviving evidence for Saxo's achievement. It was printed under the title of *Danorum Regum Heroumque Historiæ* ("The History of the Kings and Heroes of the Danes"), but is usually known by the earlier description *Gesta Danorum* (alias *De Gestis Danorum*).

Saksi was not an uncommon name in medieval Denmark, and the historian cannot be identified for sure with any who bore it. *Grammaticus* "the learned" and *Longus* "the tall" are posthumous by-names. From his own words, we learn that he came from a warrior family, and that he joined the household of King Valdemar I's foremost adviser, Absalon, bishop of Roskilde (1158–1192) and archbishop of Lund (1178–1201), who encouraged him to write history. His partiality for Zealand suggests that he came from that island. He may have been educated abroad, and his familiarity with church business argues that he became a clerk of some sort, but probably not a monk. He was also familiar with war and seamanship. In Absalon's will, "my cleric Saxo" was forgiven a small debt, and required to send two borrowed books to the Cistercians of Sorø. Saxo completed his work under the patronage of Archbishop Anders (1201–1223), probably after 1216, and dedicated it to Anders and King Valdemar II.

During Saxo's lifetime, Denmark achieved dominance over the Baltic lands; Danes also came into closer contact with the intellectual life of the southern countries their ancestors had raided. Saxo aimed to provide them with a national history in Latin comparable to those of other European peoples. The only foreign historians he mentions are Bede, Dudo of St.-Quentin, and Paulus Diaconus; he was less influenced by them in his concept of the nation than by Vergil's *Aeneid*, and by the historical abridgments of the Roman authors Valerius Maximus and Justin. His view of morals and mythology owed much to Horace, Ovid, and Cicero; and the tone of his work coincides with the humanistic scholarship of the 12th century as expounded in the schools of northern France (e.g., by William of Conches and John of Salisbury), as well as with the contemporary epics of Galterus de Castellione (*Alexandreis*) and Geoffrey of Monmouth (*Historia regum Britanniae*).

Other Danish authors (e.g., the Roskilde Chronicler, the Lejre Chronicler, Sven Aggesen) had made pioneer attempts to record the Danish past in Latin, but Saxo found them inadequate. He had no use for the annalists of Lund, nor for conventional chronology, and the northern genealogists failed to provide him with enough kings. He claimed to be restoring lost native traditions and interpreting runic memorials, but these claims seem unfounded. He took most of his legendary and heroic material from wandering Icelanders and their MSS, relocating stories from their international repertoire within Denmark. He claimed that Archbishop Absalon's own words were his main source for modern history, but he must have used other written sources now lost. His debt to biblical ideas and language was small.

The work published in 1514 begins with a preface including a geographical description of the northern world, and is divided into sixteen books of unequal length. Books 1–4 deal with the Danes before the birth of Christ, 5–8 with the period down to the establishment of the Church in Denmark. Books 9–12 cover events from the Conversion to the promotion of Lund as a metropolitan see, and 13–16 run from 1104 to 1187.

The first eight books differ from the rest in the greater fluency of the prose and the inclusion of verse in a variety of meters. The basic subdivisions are the reigns of over seventy kings. Saxo begins with the election of the eponymous Dan as the first ruler, and the dethronement of the first two kings, Humblus and Lotherus, by unjust and justified violence. Then Skioldus and Hadingus appear as types of the heroism, luck, and virtue essential for effective kingship even in a pagan world. These kings, and Frotho I in Book 2, are names derived from Old Norse poetry and invested with attributes and episodes. With Kings Ro (Book 2) and Høtherus (Book 3), he made versions of the legends now found in the

Snorra Edda and *Skjǫldunga saga*'s epitome. Amlethus, the prototype of Hamlet, whose career appears in Books 3 and 4, was imported from an undiscovered source, and served as a type of cunning hero dogged by the unkindness of fate and human corruption, a pattern for both kings and tyrannicides. The rest of Book IV tells of the patriotic duelist Uffo, already celebrated by Sven Aggesen as vindicator of the Danish frontier, and known in Anglo-Saxon sources (e.g., *Widsith, Beowulf*, and the Mercian genealogy). The heathen gods, introduced in Book 1 as malign but fallible illusionists, enslave men's minds and lust for their daughters (Baldr and Nanna, Óðinn and Rinda, Book 3).

King Frotho III, an imaginary Danish Caesar contemporary with Christ, takes up Book 5. Helped by his witty companion Erik the Eloquent, he builds an empire over the northern world and civilizes it by enforcing two law codes. His story is enlivened by romance, adventure, and horror, but illustrates the power of words over weapons. In Book 6, this power is taken to excess, when the Danes elect the rustic poet Hiarno to rule them. This same power becomes beneficial and invigorating in the case of the degenerate Ingellus (see Ingjaldr of *Skjǫldunga saga*) and his dauntless and poetic champion Starcatherus, whose satire shamed the king into doing his duty and destroying his enemies. Stories of love, magic, and murder occupy the reign of Halfdanus in Book 7, which ends with the revival of the Danish empire under Haraldus Hyldetan, who is taught the secret of military success by Óðinn. The great fight of Brávalla, in which Óðinn betrays Haraldus to his enemies, begins Book 8; and later on, Starkatherus contrives his own death after a poetic outburst on the duty of vengeance. Jarmericus (Ermanaric the Goth) then appears, as the victim of another treacherous counselor, and in the reign of Snio, famine drives the Lombards to emigrate from Denmark. In two voyages to the underworld, Danish adventurers witness the malign and morbid condition of the old gods and giants. The mighty King Gøtricus is prevented from overthrowing Charlemagne by assassination and Saxo's "Old Testament" ends with Viking heroism betrayed by the heathen gods, powerless against fate.

In Book 9, the supreme Viking Regnerus (Ragnarr loðbrók ["hairy-breeches"]) achieves empire over the whole North, including the British Isles, only to die in Ella's snake pit as a punishment for persecuting the new faith accepted by his less successful rival Haraldus. His avenging sons fail to preserve his empire, and efforts to hold England by a succession of alternately Christian and pagan kings culminate with Gormo's marrying the English heiress Thyra. The English throne falls to their sons by inheritance, but Gormo dies of grief at the death of the elder. More tribulations afflict his successors Haraldus and Sveno in Book 10 (echoes here of Adam of Bremen and the *Roskilde Chronicle*), until both king and people accept the true faith, and Sveno's son Kanutus wins a Christian empire over the whole northern world, including England. He leaves a vigorous Church and a military law code to posterity, and after his son's death the Danes show their probity by accepting the Norwegian Magnús as king in observance of a sworn pact.

In these two books, written sources are distorted and augmented by Nordic legend: tales of Ragnarr, Ívarr, Gorm, the Jómsvikingar, and Palnatoki. From 11 onward, more Latin sources were available, and in 11 to 13 the reigns of Sven II and his five sons (1047–1134) are presented with an eye to earlier accounts, modified or rejected at will. Each ruler serves as an example of good or bad kingship according to his effectiveness against the Slavs and the unruly nobility and people of Denmark. Kings purge their own guilt by spectacular penances, and the people incur death and destruction for the slaying of King Knud (Cnut) the Saint (1086) and Knud (Cnut) Lavard (1131). Book 14 (four times as long as any other) covers the period of civil wars, conspiracy, and dissension among king, bishops, and nobles from 1134 to 1178, when Valdemar I and Absalon succeeded in conquering the Rugian Slavs and restoring unity to the kingdom. Book 15 covers Absalon's first years as archbishop of Lund (1178–1182) and the rebellion of the Scanians against his authority. Book 16 relates how his political mission was fulfilled in the early years against Knud (Cnut) VI (1182–1187) by the declaration of Danish independence against the Emperor Frederick Barbarossa, and by the subjugation of the Pomeranian Slavs.

In the last three books, a copious narrative is enlivened by reported speech and digressions on Norwegian, German, and Slavic affairs. The main source may have been Absalon's own words, but Saxo and the compiler of *Knýtlinga saga* (*ca.* 1260) perhaps used an earlier written source now lost. Books 9–16 are usually supposed to have been written first, before 1201; and the earlier books in the time of Valdemar II. Much of the text must relate to contemporary issues and personalities, but it is difficult to find Saxo advocating any official policy. His patrons were the most powerful men in the kingdom, but he was an idiosyncratic critic of the times, hoping to inspire his fellow countrymen to political unity and civic virtue by the example of former days, as well as to impress learned foreigners. Simplified and excerpted versions of his work were current in Denmark in the later Middle Ages, but it was only after 1514 and the appearance of Anders Sørensen Vedel's Danish translation in 1575 that his view of the Nordic past was widely received both at home and abroad.

See also **Cnut; Sunesen, Anders; Sven Haraldsson (Forkbeard)**

Further Reading

Editions

Pedersen, Christian, ed. *Danorum Regum Heroumque Historiæ.* Paris.

Badius, 1514 [based on complete MS Books 10–16 reproduced in E. Christiansen's trans.; the whole edition was reprinted with minor alterations at Basel in 1534 and Frankfurt in 1576].

Stephanius, Stephanus J., ed. *Saxonis Grammatici Historiæ Danicæ Libri XVI.* Sørø: Crusius, 1645 [usually bound with the following work].

Stephanius, Stephanus J. *Notæ Uberiores in historian Danicam Saxonis.* Sorø: Cntsius, 1645. Reproduced (ed. H. D. Schepelem) by Museum Tusculanum, Copenhagen, 1978. [There were further editions by C. A. Klotz (Leipzig, 1771), P. E. Müller (Copenhagen, 1839, with Prolegomena and Notæ Uberiores by J. M. Velschow, 1858), and A. Holder (Strassburg, 1886).]

Olrik, Jørgen, and H. Ræder, eds. *Saxonis Gesta Danorum.* Vol. 1. Copenhagen: Levin & Munksgaard, 1931. Vol 2. *Indicem Verborum Continens*, by Franz Blatt. Copenhagen: Levin & Munksgaard, 1957. For the 14th-century abridgment, of which four MSS survive, see: Langebek, J., ed. *Thomæ Gheysmeri Compendium Historiæ Danicæ.* In SRD, vol. 2, pp. 286–400. Copenhagen: Godiche, 1773.

Gertz, M. Cl., ed. *Scriptores Minores Historiæ Danicæ.* 2 vols. Copenhagen: Gad, 1917–18. Vol. 1 rpt. by Selskabet for Udgivelse af Kilder til Dansk Historie, Copenhagen, 1970. The four Saxo MS fragments appear in facsimile in vol. 5 of Corpus Codicum Danicorum Medii Aevi. Ed. Johannes Brøndum-Nielsen. Copenhagen: Munksgaard, 1962.

Translation

Elton, Oliver, trans. *The First Nine Books of the Danish History of Saxo Grammaticus.* Folklore Society Publications, 33. London: Nutt, 1893; rpt. 2 vols. New York: Norrœna Society, 1905.

Ellis Davidson, Hilda, ed., and Peter Fisher, trans. *Saxo Grammaticus. The History of the Danes. Books I–IX.* 2 vols. Cambridge: Brewer Totowa: Rowman and Littlefield, 1979–80.

Fisher, Peter. "On Translating Saxo into English." In Friis-Jensen, Karsten, ed. *Saxo Grammaticus: A Medieval Author Between Norse and Latin Culture.* Copenhagen: Museum Tusculanum, 1981, pp. 53–64.

Christiansen, Eric, trans. *Saxo Grammaticus: Danorum Regum Heroumque Historia. Books X–XVI: The Text of the First Edition with Translation and Commentary.* 3 vols. British Archaeological Reports, International Series, vols. 84 and 118 (in two parts). Oxford: B.A.R., 1980–81

Bibliographies

A survey of the most important work done to 1930 was given by Jørgen Olrik in the Latin and Danish Prolegomena to his edition. See further: Skovgaard-Petersen, Inge. "Saxo." *KLNM* 15 (1970), 49–50, and "Saxo" in *Dansk Biografisk Lexicon* 12 (1982), 641–3.

Laugesen, Anker Teilgaard. *Introduktion til Saxo.* Copenhagen: Gyldendal, 1972, pp. 86–7 [meager].

Literature

Two collections of articles contain much recent work: Boserup, Ivan, ed. *Saxostudier. Saxo-kollokvierne ved Københavns universitet.* Copenhagen: Museum Tusculanum, 1975.

Friis-Jensen, Karsten, ed. *Saxo Grammaticus: A Medieval Author Between Norse and Latin Culture* [see above]. These are referred to below as *Saxostudier* and *Saxo-Culture.*

(a) Myth and Legend

Turville-Petre, E. O. G. *Myth and Religion of the North: The Religion of Ancient Scandinavia.* New York: Holt, Rinehart and Winston; rpt. Westpori: Greenwood, 1975, pp. 27–34.

Ellis Davidson, H. R. *Gods and- Myths of Northern Europe.* Harmondsworth: Penguin, 1964.

Dumézil, Georges. *La Saga de Hadingus.* Paris: Presses Universitaires, 1953 [trans. by D. Coltman as *From Myth to Fiction: The Saga of Hadingus* (Chicago: University of Chicago Press, 1973) and reviewed by E. O. G. Turville-Petre in *Saga-Book of the Viking Society* 14 (1953–55), 131–4].

Andersson, Theodore M. "*Niflunga saga* in Light of German and Danish Materials." *Mediaeval Scandinavia* 7 (1974), 22–30.

Dollerup, Cay. *Denmark, Hamlet and Shakespeare.* 2 vols. Salzburg Studies in English Literature, Elizabethan and Renaissance Studies, 47. Salzburg: Institut fúr englische Sprache und Literatur, Universität Salzburg, 1975.

Lukman, Niels. "Ragnar loðbrók, Sigfrid, and the Saints of Flanders." *Mediaeval Scandinavia* 9 (1976), 7–50.

Smyth, Alfred P. *Scandinavian Kings in the British Isles 850–880.* Oxford: Oxford University Press, 1977 [on Ragnarr and his sons].

Strand, Birgit. *Kvinnor och Män i Gesta Danorum.* Kvinnohistoriskt arkiv, 18. Gothenburg: [n.p.], 1980 [English summaryl

Bjarni Guðnason. "The Icelandic Sources of Saxo Grammmaticus." In *Saxo-Culture*, pp. 79–93.

Martinez-Pizarro, Joaquin. "An *Eiriks þáttr málspaka?* Some Conjectures on the Source of Saxo's Ericus Disertus." In *Saxo-Culture*, pp. 105–19.

Skovgaard-Pedersen, Inge. "The Way to Byzantium: A Study in the First Three Books of Saxo's History of Denmark" In *Saxo-Culture*, pp. 121–33.

Strand, Birgit. "Women in Gesta Danorum." In *Saxo-Culture*, pp. 135–67.

(b) History and Ideology

Skovgaard-Petersen, Inge. "Saxo, Historian of the Patria." *Mediaeval Scandinavia* 2 (1969), 54–77.

Damsholt, Nanna. "Kongeopfattelse og kongeideologi hos Saxo." In *Saxostudier*, pp. 148–55.

Riis, Thomas. "Bruddet mellem Valdemar den Store og Eskil 1161. Søborg, diplomerne og Saxo." In *Saxostudier*, pp. 156–66.

Skyum-Nielsen, Niets. "Saxo som kilde til et par centrale institutioner i samtiden." In *Saxostudier*, pp. 175–92.

Weibull, Curt. "Vem var Saxo?" *Historisk tidsskrift* (Denmark) 78 (1978) 87–96.

Riis, Thomas. *Les institutions politiques centrales du Danemark 1100–1332.* Odense University Studies in History and Social Sciences, 46. Odense: Odense University Press, 1977, pp. 14–31, 86–150.

Johannesson, Kurt. *Saxo Grammaticus. Komposition och världsbildi Gesta Danorum.* Stockholm: Almqvist & Wiksell, 1978 [in Swedish, but for an English summary see his "Order in Gesta Danorum and Order in the Creation," in *Saxo-Culture*, pp. 95–104].

Malmros, Rikke. "Blodgildet i Roskilde historiografisk belyst." *Scandia* 45 (1979), 46–66 [English summary].

Weibull, Curt. "Saxos berättelser om de danske vendertågen 1158–1185." *Historisk tidsskrift* (Denmark) 83 (1983), 35–70.

Sawyer, Birgit. "Saxo-Valdemar-Absalon." *Scandia* 51 (1985), 33–60 [English summary].

Sawyer, Birgit. "Valdemar, Absalon and Saxo: Historiography and Politics in Medieval Denmark." *Revue Belge de philologie et d'histoire* 63 (1985), 685–705

Skovgaard-Pedersen, Inge. *Da Tidernes Herre var nær. Studier i Saxos historiesyn.* Copenhagen: Den danske historiske Forening, 1987.

(c) Latinity, Verse, and Manuscripts: Blatt, Franz [Indledning and Præfatio to the Index (vol. 2) of Olrik and Ræder's 1931 edition]

Saxostudier, pp. 1–114, contains thirteen articles in Danish on the language, construction, and analogues of Saxo's work

Friis-Jensen, Karsten. *Saxo og Vergil.* Copenhagen: Museum Tusculanum, 1975 [French summary].

Boserup, Ivan. "The Angers Fragment and the Archetype of Gesta Danorum." *Saxo-Culture*, pp. 9–26.

Friis-Jensen, Karsten. "The Lay of Ingellus and Its Classical Models." *Saxo-Culture*, pp. 65–78.

Friis-Jensen, Karsten. *Saxo Grammaticus as Latin Poet: Studies in the Verse Passages of the Gesta Danorum.* Analecta Romana; Instituti Danici, Supplementum 14. Rome: Bretschneider, 1987.

Friis-Jensen, Karsten. "Was Saxo a Canon of Lund?" *Cahiers de l'institut du moyen-ge grec et latin* 59 (1989), 331–57.

ERIC CHRISTIANSEN

SCHONGAUER, MARTIN (ca. 1450–1491)

Known today primarily as an engraver, this artist, active in Colmar and the Upper Rhine area from circa 1470 until about 1491, was nicknamed Hübsch Martin (Fair Martin) by his contemporaries in praise of his abilities as a painter. He is important as an assimilator of Netherlandish art. His work was influential in Germany, and he attracted many followers, including Albrecht Dürer.

Martin Schongauer was probably born circa 1450 in Colmar, a town south of Strasbourg. Although some have proposed a birth date of about 1430, this view has not found widespread acceptance. His father, Caspar, was a goldsmith, and Martin probably first trained in his shop. His rather apparently wanted his son to become a cleric, for Schongauer's name appears in the 1465 matriculation records of the University of Leipzig. After only one semester, however, he returned to Colmar and began training as a painter. Caspar Isenmann, active in Colmar circa 1435–1472, is often cited as his teacher, but no evidence, documentary or stylistic, supports this assumption. As a journeyman, Schongauer likely traveled to Cologne, then to the Netherlands. His experience of works by the major Netherlandish masters—Roger van der Weyden, Robert Campin, Dieric Bouts, and Hugo van der Goes—is evident in his overall style and in his appropriation of Netherlandish compositions, motifs, and figure types. After his travels, Schongauer settled in Colmar, where he purchased a house in 1469 and again in 1477. He remained there until 1489, when he became a citizen of nearby Breisach. He died there in 1491.

None of Martin Schongauer's paintings are signed. The only dated work attributed to him is the Madonna of the Rose Arbor (Colmar, church of St. Martin), dated 1473 on the reverse. The figure types and detailed, naturalistic rendering of plants and birds are inspired by Netherlandish art. This work's date has been used to establish Schongauer's chronology.

Scholars agree that the earliest preserved works by Schongauer are two wings from the altarpiece commissioned by Jean d'Orlier, preceptor of the Antonite monastery of Isenheim, about 1470 (Colmar, Musée d'Unterlinden). They feature an Annunciation on the exterior, and on the interior, an Adoration and Jean d'Orlier presented by St. Anthony. Schongauer painted several small devotional paintings in the 1480s: two Holy Families (Munich, Alte Pinakothek; Vienna, Kunsthistorisches Museum), an Adoration of the Shepherds (Berlin, Gemäldegalerie), and two versions of the Virgin and Child at a Window (private collections). His last painting, a Last Judgment fresco in Breisach Minster, is based on Roger van der Weyden's Last Judgment Altarpiece of about 1445 (Beaune, Musée de l'Hôtel Dieu).

One-hundred sixteen monogrammed engravings survive, which include both religious and secular subjects. Schongauer's great contributions to the medium were his innovative use of stipling (dots), hatching (fine lines), and crosshatching to create tonal effects like those in paintings, and his adoption of complex compositions derived from paintings. The works are divided into two periods. The early engravings date to the early 1470s. Compositions, as in *Christ Carrying the Cross*, tend to be intricate and crowded with figures, and the system of modeling inconsistent. Mature works, from the late 1470s until his death, contain smaller groups, or single figures, and the modeling is more controlled and logical, as in the *Wise and Foolish Virgins*.

A number of drawings attributed to Schongauer also survive. The recent attribution of a watercolor *Study of Peonies* (private collection) provides insight into Schongauer's working methods (Koreny 1991: 591–596). It was probably executed as a preparatory study from nature for the 1473 *Madonna of the Rose Arbor*.

Further Reading

Baum, Julius. *Martin Schongauer.* Vienna: A. Schroll, 1948.

Le beau Martin: Gravures et dessins de Martin Schongauer vers 1450–1491. Colmar: Musée d'Unterlinden, 1991.

Châtelet, Albert. "Martin Schongauer et les primitifs flamands." *Cahiers alsaciens d'archéologie, d'art et d'histoire* 22 (1979): 117–142.

Dvorak, Max. "Schongauer und die niederländische Malerei," in *Kunstgeschichte als Geitstesgeschichte: Studien zur abendländischen Kunstentwicklung.* Munich: Piper, 1924, pp. 151–189.

Koreny, Fritz. "A Coloured Flower Study by Martin Schongauer and the Development of the Depiction of Nature from van der Weyden to Dürer," *Burlington Magazine* 133 (1991): 588–597.

Rosenberg, Jakob. *Martin Schongauer Handzeichnungen*. Munich: Piper, 1923.
Shestack, Alan. *The Complete Engravings of Martin Schongauer*. New York: Dover, 1969.

SUSANNE REECE

SERCAMBI, GIOVANNI
(1348–27 May 1424)

Giovanni Sercambi was born in Lucca, where his father ran a book and paper store; he thus grew up with a good library at hand. He was educated by private tutors for a government career, and he prospered by supporting the rise to power of the Guinigi family. After 1400, however, feeling neglected by the Guinigi, he withdrew from politics and began to write. Sercambi's works include *A Chronicle of the Affairs of Lucca* (from 1164–1424, including events in which he had participated); the *Monito*, a compendium of advice on finance and administration based on his own experiences in public service; and, in his final years, the *Novelle*, a collection of 155 tales.

The book of advice, dedicated to the Guinigi, advocates practical measures for maintaining control: taking a census of the citizens, forbidding them to possess arms, and ensuring that the legislative council is filled with one's own friends and relatives. The novelle, which draw in part on Sercambi's history of Lucca, are similarly hard-boiled; the collection is filled with tales of deceit, fraud, theft, clerical misbehavior, and the self-serving manipulations of lovers, parents, children, dealers, and clients. A few of the tales are about Sercambi himself, e.g., how he escaped an attack by highway robbers.

The tales are framed by an account of a plague in 1374, during which a group of men and women travel around Italy to avoid the disease. As on some of the actual penitential pilgrimages occasioned by recurring plagues, the travelers agree to pool their money, hear mass every morning, and refrain from sexual activity during the journey. Boccaccio's influence is clear in the setting (the plague), in the inclusion of occasional poems, and in more than twenty of the tales; but instead of having various members of the group narrate in turn, Sercambi's travelers appoint one storyteller to keep them entertained. This character often tells stories appropriate to the places they are visiting: stories of theft near Naples, of Roman history at Rome, of Venetian customs at Venice. Many of the stories are drawn from contemporary or recent events, as well as from Roman myth and history, popular fabliaux, and other medieval collections of tales, such as the *Disciplina clericalis* and the *Decameron*. The titles of the stories suggest the moral categories of preachers' *exempla*: "On Great Prudence," "On Supreme Avarice," "On Supreme Justice," "On Vain Lust," and so forth.

Sercambi's style is rough, and his tales were rarely mentioned before the late 1700s, when one of the two fifteenth-century manuscripts was found. However, since its first printing in Venice in 1816, the *Novelle* has been reprinted many times.

See also **Boccaccio, Giovanni**

Further Reading

Editions and Translation
Le croniche, ed. Salvatore Bongi. Rome: Fonti per la Storia d'Italia Pubblicate dall'Istituto Storico Italiano, 1892.
Italian Renaissance Tales, trans. Janet Smarr. Rochester, N.Y.: Solaris, 1983, pp. 49–68.
Novelle, ed. Giovanni Sinicropi. Scrittori d'Italia, 250–251. Bari: Laterza, 1972.
Novelle, ed. Luciano Rossi, 3 vols. Rome: Salerno, 1974.

Critical Studies
Alexanders, James W. "A Preparatory Study for an Edition of the *Novelle* of Giovanni Sercambi." Dissertation, University of Virginia, 1940.
Di Francia, Letterio. *Novellistica*, Vol. 1. Milan: Vallardi, 1924, pp. 223–260.
Di Scipio, Giuseppe Carlo. "Giovanni Sercambi's *Novelle*: Sources and Popular Traditions." *Merveilles et Contes*, 2, 1988, pp. 25–36.
The Italian Novella: A Book of Essays, ed. Gloria Allaire. New York: Routledge, 2003.
Marietti, Marina. "Imitation et transposition du *Décaméron* chez Sercambi et Sermini: Réécriture et contexte culturelle." In *Réécritures*, Vols. 1–2, *Commentaires, parodies, variations dans la littérature italienne de la Renaissance*. Paris: Université de la Sorbonne Nouvelle, 1984, Vol. 2, 9–68.
Nicholson, Peter. "The Two Versions of Sercambi's *Novelle*." *Italica*, 53, 1976, pp. 210–213.
Petrocchi, Giorgio. "Il novelliere medievale del Sercambi." *Convivium*, 17, 1949.
Plaisance, Michel. "Les rapports ville campagne dans les nouvelles de Sacchetti, Sercambi, et Sermini." In *Culture et société en Italie du Moyen Age à la Renaissance*. Paris: Université de la Sorbonne Nouvelle, 1985, pp. 61–73.
Pratt, Robert A. "Chaucer's Shipman's Tale and Sercambi." *Modern Language Notes*, 55, 1940, pp. 142–145.
Salgarolo, David. "The Jews and Conversion in the Medieval and Renaissance Italian Novella." *NEMLA Italian Studies*, 11–12, 1987–1988, pp. 27–40.
Salwa, Piotr. "Il novelliere sercambiano e il suo contesto lucchese." *Kwartalnik Neofilologiczny*, 33(2), 1986, pp. 207–225.
——. *Narrazione, persuasione, ideologia: Una lettura del "Novelliere" di Giovanni Sercambi, lucchese*. Lucca: Maria Paccini Fazzi Editore, 1991.
Swennen Ruthenberg, Myriam. "The Revenge of the Text: The Real-Ideal Relationship between Giovanni Sercambi's *Croniche* and *Novelliere*." Dissertation, New York University, 1994.
Vivarelli, Ann W. "Giovanni Sercambi's *Novelle* and the Legacy of Boccaccio." *Modern Language Notes*, 90, 1975, pp. 109–127.

JANET LEVARIE SMARR

SEUSE, HEINRICH (1295/1297–1366)

This Dominican priest served as a confessor, preacher, and teacher to religious men and women in the German south. His poetic works in the mystical tradition served to inspire those in his care.

Born into a patrician family in or near Constance, Seuse did not seek out ministerial service but followed in the footsteps of his religiously oriented mother, whose name he chose to use. At thirteen he entered the monastery at Constance. Following a general course of study there, he may have studied briefly in Strasbourg before attending the *studium generate* (early form of university education) in Cologne around 1324 or 1325, where he studied with Meister Eckhart. Seuse probably remained in Cologne until the master's death in 1327, when he returned to Constance and was appointed lector at the monastery. At the age of forty, around 1335, Seuse was told by God to abandon the ascetic practices he had followed for twenty-two years. This turning point in his personal life also marked a change in his professional career: Seuse became an itinerant preacher and spiritual adviser, concentrating his activities in Switzerland, the Alsace, and along the Upper Rhine. Because he supported the pope in a power struggle with Ludwig of Bavaria, Seuse was forced to leave Constance in 1338 or 1339; some eight years later he probably returned. Around 1348 he was transferred to the Dominican monastery in Ulm, where he remained until his death more than fifteen years later. He was canonized in 1831.

In his last years, Seuse undertook the editing of his works for publication, his *Ansgabe letzter Hand;* the works he chose make up the *Exemplar.* Included are his life *(Vita),* which chronicles in third-person narrative the life of the *Diener der ewigen Weisheit* (Servant of Eternal Wisdom), Seuse himself. The authorship of the *Vita* is disputed; the Töß sister Elsbeth Stagel, one of Seuse's spiritual charges, probably played a role in the editing, if not the writing of the work. Following are Seuse's earliest works, the *Büchlein der ewigen Weisheit (Little Book of Eternal Wisdom)* and the *Büchlein der Wahrheit (Little Book of Truth),* two of the most popular devotional tracts in the late medieval mystical tradition. Both are written as dialogues between the Servant and the personification of eternal wisdom and truth, respectively. The *Exemplar* concludes with the *Briefbüchlein (Little Book of Letters),* an edited version of Seuse's correspondence with the Dominican sisters in his charge, primarily those at the convent of Töß. The *Little Book of Love (Minnebüchlein),* whose authenticity is doubtful, and a larger collection of letters, the *Großes Briefbuch* (Great Book of Letters), also survive. Both sets of letters by Seuse are more characteristic of the homiletic rather than the epistolary genre. Indeed, few of his homiletic works are extant, although he was charged with the responsibility of preaching; only two German sermons

are accepted as authentic works of the Dominican friar, but neither is included in the *Exemplar.* The *Horologium sapientiae (Clock of Wisdom)* is the only extant work of the Dominican in Latin; it is an expanded version of the *Büchlein der ewigen Weisheit.*

The religious content of Seuse's work, which draws on the Bernhardian tradition, stands in marked contrast to the speculative mystical theology of his teacher Eckhart. Because of his poetic style and the preeminence of love imagery in his writings, Seuse often is characterized as the *Minnesänger* among the medieval German mystics.

See also **Meister Eckhart**

Further Reading

Bihlmeyer, Karl, ed. *Heinrich Seuse. Deutsche Schrifien.* 1907; rpt. Frankfurt am Main: Minerva, 1961.

Boesch, Bruno. "Zur Minneauffassung Seuses." *Festschrift Josef Quint anläßlich* seines 65. Geburtstages übefreicht, ed. Hugo Moser, Rudolf Schutzeichel, and Karl Stackmann. Bonn: Semmel, 1964, pp. 57–68.

Clark, James M. *The Great German Mystics: Eckhart, Tauler and Suso.* Oxford: Blackwell, 1949.

Colledge, Edmund, and J. C. Marler. 'Mystical' Pictures in the Suso 'Exemplar' *Ms Strasbourg 2929." Archivum Fratrurn Praedicatorum* 54 (1984): 293–354.

Filthaut, Ephrem M., ed. *Heinrich Seuse. Studien zum 600. Todestag, 1366–1966.* Cologne: Albertus Magnus, 1966.

Haas, Alois M., and Kurt Ruh. "Seuse, Heinrich OP," in *Die deutsche Literatur des Mittelalters: Verfasserlexikon,* 2d ed., ed. Kurt Ruh et al. Berlin: de Gruyter, 1992, vol. 8, cols. 1127–1129.

Hamburger, Jeffrey E. "The Use of Images in the Pastoral Care of Nuns: The Case of Heinrich Suso and the Dominicans" *Art Bulletin* 71 (1989): 20–46.

Künzle, Pius. *Heinrich Seuses Horologium sapientiae.* Spicilegium Friburgense 23. Freiburg im Breisgau: Universitätsverlag, 1977.

Stoudt, Debra L. "The Structure and Style of the Letters of Seuses *Großes Briefbuch." Neuphilologische Mitteilungen* 90 (1989): 359–367.

Tobin, Frank. "Coming to Terms with Meister Eckhart: Suso's Buch der Wahrheit." *Semper idem et novus. Festschrift for Frank Banta,* ed. Francis G. Gentry. Göppingen: Kümmerle, 1988, 321–344.

Tobin, Frank. *Henry Suso: The Exemplar, with Two German Sermons.* Mahwah, N.J.: Paulist, 1989.

Walz, Angelus. "Bibliographiae susonianae conatus." *Angelicum* 46 (1969): 430–491.

DEBRA L. STOUDT

SHEM TOV OF CARRIÓN (ca. 1290–1360)

Shem Tov Yiẕḥaq ben Arduti'el, Castilian rabbi and poet whose *Proverbios morales,* addressed to Pedro I and quoted in the Marqués de Santillana's *Prohemio e carta,* synthesizes Semitic poetics with the Spanish idiom in a permutation of a literary formula: the getting of wisdom. Its relative success has eclipsed Shem

Tov's Hebrew compositions *Ma'aseh ha-rav*, a *maqáma* featuring a debate between pen and scissors; *Vam qohelet*, a *baqashah* consisting of two thousand words beginning with the letter *mem*; and, finally, *Ha-vidui ha-gadol*, a prayer of confession for Yom Kippur. This oeuvre provides a useful frame of reference for gauging the ethical, rhetorical, and philosophical dimensions of the *Proverbios morales*. Shem Tov also translated Yisra'el ha-Yisra'eli's liturgical treatise *Miẓvot zemaniyot* from Arabic into Hebrew; the authorship of other titles sometimes attributed to him is dubious. Excluding inferences from his work, the scant known biographical information is obtained from a *dīwán* (book of poetry) written by Shmu'el ben Yosef ben Sason, and places him in Carrión de los Condes in 1338.

Drawing on the language of paremiology, medieval philosophy, the Bible, Talmud, and Arabic wisdom anthologies, *Proverbios morales* examines the ostensible dilemma posed to the individual by the unpredictability of human existence and endorses adherence to the Aristotelian mean in ethical matters, recognition of circumstances in social conduct, and ultimate faith in the Creator. Here, all things exist in complementary opposition—night and day, loss and gain, and so on; therefore wealth is ephemeral, happiness is momentary, and power mere vanity. For the individual, successful negotiation of such a world requires the perspicacious appraisal of circumstance since an action once advantageous may now be disadvantageous, as Shem Tov shows in a paradox on speech and silence. For the monarch, God's representative, duty requires that he vouchsafe truth, justice, and peace, the foundations of political order.

The poem's language is consistent in its general phonetic, morphological, and syntactic features with medieval Castilian. Its distinctive traits include homoioteleuton rhyme, complex hyperbaton, phraseological parallelism, the prevalence of parataxis over hypotaxis, and the accumulation of grammatical functions in pleonastic pronouns.

The suggestion that the poem may be a vestige of a rabbinical *mester de clerecía* (clerical poetry) could ultimately establish its otherwise uncertain generic identity. The 725 alexandrine stanzas reveal a sustained tone of self-assurance in Shem Tov's poetic voice, equally adept at evoking poignancy, melancholy, or whimsy. The antonymic parallelism of his compositional technique, derived from Arabic and Hebrew poetics, sometimes interpreted as indicative of moral relativism, serves to enunciate extremes that define a center of equilibrium.

Each of the six extant manuscripts preserves multiple variants and stanza sequences, several suggest the complex social profile a single work may possess. One is redacted in Hebrew *aljamía* (Cambridge), another includes an anonymous prose prologue (Madrid), and a third records 219 stanzas written from memory and entered into evidence during proceedings for the crime of heresy (Cuenca). The first example implies genesis of the poem's main body for purposes of Jewish education. The latter pair allude to its essentially oral performance character; the commentator advocates memorizing the work, "que todo omne la deuiera decorar. Ca esta fue la entençio del sabio rraby que las fizo," ["that each person should memorize. That was the intention of the wise rabbi who made it"] and the defendant charged with heresy swears he recorded "quantas a la memoria me han venido" ["as many as have come to memory"].

That the *Proverbios morales* were presented to Pedro I for his edification seems apparent, but the assertion that it was written specifically for a Christian audience warrants appraisal. That hypothesis relies upon the poem's redaction in Castilian, an opening apostrophe and closing reference to Pedro I, and a *captatio benevolentiae* summarizing the Jewish poet's situation when addressing a Christian audience of superior social rank. The delivery of medieval Jewish sermons in a vernacular places a correlation between language choice and intended audience here in doubt. The use of the *V(os)* form of address, required for addressing a social superior, is limited to the poem's introductory and concluding passages, the main body prefers the *T(ú)* form suitable for an equal or inferior in status. It may be inferred therefore that Shem Tov composed the *Proverbios morales* for a destinatory of equal or inferior status—that is, the Jewish community, and redacted occassional material in order to accommodate the poem for presentation before a different audience.

A subtle poetic composition, *Proverbios morales* succeeds in incorporating the complexity of human existence into a persuasive discourse on ethics and philosophy that addresses the dynamic of the individual in society.

See also **Pedro I the Cruel, King of Castile**

Further Reading

Alarcos Llorach, E. "La lengua de los *Proverbios morales* de don Sem Tob," *Revisía de Filología Española* 35 (1951), 249–309.

Perry, T. A. The *"Moral Proverbs" of Santob de Carrion: Jewish Wisdom in Christian Spain*, Princeton, N.J., 1987.

Zemke, J. *Critical Approaches to the "Proverbios Morales" of Shem Tov de Carrión*. Newark, Del., 1997.

JOHN ZEMKE

SHUSHTARĪ, AL-, ABŪ AL-ḤASAN (b. 1212)

The medieval Hispano-Arabic mystical poet Abū al-Ḥasan al-Shushtarī, who was born and who lived most of his life in Muslim Spain, introduced the colloquial *zajal* to the field of Ṣūfi (Islamic mystical) poetry. The *zajal* is the well-known strophic poem that uses the colloquial as its medium—in this case, the Andalusian medieval dialect—and particularly originated in Muslim Spain during the Middle Ages. As a "popular" art form that had not been used before or thought appropriate for sublime Ṣūfi expression, the Hispano-Arabic zajal that existed at the time was especially perfected by another Andalusian poet, Ibn Quzmān, who mainly wrote satirical and courtly love zajals. There is today enough evidence that this type of zajal was performed, sometimes by means of choral singing. In the East, Ṣūfi poets like Ibn al-Farīd of Egypt (d. 577) had been using the classical form of the Arabic *qaṣīda*, with its traditional framework of monorhyme and monorhythm and with classical Arabic language to express thoughts. In Spain, however, strophic poetry—namely the *muwashshaḥa* and the zajal—evolved in Andalusian Arabic verse, demonstrating the influence of Romance popular literature. In other words, the *muwashshaḥa* and the zajal in their inception in Arabic literature became uniquely associated with al-Andalus. But it was Al-Shushtarī who first chose the zajal for Ṣūfi purposes.

Therefore, most important about Al-Shushtarī in this context is that his strophic poetry forms a link between two areas of interest in the literature of Muslim Spain: the formal and esoteric, on the one hand (represented by the mystical philosophy of Ibn 'Arabī and Ibn Sab'īn, two Ṣūfi whom Al-Shushtarī followed), and the "popular" aspect of the Hispano-Arabic literary world (represented by the informal zajal and its master, Ibn Quzmān) on the other. Through the unity of these two strands, Al-Shushtarī sought to interpret and make accessible mystical ideas and to propound an understanding of Ṣūfism virtually synonymous with a vibrant, aesthetic perceptiveness. He therefore represents an important melding of the esoteric spirituality of Ṣūfism and a kind of emerging lay spirituality.

This yoking of a theological and an aesthetic perspective significantly illuminates the act and art of interpretation, which is the main area of concern in Al-Shushtarī's poetry. Ṣūfi scriptural (i.e., Qur'ānic) exegesis plays a fundamental role in this literary self-awareness that permeates the poetry. Consistent textual references such as "understanding" and "grasping allusions," "words," "terms," "symbols," or "signs" underline the concept of critical interpretation. Like all Ṣūfis, Al-Shushtarī did not deal with texts—scripture or otherwise—superficially. He constantly asked his audience to "untie symbols" and to "grasp ultimate meanings," urging them to think, to analyze, and to put parts of a poem together in the service of the whole, as if inviting them to join his Ṣūfi path by interpreting his

songs. Hence, this literary self-consciousness ultimately reflects a mystical self-consciousness as well, while the Ṣūfi principle of Qur'ānic exegesis shaped the way Ṣūfi poets, such as Al-Shushtarī, composed poetry and the way they expected it to be interpreted.

Al-Shushtarī utilized the means provided by this mystical tradition for symbolic expression, but his innovation in the use of the zajal for such marks his contribution in the field. He could not merely depend on the techniques provided by traditional rhetoric to achieve a combination of artistry and mysticism. In al-Shushtarī, the concept of "interpretation" in itself becomes the main concern, and the poetry comes to express the interrelation between critical perceptiveness of text and mystical views. It is this integration that Al-Shushtarī's strophic poetry fully realizes.

This relationship between the lyrical and the mystical manifests itself in three main features that act as systems of reference and regulation that afford the audience effective ways of responding spiritually as well as aesthetically to the lyrics. These reference systems are regarded from the standpoint of their mystico-aesthetic correspondence to convey Al-Shushtarī's mystical and aesthetical philosophy simultaneously.

The first aspect is the idea of the multiple levels of meaning existing within the poems—that is, the symbolism. This feature directly translates into two areas of interest: the network of Ṣūfi doctrines and symbolic terminology as well as the literary self-conscious mode characterized by direct textual references. The major reference is that of *ramz* (symbol), hence underlying the symbolic composition of the poems and suggesting the application of symbolic interpretation in order to discern the text's binary dimension. In other words, Al-Shushtarī does not merely use symbols but calls attention to this use and to symbolic critical reading.

The second major area that also displays literary self-consciousness is structure—specifically ring composition and its relation to the theme of the "reflexive." The ring structure embodies a circular principle of interpretation, which is most appropriate to the Ṣūfi mode of perception and to the tradition of composing strophic poetry. Ṣūfi exegesis, called *ta'wī*, is the internal interpretation of the Qur'ān and seeks the inner level or primary meaning through returning the outward, literal plane of scripture to its original, hidden spiritual essence—hence a circular, reflexive movement. And in strophic poetry, the nature thereof allows the poet to utilize his strophes as movable structural units, which is more feasible than dealing with single lines in the more restrictive form of a classical qasida. Al-Shushtarī could also use the interplay between the different parts of the zajal or *muwashshaḥa* (such as the *matla*, the *qufl*, and the *kharja*) to solidify the ring composition. Moreover, the phenomena of borrowing and of composing a poem based on an already established kharja (the last line in the song)—that is, starting from the end—or based on an established prosodic pattern (contrafaction) are all typical compositional techniques that enhance the circular effect. Thus, Al-Shushtarī was very conscious of specific structural patterns and their significance to the art of critical interpretation.

The third manifestation of that general literary concern lies in the element of performance itself, which is naturally realized with the pioneering use of the zajal. Because this is a poem composed to be sung or performed in public (sometimes in a choral manner), it affords the audience or recipients interaction with the art presented. The active participation involved here is what distinguishes Al-Shushtarī's mystical work, adding a new dimension to Ṣūfi poetry in general, and invigorating the whole mystical experience. Ṣūfi poetry here is thus no longer intellectually exclusive or highly theoretical and unreached, but a living part of the mystical existence. Al-Shushtarī even included within the lyrics themselves, and among his other created personalities, the persona of the *zajjal* (the zajal's composer) or singer—that is, the persona of the poet/artist.

The two other personae are the ascetic, pious *faqir* (epithet for Ṣūfi) and its symbolic counterpart, a wanton drunk. The first persona, the wandering, "ecstatic" Ṣūfi, seems to embody the character of Al-Shushtarī himself, a Ṣūfi faqir who wandered in various lands and took his zajal singing in the streets and marketplaces. At times, however, Al-Shushtarī adopts the Quzmāni wanton persona; as he says in his "Zajal 99," he literally puts on his defiant and unorthodox hat (exchanging his turban for a monk's hood). Of course, this device of putting on literary masks serves an important artistic purpose: the personalities ultimately join to form an underlying unity between literature and Ṣūfism.

As has been shown, the use of symbols and circular structure are ways of enhancing the concept of Ṣūfi exegesis and establishing the necessity of critical interpretation. In the same manner, drawing attention to performance and to various personae or voices further proves how Al-Shushtarī was aware that he presented a new art—not merely a Ṣūfi philosophical treatise or didactic poetry—and that he was interested in the intricate artistry of composition.

In the final analysis, the novel aesthetic position of Al-Shushtarī is that critical interpretation, from the Ṣūfi perspective, is a "circular" process in which an "essential," spiritual truth becomes a poem: then by means of interaction with an interpreting audience (through public performance) the poem is returned to its origins. The correspondence between the theological dimension and the aesthetic dimension has one purpose: to illuminate the nature of the process of interpretation when linked to religious hermeneutics. Al-Shushtarī's poetry illustrates his characteristic blend of appealing and melodic simplicity, on the one hand, and sophisticated and even enigmatic complexity on the other. He was able to make "perfect form" (i.e., (zajals and *muwashshaḥas*) in art indistinguishable from mystical pursuit.

See also **Ibn Quzmn**

Further Reading

Corbin, H. *Creative Imagination in the Sufism of Ibn 'Arabī.* Trans. R. Manheim. Princeton, N.J., 1969.
Monroe, J. *Hispano-Ambic Poetry.* Berkeley, 1974.
"Prolegomena to the Study of Ibn Quzmān: The Poet as Jongleur." In *The Hispanic Ballad Today: History, Comparativism, Critical Bibliography.* Ed. S. G. Armistead, A. Sanchez-Romeralo, and D. Catalán. Madrid, 1979. 77–129.
Shushtarī, al-, A. al-Ḥasan. *Dīwān.* Ed. A. S. al-Nashshar. Cairo, 1960.
Stern, S. M. *Hispano-Arabic Strophic Poetry.* Ed. L. P. Harvey. Oxford, 1974.

OMAIMA ABOU-BAKR

SIGER OF BRABANT
(ca. 1240–November 10 1284)

This scholastic philosopher, an important representative of thirteenth-century heterodox Aristotelianism, played a prominent role in the debate on the proper place of philosophy with respect to theology and Christian faith.

The details of Siger's biography are largely unknown. He was born around 1240 or shortly thereafter in Brabant and started his academic career circa 1255–1260 in Paris, where he received an M.A. in 1260–1265. On November 10, 1284, he died in Orvieto, killed by his secretary.

His oeuvre includes commentaries on Aristotle's *Physics, Metaphysics,* and *On the Soul,* and a number of separate questions dealing with logic, philosophy of nature, metaphysics, and ethics. Most of his writings resulted from his teaching as a master of arts at Paris. His published work probably dates from around 1270 and thereafter.

In his early writings, Siger professes the ideal of the pure philosopher searching for truth unaided by Christian revelation and trying to reveal the exact teachings of Aristotle, the philosopher par excellence. This attitude was seen as a serious threat to theology by a number of theologians, whose reaction was reflected in the famous Parisian Articles of 1270 and 1277, issued by Bishop Stephen Tempier. In his later work, however, Siger is less radical and steers a middle course between philosophy and Christian faith.

Of central importance was Siger's theory of the human intellect. In line with the teachings of Averröes, Siger holds that humans receive intellectual knowledge from a single, pure intellectual substance, which is the last of the hierarchy of intellectual substances and which consists of an active and a potential part. Only this pure intellectual substance is immortal; final personal responsibility therefore has no place. The theory evoked a sharp and detailed criticism of Thomas Aquinas. Toward the end of his career, Siger no longer defended it, mainly because of the attack of Thomas Aquinas, which seems to have convinced him that he was wrong.

See also **Aquinas, Thomas**

Further Reading

Philosophes Médiévaux 3 (1954): 12–14; (1972–1974): 24–25; (1981–1983) [editions of most of Siger's works].

Gauthier, R. A. "Notes sur Siger de Brabant." *Revue des sciences philosophiques et théologiques* 67 (1983): 201–232; 68 (1984): 3–49.

Hissette, Roland. *Enquête sur les 219 articles condamnés à Paris le 7 mars 1277.* Louvain: Publications Universitaires de Louvain, 1977.

Van Steenberghen, Fernand. *Maître Siger de Brabant.* Louvain: Publications Universitaires de Louvain, 1977.

——. "Publications récentes sur Siger de Brabant," in *Historia Philosophia Medii Aevi,* ed. Burkhard Mojsisch and Olaf Plua, vol. 2. Amsterdam: Grumer, 1991, pp. 1003–1011 [bibliography].

MAARTEN J. F. M. HOENEN

SIGHVATR ÞÓRÐARSON

With more than 160 stanzas and half-stanzas, Sighvatr's *oeuvre* is the most fully attested of all the skalds. Even so, the original context of many stanzas is uncertain and only one poem, *Bersǫglisvísur* ("Plain-speaking Verses"), approaches complete preservation. Although no saga centering on Sighvatr exists, his distinguished career is documented by numerous episodes, some anecdotal and perhaps dubiously reliable, in the various versions of *Óláfs saga helga*. An Icelander born near the turn of the 11th century, Sighvatr belonged to a skaldic kindred, being the son of Þórðr Sigvaldaskáld and the uncle of Óttarr svarti ("the black"). His childhood was spent independently of his father, who seems to have been attached to the Jómsvíkingar, and in a non-Snorri anecdote his legendary fluency in poetic improvisation is attributed to his having caught and eaten a miraculous fish. Following a successful petition to St. Óláfr to accept him as a court poet, his adult career began with his *Víkingarvísur* ("Verses on the Viking Expedition"; the title is editorial). Here, Sighvatr used information from eyewitnesses (including his father?) to enumerate Óláfr's battles in the Baltic, England, France, and Spain. *Nesjavisur* ("Nesjar Verses"), by contrast, is based on Sighvatr's own participation in Óláfr's victorious sea-battle against Earl Sveinn Hákonarson (1016). Sighvatr also became personally involved in peace missions. His embassy (*ca.* 1017) to Earl Rognvaldr of Västergötland

is described in *Austrfararvísur* ("Verses on a Journey to the East"). This collection of verses gives vivid, humorous, almost chatty impressions of a difficult route, inhospitable heathen people, and a favorable diplomatic outcome, although its exact documentary significance remains controversial. Subsequently, with the high rank of *stallari* ("marshall"), Sighvatr went to England to gather intelligence about Knud (Cnut) the Great's designs in Norway. He described this mission in a sparsely preserved sequence entitled *Vestrfararvísur* ("Verses on a Journey to the West"; 1025–1026). Sighvatr's close relationship with Óláfr, richly documented in the *lausavísur* and other compositions, brought him landed property and also benefited other Icelanders, including his nephew Óttarr. Tradition has it that he was instrumental in the naming of Óláfr's son Magnús, and in return the king sponsored Sighvatr's daughter at baptism. A pilgrimage to Rome (1029–1030) precluded his participation in the king's final battle at Stiklastaðir. His sorrow is expressed in some very eloquent and touching memorial *lausavísur*. His *erfidrápa* ("memorial lay"), perhaps composed some years later, appears to have focused on Óláfr's battles, sainthood, and miracles. Spurning an invitation from Sveinn, the temporary regent of Norway, Sighvatr attached himself to Óláfr's widow, Ástriðr, in exile in Sweden, and composed verses eulogizing her political efforts on behalf of Magnús, her stepson. Returning to Norway with Magnús (1035), he forestalled civil war with the poem entitled *Bersǫglisvísur*, which, by mingling candid admonition with sweet persuasion, brought the new king to recognize the grievances of Sveinn's erstwhile supporters. He also mediated between Ástriðr and Álfhildr, the mother of Magnús. Despite his declaration to Knud that he could serve only one lord at a time, Sighvatr was capable of political independence. Most notably, he composed a *drápa* and an affectionate memorial *flokkr* in honor of Erlingr Skjálgsson, Óláfr's brother-in-law and long-time foe (d. 1028). Some MSS connect his name with a poorly attested *Tryggvaflokkr* for Tryggvi Óláfsson (son of Óláfr Tryggvason, and an unsuccessful contender against Earl Sveinn); poems praising Earl Ívarr and the Swedish king Ǫnundr Jakob are also reported. His *Knútsdrápa* ("Lay in Honor of Knud") was composed after Knud's death (1035), perhaps on the occasion of Magnús's reconciliation with Hardacnut (1038). Its coverage included Knud's English campaign, the battle of Helgeå, and the king's pilgrimage to Rome. It is distinctive formally for its *klofastef* ("broken refrain") and very restrictive *tøglag* versification. Sighvatr's death probably occurred around 1043. His verse distinguishes itself by sincerity, loyalty, humor, and general strength of personality. Such is the air of spontaneity that his poems appear to be retrospective assemblages of occasional or anecdotal verses. Colloquial and proverbial touches sit side by side with foreign words, which, combined with the breadth of geographical references, give his verse a somewhat cosmopolitan feel. Mythological kennings occur seldom, except in *Erlingsflokkr*, perhaps because they were out of keeping with the newly Christian ethos. Also scarce are obscure, neologistic compound nouns and kennings, of the sort so often found in other skalds' work. The general effect is simplicity, commonly offset by a difficult word order or an intricate plaiting of several short sentences within the one *helmingr*. With Sighvatr, then, skaldic discourse seems to be both in touch with its traditions and also opening itself to international contacts, in conformity with the expansion of Norwegian and Danish hegemony during his lifetime.

See also **Cnut**

Further Reading

Editions

Finnur Jónsson, ed. *Den norsk-islandske skjaldedigtning.* Vols. 1A-2A (tekst efter håndskrifterne) and 1B-2B (rettettekst). Copenhagen and Christiania [Oslo]: Gyldendal, 1912–15; rpt. Copenhagen: Rosenkilde & Bagger, 1967 (A) and 1973 (B).

Kock, Ernst A., ed. *Den norsk-isländska skjaldedikwingen.* 2 vols. Lund: Gleerup, 1946–50 [contains some improvements on Finnur Jónsson's edition].

Jón Skaptason. "Material for an Edition and Translation of the Poems of Sigvat Þórðarson, *skáld*." Diss. State University of New York at Stony Brook, 1983.

Translations

Hollander, Lee M. *The Skalds: A Selection of Their Poems with Introduction and Notes.* Princeton: Princeton University Press, 1945; 2nd ed. Ann Arbor: Michigan University Press, 1968 [brief biography, together with translations of selected stanzas, with emphasis on *Austrfararvísur*, *Vestrfararvísur*, and *Bersglisvísur*].

Campbell, Alistair. *Skaldic Verse and Anglo-Saxon History.* London: Lewis, 1971 [translation of Sighvatr's verses on English topics and discussion of their historical value].

Turville-Petre, E. O. G. *Scaldic Poetry.* Oxford: Clarendon, 1976 [brief biography, with small selection of stanzas and translations].

Whitelock, Dorothy, ed. *English Historical Documents c. 500–1042.* 2nd ed. London and New York: Eyre Methuen Oxford University Press, 1979 [English translation of Sighvatr's verses on English topics].

Fell, Christine. "*Víkingarvísur.*" In *Specvlvm Norroenvm: Norse Studies in Memory of Gabriel Turville-Petre.* Ed. Ursula Dronke *et al.* Odense: Odense University Press, 1981, pp. 106–22 [text, translation, and discussion of *Víkingarvísur*].

Literature

Finnur Jónsson. *Den oldnorske og oldislandske Litteraturs Historie.* 3 vols. 2nd ed. Copenhagen: Gad, 1920–24 [account of Sighvatr's career and poems].

Vestlund, Alfred. "Om strofernas ursprungliga ordning i Sigvat Tordarsons *Bersøglisvísur*." *Arkiv för nordisk filologi* 46 (1929), 281–93 [analysis and rearrangement of stanza order in *Bersøglisvísur*].

Moberg, Ove. *Olav Haraldsson, Knut den Store och Sverige.*

Lund: Gleerup, 1941 [historical account of Sighvatr's verses].

Campbell, Alistair. *Encomium Emmae reginae.* Camden Society Third Series, 72. London: Royal Historical Society, 1949 [historical value of Sighvatr's verses on English topics].

Holtsmark, Anne. "Uppreistarsaga." *Maal og minne* (1958), 93–7 [the theme of betrayal in *Erfidrápa*].

Hallberg, Peter. *Den fornisländska poesien.* Verdandis skriftserie, 20. Stockholm: Bonnier, 1962 [selections, chiefly from *Ausufararvísur*].

Vries, Jan de. *Altnordische Literaturgeschichte.* 2 vols. Grundriss der germanischen Philologie, 15–6. Berlin: de Gruyter, 1941–42 rpt. 1964–67, vol. 1 [general account of Sighvatr's career and compositions].

Bóðvar Guðmundsson. "Röðin á Bersöglisvísum." *Mfmir* 9.1 (1970), 5–8 [reply to Vestlund, urging conservative approach to the prose sources].

Höskuldur Þrainsson. "Hendingar í dróttkvæðum hætti hjá Sighvati Þórðarsyni." *Mímir* 9.1 (1970), 9–29 [Sighvatr's practice with *hendingar*].

Frank, Roberta. *Old Norse Court Poetry: The* Dróttkvætt *Stanza.* Islandica, 42. Ithaca and London: Cornell University Press, 1978 [detailed analyses of selected stanzas from *Austrfararvísur*, the memorial *lausavísur*, and the *Erfidrápa*].

Fidjestøl, Bjarne. *Det norrøne fyrstediket.* Øvre Ervik: Alvheim & Eide, 1982 [discussion of stanza allocation and sequence in the known praise poems].

RUSSELL POOLE

SIMON DE MONTFORT, EARL OF LEICESTER (ca. 1208–1265)

A younger son of the Simon de Montfort who led the crusade against the Albigensian heretics in southern France, he first came to England in 1230 to pursue a ramily claim to the earldom of Leicester. Simon quickly won King Henry III's favor, secured the family inheritance, and married the king's sister in 1238. He thus aroused the resentment of established baronial families, who saw him as a self-seeking interloper. But his political career followed a path different from that of Henry's other favorites.

Simon was a proud, ambitious, and self-confident man who developed strong ecclesiastical friendships. Although he was at the center of affairs in the 1240s and 1250s, he came to despise Henry's military incapacity and to condemn his conduct of government. In 1258 he joined other magnates in imposing baronial government upon the king in the Provisions of Oxford. When Henry plotted to regain his power, Simon emerged as the chief advocate of the Provisions and Henry's implacable enemy. He rejected the arbitration of Louis IX of France and, though outnumbered, defeated Henry at the Battle of Lewes, 14 May 1264.

Simon now virtually ruled England, with the king as his prisoner, but he could not legitimize his authority. Faced with, the hostility of the pope and most of the barons, he tried to strengthen his position by including representatives of the towns and counties in

603

the parliament of January 1265, the first time they had been convened together, Simon's position weakened as some of his supporters deserted him, complaining of his arrogance and use of power to enrich his family; he was defeated and killed at the Battle of Evesham, 4 August 1265.

For some years he was popularly venerated as a saint who had died for the liberties of the realm. It was, in reality, the kings need for taxation that ensured the development of the medieval parliament, not Simon's novel expedient of convening all the interested parties, simultaneously, in 1265.

Further Reading

Bemont, Charles. *Simon de Montfort, Earl of Leicester, 1208-1265.* New ed. Trans. Ernest F. Jacob. Oxford: Clarendon, 1930.

Carpenter, DA. "Simon de Montfort: The First Leader of a Political Movement in English History." *History76* (1991): 3–23.

Knowles, C.H. *Simon de Montfort, 1265–1965.* London: Historical Association, 1965 [covers Simon's changing reputation].

Labarge, Margaret Wade. *Simon de Montfort.* London: Eyre & Spottiswoode, 1962.

Maddicott, J.R. *Simon de Montfort.* .Cambridge: Cambridge University Press, 1994 [the best account of his life].

C.H. KNOWLES

SLUTER, CLAUS (ca. 1345–1405/06)

Artist who also achieved prominence as one of Philip the Bold of Burgundy's *valets de chambre,* a position he acquired after the death of his master, Jehan de Marville, Sluter was born in Haarlem in Holland; after working in Brussels from 1379 to 1385, he became an assistant to Marville, then *valet de chambre* to Philip, in Dijon. The Chartreuse de Champmol in Dijon, a project begun by Marville and his workshop, features one of Sluter's and the workshop's finest accomplishments, the *Well of Moses* (ca. 1395–1406). Sluter also finished the tomb of Philip the Bold, now in the Musée des Beaux-Arts in Dijon, which had been begun by his predecessor. His primary achievement in his art was to free sculpture from its purely structural function, enabling the figures to dominate the architectural setting. Sluter infused his work with energy and an emotive quality unsurpassed by his contemporaries.

See also **Philip the Bold**

Further Reading

Morand, Kathleen. *Claus Sluter: Artist at the Court of Burgundy.* Austin: University of Texas Press, 1991.

Snyder, James. *Northern Renaissance Art.* New York: Abrams, 1985.

MICHELLE I. LAPINE

SNORRI STURLUSON (1178/9–1241)

Snorri Sturluson was outstanding as a man of letters, and as a man of the world. More is known about him than about most authors of his time. He figures prominently in the major events of his day as recorded by his nephew Sturla Þórðarson in his *Íslendinga saga,* the chief item in the *Sturlunga saga* collection. We also gain glimpses of Snorri from other sagas of the *Sturlunga* collection, from Sturla Þórðarson's *Hákonar saga Hákonarsonar,* and from sagas of contemporary Icelandic bishops, especially Guðmundr Arason, as well as from annals, genealogies, letters, and verses by Snorri and his contemporaries.

Snorri's intelligence and driving ambition made him exceptional, but, at the same time, his life reflects his age and its contradictions, not least that between political turbulence and intellectual achievement.

Snorri is named in a near-contemporary source among the eight most powerful laymen in Iceland while still in his twenties. In 1215–1218 and 1222–1231/5, he held the almost presidential position of lawspeaker (*Igsǫgumaðr*) to the *Alþingi,* and he became the richest man in the land.

Snorri owed his worldly success to a combination of luck and shrewd management. He was born into the clan of the Sturlungar, who took their name from his father, the chieftain Sturla Þórðarson of Hvammr (d. 1183), and gave their name to one of the most tempestuous ages in Iceland's history, the "Age of the Sturlungs." Snorri's relations with his brothers Þórðr and Sighvatr and nephew Sturla Sighvatsson varied throughout their lives, but at their worst were tragically destructive. In 1227–1228, for instance, Snorri and Þórðr ousted Sturla Sighvatsson from the family chieftainship (*goðorð*) in Dalir. In 1236, Sturla attacked Snorri's farm at Reykjaholt and had his son Órækja mutilated.

Although born into the Sturlungar, Snorri was brought up among the Oddaverjar, being fostered at Oddi, a prime center of learning, by the great chieftain Jón Loptsson (d. 1197). Partly through the agency of his foster-kinsman Særmmdr Jónsson, Snorri married Herdis, daughter of Bersi inn auðgi ("the wealthy") in 1199. He inherited Bersi's estate at Borg two years later. In 1206, Snorri moved to Reykjaholt, his main home for the rest of his life, and took over the *goðorð* there, later extending his influence (often by a shared or temporarily entrusted *goðorð*) still farther throughout the west of the country and into the northern and southern quarters. Herdis remained in Borg until her death in 1233, but before that, in 1224, Snorri had found another partner, Hallveig Ormsdóttir, a member of the Oddaverjar and the richest woman in Iceland.

Snorri also allied himself with other chieftainly families through his daughters' marriages: Hallbera's to Árni Magnússon óreiða ("the unready") of the Ámundaætt

and then to Kolbeínn ungi ("the young") of the Ásbirn-
ingar; Ingibjg's to Gizurr Þorvaldsson of the Haukdœlir;
and Þórdís's to Þorvaldr Vatnsfirðingr. But Þorvaldr was
burned to death at the instigation of Sturla Sighvatsson
in 1228, and the other three marriages turned sour, and
with them the alliances, which proved to be the death
of Snorri, because Gizurr and Kolbeinn were leaders of
the expedition that killed him.

Snorri's dealings with his fellow Icelanders, as lawspeaker, chieftain, and neighbor, and the personality that
emerges from them, are far too intricate even to outline
here. In essence, Snorri shunned violence and cherished
an ideal of peace, which, however, could not prevail
against the violence of the times or his own greed for
power and ostentatious wealth. He figures variously as
a reconciler, an equivocator, or a coward. His practical
sense and legal expertise were often put to the service of
his friends, but often used in deviously self-promoting
ways; and where legal means failed, he did not flinch
from inciting others to violence.

Snorri began early to court the favor of Scandinavian
rulers by sending youthful praise poems to the Norwegian kings Sverrir Sigurðarson and Ingi Bárðarson, and
the earl Hákon galinn ("the mad"). Hákon sent lavish
gifts in return and an invitation to Norway, but died
before Snorri was able to take up this offer. Snorri did,
however, make the journey to see Hákon's widow, Kris-
tin, now remarried in Gautland, during his Scandinavian
visit of 1218–1220. The main focus of the visit was the
Norwegian court, and Snorri spent the two winters with
Earl Skúli, regent to the young King Hákon Hákonarson,
becoming a royal retainer and receiving titles from them
culminating in *lendr maðr* ("baron," literally "landed-
man") as well as magnificent gifts. The glory and
generosity of these rulers were celebrated in Snorri's
grand metrical sampler *Háttatal,* and Snorri is credited
with two panegyrics for Skúli alone, from which only
a refrain survives. Snorri also cut a political deal in
Norway, making a promise (which he kept little or not
at all) to persuade the Icelanders to accept Norwegian
rule, while Skúli in return gave up his intention to punish
a fracas between the Oddaverjar and Norwegian traders
by invading Iceland.

Snorri again sailed to Norway in 1237, thus escaping
from the tightening web of hostility between Icelandic
clans and within his own, and there he learned of the
deaths of Sighvatr Sturluson and Sturla Sighvatsson in
the battle of Qrlygsstaðir (1238). Snorri stayed with
Earl Skúli and his son Pétr, thus taking the wrong side in
what became a fatal rift between Skúli and King Hákon.
It was later rumored in Iceland that Skúli had secretly
granted Snorri the title of "jarl," but certainly Snorri
gave Hákon grounds enough for anger and a charge of
treason by leaving Norway in defiance of his ban. The
king's anger joined that of Gizurr Þorvaldsson, Snorri's

alienated and ambitious son-in-law. Acting in delayed
response to a letter from the king that had been brought
to him by Árni óreiða, another former son-in-law, Gizurr,
led the force of seventy men that attacked Reykjaholt on
September 22, 1241. Kolbeinn ungi and one of Hallveig
Ormsdóttir's sons were also in the company. A party of
five warriors discovered Snorri hiding in the cellar and,
despite his injunction "do not strike" *(eigi skal hggva),*
killed him there.

To posterity, Snorri's role as a man of letters, a preserver of poetic, mythological, and historical traditions,
a composer of technically ingenious verse, and a writer
of at times superb prose far exceeds his importance
as magnate and statesman. Yet Sturla Þórðarson only
rarely refers to this side of his life, calling him a good
skáld, and reporting spiteful comments about Snorri's
poetic attempts to ingratiate himself with the Norwegian
monarchy and about his tendency to compose verses
rather than act. He also tells how Snorri's nephew Sturla
Sighvatsson spent a winter at Reykjaholt in 1230–31,
and had copies of Snorri's *sogubæskr* made. What saga
books these were is not clear, but Snorri probably wrote
his *Prose Edda,* his separate *Óláfs saga helga,* and
most of *Heimskringla* in the relatively peaceful decade
1220–1230. That he also composed *Egils saga* has been
argued often and persuasively, if not conclusively.

See also **Sturla Þórðarson**

Further Reading

Literature

Sigurður Nordal. *Snorri Sturluson.* Reykjavik: Þorláksson, 1920;
    rpt. Reykjavik: Helgafell, 1973
Paasche, Fredrik. *Snorre Sturlason og Sturlungeme.* Oslo: As-
    chehoug, 1922; 2nd ed. 1948
Einar Ól. Sveinsson. *The Age of the Sturlungs: Icelandic Civiliza-
    tion in the Thirteenth Century.* Trans. Jóhann S. Hannesson.
    Islandica, 36. Ithaca: Cornell University Press, 1953; rpt. New
    York: Kraus, 1966
Simon, John. "Snorri Sturluson: His Life and Times." *Parergon*
    15 (1976), 3–15
Ciklamini, Marlene. *Snorri Sturluson.* Twayne's World Authors
    Series, 493. Boston: Twayne, 1978.

DIANA EDWARDS WHALEY

SPINELLO ARETINO (c. 1350–1410)

The painter Spinello Aretino (Spinello di Luca Spinelli)
was born into a family of goldsmiths. Spinello was active in the principal towns of Tuscany, and his art, like
that of his contemporaries Agnolo Gaddi and Antonio
Veneziano, is characterized by profound insight into
Giottesque concerns with light, space, and form. To this
should be added his highly expressive treatment of line
and, in certain works, an interest in richly wrought surface textures and luminous color. His skills in narrative

composition and design were cleverly applied in the many important monumental fresco commissions that punctuate his career.

1370s–1385: Arezzo and Lucca

It would appear that Spineilo spent his formative years in Arezzo, and it is likely that he trained under the local painter Andrea di Nerio, whose influence can be detected in the austere and powerfully modeled forms of Spinello's fresco *Virgin and Child with Saints and a Donor* (1377; Arezzo, Museo Diocesano). By the early 1380s, Spinello had moved to Lucca, where the measured style of his earlier Aretine phase had evolved to take greater account of the decorative qualities of line and color; these developments suggest that he was responding to the sumptuous aspects of contemporary Lucchese artistic culture, especially the art of Angelo Puccinelli. In 1384, it is documented that Spinello had recently executed an altarpiece for the Olivetan order in Lucca; today, its principal components are generally identified as a central *Virgin and Child with Angels* (Fogg Collection, Cambridge, Massachusetts), two flanking panels of *Saint Pontianus* and *Saint Benedict* (both in the Hermitage, Saint Petersburg), and three predella scenes (Galleria Nazionale, Parma). The predella scenes were designed with a remarkable degree of spirited narrative detail, and some of the motifs indicate that Spinello was familiar with the monumental fresco cycles of the Camposanto in nearby Pisa. Spinello's sojourn in Lucca culminated in another commission from the Olivetan order: a grand polyptych for the high, altar of Santa Maria Nuova in Rome. Its central panel (now missing) was signed and dated 1385.

1386–1398: Arezzo, Florence, and Pisa

Spinello is documented in Arezzo in 1386. He was in Florence the following year, by which point he had joined the Arte dei Medici e degli Speziali and had received payment for two designs of statues intended for the cathedral facade. In this same period, he was commissioned by the Alberti family to work on two great fresco cycles: scenes from the *Life of Saint Benedict* (c. 1387–1388) for the sacristy of the Olivetan foundation of San Miniato al Monte, and episodes from the *Life of Saint Catherine of Alexandria* (c. 1390) for the private chapel of the Alberti, the Oratorio di Santa Caterina in Antella (outside Florence). Spinello's powers of narrative composition, which were already evident in the predella scenes of the Lucchese altarpieces, are fully developed in both fresco cycles, in which the facial expressions and individual gestures of the robustly modeled figures have been intelligently selected. In these years, Spinello's use of rhythmic line intensified,

as can be seen in his next project, frescoes depicting scenes from the *Lives of Saints Ephysius and Potitus* (1390–1391) in the Camposanto of Pisa. Here, Spinello emphasizes the calligraphic forms of the undulating drapery and also exhibits an interest in antique models, for his great battle scenes rely on reliefs from Roman sarcophagi for their effects. Following this commission in Pisa, Spinello returned to Florence, where he probably completed the cycle in Antella, as well as executing frescoes of episodes in the *Life of Saint John the Baptist* (now destroyed) in the Manetti Chapel in Santa Maria del Carmine. Spinello is again documented in Arezzo in 1395–1397.

1399–1411: Florence, Siena, and Arezzo

Between 1399 and 1401, Spinello was once again working in Florence, where he collaborated with Niccolò di Pietro Gerini and Lorenzo di Niccolò on the high altarpiece of Santa Felicita (1401; Accademia, Florence). Spinello's austerely designed saints from the right wing are in marked contrast to his dancing angels in the central panel, whose furious movements and fully activated drapery forms are remarkable for their expressive force. In the following years Spinello was mostly occupied with commissions in Arezzo, but by late 1404 he was in Siena to paint frescoes for the Sant'Ansano Chapel (now destroyed) in the cathedral. His years in Siena culminated in a commission, on which his son Parri Spinelli assisted him, to decorate the Sala di Balia in the Palazzo Pubblico with frescoed scenes from the *Life of Pope Alexander III* (1407–1408); these are remarkable for their engaging anecdotal elements and expressively characterized human figures.

Spinello occupies an important position in the development of Tuscan painting. His interest in the principles of Giotto's art and his competence in monumental mural painting were to influence Masaccio and others; at the same time, his lavish effects of color and pattern, decorative use of line, and freshness of narrative anticipated the late Gothic style of Lorenzo Monaco and Lorenzo Ghiberti.

See also **Giotto di Bondone**

Further Reading

Bellosi, Luciano. "Da Spinello Aretino a Lorenzo Monaco." *Paragone*, 187, 1965, pp. 18–43.

Boggi, Flavio. "Painting in Lucca from the Libertà to the Signoria of Paolo Guinigi: Observations, Proposals, and New Documents." *Arte Cristiana*, 87, March-April 1999, pp. 105–116.

Boskovits, Miklos. *Pittura fiorentina alila vigilia del rinascimento, 1370–1400*. Florence: Edam, 1975, pp. 141–147, 430–432.

Calderoni Masetti, Anna Rosa. *Spinello Aretino giovane*. Florence: Centro Di, 1973.

Fehm, Sherwood A. "Notes on Spinello's So-Called Monte Oliveto Altarpiece." *Mitteilungen des Kunsthistorischen Institutes in Florenz*, 17, 1973, pp. 257–272.

Fremantle, Richard. *Florentine Gothic Painters: From Giotto to Masaccio—A Guide to Painting in and Near Florence*. London: Secker and Warburg, 1975, pp. 343–354.

Weppelmann, Stefan. "Andrea di Nerio o Spinello Aretino?" *Nuovi Studi*, 4, 1999, pp. 5–16.

——. "Sulla pittura del trecento aretino tra le botteghe di Andrea di Nerio e Spinello Aretino." *Proporzioni*, 1, 2000, pp. 28–36.

FLAVIO BOGGI

STAINREUTER, LEOPOLD
(ca. 1340–ca. 1400)

An Austrian by birth, the cleric Leopold Stainreuter studied at the Universities of Paris and Vienna, becoming court chaplain to Duke Albrecht III of Austria (d. 1395). Stainreuter was a prominent translator of Latin theological tracts, having rendered the *Rationale divinorum officiorum* of Guilelmus Durandus (d. 1296) for the ducal court. Apparently at the behest of the duke's steward, Hans von Liechtenstein, Stainreuter translated Latin books on pilgrimage (called *Pilgerbüchlein*). Stainreuter, as translator and popular theologian, joins the so-called *Wiener Schule* (Viennese School), formed from authors with close ties both to the Habsburg court and the University of Vienna: Heinrich von Langenstein, Nikolaus von Dinkelsbühl, Thomas Peuntner, Nikolaus Kempf, and Nikolaus von Astau. (Johannes von Gelnhausen, Rudolf Wintuawer, Friedrich der Karmeliter, and Ulrich von Pottenstein are also associated, however tangentially, with the Viennese School.)

Central concerns of the authors named were religious instruction and edification, to which ends they translated Latin writings into the vernacular. Believing that literature should offer practical instruction for daily living and should promote the conversion of souls, they aimed their catechetical literature at a broad audience, embracing clerics, the laity, common people, and the nobility. Augustinianism was the theological direction of the school, Stainreuter having been active in the monastery of the Augustinian Hermits in Vienna.

Stainreuter also found his voice as historian, translating and composing dynastic history. For his 1385 translation of the *Historia tripartita*, the three-part church history by Cassiodorus, he wrote, as a type of introduction, a panegyric poem to Duke Albrecht III, labeled an "Epistel in daz lob des furstleihen herren herczog Albrechten czw Österreich" (Epistle of praise of his princely duke Albrecht of Austria). In the work Stainreuter identifies himself both as *chapplan, prueder Lewpoltz* (Brother Leopold, chaplain) and *lesmaister* (lector). Noteworthy is his employment of genealogy, a topic carried to fullness in his *Österreichische Chronik von den 95 Herrschaften* (begun in the late 1380s), an influential compendium of Austrian history borrowing the frame of world history, and commissioned by Duke Albrecht III. The *Chronik,* sometimes called the *Chronica patrie,* is a detailed, annalist prose history—based in part on the religious chronicle *Flores temporum* focusing on Austria from its earliest times through the rule of Duke Albrecht. (The concluding events are the death of the duke in 1395 and the pilgrimage of Duke Albrecht IV in 1398.) Stainreuter's *Chronik* is nourished by its vivid historical awareness, as indicated by its opening references to Seneca as helmsman, of the value of memory *(gedechtnüs),* and of history writing itself. There follows a fabulous pseudo-history, insistent in its efforts to legitimate Habsburg rule, placing Austria in a historical context that is both inventive and tendentious. As valuable as any of the Austrian historical events reported by Stainreuter is his allusion to a very early German Bible. He reports (in paragraph 388) that Queen Agnes of Hungary (d. 1364), *het ain bibel, die waz ze deütsche gemachet* (possessed a Bible written in the German tongue).

By the 1980s scholarship on Leopold Stainreuter seemed stable and serene. For all the vague remarks in the critical literature of the type that works were "ascribed" to him, a consensus had emerged that he was a translator and historian of note. Now that consensus has been shattered. Paul Uiblein recently shook Stainreuter research to its foundations, claiming Stainreuter was in fact the beneficiary of a kind of mistaken identity. Uiblein identifies our author, instead, as a certain Leopold of Vienna (Leupoldus de Wienna), a cleric of similar background who studied theology in Paris and taught the same in the theological faculty of the University of Vienna, established in 1384. At some point before this, Leopold had become court chaplain of Duke Albrecht III of Austria. Among his ducal duties was the preparation of translations; for these, as well as for his teaching at the university, he was recognized in 1385. In that year Duke Albrecht interceded on Leopold's behalf with Pope Urban VI, so that the chaplain might receive a benefice. That Leopold of Vienna already enjoyed the favor of the pope is shown by the bestowal of the title "papal honorary chaplain" in 1385.

Suffice it here to say that scholarship on Leopold Stainreuter is in flux; it is not yet certain when, or how, researchers might sort through the claims and counterclaims, and make a cogent case for the achievements of either "Leopold." Until that time, the literary patronage of the Habsburg dukes, primarily Albrecht III, will be more opaque than once believed. What is clear is that in late-fourteenth-century Austria a court historiography arose animated by nobles and confected of genealogy, historical fact, and fable.

Further Reading

Boot, Christine, ed. *Cassiodorus' Historia Ecclesiastica Tripartita in Leopold Stainreuter's German Translation MS ger. fol.1109*. 2 vols. Amsterdam: Rodopi, 1977.

Uiblein, Paul. "Leopold von Wien (Leupoldus de Wienna)," in *Die deutsche Literatur des Mittelalters. Verfasserlexikon*, 2d ed., ed. Kurt Ruh et al. Berlin: de Gruyter, 1985, vol. 5, cols. 716–723.

WILLIAM C. MCDONALD

STEPHEN II, POPE (d. 757, r. 752–757)

Pope Stephen II is sometimes identified as Stephen III—his predecessor, the original Stephen II, having died in 752 before being consecrated. Stephen became pope at a time of flux that gravely threatened the papacy. Since the late seventh century, the control of the Byzantine empire over its Italian possessions had steadily deteriorated. This decline allowed a succession of popes to assume de facto control over the duchy of Rome and to formulate an increasingly persuasive ideology justifying the right of the successors of Saint Peter to guide the orthodox in Italy, i.e., the true Romans who spurned the heretical iconoclastic policy of the emperors. However, another Italian power, the Lombard kingdom, was eager to exploit the decline of Byzantium. The Lombards became increasingly aggressive, and in 751 the Lombard king, Aistulf (r. 749–756), seized the exarchate, an important Byzantine territory around Ravenna, and threatened to occupy the duchy of Rome.

Stephen's central concern throughout his pontificate was to provide security for what was coming to be called the Republic of Saint Peter. After diplomacy failed to avert the Lombard threat and after approaches to Constantinople made clear that his theoretical overlord was incapable of protecting Rome, Stephen turned to Pepin III, king of the Franks. Pepin was perhaps grateful to the papacy, which had approved his seizure of the Frankish crown in 751, and indicated that he was willing to support Stephen's cause. Stephen thereupon journeyed to Francia in 753–754. After lengthy negotiations, the two parties entered a treaty of friendship, and Pepin agreed to protect the papacy and to restore to it extensive territories described in a written document. For his part, Stephen solidified the claim of the Carolingians to the throne by reanointing Pepin and his sons and by forbidding anyone to replace the Carolingians as kings. He also bestowed on Pepin and his sons the vague title *patricius Romanorum*, which implied that the Frankish rulers were responsible for protecting the Romans.

These negotiations resulted in a successful Frankish expedition to Italy in 755, which exacted from Aistulf a promise to restore extensive territories. However, once Pepin left Italy, Aistulf refused to respect his promise and again threatened Rome. Stephen's appeals led to a second Frankish expedition in 756 and another defeat for Aistulf. Pepin's agents now took possession of formerly Byzantine cities and territories in the exarchate and the Pentapolis and granted them to the pope, in a document known as the Donation of Pepin. Although these territories did not encompass all that Pepin had promised in 754, they and the duchy of Rome constituted the core of what was in effect an independent papal state. Stephen II followed up this success by playing a significant role in the election of Desiderius (757–774) to succeed Aistulf under terms favorable to the papacy.

When Stephen II died, there remained many uncertainties about the exact boundaries of the papal state, the future course of action of the new Lombard king, and the relationship between the papacy and the Frankish monarchy. However, Stephen's successes in expanding the republic of Saint Peter and in gaining a protector for it marked a turning point not only in papal and Italian history but also in the history of the west and its relationship with the east.

See also **Pepin III the Short**

Further Reading

Editions

Codex Carolinus, ed. Wilhelm Gundlach. Monumenta Germaniae Historica, Epistolae Merowingici et Karolini aevi, 1. Berlin: Weidmann, 1892, pp. 487–505.

Le liber pontificalis, 3 vols., ed. Louis Duchesne, 2nd ed. Bibliothèque des Écoles Françaises d'Athènes et de Rome. Paris: E. de Boccard, 1955–1957, Vol. 1, pp. 440–462.

Critical Studies

Miller, David Harry. "The Roman Revolution of the Eighth Century: A Study of the Ideological Background of the Papal Separation from Byzantium and Alliance with the Franks." *Mediaeval Studies*, 36, 1974, pp. 79–133.

Noble, Thomas F. X. *The Republic of Saint Peter. The Birth of the Papal State, 680–725*. The Middle Ages. Philadelphia: University of Pennsylvania Press, 1984, pp. 61–107.

RICHARD E. SULLIVAN

STEPHEN LANGTON (ca. 1155–1228)

Stephen Langton and his brother Simon were two of the most influential figures of their age. Stephen was born in Langton-by-Wragby, near Lincoln. His early education was probably at the Lincoln cathedral school, but ca. 1170 he moved to Paris and studied and then taught, for about twenty years, around the Petit Pont, probably at the school of Peter the Chanter. Like the Chanter and Peter Comestor, Stephen was interested in practical moral questions and in biblical studies. He was at his best when discussing, in a common-sense way, the problems of everyday life. He sided most definitely with the active rather than the contemplative life.

Stephen's fame came not from his theology but from his preaching and biblical commentaries. He was known as *Linguatonans*—thundering tongue. About 500 of his sermons survive. He is credited with the division of the Bible into more or less its present chapters; he was well known for his corrections to the text; and he commented on most of the Bible according to both the literal and spiritual senses. His commentaries circulated in a number of forms, some with only one sense, some with both. He also wrote commentaries on Peter Comestor's *Historia scholastica.*

While in Paris, he was a close friend of Lothar of Segni, who as Pope Innocent III made him a cardinal in 1206. In December 1206, Stephen was elected archbishop of Canterbury; but owing to disputes over his election between King John Lackland and the Canterbury chapter (backed by Innocent III), he was not allowed to take his seat until 1213. Until then, he lived in exile at the abbey of Pontigny.

Stephen was closely involved with Magna Carta and may have been its author. He worked hard to maintain the role of mediator during the events that led to 1215 and saw the charter not as innovation but as restatements of the rights and duties of kingship. Innocent read Langton's mediation with the barons as an indirect challenge to himself and suspended him as archbishop for two years. The dispute was eventually settled by the deaths of John and Innocent, and Stephen returned to England in 1218.

He attended the Fourth Lateran Council in 1215 and was very much in sympathy with its reforming principles. Back in England, he avidly pursued church reform, holding the first provincial council to legislate in England in 1222 in Oxford. He himself was active in administration of his see. He presided over the translation of the relics of Thomas Becket at Canterbury in 1220. He played a major role in the coronation of the boy-king Henry III (1220) and became his adviser. He died in Sussex in 1228.

See also **Innocent III, Pope; John; Peter Comestor; Peter the Chanter**

Further Reading

Stephen Langton. *Commentary on the Book of Chronicles,* ed. Avrom Saltman. Ramat-Gan:Bar-Ilan University Press, 1978.

——. *Der Sentenzenkommentar des Kardinals Stephan Langton,* ed. Artur Michael Landgraf. Münster: Aschendorff, 1952.

——. *Selected Sermons of Stephen Langton,* ed. Phyllis Barzillay Roberts. Toronto: Pontifical Institute of Mediaeval Studies, 1980.

Baldwin, John W. *Masters, Princes, and Merchants: The Social Views of Peter the Chanter and His Circle,* 2 vols. Princeton: Princeton University Press, 1970, Vol. 1, pp. 25–31.

Longère, Jean. *Œuvres oratoires de maîtres parisiens au XIIe siècle: étude historique et doctrinale.* Paris: Études Augustiniennes, 1975.

Powicke, Frederick Maurice. *Stephen Langton: Being the Ford Lectures Delivered in the University of Oxford in Hilary Term 1927.* Oxford: Clarendon, 1928.

Roberts, Phyllis Barzillay. "Master Stephen Langton Preaches to the People and Clergy: Sermon Texts from Twelfth-Century Paris." *Traditio* 36 (1980): 237–68.

——. *Stephanus de Lingua-Tonante: Studies in the Sermons of Stephen Langton.* Toronto: Pontifical Institute of Mediaeval Studies, 1968.

LESLEY J. SMITH

STOSS, VEIT (ca. 1445/1450–1533)

The famed sculptor was born in Horb am Neckar and died in Nuremberg on September 20, 1533. Virtually no documentation exists about Stoss's training and earlier years. His earliest secure sculptures show his familiarity with the heightened realism of the art of Nikolaus Gerhaert and Martin Schongauer, suggesting a stay on the Upper Rhine, perhaps in Strasbourg. Rogier van der Weyden's paintings, likely through other artistic intermediaries, also influenced the young sculptor. Although scholars have suggested the Stoss collaborated on altarpieces in Rothenburg (1466) and Nördlingen, nothing is known about his very earliest production. He certainly was an established sculptor when, in 1477, he moved to Kraków from Nuremberg, where he had married before 1476. Between 1477 and 1489 he created the Mary Altarpiece for St. Mary's in Kraków. Measuring 13.95×10.68 meters, this is probably the period's largest winged retable. Several of the apostles in the Death and Coronation of the Virgin in the corpus are about 2.8 meters tall. Here and in the relief scenes of the inner and outer wings, Stoss provides his figures with little space. Most are located within a shallow stage with a sharply tilted ground plane. Stoss's virtuosity in cutting highly animated draperies with deep, crisp folds is best observed in the richly polychromed (multicolored) and gilt corpus statues. For a project of this magnitude, the artist employed several assistants likely including a few of his seven sons. The Mary Altarpiece, the red marble Tomb of King Casimir IV Jagiello (1492) in Wawel Cathedral in Kraków, and his cast bronze Tomb Plate of Callimachus (Filippo Buonaccorsi, d. 1496) in the city's Dominican Church, among other works, exerted a tremendous influence on other artists active in Poland and eastern Prussia.

In 1496 Stoss moved back to Nuremberg. Three years later he completed stone statues of the Man of Sorrows and Mater Dolorosa plus three reliefs of the Last Supper, Christ on the Mount of Olives, and the Arrest of Christ that patrician Paulus Volckamer set in the eastern choir wall of St. Sebaldus church. The emotional appeal of the figures, notably Christ and Mary, who look beseechingly at the viewers passing in the ambulatory, coupled with a growing clarity of form define Stoss's more developed style. His career, however, was temporarily sidetracked. Having lost 1,265 guilders speculating on copper, Stoss forged a promissory note in 1503. After being convicted, he was branded on both cheeks and banned from leaving the city. In 1504 Stoss fled and worked briefly in Münnerstadt, where he polychromed Tillmann Riemenschneider's Mary Magdalene Altarpiece (1490–1492) and painted four scenes of the Martyrdom of St. Kilian on the wings. These are Stoss's only documented paintings; he also created ten engravings during this decade. Stoss returned to Nuremberg and through the intercession of Emperor Maximilian resumed his career. For the choir of St. Sebaldus, he made the limewood St. Andrew (1505–1507), in which the clear and stable pose of the apostle contrasts with the marvelous billowing drapery.

Stoss carved both small-scale and large statues throughout the 1510s and 1520s for local patrons and churches. His greatest feat was the Angelic Salutation (1517–1518), an over-life-size Annunciation suspended from the choir vault in St. Lorenz church. Supported by an angel holding *sanctus* bells, Gabriel and Mary float before the high altar. They are enframed by a giant rosary complete with roses, beads, small figured roundels, a group of joyous angels, and, at the apex, God. The ensemble included a great crown above, now lost, and Jakob Pülmann's candelabrum. Commissioned by Anton II Tucher, Nuremberg's highest official, the Angelic Salutation was covered for much of the liturgical year. With the advent of the Reformation in Nuremberg, the whole group was sheathed permanently from 1529 until circa 1806. The Reformation also affected Stoss's final great commission, the Mary Altar (1520–1523) ordered by the artist's son, Andreas Stoss, who was the prior of the local Carmelite convent. Stoss's preparatory drawing is today in the University Museum in Kraków. The sculptor had yet to be paid when the convent was dissolved in 1525.

After a long legal battle, the altarpiece was transferred by Stoss's heirs to Bamberg in 1543 and is now in the cathedral. Like several of Stoss's later carvings, the Mary Altar was stained but never polychromed. Stoss continued working at least until 1532. His impact on regional sculpture, at least before 1525, was considerable.

See also **Maximilian; Riemenschneider, Tillmann; Schongauer, Martin**

Further Reading

Baxandall, Michael. *The Limewood Sculptors of Renaissance Germany.* New Haven, Conn.: Yale University Press, 1980.

Kahsnitz, Rainer. "Veit Stoss in Nürnberg. Eine Nachlese zum Katalog und zur Ausstellung." *Anzeiger des Germanischen Nationalmuseum* (1984): 39–70.

——, ed. *Veit Stoss in Nürnberg: Werke des Meisters und seiner Schule in Nürnberg und Umgebung.* Munich: Deutscher Kunstverlag, 1983.

——, ed. *Veit Stoss: Die Vorträge des Nürnberger Symposions.* Munich: Deutscher Kunstverlag, 1985.

Lutze, Eberhard. *Veit Stoss,* 4th ed. Munich: Deutscher Kunstverlag, 1968.

Oellermann, Eike. "Die monochromen Holzbildwerke des Veit Stoss." *Maltechnik* 82 (1976): 173–182.

Sello, Gottfried. *Veit Stoss.* Munich: Hirmer, 1988.

Skubiszewski, Piotr. *Veit Stoss und Polen.* Nuremberg: Germanisches Nationalmuseum, 1983.

Soding, Ulrich. "Veit Stoss am Oberrhein: Zur Kunstgeschichtlichen Stellung der 'Isenheimer Muttergottes' im Louvre." *Jahrbuch der Staatlichen Kunstsammlungen in Baden-Württemberg* 29 (1992): 50–76.

JEFFREY CHIPPS SMITH

STRICKER, DER (ca. 1190–ca. 1250)

This itinerant poet, known only by his pseudonym, was probably born toward the end of the twelfth century in the Middle German region. A major portion of his life was spent in Austria, where he died about 1250, if the last poems for which reliable dates exist are taken as *terminus post quern.* Clearly not a member of the nobility, he seems to have worked for various audiences and patrons, although none is known to us by name. His oeuvre, consisting of nearly 170 works and spanning a wide variety of genres, attests not only to his versatility and originality but also to his considerable knowledge of theological and legal issues. He is familiar with the works of Hartmann von Aue and Wolfram von Eschenbach. The paucity of information regarding the poet extends to the chronology of his works. While it is generally assumed that his two longer works, *Daniel von dem Blühenden Tal* and *Karl der Große,* are products of his youth, it remains impossible to establish a sequence for *Pfaffe Amis,* various stories of medium length, and his vast output of short narratives consisting of fables, prayers, didactic poems, and a corpus of *Mären* (stories or tales) that constitute his actual claim to fame. *Daniel von dem Blühenden Tal,* consisting of 8,478 verses and transmitted in four extant manuscripts, is a highly original treatment of the Arthurian romance genre. Denounced by earlier scholarship, which viewed Stricker's *novum* of an unproblematic hero and an active, functioning society as a serious misunderstanding of the genre, it is recognized today as the coherent and skillful text that introduced the notion of *ratio* as a means to avoid the pitfalls of human life. The popularity of Stricker's *Karl* is attested to by twenty-four manuscripts and twenty-three fragments. Whether it was written in the wake of the Charlemagne revival or occasioned by the moving of his remains to Aachen in 1215 or by the transport of Charlemagne reliquaries to Zurich in 1233 still must be determined. Although Stricker's primary source was the *Chanson de Roland,* modern scholarship has been reluctant to label the 12,206 verse narrative simply a reworking of his source. Yet, attempts to explain it in its historical context as a political piece aimed at renewing interest in crusading efforts or as confirmation of the Hohenstaufen emperors as legitimate heirs to Charlemagne are inconclusive as well. A comprehensive interpretation remains a desideratum.

Stricker's shorter narratives are transmitted in fifty-three manuscripts and range from 10 to circa 2,500 verses. Counted among the latter are *Die Frauenehre,* Stricker's praise of women, and *Pfaffe Amis,* a cyclical narrative arranged in twelve episodes that castigates the folly of man. The thematic emphasis on *prudentia* and self-knowledge, either as underlying message or overtly stated, extends to many of the shorter works, which range from purely religious to profane, from entertaining to moralizing. Viewed as a whole, the shorter narratives present a canon of values appropriate to men and women and to all social classes.

See also **Charlemagne; Hartmann von Aue; Wolfram von Eschenbach**

Further Reading

Bartsch, Karl. *Karl der Große von dem Stricker.* Quedlin-burg: Basse, 1857; rpt. Berlin: de Gruyter, 1965.

Ehrismann, Otfrid. *Der Stricker: Erzählungen, Fabeln, Reden. Mittelhochdeutsch/Neuhochdeutsch* Stuttgart: Re-clam, 1992.

Fischer, Hanns. "Strickerstudien: Ein Beitrag zur Liter-aturge-schichte des 13. Jahrhunderts." Ph.d. diss., Lud-wig Maximil-ian-Universität, Munich, 1953.

——. *Studien zur deutschen Märendichtung.* Tübingen: Nie-meyer, 1968, 2d ed. 1983.

——. *Der Stricker: Verserzählungen I.* Tübingen: Niemeyer, l960, 4th ed. Johannes Janota, ed. 1979.

——. *Der Stricker. Verserzählungen II* Tübingen: Niemeyer, 1967, 4th, ed. Johannes Janota, 1983.

Geith, Karl-Ernst. *Carolus Magnus: Studien zur Darstellung Karls des Großen in der deutschen Literatur des 12. und 13. Jahrhunderts,* Bibliotheca Germanica 19. Bern: Francke, 1977.

Henderson, Ingeborg, *Strickers Daniel von dem Blühenden Tal: Werkstruktur und Interpretation.* Amsterdam: Benjamins, 1976.

Henne, Hermann. *Der Pfaffe Amis.* Göppingen: Kümmerle, 1991.

Hofmann, Klaus. *Strickers Frauenehre: Überlieferung, Textkri-tik, Edition, literaturgeschichtliche Einordnung.* Marburg: Elwert, 1976.

Mettke, Heinz. *Fabeln und Mären von dem Stricker.* Halle: Niemeyer, 1959.

Moelleken, Wolfgang W. *Die Kleindichtung des Strickers,* 5 vols. Göppingen: Kümmerle, 1973–1978.

Räkel, Hans-Herbert. "Die Frauenehre von dem Stricker," in *Österreichische Literatur zur Zeit der Babenberger,* ed. Alfred Ebenbauer. Vienna: Halosar, 1977.

Resler, Michael. *Der Stricker: Daniel von dem Blühenden Tal.* Tübingen: Niemeyer, 1983.

——. *Der Stricker: 'Daniel of the Blossoming Valley' (Daniel von dem Blühenden Tal).* New York: Garland, 1990.

Schwab, Ute. *Die bisher unveröffentlichten geistlichen Bispelre-den des Strickers.* Göttingen: Vandenhoeck and Ruprecht, 1959.

——. *Der Stricker, Tierbispel.* Tübingen: Niemeyer, 1960, 3d ed. 1983.

Thamert. Mark Lee. "The Medieval Novelistic 'Märe': Telling and Teaching in Works of the Stricker." Ph.d. diss., Princeton University, 1986.

Wailes, Stephen L. *Studien zur Kleindichtung des Stricker.* Berlin: Schmidt, 1981.

Ziegeler, Hans-Joachim. *Erzählen im Spätmittelalter.* Munich: Artemis, 1985.

INGEBORG HENDERSON

STURLA ÞÓRÐDARSON
(July 29, 1214–July 30, 1284)

Sturla Þórðdarson attained eminence as a historian, poet, and legal expert. His literary fame is based on his histories: *Íslendinga saga* ("History of the Icelanders"), which covers in detail the period from 1183 to 1242, and *Hákonar saga Hákonarsonar,* a chronicle of the reign of the Norwegian king Hákon Hákonarson (1217–1263). He also composed a version of *Landnámabók* ("Book of Settlements") known as *Sturlubók.* Although much of his skaldic poetry has been lost, the surviving verses are generally considered conventional rather than exceptional in inspiration and in expression. In the last two decades of his life, he was an acknowledged authority on his native law. Following Iceland's integration into Norway (1264), the Norwegian king Magnús Hákonar-son (1263–1280) appointed him a member of the commission charged with revising provincial law.

Sturla was born the illegitimate son of a major chieftain, Þórðr Sturluson, in the northwest of Iceland. Although his illegitimacy was a distinct social disadvantage, his upbringing was privileged. In his infancy, he was raised by his grandmother Guðný, a woman of remarkable intellect and energy. His father trained him early in the duties of a chieftain, which included participation in legal affairs and in armed ventures. At age thirteen, he was delegated to empower his uncle Snorri to administer his father's chieftaincy al the *Alþingi.* In his late teens, he guarded Bishop Guðmundr and his retinue of paupers during his visitation of western Iceland. Subsequently, Sturla joined his brothers in protecting their father's territory from the depredations of Snorri's son Órækja. These missions involved him in open or barely concealed enmities that would test his organizational skills and would develop his abilities as a chieftain.

In 1235, Sturla joined his uncle Snorri, the great writer and historian. A closeness developed between the two. Although Sturla would ascribe demeaning foibles to Snorri in *Íslendinga saga,* the fact remains that Snorri assigned to Sturla the administrative powers that made

Sturla, at age twenty-six, one of the foremost chieftains of western Iceland (1240). Sturla acknowledged his debt by naming his oldest son after his uncle and by joining Óraekja in seeking blood revenge for the slaying of Snorri (1241).

In the internecine struggles of the thirties and forties, the power of Sturla's clan, the Sturlungar, had been truncated. Increasingly, the Norwegian king manipulated the internal jockeying for power. Sturla was embroiled in these fights, both because two of the main contestants, Þórðr Kakali and Þorgils Skarði, were his cousin and nephew respectively, and because he felt compelled to protect his own territorial interests. His fortunes fluctuated as he participated, sometimes reluctantly, sometimes actively, in bitter feuds. Tragedy also touched his life. In 1253, Sturla had allied himself with Gizurr Þorvaldsson, the chieftain who had ordered Snorri's death. To strengthen the alliance, Sturla had affianced his daughter to Gizurr's son Hallr. At the end of the wedding celebration, Gizurr's manor, Flugumýrr, was put to the torch. The bride barely escaped in the attack that was futilely launched in revenge for the slaying of both Snorri and of Snorri's nephew, Sturla Sighvatsson. Moreover, Þorgils Skarði, for a brief time the major chieftain in northern Iceland and Sturla's close associate, was slain in 1258.

A period of uncertainty, dashed hopes, ill-fated alliances, and ventures ended in Sturla's exile to Norway in 1263. His stay at the court was prolonged. It was also an intellectually busy and fruitful time. Appointed court historian, he composed the official history of Magnús's father, King Hákon Hákonarson, a work based on eyewitness reports and on records in the royal chancery. Sturla was also busy with the revision of the provincial laws, including Icelandic law. He returned to Iceland with the first codification of the amended law, the so-called *Jámsiða* ("iron side"), in 1272. He then assumed the highest judiciary post. In 1277, his jurisdiction as lawman was restricted to northern and western Iceland. Concomitantly, he was summoned to Norway on charges that he was less active in discharging his duties than the newly appointed lawman for eastern and southern Iceland. Still, he was honored by the king, who appointed him a member of the court with the rank of knight (*skutilsveinn*). Again he assumed the post of royal biographer by writing the history of Magnus's reign, of which only one page survives. He resigned his post as lawman when he felt unable to cope with the question of jurisdiction over church property that pitted landowners against the bishop. He died in 1284, respected by his contemporaries for his scholarliness and integrity.

His literary work was extensive. He probably wrote, as a prologue to *Landnámabók*, an account of Iceland's christianization, *Kristni saga*, and also a lost version of *Grettis saga*. A 14th-century clerical author credits Sturla with a fantastic story about the troll-woman Selkolla. Less certain is the conjecture that he was responsible for the oldest versions of Icelandic annals and for a list of lawspeakers that has survived only in a MS of the 17th century.

See also **Hákon Hákonarson; Magnús Hákonarson; Snorri Sturluson**

Further Reading

The primary sources for Sturla's life are his own *Íslendinga saga*, other sagas in the collection known as *Sturlunga saga*, and *Árna saga biskups*.

Literature

Ker, William Paton. *Sturla the Historian*. The Romanes Lecture, 1906. Oxford: Oxford University Press, 1906; rpt. in *Collected Essays of W. P. Ker*. Ed. Charles Whibley. London: Macmillan, 1925.

Einar Ól. Sveinsson. *The Age of the Sturlungs: Icelandic Civilization in the Thirteenth Century*. Trans. Jóhann S. Hannesson. Islandica, 36. Ithaca: Cornell University Press, 1953; rpt. New York: Kraus, 1966.

Magerøy, Hallvard. "Sturla Tordsson." In *Norsk biografisk leksikon* 15. Oslo: Aschehoug, 1966, pp. 188–201 [contains bibliography].

Jón Jóhannesson. *A History of the Old Icelandic Commonwealth: Íslendinga saga*. Trans. Haraldur Bessason. University of Manitoba Icelandic Studies, 2. Winnipeg: University of Manitoba Press, 1974.

Ciklamini, Marlene. "Biographical Reflections in *Íslendinga saga*: A Mirror of Personal Values." *Scandinavian Studies* 55 (1983), 205–21.

Guðrún Ása Grímsdóttir and Jónas Kristjánsson, eds. *Sturlustefna. Ráðstefna haldin á sjö alda ártíð Sturlu Þórðarsonar sagnaritara 1984*. Reykjavik: Stofnun Árna Magnússonar, 1988.

MARLENE CIKLAMINI

SUCHENWIRT, PETER (FL. 14TH C.)

Neither the birth date nor death date is known for this most famous German herald of the fourteenth century. The name Suchenwirt is apparently a professional one derived from *such den wirt* (get the innkeeper); he calls himself *chnappe von den wappen* (page of the weapons, poem 30, II. 169–189). His name appears in twelve documents from 1377 to 1407, all dealing with his house in Vienna. His name also appears in a eulogy by Hugo von Montfort (1357–1423), who was with him on Duke Albrecht III's Prussian crusade of 1377. Suchenwirt's language, perspective, and sympathies suggest that he was an Austrian. The best source of information about his life is found in his poetry.

There are fifty two poems by Peter Suchenwirt extant in at least thirty three manuscripts. The main manuscript containing Suchenwirt's works, called "A," is in the National Library in Vienna (no. a3045, 503 pages from beginning of fifteenth century). The poems range in length from 57 lines to 1,540 lines. They include a number of different genres: four death laments; eighteen elegies (*Ehrenreden*); eleven historical and political occasional poems; fifteen moral allegories and spiritual didactic poems; four comic poems. The general term *Ehrenrede* was coined by Alois Primisser, Suchenwirt's first editor, and was applied to Suchenwirt's poems honoring famous Austrian nobles. These were poems that followed a strict formula: a formal expression of humility; general praise of the hero; description of hero's specific deeds; repetition of general praise; prayer for intercession of his soul (if the hero was already deceased); description of his coat of arms, both shield and helmet; name of the hero; a short closing prayer.

The subject matter of his political comments is especially enlightening. He discusses the ramifications of a division of property, the political consequences of a tax on wine, and the interrelationships among the classes; these are not generally the subject matter for chronicles or historical songs.

Suchenwirt (and a certain Gelre in the Low Lands) are unique in writing *Ehrenreden*. Their poetry places them within a long and illustrious tradition whose origins are in the death lament, the political-historical song, and in the so-called "tournament and siege poetry."

The heroes of the *Ehrenreden* follow similar life patterns with crusades against the heathens in Prussia, pilgrimages to the Holy Land, expeditions into Italy, and in the so-called numerous local campaigns in their homelands.

Further Reading

Achnitz, Wolfgang. "Peter Suchenwirts Reimtraktat 'Die zehn Gebote' im Kontext deutschsprächer Dekaloggedichte des Mittelalters. Mit Textedition und einem Abdruck der Dekalog-Auslegung des Johannes Künlin." *Beiträge zur Geschichte der deutschen Sprache und Literatur* 120 (1998): 53–102.

Blosen, Hans. "Überlegungen zur Textüberlieferung und Text-gestaltung bei einem Gedicht von Peter Suchenwirt," in *Probleme altgermanistischer Editionen*, ed. Hugo Kuhn, Karl Stackmann, and Dieter Wuttke. "Wiesbaden: Steiner, 1968.

Brinker-von der Heyde, Claudia. "Suchenwirt, Peter," in *Die deutsche Literatur des Mittelalters. Verfasserlexikon*, 2d ed., ed. Kurt Run et al. vol. 9. Berlin: de Gruyter, 1995, cols. 481–488.

Busse, Kaarl Heinrich von. "Peter Suchenwirt's Sagen über Livlane." *Mittheilungen aus dem gebiete der Geschichte Liv-, Esthh- und Kurland's,* ed. Gesellschaft für Geschichte und Altertumskund der russischen Ostsee-Provinzen. 3. Riga: Nicolai Kymmel, 1845, pp. 5–21.

Docen, Bernard Joseph. "Die Schlacht bei Sempach. 1386. Von Peter Suchenwirt." *Sammlungfür altdeutsche Literatur und Kunst* 1, no. 1 (1812): 152–160.

Friess, Godfried Edmund. "Fünf unedierte Ehrenreden Peter Suchenwirts." *Wiener Sitzungsberichte der Akademie der Wissenschaften, Phil.-hist. Klasse* 88 (1877): 99–126.

Primisser, Alois, ed. *Peter Suchenwirt's Werke aus dem vier-*

zehnten Jahrhunderte. Ein Beytrag zur Zeit- und Sittenge-schichte. Vienna: J.B. Wallishausser, 1827; rpt. Vienna: H. Geyer, 1961.

Van D'Elden, Stephanie Cain. *Peter Suchenwirt and Heraldic Poetry.* Vienna: Halosar, 1976.

STEPHANIE CAIN VAN D'ELDEN

SUGER (1081–1151)

Abbot of Saint-Denis from 1122 to 1151, Suger is one of the most interesting representatives of French monastic culture in the 12th century, combining an extraordinary devotion to his monastery with an understanding of the weaknesses and potential strengths of the kings of France. He was an ardent administrator and builder, and, if he is best remembered for his desire to adorn his church, he also reformed the liturgy and improved the life of the community, earning the praise of Bernard, abbot of Clairvaux.

Suger also stands out from most of his contemporaries because of the much clearer picture we have of his personality and achievements. He himself wrote a Latin vita of Louis VI, in which he gives a vivid picture of the king's attempts to subdue the turbulent aristocracy in the Paris region, his own role in this process, and the king's special devotion to St. Denis. He also wrote two works concerning his administration of the monastery's lands and the building and consecration of the new church. A small number of his charters and letters survive, and his image and his words are preserved in several places in the church of his abbey.

Suger was born of a modest knightly family probably not too far from Saint-Denis and was given as an oblate to the abbey. During his early years, he seems to have realized how the abbey had lost prestige, power, and wealth since the time of Charlemagne and Charles the Bald; how the reciprocal devotion of saint and king had been a strength to both; and how the church's small size and decayed furnishings no longer served the needs of the monks or the crowds of pilgrims coming there. Throughout his long life and particularly during his abbacy, it was his purpose to remedy these three lacks.

Suger tells us how as a youth he used to look at the abbey's muniments and how he was aware not only of its lost domains, but also how through mismanagement it was receiving much less revenue than it should. The first portion of his book on the administration of the abbey, *De rebus in administratione sua gestis,* described how he carefully and painstakingly tried to recover what was owed to the abbey and to increase its revenues. For example, increases came from getting more revenues from the town of Saint-Denis or acquiring a wealthy priory like Argenteuil, but they also came from clearing forests, planting new crops and vines, settling new inhabitants on the land, enforcing ancient rights against the encroachments of local lords, building houses, granges, and courts, establishing new churches, and converting cash rents into payments in kind.

Suger also learned from the monastery's history that it had been a frequent beneficiary of royal munificence. Lands, money, and precious objects had been given to Saint-Denis by kings of France from Dagobert on. He knew, too, that it was in times of peace and harmony that Saint-Denis had prospered most. An opportunity to recreate that special harmony between king and abbot arose from the fact that Louis VI, once a pupil at the abbey, had a particular devotion to the martyrs and confidence in Suger. Although Suger was to become regent while Louis VII was on crusade, and it was then that he acted as a royal "minister" of the king, it was really during the reign of Louis VI (d. 1137) that troublesome enemies of both king and abbey, like the lords of Le Puiset, were brought to heel. The ancient relationship between *regnum* and *monasterium* was not only enhanced but refashioned when Louis VI returned the crown of his father, Philip I, to Saint-Denis; took the royal standard from the abbey's altar as he left for war in 1124, declaring that if he were not king he would do homage to the abbey; granted the fair of the Lendit what amounted to an immunity from royal justice; and declared that the kings of France should be buried at Saint-Denis.

The more rigorous administration of the monastic lands and the creation of symbols that emphasized Saint-Denis's special importance for the French were antecedent to Suger's intention to tear down the old church and replace it with a larger one with more splendid hangings, stained glass, altars, crosses, and other objects. Though this must have long been planned for, Suger tells in his *De consecratione ecclesie sancti Dionisii* that once construction started the work proceeded quickly, the western narthex and towers being consecrated in 1140, and the translation of the saints to their new reliquaries and the construction of the eastern end with the new ambulatory and stained-glass windows completed in 1144. If stylistically the chevet anticipates many features of the Gothic churches of the Île-de-France, the church also incorporates many of Suger's major concerns: the preservation of the past, a harmonious adaptation of the old to the new, an emphasis on the liturgy, and most of all the exaltation of the saints.

Suger was inventive and eclectic. He reshaped and adorned objects that had been in the church; if he was not given the precious stones he needed, he bought them. So, too, he found the sources for his conception of the church in writings as diverse as saints' lives, liturgical texts, biblical commentaries, chronicles, and the writings of Pseudo-Dionysius the Areopagite, as well as in buildings he had seen.

Suger was a small man and an assertive one, and on behalf of his church he considered any means legitimate.

In his last years, as regent, he had had to spend much of his time away from Saint-Denis, and money that had been intended for the rebuilding of the nave he used for the king's needs. He died at Saint-Denis in 1151.

Further Reading

Suger. *Vie de Louis VI le Gros* (*Vita Ludovici VI*), ed. and trans. Henri Waquet. Paris: Les Belles Lettres, 1929.
——. *Abbot Suger on the Abbey Church of Saint-Denis and Its Art Treasures*, ed. and trans. Erwin Panofsky. 2nd ed. Princeton: Princeton University Press, 1979. [*Liber de rebus in administratione sua gestis*, chs. xxiv–xxxiv; *Libellus de consecratione Sancti Dionisii; Ordinatio.*]
Bur, Michel. *Suger, abbé de Saint-Denis, régent de France.* Paris: Perrin, 1991.
Cartellieri, Otto. *Abt Sugervon Saint-Denis, 1081–1151.* Berlin: Ebering, 1898.
Gerson, Paula L., ed. *Abbot Suger and Saint-Denis: A Symposium.* New York: Metropolitan Museum of Art, 1986.

THOMAS G. WALDMAN

SUNESEN, ANDERS (ca. 1160–1228)

Anders Sunesen was archbishop of Lund from 1201/2 to 1223/4. His father, Sune Ebbesen, was a cousin of Archbishop Absalon and one of the wealthiest men in Denmark. In the 1180s, Anders studied abroad. He probably received his main training in Paris (arts and theology), but also visited Italy (for law studies in Bologna?), and England (for an unknown purpose). After becoming a master of arts perhaps by 1186, and of theology some years later, he spent some time teaching, probably theology in Paris, before becoming chancellor to King Knud VI (r. 1182–1202). His first-known job as chancellor was on an embassy in 1195 that tried to reconcile Philippe Auguste of France with his Danish queen, Ingeborg. In 1201/2, Anders succeeded Absalon as archbishop of Lund and left the chancellery to his brother Peter, bishop of Roskilde, Denmark. In 1204, Anders was named papal legate to Denmark and Sweden. During the years 1206–1222, he cooperated with King Valdemar II (r. 1202–1241) in the subjugation and christianization of pagan populations in the Baltic area, in particular Estonia. Though initially reluctant, he seems in the end to have obeyed a papal summons to attend the Fourth Lateran Council in Rome in 1215. In 1222, he petitioned the pope to be relieved of his duties as archbishop due to "an incurable bodily infirmity." His successor, Peder Saksesen, was consecrated in 1224. Anders died in 1228, leaving various possessions to Lund chapter, including a collection of books.

As archbishop, Anders was an able administrator and politician on good terms with both pope and king. A later legend, modeled on the story of Moses in Exodus 17, credits him with prayer that secured Danish victory in the decisive battle against the Estonians at Lyndanis on June 15, 1219. This legend is often combined with another, according to which the Danish flag, *Dannebrog*, was sent from heaven during the battle.

Anders produced no literary works in Danish, as far as is known. Apart from administrative documents, the following Latin works have been attributed to Anders: (1) *Hexaemeron*, a theological poem in 8,040 hexameters, extant. (2) *De vii ecclesiae sacramentis*, also in hexameters, now lost. (3) Two sequences, "Missus Gabriel de celis" and "Stella solem preter morem"; "Missus," however, seems to predate Anders, and his authorship of "Stella" is also doubtful. (4) A Latin version of the Law of Scania, extant; the attribution rests on slender evidence, but is generally accepted.

The *Hexaemeron* is preserved in one medieval MS (Copenhagen, Royal Library, E don. var. 155 4to) from the second half of the 13th century, originally in the cathedral library at Roskilde. Anders probably composed the work in Paris in the early 1190s. It consists of twelve books and combines a commentary on Genesis 1–3 (Books 1–4) with an exposition of the main points of systematic theology, excluding the sacraments (5–12 plus a digression on divine names in 2–3). Main sources include, for the commentary on Genesis, Peter Comestor's *Historia scholastica* and Richard of St. Victor's *Allegorie*, and for the remaining part of the work, Stephen Langton's *Summa* and *Quaestiones*. As a whole, the *Hexaemeron* takes the reader from the Creation (1) to the Day of Judgment (12). A second proemium in Book 10 marks off two main parts: creation and fall (1–9), recreation in Christ (10–12). Anders shows great skill as a poet of hexameters. In his handling of the Latin language and of verse technique, he dissociates himself from the classicizing school represented by Saxo. The poem seems to have had a very limited diffusion, probably because so much learning is packed into it that it makes for very difficult reading.

See also **Peter Comestor; Philip II Augustus; Richard of Saint-Victor**

Further Reading

Editions

Leges Provinciales Terrae Scaniae ante annos 400 Latinæ redditae per Andream Suonis F. Ed. Arnoldus Hvitfeldius. Copenhagen, 1590.

Andreae Sunonis filii archiepiscopi Lundensis Hexameron libri duodecim. Ed. M. Cl. Genz. Copenhagen: Gyldendal, 1892 [includes edition of the sequences].

Skånske lov. Anders Sunesøns parafrase. Aakjær, S. and E. Kroman, eds. In *Danmarks gamle Landskabslovemed Kirkelovene* 1.2. Ed. Johs. Brøandum-Nielsen and Poul Johs. Jørgensen. Danish Society of Language and Literature. Copenhagen: Gyldendal, 1933.

Andreae Sunonis Filii Hexaemeron Post M. Cl. Gertz. Ed. Sten Ebbesen and L. B. Mortensen. Corpus Philosophorum Danicorum Medii Aevi, 11.1–2. Danish Society of Language and Literature. Copenhagen: Gad, 1985–88 [contains English introduction in part 1 and extensive bibliography in part 2].

Literature

Kabell, Aage. "Ueber die dem dänischen Erzbischof Anders Sunesen zugeschriebenen Sequenzen." *Archivum latinitatis medii aevi* 28 (1958), 19–30.

Christensen, A. E. "Sunesen, Anders." *Dansk Biografisk Leksikon* 14. Copenhagen: Gyldendal, 1983, pp. 208–11.

Mortensen, Lars Boje. "The Sources of Andrew Sunesen's Hexaemeron." Université de Copenhague, *Cahiers de l'Institut du moyen âge grec et latin* 50 (1985), 113–216.

Ebbesen, Sten, ed. *Anders Sunesen, stormand—teolog—administrator—digter.* Copenhagen: Gad, 1985 [contains fifteen studies on Sunesen, with English summaries and extensive bibliography].

Ebbesen, S. "Corpus Philosophorum Danicorum Medii Aevi, Archbishop Andrew (+1228), and Twelfth-Century Techniques of Argumentation." In *The Editing of Theological and Philosophical Texts from the Middle Ages.* Ed. Monika Asztalos. Acta Universitatis Stockholmiensis, Studia Latina Stockholmiensia, 30. Stockholm: Almqvist & Wikselt, 1986, pp. 267–80.

STEN EBBESEN

SVEN HARALDSSON (FORKBEARD) (r. 987–1014)

Sven Haraldsson was king of Denmark 987–1014. Sven seized power through a revolt against his father, Harald Gormsson (Bluetooth), who fled to the Wends and died of his wounds on November 1, 987. That Sven was captured and ransomed from the Wends following this revolt is highly dubious. According to Adam of Bremen, Sven's revolt was a pagan reaction, but its motives were more likely political; there is no other indication that Sven was a pagan. In Sven's time, Viking raids against England were resumed, and in 994 he led a raid together with Óláfr Tryggvason. He probably also took part in the raid in 991 and the battle of Maldon, but apparently not in the great raids of 997–1002 and 1009–1012. In 1003–1004, however, he conducted a raid, possibly to avenge the death of his sister Gunnhild and her husband, Pallig, in Æthelred's massacre of the Danes on November 13, 1002. In 1013, he led a raid that, in a strikingly short time, achieved the conquest of England, when Æthelred gave up resistance and left the country at Christmas, his subjects having acknowledged Sven as king. Sven's English reign was brief, however; he died on February 3, 1014, in Gainsborough and was buried first in England, then in Roskilde.

Sven also reasserted his father's claim to Norway, which had been seized, possibly with the help of Æthelred, by Óláfr Tryggvason around 995. Sven supported the sons of Earl Hákon, and, having married the widow of the Swedish king Erik Bjarnarson and thereby gaining influence in Sweden, he also supported his young stepson Olav (Skötkonung) Eriksson. Together with these allies, he won a decisive victory over Óláfr Tryggvason in the battle of Svlðr (Svold) and thereby restored traditional Danish overlordship over Norway.

The sources for Sven's reign are contradictory. While Thietmar and Adam of Bremen depict him as a cruel and evil ruler who was punished by the Lord with captivity, exile, and foreign conquest, and whose position was very insecure, according to the *Encomium Emmae*, he "was practically the most fortunate of all the kings of his time." Both views are obviously biased, but Sven's career to a large extent bears out the encomiast's view. To be able repeatedly to leave Denmark on prolonged campaigns, he must have enjoyed a secure position at home, suggested also by the fact that the fortifications built late in his father's reign were allowed to decay. He had remarkable political and military success in Scandinavia as well as in England.

Sven was the first Danish king to strike coins with his name on them. Only one type is known, imitating an Anglo-Saxon coin and struck by an English moneyer who apparently also worked for Óláfr Tryggvason and for Olav Eriksson. The coins of the three kings are so different, however, that they are more likely to be independent imitations than struck by the same moneyer. At the same time, imitations of English coins, but without the Danish king's name on them, began to be produced in large numbers in Lund, which developed into a town early in Sven's reign.

See also **Adam of Bremen; Óláfr Tryggvason**

Further Reading

Editions
Campbell, Alistair, ed. and trans. *Encomium Emmae Reginae*. Camden Society Third Series, 72. London: Royal Historical Society, 1949.

Thietmar von Merseburg, *Chronik*. Ed. Werner Trillmich. Ausgewähite Quellen zur deutschen Geschlchte des Mittelalters, 9. Berlin: Rütten & Loening, 1957.

Adam Bremensis. *Gesta Hammaburgensis Ecclesiae Pontificum*. In *Quellen des 9. und 11. Jahrhunderts zur Geschichte der hamburgischen Kirche und des Reiches*. Ed. Werner Trillmich and Rudolf Buchner. Ausgewähite Quellen zur deutschen Geschichte des Mittelalters, 11. Berlin: Rütten & Loening, 1978.

Translations
Adam of Bremen. *History of the Archbishops of Hamburg-Bremen*. Trans. Francis J. Tschan. Records of Civilization: Sources and Studies. New York: Columbia University Press, 1959.

Literature
Skovgaard-Petersen, Inge. "Sven Tveskseg i den ældste danske historiografi. En Saxostudie." In *Middelalderstudier tilegnede Aksel E. Christensen på tresårsdagen II. september 1966*. Ed. Tage E. Christensen *et al.* Copenhagen: Munksgaard, 1966, pp. 1–38.

Stenton, F.M. *Anglo-Saxon England*. 3rd ed. Oxford History of England, 2. Oxford: Clarendon, 1971.

Demidoff, Lene. "The Death of Sven Forkbeard—in Reality and Later Tradition." *Mediaeval Scandinavia* 11 (1978–79), 30–47.

Sobel, Leopold. "Ruler and Society in Early Medieval Western Pomerania." *Antemurale* 25 (1981), 19–142.

Andersson, Theodore M. "The Viking Policy of Ethelred the Unready." *Scandinavian Studies* 59 (1987), 284–95.

Brown, Phyllis R. "The Viking Policy of Ethelred: A Response." *Scandinavian Studies* 59 (1987), 296–8.

Sawyer, Peter. *Da Danmark blev Danmark*. Gyldendal og Politikens Danmarkshistorie, 3. Copenhagen: Gyldendal; Politiken, 1988.

Sawyer, Peter. "Swein Forkbeard and the Historians." In *Church and Chronicle in the Middle Ages*. Ed. Ian Wood and G.A. Loud. London: Hambledon, 1991, pp. 27–40.

NIELS LUND

SVERRIR SIGURÐARSON (r. 1177–1202)

King of Norway 1177–1202, Sverrir Sigurðarson was a native of the Faroe Islands, where his paternal uncle held the bishopric of Kirkebø (Kirkubæur). Here, Sverrir grew up and received his education. At the age of twenty-four, he was consecrated a priest, and his Norwegian mother revealed to him that his true father was the then long-dead King Sigurðr munnr ("mouth") Haraldsson. This revelation caused Sverrir to go to Norway in 1176, quit the clergy, and fight his way to the throne in fierce opposition to the powerful Archbishop Eysteinn, who had supported Magnús Erlingsson and crowned him king in 1164. Sverrir was proclaimed king in 1177 in Trondheim, and a few years later he had succeeded in gaining control of the larger part of the country. After the battle at Fimreiti in 1184, where King Magnús fell together with the majority of the Norwegian aristocracy, Sverrir became the sole ruler of Norway, although having constantly to fight an array of pretenders to the kingdom.

Our knowledge about Sverrir comes primarily from his saga, *Sverris saga*, which presents us with a fascinating personality, seemingly embodying great contrasts. He describes himself as being fierce as the lion and mild as the lamb, both symbols found on his royal seal. His biography does indeed exhibit his wit and down-to-earth philosophy, but also the new Christian ethics of mildness and forgiveness toward one's enemies. Sverrir's complex background and subtle mind are reflected in his irony and humor, displaying great self-confidence. Sverrir was a brilliant military leader on sea as well as on land. His ingenious tactics in warfare were so untraditional that he has been called a coward despite being victorious; his guerilla attacks were often of a kind that most Norse noblemen avoided. Sverrir had a profound knowledge of the Bible. His national-church policy brought him into lasting conflict with the Norwegian bishops; eventually, the archbishop left the country. Sverrir was excommunicated by him and later by the pope.

Sverrir's struggle with the Church is set forth in a document he himself commissioned. From his *Oratio contra clerum Norvegiae* ("Speech Against the Norwegian Clergy"), as well as the contemporary *Sverris saga*, we learn about his political ideology, drawn partly from Old Testament values. At the same time that he carried out his controversies with the international Church, Sverrir introduced those theocratic traits into his dynastic policy that are so extraordinary for the 13th-century Norwegian monarchy. During his reign, Sverrir strengthened the centralization of the king's administration, and the finances of the Crown were improved by a new system of taxation.

After the Reformation, Sverrir was celebrated as the king who had the courage to speak against the authority of Rome. In the 19th-century Norwegian struggle for national independence, Sverrir became a symbolic figure for the national identity. Present-day interest in the development of the state as an institution has made Sverrir and his royal descendants much valued as the creators of a strong and highly centralized state as early as the 13th century.

Further Reading

Literature

Cederschiöld, Gustaf. *Konung Sverre*. Lund: Gleerup, 1901.

Paasche, Frederik *Kong Sverre*. Oslo: Aschehoug, 1920.

Koht, Halvdan. *Kong Sverre*. Oslo: Aschehoug, 1952.

Gathome-Hardy, Geoffrey M. *A Royal Impostor: King Sverre of Norway*. Oslo: Aschehoug London: Oxford University Press, 1956.

Holm-Olsen, Ludvig. "Kong Sverre i sökelyset." *Nordisk tidskrift* 34 (1958), 167–81.

Helle, Knut. *Norge blir en stat, 1130–1319*. Handbok i Norges historie, 3. 2nd ed. Bergen, Oslo, and Tromsø: Universitetsforlaget, 1974.

Gunnes, Erik. *Kongens ære: Kongemagt og kirke i "En tale mot biskopene."* Oslo: Gyldendal, 1971.

Lunden, Kåre. *Norge under Sverreætten 1177–1319*. Oslo: Cappelen, 1976.

Ólafía Einarsdóttir. "Sverrir—præst og konge." In *Middelalder, Methode og Medier. Festskrift til N. Skyum-Niehen*. Ed. Karsten Fledelius *et al*. Copenhagen: Museum Tusculanum, 1981, pp. 67–93; rpt. in *Norske Historikere i Utvalg VI*. Oslo: Universitetsforlaget, 1983, pp. 126–41, 336–8.

ÓLAFÍA EINARSDÓTTIR

SYRLIN, JÖRG THE ELDER (1420/1430–1491) AND JÖRG THE YOUNGER (1455–1523)

Father and son were highly successful joiners and masons. Based in Ulm (Baden-Württemberg), they supplied furniture, altars, fountains, and other carvings for towns throughout Swabia and southern Germany. Yet were they also sculptors? The answer to this question ultimately determines the level of their fame. Recent scholarship suggests that most carvings attributed to the pair are by other Ulm sculptors with whom they collaborated. The careers of the Syrlins are relatively well documented. Jörg the Elder signed and dated (1458) an oak lectern with sculpted evangelist symbols now in the Ulmer Museum. More important, his signatures appear on the sedilia (chancel seats, 1468) and elaborate choir stalls (1469–1474) in the Minister cathedral in Ulm. This is the finest extant late Gothic cycle in Germany. It includes ninety nine exquisite oak busts and reliefs of philosophers and sibyls, each distinguished by fine facial characterizations and varied natural poses. Traditionally, scholars ascribed the sculpture and the carpentry to Jörg the Elder, though already in 1910 Georg Dehio challenged this view by arguing that Jörg's signatures and monograms pertain only to his production as a joiner. The sculpture of these and other carvings ascribed to Jörg are quite varied in their styles rather than the work of a single hand. In later-fifteenth-century Ulm, it was common for a single master to receive a commission for a complex altarpiece. This artist then engaged a collaborative team of sculptors, joiners, and painters. Between 1474 and 1481, Jörg and his colleagues created the Münster's monumental high altar. Although the altar was destroyed on July 20, 1531, during the Protestants' iconoclastic cleansing of the church, Jörg the Elder's intricate presentation drawing (81 × 231 cm; Stuttgart, Württembergisches Landesmuseum) displays his talents as a designer, notably his adept mastery of architectural ornament. The sculptor of the altar is unknown, though Michel Erhart of Ulm has been suggested.

Jörg the Younger trained with and assisted his rather before assuming control of the workshop in early 1482. Under his direction the atelier's production seems to have expanded, though again his role as sculptor is doubtful. Inscriptions and other documentation link him with projects at the Benedictine abbeys of Ochsenhausen, Zweifalten, and Blaubeuren. For Zwiefalten Jörg prepared choir stalls, a sacrament house, and seven altars between 1509 and the dedication of the choir in 1517. He was aided by Christoph Langeisen, an Ulm sculptor. Langeisen was likely just one of several participating sculptors. Little survived the rebuilding of the church in the mid-eighteenth century. Passion reliefs from one of these altars, today in the Württembergisches Landesmuseum in Stuttgart, are attributed to Nikolaus Weckmann (active 1481–1526), another Ulm sculptor to whom the majority of carvings once ascribed to Jörg the Younger are now credited. It appears that the son too was primarily a joiner and contractor. In 1493 his workshop created the elaborate choir stalls at Blaubeuren, which while loosely patterned on those in the Ulm Münster include far fewer sculpted busts.

Jörg the Younger, like his father, excelled as a designer. In 1482 one of the Syrlins completed and signed the Fish Trough fountain opposite the city hall in Ulm. The pair probably collaborated on the project; some scholars believe the showy twisting of the spire relates to other architectural drawings, such as the plan for a new western tower for the Münster, ascribed to the son. The three sandstone sculptures of knights, now in the Ulmer Museum, are by yet another hand.

See also **Erhart, Michel**

Further Reading

Baum, Julius. *Die Ulmer Plastik der Spätgotik.* Stuttgart: J. Hoffmann, 1911.

Dehio, Georg. "Über einige Künstlerinschriften des deutschen 15. Jahrhunderts." *Repertorium für Kunstwissenschaft* 33 (1910): 18–24.

Deutsch, Wolfgang. "Der ehemalige Hochaltar und das Chorgestühl, zur Syrlin- und zur Bildhauerfrage," in *600 Jahre Ulmer Münster: Festschrift,* ed. Hans Eugen Specker and Reinhard Wortmann. Forschungen zur Geschichte der Stadt Ulm 19. Ulm: Stadtarchiv, 1977, pp. 242–322.

——. "Syrlin der Jüngere oder Niklaus Weckmann?" In *Meisterwerke Massenhaft: Die Bildhauerwerkstatt des Niklaus Weckmann und die Malerei in Ulm um 1500.* Stuttgart: Württembergisches Landesmuseum, 1993, pp. 7–17.

Koepf, Hans. *Die gotischen Planrisse der Ulmer Sammlungen.* Foschungen zur Geschichte der Stadt Ulm, 18. Ulm: Stadtarchiv, 1977, nos. 8, 30, 31, 49.

Schneckenburger-Broschek, Anja. "Ein Niederländer als schwäbisches Genie: Neues zum Ulmer Chorgestühl." *Zeitschrift des deutschen Vereins für Kunstwissenschaft* 40 (1986): 40–68.

Seifert, Hans. *Das Chorgestühl im Ulmer Münster.* Königstein im Taunus: K.R. Langewiesche Nachfolger, 1958.

Vöge, Wilhelm. *Jörg Syrlin der Ältere und seine Bildwerke, 2 vols.* Berlin: Deutsche Verein für Kunstwissenschaft, 1950.

JEFFREY CHIPPS SMITH

T

TANNHÄUSER, DER (FL. MID–13TH C.)

The lyrical works of Tannhäuser, a thirteenth-century traveling singer and composer, are preserved in the famous Zurich Manesse family and Jena manuscripts of courtly love poetry known as *Minnesang*. The name is toponymic, but as several villages are called Tannhausen, the poet's place of origin cannot be determined. We know only that he was for a time at court in Vienna under the patronage of Duke Frederick II. The first song *(Leich)* can be dated to 1245, the sixth to 1264–1266. The language is South German.

The range and quality of the surviving poetry reveal Tannhäuser as a fine poet of great versatility. All three major categories of Middle High German verse are represented: *Minnesang, Leich,* and *Sangspruch*. The six *Minnelieder,* preserved in the Manesse manuscript, can be grouped as two summer songs, two winter songs—all relatively conventional—and two *Minne* (courtly love) parodies in which the poet's optimism is obviously misplaced in the face of the impossibility of his lady's absurdly exaggerated demands.

The *Leiche,* likewise in the Manesse manuscript, are probably Tannhäuser's best-known pieces. There are seven, five of them *Tanzleiche,* the earliest such dance songs in German literature. The first is a panegyric on Duke Frederick, and princes and patronage return later in *Leich* 6. *Minne* is a theme in several, and 2 and 3 both contain love stories. The shortest, 7, is a riddle. Recurring motifs are nature, May, and dancing, lending the *Leiche* a consistently jovial tone. The poet delights in references to contemporary narrative literature. A passion for geographical locations is no doubt intended to underscore the vast experience of the traveling singer, though some feel that in *Leich* no. 5 this reaches the level of parody.

There are sixteen *Sangsprüche* in three cycles in the Manesse manuscript and—though authenticity is open to question—a further cycle of four in the Jena manuscript. The principle theme of the Manesse *Sangsprüche* is the experience (and the poverty) of the traveling singer, patronage, and the death of the patron. The Jena cycle is more pious, including prayers of atonement. Other lyrical works attributed to Tannhäuser in Jena, Kolmar, and Wiltener manuscripts are at best of dubious authorship.

Tannhäuser was held in particular esteem in ensuing centuries, his love poetry being celebrated by the *Meistersänger,* who named a melody *(Tannhäuserton)* after him and cast him as the thirteenth member at the gathering of the "12 old masters." By contrast, a pious rejection of sexuality underlies the late medieval Tannhäuser legend, in which the poet endangers his soul by his service to Venus but turns to Mary in the end. In the poems *Tannhäuser und Venus* and *Tannhäuser und Frau Welt,* the Minnesinger takes his leave of the goddess despite her allure. The fifteenth-century *Tannhäuser-Ballads* develops this, with Tannhäuser then traveling to Rome to seek absolution. The pope (Urban IV) tells him he can no more be saved than the papal staff can produce life. When the dry stick begins to bud, the pope sends for Tannhäuser, but too late; the poet has returned to Venus and the pope is damned. The most familiar modern version of the legend is Wagner's opera, in which it is merged with the story of the *Wartburgkrieg.*

Further Reading

Thomas, J.W., trans. *Tannhäuser: Poet and Legend.* Chapel Hill: University of North Carolina Press, 1974.

GRAEME DUNPHY

THEODORA (c. 500–548)

Theodora became empress of Byzantium in 527. She had been born in poverty and had spent her youth as a notoriously virtuosic courtesan in Constantinople. But she reformed, and her cleverness and strong personality attracted the young Justinian, who made her his wife and, on his ascent to the throne as Justinian I, his consort.

Although Theodora differed with Justinian on theology and, as a strong adherent of Monophysitism, sometimes worked against his policies, she was his invaluable ally and counselor. Her advice helped him rescue his throne during the Nika riots (532), and her death from cancer in 548 was a grievous blow to him personally and politically.

Theodora had risen from the dregs of society and never felt totally secure on her throne; she intrigued constantly to ward off any challenge she saw to her husband or to her own standing with him. Thus, it is said, Theodora became jealous of the Ostrogothic queen of Italy, Amalasuntha, who was famous for cleverness and beauty, and—anxious lest this woman come to the capital and attract Justinian—conspired to have her murdered as a part of the dynastic tangles of the Ostrogothic court. Theodora's support of the Monophysites was played on by the Roman legate Vigilius, who promised her his aid in return for her influence in having him made pope (537). However, Vigilius found it impossible to keep his promise, and Theodora became his implacable foe. At her urging, Justinian had Vigilius abducted and brought to Constantinople to be coerced into supporting religious policies that Theodora had helped frame. Vigilius's degradation was Theodora's last triumph before her death.

Several portrait busts surviving from this period have been identified as Theodora, notably one that is now in the Castello Sforzesco in Milan. Even more striking is her austere portrayal, together with her retinue, in a famous mosaic panel in the church of San Vitale in Ravenna. Fired by the sensational account given of her by the historian Procopius, artists and writers of modern times have continued to be fascinated by her image: she has been the fanciful subject of an opera by Donizetti, a play by Sardou, numerous novels, and at least one (Italian) movie.

See also **Justinian I**

Further Reading

Bridge, Antony. *Theodora: Portrait in a Byzantine Landscape.* London: Casseil, 1978.

Browning, Robert. *Justinian and Theodora*, rev. ed. London: Thames and Hudson, 1987.

Diehl, Charles. *Theodora: Empress of Byzantium*, trans. Samuel R. Rosenbaum. New York: Ungar, 1972. (Originally published 1904.)

Procopius of Caesarea. *History of the Wars* and *Secret History.* Loeb Classical Library Series. London and Cambridge, Mass.: Heinemann/Harvard University Press, 1914–1935. (With reprints; translations.)

JOHN W. BARKER

THEODULF OF ORLÉANS (ca. 760–821)

A Goth born in Spain, Theodulf was forced to flee his homeland, coming to the court of Charlemagne in 780. By 798 he was named bishop of Orléans by Charlemagne. In 801 Pope Leo III honored him with the title of archbishop. Theodulf enjoyed high visibility and favor in the courts of Charlemagne and his successor, Louis the Pious. His luck changed, however, in 817, when he was accused of conspiring against the emperor, whereupon he was removed from his bishopric and imprisoned. He died, thus disgraced, in 821.

Although Theodulf is best known today as one of the preeminent poets of the Carolingian renaissance, he was probably more valued among his contemporaries for his theological and pastoral works. Around 800 he composed his first *Capitula*, a manual for parish priests, in an attempt to institute a reform within his diocese, and a second somewhere between 800 and 813. Forty-one copies survive throughout Europe and England, written between the 9th and 12th centuries, attesting to the popularity of the work. At Charlemagne's request he wrote the *Libri Carolini* under the pretense that it was actually the emperor's work. He also wrote *De ordine baptismi* and supervised a revision of the Bible at his scriptorium.

Theodulf's *Capitula* was widely used during the Anglo-Saxon monastic reform and survives in four English manuscripts. In Latin and English it became a standard work for the clergy and a source for Anglo-Saxon prose. Vercelli Homily III and Assmann Homilies XI and XII draw from the *Capitula*; Ælfric seems to have used it in his pastoral letters; and Wulfstan used it in composing his homilies. The *De ordine baptismi* was also known to the Anglo-Saxons. The text, surviving in BL Royal 8.C.iii, was used by Wulfstan in Homily VIII.

See also **Charlemagne; Wulfstan of York**

Further Reading

Primary Sources

Napier, Arthur S., ed. *The Old English Version of the Enlarged Rule of Chrodegang…; An Old English Version of the Capitula of Theodulf…* EETS o.s. 150. London: Kegan Paul, Trench, Trübner, 1916.

Theodulf. *Opera Omnia.* PL 105.

Secondary Sources

Gatch, Milton McC. *Preaching and Theology in Anglo-Saxon England: Ælfric and Wulfstan.* Toronto: University of Toronto Press, 1977.

Godman, Peter. *Poets and Emperors: Frankish Politics and Carolingian Poetry.* Oxford: Clarendon, 1987.

McKitterick, Rosamond, ed. *Carolingian Culture: Emulation and Innovation.* Cambridge: Cambridge University Press, 1994.

HELENE SCHECK

THIBAUT DE CHAMPAGNE (1201–1253)

The most illustrious of the trouvères and one of the most prolific, Thibaut IV, count of Champagne and king of Navarre, grandson of the great patroness of poets Marie de Champagne, was also an important political figure. After several years' education at the royal court of Philip II Augustus, young Thibaut began his life as a ruler under the regency of his mother, Blanche of Navarre. He later took part in the war of the newly crowned Louis VIII against the English, appearing at the siege of La Rochelle in 1224, and continued to serve the king, his overlord, thereafter. In 1226, however, he withdrew his support during the royal siege of Avignon and returned home in secret. Upon the king's death a few months later, Thibaut was accused of having poisoned him, but nothing came of this apparently groundless charge. The following year, he allied himself with other feudal powers in an attempt to dethrone Blanche of Castile, widow of Louis VIII and regent for their son Louis IX, but the queen succeeded in detaching him from the rebellious group and making him her defender. Attacked by his erstwhile allies, Thibaut was saved by the royal army.

Thibaut's relations with the crown, however, were unsteady, particularly after 1234, when he succeeded his uncle Sancho the Strong as king of Navarre, and it was not until 1236 that a final peace was achieved, based on the vassal's submission. Three years later, he left for the Holy Land as head of the crusade of 1239; the undertaking was marked from the start by discord among the Christian leaders and by Muslim military superiority, the result of which was Thibaut's decision in 1240 to withdraw from his charge and return to France. There, armed struggles engaged his attention through the following years, and in 1248 he made a penitent's pilgrimage to Rome. He died in Pamplona. He had been betrothed twice, married three times, divorced once, widowed once, and had fathered several children. The rumor has persisted since his day that the great love of his life was none other than Blanche of Castile, but apart from offering a tempting key to his political shifts, it seems to have no merit.

As a trouvère, Thibaut was immediately successful, seen as equaled only by his great predecessor Gace Brulé. Dante was to consider him one of the "illustrious" poets in the vernacular, and the medieval songbooks that group their contents by composer place his works before all others. The over sixty pieces ascribed to him with reasonable certainty, almost all preserved with music, show a majority of courtly chansons, none anti-conventional in theme or form but most marked by an unusual development of imagery, especially allegorical, use of refrains, or self-confident lightness of tone. The other works, revealing a style similarly characteristic of Thibaut, are *jeux-partis* (among the earliest known), debates, devotional songs (including one in the form of a *lai*), crusade songs, *pastourelles*, and a *serventois*.

See also **Blanche of Castile; Louis IX; Philip II Augustus**

Further Reading

Brahney, Kathleen J., ed. and trans. *The Lyrics of Thibaut de Champagne.* New York: Garland, 1988.

van der Werf, Hendrik, ed. *Trouvères-Melodien II.* Kassel: Bärenreiter, 1979, pp. 3–311.

Wallensköld, Axel, ed. *Les chansons de Thibaut de Champagne, roi de Navarre.* Paris: Champion, 1925.

Bellenger, Yvonne, and Danielle Quéruel, eds. *Thibaut de Champagne, prince et poète au XIIIe siècle.* Lyon: La Manufacture, 1987.

SAMUEL N. ROSENBERG

THIETMAR OF MERSEBURG (975–1008/1018)

Born into the comital house of Walbeck in eastern Saxony, Thietmar received his primary education at the royal convent of Quedlinburg. In 987, his father transferred him from Quedlinburg to the monastery of Berge, outside of Magdeburg. Thietmar remained at Berge for three years, continuing his education, apparently with the expectation that he would eventually join the community. When a place could not be obtained for him there, he was moved to the cathedral at Magdeburg (November 1, 990). Thietmar studied at the cathedral's school, then among the empire's preeminent centers of learning, and was formally admitted to the chapter circa 1000, during the reign of Archbishop Giselher. Professional advancement came to him during the reign of Giselher's successor, Archbishop Tagino. The archbishop elevated him to the priesthood in 1004 at a ceremony attended by Emperor Henry II, and thereafter he seems to have joined the archbishop's entourage. It was due to Tagino's favor, moreover, that Thietmar was chosen by Henry II to succeed the recently deceased bishop of the see of Merseburg (1008). As Bishop of Merseburg, Thietmar inherited a host of problems deriving from that diocese's troubled history. Emperor Otto I had founded the bishopric in 968, in conjunction with his elevation of Magedeburg to the status of archbishopric. For a variety of reasons, it was suppressed in 981, its property being divided among neighboring dioceses and its cathedral transformed into a proprietary monastery of the archbishops of Magdeburg. Although the diocese was restored by Henry II in 1004, its boundaries and property rights remained a matter of dispute. Thietmar seems to have occupied most of his career in attempts to regain diocesan lands ceded to neighboring dioceses during the period of Merseburg's suppression (i.e., 981–1004). Similar issues led to a long running property dispute with the Saxon ducal house of the Billunger.

Thietmar's chief gift to posterity is his history, the *Chronicon*, which he composed between 1012 and his death in 1018. The work is divided into eight books and survives in two manuscripts at Brussels and Dresden, the latter now available only in the form of a facsimile. The Dresden manuscript is particularly valuable as it was produced under Thietmar's direction and includes corrections and additions made in his own hand. In compiling the *Chronicon*, Thietmar drew heavily at times on the work of other historians, but much of his material is based on his own observations and experiences, especially in the later books. Indeed, for events in the reign of Emperor Henry II, he is often our unique informant. It is generally assumed that Thietmar's original intention was to focus on the history of his diocese. If so, his theme must have rapidly expanded to include the history and deeds of the Ottonian kings, their lineage, and other topics as well. Thietmar was nothing if not opinionated and expressed views on subjects ranging from politics to the (in his opinion) shocking character of contemporary women's fashions. He subjected monastic reform and its advocates to a withering critique and offered negative characterizations of Lotharingians, Bavarians, Italians, and others lacking the good fortune to have been born Saxon. With his detailed commentary on the career of Duke Boleslav Chrobry, Thietmar is one of the most important witnesses for the emergence of the medieval Polish state, and his detailed descriptions of Slavic social customs and religion are some of the earliest on record. Thietmar's testimony is especially valuable for the history of Ottonian policy in the east, German relations with the western Slavs, and the family histories of the east Saxon aristocracy.

See also **Otto I**

Further Reading

Chronicon (*Die Chronik des Bischofs Thietmar von Merseburg und ihre Korveier Überarbeitung*). ed. Robert Holtzmann. Monumenta Germaniae Historica, Scriptores rerum Germanicarum, nova series 9. Berlin: Weidmann, 1935.

Leyser, Karl. *The Ascent of Latin Europe*. Oxford: Clarendon Press, 1986.

Lippelt, Heinrich. *Thietmar von Merseburg. Riechsbischof und Chronist*. Mitteldeutsche Forschungen 72. Cologne: Böhlau, 1973.

Warner, David A. "Thietmar of Merseburg on Rituals of Kingship." *Viator* 26 (1995): 53–76.

——. *Ottonian Germany*. Manchester: Manchester University Press, 1999.

DAVID A. WARNER

THOMAS À KEMPIS (1379/1380–1471)

An author of spiritual writings, Thomas (Hemerken) à Kempis (also Hamerkein, Malleolus) was born some time between September 29, 1379, and July 24, 1380, at Kempen near Cologne. At the age of thirteen he left for Deventer to attend classes at the chapter's school of the Lebuinus Church. In 1399 he applied for admission to a monastery of the Canons Regular at Zwolle called St. Agnietenberg. This monastery, a daughter-house of Windesheim, was pervaded by the spirit of the *Devotio moderna* (Modern Devotion) movement. After taking the habit in 1406 and after his solemn profession in 1407, Thomas was ordained a priest in 1413 or 1414. He evolved into a prolific transcriber and author of several spiritual writings. From 1425 till 1430 (and in a second term starting in 1433), he performed the task of subprior and combined it with the assignment of a novice master. In this last quality he developed as a musician, preacher, and history teacher. For the job of procurator Thomas turned out to be less suited; he held that office for only one year in 1443. He died on either May 1 or July 24, 1471.

Thomas à Kempis is credited with thirty-one treatises, as well as three cycles of *sermones* (sermons), some *cantica* (catechetic songs), and *epistolae* (letters). Depending on the goal he had in mind or the audience he wanted to reach, he used different genres. He proved to be a pious historian in, e.g., his *Chronicon Montis sanctae Agnetis*. One can discover his qualities as a musician and writer of letters in his *Cantica* and *Epistolae*. His output consists in large part of practical-ascetic works, such as his *Libellus de disciplina claustralium*, *Vita boni monachi*, *Manuale parvulorum*, and *Doctrina iuvenum*.

His famous *De Imitatione Christi* is included in this category as well. This work deserves a wider treatment here, as it is one of the most influential spiritual texts of the late Middle Ages and can be considered the most widely read book in Christianity, with the exception of the Bible. In the centuries-old fight about the authorship of this fifteenth-century treatise, forty serious candidates have been taken into account. Among them Augustin, Bernard, Jan van Ruusbroec, Geert Grote, Joannes Gersen, abbot of Vercelli, Jean Gerson, and, finally, Thomas à Kempis, were the most prominent. On the basis of the excellent linguistic and codicological (manuscript) investigations of L.J.M. Delaissé, it is now generally accepted among scholars that Thomas à Kempis has to be regarded as the author of the four *libelli* (books) that form *De Imitatione Christi*. The first four treatises of Thomas à Kempis's autograph of 1441 (Brussels, Koninklijke Bibliotheek, manuscript no. 5855–5861) form, in this order, books I, II, IV, and III of *De Imitatione Christi*. They have the following incipits (first lines):

1. *Qui sequitur me, non ambulat in tenebris*
2. *Regnum Dei intra vos est dicit Dominus*
3. *De sacramento. Venite ad me omnes qui laboratis*
4. *Audiam quid loquator in me Dominus Deus*

In other manuscripts and incunabula, treatises I, II, and IV often appear as a unity. If one considers the contents of these works and the titles given by Thomas in his autograph of 1441, this unity is not purely a coincidence. A codex belonging to a monastery of Canons Regular at Nijmegen, now in the Royal Library in Brussels (manuscript no. 22084), makes clear that the four *libelli* of *De Imitatione Christi* already circulated in 1427, fifteen years before Thomas completed his final redaction in the autograph mentioned above.

In treatise I, *Admonitiones ad spiritualem vitam utiles*, Thomas formulates, for beginners in spiritual life, some points of advice concerning a life in silence, prayer, and study. In treatise II, *Admonitiones ad interna trahentes*, Thomas merely describes the mental state that the young religious has to develop to consider prayer as a privileged place where one is able to meet Christ personally instead of a mechanical duty. Treatise III, *De interna consolatione*, is Thomas's personal testimony of his intimate relationship with Christ in daily life of the monastic community. Thomas points out that the life of a person who is looking for God is not without obstacles. He wrote this book, furthermore, to provide consolation. Finally, treatise IV of the *De Imitatio Christi* contains reflections on the Holy Eucharist that are characteristic of the time in which the *Imitatio* was composed but not strictly coordinated with the contents of the first three books. It is especially in these books that Thomas develops the concept of a "journey" for the faithful. Here he first describes the inner disposition from which one can be open to Christ and follow Him in the most appropriate and fruitful way. From studies made after those of Delaissé mentioned above, the conclusion can be drawn that Thomas made the stylistic improvements in the *Imitatio* not because of his love for the beauty of the (Latin) language, the *latinitas*, but for catechetical reasons.

Other treatises, like the *Orationes et meditationes de vita Christi*, have a more theological character. In his *Hortulus rosarum* and *Soliloquium animae*, Thomas shows his gifts as a spiritual writer. All but one of his works were composed in Latin; he wrote a small treatise in Middle Dutch: *Van goeden woerden to horen ende die to spreken*. Finally, he compiled his *sermones* in three coherent cycles.

One can easily conclude that the quantity of scholarly contributions on the sources, style, and theology in Thomas à Kempis's *opera omnia* (complete works) stands in no proportion to the enormous amount of literature devoted to his authorship of the *Imitatio*. The study of his theology is in an early stage; up until now, no attempt has been made at a synthesis. Recent investigation has shown that Thomas's originality lies in his view that the ascetic structuring of life is explained by the mystical longing that Thomas wants to develop in each person. In his theological anthropology, mystical aspirations are exclusively nourished and purified by a realization of the self in an ascetic way of life. Furthermore, his spirituality is strongly Christ-centered.

Further Reading

Ampe, Albert, and Bernhard Spaapen. "Imitatio Christi. I. Le livre et l'auteur.—II. Doctrine," in *Dictionnaire de spiritualité*, ed. Marcel Viller. Paris: Beauchense, 1932ff, vol. 7, cols. 2338–2355.

Delaissé, L. J. M. *Le Manuscrit autographe de Thomas à Kempis et "L'Imitation." Examen archéologique et édition diplomatique du Bruxellensis 5855–5861.* 2 vols. Paris: Erasme, 1956.

Ingram, John K., ed. *The Earliest English Translation of the First Three Books of* De imitatione Christi ... London: K. Paul, Trench, Trubner, 1893.

Pohl, Michael Joseph, ed. *Thomae a Kempis canonici regularis ordinis S. Augustini Opera Omnia*, 7 vols. Freibourg im Breisgau: Herder, 1902–1922.

Puyol, Pierre-Édouard. *L'auteur du livre De Imitatione Christi. Première section: la contestation.* Paris: Retaux, 1899.

van Dijk, Rudolf, Th.M. "Thomas Hemerken à Kempis," in *Dictionnaire de spiritualité*, ed. Marcel Viller. Paris: Beauchense, 1932ff., vol. 15, cols. 817–826.

van Geest, Paul. "Thomas Hemerken a Kempis," in *Die deutsche Literatur des Mittelalters*: *Verfasserlexikon*, ed. Kurt Ruh et al., vol. 9. Berlin: de Gruyter, 1978, cols. 862–882.

——. "Introduction," in *Thomas a Kempis: La vallée des Lis*. Bégrolles-en-Mauges: Abbaye de Bellefontaine, 1992, pp. 11–48.

——. "De sermones van Thomas a Kempis; een terreinverkenning." *Trajecta* 2 (1993): 305–326.

——. *Thomas a Kempis (1379/80–1471): een studie van zijn mens- en godsbeeld: analyse en tekstuitgave van de Hortulus Rosarum en de Vallis Liliorum.* Kampen: Kok, 1996.

Weiler, Anton G. "Recent Historiography on the Modern Devotion: Some Debated Questions." *Archief voor de geschiedenis van de katholieke kerk in Nederland* 26 (1984): 161–184.

"The works of Thomas à Kempis," trans. Michael Joseph Pohl. 6 vols. Ph.d. diss., University of London, 1905–1908.

PAUL J. J. VAN GEEST

THOMAS D'ANGLETERRE (fl. 2nd half of the 12th c.)

Eight fragments totaling 3,146 octosyllabic lines, distributed among five manuscripts, are all that remain of Thomas's *Tristan*, composed ca. 1175 for the nobility of Norman England. The author may have been a clerk at the court of Henry II Plantagenêt in London. The fragments of Thomas's *Tristan* preserve essentially the last part of the story, from Tristan's exile in Brittany to the lovers' deaths. Line 3,134 of the epilogue, the adaptations by Brother Robert (Old Norse) and Gottfried von Strassburg (Middle High German), and the Oxford *Folie*, however, all indicate that Thomas had composed a complete version, one that followed the biographical structure and general movement of the original legend, though Thomas made numerous modifications to it.

Placing Arthur in the mythic past and situating the story in an England ruled over by King Marc, Thomas's reworking is dominated by rationality; the poet tones down the fantastic elements and shows a certain logic in the ordering of events and in the behavior and motivation of the characters. It is possible to suppose that Thomas would have described the *amur fine e veraie* experienced by the protagonists when Tristan first came to Ireland (see 1. 2,491), with the love potion only confirming that love. In keeping with the milieu for which he wrote, Thomas eliminated or reworked overly "realistic" episodes (harp and lyre, Iseut and the lepers, life in the forest of Morois), bringing the story into line with the new courtly ideals. A master hunter, Tristan (like his "pupil" Iseut) is also a musician and poet as well as an artist capable of creating the marvelous statues of the Hall of Images.

The principal contribution of Thomas, as scholar and moralist, is in his minute analysis of love and the other mysteries of human nature. Characters reveal themselves through monologues, debates, and lyric laments; and their self-examination is analyzed through the narrator's long interventions. The action is motivated less by exterior agents than by *inner* adventure, the wanderings of the protagonists' consciences, which, alone seems to interest Thomas. The paradox in Thomas's version is thus the narration, within the story of a love seen as absolute and perfect, of an analysis of love that shows Tristan's desire for change (*novelerie*) and his fundamental dissatisfaction. This analysis is coupled with reflections on jealousy and on Tristan's obsession with taking the place of the Other (Iseut or Marc) and feeling himself the pleasure experienced (or not) by the Other. Iseut's role is to express, in actions and lyric laments, her passion, tenderness, and pity for her lover's plight. Thomas uses the technique of "gainsaying": the quarrel between Iseut and Brangain allows the queen to reveal the positive side of *fin'amor*, which had been depicted by Brangain as folly and lechery. Characters like Cariado, Iseut of the White Hands, Tristan the Dwarf, and, undoubtedly, the faithful Kaherdin in the lost episodes, are there to fill out this "mirror" of the multiple faces of love.

The language available to Thomas was not yet as subtle and supple as his analyses. Words like *desir*, *voleir*, *poeir*, even *raisun*, whose meanings seem still too imprecise or overcharged, are significant less in themselves than through the systems of oppositions into which they fit. Repetitions bordering on redundancy, anaphora, antitheses, and rhetorical questions occur almost too frequently. Thomas, however, is capable of realistic depiction, as in the description of London, the doctors who treat Tristan, or the storm. The death scene is characterized by a rhythm wedded to the circularity of desire that conveys, in the echoing of certain rhyme pairs (*confort/mort, amur/dulur, anguissus/desirus*), the very essence of love.

Thomas makes good the ambitious program articulated in the epilogue: to complete a narrative (*l'escrit*) in which all lovers, whatever their manner of loving, can find pleasure, recall their own passion through the exemplary destiny of Tristan and Iseut, and perhaps escape—for that seems to be the moralist's ultimate goal—the torments and deceits of passion.

See also **Béroul; Gottfried von Straßburg; Henry II**

Further Reading

Thomas d'Angleterre. *Le roman de Tristan par Thomas*, ed. Joseph Bédier. 2 vols. Paris: SATF, 1902–05.
——. *Les fragments du roman de Tristan, poème du XIIe siècle*, ed. Bartina H. Wind. Geneva: Droz, 1960.
——. *Thomas of Britain: Tristran*, ed. and trans. Stewart Gregory. New York: Garland, 1991.
Baumgartner, Emmanuèle. *Tristan et Iseut: de la légende aux récits en vers*. Paris: Presses Universitaires de France, 1987.
Fourrier, Anthime. *Le courant réaliste dans le roman courtois en France au moyen âge*. Paris: 1960, pp. 19–109.
Hunt, Tony. "The Significance of Thomas' *Tristan*." *Reading Medieval Studies* 7 (1981): 41–61.

EMMANUÈLE BAUMGARTNER

THOMAS OF CELANO (c. 1190–1260)

Thomas of Celano was a Franciscan hagiographer, the author of the first two lives of Francis of Assisi. Little is known about Thomas's early life, except that he was apparently from a noble family and received a good education. He joined the Franciscan order in the first years of its existence, probably in 1215, and volunteered for the first Franciscan mission to Germany in 1221. He seems to have shown administrative talent, for the next year he was made *custos* of a substantial part of the central European province, and in 1223 he was appointed vicar for the entire province while its minister was in Italy. In 1224, Thomas returned to Italy. He may have been present when Francis died in 1226.

Thomas's reputation as a preacher and stylist and his status as a relatively early follower of Francis seem to be the reasons Pope Gregory IX commissioned him in July 1228 to write an official life of the saint. While preparing the work, Thomas amassed a huge collection of anecdotes from friars and laymen that became a source for several later lives of Francis. By February 1229, he had finished what would come to be called *Vita prima*. Written in *cursus*, or rhythmical prose, the *Vita prima* is a skillful attempt to convey the interior life of Francis as early Franciscans knew it. But in many ways it is also a conventional stereotyped hagiography. It emphasizes Francis's spiritual journey and ideals but omits some of the quirkiest and most compelling episodes of the saint's life. In 1230, Thomas edited the *Vita prima* into a liturgical epitome, the *Legenda ad usum chori*.

Although the *Vita prima* was greeted with enormous enthusiasm when it first appeared, by the early 1240s many friars were voicing dissatisfaction with it, apparently because so many favorite stories about Francis had been left out. In 1244, the Franciscan general chapter invited all friars who had known Francis ro submit their reminiscences so that a new, more complete *vita* could be composed. Thomas was once again called on to be the author. From materials he had not used in his first life and from recently submitted anecdotes, Thomas crafted the *Memoriale in desiderio animae de gestis et verbis sanctissimi patris nostri Francisci*, usually called the *Vita secunda*. Like the first life, it tells the *story* of Francis's conversion; but in its second part the anecdotes are arranged as a kind of prolonged character study of the subject. The *Vita secunda*—unlike the *Vita prima*—confronts matters of controversy within the order, especially a growing dispute over the relaxation of the rule. Thomas clearly depicts Francis as favoring a strict adherence to the rule and lamenting the corruption of his order by those who sought to relax it.

If "laxists" found the general message of the *Vita secunda* distasteful, many throughout the order complained that it gave insufficient attention to Francis's miracles, a subject that had been carefully elaborated in the *Vita prima*. To remedy this, Thomas composed a *Tractatus de miraculis* in 1255–1256 that detailed almost 200 of Francis's miracles. Thomas may also be the author of the *Legenda sanctae Clarae*, a life of Francis's friend Saint Clare written in the mid-1250s.

Thomas died in 1260 at Tagliacozzo. His works survived, despite a directive of the Franciscan chapter general of 1266 ordering that they and all other lives of Francis be destroyed to facilitate acceptance of Bonaventure's *Legenda maior* as the only official version of Francis's life.

See also **Bonaventure, Saint; Francis of Assisi, Saint**

Further Reading

Edition

Thomas of Celano. *Saint Francis of Assisi: First and Second Life of Saint Francis, with Selections from the Treatise on the Miracles of the Blessed Francis*, trans. Placid Hermann. Chicago, Ill.: Franciscan Herald, 1963.

Critical Studies

Bontempi, Pietro. *Tommaso da Celano, storico e innografo*. Rome: Scuola Salesiana del Libro, 1952.

De Beer, Francis. *La conversion de Saint François selon Thomas de Celano*. Paris: Éditions Franciscaines, 1963.

Facchinetti, Vittorino. *Tommaso da Celano: Il primo biografo di San Francesco*. Quaracchi: Collegio di San Bonaventura, 1918.

Miccoli, Giovanni. "La 'conversione' di San Francesco secondo Tommaso da Celano." *Studi Medievali* Series 3(5), 1964, pp. 775–792.

Moorman, John R. H. *Sources for the Life of Francis of Assisi*. Manchester: Manchester University Press, 1940. (Reprint, Farnborough: Gregg, 1966.)

Spirito, Silvana. *Il francescanesimo di fra Tommaso da Celano*. Assisi: Edizioni Porziuncola, 1963.

THOMAS TURLEY

THOMASÎN VON ZERCLAERE
(fl. early 12th c.)

Born into an ancient noble family in Cividale in Friulia, northern Italy, around 1185, Thomasîn was a member of the monastic cathedral of Aquileia and so later came into close contact with Wolfger von Erla, the German patriarch of Aquileia known for his patronage of such famous German poets as Walther von der Vogelweide. We might assume that Wolfger commissioned Thomasîn to compose his famous book of courtly etiquette, *Der Welsche Gast* (*The Italian Visitor*), consisting of about 14,800 verses. Thomasîn dated his Middle High German poem by telling us that he wrote it twenty-eight years after the loss of Jerusalem to the Arabs in 1187, that is, in 1215. The intention with his treatise was to improve the desolate state of the German nobility. It is the first German *Hofzucht* (courtly primer) ever written, and this by a nonnative speaker; it addresses young noblemen and women, teaching them the norms of courtly behavior. Thomasîn also added a general lesson about courtly love that he based on his *Buch von der Höfischeit* (*Book of Courtliness*), which he had previously composed in the Provençal language. In his book the poet emphasizes the value of constancy (*staete*), moderation (*mâze*), law (*reht*), and generosity (*milte*). Thomasîn drew from many different sources but mentions only the *Moralia* by Pope Gregory the Great (d. 604), a highly popular Latin moral treatise. Nevertheless, the text demonstrates Thomasîn's extensive knowledge of theological and secular literature of his time. The poet was clearly opposed to Walther von der Vogelweide's polemics against the pope, warned of the threatening spread of hereticism, and appealed to the German knighthood to embark on a new crusade. For him, knighthood must be subservient to the church and must pursue primarily religious and moral ideals. However, Thomasîn did not hesitate to recommend courtly literature as reading material for young noble people because some of the best-known protagonists in Middle High German literature would provide them with models of ideal behavior. The *Welsche Gast* proved to be an enormously popular didactic treatise and has come down to us in some two dozen manuscripts (thirteen complete, eleven as fragments), of which almost all are illustrated.

See also **Gregory VII, Pope; Walther von der Vogelweide**

Further Reading

Huber, Christoph. "Höfischer Roman als Integumentum? Das Votum Thomasîns von Zerclaere." *Zeitschrift für deutsches Altertum* 115 (1986): 79–100.

Neumann, Friedrich. "Einführung," in *Der Welsche Gast des Thomasîn von Zerclaere. Cod. Pal. Germ. 389 der Universitätsbibliothek Heidelberg*. Wiesbaden: Reichert, 1974, Kommentarband, pp. 1–65.

Röcke, Werner. *Feudale Anarchie und Landesherrschaft: Wirkungsmöglichkeiten didaktischer Literatur. Thomasîns von Zerclaere "Der Welsche Gast."* Bern: Lang, 1978.

Ruff, E. J. F. *"Der Welsche Gast" des Thomasîn von Zerclaere: Untersuchung zu Gehalt und Bedeutung einer mhd. Morallehre*. Erlangen: Palm und Enke, 1982.

Thomasîn von Zerclaria. *Der Welsche Gast*, ed., Heinrich Rückert. Quedlinburg: Basse, 1852; rpt. ed. Friedrich Neumann. Berlin: de Gruyter, 1965.

ALBRECHT CLASSEN

TORQUEMADA, TOMÁS DE (1420–1498)

Born in the town from which he drew his surname, in the province of Palencia, in 1420. He was nephew to the no less famous Cardinal Juan de Torquemada, author of the *Tractatus contra Midianitas*, written in defense of the Jewish *conversos* (Christian converts) from whom he, and correspondingly Tomás, were said to have been descended. As a young man, Tomás entered the Order of St. Dominic in the priory of San Pablo in Valladolid, and resided as a friar in the convent at Piedrahita. He was later appointed prior of the convent of Santa Cruz in Segovia, a title he retained throughout his career; and at about the same time was chosen to be a confessor of Queen Isabel and King Fernando: it is in this role that he appears in the only painting that is believed to depict him faithfully, Berruguete's *Virgin of the Catholic Kings*, in the Prado.

On 11 February 1482 he was appointed by papal bull as one of seven new inquisitors to continue the work of the recently founded Inquisition (the first two inquisitors had been appointed in 1480). In 1483 a new central council, the Consejo de la Suprema y General Inquisición, was set up by the king and queen to govern the inquisition, and Torquemada was chosen to head it as inquisitor general. On 17 October 1483 another papal bull, which conceded control of the inquisitions of the

Iberian Peninsula to the crown, also appointed Torquemada as joint inquisitor general of the three realms of Aragón, Catalonia, and Valencia. In this role, he was empowered to intervene in any part of the peninsula in a way that not even the crown was always able to. Torquemada subsequently played a key role in forcing through the introduction of the new inquisition in the realms of the Crown of Aragón, which still retained their old inquisitors from the medieval inquisition. In May 1484 Torquemada appointed new inquisitors for the eastern kingdoms, but faced enormous opposition, fundamentally because the new appointees were all Castilians and their tribunal was not subject to the laws of the kingdoms; in Aragón one of the appointees, Pedro Arbués, was murdered in 1485. To find a way out of the impasse, in February 1486 pope Innocent VII sacked all the existing papal inquisitors in the Crown of Aragón, and secured the simultaneous withdrawal of the Castilian nominees. This left the way open for Torquemada to start again with new appointees.

The important contribution made by Torquemada to the new inquisition is confirmed by the fact that he wrote its first rule book, the *Instrucciones*, first drawn up in November 1484 and then later amplified in versions of 1485, 1488, and 1498. Together with additions made in 1500, these early rules were known as the *Instrucciones Antiguas*, and laid down all the procedures of the tribunal in its early period. Torquemada must not, however, be viewed as all-powerful. As inquisitor general he was no more than chairman of the Suprema and could be overruled by it; moreover, his commission, which came from the pope, could be revoked at any time. In 1491 and again in 1494, while Torquemada was still functioning, additional and temporary (until 1504) inquisitor generals were appointed to aid the work of the inquisition, proof that he did not hold unquestioned power.

No documentary proof whatsoever exists for attributing to Torquemada the evidently anti-Semitic philosophy of the early inquisition, or responsibility for the bloody excesses of the tribunal; but neither is there any reason to question the traditional view that sees him as the driving spirit behind its early years. It is unquestionable that he was a major force behind the expulsion of the Jews in 1492: King Fernando stated expressly, in a letter that he sent to several nobles, that "the Holy Office of the Inquisition has provided that the Jews be expelled from all our realms." A story of uncertain origin states that when the Jews tried to buy their way out of the expulsion, Torquemada burst into the presence of the king and queen and threw thirty pieces of silver on the table, demanding to know for what price Christ was to be sold again.

A strong supporter of religious reform, Torquemada in 1482 founded the beautiful monastery of Santo Tomás in Avila, where he died on 16 September 1498.

Further Reading

Kamen, H. *Historia de la Inquisitión en España y América.* Madrid, 1984. Lea, H. C. *A History of the Inquisition of Spain.* 4 vols.

HENRY KAMEN

TORRE, ALFONSO DE LA (fl. mid-15th c.)

Theologian and writer in the vernacular active in the mid-fifteenth century, remembered nowadays as the author of the *Visión deleytable*, a philosophical dialogue and survey of the seven liberal arts, natural theology, and ethics. The work is in large part a cento of older texts, mostly unidentified and at times heavily amplified and supplemented by the author, and bound together by an allegorical dialogue. The *Visión* enjoyed a certain currency in its own century and in the two following. By the end of the seventeenth century it had undergone eleven printings, had been translated into Catalan and Italian and, unbelievably, back into Spanish.

What is most notable, indeed astonishing, about Torre's dialogue and the thought it expresses is the fundamentally Averroist and rationalist direction of its argument, especially of its theology. The main index to this tendency is, of course, the author's choice of sources, in some instances unremarkable, in others quite otherwise. Thus the passages on the liberal arts depend largely on Isidore of Seville and Al-Ghazāli. The pages on cosmology, on the influence of the spheres on the sublunary world, are from a source Torre calls simply "Hermes," but which is in fact the *Latin Asclepius*, very well known and influential in Western Christendom. But the matter on natural theology comes not from a Christian source, but from Maimonides's *Guide for the Perplexed*. This notable text brings to the *Vision* unaltered the Maimonidean teaching about the nature of God, eminently his existence, unity and incorporeity, but also his power, omniscience, and Providence. One should add that the passages in the *Guide* that express views at odds with what we could call common Christian theology—on providence, for example, or on the nature of evil—are preserved in the *Vision* without embarrassment. There is also in Torre's text, as we should note in fairness, a series of chapters that speak plain Christian language. But the author makes absolutely no effort to reconcile the sense of these pages with the rest of his argument, and one might indeed reasonably guess that this passage is a sop, a concession to the Christian reader, who elsewhere in the work is induced to accept views that at best are on the outer limits of orthodoxy.

The rationalist strain is sustained in the *Vision* in passages entirely separate from those directly and extensively dependent on the *Guide*. In a pair of lines early in the work Torre alludes hastily to Maimonides's theory of prophecy, roughly the view that God speaks to his prophets "mediante la lunbre yntelectual" (by means of intellectual enlightenment). In a second short passage he refers clearly to Maimonides's notion that the Bible speaks one language to the wise and learned and another to the vulgar, or in Leo Strauss's words, that Scripture "is an esoteric text, and that its esoteric teaching is akin to that of Aristotle." More important, perhaps, the *Visión's* chapters on ethics make few significant allusions to Christianity, or indeed, even to the idea of rewards and punishments in the other world.

Torre at one point says that the will of God can be understood in two senses, as what he wills directly and as what he wills virtually as he foresees the consequences of his first decision. Significantly, this theme is not Maimonidean; it savors of Christian scholasticism, and is possibly of Scotist or nominalist tendency. In other words, Torre's rationalism is not an accident. When he presents unmodified Maimonidean teachings that are at variance with those of Christian theology, the choice of doctrine is not innocent; it is certainly not made in ignorance. Torre was, as we have seen, a legitimate theologian, a *bachiller en teología*, and the knowledge of Christian divinity revealed in details of the course of the *Vision* is fully professional. His choice of themes, therefore, must have been fully deliberate. What, then, are we to think of this strange book and its author? Was Torre a crypto-Jew? Perhaps; the case is interesting. One should note that the mixture in the *Visión* of Jewish authorities and Christian is in no way alien to later medieval Jewish Averroism; the conversion of Shlomo Halevy/Pablo de Santa María was due in great part to his early familiarity with Aquinas. Torre's final plea to the Infante don Carlos not to show his book to a third person is itself revealing. Maimonides himself lays it down firmly that high doctrine should not be revealed to the vulgar.

See also **Averroës, Abu 'L-Walīd Muhammad B. Ahmad B. Rushd; Isidore of Seville, Saint; Maimonides**

Further Reading

Strauss, L. *How Fārābī Read Plato's Laws.* Damascus, 1957.
Torre, A. de la. *Visión deleytable.* 2 vols. Salamanca, 1991.

CHARLES FRAKER

TOSCANELLI, PAOLO DAL POZZO (1397–May 1482)

Noted Florentine physician, mathematician, astronomer, and leading cosmographer of his day. Born into a family of rich Florentine merchants and bankers, Toscanelli studied medicine (he is sometimes referred to as Paul the Physician) at the University of Padua, the principal seat of scientific learning in Italy. Here he acquired a sound theoretical education, which he combined with a Florentine appreciation of pragmatism and practical experience. He was a scientist with a businessman's eye for calculations. Toscanelli numbered among his close friends and acquaintances important humanists like Nicholas of Cusa, Filippo Brunelleschi, Angelo Poliziano, Cristoforo Landino, and Leon Battista Alberti; he also knew Marsilio Ficino and Giovanni Pico, although he disagreed with them on the subject of astrology.

If little has survived of Toscanelli's own writings, we know from the tributes of his contemporaries that he was held in great regard. Toscanelli was interested in a wide variety of subjects, including optics and agriculture. One surviving manuscript shows that his observations on comets were remarkably accurate for his day. Highly empirical, he founded his geographical theories more on contemporary travel accounts and his own research than on classical sources such as Ptolemy. He is reported to have interviewed travelers and visitors recently returned from Asia and Africa: he knew Marco Polo's *Divisament du monde* (c. 1298) and Niccolò dei Conti's account of Asia based on his travels (1435–1439), written by his contemporary, Poggio Bracciolini.

Early biographers of Toscanelli credit him with having theorized about the possibility of reaching the Indies via the Atlantic, and of making his idea known to King Alfonso V of Portugal (r. 1438–1481) and Christopher Columbus (1451–1506). In 1474, Toscanelli is said to have written a letter defending the notion that one could sail west from Europe and reach the spice regions of "Cathay" to Portuguese canon Fernão Martins de Reriz, a familiar at court and later cardinal. The information was meant for the king. Toscanelli and Martins had been friends of Nicholas of Cusa for many years; both had been present at his death in 1464. A world map supposed to have accompanied the letter and now also lost, greatly underestimated the true expanse of the Atlantic, showing "Cipangu" (Japan) lying 3,000 nautical miles (some 3,450 miles or 5,555 kilometers) west of the Canaries and at about the same latitude. Having learned of this letter and map, Columbus wrote to Toscanelli from Lisbon some years later (c. 1480) requesting a copy of the map. A transcription of Toscanelli's response survives in a book (*Historia Rerum Ubique Gestarum* by Aeneas Silvius [Pope Pius II]) that Columbus once owned. The veracity of this correspondence has been disputed, and even if authentic, Toscanelli's miscalculation of the earth's circumference probably only confirmed Columbus's own ideas rather than implanted them as has been claimed.

The text of the letter encourages Columbus to undertake such a westward voyage for several reasons: commercial (the East was rich in precious commodities); practical (a voyage across the Atlantic, as Toscanelli misconstrued it, would be quicker than the route around Africa); and pious (Christian Europe would be able to resurrect its mission to Asia, which had been abandoned in the fourteenth century, and mount a crusade to reconquer the Holy Land).

Years after his death, Toscanelli's fame as a scientist had not waned; in 1493, Ercole d'Este, duke of Ferrara, sent to Toscanelli's heir in Florence seeking to obtain his manuscripts and maps.

See also **Columbus, Christopher; Polo, Marco; Nicholas of Cusa**

Further Reading

La Carta perduta: Paolo dal P.T. e la cartografia delle grandi scoperte. Florence: Alinari, 1992.

Flint, Valerie I.J. *The Imaginative Landscape of Christopher Columbus.* Princeton, NJ: Princeton UP, 1992.

Garin, Eugenio. "Ritratto di Paolo dal Pozzo Toscanelli." *Belfagor* 3 [anno 12] (1957): 241–257; rpt. in *Ritratti di umanisti.* Florence, 1967, pp. 41–66.

Morison, Samuel Eliot. *Journals and Other Documents on theLife and Voyages of Christopher Columbus.* New York: Columbia UP, 1963.

Phillips, J.R.S. *The Medieval Expansion of Europe.* Oxford and New York: Oxford UP, 1988.

Revelli, Paolo. *Cristoforo Colombo e la scuola cartografica genovese.* Genoa: Consiglio Nazionale delle Ricerche, 1937.

GLORIA ALLAIRE

TRAINI, FRANCESCO (fl. 1321–1345)

The painter and illuminator Francesco Traini (Francesco di Traino) is generally considered the most important Pisan artist of the second quarter of the *Trecento*, when Pisa was under the rule of Francesco Novello della Gherardesca. Traini's career is still a focus of debate among scholars, but all would agree that he was one of the most original painters in fourteenth-century Italy. Traini's only surviving signed work is an altarpiece depicting Saint Dominic between eight scenes from his life (1344–1345; Pisa, Museo Nazionale di San Matteo). Since the nineteenth century, this altarpiece has been a valuable point of reference in attempts to identify a larger body of Traini's work.

Documented Life and Career: 1321–1345

Nothing is known about Traini's formative years; but to judge from his securely identifiable work, he was indebted to Sienese artistic traditions, especially the art of Simone Martini and Lippo Memmi, who were both active in Pisa in the early fourteenth century. This debt is evident in Traini's expressive treatment of line, his use of richly wrought surface textures, and his interest in spirited narrative detail. In addition, the Giottesque traditions of Florentine painting in general and the San Torpè Master in particular have been identified as pos-

Francesco Traini. *The Triumph of St. Thomas Aquinas.*
© Scala/Art Resource, New York.

sible sources for the more forcefully expressive elements in Traini's recognized oeuvre. Traini must already have been established as an independent painter with a certain reputation c. 1321, for in July and August 1322 it is recorded that he was paid for having decorated two important rooms in the Palazzo degli Anziani in Pisa. His success during the following decade is indicated by the fact that in December 1337 he committed himself to taking on an apprentice (by the name of Giovanni) for a period of three years. Traini is next recorded in December 1340 and February 1341, when he was involved in a commission to paint a banner for the confraternity of the Laudi of the cathedral in Pisa. In 1344 and 1345, Traini received payment for the signed Saint Dominic Altarpiece, which adorned an altar in the powerful Dominican church of Santa Caterina in Pisa. Albizzo delle Statere, a wealthy Pisan citizen who was active in public life, had allocated funds for its execu-

tion in his will of 1336; the status of this commission suggests that Traini's art was held in high regard by his contemporaries. Traini is not thought to have survived the Black Death in 1348.

Panel Paintings, Frescoes, and Illuminations: 1320s–1340s

The Saint Dominic Altarpiece is considered one of the greatest achievements of Pisan *Trecento* panel painting. It shows a monumental standing figure of the saint, whose solid form is crisply delineated and defined by robust modeling. At each side of the saint are four episodes from his life, contained within quatrefoils; these are characterized by a remarkably fresh sense of narrative. For example, in one scene—*Saint Dominic Saving Pilgrims from a Shipwreck*—the painter was careful to evoke a variety of responses ranging from a desperate struggle for life by those in the water to the gratitude of the drenched figures who have been saved. Profound insights into psychological nuances and individual characteristics are evident throughout the altarpiece and are a hallmark of Traini's style generally, as can be seen in the *Saint Anne with Virgin and Child* (1330s; Princeton University Art Museum) and the *Archangel Michael* (c. 1330s; Lucca, Museo Nazionale di Villa Guinigi). The *Saint Anne with Virgin and Child* has a highly innovative design: an immobile and matronly Anne with a wizened face is juxtaposed with a suave, youthful Virgin who tenderly supports a lithe and nimble infant. The *Archangel Michael* depicts a heroic figure whose activated pose and spirited drapery convey a powerful sense of energy.

There are still differences of opinion regarding the exact nature of Traini's activity as a fresco painter in the Camposanto of Pisa. Since 1974, when Bellosi attributed the *Triumph of Death* and stylistically similar frescoes to Bonamico Buffalmacco, some scholars have held that Traini's contribution was limited to the bold designs of the Crucifixion (1330s). Traini's career as an illuminator is less contentious, but it too is a subject of divergent critical opinions, which concern the role of collaborators or intervention by a shop. The quality of Traini's illuminations is perhaps best seen in Lucano Spinola of Genoa's copy of Dante's *Inferno* (c. 1330; Chantilly, Musée Condé), which manifests a remarkable sensitivity to glance, gesture, and the fall of drapery.

The legacy of the marked expressive power of Traini's art can be discerned in the work of a number of important younger painters active in northwestern Tuscany. These painters include Francesco Neri of Volterra and Angelo Puccinelli of Lucca, both of whom used Traini's robust chiaroscuro, powerful volumes, and eccentric characterization of figures.

See also **Martini, Simone**

Further Reading

Balberini, Chiara. "Problemi di Miniatura del Trecento a Pisa: Gli Antifonari di San Francesco." *Critica d'Arte*, 63(7), 2000, pp. 44–60.

Bellosi, Luciano. *Buffalmacco e il Trionfo della Morte.* Turin: Einaudi, 1974.

——. "Sur Francesco Traini." *Revue de l'Art*, 92, 1991, pp. 9–19.

Carli, Enzo. *Pittura pisana del Trecento*, Vol. 1. Milan: A. Martello, 1959.

——. *La pittura a Pisa dalle origini alla "Bella Maniera"* Pisa: Pacini Editore, 1994.

Dalli Regoli, Gigetta. *Miniatura pisana del Trecento.* Venice: N. Pozza, 1963.

Meiss, Millard. *Francesco Traini*, ed. Hayden B. J. Maginnis. Washington, D.C.: Decatur House, 1983.

Polzer, Joseph. "Observations on Known Paintings and a New Altarpiece by Francesco Traini." *Pantheon*, 29, 1971, pp. 379–389.

Testi Cristiani, Maria. "Francesco Traini, i 'Chompagni' di Simone Martini a Pisa e la Madonna 'Linsky' con Bambino, Santi, e Storiette del Metropolitan Museum." *Critica d'Arte*, 64(9), 2001, pp. 21–45.

FLAVIO BOGGI

TREVISA, JOHN (early 1340s?–1402)

Translator of informational works. Born probably in Cornwall, Trevisa entered Exeter College, Oxford, in 1362 and remained there until 1365. In 1369 he entered Queen's College and subsequently became a fellow. He was ordained priest in 1370. Trevisa was expelled from Queen's in 1378 for alleged misuse of college property but appears to have returned there for lengthy periods in 1383–86 and 1394–96. It was possibly after his expulsion from Queen's that he became vicar of Berkeley in Gloucestershire and chaplain to Thomas, Lord Berkeley. He was also a nonresident canon of Westbury-on-Trym, near Bristol.

Trevisa's major undertakings were his translations of several lengthy Latin works. The first that can be securely dated is his translation of Ranulf Higden's *Polychronicon*, a universal history, which he completed in 1387. His translation of the *De proprietatibus rerum*, the medieval encyclopedia of Bartholomaeus Anglicus, was finished in 1398. He produced this translation, as well as one of Giles of Rome's *De regimine principum*, a treatise on kingship, under the patronage of Thomas, Lord Berkeley. Trevisa also translated several shorter works: the apocryphal *Gospel of Nicodemus*, Richard FitzRalph's antimendicant sermon *Defensio curatorum*, and William Ockham's *Dialogus inter militem et clericum*. His only original works seem to be two brief essays on translation that preface some manuscripts of his *Polychronicon* translation: the "Dialogue between a Lord and a Clerk on Translation" and the "Epistle… Unto Lord Thomas of Barkley upon the Translation of *Polychronicon*.…"

Trevisa's achievement as a translator has several important aspects. Most obviously, he made accessible to an English audience such widely popular Latin informational works as the *Polychronicon* and *De proprietatibus rerum*. The influence of these translations was considerable. Both appear to have circulated widely (given their massive sizes) in manuscript and were printed by Caxton and de Worde, respectively, in the late 15th century. The *Polychronicon* was reprinted in the 16th century, while the *De proprietatibus* achieved an extended influence through Thomas East's revised edition in 1582 of *Batman vppon Bartholome*, a commentary on the work by Stephen Batman. In the latter form it was still being read and used in the late 17th century.

Trevisa also had a valuable role as neologizer. His translations expanded the lexical range of English, particularly in his use of new scientific and technical terminology. His fluent and generally accurate renderings of Latin prose demonstrated the possibilities of English prose as an instructional medium, thereby extending his influence into form as well as content.

Trevisa has also been credited with a role in the translation of the Wycliffite Bible. He was certainly at Oxford at the same time as Wyclif and Nicholas Hereford. However, his involvement in the Wycliffite translation remains uncertain, although there is at least some circumstantial evidence for it. His authorship has also been urged for a translation of Vegetius's *De re militari* into ME, but this seems unlikely.

See also **Caxton, William; Ockham, William of; Wyclif, John**

Further Reading

Primary Sources
Babington, Churchill, and J.R. Lumby, eds. *Polychronicon Ranulphi Higden,* 9 vols. Rolls Series. London: Longmans, 1865–86.

Perry, Aaron J., ed. *Dialogus inter Militem et Clericum*; Richard FitzRalph's Sermon: "Defensio Curatorum"; and Methodius: "Þe Bygynnyng of þe World and þe Ende of Worldes". EETS o.s. 167. London: Humphrey Milford, 1925.

Seymour, M.C., gen. ed. *On the Properties of Things*: John Trevisa's Translation of Bartholomaeus Anglicus De proprietatibus rerum. 3 vols. Oxford: Clarendon, 1975–88.

Waldron, Ronald A., ed. "Trevisa's Original Prefaces on Translation: A Critical Edition." In *Medieval English Studies Presented to George Kane*, ed. Edward Donald Kennedy et al. Woodbridge: Brewer, 1988, pp. 285–99.

Secondary Sources
New *CBEL* 1:467-68, 806.
Manual 8:2656–61, 2866–77.
Edwards, A.S.G. "John Trevisa." In *Middle English Prose: A*

Critical Guide to Major Authors and Genres, ed. A.S.G. Edwards. New Brunswick: Rutgers University Press, 1984, pp. 133–46.

Fowler, David C. *John Trevisa*. Aldershot: Variorum, 1993.

A.S.G. EDWARDS

TROTULA OF SALERNO

Trotula is the name given to a number of medical treatises on the diseases of women, most of which seem to have come from the medical university of Salerno. Whethier a twelfth-century Trotula of Salerno actually existed, whether Trotula was a woman, and what and for whom Trotula wrote have been a subject of scholarly debate for many years. Benton (1985) suggested that a female physician named Trota wrote a *Practica* (*Practice of Medicine*) containing obstetrical and gynecological material while teaching at Salerno. Unlike many other universities in the Latin west, Salerno was formed by a community of medical practitioners who were not necessarily clerics; this anomaly would probably account for the remarkable presence of a woman teacher. The *Practica*, in Latin, was not copied after c. 1200; it was supplanted by other Latin works on gynecology and cosmetics taken from various male writers. The name Trotula (probably a diminutive of Trota) was attached to these later writings, which were in turn translated into a number of European vernaculars. Benton held that the genuine writings of Trota were more practical in character than those of her fellow Salernitan physicians, but this conclusion is difficult to support.

Further Reading

Benton, John F. "Trotula, Women's Problems, and the Professionalization of Medicine in the Middle Ages." *Bulletin of the History of Medicine*, 59, 1985, pp. 30–53.

Green, Monica H. "Women's Medical Practice and Health Care in Medieval Europe." *Signs*, 14, 1989, pp. 434–473. (Reprinted in *Sisters and Workers in the Middle Ages*, ed. Judith Bennett, et al. Chicago, Ill.: University of Chicago Press, 1989, pp. 39–78.)

The Trotula: A Medieval Compendium of Women's Medicine, ed. and trans. Monica H. Green. Philadelphia: University of Pennsylvania Press, 2001.

FAYE MARIE GETZ

U

UBERTINO DA CASALE (1259–c. 1329)

The Franciscan reformer Ubertino da Casale was the author of the *Arbor vite crucifixe Jesu*—sometimes translated as *The Tree of the Crucified Life of Jesus.* This work had a strong effect on later Franciscan rigorists and on some prelates and monarchs; figures who were influenced by it include Dante, Giovanni dalle Celle, Saint Catherine of Siena, Saint Bernardino, John Brugman, and King Martin I of Aragon.

Most of our information about Ubertino until the time when he composed the *Arbor vite* in 1305 comes from its first prologue, but its chronology is not always clear. Ubertino was a native of Casale Monferrato in the diocese of Vercelli and in the Franciscan province of Genoa. He was received into the Franciscan order (Friars Minor) at age fourteen. Scholars disagree about the next period of his life. Some think that he remained in his province for a considerable time, until c. 1284 or 1285; but others—on the basis of his own testimony that he studied for nine years *et Parisius fui*—believe that after his novitiate he went to Paris and remained there until c. 1284. In any event he spent the years 1285 to 1289 (dates on which all the scholars agree) at Santa Croce in Florence. There, he was probably a subordinate lector in its *studium*, since he says that he was occupying the office of lector when he heard, at Pentecost, of John of Parma's death, which occurred in March 1289 (*Arbor vite*, 5.3).

It seems likely that Ubertino's studies in Paris had preceded this period in Florence rather than that, as some scholars hold, he went to Paris only after 1289. Ubertino associates Paris with a time when he was lax and ambitious. He tells us that his coming to Tuscany was accompanied by a conversion to a more ascetic life. Half of his four-year stay in Florence coincided with the lectorate there of the reformer who was to have the greatest influence on him, Petrus Johannis Olivi. Uber-

tino would have been exposed to Olivi's doctrine of *usus pauperi*, or "poor use," as essential to the Franciscan way of life—that is, the austere use of necessities and the avoidance of economic security and all superfluity. He must also have heard Olivi prophesy the persecution of the "spiritual" church by the "carnal" church. Ubertino's first meetings with Olivi—and with Margaret of Cortona, Cecilia of Florence, and John of Parma (who was in retirement at Greccio)—must have taken place just before or during 1285–1289. His crucial encounter with Angela of Foligno may also have been at this time. (There is conflicting evidence in the manuscripts on the date of this meeting: some say "in the twenty-fifth year of my religion.") According to Ubertino, these were the meetings that brought about his real conversion, after "almost fourteen years of external observance." It is difficult to believe that he then relapsed into what he calls laxity and ambition.

Ubertino learned a great deal from Olivi at Santa Croce; but unlike Olivi, he had no vocation to be a professional theologian, or to continue as a lector. Instead, Ubertino abandoned teaching to become a wandering preacher, traveling through Tuscany, Umbria, and the Marches, and denouncing both the heresy of the Brethren of the Free Spirit and the corruption of the official church. It is clear from the *Arbor vite* that he considered the resignation of Pope Celestine V and the subsequent election of Pope Boniface VIII illegitimate—a point on which he differed from Olivi. In the *Arbor vite* he identified Boniface, as well as Boniface's successor Pope Benedict XI, with the mystical Antichrist. How far Ubertino went in expressing these radical views in his public sermons is uncertain, but some hint of his opinions must have reached Benedict XI, because the pope summoned and arrested him. Ubertino was freed only because of the entreaties of a delegation of Perugian citizens; he was then sent by his Franciscan superiors to La Verna for an extended period of meditation. He used that time to write the *Arbor vite*, although he can hardly have composed the whole artful and almost interminable work, as he avows, in three months and seven days in 1305, without premeditation and with the aid of just a few books. Perhaps he was referring only to the nucleus of this vast work—a conjecture that might explain how Angelo Clareno could have described it as a "small" book. In any case, the more extreme opinions in the work were evidently not known to Ubertino's enemies among the Friars Minor for a long time, for they attacked only his defense of Olivi and were unable to keep Ubertino from exerting considerable influence in high ecclesiastical circles.

Ubertino also became the confidant and servant of a prominent cardinal, Napoleone Orsini, who looked kindly on the Spiritual faction of the Franciscans. Ubertino was appointed Orsini's chaplain in 1306 (though their connection seems to have begun earlier) and as late as 1324 was still doing important diplomatic work for him, helping conduct negotiations between Pisa and Aragon. In 1307, Ubertino was in Tuscany trying to further efforts on behalf of the Florentine exiles and was also undertaking juridical activity against the heretics of the Free Spirit. At about this time, he was also becoming increasingly involved in defending the interests of the Spiritual Franciscans; he served as procurator for various Spiritual groups, carrying their cases as far as Avignon.

Orsini's protection, and perhaps that of Cardinal James Colonna as well, must have been vital to Ubertino during the many years when he was able to frustrate the designs of the Franciscan leaders against him. He also seems to have elicited some sympathy from the popes to whom these leaders complained about him—Clement V and John XXII. At the time of the Council of Vienne (1310–1312), Ubertino wrote polemical treatises defending Olivi, advocating the doctrine of "poor use" for the Franciscan order, and pleading that at the very least the Spirituals should be allowed to follow the will of Francis and be free from persecution by the order. These writings were reflected to some extent in the bulls of Clement V, although in the end Clement refused to grant the Spirituals exemption from their superiors. The Spirituals fared worse under John XXII, but after their downfall Ubertino was not turned over to the authorities of the order. Instead, he secured from John a bull (20 October 1317) permitting him to enter the Benedictine house of Gembloux in the diocese of Liège, though there is no record that he ever set foot there. Ubertino was still in Avignon in 1322, when John asked him and a number of cardinals, bishops, Franciscans, Dominicans, and other clerics for their opinion on whether, as the Franciscans asserted, Christ and his apostles had owned nothing either individually or in common. The pope

eventually issued a bull condemning the Franciscans' claim that only their order, which professed corporate as well as individual poverty, fully imitated the life of Christ and his apostles; in this bull, John came very close to quoting some of Ubertino's earlier arguments against the practices of the Franciscan community.

But Ubertino's longtime defense of Olivi finally made it possible for the Franciscan community to bring him down. In 1325, in a bull directed to the Franciscans, John described Ubertino as a fugitive—Ubertino having fled from Avignon in fear of imminent condemnation—and ordered his arrest. Ubertino may have escaped to the court of Lewis of Bavaria, and he may have helped in the writing of some of Lewis's attacks on John XXII; this hypothesis rests mainly on Albertino Mussato's testimony that Ubertino and Marsilius of Padua accompanied Ludwig to Rome in 1328. There is contemporary testimony that Ubertino preached on behalf of Ludwig's Franciscan antipope Peter Corbara.

The date and manner of Ubertino's death are unknown, though a later tradition of the Fraticelli (a Spiritual Franciscan group) held that it was violent.

Ubertino was an interesting combination of ascetic, polemicist, and diplomat. He was a gifted rhetorician and, particularly in his polemical works, a brilliant satirist. He poured into the *Arbor vite* his often moving meditations on Christ's life and the similarities between Christ and Saint Francis. This work, obviously constructed in large part from Ubertino's earlier sermons and treatises, also contains a multitude of long and short extracts from various authorities: the church fathers; Bernard, Bonaventure, Olivi, and other Franciscan writers; and Thomas Aquinas. There are surely also many sources that have not yet been identified. The fifth book of the *Arbor vite*, containing Ubertino's views on ecclesiastical history, is mainly based, as Manselli (1965, 1977) has shown, on Olivi's *Postilla in Apocalypsim*. Ubertino's polemical treatises are vivid, supple, and remarkably readable, despite the technicality of their arguments. In these works, the historical dimension disappears, and "poor use" is emphasized much more than corporate expropriation. In 1322, the pope commanded Ubertino to enlarge his oral opinion on whether Christ and the apostles had possessed nothing, either individually or in common. Ubertino did so in the unpublished treatise *De altissima paupertate* (*Treatise on the Highest Poverty*), largely copied—although with significant omissions, additions, and modifications—from Olivi's question 8, *De altissima paupertate*, in the series of questions called *De perfectione evangelica*. Ubertino's summary of that treatise, *Reducendo igitur ad brevitatem*, was included in a famous collection of opinions on the question, in manuscript Vatican Latinus 3740, and attracted a marginal note in the pope's own hand. This summary drew a number of its arguments from Olivi's question 9, dealing with whether *usus pauper* was included in the Franciscan vow of evangelical poverty. Cardinal Orsini's opinion contained in the same collection follows a line of argument similar to Ubertino's and may actually have been written by Ubertino.

Ubertino's doctrines regarding poverty are the most interesting aspect of his thought. They seem to have undergone considerable development over his lifetime. In the *Arbor vite*, Ubertino accepted the official Franciscan view, shared by all factions, that as followers of evangelical perfection, if not as prelates transferring goods to the poor, they absolutely embraced corporate as well as individual poverty. To this he added Olivi's view that "poor use" was necessary to the observance of the highest poverty, and that the persecution of those who followed "poor use" was a sign of the appearance of the Antichrist and the coming of the "last age."

In Ubertino's polemical treatises, this historical dimension of his thought disappears entirely, and he is much more concerned with poor use than with corporate expropriation. In his final treatise, written when he was nominally a Benedictine, Ubertino was unwilling to accept the traditional view that the holding of collective property by monastic corporations according to human law was no breach of evangelical perfection. He did, however, clearly affirm, against the Franciscans, that possession according to natural (though not civil) law was inseparable from the use of consumable things. The Franciscans' theory, on the other hand, maintained that Franciscans had only the use of such things, whose ownership always rested with the donors or was held by the pope. Ubertino now evidently regarded this theory as a pitiful pretense. He also thought that it was ultimately inimical to Olivi's doctrine of "poor use," a doctrine to which—despite his careful editing and revision of Olivi's question concerning the highest poverty—he always remained faithful.

See also **Boniface VIII, Pope; Catherine of Siena, Saint; Celestine V, Pope; Dante Alighieri**

Further Reading

Editions

Arbor vitae crucifixae Jesu. Venice: Andrea de Bonettis de Papia, 1485. (Reprint, ed. Charles T. Davis. Turin: Bottega d'Erasmo, 1961.)

Declaratio fratris Ubertini de Casali et sociorum eius contra falsitates datas per fratrem Raymundum procuratorem et Bonagratiam da Bergamo, ed. F. Ehrle. *Archiv für Literatur und Kirchengeschichte des Mittelalters*, 3, 1887, pp. 160–195.

Decretalis etiam, ed. F. Ehrle. *Archiv für Literatur und Kirchengeschichte des Mittelalters*, 3, 1887, pp. 130–135.

Reducendo igitur ad brevitatem, ed. Charles T. Davis. In "Ubertino da Casale and His Conception of *Altissima Paupertas.*" *Studi Medievali*, Series 3(22.1), 1981, pp. 41–56.

Rotulus iste, ed. F. Ehrle. *Archiv für Literatur und Kirchengeschichte des Mittelalters*, 3, 1887, pp. 89–130.

Sanctitas vestra, ed. F. Ehrle. *Archiv für Literatur und Kirchengeschichte des Mittelalters*, 3, 1887, pp. 48–89.

Sanctitati apostolice, ed. F. Ehrle. *Archiv für Literatur und Kirchengeschichte des Mittelalters*, 2, 1886, pp. 374–416.

Super tribus scelribus Damasci, ed. A. Heysse. *Archivum Franciscanum Historicum*, 10, 1917, pp. 103–174.

Tractatus Ubertini de altissima paupertate Christi et apostolorum eius et virorum apostolicorum. Codex Vienna Staatsbibliothek, 809, fols. 128r–159v.

Critical Studies

Bihl, Michael. "Review of Biographies of Ubertino, by Huck, Knoth, and Callaey." *Archivum Franciscanum Historicum*, 4, 1911, pp. 594–599.

Blondeel, E. "L'influence d'Ubertin de Casale sur les écrits de S. Bernardin de Sienne" and "Encore l'infiuence d'Ubertin de Casale sur les écrits de S. Bernardin de Sienne." *Collectanea Franciscana*, 6, 1936, pp. 5–44, 57–76.

Callaey, Frédégand. *L'idéalisme franciscain spirituel au XIV siècle*: *Étude sur Ubertin de Casale.* Louvain, 1911.

——. "L'influence et la diffusion de l'*Arbor vitae* de Ubertini de Casale." *Revue d'Historie Ecclésiatique*, 17, 1921, pp. 533–546.

——. "L'infiltration des id–es franciscaines spirituales chez les frères mineurs capucins au XVI siècle." In *Miscellanea Francesco Ehrle*, Vol. 1. Rome: Biblioteca Apostolica Vaticana, 1924.

Colasanti, G. "I Santi Cuori di Gesùe di Maria nell'*Arbor vitae* (1305) di Ubertino da Casale, O. Min." *Miscellanea Francescana*, 59, 1959, pp. 30–69.

Damiata, Marino. *Pietà e storia nell' "Arbor vitae" di Ubertino da Casale.* Florence: Edizioni Studi Francescani, 1988, pp. 195–215.

——. "Ubertino da Casaie: Ultimo atto." *Studi Francescani*, 86, 1989, pp. 279–303.

Daniel, Randolph. "Spirituality and Poverty: Angelo da Clareno and Ubertino da Casale." *Medievalia et Humanistica*, n.s., 4, 1973, pp. 89–98.

Davis, Charles T. "Ubertino da Casaie and His Conception of *Altissima Paupertas.*" *Studi Medievali*, Series 3(22.1), 1981, pp. 1–41.

Douie, Decima L. *The Nature and the Effect of the Heresy of the Fraticelli.* Manchester: University Press, 1932, pp. 120–152. (Reprint, 1978.)

Ehrle, F. "Die Spiritualen, ihr Verhältniss zum Franzis Kanerorden und zu den Fraticelen." *Archiv für Literatur und Kirchengeschichte des Mittelalters*, 1, 1885, pp. 509–569; 2, 1886, pp. 106–164; 3, 1887, pp. 553–623; 4, 1888, pp. 1–190.

——. Zur Vorgeschichte des Konzils von Vienne." *Archiv für Literatur und Kirchengeschichte des Mittelalters*, 2, 1886, pp. 353–416; 3, 1887, pp. 1–195.

Godefroy, P. "Ubertin de Casale." *Dictionnaire de théologie catholique*, 15, 1950, pp. 2021–2034.

Guyot, B. G. "*L'Arbor vitae crucifixae Iesu* d'Ubertin de Casale et ses emprunts aux *De articulis fidei* de S. Thomas d'Aquin." In *Studies Honoring Ignatius Charles Brady, Friar Minor*, ed. Romano Stephen Almagno and Conrad L. Harkins. Saint Bonaventure, N.Y.: Franciscan Institute, 1976, pp. 293–307.

Hofer, J. "Das Gutachten Ubertins von Casale über die Armut Christi." *Franziskanische Studien*, 11, 1924, pp. 210–215.

Huck, Johann Chrysostomus. *Ubertin von Casale und dessen Ideenkreis: Ein Beitrag zum Zeitalter Dantes.* Freiburg im Breisgau: Herder, 1903.

Ini, A. M. "Nuovi documenti sugli Spirituali di Toscana." *Archivum Franciscanum Historicum*, 66, 1973, pp. 305–377.

Knoth, E. *Ubertin von Casale: Ein Beitrag zur Geschichte der Franziskaner an der Wende des 13. und 14. Jahrhunderts.* Marburg, 1903.

Manselli, Raoul. "Pietro di Giovanni Olivi ed Ubertino da Casale (a proposito della *Lectura super Apocalipsim* e dell'*Arbor vitae crucifixae Iesu*)." *Studi Medievali*, Series 3(6), 1965, pp. 95–122

———. "L'anticristo mistico: Pietro di Giovanni Olivi, Ubertino da Casale, e i papi del loro tempo." *Collectanea Franciscana*, 47, 1977, pp. 5–25.

Martini, A. "Ubertino da Casale alla Verna e la Verna nell'Arbor Vitae." *La Verna*, 11, 1913, pp. 273–344.

Oliger, Livarius. "De relatione inter Observantium querimonias Constantienses (1415) et Ubertini Casalensis quoddam scriptum." *Archivum Franciscanum Historicum*, 9, 1916, pp. 3–41.

Potestà, G. L. "Un secolo di studi sull' *Arbor vitae*: Chiesa ed escatologia in Ubertino da Casale." *Colléctanea Franciscana*, 47, 1977, pp. 217–267.

——— . *Storia ed escatologia in Ubertino da Casale.* Milan: Vita e Pensiero, 1980.

Zugaj, M. "Assumptio B. M. Virginis in *Arbor Vitae Crucifixae Jesu* (a. 1305) Fr. Ubertino de Casali, O. Min." *Miscellanea Francescana*, 46, 1946, pp. 124–156.

CHARLES T. DAVIS

UGUCCIONE DA PISA
(c. 1125 or 1130–30 April 1210)

Under the entry *Pis* in *Derivationes*, Uguccione states that he was born in Pisa—without, however, indicating the year, which has had to be estimated by his biographers. The date of his election as bishop of Ferrara is likewise uncertain. He completed his studies at Bologna, where in all probability he wrote his grammatical treatises. Later, he began to lecture on Gratian's *Decretum*, perhaps at the monastery of Saint Nabore and Saint Felice, where Gratian had taught. One of Uguccione's students was Lothar, a count of the Segni, who later became Pope Innocent III. Uguccione headed the diocese of Ferrara until his death. During his years as bishop he was given important assignments by popes Celestine III and Innocent III, his former pupil, mostly for the purpose of resolving a crisis at Nonantola, which was governed by an *abate* insufficient to the task. The archbishop of Ravenna, Guglielmo Curiano, also entrusted Uguccione with settling disputes between the inhabitants of Ravenna and those of nearby Rimini. The outline of these biographical events agrees with the traditional view according to which Uguccione da Pisa, bishop of Ferrara, was, as both lecturer on grammar and canonist, the author of all of the works mentioned below. Muller (1991, 1994) has challenged this view, arguing that the grammarian and the canonist should not be identified as the same person.

It will be useful to point out links among Uguccione's works, based on internal cross-references. The *De dubio accentu* and *Rosarium* are cited in *Derivationes* and explicitly referred to by name in the *Agiographia*, which is itself referred to by name in the *Summa decretorum*. These references constitute the writer's claim to authorship and the basis for all further critical discussion of his works.

De dubio accentu: This brief treatise provides the correct pronunciation of a number of compound words or words in which the penultimate syllable is followed by a mute plus a liquid. In a set of appendixes, Uguccione deals with more specialized issues relating, again, to pronunciation, and also to spelling. Giovanni Balbi's *Catholicon* often draws on this text, while occasionally deferring to Bene da Firenze's teachings.

Rosarium: This treatise on grammar, cited twice in the *Derivationes*, is preserved in a single manuscript dating from 1382, Erfurt Ampl. Q. 69 (252), ff, 1–63. It provides a summary of *ars grammatica*, based on the eight parts of speech. A list of conjugated verb forms, arranged alphabetically (*amo, amas*, etc. to *zelo, zelas*), appears on leaves 24ra–54rb.

Derivationes: Preserved in more than 200 extant manuscripts, this lexicon comprises the entire patrimony of *the* Latin language, classified by the principles of word derivation. It constitutes a fundamental stage in the development of medieval Latin lexicography because it organizes a large amount of linguistic data into derivational groupings and because it integrates into this scheme erudition passed down from antiquity, to be preserved and passed on to future generations. The work remains unpublished.

Agiographia: This short text also uses the word derivation format, which, in its most noteworthy section, presents a list of saints' names, arranged according to the liturgical calendar; these are then glossed with reference to traditional hagiographical aspects relating to holy deeds leading to canonization. The work serves as a bridge between Uguccione's two major texts; it is cited in the *Summa decretorum*, and it makes, in turn, an explicit reference to the *Derivationes*.

Summa decretorum: Uguccione worked on this text from 1178 to at least 1188. However, some questions arise as to whether the commentary regarding cases 23–26 is authentic or the work of one of Uguccione's continuators. Relatively recently, this text has been subjected to renewed scrutiny by historians of canon law, in an attempt to understand Uguccione's views on the thorny issue of the relationship between the two supreme authorities on earth—the papacy and the empire. According to some, Uguccione's thinking on this subject may have inspired Dante's *Monarchia*; indeed, Dante explicitly cites the *Derivationes* in his *Convivio* (4.6.5). The *Summa decretorum* also deals with a number of questions pertaining to the theology of the sacraments. For the manuscript tradition of this

Summa, still unpublished, readers should consult Leonardi (1956–1957).

Expositio de symbolo apostolorum: This text is attributed to Uguccione in Trombelli (1775) and codex 2633 in the University Library of Bologna but is not cited by him in any of his other works. It offers a commentary on the twelve articles of the *credo*, thereby constituting itself a catechism on the fundamental beliefs of the Christian faith. This brief exposition may be the fruit of Uguccione's pastoral activity, undertaken during the last twenty years of his life as bishop of Ferrara.

See also **Gratian, Innocent III, Pope**

Further Reading

Editions

De dubio accentu—Agiographia—Expositio de symbolo apostolorum, ed. Giuseppe Cremascoli. Spoleto: Centro Italiano di Studi sull'Alto Medioevo, 1978.

Derivationes. Florence: Accademia della Crusca, 2000.

Il"De dubio accentu" di Uguccione da Pisa, ed. Giuseppe Cremascoli. Bologna, 1969.

Expositio Domini Huguccionis Ferrariensis Episcopi de Symbolo Apostolorum, ed. Joannes Chrysostomus Trombelli. In *Bedae et Claudii Taurinensis itemque aliorum veterum Patrum opuscula*, Bologna, 1755, pp. 207–223.

L "Expositio de symbolo apostolorum " di Uguccione da Pisa, ed. Giuseppe Cremascoli. *Studi Medievali*, 14, 1973, pp. 364–442.

Häring, Nicholas M. "Zwei Kommentare von Huguccio, Bischof von Ferrara." *Studia Gratiana*, 19, 1976, pp. 355–416.

Critical Studies

Austin, H. D. "Glimpses of Uguiccione's Personality." *Philological Quarterly*, 26, 1947, pp. 367–377.

——. "Uguiccione Miscellany." *Italica*, 27, 1950, pp. 12–17.

Cremascoli, Giuseppe. "Saggio bibliografico." *Aevum*, 42, 1968, pp. 123–168.

Leonardi, Corrado. "La vira e l'opera di Uguccione da Pisa decretista." *Studia Gratiana*, 4, 1956–1957, pp. 37–120.

Marigo, Aristide. *I codici manoscritti delle "Derivationes" di Uguccione Pisano.* Rome: Istituto di Smdi Romani, 1936.

Müller, Wolfgang P. "Huguccio of Pisa: Canonist, Bishop, and Grammarian?" *Viator*, 22, 1991, pp. 121–152.

——. *Huguccio: The Life, Works, and Thought of a Twelfth Century Jurist.* Washington, D.C.: Catholic University of America Press, 1994.

Riessner, Claus. *Die "Magnae Derivationes" des Uguccione da Pisa und ihre Bedeutung für die romanische Philologie.* Rome: Edizioni di Storia e Letteratura, 1965.

GIUSEPPE CREMASCOLI
TRANSLATED BY RICHARD LANSING

ÚLFR UGGASON (fl. ca. 1000)

Úlfr Uggason was an Icelandic skald who flourished around the year 1000. He married Járngerðr, daughter of Þórarinn Grimkelsson and Jórunn Einarsdóttir from Stafaholt (*Landnárnabók* S76, H64). His wife's family were descendants of Hrappr, son of Bjrn buna Veðrar-Grímsson, one of the most prominent early settlers in Iceland. His father's family is unknown.

Úlfr is represented in three sagas. *Njáls saga* portrays him as a cautious man. In ch. 60, he makes a brief appearance as the loser in an inheritance claim he contests with Ásgrímr Elliða-Grimsson. In ch. 102, he refuses to commit himself openly to physical violence in the cause of the antimissionary party in the events surrounding the conversion of Iceland to Christianity. Both here and in *Kristni saga* (ch. 9), a single verse of Úlfr's is preserved in which he responds to a poetic incitement to push the foreign evangelist Þangbrandr over a cliff. Likening himself to a wily fish, he asserts that it is not his style to swallow the fly (*esat mínligt . . . flugu at gína*)!

However, Úlfr is best known for his composition of a skaldic picture poem, *Húsdrápa* ("House-lay"), which commemorates a splendid new hall that Óláfr pái ("peacock") had built at Hjarðarholt. The *drápa* celebrates both the builder of the hall and the mythological stories depicted on its carved panels, *Laxdæla saga* (ch. 29) describes the hall and the occasion upon which Úlfr delivered his poem, the marriage feast of Óláfr's daughter Þuriðr. Excellent stories (*ágætligar sgur*) were carved on the wainscoting and on the hall ceiling, and these splendid carvings surpassed the wall hangings. *Laxdæla saga* does not preserve the poem, but comments only that *Húsdrápa* was well crafted (*vel ort*) and that Úlfr received a good reward for it from Óláfr. These events are usually dated, according to the saga's chronology, to about 985.

Fortunately for posterity, Snorri Sturluson preserved fifty-six lines of *Húsdrápa* in his *Edda*, mostly as half-stanzas illustrating points of skaldic diction in *Skáldskaparmál*. Out of these verses, editors have conventionally reconstructed a *drápa* of twelve stanzas or half-stanzas, which probably had the refrain *hlaut innan svá minnum* ("within have appeared these motifs").

There are three known mythological subjects Úlfr treated in *Húsdrápa*, and there may have been more. Snorri states that Úlfr composed a long passage in the poem on the story of Baldr, of which we now have five half-stanzas (7–11 in Finnur Jónsson 1912–15). They deal with the procession of supernatural beings and their mounts riding to Baldr's funeral. In *Gylfaginning*, chs. 33–35 (Finnur Jónsson 1931: 63–8, Faulkes 1987: 48–51), Snorri gives a prose account of the funeral and other events that led up to and followed Baldr's death, for which *Húsdrápa* was probably one of his main sources.

Two other known subjects of *Húsdrápa* were Þórr's fight with the World Serpent, Miðgarðsormr, a popular choice with Viking Age skalds and sculptors (sts. 3–6), and the otherwise unrepresented myth of how the gods Heimdallr and Loki, said by Snorri to have taken the form of seals, wrestled for a "beautiful sea-kidney" (probably the necklace Brísíngamen) at a place called Singasteinn. Only one stanza (2) of this section survives, although from Snorri's summary it seems likely to have been longer in the complete *drápa*.

It may be surmised that Úlfr's pictorial praise poem in honor of Óláfr pái was, in a late 10th-century Icelandic context, something of a hearkening back to the courtly, aristocratic style of skalds like Bragi Boddason and Þjóðólfr of Hvin, who lived about a century earlier than Úlfr. Judging by *Laxdæla saga's* account of Óláfr, his splendid style of living, and Irish royal connections, he would have been flattered by an implicit comparison with Norwegian princelings and their skaldic encomiasts.

See also **Bragi Boddason; Snorri Sturluson**

Further Reading

Editions

Kahl, B. *Kristni saga. Þáttr Þorvalds ens víðfǫrla. Þáttr Ísleifs biskups Gizurarsonar. Hungrvaka.* Altnordische Saga-Bibliothek, 11. Halle: Niemeyer, 1905 [see pp. 1–57].

Finnur Jónsson, ed. *Den norske-islandske skjaldedigtning.* Vols. 1A-2A (tekst efter håndskrifterne) and 1B-2B (rettet tekst). Copenhagen and Christiania [Oslo]: Gyldendal, 1912–15; rpt. Copenhagen: Rosenkilde & Bagger, 1967 (A) and 1973 (B), vol. 1A. pp. 136–9; vol. 1B, pp. 128–30.

Finnur Jónsson, ed. *Edda Snorra Sturlusonar.* Copenhagen: Gyldendal, 1931 [lines from *Húsdrápa* pp. 89, 90, 94, 96–100, 147, 152, 165, 168].

Einar Ól. Sveinsson, ed. *Laxdæla saga,* Oslenzk fomrit, 5. Reykjavik: Hið íslenzka fornritafélag, 1934.

Einar Ól. Sveinsson, ed. *Brennu-Njáls saga.* Íslenzk fornrit, 12. Reykjavik: Hið íslenzka fomritafélag, 1954.

Jakob Benediktsson, ed. *Íslendingabók. Landnámabók.* Íslenzk fornrit, 1. Reykjavik: Hið íslenzka fornritafélag, 1968.

Turville-Petre, E. O. G. *Scaldic Poetry.* Oxford: Clarendon, 1976, pp. 67–70 [Baldr's funeral strophes from *Húsdrápa*].

Frank, Roberta. *Old Norse Court Poetry: The* Dróttkvætt *Stanza.* Islandica, 42. Ithaca and London: Cornell University Press, 1978 [texts and discussion of *Húsdrápa* pp. 104–5, 110–2, 170].

Translations

Gudbrand Vigfusson and F. York Powell, eds. and trans. "Christne saga." In *Origines Islandicae: A Collection of the More Important Sagas and Other Native Writings Relating to the Settlement and Early History of Iceland.* 2 vols. Oxford: Clarendon, 1905 rpt. Millwood: Kraus, 1976, vol. 1, pp. 370–406.

Hollander, Lee M. *The Skalds: A Selection of Their Poems, with Introductions and Notes.* New York: American-Scandinavian Foundation, 1945; 2nd ed. Ann Arbor: University of Michigan Press, 1968, pp. 49–54.

Magnús Magnússon and Hermann Pálsson, trans. *Njal's saga.* Harmondsworth: Penguin, 1960 [esp. pp. 144 and 220–1].

Magnús Magnússon and Hermann Pálsson, trans. *Laxdæla saga.* Harmondsworth: Penguin, 1960 [esp. pp. 111–3].

Faulkes, Anthony, trans. *Snorri Sturluson. Edda.* Everyman Classics. London and Melbourne: Dent, 1987 [lines from *Húsdrápa,* pp. 67–8, 71, 74–7, 116, 121, 132–3, 135].

Bibliographies

Hollander, Lee M. *A Bibliography of Skaldic Studies.* Copenhagen: Munksgaard, 1958.

Bekker-Nielsen, Hans. *Old Norse-Icelandic Studies: A Select Bibliography.* Toronto Medieval Bibliographies, 1. Toronto: University of Toronto Press, 1967.

Literature

Lie, Hallvard. "Billedbeskrivende dikt." *KLNM* 1 (1956), 542–5.

Lie, Hallvard. *"Natur" og "unatur" iskaldekunsten.* Avhandlinger utg. av Det norske Videnskaps-Akademi i Oslo. II. Hist.-filos. kl. No. 1. Oslo: Aschehoug, 1957; rpt. in his *Om sagakunst og skaldskap. Utvalgte avhandlinger.* Øvre Ervik: Alvheim & Eide, 1982, pp. 201–315.

Lie, Hallvard. "Húsdrápa," *KLNM* 7 (1962), 122–4.

Turville-Petre, E.O.G. *Myth and Religion of the North: The Religion of Ancient Scandinavia.* New York: Holt, Rinehart and Winston, 1964; rpt. Westport: Greenwood, 1975.

Strömbäck, Dag. *The Conversion of Iceland: A Survey.* Trans. and annotated by Peter Foote. Text Series, 6. London: Viking Society for Northern Research, 1975.

Schier, K. "Balder." In *Reallexikon der germanischen Altertumskvnde* 2. Gen. ed. Johannes Hoops. Berlin and New York; de Gruyter, 1976, pp. 2–7.

Schier, Kurt. "Die *Húsdrápa* von Úlfr Uggason und die bildliche Überlieferung altnordischer Mythen." In *Minjar og menntir: Afmælisrit helgað Kristjáni Eldjárn, 6 desember 1976.* Ed. Guðni Kolbeinsson *et al.* Reykjavik: Menningarsjóður, 1976, pp. 425–43.

Schier, Kurt. "Húsdrápa, 2. Heimdall, Loki und die Meerniere." In *Festgabe für Otto HMfler zum 75. Gebunstag.* Ed. Helmut Birkhan. Philologica Germanica, 3. Vienna: Braumüller, 1976, pp. 577–88.

Clover, Carol J. "Skaldic Sensibility." *Arkiv för nordisk filologi* 93 (1978), 63–81.

Clunies Ross, Margaret. "Style and Authorial Presence in Skaldic Mythological Poetry." *Saga-Book of the Viking Society* 20 (1981), 276–304.

Kuhn, Hans. *Das Dróttkvætt.* Heidelberg: Winter, 1983 [esp. pp. 295–6].

Meulengracht Sørensen, Preben. "Thor's Fishing Expedition." In *Words and Objects: Towards a Dialogue Between Archaeology and History of Religion.* Ed. Gro Steinsland. Institute for Comparative Research in Human Culture, Oslo. Ser. B: Skrifter, 71. Oslo: Norwegian University Press, 1986, pp. 257–78.

MARGARET CLUNIES ROSS

ULRICH VON ETZENBACH
(fl. 2d half of the 13th c.)

A German author who contributed to the emerging German culture at the Bohemian court in Prague of the House of the Přemysl. He began writing his *Alexander* romance around 1270 under the patronage of King Ottokar, and completed it in 1286 under King Wenzel II, Ottokar's son. The legendary romance *Wilhelm von Wenden* was written around 1290, whereas the date of Ulrich's *Herzog Ernst* version D (attribution uncertain) cannot be confirmed.

We do not know much about Ulrich apart from what

he mentions about himself in his works. He was born in Northern Bohemia (*Alexander*, vv. 27627f.) and acquired a solid education, though he probably did not become a cleric. His knowledge of Latin was very good, and so his familiarity with "classical" Middle High German literature, to which he refers often.

The *Alexander*, which has been preserved in six manuscripts and several fragments, deals with the famous history of the Macedonian ruler Alexander the Great and follows his conquest of the Persian Empire and all the lands extending to the river Indus. The text is based primarily on the Latin epic poem *Alexandreis* (thirteenth century), composed in hexametric verse by Walther of Châtillon, but then also on the *Nativitas et victoriae Alexandri Magni regis* (*Birth and Victories of Alexander the Great King*, ca. 950–970) by the Archpriest Leo (which again was based on the tenth-century *Historia preliis*).

For both Walther and Ulrich, Alexander's victories laid the foundation for the third of four secular empires that would, according to biblical traditions, come and go before Christ's return and the Day of Judgment. For religious reasons Alexander's activities are cleansed from any negative elements as in the older tradition; even murderous slaughter and killing of enemy troops are exculpated. Moreover, the important aspects of Alexander's curiosity leading to his exploration of the world (dive into the sea in a glass bubble; flight in the air with the help of griffins) are eliminated as well, because he is seen as God's instrument and made to an ideal ruler in the tradition of the *Fürstenspiegel* (didactic texts for princes). In many respects, Alexander is modeled after Ottokar II, whom Ulrich wanted to idealize through his work.

In *Wilhelm von Wenden*, preserved only in one manuscript, now in Dessau, King Wenzel II and his wife, Guta of Habsburg, are immortalized in the figure of Prince Wilhelm of Parrit and his wife, Bene (the Good One). Wilhelm secretly departs from his dukedom to make a pilgrimage to Jerusalem and to convert to a Christian. Bene accompanies him but is left behind in a foreign country after she delivers twins, whom Wilhelm sells to Christian merchants to be free of this burden on his pilgrimage. Because of Bene's virtuous lifestyle she is later elected (!) the ruler of that country, and when by chance the family eventually reunites again after many years, they all convert to Christianity and thus missionize the entire country. Both the role of the strong woman and the tolerant attitude toward non-Christian religions are remarkable. Ulrich used as his model either *Guillaume d'Angleterre* by Chrétien de Troyes, or the *Eustachius* legend in the *Legenda aurea* (*Golden Legendary*).

Herzog Ernst D finally, extant in one manuscript (Gotha, called "d"), follows the tradition of goliardic narratives (*Spielmannsepen*) in which the young Bavar-

ian duke has to leave Germany because of political and military conflicts with his father-in-law, the irrational and impetuous emperor, and explores the world of the Orient. Both this text and the *Alexander* were later translated into Czech.

See also **Walter of Châtillon**

Further Reading

Behr, Hans-Joachim. *Literatur als Machtlegitimation*. Munich: Fink, 1989.
Classen, Albrecht: "Ulrichs von Etzenbach *Wilhelm von Wenden*—ein Frauenroman?" *Literaturwissenschaftliches Jahrbuch* 30 (1989): 27–43.
Kohlmayer, Rainer: *Ulrichs von Etzenbach "Wilhelm von Wenden."* Meisenheim: Hain, 1974.
Rosenfeld, Hans-Friedrich, ed. *Ulrich von Etzenbach. "Wilhelm von Wenden."* Berlin: Akademie-Verlag, 1957.
——, ed. *Herzog Ernst D.* Tübingen: Niemeyer, 1991.
Toischer, Wendelin, ed. *Ulrich von Etzenbach: "Alexander. "* Prague: Verein für Geschichte der Deutschen in Böhmen, 1888.

ALBRECHT CLASSEN

ULRICH VON LIECHTENSTEIN (ca. 1200–1275)

Ulrich von Liechtenstein's action-filled life as a political *ministeriale* in Austria in the middle two fourths of the twelfth century is well documented in contemporary records. As a literary parallel to his life, Ulrich created with his *Frauendienst* (*Service of Ladies*), compiled around 1255, though doubtless utilizing songs composed earlier, a fictional verse romance in which his persona, the minnesinger Ulrich, woos a recalcitrant lady with songs, adventures, including a cross-country tournament for which he dresses himself as Venus, and misadventures. In one of these he disables a finger while fighting to gain his lady's approval. When he learns that she doubts he was really injured, he chops the finger off and sends it to her in a jeweled casket, accompanied by a verse booklet proclaiming his love. His misadventures, which often echo literary motifs, are recounted with rollicking humor. His attempted tryst with the lady in her chambers, in the course of which he is hoisted up to and let down (literally: let fall) from her window in a basket and is so distraught at being rejected that he tries to drown himself, forms a high point of his hapless service. Angered by her consistent rejection of him, he turns to the service of a new lady, undertaking yet another marathon tournament, this time as King Arthur. In the midst of all his feverish service of a lady, he explicitly takes some time off to enjoy the company of his wife. Whereas songs more or less punctuate the narrative in the first half of the work (though their motifs often seem to have inspired its plot), they dominate the second half.

Here, the framework often becomes little more than a poetological commentary on the songs, though as in many *razos*, or reasons (i.e., prose commentaries), of the troubadours—a possible inspiration for this part of the work—the commentary consists largely of paraphrase, and praise of the songs' excellence. Ulrich's fifty-seven songs and one *Leich* (poem), though accomplished, pale somewhat against the originality of their frame. His models were Walther von der Vogelweide (whom he quotes without attribution), Wolfram von Eschenbach (whose dawn songs he parodies), and Gottfried von Straßburg. He also doubtless learned from singers such as Gottfried von Neifen (whose use of the motif of the lady's rose-red mouth he exaggerates to comic effect) and probably influenced others in turn, such as Steinmar. A set of strophes he shares with Heinrich von Veldeke and Niune (Kraus, no. 58 XII) probably bears the former's name through scribal misascription and was adapted into two shorter songs by the latter.

In addition to the *Frauendienst*, he wrote the *Frauenbuch*, a didactic treatise in debate form in which a lady and a knight discuss who is responsible for the sad state of the world. In the end the lady is declared free of blame. Though it lacks the innovative sparkle (and the occasional narrative tedium) of the former work, its earnestness and apparent sincerity remind us that despite the ubiquity of humor and playfulness in Ulrich's larger work, he seems to have taken the exhortations to be constant, loyal, pure, and kind (good)that permeate both works to heart. Despite all the weaknesses and absurdities that he clearly recognizes in contemporary life and (especially) letters, he valorizes courtly ideals and seeks to promote *hôher muot* (courtly good cheer).

See also **Heinrich von Veldeke; Walther von der Vogelweide**

Further Reading

Bechstein, Reinhold, ed. *Ulrich's von Lichtenstein Frauendienst.* 2 vols. Leipzig: Brockhaus, 1888.

Kraus, Carl von, ed. *Deutsche Liederdichter des 13. Jahrhunderts.* 2 vols.; 2d ed. Gisela Kornrumpf. Tübingen: Niemeyer, 1978.

Lachmann, Karl, ed. *Ulrich von Lichtenstein.* Berlin: Sander, 1841; rpt. Hildesheim: Olms, 1974.

Thomas, J. W., trans. *Ulrich von Liechtenstein's Service of Ladies.* Chapel Hill: University of North Carolina Press, 1969.

HUBERT HEINEN

ULRICH VON TÜRHEIM
(fl. ca. 1230–1245)

After Gottfried von Straßburg had left his *Tristan* as a torso around 1210, two authors picked up the fragment and provided their own conclusions—Heinrich von Freiberg (ca. 1280–1290) and Ulrich von Türheim. The latter composed his *continuatio* (continuation) roughly between 1230 and 1235, adding a total of 3,730 verses. Uirich's conclusion of the *Tristan* was commissioned by the imperial cup-bearer (*Reichsschenk*), the Augsburg nobleman Konrad von Winterstetten (d. 1243). Sometime after that Ulrich wrote the continuation of Wolfram von Eschenbach's *Willehalm*, the so-called *Rennewart*, comprising more than 36,000 verses, completed before 1250. Among his earliest literary enterprises, however, we find Ulrich's short narrative *Clîges*, which is extant only in a fragment from circa 1230 and based on Chrétien de Troyes's *Cligès*.

An Ulrich von Türheim appears in the documents of the bishop and the cathedral chapter of Augsburg between 1236 and 1244. We assume that he was identical with our poet.

For his *Tristan* continuation, Ulrich relied heavily on the *Tristan* version by Eilhart von Oberg, *Tristrant*. Here, Tristan marries Isolde Whitehand, without sleeping with his newlywed. Her brother Kaedin learns about this scandalous situation and challenges Tristan, who then tells him of Isolde the Fair. Together they travel to England and meet Isolde secretly. Tristan spends one night with her alone, whereas Kaedin is duped by a chambermaid. Later Tristan is falsely accused of having failed in his service for the queen, and the latter orders him to be beaten and chased away when he shows up at court in the guise of a leper. The lovers overcome the conflict and misunderstanding, however, and Tristan can spend some time at court hidden behind his mask, until he is discovered and then returns to Arundel with Kaedin. Now Tristan fully accepts his wife and sleeps with her. When he later helps Kaedin in a secret love affair, Kaedin is killed and Tristan badly wounded. He requests help from Isolde the Fair, and asks that in case of her arrival the ship should set a white sail. When Isolde the Fair approaches the coast, jealous Isolde Whitehand deceives her husband and tells him that the sail is black. Despairing, Tristan dies, and when his true love has finally arrived at the bed, she drops dead next to him. King Marke has both buried together; a rosebush and a grapevine planted on their grave later intertwine, symbolizing the everlasting love of Tristan and Isolde the Fair.

Ulrich's *Rennewart* focuses on the history of the eponymous hero, who is, after the victory over the Saracens (described by Wolfram von Eschenbach in his *Willehalm*), baptized and married to King Loys' daughter Alise. Rennewart assumes the kingdom of Portebaliart and continues with his battles against the heathens. Alise dies at the birth of her child Malefer, who is soon after kidnapped by merchants and brought to Terramer, who wants to raise him as an opponent to Christianity, though to no avail. Rennewart, deeply grieved, joins a monastery where he lives for twenty more years. Two times he enters the battlefield again, however, and there he meets his son and entrusts him with the rulership of Portebaliart. Malefer later conquers the Oriental empire of his grandfather Terramer and marries the queen of the Amazons, Penteselie, who delivers a child with the name Johann who will continue with the religious struggle against the heathens. When Terramer's son Matribuleiz attacks France anew, Willehalm returns from his hermitage, a move that immediately convinces the Saracens, reminded of their previous defeat, to return home. Willehalm erects a monastery near Muntbasiliere where he will eventually meet his death.

This *continuatio* was, along with Wolfram's epic, highly popular and is extant in thirteen manuscripts and twenty-nine fragments. Ulrich relied in part on the French tradition of the *chansons de gestes* (heroic songs), which are focused on Guillaume d'Orange. The Augsburg citizen Otto der Bogner supplied Ulrich, as he indicates in his *Rennewart*, with the manuscripts of the French texts (vv. 10270–10282). Ulrich probably composed his works for the royal court of the Hohenstaufen family.

See also **Eilhart von Oberg; Gottfried von Straßburg; Wolfram von Eschenbach**

Further Reading

Grubmüller, Klaus. "Probleme einer Fortsetzung." *Zeitschrift für deutsches Altertum* 114 (1985): 338–348.
McDonald, William C. *The Tristan Story in German Literature of the Late Middle Ages and Early Renaissance.* Lewiston, Maine: Edwin Mellen Press, 1990.
Spiewok, Wolfgang, ed. *Das Tristan-Epos Gottfrieds von Straßburg. Mit der Fortsetzung des Ulrich von Türheim.* Berlin: Akademie-Verlag, 1989.
Ulrich von Türheim. *Rennewart*, ed. A. Hübner. Berlin: Weidmann, 1938; 2d ed., 1964.
——. *Tristan*, ed. Th. Kerth. Tübingen: Niemeyer, 1979.
Westphal-Schmidt, Christa. *Studien zum Rennewart Ulrichs von Türheim.* Frankfurt am Main: Haage und Herchen, 1979.

ALBRECHT CLASSEN

URBAN II, POPE
(c. 1035–1099, r. 1088–1099)

Pope Urban II (Odo of Lagery, Eudes de Châtillon) was a church reformer and founder of the crusading movement. Urban was a native of France and was descended from a noble family of Châtillon–sur–Marne, near Soissons; Odo was his baptismal name. During his early school days at Reims, he came under the influence of Saint Bruno, the founder of the Carthusian order, who remained a potent influence in shaping his goals and values even after he had become pope. Odo's early career followed a pattern common among young clerics of noble lineage. After becoming archdeacon of Reims

by 1160, he abandoned his career among the secular clergy and entered the monastery of Cluny. There, too, he advanced rapidly. By c. 1070 he was prior of Cluny; then Pope Gregory VII recruited him into the papal service in 1079–1080 and soon named him cardinal-bishop of Ostia.

Odo served Gregory diligently, at times at considerable peril to himself, notably when he was a papal legate in Germany during some of the darkest days of the pope's struggle against King Henry IV. When Gregory died at Salerno on 25 May 1085, Odo seemed a likely successor, but the choice fell instead on Abbot Desiderius of Monte Cassino, who reigned briefly as Pope Victor III. Shortly before his death (in 1087), Victor recommended that Odo be elected to succeed him. On 12 March 1088, the cardinals who had assembled at Terracina complied with Victor's suggestion, and Odo was crowned as Pope Urban II the same day.

The papacy was at this point in dire straits. Since Rome and the patrimony of Saint Peter were in the hands of Henry IV's supporters, papal revenues were greatly reduced, an antipope (Clement III) had the backing of the emperor, and the church reform movement seemed to be faltering. The great achievement of Urban's pontificate was to redress and, in large measure, to reverse this situation.

Urban was in many ways far more successful in implementing the papal reform program than Gregory VII had ever been. He achieved this in part by an unremitting round of meetings with bishops, the clergy, and powerful laymen, in which he preached, argued, bargained, and cajoled to induce his hearers to accept the main planks of the reformers' platform—to refrain from simoniacal appointments to church offices, to restore church property to clerical control, and to commit the clergy at every level to celibacy. At the same time, Urban sought, with considerable success, to reduce the political tension resulting from the confrontations that had marked the pontificate of Gregory VII. In place of confrontation, Urban offered negotiation; instead of demands, he advanced proposals; and he preferred to outmaneuver his opponents rather than challenge them directly.

Urban saw clearly that his reform program could succeed in the long run only if it was securely anchored in the church's legal structure. Accordingly, he devoted a great deal of time and effort to persuading church councils to adopt the principal tenets of his program as church law. He also lavished time and attention on his role as supreme judge in the ecclesiastical court system, and his decisions became an integral part of the canonical jurisprudence of later generations.

Urban is best-known, however, as the pope who proclaimed the First Crusade. At the council of Clermont on 27 November 1095, Urban called on the knights, nobles,

Council of Clermont. Arrival of Pope Urban II in France. Miniature from the Roman de Godefroi de Bouillon. 1337. Ms. fr. 22495, fol. 15. © Bridgeman-Giraudon/Art Resource, New York.

and bishops of Christendom to join in an expedition to push back Turkish armies that had occupied Asia Minor and to help the Byzantine emperor restore Christian control over the Levant. He further promised that participants in this expedition would receive spiritual rewards, as well as a share in the conquests that they achieved. The council adopted his proposals, which quickly aroused a broad and enthusiastic response—probably broader and more enthusiastic, indeed, than Urban had anticipated. The pope devoted a great deal of time and effort over the following months to spelling out the implications of his proposal and refining arrangements for its organization and implementation.

By the fall of 1096, crusaders from France, Germany, and England were on the way to their rendezvous at Constantinople. In Italy, Urban's proposal aroused interest at first mainly among the restless Norman conquerors of the south, who saw it as an opportunity to secure a foothold in Byzantine territories; and the merchants of a few maritime cities in the north, especially Genoa and Pisa, who perceived that the venture, if successful, might open up profitable commercial opportunities in the Middle East.

After the initial bands of crusaders had departed, Urban once more directed his attention to the implementation of church reform and endeavored to resolve the issues that had put the papacy at odds with the principal monarchs north of the Alps. Although he achieved some successes, his program was still incomplete when he fell ill in the summer of 1099. At the beginning of July, the crusading armies that he had dispatched to the east had taken the city of Jerusalem. News of this momentous victory had not yet reached Rome when Urban died on 19 July 1099.

See also **Gregory VII, Pope; Henry IV, Emperor**

Further Reading

Editions

The Councils of Urban II, Part 1, *Decreta Claromontensia*, ed. Robert Somervilie. Amsterdam: Hakkert, 1972.

Jaffé, Philipp. *Regesta pontificum Romanorum*, 2nd ed., 2 vols. Leipzig, 1885–1888, Vol. 1, pp. 657–701. (Reprint, Graz: Akademische Druck- U. Verlagsanstalt, 1956. Includes some of Urban's letters.)

Patrologia Latina, 151, cols. 283–558. (Texts of most of Urban's surviving letters.)

Critical Studies

Becker, Alfons. *Papst Urban II (1088–1099)*, 2 vols. Schriften der Monumenta Germanise Historica, 19. Stuttgart: A. Hiersemann, 1964–1988. Furhmann, Horst. *Papst Urban II. und der Standder Regularkanoniker.* Munich: Beck, 1984.

Gossman, Francis J. *Pope Urban II and Canon Law.* Washington, D.C.: Catholic University of America Press, 1960.

Kuttner, Stephan, "Brief Notes: Urban II and Gratian." *Traditio*, 24, 1968, pp. 504–505.

——. "Urban II and the Doctrine of Interpretation: A Turning Point?" *Studia Gratiana*, 15, 1972, pp. 53–86.

Somerville, Robert. "The Council of Clermont and the First Crusade." *Studia Gratiana*, 20, 1976, pp. 323–337.

——. "Mercy and Justice in the Early Months of Urban II's Pontificate." In *Chiesa diritto e ordinamento della "Societas Christiana" net secoli XI e XII: Atti della nona Settimana internazionale di studio, Mendola, 28 agosto–2 settembre 1983.* Milan: Vita e Pensiero, 1986, pp. 138–158.

JAMES A. BRUNDAGE

V

VALERA, DIEGO DE
(1412–c. 1488)

According to Valera himself, he was born in 1412 and lived to a ripe old age, probably dying late in 1488. His father, Alonso Chirino de Guadalajara, was the chief royal physician to Juan II of Castile and author of at least two medical treatises, one of which was printed in Seville in 1506. In 1427 Valera joined the royal court at the age of fifteen and served as one of the *donceles* of Juan II, and then Prince Enrique (the future Enrique IV). He was present at the Christian victory of La Higueruela just outside the Naṣrid capital of Granada in 1431, and was made a knight at the conquest of Huelma.

In 1437 Valera began a series of travels and adventures throughout western Europe, being included by Fernando del Pulgar in his *Claros varones de Castilla* among a select list of famous knights errant "que con ánimo de cavalleros fueron por los reinos estraños a fazer armas con qualquier cavallero que quisiese fazerlas con ellos, e por ellas ganaron honrra para sí e fama de valientes e esforçados cavalleros para los fijosdalgos de Castilla." He was present at sieges, which Charles VII of France directed against the English, traveled to Prague, helped Albert V in his campaigns against the Hussites, and was rewarded by being made a member of several chivalrous orders. Returning to Castile, it was not long before Valera was on his travels again with the king's backing and accompanied by a royal herald, this time visiting Denmark, England, and Burgundy, taking part in a famous tournament near Dijon, and returning subsequently on yet another mission to the court of Charles VII of France.

Valera took part on the royal side at the battle of Olmedo in 1445, but he was soon to fall out of favor due to his habit of preferring unsolicited advice in letters addressed to Juan II and then, subsequently, to Enrique IV. As a result he passed into the service of the count of Plasencia, Pedro de Estúñiga, for several years. By his own detailed account in his final chapter of the *Crónica abreviada*, Valera played an important role in the downfall of Álvaro de Luna, who was beheaded in Valladolid in 1453.

Apart from short periods of judicial office in Palencia and Segovia as well as some service in the noble house of Medinaceli, Valera spent most of his later life in Puerto de Santa María, from where he continued to write letters of political and military advice, in particular to Fernando the Catholic.

Valera was a prolific author whose main interests were devoted to chronicles and short treatises of a chivalrous, political, or moral nature. Carriazo established a chronological list of his works as follows: *Arbol de las Batallas*, a translation of the famous French treatise on the laws of arms by Honoré Bonet, done for Álvaro de Luna (prior to 1441); *Espejo de Verdadero Nobleza*, a treatise on the origins and nature of nobility, dedicated to Juan II (ca. 1441); *Defensa de virtuosos mugeres*, dedicated to Queen María of Castile (prior to 1443); *Exhortatión a la paz*, addressed to Juan II (ca. 1448): *Tratado de las armas*, for Afonso V of Portugal (ca. 1458–1467); *Providencia contra Fortuna*, dedicated to the marquis of Villena (ca. 1465); *Ceremonial de Príncipes*, also dedicated to the marquis of Villena (ca. 1462–1467); *Breviloquio de virtudes*, for Rodrigo Pimentel, count of Benavente; *Origen de Roma y Troya*, for Juan Hurtado de Mendoza; *Origen de la casa de Guzmán*; *Doctrinal de príncipes*, dedicated to Fernando the Catholic (ca. 1475–1476), perhaps one of Valera's more original works; *Preheminencias y cargos de los oficiales de armas*, for Fernando the Catholic; *Geneología de los Reyes de Francia*, dedicated to Juan Terrin; *Crónica abreviada de Espana* (1479–1481); *Memorial de diversas hazanas*; and *Crónica de los Reyes Católicos*.

In addition Carriazo listed another two works, a lost

work on the Estúñiga family, and another of dubious attribution, also lost, on *Ilustres varones de España*. In between all these works, the extraordinarily productive Valera also managed to write a considerable number of short poems of a moralistic or courtly love nature.

Further Reading

Pulgar, F. del. *Claros varones de Castilla*. Ed. R. B. Tate. Oxford, 1971.

Valera, M. D. de. *Crónica de los Reyes Católicos*. Ed. J. de Mata Carriazo. Madrid, 1927.

———. *Memorial de diversas hazañas*. Ed. J. de Mata Carriazo. Madrid, 1941. This edition includes the *Crónica abbreviada* as well.

ANGUS MACKAY

VAN DER WEYDEN, ROGIER (1399/1400–1464)

Flemish painter, a student of Robert Campin, known in his day as second only to Jan van Eyck, Rogier van der Weyden was born in Tournai in French-speaking Hainaut, but the economic life of the area depended heavily on Flanders rather than France. In the 1430s, rather than seek employment at the Burgundian court, he moved to Brussels as the head of a large workshop. As a guild member, he catered heavily to Germanic circles of patronage, which did not, however, prevent his appreciation of the achievements of the court painter van Eyck. The influence of his predecessor can be detected in early works such as the *Annunciation* of ca. 1435, now in the Louvre, from his attention to detail in the patterning of the floor and fabrics to the symbolic objects filling the panel with meaning. Simultaneously, van der Weyden began to move beyond van Eyck's stylistic accomplishments to create a style of his own, as exemplified by his *Lamentation* (ca. 1435–38) in the Prado. In a shallow, undefined space, van der Weyden focuses the viewer's attention upon the monumental figures actively demonstrating their grief. He rejects the disguised symbolism so favored by van Eyck in order to explore more fully the emotive capabilities of composition. Van der Weyden, although not employed directly by the Burgundian court, did produce some works for its most prominent members. An example is his *Altarpiece of the Seven Sacraments* (ca. 1453–55) in the Musée Royal des Beaux-Arts of Antwerp, executed for Jean Chevrot, bishop of Tournai, in which he expanded the Gothic cathedral interior as depicted in van Eyck's earlier *Madonna in the Church*. He and van Eyck shared a client in the person of Nicolas Rolin, chancellor of Flanders. Van der Weyden also painted a nativity altarpiece (1452–55), now in Berlin, for Pieter Bladelin, who was the chief tax collector in Flanders for Philip the Good.

See also **Campin, Robert; Van Eyck, Jan**

Further Reading

Davies, Martin. *Rogier van der Weyden*. London: Phaidon, 1972.

Panofsky, Erwin. *Early Netherlandish Painting*. New York: Harper and Row, 1971.

Snyder, James. *Northern Renaissance Art*. New York: Abrams, 1985.

MICHELLE I. LAPINE

VAN EYCK, JAN (ca. 1380–1441)

As one of the most famous painters of his day, van Eyck had the special privilege of being a *valet* to Philip the Good, duke of Burgundy. His role as court painter extended into the realm of diplomacy, as van Eyck was one of Philip's emissaries to Spain between 1424 and 1430. Van Eyck began his career in the Burgundian court after the death of his former patron, John of Bavaria. Although he served Philip directly, his production of panel painting for him went unrecorded. However, accounts of patronage do exist for members of Philip's circle. Van Eyck's reputation as a great master emerged from his superrealistic and sensual treatment of the panel, his rich and precise handling of clothing and jewels. Van Eyck fully exploited oil paint as his medium, evidenced by his exquisite details and nearly invisible brushwork. As was practiced by the majority of northern painters, van Eyck infused the objects in his world with secondary, allegorical, and christological meanings. The most obvious expression of his disguised symbolism can be found in his treatment of the Virgin and Child, a subject van Eyck repeatedly explored. His *Madonna in the Church* (ca. 1437–38), now hanging in the Gemaldegalerie-Staatliche Museen in Berlin, represents a beautifully executed example of his style and iconographic approach: the large size of the Virgin in comparison with her surroundings emphasizes her status. The *Ghent Altarpiece* (1432), which has sparked many a debate concerning attribution and assemblage, was done in collaboration with his brother Hubert and represents the only painting known by van Eyck prior to 1433.

Van Eyck produced his most renowned work for the members of the Burgundian court or people closely linked to it, particularly the two-thirds of his paintings that contain portraits. The *Arnolfini Wedding Portrait*, which rivals the altarpiece in reputation, was painted for Giovanni Arnolfini in 1434. Arnolfini settled in Flanders with his half-French wife after Philip the Good appointed him to a position at court. Baudouin de Lannoy, lord of Molembaix, commissioned a work in honor of his membership in the order of the Golden Fleece, founded by Philip in 1430. The inclusion of the order's collar in his portrait of 1435 advertises his newly acquired status. Van Eyck served Philip and the court of Burgundy for a sixteen-year stint that ended with his death in 1441. It was during his tenure as artist of the court that van Eyck developed the detailed, naturalistic style that had such a great impact on all who followed him.

See also **Van der Weyden, Rogier**

Further Reading

Dhanens, Elisabeth. *Hubert and Jan van Eyck.* New York: Alpine, 1970.

Henbison, Craig. *Jan van Eyck: The Play of Realism.* London: Reaktion, 1991.

Panofsky, Erwin. *Early Netherlandish Painting.* New York: Harper and Row, 1971.

Snyder, James. *Northern Renaissance Art.* New York: Abrams, 1985.

MICHELLE I. LAPINE

VENEZIANO, PAOLO (died c. 1362)

The earliest undisputed date for Paolo Veneziano is 1333, when he signed and dated a triptych, the *Dormition of the Virgin*, formerly at San Lorenzo in Vicenza and now in the civic museum there. An art collector in Venice mentions him in a memorandum of 1335. His *Madonna and Child Enthroned* in the Crespi collection in Milan is signed and dated August 1340. A signed deposition by Paolo of March 1341 is in the Venetian archives, where there was once a document of September 1342 commissioning a throne for use in a state festival from a painter named Paolo. This Paolo, who appears to be the same artist, enjoyed official status at the time. In April 1345, Paolo and his sons Luca and Giovanni signed and dated a panel used to protect the enamel and gold Pala d'Oro on the high altar of the basilica of San Marco. The cover, which is still in place, depicts episodes from the legend of Saint Mark, with half-figure saints and the *Man of Sorrows* above. A Venetian archival document of January 1346 records payment to Paolo fot an altarpiece for the chapel of Saint Nicholas in the ducal palace; two scenes from the life of Nicholas in the Soprintendenza at Florence may have once belonged to it. An *Enthroned Madonna and Child* at Carpineta in the Romagna bears Paolo's signature and the date 1347. A document of April 1352 in the archives at Dubrovnik relates to an altarpiece by him which is now lost. In 1358, Paolo and his son Giovanni signed and dated the *Coronation of the Virgin* now in the Frick Collection. Paolo died sometime between then and September 1362, when a Venetian archival document mentions him as deceased.

A large body of undocumented work is attributed to Paolo and his workshop, which is known to have included his sons Luca, Giovanni, and probably Marco, and at least one other artist. This body of work may be divided into two groups. One group falls within Paolo's documented career and is widely accepted, although with differences of opinion concerning chronology and autograph share; the other group is placed before that and is controversial. Important works among the former group are as follows: the votive tomb lunette of Doge Francesco Dandolo in Santa Maria dei Frari in Venice, painted around the time of the doge's death in October 1339; the *Enthroned Madonna and Child* with angels and donors in the Accademia in Venice, probably c. 1340; the polyptych from Santa Chiara in the same museum, depicting the *Coronation of the Virgin* and scenes from the lives of Christ, Saint Francis, and Saint Clare, probably from the early 1340s; a dismembered polyptych in San Giacomo Maggiore, Bologna, possibly c. May 1344, when the church was consecrated; a crucifix in the church of Saint Dominic at Dubrovnik, probably the one mentioned in a document of March 1348; dated polyptychs of 1349 at Chioggia, 1354 in the Louvre, and April 1355 formerly at Piran in Istria; and another late polyptych, dismembered, at San Severino in the Marches.

The other group of works, which is a subject of debate, should be attributed to Paolo's early period. It includes the panel masking the sarcophagus of the Blessed Leo Bembo, dated 1321, once in San Sebastiano, Venice, and now at Vodnjan in Istria; the dated *Coronation of the Virgin* of 1324 in the National Gallery in Washington; five panels from the early life of the Virgin and her parents at Pesaro; an altarpiece with half-length Madonna and child and four scenes from their lives in San Pantalon, Venice; sixteen panels from the legend of Saint Ursula in the Volterra collection in Florence; and a polyptych with an image and narrative of Saint Lucy, originally in her church at Jurandor and today in the bishop's chancellery at Krk in Dalmatia. The undated works were apparently done during the 1320s, in the order listed. The painted donor figures in a wood relief of 1310 at Murano have also been ascribed to Paolo, but they seem too early to have been painted by him and may show the hand of his master. It also has been suggested that Paolo and his workshop illuminated manuscripts and designed or executed mosaics and embroideries.

Although a long Venetian mosaic tradition survived into the fourteenth century, relatively little work on panel or in the other pictorial media was produced in the period immediately before Paolo. The traditional view is that Paolo was the founder and first great master of Venetian *Trecento* painting, and this view would have to be upheld unless the works assigned to him before his documented activity are rejected. Some of these works, particularly the panels at Pesaro, show the direct influence of Giotto's frescoes in nearby Padua; others, such as the *Coronation of the Virgin* in Washington, show the intrusion of Gothic style and iconography into the local Byzantine tradition. These same ingredients—the Byzantine, the Gothic, and the Giottesque—are the fundamental elements in Paolo's later works, in which the Gothic becomes more pronounced. The Byzantine and Gothic are so harmoniously blended as to suggest their ultimate common source in the distant classical past; the same might be said of the Giottesque. The influence of the Saint Cecilia Master and the school of Rimini may also be detected. The published literature assumes that, despite the obvious similarities, Paolo attained his style independendy of direct Sienese influence. Such examples as his Accademia *Madonna*, which is close to Duccio's in the Pinacoteca at Siena; and his figures of Saint Catherine in the Sanseverino polyptych and in a panel at Chicago, which resemble Simone Martini's fresco of that saint at Assisi, suggest otherwise. The bold patterns and glowing colors give Paolo's paintings an opulence unequaled even by the Sienese.

Paolo Veneziano had a profound influence on Venetian pictorial art, particularly panel painting, until the end of the fourteenth century. The style that he instituted was continued by Lorenzo Veneziano (whose dated works range from 1357 to 1372) and others into the fifteenth century and the international Gothic style. Paolo had relatively little influence on the mainland, which, with the exception of Istria and Dalmatia, responded to more progressive artistic stimuli.

Further Reading

Lucco, Mauro, ed. *La pittura nel Veneto: Il Trecento*. Milan: Electa, 1992.

Muraro, Michelangelo. *Paolo da Venezia*. University Park and London: Pennsylvania State University Press, 1970.

Pallucchini, Rodolfo. *La pittura veneziana del Trecento*. Venice and Rome: Istituto per la Collaborazione Culturale, 1964.

Il Trecento adriatico: Paolo Veneziano e la pittura tra oriente e occidente, ed. Francesca Flores d'Arcais and Giovanni Gentili. Milan: Silvana, 2002.

BRADLEY J. DELANEY

VILANOVA, ARNAU DE

Arnau de Vilanova is a figure of unusual interest for his role in medieval intellectual history. Though he called himself "Catalanus" and grew up in Valencia, it seems likely that he came there with his parents from a village outside Daroca (in Aragón) during the Christian resettlement of the city after its reconquest in 1237/8. We can infer his medical training at the *studium* of Montpellier in the 1260s, but it is only with the 1280s that we can begin to reconstruct his biography in detail. During that decade he was in Barcelona in medical attendance on the kings of Aragón-Catalonia, first Pedro III el Gran

and then Alfonso III. It was in this same period that his translation of Galen's *De rigore* from Arabic into Latin was finished (Barcelona, 1282); Arnau had presumably learned Arabic growing up in Aragón or Valencia. His other medical translations—of Avicenna's *De viribus cordis* and of Abulcasis's *De medicinis simplicibus*—though undated, may also have been completed in these years.

During the 1290s Arnau was apparently back at Montpellier, this time as a regent master, though occasionally he can also be found advising the new king, Jaime II, on his family's health. This was a period of great intellectual fruitfulness. Arnau composed a number of scientific works in these years, in which he developed aspects of medical theory. Simultaneously, his personal theological views were maturing along Joachimite lines; like the spiritual Franciscans with whom he was also beginning to establish close ties, he viewed the contemporary church, its institutions and orders, as corrupt, and he took that corruption to manifest the coming end of a historical age. When Jaime II sent him to Paris and to King Philip le Bel in 1300 to negotiate the status of the disputed Vail d'Aran, Arnau took the opportunity to defend these views as set out in his *De adventu antichristi* before the theologians of the Sorbonne: as a result, he was imprisoned as a heretic and released only at the intervention of the French monarch.

Seeking vindication, Arnau went now to Pope Boniface VIII, treating the pope successfully for the ailment of a stone and winning his agreement that Arnau's views, while rash, were not heterodox. With this assurance, Arnau renewed his attack on his adversaries, the scholastic theologians—Dominicans, in particular—whom he accused more harshly than ever of faithlessness, of having abandoned the study of the Bible for secular sciences. The installation of a friend as Pope Clement V in 1305 gave Arnau still more support and allowed him the calm to return to intellectual reflection and composition, in both his fields of activity. His most careful work on clinical medicinae, the *Regimen sanitatis* prepared for Jaime II, was written at this time, as was his *Speculum medicinae*, an ambitious attempt to draw current medical theory together synthetically. Yet simultaneously (1306) he was composing his *Expositio super antichristi*, doctrinally the most complex of his theological writings. He looked now to Clement as the authority destined to lead the reform of the church and society that would enable them to confront the Antichrist, and he believed that he had won over Jaime II and his brother Frederigo III of Sicily (Trinacria) to his program. But in 1309 Arnau went too far in his claims about Jaime, who thereupon broke completely with his former advisor and friend. Frederic, however, continued faithful, implementing Arnauldian spiritual principles in his kingdom even after Arnau's death in 1311.

On balance, Arnau enjoyed more success as a physician than as a theologian and reformer. A council at Tarragona condemned a dozen of his theological works in 1316, and most of the several Beguine communities inspired by his ideal of a lay spirituality dwindled away where they were not suppresssed outright. The taint of heterodoxy may have contributed to the later ascription to Arnau of many alchemical works, none with any verisimilitude. His genuine medical writings are numerous, however, and enjoyed great popularity down to the sixteenth century—particularly his *Regimen sanitatis* for Jaime II and the *Medicationis parabole* dedicated to Philip le Bel in 1300. Arnau's more abstract scientific writings are often original attempts to develop some particular aspect of medical theory and to imbed it within a broader naturophilosophical framework, and—like his *Aphorismi de gradi-bus*—they show considerable breadth of knowledge and imagination. Often harshly critical of his academic colleagues, he was particularly severe on their overdependence upon Avicenna's *Canon*, which had been the dominant authority behind the thirteenth-century schools. (To be sure, his own works are heavily marked by Avicennan problems and conclusions.) In 1309 he was one of three advisors who helped Clement V draw up a new curriculum for the medical faculty at Montpellier, one that made the works of Galen rather than Avicenna the core of medical instruction at that school. Attempts have been made to see his theological and medical positions as unified, but in many respects he seems to have been able to keep his two lives/passions compartmentalized.

See also **Avicenna; Clement V, Pope; Jaime II**

Further Reading

Arnaldi de Villanova Opera Medica Omnia. vols. 2, 3, 4, 6.1, 15, 16, 18, 19 published to date. Barcelona, 1975–.

Crisciani, C. "Exemplum Christi e Sapere. Sull'epistemologia di Arnaldo da Villanova," *Archives Internationales d'Histoire des Sciences* 28 (1978), 245–92.

García Ballester, L. "Arnau de Vilanova (c. 1240–1311) y la reforma de los estudios medicos en Montpellier (1309)," *Dynamis* 2 (1982), 97–158.

Perarnau, J. L'*"Alia Informatio Beguinorum" d'Arnau de Vilanova.* Barcelona, 1978.

Santí, F. *Arnau de Vilanova: L'obra espiritual.* Valencia, 1987.

MICHAEL MCVAUGH

VILLANI, GIOVANNI (c. 1280–1348)

The Florentine chronicler Giovanni Villani was a merchant and politician as well as a writer. He was the author of the *Nuova cronica* (*New Chronicle*), a history of Florence set in a much wider context, beginning with the tower of Babel and extending to 1348, the year when he died of the plague. In this work, he combined municipal patriotism and a cosmopolitan outlook with a passion for statistics and detail. Despite its length, it was (like Dante's *Comedy*) a great popular success, circulated in many fourteenth- and fifteenth-century manuscripts. However, although there were a number of subsequent printings, it was given a critical edition only quite recently (Porta 1990–1991).

Giovanni Villani was born into a mercantile family of some standing in Florence. Giovanni's father served a term as a prior—a member of the main governing board of the city—in 1300; and Giovanni and his three brothers were able to secure positions with two of the leading Florentine banking and commercial houses. Giovanni himself became a successful and rich businessman, though he must have lost most of his fortune in the great financial crash of the 1340s. He was also successful socially and politically. He married, as his second wife, a woman from the aristocratic Pazzi family; and he held a place in the ruling Florentine oligarchy, serving in various communal offices, including three terms as prior. His business career not only gave him intimate knowledge of the power struggles in his own city but also put him in touch with the wider world. He was able to travel extensively and receive reports from all over western Europe at a time when Florence was one of its richest and most populous cities. In this golden age, Florence enjoyed—as Giovanni observed in a meticulous statistical description of its trade and resources c. 1338—an income greater than that of many kingdoms. At this time, its banking and mercantile companies controlled and manipulated a disproportionately large concentration of capital and trade. Of these companies, the most powerful were the Bardi and the Peruzzi. As early as 1300, Giovanni was a shareholder with the Peruzzi firm, and c. 1302 he went to Bruges in its service; he was connected with it for a number of years, as were several of his relatives. Then, probably by 1312, but certainly by 1322, he transferred his activities to a new but rapidly growing firm, the Buonaccorsi, in which he and his brother Matteo became prominent—in fact, Giovanni was its codirector by 1324. Certainly by the late 1320s its operations were varied and widespread, including not only banking but also trading in many commodities, and extending over a vast area: southern and northern Italy, southern and northern France, Brabant, Flanders, England, and various parts of the Mediterranean. Although Giovanni mentions other places from time to time, it is these regions of which he seems to have had real knowledge. At least for those chapters of his chronicle that cover the period 1300–1348, we may suppose that conversations, oral reports, and merchants' letters are at least as important a source as chronicles and official documents.

Giovanni's access to both official and private documents must have made possible his unusually rich and accurate statistics about such things as armies, tax revenues, cloth production, wine consumption, coinage parities, and the number of castles in private and in communal hands. No doubt his collection of such quantitative information was greatly facilitated by the various offices and appointments entrusted to him by his city and his guild. Apart from his three priorates, these were mostly financial. As a municipal official, for example, he supervised the commune's money and the building of a stretch of the third circle of walls. As an official of the Calimala guild, he served on the *mercanzia* council of eight and oversaw the making of Andrea Pisano's bronze doors for the Baptistery. He also went on some diplomatic missions: he was sent to Cardinal Bertrand de Pouget in Bologna in 1329 and a little later to negotiate (unsuccessfully) for the surrender of Lucca. Most of his officeholding was in 1320–1330. After that, he may have been under a cloud, having been tried for barratry in 1331 for his part in building the walls, even though he was cleared of the charge. The fact that Charles of Calabria, then lord of the city, entrusted to the Buonaccorsi company the collection of the taxes from three of the six districts of Florence to pay for the building of those very walls may not have helped Villani's reputation. But real disaster came later, in 1346, after the collapse of the great Florentine commercial companies. Then Giovanni was imprisoned for alleged misconduct as the representative of the Buonaccorsi in negotiations with the communal government about their bankruptcy liabilities. Giovanni does not mention this personal disgrace, but he does express remorse for his share of responsibility in the losses of the small investors in the great companies. We do not know how long his imprisonment lasted. He died in 1348, some two years after it began, and was buried in Florence in the church of the Santissima Annunziata. His brother Matteo and his nephew Filippo continued his chronicle.

For the most part, the opinions Giovanni Villani expresses in his chronicle are remarkably balanced and moderate. His patriotism as a Florentine, for example, was real but not exaggerated. He knew that Florence was sometimes unjust to its neighbors, and though he praised its resilience and resourcefulness in times of crisis, he often deplored its lack of talent for war. He disliked *signori* and signorial government, but he could not always conceal his admiration for a despot as brilliant as Castruccio Castracani, despite the defeats Castruccio inflicted on Florence. Giovanni favored republican government and connected it with political liberty. But he bitterly condemned factional strife and considered the rule of a benevolent *signore* like King Robert of Naples sometimes necessary to restrain it. Villani was also critical of republican regimes representing one class, whether that class was aristocratic, mercantile, or (especially) artisan.

Giovanni was not only a moderate patriot and republican but also a moderate, though very loyal, Guelf. The rival Ghibelline party had been driven out of Florence in the late 1260s, before Giovanni was born, at the same time that the rule of the Ghibellines' Hohenstaufen patrons in southern Italy had given way to the rule of Charles of Anjou, called in by the pope to govern the kingdom of the Two Sicilies. The Ghibellines remained strong in the north and in some parts of Tuscany, but Guelf Florence, Angevin Naples, and the papacy, despite occasionally violent quarrels, were linked by strong economic and political bonds. For Giovanni, these bonds seem to have been ideological as well, reinforced by sincere religious feeling. He regarded Charles of Anjou as a new Charlemagne, summoned to Italy to rescue the Roman church from the Hohenstaufen Lombards. Giovanni devoted perhaps his most sustained literary effort to a long and eloquent account of Charles's Italian campaigns. He also portrayed Florence as usually an ally of the church, from the struggle between Pope Gregory VII and the Emperor Henry IV in the late eleventh century down to his own time. The intervals during the later period when the pope and Florence were at odds worried Giovanni, as did the taxation of the Florentine clergy without their consent by his own commune. At the same time, he did not hesitate to criticize individual popes and Angevin rulers for avarice and immorality, and his fellow Guelfs for factionalism. He thought that the expulsion of the White Guelfs in 1302 was disgraceful, but he was glad that their assault on the city in 1304 did not succeed. He was also glad that Henry VII failed to capture Florence in 1312, but he said that the emperor's original intention had been to deal justly with Guelfs as well as Ghibellines. Such urbane judiciousness was appropriate to a rich businessman who numbered kings and princes among his acquaintances and had wide experience of the world.

In the prologue to the *Nuova cronica*, Giovanni says that his pride in the noble origins of his city and his desire to delight and instruct his fellow citizens had impelled him to write its history. In Book 9, Chapter 36, he relates that he began to write in 1300, after returning to Florence from Rome, where he had participated in the great papal jubilee. Seeing the ancient Roman ruins, reading the ancient histories, and reflecting on the decline of Rome had inspired him to tell the story of the rise of Florence, an offspring of Rome. Whether or not Giovanni began his chronicle immediately after his return to Florence, it is evident that he wrote primarily for Florentines and that one of his main purposes was to celebrate their successes without omitting their blunders and failures. The history of no other European city except Rome had hitherto been told at such length. Giovanni also conveys a sharp awareness of developments in the physical shape and monuments of Florence—for example, its central octagonal church, the Baptistery, which he says travelers assured him was the most beautiful in the world; its other churches and public buildings, whose siting and arrangement he compared, following an old Florentine historical tradition, with those of similarly named Roman monuments; the dimensions of its walls, towers, and bridges; and even the emblems on the banners of its militia and the decoration on its war cart, or *carroccio*. He is also aware that Florence is not just a city but a European power, and his ability to see Florence as part of a greater world is one of his main merits as a historian. Giovanni also likes to include a good story or a vivid detail, from wherever it comes. He touches on such topics as astral portents, monstrous births, costumes, public feasts, civil and religious rituals, relics, epidemics, earthquakes, inscriptions, apparitions, the lions behind the communal palace in Florence, coins, Gog and Magog, Muhammad, what might have happened, famous men (like Aquinas, Dante, and Giotto, of whom he writes pocket biographies), sea battles, sermons, governments, and expedients for increasing public revenue. Given such variety, it is no wonder that many critics have accused Giovanni Villani of being episodic and lacking a unifying theme or point of view. Porta believes that Giovanni did revise the chronicle extensively but that his main purpose was probably to introduce new information at many points—a process made easier because the chronicle is for the most part organized not thematically but year by year.

Giovanni certainly wants to instruct as well as entertain and inform his readers. He says that he wants to show future Florentines which actions of their predecessors they should imitate and which they should avoid. The guidance he offers is more moral than intellectual. It is true that much shrewd commentary on business, politics, and war is scattered through his book, but he has no single large lesson to teach. His analysis of the secondary causes of a particular Florentine victory or defeat can be thorough and penetrating, as, for example, in his explanations of the failure of Florence to acquire Lucca after the death of Castruccio Castracani. Very often, however, he is content—as a devout and right-thinking Florentine Guelf—to attribute such disasters to the wrath of the deity at the wickedness of the Florentines: their pride, avarice, and envy. Giovanni knows the Old Testament well, and his God, like Yahweh, is swift to punish. Sometimes, particularly in the later books of his chronicle, he seeks scientific, or at any rate astrological, explanations; but he consistently denies that the influence of the stars negates free will or men's responsibility for their actions, and he expresses again and again his conviction that the stars are immediately and totally subject to God's commands. He does try to account rationally for one great problem in thirteenth-century and early fourteenth-century Florence: factionalism.

He does so by a literal application of Dante's metaphor about the opposition between the two peoples who, according to Florentine legend, shared in populating the city, the allegedly "noble and virtuous" Romans and the allegedly "rough and fierce" Fiesolans. For Dante, "Romans" were all those willing to submit to the emperor's laws; "Fiesolans" were those "barbarians" who resisted it. For Giovanni Villani, the two names designate two peoples who actually participated in populating Florence and whose imperfect mixing produced chronic strife. He finds the story of this mixing in the *Chronica de origine civitatis* (written before 1231) and its Italian translations. (It is very unlikely that he was able to find the origin, as some scholars have maintained, in the so-called Malispinian chronicle, which was almost certainly written after his own and was largely copied from a compendium of his work.) In the *Chronica de origine civitatis*, the Roman origins of Florence were exalted and Julius Caesar himself was included among the founders of the city; but though the Fiesolans were represented as fierce enemies of the Romans, they were not depicted as barbarians. This Giovanni could have found in no surviving work before Dante's *Inferno*, circulated c. 1314. Probably Giovanni was also paraphrasing Dante's words in *Paradiso* (15.109–111), as Aquilecchia (1965) has suggested, when he referred in Book 9, Chapter 36, to the rise of Florence and the decline of Rome.

Up to this point in his chronicle, Giovanni is mainly concerned with describing the steady ascent, despite occasional disasters, of Florence, the child of Rome. Afterward, misfortunes multiply and the direction of Florence's development is not so clear. But Giovanni retains much of his optimism until the 1340s, the imposition and overthrow of Walter de Brienne's regime, and the subsequent financial crash. Neither communal nor personal calamities slowed the chronicler's busy pen. It continued right up to his death to provide an invaluable picture of the attitudes of the fourteenth-century oligarchy of Florence toward its past and present, and, especially for the period from c. 1320 to 1348, a narrative source for medieval Florentine history of inexhaustible richness and variety.

See also **Dante Alighieri; Malispini, Ricordano**

Further Reading

Editions

Villani, Giovanni. *Cronica*, 8 vols., ed. Ignazio Moutier. Florence: Magheri 1823. (Reprinted in Florence: Coen, 1844; Milan: Borroni e Scotti, 1848.)

——. *Selections from the First Nine Books of the "Croniche Florentine" of Giovanni Villani*, trans. Rose E. Selfe, ed. Philip H. Wicksteed. Westminster: A. Constable, 1896.

——. *Cronisti del Trecento*, ed. Roberto Palmarocchi. Milan: Rizzoli, 1935, pp. 153–466.

——. *Nuova cronica*, 3 vols., ed. Giuseppe Porta. Parma: Fondazione Pietro Bembo; U. Guanda, 1990–1991.

Critical Studies

Aquilecchia, Giovanni. "Dante and the Florentine Chroniclers." *Bulletin of the John Rylands Library*, 48(1), 1965, pp. 30–55.

Arias, G. "Nuovi documenti su Giovanni Villani." *Giornale Storico della Letteratura Italiana*, 34, 1899, pp. 383–387.

Bec, Christian. "Sur l'historiographie marchande à Florence au XIVe siècle." In *La chronique et l'histoire au moyen-âge*: *Colloque des 24 et 25 mai 1982*, ed. D. Poiron. Paris, 1984, pp. 45–72.

Becker, Marvin B. *Florence in Transition*, Vol. 1, *The Decline of the Commune*. Baltimore, Md.: Johns Hopkins University Press, 1967.

Bruni, Francesco. "Identità culturale e mito delle origini: Firenze nella *Cronica* di Giovanni Villani." In *Storia delle civilta letteraria Italiana*, Vol.1, *Dalle origini al Trecento*, ed. G. Barberi Squarotti. Turin: 1990, part 2, pp. 716–728.

Castellani, A. "Sulla tradizione delk *Nuova cronica* di Giovanni Villani." *Medioevo e Rinascimento*, 2, 1988, pp. 53–118.

——. "Pera Baducci lla tradizione della *Nuova Cronica* di Giovanni Villani." *Studi di Filologia Italiana*, 48, 1990, pp. 5–13.

Cipolla, C. M. *The Monetary Policy of Fourteenth-Century Florence*. Berkeley: University of California Press, 1982.

Davis, Charles T. "Dante, Villani, and Ricordano Malispini." In *Dante and the Idea of Rome*. Oxford: Clarendon, 1957, pp. 244–262.

——. "The Malispini Question." *Studi Medievali*, Series 3(10.3), 1970, pp. 215–254. (Reprinted in *Dante's Italy and Other Essays*. Philadelphia: University of Pennsylvania Press, 1984, pp. 94–136.)

——. "Il buon tempo antico." In *Florentine Studies*: *Politics and Society in Renaissance Florence*, ed. N. Rubinstein. London, 1968, pp. 45–69. (Reprinted in *Dante's Italy and Other Essays*. Philadelphia: University of Pennsylvania Press, 1984, pp. 71–93.)

——. "Topographical and Historical Propaganda in Early Florentine Chronicles and in Villani." *Medioevo e Rinascimento*, 2, 1988, pp. 35–51.

Della Torre, A. "L'amicizia di Dante e Giovanni Villani." *Giornale Dantesco*, 12, 1904, pp. 33–44.

Del Monte, A. "La storiografia fiorentina dei secoli XII e XIII." *Bullettino dell'Istituto Storico Italiano per il Medio Evo e Archivio Muratoriano*, 62, 1950, pp. 175–282.

De Matteis, M. C. "Ancora su Malispini, Villani, e Dante: Per un riesame dei rapporti tra cultura storica e profezia etica nell'Alighieri." *Bullettino dell'Istituto Storico Italiano per il Medio Evo e Archivio Muratoriano*, 82, 1970, pp. 329–390.

——. "Malispini da Villani o Villani da Malispini? Una ipotesi sui rapporti tra Ricordano Malisini, il 'Compendiatore,' e Giovanni Villani." *Bullettino dell'Istituto Storico Italiano per il Medio Evo e Archivio Muratoriano*, 84, 1973, pp. 145–221.

Fiumi, Enrico. "La demografia fiorentina nelle pagine di Giovanni Villani." *Archivio Storico Italiano*, 108, 1950, pp. 78–158.

——. "Economia e vita privata dei fiorentini nelle rilevazioni statistiche di Giovanni Villani." *Archivio Storico Italiano*, 111, 1953, pp. 207–241.

Frugoni, Arsenio. "G. Villani *Cronica*, XI, 94." *Bullettino dell'Istituto Storico Italiano per il Medio Evo e Archivio Muratoriano*, 77, 1965, pp. 229–255.

Green, Louis. *Chronicle into History*: *An Essay on the Interpretation of History in Florentine Fourteenth-Century Chronicles*. Cambridge: Cambridge University Press, 1972.

Hartwig, Otto. *Quellen und Forschungen zur ältesten Geschichte der Stadt Florenz*, 2 vols. Marburg: N. G. Elwert'sche Verlagsbuchh., 1875–1880.

Hyde, J. K. "Medieval Descriptions of Cities." *Bulletin of the John Rylands Library*, 48(2), 1966, pp. 308–340.

Imbriani, V. "Sulla rubrica dantesca nel Villani." In *Studi danteschi*. Florence, 1891, pp. 1–175.

Lami, V. "Di un compendio inedito della cronica di Giovanni Villani nelle sue relazioni con la storia fiorentina malispiniana." *Archivio Storico Italiano*, Series 5, 1890, pp. 369–416.

Link-Heer, Ursula. "Italienische Historiographie zwischen Spätmittelalter und fruher Neuzeit." In *Grundriss der romanischen Literaturen des Mittelalters*, Vol. 11(1). Heidelberg: C. Winter Universitätsverlag, 1987, pp. 1068–1129. (See especially pp. 1078–1088.)

Luiso, F. P. "Le edizioni della *Cronica* di Giovanni Villani." *Bullettino dell'Istituto Storico Italiano per il Medio Evo e Archivio Muratoriano*, 49, 1933, pp. 279–315.

——. "Indagini biografiche su Giovanni Villani." *Bullettino dell'Istituto Storico Italiano per il Medio Evo e Archivio Muratoriano*, 51, 1936, pp. 1–64.

Luzzati, Michele. "Ricerche sulle attivita mercantili e sul fallimento di Giovanni Villani." *Bullettino dell'Istituto Storico Italiano per il Medio Evo e Archivio Muratoriano*, 81, 1969, pp. 173–235.

——. *Giovanni Villani e la compagnia dei Buonaccorsi*. Rome: Istituto della Enciclopedia Italiana, 1971.

Mattucci, Andrea. "Da Giovanni Villani al primo Guicciardini: I mondi separati della *narrazione* e del *discorso*." In *Machiavelli nella storiografia fiorentina*: *Per la storia di un genere letterario*. Florence: Olschki, 1991, pp. 3–30.

Mehl, Ernst. *Die Weltanschauung des Giovanni Villani*: *Ein Beitrag zur Geistesgeschiehte Italiens im Zeitalter Dantes*. Leipzig: Tuebner, 1927.

——. "G. Villani und die *Divina Commedia*." *Deutsches Dante-Jahrbuch*, 10, 1928, pp. 173–184.

Meissen T. "Atiia, Totila, e Carlo Magno fra Dante, Villani, Boccaccio, e Malispini: Per la genesi di due leggende erudite." *Archivio Storico Italiano*, 152, 1994, pp. 561–639.

Milanesi, G. "Documenti riguardanti Giovanni Villani e il palazzo degli Alessi in Siena." *Archivio Storico Italiano*, n.s., 4, 1856, pp. 3–12.

Morghen, Raffaello. "Dante, il Villani, e Ricordano Malispini." *Bullettino dell'Istituto Storico Italiano per il Medio Evo e Archivio Muratoriano*, 41, 1921, pp. 171–194.

——. "La storiografia fiorentina del Trecento: Ricordano Malispini, Dino Compagni, e Giovanni Villani." In *Libera cattedra di storia della civiltà fiorentina—Secoli vari: '300, '400, '500*. Florence: Sansoni, 1958, pp. 69–93.

Najemy, J. M. *Corporatism and Consensus in Florentine Electoral Politics, 1280–1400*. Chapel Hill: University of North Carolina Press, 1982.

——. "L'ultima pane tiella Nuova Cronica di Giovanni Villani." *Studi di Filologia Italiana*, 41, 1983, pp. 17–36.

Neri, F. "Dante il primo Villani." *Giornale Dantesco*, 20, 1912, pp. 1–31. Ottokar, Nicola. *Il commune di Firenze alla fine del Dugento*. Florence: Vallecchi, 1926. (See also 2nd ed. Turin: Einaudi, 1962.)

Pezzarossa, Fulvio. "La tradizione fiorentina della memorialistica." In *La "memoria" dei "mercatores"*: *Tendenze ideologiche, ricordanze, artigianato in versi nella Firenze del Quattrocento*, ed. Gian-Mario Anselmi, Fulvio Pezzarossa, and Luisa Avellini. Bologna: Pàtron, 1980, pp. 39–149.

——. "Le geste e' fatti de' Fiorentini: Riflessioni a margine di un'edizione della cronica di Giovanni Villani." *Lettere Italiane*, 45, 1993, pp. 93–115. Porta, Giuseppe. "Censimento dei manoscritti delle cronache di Giovanni, Matteo, e Filippo Villani, 1." *Studi di Filologia Italiana*, 34, 1976a, pp. 61–129.

——. "Testimonianze di volgare campano e francese in G. Villani." *Lingua Nostra*, 37, 1976b, pp. 8–9.

——. "Censimento dei manoscritti delle cronache di Giovanni, Matteo, e Filippo Villani, 2." *Studi di Filologia Italiana*, 37, 1979, pp. 93–117.

——. "Aggiunta al censimento dei manoscritti delle cronache di Giovanni, Matteo, e Filippo Villani," *Studi di Filologia Italiana*, 44, 1986a, pp. 65–67.

——. "Sul testo e la lingua di Giovanni Villani." *Lingua Nostra*, 47, 1986b, pp. 37–40.

——. "La storiografia fiorentina fra il Duecento e il Trecento." *Medioevo e Rinascimento*, 2, 1988, pp. 119–130.

——. "Giovanni Villani storico e scrittore." In *I racconti di Clio: Tecniche narrative della storiografia—Atti del Convegno di Arezzo, 6–8 novembre 1986*, ed. Roberto Bigazzi, et al. Pisa: Nistri-Lischi, 1989, pp. 147–156.

——. "Les rapports entre l'Italie et la France dans la persepective des chroniqueurs florentins du XIVe siècle." In *Die kulturellen Beziehungen zwischen Italien und den anderen Laendern Europas im Mittelalter*, ed. Danielle Buschinger and Wolfgang Spiewok. 1993a, pp. 147–156.

——. "Le varianti redazionali come strumento di verifica dell'autenticità di testi: Villani e Malispini." In *La filologia romanza e i codici: Atti del Convegno di Messina, 19–22 dicembre 1991*, Vol. 2. Messina, 1993b, pp. 481–529.

Ragone, Franca. "Le scritture parlate: Qualche ipotesi sulla redazione delle cronache volgari nel Trecento dopo l'edizione critica della *Nuova Cronica* di Giovanni Villani." *Archivio Storico Italiano*, 149, 1991, pp. 783–810.

Rubinstein, Nicolai. "The Beginnings of Political Thought in Florence." *Journal of the Warburg and Courtauld Institutes*, 5, 1942, pp. 198–227.

Santini, Pietro. *Quesiti e ricerche di storiografia fiorentina*. Florence: Seeber, 1903.

CHARLES T. DAVIS

Villard de Honnecourt (c. 1225–c. 1250). Drawing of flying buttresses of Reims Cathedral, 1230–35. © Bridgeman-Giraudon/Art Resource, New York.

VILLARD DE HONNECOURT (WILARS DEHONECORT; VILARS DEHONCORT; fl. 1220–30)

Picard artist now known only through a portfolio of thirty-three parchment leaves of drawings in Paris (B.N. fr. 19093). Some leaves have been lost from the portfolio; the maximum number that can be proven to be lost is thirteen, with the possible loss of two additional leaves.

Villard addressed his drawings to an unspecified audience, saying that his "book" contained "sound advice on the techniques of masonry and on the devices of carpentry . . . and the techniques of representation, its features as the discipline of geometry commands and instructs it." The subjects of Villard's drawings are animals, architecture, carpentry, church furnishings, geometry, humans, masonry, mechanical devices, recipes or formulae, and surveying.

Villard traveled extensively, and most of the identifiable monuments that he drew date to the first quarter of the 13th century. He drew, and perhaps visited, the ca-

thedrals of Cambrai, Chartres, Laon, Meaux, Reims, and the abbey of Vaucelles in France; the cathedral of Lausanne in Switzerland; and the abbey of Pilis in Hungary.

There is no documentary evidence that Villard designed or built any church anywhere or that he was in fact an architect. It has been proposed that he may have been "a lodge clerk with a flair for drawing" or that his training may have been in metalworking rather than masonry. It may be that Villard was not a professional craftsman but rather an inquisitive layman who had an opportunity to travel widely.

Further Reading

Barnes, Carl F., Jr. "Le 'problème' Villard de Honnecourt." In *Les batisseurs des cathédrales gothiques,* ed. Roland Recht. Strasbourg: Éditions les Musées de la Ville de Strasbourg, 1989, pp. 209–23.

——. *Villard de Honnecourt: The Artist and His Drawings, A Critical Bibliography*. Boston: Hall, 1982.

——, and Lon R. Shelby. "The Codicology of the Portfolio of Villard de Honnecourt (Paris, Bibliothèque nationale, MS fr. 19093)." *Scriptorium* 40 (1988): 20–48.

Hahnloser, Hans R. *Villard de Honnecourt: Kritische Gesamtausgabe des Bauhüttenbuches ms. fr. 19093 der Pariser Nationalbibliothek.* Vienna: Schroll, 1935; rev. ed. Graz: Akademische Druck- und Verlagsanstalt, 1972. [Best facsimile edition.]

CARL F. BARNES, JR.

VILLEHARDOUIN, GEOFFROI DE
(ca. 1150–before 1218)

Author of the *Conquête de Constantinople,* one of the earliest historical works written in French prose, and one of two eyewitness accounts of the Fourth Crusade. Villehardouin was born into a noble Champenois family. He served the count of Champagne, Thibaut III, as marshal after 1185. In this capacity, Villehardouin developed the mediating abilities that would serve him so well. We know of three disputes he mediated, one involving the count himself.

Count Thibaut III of Champagne (d. 1202) was one of the organizers of the Fourth Crusade, so Villehardouin was at the heart of the planning. He was one of the six ambassadors sent to Venice in 1201 to negotiate passage in Venetian ships. In 1203, he was sent to Isaac II, whom the crusaders had restored to the throne of Constantinople, to see that the Latins would be paid as agreed. He carried out negotiations between the emperor Baudouin and Boniface of Montferrat, the new leader of the crusade, when the two fell out. Because of his outstanding services, Villehardouin was made marshal of Romania in 1205. The rest of his life is obscure. He last appears in the records in 1212 and was certainly dead by 1218, when his son arranged a memorial for him.

The *Conquête,* which begins with the preaching of the crusade by Foulques de Neuilly and ends suddenly in 1207, was composed after the events it relates, although Villehardouin probably made notes and certainly used documentary sources. The prose is straightforward and unrhetorical. The story is told in excellent chronological order.

Villehardouin seems to have intended his work as a defense of the crusade against critics who pointed out that the crusaders attacked only the Christian cities of Zara and Constantinople and never got to Jerusalem at all. Villehardouin lays chief blame for these unfortunate facts on those who failed to join the crusade at Venice and help pay for passage, forcing the crusaders to repay Venice by attacking Zara, and those who deserted later, leaving too small a fighting force for a real holy war. He does not, however, hold blameless those who participated or remained; their sins, particularly their greed, caused further disasters and offended God.

Villehardouin's narrative was more widely read than Robert de Clari's, the other eyewitness account of the Fourth Crusade. Six manuscripts of the *Conquête* are extant, and two more were used in early editions before they disappeared. In addition, two manuscripts of an abbreviation exist. Villehardouin's work was also incorporated in the *Chronique de Baudouin d'Avesnes,* a 13th-century compilation that circulated widely.

Further Reading

Villehardouin, Geoffroi de. *La conquête de Constantinople,* ed. Edmond Faral. 2 vols. 2nd ed. Paris: Les Belles Lettres, 1937.

Joinville and Villehardouin. *Chronicles of the Crusades,* trans. Margaret Shaw. Harmondsworth: Penguin, 1963.

Beer, Jeanette M.A. *Villehardouin, Epic Historian.* Geneva: Droz, 1968.

Dufournet, Jean. *Les écrivains de la IVe croisade: Villehardouin et Clari.* 2 vols. Paris: SEDES, 1973.

LEAH SHOPKOW

VILLON, FRANÇOIS (1431–1463)

Of all the lyricists of late-medieval France, Villon is the most celebrated among both scholars and general readers. Students of premodern literature inside and outside the francophone world have encountered him in his original Middle French; and thousands of people who have little or no French have read versions of his poems in the major European languages.

It was not always thus. The circle of contemporaries who knew of Villon's literary abilities was a modest one. He tells us in his *Testament* that an earlier work, the *Lais,* is already in circulation and being referred to by a title not of his choosing. On the other hand, the number of early sources preserving his poems is small; and his readers were in general not found among the rich and powerful. Although some such personages come in for mention in his verses, it is usually in the context of appeals for money, or of distant, uneasy, or downright irreverent allusion; Villon was not a success with well-off patrons of literature. The fame he sought eluded him. He seemingly hoped for a career as a court poet and exerted himself to catch the eye of such highly placed connoisseurs as Charles d'Orléans; but for unknown reasons, he did not achieve more than a small gift of money here and there. Greater success in his lifetime, however, might well have spelled later obscurity; his *poésies de circonstance,* composed, we must assume, to curry favor, competent though they are, are by and large forgettable. Rather than spend much of his career in turning out pleasing official verse, he was driven by circumstance, and perhaps also by a jarring personality, to live by expedients, know misery, reflect on it, and write amateur poetry of a unique stamp.

The body of Villon's works is of moderate dimensions: some 3,300 lines. It comprises independent pieces in fixed form (ballades and rondeaux) and two unified compositions, the *Lais* and the *Testament.* The

Lais, dated 1456, is a series of burlesque legacies occasioned by being, as Villon asserts, crossed in love, and consequently deciding to quit Paris, perhaps never to return. The *Testament* (1461) takes up again the legacy pattern but refines it into the articles of a last will and testament, complete with legal clauses and phraseology, the fiction now being that the author is near death and bethinking himself of soul and body as well as of worldly goods. This, Villon's major work, written, in octaves (eight-line strophes of octosyllabic verse), contains fixed-form pieces as well, some of which may antedate or even postdate 1461. The whole amounts to a personal literary anthology as well as the poet's artistic testament and monument. The rest of his *œuvre* is made up of a fulsome *Louange* of Princess Marie d'Orléans, with attached double ballade and much Latin adornment; a *Ballade franco-latine,* even more latinate; a number of difficult poems in the jargon of the medieval French underworld; and some ballades made up of the rhetorical devices dear to the schoolroom and fashionable court. Jumbled in with them are some pieces so intensely felt, so personal, so perfectly marrying form and content, that they belong by right to the greatest world literature. Among these are the *Épître à ses amis*, Villon's De *profundis*; the yes-and-no meditation on fate and individual responsibility best called *Débat de Villon et de son cœur*, and the *Ballade des pendus*, with its unbearable yet inescapable vision of legally executed bodies (including the poet's?) and its reiterated solicitation of prayer for their souls. Villon's last poems appear to fit into the interval between his last imprisonment and appeal, the commutation of his death sentence to a ten-year exile, and his departure in 1463 to an unknown end.

Villon was born into a poor family (*Testament*, ll. 273–75) in 1431, the year marked by the death of Jeanne d'Arc, celebrated in the *Testament* (ll. 351–52) as ... *Jehanne la bonne Lorraine/Qu'Engloys brulerent a Rouen* ("Joan, the brave girl from Lorraine/Burned by the English at Rouen"). The Hundred Years' War was dragging on; disease, food-shortages, and protracted spells of cold, wet weather afflicted everyone, the poor especially. It was out of harsh necessity, no doubt, that the future poet's mother entrusted her child to a presumed relative, Guillaume de Villon, the kindly chaplain of the Parisian church of Saint-Benoît-le-Bétourné not far from the Sorbonne, who would be the boy's *plus que père* (*Testament*, 1. 849).

Young François, originally called de Montcorbier or des Loges, took the surname of his adoptive father, and much else besides: security, relative comfort, clerical status, and the opportunity for the best formal education then available. In 1449, he obtained the baccalaureate degree and three years later the License and the degree of Maître ès Arts. This and his connections ought to have smoothed Villon's path into the learned professions; but these were overpopulated in the mid-15th century. To enter the secular or regular clergy was apparently not for him a viable choice; nor, in the absence of an independent income or a patron, was it possible for him to become a professional writer. He turned to living by his wits, in the company of other unemployed *clercs* and even more lowly individuals; and this led him into repeated brushes with the law, mainly for theft but once for manslaughter. As an *écolier*, he was entitled to the church's protection from the full rigor of secular justice; but it looks as if he lost the benefit of clergy, as well as many months of freedom, when he was condemned to prison at Meung-sur-Loire in 1461 by the bishop of Orléans.

It was his long police record, rather than one final and spectacular crime, that drove the exasperated secular authorities in late 1462 to pass a capital sentence; the Parlement, on appeal, commuted this to a ten-year banishment from Paris and its environs. Sadly, it is owing to his activities as part-time criminal that much of the information about Villon has come to us, for the abundant records have been preserved in the Paris archives. They supplement the hints, half-truths, special pleading, and downright lies that bestrew the poet's own writings.

Such a biographical excursus is particularly indicated in Villon's case, for much of his work is highly personal without always being informative or even candid. His feelings take precedence over the exact cause for them, his hatred for his enemies overshadows the ways whereby the latter have earned his resentment, and the possibility that the poet himself might somehow have provoked or deserved rough handling is pushed far into the background. Yet the interweaving of concrete if unreliable allusions to persons and events on the one hand, of passionate response on the other, makes of Villon an autobiographical lyricist to an unusual degree.

His themes, though, are universal ones, colored by his cultural milieu and his own subjectivity. Adversity, suffering, insecurity, the hunger for love, the transitoriness of youth and of all good things, the approach of death, the faith that sees beyond it—these are the timbers of which his work is built. Through the 2,000 lines of the *Testament*, he turns these notions over and over, in a composition structured by association of ideas and shifting moods rather than logical or formal progression. This begins as early as the first stanzas, which move with great rapidity from the testator's age and mental condition to his state of health and thence to his recent hardships and the person responsible for them; and with the name of Bishop Thibaut d'Aussigny, the memory of the preceding summer's incarceration, and probable degradation from clerical status, comes flooding back, making him sacrifice syntax to sarcasm: yes, he will pray for his enemy—with a cursing psalm. For good measure, he adds a prayer for Louis, *le bon roy de France*. On he goes, intermingling complaint, piety, and half-admissions of unsatisfactory behavior. Yet a sinner in his situation is pardonable: *Neccessité fait gens mesprendre/Et fain saillir le loup du boys* ("It's need drives folks to go astray/And hunger, the wolf to leave the woods"; ll. 167–68). He has abundant grounds for lamentation. His youth has flown; he is prematurely old, poor, rejected by his kin, disappointed in love, regretting his old friends (where are they now?), knowing that death will come for him as it has for the lovely ladies and great potentates of the past. These are themes to which he returns, obsessively but not uninterruptedly; for a great number of bequests remain to be formulated and the whole apparatus of the fictitious testament to be worked in.

There is a good deal of humor in all this, of a rough, pun-filled, scabrous character; and the poet takes advantage of the safety afforded by the last-will-and-testament schema to take verbal revenge on the individuals and classes who have earned his disapproval; after all, the document, according to the poetic fiction, will not be read until after his decease. We are led once again to the theme that underlies the *Testament* as a whole. It sometimes is expressed with gentle gravity, as in the *Ballade des dames du temps jadis*; in grimmer moments, the poet's thought turns to scenes commonly beheld in Paris: the piled-up and anonymous bones in the Cemetery of the Innocents, the cadavers of executed criminals dangling from the Montfaucon gibbet, the last agony awaiting each man and woman. In the Europe of the 15th century, the body's death was but a stage in the soul's journey; prayers and allusions to Heaven and Hell throng the octaves and fixed-form pieces. In the intervals of anxiety about death and what is in store for himself and all humankind, Villon repeatedly turns to common experience, particularly its darker side. Happiness is rare and fleeting; sorrow, fear, physical discomfort, and decrepitude—these are the lot of the human race. Why had Villon, why had so many men and women known suffering? Why does a just God permit malevolent Fortune to afflict the innocent? The poet's own stance, at least as early as the independent *Épître à ses amis* (presumably composed during the 1461 incarceration at Meung-sur-Loire) is that of a blameless victim, and he cries out with the words of the archetypical righteous sufferer, Job (11. 1–2): *Ayez pictié, ayez pictié de moy/A tout le moins, s'i vous plaist, mes amis!* ("Have pity, do have pity upon me,/You at least, if you please, who are my friends"). This explicit kinship with Job is affirmed repeatedly through the *Testament*; it has become the poet's characteristic way of making sense of what has befallen him, of understanding, as well, the human condition.

Villon's themes are by no means original, nor is his use of archetypes in working them out. As an educated man, he was steeped in the Latin classics and in the Bible, those storehouses of human experience and its literary expression; to allude to traditional topoi, stories, and personages was second nature for him, as it was for other writers of the day. His preoccupation with death and decay, his frequent melancholy, his startling coarseness, his mingling of jest and seriousness, are also features common in late-medieval writing, and in the visual arts as well. What sets him apart is the immediacy of his communication with the reader. His verse revivifies the notion of lyric: not poems to be sung, but poems expressive of feeling. Unlike the conventional and impersonal *je* of much contemporary writing, Villon's *je* most frequently is his unique and unruly self, temporarily brought to order by the discipline of his octaves and his fixed-form pieces. Much 15th-century poetry treats of love, again in courtly and stereotyped ways, for the stylized worship of the lady was still very much alive. Villon writes of love, too, but mostly from his own limited experience: it is a snare and a delusion, at best a fleeting joy. By and large, women are sensual and venal (but not to be condemned, for it is *nature femeninne* [*Testament*, 1. 611] that moves them), and in any case their attractiveness soon withers. Indeed, woman's charms, such a staple among mainstream masculine writers of the period, do not feature much here except in the context of bitter reminiscence and of regret for the transitoriness of all things desirable. It would in fact not be easy to find another major poet so indifferent to beauty; but then visual description of any sort does not stand out in Villon's verses. He inclines to naming persons and places, to evoking action and speech and gesture, rather than to painting word pictures. Even his self-description is limited to a few qualifiers: *sec et noir*; *plus maigre que chimere* ("skinny and dark"; "thinner than a wraith"). What he does give us is his reactions to his experience, and a sketch of late-medieval France as he knew it. This is a world of people living by their wits and not hampered by scruples: entertainers, prostitutes, counterfeiters, tavern keepers and tavern haunters, jailers and moat cleaners, peddlers, beggars, dissolute monks—Villon's poetry opens the door upon a teeming world, lacking in grace or nobility but intensely alive. Most vital of all are the poet's own self and experience, given expression that transcends his own time and milieu so as to be at once personal and universal.

Villon's works have been preserved in a number of manuscripts and fragments, and in a printed edition of 1489, These early sources vary in completeness, from the *Lais*, the *Testament*, and numerous independent pieces, down to two or three ballades; they differ also in degree of reliability. The manuscript copies, the incunabulum, and also the many 16th-century printings of his works attest to a moderate readership over the course of about a century. Villon then, like most medieval writers, underwent an eclipse, with one edition at the end of the 1600s and three in the 1700s. The years from 1832 onward have seen an increasing flow of editions, translations, historical notes, and interpretive essays; and the stream shows no sign of drying up. Villon continues to be subject to much critical scrutiny, some of it closer to creative writing than to explication of the texts, but much of it responsible and serious. We can now read Villon's often difficult and allusive verses with a fair approximation to his own meaning.

See also **Charles d'Orléans**

Further Reading

Villon, François. *Complete Poems*, ed. and trans. Barbara N. Sargent-Baur. Toronto: Toronto University Press, 1994.

——. *Le lais Villon et les poèmes variés*, ed. Jean Rychner and Albert Henry. 2 vols. Geneva: Droz, 1977.

——. *Le Testament Villon*, ed. Jean Rychner and Albert Henry. 2 vols. Geneva: Droz, 1974–85.

——. *François Villon: Œuvres*, trans. André Lanly. 2 vols. Paris: Champion, 1969.

——. *François Villon: ballades en jargon*, trans. André Lanly. Paris: Champion, 1979.

——. *The Poems of François Villon*, trans. Galway Kinnell. New York: New American Library, 1965.

Burger, André. *Lexique complet de la langue de Villon*. 2nd ed. Geneva: Droz, 1974.

Champion, Pierre. *François Villon: sa vie et son temps*. 2nd ed. 2 vols. Paris: Champion, 1934.

Fox, John Howard. *The Poetry of Villon*. London: Nelson, 1962.

LeGentil, Pierre. *Villon*. Paris: Hatier, 1967.

Peckham, Robert D. *François Villon: A Bibliography*. New York: Garland, 1990.

Sargent-Baur, Barbara N. *Brothers of Dragons: Job dolens and François Villon*. New York: Garland, 1990.

Siciliano, Italo. *François Villon et les thèmes poétiques du moyen âge*. Paris: Nizet, 1934.

Sturm, Rudolf. *François Villon, bibliographie et matériaux littéraires (1489–1988)*. Munich: Saur, 1990.

Vitz, Evelyn Birge. *The Crossroad of Intentions: A Study of Symbolic Expressions in the Poetry of François Villon*. The Hague: Mouton, 1974.

Ziwès, Armand, and Anne de Bercy. *Le jargon de maître François Villon interprété*. 2nd ed. 2 vols. Paris: Puget, 1960.

BARBARA N. SARGENT-BAUR

VINCENT DE BEAUVAIS
(ca. 1190–ca. 1264)

The author of a most spectacular encyclopedia of medieval culture and thought, Vincent de Beauvais joined the Dominican house at Paris ca. 1220, shortly after its founding, and probably moved to the new Dominican house in his native region of Beauvais toward the end of the same decade. Vincent served as lecturer to the monks of the nearby Cistercian abbey of Royaumont, founded by King Louis IX in 1228 and through this association, mediated by Abbot Ralph, won the favor of the king and ultimately the support of the royal purse for his scholarly projects.

The first half of the 13th century was a time of intellectual "consolidation," when several scholars, Vincent among them, felt the need to integrate the results of the intellectual explosion of the 12th century with the traditional learning of western civilization. Vincent entitled his work *Speculum maius*, a mirror to the world and its truths, which he compares implicitly with, earlier attempts, perhaps the *Imago mundi* of the 12th century, sometimes attributed to Honorius of Autun. The *Speculum* originally comprised two parts: the *Naturale* and the *Historiale*. The *Naturale* beings with a treatise on theology (the triune God, archetype and creator of the universe; angels; demons; account of Creation and the exitus of all reality from God), proceeds to a consideration of the Fall, Redemption, and the sacraments of the church, and concludes with a summation of natural philosophy, including a description of the physical universe and the nature of human being. The *Historiale* gives an account of history from the Creation story of Genesis to 1244 in his earliest edition, and extended to 1254 in his later version. Its popularity is attested by several translations into the vernacular, including French, Catalan, and Dutch verse. After revising and reorganizing his work, Vincent produced a third volume, the *Doctrinale*, that contained a treatise on knowledge and the arts, including all the fields of science, from grammar and mechanics to politics, law, and medicine: in short, all that is useful to know to live a fruitful and productive life, both public and private. Although Vincent had intended to publish a fourth part, the *Morale*, he never accomplished his goal. The tract entitled *Morale* that began to circulate in the 14th century with the first three parts is in fact an anonymous compilation drawn from the *Summa theologica* of Thomas Aquinas.

In the last years of his life, Vincent composed treaties for the royal court. On the death of the dauphin Louis in January 1260, he wrote his *Epistola consolatoria super morte filii*. Within the next year or so, he published at the request of Queen Marguerite a tract on the education of princes, *De eruditione filiorum nobilium*, for the tutors of Prince Philip. Finishing this work, Vincent returned to his treatise concerning royal government requested by Louis IX. Sometime before Pentecost 1263, he presented the first part, *De morali principis institutione*, to his patron. But as with his *Speculum*, Vincent never finished this work: the second part was only supplied at a later date by a fellow Dominican, William Peraldus.

See also **Aquinas, Thomas; Louis IX**

Further Reading

Vincent de Beauvais. *De eruditione filiorum nobilium*, ed. Arpad Steiner. Cambridge: Mediaeval Academy of America, 1938.

Gabriel, Astrik. *The Educational Ideas of Vincent of Beauvais.* 2nd ed. Notre Dame: University of Notre Dame Press, 1962.

Lusignan, Serge, A. Nadeau, and M. Paulmier-Foucart, eds. *Vincent de Beauvais: Actes du Colloque de Montréal, 1988.* Montreal, 1990.

McCarthy, Joseph M. *Humanistic Emphases in the Educational Thought of Vincent of Beauvais.* Leiden: Brill, 1976.

Paulmier-Foucart, M., and Serge Lusignan. "Vincent de Beauvais et l'histoire du *Speculum majus.*" *Journal des Savants* 1990, pp. 97–124.

MARK ZIER

WACE (ca. 1100–after 1174)

Born on the island of jersey, Wace received his training first at Caen, then at Paris or, less likely, at Chartres; the influence of Hugh of Saint-Victor on his work is evident. Early in the 1130s, *maistre* Wace returned to Caen, where he occupied the position of *clerc lisant* (this term, used by Wace himself, most likely meant "reader of the lessons in the church service"); between 1165 and 1169, King Henry II of England rewarded him for his literary work with the prebend of a canon at Bayeux. He must have sojourned in England, since he knew the English language and gives precise geographical details of that country, especially of the Dorset area. Charters at Bayeux that bear his signature are not helpful in more precisely dating his life, which is known exclusively from personal remarks in his *Roman de Rou*.

Wace began his literary career with a series of hagiographical poems, of which three, signed by him, are preserved. From his stay in England, the center of St. Margaret's cult, he probably brought back a *Vie de sainte Marguerite* (742 lines), the first and stylistically by far the best of thirteen verse adaptations of this legend into French. His *Conception Nostre Dame* (1,810 lines) was designated as propaganda in favor of the establishment of the feast of the Immaculate Conception, as furthered by Abbot Anselm of Bury-Saint-Edmunds (r. 1121–46) against formidable opposition, especially from St. Bernard of Clairvaux. As a Norman, Wace would have had great interest in the life of the Virgin, for the Normans were among the first in France to establish the feast of the Immaculate Conception, which was often called the *fete aux Normands*. In the *Conception Nostre Dame*, Wace introduces the technique of grouping different episodes in one poem, in this case five that lead from the establishment of the feast to the Assumption of the Virgin. The same technique is found in his *Vie de saint Nicolas* (1,563 lines), written probably for a citizen of

Caen, Robert, son of Tiout; containing twenty-three independent episodes, without any advancement in time, it testifies to the popularity of the saint in Normandy in the first half of the 12th century. The three poems, all in rhymed octosyllabic lines, can be dated ca. 1135–50.

Wace's reputation as an adapter of Latin works on popular topics might have brought him the commission by Eleanor of Aquitaine, newly wed to Henry II, to "translate" Geoffrey of Monmouth's *Historic reg'um Britanniae* (ca. 1136). Wace could not immediately locate a copy of this text and consequently based most of his adaptation on the *Britannici sermonis liber vetustissimus* (possibly by the archdeacon Walter of Oxford, a close friend of Geoffrey of Monmouth who is mentioned by Geffrei Gaimar), written in the early 1130s with the intent of ingratiating the Celtic part of the population with the new Norman rulers by stressing the Britons' claim to Britain, tracing its history back to the Trojans, in particular to Aeneas, with the help of early Welsh chronicles and Nennius. According to these sources, Brutus (folk etymology of *Brytt* 'Briton'), Aeneas's great-grandson, led the Trojans out of Greek captivity to Britain; the *Liber vetustissimus* then depicted the legendary history of Brutus's descendants on this island through the 8th century, when the Celts had to abandon all hope of reconquering the country from the Anglo-Saxons. It was this text that Geoffrey reedited and brought to renown thanks to the interest of the Norman dynasty in the predecessors of the Anglo-Saxons, renown that also had its repercussions on Wace's *Roman de Brut*, or *Geste des Bretons* (1155), since scribes of later manuscripts constantly altered the text by increasingly modeling it on Geoffrey's work. In the critical edition, the *Roman de Brut* is narrated in 14,866 octosyllabic verses; the manuscript Durham Cathedral C. iv. 1 (Anglo-Norman; 13th c.) inserts 670 decasyllabic verses containing the prophecies of

Merlin related by a certain Elias; Lincoln Cathedral 104 (Anglo-Norman; 13th c.) adds 640 Alexandrines of the same prophecies by a certain William; and B.L. Add. 45103 (Anglo-Norman; 13th c.) contains yet another version of the prophecies, also in Alexandrines, and anonymous. B.N. fr. 1450 (Picard; 13th c.) goes even further and inserts between lines 9,798 and 9,799 Chrétien de Troyes's romances *Erec*, *Perceval*, *Cligés*, *Yvain*, and *Lancelot*, in that order.

Wace is remarkably critical of his source, frequently stressing that he is not certain of a fact; conversely, he romanticizes the dry events of history in order to make them palatable to an audience of noble laypersons. In particular, his work contains several episodes that presage the spirit of courtly love, such as King Aganippus's love "from afar" for Cordeïlle, King Leïr's youngest daughter, or Uther Pendragon's love from reputation only for Ygerne; but he also stresses the catastrophic consequences of passion, illustrated, for example, by the episodes of Locrin's and Mordred's adulterous relationships. Though he eliminates the most fantastic elements in his source, such as Merlin's prophecies, he adds many picturesque details, among them a mention of the institution of the Round Table, a detail that to date has not been satisfactorily explained. Wace's work was enormously popular (twenty-six manuscripts have preserved it in complete or fragmented, form), and ca. 1200 the priest Layamon of Raston in Worcestershire adapted it into Middle English, swelling it to nearly 30,000 lines; it is Layamon who reports that Wace had dedicated his work to Eleanor, which is possible though not mentioned in the text.

While in the *Roman de Brut* Wace was highly successful in converting pseudohistory into narrative fiction, he was less so in the *Roman de Rou* (i.e., Rollo), or *Geste des Normands* (11,440 octosyllabic lines; plus a prologue of 315 lines and the first 4,425 lines of the work, in Alexandrines; in addition, there exists the first draft of a prologue in 750 octosyllabic lines). The work was commissioned by Henry II, who wanted a poem similar to the *Brut* with respect to the history of Normandy. Wace especially had recourse to Dudo de Saint-Quentin's unreliable *De moribus et actis primorum Normanniae ducum*, from the first years of the 11th century, Guillaume de Jumièges's *Gesta Normannorum ducum* of 1071, Guillaume de Poitiers's *Gesta Guillelmi* (ca. 1078), and William of Malmesbury's *Gesta regum Anglorum* of the first half of the 12th. Wace began the project in 1160. He was uncomfortable with real history and its sources, excelling only when he narrated legendary material, such as stories about Duke Richard I, the Richard of Normandy in the *Chanson de Roland*, and events during the reigns of kings William II Rufus and Henry I (r. 1100–35), where he was a historian in his own right, drawing from personal information. Occasionally,

he also gives firsthand information concerning the reign of the Conqueror, such as details about William's fleet in 1066, having as a small child heard his father comment on it. The commission did not excite Wace: for a while, he even attempted another meter, the Alexandrine (one of the first authors, if not the first, to do so); the work thus advanced so slowly that Henry II grew impatient and commissioned the much younger Benoît de Sainte-Maure, whose *Roman de Troie* (ca. 1165) had superseded the *Brut* as a literary success, with the same task. Wace, bitterly disappointed, interrupted his work after having narrated the Battle of Tinchebrai, in which Henry I defeated his older brother Robert Curthose and annexed Normandy (1106). Since he mentions Henry II's siege of Rouen in 1174, it is assumed that he died soon after that date.

Wace is undoubtedly the most brilliant author of the first period of Norman literature; the modern reader is also struck by his conscientiousness, honesty, and—for the period—highly critical, even scholarly approach to literature.

See also **Benoît de Sainte-Maure; Bernard of Clairvaux; Chrétien de Troyes**

Further Reading

Wace. *Le roman de Brut de Wace*, ed. Ivor Arnold. 2 vols. Paris: SATF, 1938–40.
——. *The* Conception Nostre Dame *of Wace*, ed. William Ray Ashford. Chicago: University of Chicago Libraries, 1933.
——. *Le roman de Rou de Wace*, ed. Anthony J. Holden. 3 vols. Paris: Picard, 1970–73.
——, ed. *Wace: La vie de sainte Marguerite*, ed. Hans-Erich Keller. Tubingen: Niemeyer, 1990.
——.. *La vie de saint Nicolas par Wace*, *poème religieux du Xlle siècle*, ed. Einar Ronsjö. Lund: Gleerup, 1942.
Keller, Hans-Erich. *Étude descriptive sur le vocabulaire de Wace*. Berlin: Akademie, 1953.
——. "The Intellectual Journey of Wace." *Fifteenth Century Studies* 17 (1990): 185–207.
Pelan, Margaret. *L'influence du "Brut" de Wace sur les romans français de son temps*. Paris: Droz, 1931.

HANS-ERICH KELLER

WALAFRID STRABO (ca. 808–849)

A Carolingian scholar and poet, Walafrid (Strabo means "the squinter") was born in Swabia and educated at Reichenau and later at Fulda under Rabanus Maurus. He served from 829 to 838 as tutor to Louis the Pious's youngest son, Charles the Bald. After 838, he was the abbot of Reichenau; for political reasons, he was expelled by Louis the German in 840 but reinstated in 842. Walafrid died on August 18, 849, crossing the Loire to visit his former student, Charles the Bald.

To modern readers, Walafrid's most famous works are his poems, including the *Visio Wettini*, a hexameter treatment of visions of Hell, Purgatory, and Paradise written at the age of eighteen and dedicated to his former teacher, Wettin of Reichenau; and *De cultura hortorum* (or *hortulus*), a medicinal description and allegorical interpretation of twenty-three herbs and flowers. Other poems include hagiography and praises of important people (including Louis the Pious and the empress Judith, mother of Charles the Bald). In the Middle Ages, he was also famous for his exegesis, much of it based on the longer works of Rabanus Maurus, including commentaries on the Pentateuch, the Psalms, and the canonical epistles. This exegesis remains in need of further critical study. The *Glossa ordinaria*, published as a work of Walafrid in Migne's *Patrologia Latina*, Vols. 113–14, is now known to have been written in the 12th century and erroneously ascribed to Walafrid in the 15th.

See also **Louis the Pious; Rabanus Maurus**

Further Reading

Walafrid Strabo. *Poems. MGH Poetae* 2.259–473.
Traill, David A., ed. and trans. *Walahfrid Strabo's Visio Wettini: Text, Translation and Commentary.* Bern: Lang, 1974.
Duckett, Eleanor Shipley. *Carolingian Portraits: A Study in the Ninth Century.* Ann Arbor: University of Michigan Press, 1962, pp.121–60.
Godman, Peter. *Poets and Emperors: Frankish Politics and Carolingian Poetry.* Oxford: Clarendon, 1987.
Onnerfors, Alf, Johannes Rathofer, and Fritz Wagner, eds. "Über Walahfrid Strabos Psalter-Kommentar." In *Literatur und Sprache im europaischen Mittelalter: Festschrift für Karl Langosch zum 70. Geburtstag.* Darmstadt: Wissenschaftliche Buchgesellschaft, 1973, pp. 75–121.

E. ANN MATTER

WALLĀDAH BINT AL-MUSTAFKI

Wallādah, who lived in Córdoba in the eleventh century, was the daughter of Caliph Muḥammad al-Mustakfi. Her house was a meeting place for writers. She had a tempestuous relationship with the famous poet Ibn Zaydūn, who dedicated many of his poems to her. Wallādah accused him of sleeping both with her slave and his own secretary, a man by the name of 'Ali. In turn, she had affairs with Muhya, a woman poet, and with the vizir. Her relationship with Ibn Zaydūn ended badly. Most of her nine extant poems are about him. Some are delicate love poems, such as: "Expect my visit at dusk, for I find that night is the best time to hide secrets. What I feel for you is such that by its side the sun would not shine, the moon would not rise and the stars would not begin their nocturnal journey." Some are obscene satirical poems: "You are called the hexagonous, a name that will endure beyond your life: faggot, buggerer, philanderer, fucker, cuckold, thief."

Although Wallādah's lifestyle was unconventional, her poetry was not. In addition to panegyrical poems, a genre she seems not to have cultivated, satirical and love poems were very popular among the poets of al-Andalus. The works of women poets, for the most part, took the form of a dialogue with their male counterparts. In accordance with this fashion, Wallādah's love and satirical poems consist of dialogues with Ibn Zaydūn. However, if she followed established genres, she did so with originality and flair. Wallādah held her own against the best male poets of her time. Indeed, she was considered brilliant.

It is said that Wallādah had the following two verses embroidered on her tunic: "By God, I was made for glory and I proudly follow my own path" and "I offer my cheek to whomever loves me and give a kiss to whomever desires me." She seems to have followed her mottos, because she became a legendary poet and lover who has excited the imagination of readers for centuries.

See also **Ibn Zaydūn**

Further Reading

Garulo, T. *Diwan de las poetisas de al-Andalus.* Madrid, 1986.
Sobh, M. *Poetisas arábigo-andaluzas.* Granada, n.d.

CRISTINA GONZÁLEZ

WALTER OF CHÂTILLON (fl. 1160–1190)

One of most celebrated poets of the twelfth century, whose *Alexandreis* reveals the author's interest in the East and in world geography.

Despite Walter of Châtillon's reputation as an extraordinary poet in Latin, we know little about his life. He was born near Lille, then in the county of Flanders. After studying at schools in France (probably at Paris, possibly at Reims or Orléans), he taught at a number of schools in northern France, including one at Châtillon. After studying at Bologna, he joined the court of William, archbishop of Reims, who eventually made Walter a canon, probably of Amiens. In addition to numerous lyrics in Latin on a wide variety of subjects (religious, erotic, and satirical) and a treatise against the Jews, Walter wrote his best-known work, the *Alexandreis* (between 1171 and 1181), which he dedicated to Archbishop William. *The Alexandreis,* a ten-book epic in dactylic hexameters, takes its form, diction, and style from the classical epic tradition. Its primary model is Lucan's *Bellum civile,* its primary historical source, Quintus Curtius Rufus's *Historia Alexandri Magni.*

Although the *Alexandreis,* which covers the life of Alexander the Great, is more restrained than some versions of the story in the Alexander romance tradition, it nevertheless reveals Walter's considerable interest in the East. By contrast to the Alexander romance, the *Alexandreis* follows Curtius's more "realistic" depiction of the East. Alexander does not confront any of the monstrous races or exotic peoples described in the romance. For example, rather than encountering the Brahmans, the legendary inhabitants of India famed for their ascetic life and philosophy, Walter's Alexander meets the Scythians. His Scythians, however, presented as idealized primitives living in accordance with Nature's dictates, have much in common with the Brahmans of the romance.

Walter's Alexander seems to be a paradigm for crusaders—in particular for crusading kings such as Philip Augustus (r. 1180–1223). Critics have argued that he serves, on the one hand, as a positive model of prowess to be imitated and as a negative warning against pursuing the wrong things in the Holy Land: wealth and fame rather than the salvation of his soul.

A catalogue of the lands of Asia in Book 1 and a description of a map carved on the inside of the dome of the tomb of the Persian emperor Darius in Book 7 define the natural limitations of the world. This map is a typical medieval *mappamundi* of the tripartite type: the *orbis terrarum* has a circular form and is oriented to the East, with Asia filling the top half of the circle, Europe and Africa the two quarters on the bottom. The world is ringed by a surrounding Ocean. Like contemporary *mappamundi*, Walter's includes places and peoples of significance from all periods in biblical, ancient, and medieval history. Walter presents as unnatural Alexander's ambition to cross the Ocean, to see the regions of the extreme East, and to conquer the peoples of the Antipodes. When Alexander begins to fulfill this ambition by invading the Ocean, the goddess Nature intervenes and arranges his death. Although Walter's *Alexandreis* was widely known during the Middle Ages—it survives in some 200 manuscripts and was familiar to such prominent vernacular poets as Dante and Chaucer (whose Wife of Bath alludes casually to Darius's tomb in her "Prologue" [ll. 497–499])—the poem has been largely (and undeservedly) forgotten.

See also **Chaucer, Geoffrey; Dante Alighieri; Godfrey of Viterbo; Philip II Augustus**

Further Reading

Kratz, Dennis. *Mocking Epic: Waltharius, Alexandreis, and the Problem of Christian Heroism.* Madrid: José Porrúa Turanzas, 1980.

Lafferty, Maura K. "Mapping Human Limitations: The Tomb Ecphrases in Walter of Châtillon's *Alexandreis*." *Journal of Medieval Latin* 4 (1994): 64–81.

Ratkowitsch, Christine. *Descriptio Picturae: Die literarische Funktion der Beschreibung von Kunstwerken in der lateinischen Grossdichtung des 12. Jahrhunderts.* Vienna: Verlag der Österreichischen Akademie der Wissenschaften, 1991.

Walter of Chatillon. *Alexandreis*. Ed. Marvin L. Colker. Padova, Italy: Antenore, 1978.

——. *Alexandreis*. Trans. R. Telfryn Pritchard. Toronto: Pontifical Institute of Medieval Studies, 1986.

——. *Alexandreis*. Trans. David Townsend. Philadelphia: U of Pennsylvania P, 1997.

MAURA K. LAFFERTY

WALTHER VON DER VOGELWEIDE (ca. 1170–ca. 1230)

In service largely at the Hohenstaufen courts, Walther is considered the greatest of the German courtly singers of the High Middle Ages. Some would argue for his poetic primacy among European singers in any language. Internal evidence in his songs suggests he was active between the early 1190s and the late 1220s. His *Minnesang* (love singing), in which he sang the painful joy of unrequited love for a woman of high station *(hôhe minne)*, shows influences of fashionable German courtly singers such as Heinrich von Morungen and Reinmar der Alte. Walther also sang of the so-called *nidere minne* (down-to-earth love), an amorous relationship both physical and mutual that has close parallels in Latin secular love songs. His political, personal, didactic, and religious songs (*Sangspruch*) reflect the vicissitudes of his career as well as the turbulent political events of the *sacrum imperium*, known later as the Holy Roman Empire.

Extant today are over six hundred stanzas in some three dozen manuscripts. Walther's music has been entirely lost save for five melodies, two of them fragmentary and another two from manuscripts written three centuries later. Accordingly, readers must use their imaginations to re-create the conditions of performance and the effect of the melodies and their accompaniments.

Walther's name appears only once in nonliterary documents of his lifetime, a 1203 entry in the travel accounts of Bishop of Passau directing that five shillings be given the singer *(cantor)* for a fur coat. But other thirteenth-century singers and romanciers provide ample encomia, or formal praise, for this towering figure of German lyric singing. Gottfried of Straßburg in his *Tristan* (ll. 4751–4820) calls him the nightingale carrying the banner of *Minnesang*, praising Walther's high (tenor?) voice and his dexterity in the polyphonic style of the day (organum). His artistry is also celebrated by, among others, Reinmar von Zweter, Bruder Werner, and Rudolf von Ems. In the waning Middle Ages he is enthroned by the Meistersinger as one of the Twelve Old Masters. Only one contemporary provides negative criticism: Thomasin von Zerklaere castigates him as a slanderer of Pope Innocent III and a deceiver of men (*Der welsche Gast*, 11. 11091–11268).

The songs classified as *Minnesang*—the sequence can only be surmised—are normally categorized in the following major groups: early songs of elevated love *(hôhe minne)* linked to Reinmar at the Viennese court; later *Minnesang*; songs of down-to-earth love *(nidere minne)*; and late songs. Augmenting the difficulties of dating these songs is the strong possibility of revision in the course of the singer's career or changes developing from the orality of the pieces.

Walther's assumed apprenticeship at the Viennese court, in the 1190s under the tutelage of Reinmar der Alte (Reinmar von Hagenau), produced a number of early songs. Some of these have been linked to a "Reinmar feud" *(Reinmar-Fehde)*, a quasi debate revealing the outlines of a serious polemic with his former mentor on the nature of *minne*. Reinmar is the representative of the traditional (since the 1160s) ideas inherent in the troubadour lyric: his love, unrequited and unconsummated, is for an unapproachable lady of a higher station. Walther, on the other hand, hints at a more mutual love; his lady is valued not for her cold, Turandot-like majesty but for a more immediate and shared joy. The Reinmar debate began in the 1190s and seemed to continue until after Walther's departure from Vienna in 1198. Emblematic of this exchange is Walther's *Ein man verbiutet âne pfliht* (no. L. 111,22ff), a response to Reinmar's *Ich wirbe umb allez daz ein man* (*Minnesangs Frühling*, no. 159,1ff), in which, using the same melody and stanzaic form, he weaves Reinmar's key motifs into his song to produce an ironically critical response to his mentor.

It is difficult to separate what seem to be the more mature songs of the Reinmar debate from Walther's non-Reinmar–related songs of the period circa 1205–1215, a time in which he achieved mastery of language. Here the singer composed his most effective and inventive songs, sharply breaking with the traditional German *Minnesang* (as performed by Heinrich von Morungen, Reinmar, and others), with its prickling tensions and the incessant conjectures about an impossible love. Walther's style now becomes pointed, ironic, playful, and original. Though still dancing around the theme of *hôhe minne*, many of his songs now suggest an equal relationship with a young woman whose station is not of importance and whose designation increasingly becomes the generically female *wîp* (woman) rather than the socially hierarchical *frouwe* (lady). In *Si wunderwol gemachet wîp*, (L. 53,25ff), he sings of the physical attributes of a woman not of the nobility, completing his catalog of adulation with an unprecedented image of the woman, unclothed, stepping cleanly from her bath.

Among the songs of this period are some that appear outside the scope of the *Minne* theme. The so-called *Preislied* (panegyric) *Ir sult sprechen willekomen* (L. 56, 14ff) is possibly a response to the troubadour Peire Vidal (fl. ca. 1187–1205), whose unkind characterizations of German deportment probably rankled at German-speaking courts. Walther's praise of German

(tiutschiu) woman and, by extension, German culture is unique in medieval song.

During these years Walther also composed songs with bucolic settings about the real and physical love of a young woman who seems tangential to courtly circles (songs of *nidere Minne*, sometimes called *Mädchenlieder*). In "Herzeliebez frouwelîn" (L. 49, 25ff) he is charmed by a woman or girl whose glass ring he values more than the gold ring of a queen. "Nement, frowe, disen cranz" (L. 74, 20ff) projects a dream vision of his beloved, a pretty girl *(wol getânen maget)* portrayed in the scenery of the *Carmina Burana*, that is, under a blossoming tree on a meadow graced by flowers and the singing of the birds.

"Under der linden" (Beneath the Linden Tree, no. L. 39,11ff) is Walther's most celebrated love song. In the tradition of the Latin *pastourelle*, it contains the same predictable imagery as in "Nement, frowe, disen cranz." But Walther brings to this tradition a deceptively simple language expressing the essence of the lovers' joy, deftly combined with a playful and delicate web of motifs to form a song with complex levels of meaning.

Walther's position at court required him also to excel at the art of *Sangspruch*. The term pertains to songs in which love is not the primary matter: political pieces, songs of personal invective, requests for favors from a patron, crusade songs, and songs with a didactic or religious content. Each piece is normally restricted to one stanza, though in some cases several stanzas composed in the same tune (*Ton*, plural *Töne*) can be bound together to form a performance piece. Walther's *Sangspruch* provides a glimpse of the events of his life as well as the fortunes of the empire under the Hohenstaufen rulers and its ongoing struggle with the papacy. These songs were composed largely for patrons at the electoral courts—kings, dukes, counts, and bishops—who expected from the singer both workmanlike compositions and persuasive performances. Occasional songs in the best sense, they were composed about specific events or personalities. In editions of Walther they are usually grouped into cycles of stanzas of identical metrical and musical form *(Ton)*. Some, though not all, of the stanzas of a *Ton* have the same general thematic content. Modern scholarship has given them associative names that apply to some though not all of the stanzas in the *Ton*. In the "Konig-Friedrichston" (King Friedrich Tune, no. 26,3ff), for example, King Friedrich (later the emperor Friedrich II) plays a major role only in a few of the stanzas. Each of these *Töne* contains between three and eighteen stanzas.

Walther's best-known *Ton*, the "Reichston" (Imperial Tune, L. 8,4ff), may well be the earliest. A triad of long stanzas (twenty-four lines each), it begins pensively with the trademark image of Walther sitting on a stone in the pose of the philosopher (*Ich saz ûf eime steine*, I sat upon a stone). In the second song (L. 8,28), Walther moves out of the meditative mode and into the political, calling for the crowning of the true emperor, the Hohenstaufen candidate Philipp of Swabia rather than the papally sanctioned Otto of Brunswick, dynastic leader of the Welf party. With pointed imagery he declares the clergy of Rome corrupt and the times out of joint. In the third song (L. 9,16), assuming the persona of a pious hermit, he indicts the pope as being too young (Innocent III was only thirty-nine), an anomaly symptomatic of the ills besetting the curia at Rome and its imperial policy.

In 1198 Walther left Vienna and attached himself to various Hohenstaufen courts in the middle German regions, continuing both positive and negative associations with Philipp of Swabia (in the five stanzas of the first "Philippston," Philipp Tune, L. 18,29ff). Despite Walther's ardent propaganda for the imperial candidate, he complains of Philipp's parsimony. This theme of a patron's miserly qualities would become a favorite of the later generation of *Sangspruch* singers in the thirteenth century.

The "Wiener Hofton" (Viennese Court Tune, L. 20,16ff), largely composed after Walther's departure from Vienna in 1198, reveals an ambivalence about the Viennese court, combining a longing to return to this desirable venue with an uneasiness about his relations with the reigning Duke Leopold VI. Walther continues to sing in the causes of Philipp until the would-be emperor's death in 1208, but gradually in the course of the first decade of the thirteenth century, he forms new courtly associations, most prominently with Hermann, Landgrave of Thuringia, and his son-in-law, Dietrich, Margrave of Meißen. These princes are forced to change allegiance after Philipp's death, leaving the imperial candidacy open to his archrival, Otto of Brunswick. Walther reflects the new loyalties in the "Ottenton" (Otto Tune, L. 11,6ff), in which he welcomes the new kaiser to the Reichstag (imperial diet) in Frankfurt, declaring that his patron, the Margrave of Meißen, is as loyal to the emperor as an angel is to God. Less than a year later the margrave and other princes (like the fallen angels) are in open rebellion, preparing the way for a new-Hohenstaufen pretender, the young Friedrich II, grandson of Barbarossa.

As was the lot of singers employed by the courts, Walther continued the propaganda commissioned by his various patrons. In one of his sharpest and most amusing pieces, "Unmutston" (Disgruntled Tune, L. 34,4), Walther rants against that most ardent enemy of the Hohenstaufen interests, Pope Innocent III, for his collecting of German monies to finance the Albigensian Crusade in 1213, accusing the Roman clergy of feasting on capons and wine while the German laity grows lean from fasting.

There is evidence that Walther was able to gain a modicum of independence as overseer of a fief. In 1220 he composed a song of request to King Friedrich for his own house, playing on his lord's sympathy for a homeless singer whose wearisome life was a procession of one-night stands. ("König-Friedrichston," L. 28,1). Apparently Walther was successful, for in the same *Ton* (L. 28,31) he proclaims triumphantly his thanks to the king, grateful that he need no longer go begging at the courts of base lords for shelter.

Since these songs of praise and political propaganda were produced on demand to suit the shifting political alliances of a turbulent period of imperial history, one might properly ask to what extent Walther's songs reflect his own values. Many are outright propaganda, although of a kind wrought with the highest poetic skills and a deft sense of language. And yet many pieces reveal a personality sharply troubled by the woeful state of the mutable world and impelled by a desire to return to the established, predictable, and more ethical patterns of time past. The "Wiener Hofton" bewails the uncouth behavior of courtly youth (L. 24,3), marking its disparity with the days when one did not spare the rod with ill-mannered children. More personal and sadder echoes of this nostalgia permeate the "Elegie" (Elegy, L. 124,1 ff), generally held to have been composed in Walther's old age. It too complains of the uncourtly behavior of young people, but combines it with what must have been an old man's deeply personal sense of an irretrievable past. And yet, in the last stanza, it is clear that it is a song of outright propaganda, urging knights to undertake a crusade, possibly that of Frederick II in 1227. Walther was still the paid entertainer whose patron called the tune.

The manuscripts also contain a scattering of personal and religious songs of one or more stanzas that cannot properly be called *Sangspruch*. One is the "Palästina-Lied" (Palestine Song, L. 14,38ff), also a recruiting song for a crusade, containing the only complete and proven melody among Walther's songs. Another is the *Leich* (L. 3,1ff). This most virtuosic of all medieval lyric forms—derived from the liturgical sequence—is a large-format song built on a series of versicles and responses that undergo repetition and variation. It may have been specifically composed for groups of singers and instrumentalists, who would have sung and played it antiphonally in unison or possibly with rudimentary polyphony (*organum*). With its many repetitions and variations, it often approached the complexity of a fugue. This is Walther's longest single performance piece, a prayer to the Mother of God (hence called a *Marienleich*), marked by lush praise of the Virgin commingled with references to the Trinity, biblical prefigurations, and elements of Christian theology. Yet even in this, Walther's most pious work, the singer cannot refrain from references to the Roman curia and its "unchristian things" *(unchristliche dinge)*.

The legacy of Walther's *Sangspruch* was a set of models and patterns for a century of professional singers who followed. His love songs, on the other hand, marked in a sense the end of *Minnesang*. The art had soared in the songs of Morungen and Reinmar. Walther moved through the exhausted concept of *hôhe minne* and brought the love song back to earth. But after him no other Minnesinger approached his or his predecessors' mastery of the art.

See also **Frederick II; Heinrich von Morungen; Reinmar der Alte**

Further Reading

Bäuml, Franz, ed. *From Symbol to Mimesis: The Generation of Walther von der Vogelweide.* Göppingen: Kümmerle, 1984.

Bein, Thomas. *Walther von der Vogelweide.* Stuttgart: Reclam, 1997.

Brunner, Horst, et al. *Walther von der Vogelweide: Die gesamte Überlieferung der Texte und Melodien—Abbildungen, Materialien, Melodiestranskription.* Göppingen: Kümmerle, 1977.

——, et al. *Walther von der Vogelweide: Epoche—Werk—Wirkung.* Munich: Beck, 1996.

Cormeau, Christoph, ed. *Walther von der Vogelweide: Leich, Lieder, Sangsprüche.* Berlin: de Gruyter, 1996.

Goldin, Friedrich. "Walther versus Reinmar," in *The Regeneration of Poetic Language in Medieval German Literature: Vernacular Poetics in the Middle Ages,* ed. Lois Ebin. Kalamazoo: Western Michigan University, 1984, pp. 57–92.

Hahn, Gerhard. *Walther von der Vogelweide: Eine Einführung.* Munich: Artemis, 1986.

Halbach, Kurt Herbert. *Walther von der Vogelweide,* 4th ed. Stuttgart: Metzler, 1983.

Jones, George Fenwick. *Walther von der Vogelweide.* New York: Twayne, 1968.

McFarland, Timothy, and Silvia Ranawake, eds. *Walther von der Vogelweide: Twelve Studies.* Oxford: Oxford University Press, 1982.

Mück, Hans-Dieter. *Walther von der Vogelweide: Beiträge zu Leben und Werk.* Stuttgart: Stöffler and Schütz, 1989.

Müller, Jan-Dirk, and Franz Josef Worstbrock, eds. *Walther von der Vogelweide: Hamburger Kolloquium 1988 zum 65. Geburtstag von Karl-Heinz Borck.* Stuttgart: Hirzel, 1989.

Nix, Matthias. *Untersuchungen zur Funktion der politischen Spruchdichtung Walthers von der Vogelweide.* Göppingen: Kümmerle, 1993.

Scheibe, Fred Karl. *Walther von der Vogelweide, Troubadour of the Middle Ages: His Life and His Reputation in the English-Speaking Countries.* New York: Vantage, 1969.

PETER FRENZEL

WENCESLAS
(November 26, 1361–August 6, 1419)

Wenceslas IV (Václav, Wenzel, king of the Romans 1378–1400, king of Bohemia until 1419) was the eldest son of Charles IV by his third wife, Anna of Schweidnitz. Wenceslas was born on November 26, 1361, in Nuremberg. He was elected king of the Romans on June 10, 1376, and assumed control of imperial affairs as Staathalter in February of the following year. After Charles's death, he inherited the Bohemian crown. Wenceslas has not enjoyed the good reputation of his father. In particular, he has been generally condemned for his sloth, vacillation, and drunkenness.

Wenceslas was faced immediately with several serious problems. First was the Swabian City League, established July 4, 1376. The growth of the league, aimed directly against the mortgage policies of his rather, led to a major war, lasting until 1389. The second problem was the Great Schism, which broke out in the fall of 1378. Wenceslas supported the pope in Rome, Urban VI. In 1380 he traveled to Paris in an attempt to convince French King Charles V to withdraw support from the Avignon pope, Clement II. When this effort failed, on the advice of Urban VI, Wenceslas allied himself with Richard II of England. The alliance and resulting marriage between the English king and Wenceslas's sister Anna marked a total break with the traditional pro-French Luxembourg policy. Within the empire, a group of southern principalities, led by Leopold III of Austria and Archbishop Pilgrim II of Salzburg, supported Clement VII.

During the first years of his reign, Wenceslas sought to resolve the problems of the cities. The *Landfriede* (peace) of Nuremberg (1383) marks the first attempt to divide the empire into districts or counties (*Kreise*), anticipating the later reforms of Albrecht II and Maximilian I. After the league's defeat at Döffingen (1388), the *Landfriede* of Eger (1389) provided a modicum of stability for the next several decades. The political autonomy of the cities was recognized, while they were banned from making further leagues.

After 1390, problems in Bohemia consumed most of Wenceslas's energy. He tended to support the towns and lower nobility; this provoked resistance from the great nobles and higher clergy. The archbishop of Prague, Jan z Jenštejna (1379–1396) in particular proved a serious opponent of the crown. The torture and murder of the vicar general of Prague, John of Pomuk (March 20, 1393) by royal officials provoked a noble Fronde in 1394. Wenceslas's cousin, Margrave Jost of Moravia, joined with the nobles and took the king prisoner (May 8, 1394) with the collusion of Duke Albrecht III of Austria. Jost was named regent, but the intervention of Wenceslas's half-brother John of Görlitz and Ruprecht II of the Palatinate led to the king's release. As Wenceslas now turned on his opponents, a civil war broke out. The deaths of Albrecht III (August 29, 1395) and John of Görlitz (March 1, 1396) brought an end to the fighting. Wenceslas's other half-brother, king Sigismund of Hungary, was able to negotiate a peace settlement among Jost, Wenceslas, and the nobles. In return, Sigismund was recognized as Wenceslas's heir and named imperial vicar.

After the battle of Nikopolis (September 28, 1396), Sigismund turned to securing his Hungarian lands. This left Wenceslas, after a ten-year absence from Germany, faced with an angry crowd of princes at the imperial diets of Nuremberg (1397) and Frankfurt (1398). The four Rhenish electors issued a series of demands. The *Landfriede* and Schism were perennial sticking points. Wenceslas's elevation of Giangalleazzo Visconti to the duchy of Milan (April 11, 1395) also provoked the electors' ire. In June 1400 the Rhenish electors demanded that Wenceslas appear before them to answer to their complaints. Their request coincided with a renewal of hostilities among Wenceslas, Jost, and the nobles. Wenceslas's Bohemian problems did not, in the eyes of the electors, excuse his refusal to appear. On August 20, 1400, the four Rhenish electors declared Wenceslas deposed and elected the count palatine, Ruprecht III, king of the Romans.

Wenceslas refused to recognize his deposition, but he was too occupied with Bohemian affairs to do much about it. The death of Ruprecht of the Palatine in 1401 presented Wenceslas with an opportunity to regain the German throne. Unfortunately he could not count on support from his family. Indeed, both Sigismund and Jost were able to secure election to the imperial throne. Jost's death—perhaps from poison—in January 1411 cleared the way for an agreement between Sigismund and Wenceslas. The latter agreed to relinquish his German crown in return for half the imperial revenues and recognition of his position in Bohemia.

The last years of Wenceslas's reign in Bohemia saw the beginnings of a religious and political crisis that would later erupt in the Hussite revolution. Since the time of Charles IV, a series of radical preachers, among them Conrad Waldhause, Jan Milíc, and Matthew of Janov, had been attacking the higher clergy. The marriage between Anne of Bohemia and Richard II of England led to the growth of a Wycliffite faction among Czech scholars at the University of Prague. Jerome of Prague, along with his student Jan Hus, appeared as leaders of the Wycliffite Czechs. The ideological struggles were connected with political struggles in the university between the Czech minority and the three German-dominated "nations."

After the Roman pope Boniface IX (1389–1404) supported the Rhenish electors in 1400, Wenceslas turned to support the Czech reformers. He agreed to recognize the Council of Pisa (1408) and at the council of Kutná Hora ordered the German masters of the university to do so as well. The Kutná Hora decrees (January 18, 1409) broke the Germans' control over the university, giving the Czech nation three votes to one for all three of the German nations. A number of German masters left, later forming the core of the University of Leipzig.

The principal architects of the Czech victory were Jerome of Prague, Jan Hus, and Jakoubeck of Stríbro. In the wake of the Kutná Hora decrees, Archbishop Zdynek of Prague (1399–1411) excommunicated a number of royal officials and placed Prague under the interdict. Wenceslas ordered the city's clergy to ignore the decree. Zydnek agreed to submit to the king, but then fled the kingdom, seeking the aid of Emperor Sigismund. The archbishop died in Bratislava in September 1411, and after his departure, the Hussite movement became more radical. A group of reformers began calling for the administration of the cup to the laity *(utraquism)*. In 1412 Hus and Jakoubek publicly declared the Roman pontiff to be antichrist, leading to their excommunication. Along with the new archbishop, Conrad of Vechta, Wenceslas made a furtive attempt to restore Catholicism. Hus turned to the nobility for support, and at a synod in February 1413, Wenceslas again changed his mind, ordering the archbishop's commission to declare that there was no heresy in Bohemia.

In 1414 Emperor Sigismund requested that Hus appear before the Council of Constance to explain his program. Under a guarantee of safe-conduct, Hus went to Constance but soon found himself imprisoned. Over 250 Czech nobles protested this action, but to no avail. On July 6, 1415, Hus was burnt as a heretic in Constance. Reprisals against other Hussites had already begun. The German burghers of Olomouc had burned two lay preachers a week earlier; Jerome of Prague was burnt in May of the following year. Hus's death led fifty-eight Hussite nobles to form a Hussite league in September 1415. A Catholic alliance followed a month later. In 1416 Wenceslas again tried to restore Catholicism in Prague, but resistance from the university faculty and nobility forced a compromise on the question of *utraquism*.

The election of Pope Martin V in 1417 increased pressure on Wenceslas to take a hard line against the heretics. In the spring of 1419, Wenceslas arrested priests in Prague who granted the cup to the laity, and appointed Czech and German Catholics as *Bürgermeister* (mayors) in the Nové Mesto. On July 30, 1419, the radical preacher Jan Zelivsky led a procession through the city to the New Town Hall demanding the release of imprisoned Utraquist priests. A scuffle broke out, and thirteen of the council members were thrown out the window. The first defenestration of Prague led to the outbreak of a great revolt. Not long after, on August 6, 1419, Wenceslas died. While most works ascribe his death to a stroke, research by a Czech neurologist suggests that the actual cause of death was acute alcohol poisoning.

Wenceslas was married twice, to Johanna of Bavaria (d. 1386) and Sophia of Bavaria (d. 1425). He had no children and all his lands fell to Emperor Sigismund.

See also **Charles IV; Charles V the Wise; Richard II**

Further Reading

Baethgen, Friedrich. *Schisma und Konzilzeit, Reichsreform und Habsburg Aufstieg.* Munich: Deutscher Taschenbuch Verlag, 1973.

Gerlich, Alois. *Habsburg-Luxembourg-Wittelsbach im Kampf um die deutschen Königsthrone: Studien zur Vorgeschichte König-tums Ruprechts von der Pfalz.* Wiesbaden: Steiner, I960,

Hlaváek, Ivan. *Das Urkunden- und Kanzleiwesen des böhmischen und römischen Königs Wenzel (IV.) 1376–1419: Ein Beitrag zur spätmittelalterlichen Diplomatik.* Stuttgart: Hiersemann, 1970.

Kaminsky, Howard. *A History of the Hussite Revolution.* Berkeley: University of California Press, 1967.

Lindner, Theodor. *Geschichte des deutschen Reiches unter König Wenzel.* Braunschweig: C. A. Schwetschkte und Sohn, 1875/1880.

Speváek, JiYí. *Václav IV. 1361–1419. K predpokladûm hustiské revoluce.* Prague: Svoboda, 1986.

WILLIAM BRADFORD SMITH

WERNER DER GÄRTNER
(fl. circa 1250–1280)

The creator of one of the most realistic narratives of the Middle Ages, Werner der Gärtner (the gardener) composed *Helmbrecht*, a short epic of 1,934 lines written in rhyming couplets, between 1250 and 1280, although some dispute this dating. Detailing a drastic picture of contemporary life, Werner depicts the decline of chivalry as well as the moral decay of the peasantry. The work has been variously described as a *Dorfgeschichte* (village tale), *Verspredigt* (rhymed sermon), and exemplum (moral tale). *Helmbrecht* survives in two manuscripts: "A" refers to the famous *Ambras Book of Heroes* (Heldenbuch) from 1504 to 1515, a costly parchment manuscript in Vienna (Nationalbibliothek) copied by Hans Ried; and "B," the "Leombach Manuscript" (1413), a paper manuscript. A third, illustrated manuscript, now lost, was still extant at the start of the nineteenth century. Manuscript "A," regarded as the original version, points to the Austrian-Bavarian region as its place of composition. Little is known of Werner, who is generally thought to have been a cleric, a wandering minstrel, or an occasional poet. He was an educated man whose work was intended for a sophisticated, noble audience.

This moral-didactic tale centers on the generation gap between father and son, between older conservative values and newer progressive aspirations. Werner begins with a description of the elaborate and highly inappropriate cap with which Helmbrecht, the farmer's son, hopes to find acceptance among the knights. The younger Helmbrecht rejects the farmer's life and instead aspires to become a knight, a calling for which he is clearly unsuited. His mother and sister provide him with expensive clothing (a contravention of the sumptuary laws); father Helmbrecht provides him with a costly steed, but only after trying to dissuade his son from leaving the farm (vv. 233–258; 279–298; 329–360). Helmbrecht easily finds acceptance with a band of robber knights and soon becomes the worst in his gang. After a year of plundering, he returns home and tells his father about the depravity and immorality of the knights. The elder Helmbrecht again tries to convince his son to remain on the farm and offers to share all that he has with him (vv. 1098–1114). Helmbrecht scoffs at this offer and returns to his band of robber knights, taking with him his sister Gotelint, who secretly has agreed to marry his friend Lemberslint. The marriage proves ill-fated, for after the wedding breakfast the judge and his hangmen appear and try them on the spot. Helmbrecht's nine companions are summarily hanged. Helmbrecht's life is spared but only after he has been maimed and blinded as punishment for his behavior toward his parents. It is in this pitiful condition that Helmbrecht returns home for the last time. Unlike before, he does not find a compassionate father ready to help him, but rather a disdainful father who turns him out (vv. 1713–1760; 1775–1813). Helmbrecht suffers a miserable existence in the forest until he is finally captured by peasants whom he had wronged and is hung.

The three conversations between father and son mark the tale's progress. The lesson is clear: parents should be strict in educating their children; children should obey their parents (the Fourth Commandment); one should be content with one's station in life (*ordo mundi*). Whether or not Werner actually witnessed the events he describes, these events accurately reflect the social unrest occasioned by the end of the Hohenstaufen reign in the late thirteenth century. Werner addresses the major social issues of his time by depicting the collapse of the feudal system, the decline of chivalry, and the new self-assertiveness of the peasants; his social criticism is directed at peasants and knights alike.

Further Reading

Banta, Frank G. "The Arch of Action in Meier Helmbrecht." *Journal of English and German Philology* 63 (1964): 696–711.

Helmbrecht, ed. and trans. Helmut Brackert, Winfried Frey, and Dieter Seitz. Frankfurt am Main: Fischer-Taschenbuch Verlag, 1972; rpt. 1990.

Jackson, W. T .H. "The Composition of Meier Helmbrecht." *Modern Language Quarterly* 18 (1957): 44–58.

Kolb, Herbert. "Der 'Meier Helmbrecht' zwischen Epos und Drama." *Zeitschrift für deutsche Philologie* 81 (1962): 1–23.

Meier Helmbrecht von Wernher der Gartenaere, ed. Friedrich Panzer. Halle: Niemeyer, 1902; 10th ed., Hans-Joachim Ziegeler. Tübingen: Niemeyer, 1993.

Seelbach, Ulrich. *Bibliographie zu Wernher der Gartenaere.* Berlin: Schmidt, 1981.

———. *Kommentar zum Helmbrecht von Wernher dem Gartenaere.* Göppingen: Kümmerle, 1987.

Sowinski, Bernbard. *Wernher der Gartenaere: Helmbrecht. Interpretation.* Munich: Oldenbourg, 1971.

Wernher der Gartenaere: Helmbrecht, trans. Linda Parshall, ed. Ulrich Seelbach. New York: Garland, 1987.

LYNN D. THELEN

WILIGELMUS (fl. c. 1099–c. 1120)

Wiligelmus (Guglielmo, Wiligelmo) is often considered the first great Italian sculptor. His reliefs on the facade of Modena cathedral are among the first important sculptural programs of northern Italy, as part of the early development of Romanesque sculpture. His identity as the creator is known from an inscription held by the figures of the prophets Enoch and Elijah: *Inter scultores quanto sis dignis onore—Claret scultura nunc Wiligelme tua* ("How much honor you deserve among sculptors is now shown by your sculpture, Wiligelmo"). Wiligelmus's oeuvre has been identified at Modena and elsewhere through stylistic comparisons with these prophets, carved from the same block as the inscription.

Wiligelmus's principal work is the sculptural assemblage on the west facade of the cathedral of Modena, presumably executed c. 1106–1110, including the inscription plaque; four reliefs from Genesis; two reliefs of *genii* with overturned torches; numerous capitals and decorative reliefs; and the program of the central portal, containing an elaborate scroll motif and twelve reliefs of prophets. The present placement of some of the reliefs is the result of changes made to the facade in the late twelfth century by the Campionese masters, who added the lateral portals and relocated the first and fourth reliefs from Genesis above them. Some scholars hold that these reliefs were created as part of liturgical furnishings for the interior of the cathedral (Quintavalle 1964–1965), but the evidence suggests that they were originally intended as part of a sculptural program decorating the facade.

The four reliefs from Genesis flanking the central portal serve as a monumental introduction to the cathedral and constitute the first large-scale frieze devoted exclusively to biblical subjects. The general themes are the creation, the fall, and the promise of salvation as revealed in the flood. The frieze concludes with the ark as the ship of salvation—an Old Testament prefiguration of salvation and the mission of the church. *Labors of the Progenitors* and *Cain and Abel Offering to God*, which flank the main portal, present a lesson to the faithful about giving the fruits of one's labors to God (and the church). Textual similarities between the inscriptions and the liturgical drama *Ordo representacionis Ade* suggest that performance and image were intended to work together to educate audiences about the roles of church and faithful in the history of salvation. Wiligelmus's Genesis frieze should thus be seen as an important early example of the development of large-scale didactic Romanesque sculptural programs.

Wiligelmus's figures are conceived as bold, massive, vital forms of great monumentality and plasticity. They convey an impressive sense of weight, as seen in the angels holding God's *mandorla* and Abel's slumping body in *Cain Killing Abel.* Figures emerge from the relief plane and fully occupy the space that is allotted to them, even bursting into the frame of the plaque (e.g., *Enoch and Elijah).* These forms have large heads, hands, and feet; broad faces with lead–inset eyes; hair articulated by long, wavy parallel strokes; and beards punctuated with drill holes. Solemn, full of *gravitas,* these bodies express the narrative action with clear, bold gestures. Wiligelmus animates his figures with palpable human expressions (especially notable is the anguish on Cain's face as he is killed by Lamech). Most of these sculptures make prominent use of inscriptions, either identifying figures or including more extensive biblical, liturgical, or secular texts; the inscription plaque held by Enoch and Elijah is an example.

Numerous sources and models for Wiligelmus's style have been suggested, including ivory, metalwork, and manuscripts as well as early Romanesque sculpture in Aquitaine and Bari. The most direct and most apparent source of inspiration is Roman sculpture. Local, provincial Roman works clearly provided models for several of the reliefs in Modena. The *genii* with overturned torches and the arrangement of the prophets Enoch and Elijah on the inscription plaque are clearly derived from Roman sarcophagi. Wiligelmus's access to these sources can be explained by *Relation translationis carports sancti Geminiani (Account of the Translation of the Body of Saint Geminianus),* which mentions the miraculous discovery of a quarry of building materials, presumably the necropolis or other parts of the Roman city of Mutina (Modena). Wiligelmus adopted not only formal arrangements of figures from these Roman sources but also the sense of solidity and *gravitas* that distinguishes his sculptures. Furthermore, the obvious source of inspiration for the arrangement of the frieze around the central portal is the Roman triumphal arch. This suggests a certain conscious use of antique forms to connote both the venerable antiquity of Modena and the triumph of the church.

In addition to the program at Modena, Wiligelmus appears to have worked at the cathedral in Cremona before the earthquake of 1117. The four large prophets from the jamb of the portal are stylistically analogous to his work at Modena. Fragments of a frieze from the cathedral of Cremona, clearly modeled after Wiligelmus's reliefs in Modena, appear to have been executed by his workshop. Wiligelmus apparendy directed a large workshop that trained numerous sculptors who continued his work at Modena and carried his style elsewhere. The two lateral portals at Modena—Porta della Pescheria (north, by the Master of the Artù) and Porta dei Principi (south, by the Master of San Geminiano)—are products of the school of Wiligelmus. These two portals follow Wiligelmus's basic scheme from the west portal, but with smaller, less massive, though more lively figures. The Porta dei Principi is the earliest example of the northern Italian form of a two-story porch-portal supported by lions or *atlantes* bearing columns. That this form developed in the context of Wiligelmus's workshop further indicates his seminal role in the development of northern Italian Romanesque sculpture.

Additional sculpture by the workshop of Wiligelmus can be found at the Benedictine abbey of Nonantola, the cathedral of Piacenza, the Pieve di Quarantoli, and the Cluniac abbey of San Benedetto Polirole. The most noteworthy pupil of Wiligelmus is Master Nicholaus.

Further Reading

Crichton, George Henderson. *Romanesque Sculpture in Italy*. London: Routledge and Kegan Paul, 1954.

Francovich, Geza de. "Wiligelmo da Modena e gli inizii della scultura romanica in Francia e in Spagna." *Rivista dell'Istituto Nazionale di Archeologia e Storia dett'Arte*, 7, 1940, pp. 225–294.

Frugoni, Chiara. *Wiligelmo: Le sculture del duomo di Modena*. Modena: F. C. Panini, 1996.

Gandolfo, Francesco. "Note per una interpretazione iconologica delle storie del Genesi di Wiligelmo." In *Romanico padano, romanico europeo*, ed. Arturo Carlo Quintavalle. Parma: Artegrafica Silva, 1982, pp. 323–337.

Lanfranco e Wiligelmo: Il duomo di Modena (Quando le cattedrali erano bianche), 3 vols., ed. E, Castelnuovo, V. Fumigalli, A. Peroni, and A. Settis. Modena: Panini, 1984.

Porter, Arthur Kingsley. *Romanesque Sculpture of the Pilgrimage Roads*, 10 vols. Boston: Marshall Jones, 1923. (Reissue, New York, 1966.)

Quintavalle, Arturo Carlo. *La cattedrale di Modena: Problemi di romanico emiliano*, 2 vols. Modena: Editrice Bassi, 1964–1965.

——. *Da Wiligelmo a Nicola*. Parma, 1966.

——, ed. *Wiligelmo e la sua scuola*. Florence: Sadea-Sansoni, 1967.

——. *Romanico padano, civiltà d'occidente*. Florence: Marchi e Bertolli, 1969.

——. "Piacenza Cathedral, Lanfranco, and the School of Wiligelmo." *Art Bulletin*, 55, 1973, pp. 40–57.

——. *Wiligelmo e Matilda: L'officina romanica*. Milan: Electa, 1991. Salvini, Roberto. *Wiligelmo e le origini della scultura romanica.* Milan: Aldo Martello, 1956.

——. *La scultura romanica in Europa*. Milan: Garzanti, 1963.

——. *Il duomo di Modena e il romanico nel modenese*. Modena: Cassa di Risparmio di Modena, 1966.

Wiligelmo e Lanfranco nell'Europa romanica. Atti del Convegno, Modena, 24–27 ottobre 1985. Modena: Panini, 1989.

SCOTT B. MONTGOMERY

WILLEM OF HILDEGAERSBERCH (ca. 1350–1408/1409)

The most important author and performer of *sproken* (short verse narratives) in Middle Dutch literature, Willem was born around 1350 in Hillegersberg, near Rotterdam (county of Holland). He died between June 1408 and April 1409. He was not of noble heritage and seems to have received a rather restricted education. We can probably take seriously the verses in which he states that he is ashamed of his lack of knowledge of Latin. Willem was an itinerant poet, performing at aristocratic courts, in abbeys, and in towns. He maintained a close relationship with the court in The Hague, judging by his frequent appearances in the writings about the counts of Holland. Between 1383 and 1403, Willem is mentioned no fewer than thirty-two times.

Much of Willem's oeuvre survives; 120 *sproken* can be attributed to him. His name is mentioned in forty of them. Two manuscripts contain almost all known *sproken* written by him: The Hague, Koninklijke Bibliotheek (manuscript no. 128 E 6) and Brussels, Koninklijke Bibliotheek (manuscript no. 15.659–661), preserving 117 and 119 *sproken*, respectively. Fragments and *sproken* in other miscellanies prove that Willem of Hildegaersberch was very esteemed in his days.

The *sproke*, a short poetic genre, was performed from the fourteenth century onward by itinerant artists in the Middle Dutch area. It has an average length of 180 to 200 verses, but shorter as well as longer *sproken* are found. The *sproke* can be mainly narrative as well as demonstrative, mostly with no lyrical tenor. It generally implicitly or explicitly moralizes or serves a didactic purpose. Moral truth and Christian or worldly ethics are often stressed. The genre of the *sproke* is very close to the exemplum, the parable, and the sermon. Willem mostly writes rhyming couplets, but he sometimes switches to a strophic form.

Willem's poems treat a large diversity of themes. He speaks about religious subjects, such as Christian virtues or the Easter gospel. On the other hand, he does not hesitate to criticize the clergy. An important part of Willem's oeuvre was meant to be recited at court, and these texts are consequently directly addressed to the lords. Here he is concerned with worldly virtues like honor and justice, especially complaining about their decline. He considers it to be his duty to advise the lords in matters of government and to confront them with the truth. His criticism concerns especially the rogues who surround the lords and deceive them. Willem of Hildegaersberch was conscious that he depended to a very large extent on the favor of the lords. This is why he sometimes felt obliged to soften the truth. In those cases he formulated his criticism in an indirect way. Thus, no one had to feel offended, and the person in question always had the possibility to say the criticism did not apply to him or her. The way to make his criticism indirect is fiction. Willem uses dissociating elements: he wraps his criticism in exempla, allegories, or (animal) fables, for example.

Further Reading

Bisschop, Willem, and Eelco Verwijs, eds. *Gedichten van Willem van Hildegaersberch*. The Hague: Nijhoff, 1870.

Hogenelst, Dini. *Sproken en sprekers. Inleiding op en repertorium van de Middelnederlandse sproke*. 2 vols. Amsterdam: Prometheus, 1997.

Meder, Theo. *Sprookspreker in Holland. Leven en werk van Willem van Hildegaersberch (circa 1400)*. Amsterdam: Prometheus, 1991 [German summary].

van Oostrom, Frits P. *Court and Culture: Dutch Literature, 1350–1450*. Berkeley: University of California Press, 1992.

AN FAEMS

WILLIAM DURANDUS
(c. 1230 or 1231–1 November 1296)

William Durandus (Guillelmus Duranti, Guillaume Durand) is called the Elder to distinguish him from a nephew with the same name. The elder "William Durandus was born in Puimisson, near Béziers in Provence. We know practically nothing about his family or early life before his ordination as subdeacon in the cathedral of Narbonne c. 1254 and his enrollment in the list of canons at the cathedral of Maguelonne at about the same time. Not long after taking clerical orders, William began formal legal studies at the University of Bologna; he earned a doctorate in canon law there c. 1263. He may have lectured at the university before he became a papal chaplain and "general auditor" under Pope Urban IV (r. 1261–1264). Early in his long and increasingly difficult career in the service of the papal curia, William befriended the best-known canonist in Europe, Cardinal Henricus de Segusia (Henry of Susa), known as Hostiensis.

Under Pope Clement IV (1265–1268), William continued his service as papal chaplain and auditor. He also finished the first edition of his first publication, *Aureum repertorium* (c. 1264–1270), a short index and commentary on Gratian's *Decretum* (c. 1140) and on Pope Gregory IX's *Liber extra* (1234). *Aureum repertorium* was soon followed by William's massive and—during the medieval period—definitive textbook on procedural law, *Speculum Iudiciale* (c. 1271–1276). The enduring fame of this work earned William the nickname Speculator, by which he was commonly known during and after his lifetime.

In the summer of 1274, William attended the Second Council of Lyon and held the official title of *peritus* (theologian) for Pope Gregory X (1271–1276). William later assisted in the post-conciliar editing of the canons of the council, and some twenty years afterward he published the final version of *In sacrosanctum Lugdunese concilium commentarius* (c. 1293–1294), his long commentary on the council's decrees.

By 1279, William was ordained a priest and was made dean of the cathedral of Chartres by Pope Nicholas III (r. 1277–1280). In 1280, Nicholas appointed him *rector et capitaneus generalis* of a portion of the papal states (including a part of Tuscany and the diocese of Rieti). In 1281, the new pope, Martin IV (r. 1281–1285), added to William's official duties rule of the turbulent Romagna. From 1282 to 1286, William coordinated the war efforts of the papacy in the Romagna, leading the pro-papal Guelfs to a precarious interim victory over the Ghibellines.

In 1285, William submitted his resignation from the papal service to Pope Honorius IV (r. 1285–1287). Within a month, William was elected bishop of Mende in his native Provence by the cathedral chapter. He was consecrated bishop by the archbishop of Ravenna in 1286 but (inexplicably) remained in Rome for another five years before taking up residence in Mende in July 1291.

William's prolific literary production during his episcopacy demonstrates his conscientious application of his learning to pastoral care (not to mention his capability as an encyclopedic polymath). The works he published in this period include the following: *Constitutiones synodales* (c. 1292), a collection of statutes and instructions for the reform of the clergy of his diocese; *Ordinarium* (c. 1291–1293), a book regulating the liturgical services of the cathedral of Mende; his commentary on the Second Council of Lyon; *Rationale divinorum officiorum* (c. 1291–1296), a long allegorical commentary on the entire liturgy (including the mass, divine office, and church year); and *Pontificale* (*Bishop's Book*, c. 1293–1295), which provided rubrics and prayers for liturgical services performed only by a bishop. Modern scholarship has revealed that William's *Rationale* and *Pontificale* were two of the most important liturgical texts of the entire medieval period in Europe.

William had been a resident bishop for only four years when he succumbed to the persistent entreaties of his friend Benedict Gaetani, now Pope Boniface VIII (r. 1294–1303), to return to Rome and assume official duties in the papal states. In September 1295, William was appointed rector of the Anconian March and the Romagna, territories that were in a state of near-anarchy since the Ghibelline faction had mobilized itself for war with the Guelfs. William's command of the papacy's war effort failed, however, when he lost the city of Imola to the Ghibellines and presided over the defeat of a pro-papal Bolognese army in April 1296. By the end of the summer of 1296, William, who was by then in his sixties, seems to have had little if any official responsibility in the papal states. He continued to reside in Rome, where he died.

William Durandus the Elder was buried in the church of Santa Maria Sopra Minerva. A thirty-line epitaph praising his life and works was inscribed there in marble, possibly at the request of his nephew William Durandus the Younger, who succeeded him as bishop of Mende.

There are numerous incunabula and early printed editions of *Aureum repertorium super toto corpore iuris canonici*, but as of the present writing there was no modern edition. *Speculum iudiciale* survives in more than 100 medieval manuscripts; there are numerous incunabula and early printed editions but (again as of this writing) no modern edition. A manuscript (possibly written or corrected by Durandus himself) of *Constitutiones synodales* was published in a diplomatic edition (Berthelé and Valmary 1905). The only known printed edition of *In sacrosanctum Lugdunese concilium commentarius* is that of 1569. The *Pontificale* was published in the magisterial edition of Andrieu (1940). The *Rationale divinorum offciorum* survives in hundreds of medieval Latin manuscripts, as well as numerous medieval vernacular translations; the first modern critical edition is Davril and Thibodeau (1995, 1998). Although a complete modern biography of Durandus has yet to be written, the bibliography of secondary sources is voluminous; selected references are listed below.

Further Reading

Primary Sources

Andrieu, Michel, ed. *Le pontifical romain au Moyen-Âge*, Vol. 3, *Le pontifical de Guillaume Durand*. Studi e Testi, 88. Vatican City: Biblioteca Apostolica Vaticana, 1940.

Aureum repertorium super toto corpore iuris canonici. Venice: Paganinus de Paganinis, 1496–1497.

Berthelé, J., and M. Valmary, eds. "Les instructions et constitutions de Guillaume Durand le Spéculateur," *Académie des Sciences et Lettres de Montpellier: Mémoires de la Section des Lettres*, Series 2(3), 1905, pp. 1–148.

Davril, Anselme, and T. M. Thibodeau, eds. *Guillelmi Duranti Rationale divinorum officiorum I–IV, V–VI*. Corpus Christianorum, Continuatio Medieaevalis, 140 and 140A. Turnhout: Brepols, 1995; 1998.

In sacrosanctum Lugdunese concilium commentarius sub Gregorio X Guilelmi Duranti cognomeno Speculatoris commentarius, ed. Simone Maiolo. Fano: Iacobus Moscardus, 1569.

Speculum iudiciale, illustratum, et repurgatum a Giovanni Andrea et Baldo degli Ubaldi. Basel: Froben, 1574. (4 parts in 2 vols.; the best-known and most widely available text. Reprint, Darmstadt: Aalen, 1975.)

Secondary Sources

Baimelle, Marius. *Bibliographie du Gévaudan*, n.s., fasc. 3. Mende: n.p., 1966. (Pamphlet. Good though dated bibliography for the life and works of Durandus and his nephew.)

Boyle, Leonard. "The Date of the Commentary of William Duranti the Elder on the Constitutions of the Second Council of Lyons." *Bulletin of Medieval Canon Law*, n.s., 4, 1974, pp. 39–47.

Douteil, Herbert. *Studien zu Durantis "Rationale divinorum officiorum" als kirchenmusicalischer Quelle*. Kölner Beiträge zur Musikforschung, 52. Regensburg, 1969.

Dykmans, Marc. "Notes autobiographiques de Guillaume Durand le Spéculateur." In *Ius populi Dei: Miscellanea in honorem Raymundi Bidagor*. Rome, 1972, pp. 121–142.

Faletti, Louis. "Guillaume Durand." *Dictionnaire de droit canonique*, 5, 1953, pp. 1014–1075.

Gy, Pierre-Marie, ed. *Guillaume Durand, évêque de Mende (v. 1230–1296): Canoniste, liturgiste, et homme politique—Actes de la Table Ronde du CNRS Mende 24–27 mai 1990*. Paris: Centre National de la Recherche Scientifique, 1992. (Collection of papers; at the time of its publication it represented the most up-to-date research on Durandus.)

Leclerq, Victor. "Guillaume Duranti, évêque de Mende, surnommé le Spéculateur." In *Histoire Littéraire de la France*, Vol. 20. Paris: Librairies Universitaires, 1895, pp. 411–480.

Ménard, Clarence C. "William Durand's *Rationale divinorum officiorum*: Preliminaries to a New Critical Edition." Dissertation, Gregorian University (Rome), 1967. (Groundbreaking work that was the basis for a recently published edition of the *Rationale*.)

Thibodeau, Timothy M. "*Enigmata figurarum*: Biblical Exegesis and Liturgical Exposition in Durand's *Rationale*". *Harvard Theological Review*, 86, 1993, pp. 65–79.

TIMOTHY M. THIBODEAU

WILLIAM I (1027/28–1087; r. 1066–87)

First Norman king of England; known as "the Conqueror." Born in 1027 or 1028 at Falaise in Normandy, William was the only, but illegitimate, son of Duke Robert of Normandy. His mother, Herleva, was the daughter of a tanner or, more probably, an undertaker of Falaise. Subsequently Robert married her off to a minor noble from the Seine Valley, Herluin de Conteville, by whom she had two further sons, Odo, later bishop of Bayeux (from 1050), and Robert, subsequently (from ca. 1060) count of Mortain.

William became duke of Normandy at the age of seven, when his father died in July 1035 while returning from a pilgrimage to Jerusalem. That he became duke at all, given his age and illegitimacy, was probably due to the lack of other candidates. Though Robert had taken the precaution to have him formally designated duke before departing for the Holy Land, William's rule in Normandy was to face serious challenges for more than twenty years. Law and order collapsed in the duchy during his minority, ducal power and property were usurped by contending nobles, and several members of his court, including some cousins, were murdered in factional disputes. This disorder culminated in a serious rebellion in western Normandy in 1047, led by Count Guy of Brienne, suppressed only with the help of the French king Henry I, who assisted William in defeating the rebels at the Battle of Val-es-Dunes near Caen.

In the years immediately after this success the domestic situation in Normandy was stable enough for

William to start aggressive operations on his southern border, capturing the frontier fortresses of Domfront and Alençon in 1051/52. This in turn brought him into conflict with the overlord of Maine, Count Geoffrey Martel of Anjou, and with his erstwhile ally King Henry, and was also followed by renewed revolt in Normandy by a hitherto loyal supporter, his uncle Count William of Arques. The Duke's position was saved by his own military prowess and activity, and smashing defeats were inflicted on French armies at Mortemer in 1054 and Varaville in 1057. The latter marked the end of the young duke's struggle for survival.

From 1062 onward William's chief concern seems to have been the acquisition of the county of Maine, after the death of the childless Count Herbert II. He was aided in this by the fact that the new king of France, Philip I, was a minor, while Anjou was weakened by a succession struggle between the sons of Geoffrey Martel. By 1065 William had placed a garrison in Le Mans, installed a Norman bishop, secured the fealty of the leading nobles of the county, and had his eldest son, Robert, recognized as count. But his hold over Maine was never fully consolidated and was to remain a problem for the rest of his life.

In 1051 the childless king of England, Edward the Confessor, had designated William, his cousin, as his successor. One source suggests that the duke visited England in 1051. This seems unlikely, given how difficult his position was in Normandy at that time; probably Archbishop Robert of Canterbury (a Norman) had acted as intermediary while on his way to Rome in that summer. Whether Edward persisted in his intention of having William as his heir also seems doubtful; he may have changed his mind several times. William's chance of securing the succession was much enhanced when his potential rival, Harold of Wessex, Edward's brother-in-law, visited Normandy in 1064 or 1065 and was persuaded or forced to swear fealty to the duke and to support his claim. Many details remain obscure; we cannot be certain why Harold went to Normandy, whether Edward sent him or not, or even the date of his visit.

Nor did it have any immediate effect on the English succession. When Edward died on 5 January 1066 Harold succeeded him. The designation of 1051 and Harold's oath had given William a *casus belli*, and he used them to orchestrate a propaganda campaign to secure recruits from all over France and to gain papal support. The invasion was launched, after some delays, at the end of September 1066, and on 14 October the Norman and English armies met a few miles north of Hastings. After a desperate struggle the English were defeated and Harold killed. Within two months the surviving English magnates and the church leaders had surrendered, and William was crowned king of England in Westminster Abbey on Christmas Day 1066.

This merely marked the start of the conquest of England. To begin with William sought to emphasize the continuity of his rule with that of Edward, and to use Englishmen in his government. His first earl of Northumbria, Copsi, was an Englishman, and even Archbishop Stigand of Canterbury, whose appointment had been canonically dubious and who was regarded with disapproval by the papacy, was retained until 1070. But widespread rebellion, in the west and north in 1068, and more seriously in the north and in the fen country of East Anglia in 1069 and 1070¾the latter with Danish support—led to a major change in policy and the widespread replacement of English landowners by Frenchmen. The king was under obvious pressure to satisfy what Orderic Vitalis called "his envious and greedy Norman followers." So serious was the revolt of 1069 that William resorted to the harshest of measures to quell it, devastating much of Yorkshire to prevent further rebellion and thereby condemning many of the inhabitants to death by starvation. Inured as they were to violence, contemporary chroniclers were shocked by the barbarity of his actions.

But this drastic treatment worked. The last bastion of English resistance, the Isle of Ely, surrendered in 1071. Thereafter William's rule in England was not seriously threatened. There was admittedly another rebellion in 1075, led by the Norman earl Roger of Hereford and the Breton earl Ralph of Norfolk, but this was crushed by William's subordinates, under the direction of Archbishop Lanfranc, while the king remained in Normandy. Indeed, in his later years, William was largely an absentee ruler, not visiting the country at all between 1076 and 1080 and spending eleven of his last fifteen years in Normandy. In his absence England was ruled largely by his half-brother Odo of Bayeux (until his disgrace and imprisonment in 1082) and Lanfranc. Queen Matilda played a similarly crucial role in Normandy until her death in 1083.

After 1070 renewed problems on the Norman frontiers helped to keep William in the duchy. The king suffered the only serious military setback of his life at Dol on the Breton border in September 1076. Relations with the king of France, Philip, deteriorated. Maine became restive under Norman rule. And worst of all, the king's son Robert Curthose rebelled, probably in the spring of 1078. There was an indecisive battle at Gerberoi in eastern Normandy in January 1079, in which William was slightly wounded. Although there was a temporary reconciliation early in 1080, relations remained difficult and Robert went into exile again in 1084. The root of the problem seems to have been Robert's wish to have an independent role in Normandy, of which he had been designated as duke before Hastings, and William's determination to keep his son firmly under supervision.

William's last visit to England came in 1085–86, to

organize the defense of the kingdom against a threatened Danish invasion. But the most important result of this visit was the Domesday Book. Its purpose has been much debated. Probably it was a guide to both the resources of the country and the ownership of particular estates, made necessary by the large-scale redistribution of land caused by the Conquest.

The first draft of the Domesday survey was probably nearly completed when William held a court at Salisbury in August 1086, where he exacted a comprehensive oath of loyalty from his magnates and the more important of their undertenants. Eleven months later, when campaigning at Mantes on the Norman border, he was taken seriously ill. He was carried to Rouen, where he died on 9 September 1087. On his deathbed he agreed to Robert's succession as duke of Normandy, his second surviving son, William Rufus, succeeding as king of England. He was buried at the monastery of St. Étienne at Caen, which he himself had founded a quarter of a century earlier.

Much of William's success came from a partnership with a small group of Norman nobles, such men as William Fitz Osbern, Roger de Montgomery, and his own half-brothers. It was not surprising that this group of seven or eight men were the chief beneficiaries of the Conquest. In ecclesiastical matters his chief adviser was Lanfranc, abbot of St. Étienne at Caen in 1063 and archbishop of Canterbury in 1070. Though favoring the moral reform of the clergy, William was always concerned to vindicate his own control of the church and to limit papal interference. He was not above appointing his half-brother Odo as bishop when the latter was well below the canonical age. After 1066 he was generally content to adopt existing English laws and institutions but to exploit them to the full; contemporaries agreed that his government was harsh and predatory. The Anglo-Saxon Chronicle called him "stern beyond all measure to people who resisted his will."

William was tall, strong, and of harsh voice and imposing appearance, tending to corpulence in later life. He married ca. 1050 Matilda, daughter of Baldwin V of Flanders, by whom he had four sons (one of whom, Richard, died young) and four or perhaps five daughters.

See also **Edward the Confessor; Harold Godwinson; Lanfranc of Bec**

Further Reading

Primary Sources

Chibnall, Marjorie, ed. and trans. *The Ecclesiastical History of Orderic Vitalis.* 6 vols. Oxford: Clarendon, 1969–80.

Foreville, Raymonde, ed. and trans, (into French). *Histoire de Guillaume le Conquérant.* Paris: Les Belles Lettres, 1952 [the chronicle of William of Poitiers].

van Houts, Elisabeth M.C., ed, and trans. *The Gesta Normannorum Ducum of William of jumièges, Orderic Vitalis and Robert of Torigni. 2* vols. Oxford: Oxford University Press, 1992–95.

Wilson, David M., ed. *The Bayeux Tapestry*: *The Complete Tapestry in Colour.* London: Thames & Hudson; New York: Knopf, 1985 [fascinating illustrated account of the campaign of 1066].

Secondary Sources

Barlow, Frank. *Edward the Confessor.* Berkeley: University of California Press, 1970.

Bates, David. *Normandy before 1066.* London: Longman, 1982

Bates, David. *William the Conqueror.* London: Philip, 1989 [excellent bibliography].

Douglas, David C. *William the Conqueror.* London: Eyre & Spottiswoode, 1964.

John, Eric. "Edward the Confessor and the Norman Succession." *EHR94* (1979): 241-67.

Le Patourel, John. *The Norman Empire.* Oxford: Clarendon, 1976.

Loyn, H.R. *The Norman Conquest.* 3d ed. London. Hutchinson, 1982 [the best of several general books].

van Houts, Elisabeth M.C. "The Origins of Herleva, Mother of William the Conqueror." *EHR*101 (1986): 399–404.

GRAHAM A. LOUD

WILLIAM OF AUVERGNE (WILLIAM OF PARIS; 1180/90–1249)

Born in Aurillac in the Auvergne, William was canon of Notre-Dame in Paris by 1223, regent master at Paris in 1225, and bishop of Paris in 1228. A secular master himself, William was, however, an early champion of the mendicant orders, allowing Roland of Cremona to hold the first Dominican chair in theology (1229). Known for his fairness and good sense, he was confessor to Blanche of Castile and friend and adviser to Louis IX.

William left a vast corpus of works in encyclopedic style, including a series of tracts sometimes called his *Magisterium divinale* (1123–40), which included *De universo. Cur Deus homo, De fide et legibus*, and *De Trinitate*. His *De vitiis et virtutibus* rivaled that of William Peraldus (the two men were often confused) in popularity. One of the first theorists of Purgatory, he was also among the first theological users of Aristotle in Paris, and he sought out texts of Avicenna, Maimonides's *Guide*, Avicebrol, and others in the service of orthodox belief.

See also **Blanche of Castile; Louis IX**

Further Reading

William of Auvergne. *Opera omnia. 2* vols. Paris: Andraeas Pralard, 1674; repr. Frankfurt am Main: Minerva, 1963.

——. *De Trinitate*, ed. Bruno Switalski. Toronto: Pontifical Institute of Mediaeval Studies, 1976.

——. *The Immortality of the Soul = De immortalitate animae*, trans. Roland J. Teske. Milwaukee: Marquette University Press, 1991.

———. *The Trinity, or, The First Principle = De Trinitate, seu De primo principio*, trans. Roland j. Teske and Francis C. Wade. Milwaukee: Marquette University Press, 1989.

Bernstein, A.E. "Esoteric Theology: William of Auvergne on the Fires of Hell and Purgatory." *Speculum* 57 (1982): 509–31.

Marrone, Steven P. *William of Auvergne* and *Robert Grosseteste: New Ideas of Truth in the Early 13th Century.* Princeton: Princeton University Press, 1983.

Quentin, Albrecht. *Naturkenntnisse und Naturanschauungen bei Wilhelm von Auvergne.* Hildesheim: Gerstenberg, 1976.

Rohls, Jan. *Wilhelm von Auvergne und der mittelalterliche Aristotelismus: Gottesbegriff und aristotelische Philosophie zwischen Augustin und Thomas von Aquin.* Munich: Kaiser, 1980.

Valois, Noel. *Guillaume d'Auvergne, évêque de Paris (1228–1249), sa vie et ses ouvrages.* Paris: Picard, 1880.

LESLEY J. SMITH

WILLIAM OF CONCHES
(ca. 1085–ca. 1154)

Named by John of Salisbury as one of his teachers, William is most often associated with the so-called School of Chartres, as a student of Bernard of Chartres and a master there, although Richard W. Southern has called into question whether William actually taught at Chartres, as opposed to Paris. John of Salisbury calls William a grammarian, and much of William's extant work is in the form of glosses on authoritative texts widely used in the schools. He glossed Boethius's *De consolatione Philosophiae*, Macrobius's *In somnium Scipionis*, Plato's *Timaeus*, Priscian's *Institutiones grammaticae*, and Juvenal. He may be the author of *Moralium dogma philosophorum*. His gloss on *De consolatione* identified the World Soul with the Holy Spirit, although the gloss on the *Timaeus* presents the World Soul as a concept with many hidden meanings. William's glosses on Macrobius and the *Timaeus* analyze the nature of *fabula* and *integumentum* as these apply to the "cloaking" of philosophical and theological truth in words and images in literary texts and imaginative narratives. William's interest in physics and cosmology is revealed in his *Philosophia mundi* (entitled *Dragmaticon* in a later revision), a systematic treatment of physical, cosmological, geographical, and meteorological phenomena and questions, summing up scientific knowledge in the era before the translation of Aristotle's scientific works. He sought to discern the true workings of nature and shunned "miraculous" explanations, even for biblical events, when a more straightforward explanation might be found. William made use of translations-adaptations of medical works from the Arabic, such as Constantine the African's *Pantegni*.

See also **John of Salisbury; Macrobius; Martianus Capella**

Further Reading

William of Conches. *Glosae in luvenalem*, ed. Bradford Wilson. Paris: Vrin, 1980.

———. *Glosae super Platonem*, ed. Édouard Jeauneau. Paris: Vrin, 1965.

———. *Philosophia*, ed. Gregor Maurach with Heidemarie Telle. Pretoria: University of South Africa, 1980.

———. *Das Moralium dogma philosophorum des Guillaume de Conches, lateinisch, altfranzösich und mittelnieder-frankisch*, ed. John Holmberg. Uppsala: Almqvist and Wiksell, 1929.

Gregory, Tullio. *Anima mundi: la filosofia de Guglielmo di Conches e la scuola di Chartres.* Florence: Sansoni, 1955.

Häring, Nikolaus M. "Commenatry and Hermeneutics." In *Renaissance and Renewal in the Twelfth Century*, ed. Robert L. Benson and Giles Constable with Carol D. Lanham. Cambridge: Harvard University Press, 1982, pp. 173–200.

Jeauneau, Édouard. "Deux rédactions des gloses de Guillaume de Conches sur Priscien." *Recherches de théologie ancienne et médiévale* 27 (1960): 212–47.

———. "*Lectio philosophorum*": *recherches sur l'École de Chartres.* Amsterdam: Hakkert, 1973.

Parent, Joseph-Marie. *La doctrine de la création dans l'École de Chartres: études et textes.* Paris: Vrin, 1938.

Southern, Richard W. *Platonism, Scholastic Method, and the School of Chartres.* Reading: University of Reading, 1979.

Wetherbee, Winthrop. *Platonism and Poetry in the Twelfth Century: The Literary Influence of the School of Chartres.* Princeton: Princeton University Press, 1972.

GROVER A. ZINN

WILLIAM OF OCKHAM (ca. 1285–1347)

Philosopher and Franciscan theologian. William studied in London and Oxford. His writings include commentaries on the *Sentences* of Peter Lombard and lectures on Aristotle's logic and physics and reflect the influence of his fellow Franciscan John Duns Scotus (d. 1308).

Ockham was an outstanding dialectician and theologian, but his outspoken views were not without controversy. Although summoned in 1324 to the papal court at Avignon to justify his teaching on transubstantiation, there was no formal condemnation of his doctrines. His study of the papal constitutions on apostolic poverty led to his involvement in the debate over Franciscan poverty and the attack on John XXII (1316–34) as a heretic. Under the protection of Emperor Louis IV of Bavaria, the political opponent of the pope, Ockham wrote several political works, including the *Dialogue*, where he discussed his views on the errors of the papacy and its rights with respect to the Holy Roman Empire.

Ockham's doctrines marked a turning point in the history of philosophy and theology. He held that logic was separate from theology, that they are both true, and that they represent different kinds of truth. Thus theology cannot be proved by logic. This *via moderna* ("modern way") marked the separation between faith and reason and was a hallmark of late-medieval philosophy.

Ockham is usually associated with the rule of "Ockhams razor." Known also as the law of parsimony or economy, the dictum became a foundation stone of scientific method: the simpler a theory or explanation is, the less chance for error.

Ockham died 10 April 1347 in Munich and was buried in the Franciscan church. His nominalist philosophy, which emphasized the fundamental reality of individually existing things, and his political theory on the limitation of papal power, were to be highly influential in Reformation thought.

See also **Duns Scotus, John**

Further Reading

Courtenay, William J. "Nominalism and Late Medieval Thought: A Bibliographical Essay." *Theological Studies* 33 (1972): 716–34
Courtenay, William J. "Late Medieval Nominalism Revisited: 1972–1982." *Journal of the History of Ideas* 44 (1983): 159–64
Leff, Gordon. *William of Ockham*: *The Metamorphosis of Scholastic Discourse.* Manchester: Manchester University Press, 1975
William of Ockham. *Philosophical Writings*: *A Selection.* Ed. and trans. Philotheus Bohner. Edinburgh: Nelson, 1957.

PHYLLIS B. ROBERTS

WILLIAM OF SAINT-AMOUR
(ca. 1200–1272)

William is now chiefly remembered for his ferocious campaign against the mendicant orders. We know nothing of his life until he became master of arts in Paris (by 1228). By November 1238, he had received the doctorate in canon law and was also canon of Beauvais and rector of Guerville. He went on to study theology in Paris and ca. 1250 was a regent master.

From about this time, William began his attacks on the mendicant way of life, and it was through his influence that the Dominicans were suspended from teaching in 1254 for having in effect broken the closed shop of masters by ignoring the suspension of classes in the previous year and continuing to teach.

William never substantially amended his views on the mendicants, and his subsequent fate depended on who was pope at the time. Innocent IV (r. 1243–54) was sympathetic, and he flourished. Alexander IV (r. 1254–61) was cardinal protector of the Franciscans, and William was deprived of his privileges and expelled from France. Clement IV, although disagreeing, allowed him to return to Saint-Amour, where he died. His most famous polemical work is *De periculis novissimorum temporum* (1256).

Further Reading

Douie, Decima L. *The Conflict Between the Seculars and the Mendicants at the University of Paris in the Thirteenth Century*. London: Blackfriars, 1954.
Dufeil, M.M. *Guillaume de Saint-Amour et la polémique universitaire parisienne, 1250–1259*. Paris: Picard, 1972.

LESLEY J. SMITH

WILLIAM OF SAINT-THIERRY
(1070/90–1148)

Born in Liège, William of Saint-Thierry studied at the schools of Reims and perhaps at Laon under Anselm of Laon, where he may have met Peter Abélard. For unknown reasons, he renounced his studies and in 1113 became a monk in the Benedictine monastery of Saint-Nicasius in Reims. In 1118, he became abbot of Saint-Thierry, near Reims. As a close friend and admirer of Bernard of Clairvaux, he wished to change orders and become a Cistercian. However, Bernard dissuaded him until 1135, when William became a monk in the newly founded Cistercian monastery of Signy, where he died in 1148.

On several occasions, William encouraged Bernard's literary activities. Bernard's early work, the *Apologia*, a fierce attack on the traditional Benedictine monastic lifestyle, was written at William's request and dedicated to him. About 1138, William, shocked by the theological audacity of Abélard, persuaded Bernard to oppose him, adding to his request a list of Abélard's errors, published as the *Disputatio adversus Abaelardum*. Bernard's intervention resulted in Abélard's condemnation at the Council of Sens in 1141. William was also instrumental in bringing about Bernard's famous series of sermons on the Song of Songs. When both were ill, they spent some time together in the infirmary of Clairvaux, talking about the *Canticle*. William also intended to write a life of Bernard but completed only the first book, the so-called *Sancti Bernardi vita prima*.

William published many works on devotional and exegetical themes, among which are the *Expositio in epistolam ad Romanos* (in reaction to Abélard's commentary on Paul's Epistle to the Romans), the *Expositio super Cantica canticorum* (a commentary on the Song of Songs), as well as two compilations on the Song of Songs from the works of Ambrose and Gregory the Great and a treatise on the relation between body and soul (*De natura corporis et animae*). Author of *De natura et dignitate amoris* and *De contemplando Deo*, William is also considered to be the author of the famous *Epistola ad fratres de Monte Dei*, about the solitary and contemplative life.

For William, the act of faith is part of and subsumed

under mystical knowledge and contemplation. Faith is a pretaste of the vision of the divine. Reason helps faith in the process of understanding itself, raising it to the level of full mystical knowledge characterized by love. William supports his reflections on mystical knowledge with quotations from many sources, mainly patristic, while also frequently referring to profane, classical authors. He, like the "monastic theology" he helped to create, can thus be seen as part of the so-called 12th-century renaissance.

See also **Abélard, Peter; Anselm of Laon; Bernard of Clairvaux**

Further Reading

William of Saint-Thierry. *Opera. PL* 180, 184, 185.
——. *On Contemplating God*, trans. Sister Penelope. Kalamazoo: Cistercian, 1977.
——. *The Nature and Dignity of Love*, trans. Thomas X. Davis. Kalamazoo: Cistercian, 1981.
——. *On Contemplating God*; *Prayer, Meditations*, trans. Sister Penelope. Kalamazoo: Cistercian, 1971.
——. *On the Nature of the Body and the Soul*, trans. B. Clark. In *Three Treatises on Man: A Cistercian Anthropology*, ed. Bernard McGinn. Kalamazoo: Cistercian, 1977.
——. *Exposé sur le Cantique des cantiques*, ed. jean M. Déchanet, trans. Pierre Dumontier. Paris: Cerf, 1962.
——. *The Mirror of Faith*, trans. Thomas X. Davis. Kalamazoo: Cistercian, 1979.
——. *Lettre aux frères de Mont-Dieu* (*Lettre d'Or*), ed. and trans. Jean M. Déchanet. Paris: Cerf, 1975
Bell, David N. *The Image and Likeness: The Augustinian Spirituality of William of Saint-Thierry*. Kalamazoo: Cistercian, 1984.
Déchanet, Jean M. *William of Saint-Thierry: The Man and His Work*. Spencer: Cistercian, 1972.

BURCHT PRANGER

WIRNT VON GRAFENBERG
(fl. 1204–1210)

Author of the Middle High German Arthurian romance *Wigalois*, written between 1204 and 1210, Wirnt is thought to be a *ministerial* (clerical administrator) from the town of Gräfenberg north of Erlangen.

No documents associate him with any particular court at which *Wigalois* might have been written, but Berthold IV, count of Andechs and duke of Meran, is his most likely patron. References to characters from *Erec* and *Iwein* as well as the first part of *Parzival* attest to the author's familiarity with the works of his famous contemporaries Hartmann von Aue and Wolfram von Eschenbach. Although earlier treatments of the *Wigalois* story, such as Renaud de Beaujeu's *Le Bel Inconnu*, existed outside of Germany, Wirnt insists that his source was a story told by a squire. It has been suggested that the citing of an oral source served as a pretext to set

his own emphasis rather than following slavishly the demands of the genre.

The *Wigalois* romance consists of 11,708 verses and is written in rhymed couplets. The story of Gawein's son, it is divided into five distinct parts: the hero's upbringing in his mother's fairy kingdom; his arrival at Arthur's court and his adventures in the Arthurian realm; his adventures in the otherworldly realm of Korntin and ultimate triumph over the prince of darkness, the heathen King Roaz of Glois; the hero's wedding and coronation; and the avenging of the murder of a wedding guest. While earlier scholarship insisted on viewing Wirnt's hero as the unproblematic knight of fortune's wheel, more recent work detects a flawed character in need of God's mercy who submits to the will of God. It is God who provides the supreme guidance through the supernatural obstacles of Korntin and grants victory. Wirnt's novelty is the Arthurian knight as God's champion in the eschatological conflict between heaven and hell. He uses the genre to send a message of apocalyptic urgency to his contemporary society, drawing obvious parallels between that society and Wigalois's antagonist. Both have lost sight of the ultimate good, and thus the story of Wigalois serves as a vehicle to reaffirm God's grace as our only hope for salvation. Wirnt's romance has enjoyed surprising popularity, judging not only by the relatively large number of extant manuscripts but also by its influence on contemporary as well as subsequent German authors writing in the latter thirteenth and fourteenth centuries. Noteworthy later adaptations of the story include a fifteenth-century chapbook, a Yiddish rendition transmitted in manuscripts from the sixteenth century, and a nursery tale dated 1786. Wirnt himself became the hero of Konrad von Würzburg's verse narrative *Der Welt Lohn*, in which he is depicted as a knight who learns to forsake the things of the world and to serve God. The story of Wigalois has also contributed valuable material to the body of Arthurian iconography, ranging from the Wigalois frescoes in Runkelstein castle near Bolzano in South Tyrol and woodcuts illustrating the chapbook version to picture cycles in two of the manuscripts. One of these, the parchment codex no. *Ltk 537* of Leyden, is considered the only significant illuminated Arthurian manuscript of the fourteenth century.

See also **Hartmann von Aue; Konrad von Würzburg; Wolfram von Eschenbach**

Further Reading

Cormeau, Christoph. *'Wigalois' und 'Diu Crone': Zwei Kapitel zur Gattungsgeschichte des nachklassischen Aventiureromans.* Zurich: Artemis, 1977.
Freeland, Beverly M. "*Wigalois A*: A Prototype Edition of Wirnt von Gravenberg's *Wigalois*." Ph.d. diss., University of California, Los Angeles, 1993.

Henderson, Ingeborg. "Manuscript Illustrations as Generic Determinants in Wirnt von Gravenberg's *Wigalois*," in *Genres in Medieval German Literature*, ed. Hubert Heinen and Ingeborg Henderson. Göppingen: Kümmerle, 1986.

Kapteyn, J. M. N. *Wigalois, der Ritter mit dem Rade*. Bonn: Klopp, 1926.

Thomas, J. W. *Wigalois, The Knight of Fortune's Wheel*. Lincoln: University of Nebraska Press, 1977.

INGEBORG HENDERSON

WITTENWILER, HEINRICH
(ca. 1350–ca. 1450)

Author of the *Ring*, a comic-didactic verse satire of the early fifteenth century, Heinrich Wittenwiler employs chiefly High Alemannic language in the poem, with occasional Bavarianisms. As shown by his knowledge of the local dialect, which he places in the mouths of the peasants in the *Ring*, Wittenwiler probably stemmed from the Toggenburg area of Switzerland. The poem exists in only one manuscript, located in the Meiningen (Thuringia) archives.

Wittenwiler served as *advocatus curiae* at the episcopal court in Constance, where, as a high official of the bishop, he would have moved in circles favorable to the Austrian nobility and inimical to disruptive forces such as the city guilds and the Bund ob dem See (Dutch marine commerce alliance). His use of *Sachliteratur* (technical writing) shows him to have been a man of great learning and wide-ranging interests. He is mentioned in documents from the last two decades of the fourteenth century, although the composition of the *Ring* falls in the first decade of the fifteenth, probably during the episcopate of Albrecht Blarer.

Wittenwiler derived the basic structure of the *Ring* from the short force *Metzen hochzît (Metz's Wedding)*, but expanded it to almost ten thousand lines with extensive allegorical, didactic, and satirical passages. Set in the village of Lappenhausen, the first of three sections deals with Bertschi Triefnas's devotion to Mätzli Rüeren-zumph, the antipode of all ideals of courtly beauty. During his wooing, Bertschi accidentally inflicts a head wound on Mätzli, who, while receiving treatment, is impregnated by the doctor Chrippenchra. To cover up his misdeed, the doctor persuades Mätzli to marry Bertschi.

In the second section, a lengthy debate on the pros and cons of marriage, as well as instruction for Bertschi in religion, manners, virtue, hygiene, and home economics, precede the wedding. At the wedding feast, the villagers display every possible form of bad manners and finally abandon themselves to wild dancing. A minor incident at the dance leads, in the third section, to an all-out war between Lappenhausen and neighboring Nissingen. The conflict escalates until it involves most of southwestern Germany and figures from the Germanic epics. Fro Laichdenman, the local astrologer, betrays Lappenhausen to its enemies, and the village burns to the ground. Bertschi, the only survivor, laments his failure to follow the wise teachings of his mentors and moves to the Black Forest to lead the life of a hermit.

To underscore Wittenwiler's method of alternating didacticism with bucolic bawling *(gpauren gschrai)*, the manuscript differentiates by means of red or green marginal stripes those passages that can serve as stylistic models (red) from those that satirize peasant mores (green). Read as an allegorical work, the *Ring* strongly associates peasants with images of a carnal and sinful humanity; read politically, it expresses the disgust of an urban nobility faced with a series of peasant revolts.

Further Reading

Jones, George Fenwick, trans. *Wittenwiler's Ring and the Anonymous Scots Poem Colkelbie Sow*. Chapel Hill: University of North Carolina Press, 1956; rpt. New York: AMS, 1969.

Lutz, Eckhart Conrad. *Spiritualis Fornicatio*. Sigmaringen: Thorbecke, 1990.

Plate, Bernward. *Heinrich Wittenwiler*. Darmstadt: Wissenschaftliche Buchgesellschaft, 1977.

Riha, Ortrun. *Die Forschung zu Heinrich Wittenwilers "Ring" 1851–1988*. Würzburg: Königshausen and Neumann, 1990.

Wießner, Edmund. *Heinrich Wittenwilers "Ring."* Leipzig: Redam, 1931; rpt. Darmstadt: Wissenschaftliche Buchgesellschaft, 1964.

Wittenwiler, Heinrich. *Der Ring*, ed. Rolf Bräuer, George F. Jones, and Ulrich Müller. Göppingen: Kümmerle, 1990 [facsimile ed.].

JIM OGIER

WITZ, KONRAD
(ca. 1400/1410–1445/1446)

In 1896, Daniel Burckhardt of the Öffentlichen Kunstsammlung in Basle published his observations on the stylistic similarity between the panels of an incomplete Heilsspiegel Altar (Altar of Human Salvation) in Basle and the panels from the St. Peter Altar in Geneva, which are signed by Konrad Witz and dated 1444. This artist, whose distinctive style had little influence on later German art, had been forgotten since his death.

Konrad Witz was probably born in Rottweil in Württemberg circa 1400–1410; he is first documented by his entrance into the Basel painters' guild on June 21, 1434. The Council of Basle (1431–1437), which brought high church officials to the city, thus increasing the possibilities for important artistic commissions, was probably the motivation for his move. On January 10, 1435, he became a citizen of Basle, and he married shortly thereafter. In 1441 and 1442 he was paid for unknown paintings in the Kornhaus (granary). One of the wings of his altarpiece for the high altar of St. Peter in Geneva is signed and dated 1444. In 1446 he is recorded as dead, leaving his widow and five young children.

The Heilsspiegel Altar, dated circa 1435 and partially destroyed and dismembered in the iconoclasm of 1529, was painted for the choir of the church of St. Leonhard in Basle. Based on the *Speculum humanae salvationis (Mirror of Human Salvation)*, which places Old Testament an other prefigurations next to their fulfillment in the New Testament and Last Judgment, it is the earliest and largest altar in this tradition in the fifteenth century. The center and predella (lower alter panel) are lost, but seven of the eight scenes from the inner wings survive. Five are in the Kunstmuseum in Basle and the other two in the Gemäldegalerie in Berlin and the Musée des Beaux Arts in Dijon. Since they show Old Testament or historical scenes with two figures standing before a gold background, the missing center must have shown their fulfillment: an Adoration of the Magi or a *Christus Salvator* (Christ as Savior) are most often suggested. The outside panels seen on the closed altar showed single figures standing in narrow rooms. Five of the original eight survive: four in Basle and one in Dijon.

The St. Peter Altarpiece (Geneva, Musée d'Art et d'Histoire) also lacks its center and predella, probably destroyed by iconoclasts in 1535, when the remaining panels were separated. Today the inner wings show the Adoration of the Magi on the left and the donor presented to the Virgin by St. Peter on the right. The left outside wing represents the Miracle of Fishes and Calling of St. Peter, and the right outside wing the Freeing of St. Peter from Prison. The landscape of the Miracle of Fishes gives an accurate view of the shores of Lake Geneva with the Savoy Alps and Mont Blanc and is considered to be the first topographical landscape portrayed in northern European art. New research considers the connection of this panel to the politics of Savoy. Other undated paintings attributed to Wirz are the Annunciation (Nuremberg, Germanis ches Nationalmuseum), the Meeting at the Golden Gate (Basel, Kunstmuseum), and Saints Catherine and Mary Magdalene in a Church (Strasbourg, Musée de l'Oeuvre Notre-Dame).

The physical presence of figures and materials is more important in Witz's paintings than depiction of rich costumes or detailed settings. His tempera technique and strong, simple colors increase the immobility that characterizes his figures, and strong shadows help to define his space. The forms on the outside wings in their narrow rooms resemble those in some miniatures of the Utrecht school circa 1430.

Further Reading

Deuchler, Florens. "Konrad Witz, la Savoie et l'Italie: Nouvelles hypothèses à propos du retable de Genève." *Revue de l'art* 71 (1986): 7–16.

Gantner, Joseph. *Konrad Witz*. Vienna: A. Schroll, 1942.

Rott, Hans. *Quellen und Forschungen zur südwestdeutschen und schweizerischen Kunstgeschichte im XV. und XVI. Jahrhundert 3: Der Oberrhein* 2. Stuttgart: Strecker und Schröder, 1936, pp. 20–25.

Schauder, M. "Konrad Witz und die Utrechter Buchmalerei," in *Masters and Miniatures: Proceedings of the Congress on Medieval Manuscript Illumination in the Northern Netherlands (Utrecht, 10–13 December 1989)*, ed. K. van der Horst and Johann-Christian Klamt. Doornspijk: Davaco, 1991, pp. 137–147.

MARTA O. RENGER

WOLFRAM VON ESCHENBACH (fl. first half of the 13th c.)

The greatest German epic poet of the High Middle Ages, Wolfram wrote *Parzival, Willehalm, Titurel*, and nine lyric poems. Internal evidence in his works makes it likely that he composed *Parzival* between 1200 and 1210, worked on *Willehalm* after 1212, and left it unfinished sometime after 1217, possibly as late as the 1220s. Wolfram's few lyric poems, most of them amorous exchanges between two lovers ("dawn songs"), were probably completed early in his career, and the two fragments that make up *Titurel* were composed either during or after his work on *Willehalm*. Wolfram must have lived from about 1170 to the 1220s. He names himself in both *Parzival* and *Willehalm* and characteristically interjects remarks about his personal life and circumstances, so that we seem to have ample biographical information about Wolfram. Yet it is difficult to know how much of it is true or how much is only a pose.

If we take Wolfram at his word, he was a poor man, probably not a ranked administrator (*ministeralis*, ministerial), dependent on wealthy patrons for support. He must have been at the court of Landgrave Hermann of Thuringia, who, he says, provided the French source for *Willehalm*, and he claims to have been a military man with a wife and young daughter. Wolfram was probably born in the Middle Franconian town of Ober-Eschenbach, today renamed Wolframs-Eschenbach. His grave was seen there in the fifteenth century and again in the early seventeenth century, but there is no sign of it today. He was well acquainted with the works of the leading poets of his day: Heinrich von Veldeke, Hartmann von Aue, Gottfried von Straßburg, Walther von der Vogelweide, and Neidhart von Reuental. He surely knew Eilhart von Oberge's *Tristant*, the German *Alexanderlied, Rolandslied, Kaiserchronik, Nibelungenlied*, and other heroic sagas. Yet Wolfram claims not to be able to read or write (see *Parzival* strophe 115, ll. 27–30; Willehalm 2,16–22). Such remarks may well have been made in reaction to poets like Hartmann and Gottfried, who boasted of their learning and their literary abilities.

Wolfram's *Parzival*, an Arthurian romance of over 25,000 lines in rhymed couplets, is based on Chrétien de Troyes's *Perceval* (also called *Le Conte del Graal*). It is not a translation in the modern sense, rather an adaptation, expansion, and completion of Chrétien's work. There are several important differences. Chrétien's romance is unfinished. Although there are several continuations, his work stops after 9,234 lines. Wolfram provides his *Parzival* with a detailed prehistory and brings his story to a logical conclusion, while maintaining the general sequence of events found in his source. The prehistory (the first two books) deals with Parzival's father, Gahmuret, and how he eventually marries Herzeloyde, but is killed in battle. Striken by the news of Gahmuret's tragic death, Herzeloyde gives birth to Parzival and resolves to raise him in the wilderness, far from the knightly world of the court.

Wolfram takes Chrétien to task in an epilogue for not having told the story properly then goes on to say that a certain "Kyot," who told the true tale, might well be angry about that (*Parzival* 827, 1–4). Earlier Wolfram had claimed Kyot as his source on several occasions and had gone into great detail about how Kyot had found the true story of the Grail in a discarded Arabic manuscript in Toledo. In the manuscript there was a report about the Grail and the Grail family by a part-Jewish astronomer named Flegetanis, who had read about the Grail in the stars. Kyot, a Provençal Christian, had to learn Arabic to read the manuscript. Then he read in Latin chronicles and finally found the story of the Grail Family, which he eventually located in Anjou. All in all, an elaborate invention, especially since we have no real evidence of such a Kyot.

Another striking difference between Wolfram and his source is the nature of the Grail. In Chrétien it is a dish or bowl, in Wolfram a fantastic stone with the pseudo-Latin name of *lapsit exillis*. The angels, who had remained neutral during Lucifer's rebellion, were banished to the stone. Later, a human family became the guardians of the Grail and lived from the food and drink that the Grail miraculously provided. Anyone who has been in the presence of the Grail will not die for a week thereafter, only a virgin can carry the Grail, and inscriptions appear on the stone to name children who are called to the Grail. They grow up to become knights and ladies and are sent out to occupy thrones that lack rulers. The knights defend the Grail Castle and are forbidden to marry or to have a love relationship with a woman (Wolfram calls them "templars"). Only the Grail King may have a wife, but King Anfortas had been wounded by a poisoned spear while performing chivalric deeds in the service of a lady, and been kept alive by the power of the Grail, yet suffering excruciating pain. Nevertheless, although the Grail cannot be found by any seeker, an inscription on the Grail announced that a stranger would come and Anfortas would be healed if he asked the question without prompting during the first night. The stranger would then become Grail King.

Of course, Parzival is destined to be that stranger. He grows up ignorant of knighthood until he encounters some knights, riding through the forest. Impressed by their armor, Parzival is intent on becoming a knight himself. His desire for knighthood stems from the paternal side of his genetic makeup, and his mother reluctantly allows him to leave. Still, she dresses him in fool's clothing in the hope that the ridicule he will surely receive will force his return. However, Parzival's handsome appearance impresses people, and he eventually reaches King Artus's court, only to be told that he should get his own armor by attacking Ither, a knight outside the court who is feuding with Artus, if he wants to become a knight.

Parzival kills Ither with his crude javelin, unaware that Ither is a blood relative, strips him of his armor, puts it on, and rides off on Ither's horse. He arrives at the castle of Gurnemanz, who gives him a short course in knightsmanship and admonitions about how to behave as a knight. Traveling on to Pelrapeire, Parzival wins the beautiful Condwiramurs by defeating her besiegers. After some rime, Parzival leaves Condwiramurs to visit his mother, but he arrives instead unwittingly at Munsalvæsche, the Grail Castle. There he is received with great honor, sees the Grail procession and the bloody lance, hears the lamenting of the people, and receives a sword from King Anfortas, who is obviously in great pain. But Parzival, mindful of Gurnemanz's advice not to ask too many questions, remains silent. The next morning the Grail company has disappeared, and Parzival leaves to try to find them. Two days later, he comes to King Artus's court, which has been eager to meet the Red Knight, as he was called by the knights he had defeated, and sent to Artus. His arrival occasions a feast at the Round Table, and Parzival is duly admitted to that select company. At this crowning moment of Parzival's knightly career, the ugly Grail messenger, Cundrie, appears and castigates him verbally for having failed to ask about An-fortas's suffering. Publically humiliated, Parzival leaves, angrily blaming God for his shame and determined to find the Grail and rectify things.

After Parzival's humiliation by Cundrie in front of Artus and his knights, that other paragon of chivalry, Gawan, is challenged to defend his honor. He then takes over center stage of the narrative with his quest for four queens and four hundred maidens held captive at Schastel Marveile. His adventures predominate from Book VII through XIV, except for Book IX, where the story returns to Parzival. Book IX is crucial for Parzival, angry as he is at God but with his thoughts on the Grail and his wife, Condwiramurs. Four and one-half years have passed since Parzival was at the Munsalvæsche and had failed to ask the question. Now, on Good Friday, he is directed to his uncle, the hermit Trevrizent, who tells him about his family and his relationship to the Grail King Anfortas. In addition, Parzival learns all about the Grail, about his motner's death, and the fact that he had killed a relative, Ither, in his effort to become a knight. Hesitatingly, Parzival admits that he was the one who had visited the Grail Castle but had not asked the question. After this confession, Trevrizent gives Parzival a new understanding of the relationship of God and humans, so that he makes his peace with God through penance. Nevertheless, he will still wander in search of the Grail Castle.

Gawan, in the meanwhile, has cleared his family name, rescued the queens from Schastel Marveille, and won the hand of Orgeluse. He has one last task to complete: single combat with Gramoflanz in the presence of his uncle, King Arms, who arrives with all his court. Before that can happen, Gawan fights with Parzival but is spared when they recognize each other. Parzival rights in place of the wounded Gawan against Gramoflanz and defeats him. King Artus then arranges a reconciliation among all the parties involved, and a joyous nuptial celebration ensues. Parzival leaves the festivities alone and encounters his heathen half-brother, Feirefiz, in combat. Just when it appears that Parzival will be defeated, Feirefiz throws aside his sword and magnanimously discloses his identity first. Now Parzival, with his new awareness of God and having been tested to the point of death, is ready to be summoned to the Grail. Cundrie appears, announces that Parzival has been called, and they leave for Munsalvæsche accompanied by Feirefiz. There Parzival asks the question, Anfortas is healed, and a short time thereafter Parzival is reunited with Condwiramurs, who arrives at the castle with their twin sons.

In Wolfram's *Parzival* we see two ideal realms, that of King Artus and that of the Grail. The knights of Artus's Round Table represent the highest secular ideal of chivalry, epitomized in the person of Gawan. The Grail knights on the other hand have a special relationship to God. They are chosen for divine purposes. Parzival belongs to both realms by virtue of his inheritance: from his father, the skill and desire to excel in knightly combat; from his mother, his genealogical relationship to the Grail family and his destiny to succeed Anfortas as King of the Grail Castle. We see in his story first his misguided striving to become an exemplary knight, then his angry confusion when he is humiliated at what should have been his moment of highest honor. Finally, he learns to adjust his sights from the goals of his own ambition and accept the purposes that God has for him. The twofold structure of the work embodied in the figures of Gawan and Parzival shows both knights succeeding in their particular tasks of freeing two groups of people. For one it is a worldly success, for the other, a transcendent, spiritual achievement.

Wolfram's other major work, *Willehalm*, is quite different from *Parzival*. Not only is it unfinished, but it is also not an Arthurian romance. Its source is the Old French *chanson de geste*, *La Bataille d'Aliscans*, one of the twenty-four poems in the cycle about Guillaume d'Orange and his family. This is heroic poetry that revels in combat and death, Christians against heathens, good against evil. Wolfram himself takes notice of the difference when he states: "Whatever I recounted earlier about fighting [. . .] ended in some way other than in death. *This* fighting will settle for nothing less than death and loss of joy" (*Willehlm* 10, 22–26). Yet for Wolfram, love and courtly attitudes are not lacking. *Willehalm* deals with the conflict between religions and the love that makes the religious conflict tragic. It involves immense slaughter and suffering on both the Christian *and* the heathen sides, and the religious differences and the human experience of the struggle give the work a much greater depth. Although he has transformed the material of his source perhaps to an even greater extent than in *Parzival*, Wolfram still preserves the essential sequence of events of his source as far as his story goes. One final difference: the *chanson* is written in tirades—stanzas of a varying number of ten-syllable lines, with each tirade, or *laisse*, having the same assonance. Wolfram uses the rhymed couplets of the courtly romance.

Willehalm begins in the midst of the first great battle of Aliscans. The heathen emperor Terramer had summoned huge armies and landed not far from Willehalm's fortified city of Oransche. Terramer's purpose is to force the return of his daughter Arabel to her husband, Tybalt, and to the religion of her people. Arabel, now called Gyburg after her baptism, had fallen in love with Willehalm when he was a prisoner in heathendom. She had helped him escape, left Tybalt to flee with Willehalm, and converted to Christianity. Her former husband and her son have come with the Saracen forces.

In the course of the first battle, Willehalm loses all his knights, including young Vivianz, who is the outstanding fighter for the Christians. Willehalm himself is barely able to escape the slaughter by donning the armor of King Arofel, whom he had slain, and riding away through the heathen ranks, almost unnoticed. He spends the night at Oransche with Gyburg, then leaves early the next morning to seek help from King Louis. Gyburg is left to defend the fortress with her ladies and a handful of survivors.

Having arrived in Laon, Willehalm receives an extremely cold welcome. King Louis and the queen, Willehalm's sister, are most reluctant to do anything for him. Willehalm, in great rage at the insulting treatment and deeply concerned about Gyburg's fate, grabs the queen by her braids and threatens to cut her head off.

When Willehalm's rather, mother, and brothers, who are present at court, hear what has happened at Aliscans and Oransche, they immediately pledge help. Eventually, Willehalm's anger is appeased by the intervention of his niece, Alyze; Louis, whose life had also been threatened by Willehalm, is mollified so that he, too, offers to send imperial forces under Willehalm's command to raise the siege at Oransche.

Before setting out for Oransche with the French troops, Willehalm obtains from Louis the services of Rennewart, a huge young heathen who had been working as a kitchen boy, having rejected baptism. Rennewart is eager to fight, believing that his relatives had refused to ransom him after he was abducted by merchants. He asks for a gigantic club, bound with iron bands, as his weapon, but he forgets it repeatedly on the way to Oransche. (In *Aliscans*, Rainouras is a burlesque figure who eventually dominates the fighting in the second battle. Wolfram's Rennewart, however, despite some boorish acts, is portrayed as a young nobleman in undeserved circumstances. He is actually Gyburg's long-lost brother!)

Willehalm hastens back to Oransche with the French troops, only to discover that Terramer's forces had withdrawn to the coast where the air was better without having stormed the fortress successfully. Gyburg and her meager forces had been able to hold them off. One by one, Willehalm's father and his brothers arrive with their armies, and the stage is set for the second battle. However, before it begins, a meeting of all the leaders takes place, at which all voice their resolve and support for the battle. Gyburg alone adds a temporizing voice. Tearfully she expresses her sorrow that she is the cause for the huge loss of life on both sides and makes a moving plea for the Christians to spare the heathens, if possible.

In the ensuing battle the Christians are victorious, but the loss of life on both sides is immense. Rennewart, who had forcibly "persuaded" the wavering French not to desert, plays a leading role in the victory. Terramer manages to escape to his ships, and the expected confrontation between Rennewart and his father does not take place. Indeed, when the battle is over Rennewart is missing. Willehalm grieves at the apparent loss of Rennewart and about the terrible slaughter that has occurred. In a gesture of respect for the noble heathens, he gives orders to have their fallen kings embalmed and buried according to their own rites. At this point the narrative breaks off.

Most scholars believe that *Willehalm* is a fragment, basing their argument on the fact that too many narrative strands are left untied. Others feel that, for whatever reasons, Wolfram may have been unable to finish it and devised an emergency conclusion (the *Notdach* theory). Still others maintain that *Willehalm* is complete as it stands, that with the tragic quality of the poem Wolfram has put an entirely new meaning into the substance of his source and that for him any continuation of the Rennewart story had become irrelevant. One further, more recent position is that Wolfram intended it to be a fragment. No matter how one looks at the ending, or lack thereof, *Willehalm* is still a powerfully moving work, dealing with problems that have been with us, as Wolfram says: "since Jesus was plunged into the Jordan to be baptized" (*Willehalm* 4, 28f). Wolfram seems to have been deeply affected himself by the tragedy of it all, if one can judge by his numerous self-reflective remarks throughout the poem.

The two fragments usually called *Titurel* from the name of the old Grail King in the first line of the first fragment deal with the two young lovers, Schionatulander and Sigune, from Wolfram's *Parzival*. It is as if Wolfram attempted to flesh out the briefly mentioned story of their tragic love. Written in four long-line strophes that resemble the *Nibelungenlied* strophes to a limited degree, the first fragment deals with the discovery of the mutual love of the two young people, and the second fragment describes an idyll in the woods that is interrupted by the catching of a hunting dog who had been running through the woods trailing a fantastically elaborate leash with a story depicted on it. Sigune wishes to read the story to its end, but the dog escapes as she loosens the leash to read more and carries the leash away. She promises Schionatulander her love as a reward for retrieving the leash. We know from *Parzival* that Schionatulander gets killed in the attempt, and Sigune is left mourning over his dead body when Parzival meets her. A later poet named Albrecht (von Scharfenberg?) took on the task of completing *Titurel*, and he did so with a vengeance. There are over 6,000 strophes in his so-called *Jüngerer Titurel*, compared with Wolfram's 170! Although it is poetically inferior, Albrecht's work was thought for a long time to be Wolfram's because he identifies himself as Wolfram early on in the work, disclosing his own name only at almost the very end.

There are many problems in *Titurel*. These include the manuscript tradition, the precise text of the poem, and the relationship of the two fragments to each other. Even the theme of love is treated strangely, portraying the exuberance and joy of the naive young lovers trying to act so properly as courtly lovers, yet with a background of impending tragedy on the basis of family history. It is a work of changing moods with somberness predominating.

Wolfram's lyric poems generally describe the parting of lovers at dawn and follow a tradition found in Provençal and Old French poetry. For the most part the lady is the dominant figure. She is the one who is awake as dawn is breaking and must wake her lover so that he can leave without being seen. But Wolfram also includes a sympathetic watchman in several instances, and in one poem he is the dominant speaker. The poems generally end with one last embrace and then the tearful parting as the sun rises higher. Wolfram's dawn songs, among the first in German of that genre, are marked by their striking imagery and their sensitive portrayal of the lovers. His few other poems are similar to more traditional *Minnelieder* (courtly love songs) but show his complete mastery of that type.

See also **Eilhart von Oberg; Gottfried von Straß-burg; Hartmann von Aue**

Further Reading

Bumke, Joachim. *Die Wolfram von Eschenbach Forschung seit 1945. Bericht und Bibliographie.* Munich: Wilhelm Fink, 1970.

——. *Wolfram von Eschenbach*, 6th ed. Stuttgart: Metzler, 1991; 7th ed., 1997.

Gibbs, Marion E., and Sidney M. Johnson, trans. *Wolfram von Eschenbach: Willehlam.* Harmondsworth: Penguin, 1984.

Gibbs, Marion E., and Sidney M. Johnson. *Wolfram von Eschenbach: "Titurel" and the "Songs."* New York: Garland, 1988 [with English trans.].

——. *Medieval German Literature: A Companion.* New York: Garland, 1997, pp. 174–205.

Green, D. H. *The Art of Recognition in Wolfram's "Parzival."* Cambridge: Cambridge University Press, 1982.

Groos Arthur. *Romancing the Grail.* Ithaca, N.Y.: Cornell University Press, 1995 [on *Parzival*].

Hatto, Arthur T., trans. *Wolfram von Eschenbach: Parzival.* Harmondsworth: Penguin, 1980.

Heinzle, Joachim. *Stellenkommentar zu Wolframs "Titurel."* Tübingen: Niemeyer, 1972.

Heinzle, Joachim, ed. *Wolfram von Eschenbach: Willehlam.* Frankfurt am Main: Verlag Deutscher Klassiker, 1991 [with German trans.].

——, ed. *Willehalm: nach der Handschrift 857 der Stiftsbibliothek St. Gallen.* Tübingen: Niemeyer, 1994.

Kiening, Christian. "Wolfram von Eschenbach: *Willehalm*," in *Mittelhochdeutsche Romane und Heldenepen*, ed. Horst Brunner. Stuttgart: Reclam, 1993, pp. 212–232.

Kühn, Dieter, trans. *Wolfram von Eschenbach: Parzival.* Frankfurt am Main: Insel, 1986.

Lachmann, Karl, ed. *Wolfram von Eschenbach*, 6th ed. Berlin: de Gruyter, 1926 [reprinted often].

Leitzmann, Albert, ed. *Wolfram von Eschenbach*, 5 vols. Halle (Saale): Niemeyer, 1902–1906 [reprinted often].

Lofmark, Carl. *Rennewart in Wolfram's "Willehalm": A Study of Wolfram von Eschenbach and His Sources.* Cambridge, England: Cambridge University Press, 1972.

Mertens, Volker. "Wolfram von Eschenbach: *Titurel*," in *Mittelhochdeutsche Romane und Heldenepen*, ed. Horst Brunner. Stuttgart: Reclam, 1993, pp. 196–211.

Mohr, Wolfgang. *Wolfram von Eschenbach. Titurel. Lieder.* Göppingen: Kummerle, 1978, pp. 101–161.

Mustard, Helen M., and Charles E. Passage, trans. *Wolfram von Eschenbach: Parzival.* New York: Vintage Books, 1961.

Nellmann, Eberhard, ed. *Wolfram von Eschenbach: Parzival.* Frankfurt am Main: Verlag Deutscher Klassiker, 1994 [German trans. Dieter Kühn].

Passage, Charles E., trans. *Wolfram von Eschenbach: Willehlam.* New York: Ungar, 1977.

——. trans. *Wolfram von Eschenbach: Titurel.* New York: Ungar, 1984.

Poag, James F. *Wolfram von Eschenbach.* New York: Twayne, 1972 [good general introduction in English].

Pretzel, Ulrich, and Wolfgang Bachofer. *Bibliographie zu Wolfram von Eschenbach*, 2d ed. Berlin: Schmidt, 1968.

Schmidt, Elisabeth. "Wolfram von Eschenbach: *Parzival*," in *Mittelhochdeutsche Romane und Heldenepen*, ed. Horst Brunner. Stuttgart: Reclam, 1993, pp. 173–195.

Schröder, Werner, ed. *Wolfram von Eschenbach: Willehalm.* Berlin: de Gruyter, 1978 [with German trans. Dieter Kartschoke; rev. 1989].

Walshe, Maurice O'C. *Medieval German Literature.* Cambridge, Mass.: Harvard University Press, 1962, pp. 156–175 [concise treatment].

Wapnewski, Peter. *Die Lyrik Wolframs von Eschenbach: Edition. Kommentar. Interpretation.* Munich: Beck, 1972 [songs, with German trans.].

SIDNEY M. JOHNSON

WOLGEMUT, MICHAEL (1434/1437–1519)

Born in Nuremberg between 1434 and 1437, Michael Wolgemut was the city's foremost painter and printmaker in the late fifteenth century. Wolgemut trained with his father, Valentin, a painter, and worked as a journeyman with Gabriel Mälesskircher in Munich before returning to Nuremberg in 1471. A year later he married Barbara, the widow of the noted painter Hans Pleydenwurff. Whether he had collaborated earlier with Hans is uncertain. Wolgemut developed a large workshop that specialized in the production of large retables, woodcuts, and designs for stained glass windows. The artist's pupils included his stepson, Wilhelm Pleydenwurff, and Albrecht Dürer, who was in the shop from 1486 until 1489.

Wolgemut's first documented painting is the high altar completed in 1479 for the St. Marienkirche in Zwickau. This complex polyptych includes painted wings depicting the Passion of Christ (exterior) and Infancy (middle) that cover the nine life-size standing statues of saints on the inner wings and in the corpus, a painted and carved winged predella (lower altar panel), and a Last Judgment covering the back of the altar. Wolgemut employed a team of now anonymous joiners, painters, and sculptors on this and similar elaborate projects, notably the Peringsdorfer Altar made circa 1486 for the Augustinian Cloister in Nuremberg (today in the Friedenskirche) and the high altar (1506–1508) in the church of St. Johannes and St. Marrinus in Schwabach. In his paintings, including his independent portraits, such as that of Levinus Memminger circa 1485 (Madrid, Museo Thyssen-Borne-misza), Wolgemut displayed his familiarity with Netherlandish art, notably the works of Rogier van der Weyden and Dirk Bouts. His clearly defined figures are located in the extreme foreground before deep landscapes.

Today the artist is best known for his prints. In addition to independent woodcuts, Wolgemut recognized the potential of illustrating books. The artist, his stepson, and his shop supplied 96 woodcuts for Stephan Fridolin's *Schatzbehalter* (1491) and 1,809 woodcuts using 645 different blocks for Hartmann Schedel's *Liber Chronicarum* (*Nuremberg Chronicle*, 1493), both published by Anton Koberger in Nuremberg. The latter with its maps, city views, portraits, and elaborate illustrations was the century's most ambitious publishing project and was marketed across Europe.

Wolgemut's career spanned four decades. His last major picture, the *Epitaph of Anna Gross* (Nuremberg, Germanisches Nationalmuseum), dates around 1509. In 1516 Albrecht Dürer affectionately recorded his mentor's likeness in a portrait (Nuremberg, Germanisches Nationalmuseum). Wolgemut died on November 30, 1519, in Nuremberg.

Further Reading

Bellm, Richard. *Wolgemuts Skizzenbuch im Berliner Kupferstichkabinett*. Studien zur deutschen Kunstgeschichte 322. Baden-Baden: P. H. Heitz, 1959.

Fridolin, Stefan. *Der Schatzbehalter: Ein Andachts- und Erbauungsbuch aus dem Jahre 1491*, ed. Richard Bellm. 2 vols. Wiesbaden: G. Pressler, 1962.

Füssel, Stephan, ed. *500 Jahre Schedelsche Weltchronik*. Pirckheimer Jahrbuch 9. Nuremberg: Carl, 1994.

Rücker, Elizabeth. *Die Schedelsche Weltchronik: Das größte Buchunternehmen der Dürer-Zeit*, 33d rev. ed. Munich: Prestel, 1988.

Scholz, Hartmut. *Entwurf und Ausführung: Werkstattpraxis in der Nürnberger Glasmalerei der Dürerzeit*. Ph.d. diss., University of Stuttgart, 1988. Berlin: Deutscher Verlag für Kunstwissenschaft, 1989.

Stadler, Franz Izra. *Michael Wolgemut und der Nürnberger Holzschnitt im letzten Drittel des XV. Jahrhunderts*. 2 vols. Studien zur deutschen Kunstgeschichte 161. Strasbourg: J. H. E. Heitz, 1913.

Strieder, Peter. *Tafelmalerei in Nürnberg, 1350 bis 1550*. Königstein im Taunus: K. Robert, 1993, pp. 65–85, 200–219.

Wilson, Adrian. *The Making of the Nuremberg Chronicle*. Amsterdam: Nico Israel, 1976.

JEFFREY CHIPPS SMITH

WULFSTAN OF YORK (d. 1023)

Bishop of London 996–1002, bishop of "Worcester 1002–16, and archbishop of York 1002–23, who served two kings (Æthelred II and Cnut) as adviser and author of legislation while addressing the pressing moral and ecclesiastical issues of his time. One of two great stylists in the history of OE prose (with Ælfric), Wulfstan had a distinguished career as a homilist and statesman. Although educated as a Benedictine, he was very much a public figure who began signing himself "Lupus" ("Wolf") early in his career, as he developed a reputation for spoken and written eloquence and for moral reform. The 12th-century *Liber Eliensis* (*Book of Ely*) provides the only medieval information, much of riiat questionable, about his life.

When he assumed the sees of Worcester and York in plurality (holding both simultaneously) upon the death in 1002 of Archbishop Eadulf, Wulfstan had experienced the worst ravages of the Danes and the largely ineffectual responses of Æthelred's army. With its rich library and scriptorium removed from the worst of the fighting Worcester provided him an opportunity to study important patristic and canonical texts and thus to develop as a writer and reformer. Much of his work was also done at York, where he performed the functions of a leader of the church. Extant manuscripts from both centers show Wulfstan's hand in the annotations. In addition several versions of his "commonplace book" survive, containing collections of materials intended for use in his own work. Either at Worcester or York he wrote versified entries for 957 and 975 in the D version of the Anglo-Saxon Chronicle.

Wulfstan's reputation grows from his sermons. These include a series of eschatological works, impassioned calls for repentance in response to signs of the coming of Doomsday. Another series on the elements of Christian faith treats the subjects of baptism, the Creed, the gifts of the Holy Spirit, and the duties of a Christian. In both series he draws on a variety of Latin sources largely from the Carolingian period and shapes his work to specific audiences. Only two of his sermons are proper to the church year, and those address the matter of penance during Lent. Wulfstan's sermons are topical, hortative, and utilitarian messages rather than explications of the Gospels or hagiographic narratives.

The best-known sermon also seems to have been the most popular in its time: *Sermo Lupi ad Anglos* (*The Sermon of Wolf to the English*), so called from the opening words of its rubric. Surviving in five manuscript versions, this work probably was composed in 1014, the year in which Æthelred was exiled. The *Sermo Lupi* is noteworthy for drawing on themes and materials that engaged Wulfstan throughout his career, here brought together and presented urgently when it seemed that God was punishing the English at the hands of the Danes. In particular Wulfstan uses phrases from his eschatological sermons in depicting the present evils that presage the end of the world. He ends with a typical exhortation to return to the faith of baptism, where there is protection from the fires of hell.

As trusted counselor to Æthelred, and to his Danish successor Cnut, Wulfstan wrote a variety of legislation intended to reassert the laws of earlier Anglo-Saxon kings and bring order to a country that had been unsettled by war and the influx of Scandinavians. Although he put into writing edicts that had been decreed by the ruling witan, or council, Wulfstan echoed there the concerns about present conditions and the urgency for change expressed in his homiletic writings. The laws are of three distinct types: short codes addressing such specific issues as the need to christianize the Danelaw, protect the clergy and the church, and reinforce a hierarchical social order consistent with the past; drafts of legislation for Æthelred and Cnut; and a comprehensive, formal code for Cnut. Through these legal writings Wulfstan used his influence to press for social, moral, religious, and political reforms extending even to the obligations of the king.

Beginning about 1005 a remarkable interchange occurred between Wulfstan and his talented contemporary Abbot Ælfric of Eynsham. Wulfstan requested from Ælfric two pastoral letters in Latin treating duties of the secular clergy. Shortly thereafter he asked Ælfric to translate the letters into OE. Although the versions that survive today bear evidence of Wulfstan's revisions, they are important because they strongly influenced his own prescriptions for the secular clergy, the *Canons of Edgar*, as well as the code he drafted for Æthelred at Enham in 1008. These and other letters by Ælfric formed part of a group of canonistic materials including Frankish capitularies and Wulfstan's translation of Amalarius's *De regula canonicorum*, materials that underlie one of Wulfetan's sermons on baptism, his *Institutes of Polity*, and certain legal codes, in addition to the *Canons of Edgar*.

Because they provide yet another strong example of his reforming philosophy, Wulfstan's own canonistic works command interest. The *Canons of Edgar*, so-called because they hark back to better times during the reign of Edgar, provide instruction on proper conduct and training for the secular clergy and detailed instructions on their duties, including how to conduct the mass. The *Institutes of Polity* form a treatise on the organization of society, an early example of estates literature that attempts to define the duties of each class. His lengthy discussion of the bishop's role provides insight into the career Wulfstan fashioned fot himself. Wulfstan also translated prose portions of the Benedictine office into OE, presumably to help the secular clergy with their devotions.

The effectiveness of Wulfstan's writing owes much to his rhythmic style, distinctive vocabulary, and use of rhetorical figures. He usually wrote with two-stress, alliterating, sometimes rhyming phrases syntactically independent of one another, which he could use to build toward a powerful climax. His stylistic touches include a large stock of intensifying words, repeated phrases, and forceful compounds. Figures of sound as taught by medieval manuals of rhetoric appear prominently in his work. All of these tools Wulfstan used in his attempts to restore England to the order and piety it had enjoyed before the Viking depredations.

See also **Ælfric; Cnut**

Further Reading

Primary Sources
Bethurum, Dorothy, ed. *The Homilies of Wulfstan*, Oxford: Clarendon, 1957.
Fowler, Roger, ed. *Wulfstan's Canons of Edgar*. EETS o.s. 266. London: Oxford University Press, 1972.
Jost, Karl, ed. *Die "Institutes of Polity, Civil and Ecclesiastical": Ein Werk Erzbisch of Wulfstans von York*. Schweitzer anglistische Arbeiten 47. Bern: Francke, 1959.
Ure, James M., ed. *The Benedictine Office: An Old English Text*. Edinburgh University Publications in Language and Literature 11. Edinburgh: Edinburgh University Press, 1957.
Whitelock, Dorothy, ed. *Sermo Lupi ad Anglos*. 3d ed. New York: Methuen, 1966.

Secondary Sources
Bethurum, Dorothy. "Archbishop Wulfstan's Commonplace Book." *PMLA* 57 (1942): 916–29.
Bethurum, Dorothy. "Wulfstan." In *Continuations and Beginnings: Studies in Old English Literature*, ed. Eric G. Stanley. London: Nelson, 1966, pp. 210–46.
Gatch, Milton McC. *Preaching and Theology in Anglo-Saxon England: Ælfric and Wulfstan*, Toronto: University of Toronto Press, 1977.
Ker, N.R. "The Handwriting of Archbishop Wulfstan." In *England before the Conquest: Studies in Primary Sources Presented to Dorothy Whitelock*, ed. Peter Clemoes and Kathleen Hughes. Cambridge: Cambridge University Press, 1971, pp. 315–31.
Richards, Mary P. "The Manuscript Contexts of the Old English Laws: Tradition and Innovation." In *Studies in Earlier Old English Prose*, ed. Paul E. Szarmach. Albany: SUNY Press, 1986, pp. 171–92.
Stafford, Pauline. "The Laws of Cnut and the History of Anglo-Saxon Royal Promises." *ASE* 10 (1981): 173–90.
Whitelock, Dorothy. "Wulfstan's Authorship of Cnut's Laws." *EHR70* (1955): 72–85.
Wormald, Patrick, "Æthelred the Lawmaker." In *Ethelred the Unready*, ed. David Hill. BAR Brit. Ser. 59. Oxford: BAR, 1978, pp. 47–80.

MARY P. RICHARDS

WYCLIF, JOHN (ca. 1330–1384)

The most distinguished English philosopher and theologian of the later 14th century and a significant influence on the emergence of the heretical Lollard movement. His popular fame as a church reformer, however, is largely unjustified and only dates from the Reformation period.

Wyclif was probably born in Yorkshire. For most of his adult life he was a scholar and teacher at Oxford, and only in his last decade did he make any impression on a wider stage, first as a royal servant and then as the inspiration of heresy. He first appears in the records as a fellow of Merton College in 1356, as master of Balliol College in 1360, and later as warden of Canterbury Hall, an appointment that involved him in a struggle with the regular clergy. He proceeded from Arts to Theology in the late 1360s and became a doctor of theology about 1372–73. He was, it appears, a conventional academic and like most of his contemporaries was supported, as an absentee, by the revenues of various benefices, none of great value. He was granted a canonry at Lincoln in 1371, though the promise of a prebend there with substantial resources was never fulfilled. In 1374 he was granted the Leicestershire benefice of Lutterworth, which was in the gift of the crown.

This undoubtedly was a reward for services as a polemicist and a diplomat. He defended the crown's right to tax the clergy and even its violation of sanctuary in order to arrest crown debtors, and in 1374 he took part in a diplomatic mission to Bruges. By 1378 he was compelled to withdraw from politics, although his lay patrons continued to protect him from the assaults of church authorities who had secured papal condemnation of his views on the subject of civil and divine lordship. In 1381 he was forced to leave Oxford, retiring to Lutterworth, where he died of a stroke at the end of 1384. Although his enemies alleged that he had inspired the Peasant Rebellion of 1381, this view cannot be substantiated and his earlier strong royatism makes it inherently unlikely.

Increasing knowledge of the development of scholastic philosophy has enhanced Wyclif's reputation as a thinker. A man of great learning and incisive mind, he was a vigorous defender of realist metaphysics against the nominalism of William of Ockham. In this he followed the tradition active during his formative years in Oxford, but he went beyond his teachers as an independent thinker. As a philosopher his views remained acceptable, but when he began teaching theology he clashed with the authorities.

His early theological concern with questions of dominion and grace probably arose more from his activities as a royal servant than from philosophical principles. Concurrently with his royal service, however, he became involved in biblical studies, writing a commentary on the whole Bible, something none of his contemporaries did. His reverence for scripture led to a fundamentalist view of the Bible as eternally present in God and probably influenced his denial of transubstantiation in the eucharist, an opinion in accord with his metaphysical views. There has been recent debate on whether metaphysics or biblicism gave the first impetus to this opinion, the issue that led to his final breach with orthodoxy. Even by the end of his life Wyclif had probably not worked out his precise belief in the nature of the eucharist, but it may have come close to the later Lutheran doctrine of consubstantiation.

His influence survived his death, and his eucharistic views were, in a simplified form, one of the hallmarks of later Lollardy. More important perhaps was the production by his followers, under the influence of his biblicism, of two English versions of the Bible, the staple reading for heretical groups and material for works of orthodox devotion. His philosophical views were taught for a time in Oxford and spread also to Bohemia, where they influenced the thought of religious reformers. Later his theological teachings also reached Bohemia and probably contributed to the more radical wing of Hussite thought. A substantial number of Wycliffite manuscripts have survived in libraries there.

By this time the church authorities were taking steps against his writings. Forty-five articles from his works were condemned at Prague in 1403, 267 articles were condemned after Archbishop Arundel's purge at Oxford in 1409, and the attacks continued at the councils of Rome (1413) and Constance (1415). At the last a command was issued for the exhumation and burning of his body, though this part of the sentence was not carried out until 1428.

See also Ockham, William of

Further Reading

Kenny, Anthony. *Wyclif.* Oxford: Oxford University Press, 1985 [best introduction].

Kenny, Anthony, ed. *Wyclif in His Times.* Oxford: Clarendon, 1986 [valuable essays on many aspects of the man and his influence].

Leff, Gordon. *Heresy in the Later Middle Ages: The Relation of Heterodoxy to Dissent, c. 1250–c. 1450.* Manchester: Manchester University Press, 1967 [a good summary of Wyclif's teachings].

McFarlane, K.B. *John Wycliffe and the Beginnings of English Nonconformity.* London: English Universities Press, 1952 [illuminating and good for biography unfair to Wyclif as a thinker].

Thomson, Williell R. *The Latin Writings of John Wyclyf. An Annotated Catalog.* Toronto: Pontifical Institute, 1983 [the best bibliographical treatment of Wydif's writings].

Workman, Herbert B. *John Wyclif: A Study of the English Medieval Church. 2 vols.* Oxford: Clarendon, 1926 [the fullest life, though the interpretation is colored by Reformation apologetics].

J.A.F. Thomson

INDEX

Page numbers in italic indicate figure.

INDEX

INDEX

INDEX

INDEX

INDEX